Contents

What is Volume Two?	v
A typical trust entry	vi
About CAF	vii
Other publications from CAF	viii
The main register of grant making charitable trusts	**3**

16TH EDITION

The Directory of

Grant Making Trusts

REGISTER OF TRUSTS

1999–2000

VOLUME 2

EDITORIAL TEAM
Owen Bevan
Johanna Davis
David Moncrieff

CAF

© 1999 CAF

Published by CAF (Charities Aid
Foundation)
Kings Hill
West Malling
Kent ME19 4TA

Telephone
+44 (0) 1732 520000

Fax
+44 (0) 1732 520001

Website
http://www.charitynet.org

E-mail
cafpubs@caf.charitynet.org

Database management
and typesetting
The Polestar Group
(Whitefriars) Ltd

Design
Eugenie Dodd Typographics

Printed and bound in Great
Britain by Bell & Bain Ltd,
Glasgow

A catalogue record for this book
is available from the British
Library.

ISBN 1–85934–078–4
(three volumes)

What is Volume Two?

The alphabetical register of trusts found in this volume contains the core data about the individual trusts held on the CAF database.

In 1997 the Top 300 grant making trusts identified by CAF gave away approximately £1,132,877,000. In view of this total, we decided that these trusts should be covered in more detail in *Spotlight on Major Trusts* (Volume Three). However, we were unable to find financial records later than 1995 on file for 4 trusts, and there was insufficient information to write a substantive commentary for a further 12 trusts. Because of this, these trusts are included in this volume.

It is recommended that users read 'How to use the *DGMT*' on pages xvi–xix of Volume One to find out how to produce a shortlist of possible trusts.

In general the listing includes:

- trusts with an income of £13,000 or over which make grants to charities and voluntary organisations (including the National Lottery boards and Arts Councils.

We have excluded:

- trusts which fund individuals only;
- trusts which fund one organisation exclusively;
- trusts which have an income of less than £13,000 (these trusts will be included in the second edition of *The Directory of Smaller Grant Making Trusts* published in January 2000);
- trusts whose funds are demonstrably fully committed for the life of the directory;
- trusts which have ceased to exist.

Frequent users of the directory will note a change of policy regarding trusts that do not respond to unsolicited applications. These trusts are now being included in the *DGMT* because we believe that this gives fundraisers a broader overview of the grant making community.

A typical trust entry

A complete entry should contain information under the headings listed below. An explanation of the information which should appear in these fields appears alongside.

The types of project the trust will definitely not fund, eg expeditions, scholarships

The village, town, borough, parish or other geographical area the trust is prepared to fund

The smallest, largest and typical size of grant normally given

The trust's most recent financial figures including the total amount of grants given

Titles of publications the trust has produced which are of interest to grant seekers

Any information which is useful to those preparing their grant application

Charity Commission number

Full details of the types of project or activity the trust plans to fund in 1999–2000

The people, animals, etc the trust wishes ultimately to benefit (although via charities and other voluntary organisations)

The types of grant or loan the trust is prepared to give, eg one-off, recurring, interest-free loan

The top ten grants given by the trust in the last financial year

Names of the Trustees

Any other information which might be useful to grant seekers

The name and address of the person to whom applications should be sent

Year established

■ The Fictitious Trust

WHAT IS FUNDED Education and training
WHAT IS NOT FUNDED No grants to individuals
WHO CAN BENEFIT Charities benefiting children
WHERE FUNDING CAN BE GIVEN UK
TYPE OF GRANT One-off, capital, running costs
RANGE OF GRANTS £250–£5,000
SAMPLE GRANTS £5,000 to a school; £1,000 to a university; £800 to a school library; £600 to a school; £500 to a community school; £500 to a grammar school; £500 for classroom equipment; £400 towards the building of a science block; £400 to a university appeal; £250 for a wheelchair ramp
FINANCES *Year* 1997 *Income* £55,000 *Grants* £50,000
TRUSTEES Peter Brown, BA (Chairman), Mrs Mary Brown, Alistair Johnson, Miss Natalie Jones
PUBLICATIONS Annual Report and Accounts, *The Fictitious Trust – the first twenty years*
NOTES Owing to the large number of applications, some considerable time may elapse before a response is received
HOW TO APPLY In writing to the address below. A sae should be included if an acknowledgement is required
WHO TO APPLY TO Peter Brown, Chairman, The Fictitious Trust, 1 The Street, Any Town, AT13 4LY
Tel 0171-000 0000   *Fax* 0171-000 0000
E-mail person@abc.efghijklmn.org
Website http://www.efghijklmn.co.uk
CC NO 1234567   **ESTABLISHED** 1977

About CAF

CAF, Charities Aid Foundation, is a registered charity with a unique mission – to increase the substance of charity in the UK and overseas. It provides services that are both charitable and financial which help donors make the most of their giving and charities make the most of their resources.

Many of CAF's publications reflect the organisation's purpose: *Dimensions of the Voluntary Sector* offers the definitive financial overview of the sector, while the *Directory of Grant Making Trusts* provides the most comprehensive source of funding information available.

As an integral part of its activities, CAF works to raise the standards of management in voluntary organisations. This includes the making of grants by its own Grants Council, sponsorship of the Charity Annual Report and Accounts Awards, seminars, training courses and the Charities' Annual Conference, the largest regular gathering of key people from within the voluntary sector. In addition, CharityNet is now established as the leading Internet site on voluntary action.

For decades, CAF has led the way in developing tax-effective services to donors, and these are now used by more than 150,000 individuals and 2,000 of the UK's leading companies. Many are also using CAF's CharityCard, the world's first debit card designed exclusively for charitable giving. CAF's unique range of investment and administration services for charities includes the CafCash High Interest Cheque Account, two common investment funds for longer-term investment and a full appeals and subscription management service.

CAF's activities are not limited to the UK, however. Increasingly, CAF is looking to apply the same principles and develop similar services internationally, in its drive to increase the substance of charity across the world.

Other publications from CAF

Grantseeker
The interactive CD-ROM for fundraisers
£58.69 (INCL VAT)
FOR EACH
SIX-MONTHLY RELEASE

Drawing on CAF's years of experience as a publisher of *The Directory of Grant Making Trusts*, *Grantseeker* is the tailor-made solution to the information needs of trust fundraisers in the electronic age. Published for the first time as a subscription service, users will receive a completely new updated edition every six months.

Fully interactive, *Grantseeker*'s specially designed search engine will quickly scan the entire *DGMT* database on the basis of a user's own selection criteria and generate a 'hit list' of trusts whose funding preferences match their project or cause. There are two additional search functions: the ability to search on trustees' names and a key word search by town or city which allows users a more closely defined geographical search. Users' bookmarks and notes automatically carry over to each new release.

Taking full advantage of the extra options available via an electronic search tool, *Grantseeker* offers a more sophisticated matching service than can be provided by traditional methods, enabling fundraisers to save weeks of effort and frustration. A simple hypertext link can provide them with a complete *DGMT* entry on a potential funder within moments of loading the CD. The days of ultimate dependence on a paper-based directory are over.

Designed for use by fundraisers with little or no experience of electronic directories, as well as the more technically minded, *Grantseeker* provides step-by-step instructions on every stage of the search process, backed by comprehensive help files. Even the most confirmed Luddite should not be intimidated!

Grantseeker runs under Windows 3.1 or above.

The Directory of Smaller Grant Making Trusts
1st Edition
ISBN 1–85934–062–8
£29.95
Published February 1998

For many years *The Directory of Grant Making Trusts*, known colloquially as the 'fundraiser's bible', has thrown a spotlight on the funding policies and preferences of the majority of the UK's leading trusts and foundations. Of necessity, however, space constraints have meant that many of the smaller trusts have not been listed. *The Directory of Smaller Grant Making Trusts*, which is to be published every two years, has been developed to remedy this situation and ensure that grant seekers have access to the information they need on these important sources of funding.

The Directory of Smaller Grant Making Trusts contains details of over 1,000 smaller trusts with an income of less than £13,000 per annum. Many of them have not previously been included in directory listings. The individual entries demonstrate that a large number of the trusts have a particular preference for funding activities in selected local, community-based arenas, which will make the directory of particular interest to fundraisers with a regional focus.

FOCUS SERIES

Designed to make the search for funds easier still, many directories from the Focus Series collect together, in individual volumes, details of trusts which have expressed an intention to support charitable activity in a particular field or in a particular geographical area.

In addition to comprehensive details of the funding policies of the trusts listed, information is also provided on recent grants they have made.

These directories will give grant seekers working in the relevant fields a head-start in identifying sympathetic trusts and presenting well-tailored funding applications.

Environment, Animal Welfare and Heritage
ISBN 1–85934–016–4
£19.95

Social Care
ISBN 1–85934–051–2
£16.95

International
ISBN 1–85934–052–0
£19.95

Schools, Colleges and Educational Establishments
ISBN 1–85934–053–9
£19.95

Children and Youth
2nd Edition
ISBN 1–85934–072–5
£19.95

Religion 2nd Edition
ISBN 1–85934–080–6
£19.95
Published February 1999

The East Midlands
ISBN 1–85934–087–3
£19.95
Published February 1999

Museums, Galleries and the Performing Arts
2nd Edition
ISBN 1–85934–081–4
£19.95
Published March 1999

The North East
ISBN 1–85934–086–5
£19.95
Published March 1999

HOW TO SERIES

The *How To Series* has been developed for use by anyone working with smaller voluntary organisations. Whatever your background, this series is designed to provide practical one-stop guides on a variety of core activities to give both volunteers and inexperienced salaried staff essential information and guidance on good practice.

Each title provides a clear picture of the subject matter in a jargon-free format for non-specialists. The books include information on relevant legislation, contact details of useful organisations, examples of practical worksheets – all the necessary tools to help develop your understanding, step by step, of the topic being discussed.

Applying to a Grant Making Trust
Anne Villemur
ISBN 1–85934–033–4
£7.95

Effective Media Relations
Ian Gilchrist
ISBN 1–85934–063–6
£7.95

Payroll Giving
Willemina Bell
ISBN 1–85934–061–X
£7.95

Public Speaking and Presentations
Ian Gilchrist
ISBN 1–85934–064–4
£7.95

Running a Local Fundraising Campaign
Janet Hilderley
ISBN 1–85934–040–7
£9.95

Running a Public Collection
Jennie Whiting
ISBN 1–85934–060–1
£7.95

The Treasurer's Handbook
Ian Caulfeild Grant
ISBN 1–85934–018–0
£7.95

Producing Promotional Materials
Karen Gilchrist
ISBN 1–85934–084–9
£9.95

Fundraising for Education
ISBN 1–85934–083–0
£9.95
Published April 1999

Fundraising using a Database
Peter Flory
ISBN 1–85934–082–2
£11.95
Published April 1999

....

To order any of the above publications, please ring Biblios Publishers' Distribution Services Ltd on 01403 710851 or you can order online using our website: http://www.charitynet.org/bookstore/

The alphabetical register of grant making charitable trusts

This section lists the individual entries for grant making charitable trusts

A

■ The AB Charitable Trust

WHAT IS FUNDED To promote and defend the cause of human dignity

WHAT IS NOT FUNDED Medical research, animal welfare, expeditions, bursaries, conservation and environment

WHO CAN BENEFIT Institutions and charities benefiting at risk groups and those disadvantaged by poverty

WHERE FUNDING CAN BE GIVEN UK, third world countries

TYPE OF GRANT Single donations

RANGE OF GRANTS £1,000–£5,000

SAMPLE GRANTS £10,000 to Asylum Aid; £5,000 to ADFAM; £5,000 to Action Aid; £5,000 to Contact the Elderly; £5,000 to PECAN; £5,000 to Community Selfbuild Agency; £5,000 to St John's Family Resource Unit; £5,000 to Women's Therapy Centre; £5,000 to ATD Fourth World (UK) Ltd; £5,000 to Hospice of the Good Shepherd

FINANCES *Year* 1998 *Income* £190,372 *Grants* £189,000

TRUSTEES Y J M Bonavero, D Boehm, Mrs A G M-L Bonavero, Miss S Bonavero, Miss C Bonavero

HOW TO APPLY Written applications with latest certified full financial statement. Decision will be advised

WHO TO APPLY TO T M Denham, Secretary, The AB Charitable Trust, 12 Addison Avenue, London W11 4QR

CC NO 1000147   **ESTABLISHED** 1990

■ AF Trust Company

WHAT IS FUNDED Making grants for charitable purposes connected with the provision of higher education. The Company currently provides property services and leasing facilities to educational establishments on an at arms length basis

WHO CAN BENEFIT Organisations benefiting young adults and students

WHERE FUNDING CAN BE GIVEN England

TYPE OF GRANT Buildings will be considered

FINANCES *Year* 1997 *Income* £84,692

TRUSTEES K R Blanshard, R Clayton, Ms G Coley, Ms M R Deacon, Ms D Everitt, M R Hansen, M S Hedges, A J Knapp, Ms A A Reid, Ms J Ross, C R Showell, G J Sutton

NOTES No grants were given in this initial period, however, at the year end the Directors have approved donations totalling £62,500 payable in 1997–98

HOW TO APPLY To the address under Who To Apply To in writing

WHO TO APPLY TO P D Welch, Secretary, AF Trust Company, 34 Chapel Street, Thatcham, Berkshire RG18 4QL

CC NO 1060319   **ESTABLISHED** 1996

■ AGF Charitable Trust (formerly NEM Charitable Trust)

WHAT IS FUNDED Support for past and present members of AGF staff charitable initiatives. Support for charities local to AGF branches. This includes: residential facilities and services; infrastructure, support and development; religion; health care; education and training; and social care and development

WHAT IS NOT FUNDED No grants to individuals, or to national charities

WHO CAN BENEFIT Staff and pensioners of AGF. Local charitable bodies benefiting older people; academics; retired people; and students. There are few restrictions on the social circumstances of, and no restrictions on the disease or medical condition suffered by the beneficiaries

WHERE FUNDING CAN BE GIVEN Milton Keynes, Manchester, City of London

TYPE OF GRANT Single donations

RANGE OF GRANTS £100–£2,000, typical grant £250

SAMPLE GRANTS £500 to Insurance Benevolent Fund for Insurance Charities Day August 1998; £500 to Trek China – staff personal effort for Barnardo's; £340 to Children's Safety Books for local distribution of safety information to schools; £300 to Scout Hut, Apsley Guise for local scout group; £300 to Mencap for a personal initiative to raise funds

FINANCES *Year* 1996 *Income* £15,187 *Grants* £17,530

TRUSTEES A Dean, R Neal

HOW TO APPLY Applications received during a quarter normally accumulated and reviewed at the subsequent meeting of the Trustees

WHO TO APPLY TO Mrs A Ward, AGF Charitable Trust, AGF House, 500 Avebury Boulevard, Milton Keynes MK9 2LA *Tel* 01908 683260 *Fax* 01908 669783

CC NO 327671   **ESTABLISHED** 1988

■ AIIT (The Ancient India and Iran Trust)

WHAT IS FUNDED At present the Trustees' prime aim is to support the cataloguing, maintenance and conservation of their Library at Brooklands House, which is open for the use of bona fide scholars and students by appointment. In so far as circumstances permit, they make small grants to individuals and a limited number of projects for travel and research in South Asia in archaeology, art history and related subjects covered by the Trust; and sponsor lectures, seminars, publications and conferences in Cambridge, within the field of the Trust

WHAT IS NOT FUNDED Modern research topics not normally eligible for support. The Trust is restricted to research in the ancient cultures of South Asia and Iran

WHO CAN BENEFIT Scholars and graduate students and recognised projects

WHERE FUNDING CAN BE GIVEN Europe, South Asia

TYPE OF GRANT Small grants to individual research students and scholars, and to selected projects

RANGE OF GRANTS £129–£36,000

SAMPLE GRANTS £36,000 Leverhulme Trust; £22,956 to Kreitman Art Fund; £13,461 to Heritage for library cataloguing; £3,000 to Charles Wallace India Fund; £725 to individuals; £129 to Kreitman Book Fund

FINANCES *Year* 1998 *Income* £94,964

TRUSTEES Dr F R Allchin, Dr B Allchin, N Kreitman, BA, Sir N J Barrington, MA, Prof N J Sims-Williams, Dr G H R Tillotson, A Topsfield, MA, Dr R A E Coningham

PUBLICATIONS *Shahr-i Zohak and the History of the Bamiyan Valley, Afghanistan* P H B Baker and F R Allchin, Ancient India & Iran Trust Series No 1, Tempus Reparatum, 1991, *Crossroads of Asia: transformation in image and symbol in the art of ancient Afghanistan and Pakistan.* Edited by E Errington and J Cribb. Proceedings of the 13th

Biennial Conference of the European Association of South Asian Archaeologists. Brochure, *The Ancient India and Iran Trust*

HOW TO APPLY No application form, enquiries to the address under Who To Apply To in writing including a brief CV, short outline of project and budget

WHO TO APPLY TO Dr B Allchin, AIIT (The Ancient India and Iran Trust), Brooklands House, 23 Brooklands Avenue, Cambridge CB2 2BG

CC NO 276295   **ESTABLISHED** 1978

■ AM Charitable Trust

WHAT IS FUNDED General charitable purposes. The Trustees prefer to provide medium term support for a number of charities already known to them. The Trustees do not feel able to investigate appeals from individuals and therefore do not make grants to individuals

WHAT IS NOT FUNDED No grants to individuals

WHO CAN BENEFIT There are no restrictions on the age; professional and economic group; family situation; religion and culture; and social circumstances of; or disease or medical condition suffered by, the beneficiaries

WHERE FUNDING CAN BE GIVEN UK

RANGE OF GRANTS £60–£25,000

SAMPLE GRANTS £25,000 to Jerusalem Foundation; £5,000 to British Ort; £5,000 to Friends of the Hebrew University of Jerusalem; £5,000 to World Jewish Relief; £2,500 to West London Synagogue; £2,000 to British Heart Foundation; £2,000 to British Technion Society; £2,000 to Cancer Research Campaign; £2,000 to Norwood Ravenswood Child Care; £1,000 to Blond McIndoe Centre for Medical Research

FINANCES *Year* 1997 *Income* £62,953 *Grants* £56,900

TRUSTEES Kleinwort Benson Trustees Limited Directors: D H Benson, D V Clasper, K W Hotchkiss, D J McGilvray

HOW TO APPLY Only successful applicants are notified of the Trustees decision

WHO TO APPLY TO AM Charitable Trust, Kleinwort Benson Trustees Limited, PO Box 191, 10 Fenchurch Street, London EC3M 3LB

CC NO 256283   **ESTABLISHED** 1968

■ The AMW Charitable Trust

WHAT IS FUNDED A broad range of activity is supported including work with the disabled, Christian charities, historic buildings and work with young people

WHAT IS NOT FUNDED Grants are not made to individuals

WHO CAN BENEFIT Organisations benefiting young adults, disabled people and Christians

WHERE FUNDING CAN BE GIVEN Scotland

FINANCES *Year* 1996 *Income* £800,000 *Grants* £200,000

TRUSTEES R W Speirs, C Denholm, Prof R B Jack

HOW TO APPLY Applications in writing to the address below

WHO TO APPLY TO Campbell Denholm, The AMW Charitable Trust, KPMG, 24 Blythswood Square, Glasgow G2 4QS

SC NO SCO 06959   **ESTABLISHED** 1974

■ The AS Charitable Trust

WHAT IS FUNDED The Trust is sympathetic to the following projects: (a) Third world development. (b) Peace making and reconciliation. (c) Christian lay leadership. (d) Christian social action. (e) Charismatic Christian groups involved in any of the above

WHAT IS NOT FUNDED Grants to individuals or large charities are very rare. Such applications are discouraged

WHO CAN BENEFIT Preference for charities of which the Trust has special interest, knowledge or association. Christian organisations will benefit. Support may go to victims of famine, man-made or natural disasters, and war

WHERE FUNDING CAN BE GIVEN UK and overseas

FINANCES *Year* 1995 *Income* £97,552 *Grants* £35,155

TRUSTEES R St George Calvocoressi, C W Brocklebank

WHO TO APPLY TO The Administrator, The AS Charitable Trust, Bixbottom Farm, Henley-on-Thames RG9 6BH *Tel* 01491 577745

CC NO 242190   **ESTABLISHED** 1965

■ The ATP Charitable Trust

WHAT IS FUNDED Educational, religious, medical and social care

WHAT IS NOT FUNDED Expeditions are not funded

WHO CAN BENEFIT Organisations benefiting children, young adults and students, at risk groups, those disadvantaged by poverty and socially isolated people. There is no restriction on the religion of, or the disease or medical condition suffered by, the beneficiaries

WHERE FUNDING CAN BE GIVEN UK

TRUSTEES M R Bentata, J A Bentata, A G A Macfadyen

HOW TO APPLY The Trust welcomes initial telephone calls, but does not issue application forms or guidelines. There are no application deadlines. An sae is appreciated

WHO TO APPLY TO M R Bentata, The APT Charitable Trust, 31 Millharbour, Isle of Dogs, London E14 9TX *Tel* 0171-510 0623

CC NO 328408   **ESTABLISHED** 1989

■ AW Charitable Trust (177)

WHAT IS FUNDED General charitable purposes at Trustees' discretion

WHO CAN BENEFIT There are no restrictions on the age; professional and economic group; family situation; religion and culture; and social circumstances of; or disease or medical condition suffered by, the beneficiaries

WHERE FUNDING CAN BE GIVEN UK and overseas

TYPE OF GRANT At the discretion of the Trustees

FINANCES *Year* 1994–95 *Income* £364,683 *Grants* £590,723

TRUSTEES A Weis, R Weis

WHO TO APPLY TO B Olsberg, AW Charitable Trust, Messrs B Olsberg & Co, 3rd Floor, Barclay House, 35 Whitworth Street West, Manchester M1 5NG

CC NO 283322   **ESTABLISHED** 1961

■ The Aaron Charitable Trust

WHAT IS FUNDED General charitable purposes

WHO CAN BENEFIT There are no restrictions on the age; professional and economic group; family situation; religion and culture; and social circumstances of; or disease or medical condition suffered by, the beneficiaries

WHERE FUNDING CAN BE GIVEN UK and overseas

TRUSTEES P M Emanuel, S T Samuels, Ms G Samuels

WHO TO APPLY TO G Meade, The Aaron Charitable Trust, c/o Hamlin Slowe, Roxburghe House, 273–287 Regent Street, London W1A 4SQ
CC NO 1065844   **ESTABLISHED** 1997

■ Abbey National Charitable Trust

WHAT IS FUNDED (a) Support for equal opportunities for disabled people. (b) Education and employment for disadvantaged/socially excluded groups. This includes arts, culture and recreation; respite shelter; advice and information (housing); infrastructure development; community services; and playschemes. The Trustees prefer to receive requests for modest grants from well established charities to support specific projects

WHAT IS NOT FUNDED Donations will not be given to individuals or for the exclusive benefit of one religious or ethnic grouping. Only bodies or organisations with charitable status will be supported

WHO CAN BENEFIT There is a preference for appeals which will most directly benefit those in need, whether made by national, regional or local charities. Beneficiaries considered for funding include: at risk groups; disabled people; those disadvantaged by poverty; homeless and socially isolated people

WHERE FUNDING CAN BE GIVEN UK

TYPE OF GRANT One-off donations only, mostly capital. Buildings, feasibility studies, project, research, running costs, and start-up costs are also considered. Funding is available for up to one year

RANGE OF GRANTS £250–£20,000

SAMPLE GRANTS £25,000 to Family Policy Studies Centre for research on family issues; £25,000 to Middlesex Young People's Clubs for sport for disabled young people; £25,000 to Prince's Youth Business Trust for employment for disabled people; £20,000 to Almshouse Association for accommodation for disabled people; £20,000 to Barnardos for parenting support

FINANCES *Year* 1997 *Income* £900,000
Grants £900,000

TRUSTEES The Committee

HOW TO APPLY Applications by letter, should include a business plan and audited accounts where appropriate,and can be made at any time. They should be sent to the address under Who To Apply To. Initial telephone enquiries are welcome

WHO TO APPLY TO K J Taylor, DMS, Trust Secretary, Abbey National Charitable Trust, 201 Grafton Gate East, Milton Keynes, Buckinghamshire MK9 1AN *Tel* 01908 341126
CC NO 803655   **ESTABLISHED** 1990

■ Abbeydale Trust

WHAT IS FUNDED Advancement of medical research and education. Preference given to projects in which the Trustees have special interest or knowledge

WHO CAN BENEFIT Individuals, and organisations benefiting children, young adults, medical professionals, research workers, students, teachers and governesses. There is no restriction on the disease or medical condition suffered by the beneficiaries

WHERE FUNDING CAN BE GIVEN UK

SAMPLE GRANTS £10,998 to St George's Hospital Medical School; £3,000 to Birmingham University; £2,950 to Institute of Neurology; £2,000 to Camphill Trust; £1,000 to Cheltenham YFC; £300 to University of London

FINANCES *Year* 1996 *Income* £26,199
Grants £20,248

NOTES Most of the income is already allocated. We regret that unsuccessful applicants cannot be acknowledged

HOW TO APPLY To the address under Who To Apply To

WHO TO APPLY TO The Secretary, Abbeydale Trust, c/o Midland Bank plc, 2 Fargate, Sheffield, South Yorkshire S1 2JS
CC NO 217333   **ESTABLISHED** 1959

■ Abel Charitable Trust

WHAT IS FUNDED Charities working in the fields of: advice and information about housing; care in the community and Christian outreach. Orientating to resolve rather than alleviate problems

WHAT IS NOT FUNDED Applications from individuals, including students, are ineligible. Funds will not be given for building projects or to reduce extant deficits, or for vehicles, or for work with the elderly. No grants made in response to general appeals from large, National organisations

WHO CAN BENEFIT Registered charities benefiting: young adults, unemployed people, Christians, at risk groups, those disadvantaged by poverty and homeless people. Mainly emergent charities aiming to make the individual more self-sufficient and treating the person as a whole and not a malfunctioning part

WHERE FUNDING CAN BE GIVEN London

TYPE OF GRANT Recurring costs, feasibility studies and start-up costs. Funding of up to three years will be considered

RANGE OF GRANTS £200–£3,000, typical grant £1,000

SAMPLE GRANTS £2,000 to Sutton Pastoral Foundation for training teachers for counselling and support in schools; £2,000 to Charterhouse-in-Southwark for recruitment and training educators to teach young about drugs and sexual health issues; £1,500 to Together in Notre Dame for community facilities on Notre Dame Estate, Clapham; £1,500 to St John-at-Hackney for development of 'Drop-In' service; £1,500 to Operation New World for self help education charity for young unemployed

FINANCES *Year* 1996 *Income* £14,000
Grants £27,000

TRUSTEES Rev Canon I Smith-Cameron, The Ven M Baddeley, Rev A R C Arbuthnot

HOW TO APPLY By application during the months November to January

WHO TO APPLY TO The Rev D J Abel, Abel Charitable Trust, Balcombe Mill, Mill Lane, Balcombe, Haywards Heath, West Sussex RH17 6QT
CC NO 288421   **ESTABLISHED** 1983

■ The Aberdeen Endowments Trust

WHAT IS FUNDED Grants are mainly given in the form of bursaries to pupils at selected establishments. Grants are also awarded to organisations which: are educational; promote sport for young people; or give assistance to choirs, orchestras, bands, dramatic groups and the visual arts. The main outgoing is to meet the fees of beneficiaries at Robert Gordon's College

WHO CAN BENEFIT Children and young adults, young sportsmen and women, and musicians

WHERE FUNDING CAN BE GIVEN Aberdeen

FINANCES *Year* 1996 *Income* £620,000 *Grants* £460,000

TRUSTEES N R D Begg, J Cameron, R Clark, W T Fraser, W J Hunter, A C Kennedy, E A Leslie, I A McDonald, N Mackenzie, J A Porter, G S Stephen, Rev J C Stewart, J K A Thomaneck, G Thomson, Miss E F Torrance, M E Watt

PUBLICATIONS An Annual Report and Guidance Notes are available from the Trust

HOW TO APPLY Contact the Clerk at the address below for further details

WHO TO APPLY TO William Russell, Clerk, The Aberdeen Endowments Trust, 19 Albert Street, Aberdeen AB9 1QF

SC NO SCO 10507 **ESTABLISHED** 1739

■ The Henry and Grete Abrahams Charitable Foundation

WHAT IS FUNDED The Trust supports Jewish organisations and medical charities

WHAT IS NOT FUNDED No grants to individuals. Registered charities only

WHO CAN BENEFIT Registered Jewish and medical charities benefiting Jewish people and the sick. There is no restriction on the disease or medical condition suffered by the beneficiaries

WHERE FUNDING CAN BE GIVEN UK and overseas

TYPE OF GRANT Recurring, though amounts vary greatly from one year to the next

RANGE OF GRANTS £100–£5,000

SAMPLE GRANTS £5,000 to St John and Elizabeth Hospice; £1,000 to Cancer Research Campaign; £1,000 to Brainwave; £1,000 to Marie Curie Cancer Care; £1,000 to Cancer Research; £500 to Peter May Memorial Appeal; £250 to BTCV; £200 to Debra Charity; £200 to Imperial Cancer Research; £100 to Sense Charity

FINANCES *Year* 1996–97 *Income* £26,050 *Grants* £10,350

TRUSTEES Mrs G Abrahams, MBE, M H Gluckstein, D M Maislish

HOW TO APPLY Applications to the address under Who To Apply To in writing

WHO TO APPLY TO Mrs G Abrahams, The Henry and Grete Abrahams Charitable Foundation, 23 Chelwood House, Gloucester Square, London W2 2SY

CC NO 265517 **ESTABLISHED** 1973

■ The Henry and Grete Abrahams 2nd Charitable Foundation

WHAT IS FUNDED General charitable purposes. The Trust supports a wide range of charitable projects including the disabled and disadvantaged young people

WHAT IS NOT FUNDED No grants to individuals or non-registered charities

WHO CAN BENEFIT There are no restrictions on the age; professional and economic group; family situation; religion and culture; and social circumstances of; or disease or medical condition suffered by, the beneficiaries. At the discretion of the Trustees

WHERE FUNDING CAN BE GIVEN UK and overseas

TYPE OF GRANT At the discretion of the Trustees

RANGE OF GRANTS £250–£39,000

SAMPLE GRANTS £39,000 to Wingate Youth Trust; £12,500 to WIZO; £10,000 to Royal Star and Garter Home; £1,000 to Liberal Jewish Synagogue; £1,000 to Nightingale House; £250 to Police Foundation

FINANCES *Year* 1996–97 *Income* £58,044 *Grants* £63,750

TRUSTEES Mrs G Abrahams, Mark Gluckstien, David Maislish

WHO TO APPLY TO Mrs G Abrahams, The Henry and Grete Abrahams 2nd Charitable Foundation, 23 Chelwood House, Gloucester Square, London W2 2SY

CC NO 298240 **ESTABLISHED** 1987

■ Brian Abrams Charitable Trust

WHAT IS FUNDED To support Jewish organisations

WHAT IS NOT FUNDED No grants to individuals

WHO CAN BENEFIT Jewish organisations

WHERE FUNDING CAN BE GIVEN UK, Israel

RANGE OF GRANTS £100–£8,000

SAMPLE GRANTS £8,000 to ITRI Foundations; £7,500 to the Friends of the Centre for Torah Education; £6,000 to Halacha Lemoshe Trust; £5,400 to Jewish Philanthropic Association for Israel and the Middle East; £5,000 to Friends of Ohr Ahiva Institution; £4,500 to Rabbi Nachman of Breslov Charitable Foundation; £750 to King David School; £700 to The Charity Service; £625 to DFS Extension Charitable Trust; £500 to Community Security Trust

FINANCES *Year* 1996 *Income* £39,358 *Grants* £40,275

TRUSTEES Betty Abrams, Brian Abrams, Eric Abrams, Gertrude Abrams

HOW TO APPLY To the address under Who To Apply To in writing

WHO TO APPLY TO R A Taylor, Brian Abrams Charitable Trust, Alexander Layton, Chartered Accountants, 130–132 Nantwich Road, Crewe, Cheshire CW2 6AZ

CC NO 275941 **ESTABLISHED** 1978

■ Eric Abrams Charitable Trust

WHAT IS FUNDED To support Jewish organisations

WHAT IS NOT FUNDED No grants to individuals

WHO CAN BENEFIT Jewish organisations

WHERE FUNDING CAN BE GIVEN UK, Israel

RANGE OF GRANTS £100–£8,000

SAMPLE GRANTS £8,000 to ITRI Foundation; £7,500 to the Friends of the Centre for Torah Education; £6,000 to Halacha Lemoshe Trust; £5,000 to Jewish Philanthropic Association for Israel and the Middle East; £5,000 to Friends of Ohr Akiva Institution; £4,500 to Rabbi Nachman of Breslov Charitable Foundation; £1,500 to the Charity Service; £750 to King David School; £625 to DFS Extension Charitable Trust; £500 to Community Security Trust

FINANCES *Year* 1996 *Income* £38,864 *Grants* £40,275

TRUSTEES Betty Abrams, Brian Abrams, Eric Abrams, Gertrude Abrams

HOW TO APPLY To the address under Who To Apply To in writing

WHO TO APPLY TO R A Taylor, Eric Abrams Charitable Trust, Alexander Layton, Chartered Accountants, 130–132 Nantwich Road, Crewe, Cheshire CW2 6AZ *Tel* 01270 213475

CC NO 275939 **ESTABLISHED** 1978

■ Acacia Charitable Trust

WHAT IS FUNDED Educational and medical charities in the UK. Jewish charities, both in UK and the State of Israel

WHAT IS NOT FUNDED No grants to individuals

WHO CAN BENEFIT Registered charities benefiting children, young adults and Jewish people. Support may be given to medical professionals, teachers, governesses and students. There is no restriction on the disease or medical condition suffered by the beneficiaries

WHERE FUNDING CAN BE GIVEN UK and Israel

RANGE OF GRANTS £10–£31,000

SAMPLE GRANTS £31,000 to University of Reading; £27,000 to CBF World Jewish Relief; £6,500 to UK JAID; £2,000 to Jewish Care; £1,715 to Spanish and Portuguese Jews Congregation; £1,500 to the British Museum; £1,000 to Fine Art Trust; £1,000 to Immanuel College; £1,000 to Jews College London; £1,000 to Ravenswood Foundation

FINANCES *Year* 1997 *Income* £117,423
Grants £79,330

TRUSTEES K D Rubens, OBE, Mrs A G Rubens, S A Rubens

WHO TO APPLY TO Nora Howland, Secretary, Acacia Charitable Trust, 104 Wigmore Street, London W1H 9DR

CC NO 274275   **ESTABLISHED** 1977

■ Access 4 Trust

WHAT IS FUNDED Trustees focus their grant-giving primarily towards deprived children and needy families, women's organisations and adoption

WHAT IS NOT FUNDED No grants to individuals

WHO CAN BENEFIT Institutions and registered charities benefiting deprived children and needy families

WHERE FUNDING CAN BE GIVEN UK and newly developing countries

TYPE OF GRANT Single donations

FINANCES *Year* 1998 *Income* £54,473
Grants £171,846

TRUSTEES Miss S M Wates, J R F Lulham

HOW TO APPLY Apply in writing

WHO TO APPLY TO C W Sudlow, Access 4 Trust, 7 St James's Square, London SW1Y 7JU
Tel 0171-930 7621

CC NO 267017   **ESTABLISHED** 1973

■ Achiezer Association Limited

WHAT IS FUNDED People and institutions of the Orthodox Jewish religion, for: the relief of the aged, impotent and poor; advancement of education; advancement of religion; and general charitable purposes

WHO CAN BENEFIT Organisations benefiting Orthodox Jewish people, the elderly, academics, rabbis, students, teachers and governesses and those disadvantaged by poverty

WHERE FUNDING CAN BE GIVEN UK

FINANCES *Year* 1996–97 *Income* £261,908
Grants £248,864

TRUSTEES S Cherkow, A Chontow, J A Chontow

WHO TO APPLY TO D Chontow, Achiezer Association Limited, 132 Clapton Common, London E5 9AG

CC NO 255031   **ESTABLISHED** 1965

■ The Acorn Foundation

WHAT IS FUNDED Funds distributed for the benefit of the poorest people in any country of the world for the alleviation of poverty

WHO CAN BENEFIT Organisations benefiting those disadvantaged by poverty

WHERE FUNDING CAN BE GIVEN UK and overseas

TYPE OF GRANT Range of grants

FINANCES *Year* 1998 *Income* £75,478
Grants £21,699

TRUSTEES Dr P F Sands, Mrs E Edwards

NOTES The affairs of the foundation are conducted on a Christian basis

WHO TO APPLY TO M E E Wood, The Acorn Foundation, 12 Church Street, Rickmansworth, Hertfordshire WD3 1BS

CC NO 252153   **ESTABLISHED** 1966

■ Action for Blind People (formerly London Association for the Blind)

WHAT IS FUNDED To provide a grants-in-aid scheme to assist individuals of all ages, throughout the United Kingdom; where additional cash help is the most appropriate response to need. The scheme is part of a comprehensive service of general information and welfare benefits advice and casework support

WHAT IS NOT FUNDED Applicants for cash grants must be registered blind or partially sighted. Grants should be applied for through a statutory or voluntary agency

WHO CAN BENEFIT Registered blind and partially sighted people, and organisations benefiting the blind and partially sighted

WHERE FUNDING CAN BE GIVEN UK

TYPE OF GRANT Special one-off payments for specific items and low income grants paid in a lump sum to generally boost income. Criteria governing purpose and amount are published

FINANCES *Year* 1997 *Income* £9,429,000
Grants £452,000

TRUSTEES The Council: G D Neely, MA, FCA (Chair), Miss M M Biggart (Vice Chair), R P Gent, BA, FCA (Hon Treasurer), M Brace, K Deatker, W B Harding, Miss P Hart, MBE, BA, J C Jorgensen, Mrs K M Magnurson, M A F Newton, MA, B H Pearce, CBE, Mrs J L Smith, MA, P P M Wiesner

PUBLICATIONS Annual Report, Handbook of Services for Blind and Partially Sighted People, Newsletter

NOTES During 1997, £10,000 was given to the National Deaf Blind League

HOW TO APPLY By way of a simple application form for individuals (through local voluntary organisations or Social Services Department). At any time

WHO TO APPLY TO Grants Officer, Action for Blind People, 14–16 Verney Road, London SE16 3DZ

CC NO 205913   **ESTABLISHED** 1888

■ Action Research

WHAT IS FUNDED With the exception of cancer, cardiovascular and HIV/AIDs research, we support basic and clinical research leading to the (a) prevention of disability, regardless of cause or age group and (b) alleviation of existing physical handicap. Areas this Trust will consider funding are: medical studies and research; professional and specialist training under special schemes; and physics applied to medicine

WHAT IS NOT FUNDED Strictly limited to direct support of medical research. We do not support other charities. This Trust will not support basic and clinical research into cancer, cardiovascular and HIV/AIDs

WHO CAN BENEFIT University departments, hospitals and research institutes benefiting: people of all ages; medical professionals; research workers and scientists; at risk groups; and disabled people. There are few restrictions (named above) on the disease or medical condition suffered by the beneficiaries

WHERE FUNDING CAN BE GIVEN UK

TYPE OF GRANT Project grants, salaries, and competitive Research Training Fellowship scheme which is advertised annually in November. Funding is for up to or more than three years

SAMPLE GRANTS £92,350 to Brunel Institute for Bioengineering, Brunel University over eighteen months for the development of an active urine collection device; £68,493 to Department of Nephrology, Birmingham Children's Hospital and University of Birmingham and Queen Elizabeth Hospital, Birmingham over one year to study verocytotoxin-producing E. coli-induced Haemolytic syndrome; £66,365 to Department of Obstetrics and Gynaecology, University of Edinburgh, a three year fellowship to study the role of chemokines in cervical ripening and the potential implications for early diagnosis of premature labour; £48,990 to Department of Child Health, University Hospital, Nottingham and a number of other institutions over two years for a follow-up study of school children who were born prematurely; £40,862 to Departments of Haematology and Paediatrics, Imperial College School of Medicine, Hammersmith Hospital over one year for an investigation into the haemopoietic basis of the common problems of preterm babies; £33,821 to Department of Medical Physics and Bioengineering, University College London, and the Dental Institute, Royal London Hospital over one year for facial growth studies in relationship to the treatment of hemifacial microsomia & additional facial anomalies; £28,814 to Department of Medical Physics and Bioengineering, University College London over one year to investigate the feasibility of a new method for controlling stimulators which enable paraplegics to stand; £18,518 to Departments of Rheumatology and Pathological Sciences, University of Manchester and Manchester Royal Infirmary over one year for preliminary studies of the role of gonadal steroids in male osteoporosis; £9,982 to Department of Psychology, University of Leicester over five months for a study of virtual reality for disabled children; £3,660 to Bone & Joint Movement Research Group, University of Derby and Derbyshire Royal Infirmary over two years for the evaluation of Colles fracture hand therapy

FINANCES *Year* 1997 *Income* £4,617,943
Grants £4,377,152

TRUSTEES The Council of Management

PUBLICATIONS *Research in Action*

HOW TO APPLY Applicants for a project grant should submit a preliminary written outline and estimate of funding sought to assess acceptability. Closing dates are mid March, July and November

WHO TO APPLY TO Dr Tracy Swinfield, PhD, Head of Research Administration, Action Research, Vincent House, Horsham, West Sussex RH12 2DP *Tel* 01403 210406

CC NO 208701   **ESTABLISHED** 1952

■ The Acts Foundation

WHAT IS FUNDED General charitable purposes. The Trust states that What Is Funded is confidential

WHO CAN BENEFIT There are no restrictions on the age; professional and economic group; family situation; religion and culture; and social circumstances of; or disease or medical condition suffered by, the beneficiaries

WHERE FUNDING CAN BE GIVEN Overseas

FINANCES *Year* 1997 *Income* £18,453

TRUSTEES A K Watson, R H Eames

HOW TO APPLY **This Trust states that it does not respond to unsolicited applications**

WHO TO APPLY TO R H Eames, The Acts Foundation, The Well, 105 High Street, Stourbridge, West Midlands DY8 1EE

CC NO 326353   **ESTABLISHED** 1983

■ Franklin Adams Trust Foundation

This trust did not respond to CAF's request to amend its entry and, by 30 June 1998, CAF's researchers did not find financial records for later than 1995 on its file at the Charity Commission. Trusts are legally required to submit annual accounts to the Charity Commission under section 42 of the Charities Act 1993

WHAT IS FUNDED The furtherance of the study and practice of community medicine to enable student doctors or nurses or others, to be trained or otherwise assisted

WHO CAN BENEFIT Student doctors or nurses

WHERE FUNDING CAN BE GIVEN UK and overseas

TYPE OF GRANT At the discretion of the Trustees

TRUSTEES John I Franklin-Adams, James M Henderson, Thomas A Rudge

WHO TO APPLY TO Dr A J Copping, Chairman of Trustees, Franklin Adams Trust Foundation, 4 Grove Avenue, Coombe Dingle, Bristol BS9 2RN

CC NO 314191   **ESTABLISHED** 1973

■ The Adamson Trust

WHAT IS FUNDED Groups who organise holidays for needy children and individual children under the age of sixteen are given grants

WHO CAN BENEFIT Needy children, both groups and individuals

WHERE FUNDING CAN BE GIVEN Scotland

FINANCES *Year* 1996 *Income* £500,000
Grants £400,000

HOW TO APPLY Applications should be made in writing to the address below and must include details about the organisation, the proposed holiday and the numbers of children who would benefit

WHO TO APPLY TO Neil Drysdale, The Adamson Trust, Messrs Drysdale Anderson WS, 14 Comrie Street, Crieff, Perthshire PH7 4AZ

SC NO SCO 37871   **ESTABLISHED** 1946

■ The Victor Adda Foundation

WHAT IS FUNDED This Trust mainly supports the Fan Museum in Greenwich

WHERE FUNDING CAN BE GIVEN UK, in practice Greenwich

RANGE OF GRANTS £500–£52,095

SAMPLE GRANTS £52,095 to The Fan Museum Trust; £500 to Child Trust

FINANCES *Year* 1997 *Income* £240,441
Grants £52,595

TRUSTEES A V Alexander, CBE, Mrs H E Alexander, Mrs B E Hodgkinson, M I Gee, N H Smith

8

Think carefully about every application. Is it justified?

HOW TO APPLY To the address under Who To Apply To in writing

WHO TO APPLY TO A V Alexander, CBE, The Victor Adda Foundation, c/o Kleinwort Benson Trustees, PO Box 191, 10 Fenchurch Street, London EC3M 3LB

CC NO 291456 **ESTABLISHED** 1984

■ Addiscombe Neighbourhood Care Association (otherwise known as ANCA)

WHAT IS FUNDED The relief of the poor and needy and other general charitable purposes

WHO CAN BENEFIT Organisations benefiting at risk groups, those disadvantaged by poverty and socially isolated people. Otherwise, there are no restrictions on the age; professional and economic group; family situation; religion and culture; and social circumstances of; or disease or medical condition suffered by, the beneficiaries

WHERE FUNDING CAN BE GIVEN In practice Addiscombe, Croydon

FINANCES *Year* 1997 *Income* £13,219

NOTES No grants were awarded in 1997. Income was spent on projects such as shopping bus, social events for clients, staff salaries and Extend

WHO TO APPLY TO C Rutter, Addiscombe Neighbourhood Care Association, The Green Room, St Mildred's Hall, Bingham Road, Addiscombe, Croydon CRO 7EB

CC NO 1031601 **ESTABLISHED** 1993

■ Adenfirst Ltd

WHAT IS FUNDED Jewish organisations are exclusively supported

WHAT IS NOT FUNDED The Trust supports only Jewish organisations

WHO CAN BENEFIT Jews

WHERE FUNDING CAN BE GIVEN UK and overseas

RANGE OF GRANTS Below £1,000–£10,000

SAMPLE GRANTS £10,000 to Beis Yaakov Chassidic Seminary; £10,000 to Friends of United Institutions of Arad; £10,000 to Merkaz Mosdos Chinuch L'Bonos Ashdod; £8,000 to Kintergarden and Dormitory Network; £6,400 to Friends of Achiezer- Arad; £6,160 to Colel Polen Kupath Ramban; £5,000 to Bnei Emes Institute; £5,000 to Eli Siach Handicapped Homes; £5,000 to Friends of Harim Establishments; £4,000 to Central Charity Fund

FINANCES *Year* 1996 *Income* £76,608 *Grants* £93,153

TRUSTEES Mrs H F Bond, I M Cymerman, Mrs R Cymerman

NOTES The Trustees do not encourage unsolicited applications

HOW TO APPLY To the address under Who To Apply To in writing

WHO TO APPLY TO I M Cymerman, Governor, Adenfirst Ltd, 99 Grove Green Road, London E11 4EF

CC NO 291647 **ESTABLISHED** 1984

■ The Adint Charitable Trust (261 =)

This trust declined to meet CAF's researchers and failed to supply a copy of its annual report and accounts to CAF as required under section 47(2) of the Charities Act 1993. The information held on file at the Charity Commission was insufficient to enable CAF's researchers to write a substantive commentary on the trust's activities. Accordingly, despite its size, we are unable to list this trust in Spotlight on Major Trusts

WHAT IS FUNDED General charitable purposes. Grants to registered charities only

WHAT IS NOT FUNDED Grants may be made to registered charities only. No applications from individuals can be entertained under any circumstances

WHO CAN BENEFIT Registered charities only. There are no restrictions on the age; professional and economic group; family situation; religion and culture; and social circumstances of; or disease or medical condition suffered by, the beneficiaries

WHERE FUNDING CAN BE GIVEN UK

FINANCES *Year* 1995 *Income* £335,983 *Grants* £338,194

TRUSTEES Mrs M Edwards, A E Edwards, A A Davis, Mrs D Jeffery, D R Oram

WHO TO APPLY TO A A Davis, The Adint Charitable Trust, c/o BDO Stoy Hayward, 8 Baker Street, London W1M 1DA

CC NO 265290 **ESTABLISHED** 1973

■ The Adnams Charity

WHAT IS FUNDED Welfare, including community facilities and services, well woman clinics and hostels; education and training to include secondary schools and special needs education; humanities covering various arts and cultural activities, opera and dance; environmental resources; and other charitable purposes

WHAT IS NOT FUNDED No grants to individuals, students or national charities

WHO CAN BENEFIT Small local projects, innovative projects benefiting: retired people; volunteers; disabled people; those disadvantaged by poverty; and ex-offenders and those at risk of offending. Also homeless people, those living in rural areas and victims of abuse and domestic violence will be considered

WHERE FUNDING CAN BE GIVEN Within a 25-mile radius of Southwold (strictly)

TYPE OF GRANT One-off, buildings, capital, project, research and start-up costs will be considered. Funding may be given for up to one year

RANGE OF GRANTS £250–£1,500

SAMPLE GRANTS £8,000 to RSPB for the creation of a dipping pond; £5,000 to Framlington Thomas Mills School for a school maths block

FINANCES *Year* 1996 *Income* £31,000 *Grants* £31,000

TRUSTEES B Segrave-Daly, S P D Loftus, J P A Adnams, R J Nicholson, M Horn, A Rous

PUBLICATIONS Annual Report

HOW TO APPLY Trustees meet quarterly. Applications for specific grants in writing

WHO TO APPLY TO Mrs E M Utting, The Adnams Charity, Sole Bay Brewery, Southwold, Suffolk IP18 6JW *Tel* 01502 727200 *Fax* 01502 727201

CC NO 1000203 **ESTABLISHED** 1990

Does the trust you have chosen match your needs? Haphazard applications waste postage and time

9

■ Africa Advocacy Foundation

WHAT IS FUNDED Relief of poverty and sickness, particularly within the African community in Greater London; protection and preservation of health; relief of those suffering from severe shock or depression as a result of dislocation or illness among family and friends; advancement of education of children through events featuring African music, dance and drama; provision of facilities for recreation and leisure time, particularly by the provision of a community centre; and relief of the elderly and disabled

WHO CAN BENEFIT Organisations benefiting the elderly, the African community in Greater London, disabled people and those disadvantaged by poverty. There is no restriction on the disease or medical condition suffered by the beneficiaries, however, particular favour is given to those suffering from mental illness

WHERE FUNDING CAN BE GIVEN In practice, Greater London

FINANCES *Year* 1997 *Income* £15,243

TRUSTEES Ms T Darko, Ms C Harriet, Ms S Kakaji, N Karema, K Kiwanuko, Ms R Nantongo, T Ofosu, Ms M Sengooda, A Shifferaw, R Williams

WHO TO APPLY TO N Karema, Africa Advocacy Foundation, 4 Crowndale Centre, 218 Eversholt Sreet, London NW1 1BD

CC NO 1059268   **ESTABLISHED** 1996

■ Age Concern Eastwood

WHAT IS FUNDED The welfare of elderly people

WHO CAN BENEFIT To benefit elderly individuals

WHERE FUNDING CAN BE GIVEN Eastwood and district

TYPE OF GRANT Recurring

FINANCES *Year* 1994–95 *Income* £15,370 *Grants* £14,962

WHO TO APPLY TO C Dyson, Age Concern Eastwood, 6 Queens Drive, Brinsley, Nottinghamshire NG16 5DF

CC NO 518442   **ESTABLISHED** 1952

■ Aid to the Church in Need (United Kingdom)

WHAT IS FUNDED To meet needs in the Church wherever there is oppression or suffering including funding for: Christian education; missionaries and evangelists; Catholic umbrella bodies; and scholarships

WHO CAN BENEFIT Persecuted, oppressed and poor Christians, especially Roman Catholics, Russian Orthodox and refugees

WHERE FUNDING CAN BE GIVEN Mainly Eastern Europe and overseas

SAMPLE GRANTS £25,000 to Keston, Moscow, Russia for running a Christian News Agency in Moscow; £22,273 to Société des Missions Entrangères, Paris for seminarians, novices, chapels, etc in Asia; £16,190 to Société des Missions Entrangères, Paris for chapel, presbytary, etc in Burma; £10,278 to Holy Ghost Parish, Nigeria for vehicles/transport; £8,138 to Diocese of Mahenge, Tanzania for construction of formation centre; £7,500 to Diocese of Mopti, Mali for transport; £6,303 to Youth Apostelate Office, Uganda for Aids Campaign and Catholic education; £6,266 to Ameca Pastoral Institute, Kenya for repairs and renovations; £6,170 to Carmel, Philippines for repairs to buildings; £6,040 to Société des Missions Entrangères, Hong Kong for construction of a church

FINANCES *Year* 1997 *Income* £2,157,302 *Grants* £1,715,426

TRUSTEES The members of the Board

PUBLICATIONS *ACN Mirror*

NOTES Please note: (a) The focus of this Charity is on the Church overseas. (b) Individuals without the backing as required under How To Apply may not apply for funding

HOW TO APPLY All applications by individuals must have the backing of a Bishop or Religious Superior. Grants are reviewed by the International Secretariat in Königstein, Germany

WHO TO APPLY TO Mrs Mavis Perris, Grants Co-ordinator, Aid to the Church in Need, 1 Times Square, Sutton, Surrey SM1 1LF *Tel* 0181-642 8668 *Fax* 0181-661 6293

CC NO 265582   **ESTABLISHED** 1972

■ Green and Lilian F M Ainsworth and Family Benevolent Fund

WHAT IS FUNDED The Trustees have a comprehensive list of charitable objects from whom they select each year. Other applicants are made secondary to these preferred charities, including those supporting the young, elderly and the handicapped

WHAT IS NOT FUNDED Payments to registered charities only considered. The Trustees do not sponsor individuals but preference for secondary awards is given to charities whose work is in the North West of England

WHO CAN BENEFIT The young, the elderly and the handicapped preferred

WHERE FUNDING CAN BE GIVEN North West England

RANGE OF GRANTS £250–£1,400

SAMPLE GRANTS £1,400 to Benevolent Fund of Chartered Accountants; £1,400 to RSPCA; £1,400 to British Heart Foundation; £1,400 to RNLI; £1,400 to RNIB; £1,400 to NSPCC; £1,400 to Barnardo's; £1,400 to Help the Aged; £1,000 to Kirkgate Centre Trust, Cockermouth; £1,000 to Motability, North West

FINANCES *Year* 1996 *Income* £31,689 *Grants* £14,450

TRUSTEES The Royal Bank of Scotland plc

WHO TO APPLY TO Preston Trustee Office, Green and Lilian F M Ainsworth and Family Benevolent Fund, The Royal Bank of Scotland plc, Guildhall House, Guildhall Street, Preston, Lancashire PR1 3NU

CC NO 267577   **ESTABLISHED** 1974

■ The Air Charities Trust

WHAT IS FUNDED The advancement of education in all branches of aviation, especially the promotion of safety. It is the practice of the Trust to make grants only to charities linked with the work of the

Guild of Air Pilots and Air Navigators of the the City of London

WHO CAN BENEFIT Charities linked with the work of the Guild of Air Pilots and Air Navigators of the the City of London

WHERE FUNDING CAN BE GIVEN UK

FINANCES *Year* 1994–95 *Income* £121,056 *Grants* £133,000

TRUSTEES Sir Michael Cobham, CBE, C Ray Jeffs, OBE

HOW TO APPLY To the address under Who To Apply To in writing

WHO TO APPLY TO Mr Thom, The Air Charities Trust, Messrs Wilsons, Solicitors, Steynings House, Fisherton Street, Salisbury, Wiltshire SP2 7RJ

CC NO 286915   **ESTABLISHED** 1983

■ Airflow Charity Ltd

WHAT IS FUNDED The advancement of education, the relief of poverty, disabled and any other charitable purposes

WHAT IS NOT FUNDED Holidays, expeditions, and scholarships are not funded. No grants to individuals

WHO CAN BENEFIT Favours the needy and disabled, smaller charities within the geographical area. Especially organisations benefiting children and young adults, those disadvantaged by poverty and disabled people

WHERE FUNDING CAN BE GIVEN Buckinghamshire, Berkshire and Oxfordshire

TYPE OF GRANT One-off generally

RANGE OF GRANTS £100–£350

TRUSTEES I J Anderson, G C Arnold, W H Beglow, B C Blackburn, A N Blond, K R Burroughs, K E Dear, P M Downing, M J Graham, K C Miller, A J Nixon, D I Peckett, S Smith, S J Stevens, J W Wallace, K Wright

NOTES Quarterly meetings held in late January, April, July and October

HOW TO APPLY In writing

WHO TO APPLY TO W H Beglow, Company Secretary, Airflow Charity Ltd, Airflow, Lancaster Road, Cressex Business Park, High Wycombe, Buckinghamshire HP12 3QP *Tel* 01494 525252

CC NO 1069338   **ESTABLISHED** 1998

■ The Sylvia Aitken Charitable Trust

WHAT IS FUNDED Higher and further education establishments, children's charities and medical research bodies

WHO CAN BENEFIT To benefit children, young adults, students and researchers. There is no restriction on the disease or medical condition suffered by the beneficiaries

WHERE FUNDING CAN BE GIVEN UK, with a preference for Scotland

SAMPLE GRANTS £47,000 to University of Wales; £14,354 to Glasgow University; £12,500 to Respiratory Diseases Research; £10,000 to Kind Charity; £10,000 to Variety Club Children's Charity; £5,000 to Friends of the Lake District

FINANCES *Year* 1996 *Income* £140,000 *Grants* £90,000

TRUSTEES Mrs S M Aitken, J Ferguson

HOW TO APPLY To the address under Who To Apply To in writing

WHO TO APPLY TO Jim Ferguson, Trust Administrator, The Sylvia Aitken Charitable Trust, Hacker Young, Chartered Accountants, 4 Royal Crescent, Glasgow G3 7SL

SC NO SCO 10556   **ESTABLISHED** 1985

■ The Ajahma Charitable Trust

WHAT IS FUNDED Development; health, especially campaigning, advocacy and counselling; disability; poverty; women's issues; family planning; human rights; and social need

WHAT IS NOT FUNDED No support for overseas projects where the charity has an income of **less than £350,000 pa**; any charity with an income of **more than £4 million pa**; individuals; groups with a religious bias; the arts; medical research; buildings; equipment; animal rights and welfare or local groups (unless there is a demonstrated potential for wider application)

WHO CAN BENEFIT There are no restrictions on the age or the social circumstances of the beneficiaries

WHERE FUNDING CAN BE GIVEN UK and overseas

TYPE OF GRANT Core costs, project and salaries. Funding is available for up to three years

SAMPLE GRANTS £23,375 to One World Action for democracy rights and development work; £23,200 to Co-operation For Development, setting up new regional development strategies in Middle East, South and West Africa and Caribbean; £23,000 to Results Education to fund post of National Director; £20,460 to Action on Disability and Development for a mobility programme in East Africa; £20,000 to Action Health 2000 providing core funding; £17,000 to City Dysphasic Group for self advocacy and aphasia project and £2,000 towards cost of a fundraiser; £16,185 to International Health Exchange for 'Winning Over the NHS' Project; £13,899 to VSO for projects in Nigeria and Ghana; £12,000 to UNICEF for study on breastmilk substitutes; £11,184 to Oxfam for projects in Ghana and Samagra Grameena Ashram

FINANCES *Year* 1996–97 *Income* £155,523 *Grants* £314,803

TRUSTEES Ms J Sheridan, Dr E Simpson, J S Taylor, M Horsman

WHO TO APPLY TO Suzanne Hunt, Administrator, The Ajahma Charitable Trust, 4 Jephtha Road, London SW18 1QH

CC NO 273823   **ESTABLISHED** 1977

■ The Alabaster Trust

WHAT IS FUNDED General charitable purposes, particularly the advancement of the Christian faith

WHO CAN BENEFIT Organisations benefiting Christians

WHERE FUNDING CAN BE GIVEN UK and overseas

FINANCES *Year* 1997 *Income* £71,872 *Grants* £29,530

TRUSTEES G A Kendrick, Mrs F Forster, D Fellingham, Mrs J Kendrick

WHO TO APPLY TO J R Caldine, Accountant, The Alabaster Trust, 1 The Avenue, Eastbourne, East Sussex BN21 3YA

CC NO 1050568   **ESTABLISHED** 1995

■ The Albin-Dyer Bermondsey and Rotherhithe Foundation

WHAT IS FUNDED Relief of poverty and sickness and other general charitable purposes for the benefit of the community of Bermondsey and Rotherhithe

WHO CAN BENEFIT To benefit those disadvantaged by poverty. There is no restriction on the disease or medical condition suffered by the beneficiaries

WHERE FUNDING CAN BE GIVEN Bermondsey and Rotherhithe

TRUSTEES B G Albin-Dyer, F G Collins, P Darnell, J P Fletcher

WHO TO APPLY TO D M Lloyd, The Albin-Dyer Bermondsey and Rotherhithe Foundation, The Old Forge, High St, Stanwell Vilage, Staines, Middlesex TW19 7JR

CC NO 1067137   **ESTABLISHED** 1998

■ D G Albright Charitable Trust

WHAT IS FUNDED General charitable purposes

WHAT IS NOT FUNDED No grants to individuals or students

WHO CAN BENEFIT There are no restrictions on the age; professional and economic group; family situation; religion and culture; and social circumstances of; or disease or medical condition suffered by, the beneficiaries

WHERE FUNDING CAN BE GIVEN UK

TYPE OF GRANT One-off and recurrent

RANGE OF GRANTS £500–£5,000

SAMPLE GRANTS £5,000 to St Luke's Hospital for the Clergy; £3,000 to the Haven Trust; £2,000 to Gloucestershire Macmillan Cancer Service; £2,000 to the Children's Society; £2,000 to SSAFA Gloucestershire branch; £2,000 to St Andrew's Trust; £2,000 to RNIB Talking Books Service; £2,000 to PCC of Bromesberrow; £2,000 to Cheshire Homes of Gloucestershire; £1,000 to British Trust for the Ecumenical Institute

FINANCES *Year* 1997 *Income* £42,914
Grants £30,500

TRUSTEES Hon Dr G Greenall, R G Wood

WHO TO APPLY TO M J Huxley, D G Albright Charitable Trust, Johnstone Kemp Tooley Ltd, Central House, Medwin Walk, Horsham, West Sussex RH12 1AG

CC NO 277367   **ESTABLISHED** 1978

■ Aldgate and Allhallows Barking Exhibition Foundation

WHAT IS FUNDED Projects which are: initiated by schools that will enhance the National Curriculum; aimed at improving literacy and numeracy; or aimed at promoting the study of science, mathematics and the arts. Preference is given to: original developments, which are not yet part of the regular activities of an organisation; developments that are either strategic, such as practical initiatives directed towards addressing the root causes of problems, or seminal, because they seek to influence policy and practice elsewhere

WHAT IS NOT FUNDED Grants are not given for: the purchase, repair or refurbishment of buildings; basic equipment or teachers salaries, which are the responsibility of the education authorities; performances, exhibitions or festivals; youth projects or foreign travel; conferences or seminars; university or medical research; establishing funds for bursary or loans schemes; stage, film, video production costs, or commercial publications; mother tongue teaching; retrospective grants to help pay off overdrafts or loans, nor will the Foundation remedy the withdrawal or reduction of statutory funding

WHO CAN BENEFIT Schools and organisations that benefit children and young people under the age of 25, and students who have lived or worked in the City of London or Tower Hamlets for at least three years, and who are studying for a recognised qualification

WHERE FUNDING CAN BE GIVEN City of London and the London Borough of Tower Hamlets

FINANCES *Year* 1997 *Income* £231,939
Grants £190,407

NOTES The Foundation will only consider applications for specific projects where it is clear what purposes and activities grant aid is being sought

HOW TO APPLY Initial enquiries should be in the form of a letter, including details about: the organisation, its aims and objectives, legal status, brief history, staffing and management committee; a detailed financial statement for the current year listing the organisation's main source of income and expenditure; the exact purpose for which the funding is being sought, including information on who should benefit from the project; the amount required, with a breakdown of how this amount has been arrived at; information about other sources of income for the particular project proposal, if any; and plans for evaluating the results of the project (the Foundation regards this as an important element to any proposal and will always require a report on the work undertaken by organisations in receipt of grant support). These should be accompanied by: a copy of the organisation's constitution, (if applicable); the most recent Annual Report and audited Accounts; a contact name, address and telephone number; and the names of the people who will implement the project

WHO TO APPLY TO Clerk to the Governors, Aldgate and Allhallows Barking Exhibition Foundation, 31 Jewry Street, London EC3N 2EY

CC NO 312500   **ESTABLISHED** 1893

■ The Aldgate Freedom Foundation

WHAT IS FUNDED Hospitals

WHAT IS NOT FUNDED Expeditions, scholarships

WHO CAN BENEFIT Organisations benefiting older people

WHERE FUNDING CAN BE GIVEN Freedom part of the Parish of St Botolph, Aldgate

TYPE OF GRANT One-off. Funding of up to one year will be considered

RANGE OF GRANTS £100–£250

SAMPLE GRANTS £18,000 to St Botolphs Church Project for help for homeless; £500 to Royal London Hospital for specific hospital needs; £250 to St Bartholomews Hospital for specific hospital needs; £250 to Whitechapel Mission for homeless, poor and needy; £250 to Jewish Care for homeless, poor and needy; £250 Royal London Hospital for specific hospital projects; £250 to London Hospital for specific hospital projects; £250 to Mildmay Mission for specific hospital projects; £250 to St Andrews Hospital for specific hospital projects; £250 to Nari Samity for poor and needy

FINANCES *Year* 1996 *Income* £31,111

TRUSTEES Rev B J Lee (Chairman), W H Dove, Miss E Crowther, J W Marshall, S J Rowbotham, P Groom, C A Jones, Ms M Everingham

HOW TO APPLY To the address under Who To Apply To in writing

WHO TO APPLY TO H L Gledhill, Clerk to the Governers, The Aldgate Freedom Foundation, St Botolph's Church, Aldgate, London EC3N 1AB *Tel* 0171-283 1670

CC NO 207047   **ESTABLISHED** 1962

■ Aldridge Charitable Trust

WHAT IS FUNDED The provision of facilities and equipment for physically and mentally handicapped children

WHO CAN BENEFIT Physically and mentally handicapped children

WHERE FUNDING CAN BE GIVEN UK

TRUSTEES E Aldridge, A Hawkins, M Hurst

HOW TO APPLY To the address below in writing

WHO TO APPLY TO Edward Aldridge, Chairperson, Aldridge Charitable Trust, 30–34 Eagle Wharf Road, London N1 7EB

CC NO 1059942   **ESTABLISHED** 1996

■ The Alecto Trust

WHAT IS FUNDED Broad charitable purposes including Arts

WHO CAN BENEFIT Institutions and crisis appeals. Beneficiaries include: actors and entertainment professionals; musicians; textile workers and designers; and writers and poets

WHERE FUNDING CAN BE GIVEN UK and overseas

TYPE OF GRANT Mainly recurrent, but consider single donations

FINANCES *Year* 1996 *Income* £19,656
Grants £17,163

TRUSTEES J G Studholme, Mrs R Studholme, A Studholme

HOW TO APPLY To the address under Who To Apply To

WHO TO APPLY TO J Lockyer-Nibbs, Secretary, The Alecto Trust, 35 Manor Road, Wallington, Surrey SM6 0BW

CC NO 326555   **ESTABLISHED** 1984

■ The Aleh Charitable Foundation

WHAT IS FUNDED The furtherance of the educational objects and activities of the Aleh Home in Bnei Brak near Tel Aviv in Israel. For the foreseeable future funds are fully committed for this purpose

WHO CAN BENEFIT To benefit children and young adults at the Aleh Home in B'nei Brak near Tel Aviv

WHERE FUNDING CAN BE GIVEN Israel

FINANCES *Year* 1997 *Income* £81,005
Grants £80,500

TRUSTEES D H J Cohen, A Sacks

HOW TO APPLY Applications are not currently considered as the available funds are fully committed

WHO TO APPLY TO D H J Cohen, The Aleh Charitable Foundation, c/o Paisner & Co, 154 Fleet Street, Bouverie House, London EC4A 2DQ

CC NO 327766   **ESTABLISHED** 1988

■ The Alexander Charitable Trust

WHAT IS FUNDED Education of girls and women

WHO CAN BENEFIT Girls, women and students

WHERE FUNDING CAN BE GIVEN Bedfordshire

TYPE OF GRANT At the discretion of the Trustees. Mostly ongoing support

RANGE OF GRANTS £500–£200,000

SAMPLE GRANTS £200,000 to De Montfort University, Bedford for a Postgraduate Bursary Fund for research in the School of Physical Education, Sport and Leisure; £50,000 to De Montfort University, Bedford; £1,000 to Pestalozzi Children's Village Trust; £1,000 to North Bedfordshire Age Concern; £1,000 to St Gemma's Hospice; £1,000 to Wheatfield's Hospice; £1,000 to Sue Ryder Foundation for St John's Hospice; £500 to The Children's Society; £500 to Queen Elizabeth Foundation for Disabled People; £500 to Bedford Methodist Outreach

FINANCES *Year* 1997 *Income* £27,669
Grants £259,500

TRUSTEES E Alexander, P J Howell

WHO TO APPLY TO Messrs Booth and Co, The Alexander Charitable Trust, PO Box 8, Sovereign House, South Parade, Leeds LS1 1HQ

CC NO 291598   **ESTABLISHED** 1982

■ Alexandra Rose Day

WHAT IS FUNDED Grants to registered charities only who take part in the Alexandra Rose Day collections

WHO CAN BENEFIT There are no restrictions on the age; professional and economic group; family situation; religion and culture; and social circumstances of; or disease or medical condition suffered by, the beneficiaries

WHERE FUNDING CAN BE GIVEN Primarily London, UK

SAMPLE GRANTS £6,268 to Hertfordshire Association for Disabled; £5,133 to Essex Physically Handicapped; £4,386 to Norfolk Association for the Disabled; £3,804 to SW Surrey Mobile Physio Service; £3,646 to Talking Newspapers Association; £3,212 to Avon and Bristol Federation of Clubs for Young People; £3,210 to Bishop Creighton House, Lillie Road, London; £2,851 to ARD County Committee for distribution; £2,583 to Church's Action for the homeless; £2,359 to SPHERE

FINANCES *Year* 1997 *Income* £399,050
Grants £216,045

TRUSTEES The Council: Mrs A Beckman, P Beckman, Capt D Buchan, Lady Clarke, S King, Sir E Anstruther-Gough-Calthorpe, Mrs M Neal, Hon Mrs P Penny, Mrs J Pomian, Sir I Rankin, F Salvesen, Mrs D Taylor, Mrs A Travis

WHO TO APPLY TO Mrs Gillian Greenwood, National Director, Alexandra Rose Day, 2A Ferry Road, Barnes, London SW13 9RX

CC NO 211535   **ESTABLISHED** 1912

■ Alexandra Trust

WHAT IS FUNDED Relief of the poor, through provision of cheap food and shelter and the means of obtaining basic necessities. Annual donations are made to a small number of charities which are supported on an on-going basis. It is a specific policy that at least one Governor takes a personal interest in any charity considered for support

WHAT IS NOT FUNDED No grants to individuals

WHO CAN BENEFIT Organisations benefiting those disadvantaged by poverty

WHERE FUNDING CAN BE GIVEN Essentially East London

FINANCES *Year* 1996 *Income* £18,260
Grants £14,000

TRUSTEES The Governors and Executive Committee

WHO TO APPLY TO A D Screwvala, The Alexandra Trust, PO Box 436, No1 Watergate, London EC4Y 0AE

CC NO 207362   **ESTABLISHED** 1898

Does the trust you have chosen match your needs? Haphazard applications waste postage and time

13

■ The Alexis Trust

WHAT IS FUNDED Support for a variety of Christian causes

WHAT IS NOT FUNDED No restrictions as long as they fall within Objects

WHO CAN BENEFIT Individuals and organisations benefiting Christians

WHERE FUNDING CAN BE GIVEN UK and overseas

TYPE OF GRANT One-off, project and recurring costs will be considered

FINANCES *Year* 1997 *Income* £33,800
Grants £32,000

TRUSTEES Prof D W Vere, Mrs V Vere, C P Harwood, Mrs E M Harwood

NOTES (a) The Trustees do not support fee payments, especially annually recurring fees, to colleges. (b) The Trustees do not give to building appeals. (c) Most of the funds of this Trust are regularly committed

HOW TO APPLY In writing at any time

WHO TO APPLY TO Mrs A Heaphy, The Alexis Trust, Messrs Jacob Cavenagh & Skeet, 6–8 Tudor Court, Brighton Road, Sutton, Surrey SN2 5AE *Tel* 0181-643 1166

CC NO 262861   **ESTABLISHED** 1971

■ The Al-Fayed Charitable Foundation (178)

This trust declined to meet CAF's researchers and failed to supply a copy of its annual report and accounts to CAF as required under section 47(2) of the Charities Act 1993. The information held on file at the Charity Commission was insufficient to enable CAF's researchers to write a substantive commentary on the trust's activities. Accordingly, despite its size, we are unable to list this trust in Spotlight on Major Trusts

WHAT IS FUNDED General charitable purposes

WHO CAN BENEFIT There are no restrictions on the age; professional and economic group; family situation; religion and culture; and social circumstances of; or disease or medical condition suffered by, the beneficiaries

WHERE FUNDING CAN BE GIVEN UK

FINANCES *Year* 1995 *Income* £441,878
Grants £587,615

TRUSTEES M Al-Fayed, A Fayed, S Fayed

HOW TO APPLY In writing to the address below

WHO TO APPLY TO Mrs A J B Stuart, The Al-Fayed Charitable Foundation, 5th Floor, 87–135 Brompton Road, London SW1X 7XL

CC NO 297114   **ESTABLISHED** 1987

■ Alglen Ltd

WHAT IS FUNDED Jewish causes

WHAT IS NOT FUNDED Non-Jewish causes and organisations are not funded

WHO CAN BENEFIT Jewish organisations

WHERE FUNDING CAN BE GIVEN UK

RANGE OF GRANTS £150–£36,000

SAMPLE GRANTS £36,000 to Torah Vemmunah Charity Trust; £7,000 to Torah Vechased Le'ezra Vesad; £7,000 to Beis Yaacov; £5,000 to SOFT; £5,000 to Gur Trust; £5,000 to Emuno Educational Centre Ltd; £3,800 to Ponevez Yeshivah; £3,600 to Friends of Harim Establish; £3,000 to Friends of Achiezer; £2,000 to Hachnasas Kalloh Fund Aguda

FINANCES *Year* 1997 *Income* £237,682
Grants £84,550

TRUSTEES D Stieglitz, Mrs E Stieglitz, Mrs R Lipschitz

WHO TO APPLY TO Felds, Accountants, Alglen Ltd, 5 North End Road, London NW11 7RJ

CC NO 287544   **ESTABLISHED** 1983

■ The Alice Trust

WHAT IS FUNDED Support of registered charities concerned with the preservation of land and buildings in Buckinghamshire

WHO CAN BENEFIT Registered charities concerned with preservation of buildings and land in Buckinghamshire

WHERE FUNDING CAN BE GIVEN Buckinghamshire

RANGE OF GRANTS £57,991–£879,316

SAMPLE GRANTS £879,316 to The National Trust for Waddesdon Manor, running costs, repair and refurbishment; £57,991 to Water Garden, Waddesdon for refurbishment and expansion

FINANCES *Year* 1997 *Income* £1,294,896
Grants £937,307

TRUSTEES Lord Rothschild, Lady Serena Rothschild, M E Hatch, SJP Trustee Company Limited

NOTES The Trust does have a regular list of beneficiaries, but occasionally grants are made to other organisations

HOW TO APPLY To the address under Who To Apply To in writing

WHO TO APPLY TO The Clerk, The Alice Trust, Messrs Saffery Champness, Fairfax House, Fulwood Place, Grays Inn, London WC1V 6UB

CC NO 290859   **ESTABLISHED** 1984

■ The Allachy Trust

WHAT IS FUNDED (a) Provision or assistance to under developed communities becoming self sufficient. (b) Conservation of natural resources. (c) Assistance to co-operative ventures (self help) communities becoming self sufficient

WHAT IS NOT FUNDED No grant to individuals or charities that only offer short term help

WHO CAN BENEFIT Registered charities. There are no restrictions on the age; professional and economic group; family situation; religion and culture; and social circumstances of; or disease or medical condition suffered by, the beneficiaries

WHERE FUNDING CAN BE GIVEN UK and overseas

RANGE OF GRANTS £5,000–£22,000

SAMPLE GRANTS £22,000 to Action Aid; £5,000 to APT Design and Development

FINANCES *Year* 1996 *Income* £33,594
Grants £27,000

TRUSTEES A W Layton, R M Newby, J W Dolman

NOTES A substantial part of the Trustees' annual income is fully committed. Grants may be awarded out of any balance of annual income. The Trustees will award grants in the manner they think will best benefit the project or community

HOW TO APPLY Detailed prospectus accompanied by Accounts and full estimate of costs

WHO TO APPLY TO M J Day, The Allachy Trust, 1 Dean Farrer Street, Westminster, London SW1H 0DY

CC NO 326237   **ESTABLISHED** 1982

■ The Allan Charitable Trust

WHAT IS FUNDED To make payments of income or capital to such charities as the trustees decide. The Trust supports a range of projects involving young people and the homeless

WHAT IS NOT FUNDED No grants to individuals

WHO CAN BENEFIT Registered charities benefiting young people and the homeless

WHERE FUNDING CAN BE GIVEN UK and overseas with special emphasis on Inner London, particularly Islington

TYPE OF GRANT One-off

RANGE OF GRANTS £250–£2,500

FINANCES *Year* 1997 *Income* £16,671 *Grants* £19,000

TRUSTEES R B Allan, Mrs D Allan, J B Allan, J R Allan

HOW TO APPLY In writing to the address under Who To Apply To supported by 'statement of case' and audited accounts. Applications considered half yearly in January and July

WHO TO APPLY TO R B Allan, Trustee, The Allan Charitable Trust, 8 Northampton Park, London N1 2PJ *Tel* 0171-226 7440

CC NO 1045835   ESTABLISHED 1995

■ The Allen and Overy Foundation

This trust did not respond to CAF's request to amend its entry and, by 30 June 1998, CAF's researchers did not find financial records for later than 1995 on its file at the Charity Commission. Trusts are legally required to submit annual accounts to the Charity Commission under section 42 of the Charities Act 1993

WHAT IS FUNDED General charitable purposes at the discretion of the Trustees

WHAT IS NOT FUNDED No grants to individuals

WHO CAN BENEFIT At the discretion of the Trustees. There are no restrictions on the age; professional and economic group; family situation; religion and culture; and social circumstances of; or disease or medical condition suffered by, the beneficiaries

WHERE FUNDING CAN BE GIVEN UK

TYPE OF GRANT At the discretion of the Trustees

TRUSTEES J M Kennedy, W V W Norris, A J Herbert, P R J Holland, W T John, P H T Mimpress, A R Humphrey

WHO TO APPLY TO W Tudor John, Allen and Overy Foundation, 9 Cheapside, London EC2V 6AD *Tel* 0171-330 3000

CC NO 803071   ESTABLISHED 1990

■ Mrs R P Allen Charitable Trust

WHAT IS FUNDED General charitable purposes

WHO CAN BENEFIT There are no restrictions on the age; professional and economic group; family situation; religion and culture; and social circumstances of; or disease or medical condition suffered by, the beneficiaries

WHERE FUNDING CAN BE GIVEN UK

TRUSTEES J F M Cannon, H C D Moorhead, R H V Moorhead, G C Taylor

HOW TO APPLY **This Trust states that it does not respond to unsolicited applications**

WHO TO APPLY TO R H V Moorhead, Mrs R P Allen Charitable Trust, 2 Stade Street, Hythe, Kent CT2 6BD

CC NO 1068063   ESTABLISHED 1997

■ The Rita Allen Charitable Trust

WHAT IS FUNDED General charitable purposes

WHAT IS NOT FUNDED No grants to individuals

WHO CAN BENEFIT Institutions. There are no restrictions on the age; professional and economic group; family situation; religion and culture; and social circumstances of; or disease or medical condition suffered by, the beneficiaries

WHERE FUNDING CAN BE GIVEN UK

SAMPLE GRANTS £4,000 to BRACE (Alzheimer's Research); £4,000 to St John Ambulance; £3,000 to Alzheimer's Disease Society; £3,000 to the Arthritis and Rheumatism Council; £3,000 to the Royal Star and Garter Home; £2,000 to NCH Action for Children; £2,000 to Tettenhall Horse Sanctuary; £2,000 to the Nation Council of YMCAs; £2,000 to Royal National Institute for the Blind; £2,000 to The Salvation Army

FINANCES *Year* 1995 *Income* £32,452 *Grants* £33,000

TRUSTEES P B Shone, D G Allen

HOW TO APPLY By letter

WHO TO APPLY TO P B Shone, The Rita Allen Charitable Trust, Bolinge Hill Farm, Buriton, Petersfield, Hampshire GU31 4NN

CC NO 1014947   ESTABLISHED 1992

■ Dorothy Gertrude Allen Memorial Fund

WHAT IS FUNDED General charitable purposes

WHAT IS NOT FUNDED Registered charities only

WHO CAN BENEFIT Registered charities only. There are no restrictions on the age; professional and economic group; family situation; religion and culture; and social circumstances of; or disease or medical condition suffered by, the beneficiaries

WHERE FUNDING CAN BE GIVEN UK

SAMPLE GRANTS £4,000 to Windmill Hill City Farm, Bristol; £3,000 to The Talking newspaper Association; £3,000 to Great Ormond Street Children's Hospital Fund; £3,000 to National Playbus Association; £3,000 to Fairbridge in Scotland (young people at risk); £3,000 to Duke of Edinburgh's Award (Devon); £3,000 to The Rainbow Trust; £3,000 to Portsmouth Area Hospice; £3,000 to The Rural Youth Trust; £3,000 to Project Ear Foundation

FINANCES *Year* 1995 *Income* £69,579 *Grants* £45,500

TRUSTEES H B Allen, P B Shone

WHO TO APPLY TO P B Shone, Dorothy Gertrude Allen Memorial Fund, Bolinge Hill Farm, Buriton, Petersfield, Hampshire GU31 4NN

CC NO 290676   ESTABLISHED 1984

■ Mrs M H Allen Trust

WHAT IS FUNDED Military charities working in the fields of: infrastructure, support and development; health; and community facilities. The Trustees prefer to assist people (the disabled, the injured and the disadvantaged) rather than institutions or the preservation of buildings

WHAT IS NOT FUNDED No grants to any non-naval or military charities, individuals, scholarships and education generally

WHO CAN BENEFIT Registered naval and/or military charities benefiting ex-service and service people; disabled people and those disadvantaged by poverty. There is no restriction on the disease or medical condition suffered by the beneficiaries

WHERE FUNDING CAN BE GIVEN UK

TYPE OF GRANT Capital, core costs, one-off, project, research, recurring costs and salaries. Funding of up to two years

RANGE OF GRANTS £500–£25,000, typically £2,500

SAMPLE GRANTS Grants for general purposes:; £25,000 to Westminster Dragoons Benevolent Fund; £5,000 to Army Museums Ogilby Trust; £4,000 to King Edward VII's Hospital for Officers; £3,706 to The League of Remembrance; £2,500 to Airborne Forces Security Fund; £2,500 to BLESMA; £2,500 to Ex-services Mental Welfare Society; £2,500 to King George's Fund for Sailors; £2,500 to SSAFA; £2,500 to Royal Star and Garter Home
FINANCES *Year* 1997 *Income* £48,626 *Grants* £68,506
TRUSTEES A F Niekirk, A P C Niekirk, W D Niekirk
HOW TO APPLY In writing at any time. There is no formal application form
WHO TO APPLY TO Mrs M H Allen Trust, Messrs Dawson & Co, (Ref AFN), 2 New Square, Lincoln's Inn, London WC2A 3RZ *Tel* 0171-421 4800 *Fax* 0171-421 4848
CC NO 211529   **ESTABLISHED** 1924

■ Alliance Family Foundation Limited

WHAT IS FUNDED The relief of poverty and advancement of religion, education and medical knowledge
WHAT IS NOT FUNDED No grants to individuals
WHO CAN BENEFIT Organisations benefiting children, young adults, clergy and those disadvantaged by poverty. There are no restrictions on the religion or culture of, or on the disease or medical condition suffered by, the beneficiaries
WHERE FUNDING CAN BE GIVEN UK
SAMPLE GRANTS £16,000 to the University of Manchester; £7,500 to Weizmann Institute Foundation; £6,747 to Shaare Sedek Synagogue; £4,000 to After Adoption; £2,500 to Aish Ha Torah; £2,500 to Alder Trust; £2,500 to Community Security Trust; £2,500 to the Mairmondies Foundation; £2,000 to Iranian Volleyball Association; £1,200 to North Cheshire Jewish Primary School
FINANCES *Year* 1996 *Income* £184,474 *Grants* £125,852
TRUSTEES The Directors: Sir D Alliance, N Alliance, G N Alliance, Mrs S D Esterkin
WHO TO APPLY TO G N Alliance, Alliance Family Foundation Limited, c/o 12th Floor, Bank House, Charlotte Street, Manchester M1 4ET
CC NO 258721   **ESTABLISHED** 1968

■ Allied Domecq Trust (formerly the Allied-Lyons Trust)

WHAT IS FUNDED The arts, education and the environment
WHO CAN BENEFIT All types of voluntary and statutory organisations benefiting children and young adults, students, teachers and arts practioners
WHERE FUNDING CAN BE GIVEN UK and overseas
TYPE OF GRANT Normally one-off, or recurrent for up to four years
FINANCES *Year* 1996 *Income* £650,000 *Grants* £615,330
TRUSTEES A J Hales (Director), A S Pratt (Director), W E Mason (Chair)
NOTES The Board meets at approximately three monthly intervals to consider applications
HOW TO APPLY To the address under Who To Apply To, accompanied by most recent audited accounts

WHO TO APPLY TO C Burns, The Secretary, Allied Domecq Trust, 24 Portland Place, London W1N 4BB
CC NO 284358   **ESTABLISHED** 1982

■ Angus Allnatt Charitable Foundation

WHAT IS FUNDED Organisations which provide music or sailing activities for young people (13–25). Bursaries and fees will be considered
WHAT IS NOT FUNDED The Trustees do not contribute to large general appeals nor do they consider mail-shot appeals. No grants to individuals
WHO CAN BENEFIT Mostly small organisations which are registered charities benefiting: children; young adults; musicians; and those who are involved in youth sailing activities
WHERE FUNDING CAN BE GIVEN UK
TYPE OF GRANT One-off for specific needs or start-up costs. Funding is available for up to one year
RANGE OF GRANTS £250–£1,000 with a maximum of £2,000
SAMPLE GRANTS £4,750 to Raleigh International to purchase sea kayaks; £4,000 to Kirckman Concert Society towards recitals programme; £2,000 to Young Concert Artists Trust towards lunchtime recitals; £1,600 to Scottish Chamber Orchestra for schools project; £1,500 to Merseyside Council for Voluntary Service to fund music lessons
FINANCES *Year* 1998 *Income* £20,400 *Grants* £29,270
TRUSTEES Rodney Dartnall, Anthony Pritchard, Calton Younger, Marian Durban
NOTES Appeals falling outside our guidelines will not be acknowledged
HOW TO APPLY At any time. Trustees meet three times annually at present. Application by letter. No application form. The Foundation has no staff and no telephone
WHO TO APPLY TO Calton Younger, Angus Allnatt Charitable Foundation, 34 North End Road, London W14 0SH
CC NO 1019793   **ESTABLISHED** 1993

■ Pat Allsop Charitable Trust

WHAT IS FUNDED Medicine and health, welfare, education. Particularly concerned with: almshouses; housing associations; hospices; medical studies and research; schools and colleges; special needs education; and emergency care for refugees and famine
WHAT IS NOT FUNDED No grants to individuals or students
WHO CAN BENEFIT National organisations benefiting: children; those in property management; those disadvantaged by poverty; those living in urban areas; refugees and the victims of famine
WHERE FUNDING CAN BE GIVEN UK
TYPE OF GRANT One-off, project, research and recurring costs
SAMPLE GRANTS £5,500 to Jewish Care; £4,000 to National Children's Homes; £3,350 to The Story of Christmas 1996; £3,000 to College of Estate Management Benevolent Fund; £1,000 to St Barnabas-in-Soho
FINANCES *Year* 1996–97 *Income* £57,032 *Grants* £35,000
TRUSTEES J P G Randel, A P Collett, A G Butler, B C Fowler
NOTES Trust has historical connections with surveying and estate management

HOW TO APPLY Trustees meet three or four times a year

WHO TO APPLY TO J P G Randel, Pat Allsop Charitable Trust, c/o Monier Williams & Boxalls, 71 Lincoln's Inn Fields, London WC2A 3JF

CC NO 1030950　　　　**ESTABLISHED** 1973

■ Al-Masoom International Foundation Trust

WHAT IS FUNDED The Trust supports general causes, but especially the advancement of Muslim/Islam and the economically disadvantaged

WHO CAN BENEFIT To benefit Muslims and those disadvantaged by poverty

WHERE FUNDING CAN BE GIVEN UK and overseas

WHO TO APPLY TO Mrs K Khan, Chairperson, Al-Masoom International Foundation Trust, 71 Alexandra Road South, Whalley Range, Manchester M16 8GJ

CC NO 1061821　　　　**ESTABLISHED** 1997

■ The Almond Trust

WHAT IS FUNDED Support of Evangelical, Christian projects, Christian Evangelism, advancement of Scripture

WHO CAN BENEFIT Mostly individuals or organisations of which the Trustees have personal knowledge, particularly those benfiting Christian and Evangelists

WHERE FUNDING CAN BE GIVEN UK and overseas

TYPE OF GRANT Buildings, capital, core costs, one-off, project, recurring and running costs, salaries, and start-up costs. Funding is available for up to two years

FINANCES *Year* 1997–98 *Income* £326,135 *Grants* £287,700

TRUSTEES J L Cooke, Barbara H Cooke, E E Cooke

NOTES Rarely respond to uninvited grant applications

HOW TO APPLY Not generally open to applications. Trustees consider charitable matters of which they have personal knowledge

WHO TO APPLY TO J L Cooke, The Almond Trust, 111 Dulwich Village, London SE21 7BJ

CC NO 328583　　　　**ESTABLISHED** 1990

■ Almondsbury Church Lands Charities

WHAT IS FUNDED Churches, schools and relief organisations in the area Where Funding Can Be Given

WHO CAN BENEFIT Individuals and organisations benefiting: children; young adults; Christians; at risk groups; those disadvantaged by poverty; and socially isolated people

WHERE FUNDING CAN BE GIVEN Almondsbury, Patchway, Bradley Stoke North, parts of Easter Compton and Pilning

SAMPLE GRANTS £5,568 to Pilning Ecumenical Church Council; £1,500 to St Chad's Church for the Seeds Coffee Bar; £1,466 to Patchway Ecumenical Church Council; £1,100 to Patchway Festival; £900 to Patchway and Bradley Stoke Play Association; £750 to Coniston Junior School; £700 to Patchway High School; £450 to 1st Almondsbury Scouts; £373 to Patchway Community Association; £360 to Patchway Day Centre

FINANCES *Year* 1996 *Income* £42,110 *Grants* £24,201

TRUSTEES Rev R E Penn, Rev D B Harrex, Dr A G Warner, Mrs K M Hewitt, Mrs S J Cook, I Humphries, L Gray, Mrs H M Dennison, Mrs R G Hitchcock, K J Beard, A B Gaydon, R S Ames, B C Brook, R E Davies, W H Dick, G D Wilmott

NOTES The Almondsbury Church Lands Charities distribute money through the Ecclesiastical Fund, the Education Fund and the Relief Fund

HOW TO APPLY On a form available from the address under Who To Apply To

WHO TO APPLY TO T Davies, Secretary, Almondsbury Church Lands Charities, 18 Coape Road, Stockwood, Bristol BS14 8TN

CC NO 202263　　　　**ESTABLISHED** 1976

■ The Almshouse Association (The National Association of Almshouses)

WHAT IS FUNDED To make grants and loans to almshouse charities after full advantage has been taken of statutory aid

WHAT IS NOT FUNDED No grants to individuals

WHO CAN BENEFIT Almshouse charities benefiting the elderly and those disadvantaged by poverty

WHERE FUNDING CAN BE GIVEN Almshouse charities throughout the UK

TYPE OF GRANT Usually one-off grant or interest-free loan for a specific project

FINANCES *Year* 1997 *Income* £1,020,457 *Grants* £117,819

TRUSTEES Executive Committee

PUBLICATIONS Annual Report and quarterly *Almshouses Gazette*

NOTES Loans made in year £210,000

HOW TO APPLY To the Director at any time

WHO TO APPLY TO A L Leask, Director, The Almshouse Association, Billingbear Lodge, Wokingham, Berkshire RG40 5RU

CC NO 245668　　　　**ESTABLISHED** 1946

■ Altamont Ltd

WHAT IS FUNDED Jewish charitable purposes

WHO CAN BENEFIT Organisations benefiting Jewish people

WHERE FUNDING CAN BE GIVEN UK and overseas

TYPE OF GRANT Large grants were made to Jewish organisations that were grant making trusts in 1994–95, with smaller grants going direct to Jewish charities

RANGE OF GRANTS £500–£270,000

SAMPLE GRANTS £270,000 to Primerquote Limited; £150,500 to Natlas Trust; £147,500 to Fordeve Limited; £30,000 to Toldos Yacov Yosef; £25,000 to Claimworth Limited; £11,000 to Friends of Betz; £10,000 to Friends of Wiznitz; £5,000 to Friends of Bobov; £500 to BBC Children in Need

FINANCES *Year* 1994–95 *Income* £109,036 *Grants* £649,500

TRUSTEES D Last, H Last, Mrs H Kon, Mrs S Alder, Mrs G Wiesenfeld

HOW TO APPLY To the address under Who To Apply To in writing

WHO TO APPLY TO The Clerk, Altamont Ltd, Gerald Kreditor & Co, Tudor House, Llan Vanor Road, Finchley Road, London NW2 2AQ

CC NO 273971　　　　**ESTABLISHED** 1977

■ Alvi Charitable Trust Limited

WHAT IS FUNDED General charitable purposes in the UK and India

WHO CAN BENEFIT There are no restrictions on the age; professional and economic group; family situation; religion and culture; and social circumstances of; or disease or medical condition suffered by, the beneficiaries

WHERE FUNDING CAN BE GIVEN UK and India

TRUSTEES Highstone Directors Ltd, Highstone Secretaries Ltd

WHO TO APPLY TO H Mohammed, Solicitor, Alvi Charitable Trust Limited, 42 St Johns Place, Preston, Lancashire PR1 3XX

CC NO 1068922   **ESTABLISHED** 1997

■ The Amar International Charitable Foundation

WHAT IS FUNDED (a) Provision of aid to victims of breaches of human rights, natural disasters, war or civil disturbance. (b) Schools, training centres or any educational establishment or educative programme. All programmes are AMAR implemented

WHAT IS NOT FUNDED No grants to programmes not carried out by AMAR staff

WHO CAN BENEFIT Organisations benefiting at risk groups, victims of man-made or natural disasters and war, refugees, those disadvantaged by poverty, children, young adults and students

WHERE FUNDING CAN BE GIVEN UK and overseas

SAMPLE GRANTS £400,748 to ODA Fund to provide support for primary health care for Iraqi refugees in Iran; £63,753 to Parliamentary Appeal for Romanian Children to relieve poverty and sickness and provide education for children in Home No 11 and School No 6 in Bucharest; £47,393 to Amar Appeal Trust for the relief of poverty, distress and suffering in the world, in particular to needy Iraqi people

FINANCES *Year* 1996 *Income* £516,444

TRUSTEES Sir M H Caine, Rt Hon Earl Jellicoe, L Kramer, E Nicholson, A R Rowsell, D Suratgar, T J Taylor, Dr Theodore Zeldin

PUBLICATIONS Draft consultative bulletin *An Environmental and Ecological Study of the Marshlands of Mesopotamia*

WHO TO APPLY TO Emma Nicholson, Trustee, The Amar International Charitable Foundation, 2 Vincent Street, London SW1P 4LD *Tel* 0171-828 4991

CC NO 1047432   **ESTABLISHED** 1995

■ The Amberstone Trust

WHAT IS FUNDED General charitable purposes. All funds presently committed. The Trustees are not currently seeking new applications

WHAT IS NOT FUNDED No applications from individuals

WHO CAN BENEFIT There are no restrictions on the age; professional and economic group; family situation; religion and culture; and social circumstances of; or disease or medical condition suffered by, the beneficiaries

WHERE FUNDING CAN BE GIVEN UK

FINANCES *Year* 1996–97 *Income* £167,241 *Grants* £197,067

TRUSTEES Hon D S Bernstein, C A Blackman, Hon P S Zuckerman

HOW TO APPLY **All funds presently committed. The Trustees are not currently seeking new applications**

WHO TO APPLY TO The Trustees, The Amberstone Trust, c/o Buss Murton (Ref. 46), The Priory, Tunbridge Wells, Kent TN1 1JJ *Tel* 01892 510222

CC NO 279787   **ESTABLISHED** 1978

■ Ambika Paul Foundation (formerly Ambika Charitable Foundation)

WHAT IS FUNDED Main areas of interest are to do with young people and education

WHAT IS NOT FUNDED Grants are only available to children and young people's charities. Will not fund individuals or DSS requests. Will not pay individuals' salaries/running costs. Applications from individuals, including students, mainly ineligible. Funding for scholarships made direct to colleges/universities, not to individuals. No expeditions

WHO CAN BENEFIT Large organisations, registered charities, colleges and universities benefiting children, young adults and students

WHERE FUNDING CAN BE GIVEN UK, India

TYPE OF GRANT Direct donations, deeds of covenant

FINANCES *Year* 1997 *Income* £474,857 *Grants* £27,922

PUBLICATIONS Annual Report

HOW TO APPLY In writing to the Trustees at address below. Acknowledgements sent if sae enclosed. However, the Trust has no paid employees. The enormous number of requests now received has created administrative difficulties

WHO TO APPLY TO Lord Paul, Ambika Paul Foundation, Caparo House, 103 Baker Street, London W1M 1FD

CC NO 276127   **ESTABLISHED** 1978

■ The Harold Amelan Charitable Trust

WHAT IS FUNDED General charitable purposes. The Trust will support national charities, but preference will be given to local charities around the Greater Manchester area

WHAT IS NOT FUNDED No grants to individuals

WHO CAN BENEFIT There are no restrictions on the age; professional and economic group; family situation; religion and culture; and social circumstances of; or disease or medical condition suffered by, the beneficiaries

WHERE FUNDING CAN BE GIVEN UK with preference for Greater Manchester area

RANGE OF GRANTS £50–£2,500

SAMPLE GRANTS £2,500 to Hale and District Hebrew Congregation; £2,000 to JPAIME; £1,000 to JIAME; £1,000 to GRET; £1,000 to JIA

FINANCES *Year* 1996 *Income* £18,602 *Grants* £14,445

TRUSTEES R E Amelan, J F Middleweek

WHO TO APPLY TO J E Avery-Gee, The Harold Amelan Charitable Trust, c/o Kay Johnson-Gee, Griffin Court, 201 Chapel Street, Salford, Manchester M3 5EQ

CC NO 263804   **ESTABLISHED** 1972

■ The Ammco Trust

WHAT IS FUNDED Medicine and health; welfare; special needs education; humanities; environmental resources and conservation; churches; Anglican bodies; music and orchestras; cultural heritage; and the charitable purposes

WHAT IS NOT FUNDED No grants to individuals or students

WHO CAN BENEFIT Small local projects; national, new organisations; and established organisations benefiting: ex-service and service people; musicians; carers; and victims of abuse and violence, famine and war. There is no restriction on the age of the beneficiaries. A wide range of diseases and medical conditions are considered for funding

WHERE FUNDING CAN BE GIVEN Oxfordshire and adjoining counties

TYPE OF GRANT One-off and recurrent for buildings and core costs. Funding is available for up to one year

RANGE OF GRANTS £50–£5,000

SAMPLE GRANTS £2,000 to Gloucestershire Deaf Association for summer playschemes project; £2,000 to Sustrans, Bristol for safe routes to school project; £1,000 to Camphill Milton Keynes Communities Appeal to extend accommodation; £1,000 to Nancy Oldfield Trust for sailing for the disabled; £1,000 to Anthony Toby Homes Trust, Berkshire for extension appeal for accommodation for people with learning difficulties; £1,000 to Cotswold Home, Burford for DGAA home for elderly appeal; £1,000 to Nuffield Orthopaedic Centre, Oxford for building appeal; £1,000 to Spina Bifida and Hydrocephalus Association for funding appeal; £1,000 to Muscular Dystrophy Group for funding appeal; £1,000 to Crossroads for respite care

FINANCES *Year* 1997–98 *Income* £128,327 *Grants* £80,829

TRUSTEES Mrs E M R Lewis, Mrs R S E Vickers, N P Cobbold

PUBLICATIONS Annual Report

NOTES Trustees have an interest in disability

HOW TO APPLY In writing at any time. No application forms. An sae is appreciated

WHO TO APPLY TO Mrs E M R Lewis, The Ammco Trust, Glebe Farm, Hinton Waldrist, Faringdon, Oxfordshire SN7 8RX *Tel* 01865 820269 *Fax* 01865 821188

CC NO 327962   **ESTABLISHED** 1988

■ Viscount Amory Charitable Trust

WHAT IS FUNDED The income is employed mostly in the field of youth service and the elderly. The limited resources of this Trust are employed to help a number of charitable objects with which the Trust has been associated for a number of years, mostly within the county of Devon, including education and training for children and young people

WHO CAN BENEFIT There are no restrictions on the age; professional and economic group; family situation; religion and culture; and social circumstances of; or disease or medical condition suffered by, the beneficiaries. However, particular favour is given to young adults and the elderly

WHERE FUNDING CAN BE GIVEN Primarily Devon, but occasionally elsewhere in the UK

SAMPLE GRANTS £73,000 to London Sailing Project; £10,000 to St Peter's Church, Tiverton; £9,907 to Blundells School, Tiverton; £8,702 to Maynard School, Exeter; £6,921 to Eton College; £5,000 to St Paul's Church, Tiverton; £5,000 to Michael Trinick Memorial Fund; £4,500 to Sedbergh School, Cumbria; £4,000 to Mid Devon Enterprise Agency; £3,680 to Ludgrove School

FINANCES *Year* 1997 *Income* £341,529 *Grants* £244,748

TRUSTEES Sir Ian Heathcoat Amory, Bt, Sir John Palmer

WHO TO APPLY TO Sir Ian Heathcoat Amory, Trustee, Viscount Amory Charitable Trust, The Island, Lowman Green, Tiverton, Devon EX16 4LA

CC NO 204958   **ESTABLISHED** 1962

■ Sir John and Lady Heathcoat Amory's Charitable Trust (formerly Sir John Heathcoat Amory Trust)

WHAT IS FUNDED General charitable purposes

WHO CAN BENEFIT Local organisations plus a few national ones. There are no restrictions on the age; professional and economic group; family situation; religion and culture; and social circumstances of; or disease or medical condition suffered by, the beneficiaries

WHERE FUNDING CAN BE GIVEN Devon, and elsewhere in the UK

SAMPLE GRANTS £8,000 to Knightshayes Garden Trust; £4,538 to Blundells School; £4,324 to Relief for the Elderly and Infirm; £3,000 to Tiverton Girl Guides; £2,500 to Spana; £2,000 to Age Concern Tiverton; £2,000 to London Sailing Project; £2,000 to NSPCC; £2,000 to Tiverton Senior Citizens, Amory House; £1,500 to Age Concern

FINANCES *Year* 1997 *Income* £47,229 *Grants* £47,657

TRUSTEES Lady Joyce Heathcoat Amory, Sir John Palmer, Sir Ian Heathcoat Amory, Bt, Lady Palmer

WHO TO APPLY TO Sir Ian Heathcoat Amory, Sir John and Lady Heathcoat Amory's Charitable Trust, The Island, Lowman Green, Tiverton, Devon EX16 4LA

CC NO 203970   **ESTABLISHED** 1961

■ The Ampelos Trust

WHAT IS FUNDED General charitable purposes

WHO CAN BENEFIT There are no restrictions on the age; professional and economic group; family situation; religion and culture; and social circumstances of; or disease or medical condition suffered by, the beneficiaries

WHERE FUNDING CAN BE GIVEN UK

RANGE OF GRANTS £1,000–5,000

SAMPLE GRANTS £5,000 to CLIC; £5,000 to John Aspinall Appeal Fund; £1,500 to Joyce Green Hospital Radio; £1,000 to Colchester Multiple Sclerosis Society; £1,000 to North London Hospice; £1,000 to RSPCA for the Milford Haven Disaster Appeal

FINANCES *Year* 1996 *Income* £48,285 *Grants* £14,500

TRUSTEES D J Rendell, G W N Stewart

WHO TO APPLY TO G W N Stewart, Secretary, The Ampelos Trust, 9 Trinity Street, Colchester, Essex CO1 1JN

CC NO 1048778   **ESTABLISHED** 1995

■ The Ancaster Trust

WHAT IS FUNDED Welfare and environmental causes

WHO CAN BENEFIT Registered charities benefiting at risk groups, those disadvantaged by poverty and those who are socially isolated

WHERE FUNDING CAN BE GIVEN Mainly UK, occasionally overseas

TYPE OF GRANT Normally small, recurring grants

FINANCES *Year* 1997 *Income* £80,382 *Grants* £16,251

TRUSTEES Lady Willoughby de Eresby, S G Kemp

NOTES Income currently wholly committed

HOW TO APPLY In writing to the address under Who To Apply To at any time

WHO TO APPLY TO The Trustees of The Ancaster Trust, c/o Sayers Butterworth, 18 Bentinck Street, London W1M 5RL

CC NO 270822   **ESTABLISHED** 1965

■ The Andersen Consulting Foundation

WHAT IS FUNDED Education; health; community; the arts

WHO CAN BENEFIT Organisations benefiting children, young adults, students, at risk groups, those disadvantaged by poverty and socially isolated people. Actors and entertainment professionals, musicians, textile workers and designers, and writers and poets will be considered. There are no restrictions on the disease or medical condition suffered by the beneficiaries

WHERE FUNDING CAN BE GIVEN UK

TYPE OF GRANT At the discretion of the Trustees

FINANCES *Year* 1995 *Income* £1,265,810
Grants £1,019,504

TRUSTEES V C Watts, D J Mowat, I D Milner, N P Thompsell, M Vandersteen

NOTES Made donations to 563 charities in 1995

WHO TO APPLY TO C M Bremner, The Andersen Consulting Foundation, 2 Arundel Street, London WC2R 3LT

CC NO 1057696   **ESTABLISHED** 1995

■ The D A Anderson Charitable Trust

WHAT IS FUNDED Third world charities

WHO CAN BENEFIT There are no restrictions on the age; professional and economic group; family situation; religion and culture; and social circumstances of; or disease or medical condition suffered by, the beneficiaries

WHERE FUNDING CAN BE GIVEN Third world

WHO TO APPLY TO D A Anderson, The D A Anderson Charitable Trust, Ashford House, Talybont on Usk, Brecon, Powys LD3 7YR

CC NO 272958   **ESTABLISHED** 1977

■ The Anderson Foundation

WHAT IS FUNDED The relief of sickness and poverty of persons, to benefit the environment and to support educational and medical charitable purposes

WHO CAN BENEFIT To benefit children and young adults, and those disadvantaged by poverty. There is no restriction on the disease or medical condition suffered by the beneficiaries

WHERE FUNDING CAN BE GIVEN UK

TRUSTEES M Anderson

WHO TO APPLY TO A Short, The Anderson Foundation, Morison Stoneham, 805 Salisbury House, 31 Finsbury Circus, London EC2M 5SQ

CC NO 1063380   **ESTABLISHED** 1997

■ Andrew Anderson Trust

WHAT IS FUNDED Grants to evangelical and social causes

WHAT IS NOT FUNDED No applications from individuals for education or travel

WHO CAN BENEFIT Organisations benefiting: Christians and evangelists; at risk groups; carers; disabled people; those disadvantaged by poverty; socially isolated people; victims of abuse, crime and domestic violence

WHERE FUNDING CAN BE GIVEN UK

FINANCES *Year* 1996–97 *Income* £274,909
Grants £222,510

TRUSTEES A A Anderson, M S Anderson, A R Anderson, M L Anderson

WHO TO APPLY TO The Trustees, Andrew Anderson Trust, 84 Uphill Road, Mill Hill, London NW7 4QE

CC NO 212170   **ESTABLISHED** 1954

■ The James and Grace Anderson Trust

WHAT IS FUNDED Grants are given for research into alleviating those conditions which arise from cerebral palsy

WHO CAN BENEFIT Organisations benefiting cerebral palsy sufferers. Medical professionals and research workers may benefit

WHERE FUNDING CAN BE GIVEN Scotland

TYPE OF GRANT At least one grant is recurring. Project and research grants are considered. Funding is available for more than three years

SAMPLE GRANTS £18,285 to University of Edinburgh for Gait Analysis Project

FINANCES *Year* 1996–97 *Income* £28,700
Grants £18,285

TRUSTEES W Souter, FRCS (Ed), J Donald, J D M Urquhart, T D Straton

HOW TO APPLY Applications should be made in writing to the address under Who To Apply To

WHO TO APPLY TO T D Straton, The James and Grace Anderson Trust, Scott-Moncrieff Downie Wilson, 17 Melville Street, Edinburgh EH3 7PH *Tel* 0131-473 3500

SC NO SCO 04172   **ESTABLISHED** 1974

■ The Frederick Andrew Convalescent Trust

WHAT IS FUNDED Those who may be broadly described as professional women (working or retired) are helped with the cost of recuperative holidays or convalescent treatment following illness or an operation. Donations or subscriptions may also be made to convalescent homes or other institutions or organisations at or from which the beneficiaries may receive care and relief. This is to give priority to grants to individuals but if spare money is available grants are made to convalescent homes, etc

WHO CAN BENEFIT Individuals and organisations benefiting professional women. There are few restrictions on the disease or medical condition suffered by the beneficiaries

WHERE FUNDING CAN BE GIVEN UK

TYPE OF GRANT One-off grants of up to £600 to women and grants of about £5,000 each to other charities

FINANCES *Year* 1995 *Income* £60,722
Grants £124,172

TRUSTEES Dr W A Maclure, Mrs E Dudman, Rev Canon J Bayley, R W Howick, T J Kelsey, Dr H Jackson, Mrs M Elgood, Mrs L V Kirk

HOW TO APPLY Must be on our application form

WHO TO APPLY TO The Clerk, The Frederick Andrew Convalescent Trust, c/o Messrs Andrew & Co, Solicitors, St Swithin's Square, Lincoln, Lincolnshire LN2 1HB *Tel* 01522 512123 *Fax* 01522 546713

CC NO 211029   **ESTABLISHED** 1970

■ The Angel Charitable Trust

WHAT IS FUNDED General charitable purposes

WHO CAN BENEFIT There are no restrictions on the age; professional and economic group; family situation; religion and culture; and social circumstances of; or disease or medical condition suffered by, the beneficiaries

WHERE FUNDING CAN BE GIVEN UK

TRUSTEES A L Angel, R Francis, B Angel, B B Angel

WHO TO APPLY TO A L Angel, Trustee, The Angel Charitable Trust, High Trees, 8 Oaktree Close, Stanmore, Middlesex HA7 2PX

CC NO 1067819 **ESTABLISHED** 1997

■ Angler's Inn Trust

WHAT IS FUNDED To support local schools, vicarage, bowling club, playgrounds, youth clubs

WHO CAN BENEFIT Individuals and institutions benefiting children, young adults, clergy and other local facilities

WHERE FUNDING CAN BE GIVEN Kendal, Cumbria

SAMPLE GRANTS £3,098 to Burneside Organisations for computer facilities; £2,393 to Burneside School; £1,500 to Queen Katherine School; £1,500 to Kirkbie Kendal School; £1,500 to Lakes School

FINANCES *Year* 1997 *Income* £16,358 *Grants* £14,384

TRUSTEES O G D Ackland, J A Cropper, D E Willink

WHO TO APPLY TO L Buckle, Secretary, Angler's Inn Trust, c/o James Cropper plc, Burneside Mills, Kendal, Cumbria LA9 6PZ

CC NO 234193 **ESTABLISHED** 1938

■ The Anglian Water Trust Fund

WHAT IS FUNDED Two programmes of grant making: (a) to individuals in need, and (b) to improve access to independent money advice services

WHAT IS NOT FUNDED Those outside What is Funded will not be considered

WHO CAN BENEFIT People throughout the Anglian Water regions including those disadvantaged by poverty

WHERE FUNDING CAN BE GIVEN Anglian Water region: Hartlepool; Lincolnshire; Bedfordshire; Cambridgeshire; Essex; Hertfordshire; Luton; Norfolk; Peterborough; Suffolk; and parts of Leicestershire, Northamptonshire, Nottinghamshire and Rutland

TYPE OF GRANT (a) Individuals – one-off, and (b) organisations – one-off, capital and recurring. Project, running costs, salaries and start-up costs are also considered. Funding is available for up to three years

SAMPLE GRANTS £32,005 to Norwich Citizens Advice Bureau to establish money advice sessions in GPs surgeries; £31,849 to Cambridge Independent Advice Centre to deliver money advice outreach service in rural areas around Cambridge; £28,823 to Haverhill Citizens Advice Bureau to develop Bureau Money Advice Service; £28,734 to Wymondham Citizens Advice Bureau to develop Bureau Money Advice Service; £27,137 to Clacton-on-Sea Citizens Advice Bureau to develop Bureau Money Advice Service; £22,762 to Hartlepool Citizens Advice Bureau to develop Bureau Money Advice Service; £19,884 to Kettering Citizens Advice Bureau to develop Bureau Money Advice Service; £19,575 to St Neots Citizens Advice Bureau to develop Bureau Money Advice Service; £17,943 to Beccles Citizens Advice Bureau to develop debt helpline and Bureau Money Advice Service; £16,643 to Cambridge Citizens Advice Bureau to develop Bureau Money Advice Service to people with mental health problems

FINANCES *Year* 1997–98 *Income* £2,000,000 *Grants* £1,900,000

TRUSTEES Grahma Blagden, Diane Clay, Norman Guffick, Elizabeth Ingram, Stuart De Prochnow, Mary Rainey, Amanda Robertson (Treasurer), Barbara Ruffell (Chair), Chris Ure

HOW TO APPLY Individuals: No deadlines. Applications must be made on an application form. Guidelines are issued with the form. Most advice agencies in the Anglian region stock forms or they can be requested by writing to the address under Who To Apply To. Organisations: Deadlines as announced. By application from to the address under Who To Apply To

WHO TO APPLY TO The Anglian Water Trust Fund, PO Box 42, Peterborough PE1 1BN

CC NO 1054026 **ESTABLISHED** 1996

■ The Anglo Hong Kong Trust

WHAT IS FUNDED To promote the advancement of commerce and industry for the benefit of the UK, Hong Kong and China and to promote mutual educational and cultural activities in particular through development and improvement of contacts between their respective educational and cultural institutions

WHO CAN BENEFIT Institutions or organisations, particularly those benefiting children, young adults and students

WHERE FUNDING CAN BE GIVEN UK and Hong Kong

SAMPLE GRANTS $244,980 to The South Bank Centre; $16,357 to an individual for educational sponsorship; $12,495 to an individual for educational sponsorship; $12,485 to an individual for educational sponsorship; $12,000 to an individual for art sponsorship

FINANCES *Year* 1997 *Income* $2,413,952 *Grants* $318,317

TRUSTEES J G Cluff, D Tang, D J Davies, S Murray

NOTES All finances are in Hong Kong Dollars

WHO TO APPLY TO D Tang, Secretary, The Anglo Hong Kong Trust, Cluff Mining, 29 St James' Place, London SW1A 1NR

CC NO 328194 **ESTABLISHED** 1989

■ Anglo-Arab Aid Ltd

WHAT IS FUNDED The relief of poverty of Arab families (ie those born in Arab countries and those born in non-Arab countries of Arab parents) in need, in the UK and abroad

WHAT IS NOT FUNDED No grants to individuals or students

WHO CAN BENEFIT Small local projects benefiting Arab families

WHERE FUNDING CAN BE GIVEN UK, Syria and Arab countries

TYPE OF GRANT At the discretion of the Trustees

FINANCES *Year* 1995 *Income* £22,492
Grants £12,145

TRUSTEES Mrs A Zouheiri, Mrs N Al-Kutoubi, Mrs I El–Ansari, Ms H Nouss

NOTES Relieve poverty overseas but would consider UK applications

HOW TO APPLY In writing. Trustees meet three times a year

WHO TO APPLY TO Mrs R Sukkar, Anglo-Arab Aid Ltd, 5 Breamwater Gardens, Surrey TW10 7SF

CC NO 1002687 **ESTABLISHED** 1990

■ The Anglo-Catholic Ordination Candidates Fund

WHAT IS FUNDED Grants to candidates for the ordained Ministry of the Church of England, and of churches in full communion with the Church of England, whose private resources are insufficient to enable them to pay in full for their training; and for the assistance of Theological Colleges and courses or other institutions approved by the Committee

WHO CAN BENEFIT Individuals and organisations benefiting young adults, older people and students training for the ministry of the Church of England

WHERE FUNDING CAN BE GIVEN UK and overseas

TYPE OF GRANT Buildings, capital, core costs, running costs and salaries. Funding is available for up to three years

FINANCES *Year* 1997 *Income* £101,210
Grants £78,525

TRUSTEES The Committee: Rt Rev E W Kemp, Most Revand Rt Hon D M Hope, Rev C J Chessun, Rev K W Clinch, Rev C W Danes, Rev Canon M J Gudgeon, Rev Canon R J Halliburton, R Harbord, FCA, Rev R Harper, Rev Prebendary H D Moore, Rev Canon P R Strange, Rev P E Ursell

NOTES Candidates means men already selected by a Bishop and church authorities for training

WHO TO APPLY TO Rev C W Danes, Secretary, The Anglo-Catholic Ordination Candidates Fund, 31 Oakley Road, Bocking, Braintree, Essex CM7 5QS

CC NO 220121 **ESTABLISHED** 1959

■ The Animal Defence Trust

WHAT IS FUNDED Animal welfare

WHAT IS NOT FUNDED Individuals and students

WHO CAN BENEFIT National and established organisations benefiting animals

WHERE FUNDING CAN BE GIVEN UK and overseas

TYPE OF GRANT One-off and recurrent

RANGE OF GRANTS £500–£7,000

SAMPLE GRANTS £7,000 to Brooke Hospital for Animals; £6,500 to Humane Slaughter Association; £6,000 to Born Free Foundation; £5,000 to Thoroughbred Rehabilitation Centre; £5,000 to Ferne Animal Sanctuary; £5,000 to National Canine Defence League; £5,000 to Society for the Welfare of Horses and Ponies; £5,000 to C Hammond Animal Trust; £5,000 to PDSA; £5,000 to Wood Green Animal Centres

FINANCES *Year* 1996 *Income* £241,040
Grants £74,800

TRUSTEES Diana H Andrews, Marion Saunders, Alan A Meyer

PUBLICATIONS Annual Report

NOTES Grants to existing charities in the field of animal welfare

HOW TO APPLY In writing at any time

WHO TO APPLY TO A A Meyer, Halsey Meyer Higgins, 10 Carteret Street, Queen Anne's Gate, London SW1H 9DR

CC NO 263095 **ESTABLISHED** 1971

■ The Annandale Charitable Trust

WHAT IS FUNDED General charitable purposes

WHAT IS NOT FUNDED The Trustees will not consider appeals from outside organisations. They make their own decisions on those charities that are supported by the Trust

WHO CAN BENEFIT There are no restrictions on the age; professional and economic group; family situation; religion and culture; and social circumstances of; or disease or medical condition suffered by, the beneficiaries

WHERE FUNDING CAN BE GIVEN UK

TRUSTEES Ms S M Blofeld, Ms A Lee

HOW TO APPLY **This Trust states that it does not respond to unsolicited applications**

WHO TO APPLY TO C M Woodrow, Trust Manager, The Annandale Charitable Trust, Midland Trust, Cumberland House, 15/17 Cumberland Place, Southampton, Hampshire SO15 2UY
Tel 01703 531396

CC NO 1049193 **ESTABLISHED** 1995

■ The Princess Anne's Charities Trust

WHAT IS FUNDED Social welfare, medical research and care, children and youth, wildlife

WHAT IS NOT FUNDED No grants are made to individuals

WHO CAN BENEFIT Registered charities benefiting children and young adults. There is no restriction on the disease or medical condition suffered by the beneficiaries. And few restrictions on their social circumstances

WHERE FUNDING CAN BE GIVEN UK and overseas

FINANCES *Year* 1996 *Income* £241,335
Grants £110,607

TRUSTEES Lt Col Sir Peter Gibbs, KCVO, Captain T J H Laurence, MVO, RN, The Hon Mark Bridges

WHO TO APPLY TO Lt Col Sir Peter Gibbs, KCVO, The Princess Anne's Charities Trust, Buckingham Palace, London SW1A 1AA

CC NO 277814 **ESTABLISHED** 1979

■ The Anstruther Literary Trust

This trust did not respond to CAF's request to amend its entry and, by 30 June 1998, CAF's researchers did not find financial records for later than 1995 on its file at the Charity Commission. Trusts are legally required to submit annual accounts to the Charity Commission under section 42 of the Charities Act 1993

WHAT IS FUNDED The advancement of education via books, pictures and historical records of national and private libraries. The protection and repair of public and private libraries. Access to historical records for the general public

WHAT IS NOT FUNDED Educational purposes only

WHO CAN BENEFIT Educational institutions, and establishments benefiting children, young adults and students

WHERE FUNDING CAN BE GIVEN UK

TRUSTEES I F C Anstruther, S C P Anstruther, J W Dolman

HOW TO APPLY In writing, including supporting material such as an Annual Report

WHO TO APPLY TO J W Dolman, Trustees' Solicitor, The Anstruther Literary Trust, Messrs Bircham and Co, 1 Dean Farrar Street, Westminster, London SW1M 0DY

CC NO 800758 **ESTABLISHED** 1988

■ The Fagus Anstruther Memorial Trust

WHAT IS FUNDED General charitable purposes, with express powers to make grants for purposes connected with further education in the arts and sciences

WHAT IS NOT FUNDED No unsolicited applications from individuals will be considered

WHO CAN BENEFIT Organisations only. There are no restrictions on the age; professional and economic group; family situation; religion and culture; and social circumstances of; or disease or medical condition suffered by, the beneficiaries

WHERE FUNDING CAN BE GIVEN Overseas

TYPE OF GRANT Small grants, not exceeding £500

FINANCES *Year* 1995 *Income* £20,000
Grants £18,000

TRUSTEES S M Anstruther, S P C Anstruther, G S Smith, K Anstruther, E T C Anstruther

HOW TO APPLY To the address below

WHO TO APPLY TO J W Dolman, The Fagus Anstruther Memorial Trust, 1 Dean Farrar Street, Westminster, London SW1H 0DY

CC NO 275173 **ESTABLISHED** 1978

■ Ambrose & Ann Appelbe Trust

WHAT IS FUNDED General charitable purposes – junior and adult education, research into social conditions and education – improvement of educational facilities

WHAT IS NOT FUNDED Buildings are not funded

WHO CAN BENEFIT Organisations benefiting people of all ages and students

WHERE FUNDING CAN BE GIVEN UK

RANGE OF GRANTS £25–£8,500

SAMPLE GRANTS £8,500 to Educational Bursaries; £2,000 to NSPCC; £2,000 to Hill Homes; £1,735 to HLSI; £1,500 to North London Hospice; £1,000 to Tradescant Trust; £1,000 to Bloomfield Centre; £800 to IRIS Fund; £700 to Society of Friends; £600 to Gospel Oak Nursery School

FINANCES *Year* 1997 *Income* £29,232
Grants £27,140

TRUSTEES A Appelbe, F A Appelbe, V Thomas

HOW TO APPLY By letter to the address under Who To Apply To

WHO TO APPLY TO Felix Appelbe, Solicitors, Ambrose & Ann Appelbe Trust, 1 Ellerdale Close, Hampstead, London NW3 6BE

CC NO 208658 **ESTABLISHED** 1944

■ Apple Charity (UK) Limited

WHAT IS FUNDED General charitable purposes

WHO CAN BENEFIT There are no restrictions on the age; professional and economic group; family situation; religion and culture; and social circumstances of; or disease or medical condition suffered by, the beneficiaries

WHERE FUNDING CAN BE GIVEN UK

TRUSTEES N Aspinall, B Capocciama, S Tenenbaum

WHO TO APPLY TO N S Aspinall, Apple Charity (UK) Limited, 27 Ovington Square, London SW3 1LJ

CC NO 1067560 **ESTABLISHED** 1998

■ The Appleton Trust

WHAT IS FUNDED In accordance with the Trust Deed for the general benefit of the Church of England

WHAT IS NOT FUNDED The Managing Trustees may not seek to relieve the Diocesan Board of Finance or the parishes in the Diocese of normal obligations to provide the money necessary for financing the work of the Church of England in the Diocese

WHO CAN BENEFIT Individuals and charitable and religious organisations in the Diocese of Canterbury and the Parish of St John the Evangelist, Shirley, Croydon

WHERE FUNDING CAN BE GIVEN Diocese of Canterbury and the Parish of St John the Evangelist, Shirley, Croydon

RANGE OF GRANTS Below £1,000–£4,000

SAMPLE GRANTS £4,000 to Springboard Travelling School; £2,877 to Diocesan House for a chairlift; £2,500 to St Luke's Hospital for the Clergy; £2,400 to the Rose Trust; £1,500 to Family Life and Marriage Education; £1,500 to Resources Centre at Ashford Christ Church School; £1,000 to St Peter in Thanet Portland Centre; 1000 to Cautley House Trust; £1,000 to Canterbury Cyrenians

FINANCES *Year* 1996 *Income* £38,362
Grants £34,534

TRUSTEES P F Maugham, D S Kemp, Canterbury Diocesan Board of Finance

WHO TO APPLY TO Miss R A Collins, The Appleton Trust, Diocesan House, Lady Wootton's Green, Canterbury, Kent CT1 1NQ

CC NO 250271 **ESTABLISHED** 1966

■ The Appletree Trust

WHAT IS FUNDED Cancer research and care and organisations which are concerned with disabled children, blind people and heart disease

WHAT IS NOT FUNDED No grants to individuals

WHO CAN BENEFIT Organisations benefiting disabled children, and people suffering from cancer, heart disease and sight loss

WHERE FUNDING CAN BE GIVEN UK and overseas, with a particular interest in North East Fife

TRUSTEES The Royal Bank of Scotland plc, Rev W McKane, Rev J D Martin

PUBLICATIONS Accounts and an Annual Report are available from the Trust

HOW TO APPLY Applications should be made in writing to the address below

WHO TO APPLY TO Mrs R Muirhead, The Appletree Trust, The Royal Bank of Scotland plc, Private Trust and Taxation, 2 Festival Square, Edinburgh EH3 9SU

SC NO SCO 04851 **ESTABLISHED** 1982

■ Aquinas Trust

This trust did not respond to CAF's request to amend its entry and, by 30 June 1998, CAF's researchers did not find financial records for later than 1995 on its file at the Charity Commission. Trusts are legally required to submit annual accounts to the Charity Commission under section 42 of the Charities Act 1993

WHAT IS FUNDED Medicine and health, welfare, particularly children's needs, especially those that fall outside the mainstream charity aid

WHAT IS NOT FUNDED None

WHO CAN BENEFIT Small local projects helping children who have very rare or individual problems who cannot find any help through other charities

WHERE FUNDING CAN BE GIVEN Manchester and UK

TYPE OF GRANT One-off small grants of £1,000 or less

TRUSTEES S Mathis, S McCarthy, H F Riley, G Cosgrave, D Robson

HOW TO APPLY To the address under Who To Apply To in writing at any time

WHO TO APPLY TO S N McCarthy, Aquinas Trust, Holiday Inn, Crowne Plaza, Peter Street, Manchester M60 2DS

CC NO 1033098   **ESTABLISHED** 1993

■ The Arab-British Chamber Charitable Foundation

WHAT IS FUNDED The advancement of science, education for needy young people and adults, in particular, on industrial, commercial, technological and professional subjects of relevance to the Arab States. Grants given for the higher education of Arab nationals

WHO CAN BENEFIT To benefit young people, adults, students and those disadvantaged by poverty

WHERE FUNDING CAN BE GIVEN UK and overseas

FINANCES *Year* 1997 *Income* £169,766 *Grants* £83,017

TRUSTEES Rt Hon Lord Denman, Dr S N Jaroudi, Sir J Wilton, Dr A B Zahlan

WHO TO APPLY TO The Arab-British Chamber Charitable Foundation, Weathervane Cottage, Much Hadham, Hertfordshire SG10 6BY

CC NO 280487   **ESTABLISHED** 1980

■ The John M Archer Charitable Trust

WHAT IS FUNDED General charitable purposes. Grants are made to a range of organisations

WHO CAN BENEFIT There are no restrictions on the age; professional and economic group; family situation; religion and culture; and social circumstances of; or disease or medical condition suffered by, the beneficiaries

WHERE FUNDING CAN BE GIVEN UK and overseas

FINANCES *Year* 1997–98 *Income* £22,038 *Grants* £21,475

TRUSTEES G B Archer, Mrs C M Archer, R Stewart, Mrs I Morrison, Mrs A Morgan, Mrs W Grant

HOW TO APPLY Applications should be made in writing to the address under Who To Apply To

WHO TO APPLY TO Miss I C Archer, Secretary, The John M Archer Charitable Trust, 12 Broughton Place, Edinburgh EH1 3RX *Tel* 0131-556 4518

SC NO SCO 10583   **ESTABLISHED** 1969

■ The Archer Trust

WHAT IS FUNDED To relieve suffering among the aged, impotent or poor. To advance education. To advance the Christian religion. To help with charitable objects as seen fit by the Trustees. Support for the disabled and the handicapped, and to encourage handicapped people to reach their full potential. To distribute the revenue of the Trust to reinvest the capital, but this is not binding. Distribution may be made to other registered charities or direct to individuals or groups

WHAT IS NOT FUNDED The Trustees do not support animal charities and wish to keep a low profile locally

WHO CAN BENEFIT Individuals and organisations benefiting: people of all ages; retired people; those disadvantaged by poverty or disabled; those of at risk groups; are homeless or socially isolated

WHERE FUNDING CAN BE GIVEN UK and overseas

RANGE OF GRANTS £250–£2,500

SAMPLE GRANTS £3,000 to Demand for a new building for equipment making for handicapped; £2,500 to Stepney Children's Fund for pre-school appeal; £2,000 to United World College of the Atlantic for educational scholarship; £2,000 to Thames Valley Adventure Playground for the handicapped; £1,250 to RAPt for the welfare of prisoners

FINANCES *Year* 1995–96 *Income* £14,222 *Grants* £11,300

TRUSTEES Mrs C M Archer, M F Baker, J N Archer, F D R MacDougall

NOTES We do not generally give grants to individuals

HOW TO APPLY Applications will be acknowledged and guidelines sent if an sae is enclosed. A copy of accounts will be required

WHO TO APPLY TO Mrs C M Archer, The Archer Trust, Oldfield, Wadesmill, Ware, Hertfordshire SG12 0TT

CC NO 1033534   **ESTABLISHED** 1994

■ The Architectural Heritage Fund

WHAT IS FUNDED Support is given in the form of low interest loans, advice and information for the preservation of old buildings. Grants are also made for feasibility studies

WHAT IS NOT FUNDED No grants to individuals, non-charitable organisations or for projects which do not include a change of ownership or use

WHO CAN BENEFIT There are no restrictions on the age; professional and economic group; family situation; religion and culture; and social circumstances of; or disease or medical condition suffered by, the beneficiaries

WHERE FUNDING CAN BE GIVEN UK

TYPE OF GRANT Loans, feasibility study grants

FINANCES *Year* 1997 *Income* £1,426,759

TRUSTEES Dame Jennifer Jenkins (Chairman), N Baring, R Clow, M Crowder, Prof J Dunbar-Nesmith, J N C James, Sir B Jenkins, P Rumble, M Stonefrost, R Worskett, Dr R Wools

NOTES Only organisations with charitable status and preservation trusts can be considered for funding

HOW TO APPLY Applications are considered quarterly in March, June, September and December and should be submitted at least six weeks in advance. Telephone enquiries welcome. Comprehensive notes to assist applicants to complete and submit their application are available on request

WHO TO APPLY TO Lady Weir, Correspondent, The Architectural Heritage Fund, Clareville House, 26–27 Oxendon Street London SW1Y 4EL
CC NO 266780   **ESTABLISHED** 1974

■ The Ardwick Trust

WHAT IS FUNDED To support Jewish welfare, along with a wide band of non-Jewish causes to include social welfare, education, the elderly, conservation and the environment
WHAT IS NOT FUNDED No grants to individuals
WHO CAN BENEFIT Institutions and registered charities (mainly national charities) benefiting people of all ages, students and Jews. There are few restrictions by social circumstance
WHERE FUNDING CAN BE GIVEN UK, Israel and the third world
RANGE OF GRANTS £50–£2,000
FINANCES *Year* 1997 *Income* £40,515 *Grants* £19,675
TRUSTEES Mrs J B Bloch, Miss E R Wix
WHO TO APPLY TO Mrs J B Bloch, The Ardwick Trust, 6 Hocroft Avenue, London NW2 2EH *Tel* 0171-435 1602
CC NO 266981   **ESTABLISHED** 1975

■ A Arenson Charitable Trust

This trust did not respond to CAF's request to amend its entry and, by 30 June 1998, CAF's researchers did not find financial records for later than 1995 on its file at the Charity Commission. Trusts are legally required to submit annual accounts to the Charity Commission under section 42 of the Charities Act 1993

WHAT IS FUNDED General charitable purposes
WHAT IS NOT FUNDED No unsolicited applications will be considered. Registered charities only
WHO CAN BENEFIT Registered charities only. There are no restrictions on the age; professional and economic group; family situation; religion and culture; and social circumstances of; or disease or medical condition suffered by, the beneficiaries
WHERE FUNDING CAN BE GIVEN UK
TRUSTEES Mrs R J Sacks, Mrs H B Kalmanson, S D Arenson, C Wagman
HOW TO APPLY **This Trust states that it does not respond to unsolicited applications**
WHO TO APPLY TO Mrs H B Kalmanson, Trustee, A Arenson Charitable Trust, Green Verges, Priory Drive, Stanmore, Middlesex HA7 3HL
CC NO 272515   **ESTABLISHED** 1971

■ Argent Charitable Trust

This trust did not respond to CAF's request to amend its entry and, by 30 June 1998, CAF's researchers did not find financial records for later than 1995 on its file at the Charity Commission. Trusts are legally required to submit annual accounts to the Charity Commission under section 42 of the Charities Act 1993

WHAT IS FUNDED (a) To relieve the aged, impotent and infirm; (b) to advance education; (c) to advance religion, limited to the Jewish religion; (d) other general charitable purposes for the benefit of the community
WHO CAN BENEFIT Children, young adults, older people and Jewish people
WHERE FUNDING CAN BE GIVEN UK and elsewhere

WHO TO APPLY TO G R Stewart, Director of Trustee Company, Argent Charitable Trust, c/o Argent Trustees, 1 Battersea Bridge Road, London SW11 3BG
CC NO 1043969   **ESTABLISHED** 1994

■ The Arkleton Trust

WHAT IS FUNDED To study practical ways of improving the conditions of life of rural people particularly through education and rural development. It aims to stimulate discussion between politicians, administrators and practitioners on problems facing rural people throughout the world. To collaborate with other bodies which share its aims and with individuals working in the same field. To hold seminars and undertake research and studies. To publish and disseminate results of research, studies and fellowships
WHAT IS NOT FUNDED No grants to individuals seeking support for educational purposes. Applicants must conform to the requirements of each fund including closing dates (see Notes)
WHO CAN BENEFIT People living in rural areas
WHERE FUNDING CAN BE GIVEN UK and overseas
TYPE OF GRANT One-off awards from the funds listed in Notes only are available to applicants after adjudication by a selection committee
RANGE OF GRANTS £400–£5,000
FINANCES *Year* 1997 *Income* £37,285 *Grants* £10,779
TRUSTEES Sir Kenneth Alexander, A Bell, M Galsworthy, D Walton, D C Y Higgs, Lady Higgs,
PUBLICATIONS Seminar reports. Arkleton Lecture, Research Reports. Occasional publications on rural development and fellowship reports
NOTES (a) The David Moore Memorial Fund, aimed at young people engaged in the study of rural development and social change in Europe and/or Third World countries to enable them to supplement academic course work with some research/practical field investigations. Amount of award between £400 and £800. Closing date 31 January of each year. (b) The Bernard Conyers Fund to encourage an individual or small organisation to disseminate information, findings or ideas relating to the Third World, the links between Europe and the Third World, or the lessons which Europe can learn from Third World experience. More than one award may be given in any one year. Total to be awarded £6,000. Closing date 14 May of each year. (c) John Higgs Fund seeks to identify groups doing specific development, community (not playgroups) or education (not schools) work in rural areas: small awards made on a one-off basis
HOW TO APPLY Applications in writing only considered, but notes for guidance are available from the Trust for (a) and (b) above
WHO TO APPLY TO The Administrator, The Arkleton Trust, Enstone, Chipping Norton, Oxfordshire OX7 4HH *Tel* 01608 677255 *Fax* 01608 677276 *E-mail* arkleton@enstoneuk.demon.co.uk
CC NO 275153   **ESTABLISHED** 1978

■ G C Armitage Charitable Trust

WHAT IS FUNDED Charities working in the fields of: churches; music; opera; support to voluntary and community organisations; the Council for Voluntary Service; hospices; cancer research; woodlands; and horticulture
WHAT IS NOT FUNDED Individual applications will not be considered, expenses kept to absolute

Does the trust you have chosen match your needs? Haphazard applications waste postage and time

25

minimum, do not favour other than local/known charities

WHO CAN BENEFIT Organisations benefiting: musicians; seafarers and fishermen; disabled people; victims of crime; victims of war; and beneficiaries who are terminally ill or suffering from cancer

WHERE FUNDING CAN BE GIVEN Leeds, North Yorkshire, Wakefield and York

TYPE OF GRANT Funding for up to and over three years will be considered

RANGE OF GRANTS £100–£2,500; average approximately £800

SAMPLE GRANTS £2,500 to Cancer Relief for Ripon Hospital; £2,000 to RNLI; £2,000 to Wheatfields Hospice; £2,000 to St Michaels Hospice; £1,500 to St Leonards Church, Burton Leonard; £1,500 to Martin House; £1,500 to Leeds Parish Church for appeal; £1,000 to Salvation Army; £1,000 to Friends of Opera North; £1,000 to St Georges Crypt Leeds

FINANCES *Year* 1998 *Income* £32,500 *Grants* £32,700

TRUSTEES Mrs V M Armitage, Mrs C J Greig

WHO TO APPLY TO Mrs V M Armitage, G C Armitage Charitable Trust, Aldborough House, Aldborough, Boroughbridge YO51 9EY

CC NO 326418 **ESTABLISHED** 1985

■ The Armourers' & Brasiers' Gauntlet Trust

WHAT IS FUNDED Research and education in materials science

WHO CAN BENEFIT Organisations benefiting young adults, academics, research workers and students

WHERE FUNDING CAN BE GIVEN UK

FINANCES *Year* 1998 *Income* £198,269 *Grants* £170,774

TRUSTEES Details available on application

HOW TO APPLY By letter supported by tutor

WHO TO APPLY TO Cdr T J K Sloane, OBE, RN, Secretary, The Armourers' & Brasiers' Gauntlet Trust, Armourers' Hall, 81 Coleman Street, London EC2R 5BJ *Tel* 0171-606 1199 *Fax* 0171-606 7481

CC NO 279204 **ESTABLISHED** 1979

■ The Armthorpe Poors Estate Charity

WHAT IS FUNDED Welfare organisations, individuals and educational grants. Particularly charities working in the fields of: accommodation and housing; acute health care; costs of study and community service

WHO CAN BENEFIT Individuals and organisations benefiting: children; young adults; older people; retired people; students; unemployed people; those in care, fostered and adopted; one parent families; widows and widowers; at risk groups; carers; disabled people; those disadvantaged by poverty; disaster victims and homeless people

WHERE FUNDING CAN BE GIVEN Armthorpe

TYPE OF GRANT Cash grants

RANGE OF GRANTS £35–£500

SAMPLE GRANTS £1,620 to Physically disabled people for relief of need; £600 to local Parish Council for meals for the elderly infirm; £500 to an MS sufferer for part cost of vehicle; £475 to a playgroup to widen their service to under privileged children; £440 to blind people for relief of need; £250 to a single parent for beds etc; £189 to a single parent for cooker and washer; £180 to local family in need for beds for two children; £175 to a pensioner for repairs to heating system; £100 to a carer for a holiday break

FINANCES *Year* 1997–98 *Income* £134,400

TRUSTEES Miss M Colbeck, Rev J Barnes, F Paling, N H Pattinson, H Schofield

HOW TO APPLY To the address under Who To Apply To in writing or by telephone

WHO TO APPLY TO F Pratt, Clerk, The Armthorpe Poors Estate Charity, 32 Garth Avenue, Edenthorpe, Doncaster DN3 2LW *Tel* 01302 882806

CC NO 226123 **ESTABLISHED** 1963

■ The Army Benevolent Fund

WHAT IS FUNDED Support and benefit, in any charitable way, of persons serving, or who have served, in Her Majesty's Army, or their dependants. This is done directly or indirectly, by making grants to approved military charities, including Corps and Regimental Associations. The Fund does not deal direct with individual cases, these should be referred initially to the appropriate Corps or Regimental Association

WHO CAN BENEFIT National headquarters of charities and charitable funds of Corps and Regimental Associations benefiting ex-service and service people, and their dependants, such as widows, widowers, spouses and children

WHERE FUNDING CAN BE GIVEN UK

RANGE OF GRANTS £600–£225,000

SAMPLE GRANTS £225,000 to St Dunstan's; £158,219 to Forces Help Society and Lord Robert's Workshops; £150,000 to Haig Homes; £147,488 to Ex-Services Mental Welfare Society; £143,468 to SSAFA; £132,519 to Ex-Service Fellowship Centres; £128,104 to Regular Forces' Employment Association; £100,000 to British Commonwealth Ex-Services League; £100,000 to Officers' Association; £100,000 to Chaseley Trust

FINANCES *Year* 1996–97 *Income* £5,418,635 *Grants* £2,076,210

TRUSTEES Members of the Executive Committee of the ABF

NOTES Financial support given by the Fund must be directly or indirectly for the benefit of persons, or dependents of persons, who are serving, or have served, in Her Majesty's Army

WHO TO APPLY TO The Controller, The Army Benevolent Fund, 41 Queen's Gate, London SW7 5HR

CC NO 211645 **ESTABLISHED** 1944

■ Thomas Arno Bequest

WHAT IS FUNDED Assistance to poor pupils and ex-pupils of Haberdasher's schools. Grants to schools of Haberdashers' Company. Donations to hospitals, institutions

WHAT IS NOT FUNDED No grants to individuals other than those under What Is Funded

WHO CAN BENEFIT Pupils and ex-pupils of Haberdasher's schools who are disadvantaged by poverty. There is no restriction on the disease or medical condition suffered by the beneficiaries

WHERE FUNDING CAN BE GIVEN UK

Have you read How to use the DGMT *on page xvi?*

FINANCES *Year* 1997 *Income* £103,000
Grants £116,000
TRUSTEES The Haberdashers Company
WHO TO APPLY TO The Clerk to the Haberdashers'
Company, Thomas Arno Bequest, Haberdashers'
Hall, 39–40 Bartholomew Close, London
EC1A 7JN *Tel* 0171-606 0967
CC NO 230497   **ESTABLISHED** 1959

■ Jaquine Lachman Arnold Charitable Foundation

WHAT IS FUNDED Buildings of architectural or
historical importance
WHAT IS NOT FUNDED No grant for non-structural
projects/activities
WHERE FUNDING CAN BE GIVEN UK
TYPE OF GRANT Discretionary
TRUSTEES Ms J C Arnold, F Ledwidge, J C V Miles
NOTES This Trust replied to CAF's mailing. However,
by 30 June 1998, CAF's researchers did not find
any financial records filed at the Charity
Commission
WHO TO APPLY TO F Ledwidge, Trustee, Jaquine
Lachman Arnold Charitable Foundation, 7–19
Royal Avenue, Belfast BT1 1FB
Tel 01232 235600
CC NO 1043493   **ESTABLISHED** 1995

■ The Arnold Foundation

WHAT IS FUNDED Only to support local (South West
England) charities in which the Trustees have a
personal knowledge and interest. Particularly
charities working in the fields of: music; visual
arts; orchestras; theatrical companies and theatre
groups; hospices and hospitals; cancer research;
neurological research; conservation; wildlife
sanctuaries; heritage and churches
WHAT IS NOT FUNDED Registered charities only.
Applications from individuals, including students,
are ineligible. No grants made in response to
appeals from large national organisations, nor
from any organisation working outside South West
England
WHO CAN BENEFIT Small charities in SW England
personally known to the Trustees benefiting:
actors and entertainment professionals;
musicians; victims of abuse and crime; and those
suffering from Alzheimer' disease, cancers,
epilepsy, mental illness, strokes and terminally ill
people
WHERE FUNDING CAN BE GIVEN South West England
TYPE OF GRANT One-off grants funded for up to or
more than three years will be considered
RANGE OF GRANTS £250–£1,000
FINANCES *Year* 1997 *Income* £15,657
Grants £19,300
TRUSTEES J L S Arnold (Chairman), Mrs M S
Grantham, A J Meek, FRIBA, D F Smith, FCA
NOTES **Funds fully committed**
HOW TO APPLY **This Trust states that it does not
respond to unsolicited applications**
WHO TO APPLY TO The Secretary, The Arnold
Foundation, 37 Nightingale Rise, Portishead,
Bristol BS20 8LN *Tel* 01275 842414
CC NO 277430   **ESTABLISHED** 1979

■ The Arnopa Trust

WHAT IS FUNDED Support is given to deprived children
through the work of schools and colleges,
community services and religious organisations
WHAT IS NOT FUNDED Not medical research,
expeditions. No grants to individuals
WHO CAN BENEFIT Organisations benefiting deprived
children and young adults
WHERE FUNDING CAN BE GIVEN UK
TYPE OF GRANT One-off, revenue and salaries will be
considered
SAMPLE GRANTS £20,000 to Brentwood Catholic
Children's Society for a social worker to assist the
Society's work in Newham; £20,000 to
Cornerstone Church, Swansea for a youth
worker's salary; £16,000 to The Reedham Trust
for a student award scheme and scholarship fund;
£10,000 to Archdiocese of Westminster SPEC
Centre for a loft conversion for young people's
pastoral centre; £8,275 to Kulika Charitable Trust
for the salary costs of a social worker
FINANCES *Year* 1997 *Income* £508,933
Grants £74,275
TRUSTEES Charport Ltd
WHO TO APPLY TO Jane Leek, The Arnopa Trust,
1 Connaught Place, London W2 2DY *Tel* 0171-
402 5500 *Fax* 0171-298 0003
CC NO 275537   **ESTABLISHED** 1977

■ Arthritis Research Campaign

WHAT IS FUNDED To finance research into the cause
and cure of rheumatic diseases. Projects must be
relevant to rheumatology
WHAT IS NOT FUNDED Restricted to support for
research into rheumatic diseases. Applications for
welfare and social matters will not be considered
WHO CAN BENEFIT Medical schools, hospitals and
individual research workers, medical
professionals, and those suffering from arthritis,
rheumatism and allied diseases
WHERE FUNDING CAN BE GIVEN Essentially the UK
SAMPLE GRANTS £641,654 to Infection and Immunity
Research Group Kings College, London;
£377,023 to Dept of Medicine and Therapeutics
University of Aberdeen; £305,793 to Wellcome
Trust Centre for Human Genetics Nuffield
Orthapaedic Centre, Oxford; £156,861 to Division
of Medicine, Imperial College School of Medicine,
London; £156,304 to Dept of Biochemical
Pharmacology St Bartholomew's and The Royal
London Hospital, London; £155,504 to Dept of
Veterinary Basic Sciences, The Royal College of
Veterinary Surgeons, London; £153,469 to Dept
of Biochemistry, University of Oxford, Oxford;
£133,760 to Division of Medicine, Imperial
College School of Medicine, London; £124,272 to
Dept of Biochemistry and Molecular Biology Royal
Free Hospital, London; £123,224 to Anatomy Unit
School of Molecular Medicine and Bioscience,
Cardiff
FINANCES *Year* 1997 *Income* £20,899,000
Grants £15,081,000
TRUSTEES The Board of Trustees: Dr C G Barres, Sir R
Butler, Dr B M Ansell, Dr P W M Copeman, O N
Dawson, Prof P Dieppe, Prof T Duckworth, Dame
M Glen-Haigh DBE, Prof H J F Hodgson, R E
Holland, S A Maitland, J C Mausey, Prof G Nuki,
A C Tory
HOW TO APPLY Application form and guidelines
available with sae
WHO TO APPLY TO Fergus Logan, Chief Executive,
Arthritis Research Campaign, Copeman House, St
Mary's Court, St Mary's Gate, Chesterfield,
Derbyshire S41 7TD *Tel* 01246 558033
Fax 01246 558007 *E-mail* r&e@arc.org.uk
CC NO 207711   **ESTABLISHED** 1936

■ Arts and Youth Trust for Eastleigh

WHAT IS FUNDED Promotion of the arts; assistance in the provision of facilities for young people for recreation or other leisure time occupations in the interests of social welfare

WHO CAN BENEFIT Children and young adults, artists, musicians, textile workers and designers, and writers and poets

WHERE FUNDING CAN BE GIVEN Eastleigh

TRUSTEES Ms S J Bryen, B Clarke, S Cox, Mrs N Lark, M Morris, J Vaughan, J Whatley, J Wray

WHO TO APPLY TO M Morris, Chairman, Arts and Youth Trust for Eastleigh, 4 Raglan Close, Chandlers Ford, Eastleigh, Hampshire SO53 4NH

CC NO 1055297   **ESTABLISHED** 1996

■ The Arts Council of England

WHAT IS FUNDED Activities limited to visual art (including photography and arts films), dance, drama, literature, music and opera. Capital programme funded by the National Lottery. The Arts Council of England is responsible for the distribution of the arts share of Lottery funds. At present this includes grants for capital projects such as constructing new buildings

WHAT IS NOT FUNDED Support is primarily confined to professional arts organisations and artists. The Arts Council is no longer in a position to consider grants towards the cost of educational courses. No grants to individuals

WHO CAN BENEFIT Non-profit-distributing arts organisations; professional creative artists; actors and entertainment professionals; musicians; and writers and poets

WHERE FUNDING CAN BE GIVEN England

TYPE OF GRANT Buildings, capital, core costs, feasibility studies, one-off, project, research, recurring costs, running costs, salaries and start-up costs. Funding is available for up to and over three years

SAMPLE GRANTS £13,218,256 to South Bank Board; £11,955,000 to English National Opera; £11,167,000 to Royal National Theatre; £8,470,000 Royal Shakespeare Theatre; £7,954,000 to The Royal Opera; £6,455,000 to Royal Ballet; £5,417,280 to Birmingham Royal Ballet; £5,034,000 to Opera North; £4,201,500 to Welsh National Opera; £3,871,776 to English National Ballet

FINANCES *Year* 1998 *Income* £184,600,000

TRUSTEES Members of the Council (Chairman: Gerry Robinson)

PUBLICATIONS Annual Report. List of publications available on request

WHO TO APPLY TO Information Officer, The Arts Council of England, 14 Great Peter Street, London SW1P 3NQ *Tel* 0171-333 0100

CC NO 212210   **ESTABLISHED** 1946

■ The Arts Council of Wales

WHAT IS FUNDED Activities limited to arts (including visual art, dance, drama, literature, music and craft)

WHO CAN BENEFIT Arts related organisations benefiting: actors and entertainment professionals; musicians; textile workers and designers; and writers and poets

WHERE FUNDING CAN BE GIVEN Wales

TYPE OF GRANT Revenue grants, grants for arts projects, grants promoting access to and

participation in the arts and to benefit young people in particular, individual bursaries and grants towards capital expenditure

FINANCES *Year* 1996–97 *Income* £31,956,000 *Grants* £25,351,000

PUBLICATIONS Annual Report; occasional research digests; Crefft; Artists Notes, etc

HOW TO APPLY Contact the relevant art form or regional officer for details

WHO TO APPLY TO Information Officer, The Arts Council of Wales, 9 Museum Place, Cardiff CF1 3NX *Tel* 01222 376500 *Fax* 01222 221447

REGIONAL OFFICES The Arts Council of Wales also has two regional offices:
ACW, North Wales Office, Prince's Drive, Colwyn Bay LL29 8LA *Tel* 01492 533440
ACW, West Wales Office, 6 Gardd Llydaw, Jacksons' Lane, Carmarthen, Dyfed SA31 1QD *Tel* 01267 234248

CC NO 1034245   **ESTABLISHED** 1994

■ Arts Foundation

This trust did not respond to CAF's request to amend its entry and, by 30 June 1998, CAF's researchers did not find financial records for later than 1995 on its file at the Charity Commission. Trusts are legally required to submit annual accounts to the Charity Commission under section 42 of the Charities Act 1993

WHAT IS FUNDED Advancement of public education in the arts, in particular, by the exhibition of contemporary art and by an educational programme for schools

WHO CAN BENEFIT Children, young adults and artists

WHERE FUNDING CAN BE GIVEN UK

WHO TO APPLY TO Dr C Greenberg, Arts Foundation, 6 Arkwright Mansions, Finchley Road, London NW3 6DE

CC NO 1007208   **ESTABLISHED** 1991

■ The Arundell Street Fund

WHAT IS FUNDED Care and social welfare in the area Where Funding Can Be Given

WHAT IS NOT FUNDED No grants for revenue costs or to individuals

WHO CAN BENEFIT Organisations benefiting at risk groups, those disadvantaged by poverty and socially isolated people. There is no restriction on the disease or medical condition suffered by the beneficiaries

WHERE FUNDING CAN BE GIVEN City of Westminster

FINANCES *Year* 1996–97 *Income* £38,300 *Grants* £23,974

TRUSTEES Members of the Arts and Grants Sub-committee of the City of Westminster

HOW TO APPLY To the address under Who To Apply To in writing

WHO TO APPLY TO Ms Nicola Mills, Principal Grants Officer, The Arundell Street Fund, Grants and Arts Unit, 16th Floor, Westminster City Hall, Victoria Street, London SW1E 6QP

CC NO 273817   **ESTABLISHED** 1979

■ The Ascot Fire Brigade Trust

WHAT IS FUNDED General charitable purposes in the Ascot area. Particularly charities working in the fields of: volunteer bureaux; community arts and recreation; clubs; day centres; holidays and outings; and playschemes

WHAT IS NOT FUNDED Grants to schools/PTA's are unlikely to be made

WHO CAN BENEFIT The residents of Ascot. There are no restrictions on the age; professional and economic group; family situation; religion and culture; and social circumstances of; or disease or medical condition suffered by, the beneficiaries

WHERE FUNDING CAN BE GIVEN Ascot (includes Sunninghill and Sunningdale) only

TYPE OF GRANT Buildings, capital, core costs, one-off, project and recurring costs. Funding for one year or less will be considered for public purposes for the benefit of the inhabitants of Ascot and not provided out of rates or other public funds

RANGE OF GRANTS £100–£7,500, average grants £500–£1,000

SAMPLE GRANTS £7,500 to 1st South Ascot Scout Group towards new building; £2,222 to 1st Sunninghill Girl Guides for building repairs to Guide Hut; £1,760 to Ascot District Day Centre for general purposes; £1,000 to North Ascot Community Centre for building purposes; £1,000 to Paul Bevan Cancer Foundation Ascot for general purposes, eg funding Macmillan Nurses

FINANCES *Year* 1996 *Income* £19,617
Grants £18,732

TRUSTEES G E Butcher, J H Maisey, J V Meech

HOW TO APPLY To the address under Who To Apply To in writing. Trustees meet usually three or four times a year

WHO TO APPLY TO J H Maisey, Trustee, The Ascot Fire Brigade Trust, 18 Woodlands Rise, South Ascot, Berkshire SL5 9HN *Tel* 01344 23511

CC NO 245675   **ESTABLISHED** 1959

■ Ashburnham Thanksgiving Trust

WHAT IS FUNDED Only Christian work already known to the Trustees is supported, particularly evangelical overseas missionary work

WHAT IS NOT FUNDED No grants for buildings

WHO CAN BENEFIT Individuals and organisations benefiting Christians and Evangelists

WHERE FUNDING CAN BE GIVEN UK and overseas

SAMPLE GRANTS £10,170 to Interserve; £5,000 to the Cherith Trust; £3,853 to Lama Ministries; £3,715 to Lawrence Barham Memorial Trust; £3,350 to Genesis Arts Trust; £3,171 to Ashburnham and Penshurst Churches; £2,043 to Ashburnham Christian Trust; £1,713 to Christian Praise; £1,416 to TEAR Fund; £1,200 to Open Doors

FINANCES *Year* 1996 *Income* £117,329
Grants £76,198

TRUSTEES Mrs M Bickersteth, Mrs K Habershon, E R Bickersteth, R D Bickersteth

HOW TO APPLY **This Trust states that it does not respond to unsolicited applications**. Funds already fully committed

WHO TO APPLY TO Mrs J D Bickersteth, Ashburnham Thanksgiving Trust, Agmerhurst House, Ashburnham, Battle, East Sussex TN33 9NB

CC NO 249109   **ESTABLISHED** 1965

■ The Ashby Charitable Trust

WHAT IS FUNDED Young entrepreneurs commencing in business or wishing to expand an existing business, along lines similar to those of The Prince's Youth Business Trust; educational awards to educational establishments and to individuals, especially to mature students ineligible for state support; and other registered charities in the field of research and help for sufferers from cancer, leukaemia, heart disease, multiple sclerosis and spina bifida

WHO CAN BENEFIT Individuals and organisations benefiting young people, mature students, research workers and medical professionals. Support may be given to those suffering from a variety of diseases and medical conditions

WHERE FUNDING CAN BE GIVEN UK, Africa, India

TYPE OF GRANT Research and educational awards are considered

FINANCES *Year* 1997 *Income* £101,445
Grants £7,424

TRUSTEES B A Ashby, FRICS, Mrs I Ashby, D R Ashby, BSc, MBA, ARICS, R Goodwin, FCA, Viscount Tamworth, FCA

NOTES Since October 1996, the Trust has had close links with London Regional Transport to set up an Ashby Charitable Trust Award, a scheme rewarding caring and courageous acts by London Underground staff and Transport Police only. Though recommendations have been received, so far none have satisfied the criteria

WHO TO APPLY TO R Goodwin, The Ashby Charitable Trust, 7 New Street, Ledbury, Herefordshire HR8 2DX *Tel* 01531 633812
Fax 01531 634583 *E-mail* gyf@wildnet.co.uk

CC NO 276497   **ESTABLISHED** 1978

■ A J H Ashby Will Trust

WHAT IS FUNDED Education; environmental resources; children in the Lea Valley; wildlife; conservation; English heritage

WHAT IS NOT FUNDED No grants to individuals or students

WHO CAN BENEFIT Small local projects benefiting children and young adults

WHERE FUNDING CAN BE GIVEN Lea Valley, Hertfordshire only

TYPE OF GRANT One-off and recurrent range of grants

FINANCES *Year* 1995 *Income* £62,725
Grants £72,000

TRUSTEES Midland Bank Trust Co Ltd

HOW TO APPLY To the Correspondent in writing

WHO TO APPLY TO C M Woodrow, Trust Manager, A J H Ashby Will Trust, Midland Bank, Cumberland House, 15–17 Cumberland Place, Southampton SO15 2UY *Tel* 01703 531364

CC NO 803291   **ESTABLISHED** 1990

■ Michael A Ashcroft Foundation (also known as The Prospect Charitable Trust)

WHAT IS FUNDED Education, welfare, crime prevention

WHO CAN BENEFIT Support is given to children, young adults, students and teachers. Support is also given to at risk groups, those disadvantaged by poverty, socially isolated people, ex-offenders and those at risk of offending

WHERE FUNDING CAN BE GIVEN UK

SAMPLE GRANTS £2,000 to Imperial Cancer Research

FINANCES *Year* 1997 *Income* £141,235
Grants £2,000

TRUSTEES Terence W Godfrey, Llewelyn J Austen, Susan M Ashcroft

NOTES The majority of the Foundation's income is spent on staff salaries, travel expenses and motor vehicle expenses

HOW TO APPLY To the address under Who To Apply To in writing

WHO TO APPLY TO T Godfrey, Trustee, Michael A Ashcroft Foundation, 19–21 Denmark Street, Wokingham, Berkshire RG40 2QE
CC NO 802461   **ESTABLISHED** 1989

■ The Ashe Charitable Foundation

This trust did not respond to CAF's request to amend its entry and, by 30 June 1998, CAF's researchers did not find financial records for later than 1995 on its file at the Charity Commission. Trusts are legally required to submit annual accounts to the Charity Commission under section 42 of the Charities Act 1993

WHAT IS FUNDED General charitable purposes
WHO CAN BENEFIT There are no restrictions on the age; professional and economic group; family situation; religion and culture; and social circumstances of; or disease or medical condition suffered by, the beneficiaries
WHERE FUNDING CAN BE GIVEN UK
TRUSTEES C Heath, Mrs M Heath, F Akers-Douglas
WHO TO APPLY TO F A M Akers-Douglas, The Ashe Charitable Foundation, BDO Binder Hamlyn, 17 Lansdown Road, Croydon, Surrey CR9 2PL
CC NO 299936   **ESTABLISHED** 1988

■ The Ashendene Trust

WHAT IS FUNDED Small organisations, ex-offenders, socially deprived and the arts. Particularly charities working in the field of the advancement of Christianity; Anglican bodies: arts, culture and recreation; conservation of flora; the purchase of books; scholarships; and clubs and counselling
WHAT IS NOT FUNDED No large organisations, education or health
WHO CAN BENEFIT Registered charities benefiting children; clergy; musicians; writers and poets; those disadvantaged by poverty; ex-offenders and those at risk of offending and homeless people
WHERE FUNDING CAN BE GIVEN London, Oxfordshire and Berkshire
TYPE OF GRANT Capital, core costs and project. Funding available for up to three years
RANGE OF GRANTS £500–£25,000 (4 years). Average grant £2,500
FINANCES *Year* 1996–97 *Income* £28,000 *Grants* £34,000
TRUSTEES Sir Simon Hornby, Sir Edward Cazalet, A D Loehnis
NOTES This a small Trust that gives to organisations where the grant will really make an impact
WHO TO APPLY TO Sir Simon Hornby, Trustee, The Ashendene Trust, The Ham, Wantage, Oxfordshire OX12 0JA
CC NO 270749   **ESTABLISHED** 1975

■ The Ashfield Trust

WHAT IS FUNDED General charitable purposes
WHO CAN BENEFIT There are no restrictions on the age; professional and economic group; family situation; religion and culture; and social circumstances of; or disease or medical condition suffered by, the beneficiaries
WHERE FUNDING CAN BE GIVEN UK
FINANCES *Year* 1996 *Income* £13,731
TRUSTEES Ms B Jones, Ms J P Noonan, F C Noonan
NOTES No grants given in 1996
WHO TO APPLY TO F C Noonan, The Ashfield Trust, Peart Hall, Church Road, Spaxton, Bridgewater, Somerset TA5 1DA
CC NO 1041366   **ESTABLISHED** 1994

■ Bevan Ashford Charitable Trust

WHAT IS FUNDED General charitable purposes for the benefit of the inhabitants of Bristol, Cardiff and surrounding areas
WHO CAN BENEFIT There are no restrictions on the age; professional and economic group; family situation; religion and culture; and social circumstances of; or disease or medical condition suffered by, the beneficiaries
WHERE FUNDING CAN BE GIVEN Bristol, Cardiff and surrounding areas
TRUSTEES P A Cooper, N C Jarrett–Kerr, N L T Morgan, P J Scott
WHO TO APPLY TO N C Jarrett-Kerr, Solicitor, Bevan Ashford Charitable Trust, 35 Colston Avenue, Bristol BS1 4TT
CC NO 1067624   **ESTABLISHED** 1997

■ The Norman C Ashton Foundation

WHAT IS FUNDED The relief of poverty particularly amongst those connected with the company or their dependants. To assist over education. To support schools, colleges or other educational foundations recognised as charitable in law. To alleviate any national or local disaster. Each application judged on its merits. Preference around Leeds
WHO CAN BENEFIT Local organisations benefiting people of all ages, students, those disadvantaged by poverty and disaster victims
WHERE FUNDING CAN BE GIVEN Generally around Leeds
TYPE OF GRANT One-off
FINANCES *Year* 1995 *Income* £24,068 *Grants* £35,537
TRUSTEES Mrs C W Ashton, Mrs S E Sharp
HOW TO APPLY Applications by post only with sae. **Committments currently extend some years ahead**
WHO TO APPLY TO Mrs S E Sharp, The Norman C Ashton Foundation, 1 Holt Cottages, Holt Lane, Leeds LS16 7NW
CC NO 260036   **ESTABLISHED** 1969

■ The Ashworth Charitable Trust

WHAT IS FUNDED General charitable purposes. Particular emphasis is given to support for the Ironbridge Gorge Museum Trust and to humanitarian projects
WHO CAN BENEFIT Individuals and organisations. There are no restrictions on the age; professional and economic group; family situation; religion and culture; and social circumstances of; or disease or medical condition suffered by, the beneficiaries
WHERE FUNDING CAN BE GIVEN UK, with preference given to Ottery St Mary and Sidmouth for medical purposes
SAMPLE GRANTS £10,000 to Marie Curie Cancer Research; £10,000 to Ironbridge Gorge Museum Trust; £10,000 to Hospicecare; £5,000 to The Mulberry Bush School; £5,000 to The Children's Hospice for the Eastern Region; £3,000 to Re-Solv; £3,000 to Catch; £3,000 to Youth Clubs UK; £3,000 to The Tibet Relief Fund of the United Kingdom; £3,000 to British Institute for Brain Injured Children
FINANCES *Year* 1997 *Income* £344,741 *Grants* £81,148
TRUSTEES C F Bennett, Miss S E Crabtree, A Elphinston, Ms K A Gray
NOTES In 1997, £1,648 was donated in the form of five grants to individuals

WHO TO APPLY TO A Elphinston, Secretary, The Ashworth Charitable Trust, 4–6 Barnfield Crescent, Exeter, Devon EX1 1RF
CC NO 1045492   ESTABLISHED 1995

■ The Ian Askew Charitable Trust

WHAT IS FUNDED All forms of health research particularly mental health. Preservation of ancient buildings
WHAT IS NOT FUNDED No grants to individuals
WHO CAN BENEFIT Mainly headquarters organisations. There is no restriction on the disease or medical condition suffered by the beneficiaries, however particular favour is given to those with mental illness
WHERE FUNDING CAN BE GIVEN Sussex mainly
FINANCES *Year* 1995 *Income* £65,403
Grants £18,336
TRUSTEES Cleone Pengelley, J R Rank, R A R Askew, R J Wainwright, G B Ackery
NOTES Grants are mainly made to headquarters organisations
WHO TO APPLY TO c/o Kidsons Impey, The Ian Askew Charitable Trust Spectrum House, 20–26 Cursitor Street, London EC4A 1HY
CC NO 264515   ESTABLISHED 1972

■ The Dorothy Askew Trust

WHAT IS FUNDED General charitable purposes
WHAT IS NOT FUNDED No grants to individuals
WHO CAN BENEFIT There are no restrictions on the age; professional and economic group; family situation; religion and culture; and social circumstances of; or disease or medical condition suffered by, the beneficiaries
WHERE FUNDING CAN BE GIVEN Sussex charities and charities which have previously been aided
RANGE OF GRANTS £200–£1,000
SAMPLE GRANTS £1,000 to Alzheimer's Disease Society; £1,000 to Hearing Research Trust; £1,000 to Motor Neurone Disease Association; £1,000 to Schizophrenia Association of Great Britain; £1,000 to The Rainbow Trust; £1,000 to The Sussex Beacon; £500 to Anthony Nolan Bone Marrow Trust; £500 to BLISS; £500 to British Institute for Brain Injured Children; £500 to British Lung Foundation
FINANCES *Year* 1995 *Income* £27,212
Grants £27,650
TRUSTEES I V Askew, Mrs D M McAlpine, Mrs P St Q Askew, R A R Askew, B A McAlpine, G B Ackery, Mrs P St Q Pengelley, Mrs M H A Askew
WHO TO APPLY TO The Dorothy Askew Trust, Messrs Kidsons Impey, Spectrum House, 20–26 Cursitor Street, London EC4A 1HY
CC NO 286088   ESTABLISHED 1982

■ The Assair Charitable Trust

This trust did not respond to CAF's request to amend its entry and, by 30 June 1998, CAF's researchers did not find financial records for later than 1995 on its file at the Charity Commission. Trusts are legally required to submit annual accounts to the Charity Commission under section 42 of the Charities Act 1993

WHAT IS FUNDED General charitable purposes
WHO CAN BENEFIT There are no restrictions on the age; professional and economic group; family situation; religion and culture; and social circumstances of; or disease or medical condition suffered by, the beneficiaries

WHERE FUNDING CAN BE GIVEN UK, with a possible preference for Manchester
HOW TO APPLY To the address under Who To Apply To in writing
WHO TO APPLY TO B Olsberg, Accountant, The Assair Charitable Trust, 1st Floor, 35 Whitworth Street West, Manchester M1 5NG
CC NO 327558   ESTABLISHED 1987

■ The Associated Country Women of the World

WHAT IS FUNDED Education, environmental resources and other general charitable purposes will be considered
WHAT IS NOT FUNDED No grants to individuals or students
WHO CAN BENEFIT Small local projects, established organisations benefiting children, young adults and students in particular
WHERE FUNDING CAN BE GIVEN Overseas
TYPE OF GRANT One-off
RANGE OF GRANTS £2,000 or less
FINANCES *Year* 1996 *Income* £450,883
Grants £112,401
TRUSTEES Mrs L Hachet-Pain, Mrs H Stewart, Mrs M Munro, Mrs N Whamond
PUBLICATIONS *All about ACWW, Women Feed the World, Water for All*
HOW TO APPLY In writing at any time
WHO TO APPLY TO Mrs A Frost The Associated Country Women of the World, Vincent House Vincent Square London SW1P 2NB *Tel* 0171-834 8635
CC NO 290367   ESTABLISHED 1984

■ Association for the Assistance of Children at Risk Everywhere

WHAT IS FUNDED To relieve poverty, sickness and distress and any other general charitable purposes for the benefit of children living in the former Yugoslavia and Europe in particular to establish ongoing supportive links between such children and volunteer host families on a one-to-one basis
WHO CAN BENEFIT To benefit children who are sick or disadvantaged by poverty
WHERE FUNDING CAN BE GIVEN The former Yugoslavia and elsewhere in Europe
FINANCES *Year* 1996 *Income* £61,990
TRUSTEES Mrs M A Behan, Mrs A M Jamieson, Mrs J Shardlow, R Stringer
NOTES We do not, as such, give grants; we raise funds for an orphanage in Croatia to enable them to refurbish it. We also try to raise money to bring the children to England for holidays, but since the end of the war and former Yugoslavia is no longer in the news it is difficult to raise enough funds to do so
WHO TO APPLY TO R Stringer, Association for the Assistance of Children at Risk Everywhere, Roselands, Ashleigh Close, Barton, Torquay, Devon TQ2 8HP *Tel* 01803 312331/327885 *Fax* 01803 327798
CC NO 1053804   ESTABLISHED 1996

■ Asthma Allergy and Inflammation Research Trust (AIR)

WHAT IS FUNDED To research into asthma allergy and related disorders; prevention and treatment to improve quality of health care for sufferers; publish results of research for general and medical consideration and to raise awareness and raise funds, particularly at the Department of Immunopharmacology at Southampton General Hospital. Research studies, equipment, small commodities and limited support for PhD students, all of which applies on site. The development of an Asthma Centre

WHO CAN BENEFIT To benefit research workers, and PhD students particularly at the Department of Immunopharmacology at Southampton General Hospital, and asthma sufferers

WHERE FUNDING CAN BE GIVEN Medicine Department, University of Southampton/General Hospital

FINANCES *Year* 1997 *Income* £373,000
Grants £265,000

TRUSTEES Prof Stephen Holgate, Prof Jack Howell, Prof John Warner, David Archer, Mrs J Jonas, Mrs M Mitchell, F E Anderson, M K Church, P Clark, D Coggan, P H Howarth, L McMenemy

PUBLICATIONS Medical Journals, Trustees' Annual Report and Accounts

HOW TO APPLY Applications are best initiated by telephone enquiry: 01703 796891/01703 798579

WHO TO APPLY TO Frank E Anderson, Administrator to Charity, Asthma Allergy and Inflammation Research Trust, Uni Med Level D Centre Block, Southampton General Hospital, Tremona Road, Southampton, Hampshire SO16 6YD

CC NO 803715   **ESTABLISHED** 1990

■ Aston Charities Trust Ltd

WHAT IS FUNDED To support, maintain and extend its community development work through its centres and hostel in the London borough of Newham and its holiday hotel for the elderly at Westcliff on Sea. Strong preference to bodies based in the Newham area. Charities working in the fields of: advice and information on housing; emergency and short-term housing; respite; information technology and computers; publishing and printing; community development; economic regeneration schemes; support to voluntary and community organisations; and community arts and recreation will also be considered

WHAT IS NOT FUNDED Revenue funding for salaries and maintenance unlikely to be given. The Trust will be making no further grants for the foreseeable future apart from continuing to give some limited help to those it is currently assisting. No national appeals

WHO CAN BENEFIT Organisations benefiting people of all ages disadvantaged by poverty

WHERE FUNDING CAN BE GIVEN Newham and immediate surroundings

TYPE OF GRANT Buildings, capital, feasibility studies, one-off, project and research. Funding of one year or less will be considered

FINANCES *Year* 1995–96 *Income* £1,197,521
Grants £32,735

TRUSTEES Directors: D J West, The Right Rev the Lord Bishop of Chelmsford, Mrs P B Jamal, C C Keen, A F West

PUBLICATIONS Annual Report; occasional papers by Aston Community Involvement Unit

HOW TO APPLY No guidelines; no forms

WHO TO APPLY TO R J K Speyer, Aston Charities Trust Ltd, Durning Hall, Earlham Grove, Forest Gate, London E7 9AB *Tel* 0181-555 0142

CC NO 208155   **ESTABLISHED** 1930

■ The Aston Villa Charitable Trust

WHAT IS FUNDED Health and welfare

WHO CAN BENEFIT At risk groups; those disadvantaged by poverty; socially isolated people; and the sick. There are no restrictions on the disease or medical condition suffered by the beneficiaries

WHERE FUNDING CAN BE GIVEN Mainly Birmingham

FINANCES *Year* 1997 *Income* £19,522
Grants £20,802

TRUSTEES H D Ellis, J A Alderson, M J Ansell

HOW TO APPLY To the address under Who To Apply To in writing

WHO TO APPLY TO H D Ellis, Trustee, The Aston Villa Charitable Trust, Aston Villa Football Club plc, Villa Park, Birmingham B6 6HE

CC NO 327923   **ESTABLISHED** 1988

■ The Astor Foundation

WHAT IS FUNDED Medical research and helping people who are disabled by physical and mental disease. Help new and imaginative charities in their early days. Funding may be given to charities working in the fields of: accommodation and housing; the advancement of the Christian religion; arts, culture and recreation; health; conservation and environment. Support may also be considered for infrastructure, support and development; social care and development; special needs education and speech therapy

WHAT IS NOT FUNDED Positively no grants to individuals. Normally not capital building works. No grants made to post-graduates or those requiring funding for travel, etc

WHO CAN BENEFIT Mainly headquarters organisations. Innovatory projects rather than long established or well endowed ones (with some exceptions). Organisations benefiting: Christians and the Church of England; ex-service and service people; medical professionals; research workers; seafarers and fishermen; and volunteers. There is no restriction on age, family situation of, or the disease or medical condition suffered by the beneficiaries. However, there are some restrictions on their social circumstances

WHERE FUNDING CAN BE GIVEN UK and Ireland

TYPE OF GRANT Grants are usually one-off though buildings, capital, core costs, project, research and start-up costs will be considered. Salaries are rarely given. Funding may be for up to three years

RANGE OF GRANTS Smallest £250, average grant £1,500

SAMPLE GRANTS £3,500 to Invalids-at-Home; £3,500 to Help the Hospices; £3,000 to League of Friends, Middlesex Hospital; £3,000 to The Samaritans; £3,000 to Berkshire Community Trust for local charities; £3,000 to the Gurkha Welfare Trust; £2,500 to Council of the Order of St John for Kent; £2,500 to Royal National College for the Blind, Hereford; £2,000 to Royal National Lifeboat Institution; £2,000 to Alzheimer's Disease Society

FINANCES *Year* 1997 *Income* £151,000
Grants £77,750

TRUSTEES Sir William Slack, KCVO, Lord Astor of Hever, J R Astor, R H Astor, Dr H Swanton, C Money-Coutts

HOW TO APPLY Applications are eventually acknowledged. Annual Accounts whilst not necessary are useful. Initial telephone calls are not welcome

WHO TO APPLY TO The Secretary, The Astor Foundation, 5 Northview, Hungerford, Berkshire RG17 0DA

CC NO 225708　　　　　**ESTABLISHED** 1963

■ The Astor of Hever Trust

WHAT IS FUNDED To make donations to charitable bodies in the fields of the arts, medicine, religion, education, conservation, youth and sport

WHAT IS NOT FUNDED No grants to individuals

WHO CAN BENEFIT Both headquarters and local branches of charities, mainly established organisations with particular emphasis on Kent. To the benefit of: children and young adults; actors and entertainment professionals; musicians; textile workers and designers; writers and poets, students, sportsmen and women. There is no restriction on the disease or medical condition suffered by the beneficiaries, or on their religion or culture

WHERE FUNDING CAN BE GIVEN Kent given preference

FINANCES *Year* 1997 *Income* £53,251
Grants £44,825

TRUSTEES Irene, Lady Astor of Hever, Lord Astor of Hever, The Hon Philip Astor

WHO TO APPLY TO Lord Astor of Hever, The Astor of Hever Trust, Frenchstreet House, Frenchstreet, Westerham, Kent TN16 1PW

CC NO 264134　　　　　**ESTABLISHED** 1955

■ The Astra Foundation (217)

This trust failed to supply a copy of its annual report and accounts to CAF as required under section 47(2) of the Charities Act 1993. The information held on file at the Charity Commission was insufficient to enable CAF's researchers to write a substantive commentary on the trust's activities. Accordingly, despite its size, we are unable to list this trust in Spotlight on Major Trusts

WHAT IS FUNDED Medicine and health, welfare, education, sciences, general

WHO CAN BENEFIT Registered charities benefiting children and young adults. There is no restriction on the disease or medical condition suffered by the beneficiaries, and few restrictions on their social circumstances

WHERE FUNDING CAN BE GIVEN UK and regional

TYPE OF GRANT One-off

FINANCES *Year* 1993 *Income* £628,484
Grants £459,849

TRUSTEES Dr G R Barker, Dr P D I Richardson, L Kelly, N P Vigart

PUBLICATIONS Annual financial statement

HOW TO APPLY In writing. Trustees meet three times a year

WHO TO APPLY TO N P Vigart, The Astra Foundation, c/o Astra Pharmaceuticals Limited, Home Park, Kings Langley, Hertfordshire WD4 8DH

CC NO 1014774　　　　　**ESTABLISHED** 1992

■ The Atkinson Family Trust

WHAT IS FUNDED General charitable purposes

WHO CAN BENEFIT There are no restrictions on the age; professional and economic group; family situation; religion and culture; and social circumstances of; or disease or medical condition suffered by, the beneficiaries

WHERE FUNDING CAN BE GIVEN UK

TRUSTEES Ms A E Atkinson, J F Atkinson, G E Boucher, T J J Bussell, K J Greenall, G H Heathcote, A E Sayer

WHO TO APPLY TO A E Sayer, Trustee, The Atkinson Family Trust, Sterne House, Lodge Lane, Derby DE1 3WD

CC NO 1055542　　　　　**ESTABLISHED** 1996

■ The Auerbach Trust

This trust did not respond to CAF's request to amend its entry and, by 30 June 1998, CAF's researchers did not find financial records for later than 1995 on its file at the Charity Commission. Trusts are legally required to submit annual accounts to the Charity Commission under section 42 of the Charities Act 1993

WHAT IS FUNDED General at Trustees discretion

WHO CAN BENEFIT At the discretion of the Trustees. There are no restrictions on the age; professional and economic group; family situation; religion and culture; and social circumstances of; or disease or medical condition suffered by, the beneficiaries

WHERE FUNDING CAN BE GIVEN UK

TYPE OF GRANT At the discretion of the Trustees

WHO TO APPLY TO Mrs D Auerbach, The Auerbach Trust, 46 Hyde Park Gardens Mews, London W2 2NX

CC NO 263896　　　　　**ESTABLISHED** 1972

■ The Aurelius Charitable Trust

WHAT IS FUNDED Research or publications in the conservation of culture inherited from the past and the humanities field

WHAT IS NOT FUNDED No grants to individuals

WHO CAN BENEFIT Registered charities, institutions and academic bodies benefiting academics and research workers

WHERE FUNDING CAN BE GIVEN UK preferred

TYPE OF GRANT Seed-corn or completion funding not otherwise available, usually one-off

RANGE OF GRANTS generally £500–£3,000

FINANCES *Year* 1997 *Income* £70,000
Grants £70,000

TRUSTEES W J Wallis, P E Haynes

NOTES We do not encourage applications and grants seekers

HOW TO APPLY Applications will only be acknowledged if accompanied by a sae

WHO TO APPLY TO The Hon Secretary, The Aurelius Charitable Trust, 250 Waterloo Road, London SE1 8RE

CC NO 271333　　　　　**ESTABLISHED** 1975

■ The Rt Hon Herbert, Baron Austin of Longbridge Will Trust

WHAT IS FUNDED Charitable institutions or objects in England with main emphasis on the welfare of children and the care of old people and medical institutions and research. The Trustees stress that new awards are now severely limited

WHAT IS NOT FUNDED Organisations and projects in England only and limited to: (a) local charities based in Birmingham and West Midlands; (b) national organisations (but not their provincial branches). The Trustees are unable to consider appeals from, or on behalf of, individual applicants

WHO CAN BENEFIT Organisations benefiting: children and older people, at risk groups, those disadvantaged by poverty and socially isolated people. There is no restriction on the disease or medical condition suffered by the beneficiaries

WHERE FUNDING CAN BE GIVEN West Midlands

FINANCES *Year* 1995–96 *Income* £178,918
Grants £146,155

Does the trust you have chosen match your needs? Haphazard applications waste postage and time

33

TRUSTEES J M G Fea, R S Kettel, Baring Trust Co Limited
WHO TO APPLY TO David L Turfrey, Secretary, The Rt Hon Herbert, Baron Austin of Longbridge Will Trust, St Philips House, St Philips Place, Birmingham B3 2PP
CC NO 208394   **ESTABLISHED** 1937

■ The Avenue Charitable Trust

WHAT IS FUNDED General charitable purposes
WHO CAN BENEFIT Registered charities. There are no restrictions on the age; professional and economic group; family situation; religion and culture; and social circumstances of; or disease or medical condition suffered by, the beneficiaries
WHERE FUNDING CAN BE GIVEN UK and overseas
TYPE OF GRANT One-off and recurrent
SAMPLE GRANTS £33,000 to Prison Charity Shops; £29,000 to Friends of Birzeit University; £2,000 to Virginia House Settlement; £12,627 to Michael Scott Memorial Trust; £12,544 to NARCO; £12,000 to Medical Aid for Palestinians; £10,000 to Appropriate Technology for Tibetans; £10,000 to Nazareth House Children's Home; £10,000 to Palestinian Youth Association; £6,019 to Research Centre for Arab Heritage
FINANCES *Year* 1995 *Income* £46,179 *Grants* £210,242
TRUSTEES The Hon F D L Astor, The Hon Mrs B A Astor, S G Kemp
NOTES Income wholly committed to existing beneficiaries
HOW TO APPLY In writing to the address under Who To Apply To but see note above. No formal application forms. Unsuccessful applications acknowledged only if sae provided
WHO TO APPLY TO S G Kemp, The Avenue Charitable Trust, c/o Messrs Sayers Butterworth, 18 Bentinck Street, London W1M 5RL
CC NO 264804   **ESTABLISHED** 1972

■ The John Avins Trustees

WHAT IS FUNDED Medical charities in Birmingham and neighbourhood, and the following charities mentioned in the will of John Avins: Birmingham Blue Coat School; Birmingham Royal Institution for the Blind; and Middlemore Homes, Birmingham
WHAT IS NOT FUNDED No grants to individuals, non-medical charities or for purposes outside Birmingham and neighbourhood
WHO CAN BENEFIT Medical charities. There is no restriction on the disease or medical condition suffered by the beneficiaries. Support may be given to medical professionals and research workers
WHERE FUNDING CAN BE GIVEN Birmingham and neighbourhood only
SAMPLE GRANTS £5,000 to Birmingham Blue Coat School; £5,000 to Birmingham Royal Institution for the Blind; £5,000 to Middlemore Homes, Birmingham; £2,000 to Little Sisters of the Poor; £2,000 to St Mary's Hospice; £1,000 to Elizabeth Fitzroy Homes; £1,000 to Grey Gables; £1,000 to C B and A B Holinsworth Fund for Help; £1,000 to MSA for Midland People with Cerebral Palsy; £1,000 to Prospect Hall Ltd
FINANCES *Year* 1995 *Income* £46,406 *Grants* £41,840
TRUSTEES A D Martineau, M B Shaw, C F Smith, C J Timbrell

WHO TO APPLY TO J M G Fea, Martineau Johnson, Solicitors, The John Avins Trustees, St Philips House, St Philips Place, Birmingham B3 2PP
CC NO 217301   **ESTABLISHED** 1931

■ AXA Equity & Law Charitable Trust (formerly Equity & Law Charitable Trust)

WHAT IS FUNDED (a) To match donations made by employees under the Give As You Earn scheme. (b) In which employees are involved. (c) Local to AXA E & L offices. (d) To support registered charities operating on a national basis in the following principal categories: the fight against drugs and helping the disabled
WHAT IS NOT FUNDED Grants not available for the support of individuals or individual projects, nor for charities operating on a regional, local or international basis
WHO CAN BENEFIT Organisations benefiting disabled people and substance misusers in particular
WHERE FUNDING CAN BE GIVEN UK
SAMPLE GRANTS £3,000 to Business in the Community; £1,000 to Help the Hospices; £1,000 to the Insurance Benevolent Fund; £500 to the Boys' Brigade, Belfast Battalion; £500 to RUKBA; £250 to International Spinal Research Trust; £250 to New Hope Trust; £250 to Baby Lifeline, Coventry; £250 to PACE Centre, Dinton, Aylesbury; £250 to ARA Addiction Recovery Agency
FINANCES *Year* 1997 *Income* £33,222 *Grants* £35,953
TRUSTEES W M Brown, I Hird, D A Kerr (Chairman)
WHO TO APPLY TO D C R Hadley, Secretary, AXA Equity & Law Charitable Trust, Amersham Road, High Wycombe, Buckinghamshire HP13 5AL
CC NO 266163   **ESTABLISHED** 1958

■ Axbridge Parochial Charities

WHAT IS FUNDED General charitable purposes
WHAT IS NOT FUNDED Grants will only be made in the area Where Funding Can Be Given
WHO CAN BENEFIT There are no restrictions on the age, professional and economic group, family situation, religion and culture, and social circumstances of, or disease or medical condition suffered by, the beneficiaries
WHERE FUNDING CAN BE GIVEN Axbridge
RANGE OF GRANTS £250–£30,000
SAMPLE GRANTS £30,000 to Axbridge Parochial Church Council for the Church Restoration Fund; £13,854 to Axbridge Town Council for Furlong Play area; £4,508 to Axbridge Playgroup; £1,000 to Axbridge Town Trust; £600 to Axbridge Sports and Social for Christmas festivities; £500 to Axbridge Town Appeal for a Visit to Balacarat, Australia; £500 to Axbridge Sports and Social for VE Day; £250 to Friends of Houlgate Bursary
FINANCES *Year* 1995 *Income* £27,140 *Grants* £51,212
TRUSTEES J A Lukins, Mrs P A Chard, Rev J Smith, Dr M Lewis, J Chard
NOTES Subsidiaries include: J P Todd Bequest, Reverend Elias Robtier, Richard Durbin's Gift, Ecclesiastical Charity of W M Spearing, W M Spearing for the Poor, Thomas Bythersea's Charity, Mrs Mary Dunster
HOW TO APPLY To the address under Who To Apply To in writing
WHO TO APPLY TO F Jarmany, Axbridge Parochial Charities, Ochre House, Hillside, Axbridge, Somerset BS26 2AN
CC NO 233378   **ESTABLISHED** 1964

■ The Aylesfield Foundation

WHAT IS FUNDED General charitable purposes with preference to the care of disadvantaged and disabled children

WHAT IS NOT FUNDED No grants to individuals or students

WHO CAN BENEFIT Mainly charities benefiting disadvantaged and disabled children

WHERE FUNDING CAN BE GIVEN Hampshire

TYPE OF GRANT One-off and recurrent grants

RANGE OF GRANTS £500–£3,000

SAMPLE GRANTS £3,000 to Treloar Trust; £2,000 to Bulton Village; £1,000 to Cystic Fibrosis Research Trust; £1,000 to Scarba Trust; £1,000 to Royal Society for Deaf Children; £500 to Rainbow Trust; £500 to Imperial Cancer Research Fund; £500 to Underwood Foundation for Leukaemia Research

FINANCES *Year* 1997 *Income* £49,062
Grants £9,500

TRUSTEES N R Elwes, Mrs C P Elwes, A J R Elwes, P G Eaton, Mrs S C Bradbeer

HOW TO APPLY In writing to the address under Who To Apply To

WHO TO APPLY TO N R Elwes, The Aylesfield Foundation, Aylesfield, Alton, Hampshire GU34 4BY

CC NO 1019754   **ESTABLISHED** 1993

■ The Aylesford Family Charitable Trust

WHAT IS FUNDED General charitable purposes

WHO CAN BENEFIT There are no restrictions on the age; professional and economic group; family situation; religion and culture; and social circumstances of; or disease or medical condition suffered by, the beneficiaries

WHERE FUNDING CAN BE GIVEN Midlands

SAMPLE GRANTS £5,000 to St James Trust; £5,000 to AT 7 Trust; £5,000 to Birmingham Children's Hospital; £2,500 to Feel Happy; £2,500 to KIDS; £2,500 to Birmingham Association of Youth Clubs; £1,500 to Solihull Outward Bounds Association; £1,500 to FWAG; £1,250 to English Speaking Union; £1,250 to Winged Fellowship

FINANCES *Year* 1997 *Income* £52,088
Grants £64,135

TRUSTEES Lord Guernsey, Lady Guernsey

HOW TO APPLY To the address under Who To Apply To in writing

WHO TO APPLY TO H B Carslake, The Aylesford Family Charitable Trust, Martineau Johnson, St Philip's House, St Philip's Place, Birmingham B3 2PP

CC NO 328299   **ESTABLISHED** 1989

■ The BAA 21st Century Communities Trust

WHAT IS FUNDED The Trust will consider funding education, environment and economic regeneration, including hostels and residential facilities, conservation and campaigning, community transport and crime prevention. Equal opportunity campaigning and social advice centres may also be funded

WHAT IS NOT FUNDED No grants for religious or political groups

WHO CAN BENEFIT Organisations in local communities around BAA airports benefiting children, young adults, teachers and unemployed people. Also those at risk, and disabled and homeless people

WHERE FUNDING CAN BE GIVEN Local communities around BAA airports, situated in: East and West Sussex: Hampshire; Isle of Wight; Slough; Southampton; Surrey; Windsor and Maidenhead; London; Cambridgeshire; Essex; Hertfordshire; Aberdeen; Aberdeenshire; East Lothian; Edinburgh; Glasgow; and Renfrewshire

TYPE OF GRANT One-off, recurring, buildings, capital, project and start-up costs. Funding is available for up to three years

RANGE OF GRANTS £100–£50,000, typical grant £5,000–£10,000

SAMPLE GRANTS £29,375 to Surrey Youth Games; £15,000 to Fulcrum Project; £15,000 to Feltham Opportunities Centre; £14,450 to Cambridgeshire, Bedfordshire and Northamptonshire Wildlife Trust; £12,500 to Media Trust; £11,000 to RSNC; £10,416 to Uttlesford Community Travel Programme; £10,000 to Marjorie Kinnon School; £10,000 to Reflections; £10,000 to YMCA Foyer Project, Bishop Stortford

FINANCES *Year* 1997–98 *Income* £306,129

TRUSTEES D Wilson, R Everitt, A Barrell, C Hoare, Lord Wright

PUBLICATIONS *BAA Environment and Community Report 1997–98*

HOW TO APPLY In writing the the Community Relations Manager at the local BAA airport

WHO TO APPLY TO Please apply to the appropriate address below

REGIONAL OFFICES Community Relations Manager, The BAA 21st Century Communities Trust, BAA Heathrow, Heathrow Point, 234 Bath Road, Harlington, Middlesex UB3 5AP

Community Relations Manager, The BAA 21st Century Communities Trust, BAA Gatwick, Gatwick, West Sussex RH6 0HP

Public Relations Manager, The BAA 21st Century Communities Trust, BAA Glasgow, Paisley, Renfrewshire PA3 2ST

Community Liason Executive, The BAA 21st Century Communities Trust, BAA Edinburgh, Edinburgh EH12 9DN

Passenger Services Manager, The BAA 21st Century Communities Trust, BAA Aberdeen, Dyce, Aberdeenshire AB2 0DU

Community Relations Manager, The BAA 21st Century Communities Trust, BAA Stansted, Stansted, Essex CM24 1QN

Public Affairs Manager, The BAA 21st Century Communities Trust, BAA Southampton, Southampton, Hampshire SO18 2NL
CC NO 1058617   **ESTABLISHED** 1996

■ The BBA Centenary Trust

WHAT IS FUNDED General charitable purposes
WHO CAN BENEFIT There are no restrictions on the age, professional and economic group, family situation, religion and culture, and social circumstances of, or disease or medical condition suffered by, the beneficiaries
WHERE FUNDING CAN BE GIVEN UK
FINANCES *Year* 1996 *Income* £19,341
Grants £45,915
TRUSTEES G Howard, P M Duggan
WHO TO APPLY TO Julie Hotham, The BBA Centenary Trust, PO Box 18, Hunsworth Lane, Cleckheaton, West Yorkshire BD19 3UJ
CC NO 509753   **ESTABLISHED** 1988

■ BBC Radio Cambridgeshire Trustline Fund

WHAT IS FUNDED Local organisations helping elderly, disadvantaged and disabled people. Particularly charities working in the fields of: residential facilities and services; infrastructure, support and development; film, video and multimedia broadcasting; theatre; hospices and various community services
WHAT IS NOT FUNDED No grants to individuals or animals
WHO CAN BENEFIT Groups and organisations benefiting: elderly people; disadvantaged and disabled people. There is no restriction on the age or the family situation of, or disease or medical condition suffered by, the beneficiaries. There are few restrictions on their social circumstances
WHERE FUNDING CAN BE GIVEN Cambridgeshire covered by BBC Radio Cambridgeshire
TYPE OF GRANT Local charities to buy equipment to benefit the largest number of people. Core costs, one-off, project, running costs and start-up costs. Funding for up to three years will be considered
RANGE OF GRANTS £100–£1,000
SAMPLE GRANTS £1,000 to Arthur Rank Hospice for Hospice Day Centre; £1,000 to East Anglian Autistic Support Trust for centre for autistic adults; £700 to Handicapped Children's Pilgrimage Trust for local children to go to Lourdes; £500 to Riding for the Disabled Association to buy riding equipment; £500 to Sue Ryder Home, Ely for equipment for residents; £500 to Multiple Sclerosis Therapy Centre for conversion equipment for Hyperbaric Oxygen Chamber; £500 to Isle of Ely Society for the Blind funding for transport; £500 to Cog-wheel Trust for equipment storage for counsellors; £480 to Peterborough Stroke Group for minibus hire for meetings; £400 to Romsey Mill Youth and Community Centre for giant soft play box
FINANCES *Year* 1998 *Income* £27,176
Grants £21,000
TRUSTEES Michael Marshall, The Ven James Rone, The Archdeacon of Wisbech
NOTES Only charities/groups in Cambridgeshire need apply
HOW TO APPLY To the address under Who To Apply To in writing in January of each year. Grants allocated in July of each year. Applicants are advised that no initial telephone call is welcome. There is an application form and guidelines are issued. Sae helpful
WHO TO APPLY TO Mrs Sylvia Green, Administrator, BBC Radio Cambridgeshire Trustline Fund, 104 Hills Road, Cambridge CB2 1LD
Tel 01223 259696
CC NO 297555   **ESTABLISHED** 1987

■ BBC Radio Lincolnshire Charity Trust

WHAT IS FUNDED Provision of grant aid for capital items which will benefit people resident in the County of Lincolnshire
WHO CAN BENEFIT There are no restrictions on the age; professional and economic group; family situation; religion and culture; and social circumstances of; or disease or medical condition suffered by, the beneficiaries
WHERE FUNDING CAN BE GIVEN Lincolnshire
TYPE OF GRANT Capital and one-off funding for one year or less will be considered
SAMPLE GRANTS £22,154 to Red Cross, Lincolnshire Branch for fire support vehicle
FINANCES *Year* 1996 *Income* £27,000
HOW TO APPLY For more information contact the address under Who To Apply To
WHO TO APPLY TO C J Thomas, Chair, BBC Radio Lincolnshire Charity Trust, PO Box 219, Newport, Lincoln, Lincolnshire LN1 3XY
Tel 01522 511411 *Fax* 01522 511058
CC NO 52162   **ESTABLISHED** 1996

■ BCH 1971 Charitable Trust

WHAT IS FUNDED Children's and medical charities
WHAT IS NOT FUNDED No grants to individuals
WHO CAN BENEFIT Registered charities only. Children and sick people may benefit. There is no restriction on the disease or medical condition suffered by the beneficiaries. Support may be given to medical professionals and research workers
WHERE FUNDING CAN BE GIVEN Cornwall and Devon
RANGE OF GRANTS £500–£2,000
SAMPLE GRANTS £2,000 to British Red Cross Society (Disaster Fund); £2,000 to Cornwall Disabled Association; £2,000 to Cancer Relief Macmillan Fund; £1,000 to John Groom's Association for Disabled People; £1,000 to MENCAP; £1,000 to Blue Cross; £1,000 to Chailey Challenge; £1,000 to Action for Blind People; £1,000 to Cancer Care; £1,000 to Crossroads
FINANCES *Year* 1997 *Income* £40,714
Grants £31,000
TRUSTEES R C Holman, M A Hayes, Miss J M Holman
WHO TO APPLY TO M Hayes, BCH 1971 Charitable Trust, c/o Macfarlanes, 10 Norwich Street, London EC4A 1BD
CC NO 263241   **ESTABLISHED** 1971

■ BC No 9 1972 Charitable Trust

WHAT IS FUNDED General charitable purposes, in particular, donations to The Society of Friends
WHO CAN BENEFIT Charitable insitutions only. There are no restrictions on the age; professional and economic group; family situation; religion and culture; and social circumstances of; or disease or medical condition suffered by, the beneficiaries. However, particular favour is given to the Society of Friends
WHERE FUNDING CAN BE GIVEN UK

FINANCES *Year* 1995 *Income* £90,087
TRUSTEES R B Clark, Mrs S M Pedder, J D Clark
NOTES The Trustees resources are currently fully committed
WHO TO APPLY TO R J A Furneaux, Trustees Accountant, BC No 9 1972 Charitable Trust, KPMG, 15 Pembroke Road, Clifton, Bristol BS8 3BG
CC NO 264135   ESTABLISHED 1972

■ BMTA Educational and Welfare Trust Limited

WHAT IS FUNDED Relief of the poor, needy, incapacitated, infirm or otherwise in necessitous circumstances and their wives, widows, husbands, widowers, parents, children and other dependents who are employed or have been employed in the motor trade or motor industry
WHO CAN BENEFIT Individuals and organisations benefiting employees and ex-employees of the motor trade or motor industry who are poor, needy, incapacitated or infirm, and their dependants
WHERE FUNDING CAN BE GIVEN UK
SAMPLE GRANTS £1,000 to Tarporley War Memorial Hospital; £1,000 to Keston Boys' Club; £1,000 to Children's Hospice (Eastern); £1,000 to National youth Orchestra of Scotland; £1,000 to Lurgan YMCA
FINANCES *Year* 1997 *Income* £273,910
Grants £183,740
TRUSTEES T Neville, A W Wright, J A Williams, W L Sleigh, A Pearson, P N Guy
NOTES Grant payments totalled: for individuals £178,239 and for organisations £5,500
WHO TO APPLY TO Mrs Wilding, Case Secretary, BMTA Educational and Welfare Trust Limited, Arkudi House, Waterhouse Lane, Kingswood, Surrey KT20 6DT
CC NO 273978   ESTABLISHED 1977

■ The BNFL Risley Medical, Research and Charity Trust

WHAT IS FUNDED Provision of medical equipment; health; accomodation and housing; charity or voluntary umbrella bodies; special schools; special needs education; speech therapy; medical research; care in the community; community transport; and day centres
WHAT IS NOT FUNDED Individual sponsorship and revenue expenditure
WHO CAN BENEFIT Organisations benefiting: children; young adults; older people; those in care, fostered and adopted; widows and widowers; at risk groups; disabled people; those disadvantaged by poverty; disaster victims; homeless people; those living in rural and urban areas; socially isolated people; victims of crime, abuse and domestic violence; and victims of war. There are few restrictions on the disease or medical condition suffered by the beneficiaries
WHERE FUNDING CAN BE GIVEN Cheshire, Greater Manchester, Lancashire and Merseyside
TYPE OF GRANT Building, capital and research
FINANCES *Year* 1997 *Income* £52,772
TRUSTEES R J Balmer, M Howarth, M C Mackenzie
HOW TO APPLY To the address below in writing
WHO TO APPLY TO Mrs M Howarth, Secretary, The BNFL Risley Medical, Research and Charity Trust, British Nuclear Fuels plc, Risley, Warrington WA3 6AS *Tel* 01925 833211
CC NO 512584   ESTABLISHED 1982

■ The BNFL Springfields Medical Research and Charity Trust Fund

WHAT IS FUNDED Grants to hospitals and local medical and welfare charities for medical equipment
WHO CAN BENEFIT Organisations benefiting disabled people. There is no restriction on the disease or medical condition suffered by the beneficiaries
WHERE FUNDING CAN BE GIVEN Lancashire
RANGE OF GRANTS £8–£4,760
SAMPLE GRANTS £4,760 to Blackpool Bears; £3,020 to Highfield Nursery; £2,528 to Trinity Hospice; £2,068 to Heartbeat NW Cardia Centre; £1,981 to Lancashire Priority Services for Harriet McAvoy Ashworth Trading; £1,785 to Health Centre, Great Eccleston; £1,704 to Scan Mobility; £1,673 to BWF Blenheim House; £1,550 to BWF Devonshire Road Hospital; £1,482 to Moorfield School, Preston
FINANCES *Year* 1997 *Income* £108,602
Grants £35,802
TRUSTEES D Singleton, D Pine, Mrs P Goodacre
HOW TO APPLY To the address under Who To Apply To in writing
WHO TO APPLY TO The BNFL Springfields Medical Research and Charity Trust Fund, British Nuclear Fuels plc, Springfield Works, Salwick, Preston, Lancashire PR4 0XJ
CC NO 518005   ESTABLISHED 1986

■ BP Exploration Charitable Trust for the UK

WHAT IS FUNDED General charitable purposes
WHAT IS NOT FUNDED Grants will not be given to individuals, building projects, religious, sectarian or political causes
WHO CAN BENEFIT Organisations. There are no restrictions on the age; professional and economic group; family situation; religion and culture; and social circumstances of; or disease or medical condition suffered by, the beneficiaries
WHERE FUNDING CAN BE GIVEN UK
HOW TO APPLY In writing to the address below
WHO TO APPLY TO BP Exploration Charitable Trust for the UK, 301 St Vincent Street, Glasgow G2 5DD
SC NO SCO 08098

■ The BT Swimathon Foundation

WHAT IS FUNDED General charitable purposes, in particular: the protection of health; the relief of poverty and sickness; and the advancement of education and religion
WHO CAN BENEFIT Organisations benefiting those disadvantaged by poverty. There are no restrictions on the religion and culture of, or on the disease or medical condition suffered by, the beneficiaries
WHERE FUNDING CAN BE GIVEN UK
FINANCES *Year* 1997 *Income* £120,000
TRUSTEES R Broad, M Bowtell, P Stinson
WHO TO APPLY TO G Batterham, The BT Swimathon Foundation, 44 Earlham Street, London WC2H 9LA
CC NO 1060679   ESTABLISHED 1997

■ The BUPA Foundation

WHAT IS FUNDED Three areas of medical research are supported, namely: (a) surgical projects including the development in surgical practice with

Does the trust you have chosen match your needs? Haphazard applications waste postage and time

37

particular emphasis on the evaluation and economic outcomes, and identification and teaching of new surgical techniques; (b) preventive, epidemiological and health maintenance projects covering all environments, including the work place; and (c) projects covering health information and communication between health professionals and the public/patients

WHAT IS NOT FUNDED No grants are made for: (a) applications for general appeals; (b) applications from students for sponsorship through college; or (c) applications from other charitable organisations

WHO CAN BENEFIT Small local projects, national and established organisations. There is no restriction on the disease or medical condition suffered by the beneficiaries

WHERE FUNDING CAN BE GIVEN UK

TYPE OF GRANT Project, research and salaries funded for up to and over three years will be considered

FINANCES *Year* 1997 *Income* £549,188
Grants £664,107

TRUSTEES Dr A Vallance-Owen

PUBLICATIONS Annual Report

HOW TO APPLY Application form available

WHO TO APPLY TO The Administrator, The BUPA Foundation, BUPA House, 15–19 Bloomsbury Way, London WC1A 2BA *Tel* 0171-656 2951 *Fax* 0171-656 2708

CC NO 277598   **ESTABLISHED** 1979

■ The Bacta Charitable Trust

WHAT IS FUNDED Welfare charitable purposes. Generally to support causes recommended to it by members of The Amusement Machine Industry

WHAT IS NOT FUNDED Overseas charities. Religious purposes

WHO CAN BENEFIT Usually local charities benefiting: at risk groups; those disadvantaged by poverty; and socially isolated people

WHERE FUNDING CAN BE GIVEN Great Britain

TYPE OF GRANT Buildings, capital, core costs, endowment, feasibility studies, one-off, project, research, recurring costs and running costs. Funding is available for up to and over three years

FINANCES *Year* 1995 *Income* £67,000
Grants £67,000

TRUSTEES R Withers (Chairman), Sonia Meaden, C Henry, J Bollom, R Higgins, R Smith

HOW TO APPLY All applications must be supported by and made through a member of Bacta (the trade association for Britain's amusement machine industry). All applications must be made in writing

WHO TO APPLY TO J S White, Clerk to the Trustees, The Bacta Charitable Trust, Bacta House, Regents Wharf, 6 All Saints Street, London N1 9RG *Tel* 0171-713 7144 *Fax* 0171-713 0446

CC NO 328668   **ESTABLISHED** 1991

■ The Badley Memorial Trust

WHAT IS FUNDED Relief can be given to those who are sick, convalescent, disabled, handicapped or infirm in the former County Borough of Dudley, and in certain circumstances, to persons who live elsewhere in the present Dudley Metropolitan Borough area or in the Borough of Sandwell. Funding can be given for: Councils for Voluntary Service; respite; health care; special schools; and community transport

WHAT IS NOT FUNDED Holidays abroad or any request that is outside What is Funded

WHO CAN BENEFIT Individuals, local branches of national charities benefiting children; young adults

and older people; parents and children; one parent families; widows and widowers; those disadvantaged by poverty; and disabled people. There is no restriction on the disease or medical condition suffered by the beneficiaries

WHERE FUNDING CAN BE GIVEN The former County Borough of Dudley

TYPE OF GRANT One-off

RANGE OF GRANTS £25–£5,000

FINANCES *Year* 1996–97 *Income* £58,363
Grants £20,068

HOW TO APPLY To the address under Who To Apply To in writing. Initial telephone calls welcome. Guidelines and application forms are available. An sae is prefered

WHO TO APPLY TO D Underwood, Clerk, The Badley Memorial Trust, 23 Water Street, Kingswinford, West Midlands DY6 7QA *Tel* 01384 277463

CC NO 222999   **ESTABLISHED** 1983

■ Bagri Foundation

WHAT IS FUNDED General charitable purposes

WHO CAN BENEFIT Institutions and individuals. There are no restrictions on the age; professional and economic group; family situation; religion and culture; and social circumstances of; or disease or medical condition suffered by, the beneficiaries

WHERE FUNDING CAN BE GIVEN UK and overseas

TYPE OF GRANT At the discretion of the Trustees

FINANCES *Year* 1997 *Income* £113,273
Grants £46,357

TRUSTEES Lord Bagri, CBE, Hon A Bagri, Lady Bagri, R J Gatehouse

WHO TO APPLY TO Lynn Stokes, Bagri Foundation, Metdist Ltd, 80 Cannon Street, London EC4N 6EJ

CC NO 1000219   **ESTABLISHED** 1990

■ Veta Bailey Charitable Trust

WHAT IS FUNDED Training of medical and para-medical personnel in third world and developing countries

WHO CAN BENEFIT Organisations benefiting medical professionals

WHERE FUNDING CAN BE GIVEN Overseas

TYPE OF GRANT One-off grants

FINANCES *Year* 1996 *Income* £61,362
Grants £70,433

TRUSTEES B L Worth, E McClatchey

WHO TO APPLY TO B L Worth, Veta Bailey Charitable Trust, The Cottage, Tiltups End, Kersley, Stroud, Gloucestershire GL6 0QE

CC NO 1007411   **ESTABLISHED** 1981

■ R W Bailey Memorial Trust

WHAT IS FUNDED General charitable purposes and in particular the relief of the sick and the mentally or physically disabled. Go For It – in Bath provides structured voluntary work and support for a group of beneficiaries with a variety of support needs. The mobile community team has continued to carry out gardening, decorating, DIY and removals for older and disabled people

WHO CAN BENEFIT Organisations benefiting the elderly, sick and disabled people. There is no restriction on the disease or medical condition suffered by the beneficiaries

WHERE FUNDING CAN BE GIVEN UK with preference for charities operating in the South West

TYPE OF GRANT Running costs are considered

FINANCES *Year* 1997 *Income* £51,597

TRUSTEES S D Forge, N F Hammond, M J Way

WHO TO APPLY TO M Way, Secretary, R W Bailey Memorial Trust, 19 Lynmouth Road, St Werburghs, Bristol BS2 9HY
CC NO 1046422   **ESTABLISHED** 1994

■ Dr James and Dr Bozena Bain Memorial Trust Fund

WHAT IS FUNDED General charitable purposes
WHO CAN BENEFIT There are no restrictions on the age; professional and economic group; family situation; religion and culture; and social circumstances of; or disease or medical condition suffered by, the beneficiaries
WHERE FUNDING CAN BE GIVEN UK and overseas
TYPE OF GRANT One-off and recurrent
FINANCES *Year* 1994–95 *Income* £31,806 *Grants* £35,367
TRUSTEES T B Patterson, M N Patterson
WHO TO APPLY TO T B Patterson, Dr James and Dr Bozena Bain Memorial Trust Fund, Eshwood Hall, New Brancepeth, Durham DH7 7HG
CC NO 328356   **ESTABLISHED** 1989

■ The Cecile Baines Charitable Trust

WHAT IS FUNDED General charitable purposes. Medical, children and youth, maritime
WHO CAN BENEFIT Individuals and organisations benefiting: children and youth; medical researchers; and seafarers and fishermen
WHERE FUNDING CAN BE GIVEN Africa, UK and Europe
TYPE OF GRANT One-off, recurring costs, buildings, capital, core costs, project and research. Funding is available for up to and over three years
SAMPLE GRANTS £600 to Hodgkins Disease and Lymphoma Association for research
FINANCES *Year* 1997–98 *Income* £31,637 *Grants* £600
TRUSTEES R H Baines, Mrs R C Cunynghame, Mrs D Sharp
HOW TO APPLY To the address under Who To Apply To in writing
WHO TO APPLY TO Doris Sharp, Solicitor, The Cecile Baines Charitable Trust, c/o Antrak Group Limited, Marc House, 13–14 Saint Thomas Apostle, London EC4V 2BB *Tel* 0171-332 6010
CC NO 1056849   **ESTABLISHED** 1996

■ A G Bain's Trust

WHAT IS FUNDED Grants are given to a voluntary organisation in Aberdeen which works in the interests of young people in care, disabled and elderly people
WHAT IS NOT FUNDED No grants to individuals
WHO CAN BENEFIT Organisations benefiting young people in care, disabled people and elderly people
WHERE FUNDING CAN BE GIVEN Aberdeen
SAMPLE GRANTS £49,750 to Voluntary Services Aberdeen for Re-vamping to Finn Moor Residential School for renewal of windows
FINANCES *Year* 1998 *Grants* £49,750
TRUSTEES J C Chisholm, C A B Crosby, W S Crosby
PUBLICATIONS Accounts and notes are available from the Trust
HOW TO APPLY Contact J C Chisholm at the address below
WHO TO APPLY TO J C Chisholm, A G Bain's Trust, 2 Bon-Accord Crescent, Aberdeen AB1 2DH *Tel* 01224 587261
SC NO SCO 03250   **ESTABLISHED** 1990

■ The Baird Trust

WHAT IS FUNDED The Trust is chiefly concerned with supporting with grants the repair and refurbishment of the churches and halls belonging to the Church of Scotland. It also endows parishes and gives help to the Church of Scotland in its work
WHERE FUNDING CAN BE GIVEN Scotland
TYPE OF GRANT Buildings. Funding for up to one year
FINANCES *Year* 1997 *Income* £289,000 *Grants* £222,000
PUBLICATIONS Accounts are available from the Trust
HOW TO APPLY Applications should be made in writing to the address under Who To Apply To
WHO TO APPLY TO Ronald D Oakes, The Baird Trust, 182 Bath Street, Glasgow G2 4HG *Tel* 0141-332 0476
SC NO SCO 16549   **ESTABLISHED** 1873

■ Baitul Mukarram Mosque Trust

WHAT IS FUNDED Education and training. To relieve poverty and sickness, to advance the Islamic religion
WHO CAN BENEFIT Children and young adults; students; Muslims; and those disadvantaged by poverty. There is no restriction on the disease or medical condition suffered by the beneficiaries
WHERE FUNDING CAN BE GIVEN Leicester
FINANCES *Year* 1995 *Income* £64,687
TRUSTEES F H Chowdhury, L R Chowdhury, A Khair, Md M Ali, A Mukith, A Taher, H Ullah
NOTES No grants awarded in 1995
WHO TO APPLY TO F H Chowdhury, Baitul Mukarram Mosque Trust, 22–24 St Stephens Road, Leicester, Leicestershire LE2 1DQ
CC NO 1068370   **ESTABLISHED** 1993

■ The Baker Charitable Trust

WHAT IS FUNDED Priority is given to charities working in the fields of the advancement of the Jewish religion; neurological research; and welfare of elderly people; disabled people; and those suffering from diabetes and epilepsy. Preference is given to charities which the Trust has special interest, knowledge or association
WHAT IS NOT FUNDED No grants to individuals or for expeditions and scholarships
WHO CAN BENEFIT Mainly headquarters organisations benefiting: older people; Jews; disabled people and those suffering from diabetes and epilepsy
WHERE FUNDING CAN BE GIVEN UK and overseas
TYPE OF GRANT Core costs
RANGE OF GRANTS £250–£10,000, typical grant £1,000–£5,000
FINANCES *Year* 1997–98 *Income* £57,000 *Grants* £35,000
TRUSTEES Dr H Baker, Mrs A Baker
HOW TO APPLY Written applications only
WHO TO APPLY TO Dr Harvey Baker, Trustee, The Baker Charitable Trust, 16 Sheldon Avenue, Highgate, London N6 4JT
CC NO 273629   **ESTABLISHED** 1977

■ The C Alma Baker Trust

WHAT IS FUNDED Agriculture and education with an agricultural connection particularly in New Zealand and UK. (a) Agricultural research particularly New Zealand. (b) Massey University, New Zealand – Wye College, UK. Undergraduate Scheme. (c) UK YFC Scheme for young farmers to experience New

Zealand farming on the Trust's property in New Zealand. (d) Annual Travel Fellowship New Zealand-UK, UK-New Zealand. (e) Maori Language Education Scholarship, Wailato University, New Zealand

WHO CAN BENEFIT Individuals or scientific research institutions benefiting young adults, farmers, academics, research workers and students

WHERE FUNDING CAN BE GIVEN UK and overseas, particularly New Zealand

TYPE OF GRANT Range of grants, though normally one-off annual grants

RANGE OF GRANTS For education £200–£10,000, typical grant £1,600

SAMPLE GRANTS £5,792 to an individual at Massey University, New Zealand for work on parasitology in the sheep abnomasum; £4,644 to an individual at Lincoln University, New Zealand for doctoral scholarship in inorganic nitrogen in woolscour sludge; £4,633 to an individual at Massey University, New Zealand for work into efficient venison production with minimal imputs; £4,633 to an individual at Lincoln University, New Zealand for doctoral scholarship re Asochyta disease in broad beans and peas; £3,861 to an individual at Massey University, New Zealand for evaluation of once bred heifer beef production; £3,352 to an individual at Reading University, UK for travel fellowship to New Zealand Institute of Agricultural Science; £2,836 to an individual from Chipping Sodbury, UK for YFC Scheme to Limestone Down, New Zealand; £2,706 to an individual from Brecon, Powys, UK for YFC Scheme to Limestone Downs, New Zealand; £2,689 to an individual from Murchison, New Zealand for Wool Diploma Study Tour to UK textile Industry; £2,507 to an individual at Wye College, UK for Undergraduate Exchange to Massey University, New Zealand

FINANCES *Year* 1996–97 *Income* £456,416 *Grants* £64,487

TRUSTEES C R Boyes, R Moore, S F B Taylor. New Zealand Committee: C T Horton, Prof A Frampton, D J Frith, K I Lowe, Prof B MacDonald, Mrs M Millard

PUBLICATIONS Limestone Downs Annual Report in New Zealand

NOTES The Trust's main asset is Limestone Downs, a sheep and beef property in the North Island, New Zealand utilised for new ideas and development in agriculture to be explored and debated in a working farm environment

HOW TO APPLY In writing for annual grant review at the end of November each year. The Trust only has a limited number of grants available. For New Zealand applicants apply to: Professor B Macdonald, Secretary to New Zealand Committee, The C Alma Baker Trust, Massey University, Bag 11-222, Palmerston North, New Zealand. Fax: 00 64 63 505686

WHO TO APPLY TO Mrs Scott, Secretary to the Trustees, The C Alma Baker Trust, Warrens Boyes & Archer, 20 Hartford Road, Huntingdon, Cambridgeshire PE18 6QE *Fax* 01480 459012 *E-mail* wba.law@btinternet.com

CC NO 283015   **ESTABLISHED** 1981

■ The Balcraig Foundation

WHAT IS FUNDED Grants have been given to fund charitable projects in Africa

WHAT IS NOT FUNDED Applications from individuals are not usually accepted

WHO CAN BENEFIT There are no restrictions on the age; professional and economic group; family situation; religion and culture; and social circumstances of; or disease or medical condition suffered by, the beneficiaries

WHERE FUNDING CAN BE GIVEN Scotland and the third world

TRUSTEES Ann Gloag, David Mcleary, Linda Scott

PUBLICATIONS Accounts and an Annual Report are available from the Trust

HOW TO APPLY Applications, which must include an outline of the project, should be made in writing to the address below

WHO TO APPLY TO The Balcraig Foundation, Balcraig House by Scone, Perthshire PH2 7PG

SC NO SCO 20037

■ The Stanton Ballard Charitable Trust

WHAT IS FUNDED THe Trust concentrates on relieving residents in the City of Oxford, who are in conditions of need, hardship or distress as determined through social services, probation and other bodies in a position to make recommendations. Provision of clothing, holidays and medical requirements

WHAT IS NOT FUNDED No grants for buildings

WHO CAN BENEFIT Individuals and organisations benefiting older people, parents and children, one parent families, at risk groups, those disadvantaged by poverty and socially isolated people. There is no restriction on the disease or medical condition suffered by the beneficiaries. Priority is to families with children, the disabled and the elderly

WHERE FUNDING CAN BE GIVEN In practice, City of Oxford and neighbourhood

TYPE OF GRANT Small grants

FINANCES *Year* 1997 *Income* £74,753 *Grants* £41,800

TRUSTEES Michael G Ballard, Mary J Tate, Rosamund C Nicholson, June D Kimberley, J Martin, K Pawson, Rev D Pritchard

NOTES The Trustees meet on average every six weeks to discuss applications

WHO TO APPLY TO M G Ballard, The Stanton Ballard Charitable Trust, The Stables, Champ Folly, Abingdon, Oxfordshire OX13 5NX

CC NO 294688   **ESTABLISHED** 1986

■ Albert Casanova Ballard Deceased

WHAT IS FUNDED Local charities and local branches of national organisations working in the Plymouth area in the fields of health, welfare and young people provided they are registered charities. Boys entering secondary school education to assist with school uniform and books

WHAT IS NOT FUNDED No grants for anything other than that stated in What Is Funded

WHO CAN BENEFIT Boys entering secondary school education, and registered charities benefiting: children; at risk groups; those disadvantaged by poverty; and socially isolated people. There is no restriction on the disease or medical condition suffered by the beneficiaries

WHERE FUNDING CAN BE GIVEN Plymouth only

TYPE OF GRANT Recurrent

RANGE OF GRANTS Charities: £250–£1,500. Individual boys: £125–£225

SAMPLE GRANTS £1,500 to Ballard Activity Centre; £500 to Beckley Centre; £500 to Alexandra House; £500 to Devon Youth Association; £500 to Guild of Community Service; £500 to Plymouth and District Cardiology Fund; £500 to Royal British Legion Women's Section; £500 to The Samaritans; £500 to St John Ambulance West Devon Area; £400 to Shekihah Mission

FINANCES *Year* 1998 *Income* £43,299 *Grants* £35,500

TRUSTEES Kenneth J Banfield, Mrs Audrey B Houston, Mrs Margaret Pengilly, Ian D Rendle

HOW TO APPLY To the address under Who To Apply To in writing. Applications for grants for boys are made once a year in July. Applications from charities are also made once a year in November. Both grants are advertised once only in the *Western Morning News* or *Evening Herald*. Grants will NOT be entertained outside these periods

WHO TO APPLY TO I D Rendle, Albert Casanova Ballard Deceased, Blue Gates, The Galde, Crapstone, Yelverton, Devon PL20 7PR *Tel* 01822 853421

CC NO 201759   **ESTABLISHED** 1962

■ The Ballinger Charitable Trust

WHAT IS FUNDED General at the Trustees discretion

WHAT IS NOT FUNDED No grants to individuals

WHO CAN BENEFIT At the discretion of the Trustees. Registered charities only. There are no restrictions on the age; professional and economic group; family situation; religion and culture; and social circumstances of; or disease or medical condition suffered by, the beneficiaries

WHERE FUNDING CAN BE GIVEN North East England,Tyne and Wear

TYPE OF GRANT At the discretion of the Trustees

SAMPLE GRANTS £2,000 to Durham Association of Boys' Clubs; £3,750 was also given in grants of less than £1,000

FINANCES *Year* 1997 *Income* £26,466 *Grants* £5,750

TRUSTEES Martin S A Ballinger, Diana S Ballinger

WHO TO APPLY TO M Ballinger, The Ballinger Charitable Trust, Bolam Hall (East), Morpeth NE61 3UA

CC NO 1053273   **ESTABLISHED** 1994

■ The Balmore Trust

WHAT IS FUNDED Two-thirds of grants are given to overseas projects and the remainder to local projects in the UK, working with women or young people in areas of greatest social need. Holiday schemes in the UK are looked on favourably. Medical/educational projects are favoured overseas, but not generally in the UK

WHAT IS NOT FUNDED Grants are not given to individuals

WHO CAN BENEFIT Organisations benefiting those in greatest social need, especially children, young adults and women, at risk groups, those disadvantaged by poverty and victims of domestic violence

WHERE FUNDING CAN BE GIVEN Third world and UK, particularly Strathclyde

TYPE OF GRANT Grants are one-off. Core costs, project and start-up costs will be considered. Funding may be given for up to one year

RANGE OF GRANTS £50–£3,000, but larger grants to 'old friends'. New overseas grants maximum £500 and UK £200

SAMPLE GRANTS £7,600 to Sophia Mission Institute, Myanmar for capital building costs; £3,000 to Amajuba Education Fund, South Africa for educational scholarships/loans; £2,650 to Child in Need Institute, Calcutta, India for the welfare of mothers and young children; £1,200 to Eagle Trust, Dunbartonshire for social welfare work with teenagers; £1,000 to Bombolulu Workshops, Kenya for craft workshops, flood damage

FINANCES *Year* 1997 *Grants* £30,000

TRUSTEES Ms O Beauvoisin, C Brown, Ms J Brown, J Eldridge, B Holman, Ms R Jarvis, J Riches, Ms R Riches

PUBLICATIONS A twice yearly newsletter is available free from the Trust's shop, The Coach House Charity Craft Shop in Balmore, or from the address under Who To Apply To upon receipt of an sae

HOW TO APPLY Applications should be made in writing to the address under Who To Apply To. Organisations which are previously unknown to the Trust are unlikely to succeed. There are very limited funds available for new applicants with no personal connection to the Coach House/Balmore Trust. There is no application form and guidelines are issued on request. There are no deadlines, but the main disbursement is around March. Sae necessary if applicant wishes response (unless Trust wishes to make a grant

WHO TO APPLY TO The Secretary, The Balmore Trust, Viewfield, Balmore, Glasgow G64 4AE *Tel* 01360 620742

SC NO SCO 08930   **ESTABLISHED** 1980

■ The Balney Charitable Trust

WHAT IS FUNDED Trustees lean towards local appeals and ex-servicemen/women's' institutions. Particularly charities working in the fields of: residential facilities and services; churches; Anglican bodies; Free Churches; acute health care; hospices; and conservation will be considered

WHAT IS NOT FUNDED Local community projects outside North Bedfordshire and North Buckinghamshire will not be funded

WHO CAN BENEFIT Registered charities and institutions. Individuals and organisations benefiting Christians and those disadvantaged by poverty. There is no restriction on the disease or medical condition suffered by the beneficiaries

WHERE FUNDING CAN BE GIVEN North Buckinghamshire and North Bedfordshire

TYPE OF GRANT Start-up costs, capital grants; contributions to building projects, ie local churches, and research. Funding for up to three years will be considered

RANGE OF GRANTS £200–£5,000

SAMPLE GRANTS £6,000 to Raisonne on Works of Arthur Hughes for research and towards costs of publishing; £5,000 to Bunyan Church and Museum Appeal for church repairs and museum conversion; £4,000 to All Saints Church, Emberton, Buckinghamshire for church repairs; £2,000 to St Lukes Hospital for Clergy for medical requirements; £2,000 to St Dunstan's for help to the blind; £2,000 to Kew Millennium Seed Bank Appeal towards the formation of rare seed bank; £2,000 to Sherrington Church for repairs; £2,000 to 94th Bedfordshire Sea Scouts for youth service facility; £1,250 to Pre-school Learning Alliance for the establishment of local pre-school group; £1,000 to The PACE Centre a contribution towards of setting up

FINANCES *Year* 1997 *Income* £50,569 *Grants* £38,255

TRUSTEES J G B Chester, R Ruck-Keene

HOW TO APPLY Written applications only. Sae if acknowledgement is required

WHO TO APPLY TO G C Beazley, The Balney Charitable Trust, The Chicheley Estate, Bartlemas Office, Pavenham, Bedford MK43 7PF
Tel 01234 823661 *Fax* 01234 825058
CC NO 288575   **ESTABLISHED** 1983

■ The Baltic Charitable Fund

WHAT IS FUNDED To make grants to registered charities only which must be connected with the City of London or shipping or the military forces

WHAT IS NOT FUNDED Donations not made for advertising or charity dinners, etc

WHO CAN BENEFIT Registered charities benefiting residents of the City of London, seafarers, fishermen, ex-service and service people

WHERE FUNDING CAN BE GIVEN UK with preference the City of London

TYPE OF GRANT One-off

RANGE OF GRANTS £250–£25,000, typical grant £500, sometimes £1,000

SAMPLE GRANTS £25,000 to RNLI for lifeboat 'Baltic Exchange III' 2003 Appeal; £6,000 to City of London School for Boys towards a bursary; £5,700 to City of London School for Girls towards a bursary; £5,000 to Lord Mayor of City of London Appeal for British Diabetics Association and NCH Action for Children; £3,500 to City University Business School towards a bursary; £3,000 to SSAFA, a military charity; £2,600 to Lloyds Officer Cadet Scholarship as part funding; £2,000 to Royal Merchant Navy School Foundation, a naval charity; £2,000 to King George's Fund for Sailors, a general naval charity; £1,000 to Medway Missions to Seamen Trust for Pembroke House

FINANCES *Year* 1997–98 *Income* £71,897
Grants £77,183

TRUSTEES The Directors of the Exchange

HOW TO APPLY By letter. An initial telephone call is welcome

WHO TO APPLY TO Anthony Howard Ring, The Baltic Charitable Fund, The Baltic Exchange, 38 St Mary Axe, London EC3A 8BH *Tel* 0171-369 1655
Fax 0171-623 6644
E-mail broker@balticexchange.co.uk
Web Site www.balticexchange.com
CC NO 279194   **ESTABLISHED** 1979

■ The Baltic Charitable Trust

WHAT IS FUNDED The advancement of the Jewish religion; primary, junior and special schools; cultural and religious teaching; and specialist training

WHO CAN BENEFIT Organisations benefiting children, young adults and Jewish people. Support is given to at risk groups, disabled people and those disadvantaged by poverty

WHERE FUNDING CAN BE GIVEN England

TRUSTEES Baltic Trustees Ltd, J A Clare, A Yargaroff, N Fetterman, FCA

HOW TO APPLY Trustees do not welcome applications

WHO TO APPLY TO P Galloway, The Baltic Charitable Trust, 25–26 Albemarle Street, London W1X 4AD
Tel 0171-493 3900
CC NO 328629   **ESTABLISHED** 1989

■ The Bamford Charitable Trust

WHAT IS FUNDED Particularly charities working in the fields of: hostels; support to voluntary and community organisations; churches; Anglican bodies; Catholics; diocesan boards; dance and ballet; music; hospices at home; support; self help groups; health facilities and buildings; medical studies and research; church buildings; agriculture; schools and colleges; cultural and religious teaching and various community facilities and services

WHAT IS NOT FUNDED No grants to individuals

WHO CAN BENEFIT Mainly local organisations benefiting: children; young adults; older people; clergy; medical professionals; volunteers; Church of England; Methodists; Roman Catholics; at risk groups; carers; disabled people; those disadvantaged by poverty; disaster victims; homeless people; and beneficiaries suffering from cancers, hearing loss and HIV and AIDS

TYPE OF GRANT One-off

RANGE OF GRANTS £100–£5,000; typical £250

FINANCES *Year* 1997 *Income* £168,178
Grants £137,000

TRUSTEES Sir Anthony Bamford, Lady Bamford, E T D Leadbeater

HOW TO APPLY By letter only

WHO TO APPLY TO L Mitchell, The Bamford Charitable Trust, c/o J C Bamford Excavators Ltd, Rocester, Uttoxeter, Staffordshire ST14 5JP
CC NO 279848   **ESTABLISHED** 1979

■ The Banbury Charities

WHAT IS FUNDED General charitable purposes

WHAT IS NOT FUNDED No grants are made for loans, payments of ongoing costs, ie wages

WHO CAN BENEFIT Individuals and groups. There are no restrictions on the age; professional and economic group; family situation; religion and culture; and social circumstances of; or disease or medical condition suffered by, the beneficiaries

WHERE FUNDING CAN BE GIVEN Banbury

TYPE OF GRANT One-off grants

RANGE OF GRANTS £10–£15,000

SAMPLE GRANTS £15,000 to Cherwell District Council for Work Start Project; £9,000 to Home Farm Trust for soft furnishings for two new homes; £7,000 to Scouts for refurbishment of Scout Hut; £6,000 to St Paul's Church for central heating; £3,000 to The Samaritans as a donation; £2,300 to Victim Support for equipment; £2,000 to Beacon Centre (for the homeless) a donation; £2,000 to Cherwell District Council for CCTV; £2,000 to St John Ambulance for radio equipment; £1,500 to talking Newspaper for equipment

FINANCES *Year* 1997 *Income* £269,000
Grants £169,000

TRUSTEES Co-optative Trustees: Mrs J M Colgrave, J P Friswell, OBE, JP, R L Keys, MBE, Mrs J May, R P Walford. Nominative Trustees: C F Blackwell, Mrs J Justice, G A Parish

NOTES The Banbury Charities are: The Bridge Estate, Lady Arran's Charity, Banbury Arts and Educational Charity, Banbury Sick Poor Fund and the Banbury Welfare Trust. (All deal with different charitable areas)

HOW TO APPLY To the address under Who To Apply To in writing

WHO TO APPLY TO A Scott Andrews, The Banbury Charities, 36 West Bar, Banbury, Oxfordshire OX16 9RU *Tel* 01295 251234
CC NO 201418   **ESTABLISHED** 1961

◼ William P Bancroft (No 2) Charitable Trust and Jenepher Gillett Trust

WHAT IS FUNDED Grants mainly to Quaker charities or projects

WHAT IS NOT FUNDED No appeals unconnected with Quakers. No individual or student grant applications

WHO CAN BENEFIT Mainly charities benefiting Quakers

WHERE FUNDING CAN BE GIVEN UK and overseas

TYPE OF GRANT Buildings, core costs, endowment, one-off and start-up costs. Funding of up to three years will be considered

RANGE OF GRANTS £400–£6,000, average grant £2,200

SAMPLE GRANTS £6,000 to Woodbrooke College Quaker Study Centre for bursaries; £5,000 to Britain Yearly Meeting, Society of Friends for property maintenance; £4,500 to Sibford School for bursaries; £4,200 to Chainey Manor, Quaker Conference Centre for bursaries and maintenance; £2,000 to Bookham School for Development Appeal; £2,000 to Glebe House – Friends Therapeutic Community for general purposes; £2,000 to Bedford Institute Association, Quaker Social Action for general purposes; £2,000 to Quaker Council for European Affairs for general purposes; £1,500 to Cape Town Quaker Peace Centre for bursaries for staff to attend Woodbrooke College; £1,500 to Pendle Hill (Quaker College near Philadelphia, USA), a grant to British residents for one seminar

FINANCES *Year* 1997 *Income* £34,717 *Grants* £33,600

TRUSTEES J C Gillett, R Gillett, J B Sewell, G T Gillett, D S Gillett, J Moseley

NOTES Applications should only come from Quaker charities

HOW TO APPLY By letter not later than April – Trustees meet in May

WHO TO APPLY TO Dr Roger Gillett, William P Bancroft (No 2) Charitable Trust and Jenepher Gillett Trust, Fernroyd, St Margaret's Road, Altrincham, Cheshire WA14 2AW *Tel* 0161-928 5112 *Fax* 0161-928 5112 *E-mail* g.gillett@hgmp.mrc.ac.uk

CC NO 288968   **ESTABLISHED** 1984

◼ The Band Trust

WHAT IS FUNDED Available income is principally used for assisting the disabled and other disadvantaged people and for education

WHO CAN BENEFIT Organisations benefiting children, young adults, students and teachers. Support is also given to the disabled, those disadvantaged by poverty, at risk groups and the socially isolated

WHERE FUNDING CAN BE GIVEN UK

RANGE OF GRANTS £190–£105,000

SAMPLE GRANTS £105,000 to the Royal Free School of Medicine; £30,000 to the Children's Hospice Trust; £25,000 to Honourable Society Gray's Inn; £20,000 to Radcliffe Hospital; £16,950 to the Florence Nightingale Memorial Committee; £10,600 to the Neuromuscular Centre; £10,000 to the National Association of Toy and Leisure Libraries; £10,000 to the Treloar Trust; £5,833 to an individual (ex-employee); £5,500 to Disability Aid Fund

FINANCES *Year* 1996 *Income* £10,324,048 *Grants* £269,173

TRUSTEES H D Swales, The Hon Mrs Nicholas Wallop, The Hon Nicholas Wallop, R J S Mason, B G Streather

NOTES Funds are already committed to projects known to the Trustees

HOW TO APPLY **This Trust states that it does not respond to unsolicited applications**

WHO TO APPLY TO The Band Trust, Messrs Streathers, Solicitors, Sackville House, 40 Picadilly, London W1V 0PA

CC NO 279802   **ESTABLISHED** 1976

◼ Bangladesh Welfare Association Croydon

WHAT IS FUNDED (a) To relieve poverty amongst Bangladeshis in Croydon; (b) to advance education, particularly by the provision of English Language classes and supplementary school for Bangladeshi children; (c) to relieve the aged; (d) to provide facilities for recreation and leisure time; (e) to promote good race relations in Croydon; (f) to advance charitable purposes in Bangladesh

WHO CAN BENEFIT Organisations benefiting Bangladeshis in Croydon, particularly those disadvantaged by poverty, children, young adults and elderly people

WHERE FUNDING CAN BE GIVEN London Borough of Croydon, secondarily Bangladesh

FINANCES *Year* 1997 *Income* £46,452 *Grants* £651

TRUSTEES H Islam, M Islam, A Jahur, J Kabir, A A Khalique, A A M Khan, A Matin, M A Miah, S Miah, R Rahman, Mrs S J Rahman, A Tejou

NOTES The majority of the Trust's income was spent on running costs of the Association, eg salaries, rent, maintenance and activities, etc

WHO TO APPLY TO Humayun Kabir, Bangladesh Welfare Association Croydon, (BWAC), 89 London Road, West Croydon CR0 2RF

CC NO 1058085   **ESTABLISHED** 1996

◼ The Banks Educational Trust

WHAT IS FUNDED General charitable purposes at the discretion of the Trustees

WHAT IS NOT FUNDED No grants to individuals

WHO CAN BENEFIT At the discretion of the Trustees. There are no restrictions on the age; professional and economic group; family situation; religion and culture; and social circumstances of; or disease or medical condition suffered by, the beneficiaries

WHERE FUNDING CAN BE GIVEN UK

TYPE OF GRANT At the discretion of the Trustees

FINANCES *Year* 1997 *Income* £27,569

TRUSTEES A C Murdie, T M Sills, M C Banks, R L Banks, Mrs J A Clements

WHO TO APPLY TO T M Sills, The Banks Educational Trust, 6 Bedford Road, Sandy, Bedfordshire SG19 1EN

CC NO 1046289   **ESTABLISHED** 1995

◼ The Barakel Charitable Trust

WHAT IS FUNDED General charitable purposes

WHO CAN BENEFIT There are no restrictions on the age; professional and economic group; family situation; religion and culture; and social circumstances of; or disease or medical condition suffered by, the beneficiaries

WHERE FUNDING CAN BE GIVEN UK

TRUSTEES J Williams, G Williams, N MacLeod

WHO TO APPLY TO J Warin, Professional Advisor, The Barakel Charitable Trust, c/o Connor Warin, Chartered Accountant, Trinity House, Foxes Parade, Stewardstone Road, Waltham Abbey, Essex EN9 1PJ

CC NO 1069178   ESTABLISHED 1998

■ The Barber Charitable Trust

WHAT IS FUNDED Evangelical Christian causes, missionary societies, bible societies, Christian radio, Christian relief, Christian education and outreach, and church buildings

WHAT IS NOT FUNDED No grants to non-Christian causes. Grants are rarely given to individuals or unregistered charities

WHO CAN BENEFIT Mainly Evangelical Christian causes benefiting: people of all ages; Baptists, Christians; Church of England and evangelists

WHERE FUNDING CAN BE GIVEN UK, Africa, Asia, South America

TYPE OF GRANT Project, recurring costs, one-off, core costs, capital and buildings. All funding for up to two years

RANGE OF GRANTS £20–£750, typical grant £250

FINANCES *Year* 1997–98 *Income* £50,597 *Grants* £48,596

TRUSTEES E E Barber, Mrs D H Barber

NOTES The funds available to the Trust are fully committed for several years ahead

HOW TO APPLY **Unsolicited applications not invited or acknowledged**

WHO TO APPLY TO E E Barber, FCCA, The Barber Charitable Trust, Tortington Cottage, Tortington, Arundel, West Sussex BN18 OBG *Tel* 01903 882337

CC NO 269544   ESTABLISHED 1975

■ Barbour Paton Charitable Trust

WHAT IS FUNDED Environmental resources and general charitable purposes

WHO CAN BENEFIT There are no restrictions on the age; professional and economic group; family situation; religion and culture; and social circumstances of; or disease or medical condition suffered by, the beneficiaries

WHERE FUNDING CAN BE GIVEN UK and overseas

TYPE OF GRANT One-off and recurrent

RANGE OF GRANTS £50–£5,500

SAMPLE GRANTS £5,500 to RSPCA for MIllbrook Animal Centre Gala Day; £1,500 to Marie Curie Cancer Care; £700 to the Home of Rest for Horses; £700 to Royal National Lifeboat Institution; £650 to WWF UK

FINANCES *Year* 1996–97 *Income* £17,585 *Grants* £14,000

TRUSTEES M R Nathan, R V Watson

WHO TO APPLY TO G Wright, Barbour Paton Charitable Trust, Baker Tilly, Chartered Accountants, Iveco Ford House, Station Road, Watford, Hertfordshire WD1 1TG

CC NO 211470   ESTABLISHED 1962

■ The Barbour Trust

WHAT IS FUNDED (a) Relief of patients suffering from any form of illness or disease, promotion of research into causes of such illnesses. (b) Furtherance of education. (c) Preservation of buildings and countryside of environmental, historical or architectural interest. (d) Relief of persons in need. Charities working in the fields of: infrastructure development; religious umbrella bodies and animal welfare will also be considered. Applications from organisations based in the North East of England are looked at favourably, particularly those based in Tyne and Wear and County Durham. Northumberland and Cleveland are considered

WHAT IS NOT FUNDED Grants are made to registered charities only and not to individuals

WHO CAN BENEFIT The Trust likes to support local activities. The Trust also supports local branches of national charities benefiting: people of all ages; unemployed people; volunteers; parents and children; one parent families; those disadvantaged by poverty; and homeless people. Those suffering from various diseases and medical conditions will also be considered

WHERE FUNDING CAN BE GIVEN North East England (Tyne & Wear, Northumberland, Co Durham & Cleveland)

TYPE OF GRANT Capital, core costs, one-off, project, research, running costs, recurring costs, salaries and start-up costs. Funding for up to one year will be considered

FINANCES *Year* 1996 *Income* £367,158

TRUSTEES Mrs M Barbour, CBE, DL (Chairman), H J Tavroges, A A E Clenton, Helen M Barbour, BA

PUBLICATIONS A statement of the accounts of the Trust is published annually

HOW TO APPLY The Trust meets every two months to consider the applications

WHO TO APPLY TO Mrs A Harvey, The Barbour Trust, PO Box 21, Guisborough, Cleveland TS14 8YH

CC NO 328081   ESTABLISHED 1988

■ Philip Barker Charity

WHAT IS FUNDED Principally: local youth organisations; medical; health; disabled; welfare and educational charities

WHAT IS NOT FUNDED No grants to individuals who are not sponsored by a registered charity

WHO CAN BENEFIT Registered charities benefiting: children and young adults; carers; disabled people; and volunteers

WHERE FUNDING CAN BE GIVEN Cheshire

TYPE OF GRANT Principally one-off grants. Will consider contribution towards recurring costs, core costs and projects. Funding is available for up to two years

RANGE OF GRANTS £200–£1,000

FINANCES *Year* 1996–97 *Income* £78,693 *Grants* £74,696

TRUSTEES Mrs M G Mather, H J Partington, Mrs C Munday, E F G Burton, Mrs A V R Burton, Capt S P Barker

NOTES The Trustees will consider applications from individuals sponsored by registered charities, supporting youth projects, medical, health, welfare and educational objectives

HOW TO APPLY To the address under Who To Apply To in writing only

WHO TO APPLY TO Mrs M G Mather, Correspondent, Philip Barker Charity, 1a Rothesay Road, Curzon Park, Chester CH4 8AJ

CC NO 1000227   ESTABLISHED 1990

■ Peter Barker-Mill Memorial Charity

WHAT IS FUNDED General charitable purposes

WHO CAN BENEFIT There are no restrictions on the age; professional and economic group; family situation; religion and culture; and social

circumstances of; or disease or medical condition suffered by, the beneficiaries

WHERE FUNDING CAN BE GIVEN UK

SAMPLE GRANTS £5,000 to Red Cross Land Mines Appeal; £4,800 to Wessex Children's Hospice; £3,000 to North Kensington Community Care; £2,000 to RNLI; £2,000 to Chelsea and Westminster Arts Project

FINANCES *Year* 1997 *Income* £71,743 *Grants* £16,800

TRUSTEES C Gwyn-Evans, C H Hall, T Jobling, G N Knowles, F R A Wheatley

WHO TO APPLY TO C Gwyn-Evans, Trustee, Peter Barker-Mill Memorial Charity, Longdown Management Ltd, The Estate Office, Longdown, Southampton SO40 4UH

CC NO 1045479   **ESTABLISHED** 1995

■ Barnabas Charitable Trust

WHAT IS FUNDED Trustees will consider a wide range of Christian outreach including inner-city projects. Children's education including arts education; community services; and bursaries and fees

WHAT IS NOT FUNDED No grants for projects or large charities

WHO CAN BENEFIT Individuals and organisations benefiting: unemployed people; volunteers; parents and children; one parent families; at risk groups; disabled people; and ex-offenders and those at risk of offending. There is no restriction on the age, and few on the religion and culture of the beneficiaries

WHERE FUNDING CAN BE GIVEN West Midlands, North West, Sheffield and Derbyshire

TYPE OF GRANT Core costs, one-off, project, recurring costs, running costs, salaries and start-up costs. Funding is available for up to three years

RANGE OF GRANTS £100–£10,000

SAMPLE GRANTS £8,050 to Furnival Project, Sheffield for community project salary; £5,000 to Bilston Care Centre for care of the elderly; £4,000 to Urban Solidarity, Wolverhampton for salaries; £3,050 to Bilston Congregational Church for support to community project for elderly; £2,652 to Liverpool Metropolitan Cathedral for bursaries for children in choir; £2,000 to Wash Nursery School, Derbyshire for bursaries and parenting skill courses

FINANCES *Year* 1997 *Income* £38,000 *Grants* £38,000

TRUSTEES D Harding, Mrs R Harding, R L Harding

HOW TO APPLY Write with full information. There are no application forms. No reply will be sent if application is unsuccessful

WHO TO APPLY TO D Harding, Barnabas Charitable Trust, Gorstylow Farm, The Wash, High Peak SK23 0QL *Tel* 01663 750546

CC NO 299718   **ESTABLISHED** 1988

■ The Barnabas Trust

WHAT IS FUNDED Christian evangelical projects – overtly evangelical, not social, unless for a particular evangelical input. The Trust will consider funding Christian education and outreach; missionaries and evangelicals; and Anglican and Free Church bodies

WHAT IS NOT FUNDED On-going revenue costs, eg. salaries. Any building purchase, renovation, extension, refurbishment

WHO CAN BENEFIT Organisations and individuals benefiting Christians and evangelists

WHERE FUNDING CAN BE GIVEN UK and overseas. Overseas projects are supported only if they are personally known by the Trustees

TYPE OF GRANT One-off for one year or less

RANGE OF GRANTS £250–£5,000

FINANCES *Year* 1996–97 *Income* £259,735 *Grants* £321,140

TRUSTEES S M Lennard, N Brown, K C Griffiths

NOTES For clarification as to whether applications fall within current guidelines, please telephone the Trust. After support for the established giving base, there are only limited funds available for quarterly distribution

HOW TO APPLY To the address under Who To Apply To in writing giving as much detail as possible, enclosing copy of latest audited accounts, if applicable. Applications should be received a month before meetings, which take place in March, June, September and December

WHO TO APPLY TO Mrs D Edwards, The Barnabas Trust, 63 Wolsey Drive, Walton-on-Thames, Surrey KT12 3BB *Tel* 01932 220622

CC NO 284511   **ESTABLISHED** 1983

■ Lord Barnby's Foundation

WHAT IS FUNDED General charitable purposes with emphasis on preservation of the national heritage, the countryside and ancient buildings particularly the Anglican cathedrals; charities for ex-servicemen particularly Cavalry Regiments and the Sherwood Foresters; welfare of horses and those who work with them; refugees; charities for the benefit of the Polish people. Local charities preserving the amenities of the areas of Ashtead, Surrey, Blyth, Nottinghamshire and Bradford, Yorkshire, and youth organisations in those areas. Schools and colleges; purchase of books; scholarships; textiles and upholstery; community facilities; health care; residential facilities and services; arts and arts facilities; and cultural activities

WHAT IS NOT FUNDED No grants to individuals; grants to registered charities only

WHO CAN BENEFIT Registered charities benefiting: people of all ages; ex-service and service people; textile workers and designers; disabled people; those disadvantaged by poverty; disaster victims; homeless people; refugees; victims of crime; victims of famine; victims of war; victims of man-made or natural disasters; and terminally ill people. Those suffering from various diseases and medical conditions

WHERE FUNDING CAN BE GIVEN UK

TYPE OF GRANT One-off, buildings, capital, core costs, project, research. Funding is up to two years

RANGE OF GRANTS Grants range from £500 to £50,000 but are generally £1,000 to £2,000

SAMPLE GRANTS £50,000 to Therfield School, Surrey for construction of hockey pitch; £12,750 to Atlantic College for sponsoring Polish student; £20,500 to Textile Institute for computerisation of library and general funding; £10,000 to Motor Neurone Disease; £10,000 to Medical Emergency Relief International; £10,000 to Countryside Foundation; £10,000 to Royal Hospital for Children, Bristol; £10,000 to The Game Conserving Trust; £10,000 to The Langford Trust; £10,000 to Royal Commonwealth Society for the Blind

FINANCES *Year* 1998 *Income* £181,164 *Grants* £289,450

TRUSTEES Rt Hon Lord Newall, Sir John L Lowther, Sir Michael Farquhar, Bt, The Hon G Lopes, The Rt Hon Countess Peel

NOTES Annual review of permanent lists of donations and additions or deletions at Trustees' discretion. Appeals are considered three times a year in March, July and October. Once only donations to special appeals or capital projects

HOW TO APPLY Applications should be made in writing, accompanied by a set of the latest Accounts. Applicants do not need to send sae

WHO TO APPLY TO Lord Barnby's Foundation, Messrs Payne Hicks Beach, 10 New Square, Lincoln's Inn, London WC2A 3QG *Tel* 0171-465 4300 *Fax* 0171-465 4400

CC NO 251016   **ESTABLISHED** 1966

■ The Ellen Barnes Charitable Trust

WHAT IS FUNDED General charitable purposes

WHO CAN BENEFIT There are no restrictions on the age; professional and economic group; family situation; religion and culture; and social circumstances of; or disease or medical condition suffered by, the beneficiaries

WHERE FUNDING CAN BE GIVEN Weston Rhyn and adjoining parishes

FINANCES *Year* 1995 *Income* £20,605

HOW TO APPLY To the address under Who To Apply To in writing

WHO TO APPLY TO Mark Woodward, Secretary, The Ellen Barnes Charitable Trust, Messrs Crampton Pym & Lewis, The Poplars, 47 Willow Street, Oswestry, Shropshire SY11 1PR

CC NO 217344   **ESTABLISHED** 1963

■ The Barnes Ouzounian Foundation

WHAT IS FUNDED General charitable purposes

WHO CAN BENEFIT There are no restrictions on the age; professional and economic group; family situation; religion and culture; and social circumstances of; or disease or medical condition suffered by, the beneficiaries

WHERE FUNDING CAN BE GIVEN UK and overseas

TRUSTEES Miss E Barnes, National Westminster Bank plc

WHO TO APPLY TO Andrew King, Manager, The Barnes Ouzounian Foundation, NatWest plc, 2nd Floor, Western House, 56 Dingwall Road, Croydon, Surrey CR9 3HB

CC NO 1063599   **ESTABLISHED** 1997

■ Barnes Workhouse Fund

WHAT IS FUNDED The benefit of the inhabitants of the area of the Ancient Parish of Barnes as follows:
(a) The relief of the aged, impotent and poor.
(b) The relief of distress and sickness. (c) The provision and support (with the object of improving of life for the said inhabitants in the interests of social welfare) of facilities for recreation or other leisure time occupation. (d) The provision and support of educational facilities

WHO CAN BENEFIT Organisations benefiting: people of all ages who are at risk groups; disabled; disadvantaged by poverty; or socially isolated. There is no restriction on the disease or medical condition suffered by the beneficiaries

WHERE FUNDING CAN BE GIVEN Ancient Parish of Barnes only (SW13 postal district in London)

TYPE OF GRANT Buildings, capital, core costs, endowments, feasibility studies, interest free loans, one-off, project, research, running costs, recurring costs, salaries and start-up costs.

Funding for up to and over three years will be considered

RANGE OF GRANTS £25–£3,500, average grant £450

FINANCES *Year* 1995 *Income* £143,847
Grants £65,629

TRUSTEES A J Paterson, Miss B Westmorland, Rev Richard Ames-Lewis, Mrs Veronica Schroter, J Seekings, P Makower, Mrs A Style, Mrs F Hallett

HOW TO APPLY No telephone calls to office. Application forms and guidelines are available

WHO TO APPLY TO T M Sutton-Mattocks, Barnes Workhouse Fund, Bank Chambers, 1 Rocks Lane, Barnes, London SW13 0DE

CC NO 200103   **ESTABLISHED** 1970

■ Barnsbury Charitable Trust

WHAT IS FUNDED The financial support of national charities in the UK and local charities in Oxfordshire in the fields of Social Welfare, the Arts, and the Environment

WHAT IS NOT FUNDED No grants to individuals or to expeditions

WHO CAN BENEFIT Charitable bodies. There are no restrictions on the age; professional and economic group; family situation; religion and culture; and social circumstances of; or disease or medical condition suffered by, the beneficiaries. However, particular favour is given to at risk groups, those disadvantaged by poverty and socially isolated people

WHERE FUNDING CAN BE GIVEN UK, but no local charities outside Oxfordshire

RANGE OF GRANTS £35–£3,140

SAMPLE GRANTS £3,140 to St Leonards, Mayfield School; £2,000 to St Gile's Church, Lady Chapel Appeal; £1,000 to City of London Chamber Orchestra; £1,000 to Abingdon School Appeal; £1,000 to Oxford Bach Choir; £1,000 to Merrion Monotype Trust; £1,000 to Gatehouse; £1,000 to Northlands Festival, Caithness, Scotland; £1,000 to Family Nurturing Network; £1,000 to Oxfordshire Touring Theatre Company

FINANCES *Year* 1995 *Income* £25,011
Grants £20,300

TRUSTEES H L J Brunner, M R C Brunner, T E Yates

WHO TO APPLY TO Barnsbury Charitable Trust, Messrs Lawrence Graham, Solicitors, 190 Strand, London WC2R 1JN

CC NO 241383   **ESTABLISHED** 1964

■ The Barracks Trust of Newcastle-under-Lyme

WHAT IS FUNDED General charitable purposes, including: relief of the aged, impotent and poor. Relief of distress and sickness. Improving conditions of life in the interests of social welfare, facilities for recreation and other leisure-time occupation. Provision and support of educational facilities

WHAT IS NOT FUNDED No grants for the relief of public funds, taxes and rates

WHO CAN BENEFIT There are no restrictions on the age; professional and economic group; family situation; religion and culture; and social circumstances of; or disease or medical condition suffered by, the beneficiaries

WHERE FUNDING CAN BE GIVEN The former Borough of Newcastle-under-Lyme

FINANCES *Year* 1997–98 *Income* £37,036
Grants £12,940

WHO TO APPLY TO Felix R Hartley, Clerk, The Barracks Trust of Newcastle-under-Lyme, Legal & Administative Services, Civic Offices, Merrial Street, Newcastle-under-Lyme, Staffordshire ST5 2AG

CC NO 217919   ESTABLISHED 1952

■ The Misses Barrie Charitable Trust

WHAT IS FUNDED General charitable purposes at the discretion of the Trustees

WHAT IS NOT FUNDED No grants to individuals

WHO CAN BENEFIT Registered charities. There are no restrictions on the age; professional and economic group; family situation; religion and culture; and social circumstances of; or disease or medical condition suffered by, the beneficiaries

WHERE FUNDING CAN BE GIVEN UK

TYPE OF GRANT Mainly one-off

RANGE OF GRANTS £500–£13,000

SAMPLE GRANTS £13,000 to University of Dundee for research into Biochemistry and Genetic Analysis of HIV-1; £6,250 to University of Oxford for research into Molecular Immunology Group; £6,000 to London Cricket Club; £5,000 to Gardeners Exchange Trust; £5,000 to Princess Royal Trust for Carers; £5,000 to East Surrey Dial-a-Ride; £4,000 to Museum of Scotland; £3,500 to British Wireless for the Blind Fund; £2,500 to Action for Kids; £2,500 to Warlingham Almshouses

FINANCES Year 1997 Income £186,016 Grants £141,750

TRUSTEES R G Carter, MBE, FCA, R S Waddell, CA, R S Ogg, MA(Cantab)

HOW TO APPLY At any time

WHO TO APPLY TO The Misses Barrie Charitable Trust, Messrs Raymond Carter & Co, Chartered Accountants, 1b Haling Road, South Croydon, CR2 6HS

CC NO 279459   ESTABLISHED 1979

■ The Bartholomew Charitable Trust

WHAT IS FUNDED To aid the sick, the handicapped and the terminally ill particularly through respite accommodation, aftercare, hospice at home, respite care, hospices, rehabilitation centres, and cancer research

WHAT IS NOT FUNDED Registered charities only. No grants to individuals. Normally grants are not made in response to general appeals from large national charities

WHO CAN BENEFIT Registered charities benefiting disabled people. There is no restriction on the disease or medical condition suffered by the beneficiaries. Hospices are supported in preference to nursing homes

WHERE FUNDING CAN BE GIVEN UK and overseas

TYPE OF GRANT Buildings, capital, core cost and start-up costs. Funding may be given for more than three years

TRUSTEES J J Berry, Ms R K T Berry, S C Berry

HOW TO APPLY In writing. Applications reviewed periodically. Only successful applications will be acknowledged. Please do not send sae. No telephone calls will be accepted

WHO TO APPLY TO J Berry, Trustee, The Bartholomew Charitable Trust, Goddards Farm, Lindfield, West Sussex RH16 2QX

CC NO 1063797   ESTABLISHED 1997

■ Bartlett Taylor Charitable Trust

WHAT IS FUNDED General charitable purposes at Trustees' discretion

WHO CAN BENEFIT There are no restrictions on the age; professional and economic group; family situation; religion and culture; and social circumstances of; or disease or medical condition suffered by, the beneficiaries

WHERE FUNDING CAN BE GIVEN Oxfordshire

TYPE OF GRANT At the discretion of the Trustees

RANGE OF GRANTS £50–£1,000

FINANCES Year 1998 Income £49,483 Grants £32,212

TRUSTEES R Bartlett, P Burchett, B Cook, J Dingle, R Warner, I Welch

WHO TO APPLY TO I Welch, Bartlett Taylor Charitable Trust, 24 Church Green, Witney, Oxfordshire OX8 6AT Tel 01993 703941 Fax 01993 776071

CC NO 285249   ESTABLISHED 1982

■ Eleanor Barton Trust

WHAT IS FUNDED The Trustees' particular interest is in the use of the arts as therapy to enable the disadvantaged to find a new dimension to their lives. The disadvantage can be social, mental, physical and includes the elderly, those facing the challenge of AIDS and disaffected or mentally/physically disabled youth

WHAT IS NOT FUNDED No grants given for medical matters or to individuals

WHO CAN BENEFIT Usually registered charities benefiting: people of all ages; at risk groups; those disadvantaged by poverty; disabled people and socially isolated people; those suffering from HIV and AIDs; and mental illness

WHERE FUNDING CAN BE GIVEN UK

TYPE OF GRANT Usually one-off grants towards specific projects. Funding is available for up to one year or less

FINANCES Year 1997 Income £24,000 Grants £15,000

TRUSTEES R D Creed, C B Moynihan

HOW TO APPLY The Trustees are willing to receive but do not promise to respond to unsolicited applications. No initial telephone calls welcome. There are no application forms, guidelines or deadlines. No sea required

WHO TO APPLY TO Richard D Creed, Eleanor Barton Trust, Ouvry Creed & Co, Solicitors, Foresters House, Sherston, Malmesbury, Wiltshire SN16 0LQ Tel 01666 840843 Fax 01666 840001

CC NO 293212   ESTABLISHED 1985

■ The Paul Bassham Charitable Trust

WHAT IS FUNDED General charitable purposes. Preference given to Norfolk charitable causes; if funds permit, other charities with national coverage will be considered

WHAT IS NOT FUNDED Restricted to UK registered charities/charitable causes; grant payments will not be made directly to individuals

WHO CAN BENEFIT There are no restrictions on the age; professional and economic group; family situation; religion and culture; and social circumstances of; or disease or medical condition suffered by, the beneficiaries

WHERE FUNDING CAN BE GIVEN Norfolk, UK, some international charities

RANGE OF GRANTS Below £1,000–£25,000
SAMPLE GRANTS £25,000 to H J Sexton Norwich Arts Trust; £5,000 to MA Fine Art Charitable Trust; £5,000 to St John Ambulance Service; £5,000 to Norfolk Wildlife Trust; £2,000 to Norfolk Family Conciliation Service; £1,500 to the Nancy Oldfield Trust; £1,000 to UNICEF; £1,000 to The National Trust
FINANCES *Year* 1997 *Income* £82,982 *Grants* £67,510
TRUSTEES R Lovett, R J Jacob
NOTES Applications considered quarterly by Trustees (April, July, October, January)
WHO TO APPLY TO R Lovett, The Paul Bassham Charitable Trust, KPMG, Holland Court, The Close, Norwich NR1 4DY
CC NO 266842   **ESTABLISHED** 1973

■ The Batchworth Trust

WHAT IS FUNDED General charitable purposes
WHAT IS NOT FUNDED No grants to individuals
WHO CAN BENEFIT Major national and international charities. There are no restrictions on the age; professional and economic group; family situation; religion and culture; and social circumstances of; or disease or medical condition suffered by, the beneficiaries
WHERE FUNDING CAN BE GIVEN UK and overseas
RANGE OF GRANTS £1,000–£33,000
SAMPLE GRANTS £33,000 to Royal College of Surgeons; £20,000 to International Red Cross; £1,000 to Farm Africa; £1,000 to Red Herring Productions; £10,000 to Royal Commonwealth Society for the Blind; £10,000 to St Mungo's Charitable Trust; £7,500 to Magdalen College School; £7,500 to Wadham College; £5,000 to Action for Dysphasic Adults; £5,000 to African Medical Mission
FINANCES *Year* 1997 *Income* £301,724 *Grants* £213,500
TRUSTEES Lockwell Trustees Ltd
WHO TO APPLY TO M Neve, Administrative Executive, The Batchworth Trust, 33–35 Bell Street, Reigate, Surrey RH2 7AW
CC NO 245061   **ESTABLISHED** 1965

■ Nancy Bateman Charitable Trust

WHAT IS FUNDED General charitable purposes
WHO CAN BENEFIT There are no restrictions on the age; professional and economic group; family situation; religion and culture; and social circumstances of; or disease or medical condition suffered by, the beneficiaries
WHERE FUNDING CAN BE GIVEN UK
FINANCES *Year* 1997 *Income* £13,750
TRUSTEES A H Isaacs, Miss D J Bateman
NOTES Applications are discouraged and due to limited resources requests will not be acknowledged
HOW TO APPLY **This Trust states that it does not respond to unsolicited applications**
WHO TO APPLY TO J M G Markham, Nancy Bateman Charitable Trust, 34–36 Gray's Inn Road, London WC1X 8HR
CC NO 288015   **ESTABLISHED** 1983

■ The Bates Charitable Trust

WHAT IS FUNDED Gives to wide range of humanitarian causes, with particular regard to work which stands within the Evangelical tradition of the Church of England

WHAT IS NOT FUNDED No donations to individuals
WHO CAN BENEFIT Registered charities benefiting Church of England, at risk groups, those disadvantaged by poverty and socially isolated people
WHERE FUNDING CAN BE GIVEN UK
RANGE OF GRANTS £100–£2,500
SAMPLE GRANTS £2,500 to St Nicholas PCC; £2,000 to British Red Cross; £1,000 to Church Army of Africa; £1,000 to YMCA; £1,000 to Sue Ryder Foundation; £1,000 to Shelter; £1,000 to St Martin-in-the-Fields; £1,000 to Feed the Children; £1,000 to Holding Hands Appeal; £1,000 to Help the Aged
FINANCES *Year* 1996 *Income* £27,281 *Grants* £28,650
TRUSTEES Mrs A L Bates, W F Bates, J H Bates, D L Hohnen
WHO TO APPLY TO Mrs A L Bates, The Bates Charitable Trust, 30 Swinnerton House, Phyllis Court Drive, Henley-on-Thames, Oxfordshire RG9 2HU
CC NO 280602   **ESTABLISHED** 1980

■ Batten and Co Charitable Trust

WHAT IS FUNDED Religion; arts, culture and recreation; infrastructure and technical support; health; community facilities and services; advice and information on social issues; conservation and environment; schools and colleges; literacy; special needs education; training for community development; and bursaries and fees
WHO CAN BENEFIT Individuals and organisations benefiting students, unemployed people and volunteers. There are no restrictions on the age; family situation; religion and culture of; or disease or medical condition suffered by, the beneficiaries. There are few restrictions on their social circumstances
WHERE FUNDING CAN BE GIVEN Somerset and North and West Devon
TYPE OF GRANT Buildings, capital, core costs, one-off, project, recurring costs and start-up costs. Funding may be given for one year or less
FINANCES *Year* 1997 *Income* £103,325 *Grants* £4,452
TRUSTEES S R Allen, R M Edwards, D G March, R J Vaughan
NOTES 1997 the Trustees received a legacy far in excess of the usual income. In line with the wishes of the testator, this money remains invested and the income will be used for general charitable purposes
HOW TO APPLY In writing to the address below
WHO TO APPLY TO R J Gibbons, Clerk, Batten and Co Charitable Trust, Church House, Church Street, Yeovil, Somerset BA20 1HB
CC NO 293500   **ESTABLISHED** 1985

■ The Battishorne Trust

WHAT IS FUNDED General charitable purposes including: arts, culture and recreation; conservation; education and training; and community facilities and services. Hospices, hospice at home, nursing services and cancer research are also considered
WHAT IS NOT FUNDED No grants to individuals
WHO CAN BENEFIT The inhabitants of Honiton
WHERE FUNDING CAN BE GIVEN Honiton in Devon
TYPE OF GRANT Capital, core costs and one-off funding will be considered
TRUSTEES P M Martin, F E Martin, D P Steele-Perkins, E J Underdown

HOW TO APPLY By letter to D P Steele-Perkins at the address under Who To Apply To

WHO TO APPLY TO D P Steele-Perkins, Trustee, The Battishorne Trust, The Laurels, 46 New Street, Honiton Devon EX14 8BZ *Tel* 01404 43431

CC NO 1048821　　**ESTABLISHED** 1995

■ The Baxendell Charitable Trust

This trust did not respond to CAF's request to amend its entry and, by 30 June 1998, CAF's researchers did not find financial records for later than 1995 on its file at the Charity Commission. Trusts are legally required to submit annual accounts to the Charity Commission under section 42 of the Charities Act 1993

WHAT IS FUNDED General charitable purposes

WHO CAN BENEFIT There are no restrictions on the age; professional and economic group; family situation; religion and culture; and social circumstances of; or disease or medical condition suffered by, the beneficiaries

WHERE FUNDING CAN BE GIVEN UK

TRUSTEES Sir Peter Baxendell, Lady Rosemary Baxendell, Robert J Mitchell

HOW TO APPLY To the address under Who To Apply To in writing

WHO TO APPLY TO R J Mitchell, Trustee, The Baxendell Charitable Trust, Messrs Fraser & Russell, Albany House, 128 Station Road, Redhill, Surrey RH1 1ET

CC NO 1043504　　**ESTABLISHED** 1994

■ The Bay Tree Charitable Trust

WHAT IS FUNDED General charitable purposes at the discretion of the Trustees

WHAT IS NOT FUNDED No grants to individuals

WHO CAN BENEFIT At the discretion of the Trustees. There are no restrictions on the age; professional and economic group; family situation; religion and culture; and social circumstances of; or disease or medical condition suffered by, the beneficiaries

WHERE FUNDING CAN BE GIVEN UK and overseas

TYPE OF GRANT At the discretion of the Trustees

TRUSTEES G S Brown, Mrs A H Palmer

WHO TO APPLY TO G S Brown, The Bay Tree Charitable Trust, 10 New Square, Lincoln's Inn, London WC2A 3QG *Tel* 0171-465 4300

CC NO 1044091　　**ESTABLISHED** 1994

■ The Dorothy Bayles Trust

WHAT IS FUNDED Christian, general charitable purposes

WHO CAN BENEFIT Organisations benefiting Christians

WHERE FUNDING CAN BE GIVEN Lincolnshire

RANGE OF GRANTS £50–£486,000

SAMPLE GRANTS £486,000 to Dorothy Kerin Trust (from the proceeds of Chalk Farm); £11,000 to Lincoln Cathedral Fabric Fund; £5,500 to Parkinson's Disease Society; £4,000 to Lincoln MRI Scanner Appeal; £3,000 to Lincoln Ambucopter Appeal; £3,000 to the Leprosy Mission; £2,000 to St Luke's Hospital, London; £2,000 to St Barnabas Trust, Lincoln; £2,000 to the Iris Fund; £2,000 to Save the Children

FINANCES *Year* 1997 *Income* £596,018 *Grants* £572,400

TRUSTEES M Strawson

NOTES Income in 1997 includes the sale of a Trust property, Chalk Farm, resulting in large income for one year

HOW TO APPLY To the address under Who To Apply To in writing

WHO TO APPLY TO Mark Bayles Strawson, Trustee, The Dorothy Bayles Trust, Lings Farm House, Croxby Top, Market Rasen, Lincolnshire LN7 6BN

CC NO 271259　　**ESTABLISHED** 1976

■ Baylies' Educational Foundation

WHAT IS FUNDED Religious education and financial assistance to young persons to enable them to pursue their chosen educational courses up to university level and beyond. Also, the setting up of school libraries. Educational visits abroad are especially encouraged

WHO CAN BENEFIT Schools and individuals and students within the area Where Funding Can Be Given. The normal age limit is 21 years

WHERE FUNDING CAN BE GIVEN Dudley

SAMPLE GRANTS £385 to Dudley Educational Foundation

FINANCES *Year* 1997 *Income* £48,321 *Grants* £48,783

TRUSTEES A Austin, J W Abbiss, I Cleland, J Cooksey, B M Fisher, D J Hughes, H Hyde, R J Little

NOTES Applications are considered in February, April, June, September and December

HOW TO APPLY Application forms can be obtained from the address under Who To Apply To

WHO TO APPLY TO W B Owen Griffiths, Clerk, Baylies' Educational Foundation, 18 Paganel Drive, Dudley, West Midlands DY1 4AY *Tel* 01384 253513

CC NO 527118　　**ESTABLISHED** 1961

■ Bayne Benefaction

WHAT IS FUNDED To make such grants as may assist schools and priests entitled to apply for assistance. Particularly charities working in the fields of: Christian education; Diocesan boards; Church schools; cultural and religious teaching; bursaries and fees and the purchase of books

WHO CAN BENEFIT Individuals and organisations benefiting children, young adults, older people, clergy and Church of England

WHERE FUNDING CAN BE GIVEN Bracknell Forest, Buckinghamshire, Milton Keynes, Oxfordshire, Reading, Slough, West Berkshire, Windsor and Maidenhead and Wokingham

TYPE OF GRANT Endowment

FINANCES *Year* 1997 *Income* £18,741

TRUSTEES Dean of Christ Church, Bishop of Oxford, Archdeacons of Oxford, Buckingham and Berkshire

NOTES An original restriction of £100 per individual priest applying has now been raised, but sums provided are conditioned in part by the number of applicants, who must apply afresh each year, and may be required to submit details of income and reasons for application. No financial restrictions are placed upon schools, the grant made being at the Trustees' discretion

HOW TO APPLY Applications from schools to be made through the Diocesan Schools' Adviser for each county or unitary authority. Applications from Clergy by letter giving as much information as possible. To be sent to the secretary late September each year

WHO TO APPLY TO Freda Storrar, Secretary, Bayne Benefaction, 12 Eider Close, Buckingham MK18 1GL

CC NO 203262　　**ESTABLISHED** 1911

Does the trust you have chosen match your needs? Haphazard applications waste postage and time

49

■ Beacon Centre for the Blind (also known as The Wolverhampton, Dudley and Districts Institute for the Blind)

WHAT IS FUNDED Maintaining a residential home, a day centre and running employment schemes; outings; holidays; talking books and newspapers for blind and partially sighted people

WHO CAN BENEFIT Individuals and organisations benefiting the partially sighted, blind and unemployed people

WHERE FUNDING CAN BE GIVEN The Boroughs of Sandwell, Wolverhampton, Dudley (except Halesowen and Stourbridge) and parts of South Staffordshire District Council area

RANGE OF GRANTS £2,280–£319,129

SAMPLE GRANTS £391,129 to Beacon House; £247,316 to Day Centre; £68,891 to Mobile Resource Unit; £63,138 for welfare and talking newspapers; £55,442 to John Chamberlain Hall; £42,176 for a canteen; £14,436 to homeworkers; £13,585 to Charles Hayward Bungalows; £2,280 to Community Action

FINANCES Year 1997 Income £3,081,242 Grants £898,393

TRUSTEES T D T Hickman, M Machelworth, S F Chaplin, R F Ilsley, R B Bumbell, D W Evans, G E Gilbert, M K Hill, W V Jolly, R A Joseph, A H McIlreath, W T Melia, G A Oldbury, S A Portman, J K Sadler, T F Smith, M D Thomas, E A Askew, D J Flavell, A D Johnson, K Read, D M Seiboth, A J Taylor, MBE, H Fielding

HOW TO APPLY To the address under Who To Apply To in writing

WHO TO APPLY TO Director/Secretary, Beacon Centre for the Blind, Wolverhampton Road East, Wolverhampton WV4 6AZ

CC NO 216092   **ESTABLISHED** 1875

■ Beacon Trust

WHAT IS FUNDED Evangelical Protestant causes

WHAT IS NOT FUNDED No grants to individuals

WHO CAN BENEFIT Organisations benefiting evangelical Protestants, including Baptists, Anglican and Methodists. Funding is usually given to headquarters organisations

WHERE FUNDING CAN BE GIVEN Mainly UK, but also some overseas (usually in Commonwealth) and Spain and Portugal

FINANCES Year 1997 Income £72,040 Grants £111,100

TRUSTEES Mrs D J Spink, G A Stacey, Miss J M Spink

WHO TO APPLY TO G A Stacey, Beacon Trust, 2 Tongdean Avenue, Hove, East Sussex BN3 6TL

CC NO 230087   **ESTABLISHED** 1963

■ The Beale Trust

This trust did not respond to CAF's request to amend its entry and, by 30 June 1998, CAF's researchers did not find financial records for later than 1995 on its file at the Charity Commission. Trusts are legally required to submit annual accounts to the Charity Commission under section 42 of the Charities Act 1993

WHAT IS FUNDED General charitable purposes, in particular to relieve necessitous employees, former employees and their dependents in respect of Beale's Ltd and any associated companies

WHO CAN BENEFIT There are no restrictions on the age; professional and economic group; family situation; religion and culture; and social circumstances of; or disease or medical condition suffered by, the beneficiaries. However, particular favour is given to employees and ex–employees of Beale's Ltd, or any associated company, and their dependants

WHERE FUNDING CAN BE GIVEN UK and overseas

TRUSTEES A E Beale, T H Beale, Ms S D Clayton

WHO TO APPLY TO T Beale, Trustee, The Beale Trust, West Lodge Park, Hadley Wood, Barnet, Hertfordshire EN4 0PY

CC NO 1043361   **ESTABLISHED** 1995

■ The Bealey Foundation

WHAT IS FUNDED Medical research, and of the relief of physical and mental sickness and disability for the benefit of the public

WHO CAN BENEFIT Institutions, hospitals and hospices benefiting sick people, research workers and medical professionals. There is no restriction on the disease or medical condition suffered by the beneficiaries

WHERE FUNDING CAN BE GIVEN UK

TYPE OF GRANT One-off grants

TRUSTEES M D Bealey, J M Bealey, T Shaw, K Egerton

WHO TO APPLY TO Martin Bealey, Trustee, The Bealey Foundation, 6 Field Close, East Molesey, Surrey KT8 0LA

CC NO 297505   **ESTABLISHED** 1987

■ Bear Mordechai Ltd

WHAT IS FUNDED Jewish charities

WHO CAN BENEFIT Individuals, small local projects and national organisations benefiting Jewish people

WHERE FUNDING CAN BE GIVEN UK and overseas

TYPE OF GRANT Recurring costs and core costs will be considered

FINANCES Year 1997 Income £123,748 Grants £88,925

TRUSTEES Y Benedikt, C Benedikt, E S Benedikt

WHO TO APPLY TO Y Benedikt, Bear Mordechai Ltd, 50 Moresley Road, London E5 9LF

CC NO 286806   **ESTABLISHED** 1982

■ The Bearder Charity

WHAT IS FUNDED General charitable purposes

WHO CAN BENEFIT There are no restrictions on the age; professional and economic group; family situation; religion and culture; and social circumstances of; or disease or medical condition suffered by, the beneficiaries

WHERE FUNDING CAN BE GIVEN Calderdale

FINANCES Year 1997 Income £27,623 Grants £18,727

TRUSTEES J A Bearder, Mrs V Shepherd, P W Townend, T Simpson, R D Smithies, Mrs S Gee, L Smith

HOW TO APPLY To the address under Who To Apply To in writing

WHO TO APPLY TO T Simpson, Secretary, The Bearder Charity, 1 School Close, Ripponden, Sowerby Bridge HX6 4HP

CC NO 1010529   **ESTABLISHED** 1992

■ Bearwood Chapel Trust

WHAT IS FUNDED To advance the Christian faith; to relieve persons who are in conditions of need, hardship, distress or who are aged or sick; any other general charitable purposes for the benefit of the community

WHO CAN BENEFIT There are no restrictions on the age; professional and economic group; family situation; religion and culture; and social circumstances of; or disease or medical condition suffered by, the beneficiaries. However, particular favour is given to at risk groups, those disadvantaged by poverty and socially isolated people, the elderly and the sick

WHERE FUNDING CAN BE GIVEN West Midlands, UK and overseas

FINANCES *Year* 1997 *Income* £58,171

WHO TO APPLY TO Dr J Wearn, Chairman, Bearwood Chapel Trust, The Riding Light, 289 Lordswood Road, Birmingham BI7 8PR

CC NO 1049009   **ESTABLISHED** 1995

■ The Rt Hon Else Countess Beauchamp Deceased Charitable Trust

WHAT IS FUNDED Charities in Herefordshire and Worcestershire for the preservation of buildings and rural scenery. Arts and arts facilities are also considered

WHAT IS NOT FUNDED No grants to individuals or for endowments

WHERE FUNDING CAN BE GIVEN Herefordshire and Worcestershire

SAMPLE GRANTS The Elmley Foundation

FINANCES *Year* 1996–97 *Income* £200,555 *Grants* £82,000

TRUSTEES John de la Cour, Diana Johnson, S Driver White

NOTES The Trust's funds are used overwhelmingly to support the Elmley Foundation which the Trustees also control

HOW TO APPLY Payments are made only at the Trustees' instigation

WHO TO APPLY TO J de la Cour, The Rt Hon Else Countess Beauchamp Deceased Charitable Trust, West Aish, Morchard Bishop, Crediton, Devon EX17 6RX *Tel* 01363 775587

CC NO 1042208   **ESTABLISHED** 1994

■ The Beaufort House Trust

WHAT IS FUNDED To make grants for diocesan education, ministry bursaries and more general Christian beneficiaries. The furtherance of education will be considered

WHAT IS NOT FUNDED No grants to individuals

WHO CAN BENEFIT Organisation benefiting Christians, children and young adults

WHERE FUNDING CAN BE GIVEN UK

TYPE OF GRANT Some recurring, majority one-off

RANGE OF GRANTS £100–£5,000

FINANCES *Year* 1997 *Income* £1,178,379 *Grants* £88,100

TRUSTEES C Alan McLintock, M R Cornwall-Jones, B V Day, Rt Hon Viscount Churchill, Rt Rev D G Snelgrove, W H Yates

HOW TO APPLY To the address under Who To Apply To in writing

WHO TO APPLY TO R W Clayton, Secretary, The Beaufort House Trust, Beaufort House, Brunswick Road, Gloucester GL1 1JZ *Tel* 01452 528533

CC NO 286606   **ESTABLISHED** 1983

■ Beauland Ltd

WHAT IS FUNDED Healthcare charities and exclusively Jewish projects supported

WHO CAN BENEFIT To benefit Jewish people and the sick. There is no restriction on the disease or medical condition suffered by the beneficiaries

WHERE FUNDING CAN BE GIVEN Greater Manchester

FINANCES *Year* 1997 *Income* £285,567 *Grants* £204,444

TRUSTEES W Neuman, F Neuman, H Neuman, M Neuman, P Neuman, E Neuman, E Henry, M Friedlander, H Roseman, J Bleirer, R Delange

WHO TO APPLY TO W Newman, Beauland Ltd, 4 Cheltenham Crescent, Salford, Manchester M7 4FE

CC NO 511374   **ESTABLISHED** 1981

■ The Becker Family Charitable Trust

WHAT IS FUNDED General charitable purposes

WHO CAN BENEFIT There are no restrictions on the age; professional and economic group; family situation; religion and culture; and social circumstances of; or disease or medical condition suffered by, the beneficiaries

WHERE FUNDING CAN BE GIVEN UK and overseas

FINANCES *Year* 1996 *Income* £26,159 *Grants* £7,868

TRUSTEES A Becker, L Becker, Ms R Becker, Ms D Fried, C Guttentag

WHO TO APPLY TO L Becker, Trustee, The Becker Family Charitable Trust, 7 Riverside Drive, Golders Green Road, London NW11 9PU

CC NO 1047968   **ESTABLISHED** 1995

■ The Heather Beckwith Charitable Settlement

WHAT IS FUNDED Health services, medical research and studies, the arts

WHAT IS NOT FUNDED No grants to individuals unless personally known to the Trustees. Appeals from overseas will not be considered

WHO CAN BENEFIT Organisations benefiting: actors and entertainment professionals; musicians; medical professionals; research workers; textile workers and designers; writers and poets; and the sick. There is no restriction on the disease or medical condition suffered by the beneficiaries

WHERE FUNDING CAN BE GIVEN UK

TYPE OF GRANT Depends on request, but research grants are considered

SAMPLE GRANTS £9,208 to the Dragon School; £2,500 to Macmillan Nurses; £2,300 to Teenage Cancer Trust; £550 to Richmond Park Charitable Trust; £500 to Philip Lawrence Memorial Fund

FINANCES *Year* 1996 *Income* £22,545 *Grants* £16,813

TRUSTEES Mrs H M Beckwith, J L Beckwith, M R MacFadyen

HOW TO APPLY No regular dates

WHO TO APPLY TO Mrs H M Beckwith, The Heather Beckwith Charitable Settlement, Pacific Investments, 195 Knightsbridge, London SW7 1RE

CC NO 1000952   **ESTABLISHED** 1990

■ The Peter Beckwith Charitable Trust

WHAT IS FUNDED Trustees support a broad range of medical and welfare charities

WHO CAN BENEFIT Institutions and registered charities benefiting at risk groups, those disadvantaged by poverty and socially isolated people. There is no restriction on the disease or medical condition suffered by the beneficiaries

WHERE FUNDING CAN BE GIVEN UK

FINANCES *Year* 1995–96 *Income* £121,378 *Grants* £53,823

TRUSTEES P M Beckwith, Mrs P Beckwith, Mrs A Peppiatt

WHO TO APPLY TO P M Beckwith, The Peter Beckwith Charitable Trust, Hill Place House, 55a High Street, Wimbledon, London SW19 5BA

CC NO 802113 **ESTABLISHED** 1989

■ The Peter Bedford Trust

WHAT IS FUNDED The current policy of the Trustees is to make grants to the Peter Bedford Housing Association for its work in offering work, training, employment, housing and support for people starting a new life in the community

WHO CAN BENEFIT Organisations benefiting unemployed people, homeless people, disabled people and ex-offenders and those at risk of offending

WHERE FUNDING CAN BE GIVEN UK

SAMPLE GRANTS £15,479 to Peter Bedford Housing Association for PBHA's Work

FINANCES *Year* 1996–97 *Income* £75,498 *Grants* £15,479

TRUSTEES A Watson (Chair), B Allan, C Egan, M Boye-Anawonah

HOW TO APPLY To the address Under Who To Apply To in writing. **This Trust states that it does not respond to unsolicited applications**

WHO TO APPLY TO The Secretary, The Peter Bedford Trust, Legard Works, 17a Legard Road, Highbury, London N5 1DE *Tel* 0171-226 6074

CC NO 296309 **ESTABLISHED** 1990

■ The Patricia Beecham Charitable Settlement

WHAT IS FUNDED Largely Jewish causes, at Trustees' discretion

WHO CAN BENEFIT To benefit Jewish people

WHERE FUNDING CAN BE GIVEN UK

RANGE OF GRANTS £5–£11,540

SAMPLE GRANTS £11,540 to Lewis Hammerson Memorial Home; £5,406 to Hammerson House; £1,000 to British Friends of Haifa University; £750 to West London Synagogue; £500 to Nightingale Home

FINANCES *Year* 1997 *Income* £16,908 *Grants* £24,921

TRUSTEES Mrs P Beecham, A J Thompson, R J Beecham, JP

WHO TO APPLY TO Mrs P Beecham, The Patricia Beecham Charitable Settlement, Nash House, 3 Chester Terrace, Regents Park, London NW1 4ND

CC NO 294558 **ESTABLISHED** 1986

■ The David and Ruth Behrend Fund

WHAT IS FUNDED General charitable purposes. The Trust only gives funding to charities known to the Settlors

WHO CAN BENEFIT There are no restrictions on the age; professional and economic group; family situation; religion and culture; and social circumstances of; or disease or medical condition suffered by, the beneficiaries

WHERE FUNDING CAN BE GIVEN Merseyside

SAMPLE GRANTS £11,000 to Merseyside Development Foundation; £7,500 to Fair Play for Children; £2,000 to Barnstable Trust; £2,000 to FORME; £2,000 to Mustard Seed Ministries; £2,000 to Sheila Kay Fund; £1,000 to PSS; £1,000 to Merseyside Holiday Scheme; £1,000 to KIND

FINANCES *Year* 1997 *Income* £45,000 *Grants* £19,000

TRUSTEES Liverpool Council of Social Services (Inc)

PUBLICATIONS Annual Report

HOW TO APPLY **This Trust states that it does not respond to unsolicited applications**

WHO TO APPLY TO Carol Champman, Financial Services Manager, The David and Ruth Behrend Fund, Liverpool Council of Social Services (Inc), 14 Castle Street, Liverpool L2 0NJ *Tel* 0151-236 7728 *Fax* 0151-258 1153

CC NO 261567 **ESTABLISHED** 1969

■ E M Behrens Charitable Trust

WHAT IS FUNDED General charitable purposes

WHAT IS NOT FUNDED Registered charities only. No grants are made to general appeals from large national organisations

WHO CAN BENEFIT UK registered charities. There are no restrictions on the age; professional and economic group; family situation; religion and culture; and social circumstances of; or disease or medical condition suffered by, the beneficiaries

WHERE FUNDING CAN BE GIVEN UK

FINANCES *Year* 1997 *Income* £56,243 *Grants* £11,550

TRUSTEES S J Cockburn, C H W Parish, J N Behrens

NOTES Grants were distributed in 1997 under the following organisation type: disadvantaged and special needs; Music, art and education; children and young people; and medical research; environmental

HOW TO APPLY **This Trust states that it does not respond to unsolicited applications**

WHO TO APPLY TO J R Males, E M Behrens Charitable Trust, 18th Floor, Royex House, Aldermanbury Square, London EC2V 7HR

CC NO 266324 **ESTABLISHED** 1973

■ Beis Chinuch Lebonos Limited

WHAT IS FUNDED The advancement of religion in accordance with the Orthodox Jewish faith; the relief of poverty and other general charitable purposes

WHO CAN BENEFIT To benefit Jewish people and those disadvantaged by poverty

WHERE FUNDING CAN BE GIVEN London

FINANCES *Year* 1997 *Income* £214,576

TRUSTEES Y Reitzer, A Schechter, Mrs E Spitzer

WHO TO APPLY TO Mrs Spitzer, Beis Chinuch Lebonos Limited, 5 Paget Road, London N16 5ND

CC NO 1049458 **ESTABLISHED** 1993

■ The Beis Malka Trust

This trust did not respond to CAF's request to amend its entry and, by 30 June 1998, CAF's researchers did not find financial records for later than 1995 on its file at the Charity Commission. Trusts are legally required to submit annual accounts to the Charity Commission under section 42 of the Charities Act 1993

WHAT IS FUNDED Jewish education projects

WHO CAN BENEFIT Jewish children, young adults and students

WHERE FUNDING CAN BE GIVEN UK and overseas

TRUSTEES M Grossman, A Grossman, M Dresdner

WHO TO APPLY TO Mr Dresdner, The Beis Malka Trust, 93 Aicham Road, London N16 6XD

CC NO 284447   **ESTABLISHED** 1981

■ John Bell Charitable Trust

WHAT IS FUNDED General charitable purposes with a preference for youth work and aged and medical charities. This Trust also considers: ambulances and mobile units; hospices; community centres and village halls; crime prevention schemes; and playschemes

WHO CAN BENEFIT Local organisations benefiting young adults and older people. Also those suffering from Alzheimer's disease and heart disease

WHERE FUNDING CAN BE GIVEN Tyne and Wear, Northumberland and County Durham

TYPE OF GRANT Cash and one-off

SAMPLE GRANTS £2,500 to Kings School, Tynemouth for new hall appeal; £2,000 to Northumberland County Scout Council; £1,500 to British Heart Foundation; £1,000 to Cedarwood Trust; £1,000 to Crimestoppers

FINANCES *Year* 1998 *Income* £19,593
Grants £20,650

TRUSTEES R I Stewart CBE, DL, N Sherlock, DL, H Straker

HOW TO APPLY Letters only. No acknowledgements

WHO TO APPLY TO R I Stewart, CBE, DL, John Bell Charitable Trust, Brockenhurst, 2 The Broadway, Tynemouth NE30 2LD

CC NO 272631   **ESTABLISHED** 1974

■ The Barron Bell Trust and Additional Fund

WHAT IS FUNDED Providing, installing, inspecting, repairing or maintaining carillons of bells in churches in Great Britain. The Fund is relatively small in modern terms and the income commensurately so. The income is such that we try to support as many applicants as possible with sums which are an encouragement rather than any great contribution. The fund is administered within the requirements of the Trust Making Deed but also within the spirit of Emma Barron's original desires. The Trustees also endeavour to support churches where there are a minimum of six bells to form the peal. The Trustees are keen to support applications where there is an intention to increase the number of bells up to a minimum of six

WHAT IS NOT FUNDED Grants are made strictly in respect of the items covered under the objects. There is a restriction that the services held in the church should be Low Church. The Trustees also endeavour to support those applicants where at least 50 per cent of the required monies have already been accumulated

WHO CAN BENEFIT Bell restoration funds

WHERE FUNDING CAN BE GIVEN UK

FINANCES *Year* 1998 *Income* £23,940
Grants £21,200

TRUSTEES I H Walrond, N D L Kidson, Mrs A G Bryant-Fenn

PUBLICATIONS Annual Report to Register of Charities

NOTES The Trustees meet twice a year to consider applications and there is little correspondence outside these times

HOW TO APPLY To address under Who To Apply To by application form

WHO TO APPLY TO I H Walrond, FRICS, The Barron Bell Trust and Additional Fund, 71 Lower Green Road, Pembury, Tunbridge Wells, Kent TN2 4EB

CC NO 228846   **ESTABLISHED** 1925

■ The Henry Bell Trust

WHAT IS FUNDED General charitable purposes including: almshouses and sheltered accommodation; support to voluntary and community organisations; charity or voluntary umbrella bodies; churches and church bodies; arts activities and education; health facilities and buildings; conservation; bird sanctuaries; parks; heritage and wildlife; schools and colleges; and community facilities

WHAT IS NOT FUNDED No grants to individuals

WHO CAN BENEFIT To benefit: people of all ages; students; Methodists; and those disadvantaged by poverty

WHERE FUNDING CAN BE GIVEN Hexham, Hexham Low Quarter and Hexhamshire

TYPE OF GRANT Buildings, one-off and running costs. Funding is available for over three years

FINANCES *Year* 1996–97 *Income* £16,407

TRUSTEES A Brogdon, J M Clark, Canon M Nelson, M Howard, I Brogdon

HOW TO APPLY To the address under Who To Apply To in writing

WHO TO APPLY TO J M Clark, Trustee, The Henry Bell Trust, c/o Clark Scott-Harden, Market Place, Haltwhistle, Northumberland NE49 0BP
Tel 01434 320363

CC NO 702166   **ESTABLISHED** 1989

■ Bellahouston Bequest Fund

WHAT IS FUNDED Churches and charitable bodies within Glasgow; the promotion of Protestant and Evangelical religion; and the relief of poverty and disease in Glasgow

WHAT IS NOT FUNDED No grants to individuals

WHO CAN BENEFIT Churches and registered charities in Glasgow or within five miles especially those benefiting Protestant Evangelical denominations and clergy of such churches, as well as those disadvantaged by poverty

WHERE FUNDING CAN BE GIVEN Does not extend more than five miles beyond the Glasgow City boundary

TYPE OF GRANT Capital

FINANCES *Year* 1996 *Income* £130,000
Grants £100,000

HOW TO APPLY By letter. Application form for Churches

WHO TO APPLY TO E H Webster, Messrs Mitchells Roberton, George House, 36 North Hanover Street, Glasgow G1 2AD

SC NO SCO 11781   **ESTABLISHED** 1888

Does the trust you have chosen match your needs? Haphazard applications waste postage and time

53

■ The Bellinger Donnay Trust

WHAT IS FUNDED Charitable projects by organisations

WHAT IS NOT FUNDED Personal education, expeditions and financial assistance will not be funded

WHO CAN BENEFIT Individuals through charities. There are no restrictions on the age; professional and economic group; family situation; religion and culture; and social circumstances of; or disease or medical condition suffered by, the beneficiaries

WHERE FUNDING CAN BE GIVEN London and Buckinghamshire

SAMPLE GRANTS £7,550 to Wellbeing; £4,820 to Royal Academy Trust; £1,000 to Broaderers Charity Trust; £1,000 to South Buckinghamshire Riding School for Disabled; £600 to St John Ambulance; £445 to International Social Services; £350 to National Thoroughbred Trust; £250 to Beau Soleil Music Centre; £250 to National Opera Studio; £250 to Society for Autistic Children

FINANCES *Year* 1996–97 *Income* £108,877 *Grants* £20,730

TRUSTEES Sir R I Bellinger, GBE, Lady C M L Bellinger, Ms L E Bellinger-Smith, I A Bellinger

HOW TO APPLY In writing to the address under Who To Apply To

WHO TO APPLY TO Sir Robert Bellinger, GBE, The Bellinger Donnay Trust, Penn Wood, Fulmer, Buckinghamshire SL3 6JL

CC NO 289462　　　　　**ESTABLISHED** 1984

■ Belljoe Tzedoko Ltd

WHAT IS FUNDED Trustees consider applications from organisations with general charitable purposes

WHO CAN BENEFIT Registered charities and institutions. There are no restrictions on the age; professional and economic group; family situation; religion and culture; and social circumstances of; or disease or medical condition suffered by, the beneficiaries

WHERE FUNDING CAN BE GIVEN UK

RANGE OF GRANTS £15–£8,550

SAMPLE GRANTS £8,550 to Marbeh Torah Trust; £7,525 to Society of Friends of the Torah; £5,500 to Yesodey Hatorah School; £5,050 to Kollel Shomrei Hachomos; £5,000 to Keren Hatorah; £4,336 to Yeshivo Horomo; £4,000 to Hachnos Kalloh Foundation (Dowry for the Bride); £4,000 to Sinai Synagogue; £3,215 to Ponovez; £3,000 to Beis Yakov

FINANCES *Year* 1995 *Income* £61,634 *Grants* £76,332

TRUSTEES H J Lobenstein, Mrs B Lobenstein, D Lobenstein, M Lobenstein

WHO TO APPLY TO H J Lobenstein, Belljoe Tzedoko Ltd, 27 Fairholt Road, London N16 5EW

CC NO 282726　　　　　**ESTABLISHED** 1981

■ Bell's Nautical Trust

WHAT IS FUNDED Grants are given to a range of maritime institutions

WHO CAN BENEFIT Maritime institutions benefiting seafarers and fishermen

WHERE FUNDING CAN BE GIVEN Scotland, especially Leith

FINANCES *Year* 1997–98 *Income* £20,000 *Grants* £17,000

TRUSTEES R S Salvesen, S J Boyd, C W Davidson, R M Logan, J A G Lowe, W McDonald, J MacNeill, B Parker, R K Scovell, J W Sellars, J W Simpson, N C Souter, J Taylor, Captain A H F Wilks

HOW TO APPLY Applications should be made in writing to the address under Who To Apply To. Deadline is 30 November annually

WHO TO APPLY TO W H Gordon Mathison, Bell's Nautical Trust, 11 Corrennie Gardens, Edinburgh EH10 6DG *Tel* 0131-447 9859

SC NO SCO 017199　　　　**ESTABLISHED** 1984

■ The Belmont Trust

WHAT IS FUNDED Small donations for medical, welfare, environmental and musical purposes. Particularly charities working in the areas of: residential services; support for voluntary and community organisations; support for volunteers; Council for Voluntary Service; volunteer bureaux; music; health; conservation and conservation campaigning; medical research; and community facilities and services

WHAT IS NOT FUNDED Applications from individuals and for religious purposes are excluded

WHO CAN BENEFIT Organisations benefiting one parent families; musicians; carers; immigrants and refugees. There is no restriction on the disease or medical condition suffered by the beneficiaries

WHERE FUNDING CAN BE GIVEN Hampshire and adjacent counties preferred

TYPE OF GRANT No loans. Information about the Music Award (£2,000 in 1998) should be obtained from the Musicians Benevolent Fund

RANGE OF GRANTS Largest £750, typical grants £50–£150

SAMPLE GRANTS £750 to Oxfam; £200 to Age Concern; £200 to Refugee Council; £200 to Cancer Research Campaign; £200 to World Jewish Relief

FINANCES *Year* 1997–98 *Income* £21,000 *Grants* £12,000

TRUSTEES Mrs L Steel, Miss H E F Corbett, BSc

HOW TO APPLY In writing with full supporting details. Trustees regret that they cannot acknowledge unsuccessful applications. Please note that a large proportion of donations are made in March/April of each year via the Charities Aid Foundation

WHO TO APPLY TO The Belmont Trust, PO Box 89, Havant, Hampshire PO9 3YU

CC NO 265946　　　　　**ESTABLISHED** 1973

■ Belsize Charitable Trust No1

WHAT IS FUNDED (a) Nature conversation, including nature reserves and historic buildings. (b) Promotion of traditions skills. (c) Sailing charities. (d) Employment for the disabled schemes

WHAT IS NOT FUNDED No grants made to individuals

WHO CAN BENEFIT Organisations benefiting: seafarers and fishermen; unemployed people; and disabled people

WHERE FUNDING CAN BE GIVEN England

TYPE OF GRANT One-off and project

RANGE OF GRANTS Typical grant £5,000

SAMPLE GRANTS £11,000 to International Boat Building Training College for scholarships

FINANCES *Year* 1997 *Income* £27,231 *Grants* £11,000

TRUSTEES Lloyds Bank A/C 42392/CR

HOW TO APPLY All letters considered half yearly at the end of February and August. No acknowledgements issued

WHO TO APPLY TO Lloyds Private Banking Ltd, Belsize Charitable Trust No1, UK Trust Centre, The Clock House, 22–26 Ock Street, Abingdon, Oxfordshire OX14 5SW
CC NO 262535   **ESTABLISHED** 1958

■ Benfield Motors Charitable Trust

WHAT IS FUNDED Grants are given to mainly health and welfare and Christian charities
WHAT IS NOT FUNDED Expeditions, scholarships and animal charities are not funded
WHO CAN BENEFIT Neighbourhood-based community projects and national schemes benefiting Christians, at risk groups, those disadvantaged by poverty and socially isolated people. There is no restriction on the disease or medical condition suffered by the beneficiaries. Third world relief will be considered
WHERE FUNDING CAN BE GIVEN UK and overseas, with a preference for the North East of England
TYPE OF GRANT One-off
RANGE OF GRANTS £50–£25,000; typical grant £1,000
SAMPLE GRANTS £10,000 to TWF; £6,856 to Macmillan; £6,633 to St Oswalds Hospice; £2,000 to British Red Cross; £2,000 to Northumberland Coalition Against Crime; £1,250 to Northumberland Association of Boys Clubs; £1,000 to Christian Aid; £1,000 to Save the Children; £1,000 to St George's Crypt; £1,000 to the Sick Children's Trust
FINANCES *Year* 1997 *Income* £50,000
Grants £39,393
TRUSTEES John Squires, Malcolm Squires, Stephen Squires
HOW TO APPLY To the address under Who To Apply To in writing
WHO TO APPLY TO Mrs L Squires, Benfield Motors Charitable Trust, Newcastle Business Park, Newcastle upon Tyne NE4 7YD
CC NO 328149   **ESTABLISHED** 1989

■ Benham Charitable Settlement

WHAT IS FUNDED Established by the late Cedric and Hilda Benham, the Trust's policy is to make a large number of relatively small grants to groups working in many charitable fields – including charities involved in medical research, disability and handicap, the elderly, children, young people, churches, the disadvantaged, wildlife, the environment, education and the arts. The emphasis is very much on activities within Northamptonshire
WHAT IS NOT FUNDED Registered charities only. No individuals
WHO CAN BENEFIT Organisations benefiting children, young adults, older people, at risk groups, disabled people, those disadvantaged by poverty and socially isolated people. There are no restrictions on the disease or medical condition suffered by the beneficiaries. Most good causes considered, including national appeals, or branches of the same in Northamptonshire. National cathedrals supported, but only churches in Northamptonshire
WHERE FUNDING CAN BE GIVEN UK, but with special interest in Northamptonshire
TYPE OF GRANT One-off and recurring grants will be considered
RANGE OF GRANTS £50–£25,000; typically £300
FINANCES *Year* 1997–98 *Income* £147,171
Grants £138,000

TRUSTEES Mrs M M Tittle, Mrs R A Nickols, E N Langley
NOTES Only successful applications are acknowledged
HOW TO APPLY Must be in writing to the address under Who To Apply To. No telephone calls. No application forms or guidelines. Applications considered any time, but only once each year
WHO TO APPLY TO Mrs M M Tittle, Benham Charitable Settlement, Hurstbourne, Portnall Drive, Virginia Water, Surrey GU25 4NR
CC NO 239371   **ESTABLISHED** 1964

■ Hervey Benham Charitable Trust

WHAT IS FUNDED Artistic (particularly musical) activities which benefit the people of Colchester and district and which would benefit from pump-priming by the Trust and/or a contribution which enables self-help to function more effectively; individuals with potential artistic (especially musical) talent who are held back by physical, environmental or financial disability; preservation of the heritage from the past of Colchester and district and of the maritime traditions of the Essex/Suffolk coast; local history and conservation affecting the heritage and environment of the area
WHAT IS NOT FUNDED Anything not related to area Where Funding Can Be Given
WHO CAN BENEFIT Individuals or self-help organisations benefiting: children; young adults; musicians; seafarers and fishermen; students; writers and poets; those disadvantaged by poverty; and disabled people
WHERE FUNDING CAN BE GIVEN Colchester and north east Essex
TYPE OF GRANT Buildings, capital, feasibility studies, interest free loans, one-off, project, recurring costs and start-up costs. Funding is available for up to three years
RANGE OF GRANTS Grants range from £100–£5,000
SAMPLE GRANTS £5,000 to Essex Wildlife Trust for the Blue House Farm Appeal; £3,000 to Colchester Institute for bassoon scholarship, over three years; £2,000 to Colne Smack Preservation Society for the restoration of Lowe Smack Dock; £1,500 to an individual towards fees (year 3) at Elmhurst Ballet School; £1,500 to an individual towards fees (year 2) at London Studio Centre; £1,500 to Scouts Offshore for a new skipper training scheme, over 3 years; £1,247 to Victoria County History of Essex for a reprint of Tudor and Stewart Colchester; £750 to an individual to assist bassoon purchase; £500 to an individual for the Guildhall School of Music (Saturday Junior School); £500 to an individual for postgraduate violin performance, Trinity College of Music
FINANCES *Year* 1998 *Income* £43,076
Grants £24,097
TRUSTEES G W Bone, M R Carr, M Ellis, K E Mirams, A B Phillips
PUBLICATIONS Brochure
NOTES Applications from outside area Where Funding Can Be Given not considered
HOW TO APPLY In writing to the address under Who To Apply To by the normal quarterly dates
WHO TO APPLY TO J Woodman, Hervey Benham Charitable Trust, The Chase House, The Chase, Irvine Road, Colchester, Essex CO3 3TP
Tel 01206 561086 *Fax* 01206 561086
E-mail jwoodman@aspects.net
CC NO 277578   **ESTABLISHED** 1978

■ Maurice and Jacqueline Bennett Charitable Trust

This trust did not respond to CAF's request to amend its entry and, by 30 June 1998, CAF's researchers did not find financial records for later than 1995 on its file at the Charity Commission. Trusts are legally required to submit annual accounts to the Charity Commission under section 42 of the Charities Act 1993

WHAT IS FUNDED General charitable purposes

WHO CAN BENEFIT There are no restrictions on the age; professional and economic group; family situation; religion and culture; and social circumstances of; or disease or medical condition suffered by, the beneficiaries

WHERE FUNDING CAN BE GIVEN UK

TRUSTEES Maurice Bennett, Michael Bennett, Ms J Bennett

WHO TO APPLY TO M Bennett, Trustee, Maurice and Jacqueline Bennett Charitable Trust, 32–38 Scrutton Street, London EC22 4SS

CC NO 1047566　　　　　**ESTABLISHED** 1995

■ Michael and Lesley Bennett Charitable Trust

This trust did not respond to CAF's request to amend its entry and, by 30 June 1998, CAF's researchers did not find financial records for later than 1995 on its file at the Charity Commission. Trusts are legally required to submit annual accounts to the Charity Commission under section 42 of the Charities Act 1993

WHAT IS FUNDED General charitable purposes

WHO CAN BENEFIT There are no restrictions on the age; professional and economic group; family situation; religion and culture; and social circumstances of; or disease or medical condition suffered by, the beneficiaries

WHERE FUNDING CAN BE GIVEN UK

TRUSTEES Michael Bennett, Ms L Bennett, Maurice Bennett

WHO TO APPLY TO M Bennett, Trustee, Michael and Lesley Bennett Charitable Trust, 69–77 Paul Street, London EC2A 4PN

CC NO 1047611　　　　　**ESTABLISHED** 1995

■ Rowan Bentall Charity Trust

WHAT IS FUNDED To support charities in Southern England, assisting hospitals, churches, youth organisations, care of the elderly, handicapped, the armed forces, education and preservation of the environment.

WHAT IS NOT FUNDED No grants to individuals

WHO CAN BENEFIT Children; young adults; older people; those in the armed forces; students and disabled people

WHERE FUNDING CAN BE GIVEN Southern England

RANGE OF GRANTS £25–£1,500, typical grant £100

FINANCES *Year* 1997 *Income* £19,248
　　　　　Grants £16,172

TRUSTEES L Edward Bentall, FCA, Alastair R Bentall, Kate C Bentall

NOTES Trustees meet twice a year, in July and December

WHO TO APPLY TO L Edward Bentall, FCA, Rowan Bentall Charity Trust, Anstee House, Wood Street, Kingston upon Thames, Surrey KT1 1TS

CC NO 273818　　　　　**ESTABLISHED** 1960

■ The Berean Trust

WHAT IS FUNDED Christian based projects

WHO CAN BENEFIT Registered Christian charities and institutions

WHERE FUNDING CAN BE GIVEN Surrey

RANGE OF GRANTS £60–£12,000

SAMPLE GRANTS £12,000 to St Peter's Church, Newdigate; £3,600 to Bishop of Guildford's Foundation; £1,000 to Oasis Trust; £500 to Prison Fellowship; £500 to Open Doors

FINANCES *Year* 1997 *Income* £19,802
　　　　　Grants £17,860

TRUSTEES D A Newbery, Ms C J Newbery

NOTES **Trust funds are fully committed for the next two years.** No applications will be considered during this period

WHO TO APPLY TO D A Newbery, The Berean Trust, The Estate Office, Parkgate Road, Newdigate, Surrey RH5 5AH *Tel* 01306 631730

CC NO 291782　　　　　**ESTABLISHED** 1985

■ Bergqvist Charitable Trust

WHAT IS FUNDED To benefit medical research, children and young people, the arts, the preservation of historic buildings and environmental concerns

WHO CAN BENEFIT Organisations benefiting those involved in the arts, medical professionals and research workers

WHERE FUNDING CAN BE GIVEN UK

TYPE OF GRANT One-off and recurrent grants

FINANCES *Year* 1997 *Income* £50,000
　　　　　Grants £24,100

TRUSTEES Mrs P A Bergqvist, Miss J A M Bergqvist

WHO TO APPLY TO Mrs Patricia Bergqvist, Bergqvist Charitable Trust, Moat Farm, Ford, Aylesbury, Buckinghamshire HP17 8XD

CC NO 1015707　　　　　**ESTABLISHED** 1992

■ Berkshire Community Trust

WHAT IS FUNDED Local groups in the following categories: community leadership, ethnic minority access, community care, counselling services, disability, homelessness, rural deprivation, voluntary sector support training, community safety and victim support, addiction and rehabilitation of offenders

WHAT IS NOT FUNDED Normally unable to support major building appeals, individuals, animal welfare, adverts in publications, fundraising costs, or the arts and sport unless in the context of tackling wider social need

WHO CAN BENEFIT Voluntary organisations only, locally managed and providing services within Berkshire. Trustees particularly wish to encourage smaller groups. Organisations benefiting: children; young adults; older people; volunteers; those in care, fostered and adopted; parents and children; one parent families; widows and widowers; at risk groups; carers; disabled people; those disadvantaged by poverty; ex-offenders and those at risk of offending; gays and lesbians; immigrants; refugees; those living in rural areas; socially isolated people; travellers and those living in urban areas; victims of abuse, crime and domestic violence. There are no restrictions on the disease or medical condition suffered by the beneficiaries

WHERE FUNDING CAN BE GIVEN Berkshire only

TYPE OF GRANT Strategic: recurring core or project costs for activities identified as of strategic importance to the local community. Quick

Response and Project Support: specifically costed items of expenditure on a non-recurring basis. Buildings, capital and start-up costs. Funding for up to five years will be considered

RANGE OF GRANTS Three sizes of grants: Quick reponse – up to £300; Project Support – up to £2,000; Strategic – up to £15,000 annually for up to five years. One new Strategic Grant is selected each year

SAMPLE GRANTS £44,850 to Slough Foyer over three years to support worker for young people in Foyer; £2,000 to Braywick Health Scheme for outside lighting for horticultural project for people with range of special needs; £2,000 to Keep Mobile, Wokingham to upgrade seats and seatbelts in community transport vehicle; £2,000 to Relate, Reading for counsellor training; £1,750 to Maidenhead CAB towards pilot Help Desk in Magistrates' Court; £1,300 to Burghfield Friday Club for start-up costs for drop-in club for people with mental health problems; £1,000 to Reading Voluntary Action for new integrated computer software; £1,000 to Age Concern, Slough for start-up costs for lunch-club; £1,000 to Newbury Motor Project for subsidy for special needs places

FINANCES *Year* 1997–98 *Income* £461,687 *Grants* £129,436

TRUSTEES R Benyon, J Briggs, D Brooks, S Burnell, I Campbell, A Clack, A Craven, P Deigman, C Gabriel, J Heath, R Mandeville, M Newmarch, B Oatey, R Palmer, J Wates, A Md Waess, C Williams, S Southgate, Lady J G Finnie, M Jessop

PUBLICATIONS Newsletters, Corporate Brochure, Grants Policy and Guidelines, Community Needs Survey

NOTES Preliminary telephone call to Grants Administrator is encouraged, to eliminate ineligible applications and to trigger support where required. The Trust also provides the grant adminisration service for Give a Child a Chance, a grants programme for children in the radio braodcasting area of 2-TEN FM and Capital Gold 1435 AM

HOW TO APPLY On application form only. Quick response grants – year round application. Project support – deadlines 1 March and 1 October. Strategic – via written 'expression of interest'

WHO TO APPLY TO Grants Administrator, Berkshire Community Trust, Arlington Business Park, Theale, Reading RG7 4SA *Tel* 0118-930 3021 *Fax* 0118-930 4933 *E-mail* bct@patrol.i-way.co.uk *Web Site* http://www.yell.co.uk/sites/communitytrust

CC NO 294220   **ESTABLISHED** 1985

■ The Berkshire Nurses and Relief in Sickness Trust

WHAT IS FUNDED Health and welfare. To aid people in need as a result of sickness or disability; nurses and midwives previously employed as district nurses. The Trust will consider: charity or voluntary umbrella bodies; respite care and care for carers; day centres; and holidays and outings

WHAT IS NOT FUNDED On-going payments, statutory responsibilities, scholarships, training costs

WHO CAN BENEFIT People in need through illness or disability, either mental or physical. Beneficiaries include: children; young adults; older people; medical professionals, nurses and doctors; those in care, fostered or adopted; parents and children; one parent families; widows and widowers; at risk groups; carers; disabled people; those disadvantaged by poverty; disaster victims; victims of abuse; and victims of domestic

violence. There are no restrictions on the disease or medical condition suffered by the beneficiaries

WHERE FUNDING CAN BE GIVEN Berkshire and those parts of Oxfordshire which, prior to 1974, were in Berkshire

TYPE OF GRANT One-off, buildings, capital, core costs, running costs and start-up costs

RANGE OF GRANTS £25–£2,500

FINANCES *Year* 1997–98 *Income* £56,600 *Grants* £48,902

NOTES Information sheet available from the address under Who To Apply To

HOW TO APPLY On a form available from the address under Who To Apply To. Applications from individuals must be made by a member of the statutory authorities. Applications are not accepted from members of the public directly

WHO TO APPLY TO R Pottinger, Secretary, Berkshire Nurses and Relief in Sickness Trust, 26 Montrose Walk, Fords Farm, Calcot, Reading, Berkshire RG31 7YH *Tel* 0118-942 4556

CC NO 205274   **ESTABLISHED** 1983

■ The Bernadette Charitable Trust

WHAT IS FUNDED General charitable purposes. Only causes known to Trustees are considered

WHO CAN BENEFIT Institutions. There are no restrictions on the age; professional and economic group; family situation; religion and culture; and social circumstances of; or disease or medical condition suffered by, the beneficiaries

WHERE FUNDING CAN BE GIVEN UK

FINANCES *Year* 1995 *Income* £33,751

TRUSTEES J O'Hea, O'Hea Trustees Ltd

HOW TO APPLY This Trust states that it does not respond to unsolicited applications

WHO TO APPLY TO Jerome O'Hea, The Bernadette Charitable Trust, Church Farm, Oving Road, Aldingbourne, Chichester, West Sussex PO20 6UB

CC NO 1026111   **ESTABLISHED** 1993

■ Patrick Berthoud Charitable Trust

WHAT IS FUNDED (a) To provide funding for full time three year fellowships to persons in clinical neurological training in the UK who have obtained their membership and have the status of Specialist, Registrar or Clinical Lecturer for research in the field of neurological disease; (b) to assist existing peer-reviewed innovative research projects in the UK to meet, or help to meet, the cost of special equipment or defined medical research project support costs

WHO CAN BENEFIT (a) Individuals in clinical neurological training in the UK who have obtained their membership and have the status of Specialist, Registrar or Clinical Lecturer; (b) neurological research charities. (Applications from universities and NHS Trusts will not be accepted)

WHERE FUNDING CAN BE GIVEN UK

TYPE OF GRANT (a) Research fellowships, (b) one-off grants. Research is considered. Funding is available for up to one year. There will be one distribution of funds per year in December

RANGE OF GRANTS For (a) up to £50,000 per annum, and (b) £2,500–£10,000

Does the trust you have chosen match your needs? Haphazard applications waste postage and time

57

SAMPLE GRANTS £95,060 to support H Berthaud Fellows; £5,000 to Meningitis Research Foundation for molecular biology reagents; £5,000 to Motor Neurone Association for consumables; £5,000 to Multiple Sclerosis Society for laboratory consumables; £4,500 to Action Research for surgical supplies; £2,500 to International Spinal Research Trust for molecular biology reagents

FINANCES *Year* 1997–98 *Income* £160,000 *Grants* £117,060

TRUSTEES Trustees of the Charities Aid Foundation

PUBLICATIONS Information included in the CAF Grants Council Review

NOTES Priority will be given to applications from smaller charities working in less popular fields. Recurrent funding applications will not be accepted. At least two years should elapse from the receipt of a grant before a further application will be considered from a successful recipient charity. Support for salaries will not be considered except in exceptional circumstances

HOW TO APPLY (a) Applications should be made on a special application form available from CAF. Deadline for receipt of applications is 31 December. (b) Applications should be made on the standard application form available from CAF and supported by a copy of the successful application made to the organisation supporting the project, together with comments from referees and the applying charity's own statement of its medical aims

WHO TO APPLY TO Grants Administrator, Patrick Berthoud Charitable Trust, Charities Aid Foundation, Kings Hill, West Malling, Kent ME19 4TA *Tel* 01732 520031 *Fax* 01732 520001 *Web Site* http://www.charitynet.org

CC NO 268369   ESTABLISHED 1994

■ The Miss J K Bertram Memorial Trust

WHAT IS FUNDED Grants are given to organisations which carry out research into Parkinson's Disease or which care for sufferers. An endowment is made to a hospital

WHAT IS NOT FUNDED No grants to individuals

WHO CAN BENEFIT Organisations benefiting people with Parkinson's Disease

WHERE FUNDING CAN BE GIVEN Scotland with a preference for Lothian, particularly Edinburgh

TYPE OF GRANT Endowment, one-off grants

HOW TO APPLY Applications should be made on an application form which is available from the Secretary at the address below

WHO TO APPLY TO Mrs Joyce Hutchinson, Secretary, The Miss J K Bertram Memorial Trust, 1 Darnaway Street, Edinburgh EH3 6DW

SC NO SCO 18150

■ Besom Foundation

WHAT IS FUNDED General charitable purposes. The Foundation will only consider requests which are for small items of expenditure which encourage self-help at a grass roots level. The four main activities are projects, employee clusters, positive recycling and volunteering

WHAT IS NOT FUNDED No grants for salaries, training or running costs or towards relief work

WHO CAN BENEFIT Small charities, often involved in development and health, benefiting volunteers, employees and the sick. There are no restrictions

on the disease or medical condition suffered by the beneficiaries

WHERE FUNDING CAN BE GIVEN UK and overseas

TYPE OF GRANT Capital, projects and some recurring

RANGE OF GRANTS £500–£4,000

FINANCES *Year* 1996–97 *Income* £185,322 *Grants* £64,083

TRUSTEES J R B Odgers, Ms F J Ruttle, Ms E Plunkett

HOW TO APPLY To the address under Who To Apply To in writing, with as much relevant detail as possible

WHO TO APPLY TO Mrs H L Odgers, Besom Foundation, 42 Burlington Road, London W4 4BE

CC NO 297905   ESTABLISHED 1987

■ The Bestway Foundation

WHAT IS FUNDED Advancement of education, in cases of genuine hardship. Assistance by means of grants, endowments, scholarships and loans

WHAT IS NOT FUNDED No grants for trips/travel abroad

WHO CAN BENEFIT Individuals and institutions benefiting children, young adults, students and teachers and governesses

WHERE FUNDING CAN BE GIVEN UK and overseas

TYPE OF GRANT Range of grants

SAMPLE GRANTS £40,000 to Age Concern England; £16,000 to Duke of Edinburgh's Award; £15,000 to Bordesley Green Girls School; £12,500 to Francis Holland School for Graham Terrace Appeal; £10,000 to Business and Professional Women's Organisation; £10,000 to Society for the Welfare of Patients of Urology and Transplantation; £7,100 to School of Oriental and African Studies; £6,000 to National Grocers Benevolent Fund; £5,000 to Liverpool School of Tropical Medicine; £3,000 to All Pakistan Women's Association

FINANCES *Year* 1996 *Income* £468,940 *Grants* £163,476

TRUSTEES A K Bhatti, A K Chaudhary, M Y Sheikh, Z M Chaudrey, M A Pervez, Z U H Khan

HOW TO APPLY Written applications only. Brief letter. No application forms available. Sae required. Telephone calls are not welcome

WHO TO APPLY TO Ms D Taylor, The Bestway Foundation, Bestway Cash & Carry Ltd, Abbey Road, Park Royal, London NW10 7BW

CC NO 297178   ESTABLISHED 1987

■ Betard Bequest

WHAT IS FUNDED Holidays, specially adapted furniture, computers, medical aids

WHAT IS NOT FUNDED Grants are not made directly to individuals but through an appropriate charity or social worker

WHO CAN BENEFIT Registered charities only. Modest grants are made to eligible individuals through social worker or charity. Larger grants are made to welfare charities to distribute to eligible individuals. Those who can benefit include people of all ages who are disadvantaged by poverty and those suffering from arthritis and rheumatism

WHERE FUNDING CAN BE GIVEN UK

TYPE OF GRANT One-off

RANGE OF GRANTS Individuals: £100; welfare charity (for distribution): £4,500

SAMPLE GRANTS The following grants were to charities for distribution to eligible individuals:; £4,765 to Foundation for Communication for the Disabled; £3,400 to Disability Aid Fund; £3,000 to Invalids at Home; £2,458 to Ryder-Cheshire Volunteers; £2,500 to Lupus UK; £2,500 to Aidis Trust; £1,200 to Break; £1,200 to Help the Handicapped Holiday Fund; £1,000 to Arthritis Care Gateshead; £1,000 to Nightingale House

FINANCES *Year* 1997–98 *Income* £33,000 *Grants* £32,800

TRUSTEES The Trustees of Charities Aid Foundation

PUBLICATIONS Information included in the CAF Grants Council Annual Review

HOW TO APPLY Applications can be sent in at any time for quarterly consideration. Initial telephone calls by applicants are welcome. No application forms are necessary, but guidelines are issued. There are no deadlines for applications, and no sae is required

WHO TO APPLY TO Grants Administrator, Betard Bequest, Charities Aid Foundation, Kings Hill, West Malling, Kent ME19 4TA *Tel* 01732 520031 *Fax* 01732 520001 *Web Site* http://www.charitynet.org

CC NO 268369   **ESTABLISHED** 1985

■ The Bethesda Charitable Trust Fund

WHAT IS FUNDED Grants are made to Christian charities and churches for Christian education and outreach, missionaries and evangelicals. Hospices, hospice at home and the Council for Voluntary Service are also considered

WHAT IS NOT FUNDED No grants for expeditions, scholarships, housing, animal charities or personal projects

WHO CAN BENEFIT Charities which have a Christian spiritual objective together with their other aims

WHERE FUNDING CAN BE GIVEN UK and overseas

TYPE OF GRANT One-off gifts for capital and buildings

RANGE OF GRANTS Normal maximum £1,000

SAMPLE GRANTS £18,450 to Deeside Christian Fellowship Church for a building project; £6,000 to Doulos Trust; £1,000 to SIM United Kingdom

FINANCES *Year* 1997–98 *Income* £38,961 *Grants* £25,450

TRUSTEES Mrs A R P Wilson, B Wilson, J Wilson

NOTES Grants are usually made to charities where at least one of the trustees has been able to to make personal visits to assess need

HOW TO APPLY Applications should be made in writing to the address under Who To Apply To. Please send an sae

WHO TO APPLY TO Jim Wilson, The Bethesda Charitable Trust Fund, 6 Albert Place, Aberdeen AB2 4RG *Tel* 01224 626090

SC NO SCO 07968

■ Bethesda Community Charitable Trust

WHAT IS FUNDED The advancement of the Christian religion and Christian faith; the relief of poverty, suffering and distress in the community; the advancement of education; and other general charitable purposes

WHO CAN BENEFIT Organisations benefitting children; young adults; students; Christians; at risk groups; those disadvantaged by poverty; and socially isolated people. There is no restriction on the disease or medical condition suffered by the beneficiaries

WHERE FUNDING CAN BE GIVEN UK

FINANCES *Year* 1997 *Income* £59,260

WHO TO APPLY TO R W Jarritt, Bethesda Community Charitable Trust, 41 Highfield Road, Ipswich, Suffolk IP1 6DD

CC NO 1042816   **ESTABLISHED** 1994

■ Mr Thomas Betton's Charity (Educational)

WHAT IS FUNDED Grants are given for the reconstruction of schools having charitable status giving religious instruction in accordance with the principles of the Church of England or Church in Wales

WHAT IS NOT FUNDED No grants to individuals

WHO CAN BENEFIT (a) Diocesan Education Committees for their aided schools. (b) Occasionally independent schools not under the control of Diocesan Education Committees. Organisations benefiting children and young adults, the Church of England and Church in Wales

WHERE FUNDING CAN BE GIVEN (a) Greater London, (b) England and Wales

TYPE OF GRANT One-off and capital grants will be considered

RANGE OF GRANTS £1,000–£5,000

FINANCES *Year* 1997 *Income* £75,145 *Grants* £64,643

TRUSTEES Worshipful Company of Ironmongers

HOW TO APPLY Applications to arrive by 1 February. Sae required

WHO TO APPLY TO The Clerk of the Worshipful Company of Ironmongers, Mr Thomas Betton's Charity (Educational), Ironmongers' Hall, Barbican, London EC2Y 8AA *Tel* 0171-606 2725

CC NO 313632   **ESTABLISHED** 1723

■ Thomas Betton's Charity for Pensions and Relief in Need

WHAT IS FUNDED Relief in need

WHO CAN BENEFIT There are a few restrictions on the social circumstances of the beneficiaries

WHERE FUNDING CAN BE GIVEN UK

TYPE OF GRANT One-off

RANGE OF GRANTS £500–£2,000

FINANCES *Year* 1996–97 *Income* £40,024 *Grants* £31,661

TRUSTEES Ironmongers' Company

HOW TO APPLY To the address under Who To Apply To in writing

WHO TO APPLY TO The Clerk, Thomas Betton's Charity, Ironmonger's Company, Ironmongers Hall, Barbican, London EC2Y 8AA *Tel* 0171-606 2725

CC NO 280143   **ESTABLISHED** 1980

■ Miss Beveridge's Trust

WHAT IS FUNDED Grants are given to organisations which work with children

WHAT IS NOT FUNDED No grants to individuals. Grants are not given to private schools or colleges, non-registered charities, nor to projects that are eligible for statutory funding

WHO CAN BENEFIT Organisations benefiting children

WHERE FUNDING CAN BE GIVEN Lothian

TYPE OF GRANT One-off grants

FINANCES *Year* 1996 *Grants* £47,996

HOW TO APPLY Applications should be made on the application form which is available from the address below. Grants are awarded at the

Trustees' quarterly meetings in March, June, October and December

WHO TO APPLY TO The Trust Fund Administrator, Miss Beveridge's Trust, Edinburgh Voluntary Organisations Trusts, 11 Colme Street, Edinburgh EH3 6AG

SC NO SCO 17196

■ Antrobus Bewlay Charitable Trust

WHAT IS FUNDED General charitable purposes as determined by the Trustees

WHO CAN BENEFIT There are no restrictions on the age; professional and economic group; family situation; religion and culture; and social circumstances of; or disease or medical condition suffered by, the beneficiaries

WHERE FUNDING CAN BE GIVEN UK and overseas

HOW TO APPLY **This Trust states that it does not respond to unsolicited applications**

WHO TO APPLY TO Nicholas Quartly Grazebrook, Solicitor, Antrobus Bewlay Charitable Trust, Shakespeares, 10 Bennetts Hill, Birmingham B2 5RS *Tel* 0121-632 4199

CC NO 1060111   **ESTABLISHED** 1997

■ Bexley Deaf Group

WHAT IS FUNDED (a) To relieve deaf persons resident in the London Borough of Bexley by pressing for improvements in all facilities (ie medical, environmental, education and recreational) for the deaf and hard of hearing, to enable them to enjoy the same quality of life as that enjoyed by those with normal hearing. (b) To manage Bexley Deaf Centre. (c) To provide facilities for voluntary bodies in the said area

WHO CAN BENEFIT To benefit people who are deaf or hard of hearing

WHERE FUNDING CAN BE GIVEN The London Borough of Bexley

FINANCES *Year* 1997 *Income* £57,746

WHO TO APPLY TO Mrs B Constable, Bexley Deaf Group, Bexley Deaf Centre, 1A Vicarage Road, Bexley DA5 2AL

CC NO 1039183   **ESTABLISHED** 1994

■ The Mason Bibby 1981 Trust

WHAT IS FUNDED Main area of interest is the elderly but applications are considered from other groups

WHAT IS NOT FUNDED Apart from employees and ex-employees of J Bibby & Sons PLC, applications are considered from registered charities only

WHO CAN BENEFIT Priority to the elderly and employees and ex-employees of J Bibby and Sons Plc

WHERE FUNDING CAN BE GIVEN UK

RANGE OF GRANTS £250–£9,156

SAMPLE GRANTS £9,156 to Bibby employees and ex-employees, etc; £5,000 to Age Concern, Liverpool; £5,000 to Liverpool Personal Service Society; £5,000 to Age Concern, Wirral for the New Devonshire Centre Project; £2,500 to Pain Relief Foundation; £2,500 to Liverpool Council of Social Services; £2,500 to Shropshire and Mid-Wales Hospice for a special appeal; £2,000 to The Salvation Army, North West; £2,000 to Cancer Relief for the Rutland Macmillan Fund; £2,000 to Royal School for the Blind, Liverpool

FINANCES *Year* 1997 *Income* £74,154
Grants £77,206

TRUSTEES B A Jones, Dr H M Bibby, K A Allan, J B Bibby, C L Bibby, J P Wood, Mrs D M Fairclough, S W Bowman, J McPheat

PUBLICATIONS Annual Report

HOW TO APPLY At any time. Trustees meet half yearly. Applications are only acknowledged if a grant is agreed

WHO TO APPLY TO Mrs D M Fairclough, The Mason Bibby 1981 Trust, c/o Rathbone Bros & Co Ltd, Port of Liverpool Building, Pierhead, Liverpool L3 1NW

CC NO 283231   **ESTABLISHED** 1981

■ Edward Bibby Fund

WHAT IS FUNDED General charitable purposes. Preference to charities of which the Trust has special interest, knowledge or association and located on Merseyside

WHAT IS NOT FUNDED No grants to individuals

WHO CAN BENEFIT There are no restrictions on the age; professional and economic group; family situation; religion and culture; and social circumstances of; or disease or medical condition suffered by, the beneficiaries

WHERE FUNDING CAN BE GIVEN Merseyside

FINANCES *Year* 1997 *Income* £16,796
Grants £17,000

TRUSTEES Liverpool Council of Social Service (Inc), C L Bibby

WHO TO APPLY TO The Secretary, Edward Bibby Fund, Liverpool Council of Social Service (Inc), 14 Castle Street, Liverpool, Merseyside L2 ONJ

CC NO 200593   **ESTABLISHED** 1960

■ BibleLands

WHAT IS FUNDED To help Christian Mission in the lands of the Bible – help the sick, blind, poor and homeless. The Trust will consider funding: Christian outreach and education; missionaries and evangelists; religious umbrella bodies; health care; health facilities and buildings; ophthalmology; schools and colleges; professional specialist training; special needs education; speech therapy; vocational training; and community services

WHAT IS NOT FUNDED Confined to Christian led-work in the lands of the Bible (Middle East). No grants to individuals

WHO CAN BENEFIT Organisations benefiting: people of all ages; those in care, fostered and adopted; Baptist, Christians, Church of England, Methodists and Roman Catholics; disabled people; those disadvantaged by poverty; disaster victims and refugees. Those suffering from cerebral palsy; hearing loss; and sight loss. All beneficiaries must be in the Lands of the Bible

WHERE FUNDING CAN BE GIVEN Lands of the Bible, ie Middle East mainly

TYPE OF GRANT Capital, recurring, buildings, core costs, one-off, running costs and start-up costs. Funding is for up to or more than three years

FINANCES *Year* 1996 *Income* £2,296,063
Grants £2,392,977

TRUSTEES Rev David S T Izzett (President), Rev Douglas A Dennis (Chairman), Dr Cyril J Young (Vice-Chairman), K S Mills (Treasurer), and 10 other Trustees

PUBLICATIONS *The Star in the East*

HOW TO APPLY Apply in writing for an application form, giving brief outline

WHO TO APPLY TO A P Jong, BibleLands, PO Box 50, High Wycombe, Buckinghamshire HP15 7QU *Tel* 01494 521351 *Fax* 01494 462171
CC NO 226093   ESTABLISHED 1854

■ The Ken Biggs Charitable Trust

WHAT IS FUNDED General charitable purposes at the discretion of the Trustees
WHO CAN BENEFIT There are no restrictions on the age; professional and economic group; family situation; religion and culture; and social circumstances of; or disease or medical condition suffered by, the beneficiaries
WHERE FUNDING CAN BE GIVEN UK
TYPE OF GRANT At the discretion of the Trustees
RANGE OF GRANT £250–£560
SAMPLE GRANTS £560 to Camerton Parochial Church Council; £250 to Dorothy House Foundation
FINANCES *Year* 1995 *Income* £52,944 *Grants* £810
TRUSTEES K S Biggs, Mrs A M Wyatt, N J Biggs
WHO TO APPLY TO K S Biggs, The Ken Biggs Charitable Trust, Camerton Court, Camerton, Bath BA3 1PU
CC NO 1037916   ESTABLISHED 1991

■ Billingsgate Christian Mission Charitable Trust

WHAT IS FUNDED To relieve poverty, distress and sickness among persons engaged in the Fish and Fishing Industries in the UK. To advance religious and social work in accordance with the Christian Faith among persons engaged in the Fish and Fishing Industries in the UK. To advance medical science, particularly by way of grants for scholarships
WHAT IS NOT FUNDED No grants to individuals
WHO CAN BENEFIT Registered charities benefiting persons engaged in the Fish and Fishing Industries in the UK who may be sick, in distress or those disadvantaged by poverty. There is no restriction on the disease or medical condition suffered by the beneficiaries. Christians, research workers and medical professionals may also be considered
WHERE FUNDING CAN BE GIVEN UK
TYPE OF GRANT One-off
FINANCES *Year* 1997 *Income* £52,715 *Grants* £40,300
TRUSTEES The Court of the Fishmongers' Company
HOW TO APPLY To the address under Who To Apply To. Trustees meet three times a year. Latest Annual Accounts required with application
WHO TO APPLY TO K S Waters, Clerk, Billingsgate Christian Mission Charitable Trust, Fishmongers' Company, Fishmongers' Hall, London Bridge, London EC4R 9EL *Tel* 0171-626 3531 *Fax* 0171-929 1389
CC NO 1013851   ESTABLISHED 1992

■ The Billmeir Charitable Trust

WHAT IS FUNDED General charitable purposes with a preference for the Elstead and Farnham areas of Surrey
WHO CAN BENEFIT There are no restrictions on the age; professional and economic group; family situation; religion and culture; and social circumstances of; or disease or medical condition suffered by, the beneficiaries
WHERE FUNDING CAN BE GIVEN Surrey

SAMPLE GRANTS £10,000 to Edgeborough Appeal; £10,000 to United Reform Church, Elstead; £9,000 to Elstead Community Association; £6,000 to Reed School, Cobham; £6,000 to the Meath Home; £5,000 to British Homes for Incurables; £5,000 to Lord Mayor Treloar School; £5,000 to RNLI; £500 to the Hospital for Neuro-Disability; £5,000 to Tilford Institute Centenary Fund
FINANCES *Year* 1997 *Income* £151,047 *Grants* £119,000
TRUSTEES B C Whitaker, F C E Telfer, M R MacFadyen
HOW TO APPLY The Trustees meet annually to consider applications although the income is virtually fully committed
WHO TO APPLY TO Timothy T Cripps, Secretary to the Trustees, The Billmeir Charitable Trust, Moore Stephens, 1 Snow Hill, London EC1A 2EN
CC NO 208561   ESTABLISHED 1956

■ The Bingham Trust

WHAT IS FUNDED Identifiable community needs in the areas of: accommodation and housing; building services; information and computer technology; infrastructure and development; charity or voluntary umbrella bodies; religion; arts, culture and recreation; health; conservation and environment; education and training; community facilities and services; and other charitable purposes
WHAT IS NOT FUNDED Generally, limited to the town of Buxton and district
WHO CAN BENEFIT Primarily charitable organisations benefiting people of all ages; volunteers; those in care, fostered and adopted; parents and children; one parent families; widows and widowers; at risk groups; carers; disabled people; those disadvantaged by poverty; ex-offenders and those at risk of offending; those living in rural areas; socially isolated people; and victims of abuse, crime and domestic violence. There is no restriction on the disease or medical condition suffered by the beneficiaries. Occasionally individuals
WHERE FUNDING CAN BE GIVEN Buxton, Derbyshire
TYPE OF GRANT One-off, capital, buildings, project, running costs, salaries and start-up costs. Funding is for up to three years
RANGE OF GRANTS £50–£15,000
FINANCES *Year* 1997 *Income* £63,729 *Grants* £62,960
TRUSTEES J I Fraser, R A Horne, Mrs J H Cawton, Rev P J Meek, Dr R G B Willis
HOW TO APPLY Apply in writing on not more than two sides of A4 paper stating total cost of the project and sources of other funding. Apply before the end of June, September, December and February each year
WHO TO APPLY TO The Bingham Trust, Bennett Brooke-Taylor & Wright, 4 The Quadrant, Buxton, Derbyshire SK17 6AW
CC NO 287636   ESTABLISHED 1977

■ Binsted Holy Cross Church Trust

WHAT IS FUNDED Advancement of the Christian religion, in particular, the maintenance and repair of, and provision for, the fabric of the Holy Cross Church, Binsted. Other general charitable purposes for the benefit of the Holy cross Church or the Parish of Binsted
WHO CAN BENEFIT Christians and others living in the Parish of Binsted

WHERE FUNDING CAN BE GIVEN In practice, the Parish of Binsted
FINANCES *Year* 1998 *Income* £17,723
WHO TO APPLY TO Col J A De Benham-Crosswell, Binsted Holy Cross Church Trust, Cheriton Mill, Alresford, Hampshire SO24 0NG
CC NO 1046007   ESTABLISHED 1995

■ Birdlife International

WHAT IS FUNDED To conserve all bird species on earth and their habitats, and through this work for the world's biological diversity and the sustainability of human use of natural resources
WHAT IS NOT FUNDED 50 per cent of any funds granted must be used for the involvement of national counterparts. No longer consider applications from individuals applying for funding to join an expedition, ie only consider the whole expedition team
WHO CAN BENEFIT Teams should be of undergraduates with at least one graduate in life sciences
WHERE FUNDING CAN BE GIVEN Expeditions to and from anywhere in the world
TYPE OF GRANT Four main grants of £3,000 are awarded, one each, to projects with the themes of globally threatened species; oceanic islands and marine habitats; tropical forests; wetlands, grasslands, savannahs and deserts. Eight runners-up are each awarded £1,500. To encourage on-going conservation work a single award of £10,000 is given to the best follow-up proposal from a previous winning project
RANGE OF GRANTS £1,500–£10,000
FINANCES *Year* 1996 *Income* £3,202,229 *Grants* £2,902,316
TRUSTEES Directors of Birdlife International: Dr D Baker-Gabb, Dr G A Bertrand, Dr E Bucher, S D Eccles, Dr J Fjeldsa, S A Hussain, Dr G H Fenwick, R Gauto, A P Leventis, P Iankov, Dr B F Master, Dr Y Ntiamoa-Baidu, Mrs L Sharaf, J Sultana, B Young
PUBLICATIONS *World Birdwatch*, *The Birdlife Conservation Series*, *Bird Conservation International*, *Birdlife in Europe*, *Birdlife in the Americas*
HOW TO APPLY Awards are granted annually. Applications should be received by 31 December. Contact the Birdlife Expeditions Officer for guidelines for applicants and application forms
WHO TO APPLY TO Michael Rands, Director and Chief Executive, Birdlife International, Wellbrook Court, Girton Road, Cambridge CB3 0NA *Web Site* http://www.bp.co/conservation
CC NO 1042125   ESTABLISHED 1994

■ Birmingham Bodenham Trust

WHAT IS FUNDED Grants are made for the benefit of the education of people under the age of 19
WHO CAN BENEFIT Children and young adults under the age of 19
WHERE FUNDING CAN BE GIVEN Birmingham
FINANCES *Year* 1995 *Income* £17,002 *Grants* £9,575
HOW TO APPLY To the address under Who To Apply To in writing
WHO TO APPLY TO Miss K Heath, Birmingham Bodenham Trust, Education Finance, 38–50 Orphanage Road, Erdington, Birmingham B24 9HN *Tel* 0121-303 2525
CC NO 528902   ESTABLISHED 1989

■ Birmingham District Nursing Charitable Trust

WHAT IS FUNDED To benefit sick people, aid to medical institutions and hospital amenities
WHAT IS NOT FUNDED No grants made to individuals
WHO CAN BENEFIT Local organisations benefiting medical professionals. There is no restriction on the disease or medical condition suffered by the beneficiaries. Grants may be made to local branches of national organisations
WHERE FUNDING CAN BE GIVEN In or near city of Birmingham
FINANCES *Year* 1996 *Grants* £36,500
TRUSTEES Prof J I Brooking, C L Chatwin, G R De'Ath, Miss B Holmes, Prof W A Littler, Dr J R Mann, A D Martineau, H W Tuckey
HOW TO APPLY Applicants must provide a copy of the latest Annual Accounts if grants are to be made
WHO TO APPLY TO Gay de Ath, c/o Messrs Shakespeares, Solicitors, 10 Bennetts Hill, Birmingham, West Midlands B2 5RS
CC NO 215652   ESTABLISHED 1960

■ The Birmingham Foundation

WHAT IS FUNDED The relief of poverty and sickness; the protection and preservation of good health, both mental and physical; and the advancement of education. Generation of lasting and creative alliances between those who, in their private or commercial lives, influence the use of financial and human resources and those who are, at present, excluded from most of the benefits of life in Birmingham
WHO CAN BENEFIT Organisations benefiting children, young adults, students, teachers and governesses. Support is given to those disadvantaged by poverty. There is no restriction on the disease or medical condition suffered by the beneficiaries
WHERE FUNDING CAN BE GIVEN Birmingham and surrounding area
FINANCES *Year* 1996 *Income* £44,502
TRUSTEES R Taylor, Lord Lieutenant of the County of the West Midlands (President), P Cheesewright, Mrs S Humphreys, Sir P Lawrence, P Morley, J M Munn, P J Richardson, C J Timbrell, Hon Ald C Wilkinson, Mrs A P Worley
NOTES No grants were made in 1996
HOW TO APPLY To the address under Who To Apply To in writing
WHO TO APPLY TO Ms Debbie Byrne, Chief Executive, The Birmingham Foundation, 16 Westbourne Road, Edgbaston, Birmingham B15 3TR *Tel* 0121-456 3293 *Fax* 0121-456 3286 *E-mail* birmingham.foundation@pertemps.co.uk
CC NO 1048160   ESTABLISHED 1995

■ Birmingham Hospital Saturday Fund Medical Charity and Welfare Trust

WHAT IS FUNDED To maintain an efficient convalescence service, provide comforts and amenities for patients or staff in hospital and medical charities, assist medical research, education and science, and support charitable organisations concerned with the sick or disadvantaged. The Trust will consider funding: health; speech therapy; scholarships; building services; information technology and computers; publishing and printing; and health professional bodies

WHAT IS NOT FUNDED (a) Administration expenditure including salaries; (b) bank loans/deficits/mortgages; (c) items or services which would normally be publicly funded; (d) vehicle operating costs; (e) motor vehicles for infrequent use and where subsidised share schemes are available to charitable organisations; (f) part contributions to large appeals; or (g) grants to individuals

WHO CAN BENEFIT Registered medical charities, NHS hospitals, medical research organisations benefiting children; young adults; older people; medical professionals, and nurses and doctors; at risk groups; and disabled people. There are few restrictions on the disease or medical condition suffered by the beneficiaries

WHERE FUNDING CAN BE GIVEN Birmingham and UK

TYPE OF GRANT One-off grants, capital, project and research, all funded for up to one year

RANGE OF GRANTS Up to £5,000

SAMPLE GRANTS £13,470 to St Mary's Hospice to refurbish bedroom for palliative care; £5,100 to West Midlands NHS Executive for nurse travel scholarships and book prizes; £5,000 to Edgwood Court Day Centre to replace furniture for the elderly; £4,007 to Birmingham Royal Institute for the Blind for low vision equipment/training aids; £4,000 to Nursing Times, London for nurse travel scholarships; £3,600 to Birmingham Medical Institute for Gamgee lecture and books; £3,400 to South and West NHS Executive, Bristol for nurse travel scholarship and book prizes; £3,000 to Birmingham Oncology Centre for medically prescribed wigs; £2,500 to Birmingham Retirement Council for refurbishing premises; £2,500 to City Hospital NHS Trust for operating theatre artwork

FINANCES *Year* 1997 *Income* £1,294,000 *Grants* £95,790

TRUSTEES Sir David Perris, Dr P Kanas, S G Hall

HOW TO APPLY On a form available from the address under Who To Apply To

WHO TO APPLY TO P J Peers, Secretary, Birmingham Hospital Saturday Fund Medical Charity and Welfare Trust, Gamgee House, 2 Darnley Road, Birmingham B16 8TE *Tel* 0121-454 3601

CC NO 502428   **ESTABLISHED** 1972

■ The Birnie Trust

WHAT IS FUNDED To award grants to Scottish charities and some international projects

WHAT IS NOT FUNDED No grants to individuals

WHO CAN BENEFIT There are no restrictions on the age; professional and economic group; family situation; religion and culture; and social circumstances of; or disease or medical condition suffered by, the beneficiaries

WHERE FUNDING CAN BE GIVEN UK and overseas, with a preference for Scotland

TRUSTEES D A Connell, Mrs E A G Gordon, Lt Col E F Gordon, Dr L J King

PUBLICATIONS Accounts are available from the Trust

HOW TO APPLY Applications should be made in writing to the address below

WHO TO APPLY TO The Correspondent, The Birnie Trust, Messrs Dundas & Wilson, Saltire Court, 20 Castle Terrace, Edinburgh EH1 2EN

SC NO SCO 05509   **ESTABLISHED** 1986

■ The Bisgood Trust

WHAT IS FUNDED General charitable purposes. Main grants have been and will be concentrated on following categories: (a) operating under Roman Catholic auspices; (b) operating in the County of

Dorset; (c) national (not local) charities concerned with the elderly

WHAT IS NOT FUNDED No grants to individuals or to organisations other than registered charities. No grants to local projects outside Dorset unless under Roman Catholic auspices

WHO CAN BENEFIT Registered charities benefiting Roman Catholics and the elderly. Otherwise, there are no restrictions on the age; professional and economic group; family situation; religion and culture; and social circumstances of; or disease or medical condition suffered by, the beneficiaries

WHERE FUNDING CAN BE GIVEN UK and overseas

RANGE OF GRANTS £20–£2,500

SAMPLE GRANTS £2,500 to CAFOD; £2,000 to Sight Savers; £2,000 to St Joseph's Missionary Society; £2,000 to the White Fathers; £1,500 to Intermediate Technology; £1,500 to International Refugee Trust; £1,500 to Columbian Fathers; £1,500 to De Paul Trust; £1,250 to Research into Ageing; £1,000 to Society of the Holy Child Jesus

FINANCES *Year* 1996–97 *Income* £46,252 *Grants* £26,520

TRUSTEES Miss J M Bisgood, P Schulte, P J K Bisgood

NOTES Grants for overseas projects can only made to UK-based charities

HOW TO APPLY Applications without charity registration number will not be considered. Regret applications cannot be acknowledged

WHO TO APPLY TO Miss J M Bisgood, CBE, The Bisgood Trust, 12 Water's Edge, Brudenell Road, Canford Cliffs, Poole, Dorset BH13 7NN

CC NO 265403   **ESTABLISHED** 1973

■ Miss Jeanne Bisgood's Charitable Trust

WHAT IS FUNDED General charitable purposes. Main grants have been and will be concentrated on following categories: (a) operating under Roman Catholic auspices; (b) operating in the County of Dorset; (c) national (not local) charities concerned with the elderly. Support may also be given to education

WHAT IS NOT FUNDED No grants to individuals or to organisations other than registered charities. No grants to local projects outside Dorset unless under Roman Catholic auspices

WHO CAN BENEFIT There are no restrictions on the age; professional and economic group; family situation; religion and culture; and social circumstances of; or disease or medical condition suffered by, the beneficiaries. However, particular favour is given to Roman Catholics, the elderly, children, young adults, students and teachers

WHERE FUNDING CAN BE GIVEN Grants are to UK charities only but include those operating outside the UK

SAMPLE GRANTS £2,000 to CAFOD; £1,250 to St Francis Leprosy Guild; £1,250 to Bourne Trust; £1,250 to Survive-Miva; £1,000 to Intercare; £1,000 to Sue Ryder Foundation; £1,000 to Help the Hospices; £1,000 to Sylvia Wright Trust; £1,000 to Victoria School Appeal; £1,000 to Aid to the Church in Need

FINANCES *Year* 1996–97 *Income* £34,138 *Grants* £37,265

TRUSTEES J M Bisgood, P Schulte, P J K Bisgood

HOW TO APPLY Applications without charity registration number will not be considered. Regret applications cannot be acknowledged

WHO TO APPLY TO Miss J M Bisgood, CBE, Miss
Jeanne Bisgood's Charitable Trust, 12 Water's
Edge, Brudenell Road, Canford Cliffs, Poole,
Dorset BH13 7NN
CC NO 208714   ESTABLISHED 1962

■ The Bishop of Birmingham's Charitable Trust

WHAT IS FUNDED General charitable purposes at the
discretion of the Trustees

WHO CAN BENEFIT There are no restrictions on the
age; professional and economic group; family
situation; religion and culture; and social
circumstances of; or disease or medical condition
suffered by, the beneficiaries

WHERE FUNDING CAN BE GIVEN Birmingham

TRUSTEES The Rt Rev J M Austin, H B Carslake, The
Rt Rev M Santer

WHO TO APPLY TO Secretary to the Bishop, The Bishop
of Birmingham's Charitable Trust, Bishops Croft,
Old Church Road, Harborne, Birmingham B17 1BG
CC NO 1058628   ESTABLISHED 1996

■ The Bishop's Development Fund

WHAT IS FUNDED The Fund will support diocesan
mission and seek to specifically encourage:
(a) Congregational growth – projects which will
provide new facilities or initiatives to encourage
more people to attend and support church.
(b) Attracting younger people – new facilities or
initiatives to attract and retain young people.
(c) Community outreach – new projects which will
bring benefits to the wider local community. The
aim is to support locally-based projects where
mission and not maintenance is keynote of church
life

WHAT IS NOT FUNDED Any application which does not
meet the criteria under What is Funded

WHO CAN BENEFIT Organisations benefiting children,
young adults and Christians

WHERE FUNDING CAN BE GIVEN The Diocese of
Wakefield

TYPE OF GRANT Capital grants at the discretion of the
Fund's Trustees

RANGE OF GRANTS £1,000–£3,000, maximum grant
is £5,000, average grant £2,300

SAMPLE GRANTS £5,000 to All Saints Church, Halifax;
£3,500 to Christ Church, Moldgreen,
Huddersfield; £3,000 to St Mary's Church,
Longley, Huddersfield; £3,000 to St Catherine's
Church, Sandal, Wakefield; £2,000 to St James's
Church, Rawthorpe; £2,000 to St George's
Church, Halifax; £2,000 to St Augustine's Church,
Halifax; £2,000 to St Luke's Church, Sharlston;
£1,400 to St Hilda's Church, Halifax; £1,000 to
St Philip's Church, Birchencliffe, Huddersfield

FINANCES Year 1996–97 Income £76,504
Grants £33,065

TRUSTEES R Carbutt, Rev Canon I Gaskell, Rev Canon
R Giles, Mrs C M Haigh, R Holmes, The Ven
Archdeacon of Halifax, R Inwood, Mrs M Judkins,
Mrs C Leckie, Mrs A E Lee, Rt Rev Bishop of
Wakefield, N McCulloch, The Ven Archdeacon of
Pontefract, T Robinson, R Sanderson, S W
Williamson, QC

HOW TO APPLY To the address under Who To Apply To
in writing. Only applications formally approved by
the Parochial Church Councils of Church of
England churches in the Diocese of Wakefield will
be considered

WHO TO APPLY TO The Secretary/Administrator, The
Bishop's Development Fund, Church House,
1 South Parade, Wakefield WF1 1LP
Tel 01924 371802
CC NO 700588   ESTABLISHED 1988

■ The Bishopsdown Trust

WHAT IS FUNDED The Trustees have a specific interest
in Keston College (Oxford) and the disabled in
relation to sports activities, also supporting links
with Russian Christians. Charitable bodies
promoting the advancement of education in
religion or in the history of religion. The
advancement of aesthetic education with respect
to music, particularly the promotion of the practice
and performance of choral works by local choirs or
orchestras and the advancement of church music

WHO CAN BENEFIT Individuals, registered charities and
institutions benefiting: children; young adults;
musicians; choir singers; sportsmen and women;
Christians and disabled people

WHERE FUNDING CAN BE GIVEN Mainly Oxford

TYPE OF GRANT Buildings, capital, feasibility studies,
interest free loans, project, research, and start-up
costs. Funding may be given for up to three years

RANGE OF GRANTS £13–£6,862

SAMPLE GRANTS £6,862 to Keston Institute; £600 to
Lilit Danielian; £525 to Iffley Festival; £500 to an
individual for help in disabled sporting activities;
£500 to British Deaf Sports; £500 to SADA; £404
to an individual; £250 to Leeds and District SSCB;
£250 to Airspace; £250 to Church in Wales

FINANCES Year 1996 Income £343,089
Grants £11,136

TRUSTEES Rev Canon Michael Bourdeaux, Mrs L
Bourdeaux, K Grant, Ms K Barnes, R Bryan

WHO TO APPLY TO R L Bryan, Secretary and Trustee,
The Bishopsdown Trust, 7 Bradford Drive, Ewell,
Epsom, Surrey KT19 0AQ
CC NO 326725   ESTABLISHED 1984

■ Bishopsgate Foundation

WHAT IS FUNDED Support of the Bishopsgate
Institute, library and public hall, relief of need

WHO CAN BENEFIT Individuals, and organisations
benefiting at risk groups, those disadvantaged by
poverty and the socially isolated

WHERE FUNDING CAN BE GIVEN Parishes of St Botolph;
Christchurch Spitalfields; St Leonards Shoreditch

FINANCES Year 1998 Income £978,000
Grants £37,000

TRUSTEES William Dove (Chairman), Deputy E Patrick
Roney, CBE, Alderman Michael Oliver (Alderman of
the Ward of Bishopsgate), John R Perring, Anthony
Graves, Peter Luscombe, Roger Payton, Edwin
Tarry, David Paton (Rector of St Botolph without
Bishopsgate), Eugenie Maxwell (Vice Chairman),
Patrick Wright, John Davis-French, Michael Roberts

HOW TO APPLY To the address under Who To Apply To
in writing

WHO TO APPLY TO A Fuller, Finance Director,
Bishopsgate Foundation, 230 Bishopsgate,
London EC2M 4QH
CC NO 208874   ESTABLISHED 1894

■ Edna Black Charitable Trust

WHAT IS FUNDED Welfare and relief of aged, impotent
and poor – relief of distress by social and spiritual
agencies – preservation of child life – relief of child
and old age distress by provision of material

64

Think carefully about every application. Is it justified?

needs. Christian work with emphasis on evangelism

WHAT IS NOT FUNDED No grants to individuals

WHO CAN BENEFIT To benefit: children and the elderly; Christians and Evangelists; at risk groups; those disadvantaged by poverty; and socially isolated people

WHERE FUNDING CAN BE GIVEN Overseas

FINANCES *Year* 1997 *Income* £52,759 *Grants* £48,400

TRUSTEES A W Black, K R Crabtree, Mrs J D Crabtree

WHO TO APPLY TO The Secretary, Edna Black Charitable Trust, 6 Leopold Road, Wimbledon, London SW19 7BD

CC NO 253578   **ESTABLISHED** 1965

■ Peter Black Charitable Trust

WHAT IS FUNDED Support for Jewish organisations is favoured

WHO CAN BENEFIT Regional, national and Jewish charities

WHERE FUNDING CAN BE GIVEN UK and overseas

TYPE OF GRANT One-off and recurrent grants

RANGE OF GRANTS £24–£7,500

SAMPLE GRANTS £7,500 to Imperial War Museum; £5,076 to the Dales Centre; £5,000 to the Ashken Trust; £5,000 to Cookridge Cancer Centre Appeal; £2,500 to Asygarth School Appeal; £2,000 to Yorkshire Ballet Seminars; £2,000 to One to One Peace Talks; £1,000 to Quest Cancer Research; £1,000 to Bootham School; £1,000 to Ardenlea Marie Curie Centre

FINANCES *Year* 1997 *Income* £83,445 *Grants* £41,121

TRUSTEES T S S Black, G L Black, A S Black

WHO TO APPLY TO T Dunn, Peter Black Charitable Trust, Peter Black Holdings plc, Lawkholme Lane, Keighley, West Yorkshire BD21 3BB

CC NO 264279   **ESTABLISHED** 1972

■ Sydney Black Charitable Trust

WHAT IS FUNDED Donations are made to religious, medical and other institutions, such as those helping disadvantaged and handicapped people

WHAT IS NOT FUNDED No grants to individuals

WHO CAN BENEFIT To benefit disabled and disadvantaged people. There is no restriction on the religion or culture of, or on the disease or medical condition suffered by, the beneficiaries

WHERE FUNDING CAN BE GIVEN Overseas

FINANCES *Year* 1997 *Income* £49,464 *Grants* £41,800

TRUSTEES A W Black, K R Crabtree, Mrs J D Crabtree

WHO TO APPLY TO M B Pilcher, The Secretary, Sydney Black Charitable Trust, 6 Leopold Road, Wimbledon, London SW19 7BD

CC NO 219855   **ESTABLISHED** 1949

■ The Bertie Black Foundation

WHAT IS FUNDED The relief and assistance of the poor and needy, the advancement of education and religion and other charitable purposes

WHO CAN BENEFIT Children, young adults and those disadvantaged by poverty

WHERE FUNDING CAN BE GIVEN Dorset

SAMPLE GRANTS £5,000 to Jewish Care; £1,000 to Communal Security Trust; £500 to Ravenswood Foundation; £200 to New North London Synagogue

FINANCES *Year* 1995 *Income* £131,843 *Grants* £38,592

TRUSTEES I B Black, Mrs D Black, H S Black, Mrs I R Broido

HOW TO APPLY **The Foundation does not welcome unsolicited approaches** and tends to support sources which fall within one of the following categories: (a) those known to the Trustees, or (b) where long-term commitments have been entered into. **The Foundation is fairly fully committed at the present time**

WHO TO APPLY TO S J Jones, The Bertie Black Foundation, 3rd Floor, Beacon House, 15 Christchurch Road, Bournemouth, Dorset BH1 3LB

CC NO 245207   **ESTABLISHED** 1965

■ Isabel Blackman Foundation

WHAT IS FUNDED The elderly, blind, disabled, hospitals, churches, voluntary charitable bodies, youth organisations, education. Grants are restricted to applicants from Hastings & District

WHAT IS NOT FUNDED Please note only applications from Hastings and District are considered

WHO CAN BENEFIT Organisations benefiting: children, young adults, older people, retired people, disabled people, Christians and beneficiaries suffering from sight loss and blindness

WHERE FUNDING CAN BE GIVEN Hastings & District only

TYPE OF GRANT One-off

RANGE OF GRANTS £100–£50,000

FINANCES *Year* 1996–97 *Income* £212,294 *Grants* £192,645

TRUSTEES Mrs W M Mabbett, R A Vint, R T Mennell, D J Jukes, Mrs M Haley

HOW TO APPLY By letter

WHO TO APPLY TO R A Vint, Secretary to the Managing Trustees, Isabel Blackman Foundation, 13 Laton Road, Hastings, East Sussex TN34 2ES *Tel* 01424 431756

CC NO 313577   **ESTABLISHED** 1966

■ The Charity of John Blacknall

WHAT IS FUNDED Welfare (relief in need) and church upkeep

WHO CAN BENEFIT Individuals and organisations benefiting Christians, at risk groups, those disadvantaged by poverty and socially isolated people

WHERE FUNDING CAN BE GIVEN The ancient parishes of St Helens and St Nicholas; the Borough of Abingdon

FINANCES *Year* 1995 *Income* £24,424 *Grants* £19,775

HOW TO APPLY To the address under Who To Apply To in writing

WHO TO APPLY TO Mrs A J Claridge, Clerk, The Charity of John Blacknall, 1 Old Station Yard, Abingdon, Oxfordshire OX14 3LQ *Tel* 01235 526487

CC NO 206803   **ESTABLISHED** 1971

■ Sir Alec Black's Charity

WHAT IS FUNDED Primarily to benefit former employees and to provide bedlinen and pillows to hospitals. Secondarily to benefit sick poor fishermen and dockworkers of Grimsby

WHO CAN BENEFIT Organisations benefiting ex-employees, hospital patients and poor fishermen and dockworkers of Grimsby

WHERE FUNDING CAN BE GIVEN Grimsby

RANGE OF GRANTS £50–£9,198

Does the trust you have chosen match your needs? Haphazard applications waste postage and time

65

SAMPLE GRANTS The following grants were made to help with the costs of bedlinen:; £9,198 to Queen Elizabeth's Foundation; £3,840 to St Gemma's Hospice; £3,199 to Jewish Care; £2,942 to Butterwick House; £2,704 to Burlingham House; £2,589 to John Groom's Association for the Disabled; £2,254 to St Oswald's Hospice; £2,242 to Winged Fellowship; £2,092 to LOROS; £1,750 to St Michael's Hospice

FINANCES *Year* 1997 *Income* £69,163 *Grants* £59,845

TRUSTEES G H Taylor, J N Harrison, S Wilson, P A Mounfield, Dr D F Wilson

NOTES The Trustees give preference to aid for primary causes

WHO TO APPLY TO The Trustees, Sir Alec Black's Charity, 17–19 Osborne Street, Grimsby, North East Lincolnshire DN31 1HA

CC NO 220295   **ESTABLISHED** 1942

■ The Blackstock Trust

WHAT IS FUNDED Grants are made to institutions and charitable bodies providing care and attention for the elderly or disabled and to individuals. Holidays and outings will be considered

WHO CAN BENEFIT Elderly or disabled people and those suffering from a variety of diseases or medical conditions

WHERE FUNDING CAN BE GIVEN The counties of Roxburgh, Berwick and Selkirk in Scotland

TYPE OF GRANT One-off

RANGE OF GRANTS Maximum £500

SAMPLE GRANTS The following grants were to individuals:; £750 for a garden shed; £750 for carpeting and household goods; £500 for a television; £500 towards electric wheelchair

FINANCES *Year* 1997 *Grants* £25,000

HOW TO APPLY Applications should be made in writing to the address under Who To Apply To

WHO TO APPLY TO William Windram, Secretary, The Blackstock Trust, Messrs Pike & Chapman, 36 Bank Street, Galashiels TD1 1ER *Tel* 01896 752379

SC NO SCO 14309

■ The Morgan Blake Charitable Trust

WHAT IS FUNDED General charitable purposes. Consider most projects

WHAT IS NOT FUNDED No grants to individuals

WHO CAN BENEFIT Most applications considered. There are no restrictions on the age; professional and economic group; family situation; religion and culture; and social circumstances of; or disease or medical condition suffered by, the beneficiaries

WHERE FUNDING CAN BE GIVEN UK

RANGE OF GRANTS £1,000–£5,000

SAMPLE GRANTS £5,000 to Quidenham Children's Hospice; £2,000 to St Dunstans; £2,000 to Northampton Volunteer Reading Help; £2,000 to the Norfolk Boat; £2,000 to Great Dunham Primary School

FINANCES *Year* 1997 *Income* £22,513 *Grants* £28,000

TRUSTEES J P Hall, J F Whigham

WHO TO APPLY TO J F Whigham, Solicitor, The Morgan Blake Charitable Trust, Wood Farmhouse, Little Fransham, Dereham, Norfolk NR19 2JX

CC NO 293706   **ESTABLISHED** 1985

■ The Blakemore Foundation

WHAT IS FUNDED Medicine and health, welfare, education, the sciences, humanities and environmental resources. Also supported are community businesses, community development, economic regeneration schemes, job creation, small enterprises and support to voluntary and community organisations and volunteers. Community facilities and services are considered, as are environmental conservation and campaigning causes

WHO CAN BENEFIT Individuals and registered charities, both local and national, benefiting children, young adults, scientists, students, teachers, governesses and volunteers. Support is also given to at risk groups, those disadvantaged by poverty and socially isolated people

WHERE FUNDING CAN BE GIVEN UK and overseas. Priority is given to the West Midlands and to areas of A F Blakemore & Sons Ltd operations

TYPE OF GRANT One-off and recurrent small grants

RANGE OF GRANTS £1,000 or less

FINANCES *Year* 1996 *Income* £27,210 *Grants* £11,086

TRUSTEES P F Blakemore, G M Blakemore, J M J Tonks

NOTES The Foundation prefers to donate to charities/institutions in the areas in which the main company operates

HOW TO APPLY In writing at any time

WHO TO APPLY TO P F Blakemore, The Blakemore Foundation, A F Blakemore & Son Ltd, Long Acres Industrial Estate, Rosehill, Willenhall, West Midlands WV13 2JP *Tel* 01902 366066

CC NO 1015938   **ESTABLISHED** 1992

■ Lady Blakenham's Charity Trust

WHAT IS FUNDED Grants to general charities – emphasis on assistance to aged, blind, physically incapacitated. Relief of poverty. Not intended for the advancement of education or religion. Assistance is given towards holidays for those with physically disabled dependants

WHAT IS NOT FUNDED The Trust does not support religious or educational charities

WHO CAN BENEFIT Care of elderly, medical research, holiday homes for the disabled. Organisations benefiting: children; young adults; older people; retired people; research workers; at risk groups; disabled people; those disadvantaged by poverty; and socially isolated people

WHERE FUNDING CAN BE GIVEN UK and overseas only in special circumstance

FINANCES *Year* 1997 *Income* £25,350 *Grants* £21,280

TRUSTEES Viscount Blakenham, T M Sergison-Brooke

NOTES Trustees respond to applications. No covenants – donations reviewed annually

HOW TO APPLY Applications reviewed on appeal and annually

WHO TO APPLY TO T Sergison-Brooke, Lady Blakenham's Charity Trust, Chipping Warden Manor, Banbury, Oxon OX17 1LA

CC NO 266198   **ESTABLISHED** 1973

■ The Celia and Conrad Blakey Charitable Trust

WHAT IS FUNDED Main areas of interest are medical, music, sport, youth and the sea

WHAT IS NOT FUNDED No grants to individuals. No grants to national appeals. Grants rarely made to bodies outside Kent

WHO CAN BENEFIT Registered charities benefiting: children; young adults; musicians; seafarers and fishermen; sportsmen and women. There is no restriction on the disease or medical condition suffered by the beneficiaries

WHERE FUNDING CAN BE GIVEN South East Kent

RANGE OF GRANTS £250–£5,000

SAMPLE GRANTS £5,000 to Save the Children Fund; £4,500 to Folkestone and District Sports Centre Trust Limited; £2,500 to the Kent Foundation; £2,000 to Duke of Edinburgh's Award Scheme; £1,000 to the Paula Carr Trust

FINANCES *Year* 1997 *Income* £24,165 *Grants* £19,500

TRUSTEES Mrs C Blakey, C C Blakey, Miss J S Portrait

WHO TO APPLY TO Miss J S Portrait, The Celia and Conrad Blakey Charitable Trust, Messrs Protrait, 1 Chancery Lane, Clifford's Inn, London WC2A 1LF

CC NO 263482   **ESTABLISHED** 1971

■ The Blanchminster Trust *(formerly the Blanchminster Charity)*

WHAT IS FUNDED Charities working in the fields of: infrastructure, support and development; religious buildings; arts, culture and recreation; health facilities and buildings; education and training; community services and facilities; and advice and information. Applicants must reside within the area Where Funding Can Be Given and give proof of financial need

WHAT IS NOT FUNDED Applications from Bude/Stratton only will be considered

WHO CAN BENEFIT Organisations or individuals having residential qualifications as above and showing proof of financial need. Organisations benefiting children; young adults; older people; academics; students; actors and entertainment professionals; and musicians may be considered

WHERE FUNDING CAN BE GIVEN The former Urban District of Bude-Stratton as constituted on 31.3.74

TYPE OF GRANT Cash or equipment. Cash may be grant or loan, equipment normally 'permanent loan'. Buildings, capital, core costs, feasibility studies, interest free loans, one-off, project, running costs and start-up costs. Funding will be considered for one year or less

SAMPLE GRANTS £9,000 to Bude Hockey Club for equipment; £3,864 to Hartland Primary School for computer equipment; £1,123 to Bude Fire Cadets for equipment; £750 to Bude September Festival for running costs; £500 to North Cornwall Arts for arts workshops in Bude; £400 to Bude and District Mencap for holiday funds; £300 to Bude Infants' School for repairs to play area; £154 to Hope (UK) for Community School Drugs Publicity

FINANCES *Year* 1997 *Income* £279,276 *Grants* £79,821

TRUSTEES A N Benney, C B Cornish, Miss M H Clowes, J E Gardiner, W J Keat, JP, J Richardson, R S Thorn, L M J Tozer, P Truscott, Mrs J M Shepherd, Mrs V A Newman, B Rowlands, G C Rogers

HOW TO APPLY To Clerk by letter. Applications considered at monthly meetings. All applications acknowledged

WHO TO APPLY TO O A May, Clerk, The Blanchminster Trust, Blanchminster Building, 38 Lansdown Road, Bude, Cornwall EX23 8EE *Tel* 01288 352851 *Fax* 01288 352851

CC NO 202118   **ESTABLISHED** 1421

■ The Solomon & Isabel Blankstone Charitable Trust

WHAT IS FUNDED Charities working in the fields of the advancement of the Jewish religion, synagogues, Jewish religious umbrella bodies, fine arts, music, orchestras, ambulances and mobile units, hospitals, secondary schools, and art galleries and cultural centres

WHAT IS NOT FUNDED No grants to individuals

WHO CAN BENEFIT Organisations benefiting young adults, musicians, Jews and those suffering from autism and tropical diseases

WHERE FUNDING CAN BE GIVEN North-West England

TYPE OF GRANT One-off funding for one year or less

FINANCES *Year* 1997 *Income* £17,807 *Grants* £9,845

TRUSTEES M D Blankstone, Mrs A Blankstone, M L Blankstone, N S Blankstone

HOW TO APPLY In writing to the address under Who To Apply To

WHO TO APPLY TO M D Blankstone, The Solomon & Isabel Blankstone Charitable Trust, 71 Woolton Hill Road, Liverpool L25 4RD *Tel* 0151-707 1707 (daytime only)

CC NO 282244   **ESTABLISHED** 1980

■ The Michael Blanning Trust

WHAT IS FUNDED Provision of housing for elderly, and relief and assistance of the elderly are the main areas of concern for the Trustees

WHO CAN BENEFIT Individuals, registered charities and institutions benefiting the elderly who are at risk, disadvantaged by poverty or socially isolated

WHERE FUNDING CAN BE GIVEN UK

FINANCES *Year* 1996 *Income* £21,699

TRUSTEES H R Johnson, K R James, R M Oulsnam, Mrs A Bradley, A Bradley, T G Wakeley

NOTES The Trust is accumulating income at present and has almost completed the development of flats and bungalows at Four Ashes, Solihull and hopes to develop a further site through a housing association set up by the Trustees

WHO TO APPLY TO R Johnson, The Michael Blanning Trust, Charles Wakeling & Co, c/o Mercury House, 195 Knightsbridge, London SW7 1RE

CC NO 266691   **ESTABLISHED** 1973

■ Neville & Elaine Blond Charitable Trust

WHAT IS FUNDED General charitable purposes, with particular emphasis on Jewish Charities

WHO CAN BENEFIT There are no restrictions on the age; professional and economic group; family situation; religion and culture; and social circumstances of; or disease or medical condition suffered by, the beneficiaries. However, particular favour is given to Jewish Charities

WHERE FUNDING CAN BE GIVEN Mainly Israel

FINANCES *Year* 1997 *Income* £95,103 *Grants* £95,200

TRUSTEES Mrs A E Susman, Dame Simone Prendergast, P Blond, S N Susman, Mrs J Skidmore

HOW TO APPLY Funds already committed to charities known to Trustees

WHO TO APPLY TO H W Fisher & Co, Neville & Elaine Blond Charitable Trust, Acre House, 11–15 William Road, London NW1 3ER

CC NO 206319 **ESTABLISHED** 1953

■ The Patsy Bloom Charitable Trust

WHAT IS FUNDED General charitable purposes at the discretion of the Trustees

WHO CAN BENEFIT At the discretion of the Trustees. There are no restrictions on the age; professional and economic group; family situation; religion and culture; and social circumstances of; or disease or medical condition suffered by, the beneficiaries

WHERE FUNDING CAN BE GIVEN UK

TYPE OF GRANT At the discretion of the Trustees

FINANCES *Year* 1997 *Income* £545,077 *Grants* £32,243

TRUSTEES I A Brecher, P Bloom, A L Bloom

HOW TO APPLY **This Trust states that it does not respond to unsolicited applications**

WHO TO APPLY TO Mark Deller, The Patsy Bloom Charitable Trust, PO Box 11217, London NW1 4WE

CC NO 1054034 **ESTABLISHED** 1996

■ The Bluff Field Charitable Trust

WHAT IS FUNDED General charitable purposes

WHO CAN BENEFIT There are no restrictions on the age; professional and economic group; family situation; religion and culture; and social circumstances of; or disease or medical condition suffered by, the beneficiaries

WHERE FUNDING CAN BE GIVEN UK

WHO TO APPLY TO Peter Field, Chairman, The Bluff Field Charitable Trust, c/o Risk Publications, 104–112 Marylebone Lane, London W1M 5FU

CC NO 1057992 **ESTABLISHED** 1996

■ The Bluston Charitable Settlement

WHAT IS FUNDED General charitable purposes

WHAT IS NOT FUNDED No grants to individuals

WHO CAN BENEFIT There are no restrictions on the age, professional and economic group, family situation, religion and culture, and social circumstances of, or disease or medical condition suffered by, the beneficiaries

WHERE FUNDING CAN BE GIVEN UK

SAMPLE GRANTS £30,000 to Jewish Care; £30,000 to Nightingale House Home for the Aged; £30,000 to Norwood Ravenswood; £10,000 to Children's Trust; £7,000 to Family Welfare Association; £5,000 to St Mary's 150th Anniversary Appeal; £5,000 to Variety Club Children's Charity Ltd; £4,000 to North London Hospice; £3,000 to CHAI Lifeline; £3,000 to Samaritans

FINANCES *Year* 1997 *Income* £135,398 *Grants* £141,020

TRUSTEES Messrs BDO Stoy Hayward

WHO TO APPLY TO The Trustees, The Bluston Charitable Settlement, c/o BDO Stoy Hayward, 8 Baker Street, London W1M 1DA

CC NO 256691 **ESTABLISHED** 1968

■ Enid Blyton Trust for Children

WHAT IS FUNDED Special schools and special needs education; literacy; playschemes; arts activities and arts education. Particularly small projects or on-going requirements of small charities

WHAT IS NOT FUNDED No grants for further education, private education or for the benefit of anyone over the age of 16

WHO CAN BENEFIT Children up to the age of 16 where there is a need not supplied from the non-charitable sector. Including children who are in care, fostered and adopted; and those suffering from cancers, cerebral palsy, mental illness, and paediatric diseases

WHERE FUNDING CAN BE GIVEN UK and overseas

TYPE OF GRANT Usually one-off, occasionally recurring. Also project

RANGE OF GRANTS £200–£2,000

SAMPLE GRANTS £12,000 to Candlelight Appeal (Children with Cancer) for research and development at St James Hospital, Leeds; £1,500 to REACH Resource Centre for reading for disabled children; £750 to Children of the Andes for homeless children in South America; £650 to Cricket Green School for their art project; £500 to Avalon School towards the cost of a new minibus; £500 to Children's Adventure Farm for Leapfrog Appeal; £500 to Commonwealth Society for the Deaf for Soundseekers Appeal; £500 to North Eastern Prisoner After Care Society for children's playroom for visitors; £500 to Sussex Association for Spina Bifida and Hydrocephalus for support work

FINANCES *Year* 1997–98 *Income* £28,067 *Grants* £20,600

TRUSTEES Miss Sophie Smallwood, Dr Sian Baverstock, John Blyton, R Wood, Mrs I M Smallwood

NOTES The grant of £12,000 to candlelight Appeal was part of a five year programme of grants (totalling £60,000) which was agreed in 1995 by previous trustees. This size grant is unlikely to be repeated

HOW TO APPLY In writing to the address below, including Annual Accounts or at least good financial details. The Trustees meet three times a year, usually in March, July and at the end of November. Applications should be received by the previous month

WHO TO APPLY TO Ms S Smallwood, Enid Blyton Trust for Children, 98 Bomeville Gardens, London SW4 9LE *Tel* 0181-675 6836

CC NO 284999 **ESTABLISHED** 1982

■ Bernard Richard Body Charitable Trust

WHAT IS FUNDED For the protection and benefit of animals, particularly for our own animal sanctuary in Berkshire. Some other charities on a regular basis

WHAT IS NOT FUNDED No grants for scholarships or expeditions

WHERE FUNDING CAN BE GIVEN UK and overseas

TYPE OF GRANT Regular grants given to certain charities. Only restricted funds available for further grants

RANGE OF GRANTS Some annual grants of £1,000 or less; one-off grants of £500 or less

SAMPLE GRANTS £1,000 to Centre for European Studies; £500 to Brooke Hospital for Animals; £500 to Pilgrim Scanner Appeal, Boston; £500 to Society of Friends; £250 to Action against Breast Cancer

FINANCES *Year* 1996–97 *Income* £17,000 *Grants* £4,270

TRUSTEES B R Body, Mrs A Burfoot, J Coleman

HOW TO APPLY To the address under Who To Apply To in writing

WHO TO APPLY TO Lady Body, Bernard Richard Body Charitable Trust, Jewells Farm, Stanford Dingley, Reading, Berkshire RG7 6LX

CC NO 800320　　　　**ESTABLISHED** 1988

■ The Body Shop Foundation

WHAT IS FUNDED Innovative, grassroots projects in the fields of human rights and environmental protection

WHAT IS NOT FUNDED No grants to individuals, sport or the arts, capital investment, low likelihood of substainability, emergency aid, dependent relationships

WHO CAN BENEFIT Registered charities benefiting refugees, socially isolated people and victims of domestic violence

WHERE FUNDING CAN BE GIVEN UK and overseas

TYPE OF GRANT Buildings, capital, one-off, project and research. Funding of up to three years will be considered

RANGE OF GRANTS Up to £10,000

SAMPLE GRANTS £50,000 to Unrepresented Nations and Peoples Organisation to establish fund-raising base; £47,570 to Body and Soul for advice and support for women and families with AIDs and HIV; £39,000 to Global Witness for research costs into the deforestation of Cambodia; £35,180 to Cambridge Female Education Trust for education of girls in Zimbabwe; £33,163 to Citizens Fund to provide information on pesticides in foods in USA; £30,000 to MEIC for medical research; £26,126 to TASO UK for students in Uganda using aromatherapy for HIV/AIDs sufferers; £25,000 to World Society for the Protection of Animals to help reintroduce spectacled bears into the wild; £24,310 to Childhope UK for street children project in the Philippines; £21,200 to Environmental Investigation Agency to investigate the trade of endangered species in Northern India

FINANCES *Year* 1997 *Income* £1,118,146 *Grants* £701,980

TRUSTEES Mrs A Roddick, G Roddick, M Barrett, R Cockerill, R Godfrey, J Floodgate, A Kinney-Eiltinger, S Scott

HOW TO APPLY **This Trust states that it does not respond to unsolicited applications**

WHO TO APPLY TO The Body Shop Foundation Watersmead, Littlehampton, West Sussex BN17 6LS

CC NO 802757　　　　**ESTABLISHED** 1988

■ The Bohm Foundation

WHAT IS FUNDED General charitable purposes, particularly the arts

WHO CAN BENEFIT Individuals and organisations, particularly those involved in the arts

WHERE FUNDING CAN BE GIVEN UK and overseas

TYPE OF GRANT Capital

SAMPLE GRANTS £5,000 to an individual for a project on fabric form and place; £2,678 to Northern Centre for Contemporary Art; £500 to the Hillel Foundation

FINANCES *Year* 1996 *Income* £25,023 *Grants* £8,178

TRUSTEES Dorothy Bohm, Charles Green

HOW TO APPLY To the address under Who To Apply To in writing

WHO TO APPLY TO D Graham, The Bohm Foundation, Messrs Bristows, Cooke & Carpmeal Solicitors, 10 Lincoln's Inn Fields, London WC2A 3BP

CC NO 280421　　　　**ESTABLISHED** 1980

■ The Boltons Trust

WHAT IS FUNDED Relief of suffering; cultural and religious teaching; bursaries and fees; and international rights of the individual and other charitable purposes

WHAT IS NOT FUNDED No grants to individuals

WHO CAN BENEFIT Organisations benefiting: children; young adults; older people; Jews; carers and disaster victims

WHERE FUNDING CAN BE GIVEN UK and overseas

TYPE OF GRANT Generally single grants for core costs, project, recurring costs and running costs. Funding is available for one year or less

SAMPLE GRANTS £50,000 to Conciliation Resources for peace studies; £50,000 to Council of Christians and Jews for interfaith understanding; £50,000 to Dulwich Art Gallery for general funding; £50,000 to Jerusalem Foundation for educational/medical projects in Jerusalem; £50,000 to Jewish Childs Day for victims of the Chernobyl disaster; £40,000 to POWER for prosthetics and orthotics, education and relief - mine victims of Laos and Mozambique; £25,000 to Norwood - Childcare for child welfare; £20,000 to City University for stroke and speech impediment; £20,000 to Thames Valley University for support for university; £15,000 to Nightingale House for homes for the aged

FINANCES *Year* 1997 *Income* £118,977 *Grants* £528,000

TRUSTEES C M Marks, Mrs C Albuquerque, H B Levin

HOW TO APPLY Absolutely no personal callers or telephone enquiries. Applications must be made in writing. It is unlikely that unsolicited applications will be successful. Applicants should enclose an sae for response

WHO TO APPLY TO C M Marks, FCA, The Boltons Trust, 44a New Cavendish Street, London W1M 7LG

CC NO 257951　　　　**ESTABLISHED** 1967

■ The John and Celia Bonham Christie Charitable Trust

WHAT IS FUNDED Grants are generally small and made to medical charities and organisations, though smaller grants are made to a wide range of other organisations

WHO CAN BENEFIT Individuals, local and national organisations. There are no restrictions on the disease or medical condition suffered by the beneficiaries

WHERE FUNDING CAN BE GIVEN UK, with a preference for the Avon area

TYPE OF GRANT Recurrent, over three to five years

RANGE OF GRANTS £200–£2,000

Does the trust you have chosen match your needs? Haphazard applications waste postage and time

69

SAMPLE GRANTS £2,000 to Bath Abbey; £1,000 to Multiple Sclerosis Society; £1,000 to Monkton Combe School; £800 to St Luke's Hospice; £600 to Hospice of the Good Shepherd; £600 to National Eye Research Centre; £600 to Rainbow Trust; £500 to Devon County Association for Blind; £500 to Freeway Association; £500 FWA

FINANCES *Year* 1997 *Income* £41,444
Grants £38,400

TRUSTEES R Bonham Christie, P R Fitzgerald, R Ker, Celia Bonham Christie

NOTES £1,500 was given in grants to four individuals

HOW TO APPLY To the address under Who To Apply To in writing. The Trustees regret that the income is fully allocated for the foreseeable future. Only a small number of new applications are supported each year

WHO TO APPLY TO P R Fitzgerald, Trustee, John and Celia Bonham Christie Charitable Trust, c/o Messrs Wilsons, Steynings House, Chapel.Place, Fisherton Street, Salisbury, Wiltshire SP2 7RJ *Tel* 01722 412412

CC NO 326296   **ESTABLISHED** 1983

■ The Charlotte Bonham-Carter Charitable Trust

WHAT IS FUNDED General charitable purposes which were of particular concern to Lady Charlotte Bonham-Carter during her lifetime

WHAT IS NOT FUNDED No grants to individuals

WHO CAN BENEFIT There are no restrictions on the age; professional and economic group; family situation; religion and culture; and social circumstances of; or disease or medical condition suffered by, the beneficiaries

WHERE FUNDING CAN BE GIVEN Hampshire

FINANCES *Year* 1997 *Income* £106,978
Grants £92,299

TRUSTEES Sir Matthew Farrer, GCVO, N A Bonham-Carter, N B Wickham-Irving

NOTES Grants are not given to individuals

HOW TO APPLY In writing. Trustees meet twice annually. Applications will only be acknowledged if sae enclosed. Successful applicants only will be notified. There are no application forms

WHO TO APPLY TO Sir Matthew Farrer, GCVO, The Charlotte Bonham-Carter Charitable Trust, Messrs Farrer & Co, 66 Lincoln's Inn Fields, London WC2A 3LH *Tel* 0171-242 2022

CC NO 292839   **ESTABLISHED** 1985

■ Bonhomie United Charity Society

WHAT IS FUNDED The elderly and disabled. The Trust will consider funding: hospices; MS research; special schools and special needs education; holidays and outings; and playschemes. The conservation of monuments will also be considered

WHAT IS NOT FUNDED No grants to individuals directly, only through voluntary organisations or social services

WHO CAN BENEFIT Local organisations in Southampton benefiting the elderly and the disabled. Those suffering from a range of diseases and medical conditions will be considered for funding

WHERE FUNDING CAN BE GIVEN Southampton

TYPE OF GRANT One-off for buildings and capital

FINANCES *Year* 1997 *Income* £65,106
Grants £54,514

TRUSTEES B J Davies, S Davies, J Davies, R Davies

NOTES The Trust's funds are fully committed

WHO TO APPLY TO B J Davies, Trustee, Bonhomie United Charity Society, 9 Bassett Heath Avenue, Bassett, Southampton SO16 7PG

CC NO 247816   **ESTABLISHED** 1966

■ The Book Aid Charitable Trust

WHAT IS FUNDED General charitable purposes including the advancement of the Christian religion through the provision of bibles and books

WHAT IS NOT FUNDED No financial grants

WHO CAN BENEFIT To benefit people and projects in countries with a shortage of books, especially Christians

WHERE FUNDING CAN BE GIVEN Developing countries

TYPE OF GRANT For books and bibles only, mainly secondhand from single cartons to containers of books

FINANCES *Year* 1997 *Income* £119,106

TRUSTEES S Green, B Hiley, A Hiley, M Silver

PUBLICATIONS Newsletter occasionally

NOTES Books have been supplied in Nigeria, Malawi, Zimbabwe, Kenya, Ghana, Tanzania, Liberia and India

HOW TO APPLY In writing with an sae

WHO TO APPLY TO J R Hiley, The Book Aid Charitable Trust, 271 Church Road, London SE19 2QQ *Tel* 0181-857 7794

CC NO 1039484   **ESTABLISHED** 1994

■ Boots Charitable Trust

WHAT IS FUNDED Health, family, maternity and child welfare, education, economic development, residential facilities and services; and social advice and information

WHAT IS NOT FUNDED Individuals, private fund-raising groups and organisations which are not registered with the Charity Commission are ineligible

WHO CAN BENEFIT Small local projects, innovative projects, new and established organisations benefiting: people of all ages; at risk groups; carers, disabled people; those disadvantaged by poverty; disaster victims; homeless people; those living in rural and urban areas; socially isolated people; victims of abuse, crime and domestic violence. There is no restriction on the disease or medical condition suffered by the beneficiaries

WHERE FUNDING CAN BE GIVEN Nottinghamshire

TYPE OF GRANT One-off, recurrent, buildings, capital, core costs, project, running costs, salaries and start-up costs. Funding is for up to three years

SAMPLE GRANTS £16,400 to Age Concern, Nottinghamshire; £10,000 to Macedon as the first of a three part grant; £10,000 to WISH (Women in Special Hospitals) as the second of a three part grant; £9,000 to Nottinghamshire Royal Society for the Blind; £7,500 to Nottinghamshire Hospice; £7,500 to Landmarks; £6,000 to National Society for Epilepsy as the first of a three part grant; £5,000 to Ecoworks as the third of a three part grant; £5,000 to Shelter (Nottinghamshire Housing Advice Service); £5,000 to Home Farm Trust (Nottinghamshire)

FINANCES *Year* 1997–98 *Income* £485,735
Grants £486,954

TRUSTEES The Boots Co Plc, The Boots Co Nominees Ltd

PUBLICATIONS Annual Report

HOW TO APPLY In writing to either M Haworth or Ms S Smith at the address below. Applications are acknowledged

WHO TO APPLY TO Ms S Smith, The Boots Charitable Trust, The Boots Company Plc, Queens Road, Nottingham NG2 3AA *Tel* 0115-949 2185 *Fax* 0115-949 2120
CC NO 1045927   ESTABLISHED 1971

■ Salo Bordon Charitable Trust

WHAT IS FUNDED Jewish organisations, religious education and social welfare
WHO CAN BENEFIT Organisations, primarily Jewish, benefiting: at risk groups, those disadvantaged by poverty and socially isolated people
WHERE FUNDING CAN BE GIVEN UK and overseas
RANGE OF GRANTS £15–£7,867
SAMPLE GRANTS £7,867 to Society of Friends of Torah; £3,521 to Golders Green Beth Hamedrash; £3,110 to Beis Abraham Synagogue; £3,000 to Federation of Synagogues; £3,000 to MIR; £2,200 to Ohr Elchonon; £2,000 to Hamaayan; £1,785 to Lolev Trust; £1,500 to Pischei Teshuvah; £1,427 to Ponevez
FINANCES *Year* 1996–97 *Income* £654,969 *Grants* £52,668
TRUSTEES S Bordon, Mrs L Bordon, M Bordon, D Bordon, M Bordon
HOW TO APPLY To the address under Who To Apply To in writing
WHO TO APPLY TO S Bordon, Trustee, Salo Bordon Charitable Trust, 78 Corringham Road, London NW11 7EB
CC NO 266439   ESTABLISHED 1973

■ Sir William Boreman's Foundation

WHAT IS FUNDED Providing educational awards to people under 25, and to organisations benefiting eligible individuals, including youth clubs, colleges and educational projects in the area Where Funding Can Be Given
WHAT IS NOT FUNDED No grants to subsidise or replace statutory funding
WHO CAN BENEFIT People/organisations concerned with people under 25, resident in the London Boroughs of Lewisham or Greenwich, for three years or more, in financial need
WHERE FUNDING CAN BE GIVEN Greenwich, Lewisham, Deptford and Woolwich, (with a preference for Greenwich)
TYPE OF GRANT One-off
FINANCES *Year* 1997–98 *Income* £145,000 *Grants* £100,000
TRUSTEES The Draper's Company
NOTES Administered by the Draper's Company, the Foundation was founded under the Will of Sir William Boreman dated 1684
HOW TO APPLY To the address under Who To Apply To in writing. The application should include: an sae; a description of your organisation, its work and existing sources of funding; an account of the proposed project in detail including where else you have or will be applying; funds already raised; amount you are applying for from the Foundation; details of how the project will benefit its intended beneficiaries; details of previous applications to and grants from the Foundation; an Annual Report and latest set of audited accounts.
Individuals should write to or telephone the Clerk to the Governors for an application form. Evidence of income will need to be provided. Parental joint income must not exceed £17,000 gross per annum. Evidence of age and an academic reference are also required

WHO TO APPLY TO Miss D J Thomas, Clerk to the Governors, Sir William Boreman's Foundation, Clerk's Office, Draper's Company, Draper's Hall, London EC2N 2DQ *Tel* 0171-588 5001
CC NO 312796   ESTABLISHED 1962

■ The Born Free Foundation

WHAT IS FUNDED Preservation and conservation of animal species in their natural habitats, on an international basis. The Foundation undertakes all relevant educational and research activities and publishes the useful results of such research. Prevention of all types of cruelty and abuse of animals and wildlife, particularly in zoos and other places where animals are kept in captivity
WHERE FUNDING CAN BE GIVEN UK and overseas
FINANCES *Year* 1996 *Income* £615,097
WHO TO APPLY TO Miss Alison Hood, Trustee, The Born Free Foundation, 3 Grove House, Foundry Lane, Horsham, West Sussex RH13 5PL
CC NO 296024   ESTABLISHED 1987

■ A Bornstein Charitable Settlement

WHAT IS FUNDED Jewish organisations, mainly in Israel concentrating on disabled and disadvantaged people of all ages
WHAT IS NOT FUNDED No grants for non-Jewish organisations
WHO CAN BENEFIT Jewish organisations benefiting disabled people and disadvantaged people
WHERE FUNDING CAN BE GIVEN UK and Israel
RANGE OF GRANTS £50–£100,000
SAMPLE GRANTS £100,000 to Norwood Ravenswood; £14,000 to Jewish Philanthropic Association for Israel and the Middle East; £11,000 to British Olim Society Charitable Trust; £10,000 to World Jewish Relief; £10,000 to UJA Federation; £8,000 to Shaare Zadek Hospital; £5,000 to Jewish Federation of Rhode Island; £2,000 to The Torah Centre; £2,000 to Chabad House; £2,000 to Bar Ilan University - School of Social Work
FINANCES *Year* 1997 *Income* £115,648 *Grants* £164,450
TRUSTEES N P Bornstein, M Hollander
HOW TO APPLY To the Trustees in writing
WHO TO APPLY TO The Trustees, A Bornstein Charitable Settlement, c/o Morley & Scott, Lynton House, 7–12 Tavistock Square, London WC1H 9LT
CC NO 262472   ESTABLISHED 1967

■ The Oliver Borthwick Memorial Trust

WHAT IS FUNDED Currently the main areas of interest are to provide shelter and help for the homeless
WHAT IS NOT FUNDED Applications from individuals, including students, are ineligible
WHO CAN BENEFIT Registered charities benefiting: the homeless; and those disadvantaged by poverty. In particular the Trustees welcome applications from small but viable charities in deprived inner city areas
WHERE FUNDING CAN BE GIVEN UK
FINANCES *Year* 1997 *Grants* £33,000
TRUSTEES Earl Bathurst, R Marriott, H de Quetteville, M H R Bretherton, R Graham, I J Macdonald, J R Marriott
WHO TO APPLY TO The Trust Department, The Oliver Borthwick Memorial Trust, Charities Aid

Foundation, Kings Hill, West Malling, Kent
ME19 4TA *Tel* 01732 520083
Fax 01732 520001
E-mail tmcbride@caf.charitynet.org
cc no 256206   **established** 1968

■ The Boston Green Trust

what is funded General charitable purposes
including the advancement of the Christian faith,
the advancement of education and the relief of the
poor, the needy, the sick and the elderly
who can benefit There are no restrictions on the
age; professional and economic group; family
situation; religion and culture; and social
circumstances of; or disease or medical condition
suffered by, the beneficiaries
where funding can be given UK and overseas
trustees B T Feechan, C A Feechan
who to apply to Bede Thomas Feechen, The Boston
Green Trust, 2 Martindale, Swallow Street, Ivor
Heath, Buckinghamshire SL0 0HY
cc no 1064761   **established** 1997

■ The Camelia Botnar Foundation

what is funded To help and educate children and
young people under the age of 21 years who are
considered to be in special need of care and
attention by reason of sickness, physical or
mental disablement, poverty or social and
economic circumstances so as to develop their
physical and mental capacities that they may grow
to full maturity as individuals and members of
society and that their conditions of life may be
improved
who can benefit Charities, voluntary bodies and
statutory authorities benefiting children and young
adults under the age of 21, at risk groups,
disabled people, those disadvantaged by poverty
and socially isolated people. Those suffering from
many diseases or medical conditions will be
supported
where funding can be given UK
sample grants £5,000,000 to Great Ormond Street
Hospital for projects including a hydro-therapy pool
and improved renal unit; £396,667 to Camelia
Botnar Children's Centre; £228,493 to Angmering
School
finances *Year* 1996 *Income* £2,423,323
Grants £5,743,416
trustees Miss D P Lawson, J S H North, B A Groves,
Mrs M C Botnar
notes The Foundation has established a residential
training and working estate in Cowfold and also
funds the Camelia Botnar Children's Centre in
Worthing. The Foundation invites referrals of young
people from other organisations
who to apply to Stephen Hibbin, FCCA, The Camelia
Botnar Foundation, Maplehurst Road, Cowfold,
Horsham, West Sussex RH13 8DQ
cc no 277275   **established** 1979

■ Harry Bottom Charitable Trust

what is funded Income applied mainly in the
Yorkshire and Derbyshire area towards the
advancement of religion, relief of the aged or sick,
advancement of education, relief of chronic
diseases and research into the cause, relief or
cure of chronic diseases and general charitable
purposes
what is not funded No grants to individuals

who can benefit Registered charities benefiting
people of all ages and students. There is no
restriction on the religion and culture of, or the
disease and medical condition suffered by, the
beneficiaries
where funding can be given Yorkshire and
Derbyshire area
finances *Year* 1997 *Income* £196,059
Grants £89,175
trustees J G Potter, J M Kilner, G T Edwards, Prof
H F Woods
notes Donations made for medical activities
£28,500; religious activities £33,000; and
educational and other activities £27,675
how to apply In writing. Sae not required
who to apply to D R Proctor, Harry Bottom
Charitable Trust, Westons, Queen's Buildings, 55
Queen Street, Sheffield, South Yorkshire S1 2DX
cc no 204675   **established** 1960

■ The Boughton Trust

what is funded All grants have been made to
charities known to the Trustees that fall within the
catergories of: the elderly; the disabled; or the
environment
who can benefit Organisations known to the
Trustees, benefiting the elderly and the disabled
where funding can be given UK
type of grant One-off grants
sample grants £4,000 to Winston Churchill
Memorial Trust for travelling scholarship; £2,500
to Hospice in the Weald for Egerton Paragon bed;
£1,500 to St Andrew Church, Compton; £1,500 to
Freeway Trust; £1,000 to the London Sailing Trust
finances *Year* 1997 *Income* £24,939
Grants £19,231
trustees P M Williams, G J M Wilding, C J T Harris
notes Grants are only made to charities known to the
Trustees
how to apply In writing to the address under Who To
Apply To
who to apply to Clerk to the Trustees, The
Boughton Trust, c/o Kidd Rapinet, Solicitors, 14
and 15 Craven Street, London WC2N 5AD
cc no 261413   **established** 1968

■ The A H and M A Boulton Trust

*This trust did not respond to CAF's request to amend its
entry and, by 30 June 1998, CAF's researchers did not
find financial records for later than 1995 on its file at the
Charity Commission. Trusts are legally required to
submit annual accounts to the Charity Commission
under section 42 of the Charities Act 1993*

what is funded The erection of buildings for religious
purposes of preaching the gospel and of teaching
the doctrines. General charitable purposes
who can benefit There are no restrictions on the
age; professional and economic group; family
situation; religion and culture; and social
circumstances of; or disease or medical condition
suffered by, the beneficiaries
where funding can be given UK
trustees Mrs E Boulton, Mrs J R Gopsill, F P Gopsill
who to apply to J Glashby, The A H and M A Boulton
Trust, Moore Stephen, 49 North John Street
Liverpool L2 6TG
cc no 225328   **established** 1935

72

Think carefully about every application. Is it justified?

The P G and N J Boulton Trust

WHAT IS FUNDED Relief work at home and overseas. Christian missionary work

WHAT IS NOT FUNDED No grants to individuals, environment/conservation, heritage, animal welfare

WHO CAN BENEFIT Charitable bodies of particular interest to the Trustees. Particularly organisations benefiting: carers; disabled people; homeless people; refugees; victims of abuse; victims of famine; victims of man-made or natural disasters; and victims of war

WHERE FUNDING CAN BE GIVEN UK and overseas

TYPE OF GRANT One-off

RANGE OF GRANTS Normally in range £200–£500

SAMPLE GRANTS £8,000 Intercessors for Britain; £5,270 to Worldwide Christian Outreach; £3,850 to Open Doors; £2,600 to Youth with a Mission; £2,600 to Operation Mobilisation; £1,600 to Christian Friends of Israel; £1,600 to Ebenezer Emergency Fund; £1,500 to Youth With a Mission; £1,500 to Wirral Christian Centre; £1,300 to Samaritan's Purse International

FINANCES *Year* 1997 *Income* £68,937 *Grants* £77,820

TRUSTEES Miss N J Boulton, L J Marsh, A L Perry, Mrs S Perry

HOW TO APPLY No application form. No telephone requests

WHO TO APPLY TO Miss N J Boulton, The P G and N J Boulton Trust, 28 Burden Road, Moreton, Wirral, Merseyside L46 6BQ *Web Site* http://members.aol.com/pgnjbt/

CC NO 272525   **ESTABLISHED** 1976

The M Bourne Charitable Trust

WHAT IS FUNDED Trustees favour Jewish causes

WHO CAN BENEFIT Individuals and institutions benefiting Jewish people

WHERE FUNDING CAN BE GIVEN UK

RANGE OF GRANTS £50–£3,000

SAMPLE GRANTS £3,000 to King Solomon School; £2,595 to Jewish Care; £450 to Ravenswood Foundation; £300 to Norwood; £250 to Chigwell Sunset; £250 to Helen Harris Trust; £250 to Community Security Trust; £150 to Jewish National Fund; £150 to Children in Need; £100 to HGS Trust

FINANCES *Year* 1997 *Income* £50,152 *Grants* £8,270

TRUSTEES C J Bourne, Mrs J H Bourne, D M Morein

WHO TO APPLY TO D M Morein, The M Bourne Charitable Trust, Seabourne Express, Purlieu House, 11 Station Road, Epping CM16 9HA

CC NO 290620   **ESTABLISHED** 1984

The Anthony Bourne Foundation

WHAT IS FUNDED Youth related activities. Particularly charities working in the fields of: social care professional bodies; volunteer bureaux; hostels; hospices; and community issues

WHAT IS NOT FUNDED No grants to individuals

WHO CAN BENEFIT Institutions benefiting: children; young adults; disabled people; those disadvantaged by poverty; ex-offenders and those at risk of offending; homeless people and those living in urban areas

WHERE FUNDING CAN BE GIVEN UK

TYPE OF GRANT One-off grants for buildings, capital, core costs and start-up costs. Funding of up to three years will be considered

RANGE OF GRANTS £1,000–£25,000. Generally £2,000

SAMPLE GRANTS £25,000 to Shakespeare Hospice for construction of new hospice; £12,000 to Bourne Youth Challenge for working with Youth Clubs in the Warwickshire area; £5,000 to Centrepoint; £1,000 to IRIS; £1,000 to Raleigh International

FINANCES *Year* 1997–98 *Income* £22,443 *Grants* £44,000

TRUSTEES Mrs V A Bourne, A B V Hughes, R F V Jeune

HOW TO APPLY In writing accompanied by a set of latest Accounts

WHO TO APPLY TO A B V Hughes, The Anthony Bourne Foundation, Payne Hicks Beach, Solicitors, 10 New Square, Lincoln's Inn, London WC2A 3QG *Tel* 0171-465 4300 *Fax* 0171-465 4400

CC NO 1015759   **ESTABLISHED** 1994

The Bouverie Trust

WHAT IS FUNDED General charitable purposes. Select their own beneficiaries in response to approaches made from a variety of sources

WHAT IS NOT FUNDED Educational fees or other ongoing commitments

WHO CAN BENEFIT Charitable organisations. There are no restrictions on the age; professional and economic group; family situation; religion and culture; and social circumstances of; or disease or medical condition suffered by, the beneficiaries

WHERE FUNDING CAN BE GIVEN UK

RANGE OF GRANTS £3–£500

SAMPLE GRANTS £500 to Glyndebourne Arts; £150 to Council of Christians and Jews; £120 to the London Library; £25 to Friends of UCL; £15 to Friends of National Library

FINANCES *Year* 1996 *Income* £17,486 *Grants* £813

TRUSTEES P Chody, Mrs D M Rawstron

HOW TO APPLY **This Trust states that it does not respond to unsolicited applications**

WHO TO APPLY TO Philip Chody, The Bouverie Trust, 90 Fetter Lane, London EC4A 1EQ

CC NO 275853   **ESTABLISHED** 1978

The Bowerman Memorial Trust

WHAT IS FUNDED Religion, humanities, medicine, health and education

WHO CAN BENEFIT Organisations benefiting children and young adults, medical professionals, research workers and students. Also support for people of many different religions and cultures

WHERE FUNDING CAN BE GIVEN UK

TYPE OF GRANT One-off and recurrent

FINANCES *Year* 1997 *Income* £284,033 *Grants* £133,891

TRUSTEES D W Bowerman, Mrs C M Bowerman, Mrs J M Taylor, Miss K E Bowerman, Mrs A M Downham

WHO TO APPLY TO D W Bowerman, Trustee, The Bowerman Memorial Trust, Champs Hill, Coldwatham, Pulborough, West Sussex RH20 1LY

CC NO 289446   **ESTABLISHED** 1984

The Bowland Charitable Trust

WHAT IS FUNDED Preference to help young people, educational or for leisure

WHO CAN BENEFIT Individuals, institutions, and registered charities benefiting, in general, children and young adults. Students may be considered

WHERE FUNDING CAN BE GIVEN UK and overseas

Does the trust you have chosen match your needs? Haphazard applications waste postage and time

73

TYPE OF GRANT Grant size depends on circumstances/application

FINANCES *Year* 1997 *Income* £233,506

TRUSTEES R A Cann, H A Cann, D L Walmsley

HOW TO APPLY In writing, telephone applications are not accepted

WHO TO APPLY TO Mrs Carole Fahy, The Bowland Charitable Trust, TDS House, Lower Phillips Road, Whitebirk Estate, Blackburn BB1 5TH *Tel* 01254 676921

CC NO 292027   **ESTABLISHED** 1985

■ Bowness and Windermere Community Care Trust

WHAT IS FUNDED The relief of those in need who are poor, aged or disabled in Windermere and the surrounding area; other general charitable purposes

WHO CAN BENEFIT Organisations benefiting older people, those disadvantaged by poverty and disabled people

WHERE FUNDING CAN BE GIVEN Windermere and the surrounding area

TYPE OF GRANT Running costs and salaries are considered

FINANCES *Year* 1997 *Income* £20,730 *Grants* £301

WHO TO APPLY TO Clive W Langley, Bowness and Windermere Community Care Trust, Oak Ridge, Meadowcroft Lane, Bowness on Windermere LA23 3JJ

CC NO 1056802   **ESTABLISHED** 1996

■ The Viscountess Boyd Charitable Trust

WHAT IS FUNDED General charitable purposes in Devon and Cornwall including support to voluntary and community organisations; support to volunteers; professional bodies; charity or voluntary umbrella bodies; churches; arts, culture and recreation; health; conservation; animal welfare; bird sanctuaries; wildlife sanctuaries; schools and colleges; education and training; purchase of books; medical research; science and technology; specialist research and social care and development

WHO CAN BENEFIT Children; young adults and older people; those in care, fostered and adopted; parents and children; one parent families; widows and widowers; disabled people; and those living in both urban and rural areas

WHERE FUNDING CAN BE GIVEN South West England

TYPE OF GRANT Capital, core costs, endowment, feasibility studies and one-off funding. Grants can be funded for up to three years and for over three years will also be considered

SAMPLE GRANTS £2,000 to St Stephen-by-Saltash parish Church for Roof Restoration Fund; £1,000 to The Rowing Foundation towards the Rupert Guinness Centenary Training Camp; £1,000 to Ampthill Feoffee Estate Charity's Almshouse Appeal; £1,000 to El Shaddai Orphanage Trust for general purposes; £500 to Saltash and District Age Concern for Minibus Appeal

FINANCES *Year* 1997–98 *Income* £19,736 *Grants* £34,000

TRUSTEES The Iveagh Trustees Limited, Viscountess Boyd, Viscount Boyd

NOTES The Trustees are particularly interested in organisations from the Devon and Cornwall areas. Only applications enclosing an sae are ensured of a reply

HOW TO APPLY First of the month, no application form is used

WHO TO APPLY TO Miss Yvonne White, The Viscountess Boyd Charitable Trust, The Iveagh Trustees Limited, Iveagh House, 41 Harrington Gardens, London SW7 4JU

CC NO 284270   **ESTABLISHED** 1982

■ Miss Margaret Boyd's Charitable Trust

WHAT IS FUNDED General charitable purposes

WHO CAN BENEFIT Registered charities. There are no restrictions on the age; professional and economic group; family situation; religion and culture; and social circumstances of; or disease or medical condition suffered by, the beneficiaries

WHERE FUNDING CAN BE GIVEN UK

WHO TO APPLY TO Miss Margaret Boyd's Charitable Trust, 105 West George Street, Glasgow G2 1QP

SC NO SCO 10801

■ Brackley United Feoffee Charity

WHAT IS FUNDED Grants are made to individuals in need, individuals for educational purposes, local schools and the parish church in Brackley

WHO CAN BENEFIT The people of Brackley. There is no restriction on the age of the beneficiaries though there may be a few restrictions on their social circumstances

WHERE FUNDING CAN BE GIVEN Brackley

TYPE OF GRANT Buildings, capital, core costs, endowment, feasibility studies, interest free loans, one-off, project, research, recurring costs, running costs, salaries and start-up costs. Funding for up to and over three years will be considered

RANGE OF GRANTS £20–£4,500; typical £200

SAMPLE GRANTS £3,500 to St Peter's Church for fabric; £1,000 to each of the five LEA schools in Brackley for IT and books; £850 to local resident for loan of vehicle; £500 to local resident for loan of vehicle; £200 to Police for Action against Crime

FINANCES *Year* 1995–96 *Income* £15,192 *Grants* £7,427

TRUSTEES Cllr C Billingham, Cllr G Britchfield, Cllr J Broomfield, K Bunker, Cllr C Cartmell, Cllr T Gregory, Cllr B Stimpson, C C Wheatcroft, Cllr G Wilkins, Rev Canon P Woodward

HOW TO APPLY To the address under Who To Apply To in writing

WHO TO APPLY TO Mrs R Hedges, Brackley United Feoffee Charity, 7 Easthill Close, Brackley, Northamptonshire NN13 7BS *Tel* 01280 702420

CC NO 238067   **ESTABLISHED** 1886

■ The Seventh Earl of Bradford's 1981 Charitable Trust (also known as The Lord Bradford 1981 Charitable Trust)

WHAT IS FUNDED Conservation, agriculture, the purchase of books for education, community facilities and crime prevention schemes

WHO CAN BENEFIT To benefit children, young adults, students, ex-offenders and those at risk of offending

WHERE FUNDING CAN BE GIVEN The Midlands

TYPE OF GRANT One-off, recurrent and buildings are considered

FINANCES *Year* 1994–95 *Income* £13,789 *Grants* £11,700

TRUSTEES Lord Bradford, Lady Bradford, P E J Clerk

HOW TO APPLY In writing. Grants are only awarded at the AGM normally held in November. Sae essential

WHO TO APPLY TO Mrs J Woodward, The Seventh Earl of Bradford's 1981 Charitable Trust, Bradford Estate Office, Weston under Lizard, Shifnal, Shropshire TF11 8JU

CC NO 284689   **ESTABLISHED** 1982

■ The Brading Town Trust

WHAT IS FUNDED General charitable objectives benefiting building services; community development; support to voluntary and community organisations; churches; arts activities; arts education; cultural activity; hospices; medical centres; cancer research; conservation; heritage; primary schools; community facilities; day centres, community issues and development proposals

WHAT IS NOT FUNDED No grants to individuals

WHO CAN BENEFIT Organisations benefiting children; young adults and older people; retired people; students; sportsmen and women; Church of England; Methodists and those suffering from Alzheimer's disease; cancer; and arthritis and rheumatism within the area Where Funding Can Be Given

WHERE FUNDING CAN BE GIVEN Brading, Isle of Wight

TYPE OF GRANT Buildings, one-off grants and project. Funding is available for up to one year

SAMPLE GRANTS £2,087 to Brading Community Association for refurbishment of and equipment for youth club project; £652 to Town Square and Primary School for new flagpole and flags; £385 to Brading Youth club for a table tennis table; £350 to St Mary's Church towards the costs of repairing the clock and steeple; £350 to Methodist Church towards the cost of central heating

FINANCES *Year* 1995 *Income* £14,257
Grants £15,900

TRUSTEES Betty Howell (Chairman), Margaret Wetherick, Peter Wright, Paul Eccles, Roger Woodcock

HOW TO APPLY To the address under Who To Apply To in writing

WHO TO APPLY TO J Lee, Clerk, The Brading Town Trust, 42 High Street, Brading, Isle of Wight PO36 0DJ *Tel* 01983 407560

CC NO 202053   **ESTABLISHED** 1898

■ The Braemar Charitable Foundation

This trust did not respond to CAF's request to amend its entry and, by 30 June 1998, CAF's researchers did not find financial records for later than 1995 on its file at the Charity Commission. Trusts are legally required to submit annual accounts to the Charity Commission under section 42 of the Charities Act 1993

WHAT IS FUNDED General charitable purposes

WHO CAN BENEFIT There are no restrictions on the age; professional and economic group; family situation; religion and culture; and social circumstances of; or disease or medical condition suffered by, the beneficiaries

WHERE FUNDING CAN BE GIVEN UK

TRUSTEES M Noble, P Noble

WHO TO APPLY TO R J Whitelaw, The Braemar Charitable Foundation, 1A Dukes Way Court, Team Valley, Gateshead, Newcastle upon Tyne NE11 0PJ

CC NO 298896   **ESTABLISHED** 1987

■ The William Brake Charitable Trust

WHAT IS FUNDED General charitable purposes

WHO CAN BENEFIT There are no restrictions on the age; professional and economic group; family situation; religion and culture; and social circumstances of; or disease or medical condition suffered by, the beneficiaries

WHERE FUNDING CAN BE GIVEN Kent

FINANCES *Year* 1997 *Income* £18,118
Grants £16,280

TRUSTEES Bruce Rylands, Michael Philpott, David Richardson

HOW TO APPLY To the address under Who To Apply To in writing

WHO TO APPLY TO B Rylands, Solicitor, The William Brake Charitable Trust, Gill Turner & Tucker, Colman House, King Street, Maidstone, Kent ME14 1JE *Tel* 01622 759051

CC NO 1023244   **ESTABLISHED** 1984

■ The Tony Bramall Charitable Trust

WHAT IS FUNDED To provide support to local charities within the county of Yorkshire and national medical institutions, in particular those concerned with child health

WHO CAN BENEFIT There are no restrictions on the age; professional and economic group; family situation; religion and culture; and social circumstances of; or disease or medical condition suffered by, the beneficiaries

WHERE FUNDING CAN BE GIVEN UK

SAMPLE GRANTS £11,000 to St Oswalds Hospice, Gosforth; £5,000 to Cookridge Cancer Centre Appeal; £3,000 to The Hospital Heartbeat Appeal; £3,000 to Starlight Foundation for play centre for children in hospital; £3,000 to Gloucester County Association for the Blind for computer equipment; £2,500 to Derian House Children's Hospice; £2,500 to War on Cancer; £2,500 to Chris Fund Ltd, a Children's Appeal; £1,000 to National Association of Almshouses; £1,000 to Childline

FINANCES *Year* 1998 *Income* £66,000
Grants £46,000

TRUSTEES D C A Bramall, K S Bramall Ogden, M J Foody, G M Tate, A Bramall

HOW TO APPLY To the address under Who To Apply To in writing

WHO TO APPLY TO J R Illingworth, Secretary to the Trustees, The Tony Bramall Charitable Trust, Harlow Court, Otley Road, Harrogate, North Yorkshire HG3 1PU

CC NO 1001522   **ESTABLISHED** 1990

■ The Bramhope Trust

WHAT IS FUNDED General charitable purposes. Individuals and organisations in the village of Bramhope

WHAT IS NOT FUNDED Organisations and individuals who do not reside in the Parish of Bramhope

WHO CAN BENEFIT There are no restrictions on the age; professional and economic group; family situation; religion and culture; and social circumstances of; or disease or medical condition suffered by, the beneficiaries

WHERE FUNDING CAN BE GIVEN Bramhope in Leeds

TYPE OF GRANT Gifts are given according to circumstances

SAMPLE GRANTS £5,000 to Village Hall for renewal of curtains; £2,500 to St Giles Parish Church for double glazing some of the windows; £2,500 to Bramhope Methodist Church to support a project for access for the disabled; £2,500 to Parish Council towards renewal of play area; £2,000 to Wheatfields Hospice

FINANCES *Year* 1995–96 *Income* £21,549
Grants £25,000

TRUSTEES B D Blundey, Mrs A R Schofield, Mrs M I B Drayton, A J Hodgetts, A L Thompson

HOW TO APPLY To the address under Who To Apply To in writing

WHO TO APPLY TO Mrs Anne Schofield, Trustee, The Bramhope Trust, Wharfe Croft, 51 Breary Lane East, Bramhope, Leeds LS16 9EU *Tel* 0113-267 8813

CC NO 504190   ESTABLISHED 1975

■ The Brampton Trust

WHAT IS FUNDED Roman Catholic Charities
WHO CAN BENEFIT Roman Catholics
WHERE FUNDING CAN BE GIVEN England
FINANCES *Year* 1997 *Income* £126,384
Grants £88,866
HOW TO APPLY Funds are fully committed. No grants available
WHO TO APPLY TO C M S Eldridge, Secretary, The Brampton Trust, Windingwood Farmhouse, Hungerford, Berkshire RG17 9RN
CC NO 242326   ESTABLISHED 1909

■ The Brand Trust

WHAT IS FUNDED General charitable purposes in accordance with the wishes of the Settlor. Particular favour is given to health, welfare and the arts
WHAT IS NOT FUNDED No grants to individuals
WHO CAN BENEFIT Registered charities. There are no restrictions on the age; professional and economic group; family situation; religion and culture; and social circumstances of; or disease or medical condition suffered by, the beneficiaries. However, particular favour is given to at risk groups, those disadvantaged by poverty, socially isolated people, and those involved in the arts
WHERE FUNDING CAN BE GIVEN UK, Romania, third world
RANGE OF GRANTS £50–£200
SAMPLE GRANTS £200 to Royal Exchange Theatre; £150 to Prisoners' Families Services; £120 to Action Aid; £100 to National Deaf Children's Society; £100 to Tower Hamlets Mission
FINANCES *Year* 1997 *Income* £17,547
Grants £17,270
TRUSTEES M L Meyer, E Meyer, I Dunlop
WHO TO APPLY TO M L Meyer, The Brand Trust, 4 Montague Square, London W1H 1RA
CC NO 274704   ESTABLISHED 1977

■ The Breast Cancer Research Trust

WHAT IS FUNDED Applications only for medical research mainly into breast cancer and diagnosis
WHAT IS NOT FUNDED No grants to students
WHO CAN BENEFIT National and established organisations, innovative projects benefiting medical professionals, research workers and those suffering from breast cancer
WHERE FUNDING CAN BE GIVEN UK

TYPE OF GRANT Research funding of up to three years will be considered
SAMPLE GRANTS £16,700 to Royal Marsden Hospital for histological grading by cytology and subsequent treatment; £13,271 to Charing Cross Hospital and Westminster Medical School for biological research into breast cancer; £6,925 to Queens University, Belfast for biological research into breast cancer; £5,000 to Breast Cancer Clinic in Brighton
FINANCES *Year* 1995 *Income* £77,406
Grants £36,095
TRUSTEES Vera Lynn, Jean-Claude Gazet
PUBLICATIONS Annual Report
HOW TO APPLY Application form available
WHO TO APPLY TO J C Gazet, The Breast Cancer Research Trust, 104 Harley Street, London W1N 1AF *Tel* 0171-935 0427 *Fax* 0171-935 5438
CC NO 272214   ESTABLISHED 1961

■ The Brecher & Co Charitable Trust

This trust did not respond to CAF's request to amend its entry and, by 30 June 1998, CAF's researchers did not find financial records for later than 1995 on its file at the Charity Commission. Trusts are legally required to submit annual accounts to the Charity Commission under section 42 of the Charities Act 1993

WHAT IS FUNDED Jewish charities, and other charitable purposes
WHAT IS NOT FUNDED Applications are not invited and are not considered for individuals
WHO CAN BENEFIT Registered charities benefiting Jewish needs. There are no restrictions on the age; professional and economic group; family situation; religion and culture; and social circumstances of; or disease or medical condition suffered by, the beneficiaries
WHERE FUNDING CAN BE GIVEN UK
TRUSTEES D J Brecher, H A Brecher
WHO TO APPLY TO H A Brecher, The Brecher & Co Charitable Trust, Brecher Abram Solicitors, Broadbent House, 64/65 Grosvenor Street, London W1X 9DB
CC NO 266462   ESTABLISHED 1973

■ Brent Irish Advisory Service

WHAT IS FUNDED To promote welfare and relieve poverty for those in need due to physical or social conditions. To provide recreational facilities. To advance education
WHO CAN BENEFIT To benefit Irish people in Britain who are at risk, those disadvantaged by poverty and socially isolated people. Children, young adults and students may benefit. There is no restriction on the disease or medical condition suffered by the beneficiaries
WHERE FUNDING CAN BE GIVEN London Borough of Brent
FINANCES *Year* 1997 *Income* £192,321
Grants £175,747
TRUSTEES M Dalton, T Donnellan, M Gallagher, J Glackin, D MacGraith, M MacNamara, C Moloney, J Smith
WHO TO APPLY TO J Glackin, Brent Irish Advisory Service, B I A S, Premier House, 313 Kilburn Lane, London W9 3ES
CC NO 1059801   ESTABLISHED 1996

■ The Brewcroft Trust

WHAT IS FUNDED Education, religion

WHO CAN BENEFIT Projects known to the Trustees benefiting children, young adults, older people and students

WHERE FUNDING CAN BE GIVEN UK and overseas

TYPE OF GRANT One-off, project and recurring costs

RANGE OF GRANTS Grants of £1,000 or less

FINANCES *Year* 1995 *Income* £13,159

TRUSTEES G A Rawlinson, C J Rawlinson, D D C Monro

HOW TO APPLY **This Trust states that it does not respond to unsolicited applications**

WHO TO APPLY TO G A Rawlinson, The Brewcroft Trust, 10 Deepdale, Wimbledon, London SW19 5EZ *Tel* 0181-946 4818

CC NO 1046971   **ESTABLISHED** 1995

■ The Brewers' Company General Charitable Trust

WHAT IS FUNDED General charitable purposes

WHO CAN BENEFIT There are no restrictions on the age; professional and economic group; family situation; religion and culture; and social circumstances of; or disease or medical condition suffered by; the beneficiaries

WHERE FUNDING CAN BE GIVEN UK

FINANCES *Year* 1997 *Income* £27,280 *Grants* £26,920

TRUSTEES The Brewers Company

WHO TO APPLY TO The Clerk to the Brewers' Company, The Brewers' Company General Charitable Trust, Brewers' Hall, Aldermanbury Square, London EC2V 7HR *Tel* 0171-606 1301

CC NO 1059811   **ESTABLISHED** 1996

■ The Bridge House Trust – Non-Ecclesiastical

WHAT IS FUNDED Organisations within the area of the Ancient Parish of Datchet. Particularly charities working in the fields of: information technology and computers; support to voluntary and community organisations; theatrical companies and theatre groups; primary schools; secondary schools; the purchase of books; clubs; community centres and village halls; parks and playgrounds

WHAT IS NOT FUNDED Applications from individuals or from organisations outside the Parish of Datchet

WHO CAN BENEFIT Inhabitants of the Parish of Datchet. Organisations benefiting children; young adults; and actors and entertainment professionals

WHERE FUNDING CAN BE GIVEN The Ancient Parish of Datchet

TYPE OF GRANT Capital project only. Funding can be given for up to one year

RANGE OF GRANTS £50–£6,000 (the highest grant to date)

SAMPLE GRANTS £6,000 to Datchet Hall Management Committee for provision of a new floor for the Hall; £5,000 to Churchmead School, Datchet for provision of computers; £2,000 to Datchet Parish Council for council development scheme; £1,998 to 1st Datchet Sea Scouts Group for provision of new kayaks (canoes); £1,500 to Datchet Women's Institute for provision of new chairs and tables

FINANCES *Year* 1997–98 *Income* £18,036 *Grants* £18,885

TRUSTEES A W Griffiths (Chairman), M J Fisher, D V Allen, J A Smith, G A S Symonds

NOTES Applications from outside the Parish of Datchet connot be entertained

HOW TO APPLY In writing to either the Chairman, A W Griffiths, at 127 Slough Road, Datchet, Berkshire SL3 9AE or the Clerk, W Middlemass, at the address below. No application forms. No sae required. Invoices for expenditure must be produced. Invoices usually required within six months of approval of application

WHO TO APPLY TO W Middlemass, Clerk, The Bridge House Trust – Non-Ecclesiastical, 16 Buccleuch Road, Datchet, Berkshire SL3 9BP *Tel* 01753 542035

CC NO 248190   **ESTABLISHED** 1966

■ The Bridge Trust

WHAT IS FUNDED Organisations working in the fields of music, hospices, ambulances and mobile units, and voluntary bodies will be considered. Church and historic buildings, schools and colleges, and community facilities and services and other charitable purposes may also be given funding.

WHAT IS NOT FUNDED No grants to individuals, other than referral through caring agency

WHO CAN BENEFIT Local organisations benefiting: at risk groups; disabled people; those disadvantaged by poverty; homeless people and victims of crime and abuse. There is no restriction on the age or family situation of the beneficiaries

WHERE FUNDING CAN BE GIVEN Barnstaple and immediate neighbourhood (five mile radius)

TYPE OF GRANT Buildings, capital, core costs, one-off, project, research, running costs, recurring costs and start-up costs will be considered. Funding may be given for up to one year

RANGE OF GRANTS Up to £15,000

FINANCES *Year* 1997 *Income* £153,859 *Grants* £125,409

TRUSTEES Comprise 16 local Trustees of which five are nominated by Barnstaple Town Council

WHO TO APPLY TO C J Bartlett, FCA, Clerk, The Bridge Trust, 7 Bridge Chambers, Barnstaple, Devon EX31 1HB *Tel* 01271 43995

CC NO 201288   **ESTABLISHED** 1961

■ The Dick Bridgeman TRA Foundation (formerly TRA Charitable Trust)

WHAT IS FUNDED Benefit of schools, colleges, universities and any other educational establishment. Benefit of any training establishment of any branch of the armed forces. Education/training of persons intending to teach at any educational establishment

WHAT IS NOT FUNDED No grants to individuals

WHO CAN BENEFIT Registered charities only benefiting: people of all ages; ex-service and service people; teachers and governesses and students

WHERE FUNDING CAN BE GIVEN UK

SAMPLE GRANTS £5,000 to Bridport and Dorset Sports Trust; £2,917 to Malvern College; £2,300 to Cheltenham College; £1,810 to Clifton College; £1,666 to Rugby School

FINANCES *Year* 1997 *Income* £16,786 *Grants* £14,323

TRUSTEES The Rt Hon Baron Aberdare, J R Greenwood, A N W Beeson, N W Smith

WHO TO APPLY TO N W Smith, The Dick Bridgeman TRA Foundation, Messrs Currey & Co, 21 Buckingham Gate, London SW1E 6LS

CC NO 313843   **ESTABLISHED** 1965

■ The Harold Bridges Foundation

WHAT IS FUNDED General charitable purposes, particularly the young, the elderly and supporting village activities

WHAT IS NOT FUNDED No grants to individuals

WHO CAN BENEFIT There are no restrictions on the age; professional and economic group; family situation; religion and culture; and social circumstances of; or disease or medical condition suffered by, the beneficiaries. However, particular favour is given to children young adults, the elderly and village activities

WHERE FUNDING CAN BE GIVEN Preference to the North West of England (as far south as Preston)

RANGE OF GRANTS £500–£5,000

SAMPLE GRANTS £5,000 to St Martin's College, Lancaster; £5,000 to The Airborne Forces Security Fund; £5,000 to Kirby Lonsdale Rugby Club; £2,000 to St John's Churchyard Fund, Tunstall; £2,000 to Cowan Bridge Youth Centre; £1,000 to The Army Benevolent Fund; £1,000 to Quermore Recreation Club; £1,000 to Lonsdale and District Scout Council; £1,000 to Vernon Carus Cricket Club, Penwortham; £1,000 to Kirby Lonsdale Brass Band

FINANCES *Year* 1997 *Income* £87,792 *Grants* £33,000

TRUSTEES The Royal Bank of Scotland plc, R N Hardy, J W Greenwood

NOTES The Trustees have a comprehensive list of charitable objects whom they benefit each year. Other applicants are secondary to these preferred charities

HOW TO APPLY In writing

WHO TO APPLY TO The Trust Manager, The Harold Bridges Foundation, Royal Bank of Scotland plc, Private Trust and Taxation, PO Box 356, 45 Moseley Street, Manchester M60 2BE

CC NO 236654   **ESTABLISHED** 1963

■ The Bridgewater Charitable Trust

WHAT IS FUNDED General charitable purposes

WHO CAN BENEFIT There are no restrictions on the age; professional and economic group; family situation; religion and culture; and social circumstances of; or disease or medical condition suffered by, the beneficiaries

WHERE FUNDING CAN BE GIVEN UK

WHO TO APPLY TO A Bridgewater, The Bridgewater Charitable Trust, Linquenda, 447 Unthank Road, Norwich, Norfolk NR4 7QN

CC NO 1068974   **ESTABLISHED** 1998

■ Briess Family Charitable Trust (formerly HJB Charitable Trust)

WHAT IS FUNDED General charitable purposes

WHO CAN BENEFIT There are no restrictions on the age; professional and economic group; family situation; religion and culture; and social circumstances of; or disease or medical condition suffered by, the beneficiaries

WHERE FUNDING CAN BE GIVEN UK

TYPE OF GRANT Usually recurrent operational expenses

RANGE OF GRANTS £50–£3,300

SAMPLE GRANTS £3,300 to JPA for Israel and Middle East; £2,480 to British ORT; £1,500 to World Jewish Relief; £1,100 to Jewish Care; £1,000 to JNF

FINANCES *Year* 1997–98 *Income* £20,594 *Grants* £17,802

TRUSTEES S A Rayner, P Briess

WHO TO APPLY TO S A Rayner, (Ref SAR/B00457), Briess Family Charitable Trust, Messrs Rayner de Wolfe, Solicitors, 31 Southampton Row, London WC1B 5HJ

CC NO 272721   **ESTABLISHED** 1976

■ The Briggs Animal Welfare Trust

WHAT IS FUNDED Animal welfare including Royal Society for the Prevention of Cruelty to Animals; Reystede Animal Sanctuary, Ringmer; Brooke Hospital for Animals, Cairo; Care of British Columbia House; and the Society for the Protection of Animals, North Africa

WHERE FUNDING CAN BE GIVEN UK and overseas

SAMPLE GRANTS £1,000 to RSPCA; £1,000 to Brooke Hospital for Animals, Cairo; £1,000 to Born Free Foundation; £1,000 to Cranmer Cat Sanctuary; £1,000 to North Clwyd Animal Rescue; £1,000 to Sebakwe Black Rhino; £1,000 to Thoroughbred Rehabilitation Centre; £1,000 to Bleakholt Sanctuary; £1,000 to CEWA Hammond Trust; £1,000 to Woodside Animal Welfare

FINANCES *Year* 1997 *Income* £31,818 *Grants* £31,000

WHO TO APPLY TO Mrs A J Hartnett, The Briggs Animal Welfare Trust, Belmoredean. Maplehurst Road, West Grinstead, West Sussex RH13 6RN

CC NO 276459   **ESTABLISHED** 1978

■ The Brighton District Nursing Association Trust

WHAT IS FUNDED Health, the relief of sickness, respite

WHO CAN BENEFIT Both individuals and organisations benefiting the sick and carer. There is no restriction on disease or medical condition suffered by the beneficiaries

WHERE FUNDING CAN BE GIVEN Brighton and Hove

TYPE OF GRANT One-off and funding for one year or less may be considered

FINANCES *Year* 1996 *Income* £65,000 *Grants* £57,000

HOW TO APPLY To the address under Who To Apply To in writing

WHO TO APPLY TO Anthony Druce, Secretary, The Brighton District Nursing Association Trust, c/o Fitzhugh Gates, 3 Pavilion Parade, Brighton BN2 1RY *Tel* 01273 686811

CC NO 213851   **ESTABLISHED** 1963

■ Bristol Initiative Trust

WHAT IS FUNDED Supports the Bristol Cultural Development Partnership whose role is to develop culture and encourage the general publics participation in cultural activities. Supports the Broadmead Initiative whose aim is to improve the City Centre

WHO CAN BENEFIT Organisations encouraging participation in cultural activities

WHERE FUNDING CAN BE GIVEN Bristol

SAMPLE GRANTS £18,141 to Cultural Development Partnership; £5,380 to Sports Action Group; £4,840 to Hartcliffe Leisure Ltd; £4,000 to Broadmead; £3,234 to Food vouchers for the needy

FINANCES *Year* 1995 *Income* £42,015 *Grants* £35,595

TRUSTEES A Hurley, B Rogerson (Bishop of Bristol), P Gregory, A Ewens

HOW TO APPLY To the address under Who To Apply To in writing
WHO TO APPLY TO Alec Ewens, Chairman, Bristol Initiative Trust, Leigh Court, Abbots Leigh, Bristol BS8 3RA *Tel* 0117-973 7373
CC NO 1015222 **ESTABLISHED** 1992

■ The Bristol Municipal Charities

WHAT IS FUNDED Education, relief of sickness, relief of need
WHO CAN BENEFIT Individuals and organisations benefiting children, young adults and students, at risk groups, those disadvantaged by poverty and socially isolated people. There is no restriction on the disease or medical condition suffered by the beneficiaries
WHERE FUNDING CAN BE GIVEN Within a ten mile radius of Bristol City centre
RANGE OF GRANTS £35–£10,000, average grant £200
SAMPLE GRANTS £50,072 to Total Group A; £42,738 to Bristol Guild of the Handicapped Trust; £20,417 to Richard Reynold's Charity; £11,982 to Bristol Dispensary; £10,640 to Rev Dr T White's Essex Estates; £4,895 to Clifton Dispensary; £4,471 to Rev Dr T White's Grays Inn Lane Trust; £4,551 to Old; £4,210 to Shirehampton Temperance Society; £3,120 to Bristol District Nursing Association
FINANCES *Year* 1997 *Income* £948,271 *Grants* £179,437
TRUSTEES Clive Halton (Chairman), James Ackland, Dinah Bernard, Mrs A Bryant, John Cottrell, Kenneth Crawford, Bernard Cripps, Richard Hill, Patrick Lucas, Jeffery Mason, Miss C Mercer, Prof Peter Robinson, Martin Sisman, Mrs V Stone, Vanessa Stevenson, C Sweet, Derek Tedder, Stephen Thomas, D Watts
HOW TO APPLY To the address under Who To Apply To in writing. Individuals need to complete an application form and have it sponsored by a responsible person
WHO TO APPLY TO R S Hawkins, Secretary General, The Bristol Municipal Charities, Orchard Street, Bristol BS1 5EQ *Tel* 0117-929 0084/0117-930 0303
CC NO 204665 **ESTABLISHED** 1960

■ Britannia Building Society Foundation

WHAT IS FUNDED Initiatives and projects that will make a difference to local communities. Priorities are: homelessness, including helping people to stay in their homes; educational achievement and aspirations; community safety, including crime prevention schemes; encouraging prudent money management, by improving financial literacy and money advice services. Infrastructure development is also considered
WHAT IS NOT FUNDED No grants to: individuals, including expeditions and overseas travel; hospitals; medical centres; medical treatment or medical research
WHO CAN BENEFIT Organisations benefiting: homeless people; and those in need of training, especially in financial matters
WHERE FUNDING CAN BE GIVEN Within 25 miles of Leek, in the counties of Staffordshire, Cheshire and Derbyshire
TYPE OF GRANT Any, but preferably special items, and not general contributions towards large appeals. Funding for core costs normally restricted to

maximum of three years. Buildings, capital, feasibility studies, one-off, project, research, recurring costs, running costs, salaries and start-up costs are all considered for funding
RANGE OF GRANTS £250–£25,000
FINANCES *Year* 1998 *Income* £225,000
TRUSTEES G Brown, J Bullock, C Connolly, E Filkin (Chairman), J Gifford, G Gregory, G H Stow
PUBLICATIONS Grants and Donations Policy leaflet
HOW TO APPLY Copy of Grants and Donations Policy and application form on request from the Secretary. We welcome initial telephone calls
WHO TO APPLY TO L Mullinger, Secretary, Britannia Building Society Foundation, Britannia House, Leek, Staffordshire ST13 5RG *Tel* 01538 391460 *Fax* 01538 399261
CC NO 1069081 **ESTABLISHED** 1998

■ British Council for Prevention of Blindness (known in appeals as See – Save Eyes Everywhere)

WHAT IS FUNDED Research into eye disease, sight restoration and prevention of blindness throughout the world. Grants are made to hospitals and research workers investigating the causes of blindness, and to those taking steps to cure blindness caused by malnutrition. Support is also given to the organisation of sight-restoration operations, eg for cataracts
WHAT IS NOT FUNDED BCPB does not make grant towards the welfare of blind individuals or for UK medical students to travel abroad
WHO CAN BENEFIT Organisations benefiting those suffering from sight loss, and medical professionals, research workers and scientists in the field
WHERE FUNDING CAN BE GIVEN UK and developing world
TYPE OF GRANT For scientific personnel, consumables and equipment
RANGE OF GRANTS £480–£22,466
SAMPLE GRANTS £22,466 to Western General Hospital and University of Edinburgh for research into novel approaches to glucocorticoid sensitivity in disorders relating to intra-ocular pressure; £17,185 to International Centre for Eye Health for trials testing chlorhexidine gel as a primary treatment for suppurative keratitis in Ghana; £15,220 to University of East Anglia for study into prevention of lens posterior capsule opacification; £15,104 to Institute of Opthalmology for research into identification and prevention of onchoceral blindness; £12,292 to London School of Hygiene and Tropical Medicine for studies into congenital anophtalmia and microphtalmia in England; and phenotypic and aetiologic heterogeneity – significance as a cause of blindness; £12,000 to University of Nottingham for invitro studies in blood group ABO matching in corneal transplantation; £11,754 to Bristol Eye Hospital for a prospective study of tissue typing and matching in corneal grafting; £6,076 to Queen's University, Belfast, for research into blood retinal barrier breakdown in diabetic retinopathy; £5,914 to International Centre for Eye Health for study into screening methods for angle closure glaucoma; £5,138 to University of Birmingham, Academic Unit of Opthalmology for research into visual acuity measurements in childhood visual disorders
FINANCES *Year* 1997 *Income* £275,396 *Grants* £121,406
PUBLICATIONS Annual Report
HOW TO APPLY Council meets in January, June and September. The closing date is about four weeks

before a meeting. Phone to confirm dates. All applications are considered on merit. Applications must be for detailed, costed projects on eye research or sight restoration and must be on a form obtainable from the Director
WHO TO APPLY TO Rachel Carr-Hill, Director, British Council for Prevention of Blindness, 12 Harcourt Street, London W1H 1DS
CC NO 270941   **ESTABLISHED** 1976

■ The British Diabetic Association

WHAT IS FUNDED To promote and fund research and experimental work into: (a) the causes and effects of diabetes, (b) the treatment and alleviation of the effects of diabetes to minimise the potential serious complications that can arise. To initiate and fund development work to progress successful research. To provide support, and an advisory service for all suffering from diabetes in the UK. To provide a framework within which: (a) communication and self-help between people with diabetes and those that help them is stimulated, (b) the views and ideas, at all levels, of those interested in research into education in and treatment of diabetes may be effectively exchanged. To mobilise the influence and interest of the general public in the achievement of these objectives
WHO CAN BENEFIT Individuals and organisations benefiting: people of all ages; academics; medical professionals; research workers and scientists. Beneficiaries suffering from diabetes, heart disease, kidney disease, paediatric diseases, sight loss and strokes. Prenatal care will also be considered
WHERE FUNDING CAN BE GIVEN UK
TYPE OF GRANT Project, equipment, small grants, fellowships, research grants and studentships will be considered
RANGE OF GRANTS £5,000–£40,000
FINANCES *Year* 1997 *Income* £13,165,000
Grants £4,635,000
TRUSTEES Dr M S Hall, Prof K G M M Alberti, T Guppy, M Higgins, Sir Michael W Hirst, Ms K Addington, Dr P Bell, Prof S Bloom, Dr S Bootle, Dr D Borsey, Dr F Burden, Mrs B Bury, Mrs P Card, Mrs D Cartwright, Mrs S Craddock, P Doherty, Mrs A Felton, B Finney, S Freel, Dr O Gibby, Lord Gladwin of Clee, Dr R Holland, T Hoy, Mrs M Hunter, Dr I Jefferson, Dr S Marshall, Dr D Matthews, Sir Humphrey Maud, Dr D Rothman, Prof D Shaw, A Webber, T Westwell
PUBLICATIONS Grants and Fellowships Booklet
HOW TO APPLY Telephone for a form
WHO TO APPLY TO Dr M Murphy, Research Director, British Diabetic Association, 10 Queen Anne Street, London W1M 0BD *Tel* 0171-323 1531
CC NO 215199   **ESTABLISHED** 1934

■ The British Dietetic Association General and Education Trust Fund

WHAT IS FUNDED (a) To encourage the development of the scientific knowledge base for the discipline of dietetics through funding of relevant research. (b) To support the profession's development of pre- and post-registration education structures and standards. (c) To fund an annual travel bursary for student and newly qualified dietitians
WHAT IS NOT FUNDED Direct support of postgraduate qualifications for individuals – ie the Trust will not pay postgraduate fees/expenses

WHO CAN BENEFIT (a) Individuals/research groups of state registered dietitians (and colleagues in related disciplines). (b) Professional bodies concerned with dietetics. There are few restrictions on the disease or medical condition suffered by the beneficiaries
WHERE FUNDING CAN BE GIVEN UK
TYPE OF GRANT Project, one-off, research, recurring costs, salaries, start-up costs, interest free loans and running costs. Funding can be given up to and over three years
SAMPLE GRANTS £15,812 to Professional Association – The British Dietetic Association for a project: Raising professional awareness of clinical effectiveness; £11,070 to State Registered Dietitians for research comparing efficiency of nasogastric feeding and parental nutrition during bone marrow transplantation; £3,850 to Professional Association - The British Dietetic Association for a project: Key characteristics pilot study; £3,428 to an individual State Registered Dietitian for research evaluating methods of assessing body composition of patients with cirrhosis; £1,000 to student dietitians as travel bursaries
FINANCES *Year* 1997–98 *Income* £80,380
Grants £72,992
TRUSTEES Mrs A M Dobson, SRD, MBA, Dame Barbara Clayton, DBE, Mrs Christine Rudd, SRD, W T Seddon, P Brindley, Miss Creina Murland, SRD
HOW TO APPLY Guidelines and an application form are sent to prospective applicants. All applications are acknowledged
WHO TO APPLY TO J C J Grigg, Secretary to the Trustees, The British Dietetic Association General and Education Trust Fund, 7th Floor, Elizabeth House, 22 Suffolk Street, Queensway, Birmingham B1 1LS *Tel* 0121-631 4551
Fax 0121-633 4399 *E-mail* bda@dial.pipex.com
CC NO 282553   **ESTABLISHED** 1981

■ British Fashion Council Princess of Wales Charitable Trust

WHAT IS FUNDED Scholarships
WHO CAN BENEFIT BA Fashion Design Gaduates
WHERE FUNDING CAN BE GIVEN UK
TRUSTEES A Harvey, B Godbold, J Wilson
HOW TO APPLY Direct or through college/university
WHO TO APPLY TO J R Wilson, Trustee, British Fashion Council Princess of Wales Charitable Trust, 5 Portland Place, London W1N 3AA *Tel* 0171-636 7788 *Fax* 0171-636 7515
CC NO 1064820   **ESTABLISHED** 1997

■ The British Friends of Chinuch Atzmai Trust

WHAT IS FUNDED Advancement of education of Jewish children in any part of the world (particularly in Israel) in accordance with Orthodox Jewish religion
WHO CAN BENEFIT To benefit Jewish children
WHERE FUNDING CAN BE GIVEN UK and overseas
FINANCES *Year* 1996 *Income* £74,762
TRUSTEES H Feldman, I Kraus
NOTES The income of the Trust is largely spent on travelling, meeting and reception expenses
WHO TO APPLY TO Louis Tiefenbrun, The British Friends of Chinuch Atzmai Trust, 23B Springfield, London E5 9EF
CC NO 313904   **ESTABLISHED** 1964

Think carefully about every application. Is it justified?

■ British Heart Foundation

WHAT IS FUNDED BHF funds medical research into all aspects of heart disease – causes, prevention, diagnosis and treatment. Grants are awarded to postgraduate researchers and chairs of cardiology. Funds are also spent on educating the public and medical profession, and on life-saving cardiac equipment. BHF also helps heart patients return to a full and active way of life through rehabilitation centres, nursing care and heart support groups

WHO CAN BENEFIT Organisations benefiting people of all ages; academics; medical professionals; students and those suffering from heart disease

WHERE FUNDING CAN BE GIVEN UK

FINANCES *Year* 1997–98 *Income* £56,000,000 *Grants* £48,000,000

TRUSTEES The Council

HOW TO APPLY Application forms and criteria are available for BHF for those seeking grants in line with the Charity's objects

WHO TO APPLY TO Medical Division, British Heart Foundation, 14 Fitzhardinge Street, London W1H 4DH *Tel* 0171-935 0185 *Fax* 0171-486 5820 *Web Site* www.bhf.org.uk

CC NO 225971   **ESTABLISHED** 1961

■ British Humane Association

WHAT IS FUNDED To operate Individual Grant Scheme for relief of personal and family distress with co-operation of: The Order of St John, Professional Classes Aid Council, Artists' General Benevolent Institution, Church Lads and Girls Brigade, Guild of Aid for Gentlepeople, St Luke's Hospital for Clergy

WHAT IS NOT FUNDED No grants to individuals

WHO CAN BENEFIT As recommended by charitable bodies under What is Funded. Organisations benefiting people of all ages; clergy; at risk groups; disabled people; those disadvantaged by poverty; and socially isolated people. There is no restriction on the disease or medical condition suffered by the beneficiaries

WHERE FUNDING CAN BE GIVEN UK

TYPE OF GRANT One-off, capital and recurring grants will be considered

RANGE OF GRANTS £1,000–£10,000

SAMPLE GRANTS £20,000 to Professional Classes Aid Council for income support for individuals; £20,000 to Medical Foundation for caring for victims of torture; £7,000 to Ophthalmic Hospital Jerusalem for sponsorship of a doctor; £5,000 to Friends of the Elderly for repairs to homes; £5,000 to Guild of Aid for Gentlepeople for support to individuals; £5,000 to St Lukes Hospital for Clergy for running costs; £5,000 Unleash for help for the homeless (Church Action); £5,000 to Craighead Centre for rehabilitation of criminals; £2,500 to Greater London Scout County for training for youth leaders; £2,500 to Church Lads and Church Girls Brigade for support to youth groups

FINANCES *Year* 1997 *Income* £119,631 *Grants* £82,000

TRUSTEES Board or Council of Management

HOW TO APPLY Through registered charities

WHO TO APPLY TO C A E Butler, FCA, British Humane Association, 24 Craddocks Avenue, Ashtead, Surrey KT21 1PB

CC NO 207120   **ESTABLISHED** 1922

■ British Institute of Archaeology at Ankara

WHAT IS FUNDED Research into archaeology and associated subjects of Turkey from Prehistoric until Islamic times. Grants made to undergraduates and graduates in archaeology wishing to specialise in archaeology and allied subjects of Anatolia, who are studying or travelling in Turkey. The Trust will consider funding: arts, culture and recreation; religious buildings; publishing and printing; professional bodies; charity or voluntary umbrella bodies; conservation; botany; natural history; heritage; postgraduate, tertiary and higher education; fellowships; academic subjects; science and research; and libraries and museums

WHAT IS NOT FUNDED No grants to non-British Commonwealth citizens

WHO CAN BENEFIT British Commonwealth students and academics of archaeology and associated fields. This includes academics, the retired and scientists

WHERE FUNDING CAN BE GIVEN UK and Turkey

TYPE OF GRANT Travel, research, capital, feasibility studies, one-off, project, recurring costs, salaries and start-up costs. All funding of up to and over three years

RANGE OF GRANTS Research grants £450–£25,000. Travel grants £250–£500

SAMPLE GRANTS £25,450 to University of Cambridge for Kilistepe research project; £16,000 to University of Cambridge for Gataluöyük research project; £14,000 to University of Warwick for Giftlik Rescue Excavation; £11,200 to an individual for Rerkenes Dağ research project; £10,635 to an individual for Tille excavations publication project; £7,950 to an individual for Project Paphlagonia; £7,000 to an individual for Amorium project; £5,080 to University of Newcastle for Anastasia Wall project; £4,446 to an individual for survey of mediaeval castles; £4,000 to an individual for Madra Gay project

FINANCES *Year* 1997 *Income* £360,000 *Grants* £151,000

TRUSTEES Council of Management

PUBLICATIONS *Anatolian Studies* and *Anatolian Archaeology*. Both annual publications

NOTES Guidelines available

HOW TO APPLY Initial telephone calls welcome. Application forms and guidelines are available on request

WHO TO APPLY TO The London Secretary, British Institute of Archaeology at Ankara, Senate House, Malet Street, London WC1E 7HU *Tel* 0171-862 8734 *Fax* 0171-862 8734

CC NO 313940   **ESTABLISHED** 1948

■ British Record Industry Trust

WHAT IS FUNDED The setting up initially, and now the running, of the London School of Performing Arts and Technology. To encourage young people in the exploration and pursuit of educational, cultural or therapeutic benefits emanating from music. Other charitable purposes

WHO CAN BENEFIT Individuals and organisations benefiting young people involved in the arts

WHERE FUNDING CAN BE GIVEN UK

RANGE OF GRANTS Below £500–£162,180

Does the trust you have chosen match your needs? Haphazard applications waste postage and time

81

SAMPLE GRANTS £162,180 to Nordoff Robbins; £70,619 to British School for the Performing Arts and Technology; £15,000 to Commission for Racial Equality; £5,000 to Terence Higgins Trust; £5,000 to Chicken Shed Theatre Company; £3,000 to Pimlico School; £1,100 to two individuals; £500 for miscellaneous needs

FINANCES *Year* 1995–96 *Income* £506,456 *Grants* £262,399

TRUSTEES S Alder, P Burger, J Craig, J Deacon, R Perry, J Preston

NOTES This Trust is actively seeking other causes to support

HOW TO APPLY To the address under Who To Apply To in writing

WHO TO APPLY TO Margaret Crowe, British Record Industry Trust, BPI, 25 Saville Row, London W1X 1AA

CC NO 1000413   **ESTABLISHED** 1989

■ British Schools and Universities Foundation (Inc)

WHAT IS FUNDED The Foundation applies the following criteria in selecting institutions and individuals: The applicant institution should have an appeal under way for clearly defined specific projects; acceptability of these projects should be demonstrated by the efforts and support of its alumni and friends in the United States. Student applicants should have excellent educational qualifications, proof of financial need, and a convincing reason for the choice of study offshore

WHAT IS NOT FUNDED No grants for commercial research, religious appeals and other projects outside the Foundation Charter, nor for short-term visits, eg conferences, electives, travel, etc

WHO CAN BENEFIT Schools, colleges, universities and other educational, scientific and literary institutions. Individual scholars. UK citizens to USA and vice versa. Students with financial needs

WHERE FUNDING CAN BE GIVEN United States of America and UK

TYPE OF GRANT One-off for specific projects

FINANCES *Year* 1995 *Income* £985,000 *Grants* £230,000

TRUSTEES The Board of Directors, Suite 1006, 575 Madison Avenue, New York, NY 10022–2511, USA

PUBLICATIONS Annual Report

HOW TO APPLY Apply for guidelines and application form to the address under Who To Apply To enclosing sae

WHO TO APPLY TO Mrs S Wiltshire, OBE, BSc, Hon UK Representative, BSUF, 6 Windmill Hill, Hampstead, London NW3 6RU

CC NO FED ID:13 **ESTABLISHED** 1961
6161189

■ British Sugar Foundation (formerly Bristar Foundation)

WHAT IS FUNDED General charitable purposes, but the main areas of interest are environment, education, healthcare and enterprise. These include: literacy; special needs education; nature reserves; libraries and museums; and community services

WHAT IS NOT FUNDED Generally not large national organisations. Applications from individuals, including students are not eligible. No overseas aid

WHO CAN BENEFIT Volunteer organisations only. There are no restrictions on the age; professional and economic group; family situation; religion and culture; and social circumstances of; or disease or medical condition suffered by, the beneficiaries

WHERE FUNDING CAN BE GIVEN Communities local to British Sugar sites only. Areas include Nottinghamshire, Worcestershire, Norfolk, Peterborough, Suffolk and York

TYPE OF GRANT Usually one-off for specific project

FINANCES *Year* 1997 *Income* £94,000 *Grants* £94,000

PUBLICATIONS Policy and Guidelines

NOTES Projects inspired by company employees and benefiting the communities in which company employees and their families live will receive special attention

HOW TO APPLY At any time

WHO TO APPLY TO The Secretary, British Sugar Foundation, Oundle Road, Peterborough, Cambridgeshire PE2 9QU *Tel* 01733 422902 *Fax* 01733 422487 *E-mail* amacdoug@britishsugar.co.uk

CC NO 290966   **ESTABLISHED** 1984

■ British Turned Parts Manufacturers' Charitable Company Limited

WHAT IS FUNDED The advancement of the education of the public in all aspects of the turned parts industry and the provision of education and training for persons associated with the industry

WHO CAN BENEFIT The general public and individuals associated with the turned parts industry

WHERE FUNDING CAN BE GIVEN UK

HOW TO APPLY To the address under Who To Apply To in writing

WHO TO APPLY TO Dr K T Lee, Secretary, British Turned Parts Manufacturers' Charitable Company Limited, 91 Erdington Road, Aldridge, Walsall WS9 0RN

CC NO 1064213   **ESTABLISHED** 1997

■ The Britland Charitable Trust

WHAT IS FUNDED For the benefit of those engaged in mission, and in particular to support Christian education and training

WHO CAN BENEFIT Individuals and institutions benefiting Christians and Evangelists

WHERE FUNDING CAN BE GIVEN UK and overseas

TYPE OF GRANT At the discretion of the Trustees

RANGE OF GRANTS £50–£85,000

SAMPLE GRANTS £85,000 to Philo Trust; £4,000 to St Marks Church, Battersea Rise; £1,000 to Care Trust; £750 to Nehemiah Project; £500 to Manna Counselling Service; £500 to Mark Perrot World's End Church; £500 to an individual; £375 to The Arbour; £250 to Heworth Parish Church; £90 to Broomwood Hall School Charity

FINANCES *Year* 1997 *Income* £93,822 *Grants* £93,215

TRUSTEES J M P Colman, S E Colman, R G O Bell

WHO TO APPLY TO J M P Colman, The Britland Charitable Trust, 20 Henderson Road, Wandsworth, London SW18 3RR

CC NO 1014956   **ESTABLISHED** 1992

■ The J and M Britton Charitable Trust

WHAT IS FUNDED General charitable purposes with preference given to organisations in the Bristol and Avon area

WHAT IS NOT FUNDED No grants to individuals

WHO CAN BENEFIT Registered charities. There are no restrictions on the age; professional and economic group; family situation; religion and culture; and social circumstances of; or disease or medical condition suffered by, the beneficiaries

WHERE FUNDING CAN BE GIVEN Bristol and Avon

TYPE OF GRANT One-off

RANGE OF GRANTS £200–£10,000

TRUSTEES R E J Bernays, R O Bernays, Lady M Merrison, J E D Wilcox, Mrs S Morgan (Secretary)

NOTES Decisions are subjective and made in the light of the Trustees opinion as to deserts

WHO TO APPLY TO R E J Bernays, The J and M Britton Charitable Trust, Old Down House, Tockington, Bristol BS12 4PG

CC NO 12175   **ESTABLISHED** 1961

■ The Brixton Estate Charitable Trust

WHAT IS FUNDED General charitable purposes. Priority is given to charities in the geographical areas in which the Company operates, and national charities

WHAT IS NOT FUNDED No grants to individuals. Local branches of national charities and charities whose main object is to support other charities are not supported

WHO CAN BENEFIT Registered charities. There are no restrictions on the age; professional and economic group; family situation; religion and culture; and social circumstances of; or disease or medical condition suffered by, the beneficiaries

WHERE FUNDING CAN BE GIVEN UK

FINANCES *Year* 1997 *Income* £60,246
Grants £51,800

TRUSTEES Sir R B Wilbraham, D F Gardner, D E Marlow, T J Nagle

WHO TO APPLY TO R H J Tanner, The Brixton Estate Charitable Trust, c/o 22–24 Ely Place, London EC1N 6TQ

CC NO 266348   **ESTABLISHED** 1963

■ Broadfield Trust (273)

This trust failed to supply a copy of its annual report and accounts to CAF as required under section 47(2) of the Charities Act 1993. The information held on file at the Charity Commission was insufficient to enable CAF's researchers to write a substantive commentary on the trust's activities. Accordingly, despite its size, we are unable to list this trust in Spotlight on Major Trusts

WHAT IS FUNDED General charitable purposes at the discretion of the Trustees

WHAT IS NOT FUNDED No grants to individuals

WHO CAN BENEFIT At the discretion of the Trustees. There are no restrictions on the age; professional and economic group; family situation; religion and culture; and social circumstances of; or disease or medical condition suffered by, the beneficiaries

WHERE FUNDING CAN BE GIVEN UK

TYPE OF GRANT At the discretion of the Trustees

FINANCES *Year* 1996–97 *Income* £246,268
Grants £686,400

TRUSTEES Hon Edward R Hamilton Wills, J R Henderson, Sir Ashley Ponsonby, P N Houldsworth Gibbs, C A Hamilton Wills, P J Hamilton Wills

WHO TO APPLY TO T Davies, Broadfield Trust, c/o Kidsons Impey, Elgar House, Holmer Road, Hereford HR4 9SF

CC NO 206623   **ESTABLISHED** 1961

■ The Charles and Edna Broadhurst Charitable Trust

WHAT IS FUNDED Grants are mainly given to social welfare, medical, academic research and Christian causes

WHAT IS NOT FUNDED No grants to individuals

WHO CAN BENEFIT Academics; research workers; Christians; at risk groups; those disadvantaged by poverty; and socially isolated people. There are no restrictions on the disease or medical condition suffered by the beneficiaries

WHERE FUNDING CAN BE GIVEN Southport

RANGE OF GRANTS £250–£6,000

SAMPLE GRANTS £6,000 to Wesley Southbank Road Methodist Church; £2,000 to Winged Fellowship; £2,000 to Birkdale School for Hearing Impaired Children; £2,000 to Light for Life; £2,000 to Ellerslie Court; £2,000 to KGV College; £1,250 to Southport Music Festival; £1,000 to Merseyside Drugs Council; £1,000 to Ainsdale Community Care; £1,000 to NSPCC

FINANCES *Year* 1997 *Income* £31,566
Grants £25,000

TRUSTEES H G Highton (Chairman), D H Hobley, Mrs J Carver, Mrs M P Smith, Mrs G Edmundson

HOW TO APPLY To the address under Who To Apply To in writing. Applications are considered twice a year, usually in June and November

WHO TO APPLY TO D H Hobley, The Charles and Edna Broadhurst Charitable Trust, 399 Lord Street, Southport PR9 0AS

CC NO 702543   **ESTABLISHED** 1988

■ The Broadley Charitable Trust

WHAT IS FUNDED Arts, health, education, all on personal recommendation

WHAT IS NOT FUNDED No grants to individuals

WHO CAN BENEFIT Registered charities benefiting: children and young adults; actors and entertainment professionals; musicians; students; textile workers and designers; writers and poets; and the sick. There is no restriction on the disease or medical condition suffered by the beneficiaries

WHERE FUNDING CAN BE GIVEN UK

TYPE OF GRANT Capital

RANGE OF GRANTS £300–£3,000

SAMPLE GRANTS £3,000 to Lant Trust; £2,025 to Victoria and Albert Museum; £2,000 to St Giles Church; £2,000 to HAC Biographical Dictionary; £750 to Radio Lollipop

FINANCES *Year* 1997 *Income* £22,880
Grants £11,075

TRUSTEES R B Tiley, P G K Hudson

NOTES Mail shots usually fail

HOW TO APPLY No guidelines issued. Applications are not acknowledged in the interests of economy and Annual Accounts are normally requested

WHO TO APPLY TO R B Tiley, The Broadley Charitable Trust, 43 Victoria Road, London W8 5RH

CC NO 291352   **ESTABLISHED** 1985

■ The Broadway Cottages Trust

WHAT IS FUNDED Health and welfare. The provision of financial assistance to persons, hospitals and charitable institutions. The provision of housing at rents within people's means

WHO CAN BENEFIT Organisations benefiting at risk groups, those disadvantaged by poverty and socially isolated people. There is no restriction on the disease or medical condition suffered by the beneficiaries

WHERE FUNDING CAN BE GIVEN UK, with a preference for Kettering

RANGE OF GRANTS £100–£1,000

SAMPLE GRANTS £1,000 to Northamptonshire Grammar School; £850 to Kettering and District Society for Mentally Handicapped Children; £850 to Macmillan Nurses Appeal; £850 to Northampton and County Association for the Blind; £800 to Community Patients' Welfare Fund; £700 to Winged Fellowship Trust; £600 to Barnardo's; £600 to Kingston Trust; £600 to NSPCC; £600 to Northamptonshire Samaritans

FINANCES *Year* 1996 *Income* £39,994
Grants £28,744

TRUSTEES P J Wilson, Mrs C Upton, A P S Everard, N J Drake-Lee, D E M Kearley

HOW TO APPLY To the address under Who To Apply To in writing

WHO TO APPLY TO P J Wilson, Trustee, The Broadway Cottages Trust, Wilson Browne, 41 Meadow Road, Kettering, Northamptonshire NN16 8TN

CC NO 203763   **ESTABLISHED** 1965

■ The Bromley Trust

WHAT IS FUNDED (a) Combat violations of human rights; and help victims of torture, refugees from oppression and those who have been falsely imprisoned. (b) Help those who have suffered severe bodily or mental hurt through no fault of their own, and if need be help their dependants: try in some small way to offset man's inhumanity to man. (c) Oppose the extinction of the world's fauna and flora and the destruction of the environment for wildlife and for mankind worldwide. By far the greatest part of our income goes to those charities that are concerned with human rights, a comparitively small prportion being paid to charities concerned with the preservation of the world environment

WHAT IS NOT FUNDED Non-registered charities and individuals. (And anything outside our stated objectives)

WHO CAN BENEFIT National schemes and organisations, and international organisations benefiting immigrants, refugees and torture victims

WHERE FUNDING CAN BE GIVEN UK and overseas

TYPE OF GRANT Mainly recurrent: one-off grants are ocasionally made, but these are rare. It is our declared policy to give larger amounts to fewer charities rather than to spread our income over a large number of small grants. Buildings, capital, project, research, running costs, salaries and start-up costs will be considered. Funding can be given for any length of time

RANGE OF GRANTS £250–£10,000

SAMPLE GRANTS £9,800 to Medical Foundation for the Care of Victims of Torture; £8,600 to Population Concern; £8,500 to Anti-Slavery International; £8,000 to Amnesty International (UK Section); £8,000 to Worldwide Land Conservation Trust; £7,400 to Prisoners of Conscience; £7,400 to Survival International; £7,400 to Manic Depression Fellowship; £7,000 to Ockenden Venture; £5,900 to Greenpeace Environmental Trust

FINANCES *Year* 1997–98 *Income* £168,624
Grants £163,050

TRUSTEES Keith Bromley, Anna Home OBE, Alan P Humphries, Lady Ann Wood, Lady Anne Prance, Peter Winfield

NOTES The Trustees meet twice a year, usually in April and October. Urgent appeals may be dealt with at any time

HOW TO APPLY To the address under Who To Apply To in writing. Single general information sheet sent on request

WHO TO APPLY TO Keith Bromley, The Bromley Trust, Ashley Manor, King's Somborne, Stockbridge, Hampshire SO20 6RQ *Tel* 01794 388241 *Fax* 01794 388264

CC NO 801875   **ESTABLISHED** 1989

■ The F V and E Brook Charitable Trust

WHAT IS FUNDED General charitable purposes

WHO CAN BENEFIT There are no restrictions on the age; professional and economic group; family situation; religion and culture; and social circumstances of; or disease or medical condition suffered by, the beneficiaries

WHERE FUNDING CAN BE GIVEN UK and overseas

TRUSTEES Mrs H N Mills, Mrs C F Savage, S C Mills, R J Mills

WHO TO APPLY TO Mrs C F Savage, Chairperson, The F V and E Brook Charitable Trust, 31 Norwood Park, Birkby, Huddersfield HD2 2DU

CC NO 1068335   **ESTABLISHED** 1997

■ William Brooke Benevolent Fund

WHAT IS FUNDED Local charities working in the fields of: the relief of poverty; welfare; the advancement of the Christian religion; arts, culture and recreation; and education and training

WHAT IS NOT FUNDED No grants to national charities or students

WHO CAN BENEFIT Individuals and local organisations benefiting: people of all ages; retired people; Christians; disabled people; those disadvantaged by poverty; and textile workers and designers who are ex-employees of John Brooke and Sons Ltd

WHERE FUNDING CAN BE GIVEN Local (Huddersfield area)

TYPE OF GRANT Core costs, one-off, running costs, salaries and start-up costs. Funding of up to two years will be considered

RANGE OF GRANTS £50–£4,000; typical grant £250

84

Think carefully about every application. Is it justified?

SAMPLE GRANTS £14,200 to Bridgewood Trust for people with learning difficulties; £5,000 to Armitage Bridge Church for bells appeal and 150th Anniversary; £5,000 to Huddersfield Hospice, Kirkwood; £3,000 to Cephas Project, Dalton for welfare through joint churches; £500 to All Saints Church, Keighley for reordering; £500 to Alliance Asian Christians for general Christian education; £500 to Yorkshire Wildlife Trust; £500 to Netherton Junior Football Club; £250 to Longley Baptist Church for reordering; £250 to Armitage Bridge Cricket Club for returfing

FINANCES *Year* 1996–97 *Income* £65,228 *Grants* £30,000

TRUSTEES E L M Brooke, M R H Brooke

NOTES The Charity runs The William Brooke Academy for Arts Education

HOW TO APPLY In writing with an sae. Trustees meet in November

WHO TO APPLY TO M R H Brooke, William Brooke Benevolent Fund, Armitage Bridge Mills, Huddersfield, HD4 7NR *Tel* 01484 661281

CC NO 209138   **ESTABLISHED** 1912

■ The Charles Brotherton Trust

WHAT IS FUNDED Advancement of education including the establishment and maintenance of scholarships and the recreational training and education of young persons – furtherance of medical and surgical research – support of medical or surgical charities. Charities working in the fields of: housing and accommodation; arts; culture and recreation; conservation and environment; and community facilities and services will be considered. Support may also go to community development, volunteers and voluntary organisations, churches and religious ancillary buildings

WHAT IS NOT FUNDED No grants to individuals – only to registered charities and recognised bodies

WHO CAN BENEFIT Organisations benefiting: chemists; ex-service and service people; research workers; scientists; students; volunteers; carers and disabled people. There may be a few restrictions on the disease or medical condition of the beneficiaries

WHERE FUNDING CAN BE GIVEN Birmingham, Liverpool, Wakefield, York, Leeds, Borough of Bebington (Cheshire)

TYPE OF GRANT Buildings, capital, core costs, one-off and research will be considered. Funding may be given for up to three years

RANGE OF GRANTS £100–£350

FINANCES *Year* 1996 *Income* £88,000 *Grants* £80,000

TRUSTEES D R Brotherton (Custodian), S B Turner, C M Brotherton-Ratcliffe, J S Riches, Management: D R Brotherton, Mrs A Henson, Mrs P L M H Seeley, C M Brotherton-Ratcliffe, S B Turner

HOW TO APPLY Applicants annual accounts required. Applications not acknowledged. Distribution made annually in June for successful applications received by 31 January. Applications for student grants and scholarships should be made to the Bursar at the Universities of Leeds and Liverpool, the Registrar at York University and the Students Welfare Adviser at Birmingham University

WHO TO APPLY TO C Brotherton-Ratcliffe, Secretary, The Charles Brotherton Trust, PO Box 374, Harrogate, North Yorkshire HG1 4YW

CC NO 227067   **ESTABLISHED** 1940

■ Joseph Brough Charitable Trust

WHAT IS FUNDED There is a regular donation of £24,000 to the Brough Benevolent Association which helps individuals in need. Other grants are for a wide range of charitable purposes in the area Where Funding Can Be Given. Grants are usually between £500–£1,000 and usually for a specific purpose where a contribution of up to £1,000 will make a difference. Contributions to appeals are only considered when a project is within £10,000 of its target. Most grants are small contributions where the total costs are less than £5,000. There is a specific interest in Methodist appeals

WHAT IS NOT FUNDED Applications outside the area Where Funding Can Be Given. National appeals and major appeals are unlikely to be successful. No grants to individuals

WHO CAN BENEFIT Voluntary organisations with a special interest in Methodist appeals that benefit the wider community

WHERE FUNDING CAN BE GIVEN The historic counties of Northumberland and Durham

TYPE OF GRANT Buildings, capital, one-off, project, running costs and start-up costs. Funding is available for up to one year

RANGE OF GRANTS £500–£1,000

SAMPLE GRANTS £1,000 to Teeside Lions Wheelchair Basketball Club for running costs; £584 to South Tyneside Multi Cultural Project for equipment for English lessons; £560 to Asian Women's Sewing Group for creche costs

FINANCES *Year* 1997 *Income* £35,406 *Grants* £39,574

TRUSTEES Tyne & Wear Foundation

HOW TO APPLY Telephone enquiries are welcomed. Applicants should send a letter outlining their request for support and provide supporting financial information

WHO TO APPLY TO Maureen Fligh, Joseph Brough Charitable Trust, Tyne & Wear Foundation, 9th Floor, Cale Cross House, 156 Pilgrim Street, Newcastle upon Tyne NE1 6SU *Tel* 0191-222 0945 *Fax* 0191-230 0689 *E-mail* TWF@onyxnet.co.uk

CC NO 227332   **ESTABLISHED** 1940

■ Miss Marion Broughton's Charitable Trust

WHAT IS FUNDED Grants are made to charities and organisations which are dedicated to helping elderly and disabled people and also children

WHAT IS NOT FUNDED No grants to individuals

WHO CAN BENEFIT Organisations benefiting children, older people and disabled people

WHERE FUNDING CAN BE GIVEN Scotland, especially Lothian

FINANCES *Year* 1996 *Income* £40,000 *Grants* £30,000

TRUSTEES E J Cuthbertson, A M C Dalgleish

PUBLICATIONS Accounts are available from the Trust

HOW TO APPLY Applications should be made in writing to the address below

WHO TO APPLY TO E J Cuthbertson, Miss Marion Broughton's Charitable Trust, Messrs Brodies, Solicitors, 15 Atholl Crescent, Edinburgh EH3 8HA

SC NO SCO 09781   **ESTABLISHED** 1975

■ Mrs E E Brown Charitable Settlement

WHAT IS FUNDED General charitable purposes

WHAT IS NOT FUNDED No individuals

WHO CAN BENEFIT Registered charities. There are no restrictions on the age; professional and economic group; family situation; religion and culture; and social circumstances of; or disease or medical condition suffered by, the beneficiaries

WHERE FUNDING CAN BE GIVEN UK, Israel

TYPE OF GRANT Recurring and one-off

RANGE OF GRANTS £10–£5,000; typical £500

SAMPLE GRANTS £5,000 to LFCYP Woodrow High House; £1,000 to Friends of Earth; £1,000 to Georges Jewish Settlement; £1,000 to St Johns Opthal Hospital; £1,000 to Anna Scher Theatre; £1,000 to Musicians Fund; £1,000 to Ben Uri Art Society

FINANCES *Year* 1997 *Income* £25,733 *Grants* £17,840

TRUSTEES Mrs E E Brown, M D Brown, Sir Simon Brown

NOTES The Trustees are not considering any new application at present

HOW TO APPLY Written application for Trustees consideration periodically

WHO TO APPLY TO J Rowan, Mrs E E Brown Charitable Settlement, Barber Harrison & Platt, Accountants, 2 Rutland Park, Sheffield S10 2PD *Tel* 0114-266 7171 *Fax* 0114-266 9846 *E-mail* info@bhp.co.uk

CC NO 261397   **ESTABLISHED** 1970

■ The Brown Family Charitable Trust

WHAT IS FUNDED General charitable purposes

WHO CAN BENEFIT There are no restrictions on the age; professional and economic group; family situation; religion and culture; and social circumstances of; or disease or medical condition suffered by, the beneficiaries

WHERE FUNDING CAN BE GIVEN In practice, the City of York and county of North Yorkshire

TRUSTEES F H Brown, J D Brown, D Brown, K I Brown, D H Brown

WHO TO APPLY TO F H Brown, The Brown Family Charitable Trust, The Old Cottage, Askham Bryan, York YO2 3QS

CC NO 1064657   **ESTABLISHED** 1997

■ R S Brownless Charitable Trust

WHAT IS FUNDED At Trustees' discretion, especially disabled, disadvantaged and seriously ill. Charities working in the fields of: accommodation and housing; job creation; voluntary work; Christian education; community arts and recreation will be considered. Support will go to health and community services

WHAT IS NOT FUNDED No grants for scholarships or expeditions and rarely for conservation or education

WHO CAN BENEFIT At the discretion of the Trustees. However, children and young adults, Christians and disabled people will be considered. There is no restriction on the disease or medical condition suffered by, but some restriction on the social circumstances of the beneficiaries who will be supported

WHERE FUNDING CAN BE GIVEN UK, rarely overseas

TYPE OF GRANT Usually one-off, sometimes annually. Buildings, capital, core costs, project, research

and start-up costs are considered. Funding may be given for up to three years

RANGE OF GRANTS Up to £2,000, usually £100–£500

FINANCES *Year* 1997–98 *Income* £45,000 *Grants* £50,000

TRUSTEES Mrs J E Barrett, Mrs P M Nicolai, Mrs F A Plummer

HOW TO APPLY In writing to the Trustees. No application form

WHO TO APPLY TO Mrs P Nicolai, R S Brownless Charitable Trust, Hennerton Holt, Wargrave, Reading, Berkshire RG10 8PD

CC NO 1000320   **ESTABLISHED** 1990

■ The J H K Brunner Charitable Settlement

WHAT IS FUNDED General charitable purposes

WHO CAN BENEFIT There are no restrictions on the age; professional and economic group; family situation; religion and culture; and social circumstances of; or disease or medical condition suffered by, the beneficiaries

WHERE FUNDING CAN BE GIVEN UK

WHO TO APPLY TO T Thornton Jones, The J H K Brunner Charitable Settlement, 190 Strand, London WC2R 1JN

CC NO 268085   **ESTABLISHED** 1973

■ T B H Brunner's Charitable Trust

WHAT IS FUNDED Arts, education and other charitable purposes

WHO CAN BENEFIT To benefit children; young adults; actors and entertainment professionals; musicians; textile workers and designers; and writers and poets

WHERE FUNDING CAN BE GIVEN UK

RANGE OF GRANTS £25–£2,500

SAMPLE GRANTS £2,500 to the Institute for Economic Affairs; £1,500 to Rotherfield Grey PCC; £1,000 to the Kensington Society; £1,000 to the Minority Rights Group; £1,000 to Portobello Trust; £1,000 to the Royal Opera House Trust; £1,000 to the Westminster Pastoral Foundation; £1,000 to York Early Music Festival; £1,000 to York Minster Fund; £750 to Live Music Now

FINANCES *Year* 1995 *Income* £28,235 *Grants* £23,823

TRUSTEES T B H Brunner, Helen U Brunner

WHO TO APPLY TO T B H Brunner, T B H Brunner's Charitable Trust, Flat 4, 2 Inverness Gardens, London W8 4RN

CC NO 260604   **ESTABLISHED** 1969

■ Sir Felix Brunner's Sons' Charitable Trust

WHAT IS FUNDED General charitable purposes, particularly educational institutions and churches

WHO CAN BENEFIT Organisations benefiting children, young adults, students and Christians

WHERE FUNDING CAN BE GIVEN UK

RANGE OF GRANTS £500–£10,000

SAMPLE GRANTS £10,000 to The National Trust; £10,000 to Rugby School Development Campaign; £5,000 to Mental Health Research; £5,000 to St Edward's School; £5,000 to the Open Spaces Society; £5,000 to Friends of St Mary's, Bampton; £2,500 to Greys PCC; £2,000 to the Institute of Economic Affairs; £2,000 to the Cothill House Bursary; £2,000 to St Giles Church, Oxford

FINANCES *Year* 1995 *Income* £61,522 *Grants* £56,500

TRUSTEES J H K Brunner, T B H Brunner, H L J Brunner

WHO TO APPLY TO T B H Brunner, Sir Felix Brunner's Sons' Charitable Trust, Flat 4, 2 Inverness Gardens, Kensington, London W8 4RN

CC NO 260602 **ESTABLISHED** 1969

■ The Brunswick Trust

WHAT IS FUNDED General charitable purposes

WHO CAN BENEFIT There are no restrictions on the age; professional and economic group; family situation; religion and culture; and social circumstances of; or disease or medical condition suffered by, the beneficiaries

WHERE FUNDING CAN BE GIVEN UK

FINANCES *Year* 1996 *Income* £13,722

TRUSTEES Ms A Gibson, The Dickinson Trust Limited

WHO TO APPLY TO R E Webb, The Brunswick Trust, Pollen House, 10–12 Cork Street, London W1X 1PD

CC NO 1046416 **ESTABLISHED** 1995

■ The Jack Brunton Charitable Trust

WHAT IS FUNDED General charitable purposes. All applications are considered

WHAT IS NOT FUNDED Individuals are only considered in exceptional circumstances

WHO CAN BENEFIT Registered charities and individuals. There are no restrictions on the age; professional and economic group; family situation; religion and culture; and social circumstances of; or disease or medical condition suffered by, the beneficiaries

WHERE FUNDING CAN BE GIVEN Old North Riding area of Yorkshire only

TYPE OF GRANT One-off

FINANCES *Year* 1996–97 *Income* £133,145 *Grants* £143,500

TRUSTEES Lady Diana Brittan, Mrs A J Brunton, J G Brunton, B E M Jones, E Marquis, D W Noble, P Reed

HOW TO APPLY In writing giving full details including costings if appropriate

WHO TO APPLY TO D A Swallow, FCA, Administrator, The Jack Brunton Charitable Trust, 10 Bridge Road, Stokesley, North Yorkshire TS9 5AA *Tel* 01642 711407

CC NO 518407 **ESTABLISHED** 1986

■ Brushmill Ltd

WHAT IS FUNDED Jewish charitable purposes

WHO CAN BENEFIT Organisations benefiting Jewish people

WHERE FUNDING CAN BE GIVEN UK

FINANCES *Year* 1996 *Income* £133,561 *Grants* £217,276

TRUSTEES J Weinberger, Y Getter, Mrs E Weinberger

WHO TO APPLY TO C Getter, Brushmill Ltd, Fairholt Road, London NW6 5HN

CC NO 285420 **ESTABLISHED** 1981

■ The Bryant Trust

WHAT IS FUNDED General charitable purposes. A large proportion of the Trust's income is committed to organisations in which the Trustees have a special interest. Charities working in the fields of community arts and recreation, cultural activity, hostels, voluntary and community organisations, respite care, self help groups, heritage, education, campaigning, advice centres and various community services and facilities will be considered

WHAT IS NOT FUNDED No grants to non-registered charities, animal welfare or individuals. National charities based outside of Birmingham are rarely funded

WHO CAN BENEFIT At the discretion of the Trustees. There is no restriction on the age of the beneficiaries; carers, disabled people, those disadvantaged by poverty, the homeless and victims of crime will be considered

WHERE FUNDING CAN BE GIVEN Roughly the Birmingham conurbation within about ten mile radius off the City Centre, but only east of the M6 (to include Solihull and Sutton Coldfield)

TYPE OF GRANT Capital projects are preferred to core funding. Buildings, one-off, project, research, salaries, start-up costs will be considered. Funding is available for up to three years

RANGE OF GRANTS About 20 per cent of grants are part of a Small Grants Scheme where a typical grant is £200–£500

SAMPLE GRANTS £17,000 to Emmaus UK for expansion of self help community of disabled; £13,000 to Birmingham Settlement for a variety of social work in inner city; £13,000 to YMCA for specific property improvements; £10,000 to Rehabilitation for Addicted Prisoners Trust to fund counselling training; £7,000 to Birmingham Settlement for specific property improvements; £7,000 to YMCA for specific property improvements; £5,000 to Midlands Arts Centre for specific arts projects; £5,000 to Rehabilitation for Addicted Prisoners Trust for specific arts projects; £5,000 to Relate for general funds; £5,000 to Trinity Centre for specific project at Home for Homeless

FINANCES *Year* 1997–98 *Income* £132,000 *Grants* £129,300

TRUSTEES J R Clemishaw, T J Cole, V K Houghton, D M Newton, J R L Smith, M C G Smith, A R Thomas

HOW TO APPLY To the address under Who To Apply To in writing with a copy of the accounts and, where applicable, budget. Only two meetings are held each year. Appeals should be received either by mid March or mid October

WHO TO APPLY TO J R Clemishaw, The Bryant Trust, PO Box 1624, Shirley, Solihull, West Midlands B90 4QZ

CC NO 501450 **ESTABLISHED** 1972

■ Buccleuch Place Trust

WHAT IS FUNDED Financial assistance to charitable organisations of Edinburgh (Lothian). All organisations must be recognised as charitable by the Inland Revenue

WHAT IS NOT FUNDED No applications outside Edinburgh (Lothian) will be considered or acknowledged, whatever their worth

WHO CAN BENEFIT Local organisations. There are no restrictions on the age; professional and economic group; family situation; religion and culture; and social circumstances of; or disease or medical condition suffered by, the beneficiaries

WHERE FUNDING CAN BE GIVEN Edinburgh (Lothian) exclusively

TYPE OF GRANT One-off

TRUSTEES Bishop R Holloway (Chairman), R Graeme Thom, M J Malcolm

PUBLICATIONS Incorporated in Annual Report of the Edinburgh Voluntary Organisations Council

HOW TO APPLY Applications for large grants (over £200) are considered quarterly. Forms are available from the Trust Fund Administrator. Applications for small grants (under £200) must be made, on form available, through social workers, health visitors, etc who work in welfare agencies, either local authorities or voluntary bodies

WHO TO APPLY TO The Trust Fund Administrator, Buccleuch Place Trust, Council of Social Services, Anslie House, 11 St Colme Street Edinburgh EH3 6AG

SC NO SCO 04029   **ESTABLISHED** 1950

■ Buckingham Trust

WHAT IS FUNDED Advancement of religion (including missionary activities) – relief of the poor, sick and aged

WHO CAN BENEFIT Organisations bnefiting the elderly, those disadvantaged by poverty, medical professionals and missionaries. There is no restriction on the disease or medical condition suffered by the beneficiaries

WHERE FUNDING CAN BE GIVEN UK

FINANCES *Year* 1996 *Income* £149,967 *Grants* £114,090

TRUSTEES D J Hanes, D H Benson, R W D Foot, P R Edwards

NOTES Preference is given to charities of which the Trustees have personal interest, knowledge, or association. The Trust acts mainly as an agency charity and in 1996 acted on behalf of 54 donors

WHO TO APPLY TO Buckingham Trust, Messrs Foot Davson & Co, 17 Church Road, Tunbridge Wells, Kent TN1 1LG

CC NO 237350   **ESTABLISHED** 1962

■ Buckinghamshire Historic Churches Trust

WHAT IS FUNDED The preservation, repair, maintenance, upkeep, and reconstruction of churches or chapels in Buckinghamshire. Grants are made to churches and chapels embarking upon restoration

WHAT IS NOT FUNDED Churches and chapels not in use for public worship

WHO CAN BENEFIT Parochial Church Councils or Trustees of Christian churches and chapels, including Baptist, Anglican, Methodist and Catholic

WHERE FUNDING CAN BE GIVEN Buckinghamshire only

FINANCES *Year* 1997 *Income* £44,633 *Grants* £42,500

TRUSTEES The Lord Lieutenant of Buckinghamshire (President), The Suffragan Bishop of Buckingham (Vice-President) and up to 20 other Trustees appointed by the Lord Lieutenant

PUBLICATIONS Newsletter

WHO TO APPLY TO B F Davis, Buckinghamshire Historic Churches Trust, Chiltern House, Oxford Road, Aylesbury, Buckinghamshire HP19 3EQ

CC NO 206471   **ESTABLISHED** 1957

■ Buckinghamshire Masonic Centenary Fund

WHAT IS FUNDED General charitable purposes, in particular health, education, community services and community centres and village halls

WHAT IS NOT FUNDED No grants to individuals, for expeditions or youth work overseas

WHO CAN BENEFIT Registered charities and institutions particularly those benefiting: children and young adults; medical professionals; research workers; disabled people and victims of crime and abuse. There is no restriction on the disease or medical condition suffered by the beneficiaries

WHERE FUNDING CAN BE GIVEN Mainly Buckinghamshire (Milton Keynes, Slough, Windsor and Maidenhead considered)

TYPE OF GRANT One-off

RANGE OF GRANTS £1,000–£5,000

SAMPLE GRANTS £5,000 to Pheonix Lodge Hospice, Milton Keynes for start-up work; £5,000 to Cancer Care, Stoke Mandeville for work in this part of the hospital; £2,000 to Stokenchurch Transport for community transport; £2,000 to Victim Support, Aylesbury for aid to crime victims; £2,000 to Victim Support, Amersham for aid to crime victims; £2,000 to Cot Death Society for alarm monitors; £1,700 to High Wycombe Women's Aid for charitable work; £1,500 to Slough Branch Parkinson's Disease Society; £1,436 to Keats Ward, Tindal Hospital, Aylesbury for refurbishment; £1,000 to Marie Curie Cancer Care for Aylesbury areas patient work

FINANCES *Year* 1997 *Income* £36,000 *Grants* £35,000

TRUSTEES Dr R G Fender, D G Varney, Rt Hon Lord Burnham, Dr E W Hall

NOTES Small resources, numerous applicants

HOW TO APPLY In writing. Set out aims and objectives on one page of A4. Audited accounts if available

WHO TO APPLY TO A R Chalk, Buckinghamshire Masonic Centenary Fund, 48a Townside, Haddenham, Aylesbury, Buckinghamshire HP17 8BQ *Tel* 01844 292263

CC NO 1007193   **ESTABLISHED** 1991

■ The Buckle Family Charitable Trust

WHAT IS FUNDED General charitable purposes

WHO CAN BENEFIT There are no restrictions on the age; professional and economic group; family situation; religion and culture; and social circumstances of; or disease or medical condition suffered by, the beneficiaries

WHERE FUNDING CAN BE GIVEN UK with preference for Suffolk

RANGE OF GRANTS £50–£27,967, average grant of £1,000

SAMPLE GRANTS £27,967 to Charing Cross and Westminster Medical School; £10,000 to an individual; £3,000 to Suffolk Parish Churches (£500 each to Chesworth, Whatfield, Elmsett, Bidleston, Naughton and Semer); £1,000 to Nedging Parish Church, Suffolk; £1,000 to Hadleigh High School, Suffolk; £300 to Aldham Parish Church, Suffolk; £250 to Riding for the Disabled, Hadleigh Group; £250 to People's Trust for Endangered Species, Mammals; £250 to Trevor Jones Tetraplegic Trust; £250 to RDA
FINANCES *Year* 1994–95 *Income* £40,000 *Grants* £45,804
TRUSTEES B K D Buckle, G M L Buckle, J K Buckle, J L Buckle, G W N Stewart
WHO TO APPLY TO G W N Stewart, Secretary and Solicitor, The Buckle Family Charitable Trust, 9 Trinity Street, Colchester CO1 1JN
CC NO 1001962 **ESTABLISHED** 1991

■ The Rosemary Bugden Charitable Trust

WHAT IS FUNDED To promote and support the performing arts in the UK
WHO CAN BENEFIT Individuals and organisations involved with the performing arts
WHERE FUNDING CAN BE GIVEN UK
RANGE OF GRANTS £30–£4,112
SAMPLE GRANTS £4,112 to two individuals for college fees; £3,500 to Great Elm Festival for prize money; £3,253 to an individual for college fees; £2,516 to an individual; £2,129 to an individual for college fees; £2,005 to an individual for college fees; £1,463 to an individual for college fees; £1,456 to Patchway CE Primary School; £1,429 to an individual for college fees; £1,371 to an individual for school fees
FINANCES *Year* 1997 *Income* £48,700 *Grants* £38,781
TRUSTEES Mrs E Frimston, J W Sharpe, D H Drew
HOW TO APPLY Write to J W Sharpe at address under Who To Apply To
WHO TO APPLY TO J W Sharpe, The Rosemary Bugden Charitable Trust, Osborne Clarke, 50 Queen Charlotte Street, Bristol BS1 4HE
CC NO 327626 **ESTABLISHED** 1987

■ Henry Robert Bull Charitable Trust

WHAT IS FUNDED Grants are made in the area of agriculture and hospitals in Oxfordshire and Gloucestershire
WHAT IS NOT FUNDED The Trustees are not empowered to make grants to individual applicants or to students
WHO CAN BENEFIT Organisations benefiting medical professionals. There is no restriction on the disease or medical condition suffered by the beneficiaries
WHERE FUNDING CAN BE GIVEN Oxfordshire, Gloucestershire
FINANCES *Year* 1996 *Income* £20,145 *Grants* £5,500
TRUSTEES W G Davies, H G Davies, M J Oughton, C H Arkell
WHO TO APPLY TO W G Davies, Messrs Kendall & Davies, Solicitors, Bourton on the Water, Cheltenham, Gloucestershire GL54 2AA
CC NO 296133 **ESTABLISHED** 1987

■ The Bulldog Trust

WHAT IS FUNDED General charitable purposes
WHO CAN BENEFIT There are no restrictions on the age; professional and economic group; family situation; religion and culture; and social circumstances of; or disease or medical condition suffered by, the beneficiaries
WHERE FUNDING CAN BE GIVEN UK
RANGE OF GRANTS £100–£22,387
SAMPLE GRANTS £22,387 to Ampleforth College; £10,000 to Haig Homes; £10,000 to The Prince's Trust; £10,000 to Project Scholastic Acorn; £7,243 to Ampleforth Abbey Trust; £7,013 to Nilgiri's Association Centenary Trust; £5,500 to GAMPA; £5,000 to Basingstoke YMCA; £2,500 to Great Massingham PCC; £2,500 to The Tylehurst School Trust
FINANCES *Year* 1996 *Income* £434,595 *Grants* £118,476
TRUSTEES R Hoare, Messrs Hoare Trustees
WHO TO APPLY TO R Hoare, The Bulldog Trust, Messrs Hoare Trustees, 37 Fleet Street, London EC4P 4DQ
CC NO 326292 **ESTABLISHED** 1983

■ Becket Bulmer Charitable Trust

WHAT IS FUNDED Arts; broadening the education and experiences of young people; improvement of the environment
WHO CAN BENEFIT Individuals and small local projects benefiting children, young adults and students. Actors, entertainment professionals, musicians, textile workers, designers, writers and poets will be considered
WHERE FUNDING CAN BE GIVEN Hereford, Herefordshire
TYPE OF GRANT One-off
RANGE OF GRANTS Typically £200–£400
SAMPLE GRANTS £8,500 to Cider Museum Donations; £2,000 to Barrs Court School; £500 to Chandes Symphony Orchestra; £450 to Celebrating Creative Festival Association; £400 to British School of Osteopathy
FINANCES *Year* 1997 *Income* £16,884 *Grants* £15,267
TRUSTEES G H Bulmer, Dr R B Bulmer, G H Maude, S J Bulmer, A J M Patten
PUBLICATIONS Guidelines
HOW TO APPLY In writing at any time
WHO TO APPLY TO A J M Patten, c/o The Becket Bulmer Charitable Trust, The Old Rectory, Credenhill, Hereford HR4 7DJ
CC NO 517682 **ESTABLISHED** 1986

■ The Howard Bulmer Charitable Trust

WHAT IS FUNDED General charitable purposes. Trustees favour causes in Herefordshire, home of the Bulmer family
WHO CAN BENEFIT There are no restrictions on the age, professional and economic group, family situation, religion and culture, and social circumstances of, or disease or medical condition suffered by, the beneficiaries
WHERE FUNDING CAN BE GIVEN Herefordshire
FINANCES *Year* 1997 *Income* £36,648 *Grants* £41,510
TRUSTEES J E Bulmer, D E Bulmer, J C Bulmer
HOW TO APPLY Written details of purpose/projects for which funding is sought

WHO TO APPLY TO Ref TDM 184365, The Howard
Bulmer Charitable Trust, Macfarlanes, Solicitors,
10 Norwich Street, London EC4A 1BD *Tel* 0171-
831 9222
CC NO 292437   ESTABLISHED 1984

■ The Bura Charitable Trust

WHAT IS FUNDED Infrastructure, campaigning and
advocacy, arts activities and arts education
WHAT IS NOT FUNDED Charitable institutions only
WHO CAN BENEFIT This Trust will consider
organisations benefiting: those involved in the
arts; campaigners and at risk groups
WHERE FUNDING CAN BE GIVEN UK
FINANCES *Year* 1996–97 *Income* £16,027
Grants £10,000
WHO TO APPLY TO J S Francis, Trust Treasurer, The
Bura Charitable Trust, Lindeyer Francis Ferguson,
North House, 198 High Street, Tonbridge, Kent
TN9 1BE
CC NO 802176   ESTABLISHED 1989

■ The Burall Charitable Trust

WHAT IS FUNDED To benefit communities where the
Burall Company operates, with an interest in
education, health relief, hardship or purposes for
that benefit of the community. In particular they
are interested in charitable activity that benefits
youth, sporting or cultural projects where they are
also of an educational nature
WHO CAN BENEFIT Children, young adults and
students, those disadvantaged by poverty, at risk
groups, disabled people, socially isolated people,
and victims of abuse, crime and domestic violence
WHERE FUNDING CAN BE GIVEN UK and overseas,
although the Trustees have been asked to give
preference to communities where Burall Business
operates: Cambridgeshire, Merseyside and Leeds
HOW TO APPLY Please send a letter outlining your
work and interests before writing a letter of
application
WHO TO APPLY TO Colin Arnold, The Burall Charitable
Trust, Frasers, 29 Old Market, Wisbech,
Cambridgeshire PE13 1ND *Tel* 01945 468700
Fax 01945 468709
CC NO 1069455   ESTABLISHED 1998

■ H M Burdall Charity

WHAT IS FUNDED To relieve persons aged 70 years
and over resident in the City of Sheffield in
conditions of need, hardship or distress. To make
grants to institutions or organisations rather than
to individuals providing community services
WHAT IS NOT FUNDED (a) None of the income shall be
applied directly in relief of rates, taxes or other
public funds but it may be applied in
supplementing relief or assistance provided out of
public funds. (b) The Trustees shall not commit
themselves to repeat or renew the relief granted
on any occasion in any case. (c) No grants to
individuals
WHO CAN BENEFIT Residents of the City of Sheffield
aged 70 years or over in conditions of need,
hardship or distress
WHERE FUNDING CAN BE GIVEN City of Sheffield
TYPE OF GRANT Grants made for capital, one-off,
recurring costs and start-up costs. Funding
available for one year or less
FINANCES *Year* 1997 *Income* £20,428
Grants £18,550

TRUSTEES Mrs P Sims, Mrs J Tyzack, A E H Roberts,
Mrs J A Lee, Mrs R Viner, Mrs S E Wilson, A J
Riddle, R D Cheetham, Mrs P Heath, Miss E
Murray
HOW TO APPLY In writing to reach the Clerk by the
following dates: 31 January, 30 April, 31 July or
31 October. Guidelines available. Applications
acknowledged. Accounts required
WHO TO APPLY TO R H M Plews, FCA, Clerk to the
Trustees, H M Burdall Charity, Knowle House,
4 Norfolk Park Road, Sheffield S2 3QE *Tel* 0114-
276 7791 *Fax* 0114-275 3538
CC NO 514273   ESTABLISHED 1986

■ The Burden Trust

WHAT IS FUNDED Medical research; hospitals; schools
and training institutions; homes for and care of the
infirm, aged and necessitous persons; children's
homes and care. There is an overall adherence to
the tenents and principles of the Church of
England. The main funding is likely to support
research in neurosciences
WHAT IS NOT FUNDED As a matter of policy we do not
support applications from individuals
WHO CAN BENEFIT A bias towards the Anglican Church
(as laid down in the Trust Deeds). Beneficiaries
include: children and older people; medical
professionals; Church of England; those in care,
fostered and adopted; and at risk groups
WHERE FUNDING CAN BE GIVEN UK and overseas
TYPE OF GRANT Recurring and one-off
RANGE OF GRANTS £1,000–£45,000
SAMPLE GRANTS £45,000 to Burden Neurological
Institute for neurological research; £17,500 to
Trinity College, Bristol for theological training;
£15,000 to Chescombe Trust for sheltered
housing; £15,000 to Monkton Combe School for
bursaries for children of clergy; £15,000 to
Overseas Missionary Fellowship special work at
missionary retirement home; £12,000 to Oxford
Centre for Mission Studies for technology projects;
£10,000 to Faculté Libre de Théologie
Evangélique for theological training; £10,000 to
Association for Theological Education by Extension
for post-graduate programme in Applied Theology;
£10,000 to St Peter's Hospice, Bristol for new
building project
FINANCES *Year* 1998 *Income* £240,000
Grants £205,000
TRUSTEES Dr M G Barker (Chair), R E J Bernays
(Deputy Chair), A C Miles, Prof G M Stirrat, Lady
Elizabeth White, M C Tosh
NOTES All applications sent to Trust office at the
address under Who To Apply To are acknowledged
provided an sae is enclosed
HOW TO APPLY We prefer applications to be in writing;
these must reach the Hon Secretary by 31 March
in order to be considered for the ensuing year
WHO TO APPLY TO M C Tosh, CA, Hon Secretary, The
Burden Trust, Little Clandon, West Clandon,
Surrey GU4 7ST *Tel* 01483 222561
Fax 01483 224187
CC NO 235859   ESTABLISHED 1913

■ The Michael Burgess Trust

WHAT IS FUNDED Disaster relief funds. for the relief of
people, particularly UK citizens, who are in
conditions of hardship or distress as a result of
local, national or international disasters
WHO CAN BENEFIT Institutions benefiting victims of
man-made or natural disasters
WHERE FUNDING CAN BE GIVEN UK

TRUSTEES Mrs M Burgess, J R F Coldstream, C P Masters, A P Higham
WHO TO APPLY TO C P Masters, The Michael Burgess Trust, Grant Thornton, Wall Tree Court, St Peter's Road, Petersfield, Hampshire GU32 3HY
CC NO 1018545   ESTABLISHED 1993

■ The Burghley Charitable Trust

WHAT IS FUNDED The Trust will consider funding: church buildings, community facilities, and community services, in the Area Where Funding Can Be Given
WHAT IS NOT FUNDED Animal charities. No grants to individuals
WHO CAN BENEFIT Organisations benefiting children, young adults, older people and ex-service and service people
WHERE FUNDING CAN BE GIVEN Lincolnshire, Rutland and Peterborough
TYPE OF GRANT One-off, recurring, buildings, capital, core costs, running costs and start-up costs. Funding is given for more than three years
RANGE OF GRANTS £100–£1000. The average is £350
FINANCES Year 1995–96 Income £14,000 Grants £11,500
HOW TO APPLY To the address under Who To Apply To in writing
WHO TO APPLY TO S P Leatham, Trustee, The Burghley Charitable Trust, Burghley House, Stamford, Lincolnshire PE9 3JY Tel 0171-491 4294
CC NO 258928   ESTABLISHED 1969

■ The Dorothy Burns Charity

WHAT IS FUNDED Humanities, medicine and health, youth
WHAT IS NOT FUNDED No grants to individuals
WHO CAN BENEFIT Registered charities benefiting children and young adults. There is no restriction on the disease or medical condition suffered by the beneficiaries
WHERE FUNDING CAN BE GIVEN UK and overseas
TYPE OF GRANT Primarily one-off, but some recurring
RANGE OF GRANTS £1,000–£26,000
SAMPLE GRANTS £26,000 to United World College of the Atlantic; £16,000 to Royal Society of Edinburgh; £15,440 to Slade School of Art; £10,000 to Royal Postgraduate Medical School; £9,510 to London Academy of Music and Drama; £7,500 to Attlee Foundation; £6,000 to St Edmunds Hall; £5,000 to Kings Medical Research; £5,000 to Royal National Institute for the Deaf; £5,000 to ENO-Baylis Programme
FINANCES Year 1996–97 Income £58,731 Grants £190,862
TRUSTEES Lady Balfour of Burleigh, C Campbell, CBE, Prof B Cohen, Miss E A Minogue, Lady Tummin, OBE
NOTES New applications can rarely be considered
WHO TO APPLY TO A J M Baker, The Dorothy Burns Charity, Fladgate Fielder, Heron Place, 3 George Street, London W1H 6AD
CC NO 290497   ESTABLISHED 1984

■ The Hon Dorothy Burns Charity

WHAT IS FUNDED A small number of scholarships are funded each year; support is given to certain hospitals, medical charities and medical research organisations. Other organisations are supported in the fields of arts and youth and also in Jamaica
WHAT IS NOT FUNDED No grants to individuals

WHO CAN BENEFIT Organisations benefiting: children and young adults; medical professionals and research workers. There is no restriction on the disease or medical condition suffered by the beneficiaries
WHERE FUNDING CAN BE GIVEN UK and Jamaica
TYPE OF GRANT Some recurrent
FINANCES Year 1995–96 Income £95,000 Grants £250,000
TRUSTEES Lady Balfour of Burleigh, Christopher Campbell, Prof Bernard Cohen, Miss Ann Minogue, Lady Tumin
HOW TO APPLY To the address under Who To Apply To in writing
WHO TO APPLY TO The Clerk, The Hon Dorothy Burns Charity, Fladgate Fielder, Trustees' Solicitor, Heron Place, 3 George Street, London W1H 6AD Tel 0171-486 9231
CC NO 294225   ESTABLISHED 1986

■ The Alan & Rosemary Burrough Charitable Trust

WHAT IS FUNDED Particular interest in organisations concerned with rowing and disablement
WHAT IS NOT FUNDED No grants for foreign travel
WHO CAN BENEFIT Disabled people and those involved with rowing
WHERE FUNDING CAN BE GIVEN UK
RANGE OF GRANTS £15–£34,000
SAMPLE GRANTS £34,000 to Cambridge Rowing Trust; £4,500 to Hertford College, Oxford; £2,500 to University Athletics Central Committee CUBC Appeal; £1,200 to Remenham Parish Church; £1,000 to Jesus College Boat Club; £800 to NSPCC; £500 to Alzheimer's Research Trust; £500 to Rosanna Hospital; £500 to Rowing Foundation; £500 to Theatre Royal
FINANCES Year 1997 Income £49,521 Grants £50,615
TRUSTEES A Burrough, CBE, B R H Burrough, A C C Burrough
HOW TO APPLY In writing to the address under Who To Apply To
WHO TO APPLY TO Alan Burrough, The Alan & Rosemary Burrough Charitable Trust, Manor Garden, Henley-on-Thames, Oxfordshire RG9 2NH
CC NO 328150   ESTABLISHED 1989

■ James Burrough Distillers Charitable Trust (formerly known as Long John International Charitable Trust)

This trust did not respond to CAF's request to amend its entry and, by 30 June 1998, CAF's researchers did not find financial records for later than 1995 on its file at the Charity Commission. Trusts are legally required to submit annual accounts to the Charity Commission under section 42 of the Charities Act 1993

WHAT IS FUNDED To make grants mainly to charities dealing with children (especially with disabilities), young people and the aged
WHAT IS NOT FUNDED Registered charities only. Unable to aid individuals
WHO CAN BENEFIT Registered charities benefiting children (particularly those with disabilities), young adults and older people
WHERE FUNDING CAN BE GIVEN Scotland
TYPE OF GRANT Cash donation
TRUSTEES J Hooper, A M Dewar-Durie
HOW TO APPLY To the Secretary in writing. Meetings held biannually in June and December

WHO TO APPLY TO J S Montgomery, Assistant
Secretary, James Burrough Distillers Charitable
Trust, 2 Glasgow Road, Dumbarton G82 1ND
CC NO 253102   ESTABLISHED 1967

■ The Burry Charitable Trust

WHAT IS FUNDED Medicine and health
WHAT IS NOT FUNDED No grants to individuals or
students
WHO CAN BENEFIT Institutions. There is no restriction
on the disease or medical condition suffered by
the beneficiaries. Medical professionals and
research workers may be considered
WHERE FUNDING CAN BE GIVEN UK
TYPE OF GRANT Range of grants
FINANCES *Year* 1995–96 *Income* £27,968
Grants £54,000
TRUSTEES R J Burry, Mrs J A Knight, A John
HOW TO APPLY **This Trust states that it does not
respond to unsolicited applications**
WHO TO APPLY TO J Burry, The Burry Charitable Trust,
261 Lymington Road, Highcliffe, Christchurch,
Dorset BH23 5EE
CC NO 281045   ESTABLISHED 1961

■ The A J Burton 1956 Charitable Trust

WHAT IS FUNDED General charitable purposes
WHAT IS NOT FUNDED No support to charities not
already known by the Trust
WHO CAN BENEFIT There are no restrictions on the
age; professional and economic group; family
situation; religion and culture; and social
circumstances of; or disease or medical condition
suffered by, the beneficiaries
WHERE FUNDING CAN BE GIVEN UK and overseas
SAMPLE GRANTS £25,000 to World Jewish Relief for
poverty in mainly former USSR; £25,000 to
Institute of Ophthalmology for Fight for Sight;
£25,000 to Marie Stopes International for
population and health; £10,000 to Leeds
Education 2000; £10,000 to Leeds Jewish
Welfare Board; £10,000 to School Field, Rugby;
£5,000 to SUSTRANS for sustainable transport;
£5,000 to National Hospital DF; £5,000 to The
National Trust; £5,000 to Psychiatry Research
Trust
FINANCES *Year* 1996–97 *Income* £200,525
Grants £234,811
TRUSTEES A J Burton, M T Burton, J J Burton
HOW TO APPLY **The Trust's funds are already
committed to our existing list of 200 registered
charities. This Trust states that it does not
respond to unsolicited applications**
WHO TO APPLY TO Keith Pailing, The A J Burton 1956
Charitable Trust, Trustee Management Ltd, Trust
Managers, 27 East Parade, Leeds LS1 5SX
CC NO 1020986   ESTABLISHED 1956

■ R M Burton 1956 Charitable Trust

WHAT IS FUNDED Jewish charities, education, the arts,
medicine and conservation are the areas which
have priority
WHAT IS NOT FUNDED No grants to individuals. No
appeals from local charities outside Yorkshire and
Humberside
WHO CAN BENEFIT Organisations benefiting: actors
and entertainment professionals; musicians;
students; textile workers and designers; writers
and poets; and Jews. There is no restriction on the
disease or medical condition suffered by the
beneficiaries
WHERE FUNDING CAN BE GIVEN England with a
preference for Leeds and Yorkshire, also Israel
RANGE OF GRANTS £50–£100,000
FINANCES *Year* 1997 *Income* £295,059
Grants £274,781
TRUSTEES R M Burton, A J Burton, Mrs P N Burton
WHO TO APPLY TO R M Burton 1956 Charitable Trust,
c/o Trustee Management Ltd, 27 East Parade,
Leeds LS1 5SX
CC NO 253421   ESTABLISHED 1956

■ The Burton Breweries Charitable Trust

WHAT IS FUNDED Youth and youth organisations in the
geographical area of Burton and East
Staffordshire. Funding is given in areas such as
residential facilities and services; community
facilities; and extra curricular education and
training
WHAT IS NOT FUNDED Children under 11 years old and
organisation which benefit children under 11 years
or adults (over 21 years). Education where there is
provision by State
WHO CAN BENEFIT Young people (11–21 years), youth
and community organisations. Young people from
a wide range of social circumstances are
considered for funding
WHERE FUNDING CAN BE GIVEN Geographical area of
East Staffordshire District and the County
boundaries of Burton on Trent
TYPE OF GRANT Buildings, capital, core costs, interest
free loans, one-off, project, recurring costs,
running costs, salaries and start-up costs. Funding
is available for up to two years
RANGE OF GRANTS £100–£5,000
FINANCES *Year* 1998 *Income* £35,000
Grants £30,000
TRUSTEES Janet Dean MP, Michael Hurdle, Martin
Thomas, John McKeown
HOW TO APPLY By letter. Terms of Reference available
WHO TO APPLY TO B E Keates FCA, Secretary to the
Trustees, The Burton Breweries Charitable Trust,
Studio 2, Waterside Court, Third Avenue, Centrum
100, Burton on Trent, Staffordshire DE14 2WQ
Tel 01283 740600
CC NO 1068847   ESTABLISHED 1998

■ The Geoffrey Burton Charitable Trust

WHAT IS FUNDED General charitable purposes of a
welfare nature, and environment. Particularly
charities working in the fields of: holiday
accommodation; cemeteries and burial grounds;
churches; hospices; conservation; community
centres and village halls; libraries and museums;
and recreation grounds
WHAT IS NOT FUNDED No grants to individuals
WHO CAN BENEFIT Organisations benefiting Christians
and those disadvantaged by poverty. There is no
restriction on the disease or medical condition
suffered by the beneficiaries
WHERE FUNDING CAN BE GIVEN Suffolk
TYPE OF GRANT 37 grants in year, largest to Blond
McIndoe. Buildings, core costs, funding for one
year or less will be considered

Think carefully about every application. Is it justified?

SAMPLE GRANTS £15,000 to Blond McIndoe funding Research Registrar; £4,000 to St Johns Church, Needham Market towards Restoration Project; £4,000 to Suffolk Wildlife Trust for butterfly project; £2,500 to Needham Market Playgroup for building fund; £2,000 Suffolk Wildlife Trust for upkeep of Bonny Wood; £2,000 to Suffolk Wildlife Trust towards purchase of Foxburrow Farm; £1,000 to John Grooms for Icanho Centre Project; £700 to Ormiston Trust for repairs at Robert Milne House; £600 to Ipswich Sea Cadets Corps to purchase two canoes; £500 to Marie Curie towards nurses in Suffolk

FINANCES *Year* 1996–97 *Income* £48,490 *Grants* £41,436

TRUSTEES E de B Nash, E E Maule

HOW TO APPLY To the address under Who To Apply To in writing

WHO TO APPLY TO E E Maule, The Geoffrey Burton Charitable Trust, 1 Gainsborough Road, Felixstowe, Suffolk IP11 7HT *Tel* 01394 285537 *Fax* 01394 670073

CC NO 290854   **ESTABLISHED** 1984

■ Consolidated Charity of Burton on Trent

WHAT IS FUNDED To benefit poor, sick and needy residents of Burton on Trent; to provide recreational and educational facilities, including those for social and physical training

WHO CAN BENEFIT Poor, sick and needy residents of Burton on Trent

WHERE FUNDING CAN BE GIVEN Burton on Trent together with Branston and Stretton

FINANCES *Year* 1997 *Income* £508,510 *Grants* £191,458

HOW TO APPLY Contact the address below for an application form

WHO TO APPLY TO G W Simnett, Consolidated Charity of Burton on Trent, Messrs Talbot & Co, 148 High Street, Burton-on-Trent DE14 1JY

CC NO 239072   **ESTABLISHED** 1981

■ Sir Matt Busby Charities Fund

WHAT IS FUNDED General charitable purposes to support local charities

WHO CAN BENEFIT Registered charities. There are no restrictions on the age; professional and economic group; family situation; religion and culture; and social circumstances of; or disease or medical condition suffered by, the beneficiaries

WHERE FUNDING CAN BE GIVEN Greater Manchester

SAMPLE GRANTS £1,000 to Rainbow Trust; £1,000 to Dehon House; £1,000 to Henshaws Society for the Blind; £1,000 to Sense; £500 to Childline

FINANCES *Year* 1995 *Income* £24,414 *Grants* £5,750

TRUSTEES D McMorrow (Treasurer), M W Sweeney (Secretary)

HOW TO APPLY To the address under Who To Apply To in writing

WHO TO APPLY TO John Doherty, Secretary, Sir Matt Busby Charities Fund, 4 Beaulieu, Leicester Road, Hale, Altruncham, Cheshire WA15 9QA

CC NO 1008119   **ESTABLISHED** 1991

■ The Bute Charitable Trust

WHAT IS FUNDED General charitable purposes. Funds are at present fully committed and no reply can be made to unsolicited applications

WHO CAN BENEFIT There are no restrictions on the age; professional and economic group; family situation; religion and culture; and social circumstances of; or disease or medical condition suffered by, the beneficiaries

WHERE FUNDING CAN BE GIVEN UK

FINANCES *Year* 1996 *Income* £32,267

TRUSTEES Lady Sophia Crichton-Stuart, J A W Jennings

WHO TO APPLY TO The Bute Charitable Trust, 39 Cloth Fair, Messrs Steele, Robertson & Co, London EC1A 7JQ

CC NO 285226   **ESTABLISHED** 1981

■ Bill Butlin Charity Trust

WHAT IS FUNDED Normally to assist handicapped children, and old and needy people through recognised institutions

WHAT IS NOT FUNDED Grants to registered charities only

WHO CAN BENEFIT Registered charities benefiting children, older people, the handicapped and needy

WHERE FUNDING CAN BE GIVEN UK

RANGE OF GRANTS £500–£20,000

SAMPLE GRANTS £20,000 to Canadian Veterans Association (UK); £10,000 to Liver Research; £10,000 to British Institute for Brain Injured Children (BIBIC); £10,000 to SOS School for Parents; £5,000 to St Wilfrid's Hospice; £5,000 to Barnados, Queens Road, Bradford Appeal; £3,000 to Victims of Violence; £2,500 to Cup of Kindness Fund; £2,500 to Chichester Cathedral Trust; £2,500 to Chagford Recreational Trust

FINANCES *Year* 1997 *Income* £117,563 *Grants* £93,250

TRUSTEES R F Butlin, F T Devine, P A Hetherington, Mrs S I Meaden, T Watts Snr, Lady Sheila Butlin, T Watts Jnr

HOW TO APPLY By letter to the address under Who To Apply To

WHO TO APPLY TO The Secretary, Bill Butlin Charity Trust, 3rd Floor, Eagle House, 110 Jermyn Street, London SW1Y 6RH

CC NO 228233   **ESTABLISHED** 1963

■ The Byfleet United Charity

WHAT IS FUNDED Help is given to those in need

WHO CAN BENEFIT Individuals and organisations benefiting those in need

WHERE FUNDING CAN BE GIVEN Byfleet

SAMPLE GRANTS £93,811 to pensioners; £13,107 to organisations and individuals

FINANCES *Year* 1996 *Income* £204,195 *Grants* £106,918

TRUSTEES Rev L S Smith, D M Forsyth, Mrs J P Mackintosh, B F Smith, Mrs P Acheson, Mrs M K Henderson, Rev R D Trumper

PUBLICATIONS Leaflets outlining the Trust's activities are available in libraries and other public places

HOW TO APPLY To the address under Who To Apply To in writing. Applications are received through a variety of routes including social services, Citizens Advice Bureau, doctors' surgeries and churches

WHO TO APPLY TO The Clerk, The Byfleet United Charity, Stoop Court, Leisure Lane, West Byfleet, Surrey KT14 6HF

CC NO 200344   **ESTABLISHED** 1989

Does the trust you have chosen match your needs? Haphazard applications waste postage and time

93

■ CAFOD (Catholic Fund for Overseas Development)

WHAT IS FUNDED The relief of poverty throughout the world, the advancement of education throughout the world, the advancement of the Christian Religion throughout the world, the relief and prevention of sickness, disease and physical or mental disability throughout the world. Grants are not made to other charities as such. The charities concerned with self-help development in the developing world may be partners of CAFOD in joint development projects

WHAT IS NOT FUNDED Projects submitted to CAFOD for funding normally come through a Church source, ie, a Catholic diocesan secretariat, in a developing country, or an ecumenical body. The beneficiaries, however, would be without discrimination of race, creed or colour

WHO CAN BENEFIT Poor communities overseas in developing countries. There is no restriction by age, culture and religion, or disaese and medical condition suffered by the beneficiaries

WHERE FUNDING CAN BE GIVEN Third world countries

TYPE OF GRANT Project

FINANCES *Year* 1997 *Income* £16,800,000 *Grants* £12,100,000

TRUSTEES Miss Mildred Nevile, MBE, MA, Most Rev Patrick Kelly, Archbishop of Liverpool, Rt Rev John Crowley (Chairman), His Honour Judge Peter Langan, QC

WHO TO APPLY TO The Director, J Filochowski, CAFOD, Romero Close, Stockwell Road, London SW9 9TY *Tel* 0171-733 7900 *Fax* 0171-274 9630

CC NO 285776   **ESTABLISHED** 1962

■ The C & A Charitable Trust

WHAT IS FUNDED The C&A Charitable Trust operates primarily through the local C&A stores. Staff take the initiative both in selecting the small number of registered charities to benefit in their area and in helping to raise funds for them. Preferred charities directly benefit children, the elderly or the disadvantaged within the UK. Brochure appeals are not supported. The Trust is therefore unable to respond to unsolicited appeals

WHO CAN BENEFIT Registered charities including religious organisations, hospitals and other medical bodies, schools, community projects, child welfare organisations and homes for the aged. Organisations benfiting: children; young adults; those in care, fostered and adopted; parents and children; one parent families; and those disadvantaged by poverty

WHERE FUNDING CAN BE GIVEN UK with preference to areas where C&A stores operate

RANGE OF GRANTS £50–£7,000; typical £1,000

SAMPLE GRANTS £39,249 to Childline; £30,744 Cot Death Society; £17,396 to Whizz Kids; £8,000 to Institute of Child Health; £6,011 to British Kidney Patient Association

FINANCES *Year* 1996–97 *Income* £344,323 *Grants* £279,270

TRUSTEES C&A Charitable Trustees

HOW TO APPLY Through stores and London charity committees. **This Trust states that it does not respond to unsolicited applications**

WHO TO APPLY TO The Secretary, C & A Charitable Trust, 20 Old Bailey, London EC4M 7BH

CC NO 269881   **ESTABLISHED** 1975

■ The CBSO Development Trust

WHAT IS FUNDED To apply the income towards financial support of the City of Birmingham Symphony Orchestra (CBSO) Society Limited

WHO CAN BENEFIT The City of Birmingham Symphony Orchestra

WHERE FUNDING CAN BE GIVEN City of Birmingham

SAMPLE GRANTS £92,867 to CBSO

FINANCES *Year* 1997 *Income* £146,395 *Grants* £92,867

TRUSTEES Sir M Checkland, M Corbett, Ms C Gentry, R Hartshorn, P Monahan, M Phillips, E Smith, R York

WHO TO APPLY TO Ms C Gentry, The CBSO Development Trust, c/o CBSO Society Limited, CBSO Centre, Berkley Street, Birmingham B1 2LF

CC NO 1042296   **ESTABLISHED** 1994

■ CfBT Education Services

WHAT IS FUNDED To give priority to the support of projects, which are distinctive, integrated and growing out of actual or prospective CfBT activities at home and abroad, likely to have a multiplier effect, and have a clear measurable outcome. Areas of particular interest are: the development and management of schools; English language teaching and learning; educational and project management; teacher education; careers guidance. Other charitable purposes will be considered

WHAT IS NOT FUNDED Grants will not be made for: general appeals; buildings or capital costs; research of a mainly theoretical nature; day-to-day running costs; to replace statutory funding; the arts; religion; sports and recreation; conservation; heritage or environmental projects; animal rights or welfare; expeditions; travel; adventure/holiday projects; educational exchanges between institutions; staff salaries

WHO CAN BENEFIT Individuals and organisations involved in education in areas where CfBT is involved. Including organisations benefiting: children and young adults; research workers; students; teachers and governesses; and those disadvantaged by poverty

WHERE FUNDING CAN BE GIVEN UK and countries abroad where CfBT is actively involved

TYPE OF GRANT Grants and awards which satisfy the stated criteria in the form of grants for feasibility studies, one-off, project and research. Funding for up to and over three years will be considered

FINANCES *Year* 1997 *Income* £1,410,000 *Grants* £720,000

TRUSTEES A C Stuart, CMG (Chairman), Mrs A M C Fitzpatrich, OBE, Prof R O Iredale, Ms S A Lock, I McArthur, J E Parr

PUBLICATIONS Six-monthly reports issued. Annual Report

HOW TO APPLY Application forms and further details can be obtained from CfBT offices. The Trustees meet quarterly to consider applications received from organisations, and annually to consider those from individuals

WHO TO APPLY TO Richard Birhett, Development Fund Manager, CfBT Education Services, 1 The Chambers, East Street, Reading, Berkshire RG1 4JF *Tel* 0118-952 3900 *Fax* 0118-952 3939 *E-mail* kgristock@cfbt-hq.org.uk *Web Site* www.cfbt.co.uk
CC NO 270901 **ESTABLISHED** 1965

■ CI Educational Trust Company

WHAT IS FUNDED The advancement of public education at Chichester Institute by the provision of facilities, and other general charitable purposes
WHAT IS NOT FUNDED Anything that does not take place at Chichester Institute. No grants to individuals
WHO CAN BENEFIT Students, staff and other users of Chichester Institute's facilities
WHERE FUNDING CAN BE GIVEN West Sussex
TYPE OF GRANT Buildings and capital. Funding is available for up to one year or less
WHO TO APPLY TO P E D Robinson, CI Educational Trust Company, Bishop Otter College, College Lane, Chichester, West Sussex PO19 4PE *Tel* 01243 816050 *Fax* 01243 816053
CC NO 1063307 **ESTABLISHED** 1997

■ CLA Charitable Trust

WHAT IS FUNDED (a) Provision of facilities for recreation and leisure in the countryside for the disabled. (b) Advancement of education in agriculture and conservation. (c) Relief of poverty
WHAT IS NOT FUNDED Individuals and students
WHO CAN BENEFIT Small local projects, innovative projects and new established projects benefiting disabled people and those disadvantaged by poverty
WHERE FUNDING CAN BE GIVEN England and Wales
TYPE OF GRANT Buildings, capital, one-off and project. Funding is available for up to one year
SAMPLE GRANTS £10,000 to Country Trust for school children's visits to farms; £7,500 to Farming and Wildlife Advisory Group for improvement of conservation techniques; £2,500 to Ramblers Association for improved footpath surfacing; £2,000 to Bruce Trust for rebuilding boat for disabled; £2,000 to Norfolk Association for Disabled for mobility equipment; £2,000 to Nancy Oldfield Trust for repairs to boat for disabled; £2,000 to Waverney Stardust for repairs to boat for disabled; £1,650 to Carousel for equipment for disabled art bookshop; £1,500 to RDA for vehicle for disabled; £1,000 to Rainbow Riding Oppurtunities for fittings for riding school for disabled
FINANCES *Year* 1996–97 *Income* £100,600 *Grants* £81,200
TRUSTEES M A Gregory, OBE, LLB, A Duckworth-Chad, DL, P R de L Giffard, DL, A H Duberly, CBE, DL
PUBLICATIONS Annual Report
HOW TO APPLY In writing at any time
WHO TO APPLY TO Col A F MacKain-Bremner, OBE, CLA Charitable Trust, Summerlea, The Street, East Knoyle, Salisbury SP3 6AJ *Tel* 01747 830410
CC NO 228064 **ESTABLISHED** 1980

■ CSF Charitable Trust

WHAT IS FUNDED General charitable purposes
WHO CAN BENEFIT Registered charities. There are no restrictions on the age; professional and economic group; family situation; religion and culture; and social circumstances of; or disease or medical condition suffered by, the beneficiaries
WHERE FUNDING CAN BE GIVEN UK
FINANCES *Year* 1997 *Income* £25,468 *Grants* £3,149
TRUSTEES P A Beer, M Cohen, D M Greenberg, M J Northall
NOTES During 1997 the Trust supported the following charities: Crisis, Duke of Edinburgh Trust; Northampton Cancer Support; Radar
WHO TO APPLY TO C Keeble, Financial Controller, CSF Charitable Trust, c/o CSF Group plc, Alliance House, 47–51 East Road, London N1 6AH
CC NO 1047624 **ESTABLISHED** 1995

■ CVCC Limited

This trust did not respond to CAF's request to amend its entry and, by 30 June 1998, CAF's researchers did not find financial records for later than 1995 on its file at the Charity Commission. Trusts are legally required to submit annual accounts to the Charity Commission under section 42 of the Charities Act 1993

WHAT IS FUNDED (a) The advancement of the Christian faith; (b) the relief of persons who are in conditions of need, hardship or distress who are aged or sick; (c) the advancement of education. The Trust supports projects in the developing world emphasising releasing nationals within their own countries through leadership training programmes and broadcast media work
WHO CAN BENEFIT Organisations benefiting people of all ages, students, at risk groups, those disadvantaged by poverty, and socially isolated people. There is no restriction on the disease or medical condition suffered by the beneficiaries
WHERE FUNDING CAN BE GIVEN UK and overseas
FINANCES *Year* 1997 *Income* £713,758 *Grants* £594,387
TRUSTEES I P Baker, R N Edmiston, T J Spicer
NOTES The Trust is connected to the Christian Vision Charity and was set up to support their work. It gives direct support to the projects initiated by Christian Vision in various parts of the developing world. In 1997 grants were made in the following geographical areas: £505,838 in the UK; £69,801 in Zambia; £15,804 in Chile; and £2,944 in Mozambique
WHO TO APPLY TO Ms T Spicer, CVCC Limited, Ryder Street, West Bromwich, West Midlands B70 0EJ
CC NO 1031031 **ESTABLISHED** 1993

■ Christopher Cadbury Charitable Trust

WHAT IS FUNDED To support approved charities by annual contribution
WHAT IS NOT FUNDED No funding for individuals, expeditions or scholarships
WHO CAN BENEFIT Registered charities only. There are no restrictions on the age; professional and economic group; family situation; religion and culture; and social circumstances of; or disease or medical condition suffered by, the beneficiaries
WHERE FUNDING CAN BE GIVEN Bias towards the Midlands
TYPE OF GRANT Recurring grants up to seven years
RANGE OF GRANTS £200–£14,500

SAMPLE GRANTS £14,500 to Royal Society for Nature Conservation; £7,500 to Playthings Past Museum Trust; £5,000 to Croft Trust; £5,000 to Norfolk Naturalists Trust; £4,500 to Fircroft College; £4,000 to Worcestershire Wildlife Trust

FINANCES *Year* 1998 *Income* £68,561
Grants £63,450

TRUSTEES Dr C J Cadbury, R V J Cadbury, Mrs V B Reekie, Dr T N D Peet, P H G Cadbury, Mrs C V E Benfield

PUBLICATIONS Annual Trustees Report including Accounts

NOTES All funds are committed

HOW TO APPLY The Trustees have fully committed funds for projects presently supported and cannot respond positively to any further applications

WHO TO APPLY TO R Harriman, Trust Administrator, Christopher Cadbury Charitable Trust, New Guild House, 45 Great Charles Street, Queensway, Birmingham B3 2LX *Tel* 0121-212 2222

CC NO 231859   **ESTABLISHED** 1922

■ G W Cadbury Charitable Trust

WHAT IS FUNDED General charitable purposes with a bias towards population control and conservation. £77,324 given to support family planning and welfare in 1998

WHAT IS NOT FUNDED Individuals and scholarships not funded. Registered charities only

WHO CAN BENEFIT Organisations benefiting: at risk groups; those disadvantaged by poverty; and the socially isolated

WHERE FUNDING CAN BE GIVEN UK (67.3 per cent), USA (22.4 per cent) and Canada (10.3 per cent)

RANGE OF GRANTS Up to £30,000. 22 grants over £1,000 and 50 below £1,000

SAMPLE GRANTS £30,000 to World Development Movement Trust; £24,032 to Gloucester Adventure (Massachussetts); £12,000 to Birth Control Trust; £10,000 to Belfast Brook Advisory Trust; £10,000 to Brook Advisory Centres; £10,000 to Maternity Alliance Educational and Research Trust; £10,000 to Family Planning Association; £10,000 to Population Concern; £9,028 to Planned Parenthood Federation of Canada; £7,000 to Worldwide Fund for Nature

FINANCES *Year* 1998 *Income* £197,702
Grants £178,102

TRUSTEES Mrs C A Woodroffe, Mrs L E Boal, Miss J C Boal, P C Boal, Miss J L Woodroffe, N B Woodroffe

PUBLICATIONS Trustees Annual Report is included in the Accounts

HOW TO APPLY This Trust states that it does not respond to unsolicited applications

WHO TO APPLY TO R Harriman, Trust Administrator, G W Cadbury Charitable Trust, New Guild House, 45 Great Charles Street, Queensway, Birmingham B3 2LX *Tel* 0121-212 2222

CC NO 231861   **ESTABLISHED** 1922

■ H T and L B Cadbury Charitable Trust

WHAT IS FUNDED Charities working in the fields of healthcare; rehabilitation centres; community services; community issues; development proposals; and racial equality, discrimination and relations. No requests considered as funds are already allocated. Income of Trust donated each year

WHAT IS NOT FUNDED Registered charities only. Unsolicited and personal appeals will not be accepted or acknowledged

WHO CAN BENEFIT Registered charities only. There is no restriction on the social circumstances of the beneficiaries

WHERE FUNDING CAN BE GIVEN UK and overseas

SAMPLE GRANTS Grants for general funds; £1,500 to Woodbrooke; £1,500 to Macmillan Nurses; £1,500 to Battle against Tranquilizers; £1,250 to Refugee Council; £1,250 to London Cyclists Trust; £1,000 to NSPCC Middlesbrough; £1,000 to Action for Disability and Development; £1,000 to Road Peace; £1,000 to Victim Support; £1,000 to Carers National Association

FINANCES *Year* 1995 *Income* £32,013
Grants £21,750

TRUSTEES M B Gillett, K M Charity, E Rawlins, C Gillett, R Charity, B S Cadbury, V Franks

HOW TO APPLY This Trust states that it does not respond to unsolicited applications. Funds are already allocated

WHO TO APPLY TO V Franks, H T and L B Cadbury Charitable Trust, BCM 2024, London WC1N 3XX

CC NO 280314   **ESTABLISHED** 1924

■ J & L A Cadbury Charitable Trust

WHAT IS FUNDED Main areas of interest are conservation; social welfare; environment; education (Quaker and local schools only); local or historic churches. Local charities who support hospices, emergency and short term housing, hostels, housing associations, voluntary and community organisations and various community facilities and services will be considered

WHAT IS NOT FUNDED Registered charities only. No grants to individuals or London (local) charities. Not overseas

WHO CAN BENEFIT Mainly local organisations benefiting children; young adults and older people; those in care, fostered and adopted; one parent families; Christians, Church of England; Quakers; victims of abuse, crime and domestic violence will be considered

WHERE FUNDING CAN BE GIVEN Preference towards activities in the West Midlands

TYPE OF GRANT Usually one-off

RANGE OF GRANTS £50–£500, usually £100–£250

SAMPLE GRANTS £500 to Birmingham Settlement; £500 to Traidcraft Exchange; £500 to Royal Orthopaedic Hospital, Birmingham; £500 to Elizabeth Fitzroy Homes; £500 to Worcestershire Wildlife Trust; £300 to Society of Friends for Swarthmore Appeal; £250 to Medical Foundation for Victims of Torture; £250 to Bordesley Green Centre, Birmingham; £250 to Kings Heath and Moseley Baptist Church

FINANCES *Year* 1997 *Income* £32,750
Grants £27,230

TRUSTEES Mrs L A Cadbury, W J B Taylor, Mrs S M Gale

HOW TO APPLY By letter with details, estimated costs/budget if possible. No official form. Applications are considered monthly. No circular, undated or unsigned appeals will be considered

WHO TO APPLY TO The Secretary, J & L A Cadbury Charitable Trust, 2 College Walk, Birmingham B29 6LQ

CC NO 241895   **ESTABLISHED** 1965

96

Think carefully about every application. Is it justified?

■ Richard Cadbury Charitable Trust

WHAT IS FUNDED This Trust is willing to support: community centres and village halls; libraries and museums; counselling; crime prevention; play schemes; gay and lesbian rights; racial equality, discrimination and relations; social advocacy; health care; hospices and rehabilitation centres; cancer and prenatal research; health promotion; and health related volunteer schemes. It will also consider the fields of: accommodation and housing; infrastructure support and development; conservation and environment; and religion

WHAT IS NOT FUNDED Registered charities only. No student grants or support of individuals

WHO CAN BENEFIT Organisations benefiting: children; young adults; the elderly; those in care, fostered and adopted; parents and children; and one parent families. People with many different social circumstances and suffering from diseases and medical conditions will be considered

WHERE FUNDING CAN BE GIVEN Mainly local to Birmingham, Worcester and Coventry

TYPE OF GRANT One-off for capital and buildings (preferred). Funding is available for one year or less

RANGE OF GRANTS £200–£1,000

SAMPLE GRANTS £1,000 to Centrepoint, Soho for youth work; £1,000 to Coventry Cyrenians for homelessness shelter; £1,000 to Oxfam for third world support; £1,000 to Shelter, West Midlands for homelessness; £800 to Children's Society for family support; £800 to YMCA, Birmingham for community support; £600 to Youth Aid for youth services and support; £600 to The Salvation Army, Birmingham; £500 to Prison Fellowship for prison visiting support; £500 to Quaker Peace and Service for general Quaker support worldwide

FINANCES *Year* 1997 *Income* £43,534 *Grants* £42,000

TRUSTEES R B Cadbury, Mrs M M Eardley, D G Slora, Miss J A Slora

NOTES Restricted from small unregistered groups. However, help can be offered through recognised religious or educational bodies in exceptional circumstances

HOW TO APPLY By letter including costings and current set of accounts if appropriate. Trustee meetings held February, June and October

WHO TO APPLY TO Mrs M M Eardley, Administrator, Richard Cadbury Charitable Trust, 6 Middleborough Road, Coventry, West Midlands CV1 4DE

CC NO 224348   **ESTABLISHED** 1948

■ C James Cadbury Charity

WHAT IS FUNDED General charitable purposes

WHO CAN BENEFIT There are no restrictions on the age; professional and economic group; family situation; religion and culture; and social circumstances of; or disease or medical condition suffered by, the beneficiaries

WHERE FUNDING CAN BE GIVEN UK and overseas

TRUSTEES H B Carslake, Mrs J Cadbury, P H G Cadbury

WHO TO APPLY TO H B Carslake, C James Cadbury Charity, Martineau Johnson Solicitors, St Philips House, St Philips Place, Birmingham B3 2PP

CC NO 270609   **ESTABLISHED** 1969

■ The Cadbury Schweppes Foundation

WHAT IS FUNDED At the discretion of the Trustees but especially education and enterprise, health and welfare, the environment and equal opportunities

WHO CAN BENEFIT Organisations benefiting children, young adults, at risk groups, those disadvantaged by poverty and socially isolated people. There is no restriction on the disease or medical condition suffered by the beneficiaries

WHERE FUNDING CAN BE GIVEN UK

FINANCES *Year* 1995 *Income* £306,033 *Grants* £372,385

TRUSTEES N D Cadbury, D N Makin, N M Boultwood, D G McCabe, L R Todd

WHO TO APPLY TO Ms C Forest, Finance Administrator, The Cadbury Schweppes Foundation, Cadbury Schweppes plc, 25 Berkeley Square, London W1X 6HT

CC NO 1050482   **ESTABLISHED** 1994

■ The Barrow Cadbury Trust

WHAT IS FUNDED The Trust runs programmes of national importance in Civil Rights, Community Democracy, Disability, Gender, Penal Affairs and Racial Justice, but Trust programmes are increasingly proactive and unallocated funds are scarce

WHAT IS NOT FUNDED All fields outside the focus of the above programmes including grants for individuals

WHO CAN BENEFIT Charities and voluntary organisations who benefit children, young adults, older people, disabled people, immigrants and refugees

WHERE FUNDING CAN BE GIVEN The UK with a preference for the West Midlands, Armagh, Fermanagh and Omagh

TYPE OF GRANT Core costs, project, recurring costs, running costs, salaries and start-up costs, for more than three years

SAMPLE GRANTS £165,000 to Citizen Organising Foundation for core costs and local organisation training; £110,000 to CRIS Trust, Birmingham for running costs; £65,000 to Women Acting in Today's Society for running costs and training; £55,000 to Prison Reform Trust for running costs and research; £50,000 to Fermanagh Trust for grants programme; £40,000 to Circles Network for running costs; £40,000 to CENTRIS for running costs; £40,000 to Department of Peace Studies, Bradford for salaries and bursaries; £33,500 to Searchlight Educational Trust for salaries and running costs; £30,000 to Trillick Enterprise Group for building costs

FINANCES *Year* 1996–97 *Income* £2,096,198 *Grants* £2,092,765

TRUSTEES Catherine R Hickinbotham, Charles L Cadbury, Philippa H Southall, Roger P Hickinbotham, Anna C Southall, Richard G Cadbury, Ruth M Cadbury, Erica R Cadbury, James E Cadbury, Candia H Compton, Thomas S Cadbury, Helen R Cadbury, Nicola J Cadbury

PUBLICATIONS Annual Report

HOW TO APPLY Initial enquiry by telephone is preferred. Guidelines are available, but there are no application forms and no deadlines

WHO TO APPLY TO Eric Adams, Director, The Barrow Cadbury Trust, 2 College Walk, Selly Oak, Birmingham B29 6LQ *Tel* 0121-472 0417 *Fax* 0121-471 3130

CC NO 226331   **ESTABLISHED** 1920

■ The Edward & Dorothy Cadbury Trust (1928)

WHAT IS FUNDED To continue to support, where appropriate, the interests of the Founders and the particular charitable interests of the Trustees. A special preference for West Midlands appeals for health, education and the arts

WHAT IS NOT FUNDED Registered charities only. Grants not made to individuals

WHO CAN BENEFIT Registered charities benefiting: children and young adults; actors and entertainment professionals; musicians; textile workers and designers; and writers and poets. There is no restriction on the disease or medical condition suffered by the beneficiaries

WHERE FUNDING CAN BE GIVEN West Midlands

TYPE OF GRANT On-going funding commitments rarely considered

RANGE OF GRANTS £250–£1,000

SAMPLE GRANTS £5,000 to Age Concern Bromsgrove; £5,000 to Edwards Trust; £3,500 to Bromsgrove Festival; £2,500 to Disability West Midlands; £2,350 to Bromsgrove Concerts; £2,000 to Centre for Black and White; £2,000 to Glen Project; £2,000 to Mountview Conservatiore; £2,000 to Prospect Hall Ltd; £1,500 to Acorns Children's Hospital

FINANCES *Year* 1998 *Income* £106,805
Grants £82,536

TRUSTEES Mrs P A Gillett, Dr C M Elliott, Mrs P S Ward

HOW TO APPLY At any time but allow three months for a response. The Trust does not have an application form. Applications should be made in writing to the address under Who To Apply To. They should clearly and concisely give relevant information concerning the project and its benefits, an outline budget and how the project is to be funded initially and in the future. Up to date accounts and the organisation's latest Annual Report are also required. Applications that do not come within What is Funded above, as stated above, will not be considered or acknowledged

WHO TO APPLY TO Mrs M Walton, The Edward & Dorothy Cadbury Trust, Elmfield, 2 College Walk, Selly Oak, Birmingham B29 6LE

CC NO 221441   **ESTABLISHED** 1928

■ The George Cadbury Trust (Edward Cadbury Section) (George Cadbury Fund A Account)

WHAT IS FUNDED The Trust is for general charitable purposes for Quaker charities and organisations and Society of Friends activities only

WHAT IS NOT FUNDED Non-Quaker projects cannot benefit

WHO CAN BENEFIT Organisations benefiting Quakers

WHERE FUNDING CAN BE GIVEN UK

TYPE OF GRANT At the discretion of the Trustees

RANGE OF GRANTS £50–£19,240

SAMPLE GRANTS £19,240 to Woodbrooke for buildings appeal, bursaries and general funds; £11,000 to Quaker Peace Studies Trust; £6,500 to Selly Oak Colleges for maintenance of the George Cadbury Hall; £5,205 to Bryony House; £4,815 to Leighton Park Trust for bursaries and library; £4,350 to Society of Friends Warwick Meeting for development appeal; £4,000 to Ironbridge Gorge Museum Trust for Quaker houses; £3,000 to Society of Friends St Albans Meeting for building fund; £2,000 to Quaker Home Services; £2,000 to Society of Friends Junior Yearly Meeting

FINANCES *Year* 1998 *Income* £92,381
Grants £68,010

TRUSTEES Peter E Cadbury, Annette L K Cadbury, Robin N Cadbury, Sir Adrian Cadbury, Roger V J Cadbury

PUBLICATIONS Annual Report is included in the Accounts

HOW TO APPLY To the address under Who To Apply To in writing

WHO TO APPLY TO R Harriman, The George Cadbury Trust, New Guild House, 45 Great Charles Street, Queensway, Birmingham B3 2LX *Tel* 0121-212 2222

CC NO 1040998   **ESTABLISHED** 1924

■ The George Cadbury Trust (George Henry T and Laurence J Cadbury Section)(George Cadbury Fund B Account)

WHAT IS FUNDED General charitable purposes at the Trustees' discretion

WHAT IS NOT FUNDED Appeals from individuals for projects or courses of study, including expeditions and sporting tours, or from overseas will not be considered

WHO CAN BENEFIT UK-based charities. There are no restrictions on the age; professional and economic group; family situation; religion and culture; and social circumstances of; or disease or medical condition suffered by, the beneficiaries

WHERE FUNDING CAN BE GIVEN UK, preferably the Midlands, Hampshire and Gloucestershire

TYPE OF GRANT At the discretion of the Trustees subject to the restrictions in What Is Not Funded

RANGE OF GRANTS £5–£30,000

SAMPLE GRANTS £30,120 to Cheltenham College; £16,000 to World Wildlife Fund; £6,000 to Bouler Trust; £6,000 to C James Cadbury Charitable Trust; £6,000 to P H G Cadbury Charitable Trust; £6,000 to R V J Cadbury Charitable Trust; £6,000 to R A and V B Reeke Trust; £6,000 to Sarnia Charitable Trust; £5,213 to St John's Ophthalmic Hospital, Jerusalem; £5,000 to Guide Association, Gold Appeal

FINANCES *Year* 1998 *Income* £253,761
Grants £227,302

TRUSTEES Peter E Cadbury, Annette L K Cadbury, Robin N Cadbury, Sir Adrian Cadbury, Roger V J Cadbury

PUBLICATIONS Annual Report is included in the Accounts

NOTES Trustees have a tendency to support charities on a results basis and also to support charities of a local nature (The Midlands, Hampshire and Gloucestershire). Although applications for funding will be considered each quarter, preference is given as instructed and **unsolicited requests are not usually successful**

HOW TO APPLY In writing to the address under Who To Apply To

Have you read How to use the DGMT *on page xvi?*

WHO TO APPLY TO R Harriman, The George Cadbury Trust, New Guild House, 45 Great Charles Street, Queensway, Birmingham B3 2LX *Tel* 0121-212 2222
CC NO 1040999   **ESTABLISHED** 1924

■ P H G Cadbury Trust

WHAT IS FUNDED General charitable purposes
WHO CAN BENEFIT There are no restrictions on the age; professional and economic group; family situation; religion and culture; and social circumstances of; or disease or medical condition suffered by, the beneficiaries
WHERE FUNDING CAN BE GIVEN UK and overseas
RANGE OF GRANTS £24–£2,000
SAMPLE GRANTS £2,000 to Get Ahead; £1,530 to Friends of Victoria and Albert Museum; £1,500 to Friends of the Tate Gallery; £1,500 to Helen House; £1,500 to National Art Collection Fund; £1,500 to Royal School of Needlework; £1,500 to Garsington Opera Ltd; £1,000 to Multiple Sclerosis; £1,000 to Friends of Royal Academy; £1,000 to St Martins in the Fields
FINANCES *Year* 1997 *Income* £27,154 *Grants* £17,731
TRUSTEES P H G Cadbury, S G A Roberts, R V J Cadbury
NOTES Unlikely that any new applications can be granted
WHO TO APPLY TO Derek Larder, P H G Cadbury Trust, PO Box 4UD, London W1A 4UD
CC NO 327174   **ESTABLISHED** 1986

■ The Cadell-Samworth Foundation (otherwise known as Chetwode Samworth Charitable Trust)

WHAT IS FUNDED General charitable purposes
WHAT IS NOT FUNDED Registered charities only. No grants to individuals
WHO CAN BENEFIT There are no restrictions on the age; professional and economic group; family situation; religion and culture; and social circumstances of; or disease or medical condition suffered by, the beneficiaries
WHERE FUNDING CAN BE GIVEN Preference to charities located in Nottinghamshire, Derby, Leicestershire areas
FINANCES *Year* 1997 *Income* £1,166,644 *Grants* £126,245
TRUSTEES T J Barker, Mrs C L Frostwick
HOW TO APPLY In writing to the address under Who To Apply To
WHO TO APPLY TO Mrs C Frostwick, The Cadell-Samworth Foundation, Chetwode House, Leicester Road, Melton Mowbray, Leicestershire
CC NO 265647   **ESTABLISHED** 1973

■ The Beatrice A V Cadman Charitable Trust

WHAT IS FUNDED General charitable purposes
WHAT IS NOT FUNDED No grants are made to individuals
WHO CAN BENEFIT Registered charities. There are no restrictions on the age; professional and economic group; family situation; religion and culture; and social circumstances of; or disease or medical condition suffered by, the beneficiaries
WHERE FUNDING CAN BE GIVEN UK with some preference being given to North West Wales, Yorkshire and West Midlands

TYPE OF GRANT Both capital projects and running expenses are considered
RANGE OF GRANTS £100–£500
FINANCES *Year* 1996 *Income* £15,099 *Grants* £15,850
TRUSTEES Mrs B A V Cadman, P H B Cadman
HOW TO APPLY In writing to the address under Who To Apply To at any time. Unsolicited applications will not be acknowledged unless accompanied by an sae
WHO TO APPLY TO P H B Cadman, The Beatrice A V Cadman Charitable Trust, 19 Tudor Hill, Sutton Coldfield, West Midlands B73 6BD
CC NO 326324   **ESTABLISHED** 1982

■ The Cairns Charitable Trust

WHAT IS FUNDED Medicine and health; welfare; education; sciences; humanities; religion; environmental resources; international; and other general charitable purposes
WHAT IS NOT FUNDED No grants to individuals
WHO CAN BENEFIT Small local projects; new, national and established organisations. There are no restrictions on the age; professional and economic group; family situation; religion and culture; and social circumstances of; or disease or medical condition suffered by, the beneficiaries
WHERE FUNDING CAN BE GIVEN UK and overseas
TYPE OF GRANT One-off and recurrent
SAMPLE GRANTS £1,000 to John Muir Trust Appeal; £500 to Hospital for Tropical Diseases Appeal; £500 to Kyabobo Conservation Project; £500 to Endsleigh Charitable Trust; £500 to NCC PG Garden Heritage Fund
FINANCES *Year* 1996 *Income* £21,506 *Grants* £6,845
TRUSTEES The Rt Hon the Earl Cairns, Countess Cairns, Sir John Chance Palmer
HOW TO APPLY In writing
WHO TO APPLY TO The Cairns Charitable Trust, c/o Ernst & Young, Broadwalk House, Southernhay, West Exeter, Devon EX1 1LF
CC NO 295662   **ESTABLISHED** 1986

■ Caistor Limited

WHAT IS FUNDED General charitable purposes
WHO CAN BENEFIT There are no restrictions on the age; professional and economic group; family situation; religion and culture; and social circumstances of; or disease or medical condition suffered by, the beneficiaries
WHERE FUNDING CAN BE GIVEN Caistor and surrounding area
FINANCES *Year* 1996 *Income* £55,945
WHO TO APPLY TO N Love, Secretary, Caistor Limited, 20 The Buttermarket, Caistor, Lincolnshire LN7 6UB
CC NO 1044892   **ESTABLISHED** 1995

■ Calderdale Community Foundation

WHAT IS FUNDED Grants are made to families and individuals in need and to community groups and voluntary organisations promoting the arts, education, leisure activities, environmental awareness and support for disabled or disadvantaged people. Advancement of religion
WHO CAN BENEFIT Individuals and organisations benefiting: children and young adults; actors and entertainment professionals; musicians; textile

workers and designers; writers and poets; students; at risk groups, those disadvantaged by poverty and socially isolated people. There is no restriction on the religion or culture of the beneficiaries

WHERE FUNDING CAN BE GIVEN Calderdale

TYPE OF GRANT Revenue, capital, one-off

FINANCES *Year* 1996 *Income* £146,016 *Grants* £64,763

TRUSTEES M Aslam, Mrs J M Crabtree, Mrs J Stark, A Gartland, Sir E Hall, OBE, DL, R A Harvey, T D Lodge, M R Olive, W T Rooney, OBE, Cllr Mrs P J Warhurst, Dr P M Humberstone, M Ellison, G R Lawrence, JP, D T Shutt, OBE, Mrs F H Tighe, E N Wood

PUBLICATIONS *Calderdale Communicator*, Annual Report, *Calderdale Matters – A Community Profile*, *Researching the Community* a report of research undertaken in Calderdale into the training, advice and support needs of the voluntary sector

HOW TO APPLY Application forms and guidelines are available from the address under Who To Apply To

WHO TO APPLY TO Mrs Megan Vickey, Administrator, Calderdale Community Foundation, Dean Clough Industrial Park, Halifax HX3 5AX *Tel* 01422 349700 *Fax* 01422 350017 *E-mail* CCFoundatn@aol.com

CC NO 1002722   **ESTABLISHED** 1991

■ Callander Charitable Trust

WHAT IS FUNDED General charitable purposes

WHAT IS NOT FUNDED Gives only in Falkirk and surrounding area

WHO CAN BENEFIT There are no restrictions on the age; professional and economic group; family situation; religion and culture; and social circumstances of; or disease or medical condition suffered by, the beneficiaries

WHERE FUNDING CAN BE GIVEN Falkirk and surrounding area

HOW TO APPLY No specific dates. Applicants should state briefly in writing: (a) Details of project they require funded. (b) How long project will last. (c) How much cash they will require annually and in total. (d) Name and brief details of person in charge of project. (e) Can this person send short but factual reports every six months including financial details? (f) Will project receive matching ODA grant?

WHO TO APPLY TO Callander Charitable Trust, Messrs A J & A Graham, 110 West George Street, Glasgow G2 1QA

SC NO SCO 16609

■ The Calliandra Foundation

WHAT IS FUNDED General charitable purposes

WHO CAN BENEFIT There are no restrictions on the age; professional and economic group; family situation; religion and culture; and social circumstances of; or disease or medical condition suffered by, the beneficiaries

WHERE FUNDING CAN BE GIVEN UK

TRUSTEES I S Anderson, Ms J S Anderson, A W M Mitchell, P A Thorn

WHO TO APPLY TO A W M Mitchell, Trustee and Solicitor, The Calliandra Foundation, Burges Salmon, Narrow Quay House, Narrow Quay, Bristol BS1 4AH

CC NO 1064235   **ESTABLISHED** 1996

■ Roland Callingham Foundation

WHAT IS FUNDED General charitable purposes. Tend to give to charities already known to the Trustees

WHO CAN BENEFIT Registered charities. There are no restrictions on the age; professional and economic group; family situation; religion and culture; and social circumstances of; or disease or medical condition suffered by, the beneficiaries

WHERE FUNDING CAN BE GIVEN Especially Beaconsfield

TYPE OF GRANT Recurrent donations

SAMPLE GRANTS £1,200 to the Chartered Accountants' Benevolent Association

FINANCES *Year* 1997 *Income* £32,327 *Grants* £31,200

TRUSTEES N J Heaton, P R Holgate, T K H Robertson, W S Callingham

WHO TO APPLY TO N J Heaton, Senior Trustee, Roland Callingham Foundation, Devonshire House, 60 Goswell Road, London EC1M 7AD

CC NO 270129   **ESTABLISHED** 1975

■ Calypso Browning Trust

WHAT IS FUNDED Animal welfare and homeless people. Regular grants made to some chosen charities but do include occasional new charities in line with trust objects

WHO CAN BENEFIT Organisations benefiting homeless people and animals

WHERE FUNDING CAN BE GIVEN UK

TYPE OF GRANT One-off and recurrent

RANGE OF GRANTS £500–£4,664

SAMPLE GRANTS £4,664 to Shelter; £4,664 to Housing Association Charitable Trust; £3,887 to Nottinghill Housing Trust; £2,332 to YMCA; £1,554 to SPEAR; £1,554 to Brighton Housing Trust; £1,000 to Kensington Housing Trust; £1,000 to People's Dispensary for Sick Animals; £1,000 to RSPCA; £500 to the Donkey Sanctuary

FINANCES *Year* 1997 *Income* £33,159 *Grants* £22,659

TRUSTEES A B S Weir, Mrs J M Kapp

HOW TO APPLY By letter to the address under Who To Apply To

WHO TO APPLY TO Calypso Browning Trust, Tweedie & Prideaux, Solicitors, 5 Lincoln's Inn Fields, London WC2A 3BT

CC NO 281986   **ESTABLISHED** 1979

■ The Camelot Foundation

WHAT IS FUNDED Equipment; training for project users, volunteers, staff, volunteer support; Alzheimer's disease and other dementias; carers; people leaving care; domestic violence; refugees; and rural transport

WHAT IS NOT FUNDED No grants to individuals. No projects aimed at children. No salary costs

WHO CAN BENEFIT Organisations that help disabled and disadvantaged people play a fuller role in society

WHERE FUNDING CAN BE GIVEN UK

TYPE OF GRANT One-off, core costs, project and running costs. Funding is available for up to one year

FINANCES *Year* 1998 *Income* £3,000,000

TRUSTEES Sir Clive Whitmore, GCB, CVO, Sir Peter Imbert, QPM, DL, Usha Prashar, CBE, Tim Holley, Trevor Phillips, Jane Tewson, Sue Shipman, Richard Brown, Louise White

NOTES Three funding aims: charitable projects (large, innovative); community support (grants up to £5,000); and employee participation (Camelot Group Staff)

100

Think carefully about every application. Is it justified?

HOW TO APPLY Sae from applicants for community support. Telephone enquiry for charitable projects

WHO TO APPLY TO The Trustees, The Camelot Foundation, 1 Derry Street, London W8 5HY *Tel* 0171-937 5594 *Fax* 0171-937 0574 *Minicom* 0171-937 5471

CC NO 1060606　　　**ESTABLISHED** 1996

■ The Ellis Campbell Charitable Foundation

WHAT IS FUNDED (a) Education/assistance of persons under 25. (b) Preservation/protection/improvement of items of architectural/structural heritage. This includes: architecture; combined arts and arts activities; conservation and heritage

WHAT IS NOT FUNDED No grants to individuals. No applications more regularly than every other year

WHO CAN BENEFIT Organisations benefiting: children and young adults; at risk groups; and disabled people. Those suffering from: autism; blood disorders and haemophilia; cerebral palsy; Crohn's disease; cystic fibrosis; Friedrichs Ataxia; head and other injuries; motor neurone disease; multiple sclerosis; muscular dystrophy; spina bifida and hydrocephalus; and strokes

WHERE FUNDING CAN BE GIVEN Hampshire, Perth and Kinross

TYPE OF GRANT One-off funding for over three to five years

RANGE OF GRANTS £25–£10,000, typical grant £500–£1,000

SAMPLE GRANTS £10,000 to The Treloar Trust for new residential building; £1,500 to Edward Barnsley Educational Trust for apprenticeship in fine furniture making; £1,500 to Society for Protection of Ancient Buildings for training scheme for four architectural craftsmen and women; £1,300 to CSV Network for young volunteers for care in the community; £1,000 to Jubilee Sailing Trust for second training ship for able and disabled; £1,000 to Abernethy Trust for Ardenoig Outdoor Centre; £1,000 to Avon Tyrrell Youth Clubs, UK for New Forest Residential Centre; £1,000 to Children's Hospice Association Scotland (CHAS) to provide support for 200 families per annum; £1,000 to Fordingbridge Youth Action Group for Drop-in Centre and organised activities; £1,000 to British Wheelchair Sports Foundation for promotion for disabled to participate

FINANCES *Year* 1997 *Income* £91,480 *Grants* £42,001

TRUSTEES M D C C Campbell, Mrs L F Campbell, Mrs D Campbell, J Campbell, Mrs A Andrew, T M Aldridge

PUBLICATIONS Annual Report

HOW TO APPLY To the address under Who To Apply To in writing. There is no application form. Trustees meet March, July and October. Applications by first of preceding month

WHO TO APPLY TO Michael D C C Campbell, DL, The Ellis Campbell Charitable Foundation, Shalden Park Steading, Shalden, Alton, Hampshire GU34 4DS *Tel* 01256 381821 *Fax* 01256 381921

CC NO 802717　　　**ESTABLISHED** 1989

■ Cancer Research Campaign

WHAT IS FUNDED Grants are made to universities, medical schools, hospitals and research institutes throughout the UK for research into how to attack and defeat the disease of cancer in all its forms, investigation of its causes, distribution, symptoms, pathology and treatment and promotion of its cure

WHAT IS NOT FUNDED Expenditure is confined to research; no funds are spent on relief or patient support

WHO CAN BENEFIT Organisations benefiting medical professionals, research workers and scientists engaged in research into cancer

WHERE FUNDING CAN BE GIVEN UK

TYPE OF GRANT Grants are given over three or five years

FINANCES *Year* 1996 *Income* £66,221,000 *Grants* £48,251,000

TRUSTEES Council, Mrs Judy Hurd

PUBLICATIONS Scientific Yearbook, Annual Review

WHO TO APPLY TO M Harries, Cancer Research Campaign, 6–10 Cambridge Terrace, London NW1 4JL

CC NO 225838　　　**ESTABLISHED** 1923

■ The Candap Trust

WHAT IS FUNDED Evangelistic organisations, individuals in overseas mission, housing needs

WHO CAN BENEFIT Individuals and organisations benefiting Evangelists, people in missions and those in need of housing

WHERE FUNDING CAN BE GIVEN UK, regional and overseas

TYPE OF GRANT One-off and recurring costs will be considered

RANGE OF GRANTS £1,500 or less

FINANCES *Year* 1995 *Income* £13,656 *Grants* £14,090

TRUSTEES Rev Christopher Poulard, FCA, Mrs A Poulard, S R Poulard, M P Poulard

PUBLICATIONS Annual Report

HOW TO APPLY In writing at any time

WHO TO APPLY TO Rev C Poulard, The Candap Trust, The Rectory, Haddiscoe, Norwich NR14 6PG

CC NO 295437　　　**ESTABLISHED** 1986

■ The Canewdon Educational Foundation

WHAT IS FUNDED Grants are given for the benefit of people under the age of 25 for educational purposes

WHO CAN BENEFIT Individuals and organisations benefiting children, young adults and students under the age of 25

WHERE FUNDING CAN BE GIVEN Canewdon

RANGE OF GRANTS £26–£1,988

SAMPLE GRANTS £1,988 to a school; £1,920 to a school for a patio; £1,888 to 22 individuals for music lessons; £1,412 to four individuals for extra tuition; £1,288 to 21 individuals for school trips and holidays; £1,160 to four individuals for course fees and assistance; £1,011 to 14 individuals for dance and drama lessons; £847 to 27 individuals for swimming tuition; £493 to seven individuals for riding lessons; £483 to a youth club

FINANCES *Year* 1996 *Income* £36,309 *Grants* £14,455

TRUSTEES Rev N Kelly, J D Smith, M H Wright, T C Stewart, D W Squirer, M Stalker, J Windsor, I Puzey, J Ralph, N Whalley, A Bromiley

HOW TO APPLY To the address under Who To Apply To in writing

WHO TO APPLY TO Charles Aldridge, Clerk, The Canewdon Educational Foundation, Roundabout, Anchor Lane, Canewdon, Essex SS4 3PB

CC NO 310718　　　**ESTABLISHED** 1965

Does the trust you have chosen match your needs? Haphazard applications waste postage and time

101

■ The Canine Supporters Charity

WHAT IS FUNDED Academic and practical study and opportunities to bring people together to discuss dogs

WHO CAN BENEFIT Registered charities and organisations associated with dogs

WHERE FUNDING CAN BE GIVEN UK

FINANCES *Year* 1996–97 *Income* £20,528 *Grants* £18,500

TRUSTEES The Committee: Mrs H Morse, Mrs K le Mare, K Forrest, M Harvey, Mrs B Harvey, M Mcmillan, G Payne, Mrs L Skeritt, Mrs L Burtenshaw, P Burtenshaw, Mrs S Clark, Ms A Messenger

WHO TO APPLY TO K M Forrest, The Canine Supporters Charity, Wey Farm, Guildford Road, Ottershaw, Surrey KT16 0QW

CC NO 289046   **ESTABLISHED** 1984

■ The Archbishop of Canterbury's Charitable Trust

WHAT IS FUNDED The training for the Ministry and work of the Church, for the maintenance of the Clergy, provision of pensions and for the benefit of ministers, teachers and workers of the Church and their families and dependants. The extension of education in and knowledge of the faith and practice of the Church of England, the development of any work of such Church Union of Churches to further the Christian religion generally

WHO CAN BENEFIT Organisations benefiting the clergy and their dependants and other followers of the Church of England. Named charitable funds have been recipients in the past

WHERE FUNDING CAN BE GIVEN UK and overseas

SAMPLE GRANTS £127,391 to General Fund; £2,788 to Michael Ramsey Chair Income Fund, an endowment towards the Michael Ramsey Chair in Anglican and Ecumenical Theology at University of Kent; £200 to Living Memory Rogers Harrison L020 Fund for British born ministerial students for the priesthood of the Church of England and for British born retired Anglican bishops, priests and their widows and heirs, the poor, blind, the elderly and crippled residents of Greater London

FINANCES *Year* 1997 *Income* £479,464 *Grants* £130,379

TRUSTEES Most Rev The Lord Archbishop of Canterbury, Sir J Owen, Dr A Purkis, Rt Rev F Sargeant

NOTES **Funds are allocated for several years ahead. Therefore no new applications can be considered**

HOW TO APPLY To the address under Who To Apply To in writing, but see Notes above

WHO TO APPLY TO P E B Beesley, Registrar, The Archbishop of Canterbury's Charitable Trust, 1 The Sanctuary, Westminster, London SW1P 3JJ

CC NO 287967   **ESTABLISHED** 1983

■ The H and L Cantor Trust

WHAT IS FUNDED General charitable purposes, with particular consideration to be given to Jewish charities

WHO CAN BENEFIT To benefit Jewish people

WHERE FUNDING CAN BE GIVEN UK, especially Sheffield

RANGE OF GRANTS £10–£970

SAMPLE GRANTS £970 to Sheffield Jewish Congregation and Centre; £850 to Friends of the Royal Academy; £170 to Sheffield Jewish Welfare Organisation; £130 to Society of Friends of the Federation of Women Zionists; £125 to Sheffield and District Reform Jewish Congregation; £100 to Sheffield Friends of Alyn Hospital; £100 to FTBA; £100 to NSPCC; £100 to World Jewish Relief; £100 to Ravenswood

FINANCES *Year* 1997 *Income* £50,350 *Grants* £5,241

TRUSTEES L Cantor, H Cantor

HOW TO APPLY **This Trust states that it does not respond to unsolicited applications**

WHO TO APPLY TO Irwin Mitchell, The H and L Cantor Trust, St Peter's House, Hartshead, Sheffield S1 2EL

CC NO 220300   **ESTABLISHED** 1959

■ Laura Capel Charitable Trust

WHAT IS FUNDED General charitable purposes, with particular attention to institutions for the benefit of ex-servicemen disabled in body or mind

WHO CAN BENEFIT Local and national charities. There are no restrictions on the age; professional and economic group; family situation; religion and culture; and social circumstances of; or disease or medical condition suffered by, the beneficiaries

WHERE FUNDING CAN BE GIVEN South East England

RANGE OF GRANTS Below £1,000–£4,000

SAMPLE GRANTS £7,750 for miscellaneous grants; £4,000 to Birling Church; £2,000 to Osbournby Parish Church

FINANCES *Year* 1996–97 *Income* £137,477 *Grants* £13,750

TRUSTEES P H Byam-Cook, J V Balfour, J R Fischel

HOW TO APPLY To the address under Who To Apply To in writing

WHO TO APPLY TO Laura Capel Charitable Trust, c/o The Hedley Foundation, 9 Dowgate Hill, London EC4R 2SU

CC NO 214658   **ESTABLISHED** 1962

■ The Capenhurst Medical and Research Charity Trust Fund

WHAT IS FUNDED Medical equipment for medical research establishments, hospitals, nursing homes, doctors' surgeries or other medical establishments

WHAT IS NOT FUNDED Preference for actually purchasing needed equipment rather than making cash donations as contributions, although this is possible exceptionally. Expeditions and scholarships are not funded

WHO CAN BENEFIT Organisations benefiting medical professionals and research workers

WHERE FUNDING CAN BE GIVEN Cheshire, Denbyshire, Flintshire and Wrexham

TYPE OF GRANT One-off, capital and recurrent grants will be considered

RANGE OF GRANTS £5,000–£10,000. Grants in excess of £10,000 unlikely

SAMPLE GRANTS £2,000 to Manor Hospital, Wrexham, the Special Baby Care Unit towards a ventilator; £1,541 to an individual (relative of former employee) for electric wheelchair; £1,000 to Roy Castle Cause for Hope Foundation; £1,000 to the Royal School for the Blind; £850 to an individual (ex-employee) for a second-hand electric scooter; £729 to British Red Cross, Merseyside Branch for two Resusci junior dolls; £664 to The Cot Death Society for two apnoea/respiration monitors; £500 to LUPUS (UK) for assistance with purchase of a computer; £500 to West Cheshire Project for assistance with purchase of a computer; £366 to an individual (wife of employee) for a portable air conditioning unit

FINANCES *Year* 1997 *Income* £26,300 *Grants* £9,807

TRUSTEES P T Farrington, D Kilfoyle, D Upton, J Edwards, D Bond, L Taylor, D Knight, J G Williams

HOW TO APPLY To the address under Who To Apply To in writing, stating the purpose of the equipment wanted and what the medical benefits are. The committee meets quarterly

WHO TO APPLY TO P T Farrington, The Capenhurst Medical and Research Charity, Urenco (Capehurst) Limited, Capenhurst Works, Chester CH1 6ER *Tel* 0151-347 3618

CC NO 513722 **ESTABLISHED** 1983

■ Alfred Caplin Charity Settlement

WHAT IS FUNDED Medical, welfare and Jewish charitable purposes

WHO CAN BENEFIT Jewish people; at risk groups; those disadvantaged by poverty; and socially isolated people. There are no restrictions on the disease or medical condition suffered by the beneficiaries

WHERE FUNDING CAN BE GIVEN UK

FINANCES *Year* 1995–96 *Income* £27,195

HOW TO APPLY To the address under Who To Apply To in writing

WHO TO APPLY TO C Caplin, Alfred Caplin Charity Settlement, c/o Messrs Charles Caplin and Co, Dolcis House, 87–91 New Bond Street, London W1Y 9AL

CC NO 254328 **ESTABLISHED** 1967

■ The Ron Carbutt Trust Fund

WHAT IS FUNDED General charitable purposes. Local charities in which the Trustees have a special interest

WHAT IS NOT FUNDED No grants to national charities

WHO CAN BENEFIT There are no restrictions on the age; professional and economic group; family situation; religion and culture; and social circumstances of; or disease or medical condition suffered by, the beneficiaries

WHERE FUNDING CAN BE GIVEN Primarily South Yorkshire

SAMPLE GRANTS £10,000 to Wakefield 'Mara' Appeal; £5,000 to Prince's Youth Business Trust; £5,000 to Rotherham Metropolitan BC Schools; £5,000 to Bishops Development Fund; £1,000 to Anthony Nolan Bone Marrow Trust; £1,000 to Grimethorpe Neighbourhood Community Trust; £1,000 to Cawthorne Primary School; £1,000 to Church in Community; £1,000 to Cawthorne Parish Church; £1,000 to an individual

FINANCES *Year* 1997 *Income* £33,500 *Grants* £45,000

TRUSTEES Ron Carbutt, Margaret Carbutt, David Burkinshaw

HOW TO APPLY To the address under Who To Apply To in writing. No telephone calls

WHO TO APPLY TO Ron Carbutt, Trustee, The Ron Carbutt Trust Fund, Hollyhock Cottage, Bark House Lane, Cawthorne, Barnsley, South Yorkshire S75 4AW

CC NO 328120 **ESTABLISHED** 1989

■ The Cardy Beaver Foundation

This trust did not respond to CAF's request to amend its entry and, by 30 June 1998, CAF's researchers did not find financial records for later than 1995 on its file at the Charity Commission. Trusts are legally required to submit annual accounts to the Charity Commission under section 42 of the Charities Act 1993

WHAT IS FUNDED General charitable purposes. Trustees are interested in applications from smaller charities

WHO CAN BENEFIT Small charities. There are no restrictions on the age; professional and economic group; family situation; religion and culture; and social circumstances of; or disease or medical condition suffered by, the beneficiaries

WHERE FUNDING CAN BE GIVEN UK

TYPE OF GRANT Small grants over two years, large ones decided biannually

TRUSTEES J L Cardy, D J Hare, G R Coia

WHO TO APPLY TO G R Coia, The Cardy Beaver Foundation, Brannan's, 63 Stowe Road, London W12 8BE *Tel* 0181-749 2575

CC NO 265763 **ESTABLISHED** 1973

■ The W A Cargill Charitable Trust

WHAT IS FUNDED Social services and relief in a local area; hospices; Christians; medical research and specific conditions; youth recreational organisations; people with visual impairments; primary and secondary education; animals and wildlife; and lifeboat services

WHO CAN BENEFIT Children and young adults, medical professionals, teachers and Christians. There is no restriction on the disease or medical condition suffered by the beneficiaries, and few restrictions on their social circumstances

WHERE FUNDING CAN BE GIVEN Scotland

FINANCES *Year* 1996 *Income* £90,000 *Grants* £80,000

TRUSTEES A C Fyfe, W G Peacock, N A Fyfe, Mirren E Graham

HOW TO APPLY Applications should be made in writing to the address below

WHO TO APPLY TO Alexander C Fyfe, The W A Cargill Charitable Trust, 190 St Vincent Street, Glasgow G2 5SP

SC NO SCO 12076 **ESTABLISHED** 1954

■ The D W T Cargill Fund

WHAT IS FUNDED General charitable purposes

WHO CAN BENEFIT There are no restrictions on the age; professional and economic group; family situation; religion and culture; and social circumstances of; or disease or medical condition suffered by, the beneficiaries

WHERE FUNDING CAN BE GIVEN UK, in particular Scotland

HOW TO APPLY Applications should be made in writing to the address below

WHO TO APPLY TO Alexander C Fyfe, The D W T Cargill Fund, 190 St Vincent Street, Glasgow G2 5SP

SC NO SCO 12703

The W A Cargill Fund

WHAT IS FUNDED Medical associations and societies; welfare of the aged; welfare of the family; Christian causes; welfare of service and ex-service personnel; dance, music and opera; youth recreational organisations; medical research and specific conditions; welfare of the young; and primary and secondary education

WHO CAN BENEFIT Children, young adults and older people, ex-service and service people, musicians, teachers, parents and children, and one parent families. There are no restrictions on the disease or medical condition suffered by the beneficiaries, and few restrictions on their social circumstances

WHERE FUNDING CAN BE GIVEN West of Scotland

FINANCES *Year* 1996 *Income* £290,000
Grants £190,000

TRUSTEES A C Fyfe, W G Peacock, N A Fyfe, Mirren E Graham

PUBLICATIONS Little information has been made available

HOW TO APPLY Applications should be made in writing to the address below

WHO TO APPLY TO Alexander C Fyfe, The W A Cargill Fund, 190 St Vincent Street, Glasgow G2 5SP

SC NO SCO 08456   **ESTABLISHED** 1962

Caring For People

WHAT IS FUNDED Relief of poverty and economic deprivation in India. Relief of mental illness within the UK. For housing and medical development. To fund already selected projects

WHO CAN BENEFIT Organisations benefiting those disadvantaged by poverty in India, and those suffering from mental illness in the UK

WHERE FUNDING CAN BE GIVEN UK and India

FINANCES *Year* 1997 *Income* £14,806
Grants £15,030

TRUSTEES G G Plumb

HOW TO APPLY No applications considered, all funding already allocated

WHO TO APPLY TO Jenny Hardman, Caring For People, c/o Unravel Mills (Preston) Ltd, Broomfield Mill, Broomfield Mill Street, Preston PR1 1NQ
Tel 01772 259065 *Fax* 01772 881398

CC NO 275195   **ESTABLISHED** 1977

Carlee Ltd

WHAT IS FUNDED The advancement of religion in accordance with the Orthodox Jewish faith. The relief of poverty. General charitable purposes

WHO CAN BENEFIT Talmudical scholars and Jewish people

WHERE FUNDING CAN BE GIVEN UK and overseas

FINANCES *Year* 1996–97 *Income* £214,480
Grants £210,045

TRUSTEES H Grunhut, Mrs P Grunhut

HOW TO APPLY To the address under Who To Apply To in writing

WHO TO APPLY TO The Secretary, Carlee Ltd, 6 Grangecourt Road, London N16 5EG

CC NO 282873   **ESTABLISHED** 1981

The Carlton House Charitable Trust

WHAT IS FUNDED Mostly Jewish organisations. The advancement of education, research work and fellowships. Other general charitable purposes will be considered

WHO CAN BENEFIT Organisations benefiting children and young adults, academics, research workers, students and Jewish people

WHERE FUNDING CAN BE GIVEN UK and overseas

TYPE OF GRANT One-off

RANGE OF GRANTS £35–£10,070

SAMPLE GRANTS £10,070 to B'nai B'rith District 15 Charities Fund; £2,514 to Western Marble Arch Synagogue; £1,000 to B'nai B'rith Hillel Foundation; £1,000 to Jewish Care; £600 to B'nai B'rith First Lodge Charitable Trust; £500 to Board of Deputies Charitable Foundation; £500 to British Friends of the Israel Arts Museums; £500 to British Technion Society; £500 to Diapora Yeshivah Toras Israel; £500 to Jewish Music Heritage Trust

FINANCES *Year* 1997 *Income* £49,040
Grants £20,764

TRUSTEES Stewart S Cohen, Pearl C Cohen, Fiona A Cohen

HOW TO APPLY To the address under Who To Apply To in writing

WHO TO APPLY TO Stewart S Cohen, Trustee, The Carlton House Charitable Trust, Craven House, 121 Kingsway, London WC2B 6PA

CC NO 296791   **ESTABLISHED** 1986

Carlton Television Trust

WHAT IS FUNDED Educational projects for children and young people who have special needs or are disadvantaged. Includes theatre-in-education, ESOL, employment training, literacy and numeracy, etc. Community facilities; counselling; playschemes; and arts, culture and recreation are also considered. Both organisation and project must be based in the area Where Funding Can Be Given. Grants are only made to registered charities so non-registered groups must find a charity willing to endorse their application and receive any cheque on their behalf

WHAT IS NOT FUNDED Individuals cannot apply. No grants are made for: general appeals, deficit funding, distribution to other organisations, retrospective funding, relief of statutory responsibilities, conferences and seminars, ongoing salaries and running costs

WHO CAN BENEFIT Properly constituted non profit-making organisations and registered charities. Low priority is given to appeals from statutory services and local authorities. The Trust will considered benefiting: children, young adults and students; unemployed people; and volunteers. There are no restrictions on the family situation. A wide range of religion and cultures of; social circumstances of; and diseases or medical conditions suffered by, the beneficiaries are also considered for funding

WHERE FUNDING CAN BE GIVEN Carlton Television transmission area: Greater London and parts of Essex, Hertfordshire, Buckinghamshire, Bedfordshire, Oxfordshire, Berkshire, Surrey, East & West Sussex and Kent

TYPE OF GRANT One-off, capital or project grants. Exceptionally salaries and running costs may be considered for two/three years if this will establish new ways of meeting need or to become more effective. Start-up costs also considered

RANGE OF GRANTS £200–£30,000, average grant £4,000, mostly £1,000–£5,000

SAMPLE GRANTS £30,000 to Royal Academy of Dramatic Art (RADA) for their Centenary Appeal, bursary fund for students; £20,000 to MENCAP towards salary of Southwark family advisor; £20,000 to Sportsaid Trust for sports training grants for 12–19 year olds; £14,684 to Harington Scheme for the salary of training supervisor; £13,000 to Ealing Pre-school Learning Alliance for the salaries of three creche workers for one year; £11,302 to Advisory Centre for Education (ACE) Ltd for 50 per cent of cost of providing exclusions helpline; £10,000 to Centrepoint towards refuge for under 16s; £10,000 to London Disability Arts Forum for mobile culture clubs for special needs children; £10,000 to London Connection for the part salary of playspace project worker; £10,000 to Science Museum towards education and outreach work

FINANCES *Year* 1997 *Income* £525,000
Grants £505,501

TRUSTEES Nigel Walmsley (Chairman), Michael Green, Colin Stanbridge, The Hon Sara Morrison, Karen McHugh, Baroness Jay of Paddington, Erica De'Ath

PUBLICATIONS Annual Report and Accounts, Annual Review, Five Year Review 1993–1997

HOW TO APPLY The Trust opens from early April to early June only, when application forms and information leaflets are available by sending a large sae with two first class stamps to: Carlton Television Trust, PO Box 1, London W12 8UB. Applications returned after the closing date shown on the form will not be considered. All applicants will receive written notification of the Trustees' decisions by 30 November

WHO TO APPLY TO Liz Delbarre, Administrator, Carlton Television Trust, 101 St Martin's Lane, London WC2N 4AZ *Tel* 0171-615 1641

CC NO 1019628   **ESTABLISHED** 1993

■ The Carmelite Monastery Ware Trust

WHAT IS FUNDED To advance the religious and other charitable work carried out at Ware for the benefit of the public

WHO CAN BENEFIT Individuals and organisations. There are no restrictions on the age; professional and economic group; family situation; religion and culture; and social circumstances of; or disease or medical condition suffered by, the beneficiaries

WHERE FUNDING CAN BE GIVEN UK with preference for Ware, and overseas

RANGE OF GRANTS Below £1,000–£5,200

SAMPLE GRANTS £5,200 to Westminster Ecclesiastical Education Fund; £5,000 to Association of British Carmels; £5,000 to Westminster Roman Catholic Diocesan Trust, Trinity Fund; £2,900 to Catholic Fund for Overseas Development; £1,250 to Sion Evangelisation Centre for National Training

FINANCES *Year* 1997 *Income* £14,275
Grants £42,000

TRUSTEES Patricia E McGee, Carole A Henderson, Maureen M E Pike, Theresa M Linforth, Helen M Quinn, Mary J Richardson

WHO TO APPLY TO D J Clerk, The Carmelite Monastery Ware Trust, 28 Ely Place, London EC1N 6RL

CC NO 298379   **ESTABLISHED** 1987

■ The Carmichael-Montgomery Charitable Trust

WHAT IS FUNDED Support is given chiefly to URC or ecumenical projects, with some consideration given to individuals known personally to the Trustees. This includes Christian education, Christian outreach and Free Church umbrella bodies

WHAT IS NOT FUNDED Grants are not made for medical aid or individuals

WHO CAN BENEFIT United Reformed Church

WHERE FUNDING CAN BE GIVEN UK

TYPE OF GRANT Capital, buildings, one-off, project and start-up costs. Funding is available for one year or less

RANGE OF GRANTS Average £2,000

FINANCES *Year* 1995 *Income* £57,000
Grants £49,000

TRUSTEES Mrs B Baker, Mrs N Johnson, D Carmichael, Miss B Exley, K Forrest, P Maskell, Mrs S Nicholson, Rev M G Hanson

HOW TO APPLY Applications are normally reviewed in March and October. There is no official application form. Only successful applications are acknowledged. Annual accounts required

WHO TO APPLY TO Mrs N Johnson, The Carmichael-Montgomery Charitable Trust, 3 Bear Close, Henley-in-Arden, Warwickshire B95 5HS

CC NO 200842   **ESTABLISHED** 1961

■ Carnegie Dunfermline Trust

WHAT IS FUNDED Social, educational, cultural and recreational purposes in Dunfermline and its immediate environs. This includes: information technology and computers; infrastructure development, Council for Voluntary Service; volunteer bureaux; arts, culture and recreations; historic buildings; waterways, woodlands; animal homes; bird sanctuaries; schools and colleges; community facilities and services; and other charitable purposes

WHAT IS NOT FUNDED Operates only within Dunfermline and its immediate environs. Grants rarely given to individuals

WHO CAN BENEFIT Local clubs and societies, and special projects benefiting: people of all ages; actors and entertainment professionals; musicians; students; textile workers and designers; and writers and poets. There are few restrictions on their social circumstances

WHERE FUNDING CAN BE GIVEN Dunfermline and its immediate environs only

TYPE OF GRANT Buildings, capital, feasibility studies, one-off and project. Funding is for one year or less

RANGE OF GRANTS £100–£75,000. Typical grant £500–£1,000

FINANCES *Year* 1997 *Income* £364,000
Grants £165,000

TRUSTEES Appointed in terms of Royal Charter

HOW TO APPLY To the address under Who To Apply To. Initial telephone calls are welcome. Application forms and guidelines available. There are no deadlines for applications. Sae is not required

WHO TO APPLY TO The Secretary, Carnegie Dunfermline Trust, Abbey Park House, Dunfermline, Fife KY12 7PB *Tel* 01383 723638 *Fax* 01383 721862

SC NO SCO 00729   **ESTABLISHED** 1903

Does the trust you have chosen match your needs? Haphazard applications waste postage and time

105

■ Carpenter Charitable Trust

WHAT IS FUNDED Local Christian based outreach charities preferred

WHAT IS NOT FUNDED No grants to individuals

WHO CAN BENEFIT Local Christian organisations

WHERE FUNDING CAN BE GIVEN UK and overseas

TYPE OF GRANT One-off

RANGE OF GRANTS £500–£1,000

SAMPLE GRANTS £1,500 to Orbis International; £1,000 to Blue Cross; £1,000 to The Brooke Hospital; £1,000 to Crisis; £1,000 to Cats Protection League; £1,000 to Great St Helen's Trust; £1,000 to Isle of Eigg Trust; £1,000 to Mission Aviation Fellowship; £1,000 to the Salvation Army; £500 to Colon Cancer Campaign

FINANCES *Year* 1996–97 *Income* £27,188 *Grants* £17,500

TRUSTEES M S E Carpenter, Mrs G M L Carpenter

HOW TO APPLY Applications not required –Trustees are having a strategic review over the next 18 months – in the meantime **the funds are fully committed**

WHO TO APPLY TO M S E Carpenter, Carpenter Charitable Trust, The Old Vicarage, Hitchin Road, Kimpton, Hitchin, Hertfordshire SG4 8EF

CC NO 280692   **ESTABLISHED** 1980

■ The Carpenters' Company Charitable Trust

WHAT IS FUNDED To support the carpentry craft

WHO CAN BENEFIT Individuals and schools, colleges, universities and other charitable organisations promoting the craft of carpentry

WHERE FUNDING CAN BE GIVEN UK

SAMPLE GRANTS £64,474 to Carpenter's Road School; £20,000 to Carpenters and Docklands Centre; £6,647 to Richard Wyatt's Almshouses; £2,001 to King Edward's School, Witley; £1,500 to City of London Freeman's School; £1,500 to City of London School; £1,000 to City University

FINANCES *Year* 1997 *Income* £279,840 *Grants* £245,488

TRUSTEES V F Browne, Dr W F Felton, M R Francis, P C Osborne, D R Stuckey

HOW TO APPLY Apply in advance in writing to the Clerk. No retrospective grants given

WHO TO APPLY TO The Clerk, The Carpenters' Company, Carpenters' Hall, 1 Throgmorton Avenue, London EC2N 2JJ

CC NO 276996   **ESTABLISHED** 1978

■ The Carriejo Charitable Trust

WHAT IS FUNDED General charitable purposes

WHO CAN BENEFIT There are no restrictions on the age; professional and economic group; family situation; religion and culture; and social circumstances of; or disease or medical condition suffered by, the beneficiaries

WHERE FUNDING CAN BE GIVEN UK and overseas

TRUSTEES Ms C M Chichester, Countess of Belfast, Ms J C Lascelles, Ms M C A Philipson

WHO TO APPLY TO Miss L J Cousins, Secretary, The Carriejo Charitable Trust, 10 Fenchurch St, London EC3M 3LB

CC NO 1066520   **ESTABLISHED** 1997

■ The Carrington Charitable Trust

WHAT IS FUNDED General charitable purposes. Prefer local charities

WHAT IS NOT FUNDED No grants given to individuals

WHO CAN BENEFIT Local branches of a wide range of charities. There are no restrictions on the age, professional and economic group, family situation, religion and culture, and social circumstances of, or disease or medical condition suffered by, the beneficiaries

WHERE FUNDING CAN BE GIVEN Aylesbury, Buckinghamshire

SAMPLE GRANTS £50,000 to Hammersmith Hospital (Leukaemia Research Fund) for medical research; £7,879 towards running costs for old people's homes; £5,000 to Cancer Care and Haematology Fund (Stoke Mandeville Hospital) for medical research

FINANCES *Year* 1996 *Income* £60,902 *Grants* £68,043

TRUSTEES Rt Hon Lord Carrington, KG, J A Cloke

WHO TO APPLY TO J A Cloke, The Carrington Charitable Trust, Messrs Cloke & Co, Warnford Court, Throgmorton Street, London EC2N 2AT *Tel* 0171-638 8992

CC NO 265824   **ESTABLISHED** 1973

■ The Carroll-Marx Charitable Foundation

WHAT IS FUNDED General charitable purposes

WHO CAN BENEFIT There are no restrictions on the age; professional and economic group; family situation; religion and culture; and social circumstances of; or disease or medical condition suffered by, the beneficiaries

WHERE FUNDING CAN BE GIVEN UK and overseas

RANGE OF GRANTS £500–£4,000

SAMPLE GRANTS £4,000 to Ajex; £3,000 to Jewish Care; £2,000 to GRET; £2,000 to Jewish Aids Trust; £2,000 to Jewish Lads and Girls Brigade; £2,000 to World Jewish Relief; £2,000 to Norwood Ravenswood; £1,000 to British Retinitis Pigmentosa Society; £1,000 to Council of Christians and Jews; £1,000 to Jewish Deaf Association

FINANCES *Year* 1996 *Income* £28,133 *Grants* £32,620

WHO TO APPLY TO C Ward, The Carroll-Marx Charitable Foundation, New Court, St Swithin's Lane, London EC4P 4DU

CC NO 212605   **ESTABLISHED** 1960

■ The Carron Charitable Trust

WHAT IS FUNDED Applications from charities linked to wildlife, education, medicine, the countryside, printing and publishing will be considered, including charities working in the fields of health professional bodies, health campaigning and advocacy, conservation, wildlife parks and sanctuaries, natural history, endangered species, education and training, costs of study and academic research

WHAT IS NOT FUNDED No grants to individuals

WHO CAN BENEFIT Organisations benefiting academics, medical professionals, nurses and doctors, research workers and students. There are no restrictions on the age of, or the disease or medical condition suffered by, the beneficiaries

WHERE FUNDING CAN BE GIVEN UK and overseas

TYPE OF GRANT Project, research, running costs and salaries. Funding of up to three years may be considered

SAMPLE GRANTS £2,500 to The Henley Centre for research on executive stress; £2,000 to The Dornock Academy to set up the Duke of Edinburgh Scheme

FINANCES *Year* 1997 *Income* £17,282 *Grants* £13,140

TRUSTEES P G Fowler, Mrs J Wells, W M Allen, D L Morgan, FCA

HOW TO APPLY **Almost all of the Charity's funds are committed for the foreseeable future and the Trustees therefore do not invite applications from the general public**

WHO TO APPLY TO Mrs C S Cox, The Carron Charitable Trust, Messrs Rothman Pantall & Co, 10 Romsey Road, Eastleigh, Hampshire SO50 9AL *Tel* 01703 614555

CC NO 289164   ESTABLISHED 1984

■ The Leslie Mary Carter Charitable Trust

WHAT IS FUNDED General charitable purposes. Trustees prefer well thought-out applications for larger gifts, than many applicants for smaller grants. The preferred areas for grant giving are nature conservation and wildlife. Other applications will be considered but acknowledgements may not always be sent

WHAT IS NOT FUNDED Applications for grants from individuals will not be entertained

WHO CAN BENEFIT There are no restrictions on the age; professional and economic group; family situation; religion and culture; and social circumstances of; or disease or medical condition suffered by, the beneficiaries

WHERE FUNDING CAN BE GIVEN UK with preference to East Anglia

TYPE OF GRANT Buildings, capital, core costs, one-off, project, research, running costs and recurring costs will be considered

RANGE OF GRANTS £500–£5,000, typical grant £4,000

FINANCES *Year* 1997 *Income* £66,640 *Grants* £59,500

TRUSTEES Miss L M Carter, S R M Wilson

HOW TO APPLY Telephone calls are not welcome. There is no application form, guidelines, deadlines for applications or a requirement for a sae, unless the applicant wishes to have material returned

WHO TO APPLY TO S R M Wilson, The Leslie Mary Carter Charitable Trust, Messrs Birketts, 24–26 Museum Street, Ipswich, Suffolk IP1 1HZ

CC NO 284782   ESTABLISHED 1982

■ Carters Educational Foundation

WHAT IS FUNDED The Trust primarily supports the South Wilford Endowed Church of England School. Some grants may be given to individuals under the age of 25 living in the area Where Funding Can Be Given and organisations with a broadly educational nature which benefit such people

WHO CAN BENEFIT Organisations benefiting children and young adults in the Parish of Wilford in Nottingham

WHERE FUNDING CAN BE GIVEN Wilford Parish in the City of Nottingham

TYPE OF GRANT One-off

RANGE OF GRANTS £25–£300

FINANCES *Year* 1997 *Income* £104,827 *Grants* £2,200

TRUSTEES Mrs J A Buckland, Mrs M Hall, R A D Nettleship, Rev P Newton, F J Scott, R W Stanley, A Wheelhouse

HOW TO APPLY Application forms are available from the address under Who To Apply To each year at Easter. Completed forms must be returned by 31 May. Applicants are requested to write in and Clerk will telephone them if necessary

WHO TO APPLY TO Mrs C M Byers, Clerk, Carters Educational Foundation, Pennine House, 8 Stanford Street, Nottingham NG1 7BQ *Tel* 0115-958 6262 *Fax* 0115-958 9700

CC NO 528161   ESTABLISHED 1888

■ The Carvill Trust

WHAT IS FUNDED General charitable purposes

WHO CAN BENEFIT There are no restrictions on the age; professional and economic group; family situation; religion and culture; and social circumstances of; or disease or medical condition suffered by, the beneficiaries

WHERE FUNDING CAN BE GIVEN UK

SAMPLE GRANTS £10,000 to Mary Hare Foundation; £5,000 to Downs Syndrome Association; £750 to Pattaya Orphanage; £115 to Lords Taverners

FINANCES *Year* 1997 *Income* £116,738 *Grants* £15,865

TRUSTEES R K Carvill, R E Pooley, K D Tuson

WHO TO APPLY TO K D Tuson, The Carvill Trust, Alto House, 29–30 Newbury Street, London EC1A 7HU

CC NO 1036420   ESTABLISHED 1994

■ The Casey Trust

WHAT IS FUNDED General charitable purposes

WHO CAN BENEFIT There are no restrictions on the age; professional and economic group; family situation; religion and culture; and social circumstances of; or disease or medical condition suffered, the beneficiaries

WHERE FUNDING CAN BE GIVEN UK

TRUSTEES R H Glick, E D Green, K C Howard

WHO TO APPLY TO Kenneth Howard, Trustee, The Casey Trust, 27 Arkwright Road, London NW3 6BJ

CC NO 1055726   ESTABLISHED 1996

■ Cash for Kids (formerly BRMB – Birmingham Walkathon)

WHAT IS FUNDED The Charity aims to help disadvantaged children and young people (under 18's) living within Birmingham and the West Midlands area. Supports relief of poverty or deprivation and the general welfare of children

WHAT IS NOT FUNDED No grants outside the area Where Funding Can Be Given. No grants to individuals or for: research; trips abroad; medical treatment; deficit funding or repayment of loans; distribution to other organisations, administration costs; or unspecified expenditure

WHO CAN BENEFIT Organisations benefiting young people

WHERE FUNDING CAN BE GIVEN West Midlands only (50 mile radius of Birmingham)

TYPE OF GRANT One-off

FINANCES *Year* 1996–97 *Income* £118,746 *Grants* £103,623

TRUSTEES David Bagley, John Buckingham, Peter Langard, Dr Barry Roseman

PUBLICATIONS Brief guide to Cash for Kids

HOW TO APPLY On a form available from the address under Who To Apply To. Applications must be received between 1 March and 1 July
WHO TO APPLY TO Mike Owen, Cash for Kids, BRMB Radio Group, Radio House, Aston Road North, Aston, Birmingham B6 4BX
CC NO 1042820   **ESTABLISHED** 1994

■ Cash for Kids at Christmas Charitable Trust

WHAT IS FUNDED Christmas presents, food, pantomime trips, clothing and other tangible items are given to sick or underprivileged children via Strathclyde Regional Council's Social Work Department and through community and voluntary groups
WHAT IS NOT FUNDED Grants are not given for summer or Easter trips, equipment or salaries. Children benefiting must be aged up to sixteen
WHO CAN BENEFIT Children and young adults up to the age of sixteen, including those in care, fostered and adopted. There is no restriction on the disease or medical condition suffered by the beneficiaries, and few restrictions on their social circumstances
WHERE FUNDING CAN BE GIVEN West and Central Scotland
FINANCES *Year* 1997 *Income* £550,000 *Grants* £480,000
TRUSTEES John R Bowman, Robert F Caldwell, Alex Dickson, OBE
PUBLICATIONS Accounts and guidelines for applicants are available from the Trust
HOW TO APPLY Applications should be made on an application form which is available from the address below
WHO TO APPLY TO Cash for Kids at Christmas Charitable Trust, CSV Media, Clyde Action, 236 Clyde Street, Glasgow G1 4JH
SC NO SCO 03334   **ESTABLISHED** 1984

■ Sir Ernest Cassel Educational Trust *(Grants for Educational Purposes)*

WHAT IS FUNDED To make grants for educational purposes to institutions or organising bodies (eg in adult education) but not individuals
WHAT IS NOT FUNDED No grants to individuals. General appeals will not be funded
WHO CAN BENEFIT Institutions of higher education, colleges or organising bodies (eg in adult education) benefiting young adults, students and academics
WHERE FUNDING CAN BE GIVEN UK
TYPE OF GRANT One-off or recurrent grants will be considered. Funding may be given for up to three years
RANGE OF GRANTS £500–£5,000

SAMPLE GRANTS £25,600 to the Mountbatten Memorial Grants to Commonwealth Students (£14,400 as block grants and £11,200 as exceptional grants); £5,000 to Overseas Research Grants (British Academy); £1,500 to Burnbake Trust Arts Centre; £1,500 to Centre for Cross-Cultural Research on Women, University of Oxford; £1,500 to Edinburgh University, Fund for Commonwealth Postgraduate Students; £1,500 to Lucy Cavendish College, Cambridge; £1,500 to St Hugh's College, Oxford; £1,500 to University of Leicester, Richard Attenborough Centre for Disability and the Arts; £1,000 to Project Trust; £1,000 to the Marine Society
FINANCES *Year* 1998 *Income* £61,088 *Grants* £45,500
TRUSTEES Countess Mountbatten of Burma, CBE, CD, JP, DL (Chairman), Lord Annan, Lord Desai, Ms A S Kennedy, Dr O S O'Neill, H J Renton, Sir S Sutherland, Sir R Way
HOW TO APPLY In writing with supporting documents but not Annual Accounts
WHO TO APPLY TO R Le Fanu, OBE, Sir Ernest Cassel Educational Trust, 8 Malvern Terrace, Islington, London N1 1HR
CC NO 313820   **ESTABLISHED** 1919

■ The Elizabeth Casson Trust

WHAT IS FUNDED 75 per cent to support Oxford Brookes University occupational therapy courses. 25 per cent to support other occupational therapy school/departments and individual occupational therapists
WHO CAN BENEFIT Oxford Brookes University, other occupational schools and departments, and individual occupational therapists
WHERE FUNDING CAN BE GIVEN Oxford Brookes University and UK
TYPE OF GRANT Research projects, courses/travel bursaries that will benefit the profession as well as the individual
SAMPLE GRANTS £500 to occupational therapist attending paediatric Bobath course; £500 to occupational therapist towards MSc/BPhil course; £250 to occupational therapist attending World Federation of Occupational Therapy congress in Canada; £250 to occupational therapist attending International Conference in Austria
FINANCES *Year* 1996 *Income* £187,434
TRUSTEES B M Mandlebrote, MA, FRCP, DPM (Chairman), Prof W Couchman, BA, MSc, CSS, K D Grevling, LIB, BCI, D.Phil, B E Hulse, OBE, CPFA, Miss M A Mendez, OBE, FCOT, Mrs C Rutland, DipCOT, D T Wade, MD, FRCP, Lady Williams
NOTES The Trust was founded in 1930 as the Dorset House School of Occupational Therapy (a registered company). In 1948 the Founder Dr Elizabeth Casson registered this Trust and an associated trust, The Casson Trust, under the same number at the Charity Commission. In 1992 Dorset House site was leased to Oxford Brookes University and in 1993 the company changed its name to The Elizabeth Casson Trust
HOW TO APPLY On the Trust's application form which can be obtained from the address under Who To Apply To
WHO TO APPLY TO B A Davies, Secretary, The Elizabeth Casson Trust, 20 Chaundy Road, Tackley, Kidlington, Oxfordshire OX5 3BJ
CC NO 227166   **ESTABLISHED** 1930

■ H and M Castang Charitable Trust

WHAT IS FUNDED Trustees are particularly interested in giving to research into mental and physical disability

WHO CAN BENEFIT Registered charities benefiting medical professionals, research workers and those with physical or mental disability

WHERE FUNDING CAN BE GIVEN UK

RANGE OF GRANTS £10,000–£12,000

SAMPLE GRANTS £12,000 to the Kerland Foundation for an occupational therapy unit and physical evaluation research laboratory; £10,000 to The Little Foundation for a research programme

FINANCES *Year* 1995–96 *Income* £25,426 *Grants* £22,000

TRUSTEES H A Castang, I A Burman, M B Glynn, Dr I StJ Kemm

HOW TO APPLY To the address under Who To Apply To

WHO TO APPLY TO I A Burman, H and M Castang Charitable Trust, Carmelite House, 50 Victoria Embankment, Blackfriars, London EC4Y 0LS

CC NO 1003867   **ESTABLISHED** 1991

■ Catholic Charitable Trust

WHAT IS FUNDED To support the traditional teachings of the Roman Catholic faith. The Trust income is usually fully committed

WHAT IS NOT FUNDED No grants to individuals

WHO CAN BENEFIT Traditional Catholic organisations and Roman Catholics

WHERE FUNDING CAN BE GIVEN America and Europe

FINANCES *Year* 1997 *Income* £34,000 *Grants* £59,000

TRUSTEES J C Vernor Miles, R D D Orr

WHO TO APPLY TO J C Vernor Miles, Catholic Charitable Trust, Messrs Vernor, Miles & Noble, 5 Raymond Buildings, Gray's Inn, London WC1R 5DD

CC NO 215553   **ESTABLISHED** 1935

■ Catholic Education Service for England and Wales

WHAT IS FUNDED To consider applications from (a) Proprietors of Roman Catholic schools which receive no assistance from rates or taxes, (b) Roman Catholic Parishes for assistance with cost of transport of pupils to Catholic schools

WHO CAN BENEFIT Proprietors of Roman Catholic schools and the children and young adults attending such schools

WHERE FUNDING CAN BE GIVEN England and Wales

FINANCES *Year* 1997 *Income* £659,083

TRUSTEES Rt Rev D Konstant, Rt Rev V Nichols

WHO TO APPLY TO Mrs M M Smart, Catholic Education Service, 39 Eccleston Square, London SW1V 1BX

CC NO 313147   **ESTABLISHED** 1965

■ Catholic Foreign Missions

WHAT IS FUNDED Advancement of the Roman Catholic religion by maintenance, support and upkeep of Missions in any part of the world

WHO CAN BENEFIT Roman Catholics

WHERE FUNDING CAN BE GIVEN UK and overseas

FINANCES *Year* 1997 *Income* £750,461 *Grants* £1,118,251

TRUSTEES The Council of Management

WHO TO APPLY TO Secretary, Catholic Foreign Missions, c/o Witham Weld, Solicitors, 70 St George's Square, London SW1V 3RD

CC NO 249252   **ESTABLISHED** 1941

■ The Cattanach Charitable Trust

WHAT IS FUNDED General charitable purposes. Grants are made to a range of charities

WHO CAN BENEFIT There are no restrictions on the age; professional and economic group; family situation; religion and culture; and social circumstances of; or disease or medical condition suffered by, the beneficiaries

WHERE FUNDING CAN BE GIVEN UK

TRUSTEES The Royal Bank of Scotland plc, R M Barge, C H K Corsar, F W Fletcher, Lord M MacLay

PUBLICATIONS Annual Report and Accounts are available from the Trust

HOW TO APPLY Applications should be made in writing to the address below

WHO TO APPLY TO The Trust Officer, The Cattanach Charitable Trust, The Royal Bank of Scotland plc, Private Trust and Taxation, 36 St Andrew Square, Edinburgh EH2 2YB

SC NO SCO 20902   **ESTABLISHED** 1992

■ The Joseph and Annie Cattle Trust

WHAT IS FUNDED General charitable purposes

WHAT IS NOT FUNDED No grants to individuals, national societies (except for work in North Humberside area) or professional appeals (where agents and appeal staff are employed or paid)

WHO CAN BENEFIT Handicapped disabled, especially aged and young and local charities

WHERE FUNDING CAN BE GIVEN North Humberside

TYPE OF GRANT One-off, capital, recurring and interest free loans are considered

RANGE OF GRANTS £200–£10,000

FINANCES *Year* 1998 *Income* £342,000 *Grants* £280,000

TRUSTEES R Waudby, Mrs J A Collier, M T Gyte

HOW TO APPLY Initial telephone calls are welcome. There are no application forms, guidelines or deadlines. An sae is required

WHO TO APPLY TO R C Waudby, The Joseph and Annie Cattle Trust, Morpeth House, 114 Spring Bank, Hull HU3 1QJ *Tel* 01482 653250

CC NO 262011   **ESTABLISHED** 1970

■ The Thomas Sivewright Catto Charitable Settlement

WHAT IS FUNDED General charitable purposes

WHAT IS NOT FUNDED To registered charities only. The Trust does not support expeditions or travel bursaries; nor unsolicited applications from churches of any denomonation. The areas of community care; playschemes; and drug abuse are unlikely to be considered; as are applications from area branches of national organisations, eg Scout Groups

WHO CAN BENEFIT Registered charities only. There are no restrictions on the age; professional and economic group; family situation; religion and culture; and social circumstances of; or disease or medical condition suffered by, the beneficiaries

WHERE FUNDING CAN BE GIVEN UK

TYPE OF GRANT Donation

FINANCES *Year* 1997 *Income* £89,046 *Grants* £96,870

Does the trust you have chosen match your needs? Haphazard applications waste postage and time

109

TRUSTEES Hon Mrs Ruth Bennett, Lord Catto, Miss Zoe Richmond-Watson
HOW TO APPLY To the address under Who To Apply To with sae
WHO TO APPLY TO Miss Ann Uwins, The Thomas Sivewright Catto Charitable Settlement, 23 Great Winchester Street, London EC2P 2AX
CC NO 279549   **ESTABLISHED** 1979

■ The Wilfred and Constance Cave Foundation

WHAT IS FUNDED General charitable purposes
WHAT IS NOT FUNDED No grants to individuals
WHO CAN BENEFIT There are no restrictions on the age; professional and economic group; family situation; religion and culture; and social circumstances of; or disease or medical condition suffered by, the beneficiaries
WHERE FUNDING CAN BE GIVEN Chiefly Wiltshire and Berkshire
RANGE OF GRANTS £150–£15,000
SAMPLE GRANTS £15,000 to Camp Mohawk; £5,000 to West of England School; £5,000 to Farms for City Children; £5,000 to National Playbus Association; £5,000 to Childline; £5,000 to Midshire Caring Trust; £5,000 to National Memorial Arboretum Appeal; £4,500 to Nuneaton and Warwickshire Equestrian Centre; £4,000 to Breakthrough Cancer; £4,000 to Sustrans
FINANCES *Year* 1997 *Income* £218,003 *Grants* £135,825
TRUSTEES F Jones, Rev P Buckler, OBE, Mrs T Ellis, Mrs T Jones, M Pickin, Mrs J Pickin, Mrs G Stratton, Mrs N Thompson, Mrs J Thorne
NOTES Only local charities or charities of which the Trustees have personal knowledge, interest, or association are considered. No applications from individuals or postal applications will be considered
WHO TO APPLY TO W Varney, The Wilfred and Constance Cave Foundation, c/o New Lodge Farm, Drift Road, Winkfield, Windsor, Berkshire SL4 4QQ
CC NO 241900   **ESTABLISHED** 1965

■ The B G S Cayzer Charitable Trust

WHAT IS FUNDED General charitable purposes
WHO CAN BENEFIT There are no restrictions on the age; professional and economic group; family situation; religion and culture; and social circumstances of; or disease or medical condition suffered by, the beneficiaries
WHERE FUNDING CAN BE GIVEN UK
RANGE OF GRANTS £50–£25,000
SAMPLE GRANTS £25,000 to Westerkirk Parish Trust; £20,000 to the Feathers Club Association; £5,000 to the Game Conservancy Trust; £3,500 to the Royal Horticultural Society; £3,000 to Woking Hospice Appeal; £3,000 to the Museum of Scotland; £2,500 to NSPCC; £2,500 to Arthritis Research; £1,000 to the Neo-Natal Trust Fund; £900 to Notting Hill Housing Trust
FINANCES *Year* 1996 *Income* £439,586 *Grants* £75,410
TRUSTEES P N Buckley, P R Davies
HOW TO APPLY **This Trust states that it does not respond to unsolicited applications**

WHO TO APPLY TO J H Sefton, The B G S Cayzer Charitable Trust, c/o The Cayzer Trust Co Ltd, Cayzer House, 1 Thomas More Street, London E1 9AR
CC NO 286063   **ESTABLISHED** 1982

■ The Raymond Cazalet Charitable Trust

WHAT IS FUNDED Large educational/medical charities
WHAT IS NOT FUNDED No grants to individuals
WHO CAN BENEFIT Large educational and medical charities benefiting children, young adults and students. There is no restriction on the disease or medical condition suffered by the beneficiaries. Medical professionals and research workers may be considered for funding
WHERE FUNDING CAN BE GIVEN Mainly UK
TYPE OF GRANT Research grants may be considered
SAMPLE GRANTS £5,000 to the Tropical Health and Education Trust; £2,500 to Youth for Britain; £2,500 to the Stroke Association; £2,500 to Sequal Trust; £2,500 to Fairbridge; £2,500 to the Friends of Christ Church, Spitalfields; £2,500 to Sight Savers International; £2,500 to the British Kidney Patients Association; £2,500 to Survival International; £2,500 to Uppingham School
FINANCES *Year* 1996 *Income* £43,827 *Grants* £28,500
TRUSTEES B J Leach, C J Cazalet, M J Cazalet, R H Cazalet
WHO TO APPLY TO B J Leach, The Raymond Cazalet Charitable Trust, 12 New Fetter Lane, London EC4A 1AP
CC NO 327685   **ESTABLISHED** 1987

■ The Celebrities Guild of Great Britain

WHAT IS FUNDED The purchasing of equipment, training or other educational purposes. The establishment and maintenance of homes and hostels. Allowances for medical treatment and care. Workshops for occupational therapy. Donations to hospitals
WHO CAN BENEFIT Individuals and organisations benefiting children and young adults, disabled and homeless people. There is no restriction on the disease or medical condition suffered by the beneficiaries
WHERE FUNDING CAN BE GIVEN UK and overseas
TYPE OF GRANT Periodical allowances, grants and loans
RANGE OF GRANTS £48–£2,303
SAMPLE GRANTS £2,303 to two quadriplegic individuals for a specially adapted computer; £2,000 to Thorne House Autistic Community, Doncaster for two computers and accessories; £1,000 to Guy's Hospital for the Paediatric Intensive Care Ward; £1,000 to Lancaster University for Cardio Information Service; £1,000 to Carlton Athletic Recovery Group; £1,000 Stoke Mandeville for the Microbiology Department; £1,000 to London Taxi Drivers' Fund for underprivileged children; £1,000 to Calvert Trust for outdoor activities for the disabled; £1,000 to Canine Partners for Independence for the Deaf; £1,000 to Borth Coastguard Association
FINANCES *Year* 1997 *Income* £28,657 *Grants* £15,727
TRUSTEES R Short, E Glazer, MBE, M Freedland, R Rietti, B Spear

WHO TO APPLY TO Mrs Ella Glazer, The Celebrities Guild of Great Britain, Knight House, 29–31 East Barnet Road, East Barnet, Hertfordshire EN4 8RN

CC NO 282298   **ESTABLISHED** 1981

■ Central & Eastern European Fellowship

WHAT IS FUNDED For Christian evangelical organisations in central and eastern Europe

WHO CAN BENEFIT National and established Christian evangelical organisations

WHERE FUNDING CAN BE GIVEN UK and overseas

TYPE OF GRANT Range of grants

RANGE OF GRANTS £164–£5,775

SAMPLE GRANTS £5,775 to Romania for general purposes; £5,727 to Romania for music equipment; £4,667 to Romania for church equipment; £3,824 to Hungary for building; £3,479 to Romania towards relief; £3,224 to Poland towards relief; £2,322 to Yugoslavia towards relief; £2,319 to Student support; £2,133 to Slovakia towards relief; £2,000 to Slovakia for building

FINANCES *Year* 1996–97 *Income* £70,224 *Grants* £42,714

TRUSTEES N Jones, T W O Matheson, H Moore

WHO TO APPLY TO W E Grunbaum, Central & Eastern European Fellowship, 4 Northover Road, Lymington, Hampshire SO41 8GW

CC NO 263723   **ESTABLISHED** 1971

■ The Amelia Chadwick Trust

WHAT IS FUNDED The Trust has a preference for Merseyside with a wide range of charities supported

WHO CAN BENEFIT Neighbourhood-based community projects, some national organisations. There are no restrictions on the age; professional and economic group; family situation; religion and culture; and social circumstances of; or disease or medical condition suffered by, the beneficiaries

WHERE FUNDING CAN BE GIVEN UK, especially Merseyside

TYPE OF GRANT Recurring

RANGE OF GRANTS £200–£29,750

SAMPLE GRANTS £29,750 to Merseyside Development Foundation; £7,500 to Fair Play for Children; £6,500 to St Helens Women's Aid; £6,500 to Liverpool PSS; £2,700 to European Playworkers; £2,000 to Centrepoint; £2,000 to Garston Adventure Playground; £2,000 to Rotunda Community College; £1,500 to Merseyside Holiday Service; £1,000 to Neston Nomads Junior Football Club

FINANCES *Year* 1997 *Income* £94,716 *Grants* £86,251

TRUSTEES J R McGibbon, J C H Bibby

NOTES The Trust's funds are fully committed

HOW TO APPLY To the address under Who To Apply To in writing. The Trust does not welcome telephone calls. There is no application form or guidelines, and no deadlines for applications. No sae is required

WHO TO APPLY TO J R M McGibbon, Partner, The Amelia Chadwick Trust, Layton & Co, Victoria House, 20 Hoghton Street, Southport PR9 0NX *Tel* 01704 547117

CC NO 213795   **ESTABLISHED** 1960

■ Challenge Adventure Charities

WHAT IS FUNDED General charitable purposes

WHO CAN BENEFIT There are no restrictions on the age; professional and economic group; family situation; religion and culture; and social circumstances of; or disease or medical condition suffered by, the beneficiaries

WHERE FUNDING CAN BE GIVEN UK

FINANCES *Year* 1997 *Income* £125,973 *Grants* £125,973

TRUSTEES S Derrick, S Mason-Elliott, C Saltrick

WHO TO APPLY TO C Saltrick, Secretary, Challenge Adventure Charities, 2 Lion's Gate, 33–39 High Street, Fordingbridge, Hampshire SP6 1AX

CC NO 1057920   **ESTABLISHED** 1996

■ The Challenge Trust

WHAT IS FUNDED Gifts are given to organisations concerned with distributing Bibles, missionary work and other mainly Christian activities

WHAT IS NOT FUNDED No grants to individuals

WHO CAN BENEFIT Organisations benefiting Christians

WHERE FUNDING CAN BE GIVEN UK and overseas

TRUSTEES A Naismith, J L MacLellan, Ms R A MacLellan

PUBLICATIONS Annual Report

HOW TO APPLY **This Trust states that it does not respond to unsolicited applications**

WHO TO APPLY TO A Naismith, Honorary Treasurer, The Challenge Trust, Orchardlea, Craigerne Lane, Peebles EH45 9HQ

SC NO SCO 16121

■ The Challice Trust

WHAT IS FUNDED This Trust will consider: social care professional bodies; volunteer bureaux; Christian outreach; community arts and activities; cultural activities; health buildings and facilities; cancer research; conservation; animal homes and welfare; special needs education; community facilities and services; and social advice centres. Help for local needs has priority

WHAT IS NOT FUNDED Only local students helped

WHO CAN BENEFIT Local organisations and individuals benefiting: academics; ex-service and service people; sportsmen and women; students; volunteers; and cancer sufferers. There is no restriction on age, and few on social circumstances of the beneficiaries

WHERE FUNDING CAN BE GIVEN Surrey

TYPE OF GRANT Small capital and maintenance

SAMPLE GRANTS £2,228 to local residents for coal and fuel; £1,000 to King Edward VII Hospital towards a hospice

FINANCES *Year* 1998 *Income* £13,282 *Grants* £11,362

TRUSTEES P W Smith, Mrs B Munro Thomson, R W Edmondson, B E Farley

HOW TO APPLY By brief letter. The are no deadline dates

WHO TO APPLY TO P W Smith, The Challice Trust, 29 Poltimore Road, Guildford, Surrey GU2 5PR

CC NO 222360   **ESTABLISHED** 1962

■ The Chamberlain Foundation

WHAT IS FUNDED Relief of poor, aged and infirm, advancement of education and religion, and other general charitable purposes for the benefit of the community

WHO CAN BENEFIT Individuals and organisations benefiting people of all ages, infirm people and those disadvantaged by poverty. Beneficiaries of many religions may be considered
WHERE FUNDING CAN BE GIVEN UK
RANGE OF GRANTS £50–£7,000
SAMPLE GRANTS £7,000 to Community of St Mary at the Cross; £5,000 to Cancer Vaccine Campaign; £5,000 to Eurograd Promotion Chelation; £3,000 to Winged Fellowship Trust; £2,000 to St Luke's Special School; £2,000 to Keystone Appeal YMCA; £2,000 to Quidenham Children's Hospice; £2,000 to St Mary-le-Bow Church towards Young Homelessness Project; £2,000 to Rainbow Trust; £2,000 to the Farimir Trust
FINANCES *Year* 1996 *Income* £90,929 *Grants* £127,747
TRUSTEES Mrs M J Spears, Mrs G M Chamberlain, G R Chamberlain, A G Chamberlain, Mrs S J Kent, Mrs C M Lester, Mrs L A Churcher
NOTES Total amount of gifts and grants to individuals was £72,330 for the year 1996. Trustees visit individuals who are shown to have need of support
WHO TO APPLY TO Ms C Elmer, Secretary, The Chamberlain Foundation, Devon House, The Green, Winchmore Hill, London N21 1SA
CC NO 1033995 **ESTABLISHED** 1949

■ The Pamela Champion Foundation

WHAT IS FUNDED General charitable purposes at Trustees' discretion. Grants are made to all or any of the following: National Council for the Single Woman and Her Dependants; The Salvation Army; Church Army; Royal United Kingdom Beneficent Association; Wood Green Animal Shelter; Help the Aged; NSPCC: Marie Curie Memorial Foundation; and other charitable causes
WHO CAN BENEFIT There are no restrictions on the age; professional and economic group; family situation; religion and culture; and social circumstances of; or disease or medical condition suffered by, the beneficiaries
WHERE FUNDING CAN BE GIVEN UK
TYPE OF GRANT At the discretion of the Trustees
FINANCES *Year* 1996 *Income* £40,542 *Grants* £23,500
TRUSTEES M Stanlake, C Winser, J G Bower, J E Richardson
WHO TO APPLY TO J E Richardson, Trustee, The Pamela Champion Foundation, Brant Wood, Hobson House, 155 Gower Street, London WC1E 6BJ
CC NO 268819 **ESTABLISHED** 1974

■ The Chandris Foundation

WHAT IS FUNDED Medicine and health; welfare; religion
WHAT IS NOT FUNDED No grants to individuals
WHO CAN BENEFIT Established and national organisations benefiting at risk groups, those disadvantaged by poverty and socially isolated people. There is no restriction on the religious or cultural background of, or the disease or medical condition suffered by the beneficiaries
WHERE FUNDING CAN BE GIVEN UK and overseas
TYPE OF GRANT One-off and recurrent
RANGE OF GRANTS £60–£5,200

SAMPLE GRANTS £5,200 to Action on Addiction; £5,000 to Hellenic College of London; £5,000 to Cycladic AA Foundation; £1,000 to SMH Special Trustees Fundraising; £970 to Royal Marsden Hospital; £500 to Frangiskatos book; £500 to St Sophia School; £500 to Malcolm Sargent Cancer Fund for Children; £500 to Teenage Cancer Trust Appeal; £500 to War on Cancer
FINANCES *Year* 1997 *Income* £44,436 *Grants* £28,900
TRUSTEES Chandris Foundation Trustees Ltd, M D Chandris, J D Chandris, R H Hall
HOW TO APPLY In writing
WHO TO APPLY TO R H Hall, Chandris Foundation Trustees Ltd, 17 Old Park Lane, London W1Y 3LG
CC NO 280559 **ESTABLISHED** 1980

■ Chapman Charitable Trust

WHAT IS FUNDED General charitable purposes. Main areas supported are culture and recreation; education and research; health; social services; environment; heritage; and religion
WHAT IS NOT FUNDED No grants to individuals
WHO CAN BENEFIT There are no restrictions on the age; professional and economic group; family situation; religion and culture; and social circumstances of; or disease or medical condition suffered by, the beneficiaries. However, particular favour is given to children, young adults, clergy, students, medical professionals, research workers and teachers and governesses. Support is also given to at risk groups, those disadvantaged by poverty and socially isolated people
WHERE FUNDING CAN BE GIVEN UK
TYPE OF GRANT Any, except new recurring ones
RANGE OF GRANTS £500–£25,000
SAMPLE GRANTS £25,000 to Aldeburgh Foundation; £10,000 to Field Studies Council for Juniper Hall Field Centre; £10,000 to Methodist Homes for the Aged; £10,000 to NCH Action for Children; £10,000 to Queen Alexandra's Hospital Home; £10,000 to St Bridget's Cheshire Home; £2,500 to Courtauld Institute of Art; £2,500 to The National Trust for Scotland; £2,000 to Fragile X Society; £2,000 to National Playing Fields Association
FINANCES *Year* 1997 *Income* £160,000 *Grants* £16,000
TRUSTEES Roger S Chapman, W John Chapman, Richard J Chapman, Bruce D Chapman
NOTES No guidelines are issued other than those appearing here. Grants are normally made only to recognised charities, mainly those in which the late Settlor and/or the Trustees have a personal interest or concern
HOW TO APPLY In writing at any time. The Trustees currently meet twice a year at the end of September and March. They receive a great many applications and regret that they cannot acknowledge receipt of them. The absence of any communication for six months means that an application must have been unsuccessful
WHO TO APPLY TO R S Chapman, Chapman Charitable Trust, Messrs Crouch Chapman, 62 Wilson Street, London EC2A 2BU
CC NO 232791 **ESTABLISHED** 1963

■ The Charities Advisory Trust

WHAT IS FUNDED General charitable purposes, particularly: income generation projects; homelessness; museums; cancer research and treatment

WHAT IS NOT FUNDED No grants for expeditions, scholarships and missionary activities (any denomination)

WHO CAN BENEFIT Homeless people, those disadvantaged by poverty and those suffering from cancer

WHERE FUNDING CAN BE GIVEN Worldwide, particularly in India and UK

TYPE OF GRANT Buildings, capital, core costs, endowments, feasibility studies, interest free loans; one-off, project, research, running costs, recurring costs, salaries and start-up costs. Funding is available for up to and over three years

RANGE OF GRANTS £500–£20,000, typically £5,000

SAMPLE GRANTS £15,000 to Vrindairau Society, India to establish an embroidery museum; £10,000 to Green Motel, Mysore for a model sustainable tourist project; £10,000 to British Refugee Council for hardship fund for asylum seekers; £5,000 to Ko'olot Ba'aw for peace and reconciliation work in Israel; £5,000 to Diabetes Specialist Nursing Fund at the Royal Free Hospital helping diabetics; £5,000 to Hammersmith Hospital, Department of Chemical Oncology for cancer patients – complementary therapies, eg massage; £5,000 to Colon Cancer Concern for research; £5,000 to Birmingham Settlement for hardship fund; £4,729 to National Theatre, Education Department for work with primary schools in Southwark

FINANCES *Year* 1996–97 *Income* £1,644,842 *Grants* £298,784

TRUSTEES Dr Cornelea Navar, Dr Carolynne Deauts, Prof Bob Holwan, Ms Dawn Peuso

NOTES We will consider anything but generally are pro-active in our funding

HOW TO APPLY No application form or guidelines. Unsolicited applications are not acknowledged

WHO TO APPLY TO The Charities Advisory Trust, Radius Works, Back Lane, London NW3 1HL *Tel* 0171-794 9835

CC NO 1040487   **ESTABLISHED** 1994

■ The Charities Aid Fund of the City of Glasgow Society of Social Service

WHAT IS FUNDED General charitable purposes

WHO CAN BENEFIT There are no restrictions on the age; professional and economic group; family situation; religion and culture; and social circumstances of; or disease or medical condition suffered by, the beneficiaries

WHERE FUNDING CAN BE GIVEN Glasgow

SAMPLE GRANTS £3,500 to Lodging House Mission (Church of Scotland); £2,500 to Glasgow Children's Holiday Scheme; £2,500 to Erskine House; £2,500 to Scottish Episcopal Church (Social Responsibility Unit); £2,500 to Springburn Youth and Community Project; £2,000 to Church House (St Francis in the East); £2,000 to Sense Scotland (Deaf, Blind and Rubella); £2,000 to Children First (RSPCC); £1,500 to Glasgow University Settlement; £1,500 to Glasgow Women's Aid

FINANCES *Year* 1997 *Income* £231,912 *Grants* £192,222

TRUSTEES Daniel J Brewster, Robert L Cromar, Ronald G Fulton, Alexander C Fyfe, Ian Jonstone, Mrs Grace Keele, John Keith, Donald J M Marshall, James MacDonald, John MacFarlan, William McInnes, Dr Sarah Orr, James Smillie, Mrs Joyce Stevenson

HOW TO APPLY Applications should be made in writing to the address under Who To Apply To

WHO TO APPLY TO James Smillie, Secretary, The Charities Aid Fund of the City of Glasgow, The City of Glasgow Society of Social Service, 30 George Square, Glasgow G2 1EG *Tel* 0141-248 3535

SC NO SCO 00906 (number for The City of Glasgow Society of Social Service)

■ Charities Fund

WHAT IS FUNDED (a) The provision of amenities for hospital patients. (b) The making of grants to charitable associations. (c) The making of grants to or for the relief and assistance of needy, sick and elderly persons

WHAT IS NOT FUNDED No grants to individuals

WHO CAN BENEFIT Generally local organisations benefiting older people, at risk groups, those disadvantaged by poverty and socially isolated people. There is no restriction on the disease or medical condition suffered by the beneficiaries

WHERE FUNDING CAN BE GIVEN UK with preference for the Yorkshire area, primarily areas covered by Sovereign Health Care

SAMPLE GRANTS £42,000 to War on Cancer; £10,000 to Manorlands; £10,000 to Stepping Stones; £10,000 to Rainbow Appeal; £10,000 to Sue Ryder Foundation; £7,500 to National Heart Research Fund; £7,000 to Bradford NHS Trust Team of the Year for equipment and research; £6,500 to Cancer Support Centre; £6,000 to The Samaritans; £5,000 to Macmillan Cancer Research for research

FINANCES *Year* 1997 *Income* £262,995

TRUSTEES Executive Committee of Sovereign Health Care

HOW TO APPLY In writing only. The Trust does not issue an application form

WHO TO APPLY TO The Secretary, Charities Fund, Sovereign Health Care, Royal Standard House, 26 Manningham Lane, Bradford, West Yorkshire BD1 3DN

CC NO 227355   **ESTABLISHED** 1955

■ Charity Association Manchester Ltd (164)

This trust failed to supply a copy of its annual report and accounts to CAF as required under section 47(2) of the Charities Act 1993. The information held on file at the Charity Commission was insufficient to enable CAF's researchers to write a substantive commentary on the trust's activities. Accordingly, despite its size, we are unable to list this trust in Spotlight on Major Trusts

WHAT IS FUNDED Jewish charities

WHO CAN BENEFIT Charities benefiting Jewish people

WHERE FUNDING CAN BE GIVEN UK and Israel

HOW TO APPLY To the address under Who To Apply To in writing

WHO TO APPLY TO P Koppenheim, Charity Association Manchester Ltd, 134 Leicester Road, Salford, Manchester M7 0HB

CC NO 257576   **ESTABLISHED** 1969

Does the trust you have chosen match your needs? Haphazard applications waste postage and time

113

■ Charity for Change

This trust did not respond to CAF's request to amend its entry and, by 30 June 1998, CAF's researchers did not find financial records for later than 1995 on its file at the Charity Commission. Trusts are legally required to submit annual accounts to the Charity Commission under section 42 of the Charities Act 1993

WHAT IS FUNDED The relief of poverty, advancement of education, advancement of religion and other charitable purposes at the discretion of the Trustees

WHO CAN BENEFIT At the discretion of the Trustees. There are no restrictions on the age; professional and economic group; family situation; religion and culture; and social circumstances of; or disease or medical condition suffered by, the beneficiaries

WHERE FUNDING CAN BE GIVEN Lancashire, UK and overseas

TYPE OF GRANT At the discretion of the Trustees

TRUSTEES F C Collins, A T Eastham, D R Watkinson

WHO TO APPLY TO A Eastham, Charity for Change, Eastham Solicitors, Continental House, 292–302 Church Street, Blackpool, Lancashire FY1 3QA

CC NO 1050388 **ESTABLISHED** 1994

■ The Charity People Trust

WHAT IS FUNDED General charitable purposes by the direction of the Founder, decided by representatives of the staff of Charity People Ltd. Charities working in the fields of: personnel and human resources; recruitment services; infrastructure development; education and training; campaigning and advocacy for social issues will be considered

WHAT IS NOT FUNDED No funding for non-people issues

WHO CAN BENEFIT Organisations benefiting children, young adults and volunteers

WHERE FUNDING CAN BE GIVEN UK

TRUSTEES D J Lale, S A Lale

WHO TO APPLY TO David Lale, Chairman, The Charity People Trust, c/o Charity People, 38 Bedford Place, London WC1B 5JH

CC NO 1057676 **ESTABLISHED** 1996

■ The Charles Trust

WHAT IS FUNDED Advancement of Christian religion as directed by Settlor

WHO CAN BENEFIT Organisations benefiting Christians

WHERE FUNDING CAN BE GIVEN UK and overseas

HOW TO APPLY This Trust states that it does not respond to unsolicited applications

WHO TO APPLY TO Mr Wakeling, The Charles Trust, UKET, PO Box 99, Loughton, Essex IG10 3QJ *Tel* 0181-502 5600

CC NO 1053160 **ESTABLISHED** 1995

■ The Charter 600 Charity

WHAT IS FUNDED General charitable purposes

WHO CAN BENEFIT There are no restrictions on the age; professional and economic group; family situation; religion and culture; and social circumstances of; or disease or medical condition suffered by, the beneficiaries

WHERE FUNDING CAN BE GIVEN UK

SAMPLE GRANTS £9,450 to Nairobi Hospice Charitable Trust; £1,000 to Prestbury Memorial Home Trust; £1,000 to Echo Polish Foundation for the Deaf; £1,000 to Nine Acres School; £600 to Nympsfield Village Hall; £500 to Oxford Council for Voluntary Action; £500 to Newbury Dyslexia Support Group; £500 to COMPAID Trust; £500 to Little Gaddesden Village Hall; £500 to Rendezvous Social Centre

FINANCES *Year* 1997 *Income* £99,864 *Grants* £19,150

WHO TO APPLY TO The Administrator, The Charter 600 Charity, Mercers' Hall, Ironmongers Lane, London EC2V 8HE *Tel* 0171-726 4991

CC NO 1051146 **ESTABLISHED** 1995

■ The Chartered Institute of Management Accountants' Research Foundation

WHAT IS FUNDED The Charitable Trust exists to promote research and education in the field of cost and management accounting and normally finances specific projects of this nature. It has not in the past made grants to other bodies to be spent at their discretion

WHO CAN BENEFIT Researchers in management accountancy

WHERE FUNDING CAN BE GIVEN UK

TYPE OF GRANT Project

FINANCES *Year* 1996 *Income* £350,721 *Grants* £342,500

TRUSTEES The Institute of Cost and Works Accountants' Charities Ltd Trustees: B Epsley, E N C Eustance, B R S Hulatt, D C Johnson, C Pinder, M C B Strickland, R M Sykes

WHO TO APPLY TO The Chartered Institute of Management Accountants' Research Foundation, 63 Portland Place, London W1N 4AB

CC NO 257749 **ESTABLISHED** 1968

■ The Charterhouse Charitable Trust

WHAT IS FUNDED Donations to registered charities dealing with inner city welfare, eg homelessness, drug or alcohol dependency, major educational charities, specific appeals and other charitable organisations

WHAT IS NOT FUNDED No donations to individuals. No sponsorships or advertising. No funding for politically motivated groups

WHO CAN BENEFIT Registered charities benefiting: children, young people and students; at risk groups; those disadvantaged by poverty; socially isolated and homeless people; and those suffering from drug or alcohol dependency

WHERE FUNDING CAN BE GIVEN London

TYPE OF GRANT Exclude 'starter financing', some regular annual donations

RANGE OF GRANTS £200–£30,000

SAMPLE GRANTS £30,000 to the London Connection; £10,000 to Macmillan Cancer Relief; £10,000 to St Mary's 150th Anniversary Appeal Charity; £7,500 to Wellbeing; £4,000 to the City of London Endowment Trust for St Paul's Cathedral; £2,500 to Crimestoppers Trust; £2,500 to Fight for Sight; £2,500 to the Royal Hospital for Neuro-Disability; £2,000 to The Duke of Edinburgh's Award; £2,000 to Jewish Care

FINANCES *Year* 1996–97 *Income* £133,011 *Grants* £97,950

TRUSTEES M V Blank, E G Cox

HOW TO APPLY To the Secretary, in writing, for the quarterly meeting of the Trustees

WHO TO APPLY TO The Secretary, The Charterhouse Charitable Trust, 1 Paternoster Row, St Paul's, London EC4M 7DH

CC NO 210894   **ESTABLISHED** 1954

■ The Chasah Trust

WHAT IS FUNDED The encouragement of missionary activity as well as the advancement of the evangelical tenets of Christianity

WHAT IS NOT FUNDED Buildings or general appeals

WHO CAN BENEFIT Evangelists and Christians

WHERE FUNDING CAN BE GIVEN UK, especially Greater London

FINANCES *Year* 1996–97 *Income* £50,000 *Grants* £50,000

TRUSTEES Karen Collier-Keywood, Richard Collier-Keywood, Glyn William

HOW TO APPLY To the address under Who To Apply To in writing

WHO TO APPLY TO R D Collier-Keywood, The Chasah Trust, Glydwish Hall, Fontridge Lane, Burwash, East Sussex TN19 7DG *Tel* 0171-213 3997

CC NO 294898   **ESTABLISHED** 1986

■ The Chase Charity

WHAT IS FUNDED The Trustees do not contribute to large general appeals, nor to annual running costs. They work over a wide field but projects in rural areas of particular interest together with strengthening vulnerable groups. They try to make an impact with each grant. Starter finance, unforeseen capital or other expenditure, even help over a bad patch are considered. Small charities and projects are preferred. This Trust considers funding: accommodation and housing; infrastructure development; churches; religious umbrella bodies; arts, culture and recreation; respite care for carers; church buildings; historical buildings; nature reserves; literacy; training for personal development; community facilities; care in the community; day centres; and individual rights

WHAT IS NOT FUNDED No grants are made for projects abroad or in Greater London; individuals; travel; expeditions; sport; endowment funds; hospices; the advancement of religion; animal welfare; medical research; formal education; festivals; individual youth clubs and uniformed youth groups; holidays; projects in receipt of Millennium Lottery Board funding; and other grant making bodies

WHO CAN BENEFIT Mostly small organisations often in rural areas. This includes: actors and entertainment professionals; musicians; research workers; scientists; retired and unemployed people; volunteers; and writers and poets. There is no restriction on the age or family situation, and some restrictions on the religion or culture and social circumstances of, and the disease or medical condition suffered by the beneficiaries

WHERE FUNDING CAN BE GIVEN Great Britain, except London

TYPE OF GRANT Buildings, capital, core costs, one-off, project, research, salaries and start-up costs. Funding is available for up to three years

RANGE OF GRANTS £1,000–£10,000

SAMPLE GRANTS £5,000 to the Griffin Almshouse, Alphington, Devon towards the cost of replacing windows; £5,000 to Deckham Community Centre, Gateshead for replacing roof; £4,000 to St Mark's Church Community Centre, Bedford for purchasing Portakabin as base for local autistic society; £4,000 to South Leeds Team Ministry Charity Ltd, Belle Isle, Leeds to refurbish and extend Belle Isle Day Centre for elderly people; £4,000 to Bridge Accommodation Project, Rushden, Northamptonshire to expand service for homeless people into rural areas, an 18 month pilot scheme; £4,000 to Voluntary Hostels Group, Norwich to establish a register of hostel workers as a one year pilot scheme; £3,500 to Lochaber Community Care Forum, Fort William, Scotland to help establish a 20 week pilot scheme involving visually impaired people; £3,120 to Community Campus '87, Middlesbrough to run evening tenant participation sessions for young people; £3,000 to Art Discovery, The Orkneys towards the cost of Ancient Minds – Modern Art Project with school children; £2,200 to the Crumbs Project, Bournemouth to open the kitchen for a third day to involve more people with mental health problems

FINANCES *Year* 1996–97 *Income* £289,476 *Grants* £207,770

TRUSTEES The Council of Management: A Ramsay Hack (Chairman), Gordon Halcrow, Richard Mills, Elizabeth Moore, Ninian Perry, Ann Stannard

PUBLICATIONS Annual Report; *How to Apply for a Grant*

HOW TO APPLY At any time. The Trustees meet quarterly, but there is a waiting list so projects are not often considered within three months of applying

WHO TO APPLY TO Ailsa Hornsby, The Chase Charity, 2 The Court, High Street, Harwell, Didcot, Oxfordshire OX11 0EY *Tel* 01235 820044

CC NO 207108   **ESTABLISHED** 1962

■ The Frank Chase Trust

WHAT IS FUNDED Education and training of unemployed people, relief of poverty; general charitable purposes at the discretion of the Trustees

WHO CAN BENEFIT There are no restrictions on the age; professional and economic group; family situation; religion and culture; and social circumstances of; or disease or medical condition suffered by, the beneficiaries. However particular favour is given to the unemployed and to those disadvantaged by poverty

WHERE FUNDING CAN BE GIVEN UK

TRUSTEES R Maxwell Justice, N Maxwell Chase

WHO TO APPLY TO Secretary to the Trustees, The Frank Chase Trust, Kelly's Secretariat, Washington House, PO Box 112, Reigate, Surrey RH2 9FT

CC NO 1053546   **ESTABLISHED** 1996

■ Chechen Appeal Foundation

WHAT IS FUNDED General charitable purposes to relieve poverty, sickness, to protect and preserve good health, and to advance education

WHO CAN BENEFIT Organisations benefiting children, young adults and students, those disadvantaged by poverty and socially isolated people. There is no restriction on the disease or medical condition suffered by the beneficiaries. Support may be given to medical professionals and research workers

WHERE FUNDING CAN BE GIVEN Overseas and Chechenya

FINANCES *Year* 1996 *Income* £38,441
Grants £27,100

WHO TO APPLY TO A R Bougara, Chechen Appeal Foundation, 12 Severn Road, Broomhill, Sheffield S10 2SU

CC NO 1056170   ESTABLISHED 1996

■ The Chelsea Square 1994 Trust

WHAT IS FUNDED Chiefly animals, the aged and the underprivileged. General charitable purposes

WHO CAN BENEFIT Organisations benefiting elderly people, at risk groups, those disadvantaged by poverty and socially isolated people. Otherwise, there are no restrictions on the age; professional and economic group; family situation; religion and culture; and social circumstances of; or disease or medical condition suffered by, the beneficiaries

WHERE FUNDING CAN BE GIVEN Southern England and to a limited extent overseas

TYPE OF GRANT One-off grants

FINANCES *Year* 1997 *Income* £49,287
Grants £59,610

HOW TO APPLY By letter with report and accounts

WHO TO APPLY TO J B Talbot, MC, The Chelsea Square 1994 Trust, The Middle House, Chapel Road, Rowledge, Farnham, Surrey GU10 4AN

CC NO 1040479   ESTABLISHED 1994

■ Chelsea Youth Opportunity Trust Ltd

WHAT IS FUNDED General charitable purposes

WHO CAN BENEFIT There are no restrictions on the age; professional and economic group; family situation; religion and culture; and social circumstances of; or disease or medical condition suffered by, the beneficiaries

WHERE FUNDING CAN BE GIVEN UK

TRUSTEES Hallmark Secretaries Ltd, Hallmark Registrars Ltd

WHO TO APPLY TO A L Shaw, Chelsea Youth Opportunity Trust Ltd, c/o Chelsea Village plc, Stamford Bridge, Fulham Road, London SW6 1HS

CC NO 1066875   ESTABLISHED 1997

■ Chernobyl Children's Challenge

WHAT IS FUNDED Relief of poverty for the benefit of the children in the Ukraine who have been affected by the explosion at the nuclear power plant in Chernobyl. Health care may be funded

WHO CAN BENEFIT Children affected by the explosion at the nuclear plant in Chernobyl, especially those disadvantaged by poverty

WHERE FUNDING CAN BE GIVEN Ukraine

SAMPLE GRANTS £8,485 to Chernigor Rehabilitation Centre; £1,252 to Keiv Hospital Immunology

FINANCES *Year* 1997 *Income* £34,297
Grants £9,738

TRUSTEES M Frohn, C J Frohn, Dr T A Hussell, V Kubik, L J C Frohn, M G W Frohn

WHO TO APPLY TO M Frohn, Trustee, Chernobyl Children's Challenge, Oakwood House, 22 Rectory Close, Woodchurch, Ashford, Kent TN26 3QD

CC NO 1064422   ESTABLISHED 1997

■ The Chertsey Combined Charity

WHAT IS FUNDED Charities working in the fields of: infrastructure, support and development; religion; self help groups; ambulances and mobile units; special needs education; speech therapy; and community services will be considered. Other charitable purposes are funded

WHO CAN BENEFIT Organisations benefiting: volunteers; Christians; Church of England; Roman Catholics; at risk groups; disabled people; those disadvantaged by poverty; and victims of abuse, crime and domestic violence. There is no restriction on age or family situation of the beneficiaries

WHERE FUNDING CAN BE GIVEN Former Urban District of Chertsey

TYPE OF GRANT Buildings, capital, core costs, one-off, recurring costs and start-up costs will be considered. Funding may be given for up to one year

RANGE OF GRANTS £15–£10,000

SAMPLE GRANTS £12,884 to various local organisations for Christmas festivities; £10,020 to various local residents for part payment of fuel bills; £7,500 to the Salvation Army for building; £2,000 to Ottershaw Playgroup for a garden; £1,000 to Relate for a computer; £500 to Splash towards playscheme

FINANCES *Year* 1997–98 *Income* £39,384
Grants £41,043

TRUSTEES Y Barnes, J M Edwards, C J Norman, R Fleming, D Harding, Canon D Head, G Hobbs, J Gooderham, Mrs M Lowther, M Everett, P Austin, P Anderson, M Loveday

NOTES Potential assistance of £1,000 or more requires formal presentation at Trustee meeting

HOW TO APPLY To the address under Who To Apply To in writing

WHO TO APPLY TO M R O'Sullivan, Secretary, The Chertsey Combined Charity, PO Box 89, Weybridge, Surrey KT13 8HW

CC NO 200186   ESTABLISHED 1987

■ The Cheshire Provincial Fund of Benevolence

WHAT IS FUNDED The relief of masons and their dependants, masonic charities and other charities, especially medical

WHO CAN BENEFIT Individuals and organisations benefiting masons and their families. There is no restriction on the disease or medical condition suffered by the beneficiaries

WHERE FUNDING CAN BE GIVEN Cheshire

SAMPLE GRANTS £7,000 to PGM Charity Account; £1,500 to St Luke's Hospice; £1,500 to St Ann's Hospice; £1,500 to East Cheshire Hospice; £1,500 to St John's Hospice; £1,500 to Hospice of the Good Shepherd; £1,500 to Rainbow Family Trust; £1,500 to Hope House Children's Respite Hospice; £1,500 to Beechwood Cancer Care Centre; £1,500 to Tameside and Glossop Hospice

FINANCES *Year* 1997 *Income* £322,663
Grants £237,501

TRUSTEES J A T Collins, A E Cross, G Glover, G R Humphries, P W Wellings, J Williams

NOTES In 1997, payments of £26,251 were made to individuals, £177,500 were made to masonic charities, and £33,750 were made to non-masonic charities

HOW TO APPLY To the address under Who To Apply To in writing

WHO TO APPLY TO J A T Collins, Provincial Grand Secretary, The Cheshire Provincial Fund of Benevolence, Ashcroft House, 36 Clay Lane, Timperley, Altrincham WA15 7AB
CC NO 219177   **ESTABLISHED** 1963

....

■ The Cheshire Provincial Grand Lodge of Mark Master Mason's Fund of Benevolence

WHAT IS FUNDED Masonic charities, the relief of poor masons and their families and other charitable purposes
WHO CAN BENEFIT Charities and other organisations benefiting masons, individual masons and their families
WHERE FUNDING CAN BE GIVEN Cheshire, Merseyside and Greater Manchester
RANGE OF GRANTS £100–£1,500
SAMPLE GRANTS £1,500 to Masonic Dorset Festival 1997; £1,182 to Cheshire Scouts and Guides; £1,000 to Masonic West Lancashire Festival 2005; £1,000 to Masonic Cheshire Festival 2000; £500 to Hospice of the Good Shepherd; £500 to Children's Heart Foundation; £400 to Distressed Brethren as three grants; £100 to St Johns Hospice
FINANCES *Year* 1997 *Income* £33,453 *Grants* £6,182
TRUSTEES H Statter (Chairman), J T Crompton, C J MacDonald
HOW TO APPLY To the address under Who To Apply To in writing. Applications from non-Masonic charities are considered once a year at the AGM
WHO TO APPLY TO J A T Collins, Provincial Grand Secretary, The Cheshire Provincial Grand Lodge of Mark Master Mason's Fund of Benevolence, Ashcroft House, 36 Clay Lane, Timperley, Altrincham WA15 7AB
CC NO 512541   **ESTABLISHED** 1982

....

■ Chest Heart and Stroke Scotland

WHAT IS FUNDED Grants are given for medical research into all aspects of the aetiology, diagnosis, prevention, treatment and social impact of chest, heart and stroke illness. Grants are also given to individuals in financial difficulty because of these conditions
WHO CAN BENEFIT Organisations benefiting: people suffering or at risk of chest, heart or stroke illness; at risk groups; carers; disabled people; and those disadvantaged by poverty. Funding is given to academics, research workers and medical professionals
WHERE FUNDING CAN BE GIVEN Scotland
TYPE OF GRANT Research fellowships, project grants, travel and equipment grants, career development awards, research secondments, student electives, welfare grants. Funding may be given for up to two years
RANGE OF GRANTS Research grants up to £60,000. Welfare grants up to £200

SAMPLE GRANTS £117,146 to a doctor at University of Glasgow for research into stroke rehabilitation; £57,565 to a research team at Ruchill Hospital, Glasgow for work focusing on reducing the risks of strokes in women and poorer socio-economic groups; £55,034 to a research team at Western Infirmary, Glasgow for work focusing on genetic determinants of left ventricular hypertrophy; £40,490 to two doctors at City Hospital, Edinburgh for research into respiratory infection; £28,865 to a doctor at Western General Hospital, Edinburgh for research into balloon angioplasty; £28,834 to a team of doctors at the Royal Infirmary, Edinburgh for research into the prevalence of chlamydia pneumonia; £27,945 to a research team at the University of Glasgow for work focusing on the influence of pressure on vascular structure; £26,050 to a research team at the Royal Infirmary, Aberdeen for work focusing on the use of a novel MRI technique; £18,900 to two individuals at the University of Dundee for flow cytometer; £15,000 to CRAG and the Royal College of Physicians and Surgeons for a national audit of Scottish stroke services
FINANCES *Year* 1997–98 *Income* £2,412,543 *Grants* £613,106
TRUSTEES Prof Charles Forbes, FRCP, FRSEd (Chairman), Dr Gavin Boyd, MD, FRCP (Vice Chairman), Colin McLean, MA, FFA (Vice Chairman), Dr John Callander, FRCGP, Sir John Crofton, MD, FRCP FRCPE, Dr Martin Dennis, Kenneth Dick, MVO, Duncan A Ferguson, FCIBS, Dr Peter Langhorne, BSc, PhD, MRCP, Miss Valerie Lobban, Alasdair Macdonald, Dr Hazel McHaffie, PhD, SRN, RM, Dr David Player, FRCPEd, FRCPsych, FFCM, Prof Lewis D Ritchie, MD, MSc, FFPHM, MRCGP, Graham T Ross, LVO, OBE, Mrs Christina Seiler, MA, Dr Roger G Smith, MB, FRCP, FRCPE, Dr Michael F Sudlow, MB, FRCP, FRCPE, James Williamson, CBE, FRCPE, DSc
PUBLICATIONS Annual Report
HOW TO APPLY Grants are awarded only to researchers living and working in Scotland; welfare grants are administered through social work authorities. For research grants contact: Fiona Swann-Skimming; for welfare grants contact: Helen McBain at the address under Who To Apply To
WHO TO APPLY TO Chest Heart and Stroke Scotland, 25 North Castle Street, Edinburgh EH2 3LT *Tel* 0131-225 6963 *Fax* 0131-220 6313 *E-mail* chss@dial.pipex.com
SC NO SCO 18761   **ESTABLISHED** 1990

....

■ Chester Diocesan Moral Aid Charity (St Bridget's Trust)

WHAT IS FUNDED Societies supporting women in moral danger and their children
WHAT IS NOT FUNDED No grants to individuals
WHO CAN BENEFIT Women (and their children), particularly those in care, fostered and adopted, and victims of abuse
WHERE FUNDING CAN BE GIVEN Cheshire
TYPE OF GRANT Core costs
RANGE OF GRANTS £1,100pa–£11,000pa; typical £1,800pa

Does the trust you have chosen match your needs? Haphazard applications waste postage and time

117

SAMPLE GRANTS £11,400 to Chester Diocese Adoption Services for core costs; £9,100 to Chester Diocese Committee for Social Responsibility for family services; £1,800 to Chester Womens Aid for abused women and children; £1,800 to Macclesfield Cradle Concern to support their care for unmarried mothers and babies; £1,600 to Save the Family for work with unmarried mothers and their children; £1,100 to YWCA Winsford to support their care for unmarried mothers and babies

FINANCES *Year* 1997–98 *Income* £28,092 *Grants* £26,800

TRUSTEES R Biggins, R L Jones, Rt Rev P Foster, Rev R M Powley, Canon G Robinson, Rev C J Samuels, Ms W Steadman

NOTES **All our income is fully committed**

HOW TO APPLY To the address under Who To Apply To in writing with an initial telephone call

WHO TO APPLY TO Canon G V M Robinson, Clerk, Chester Diocesan Moral Aid Charity, 69 Marian Drive, Great Boughton, Chester, Cheshire CH3 5RY *Tel* 01244 315828

CC NO 213298   **ESTABLISHED** 1962

■ Chesterfield General Charitable Fund

WHAT IS FUNDED Donations fall into four categories: specialised medical equipment; building restoration; recreational activities; and educational support

WHO CAN BENEFIT Individuals and institutions, especially those benefiting children and young adults

WHERE FUNDING CAN BE GIVEN The Parliamentary Constituency containing Chesterfield

SAMPLE GRANTS £15,250 to Duke of Edinburgh's Award Scheme; £4,000 to Derbyshire Life Appeal; £1,000 to DRFU; £500 to Birdholme School, Chesterfield for computer equipment; £500 to Dynah (Do you need a hand) towards a minibus appeal

FINANCES *Year* 1997 *Income* £24,888 *Grants* £24,275

TRUSTEES Mrs S Walker, P B Robinson, M Hadfield, Mrs G Goucher, D Botham, R Mansell, J Bown, K Unwin, J Husband

HOW TO APPLY To the address under Who To Apply To in writing

WHO TO APPLY TO Michael A Hadfield, Chesterfield General Charitable Fund, Commerce House, 658B Chatsworth Road, Chesterfield S40 3JZ *Tel* 01246 566667

CC NO 511375   **ESTABLISHED** 1981

■ The Chesterfield/Tsumeb Trust

WHAT IS FUNDED The relief of poverty, sickness and the advancement of education within the area of Tsumeb (Namibia) and among the inhabitants of Chesterfield. Sheltered accommodation and community clubs will be considered

WHO CAN BENEFIT Inhabitants of Tsumeb (and Chesterfield). Support will be considered for children, older people, retired people, students, widows and widowers. Funding may be given to those disadvantaged by poverty and homeless people

WHERE FUNDING CAN BE GIVEN Tsumeb (Namibia) and Chesterfield

TYPE OF GRANT One-off, capital, recurring and buildings will be considered. Funding may be given for more than three years

RANGE OF GRANTS £100–£5,000

FINANCES *Year* 1997–98 *Income* £3,320

TRUSTEES R Hennelly, G Lyndon, S Niblock, C Rose, D R Shaw, P Stone, D A Wain

NOTES Funds are very restricted and in the early years are likely to be limited to known, established recipients

HOW TO APPLY A telephone call to the Borough Council Twinning Officer on 01246 345236 will save unnecessary applications

WHO TO APPLY TO D R Shaw, Town Clerk and Chief Executive, The Chesterfield/Tsumeb Trust, Town Clerk and Chief Executive Dept, Town Hall, Chesterfield, Derbyshire S40 1LP *Tel* 01246 345312

CC NO 1063932   **ESTABLISHED** 1997

■ The Chetwode Foundation

WHAT IS FUNDED General charitable purposes

WHO CAN BENEFIT There are no restrictions on the age; professional and economic group; family situation; religion and culture; and social circumstances of; or disease or medical condition suffered by, the beneficiaries

WHERE FUNDING CAN BE GIVEN Preference to Notts, Derby and Leicestershire areas

RANGE OF GRANTS £40–£2,000

SAMPLE GRANTS £2,000 to St Paul's Church; £1,300 to Tythby and Cropwell Butler PCC; £517 to Nottingham County Show; £500 to Cricket Federation for People with Disabilities; £500 to Edwalton Parish Church; £500 to Council for Voluntary Service; £500 to St Peter's Church; £250 to Bingham Methodist Church; £50 to National Trust for Scotland; £50 to Helen Hurst Charity Fund

FINANCES *Year* 1996 *Income* £38,674 *Grants* £6,207

TRUSTEES J G Ellis, R N J S Price

WHO TO APPLY TO J G Ellis, The Chetwode Foundation Samworth Brothers Limited, Fields Farm, Cropwell Butler, Nottingham NG12 3AP

CC NO 265950   **ESTABLISHED** 1973

■ The Chevras Ezras Nitzrochim Trust

WHAT IS FUNDED Orthodox Jewish organisation set up to raise money to help the poor in Jewish communities

WHO CAN BENEFIT Organisations benefiting Jewish people who are disadvantaged by poverty

WHERE FUNDING CAN BE GIVEN UK

FINANCES *Year* 1996 *Income* £212,156 *Grants* £205,834

TRUSTEES H Kahan, The Very Rev D L Edwards, DD, Rev Canon R White, A N Russell

WHO TO APPLY TO H Kahan, The Chevras Ezras Nitzrochim Trust, 53 Heathland Road, London N16 5PQ

CC NO 275352   **ESTABLISHED** 1978

■ The Chickadee Trust

WHAT IS FUNDED Relief of poverty, advancement of education, promotion of the Christian faith and other charitable purposes will be considered

WHO CAN BENEFIT Small local projects, national and established organisations benefiting children, young adults, Christians and those disadvantaged by poverty

WHERE FUNDING CAN BE GIVEN UK and overseas

Have you read How to use the DGMT *on page xvi?*

TYPE OF GRANT One-off and recurrent
RANGE OF GRANTS £100–£26,000
SAMPLE GRANTS £26,000 to Overseas Missionary Fellowship; £19,520 to Andamio (Spanish Evangelical Publishing House); £14,684 Meadowridge School; £11,000 to Tear Fund; £8,000 to an individual; £4,000 to St Marks Church; £3,600 to Proclamation Trust; £2,000 the Titus Trust; £1,800 to an individual; £1,100 to an individual
FINANCES *Year* 1997 *Income* £34,907 *Grants* £96,272
TRUSTEES Rupert Mackay, Peter Mackay, Stephen Mackay, David D C Munro
WHO TO APPLY TO R Mackay, The Chickadee Trust, 5 Albert Square, London SW8 1BU
CC NO 328560   ESTABLISHED 1989

■ Child Growth Foundation

WHAT IS FUNDED (a) The Foundation seeks to ensure that the growth of every UK child is regularly assessed and that any child growing excessively slowly or fast is referred for medical attention as soon as possible. (b) The Foundation seeks to ensure that no child will be denied the drugs they need to correct their stature. (c) The Foundation supports institutions researching the cause/cures of growth conditions. (d) The Foundation maintains a network of families to offer support/advice for any family concerned/diagnosed with a growth problem
WHO CAN BENEFIT Institutions researching child/adult growth disorders and sufferers of such diseases
WHERE FUNDING CAN BE GIVEN UK
TYPE OF GRANT Research
FINANCES *Year* 1997 *Income* £365,189 *Grants* £272,085
TRUSTEES Management Committee: P Ballinger, Ms B Dudman, Ms R Chaplin, T Fry, C Hermon, Ms C Matthews, D Oram, M Silver, Ms A Smyth
PUBLICATIONS Patient information booklets, newsletters
WHO TO APPLY TO R I Chaplin, Hon Treasurer, Child Growth Foundation, 13 Chestnut Avenue, Edgware, Middlesex HA8 7RA
CC NO 274325   ESTABLISHED 1977

■ Child Resettlement Trust Fund – Emunah

WHAT IS FUNDED To provide funds for the welfare of underprivileged children in Israel, and for their education according to Jewish law and tradition, helping senior citizens and new immigrants
WHO CAN BENEFIT Jewish children and senior citizens in Israel who are at risk, disadvantaged by poverty or socially isolated, New immigrants may also be supported
WHERE FUNDING CAN BE GIVEN Israel
SAMPLE GRANTS £673,773 to British Emunah Projects in Israel
FINANCES *Year* 1997 *Income* £775,488 *Grants* £973,773
TRUSTEES Mrs G Grahame, H Kaufman, Mrs G Compton, Mrs R Selby, Mrs L Brodie
WHO TO APPLY TO Mrs Helen French, Child Resettlement Trust Fund, Norwood House, Harmony Way (off Victoria Road), London NW4 2DR *Tel* 0181-203 6066
CC NO 215398   ESTABLISHED 1950

■ Children First

WHAT IS FUNDED General charitable purposes
WHO CAN BENEFIT There are no restrictions on the age; professional and economic group; family situation; religion and culture; and social circumstances of; or disease or medical condition suffered by, the beneficiaries
WHERE FUNDING CAN BE GIVEN UK
FINANCES *Year* 1996 *Income* £106,262
TRUSTEES Miss E McGreevy, Miss K McGreevy
WHO TO APPLY TO K P M G, Children First, Richmond Park House, 15 Pembroke Road, Clifton, Bristol BS8 3BG
CC NO 1046266   ESTABLISHED 1995

■ The Children's Charter

WHAT IS FUNDED Local projects which guarantee care, treatment, rehabilitation, education and healthy activity programmes for abused and disabled children and young people
WHO CAN BENEFIT Organisations benefiting children and young adults, who are disabled or victims of abuse
WHERE FUNDING CAN BE GIVEN UK, but money raised in one county will be spent in that county
TYPE OF GRANT Running costs to already established but financially stretched projects
HOW TO APPLY To the address under Who To Apply To in writing. Funds are allocated on an annual basis at the end of each financial year
WHO TO APPLY TO Ms S Keating-Cairnes, Founder, The Children's Charter, Sanders House, 48 Oldfield Circus Whitton Avenue West, Northolt, Middlesex UB5 4RR
CC NO 1056701   ESTABLISHED 1996

■ The Children's Research Fund

WHAT IS FUNDED Promoting, encouraging and fostering research into all aspects of diseases in children, child health and prevention of illness in children. Support of research centres and research units by grants to academic institutions, hospitals and other bodies with similar aims and objects to the Fund. Support after the first year dependent on receipt of satisfactory report
WHO CAN BENEFIT Institutes of child health and university child health departments benefiting sick children. Academics, medical professionals, research workers and students may benefit
WHERE FUNDING CAN BE GIVEN UK
TYPE OF GRANT Research
SAMPLE GRANTS £65,833 to Institute of Child Health, University of Liverpool; £50,000 to University of Southampton Therapist Course; £30,000 to University of Leicester; £17,500 to University of Essex; £14,905 to Institute of Epidemiology, University of Leeds; £14,000 to Pain Relief Foundation; £11,407 to Wessex Medical School Trust; £10,500 to Great Ormond Street Hospital; £5,439 to University of Glasgow; £3,877 to Glasgow Royal Hospital
FINANCES *Year* 1997 *Income* £231,543 *Grants* £226,611
TRUSTEES The Council: H Greenwood, H E Greenwood, G W Inkin, Prof J Lister, Rt Hon A Morris, Dr G J Piller, Ms E Theobald
WHO TO APPLY TO Hugh Greenwood, Chairman, The Children's Research Fund, 6 Castle Street, Liverpool L2 0NA
CC NO 226128   ESTABLISHED 1962

■ The Childs Charitable Trust

WHAT IS FUNDED To support Christian activity at home and overseas, especially the furtherance of the Christian Gospel

WHO CAN BENEFIT Churches or Christian organisations

WHERE FUNDING CAN BE GIVEN UK and overseas. Contacts are particularly strong with South America and the Philipines

FINANCES _Year_ 1995 _Income_ £234,773 _Grants_ £158,267

TRUSTEES D N Martin, Mrs H V Childs, R H Williams, A B Griffiths

NOTES It is the policy of the Trustees that one of their number visit funding locations to ensure that their money is correctly used

WHO TO APPLY TO D Martin, The Childs Charitable Trust, 2–4 Saffrons Road, Eastbourne, East Sussex BN21 1DG

CC NO 234618   **ESTABLISHED** 1962

■ The Chiltern Trust Fund

WHAT IS FUNDED Mainly evangelical Christian causes

WHO CAN BENEFIT Individuals and societies benefiting Evangelists and Christians

WHERE FUNDING CAN BE GIVEN UK

TRUSTEES G R Norden, P L Harden

HOW TO APPLY **This Trust states that it does not respond to unsolicited applications**

WHO TO APPLY TO G R Norden, The Chiltern Trust Fund, 13 Redlands Road, Sevenoaks, Kent TN13 2JZ

CC NO 267183   **ESTABLISHED** 1958

■ The Chilton Charitable Trust

WHAT IS FUNDED General charitable purposes at the discretion of the Settlor

WHO CAN BENEFIT There are no restrictions on the age; professional and economic group; family situation; religion and culture; and social circumstances of; or disease or medical condition suffered by, the beneficiaries

WHERE FUNDING CAN BE GIVEN UK

TRUSTEES A Garfield, D Kossof, L Kossof, S B Sylvester

WHO TO APPLY TO A M Garfield, Trustee, The Chilton Charitable Trust, 120 Salmon Street, Kingsbury, London NW9 8NL

CC NO 1051738   **ESTABLISHED** 1995

■ Chinak Charitable Trust

WHAT IS FUNDED Relief of poverty, particularly the provision of grants to women setting up small businesses and co-operatives; the provision of educational materials overseas

WHO CAN BENEFIT Organisations benefiting children, women and those disadvantaged by poverty

WHERE FUNDING CAN BE GIVEN UK and overseas

TRUSTEES B C Akigwe, I N Akigwe, J E Akigwe

WHO TO APPLY TO J E Akigwe, Chairman, Chinak Charitable Trust, 45 Fairholme Road, Harrow, Middlesex HA1 2TL

CC NO 1058010   **ESTABLISHED** 1996

■ The Chippenham Borough Lands Charity

WHAT IS FUNDED Benefiting the inhabitants of Chippenham, especially the aged, sick, disabled or poor, provision of facilities for recreation and other leisure time occupation, and advancement of education

WHAT IS NOT FUNDED All considered except retrospective applications

WHO CAN BENEFIT Residents of the Parish. Organisations benefiting children, young adults, older people, retired, those disadvantaged by poverty and disabled people. There is no restriction on the disease or medical condition suffered by, the beneficiaries

WHERE FUNDING CAN BE GIVEN Chippenham

RANGE OF GRANTS £5–£50,000

FINANCES _Year_ 1995–96 _Income_ £251,498

TRUSTEES Mrs R Angill (Chairman), C Grace, Mrs E Taylor, Mrs J Wood, M Braun and others

PUBLICATIONS Annual Report

HOW TO APPLY To the address under Who To Apply To in writing

WHO TO APPLY TO B D Coombs, Chief Executive, The Chippenham Borough Lands Charity, 16 Market Place, Chippenham, Wiltshire SN15 3HW _Tel_ 01249 658180

CC NO 270062   **ESTABLISHED** 1990

■ The Chipping Sodbury Town Lands Charity

WHAT IS FUNDED Relief in need and educational purposes. Charities working in the fields of: dance and ballet; music and the theatre; arts education; church buildings and historic buildings; and health education will also be considered

WHO CAN BENEFIT Both individuals and organisations benefiting: one parent families; widows and widowers; disabled people; those disadvantaged by poverty; and disaster victims. People with a variety of diseases and medical conditions will be considered. Support may also go to actors and entertainment professionals and musicians

WHERE FUNDING CAN BE GIVEN Chipping Sodbury and Old Sodbury

TYPE OF GRANT Buildings, capital, one-off and recurring costs will be considered

SAMPLE GRANTS £16,500 to a local church for repairs; £9,000 to a local senior school for computer equipment; £7,500 to a local school for music fees and books for FE; £2,500 to a local football club for improvements to building; £2,156 to a local junior school for computer equipment; £1,800 to a local disabled child for a special bed; £1,000 to a playscheme for equipment; £1,000 to a local church for repairs to lych gate; £800 to the village hall for repairs; £552 to Abbeyfield Residents Association for outings for the residents

FINANCES _Year_ 1997 _Income_ £213,453 _Grants_ £54,488

TRUSTEES W J Ainsley, OBE, P J Elsworth, C A R Matfield, W S King, D Shipp, P L Tily, E J J Williams, C Wilmore

HOW TO APPLY To the address under Who To Apply To in writing. The Trustees meet on the third week of each month except August

WHO TO APPLY TO The Clerk to the Trustees, The Chipping Sodbury Town Lands Charity, Town Hall, 57–59 Broad Street, Chipping Sodbury, South Gloucestershire BS37 6AD _Tel_ 01454 852223

CC NO 236364   **ESTABLISHED** 1977

■ The Chiron Trust

WHAT IS FUNDED Support is given in the fields of conservation and environment, health facilities, vocational training, advice centres, and support for volunteers and voluntary organisations

WHAT IS NOT FUNDED No funding for expeditions or travel bursaries

WHO CAN BENEFIT Registered charities benefiting: volunteers; at risk groups; those disadvantaged by poverty; socially isolated people; victims of famine, war and man-made or natural disasters, and those who are terminally ill

WHERE FUNDING CAN BE GIVEN England, particularly North East, North West and Eastern regions and London

TYPE OF GRANT Buildings, core costs, running costs and start-up costs will be considered. Funding is available for up to three years

RANGE OF GRANTS £250–£1,000

FINANCES *Year* 1997 *Income* £113,747 *Grants* £144,323

TRUSTEES D M Tinson, C J Du B Tinson, I R Marks

NOTES In writing, no application forms

WHO TO APPLY TO Mrs D M Tinson, The Chiron Trust, 30 Fitzwalter Road, Colchester, Essex CO3 3SY

CC NO 287062   **ESTABLISHED** 1983

■ The Chownes Foundation

WHAT IS FUNDED Medicine and health, welfare, education, religion. These include: Christian education; catholic bodies; training for personal development; bursaries, fees and scholarships; international rights of the individual; penal reform; and health counselling

WHO CAN BENEFIT Small local projects, national and established organisations, individuals requiring finance for education or the relief of poverty. This includes: children; young adults; retired people; students; parents and children; Roman Catholics; and those disadvantaged by poverty. Also those suffering from: asthma, mental illness, and spina bifida and hydrocephalus

WHERE FUNDING CAN BE GIVEN Preference for Sussex

TYPE OF GRANT One-off, recurrent, buildings, capital, core costs, research and running costs. Funding is available for up to and over three years

SAMPLE GRANTS £5,650 to an individual for relief of poverty; £5,000 to Amnesty International for social purposes; £3,500 to the Abbot of Worth for religious purposes; £3,000 to an individual for educational purposes; £2,500 to an individual for relief of poverty; £2,486 to an individual for relief of poverty; £2,000 to Friends of the Samaritans for social purposes; £2,000 to Howard League for Penal Reform for social purposes; £2,000 to St Anne's Convent for religious purposes; £2,000 to an individual for relief of poverty

FINANCES *Year* 1997–98 *Income* £100,811 *Grants* £105,186

TRUSTEES C R P Stonor, The Rt Rev S Ortiger The Abbot of Worth, Mrs U Hazeel

HOW TO APPLY In writing. Applications not always acknowledged. No guidelines issued

WHO TO APPLY TO R A Brooker, The Chownes Foundation, The Courtyard, Beeding Court, Steyning, West Sussex BN44 3TN *Tel* 01903 816699

CC NO 327451   **ESTABLISHED** 1987

■ The Chrimes Family Charitable Trust

WHAT IS FUNDED Infrastructure development; hospice at home; and respite and care for carers. The Trustees give preference to support of community welfare on Merseyside and North Wales. Elsewhere only work, in this field, of originality or outstanding excellence is supported

WHAT IS NOT FUNDED No grants to individuals, arts, conservation or education and training

WHO CAN BENEFIT Volunteers; carers and disabled people. Those suffering from arthritis and rheumatism; asthma; autism; cancers; hearing and sight loss; and terminal illnesses

WHERE FUNDING CAN BE GIVEN Priority to Merseyside, Wirral, Conwy and Gwynedd

RANGE OF GRANTS £50–£500

FINANCES *Year* 1997 *Income* £18,396 *Grants* £21,984

TRUSTEES Mrs Anne Williams, Mrs H G Kirkham Prosser

HOW TO APPLY No application form. Letters appreciated. No deadlines

WHO TO APPLY TO Mrs Anne Williams, The Chrimes Family Charitable Trust, Northfield, Upper Raby Road, Neston, South Wirral L64 7TZ

CC NO 210199   **ESTABLISHED** 1955

■ The Christadelphian Samaritan Fund

WHAT IS FUNDED Prefer human causes and aid to third world

WHAT IS NOT FUNDED No grants to individuals

WHO CAN BENEFIT Registered charities and organisations in the third world. There are no restrictions on the age; professional and economic group; family situation; religion and culture; and social circumstances of; or disease or medical condition suffered by, the beneficiaries

WHERE FUNDING CAN BE GIVEN UK and overseas

TYPE OF GRANT Single donations

SAMPLE GRANTS £2,400 to Red Cross in response to North Korea Appeal; £1,000 to Red Cross Iran Appeal after earthquake; £500 to Leper Colony, India; £500 Oxfam for North Korea; £400 to Turning Point; £400 to Camphill Village Trust

FINANCES *Year* 1997 *Income* £46,045 *Grants* £40,065

TRUSTEES The Committee

HOW TO APPLY In writing

WHO TO APPLY TO K H A Smith (Treasurer), The Christadelphian Samaritan Fund, 1 Sherbourne Road, Acocks Green, Birmingham B27 6AB *Tel* 0121-706 6100

CC NO 1004457   **ESTABLISHED** 1991

■ The Christendom Trust

WHAT IS FUNDED Promotion of research and application of research in the area of Christian social thought, education and training and costs of study

WHAT IS NOT FUNDED Grants are not normally made to individuals pursuing research for university degrees; nor are grants given to maintain already-existing projects

WHO CAN BENEFIT The principal beneficiary is the Maurice Reckitt Community Theologian at St Botolph's, Aldgate. Grants have also been made to Christian Aid (Education Sector), the Irish School of Ecumenics, research projects associated with Church Action on Poverty and the

Does the trust you have chosen match your needs? Haphazard applications waste postage and time

121

Institute for the Study of Christianity and Sexuality. More generally, individuals or organisations benefiting children, young adults, older people, academics, clergy, volunteers, Christians and those disadvantaged by poverty

WHERE FUNDING CAN BE GIVEN UK and overseas

TYPE OF GRANT Feasibility studies, one-off, project, research, running costs, salaries and start-up costs. Funding is considered for up to three years

SAMPLE GRANTS £10,000 to St Botolph's, Aldgate, London for M B Reckitt Community Theologian; £4,500 to Centre for Theology and Public Issues, Edinburgh for research project; £3,000 to Manchester Development Education Project for Values and Vision education research project; £3,000 to Kainos Europa towards costs of European grass roots campaign; £2,500 to Ecumenical Spirituality Project for Spirituality in Conversation Project

FINANCES *Year* 1997 *Income* £25,000 *Grants* £30,000

TRUSTEES Mrs Angela Cunningham, William Fuge, Rev Ermal Kirby, Prof Andrew Louth, Rev Christopher Martin, Dr David Ormrod, Rev Alyson Peberdy, Dr R C Towler, Dr Stephen Yeo, Mrs Angela West

HOW TO APPLY Applications for guidelines should be sent to the address below. The Trust meets three times per annum to consider applications, which should be sent to the Hon Secretary by the end of January, May and September

WHO TO APPLY TO Angela Cunningham, Hon Secretary, The Christendom Trust, 24 Westbourne Road, Lancaster LA1 5DD

CC NO 262394   **ESTABLISHED** 1971

■ Christian Aid

WHAT IS FUNDED Christian Aid works in four main areas: (a) it supports the poorest communities in their struggle to achieve a better life; (b) through advocacy, campaigning and education, mainly in Britain and Ireland but also in the world's poorest countries, it addresses the root causes of poverty and works to change the context in which those communities struggle: (c) by communication work on as broad a front as possible it tells the stories of those communities, the realities they face, and the work that they and Christian Aid achieve together; (d) it raises funds in order to direct as much money as possible to the world's poorest people. Trustees appointed by sponsoring churches and ecumenical instruments

WHAT IS NOT FUNDED No grants to individuals for any purpose or for political purposes or to organisations whose aims are primarily political

WHO CAN BENEFIT Councils of Churches, other ecumenical bodies, development and relief groups, UN agencies benefiting: at risk groups; those disadvantaged by poverty; homeless people; refugees; immigrants; socially isolated people; victims of famine, man-made or natural disasters, and war. There is no restriction on the age; family situation or religion and culture of the beneficiaries

WHERE FUNDING CAN BE GIVEN Mainly third world but also limited assistance for development education projects in the UK

FINANCES *Year* 1996–97 *Income* £39,344,000 *Grants* £37,424,000

TRUSTEES Board of Christian Aid appointed by sponsoring churches and ecumenical instruments

PUBLICATIONS Publications list available

WHO TO APPLY TO The Director, Christian Aid, PO Box 100, London SE1 7RT *Tel* 0171-620 4444 *Fax* 0171-620 0719 *E-mail* caid@gn.apc.org

CC NO 258003   **ESTABLISHED** 1945

■ The Christian Renewal Trust

WHAT IS FUNDED Advancement of Christian religion, churches, relief of the poor, relief of the sick and the aged in need. However, no funds are available for the foreseeable future

WHO CAN BENEFIT Churches. Organisations benefiting older people and those disadvantaged by poverty. There is no restriction on the disease or medical condition suffered by the beneficiaries

WHERE FUNDING CAN BE GIVEN UK and overseas

TYPE OF GRANT One-off donations

FINANCES *Year* 1994–95 *Income* £23,165 *Grants* £22,289

TRUSTEES A S Robinson, M Robinson, I MacRoberts, P Seadon

HOW TO APPLY **There are no funds available for the foreseeable future**

WHO TO APPLY TO M Cole, Accountant, The Christian Renewal Trust, Watson Saunders & Cole, 10 Peacock Lane, Leicester LE1 5PW

CC NO 276496   **ESTABLISHED** 1978

■ Christian Vision

WHAT IS FUNDED Christian faith, relief of poverty and sickness, Christian education

WHAT IS NOT FUNDED Buildings, land, scholarships, expeditions

WHO CAN BENEFIT Institutions benefiting Christians, Evangelists and those disadvantaged by poverty. There are no restrictions on the disease or medical condition suffered by the beneficiaries

WHERE FUNDING CAN BE GIVEN Primarily overseas; some UK

TYPE OF GRANT One-off, recurrent and project. Funding for more than three years will be considered

SAMPLE GRANTS £880,101 to Christian Vision (Zambia) for running Christian Radio Station, establishing Christian Bible college/school; £691,334 to Emisora Christian Vision (Chile) for setting up Christian Radio Station; £333,016 to Visao Crista Mocambique for Church planting project

FINANCES *Year* 1996 *Income* £4,492,499 *Grants* £2,340,615

TRUSTEES R N Edmiston, I P Baker, T J Spicer, N Cuthbert

HOW TO APPLY In writing. Trustees meet three times a year

WHO TO APPLY TO R N Edmiston, Trust Director, Christian Vision, Ryder Street, West Bromwich, West Midlands B70 0EJ *Fax* 0121-522 6083 *E-mail* christian_vision@compuserve.com

CC NO 1031031   **ESTABLISHED** 1988

■ Christ's Hospital Endowment at Potter Hanworth

WHAT IS FUNDED Educational purposes in the area Where Funding Can Be Given

WHO CAN BENEFIT Individuals and schools benefiting children, young adults and students under the age of 25 in the area Where Funding Can Be Given

WHERE FUNDING CAN BE GIVEN Potterhanworth

FINANCES *Year* 1997 *Income* £16,709 *Grants* £10,000

HOW TO APPLY To the address under Who To Apply To in writing

WHO TO APPLY TO Mrs Y Woodcock, Clerk, Christ's Hospital Endowment at Potter Hanworth, The Conifers, Barff Road, Potterhanworth, Lincoln LN4 2DU *Tel* 01522 790942
CC NO 527669   **ESTABLISHED** 1961

■ Chubb Employees Charities Fund

WHAT IS FUNDED Sickness, elderly people, equipment for local causes, local charities
WHO CAN BENEFIT Organisation benefiting: older people, retired people and the local community. There are no restrictions on the disease or medical condition suffered by the beneficiaries
WHERE FUNDING CAN BE GIVEN UK, especially Wolverhampton and the surrounding area
TYPE OF GRANT Capital grants will be considered
FINANCES *Year* 1996–97 *Income* £23,018
Grants £10,599
HOW TO APPLY To the address under Who To Apply To in writing
WHO TO APPLY TO T E Dulson, Secretary Charities Committee, Chubb Employees Charities Fund, Chubb Locks Ltd, PO Box 197, Wednesfield Road, Wolverhampton WV10 0ET
CC NO 273642   **ESTABLISHED** 1977

■ Bruce Church Charitable Trust

WHAT IS FUNDED General charitable purposes, in particular, the education in the United States or the United Kingdom of painters of promise who work in the School of Figurative Art
WHO CAN BENEFIT To benefit painters of promise who work in the School of Figurative Art
WHERE FUNDING CAN BE GIVEN UK and USA
FINANCES *Year* 1996 *Income* £43,055
HOW TO APPLY All grants are made through Camberwell College
WHO TO APPLY TO R A Cassells, Bruce Church Charitable Trust, Brian Cave, LLP, 29 Queen Anne's Gate, London SW1H 9BU *Tel* 0171-896 1941
CC NO 1042327   **ESTABLISHED** 1994

■ The Church Houses Relief in Need Charity (also known as St Michael's and All Saints Charities Relief Branch)

WHAT IS FUNDED Hospitals and nursing homes; relief in sickness; relief for the disabled, for the homeless and the destitute; social services
WHAT IS NOT FUNDED No grants to individuals
WHO CAN BENEFIT Institutions and organisations benefiting disabled people, those disadvantaged by poverty and homeless people. There is no restriction on the disease or medical condition suffered by the beneficiaries
WHERE FUNDING CAN BE GIVEN Oxford
TYPE OF GRANT Recurrent
RANGE OF GRANTS £150–£5,000
SAMPLE GRANTS £5,000 to Nuffield Orthoptics Appeal; £3,200 to Oxford Home Start; £2,000 to Oxford and District MENCAP; £2,000 to Oxford Victim Support Scheme; £1,750 to PARASOL (Children's and Young People's Special Needs); £1,650 to Oxford OAP Club; £1,500 to Lincoln College Vacation Project; £1,500 to Restore; £1,000 to Abbeyfield Oxenford Extra Care Society; £1,000 to Fairfield Home
FINANCES *Year* 1995 *Income* £55,235
Grants £51,850

TRUSTEES Rev Dr S Pix, Dr E Anderson, Dr A Pilkington, C Burton, M Lear, J Cole, W Earl, R Hawes, R Earl, P Eldridge
HOW TO APPLY To the address under Who To Apply To in writing
WHO TO APPLY TO P W Beavis, The Church Houses Relief in Need Charity, St Michael's Church Centre, Cornmarket Street, Oxford OX1 3EY
CC NO 202750   **ESTABLISHED** 1980

■ Church Institute

WHAT IS FUNDED The promotion of religious work and the advancement of education
WHO CAN BENEFIT To benefit children, young adults, students and Church of England
WHERE FUNDING CAN BE GIVEN Littleham with Exmouth parish
RANGE OF GRANTS £445–£6,819
SAMPLE GRANTS £6,819 to Littleham Leisure Centre
FINANCES *Year* 1996 *Income* £19,167
Grants £13,264
TRUSTEES Rev K Middleton, A Tuckett, A Pearson, R Clark, Mrs A Sargeant, A Streat, Maj R Wynter
HOW TO APPLY To the address under Who To Apply To in writing
WHO TO APPLY TO Mrs Pauline Martin, Secretary, Church Institute, Parish Office, Holy Trinity Church, Rolle Street, Exmouth, Devon EX8 2AB
CC NO 251170   **ESTABLISHED** 1921

■ The Church of Scotland Priority Areas Fund

WHAT IS FUNDED Local church and community projects which address specific needs and issues within the community. Priority is given to urban and rural areas of deprivation as defined by the 1991 census. Arts activities; training for community development; community centres and village halls; community services; and advice centres are all considered for funding
WHAT IS NOT FUNDED The following will not be considered for funding: (a) normal church activities for the benefit of the existing congregation; (b) renovation/building costs except where essential to wider community projects; (c) grants to individuals; and (d) the total costs of a project
WHO CAN BENEFIT Mainly disadvantaged groups within priority areas, particularly church and community organisations working together for the benefit of the wider community in rural and urban areas
WHERE FUNDING CAN BE GIVEN Scotland. Priority is given to areas of greatest deprivation
TYPE OF GRANT Capital and initial set-up costs (maximum £3,000); revenue costs (maximum £12,000 over a four year period); training allowances allocated in addition to main grant awards. Funding can be given as one-off and recurrent grants for projects, salaries, core costs and running costs as well
SAMPLE GRANTS Go For It (Bellsmyre Children's Project); Mid Craigie Parish Project; Garnock Valley Family Care; Govan Ecumenical Youth Association; West End Churches Key Fund; Viewpark Family Centre Association; Neilston Youth Project; Whitfield Church of Scotland; St Pauls Youth Association; Colston Milton Church of Scotland
FINANCES *Year* 1997 *Income* £273,069
Grants £128,860
TRUSTEES Barbara Kelly, CBE (Convener), Rev Martin Johnstone (Vice Convener), D Beckett, I Bristow, S Carter, I Fraser, E Henderson, B Murray, M Fair, A

Varwell, S Wright, J Cowie, G Kitcheman, D McCann, C Payn, J Thain, F Falconer

PUBLICATIONS Annual Report. *Good News for a Change* by the Church of Scotland (£3.50)

NOTES The Foundation seeks to enter into a constructive partnership with local organisations rather than simply providing a quick fix solution to funding problems, The final disbursement of the Fund is in 1999–2000, after this the Foundation may become part of an ecumenical fund for community development in Scotland

HOW TO APPLY Guidelines and application forms are available from the address under Who To Apply To. Initial enquiries are welcome. Trustees meet in August, October, January and April. Deadlines are the first weeks of July, September, December and January respectively

WHO TO APPLY TO Iain Johnston, Development and Training Officer, The Church of Scotland Priority Areas Fund, 121 George Street, Edinburgh EH2 4YN *Tel* 0131-225 5722 *Fax* 0131-226 6121

SC NO SCO 11353   ESTABLISHED 1995

■ Church Urban Fund

WHAT IS FUNDED Main emphasis is on places which suffer from social disintegration. The projects supported in these areas arise directly from local needs. Both innovative and proven ideas are supported

WHAT IS NOT FUNDED No grants to individuals

WHO CAN BENEFIT Organisations benefiting those disadvantaged by poverty, socially isolated people and those living in urban areas. Church-based community initiatives in the Urban Priority Areas of England which address issues of urban regeneration, social marginalisation, isolation, and poverty. Projects which work ecumenically and work in partnership with other agencies and faiths in the community

WHERE FUNDING CAN BE GIVEN Urban priority areas in England

TYPE OF GRANT Revenue and capital funding. Revenue grants are usually for three years. Small Grants Scheme

SAMPLE GRANTS £45,000 to St Nicholas Church Site, Poplar towards the redevelopment of the community centre as a focal point for people on this isolated estate; £33,000 to Black Women's Resource Centre, Sheffield towards salary costs; £24,000 to St Thomas' Community Links Project, Oldham towards salary costs. Play group serving a predominantly Bengali and Pakistani population which helps to overcome cultural and social differences in education. Involves the parents in the education of their children; £21,000 to Generation Link, London towards the salary costs of a co-ordinator. The project involves the older women in the area with lone parents as surrogate grandparents; £20,000 to The Light of the World Gospel Church, Bradford – capital grant to build a community centre which will include a drop-in centre for the elderly and a creche

FINANCES *Year* 1995 *Income* £2,716,000 *Grants* £2,871,000

TRUSTEES The Archbishop of Canterbury (Chair), Stephen O'Brien (Vice-Chair), Ruth McCurry, Canon John Stanley, Alan McLintock, Ven Granville Gibson, Rev Eileen Lake, Richard Farnell, Mark Cornwall-Jones, Michael Mockridge, Elaine Appelbee

HOW TO APPLY Through the relevant Diocesan office

WHO TO APPLY TO Chief Executive, Church Urban Fund, 2 Great Peter Street, London SW1P 3LX

CC NO 297483   ESTABLISHED 1988

■ Churchlands and John Johnson's Estate Charities

WHAT IS FUNDED The Trust has a preference for welfare causes, particularly ex-service, cancer, blind/disability and church related appeals

WHO CAN BENEFIT Organisations benefiting ex-service and service people, Christians, at risk groups, disabled people, those disadvantaged by poverty and socially isolated people. Beneficiaries suffering from cancers and blindness are given priority

WHERE FUNDING CAN BE GIVEN Berkshire, especially Reading

FINANCES *Year* 1996 *Income* £131,558 *Grants* £60,722

HOW TO APPLY To the address under Who To Apply To in writing. The Trustees meet in April and in November

WHO TO APPLY TO John Michael James, Treasurer, Churchlands and John Johnson's Estate Charities, c/o Vale and West, Victoria HOuse, 26 Queen Victoria Street, Reading, Berkshire RG1 1TG *Tel* 01734 537238

CC NO 272566   ESTABLISHED 1941

■ Churchlands or Parish Lands

WHAT IS FUNDED The upkeep of the parish church, local churches

WHERE FUNDING CAN BE GIVEN Buckfastleigh

TYPE OF GRANT Buildings

FINANCES *Year* 1996 *Income* £29,347 *Grants* £800

NOTES £11,239 was given to the Parish Church Council, of which £10,000 was spent on the rehanging of bells at Holy Trinity Church

HOW TO APPLY To the address under Who To Apply To in writing

WHO TO APPLY TO Janet James, Secretary, Churchlands or Parish Lands, 68 Barn Park, Buckfastleigh, Devon TQ11 0AT

CC NO 254697   ESTABLISHED 1895

■ The Cinderford Charitable Trust

WHAT IS FUNDED The bulk of the income is given to charities which have been supported over many years. Main areas medical, the arts and wildlife

WHAT IS NOT FUNDED No grants to individuals

WHO CAN BENEFIT Organisations benefiting: actors and entertainment professionals; musicians; textile workers and designers; and writers and poets. There is no restriction on the disease or medical condition suffered by the beneficiaries

WHERE FUNDING CAN BE GIVEN UK

TYPE OF GRANT Buildings, capital, core costs, endowments, feasibility studies, interest free loans, one-off, project, research, recurring costs, running costs, salaries and start-up costs. Funding for up to and over three years is available

SAMPLE GRANTS £7,883 to St Wilfred's Hospice; £7,883 to Save the Children Fund; £7,883 to Musicians' Benevolent Fund; £7,883 to Barnardo's; £7,883 to World Wildlife Fund; £7,883 to the Salvation Army; £7,883 to NSPCC; £7,883 to Scope; £5,067 to British Stroke Association; £5,067 to Cancer Relief Macmillan Fund

FINANCES *Year* 1997 *Income* £162,357 *Grants* £192,750

TRUSTEES R J Clark, R McLeod

WHO TO APPLY TO R J Clark, The Cinderford Charitable Trust, 2 Bloomsbury Street, London WC1B 3ST

CC NO 286525   ESTABLISHED 1983

■ The City and Metropolitan Welfare Charity

WHAT IS FUNDED To assist deserving persons who by reason of age, ill-health, accident, infirmity or straitened financial circumstances are in need of assistance. Grants are made to institutions or organisations providing welfare services established for the care and relief of such persons, with a preference for institutions or organisations which are administered in or in connection with the City of London, or are located in Greater London. Funds fully allocated or committed

WHAT IS NOT FUNDED No grants to individuals or for research purposes

WHO CAN BENEFIT Organisations benefiting: the aged; at risk groups; those disadvantaged by poverty; and the sick. There is no restriction on the disease or medical condition suffered by the beneficiaries

WHERE FUNDING CAN BE GIVEN London

RANGE OF GRANTS £1,000–£3,000

SAMPLE GRANTS £3,000 to Ex Vinculis Trust; £2,000 to Bourne Trust; £2,000 to Crimestoppers Trust; £2,000 to London Action Trust; £2,000 to Markfield Project; £2,000 to One Small Step Trust; £2,000 to Rehabilitation for Addicted Prisoners; £2,000 to Universal Beneficent Society; £2,000 to Weston Spirit; £2,000 to Sheriff's and Recorders' Fund

FINANCES *Year* 1997 *Income* £32,235
Grants £31,800

TRUSTEES R A Eve, B C Gothard, Sir M Harrison, R A R Hedderwick, Maj D Ide-Smith, H S Johnson, W P Martineau, G H J Nicholson, J P C Palmer, R S Whitmore

HOW TO APPLY By letter

WHO TO APPLY TO The Clerk to the Trustees, The City and Metropolitan Welfare Charity, Mercers' Hall, Ironmonger Lane, London EC2V 8HE

CC NO 205943　　　**ESTABLISHED** 1961

■ The City Educational Trust Fund

WHAT IS FUNDED A variety of educational groups and institutions in London, especially City University. Also science, technology, business management, commerce, biology, ecology and the cultural arts by promoting study, teaching and training in such areas

WHO CAN BENEFIT Institutions in London benefiting young adults, research workers, students and teachers

WHERE FUNDING CAN BE GIVEN Generally within London, in practice the catchment area of the University

TYPE OF GRANT One-off, on-going and fixed period grants

RANGE OF GRANTS £100–£21,000

SAMPLE GRANTS £21,000 to City University for joint research post – Head of Speech and Language Therapy; £20,300 to Guildhall School of Music and Drama for the maintenance of three students; £20,000 to St Paul's Cathedral Choir School; £10,000 to Foundation for Public Service Interpreting; £5,000 to Foundation for Communication of the Disabled; £5,000 to Foundation for Young Musicians; £1,400 to Beside Befriending Scheme; £100 to Union of Capital Cities of the European Union Meeting of Young People for City Schools Trip

FINANCES *Year* 1997 *Income* £145,270
Grants £82,800

TRUSTEES Corporation of London

HOW TO APPLY To the address under Who To Apply To in writing

WHO TO APPLY TO Town Clerk, The City Educational Trust Fund, Corporation of London, PO Box 270, Guildhall, London EC2P 2EJ

CC NO 290840　　　**ESTABLISHED** 1967

■ City Faith Ministries Trust

WHAT IS FUNDED General charitable purposes in particular to advance the Christian faith; to relieve persons in conditions of need, hardship or who are aged or sick in the area of Greater London and the UK

WHO CAN BENEFIT Organisations benefiting older people, Chistians, at risk groups, those disadvantaged by poverty and socially isolated people. There is no restriction on the disease or medical condition suffered by the beneficiaries

WHERE FUNDING CAN BE GIVEN UK with preference for Greater London

FINANCES *Year* 1996 *Income* £77,666

WHO TO APPLY TO Chair of Trustees, City Faith Ministries Trust, 166 Greenbay Road, London SE7 8PU

CC NO 1045627　　　**ESTABLISHED** 1995

■ City Gates Church Trust

WHAT IS FUNDED Advancement of the Christian faith; relief of persons who are in conditions of need, hardship, distress or who are aged or sick; any other general charitable purposes will be considered

WHO CAN BENEFIT Organisations benefiting elderly people, at risk groups, those disadvantaged by poverty and socially isolated people. There is no restriction on the disease or medical condition suffered by the beneficiaries

WHERE FUNDING CAN BE GIVEN UK with preference for Gloucestershire

SAMPLE GRANTS £1,197 as mission gifts

FINANCES *Year* 1996–97 *Income* £20,541
Grants £1,197

TRUSTEES D Kelly, K Tripp, K Martin, D Marshall

WHO TO APPLY TO K P Martin, City Gates Church Trust, c/o City Gates Church, PO Box 230, Gloucester GL4 6ZA

CC NO 1057322　　　**ESTABLISHED** 1996

■ The City of London School Charitable Trust

WHAT IS FUNDED General charitable purposes

WHO CAN BENEFIT There are no restrictions on the age; professional and economic group; family situation; religion and culture; and social circumstances of; or disease or medical condition suffered by, the beneficiaries

WHERE FUNDING CAN BE GIVEN UK

TYPE OF GRANT One-off grants

FINANCES *Year* 1997 *Income* £33,339
Grants £24,400

TRUSTEES Committee of Staff/Governors: B F Catt, R M Dancey, E M Hartley, T Y Heard, C Pearce

HOW TO APPLY In writing to the address under Who To Apply To by 30 April each year

WHO TO APPLY TO E M Hatley, The City of London School Charitable Trust, The City of London School, Queen Victoria Street, London EC4V 3AL

CC NO 1020824　　　**ESTABLISHED** 1993

Does the trust you have chosen match your needs? Haphazard applications waste postage and time

125

■ City of Westminster Charitable Trust

WHAT IS FUNDED General charitable purposes. Grants to organisations benefiting the City of Westminster

WHAT IS NOT FUNDED Organisations outside the area Where Funding Can Be Given will not be funded

WHO CAN BENEFIT City of Westminster and/or its residents. There are no restrictions on the age; professional and economic group; family situation; religion and culture; and social circumstances of; or disease or medical condition suffered by, the beneficiaries

WHERE FUNDING CAN BE GIVEN City of Westminster

TYPE OF GRANT One-off

FINANCES *Year* 1996–97 *Income* £34,057 *Grants* £45,628

TRUSTEES Lord Mayor, W Roots, C T Wilson, Cllr C Nemeth, Cllr R Bramble, Cllr J Bianco

PUBLICATIONS Annual Report

HOW TO APPLY Applications should be made in September/October

WHO TO APPLY TO Ms S Carter, City of Westminster Charitable Trust, Westminster City Council, Westminster City Hall, 18th Floor, 64 Victoria Street, London SW1E 6QP

CC NO 296091   **ESTABLISHED** 1987

■ The Citymark Charitable Trust

WHAT IS FUNDED Grants to charitable organisations to further the health of young people in the Bristol area; to help the development of the spiritual, mental and physical capabilities of young people through leisure activities, so that they may grow to full maturity as individuals and members of society

WHO CAN BENEFIT Organisations benefiting children and young adults

WHERE FUNDING CAN BE GIVEN Bristol area

WHO TO APPLY TO M Incledon, Secretary, The Citymark Charitable Trust, 2–6 Kings Parade Mews, Clifton, Bristol BS8 2RE

CC NO 1056143   **ESTABLISHED** 1996

■ The Civil Service Benevolent Fund

WHAT IS FUNDED Financial assistance and support in finding and financing good quality 24 hour care in residential and nursing homes. While the assistance is predominantly to individuals, in exceptional circumstances grants are made to other charities where there are special links with civil servants or their dependants. Charities working in the fields of: information technology and computers; health care; care in the community; community transport; and playschemes will also be considered

WHAT IS NOT FUNDED Assistance falling outside the Policy Guide

WHO CAN BENEFIT Serving, former, and retired Civil Servants and Associated Organisations and their dependants. There are no restrictions on the age, family situation, and religion and culture of, or disease or medical condition suffered by, the beneficiaries, although there may be a few restrictions on their social circumstances

WHERE FUNDING CAN BE GIVEN UK

TYPE OF GRANT Assistance is given by lump sum grants, repayable grants and time limited allowances for childcare and community service costs, and residential and nursing home fees, subject to guidelines agreed by the Committee of Management. Buildings, capital, one-off, project and running costs will also be considered

FINANCES *Year* 1997 *Income* £10,963,000 *Grants* £4,397,000

TRUSTEES Administered by a Committee of Management

PUBLICATIONS Annual Report and Statement of Accounts published in May. *Fund News* published in August

NOTES Funding to provide nursing convalescent care will change in the future, homes are currently being sold, support will be offered in finding nursing homes for beneficiaries. This Fund is not registered with the Charity Commission. However, it is Registered Friendly Society No 26BEN with charitable status

HOW TO APPLY In assisting when need arises. Application for Assistance form assesses financial need and circumstances. Welfare officer/social worker/voluntary visiting officer report sometimes required. Assistance given subject to Policy Guide. Help and Advisory Services Enquiry Line 0181–240 2452

WHO TO APPLY TO Miss Rosemary Doidge, MSc, Director, The Civil Service Benevolent Fund, Fund House, Anne Boleyn's Walk, Cheam Sutton, Surrey SM3 8DY *Tel* 0181-240 2400 *Fax* 0181-240 2401

CC NO See Notes   **ESTABLISHED** 1886

■ Clapman Charitable Trust

WHAT IS FUNDED For the relief and assistance of poor and needy persons. General charitable purposes

WHAT IS NOT FUNDED We will not consider applications from abroad or students

WHO CAN BENEFIT Institutions. There are no restrictions on the age; professional and economic group; family situation; religion and culture; and social circumstances of; or disease or medical condition suffered by, the beneficiaries

WHERE FUNDING CAN BE GIVEN UK

RANGE OF GRANTS £50–£300

SAMPLE GRANTS £300 to Nightingale House for part of a building project; £200 to Nightingale House; £150 to Jewish Children's Holiday Fund (JCHF); £150 to World Jewish Fund; £100 to Children's Centre Fund (NPH)

FINANCES *Year* 1997 *Income* £17,924 *Grants* £2,950

TRUSTEES J Clapman, P Enfield

WHO TO APPLY TO Phyllis Enfield, Clapman Charitable Trust, Green Tiles, Green Lane, Stanmore, Middlesex HA7 3AH

CC NO 208220   **ESTABLISHED** 1961

■ Clark Charitable Trust

WHAT IS FUNDED Support is given for such purposes as are charitable in law or to such institutions, societies, foundations or funds as are charitable in law at the Trustees' absolute discretion

WHAT IS NOT FUNDED Unable to assist non-charitable bodies or individuals

WHO CAN BENEFIT Charitable bodies only. There are no restrictions on the age; professional and economic group; family situation; religion and culture; and social circumstances of; or disease or medical condition suffered by, the beneficiaries

WHERE FUNDING CAN BE GIVEN UK and overseas

SAMPLE GRANTS £5,000 to Oxfam; £4,300 to Oxfam for work in Zaire; £1,000 to The National Trust for Scotland; £1,000 to Alzheimer's Disease Society; £750 to the Sylvia Wright Trust

FINANCES *Year* 1997 *Income* £24,200 *Grants* £22,600

TRUSTEES Barclays Bank Trust Co Ltd, Rev D E R Isitt

WHO TO APPLY TO Barclays Bank Trust Company Limited, Clark Charitable Trust, Executorship and Trustee Service, Osborne Court, Gadbrook Park, Rudheath, Northwich, Cheshire CW9 7UE

CC NO 274300   **ESTABLISHED** 1977

■ Hilda & Alice Clark Charitable Trust

WHAT IS FUNDED Grants mainly to Society of Friends. Educational charities. General charitable purposes

WHO CAN BENEFIT There are no restrictions on the age; professional and economic group; family situation; religion and culture; and social circumstances of; or disease or medical condition suffered by, the beneficiaries. However particular favour is given to the Society of Friends (Quakers) and to children and young adults

WHERE FUNDING CAN BE GIVEN UK

TYPE OF GRANT Donations

FINANCES *Year* 1995 *Income* £24,910 *Grants* £27,250

TRUSTEES R B Clark, A T Clothier, T A Clark, Ms A Clark, M Lovell

HOW TO APPLY Any time during year by letter. Trustees meet in December

WHO TO APPLY TO The Trustees, Hilda & Alice Clark Charitable Trust, c/o KPMG, 15 Pembroke Road, Bristol, Avon BS8 3BG

CC NO 290916   **ESTABLISHED** 1953

■ J A Clark Charitable Trust

WHAT IS FUNDED Projects oriented towards social change in areas of health, education, peace, preservation of the earth and the arts. Preference for the work of small, new, innovative projects and for young people. Charities working in the fields of community development, arts and arts facilities, arts education, alternative healthcare, conservation of fauna and flora, environmental issues, transport and alternative transport, training for community development, crime prevention schemes, family support and community issues

WHAT IS NOT FUNDED No support for independent schools (except special needs), conservation of buildings or for individuals

WHO CAN BENEFIT Organisations benefiting children, young adults, parents and children, one parent families, Quakers, those disadvantaged by poverty, ex-offenders and those at risk of offending, the homeless and victims of abuse

WHERE FUNDING CAN BE GIVEN The south west of England and overseas

TYPE OF GRANT One-off for up to three years, including start-up costs

RANGE OF GRANTS £500–£10,000

SAMPLE GRANTS £23,450 to Students International for scholarship in Zimbabwe; £10,000 to Marie Stopes for outreach project in Madagascar; £7,000 to Quaker Peace Service in Sri Lanka; £7,000 to Turning Point for complementary therapy for HIV and drug users; £7,000 to Inner City Scholarship Fund for assistance to ex-prisoners, refugees for qualifications and employment; £6,000 to Ashoka for an individual in Thailand; £5,000 to Yeovil Foyer; £5,000 to Take Art for artist in residence at Chard Hospital; £4,900 to Network Foundation for Social Change for various projects; £1,000 to British Trust for Conservation Volunteers for training conservation volunteers

FINANCES *Year* 1997 *Income* £171,125 *Grants* £141,637

TRUSTEES Lancelot Pease Clark, John Cyprus Clark, Thomas Aldenham Clark, Caroline Pym, Aidan J R Pelly

HOW TO APPLY Written application with project details plus most recent accounts. Receipt of applications will not be acknowledged. All applications are, however, considered and a small number are contacted with a request for a formal application. Trustees grant allocation meeting October/November

WHO TO APPLY TO The Secretary, J A Clark Charitable Trust, PO Box 1704, Glastonbury, Somerset BA16 0YB

CC NO 1010520   **ESTABLISHED** 1992

■ Roger and Sarah Bancroft Clark Charitable Trust

This trust did not respond to CAF's request to amend its entry and, by 30 June 1998, CAF's researchers did not find financial records for later than 1995 on its file at the Charity Commission. Trusts are legally required to submit annual accounts to the Charity Commission under section 42 of the Charities Act 1993

WHAT IS FUNDED General charitable purposes

WHO CAN BENEFIT Society of Friends, registered charities, general, individuals. There are no restrictions on the age; professional and economic group; family situation; religion and culture; and social circumstances of; or disease or medical condition suffered by, the beneficiaries. Preference given to local appeals

WHERE FUNDING CAN BE GIVEN UK

TRUSTEES Eleonor C Robertson, Roger S Goldby, Mary P Lovell, S Clark, S Caroline Gould

NOTES Time limit to 2020

HOW TO APPLY Income fully allocated

WHO TO APPLY TO Mrs B L Gunson, Roger & Sarah Bancroft Clark Charitable Trust, 40 High Street, Street, Somerset BA16 0YA

CC NO 211513   **ESTABLISHED** 1960

■ Clark Foundation II

This trust did not respond to CAF's request to amend its entry and, by 30 June 1998, CAF's researchers did not find financial records for later than 1995 on its file at the Charity Commission. Trusts are legally required to submit annual accounts to the Charity Commission under section 42 of the Charities Act 1993

WHAT IS FUNDED The advancement of higher education for those in need. The promotion of education. The provision of facilities for public benefit for social welfare and recreation

WHAT IS NOT FUNDED It is not the policy of the Trustees to give grants to individual students or

National charities unless there is a strong local connection

WHO CAN BENEFIT Registered charities benefiting children, young adults and students. There are few restrictions on the social circumstances of the beneficiaries

WHERE FUNDING CAN BE GIVEN Somerset and the West of England

TRUSTEES W Bancroft-Clark, J Daniel Clark, J Anthony Clark, JP, Anthony T Clothier

WHO TO APPLY TO Richard Clark, Secretary, The Clark Foundation, C & J Clark Ltd, Street, Somerset BA16 0YA

CC NO 313143   **ESTABLISHED** 1959

■ The Clarke Charitable Settlement

WHAT IS FUNDED The advancement of Christian religion, medical research and hospices

WHO CAN BENEFIT At the discretion of the Trustees. Funding may be considered for Christians, research workers and medical professionals. Those suffering from various different diseases and medical conditions will be supported

WHERE FUNDING CAN BE GIVEN Priority to Staffordshire area

TYPE OF GRANT At the discretion of the Trustees

RANGE OF GRANTS £20–£5680

SAMPLE GRANTS £5,680 to British Red Cross; £5,000 to Animal Health Trust; £4,112 to Duke of Edinburgh's Award; £2,500 to De Ferrer's High School; £1,000 to Thomas Russell Infants School; £1,000 to Yellow Brick Road; £965 to Needwood Singers; £600 to NSPCC; £500 to Spalding Leukaemia Fund; £500 to Action on Addiction

FINANCES *Year* 1996 *Income* £34,829
Grants £36,230

TRUSTEES Stanley William Clarke, CBE, Hilda Joan Clarke, Sally Ann Hayward, Mary Elizabeth MacGregor

WHO TO APPLY TO Mr & Mrs S W Clarke, The Clarke Charitable Settlement, The Knoll, Barton Under Needwood, Staffordshire DE13 8AB

CC NO 702980   **ESTABLISHED** 1990

■ The Late Miss Doris Evelyn Clarke's Charitable Trust

WHAT IS FUNDED Donations primarily made to animal charities chosen from a list provided by the settlor

WHO CAN BENEFIT Established organisations

WHERE FUNDING CAN BE GIVEN UK

TYPE OF GRANT Recurrent

RANGE OF GRANTS £205–£4,285

SAMPLE GRANTS £4,285 to Royal Society for the Prevention of Cruelty to Animals; £1,920 to the Cats' Protection League; £1,920 to the Donkey Sanctuary; £1,920 to Blue Cross Animals' Hospital; £445 to the Guide Dogs for the Blind Association

FINANCES *Year* 1996 *Income* £13,555
Grants £13,659

TRUSTEES The Royal Bank of Scotland plc

PUBLICATIONS Annual Accounts

HOW TO APPLY In writing at any time

WHO TO APPLY TO The Royal Bank of Scotland plc, The Late Miss Doris Evelyn Clarke's Charitable Trust, 2nd Floor, Guildhall House, Guildhall Street, Preston, Lancashire PR1 3NU

CC NO 281282   **ESTABLISHED** 1979

■ The Classic FM Charitable Trust

WHAT IS FUNDED The promotion of education and training of members of the public in music, the relief of financial need and the relief of sickness

WHAT IS NOT FUNDED No grants to individuals

WHO CAN BENEFIT Established organisations benefiting musicians and those disadvantaged by poverty. There is no restriction on the disease or medical condition suffered by the beneficiaries

WHERE FUNDING CAN BE GIVEN UK

TYPE OF GRANT One-off

SAMPLE GRANTS £60,000 to the National Appeal for Music Therapy

FINANCES *Year* 1997 *Income* £88,389
Grants £60,000

TRUSTEES Mrs V L Duffield, CBE, Prof Stanley Glasser, Robert O'Dowd, John McLaren, Robin Ray, John Spearman, Douglas Thackway, Andrew Tuckey

PUBLICATIONS Annual Report

NOTES Select one grant per year associated with music

WHO TO APPLY TO R O'Dowd, The Classic FM Charitable Trust, Classic FM plc, Academic House, 24–28 Oval Road, London NW1 7DQ *Tel* 0171-284 3000

CC NO 1028531   **ESTABLISHED** 1993

■ Robert Clayton's Charitable Settlement

This trust did not respond to CAF's request to amend its entry and, by 30 June 1998, CAF's researchers did not find financial records for later than 1995 on its file at the Charity Commission. Trusts are legally required to submit annual accounts to the Charity Commission under section 42 of the Charities Act 1993

WHAT IS FUNDED General charitable purposes

WHAT IS NOT FUNDED Time charity to 2022

WHO CAN BENEFIT There are no restrictions on the age; professional and economic group; family situation; religion and culture; and social circumstances of; or disease or medical condition suffered by, the beneficiaries

WHERE FUNDING CAN BE GIVEN UK

TRUSTEES R A Romain, G Phillips, A H Clayton

HOW TO APPLY **This Trust states that it does not respond to unsolicited applications**

WHO TO APPLY TO Robert Clayton's Charitable Settlement, Kershaw, Gassman and Matthews, 32 Hans Road, Knightsbridge, London SW3 1RP

CC NO 264102   **ESTABLISHED** 1972

■ The Cleaford Christian Trust

WHAT IS FUNDED To relieve the poor and needy in Romania by providing food, clothing, literature and medical equipment. Charities working in the fields of: health; church and primary schools; cultural and religious teaching; the advancement of the Christian religion; churches; and information technology and computers will be considered

WHO CAN BENEFIT Individuals and organisations benefiting: clergy; medical professionals; students, teachers and governesses; Baptists and Christians. Support will also be given to those in care, fostered and adopted, carers, those disadvantaged by poverty, homeless people and those suffering from asthma

WHERE FUNDING CAN BE GIVEN Romania

TYPE OF GRANT Buildings, capital, core costs, interest free loans, project, salaries and start-up costs. Funding may be given for more than three years

Think carefully about every application. Is it justified?

SAMPLE GRANTS £4,000 to village and city schools in Brasov area for equipment; £3,500 to UK carriers for transportation of aid items; £2,600 to Houghiton Christian Camp for wages and gas; £2,500 to Brasov Children's Hospital for medications and equipment; £500 to Baptist pastor for general ministry

FINANCES *Year* 1998 *Income* £30,000 *Grants* £25,000

TRUSTEES Angus Cleaver, Abigail Cleaver, Phil Dunford, Tom Dunford, Roger Guy, Pat Guy, David Stickland

HOW TO APPLY Letter of recommendation from the Hungarian Baptist Church in Brasov, Romania

WHO TO APPLY TO A R Cleaver, The Cleaford Christian Trust, 46 Hazell Road, Farnham, Surrey GU9 7BP *Tel* 01252 717166

CC NO 1039861 **ESTABLISHED** 1994

■ Cleary Foundation

WHAT IS FUNDED Principally to apply the income of the Foundation for various selected charities. The relief of pain and hardship and conservation. These include: civil society development; community development; social care professional bodies; churches; music; visual art; arts activities; dance and ballet; dance groups; theatrical companies and theatre groups; horticulture; special schools; community centres and village halls; and parks

WHAT IS NOT FUNDED No grants are made to individuals who require aid with further education

WHO CAN BENEFIT Registered charities benefiting: children; older people; ex-service and service people; seafarers and fishermen; Christians; Church of England; disabled people; and those disadvantaged by poverty

WHERE FUNDING CAN BE GIVEN Kent

TYPE OF GRANT Core costs and one-off

SAMPLE GRANTS £42,000 to Ripple Down House Trust; £500 to Canterbury Festival; £250 to Canterbury Choral Society; £250 to St Martins Emmaus Dover; £200 to CRUSE, Dover Counselling Centre; £200 to National Gardens Scheme Charitable Trust; £110 to The Gardeners Royal Benevolent Society; £100 to National Society for Prevention of Cruelty to Children

FINANCES *Year* 1997 *Income* £35,878 *Grants* £43,610

TRUSTEES Mrs P M Gould, K A F Phillips, M R Thody, A T F Gould, P A Took

PUBLICATIONS Annual Report

WHO TO APPLY TO C Fronty, The Cleary Foundation, South Sands House, St Margaret's Bay, Dover, Kent CT15 6DZ *Tel* 01304 852764 *Fax* 01304 853626

CC NO 242675 **ESTABLISHED** 1965

■ The John & Heather Clemence Charitable Settlement

WHAT IS FUNDED General charitable purposes. The Trust has a number of ongoing commitments

WHO CAN BENEFIT There are no restrictions on the age; professional and economic group; family situation; religion and culture; and social circumstances of; or disease or medical condition suffered by, the beneficiaries

WHERE FUNDING CAN BE GIVEN UK

TYPE OF GRANT Recurrent

RANGE OF GRANTS £25–£1,440

SAMPLE GRANTS £1,440 to the Cleary Foundation; £750 to Burdett-Coutts and Townshead Foundation CE Primary School; £600 to St Giles Church, Shipbourne; £550 to New Beacon Educational Trust; £500 to the Gordon Highlanders Museum Campaign

FINANCES *Year* 1997 *Income* £16,954 *Grants* £19,290

TRUSTEES J A Clemence, TD, FCA, Mrs H M K Clemence, R D Holliday, TD, W J Clemence

WHO TO APPLY TO J A Clemence, Trustee, John & Heather Clemence Charitable Settlement, 8 Baker Street, London W1M 1DA

CC NO 283114 **ESTABLISHED** 1981

■ Cleopatra Trust

WHAT IS FUNDED Support is given to: emergency and short-term housing; holiday accommodation; hostels; health counselling and education; respite care; hospices; environmental issues; renewable energy; care in the community; and crime prevention schemes

WHAT IS NOT FUNDED No grants to individuals, or for expeditions, research or scholarships

WHO CAN BENEFIT Registered charities benefiting people of all ages; those disadvantaged by poverty; homeless people; and victims of crime and domestic violence. Also those suffering from various diseases and medical conditions

WHERE FUNDING CAN BE GIVEN UK, the Trustees sometimes consider overseas projects carried out by UK charities

TYPE OF GRANT Capital, projects and one-off. Funding is for one year or less

RANGE OF GRANTS £500–£10,000

SAMPLE GRANTS · £10,000 to Sense for holidays for deaf/blind children; £10,000 to Centrepoint towards resettlement work; £10,000 to Foundation for Conductive Education for funding for two children at the school; £10,000 to Intermediate Technology loan scheme in Peru for hydro-power; £10,000 to National Kidney Research Fund to upgrade equipment at Hammersmith Hospital; £5,000 to National Asthma Campaign for running cost of helpline; £5,000 to Break for respite holidays for special needs children; £3,000 to Guild of Disabled Homeworkers for administration costs to answer calls for help; £2,000 to British Tinitus Association for production of 'Quiet' magazine; £2,000 to Look Ahead Housing Association for developing a lifeskills flat

FINANCES *Year* 1996 *Income* £154,000 *Grants* £93,000

TRUSTEES Dr C Peacock, C Peacock, Mrs B Bond

HOW TO APPLY In writing only to the address under Who To Apply To. Applications are normally considered in July and December. A copy of latest Annual Report and Accounts must accompany any application

WHO TO APPLY TO Mrs Barbara Davis, Senior Information Officer, Cleopatra Trust, c/o CAF, Kings Hill, West Malling, Kent ME19 4TA *Tel* 01732 520081 *Fax* 01732 520001 *E-mail* bdavis@caf.charitynet.org

CC NO 1004551 **ESTABLISHED** 1990

■ The Clergy Rest Fund

WHAT IS FUNDED The Trustees carry out their duties by making annual distributions to each of the Bishops of the Dioceses of the Church of England and by allocating a sum for personal distribution by each of the three Trustees for worthy causes or

Does the trust you have chosen match your needs? Haphazard applications waste postage and time

129

individual needs in accordance with the terms of the Trust

WHO CAN BENEFIT The clergy of the Church of England

WHERE FUNDING CAN BE GIVEN UK

TYPE OF GRANT Recurrent

RANGE OF GRANTS £500–£1,000

FINANCES *Year* 1997 *Income* £113,883
Grants £48,000

TRUSTEES His Honour Judge Q T Edwards, J G Underwood, Dr F E Robson

WHO TO APPLY TO The Secretary, The Clergy Rest Fund, Winckworth & Pemberton Solicitors, 35 Great Peter Street, Westminster, London SW1P 3LR

CC NO 233436   **ESTABLISHED** 1919

■ The Clerkenwell Charities

WHAT IS FUNDED Local churches and organisations

WHO CAN BENEFIT Christians and members of the local community

WHERE FUNDING CAN BE GIVEN Clerkenwell

FINANCES *Year* 1996–97 *Income* £25,278
Grants £22,800

TRUSTEES Mayor of Islington, Rev P Baggott, J H Fitt, Cllr P Haynes, Rev A J Salter, Rev J Thomas, G A Wrigglesworth

HOW TO APPLY To the address under Who To Apply To in writing

WHO TO APPLY TO P S Rust, Secretary, The Clerkenwell Charities, 61 West Smithfield, London EC1A 9EA

CC NO 209326   **ESTABLISHED** 1977

■ Cleveland Community Foundation

WHAT IS FUNDED To improve the quality of life of the people of Cleveland by supporting a wide range of charitable organisations working to benefit the community, particularly in support of those deprived by social, environmental and economic factors. We seek to support smaller, locally based groups working in: education and training; schools and colleges; conservation; social care and development; arts, culture and recreation; religious umbrella bodies; hospices; community development; support to community and voluntary organisations; and Council for Voluntary Service

WHAT IS NOT FUNDED Applications are not usually considered for major appeals, sponsored events, holidays and social outings, or for individuals

WHO CAN BENEFIT All registered charities or bonafide voluntary/community groups, provided the purpose of the grant is wholly charitable and for the benefit of people in Cleveland. To benefit: young adults and older people; at risk groups; carers, disabled people; those disadvantaged by poverty; socially isolated people; and those living in urban areas

WHERE FUNDING CAN BE GIVEN County of Cleveland and neighbourhood

TYPE OF GRANT Capital or revenue

SAMPLE GRANTS £5,000 to Skillshare, Hartlepool; £5,000 to St Mary's Centre; £5,000 to the Hope Foundation; £5,000 to Joe Walton's Youth Centre, Middlesbrough; £4,000 to Azaad Youth Project, Middlesbrough; £3,800 to Stockton Speech After Stroke; £3,354 to Xpress Youth, Hemlington; £2,500 to Cleveland Family Mediation Service; £2,000 to CDF Independent Living Project; £2,000 to Friends of Alderman William Jones Primary School

FINANCES *Year* 1997 *Income* £1,770,000
Grants £377,000

TRUSTEES Sir Ron Norman, Dr A J Gillham, J Bennett, J Bloom, J Foster, C Hope, M Houseman, A Kitching, J Ord, R Sale, P Sole, M Stewart, S Still, B Storey, K Taylor

PUBLICATIONS Annual Report and Accounts in July and periodic newsletter

HOW TO APPLY Yearly application. Apply to the Foundation for an application form and guidelines for applicants. Applications accepted at any time and considered in February, June and October each year

WHO TO APPLY TO Kevin Ryan, Director, Cleveland Community Foundation, Southlands Business Centre, Ormesby Road, Middlesborough TS3 0HB *Tel* 01642 314200
Fax 01642 313700 *E-mail* ccftrust@yahoo.com

CC NO 700568   **ESTABLISHED** 1988

■ Clifton Charitable Trust

WHAT IS FUNDED General charitable purposes

WHO CAN BENEFIT There are no restrictions on the age; professional and economic group; family situation; religion and culture; and social circumstances of; or disease or medical condition suffered by, the beneficiaries

WHERE FUNDING CAN BE GIVEN UK and overseas

RANGE OF GRANTS £10–£15,000

SAMPLE GRANTS £15,000 to Greater Bristol Trust; £10,000 to Bristol Dyslexia School; £7,750 to Bras Manuel Alexio for relief of poverty in Mozambique; £1,000 to Bristol Cathedral Trust; £250 to Quest

FINANCES *Year* 1996 *Income* £18,647
Grants £35,250

TRUSTEES Avon Executor and Trustee Company

NOTES The Craig Fund is part of the Clifton Charitable Trust; however it has separate finances

WHO TO APPLY TO Clifton Charitable Trust, 15 Pembroke Road, Clifton, Bristol BS8 3BG

CC NO 285564   **ESTABLISHED** 1970

■ Lord Clinton's Charitable Trust

WHAT IS FUNDED Young people and the encouragement of youth activities, physically handicapped and disabled people, support for the elderly, medical aid and research, maritime charities. Respite and sheltered accommodation; churches; information technology and computers; personnel and human resources; support to voluntary and community organisations and volunteers; professional bodies; community centres and village halls; clubs; holidays and outings are all considered for funding

WHAT IS NOT FUNDED Registered charities only. No grants made in response to general appeals from large national organisations nor to smaller bodies working in areas other than those set out above

WHO CAN BENEFIT Registered charities benefiting: people of all ages; ex-service and service people; seafarers and fishermen; sportsmen and women; volunteers; parents and children; disabled people;

and victims of man-made or natural disasters. Those suffering from: cancers; paediatric diseases; sight loss and those who are terminally ill

WHERE FUNDING CAN BE GIVEN County of Devon only

TYPE OF GRANT For projects, recurring costs and start-up costs. Funding is available for one year or less

SAMPLE GRANTS £1,000 to North Devon Cancer Care for the relief of cancer sufferers in North Devon; £500 to South Devon Sports for the Disabled for the provision of sports equipment; £500 to the Parnham Trust for youth training; £500 to National Blind Children's Society for equipment; £500 to Devon Community Foundation

FINANCES *Year* 1997–98 *Income* £24,553 *Grants* £22,605

TRUSTEES The Hon Charles F Trefusis, R A L Waller, FRICS

NOTES Applications not falling within the Trust's objects and funding priorities will not be considered or acknowledged

HOW TO APPLY To the address under Who To Apply To in writing

WHO TO APPLY TO R A L Waller, FRICS, Lord Clinton's Charitable Trust, Rolle Estate Office, East Budleigh, Budleigh Salterton, Devon EX9 7DP *Tel* 01395 443881 *Fax* 01395 446126

CC NO 268061　　　**ESTABLISHED** 1974

■ The Clio Trust

WHAT IS FUNDED General charitable purposes

WHO CAN BENEFIT There are no restrictions on the age; professional and economic group; family situation; religion and culture; and social circumstances of; or disease or medical condition suffered by, the beneficiaries

WHERE FUNDING CAN BE GIVEN UK

TRUSTEES Sir John Elliott, Lady Elliott, W L G Swan

NOTES At present the Trustees' resources are fully committed and they will not consider applications from third parties for the time being

HOW TO APPLY This Trust states that it does not respond to unsolicited applications

WHO TO APPLY TO Sir John Huxtable Elliott, Trustee, The Clio Trust, 122 Church Way, Oxford OX4 4EG *Tel* 01865 716703

CC NO 1059390　　　**ESTABLISHED** 1996

■ The Clockmakers' Charity

WHAT IS FUNDED General charitable purposes and particularly training in horology. The appeals made by the Lord Mayor of London

WHO CAN BENEFIT Individuals and organisations benefiting clockmakers

WHERE FUNDING CAN BE GIVEN London

TYPE OF GRANT One-off

RANGE OF GRANTS £250–£5,100

SAMPLE GRANTS £5,100 to an individual for horological training; £5,000 to an individual for horological training; £2,750 to an individual for horlogical training; £1,500 to an individual for horological training; £1,250 to an individual for horological training

FINANCES *Year* 1998–99 *Income* £23,700 *Grants* £23,700

TRUSTEES Clockmakers' Company

HOW TO APPLY To the address under Who To Apply To in writing

WHO TO APPLY TO Peter H Gibson, Clerk, The Clockmakers' Charity, Room 66–67 Albert Buildings, 49 Queen Victoria Street, London EC4N 4SE *Tel* 0171-236 0070

CC NO 275380　　　**ESTABLISHED** 1978

■ Miss V L Clore's 1967 Charitable Trust

WHAT IS FUNDED General charitable purposes

WHO CAN BENEFIT There are no restrictions on the age; professional and economic group; family situation; religion and culture; and social circumstances of; or disease or medical condition suffered by, the beneficiaries

WHERE FUNDING CAN BE GIVEN UK

RANGE OF GRANTS £200–£10,000

SAMPLE GRANTS £10,000 to English Touring Opera; £4,000 to Starlight Foundation; £3,000 to Cancer Relief Macmillan Fund; £3,000 to Cancer Research Campaign; £2,000 to The National Tenants' Resource Centre; £2,000 to NSPCC in London; £1,000 to Cancerkin – The Royal Free Hospital Appeal Trust; £1,000 to Design Museum; £1,000 to Foundation Friends of Warsaw and Help Poland Fund; £1,000 to KIDS for work with children with special needs

FINANCES *Year* 1997 *Income* £44,697 *Grants* £37,520

TRUSTEES Mrs V L Duffield, CBE, D T D Harrel, Sir Jocelyn Stevens, CVO, Mrs Caroline Deletra

NOTES Only charities personally known to the Trustees are considered. Funds are fully allocated at this time

HOW TO APPLY Applications are not acknowledged

WHO TO APPLY TO Miriam Harris, Miss V L Clore's 1967 Charitable Trust, 3 Chelsea Manor Studios, Flood Street, London SW3 5SR

CC NO 253660　　　**ESTABLISHED** 1967

■ Closehelm Ltd

WHAT IS FUNDED The advancement of religion in accordance with the Jewish faith, the relief of poverty and general charitable purposes

WHO CAN BENEFIT Individuals and institutions benefiting Jewish people and those disadvantaged by poverty

WHERE FUNDING CAN BE GIVEN UK

FINANCES *Year* 1996 *Income* £159,853 *Grants* £254,312

TRUSTEES A Van Praagh, H W Van Praagh, H R Van Praagh

WHO TO APPLY TO A Van Praagh, Closehelm Ltd, 30 Armitage Road, London NW11 8RD

CC NO 291296　　　**ESTABLISHED** 1983

■ The P T & V O Clothier Charitable Trust

WHAT IS FUNDED General charitable purposes in Street and the surrounding areas

WHO CAN BENEFIT Institutions. There are no restrictions on the age, professional and economic group, family situation, religion and culture, and social circumstances of, or disease or medical condition suffered by, the beneficiaries

WHERE FUNDING CAN BE GIVEN UK, with a preference for Street and the surrounding areas

TYPE OF GRANT One-off and recurrent

SAMPLE GRANTS £500 to Holy Trinity Parochial Church, Street

FINANCES *Year* 1995 *Income* £24,810 *Grants* £500

TRUSTEES A T Clothier, J C Clothier, G O Edwards

WHO TO APPLY TO The P T & V O Clothier Charitable Trust, KPMG, 15 Pembroke Road, Clifton, Bristol BS8 3BG

CC NO 262395　　　**ESTABLISHED** 1971

■ Robert Clutterbuck Charitable Trust

WHAT IS FUNDED Personnel within the armed forces and ex-services men and women. Sport and recreational facilities. Natural history. The welfare, protection and preservation of animal life

WHAT IS NOT FUNDED Applications for payments to individuals are not considered

WHO CAN BENEFIT The Trustees only consider applications from registered charities. Organisations benefiting ex-service and service people, and sportsmen and women

WHERE FUNDING CAN BE GIVEN Mainly UK. Special consideration will be given to charities associated with the counties of Cheshire and Hertfordshire

TYPE OF GRANT Payments normally from income, generally for the purchase of specific items

RANGE OF GRANTS £130–£20,000; typical £2,000–£3,000

SAMPLE GRANTS £4,810 to Barrowmore, Great Barrow, Chester for conversion of a flat for a disabled woman; £4,500 to College of St Barnabas Centenary Appeal, Lingfield, Surrey for cost of new staircase; £3,500 to Trefoil House, Edinburgh for new floor in games room; £3,325 to Training Ship Stirling, Edinburgh for sponsorship of 25 sea cadets for one week on sail training ship; £3,000 to St John the Baptist Church at Godley-Cum-Newton Green, Cheshire for new floor for the conversion of a former school to a community centre; £3,000 to Buckmore Park Scout Centre, Chatham for purchase of a second hand land rover; £2,300 to Coventry Boys' Club for extension of internal games area and purchase of camping and sports equipment; £2,000 to SSAFA Forces Help, Cheshire Branch for administration expenses; £2,000 to David Lewis Organisation, Alderley Edge for grant towards cost of recreation/relaxation room; £2,000 to Royal Schools for the Deaf, Manchester for contribution to cost of multi sensory hydrotherapy pool

FINANCES *Year* 1997–98 *Income* £49,897 *Grants* £44,985

TRUSTEES Major R G Clutterbuck, C N Lindsell, A C Humphries, OBE

HOW TO APPLY To B C Berryman who will acknowledge them. Applications are only considered by Trustees at their meetings. They meet three times a year

WHO TO APPLY TO B C Berryman, Robert Clutterbuck Charitable Trust, Ashleigh Cottage, 207 Staines Road, Laleham, Staines, Middlesex TW18 2RS *Tel* 01784 451651

CC NO 1010559   **ESTABLISHED** 1992

■ County Council of Clwyd Welsh Church Charity Fund

WHAT IS FUNDED Preservation of listed buildings including churches, community groups, scout halls, Eisteddfodan. Individuals may also be supported for example, those with outstanding sporting ability

WHAT IS NOT FUNDED Non-listed buildings will not be funded

WHO CAN BENEFIT Individuals and local organisations. There are no restrictions on the age; professional and economic group; family situation; religion and culture; and social circumstances of; or disease or medical condition suffered by, the beneficiaries. Particular favour may be given to those with outstanding sporting ability

WHERE FUNDING CAN BE GIVEN Wales, especially Clwyd

RANGE OF GRANTS £50–£5,000

SAMPLE GRANTS £5,000 to National Eisteddfod; £2,000 to Urdd Gobaith Cymru Bro Maelor; £1,000 to Clwyd Fine Arts Trust; £1,000 to Cambrian Educational Foundation for Deaf Children; £750 to Shelter Cymru; £500 to Rhyl and District Arts Festival Association; £500 to Denbighshire Historical Society; £500 to Cyllun Casetiow Cymraeg I'r Dellion; £500 to Cymru Cymraeg a Dysgwyr ar Y Cyd; £500 to Royal Welsh Agricultural Society

FINANCES *Year* 1995 *Income* £34,369 *Grants* £25,361

TRUSTEES Finance sub-committee

HOW TO APPLY Application forms are available from the address under Who To Apply To. The Trustees meet in June and December

WHO TO APPLY TO David Ledsham, Accountant, County Council of Clwyd Welsh Church Charity Fund, Finance Dept Flintshire County Council, Count Hall, Mold, Flintshire CH7 6NR

CC NO 504476   **ESTABLISHED** 1975

■ Clyde Shipping Co Charitable Trust

WHAT IS FUNDED General charitable purposes

WHO CAN BENEFIT Mainly registered charities. There are no restrictions on the age; professional and economic group; family situation; religion and culture; and social circumstances of; or disease or medical condition suffered by, the beneficiaries

WHERE FUNDING CAN BE GIVEN UK, with preference for Scotland

WHO TO APPLY TO Mrs A Henphill, Trust Secretary, Clyde Shipping Co Charitable Trust, Cumbrae House, 15 Carlton Street, Glasgow G5 9JP

SC NO SCO 01402

■ Clydpride Ltd

WHAT IS FUNDED Advancement of the Orthodox Jewish faith. Relief of poverty. General charitable purposes

WHO CAN BENEFIT Individuals and institutions benefiting Jewish people and those disadvantaged by poverty

WHERE FUNDING CAN BE GIVEN UK

TYPE OF GRANT At the discretion of the Trustees

FINANCES *Year* 1996 *Income* £773,610 *Grants* £134,184

TRUSTEES L Faust, D Faust

WHO TO APPLY TO L Faust, Secretary to the Trustees, Clydpride Ltd, 144 Bridge Lane, London NW11 9JS

CC NO 295393   **ESTABLISHED** 1982

■ The Francis Coales Charitable Foundation

WHAT IS FUNDED The repair/restoration of any ecclesiastical buildings built before 1875

WHAT IS NOT FUNDED No grants for improvements, heating, wiring, etc

WHERE FUNDING CAN BE GIVEN UK, especially Bedfordshire, Buckinghamshire, Hertfordshire and Northamptonshire. Other areas not excluded if important building

TYPE OF GRANT Largely one-off or recurring if for an on-going application

RANGE OF GRANTS £250–£10,000, typical grant £1,000–£2,500

132

Think carefully about every application. Is it justified?

SAMPLE GRANTS £7,000 to Ely Cathedral for archivist to calendar modern archives; £5,000 to Pilton, Northamptonshire for church spire; £5,000 to Offley, Hertfordshire for restoration of church; £5,000 to Cockayne Hatley, Bedfordshire for conservation of church woodwork; £3,500 to Claybrooke, Leicestershire for chancel and roof repairs; £3,000 to Charwelton, Northamptonshire for church restoration; £3,000 to British Archaeological Association for publication of volume on Bury St Edmunds; £3,000 to Lilbourne, Northamptonshire for tower repairs; £3,000 to Harlestone, Northamptonshire for stonework restoration; £3,000 to Staverton, Northamptonshire for repairs to window tracery

FINANCES *Year* 1997 *Income* £117,895
Grants £103,301

NOTES Grants are made for monuments in churches irrespective of location

HOW TO APPLY To the address under Who To Apply To in writing for an application form with brief outline of request. Full details will be required on return of application form

WHO TO APPLY TO T H Parker, Administrator, The Francis Coales Charitable Foundation, The Bays, Hillcote, Bleadon Hill, Weston-Super-Mare, Somerset BS24 9JS *Tel* 01934 814009

CC NO 270718   **ESTABLISHED** 1975

■ The Coates Charitable Settlement

WHAT IS FUNDED Medicine and health, welfare, education, humanities

WHAT IS NOT FUNDED No grants to individuals or students

WHO CAN BENEFIT To benefit children and young adults. Support is given to those from many different social backgrounds. There is no restriction on the disease or medical condition suffered by the beneficiaries

WHERE FUNDING CAN BE GIVEN UK and Leicestershire

TYPE OF GRANT Range of grants

RANGE OF GRANTS £12,500–£125,000

SAMPLE GRANTS £125,000 to Macmillan Green Ribbon Appeal; £41,000 to Glenfield Hospital Department of Cardiology; £35,000 to Royal Leicestershire, Rutland and Wycliffe Society for the Blind; £12,500 to Leicester Charity Organisation Society for a palliative care project

FINANCES *Year* 1997 *Income* £25,227
Grants £213,500

TRUSTEES W C Coates, B M Coates, M A Chamberlain

HOW TO APPLY In writing

WHO TO APPLY TO M A Chamberlain, The Coates Charitable Settlement, KPMG, 1 Waterloo Way, Leicester LE1 6LP

CC NO 1015659   **ESTABLISHED** 1992

■ Lance Coates Charitable Trust 1969

WHAT IS FUNDED Promotion of biological and ecological approach to food production with the object of: (a) maintaining soil fertility for future generations; (b) improving health; (c) safeguarding scarce resources; and (d) minimising pollution

WHAT IS NOT FUNDED No grants to individuals

WHO CAN BENEFIT There are no restrictions on the age; professional and economic group; family situation; religion and culture; and social circumstances of; or disease or medical condition suffered by, the beneficiaries. Local activities often preferred

WHERE FUNDING CAN BE GIVEN UK

RANGE OF GRANTS £100–£5,000

SAMPLE GRANTS £5,000 to Country Trust; £5,000 to Springhill Cancer Rehabilitation Centre; £500 to Whitchurch PCC; £500 to Farm Africa; £500 to St Luke's Hospital for the Clergy; £150 to St Catherine's Church, Holworth; £100 to Cult Information Centre

FINANCES *Year* 1996 *Income* £29,017
Grants £11,750

TRUSTEES H L T Coates, E P Serjeant, Mrs S M Coates

WHO TO APPLY TO D Nye, Trustee, Lance Coates Charitable Trust 1969, Hillier Hopkins, 77–79 Marlows, Hemel Hempstead, Hertfordshire HP1 1LW

CC NO 261521   **ESTABLISHED** 1969

■ The John Coates Charitable Trust

WHAT IS FUNDED Preference is given to educational foundations, medical charities (especially those sponsoring research into the causes of Ankylosing Spondylitis, the rheumatic diseases generally and non-specific back pain), charities associated with preservation of the environment, charities sponsoring research into government fiscal and economic policies. Distributions are made to institutions and not to individuals

WHAT IS NOT FUNDED No grants to individuals

WHO CAN BENEFIT Institutions either national or of personal or local interest to one or more of the Trustees benefiting children and young adults, medical professionals, research workers and students will be considered. There is no restriction on the disease or medical condition suffered by the beneficiaries

WHERE FUNDING CAN BE GIVEN Mainly southern England

TYPE OF GRANT Capital and recurring

RANGE OF GRANTS £250–£15,000

SAMPLE GRANTS £15,000 to Lymington Museum; £12,000 to Painshill Park Trust; £10,000 to Chichester Cathedral; £10,000 to Chichester Festival Theatre; £10,000 to Mary Rose Trust; £10,000 to Royal Botanic Gardens, Kew; £10,000 to St Mungo's Association; £10,000 to Shelter; £6,000 to Selwyn College, Cambridge; £5,000 to St Bride's Church

FINANCES *Year* 1997 *Income* £222,484
Grants £260,100

TRUSTEES Mrs V E Coates, Mrs P G F McGregor, Mrs C Kesley, Mrs R J Lawes

HOW TO APPLY No guidelines. No acknowledgement unless sae

WHO TO APPLY TO Mrs P L Youngman, The John Coates Charitable Trust, Crockmore House, Fawley, Henley-on-Thames, Oxfordshire RG9 6HY

CC NO 262057   **ESTABLISHED** 1969

■ Coats Viyella Foundation Trust

WHAT IS FUNDED Preference is given, but not specifically restricted, to applicants from the textile related training courses. Community facilities will also be considered for funding

WHO CAN BENEFIT Individuals and organisations benefiting students on the textile and upholstery training courses

WHERE FUNDING CAN BE GIVEN UK

TYPE OF GRANT One-off grants, project and research will be considered

RANGE OF GRANTS £520–£5,000

FINANCES *Year* 1997 *Income* £64,898
Grants £37,920

Does the trust you have chosen match your needs? Haphazard applications waste postage and time

133

TRUSTEES S Dow, Sir H A S Djanogly, CBE, A H Macdiamid, W D Shardlow, R K Stephenson

NOTES Only applicants enclosing an sae will receive a reply

HOW TO APPLY Please write, enclosing a CV and sae, giving details of circumstances and the nature and amount of funding required. There is no formal application form

WHO TO APPLY TO S P Stephen, Coats Viyella Foundation Trust, Coats Viyella Plc, (Pension Office), Pacific House, 70 Wellington Street, Glasgow G2 6UB

CC NO 268735   **ESTABLISHED** 1974

■ Cobb Charity

WHAT IS FUNDED The encouragement of co-operative values and support of a more sustainable environment with eco-friendly technologies and the promotion of education. The Charity will consider: research; food/health; recycling; organic food production; country and traditional skills; cycle routes; and educational projects. Support will be given to: publishing and printing; small enterprises; voluntary and community organisations; and volunteers working in these areas

WHAT IS NOT FUNDED Registered charities only, no individuals. No medical organisations, no student expeditions, no building restorations

WHO CAN BENEFIT Ecological causes in the UK, related educational and co-operative projects

WHERE FUNDING CAN BE GIVEN UK, but only smaller charities need apply

TYPE OF GRANT Capital, core costs, feasibility studies, one-off, project, research, running costs, recurring costs, salaries and start-up costs. Funding is available for more than three years

SAMPLE GRANTS £1,250 to Forum for the Future for training leaders in sustainability; £750 to Sustrans for routes for schools; £750 to Transport 2000 for transforming the way we travel; £750 to City farms for food and farming resources, and for children; £750 to Elm Farm Research Centre raising environmental awareness; £750 to Tree Aid for tree planting; £750 to Soil Association for information to local authorities on buying ethical timber; £750 to The Good Gardeners Association for the promotion of health through right food; £750 to Turntable Furniture Award for recycling furniture; £750 to Global Action Plan for environmental protection through education

FINANCES *Year* 1997 *Income* £34,000 *Grants* £28,000

TRUSTEES E Allitt, F Appelbe, C Cochran, M Wells

HOW TO APPLY Preferably in September or February. No phone calls. As yet no guidelines or applications forms are available

WHO TO APPLY TO Eleanor Allitt, Cobb Charity, 108 Leamington Road, Kenilworth, Warwickshire CV8 2AA

CC NO 248030   **ESTABLISHED** 1964

■ The Cobtree Charity Trust Ltd

WHAT IS FUNDED The maintenance and development of Cobtree Manor Estate; and other general charitable purposes by other charities in the Maidstone and district area

WHAT IS NOT FUNDED No grants to individuals or to non-registered charities

WHO CAN BENEFIT There are no restrictions on the age; professional and economic group; family situation; religion and culture; and social circumstances of; or disease or medical condition suffered by, the beneficiaries

WHERE FUNDING CAN BE GIVEN Maidstone and district

TYPE OF GRANT Largely recurrent

SAMPLE GRANTS £25,400 to Cheshire Homes, Maidstone; £1,500 to Heart of Kent Hospice; £1,250 to NSPCC; £1,000 to Friends of Kent Churches (1993/94)

FINANCES *Year* 1994–95 *Income* £119,611

TRUSTEES E F Clifford, R J Corben, J H Day, G Fletcher, J Fletcher

HOW TO APPLY To the address under Who To Apply To in writing

WHO TO APPLY TO G M Davis, Secretary, The Cobtree Charity Trust Ltd, 5 Salts Avenue, Loose, Maidstone, Kent ME15 0AY *Tel* 01622 743566

CC NO 208455   **ESTABLISHED** 1961

■ Charity Established by the Will of Joan Mearnie Cocheme

WHAT IS FUNDED General charitable purposes

WHO CAN BENEFIT There are no restrictions on the age; professional and economic group; family situation; religion and culture; and social circumstances of; or disease or medical condition suffered by, the beneficiaries

WHERE FUNDING CAN BE GIVEN UK

TRUSTEES C H Woodbine Parish, N S Heslop, M L Swiney

WHO TO APPLY TO C H W Parish, Trustee, Charity Established by the Will of Joan Mearnie Cocheme, 9 Dowgate Hill, London EC2R 2SU

CC NO 1068458   **ESTABLISHED** 1996

■ The Cockenzie Charitable Trust

WHAT IS FUNDED General religious purposes, with particular reference to literary and mission work

WHAT IS NOT FUNDED Applications for grants for educational objectives are seldom successful

WHO CAN BENEFIT There is no restriction on the beneficiaries by religion or culture

WHERE FUNDING CAN BE GIVEN UK and overseas

FINANCES *Year* 1996 *Income* £19,946 *Grants* £18,717

TRUSTEES D W Paterson, M P Paterson, A Hill

HOW TO APPLY Requests for grants are not always acknowledged

WHO TO APPLY TO Dr D W Paterson, The Cockenzie Charitable Trust, 42 Chancellors Close, Birmingham B15 3UJ

CC NO 232083   **ESTABLISHED** 1963

■ The Coffey Charitable Settlement

WHAT IS FUNDED (a) The relief of poverty; (b) the advancement of education; (c) the advancement of Christian religion; (d) any other charitable purpose beneficial to the community

WHO CAN BENEFIT To benefit children, young adults, Christians and those disadvantaged by poverty

WHERE FUNDING CAN BE GIVEN UK

RANGE OF GRANTS £250–£6,439

SAMPLE GRANTS £6,439 to a full-time Christian worker for expenses; £1,950 to Oasis Trust; £1,500 to an individual in hardship; £600 to Woodley Baptist Church for support of youth ministry; £500 to church pastor

FINANCES *Year* 1997 *Income* £13,632 *Grants* £12,489

TRUSTEES C Coffey, Ms W L Coffey, D J Stephenson

Have you read How to use the DGMT *on page xvi?*

NOTES Funds of the Trust are fully committed for the foreseeable future

WHO TO APPLY TO D J Stephenson, Trustee, The Coffey Charitable Settlement, Bourbon Court, Nightingales Corner, Little Chalfont, Buckinghamshire HP7 9QS *Tel* 01494 765428

CC NO 1043549   **ESTABLISHED** 1994

■ Sylvia Cohen No1 Charitable Foundation

WHAT IS FUNDED General charitable purposes

WHO CAN BENEFIT There are no restrictions on the age; professional and economic group; family situation; religion and culture; and social circumstances of; or disease or medical condition suffered by, the beneficiaries

WHERE FUNDING CAN BE GIVEN UK

TRUSTEES Ms S Cohen, B J R Cohen, Ms L Cohen, M F Williams

WHO TO APPLY TO M Williams, Professional Advisor, Sylvia Cohen No1 Charitable Foundation, 17 Lady Jane Court, Grosvenor Road, Caversham, Berkshire RG4 5EH

CC NO 1059560   **ESTABLISHED** 1996

■ The Cohen Charitable Trust

WHAT IS FUNDED General charitable purposes

WHO CAN BENEFIT There are no restrictions on the age; professional and economic group; family situation; religion and culture; and social circumstances of; or disease or medical condition suffered by, the beneficiaries

WHERE FUNDING CAN BE GIVEN UK

FINANCES *Year* 1996 *Income* £33,972
Grants £3,212

TRUSTEES I Cohen, B Karet

WHO TO APPLY TO I Cohen, Secretary, The Cohen Charitable Trust, 8 Darenth Road, Stamford Hill, London N16 6EJ

CC NO 278703   **ESTABLISHED** 1979

■ The Andrew Cohen Charitable Trust

WHAT IS FUNDED General charitable purposes, at the Trustees' discretion

WHO CAN BENEFIT There are no restrictions on the age; professional and economic group; family situation; religion and culture; and social circumstances of; or disease or medical condition suffered by, the beneficiaries

WHERE FUNDING CAN BE GIVEN UK and overseas

RANGE OF GRANTS £2,873–£112,000

SAMPLE GRANTS £112,000 to JIA; £10,000 to Jewish Care; £2,873 to L'Chaim Society Oxford

FINANCES *Year* 1994–95 *Income* £72,250
Grants £124,873

TRUSTEES J A Lewis, A L Cohen, Ms W P Cohen, I Lewis

WHO TO APPLY TO A L Cohen, The Andrew Cohen Charitable Trust, Lynton House, 5 Stanmore Hill, Stanmore, Middlesex HA7 3DP

CC NO 1033283   **ESTABLISHED** 1994

■ The Denise Cohen Charitable Trust

WHAT IS FUNDED Education; health and welfare of the aged, infirm and of children; encouragement of the arts and grants-giving to major national centres for the performing arts

WHO CAN BENEFIT Children and older people; actors and entertainment professionals; musicians; textile workers and designers; students; writers and poets; at risk groups; those disadvantaged by poverty and socially isolated. There is no restriction on the disease or medical condition suffered by the beneficiaries

WHERE FUNDING CAN BE GIVEN UK

SAMPLE GRANTS £5,500 to Child Resettlement Fund; £4,850 to Nightingale Home for Aged Jews; £4,500 to Royal Opera House

FINANCES *Year* 1996–97 *Income* £40,569
Grants £42,536

TRUSTEES Mrs D Cohen, Sara Cohen, M D Paisner

HOW TO APPLY To the address under Who To Apply To in writing. **The Trustees generally do not consider unsolicited applications**

WHO TO APPLY TO The Denise Cohen Charitable Trust, Hacker Young, St Alphage House, 2 Fore Street, London EC2Y 5DH *Tel* 0171-353 0299

CC NO 276439   **ESTABLISHED** 1977

■ The Joy Cohen Charitable Trust

WHAT IS FUNDED General charitable purposes

WHO CAN BENEFIT There are no restrictions on the age; professional and economic group; family situation; religion and culture; and social circumstances of; or disease or medical condition suffered by, the beneficiaries

WHERE FUNDING CAN BE GIVEN UK

TRUSTEES D J Brecher, Mrs J A Cohen, S S Cohen

WHO TO APPLY TO M Jacobs, Solicitor, The Joy Cohen Charitable Trust, Nicholson, Graham and Jones, 110 Cannon Street, London EC4N 6AR

CC NO 1065471   **ESTABLISHED** 1997

■ The Ruth & Harvey Cohen Charitable Trust

This trust did not respond to CAF's request to amend its entry and, by 30 June 1998, CAF's researchers did not find financial records for later than 1995 on its file at the Charity Commission. Trusts are legally required to submit annual accounts to the Charity Commission under section 42 of the Charities Act 1993

WHAT IS FUNDED General charitable purposes

WHO CAN BENEFIT There are no restrictions on the age; professional and economic group; family situation; religion and culture; and social circumstances of; or disease or medical condition suffered by, the beneficiaries

WHERE FUNDING CAN BE GIVEN UK

TRUSTEES H Cohen, Mrs H Cohen, A H Grant

HOW TO APPLY Trustees do not welcome applications

WHO TO APPLY TO A H Grant, The Ruth & Harvey Cohen Charitable Trust, 18 Bourne End Road, Northwood, Middlesex HA6 3BS *Tel* 01923 823478

CC NO 299837   **ESTABLISHED** 1988

■ The Stanley Cohen Charitable Trust

WHAT IS FUNDED General charitable purposes

WHO CAN BENEFIT There are no restrictions on the age; professional and economic group; family situation; religion and culture; and social circumstances of; or disease or medical condition suffered by, the beneficiaries

WHERE FUNDING CAN BE GIVEN UK

TRUSTEES D J Brecher, Mrs J A Cohen, S S Cohen

WHO TO APPLY TO M Jacobs, The Stanley Cohen Charitable Trust, c/o Nicholson Graham & Jones, 110 Cannon Street, London EC4N 6AR

CC NO 1065470   **ESTABLISHED** 1997

■ The Vivienne and Samuel Cohen Charitable Trust

WHAT IS FUNDED General charitable purposes in Israel and the UK, mainly education, medical causes and welfare. Particular emphasis is given to Jewish causes

WHAT IS NOT FUNDED No grants to individuals

WHO CAN BENEFIT Institutions benefiting Jewish people, children and young adults. Support is given to at risk groups, those disadvantaged by poverty and socially isolated people. Medical professionals, research workers, students, teachers and governesses may also be supported. There is no restriction on the disease or medical condition suffered by the beneficiaries

WHERE FUNDING CAN BE GIVEN UK and overseas, particularly Israel

RANGE OF GRANTS £50–£25,000

SAMPLE GRANTS £25,000 to Maaleh Adumin Foundation; £10,000 to World Jewish Relief; £5,000 to British Friends of Jerusalem Mental Hospital; £5,000 to British Friends of Sarah Herzog Memorial Hospital; £5,000 to Variety Club; £4,000 to Maaleh Hatorah School; £3,000 to British and European Machal Association; £2,000 to Jewish Marriage Council; £2,000 to Jewish Care; £2,000 to JAMI

FINANCES *Year* 1997 *Income* £91,607 *Grants* £96,053

TRUSTEES Dr V L L Cohen, Michael Y Ben-Gershon, D H J Cohen, J S Lauffer, Gershon Cohen

WHO TO APPLY TO Dr Vivienne L L Cohen, The Vivienne and Samuel Cohen Charitable Trust, 9 Heathcroft, Hampstead Way, London NW11 7HH

CC NO 255496   **ESTABLISHED** 1965

■ The David Cohen Family Charitable Trust

WHAT IS FUNDED The promotion of literature, theatre, music and art, with some emphasis on contemporary work

WHAT IS NOT FUNDED No grants to individuals

WHO CAN BENEFIT Registered charities. There is no restriction on the age of the beneficiaries

WHERE FUNDING CAN BE GIVEN UK

TYPE OF GRANT Core costs, one-off, project, recurring costs and salaries. Funding is available for up to two years

RANGE OF GRANTS Normally £50–£5,000

SAMPLE GRANTS £15,000 to Arts Council of England for David Cohen British Literature Prize; £3,000 to National Portrait Gallery for 'Pursuit of Beauty' educational programme; £3,000 to Royal Academy of Music for a one year piano residency; £3,000 to Spitalfields Market Opera for new staffing requirements; £2,200 to Glyndebourne Festival Opera for a founder member; £2,000 to The National Trust for works of art at 2 Willow Road, Hampstead; £2,000 to Serpentine Gallery for educational and disability needs; £1,500 to English Touring Theatre for outreach programme; £1,500 to Tricycle Theatre for youth education programme

FINANCES *Year* 1995–96 *Income* £54,849 *Grants* £44,245

TRUSTEES Dr David Cohen, Mrs Veronica Cohen, Miss Imogen Cohen, Miss Olivia Cohen

HOW TO APPLY To be be submitted to the address under Who To Apply To. No response is made to unsuccessful applications

WHO TO APPLY TO Duncan Haldane, Administrator, The David Cohen Family Charitable Trust, 85 Albany Street, London NW1 4BT *Tel* 0171-486 1117 *Fax* 0171-486 1118

CC NO 279796   **ESTABLISHED** 1980

■ The Alfred S Cohen Foundation

WHAT IS FUNDED General charitable purposes. The annual support of a number of registered charities selected by the Settlor

WHAT IS NOT FUNDED No grants to individuals

WHO CAN BENEFIT Small registered charities. There are no restrictions on the age; professional and economic group; family situation; religion and culture; and social circumstances of; or disease or medical condition suffered by, the beneficiaries

WHERE FUNDING CAN BE GIVEN UK

RANGE OF GRANTS £50–£3,500

SAMPLE GRANTS £3,500 to JNF Charitable Trust; £2,500 to Elsie and Barnett Janner Charitable Trust; £1,300 to Ravenswood; £1,000 to JPA; £1,000 to the Prince's Trust

FINANCES *Year* 1997 *Income* £19,623 *Grants* £16,520

TRUSTEES P C Cohen

NOTES The income from this Trust is small. Regular annual contributions are made to certain charities. Individuals will not be funded

HOW TO APPLY At any time

WHO TO APPLY TO P C Cohen, The Alfred S Cohen Foundation, The Brass Bell, Warren Road, Kingston-upon-Thames KT2 7HR

CC NO 273879   **ESTABLISHED** 1977

■ Richard J Cohen Third Charitable Trust

WHAT IS FUNDED General charitable purposes. The Trustees are more inclined to support smaller charities than big national ones

WHO CAN BENEFIT There are no restrictions on the age; professional and economic group; family situation; religion and culture; and social circumstances of; or disease or medical condition suffered by, the beneficiaries

WHERE FUNDING CAN BE GIVEN UK

TYPE OF GRANT Project rather than core funds. Capital projects might be included but applicants should remember this is a new trust with limited funds at present

RANGE OF GRANTS Up to £1,000

HOW TO APPLY In writing. The Trustees make decisions on an ad hoc basis
WHO TO APPLY TO Maurice Williams, Richard J Cohen Third Charitable Trust, 17 Lady Jane Court, Grosvenor Road, Caversham, Reading, Berkshire RG4 5EH *Tel* 0118-948 1489
CC NO 1070637 **ESTABLISHED** 1998

■ The Colchester and Tendring Community Trust

WHAT IS FUNDED General charitable purposes
WHAT IS NOT FUNDED No grants to individuals
WHO CAN BENEFIT There are no restrictions on the age; professional and economic group; family situation; religion and culture; and social circumstances of; or disease or medical condition suffered by, the beneficiaries
WHERE FUNDING CAN BE GIVEN The Borough of Colchester and the district of Tendring
RANGE OF GRANTS £50–£1,000. Average grant £200–£300
FINANCES *Year* 1996–97 *Income* £22,694 *Grants* £13,900
TRUSTEES W Bleakley, B H M Davenport, M A Lambert, R Roberts, K J Scott, J P Sheppard, W E Sandford, D D Triolo
HOW TO APPLY Applications should be made on a form available from the address under Who To Apply To. The Trustees meet twice a year to consider applications. Closing dates for grant rounds 30 April and 31 October
WHO TO APPLY TO G Posner, Trust Manager, The Colchester and Tendring Community Trust, Winsleys House, High Street, Colchester, Essex CO1 1UG *Tel* 01206 769892
CC NO 803193 **ESTABLISHED** 1989

■ Colchester Catalyst Charity

WHAT IS FUNDED Provision of support by direct contributions to health organisations for specific and well designed projects in order to improve healthcare
WHAT IS NOT FUNDED No support for general funding, staff or running costs. Retrospective funding is not considered
WHO CAN BENEFIT Health organisations. There are no restrictions on the disease or medical condition suffered by the beneficiaries
WHERE FUNDING CAN BE GIVEN North East Essex, particularly Colchester
TYPE OF GRANT One-off
SAMPLE GRANTS £213,641 to charities; £56,926 for respite care; £53,148 for equipment pools; £30,000 to individuals
FINANCES *Year* 1996–97 *Income* £409,717 *Grants* £353,715
TRUSTEES Directors: C F Pertwee (Chairman), A C Blaxill, R W Whybrow, FRICS, Dr R W Griffin, MB, ChB, FRCA, A H Frost, A R W Tomkins, P W E Fitt, FCA, Dr E Hall, MBBS, DRCOG, JP
HOW TO APPLY To the address under Who To Apply To in writing
WHO TO APPLY TO P Fitt, Colchester Catalyst Charity, 15 High Street, West Mersea, Essex CO5 8QA
CC NO 228352 **ESTABLISHED** 1959

■ The John Coldman Charitable Trust

WHAT IS FUNDED General charitable purposes
WHO CAN BENEFIT There are no restrictions on the age; professional and economic group; family situation; religion and culture; and social circumstances of; or disease or medical condition suffered by, the beneficiaries
WHERE FUNDING CAN BE GIVEN UK
RANGE OF GRANTS £250–£62,500
SAMPLE GRANTS £62,500 to Oasis Trust; £13,250 to Hever Church of England Primary School; £10,000 to NSPCC, Penge Project; £5,000 to Hever PCC; £3,250 to Cypress Junior School Fund; £2,500 to Broomhill Opera Trust; £2,500 to Centrepoint; £2,300 to St Peter and St Paul, Edenbridge; £2,000 to Hartfield Group, Riding for the Disabled; £855 to Parish Office for a personal computer
FINANCES *Year* 1997 *Income* £136,103 *Grants* £108,655
TRUSTEES D J Coldman, G E Coldman, C J Warner
WHO TO APPLY TO D J Coldman, Trustee, The John Coldman Charitable Trust, Polebrook, Hever, Edenbridge, Kent TN8 7NJ
CC NO 1050110 **ESTABLISHED** 1995

■ The Cole Charitable Trust

WHAT IS FUNDED Poverty, homelessness, refugees, self-help, particularly in the Greater Birmingham area
WHAT IS NOT FUNDED No grants to national organisations; religion; education; animal welfare; or to individuals not backed by a charity
WHO CAN BENEFIT Individuals, and local community projects or local branches of larger organisations benefiting those disadvantaged by poverty, the homeless and refugees
WHERE FUNDING CAN BE GIVEN Mainly Greater Birmingham, Cambridgeshire, Kent
TYPE OF GRANT Small capital or project grants, normally one-off
RANGE OF GRANTS £250–£6,000
SAMPLE GRANTS £6,000 to Bridget's Trust; £5,000 to Emmaus; £5,000 to Link House Trust; £3,500 to Daneford Trust; £2,000 to Medical Foundation for the Care of Victims of Torture; £1,000 to Birmingham Settlement; £1,000 to British Retinitis Pigmentosa Society; £1,000 to CARES; £1,000 to Immigrants Aid Trust; £1,000 to MIND
FINANCES *Year* 1997 *Income* £50,765 *Grants* £53,050
TRUSTEES Dr T J Cole, G N Cole, Dr J L Cole, Mrs D M Newton
HOW TO APPLY No guidelines. Sorry no acknowledgement of applications. No envelopes please. Annual Accounts required. Three meetings per year; deadlines for applications mid-April, August and December
WHO TO APPLY TO Dr J L Cole, The Cole Charitable Trust, 128 Tamworth Road, Sutton Coldfield, West Midlands B75 6DH
CC NO 264033 **ESTABLISHED** 1972

■ The John and Freda Coleman Charitable Trust

WHAT IS FUNDED Training young people to equip them with practical, manual skills and relevant technical knowledge in order to prepare them for employment. Particularly charities working in the fields of: economic regeneration; job creation; small enterprises; IT training; engineering

Does the trust you have chosen match your needs? Haphazard applications waste postage and time

137

research and research into science and technology

WHAT IS NOT FUNDED Extremely unlikely to fund expeditions or individual scholarships

WHO CAN BENEFIT Education and training centres benefiting children, young adults, older people, disabled people and those disadvantaged by poverty

WHERE FUNDING CAN BE GIVEN UK, with a preference for Surrey and Hampshire

TYPE OF GRANT Loans not given. Grants to 'kick start' relevant projects

RANGE OF GRANTS £200 to over £30,000

SAMPLE GRANTS £50,000 to Perins School for re-equipment in technical areas; £32,000 to Surrey Satro for young engineers/entrepreneurs; £10,000 to Treloar College (Lord Mayor Treloar College) for equipment for severely disabled children; £10,000 to Thames Heritage for practical work by youngsters on the Thames; £2,000 to Science and Technology Guildford for training in science and technology for youngsters in Guildford

FINANCES *Year* 1996–97 *Income* £70,000 *Grants* £108,000

TRUSTEES A J Coleman, B R Coleman, Mrs F M K Coleman, J P Coleman, L P Fernander, P B Sparks

NOTES We always take an active interest in the activities of those helped

HOW TO APPLY To the address under Who To Apply To in writing. No telephone calls welcome

WHO TO APPLY TO John Round, Administrator, The John and Freda Coleman Charitable Trust, Tanglewood, Bullbeggars Lane, Horsell, Woking, Surrey GU21 4SH

CC NO 278223   **ESTABLISHED** 1979

■ College Estate

WHAT IS FUNDED General charitable purposes to benefit the people of the town of Stratford-upon Avon

WHAT IS NOT FUNDED Very few grants are made to individuals, no education grants are made to individuals

WHO CAN BENEFIT There are no restrictions on the age; professional and economic group; family situation; religion and culture; and social circumstances of; or disease or medical condition suffered by, the beneficiaries

WHERE FUNDING CAN BE GIVEN The town of Stratford-upon-Avon

TYPE OF GRANT One-off and recurring costs will be considered

SAMPLE GRANTS £46,264 to 50th Anniversary World War II; £38,895 for bus passes; £36,001 for educational grants; £26,928 for special grants; £26,215 for grants to local organisations; £22,994 for Christmas lighting and trees; £19,500 to Stratford in Bloom; £19,000 to Stratford-upon-Avon Festival and Carnival; £8,000 to Minor Injuries Unit; £7,000 to Baptist Church

FINANCES *Year* 1996 *Income* £636,491 *Grants* £279,920

TRUSTEES The Town Council

HOW TO APPLY Applications are considered once a year only at the end of May or early June, and must be on the official application form

WHO TO APPLY TO Town Clerk, College Estate, Stratford-upon-Avon Town Council, 14 Rother Street, Stratford-upon-Avon CV37 6LU

CC NO 217485   **ESTABLISHED** 1911

■ The George Henry Collins Charity

WHAT IS FUNDED Wide, but the relief of suffering from illness, infirmity, old age or loneliness to take preference. Trustees will consider donating one-tenth annual income to charities for use overseas

WHAT IS NOT FUNDED No grants to individuals

WHO CAN BENEFIT Local charities and local branches of registered national charities in Birmingham benefiting older people, the socially isolated, and those suffering from illness. There is no restriction on the disease or medical condition suffered by the beneficiaries

WHERE FUNDING CAN BE GIVEN 50 mile radius of Birmingham

TYPE OF GRANT One-off

RANGE OF GRANTS £100–£1,000

FINANCES *Year* 1996–97 *Income* £57,477 *Grants* £40,300

TRUSTEES A D Martineau, H Kenrick, Mrs E A Davies, A A Waters, A Collins, M S Hansell

HOW TO APPLY By letter. There are no application forms

WHO TO APPLY TO David L Turfrey, The George Henry Collins Charity, St Philips House, St Philips Place, Birmingham B3 2PP

CC NO 212268   **ESTABLISHED** 1959

■ The Norman Collinson Charitable Trust

WHAT IS FUNDED This Trust will consider funding: infrastructure and development; charity or voluntary bodies; Christian outreach; arts, culture and recreation; health; and community services. Community centres, village halls, playgrounds and other charitable purposes are also considered

WHAT IS NOT FUNDED The Trustees have found it necessary to place a geographical restriction and confine grants to helping people in York and district. We do however make a limited number of grants to national charities, particularly where they can demonstrate the beneficiaries reside in the York area. No grants to individuals

WHO CAN BENEFIT We generally restrict grants to young people, the aged, infirm and the handicapped or to individuals or organisations who provide help for such people. Also considered are Christians; at risk groups; those disadvantaged by poverty; carers; disaster victims; the homeless and victims of abuse

WHERE FUNDING CAN BE GIVEN York area

TYPE OF GRANT Core costs, one-off, project and running costs are funded for up to one year. We do not enter into on-going commitments. Grants are reconsidered each year

RANGE OF GRANTS No upper or lower limit

SAMPLE GRANTS £10,000 to York Council for Voluntary Services for new accommodation; £6,000 to York and District CAB; £3,500 to the Salvation Army, York; £3,000 to Abbeyfield Society; £2,500 to York Boys Club; £2,000 to Copmanthorpe Scout Group for new premises; £1,500 to Camphill Village Trust, Bolton; £1,250 to Relate, York; £1,250 to Peasholme Centre, York for the homeless; £1,200 to SNAPPY, York for disabled children

FINANCES *Year* 1997 *Income* £86,360 *Grants* £155,967

TRUSTEES B Catton, F E Dennis, D C Fotheringham, D B Holman, J M Saville

NOTES Applications from organisations should give details of their officers and recent accounts and/or budget. (Applications from individuals should be through recognised agencies)

HOW TO APPLY The Trustees meet monthly to consider applications, normally on the second Tuesday in the month. Deadline is seven days before meeting

WHO TO APPLY TO M H Miller, The Norman Collinson Charitable Trust, 42 Briergate, Haxby, York YO32 3YP

CC NO 277325 **ESTABLISHED** 1979

■ Robert Hickson Collis Charity

WHAT IS FUNDED General charitable purposes. Annual grants are made to numerous specified charities

WHAT IS NOT FUNDED No grants to individuals

WHO CAN BENEFIT Both headquarters and local organisations. There are no restrictions on the age; professional and economic group; family situation; religion and culture; and social circumstances of; or disease or medical condition suffered by, the beneficiaries

WHERE FUNDING CAN BE GIVEN UK

FINANCES *Year* 1996 *Income* £17,300 *Grants* £8,890

TRUSTEES The Trustees of Charities Aid Foundation

WHO TO APPLY TO Miss E H Collis, c/o CAF, Trust Dept, Kings Hill, West Malling, Kent ME19 4TA

CC NO 268369 **ESTABLISHED** 1966

■ The E Alec Colman Charitable Fund Ltd

WHAT IS FUNDED Relief of poverty; advancement of education; and advancement of religion. The Trust aims to pinpoint areas of interest and take the initiative in funding organisations working in these fields

WHAT IS NOT FUNDED No grants to individuals

WHO CAN BENEFIT Organisations benefiting children, young adults, students, teachers and governesses. Support is given to those disadvantaged by poverty and to the clergy. Support may also be given to people of different religions and particular favour is given to Jewish people

WHERE FUNDING CAN BE GIVEN Great Britain and Israel

TYPE OF GRANT Recurring

RANGE OF GRANTS £23–£1,000

SAMPLE GRANTS £1,000 to Ben Gurion University Federation; £500 to Friends of Bar-Ilan University; £400 to JNF Charitable Trust; £150 to Jewish Childs Day; £150 to World Jewish Relief; £120 to Friends of Alyn Orthopaedic Hospital; £120 to Central Synagogue; £100 to Children Nationwide Cancer Campaign; £100 to British Friends of Ohel Sarah; £100 to Jewish Blind and Physically Handicapped Society

FINANCES *Year* 1996 *Income* £49,527 *Grants* £3,773

TRUSTEES The Council of Management: S H Colman, Mrs E A Colman, M Harris

NOTES This is a small charity. New beneficiaries are only considered in exceptional circumstances

WHO TO APPLY TO A N Carless, Secretary, The E Alec Colman Charitable Fund Ltd, Colman House, 121 Livery Street, Birmingham B3 1RS

CC NO 243817 **ESTABLISHED** 1965

■ Col-Reno Ltd

WHAT IS FUNDED Jewish religion and education

WHO CAN BENEFIT Religious and educational institutions benefiting children, young adults, students and Jewish people

WHERE FUNDING CAN BE GIVEN UK, Israel, USA

RANGE OF GRANTS £180–£15,000

SAMPLE GRANTS £15,000 to Agudas Yisroel of California; £6,330 to JSSM; £2,800 to SOFOT; £2,550 to Friends of Touro College; £1,000 to Jerusalem Foundation; £750 to Ulpanit Zvia Torah Programme; £180 to British Friends of Chinuch Atzmai in Israel; £180 to British Council Shaarei Zedek Medical Centre

FINANCES *Year* 1997 *Income* £43,937 *Grants* £28,790

TRUSTEES M H Stern, A E Stern, Mrs C Stern

HOW TO APPLY To the address under Who To Apply To in writing

WHO TO APPLY TO M H Stern, Col-Reno Ltd, 15 Shirehall Gardens, Hendon, London NW4 2QT

CC NO 274896 **ESTABLISHED** 1977

■ The J I Colvile Charitable Trust

WHAT IS FUNDED General charitable purposes

WHAT IS NOT FUNDED No grants to animal charities

WHO CAN BENEFIT There are no restrictions on the age; professional and economic group; family situation; religion and culture; and social circumstances of; or disease or medical condition suffered by, the beneficiaries

WHERE FUNDING CAN BE GIVEN UK and overseas

TYPE OF GRANT One-off for running costs, modest in size. Funds are available for up to one year

HOW TO APPLY By letter. Trustees will meet each March and September

WHO TO APPLY TO M S Lee-Browne, Solicitor, The J I Colvile Charitable Trust, Wilmot & Co Solicitors, High Street, Fairford, Gloucestershire, GL7 4AE *Tel* 01285 712207

CC NO 1067274 **ESTABLISHED** 1998

■ Colwinston Charitable Trust

This trust did not respond to CAF's request to amend its entry and, by 30 June 1998, CAF's researchers did not find financial records for later than 1995 on its file at the Charity Commission. Trusts are legally required to submit annual accounts to the Charity Commission under section 42 of the Charities Act 1993

WHAT IS FUNDED General charitable purposes

WHO CAN BENEFIT There are no restrictions on the age; professional and economic group; family situation; religion and culture; and social circumstances of; or disease or medical condition suffered by, the beneficiaries

WHERE FUNDING CAN BE GIVEN Cardiff

TRUSTEES M D Paisner, Ms A A Prichard, J C Prichard, M C T Prichard

WHO TO APPLY TO M Prichard, Trustee, Colwinston Charitable Trust, Booker Entertainment, 141 Sloane Street, London SW1X 9AY

CC NO 1049189 **ESTABLISHED** 1995

■ The Comic Heritage Charitable Trust

WHAT IS FUNDED General charitable purposes

WHO CAN BENEFIT There are no restrictions on the age; professional and economic group; family situation; religion and culture; and social circumstances of; or disease or medical condition suffered by, the beneficiaries

WHERE FUNDING CAN BE GIVEN UK

FINANCES *Year* 1996 *Income* £21,200 *Grants* £21,200

TRUSTEES P D C Collins, LVO, D A Graham, C N Parsons, Sir H D Secombe, L V Waumsley
WHO TO APPLY TO L V Waumsley, The Comic Heritage Charitable Trust, 23 Highcroft, North Hill, Highgate, London N6 4RD
CC NO 1031027   **ESTABLISHED** 1993

■ Commonwealth Relations Trust

WHAT IS FUNDED Contributing towards a Commonwealth Programme with Nuffield Foundation. Programme funds advanced education and training schemes which support change in developing Commonwealth countries focusing on education; science; access to justice; health; child protection; legal services; professional bodies; and advice and information
WHAT IS NOT FUNDED No grants to individuals. No grants for formal qualifications. No grants for attendance at conferences. No contributions to appeals
WHO CAN BENEFIT UK non-governmental organisations and education providers benefiting children; young adults and older people; legal professionals; medical professionals, nurses and doctors; students; scientists; teachers and governesses; those disadvantaged by poverty; disabled people and refugees
WHERE FUNDING CAN BE GIVEN Developing Commonwealth countries. Priorty to Eastern and Southern Africa
TYPE OF GRANT Project costs for up to three years
SAMPLE GRANTS £222,715 to final year of professional exchange programme; £56,910 to High/Scope UK for training of pre-school trainers in South Africa; £56,810 to International Extension College for development of distance education at University of Namibia
FINANCES *Year* 1996 *Income* £268,000 *Grants* £223,000
TRUSTEES Dr Onora O'Neill, The Hon Dame Brenda Hale, Sir John Banham, Prof Sir Michael Rutter, CBE, MD, FRCP, FRCPysch, FRS, Mrs Anne Sofer, Prof A B Atkinson
NOTES Telephone enquiries via Nuffield Foundation Tel: 0171–631 0566 Fax: 0171–323 4877
HOW TO APPLY Interested organisations should first approach by telephone or short enquiry letter
WHO TO APPLY TO Ms S Lock, Commonwealth Relations Trust, Nuffield Foundation Commonwealth Programme, 28 Bedford Square, London WC1B 3EG
CC NO 205551   **ESTABLISHED** 1937

■ Community Aid For Children and the Elderly (working name: Bright Lites)

WHAT IS FUNDED General charitable purposes
WHO CAN BENEFIT There are no restrictions on the age; professional and economic group; family situation; religion and culture; and social circumstances of; or disease or medical condition suffered by, the beneficiaries
WHERE FUNDING CAN BE GIVEN UK
FINANCES *Year* 1998 *Income* £25,017 *Grants* £300
TRUSTEES H S Batlye, D Griffiths, S Rushworth
WHO TO APPLY TO A Baxter, Community Aid For Children and the Elderly, The Town Hall, Thornton Square, Brighouse, West Yorkshire HD6 1EF
CC NO 1045797   **ESTABLISHED** 1995

■ The Foundation for Community Awareness

WHAT IS FUNDED The furtherance of education, learning and research through the promotion of lectures; study groups; seminars and discussions; the publication of books, articles, newsletters and cassettes; training and employment of people to carry out such objects
WHO CAN BENEFIT Individuals and organisations benefiting research workers, students and teachers
WHERE FUNDING CAN BE GIVEN UK and overseas
TYPE OF GRANT Recurring/educational
SAMPLE GRANTS £8,083 to Centre European Juif d'Information
FINANCES *Year* 1997 *Income* £13,050 *Grants* £8,083
TRUSTEES The Lord Weidenfeld of Chelsea, Sir Trevor Chinn, MVO
WHO TO APPLY TO D Clayton, The Foundation for Community Awareness, Charles House, 108–110 Finchley Road, London NW3 5JJ
CC NO 328343   **ESTABLISHED** 1989

■ The Community Trust for Greater Manchester

WHAT IS FUNDED Medicine and health, welfare, education, religion, arts, conservation and environment, people with disabilities, elderly, animal welfare, youth and children. Other charitable purposes will be considered
WHAT IS NOT FUNDED No grants to individuals, or for political organisations
WHO CAN BENEFIT Small local projects, new and established organisations and innovative projects benefiting children, young adults and elderly people, disabled people, at risk groups, those disadvantaged by poverty and socially isolated people. There is no restriction on the disease or medical condition suffered by the beneficiaries
WHERE FUNDING CAN BE GIVEN Greater Manchester
TYPE OF GRANT One-off grants
RANGE OF GRANTS Up to £1,000
FINANCES *Year* 1996–97 *Income* £195,352 *Grants* £121,644
TRUSTEES His Grace The Duke of Westminster, OBE, TD, DL, Alan Rudden, R Gordon Humphreys, A J Farnworth, John Sandford, C Smith, M Eileen Polding, Lorraine Worsley, Jack Buckley, W T Risby, C Chan, A A Downie
PUBLICATIONS Annual Report. Guidelines. Information Packs
HOW TO APPLY In writing. Application form available
WHO TO APPLY TO R J Carter, The Community Trust for Greater Manchester, PO Box 63, Beswick House, Beswick Row, Manchester M4 4JY *Web Site* http://www.scanline.com/intersect/community/
CC NO 1017504   **ESTABLISHED** 1993

■ The Community Trust – Milton Keynes

WHAT IS FUNDED The Trust's main priority is to help those in the Milton Keynes Council area who miss out because of poverty, ill health, disability or disadvantage. It also supports important initiatives in the spheres of the arts and leisure. Charities working in the fields of: information technology and computers; publishing and printing; community development; economic regeneration schemes; support to voluntary and community organisations; charity or voluntary umbrella bodies; family planning clinics; respite carer, care for carers; support and self help groups; community centres and village halls; historic buildings; training for community development; counselling on social issues; playschemes and advice centres will be considered

WHAT IS NOT FUNDED Grants from the Community Fund are not normally given to the following: individuals, animals, equipment which would become the responsibility of a statutory authority. Nor will the Trust replace statutory funding, support those applying for ongoing costs, such as salaries and rents (except in exceptional circumstances) or through development funding. Political, campaigning and narrowly religious activities are not eligible and the Trust will not make grants to cover costs already incurred prior to application deadlines

WHO CAN BENEFIT Organisations benefiting: people of all ages; volunteers; at risk groups; carers; disabled people; those disadvantaged by poverty; homeless people; and victims of abuse, crime and domestic violence. The Trust's Community Fund will only make grants to voluntary groups with a local-based committee whose work is in Milton Keynes. In addition, the Arts Fund does occasionally make grants to individuals and other less formally constituted groups

WHERE FUNDING CAN BE GIVEN The Milton Keynes Council area only

TYPE OF GRANT (a) Community Fund Grants: (i) Small Grants up to £1,000. (ii) General Grants from £1,001 to £5,000 can cover equipment costs, projects and minor building work, training, publicity and one-off activity costs. (iii) Development Grants, typically around £7,000 to £18,000 per year for up to three years generally for discrete project work; can include salaries, rents and other overheads. (iv) Umbrella grants: start-up new initiative £80 to £300. (b) Arts Fund Grants: minimum £1,000 awarded for artistic and cultural activities of high quality and originality. A typical grant might be £2,000

RANGE OF GRANTS £80–£18,000 depending on grant type

SAMPLE GRANTS £15,000 to Drug and Alcohol Support Services for one-stop information point; £10,000 to People Establishing a Caring Environment for a development worker; £5,000 to MADCAP Trust for building work; £5,000 to Victim Support Milton Keynes for volunteer training programme; £5,000 to MK Council of Voluntary Organisations for training courses for voluntary sector; £4,300 to MK International Folk Art Festival for access and participation by elderly or disabled people; £4,154 to Shelter Housing Aid Centre for building work at offices; £4,080 to Cornerstone Accommodation for furniture for a house for homeless young people; £4,000 to Woolstones Community Centre to replace heating system; £3,842 to Inter-Action for diesel engine for a narrowboat

FINANCES *Year* 1997–98 *Income* £448,592
Grants £271,038

TRUSTEES Naomi Eisenstadt, Rob Gifford, Richard Hall, Brian Hocken, Chris Hopkinson, Simon Ingram, Andrew Jones, Peter Kara, Juliet Murray, Michael Murray, Stephen Norrish, Francesca Skelton, Lady Tudor Price, Dr Tony Walton, Philippa Eccles

PUBLICATIONS *What is the Community Trust?*, quarterly newsletter, Policy Document, Guide to Grants, Community Fund Grants leaflet, Arts Fund Grant leaflet

HOW TO APPLY (a) Community Fund Grants: (i) Small grants: monthly, deadline being the last Friday of each month. (ii) General grants: quarterly, deadline being first Friday in February, May, August and November. (iii) Development Grants: annually, deadline being mid-November. (iv) Umbrella grants: form from the appropriate umbrella group. (b) Arts Fund Grants: Three times a year, deadline being 15 January, 15 May, 15 September. Form from Arts Fund Consultant, Maggie Nevitt at the address under Who To Apply To. Initial telephone calls are encouraged. Application forms are required for all grants

WHO TO APPLY TO Linda Whyte, Community Grants Co-ordinator, The Community Trust – Milton Keynes, Acorn House, 381 Midsummer Boulevard, Central Milton Keynes MK9 3HP *Tel* 01908 690276 *Fax* 01908 233635

CC NO 295107   **ESTABLISHED** 1987

■ The Company of Chartered Surveyors Charitable Trust Fund

WHAT IS FUNDED (a) The relief of poverty of members of the surveyors profession, or any other recognised profession, and of their dependents. Particular favour is given to members of the Company and their dependents. (b) The advancement of education of people desiring to become surveyors, or practise any other recognised profession, or of people desiring to become qualified for professional or administrative posts in national, public or local authorities, or in commerce. The latter must be done in a manner which is deemed to be charitable by law

WHAT IS NOT FUNDED Grants are not made to students from outside the field of surveying

WHO CAN BENEFIT Grants are made in the educational sphere only to students in the field of surveying. Individuals and organisations benefiting young adults, students and surveyors, and their dependants. Parents and children and widows and widowers may be supported as are those who are disadvantaged by poverty

WHERE FUNDING CAN BE GIVEN UK

TYPE OF GRANT Grants made in accordance with the following guidelines: (a) amount of the Trust Fund income only sufficient to contribute to genuine City Appeals, those arising out of bona fide City interests, those relating to members of the Livery and those relating to education and other purposes connected with the Ordnances of the Trust; (b) the financial resources of the Trust are not large enough to contribute to appeals for large amounts of money, although exceptions would be considered; (c) where possible support should be given to appeals supported by the Great Twelve Companies

FINANCES *Year* 1995 *Income* £17,501
Grants £5,050

TRUSTEES A Gordon-James, Sir Brian Hill, M K Ridley, M P L Baker, Alderman P A Bull, R S Broadhurst, M G Clark, M O Coates, P E Davidson, J R Turstram Eve, G M F Gillon, E T Hartill, Stuart Hibberdine, J N C James, C W Jonas, L W Kinney, John Leaning, Miss D F Patman, D H Pepper, T J L Roberton, Robert Steel, H D C Stebbing, FRICS

NOTES At the moment it is the policy of the Trustees to conserve its funds to build up the Trust Fund for the future. The Trust also administers the Sydney Smith Trust whose objects are also to provide financial assistance to students preparing for the examinations of the Royal Institution of Chartered Surveyors or at full-time colleges with courses which provide exemption from RICS qualifications the grants being towards living costs, books, etc. The Clerk will deal with telephone enquiries in the first instance

HOW TO APPLY Applications to be submitted at any time

WHO TO APPLY TO Mrs A Jackson, Clerk, Worshipful Company of Chartered Surveyors, 16 St Mary-at-Hill, London EC3R 8EE

CC NO 275512   **ESTABLISHED** 1977

■ The Company of Chartered Surveyors Charitable Trust Fund 1992

WHAT IS FUNDED Advancement of education; relief of poverty. Prizes to educational establishments, financial assistance to students training in surveying profession

WHO CAN BENEFIT Registered charities benefiting children, young adults, students and those disadvantaged by poverty

WHERE FUNDING CAN BE GIVEN UK

TYPE OF GRANT One-off and recurrent

FINANCES *Year* 1995 *Income* £105,524
Grants £8,371

TRUSTEES T J L Roberton, FRICS, Anthony Gordon-James, Sir Brian Hill, FRICS, M K Ridley, M P L Baker, R S Broadhurst, Ald P A Bull, M G Clark, M O Coates, P E Davidson, J R Turstram Eve, G M F Gillon, E T Hartill, S Hibberdine, J N C James, C W Jonas, L W Kinney, J Leaning, Miss D F Patman, D H Pepper, R Steel, H D C Stebbing

HOW TO APPLY In writing at any time. Application form available

WHO TO APPLY TO Mrs A L Jackson, The Company of Chartered Surveyors Charitable Trust Fund 1992, 16 St Mary at Hill, London EC3R 8EE

CC NO 1012227   **ESTABLISHED** 1992

■ The Company of Tobacco Pipe Makers and Tobacco Blenders Benevolent Fund

WHAT IS FUNDED (a) To assist in the education of those who would not otherwise be able to afford it. (b) To support only those charities with which the Company can have an active relationship. No applications from individuals will be accepted. Please do not apply individually

WHAT IS NOT FUNDED No grants to individuals

WHO CAN BENEFIT Educational establishments benefiting: children; young adults; students and those disadvantaged by poverty

WHERE FUNDING CAN BE GIVEN City of London and Sevenoaks School

TYPE OF GRANT On going scholarships

RANGE OF GRANTS £1,000–£3,000

SAMPLE GRANTS £35,000 to Sevenoaks School for scholarships; £5,000 to Guildhall School of Music for scholarships; £3,000 to Arundel Castle Cricket Foundation for scholarships; £2,500 to Riding for the Disabled for ponies feedstore; £2,000 to St Bartholomew's Hospital Medical School for scholarships

FINANCES *Year* 1998 *Income* £50,000
Grants £56,000

TRUSTEES O R Siemssen, J J Adler, J W Solomon, N D J Freeman, D P C Harris, S L Preedy, J A G Murray

WHO TO APPLY TO J E Maxwell, FCA, The Company of Tobacco Pipe Makers & Tobacco Blenders Benevolent Fund, 5 Cliffe House, Radnor Cliff, Folkestone, Kent CT20 2TY

CC NO 200601   **ESTABLISHED** 1961

■ Concern Universal

WHAT IS FUNDED Water, medical/health, educational and women's projects in the third world

WHO CAN BENEFIT International and UK schemes and organisations benefiting children, young people and women. Support is given to medical professionals, teachers, governesses and students. At risk groups and those disadvantaged by poverty are also supported. There is no restriction on the disease or medical condition suffered by the beneficiaries

WHERE FUNDING CAN BE GIVEN Overseas, especially Africa and South America

FINANCES *Year* 1995–96 *Income* £3,586,759

TRUSTEES Don McLeish (Chair), Friedenstern Howard, Rachel Shirley, Josephine Hughes, Finbarr O'Donavan, Colm Lennon, Bishop Donald Arden, Joan McGee, Fr Tiziano Laurenti

HOW TO APPLY To the address under Who To Apply To in writing. Projects must receive the approval of the appropriate local, regional and national authorities and be evaluated by the Concern Universal committee

WHO TO APPLY TO Alo Donnelly, Executive Director, Concern Universal, 14 Manor Road, Chatham, Kent ME4 6AN

CC NO 272465   **ESTABLISHED** 1976

■ The Confidential Fund, Lishkas Chasho'in

WHAT IS FUNDED General charitable purposes

WHO CAN BENEFIT There are no restrictions on the age; professional and economic group; family situation; religion and culture; and social circumstances of; or disease or medical condition suffered by, the beneficiaries

WHERE FUNDING CAN BE GIVEN UK

FINANCES *Year* 1997 *Income* £31,373
Grants £27,606

TRUSTEES Rabbi D Kahn, Rabbi M Levy, Rabbi S R Lewis

WHO TO APPLY TO Rabbi D Kahn, Trustee, The Confidential Fund, Lishkas Chasho'in, 25 St Kilda's Road, London N16 5BS *Tel* 0181-809 4770 *Fax* 0181-809 4777

CC NO 1055558   **ESTABLISHED** 1996

■ The Congleton Inclosure Trust

WHAT IS FUNDED The relief of the aged, impotent and poor; the relief of distress and sickness; the provision and support of facilities for recreation or other leisure-time activities; the provision and support of educational facilities; and any other charitable purpose

WHAT IS NOT FUNDED No grants to projects and applicants resident outside the area Where Funding Can Be Given (Congleton)

WHO CAN BENEFIT Local organisations; national organisations with projects in the area Where Funding Can Be Given. Funding may be given to people with many differing social circumstances. There is no restriction on the age or family situation of the beneficiaries, or on their disease or medical condition

WHERE FUNDING CAN BE GIVEN Congleton and the parishes of Hulme Walfield and Newbold with Astbury

TYPE OF GRANT Buildings, capital, core costs, feasibility studies, salaries and start-up costs will be considered. Funding may be given for up to one year

RANGE OF GRANTS £100–£10,000

SAMPLE GRANTS £10,000 to Astbury National Schools for a building project; £8,000 to Mossley Cricket Club for a building project; £4,000 to Congleton Brass towards instruments for local brass band; £3,500 to Congleton Community Trust for educational workshops for young people; £3,500 to Outreach Team for welfare work in the community; £2,500 to VISYON towards supporting young people under stress; £1,500 to Stepping Stones for equipment for pre-school project; £1,000 to Congleton Borough Council to the Mayor for Christmas charity for the elderly

FINANCES *Year* 1997 *Income* £66,000 *Grants* £37,830

TRUSTEES G Taylor (Chairman), D Bibbey, K P Boon, Rev E Brazier, J C Dale, A Horton, G Humphreys, R Painter, E G Pedley, M A S Roy, E R Tansley, Rev M Walters, A B Watson

HOW TO APPLY Applications should be made on a form available from the address under Who To Apply To. Applications are considered by the Trustees in January, April, July and October and should be received by the first day of the month in which the Trustees meet

WHO TO APPLY TO D A Daniel, Clerk, The Congleton Inclosure Trust, PO Box 138, Congleton, Cheshire CW12 3SZ *Tel* 01260 273180

CC NO 244136   **ESTABLISHED** 1795

■ The Congleton Town Trust

WHAT IS FUNDED The scheme provides that after defraying the cost of administration and managing the charity and it's property the Trustees are to apply their income in making grants, generally or individually, to persons resident within the area administered by the Congleton Town Council (or who can be treated as being so resident) who are in conditions of need, hardship or distress or to organisations able to provide facilities for such persons. This can be given in the areas of: accommodation and housing; support to volunteers, professional bodies; health care; health facilities and buildings; special needs education; training for work; and community services

WHO CAN BENEFIT Individuals and organisations benefiting disabled people; those disadvantaged by poverty; disaster victims; homeless people; and victims of abuse. There is no restriction on the age or family situation of the beneficiaries

WHERE FUNDING CAN BE GIVEN Congleton

TYPE OF GRANT One-off, capital, buildings, core costs, project, salaries and start-up costs. Funding is available for one year or less

SAMPLE GRANTS £9,505 to Heathfield Sports Trust for facilities for the disabled; £3,000 to youth project supporting a youth information shop; £2,500 to Town Mayor Christmas charities; £2,000 to NSPCC for a single parents project in Congleton; £1,500 to XYZ for personal grants for home improvements for a disabled child

FINANCES *Year* 1997 *Income* £22,500 *Grants* £20,500

TRUSTEES Six members nominated by Congleton Town Council and five co-opted members. G Baxendale, M J Cooper, P Copestick, J Fuller, A J Hurst, Mrs M Johnson, P Mason, J E Thompson,

C M Thompson, Mrs J Vale, R Whiston, Mrs M Williamson, D Parker

HOW TO APPLY To the address under Who To Apply To in writing

WHO TO APPLY TO D A Daniel, Clerk, The Congleton Town Trust, Copperfields, Peel Lane, Astbury, Congleton, Cheshire CW12 4RE *Tel* 01260 273180

CC NO 1051122   **ESTABLISHED** 1884

■ Martin Connell Charitable Trust

WHAT IS FUNDED General charitable purposes

WHO CAN BENEFIT Registered charities. There are no restrictions on the age; professional and economic group; family situation; religion and culture; and social circumstances of; or disease or medical condition suffered by, the beneficiaries

WHERE FUNDING CAN BE GIVEN Scotland

WHO TO APPLY TO The Trustees, Martin Connell Charitable Trust, Messrs Ernst & Young, George House, 50 George Square, Glasgow G2 1RR

SC NO SCO 09842

■ The Connop Trust

WHAT IS FUNDED General charitable purposes

WHO CAN BENEFIT There are no restrictions on the age; professional and economic group; family situation; religion and culture; and social circumstances of; or disease or medical condition suffered by, the beneficiaries

WHERE FUNDING CAN BE GIVEN UK

TRUSTEES G M Cook, R Fleming, K C Connop

WHO TO APPLY TO K C Connop, The Connop Trust, Birney Wood, Stamfordham Road, Newcastle NE15 9RB

CC NO 1068365   **ESTABLISHED** 1997

■ The Conservation Foundation

WHAT IS FUNDED Creation and management of environmental and conservation orientated projects funded by sponsorship. Income generated to pay for the costs of managing charitable projects and supporting activities

WHO CAN BENEFIT Registered charities

WHERE FUNDING CAN BE GIVEN UK and overseas

TYPE OF GRANT One-off

SAMPLE GRANTS Material Projects supported: Environmental Law Programme – educational programme for professional environmentalists; Wessex Watermark Awards – awards to projects in Wessex Water Region; Environmental Media Diary – monthly list of environmental events and activities; Network 21 – magazine providing news and information about activities and developments around the world; Yews for the Millennium – aims to provide Yews to every parish in the country; Millennium Elms – programme to research into Elms surviving Dutch Elm disease; Masterclasses – bringing together those who have environmental responsibilities; Niger Delta Environment Survey – advises the oil industry on dealing with the environment of the Niger Delta; Pacific and Asia Travel Association – Duncan Sandys Scholarship; British Homes and Holiday Parks Environmental Audit – pilot audit of environmental compliance on BHHPA sites

FINANCES *Year* 1996 *Income* £142,018 *Grants* £14,862

TRUSTEES Dr R E Close, CBE, D A Shreeve, G W Arthur, Dr B Baxter, MBE, Prof D J Bellamy, OBE,

J B Curtis, W M Pybus, B Wadley-Smith, Sir John Chapple, GCB, CBE, DL, W F Moloney
PUBLICATIONS *Network 21*, Environmental Media Diary
HOW TO APPLY In writing
WHO TO APPLY TO W F Moloney, The Conservation Foundation, Lowther Lodge, 1 Kensington Gore, London SW7 2AR
CC NO 284656   **ESTABLISHED** 1982

■ Consortium on Opportunities for Volunteering

WHAT IS FUNDED To improve opportunities for members of the public to undertake voluntary work for the benefit of all sections of the community in connection with: (a) the relief of poverty, sickness and disability (including mental); (b) the advancement of education and training; (c) the provision of facilities for recreation and leisure-time and community activities; (d) the elimination of discrimination, the promotion of equality of opportunity and racial harmony; (e) the preservation of the environment and other charitable purposes

WHAT IS NOT FUNDED No grants to individuals, or for anything that is not within a voluntary organisation, or does not include volunteers, or is not about health and social care needs

WHO CAN BENEFIT To benefit volunteers and volunteer involving projects. Particularly unemployed volunteers. Local communities with health and social care needs. Support may be given to children and older people, parents and children, one parent families and those living in rural areas

WHERE FUNDING CAN BE GIVEN England

TYPE OF GRANT Capital during first year only and up to a maximum of £2,500. Revenue to a maximum of £30,000 for up to three years. Project, running costs and salaries will be considered

RANGE OF GRANTS £4,000–£30,000, most grants are near the £30,000 maximum

SAMPLE GRANTS £32,620 to Refugee Volunteer Project for Africa Research and Information Bureau; £32,019 to Volunteering Project; £31,426 to Manchester Rape Crisis for a black women's service; £31,184 to Hull Women's Centre; £31,184 to One Stop; £31,141 to Home Start, Okehampton; £31,120 to Asian Women's Resource Centre; £31,120 to Pechett Well College; £31,110 to Trunkwell Garden Project; £30,926 to Derby Homeless Advocacy Project

FINANCES *Year* 1996–97 *Income* £2,913,361 *Grants* £2,635,832

TRUSTEES D Littlemore, N Davies, I Manley, D Obaze, M Stuart, S Williams, V Fallows, H Huish, H Reeve, P Rossetter, A Ghese, A Zavala

NOTES The Foundation awards grants on a three year cycle. Further grants are not available until April 2001 with application May–September 2000

HOW TO APPLY By application form. Address to be provided during promotion period

WHO TO APPLY TO Ms J M J Foster, Manager, Consortium on Opportunities for Volunteering, 4th Floor, 35–37 William Road, London NW1 3ER *Tel* 0171-387 1673

CC NO 1066973   **ESTABLISHED** 1997

■ The Construction Industry Trust for Youth (formerly The Building Industry Youth Trust)

WHAT IS FUNDED To improve the condition of life by sponsorship of youth training in the construction industry and by assisting in providing buildings for recreational use and occupational training. Grants for building projects will only be given to organisations which have no restrictions as to colour, class, creed or sect and only for the provision of permanent buildings for the use of youth between the ages of 8 and 25 years or for sponsorship in training disadvantaged young people under 25 who wish to enter the construction industry

WHAT IS NOT FUNDED Not for equipment, furniture, maintenance, repairs, decorating, transport or running costs. Training outside the construction industry and associated trades and professions is not considered

WHO CAN BENEFIT Any youth organisation for building projects benefiting: students; unemployed people; those disadvantaged by poverty and those living in both rural and urban areas. Individuals under 25 can be considered for sponsorship for training in the construction industry

WHERE FUNDING CAN BE GIVEN UK

TYPE OF GRANT One-off for buildings. Funding can be given for up to one year, or up to three years for training

RANGE OF GRANTS £2,000–£5000

FINANCES *Year* 1997 *Income* £78,000 *Grants* £50,000

TRUSTEES 20 senior representatives of the building and construction industries

HOW TO APPLY Apply to the address under Who To Apply To for an application form with an outline of request

WHO TO APPLY TO The Hon Secretary, The Construction Industry Trust for Youth, 11 Upper Belgrave Street, London SW1 *Tel* 0171-823 1393

CC NO 1029361   **ESTABLISHED** 1961

■ Gordon Cook Foundation

WHAT IS FUNDED The Foundation is dedicated to the advancement of all aspects of education and training which are likely to promote character development and citizenship. In recent years the Foundation has adopted the term 'Values Education' to denote the wide range of activity it seeks to support

WHAT IS NOT FUNDED Individuals are unlikely to be funded

WHO CAN BENEFIT To benefit children and young adults

WHERE FUNDING CAN BE GIVEN UK

TYPE OF GRANT One-off and recurring for projects and research. Funding may be given for more than three years

FINANCES *Year* 1997 *Income* £350,000 *Grants* £300,000

HOW TO APPLY The Foundation does not accept applications. The Trustees now invite bodies to undertake projects in line with their current proactive policies as announced from time to time

WHO TO APPLY TO Marianne Knight, Executive Officer, Gordon Cook Foundation, Hilton Place, Aberdeen AB24 4FA *Tel* 01224 183704 *Fax* 01224 485457 *E-mail* m.knight@norcol.ac.uk

SC NO SCO 17455   **ESTABLISHED** 1974

■ The Cooks Charity

WHAT IS FUNDED Grants to projects concerned with catering. Any charitable purpose in the City of London

WHO CAN BENEFIT At the discretion of the Trustees

WHERE FUNDING CAN BE GIVEN UK and London

TYPE OF GRANT Large grants

SAMPLE GRANTS £50,210 to Bournemouth University; £3,179 to Hotel and Catering Benevolent Society

FINANCES *Year* 1995 *Income* £241,992 *Grants* £55,789

TRUSTEES M V Kenyon, A W Murdoch, H F Thornton

WHO TO APPLY TO M C Thatcher, The Cooks Charity, 35 Great Peter Street, Westminster, London SW1P 3LR

CC NO 297913   **ESTABLISHED** 1987

■ The Cooksey Foundation

WHAT IS FUNDED General charitable purposes

WHO CAN BENEFIT There are no restrictions on the age; professional and economic group; family situation; religion and culture; and social circumstances of; or disease or medical condition suffered by, the beneficiaries

WHERE FUNDING CAN BE GIVEN UK and overseas

TRUSTEES D J S Cooksey, Ms J C B Cooksey, Ms A J Wardell-Yerburgh

WHO TO APPLY TO Lady Cooksey, Trustee, The Cooksey Foundation, Brooklands, Sarisbury Green, Southampton SO31 7EE

CC NO 1069334   **ESTABLISHED** 1997

■ Cooper Charitable Trust

WHAT IS FUNDED The physically handicapped and the deprived. Medical research projects and Jewish charities including; nursing services; respite care and care for carers; support and self help groups; convalescent homes and rehabilitation centres

WHAT IS NOT FUNDED No grants to individuals

WHO CAN BENEFIT National charities benefiting: disabled people and those suffering from epilepsy; head injuries and other injuries; muscular dystrophy and strokes

WHERE FUNDING CAN BE GIVEN EC and Israel

TYPE OF GRANT One-off and research. Funding available for up to two years

FINANCES *Year* 1996 *Income* £161,587 *Grants* £115,000

TRUSTEES Sally Roter, Judith Portrait, Tracy Cooper

HOW TO APPLY In writing, applications are not acknowledged

WHO TO APPLY TO Cooper Charitable Trust, 54 Regents Park Road, London NW1 7SX

CC NO 206772   **ESTABLISHED** 1962

■ The Cooper Charitable Trust

WHAT IS FUNDED Preference to charities with little State funding in the areas of: residential facilities; arts, culture and recreation; conservation; bird and wildlife sanctuaries, wildlife parks, endangered species and heritage; education and training and community facilities and services; infrastructure and development; and charity or voluntary umbrella bodies

WHAT IS NOT FUNDED Seldom to individuals

WHO CAN BENEFIT Well organised local causes and institutions benefiting: actors and entertainment professionals; musicians; retired people; students; textile workers and designers; unemployed people; writers and poets; those in

care, fostered and adopted; parents and children; one parent families; widows and widowers; at risk groups; and carers

WHERE FUNDING CAN BE GIVEN Preference to Oxford and the surrounding area

TYPE OF GRANT Single donations

RANGE OF GRANTS £100–£10,000, typical grant £500

FINANCES *Year* 1997 *Income* £18,380 *Grants* £32,600

TRUSTEES G R Cooper, A R Cooper

HOW TO APPLY To the address under Who To Apply To in writing. Accounts or financial statements required

WHO TO APPLY TO G R Cooper, The Cooper Charitable Trust, Shepherd's Close, Hinksey Hill, Oxford OX1 5BQ

CC NO 249879   **ESTABLISHED** 1966

■ The Mabel Cooper Charity

WHAT IS FUNDED General charitable purposes. Trustees do not appreciate repeated applications from charities. We are attracted to projects with low overheads

WHAT IS NOT FUNDED The Trustees do not make grants to general applicants and do not respond to mailing campaigns

WHO CAN BENEFIT There are no restrictions on the age; professional and economic group; family situation; religion and culture; and social circumstances of; or disease or medical condition suffered by, the beneficiaries

WHERE FUNDING CAN BE GIVEN UK

SAMPLE GRANTS £15,000 to Kingsbridge Methodist Church Building Fund; £11,000 to Kinsbridge Swimming Pool Fund; £5,000 to Sidney Hill Cottage Houses; £3,000 to Crisis; £2,000 to St Martins BBC Christmas Appeal; £1,000 to Christian Aid

FINANCES *Year* 1997 *Income* £48,551 *Grants* £41,800

TRUSTEES A E M Harbottle, Mrs J Harbottle

WHO TO APPLY TO A E Harbottle, The Mabel Cooper Charity, Lambury Cottage, East Portlemouth, Salcombe, Devon TQ8 8PU

CC NO 264621   **ESTABLISHED** 1972

■ Cooper Gay Charitable Trust

WHAT IS FUNDED General charitable purposes

WHO CAN BENEFIT There are no restrictions on the age; professional and economic group; family situation; religion and culture; and social circumstances of; or disease or medical condition suffered by, the beneficiaries

WHERE FUNDING CAN BE GIVEN UK

RANGE OF GRANTS £500–£5,000

SAMPLE GRANTS £5,000 to Churchill Hospital Research Department; £5,000 to Mountbatten Centre, Kent and Canterbury Hospital; £3,000 to Downs Syndrome Association; £3,000 to Evelina Children's Unit; £3,000 to Guillain-Barne Syndrome Support Group; £3,000 to Hospice of Our Lady and St John; £3,000 to Institute of Cancer Research; £3,000 to National Ankylosing Spondylitis Society; £3,000 to Petersfeld Society for Handicapped Children; £3,000 to Robert Owen Foundation

FINANCES *Year* 1996 *Income* £106,175 *Grants* £85,000

TRUSTEES D A Allen, M D Conway, S M Gillick, A A Mason, D G Staplehurst

Does the trust you have chosen match your needs? Haphazard applications waste postage and time

145

WHO TO APPLY TO D G Staplehurst, Cooper Gay Charitable Trust, c/o Cooper Gay (Holdings) Ltd, International House, 26 Creechurch Lane, London EC3A 5EH
CC NO 327514   ESTABLISHED 1987

■ The Marjorie Coote Animal Charity Fund

WHAT IS FUNDED The care and protection of horses, dogs and other animals and birds. It is the policy of the Trustees to concentrate on research into animal health problems and on the protection of species, whilst continuing to apply a small proportion of the income to general animal welfare, including sanctuaries
WHAT IS NOT FUNDED No grants to individuals
WHO CAN BENEFIT Registered charities for the benefit of animals
WHERE FUNDING CAN BE GIVEN UK and overseas
RANGE OF GRANTS £500–£25,000
SAMPLE GRANTS £26,000 to Animal Health Trust; £25,000 to Langford Trust for Animal Welfare; £5,000 to British Horse Society for welfare; £5,000 to FRAME; £5,000 to Friends of Conservation; £5,000 to Guide Dogs for the Blind; £5,000 to World Wildlife Fund for Nature; £5,000 to Cambridge University Veterinary School; £5,000 to Project Life Lion; £5,000 to University of Edinburgh for a new teaching hospital for small animals
FINANCES *Year* 1998 *Income* £129,744
Grants £116,250
TRUSTEES Sir Hugh Neill, Mrs J P Holah, N H N Coote
HOW TO APPLY Applications must be received during September
WHO TO APPLY TO Sir Hugh Neill, Barn Cottage, Lindrick Common, Worksop, Nottingham S81 8BA
CC NO 208493   ESTABLISHED 1954

■ Nicholas Coote Charitable Trust

WHAT IS FUNDED General charitable purposes. Charities for the benefit of the residents of Sheffield and charities elsewhere connected with the Catholic religion
WHAT IS NOT FUNDED Grants not made to individuals
WHO CAN BENEFIT Established charities benefiting Catholics and people living in Sheffield
WHERE FUNDING CAN BE GIVEN Sheffield and (restricted) worldwide
RANGE OF GRANTS £500–£12,500
SAMPLE GRANTS £12,500 to South Yorkshire Community Foundation; £5,435 to Heythrop College; £5,000 to Voluntary Action Sheffield; £3,500 to Blackfriars Priory; £2,000 to Vincentian Volunteers; £2,000 to Good Shepherd Trust; £2,000 to Spiritual Exercises Network; £1,000 to Salvation Army; £1,000 to Dominican Sisters of St Joseph; £1,000 to Sion Catholic Community
FINANCES *Year* 1997–98 *Income* £37,470
Grants £44,000
TRUSTEES N H N Coote, Sir Hugh Neill, Mrs P J Coote
HOW TO APPLY By latter, to reach the address under Who To Apply To during the month of June
WHO TO APPLY TO Sir Hugh Neill, Nicholas Coote Charitable Trust, Barn Cottage, Lindrick Common, Worksop, Nottinghamshire S81 8BA
CC NO 241955   ESTABLISHED 1965

■ The Marjorie Coote Old People's Charity Fund

WHAT IS FUNDED To concentrate their support on the established charitable organisations which work actively for the benefit of old people in the area of jurisdiction. At the same time, the Trustees are prepared to consider providing start-up finance for new initiatives by other organisations in South Yorkshire
WHAT IS NOT FUNDED No grants to individuals
WHO CAN BENEFIT Old people of small means
WHERE FUNDING CAN BE GIVEN South Yorkshire
TYPE OF GRANT Start-up costs
RANGE OF GRANTS £500–£35,000
SAMPLE GRANTS £35,000 to Age Concern Sheffield; £15,000 to Age Concern Rotherham; £15,000 to Voluntary Action Sheffield; £15,000 to St Lukes Hospice Sheffield; £13,000 to British Red Cross, South Yorkshire; £10,000 to The Cavendish Fellowship in Hip Surgery; £5,000 to SADACCA Day Care Appeal; £5,000 to South Yorkshire Community Foundation; £1,000 to The Cavendish Centre Sheffield; £1,000 to Counsel and Care for the Elderly
FINANCES *Year* 1997–98 *Income* £122,829
Grants £115,500
TRUSTEES Sir Hugh Neill, Mrs J A Lee, Lady Neill
HOW TO APPLY In writing to the address under Who To Apply To, to arrive during the month of May
WHO TO APPLY TO Sir Hugh Neill, The Marjorie Coote Old People's Charity Fund, Barn Cottage, Lindrick Common, Nr Worksop, Nottinghamshire S81 8BA
CC NO 226747   ESTABLISHED 1958

■ The Coppings Trust

WHAT IS FUNDED Regrettably the Trust is fully committed and is unable to respond to unsolicited applications. The Trust supports charities working in the fields of: advice and information on housing; emergency and short-term housing; personnel and human resource services; support to voluntary and community organisations; orchestras; cultural activity; health counselling; hospices at home; cultural and religious teaching; social issues counselling; emergency care, refugees and famine and international rights of the individual; racial equality, discrimination and relations; advice centres and other charitable purposes will be considered
WHO CAN BENEFIT Organisations benefiting people of all ages; ethnic minority groups; disabled people; homeless people; immigrants and refugees; victims of domestic violence, victims of war; and those suffering from HIV and AIDs
WHERE FUNDING CAN BE GIVEN UK
TYPE OF GRANT Core costs, one-off, projects, recurring costs, running costs, salaries and start-up costs. Funding for up to three years may be considered
SAMPLE GRANTS £25,000 to Prisoners Abroad; £20,000 to Yigal Allon Education Trust; £20,000 to Institute of Family Therapy; £17,000 to Jewish Literary Trust for education/literature; £10,000 to Exploring Parenthood; £5,000 to Immigrants Aid Trust for immigrant support; £5,000 to Richmond Fellowship for mental health; £5,000 to Emmaus UK for homelessness; £5,000 to Botton Village Appeal Fund for handicapped children; £3,000 to Foundation for the Care of Victims of Apartheid
FINANCES *Year* 1997 *Income* £70,377
Grants £119,059
TRUSTEES C M Marks, Dr R M E Stone, T P Bevan
NOTES All funds have been fully allocated

HOW TO APPLY This Trust states that it does not respond to unsolicited applications

WHO TO APPLY TO Clive M Marks, FCA, The Coppings Trust, 44a New Cavendish Street, London W1M 7LG

CC NO 1015435   **ESTABLISHED** 1966

■ Frank Copplestone Trust

WHAT IS FUNDED To advance the education of the public in Cornish culture by providing grants and bursaries to individuals and organisations undertaking relevant media projects, who are in need of financial assistance

WHO CAN BENEFIT Students on postgraduate and degree level higher education courses (they must be from Cornwall) and cultural media and media research projects in Cornwall. (Applicants for media and research projects must be resident in Cornwall)

WHERE FUNDING CAN BE GIVEN Cornwall

TYPE OF GRANT One-off

TRUSTEES Dr Barbara Hosking, OBE, James St Aubyn, Fenella Copplestone, Judith Higginbottom, Mark Haskell, Lady Carol Holland, Keith McDowall, Chris Denham, Eve Turner

HOW TO APPLY As we are a new charity people enquiring should write or telephone for further information

WHO TO APPLY TO Ms J Higginbottom, Secretary to the Trustees, Frank Copplestone Trust, 59 Prince Street, Bristol BS1 4QH *Tel* 0117-927 3226 *Fax* 0117-922 6216

CC NO 1066019   **ESTABLISHED** 1997

■ J Reginald Corah Foundation Fund

WHAT IS FUNDED General charitable purposes, particularly for the benefit of employees and ex-employees of hosiery firms carrying on business in the City or County of Leicester

WHAT IS NOT FUNDED No educational/professional applications from individuals

WHO CAN BENEFIT There are no restrictions on the age; professional and economic group; family situation; religion and culture; and social circumstances of; or disease or medical condition suffered by, the beneficiaries. However, particular favour is given to hosiery firms carrying out their business in the City or County of Leicester

WHERE FUNDING CAN BE GIVEN City and County of Leicester

SAMPLE GRANTS £7,800 to Leicester Grammar School; £5,000 to University of Leicester Clinical Services Library; £4,750 to Leicester Charity Organisation for small cases; £4,500 to British Red Cross, Leicestershire for Toy Brick Appeal; £2,625 to LOROS; £2,625 to Leicester Charity Organisation; £2,000 to Leicester Children's Keyhole Surgery; £1,050 to Roecliffe Manor Cheshire House; £1,000 to Leicester Boys and Girls Summer Camps; £1,000 to The Salvation Army

FINANCES *Year* 1995 *Income* £110,340 *Grants* £58,040

TRUSTEES H P Corah, D P Corah, R Bowder, G S Makings

WHO TO APPLY TO Miss L A Atterbury, J Reginald Corah Foundation Fund, Harvey Ingram, Solicitors, 20 New Walk, Leicester, Leicestershire LE1 6TX

CC NO 220792   **ESTABLISHED** 1953

■ Thomas Corbett's Charity

WHAT IS FUNDED The Charity has currently committed all its available funds to a long-term maintenance and repair programme of the Corbett Almshouses at Wychbold, therefore, no grants are being made for the foreseeable future

WHO CAN BENEFIT To benefit those disadvantaged by poverty and the Corbett Almshouses at Wychbold

WHERE FUNDING CAN BE GIVEN Counties of Worcester, Staffordshire and the City of Birmingham

TYPE OF GRANT Buildings

FINANCES *Year* 1995 *Income* £15,504

TRUSTEES M A C Brinton, Mrs E Anton, Lady Penelope Cobham, W R Webb, M G L Thomas

NOTES In 1995 grants were restricted because of repairs to Wychbold Almshouses

WHO TO APPLY TO A G Duncan, Thomas Corbett's Charity, 16 The Tything, Worcester, Hereford and Worcester WR1 1HD

CC NO 202032   **ESTABLISHED** 1933

■ Cyril Corden Trust

WHAT IS FUNDED A self contained project designed to improve the work of a charity which aims to encourage vegetarian education, animal welfare, humanitarian causes. Particularly charities working in the fields of: arts activities; arts education; alternative health care; health issues; and animal facilities and services

WHAT IS NOT FUNDED Applications for general funds are not normally considered. No grants to individuals

WHO CAN BENEFIT Any suitable charity, particularly those benefiting vegetarians

WHERE FUNDING CAN BE GIVEN UK

TYPE OF GRANT Award to one project not exceeding £10,000. Capital, feasibility studies, one-off and project funding for one year or less will be considered

RANGE OF GRANTS Up to £10,000

SAMPLE GRANTS £10,000 to Music Research Institute for music therapy researcher; £4,000 to League of Venturers for minibus for disabled transport; £2,700 to The Leaveners Theatre Company for electronic keyboard for community performances; £1,000 to National Institute of Medical Herbalists for equipment for training clinic; £844 to Electric Rainbow Arts for musical instruments for disabled use

FINANCES *Year* 1997 *Income* £23,630 *Grants* £18,672

TRUSTEES H Bland, P Corden, Ms D Craddock, N T Gale, J Kipling

NOTES Charities must be prepared to wait for a decision

HOW TO APPLY At any time with current statement of accounts

WHO TO APPLY TO Cyril Corden Trust, c/o Ravensdale, Sally Deards Lane, Rabley Heath, Welwyn, Hertfordshire AL6 9UE

CC NO 297595   **ESTABLISHED** 1987

■ The Muriel and Gershon Coren Charitable Foundation

WHAT IS FUNDED General charitable purposes

WHO CAN BENEFIT There are no restrictions on the age; professional and economic group; family situation; religion and culture; and social circumstances of; or disease or medical condition suffered by, the beneficiaries

WHERE FUNDING CAN BE GIVEN UK

SAMPLE GRANTS £1,000 to Yesodah Hatorah School; £250 to Greater London Fund for the Blind; £150 to Sue Ryder Foundation; £100 to CARE
FINANCES *Year* 1995 *Income* £38,127 *Grants* £16,383
TRUSTEES G Coren, Mrs M Coren
WHO TO APPLY to G Coren, Muriel & Gershon Coren Charitable Foundation, 263 Upper Street, Islington, London N1 2UJ
CC NO 257615 **ESTABLISHED** 1968

■ The Holbeche Corfield Charitable Settlement

WHAT IS FUNDED General charitable purposes, with emphasis on museums, religious bodies and environmental projects
WHAT IS NOT FUNDED No grants to individuals or for expeditions or research projects
WHO CAN BENEFIT Registered charities. There are no restrictions on the age; professional and economic group; family situation; religion and culture; and social circumstances of; or disease or medical condition suffered by, the beneficiaries. However, particular favour is given to religious bodies
WHERE FUNDING CAN BE GIVEN UK and overseas
RANGE OF GRANTS £100–£25,000
SAMPLE GRANTS £10,000 to Royal Artillery Heritage Campaign; £4,500 to Shaw Trust; £3,500 to The National Trust; £3,000 to St Paul's Church Truro Vicars and Churchwardens Association; £3,000 to Yeovil College; £2,500 to RSPB; £2,000 to Fenland Archaeological Trust; £2,000 to Hereford Cattle Society; £2,000 to Ironbridge Gorge Development Trust; £2,000 to Royal Corps of Signals Museums
FINANCES *Year* 1998 *Income* £30,755 *Grants* £87,050
TRUSTEES C H Corfield-Moore, S J H Corfield, K Corfield-Moore
HOW TO APPLY **Funds are fully committed**
WHO TO APPLY TO C H Corfield-Moore, The Holbeche Corfield Charitable Settlement, Greenoaks, Bradford Road, Sherborne, Dorset DT9 6BW
CC NO 258625 **ESTABLISHED** 1969

■ The Sue Cormack Memorial Fund

WHAT IS FUNDED General charitable purposes. The Trustees do not welcome unsolicited requests for aid
WHO CAN BENEFIT There are no restrictions on the age; professional and economic group; family situation; religion and culture; and social circumstances of; or disease or medical condition suffered by, the beneficiaries
WHERE FUNDING CAN BE GIVEN UK
FINANCES *Year* 1997 *Income* £804,458
TRUSTEES I D Cormack, J M I Cormack, J D G Holme, R N Blair
HOW TO APPLY **This Trust states that it does not respond to unsolicited applications**, and will not enter into any correspondence
WHO TO APPLY TO M H Lewis, The Sue Cormack Memorial Fund, Verulam Gardens, 70 Gray's Inn Road, London WC1X 8NF *Tel* 0171-404 5566
CC NO 1041735 **ESTABLISHED** 1994

■ Molly Corman Charitable Trust

WHAT IS FUNDED General charitable purposes. The Trust is wholly committed to its existing projects and cannot respond to any new applications
WHO CAN BENEFIT Registered charities only. There are no restrictions on the age; professional and economic group; family situation; religion and culture; and social circumstances of; or disease or medical condition suffered by, the beneficiaries
WHERE FUNDING CAN BE GIVEN UK and overseas
TYPE OF GRANT One-off
RANGE OF GRANTS £100–£5,000, typical grant £250
SAMPLE GRANTS £5,000 to Lubavitch Foundation for education; £2,000 to Kadima for health; £1,000 to Jewish Marriage Council for education; £1,000 to British Israel Arts Foundation for arts; £850 to DAAT Foundation for education
FINANCES *Year* 1996–97 *Income* £20,966 *Grants* £17,580
TRUSTEES C L Corman, Mrs R S Morris
HOW TO APPLY **This Trust states that it does not respond to unsolicited applications**
WHO TO APPLY TO C L Corman, Molly Corman Charitable Trust, 24 Daleham Gardens, London NW3 5DA
CC NO 214221 **ESTABLISHED** 1962

■ Edwin Cornforth 1983 Charity Trust

WHAT IS FUNDED General funds held for benefit of any charity which the bank in its absolute discretion thinks fit. Preference is given to Christian science organisations
WHAT IS NOT FUNDED No grants to individuals
WHO CAN BENEFIT Eight charities as stated in the Will. There are no restrictions on the age; professional and economic group; family situation; religion and culture; and social circumstances of; or disease or medical condition suffered by, the beneficiaries. Preference is given to Christian science organisations
WHERE FUNDING CAN BE GIVEN UK
TYPE OF GRANT Recurrent
FINANCES *Year* 1994–95 *Income* £27,711 *Grants* £34,000
TRUSTEES Lloyds Bank Plc
HOW TO APPLY In writing
WHO TO APPLY TO Mrs J L Cain, Edwin Cornforth 1983 Charity Trust, Lloyds Private Banking Limited, UK Trust Centre, The Clock House, 22–26 Ock Street, Abingdon, Oxfordshire OX14 5SW
CC NO 287196 **ESTABLISHED** 1983

■ The Duke of Cornwall Benevolent Fund

WHAT IS FUNDED (a) The relief of persons in need of assistance because of sickness, poverty or age; (b) the provision of almshouses, homes of rest, hospitals and convalescent homes; (c) the advancement of education; (d) the advancement of the arts and religion; and (e) the preservation for the benefit of the public of lands and buildings
WHO CAN BENEFIT Organisations benefiting people of all ages, those disadvantaged by poverty and homeless people. Actors and entertainment professionals, musicians, textile workers and designers; writers and poets will be considered. There is no restriction on the disease or medical condition suffered by the beneficiaries
WHERE FUNDING CAN BE GIVEN South West England
RANGE OF GRANTS £1,000–£8,000

SAMPLE GRANTS £8,000 to the Prince of Wales' Institute of Architecture; £5,000 to the Covent Garden Development Appeal; £5,000 to Philharmonia Orchestra; £5,000 to English Chamber Orchestra; £5,000 to the Gordon Highlanders Museum Campaign; £4,000 to Diocesan Board of Finance; £3,000 to Peterborough Cathedral Trust; £3,000 to the National Osteoporosis Society; £2,500 to Trustees of the Edington Foundation; £2,000 to Royal Agricultural Society of England
FINANCES *Year* 1997 *Income* £133,992 *Grants* £87,127
TRUSTEES The Rt Hon the Earl Cairns, Walter R A Ross
WHO TO APPLY TO The Secretary, The Duke of Cornwall Benevolent Fund, 10 Buckingham Gate, London SW1E 6LA
CC NO 269183   **ESTABLISHED** 1975

■ The Cornwall Heritage Trust Ltd

WHAT IS FUNDED To preserve and restore buildings, and land of particular beauty, historical, cultural and religious significance in the area Where Funding Can Be Given and artefacts of similar significance
WHAT IS NOT FUNDED Political causes will not be supported
WHO CAN BENEFIT The general public, especially that of Cornwall
WHERE FUNDING CAN BE GIVEN Cornwall and the Isles of Scilly
TYPE OF GRANT One-off grants and interest free loans
RANGE OF GRANTS £500–£3,000, typically £1,000
SAMPLE GRANTS £3,000 to Cornwall Archaeological Unit for preservation and maintenance of CCC Monument Management Project; £500 to Kesked Kernow (450th Anniversary of March to London) for administrative expenses; £500 to Newquay Rowing Club to restore the gig 'Treffry'; £500 to Bodmin Parish Church for security of St Petroc's Reliquary
FINANCES *Year* 1996–97 *Income* £27,000 *Grants* £6,350
TRUSTEES Brig M G R Anderson, R C Bailey, A J P Blackman, A W Bryce, Mrs J Carter, Ms D Clark, B L A Driscoll, H Dunn, Mrs S Edward-Collins, J B Lewis, R C Loveridge, J Oates, F C Roberts, Dr M Ripley, D Rawe, Dr W J Rowe, A G Steer, Mrs J Stevenson, Mrs L G Sutherland, Mrs M Tangye, Dr A K Thould, Sir Richard Trant, D T Wall, B Young
PUBLICATIONS Quarterly Newsletter to membership
HOW TO APPLY To the address under Who To Apply To in writing
WHO TO APPLY TO R C Bailey, The Cornwall Heritage Trust Ltd, 6a Church Street, Mevagissey, St Austell, Cornwall PL26 6SP *Tel* 01726 842911
CC NO 291607   **ESTABLISHED** 1985

■ The Cornwall Historic Churches Trust

This trust did not respond to CAF's request to amend its entry and, by 30 June 1998, CAF's researchers did not find financial records for later than 1995 on its file at the Charity Commission. Trusts are legally required to submit annual accounts to the Charity Commission under section 42 of the Charities Act 1993

WHAT IS FUNDED The upkeep of churches in the area Where Funding can be Given of architectural or historical merit; the preservation, repair and improvement of churches and chapels

WHAT IS NOT FUNDED The Trust is unlikely to give grants for schemes which alter the original character of the building
WHERE FUNDING CAN BE GIVEN Cornwall
TYPE OF GRANT Building
TRUSTEES HM Lord Lieutenant for Cornwall (President), Lord Bishop of Truro (Vice President), Viscountess Body of Merton, C F Hall, Prof A C Thomas, Mrs J H Pethybridge, G J Holborow, Mrs N Colville, Major D G F Hall, D Treffy
HOW TO APPLY To the address under Who To Apply To in writing
WHO TO APPLY TO R G Purser, Hon Secretary, The Cornwall Historic Churches Trust, 17 Higher Trehaverne, Truro, Cornwall TR1 3RW *Tel* 01872 74081
CC NO 218340   **ESTABLISHED** 1955

■ The Cornwell Charitable Trust

WHAT IS FUNDED General charitable purposes, funding projects and individuals specifically and primarily in the Cornwall area
WHAT IS NOT FUNDED Travel, expeditions, university grants
WHO CAN BENEFIT National schemes. There are no restrictions on the age; professional and economic group; family situation; religion and culture; and social circumstances of; or disease or medical condition suffered by, the beneficiaries
WHERE FUNDING CAN BE GIVEN Cornwall
TYPE OF GRANT Project and capital
FINANCES *Year* 1997 *Income* £417,842 *Grants* £64,300
TRUSTEES D J M Cornwell, V J Cornwell, G C Smith
HOW TO APPLY Written applications only
WHO TO APPLY TO G C Smith, The Cornwell Charitable Trust, Devonshire House, 1 Devonshire Street, London W1N 2DR *Tel* 0171-304 2000 *Fax* 0171-304 2020
CC NO 1012467   **ESTABLISHED** 1992

■ The Sidney and Elizabeth Corob Charitable Trust

WHAT IS FUNDED Jewish care and welfare organisations, Jewish educational institutions
WHO CAN BENEFIT Jewish organisations and educational institutions benefiting: children; young adults; Jewish people; at risk groups; those disadvantaged by poverty; and socially isolated people
WHERE FUNDING CAN BE GIVEN UK
RANGE OF GRANTS Below £1,000–£75,000
SAMPLE GRANTS £75,000 to University College; £25,000 to Oxford Centre for Postgraduate Hebrew Studies; £15,000 to Oxford Centre for Hebrew and Jewish Studies; £13,500 to Jews College; £12,500 to United Synagogues; £10,000 to Jewish Care; £10,000 to Ravenswood Foundation; £8,500 to B'nai B'rith Foundation; £7,960 to University of Birmingham; £7,500 to Immanuel College
FINANCES *Year* 1995–96 *Income* £144,151 *Grants* £330,277
TRUSTEES S Corob, E Corob, S Berg
HOW TO APPLY To the address under Who To Apply To in writing
WHO TO APPLY TO Mrs S Berg, Sidney and Elizabeth Corob Charitable Trust, 62 Grosvenor Street, London W1X 9DA
CC NO 266606   **ESTABLISHED** 1973

■ The Corona Charitable Trust

WHAT IS FUNDED General charitable purposes, in particular, the relief of the needy and the advancement of education in any part of the world including, without limitation, Jewish religious education

WHO CAN BENEFIT Children, young adults, those disadvantaged by poverty and Jewish people

WHERE FUNDING CAN BE GIVEN UK

TRUSTEES A Levy, Ms A B Levy, B Levy

WHO TO APPLY TO A Levy, Trustee and Secretary, The Corona Charitable Trust, 16 Mayfield Gardens, Hendon, London NW4 2QA

CC NO 1064320   **ESTABLISHED** 1997

■ The Tabby and John Corre Charitable Trust

WHAT IS FUNDED General charitable purposes

WHO CAN BENEFIT There are no restrictions on the age; professional and economic group; family situation; religion and culture; and social circumstances of; or disease or medical condition suffered by, the beneficiaries

WHERE FUNDING CAN BE GIVEN UK

FINANCES *Year* 1994–95 *Income* £18,000 *Grants* £18,300

TRUSTEES T Corre, J H Corre

HOW TO APPLY To the address under Who To Apply To in writing

WHO TO APPLY TO J H Corre, Trustee, The Tabby and John Corre Charitable Trust, c/o Auerbach Hope, 58–60 Berners Street, London W1P 4JS

CC NO 1002935   **ESTABLISHED** 1990

■ Corton Poor's Land Trust

WHAT IS FUNDED The relief of the people in need in the area Where Funding Can Be Given. Particularly charities working in the fields of: almshouses; respite; support to voluntary and community organisations; professional bodies; care in the community; income support and maintenance and health

WHO CAN BENEFIT Any person in need in the area Where Funding Can Be Given. Any organisation which acts on the behalf of the charity. Individuals and organisations benefiting: children; young adults; older people; at risk groups; carers; disabled people; those disadvantaged by poverty; disaster victims; ex-offenders and those at risk of offending; gays and lesbians; homeless people; socially isolated people and victims of crime. There is no restrictions on the family situation of, or on the disease or medical condition suffered by the beneficiaries

WHERE FUNDING CAN BE GIVEN The Ancient Parish of Corton

TYPE OF GRANT Any appropriate grant. One-off and running costs will be considered

RANGE OF GRANTS Varies according to need

SAMPLE GRANTS £2,680 to individual beneficiaries for Christmas Benefit

FINANCES *Year* 1996–97 *Income* £14,015 *Grants* £3,933

TRUSTEES M J S Edwards, D L Ayers, J F Hoyes, A H F Lewars, Mrs W S Rodgers, Rev J Simpson, F L Taylor

NOTES The Trustees and Secretary are also Trustees and Secretary of Corton Almshouse Charity which maintains and administers fourteen almshouse bungalows

HOW TO APPLY To the address under Who To Apply To in writing

WHO TO APPLY TO B N H Blake, Secretary, Corton Poor's Land Trust, 28 Long Lane, Corton, Lowestoft, Suffolk NR32 5HA *Tel* 01502 730665

CC NO 206067   **ESTABLISHED** 1962

■ The Cotton Trust

WHAT IS FUNDED The relief of suffering and the elimination and control of disease. Handicapped, disabled and disadvantaged people of all ages. Capital projects are funded to meet these aims

WHAT IS NOT FUNDED No grants are made for conservation, environment, animals, arts, expeditions, travel, further education, non-registered charities, individuals, running costs except in exceptional circumstances, or charities less than one year old

WHO CAN BENEFIT Registered charities benefiting people of all ages, disabled people and those disadvantaged by poverty. There is no restriction on the disease or medical condition suffered by the beneficiaries

WHERE FUNDING CAN BE GIVEN UK and overseas

TYPE OF GRANT Defined capital projects excluding building construction. Running costs and salaries only considered in exceptional cases

FINANCES *Year* 1997 *Income* £259,062 *Grants* £227,334

TRUSTEES Details available on request

NOTES Essential that the information detailed under How to Apply is provided for an application to be considered. The Trustees only accept one application in a 12-month period

HOW TO APPLY In writing enclosing a detailed budget, a full set of accounts and details of funds raised so far. Guidelines available with sae. Deadline for applications is end of June, end of October and the end of February with successful applicants being notified within two months of these dates. It is regretted that only successful applications can be answered

WHO TO APPLY TO I Stilwell, The Cotton Trust, PO Box 211, Southam, Leamington Spa, Warwickshire CV33 0WX

CC NO 222995   **ESTABLISHED** 1956

■ The Coulthurst Trust

WHAT IS FUNDED Principally to make recurring donations to specific charities with surplus funds being used towards the support of specific charitable objects in the North Yorkshire Area and then, at discretion, occasionally funding will be provided towards national appeals

WHAT IS NOT FUNDED No grants to individuals

WHO CAN BENEFIT There are no restrictions on the age; professional and economic group; family situation; religion and culture; and social circumstances of; or disease or medical condition suffered by, the beneficiaries

WHERE FUNDING CAN BE GIVEN Yorkshire

RANGE OF GRANTS £12–£1,000

SAMPLE GRANTS £1,000 to Cleveland Bay Horse Society; £1,000 to Rylstone District War Memorial Trust; £1,000 to RNLI; £1,000 to St Andrews Church, Gargrave; £1,000 to Sir Leonard Hutton Foundation; £750 to Farming and Wildlife Advisory Group, Yorkshire; £750 to the Arthritis and Rheumatism Council; £590 to Yorkshire Ballet Seminars; £500 to Atlantic Salmon Trust; £500 to the Craven Trust

FINANCES *Year* 1997 *Income* £45,274 *Grants* £34,427

TRUSTEES Coutts & Co, Mrs S H Fenwick, M J Fenwick

WHO TO APPLY TO The Coulthurst Trust, Coutts & Co, Trustee Dept, 440 Strand, London WC2R 0QS

CC NO 209690   ESTABLISHED 1947

■ Countryside Business Group Charitable Trust

WHAT IS FUNDED The protection, maintenance or preservation of the countryside, to educate the public and promote any object that will benefit the countryside

WHERE FUNDING CAN BE GIVEN UK

FINANCES *Year* 1997 *Income* £47,710

TRUSTEES Lt Col J Charteris, C Goodson-Wickes, The Earl of Stockton

NOTES Funds have been raised in 1997 to pay for the Trust's 1998 environmental project on Red Deer. This will be carried out at the Royal Veterinary College and will cost approximately £40,000

WHO TO APPLY TO Dr Charles Goodson-Wickes, Chairman, Countryside Business Group Charitable Trust, Countryside Alliance, The Old Town Hall, 367 Kennington Road, London SE11 4PT

CC NO 1060040   ESTABLISHED 1996

■ The Countryside Trust

WHAT IS FUNDED At present the Trustees only offer grants for fundraising campaigns where the money raised benefits practical conservation projects of local rather than national significance

WHAT IS NOT FUNDED Applications from individuals are ineligible. Trustees wish to assist small scale, local initiatives and have set an upper limit of £5,000 for each grant

WHO CAN BENEFIT Community or voluntary bodies concerned with the care of the local countryside of England

WHERE FUNDING CAN BE GIVEN England

TYPE OF GRANT One-off payment towards a specific fundraising project. Core funding and/or salary costs are unlikely to be considered

RANGE OF GRANTS Up to £5,000

SAMPLE GRANTS £3,000 to Yorkshire Wildlife Trust - 50 Year Appeal; £1,212 to Devon Wildlife Trust for a fete and fayre; £1,172 to Yorkshire Dales Millennium Trust - Corporate Appeal; £1,000 to BTCV, Skelton for a video; £1,000 to Northumberland Wildlife Trust for a Wildlife Art Auction; £1,000 to Nottingham Wildlife Trust for a Countryside Festival; £1,000 to Silvanus for display materials; £976 to Dandelion Trust for a woodland scheme; £597 to Suffolk Wildlife Trust for a corporate pack; £555 to Lancashire Wildlife Trust for Green Krypton Factor Challenge

FINANCES *Year* 1996–97 *Income* £47,723 *Grants* £14,979

TRUSTEES R Simmonds, R Wakeford, J L Evans

HOW TO APPLY Trustees meet twice yearly, in February and August, to consider applications. Applications can be sent in at any time but must be received by the end of December and the end of June respectively for consideration at those meetings

WHO TO APPLY TO Mrs Sarah Stone, Secretary, The Countryside Trust, John Dower House, Crescent Place, Cheltenham, Gloucestershire GL50 3RA *Tel* 01242 521381 *Fax* 01242 584270

CC NO 803496   ESTABLISHED 1990

■ County Durham Foundation

WHAT IS FUNDED Accommodation and housing; infrastructure, support and development; religion; arts, culture and recreation; conservation; education and training; bursaries and fees; purchase of books; and community facilities and services

WHAT IS NOT FUNDED Projects outside County Durham or Darlington, individuals (unless qualifying for a themed grants programme), general large appeals, fee paying schools, medical research and equipment, substitution of statutory funding or projects which are a statutory responsibility, deficit or retrospective funding, computers, umbrella group management charges, sponsored events, promotion of religious or party political causes, animal welfare, vehicle costs, sports/arts without a charitable element

WHO CAN BENEFIT Community groups and grass roots organisations seeking to improve the quality of life in their local area, particularly those aiming to combat poverty and disadvantage or promote a more equitable and just society. Applications from national organisations will only be considered if they are able to demonstrate active local involvement. This Trust considers funding: people of all ages; at risk groups; disabled people; carers; disaster victims; ex-offenders and those at risk of offending; gays and lesbians; homeless people; those living in rural and urban areas; socially isolated people; victims of abuse, crime and domestic violence

WHERE FUNDING CAN BE GIVEN County Durham and Darlington

TYPE OF GRANT Community Action Grants are divided into two levels of support: Fast track grants (up to £750) there are no application deadlines and a decision will usually be made within six weeks of application; and Project support grants (£750–£3,000) will be assessed during September, December, March and June. All applications should be received by the end of the previous month and a decision will usually be made within eight weeks of application. Themed Grant Programmes currently addressing improving the local environment, waste management, young people and children plus community leaders of the future. Additional themed programmes are planned and availability varies during the year. Up to date details are available on request. At the present time we can make one-off grants for capital, core costs, feasibility studies, project, research, recurring costs, salaries and start-up costs. Funding is available for up to one year

RANGE OF GRANTS Grants are usually awarded from between £200 and £3,000

SAMPLE GRANTS £14,250 to Centrepoint for funding towards a regional development project; £4,925 to Dawdon Detached Youth Project for six months running costs for a young persons project; £4,325 to East Durham CDI for contribution towards funding a detached youth project; £1,900 to Pride Youth Project for funding towards a support worker; £1,900 to East Durham Development Group towards running costs; £1,000 to Arts Programme to fund four art projects for disabled people; £1,000 to Gateway Wishing Well Drama Group to fund a theatre skills course for the disabled; £1,000 to Safer Spennymoor Partnership to fund a community safer mural with special needs children; £1,000 to Artworks to provide art/craft workshops for special needs groups; £1,000 to Bearpark Artists Co-operative to enable a group of adults with learning difficulties to produce paintings for an exhibition
FINANCES *Year* 1997–98 *Income* £421,638 *Grants* £54,737
TRUSTEES H Barrie, D J B Brown, Prof J I Clarke, P M Cook (Vice-Chairman), N Fairclough, D J Grant (President), T Greensmith, K F Hawkridge, J Lund, A MacConachie, Sir P D Nicholson (Chairman), S Nicholson, K Richards, B Robinson, D Robson, K W Smith, D Thompson, Major W K Trotter, D J Watson, R Wilkinson (Treasurer)
PUBLICATIONS Annual Review, newsletter, information leaflets, grant guidelines and application forms are available on request
NOTES County Durham Foundation works with individuals, companies and other charities or trusts to improve the quality of life for local people in County Durham and Darlington. Our support to grass roots organisations ensures that everyone has as full a chance as possible of enjoying and contributing to the development of their local community. We have built a £2,000,000 endowment fund in three years
HOW TO APPLY Application forms, criteria and guidelines are available on request
WHO TO APPLY TO Gillian Stacey, Director, County Durham Foundation, Aykley Vale Chambers, Durham Road, Aykley Heads, Durham DH1 5NE *Tel* 0191-383 0055 *Fax* 0191-383 2969
CC NO 1047625   **ESTABLISHED** 1995

■ County of Gloucestershire Community Foundation

WHAT IS FUNDED General charitable purposes
WHO CAN BENEFIT There are no restrictions on the age; professional and economic group; family situation; religion and culture; and social circumstances of; or disease or medical condition suffered by, the beneficiaries
WHERE FUNDING CAN BE GIVEN Gloucestershire
TYPE OF GRANT Buildings, capital, core costs, feasibility studies, interest free loans, one-off, projects, research, recurring costs, running costs, salaries and start-up costs will be considered. Funding can be given for up to and over three years
SAMPLE GRANTS £1,300 to 'Jump Start' Programme for purchase of moped and insurance for use by the unemployed in rural areas to enable them to actively seek work
FINANCES *Year* 1996–97 *Income* £42,000 *Grants* £1,300
TRUSTEES A Cadbury, OBE, JP, DL, Cllr H J Chamberlayne, J Downs, D Drew, MP, C Green, J Harvie, S M H Herdman, C R C Nichols, D Seed, J Trotter, OBE, E Wilson, C Wakeman, R Western, S Wright

PUBLICATIONS *Guides to the Grant-making Charities of Cheltenham, Tewkesbury, Stroud, Cotswolds, Forest of Dean, Gloucester City and County areas*
HOW TO APPLY In writing
WHO TO APPLY TO County of Gloucestershire Community Foundation, 15 College Green, Gloucester GL1 2LZ *Tel* 01452 528491 *Fax* 01452 528493
CC NO 900239   **ESTABLISHED** 1989

■ The Peter Courtauld Charitable Trust (formerly the Petercourt Trust)

WHAT IS FUNDED General charitable purposes. Preference to charities of which the Trust has special interest, knowledge or association
WHAT IS NOT FUNDED UK registered charities only. Applications from individuals, including students, are ineligible
WHO CAN BENEFIT UK registered charities. There are no restrictions on the age; professional and economic group; family situation; religion and culture; and social circumstances of; or disease or medical condition suffered by, the beneficiaries
WHERE FUNDING CAN BE GIVEN UK
RANGE OF GRANTS £500–£2,000
SAMPLE GRANTS £2,000 to Wellbeing; £1,000 to Sue Ryder Foundation; £1,000 to St Christopher's Fellowship; £750 to Chailey Heritage; £500 to Fairbridge
FINANCES *Year* 1997 *Income* £18,712 *Grants* £9,250
TRUSTEES W O Farrer, Mrs S M Courtauld, D A Lockhart, S P Courtauld
NOTES Applications will not necessarily be acknowledged. No telephone calls
HOW TO APPLY To the address under Who To Apply To at any time
WHO TO APPLY TO S P Courtauld, The Peter Courtauld Charitable Trust, c/o Farrer & Co, 66 Lincoln's Inn Fields, London WC2A 3LH
CC NO 258827   **ESTABLISHED** 1969

■ The Augustine Courtauld Trust

WHAT IS FUNDED General charitable purposes. Preference to charities in Essex of which the Trust has special interest, knowledge or association
WHAT IS NOT FUNDED Applications from individuals will not be considered
WHO CAN BENEFIT Registered charities. There are no restrictions on the age; professional and economic group; family situation; religion and culture; and social circumstances of; or disease or medical condition suffered by, the beneficiaries
WHERE FUNDING CAN BE GIVEN Mainly Essex
FINANCES *Year* 1996 *Income* £79,741 *Grants* £77,000
TRUSTEES The Rt Rev the Lord Bishop of Chelmsford, Rev A C C Courtauld, MA, The Lord Lieutenant of Essex, J Courtauld, Lord Tanlaw, Mrs P Fordham
WHO TO APPLY TO Birkett Long, The Augustine Courtauld Trust, Red House, Halstead, Essex CO9 2DZ
CC NO 226217   **ESTABLISHED** 1956

■ The Courtyard Farm Trust

WHAT IS FUNDED Conservation of the countryside and the natural habitats of wild flora and fauna for the education of the public; general charitable purposes in the area Where Funding Can Be Given

WHAT IS NOT FUNDED Large scale or general appeals; individuals; expeditions; any non-conservation work outside Norfolk (usually outside Ringstead)

WHO CAN BENEFIT There are no restrictions on the age; professional and economic group; family situation; religion and culture; and social circumstances of; or disease or medical condition suffered by, the beneficiaries

WHERE FUNDING CAN BE GIVEN Norfolk, especially the Parish of Ringstead

TYPE OF GRANT Buildings, capital, core costs, endowment, feasibility studies, interest free loans, one-off, project, research, recurring costs, running cots, salaries, and start-up costs. Funding for up to and over three years will be considered

RANGE OF GRANTS £1,000–£2,000

FINANCES *Year* 1996–97 *Income* £13,500 *Grants* £7,800

TRUSTEES S Housden, P Melchett, C Wedd

NOTES Unsolicited appeals generally not considered – none from outside Norfolk considered

HOW TO APPLY In writing only

WHO TO APPLY TO Peter Melchett, Trustee, The Courtyard Farm Trust, Courtyard Farm, Ringstead, Hunstanton, Norfolk PE36 5LQ

CC NO 282439   **ESTABLISHED** 1981

■ The Coutts Charitable Trust

WHAT IS FUNDED The Trustees do not consider personal appeals or make grants to individuals and their support is, in the main, directed towards charities involved with the homeless, disadvantaged and disabled children and adults, those dealing with rehabilitation and teaching self-help, youth organisations and the relief of poverty. The Trustees will also consider applications from special schools, for special needs education, health education, training for community developmenta and work, vocational training and specialist research. Where possible, the Trustees continue support for those charities to which they have traditionally given over a number of years and they also prefer to support organisations in areas where Coutts & Co has a physical presence

WHAT IS NOT FUNDED Applications from individuals, including students, are ineligible. No overseas projects considered

WHO CAN BENEFIT UK registered charities benefiting children and young adults, older people, medical professionals, scientists, unemployed people, substance misusers, at risk groups, disabled people, those disadvantaged by poverty and homeless people

WHERE FUNDING CAN BE GIVEN UK

TYPE OF GRANT Regular annual grants and one-off for specific projects

RANGE OF GRANTS £100–£10,000

SAMPLE GRANTS £10,000 to John Grooms Association for Disabled People; £5,000 to Reed's School Foundation; £3,000 to Almshouse Association; £2,500 to London Connection; £2,000 to British Performing Arts Medicine Trust; £2,000 to Hackney Employment Link Project; £2,000 to Prince's Trust; £1,150 to Imperial Cancer Research Fund; £1,000 to Co-operation Ireland; £1,000 to Kilburn Night Shelter Project

FINANCES *Year* 1997 *Income* £152,875 *Grants* £117,645

TRUSTEES Sir Ewen A J Fergusson, GCMG, GCVO, H Post, The Hon N Assheton, R Stemmons

HOW TO APPLY At any time. All applications should be sent to the address under Who To Apply To and must include clear details of the purpose for which the grant is required. No guidelines or application forms issued

WHO TO APPLY TO Mrs P A Varga, The Coutts Charitable Trust, 440 Strand, London WC2R 0QS

CC NO 1000135   **ESTABLISHED** 1987

■ Coventry Church (Municipal) Charities

WHAT IS FUNDED The administration of the almshouses; care of the elderly; homelessness

WHO CAN BENEFIT Organisations benefiting older people, those disadvantaged by poverty and homeless people

WHERE FUNDING CAN BE GIVEN Coventry

FINANCES *Year* 1995 *Income* £311,753

TRUSTEES S G Creed, Mrs H A Freeman, S Gough, J Harrison, Mrs C M Hubbard, V W Keen, R M B Kenyon, Mrs E A Kidner, Mrs M Lancaster, Mrs W Larkin, A V N Richards, Mrs J A Thomas

HOW TO APPLY To the address under Who To Apply To in writing

WHO TO APPLY TO R B K Dyott, Coventry Church (Municipal) Charities, Godfrey Payton, Old Bablake, Hill Street, Coventry CV1 4AN

CC NO 228486   **ESTABLISHED** 1964

■ The Barbara and Harold Cowan Charitable Trust

WHAT IS FUNDED General charitable purposes

WHO CAN BENEFIT There are no restrictions on the age; professional and economic group; family situation; religion and culture; and social circumstances of; or disease or medical condition suffered by, the beneficiaries

WHERE FUNDING CAN BE GIVEN UK

WHO TO APPLY TO H Cowan, Chairperson, The Barbara and Harold Cowan Charitable Trust, 1 The Knap, Dawstone Road, Heswall, Wirral, Merseyside L60 0EX

CC NO 1064876   **ESTABLISHED** 1997

■ The John Cowan Foundation

WHAT IS FUNDED General charitable purposes

WHO CAN BENEFIT There are no restrictions on the age; professional and economic group; family situation; religion and culture; and social circumstances of; or disease or medical condition suffered by, the beneficiaries

WHERE FUNDING CAN BE GIVEN UK

FINANCES *Year* 1997 *Income* £44,901

TRUSTEES J L H Cowan, C E Foster, S J Arkoulis

WHO TO APPLY TO J L H Cowan, The John Cowan Foundation, Lane End, Tydcombe Road, Warlingham, Surrey CR6 9LU

CC NO 327613   **ESTABLISHED** 1987

■ The Coward Trust

WHAT IS FUNDED Medical charities

WHAT IS NOT FUNDED Applications from individuals are unlikely to be successful

WHO CAN BENEFIT National and local organisations benefiting the visually impaired, and those suffering from cancers, diabetes, and motor neurone disease

WHERE FUNDING CAN BE GIVEN Lancashire

TYPE OF GRANT One-off

RANGE OF GRANTS £1,000–£4,000

Does the trust you have chosen match your needs? Haphazard applications waste postage and time

153

SAMPLE GRANTS £4,000 to Barnardos; £4,000 to British Diabetic Association for research; £4,000 to Derian House Children's Hospice; £4,000 to League of Friends of Teddington Memorial Hospital; £3,000 to Christie Hospital NHS Trust for cancer research; £3,000 to the Leonard Cheshire Foundation; £2,000 to Red Rose Community Trust; £2,000 to St Dunstan's; £1,000 to Motor Neurone Disease Association; £1,000 to Quidenham Children's Hospice

FINANCES *Year* 1997–98 *Income* £25,171 *Grants* £30,000

TRUSTEES Norman Jamieson, David Sharples, Gerald Sharples

HOW TO APPLY To the address below in writing. The Trustees meet to decide on grants in December each year

WHO TO APPLY TO N Jamieson, FCA, The Coward Trust, 58 Riverside Mead, Stanground, Peterborough, Cambridgeshire PE2 8JN *Tel* 01733 345800

CC NO 519341   **ESTABLISHED** 1987

■ The Cowley Charitable Foundation

WHAT IS FUNDED Health, environment and heritage

WHO CAN BENEFIT There is no restriction on the disease or medical condition suffered by the beneficiaries

WHERE FUNDING CAN BE GIVEN UK and London

TYPE OF GRANT Range of grants

RANGE OF GRANTS £25–£82,100

SAMPLE GRANTS £82,100 to British Museum; £20,000 to St Petersburg Trust; £3,000 to George Galitzine Memorial Library; £1,000 to Buckinghamshire Age Concern; £1,000 to Disabled Housing Trust; £1,000 to Friends of the Elderly; £1,000 to PACE; £1,000 to St Mungo Emergency Shelter; £1,000 to YMCA; £600 to Institute of Economic Affairs

FINANCES *Year* 1997 *Income* £81,563 *Grants* £112,725

TRUSTEES The 140 Trustee Company, Lord Hartwell, C H Rawlings

WHO TO APPLY TO The Secretary, The Cowley Charitable Foundation, The 140 Trustee Company, 36 Broadway, London SW1H 0BH

CC NO 270682   **ESTABLISHED** 1973

■ Sir William Coxen Trust Fund

WHAT IS FUNDED Benefit of hospitals and other institutions in England carrying out treatment of orthopaedic defects, particularly in respect of children

WHAT IS NOT FUNDED Grants to hospitals or institutions only. No grants to individuals

WHO CAN BENEFIT Hospitals and institutions benefiting, primarily, children suffering from orthopaedic defects

WHERE FUNDING CAN BE GIVEN England

TYPE OF GRANT One-off grants

FINANCES *Year* 1997 *Income* £50,070 *Grants* £36,586

TRUSTEES The Court of Aldermen of the City of London

NOTES Strictly orthopaedic purposes only

HOW TO APPLY In writing providing full information and details

WHO TO APPLY TO David Haddon, City Secretary's Office, Sir William Coxen Trust Fund, Corporation of London, PO Box 270, Guildhall, London EC2P 2EJ

CC NO 206936   **ESTABLISHED** 1940

■ The Lord Cozens-Hardy Trust

WHAT IS FUNDED The Trust has a preference for supporting national, Norfolk and Merseyside charities for medicine, health and welfare

WHAT IS NOT FUNDED Grants only to registered charities, see Where Funding Can Be Given

WHO CAN BENEFIT Organisations benefiting at risk groups, those disadvantaged by poverty and socially isolated people. Research workers and medical professionals may be considered. There is no restriction on the disease or medical condition suffered by the beneficiaries

WHERE FUNDING CAN BE GIVEN UK with a preference for Norfolk and Merseyside

TYPE OF GRANT At the discretion of the Trustees mostly small payments

RANGE OF GRANTS £100–£11,500

SAMPLE GRANTS £11,500 to BMA Medical Education Trust Fund; £1,500 to Lancashire Constabulary – the Lord Cozens-Hardy Travelling Fellowship; £1,250 to Raleigh International; £1,000 to Cley Church; £1,000 to Greshams School General Charitable Trust; £1,000 to Holt and Neighbourhood Housing Society Ltd; £1,000 to Incorporated Liverpool School of Tropical Medicine; £1,000 to Order of St John; £1,000 to Order of St John Hospital; £1,000 to Royal Liverpool Philanthropic Society

FINANCES *Year* 1997 *Income* £80,596 *Grants* £65,750

TRUSTEES Hon Beryl Cozens-Hardy, Hon Helen R Phelps, John E V Phelps, Mrs L F Phelps

WHO TO APPLY TO The Hon Beryl Cozens-Hardy, OBE, The Lord Cozens-Hardy Trust, The Glebe, Letheringsett, Holt, Norfolk NR25 7YA

CC NO 264237   **ESTABLISHED** 1972

■ The Crag House Charitable Trust

WHAT IS FUNDED General charitable purposes

WHO CAN BENEFIT There are no restrictions on the age; professional and economic group; family situation; religion and culture; and social circumstances of; or disease or medical condition suffered by, the beneficiaries

WHERE FUNDING CAN BE GIVEN The Winster and Windermere areas of Cumbria

TYPE OF GRANT Mainly one-off

RANGE OF GRANTS £50–£6,000; typical £200

FINANCES *Year* 1998 *Income* £14,073 *Grants* £10,324

TRUSTEES J M Hopkinson, Mrs E J Hopkinson, Mrs L C Sefton,

NOTES **The Trustees will mainly select grant recipients from amongst causes already known to them**

HOW TO APPLY Small, local charities may approach the Trust with a brief letter, but a response will not necessarily be forthcoming

WHO TO APPLY TO J M Hopkinson, Trustee, The Crag House Charitable Trust, Crag House, Winster, Windermere, Cumbria LA23 3NS *Tel* 01539 720049

CC NO 1054944   **ESTABLISHED** 1996

■ The Cranbury Foundation

WHAT IS FUNDED General charitable purposes

WHAT IS NOT FUNDED No grants to individuals or students

WHO CAN BENEFIT Small local projects. There are no restrictions on the age; professional and economic group; family situation; religion and culture; and social circumstances of; or disease or medical condition suffered by, the beneficiaries

WHERE FUNDING CAN BE GIVEN UK, Canada, Australia, New Zealand, Pakistan, Sri Lanka, india and any other part of the British Commonwealth and the USA

TYPE OF GRANT One-off grants

RANGE OF GRANTS £10–£30,000

SAMPLE GRANTS £30,000 to Winchester Diocesan Board of Finance; £10,000 to Muscular Dystrophy Group; £5,000 to Winchester Cathedral Trust; £1,000 to HABC; £625 to Queen's Nursing Institution; £500 to Project Scholastic; £500 to Cedar School; £250 to RAF Wings; £200 to Perbury Plodders; £200 to Ancient Building Trust

FINANCES *Year* 1996 *Income* £31,847 *Grants* £49,970

TRUSTEES O F Gradidge, Lord Lifford, H D Y Faulkner

HOW TO APPLY In writing

WHO TO APPLY TO The Agent/Hon Treasurer, The Cranbury Foundation, The Chamberlayne Estate, Cranbury Park, Winchester, Hampshire SO21 2HN

CC NO 314105   **ESTABLISHED** 1970

■ Craps Charitable Trust

WHAT IS FUNDED General charitable purposes. It is not the policy of the Trustees to make grants in response to appeals addressed to them, and applications will not be acknowledged

WHO CAN BENEFIT Organisations. There are no restrictions on the age; professional and economic group; family situation; religion and culture; and social circumstances of; or disease or medical condition suffered by, the beneficiaries

WHERE FUNDING CAN BE GIVEN UK and overseas

RANGE OF GRANTS £750–£17,000

SAMPLE GRANTS £17,000 to Jewish Care; £15,000 to Friends of the Federation of Women Zionists; £13,000 to Home for Aged Jews; £5,000 to the Arthritis and Rheumatism Council; £3,000 to Ben Gurion University Foundation; £3,000 to British Friends of Haifa University; £2,000 to Ravenswood Foundation; £2,000 to Friends of Israel Educational Trust; £2,000 to Scopus; £1,500 to Friends of the Earth

FINANCES *Year* 1997 *Income* £95,592 *Grants* £67,250

TRUSTEES C E Shanbury, Miss C S Dent, J P M Dent

HOW TO APPLY **This Trust states that it does not respond to unsolicited applications**

WHO TO APPLY TO C Shanbury, Craps Charitable Trust, Robson Rhodes, The Gallena, Station Road, Crawley, West Sussex RH10 1HY

CC NO 271492   **ESTABLISHED** 1976

■ The Craven Trust

WHAT IS FUNDED Community-based projects. Charities working in the fields of: accommodation and housing; arts, culture and recreation; religion; and social care and development. Funding may also be given to information technology and computers, publishing and printing, infrastructure development, voluntary umbrella bodies, healthcare, health education and promotion, education and training, conservation and campaigning

WHAT IS NOT FUNDED The Trust will not make grants to animal charities and national charities (with some exceptions), or to medical charities/fundraising activities, students, or for foreign travel

WHO CAN BENEFIT Registered charities and voluntary organisations benefiting people of all ages with many different social circumstances. There is no restriction on the family situation, or religion and culture of, or the disease or medical condition suffered by, the beneficiaries

WHERE FUNDING CAN BE GIVEN The area of the Archdeaconry of Craven in the Bradford diocese

TYPE OF GRANT One-off grants. Applications for capital expenditure are preferred. Buildings, core costs, feasibility studies, projects, running costs, recurring costs, salaries and start-up costs. Funding may be given for up to one year

RANGE OF GRANTS £100–£500, larger amounts may be considered

SAMPLE GRANTS £500 to Beamsley Project for furniture for disabled holiday accommodation; £500 to CVA Furniture Store towards running costs, petrol expenses, etc; £320 to Craven Advocacy for office equipment; £300 to Keighley and District Association for the Blind for computer equipment for training partially sighted people; £250 to Age Concern, North Craven towards running costs of drop-in facility; £250 to Howgill Baby and Toddler Group for play equipment; £250 to North Craven Women's Group for the redecoration costs of meeting hall; £250 to Settle Out-of-School Club for computer equipment; £250 to The Dales Playschool for storage facilities and equipment; £250 to Linton-in-Craven Parochial Church Council towards repairs to church house

FINANCES *Year* 1998 *Income* £80,959 *Grants* £3,470

TRUSTEES Dr B Fisher, Ven M Grundy, J Mackrell, P J D Marshall, C Reeder, P Robertshaw, C M Schwaller, J M Sheard

NOTES Grants are usually made twice a year, in March and September

HOW TO APPLY Telephone calls welcomed. Application forms and guidelines available from registered address. Deadlines for applications stated in guidelines. Saes not essential

WHO TO APPLY TO C Reeder, The Craven Trust, c/o Charlesworth, Wood & Brown, 23 Otley Street, Skipton, North Yorkshire BD23 1DY *Tel* 01756 793333

CC NO 1045419   **ESTABLISHED** 1995

■ Michael Crawford Children's Charity

WHAT IS FUNDED The benefit of children and young people and in particular the relief of sickness and the relief of poverty

WHO CAN BENEFIT To benefit children and young adults, especially those disadvantaged by poverty. There is no restriction on the disease or medical condition suffered by the beneficiaries

WHERE FUNDING CAN BE GIVEN UK

FINANCES *Year* 1995 *Income* £422,183

TRUSTEES M D Paisner, M P Crawford, I B Paul, A Clark

NOTES Trustees are continuing to accumulate funds so that a significant capital project can be financed in the foreseeable future

WHO TO APPLY TO M D Paisner, Michael Crawford Children's Charity, Bouverie House, 154 Fleet Street, London EC4A 2DQ

CC NO 1042211   **ESTABLISHED** 1994

■ The Crescent Trust

WHAT IS FUNDED Grants to large museums and arts, occasional health and education

WHO CAN BENEFIT Organisations benefiting children, young adults, medical professionals, students, teachers and arts practitioners

WHERE FUNDING CAN BE GIVEN UK

TYPE OF GRANT One-off and recurrent

RANGE OF GRANTS £1,000–60,000

SAMPLE GRANTS £60,000 to Victoria and Albert Museum; £17,500 to the Attingham Trust; £12,500 to The National Trust; £7,000 to the Furniture History Society; £1,000 to the Asthma Gift Fair

FINANCES *Year* 1995 *Income* £22,660 *Grants* £99,000

TRUSTEES J C S Tham, R A F Lascelles

WHO TO APPLY TO Ms C Akehurst, The Crescent Trust, 27a Sloane Square, London SW1W 8AB

CC NO 327644   **ESTABLISHED** 1987

■ Lord Crewe's Charity

WHAT IS FUNDED The repair and construction of churches; support of clergy and their dependants who are in need; relief of sickness and other charitable purposes in the area Where Funding Can Be Given

WHO CAN BENEFIT Organisations benefiting clergy, widows and widowers. There is no restriction on the disease or medical condition suffered by the beneficiaries

WHERE FUNDING CAN BE GIVEN Dioceses of Newcastle and Durham

FINANCES *Year* 1997 *Income* £313,293

TRUSTEES Ven P Elliott (Chairman), John Brown-Swinburne (Vice Chairman), Ven G G Gibson, Ven J D Hodgson, W F P Hugonin, Hon Harry Vane Ex Officio: Rector of Lincoln College, Oxford

HOW TO APPLY Applications should be made on a form available from the address under Who To Apply To. Applications are considered by the Trustees in May and November

WHO TO APPLY TO The Clerk, Lord Crewe's Charity, The Chapter Office, Durham Cathedral, Durham DH1 3EH *Tel* 0191-386 4266

CC NO 230347   **ESTABLISHED** 1963

■ Criffel Charitable Trust

WHAT IS FUNDED Residential facilities and services; building services; infrastructure development; professional bodies; Christian religion; film, video and multimedia broadcasting; music, orchestras, theatres, theatrical companies and theatre groups; health; conservation; bird and wildlife sanctuaries; endangered species; heritage; education and training; community centres and village halls; and community services

WHAT IS NOT FUNDED No personal applications

WHO CAN BENEFIT To benefit: the clergy; medical professionals; musicians; research workers; seafarers and fisherman; unemployed people; volunteers; Christians; Church of England; Evangelists; and Methodists. There is no restriction on the age or family situation. A wide range of social circumstances and diseases or medical conditions suffered by the beneficiaries will be considered for funding

WHERE FUNDING CAN BE GIVEN UK, Europe, Asia and Africa

TYPE OF GRANT Buildings, capital, core costs, one-off, projects, research, recurring costs and running

costs. Funding is available for more than three years

FINANCES *Year* 1997 *Income* £58,404 *Grants* £51,120

TRUSTEES Mrs J I Harvey, Mrs J C Lees, J C Lees

HOW TO APPLY **This Trust states that it does not respond to unsolicited applications**

WHO TO APPLY TO J C Lees and Mrs J E Lees, Criffel Charitable Trust, 4 Wentworth Road, Sutton Coldfield, West Midlands B74 2SG *Tel* 0121-308 1575

CC NO 1040680   **ESTABLISHED** 1994

■ The Cromarty Trust

WHAT IS FUNDED Grants are given largely to organisations which work to preserve the widlife and the historically or architecturally important buildings of Cromarty or which seek to educate the public about these and the history of Cromarty

WHO CAN BENEFIT Organisations benefiting Cromarty

WHERE FUNDING CAN BE GIVEN Mainly the Parish of Cromarty

FINANCES *Year* 1997 *Income* £22,778 *Grants* £17,466

TRUSTEES J Nightingale, Michael Nightingale of Cromarty, Miss E V de B Murray

HOW TO APPLY **Applications are not invited**

WHO TO APPLY TO Michael Nightingale of Cromarty, The Cromarty Trust, Wormshill Court, Sittingbourne, Kent ME9 0TS *Tel* 01622 884235

CC NO 272843   **ESTABLISHED** 1976

■ The John and Edythe Crosfield Charitable Trust

WHAT IS FUNDED To help deprived children and deprived adults who are sick or old. To support medical research and preserve the ecology. Our income is fixed and we give regularly to the same charities each year

WHO CAN BENEFIT Organisations benefiting: children; young adults; at risk groups; those disadvantaged by poverty and socially isolated people. There is no restriction on the disease or medical condition suffered by the beneficiaries. Research workers and medical professionals may benefit

WHERE FUNDING CAN BE GIVEN UK

SAMPLE GRANTS £1,000 to Sight Savers; £1,000 to Look Ahead Housing; £700 to Harborough School; £700 to Coleworth School; £500 to Tomlinson Trust

FINANCES *Year* 1997 *Income* £17,715 *Grants* £8,200

TRUSTEES J F Crosfield, CBE, Mrs E M Crosfield, R J Crosfield

HOW TO APPLY **Funds fully committed, new applications cannot be considered**

WHO TO APPLY TO J F Crosfield, Hon Treasurer, The John and Edythe Crosfield Charitable Trust, 45 Netherall Gardens, First Floor, Hampstead, London NW3 5RL

CC NO 268527   **ESTABLISHED** 1974

■ The Cross Trust

WHAT IS FUNDED Charities and individuals carrying out Christian work overseas and in the UK

WHO CAN BENEFIT Individuals and organisations benefiting Christians

WHERE FUNDING CAN BE GIVEN UK and overseas

TYPE OF GRANT Some recurrent

RANGE OF GRANTS £1,000–£13,104

156

Think carefully about every application. Is it justified?

SAMPLE GRANTS £13,104 to Rock Foundation for TNT Ministries; £12,980 to Areopagus Trust; £11,239 to an individual at Spurgeons College; £9,250 to an individual for Lugoj Baptist Church and relief of hardship of Christians in Romania; £6,840 to an individual; £6,000 to an individual for support for training at London Bible College on a three year theology degree course; £3,500 to an individual overseas student at London City Mission; £3,000 to Michael Hawkins Trust for school fees for clergy child; £3,000 to Breadline for Moldovan children; £2,500 to individual at London Bible College

FINANCES *Year* 1997 *Income* £103,216
Grants £84,068

TRUSTEES Ms Farmer, Mrs J D R Farmer, D J Olsen

NOTES Funds are fully committed for the foreseeable future

HOW TO APPLY To the address under Who To Apply To in writing

WHO TO APPLY TO D J Stephenson, The Cross Trust, Bourbon Court, Nightingale Corner, Little Chalfont, Buckinghamshire HP7 9QS

CC NO 298472   **ESTABLISHED** 1987

■ The Cross Trust

WHAT IS FUNDED Grants are given to fund activities such as research, training or travel which will help to foster a career or a special interest

WHAT IS NOT FUNDED Applicants must be between 16 and 35 years and of Scottish birth or parentage. Grants are not generally offered for post-graduate studies

WHO CAN BENEFIT Young people and students

WHERE FUNDING CAN BE GIVEN UK and overseas

TRUSTEES Rev Hon R D Buchanan-Smith (Chairman), Dr A E Ritchie, CBE, Mrs C M Orr, D R G Philip, Dr A R MacGregor, M Webster, Dr R H MacDougall

PUBLICATIONS Guidance notes are available from the address below

HOW TO APPLY The Assistant Secretary will provide details of the application procedure for charities

WHO TO APPLY TO Mrs Barbara Anderson, Assistant Secretary, The Cross Trust, PO Box 17, 25 South Methven Street, Perth PH1 5ES

SC NO SCO 08620   **ESTABLISHED** 1943

■ Crossfield Charitable Fund

WHAT IS FUNDED Payments for charitable purposes to registered charitable organisations – national and local

WHAT IS NOT FUNDED No grants to individuals

WHO CAN BENEFIT Charitable organisations only. There are no restrictions on the age; professional and economic group; family situation; religion and culture; and social circumstances of; or disease or medical condition suffered by, the beneficiaries

WHERE FUNDING CAN BE GIVEN UK

FINANCES *Year* 1996 *Income* £17,300
Grants £13,000

TRUSTEES Mrs M Crossfield, J Hargreaves

WHO TO APPLY TO The Manager, Crossfield Charitable Fund, Barclays Bank Trust Co Ltd, Executorship & Trustee Service, Osborne Court, Gadbrook Park, Rudheath, Northwich, Cheshire CW9 7UE

CC NO 219399   **ESTABLISHED** 1959

■ Croydon Relief in Need Charities

This trust did not respond to CAF's request to amend its entry and, by 30 June 1998, CAF's researchers did not find financial records for later than 1995 on its file at the Charity Commission. Trusts are legally required to submit annual accounts to the Charity Commission under section 42 of the Charities Act 1993

WHAT IS FUNDED Health and welfare of the sick and elderly

WHO CAN BENEFIT Older people. There are no restrictions on the disease or medical condition suffered by the beneficiaries

WHERE FUNDING CAN BE GIVEN Croydon

TRUSTEES Cllr Mrs B Saunders (Chair), T S Rogers (Vice Chair), Cllr J L Aston, Cllr M A Fowler, C P Clements, Mrs B E Cripps, D J Cropps, N P Hepworth, Rev Canon C A L Hill, R J Horden, Mrs D Pickard, D M Rawling, Mrs T G Stewart, Mrs C D A Trower, E N Trower, Lady I Walker, K A Wells, Mrs S U M Wills, P T Pearce

HOW TO APPLY To the address below in writing

WHO TO APPLY TO W B Rymer, Clerk, Croydon Relief in Need Charities, 74 High Street, Croydon CR9 2UU

CC NO 810114   **ESTABLISHED** 1962

■ The Mollie Croysdale Charitable Trust

WHAT IS FUNDED General charitable purposes

WHO CAN BENEFIT There are no restrictions on the age; professional and economic group; family situation; religion and culture; and social circumstances of; or disease or medical condition suffered by, the beneficiaries

WHERE FUNDING CAN BE GIVEN In practice, the area comprised in the former county of Yorkshire

FINANCES *Year* 1997 *Income* £108,051
Grants £2,340

TRUSTEES T D Coates, P M Croysdale, D P Griffiths, R A Hellawell

WHO TO APPLY TO Miss P M Croysdale, The Mollie Croysdale Charitable Trust, 20 Hallgarth, Pickering, North Yorkshire YO18 7AW

CC NO 1055107   **ESTABLISHED** 1996

■ The Culra Charitable Trust

WHAT IS FUNDED General charitable purposes with accent on Highland and Kent charities

WHAT IS NOT FUNDED No grants to individuals

WHO CAN BENEFIT Registered charities only. There are no restrictions on the age; professional and economic group; family situation; religion and culture; and social circumstances of; or disease or medical condition suffered by, the beneficiaries

WHERE FUNDING CAN BE GIVEN Scottish Highlands and Kent

SAMPLE GRANTS £5,000 to Bedford School Trust; £3,050 to St Mary the Virgin, West Malling

FINANCES *Year* 1997 *Income* £26,996
Grants £25,087

TRUSTEES Mrs A Byam-Cook, P J Sienesi, C H Byam-Cook

HOW TO APPLY To the address under Who To Apply To in writing

WHO TO APPLY TO P H Byam-Cook, The Culra Charitable Trust, c/o The Hedley Foundation, 9 Dowgate Hill, London EC4R 2SU

CC NO 274612   **ESTABLISHED** 1977

Does the trust you have chosen match your needs? Haphazard applications waste postage and time

157

■ The Cumber Family Charitable Trust

WHAT IS FUNDED Health, homelessness, disability and welfare, rural development, housing, overseas aid, Christian aid, agricultural development, youth and children's welfare, education

WHAT IS NOT FUNDED No grants for animal welfare or individuals without local connections. Local appeals outside the area Where Funding Can Be Given are rarely supported

WHO CAN BENEFIT Individuals and organisations benefiting children, young adults and a wide range of social circumstances are considered for funding. There is no restriction on the disease or medical condition suffered by the beneficiaries

WHERE FUNDING CAN BE GIVEN UK and overseas, with a preference for Berkshire and Oxfordshire

RANGE OF GRANTS £200–£3,000

SAMPLE GRANTS £3,000 to John Simmonds Trust; £2,000 to Oxford Macmillan Nurse Appeal; £2,000 to Intermediate Technology; £2,000 to APT Enterprise Development; £2,000 to Refugee Council; £2,000 to St Barnabas Hospice, Worthing; £2,000 to Marie Stopes International; £2,000 to Shelter; £2,000 to Barnardos; £2,000 to Farm Africa

FINANCES *Year* 1997 *Income* £52,923
Grants £54,954

TRUSTEES Miss M Cumber, A R Davey, W Cumber, Mrs M J Cumber, M J Freeman, M E Tearney

HOW TO APPLY To the address under Who To Apply To in writing. Applications are considered in February and September

WHO TO APPLY TO Mrs M J Cumber, The Cumber Family Charitable Trust, Manor Farm, Marcham, Abingdon, Oxfordshire OX13 6NZ

CC NO 291009   **ESTABLISHED** 1985

■ The Cumberland and Westmorland Provincial Grand Lodge Benevolent Fund

WHAT IS FUNDED The Trust's grant total is distributed amongst masons and their dependants, and to masonic and other charities

WHO CAN BENEFIT Mainly masons and their families

WHERE FUNDING CAN BE GIVEN Cumbria

FINANCES *Year* 1997 *Income* £258,675
Grants £44,268

TRUSTEES J H Gale, J Hale, A F Sewell, J W Tyson

HOW TO APPLY To the address under Who To Apply To in writing

WHO TO APPLY TO K Graham, Secretary, The Cumberland and Westmorland Provincial Grand Lodge Benevolent Fund, Hoylands, Bowscar, Penrith, Cumbria CA11 8RS *Tel* 01768 863860

CC NO 213203   **ESTABLISHED** 1927

■ The Cumberland Trust

WHAT IS FUNDED Charities working in the fields of: Christian education, Christian outreach, missionaries and evangelists. Prefer to give to a selected list of beneficiaries

WHAT IS NOT FUNDED In future, the Trust will only make grants to organisations and individuals known personally to the Trustees

WHO CAN BENEFIT Registered charities and institutions benefiting Christians and those suffering from leprosy

WHERE FUNDING CAN BE GIVEN UK and Africa

TYPE OF GRANT Recurrent, occasional single donations and start-up costs, funding for up to three years will be considered

SAMPLE GRANTS £1,250 to Ashley Baptist Church for re-building programme; £1,225 to CARE Trust for family support; £1,220 to Crossfire Trust for Northern Ireland Christian Trust; £1,210 to IWAF for flying programmes to help missionaries; £1,150 to Tear Fund for general aid at home and overseas; £1,000 to East Holton Charity for disabled people care; £1,000 to Inter-Health for medical programme expansion; £1,000 to Mount Zion Church for small village church in Redbourn; £1,000 to Redbourn Missionary Trust for housing missionaries on leave; £1,000 to Rivendell Retreat Project for start-up help

FINANCES *Year* 1997 *Income* £47,000
Grants £26,000

TRUSTEES B J Hosking, C A Hoskings, Mrs E Hosking

HOW TO APPLY No initial telephone calls welcome. No application form, guidelines or deadlines for applications. Sae from applicants required

WHO TO APPLY TO Mrs E Hosking, The Cumberland Trust, Holly Cottage, 34 Tywford Road, Willington, Derby DE65 6DE

CC NO 266475   **ESTABLISHED** 1973

■ The Erskine Cunningham Hill Trust

WHAT IS FUNDED The Church of Scotland is the largest single focus of the Trust's interest (50 per cent of annual income). Other grants are restricted to charitable work with the elderly; young people; ex-servicemen and women; seamen; Scottish interests; with priority given to charities administered by voluntary or honorary officials

WHAT IS NOT FUNDED No grants are made to individuals

WHO CAN BENEFIT Organisations benefiting: elderly people; young people; ex-service men and women; seamen; volunteers and the Church of Scotland

WHERE FUNDING CAN BE GIVEN UK

TYPE OF GRANT Recurring grants are made to the Church of Scotland, one-off grants are made elsewhere

RANGE OF GRANTS £1,000 each to individual charities

SAMPLE GRANTS £22,000 to Church of Scotland for central funds; £1,000 to 23 individual charities for various purposes

FINANCES *Year* 1997 *Income* £45,000
Grants £45,000

TRUSTEES G W Burnett, H Cole, A C E Hill, Very Rev Dr W B Johnston, D F Ross, D F Stewart

PUBLICATIONS Annual Report and Accounts are available

NOTES There is a two year time bar on repeat grants

HOW TO APPLY Applications should be made in writing to the address under Who To Apply To

WHO TO APPLY TO Donald F Ross, Secretary, The Erskine Cunningham Hill Trust, 121 George Street, Edinburgh EH2 4YN *Tel* 0131-225 5722

SC NO SCO 01853   **ESTABLISHED** 1955

■ The Cunningham Trust

WHAT IS FUNDED Grants are made to university departments which are carrying out academic research in the field of medicine

WHAT IS NOT FUNDED Grants are unlikely to be made available to non-regular beneficiaries

WHO CAN BENEFIT Organisations benefiting academics and research workers. There is no

restriction on the disease or medical condition suffered by the beneficiaries

WHERE FUNDING CAN BE GIVEN Scotland

TYPE OF GRANT A number of the grants made are recurring

FINANCES *Year* 1996 *Income* £220,000
Grants £400,000

TRUSTEES Mrs O M Anderson, Prof C Blake, A C Caithness

PUBLICATIONS Accounts are provided by the Trust

NOTES Grants are almost exclusively made to established beneficiaries

HOW TO APPLY Applications should be made in writing to the address below. Up-to-date information about deadlines and the procedures for submitting applications is made available to the Deans of Faculty

WHO TO APPLY TO Cantley & Caithness, Solicitors, The Cunningham Trust, Inchcape House, St Mary's Place, St Andrews, Fife KY16 9QP

SC NO SCO 13499   **ESTABLISHED** 1984

■ Curriers Company Charitable Fund

WHAT IS FUNDED The main areas of interest are projects concerning the young, the elderly, and the infirm; specific projects providing educational facilities are also considered

WHAT IS NOT FUNDED Applications from individuals, including students, are ineligible. No grants are made in response to general appeals from large national organisations, nor from smaller bodies involved in areas not included in the charity's areas of interest

WHO CAN BENEFIT Small local charities and community projects benefiting: people of all ages; retired people and students. There is only limited support for education

WHERE FUNDING CAN BE GIVEN London

TYPE OF GRANT One-off capital grants; some recurring grants

FINANCES *Year* 1997 *Income* £17,000
Grants £17,000

TRUSTEES The Worshipful Company of Curriers

PUBLICATIONS Annual Report

HOW TO APPLY **This Trust states that it does not respond to unsolicited applications**. Guidelines are not issued. Applications not always acknowledged

WHO TO APPLY TO The Clerk, Curriers Company Charitable Fund, Kestrel Cottage, East Knoyle, Salisbury, Wiltshire SP3 6AD. *Tel* 01747 830017

CC NO 261405   **ESTABLISHED** 1970

■ Dennis Curry Charitable Trust

WHAT IS FUNDED General charitable purposes with particular interest in the environment and education

WHO CAN BENEFIT To benefit children, young adults and students

WHERE FUNDING CAN BE GIVEN UK

RANGE OF GRANTS £500–£20,000

SAMPLE GRANTS £20,000 to Galapogos Conservation; £15,900 to University of Cambridge; £10,000 to Geographical Association; £7,600 to Council for Wildlife Parks; £4,000 to University of Bristol; £1,000 to Cumbria Wildlife Trust; £950 to Science Teachers Association; £500 to ISST

FINANCES *Year* 1996–97 *Income* £127,695
Grants £59,950

TRUSTEES M Curry, Mrs A S Curry, Mrs M Curry Jones, Mrs P R Edmond

HOW TO APPLY To the address under Who To Apply To in writing

WHO TO APPLY TO N J Armstrong, Dennis Curry Charitable Trust, Messrs Alliotts, 5th Floor, 9 Kingsway, London WC2B 6XF

CC NO 263952   **ESTABLISHED** 1971

■ D A Curry's Charitable Trust

WHAT IS FUNDED General charitable purposes in accordance with the Settlor's wishes

WHAT IS NOT FUNDED No grants to individuals

WHO CAN BENEFIT Registered charities. There are no restrictions on the age; professional and economic group; family situation; religion and culture; and social circumstances of; or disease or medical condition suffered by, the beneficiaries

WHERE FUNDING CAN BE GIVEN UK

SAMPLE GRANTS £6,000 to The National Trust; £5,000 to Lord Major Treloar Trust; £5,000 to RNLI; £5,000 to The Leonard Cheshire Foundation; £5,000 to The Samaritans, Torbay and South Devon Branch

FINANCES *Year* 1997 *Income* £15,085
Grants £68,900

TRUSTEES Mrs L E Curry, A Curry, N J Armstrong, FCA

HOW TO APPLY In writing

WHO TO APPLY TO N J Armstrong, FCA, D A Curry's Charitable Trust, Messrs Alliotts, 5th Floor, 9 Kingsway, London WC2B 6XF

CC NO 214751   **ESTABLISHED** 1962

■ The Thomas Curtis Charitable Trust

WHAT IS FUNDED General charitable purposes and in particular to relieve and support children with physical or learning difficulties

WHAT IS NOT FUNDED Applications not related to above objects, and for assistance with university education are not considered

WHO CAN BENEFIT Preference given to local persons and organisations for special projects, particularly in the area of special needs

WHERE FUNDING CAN BE GIVEN High Wycombe area

TYPE OF GRANT One-off lump sum for a specific project or part of a project

FINANCES *Year* 1995 *Income* £30,447
Grants £8,484

TRUSTEES J R Curtis, Mrs M A Curtis, Ms M J–M Taylor-Rose

HOW TO APPLY At any time. Trustees meet three or four times a year. Applications should include clear details of the project and how funds are to be applied

WHO TO APPLY TO J R Curtis, The Thomas Curtis Charitable Trust, Hartlands, 28 Amersham Hill Drive, High Wycombe, Buckinghamshire HP13 6QY

CC NO 293065   **ESTABLISHED** 1985

■ Suzanne and Raymond Curtis Foundation

WHAT IS FUNDED General charitable purposes including the provision of relief for persons suffering hardship or distress by reason of age, infirmity, disablement, poverty or social economic circumstances

WHO CAN BENEFIT To benefit older people, disabled people, and those disadvantaged by poverty.

There are no restrictions on the professional and economic group; family situation; religion and culture; and social circumstances of; or disease or medical condition suffered by, the beneficiaries

WHERE FUNDING CAN BE GIVEN UK

RANGE OF GRANTS £150–£4,045

SAMPLE GRANTS £4,045 to Variety Club Events Ltd; £3,600 to Variety Club; £2,700 to Babes in Arms; £2,000 to Jami; £1,500 to Comic Heritage

FINANCES *Year* 1998 *Income* £22,850 *Grants* £22,760

TRUSTEES R Curtis, Ms S Curtis, A Freeman

WHO TO APPLY TO R Curtis, Trustee, Suzanne and Raymond Curtis Foundation, Glebe Farm, Ufton Nervet, Reading, Berkshire RG7 4EP

CC NO 1050295   **ESTABLISHED** 1995

■ The Wallace Curzon Charitable Trust

WHAT IS FUNDED The over-riding emphasis is on children, ie relief of poverty and sickness of children, as well as their education. This includes: child-based charity or voluntary umbrella bodies; music, theatre, opera and opera companies and groups; medical research into paediatric diseases; health education; hospices; and alternative health care

WHAT IS NOT FUNDED Appeals from individuals are not accepted

WHO CAN BENEFIT Other charitable institutions either nationally known or of which Trustees have direct personal knowledge, benefiting children disadvantaged by poverty or suffering from sickness and disease

WHERE FUNDING CAN BE GIVEN UK, particularly South and South West of England, and overseas

FINANCES *Year* 1997 *Income* £24,158 *Grants* £28,750

TRUSTEES R Spooner, P G D Curzon, F G D Curzon

NOTES A small percentage of grants go to musical/educational connections, eg for allocation to specific pupils with a need or to help enable productions involving school children. As we tend to repeat grants, only about one in thirty applications meets a modest, positive response

HOW TO APPLY In order to reduce outgoings to a minimum (and to maximise grants) we only respond to applications including an sae. Please-keep applications simple and inexpensive

WHO TO APPLY TO Fritz Curzon, Secretary, The Wallace Curzon Charitable Trust, Homanton House, Shrewton, Salisbury, Wiltshire SP3 4ER

CC NO 294508   **ESTABLISHED** 1986

■ The Manny Cussins Foundation

WHAT IS FUNDED General charitable purposes. Preference is given to charities of which the Trust has special interest, knowledge or association

WHO CAN BENEFIT There are no restrictions on the age; professional and economic group; family situation; religion and culture; and social circumstances of; or disease or medical condition suffered by, the beneficiaries

WHERE FUNDING CAN BE GIVEN UK

SAMPLE GRANTS £14,805 to Brodestky School; £5,500 to Angels International; £5,000 to Gallery of Contemporary Architecture and Design; £4,050 to Leeds Jewish Welfare Board; £2,000 to Cookridge Cancer Centre Appeal; £1,526 to United Hebrew Congregation; £1,500 to St James University Hospital Trust; £1,090 to Leeds Ladies Aid Society; £1,000 to Yorkshire Spinal Deformity Trust; £1,000 to Music Therapy Charity

FINANCES *Year* 1997 *Income* £53,796 *Grants* £54,719

TRUSTEES A Cussins, A Cussins, J R Cussins, Mrs A Reuben, A Reuben, OBE, JP, MA (Chair)

HOW TO APPLY **This Trust states that it does not respond to unsolicited applications**

WHO TO APPLY TO A Reuben, OBE, JP, MA, The Manny Cussins Foundation, Stone Acre, Harrogate Road, Leeds LS17 8EP

CC NO 219661   **ESTABLISHED** 1962

■ The Cwmbran Trust

WHAT IS FUNDED Grants are made to provide social amenities for the advancement of education and the relief of poverty and sickness in the urban area of Cwmbran town. Particularly charities working in the fields of: community development; support to volunteers, voluntary organisations; Christian education; arts, culture and recreation; health care; hospices; rehabilitation centres; church buildings; memorials and monuments; animal homes and welfare; campaigning for environmental issues; education and training; community facilities and services

WHAT IS NOT FUNDED No grants are made outside of Cwmbran in Gwent

WHO CAN BENEFIT Neighbourhood-based community projects benefiting people of all ages; ex-service and service people; musicians; retired people; sportsmen and women; students; unemployed people; volunteers; those in care, fostered and adopted; parents and children; one parent families; widows and widowers; at risk groups; disabled people; those disadvantaged by poverty; homeless people; and victims of domestic violence. There is no restriction on the disease or medical condition suffered by the beneficiaries

WHERE FUNDING CAN BE GIVEN Cwmbran

TYPE OF GRANT Capital, core costs, interest free loans, one-off, project, running costs, recurring costs and start-up costs. Funding for up to two years will be considered

RANGE OF GRANTS £100–£10,000

SAMPLE GRANTS £6,576 to Teen Challenge for drug rehabilitation; £3,558 to Henlleys Playpark Project; £2,223 to an individual for equipment; £2,200 to Llaysavon Primary School for computer work station; £2,200 to an individual for home adoption for disabled; £2,160 to an individual for a stair lift; £2,050 to an individual for a motorised scooter; £1,880 to Woodlands Road Junior School for security equipment; £1,800 to Scope for equipment for disabled centre; £1,779 to Torfaen Community Transport for disabled transport repairs

FINANCES *Year* 1997 *Income* £65,543 *Grants* £47,564

TRUSTEES B Cunningham, P M Harris, K L Maddox, A Rippon, B E Smith, K S Strangward

HOW TO APPLY To the address under Who To Apply To in writing. The Trustees usually meet every two months, starting at the end of February

WHO TO APPLY TO K L Maddox, The Cwmbran Trust, Grange Road, Cwmbran, Gwent NP44 3XU *Tel* 01633 834040

CC NO 505855   **ESTABLISHED** 1976

■ Itzchok Meyer Cymerman Trust Limited (241 =)

This trust declined to meet CAF's researchers and failed to supply a copy of its annual report and accounts to CAF as required under section 47(2) of the Charities Act 1993. The information held on file at the Charity Commission was insufficient to enable CAF's researchers to write a substantive commentary on the trust's activities. Accordingly, despite its size, we are unable to list this trust in Spotlight on Major Trusts

WHAT IS FUNDED To advance religion in accordance with the Orthodox Jewish faith and other charitable purposes

WHO CAN BENEFIT Jewish people

WHERE FUNDING CAN BE GIVEN UK

FINANCES *Year* 1993 *Income* £604,749 *Grants* £388,429

TRUSTEES Council of Management

WHO TO APPLY TO I M Cymerman, Itzchok Meyer Cymerman Trust Limited, 22 Overlea Road, London E5 9BG

CC NO 265090   **ESTABLISHED** 1972

■ Cystic Fibrosis Trust

WHAT IS FUNDED Research to find better treatments and to find a cure for Cystic Fibrosis. Clinical support for selected hospitals providing specialist care for children and adults with Cystic Fibrosis. Information, advice and direct welfare support to individuals and families coping with Cystic Fibrosis

WHAT IS NOT FUNDED Projects with very little relevance to Cystic Fibrosis or items which are properly the responsiblity of the NHS

WHO CAN BENEFIT Individuals and families coping with Cystic Fibrosis, directly and via the National Health Service and professional who offer medical and social care. Most grants go to Doctors and Scientists in hospitals or universities with a recognised interest in, and committment to, Cystic Fibrosis

WHERE FUNDING CAN BE GIVEN Limited to UK

TYPE OF GRANT Research projects and clinical support to Cystic Fibrosis Specialist Centres. Funding is available for up to and over three years

RANGE OF GRANTS 57 research grants from £4,200–£707,788. Average £96,000. 41 clinical support and improvement grants from £9,500–£48,000. Average £39,000

SAMPLE GRANTS £707,000 for Application of gene therapy to the lungs of Cystic Fibrosis subjects; £250,000 for identification of genetic factors which modify the Cystic Fibrosis disease phenotype in the CFTRM IHGU; £185,000 for CF study of Repiratory Function

FINANCES *Year* 1996–97 *Income* £4,536,000 *Grants* £2,070,000

TRUSTEES P Levy, BSc, OBE, FRICS, D Bluck, CBE, N Benson, FCA (Treasurer), Sir Robert Johnson, P Levy, OBE, FRICS, R Luff, OStJ, Hon FRCP, CBE

PUBLICATIONS CF News (issued free to families and carers). Annual Review and Financial Statement. Information booklet/audiotape series on all aspects of Cystic Fibrosis including campaigning issues

HOW TO APPLY For a research grant, please telephone for an application form. Grants are issued twice a year. An initial telephone call to discuss a possible grant is very welcome

WHO TO APPLY TO Dr Martin Scott, Medical and Scientific Director, Cystic Fibrosis Trust, 11 London Road, Bromley, Kent BR1 1BY *Tel* 0181-464 7211 *Fax* 0181-313 0472

CC NO 281287   **ESTABLISHED** 1964

■ DAG Charitable Trust

WHAT IS FUNDED General charitable purposes and education, principally Jewish

WHO CAN BENEFIT Charitable and educational institutions benefiting children, young adults and Jewish people

WHERE FUNDING CAN BE GIVEN Manchester

FINANCES *Year* 1997 *Income* £33,420 *Grants* £28,459

TRUSTEES A Vaisfiche, E Vaisfiche

HOW TO APPLY To the address under Who To Apply To in writing

WHO TO APPLY TO The Trustees, DAG Charitable Trust, Messrs Lopian Barnett & Co, Harvester House, 37 Peter Street, Manchester M2 5QD

CC NO 290020   **ESTABLISHED** 1984

■ DG Charitable Trust

WHAT IS FUNDED General charitable purposes

WHO CAN BENEFIT There are no restrictions on the age; professional and economic group; family situation; religion and culture; and social circumstances of; or disease or medical condition suffered by, the beneficiaries

WHERE FUNDING CAN BE GIVEN UK

RANGE OF GRANTS £500–£50,000

SAMPLE GRANTS £50,000 to Crisis; £15,000 to Amnesty International UK Charitable Trust; £5,000 to Bedales Oliver Theatre Appeal; £5,000 to Hedley Roberts Trust; £5,000 to Imperial Cancer Research Fund; £5,000 to Tibet Relief Fund; £5,000 to Medical Foundation for the Care of Victims of Torture; £5,000 to the Foundation for Children with Leukaemia; £2,000 to Alzheimer's Disease Society; £2,000 to British Red Cross

FINANCES *Year* 1997 *Income* £28,413 *Grants* £119,500

TRUSTEES D J Gilmour, P Grafton-Green

WHO TO APPLY TO Ms P A Samson, DG Charitable Trust, 43 Portland Road, London W11 4LJ

CC NO 1040778   **ESTABLISHED** 1994

■ The DLM Charitable Trust

WHAT IS FUNDED To support charities operating in Oxford and the surrounding areas, particularly charities working in the fields of: arts, culture and recreation; religious buildings; self help groups; the conservation of historic buildings; memorials; monuments and waterways; schools; community centres and village halls; parks; various community services and other charitable purposes

WHAT IS NOT FUNDED No grants to individuals

WHO CAN BENEFIT Organisations benefiting children; young adults; older people; medical professionals, nurses and doctors; and sufferers of head and other injuries; heart disease and blindness

WHERE FUNDING CAN BE GIVEN Oxfordshire

TYPE OF GRANT Feasibility studies, one-off, research, recurring costs, running costs and start-up costs. Funding of up to three years will be considered

SAMPLE GRANTS £5,000 to Driving for the Disabled, Shifford Branch for general support; £5,000 to Oxfordshire Scouts for general support; £2,500 to BLISS for cot monitors for Oxford area; £2,000 to Friends of Sobell House Hospice for general support; £2,000 to Oxfordshire Association for the Blind for general support; £2,000 to Talking Newspapers for the Blind for general support; £2,000 to Cot Death Society for general support; £2,000 to Enstone Playgroup for general support; £2,000 to Marlborough School, Woodstock for general support; £1,000 to Oxford City Football Club Trust for general support
FINANCES *Year* 1996 *Income* £102,480 *Grants* £37,509
TRUSTEES Dr E A de la Mare, Mrs P Sawyer, J A Cloke
WHO TO APPLY TO J A Cloke, The DLM Charitable Trust, Messrs Cloke & Co, Warnford Court, Throgmorton Street, London EC2N 2AT
CC NO 328520 **ESTABLISHED** 1990

■ DMF Trust

This trust did not respond to CAF's request to amend its entry and, by 30 June 1998, CAF's researchers did not find financial records for later than 1995 on its file at the Charity Commission. Trusts are legally required to submit annual accounts to the Charity Commission under section 42 of the Charities Act 1993

WHAT IS FUNDED Education, research, Jewish and other charitable causes including art, art galleries, museums, music, cancer research. Preference to charities of which the Trust has special interest, knowledge or association including humanities and welfare
WHAT IS NOT FUNDED No new applications. Applications from individuals are ineligible. No mailshot adverts from large national organisations, nor to smaller bodies working in areas other than those set out above
WHO CAN BENEFIT Registered charities benefiting children and young adults, musicians, research workers, artists, Jews and people suffering from cancer
WHERE FUNDING CAN BE GIVEN UK
TRUSTEES M R Franklin, S J Franklin, N D Franklin
WHO TO APPLY TO Mrs M Franklin-Ellenbogen, DMF Trust, 83 Apsley House, Finchley Road, London NW3 0NZ
CC NO 210897 **ESTABLISHED** 1957

■ Dahlia Charitable Trust

WHAT IS FUNDED General charitable purposes as directed by the Trustees
WHO CAN BENEFIT There are no restrictions on the age; professional and economic group; family situation; religion and culture; and social circumstances of; or disease or medical condition suffered by, the beneficiaries
WHERE FUNDING CAN BE GIVEN UK
WHO TO APPLY TO Felix Posen, Trustee, Dahlia Charitable Trust, 24 Kensington Gate, London W8 5NA
CC NO 1060079 **ESTABLISHED** 1997

■ The Daily Prayer Union Trust Ltd

WHAT IS FUNDED Evangelical Christian purposes
WHAT IS NOT FUNDED No grants for bricks and mortar
WHO CAN BENEFIT To benefit Christians and Evangelists
WHERE FUNDING CAN BE GIVEN UK

SAMPLE GRANTS £7,000 to Monkton Coombe School; £5,000 to IFES; £4,000 to Radstock Ministry; £2,000 to Jesus Lane Trust; £2,000 to ISCS; £2,000 to Henry Shaheen; £2,000 to St Andrew's Church, Kendray; £2,000 to EFAL; £1,500 to MMT; £1,000 to Evangelical Literature Trust
FINANCES *Year* 1997 *Income* £72,322 *Grants* £64,960
TRUSTEES Bishop T Dudley-Smith, R J Knight, Rev G C Grinham, Canon J Tiller, Sir T Hoare, Rev J Eddison, Mrs E Bridger, Mrs A Tompson, Rev H Palmer, Mrs F M Ashton, Mrs R K Harley
HOW TO APPLY **Unsolicited applications are unlikely to be successful**
WHO TO APPLY TO Sir Timothy Hoare, Trustee, The Daily Prayer Union Trust Ltd, 10 Belitha Villas, London N1 1PD
CC NO 284857 **ESTABLISHED** 1983

■ Daily Telegraph Charitable Trust

WHAT IS FUNDED Emphasis is given to charities in the fields of education and the newspaper industry
WHAT IS NOT FUNDED Applications from individuals, including students, are ineligible
WHO CAN BENEFIT Registered charities benefiting children, young adults and those working in the newspaper industry will be considered
WHERE FUNDING CAN BE GIVEN UK
FINANCES *Year* 1995 *Income* £150,000 *Grants* £150,000
TRUSTEES D J Alder, A J Davies, C I Dolphin
HOW TO APPLY All applications must be in writing
WHO TO APPLY TO Katie O'Brien, Corporate Relations Manager, The Daily Telegraph Charitable Trust, Telegraph Group Limited, 1 Canada Square, Canary Wharf, London E14 5DT
CC NO 205296 **ESTABLISHED** 1944

■ The Daisy Foundation

This trust did not respond to CAF's request to amend its entry and, by 30 June 1998, CAF's researchers did not find financial records for later than 1995 on its file at the Charity Commission. Trusts are legally required to submit annual accounts to the Charity Commission under section 42 of the Charities Act 1993

WHAT IS FUNDED General charitable purposes
WHO CAN BENEFIT There are no restrictions on the age; professional and economic group; family situation; religion and culture; and social circumstances of; or disease or medical condition suffered by, the beneficiaries
WHERE FUNDING CAN BE GIVEN UK
TRUSTEES Ms D W Davies, C J Russell
WHO TO APPLY TO C J Russell, Trustee, The Daisy Foundation, Reynolds, Porter, Chamberlain, Chichester House, 278–282 High Holborn, London WC1V 7HA
CC NO 1045525 **ESTABLISHED** 1995

■ The Daiwa Anglo-Japanese Foundation

WHAT IS FUNDED The education of citizens of the UK and Japan in each other's culture, institutions, arts, etc. Scholarships, bursaries and maintenance allowances to enable students and academics in the UK and Japan to pursue their education abroad. Grants to charitable institutions promoting education in the UK or Japan, and research. The granting of Daiwa Scholarships to five postgraduates each year to enable them to study Japanese for two years in the UK and Japan. Support of Japanese studies and Japanese language teaching in the UK. Activities based at Daiwa Foundation Japan House, a centre for those interested in non-governmental Anglo-Japanese relations

WHO CAN BENEFIT Individuals and institutions (UK or Japanese) benefiting young adults, students and Japanese people

WHERE FUNDING CAN BE GIVEN UK and Japan

TYPE OF GRANT Outright grant, staged grant, paid in sterling or Japanese yen

SAMPLE GRANTS £30,000 to University of Hull towards cost of Japanese language tutor; £15,000 to Pembroke College, Cambridge towards five year Fellowship in Japanese Studies; £15,000 to Birkbeck College, London towards five year Fellowship in Japanese Studies; £12,000 to Reuter Foundation towards costs of Fellowship for Japanese journalists; £8,000 to the Choral Group 'Choir Family', Japan towards costs of tour of London and Europe; £8,000 to Kanazawa Institute of Technology, Japan towards joint research at the Department of Materials, Oxford University; £6,000 to SOAS towards cost of three-year research project on the Kansai area of Japan; £6,000 to London University Institute of Education ACE Project towards cost of primary and secondary schools group for British Museum Utamaro Exhibition; £6,000 to the Cheshire Education Management Programme towards cost of visit to Japan by three representatives of a consortium of VI Form Colleges in Hampshire and Cheshire; £6,000 to GAP towards four GAP volunteers attending the Kobokan Community Centre, Tokyo

FINANCES *Year* 1995–96 *Income* £1,421,262 *Grants* £258,000

TRUSTEES Lord Roll, KCMG, CB (Chair), Yoshitoki Chino, KBE (Vice Chair), Lady Adrian, Prof Alec Broers, FRS, Rt Hon Lord Carrington, KG, N P Clegg, Akio Morita, KBE

PUBLICATIONS *Managing Across Borders: Culture and Communications, Issues for British and Japanese Businesses*

NOTES Average annual grants expected to be approximately £300,000 (exclusive of funds for Daiwa Scholarships and activities based at Daiwa Foundation Japan House)

HOW TO APPLY No special forms. Applications in writing in applicant's own style outlining project, budget, etc, either to Mr Everett, the Director General in London or in Japan to Mr Masanobu Mark Nakamura, Nishi Gotanda, 7–13–5 Shinagawa-Ku, Tokyo 141. Tel: 00 813 3494 7881, Fax: 00 813 3494 7897. Mr Everett and Mr Nakamura welcome telephone enquiries and visits

WHO TO APPLY TO C H D Everett, CBE, Director General, The Daiwa Anglo-Japanese Foundation, Japan House, 13–14 Cornwall Terrace, London NW1 4QP *Web Site* http://www.daiwa-foundation.org.uk

CC NO 299955   **ESTABLISHED** 1988

■ Oizer Dalim Trust

This trust did not respond to CAF's request to amend its entry and, by 30 June 1998, CAF's researchers did not find financial records for later than 1995 on its file at the Charity Commission. Trusts are legally required to submit annual accounts to the Charity Commission under section 42 of the Charities Act 1993

WHAT IS FUNDED General charitable purposes

WHO CAN BENEFIT There are no restrictions on the age; professional and economic group; family situation; religion and culture; and social circumstances of; or disease or medical condition suffered by, the beneficiaries

WHERE FUNDING CAN BE GIVEN UK

FINANCES *Income* £96,053

WHO TO APPLY TO Mordechai C I K, Oizer Dalim Trust, 68 Osbaldeston Road, London N16 7DR

CC NO 1045296   **ESTABLISHED** 1994

■ The Dalmia Foundation

WHAT IS FUNDED General charitable purposes. Trustees review all applications

WHAT IS NOT FUNDED No grants to individuals

WHO CAN BENEFIT There are no restrictions on the age; professional and economic group; family situation; religion and culture; and social circumstances of; or disease or medical condition suffered by, the beneficiaries

WHERE FUNDING CAN BE GIVEN UK

SAMPLE GRANTS £1,000 to Manchester Royal Infirmary; £500 to Gifts Day Hospice for extension to existing premises; £500 to Grantham Initiative for the Terminally Sick

FINANCES *Year* 1997 *Income* £41,214 *Grants* £2,521

TRUSTEES L S Vaidyanathan, Mrs S Vaidyanathan, R Kaufman

HOW TO APPLY In writing. Trustees meet four times a year

WHO TO APPLY TO R Kaufman, The Dalmia Foundation, 3 Ellesmere Street, Manchester M15 4JY

CC NO 1000510   **ESTABLISHED** 1990

■ The Damont Charitable Trust

WHAT IS FUNDED Normally only for The Association for Jewish Youth. No capital can be applied so long as The Association for Jewish Youth remains in existence and recognised as a charity

WHAT IS NOT FUNDED At present exclusively for the Association for Jewish Youth Inc

WHO CAN BENEFIT To benefit Jewish youth

WHERE FUNDING CAN BE GIVEN UK

SAMPLE GRANTS £95,460 to the Association for Jewish Youth Incorporated

FINANCES *Year* 1996–97 *Income* £65,030 *Grants* £95,460

TRUSTEES E D Green, P R Jacobson, R P Tenzer, J D M Lew

WHO TO APPLY TO Mrs L Davis, The Damont Charitable Trust, Broadway House, 80–82 The Broadway, Stanmore, Middlesex HA7 4HB

CC NO 232018   **ESTABLISHED** 1963

■ R J and A H Daniels Charitable Trust

WHAT IS FUNDED General charitable purposes

WHO CAN BENEFIT There are no restrictions on the age; professional and economic group; family situation; religion and culture; and social circumstances of; or disease or medical condition suffered by, the beneficiaries

WHERE FUNDING CAN BE GIVEN UK

FINANCES *Year* 1997 *Income* £25,025

TRUSTEES Kleinwort Benson Trustees Ltd, R J Daniels, Mrs A H Daniels

NOTES The Trustees wish to let the Trust establish itself, and then they will decide whether to accumulate or donate the income accrued

WHO TO APPLY TO The Secretary, R J and A H Daniels Charitable Trust, c/o Kleinwort Benson Trustees Ltd, PO Box 191, 10 Fenchurch Street, London EC3M 3LB
CC NO 1050703   ESTABLISHED 1994

■ Doctor and Mrs Alfred Darlington Charitable Trust

WHAT IS FUNDED Mainly medical, disability, welfare or conservation

WHAT IS NOT FUNDED Applications from individuals, including students, are unlikely to be successful

WHO CAN BENEFIT Only registered charities benefiting: at risk groups; disabled people; socially isolated people. There is no restriction on the disease or medical condition suffered by the beneficiaries

WHERE FUNDING CAN BE GIVEN Devon, particularly Sidmouth and East Devon area

TYPE OF GRANT One-off, some recurring

SAMPLE GRANTS £10,000 to The Abbeyfield Sidmouth Society Ltd towards the purchase and conversion of a Torbay hotel; £7,500 to Healthy Heart Trust for research into heart disease; £6,000 to FORGE towards funding of cancer research; £6,000 to Devon Wildlife Trust towards cost of employing a surveyor; £3,000 to Arthritis Care for the refurbishment of Waring Bowen Home Hotel Fund; £2,000 to Devon County Association for the Blind a general donation; £2,000 to West of England School for the Deaf for equipment; £2,000 to Woodland Trust for the purchase of woodland; £2,000 to Motor Neurone Disease Association to purchase a light writer; £1,300 to Whipton Community Association for assistance with lunch club

FINANCES *Year* 1997 *Income* £87,768 *Grants* £51,564

TRUSTEES Lloyds Bank plc, V A Donson

PUBLICATIONS Annual return to the Charity Commission

HOW TO APPLY To the address under Who To Apply To in writing. Trustees meet quarterly in March, June, September and December. The Trustees regret that they cannot send replies to unsuccessful applicants

WHO TO APPLY TO V A Donson, Dr and Mrs A Darlington Charitable Trust, Ford Simey Daw Roberts, 8 Cathedral Close, Exeter EX1 1EW
Tel 01392 274126 *Fax* 01392 410933
CC NO 283308   ESTABLISHED 1981

■ Darnall Area Trust Fund

WHAT IS FUNDED For the benefit of the inhabitants of the Darnall area to advance education and assist in the provision of facilities for education, social welfare, recreation and leisure time occupation

WHO CAN BENEFIT Organisations benefiting: children, young adults; at risk groups; those disadvantaged by poverty and socially isolated people

WHERE FUNDING CAN BE GIVEN Darnall

SAMPLE GRANTS £300 to Bangladeshi Young Girls; £300 to St Albans Junior Club; £300 to Agaaz; £300 to Bangladeshi Welfare Project; £300 to Cosy Corner Lunch Club

FINANCES *Year* 1996 *Income* £14,589 *Grants* £6,335

TRUSTEES Cllr K Walayat, M Taylor, M Iqbal, L Hanson, A Liddell, M Fudger

HOW TO APPLY To the address under Who To Apply To in writing

WHO TO APPLY TO Miss B Ashman, Darnall Area Trust Fund, 546 Attercliffe Road, Sheffield S9 3QP
Tel 0114-249 4111
CC NO 1016283   ESTABLISHED 1992

■ Iris Darnton Foundation

WHAT IS FUNDED Fund educational and research projects only. Research into habitat and species protection and conservation. Promoting by educational means the aesthetic appreciation of flora and fauna, and to promote public morality and advancement of humanitarian principles in relation to wildlife and its preservation

WHO CAN BENEFIT Institutions benefiting academics, research workers and students

WHERE FUNDING CAN BE GIVEN UK and overseas

RANGE OF GRANTS £1,000–£7,000

SAMPLE GRANTS £7,000 to Whitley/Darnton Prizes; £6,500 to Oxford Wildlife Conservation; £5,000 to Dian Fossey Gorilla Fund UK; £2,000 to the National Pony Society; £2,000 to Mauritian Wildlife Appeal

FINANCES *Year* 1997 *Income* £24,836 *Grants* £34,250

TRUSTEES J Teacher, MA, FLS (Chairman), Miss A D Darnton, Mrs C Hardy, VMH, Mrs H Robinson, OBE

WHO TO APPLY TO J Toth, Solicitor, Iris Darnton Foundation, Buss Murton Solicitors, The Priory, Tunbridge Wells, Kent TN1 1JJ
CC NO 252576   ESTABLISHED 1966

■ Dartmouth United Charities

WHAT IS FUNDED General charitable purposes

WHO CAN BENEFIT There are no restrictions on the age; professional and economic group; family situation; religion and culture; and social circumstances of; or disease or medical condition suffered by, the beneficiaries

WHERE FUNDING CAN BE GIVEN Dartmouth

FINANCES *Year* 1997 *Income* £75,569

TRUSTEES J Cutter, D W R Webb, Mrs D Morris, L Manley, P Darby, R Davies, Mrs P R J Norton, R M Hannaford, D R A Gerrard, E C Weatherley, G Farr, T K Ellwood, J H Smith, B G Ridalls

HOW TO APPLY To the address under Who To Apply To in writing

WHO TO APPLY TO D M Scorer, Dartmouth United Charities, 1st Floor, 3 The Quay, Dartmouth TQ6 9PS
CC NO 203399   ESTABLISHED 1987

■ Datnow Limited

This trust did not respond to CAF's request to amend its entry and, by 30 June 1998, CAF's researchers did not find financial records for later than 1995 on its file at the Charity Commission. Trusts are legally required to submit annual accounts to the Charity Commission under section 42 of the Charities Act 1993

WHAT IS FUNDED General charitable purposes

WHAT IS NOT FUNDED No religious or affiliated bodies. Registered charities only

WHO CAN BENEFIT Registered charities only. There are no restrictions on the age; professional and economic group; family situation; religion and culture; and social circumstances suffered by, the beneficiaries

WHERE FUNDING CAN BE GIVEN UK and overseas

TRUSTEES The Council of Management, Mrs E M Datnow, E L Datnow, J A Datnow, A D Datnow

WHO TO APPLY TO A D Datnow, Datnow Limited, 130 Holland Park Avenue, London W11 4UE
CC NO 247183 **ESTABLISHED** 1966

■ David Charitable Trust

WHAT IS FUNDED Health and welfare, children, the aged and infirm, educational institutions, the arts

WHO CAN BENEFIT To benefit: actors and entertainment professionals; musicians; textile workers and designers; students; writers and poets; at risk groups; those disadvantaged by poverty; and socially isolated people. There is no restriction on the age of, or the disease and medical condition suffered by, the beneficiaries

WHERE FUNDING CAN BE GIVEN UK

SAMPLE GRANTS £50,000 to the Lady Hoare Trust; £4,000 to Royal College of Art

FINANCES *Year* 1996 *Income* £16,821 *Grants* £56,500

HOW TO APPLY To the address under Who To Apply To in writing

WHO TO APPLY TO David Charitable Trust, Payne Hicks Beach, Solicitors, 10 New Square, Lincoln's Inn, London WC2A 3QG
CC NO 1015509 **ESTABLISHED** 1990

■ The Lesley David Trust

WHAT IS FUNDED Preference to charities of which the Trust has special interest, knowledge or association including those involved with accommodation and housing; religious buildings; architecture; fine art and visual arts; conservation; academic subjects, sciences and research, and community facilities

WHAT IS NOT FUNDED No grants to individuals

WHO CAN BENEFIT Mainly trusts for restoration and preservation of historic buildings and nature reserves; and organisations benefiting: young adults; legal professionals and clergy

WHERE FUNDING CAN BE GIVEN UK, particularly London, Essex, England and Northern Ireland

TYPE OF GRANT One-off or annual subscription for buildings. Grants are made for one year or less

RANGE OF GRANTS £25–£1,000

SAMPLE GRANTS £2,000 to Thomas Rose Picture Trust for restoration and installation of a picture; £1,000 to William and Jane Morris Fund for restoration of churches; £1,000 to Newnham College for development; £1,000 to St Albans Cathedral; £1,000 to Georgian Group for care of Georgian buildings

FINANCES *Year* 1996 *Income* £13,840 *Grants* £11,963

TRUSTEES Lesley Lewis, Jane Lewis

NOTES Preference to small charities to which relatively small grants are useful and where there is voluntary effort. Only registered charities are considered for funding

HOW TO APPLY Initial telephone welcome. Sae preferred

WHO TO APPLY TO Lesley Lewis, The Lesley David Trust, 38 Whitelands House, Cheltenham Terrace, London SW3 4QY *Tel* 0171-730 6030
CC NO 262760 **ESTABLISHED** 1971

■ The Alderman Joe Davidson Memorial Trust

WHAT IS FUNDED The Trust Deed allows for annual maintenance of one block of flats owned by the Trust. The balance of the income is distributed as follows: (a) The provision of homes for over 70's in need; (b) Charitable donations to specific organisations as detailed in the Trust Deed; (c) annual grants to needy people nominated by Age Concern; (d) Christmas Parties each year for the elderly and children; and (e) presentation of watches to school children for regular attendance

WHO CAN BENEFIT Local and specific national organisations and individuals benefiting children; older people, nominated by Age Concern; and Jews

WHERE FUNDING CAN BE GIVEN Portsmouth, Hampshire

TYPE OF GRANT Recurring grants given to specific organisations

FINANCES *Year* 1996–97 *Income* £37,093 *Grants* £36,747

TRUSTEES Mrs S Allison, Miss M A Ashton, Hon Ald Cockerill, K Crabbe, Lady Daley, MBE, C Davidson, J Klein, Ald Mrs M B E Leonard, E Thompson

HOW TO APPLY Applications not accepted if outside the interests of the Trust as detailed above

WHO TO APPLY TO John Stock, Trustees' Secretary, The Alderman Joe Davidson Memorial Trust, Committee Services, Civic Offices, Portsmouth, Hampshire PO1 2AL *Tel* 01705 834797
CC NO 202591 **ESTABLISHED** 1962

■ Richard Davies Charitable Foundation

WHAT IS FUNDED General charitable purposes, particular help for small organisations for start-up and self-help

WHAT IS NOT FUNDED No grants to individuals or national appeals

WHO CAN BENEFIT Preference will be given to appeals for operational assistance and innovatory projects. There are no restrictions on the age; professional and economic group; family situation; religion and culture; and social circumstances of; or disease or medical condition suffered by, the beneficiaries

WHERE FUNDING CAN BE GIVEN Bristol

TYPE OF GRANT The Foundation will not enter into long term funding but will consider recurrent grants for up to five years. Buildings, capital, core costs, endowments, feasibility studies, interest free loans, one-off, project, research, running costs, recurring costs, salaries and start-up costs. Funding can be for up to or over three years

RANGE OF GRANTS From £25. Typical grants £250–£500

SAMPLE GRANTS £4,000 to Harvest Trust for adventure holidays for deprived Bristol children; £3,000 to Fairbridge in Avon for venture sailing for 'endangered' young people; £2,000 to St Peter's Hospice, a cancer hospice; £1,200 to Bristol Debt Advice Centre for running costs; £888 to an individual for a remedial operation for a deprived young boy; £624 to Wheels Project for work with young people at risk; £600 to CSV Environment for introduction of inner city kids to green issues; £500 to Bristol Drugs Project for evident anti-drug use initiative; £500 to Victim Support Bristol for support to victims of crime; £500 to Bristol Cyrenians for running costs of housing support for homeless

FINANCES *Year* 1997 *Income* £28,246 *Grants* £22,357

TRUSTEES R E Davies, K M Davies, J M Coles, T E Pyper, R A Powell, G J Coles

NOTES Please apply in writing, with full details

HOW TO APPLY In writing to the address under Who To Apply To. Applications considered at next meeting.

Does the trust you have chosen match your needs? Haphazard applications waste postage and time

165

Meetings held bi-monthly on second Wednesday. No formal application procedures/forms

WHO TO APPLY TO R A Powell, Richard Davies Charitable Foundation, 298 Canford Lane, Westbury-on-Trym, Bristol BS9 3PL *Tel* 0117-949 8571

CC NO 279380   **ESTABLISHED** 1979

■ Michael Davies Charitable Settlement

WHAT IS FUNDED General charitable purposes at the Trustees' discretion

WHO CAN BENEFIT There are no restrictions on the age; professional and economic group; family situation; religion and culture; and social circumstances of; or disease or medical condition suffered by, the beneficiaries

WHERE FUNDING CAN BE GIVEN UK

TYPE OF GRANT At the discretion of the Trustees

RANGE OF GRANTS £500–£10,000

SAMPLE GRANTS £10,000 to Camden Arts Centre; £10,000 to North London Hospice; £5,633 to Royal Albert Dock Trust; £5,000 to Arkwright Arts Trust; £5,000 to Save the Children; £3,000 to Aviation Ball; £2,222 to Architectural; £2,000 to St John Ambulance; £2,000 to the Uphill Ski Class; £2,000 to Family Holiday Association

FINANCES *Year* 1997 *Income* £48,314 *Grants* £54,355

TRUSTEES M Davies, G H Camamile

WHO TO APPLY TO K Hawkins, Michael Davies Charitable Settlement, Lee Associates, 5 Southampton Place, London WC1A 2DA

CC NO 1000574   **ESTABLISHED** 1990

■ J Davies Charities Limited

This trust did not respond to CAF's request to amend its entry and, by 30 June 1998, CAF's researchers did not find financial records for later than 1995 on its file at the Charity Commission. Trusts are legally required to submit annual accounts to the Charity Commission under section 42 of the Charities Act 1993

WHAT IS FUNDED Jewish charities

WHAT IS NOT FUNDED No grants to individuals

WHO CAN BENEFIT Organisations benefiting Jewish people

WHERE FUNDING CAN BE GIVEN UK and overseas

TRUSTEES Governors: F Davies, M Kayne, G Munitz, S L Orenstein, M Rabin

WHO TO APPLY TO M Rabin, FCA, J Davies Charities Limited 22 Hillcrest Avenue, Edgware, Middlesex HA8 8PA

CC NO 248270   **ESTABLISHED** 1966

■ The John Grant Davies Trust

WHAT IS FUNDED Financial support is given for combating poverty, to community groups, voluntary organisations and faith communities in the area Where Funding Can Be Given. Preference is given to small grassroots organisations. This includes: infrastructure development; charity or voluntary umbrella bodies; community arts and recreation; health counselling; health education; environmental issues; transport and alternative transport; IT training; literacy; training for community development; playgrounds and recreation grounds; community services; campaigning for social issues; equal opportunities; and advice and information

WHAT IS NOT FUNDED No grants for buildings or holidays or to individuals

WHO CAN BENEFIT Organisations benefiting: people of all ages; unemployed people; and volunteers. There are a few restrictions on the social circumstances of the beneficiaries

WHERE FUNDING CAN BE GIVEN Greater Manchester

TYPE OF GRANT One-off, capital, core costs, feasibility studies, project, research, salaries and start-up costs. Funding is available for up to three years

RANGE OF GRANTS £100–£3,000

SAMPLE GRANTS £2,200 to Old Trafford Community Development Project towards employing a second community development worker; £2,000 to Hulwe Action Resources project towards drop in/advice centre; £2,000 to The Furniture Station for collecting and refurbishing furniture for poor people; £2,000 to After Adoption funding part of salary for worker with women in Styal Prison who are losing or have lost a child; £2,000 to St Ambrose Young Families, Salford towards core costs; £1,800 to Salford Racial Harassment Project to help fund sessional work for self help support groups; £1,500 to STEP (Strategies to Elevate People) for costs of Saturday School for black children; £1,500 to NACRO Football Community Link funding football coaching sessions using local volunteers and local children; £1,500 Copperdale Trust, Benchill towards costs and salaries for community development project; £1,500 to Old Moat Youth Outreach for costs of drop in centre

FINANCES *Year* 1996–97 *Income* £39,900 *Grants* £31,745

TRUSTEES Jonathan Dale, Katherine Davies, Nora Davies, Craig Russell

NOTES Policy statement accompanies application form

HOW TO APPLY Applications should be made on a form available from the address under Who To Apply To. Grants are made quarterly and deadlines are given

WHO TO APPLY TO Dr N Davies, The John Grant Davies Trust, 1462 Ashton Old Road, Manchester M11 1HL *Tel* 0161-301 5119

CC NO 1041001   **ESTABLISHED** 1994

■ The Morriston Davies Trust

WHAT IS FUNDED Grants are given for research into and education on prevention, treatment and the cure of tuberculosis and other respiratory diseases

WHO CAN BENEFIT People who are at risk from respiratory diseases, particularly tuberculosis. Also medical professionals

WHERE FUNDING CAN BE GIVEN Scotland

TRUSTEES I A Campbell, R D H Monie, A R Somner

PUBLICATIONS Accounts are available from the Trust

HOW TO APPLY Applications should be made in writing to the address below

WHO TO APPLY TO The Trustees, The Morriston Davies Trust, Bank of Scotland, Trustee Department, PO Box 41, 101 George Street, Edinburgh EH2 3JH

SC NO SCO 04937

■ The Sarah D'Avigdor Goldsmid Charitable Trust

WHAT IS FUNDED No specific policy, but see What Is Not Funded. Conservation and environment, and head injuries and other injuries will be considered

Have you read How to use the DGMT *on page xvi?*

WHAT IS NOT FUNDED Applications by individuals not considered. Unsuccessful applications not acknowledged. Needs of the County of Kent favoured

WHO CAN BENEFIT Registered charities only. Those suffering from head and other injuries will be considered

WHERE FUNDING CAN BE GIVEN Kent

TYPE OF GRANT One-off

RANGE OF GRANTS £25–£1,000; typical grant £50–£100

SAMPLE GRANTS £2,500 to Glyndebourne; £1,560 to an individual; £1,500 to Kent Trust for Nature Conservation; £1,442 to an individual; £1,350 to Headway; £1,000 to Game Conservancy Scottish Research Trust; £1,000 to International Spinal Research Trust; £1,000 to an individual; £1,000 to Mark Davies Injured Riders Fund; £1,000 to Wallenberg Appeal

FINANCES *Year* 1997 *Income* £27,387 *Grants* £26,646

TRUSTEES A J M Teacher Mrs A J M Teacher

PUBLICATIONS Accounts

HOW TO APPLY By post only

WHO TO APPLY TO James Teacher, The Sarah D'Avigdor Goldsmid Charitable Trust, Hadlow Place Farm, Golden Green, Tonbridge, Kent TN11 0BW

CC NO 233083   **ESTABLISHED** 1963

■ Lily and Henry Davis Charitable Foundation

WHAT IS FUNDED General charitable purposes

WHAT IS NOT FUNDED No grants to individuals

WHO CAN BENEFIT Registered charities. Preference for national and Jewish charities. There are no restrictions on the age; professional and economic group; family situation; religion and culture; and social circumstances of; or disease or medical condition suffered by, the beneficiaries

WHERE FUNDING CAN BE GIVEN UK

RANGE OF GRANTS £50–£1,000

SAMPLE GRANTS £1,000 to Jewish Care; £800 to Winged Fellowship Trust; £600 to Jewish Deaf Association; £600 to Jewish Home and Hospital at Tottenham; £600 to Jewish Philanthropic Association for Israel and the Middle East

FINANCES *Year* 1997 *Income* £19,608 *Grants* £18,800

TRUSTEES Mrs E B Rubens, J A Clemence

NOTES Follow policy established by the founder – new charities rarely considered

HOW TO APPLY To the address under Who To Apply To in writing only

WHO TO APPLY TO John A Clemence, Trustee, Lily and Henry Davis Charitable Foundation, 8 Baker Street, London W1M 1DA

CC NO 263662   **ESTABLISHED** 1971

■ Wilfrid Bruce Davis Charitable Trust

WHAT IS FUNDED The support of cancer, kidney dialysis patients and others with improved nursing care, counselling and provision of holidays are the main aims

WHAT IS NOT FUNDED No applications from individuals considered

WHO CAN BENEFIT Voluntary groups and registered charities benefiting those suffering from cancers, head and other injuries, kidney disease, motor neurone disease, strokes and the terminally ill

WHERE FUNDING CAN BE GIVEN Mainly Cornwall

TYPE OF GRANT All funding is for up to three years

SAMPLE GRANTS £30,230 to St Michaels Hospital, Hayle Cornwall for training facility for improving well being of patients; £10,000 to St Julia's Hospice for families and staff; £5,000 to Pathway for stroke day centre in Truro; £5,000 to Cornwall Mobility Centre for running costs; £2,700 to British Kidney Patient Association as an annual grant

FINANCES *Year* 1997 *Income* £63,696 *Grants* £52,169

TRUSTEES W B Davis, MBE, Mrs D F Davis, Mrs D S Dickens

PUBLICATIONS Annual Report

HOW TO APPLY The budget for grants is filled for several years ahead and, therefore, there is little point in making applications

WHO TO APPLY TO W Bruce Davis, MBE, Wilfrid Bruce Davis Charitable Trust, La Feock Grange, Feock, Truro, Cornwall TR3 6RG

CC NO 265421   **ESTABLISHED** 1967

■ The J Davy Foundation

WHAT IS FUNDED Education, universities, schools and hospitals

WHO CAN BENEFIT To benefit children, young adults and students. There is no restriction on the disease or medical condition suffered by the beneficiaries

WHERE FUNDING CAN BE GIVEN UK

TYPE OF GRANT At the discretion of the Trustees

FINANCES *Year* 1996 *Income* £17,652

TRUSTEES T J Grove, D G Roberts, W G Short

NOTES No grants were given in 1996 due to pending decision on future policy. Previous year showed grants given as £27,500

WHO TO APPLY TO T J Grove, The J Davy Foundation, 4 Monahan Avenue, Purley, Surrey CR8 3BA

CC NO 1014511   **ESTABLISHED** 1992

■ The Charity of Thomas Dawson

WHAT IS FUNDED To provide general charitable purposes for youth, community projects, and education and training

WHAT IS NOT FUNDED No expeditions or medical requests considered

WHO CAN BENEFIT Individuals and organisations benefiting students and the unemployed. There is no restriction on the age of the beneficiaries

WHERE FUNDING CAN BE GIVEN City of Oxford only

TYPE OF GRANT One-off for up to one year

SAMPLE GRANTS £1,500 to St Clement's Family Centre; £1,000 to Oxford Youth Works

FINANCES *Year* 1995 *Income* £138,246

PUBLICATIONS Annual Accounts

NOTES Grants are allocated to educational requests only. Applicants must have been resident in the City of Oxford for at least three years

HOW TO APPLY To the address under Who To Apply To in writing only. Applicants are required to foward an sae

WHO TO APPLY TO Mrs K Lacey, Clerk and Receiver, The Charity of Thomas Dawson, 56 Poplar Close, Garsington, Oxford OX44 9BP

CC NO 213258   **ESTABLISHED** 1962

■ Thomas Dawson Educational Foundation

WHAT IS FUNDED Education and continuing education

WHAT IS NOT FUNDED No expeditions or medical requests considered

WHO CAN BENEFIT Small local projects, new and established organisations and individuals benefiting: students and the unemployed. There is no restriction on the age of the beneficiaries

WHERE FUNDING CAN BE GIVEN City of Oxford only

TYPE OF GRANT One-off for up to one year

FINANCES *Year* 1996 *Income* £138,246

PUBLICATIONS Annual Accounts

NOTES Grants are allocated to educational requests only. Applicants must have been resident in the City of Oxford for at least three years

HOW TO APPLY To the address under Who To Apply To in writing only. Applicants are requested to send an sae

WHO TO APPLY TO Mrs K Lacey, Thomas Dawson Educational Foundation, 56 Poplar Close, Garsington, Oxford OX44 9BP

CC NO 309288   **ESTABLISHED** 1966

■ The de Avenley Foundation

This trust did not respond to CAF's request to amend its entry and, by 30 June 1998, CAF's researchers did not find financial records for later than 1995 on its file at the Charity Commission. Trusts are legally required to submit annual accounts to the Charity Commission under section 42 of the Charities Act 1993

WHAT IS FUNDED Arts, especially music and setting up concerts

WHAT IS NOT FUNDED No grants to individuals

WHO CAN BENEFIT Registered charities benefiting musicians, artists, textile workers and designers, and writers and poets

WHERE FUNDING CAN BE GIVEN Cumbria and UK

TRUSTEES P R Gibson, P J Bond, B Ainley

WHO TO APPLY TO P R Gibson, The de Avenley Foundation, Stone Cross Mansion, Ulverston, Cumbria LA12 7RY

CC NO 1048672   **ESTABLISHED** 1995

■ The De Clermont Charitable Company Limited

WHAT IS FUNDED General charitable purposes. The aid and support of those charities that are of special interest to the Founders of this Company

WHAT IS NOT FUNDED No grants to individuals

WHO CAN BENEFIT Both headquarters organisations and local organisations but with regard to the latter we do not have funds available for areas outside the North East and Scotland

WHERE FUNDING CAN BE GIVEN UK

RANGE OF GRANTS £28–£1,500

SAMPLE GRANTS £1,500 to Mawden Hall Appeal; £350 to Northumberland National Park Search and Rescue Team; £300 to Royal Star and Garter Home Benevolent Fund; £300 to Northumberland Wildlife Trust; £150 to Hunt Servants Benevolent Society; £250 to Tweed Foundation; £200 to the Berwick Nursing Home; £200 to British Red Cross Society; £200 to the Royal College of Radiologists Research Appeal; £200 to RNLI

FINANCES *Year* 1997 *Income* £33,088
Grants £24,534

TRUSTEES The Directors: Mrs E K de Clermont, H S Orpwood

WHO TO APPLY TO Mrs E K de Clermont, The De Clermont Charitable Company Limited, Morris Hall, Norham, Berwick-upon-Tweed, Northumberland TD15 2JY

CC NO 274191   **ESTABLISHED** 1977

■ The Helen and Geoffrey de Freitas Charitable Trust

WHAT IS FUNDED The Trustees wish to benefit other charitable organisations and bodies. Most of the Trust income is destined for educational charities and in the preservation of wildlife and rural England. Particularly charities working in the fields of: accommodation and housing; infrastructure development; charity or voluntary umbrella bodies; community arts and recreation; cultural heritage; conservation and environment; education and training; various community facilities and services; and advice centres

WHAT IS NOT FUNDED No medical causes or charities. No grants to individuals. Registered charities only

WHO CAN BENEFIT Mainly headquarters organisations benefiting: people of all ages; research workers; unemployed people; volunteers; those in care, fostered and adopted; parents and children; one parent families; widows and widowers; at risk groups; carers; those disadvantaged by poverty; homeless people; immigrants; refugees; those living in urban areas; victims of famine, disaster and war

WHERE FUNDING CAN BE GIVEN UK and overseas

TYPE OF GRANT Feasibility studies; one-off; project and start-up costs. Funding for one year or less will be considered

RANGE OF GRANTS £1,000–£5,000

SAMPLE GRANTS £5,000 to International Social Service for Great Britain

FINANCES *Year* 1997 *Income* £20,000
Grants £15,850

TRUSTEES R C Kirby, Frances de Freitas, Roger de Freitas

HOW TO APPLY In writing only. Initial telephone calls are not welcome. No application form or guidelines. Trustees meet only twice a year. No sae required

WHO TO APPLY TO R C Kirby, The Helen and Geoffrey de Freitas Charitable Trust, Bouverie House, 154 Fleet Street, London EC4A 2HX *Tel* 0171-353 3290 *Fax* 0171-353 4825
E-mail speechlys@speechlys.co.uk

CC NO 258597   **ESTABLISHED** 1969

■ De Haan Charitable Trust

WHAT IS FUNDED General charitable purposes

WHO CAN BENEFIT There are no restrictions on the age; professional and economic group; family situation; religion and culture; and social circumstances of; or disease or medical condition suffered by, the beneficiaries

WHERE FUNDING CAN BE GIVEN UK

RANGE OF GRANTS Below £1,000–£125,000

SAMPLE GRANTS £125,000 to Westbrook House Preparatory School; £100,000 to Dover College Preparatory School Charitable Trust; £14,000 to Age Concern, Tenterden; £11,000 to the Sidney De Haan Charity; £10,000 to Research into Ageing; £1,000 to Progressive Supranuclear Palsy Association; £1,000 to St Peter's Hospice

FINANCES *Year* 1997 *Income* £240,000
Grants £265,000

TRUSTEES P C De Haan, R M De Haan, Mrs M De Haan

168

Think carefully about every application. Is it justified?

WHO TO APPLY TO P C De Haan, De Haan Charitable Trust, The Saga Building, Middleburg Square, Folkestone, Kent CT20 1AZ
CC NO 276274   **ESTABLISHED** 1978

■ De La Rue Charitable Trust (formerly
The De La Rue Jubilee Trust)

WHAT IS FUNDED Allocation of funds, in line with the Per Cent Club, to charitable and good causes that fall within policy categories, ie education, international understanding, relief of suffering, the hospice movement and for special community projects and institutions close to De La Rue locations and within its national and international markets
WHAT IS NOT FUNDED No grants to small local charities or interests which are not in the vicinity of De La Rue industrial and business locations. No grants to individuals
WHO CAN BENEFIT Registered charities benefiting children and young adults, students and teachers. at risk groups, those disadvantaged by poverty and socially isolated people are also supported. People in hospices are benefited, such as the terminally ill and those suffering from cancer
WHERE FUNDING CAN BE GIVEN Internationally within given categories
TYPE OF GRANT Usually one-off for a specific project or part thereof
FINANCES *Year* 1996 *Grants* £300,000
TRUSTEES The Rt Hon The Earl of Limerick, KBE, DL (Chairman), Keith Knox (Transaction Systems Division), Terry McWilliams (Cash Systems Division), Nicol McGregor (Security Paper & Print Division), Stephen Hoffman Womersley (Head of Corporate Affairs)
WHO TO APPLY TO Spencer Davies, De La Rue Charitable Trust, 6 Agar Street, London WC2N 4DE
CC NO 274052   **ESTABLISHED** 1977

■ R E F De Pass Charitable Trust

This trust did not respond to CAF's request to amend its entry and, by 30 June 1998, CAF's researchers did not find financial records for later than 1995 on its file at the Charity Commission. Trusts are legally required to submit annual accounts to the Charity Commission under section 42 of the Charities Act 1993

WHAT IS FUNDED General charitable purposes
WHO CAN BENEFIT There are no restrictions on the age; professional and economic group; family situation; religion and culture; and social circumstances of; or disease or medical condition suffered by, the beneficiaries
WHERE FUNDING CAN BE GIVEN UK
TRUSTEES P R De Pass, R E F De Pass
WHO TO APPLY TO R E F De Pass, Trustee, R E F De Pass Charitable Trust, New Grove, Petworth, West Sussex GU28 0BD
CC NO 1046557   **ESTABLISHED** 1995

■ Edmund De Rothschild Charitable Trust

WHAT IS FUNDED General charitable purposes
WHAT IS NOT FUNDED No grants to individuals
WHO CAN BENEFIT There are no restrictions on the age; professional and economic group; family situation; religion and culture; and social circumstances of; or disease or medical condition suffered by, the beneficiaries

WHERE FUNDING CAN BE GIVEN UK
RANGE OF GRANTS £5–£4,197
SAMPLE GRANTS £4,197 to Exbury Gardens; £2,500 to Hampshire County Scouts Council; £2,500 to Royal Artillery Museum Fund; £2,481 to Wessex Heartbeat; £1,000 to Clean Rivers Trust
FINANCES *Year* 1997 *Income* £24,242 *Grants* £20,066
TRUSTEES E L de Rothschild, N de Rothschild, Rothschild Trust Co Ltd
NOTES The Trust supports only those charities which are of special interest to the Trustees
WHO TO APPLY TO The Trustees, Edmund de Rothschild Charitable Trust, PO Box 185, New Court, St Swithins Lane, London EC4P 4DU
CC NO 247815   **ESTABLISHED** 1966

■ The Leopold De Rothschild Charitable Trust

WHAT IS FUNDED General charitable purposes
WHO CAN BENEFIT Registered charities only. There are no restrictions on the age; professional and economic group; family situation; religion and culture; and social circumstances of; or disease or medical condition suffered by, the beneficiaries
WHERE FUNDING CAN BE GIVEN UK
RANGE OF GRANTS £600–£25,100
SAMPLE GRANTS £25,100 to English Chamber Orchestra and Music Society; £5,200 to American Museum in Britain; £5,000 to Saddlers Wells; £5,000 to Jewish Child Day; £5,000 to Child Southbank Foundation; £4,450 to Royal College of Music; £1,865 to Liberal Jewish Synagogue; £1,550 to Exbury Gardens; £1,000 to Border Crossings; £1,000 to Merchant Navy
FINANCES *Year* 1997 *Income* £62,278 *Grants* £78,578
TRUSTEES Rothschild Trust Corporation Ltd
NOTES Only registered charities are considered
WHO TO APPLY TO The Leopold De Rothschild Charitable Trust, Rothschild Trust Corporation Ltd, New Court, St Swithin's Lane, London EC4P 4DU
CC NO 212611   **ESTABLISHED** 1959

■ The Margaret De Sousa Deiro Fund

WHAT IS FUNDED Treatment, care, rehabilitation, and after-care of gentlewomen suffering from TB or other diseases
WHO CAN BENEFIT Women suffering from TB or other diseases
WHERE FUNDING CAN BE GIVEN UK
TYPE OF GRANT One-off
RANGE OF GRANTS £100–£300
FINANCES *Year* 1996–97 *Income* £73,313 *Grants* £65,598
TRUSTEES Mrs D E Hood, A P P Honigmann, W R I Crewdson
HOW TO APPLY In writing through a local authority or hospital social worker
WHO TO APPLY TO The Secretaries, The Margaret de Sousa Deiro Fund, c/o Messrs Field Fisher Waterhouse, 41 Vine Street, London EC3N 2AA
CC NO 210615   **ESTABLISHED** 1927

Does the trust you have chosen match your needs? Haphazard applications waste postage and time

169

■ The De Vere Hunt Charitable Trust

WHAT IS FUNDED Charities working in the fields of: alternative healthcare; respite care; health related volunteer schemes; adoption and fostering services; holiday and outings; and playschemes

WHAT IS NOT FUNDED No grants to individuals, gap year students, student grants, or for expeditions or scholarships

WHO CAN BENEFIT Charitable organisations benefiting young adults; those in care, fostered and adopted; at risk groups; ex-offenders and those at risk of offending; and homeless people

WHERE FUNDING CAN BE GIVEN England with preference for London and Oxford

TYPE OF GRANT One-off and recurrent grants will be considered. Funding may be given for up to one year

RANGE OF GRANTS £500–£5,000, typical grant £1,000

SAMPLE GRANTS £2,000 to Oxford Homeless Medical Fund towards new premises; £2,000 to Macmillan Cancer Relief; £1,500 to ANWAB for computer for braille; £1,000 to Osteopathic Centre for Children towards new building; £1,000 to The Salvation Army

FINANCES *Year* 1995–96 *Income* £15,000
Grants £10,500

TRUSTEES P A de Vere Hunt

HOW TO APPLY In writing only. No reply without an sae

WHO TO APPLY TO P De Vere Hunt, The De Vere Hunt Charitable Trust, Thrupp Farm, Littleworth, Faringdon, Oxfordshire SN7 8JY

CC NO 285553   **ESTABLISHED** 1982

■ The Miriam Dean Refugee Trust Fund

WHAT IS FUNDED For the benefit of such persons abroad whether orphans, sick, aged or otherwise, who are in need of assistance by reason of war, disaster, pestilence or otherwise, or any organisation engaged in the relief of suffering humanity abroad as the Trustees in their absolute discretion select. Projects are usually only considered if personally investigated by Trustees

WHAT IS NOT FUNDED No direct grants to individuals for scholarships or travel abroad etc, or to the major international aid agencies

WHO CAN BENEFIT No particular preferences, however, orphans; the sick; the aged; refugees; victims of disasters, war and famine will be considered, but individual UK residents excluded

WHERE FUNDING CAN BE GIVEN Mainly Tanzania and India

FINANCES *Year* 1997 *Income* £177,313
Grants £180,577

TRUSTEES H Capon, T Dorey, V Dorey, J Budd, G Livermore

WHO TO APPLY TO The Rev Dorey, The Miriam Dean Refugee Trust Fund, The Vicarage, Manaccan, Helston, Cornwall TR12 6HA

CC NO 269655   **ESTABLISHED** 1964

■ Dearne Valley Community Forum

WHAT IS FUNDED Projects which promote self-help, community regeneration, enterprise and collaborative ways of working particularly focusing on safer communities initiatives, anti-poverty initiatives and start-up grants. Support will also be given to conservation and campaigning, pre-school education; arts, culture and recreation; aftercare; counselling on health issues; advice and information on housing and other charitable purposes

WHAT IS NOT FUNDED No support for services which are the responsibility of a statutory body, mainstream school activities, or private and religious activity

WHO CAN BENEFIT Residents of the Dearne Valley area. Organisations benefiting: unemployed people; volunteers, at risk groups; carers, disabled people; those disadvantaged by poverty; ex-offenders and those at risk of offending; socially isolated people; and victims of abuse, crime and domestic violence. There are no restrictions on the age or family situation of the beneficiaries or on their disease or medical condition

WHERE FUNDING CAN BE GIVEN Dearne Valley, including the Bolton-On-Dearne, Goldthorpe and Thurnscoe areas of Barnsley and the Conisbrough, Denaby and Mexborough areas of Doncaster and Swinton, Kilnhurst, Wath and Bramron areas of Rotherham

TYPE OF GRANT One-off, recurring, core costs, feasibility studies, projects, research, running costs, salaries and start-up costs will be considered. Funding may be for up to three years

RANGE OF GRANTS Typical grant £500–£3,000, some grants of up to £8,000

FINANCES *Year* 1998 *Income* £90,000

HOW TO APPLY Telephone for an application form

WHO TO APPLY TO Ms J C Bibby, Secretary, Dearne Valley Community Forum, Manvers House, PO Box 109, Wath Upon Dearne, Rotherham, South Yorkshire S63 7YZ *Tel* 01709 760207

CC NO 0164193   **ESTABLISHED** 1997

■ Debmar Benevolent Trust Limited

WHAT IS FUNDED Jewish charitable purposes

WHO CAN BENEFIT To benefit Jewish people

WHERE FUNDING CAN BE GIVEN UK

FINANCES *Year* 1995 *Income* £273,764
Grants £139,499

TRUSTEES G Klein, H Olsberg, M Weisz

HOW TO APPLY To the address under Who To Apply To in writing

WHO TO APPLY TO Johnny Myers, Debmar Benevolent Trust Limited, Hafner Hoff & Co, 3rd Floor, Manchester House, 86 Princess Street, Manchester M1 6NP

CC NO 283065   **ESTABLISHED** 1979

■ Debtors' Relief Funds Charity

WHAT IS FUNDED Grants awarded to appropriate organisations who have applied in current year. Social care professional bodies will be considered

WHAT IS NOT FUNDED Not to be applied in relief of rates, taxes or other public funds, no grants to individuals

WHO CAN BENEFIT Organisations benefiting young adults, ex-offenders and those at risk of offending. General preference given to innovatory programmes or capital projects

WHERE FUNDING CAN BE GIVEN England and Wales

TYPE OF GRANT Capital, one-off, project and start-up costs. Funding for more than three years will be considered

RANGE OF GRANTS Most grants will be £1,000 or less

SAMPLE GRANTS £7,000 to National Association for the Care and Rehabilitation of Offenders for the welfare of ex-offenders to reintegrate in to society; £1,000 to Cotswold Canals Trust helping Category D prisoners restore canal and towpath; £500 to Apex Trust for helping ex-offenders prepare for and find work; £500 to Cleanbreak Theatre Company to help women ex-offenders to build self esteem; £500 to Fine Cell Work helping inmates earn income by making products in their cells

FINANCES *Year* 1997 *Income* £16,900 *Grants* £14,500

TRUSTEES Sir John B Riddell, Bt, (President), The Earl of Cranbrook, Major the Earl of Romney, Mrs R Battye, G J Hans Hamilton, J C Marsham, Lady Flora Gathorne-Hardy

HOW TO APPLY Applications should be placed before the end of February. Applications are acknowledged

WHO TO APPLY TO Mrs M R Cox, Debtors' Relief Funds Charity, 34 Carew Close, Old Coulsdon, Surrey CR5 1QS *Tel* 0181-668 2643

CC NO 234144   **ESTABLISHED** 1842

■ The Lord Deedes of Aldington Charitable Trust

WHAT IS FUNDED General charitable purposes. The Trust funds international relief and development projects worldwide with special emphasis on Africa

WHAT IS NOT FUNDED No support for projects not concerned with the developing world

WHO CAN BENEFIT People in developing countries worldwide, especially Africa, who are: disadvantaged by poverty; suffering from tropical diseases; refugees; victims of famine, man-made or natural disasters, and war

WHERE FUNDING CAN BE GIVEN Overseas, developing countries worldwide, especially Africa

TYPE OF GRANT One-off, recurring or core costs. Funding is available for up to three years

TRUSTEES J Armitage, A Colman, L Whaley

HOW TO APPLY No initial telephone calls. No application form is available. Guidelines are available. There are no deadlines for applications. An sae would be appreciated

WHO TO APPLY TO Mrs A Colman, Lord Deedes of Aldington Charitable Trust, Gate House Farm, Fairmans Lane, Brenchley, Kent TN12 7AD *Tel* 01892 722912

CC NO 1069234   **ESTABLISHED** 1998

■ Deeping St James United Charities

WHAT IS FUNDED Education, medical equipment for a health centre, relief in need, relief in sickness, community initiatives/public purposes

WHO CAN BENEFIT Individuals and organisations benefiting: children, young adults and students; at risk groups; those disadvantaged by poverty; and the sick. There is no restriction on the disease or medical condition suffered by the beneficiaries

WHERE FUNDING CAN BE GIVEN The Ecclesiastical Parish of St James, Deeping

FINANCES *Year* 1996 *Income* £30,761 *Grants* £15,551

TRUSTEES The Vicar of Deeping St James, three appointees of Deeping St James Parish Council, two appointees of South Kesteven District Council, two co-opted

HOW TO APPLY To the address under Who To Apply To in writing. Applications are considered by the Trustees in March, June, September and December

WHO TO APPLY TO R Moulsher, Deeping St James United Charities, 3 High Street, Market Deeping, Peterborough PE6 8AD

CC NO 248848   **ESTABLISHED** 1966

■ Charity of Theresa Harriet Mary Delacour

WHAT IS FUNDED Catholic charities in North-East England

WHO CAN BENEFIT Catholic charities

WHERE FUNDING CAN BE GIVEN Mainly North East England

SAMPLE GRANTS £3,000 to Catholic Care North East for School Community Project; £3,000 to St Peter's Community Hall, Gateshead; £3,000 to St Thomas's Church, Wolsingham towards central heating; £2,500 to St Edmund Campion School Gateshead towards the 'Machine Tools Project'; £2,500 to Hexham and Newcastle Diocesan Deaf Service for the 'Three Year Project'; £2,500 to Hexham and Newcastle Diocesan Deaf Service for the 'The Garden Project'; £2,000 to Society of St Vincent de Paul for industrial washing machine for Matt Talbot Hostel; £2,000 to Catholic Youth Centre, Sunderland; £2,000 to St Anne's Parish Hall, Sunderland; £1,750 to Society of St Vincent de Paul for freezer and television for the 'Pop In' Centre

FINANCES *Year* 1997 *Income* £51,884 *Grants* £30,250

TRUSTEES J W Dolman, Lady Patricia Talbot of Malahide, Mrs Z F A Richards

WHO TO APPLY TO J W Dolman, Charity of Theresa Harriet Mary Delacour, Messrs Bircham & Co, 1 Dean Farrar Street, London SW1H 0DY

CC NO 222292   **ESTABLISHED** 1926

■ The William Delafield Charitable Trust

WHAT IS FUNDED General at Trustees' discretion, but where charity's work is known to the Trustees. Churches, church buildings and architectural research

WHAT IS NOT FUNDED No grants for expeditions or scholarships

WHO CAN BENEFIT Archival establishments and architectural research workers

WHERE FUNDING CAN BE GIVEN Generally Bedfordshire, Buckinghamshire and Oxfordshire

TYPE OF GRANT One-off and recurrent

RANGE OF GRANTS £3,500–£10,000, typical grant £4,000–£5,000

SAMPLE GRANTS £10,000 to All Saints Church, Leighton Buzzard for spire appeal

FINANCES *Year* 1996–97 *Income* £22,924 *Grants* £21,723

TRUSTEES W H Delafield, R F B Gilman, C J Gee

HOW TO APPLY **Grants only given to charities known to the Trustees**

WHO TO APPLY TO MacIntyre Hudson, The William Delafield Charitable Trust, 31 Castle Street, High Wycombe, Buckinghamshire HP13 6RU

CC NO 328022   **ESTABLISHED** 1988

■ The Delfont Foundation

WHAT IS FUNDED General charitable purposes

WHO CAN BENEFIT There are no restrictions on the age; professional and economic group; family

situation; religion and culture; and social circumstances of; or disease or medical condition suffered by, the beneficiaries

WHERE FUNDING CAN BE GIVEN UK

TYPE OF GRANT Usually one-off for specific purposes

FINANCES *Year* 1996 *Income* £40,668
  Grants £25,300

TRUSTEES Lady Delfont, D Delfont, Miss J Delfont, Miss S Delfont, P Ohrenstein, G Parsons

HOW TO APPLY At any time

WHO TO APPLY TO The Delfont Foundation, 17 Lewes Road, Haywards Heath, West Sussex RH17 7SB

CC NO 298047   **ESTABLISHED** 1987

■ The Delius Trust

WHAT IS FUNDED To promote the music of Delius by financing recordings; by giving grants for performances where the making of profit is not an object; by financing the issue of a uniform edition of Delius' music; acquiring material for the Trust's Archives; the preserving and making available to the public and improving and diffusing knowledge of his life and works

WHO CAN BENEFIT Individuals and organisations benefiting young adults, older people and musicians

WHERE FUNDING CAN BE GIVEN UK and overseas

TYPE OF GRANT Project funding for more than three years will be considered

FINANCES *Year* 1997 *Income* £143,420
  Grants £51,950

TRUSTEES Musicians Benevolent Fund (Representative: Helen Faulkner), David Lloyd-Jones, Martin Williams

PUBLICATIONS *A Descriptive Catalogue of the Works of Frederick Delius* by Robert Threlfall. *A Descriptive Catalogue with Checklists of the Letters and Related Documents in the Delius Collection of the Grainger Museum, University of Melbourne, Australia* by Rachel Lowe. A supplementary catalogue by Robert Threlfall. *The Collected Edition of the works of Frederick Delius*. Brochure – *Delius, 1862–1934: A Short Guide to his Life and Works*

HOW TO APPLY In writing for consideration by the Trustees and the Panel of Advisers (Felix Aprahamian, Dr Lional Carley, Robert Montgomery, Robert Threlfall). Notes on application procedure available from the Secretary

WHO TO APPLY TO Marjorie Dickinson, Secretary to the Trust, The Delius Trust, 16 Ogle Street, London W1P 8JB *Tel* 0171-436 4816 *Fax* 0171-637 4307
  E-mail Delius_Trust@compuserve.com
  Web Site www.delius.org.uk

CC NO 207324   **ESTABLISHED** 1935

■ The Delves Charitable Trust

WHAT IS FUNDED General charitable purposes. To support approved charities by annual contributions

WHAT IS NOT FUNDED Registered charities only. Expeditions, scholarships and personal sponsorship is definitely not funded

WHO CAN BENEFIT General approved charities. There are no restrictions on the age; professional and economic group; family situation; religion and culture; and social circumstances of; or disease or medical condition suffered by, the beneficiaries

WHERE FUNDING CAN BE GIVEN UK

RANGE OF GRANTS £100–£19,000

SAMPLE GRANTS £19,000 to British Heart Foundation; £10,000 to Intermediate Technology; £10,000 to SEQUAL; £9,000 to Liverpool School of Tropical Medicine; £8,000 to Quaker Peace and Service; £7,000 to Water Aid; £6,000 to National Society for Cancer Relief (Macmillan Nurses)

FINANCES *Year* 1998 *Income* £206,831
  Grants £161,100

TRUSTEES Mrs M Breeze, J Breeze, G Breeze, Miss E Breeze, Dr C Breeze, R Harriman

PUBLICATIONS Annual Report is included in the Accounts

HOW TO APPLY This Trust states that it does not respond to unsolicited applications

WHO TO APPLY TO R Harriman, Trust Administrator, The Delves Charitable Trust, New Guild House, 45 Great Charles Street, Queensway, Birmingham B3 2LX *Tel* 0121-212 2222

CC NO 231860   **ESTABLISHED** 1922

■ Denman Charitable Trust

WHAT IS FUNDED General charitable purposes

WHO CAN BENEFIT There are no restrictions on the age; professional and economic group; family situation; religion and culture; and social circumstances of; or disease or medical condition suffered by, the beneficiaries

WHERE FUNDING CAN BE GIVEN UK

RANGE OF GRANTS £30–£100

SAMPLE GRANTS £100 to St John's College, Cambridge; £100 to Shelter; £75 to Ladies' Home; £50 to Association of Jewish Refugees in Great Britain; £50 to Dr Barnardos

FINANCES *Year* 1997 *Income* £17,746
  Grants £15,629

TRUSTEES P F A Denman, Miss F M-C Denman

NOTES Funds are fully allocated or committed to supporting charities and individuals of special interest to the Trustees

HOW TO APPLY This Trust states that it does not respond to unsolicited applications

WHO TO APPLY TO F J Mulhearn, Denman Charitable Trust, 37 Great James Street, London WC1N 3HB

CC NO 265601   **ESTABLISHED** 1965

■ Denman Charitable Trust

WHAT IS FUNDED Medical research, health and welfare

WHO CAN BENEFIT To benefit: research workers; at risk groups; those disadvantaged by poverty; and socially isolated people. There is no restriction on the disease or medical condition suffered by the beneficiaries

WHERE FUNDING CAN BE GIVEN UK, especially the South West of England

TYPE OF GRANT Research

RANGE OF GRANTS £42–£19,167

SAMPLE GRANTS £19,167 to University of Bristol for Cancer Research Campaign to appoint an organiser; £10,000 to Pathway Star for hostel renovations; £5,000 to University of Bristol for oral cancer studies; £2,000 to Julian House hostel for the homeless; £1,000 to SCEP to assist Asian women in the St Paul's area; £500 to Gloucestershire Society; £500 to the Dolphin Society; £200 to Radcliffe Hospital for Neurological Research Fund; £200 to Cancer Research Campaign; £200 to British Heart Foundation

FINANCES *Year* 1996–97 *Income* £46,605
  Grants £39,536

TRUSTEES A G Denman, Mrs D M Denman, D J Marsh

HOW TO APPLY To the address under Who To Apply To in writing

WHO TO APPLY TO Mrs D M Denman, Denman Charitable Trust, c/o Steeple House, 59 Old Market Street, Bristol BS2 0HF

CC NO 326532   **ESTABLISHED** 1983

■ Dent Charitable Trust

WHAT IS FUNDED General charitable purposes

WHO CAN BENEFIT There are no restrictions on the age; professional and economic group; family situation; religion and culture; and social circumstances of; or disease or medical condition suffered by, the beneficiaries

WHERE FUNDING CAN BE GIVEN UK

RANGE OF GRANTS £25–£30,000

SAMPLE GRANTS £30,000 to British Technion Society; £26,000 to Friends of the Hebrew University; £7,000 to Jerusalem Foundation; £6,079 to Glyndebourne; £3,000 to British ORT; £3,000 to Sarah Herzog Memorial Hospital; £3,000 to Shaare Zedek Medical Centre; £3,000 to Save the Children; £3,000 to MIND; £2,000 to JNF Charitable Fund

FINANCES *Year* 1997 *Income* £70,233
Grants £91,054

TRUSTEES C E Shanbury, C S Dent, J P M Dent

NOTES The Trust regularly supports the following organisations: the Friends of the Hebrew University of Jerusalem, Children and Youth Aliyah Committee for Great Britain, Norwood Home for Jewish Children, the British Technion Society, the Society of Friends of Jewish Refugees, the Home and Hospital for Jewish Incurables, Joint Palestine Appeal and the Relief of the Jewish Poor Registered

HOW TO APPLY **This Trust states that it does not respond to unsolicited applications**

WHO TO APPLY TO C E Shanbury, Dent Charitable Trust, c/o Robson Rhodes, The Galleria, Station Road, Crawley, West Sussex RH10 1HY

CC NO 271512   **ESTABLISHED** 1976

■ The Denton Charitable Trust

WHAT IS FUNDED In practice, particular interest in children, cancer charities, research, care, the arts and local causes

WHO CAN BENEFIT Small local and national organisations particularly interested in benefiting: children; research workers; at risk groups; those disadvantaged by poverty; socially isolated people and beneficiaries suffering from cancer

WHERE FUNDING CAN BE GIVEN UK with preference to West Yorkshire

TYPE OF GRANT One-off preferred

RANGE OF GRANTS £150–£1,000

SAMPLE GRANTS £5,000 to Yorkshire Cancer Research; £5,000 to St Michael's Hospice; £5,000 to Martin House children's Hospice; £5,000 to the Stroke Association; £5,000 to NSPCC; £1,000 to Marie Curie, Ilkley; £1,000 to STA Tall Ships (Liverpool); £992 to One Hundred Hours, Todmorden; £500 to The Warren Centre, Hull; £500 to Base 10, Leeds

FINANCES *Year* 1997 *Income* £38,634
Grants £3,000

TRUSTEES J A J Wood, S J Wood, T C J Wood, D C Wilson

NOTES Grants are made in November and May

HOW TO APPLY In writing

WHO TO APPLY TO Mrs S J Wood, Trustee and Secretary, The Denton Charitable Trust, c/o Garbutt & Elliott, Chartered Accountants, Monkgate House, 44 Monkgate, York YO3 7HF
Tel 01904 654656 *Fax* 01904 610015

CC NO 1054546   **ESTABLISHED** 1996

■ Derbyshire Asian Horticultural Resource Training Initiative

WHAT IS FUNDED General charitable purposes, particularly the furtherance of the education of Derby residents aged 24 or less, the relief of Derby residents aged 24 or less in cases of financial need, hardship or distress by virtue of their youth or social economic circumstances

WHO CAN BENEFIT Derby residents aged 24 or less who are at risk, disadvantaged by poverty or socially isolated. Students may be considered

WHERE FUNDING CAN BE GIVEN In practice Derby

FINANCES *Year* 1995 *Income* £59,800
Grants £16,343

TRUSTEES M Akhtar, M Ansar

WHO TO APPLY TO A Passmore, Derbyshire Asian Horticultural Resource Training Initiative, Beightons, 192 Duffield Road, Derby DE22 1BJ

CC NO 1046158   **ESTABLISHED** 1993

■ The Derbyshire Churches and Chapels Preservation Trust

WHAT IS FUNDED The restoration, preservation, repair and maintenance of churches and chapels in the area Where Funding Can Be Given

WHERE FUNDING CAN BE GIVEN Derbyshire

TYPE OF GRANT Buildings

RANGE OF GRANTS £500–£2,000

SAMPLE GRANTS £2,000 to St Giles, Killamarsh; £2,000 to St Michael's, Sutton on the Hill; £1,000 to All Saints, Glossop; £1,000 to St Mary Magdalene, Creswell; £1,000 to St Michael and All Angels, Alvaston

FINANCES *Year* 1996–97 *Income* £20,171
Grants £10,044

TRUSTEES W A W Bemrose, Mgr M Cummins, Ven D C Garnett, MA, Ven I Gatford, AKC, M A B Mallender, LLB, Rev Canon R J Ross, MA, P Strange, PhD, R C Theobald, BA

HOW TO APPLY Applications should be made on a form available from the address under Who To Apply To. There are meetings of the grants panel in April and October

WHO TO APPLY TO Dr P Strange, Trustee, The Derbyshire Churches and Chapels Preservation Trust, 1 Greenhill, Wirksworth, Derbyshire DE4 4EN

CC NO 1010953   **ESTABLISHED** 1992

■ Derbyshire Community Foundation

WHAT IS FUNDED Community groups and voluntary organisations working to tackle disadvantage and improve quality of life. Likely priority themes as follows: supporting families; getting back to work; health and well being; young people; helping groups work; and creative community

WHAT IS NOT FUNDED No grants to individuals; work that replaces statutory funding; animal welfare; party politics or religious evangelism; general appeals; or national charities (unless it is a local project)

Does the trust you have chosen match your needs? Haphazard applications waste postage and time

173

WHO CAN BENEFIT Voluntary groups and volunteers and the people they work with in Derbyshire across a wide spectrum of activity tackling disadvantage and promoting quality of life. Organisations benefiting unemployed people. There is no restriction on the age, family situation, religion and culture of, or on the disease or medical condition suffered by the beneficiaries. There may be few restrictions on their social circumstances

WHERE FUNDING CAN BE GIVEN Derby City and Derbyshire. We have exceptionally made grants outside the county for one donor but it required special arrangement and is unlikely to be repeated

TYPE OF GRANT Usually one-off, though depending on the programme and donor's wishes, we may give more than one grant to the same group for different projects or items. Capital, core costs, feasibility studies, research, running costs, salaries and start-up costs. Funding for up to one year will be considered

RANGE OF GRANTS Usually up to £1,000

SAMPLE GRANTS £5,712 to Third Ware for skills training and confidence building for socially excluded people and neighbourhood crime prevention forums; £4,797 to Derby Domestic Violence Action Group for training; production of directory; preventative work with perpetrators and young people; £3,163 to Alternatives Activity Centre for a range of imaginative work with adults with learning disabilities; £2,520 to St Bartholemews Project for good community development and training; £2,214 to New Life Christians Centre for support for homeless, especially young homeless people; £2,000 to Anjuman Kharateen to BSL training for non-English speaking mothers of deaf Asian children; £2,000 to Sebian Orthodox Community Group for conversion of premises for use by refugees, mostly Bosnian children and elderly people; £2,000 to East Midlands Christain Fellowship for brilliant outreach work with socially excluded youngsters; £1,739 to Karma Nirvana to women's health day and swimming classes for Asian women; £1,700 to Sports 2000 for kit, equipment and support for inner city sports group

FINANCES *Year* 1997–98 *Income* £368,269 *Grants* £81,355

TRUSTEES B A Ashby (Chair), B Archbold, C J Baker, R Beck, P R Binks, A Blackwood, A Borkowski, D Forman, G R Ingram, K Martin, M McGlade, D G W Moss, E Quicke, J Rivers, C E Wilkinson

NOTES Nearly all grantmaking to date has been administration of grant programmes for other donors, who set their own criteria. By 1999 we hope to make our first grants using our own policy, with funds generated by our infant endowment fund

HOW TO APPLY Please contact our office. It is worth phoning first to check that we have a pot of money suitable for your needs. We have a standard form and we will tell you the deadline for current round. Grants are usually made in two annual rounds, with applications invited from April and October

WHO TO APPLY TO Hilary Gilbert, Director, Derbyshire Community Foundation, The Arkwright Suite, University of Derby, Kedleston Road, Derby DE22 1EB *Tel* 01332 621348 *Fax* 01332 621348

CC NO 1039485 **ESTABLISHED** 1994

■ J N Derbyshire Trust

WHAT IS FUNDED General charitable purposes, including the promotion of health; the development of physical improvement; the advancement of education; and the relief of poverty, distress and sickness. Local charities receive preferential consideration

WHAT IS NOT FUNDED No grants to individuals. Costs of study are not funded

WHO CAN BENEFIT Organisations with charitable status. There are no restrictions on the age; professional and economic group; family situation; religion and culture; and social circumstances of; or disease or medical condition suffered by, the beneficiaries

WHERE FUNDING CAN BE GIVEN The City of Nottingham and Nottinghamshire

TYPE OF GRANT Buildings, capital, core costs, project, research, recurring and running costs, salaries, and start-up costs will be considered. Funding may be given for up to three years

FINANCES *Year* 1998 *Income* £170,171 *Grants* £150,500

TRUSTEES The Council

HOW TO APPLY Obtain application form from the address under Who To Apply To

WHO TO APPLY TO P R Moore, FCA, J N Derbyshire Trust, Foxhall Lodge, Gregory Boulevard, Nottingham, Nottinghamshire NG7 6LH *Tel* 0115-955 2000 *Fax* 0115-969 1043

CC NO 231907 **ESTABLISHED** 1944

■ The Richard Desmond Charitable Trust

WHAT IS FUNDED The relief of poverty and sickness, particularly among children and such other policies as the Trustees shall determine

WHO CAN BENEFIT Organisations benefiting children, the sick and those disadvantaged by poverty. There is no restriction on the disease or medical condition of the the beneficiaries

WHERE FUNDING CAN BE GIVEN UK and overseas

TYPE OF GRANT At the discretion of the Trustees

FINANCES *Year* 1996 *Income* £87,100 *Grants* £84,607

TRUSTEES R C Desmond, Mrs J Desmond

WHO TO APPLY TO S Smith, Secretary, The Richard Desmond Charitable Trust, c/o The Northern and Shell Tower, City Harbour, London E14 9GL

CC NO 1014352 **ESTABLISHED** 1992

■ Devon Association for the Blind

WHAT IS FUNDED Direct help for individual blind people and self help groups

WHAT IS NOT FUNDED Financial grants restricted to people who are registered visually handicapped

WHO CAN BENEFIT To benefit those registered blind or registered partially sighted

WHERE FUNDING CAN BE GIVEN County of Devon less the cities of Exeter and Plymouth

FINANCES *Year* 1995 *Income* £38,124 *Grants* £57,335

TRUSTEES Chairman and Vice-Chairman

WHO TO APPLY TO Mrs B A Barnes, MBE, Devon County Association for the Blind, Station House, Holman Way, Topsham, Exeter, Devon EX3 0EN

CC NO 203044 **ESTABLISHED** 1928

■ Devon Community Foundation

WHAT IS FUNDED Support primarily for voluntary and community organisations, particularly those working to relieve the effects of poverty and disadvantage

WHAT IS NOT FUNDED No funding for: individuals, religious causes, statutory agencies or responsibilities, party political activities, medical research, animal welfare or projects outside Devon

WHO CAN BENEFIT Voluntary and community groups in Devon benefiting: carers; disabled people; those disadvantaged by poverty; homeless and socially isolated people; and those living in both rural and urban areas

WHERE FUNDING CAN BE GIVEN County of Devon only

TYPE OF GRANT Predominantly one-off small grants for core costs. Running costs and start-up costs will be considered. Funding may be given for up to one year

RANGE OF GRANTS £50–£2,000 at present, typical grant £200

SAMPLE GRANTS These are the Foundation's nine inaugural grants made in May 1998; £2,000 to Devon Co-operative Development Agency – specialist training throughout Devon in setting up Credit Unions for assistance with travel costs; £1,000 to Hamoaze House, Plymouth towards a community centre to support families of those recovering from drug addiction; £1,000 to the Beckly centre, Plymouth for musical instruments for children with a learning or physical disability; £650 to Exeter Homes Committee for a rent deposit and loan guarantee scheme for homeless people; £250 to Bradford Pre-School, West Devon for new chairs and tables for the children in this rural community playgroup; £250 to Age Concern, Seaton for basic equipment for pop-in centre for elderly people; £100 to Dawlish Gardens Trust towards garden equipment for this sheltered working environment for people with disabilities; £100 to Forget-Me-Not, North Devon for equipment for respite care home in support of carers of mentally handicapped adults; £50 to Lapford Youth Club, Mid Devon for sports equipment for young people

FINANCES *Year* 1998–99 *Income* £49,000 *Grants* £20,000

TRUSTEES Sir Ian Amory, The Countess of Arran, M H Gee, G Gilbert, G Halliday, R Harris, Sir Peter Laurence, T Legood, D Macklin, N Maxwell-Lawford, I Mercer, W Pybus (Chairman), S Rous, G Sturtridge, J Trafford, N J Wollen

PUBLICATIONS Annual Report and Accounts

NOTES The Foundation was launched in May 1998 at present it can only offer small grants

HOW TO APPLY Telephone calls welcome. Application form and current guidelines are available on request. No sae required

WHO TO APPLY TO Mrs A Sanders, Director, Devon Community Foundation, PO Box 272, Exeter, Devon EX1 1YB *Tel* 01392 252252 *Fax* 01392 252254 *E-mail* 101717.2615@compuserve.com

CC NO 1057923   **ESTABLISHED** 1996

■ Devon Local Development Agencies Forum

WHAT IS FUNDED Improvement of the efficiency of the administration of Devon Charities, in particular, by the provision of advice, management and technical support, training facilities and services to charitable organisations within Devon

WHO CAN BENEFIT Charitable organisations. There are no restrictions on the age; professional and economic group; family situation; religion and culture; and social circumstances of; or disease or medical condition suffered by, the beneficiaries

WHERE FUNDING CAN BE GIVEN Devon

FINANCES *Year* 1996–97 *Income* £75,359 *Grants* £23,125

WHO TO APPLY TO Devon Local Development Agencies Forum, c/o Wat Tyler House, King William Street, Exeter, Devon EX4 6PD

CC NO 1060153   **ESTABLISHED** 1996

■ The Duke of Devonshire's Charitable Trust

WHAT IS FUNDED General charitable purposes. Registered charities only

WHO CAN BENEFIT Registered charities only. There are no restrictions on the age, professional and economic group, family situation, religion and culture, and social circumstances of, or disease or medical condition suffered by, the beneficiaries

WHERE FUNDING CAN BE GIVEN UK and overseas

TYPE OF GRANT Buildings, capital, core costs, endowments, feasibility studies, interest free loans, one-off, project, research, recurring costs, running costs, salaries and start-up costs will be considered. Funding can be given for any length of time

RANGE OF GRANTS £50–£322,325

FINANCES *Year* 1997 *Income* £498,879 *Grants* £428,220

TRUSTEES The Marquess of Hartington, R G Beckett, N W Smith

WHO TO APPLY TO Messrs Currey & Co, Solicitors, The Duke of Devonshire's Charitable Trust, 21 Buckingham Gate, London SW1E 6LS

CC NO 213519   **ESTABLISHED** 1949

■ The Sandy Dewhirst Charitable Trust

WHAT IS FUNDED Preservation and restoration of church buildings; community service. Relieving poor persons, particularly those who are or were connected with I J Dewhirst Holdings Limited and their dependants

WHO CAN BENEFIT To benefit, in particular, those connected with I J Dewhirst Holdings Limited and their dependants who are in need

WHERE FUNDING CAN BE GIVEN UK, particularly the North and East of Yorkshire

RANGE OF GRANTS £500–£10,000

SAMPLE GRANTS £10,000 to Driffield Parochial Church Council; £5,000 to Bramcote School Centenary Appeal; £5,000 to an Individual; £5,000 to the Cornerstone Trust; £5,000 to York Minster Fund; £2,500 to Driffield Parish Church Tower Appeal; £2,500 to Driffield and District Community Service; £2,500 to The Salvation Army; £2,000 to Nafferton Parochial Church Council; £2,000 to the Army Benevolent Fund

FINANCES *Year* 1996 *Income* £52,314 *Grants* £56,500

TRUSTEES T C Dewhirst, M S Dewhirst, J A R Dewhirst, P J Howell

HOW TO APPLY To the address under Who To Apply To in writing

WHO TO APPLY TO Paul J Howell, Trustees' Solicitor, The Sandy Dewhirst Charitable Trust, Sovereign House, South Parade, Leeds LS1 1HQ

CC NO 279161   **ESTABLISHED** 1979

■ The Laduma Dhamecha Charitable Trust

WHAT IS FUNDED General charitable purposes

WHO CAN BENEFIT Organisations. There are no restrictions on the age; professional and economic group; family situation; religion and culture; and social circumstances of; or disease or medical condition suffered by, the beneficiaries

WHERE FUNDING CAN BE GIVEN UK and overseas

FINANCES *Year* 1997 *Income* £65,748
Grants £11,567

HOW TO APPLY To the address under Who To Apply To in writing

WHO TO APPLY TO Pradip Dhamecha, Trustee, The Laduma Dhamecha Charitable Trust, 2 Hathaway Close, Stanmore, Middlesex HA7 3NR

CC NO 328678   **ESTABLISHED** 1990

■ Diageo Foundation

WHAT IS FUNDED Focus areas which reflect the needs of communities where skills and business knowledge contribute to make the most positive impact on society. Support concentrates on the following: (a) Water of Life – a humanitarian and environmental initiative supporting projects with a water theme; (b) Skills for Life – giving people of all ages and cultures practical opportunities to gain skills which enable them to fulfil their potential and improve their life prospects; (c) Local Citizens – (i) local regeneration in locations where our business has a major presence and where we are able to make a difference on issues such as homelessness, unemployment and disability, (ii) culture with emphasis on local community arts initiatives; (d) Our People – concentrating on employee involvement and matched giving

WHAT IS NOT FUNDED The main areas consider to be outside the Foundation's guidelines are: (a) organisations which are not registered charities; (b) individuals; (c) loans or business finance; (d) medical charities or hospitals; (e) animal welfare; (f) endowment funds; (g) expeditions or overseas travel; (h) political organisations; (i) promotion of religion

WHO CAN BENEFIT Excluded and disadvantaged people who, with support, can help themselves to transform their own lives

WHERE FUNDING CAN BE GIVEN UK

TYPE OF GRANT Kick start funding to get business and people involved. There will be a three year limit on any funding commitment

HOW TO APPLY In writing to the address below. The Foundation will require appropriate reports and evaluation on the outcomes of the project or organisation which has been funded, identifying the effectiveness and benefits to both community and business

WHO TO APPLY TO Julie Hodsden, Administrator, Diageo Foundation, 8 Henrietta Place, London W1M 9AG *Tel* 0171-927 5627 *Fax* 0171-927 4798

CC NO 1014681   **ESTABLISHED** 1998

■ The Diamond Industry Educational Charity

WHAT IS FUNDED Trustees will consider applications only for educational projects, including training for employment or engagement in any profession or occupation

WHO CAN BENEFIT Up to three quarters of the income and capital in any year can be put towards the educational needs of children of those currently or formerly employed in the mining, cutting, polishing, marketing or broking of diamonds. Other grants to educational establishments

WHERE FUNDING CAN BE GIVEN UK and overseas

RANGE OF GRANTS £100–£11,500

SAMPLE GRANTS £11,500 to Friends of Guys Hospital; £1,200 to Harrow School; £1,000 to King Edward's School for a bursary; £1,000 to the Leys School for a bursary; £1,000 to Jesus College, Cambridge for a bursary; £1,000 to Cobham Hall for a bursary; £1,000 to Modern School, New Delhi; £500 to Charutar Arogya Mandal; £500 to London School of Hygiene and Tropical Medicine; £400 to Churchill College

FINANCES *Year* 1996–97 *Income* £74,010
Grants £19,700

TRUSTEES Sir Christopher Collet, Field Marshal the Lord Bramall, KG, GCB, OBE, MC, JP, T W H Capon, E G J Dawe, G L S Rothschild, G I Watson

NOTES Fees payable for student scholarships amounted to £33,903 in 1996–97

WHO TO APPLY TO R George, The Diamond Industry Educational Charity, 1 Charterhouse Street, London EC1P 1BL

CC NO 277447   **ESTABLISHED** 1979

■ The Diana Memorial Trust

WHAT IS FUNDED General charitable purposes

WHO CAN BENEFIT Institutions. There are no restrictions on the age; professional and economic group; family situation; religion and culture; and social circumstances of; or disease or medical condition suffered by, the beneficiaries

WHERE FUNDING CAN BE GIVEN UK

TYPE OF GRANT One-off and recurrent

RANGE OF GRANTS £300–£7,500

SAMPLE GRANTS £7,500 to Ratcliffe College Appeal; £2,000 to CHAS; £2,000 to Ohas; £1,200 to Cardinal Hume Centre; £1,000 to Brainwave

FINANCES *Year* 1994–95 *Income* £19,320
Grants £28,700

TRUSTEES C B Cunningham, J M Tierney, P Heren

WHO TO APPLY TO Father C Cunningham, The Diana Memorial Trust, St Etheldreda's, 14 Ely Place, London EC1N 6RY

CC NO 802078   **ESTABLISHED** 1989

■ The Diana, Princess of Wales Memorial Fund

WHAT IS FUNDED (a) Displaced people; (b) people at the margins of society; (c) survivors of conflict; and (d) the dying and bereaved. For UK projects in 1999, particularly children and young people between the ages of 12–18 years who, through bereavement or other circumstances, have suffered the loss of a close family member. Including (i) children/young people whose parent/prime carer or sibling has died; (ii) young carers who have lost the person for whom they cared; (iii) children/young people who have lost a family member as a result of extreme violence; (iv) children/young people in care, sometimes known as 'looked after' children. For international work criteria will be announced early in 1999

WHAT IS NOT FUNDED (a) Projects which fall outside the funding policies of the Fund; (b) activities which are the responsibility of any statutory agency; (c) organisations that are primarily fundraising bodies; (d) individuals; (e) pure research; (f) sporting activities which give little benefit in terms of social inclusion; (g) schools, colleges and hospitals; (h) repayment of loans; (i) repayment of debts; (j) retrospective funding; (k) rapid response to emergency situations; (l) promotion of religious beliefs and religious buildings. Disease or institution-specific projects will also not be included in this round

WHO CAN BENEFIT In the UK, organisations benefiting bereaved children and young people, young carers, refugee children, and those who are in care. Overseas, to be announced

WHERE FUNDING CAN BE GIVEN UK and overseas

TYPE OF GRANT Revenue: core and project costs, capital; one-off grants. Funding may be given for 3–5 years

RANGE OF GRANTS £15,000–£100,000 per annum

SAMPLE GRANTS £1,100,000 to Elton John AIDs Foundation; £1,000,000 to Centrepoint; £1,000,000 to Osteopathic Centre for Children; £1,000,000 to Leonard Cheshire Foundation; £998,500 to National AIDs Trust; £990,000 to English National Ballet; £889,000 to the Leprosy Mission

FINANCES *Year* 1998 *Income* £85,000,000 *Grants* £5,000,000

TRUSTEES Lady Sarah McCorquodale (President), Anthony Julius (Chairman), Michael Gibbins, LVO (Treasurer), Rt Hon The Earl Cairns, CBE, John Eversley, Baroness Pitkeathley, OBE, John Reizenstien, Christopher Spence, MBE, Nalini Varma

NOTES For further information please contact either Vanessa Corringham or Jo Greensted on Tel: 0171–902 5599 or Fax: 0171–902 5535

HOW TO APPLY Details of the full criteria and application forms are available by sending a self addressed A4 envelope with a 39p stamp to: The Grants Department, The Diana, Princess of Wales Memorial Fund, First Floor, The County Hall, Westminster Bridge Road, London SE1 7PB

WHO TO APPLY TO Dr Andrew Purkis, Chief Executive, The Diana, Princess of Wales Memorial Fund, First Floor, The County Hall, Westminster Bridge Road, London SE1 7PB *Tel* 0171-902 5000 *Fax* 0171-902 5511

CC NO 1064238   **ESTABLISHED** 1997

■ Dibb Lupton Broomhead Charitable Trust

WHAT IS FUNDED General charitable purposes

WHO CAN BENEFIT There are no restrictions on the age; professional and economic group; family situation; religion and culture; and social circumstances of; or disease or medical condition suffered by, the beneficiaries

WHERE FUNDING CAN BE GIVEN UK

TYPE OF GRANT Mainly single donations

FINANCES *Year* 1997 *Income* £28,545

TRUSTEES A G Chappell, N G Knowles, A Bugg

WHO TO APPLY TO A G Chappell, Dibb Lupton Broomhead Charitable Trust, Dibb Lupton Broomhead, Arndale House, Charles Street, Bradford BD1 1UN

CC NO 327280   **ESTABLISHED** 1986

■ Thomas Peter Dibdin Foundation

WHAT IS FUNDED Trustees will only consider applications from Christian and evangelical causes

WHO CAN BENEFIT Organisations benefiting Christians and Evangelists

WHERE FUNDING CAN BE GIVEN UK

FINANCES *Year* 1996–97 *Income* £944,000 *Grants* £176,000

TRUSTEES N J Barnett, D Dibdin

WHO TO APPLY TO I H Davey, Administrator, Thomas Peter Dibdin Foundation, c/o Insulated Structures, Normanby Park Works, Scunthorpe, North Lincolnshire DN15 8RQ *Tel* 01724 282020

CC NO 283524   **ESTABLISHED** 1982

■ The Dibs Charitable Trust

WHAT IS FUNDED Grants are made for the benefit of individuals for the relief of distress caused by poverty, sickness or misfortune but applications must be made on their behalf by social services, Citizens Advice Bureaux and similar organisations

WHAT IS NOT FUNDED The Trustees will not, in any circumstances, commit the Charitable Trust funds for payment of pensions or annuities of any description or for any other type of ongoing payments. Additionally, the Trustees will not commit funds for educational purposes or to meet the cost of travel abroad, clothing, redecoration, funeral or associated charges

WHO CAN BENEFIT Organisations benefiting people of all ages; at risk groups; disabled people; those disadvantaged by poverty and socially isolated people

WHERE FUNDING CAN BE GIVEN UK

TYPE OF GRANT One-off to assist relief of distress

FINANCES *Year* 1995 *Income* £23,925 *Grants* £18,314

TRUSTEES Coutts & Co, D H Isaacs, Mrs L Bloch, A Davis, K Davis

WHO TO APPLY TO A M W Davis, Dibs Charitable Trust, Angel House, 20–32 Pentonville Road, London N1 9XD

CC NO 257709   **ESTABLISHED** 1968

■ Dickson Charitable Trust

This trust did not respond to CAF's request to amend its entry and, by 30 June 1998, CAF's researchers did not find financial records for later than 1995 on its file at the Charity Commission. Trusts are legally required to submit annual accounts to the Charity Commission under section 42 of the Charities Act 1993

WHAT IS FUNDED General charitable purposes

WHO CAN BENEFIT Registered charities. There are no restrictions on the age; professional and economic group; family situation; religion and culture; and social circumstances of; or disease or medical condition suffered by, the beneficiaries

WHERE FUNDING CAN BE GIVEN UK

TRUSTEES J P Dickson, M S Dickson, J H Dickson, R J M Dickson, A J E Dickson

WHO TO APPLY TO John Park Dickson (Trustee), Dickson Charitable Trust, CS3 San Remo Towers, Sea Road, Boscombe BH5 1JT

CC NO 282813   **ESTABLISHED** 1981

■ The Digbeth Trust Ltd

WHAT IS FUNDED Feasibility studies for new projects

WHAT IS NOT FUNDED General appeals, core costs, medical research and grants for individuals not considered

WHO CAN BENEFIT Small local groups, new and established organisations and innovative projects benfiting people living in urban areas

WHERE FUNDING CAN BE GIVEN Birmingham

TYPE OF GRANT One-off for feasibility studies

RANGE OF GRANTS £1,00–£5,000 approximately

FINANCES *Year* 1997–98 *Income* £99,278 *Grants* £71,216

Does the trust you have chosen match your needs? Haphazard applications waste postage and time

177

TRUSTEES M Almasyabi, R Brackwell, J Burrows, T Clark, G De'Ath, G Macaulay, R Osei, N Sheikh, M Smith, T Wouhra

PUBLICATIONS Annual Report and guidelines

HOW TO APPLY Trustees meet every month except August. The Trust welcomes initial telephone calls to discuss application. Application form and guidance notes are available. Development worker support is offered to eligible groups. An sae would be appreciated

WHO TO APPLY TO Kate Hazlewood, The Digbeth Trust Ltd, Unit 321,The Custard Factory, Gibb Street, Digbeth, Birmingham B9 4AA *Tel* 0121-753 0706 *Fax* 0121-248 3323

CC NO 517343   ESTABLISHED 1984

■ Simon Digby Charitable Trust

WHAT IS FUNDED Religious, medical and educational causes

WHAT IS NOT FUNDED Training and education for individuals generally not funded

WHO CAN BENEFIT No specific type, but tend to be local organisations in the area Where Funding Can Be Given. Children, young adults and students will be considered. There is no restriction on the disease or medical condition suffered by the beneficiaries or on their religious and cultural background

WHERE FUNDING CAN BE GIVEN Mainly the Sherborne district of Dorset and the Coleshill district of North Warwickshire

TYPE OF GRANT Mainly one-off

SAMPLE GRANTS £2,000 to Sherborne Scout Group for a new minibus; £2,000 to Bishops Caundle All Saints Playgroup; £2,000 to Sherborne Youth Resource Centre; £1,000 to Sherborne Museum; £1,000 to Sherborne Abbey Primary School

FINANCES *Year* 1997 *Income* £13,675 *Grants* £16,700

TRUSTEES K S D Wingfield Digby, R C Hardy, J K Wingfield Digby, K G Wingfield Digby

HOW TO APPLY By letter only, all of which will be acknowledged; applications reviewed twice a year

WHO TO APPLY TO c/o The Resident Agent, The Simon Digby Charitable Trust, Digby Estate Office, 9 Cheap Street, Sherborne, Dorset DT9 3PY

CC NO 285548   ESTABLISHED 1981

■ The Simon Digby Sherborne Trust

WHAT IS FUNDED General charitable purposes for the benefit of those in Sherbourne and the neighbourhood

WHO CAN BENEFIT There are no restrictions on the age; professional and economic group; family situation; religion and culture; and social circumstances of; or disease or medical condition suffered by, the beneficiaries

WHERE FUNDING CAN BE GIVEN Sherborne and surrounding areas

FINANCES *Year* 1996–97 *Income* £57,117 *Grants* £22,220

HOW TO APPLY To the address under Who To Apply To in writing

WHO TO APPLY TO P J Langridge, Town Clerk, The Simon Digby Sherborne Trust, The Manor House, Newland, Sherborne, Dorset DT9 3JL

CC NO 801462   ESTABLISHED 1989

■ The Digital Equipment Co Ltd Charitable Society

WHAT IS FUNDED Advancement of education, relief of poverty, malnutrition, old age, disability, advancement of religion

WHO CAN BENEFIT Organisations benefiting: people of all ages; students; disabled people; those disadvantaged by poverty; victims of famine and malnourished people

WHERE FUNDING CAN BE GIVEN UK and overseas

RANGE OF GRANTS £100–£3,250

SAMPLE GRANTS £3,250 to Action Aid (Third World); £3,000 to Multiple Sclerosis for respite care in York; £3,000 to NSPCC; £3,000 to Save the Children; £2,500 to Barnardo's for children leaving Homes and needing financial support; £2,000 to Cancer Research; £2,000 to Duchess of Kent House a cancer hospice; £2,000 to John Radcliffe Hospital Cancer Unit; £1,500 to Oxfam; £1,350 to Friends of Freemantles School for autism

FINANCES *Year* 1995 *Income* £50,241 *Grants* £65,550

TRUSTEES The Council of the Society

HOW TO APPLY In writing. Applications are considered each year

WHO TO APPLY TO Mrs C Nash, Treasurer, The Digital Equipment Co Ltd Charitable Society, Digital Equipment Co Ltd, Digital Park, PO Box 115, Reading RG2 0TT

CC NO 326877   ESTABLISHED 1985

■ The Richard Dimbleby Cancer Fund

WHAT IS FUNDED Cancer research. Provision of financial support to maintain the Richard Dimbleby Laboratory at St Thomas's Hospital in conjunction with the Medical School and the Richard Dimbleby Day Care Centre at St Thomas's. Support may be given for personnel and human resource services, to voluntary and community organisations, and to health and social care professional bodies

WHAT IS NOT FUNDED No grants to individuals

WHO CAN BENEFIT Research programme at St Thomas' Hospital and relief to those suffering from cancer. Carers and research workers may benefit. There are no restrictions on the age or the religion or culture of the beneficiaries

TYPE OF GRANT One-off and research grants will be considered. Funding is available for up to one year

SAMPLE GRANTS £100,000 to Richard Dimbleby Laboratory, St Thomas's Hospital for research on papillomaviruses and cervical cancer; £70,000 to St Thomas's Hospital for a automated DNA sequencer; £50,960 to Torbay Hospital, Devon towards the cost of cancer support team; £41,470 to Department of Virology, St Thomas's Hospital for funding for senior lecturership and cancer research; £5,000 to Breast Cancer Care

FINANCES *Year* 1997 *Income* £280,852 *Grants* £267,430

TRUSTEES Mrs S Christensen, D Dimbleby, D R Dimbleby, E Dimbleby, H Dimbleby, J Dimbleby, J Dimbleby, K Dimbleby, L Dimbleby, N Dimbleby, Mrs R Travers

HOW TO APPLY Letters only

WHO TO APPLY TO Ronald Travers, OBE, The Richard Dimbleby Cancer Fund, 14 King Street, Richmond, Surrey TW9 1NF *Tel* 0181-940 6668 *Fax* 0181-332 1356

CC NO 247558   ESTABLISHED 1966

■ Dinam Charity

WHAT IS FUNDED Support for organisations dealing with international understanding, famine relief, child welfare, environmental protection, and animal welfare

WHAT IS NOT FUNDED No grants to individuals

WHO CAN BENEFIT Charitable organisations benefiting children, at risk groups, those disadvantaged by poverty, socially isolated people and victims of famine

WHERE FUNDING CAN BE GIVEN Wales

SAMPLE GRANTS £90,500 to David Davies Memorial Institute; £23,730 for general grants; £2,900 to Hackelator Fund

FINANCES *Year* 1996 *Income* £178,143 *Grants* £117,130

TRUSTEES The Hon Mrs Mary M Noble, The Hon Mrs G R Jean Cormack, The Hon Edward D G Davies, J S Tyres

WHO TO APPLY TO The Hon J H Davies, Dinam Charity, 8 Southampton Place, London WC1A 2EA

CC NO 231295   **ESTABLISHED** 1926

■ Dinwoodie 1968 Settlement

WHAT IS FUNDED Postgraduate medical education and research

WHO CAN BENEFIT Organisations benefiting academics, research workers and students. There is no restriction on the medical condition suffered by the beneficiaries

WHERE FUNDING CAN BE GIVEN UK

TYPE OF GRANT Building projects will be considered

FINANCES *Year* 1996–97 *Income* £335,779 *Grants* £122,243

TRUSTEES W A Fairbairn, Dr J M Fowler, Miss C Webster

NOTES Annual figures for grants versus income may vary substantially as payments towards building costs of each project usually absorb more than one years available income

HOW TO APPLY To the address under Who To Apply To in writing

WHO TO APPLY TO The Clerk to the Trustees, Dinwoodie 1968 Settlement, 5 East Pallant, Chichester, West Sussex PO19 1TS *Tel* 01243 786111

CC NO 255495   **ESTABLISHED** 1968

■ Diocese of Johannesburg Charitable Trust

WHAT IS FUNDED General charitable purposes

WHO CAN BENEFIT There are no restrictions on the age; professional and economic group; family situation; religion and culture; and social circumstances of; or disease or medical condition suffered by, the beneficiaries

WHERE FUNDING CAN BE GIVEN UK

WHO TO APPLY TO B G Streather, Trustee, Diocese of Johannesburg Charitable Trust, Streathers, Sackville House, 40 Picadilly, London W1V 9PA

CC NO 1062569   **ESTABLISHED** 1997

■ C H Dixon Charitable Trust

WHAT IS FUNDED The Trust will consider funding the following: education; music; medical research; animal welfare and social work. Particularly: emergency housing and short term housing; sheltered accommodation; arts education; orchestras; convalescent homes and rehabilitation centres; conservation; animal facilities and services; primary schools, special schools, education and training; libraries and museums; playgrounds and day centres

WHO CAN BENEFIT People of all ages; musicians; students; disabled people, homeless people; and those suffering from Alzheimer's disease, hearing loss and mental illness

WHERE FUNDING CAN BE GIVEN England

TYPE OF GRANT One-off

RANGE OF GRANTS £100–£2,000

SAMPLE GRANTS £1,500 to Treloar Trust for education; £1,200 to Stoneleigh Youth Orchestra for education; £1,000 to Sherbourne School for education; £1,000 to Glyndebourne Arts Trust for education; £950 to Grail Trust India for education

FINANCES *Year* 1997 *Income* £18,146 *Grants* £9,750

TRUSTEES Miss A Dixon, R M Robinson

HOW TO APPLY In writing to R M Robinson at the address under Who To Apply To

WHO TO APPLY TO R M Robinson, C H Dixon Charitable Trust, Messrs Dixon Ward, 16 The Green, Richmond, Surrey TW9 1QD

CC NO 282936   **ESTABLISHED** 1981

■ F E Dixon Charitable Trust

WHAT IS FUNDED Capital projects and special events aimed at improving facilities and services offered by recipient organisations. Community-based activities in sporting, cultural, charitable and educational spheres. Examples are sporting clubs, arts and crafts, schools, playgroups, old people's welfare

WHAT IS NOT FUNDED Unlikely to support individuals. Applicants must demonstrate financial and functional viability. Not political or religious causes or activities which should be provided by central or local government

WHO CAN BENEFIT There are no restrictions on the age; professional and economic group; family situation; religion and culture; and social circumstances of; or disease or medical condition suffered by, the beneficiaries

WHERE FUNDING CAN BE GIVEN Basildon in Berkshire; organisations located in adjacent areas of Reading and West Berkshire Districts may be assisted where applicant can show that some tangible benefit to residents of Basildon will result

TYPE OF GRANT Capital and project. Normally up to 50 per cent of cost

FINANCES *Year* 1997–98 *Income* £19,800 *Grants* £16,000

TRUSTEES J A Bunn, R L Bass, S Clare, J Delury, P Johnson

HOW TO APPLY By 28 February each year. To the address under Who To Apply To with supporting data

WHO TO APPLY TO Mr J A Bunn, F E Dixon Charitable Trust, 6 Captains Gorse, Upper Basildon, Reading RG8 8SZ

CC NO 271066   **ESTABLISHED** 1976

■ Henry Dixon's Foundation for Apprenticing

WHAT IS FUNDED Funding is made available for educational purposes

WHO CAN BENEFIT Students

WHERE FUNDING CAN BE GIVEN UK

FINANCES *Year* 1996–97 *Income* £75,811 *Grants* £90,870

TRUSTEES The Drapers' Company

HOW TO APPLY This Trust states that it does not respond to unsolicited applications
WHO TO APPLY TO Accountant to the Trustees, Henry Dixon's Foundation for Apprenticing, Clerk's Office, Drapers' Company, Drapers' Hall, Throgmorton Avenue, London EC2N 2DQ *Tel* 0171-588 5001
CC NO 314292 **ESTABLISHED** 1696

■ The Dixons Foundation

WHAT IS FUNDED General charitable purposes
WHO CAN BENEFIT There are no restrictions on the age; professional and economic group; family situation; religion and culture; and social circumstances of; or disease or medical condition suffered by, the beneficiaries
WHERE FUNDING CAN BE GIVEN UK
TRUSTEES Dixons Group plc, G D Budd, Sir S Kalms, M J Souhami
WHO TO APPLY TO Geoffrey Budd, Trustee, The Dixons Foundation, c/o Dixons Group plc, Maylands Avenue, Hemel Hempstead, Hertfordshire HP2 7IG
CC NO 1053215 **ESTABLISHED** 1996

■ The Raphael Djanogly Charitable Trust

This trust did not respond to CAF's request to amend its entry and, by 30 June 1998, CAF's researchers did not find financial records for later than 1995 on its file at the Charity Commission. Trusts are legally required to submit annual accounts to the Charity Commission under section 42 of the Charities Act 1993

WHAT IS FUNDED General at the Trustees discretion
WHO CAN BENEFIT There are no restrictions on the age; professional and economic group; family situation; religion and culture; and social circumstances of; or disease or medical condition suffered by, the beneficiaries
WHERE FUNDING CAN BE GIVEN UK and overseas
TYPE OF GRANT At the discretion of the Trustees
TRUSTEES Raphael Djanogly, David Djanogly, Norman Charles S Barling, Victor Mishcon
WHO TO APPLY TO R Djanogly, The Raphael Djanogly Charitable Trust, Flat 29, Sandyfield, 26 Manor Road, Bournemouth, Dorset BH1 3EZ
CC NO 274700 **ESTABLISHED** 1977

■ The Dudley Dodd Charitable Trust

WHAT IS FUNDED General charitable purposes
WHO CAN BENEFIT Registered charities. There are no restrictions on the age; professional and economic group; family situation; religion and culture; and social circumstances of; or disease or medical condition suffered by, the beneficiaries
WHERE FUNDING CAN BE GIVEN UK
TYPE OF GRANT Mainly single gifts
SAMPLE GRANTS £3,675 to the Royal Academy; £750 to the Friends of Leynton House; £500 to the Shipton-under-Wychwood Village Hall Appeal; £250 to The National Trust; £200 to St Mary the Virgin, Shipton-under-Wychwood
FINANCES *Year* 1997 *Income* £18,619 *Grants* £5,375
TRUSTEES D A R Dodd, K M Dodd, J W Sharpe
HOW TO APPLY In writing only to the address under Who To Apply To. No telephone enquiries

WHO TO APPLY TO J W Sharpe, The Dudley Dodd Charitable Trust, Osborne Clarke, 50 Queen Charlotte Street, Bristol BS1 4HE
CC NO 327980 **ESTABLISHED** 1988

■ Domepride Ltd

WHAT IS FUNDED Jewish, welfare, general charitable purposes
WHO CAN BENEFIT To benefit Jewish people, at risk groups, those disadvantaged by poverty and socially isolated people
WHERE FUNDING CAN BE GIVEN UK and overseas
FINANCES *Year* 1995 *Income* £57,010 *Grants* £43,746
TRUSTEES J Padwa, G Padwa, A J Cohen
HOW TO APPLY To the address under Who To Apply To in writing
WHO TO APPLY TO Mr Ulman, Accountant, Domepride Ltd, c/o Haffner Hoff & Co, 3rd Floor, Manchester House, 86 Princess Street, Manchester M1 6NP
CC NO 289426 **ESTABLISHED** 1983

■ Donatewell Ltd

WHAT IS FUNDED General charitable purposes at the discretion of the Trustees
WHO CAN BENEFIT There are no restrictions on the age; professional and economic group; family situation; religion and culture; and social circumstances of; or disease or medical condition suffered by, the beneficiaries
WHERE FUNDING CAN BE GIVEN UK
FINANCES *Year* 1994–95 *Income* £102,852 *Grants* £136,000
TRUSTEES M Halstak, Mrs R Halstak, J Halstak
WHO TO APPLY TO M Halstak, Trustee, Donatewell Ltd, 20 Leadale Road, London N16 6DA
CC NO 286973 **ESTABLISHED** 1983

■ The Doncaster Depot Charity Fund

WHAT IS FUNDED Relief in need, particularly for British Rail maintenance staff, both past and present; local welfare causes
WHO CAN BENEFIT Individuals and local organisations benefiting: young adults and older people; retired people; at risk groups; those disadvantaged by poverty; disabled people; homeless people and socially isolated people
WHERE FUNDING CAN BE GIVEN Doncaster and the surrounding area
FINANCES *Year* 1994–95 *Income* £19,351
TRUSTEES D W R Hall (Chairman)
HOW TO APPLY To the address under Who To Apply To in writing
WHO TO APPLY TO D W R Hall, The Doncaster Depot Charity Fund, c/o Adtranz, PO Box 165, Hexthorpe, Doncaster DN4 0AF
CC NO 1008599 **ESTABLISHED** 1992

■ The Dorcas Trust

WHAT IS FUNDED General at trustees discretion. To advance the Christian religion, relieve poverty and advance education
WHO CAN BENEFIT To benefit: children; young adults; students; Christians and those disadvantaged by poverty
WHERE FUNDING CAN BE GIVEN UK
TYPE OF GRANT At the discretion of the Trustees

RANGE OF GRANTS £250–£18,461

SAMPLE GRANTS £18,461 to the Navigators; £1,300 to an individual for counselling; £1,200 to Church Army; £1,000 to Mildmay Hospital; £500 to Shaftsbury Society; £500 to 2 Timothy Two Trust; £500 to Macmillan Fund; £250 to Through Faith Missions; £250 to Evangelical Alliance

FINANCES *Year* 1996 *Income* £47,568 *Grants* £24,211

TRUSTEES J C L Broad, J D Broad, P L Butler

WHO TO APPLY TO I Taylor, The Dorcas Trust, Rathbone Taxation Services, Port of Liverpool Building, Pierhead, Liverpool L3 1NW

CC NO 275494 **ESTABLISHED** 1978

■ The Dorema Charitable Trust

WHAT IS FUNDED Medicine, health, welfare, education and religion

WHAT IS NOT FUNDED Unsolicited applications

WHO CAN BENEFIT Organisations benefiting: children; young adults; older people; at risk groups and socially isolated people. There is no restriction on the religion and culture of, or medical condition suffered by the beneficiaries

WHERE FUNDING CAN BE GIVEN UK

TYPE OF GRANT One off and recurrent

FINANCES *Year* 1997 *Income* £36,047 *Grants* £15,600

TRUSTEES D S M Nussbaum, G B Nussbaum

HOW TO APPLY **This Trust states that it does not respond to unsolicited applications**

WHO TO APPLY TO D S M Nussbaum, The Dorema Charitable Trust, 4 Church Grove, Amersham, Buckinghamshire HP6 6SH

CC NO 287001 **ESTABLISHED** 1983

■ The Dorset Historic Churches Trust

WHAT IS FUNDED The restoration, preservation, repair of churches of all denominations and churchyards in the Dorset area

WHO CAN BENEFIT Any church in Dorset

WHERE FUNDING CAN BE GIVEN Dorset

TYPE OF GRANT One-off, interest free loans, buildings and funding for up to two years will be considered

RANGE OF GRANTS Up to £8,000

SAMPLE GRANTS £10,000 to Yetminster for church repairs; £5,000 to Hazelbury Poryan for church repairs; £5,000 to Canford Magna for church repairs; £4,000 to Sydling St Nicholas for church repairs; £3,000 to Winterborne Kingston for church repairs; £2,500 to Charminster for church repairs; £2,500 to Over Compton for church repairs; £2,000 to Stourton Caundle for church repairs; £1,500 to Blandford Methodist for church repairs; £1,250 to Winterborne Monkton for church repairs

FINANCES *Year* 1997 *Income* £78,457 *Grants* £47,750

TRUSTEES Bishop of Salisbury, Lord Lieutenant for Dorset, Bishop of Sherborne, Archdeacon of Dorset, Archdeacon of Sherborne, General J O C Alexander, R D Allan, Lord Cranborne, C G Dean, Sir Michael Hanham, Dr Stephen Law, Major Mansel, The Hon Mrs Marten, Lady May, P Mayne, N C McClintock, Lady Morshead, P Moule, Anthony Pitt Rivers, K G S Smith, A C Stuart, Capt N T L Thimbley, Sir Philip Williams

HOW TO APPLY To the address under Who To Apply To in writing

WHO TO APPLY TO N N McClintock, CBE, The Dorset Historic Churches Trust, Lower Westport, Wareham, Dorset BH20 4PR *Tel* 01929 553252

CC NO 282790 **ESTABLISHED** 1971

■ Dorus Trust

WHAT IS FUNDED Funding specific projects. Charities working in the fields of: emergency and short-term housing; holiday accommodation and hostels; health counselling and education; respite, care for carers; and hospices. Support also for environmental issues; renewable energy and power; care in the community and crime prevention schemes

WHAT IS NOT FUNDED No grants to individuals, or for expeditions, research or scholarships

WHO CAN BENEFIT Registered charities only benefiting: people of all ages; disabled people; those disadvantaged by poverty; homeless people; and victims of crime and domestic violence. Beneficiaries suffering from various diseases and medical conditions are also considered for support

WHERE FUNDING CAN BE GIVEN UK. The Trustees sometimes consider overseas projects carried out by UK charities

TYPE OF GRANT Normally one-off and project grants. Funding for up to one year will be considered

RANGE OF GRANTS £500–£10,000

SAMPLE GRANTS £10,000 to Action on Addiction for new computer equipment; £10,000 to AFASIC for information sheet and newsletter; £10,000 to Children's Society for information materials for safe house; £10,000 to Divert Trust towards cost of conference; £10,000 to Intermediate Technology for help setting up loan scheme for micro hydro project in Peru; £10,000 to Sightsavers International towards cost of student hostel at eye hospital; £5,000 to British Deaf Association towards advocacy project; £5,000 to Lupus UK for welfare fund; £5,000 to Motor Neurone Disease Association towards cost of respite care initiative; £5,000 to National Library for the Blind for two ways books (print/Braille)

FINANCES *Year* 1996 *Income* £154,000 *Grants* £98,000

TRUSTEES C Peacock, B Bond, M Bond

HOW TO APPLY In writing only to the address under Who To Apply To. Applications are normally considered in July and December. A copy of latest Annual Report and Accounts must accompany any application

WHO TO APPLY TO Mrs B Davis, Senior Information Officer, Dorus Trust, c/o CAF, Kings Hill, West Malling, Kent ME19 4TA *Tel* 01732 520081 *Fax* 01732 520001 *E-mail* bdavis@caf.charitynet.org

CC NO 328724 **ESTABLISHED** 1990

■ Double 'O' Charity Ltd

WHAT IS FUNDED The Charity considers all requests for aid

WHO CAN BENEFIT Registered charities. There are no restrictions on the age; professional and economic group; family situation; religion and culture; and social circumstances of; or disease or medical condition suffered by, the beneficiaries

WHERE FUNDING CAN BE GIVEN UK and overseas

TYPE OF GRANT Preferably one-off

Does the trust you have chosen match your needs? Haphazard applications waste postage and time

181

SAMPLE GRANTS £5,625 to Avtar Meher Baba Perpetual Charitable Trust; £5,000 to Oxfam; £5,000 to Royal Court Theatre; £2,500 to Knee High Theatre; £1,125 to a refuge

FINANCES *Year* 1997 *Income* £59,739 *Grants* £34,250

TRUSTEES P D B Townshend, Mrs K Townshend, N R Goderson

WHO TO APPLY TO N Goderson, Double 'O' Charity Ltd, The Boathouse, Ranelagh Drive, Twickenham, Middlesex TW1 1QZ

CC NO 271681   **ESTABLISHED** 1976

■ The Garth Doubleday Trust

WHAT IS FUNDED General charitable purposes. Mainly supports Kent charities

WHO CAN BENEFIT There are no restrictions on the age; professional and economic group; family situation; religion and culture; and social circumstances of; or disease or medical condition suffered by, the beneficiaries

WHERE FUNDING CAN BE GIVEN Kent

TYPE OF GRANT Annual by standing order. Funding for more than three years will be considered

RANGE OF GRANTS £150–£1,800

FINANCES *Year* 1997 *Income* £20,409 *Grants* £8,850

TRUSTEES E G Doubleday, Mrs C T Motley

HOW TO APPLY To the address under Who To Apply To at any time. Applications received by the beginning of January, May, September, are considered in March, July, and November respectively. Applications should include clear details of the need the intended project is designed to meet plus an outline budget. Applications are not acknowledged except when further information may be requested. No sae please

WHO TO APPLY TO B W Elvy, The Garth Doubleday Trust, Brian Elvy & Co, 1A High Street, Sittingbourne, Kent ME10 4AY

Tel 01795 479222 *Fax* 01795 476670

CC NO 249692   **ESTABLISHED** 1966

■ The Doughty Charity Trust

WHAT IS FUNDED To promote: (a) the Orthodox Jewish Religion, (b) Orthodox Jewish education and (c) institutions for poor, ill and aged Jews

WHAT IS NOT FUNDED No grants to individuals

WHO CAN BENEFIT Jewish organisations benefiting those disadvantaged by poverty and the sick. There are no restrictions on the age of, or the disease or medical condition suffered by, the beneficiaries

WHERE FUNDING CAN BE GIVEN England, Israel

TYPE OF GRANT Loan or grant £1,000 or less

RANGE OF GRANTS £100–£5,000

SAMPLE GRANTS £5,000 to Menorah Grammar School; £5,000 to Jewish Secondary School Movement; £4,400 to Woodstock/Sinclair; £2,250 to JSSM Building Fund; £2,060 to Sinai Synagogue; £1,000 to an individual for the relief of poverty; £1,000 to Sharrei Torah; £620 to GGBH; £555 to Jewish Teachers Training Seminary; £500 to Friends of Mir

FINANCES *Year* 1997 *Income* £25,681 *Grants* £26,009

TRUSTEES G B Halibard, Mrs M Halibard

HOW TO APPLY By letter to the address under Who To Apply To

WHO TO APPLY TO G B Halibard, The Doughty Charity Trust, 22 Ravenscroft Avenue, Golders Green, London NW11 0RY

CC NO 274977   **ESTABLISHED** 1977

■ The Douglas Charitable Trust

WHAT IS FUNDED Scottish universities and church restoration projects are the main interests of the Trust. Grants are also made to charities which help the deprived and homeless, and those in the third world

WHO CAN BENEFIT Academics, students, young adults, disabled people and homeless people

WHERE FUNDING CAN BE GIVEN Scotland and the third world

FINANCES *Year* 1994–95 *Grants* £33,000

TRUSTEES Rev Prof D Shaw, D Connell, E Cameron

PUBLICATIONS Accounts are available from the Trust

HOW TO APPLY Applications should be made in writing to the address below

WHO TO APPLY TO The Secretary, The Douglas Charitable Trust, Messrs Dundas & Wilson, Saltire Court, 20 Castle Terrace, Edinburgh EH1 2EN

SC NO SCO 19840

■ R M Douglas Charitable Trust

WHAT IS FUNDED Registered charities at discretion of Trustees

WHAT IS NOT FUNDED Individuals, scholarships, participation in expeditions or adventurous activities

WHO CAN BENEFIT Registered charities benefiting clergy; ex-service and service people; medical professionals; research workers; scientists; seafarers and fishermen; parents and children; widows and widowers; and Christians. A wide range of social circumstances and diseases and medical conditions are considered for funding. There is no restriction on the age of the beneficiaries

WHERE FUNDING CAN BE GIVEN Staffordshire a priority, but the West Midlands, South Wales, Europe, Asia, Africa and Ireland are also considered

TYPE OF GRANT Mostly small grants at the discretion of Trustees including buildings, capital, core costs, one-off, research, and recurring costs. Funding is available for over three years

RANGE OF GRANTS £50–£5,000. Typically £200–£250

FINANCES *Year* 1997 *Income* £55,453 *Grants* £46,350

TRUSTEES J R T Douglas, OBE, F W Carder TD, Mrs J E Lees

NOTES New applications not normally considered

HOW TO APPLY By letter. Not all acknowledged. No application form or guidelines

WHO TO APPLY TO The Administrator, R M Douglas Charitable Trust, 68 Liverpool Road, Stoke-on-Trent ST4 1BG

CC NO 248775   **ESTABLISHED** 1966

■ Dove-Bowerman Trust

WHAT IS FUNDED Small grants are made to fund women in further education or vocational training

WHO CAN BENEFIT Registered charities, individual women in further education. There are few restrictions on the professional and economic groups of the beneficiaries

WHERE FUNDING CAN BE GIVEN Mainly UK applicants for education in the UK

TYPE OF GRANT Mostly one-off grants. No loans. Research and running costs are considered. Funding may be given for up to three years

RANGE OF GRANTS £50–£350

SAMPLE GRANTS Grants of £350 were given to individual women for the following courses:; An MSc in Clinical Communications at City University London; An MSc in Psychology at Heriot Watt; Postgraduate Occupational Therapy at Bart's; A Certificate of Social Studies at University of Wales, Cardiff; To study Medicine at Queen's, Belfast; An MSc in Dietetics at University of Wales, Cardiff; An MSc in Community Disability at University College, London; A Dip HE in Nursing at Plymouth University; An MA in Medical Anthropology at the School of Oriental and African Studies; A Diploma in Integrative Arts Psychotherapy at Institute for Arts in Therapy and Education

FINANCES *Year* 1996–97 *Income* £69,656 *Grants* £48,008

TRUSTEES Rev Mrs C Canti, Mrs K Alderson, W P W Barnes, Dr M Anderson, Mrs G Fletcher-Watson, Mrs C Davis, P Wolton, J Stewart, Mrs C Archer, Mrs L Packman, C Atkins

NOTES The Trustees are concerned by the number of applications they are not in a position to support according to the terms of the Trust Deed, resources being limited and virtually all earmarked. Letters will not be acknowledged unless there is a possibility of a grant being given

HOW TO APPLY Applications close on April 30. Application forms and guidelines sent if sae enclosed

WHO TO APPLY TO Mrs J Kingsley, Dove-Bowerman Trust, Fawney, Whitchurch-on-Thames, Pangbourne, Reading RG8 7DD

CC NO 262888   **ESTABLISHED** 1971

■ The D'Oyly Carte Charitable Trust

WHAT IS FUNDED Mainly to support the arts, medical/welfare charities and the environment

WHAT IS NOT FUNDED No grants are made to individuals

WHO CAN BENEFIT Organisations benefiting: at risk groups; those disadvantaged by poverty; socially isolated people; and the sick. There is no restriction on the disease or medical condition suffered by the beneficiaries

WHERE FUNDING CAN BE GIVEN UK

TYPE OF GRANT Specific charities in which Dame Bridget D'Oyly Carte took a special interest during her lifetime are supported annually; other grants are one-off. Five major arts scholarships are given annually to Colleges; these are awarded at the discretion of the Principals of the Colleges, not the Trust

SAMPLE GRANTS £10,000 to Parkinson's Disease Society; £6,000 to Actor's Charitable Trust, Denville Hall; £6,000 to Arts Educational London Schools; £6,000 to Breakthrough Trust for the Deaf; £6,000 to City and Guilds of London Art School; £6,000 to Crafts Council; £6,000 to Help the Hospices; £6,000 to Royal ballet Schools; £6,000 to Royal Northern College of Music; £5,000 to Council for the Protection of Rural England

FINANCES *Year* 1997 *Income* £222,068 *Grants* £192,050

TRUSTEES Sir John Batten, KCVO, Sir Martyn Beckett, Bt, MC, BA, RIBA, E J P Elliott, Mrs J Sibley, Mrs F Radcliffe

NOTES Apart from child health and kidney disease, all other medical grants are made to national charities (one per field) supported annually. Regional appeals are not considered

HOW TO APPLY In writing to the address under Who To Apply To. The Trustees meet twice a year, in June and December and applications for consideration should be submitted one month in advance

WHO TO APPLY TO Mrs Jane Thorne, The D'Oyly Carte Charitable Trust, 1 Savoy Hill, London WC2R 0BP

CC NO 265057   **ESTABLISHED** 1972

■ The Drapers' Consolidated Charity

WHAT IS FUNDED Educational and social welfare organisations are the major recipients of grants

WHO CAN BENEFIT Children; young adults; students; at risk groups; those disadvantaged by poverty; and socially isolated people

WHERE FUNDING CAN BE GIVEN UK

FINANCES *Year* 1996–97 *Income* £289,066 *Grants* £210,300

TRUSTEES The Drapers' Company

HOW TO APPLY **This Trust states that it does not respond to unsolicited applications**

WHO TO APPLY TO Clerk to the Drapers' Company, The Drapers' Consolidated Charity, Drapers' Company, Drapers' Hall, Throgmorton Avenue, London EC2N 2DQ *Tel* 0171-588 5001

CC NO 209844   **ESTABLISHED** 1903

■ The George Drexler Foundation

WHAT IS FUNDED Medical research, education and charities working for the benefit of the old and incapacitated. Pensions paid to former employees of the Ofrex Group

WHO CAN BENEFIT Individuals and organisations benefiting people of all ages, students and ex-employees of the Ofrex Group

WHERE FUNDING CAN BE GIVEN UK

RANGE OF GRANTS Organisations: £400–£8,000, for individuals (educational): £1,500–£6,000 and for Ofrex pensioners: £564–£2,564

SAMPLE GRANTS £8,000 to British Red Cross Society; £6000 to an individual for education; £5,850 to an individual for education; £5,000 to London Philharmonic Orchestra; £5,000 to PACE; £5,000 to Royal Philharmonic Orchestra; £4,500 to Royal Opera House; £4,000 to Abbeyfield Development Trust; £4,000 to Imperial Cancer Research Fund; £4,000 to NSPCC

FINANCES *Year* 1996 *Income* £213,185 *Grants* £146,791

TRUSTEES L M Dresher, H P Hartley, Mrs C A Phillips

WHO TO APPLY TO The George Drexler Foundation, PO Box 338, Granborough, Buckinghamshire MK18 3YT

CC NO 313278   **ESTABLISHED** 1959

■ The Dromintee Trust

This trust did not respond to CAF's request to amend its entry and, by 30 June 1998, CAF's researchers did not find financial records for later than 1995 on its file at the Charity Commission. Trusts are legally required to submit annual accounts to the Charity Commission under section 42 of the Charities Act 1993

WHAT IS FUNDED General charitable purposes

WHO CAN BENEFIT There are no restrictions on the age; professional and economic group; family situation; religion and culture; and social circumstances of; or disease or medical condition suffered by, the beneficiaries

WHERE FUNDING CAN BE GIVEN UK and overseas

TRUSTEES H P Murphy, Ms M A Murphy, R H Smith, P Tiernan

WHO TO APPLY TO H Murphy, The Dromintee Trust, The Manor House, Main Street, Thornby LE7 9PN

CC NO 1053956   **ESTABLISHED** 1995

■ The Drum Trust

WHAT IS FUNDED General charitable purposes
WHO CAN BENEFIT There are no restrictions on the age; professional and economic group; family situation; religion and culture; and social circumstances of; or disease or medical condition suffered by, the beneficiaries
WHERE FUNDING CAN BE GIVEN UK
FINANCES *Year* 1996 *Income* £13,708
TRUSTEES J T Gibson, The Dickinson Trust Ltd
WHO TO APPLY TO R E Webb, Secretary, The Drum Trust, Pollen House, 10–12 Cork Street, London W1X 1PD
CC NO 1048322   **ESTABLISHED** 1995

■ The Drummond Trust (incorporating Stirling Tract Enterprise)

WHAT IS FUNDED To provide financial assistance for the publication of works of sound Christian doctrine and evangelical purpose. Support of Christian evangelical outreach and education; missionaries and evangelicals
WHAT IS NOT FUNDED No grants for church buildings or scholarships
WHO CAN BENEFIT Individuals or religious publishing houses; evangelists; clergy and Christians
WHERE FUNDING CAN BE GIVEN UK and overseas
TYPE OF GRANT Single projects; interest free loans; and one-off grants all for up to two years
FINANCES *Year* 1997 *Income* £20,000
Grants £15,000
TRUSTEES J F Sinclair (Chairman), Rev A S Blount, D B Cannon, Rev G Richards, J K Sinclair, Rev B W Dunsmore, Miss M J S Henderson, A J Skilling, Rev A A S Reid
HOW TO APPLY End of January and July. Application forms available from the address under Who To Apply To
WHO TO APPLY TO The Drummond Trust, Messrs Hill & Robb, Solicitors, 3 Pitt Terrace, Stirling FK8 2EY *Tel* 01786 450985 *Fax* 01786 451360
CC NO CR 20155   **ESTABLISHED** 1848

■ Isaac Duckett's Charity for Poor Maidservants

WHAT IS FUNDED For the benefit of needy and deserving men and women with preference to those who are or have been servants, housekeepers or residential caretakers
WHO CAN BENEFIT Organisations benefiting those who are or have been servants, housekeepers or residential caretakers and who are needy or deserving
WHERE FUNDING CAN BE GIVEN St Andrew, Holborn, St Clement Danes
SAMPLE GRANTS £32,000 allocated to St Andrew Holborn; £32,000 to allocated to St Clement Danes, Strand; £400 to ST Pauline's Church of England School, Crayford, Kent
FINANCES *Year* 1996 *Income* £135,478
Grants £64,400
TRUSTEES B Dunn, E Elstob, N Maltby, P Maplestone, R Morris, M Radcliffe, J Sofer, E Tatham, M Thatcher, D White, C Young
WHO TO APPLY TO I Gray, Isaac Duckett's Charity for Poor Maidservants, St Andrew's Vicarage, 5 St Andrew's Street, London EC4
CC NO 213716   **ESTABLISHED** 1974

■ Dudley Stationery Charitable Trust

WHAT IS FUNDED General charitable purposes
WHO CAN BENEFIT There are no restrictions on the age; professional and economic group; family situation; religion and culture; and social circumstances of; or disease or medical condition suffered by, the beneficiaries
WHERE FUNDING CAN BE GIVEN UK
FINANCES *Year* 1997 *Income* £529,373
TRUSTEES F A M Brient, Ms J O Brient, Ms M J Brient
WHO TO APPLY TO N Fairbairn, Secretary, Dudley Stationery Charitable Trust, Dudley Stationery Ltd, Crown Close, Wick Lane, London E3 2JT
CC NO 1050574   **ESTABLISHED** 1995

■ William Dudley Trust

WHAT IS FUNDED (a) Assistance to young people studying in Birmingham (restricted area of work-no applications invited). (b) Assistance to elderly tradespeople who have fallen on hard times (restricted area of work no applications invited). (c) Grants to charitable organisations in Birmingham towards general alleviation of need, hardship and distress
WHAT IS NOT FUNDED General appeals or individuals not considered
WHO CAN BENEFIT Charitable organisations benefiting: children; young adults; older people; and those disadvantaged by poverty. the Trust prioritises smaller local charities benefiting older people
WHERE FUNDING CAN BE GIVEN Birmingham
TYPE OF GRANT One-off, capital, core costs, project, recurring costs, running costs and start-up costs. Funding is available for up to one year
RANGE OF GRANTS £250–£2,500; average £600
FINANCES *Year* 1997 *Income* £27,904
Grants £50,825
TRUSTEES J Best, A Bhalla, J Blythe, A N Mabe, Mrs M E Scrimshaw, P H D White, Cllr R Spector
NOTES Guidelines are available
HOW TO APPLY The Trust welcomes initial telephone calls to discuss applications. There is no application form, but guidance notes are available. Trustees meet five times each year. Check with Trust for next available date
WHO TO APPLY TO Ms Kate Hazlewood, William Dudley Trust, Unit 321, The Custard Factory, Gibb St, Birmingham B9 4AA *Tel* 0121-753 0706 *Fax* 0121-248 3323
CC NO 214752   **ESTABLISHED** 1875

■ The Dugdale Charitable Trust

WHAT IS FUNDED General charitable purposes, particularly the advancement of the Methodist religion and Christian education
WHO CAN BENEFIT Methodists and Christians
WHERE FUNDING CAN BE GIVEN UK (particularly Hampshire and Westy Sussex) and overseas
SAMPLE GRANTS £78,415 to Waltham Chase Methodist Church for building a new church; £30,000 to the Kings School (Hampshire Christian Education Trust); £150 to Overseas Mission Society; £50 to Africa Inland Mission
FINANCES *Year* 1997 *Income* £45,114
Grants £108,615
TRUSTEES R A Dugdale, Mrs B Dugdale
WHO TO APPLY TO R Dugdale, Trustee, The Dugdale Charitable Trust, Harmsworth Farm, Botley Road, Curbridge, Hampshire SO30 2HB
CC NO 1052941   **ESTABLISHED** 1995

■ The P B Dumbell Charitable Trust

WHAT IS FUNDED General charitable purposes. Trustees favour local applicants

WHAT IS NOT FUNDED Grants for educational purposes only

WHO CAN BENEFIT Institutions and individuals. There are no restrictions on the age; professional and economic group; family situation; religion and culture; and social circumstances of; or disease or medical condition suffered by, the beneficiaries

WHERE FUNDING CAN BE GIVEN West Midlands

SAMPLE GRANTS £2,500 to Abbeyfield (Wolverhampton) Society Ltd for old people's housing; £2,500 to Beacon Centre for the Blind; £2,500 to Compton Hospice; £2,500 to Ironbridge Gorge Museum Development Trust; £2,000 to Bromesberrow Church; £2,000 to Clunbury Church; £2,000 to Worfield Church; £1,500 to Age Concern Wolverhampton; £1,500 to The Salvation Army; £1,500 to Wolverhampton Multiple Sclerosis Society

FINANCES *Year* 1998 *Income* £44,234 *Grants* £28,150

TRUSTEES M H Gilbert, C F Dumbell

HOW TO APPLY By letter. No telephone calls, no application forms available. Prefer sae

WHO TO APPLY TO M H Gilbert, The P B Dumbell Charitable Trust, B D O Stoy Hayward, Mander House, Wolverhampton, West Midlands WV1 3NF *Tel* 01902 714828

CC NO 232770   **ESTABLISHED** 1964

■ Dumbreck Charity

WHAT IS FUNDED General charitable purposes. Emphasis on assisting the blind and disabled, children, animals and conservation mainly in the West Midlands

WHAT IS NOT FUNDED No grants to individuals

WHO CAN BENEFIT Charitable bodies benefiting the residents of the West Midlands. Priority is given to blind people, disabled people and children

WHERE FUNDING CAN BE GIVEN West Midlands

TYPE OF GRANT Recurring and one-off grants

RANGE OF GRANTS £500–£5,000, typical grant £500

SAMPLE GRANTS £5,000 to Elizabeth Fitzroy Homes; £5,000 to Maggs Daycare Centre; £5,000 to Relate – Worcestershire Marriage Guidance; £3,000 to Brooke Hospital for Animals Cairo; £3,000 to Honiley Dog Rescue (Canine Defence League); £2,000 to Save the Children Fund; £2,000 to the Jennifer Trust for Spinal Muscular Atrophy; £2,000 to Birmingham Royal Institute for the Blind; £1,500 to Worcester Cathedral Choir Association; £1,500 to St Mary's Hospice, Birmingham

FINANCES *Year* 1997 *Income* £86,652 *Grants* £112,250

TRUSTEES A C S Hordern, Miss B Y Mellor, H B Carslake

NOTES Trustees meet annually, usually in May/June

HOW TO APPLY In writing to the address under Who To Apply To. No application form. Applications are not acknowledged

WHO TO APPLY TO A C S Horden, Dumbreck Charity, PriceWaterhouseCoopers, Cornwall Court, 19 Cornwall Street, Birmingham B3 2DT

CC NO 273070   **ESTABLISHED** 1976

■ Ronald Duncan Literary Fund

WHAT IS FUNDED Trustees aim to promote literature through the works of Ronald Duncan and others

WHO CAN BENEFIT Those promoting literature

WHERE FUNDING CAN BE GIVEN UK

FINANCES *Year* 1996 *Income* £22,303 *Grants* £5,000

TRUSTEES D Clarke (Chairman), Mrs K H Cairns, R Duncan, Mrs B Lawson

HOW TO APPLY At any time. Trustees meet half-yearly

WHO TO APPLY TO Colin B Edwards, Chartered Accountant, Ronald Duncan Literary Fund, Little Rushford, Lingfield, Surrey RH7 6DA

CC NO 266559   **ESTABLISHED** 1973

■ Dunecht Charity Trust

WHAT IS FUNDED General charitable purposes

WHAT IS NOT FUNDED No grants to individuals

WHO CAN BENEFIT Registered charities only. There are no restrictions on the age; professional and economic group; family situation; religion and culture; and social circumstances of; or disease or medical condition suffered by, the beneficiaries

WHERE FUNDING CAN BE GIVEN UK

RANGE OF GRANTS £100–£29,716

SAMPLE GRANTS £29,716 to Third Viscount Cowdray Charitable Trust; £1,000 to Banchory Ternan East Church; £1,000 to Haddo House Arts Trust; £600 to Dunecht Hall; £500 to University of Aberdeen

FINANCES *Year* 1996 *Income* £16,641 *Grants* £35,266

TRUSTEES The Cowdray Trust

WHO TO APPLY TO The Secretary, Dunecht Charity Trust, The Cowdray Trust, Pollen House, 10–12 Cork Street, London W1X 1PD

CC NO 265155   **ESTABLISHED** 1972

■ Dunn and Whieldon Charitable Trust

This trust did not respond to CAF's request to amend its entry and, by 30 June 1998, CAF's researchers did not find financial records for later than 1995 on its file at the Charity Commission. Trusts are legally required to submit annual accounts to the Charity Commission under section 42 of the Charities Act 1993

WHAT IS FUNDED General charitable purposes

WHO CAN BENEFIT There are no restrictions on the age; professional and economic group; family situation; religion and culture; and social circumstances of; or disease or medical condition suffered by, the beneficiaries

WHERE FUNDING CAN BE GIVEN UK

TRUSTEES J Dunn, I D Paterson, A G Whieldon

WHO TO APPLY TO A G Whieldon, Trustee, Dunn and Whieldon Charitable Trust, 23 St James Garden, London W11 4RE

CC NO 1049097   **ESTABLISHED** 1995

■ The Harry Dunn Charitable Trust

WHAT IS FUNDED To pursue own concerns in the locality, mainly in relation to the sick and disabled or to environmental charities. Particularly charities working in the fields of: health facilities and buildings; support to voluntary and community organisations, MS research; conservation; bird sanctuaries and ecology

WHAT IS NOT FUNDED Only to causes known to the Trustees personally and never to individual applicants

Does the trust you have chosen match your needs? Haphazard applications waste postage and time

185

WHO CAN BENEFIT Organisations benefiting sufferers of multiple sclerosis

WHERE FUNDING CAN BE GIVEN Nottinghamshire

TYPE OF GRANT Core costs and one-off, funding for one year or less will be considered

RANGE OF GRANTS £500–£5,000

FINANCES *Year* 1998 *Income* £68,075
Grants £29,000

TRUSTEES A H Dunn, C N Dunn, A J Kennedy, N A Dunn, R M Dunn

WHO TO APPLY TO A J Kennedy, The Harry Dunn Charitable Trust, Messrs Cooper-Parry, 56 High Pavement, Nottingham NG1 1HX

CC NO 297389   **ESTABLISHED** 1987

■ The Mrs C T M Dunn Foundation

WHAT IS FUNDED General charitable purposes

WHAT IS NOT FUNDED No grants to individuals

WHO CAN BENEFIT There are no restrictions on the age; professional and economic group; family situation; religion and culture; and social circumstances of; or disease or medical condition suffered by, the beneficiaries

WHERE FUNDING CAN BE GIVEN UK

TRUSTEES J J Russell, D C Chetwood

NOTES Preference is given to local charities and those of particular interest to the Trustees and the Founder

WHO TO APPLY TO D C Chetwood, The Mrs C T M Dunn Foundation, Russell & Hallmark, Solicitors, Holland House, Church Street, Malvern, Hereford and Worcester WR14 2AH

CC NO 262201   **ESTABLISHED** 1971

■ The W E Dunn Trust

WHAT IS FUNDED The funding priorities of the Trust are to benefit persons who are sick or in adversity and resident in the Midlands area, particularly in Wolverhampton, Wednesbury, North Staffordshire and neighbouring localities. The Trustees have full discretion and in addition to dealing with local personal requests through Social Services Departments, they make donations to local charities and occasionally to national charities. The Trustees particularly wish to assist the elderly and the very young but they will not make grants to settle or reduce debts already incurred. They are prepared to assist students from the Midlands to further their education but who have special difficulties which prevent them from doing so. The Trust will consider funding: accommodation and housing; infrastructure, support and development; community arts and recreation; health; church buildings; animal welfare; environmental issues; education and training; costs of study; community facilities and services, and other charitable purposes

WHO CAN BENEFIT Children; young people; older people; clergy; ex-service and service people; medical professionals, nurses and doctors; musicians; sportsmen and women; students; unemployed people; volunteers; those in care, fostered and adopted; parents and children; one parent families; Widows and widowers; at risk groups; carers; disabled people; ex-offenders and those at risk of offending; homeless people; socially isolated people; those living in urban areas; and victims of abuse, crime and domestic violence

WHERE FUNDING CAN BE GIVEN Mainly in the Midlands area

TYPE OF GRANT Buildings, capital, core costs, one-off, project and start-up costs. All funding is for up to three years

SAMPLE GRANTS £40,000 to Keele University W E Dunn Heart Unit; £3,500 to Jubilee Sailing Trust; £2,000 to St Mary's Hospice; £2,000 to Children's Hospital Appeal; £2,000 to Children's Nationwide; £1,000 to Birmingham Young Volunteers; £1,000 to Elizabeth Fitzroy Homes; £1,000 to Nechells Child Minder Trust; £1,000 to Phoenix Sheltered Workshop; £1,000 to SENSE

FINANCES *Year* 1997 *Income* £153,979
Grants £115,579

TRUSTEES C E Corney, D J Corney, D F Perkins, L H Smethurst

WHO TO APPLY TO A H Smith, The W E Dunn Trust, Trust Office, 30 Bentley Heath Cottages, Tilehouse Green Lane, Knowle, Solihull B93 9EL

CC NO 219418   **ESTABLISHED** 1958

■ The Duveen Trust

WHAT IS FUNDED To support projects of individual initiative by young people where self help on its own has proved insufficient

WHAT IS NOT FUNDED Grants towards running costs of projects including salaries and bursaries nor grants to enable people to follow courses of formal education will be considered for funding

WHO CAN BENEFIT Individual young people and registered charities. These include students, the unemployed and those suffering from hearing loss. There are no restrictions on the family situation or the religion and culture of the beneficiaries

WHERE FUNDING CAN BE GIVEN UK

TYPE OF GRANT One-off grants for individual projects

FINANCES *Year* 1997 *Income* £14,064
Grants £19,631

TRUSTEES Mrs L Barden, I Berkoff, S Cotsen, A Greenbat (Chairman), G Matthews, Ms G Murray, P Sollosi

NOTES This is a small family trust with approximately £20,000 pa to distribute. The number of applications is well in excess and we do our best to balance 'need' with 'availability'

HOW TO APPLY By application form which will be sent with guidelines. The Trustees meet three times a year and grants are not given in retrospect

WHO TO APPLY TO Mrs S Packman, The Duveen Trust, 26 Beechwood Avenue, London N3 3AX
Fax 0181-349 9649

CC NO 326823   **ESTABLISHED** 1985

■ The Dwek Family Charitable Trust

WHAT IS FUNDED The advancement of Judaism and charitable purposes of benefit to the community

WHO CAN BENEFIT Jewish people and community organisations

WHERE FUNDING CAN BE GIVEN Manchester

SAMPLE GRANTS £18,600 to Bodycote Educational Trust; £5,500 to Ta'ali-A History; £5,000 to JNF Charitable Trust; £5,000 to Manchester Jewish Social Services; £3,000 to North Cheshire Jewish School; £2,694 to Jewish Cultural Centre; £1,850 to Barnardo's; £1,500 to Shaare Sedek Synagogue; £1,250 to Delamere Forest School; £1,250 to Withington Congregation of Spanish and Portuguese Jews

FINANCES *Year* 1997 *Income* £151,028
Grants £66,013

TRUSTEES J C Dwek, J Dwek, A J Leon

HOW TO APPLY To the address under Who To Apply To in writing

WHO TO APPLY TO J C Dwek, Trustee, The Dwek Family Charitable Trust, Suite One, Courthill House, 66 Water Lane, Wilmslow, Cheshire SK9 5AP

CC NO 1001456   **ESTABLISHED** 1989

■ EAGA Charitable Trust

WHAT IS FUNDED Projects and research which assist to clarify the nature, extent and consequences of fuel poverty; and offer insights into opportunities for the energy efficient and cost-effective relief of fuel poverty in the UK. Medical research and academic subjects, science and research are also considered

WHAT IS NOT FUNDED No grants to individuals

WHO CAN BENEFIT Institutions benefiting research workers, academics and medical professionals

WHERE FUNDING CAN BE GIVEN UK

TYPE OF GRANT One-off for projects and research. Funding is available for up to and over three years

RANGE OF GRANTS £5,000–£30,000

SAMPLE GRANTS £31,300 to National Right to Fuel Campaign, Centre for Sustainable Energy for South West England Gas Market: impact on low income households; £29,850 to National Right to Fuel Campaign, Centre for Sustainable Energy for South West England Gas Market: impact on low income households; £25,000 to Centre for Management Under Regulation, University of Warwick for cost of gas and electricity prepayment meters; £22,000 to Energy Inform, Oxford University for evaluation of effectiveness of energy advice to low income households; £17,625 to NEA for improving standards of service provided by fuel suppliers for low income customers; £15,000 to NEA for assessment and identification of specific energy needs of visually impaired people; £11,138 to Centre for Management Under Regulation, University of Warwick for South West England pilot survey: monitoring liberalisation of gas and electricity

FINANCES *Year* 1996–97 *Income* £206,000 *Grants* £176,000

TRUSTEES Prof J H Chesshire, J Clough, R Jones, M Keay, A Mallen, Prof G Manners, J Stephenson

HOW TO APPLY To the Administrator. Trustees assess grant applications about three times per year. The Administrator can supply application deadlines and an information pack

WHO TO APPLY TO Dr N Brown, Trust Administrator, EAGA Charitable Trust, 20 Blencathra Street, Keswick, Cumbria CA12 4HP

CC NO 1017836   **ESTABLISHED** 1993

■ The EMI Sound Foundation (working name The Music Sound Foundation)

WHAT IS FUNDED The purchase of instruments and equipment; scholarships to music college and other musically oriented institutions; music courses for teachers and music research

WHO CAN BENEFIT Individuals and organisations benefiting: children and young adults; actors and entertainment professionals; musicians; students; teachers and governesses

WHERE FUNDING CAN BE GIVEN UK

TYPE OF GRANT Capital, core costs, one-off, project, research and salaries. Funding may be given for up to one year

SAMPLE GRANTS £100,000 to Bishopshalt School, Hillingdon which was sponsored to become an art college; £3,775 to Bedlingtonshire High School, Northumberland towards instrument tuition for children; £3,269 to Sound Minds, Battersea towards an equipment purchase for mental health centre; £3,500 to an individual in Nottingham towards an equipment purchase for local youth centre; £2,500 to English Touring Opera as a subsidy for opera summer school

FINANCES *Year* 1998 *Grants* £254,247

TRUSTEES J Beach, W Cavendish, Ms R Edge, L Hill, D Hughes, R Perry, P Reichardt, S O'Rouke, Sir C Southgate, K Townsend

NOTES Also known as The Music Sound Foundation

WHO TO APPLY TO Ms J Orr, Administrator, The EMI Sound Foundation, c/o 4 Tenterden Street, Hanover Square, London W1A 2AY *Tel* 0171-355 4848

CC NO 1055434   **ESTABLISHED** 1996

■ ET Charitable Trust

WHAT IS FUNDED General charitable purposes

WHO CAN BENEFIT There are no restrictions on the age; professional and economic group; family situation; religion and culture; and social circumstances of; or disease or medical condition suffered by, the beneficiaries

WHERE FUNDING CAN BE GIVEN UK

WHO TO APPLY TO JC Pears, ET Charitable Trust, Hedleys & Co Solicitors, 78 Sea Road, Fulwell, Sunderland, Tyne and Wear SR6 9DB

CC NO 1067215   **ESTABLISHED** 1998

■ Audrey Earle Charitable Trust

WHAT IS FUNDED Mostly animal charities

WHO CAN BENEFIT Animal charities

WHERE FUNDING CAN BE GIVEN UK and overseas

TYPE OF GRANT Small one-off and recurrent range of grants

RANGE OF GRANTS Usually £1,000 or less

FINANCES *Year* 1996 *Income* £16,944

TRUSTEES J F Russell Smith, John W H Carey, C R L Coubrough

NOTES No further applications to be considered at present. Existing commitments to be continued

WHO TO APPLY TO Audrey Earle Charitable Trust, Messrs Moon Beever & Hewlett 24 Bloomsbury Square London WC1A 2PL *Tel* 0171-637 0661

CC NO 290028   **ESTABLISHED** 1984

■ The Earley Charity

WHAT IS FUNDED To give aid to: the disabled; those with housing need; those caring for elderly parents or relatives; widows/widowers, single elderly and single parents with families; those undertaking vocational training or apprenticeships; appropriate local charities and community organisations; arts, culture and recreation; health; conservation and campaigning; schools and collages; costs of study; studies in engineering; physics, science and technology; and social care and development

WHAT IS NOT FUNDED Educational grants are for vocational courses only. No grants to university undergraduates. Persons aided should normally be resident within the area Where Funding Can Be Given. No national or international appeals are considered

WHO CAN BENEFIT Individuals in need and charitable and community organisations living or operating in the area Where Funding Can Be Given. There are

no restrictions on the age or family situation of the beneficiaries. A wide range of social circumstances will be considered for funding

WHERE FUNDING CAN BE GIVEN Earley and East Reading and the immediate neighbourhood

TYPE OF GRANT One-off, project and start-up costs. Funding is available for up to one year

RANGE OF GRANTS £30–£2,500 for individuals, and £250–£40,000 for organisations

FINANCES *Year* 1996 *Income* £390,593 *Grants* £202,348

TRUSTEES R E Ames, D J Chilvers, Dr D G Jenkins, C A Nichols, I M Robertson, Mrs M Eastwell, D C Sutton, L G Norton

PUBLICATIONS Annual Report

HOW TO APPLY In writing only, at any time, to the address under Who To Apply To. Telephone if you wish to confirm residential qualification

WHO TO APPLY TO J D T Evans, Clerk to the Trustees, The Earley Charity, The Liberty of Earley House, Strand Way, Earley, Reading RG6 4EA *Tel* 0118-975 5663

CC NO 244823   **ESTABLISHED** 1820

■ The Earmark Trust

WHAT IS FUNDED The Trustees normally support charities in which they are personally interested, and favour those charities which are concerned with the advancement of the Christian faith, the disabled, children in need and cancer research and care

WHAT IS NOT FUNDED Applications on behalf of individuals are seldom considered. Neither are applications from large scale charities nor church/cathedral restoration or rebuilding projects

WHO CAN BENEFIT Organisations benefiting: children in need; Christians; at risk groups; disabled people and those suffering from cancers

WHERE FUNDING CAN BE GIVEN UK but local charities are given priority

TYPE OF GRANT Both one-off and regular grants are given

SAMPLE GRANTS £750 to Royal London Society for the Blind; £540 to Combe Bank School; £450 to Royal Alexandra and Albert School; £300 to Bushey Place; £250 to British Red Cross

FINANCES *Year* 1997 *Income* £15,292 *Grants* £9,540

TRUSTEES F C Raven, A C M Raven

HOW TO APPLY By letter to the address under Who To Apply To. Trustees' meetings are held quarterly

WHO TO APPLY TO F C Raven, The Earmark Trust, The Knoll, Ightham, Kent TN15 9DY

CC NO 267176   **ESTABLISHED** 1974

■ Earwicker Trust

WHAT IS FUNDED General charitable purposes. Regular committed giving to registered charities

WHAT IS NOT FUNDED No grants to individuals

WHO CAN BENEFIT Registered charities. There are no restrictions on the age; professional and economic group; family situation; religion and culture; and social circumstances of; or disease or medical condition suffered by, the beneficiaries

WHERE FUNDING CAN BE GIVEN Nottingham

TYPE OF GRANT Single donations

RANGE OF GRANTS £100–£10,200

SAMPLE GRANTS £10,200 to Wollaton Parish Church; £2,400 to Macedon Trust; £1,200 to Christian Aid; £1,200 to Crisis at Christmas; £1,200 to Potters House Trust

FINANCES *Year* 1997 *Income* £20,366 *Grants* £21,000

TRUSTEES S C Earwicker, H M Earwicker, J H Parkin
NOTES Mostly fully committed to regular giving
WHO TO APPLY TO Dr H M Earwicker, Earwicker Trust, 3 Normanby Road, Wollaton, Nottinghamshire NG8 2TA
CC NO 1015667   **ESTABLISHED** 1990

■ **East Kent Provincial Charities Association**

WHAT IS FUNDED Organisations working for the relief of poverty of children and the elderly, the advancement of education, the care of the sick and elderly and other charitable purposes
WHO CAN BENEFIT Organisations benefiting: children; young adults; older people; retired people; students; and those disadvantaged by poverty. There are no restrictions on the disease or medical condition suffered by the beneficiaries
WHERE FUNDING CAN BE GIVEN UK
FINANCES *Year* 1997 *Income* £153,104 *Grants* £91,067
HOW TO APPLY Donations are decided by individual members - it is not practicable to respond to requests for funds from non-members
WHO TO APPLY TO Hugh Pierce, Secretary, East Kent Provincial Charities Association, Masonic Centre, Tovil, Maidstone, Kent ME15 6QS *Tel* 01622 766212
CC NO 1023859   **ESTABLISHED** 1993

■ **The East Lancashire Masonic Benevolent Institution (Incorporated)**

WHAT IS FUNDED Masonic charities and medical, disability and welfare charities in the area Where Funding Can Be Given
WHO CAN BENEFIT Organisations benefiting: at risk groups; disabled people; those disadvantaged by poverty and socially isolated people. There are no restrictions on the disease or medical condition suffered by the beneficiaries
WHERE FUNDING CAN BE GIVEN East Lancashire
SAMPLE GRANTS £4,500 to Province of West Lancashire 1997 MTGB Festival; £4,000 to Province of Cumberland and Westmorland 1997 Grand Charity Festival; £2,500 to Province of Hertfordshire 1998 RMBI Festival; £1,000 to Tameside Hospice Appeal; £750 to Highfield Hall Community Association; £750 to Manchester Initiative (Help the Redundant); £525 Ocean Youth Club; £500 to Age Concern; £500 to Beechwood Cancer Care; £500 to Boys and Girls Welfare Society
FINANCES *Year* 1997 *Income* £565,927 *Grants* £195,714
HOW TO APPLY To the address under Who To Apply To in writing
WHO TO APPLY TO C Wood, Hon Secretary, The East Lancashire Masonic Benevolent Institution, Freemasons Hall, Bridge Street, Manchester M3 3BT *Tel* 0161-832 6256
CC NO 225151   **ESTABLISHED** 1964

■ **East London Nursing Society Trust**

WHAT IS FUNDED (a) Nursing and hospital services; (b) education and special educational needs; (c) voluntary groups serving young people with special needs; (d) addiction recovery programmes; and (e) sick, elderly and handicapped
WHO CAN BENEFIT Voluntary and statutory bodies benefiting people of all ages and those who are disabled. There is no restriction on the disease or medical condition suffered by the beneficiaries
WHERE FUNDING CAN BE GIVEN London Borough of Tower Hamlets
RANGE OF GRANTS Normally £1,000–£500. Only in exceptional circumstances are grants made to a maximum of £1,000
SAMPLE GRANTS £1,000 x 2 to Tower Hamlets Healthcare NHS Trust for social work team in hospitals as funds for emergency needs; £1,000 and £900 to Tower Hamlets Healthcare NHS Trust for community nurses as funds for emergency needs; £785 to Beatrice Tate Special School for swimming sessions; £614 to Stephen Hawking Special School for mobile playground shelters; £500 to Marie Curie Cancer Care for home nursing scheme in Tower Hamlets
FINANCES *Year* 1997–98 *Income* £13,752 *Grants* £12,532
TRUSTEES Mrs M Chambers (Chair), B Blandford, Mrs L Brazier, D Collins (Hon Secretary), Ms J Clemerson, R H Davies, Ms J Ellwood, A Jacob, Ms N Kilne, Mrs P Mason, Miss S Mowat, Mrs M Rintoul, A Roffey, Miss O Wagstaff
HOW TO APPLY To the address below in writing
WHO TO APPLY TO Desmond Collins, Secretary, East London Nursing Society Trust, 92 Crown Woods Way, Eltham, London SE9 2NN *Tel* 0181-850 7993
CC NO 210928   **ESTABLISHED** 1973

■ **The East Lothian Educational Trust**

WHAT IS FUNDED Education. Grants are given to schools and to individuals
WHO CAN BENEFIT Children, young adults and teachers
WHERE FUNDING CAN BE GIVEN The former county of East Lothian
FINANCES *Year* 1994–95 *Grants* £32,000
HOW TO APPLY Applications should be made on an application form which is available from the address below
WHO TO APPLY TO George Russell, Clerk, The East Lothian Educational Trust, 26 Clifford Road, North Berwick, East Lothian EH39 4PP
SC NO SCO 10587

■ **East Midlands Arts Board Ltd**

WHAT IS FUNDED The promotion of arts and media in society for the benefit of the inhabitants of the East Midlands and elsewhere by developing public appreciation of the Arts and by improving public access to, and the quality of, the Arts. Priority for support of regional work, new developments, neglected areas, individual artists
WHAT IS NOT FUNDED Grants are given in connection with professional arts activities only. Students in full-time education are not funded
WHO CAN BENEFIT Individuals and organisations in the arts benefiting: people of all ages; actors and entertainment professionals; musicians; textile workers and designers; writers and poets
WHERE FUNDING CAN BE GIVEN Leicestershire, Rutland, Northamptonshire, Nottinghamshire, Derbyshire (excluding the High Peak)

Does the trust you have chosen match your needs? Haphazard applications waste postage and time

189

TYPE OF GRANT Capital, one-off, project, research and start-up costs. Funding for one year or less will be considered
FINANCES *Year* 1997 *Income* £4,954,041 *Grants* £4,036,984
TRUSTEES The Directors of the Board
PUBLICATIONS *Grants and Schemes*, Annual Leaflet, General Policy Guidelines
HOW TO APPLY Telephone for information
WHO TO APPLY TO Deborah Duggan, Customer Service Officer, East Midlands Arts, Mountfields House, Epinal Way, Loughborough, Leicestershire LE11 0QE *Tel* 01509 218292
CC NO 1004183   **ESTABLISHED** 1969

■ East Riding of Yorkshire Disabled Sports Association

WHAT IS FUNDED The promotion and development of sport and leisure opportunities for people with any disabilities
WHO CAN BENEFIT To benefit people with disabilities
WHERE FUNDING CAN BE GIVEN Yorkshire
TRUSTEES G Williams, D Green, E Blacher, V Longden, G Sunley, M Swift, S Blanchard, L Pratt, R Green, E Toole, J Frere, C Zacharias, B Green, H Clarke
HOW TO APPLY To the address under Who To Apply To in writing
WHO TO APPLY TO D S Green, Secretary, East Riding of Yorkshire Disabled Sports Association, 155 Danube Road, Off Wold Road, Kingston Upon Hull, East Riding of Yorkshire, HU5 5UX
CC NO 1064201   **ESTABLISHED** 1997

■ Eastern Arts Board

WHAT IS FUNDED Professional arts activities in the Eastern region of England
WHAT IS NOT FUNDED No grants to students
WHO CAN BENEFIT Non-profit distributing constituted organisations and individual artists
WHERE FUNDING CAN BE GIVEN Bedfordshire, Cambridgeshire, Essex, Hertfordshire, Lincolnshire, Norfolk and Suffolk
TYPE OF GRANT The projects and schemes funds are available to individual artists and organisations for one-off projects. Other schemes may be appropriate for regular funded clients. Please ask for more information
RANGE OF GRANTS £628–£346,000
SAMPLE GRANTS £346,000 to Eastern Orchestral Board; £322,750 to Wolsey Theatre, Ipswich; £230,000 to Mercury Theatre, Colchester; £204,500 to Palace Theatre, Watford; £175,000 to Aldeburgh Foundation; £170,000 to Eastern Touring Agency; £133,787 to Animateurs; £100,000 to Arts 2000; £76,000 to Eastern Angles; £71,650 to Kettle's Yard Gallery
FINANCES *Year* 1997 *Income* £5,779,657 *Grants* £5,617,342
TRUSTEES Prof B Black, Cllr S Bostock, D Cargill, Cllr B Chappell, G Creelman, R Deakin, Ms S Dyke, Cllr B Ferris, Mrs J George, J Gleadell, Sir D Harrison, CBE, Cllr J Jones, Mrs J Lyon, Cllr T Mitchell, Cllr J Seaman, Ms S Smith, Mrs R Willis Taylor
PUBLICATIONS Annual Report and Accounts, *Eastern Arts News*, *Building the Future* – the Eastern Regions plan for capital investment in the arts
HOW TO APPLY Deadlines for funding schemes are available on request
WHO TO APPLY TO Eastern Arts Board, Cherry Hinton Hall, Cherry Hinton Road, Cambridge CB1 4DW *Tel* 01223 215355
CC NO 1009835   **ESTABLISHED** 1991

■ Sir John Eastwood Foundation

WHAT IS FUNDED General charitable purposes at sole discretion of Trustees
WHAT IS NOT FUNDED No grants to individuals
WHO CAN BENEFIT Local organisations. There are no restrictions on the age; professional and economic group; family situation; religion and culture; and social circumstances of; or disease or medical condition suffered by, the beneficiaries
WHERE FUNDING CAN BE GIVEN Mainly Nottinghamshire
RANGE OF GRANTS £10–£100,000
SAMPLE GRANTS £100,000 to Nottingham Community Housing Association; £25,000 to Portland College; £25,000 to Winged Fellowship; £20,000 to The Salvation Army; £15,000 to MPS Society; £10,000 to Newark and Nottinghamshire Agricultural Society; £5,000 to Warsop Youth Club; £5,000 to Jenny Farr Centre; £5,000 to Lincolnshire Rural Activities Centre; £5,000 to Yeoman Park School
FINANCES *Year* 1996 *Income* £295,411 *Grants* £386,839
TRUSTEES Mrs C B Mudford, Mrs D M Cottingham, G Raymond, Mrs V Hardingham, P Spencer
WHO TO APPLY TO G Raymond, Sir John Eastwood Foundation, Burns Lane, Warsop, Mansfield, Nottinghamshire NG20 0QG
CC NO 235389   **ESTABLISHED** 1964

■ Ebenezer Trust

WHAT IS FUNDED Advancement of Protestant and Evangelical tenets of the Christian faith. Activities in which the Trustees are personally interested/ involved
WHAT IS NOT FUNDED No grants to individuals
WHO CAN BENEFIT Registered charities benefiting Baptists and Evangelists
WHERE FUNDING CAN BE GIVEN UK and overseas
TYPE OF GRANT Occasionally interest free loans
RANGE OF GRANTS £50–£1,000
SAMPLE GRANTS £13,000 to Brentwood Baptist Church; £5,000 to TEAR Fund; £3,300 to Pilgrims Hatch Baptist Church; £3,000 to Banchory – Ternan East Parish Church; £2,700 to Baptist Missionary Society; £2,000 to Scripture Union; £2,000 to Spurgeon's College; £1,500 to St Francis Hospice; £1,500 to Brentwood Schools Christian Worker; £1,500 to Interserve
FINANCES *Year* 1997 *Income* £61,791 *Grants* £52,547
TRUSTEES N T Davey, FCA, R M Davey
NOTES Unsolicited applications are rarely successful
WHO TO APPLY TO N T Davey, Ebenezer Trust, 31 Middleton Road, Brentwood, Essex CM15 8DJ *Tel* 0171-303 3022
CC NO 272574   **ESTABLISHED** 1976

■ Frank Eccleshare Trust

WHAT IS FUNDED General charitable purposes, welfare
WHO CAN BENEFIT At risk groups; those disadvantaged by poverty; and socially isolated people
WHERE FUNDING CAN BE GIVEN Lincoln
FINANCES *Year* 1997 *Income* £30,050
TRUSTEES F R Eccleshare, R Chapman, R L Russell, J T Little
NOTES In 1995 grants totalling £658 were made
HOW TO APPLY To the address under Who To Apply To in writing

WHO TO APPLY TO F Eccleshare, Chairman, Frank Eccleshare Trust, Epton and Co Solicitors, 2 Bank Street, Lincoln LN2 1DR

CC NO 500021   ESTABLISHED 1969

■ The Ecclesiastical Music Trust

WHAT IS FUNDED Promotion of the study, practice and appreciation of Ecclesiastical Music. The creation and spreading of interest in Ecclesiastical Music

WHAT IS NOT FUNDED No grant for any appeal unrelated to Ecclesiastical Music

WHO CAN BENEFIT Individuals and organisations benefiting children, young adults and musicians. More specifically, choirs and choristers, churches and societies concerned with church music are supported. Support may also be given to Christians, including Baptists, Anglicans, Methodists and Roman Catholics

WHERE FUNDING CAN BE GIVEN UK

RANGE OF GRANTS £150–£5,000

SAMPLE GRANTS £5,000 to Friends of Cathedral Music; £900 to an individual for choir school fees at King's, Cambridge; £750 to an individual for choir school fees at Canterbury Cathedral Choir School; £750 to an individual for choir school fees at St George's, Windsor; £600 to an individual for choir school fees at King's School, Rochester

FINANCES Year 1997 Income £15,858
Grants £13,350

TRUSTEES Canon A D Caesar, The Ven G B Timms, M P M Fleming, C F D Moore

HOW TO APPLY In writing to the address under Who To Apply To by 30 April each year. Applications will not be acknowledged

WHO TO APPLY TO Miss G Yeatman, BSc, FCA, The Ecclesiastical Music Trust, Orchard House, Cot Lane, Chidham, Chichester PO18 8ST

CC NO 235248   ESTABLISHED 1950

■ The Ecological Foundation

WHAT IS FUNDED Conservation, wildlife sanctuaries, organic food production, environmental issues, renewable energy, and transport and alternative transport

WHO CAN BENEFIT Individuals and voluntary organisations

WHERE FUNDING CAN BE GIVEN UK and overseas

TYPE OF GRANT Feasibility studies, project and research. Funding can be given for up to two years

FINANCES Year 1997 Income £54,755
Grants £85,051

TRUSTEES The Marquis of Londonderry, John Aspinall, R Hanbury-Tension, E R Goldsmith

HOW TO APPLY To the address under Who To Apply To in writing

WHO TO APPLY TO J Faull, Director, The Ecological Foundation, Lower Bosneives, Withiel, Bodmin, Cornwall PL30 5NQ Tel 01208 831236 Fax 01208 831083

CC NO 264947   ESTABLISHED 1972

■ John Eddleston's Charity

WHAT IS FUNDED Funding is divided between the advancement of religion, relief in need and educational grants, both to schools and individuals under 25

WHO CAN BENEFIT Individuals (under 25) and organisations benefiting children, young adults, students, and those in need. There is no restriction on the religion or culture of the beneficiaries

WHERE FUNDING CAN BE GIVEN The Ecclesiastical Parish of St Aidan, Billinge

RANGE OF GRANTS £150–£11,824

SAMPLE GRANTS £11,824 for upkeep of land; £5,000 to Billinge Parish Council; £3,500 to St Aidans School; £3,000 to an individual; £2,000 to Billinge County Primary School; £1,661 to an individual; £1,500 to Billinge Chapel End Primary School; £1,500 to Billinge and Winstanley St Mary's CP School; £1,498 for legal fees for an individual; £500 to 5th Wigan Brownie Guides; £500 to Billinge and Winstanley RC School

FINANCES Year 1996 Income £130,032
Grants £44,435

TRUSTEES T R Ellis, Canon K M Forrest, C E Mather, C Stockley, W N Tyrer, N F Wilson, E M Wright

HOW TO APPLY To the address under Who To Apply To in writing. Applications are considered by the Trustees in March

WHO TO APPLY TO A H Leech & Sons, Secretaries to the Trustees, John Eddleston's Charity, Greenbank House, 152 Wigan Lane, Wigan WN1 2LA

CC NO 503695   ESTABLISHED 1987

■ Eden Arts Trust

WHAT IS FUNDED To promote and develop the arts and art projects involving the community; to encourage new groups

WHAT IS NOT FUNDED Artists and community groups who are not based within Eden District or whose work is not for the benefit of the residents of Eden District

WHO CAN BENEFIT Individuals and organisations benefiting: young adults and older people; actors and entertainment professionals; musicians; textile workers and designers; volunteers; and writers and poets

WHERE FUNDING CAN BE GIVEN Eden district, Cumbria

TYPE OF GRANT Small local arts and crafts projects, days and events, feasibility studies

RANGE OF GRANTS £50–£2,000, average grant £500

SAMPLE GRANTS £2,300 to Appleby Jazz Society for Appleby Jazz Festival; £2,000 to Quondam Theatre for development work; £1,500 to East Cumbria Countryside Commission for public art project; £1,300 to Penrith Music Club towards annual programme; £1,000 to Upfront for exhibition programme

FINANCES Year 1997 Income £65,622
Grants £18,619

TRUSTEES Mrs E Thomson

WHO TO APPLY TO N Jones, Eden Arts Trust, 2 Sandgate, Penrith, Cumbria CA11 7TP Tel 01768 899444

CC NO 1000476   ESTABLISHED 1990

■ James Eden's Foundation

WHAT IS FUNDED Individuals in further education receive the majority of the grant total, while children and youth charities in the area Where Funding Can Be Given also benefit

WHO CAN BENEFIT Individuals and local organisations benefiting children, young adults and students

WHERE FUNDING CAN BE GIVEN The Metropolitan Borough of Bolton

TYPE OF GRANT One-off and recurrent

SAMPLE GRANTS £1,200 to an individual for further education; £1,000 to an individual for further education; £700 each to three individuals for further education; £650 to Bolton Lads and Girls Club; £450 to Bolton YMCA

FINANCES *Year* 1996–97 *Income* £13,112
Grants £9,100

TRUSTEES N G Coates (Chairman), A J Mitchell, B H Leigh-Bramwell, P J Senior, E R Walker, T J Arkwright, A R Taylor

HOW TO APPLY To the address under Who To Apply To in writing

WHO TO APPLY TO J G Smith, Secretary, James Eden's Foundation, Deloitte and Touche Private Clients Ltd, PO Box 500, 201 Deansgate, Manchester M60 2AT *Tel* 0161-455 8283

CC NO 526265   **ESTABLISHED** 1964

■ **The Gilbert and Eileen Edgar Foundation**

WHAT IS FUNDED Only charities in which the Trustees are personally interested will be supported. Preferences is given to medical research; care and support of the young, the old and the needy; the promotion of fine arts and education in the fine arts; the promotion of academic education, religion; and the provision of recreational facilities

WHO CAN BENEFIT Charitable organisations benefiting people of all ages, artists, academics, at risk groups, those disadvantaged by poverty and socially isolated people. Support may be given for medical professionals and research workers. People of many religions and cultures will also be supported

WHERE FUNDING CAN BE GIVEN UK and occasionally overseas

RANGE OF GRANTS £250–£5,000

SAMPLE GRANTS £5,000 to Save Our Churches Appeal, Hambledon Church; £2,702 to Royal National Theatre; £1,175 to English National Ballet; £1,004 to Sheriffs and Recorders' Fund; £1,000 to British Brain and Spine Foundation; £1,000 to Research into Ageing; £1,000 to Concern Worldwide; £1,000 to Marie Curie Cancer Care; £1,000 to St Mungo Community Trust; £1,000 to Thames Valley Hospice

FINANCES *Year* 1995 *Income* £78,731
Grants £70,031

TRUSTEES A E Gentilli, J G Matthews

NOTES The total grants given in 1995 were: to medical and surgical research £10,800; to care and support £36,654; to the fine arts £6,877; to education in the fine arts £3,000; to academic education £1,500; and to religion, recreation, conservation and heritage £11,200

WHO TO APPLY TO Mrs A Hallam, The Gilbert and Eileen Edgar Foundation, Messrs Chantrey Vellacott, 23–25 Castle Street, Reading, Berkshire RG1 7SB

CC NO 241736   **ESTABLISHED** 1965

■ **The Gilbert Edgar Trust**

WHAT IS FUNDED Only charities which the Trustees find worthwhile will be supported. Support of detailed medical research, children, UK hospices, surgical aids and mental health

WHAT IS NOT FUNDED No grants will be made to individual applicants

WHO CAN BENEFIT Registered charities, educational or cultural bodies benefiting: children; medical professionals and research workers. There is no restriction on the disease or medical condition suffered by the beneficiaries

WHERE FUNDING CAN BE GIVEN Predominantly UK, limited overseas

TYPE OF GRANT Research will be considered

FINANCES *Year* 1997 *Income* £41,408
Grants £45,000

TRUSTEES S C E Gentilli, A E Gentilli, Dr R E B Solomons

NOTES We rely on brochures, sent in before November, each year. We do not particularly like the large glossy expensive brochures. We like to know when targets have been achieved

HOW TO APPLY Brochure by post

WHO TO APPLY TO S C E Gentilli, The Gilbert Edgar Trust, Huttons Farm, Hambleden, Henley-on-Thames, Oxfordshire RG9 6NE

CC NO 213630   **ESTABLISHED** 1955

■ **The Edge and Ellison Charitable Trust**

WHAT IS FUNDED General charitable purposes

WHO CAN BENEFIT There are no restrictions on the age; professional and economic group; family situation; religion and culture; and social circumstances of; or disease or medical condition suffered by, the beneficiaries

WHERE FUNDING CAN BE GIVEN UK

TRUSTEES Partners at Edge & Ellison Solicitors

WHO TO APPLY TO Ms S Thompson, The Edge and Ellison Charitable Trust, Rutland House, 148 Edmund Street, Birmingham B3 2JR

CC NO 1064028   **ESTABLISHED** 1997

■ **The Edinburgh Children's Holiday Fund**

WHAT IS FUNDED Grants are awarded to charities which are concerned with children's welfare or which provide holidays for disadvantaged children

WHO CAN BENEFIT Children, especially those who are in care, fostered and adopted, from one parent families, at risk, disadvantaged by poverty or living in urban areas

WHERE FUNDING CAN BE GIVEN Edinburgh and Lothian

TYPE OF GRANT One-off grants funded for up to one year

SAMPLE GRANTS £8,500 to City of Edinburgh Council, Social Work Department; £7,500 to Children 1st; £4,500 to Family Care; £3,675 to Roses Charitable Trust; £3,500 to Sense Scotland

FINANCES *Year* 1997 *Income* £69,000
Grants £56,000

TRUSTEES Mrs P Balfour, Lady Clerk, W G Waterston

HOW TO APPLY Applications should be made in writing to the address under Who To Apply To by the 30 November

WHO TO APPLY TO The Edinburgh Children's Holiday Fund, Bryce, Wilson & Co, Chartered Accountants, 13a Manor Place, Edinburgh EH3 7DH *Tel* 0131-225 5111 *Fax* 0131-220 0283

SC NO SCO 10312

■ **Edinburgh Night Shelter Trust**

WHAT IS FUNDED Trustees' policy is to support organisations that provide emergency accommodation for homeless people

WHO CAN BENEFIT Registered charities benefiting homeless people

WHERE FUNDING CAN BE GIVEN Edinburgh and Lothian area

WHO TO APPLY TO E A Matthews, Secretary, Edinburgh Night Shelter Trust, Council of Social Service, Ainslie House, 11 St Colme Street, Edinburgh EH3 6AG
SC NO SCO 09339

■ Edinburgh Trust, No 2 Account

WHAT IS FUNDED General charitable purposes, but the trust fund and the income may be applied for the promotion and advancement of education and of the efficiency of the armed services of the Crown. Scientific expeditions
WHAT IS NOT FUNDED No grants to individuals, only scientific expeditions are considered with the backing of a major society
WHO CAN BENEFIT Registered charities only. There are no restrictions on the age; professional and economic group; family situation; religion and culture; and social circumstances of; or disease or medical condition suffered by, the beneficiaries
WHERE FUNDING CAN BE GIVEN UK
FINANCES *Year* 1998 *Income* £65,000
Grants £62,000
TRUSTEES Sir Brian McGrath, KCVO, C Woodhouse
WHO TO APPLY TO G D Partington, Edinburgh Trust, Buckingham Palace, London SW1A 1AA
CC NO 227897   **ESTABLISHED** 1959

■ Education Services

WHAT IS FUNDED (a) Promotion of education and provision of facilities for experiment and training in educational principle and method, with particular emphasis on the co-operative and contributive motives. (b) Promotion of research into and instruction in monetary theory and the practice of banking. Most support is given to charities of special interest to the Council of Education Services and to research and study programmes. Support may also be given to children
WHAT IS NOT FUNDED Grants are not normally made for post-graduate or first degree courses
WHO CAN BENEFIT Organisations and individuals engaged in educational and monetary research, especially innovative projects. Support may be given to students, academics and children
WHERE FUNDING CAN BE GIVEN UK
TYPE OF GRANT Project and research grants
SAMPLE GRANTS £9,000 to Cambridge University Marshall Library; £250 to Farm and Food Society; £200 to World Education Fellowship; £150 to CAIPE; £100 to Commonwealth Human Ecology Council
FINANCES *Year* 1995 *Income* £15,977
Grants £15,023
TRUSTEES J Owen Jones, R D Sawtell
NOTES Most of the donations are to individuals. Funds are mainly committed to the support of charities which are of special interest to the Council of Education Services, and to research and study programmes
WHO TO APPLY TO Mrs Philippa Franks, Education Services, 364 Woodstock Road, Oxford OX2 8AE
CC NO 313026   **ESTABLISHED** 1930

■ The Educational Charity of the Stationers' and Newspaper Makers' Company

WHAT IS FUNDED The education of people wishing to enter the printing, stationers' or newspaper makers' trades, the installation of printing departments in schools
WHAT IS NOT FUNDED Applications from persons not associated with the industries connected with the Stationers' company
WHO CAN BENEFIT Individuals and organisations benefiting children and young adults under the age of 25
WHERE FUNDING CAN BE GIVEN UK and Greater London
TYPE OF GRANT One-off, capital and funding of one year or less
RANGE OF GRANTS £200–£2,500
FINANCES *Year* 1996–97 *Income* £91,000
Grants £72,000
TRUSTEES Stationers' and Newspaper Makers' Company
HOW TO APPLY Application forms are available from the address under Who To Apply To
WHO TO APPLY TO P Thornton, Secretary, The Educational Charity of the Stationers' and Newspaper Makers' Company, Inglewood, Oving, Aylesbury, Buckinghamshire HP22 4HD
Tel 01296 641858
CC NO 312633   **ESTABLISHED** 1985

■ Dr Edwards' and Bishop King's Fulham Charity

WHAT IS FUNDED To provide pensions for people who have resided in the area Where Funding Can Be Given for not less than two years who are in need, hardship or distress. Grants to individuals on low incomes for essential items for daily living, either through local statutory or welfare agencies or directly. Weekly payments to people on low incomes who are on a register of pensioners. Grants to organisations who help people in need. Grants for aids for disabled people. Educational grants for vocational training access courses and other educational needs
WHO CAN BENEFIT Individuals and organisations benefiting young adults, older people, disabled people and those disadvantaged by poverty
WHERE FUNDING CAN BE GIVEN Former Metropolitan Borough of Fulham as in 1965
TYPE OF GRANT Mainly one-off grants
RANGE OF GRANTS £60–£51,767
SAMPLE GRANTS £51,767 to Townmead Youth Club for structural repairs; £15,000 to London Cyrenians for a Sunday Club running costs; £12,921 to FULPAC for fire and emergency safety work; £6,312 to Fulham Good Neighbour Service for a group work project; £6,165 to Furnish for new beds for clients; £5,000 to Sands End Adventure Playground for running costs; £3,000 to Bishop Creighton House; £3,000 to Fulham Citizens Advice Bureau; £3,000 to Fulham Legal Advice Centre; £3,000 to Fulham Money Advice Centre
FINANCES *Year* 1998 *Income* £362,819
Grants £153,215
TRUSTEES Mrs J Fortune, I Gray, Mrs R House, A Lott, Mrs V Lukey, A M Norridge, J Pearce, A Russell-Smith, Mrs M Sondergaard, Mrs S Spiers, Cllr C Treloggan, S W Unwin, M Waymouth
NOTES In 1998: pensions £36,504; pensioners Christmas vouchers £1,816; and relief in need £150,350

Does the trust you have chosen match your needs? Haphazard applications waste postage and time

193

WHO TO APPLY TO Mrs M Blackmore, Clerk to the Trustees, Dr Edwards' and Bishop King's Fulham Charity, 33–35 Dawes Road, London SW6 7DT
CC NO 247630 **ESTABLISHED** 1966

■ W G Edwards Charitable Foundation

WHAT IS FUNDED Housing for the elderly, other areas of care for the elderly
WHO CAN BENEFIT Neighbourhood-based community projects benefiting older people
WHERE FUNDING CAN BE GIVEN UK
TYPE OF GRANT Capital
RANGE OF GRANTS £1,000–£50,000
SAMPLE GRANTS £50,000 to Age Concern, Tower Hamlets; £50,000 to Griffin Community; £30,000 to Age Concern, Merstham; £30,000 to Shropshire Rural Housing Association; £21,000 to St Richards Hospice; £1,000 to Voluntary Reading
FINANCES *Year* 1997 *Income* £212,770
Grants £182,000
TRUSTEES Mrs M E O Edwards, Prof W D Savage, S K Phillips, Mrs J Edwards
HOW TO APPLY To the address under Who To Apply To in writing
WHO TO APPLY TO S K Phillips, W G Edwards Charitable Foundation, Wedge Property Co Ltd, 123a Station Road East, Oxted, Surrey RH8 0QE *Tel* 01883 714412
CC NO 293312 **ESTABLISHED** 1985

■ William Edwards Educational Charity (otherwise known as The School Charity of William Edwards at Kenilworth)

WHAT IS FUNDED Schools and education for those under 25 years of age
WHO CAN BENEFIT Schools and institutions benefiting children, young adults, academics and students under the age of 25
WHERE FUNDING CAN BE GIVEN Kenilworth
SAMPLE GRANTS £50,630 to other institutions; £44,238 to 263 individuals; £33,960 to Kenilworth School; £27,153 to postgraduates for bursaries; £10,412 to St John's County Primary School
FINANCES *Year* 1996–97 *Income* £201,872
Grants £166,393
TRUSTEES K Rawnsley, J Halfield, Dr R L J Lovick, Cllr Mrs P Edwards, Cllr Mrs M L Harrison, Dr G Roper, Cllr H A Thomas, Cllr L G Windybank, Cllr R R Wooller
HOW TO APPLY To the address under Who To Apply To in writing
WHO TO APPLY TO J M P Hathaway, Clerk, William Edwards Educational Charity, Messrs Heath Blenkinsop, 13 Old Square, Warwick CV34 4RA
CC NO 528714 **ESTABLISHED** 1981

■ The Eighty Eight Charitable Trust (formerly L G M Hannen Charitable Trust)

WHAT IS FUNDED General charitable purposes
WHO CAN BENEFIT There are no restrictions on the age; professional and economic group; family situation; religion and culture; and social circumstances of; or disease or medical condition suffered by, the beneficiaries
WHERE FUNDING CAN BE GIVEN UK and overseas
RANGE OF GRANTS £50–£25,000

SAMPLE GRANTS £25,000 to Peterborough Cathedral Trust; £15,000 to Foresight; £5,000 to Dulwich Picture Gallery; £2,500 to Friends of Edward VII Hospital, Midhurst; £2,000 to 9/12 Royal Lancers Association; £1,996 to AIDIS Trust; £1,000 to King Edward VII Hospital for Officers; £1,000 to the Dioces in Europe (Majorca); £500 to the Army Benevolent Fund; £500 to Dr Barnardos
FINANCES *Year* 1997 *Income* £63,406
Grants £71,940
TRUSTEES L G M Hannen, Mrs B Hannen
WHO TO APPLY TO Ms A Latimer, Accountant, The Eighty Eight Charitable Trust, Messrs Pannell Kerr Foster, Pannell House, Charter Court, Severalls Business Park, Colchester, Essex CO4 4YA
CC NO 296777 **ESTABLISHED** 1987

■ Elanore Ltd

WHAT IS FUNDED To advance religion in accordance with the Orthodox Jewish faith and the relief of poverty
WHO CAN BENEFIT Jewish people and those disadvantaged by poverty
WHERE FUNDING CAN BE GIVEN UK
TYPE OF GRANT At the discretion of the Trustees
FINANCES *Year* 1996 *Income* £33,230
Grants £2,500
TRUSTEES J Beck, Mrs D Beck
WHO TO APPLY TO J Beck, Elanore Ltd, 25 Highfield Gardens, London NW11 9HD
CC NO 281047 **ESTABLISHED** 1980

■ The Eleos Charitable Trust

WHAT IS FUNDED General charitable purposes
WHO CAN BENEFIT There are no restrictions on the age; professional and economic group; family situation; religion and culture; and social circumstances of; or disease or medical condition suffered by, the beneficiaries
WHERE FUNDING CAN BE GIVEN England and overseas
FINANCES *Year* 1997 *Income* £18,887
Grants £12,700
TRUSTEES I J Cooke, E J Green, J S Haines
NOTES The principal payment, for 1997, of £7,050 was for the purchase of a minibus to support the work amongst children, old people and members of the London homeless community
WHO TO APPLY TO I J Cooke, The Eleos Charitable Trust, 27 Spice Court, Asher Way, London E1 9JD
CC NO 1037105 **ESTABLISHED** 1994

■ Elephant Jobs Charity

WHAT IS FUNDED Support of young people for employment and training
WHO CAN BENEFIT Organisations benefiting young people seeking employment
WHERE FUNDING CAN BE GIVEN South East London, especially Southwark and Lambeth
TYPE OF GRANT At the discretion of the Trustees
FINANCES *Year* 1994–95 *Income* £55,655
Grants £16,850
TRUSTEES P B Challen, J Underwood, R Park
WHO TO APPLY TO Richard Martin, The Administrator, Elephant Jobs Charity, Winchcombe Business Centre, Lydney Close, London SE15 6QW
CC NO 282417 **ESTABLISHED** 1961

■ The Elephant Trust

WHAT IS FUNDED To extend the frontiers of creative endeavour and initiative, encourage the experimental, unconventional and imaginative and within its limited resources to make it possible for artists and those presenting artistic projects to realise and complete such works

WHAT IS NOT FUNDED No student or other study grants

WHO CAN BENEFIT Individuals and organisations concerned with the arts

WHERE FUNDING CAN BE GIVEN UK

TYPE OF GRANT One-off contributions to specific projects

RANGE OF GRANTS £1,000–£34,511

SAMPLE GRANTS £34,511 to 17 individuals; £4,000 to the Tate Gallery; £3,000 to English National Opera; £3,000 to Redstone Atlas; £3,000 to Camden Arts Centre; £2,000 to Chesil Gallery, Chiswell, Dorset; £2,000 to Eagle Graphics; £2,000 to Girls High; £2,000 to O & I Organisation and Imagination; £2,000 to the Whitworth Art Gallery, Manchester

FINANCES *Year* 1997 *Income* £141,838 *Grants* £77,571

TRUSTEES Lord Hutchinson of Lullington, John Bodley, Joanna Drew, Antony A Forwood, John Golding, Julie Lawson

PUBLICATIONS Guidelines are issued

NOTES The Trustees also administer the George Melhuish Bequest which has similar objectives

HOW TO APPLY In writing to the address under Who To Apply To, together with an sae. The Trustees normally meet four times a year

WHO TO APPLY TO A Forwood, Trustee, The Elephant Trust, 20 Furnival Street, London EC4A 1BN

CC NO 269615   **ESTABLISHED** 1975

■ E V Elias Charitable Settlement

WHAT IS FUNDED General charitable purposes, with particular favour given to Jewish charitable organisations

WHAT IS NOT FUNDED Registered charities only

WHO CAN BENEFIT There are no restrictions on the age; professional and economic group; family situation; religion and culture; and social circumstances of; or disease or medical condition suffered by, the beneficiaries. However, particular favour is given to Jewish people and Jewish charitable organisations

WHERE FUNDING CAN BE GIVEN UK

RANGE OF GRANTS £35–£2,000

SAMPLE GRANTS £2,000 to Sussex House School; £1,000 to Friends of King Edward VII Hospital; £1,000 to the Society of Friends of the Torah; £1,000 to CHIC (Community House Information Centre); £800 to Friends of the Children of Great Ormond Street; £168 to British Wheelchair Sports; £125 to Tommy's Campaign; £100 to British Trust Fomyelin Project; £100 to British Heart Foundation; £65 to NSPCC

FINANCES *Year* 1997 *Income* £34,573 *Grants* £6,393

TRUSTEES The Royal Bank of Scotland plc and others, including David W Elias

NOTES Time charity for sixty years from 27 February 1968

WHO TO APPLY TO The Royal Bank of Scotland plc, E V Elias Charitable Settlement, Private Trust & Taxation, 45 Mosley Street, Manchester M60 2BE

CC NO 255735   **ESTABLISHED** 1968

■ George Elias Charitable Trust

WHAT IS FUNDED Mainly Jewish causes, some smaller donations (£100 to £750) to more general charitable causes, including educational needs and the fight against poverty

WHO CAN BENEFIT Organisations benefiting children, young adults, those disadvantaged by poverty and Jewish people

WHERE FUNDING CAN BE GIVEN UK and Israel

TYPE OF GRANT Capital

FINANCES *Year* 1996–97 *Income* £102,779 *Grants* £85,308

TRUSTEES G H Elias, Mrs D Elias, E C Elias, S E Elias

HOW TO APPLY To the address under Who To Apply To in writing

WHO TO APPLY TO N G Denton, George Elias Charitable Trust, Elitex House, Moss Lane, Hale, Altrincham, Cheshire WA15 8AD

CC NO 273993   **ESTABLISHED** 1977

■ Eling Trust

WHAT IS FUNDED (a) The advancement of the Christian religion more particularly according to the teaching and usage of the Orthodox Churches of the East. (b) The advancement of medical research and the study of medicine. (c) The relief of sickness and/or poverty. (d) General charitable purposes

WHAT IS NOT FUNDED No grants to individuals

WHO CAN BENEFIT Organisations primarily benefiting young adults, students, those disadvantaged by poverty and Christians, in particularly Eastern Orthodox Christians. There is no restriction on the disease or medical condition suffered by the beneficiaries. Otherwise there are no restrictions on the age; professional and economic group; family situation; religion and culture; and social circumstances of the beneficiaries

WHERE FUNDING CAN BE GIVEN UK

RANGE OF GRANTS £1,000 –£6,000

SAMPLE GRANTS £6,000 to Convent of the Annunciation; £5,000 to Kellogg College

FINANCES *Year* 1997 *Income* £21,260 *Grants* £12,000

TRUSTEES D A W Gardiner, C J Pratt, FRICS, Rev Canon C T Scott-Dempster

WHO TO APPLY TO C J Pratt, FRICS, Eling Trust, Eling Estate Office, Hermitage, Newbury, Berkshire RG16 9UF

CC NO 255072   **ESTABLISHED** 1968

■ Queen Elizabeth Charitable Trust

WHAT IS FUNDED General charitable purposes at the discretion of the Trustees

WHO CAN BENEFIT There are no restrictions on the age; professional and economic group; family situation; religion and culture; and social circumstances of; or disease or medical condition suffered by, the beneficiaries

WHERE FUNDING CAN BE GIVEN UK

TRUSTEES Major Sir R Anstruther, Marsom H Boyd-Carpenter, The Rt Hon The Earl of Home, The Hon Sir A Ogilvy

WHO TO APPLY TO M Henry Boyd-Carpenter, CVO, Queen Elizabeth Charitable Trust, 66 Lincoln's Inn Fields, London WC2A 3LH

CC NO 1059721   **ESTABLISHED** 1996

■ Queen Elizabeth's Grant

WHAT IS FUNDED The parish church of St Mary's, education, medical and social projects. Particularly charities working in the fields of: Christian education; cemeteries and burial grounds; churches; Anglican bodies; Free Church; church buildings; church schools; community centres and village halls; care in the community and sheltered accommodation

WHAT IS NOT FUNDED No grants to individuals

WHO CAN BENEFIT Organisations benefiting children, young adults, Christians and carers

WHERE FUNDING CAN BE GIVEN The Borough of Stafford as defined in 1974

TYPE OF GRANT One-off, project and running costs. Funding for one year or less will be considered

RANGE OF GRANTS £250–£2,000

SAMPLE GRANTS £6,782 to St Mary's Church as the main object of the Trust; £1,500 to John Young Foundation for general expenditure; £1,150 to TS Superb (Sea Cadets) for purchase of a boat; £500 to Bethany Project for temporary accommodation for homeless; £500 to Mayor's Charities

FINANCES *Year* 1996–97 *Income* £14,475 *Grants* £10,762

TRUSTEES F S Bailey, Mayor of Stafford, Rector of Stafford, E M Riley, F E Wilkinson

HOW TO APPLY To the address under Who To Apply To in writing

WHO TO APPLY TO E V Aspin, Receiver to the Trustees, Queen Elizabeth's Grant, 38 Park Avenue, Stafford, Staffordshire ST17 9RB *Tel* 01785 212762

CC NO 250780   **ESTABLISHED** 1835

■ The Wilfred & Elsie Elkes Charity Fund

WHAT IS FUNDED The Trustees have a particular interest in child welfare, the welfare of the elderly, organisations working with deaf people and medical charities involved with deafness, Alzheimer's disease, Parkinson's disease and a range of other diseases. Animal welfare; infrastructure development; charity or voluntary umbrella bodies; accommodation and housing; and community facilities and services are also considered

WHAT IS NOT FUNDED The Trustees normally only make donations to other charitable organisations, and only exceptionally direct to individuals

WHO CAN BENEFIT Organisations benefiting retired people. There is no restriction on the age or family situation of, and some restrictions on the social circumstances and the diseases or medical conditions suffered by, the beneficiaries

WHERE FUNDING CAN BE GIVEN Particular emphasis on Staffordshire, Birmingham, Coventry, Dudley, Stoke-on-Trent, Walsall and Wolverhampton

TYPE OF GRANT Recurrent grants are given in a number of cases but more normally the grant is a one-off payment. Grants can be made for buildings, capital, core costs, project, research, running costs, salaries and start-up costs. Funding is available for up to and over three years

SAMPLE GRANTS £5,000 to Staffordshire University for the 'handy-one' Robotic dial for the disabled; £4,500 to Wilfred Home, Uttoxeter for essential maintenance; £3,500 to Consall Scout Camp for improvements; £3,000 to Commonwealth Society for the Deaf for the supply of specialist equipment; £2,000 to the Belhony Project; £2,000 to Uttoxeter District Scout Council; £2,000 to Uttoxeter General Charities

FINANCES *Year* 1996–97 *Income* £96,192 *Grants* £51,150

TRUSTEES Royal Bank of Scotland plc, F A Barnes

HOW TO APPLY Any time, but Trustees meetings are only held at approximately quarterly intervals

WHO TO APPLY TO The Trust Officer, Trustee & Taxation Office, The Wilfred & Elsie Elkes Charity Fund, Royal Bank of Scotland plc, PO Box 356, 45 Mosley Street, Manchester M60 2BE

CC NO 326573   **ESTABLISHED** 1984

■ The Elkhaven Charitable Trust

WHAT IS FUNDED General charitable purposes

WHO CAN BENEFIT There are no restrictions on the age; professional and economic group; family situation; religion and culture; and social circumstances of; or disease or medical condition suffered by, the beneficiaries

WHERE FUNDING CAN BE GIVEN UK and overseas

TRUSTEES Ms F M Allen, C P Jackson, Ms E M Jackson

WHO TO APPLY TO Mrs F Allen, Professional Advisor, The Elkhaven Charitable Trust, 38 Meer Street, Stratford upon Avon, Warwickshire CV37 6QB

CC NO 1058142   **ESTABLISHED** 1996

■ Ellinson Foundation Limited

WHAT IS FUNDED Institutions of higher learning

WHAT IS NOT FUNDED No grants to individuals

WHO CAN BENEFIT Institutions of higher learning, benefiting young adults, students and teachers

WHERE FUNDING CAN BE GIVEN UK and overseas

TYPE OF GRANT Capital and recurring grants

RANGE OF GRANTS £25–£20,000

SAMPLE GRANTS £20,000 to Friends of United Institution of Arab; £16,000 to Friends of Neve Yersholayim; £10,500 to Emuno Education Centre; £10,300 to Yeshiva L'Zeihim, Gateshead; £8,000 to British Friends of Brisher Yeshiva Jerusalem; £7,500 to Jewish Educational Trust; £7,350 to Society of Friends of Torah; £7,000 to British Friends of Chazonish Institution; £5,550 to Gateshead Jewish Boarding School; £5,000 to Tore Ohr Seminary

FINANCES *Year* 1997 *Income* £185,809 *Grants* £151,010

TRUSTEES C O Ellinson, Mrs E Ellinson, A Ellinson, A Z Ellinson, U Ellinson

WHO TO APPLY TO Ellinson Foundation Limited, Messrs Robson Laidler & Co, Accountants, 101 Jesmond Road, Newcastle upon Tyne NE2 1NH

CC NO 252018   **ESTABLISHED** 1967

■ Edith M Ellis 1985 Charitable Trust

WHAT IS FUNDED General charitable purposes including religious and educational projects (but not personal grants for religious or secular education nor grants for Church Buildings) and projects in international fields specially related to economic, social and humanitarian aid to

196

Think carefully about every application. Is it justified?

developing countries. Ecumenical and Quaker interests

WHAT IS NOT FUNDED No grants to individuals

WHO CAN BENEFIT Registered charities benefiting Quakers, at risk groups, those disadvantaged by poverty and socially isolated people. Support is also given to victims of disasters, famine and war, and refugees

WHERE FUNDING CAN BE GIVEN UK and overseas

TRUSTEES A P P Honigmann, E H Milligan

WHO TO APPLY TO A P P Honigmann, Edith M Ellis 1985 Charitable Trust, Messrs Field Fisher Waterhouse, 41 Vine Street, London EC3N 2AA

CC NO 292835   **ESTABLISHED** 1985

■ The James Ellis Charitable Trust

WHAT IS FUNDED Mainly relief of, or research into human disease or suffering

WHAT IS NOT FUNDED No grants to individuals

WHO CAN BENEFIT Organisations benefiting sick and disabled people. There is no restriction on the disease or medical condition suffered by the beneficiaries. Medical professionals and research workers may be considered for funding

WHERE FUNDING CAN BE GIVEN Mainly UK

TYPE OF GRANT One-off gifts and research will be considered

RANGE OF GRANTS £100–£5,000

SAMPLE GRANTS £5,000 to National Meningitis Trust; £5,000 to Kirkwood Hospice; £5,000 to Macmillan Cancer Relief; £3,000 to Arthritis Research Campaign; £2,000 to Imperial Cancer Research

FINANCES *Year* 1997–98 *Grants* £25,000

HOW TO APPLY By letter to the address under Who To Apply To

WHO TO APPLY TO S Ellis, Settlor, The James Ellis Charitable Trust, Barn Cottage, Botany Lane, Lepton, Huddersfield, Yorkshire HD8 0NE *Tel* 01484 514212

CC NO 1055617   **ESTABLISHED** 1996

■ The Shirley Ellis Charity Trust

This trust did not respond to CAF's request to amend its entry and, by 30 June 1998, CAF's researchers did not find financial records for later than 1995 on its file at the Charity Commission. Trusts are legally required to submit annual accounts to the Charity Commission under section 42 of the Charities Act 1993

WHAT IS FUNDED General charitable purposes

WHO CAN BENEFIT There are no restrictions on the age; professional and economic group; family situation; religion and culture; and social circumstances of; or disease or medical condition suffered by, the beneficiaries

WHERE FUNDING CAN BE GIVEN UK and overseas

TRUSTEES A Ellis, A M Ellis, Mrs S Ellis

WHO TO APPLY TO Mrs S Ellis, Trustee, The Shirley Ellis Charity Trust, 46 Higher Lane, Whitefield, Manchester M45 7UY

CC NO 1051022   **ESTABLISHED** 1995

■ Elman Charitable Trust

WHAT IS FUNDED Preference for Jewish organisations

WHO CAN BENEFIT Jewish charities and organisations benefiting Jewish people

WHERE FUNDING CAN BE GIVEN UK and overseas, especially Israel

TYPE OF GRANT A range of grants

SAMPLE GRANTS £96,000 to Emunah National Religions Women's Organisation in Israel; £50,000 to Jewish Care; £50,000 to Friends of Assaf Harofeh Medical Centre; £11,000 to Ner Yisrael Educational Trust; £6,000 to Friends of OHR Somayach; £5,300 to Our Future for the Poor of Herzlia; £5,000 to British Friends of Aleh; £5,000 to Discovery (UK); £5,000 to Ohel Moshe Synagogue; £4,000 to Friends of the Israeli Opera

FINANCES *Year* 1997 *Income* £157,931 *Grants* £260,050

TRUSTEES C Elman, K Elman, C Elman

HOW TO APPLY **This Trust states that it does not respond to unsolicited applications**

WHO TO APPLY TO C Elman, Trustee, Elman Charitable Trust, 1 Chadwick Road, Westcliffe-on-Sea, Essex SS0 8LS

CC NO 261733   **ESTABLISHED** 1970

■ The Elmchurch Trust

WHAT IS FUNDED Music and music education in the area Where Funding Can Be Given, particularly through schools and colleges, and provision of bursaries and fees

WHO CAN BENEFIT Mainly registered charities benefiting children, young adults, musicians and students

WHERE FUNDING CAN BE GIVEN Suffolk

FINANCES *Year* 1997 *Income* £34,589 *Grants* £25,900

TRUSTEES A Jackson, N A Ridley

HOW TO APPLY In writing only, to the Secretary

WHO TO APPLY TO David G Heckels, Secretary, The Elmchurch Trust, 11 Dale Hall Lane, Ipswich, Suffolk IP1 3RX *Tel* 01473 251494 *Fax* 01473 289705

CC NO 289406   **ESTABLISHED** 1984

■ Elmgrant Trust

WHAT IS FUNDED Encouragement of local life through education, the arts and the social sciences, and support for individuals wanting to make a change of direction in their lives

WHAT IS NOT FUNDED Postgraduate study and expedition/travel grants not considered. Applications for 'change of direction' only applicable to Devon and Cornwall and in response to annual local advertisements in the spring

WHO CAN BENEFIT Individuals and organisations. There are few restrictions on the social circumstances of the beneficiaries

WHERE FUNDING CAN BE GIVEN Primarily Devon and Cornwall

TYPE OF GRANT Primarily one-off, occasionally recurring; core funding; no loans

RANGE OF GRANTS £50–£2,000 (very occasionally over this). Typically £500

SAMPLE GRANTS £5,000 to The Open School for early literacy programme; £3,000 to The Dhama School towards general running costs; £3,000 to Dartington International Summer School towards Indian Music Week pilot project; £2,500 to Elmhirst Institute of Community Studies (India) for food processing and training unit; £1,600 to University of Exeter towards publication costs of mathematics professor's research and memoirs; £1,500 to Totnes Natural Health Centre towards disabled access; £1,500 to Stevenson College towards fees for Tibetan student

FINANCES *Year* 1996–97 *Income* £131,000 *Grants* £122,685

TRUSTEES Maurice Ash (Chairman), Michael Young, Claire Ash Wheeler, Sophie Young

HOW TO APPLY Initial telephone call if advice is needed. There are no application forms, except for the fellowship scheme. Guidelines are issued. Sae would be very helpful, although this is not obligatory

WHO TO APPLY TO Mrs M B Nicholson, Secretary, Elmgrant Trust, Elmhirst Centre, Dartington Hall, Totnes, Devon TQ9 6EL *Tel* 01803 863160

CC NO 313398   **ESTABLISHED** 1936

■ The Dorothy Whitney Elmhirst Trust

WHAT IS FUNDED General charitable purposes

WHO CAN BENEFIT There are no restrictions on the age; professional and economic group; family situation; religion and culture; and social circumstances of; or disease or medical condition suffered by, the beneficiaries

WHERE FUNDING CAN BE GIVEN UK

TRUSTEES W K Elmhirst, Mrs H A Elmhirst

WHO TO APPLY TO W K Elmhirst, Trustee, The Dorothy Whitney Elmhirst Trust, Applegreen Court, Bossington Lane, Porlock, Somerset TA24 8HD

CC NO 1064069   **ESTABLISHED** 1997

■ The Elmley Foundation

WHAT IS FUNDED Arts activity in Herefordshire and Worcestershire

WHAT IS NOT FUNDED Endowments, loans and general appeals are not considered

WHO CAN BENEFIT Individuals and organisations benefiting: actors and entertainment professionals; musicians; writers and poets; and textile workers and designers

WHERE FUNDING CAN BE GIVEN Herefordshire and Worcestershire

TYPE OF GRANT Buildings, capital, core costs, feasibility studies, one-off, project, research, recurring costs, running costs, salaries and start-up costs. Funding of up to three years will be considered

RANGE OF GRANTS £500–£20,000

SAMPLE GRANTS Hereford and Worcester Arts Education Agency; Pentabus Theatre; Bromsgrove Concerts; Countess of Huntingdon's Hall; Hay Festival; Ledbury Poetry Festival; Hereford College of Art and Design; Collar and Tie Theatre Company; Rural Media Company; Elgar School of Music

FINANCES *Year* 1997–98 *Income* £280,000 *Grants* £230,000

TRUSTEES Diana Johnson, S Driver White, John de la Cour

NOTES The Trustees also control a private charitable trust whose income goes to The Elmley Foundation

HOW TO APPLY By letter, to include a budget, and showing other possible or existing sources of support

WHO TO APPLY TO John de la Cour, The Elmley Foundation, The Old Mill, Sandford, Crediton, Devon EX17 4NP *Tel* 01363 775587

CC NO 1004043   **ESTABLISHED** 1991

■ Elshore Limited

WHAT IS FUNDED Advancement of religion, relief of poverty

WHO CAN BENEFIT Those disadvantaged by poverty. There are no restrictions on the religion and culture of the beneficiaries

WHERE FUNDING CAN BE GIVEN UK and overseas

TYPE OF GRANT At the discretion of the Trustees

FINANCES *Year* 1994–95 *Income* £218,156 *Grants* £108,927

TRUSTEES H Lerner, A Lerner

WHO TO APPLY TO H Lerner, Elshore Limited, 10 West Avenue, London NW4 2LY

CC NO 287469   **ESTABLISHED** 1983

■ The Monica Elwes Shipway Sporting Foundation

WHAT IS FUNDED Support for educational and sporting establishments for young people. Provision of equipment, courses, lectures, demonstrations, coaching, recreation grounds and sports centres. Support is given to various schools and colleges. Professional, specialist training and training for personal development are funded, as are bursaries, fees and scholarships

WHO CAN BENEFIT To benefit children and students

WHERE FUNDING CAN BE GIVEN England

TYPE OF GRANT One-off grants

TRUSTEES Simon Goldring, Gillian S Williams

WHO TO APPLY TO Simon Goldring, Trustee, The Monica Elwes Shipway Sporting Foundation, Messrs Goldring & Co, 201 Bredhurst Road, Wigmore, Gillingham, Kent ME8 0QX *Tel* 01634 260012

CC NO 1054362   **ESTABLISHED** 1996

■ The Vernon N Ely Charitable Trust

WHAT IS FUNDED General charitable purposes

WHAT IS NOT FUNDED No grants to individuals

WHO CAN BENEFIT There are no restrictions on the age; professional and economic group; family situation; religion and culture; and social circumstances of; or disease or medical condition suffered by, the beneficiaries

WHERE FUNDING CAN BE GIVEN UK

RANGE OF GRANTS £100–£6,116

SAMPLE GRANTS £6,116 to Cottage Homes; £3,700 to London Playing Fields Association; £3,000 to Methodist Church, Epsom; £2,102 to Merton Voluntary Association for the Blind; £1,500 to Christchurch United Reformed Church; £1,200 to Cancer Relief Macmillan Fund; £1,175 to British Red Cross; £1,050 to Royal Marsden Cancer Appeal; £1,000 to Oxfam; £1,000 to Save the Children

FINANCES *Year* 1996 *Income* £53,172 *Grants* £50,795

TRUSTEES J S Moyle, D P Howorth, R S Main

NOTES No further appeals can be considered as all available funds are earmarked for distribution to charities well known to the Trustees

HOW TO APPLY **This Trust states that it does not respond to unsolicited applications**

WHO TO APPLY TO D P Howorth, The Vernon N Ely Charitable Trust, Grosvenor Gardens House, 35–37 Grosvenor Gardens, London SW1W 0BY

CC NO 230033   **ESTABLISHED** 1962

■ Ralph and Muriel Emanuel Charitable Settlement

WHAT IS FUNDED General charitable purposes

WHAT IS NOT FUNDED No grants to individuals or to local charities

WHO CAN BENEFIT Registered charities. There are no restrictions on the age; professional and economic group; family situation; religion and culture; and social circumstances of; or disease or medical condition suffered by, the beneficiaries

WHERE FUNDING CAN BE GIVEN UK and overseas

RANGE OF GRANTS £20–£2,000

SAMPLE GRANTS £2,000 to Jewish Care; £2,000 to World Jewish Relief Association; £1,000 to B'nei B'rith Hillel Foundation; £1,000 to B'nei B'rith First Lodge Charity Trust; £700 to United Synagogue

FINANCES *Year* 1997 *Income* £14,288 *Grants* £12,715

TRUSTEES R N Emanuel, Mrs M H Emanuel, M S Emanuel, L R Goodman

HOW TO APPLY No new applications will normally be considered as the Trustees concentrate their grants on those charities to which they are committed

WHO TO APPLY TO R N Emanuel, Ralph and Muriel Emanuel Charitable Settlement, 61 Redington Road, London NW3 7AB

CC NO 266944   **ESTABLISHED** 1974

■ The Emerging Markets Charity for Children

WHAT IS FUNDED Children in developing countries. The relief of poverty, deprivation and distress. The advancement of education and training in all aspects of knowledge by means of (but not limited to) grants, including the establishment of scholarships and prizes, and other like awards. Other general charitable purposes

WHO CAN BENEFIT Children's organisations benefiting those disadvantaged by poverty, deprivation and distress. Education institutions

WHERE FUNDING CAN BE GIVEN UK and overseas, especially developing countries

FINANCES *Year* 1996 *Income* £365,613 *Grants* £102,000

TRUSTEES A Abrahams, S Field, D Kantorowicz-Toro, E Littlefield, M Quinton-Archard, H Snell, B Nicoll

HOW TO APPLY To the address under Who To Apply To in writing

WHO TO APPLY TO Stephanie Field, Director, The Emerging Markets Charity for Children, c/o Sidley & Austin, Solicitors, 1 Threadneedle Street, London EC2R 8AW

CC NO 1030666   **ESTABLISHED** 1993

■ Emerton-Christie Charity

WHAT IS FUNDED General charitable purposes. Preference is given to assist the aged and the young, particularly those who are disabled and disadvantaged

WHO CAN BENEFIT There are no restrictions on the age; professional and economic group; family situation; religion and culture; and social circumstances of; or disease or medical condition suffered by, the beneficiaries. However, particular favour is given to the elderly and the young, at risk groups, those disadvantaged by poverty and socially isolated people. Applications are occasionally entertained from individuals if supported by a registered charity

WHERE FUNDING CAN BE GIVEN UK

TYPE OF GRANT Donations for capital projects and/or income requirements

FINANCES *Year* 1995 *Income* £59,661 *Grants* £53,209

TRUSTEES A F Niekirk, D G Richards, Dr N A Walker

NOTES Only registered charities are considered for funding

HOW TO APPLY In writing to Messrs Dawson & Co, (ref AFN) at the address under Who To Apply To at any time. A demonstration of need based on budgetary principles is required and applications will not be acknowledged unless accompanied by an sae. Trustees normally meet once a year in the Autumn to select charities to benefit

WHO TO APPLY TO Messrs Dawson & Co, (Ref AFN), Emerton-Christie Charity, 2 New Square, Lincoln's Inn, London WC2A 3RZ

CC NO 262837   **ESTABLISHED** 1971

■ Emmandjay Charitable Trust

WHAT IS FUNDED General charitable purposes, with particular favour given to helping disadvantaged people. Many different projects are supported, for example, caring for the physically and mentally disabled and the terminally ill, work with young people and medical research. Projects which reach a lot of people are favoured

WHAT IS NOT FUNDED The Trust will not pay debts and does not respond to circulars. No grants to individual students

WHO CAN BENEFIT There are no restrictions on the age; professional and economic group; family situation; religion and culture; and social circumstances of; or disease or medical condition suffered by, the beneficiaries. However, particular favour is given to at risk groups, those disadvantaged by poverty and socially isolated people

WHERE FUNDING CAN BE GIVEN UK, with preference given to West Yorkshire

FINANCES *Year* 1998 *Income* £236,000 *Grants* £215,000

TRUSTEES Mrs S Clegg, J A Clegg, Mrs S L Worthington, Mrs E A Riddell

WHO TO APPLY TO Mrs A E Johnson, Emmandjay Charitable Trust, PO Box 31, Bradford BD1 5NH

CC NO 212279   **ESTABLISHED** 1962

■ Emmanuel Christian Centre

WHAT IS FUNDED The advancement of the Christian religion and to provide help for those in need and suffering from hardship or distress

WHO CAN BENEFIT The elderly and Christians. A wide range of social circumstances will be considered

WHERE FUNDING CAN BE GIVEN Cliffe Woods and surrounding area, Kent

TYPE OF GRANT Recurring

FINANCES *Year* 1997 *Income* £13,864 *Grants* £1,092

TRUSTEES David Webster, Rod Langston, Kenneth Black, Arthur Hall

WHO TO APPLY TO David Webster, Emmanuel Christian Centre, 21 Goodwin Road, Cliffe Woods, Rochester, Kent ME3 8HR *Tel* 01634 221360

CC NO 1004896   **ESTABLISHED** 1991

■ The Endowment Fund

WHAT IS FUNDED Relief of poverty. Charities working in the fields of: infrastructure development; charity or voluntary umbrella bodies; advice and information on housing; respite care; and various community services

WHAT IS NOT FUNDED Applications for grants for educational purposes or expeditions will not be considered

WHO CAN BENEFIT Individuals and organisations benefiting: people of all ages; retired people; unemployed people; those in care, fostered and adopted; parents and children; one parent families; widows and widowers; carers; disabled people and those disadvantaged by poverty

WHERE FUNDING CAN BE GIVEN Nottinghamshire and the surrounding areas

TYPE OF GRANT Capital, core costs, interest free loans, one-off, project, research, and start-up costs. Funding of up to and over three years will be considered

RANGE OF GRANTS £100–£3,000

FINANCES *Year* 1996 *Income* £99,000 *Grants* £68,000

TRUSTEES Rev G B Barrodale, M A Foulds, D R Piell, E A Randall

HOW TO APPLY To the address under Who To Apply To in writing

WHO TO APPLY TO S J Moore, Clerk, The Endowment Fund, Nelsons, Pennine House, 8 Standford Street, Nottingham NG1 7BQ *Tel* 0115-958 6262

CC NO 214421　　　　**ESTABLISHED** 1963

■ The Englass Charitable Trust

WHAT IS FUNDED The main objective is the relief of hardship of Englass Group employees, ex-employees and their dependants. The Trustees are prepared to make a limited amount of grants for the relief of people in need outside that group, but favour local rather than national charities. Funding is given to charity or voluntary umbrella bodies

WHAT IS NOT FUNDED Other than Englass Group employees and ex-employees and their dependants, the Trustees will not normally make grants to individuals or non-registered charities

WHO CAN BENEFIT Englass Group employees, ex-employees and their dependants

WHERE FUNDING CAN BE GIVEN UK

TYPE OF GRANT Usually an annual grant payable by instalments over the year. Buildings, capital, core costs, one-off, project and research will also be considered. Funding may be given for up to one year

SAMPLE GRANTS £4,790 to Wigston CFE for education; £2,500 to Loros for care of terminally ill patients; £1,000 to Leicester Education Business Partnership for education; £400 each to two individuals for relief of hardship of ex-employees; £200 to Arthritis/Rheumatism Council

FINANCES *Year* 1996 *Income* £16,358 *Grants* £24,026

TRUSTEES T J Lawson, H A Matthews, R J Piasecki, S E Case, M Marvell

HOW TO APPLY By letter giving details of past residence and current financial circumstances

WHO TO APPLY TO S E Case, The Englass Charitable Trust, Englass Group, Scudamore Road, Leicester LE3 1UG

CC NO 291786　　　　**ESTABLISHED** 1985

■ The Englefield Charitable Trust

WHAT IS FUNDED Charitable organisations in Berkshire. Particularly charities working in the fields of: infrastructure development; religion; residential facilities and services; arts, culture and recreation; health; conservation; education and training; and various community facilities and services

WHAT IS NOT FUNDED Applications from individuals for study or travel will not be considered. No grants to gays and lesbians or travellers

WHO CAN BENEFIT There are no restrictions on the age, family situation, religion and culture of, or disease or medical condition suffered by, the

beneficiaries. There are few restrictions on their professional and economic group and social circumstances

WHERE FUNDING CAN BE GIVEN Berkshire

TYPE OF GRANT Buildings, capital, interest free loans, research, running costs, salaries and start-up costs. Funding for one year or less will be considered

RANGE OF GRANTS £250–£40,000. Average grant £1,000

SAMPLE GRANTS £41,000 to St Mary the Virgin Church, Reading for restoration; £17,500 to Berkshire Association for Young people for youth projects; £10,000 to Douglas Martin Trust for assistance to young offenders in Berkshire; £12,000 to Order of Christian Unity; £100,000 to Padworth Village Hall, Berkshire for extension; £10,000 to St Mary the Virgin, Hampstead for restoration; £10,000 to St Peters De Beauvoir Town Hackney for restoration; £10,000 to Theale Green School, Berkshire to fund special teaching unit; £10,000 to West Berkshire Education Bursaries Partnership; £5,000 to Newbury Festival Education Project

FINANCES *Year* 1997–98 *Income* £398,000 *Grants* £355,000

TRUSTEES Sir William Benyon, Lady Benyon, Richard Benyon, James Shelley, Catherine Haig

NOTES Finances: funds are being withheld in addition to the figure for Grants as follows: £41,000 for St Mary the Virgin, Reading and £20,000 for St Mary the Virgin, Burghfield

HOW TO APPLY Unsuccessful applications will not be acknowledged. Trustees meet June and December

WHO TO APPLY TO The Secretary, The Englefield Charitable Trust, Englefield Estate Office, Theale, Reading RG7 5DU *Tel* 01734 302504 *Fax* 01734 323748

CC NO 258123　　　　**ESTABLISHED** 1968

■ The English China Clays Group Charitable Trust

WHAT IS FUNDED Large grants are regularly given to the St Austell China Clay Museum, other grants are made in the areas of youth, community, schools, education and disability

WHO CAN BENEFIT Regional and local organisations benefiting children, young adults, students and disabled people

WHERE FUNDING CAN BE GIVEN Berkshire, South West England and Staffordshire

FINANCES *Year* 1996 *Income* £112,291 *Grants* £87,088

TRUSTEES ECC Trustees Ltd

HOW TO APPLY To the address under Who To Apply To in writing

WHO TO APPLY TO S H Warren, The English China Clays Group Charitable Trust, English China Clays plc, 1015 Arlington Business Park, Theale, Reading RG7 4SA

CC NO 326184　　　　**ESTABLISHED** 1982

■ The English Schools' Football Association

WHAT IS FUNDED Mental, moral and physical development of schoolboys through Association Football. Assistance to teacher charities. General charitable purposes

WHAT IS NOT FUNDED Grants are restricted to membership and teacher charities

WHO CAN BENEFIT Members of the Association and organisations benefiting children and young adults, sportsmen and women and teachers. Otherwise, there are no restrictions on the age; professional and economic group; family situation; religion and culture; and social circumstances of; or disease or medical condition suffered by, the beneficiaries

WHERE FUNDING CAN BE GIVEN England

SAMPLE GRANTS £850 in support grants; £30 as floral tributes and presentations

FINANCES *Year* 1995 *Income* £329,072 *Grants* £880

TRUSTEES K W Blood, D Oliver, D C Palmer

PUBLICATIONS Referees Charts, *Guide to Teaching Soccer in Schools*, International Honours List, Handbooks

WHO TO APPLY TO A Rice, English Schools Football Association, 1–2 Eastgate Street, Stafford, Staffordshire ST16 2NQ

CC NO 306003   **ESTABLISHED** 1904

■ Enkalon Foundation

WHAT IS FUNDED To improve the quality of life in Northern Ireland. Funding is given to cross-community groups. self help, assistance to the unemployed and groups helping the disadvantaged

WHAT IS NOT FUNDED No grants made to projects outside Northern Ireland. No grants can be made to individuals except possibly ex-employees of British Enkalon Ltd

WHO CAN BENEFIT Cross-community groups, self-help, assistance to the unemployed, groups helping the disadvantaged. People with many different social circumstances may benefit

WHERE FUNDING CAN BE GIVEN Grants made only to organisations for projects inside Northern Ireland

TYPE OF GRANT Mainly for starter finance, single projects or capital projects

RANGE OF GRANTS Up to £6,000 maximum

FINANCES *Year* 1994–95 *Income* £98,000 *Grants* £94,500

TRUSTEES R L Schierbeek, CBE, J A Freeman, D H Templeton, OBE

PUBLICATIONS Guidelines for applicants available on request. Report and Statement of Accounts produced

HOW TO APPLY Four monthly meetings for grant applications. To follow the headings set out in guidelines

WHO TO APPLY TO J W Wallace, Secretary, Enkalon Foundation, 25 Randalstown Road, Antrim, Northern Ireland BT41 4LJ *Tel* 018494 63535

IR NO XN62210A   **ESTABLISHED** 1985

■ The Enterprise Foundation

This trust did not respond to CAF's request to amend its entry and, by 30 June 1998, CAF's researchers did not find financial records for later than 1995 on its file at the Charity Commission. Trusts are legally required to submit annual accounts to the Charity Commission under section 42 of the Charities Act 1993

WHAT IS FUNDED General charitable purposes, particularly: (i) the relief of the aged, the disabled and the poor, (ii) unemployed poor people by providing grants to enable them to establish themselves in a business activity which provides employment; (iii) the advancement of knowledge and education in all aspects of effective small business management, support and workplace management through research, training and work experience; (iv) the support of young tradesmen

and handicraftsmen; and (v) the promotion of industry and commerce

WHO CAN BENEFIT There are no restrictions on the age; professional and economic group; family situation; religion and culture; and social circumstances of; or disease or medical condition suffered by, the beneficiaries

WHERE FUNDING CAN BE GIVEN UK and overseas

TRUSTEES G M Cook, The Chase Family Trust, D G S Platt, M H Bradley

WHO TO APPLY TO M H Bradley, Secretary, The Enterprise Foundation, Christy House, Church Lane, Bocking, Essex CM7 5RX

CC NO 1048640   **ESTABLISHED** 1995

■ Entindale Ltd

WHAT IS FUNDED Orthodox Jewish charitable organisations

WHO CAN BENEFIT Organisations benefiting Orthodox Jews

WHERE FUNDING CAN BE GIVEN UK

TYPE OF GRANT Capital

SAMPLE GRANTS £85,000 to Menora Grammar School; £30,300 to Society of Friends of the Torah; £26,630 to British Friends of Ohr Someiach; £22,150 to Berr Avrohom UK Trust; £20,000 to YH Training Enterprise; £18,100 to British Friends of Neve Yermbolayin; £18,000 to Tetz Talmudical Academy Trust; £18,000 to Gevurath Ari Torah Academy Trust; £15,000 to Friends of Nachalat Osher; £11,000 to Scopus

FINANCES *Year* 1996–97 *Income* £994,621 *Grants* £525,975

TRUSTEES Mrs B A B Sethill, Mrs Bridgeman, S J Goldberg, A Becker

NOTES Not at present entertaining grant applications from the public

HOW TO APPLY In writing to the address under Who To Apply To

WHO TO APPLY TO The Trustees, Entindale Ltd, Equity House, 86 West Green Road, London N15 5NS

CC NO 277052   **ESTABLISHED** 1978

■ The Ben Entwistle Charitable Settlement

WHAT IS FUNDED General charitable purposes

WHO CAN BENEFIT There are no restrictions on the age; professional and economic group; family situation; religion and culture; and social circumstances of; or disease or medical condition suffered by, the beneficiaries

WHERE FUNDING CAN BE GIVEN UK

TRUSTEES C Daniels, B Entwistle, E Nobes

WHO TO APPLY TO B Entwistle, Trustee, The Ben Entwistle Charitable Settlement, 32 Palace Gardens Terrace, London W8 4RP

CC NO 1049677   **ESTABLISHED** 1995

■ Entwood Charities Ltd

WHAT IS FUNDED Jewish organisations for general charitable purposes

WHO CAN BENEFIT Jewish people

WHERE FUNDING CAN BE GIVEN UK and overseas

TRUSTEES D Feldman

HOW TO APPLY To the address under Who To Apply To in writing

WHO TO APPLY TO H Feldman, Director, Entwood Charities Ltd, 23 Overlea Road, Springfield Park, London E5 9BG

CC NO 280555   **ESTABLISHED** 1990

Does the trust you have chosen match your needs? Haphazard applications waste postage and time

201

■ Epigoni Trust

WHAT IS FUNDED Funding specific projects. Charities working in the fields of: emergency and short-term housing, holiday accommodation and hostels; health counselling and education; respite, care for carers; and hospices. Support for environmental issues; renewable energy and power; care in the community; and crime prevention schemes will also be considered

WHAT IS NOT FUNDED No grants to individuals, or for expeditions, research or scholarships

WHO CAN BENEFIT Registered charities only benefiting: people of all ages; those disadvantaged by poverty and homeless people; victims of crime and domestic violence. Support will also be given to those suffering from various diseases and medical conditions

WHERE FUNDING CAN BE GIVEN UK. The Trustees sometimes consider overseas projects carried out by UK charities

TYPE OF GRANT Normally one-off and project grants for up to two years will be considered

RANGE OF GRANTS £500–£10,000

SAMPLE GRANTS £10,000 to Chichester and Bognor Mental Health for cost of furniture and equipment; £10,000 to London Lighthouse for building and equipment for children's centre; £10,000 to Sight Savers International for student hostel at LV Prasad Eye Institute; £10,000 to Rainbow Family Trust for respite holidays for children; £10,000 to Scottish Bobath Association for treatment for ten children with cerebral palsy; £5,000 to Suzy Lamplugh Trust for booklet on personal safety; £5,000 to Action for Blind People to update speech assistance resources; £5,000 to Mildmay International for palliative care centre for AIDs in Uganda; £2,500 to Kith and Kids for volunteer training; £2,000 to Exeter Women's Aid for holidays for children at a refuge

FINANCES *Year* 1996 *Income* £155,000
Grants £93,000

TRUSTEES C Peacock, B Bond, M Bond

HOW TO APPLY In writing only to the address under Who To Apply To. Applications are normally considered in July and December. A copy of the latest Annual Report and Accounts must accompany any application

WHO TO APPLY TO Mrs B Davis, Senior Information Officer, Epigoni Trust, c/o CAF, Kings Hill, West Malling, Kent ME19 4TA *Tel* 01732 520081 *Fax* 01732 520001 *E-mail* bdavis@caf.charitynet.org

CC NO 328700   **ESTABLISHED** 1990

■ The Epilepsy Research Foundation (formerly British Epilepsy Research Foundation)

WHAT IS FUNDED Junior clinical and non-clinical fellowships, postgraduate studentships, projects, equipment and biomedical technology. All must be linked to epilepsy

WHAT IS NOT FUNDED Grants available only for basic and clinical scientific research in the field of epilepsy

WHO CAN BENEFIT All those with epilepsy

WHERE FUNDING CAN BE GIVEN UK

TYPE OF GRANT Projects, fellowship, research and equipment. Funding is for up to three years

RANGE OF GRANTS Small equipment grants £2,000–£35,000 for projects

SAMPLE GRANTS £37,200 to an individual through the Hastings Fellowships for research into SUDEP; £30,000 to University of Southampton for an individual for two years student salary for a project; £30,000 to Institute of Psychiatry for an individual for a project for one year; £20,000 to Kent and Canterbury Hospital for an individual for collaborative project – two years research assistant's salary; £16,676 to University of Southampton to an individual – Sir Desmond Pond Fellowship; £15,000 to University of Liverpool to an individual for the Epilepsy Brain Bank; £11,200 to Glasgow University to an individual for equipment; £6,058 to Institute of Neurology to an individual for equipment; £5,388 to St Thomas' hospital to an individual from the Contingency Fund; £3,000 to Radcliffe Infirmary to an individual for equipment

FINANCES *Year* 1997 *Income* £231,967
Grants £178,522

TRUSTEES Prof A Richens (Chairman), A Aspinall, Dr F Besag, Prof C Binnie, J Bowis, Dr S Brown, Mrs J Cochrane, Prof T Jones, M Stevens, H N M Thompson, J Wilson

PUBLICATIONS Newsletter. List of grants awarded

NOTES For research enquiries Tel: 0181–400 6108

HOW TO APPLY Guidelines are available on request

WHO TO APPLY TO Mrs I Little, Secretary, Epilepsy Research Foundation, PO Box 3004, London W4 1XT *Tel* 0181-995 4781 *Fax* 0181-995 4781 *E-mail* erf@geo2.poptel.org.uk

CC NO 326836   **ESTABLISHED** 1985

■ Epsom Parochial Charities

WHAT IS FUNDED Charities working in the fields of: almshouses; Christian education; hospices; schools and colleges; bursaries and fees; the purchase of books; academic subjects; sciences and research; and advancement in life

WHO CAN BENEFIT Residents in Ancient Parish of Epsom. Organisations benefiting: children; young adults; older people; academics; research workers; scientists; students; Christians and those disadvantaged by poverty

WHERE FUNDING CAN BE GIVEN Epsom and Ewell

TYPE OF GRANT One-off

RANGE OF GRANTS £50–£4,000; typical £300

SAMPLE GRANTS £4,500 to Epsom and Ewell Boys' Club towards the re-development of Stephen Woods Centre; £1,000 to Princess Alice Hospice for care for patients resident in Epsom and Ewell; £800 to an individual for contribution towards Legal Secretary's Course; £500 to an individual for contribution towards clothing and household items; £415 to Stamford Green Primary school for residential school trip tor three children; £398 to Epsom County Primary School for residential school trip for two children; £255 to an individual for contribution towards Disabled Facilities Grant; £250 to an individual for essential tools for BA Course, Surrey Institute of Art and Design; £120 to an individual for contribution towards fridge/freezer; £80 to an individual for one year's prescription certificate

FINANCES *Year* 1996 *Income* £58,000

TRUSTEES Mrs F Allen, W R Carpenter, Mrs E M F Catmur, Mrs M V De Lyon, Miss J Harridge, Mrs G I Heym, P N Linscott, Rev D Smethurst, J A Stewart, Sir J E P Titman

HOW TO APPLY Applications should be made on a form available from the address under Who To Apply To. Applications are considered quarterly by the Trustees; in the first week of March, June, September and December

WHO TO APPLY TO Mrs M West, Clerk, Epsom Parochial Charities, 38 Woodcote Hurst, Epsom, Surrey KT18 7DT *Tel* 01372 721335
CC NO 200571   **ESTABLISHED** 1988

■ The Equity Trust Fund

WHAT IS FUNDED To help professional performers in genuine need, with special reference to members, past and present, of the Union EQUITY. Also to promote, maintain, improve and advance education particularly by the encouragement of the arts and its development
WHAT IS NOT FUNDED Must be a professional performer or professional theatre company/venue
WHO CAN BENEFIT Individuals and organisations benefiting actors and entertainment professionals
WHERE FUNDING CAN BE GIVEN UK
TYPE OF GRANT No project/production costs
SAMPLE GRANTS £115,015 for education grants; £75,475 for welfare and benevolence; £51,517 for theatre grants; £39,000 for loans – provision and write-offs
FINANCES *Year* 1997 *Income* £362,625 *Grants* £281,007
TRUSTEES J Barron, D Bond, N Davenport, Barbara Hyslop, M Johns, C Baker, J Johnston, P Plouviez, Gillian Raine, H Manning, J Wickham, N Mitchell, F Williams, I McGarry, J Ainslie, H Landis, G Hamilton, F Pyne, A Bright, Anne Mitchell
HOW TO APPLY Meetings held every six weeks
WHO TO APPLY TO The Secretary, The Equity Trust Fund, Suite 222, Africa House, 64 Kingsway, London WC2B 6BD
CC NO 328103   **ESTABLISHED** 1989

■ Ericson Trust

WHAT IS FUNDED The Trust will consider funding: accommodation and housing; infrastructure and technical support; infrastructure development; Council for Voluntary Services (CVS); community arts and recreation; psychiatric rehabilitation centres; environmental issues; transport and alternative transport; training for community development; specialist research; community centres and village halls; care in the community; crime prevention schemes; emergency care; refugees and famine; community issues; international rights of the individual; and prison reform
WHAT IS NOT FUNDED Charities concerned with illness (except psychiatric) or disability, children's and youth clubs/centres or religious bodies, except in their social project, will not be considered. No grants to individuals
WHO CAN BENEFIT Organisations benefiting: middle aged and older people; carers; those disadvantaged by poverty; ex-offenders and those at risk of offending; homeless people; immigrants and refugees; socially isolated people; those living in urban areas; victims of domestic violence and of war; those suffering from mental illness
WHERE FUNDING CAN BE GIVEN UK and overseas
TYPE OF GRANT Buildings, capital, core costs, feasibility studies, one-off, project, research, running costs, salaries and start-up costs. All funding is for up to two years
RANGE OF GRANTS £1,000–£2,000

SAMPLE GRANTS £15,000 to University of Nottingham Voluntary Organisation Research Project for latest phase of on-going research into voluntary organisations; £4,000 to The Refugee Council towards a single stop building for refugee advice, etc; £3,000 to The Mental Health Foundation; £3,000 to Bede Home Association for community projects/general running of the centre; £2,500 to The Relatives Association for developments concerning Afro-Caribbean housing for the elderly; £2,000 to Psychiatric Rehabilitation Association; £2,000 to Anti-Slavery International; £2,000 to UNAIS; £2,000 to The Medical Foundation; £2,000 to The Howard League
FINANCES *Year* 1996 *Income* £28,668 *Grants* £9,500
TRUSTEES Mrs V J Barrow, Mrs A M C Cotton, Ms R C Cotton, A Weston
HOW TO APPLY Guidelines are available for applicants
WHO TO APPLY TO Mrs A M C Cotton, Ericson Trust, Flat 2, 53 Carleton Road, London N7 0ET
CC NO 219762   **ESTABLISHED** 1962

■ Eritrean Community in Lambeth

WHAT IS FUNDED The principal activity of the Trust is to support voluntary or self help social and welfare orientated non-profit organisations
WHO CAN BENEFIT Organisations benefiting at risk groups, those disadvantaged by poverty, socially isolated people and volunteers
WHERE FUNDING CAN BE GIVEN Lambeth and surrounding boroughs
FINANCES *Year* 1997 *Income* £30,413
TRUSTEES Z Abraha, M Abraham, T Abay, T Fesahassion, F N Kahasa, A Yohannes, M Tekle
WHO TO APPLY TO D Haile, Eritrean Community in Lambeth, 365 Brixton Road, London SW9 7DA
CC NO 1053428   **ESTABLISHED** 1992

■ Erycinus Charitable Trust

WHAT IS FUNDED To handle all charitable donations on behalf of Heath Group plc. Priority is given to national charities supporting medical research or capital projects for the diagnosis and treatment of human disease. A local charity may be supported where Heath Group has a presence
WHAT IS NOT FUNDED Under no circumstances will grants be awarded to individual students or in respect of university expeditions. National charities are given priority. Contributions not normally made more than once in any three year period to any individual charity
WHO CAN BENEFIT Registered charities. There are no restrictions on the disease or medical condition suffered by the beneficiaries
WHERE FUNDING CAN BE GIVEN UK
FINANCES *Year* 1997 *Income* £25,000
TRUSTEES T P Newbery, M H Kier, N Rowe
WHO TO APPLY TO N Rowe, Company Secretary, Erycinus Charitable Trust, Heath Group plc, 133 Houndsditch, London EC3A 7AH *Tel* 0171-234 4739 *Fax* 0171-234 4181
CC NO 265100   **ESTABLISHED** 1972

■ The Esher House Charitable Trust

WHAT IS FUNDED Advancement of religion, health, educational Jewish charitable causes
WHAT IS NOT FUNDED No grants to individuals
WHO CAN BENEFIT Organisation benefiting children, young adults, older people and Jews. There is no

restriction on the disease or medical condition suffered by the beneficiaries
WHERE FUNDING CAN BE GIVEN UK
TYPE OF GRANT Range of grants
RANGE OF GRANTS £10–£1,000
FINANCES *Year* 1997 *Income* £35,000 *Grants* £18,596
TRUSTEES M B Conn, H R Conn, D G Conn
HOW TO APPLY In writing only to the address under Who To Apply To
WHO TO APPLY TO Mr M Conn, The Esher House Charitable Trust, 845 Finchley Road, London NW11 8NA *Tel* 0181-455 1111 *Fax* 0181-455 9191
CC NO 276183   **ESTABLISHED** 1978

■ The Guthrie Essame Charitable Trust

WHAT IS FUNDED General charitable purposes
WHO CAN BENEFIT Well known public charities. There are no restrictions on the age; professional and economic group; family situation; religion and culture; and social circumstances of; or disease or medical condition suffered by, the beneficiaries
WHERE FUNDING CAN BE GIVEN UK
FINANCES *Year* 1997 *Income* £14,789
TRUSTEES J G Essame, Miss M G Essame, K P Pool
HOW TO APPLY Funds are fully committed
WHO TO APPLY TO The Guthrie Essame Charitable Trust, Hunters Solicitors, 9 New Square, Lincoln's Inn, London WC2A 3PN
CC NO 271022   **ESTABLISHED** 1976

■ The Mihran Essefian Charitable Trust (The Mihran & Azmir Essefian Charitable Trust)

WHAT IS FUNDED The Trustees offer scholarship grants to university students of Armenian origin and grants to organisations and institutions to promote specific educational, cultural and charitable activities for the benefit of the Armenian community throughout the world
WHO CAN BENEFIT Individuals, universities, institutions and organisations benefiting Armenians, especially children, young adults and students
WHERE FUNDING CAN BE GIVEN UK and overseas
RANGE OF GRANTS Organisations: £50–£2,000, individuals: £107–£4,500
SAMPLE GRANTS £2,000 to St Tarkmanchats School, Jerusalem; £2,000 to Hayastan All-Armenian Charitable Fund; £2,000 to Armenian Musical Assembly Yerevan; £1,750 to Armenian elementary text books, Yerevan; £1,500 to Holegate School for pupils visit to Armenia; £1,000 to Surp Pirgic Hospital, Istanbul; £1,000 to Armenian Language Saturday Studies, London; £975 to English Speaking Union of Armenia; £50 to St Peter's Armenian Church; £50 to St Sarkis Armenian Church
FINANCES *Year* 1997 *Income* £100,777 *Grants* £65,443
TRUSTEES M S Kalindjian, E Kurkdjian, H Abadjian, B P Gulbenkian
NOTES The grants shown are only for organisations and not individuals
HOW TO APPLY In writing by 30 June each year
WHO TO APPLY TO S Ovanessoff, The Mihran Essefian Charitable Trust, 15 Elm Crescent, Ealing, London W5 3JW
CC NO 275074   **ESTABLISHED** 1977

■ Essex Community Foundation

WHAT IS FUNDED General charitable purposes for the benefit of the community in the County of Essex, in particular, the advancement of education, the protection of mental and physical health, the relief of poverty and sickness
WHAT IS NOT FUNDED Organisations with no permanent presence in Essex, or project operating outside Essex are not funded. No grants to individuals, political activities or statutory bodies
WHO CAN BENEFIT Any voluntary and community group, or any non-profit making organisation working in partnership, for the benefit of people living in Essex. Support is for those, due to their circumstances, are in need of social welfare
WHERE FUNDING CAN BE GIVEN Essex
TYPE OF GRANT One-off, capital, support costs, project costs, core costs, research, running costs, salaries and start-up cost will be considered. Funding may be given for up to one year
RANGE OF GRANTS £200–£10,000
SAMPLE GRANTS £5,800 to Kids Club, Uttlesford to employ an extra playworker; £5,000 to Little Pals Opportunity Pre-school, Jaywick to provide play equipment; £5,000 to Southend Action Group for the Homeless towards emergency night shelter costs; £5,000 to Home-Start, Basildon to maintain and expand family support groups; £5,000 to Crossroads Care, Castle Point for young carers project; £5,000 to Ramsden Bellhouse Village Hall towards refurbishment; £5,000 to Royal Association in Aid of Deaf People, Colchester to provide staff costs for group sessions; £4,500 to Colchester Furniture Project (the Shake Trust) towards running costs of furniture project; £4,400 to TCVS Tendring Furniture Scheme towards workshop and materials costs; £3,000 to Chelmsford YMCA and Alzheimer's Society towards cost of shared offices
FINANCES *Year* 1997–98 *Income* £406,548 *Grants* £85,545
TRUSTEES J Burrow, CBE, C Clark, M Clegg, S Drummond, R Erith, TD, P Fitt, Rt Rev Dr L Green, I Marks, CBE, C Pertwee, DL, Lord Petre of Writtle, DL, N Shuttleworth, C Stanger, W Tolhurst
HOW TO APPLY Contact the Foundation's office for an application form and Guidelines and to ascertain deadline dates
WHO TO APPLY TO Ms L Warren, Chief Executive, Essex Community Foundation, 52A Moulsham Street, Chelmsford, Essex CM2 0JA *Tel* 01245 355947 *Fax* 01245 251151 *E-mail* EssexCF@compuserve.com
CC NO 1052061   **ESTABLISHED** 1996

■ The Essex Fairway Charitable Trust

WHAT IS FUNDED General charitable purposes
WHO CAN BENEFIT There are no restrictions on the age; professional and economic group; family situation; religion and culture; and social circumstances of; or disease or medical condition suffered by, the beneficiaries
WHERE FUNDING CAN BE GIVEN UK
FINANCES *Year* 1998 *Income* £100,784 *Grants* £500
TRUSTEES P W George, T J Hitchcock, Mrs N Hitchcock, K H Larkman
WHO TO APPLY TO K H Larkman, The Essex Fairway Charitable Trust, c/o Birkett Long, 42 Crouch Street, Colchester, Essex CO3 3HH
CC NO 1066858   **ESTABLISHED** 1997

■ Essex Heritage Trust

WHAT IS FUNDED Grants to bodies or individuals undertaking specific work in accord with the objects of the Trust including publication or preservation of Essex History and restoration of monuments, significant structures, artefacts and church decorations and equipment

WHAT IS NOT FUNDED At this stage of the Trust's development, the Trustees are not in a position to make awards towards the repair of the fabric of churches or to what might be construed as the routine maintenance of buildings. The object of the grant must be to the benefit of the public in Essex. Applications will not be considered retrospective of the work being completed

WHO CAN BENEFIT Any organisation, body or individual whose project will be to the benefit of the people of Essex

WHERE FUNDING CAN BE GIVEN Strictly within the Electoral County of Essex

TYPE OF GRANT Usually one-off starter finances for specific heritage projects falling within the Trust's objectives. These may include a contribution to capital expenses or buildings

SAMPLE GRANTS £15,000 to Uttlesford District Council for restoration of decorative panels; £5,000 to Victoria History of the County of Essex a contribution to appeal; £5,000 to Essex County Council for World War II defences survey; £4,000 to Saffron Walden Museum for documentation and restoration of tapestry; £2,500 to Essex County Council (Cressing Temple) for repairs to Barley Barn Plinth; £2,000 to Essex Society for Archaeology and History for recording field names; £2,000 to St Mary's Church, Wirenhos for repairing church bells; £2,000 to St Peter and St Paul Church, Horndon on the Hill for repairing footpaths; £1,634 to Victor Batte-Lay Trust for restoration of folly; £1,500 to St Giles Church, Great Maplestead for organ repair

FINANCES *Year* 1997–98 *Income* £54,297 *Grants* £30,414

TRUSTEES Mrs Kathleen Nolan, DL, Sir Terence Beckett, KBEDL, Sir Denis Forman, OBE, K W S Ashurst, Lord Braybrooke, The Lord Lieutenant of Essex, R J L Watson

PUBLICATIONS Annual Report

HOW TO APPLY At any time by letter in the first instance. It is not policy to reply to all letters but an application form will be returned for detailed completion with estimates if it is considered that the project falls within the Trust's objectives. Where appropriate, the project is inspected before submission to the Trustees who usually meet three times a year in March, July and November. Emergency applications may be considered

WHO TO APPLY TO Mrs G Walsh, Essex Heritage Trust, Cressing Temple, Witham Road, Braintree Road, Braintree CM7 8PD *Tel* 01376 584903 *Fax* 01376 584864

CC NO 802317   **ESTABLISHED** 1989

■ Essex Provincial Charity Fund

WHAT IS FUNDED General charitable purposes. Trustees favour masonic charities

WHO CAN BENEFIT There are no restrictions on the age; professional and economic group; family situation; religion and culture; and social circumstances of; or disease or medical condition suffered by, the beneficiaries

WHERE FUNDING CAN BE GIVEN Essex

FINANCES *Year* 1997 *Income* £123,821 *Grants* £66,696

TRUSTEES J P Rundlett, F A D Harris, A E Kemp, C G Williams, A P Bishop

WHO TO APPLY TO K Harvey, Secretary, Essex Provincial Charity Fund, 2 Station Court, Station Approach, Wickford, Essex SS11 7AT

CC NO 215349   **ESTABLISHED** 1932

■ The Essex Radio Helping Hands Trust

WHAT IS FUNDED Grants within Essex for the relief of physically or mentally disabled children or the aged within the County of Essex and in particular within the area of broadcast of Essex Radio

WHO CAN BENEFIT Disadvantaged, disabled, young and elderly within Essex

WHERE FUNDING CAN BE GIVEN Essex

TYPE OF GRANT Trustees unlikely to make grants for running costs. Mostly for capital equipment

SAMPLE GRANTS £24,396 to Cash for Kids grants; £17,461 to Helping Hands grants

FINANCES *Year* 1996 *Income* £72,894 *Grants* £42,857

TRUSTEES J Bouser, C Reeve, K Twitchen, Prof C J C Green, M Franks, G Harris

HOW TO APPLY Trustees meet every three months to discuss applications

WHO TO APPLY TO Mick Garrett, The Essex Radio Helping Hands Trust, c/o Essex Radio, Radio House, 19–20 Clifftown Road, Southend-on-Sea, Essex SS1 1SX

CC NO 290078   **ESTABLISHED** 1984

■ Euroclydon Trust (formerly H W Cross Charitable Settlement)

WHAT IS FUNDED General charitable purposes

WHO CAN BENEFIT There are no restrictions on the age; professional and economic group; family situation; religion and culture; and social circumstances of; or disease or medical condition suffered by, the beneficiaries

WHERE FUNDING CAN BE GIVEN UK

RANGE OF GRANTS £300–£21300

SAMPLE GRANTS £21,300 to Missionary Aviation Fellowship; £10,500 to Covenanters; £4,600 to Timothy Trust; £4,300 to Ambassadors for Christ, India; £4,300 to Echoes of Service; £3,000 to London Institute; £2,500 to Langham Trust; £2,000 to Millgrove Children's Home; £2,000 to Prison Fellowship; £1,800 to Operation Concern

FINANCES *Year* 1997 *Income* £57,741 *Grants* £62,000

TRUSTEES UKET

HOW TO APPLY October each year

WHO TO APPLY TO A E Waheling, Manager at UKET, Euroclydon Trust, PO Box 99, Loughton, Essex LG10 3QJ

CC NO 290382   **ESTABLISHED** 1977

■ European Cultural Foundation (UK Committee)

WHAT IS FUNDED Representation in the UK of the European Cultural Foundation of Amsterdam, primarily by facilitating its grant-making programme for projects originating in this country, including, in particular, the advancement of learning and the raising of artistic taste by the encouragement of fine arts. The Foundation works to promote multi-culturalism in Central and Eastern Europe and the Mediterranean.

Does the trust you have chosen match your needs? Haphazard applications waste postage and time

205

Community arts and recreation and cultural activity are supported

WHAT IS NOT FUNDED The following will not be considered: projects of a scientific (including medical) or commercial nature, projects in the field of academic politics; research; any project set-up for purely individual purposes; individuals or students

WHO CAN BENEFIT Projects of a European character, involving multinational European participation (by non-profit-making bodies in at least three, preferably more, European countries). Immigrants, refugees and travellers are supported

WHERE FUNDING CAN BE GIVEN UK and Europe

TYPE OF GRANT Project and one-off grants

RANGE OF GRANTS £3,000–£7,000

SAMPLE GRANTS £5,000 to Gate Theatre, Europe, towards cost of workshops

FINANCES *Year* 1996 *Income* £13,144

TRUSTEES Prof John Pinder, OBE (Chairman), D Barton, Nigel Haigh, OBE

HOW TO APPLY (a) Guidelines are published, (b) applications are acknowledged, (c) copy of accounts is required

WHO TO APPLY TO Geoffrey Denton, Director, European Cultural Foundation (UK Committee), 11 Oakhill Avenue, London NW3 7RD *Tel* 0171-794 5955 *Fax* 0171-794 5955

CC NO 257273   **ESTABLISHED** 1969

■ The Alice Evans Charitable Trust

WHAT IS FUNDED General charitable purposes at the direction of the Founder; also the provision of support for people with physical disabilities

WHO CAN BENEFIT There are no restrictions on the age; professional and economic group; family situation; religion and culture; and social circumstances of; or disease or medical condition suffered by, the beneficiaries. However particular favour is given to the disabled and their carers

WHERE FUNDING CAN BE GIVEN UK

TRUSTEES Ms H M Buhler, J F Edmondson

WHO TO APPLY TO Ian Macfarlane, Accountant, The Alice Evans Charitable Trust, c/o Messrs Kidsons Impey, Spectrum House, 2–26 Cursitor Street, London EC4A 1HY

CC NO 1055937   **ESTABLISHED** 1996

■ The Alan Evans Memorial Trust

WHAT IS FUNDED The purchase of land and the planting of trees, shrubs and plants. The restoration of cathedrals, churches and other buildings of beauty or interest, to which the public can have access

WHAT IS NOT FUNDED No grants to individuals. No grants for management or running expenses. Any appeal falling outside the Trust criteria will not be acknowledged

WHO CAN BENEFIT Registered charities only

WHERE FUNDING CAN BE GIVEN UK

RANGE OF GRANTS £1,000–£5,000

SAMPLE GRANTS £5,000 to The John Muir Trust; £5,000 to The National Trust for Yealm Estuary; £3,000 to Royal Society for the Protection of Birds; £3,000 to Wildlife Trust for Bedfordshire; £2,250 to The National Trust for Prior Park Appeal; £2,500 to Ealing Abbey Centenary Appeal; £2,500 to Lincoln Cathedral Preservation Council; £2,500 to The North West Ecological Trust; £2,250 to The National Trust for Scotland; £1,500 to Somerset Building Preservation

FINANCES *Year* 1996 *Income* £209,278 *Grants* £98,250

TRUSTEES Coutts & Co, John W Halfhead

HOW TO APPLY To the address under Who To Apply To

WHO TO APPLY TO The Alan Evans Memorial Trust, Messrs Coutts & Co, Trustee Dept, 440 Strand, London WC2R 0QS

CC NO 326263   **ESTABLISHED** 1979

■ The Eric Evans Memorial Trust

WHAT IS FUNDED This Trust will consider funding sporting and educational activities, parks, recreation grounds, sports centres and the conservation of waterways

WHO CAN BENEFIT Sportsmen and women, children and young adults

WHERE FUNDING CAN BE GIVEN Islington, East London and East Anglia

TYPE OF GRANT One-off

RANGE OF GRANTS £100–£400

FINANCES *Year* 1997 *Income* £98,854

TRUSTEES D Boehm, Mrs O Evans, J M Kinder

WHO TO APPLY TO J M Kinder, Trustee, The Eric Evans Memorial Trust, 55 Thornhill Square, London N1 1BE *Tel* 0171-285 3007

CC NO 1047709   **ESTABLISHED** 1995

■ Sir John Evelyn's Charity

WHAT IS FUNDED Pensions and grants to organisations working to relieve poverty in the area Where Funding Can Be Given

WHO CAN BENEFIT To benefit those disadvantaged by poverty

WHERE FUNDING CAN BE GIVEN The Ancient Parish of St Nicholas, Deptford and St Luke, Deptford

SAMPLE GRANTS £80,589 to groups; £24,765 to individuals for pensions; £18,762 to individuals; £3,816 to pensioners for holidays

FINANCES *Year* 1995 *Income* £87,654 *Grants* £127,932

TRUSTEES Ms J Barnett, Rev G Corneck, Ms M House, Ms E Hudson, I Jolly, Rev J K Lucas, J Murray, Ms M Vitler

HOW TO APPLY To the address under Who To Apply To in writing

WHO TO APPLY TO Mrs M Baulson, Clerk, Sir John Evelyn's Charity, 40 Rutland Avenue, Sidcup, Kent DA15 9DZ

CC NO 225707   **ESTABLISHED** 1974

■ The Eventhall Family Charitable Trust

WHAT IS FUNDED General charitable purposes

WHAT IS NOT FUNDED Student grants cannot be provided

WHO CAN BENEFIT Institutions and individuals. There are no restrictions on the age; professional and economic group; family situation; religion and culture; and social circumstances of; or disease or medical condition suffered by, the beneficiaries

WHERE FUNDING CAN BE GIVEN North West England

FINANCES *Year* 1997 *Income* £159,877 *Grants* £66,772

TRUSTEES L Eventhall, C Eventhall, D Eventhall

NOTES The largest donation made in 1997 was to the Heathlands Village and will be continuing support for the next two year. Donations were also made to other charities

WHO TO APPLY TO L H Eventhall, The Eventhall Family Charitable Trust, Greenlands, 23 Beeston Road, Sale, Cheshire M33 5AQ

CC NO 803178   **ESTABLISHED** 1989

■ The Everard Foundation

WHAT IS FUNDED General charitable purposes. To help local charities of all sizes

WHAT IS NOT FUNDED Grants to individuals unlikely

WHO CAN BENEFIT There are no restrictions on the age; professional and economic group; family situation; religion and culture; and social circumstances of; or disease or medical condition suffered by, the beneficiaries. If national organisation, donation must go to something tangible, locally

WHERE FUNDING CAN BE GIVEN Leicestershire

TYPE OF GRANT One-off

SAMPLE GRANTS £10,000 to Leicestershire Police for fighting crime/victims support suite; £10,000 to Sir Andrew Martin Trust for young people/youth organisations; £5,000 to Lords towards new development; £5,000 to Age Concern for training room at Lansdowne House; £4,500 to Homestart for an auction/Jubilee Ball; £4,375 to Born Free Foundation for chimpanzee rescue; £3,500 to St Mary's School, Wantage for fundraising in Jubilee Year; £2,000 to Defeating Deafness for research into deafness and tinnitus; £1,500 to Noseley Chapel for repairs; £1,000 to Countryside Alliance for a fundraising dinner

FINANCES *Year* 1996 *Income* £66,215

TRUSTEES R A S Everard, N W Smith, Mrs A C Richards

HOW TO APPLY Applications by post

WHO TO APPLY TO The Everard Foundation, Castle Acres, Narborough, Leicestershire LE9 5BY

CC NO 272248 **ESTABLISHED** 1976

■ The Norman Evershed Trust

WHAT IS FUNDED Christian work, famine relief. Primarily causes personally known to the Trustees

WHO CAN BENEFIT Christians and victims of famine

WHERE FUNDING CAN BE GIVEN UK and overseas

TYPE OF GRANT Various

FINANCES *Year* 1995 *Income* £29,978
Grants £28,810

TRUSTEES Mrs J S Evershed, R J Evershed, Mrs C A Evershed

NOTES Funds are fully committed at present

HOW TO APPLY **This Trust states that it does not respond to unsolicited applications**

WHO TO APPLY TO Mrs J S Evershed, The Norman Evershed Trust, 2 Borodale, Kirkwick Avenue, Harpenden, Hertfordshire AL5 2QW

CC NO 271318 **ESTABLISHED** 1976

■ Douglas Heath Eves Charitable Trust

WHAT IS FUNDED Charities supporting medical and paramedical projects, those which benefit young people (particularly educational), the elderly, those which support the arts and those which benefit the environment

WHAT IS NOT FUNDED Grants never made to individuals. Registered charities only

WHO CAN BENEFIT Organisations benefiting: people of all ages; actors and entertainment professionals; musicians; textile workers and designers; writers and poets; students and disabled people. There is no restriction on the disease or medical condition suffered by the beneficiaries

WHERE FUNDING CAN BE GIVEN UK and occasionally overseas

TYPE OF GRANT One-off single non-continuing

RANGE OF GRANTS £50–£250

FINANCES *Year* 1997 *Income* £25,125
Grants £18,812

TRUSTEES D H Eves, Mrs M Alderdice, P J Sheahan

WHO TO APPLY TO Douglas Heath Eves, Douglas Heath Eves Charitable Trust, Cocklands, Lower Basildon, Reading, Berkshire RG8 9PD

CC NO 248003 **ESTABLISHED** 1964

■ Beryl Evetts & Robert Luff Animal Welfare Trust

WHAT IS FUNDED The protection and shelter of lost or starving birds or animals. The promotion of hospitals for animals or birds (permanent site or mobile). The funding of veterinary research

WHO CAN BENEFIT Registered charities

WHERE FUNDING CAN BE GIVEN UK

RANGE OF GRANTS £100–£35,000

SAMPLE GRANTS £35,000 to Animal Health Trust; £26,000 to Royal Veterinary College; £1,000 to National Equine (and smaller animals) Defence League; £1,000 to People's Dispensary for Sick Animals; £500 to Pet Search; £100 to Paignton Zoo; £100 to Tusk Trust; £100 to National Federation of Badgers

FINANCES *Year* 1997 *Income* £88,771
Grants £63,800

TRUSTEES R C W Luff, CBE, Sir Robert Johnson, M Tomlinson, Mrs J Tomlinson, Lady Johnson, R P J Price, Ms G Favot, B D Nicholson

WHO TO APPLY TO M D Lock, Beryl Evetts & Robert Luff Animal Welfare Trust, c/o Parker Cavendish, 28 Church Road, Stanmore, Middlesex HA7 4XR

CC NO 283944 **ESTABLISHED** 1981

■ Evulot Limited

WHAT IS FUNDED General charitable purposes, in particular the advancement of the Orthodox Jewish Faith and the relief of poverty

WHO CAN BENEFIT Organisations benefiting Jewish people and those disadvantaged by poverty. Otherwise, there are no restrictions on the age; professional and economic group; family situation; religion and culture; and social circumstances of; or disease or medical condition suffered by, the beneficiaries

WHERE FUNDING CAN BE GIVEN UK

WHO TO APPLY TO A Lipschitz, Evulot Limited, 6 Durley Road, London N16 5JS

CC NO 1059735 **ESTABLISHED** 1996

■ Ewell Parochial Trusts (Relief in Need)

WHAT IS FUNDED To provide relief for those in need. Charities working in the fields of: education and training will be considered

WHO CAN BENEFIT Individuals and organisations benefiting those disadvantaged by poverty. There is no restriction on the age or family situation of the beneficiaries

WHERE FUNDING CAN BE GIVEN Ewell and Kingswood, Surrey

TYPE OF GRANT Funding may be given for up to one year

FINANCES *Year* 1997 *Income* £32,000
Grants £32,000

HOW TO APPLY To the address under Who To Apply To in writing

WHO TO APPLY TO G Berry, Clerk, Ewell Parochial Trusts (Relief in Need), 2 Portway Crescent, Ewell, Epsom, Surrey KT17 1SX *Tel* 0181-393 5979 *Fax* 0181-393 5979
CC NO 201623   **ESTABLISHED** 1961

■ Exclusive Charities Haggerston Owners

WHAT IS FUNDED The relief of disabled persons in the area of Northumberland by the provision of facilities for recreation and leisure time; other general charitable purposes in Northumberland
WHO CAN BENEFIT Organisation benefiting disabled people
WHERE FUNDING CAN BE GIVEN Northumberland
TRUSTEES D G Edgar, M McCully, J Shaw, J Brown
WHO TO APPLY TO D G Edgar, Chairperson, Exclusive Charities Haggerston Owners, Lakefield 8, Haggerston Castle, Beal, Northumberland TD15 2PA
CC NO 1064455   **ESTABLISHED** 1997

■ Exeter Dispensary and Aid in Sickness Fund

WHAT IS FUNDED The sick poor in the area Where Funding Can Be Given, either directly through grants to individuals or through local organisations. Provides grants for medical aids and appliances, chiropody, heating, bedding, warm clothing, costs of convalescence and relief of suffering generally
WHAT IS NOT FUNDED Grants are only made to people who are sick and poor
WHO CAN BENEFIT Individuals and organisations benefiting those disadvantaged by poverty who are suffering. There is no restriction on the disease or medical condition suffered by the beneficiaries
WHERE FUNDING CAN BE GIVEN Exeter
TYPE OF GRANT Often recurrent
SAMPLE GRANTS £3,300 to Exeter Age Concern; £1,650 to Hospiscare; £1,000 to Macmillan Cancer Relief an appeal for nurse at RD and E Hospital (Wonford); £715 to Honeylands Children's Centre; £550 to Friends of RD and E Hospital (Wonford); £500 to Shopmobility; £385 to Exeter and District Stroke Club; £250 to Disabled Young Adults Centre
FINANCES *Year* 1997 *Income* £29,189 *Grants* £22,821
TRUSTEES G F Cornish, A J Eveleigh, Mrs A Gundry, Dr W L Clarke, Ald S R Honeywill, J F G Michelmore, Dr A K Midgley, Dr M Mitchell, J Parkin, Miss J N Wiles
NOTES In 1997 convalescent grants given, were £10,302, a further £2,900 was given to individuals
HOW TO APPLY To the address under Who To Apply To in writing. Applications should be supported by a doctor or social worker, displaying evidence of both financial and medical need. Applications for medical equipment are considered in March and November
WHO TO APPLY TO D W Fanson, Hon Secretary, Exeter Dispensary and Aid in Sickness Fund, 85 Beacon Lane, Whipton, Exeter, Devon EX4 8LL
CC NO 205611   **ESTABLISHED** 1954

■ The Exilarch's Foundation

WHAT IS FUNDED Mainly Jewish organisations, some medical and welfare charities
WHO CAN BENEFIT Jewish people; at risk groups; disabled people; those disadvantaged by poverty and socially isolated people. There is no restriction on the disease or medical condition suffered by the beneficiaries
WHERE FUNDING CAN BE GIVEN UK
FINANCES *Year* 1996 *Income* £65,355
TRUSTEES N E Dangoor, D A Dangoor, M J Dangoor, E V B Dangoor, R S Dangoor
HOW TO APPLY To the address under Who To Apply To in writing
WHO TO APPLY TO H H The Exilarch, The Exilarch's Foundation, 4 Carlos Place, Mayfair, London W1Y 5AE *Tel* 0171-399 0850
CC NO 275919   **ESTABLISHED** 1978

■ Extonglen Ltd

This trust did not respond to CAF's request to amend its entry and, by 30 June 1998, CAF's researchers did not find financial records for later than 1995 on its file at the Charity Commission. Trusts are legally required to submit annual accounts to the Charity Commission under section 42 of the Charities Act 1993

WHAT IS FUNDED Advancement of Orthodox Jewish faith, relief of poverty and general charitable purposes
WHO CAN BENEFIT Jewish people and those disadvantaged by poverty. There are no restrictions on the age; professional and economic group; family situation; religion and culture; and social circumstances of; or disease or medical condition suffered by, the beneficiaries
WHERE FUNDING CAN BE GIVEN UK
TRUSTEES M Levine, Mrs C Levine, B B Rapaport
WHO TO APPLY TO J Schwarz, Extonglen Ltd, Arnold Cohen & Co, Accountants, 13–17 New Burlington Place, Regent Street, London W1X 2ZP
CC NO 286230   **ESTABLISHED** 1982

■ FC Charitable Trust (formerly J J M

Fletcher Charitable Trust)

WHAT IS FUNDED The advancement of Christian faith, missions, relief of hardship of individuals and communities in any part of the world
WHAT IS NOT FUNDED No scholarships. No grants to individuals
WHO CAN BENEFIT Registered charities benefiting Christians and those disadvantage by poverty
WHERE FUNDING CAN BE GIVEN UK and overseas
FINANCES *Year* 1997 *Income* £21,000
Grants £25,000
TRUSTEES M Fletcher, J C V Miles
HOW TO APPLY **The Trust's income is fully committed**
WHO TO APPLY TO J C Vernor Miles, FC Charitable Trust, Messrs Vernor, Miles and Noble, 5 Raymond Buildings, Gray's Inn, London WC1R 5DD
CC NO 277686 **ESTABLISHED** 1978

■ The Faber Charitable Trust

WHAT IS FUNDED General charitable purposes
WHO CAN BENEFIT Charitable institutions and individuals. There are no restrictions on the age; professional and economic group; family situation; religion and culture; and social circumstances of; or disease or medical condition suffered by, the beneficiaries
WHERE FUNDING CAN BE GIVEN UK
TYPE OF GRANT As appropriate to the project
SAMPLE GRANTS £5,545 to eight individuals in aggregate value of grants; £1,500 to Society of Friends for Jewish Refugees; £1,380 to Hendon Adath Yisroel Congregation; £1,000 to Kollol Trust; £1,000 to Service to the Aged; £1,000 to Hasmonean High School
FINANCES *Year* 1997 *Income* £39,999
Grants £20,821
TRUSTEES B Faber, Mrs F Faber, H Kramer
PUBLICATIONS Annual Report and Accounts
HOW TO APPLY No application forms. Informal enquiry by telephone or for programme guidelines is encouraged before formal application is made. Unsolicited applications outside the Trust's programme areas will not be acknowledged. For civil rights, gender and racial justice programmes, applications should be addressed to Dipali Chandra, for other programmes to Eric Adams. Trustees meet termly, usually in March, July and November
WHO TO APPLY TO H Kramer, The Faber Charitable Trust, Devonshire House, 1 Devonshire Street, London W1N 2DR
CC NO 294820 **ESTABLISHED** 1986

■ The Fairbairn Charitable Trust

WHAT IS FUNDED Mainly Christian mission and education, churches and Christian umbrella bodies
WHAT IS NOT FUNDED No grants to individuals
WHO CAN BENEFIT Organisations benefiting children, older people and Christians
WHERE FUNDING CAN BE GIVEN UK and overseas

TYPE OF GRANT One–off grants, projects, research, and recurring costs will be considered. Funding may be given for up to three years
TRUSTEES J A Fairbairn, Ms S P Fairbairn, Ms A Saunders
HOW TO APPLY By post, with sae
WHO TO APPLY TO Rev J A Fairbairn, Trustee, The Fairbairn Charitable Trust, 36 Gunton Church Lane, Lowestoft, Suffolk NR32 4LF
CC NO 1059697 **ESTABLISHED** 1996

■ The Fairway Trust

WHAT IS FUNDED Support of universities, colleges, schools in UK and abroad; scholarships; grants to postgraduates and undergraduates; grants to help religious purposes; support of clubs and recreational facilities for children and young persons
WHAT IS NOT FUNDED No grants to individuals
WHO CAN BENEFIT Charities only
WHERE FUNDING CAN BE GIVEN UK and overseas
FINANCES *Year* 1995 *Income* £85,713
Grants £83,257
TRUSTEES Janet Grimstone, Ms K V M Suenson-Taylor
NOTES Applications are not acknowledged
HOW TO APPLY **This Trust states that it does not respond to unsolicited applications**
WHO TO APPLY TO P V Turner, Secretary, The Fairway Trust, c/o Macfarlane & Co, 2nd Floor, Cunard Building, Water Street, Liverpool L3 1DS
CC NO 272227 **ESTABLISHED** 1976

■ The Falkland Community Trust

WHAT IS FUNDED Grants are made to organisations which work for the benefit of poor or marginalised people, particularly in deprived areas. Preference is shown towards projects that involve their users by sharing responsibilities with them. Projects that work for social justice, peace and equality in gender and race are also supported
WHAT IS NOT FUNDED Grants are not given to national organisations, capital building projects, projects that are eligible for statutory funding, publications, or research
WHO CAN BENEFIT Organisations benefiting poor or marginalised people
WHERE FUNDING CAN BE GIVEN Scotland
TYPE OF GRANT Requests for revenue funding for more than one year may be considered in specific circumstances
TRUSTEES Ms M Bremner, Ms S Kerr, F McGachy, J Norman, Ms H Steven, Ms M Stuart
PUBLICATIONS Accounts and guidelines for applicants are available from the Trust
HOW TO APPLY Applications should be made on an application form which is available from the address below. The Trustees meet every three to four months but smaller grants (e.g. up to £300) which are required urgently may be awarded between meetings
WHO TO APPLY TO John Norman, The Falkland Community Trust, Messrs Norman Downie & Kerr, 122 Constitution Hill, Edinburgh EH6 6AW
SC NO SCO 09577

■ The Family Foundations Trust

WHAT IS FUNDED All Jewish causes
WHO CAN BENEFIT Jewish people
WHERE FUNDING CAN BE GIVEN UK
RANGE OF GRANTS £30–£10,300

Does the trust you have chosen match your needs? Haphazard applications waste postage and time

209

SAMPLE GRANTS £10,300 to Jewish Care; £5,000 to friends of Bar Llan University; £2,500 to Community Security Trust; £2,400 to Western Marble Arch Synagogue; £1,500 to Nightingale House; £1,000 to Chief Rabbinate Charitable Trust; £1,000 to British ORT; £1,000 to Well Being; £1,000 to Friends of Hebrew University of Jerusalem; £850 to Norwood Ravenswood
FINANCES *Year* 1997 *Income* £140,073 *Grants* £32,385
TRUSTEES R B Mintz, P G Mintz
WHO TO APPLY TO Simon Hosier, The Family Foundations Trust, Gerald Elderman Chartered Accountants, 25 Harley Street, London W1N 2BR
CC NO 264014   ESTABLISHED 1972

■ The Family Trust

WHAT IS FUNDED Promotion of Christian faith, relief of the sick and aged and relief of poverty
WHO CAN BENEFIT Organisations benefiting the elderly, Christians and those disadvantaged by poverty. There is no restriction on the disease or medical condition suffered by the beneficiaries
WHERE FUNDING CAN BE GIVEN Colchester and surrounding area
TRUSTEES A C Green, J M Green, R Borgonan
WHO TO APPLY TO N Reynolds, The Family Trust, Reynolds & Co, Accountants, Hardy House, 404 Hale End Road, London E4 9PB
CC NO 1001105   ESTABLISHED 1990

■ Famos Foundation Trust

WHAT IS FUNDED Education, religion, international organisations, and general charitable purposes. The Trust will consider funding: the advancement of the Jewish religion; synagogues; Jewish umbrella bodies; church schools; cultural and religious teaching and religious studies
WHAT IS NOT FUNDED Individuals, students
WHO CAN BENEFIT Small local projects and established organisations benefiting children, young adults, clergy and Jews
WHERE FUNDING CAN BE GIVEN UK and overseas, particularly Gateshead, Manchester City, Salford and London
TYPE OF GRANT One-off, core costs and running costs. Funding is given for one year or less
RANGE OF GRANTS £1,000 or less
FINANCES *Year* 1996 *Income* £88,778 *Grants* £42,272
TRUSTEES Rabbi S M Kaputz
HOW TO APPLY In writing at any time
WHO TO APPLY TO Rabbi S M Kaputz, Famos Foundation Trust, 4 Hanover Gardens, Salford, Lancashire M7 4FQ *Tel* 0161-740 5735
CC NO 271211   ESTABLISHED 1976

■ The Edmund Fane Research Trust

WHAT IS FUNDED Income of funds largely committed to long-term projects in connection with cancer, multiple sclerosis, neurological and leukaemia research, and immunology
WHAT IS NOT FUNDED The Trustees have decided not to make grants to members of the medical profession doing 'electives' or service overseas, or engaging in individual research projects. They have also decided not to make grants to medical students either before or after qualification
WHO CAN BENEFIT Organisations benefiting sufferers of cancer, leukaemia and multiple sclerosis
WHERE FUNDING CAN BE GIVEN England

TYPE OF GRANT Long-term commitment to regular grants for projects; occasional one-off grants in the event of a surplus
FINANCES *Year* 1997 *Income* £30,000 *Grants* £37,000
TRUSTEES J L Norton, J J Dilger, Dr K Newton, A de Brye
WHO TO APPLY TO J J Dilger, The Edmund Fane Research Trust, Macfarlanes, (Ref 102134), 10 Norwich Street, London EC4A 1BD *Tel* 0171-831 9222 *Fax* 0171-831 9607
CC NO 262747   ESTABLISHED 1971

■ Lord Faringdon Charitable Trust

WHAT IS FUNDED Educational scholarships and grants, hospitals and the provision of medical treatment, purchase of antiques and artistic objects for collections with public access, care and assistance of aged or infirm, development and assistance of arts and sciences, physical recreation and drama, research and support of matters of public interest, relief of poverty, maintaining and developing the Faringdon Collection
WHAT IS NOT FUNDED No grants to individuals
WHO CAN BENEFIT Registered charitable institutions benefiting people of all ages. Support is given to those disadvantaged by poverty; actors and entertainment professionals; medical professionals; research workers; scientists; students; teachers and governesses. Support may also be given to sportsmen and women. There is no restriction on the disease or medical condition suffered by the beneficiaries
WHERE FUNDING CAN BE GIVEN UK
RANGE OF GRANTS £1,000–£25,000
SAMPLE GRANTS £25,000 to The National Trust Buscot Centenary and Millennium Fund; £10,000 to Botanic Gardens Conservation; £5,000 to Royal College of Art; £5,000 to The Samaritans; £5,000 to Peper Haron Foundation; £4,000 to Link Lectures Institute of Cancer Research; £2,500 to Tunbridge Wells Counselling Centre; £2,500 to Scriveners Company; £2,500 to St Lawrence Lechdale for restoration; £2,500 to Royal Academy of Arts
FINANCES *Year* 1996 *Income* £78,110 *Grants* £66,500
TRUSTEES H S S Trotter, A D A W Forbes
WHO TO APPLY TO Trustees, Lord Faringdon Charitable Trust, c/o William Sturges & Co, Alliance House, 12 Caxton Street, London SW1H 0QY
CC NO 206878   ESTABLISHED 1962

■ Lord Faringdon Second Charitable Trust

WHAT IS FUNDED Educational scholarships and grants, hospitals and the provision of medical treatment, purchase of antiques and artistic objects for collections with public access, care and assistance of aged or infirm, development and assistance of arts and sciences, physical recreation and drama, research and support of matters of public interest, relief of poverty, maintaining and developing the Faringdon Collection
WHAT IS NOT FUNDED No grants to individuals
WHO CAN BENEFIT Registered charitable institutions benefiting people of all ages. Support is given to those disadvantaged by poverty; actors and entertainment professionals; medical professionals; research workers; scientists;

students; teachers and governesses. Support may also be given to sportsmen and women. There is no restriction on the disease or medical condition suffered by the beneficiaries

WHERE FUNDING CAN BE GIVEN UK

RANGE OF GRANTS £500–£17,500

SAMPLE GRANTS £17,500 to Royal Botanic Gardens, Kew; £15,000 to St Katherine's House, Wantage; £5,000 to Royal Choral Society; £3,600 to Queen Elizabeth Foundation for the Disabled; £2,500 to St Mungo Association Charitable Trust; £1,000 to Willow Trust; £1,000 to Pearson's Holiday Fund; £1,000 to Gino Watkins Memorial Fund; £1,000 to Suffolk Deaf Association; £1,000 to Reeds School, Cobham

FINANCES *Year* 1996 *Income* £63,612 *Grants* £49,100

TRUSTEES H S S Trotter, A D A W Forbes

WHO TO APPLY TO Trustees, Lord Faringdon Second Charitable Trust, c/o William Sturges & Co, Alliance House, 12 Caxton Street, London SW1H 0QY

CC NO 237974　　**ESTABLISHED** 1964

■ The Farmers' Company Charitable Fund

WHAT IS FUNDED Promotion of agriculture research and education, including scholarships. Providing relief to members of The Farmers' Company in hardship or distress. Providing funds for British students travelling abroad to study agriculture

WHO CAN BENEFIT Individuals and organisations benefiting students, members of the Farmer's Company who are disadvantaged by poverty or in distress, socially isolated or at risk

WHERE FUNDING CAN BE GIVEN UK

FINANCES *Year* 1995 *Income* £82,508

TRUSTEES The Court of Assistants of the Worshipful Company of Farmers

WHO TO APPLY TO The Clerk, The Farmers' Company Charitable Fund, Worshipful Company of Farmers, Pel House, 35 Station Square, Petts Wood, Kent BR5 1LZ

CC NO 258712　　**ESTABLISHED** 1969

■ Samuel William Farmer's Trust

WHAT IS FUNDED Charities working in the fields of residential facilities and services, infrastructure development, churches, hospices, healthcare, medical studies and research, conservation, environmental and animal sciences, education and various community facilities and services. African agriculture may be considered

WHAT IS NOT FUNDED No grants to students, or for schools and colleges, endowments, inner city welfare or housing

WHO CAN BENEFIT Registered charities benefiting children and older people. There is no restriction on the disease or medical condition suffered by the beneficiaries, however there are some restrictions on their social circumstances

WHERE FUNDING CAN BE GIVEN Wiltshire and occasionally Africa

TYPE OF GRANT One-off and recurrent. Buildings, project, research, running costs, salaries and start-up costs. Funding is available for up to three years

RANGE OF GRANTS £100–£10,000

SAMPLE GRANTS £20,000 to Wessex Children's Hospice; £20,000 to Dauntsey's School; £10,000 to Wiltshire Community Foundation; £5,000 to Dorothy House; £5,000 to Prospect Hospice; £5,000 to Salisbury Hospice; £2,000 to Great Bedwyn School; £2,000 to British Heart Foundation; £1,500 to Wishbone Trust; £1,500 to Royal Veterinary College Animal Care Trust

FINANCES *Year* 1997 *Income* £80,603 *Grants* £83,130

HOW TO APPLY In writing only, at any time

WHO TO APPLY TO Mrs J Simpson, Samuel William Farmer's Trust, 33 The Fairway, Devizes, Wiltshire SN10 5DX

CC NO 258459　　**ESTABLISHED** 1929

■ The Thomas Farr Charitable Trust

WHAT IS FUNDED General charitable purposes

WHAT IS NOT FUNDED No grants to individuals

WHO CAN BENEFIT Registered charities only. There are no restrictions on the age; professional and economic group; family situation; religion and culture; and social circumstances of; or disease or medical condition suffered by, the beneficiaries

WHERE FUNDING CAN BE GIVEN Mainly Nottinghamshire

RANGE OF GRANTS £250–£20,000

SAMPLE GRANTS £20,000 to Bassetlaw CVS; £20,000 to Skylarks Winged Fellowship Appeal; £15,000 to Paediatric Cystic Fibrosis Fund, City Hospital, Nottingham; £7,500 to Bassetlaw Hospital Mammography Appeal; £5,000 to 47th Nottingham Scout Group; £5,000 to Age Concern; £5,000 to Motor Neurone Disease Research Fund; £5,000 to Youth Hostels Association (England and Wales); £2,000 to Ash Lee School, Cotgrove, Nottinghamshire; £2,000 to Children Nationwide Medical Research Fund

FINANCES *Year* 1997 *Income* £186,529 *Grants* £112,335

TRUSTEES B H Farr, Mrs E M Astley-Arlington, Mrs P K Myles, Kleinwort Benson Trustees Ltd

WHO TO APPLY TO B Davys, The Thomas Farr Charitable Trust, Kleinwort Benson Trustees Ltd, PO Box 191, 10 Fenchurch Street, London EC3M 3LB

CC NO 328394　　**ESTABLISHED** 1989

■ Farrer-Brown Charitable Trust

WHAT IS FUNDED General charitable purposes. Trustees prefer new projects for the common good

WHO CAN BENEFIT There are no restrictions on the age; professional and economic group; family situation; religion and culture; and social circumstances of; or disease or medical condition suffered by, the beneficiaries

WHERE FUNDING CAN BE GIVEN UK

FINANCES *Year* 1997 *Income* £22,308

TRUSTEES M F Brown, G F Brown, J F Brown, M F Brown, R F Brown

WHO TO APPLY TO Mrs J A Farrer-Brown, Farrer-Brown Charitable Trust, Radnage Bottom Farm, Radnage Lane, Radnage, Buckinghamshire HP14 4DX

CC NO 265992　　**ESTABLISHED** 1973

■ The Farthing Trust

WHAT IS FUNDED General charitable purposes at the sole discretion of the Trustees, generally assistance is given to people on humanitarian grounds rather than property

WHO CAN BENEFIT Individuals and charitable organisations. There are no restrictions on the age; professional and economic group; family situation; religion and culture; and social circumstances of; or disease or medical condition suffered by, the beneficiaries

WHERE FUNDING CAN BE GIVEN UK and overseas

TYPE OF GRANT One-off and recurring grant

RANGE OF GRANTS £905–£27,750

FINANCES *Year* 1997 *Income* £123,872 *Grants* £95,875

TRUSTEES C H Martin, Mrs E Martin, Miss J Martin, BEd, Mrs A White, BSc

NOTES Priority is given to those personally known or personally recommended to the Trustees

HOW TO APPLY In writing to the address under Who To Apply To. Applicants will only be notified of a refusal if an sae is enclosed

WHO TO APPLY TO C H Martin, MA, The Farthing Trust, 48 Ten Mile Bank, Littleport, Ely, Cambridgeshire CB6 1EF

CC NO 268066   **ESTABLISHED** 1974

■ Walter Farthing (Trust) Limited

WHAT IS FUNDED Initiation or assistance of the development of projects by undertaking or grant aiding the acquisition, erection or adaptation of buildings and the provision of initial equipment

WHAT IS NOT FUNDED The Council does not ordinarily grant aid to headquarters organisations of national charities, services which public authorities are empowered to provide, individuals or current expenditure of any nature or description

WHO CAN BENEFIT Organisations enlarging the range (including innovative projects) and/or volume of charitable services provided in the locality. There are no restrictions on the age; professional and economic group; family situation; religion and culture; and social circumstances of; or disease or medical condition suffered by, the beneficiaries

WHERE FUNDING CAN BE GIVEN Chelmsford, Essex

RANGE OF GRANTS £250–£99,862

SAMPLE GRANTS £99,862 to Acorn Village; £50,000 to St Clare's Day Hospice; £18,000 to Shaftesbury Society; £12,000 to Farthing Centre; £5,600 to St John Ambulance; £5,000 to YMCA; £5,000 to Cirdan Trust; £2,000 to Downs Syndrome; £1,000 to Gideon International; £1,000 to Wifford Parish Church

FINANCES *Year* 1995 *Income* £32,371 *Grants* £201,029

TRUSTEES The Council of Management

WHO TO APPLY TO R A Knappett, Walter Farthing (Trust) Limited, Mill House, Margaretting Road, Galleywood, Chelmsford, Essex CM2 8TS

CC NO 220114   **ESTABLISHED** 1957

■ The Fassnidge Memorial Trust

WHAT IS FUNDED Welfare of elderly people and families in the London Borough of Hillingdon. Particularly charities working in the fields of: care in the community; day centres and meals provision

WHAT IS NOT FUNDED Applications from persons or organisations outside the London Borough of Hillingdon

WHO CAN BENEFIT Individuals and organisations benefiting children, older people, parents and children, carers, disabled people and victims of domestic violence

WHERE FUNDING CAN BE GIVEN The London Borough of Hillingdon

TYPE OF GRANT Small one-off grants and start-up costs. Funding of one year or less will be considered

RANGE OF GRANTS £100–£5,000

SAMPLE GRANTS £7,500 to Uxbridge Old People's Welfare Association for day centre; £5,000 to Age Concern, Hillingdon for gardening project for the elderly; £2,050 to Uxbridge Shopmobility for disabled persons shopping assistance; £500 to SCOPE for individual child's needs; £300 to AIDIS Trust for individual child's needs

FINANCES *Year* 1997–98 *Income* £72,600 *Grants* £22,300

TRUSTEES Seven appointees of the Council of London Borough of Hillingdon and two co-opted

PUBLICATIONS Annual Report

HOW TO APPLY To the Clerk in writing

WHO TO APPLY TO F Johnson, Clerk, The Fassnidge Memorial Trust, Orchard Bungalow, Bellswood Lane, Iver, Buckinghamshire SL0 0LU *Tel* 01753 655565

CC NO 303078   **ESTABLISHED** 1963

■ The Guy Fawkes Charitable Trust

WHAT IS FUNDED General charitable purposes

WHO CAN BENEFIT There are no restrictions on the age; professional and economic group; family situation; religion and culture; and social circumstances of; or disease or medical condition suffered by, the beneficiaries

WHERE FUNDING CAN BE GIVEN UK

RANGE OF GRANTS £50–£30,000

SAMPLE GRANTS £30,000 to Christian International Peace Service; £6,000 to Langley Home Trust; £6,000 to Multiple Sclerosis Society; £5,000 to Council for Music in Hospitals; £2,000 to Finton House Educational Trust; £1,500 to Handicapped Playground Adventure Association Limited; £1,000 to Afghan Children's Appeal; £1,000 to National Eye Research Centre; £500 to British Wheelchair Sports Foundation; £500 to Contact the Elderly

FINANCES *Year* 1996 *Income* £27,156 *Grants* £56,450

TRUSTEES Miss Y F Calvocoressi, R St G Calvocoressi

WHO TO APPLY TO Miss Y Calvocoressi, The Guy Fawkes Charitable Trust, 26 Quarrenden Street, Fulham, London SW6 3SU

CC NO 258045   **ESTABLISHED** 1969

■ George Fearn Trust

WHAT IS FUNDED The support of St George's Church and St George's Schools in Stockport

WHO CAN BENEFIT St George's Church and schools benefiting children and young adults

WHERE FUNDING CAN BE GIVEN The County Borough of Stockport

TYPE OF GRANT At the Trustees' discretion

FINANCES *Year* 1997–98 *Income* £19,994 *Grants* £20,233

TRUSTEES R J B Green (Chairman), F Gregg, S B Berry, A J Garlick, P R Ball, J R Hardy

HOW TO APPLY To the address under Who To Apply To in writing

WHO TO APPLY TO F Gregg, Secretary, George Fearn Trust, 2 Mount Street, Albert Square, Manchester M2 5NX *Tel* 0161-834 7428

CC NO 223212   **ESTABLISHED** 1911

■ Federation of Jewish Relief Organisations

WHAT IS FUNDED The relief of Jewish victims of war and persecution and to help wherever Jewish need exists

WHO CAN BENEFIT Jewish people, particularly those disadvantaged by poverty, socially isolated or in at risk groups, and those who are victims of war

WHERE FUNDING CAN BE GIVEN Mainly Israel

RANGE OF GRANTS £11,632–£100,033

SAMPLE GRANTS £100,033 in grants to Israel, etc towards kindergartens, youth centres, education and medical equipment; £35,300 for clothing and relief goods shipped to Israel; £11,632 for collection, packaging, insurance and freight of clothing, food, medicaments and other relief supplies

FINANCES *Year* 1997 *Income* £1,197,751
Grants £146,965

TRUSTEES The Executive Committee: Dr W Schindler, M Katz, A Garfield

NOTES Founded in 1919 to assist victims of war and persecution in Europe and the Eastern Bloc. Since 1948 it has been concerned mainly in Israel with the rehabilitation, clothing, feeding and education of children of immigrant families

WHO TO APPLY TO Mrs R Gluckstein, Federation of Jewish Relief Organisations, 143 Brondesbury Park, London NW2 5JL

CC NO 250006   **ESTABLISHED** 1919

■ Feed the Minds (formerly Association for Christian Communication)

WHAT IS FUNDED The Trustees of Feed the Minds make grants to developing countries and Eastern Europe to support Christian literature and communication programmes

WHAT IS NOT FUNDED No grants to individuals

WHO CAN BENEFIT Developing countries and Eastern European Church organisations benefiting Christians

WHERE FUNDING CAN BE GIVEN Developing countries and eastern Europe

TYPE OF GRANT Capital and project grants to develop new work and increase overall potential of organisation, for periods from one to three years

RANGE OF GRANTS Most grants in the range of £1,000–£5,000 pa

SAMPLE GRANTS £12,000 to CCDB, Bangladesh for production of literacy materials; £8,900 to Coptic Evangelical Organisation, Egypt to set up village libraries; £6,500 to MAP International, Ecuador for radio programme 'Health without Frontiers'; £6,350 to STEP Publishers, Ghana for children's magazine *Surprise*; £6,000 to Certeza, Argentina for Christian publishing; £6,000 to IDEA, Nepal for printing machine; £6,000 to Scripture Union, South Africa for literature on AIDS for young people; £6,000 to CBFC, Congo/Zaire for hymn book publishing; £5,000 to Asian Institute for Liturgy and Music, Philippines for contextualised worship material; £5,000 to Victory Books, Papua New Guinea for Christian publishing

FINANCES *Year* 1997 *Income* £413,973
Grants £315,047

TRUSTEES Rev Canon John Lowe, Rev Dr C Elliott, Christopher Bayne, John Clark

PUBLICATIONS *Theological Book Review*

HOW TO APPLY Preferably by March and September

WHO TO APPLY TO Dr Alwyn Marriage, Director, Feed the Minds, Albany House, 67 Sydenham Road, Guildford, Surrey GU1 3RY *Tel* 01483 888580
Fax 01483 888581
E-mail feedtheminds@gn.apc.org
CC NO 291333   **ESTABLISHED** 1964

■ The John Feeney Charitable Bequest

WHAT IS FUNDED Benefit of public charities in Birmingham only. Promotion of art in Birmingham only. Acquisition and maintenance of open spaces near Birmingham. Capital projects preferred

WHAT IS NOT FUNDED Nothing political or denominational

WHO CAN BENEFIT To benefit artists and the residents of Birmingham

WHERE FUNDING CAN BE GIVEN Birmingham

TYPE OF GRANT Capital

FINANCES *Year* 1995 *Income* £33,539
Grants £31,800

TRUSTEES H Kenrick, Mrs M Smith, Rev Canon R S Stevens

HOW TO APPLY In writing. There is no application form and no sae is required. Applications should be submitted by March of each year

WHO TO APPLY TO M J Woodward, The John Feeney Charitable Bequest, Messrs Lee Crowder, 39 Newhall Street, Birmingham B3 3DY *Tel* 0121-236 4477 *Fax* 0121-236 4710

CC NO 214486   **ESTABLISHED** 1906

■ The Felicitas Trust

WHAT IS FUNDED General charitable purposes at Trustees' discretion

WHO CAN BENEFIT Institutions and individuals. There are no restrictions on the age, professional and economic group, family situation, religion and culture, and social circumstances of, or disease or medical condition suffered by, the beneficiaries

WHERE FUNDING CAN BE GIVEN UK

TYPE OF GRANT One-off and recurrent

RANGE OF GRANTS £50–£7,500

SAMPLE GRANTS £7,500 to an individual for education; £5,675 to Institute of Theology; £2,500 to British Heart Foundation; £2,000 to East Acton Primary School; £2,000 to Medical Foundation; £2,000 to NSPCC; £1,000 to Chemical Depending Centre; £1,000 to Church of St Benet, Kemerton; £1,000 to Church of St Nicholas, Winchcombe; £1,000 to Malvern College

FINANCES *Year* 1995 *Income* £42,739
Grants £29,125

TRUSTEES J M Simpson, Ms P A M Simpson, R Luff, A M A Skrine

WHO TO APPLY TO A M A Skrine, The Felicitas Trust, 9 New Square, Lincoln's Inn, London WC2A 3QN

CC NO 327321   **ESTABLISHED** 1986

■ Fellowship Charitable Trust

WHAT IS FUNDED General charitable purposes

WHO CAN BENEFIT There are no restrictions on the age; professional and economic group; family situation; religion and culture; and social circumstances of; or disease or medical condition suffered by, the beneficiaries

WHERE FUNDING CAN BE GIVEN UK

HOW TO APPLY This Trust states that it does not respond to unsolicited applications

Does the trust you have chosen match your needs? Haphazard applications waste postage and time

213

WHO TO APPLY TO D Heena, Chairman, Fellowship Charitable Trust, 21 Gotherington Lane, Bishop Cleeve, Cheltenham, Gloucestershire GL52 4EN
CC NO 1059541   **ESTABLISHED** 1996

■ The Feltmakers Charitable Foundation

WHAT IS FUNDED General charitable purposes
WHO CAN BENEFIT There are no restrictions on the age; professional and economic group; family situation; religion and culture; and social circumstances of; or disease or medical condition suffered by, the beneficiaries
WHERE FUNDING CAN BE GIVEN UK and overseas
RANGE OF GRANTS £250–£1,480
SAMPLE GRANTS £1,480 to Feltmakers Award; £1,000 to Lord Mayor's Appeal; £500 to King George V Fund for Sailors; £500 to Providence Row; £500 to Sheriffs and Recorders Fund
FINANCES *Year* 1995 *Income* £17,392 *Grants* £6,980
TRUSTEES P P Keens, JP, M J Harper, OBE, B D S Burgess, P A Grant
WHO TO APPLY TO Lt Col C J Holroyd, Clerk to the Company, The Feltmakers Charitable Foundation, Providence Cottage, Chute Cadley, Andover, Hampshire SP11 9EB
CC NO 259906   **ESTABLISHED** 1969

■ Fentham Birmingham Trust

WHAT IS FUNDED Allocations for general grants are made following the annual meeting of Trustees. Educational grants to bona fide residents of Birmingham (three year minimum) under 25 years of age (September to April, ie academic year). Particularly charities working in the fields of: tertiary and higher education, and various community services and facilities will be considered
WHO CAN BENEFIT Individuals and organisations benefiting young adults and those disadvantaged by poverty in the Birmingham City area
WHERE FUNDING CAN BE GIVEN City of Birmingham only
FINANCES *Year* 1996 *Income* £104,512 *Grants* £90,829
TRUSTEES As appointed by City of Birmingham local authorities
HOW TO APPLY There is an application form available for educational grants
WHO TO APPLY TO Mrs Anne E Holmes, Fentham Birmingham Trust, Messrs Lee, Crowder, 39 Newhall Street, Birmingham, B3 3DY *Tel* 0121-236 4477
CC NO 214487   **ESTABLISHED** 1907

■ Fenton Trust

This trust did not respond to CAF's request to amend its entry and, by 30 June 1998, CAF's researchers did not find financial records for later than 1995 on its file at the Charity Commission. Trusts are legally required to submit annual accounts to the Charity Commission under section 42 of the Charities Act 1993

WHAT IS FUNDED Applications will only be considered from students in the last year of a course or if temporary unforeseen difficulty arises. Grants are once only and normally of £200 maximum
WHO CAN BENEFIT Students belonging to the professional classes
WHERE FUNDING CAN BE GIVEN UK
TYPE OF GRANT One-off

TRUSTEES Family Welfare Association
WHO TO APPLY TO The Grants Administrator, Fenton Trust, Family Welfare Association, 501–505 Kingsland Road, Dalston, London E8 4AU
CC NO 247552   **ESTABLISHED** 1955

■ The A M Fenton Trust

WHAT IS FUNDED General charitable purposes. To support mainly one-off national appeals and local appeals
WHAT IS NOT FUNDED The Trust is unlikely to assist those wishing to take higher degrees
WHO CAN BENEFIT There are no restrictions on the age; professional and economic group; family situation; religion and culture; and social circumstances of; or disease or medical condition suffered by, the beneficiaries
WHERE FUNDING CAN BE GIVEN UK and overseas
RANGE OF GRANTS £100–£20,000
SAMPLE GRANTS £20,000 to Yorkshire County Cricket Club Charitable Youth Trust; £10,000 to Hipperholme Grammar School; £5,000 to Dewsbury and District League of Friendship for Disabled Persons; £3,000 Herridge Kate Educational; £2,500 to Kenmore Cheshire Home; £2,500 to Tweed Foundation; £2,000 to Macmillan Appeal; £2,000 to West Yorkshire Association for the Disabled; £1,969 to Citizens Advice Bureau, Harrogate; £1,500 to Drake Music Project
FINANCES *Year* 1996 *Income* £133,127 *Grants* £67,969
TRUSTEES J L Fenton, C M Fenton
WHO TO APPLY TO J L Fenton, The A M Fenton Trust, 14 Beech Grove, Harrogate, Yorkshire HG2 0EX
CC NO 270353   **ESTABLISHED** 1975

■ Ferguson Benevolent Fund Limited

WHAT IS FUNDED To give grants for such charitable purposes as they deem worthy of their support and, in particular, are connected with the Methodist Church. Preference to charities of which the Trust has special interest, knowledge or association. These include: residential facilities; respite and sheltered accommodation; information technology and computers; infrastructure development; Methodist umbrella bodies; acute health care; respite care and care for carers; support and self help groups; special schools; education and training; and community services
WHAT IS NOT FUNDED No support for trade unions and like bodies. No support to individuals for medical electives, postgraduate studies, expeditions or for private schooling
WHO CAN BENEFIT Mainly to cases of social, medical and educational need, usually through charitable bodies working in fields of social and medical need in the areas specified. Organisations benefiting: people of all ages; unemployed people; those in care, fostered and adopted; Methodists; at risk groups; carers; those disadvantaged by poverty; homeless people; those living in rural and urban areas; and victims of domestic violence. Those suffering from Alzheimer's disease, asthma, diabetes, hearing loss, heart disease, leprosy and polio
WHERE FUNDING CAN BE GIVEN North West England, Greater Manchester, Jersey and overseas

TYPE OF GRANT Buildings, capital, endowments, one-off, project, research and start-up costs. All funding is for up to two years

RANGE OF GRANTS £500–£10,000

SAMPLE GRANTS £3,000 to Children's Hospital Appeal for intensive care equipment in children's hospital; £2,000 to Action and Research for MS for a day centre for physiotherapy and helpline; £2,000 to Henshaws Society for the Blind for refurbishing two homes for blind people in Salford and Blackley; £2,000 to Contact for training and help for single girls' home; £2,000 to Ferries and Port Sunlight Family Groups for all sorts of back up for local families; £2,000 to Share and Care Fleetwood for Christian support for elderly house bound; £2,000 to International Childcare Trust for children on the streets in Kenya; £2,000 to Orbis for flying eye hospital for the third world; £1,000 to Opportunities and Activities for adult education in Fallowfield; £1,000 to Traidcraft for empowering women to do business in Africa

FINANCES *Year* 1997 *Income* £31,000
Grants £47,500

TRUSTEES Mrs E Higginbottom (Chair), Mrs C M A Metcalfe, Ms S Ferguson (Secretary), Mrs P Dobson, P A L Holt, S M Higginbottom

HOW TO APPLY By letter only. No telephone calls

WHO TO APPLY TO Mrs E Higginbottom, Ferguson Benevolent Fund Limited, PO Box 16, Ambleside, Cumbria LA22 9GD

CC NO 228746   **ESTABLISHED** 1963

■ The Ferguson Bequest Fund

WHAT IS FUNDED Grants are given to churches for repairs, educational activities and for the benefit of individuals connected with the church

WHO CAN BENEFIT Churches in South West Scotland and individuals connected with the church

WHERE FUNDING CAN BE GIVEN South West Scotland

TYPE OF GRANT Buildings. Funding for up to one year

FINANCES *Year* 1997 *Income* £172,000
Grants £130,000

PUBLICATIONS Accounts are available from the Trust

HOW TO APPLY Applications should be made in writing to the address under Who To Apply To

WHO TO APPLY TO Ronald D Oakes, Secretary, The Ferguson Bequest Fund, 182 Bath Street, Glasgow G2 4HG *Tel* 0141-332 0476

SC NO SCO 09305   **ESTABLISHED** 1869

■ The Ferraris Charitable Trust

WHAT IS FUNDED General charitable purposes at the Trustees' discretion

WHAT IS NOT FUNDED No grants to individuals

WHO CAN BENEFIT Institutions. There are no restrictions on the age; professional and economic group; family situation; religion and culture; and social circumstances of; or disease or medical condition suffered by, the beneficiaries

WHERE FUNDING CAN BE GIVEN UK and overseas

FINANCES *Year* 1998 *Income* £124,147
Grants £136,200

TRUSTEES Alfred H Ferraris, Andrew P Ferraris, Robert F Ferraris, Joanna M Gordon Ferraris, John R Ferraris

NOTES The Trust has its own list of preferred charities that it will continue to support, and it is unlikely that the Trustees will wish to make any increase to that list

HOW TO APPLY The Trustees are not looking to receive applications for grants, as it is anticipated that the Trust's income will normally be fully absorbed

WHO TO APPLY TO A H Ferraris, The Ferraris Charitable Trust, c/o A Ferraris Ltd, Strata House, 34a Waterloo Road, London NW2 7UH *Tel* 0181-452 3434

CC NO 1049563   **ESTABLISHED** 1995

■ Festival Church Trust Limited

WHAT IS FUNDED To advance the Christian religion, especially through the medium of broadcasting, conference and seminars, and to religious persons in conditions of need, hardship or distress by the provision of advice, counselling and support service. From a practical point of view, we are reaching out to thousands of people through the medium of broadcasting, producing over 11 hours of live radio programmes each week

WHAT IS NOT FUNDED Unfortunately we are not yet mature enough to be in a position to make sizeable grants. Our aim is to continue with the vision until we reach a point of maturity

WHO CAN BENEFIT We are in a position to offer a limited amount of help and training to those people who are interested in Christian broadcasting. Religious people from many different social circumstances are considered for advice, counselling and support services

WHERE FUNDING CAN BE GIVEN South Wales

FINANCES *Year* 1997 *Income* £19,806
Grants £12,609

TRUSTEES Rev M J Curtis (Chairman), Mrs D Curtis (Secretary), Rev P Hodge, Mrs M E Morton, Miss J Winwood

WHO TO APPLY TO Rev M J Curtis, Festival Church Trust Limited, 25 Brynhyfrd Brynithel, Abertillery, Gwent NP3 2HL *Tel* 01495 217243

CC NO 1044238   **ESTABLISHED** 1995

■ Fiat Auto (UK) Charity

WHAT IS FUNDED General charitable purposes including: children; the aged; physically and mentally handicapped persons; the advancement of education; relief of poverty and sickness; elimination of social and religious discrimination

WHAT IS NOT FUNDED No grants to individuals, animals, expeditions or scholarships

WHO CAN BENEFIT Organisations benefiting: people of all ages; disabled people; those in care, fostered and adopted; widows and widowers. People of many different social circumstances will be considered. There is no restriction on the disease or medical condition suffered by the beneficiaries

WHERE FUNDING CAN BE GIVEN UK

TYPE OF GRANT Buildings, capital, core costs, feasibility studies, one-off, project, research, running costs, recurring costs, salaries and start-up costs. Funding may be given for more than three years

RANGE OF GRANTS £5,000–£100,000 per annum

SAMPLE GRANTS £100,000 to Children's Society; £56,622 to Motor Trade Benevolent Fund; £10,000 to York Hill; £10,000 to Sick Kids Friends Foundation; £10,000 to NICCP; £5,000 to Princess of Wales Foundation

FINANCES *Year* 1997 *Income* £163,000
Grants £192,000

TRUSTEES L Osbourne, D Birch, A Dopudi

NOTES Long-term donations only

HOW TO APPLY By letter only

WHO TO APPLY TO L Osbourne, Secretary, Fiat Auto (UK) Charity, c/o Fiat House, 266 Bath Road, Slough, Berkshire SL1 4HJ

CC NO 1059498   **ESTABLISHED** 1996

■ The Clive Fiddler Charitable Trust

WHAT IS FUNDED General charitable purposes

WHO CAN BENEFIT There are no restrictions on the age; professional and economic group; family situation; religion and culture; and social circumstances of; or disease or medical condition suffered by, the beneficiaries

WHERE FUNDING CAN BE GIVEN Beverley, Humberside

TRUSTEES G Bawden, C Fidler, R Fydler, R Kemsley

WHO TO APPLY TO D Fudicott, Solicitor, The Clive Fiddler Charitable Trust, c/o Shoosmiths and Harrison, 52–54 The Green, Banbury, Oxfordshire OX16 9AB

CC NO 1058396 **ESTABLISHED** 1996

■ The Fidelity UK Foundation

WHAT IS FUNDED General charitable purposes. Trustees review all applications received. Particularly charities working in the fields of: accommodation and housing; community development; support to voluntary and community organisations; volunteer bureaux; health; special schools and special needs education; community centres and village halls; and various community services

WHO CAN BENEFIT Organisations benefiting; people of all ages; medical professionals; volunteers; those in care, fostered and adopted; at risk groups; carers; disabled people, those disadvantaged by poverty; disaster victims; ex-offenders and those at risk of offending; homeless people; socially isolated people; victims of abuse, crime and domestic violence. There is no restriction on the religion or culture of the beneficiaries, though there may be a few restrictions on the disease or medical condition suffered

WHERE FUNDING CAN BE GIVEN UK, Europe and Ireland

TYPE OF GRANT Buildings, capital, core costs, one-off, project, recurring costs and running costs. Funding for less than one year is considered

SAMPLE GRANTS £5,000 to Spadework towards the new horticultural training centre for the disabled; £5,000 to The Children's Trust for special care for severely disabled children; £5,000 to Richard House Trust towards building the Children's Hospice; £5,000 to The Ditchling Foundation for conferences on economic and social themes; £4,227 to Comic Relief; £3,000 to BLISS for a SA02 baby monitor for Pembury Hospital; £3,000 to John Grooms Association of Disabled People for new homes for disabled in Southborough; £2,500 to Great Weald Enterprise Agency for start-up help and advice to business; £2,000 to provide equipment for disabled children; £1,000 to Hospice in the Weald for new hospice in Kent Weald

FINANCES *Year* 1997 *Income* £238,318
Grants £78,947

TRUSTEES E C Johnson III, M P Cambridge, A J Bolton, B R J Bateman, R Milotte

HOW TO APPLY Applications should be made in writing giving details of the charity and any special projects

WHO TO APPLY TO Miss J Martin, The Fidelity UK Foundation, Oakhill House, 130 Tonbridge Road, Hildenborough, Kent TN11 9DZ
Tel 01732 361144

CC NO 327899 **ESTABLISHED** 1988

■ Doris Field Charitable Trust

WHAT IS FUNDED Medical, welfare, education and general charitable purposes

WHO CAN BENEFIT Organisations benefiting children and young adults; at risk groups; those disadvantaged by poverty; and socially isolated people. There is no restriction on the disease or medical condition suffered by the beneficiaries

WHERE FUNDING CAN BE GIVEN UK, with a preference for Oxfordshire, and overseas

TYPE OF GRANT One-off

RANGE OF GRANTS £100–£19,076

SAMPLE GRANTS £19,076 for costs in connection with the bells at Lundy; £15,000 to Oxfordshire County Scout Council for Youlbury Camp Site; £11,625 to Pastoral Centre; £10,000 to Friends of Sobell House; £6,500 to Kings School, Rochester; £5,000 to Friends of the Charlton Centre; £5,000 to Mulberry Bush School; £2,500 to the Kerland Foundation; £2,500 to Porthcawl District Guide Hall; £2,500 to Compaid Trust

FINANCES *Year* 1995–96 *Income* £173,553
Grants £145,248

TRUSTEES E E Church, N A Harper, W G S Crouch

HOW TO APPLY On an application form available from the address under Who To Apply To

WHO TO APPLY TO Mrs K Knight, Doris Field Charitable Trust, Ref KCK, Cole & Cole, Solicitors, Buxton Court, 3 West Way, Oxford OX2 0SZ

CC NO 328687 **ESTABLISHED** 1990

■ The Fifty Fund

WHAT IS FUNDED Relief of poverty. Charities working in the fields of: infrastructure development; charity or voluntary umbrella bodies; advice and information on housing; respite care; and various community services

WHAT IS NOT FUNDED Applications for grants for travel, expeditions or education will not be considered

WHO CAN BENEFIT Individuals and organisations benefiting: people of all ages; retired people; unemployed people; those in care, fostered and adopted; parents and children; one parent families; widows and widowers; carers; disabled people; and those disadvantaged by poverty

WHERE FUNDING CAN BE GIVEN Nottinghamshire and surrounding area

TYPE OF GRANT Capital, core costs, interest free loans, one-off, project, research and start-up costs. Funding of up to and over three years will be considered

RANGE OF GRANTS £100–£3,000

FINANCES *Year* 1996 *Income* £156,000
Grants £92,000

TRUSTEES D R Piell, M A Foulds, Rev G B Barrodale, E A Randall

NOTES Individuals have priority in allocation of funds

HOW TO APPLY To the address under Who To Apply To in writing

WHO TO APPLY TO S J Moore, The Fifty Fund, Nelson Johnson & Hastings, Pennine House, 8 Stanford Street, Nottingham NG1 7BQ *Tel* 0115-958 6262

CC NO 214422 **ESTABLISHED** 1963

■ The Finchley Charities

WHAT IS FUNDED The Trust's primary purpose is to maintain a group of almshouses. Also the upkeep and repair of the fabric of parish churches in Finchley

WHO CAN BENEFIT Churches in Finchley and those disadvantaged by poverty

WHERE FUNDING CAN BE GIVEN Finchley

SAMPLE GRANTS £11,369 to organisations and individuals in need; £5,000 to churches in Finchley

FINANCES *Year* 1997 *Income* £385,369 *Grants* £16,369

TRUSTEES Rector of the Parish of St Mary-at-Finchley, Cllr B Langstone, Cllr D Williams, R Chapman, C Rogers, Mrs A Allen, I Anderson, Rev D Gordon, A Hollis, J Huckstep, M Piercy, D Smith, Cllr L Sussman, Cllr J Tiplady, F Wilshire

HOW TO APPLY To the address under Who To Apply To in writing

WHO TO APPLY TO Mrs Jean Field, Manager, The Finchley Charities, 41a Wilmot Close, East Finchley, London N2 8HP

CC NO 206621   **ESTABLISHED** 1982

■ The Dixie Rose Findlay Charitable Trust

WHAT IS FUNDED Homes for the aged and children's charities including those working in the fields of accommodation and housing; arts, culture and recreation; health; social care and development; and education and training

WHAT IS NOT FUNDED No grants to individuals

WHO CAN BENEFIT An established list of registered charities benefiting children; older people; retired people; disabled people; those in care, fostered and adopted. There is no restriction on the disease or medical condition suffered by the beneficiaries

WHERE FUNDING CAN BE GIVEN UK

FINANCES *Year* 1995 *Income* £13,863 *Grants* £12,000

TRUSTEES Miss Dixie R Findlay and Midland Bank Trust Company Limited

WHO TO APPLY TO C M Woodrow, Trust Manager, The Dixie Rose Findlay Charitable Trust, Midland Trusts, Cumberland House, 15–17 Cumberland Place, Southampton SO15 2UY

CC NO 251661   **ESTABLISHED** 1967

■ Charity of F P Finn

WHAT IS FUNDED Youth, the elderly and social welfare

WHO CAN BENEFIT Organisations benefiting people of all ages, at risk groups, those disadvantaged by poverty and socially isolated people

WHERE FUNDING CAN BE GIVEN Kingston-upon-Hull and the East Riding of Yorkshire

TYPE OF GRANT One-off and recurrent

FINANCES *Year* 1998 *Income* £14,394 *Grants* £9,720

TRUSTEES G E Coyle, D M Scanlan

HOW TO APPLY To the address under Who To Apply To in writing

WHO TO APPLY TO Rollit Farrell & Bladon, Charity of F P Finn, Wilberforce Court, High Street, Hull HU1 1YJ

CC NO 218369   **ESTABLISHED** 1963

■ The Finnart House School Trust

WHAT IS FUNDED Jewish children in need; respite accommodation; special needs education; speech therapy; playgrounds and recreation grounds; holidays and outings; and care in the community

WHO CAN BENEFIT Children and young adults; Jews; those in care, fostered and adopted; at risk groups; disabled people; those disadvantaged by poverty; immigrants and refugees

WHERE FUNDING CAN BE GIVEN UK and overseas

TYPE OF GRANT Buildings, capital, one-off and project. Funding is available for up to two years

RANGE OF GRANTS £100–£20,000; typical grant £5,000

SAMPLE GRANTS £25,000 to Langdon College, Manchester to produce more accommodation, better education facilities and independent living training flat; £20,000 to Manchester Jewish Federation towards 'Project Smile' domicillary support service for children with disabilities; £20,000 to Leeds Jewish Welfare Board for independent living flatlets for homeless young people; £10,000 to Hamifal – Educational Children's Home, Israel for provision of dental care; £5,000 to Beth Hayeled, London for pool therapy provision for handicapped children; £5,000 to Redbridge Jewish Youth and Community Centre, Essex for school holiday programmes subsidies; £5,000 to Hasmonean High School, London towards cost of supportive studies unit; £5,000 to Keren Klita, Jerusalem for 'Youth in Distress' project for high risk Russian immigrant youth; £5,000 to Habonim Dror, UK as subsidies for participants in camps; £5,000 to Pelech Religious Experimental High School for Girls, Israel for educational enrichment programme for under achieving disadvantaged girls

FINANCES *Year* 1996–97 *Income* £183,614 *Grants* £140,570

TRUSTEES Robert Cohen, David Fobel, Jane Grabiner, Lilian Hochhauser, Dr Amanda Kirby, Jane Leaver, Dr Louis Mark, Hilary Norton, Mark Sebba

HOW TO APPLY On an application form available from the address under Who To Apply To enclosing a copy of the latest Accounts and Annual Report

WHO TO APPLY TO Peter Shaw, Clerk, The Finnart House School Trust, 5th Floor, 707 High Road, North Finchley, London N12 0BT *Tel* 0181-445 1670 *Fax* 0181-446 7370 *E-mail* finnart@ort.org

CC NO 220917   **ESTABLISHED** 1901

■ The David Finnie and Alan Emery Charitable Trust

WHAT IS FUNDED Support is mainly for national organisations working in the medical, health, welfare, and education and training fields, together with a number of benevolent funds which are regular beneficiaries. A few local organisations are also supported together with individuals for temporary relief of hardship and advancement of education, personal achievement and development

WHAT IS NOT FUNDED Where alternative funding was or should be made available by other agencies, government or otherwise

WHO CAN BENEFIT Individuals and organisations benefiting: at risk groups; carers; disabled people; those disadvantaged by poverty; socially isolated people; victims of abuse, crime and domestic violence; and beneficiaries suffering from Alzheimer's disease; arthritis and rheumatism; cancers; diabetes; hearing loss; heart disease; sight loss; strokes; and terminal illness. There is no restriction on the age, profession and economic group, family situation or religion and culture of the beneficiaries

WHERE FUNDING CAN BE GIVEN UK

TYPE OF GRANT One-off and recurrent (where circumstances warrent). Capital, project and research. Funding for up to three years will be considered

RANGE OF GRANTS £500–£5,600; average £1,000

FINANCES *Year* 1997–98 *Income* £57,000
Grants £59,000

TRUSTEES J A C Buck, Mrs N R Barnes, R J Emery, Mrs S A Hyde

NOTES Trustees usually meet in April and October each year to consider grants

HOW TO APPLY To the address under Who To Apply To in writing. Replies will be sent to applicants who include an sae

WHO TO APPLY TO The David Finnie and Alan Emery Charitable Trust, 4 De Grosmont Close, Abergavenny, Monmouthshire NP7 9JN
Tel 01873 855815

CC NO 258749   **ESTABLISHED** 1969

■ The Finsbury Park Community Trust

WHAT IS FUNDED The main work of the Trust involves setting up and running its own community projects in economic, environmental and social improvement. Grants are also available to local organisations

WHO CAN BENEFIT Organisations benefiting the local community

WHERE FUNDING CAN BE GIVEN London boroughs of Hackney, Islington and Haringey

RANGE OF GRANTS Usually up to £500

FINANCES *Year* 1997 *Income* £706,949

TRUSTEES T Mahmout (Chairman), Cllr P Kenyon, P Morris, R Bairham, G Smithson, I Bawa, J Bilson, R Scipio, Dr E Neufeld, M Ukandu, I Malik, S Nathoo

NOTES No small grants were given during 1996–97 but arrangements were made for the following year

HOW TO APPLY To the address under Who To Apply To in writing

WHO TO APPLY TO P Qureshi, The Finsbury Park Community Trust, Park Gate House, 306 Seven Sisters Road, London N4 2AQ

CC NO 293513   **ESTABLISHED** 1986

■ Gerald Finzi Charitable Trust

WHAT IS FUNDED In their work, the Trustees aim to reflect the ambitions and philosophy of the composer Gerald Finzi (1901–56), which included the general promotion of 20th century British music through assisting and promoting festivals, recordings and performances of British music. A limited number of modest grants are also offered to young musicians towards musical training

WHO CAN BENEFIT No beneficiary would be turned away for any policy reason except that due to the small size of the Trust it prefers to make grants to those to whom a small amount of money would be particularly appreciated, such as students

WHERE FUNDING CAN BE GIVEN UK

SAMPLE GRANTS To National Youth Orchestra

FINANCES *Year* 1995–96 *Grants* £33,422

TRUSTEES Christopher Finzi, Nigel Finzi, Jean Finzi, Andrew Burn, Robert Gower, J Dale Roberts, Paul Spicer, Michael Salmon, Christian Alexander

HOW TO APPLY No guidelines are issued

WHO TO APPLY TO Mrs Elizabeth Pooley, Gerald Finzi Charitable Trust, Hillcroft, Shucknall Hill, Hereford HR1 3SL

CC NO 313047   **ESTABLISHED** 1969

■ The Firdale Christian Trust

WHAT IS FUNDED Sponsorship of volunteers with Christian relief organisations or Christian missionaries and those training at theological college or university

WHAT IS NOT FUNDED Capital construction, extension or redevelopment projects

WHO CAN BENEFIT Small groups and individuals in UK and abroad in need of help and advice to help themselves. Organisations benefiting young adults, students, volunteers and Christians

WHERE FUNDING CAN BE GIVEN UK and third world

TYPE OF GRANT One-off and recurrent small grants, capital and core costs. Funding of up to three years will be considered

RANGE OF GRANTS £50–£250; typical £100

SAMPLE GRANTS £2,580 to St Martins Church, Lower Bourne for general church purposes; £1,000 to Youth with a Mission, Sao Paulo for missionary outreach to young people in Brazil; £250 to Wycliffe Bible Translaters for sponsorship of translaters in Mali, Africa; £200 to Bible Society for printing and distribution of Bibles; £200 to Christian Aid for relief of poverty

FINANCES *Year* 1997–98 *Income* £15,000
Grants £8,700

TRUSTEES K J Milburn, O M Milburn, P J Milburn, J W Milburn, M K Milburn, J R Parker

HOW TO APPLY In writing, no application form. No deadlines, sae preferred

WHO TO APPLY TO K J Milburn, The Firdale Christian Trust, Firdale House, 11 Old Frensham Road, Lower Bourne, Farnham, Surrey GU10 3PT

CC NO 1011863   **ESTABLISHED** 1992

■ The First Choice Holidays plc Charitable Trust

WHAT IS FUNDED General charitable purposes, principally support of the disabled and disadvantaged to help them experience the benefits and pleasure that a holiday can bring. Others who through personal circumstances are physically unable to take a holiday may also be considered

WHO CAN BENEFIT Organisations benefiting disabled and disadvantaged people

WHERE FUNDING CAN BE GIVEN UK and overseas

SAMPLE GRANTS £77,107 to UK charities; £26,724 to local charities at holiday resorts

FINANCES *Year* 1995 *Income* £104,301
Grants £103,831

TRUSTEES K W Smith, A T Coleman

WHO TO APPLY TO Ms K Murphy, Group Accountant, The First Choice Holidays plc Charitable Trust, First Choice House, London Road, Crawley, West Sussex RH10 2GX

CC NO 1049084   **ESTABLISHED** 1995

■ First Church of Christ, Scientist (Winchester)

WHAT IS FUNDED The promotion of Christian Science

WHO CAN BENEFIT Organisations benefiting Christian Scientists

WHERE FUNDING CAN BE GIVEN Winchester and district

TYPE OF GRANT Recurring

RANGE OF GRANTS £50–£1,000

Have you read How to use the DGMT *on page xvi?*

SAMPLE GRANTS £1,000 to The Mother Church; £250 to CS Monitor Operating Fund; £200 to London Airports Committee; £108 to CSM for Ref Lib and Prison; £100 to Visiting Nurse Southern

FINANCES *Year* 1996 *Income* £21,091
Grants £2,108

TRUSTEES C Fell (Chairman), G Lewis (Treasurer)

WHO TO APPLY TO The Clerk, First Church of Christ, Scientist (Winchester), 58 Tower Street, Winchester, Hampshire SO23 8TA

CC NO 229546   **ESTABLISHED** 1949

■ The Firtree Trust

WHAT IS FUNDED Support for Christian causes

WHAT IS NOT FUNDED Individuals only if application supported by local church

WHO CAN BENEFIT Individuals and organisations benefiting Christians, missionaries and evangelists

WHERE FUNDING CAN BE GIVEN UK

TYPE OF GRANT Project, one-off funding for one year or less will be considered

RANGE OF GRANTS £50–£300, typical grant £100

SAMPLE GRANTS £1,870 to Purley Baptist Church; £550 to Tear Fund for overseas relief work; £300 to Bible Society; £300 to Evangelical Alliance; £264 to Crusade for World Revival

FINANCES *Year* 1995 *Income* £23,000
Grants £16,000

TRUSTEES M J Turner, M H Turner

HOW TO APPLY Applications will only be considered in April and October. Please submit appropriately

WHO TO APPLY TO Mrs Anne Heathey, The Firtree Trust, Messrs Jacob, Cavenagh & Skeet, Chartered Accountants, 6–8 Tudor Court, Sutton, Surrey SM2 5AE

CC NO 282239   **ESTABLISHED** 1981

■ The Sir John Fisher Foundation

WHAT IS FUNDED General charitable purposes

WHO CAN BENEFIT There are no restrictions on the age; professional and economic group; family situation; religion and culture; and social circumstances of; or disease or medical condition suffered by, the beneficiaries

WHERE FUNDING CAN BE GIVEN UK, with preference for Cumbria

FINANCES *Year* 1997 *Income* £415,419

TRUSTEES B G Robinson, R F Hart Jackson, Mrs D S Meacock

WHO TO APPLY TO R F Hart Jackson, Secretary, The Sir John Fisher Foundation, 8–10 New Market Street, Ulverston, Cumbria LA12 7LW

CC NO 277844   **ESTABLISHED** 1979

■ Fisons Charity Trust

This trust did not respond to CAF's request to amend its entry and, by 30 June 1998, CAF's researchers did not find financial records for later than 1995 on its file at the Charity Commission. Trusts are legally required to submit annual accounts to the Charity Commission under section 42 of the Charities Act 1993

WHAT IS FUNDED General charitable purposes

WHAT IS NOT FUNDED Consideration is not given to individuals seeking sponsorship or grants for any purpose

WHO CAN BENEFIT Registered charities or institutions with charitable status. There are no restrictions on the age; professional and economic group; family situation; religion and culture; and social

circumstances of; or disease or medical condition suffered by, the beneficiaries

WHERE FUNDING CAN BE GIVEN UK

TRUSTEES P V M Egan, Sir Philip Harris, Sir Walter Bodmer

WHO TO APPLY TO D Nicholls, Fisons Charity Trust, Rhone-Poulenc-Rhorer, RPR House, 50 Kings Hill Avenue, Kings Hill, West Malling, Kent ME19 4AH

CC NO 247009   **ESTABLISHED** 1966

■ Marc Fitch Fund Limited

WHAT IS FUNDED Improvement and diffusion of knowledge, promotion and study of education and research in archaeology, historical geography, history of art and architecture, heraldry, genealogy, surnames, catalogues of and use of archives (especially ecclesiastical) and other antiquarian, archaeological or historical studies

WHAT IS NOT FUNDED (a) Grants are not awarded for foreign travel or for research outside Great Britain unless the circumstances are very exceptional. (b) Assistance not for persons reading full-time higher degrees

WHO CAN BENEFIT Both individual or societies benefiting young adults, research workers and students

WHERE FUNDING CAN BE GIVEN Great Britain

TYPE OF GRANT Loans, guarantees or grants

RANGE OF GRANTS Institutions: £1,000–£26,335

SAMPLE GRANTS £26,335 to University of Leicester; £5,000 to Historic Towns Trust; £5,000 to the British Museum as a loan; £4,000 to Northamptonshire VCH Trust; £4,000 to Norfolk Museums Service; £3,000 to Buildings of Scotland Trust; £3,000 to the Buildings Book Trust; £3,000 to Ulster Architectural Heritage Society as a loan; £2,603 to Sir John Soanes Museum; £2,000 to More Parish Library

FINANCES *Year* 1997 *Income* £236,155
Grants £95,361

TRUSTEES Council of Management: The Duke of Norfolk, EM, J L Cornforth, Hon N Assheton, A S Bell, Prof J P Barron, A J Camp, Prof C R Elrington, Dr J I Kermode, Prof D M Palliser, J Porteous, Dr R M Smith, A A R Stephens

PUBLICATIONS *Record 1956–1987, Record 1988–1992*

WHO TO APPLY TO Roy Stephens, Director and Secretary, Marc Fitch Fund Limited 7 Murray Court, 80 Banbury Road, Oxford OX2 6LQ
Tel 01865 553369

CC NO 313303   **ESTABLISHED** 1956

■ The Fitton Trust

WHAT IS FUNDED General charitable purposes

WHAT IS NOT FUNDED No grants to individuals

WHO CAN BENEFIT There are no restrictions on the age; professional and economic group; family situation; religion and culture; and social circumstances of; or disease or medical condition suffered by, the beneficiaries

WHERE FUNDING CAN BE GIVEN UK

RANGE OF GRANTS £100–£250, occasionally £1,000

SAMPLE GRANTS £3,500 to St Mary's Hospital Medical School, Imperial College; £1,900 to Kings Medical Research Trust; £1,500 to Imperial College of Science, Technology and Medicine; £1,000 to Young People's Trust for the Environment

FINANCES *Year* 1997 *Income* £104,797
Grants £76,800

TRUSTEES Dr R P A Rivers, MA, MRCP, D M Lumsden, D V Brand, MA, ACA

NOTES Alternative address for applications: The Secretary, Fitton Trust, PO Box 649, London SW3 4LA. No replies will be sent to unsolicited applications whether from individuals, charities or other bodies

HOW TO APPLY No formal application required; no application considered unless accompanied by fully audited accounts

WHO TO APPLY TO The Fitton Trust, Messrs Walker Martineau, 64 Queen Street, London EC4R 1AD

CC NO 208758   **ESTABLISHED** 1928

■ The Fitzmaurice Charitable Trust

WHAT IS FUNDED For people living in or around Norwich to help with individual immediate needs – to support local schools, local charities and local needs. Particularly charities working in the fields of: support for voluntary and community organisations and to volunteers; volunteer bureaux; Christian outreach; churches; Catholic bodies; music; English literature; cancer, MS and prenatal research; historic buildings; schools and colleges; literacy; special needs education; purchase of educational books; community centres and village halls; care in the community; emergency care; refugees, famine; playscheme; community issues; and advice centres

WHAT IS NOT FUNDED No large national charities

WHO CAN BENEFIT Individuals and small voluntary organisations benefiting people of all ages; students; those in care, fostered and adopted; parents and children; one parent families; widows and widowers; Roman Catholics; disabled people; those disadvantaged by poverty; victims of famine, man-made and natural disasters and war. Those suffering from various diseases and medical conditions

WHERE FUNDING CAN BE GIVEN Norwich and Norfolk

TYPE OF GRANT Small one-off grants

RANGE OF GRANTS £25–£1,000, typical grant £100

SAMPLE GRANTS £1,000 to Schools Outreach, Norwich for help to deprived/problem pupils; £1,000 to Eaton Vale Activity Centre Appeal for Scout and Guiding activities in Norfolk; £500 to University of East Anglia for Alec Rowley Music Scholarship Fund; £300 to Norwich YMCA Services Ltd for helping young people; £250 to St John's Church Flower Festival for Life Group in Norwich

FINANCES *Year* 1996 *Income* £14,923
Grants £10,755

TRUSTEES D K Fitzmaurice, K J Fitzmaurice, T P B Fitzmaurice

HOW TO APPLY In writing only to the address under Who To Apply To

WHO TO APPLY TO Mrs T M Fitzmaurice, Secretary, The Fitzmaurice Charitable Trust, Marlpit House, Wroxham Road, Coltishall, Norwich NR12 7AF

CC NO 326729   **ESTABLISHED** 1984

■ The Earl Fitzwilliam Charitable Trust

WHAT IS FUNDED Preference for charitable projects in areas with historical family connections. Chiefly in Cambridgeshire, Northamptonshire and Yorkshire. Particularly charities working in the fields of: accommodation and housing; infrastructure, support and development; Christian outreach; churches; religious umbrella bodies; arts, culture and recreation; health facilities and buildings; cancer research; conservation and environment;

schools and colleges; and various community facilities and services

WHAT IS NOT FUNDED No grants to individuals on a personal basis

WHO CAN BENEFIT Organisations benefiting: children and young adults; clergy; ex-service and service people; volunteers; Christians; Church of England; at risk groups; disabled people; those living in rural areas; victims of abuse and crime; victims of man-made and natural disasters; and beneficiaries suffering from cancers, diabetes, head and other injuries, leprosy, mental illness, spina bifida and hydrocephalus. Projects and charities connected in some way with or which will benefit rural life and communities including churches

WHERE FUNDING CAN BE GIVEN Priority given to Cambridgeshire, Northamptonshire and Yorkshire

TYPE OF GRANT Buildings, capital, endowments, one-off, project and research. Funding of one year or less will be considered

SAMPLE GRANTS £25,000 to Peterborough Cathedral Development Trust for restoration and development appeal; £10,000 to Fenland Archaeological Trust to develop the Flag Fen Project; £10,000 to Peterborough MRI Cancer Scanner Appeal at Peterborough Hospital; £10,000 to Ryedale Cameras in Action for anti vandalism and crime scheme Malton, Yorkshire; £10,000 to St Mary's Priory Church, Old Malton for development of church and church hall; £10,000 to St Michael's Church, New Malton for church restoration and new hall; £5,000 CAMVET, Cambridge for Veterinary College Research and Development Appeal; £5,000 to St Matthew's Church, Hutton Buscel, North Yorkshire for church restoration; £5,000 to Pepys House Trust, Brampton for restoration; £5,000 to The Countryside Foundation for Educational Trust for Urban Children

FINANCES *Year* 1997 *Income* £175,000
Grants £129,000

TRUSTEES Sir Philip Naylor-Leyland, BT, Lady Isabella Naylor-Leyland

HOW TO APPLY All are acknowledged – no telephone applications

WHO TO APPLY TO J M S Thompson, Secretary to the Trustees, The Earl Fitzwilliam Charitable Trust, Estate Office, Milton Park, Peterborough PE6 7AH

CC NO 269388   **ESTABLISHED** 1975

■ Bud Flanagan Leukaemia Fund

WHAT IS FUNDED Relief of persons suffering from leukaemia and allied diseases and the relief of poverty and distress among their families and dependants. Promotion of clinical research into the treatment and possible cure of leukaemia and allied diseases and the publication of the results of all such research. £1,000,000 is pledged to the Royal Marsden Hospital. The Policy is to give principal support to the Royal Marsden Hospital and the Christian Lewis Trust in their work arranging Christmas parties for children with cancer and their families

WHO CAN BENEFIT Organisations, principally the Royal Marsden Hospital and the Christian Lewis Trust, benefiting those suffering from leukaemia and their families and dependants, such as children, parents and spouses. Support is also given to at risk groups, those disadvantaged by poverty and socially isolated people

WHERE FUNDING CAN BE GIVEN UK

RANGE OF GRANTS £500–£502,000

SAMPLE GRANTS £502,000 to Royal Marsden
Hospital for the reprovision of the haemato-
oncology unit; £500 to Christian Lewis Trust for
support

FINANCES *Year* 1997 *Income* £205,618
Grants £502,500

TRUSTEES B Coral, S Coventry, T Robinson, R Powles,
T Richardson, The Countess of Normanton, D
Kaye, D Nimmo, M Weitzmann, H Poltnek, A
Kitcherside, R Parsons, J Goodman, R Fagan, R
Driver, D Glancy, A Kingston, A Love

WHO TO APPLY TO J Bernard Jones, FCA, Bud Flanagan
Leukaemia Fund, 40 Redwood Glade, Leighton
Buzzard, Bedfordshire LU7 7JT

CC NO 259670   ESTABLISHED 1969

....

■ Rose Flatau Charitable Trust

WHAT IS FUNDED General charitable purposes

WHAT IS NOT FUNDED No grants to individuals

WHO CAN BENEFIT Headquarters organisations. There
are no restrictions on the age; professional and
economic group; family situation; religion and
culture; and social circumstances of; or disease or
medical condition suffered by, the beneficiaries

WHERE FUNDING CAN BE GIVEN UK

RANGE OF GRANTS £104–£10,000

SAMPLE GRANTS £10,000 to Ravenswood
Foundation; £10,000 to Victoria Community;
£6,250 to Royal Hospital for Neuro-disability;
£5,000 to Anglo Jewish Association; £5,000 to
Bobath Centre; £5,000 to Cancer Research
Campaign; £5,000 to Crisis; £5,000 to Jewish
Aged Needy Pension Society; £5,000 to Jewish
Care; £5,000 to Queen ELizabeth Foundation for
the Disabled

FINANCES *Year* 1997 *Income* £67,383
Grants £118,604

TRUSTEES Michael E G Prince, Anthony E Woolf,
Nicholas L Woolf

NOTES Funds are fully committed to the support of
charities which are of special interest to the
Trustees

HOW TO APPLY **This Trust states that it does not
respond to unsolicited applications**

WHO TO APPLY TO M E G Prince, Rose Flatau
Charitable Trust, 5 Knott Park House, Wrens Hill,
Oxshott, Leatherhead, Surrey KT22 OHW

CC NO 210492   ESTABLISHED 1959

....

■ The Ian Fleming Charitable Trust

WHAT IS FUNDED Income is allocated equally between:
(a) Donations to national charities actively
operating for the support, relief and welfare of
men, women and children who are disabled or
otherwise in need of help, care and attention, and
charities actively engaged in research on human
diseases; (b) Music Education Awards under a
scheme administered by the Musicians
Benevolent Fund and advised by a committee of
experts in the field of music

WHAT IS NOT FUNDED No grants to individuals except
under Music Education Award Scheme. No grants
to purely local charities

WHO CAN BENEFIT Individual musicians, and
registered charities benefiting medical
professionals, research workers and scientists.
Support is also given to the disabled, those
disadvantaged by poverty, at risk groups and the
socially isolated. There is no restriction on the
disease or medical condition suffered by the
beneficiaries

WHERE FUNDING CAN BE GIVEN UK

SAMPLE GRANTS £49,000 to Music Education
Awards; £2,000 to National Asthma Campaign;
£1,500 to British Heart Foundation; £1,500 to
British Home and Hospital for Incurables; £1,500
to Cancer Research Campaign; £1,500 to Crisis;
£1,500 to the Horder Centre for Arthritis; £1,500
to Mental Health Foundation; £1,500 to the
Migraine Trust; £1,500 to the Queen Alexander
Hospital Home

FINANCES *Year* 1996 *Income* £115,830
Grants £98,000

TRUSTEES A A I Fleming, N A M McDonald, A W W
Baldwin, A H Isaacs

NOTES Only registered charities are considered

WHO TO APPLY TO A A I Fleming, The Ian Fleming
Charitable Trust, Messrs Hays Allan, Southampton
House, 317 High Holborn, London WC1V 7NL

CC NO 263327   ESTABLISHED 1971

....

■ The Joyce Fletcher Charitable Trust

WHAT IS FUNDED Music in the community and in a
special needs context, children's welfare, and
charities in the South West. Currently main areas
of interest are institutions and organisations
specialising in music education training, special
needs education and performance involving
music, and charities for children's welfare. Arts,
culture and recreation; art galleries and cultural
centres; community centres and village halls;
theatres and opera houses; and other charitable
purposes are all considered for funding

WHAT IS NOT FUNDED Grants to individual students are
extremely rare. Purely commercial music
performances, activities which are primarily a local
authority responsibility will not be funded

WHO CAN BENEFIT National and local charities. This
Trust will consider funding to the benefit of all
ages: academics; musicians; volunteers; those in
care, fostered and adopted; one parent families;
parents and children; disabled people; those living
in rural areas; and socially isolated people

WHERE FUNDING CAN BE GIVEN England, especially the
South West counties

TYPE OF GRANT Recurring expenses, capital or new
projects. £500–£1,000 usually

RANGE OF GRANTS £250–£10,000

SAMPLE GRANTS £10,000 to Live Music Now! in the
South West for concerts/workshops in special
venues; £3,000 to Share Music which provides
music holiday workshops for physically disabled;
£1,000 to Bath Area Play Project for holiday clubs;
£1,000 to NSPCC; £1,000 to Children's Hospice
in the South West; £1,000 to Royal National
Theatre for 'Oh What a Lovely War' workshops;
£1,000 to St John's PCC, Baildon, Yorkshire for
organ fund; £1,000 to Greater Bristol Foundation;
£1,000 to Dorchester Festival for a music
workshop for special education teachers; £1,000
to English Touring Opera for workshops in schools

FINANCES *Year* 1998 *Income* £40,000
Grants £35,000

TRUSTEES R A Fletcher, W D R Fletcher, A V Fretwell

HOW TO APPLY By 1 November annually. Preliminary
telephone call advisable. Application by letter.
Acknowledgements only if being considered

WHO TO APPLY TO Andrew Fletcher, The Joyce Fletcher
Charitable Trust, 17 Westmead Gardens, Upper
Weston, Bath BA1 4EZ *Tel* 01225 314355

CC NO 297901   ESTABLISHED 1987

Does the trust you have chosen match your needs? Haphazard applications waste postage and time

221

■ Roy Fletcher Charitable Trust

WHAT IS FUNDED General charitable purposes. Preference for youth, elderly and disadvantaged organisations

WHAT IS NOT FUNDED Unlikely to fund projects eligible for statutory funding

WHO CAN BENEFIT Dependent on Trustees' assessment of merit. To benefit: people of all ages; at risk groups; those disadvantaged by poverty and socially isolated people

WHERE FUNDING CAN BE GIVEN Shropshire

TYPE OF GRANT Preference for one-off grants

RANGE OF GRANTS £15–£500 (excluding grant to the Roy Fletcher Centre)

SAMPLE GRANTS £706,045 to the Roy Fletcher Centre which was established by the Trust to provide a centre to house caring agencies and provide office space, meeting rooms and counselling rooms; £500 to the Gateway Adult Education Centre for the Roy Fletcher Memorial Lecture; £300 to Shropshire Dyslexia Association; £250 to British Red Cross; £15 to Harlescott Local Charities

FINANCES *Year* 1997 *Income* £582,120 *Grants* £1,065

TRUSTEES D N Fletcher, Mrs G M Mathias, Mrs R A Coles, Mrs E F Cooper

HOW TO APPLY In writing to the Secretary. Trustees meet quarterly

WHO TO APPLY TO Mrs P Diamond, Secretary, Roy Fletcher Charitable Trust, 95 Mount Pleasant Road, Shrewsbury, Shropshire SY1 3EL

CC NO 276498   **ESTABLISHED** 1978

■ Florence's Charitable Trust

WHAT IS FUNDED The establishment, maintenance and support of places of education. Relief of the elderly. Relief of poverty of any person employed or formerly employed in the shoe trade

WHO CAN BENEFIT Mainly local organisations, or local branches of national organisations, benefiting the elderly, employees or former employees of the shoe trade and those disadvantaged by poverty. Support may be given to children and young adults

WHERE FUNDING CAN BE GIVEN UK, especially Lancashire

TYPE OF GRANT Mainly recurrent grants

RANGE OF GRANTS £50–£25,000

SAMPLE GRANTS £25,000 to St Mary's Church Hall, Bacup; £12,000 to All Saints School; £10,500 to St Mary's RC School, Bacup; £10,000 to Age Concern Victim Support, Rossendale; £2,600 to Fearns High School; £2,500 to Friends of Stacksteads Surgery; £2,500 to Stacksteads Freestyle Karate Club; £1,825 to MENCAP promotions; £1,800 to an individual for the Open University; £1,650 to Waterfoot FC Youth

FINANCES *Year* 1997 *Income* £134,927 *Grants* £111,779

TRUSTEES C C Harrison (Chairman), R Barker, A Connearn, G D Low, J Mellows, M Thurlwell, R D Uttley

HOW TO APPLY To the address under Who To Apply To in writing

WHO TO APPLY TO A Connearn, Florence's Charitable Trust, 6 Greave Crescent, Bacup, Lancashire OL13 9HH

CC NO 265754   **ESTABLISHED** 1973

■ John Anthony Floyd Charitable Trust

WHAT IS FUNDED General charitable purposes at the Trustees' discretion

WHO CAN BENEFIT Institutions. There are no restrictions on the age; professional and economic group; family situation; religion and culture; and social circumstances of; or disease or medical condition suffered by, the beneficiaries

WHERE FUNDING CAN BE GIVEN UK

SAMPLE GRANTS £5,150 to Queen Elizabeth Foundation for Disabled People; £5,500 to Ecchinswell Village Hall Fund; £5,000 to National Gallery; £2,000 to St Lawrence Church for Edifice Fund; £525 to Ecchinswell PCC; £500 to Heritage of London Trust Ltd; £500 to Newbury Spring Festival; £250 to American Museum in Britain; £250 to International Spinal Research Trust; £250 to Marie Curie Cancer Care

FINANCES *Year* 1996 *Income* £26,316 *Grants* £21,980

TRUSTEES J A Floyd, Miss E J Floyd, Mrs C P Coaker

WHO TO APPLY TO J A Floyd, Trustee, John Anthony Floyd Charitable Trust, Ecchinswell House, Ecchinswell, Newbury, Berkshire RG15 8UA

CC NO 327426   **ESTABLISHED** 1987

■ The Gerald Fogel Charitable Trust (supercedes the J G Fogel Charitable Trust)

WHAT IS FUNDED Deserving charities or appeal funds. Support may be given to charities working in the fields of: the advancement of the Jewish religion; synagogues; and cultural and religious teaching. This Trust may also fund residential facilities, arts activities, care in the community, hospices, hospitals, cancer research and campaigning on health issues

WHAT IS NOT FUNDED No grants to individuals or non-registered charities

WHO CAN BENEFIT Mainly headquarters organisations benefiting: children and older people, those in care, fostered and adopted, Jews and homeless people. Beneficiaries suffering from Alzheimer's disease and cancers will be considered

WHERE FUNDING CAN BE GIVEN UK

TYPE OF GRANT Some recurrent, some one-off

SAMPLE GRANTS £12,000 to Ravenswood Foundation; £10,000 to Jewish Care; £5,000 to Spiro Institute; £1,000 to Cancer Relief; £1,000 to Imperial Cancer Research; £1,000 to Jewish Blind and Physically Handicapped; £1,000 to King Edward VII Hospital; £1,000 to Marie Curie Cancer Care; £1,000 to NSPCC; £1,000 to World Jewish Relief

FINANCES *Year* 1995 *Income* £33,906 *Grants* £49,565

TRUSTEES J G Fogel, B Fogel, S Fogel, D Fogel

WHO TO APPLY TO J G Fogel, JP, The Gerald Fogel Charitable Trust, 23 West Hill Park, Highgate, London N6 6ND

CC NO 1004451   **ESTABLISHED** 1991

■ Sarah Wood Fogwell's Charity

WHAT IS FUNDED General charitable purposes. To support local projects in South Devon

WHO CAN BENEFIT Generally registered charities. There are no restrictions on the age; professional and economic group; family situation; religion and culture; and social circumstances of; or disease or medical condition suffered by, the beneficiaries

WHERE FUNDING CAN BE GIVEN Mainly South Devon

SAMPLE GRANTS £1,000 to Leonard Cheshire Home, Brixham
FINANCES *Year* 1996 *Income* £23,749
Grants £4,000
TRUSTEES P G D Breton, C M Pett, T D Kellock, T J B Kellock
WHO TO APPLY TO J H J K Pett, Sarah Wood Fogwell's Charity, Messrs Kellock & Johnson, 8 High Street, Totnes, Devon TQ9 5SA
CC NO 254738   **ESTABLISHED** 1967

■ Folkestone Municipal Charity

WHAT IS FUNDED Pensions, relief in need, the sick and infirm, support to voluntary and community organisations and other charitable purposes
WHAT IS NOT FUNDED Grants are not made for educational purposes
WHO CAN BENEFIT Mainly individuals and some local organisations benefiting: people of all ages; unemployed people; volunteers; those in care, fostered and adopted; parents and children; one parent families; widows and widowers; at risk groups; disabled people; those disadvantaged by poverty; victims of crime and domestic violence
WHERE FUNDING CAN BE GIVEN Folkestone only
TYPE OF GRANT One-off, capital and core costs. All funding is for more than three years. No loans are given
RANGE OF GRANTS £20–£2,000, typical grant £100–£250
FINANCES *Year* 1995–96 *Income* £81,904
HOW TO APPLY To the address under Who To Apply To in writing
WHO TO APPLY TO M Laker, Secretary, Folkestone Municipal Charity, Macsanann, The Row, Elham, Canterbury, Kent CT4 6UN *Tel* 01303 840471
CC NO 211528   **ESTABLISHED** 1984

■ The Follett Trust

WHAT IS FUNDED Social deprivation, education, the arts
WHO CAN BENEFIT Individuals and organisations benefiting children and young adults; actors and entertainment professionals; musicians; textile workers and designers; writers and poets; at risk groups; and those disadvantaged by poverty
WHERE FUNDING CAN BE GIVEN UK and overseas
TYPE OF GRANT Single donations
RANGE OF GRANTS £50–£13,900
SAMPLE GRANTS £13,900 to an individual; £13,759 to Canon Collins Trust; £10,000 to Friends UK (Mandela); £10,000 to University College London Development Fund; £10,000 to Donald Woods South African Project; £9,320 to an individual; £6,667 to IPPR; £5,000 to Centre for Research into Economics and Finance in South Africa; £3,500 to Khulumani; £3,500 to Action on Pre-Eclampsia
FINANCES *Year* 1997 *Income* £144,926
Grants £105,300
TRUSTEES M D Follett, K Follett, B Follett, MP
WHO TO APPLY TO M D Follett, The Follett Trust, 17 Chescombe Road, Yatton, North Somerset BS19 4EE
CC NO 328638   **ESTABLISHED** 1990

■ The Football Association National Sports Centre Trust

WHAT IS FUNDED Provision of football facilities
WHO CAN BENEFIT Hard surface play area schemes at clubs, schools and community centres
WHERE FUNDING CAN BE GIVEN UK
TYPE OF GRANT One-off
RANGE OF GRANTS £5,000–£25,000
SAMPLE GRANTS The following grants were for the provision of hard surface play areas:; £25,000 to Alumwell Community Association; £25,000 to Bexhill College; £25,000 to Devon County Council; £25,000 to Lancashire County Council; £25,000 to LB Bromley; £25,000 to Middlewich Ground Trust; £25,000 to North Teeside Sports Complex; £25,000 to Radcliffe Borough FC; £20,000 to Shenley Lane Community Association; £15,000 to Ashford Amateurs FC
FINANCES *Year* 1996 *Income* £1,405,694
Grants £662,695
TRUSTEES K St J Wiseman (Chairman), W T Annable, A W Brett, A D McMullen, MBE, E M Parry
HOW TO APPLY On a form available from the address under Who To Apply To (detailing which clubs/organisations are eligible)
WHO TO APPLY TO M Day, Secretary to the Trustees, The Football Association National Sports Centre Trust, 16 Lancaster Gate, London W2 3LW
CC NO 265132   **ESTABLISHED** 1972

■ The Football Association Youth Trust

WHAT IS FUNDED The furtherance of education of schools and universities encouraging football or other sports to ensure that due attention is given to the physical education and character development of pupils
WHO CAN BENEFIT County associations, schools and universities benefiting young people who play football or other sports
WHERE FUNDING CAN BE GIVEN UK
TYPE OF GRANT One-off
RANGE OF GRANTS £1,123–£50,621
SAMPLE GRANTS £50,621 to English Schools FA; £11,984 as payments to other institutions; £7,500 to Independent Schools FA; £7,500 to British University Sports Association; £4,000 to Cambridge University FC; £4,000 to Oxford University FC; £1,825 to Birmingham FA; £1,825 to Cheshire FA; £1,825 to Essex FA; £1,825 to Essex Happening Back
FINANCES *Year* 1997 *Income* £601,089
Grants £153,251
TRUSTEES Chairman of the Football Association and a committee appointed by the Executive Committee of the Football Association, K St J Wiseman (Chairman), W T Annable, A W Brett, A D McMullen, MBE, E M Parry
HOW TO APPLY To the Chairman of the Trust in writing, including a copy of the most recent Accounts
WHO TO APPLY TO Mark Day, Chief Accountant, The Football Association Youth Trust, 16 Lancaster Gate, London W2 3LW
CC NO 265131   **ESTABLISHED** 1972

■ The Forbes Trust

WHAT IS FUNDED To support education, health, arts, inner city unemployment
WHAT IS NOT FUNDED No grants for capital expenditure
WHO CAN BENEFIT Voluntary organisations benefiting children, young adults, students, teachers,

unemployed people and those living in urban areas. Actors and entertainment professionals, musicians, textile workers and designers, writers and poets, and medical professionals may be considered. There is no restriction on the disease or medical condition suffered by the beneficiaries

WHERE FUNDING CAN BE GIVEN UK

TYPE OF GRANT For projects in education, art, health and evaluation

RANGE OF GRANTS Below £1,000–£6,000

SAMPLE GRANTS £6,000 to Charities Evaluation Service; £5,000 to Abantu; £1,000 to East London Partnership; £1,000 to Business in the Community; £7,697 to consultancy to other charities

FINANCES *Year* 1995 *Income* £50,828 *Grants* £24,049

TRUSTEES Amir Bhatia (Chairman), Sir Hugh Casson, Prof Sir Bryan Thwaites, Mrs N Bhatia

PUBLICATIONS *Evaluation in the Voluntary Sector* by Mog Ball; *Art of Dying*

HOW TO APPLY At any time. No application form

WHO TO APPLY TO Amir Bhatia, The Forbes Trust, 9 Artillery Lane, London E1 7LP

CC NO 327358   **ESTABLISHED** 1987

■ Forbesville Limited

WHAT IS FUNDED Support for orthodox Jewish organisations, educational and charitable institutions both in the UK and abroad

WHO CAN BENEFIT At the discretion of the Trustees, but children, young adults, students and Jewish people will be considered

WHERE FUNDING CAN BE GIVEN UK and overseas

TYPE OF GRANT At the discretion of the Trustees

FINANCES *Year* 1996 *Income* £21,085 *Grants* £62,212

TRUSTEES Mrs J S Kritzler, M Berger, D B Kritzler

WHO TO APPLY TO M Berger, The Director, Forbesville Limited, Holborn House, 219 Golders Green Road, London NW11 9DD

CC NO 269898   **ESTABLISHED** 1975

■ The Nancy & Harold Ford Charitable Trust

WHAT IS FUNDED General charitable purposes

WHO CAN BENEFIT There are no restrictions on the age; professional and economic group; family situation; religion and culture; and social circumstances of; or disease or medical condition suffered by, the beneficiaries

WHERE FUNDING CAN BE GIVEN UK

TRUSTEES G Bloom, N H Davis, R M Baskin

NOTES General private charitable institutions are considered for funding

WHO TO APPLY TO N H Davis, The Nancy & Harold Ford Charitable Trust, Lane Heywood Davis, Chartered Accountants, Anchor Brew House, 50 Shad Thames, London SE1 2YB *Tel* 0171-403 4403

CC NO 326650   **ESTABLISHED** 1983

■ Oliver Ford Foundation

WHAT IS FUNDED To educate the general public and advance knowledge of the history and techniques of interior decoration, the design of fabrics and other decorative materials and landscape gardening. Also mental disability

WHO CAN BENEFIT Neighbourhood-based community projects, students and institutions. Those

suffering from mental illness will be considered for funding

WHERE FUNDING CAN BE GIVEN UK

TYPE OF GRANT One-off

SAMPLE GRANTS £15,000 to Acorn Village; £10,000 to MENCAP; £9,684 to Victoria and Albert Museum for tuition fees for students; £7,360 to Victoria and Albert Museum for grants to students; £6,000 to Harington Scheme; £5,639 to Kingston Maurward College, Dorset for maintenance grants for students and tuition fees; £5,000 to Ravenswood; £5,000 to Camphill Village Trust; £5,000 to Menter Foundation; £5,000 to Byways Trust

FINANCES *Year* 1997 *Income* £103,719 *Grants* £96,943

TRUSTEES Derek Hayes, Lady Wakeham, Valerie Profumo, George Levy, Johnathan Norton

HOW TO APPLY To the address under Who To Apply To in writing

WHO TO APPLY TO D Hayes, Oliver Ford Foundation, MacFarlanes, 10 Norwich Street, London EC1A 1BD

CC NO 1026551   **ESTABLISHED** 1993

■ Ford of Britain Trust

WHAT IS FUNDED Currently the main areas of interest are children and young people (with emphasis on education, special needs children, youth organisations); community service; the disabled; social welfare; community arts and recreation; cultural heritage; accommodation and housing; respite care for carers; support and self help groups; ambulances and mobile units; hospices; and social advice centres

WHAT IS NOT FUNDED Organisations outside the area Where Funding Can Be Given and national charities are rarely assisted, except for specific projects in Ford areas. Applications in respect of individuals (including students), charities requiring funds for overseas projects, and wholly religious or politically orientated projects are ineligible. Major building projects and research projects (including medical) are rarely assisted

WHO CAN BENEFIT Organisations benefiting: children; young adults; older people; unemployed people; volunteers; at risk groups; carers; disabled people; those disadvantaged by poverty; ex-offenders and those at risk of offending; homeless people; victims of crime, domestic violence and abuse. There are few restrictions on the disease or medical condition suffered by the beneficiaries

WHERE FUNDING CAN BE GIVEN Charities located in close proximity to Ford Motor Company Limited plants in UK. This includes: Halton, Knowsley, Liverpool City, St Helens, Sefton, Wirral, Northamptonshire, Warwickshire, Essex, Southend, Thurrock, Southampton, Barking and Dagenham, Croydon, Enfield, Hackney, Havering, Redbridge, Tower Hamlets, Waltham Forest, Belfast, Carrickfergus, Craigavon, Lisburn, Newtownabbey, Bridgend, Caerphilly, Cardiff, Vale of Glamorgan, Merthyr Tydfil, Neath and Port Talbot, Rhondda Cynon Taff, Swansea

TYPE OF GRANT Capital, buildings, one-off, running costs, and start-up costs. Funding is available for one year or less

RANGE OF GRANTS Most grants range between £100 and £5,000

FINANCES *Year* 1998 *Income* £598,791 *Grants* £399,487

TRUSTEES I G McAllister, CBE (Chairman), R A Hill, W G F Brooks, M J Callaghan, Prof Ann P Dowling, J H M Norris, CBE, VL, P G Knight

224

Think carefully about every application. Is it justified?

HOW TO APPLY By letter to the address under Who To Apply To. Guidelines are available

WHO TO APPLY TO R M Metcalf, Director, Ford of Britain Trust, c/o Ford Motor Co Ltd, 1–661 Eagle Way, Brentwood, Essex CM13 3BW
Tel 01277 252551

CC NO 269410   **ESTABLISHED** 1975

■ The Ford Trust

WHAT IS FUNDED General charitable purposes. Grants are mainly recurrent, so appeals from other charities or individuals are inappropriate

WHAT IS NOT FUNDED No grants to individuals

WHO CAN BENEFIT Registered charities only. There are no restrictions on the age; professional and economic group; family situation; religion and culture; and social circumstances of; or disease or medical condition suffered by, the beneficiaries

WHERE FUNDING CAN BE GIVEN UK

TYPE OF GRANT Recurrent

RANGE OF GRANTS £250–£2,000

SAMPLE GRANTS £2,000 to Children in Distress; £2,000 to Warham Trust; £1,900 to St Christopher's Anglican/RC Aided Primary School Fund; £1,500 to Oxford Homeless Medical Fund; £1,000 to African Enterprise

FINANCES *Year* 1997 *Income* £21,421
Grants £20,650

TRUSTEES J H Ford, J L Bretherton, A C O Bell

NOTES The Trustees have agreed that the Trust will be run down by the year 2002, unless another alternative arises in the meantime

HOW TO APPLY **This Trust states that it does not respond to unsolicited applications**

WHO TO APPLY TO Mrs D Ford, The Ford Trust, The Old Vicarage, Greywell Street, Greywell, Hook, Hampshire RG29 1BZ

CC NO 237976   **ESTABLISHED** 1962

■ The Forde Park Educational Trust

WHAT IS FUNDED The education of people under the age of 25

WHAT IS NOT FUNDED Grants will not be given for higher degrees or school fees

WHO CAN BENEFIT Primarily individuals living in Devon, or whose parents live in Devon. Individuals, and organisations benefiting children, young adults and students

WHERE FUNDING CAN BE GIVEN Devon

RANGE OF GRANTS £100–£200. Exceptional grant £500 maximum

FINANCES *Year* 1997 *Income* £30,000
Grants £25,000

HOW TO APPLY To the address under Who To Apply To in writing for an application form. Applications are considered by the Trustees in March, July and November and should be received by the Correspondent four weeks prior to each meeting

WHO TO APPLY TO The Clerk, The Forde Park Educational Trust, PO Box 9, Tiverton EX16 6YG

CC NO 220921   **ESTABLISHED** 1964

■ Fordeve Limited

WHAT IS FUNDED Jewish causes and relief of needy people

WHO CAN BENEFIT Organisations benefiting Jewish people, the unemployed, at risk groups, those disadvantaged by poverty and socially isolated people. Support may also be given to the disabled, the homeless, immigrants and refugees

WHERE FUNDING CAN BE GIVEN UK

FINANCES *Year* 1995 *Income* £358,751
Grants £103,601

TRUSTEES J Kon, Ms H Kon

WHO TO APPLY TO Fordeve Limited, Gerald Kreditor & Co, Tudor House, Llanvanor Road, London NW2 2AQ

CC NO 1011612   **ESTABLISHED** 1992

■ The Russell and Mary Foreman 1980 Charitable Trust

WHAT IS FUNDED Distributions are made in March each year to a number of registered charities. Special areas of interest are ecology, famine relief, children and animals

WHAT IS NOT FUNDED Grants to registered charities only. No grants to individuals

WHO CAN BENEFIT Registered charities benefiting children and victims of famine

WHERE FUNDING CAN BE GIVEN UK and overseas

TYPE OF GRANT Cash donations only. Yearly donations

SAMPLE GRANTS £250 to Compassion in World Farming

FINANCES *Year* 1996 *Income* £13,033 *Grants* £650

TRUSTEES Royal Bank of Scotland plc

HOW TO APPLY To the address under Who To Apply To in writing at any time. No acknowledgements will be sent

WHO TO APPLY TO The Senior Trust Officer (Ref 7980), Russell and Mary Foreman 1980 Charitable Trust, Royal Bank of Scotland plc, Private Trust & Taxation, PO Box 356, 45 Mosley Street, Manchester M60 2BE

CC NO 281543   **ESTABLISHED** 1980

■ The Carl & Eve Foreman Foundation

WHAT IS FUNDED Awards are granted known as 'The Carl Foreman Awards' which are administered in conjunction with the British Academy of Film and Television Arts. Each award enables a UK citizen (under the age of 32) to follow a scriptwriting course in the USA. Funding is also given to individuals and charitable organisations involved in the health of the public

WHO CAN BENEFIT To benefit those interested in scriptwriting and the sick. There is no restriction on the disease or medical condition suffered by the beneficiaries

WHERE FUNDING CAN BE GIVEN UK and overseas

RANGE OF GRANTS Organisations: £25–£1,350

SAMPLE GRANTS £1,350 to The Sound Foundation; £600 to Royal National Theatre; £600 to British Red Cross Society; £500 to Friends of the Hebrew University of Jerusalem; £400 to Fullbright Foundation; £240 to Royal Horticultural Society; £200 to Multiple Sclerosis Therapy Centre; £180 to Imperial Cancer Research Campaign; £130 to Make-a-Wish Foundation; £100 to West London Synagogue Charities Fund

FINANCES *Year* 1996 *Income* £25,324
Grants £26,794

TRUSTEES Prof A R Mellows, TD, PhD, LLD, Miss A L Foreman, J E Foreman, Mrs E R Williams-Jones

NOTES The amount expended for the Carl Foreman Awards totalled £22,069 in 1996

HOW TO APPLY The Carl Foreman Awards are made by open competition and applications are considered by a panel, the majority of whom are engaged in film or television, who interview candidates and make their recommendation to the Trustees

---

Does the trust you have chosen match your needs? Haphazard applications waste postage and time

225

WHO TO APPLY TO Mrs E R Williams-Jones, The Carl & Eve Foreman Foundation, 11 Kingston House South, Ennismore Gardens, London SW7 1NF
CC NO 1005666   **ESTABLISHED** 1991

■ Forest Hill Charitable Trust

WHAT IS FUNDED Mainly Christian outreach and relief organisations in the UK and developing countries. Small charitable organisations in the UK and abroad working for deprived and disabled people
WHAT IS NOT FUNDED Expeditions, scholarships and the arts are not funded
WHO CAN BENEFIT Charitable organisations benefiting deprived and disabled people will be considered. Christian outreach charities will be supported
WHERE FUNDING CAN BE GIVEN UK and overseas
RANGE OF GRANTS £100–£2,000, small grants £100–£500 yearly or six monthly
SAMPLE GRANTS £2,000 to Great Parks Chapel; £300 to Harvest Trust; £200 to Shaftesbury Society for general relief; £200 to ICAN to a special needs school; £200 to Hope Now for evangelist outreach
FINANCES *Year* 1997 *Income* £17,890
   Grants £7,900
TRUSTEES I B Calkin, Dr H F Pile, Mrs P J Pile
HOW TO APPLY Initial telephone calls from applicants are not welcome. No application form, but guidelines are issued. There are no deadlines for applications and an sae is not required
WHO TO APPLY TO Dr and Mrs H F Pile, Trustees, Forest Hill Charitable Trust, Eastover, 83 Rea Barn Road, Brixham, Devon TQ5 9EE
   Tel 01803 852857
CC NO 1050862   **ESTABLISHED** 1995

■ The Forester Health Charitable Trust

WHAT IS FUNDED General charitable purposes
WHO CAN BENEFIT There are no restrictions on the age; professional and economic group; family situation; religion and culture; and social circumstances of; or disease or medical condition suffered by, the beneficiaries
WHERE FUNDING CAN BE GIVEN UK
FINANCES *Year* 1996 *Income* £113,000
   Grants £80,000
TRUSTEES A Barnes, M Bearcroft, G Fyles, Dr A Kitts
WHO TO APPLY TO M Bearcroft, Trustee, The Forester Health Charitable Trust, The Manor House, Squires Hill, Rothwell, Northamptonshire NN14 6BQ *Tel* 01536 713713
CC NO 1048036   **ESTABLISHED** 1995

■ The Foresters' Charity Stewards UK Trust

WHAT IS FUNDED To improve quality of life for the elderly and handicapped and the environment of the community at large
WHO CAN BENEFIT Individuals and institutions benefiting the elderly, disabled people and communities as a whole
WHERE FUNDING CAN BE GIVEN UK
RANGE OF GRANTS £50–£750

SAMPLE GRANTS £750 to FSCH Donation; £750 to AOF Yorkshire Convalescent Home; £750 to AOF Foresters' Home; £750 to AOF Education Awards Fund; £313 to Marwood Guest House, Eastbourne; £300 to RNLI; £3,000 to Taste for Adventure; £3,000 to Abbeyfield, Potters Bar; £250 to Mayor of Scarborough's Charity; £200 to North Middlesex Hospital
FINANCES *Year* 1996 *Income* £59,487
   Grants £9,113
TRUSTEES A H W Overington, R J Overington, M F Penfold, F G Miller, M Prechner, M S Miller, G Penfold
WHO TO APPLY TO A H W Overington, The Foresters' Charity Stewards UK Trust, Springfield, 6 Halstead Road, Winchmore Hill, London N21 3EH
CC NO 328604   **ESTABLISHED** 1990

■ The Forrest and Grinsell Foundation

WHAT IS FUNDED To help the young achieve their educational goals
WHAT IS NOT FUNDED No grants for educational fees. Transient residents of the City of Westminster are excluded
WHO CAN BENEFIT Primarily individuals: children and young adults who are long-term residents of the City of Westminster
WHERE FUNDING CAN BE GIVEN City of Westminster
TYPE OF GRANT Usually non-recurring
FINANCES *Year* 1997 *Income* £36,000
   Grants £36,000
HOW TO APPLY To the address under Who To Apply To in writing
WHO TO APPLY TO Cmdr Roger Walker, LVO, RN, Clerk, The Forrest and Grinsell Foundation, United Westminster Almshouse Group of Charities, Warden's House, 42 Rochester Row, London SW1P 1BU *Tel* 0171-828 3131
CC NO 312807   **ESTABLISHED** 1889

■ Donald Forrester Trust (201 =)

This trust declined to meet CAF's researchers and failed to supply a copy of its annual report and accounts to CAF as required under section 47(2) of the Charities Act 1993. The information held on file at the Charity Commission was insufficient to enable CAF's researchers to write a substantive commentary on the trust's activities. Accordingly, despite its size, we are unable to list this trust in Spotlight on Major Trusts

WHAT IS FUNDED General charitable purposes
WHAT IS NOT FUNDED No applications for grants are accepted
WHO CAN BENEFIT There are no restrictions on the age; professional and economic group; family situation; religion and culture; and social circumstances of; or disease or medical condition suffered by, the beneficiaries
WHERE FUNDING CAN BE GIVEN UK
FINANCES *Year* 1996 *Income* £363,824
TRUSTEES G M Forrester, W J Forrester, A J Smee, M B Jones
HOW TO APPLY **This Trust states that it does not respond to unsolicited applications**
WHO TO APPLY TO Ms B G Ward, Donald Forrester Trust, Room 231, Linen Hall, 156–170 Regent Street, London W1R 5TA
CC NO 295833   **ESTABLISHED** 1986

■ The Forte Charitable Trust

WHAT IS FUNDED Education, disability, Roman Catholic, Jewish and other charitable purposes

WHO CAN BENEFIT Community-based projects and national organisations and institutions benefiting primarily children, young adults, disabled people, Roman Catholics and Jews

WHERE FUNDING CAN BE GIVEN UK and overseas

TYPE OF GRANT One-off

RANGE OF GRANTS £250–£5,000

FINANCES *Year* 1997–98 *Income* £160,000 *Grants* £65,000

TRUSTEES Hon Sir Rocco Forte, Hon Mrs Omla Pilizzi di Sorrentino, CBE, G F L Proctor

HOW TO APPLY To the address under Who To Apply To in writing

WHO TO APPLY TO Mrs Sarah Syborn, The Forte Charitable Trust, Lowndes House, Lowndes Place, Belgrave Square, London SW1X 8DB

CC NO 326038   **ESTABLISHED** 1982

■ Fortuna Charitable Trust

WHAT IS FUNDED General charitable purposes for children and youth

WHAT IS NOT FUNDED Individuals and students

WHO CAN BENEFIT Small local projects newly established and national organisations benefiting children and young adults

WHERE FUNDING CAN BE GIVEN Preference for Bristol

TYPE OF GRANT Small grants

FINANCES *Year* 1997 *Income* £58,954 *Grants* £30,430

TRUSTEES A V Tidmarsh, J N Tidmarsh

NOTES The Trustee's Funds are committed to charities already known to them and no further applications are requested

HOW TO APPLY **This Trust states that it does not respond to unsolicited applications**

WHO TO APPLY TO T Markoby, Fortuna Charitable Trust, 8 Prince's Street, Clifton, Bristol BS8 4LB

CC NO 291741   **ESTABLISHED** 1984

■ Four Acre Trust

WHAT IS FUNDED Supporting charities that provide a service to individuals: holiday and respite care; infrastructure development; hospice at home; respite care and care for carers; vocational training; holidays and outings. Funding is given to property infrastructure costs and specific programme costs

WHO CAN BENEFIT Charities benefiting at risk groups; carers; those disadvantaged by poverty; disabled people; homeless people; socially isolated people; and those living in urban areas. Those suffering from Alzheimer's disease and sight loss

WHERE FUNDING CAN BE GIVEN UK and overseas

TYPE OF GRANT Provision of premises, project, capital, interest free loans and one-off funding. Funding is available for up to three years

RANGE OF GRANTS £1,981–£70,928

FINANCES *Year* 1998 *Income* £918,000 *Grants* £116,600

TRUSTEES Mary A Bothamley, Jennifer J Bunner, John P Bothamley

HOW TO APPLY In writing with details of specific project or proposal and latest annual accounts

WHO TO APPLY TO John Bothamley, Four Acre Trust, 56 Leslie Grove, Croydon, Surrey CR0 6TG *Tel* 0181-680 3100 *Fax* 0181-760 0269

CC NO 1053884   **ESTABLISHED** 1996

■ The Four Lanes Trust

WHAT IS FUNDED Charities working in the fields of: information technology and computers; publishing and printing; community development; support to voluntary and community organisations and volunteers; professional bodies; charity or voluntary umbrella bodies; arts, culture and recreation; health facilities and buildings; schools and colleges; community issues; development proposals; various community facilities and services; and other charitable purposes will be considered. Personal and small initiatives are particularly welcomed

WHAT IS NOT FUNDED No grants to individuals or for general appeals

WHO CAN BENEFIT Organisations benefiting: people of all ages; actors and entertainment professionals; musicians; textile workers and designers; writers and poets; at risk groups; those disadvantaged by poverty; and socially isolated people. There is no restriction on the disease or medical condition suffered by the beneficiaries. The Trust does not exclude helping any person or institution whose application is within the parameter of the Trust

WHERE FUNDING CAN BE GIVEN Basingstoke and Deane District Council

TYPE OF GRANT Buildings, capital, core costs, one-off, project, running costs, recurring costs, salaries and start-up costs. Funding for up to three years will be considered

SAMPLE GRANTS £40,000 to Central Studio, Basingstoke for theatre equipment; £2,659 to Basingstoke Consortium Science Centre for equipment; £2,200 to Relate, Basingstoke and District for sound-masking equipment; £1,877 to Age Concern, Basingstoke for computer and printer; £1,860 to Wel-Care for group running costs; £1,132 to London Street United Reformed Church, Basingstoke for acoustic ceiling tiles; £1,000 to Testbourne Community School, Whitchurch for sports hall floor; £1,000 to East Woodham Village Hall for induction loop system; £1,000 to Cavalier Marching Brass for instruments; £1,000 to Basingstoke and North Hampshire Cricket Club for practice nets

FINANCES *Year* 1995 *Income* £37,000 *Grants* £33,000

TRUSTEES The Hon Dwight Makins, The Hon Virginia Shapiro, D Roberts, Mrs G Evans

HOW TO APPLY No application form. Apply by letter. Initial telephone calls welcome

WHO TO APPLY TO Len Treglown, The Four Lanes Trust, 5 Caithness Close, Oakley, Basingstoke, Hampshire RG23 7NG

CC NO 267608   **ESTABLISHED** 1974

■ The Four Winds Trust

WHAT IS FUNDED Charities working in the fields of: (a) furtherance of Protestant Evangelical and secular education. (b) Advancement of the Protestant and Evangelical tenets of the Christian faith. (c) Encouragement of missionary activity. (d) The relief of the poor and needy. (e) The help of the sick and aged. (f) Other charitable purposes. The Trust's funds are used for the benefit of charities and objectives in which the Trustees have a personal interest

WHO CAN BENEFIT Organisations benefiting: people of all ages; Protestants; Evangelists; and those disadvantaged by poverty. There is no restriction on the disease or medical condition suffered by the beneficiaries

WHERE FUNDING CAN BE GIVEN Overseas

FINANCES *Year* 1997 *Income* £27,588
Grants £28,943
TRUSTEES P A Charters, Mrs M E Charters, P J Charters
HOW TO APPLY **This Trust states that it does not respond to unsolicited applications**
WHO TO APPLY TO P A Charters, Four Winds Trust, Four Winds, Ashbury, Swindon, Wiltshire SN9 8LZ
CC NO 262524   ESTABLISHED 1971

■ Four Winds Trust

WHAT IS FUNDED Conservation of the countryside and encouragement of its use by people of all ages and abilities
WHAT IS NOT FUNDED No individuals, capital projects, buildings, expeditions, overseas projects
WHO CAN BENEFIT National and local registered charities
WHERE FUNDING CAN BE GIVEN UK
TYPE OF GRANT Project
RANGE OF GRANTS £100–£1,500
SAMPLE GRANTS £1,500 to British Trust for Conservation Volunteers; £1,500 to Harvest Trust; £1,010 to Dragonfly Holidays; £1,000 to Birmingham PHAB; £1,000 to Children's County Holiday Fund
FINANCES *Year* 1996 *Income* £22,014
Grants £26,200
TRUSTEES Mrs E Hambly, Mrs L Insall, Mrs K M Charity, Mrs Jane Simmons, J Gillett, Mrs L Craig-Wood
HOW TO APPLY Apply in writing by 31 January. Details: who will benefit, why, dates (if applicable), funding available and requested
WHO TO APPLY TO Mrs Jane Simmons, Four Winds Trust, Woodlands, Park Lane, The Raise, Alston, Cumbria CA9 3AB
CC NO 223794   ESTABLISHED 1943

■ The Fowler Memorial Trust

WHAT IS FUNDED General charitable purposes undertaken by Essex charities
WHAT IS NOT FUNDED No grants to individuals
WHO CAN BENEFIT Essex registered charities. There are no restrictions on the age; professional and economic group; family situation; religion and culture; and social circumstances of; or disease or medical condition suffered by, the beneficiaries
WHERE FUNDING CAN BE GIVEN Essex
RANGE OF GRANTS £1,000–£2,000
SAMPLE GRANTS £2,000 to Imperial Cancer Research Fund; £2,000 to The Salvation Army; £2,000 to Royal National Lifeboat Institution; £2,000 to Royal Agricultural Benevolent Association; £2,000 to Basildon and District Camping Group; £1,500 to HYP Holidays; £1,000 to Eastwood Parochial Church Council; £1,000 to St David's Church Parochial Council
FINANCES *Year* 1996 *Income* £126,568
Grants £13,500
TRUSTEES J E Tolhurst, W J Tolhurst, P J Tolhurst
WHO TO APPLY TO J E Tolhurst, The Fowler Memorial Trust, Messrs Tolhurst & Fisher, Trafalgar House, Nelson Street, Southend-on-Sea, Essex SS1 1EF
CC NO 269782   ESTABLISHED 1975

■ Fox Memorial Trust

WHAT IS FUNDED Support will be given to conservation and environment, health and various community facilities and services. Grants may be given towards costs of study and voluntary organisations. Other general charitable purposes will be considered
WHO CAN BENEFIT General charities benefiting: people of all ages who are carers; disabled; disadvantaged by poverty; at risk groups; disaster victims; ex-offenders and those at risk of offending; and victims of crime and abuse. There are some restrictions on the disease or medical condition suffered by the beneficiaries
WHERE FUNDING CAN BE GIVEN England and Scotland
RANGE OF GRANTS £250–£3000, typical grant £500
SAMPLE GRANTS £3,500 to Dean Close School for support to individual pupils; £3,000 to King Edward's School, Witley for support to individual pupils; £2,000 to Manchester High School for Girls for support to individual pupils; £1,500 to Longridge Towers School for support to individual pupils; £1,000 to British Brain and Spine Foundation; £1,000 to Lord Mayor's Appeal in Aid of CRC; £1,000 to Northallerton Health Services Charitable Funds; £1,000 to Quest Cancer Research; £1,000 to South American Mission Society for school fees; £1,000 to University of Edinburgh for support to individual veterinary student
FINANCES *Year* 1997–98 *Income* £43,716
Grants £53,032
TRUSTEES Sir Murray Fox, GBE, MA, Miss S M Crichton, Mrs F M Davies, Miss A M Fox, Miss C H Fox
HOW TO APPLY Initial telephone calls are not welcome. Sae will guarantee a response
WHO TO APPLY TO Mrs C Hardy, Fox Memorial Trust, 5 Audley Court, 32–34 Hill Street, London W1X 7FT
CC NO 262262   ESTABLISHED 1970

■ Charles Henry Foyle Trust

WHAT IS FUNDED General charitable purposes and particularly to encourage new forms of social work, research into social conditions and education, improvement of educational facilities. The provision of medical, dental and nursing facilities for the working classes, the assistance of junior or adult education, the encouragement of educational travel. Preference given to projects in and for the Birmingham and NE Worcestershire areas
WHAT IS NOT FUNDED Not to established bodies; mainly for particular projects, ie not running costs
WHO CAN BENEFIT Registered charities for new projects benefiting children and adults; students; at risk groups; those disadvantaged by poverty; and the sick. There is no restriction on the disease or medical condition suffered by the beneficiaries
WHERE FUNDING CAN BE GIVEN UK, particularly Birmingham and NE Worcestershire
TYPE OF GRANT Project, research and start-up costs
RANGE OF GRANTS Below £500–£6,000

SAMPLE GRANTS £6,000 to Stitched Textile Awards for 1997 on the theme of 'Intriguing Technology'; £5,000 to Birmingham Brook Advisory Centre for setting up reception and waiting area; £5,000 to Reddith Wheels Project; £3,000 to Huntington's Disease Association to fund a care advisor; £2,000 to CBSO for music education project for children with partial hearing; £1,600 to Acorns Children's Hospice for air conditioning unit and residential weekend; £1,500 to Birmingham Brook Advisory Centre for replacement gynaecological couches; £1,500 to Step Out Drop In for refurbishment of home for homeless people; £1,500 to Urban Wildlife Trust/Centre of the Earth for Enviorchange Project; £1,304 to Birmingham Rathbone Society for musical instruments/project with CBSO

FINANCES *Year* 1997 *Income* £88,349
Grants £64,565

TRUSTEES R K Booth, Mrs B Morris, Cllr M Francis, Prof D Thomas

WHO TO APPLY TO Mrs B Horton, Trust Administrator, Charles Henry Foyle Trust, c/o Boxfoldia Ltd, Merse Road, Redditch, Worcestershire B98 9HB

CC NO 220446   **ESTABLISHED** 1940

■ The David Frampton Charitable Trust

This trust did not respond to CAF's request to amend its entry and, by 30 June 1998, CAF's researchers did not find financial records for later than 1995 on its file at the Charity Commission. Trusts are legally required to submit annual accounts to the Charity Commission under section 42 of the Charities Act 1993

WHAT IS FUNDED Missionary societies and church organisations at Trustees' discretion

WHO CAN BENEFIT Missionary societies and church organisations benefiting clergy. There is no restriction on the religion and culture of the beneficiaries

WHERE FUNDING CAN BE GIVEN UK and overseas

TRUSTEES D H Frampton, S J Frampton

WHO TO APPLY TO J C Seabrook, The David Frampton Charitable Trust, Selsdon House, 212–220 Addington Road, Selsdon, South Croydon, Surrey CR2 8LD

CC NO 1002385   **ESTABLISHED** 1990

■ France's Charity

WHAT IS FUNDED The welfare of sick and elderly people, support groups for people in need, schools and hospitals in the local area

WHO CAN BENEFIT To benefit people of all ages and those in need. There is no restriction on the disease or medical condition suffered by the beneficiaries

WHERE FUNDING CAN BE GIVEN Leigh

RANGE OF GRANTS £200–£450

SAMPLE GRANTS £450 to Westleigh Old Age Pensioners; £450 to Bedford Old Age Pensioners; £450 to Plank Lane Old Age Pensioners; £450 to St Joseph's Area Citizens; £450 to Higher Fold Old Age Pensioners; £450 to Wigan Road Old People's Welfare Centre; £450 to Hourigan House; £450 to Lyndurst Home; £450 to Abbeyfield Society; £330 to Westleigh High School

FINANCES *Year* 1996 *Income* £45,816
Grants £6,910

HOW TO APPLY To the address under Who To Apply To in writing

WHO TO APPLY TO Mrs O E Williams, Secretary, France's Charity, Stephensons Solicitors, 26 Union Street, Leigh, Lancashire WN7 1AT

CC NO 224803   **ESTABLISHED** 1901

■ The Timothy Franey Charitable Foundation

WHAT IS FUNDED Charities working in the fields of: music; arts education and activities; hospices; hospitals; cancer research; bursaries and fees; and holidays and outings

WHAT IS NOT FUNDED No grants to individuals unless supported by a recognised charity

WHO CAN BENEFIT Organisations benefiting: children; young adults; unemployed people; those disadvantaged by poverty; victims of abuse; victims of war and those suffering from cancers, hearing loss, HIV and AIDs, motor neurone disease and sight loss. Not limited, but mainly the young – educational, health and the displaced

WHERE FUNDING CAN BE GIVEN Mainly UK, although approximately 10 per cent goes on overseas support

TYPE OF GRANT One-off, core costs and running costs. Funding for up to two years will be considered

RANGE OF GRANTS £100–£10,000

SAMPLE GRANTS £7,600 to Malcolm Sargent Cancer Fund for general support; £5,000 to Dulwich College Bursary Appeal for educational fees support; £5,000 to The Vasari Singers for arts support; £2,000 to The Dulwich Festival for arts support; £2,000 to Merseyside Drugs Council for general purposes; £1,500 to Horniman Museum for educational purposes; £1,100 to King's Hospital Appeal for Health; £1,034 to Echo International Health for overseas health; £1,000 to MND Association for health; £1,000 to National Missing Persons Helpline for general purposes

FINANCES *Year* 1997 *Income* £38,700
Grants £40,500

TRUSTEES T Franey, S Franey, P Morrison

HOW TO APPLY In writing with financial statements (annual accounts, etc). No application form. No guidelines or deadlines. Please send sae

WHO TO APPLY TO T Franey, The Timothy Franey Charitable Foundation, 32 Herne Hill, London SE24 9QS *Tel* 0171-733 7168 *Fax* 0171-733 9461

CC NO 802189   **ESTABLISHED** 1987

■ The Isaac and Freda Frankel Memorial Charitable Trust

WHAT IS FUNDED Medicine and health, education, religion and the relief of poverty

WHAT IS NOT FUNDED No grants to individuals or students, for expeditions or scholarships

WHO CAN BENEFIT Established organisations benefiting children, young adults and those disadvantaged by poverty. People of many different religions and cultures will be funded, but preference is given to Jewish people. There is no restriction on the disease or medical condition suffered by the beneficiaries. Medical professionals and research workers may be considered

WHERE FUNDING CAN BE GIVEN UK and overseas, particularly Israel

TYPE OF GRANT One-off and recurrent grants will be considered

RANGE OF GRANTS £1,000 or less

FINANCES *Year* 1996 *Income* £34,443
Grants £23,225

Does the trust you have chosen match your needs? Haphazard applications waste postage and time

229

TRUSTEES M D Frankel, G Frankel, G J Frankel

NOTES Preference for Jewish charities

HOW TO APPLY In writing

WHO TO APPLY TO M D Frankel, Secretary, The Isaac & Freda Frankel Memorial Charitable Trust, c/o Messrs Davis Frankel Mead, 33 Welbeck Street, London W1M 8LX

CC NO 1003732   **ESTABLISHED** 1991

■ Sydney E Franklin Deceased's New Second Charity

WHAT IS FUNDED Donations mainly given to small charities with low overheads; focusing on third world self help projects, endangered species and those disadvantaged by poverty

WHAT IS NOT FUNDED No grants to individuals or for scholarships. No grants to large umbrella charities

WHO CAN BENEFIT Smaller charities with low overheads dealing with third world self help projects or endangered species. Funding may be given to those disadvantaged by poverty, victims of famine, man-made or natural disasters and war

WHERE FUNDING CAN BE GIVEN Worldwide. Priority, but not exclusively, to third world projects

RANGE OF GRANTS £500–£5,000, typical grant £1,000–£3,000

SAMPLE GRANTS £4,500 to Kerala Federation for the Blind; £4,000 to SOS Appeal for Life towards Yugoslav refugee fund; £3,000 to Womenkind Worldwide; £2,000 to Serbian Orthodox Church of St Sava Refugee Fund; £2,000 to Medical Aid for Palestinians; £2,000 to Water for Kids; £1,500 to Bernard St George's Jewish Settlement; £1,500 to Norwood Ravenswood; £1,500 to Survival International; £1,000 to Diana Fossey Gorilla Fund

FINANCES *Year* 1997–98 *Income* £25,800 *Grants* £26,500

TRUSTEES A Franklin, Dr R C G Franklin, Ms T N Franklin

HOW TO APPLY Donations may only be requested by letter, and these are placed before the Trustees at their meeting which is normally held at the end of each year. Applications are not acknowledged

WHO TO APPLY TO Dr R C G Franklin, Sydney E Franklin Deceased's New Second Charity, c/o 88 Carlton Hill, London NW8 OER

CC NO 272047   **ESTABLISHED** 1973

■ Jill Franklin Trust

WHAT IS FUNDED The Trustees' current concerns are advice (particularly for those with a health or mental health disability, their carers, parents, etc); respite care and holidays (in the UK only); access and mobility for people with disabilities; encouraging and training volunteers in helping the above; recycling schemes for furniture for those being rehoused; the restoration of churches of architectural importance, but not their 'improvement'; education and training for prisoners to prepare them for a job on release. Overseas our interests are in special projects with low overheads that will deliver; our main interest is in the Commonwealth. Charities working in the fields of: residential facilities and services; arts, culture and recreation; care in the community; counselling on social issues; crime prevention schemes; playschemes; and transport and alternative transport will also be considered

WHAT IS NOT FUNDED The Trust does not fund building, endowment funds, heritage schemes, religious organisations, animals, students, travel and exploration, nor any work which should be done by Government, local Government or Health Authorities and NHS Trusts. No grants to individuals

WHO CAN BENEFIT Charitable organisations, not necessarily registered charities, benefiting: actors and entertainment professionals; textile workers and designers; writers and poets; disabled people; carers; ex-offenders and those at risk of offending; and those suffering from mental illness

WHERE FUNDING CAN BE GIVEN UK and overseas

TYPE OF GRANT One-off, project, recurring costs, running costs and start-up costs. Funding for up to three years will be considered

RANGE OF GRANTS £100–£1,000

SAMPLE GRANTS £9,750 to Camden City and Islington Bereavement Services; £5,691 to Friends of Zibonele for running community health centre in South Africa; £3,500 to Disability Action Westminster for equipment; £2,500 to National Art Collection Fund; £2,000 to Sustrans for work on North Tyne Waggonways cycle tracks; £1,500 to Centre for Architectural History Edinburgh for cataloguing; £1,000 to Inside Out Trust for work with prisoners; £1,000 to St Marks College South Africa for a bursary to a student; £1,000 to One World Action in Namibia; £1,000 to Medical Foundation for Victims of Torture for help to refugees

FINANCES *Year* 1998 *Income* £98,875 *Grants* £91,983

TRUSTEES N Franklin, S P Franklin, A C Franklin, T N Franklin, S A Franklin

PUBLICATIONS Annual Report, guidelines

NOTES This Trust was incorporated with the Norman Franklin Trust in January 1998

HOW TO APPLY The Trustees tend to look more favourably on an appeal which is simply and economically prepared, enclosing, budget and accounts and a clear statement of purpose. No acknowledgement is given of unsolicited enquiries, except where an sae is enclosed

WHO TO APPLY TO N Franklin, Jill Franklin Trust, 78 Lawn Road, London NW3 2XB *Tel* 0171-722 4543 *Fax* 0171-722 4543

CC NO 259774   **ESTABLISHED** 1988

■ The Gordon Fraser Charitable Trust

WHAT IS FUNDED At present the Trustees are particularly interested in help for children or young people in need, the environment and in assisting organisations associated with the visual arts. Other charitable purposes will also be considered

WHAT IS NOT FUNDED Excluded are organisations which are not registered as charities in England and Wales or registered with the Inland Revenue in Scotland. Applications from individuals are ineligible

WHO CAN BENEFIT The Trustees have absolute discretion as to the charities or organisations to be assisted. There are no restrictions on the age; professional and economic group; family situation; religion and culture; and social circumstances of; or disease or medical condition suffered by, the beneficiaries

WHERE FUNDING CAN BE GIVEN UK, applications from Scotland will receive favourable consideration, but not to the exclusion of applications from elsewhere

TYPE OF GRANT Grants are usually one-off though funding for up to three years may be considered

RANGE OF GRANTS £100–£15,000, typical grant £250–£750

SAMPLE GRANTS £5,500 to Ballet West for funding of student bursaries; £5,000 to Scottish Museums Council for conservation of works on paper; £4,000 to London Children's Flower Society purchase of seeds and bulbs; £3,650 to Royal Botanic Gardens, Edinburgh for collating of Hebridean flower data; £3,450 to Artlink Central for funding of artist working with residents at Bellsdyke Hospital; £3,000 to The Buildings of Scotland Trust for funding of research; £3,000 to Hunterian Art Gallery for the renovation technical equipment; £3,000 to Museum of Scotland as part of a four year £12,000 donation for restoration work on the Dean Panels; £3,000 to Waverley Care Trust for Milestone House caring for AIDs sufferers; £2,500 to Braendam Family House for general expenses or family respite centre

FINANCES *Year* 1997 *Income* £116,578
Grants £125,400

TRUSTEES Mrs M A Moss, W F T Anderson

NOTES All applications are acknowledged; an sae is therefore appreciated

HOW TO APPLY For consideration in January, April, July and October. No initial telephone call is welcome. There is no application form though guidelines are issued

WHO TO APPLY TO Mrs M A Moss, The Gordon Fraser Charitable Trust, Holmhurst, Westerton Drive, Bridge of Allan, Scotland FK9 4QL

CC NO 260869   **ESTABLISHED** 1966

■ The Hugh Fraser Foundation

WHAT IS FUNDED Grants are made to assist medical research and improve medical facilities; also to relieve the conditions of old age, ill health and poverty. Support is provided for the education, training and development of young people and for music and the arts. Other charitable causes are considered

WHAT IS NOT FUNDED Grants are neither made to individuals nor, usually, to high-profile appeals

WHO CAN BENEFIT To benefit students and those disadvantaged by poverty. There is no restriction on the age or the disease or medical condition suffered by the beneficiaries

WHERE FUNDING CAN BE GIVEN Scotland, in particular the West of Scotland and deprived areas, but grants are also made to charitable organisations based outside Scotland

FINANCES *Year* 1997–98 *Income* £1,310,335
Grants £1,213,850

TRUSTEES Dr K Chrystie (Chairman), Lady Fraser of Allander, Hon Ms A L Fraser, Ms P L Fraser, B Smith

PUBLICATIONS Accounts are available from the Trust

HOW TO APPLY Applications should be made in writing to the address under Who To Apply To and are considered by the Trustees on a quarterly basis

WHO TO APPLY TO The Hugh Fraser Foundation, Turcan Connell, Saltire Court, 20 Castle Terrace, Edinburgh EH1 2EF *Tel* 0131-228 8111

SC NO SCO 9303   **ESTABLISHED** 1960

■ The Fraser Trust

WHAT IS FUNDED Charitable purposes within or similar to the objects of St Dunstan's (for men and women blinded in the services) or other charitable purposes which may appear to St Dunstan's to be incidental or conducive to the attainment of its objects. Assistance with aids for, and exceptional grants to blind persons

WHO CAN BENEFIT Only men and women blinded in the Services who are known to St Dunstan's

WHERE FUNDING CAN BE GIVEN UK

FINANCES *Year* 1997 *Income* £24,797
Grants £24,292

TRUSTEES St Dunstan's

HOW TO APPLY **This Trust states that it does not respond to unsolicited applications**

WHO TO APPLY TO W C Weisblatt, LLB, Sec, The Fraser Trust, St Dunstan's, PO Box 4XB, 12–14 Harcourt Street, London W1A 4XB *Tel* 0171-723 5021

CC NO 215338   **ESTABLISHED** 1943

■ The Emily Fraser Trust

WHAT IS FUNDED Grants are made primarily to individuals connected to the retail trade in Scotland, but are also given to small charities which are dedicated to relieving poverty, illness and the condition of the elderly. Other charitable purposes are considered

WHAT IS NOT FUNDED Applicants already receiving grants from the Hugh Fraser Foundation will not be eligible

WHO CAN BENEFIT Funding is primarily given to individuals and organisations benefiting elderly people and those disadvantaged by poverty. There are some restrictions on the disease or medical condition suffered by the beneficiaries

WHERE FUNDING CAN BE GIVEN UK with a preference for Scotland

FINANCES *Year* 1997–98 *Income* £92,761
Grants £109,850

TRUSTEES Dr K Chrystie (Chairman), Lady Fraser of Allander, Hon A L Fraser, Ms P L Fraser, B Smith

PUBLICATIONS Accounts are available from the Trust

HOW TO APPLY Applications should be made in writing to the address under Who To Apply To

WHO TO APPLY TO The Emily Fraser Trust, Turcan Connell, Saltire Court, 20 Castle Terrace, Edinburgh EH1 2EF *Tel* 0131-228 1811

SC NO SCO 07288   **ESTABLISHED** 1971

■ The Frazer Charities Trust

WHAT IS FUNDED Mainly medical, including hospices, sailors and seamen and RNLI. The Trust's policies are constantly under review

WHAT IS NOT FUNDED Registered charities only. Applications from individuals are ineligible

WHO CAN BENEFIT Registered charities benefiting sailors and seamen and the sick. There is no restriction on the disease or medical condition suffered by the beneficiaries

WHERE FUNDING CAN BE GIVEN UK, but Yorkshire preference

TYPE OF GRANT General as long as to registered charities

RANGE OF GRANTS £100–£5,000

SAMPLE GRANTS £5,000 to Queen Alexandra Hospital Home; £2,000 to Wheatfields Hospice; £1,000 to Research into Ageing; £1,000 to the Anthony Nolan Bone Marrow Trust; £1,000 to RNLI Humber Lifeboat Appeal

FINANCES *Year* 1997 *Income* £20,632
Grants £53,270

TRUSTEES A F Sergeant, FCA, Miss A Webb

NOTES Privately administered by Trustees. Accounts prepared annually and submitted to the Charity Commissioners and the Inland Revenue

HOW TO APPLY At any time. Trustees cannot undertake to respond to submissions

WHO TO APPLY TO Miss A Webb, The Frazer Charities Trust, 70 Shadwell Walk, Moortown, Leeds, West Yorkshire LS17 6EG

CC NO 272303   **ESTABLISHED** 1976

■ Joseph Strong Frazer Trust

WHAT IS FUNDED General charitable purposes
WHAT IS NOT FUNDED No grants to individuals
WHO CAN BENEFIT Registered charities only in England and Wales. There are no restrictions on the age; professional and economic group; family situation; religion and culture; and social circumstances of; or disease or medical condition suffered by, the beneficiaries
WHERE FUNDING CAN BE GIVEN England and Wales
TYPE OF GRANT One-off, capital and recurring costs
RANGE OF GRANTS £250–£2,000
SAMPLE GRANTS £7,000 to Hill Homes; £7,000 to The Salvation Army; £6,000 to Bearwood College Charitable Bursary Fund; £5,000 to Royal Theatrical Fund; £4,000 to British Institute for Brain Injured Children; £4,000 to Royal Merchant Navy School Foundation; £4,000 to St Michael's Church, Tongwynlais; £4,000 to Stroke Association; £4,000 to Tphafen; £3,000 to All Hallows-by-the-Tower
FINANCES *Year* 1997 *Income* £465,773 *Grants* £355,750
TRUSTEES Sir William A Reardon Smith, Bt, Mrs R M Gibson, D A Cook, R M H Read
HOW TO APPLY By writing to the address under Who To Apply To. Trustees meet twice a year, usually in March and September. Application forms are not necessary but it is helpful if applicants are concise in their appeal letters which must include a sae if acknowledgement is required
WHO TO APPLY TO Joseph Strong Frazer Trust, Scottish Provident House, 31 Mosley Street, Newcastle upon Tyne, Tyne and Wear NE1 1HX
CC NO 235311   **ESTABLISHED** 1940

■ Free Computers for Education

WHAT IS FUNDED The re-distribution of computers that are scrapped by companies, to schools that require them
WHO CAN BENEFIT Schools only
WHERE FUNDING CAN BE GIVEN UK
FINANCES *Year* 1996 *Income* £250,000
HOW TO APPLY Write, requesting an application form, to the address under Who To Apply To. You will then be logged onto the Trust's database and join a growing queue
WHO TO APPLY TO Christopher Harris, Interim Director, Free Computers for Education, 1–3 Brigstock Parade, Thornton Heath, Surrey CR7 7HW
CC NO 1059116   **ESTABLISHED** 1996

■ The Louis Freedman Charitable Trust

WHAT IS FUNDED General charitable purposes. Significant endowments to charities of the Founder's choosing, and small grants to national charities
WHAT IS NOT FUNDED No grants to individuals
WHO CAN BENEFIT There are no restrictions on the age; professional and economic group; family situation; religion and culture; and social circumstances of; or disease or medical condition suffered by, the beneficiaries
WHERE FUNDING CAN BE GIVEN UK
RANGE OF GRANTS £50–£5,000

SAMPLE GRANTS £5,000 to St Marks Hospital; £1,000 to National Association of Almshouses; £1,000 to ORT; £600 to Summerfields School; £250 to Hearing Dogs for the Deaf; £250 to NCDL; £250 to Racing Welfare; £250 to St Mark's Church, Tunbridge Wells; £250 to United Synagogue; £250 to Woodside Animal Welfare Trust
FINANCES *Year* 1997 *Income* £57,795 *Grants* £11,090
TRUSTEES Mrs V Freedman, F H Hughes
HOW TO APPLY No telephone calls. Brief written details are required. There is no application form and unsuccessful applicants will not be notified
WHO TO APPLY TO F H Hughes, The Louis Freedman Charitable Trust, Messrs Thomas B Hughes, 25 Chargate Close, Burwood Park, Walton-on-Thames, Surrey KT12 5DW
CC NO 271067   **ESTABLISHED** 1976

■ A J Freeman Charitable Trust

WHAT IS FUNDED General charitable purposes
WHO CAN BENEFIT Registered charities. There are no restrictions on the age; professional and economic group; family situation; religion and culture; and social circumstances of; or disease or medical condition suffered by, the beneficiaries
WHERE FUNDING CAN BE GIVEN Mainly Manchester
TYPE OF GRANT Single donations towards specific objects
FINANCES *Year* 1996 *Income* £45,260
TRUSTEES A J Freeman, J M Levy
WHO TO APPLY TO J M Levy, A J Freeman Charitable Trust, Kuit Steinart Levy & Co, 3 St Mary's Parsonage, Manchester M3 2RD
CC NO 279522   **ESTABLISHED** 1979

■ Freemans Trust Ltd

WHAT IS FUNDED General charitable purposes. To assist Freemans employees and retired staff and charities for which they are working
WHAT IS NOT FUNDED No other charities will be considered
WHO CAN BENEFIT There are no restrictions on the age; professional and economic group; family situation; religion and culture; and social circumstances of; or disease or medical condition suffered by, the beneficiaries. However, they must be Freemans employees or ex-employees, or charities which they are connected to
WHERE FUNDING CAN BE GIVEN UK
FINANCES *Year* 1997 *Income* £143,000 *Grants* £135,000
TRUSTEES Council of Management
NOTES Applications from grant seekers will not be considered
HOW TO APPLY Five copies of applications to the address under Who To Apply To
WHO TO APPLY TO J Pearce, Freemans Trust Ltd, 139 Clapham Road, London SW99 0HR *Tel* 0171-820 2722
CC NO 1160176   **ESTABLISHED** 1974

■ The Thomas Freke and Lady Norton Charity

WHAT IS FUNDED To provide funding aid in the form of buildings or equipment for churches, schools, youth and community facilities in the area Where Funding Can Be Given. Willing to consider emergency or unforeseen expenditure. Funding may also be given to community centres, village halls, recreation grounds and sports centres

WHAT IS NOT FUNDED No grants are given for ordinary running expenses. No applications considered from outside the area Where Funding Can Be Given

WHO CAN BENEFIT Local communities and organisations benefiting children, young adults and Christians

WHERE FUNDING CAN BE GIVEN Parishes for Hannington, Inglesham, Highworth, Stanton Fitzwarren, Blunsdon St Leonards and Castle Eaton

TYPE OF GRANT Capital

FINANCES *Year* 1996–97 *Income* £107,798 *Grants* £130,114

TRUSTEES Mrs M G Hussey-Freke, Mrs V J Davies, R G Higgins, Dr K T Scholes, J M E Scott

HOW TO APPLY To the address under Who To Apply To in writing, enclosing project details, projected costs and statement of funds in hand or anticipated from other sources

WHO TO APPLY TO S J Whiteman, The Thomas Freke and Lady Norton Charity, 22 Queens Road, Hannington, Swindon, Wiltshire SN6 7RS *Tel* 01793 765058

CC NO 200824 **ESTABLISHED** 1990

■ Charles S French Charitable Trust

WHAT IS FUNDED Strong preference for Essex, East Anglia, and North East London area. Very few grants made for purposes outside these areas

WHAT IS NOT FUNDED No grants to individuals. Only very occasional grants for educational purposes and only when first approached by a school or college, not by a student. Such grants are concentrated on schools in the SW Essex or NE London area, for pupils coming from the same area

WHO CAN BENEFIT Charities, especially children's charities, and charities in Essex, East Anglia and North East London area

WHERE FUNDING CAN BE GIVEN Cambridgeshire, Essex, East Anglia, Hertfordshire and the London boroughs of Barking and Dagenham, Enfield, Hackney, Havering, City of London, Newham, Redbridge, Tower Hamlets and Waltham Forest

FINANCES *Year* 1996–97 *Income* £143,000 *Grants* £167,000

TRUSTEES W F Noble, R L Thomas, D B Shepperd

WHO TO APPLY TO R L Thomas, Charles S French Charitable Trust, 169 High Road, Loughton, Essex IG10 4LF *Tel* 0181-502 3575

CC NO 206476 **ESTABLISHED** 1959

■ Anne French Memorial Trust

WHAT IS FUNDED Any charitable purpose in the area Where Funding Can Be Given, especially church-related causes

WHO CAN BENEFIT To benefit Christians, clergy and locally-based charities

WHERE FUNDING CAN BE GIVEN The Diocese of Norwich, Norfolk

RANGE OF GRANTS £30–£59223

SAMPLE GRANTS £59,223 was given to members of the clergy as holiday gifts; £25,000 to parsonages for repairs and maintenance; £11,550 to members of the clergy for general purposes; £10,000 to Fabric Fund Trust; £9,088 to Granary Court for repairs and maintenance; £7,077 for education, youth work and training to ordination; £5,500 to members of the clergy for courses following ordination; £4,884 to archidiaconal for suffragan and assistant bishop's expenses; £3,800 to Ordinands in training for education, youth work and training to ordination; £3,780 to members of the clergy during illness

FINANCES *Year* 1996–97 *Income* £224,491 *Grants* £201,165

TRUSTEES Lord Bishop of Norwich

NOTES In 1996–97, £3,400 was given to Norwich charities and £3,200 to Norfolk charities

HOW TO APPLY To the address under Who To Apply To in writing

WHO TO APPLY TO B O L Prior, Secretary, Anne French Memorial Trust, 4 Eaton Road, Norwich, Norfolk NR4 6PY *Tel* 01603 451877

CC NO 254567 **ESTABLISHED** 1963

■ Freshfield Foundation

This trust did not respond to CAF's request to amend its entry and, by 30 June 1998, CAF's researchers did not find financial records for later than 1995 on its file at the Charity Commission. Trusts are legally required to submit annual accounts to the Charity Commission under section 42 of the Charities Act 1993

WHAT IS FUNDED General charitable purposes

WHO CAN BENEFIT All applications considered. There are no restrictions on the age; professional and economic group; family situation; religion and culture; and social circumstances of; or disease or medical condition suffered by, the beneficiaries

WHERE FUNDING CAN BE GIVEN UK and overseas

TRUSTEES P A Moores, A Moores (Settlor), Mrs E J Potter

WHO TO APPLY TO Messrs MacFarlane & Co, Freshfield Foundation, 2nd Floor, Cunard Building, Water Street, Liverpool L3 1DS *Tel* 0151 236 6161

CC NO 1003316 **ESTABLISHED** 1991

■ The Freshgate Trust Foundation

WHAT IS FUNDED Local appeals working in the fields of arts and community services and facilities

WHAT IS NOT FUNDED The Trust restricts its grants to charitable organisations and does not deal with applications from individuals, national appeals or for church fabric unless used for a wider community purpose

WHO CAN BENEFIT Organisations benefiting: people of all ages; actors and entertainment professionals; musicians; textile workers and designers; writers and poets; at risk groups; those disadvantaged by poverty and socially isolated people. Mainly charitable organisations in South Yorkshire. Both innovatory and established bodies may be considered

WHERE FUNDING CAN BE GIVEN Mainly Sheffield and South Yorkshire

TYPE OF GRANT Buildings, capital, core costs, endowments, feasibility studies, interest free loans, one-off, project, research, running costs, recurring costs, salaries and start-up costs. Funding for up to three years will be considered

SAMPLE GRANTS £4,000 to Sheffield Family Service Unit; £3,750 to Sheffield Family Holiday Fund; £3,740 to Brown Bayleys Steels Limited – Old Age Pensioners; £3,500 to Boys' Clubs of South Yorkshire and Humberside; £3,500 to Sheffield Council Girl Guides; £2,500 to Relate, Sheffield; £2,200 to Youth Association of South Yorkshire; £1,500 to Sheffield Council for Voluntary Service; £1,500 to Sheffield and District YMCA

FINANCES *Year* 1997 *Income* £126,287 *Grants* £91,649

TRUSTEES Council of Management Governing Body: M P W Lee, H Bull, Dr F P A Garton, Mrs A C Martin, J F B Hopkins, J E Parkin, A J Coombe, Miss E S Murray, D R Stone

WHO TO APPLY TO J H Robinson, Secretary, The Freshgate Trust Foundation, 346 Glossop Road, Sheffield, South Yorkshire S10 2HW *Tel* 0114-273 8551

CC NO 221467   **ESTABLISHED** 1962

■ The Mark Frey Charitable Settlement

This trust did not respond to CAF's request to amend its entry and, by 30 June 1998, CAF's researchers did not find financial records for later than 1995 on its file at the Charity Commission. Trusts are legally required to submit annual accounts to the Charity Commission under section 42 of the Charities Act 1993

WHAT IS FUNDED General charitable purposes

WHO CAN BENEFIT There are no restrictions on the age; professional and economic group; family situation; religion and culture; and social circumstances of; or disease or medical condition suffered by, the beneficiaries

WHERE FUNDING CAN BE GIVEN UK

TRUSTEES M D Frey, Ms M Frey

WHO TO APPLY TO M Frey, Trustee, The Mark Frey Charitable Settlement, The Willows, Potten End Hill, Water End, Hemel Hempstead, Hertfordshire HP1 3BN

CC NO 1046285   **ESTABLISHED** 1994

■ Friarsgate Trust

WHAT IS FUNDED General charitable purposes contributing to welfare of children and young persons, care of the aged and of the needy and sick. Existing rather than new causes are funded

WHO CAN BENEFIT Organisations benefiting people of all ages, at risk groups, those disadvantaged by poverty and socially isolated people. There is no restriction on the disease or medical condition suffered by the beneficiaries

WHERE FUNDING CAN BE GIVEN UK with preference for West Sussex

RANGE OF GRANTS £200–£3,000

SAMPLE GRANTS £3,000 to CYAT; £2,600 to Children's Family Trust; £2,600 to Arthritis and Rheumatism Council; £2,600 St Christopher's Fellowship; £2,600 Institute of Ophthalmology; £2,600 Friends of Chichester Hospitals; £2,080 Chichester Marriage Guidance Council; £1,420 to Citizens Advice Bureau; £1,420 to St Wilfrid's Hospice; £1,310 to Royal Commonwealth Society for the Blind

FINANCES *Year* 1997 *Income* £69,606 *Grants* £59,020

TRUSTEES R F Oates, H R Whittle, G N M Scoular

WHO TO APPLY TO G N M Scoular, Friarsgate Trust, Thomas Eggar Verrall Bowles, Sussex House, North Street, Horsham RH12 1BJ

CC NO 220762   **ESTABLISHED** 1955

■ The Friday Charitable Trust

WHAT IS FUNDED General charitable purposes. Preference to charitable objects of which Trustees have direct knowledge. This uses the available funds fully

WHAT IS NOT FUNDED No grants to general public appeals, building projects, restoration funds, major educational objects

WHO CAN BENEFIT There are no restrictions on the age, professional and economic group, family situation, religion and culture, and social circumstances of, or disease or medical condition suffered by, the beneficiaries. Exclude major charities

WHERE FUNDING CAN BE GIVEN UK

TYPE OF GRANT One-off and recurring

FINANCES *Year* 1997 *Income* £31,977 *Grants* £30,781

TRUSTEES J M Livingstone, J L Houlden, P J Sturrock, S G Platten, J D S Booth

HOW TO APPLY **This Trust states that it does not respond to unsolicited applications**

WHO TO APPLY TO J L Houlden, The Friday Charitable Trust, 33 Raleigh Court, Lymer Avenue, London SE19 1LS

CC NO 260781   **ESTABLISHED** 1969

■ A Friend Indeed

WHAT IS FUNDED The advancement of the Orthodox Jewish religion and religious education, the relief of poverty amongst persons of the Jewish faith

WHO CAN BENEFIT Jewish people, especially those disadvantaged by poverty

WHERE FUNDING CAN BE GIVEN UK

HOW TO APPLY To the address under Who To Apply To in writing

WHO TO APPLY TO Jacob Lipschitz, A Friend Indeed, 139 Holmleigh Road, London N16 5QA

CC NO 1064218   **ESTABLISHED** 1997

■ Friends of Biala Ltd

WHAT IS FUNDED The furthering of religious institutions. General charitable purposes may also be considered

WHO CAN BENEFIT There are no restrictions on the age; professional and economic group; family situation; religion and culture; and social circumstances of; or disease or medical condition suffered by, the beneficiaries. However, particular favour is given to to beneficiaries of religious causes

WHERE FUNDING CAN BE GIVEN UK and overseas

FINANCES *Year* 1997 *Income* £145,306 *Grants* £179,760

TRUSTEES B Z Rabinovitch, Mrs T Weinberg

WHO TO APPLY TO The Secretary, Friends of Biala Ltd, c/o 5 Rodsley Avenue, Gateshead NE8 4JY

CC NO 271377   **ESTABLISHED** 1964

■ The Friends of Essex Churches *(formerly Association of Friends of Essex Churches)*

WHAT IS FUNDED To grant money to churches, irrespective of denomination, where the repairs necessary are beyond parish resources

WHAT IS NOT FUNDED Grants are only permitted by charter for fabric repairs; thus work on decorations, bells and organs cannot be helped. No grants to individuals

WHO CAN BENEFIT Parochial Church Councils or where none exists then the church itself

WHERE FUNDING CAN BE GIVEN Diocese of Chelmsford (Greater Essex)

TYPE OF GRANT One-off (but may apply again in subsequent years) and buildings

RANGE OF GRANTS £250–£20,000 (from Special Projects Fund)

SAMPLE GRANTS £20,000 to St Nicholas, Canewdon for repairs to fabric of church; £20,000 to St Francis of Assisi, Stratford for repairs to fabric of church; £17,000 to St John Baptist, Clacton on Sea for repairs to fabric of church; £8,000 to St Patrick, Barking for repairs to fabric of church; £5,000 to St Elisabeth, Becontree for repairs to fabric of church; £5,000 to St Andrews, Halstead for repairs to fabric of church; £4,000 to St Andrew, Boreham for repairs to fabric of church; £4,000 to URC, Chadwell Heath for repairs to fabric of church; £4,000 to St Andrew, Fingringhoe for repairs to fabric of church

FINANCES *Year* 1997 *Income* £128,700 *Grants* £137,400

TRUSTEES The Council

PUBLICATIONS *Essex Churches. A Handbook for Parishes*, cost £1.50. Notes from seminar held in 1997, cost £3

HOW TO APPLY Application forms will be sent to those applying for a grant

WHO TO APPLY TO Mrs M S Blaxall, The Friends of Essex Churches, 5 Brookhurst Close, Springfield Road, Chelmsford, Essex CM2 6DX *Tel* 01245 354745

CC NO 236033   **ESTABLISHED** 1952

■ Friends of Kent Churches

WHAT IS FUNDED To assist in the preservation of Kent's ancient churches by contributing to the cost of repairs of fabric and fittings

WHAT IS NOT FUNDED No grants made towards cost of redecorations, heating, lighting and organ repairs

WHO CAN BENEFIT Ancient and historic churches of all denominations in Kent

WHERE FUNDING CAN BE GIVEN County of Kent, in the dioceses of Canterbury and Rochester

RANGE OF GRANTS £250–£4,500

SAMPLE GRANTS £4,500 to Holy Trinity, Milton Regis; £3,000 to St Matrin, Cheriton; £3,000 to Holy Trinity, Dartford; £3,000 to Holy Cross, Goodnestone; £2,500 to St John, Gravesend; £2,500 to All Saints, Iwade; £2,500 to St Augustine, Northbourne; £2,000 to St Paul, Beckenham; £2,000 to St Mildred, Canterbury; £2,000 to St Paul, Four Elms

FINANCES *Year* 1996 *Income* £118,422 *Grants* £56,000

TRUSTEES Executive Committee

WHO TO APPLY TO N B Whitehead, Hon Secretary, Friends of Kent Churches, Beemans, High Street, Cranbrook, Kent TN17 3DT

CC NO 207021   **ESTABLISHED** 1950

■ The Friends of Ta'ali

WHAT IS FUNDED Provision of funds and other monies for the advancement of the health of all the citizens of the State of Israel. Relief of poverty in all parts of the world; advancement of public education about Jews amongst Jews and non-Jews; advancement of the Jewish religion in all parts of the world

WHO CAN BENEFIT Jewish people, those disadvantaged by poverty and non-Jews. There is no restriction on the disease or medical condition suffered by the beneficiaries

WHERE FUNDING CAN BE GIVEN Israel, UK and overseas

TRUSTEES L J Tamman, E D Ishag, C Rayden

NOTES Limited provision for grants

HOW TO APPLY To the address under Who To Apply To by letter

WHO TO APPLY TO Sidney L Shipton, The Friends of Ta'ali, New House, 67–8 Hatton Garden, London EC1N 8JY *Tel* 0171-242 4556

CC NO 327953   **ESTABLISHED** 1988

■ Friends of the Animals

WHAT IS FUNDED Animal welfare and animal rescue are the main interests, particularly to aid animals in distress and to arrange veterinary treatment. To find new homes for animals. To educate the public in the aid of animals

WHERE FUNDING CAN BE GIVEN West Midlands

FINANCES *Year* 1997 *Income* £195,713 *Grants* £2,187

TRUSTEES D E Rice, CEng, MIM, D K Stokes, Mrs R Dyson, M J Gomez, F Ridler

NOTES The Charity co-operates with the charity K9 enabling them both to pursue their objectives, and also shares certain running costs with the Caring Cancer Trust

HOW TO APPLY In writing with detailed accounts and history to the address under Who To Apply To

WHO TO APPLY TO M Gomez, Treasurer, Friends of the Animals, 408 Bearwood Road, Smethwick, Warley B66 4EX

CC NO 1000249   **ESTABLISHED** 1990

■ Friends of the Green Howards Trust

WHAT IS FUNDED General charitable purposes

WHO CAN BENEFIT There are no restrictions on the age; professional and economic group; family situation; religion and culture; and social circumstances of; or disease or medical condition suffered by, the beneficiaries

WHERE FUNDING CAN BE GIVEN UK

FINANCES *Year* 1995 *Income* £94,673

WHO TO APPLY TO Major W A Laws, Friends of the Green Howards Trust, Registered Headquarters The Green Howards, Trinity Church Square, Richmond, North Yorkshire DL10 4QN *Tel* 01748 822133

CC NO 291931   **ESTABLISHED** 1985

■ Friends of Wiznitz Limited

WHAT IS FUNDED General support to charitable institutions

WHO CAN BENEFIT There are no restrictions on the age; professional and economic group; family situation; religion and culture; and social circumstances of; or disease or medical condition suffered by, the beneficiaries

WHERE FUNDING CAN BE GIVEN UK and overseas

FINANCES *Year* 1996 *Income* £205,040 *Grants* £158,076

TRUSTEES H Feldman, E Kahan, R Bergmann, S Feldman

WHO TO APPLY TO H Feldman, Friends of Wiznitz Limited, 23 Overlea Road, London E5 9BG

CC NO 255685   **ESTABLISHED** 1948

■ The Nina Frigenti Charitable Trust

This trust did not respond to CAF's request to amend its entry and, by 30 June 1998, CAF's researchers did not find financial records for later than 1995 on its file at the Charity Commission. Trusts are legally required to submit annual accounts to the Charity Commission under section 42 of the Charities Act 1993

WHAT IS FUNDED General charitable purposes

WHO CAN BENEFIT There are no restrictions on the age; professional and economic group; family situation; religion and culture; and social circumstances of; or disease or medical condition suffered by, the beneficiaries

WHERE FUNDING CAN BE GIVEN UK

TRUSTEES J R G Flynn, Mrs M Corry, D Sutton, M Zaroovabeli

WHO TO APPLY TO The Nina Frigenti Charitable Trust, Purcells, 4 Quex Road, London NW6 4PJ

CC NO 802828　　　**ESTABLISHED** 1990

■ Frognal Trust

WHAT IS FUNDED The Trustees current grant making policy is to make relatively small grants to as many qualifying charities as possible. Particularly charities working in the fields of: residential facilities and services; cultural heritage; hospices; nursing homes; ophthalmological research; conservation ; heritage; parks; and community services. Other charitable purposes will be considered

WHAT IS NOT FUNDED No grants to charities for the benefit of animals, people living outside the UK or for the propagation of religious beliefs. The Trustees do not make grants for educational/ research trips overseas

WHO CAN BENEFIT Registered charities benefiting older people, disabled people and those suffering from sight loss

WHERE FUNDING CAN BE GIVEN UK

TYPE OF GRANT Buildings, capital, one-off, research and start-up costs will be considered. Funding is available for up to two years

RANGE OF GRANT £500–£3,800

SAMPLE GRANTS £3,800 to Central and Cecil Housing Trust; £3,500 to Huntingtons Disease Society; £3,000 to League of Friends of Osborne House; £3,000 to Society for the Study of Inborn Errors of Metabolism; £3,000 to Woodland Trust; £3,000 to Crohns in Childhood Research Association; £1,500 to Alone in London Service; £1,500 to Demand Design and Manufacture for Disability; £1,500 to Alzheimer's Research Trust; £1,500 to Pearsons Holiday Fund

FINANCES *Year* 1997 *Income* £69,569 *Grants* £60,855

TRUSTEES Mrs P Blake-Roberts, J P van Montagu, P Fraser

WHO TO APPLY TO The Grants Administrator, Frognal Trust, Charities Aid Foundation, Kingshill, West Malling, Kent ME19 4TA

CC NO 244444　　　**ESTABLISHED** 1964

■ Frome Christian Fellowship

WHAT IS FUNDED To give to overseas and UK ministries

WHO CAN BENEFIT Organisations benefiting Christians

WHERE FUNDING CAN BE GIVEN UK and overseas

FINANCES *Year* 1996 *Income* £22,119

TRUSTEES D S Hawes, R Bird, B Reed

WHO TO APPLY TO Brian Reed, Frome Christian Fellowship, 19 Charles Road, Frome, Somerset BA17 1NT

CC NO 291173　　　**ESTABLISHED** 1985

■ T F C Frost Charitable Trust

WHAT IS FUNDED Research in ophthalmology by establishing research fellowships and supporting specific projects

WHAT IS NOT FUNDED There are no available resources for the relief of blind persons or persons suffering from diseases of the eye

WHO CAN BENEFIT Research associates of recognised centres of excellence in ophthalmology. Individuals and organisations benefiting academics, medical professionals, research workers and those suffering from sight loss

WHERE FUNDING CAN BE GIVEN UK and overseas

RANGE OF GRANTS £12,673–£44,821

SAMPLE GRANTS £44,821 to Institute of Ophthalmology; £32,856 to National Hospital for Neurology and Neurosurgery; £31,262 to Bascom Palmer Eye Institute, Florida, USA; £28,470 to the Wills Eye Hospital, Philadelphia, USA; £13,875 to Nuffield Laboratory of Ophthalmology; £12,673 to Lancaster University

FINANCES *Year* 1996 *Income* £132,417 *Grants* £163,957

TRUSTEES Mrs S E Frost, T A F Frost, FCA, M D Sanders, MB, BS, FRCS, FRCP, M H Miller, MD, FRCS, FCOphth

WHO TO APPLY TO Holmes & Co, Accountants, T F C Frost Charitable Trust, 10 Torrington Road, Claygate, Esher, Surrey KT10 0SA

CC NO 256590　　　**ESTABLISHED** 1966

■ The Patrick Frost Foundation

WHAT IS FUNDED The making of donations or grants at the Trustees' discretion to charitable organisations for charitable purposes including the relief and welfare of persons of small means and the less fortunate members of society and assistance for small organisations where a considerable amount of self-help and voluntary effort is required

WHAT IS NOT FUNDED No grants to individuals

WHO CAN BENEFIT Registered charities. There are no restrictions on the age, professional and economic group, family situation, religion and culture, and social circumstances of, or disease or medical condition suffered by, the beneficiaries

WHERE FUNDING CAN BE GIVEN UK and overseas

TYPE OF GRANT One-off donations

RANGE OF GRANTS £1,000–£5,000

SAMPLE GRANTS £5,000 to The Family Holiday Association; £5,000 to Universities Settlement in East London (Toynbee Hall); £5,000 to The Camphill Village Trust, Botton Village; £5,000 to Whitefield Christian Trust; £3,000 to Canine Partners for Independence; £2,000 to Chance for Children Trust; £2,000 to Action for Blind People; £2,000 to Lifestyle 1998 Humberside Police; £2,000 to Sharing and Caring; £2,000 to Merthyr Tydfil Shopmobility towards computer printer

FINANCES *Year* 1996–97 *Income* £46,439 *Grants* £22,000

TRUSTEES Mrs H Frost, D Jones, L Valner, J Chedzoy

HOW TO APPLY In writing to the address under Who To Apply To. Due to the large number of applications they receive the Trustees regret they are unable to acknowledge unsuccessful applications

236

Think carefully about every application. Is it justified?

WHO TO APPLY TO Mrs H M Frost, (Ref LHV), The Patrick Frost Foundation, c/o Trowers & Hamlins, Sceptre Court, 40 Tower Hill, London EC3N 4BN *Tel* 0171-423 8000 *Fax* 0171-423 8001
CC NO 1005505   **ESTABLISHED** 1991

■ Maurice Fry Charitable Trust

WHAT IS FUNDED General charitable purposes. Currently the main areas of interest are; medicine and health, welfare, humanities, environmental resources, and international causes

WHAT IS NOT FUNDED No grants to individuals

WHO CAN BENEFIT Registered charities benefiting at risk groups, those disadvantaged by poverty and socially isolated people. Support is given to medical professionals, research workers, scientists, academics and writers and poets. Support may also be given to refugees, and victims of famine, man-made or natural disasters and war. Otherwise, there are no restrictions on the age; professional and economic group; family situation; religion and culture; and social circumstances of; or disease or medical condition suffered by, the beneficiaries

WHERE FUNDING CAN BE GIVEN UK and overseas

RANGE OF GRANTS £200–£3,000

SAMPLE GRANTS £3,000 to Tree Aid; £2,500 to Intermediate Technology; £2,500 to Medical Foundation; £2,500 to Marie Stopes International; £1,500 to Fleet Carers; £1,500 to NSPCC; £1,300 to Childline; £1,200 to Island Trust; £1,050 to Shelter

FINANCES *Year* 1995 *Income* £31,701 *Grants* £26,250

TRUSTEES L E A Fry, A Fry, Mrs F Cooklin, Mrs L Weaks

NOTES This Trust supersedes the original Maurice Fry Charitable Trust (CC No 211514) which has now wound up

HOW TO APPLY **This Trust states that it does not respond to unsolicited applications**

WHO TO APPLY TO L Fry, Maurice Fry Charitable Trust, 98 Savernake Road, London NW3 2JR

CC NO 327934   **ESTABLISHED** 1988

■ Mejer and Gertrude Miriam Frydman Foundation

WHAT IS FUNDED New and established charitable projects for study and research, including scholarships, fellowships, professorial chairs, lectureships, prizes, awards and the cost of purchasing or erecting any building or land required for such projects

WHO CAN BENEFIT Organisations benefiting: children, young adults; students; teachers and governesses. Support is given to Jewish people, and particular favour is given to Jewish charities

WHERE FUNDING CAN BE GIVEN UK and overseas

RANGE OF GRANTS £300–£7,000

SAMPLE GRANTS £7,000 to Friends of Yeshiva Ohr Elechonon; £6,500 to North West London Jewish Day School; £6,000 to British Friends of Ariel; £5,000 to Friends of Ramot Shapira; £2,000 to Classic Charitable Trust; £1,200 to Mifal Hatorah Medical Aid Fund in Israel; £1,000 to Friends of Ohel Torah Trust; £750 to Yeshivath Meharash Engel Radomishl; £300 to Kesser Torah

FINANCES *Year* 1997 *Income* £28,397 *Grants* £29,750

TRUSTEES L J Frydman, G B Frydman, D H Frydman

WHO TO APPLY TO M Frydman, Mejer and Gertrude Miriam Frydman Foundation, c/o Messrs Westbury Schotness & Co, 145–157 St John Street, London EC1V 4PY

CC NO 262806   **ESTABLISHED** 1971

■ Fund for Human Need

WHAT IS FUNDED The relief of hunger, distress, poverty, deprivation and oppression in any part of the world without consideration of creed, race or politics

WHAT IS NOT FUNDED No grants to individuals. No grants to projects in the UK or to very large organisations

WHO CAN BENEFIT Organisations benefiting: victims of famine; refugees; the socially isolated; those disadvantaged by poverty and at risk groups. Support may also be given to disaster victims, the homeless and the victims of war

WHERE FUNDING CAN BE GIVEN Overseas

SAMPLE GRANTS £6,637 to Colon Methodist School, Panama; £3,000 to Amaudo Itumbauzo Centre, Nigeria for a water borehole; £3,000 to Volunteer Project Pakrac, Former Yugoslavia for peace building; £2,500 to Nijera Shikhi Literacy Programme, Bangladesh; £2,500 to Living Stones, UK; £2,000 to Francisco Rojas School, Peru; £2,000 to the Refugee Council, UK; £1,500 to Boys' Town, Kingston, Jamaica; £1,000 to Seva Mandir, India for a health programme; £1,000 to Africa 150, Uganda for a Queen's University, Belfast student team

FINANCES *Year* 1995 *Income* £40,819 *Grants* £29,400

TRUSTEES c/o The Methodist Church: Division of Social Responsibility

WHO TO APPLY TO The Secretary, Fund for Human Need, DSR, 1 Central Buildings, London SW1H 9NH

CC NO 208866   **ESTABLISHED** 1960

■ J G Fyfe Charitable Trust

WHAT IS FUNDED General charitable purposes

WHO CAN BENEFIT Registered charities. There are no restrictions on the age; professional and economic group; family situation; religion and culture; and social circumstances of; or disease or medical condition suffered by, the beneficiaries

WHERE FUNDING CAN BE GIVEN Scotland

WHO TO APPLY TO J G Fyfe Charitable Trust, The Manager, Bank of Scotland Trustee Department, PO Box 41, 101 George Street, Edinburgh EH2 3JH

SC NO SCO 00828

■ GABO Trust for Sculpture Conservation

WHAT IS FUNDED Education and other projects to promote the conservation of sculpture and training of sculpture conservators

WHAT IS NOT FUNDED Students

WHO CAN BENEFIT Innovative projects, established and national organisations and individuals

WHERE FUNDING CAN BE GIVEN UK

TYPE OF GRANT One-off, recurrent, capital, projects and research. Funding is available for up to three years

SAMPLE GRANTS £12,000 to an individual for Gabo Intern, Tate Gallery; £4,000 to an individual for internship, National Gallery, Washington; £2,233 to an individual for travelling scholarship, Plaster Cast Conservation; £850 to an individual for laser cleaning course, Liverpool

FINANCES *Year* 1996–97 *Income* £32,760 *Grants* £19,083

TRUSTEES N S Williams, G R Williams, M Harrison

PUBLICATIONS Statement describing the Trust and its policies is available

HOW TO APPLY In writing at any time

WHO TO APPLY TO A Dempsey, Secretary, GABO Trust for Sculpture Conservation, 92 Lenthall Road, London E8 3JN

CC NO 298715   **ESTABLISHED** 1988

■ GIFT (Helping Grandparents, Infants, Families and Teenagers)

WHAT IS FUNDED General charitable purposes, in paritcular, the relief of the needy and elderly, the advancement of education, and the provision of facilities for recreation and leisure-time

WHO CAN BENEFIT Organisations benefitting children, young adults, elderly people, students, at risk groups, those disadvantaged by poverty and socially isolated people

WHERE FUNDING CAN BE GIVEN UK

TRUSTEES A P Crossland, W J Hampson, K Thorpe

WHO TO APPLY TO A P Crossland, GIFT, 5 Verbena Way, Worle, Weston-Super-Mare, North Somerset BS22 0RF

CC NO 1064433   **ESTABLISHED** 1997

■ GMC Trust

WHAT IS FUNDED General charitable purposes, but preclaiment health care and medical research

WHAT IS NOT FUNDED The Trust does not make grants to individuals

WHO CAN BENEFIT Organisations benefiting: children, young adults and older people. There are no restrictions on the disease or medical condition suffered by the beneficiaries

WHERE FUNDING CAN BE GIVEN The UK, predominantly the West Midlands

TYPE OF GRANT One-off

RANGE OF GRANTS Grants of up to £10,000; typically £500

SAMPLE GRANTS £10,000 to CRAB Appeal; £10,000 to Macmillan Nurses; £10,000 to Mental Health Foundation; £7,600 to Acorns Children's Hospice; £2,500 to Oasis Appeal; £2,500 to Runnymede Trust

FINANCES *Year* 1998 *Income* £48,000 *Grants* £60,000

TRUSTEES Sir Adrian Cadbury, Benedict Edmund St John Cadbury

NOTES Income for 1999–2000 is substantially committed

HOW TO APPLY The Trust will only consider written applications

WHO TO APPLY TO Rodney Pitts, GMC Trust, 4 Fairways, 1240 Warwick Road, Knowle, Solihull, West Midlands B93 9LL

CC NO 288418   **ESTABLISHED** 1965

■ GNC Trust

WHAT IS FUNDED To support those charities of which the Trustees have special interest, knowledge or association, particularly of a medical or educational nature

WHAT IS NOT FUNDED No grants to individuals

WHO CAN BENEFIT Charitable bodies. There are no restrictions on the age; professional and economic group; family situation; religion and culture; and social circumstances of; or disease or medical condition suffered by, the beneficiaries

WHERE FUNDING CAN BE GIVEN Midlands, Hampshire and Cornwall

RANGE OF GRANTS £5–£10,000

SAMPLE GRANTS £10,000 to Foundation for Conductive Education; £5,000 to Downing College Foundation Fund; £5,000 to Mediation UK; £5,000 to the Woodland Trust; £2,500 to ASBAH; £2,500 to Light Railway; £2,500 to The Prince's Trust, Southern Counties; £2,000 to Bournville Village Trust; £2,000 to Royal National Rose Society; £1,800 to Society of Friends

FINANCES *Year* 1995 *Income* £68,725 *Grants* £59,816

TRUSTEES R N Cadbury, Mrs J E B Yelloly, G T E Cadbury

HOW TO APPLY In writing to the address under Who To Apply To. There is no application form. Applications are not acknowledged

WHO TO APPLY TO Mrs P M Spragg, GNC Trust, Messrs Price Waterhouse, Cornwall Court, 19 Cornwall Street, Birmingham B3 2DT

CC NO 211533   **ESTABLISHED** 1960

■ GRP Charitable Trust

WHAT IS FUNDED General charitable purposes. The Trustees prefer to provide medium term support for a number of charities already known to them. The Trustees do not feel able to investigate appeals from individuals and therefore do not make grants to individuals

WHAT IS NOT FUNDED No grants to individuals

WHO CAN BENEFIT There are no restrictions on the age; professional and economic group; family situation; religion and culture; and social circumstances of; or disease or medical condition suffered by, the beneficiaries

WHERE FUNDING CAN BE GIVEN UK and overseas

TYPE OF GRANT Some charities are supported for more than one year

RANGE OF GRANTS £60–£106,678

Have you read How to use the DGMT *on page xvi?*

SAMPLE GRANTS £106,678 to Oxford Centre for Hebrew and Jewish Studies; £70,500 to British Technion Society; £12,000 to Canterbury Area Crime Prevention Panel; £1,000 to Jewish Care; £7,665 to Anglo-Israel Association; £5,500 to Council for Christians and Jews; £3,000 to Friends of Boys Town Jerusalem in Great Britain; £2,000 to Institute of Jewish Policy Research; £1,500 to Israel Diaspora Trust; £1,340 to Royal Opera House Trust

FINANCES *Year* 1997 *Income* £190,767 *Grants* £226,294

TRUSTEES Kleinwort Benson Trustees Limited Directors: D H Benson, D V Clasper, K W Hotchkiss, D J McGilvray

HOW TO APPLY Only successful applicants are notified of the Trustees' decision

WHO TO APPLY TO GRP Charitable Trust, Kleinwort Benson Trustees Limited, PO Box 191, 10 Fenchurch Street, London EC3M 3LB

CC NO 255733   **ESTABLISHED** 1968

■ GWR Community Trust

WHAT IS FUNDED Furtherance of the work of charitable organisations, voluntary groups and community groups. Encouragement of new initiatives within local communities

WHO CAN BENEFIT There are no restrictions on the age; professional and economic group; family situation; religion and culture; and social circumstances of; or disease or medical condition suffered by, the beneficiaries. However, particular favour is given to volunteers

WHERE FUNDING CAN BE GIVEN Bristol, Swindon, Bath and environs, Wiltshire and radio transmission area of GWR Radio

TYPE OF GRANT For specific projects rather than for recurring expenses

FINANCES *Year* 1995 *Income* £144,119 *Grants* £70,482

TRUSTEES R MacDonnel (Chair), J Sutton (Treasurer), N Cooper, S Cooper, E Nickolls, G Gray, S Matthews, T Turvey, M Tiller, S Bateman, E Waddington, D John, N Rylance

HOW TO APPLY Application forms are available on request (send sae). Deadline for applications: 31 January – statement of accounts is required

WHO TO APPLY TO R MacDonnel, GWR Community Trust, Ivy Lodge, Frint Street, Churchill, Bristol BS19 5NB

CC NO 291284   **ESTABLISHED** 1985

■ Gabbitas, Truman and Thring Educational Trust

WHAT IS FUNDED The maintenance of an educational advisory service for students or parents or other persons or bodies responsible for the education of children or young persons. Encouragement and promotion of scholastic education by providing bursaries for children at school

WHO CAN BENEFIT Organisations benefiting children, young adults and students. Support may also be given to teachers

WHERE FUNDING CAN BE GIVEN UK

FINANCES *Year* 1997 *Income* £68,143 *Grants* £6,281

TRUSTEES J M E Bryer, R E Lucas, J B Shelly, Sir M Swann

WHO TO APPLY TO R E Lucas, Secretary, Gabbitas, Truman and Thring Educational Trust, Carrington House, 126–130 Regent Street, London W1R 6EE

CC NO 313116   **ESTABLISHED** 1963

■ Horace and Marjorie Gale Charitable Trust

WHAT IS FUNDED General charitable purposes. Trustees support Bedfordshire based charities

WHO CAN BENEFIT Registered charities. There are no restrictions on the age; professional and economic group; family situation; religion and culture; and social circumstances of; or disease or medical condition suffered by, the beneficiaries

WHERE FUNDING CAN BE GIVEN Bedfordshire, particularly North Bedfordshire

RANGE OF GRANTS £500–£11,000

SAMPLE GRANTS £11,000 to total donations to general charities; £9,000 to Bunyan Meeting Free Church – 1996; £5,000 to St Paul's Church, Bedford; £5,000 to Bedford Hospitals Charity Cygnet Appeal; £2,500 to Bedford Hospitals Trust Endowment Fund (Cardiac Department); £2,000 to Riding for the Disabled Association; £2,000 to Bedford Modern School Sixth Form appeal; £1,000 to the Baptist Union – Home Mission Fund; £1,000 to Baptist Missionary Society; £1,000 to Bedfordshire Baptist Association

FINANCES *Year* 1996 *Income* £46,722 *Grants* £50,000

TRUSTEES G D Payne, Rev R A Freestone, K Fletcher, P H Tyley

WHO TO APPLY TO M H T Johnson, Horace and Marjorie Gale Charitable Trust, 49 Brecon Way, Bedford MK41 8DD

CC NO 289212   **ESTABLISHED** 1984

■ R G Gale Charitable Trust

WHAT IS FUNDED General charitable purposes. Trustees support Bedfordshire based charities

WHO CAN BENEFIT Registered charities. There are no restrictions on the age; professional and economic group; family situation; religion and culture; and social circumstances of; or disease or medical condition suffered by, the beneficiaries

WHERE FUNDING CAN BE GIVEN Bedfordshire

RANGE OF GRANTS £500–£7,000

SAMPLE GRANTS £7,000 to Bunyan Meeting Free Church; £2,000 to Bedford Modern School Prize Fund; £1,000 to Bunyan Meeting Appeal Fund; £1,000 to St Marks Church Centre, Bedford; £1,000 to Bedfordshire NSPCC Child Protection Appeal

FINANCES *Year* 1995 *Income* £14,738 *Grants* £14,500

TRUSTEES A J Ormerod, D Watson, R G Gale, G D Payne

WHO TO APPLY TO M H T Johnson, R G Gale Charitable Trust, 49 Brecon Way, Bedford MK41 8DD

CC NO 290889   **ESTABLISHED** 1984

■ Angela Gallagher Memorial Fund

WHAT IS FUNDED Grants will be made primarily to registered charities. The aim of the fund is to help children and young people within the United Kingdom. The fund will also consider Christian, humanitarian and educational projects worldwide. Particularly charities working in the fields of: pre-school education; playgrounds and playschemes; recreation grounds; day centres; holidays and outings; Catholic bodies; social care professional bodies and community organisations will be considered

WHAT IS NOT FUNDED Donations will not be made to the following: the elderly; scientific research; hospitals and hospices; artistic and cultural appeals; animal welfare or building and equipment appeals. No grants to individuals

WHO CAN BENEFIT Registered charities benefiting: children; Christians, Roman Catholics and those suffering from paediatric diseases. Support will go to those disadvantaged by poverty; victims of war, famine and disasters; and victims of abuse

WHERE FUNDING CAN BE GIVEN UK and international organisations based in the UK

RANGE OF GRANTS Sums of £500–£3,000 are given to charities which help children. Medium sized charities which do not have access to large corporate donors are given priority

SAMPLE GRANTS £2,000 to Cardinal Hume Centre for homeless people; £1,000 to Care International; £1,000 to Casa Asuncion, Adelfos, Paraguay for street children; £1,000 to Chain of Hope for an orphanage in Eastern Europe; £1,000 to The De Paul Trust for homeless young people; £1,000 to Children with Cystic Fibrosis for holidays; £1,000 to Roses Charitable Trust; £1,000 to World Vision UK; £1,000 to Ski Tracks for children's holidays; £1,000 to West of England School for Children

FINANCES *Year* 1997 *Income* £90,667 *Grants* £39,850

TRUSTEES N A Maxwell-Lawford, OBE, Miss M E Northcote, P Mostyn, P A Wolrige Gordon

HOW TO APPLY In writing with supporting Accounts where possible. Applications will not be acknowledged

WHO TO APPLY TO N A Maxwell-Lawford, OBE, Angela Gallagher Memorial Fund, The Old Rectory, Buckerell, Honiton, Devon EX14 0EJ

CC NO 800739 **ESTABLISHED** 1989

■ The Gamlen Charitable Trust

WHAT IS FUNDED To provide for the financial assistance of law students and trainee solicitors. The relief of poverty and the advancement of education

WHO CAN BENEFIT Organisations benefiting law students, trainee solicitors, children, young adults and those disadvantaged by poverty

WHERE FUNDING CAN BE GIVEN UK

SAMPLE GRANTS £9,760 to LMH EEC Law Fellowship

FINANCES *Year* 1997 *Income* £22,228

TRUSTEES J W M Chadwick, R G Stubblefield, I R Ponsford, DFC, AFC

NOTES The Trust funds the Penningtons EC Law Fellowship at Lady Margaret Hall, Oxford

WHO TO APPLY TO R G Stubblefield, The Gamlen Charitable Trust, c/o Penningtons, Highfield, Brighton Road, Godalming, Surrey GU7 1NS

CC NO 327977 **ESTABLISHED** 1988

■ Gamma Trust

WHAT IS FUNDED General charitable purposes

WHAT IS NOT FUNDED No grants to individuals

WHO CAN BENEFIT Registered charities. There are no restrictions on the age; professional and economic group; family situation; religion and culture; and social circumstances of; or disease or medical condition suffered by, the beneficiaries

WHERE FUNDING CAN BE GIVEN Scotland

FINANCES *Year* 1998 *Grants* £54,000

HOW TO APPLY In writing to the address below

WHO TO APPLY TO Gamma Trust, c/o Clydesdale Bank, Trust and Executry Unit, PO Box 102, Brunswick House, 51 Wilson Street, Glasgow G1 1UZ

SC NO SCO 04330

■ The Ganton Furze Settlement

WHAT IS FUNDED General specifically named charities

WHO CAN BENEFIT There are no restrictions on the age; professional and economic group; family situation; religion and culture; and social circumstances of; or disease or medical condition suffered by, the beneficiaries

WHERE FUNDING CAN BE GIVEN UK

TYPE OF GRANT At the discretion of the Trustees

FINANCES *Year* 1997 *Income* £35,687 *Grants* £42,000

TRUSTEES David Evans, James Campbell

WHO TO APPLY TO D Evans, The Ganton Furze Settlement, 41 Park Square, Leeds LS1 2NS *Tel* 0113-244 5000

CC NO 326719 **ESTABLISHED** 1984

■ Ganzoni Charitable Trust

WHAT IS FUNDED General charitable purposes

WHAT IS NOT FUNDED Grants to individuals will not be considered

WHO CAN BENEFIT There are no restrictions on the age; professional and economic group; family situation; religion and culture; and social circumstances of; or disease or medical condition suffered by, the beneficiaries

WHERE FUNDING CAN BE GIVEN Suffolk

TYPE OF GRANT A number of the grants are recurring, the remainder will normally be one-off

RANGE OF GRANTS £50–£10,000

FINANCES *Year* 1996–97 *Income* £56,665 *Grants* £468,880

TRUSTEES Hon Mary J Ganzoni, Rt Hon John Julian (Second Baron Belstead of Ipswich), Stephen Wilson, Hon Charles Boscawen

NOTES Applications from outside Suffolk are not normally considered and will not be acknowledged

HOW TO APPLY To the address under Who To Apply To in writing. Telephone calls not encouraged. There is no application form, guidelines or deadlines. No sae is required unless material is to be returned

WHO TO APPLY TO S R M Wilson, Ganzoni Charitable Trust, Messrs Birketts, 24–26 Museum Street, Ipswich, Suffolk IP1 1HZ *Tel* 01473 232300

CC NO 263583 **ESTABLISHED** 1971

■ The Gapper Trust

WHAT IS FUNDED General charitable purposes, however the Trustees do not welcome applications

WHAT IS NOT FUNDED Applications from individuals and organisations not previously selected by the Trustees

WHO CAN BENEFIT Individuals and organisations previously selected by the Trustees. There are no restrictions on the age; professional and economic group; family situation; religion and culture; and social circumstances of; or disease or medical condition suffered by, the beneficiaries

WHERE FUNDING CAN BE GIVEN UK

FINANCES *Year* 1998 *Income* £25,000 *Grants* £15,000

TRUSTEES R P Gapper, R F Gapper, M C Gapper

HOW TO APPLY **This Trust states that it does not respond to unsolicited applications**

WHO TO APPLY TO R P Gapper, The Gapper Trust, 2 Millers Court, Chiswick Mall, London W4 2PF

CC NO 328623 **ESTABLISHED** 1990

■ The Bernard & Vera Garbacz Charitable Trust

WHAT IS FUNDED In practice largely Jewish caring and educational charities. Funding may also be given to opera companies and orchestras, information technology and computers

WHAT IS NOT FUNDED No grants for travel bursaries

WHO CAN BENEFIT Institutions benefiting people of all ages, students and Jewish people

WHERE FUNDING CAN BE GIVEN UK

TYPE OF GRANT One-off

SAMPLE GRANTS £5,250 to Hasmonean Boys Grammar School for an Information Technology Unit; £3,574 to Finchley Synagogue for general amenities; £1,410 to Child Resettlement Fund for welfare of young children; £1,196 to Jewish Care for care of the elderly; £1,115 to North West London Jewish Day School for general amenities

FINANCES *Year* 1997 *Income* £22,714
Grants £20,486

TRUSTEES Mrs V Garbacz, D J Garbacz

WHO TO APPLY TO Mrs V Garbacz, The Bernard & Vera Garbacz Charitable Trust, 1 Chessington Avenue, Finchley, London N3 3DS

CC NO 274766   **ESTABLISHED** 1980

■ Gardner's Trust for the Blind

WHAT IS FUNDED To assist blind persons and where possible organisations for the blind in England and Wales. (The Trustees give first priority to poor lonely blind people)

WHO CAN BENEFIT Registered blind and partially sighted persons in England and Wales, with occasional help to organisations for the blind

WHERE FUNDING CAN BE GIVEN England and Wales

FINANCES *Year* 1997 *Income* £70,097
Grants £46,834

TRUSTEES The Rt Hon The Earl of Shannon, A M Burnett Brown, The Rt Hon The Viscount Gough, D F A Trewby

NOTES Grants awarded in 1997: music grants £162; education and trade grants £17,230; general aid £2,493; Gardner pensions £24,135; Lord pensions £2,554; and Rashdale pensions £260

WHO TO APPLY TO Miss Angela Stewart, Gardner's Trust for the Blind, St Bartholomew Chambers, 61 West Smithfield, London EC1A 9DY

CC NO 207233   **ESTABLISHED** 1882

■ Gargrave Poor's Land

WHAT IS FUNDED Welfare particularly charities working in the fields of: the relief of sickness; help with travel expenses; the provision of holiday relief: the provision of essential items of bedding, furniture, fuel or food, etc; costs of study; and the relief of temporary distress

WHO CAN BENEFIT Individuals and organisations benefiting: people of all ages and those disadvantaged by poverty. There is no restriction on the disease or medical condition suffered by the beneficiaries. Residents of Gargrave and adjoining parishes only

WHERE FUNDING CAN BE GIVEN The parishes of Gargrave, Flasby, Eshton, Winterburn, Bank Newton and Coniston Cold

TYPE OF GRANT Capital, one-off, recurring and running costs will be considered

SAMPLE GRANTS £11,080 for distribution at Christmas to the poor, needy and elderly; £612 to cover playgroup fees enabling needy children to be looked after; £400 to CAB; £225 for assistance to children for school dinners, etc; £160 for a ramp for the disabled

FINANCES *Year* 1995 *Income* £20,747
Grants £12,462

TRUSTEES Rev M Bull, MA, J Collis, Mrs V G Fletcher, J Maud, Mrs B M Wood

HOW TO APPLY To the address under Who To Apply To in writing

WHO TO APPLY TO Mrs B M Wood, Gargrave Poor's Land, 9 Meadow Croft, Gargrave, Skipton, North Yorkshire BD23 3SN *Tel* 01756 749466

CC NO 225067   **ESTABLISHED** 1964

■ The Garnett Charitable Trust

WHAT IS FUNDED Health aid; hospices; environmental causes; arts, culture and recreation

WHAT IS NOT FUNDED No grants to individuals

WHO CAN BENEFIT To benefit actors and entertainment professionals; musicians; textile workers and designers; writers and poets. There is no restriction on the disease or medical condition suffered by the beneficiaries

WHERE FUNDING CAN BE GIVEN South West, Channel Islands and Northern Ireland

RANGE OF GRANTS £5–£10,000

SAMPLE GRANTS £10,000 to Bristol Initiative Charitable Trust; £5,000 to Bristol Community Growth and Support; £4,030 to Jackdaws Educational Trust; £3,500 to Fundacion Yannich Y Ben Jahober; £2,000 to the Royal Opera House; £1,000 to St Michael's Parish; £1,000 to St Vincent de Paul; £1,000 to Ireland Fund; £1,000 to the Ireland Fund of Great Britain; £600 to Shelter

FINANCES *Year* 1997 *Income* £28,455
Grants £26,980

TRUSTEES A J F Garnett, Mrs P Garnett, J W Sharpe

HOW TO APPLY In writing

WHO TO APPLY TO J W Sharpe, The Garnett Charitable Trust, Osborne Clarke Solicitors, 50 Queen Charlotte Street, Bristol BS1 4HE *Tel* 0117-923 0220

CC NO 327847   **ESTABLISHED** 1988

■ The John and Daisy Garrod Memorial Charitable Trust

WHAT IS FUNDED The general benefit of the Parochial Church Council of St. Catherines, Preston-next-Faversham and other charitable purposes at the discretion of the Trustees

WHO CAN BENEFIT At the discretion of the Trustees. There are no restrictions on the age; professional and economic group; family situation; religion and culture; and social circumstances of; or disease or medical condition suffered by, the beneficiaries

WHERE FUNDING CAN BE GIVEN UK and overseas

TYPE OF GRANT At the discretion of the Trustees

FINANCES *Year* 1995 *Income* £40,383

TRUSTEES G L Mead, M S Day, Rev C S Wilson, J M Matthews, K Tullett

WHO TO APPLY TO S E A Wolfe, The John and Daisy Garrod Memorial Charitable Trust, Furley, Page, Fielding & Barton Solicitors, 39 St Margarets Street, Canterbury, Kent CT1 2TX

CC NO 1052848   **ESTABLISHED** 1996

■ Garthgwynion Charities

WHAT IS FUNDED The Trustees' main areas of interest are: (a) the leading national charities conducting research into cancer, sight or disorders of the nervous system; (b) community projects or individuals with a Welsh (better still Mid-Wales) link, having either a social or artistic purpose

WHO CAN BENEFIT Organisations benefiting those suffering from various diseases and medical conditions, including Alzheimer's disease, cancers and Parkinson's disease. Support is also given to at risk groups, those disadvantaged by poverty and socially isolated people

WHERE FUNDING CAN BE GIVEN Primarily parishes of Isygarreg and Uwchygarreg at Machynlleth, Powys

RANGE OF GRANTS £250–£30,000

SAMPLE GRANTS £30,000 to Machynlleth Tabernacle Trust; £1,000 to Montgomeryshire Society Schools Appeal; £500 to Montgomeryshire Music Festival; £500 to Independent Chapel, Gaspwll; £500 to Equilibre; £500 to Citizens Advice Bureau; £5,000 to Powys Challenge Trust; £250 to Manafon Church Appeal Fund; £250 to Upper Montgomeryshire Presbytery

FINANCES *Year* 1997 *Income* £39,854
Grants £34,000

TRUSTEES Mrs E R Lambert, D H O Owen, E C O Owen

WHO TO APPLY TO The Secretary, Garthgwynion Charities, 13 Osborne Close, Hanworth, Middlesex TW13 6SR

CC NO 229334   **ESTABLISHED** 1963

■ The Cecil Gee Charitable Trust

WHAT IS FUNDED Trustees prefer Jewish causes
WHO CAN BENEFIT To benefit Jewish people
WHERE FUNDING CAN BE GIVEN UK and overseas
RANGE OF GRANTS £100–£3,925
SAMPLE GRANTS £3,925 to United Synagogue; £3,065 to British ORT; £3,000 to Norwood Ravenswood; £2,450 to Jewish Care; £1,000 to Friends of the Hebrew University of Jerusalem
FINANCES *Year* 1997 *Income* £16,231
Grants £14,932
TRUSTEES A Gee, M J Gee, FCA, R J Gee, N D Gee, D F Sharpe, FCA
HOW TO APPLY Telephone or written requests rarely receive much attention
WHO TO APPLY TO D F Sharpe, The Cecil Gee Charitable Trust, Messrs Sharpe Fairbrother, 67–69 George Street, London W1H 5PJ
CC NO 290421   **ESTABLISHED** 1984

■ The Jacqueline and Michael Gee Charitable Trust

WHAT IS FUNDED General charitable purposes
WHO CAN BENEFIT There are no restrictions on the age; professional and economic group; family situation; religion and culture; and social circumstances of; or disease or medical condition suffered by, the beneficiaries
WHERE FUNDING CAN BE GIVEN UK
WHO TO APPLY TO M J Gee, FCA, Chairperson, The Jacqueline and Michael Gee Charitable Trust, 27 Berkeley House, Hay Hill, Berkeley Square, London W1X 7LG
CC NO 1062566   **ESTABLISHED** 1997

■ The Gelston Charitable Trust

WHAT IS FUNDED The promotion of the Christian Gospel, compassion for individuals, this includes campaigning on social issues
WHAT IS NOT FUNDED No building appeals, general appeals, appeals from the South of England
WHO CAN BENEFIT Individuals who are engaged in promoting the Christian gospel and compassionate work including people of all ages; academics; clergy; medical professionals, musicians; students, teachers and governesses; unemployed people; volunteers; those in care, fostered and adopted; parents and children; one parent families; widows and widowers; Baptists; Christians; Church of England; Evangelists; Methodists and Roman Catholics
WHERE FUNDING CAN BE GIVEN Projects originating in Scotland
TYPE OF GRANT One-off, project, recurring and running costs. Support is given for up to or more than three years
RANGE OF GRANTS £600–£10,000
SAMPLE GRANTS £10,000 to MECO Middle East Christian Outreach for work in the Middle East; £8,500 to YWAM/Wycliff Translators to support individuals; £4,000 to 2 Timothy 2 Trust for work in Africa; £2,000 to YWAM Youth with a Mission for a project in Nepal; £2,000 to YWAM Youth with a Mission for work in Romania; £1,200 to YWAM Youth with a Mission for work in Scotland; £200 to National Children's Safety for Drugs Education in local schools
FINANCES *Year* 1997 *Income* £30,000
Grants £33,715
TRUSTEES A D Scott, Mrs A D Scott
NOTES **Most funds are currently committed to long term projects**
HOW TO APPLY No application form needed. The Trustees meet bi-annually and do not acknowledge all applications
WHO TO APPLY TO Mrs A D Scott, The Gelston Charitable Trust, Gelston House, Castle Douglas, Kirkcudbright DG7 1QE
CC NO 801450   **ESTABLISHED** 1987

■ Gemini Radio Charitable Trust

WHAT IS FUNDED Capital projects for a specific purpose, eg items of equipment, to the benefit of the maximum number of people. Priority is given to disabled people, elderly people and youth. Funding will be given to charities working in the fields of: education and training; community services and facilities; health facilities and buildings; and the arts. Support may also go to information technology and computers; community development; support of voluntary and community organisations; social care professional bodies and volunteer bureaux
WHAT IS NOT FUNDED No grants to individuals
WHO CAN BENEFIT Organisations benefiting people of all ages, volunteers and disabled people
WHERE FUNDING CAN BE GIVEN Devon, Dorset and Somerset within the listening area of Gemini Radio
TYPE OF GRANT Capital for a specific purpose. One-off and project may be considered. Funding can be given for up to one year
RANGE OF GRANTS £50–£3,000, average grant £750

SAMPLE GRANTS £3,000 to FLEET for ambulance equipment; £1,346 to DYAL towards IT equipment for disabled; £1,300 to SPLASH for play equipment; £1,000 to Sidmouth Inshore Rescue Service for life saving equipment; £1,000 to Exeter Children's Orchestra for instruments

FINANCES *Year* 1997–98 *Income* £23,117 *Grants* £10,680

TRUSTEES M Anstey, C Edwards, K Kane, G P Lawrence, M O'Brien, R D Pocock, C Slade

HOW TO APPLY In writing giving details of beneficiary and requirement

WHO TO APPLY TO Lt Col G P Lawrence, Gemini Radio Charitable Trust, c/o Gemini Radio Ltd, Hawthorn House, Exeter Business Park, Exeter, Devon EX1 3QS *Tel* 01392 444444

CC NO 1045212   **ESTABLISHED** 1995

■ The General Nursing Council for England and Wales Trust

WHAT IS FUNDED To make grants where appropriate, to public bodies undertaking research into matters directly affecting nursing or the nursing profession

WHAT IS NOT FUNDED No grants to individuals

WHO CAN BENEFIT Universities and other public bodies benefiting nurses

WHERE FUNDING CAN BE GIVEN England and Wales

TYPE OF GRANT One-off or annually towards research costs

FINANCES *Year* 1997 *Income* £171,869 *Grants* £101,500

TRUSTEES Dr Z E Oxlade, CBE (Chairman), Prof J E Hooper, CBE, Miss M E Uprichard, OBE, S W Jones, OBE, Prof W de Witt

PUBLICATIONS Annual Report

HOW TO APPLY By September each year

WHO TO APPLY TO Mrs P A Bovington, The General Nursing Council for England and Wales Trust, 36 Sunningdale Avenue, Eastcote, Ruislip, Middlesex HA4 9SR

CC NO 288068   **ESTABLISHED** 1983

■ The Gertner Charitable Trust

WHAT IS FUNDED Jewish organisations and individuals

WHO CAN BENEFIT Jewish people

WHERE FUNDING CAN BE GIVEN UK and overseas

TYPE OF GRANT One-off

RANGE OF GRANTS £36–£86,000

SAMPLE GRANTS £86,000 to American Friends of Yad Haron; £17,500 to Tzemach Tzedek; £12,850 to Beis Yechiel; £10,250 to Torah and Chesed Limited; £10,120 to Emuna Educational Centre; £6,000 to Jewish Educational Fund; £5,200 to Yad Aharon; £4,000 to Pardes House School; £3,980 to Kisharon; £3,000 to Aneni

FINANCES *Year* 1997 *Income* £352,744 *Grants* £188,258

TRUSTEES Mrs M Gertner, M Gertner, E Moshan

HOW TO APPLY To the address under Who To Apply To in writing

WHO TO APPLY TO Mrs M Gertner, The Gertner Charitable Trust, Fordgate, 1 Allsop Place, London NW1 5LF

CC NO 327380   **ESTABLISHED** 1987

■ The Gibbins Trust

WHAT IS FUNDED This Trust will consider funding: residential facilities and services; personnel and human resources; support to voluntary and community organisations; social care and

professional bodies; hospices, medical centres and rehabilitation centres; cancer and MS research; special schools and special needs education. Community services, community centres and village halls are also considered. Grants to organisations principally in the County of Sussex but also at national level, within England and Wales. Not Scotland or overseas

WHAT IS NOT FUNDED Time Charity. No grants to individuals

WHO CAN BENEFIT Medicine and health in general including the handicapped and carers. Charities active in the relief of hardship particularly those aimed at the very young and the very old

WHERE FUNDING CAN BE GIVEN Mainly Sussex, but also national level within England and Wales

TYPE OF GRANT Recurring and one-off grants. Funding is available for up to and over three years

RANGE OF GRANTS £50–£10,000, typical grant £300

SAMPLE GRANTS £5,600 to Carr Gomm Society for Hyde Gardens, Eastbourne, home for the homeless; £5,000 to Juvenile Diabetes Foundation UK for special grants to research programme; £2,250 to St Barnabas Home for their Centenary Appeal; £2,000 to Chichester Cathedral Trust as a regular donation; £2,000 to Sussex Housing Association for the Aged for their Anniversary Appeal; £1,500 to Age Concern, East Sussex as a regular donation; £1,500 to Age Concern, West Sussex as a regular donation; £1,350 to West Sussex Association for the Blind as a regular donation; £1,350 to League of Friends Lewes Victoria Hospital as a regular donation; £1,300 to Counsel 4 Care for the Elderly for the Elderly Invalids Fund

FINANCES *Year* 1998 *Income* £47,092 *Grants* £60,500

TRUSTEES R F Ash, R S Archer, P M Archer

NOTES The Trustees meet twice yearly, normally in May and November, when appeals are considered

HOW TO APPLY In writing to the address under Who To Apply To with full details of their organisation including accounts available. Applications will not be acknowledged

WHO TO APPLY TO R F Ash, The Gibbins Trust, 5 East Pallant, Chichester, West Sussex PO19 1TS *Tel* 01243 786111 *Fax* 01243 532001

CC NO 244632   **ESTABLISHED** 1965

■ The Gibbs Charitable Trusts

WHAT IS FUNDED Primarily to support Methodist charities; also areas of social or educational concern. Grants are normally made to projects of which the Trustees have personal knowledge

WHAT IS NOT FUNDED Individuals cannot be supported

WHO CAN BENEFIT Organisations benefiting Methodists

WHERE FUNDING CAN BE GIVEN Africa. Bristol and Lambeth in the UK

TYPE OF GRANT Buildings, capital and project will be considered

RANGE OF GRANTS Almost all grants in range £500–£10,000

SAMPLE GRANTS £10,000 to Charles Wesley Heritage Centre, Bristol for purchase of harpsichord; £10,000 to Riding Lights for purchase of premises; £10,000 to Rowledge Methodist Church for property restoration and development; £8,000 to Archives and History Committee for purchase of portrait for Charles Wesley Heritage Centre; £8,000 to Christian Aid especially regarding Jubilee 2000; £7,500 to Friends of Glyn Vivian Art Gallery for support for publication; £5,000 to Farrington's School Special Fund for Eastern Europe for scholarship; £5,000 to Amelia Farm Trust for support of worker with community for disadvantaged; £4,300 to Victoria Methodist Church, Bristol for lighting equipment and church funds; £3,000 to OXFAM for project in Malawi
FINANCES *Year* 1998 *Income* £78,006 *Grants* £105,200
TRUSTEES Mrs S M N Gibbs, J M Gibbs, J N Gibbs, A G Gibbs, W M Gibbs, J E Gibbs, S E Gibbs
HOW TO APPLY No calls, no forms, no guidelines, no deadlines. Sae's not necessary. Normally only successful applicants receive letters
WHO TO APPLY TO Dr James Gibbs, Secretary, The Gibbs Charitable Trust, 8 Victoria Square, Clifton, Bristol BS8 4ET
CC NO 207997　　　　**ESTABLISHED** 1946

■ The William Gibbs Trust

WHAT IS FUNDED To advance education amongst children and young persons. The provision of scholarships, assisting parents with school fees, the payment of travel expenses for educational purposes, the provision of equipment and books for schools
WHO CAN BENEFIT Individuals and organisations benefiting children and young adults
WHERE FUNDING CAN BE GIVEN UK
SAMPLE GRANTS £2,500 to an individual; £2,000 to National Hospitals College for speech science; £2,000 to an individual; £1,000 to an individual; £593 to an individual
FINANCES *Year* 1995 *Income* £14,727 *Grants* £8,593
TRUSTEES Lady Aldenham, Mrs A Johnson
HOW TO APPLY To the address under Who To Apply To in writing
WHO TO APPLY TO Mrs Antonia Johnson, The William Gibbs Trust, Manor Farm, Middle Chinnock, Crewkerne, Somerset TA18 7PN
CC NO 282957　　　　**ESTABLISHED** 1981

■ Edith Bessie Gibson Trust

WHAT IS FUNDED Depending on the funds available, donations are made to specific Catholic causes usually of an educational nature
WHAT IS NOT FUNDED No grants to individuals
WHO CAN BENEFIT Only persons or causes whose applications come under the terms of the Trust are considered. In future grants will be made only to Catholic colleges, not private individuals (ie students would need to apply to, eg a college bursar)
WHERE FUNDING CAN BE GIVEN UK
TYPE OF GRANT One-off, project and research will be considered
RANGE OF GRANTS £500–£1,000
FINANCES *Year* 1997–98 *Grants* £5,000
NOTES This Trust is already heavily committed
HOW TO APPLY By letter only, include sae
WHO TO APPLY TO Edith Gibson Trust, Carmelite Monastery, Quidenham, Norfolk NR16 2PH
CC NO 233277　　　　**ESTABLISHED** 1947

■ The Hon H M T Gibson's Charity Trust

WHAT IS FUNDED General charitable purposes
WHAT IS NOT FUNDED No grants to individuals
WHO CAN BENEFIT Registered charities only. There are no restrictions on the age; professional and economic group; family situation; religion and culture; and social circumstances of; or disease or medical condition suffered by, the beneficiaries
WHERE FUNDING CAN BE GIVEN UK and overseas
RANGE OF GRANTS £16–£5,370
SAMPLE GRANTS £5,370 to London City Ballet; £5,000 to National Arts Collection; £1,250 to Derby Children's Hospital; £150 to Derby Cathedral Endowment Fund; £100 to Scottish Conservation Projects
FINANCES *Year* 1996 *Income* £14,034 *Grants* £12,227
TRUSTEES The Cowdray Trust Limited
NOTES The Trust's funds are currently fully allocated
HOW TO APPLY **This Trust states that it does not respond to unsolicited applications**
WHO TO APPLY TO The Secretary, The Hon H M T Gibson's Charity Trust, The Cowdray Trust Limited, Pollen House, 10–12 Cork Street, London W1X 1PD
CC NO 264327　　　　**ESTABLISHED** 1972

■ The Hon W K Gibson's Charity Trust

WHAT IS FUNDED General charitable purposes
WHAT IS NOT FUNDED No grants to individuals. Registered charities only
WHO CAN BENEFIT Registered charities only. There are no restrictions on the age; professional and economic group; family situation; religion and culture; and social circumstances of; or disease or medical condition suffered by, the beneficiaries
WHERE FUNDING CAN BE GIVEN UK
RANGE OF GRANTS £16–£500
SAMPLE GRANTS £500 to Great Ormond Street Children's Hospital; £500 to NSPCC; £500 to Notting Hill Housing Trust; £500 to Runnymede Trust; £500 to Soane Monuments Trust
FINANCES *Year* 1996 *Income* £14,179 *Grants* £3,616
TRUSTEES The Cowdray Trust Limited
NOTES Applications for grants will only be acknowledged if a donation is to be sent
HOW TO APPLY Appeal letters should be sent to the address under Who To Apply To
WHO TO APPLY TO The Secretary, The Hon W K Gibson's Charity Trust, The Cowdray Trust Limited, Pollen House, 10–12 Cork Street, London W1X 1PD
CC NO 268846　　　　**ESTABLISHED** 1974

■ The Miss Agnes Gilchrist Adamson's Trust

WHAT IS FUNDED The provision of grants to organisations providing holidays for groups or individual children aged 16 years and under with a physical or mental disability
WHAT IS NOT FUNDED Beneficiaries must be aged 16 years and under
WHO CAN BENEFIT Disabled children under the age of 16
WHERE FUNDING CAN BE GIVEN Scotland
TYPE OF GRANT One-off
FINANCES *Year* 1996 *Income* £50,000 *Grants* £40,000

244

Think carefully about every application. Is it justified?

HOW TO APPLY To the address under Who To Apply To in writing, including details of the organisation, the number of children who will benefit and the proposed holiday

WHO TO APPLY TO Neil Drysdale, The Miss Agnes Gilchrist Adamson's Trust, Messrs Drysdale Anderson WS, 14 Comrie Street, Crieff, Perthshire PH7 4AZ

SC NO SCO 37871   **ESTABLISHED** 1946

■ Gilchrist Educational Trust

WHAT IS FUNDED May be varied from time to time but at present: (a) applications are considered from students who are within sight of the end of a degree or higher education course and are facing unexpected financial difficulties which may prevent completion of it: also from students who are required to spend a short period studying abroad as part of their course; (b) funds are offered to recognised British University Expeditions; (c) the Gilchrist Expedition Award of £10,000 is offered every two years for the best overseas research proposal by a small team of qualified scientists or academics; (d) funds are available for pioneer educational organisations

WHAT IS NOT FUNDED Assistance is not offered to part-time students; students who are entitled to a mandatory grant or loan; students seeking help in meeting the cost of maintaining dependants; students who have to complete part of a course at their own expense because they have used up part of a mandatory grant on earlier, unsuccessful studies; students who are obliged to re-take part of their course; those seeking funds to enable them to take up a place on a degree or higher education course; those wishing to go abroad on exploratory or educational projects such as Operation Raleigh

WHO CAN BENEFIT Individuals and organisations benefiting students, academics and research workers

WHERE FUNDING CAN BE GIVEN UK and overseas, but Trust's power to apply funds outside the UK is very rarely exercised

TYPE OF GRANT One-off and research

RANGE OF GRANTS In 1997–98, 41 individual students were awarded Adult Study Grants – average £504; 11 individual students were awarded Travel Study Grants – average £295; 33 university expeditions were awarded grants – average £455; 11 organisations received awards – average £1,090

FINANCES *Year* 1997–98 *Income* £77,070
Grants £53,810

TRUSTEES The Rt Hon Lord Holderness (Chairman), Miss J M Sims, MA, Lord Shuttleworth, DL, FRICS, Dr John Hemming, CMG, DLitt

NOTES All applicants are advised to write in preference to telephoning, as the office is staffed part-time only

HOW TO APPLY Individual grant-seekers should send a brief description of their circumstances, enclosing an sae. Those who appear to be eligible will be sent a list of information needed to enable an application to be considered in detail. Applications from individuals are considered throughout the year. University expeditions should write requesting an application form, which must be completed and returned by 28 February. Applications for the Gilchrist £10,000 Expedition Award must be submitted by 15 March in even-numbered years; guidelines are available. The deadline for applications from organisations is 31 March

WHO TO APPLY TO Mrs Everidge, Secretary, Gilchrist Educational Trust, Mary Trevelyan Hall, 10 York Terrace East, London NW1 4PT

CC NO 313877   **ESTABLISHED** 1865

■ The Gilgal Project

WHAT IS FUNDED Promoting Christian spiritual teaching; relieving single homeless women; relieving children who are in conditions of need, hardship and distress; relieving persons suffering from disabilities of old age or physical handicap; providing suitable accommodation for those in need or adapting housing to meet the needs of the disabled

WHO CAN BENEFIT Organisations benefiting children in need, Christians, elderly people, disabled people and single homeless women

WHERE FUNDING CAN BE GIVEN Birmingham

SAMPLE GRANTS £40,935 to Mercian Housing Association

FINANCES *Year* 1997 *Income* £57,137
Grants £40,935

WHO TO APPLY TO B M Nicholls, The Gilgal Project, 370 Court Oak Road, Harbourne, Birmingham B32 2DY

CC NO 1045812   **ESTABLISHED** 1991

■ The Gilks Trust

WHAT IS FUNDED Medical equipment for hospitals and health centres in the area Where Funding Can Be Given. Schools are also considered for funding

WHO CAN BENEFIT Individuals, organisations, local hospitals and medical centres benefiting people of all ages. There is no restriction on the disease or medical condition suffered by the beneficiaries

WHERE FUNDING CAN BE GIVEN West Yorkshire

RANGE OF GRANTS £86–£3,500

SAMPLE GRANTS £3,500 to Pinderfields Day Care Centre; £2,378 to Normanton Talking Newspaper; £1,895 to an individual for a chairlift; £1,560 to Mayor of Wakefield's Appeal for syringe and pump; £1,100 to Field Lane School

FINANCES *Year* 1997 *Income* £18,942
Grants £17,673

TRUSTEES Mrs L M Box, S Gilks, J Walkden

HOW TO APPLY To the address under Who To Apply To in writing

WHO TO APPLY TO Mrs L M Box, Clerk, The Gilks Trust, Bank House, Burton Street, Wakefield WF1 2DA

CC NO 1041285   **ESTABLISHED** 1994

■ The L & R Gilley Charitable Trust

WHAT IS FUNDED Preference for care of the elderly, the ill and the handicapped

WHAT IS NOT FUNDED No grants to individuals

WHO CAN BENEFIT Registered charities benefiting older people; retired and disabled people. There is no restriction on the disease or medical condition suffered by the beneficiaries

WHERE FUNDING CAN BE GIVEN Primarily Devon and Birmingham

SAMPLE GRANTS £100,000 to Age Concern; £1,000 to Motor Neurone Disease Association; £10,000 to RNIB; £7,500 to Precinct Project; £7,500 to Midland Spastic Association; £7,500 to Torbay Hospital League of Friends; £5,000 to Cancer Research Campaign; £3,000 to Torbay Blind Persons Club

FINANCES *Year* 1996 *Income* £59,000
Grants £63,080

Does the trust you have chosen match your needs? Haphazard applications waste postage and time

245

TRUSTEES J R Bettinson, R A Bettinson, Yvonne Garfield-Smith

HOW TO APPLY Each July. Not acknowledged

WHO TO APPLY TO Miss C M Tempest, The L & R Gilley Charitable Trust, 6 The Farthings, Harborne, Birmingham B17 0HQ *Tel* 0121-244 3258 *Fax* 0121-244 3269

CC NO 297127   ESTABLISHED 1987

■ The Gillham Charitable Trust

WHAT IS FUNDED Christian, welfare, medical and educational charitable purposes. Particularly charities working in the fields of: Christian education; Christian outreach; hospitals; and engineering research

WHO CAN BENEFIT Organisation benefiting: academics; clergy; medical professionals; research workers; students and Church of England

WHERE FUNDING CAN BE GIVEN UK, especially north east England

RANGE OF GRANTS £200–£1,000

FINANCES *Year* 1996–97 *Income* £17,000 *Grants* £11,000

TRUSTEES A J Gillham, Mrs S M Gillham

HOW TO APPLY To the address under Who To Apply To in writing

WHO TO APPLY TO A J Gillham, Trustee, The Gillham Charitable Trust, The Grange, Chop Gate, Middlesbrough, Cleveland TS9 7LB *Tel* 01439 798351

CC NO 1000727   ESTABLISHED 1990

■ Horace Gillman's Trust

WHAT IS FUNDED Grants are given to support the work of several bird charities, reserves and an observatory

WHERE FUNDING CAN BE GIVEN UK, particularly Scotland, also Ireland

FINANCES *Year* 1997 *Income* £20,000 *Grants* £10,000

TRUSTEES J K Burleigh, R G Ritchie, F Hamilton

HOW TO APPLY Applications should be made in writing to the address below

WHO TO APPLY TO J K Burleigh, Horace Gillman's Trust, 31–32 Moray Place, Edinburgh EH3 6BZ

SC NO SCO 17672   ESTABLISHED 1979

■ The John Gilpin Trust

WHAT IS FUNDED Preference is given to charities carrying out work in the Cumbria and Merseyside areas

WHAT IS NOT FUNDED Unsolicited applications will usually not be considered as funds are normally committed to projects known to the Trustees. No applications are entertained from individuals

WHO CAN BENEFIT There are no restrictions on the age; professional and economic group; family situation; religion and culture; and social circumstances of; or disease or medical condition suffered by, the beneficiaries

WHERE FUNDING CAN BE GIVEN England

TYPE OF GRANT Both recurrent and one-off

RANGE OF GRANTS £300–£1,500

SAMPLE GRANTS £1,500 to 1st Southwold Scout Group; £1,500 to Southwold and Alderburgh Theatre Trust; £500 to Suffolk Deaf Association; £500 to RNLI; £500 to Wallasey Scout Group; £500 to Liverpool One Parent Family; £500 to St Vincents School for the Blind and Partially Sighted Children; £500 to Kensington Citizens Advice Bureau; £500 to Tranmere Alliance; £500 to Victims of Alliance

FINANCES *Year* 1997 *Income* £26,422 *Grants* £10,900

TRUSTEES D J Gaffney, A T Powley

NOTES Assistance to Service and museum appeals are of interest

HOW TO APPLY Trustees will not normally consider unsolicited applications. The Trustees regret that they are not able to reply to unsuccessful applications. No saes please

WHO TO APPLY TO J Gaffney, The John Gilpin Trust, 1 Market Place, Southwold, Suffolk IP18 6DY

CC NO 276710   ESTABLISHED 1959

■ The Girdlers' Company Charitable Trust

WHAT IS FUNDED Trustees prefer medical and educational charities

WHAT IS NOT FUNDED No grants to individuals

WHO CAN BENEFIT Registered charities benefiting children, young adults, academics, students and teachers. There is no restriction on the disease or medical condition suffered by the beneficiaries

WHERE FUNDING CAN BE GIVEN UK

FINANCES *Year* 1996 *Income* £156,343 *Grants* £12,500

TRUSTEES The Master and Wardens or Keepers of the Art or Mystery of Girdlers, London: C E Grace, Sir Gordon Pirie, CVO, CBE, DL, D R L James, A R Westall, M H Sherrard, Sir David Burnett, MBE, TD, Sir Michael Newton, Bart, Col L A T Dennis, MBE, TD, MW, N K Maitland, B D Moul, Dr D N Seaton, A J R Fairclough, Rt Hon Viscount Brentford, I P R James, Capt G M A James, RN, T J Straker, P F D Trimingham, J S Maitland, P V Straker, Sir Thomas Crawley-Boevey, Bart, I W Fairclough, J P F Reeve, MA, FRSA, S V Straker, J Westall

WHO TO APPLY TO The Clerk to The Girdlers' Company, The Girdlers' Company Charitable Trust, Girdlers' Hall, Basinghall Avenue, London EC2V 5DD

CC NO 328026   ESTABLISHED 1988

■ The Gladiator Trust

WHAT IS FUNDED The advancement of the Christian religion in the City of Oxford

WHO CAN BENEFIT Local organisations benefiting Christians

WHERE FUNDING CAN BE GIVEN Oxford

FINANCES *Year* 1997 *Income* £14,887 *Grants* £1,500

HOW TO APPLY To the address under Who To Apply To

WHO TO APPLY TO J Joyce, Secretary, The Gladiator Trust, 102 Cherwell Drive, Old Marston, Oxford OX3 0NA

CC NO 236740   ESTABLISHED 1960

■ The E W Gladstone Charitable Trust

WHAT IS FUNDED General charitable purposes. Charities founded by or connected with members of the Gladstone family

WHAT IS NOT FUNDED No grants to individuals or for expeditions

WHO CAN BENEFIT Registered charities. There are no restrictions on the age; professional and economic group; family situation; religion and culture; and social circumstances of; or disease or medical condition suffered by, the beneficiaries

WHERE FUNDING CAN BE GIVEN Mainly Flintshire and Kincardineshire

RANGE OF GRANTS £25–£3,000

FINANCES *Year* 1996–97 *Income* £15,310 *Grants* £15,110

TRUSTEES Sir William Gladstone, Lady R A Gladstone

NOTES No reply signifies no grant

HOW TO APPLY In writing. Telephone calls are not welcome

WHO TO APPLY TO Sir William Gladstone, The E W Gladstone Charitable Trust, Hawarden Castle, Flintshire CH5 3PB

CC NO 260417   **ESTABLISHED** 1969

■ The Glasgow-Kilmun Society

WHAT IS FUNDED Grants are given in order to provide recuperative holidays and places in convalescent homes via organisations and directly to individuals

WHO CAN BENEFIT Disabled people and those disadvantaged by poverty. There are no restrictions on the age of, or disease or medical condition suffered by, the beneficiaries

WHERE FUNDING CAN BE GIVEN Glasgow

FINANCES *Year* 1994–95 *Income* £13,000 *Grants* £15,000

HOW TO APPLY Applications should be made in writing to the address below

WHO TO APPLY TO James Smillie, Secretary, The Glasgow-Kilmun Society, The City of Glasgow Society of Social Service, 30 George Square, Glasgow G2 1EG

SC NO SCO 10175

■ Glass House Trust

WHAT IS FUNDED Childcare services, mental health of children and young people, research and policy development in fields of children and education, family welfare and parenting

WHO CAN BENEFIT Organisations working with children and families

WHERE FUNDING CAN BE GIVEN UK

RANGE OF GRANTS £300–£66,050

SAMPLE GRANTS £66,050 to Kaleidoscope Project; £52,408 to the Jerusalem Trust; £52,408 to the Headley Trust; £44,488 to Thomas Coram Foundation for Children; £30,000 to Young Minds; £30,000 to National Children's Bureau; £30,000 to Home-Start; £21,000 to Gingerbread; £20,000 to The Place To Be; £20,000 to Civic Trust

FINANCES *Year* 1997 *Income* £503,680 *Grants* £485,480

TRUSTEES A J Sainsbury, Miss J M Sainsbury, T J Sainsbury, Miss J S Portrait

HOW TO APPLY To the address under Who To Apply To in writing

WHO TO APPLY TO Michael Pattison, Glass House Trust, 9 Red Lion Court, London EC4A 3EF

CC NO 1017426   **ESTABLISHED** 1993

■ The B & P Glasser Charitable Trust

WHAT IS FUNDED General charitable purposes

WHAT IS NOT FUNDED No grant to individuals or to students

WHO CAN BENEFIT There are no restrictions on the age; professional and economic group; family situation; religion and culture; and social circumstances of; or disease or medical condition suffered by, the beneficiaries

WHERE FUNDING CAN BE GIVEN UK

RANGE OF GRANTS £500–£10,000

SAMPLE GRANTS £10,000 to Nightingale House; £5,000 to Royal National Institute for the Blind; £3,000 to Norwood Children's Home; £2,000 to Ravenswood Foundation; £2,000 to Central British Fund for Jewish World Relief; £2,000 to Friends of Boys' Town, Jerusalem; £2,000 to Friends of Magen David Adom; £2,000 to British Council of the Shaare Zadek Medical Centre; £2,000 to Abbeyfield Homes, Wendover; £2,000 to Abbeyfield

FINANCES *Year* 1996 *Income* £73,550 *Grants* £43,000

TRUSTEES B Glasser, H Glasser, J C Belfrage, J D H Cullingham, M J Glasser, J A Glasser

WHO TO APPLY TO J C Belfrage, The B & P Glasser Charitable Trust, Stafford Young Jones, The Old Rectory, 29 Martin Lane, London EC4R 0AU

CC NO 326571   **ESTABLISHED** 1984

■ R L Glasspool Trust

WHAT IS FUNDED Help to the poor, sick and necessitous persons individually provided their application is properly referred through social services, voluntary bodies or statutory services. Temporary assistance is only given when a person is in particular difficulty

WHAT IS NOT FUNDED No grants to individuals unless through proper channels – see Notes

WHO CAN BENEFIT Support is given to at risk groups, those disadvantaged by poverty and socially isolated people. Otherwise, there are no restrictions on the age; professional and economic group; family situation; religion and culture; and social circumstances of; or disease or medical condition suffered by, the beneficiaries

WHERE FUNDING CAN BE GIVEN London postal area, Essex, Hertfordshire, Home Counties

FINANCES *Year* 1996 *Income* £318,010 *Grants* £269,968

TRUSTEES Miss P M Mitchell, ASW (Chairman), J H S Arnold, MRCVS, DVSM, J C Pearcey, QGM, FSVA, Mrs M Jessop, SRN, M R Wylde, RMN, CQSW

NOTES Only cases referred to the Trust by social services, voluntary bodies and statutory services are considered

WHO TO APPLY TO Mrs F Moore, Administrator, R L Glasspool Trust, 298 Hoe Street, Walthamstow, London E17 9QD

CC NO 214648   **ESTABLISHED** 1939

■ The Glaziers' Trust

WHAT IS FUNDED The support of artists studying the craft of stained glass and the conservation of stained glass of historic importance

WHO CAN BENEFIT To benefit those involved in the craft of stained glass

WHERE FUNDING CAN BE GIVEN UK and Greater London

FINANCES *Year* 1997 *Income* £24,533 *Grants* £2,050

TRUSTEES The Glaziers' Company: P H Trollope, Mrs C M Benyon, A W Anderson, P R Bachelor, P F B Beesley, G C Bond, Dr W C Cole, A R Fisher, S J Graham, R F Lane, D Lawrence, P G Lowe, M C Tosh, T Carlile

HOW TO APPLY To the address under Who To Apply To in writing

WHO TO APPLY TO P R Batchelor, Clerk, The Glaziers' Trust, Glaziers' Company, Glaziers' Hall, 9 Montague Close, London SE1 9DD *Tel* 0171-403 3300

CC NO 251663 **ESTABLISHED** 1966

■ Glebe Charitable Trust

WHAT IS FUNDED Education and welfare of disabled and disadvantaged children and young people

WHAT IS NOT FUNDED Grants are not made towards: (a) school buildings; (b) fees for higher education save in the most exceptional circumstances; (c) 'gap year' activities; or (d) charities whose work is not exclusively for under 25s

WHO CAN BENEFIT Individuals and registered charities benefiting children and young adults who are disabled, disadvantaged, in care, fostered and adopted. One parent families will be considered. Support for those for different social circumstances, and those suffering from various diseases and medical conditions

WHERE FUNDING CAN BE GIVEN UK and overseas

TYPE OF GRANT Capital, core costs, one-off, project, recurring and running costs and salaries will be considered. Funding is available for up to two years

RANGE OF GRANTS £100–£1,500

FINANCES *Year* 1997 *Income* £21,600 *Grants* £29,000

TRUSTEES Mrs H D Ewart, Mrs T C Ewart, T K H Robertson

HOW TO APPLY Applications should be submitted, by letter, no later than one month before the Trustees' meetings in January and July each year. No application will be considered without Annual Accounts or appropriate financial information. There are no published guidelines and no application form

WHO TO APPLY TO T K H Robertson, Glebe Charitable Trust, Tweedie & Prideaux, 5 Lincoln's Inn Fields, London WC2A 3BT *Tel* 0171-242 9231/405 1234 *Fax* 0171-831 1525

CC NO 803495 **ESTABLISHED** 1989

■ Glendoune Charitable Trust

WHAT IS FUNDED To support a limited number of causes, mainly army based charities.

WHO CAN BENEFIT Mainly army based charities

WHERE FUNDING CAN BE GIVEN Ayrshire

WHO TO APPLY TO Glendoune Charitable Trust, Messrs A J & A Graham, 110 West George Street, Glasgow G2 1QA

SC NO SCO16249

■ The Glenvilla Charity Trust

WHAT IS FUNDED General charitable purposes

WHO CAN BENEFIT There are no restrictions on the age; professional and economic group; family situation; religion and culture; and social circumstances of; or disease or medical condition suffered by, the beneficiaries

WHERE FUNDING CAN BE GIVEN UK

TRUSTEES J J Reich, S Reich, J Tendler

WHO TO APPLY TO Ms N Tendler, Secretary, The Glenvilla Charity Trust, 33 Upper Park Road, Salford, Manchester M7 4JB

CC NO 1054584 **ESTABLISHED** 1996

■ Global Care

WHAT IS FUNDED Trustees favour children's charities already supported by them working in the poorest countries and the advancement of Christian education

WHAT IS NOT FUNDED Funding committed to the Charity's own projects only

WHO CAN BENEFIT Children and families in poorest countries through relief and development. People of many religions, cultures and social circumstances will be supported

WHERE FUNDING CAN BE GIVEN Overseas

TYPE OF GRANT One-off and recurring costs will be considered. Funding is available for up to two years

FINANCES *Year* 1998 *Grants* £224,000

TRUSTEES S D Wood, J Bull, N Lochhead

PUBLICATIONS Annual Reviews and News Updates

NOTES **Funds are fully allocated, and new grants cannot be considered**

HOW TO APPLY Applications are not welcome. Trustees seek out projects to support

WHO TO APPLY TO R F Newby, Trust Secretary and Chief Executive, Global Care, 2 Dugdale Road, Coventry CV6 1PB *Tel* 01203 601800 *Fax* 01203 601800 *E-mail* 100347.1506@compuserve.com

CC NO 1054008 **ESTABLISHED** 1996

■ Gloucestershire Environmental Trust Company

WHAT IS FUNDED Any project falling within the criteria for Project Approval by ENTRUST, particularly: conservation and environment; community facilities; infrastructure development; charity and voluntary umbrella bodies; religious buildings; religious umbrella bodies; and research into waste management

WHAT IS NOT FUNDED Anything not approved by ENTRUST

WHO CAN BENEFIT Any bona fide body whose objects include any of the approved objects under the Landfill Tax Regulations, eg churches, community groups, wildlife trusts, village hall committees, historic buildings, waste management research establishments. There are no restrictions on the age; professional and economic group; religion and culture of the beneficiaries

WHERE FUNDING CAN BE GIVEN Projects in Gloucestershire only

TYPE OF GRANT Buildings, feasibility studies, one-off, project, research, running costs, salaries, and start-up costs. Funding may be given for up to two years

RANGE OF GRANTS Maximum grants £100,000 per project, a maximum limit of £100,000 for an individual organisation per annum

TRUSTEES Jonathon Porritt (Chairman), David Ball, David Burton, Paul Holliday, Gordon McGlone, Jack Newell

PUBLICATIONS Leaflets: *Applying for a Grant*, *Notes on Application for Grants* and application form

NOTES The Trust receives its income through a scheme set up by Cory Environmental under the Landfill Tax Regulations. Preferential consideration is given to projects close to

··········
248

Think carefully about every application. Is it justified?

Hempsted, Stoke Orchard and Elmstone Hardwicke operations

HOW TO APPLY In the first instance the the Trust Secretary for an application form

WHO TO APPLY TO Mrs Lynne Garner, Secretary, Gloucestershire Environmental Trust Company, Moorend Cottage, Watery Lane, Upton St Leonards, Gloucestershire GL4 8DW *Tel* 01452 615110 *Fax* 01452 613817

CC NO Pending　　　　**ESTABLISHED** 1997

■ The Gloucestershire Historic Churches Preservation Trust

WHAT IS FUNDED The restoration, preservation, repair and improvement of churches, including monuments, fittings and furniture, in the area Where Funding Can Be Given

WHAT IS NOT FUNDED No grants for routine maintenance and decorations

WHERE FUNDING CAN BE GIVEN Gloucestershire, including South Gloucestershire

TYPE OF GRANT One-off, but repeat applications will be considered

RANGE OF GRANTS £100–£5,000, typical grant £2,000

SAMPLE GRANTS £5,000 to St Mary the Virgin Church, Berkeley for restoration work; £5,000 to St Mary's Church, Fairford for restoration work; £5,000 to Tewkesbury Abbey for restoration work; £4,000 to St John's Church for restoration work; £4,000 to St George's Church for restoration work; £4,000 to St Stephen's Church, Cheltenham for restoration work; £3,500 to St George's Church, Hanham Abbots for roofing repairs; £3,000 to St Lawrence Church, Lechdale for windows and stained glass repairs; £3,000 to St Mary's Church, Lower Slaughter for roofing repair; £2,500 to Holy Rood Church, Haglingworth for stonework renewal

FINANCES *Year* 1997 *Income* £116,600 *Grants* £53,100

TRUSTEES J A Cannan, R H J Steel, D W Turner, S Ward

HOW TO APPLY Preferably in writing for a detailed application form

WHO TO APPLY TO J A Cannan, Chairman of Grants Committee, Gloucestershire Historic Churches Trust, Bevelston House, Tetbury, Gloucestershire GL8 8TT *Tel* 01666 502595

CC NO 280879　　　　**ESTABLISHED** 1980

■ Susan Glover (No 2) Trust

WHAT IS FUNDED (a) The relief of persons in need by reasons of infirmity, sickness, poverty or social or economic purposes (b) the relief of people who have been adopted, children and their adoptive and birth parents

WHO CAN BENEFIT Organisations benefiting those in care, fostered and adopted; parents and children; at risk groups, those disadvantaged by poverty and socially isolated people. There is no restriction on the disease or medical condition suffered by the beneficiaries

WHERE FUNDING CAN BE GIVEN UK

FINANCES *Year* 1997 *Income* £450,980 *Grants* £133,649

TRUSTEES R Anstis, J R A Bishop, Ms J L Bretherton, Lady I Carrington, Mrs B Forbes, Lady J Foster, P Manwaring-Robertson, Lady A Spooner

WHO TO APPLY TO J R A Bishop, Susan Glover (No 2) Trust, 52 Clarendon Road, London W11 2HH

CC NO 1048976　　　　**ESTABLISHED** 1995

■ Avraham Yitzchak Gluck Charitable Trust

WHAT IS FUNDED Advancement of Jewish religion and relief of poverty

WHO CAN BENEFIT Individuals in distress, institutions, students, those disadvantaged by poverty and Jewish people

WHERE FUNDING CAN BE GIVEN UK, Eastern and Western Europe

TYPE OF GRANT At the discretion of the Trustees

FINANCES *Year* 1997 *Grants* £2,519

TRUSTEES Mrs Natalie Gluck, Rabbi Herschel Gluck, Mrs Pessie Gluck

WHO TO APPLY TO Mrs N Gluck, Avraham Yitzchak Gluck Charitable Trust, 20 Fountayne Road, London N16 7DX

CC NO 1015214　　　　**ESTABLISHED** 1992

■ James Glyn Charitable Trust

WHAT IS FUNDED General charitable purposes

WHAT IS NOT FUNDED No grants to individuals or to purely local causes

WHO CAN BENEFIT Registered charities. There are no restrictions on the age; professional and economic group; family situation; religion and culture; and social circumstances of; or disease or medical condition suffered by, the beneficiaries

WHERE FUNDING CAN BE GIVEN UK

TYPE OF GRANT Gifts not more frequently than once a year to any cause

RANGE OF GRANTS £25–£13,430

SAMPLE GRANTS £13,430 to Jewish Care; £4,975 to Western MArble Arch Synagogue; £2,600 to Kisharon; £1,175 to WIZO; £1,010 to British ORT; £1,000 to Friends of the Hebrew University Jerusalem; £600 to Nightingale House; £500 to Friends of VJS; £500 to Norwood Child care; £500 to Society of Friends of Federation of Women Zionists

FINANCES *Year* 1997 *Income* £31,913 *Grants* £33,270

TRUSTEES J Glyn, Mrs S C Glyn, S Glyn, T M Glyn

WHO TO APPLY TO J Glyn, James Glyn Charitable Trust, 4 Harley Street, London W1N 1AA

CC NO 266245　　　　**ESTABLISHED** 1973

■ The Glyn Foundation

WHAT IS FUNDED Relief of sickness

WHAT IS NOT FUNDED Grants are made only to causes known personally to the Trustees

WHO CAN BENEFIT There is no restriction on the disease or medical condition suffered by the beneficiaries

WHERE FUNDING CAN BE GIVEN England

TYPE OF GRANT One-off grants and interest free loans will be considered

SAMPLE GRANTS Two grants towards the rebuilding of a village hall; To Arthritis Care; To Alzheimer's Research; To Foot and Mouth Painting Activity; To The Samaritans

TRUSTEES Dr J H Glyn, Mrs G Readman, D A Pyke

HOW TO APPLY Initial telephone calls are not welcome from applicants. Please send an sae if a reply is required

WHO TO APPLY TO Dr J H Glyn, The Glyn Foundation, 35 Sussex Square, London W2 2PS

CC NO 1007701　　　　**ESTABLISHED** 1991

■ Mrs Godfrey-Payton Trust

WHAT IS FUNDED Particular interests are: (a) Projects that benefit Warwick and the inhabitants thereof, for example, arts, almshouses and youth clubs. (b) Projects (non-medical) designed to help the elderly retain their independence. (c) Projects known to the Trustees

WHAT IS NOT FUNDED No grants to individuals

WHO CAN BENEFIT Registered charities benefiting people of all ages, retired people and those disadvantaged by poverty

WHERE FUNDING CAN BE GIVEN Mainly Warwick

TYPE OF GRANT Usually one-off. Buildings, capital, core costs, feasibility studies, projects and funding for up to one year will be considered

FINANCES *Year* 1997 *Income* £50,000 *Grants* £30,000

TRUSTEES R D Creed, C B Moynihan

HOW TO APPLY To the address under Who To Apply To

WHO TO APPLY TO R D Creed, Clerk, Mrs Godfrey-Payton Trust, Ouvry Creed & Co, Foresters House, Sherston, Malmesbury, Wiltshire SN16 0LQ *Tel* 01666 840843 *Fax* 01666 840001

CC NO 1005851   **ESTABLISHED** 1991

■ The Godinton Charitable Trust

WHAT IS FUNDED General charitable purposes. A regular payment is made to the Godinton House Preservation Trust

WHAT IS NOT FUNDED No grants to individuals

WHO CAN BENEFIT There are no restrictions on the age; professional and economic group; family situation; religion and culture; and social circumstances of; or disease or medical condition suffered by, the beneficiaries

WHERE FUNDING CAN BE GIVEN UK

SAMPLE GRANTS £140,875 to Godinton House Preservation Trust; £10,000 to Wye Rural Museum Trust; £5,000 to Glynebourne Arts Trust; £2,000 to Blonde McIndoe Centre for Medical Research; £2,000 to Charities Aid Foundation; £2,000 to English National Opera; £2,000 to Home Farm Trust; £2,000 to the Leonard Cheshire Foundation; £2,000 to Royal Commonwealth Society for the Blind; £2,000 to SCOPE

FINANCES *Year* 1996 *Income* £255,758 *Grants* £262,045

TRUSTEES Moran Caplat, CBE, M F Jennings, Hon W G Plumptre, Hon J D Leigh-Pemberton, L H Parsons

HOW TO APPLY **This Trust states that it does not respond to unsolicited applications.** It cannot support those charities that may have received donations in the past

WHO TO APPLY TO Michael F Jennings,Trustee, The Godinton Charitable Trust, 1 St Pauls Churchyard, London EC4M 8SH

CC NO 268321   **ESTABLISHED** 1974

■ The Isaac Goldberg Charity Trust

WHAT IS FUNDED The Trust will consider funding the following: holiday accommodation; small enterprises; support to voluntary and community organisations; the advancement of the Jewish religion, synagogues and Jewish umbrella bodies. Community arts and recreation; ambulances and mobile units; hospices; rehabilitation centres, medical studies and research; special needs education and speech therapy. Community centres and village halls, and community services

WHAT IS NOT FUNDED No grants for expeditions, scholarships and business ventures of any sort

WHO CAN BENEFIT Any requests considered but not those for personal benefit. Individuals and organisations benefiting: people of all ages; those in care, fostered and adopted; parents and children; one parent families and widows and widowers. Christians, Church of England and Jews. Carers; disabled people; those disadvantaged by poverty; ex-offenders and those at risk of offending; Gays and lesbians; homeless people; immigrants and refugees; victims of abuse, crime and domestic violence, and victims of man-made and natural disasters, famine and war. There is no restriction on the disease or medical condition suffered by the beneficiaries

WHERE FUNDING CAN BE GIVEN Europe, Asia, Africa and America

TYPE OF GRANT Recurrent and one-off

RANGE OF GRANTS £100–£250

SAMPLE GRANTS £600 to Rudolph Steiner Schools for education; £600 to Ravenswood Foundation for care of the elderly; £500 to Independent Education Association for education; £500 to Jewish Care; £500 to Nightingale House for the care of elderly people

FINANCES *Year* 1996 *Income* £15,800 *Grants* £10,700

TRUSTEES D Goldberg, C Solomons, W Rose, R Colover, Dr J McRae

HOW TO APPLY To the address under Who To Apply To prior to April of each year when Trustees meet. No initial telephone calls welcome. There are no application forms, guidelines or deadlines. No sae required

WHO TO APPLY TO David Goldberg, The Isaac Goldberg Charity Trust, 38 Copthall Drive, Mill Hill, London NW7 2NB

CC NO 801869   **ESTABLISHED** 1989

■ The Sydney and Phyllis Goldberg Memorial Trust

WHAT IS FUNDED Medical research, welfare and disability

WHO CAN BENEFIT Organisations benefiting: research workers; at risk groups; disabled people; those disadvantaged by poverty and socially isolated people. There is no restriction on the disease or medical condition suffered by the beneficiaries

WHERE FUNDING CAN BE GIVEN UK

TYPE OF GRANT One-off, some recurrent

FINANCES *Year* 1995–96 *Income* £43,885

TRUSTEES H Vowles, C J Pexton, M J Church

HOW TO APPLY To the address under Who To Apply To in writing

WHO TO APPLY TO M J Church, Trustee, The Sydney and Phyllis Goldberg Memorial Trust, Coulthards MacKenzie, 17 Pork Street, Camberley, Surrey GU15 3PQ

CC NO 291835   **ESTABLISHED** 1985

■ Morris and Fay Goldblum Charitable Trust

WHAT IS FUNDED The advancement of the Orthodox Jewish religion. The relief of poverty and sickness. Grants to schools, Yeshivas, Orthodox Synagogues, hospitals, old people's homes in UK or Israel or elsewhere

WHO CAN BENEFIT Individuals and Jewish organisations benefiting people of all ages and those disadvantaged by poverty. There is no

restriction on the disease or medical condition suffered by the beneficiaries

WHERE FUNDING CAN BE GIVEN UK and overseas with preference for Israel

RANGE OF GRANTS Single grants £2–£2,000, some organisations may receive more than one grant

SAMPLE GRANTS £2,000, £1,750 and £1,250 to Pisga Charitable Trust

FINANCES *Year* 1996 *Income* £20,933 *Grants* £17,125

TRUSTEES Mrs E F Cohen, H J Goldblum

WHO TO APPLY TO Mrs E F Cohen, Morris and Fay Goldblum Charitable Trust, 19 Gresham Gardens, London NW11 8NX

CC NO 241777 **ESTABLISHED** 1965

■ Golden Bottle Trust

WHAT IS FUNDED General charitable purposes. The Trustees only make grants to registered charities

WHAT IS NOT FUNDED Applications from individuals are not considered. Applications without existing connection with C Hoare & Co, Bankers, are unlikely to be considered

WHO CAN BENEFIT There are no restrictions on the age; professional and economic group; family situation; religion and culture; and social circumstances of; or disease or medical condition suffered by, the beneficiaries

WHERE FUNDING CAN BE GIVEN UK

FINANCES *Year* 1996 *Income* £1,467,068 *Grants* £203,600

TRUSTEES Messrs Hoare Trustees

WHO TO APPLY TO The Secretary, Golden Bottle Trust, Messrs Hoare Trustees, 37 Fleet Street, London EC4P 4DQ

CC NO 327026 **ESTABLISHED** 1985

■ Golden Charitable Trust

WHAT IS FUNDED Literature, English Literature, the conservation of printed books and manuscripts, and libraries and museums

WHAT IS NOT FUNDED No grants to individuals

WHERE FUNDING CAN BE GIVEN UK

TYPE OF GRANT Endowment, sometimes recurring

RANGE OF GRANTS From £50–£100,000; typically £1,000

SAMPLE GRANTS £100,000 to The Chichester Cathedral Millennium Endowment Trust for endowment to yield restoration income; £50,000 to Petworth Cottage Nursing Home for endowment in general; £10,000 to National Manuscripts Conservation Trust for endowment in general; £7,500 to The London Library for endowment in general; £1,100 to Petworth Festival for sponsoring 1997 festival events

FINANCES *Year* 1997–98 *Income* £20,154 *Grants* £173,700

TRUSTEES Mrs S J F Solnick, J M F Golden

HOW TO APPLY Simply write in

WHO TO APPLY TO Lewis Golden, Golden Charitable Trust, Little Leith Gate, Angel Street, Petworth, West Sussex GU28 0BG

CC NO 263916 **ESTABLISHED** 1972

■ Charity of Fred Goldfinch

WHAT IS FUNDED General charitable purposes with a tendency to support the disabled and charities well known to the Trustees

WHAT IS NOT FUNDED No grants to individuals. The Trust is unlikely to assist evangelical appeals

WHO CAN BENEFIT Charities. There are no restrictions on the age; professional and economic group; family situation; religion and culture; and social circumstances of; or disease or medical condition suffered by, the beneficiaries

WHERE FUNDING CAN BE GIVEN Priority to Whitstable and Kent

RANGE OF GRANTS £200–£2,000

SAMPLE GRANTS £2,000 to CARE, Ide Hill; £200 to St Dunstan's Organ Fund

FINANCES *Year* 1994–95 *Income* £25,964 *Grants* £2,200

TRUSTEES W C Harvey, U H B Alexander

NOTES Very rarely respond to written appeals

WHO TO APPLY TO Charity of Fred Goldfinch, Messrs Furley Page Fielding & Barton, Solictors, 52–54 High Street, Whitstable, Kent CT5 1BG

CC NO 219162 **ESTABLISHED** 1956

■ Jack Goldhill Charitable Trust

WHAT IS FUNDED To support human need causes and visual arts

WHAT IS NOT FUNDED No grants to individuals. No unsolicited applications are required

WHO CAN BENEFIT Registered charities benefiting those in need

WHERE FUNDING CAN BE GIVEN UK

RANGE OF GRANTS £30–£27,000

SAMPLE GRANTS £27,000 to Jack Goldhill Sculpture Award Fund; £18,250 to Jewish Care; £3,500 to CST; £3,000 to Royal London Hospital; £2,250 to Joint Jewish Charitable Trust; £2,000 to Inclusion; £2,000 to Tate Gallery; £2,000 to Tricycle Theatre Co; £1,450 to West London Synagogue; £1,000 to Atlantic College

FINANCES *Year* 1997 *Income* £73,417 *Grants* £78,054

TRUSTEES G Goldhill, J A Goldhill

HOW TO APPLY **This Trust states that it does not respond to unsolicited applications**

WHO TO APPLY TO J Goldhill, Jack Goldhill Charitable Trust, 85 Kensington Heights, Camden Hill Road, London W8 7BD

CC NO 267018 **ESTABLISHED** 1974

■ The Goldsmiths' Arts Trust Fund

WHAT IS FUNDED The support and encouragement of the craft of silversmithing and precious metal jewellery through the finance of exhibitions, education and grants to arts organisations

WHO CAN BENEFIT Individuals and organisations benefiting silversmiths and those crafting precious metal jewellery

WHERE FUNDING CAN BE GIVEN Greater London and UK

SAMPLE GRANTS £20,000 to Goldsmiths' Craft Council for competition expenses; £2,000 to Arkwright Scholarships for scholarship; £2,000 to Clerkenwell Green Association for workshop space for emerging craftsmen

FINANCES *Year* 1996–97 *Income* £448,565 *Grants* £447,378

TRUSTEES The Goldsmiths' Company, N G Fraser

HOW TO APPLY To the address under Who To Apply To in writing

WHO TO APPLY TO The Clerk, The Goldsmiths' Arts Trust Fund, The Goldsmiths' Company, Goldsmiths' Hall, Foster Lane, London EC2V 6BN *Tel* 0171-606 7010

CC NO 313329 **ESTABLISHED** 1963

■ The Good Company Trust

WHAT IS FUNDED So far donations have made exclusively to the theatre in education activities of the Everyday Theatre Company and associated production companies and that is likely to continue indefinitely

WHAT IS NOT FUNDED Funding will not be given to anything except theatre in education

WHO CAN BENEFIT To benefit actors and entertainment professionals linked with the Everyday Theatre Company

WHERE FUNDING CAN BE GIVEN UK

TYPE OF GRANT One-off grants

RANGE OF GRANTS £2,000–£10,000, average grant £5,000

SAMPLE GRANTS £31,800 to the Good Company (Pride and Prejudice) Ltd

FINANCES *Year* 1996 *Income* £42,125 *Grants* £31,800

TRUSTEES K Carey, D Chivers, P Rogers, Peter Godfrey, Jane Peterson, L Gwyn Jones

NOTES During the next three years the Trust is highly unlikely to make any grants at all, except those to the theatre in education activities of the Everyday Theatre Company and associated production companies

HOW TO APPLY Please include an sae

WHO TO APPLY TO Kevin Carey, The Good Company Trust, 46 Quebec Street, Brighton, East Sussex BN2 2UZ *Tel* 01273 606652

CC NO 1008182   **ESTABLISHED** 1992

■ Good Deed Foundation

WHAT IS FUNDED General charitable purposes

WHO CAN BENEFIT There are no restrictions on the age; professional and economic group; family situation; religion and culture; and social circumstances of; or disease or medical condition suffered by, the beneficiaries

WHERE FUNDING CAN BE GIVEN UK

FINANCES *Year* 1996 *Income* £19,318 *Grants* £107,876

TRUSTEES C J Smith, M Weiss, A J Winter

WHO TO APPLY TO P Willoughby, Good Deed Foundation, c/o Manro Haydan Trading, 1 Knightsbridge, London SW1X 7LX

CC NO 1041053   **ESTABLISHED** 1994

■ The Good Neighbours Trust

WHAT IS FUNDED Principally in respect of specific projects for the relief of the mentally and physically handicapped, including: acute health care; respite and care for carers; special needs education; speech therapy; and care in the community

WHAT IS NOT FUNDED Registered charities assisting physically and mentally disabled only. No grants to religious or environmental projects except for those benefiting mentally and physically handicapped people. No grants to individuals or work overseas. No grants to general community projects

WHO CAN BENEFIT Registered charities assisting the physically and mentally disabled only. This includes: people of all ages. Those suffering from: Alzheimer's disease; arthritis and rheumatism; autism; cerebral palsy; cystic fibrosis; Friedrichs Ataxia; head and other injuries; motor neurone disease; multiple sclerosis; muscular dystrophy; paediatric diseases; Parkinson's disease; sight loss; spina bifida and hydrocephalus and strokes

WHERE FUNDING CAN BE GIVEN UK and Northern Ireland, Bristol

TYPE OF GRANT Project and capital. Funding is available for up to one year

SAMPLE GRANTS £25,000 to Children's Hospital, Bristol for facilities; £8,000 to Society of Stars, Buckinghamshire for projects for the disabled; £2,500 to Help the Hospices, London for training funding; £2,000 to Foundation for Communication for the Disabled, Surrey for computerised equipment for disabled people; £2,000 to Kerland Foundation, Bridgewater for the treatment of brain injured children; £1,000 to Disabled Young Adults Centre, Exeter for computer equipment for education of young disabled adults

FINANCES *Year* 1997 *Income* £91,000 *Grants* £100,850

TRUSTEES G V Arter (Chairman), R T Sheppard, P S Broderick, J C Gurney

HOW TO APPLY By letter with accounts and support information. Notes for Guidance are available. Applications are acknowledged. No sae is required and there are no deadlines. Initial telephone calls are not welcome

WHO TO APPLY TO Peter S Broderick, Secretary, The Good Neighbours Trust, 16 Westway, Nailsea, Bristol BS48 2NA

CC NO 201794   **ESTABLISHED** 1960

■ Sir Nicholas & Lady Goodisons Charitable Settlement

WHAT IS FUNDED Arts, arts education, mostly committments to previously supported charities. General at Trustees' discretion

WHAT IS NOT FUNDED No grants to individuals

WHO CAN BENEFIT Organisations benefiting: actors and entertainment professionals; musicians and singers; and textile workers and designers

WHERE FUNDING CAN BE GIVEN UK

TYPE OF GRANT At the discretion of the Trustees. One-off grants may be considered

SAMPLE GRANTS £10,000 to English National Opera for partly the Baylis Programme; £4,808 to Fitzwilliam Museum for craft collection; £1,500 to British Museum for gifts; £1,000 to National Gallery for gifts; £1,000 to National Art Collections Fund for gifts; £1,000 to Courtauld Institute for gifts

FINANCES *Year* 1996–97 *Income* £27,567 *Grants* £23,133

TRUSTEES Sir Nicholas Goodison, Lady Judith Goodison, Miss Katharine Goodison

WHO TO APPLY TO Sir N Goodison, Sir Nicholas & Lady Goodisons Charitable Settlement, 71 Lombard Street, London EC3P 3BS *Tel* 0171-356 2074

CC NO 1004124   **ESTABLISHED** 1991

■ The Everard and Mina Goodman Charitable Foundation

WHAT IS FUNDED The relief of poverty; the advancement of education; the advancement of religion; attention to needs of children and youth; medicine; health; rehabilitation and training

WHAT IS NOT FUNDED It is not the policy of the Trustees to make grants to individuals

WHO CAN BENEFIT Organisations benefiting: children and youth; students; at risk groups; those disadvantaged by poverty; socially isolated people; and the sick. There is no restriction on the religion or culture of, or the disease or medical condition suffered by, the beneficiaries

WHERE FUNDING CAN BE GIVEN UK

SAMPLE GRANTS £4,700 to Western Marble Arch Synagogue; £2,000 to Huntingdon Foundation; £1,200 to British Red Cross; £1,000 to British ORT; £1,000 to Community Security Trust; £1,000 to Foundation for Education; £1,000 to St John Ambulance; £875 to Jewish Care; £750 to British Friends of the Art Museums of Israel; £750 to Sidney Sussex College

FINANCES *Year* 1997 *Income* £39,955 *Grants* £16,655

TRUSTEES E N Goodman, FCA, M Goodman, M P Goodman, S J Goodman

WHO TO APPLY TO E N Goodman, FCA, The Everard and Mina Goodman Charitable Foundation, 5 Bryanston Court, George Street, London W1H 7HA

CC NO 220474   **ESTABLISHED** 1962

■ The Jordan Max Goodman Charitable Trust

WHAT IS FUNDED General charitable purposes

WHO CAN BENEFIT There are no restrictions on the age; professional and economic group; family situation; religion and culture; and social circumstances of; or disease or medical condition suffered by, the beneficiaries

WHERE FUNDING CAN BE GIVEN UK

FINANCES *Year* 1997 *Income* £19,736 *Grants* £3,025

TRUSTEES A G Goodman, Ms I Goodman, H Lask

WHO TO APPLY TO H M Lask, Trustee, The Jordan Max Goodman Charitable Trust, 8–10 Bulstrode Street, London W1M 6AH

CC NO 1053984   **ESTABLISHED** 1996

■ The S & F Goodman Trust

WHAT IS FUNDED Charitable work, anywhere in the world, for the care, maintenance, education or welfare of children and adults suffering from any physical or mental disability or disorder

WHAT IS NOT FUNDED No grants to individuals

WHO CAN BENEFIT Organisations benefiting children and adults who are disabled or suffering from hearing loss, sight loss, or mental illness. Support may also be given to carers

WHERE FUNDING CAN BE GIVEN UK and overseas

FINANCES *Year* 1997 *Income* £23,918

TRUSTEES C Goodman, Mrs D Talalay

NOTES Preference is given to charities of which the Trustees have special interest, knowledge or association; the Trustees do respond to applications

WHO TO APPLY TO Mrs Deborah Talalay, Trustee, The S & F Goodman Trust, 6 Stamford Brook Avenue, London W6 0YD

CC NO 260908   **ESTABLISHED** 1969

■ The Mike Gooley Trailfinder Charity

WHAT IS FUNDED We wish to identify probably three major causes of which the Prostate Cancer Charity is the first for major support. We generally do not wish to give out a lot of minor bequests without a particular reason such as a personal request. Alongside funding for medical research, support may be given for research into physics, science and technology and specialist research

WHAT IS NOT FUNDED No funding for overseas organisations

WHO CAN BENEFIT Organisations benefiting: children and young adults; ex-service and service people; research workers; scientists; and sportsmen and women. Funding may be given to those suffering from Alzheimer's disease, cancers, heart disease and tropical diseases

WHERE FUNDING CAN BE GIVEN All UK and Ireland

TYPE OF GRANT Any type considered. Research is the main grant given

RANGE OF GRANTS £100–£600,000

SAMPLE GRANTS £200,000 to the Prostate Cancer Charity – 90 per cent research and 10 per cent information and support; £1,000 to Westminster Boating Base for youth activities on the Thames; £500 to George Thomas Hospice Care for terminally ill; £260 to Refresh for polio victims; £250 to Princess Alice Hospice for elderly people; £250 to St George's School, windsor for restoration and development; £250 to DGAA Homelife for elderly people; £250 to an individual autistic child; £250 to Divert towards changing young lives; £200 to Royal British Legion for ex-servicemen

FINANCES *Year* 1997–98 *Income* £105,275 *Grants* £219,159

TRUSTEES M Bannister, M D W Gooley, Ms B M Gooley, T P Gooley

HOW TO APPLY Written applications only

WHO TO APPLY TO M D W Gooley, Trustee, The Mike Gooley Trailfinder Charity, 9 Abingdon Road, London W8 6AH *Tel* 0171-938 3143

CC NO 1048993   **ESTABLISHED** 1995

■ The Gothold Family Charitable Trust

WHAT IS FUNDED General charitable purposes

WHO CAN BENEFIT There are no restrictions on the age; professional and economic group; family situation; religion and culture; and social circumstances of; or disease or medical condition suffered by, the beneficiaries

WHERE FUNDING CAN BE GIVEN UK

TRUSTEES A J Gothold, Ms E G Gothold, Ms R L Gothold

WHO TO APPLY TO Anthony Gothold, The Gothold Family Charitable Trust, 44 Shirehall Lane, Hendon, London NW4 2PS

CC NO 1053556   **ESTABLISHED** 1996

■ The Gough Charitable Trust

WHAT IS FUNDED Youth projects; Episcopal or Church of England projects; preservation of countryside. Applications considered on merit

WHAT IS NOT FUNDED Registered charities only. Applications from individuals, including students, are ineligible

WHO CAN BENEFIT Registered charities, usually working in areas outlined under What Is Funded selected by Settlor and Trustees, benefiting children, young adults and Church of England

WHERE FUNDING CAN BE GIVEN Preference for Scotland

TYPE OF GRANT Usually one-off but some ongoing

FINANCES *Year* 1997 *Income* £45,135

TRUSTEES Lloyds Bank plc, Nigel Guy de Laval Harvie

HOW TO APPLY At any time. Awards are considered quarterly. No application forms provided. No acknowledgements sent

WHO TO APPLY TO Mrs E D Osborn-King, The Gough Charitable Trust, Thames Valley Area Office, The Clock House, 22–26 Ock Street, Abingdon, Oxfordshire OX14 5SW

CC NO 262355   **ESTABLISHED** 1970

Does the trust you have chosen match your needs? Haphazard applications waste postage and time

253

■ The Gould Charitable Trust

WHAT IS FUNDED General charitable purposes

WHO CAN BENEFIT There are no restrictions on the age; professional and economic group; family situation; religion and culture; and social circumstances of; or disease or medical condition suffered by, the beneficiaries

WHERE FUNDING CAN BE GIVEN UK

RANGE OF GRANTS £24–£22,000

SAMPLE GRANTS £22,000 to JJCT Charity; £7,100 to Childhope UK; £600 to WPF Counselling; £200 to JNF Charitable Trust; £200 to RNIB; £100 to Chicks; £100 to St Mungo's Association; £100 to Walking for Health; £100 to Youth Aliyah; £50 to MIND

FINANCES *Year* 1997 *Income* £36,177
Grants £30,624

TRUSTEES Mrs J B Gould, L J Gould, M S Golud, S Gould, S H Gould

WHO TO APPLY TO S Gould, The Gould Charitable Trust, Cervantes, Pinner Hill, Pinner, Middlesex HA5 3XU

CC NO 1035453   **ESTABLISHED** 1993

■ The Charities of George Goward and John Evans

WHAT IS FUNDED Aiding children and youth organisations and local community organisations within the area Where Funding Can Be Given. this includes education and training, music and Christian education. The Charity also funds relief in need covering areas such as health care; holiday and respite accommodation; and community services

WHO CAN BENEFIT Individuals and organisations benefiting people of all ages, students and those in need

WHERE FUNDING CAN BE GIVEN Lakenheath

TYPE OF GRANT One-off for start-up costs

RANGE OF GRANTS £300–£1,000

FINANCES *Year* 1997 *Income* £13,500
Grants £12,500

TRUSTEES J Gentle, Rev M Higgins, Rev J Mather, H Parsons, Mrs G Phipp, Mrs P Shipp, W Smith, G Worley

HOW TO APPLY To the address under Who To Apply To in writing

WHO TO APPLY TO Mrs E M Crane, Clerk, The Charities of George Goward and John Evans, 3 Roughlands, Lakenheath, Brandon, Suffolk IP27 9HA *Tel* 01842 860445

CC NO 253727   **ESTABLISHED** 1886

■ The Gradel Foundation

WHAT IS FUNDED The main interest is in medical charities, especially those dealing with heart problems, children and disability issues. Jewish and non-Jewish charities

WHAT IS NOT FUNDED No individuals or political causes

WHO CAN BENEFIT Institutions, both large national charities and smaller specific charities benefiting children, the disabled and Jewish people. There are no restrictions on the disease or medical condition suffered by the beneficiaries, but priority is given to heart problems

WHERE FUNDING CAN BE GIVEN UK and overseas

TYPE OF GRANT Small and large grants

RANGE OF GRANTS £25–£3,500

SAMPLE GRANTS £3,500 to Friends of the Jerusalem Academy Trust; £3,000 to Higher Crumpsall and Higher Broughton Hebrews Congregation; £3,000 to Jerusalem Academy Trust; £1,500 to Wallenberg Appeal; £1,250 to Community Security Trust

FINANCES *Year* 1997 *Income* £12,116
Grants £18,728

TRUSTEES J Gradel, Ms R Gradel, Ms M Gradel, D Gradel, A Gradel

HOW TO APPLY In writing only

WHO TO APPLY TO A Gradel, The Gradel Foundation, 5th Floor, Manchester House, Bridge Street, Manchester M3 3BN

CC NO 274098   **ESTABLISHED** 1977

■ Graff Foundation

WHAT IS FUNDED General charitable purposes

WHO CAN BENEFIT There are no restrictions on the age; professional and economic group; family situation; religion and culture; and social circumstances of; or disease or medical condition suffered by, the beneficiaries

WHERE FUNDING CAN BE GIVEN Overseas

FINANCES *Year* 1995 *Income* £333,678

TRUSTEES L Graff, F X Graff, A D Kerman

HOW TO APPLY This Trust states that it does not respond to unsolicited applications

WHO TO APPLY TO A D Kerman, Graff Foundation, 79 New Cavendish Street, London W1M 8AQ

CC NO 1012859   **ESTABLISHED** 1991

■ Reginald Graham Charitable Trust

WHAT IS FUNDED Currently the main area of interest is cancer research; fine art; literature; music; special schools; and tertiary and higher education

WHAT IS NOT FUNDED Charities must be registered. No grants to individuals

WHO CAN BENEFIT Registered charities benefiting: children and young adults; academics; sportsmen and women; students; Methodists; at risk groups; victims of abuse and domestic violence. Those suffering from cancers, cystic fibrosis and muscular dystrophy

WHERE FUNDING CAN BE GIVEN England

TYPE OF GRANT One-off, core costs, buildings and capital. Funding is available for up to and over three years

RANGE OF GRANTS £50–£5,000, typical grant £1,000

SAMPLE GRANTS £15,869 to Pembroke College for Rowing Club and Blackstone Lecture; £5,000 to SABC Clubs for Young People; £5,000 to English Chamber Orchestra; £3,500 to King Edward VII Hospital for Officers; £3,000 to St Dunstans; £1,500 to King George's Fund for Sailors; £1,500 to Friends of Israel; £1,000 to Peter May Memorial Trust; £1,000 to Royal Academy; £1,000 to Victory Services

FINANCES *Year* 1995 *Income* £131,043
Grants £60,532

TRUSTEES M D Wood, R Graham, J W Dolman, Mrs M Boyd

NOTES **Trustees will not be accepting applications until 2000**

HOW TO APPLY At any time after 1999 to the address under Who To Apply To

WHO TO APPLY TO M D Wood, Reginald Graham Charitable Trust, 1 Dean Farrar Street, London SW1H 0DY *Tel* 0171-222 8044

CC NO 212428   **ESTABLISHED** 1957

■ The Grahame Charitable Foundation

WHAT IS FUNDED Charities working in the fields of: the advancement of the Jewish religion; health facilities and buildings, medical studies and research; special schools, cultural and religious teaching and community services. Funds fully committed for the next four to five years. The Trustees allocate funds on a long term basis and therefore have none available for other applicants

WHAT IS NOT FUNDED Donations restricted to charitable institutions, no grants to individuals

WHO CAN BENEFIT Organisations benefiting: children, young adults, older people and Jews. There are no restrictions on the disease or medical condition suffered by the beneficiaries

WHERE FUNDING CAN BE GIVEN UK and Worldwide

TYPE OF GRANT Capital, core costs, interest free loans, one-off, recurring costs and start-up costs. Funding for up to two years may be considered

FINANCES *Year* 1996 *Income* £54,152
Grants £80,969

TRUSTEES J M Greenwood, G Grahame

WHO TO APPLY TO Mrs S Brooks, Secretary, The Grahame Charitable Foundation, 5 Spencer Walk, Hampstead High Street, London NW3 1QZ

CC NO 259864   **ESTABLISHED** 1969

■ The Granada Foundation (formerly Northern Arts and Sciences Foundation)

WHAT IS FUNDED Favourable consideration is given to projects of potential benefit to a wide public (eg artists in residence). Fine arts, including painting, drawing, architecture, sculpture, literature, music, opera, drama, ballet and cinema

WHAT IS NOT FUNDED Not able to help individual students with the costs of a course of study or expeditions. Does not support youth clubs and community associations. No general appeals

WHO CAN BENEFIT Arts centres, theatres, galleries, performance groups benefiting: actors and entertainment professionals; musicians; textile workers and designers; and writers and poets

WHERE FUNDING CAN BE GIVEN Preference to North West of England

RANGE OF GRANTS £500–£25,000

SAMPLE GRANTS £25,000 to National Museum and Galleries in Merseyside for the completion of a display gallery in the Conservation Centre, Liverpool; £25,000 to Royal Liverpool Philharmonic Society for refurbishment of great organ and cinema screen in Philharmonic Hall; £18,562 to the 'Granada Power Game' for annual competitive project for young engineers in schools; £12,500 to the Tate Gallery, Liverpool for Phase 2 of the development plan; £7,000 to Brouhaha International Festival (1997), Liverpool; £7,000 to Buxton Festival (1997) for opera productions; £5,000 to North West Museums Service, Blackburn for conservation work for galleries and museums; £5,000 to Manchester Camerata for an educational project; £4,000 to Positive Solutions, Liverpool for training in art organisations; £3,000 to Africa Oye, Liverpool for musical events in parks across Merseyside

FINANCES *Year* 1997 *Income* £148,190
Grants £136,162

TRUSTEES Alexander Bernstein, Robert Scott

WHO TO APPLY TO Mrs Irene Langford, The Granada Foundation, Bridgegate House, 5 Bridge Place, Lower Bridge Street, Chester CH1 1SA

CC NO 241693   **ESTABLISHED** 1965

■ The Grand Charity

WHAT IS FUNDED Consideration is only given to: (a) charities whose work covers the whole of England and Wales; (b) London charities (no other local charities should apply); and (c) indigent Freemasons of the United Grand Lodge of England, their widows and certain other dependants. Welfare and medical charities, and some emergency aid charities will be considered. Support will go to elderly and distressed people

WHO CAN BENEFIT Individuals who are elderly or distressed, and charities benefiting Freemasons of the United Grand Lodge of England and their dependants, at risk groups, those disadvantaged by poverty and socially isolated people. Victims of famine, war and natural or man-made disasters may be considered

WHERE FUNDING CAN BE GIVEN UK and overseas, with preference for England and Wales

RANGE OF GRANTS £5,000–£240,000

SAMPLE GRANTS £240,000 to Royal Shakespeare Theatre Trust to improve young people's access to the RSC; £200,000 to Outward Bound Trust to enable young people to attend adventure training courses; £100,000 to Cancer Relief Macmillan Fund for paediatric nursing services; £100,000 to Age Concern and Help the Aged for home alarms for the elderly; £36,000 to Royal Liverpool University Hospital for two special cutting instruments for its anorectal speciality group; £30,000 to Doncaster College for the Deaf towards a Learning for Life Project; £25,000 to Queen's Medical Centre, Nottingham for a vascular surgery unit for treatment of abdominal aortic aneurisms; £25,000 to Yorkshire, North and East Ridings Millennium Appeal for the St William Window in York Minster; £25,000 to Worcester Cathedral Stonemason's Yard for the training of an apprentice operative mason; £20,000 to Philippine National Red Cross towards emergency relief following storms in 1995

FINANCES *Year* 1997 *Income* £4,289,700

TRUSTEES Masonic Charity Trustee Limited

PUBLICATIONS Booklet *Information on Masonic Charities*; Annual Report and Accounts

HOW TO APPLY (a) Charities should apply in writing to be received by 30 June. A copy of the latest accounts should be enclosed which should not be more than 15 months old by that date.
(b) Individuals may apply direct but will eventually have to go through the appropriate Lodge or other local Masons

WHO TO APPLY TO Dudley M Wensley, Secretary, The Grand Charity, 60 Great Queen Street, London WC2B 5AZ

CC NO 281942   **ESTABLISHED** 1980

■ Grand Order of the Water Rats Charities Fund

WHAT IS FUNDED To assist needy members of the variety and light entertainment profession. Also to supply medical equipment to certain hospitals and institutions

WHAT IS NOT FUNDED No grants to students

WHO CAN BENEFIT Actors and entertainment professionals; musicians; those disadvantaged by poverty

WHERE FUNDING CAN BE GIVEN UK

TYPE OF GRANT One-off and recurrent

FINANCES *Year* 1997 *Income* £77,799
Grants £97,889

TRUSTEES David Berglas, Wyn Calvin, Declan Cluskey, Roy Hudd, Bert Weedon

HOW TO APPLY To the address under Who To Apply To in writing

WHO TO APPLY TO John Adrian, Secretary to the Trustees, Grand Order of the Water Rats Charities Fund, 328 Gray's Inn Road, London WC1X 8BZ
Tel 0171-278 3248

CC NO 292201   **ESTABLISHED** 1889

■ Grange Farm Centre Trust

This trust did not respond to CAF's request to amend its entry and, by 30 June 1998, CAF's researchers did not find financial records for later than 1995 on its file at the Charity Commission. Trusts are legally required to submit annual accounts to the Charity Commission under section 42 of the Charities Act 1993

WHAT IS FUNDED The provision or the assistance in the provision of facilities for recreation and leisure-time occupation of the inhabitants of the area of benefit and the public generally – preference is given to youth, the aged and the disadvantaged

WHAT IS NOT FUNDED No general purposes grants. No grants to private clubs or individuals

WHO CAN BENEFIT Mainly registered charities or organisations known to the Trustees benefiting children, young adults, elderly people and disadvantaged people

WHERE FUNDING CAN BE GIVEN London metropolitan police district and the Epping Forest district council area

TYPE OF GRANT Donations out of income of charity only and normally for single specific projects

TRUSTEES A T J Bryant (Chairman), B H Gunby, R J Pocock, B M Cox, A Pelican, R C O'Malley, A T Twynham, D R Springett

HOW TO APPLY To address under Who To Apply To for consideration at Trustees meetings in September and March, accompanied by latest Annual Report and Accounts and description and cost of project

WHO TO APPLY TO N E Gadsby, Clerk to the Trust, Grange Farm Centre Trust, Foskett Marr Gadsby & Head, 181 High Street, Epping, Essex CM16 4BQ

CC NO 285162   **ESTABLISHED** 1984

■ The Grant Charitable Trust

WHAT IS FUNDED To assist local groups who are working with: (a) children suffering from a physical disability, (b) orphans, (c) families which require help to improve the long-term nutrition of their children, (d) rural medical services connected with mother and child welfare. African charities working in the fields of healthcare, special education and vocational training

WHAT IS NOT FUNDED The Trustees will not consider applications relating to areas other than those mentioned under Where Funding Can Be Given and do not reply to applications relating to any other area. They do not give grants to young people intending to travel overseas (whether within or outside the area Where Funding Can Be Given) nor do they give grants for a student's education. They do not reply to letters making such requests. No grants to individuals

WHO CAN BENEFIT (a) Hospitals, schools, health centres, (b) projects assisting the stated objectives. Organisations in East and Central Africa benefiting children; young adults; parents; those in care, fostered and adopted; disabled people; those disadvantaged by poverty; homeless people; refugees; victims of famine, war, man-made and natural disasters. The main diseases and medical conditions suffered by the beneficiaries which are considered are autism,

hearing loss, HIV and AIDs, polio, sight loss and tropical diseases

WHERE FUNDING CAN BE GIVEN Main geographical focus is East and Central Africa but sub-Saharan Africa may also be considered

TYPE OF GRANT (a) One-off grants of up to £4,000, (b) annual programme of on-going support at up to £4,000 pa for up to three years to assist with the establishment and maintenance of a longer term programme. Buildings, and start-up costs are also considered

RANGE OF GRANTS £500–£9,500, typical grant £3,000

SAMPLE GRANTS £9,500 to School for Deaf Children, Embangweni, Malawi for the costs of building three teachers' houses; £9,000 to TOSE Respite Care Home, Harare, Zimbabwe to help with running costs (£4,000) and window and boundary protection; £8,500 to Bethany Crippled Children's Foundation, Kijabe, Kenya for flyout programme for one year to bring surgeons to outlying hospitals; £8,000 to Salvation Army, Limbi, Malawi for running costs of Orphans Project; £6,000 to North Kigezi Orphan and Disabled Children's Project, Uganda for income generating project to help 2,500 orphans and 1,000 disabled children

FINANCES *Year* 1998 *Income* £20,000
Grants £127,000

TRUSTEES M C Alexander, Rev C L J Carey, Mrs A D G Carr, S J Carr, G A Hill, M B Nunn

HOW TO APPLY If your group fulfils the conditions outlined in What is Funded, Who Can Benefit and Where Funding Can Be Given, please apply for an application form to the address under Who To Apply To

WHO TO APPLY TO Geoffrey A Hill, The Grant Charitable Trust, 5 Lineacre Close, Grange Park, Swindon SN5 6DA

CC NO 297290   **ESTABLISHED** 1987

■ The Grantham Yorke Trust

WHAT IS FUNDED Grants are given for education; to individuals in need and youth organisations. In advancing the education, physical and social training, financial assistance, in providing outfits, clothing, tools, instruments, equipment or books to help such persons on leaving school, university, etc to prepare for, or enter a profession or trade

WHO CAN BENEFIT Persons under the age of 25 who are in need

WHERE FUNDING CAN BE GIVEN West Midlands, in particular the Birmingham area

RANGE OF GRANTS £182–£15,000

SAMPLE GRANTS £15,000 to Galton Village Peace Project; £10,000 to Birmingham Settlement; £10,000 to Foundation for Conductive Education; £10,000 to St Thomas' Community Project; £10,000 to SENSE Midlands; £9,500 to St Basil's Centre; £9,000 to County of Birmingham Scouts Association; £7,000 to Sandwell Lifestyles; £5,000 to Birmingham Brook Advisory Centre; £5,000 to Birmingham Young Volunteers

FINANCES *Year* 1995–96 *Income* £339,342
Grants £281,255

TRUSTEES P Varcoe, Ven J L Cooper, E Insch, F Jephcott, D Macdonald, Rev R Morris, N Paul, B Welford, Very Rev P Berry

NOTES £41,226 was given in donations to 81 individuals

HOW TO APPLY To the address under Who To Apply To in writing

WHO TO APPLY TO D L Turfrey, The Grantham Yorke Trust, Martineau Johnson, St Philip's House, St Philip's Place, Birmingham B3 2PP

CC NO 228466   **ESTABLISHED** 1975

■ Lady Virginia Grant-Lawson Charitable Trust

WHAT IS FUNDED To favour small local charities concerned with young people and the disabled

WHAT IS NOT FUNDED No grants to conservation and environment, or for costs of study or academic research

WHO CAN BENEFIT Mainly registered charities benefiting children, young adults and disabled people

WHERE FUNDING CAN BE GIVEN Mainly Somerset

TYPE OF GRANT Mainly one-off for specific purpose

RANGE OF GRANTS £100–£5,000

FINANCES *Year* 1996–97 *Income* £23,174 *Grants* £19,700

TRUSTEES M C Lewin-Harris, M S Costerton

HOW TO APPLY Applications considered annually in February/March by Trustees. No acknowledgement normally sent

WHO TO APPLY TO M C Lewin-Harris, Conquest Farm, Norton Fitzwarren, Taunton, Somerset TA2 6PN

CC NO 1023276   **ESTABLISHED** 1993

■ J G Graves Charitable Trust

WHAT IS FUNDED Charities working in the fields of: advice and information on housing; holiday accommodation; respite accommodation; charity or voluntary umbrella bodies; arts, culture and recreation; and conservation; The income is mainly applied to local (Sheffield) charities for capital purposes rather than running costs

WHAT IS NOT FUNDED No grants to individuals

WHO CAN BENEFIT Charities who have similar objectives benefiting children, young adults and older people. There is no restriction on the social circumstances of the beneficiaries

WHERE FUNDING CAN BE GIVEN Mainly Sheffield

FINANCES *Year* 1997 *Income* £153,036 *Grants* £119,561

TRUSTEES G F Young, CBE, JP, LLD, Mrs A C Womack, G W Bridge, R S Sanderson, FCA, Mrs A H Tonge, T H Reed, R T Graves, S McK Hamilton, D S W Lee, Cllr P Price, Dr D R Cullen

HOW TO APPLY In writing to reach Secretary by 31 March, 30 June, 30 September, 31 December. Guidelines available. Applications acknowledged. Accounts required

WHO TO APPLY TO R H M Plews, FCA, Secretary, J G Graves Charitable Trust, Knowle House, 4 Norfolk Park Road, Sheffield S2 3QE *Tel* 0114-276 7991 *Fax* 0114-275 3538

CC NO 40138   **ESTABLISHED** 1930

■ R B Gray Charitable Trust

WHAT IS FUNDED Hospices

WHAT IS NOT FUNDED No grants to individuals or students

WHO CAN BENEFIT Small local projects benefiting those suffering from various diseases and medical conditions

WHERE FUNDING CAN BE GIVEN Leeds

TYPE OF GRANT One-off and core costs. Funding is available for more than three years

RANGE OF GRANTS £1,000 or less

SAMPLE GRANTS £1,000 to Arthritis and Rheumatism Council for Research for general purposes; £1,000 to Spofforth Cheshire Home to put towards funding of new location; £1,000 to West Yorkshire MS Therapy Centre to improve lighting in hyperbaric chamber; £1,000 to Wheatfields Hospice for general purposes and development of day centre; £1,000 to Candlelighters Trust towards cost of a PCR workstation

FINANCES *Year* 1996 *Income* £24,674 *Grants* £8,000

TRUSTEES R B Gray, W M Gray, Mrs J E Fairfoot

HOW TO APPLY In writing. Initial telephone calls not welcome. There are no application forms, guidelines or deadlines. No sae is required

WHO TO APPLY TO R B Gray, R B Gray Charitable Trust, 33 West Park Avenue, Leeds LS8 2EB

CC NO 1008160   **ESTABLISHED** 1992

■ The Gray Trust

WHAT IS FUNDED The Trustees give preference to charities based in Nottinghamshire and charities concerned with the welfare of the elderly, handicapped and disabled and ex-service personnel and their dependants

WHAT IS NOT FUNDED Grants are not made to individuals and seldom for applications from outside Nottinghamshire

WHO CAN BENEFIT Organisations benefiting: older people; retired people; ex-service and service people; those disadvantaged by poverty and disabled people

WHERE FUNDING CAN BE GIVEN Nottinghamshire

FINANCES *Year* 1997 *Income* £208,342 *Grants* £212,300

TRUSTEES John Davenport Radford, Bella St Clair Harlow, S Basil Trease, Claire Hardstaff, R B Stringfellow, Rev K Turner

HOW TO APPLY By letter of application together with most recent accounts. Unsuccessful applicants not notified

WHO TO APPLY TO The Trustees, The Gray Trust, 1 Royal Standard Place, Nottingham NG1 6FZ

CC NO 210914   **ESTABLISHED** 1962

■ The Gordon Gray Trust

WHAT IS FUNDED General charitable purposes. Funds fully committed at present

WHAT IS NOT FUNDED No grants to individuals, students, scholarships or expeditions

WHO CAN BENEFIT There are no restrictions on the age; professional and economic group; family situation; religion and culture; and social circumstances of; or disease or medical condition suffered by, the beneficiaries

WHERE FUNDING CAN BE GIVEN Preference given to local (Gloucestershire) appeals or national charities of a particular personal involvement

TYPE OF GRANT One-off, selected on annual basis

RANGE OF GRANTS £25–£500

SAMPLE GRANTS £500 to NSPCC; £500 to British Diabetic Association; £500 to Salters Hill; £500 to Marie Curie Cancer Care; £500 to Action Research; £500 to Alzheimer's Disease Society; £500 to Cotswold Cheshire Home; £500 to Sue Ryder Foundation; £500 to Willow Trust; £250 to James Hopkins Trust

FINANCES *Year* 1997 *Income* £30,930 *Grants* £11,025

TRUSTEES G Gray, Dr B Gray, J Urry, M M Gray

HOW TO APPLY Postal applications only

Does the trust you have chosen match your needs? Haphazard applications waste postage and time

257

WHO TO APPLY TO The Clerk to the Trustees, The Gordon Gray Trust, Grange Farm, Bredon, Tewkesbury, Gloucestershire GL20 7EL
CC NO 213935   **ESTABLISHED** 1960

■ The Great Commission Ministry

WHAT IS FUNDED To advance the Christian faith, to relieve the aged, sick or needy and other general charitable purposes. Donations are given to help needy church members

WHO CAN BENEFIT To benefit older people, Christians and those disadvantaged by poverty. There is no restriction on the disease or medical condition suffered by the beneficiaries

WHERE FUNDING CAN BE GIVEN London and elsewhere

FINANCES *Year* 1997 *Income* £56,858 *Grants* £2,074

TRUSTEES Ms C Dorada, D Eustaquio, Ms A Ibale, P Vistan

NOTES The majority of the Trust's income is spent on accommodation, salaries, travel, etc

WHO TO APPLY TO Pastor R G Bolor, The Great Commission Ministry, 63 Prince Thorpe House, Warwick Estate, London W2 5SX
CC NO 1056124   **ESTABLISHED** 1995

■ The Great Stone Bridge Trust of Edenbridge

WHAT IS FUNDED Education and general charitable purposes in the Parish of Edenbridge

WHO CAN BENEFIT There are no restrictions on the age; professional and economic group; family situation; religion and culture; and social circumstances of; or disease or medical condition suffered by, the beneficiaries

WHERE FUNDING CAN BE GIVEN The Parish of Edenbridge

TYPE OF GRANT Some recurrent

FINANCES *Year* 1995–96 *Income* £109,000 *Grants* £41,000

TRUSTEES Mrs C Burges, A Dell, R Drew, J Harris, D Leigh, Mrs R Parsons, Dr A Russell, T Smith, N Young

HOW TO APPLY To the address under Who To Apply To in writing

WHO TO APPLY TO W M Ross, Clerk, The Great Stone Bridge Trust of Edenbridge, 8 Church Lane, East Grinstead, West Sussex RH19 3BA
Tel 01342 323687
CC NO 224309   **ESTABLISHED** 1964

■ Great Torrington Town Lands and Poors Charity

WHAT IS FUNDED Relief in need, the arts, community organisations in the area Where Funding Can Be Given

WHO CAN BENEFIT Individuals and organisations benefiting: actors and entertainment professionals; musicians; textile workers and designers; writers and poets; and those in need

WHERE FUNDING CAN BE GIVEN Great Torrington

SAMPLE GRANTS £11,427 for public purposes; £4,750 to the Church; £4,000 to Bedford Arts Centre; £3,200 distributed to the poor

FINANCES *Year* 1994–95 *Income* £114,279 *Grants* £23,377

TRUSTEES T R Sutton, Mrs G A Armstrong, W J Brook, Dr H E Cramp, R Davey, B M Davies, Rev J D Hummerstone, E W J Kelly, J B Nash, Mrs D

Rollinson, P Shepherd, A J Stacey, R Sussex, Mrs E Weeks, H R F Young

HOW TO APPLY To the address under Who To Apply To in writing

WHO TO APPLY TO C J Styles, Great Torrington Town Lands and Poors Charity, Town Hall Office, High Street, Torrington, Devon EX38 8HN
CC NO 202801   **ESTABLISHED** 1971

■ Greater Bristol Foundation

WHAT IS FUNDED Funding emphasis is on projects focusing on youth, disablement, isolation, homelessness and safer community environments. Projects of direct benefit to the community will be considered. This Foundation may also give grants to charities working in the fields of: arts activities; arts education; environmental issues; pre-school education and training for personal and community development

WHAT IS NOT FUNDED No grants to individuals

WHO CAN BENEFIT Any charity aimed at increasing opportunities and enhancing the quality of life in the area, particularly smaller, low profile community groups and those at a particular disadvantage through discrimination. Beneficiaries of all ages and a variety of social circumstances will be considered

WHERE FUNDING CAN BE GIVEN Greater Bristol (a ten mile radius of the City centre)

TYPE OF GRANT (a) Express programme up to £1,500 at any time. (b) Catalyst programme matching designated funds to projects. (c) Impact programme £20,000 per three for five years. (d) Range of special advised funds. (e) Donor advised funds

SAMPLE GRANTS £30,300 to BYCA-Bristol Youth community Action for youth projects addressing community safety issues; £15,000 to the Southmead Project for new approaches to helping young people with addiction problems; £5,000 to Bristol Care and Repair for arts and volunteer project with elderly people; £3,600 to Southmead Wheels Project for diversionery activities for young people; £2,998 to Citizens' Advice Bureau for debt counselling at fines court; £2,900 to Dundry Hill Group for Litter Campaign with local school children; £1,500 to Care Network B&NES for a support group for women with mental health problems; £1,500 to ACTA for a theatre production by young disabled people; £1,500 to Filtor Community Profile for developing services for elderly people; £1,500 to Somali Refugee Rehabilitation Project for basic running costs

FINANCES *Year* 1997 *Income* £248,680 *Grants* £164,965

TRUSTEES Ms J Bryant-Pearson, J Burke, D Claisse, Gillian Camm, G Ferguson, Mrs M Jackson, Alfred Morris (Chairman), D Parkes, J Pontin, Brig H Pye, The Rt Rev B Rogerson, Bishop of Bristol, T Stevenson, S Storvik, A Thornhill, QC, J Tidmarsh, MBE, LL, JP, H Webber, Heather Wheelhouse, Ms D Wood

PUBLICATIONS Annual Report, two newsletters per year, grant making policy and guidelines

HOW TO APPLY Application forms and guidelines on request. Applicants will be informed of deadlines. An initial telephone enquiry recommended and welcome. Express programme considered on a rolling basis. Enquire to Foundation for other programmes

WHO TO APPLY TO Helen Moss, Director, Greater Bristol Foundation, PO Box 383, 16 Clare Street, Bristol BS99 5JG *Tel* 0117-921 1311 *Fax* 0117-929 7965 *Web Site* http://www.bristol.digitalcity.org/org/community/gbf/index.htm
CC NO 295797 **ESTABLISHED** 1987

■ J C Green Charitable Trust

WHAT IS FUNDED General charitable purposes
WHO CAN BENEFIT Registered charities. There are no restrictions on the age; professional and economic group; family situation; religion and culture; and social circumstances of; or disease or medical condition suffered by, the beneficiaries
WHERE FUNDING CAN BE GIVEN UK
FINANCES *Year* 1995 *Income* £34,000 *Grants* £22,000
TRUSTEES J C Green, M C Green
WHO TO APPLY TO J C Green, J C Green Charitable Trust, Calamansac House, Port Navas, Constantine, Falmouth TR11 5RN
CC NO 291254 **ESTABLISHED** 1984

■ The Green Foundation

WHAT IS FUNDED Social welfare
WHAT IS NOT FUNDED No grants will be given to political bodies
WHO CAN BENEFIT Funding will be given to beneficiaries of many different social circumstances
WHERE FUNDING CAN BE GIVEN UK and overseas
TYPE OF GRANT One-off
RANGE OF GRANTS £12–£20,480
FINANCES *Year* 1998 *Income* £120,000 *Grants* £90,004
TRUSTEES Mrs Toby Lawson (Chairman), Mrs Kate Birk, H Richard Green, David R Green
HOW TO APPLY To the address under Who To Apply To before May and November annually. The Trustees will rarely entertain postal applications which can only be from authorised charities. Applications will not be acknowledged
WHO TO APPLY TO D Green, The Green Foundation, Powerbreaker House, South Road, Harlow, Essex CM20 2BG
CC NO 802876 **ESTABLISHED** 1990

■ Constance Green Foundation

WHAT IS FUNDED Some preference is given to charities operating in Yorkshire. In previous years grants have been made mainly, but not exclusively, to national organisations in the fields of social welfare and medicine, with special emphasis on support of young people in need and both mentally and physically disabled persons. Particularly charities working in the fields of residential facilities and services, health professional bodies, social care professional bodies, health, Council for Voluntary Services, church and special schools, special needs education, medical research and various community facilities and services
WHAT IS NOT FUNDED Trustees will not respond to individuals (including students)
WHO CAN BENEFIT Registered charities, and organisations recognised as charitable by the Laws of England, benefiting children; young adults and older people; ex-service and service people; medical professionals, nurses and doctors; seafarers and fishermen; unemployed people; those in care, fostered and adopted; at risk groups; disabled people; those disadvantaged by poverty; homeless; victims of famine and war; and those suffering from autism, cancers, epilepsy, head and other injuries, multiple sclerosis, prenatal conditions, terminal illness and tropical diseases will be consider
WHERE FUNDING CAN BE GIVEN UK with a preference for Yorkshire and Humberside
TYPE OF GRANT Capital, special project, buildings and one-off funding of one year or less
RANGE OF GRANTS £1,000–£250,000
SAMPLE GRANTS £170,000 to St Aidans C of E High School for a new chapel/hall; £6,000 to Harrogate Shopmobility; £6,000 to Orbis International; £6,000 to Children in Hospital; £5,000 to Queen Elizabeth Hospital for Children; £5,000 to Salvation Army, Leeds; £5,000 to St John Ambulance, Jersey; £5,000 to St Martin-in-the-Fields; £2,000 to Dream Holidays; £2,000 to Northern Ireland Women's Aid Federation
FINANCES *Year* 1997 *Income* £322,000 *Grants* £235,000
TRUSTEES M Collinson, MA (Cantab), Col H R Hall, OBE, TD, DL, N Hall, A G Collinson, BA
HOW TO APPLY No special form required. Not acknowledged unless sae provided. Guidelines issued on request
WHO TO APPLY TO M Collinson, Constance Green Foundation, Corner Cottage, 1 Trimmingham Lane, Halifax HX2 7PT
CC NO 270775 **ESTABLISHED** 1976

■ Green Hills Christian Youth Conference Centre Limited

WHAT IS FUNDED Centre for the Christian education and training of young people; provision of facilities and equipment for the spiritual, social and physical recreation and training of young people in Christian leadership for citizenship and Christian and social service; promotion of conferences, rallies, holidays, courses and other events connected with the above and generally with the object of advancing the Kingdom of Jesus Christ among young people
WHO CAN BENEFIT Organisations benefiting young people and Christians, including Baptists, Anglicans, Methodists, Roman Catholics and clergy
WHERE FUNDING CAN BE GIVEN UK
TYPE OF GRANT Recurring
WHO TO APPLY TO D Woodhouse, Green Hills Christian Youth Conference Centre Ltd, North Haven, Foxhill, Haywards Heath, West Sussex RH16 4QY
CC NO 305954 **ESTABLISHED** 1962

■ J H F Green

WHAT IS FUNDED General charitable purposes at the Trustees' discretion
WHO CAN BENEFIT There are no restrictions on the age; professional and economic group; family situation; religion and culture; and social circumstances of; or disease or medical condition suffered by, the beneficiaries
WHERE FUNDING CAN BE GIVEN UK
TYPE OF GRANT At the discretion of the Trustees
RANGE OF GRANTS £9–£2,000

SAMPLE GRANTS £2,000 to NCVO; £1,000 to Crisis; £1,000 to Notting Hill Housing Trust; £1,000 to Church of England Pensions Board; £1,000 to Intermediate Technology
FINANCES *Year* 1997 *Income* £18,102 *Grants* £15,345
TRUSTEES National Council for Voluntary Organisations
WHO TO APPLY TO Head of Finance, J H F Green, NCVO, Regents Wharf, 8 All Saints Street, London N1 9RL
CC NO 264060   **ESTABLISHED** 1972

■ The Barry Green Memorial Fund

WHAT IS FUNDED Preference for smaller charities rescuing and caring for cruelly treated animals; animal homes; animal welfare; cats, catteries and other facilities for cats; dogs, kennels and other facilities for dogs; and horses, stables and other facilities for horses
WHAT IS NOT FUNDED No expeditions, scholarships, work outside the UK or individuals
WHO CAN BENEFIT All, but the Trustees have a preference towards smaller charities working at grass roots level
WHERE FUNDING CAN BE GIVEN UK, with preference towards Yorkshire and Lancashire
TYPE OF GRANT Buildings, core costs, one-off, recurring costs, running costs and start-up costs. Funding available for more than three years
RANGE OF GRANTS £100–£15,000
FINANCES *Year* 1997 *Income* £165,584 *Grants* £42,799
TRUSTEES R Fitzgerald-Hart, M Fitzgerald-Hart
HOW TO APPLY Any time, in writing only
WHO TO APPLY TO Clerk to the Trustees, The Barry Green Memorial Fund, Claro Chambers, Horsefair, Boroughbridge, York YO5 9LD
CC NO 1000492   **ESTABLISHED** 1990

■ The Greencard Charitable Trust

WHAT IS FUNDED Purchase of equipment and materials for environmental projects
WHAT IS NOT FUNDED No grants to individuals
WHO CAN BENEFIT Local, regional and international environmental charities and credible projects
WHERE FUNDING CAN BE GIVEN UK and overseas
TYPE OF GRANT A range of cash grants
RANGE OF GRANTS Up to £5,000
SAMPLE GRANTS £21,000 to Biodiversity Challenge as payments to various wildlife trusts; £10,000 to Herpetological Conservation Trust; £5,000 to Royal Geographical Society; £3,300 to London Wildlife Trust; £1,750 to Farm Africa
FINANCES *Year* 1997 *Income* £45,600 *Grants* £44,000
TRUSTEES A C Humphries, Dr J Hemming, D Williams-Jones, Dr N Chalmers, D Nimmo, J Pettifer, Prof Sir G Prance
HOW TO APPLY Guidelines will be issued for application
WHO TO APPLY TO Suzie Lawrence, Administrator, The Greencard Charitable Trust, Transnational Financial Services Ltd, 33 Blagrave Street, Reading, Berkshire RG1 1PW *Tel* 0118-956 8444
CC NO 803506   **ESTABLISHED** 1990

■ Mrs H R Greene Charitable Settlement

WHAT IS FUNDED Welfare and general charitable purposes
WHO CAN BENEFIT Individuals and institutions. Particularly those benefiting at risk groups, those disadvantaged by poverty and socially isolated
WHERE FUNDING CAN BE GIVEN UK with preference for Shropshire and Wistanstow
TYPE OF GRANT At the discretion of the Trustees
FINANCES *Year* 1997 *Income* £92,709 *Grants* £60,374
TRUSTEES A C Boston, Rev J B Boston, N J Moore
HOW TO APPLY **This Trust states that it does not respond to unsolicited applications**
WHO TO APPLY TO J Perowne, Secretary, Mrs H R Greene Charitable Settlement, Eversheds, Paston House, Princes Street, Norwich, Norfolk NR3 1BD
CC NO 1050812   **ESTABLISHED** 1845

■ Ann Jane Green's Trust

WHAT IS FUNDED Grants are given to support hospitals, appeals and organisations which provide help for children, the sick and those in need
WHAT IS NOT FUNDED Grants are not made to individuals
WHO CAN BENEFIT Organisations benefiting children, the sick and those in need
WHERE FUNDING CAN BE GIVEN UK, Scotland in particular
TRUSTEES Ms Jaqueline Barchan, George Green, Douglas Harvey
PUBLICATIONS Accounts are available from the Trust
HOW TO APPLY Applications should be made in writing to the address below
WHO TO APPLY TO Ann Jane Green's Trust, 135 Buchanan Street, Glasgow G1 2JH
SC NO SCO 09410

■ The Denis Greenwood Charitable Settlement

WHAT IS FUNDED General charitable purposes. Grants are made within the guidelines of the Charity Commission
WHAT IS NOT FUNDED No grants made to individual students. No foreign grants are made; community/church projects limited to Leeds and Bradford area
WHO CAN BENEFIT There are no restrictions on the age; professional and economic group; family situation; religion and culture; and social circumstances of; or disease or medical condition suffered by, the beneficiaries
WHERE FUNDING CAN BE GIVEN UK
TYPE OF GRANT One-off and short term. Recurrent up to five years
RANGE OF GRANTS £10–£1,000
SAMPLE GRANTS £1,000 to Woodhouse Grove School Development Fund; £826 to Opera North; £500 to the Daisy Hill Centre; £500 to MENCAP; £300 to Macmillan Cancer Fund
FINANCES *Year* 1996 *Income* £467 *Grants* £7,484
TRUSTEES S C Rawson, J A J Hanson
NOTES All applications in writing, apart from those stated in What Is Not Funded, are considered by the Trustees
HOW TO APPLY Apply to the Trustees at address below in writing only

WHO TO APPLY TO S C Rawson, The Denis Greenwood Charitable Settlement, East End, Norwood, Harrogate, North Yorkshire HG3 1TA
CC NO 274705   **ESTABLISHED** 1977

■ Naomi and Jeffrey Greenwood Charitable Trust

WHAT IS FUNDED Trustees favour mainly Jewish charities
WHO CAN BENEFIT Registered charities especially those benefiting Jewish people
WHERE FUNDING CAN BE GIVEN UK and overseas
RANGE OF GRANTS £25–£10,000
SAMPLE GRANTS £10,000 to Jewish Care; £1,250 to Institute for Jewish Policy Research; £950 to Norwood Ravenswood; £750 to Holocaust Education Trust; £736 to United Synagogue
FINANCES *Year* 1997 *Income* £23,226
Grants £19,712
TRUSTEES J M Greenwood, Mrs N Greenwood
WHO TO APPLY TO J M Greenwood, Naomi and Jeffrey Greenwood Charitable Trust, 50 Stratton Street, London W1X 5FL
CC NO 275633   **ESTABLISHED** 1978

■ Greggs Trust

WHAT IS FUNDED Applications from small community-led organisations and self-help groups are more likely to be successful than those from larger and well-staffed organisations and those which have greater fund-raising capacity. Exceptions may be made where innovative work is being developed by established agencies or where such agencies are providing services to smaller or local groups. Projects in the fields of the arts, the environment, conservation, education and health will be considered so long as they have a social welfare focus and/or are located in areas of deprivation
WHAT IS NOT FUNDED The following will not be funded: academic research; animal welfare; capital appeals or running costs of fee-charging residential homes and nurseries; commercial charity reference books/directories; conferences/seminars/exhibitions/publications; festivals, performances and other arts and entertainment activity, unless of specific educational value and involving groups from areas of greater social need or disadvantaged by low-income or disability; foreign travel/expeditions/holidays and outings other than for disadvantaged groups; fundraising organisations, general fundraising appeals, fundraising events and sponsorship; hospitals, Health Service Trusts, medically related appeals and medical equipment; loans, repayment of loans or retrospective funding; national appeals and general appeals of established regional organisations; medical research; mini-buses and vehicles, other than community transport schemes which serve a combination of groups in a wide geographical area; overseas projects or organisations working abroad; purchase, conversion and restoration of buildings other than community-based projects serving areas of greater social need and/or particularly disadvantaged or at-risk groups; religious advancement or religious buildings. Community aspects of church-based or other religious projects may be considered if projects show outreach into the community and provide services of benefit to the community as a whole or to particularly disadvantaged or at-risk groups; restoration and conservation of historic buildings and the purchase or conservation of furnishings, paintings, other artefacts or historic equipment; school appeals other than for projects at LEA schools in areas of greater social need, eg, after school clubs and activities promoting parental and community involvement; sports buildings, equipment and sporting activities other than where particularly disadvantaged groups ore involved and where the activity is ongoing rather than 'one-off'; statutory agencies and activities that are primarily the responsibility of statutory agencies; uniformed organisations (Scouts, Guides, Sea Cadets, etc) and organisations associated with the armed services other than in areas of greater social need where projects involve outreach into the community and wider community benefit
WHO CAN BENEFIT The Trustees are committed to equal opportunities and anti-discriminatory practice and wish to encourage applications from disadvantaged groups of all kinds including ethnic minorities, people with disabilities and other minorities, without prejudice as to racial origin, religion, age, gender or sexual orientation. Recent grants have included support for work with homeless people, older people, young people, children and women, including unemployed, and for people with disabilities
WHERE FUNDING CAN BE GIVEN North East of England, ie in the counties of Northumberland, Tyne & Wear, Co Durham and the former county of Cleveland
TYPE OF GRANT Core costs, running costs, project, start-up costs, buildings, capital other than building (computers, etc), recurring costs, salaries, one-off. Funding may be given for up to three years
RANGE OF GRANTS Major grants: more than £1,000 approved by Trustees at meetings held in May and November. Small grants: in most cases to a maximum of £500, approved monthly. Hardship payments: to families and individuals in need through the Hardship Fund scheme – £50 per individual and a maximum of £200 per family. Applications must be made via a welfare agency on an application form which is available from the Trust

Does the trust you have chosen match your needs? Haphazard applications waste postage and time

261

SAMPLE GRANTS £10,000 to the People's Kitchen, Newcastle for refurbishment at the Alison Centre – their new base acquired because of road widening – which provides support for homeless and rootless people; £10,000 to Scotswood Area Strategy Youth Project, Newcastle towards the purchase and conversion of shop premises for a centre to be run by young people; the grant helped to 'lever' a major contribution from English Partnerships; £10,000 pa for two years Northern Initiative on Women and Eating, Newcastle to increase the hours of the co-ordinator in order to raise the profile of NIWE and to enable them to negotiate more contracts with health service funders in the region; £10,000 to St Margaret's Church, Scotswood towards the conversion and refurbishment of the church for a wide range of purposes of benefit to the community; £6,500 to St Simon's Community Project, Jobs, Education and Training, South Shields towards operating costs of this scheme which benefits young and older unemployed people; £5,000 to 'F' Troop, Herrington Burn YMCA, Houghton-le-Spring, Sunderland towards the renovation of a cottage owned by the YMCA at Otterburn Hall, for use by young people and volunteers from Sunderland; £5,000 to Laurel Avenue Community Association, Sherburn Estate, Durham towards improvements at the Community Centre; £5,000 to Shopmobility, South Shields towards the costs of providing a suitably adapted building and surrounds for this new shopping scheme for disabled people in South Tyneside; £5,000 pa to The Willows Community Art and Education Project, Portrack & Tilery, Stockton-on-Tees towards the matching funds needed to qualify for an EC grant for two years for a skills training project; £5,000 pa for two years to Caring Hands, Shieldfield, Newcastle towards the running costs of a project supporting older and disabled residents in the east end of the city

FINANCES *Year* 1997 *Income* £498,957 *Grants* £583,095

TRUSTEES Andrew Davison, Felicity Deakin, Ian Gregg, Jane Gregg, Fiona Nicholson

NOTES Applicants not need to be a registered charity. The Administrator is not generally available to deal with telephone enquiries. Urgent messages may be left by telephone or fax. All messages and correspondence will be dealt with as quickly as possible

HOW TO APPLY Applications should be made to the Administrator in writing. There is no application form but the Trust does supply Guidelines and organisations should refer to these before applying for a grant

WHO TO APPLY TO Ms Jenni Wagstaff, Trust Administrator, Greggs Trust, Fernwood House, Clayton Road, Jesmond, Newcastle upon Tyne NE2 1TL *Fax* 0191-281 1444

CC NO 296950   **ESTABLISHED** 1987

■ The Greibach Charitable Trust

WHAT IS FUNDED General charitable purposes

WHO CAN BENEFIT There are no restrictions on the age, professional and economic group, family situation, religion and culture, and social circumstances of, or disease or medical condition suffered by, the beneficiaries

WHERE FUNDING CAN BE GIVEN UK

FINANCES *Year* 1996 *Income* £27,069 *Grants* £21,930

TRUSTEES J Greibach, F H Greibach, C F Greibach

WHO TO APPLY TO F H Greibach, The Greibach Charitable Trust, M R Rector Limited, Rectella House, Railway Road, Chorley, Lancashire PR6 0HL

CC NO 803144   **ESTABLISHED** 1989

■ The Gresham Charitable Trust

WHAT IS FUNDED General charitable purposes

WHO CAN BENEFIT Registered charities only. There are no restrictions on the age; professional and economic group; family situation; religion and culture; and social circumstances of; or disease or medical condition suffered by, the beneficiaries

WHERE FUNDING CAN BE GIVEN UK

RANGE OF GRANTS Typical grant £3,000

SAMPLE GRANTS £3,000 to Age Concern; £3,000 to Baker Street Charitable Trust; £3,000 to Barnardos; £3,000 to Chiltern Hills Charitable Trust for Rushymead Hospice; £3,000 to Christians in Sport; £3,000 to Ex-Services Mental Welfare Society; £3,000 to Help the Aged; £3,000 to John Groom's Association for the Disabled; £3,000 to Methodist Church, Little Chalfont for organ fund; £3,000 to Methodist Church for West London Mission

FINANCES *Year* 1998 *Income* £61,353 *Grants* £78,000

TRUSTEES R Taylor, FCA, P S Vaines, FCA

HOW TO APPLY The Trustees only consider grant applications received in response to invitations issued by them to prospective charitable beneficiaries

WHO TO APPLY TO F G A Flynn, FCA, The Gresham Charitable Trust, 92 Bell Lane, Little Chalfont, Amersham, Buckinghamshire HP6 6PE *Tel* 01494 762224

CC NO 257036   **ESTABLISHED** 1965

■ The Greystoke Trust

WHAT IS FUNDED The relief of poverty, schools, colleges and other educational foundations which are charities, national or local disaster funds and the advancement of religion

WHAT IS NOT FUNDED No grants to individuals, especially students. No grants for expeditions or general appeals

WHO CAN BENEFIT Organisations benefiting children and young adults, those disadvantaged by poverty, victims of famine and man-made or natural disasters

WHERE FUNDING CAN BE GIVEN UK and overseas

RANGE OF GRANTS £100–£12,000

SAMPLE GRANTS £12,000 to Land Aid Charitable Trust

FINANCES *Year* 1996 *Income* £16,211 *Grants* £18,100

TRUSTEES Finblood Limited

HOW TO APPLY **This Trust states that it does not respond to unsolicited applications**

WHO TO APPLY TO Finblood Limited, The Greystoke Trust, 25 Harley Street, London W1N 2BR

CC NO 263597   **ESTABLISHED** 1972

■ Griffith UK Foundation

WHAT IS FUNDED Christian missionary organisations, the advancement of the Catholic Church, local charitable organisations

WHO CAN BENEFIT Christian organisations, and local organisations, particularly those benefiting Roman Catholics

WHERE FUNDING CAN BE GIVEN Derbyshire and Eastern Europe

TYPE OF GRANT Recurring and one-off grants will be considered

RANGE OF GRANTS £100–£9,505

SAMPLE GRANTS £9,505 to Christian Associates; £4,840 to Raynes Park Methodist Church; £4,403 to Eastern Europe Bible Mission; £2,516 to Executive Outreach; £1,000 to Southern Derbyshire Midlands Games

FINANCES *Year* 1994–95 *Income* £16,734 *Grants* £27,493

TRUSTEES D B G Bishop, B G Dinsmore, D L Griffith, J Moslick

HOW TO APPLY To the address under Who To Apply To in writing

WHO TO APPLY TO B G Dinsmore, Griffith UK Foundation, Griffith Laboratories Ltd, Cotes Park Farm, Somercotes, Alfreton, Derbyshire DE55 4NN *Tel* 01773 837000

CC NO 1005300   **ESTABLISHED** 1991

■ The Grimley Charity

WHAT IS FUNDED Charities working with the elderly and disabled, hospices and nursing homes

WHAT IS NOT FUNDED No grants to individuals

WHO CAN BENEFIT Registered charities benefiting young adults and the elderly and disabled people. There may be a few restrictions on the disease or medical condition suffered by the beneficiaries

WHERE FUNDING CAN BE GIVEN Worcestershire

FINANCES *Year* 1995–96 *Income* £26,600 *Grants* £2,500

TRUSTEES Sir H B Huntington-Whiteley, Bt, H B Carslake, J M G Fea

WHO TO APPLY TO J M G Fea, The Grimley Charity, Messrs Martineau Johnson, St Philips House, St Philips Place, Birmingham B3 2PP

CC NO 245250   **ESTABLISHED** 1967

■ Grimmitt Trust

WHAT IS FUNDED General charitable purposes

WHO CAN BENEFIT There are no restrictions on the age; professional and economic group; family situation; religion and culture; and social circumstances of; or disease or medical condition suffered by, the beneficiaries

WHERE FUNDING CAN BE GIVEN UK

SAMPLE GRANTS £35,034 to the community; £20,382 to children and youth causes; £15,490 to cultural and educational causes; £10,530 to medical and handicapped causes; £8,235 to support overseas; £3,200 to Methodist Relief Fund; £3,200 to Water Aid; £3,100 to Demelza House Children's Hospice; £3,000 to Magic Carpet Playbus; £2,500 to Coldingley Prison Drug Abuse Scheme

FINANCES *Year* 1997 *Income* £206,733 *Grants* £90,321

TRUSTEES P W Welch, Mrs M E Welch, D W Everitt, J S Sykes, D C Davies, J C Lees, Mrs C E Chase, P B Hyland, M G Fisher, P Quigley, D Collins, C Hughes Smith

WHO TO APPLY TO D Everitt, Trustee, Grimmitt Trust, Grimmitt Holdings, Woodgate Business Park, Kettles Wood Drive, Birmingham B32 3GH

CC NO 801975   **ESTABLISHED** 1989

■ Grimsdale Charitable Trust

WHAT IS FUNDED Aid and religious causes

WHAT IS NOT FUNDED No grants to individuals

WHO CAN BENEFIT Aid charities and religious charities benefiting at risk groups, those disadvantaged by poverty, socially isolated people and Christians

WHERE FUNDING CAN BE GIVEN UK

RANGE OF GRANTS £1,000–£6,000

SAMPLE GRANTS £6,000 to Intermediate Technology; £3,000 to Water Aid; £2,000 to Bible Society; £1,100 to Methodist Church; £1,000 to Christian Aid

FINANCES *Year* 1997 *Income* £22,994 *Grants* £15,100

TRUSTEES Mrs M Grimsdale, M P Grimsdale

WHO TO APPLY TO Mrs M Grimsdale, Grimsdale Charitable Trust, 6 Chapel Close, Castle Cary, Somerset BA47 7AX

CC NO 327118   **ESTABLISHED** 1985

■ Grocers' Charity

WHAT IS FUNDED Within broad aims which are reflected in the wide pattern of grants, the Trustees currently have a special interest in the relief of poverty (including youth) and the disabled, favouring smaller charities. Accommodation and housing; charity or voluntary umbrella bodies; arts, culture and recreation; health; conservation; heritage and community services and facilities will be considered

WHAT IS NOT FUNDED Organisations which are not registered charities are not funded. No support for churches, educational establishments, expeditions, hospices or research projects. Restricted to those having specific close and long standing connections with The Grocers' Company. Donations will not be made to individuals (but may be paid through registered charities)

WHO CAN BENEFIT Registered charities only. There are no restrictions on the age, family situation, social circumstances of, or disease or medical condition suffered by, the beneficiaries

WHERE FUNDING CAN BE GIVEN UK

TYPE OF GRANT Both capital and revenue projects. Non-recurring grants of limited size. Core costs, one-off, running costs and salaries will be considered, Funding may be given for up to one year

SAMPLE GRANTS £2,500 to St John's Smith Square, London towards disabled access; £2,000 to PHAB for general funds – 40th Anniversary; £1,500 to the College of Arms Trust, London towards cost of re-roofing building; £1,500 to Royal National Theatre, London to the education department; £1,500 to East London Schools Fund to the provision of school-home support worker; £1,500 to Community Links, London towards creation of multi-sensory room at Newham facility; £1,250 to Emmanuel Night Shelter, London towards facilities for the homeless; £1,108 to SENSE towards the provision of holidays for deaf-blind children; £1,000 to British Dyslexia Association towards cost of national telephone helpline; £1,000 to Royal Northern College of Music for junior strings project bursary fund

FINANCES *Year* 1997–98 *Income* £369,000 *Grants* £328,000

TRUSTEES The Grocers' Trust Company Ltd

PUBLICATIONS Annual Report

HOW TO APPLY In writing to the address under Who To Apply To. Trustees meet four times a year in January, April, June and November. Informal telephone inquiries encouraged. Applications are not acknowledged, but are informed of outcome in due course. Copy of latest annual accounts must accompany application

WHO TO APPLY TO Miss Anne Blanchard, Charity Administrator, Grocers' Charity, Grocers' Hall, Princes Street, London EC2R 8AD *Tel* 0171-606 3113 *Fax* 0171-600 3082

CC NO 255230   **ESTABLISHED** 1968

■ M and R Gross Charities Limited

WHAT IS FUNDED To make grants to establishments set up to assist the Jewish religion and Jewish education

WHO CAN BENEFIT Jewish organisations benefiting Jewish people, in particular children and young adults. Support may be given to Rabbis

WHERE FUNDING CAN BE GIVEN UK and overseas

FINANCES *Year* 1996 *Income* £1,608,308 *Grants* £602,443

TRUSTEES The Council

WHO TO APPLY TO M and R Gross Charities Limited, Messrs Cohen, Arnold and Co, Accountants/Auditors, 13–17 New Burlington Place, London W1X 2JP

CC NO 251888   **ESTABLISHED** 1967

■ The Grove Charitable Trust

WHAT IS FUNDED Organisations advancing education in and the religion of Orthodox Jewish faith, and the relief of poverty

WHO CAN BENEFIT To benefit Jews and those disadvantaged by poverty

WHERE FUNDING CAN BE GIVEN UK and overseas

RANGE OF GRANTS £50–£10,000

SAMPLE GRANTS £10,000 to Friends of Laniado Hospital; £5,000 to Pardes House School; £3,500 to Achisomoch Aid Co Ltd; £3,000 to Society of Friends of the Torah; £2,000 to Friends of Mir Yeshiva; £1,200 to Beth Shmnel Synagogue; £1,200 to Keren Hatorah; £500 to Friends of Bobor; £500 to Gertner Charitable Trust; £360 to Emuua Education Centre

FINANCES *Year* 1997 *Income* £28,047 *Grants* £29,210

TRUSTEES Mrs R Bodner (Chairman), B Bodner, M Bodner, Mrs S Bodner

WHO TO APPLY TO A L Bodner, The Grove Charitable Trust, 40 Highfield Gardens, London NW11 9HB

CC NO 279110   **ESTABLISHED** 1979

■ Mary Isobel Grove Charitable Trust

WHAT IS FUNDED General charitable purposes

WHO CAN BENEFIT There are no restrictions on the age; professional and economic group; family situation; religion and culture; and social circumstances of; or disease or medical condition suffered by, the beneficiaries

WHERE FUNDING CAN BE GIVEN UK

RANGE OF GRANTS £150–£40,000

SAMPLE GRANTS £40,000 to Myton Hospice; £20,000 to Acorn Hospice; £5,000 to Cornerstone Christian Charity; £280 to Warwickshire Association of Youth Clubs; £150 to Riding for the Disabled

FINANCES *Year* 1995 *Income* £74,733 *Grants* £65,430

TRUSTEES R W Ollis, I Ollis, L F Grove

WHO TO APPLY TO R W Ollis, Mary Isobel Grove Charitable Trust, Windsor House, Temple Row, Birmingham B2 5LF

CC NO 1016113   **ESTABLISHED** 1992

■ The Groves Charitable Trust

WHAT IS FUNDED This Trust will consider funding: Christian education; Christian outreach; missionaries and evangelicals; cultural and religious teaching; bursaries and fees; religious studies; and emergency care, refugees and famine. Majority of income allocated on regular basis to Christian work, missionary societies, etc

WHAT IS NOT FUNDED Mainly restricted to evangelical Christian causes

WHO CAN BENEFIT Missionary work at home and overseas. Christian relief work. Training for Christian ministry. The main beneficiaries are Christians and evangelists

WHERE FUNDING CAN BE GIVEN UK and overseas

TYPE OF GRANT Core costs, one-off and recurring. Funding can be given for up to three years

RANGE OF GRANTS £200–£1,000. Typically £200 to individuals, £300 to organisations

SAMPLE GRANTS £2,000 to Great St Helen's Trust; £1,600 to Evenlode PCC; £1,000 to Aeropagus Trust; £1,000 to Proclamation Trust; £1,000 to Lambeth Fund

FINANCES *Year* 1997 *Income* £21,033 *Grants* £21,466

TRUSTEES W H D Scott, Mrs A J Scott, L J Leppard, R A Scott

HOW TO APPLY In writing, December and May preferred. Only applications enclosing sae will be acknowledged

WHO TO APPLY TO R Humphrey, The Groves Charitable Trust, Messrs Grant Thornton, 125 High Street, Crawley, West Sussex RH10 1DQ

CC NO 263811   **ESTABLISHED** 1972

■ The David and Marie Grumett Foundation

WHAT IS FUNDED General charitable purposes

WHO CAN BENEFIT There are no restrictions on the age; professional and economic group; family situation; religion and culture; and social circumstances of; or disease or medical condition suffered by, the beneficiaries

WHERE FUNDING CAN BE GIVEN UK

RANGE OF GRANTS £500–£5,000

SAMPLE GRANTS £5,000 to the Jesuit Missions; £4,200 to Diocese of Arundel and Brighton; £3,000 to Centrepoint, Soho; £3,000 to the Bourne Trust; £2,000 to the Passage Day Centre; £2,000 to LIFE; £2,000 to Providence Row; £1,000 to The Samaritans; £1,000 to St Thomas Fund for Homeless; £500 to St Barnabas Society

FINANCES *Year* 1996 *Income* £42,175 *Grants* £23,700

TRUSTEES D T McA Grumett, Mrs M Grumett

WHO TO APPLY TO The David and Marie Grumett Foundation, Bank of Scotland, Trustee Department, PO Box No 41, 101 George Street, Edinburgh EH2 3JH

CC NO 288826   **ESTABLISHED** 1984

■ The N and R Grunbaum Charitable Trust

WHAT IS FUNDED General charitable purposes
WHO CAN BENEFIT There are no restrictions on the age; professional and economic group; family situation; religion and culture; and social circumstances of; or disease or medical condition suffered by, the beneficiaries
WHERE FUNDING CAN BE GIVEN UK and Israel
TRUSTEES N N Grunbaum, R Grunbaum, D Grunbaum
WHO TO APPLY TO N Grunbaum, The N and R Grunbaum Charitable Trust, 7 Northdene Gardens, London N15 6LX
CC NO 1068524　　**ESTABLISHED** 1998

■ The Stanley Grundy Foundation

WHAT IS FUNDED General charitable purposes. To promote local goodwill in the facility of Grundy Group companies by sponsoring local projects and charities
WHO CAN BENEFIT Local to Grundy Group companies in Teddington. There are no restrictions on the age; professional and economic group; family situation; religion and culture; and social circumstances of; or disease or medical condition suffered by, the beneficiaries
WHERE FUNDING CAN BE GIVEN Teddington
TYPE OF GRANT Cash donations or sponsorship of project
SAMPLE GRANTS £50,000 to National Back Pain Association for support to charity founded by Mr Grundy; £25,487 Rotary Chess Initiative for support to charity founded by Mr Grundy
FINANCES *Year* 1995–96 *Income* £68,054 *Grants* £69,688
TRUSTEES Mrs S Greenhill, L L Allum
HOW TO APPLY In writing to Stanley Grundy Foundation
WHO TO APPLY TO The Stanley Grundy Foundation, 16 Elmtree Road, Teddington, Middlesex TW11 8ST
CC NO 231755　　**ESTABLISHED** 1961

■ The Grut Charitable Trust

WHAT IS FUNDED Help to individuals suffering from the effects of illness or poverty
WHO CAN BENEFIT Individuals supported by recognised voluntary bodies, local authorities or social welfare organisations. Also organisations benefiting those disadvantaged by poverty. There is no restriction on the disease or medical condition suffered by the beneficiaries
WHERE FUNDING CAN BE GIVEN UK and overseas
SAMPLE GRANTS £5,000 to Wiener Library; £1,000 to New Israel Fund; £500 to United World College of the Atlantic Charity; £250 to Norwood Child Care; £250 to Council of Christians and Jews; £250 to Nightingale House; £250 to British Red Cross; £250 to Help the Aged; £250 to Imperial Cancer Research Fund; £250 to Notting Hill Housing Trust
FINANCES *Year* 1996–97 *Income* £29,977 *Grants* £31,980
TRUSTEES A C R G Montefiore, J M Bogaardt
NOTES In 1996–97 an unspecified amount was given in grants to individuals
HOW TO APPLY All requests for funding or for information must be submitted in writing
WHO TO APPLY TO Messrs Poole & Co, The Grut Charitable Trust, Dolphin House, 21 Hendford, Yeovil, Somerset BA20 1TP
CC NO 287947　　**ESTABLISHED** 1983

■ The Guardian Foundation

WHAT IS FUNDED Education, international. To promote the development of journalism particularly in Eastern European countries and to support free speech
WHO CAN BENEFIT To benefit children, young adults, students and journalists
WHERE FUNDING CAN BE GIVEN UK and overseas
TYPE OF GRANT One-off
FINANCES *Year* 1996 *Income* £65,199 *Grants* £21,400
TRUSTEES H J S Young, H J Roche, M J Scott, P J Preston, M R Unger, J P Scott, A W Phillips, A Sampson, J M Dean, A Lapping
WHO TO APPLY TO Michael Unger, Trustee, The Guardian Foundation, 164 Deansgate, Manchester M60 2RR
CC NO 1027893　　**ESTABLISHED** 1993

■ The Guardian Royal Exchange Charitable Trust

WHAT IS FUNDED Charities working in the fields of health, welfare, arts and the environment. Each application on its merits but to people rather than animals or buildings
WHAT IS NOT FUNDED Individuals, including students, are ineligible
WHO CAN BENEFIT Registered and established charities only, benefiting actors and entertainment professionals; musicians; textile workers and designers; writers and poets; at risk groups; disabled people; those disadvantaged by poverty and socially isolated people. There is no restriction on the disease or medical condition suffered by the beneficiaries
WHERE FUNDING CAN BE GIVEN UK
TYPE OF GRANT One-off or recurrent
SAMPLE GRANTS £3,000 to British Heart Foundation for medical research; £3,000 to Royal Academy of Music; £2,500 to Royal Academy of Dancing; £2,500 to British Home and Hospital for Incurables for medical research; £2,500 to Lord Mayor's Appeal for St Paul's Cathedral; £2,000 to GAP Activity Projects Ltd for welfare; £1,500 to NSPCC for welfare; £1,500 to Retired and Senior Volunteer Programme CSV for welfare; £1,500 to Royal Air Force Association for welfare; £1,500 to Percy Hedley Centre for medical research
FINANCES *Year* 1997 *Income* £259,283 *Grants* £234,381
TRUSTEES The Hon G E Adeane, CVO, Sir Paul Newally, J Sinclair, J R W Clayton
NOTES When telephoning please ask for ext 723 2365
HOW TO APPLY By post. Reviewed continuously. Include latest accounts
WHO TO APPLY TO C V Foster, Appeals Secretary, The Guardian Royal Exchange Charitable Trust, Guardian Royal Exchange Assurance plc, Royal Exchange, London EC3V 3LS *Tel* 0171-283 7101
CC NO 326003　　**ESTABLISHED** 1981

■ Mrs Margaret Guido's Charitable Trust

WHAT IS FUNDED The preservation of the built and natural environment and the promotion of the arts, especially music
WHO CAN BENEFIT Organisations benefiting actors, and entertainment professionals; musicians; textile workers and designers; writers and poets
WHERE FUNDING CAN BE GIVEN UK and overseas

FINANCES *Year* 1997–98 *Income* £22,340
Grants £22,850
TRUSTEES Coutts & Co
HOW TO APPLY To the address under Who To Apply To in writing
WHO TO APPLY TO Mrs Margaret Guido's Charitable Trust, The Trustee Department, c/o Coutts & Co, 440 Strand, London WC2R 0QS *Tel* 0171-753 1000
CC NO 290503   ESTABLISHED 1984

■ The Bishop of Guildford's Foundation

WHAT IS FUNDED The relief of poverty and isolation; the advancement of education and other charitable purposes beneficial to the community
WHAT IS NOT FUNDED The total cost of the project will not be funded. No grants to individuals
WHO CAN BENEFIT Independent organisations whose aims are charitable to help other people in need. Volunteers, unemployed people and those with many different social circumstances will be considered. There is no restriction on age or family situation of those funded
WHERE FUNDING CAN BE GIVEN The Diocese of Guildford
TYPE OF GRANT Buildings, capital, core costs, interest free loans, one-off, project, recurring costs, running costs, salaries and start-up costs. Funding may be given for up to three years
RANGE OF GRANTS £300–£10,000, typical grant £2,000
SAMPLE GRANTS £59,850 to Oakleaf Enterprises, Guildford towards support for people with mental health problems; £20,323 to St Marks Community, Godalming for the provision of church community centre; £11,217 to North Guildford Project for a community project/employment initiative; £10,000 to All Saints Nursery School, Leatherhead for a nursery class; £9,799 to Befrienders and Carers Scheme, West Surrey for befriending people with mental health problems; £8,000 to Park Barn, Guildford for a community worker; £7,700 to YMCA, Guildford for a foyer and youth cafe project; £5,530 to Connect Christian Counselling, Camberley for a counselling service; £3,200 to Youth Project, Chertsey for a drop in centre for teenagers; £3,000 to After School Club, Headley for after school and holiday clubs
FINANCES *Year* 1998 *Income* £182,354
Grants £152,170
TRUSTEES Bishop of Guildford, Lord Lane of Hossell, Bishop of Dorking, Alan Foster, Michael Young
NOTES Beneficiaries must have a bank or building society account
HOW TO APPLY Information pack with guidelines for applicants is issued
WHO TO APPLY TO Patrick Hodson, Chief Executive, The Bishop of Guildford's Foundation, Diocesan House, Quarry Street, Guildford, Surrey GU1 3XG *Tel* 01483 304000 *Fax* 01483 567896 *E-mail* Patrick.Hodson@cofeguildford.org.uk
CC NO 1017385   ESTABLISHED 1993

■ Guildhall Feoffment

WHAT IS FUNDED The principal activity of the Trust is the provision and upkeep of its almshouses. Education, health and charitable purposes which benefit the inhabitants of Bury St Edmonds are also considered
WHO CAN BENEFIT Organisations benefiting children and young adults; those disadvantaged by poverty;

homeless people; and the inhabitants of Bury St Edmonds. There is no restriction on the disease or medical condition suffered by the beneficiaries
WHERE FUNDING CAN BE GIVEN Bury St Edmonds
FINANCES *Year* 1995 *Income* £100,093
Grants £46,607
TRUSTEES A S V Williams (Chairman), M J Ames, Very Rev J E Atwell, G D R Cochram, Mrs M Dunlop-Johnson, Canon J D Hayden, Mrs M M L Horbury, F S Jepson, Miss M M P MacRae, S F Pott, F Robinson, Mrs M Statham, E G Steele, Mrs G F Tennant, J H Warren
NOTES £17,289 is spent on the maintenance of the almshouses
HOW TO APPLY To the address under Who To Apply To in writing
WHO TO APPLY TO M R Leftwich, Clerk, Guildhall Feoffment, 1 Albert Crescent, Bury St Ednonds, Suffolk IP33 3DX
CC NO 211060   ESTABLISHED 1988

■ The Guineas Ball Charitable Trust

WHAT IS FUNDED General charitable purposes
WHO CAN BENEFIT There are no restrictions on the age; professional and economic group; family situation; religion and culture; and social circumstances of; or disease or medical condition suffered by, the beneficiaries
WHERE FUNDING CAN BE GIVEN The Town of Newmarket and surrounding villages
WHO TO APPLY TO Mrs S M C Keever, The Guineas Ball Charitable Trust, Rook Tree Farm House, Great Wratting, Haverhill, Suffolk CB9 7HD
CC NO 1068592   ESTABLISHED 1998

■ The Walter Guinness Charitable Trust

WHAT IS FUNDED Unlikely to be able to support anything we are not already in touch with, but would be interested to hear from charities concerned with research, education, communities and ecology
WHAT IS NOT FUNDED No grants to individuals
WHO CAN BENEFIT Organisations benefiting: people of all ages; research workers; students; those in care, fostered and adopted; one parent families; widows and widowers; and disabled people
WHERE FUNDING CAN BE GIVEN Especially Wiltshire
TYPE OF GRANT Normally one-off
RANGE OF GRANTS Variable
SAMPLE GRANTS £17,600 to Department of Zoology Cambridge University for research; £10,000 to Enham for disabled people; £10,000 to Queen Elizabeth Foundation for the Disabled; £9,000 to UNIPAL (Palestine) for education; £9,000 to NSPCC (Ashdown Family Centre) for education and child care; £6,500 to Fairbridge for youth; £3,500 to OMSET for education/medical purposes; £3,470 to CPRE for environment/aesthetics; £2,500 to Scouts Hall, Ludgershall for the community; £2,000 to Kingston Maurward College for education
FINANCES *Year* 1997 *Income* £192,908
Grants £158,510
TRUSTEES F B Guinness, Mrs Rosaleen Mulji
HOW TO APPLY Please apply in writing. We only reply when there is a positive decision. Initial telephone calls are not welcome. There are no application forms, guidelines or deadlines. No sae required

WHO TO APPLY TO The Secretary, The Walter Guinness Charitable Trust, Biddesden House, Biddesden, Andover, Hampshire SP11 9DN
CC NO 205375 **ESTABLISHED** 1961

■ Calouste Gulbenkian Foundation (Lisbon) United Kingdom Branch

WHAT IS FUNDED Community development; support to volunteers, charity or voluntary umbrella bodies; arts, culture and recreation; schools and colleges
WHAT IS NOT FUNDED Certain general limits apply to all the programmes, and within each programme there are priorities which mark out the current areas for grant-giving. Limits and priorities are set out in a leaflet *Advice to applicants for grants*. Please read these guidelines before making an application. Please note no grants for individuals' education, training or exhibitions etc, nor for any general appeal or conferences
WHO CAN BENEFIT To or through registered charities
WHERE FUNDING CAN BE GIVEN For programmes (a), (b), (c) and (d) the United Kingdom (preference given to areas other than south east England) and the Republic of Ireland. All other areas in the world are dealt with by the Foundation's Lisbon headquarters
TYPE OF GRANT Rarely more than £5,000 for any one project. Grants for specific significant developments, never general appeals, nor established recurrent running or building costs, nor scholarships, etc for individuals, nor exhibitions, etc
SAMPLE GRANTS £10,000 to the Young Builders' Trust to help train disadvantaged unemployed and homeless people to build houses; £7,500 to the Directory of Social Change to publish an independent study evaluating the work of the Foundation's Social Welfare programme over 30 years; £7,000 to 'The Big Issue' in Scotland to help train homeless people in new skills; £5,500 over two years for workshops for teachers working in multi-denominational schools in the Republic of Ireland; £4,000 to the Cultural Traditions Group (Arts Council of N Ireland) to organise a prize competition for a Peace Song for Northern Ireland
FINANCES *Year* 1997 *Grants* £2,023,899
TRUSTEES International Foundation with a Board of Trustees in Lisbon
PUBLICATIONS *Advice to applicants for grants* and Annual Report (both free). List of other publications free on request
HOW TO APPLY See *Advice to applicants for grants* obtainable free from the Foundation. Applications should be made in writing, but there is no formal application form. Evaluations will be particularly encouraged
WHO TO APPLY TO The Director, Calouste Gulbenkian Foundation (Lisbon) United Kingdom Branch, 98 Portland Place, London W1N 4ET *Tel* 0171-636 5313 *Fax* 0171-637 3421
ESTABLISHED 1956

■ The Gunter Charitable Trust

WHAT IS FUNDED General charitable purposes. To support organisations known to the Trust
WHO CAN BENEFIT There are no restrictions on the age; professional and economic group; family situation; religion and culture; and social circumstances of; or disease or medical condition suffered by, the beneficiaries
WHERE FUNDING CAN BE GIVEN UK and overseas
RANGE OF GRANTS £100–£12,140

SAMPLE GRANTS £12,140 to Liverpool School of Tropical Medicine to six individuals; £6,000 to Dandelion Trust; £3,000 to Friends of Dr Pearay Lal Charity Hospital; £2,900 to Survival International; £2,500 to Marie Stopes International; £2,500 to the Hunter Trust; £2,200 to Intermediate Technology Development Group; £1,900 to Oxfam; £1,900 to Refugee Council; £1,600 to National Schizophrenia Fellowship
FINANCES *Year* 1997 *Income* £162,177 *Grants* £76,654
TRUSTEES J de C E Findlay, H R D Billson
HOW TO APPLY **This Trust states that it does not respond to unsolicited applications**
WHO TO APPLY TO S J Atkinson, The Gunter Charitable Trust, Forsters, 67–68 Grosvenor Street, London W1X 9DB
CC NO 268346 **ESTABLISHED** 1974

■ The Gur Trust (209 =)

This trust declined to meet CAF's researchers and failed to supply a copy of its annual report and accounts to CAF as required under section 47(2) of the Charities Act 1993. The information held on file at the Charity Commission was insufficient to enable CAF's researchers to write a substantive commentary on the trust's activities. Accordingly, despite its size, we are unable to list this trust in Spotlight on Major Trusts

WHAT IS FUNDED Advancement of education and the orthodox Jewish religion
WHO CAN BENEFIT Individuals and organisations benefiting children, young adults, students and Jewish people
WHERE FUNDING CAN BE GIVEN UK
TYPE OF GRANT At the discretion of the Trustees
FINANCES *Year* 1995 *Income* £592,461 *Grants* £489,587
TRUSTEES J Schrieber
WHO TO APPLY TO J Schreiber, The Gur Trust, 16 Grangecourt Road, London N16 5EG
CC NO 283423 **ESTABLISHED** 1961

■ Gurunanak

WHAT IS FUNDED Relief of poverty and general charitable purposes at the Trustees' discretion
WHO CAN BENEFIT Organisations, particularly those benefiting people disadvantaged by poverty
WHERE FUNDING CAN BE GIVEN UK, with preference for Greater Manchester
FINANCES *Year* 1996 *Income* £14,496 *Grants* £16,486
TRUSTEES J S Kholi, B S Kohli, A S Dhody, H S Chadha
WHO TO APPLY TO J S Kohli, Gurunanak, NIJ Than, 23a Upper Park Road, Salford M7 0HY
CC NO 1017903 **ESTABLISHED** 1993

■ Gus Charitable Trust

WHAT IS FUNDED General charitable purposes
WHO CAN BENEFIT There are no restrictions on the age; professional and economic group; family situation; religion and culture; and social circumstances of; or disease or medical condition suffered by, the beneficiaries
WHERE FUNDING CAN BE GIVEN UK
TRUSTEES The Great Universal Store plc, M V Blank, D Morris, Lady Patten of Wincanton

WHO TO APPLY TO D Morris, Gus Charitable Trust, The Great Universal Stores plc, PO Box 99, Universal House, Devonshire Street, Manchester M60 1XA
CC NO 1066511   ESTABLISHED 1997

■ Tom Gutteridge Foundation

WHAT IS FUNDED General charitable purposes
WHO CAN BENEFIT There are no restrictions on the age; professional and economic group; family situation; religion and culture; and social circumstances of; or disease or medical condition suffered by, the beneficiaries
WHERE FUNDING CAN BE GIVEN UK
TRUSTEES T M G Gutteridge, J Challis, D Leach, M Rowland
WHO TO APPLY TO T Gutteridge, Tom Gutteridge Foundation, Mentorn House, 140 Wardour Street, London W1V 4LJ
CC NO 1069096   ESTABLISHED 1998

■ Gwynedd County Council Welsh Church Fund

This trust did not respond to CAF's request to amend its entry and, by 30 June 1998, CAF's researchers did not find financial records for later than 1995 on its file at the Charity Commission. Trusts are legally required to submit annual accounts to the Charity Commission under section 42 of the Charities Act 1993

WHAT IS FUNDED General charitable purposes. Applications which are of direct benefit to the County and inhabitants of Gwynedd only are considered
WHAT IS NOT FUNDED (a) Personal applications are not entertained. (b) Only registered charities can receive financial assistance
WHO CAN BENEFIT Local organisations, local branches of national organisations, or specific local projects run by national organisations. There are no restrictions on the age; professional and economic group; family situation; religion and culture; and social circumstances of; or disease or medical condition suffered by, the beneficiaries
WHERE FUNDING CAN BE GIVEN The County of Gwynedd
TRUSTEES Gwynedd Council
WHO TO APPLY TO Mrs J Hughes, Secretary and Solicitor, Gwynedd County Council Welsh Church Fund, Gwynedd Council, Caernarfon, Gwynedd LL55 1SH
CC NO 221004   ESTABLISHED 1974

■ HACT (The Housing Association's Charitable Trust)

WHAT IS FUNDED The Trust focuses its grant-making in five key areas: (a) single homeless people with support needs, (b) people with special needs, (c) older people, (d) refugee-led groups, (e) black and minority ethnic communities. The Trustees aim to support innovative projects but will at all times adopt a flexible approach to applicants. The Trustees have adopted an equal opportunities policy and are committed to acting positively to promote equal opportunities and to counteract direct and indirect discrimination. All applicants are required to consider this issue seriously. The HACT helps housing associations and voluntary housing organisations throughout the United Kingdom to provide high quality housing and other related services for people who are homeless or badly housed. HACT works to achieve this by: (a) providing grants, loans and fund-raising advice to voluntary organisations; (b) assisting other charitable trusts on ways in which they can fund housing projects most effectively
WHAT IS NOT FUNDED No grants to individuals. The Trust will not support projects which are eligible for statutory funding
WHO CAN BENEFIT Voluntary housing organisations
WHERE FUNDING CAN BE GIVEN UK
TYPE OF GRANT Developmental and start-up revenue grants; capital grants are rare
RANGE OF GRANTS Below £7,500–£25,000
SAMPLE GRANTS £25,000 to Tung Sing (Orient) Housing Association; £23,000 to Age Concern, Nottinghamshire; £20,000 to Abbeyfield Cambs/ Vietnamese; £20,000 to Almshouse Association; £20,000 to Harrow Churches; £20,000 to Hibiscus Caribbean and African Elders; £20,000 to Kensington and Chelsea Staying Put; £20,000 to SHACT; £17,000 to FBHO; £17,000 to Say Women
FINANCES *Year* 1996 *Income* £1,184,473 *Grants* £878,482
TRUSTEES HACT's 20 trustees are drawn from housing, charitable, corporate and professional fields, serving on either the Grant-Making Committee or the Resources Committee
PUBLICATIONS Two newsletters per year, Annual Review and occasional briefing reports on urgent housing issues, for example: *Dementia, A Cause for Concern* (1995); *Supported Housing in Rural Areas: An Agenda for Action* (1996)
HOW TO APPLY Please telephone one of HACT's Advisers on 0171–336 7877 to discuss any possible application. Comprehensive guidelines are provided for applicants and applications can only be made on HACT's application form
WHO TO APPLY TO The Director, HACT, Yeoman House, 168–172 Old Street, London EC1V 9BP
CC NO 256160   ESTABLISHED 1960

■ HCD Memorial Fund

WHAT IS FUNDED Health, development and disaster aid abroad, residential facilities and services, disabled, and other social and educational work in the UK. Support may also be given towards: economic regeneration schemes; job creation;

small enterprises; support to voluntary and community organisations; woodlands; organic food production and transport and alternative transport

WHAT IS NOT FUNDED Not usually for animals or objects. No grants to individuals

WHO CAN BENEFIT Organisations benefiting: unemployed people; those in care, fostered and adopted; parents and children. Support may also be given to disabled people, those disadvantaged by poverty, homeless people, disaster victims and victims of war. Funding is considered for those suffering from HIV and AIDs, mental illness and those who are terminally ill

WHERE FUNDING CAN BE GIVEN UK and overseas

TYPE OF GRANT Can be one-off or recurring, including core costs, buildings and start-up costs. Funding may be given for up to three years

RANGE OF GRANTS £1,000–£150,000, typical grant £20,000

FINANCES *Year* 1996–97 *Income* £491,148 *Grants* £662,689

TRUSTEES C Debenham, J Debenham, N Debenham, C Flinn, Dr C Sherman

NOTES Have a preference for seeking our own projects; do not usually respond to general appeals

HOW TO APPLY In writing, no special form

WHO TO APPLY TO J Debenham, HCD Memorial Fund, Reeds Farm, Sayers Common, Hassocks, West Sussex BN6 9JQ *Tel* 01273 832173

CC NO 1044956   **ESTABLISHED** 1995

■ Haberdashers' Eleemosynary Charity

WHAT IS FUNDED Those persons in need, hardship or distress, and Freemen of the Haberdasher's Company and the City of London

WHAT IS NOT FUNDED No grants to individuals other than Freemen and their dependants. Local branches of national charities are unlikely to be supported

WHO CAN BENEFIT Freemen of the Haberdasher's Company; at risk groups; those disadvantaged by poverty; homeless people; victims of abuse; victims of crime; and victims of domestic violence

WHERE FUNDING CAN BE GIVEN UK, and especially the City of London

TYPE OF GRANT Mainly one-off

FINANCES *Year* 1997 *Income* £289,000 *Grants* £267,000

TRUSTEES The Haberdashers' Company

HOW TO APPLY To the Clerk to the Haberdashers' Company

WHO TO APPLY TO The Clerk, Haberdashers' Eleemosynary Charity, The Haberdashers' Company, 39–40 Bartholomew Close, London EC1A 7JN *Tel* 0171-606 0967

CC NO 230530   **ESTABLISHED** 1978

■ D K A Hackney Charitable Trust

WHAT IS FUNDED General charitable purposes

WHO CAN BENEFIT There are no restrictions on the age; professional and economic group; family situation; religion and culture; and social circumstances of; or disease or medical condition suffered by, the beneficiaries

WHERE FUNDING CAN BE GIVEN UK

FINANCES *Year* 1995 *Income* £28,740 *Grants* £10,510

TRUSTEES Mrs D K A Hackney, Mrs D P M Schiffer, J A Krafft

HOW TO APPLY This Trust states that it does not respond to unsolicited applications

WHO TO APPLY TO Jame J Krafft, D K A Hackney Charitable Trust, Thomson Snell & Passmore, 3 Lonsdale Gardens, Tunbridge Wells, Kent TN1 1NX *Tel* 01892 510000

CC NO 1021109   **ESTABLISHED** 1993

■ The Hackney Parochial Charities

WHAT IS FUNDED Community and education projects which benefit poor people in the area Where Funding Can Be Given

WHO CAN BENEFIT Organisations benefiting children, young adults and those disadvantaged by poverty may be considered. Community organisations may benefit

WHERE FUNDING CAN BE GIVEN The London Borough of Hackney

SAMPLE GRANTS £43,155 to Rector's Discretionary Fund; £20,000 to Hackney Quest; £11,500 to Hackney Free and Parochial Schools Foundation; £10,324 to London Borough of Hackney; £7,500 to Uganda Refugee Welfare; £6,500 to Disabled Soldiers and Sailors (Hackney) Foundation; £5,000 to St John-at-Hackney Community Space Project; £4,700 to Homerton Space Project; £4,000 to Hackney Outreach Project; £4,000 to Morpeth School's Fund

FINANCES *Year* 1996 *Income* £418,128 *Grants* £201,299

HOW TO APPLY To the address under Who To Apply To in writing

WHO TO APPLY TO A D M Sorrell, The Hackney Parochial Charities, Messrs Craigen Wilders Sorrell, 81–83 High Road, Wood Green, London N22 6BE

CC NO 219876   **ESTABLISHED** 1904

■ William Haddon Charitable Trust

WHAT IS FUNDED Medicine, religion, conservation and animal welfare including cemeteries and burial grounds; churches; music; hospices; hospitals; medical centres; parks; and crime prevention schemes

WHAT IS NOT FUNDED No grants to individuals

WHO CAN BENEFIT Registered charities benefiting: young adults; academics; clergy; ex-service and service people; musicians; research workers; scientists; seafarers and fishermen; stroke victims; terminally ill; disabled people; victims of crime; and those suffering from Alzheimer's disease, arthritis and rheumatism, asthma, diabetes, hearing loss, heart disease, HIV and AIDs, kidney disease, Parkinson's disease and sight loss

WHERE FUNDING CAN BE GIVEN UK and overseas

TYPE OF GRANT One-off grants of £1,000 or less for buildings, project and research

RANGE OF GRANTS £50–£1,000

SAMPLE GRANTS £1,000 to Fauna and Flora International for gorilla conservation; £1,000 to World Parrot Trust conservation of hyacinth macaws; £750 to International Primate Protection League, veterinary help for Cameroon; £750 to International Otter Survival Fund to otters in Britain; £500 to St Dunstan's for war-blinded servicemen

FINANCES *Year* 1995–96 *Income* £14,955 *Grants* £11,250

TRUSTEES Ms Margaret Haddon, Mrs Catherine Johnson, Mrs Joyce Haddon, Ms Celia Haddon

HOW TO APPLY In writing only. There are no application forms

Does the trust you have chosen match your needs? Haphazard applications waste postage and time

269

WHO TO APPLY TO Ms M A Haddon, William Haddon Charitable Trust, Manor Garden, Sibbertoft, Market Harborough, Leicestershire LE16 9UA
CC NO 326540 **ESTABLISHED** 1984

■ The Hadfield Charitable Trust

WHAT IS FUNDED Charities concerned with social needs, youth employment, help for the aged, the arts and the environment, particularly those working in the fields of: accommodation and housing; support and development; arts, culture and recreation; health; conservation; education and training; and social care and development

WHAT IS NOT FUNDED No grants made for projects which are political, religious or sectarian, except churches and places of worship. No grants to individuals

WHO CAN BENEFIT Organisations benefiting children; young adults and older people; unemployed; parents and children; one parent families; and widows and widowers. There is no restriction on the disease or medical condition suffered by the beneficiaries, however there are some restrictions on their social circumstances

WHERE FUNDING CAN BE GIVEN The County of Cumbria

TYPE OF GRANT Capital projects preferred, buildings will be considered and funding is generally for one year or less

RANGE OF GRANTS Minimum £500

SAMPLE GRANTS £10,000 to Life Education Centre for Cumbria for Life Education vehicle; £5,000 to Age Concern, Carlisle for a minibus; £5,000 to The National Trust for Junior Wardens Scheme in Cumbria; £4,000 to Cumbria Association of Youth Clubs; £4,000 to Calvert Trust, Penrith; £3,000 to Abbeyfield (Lakeland Extra-Care) for building extension; £2,000 to Ulverston and North Lonsdale Citizens Advice Bureau for IT equipment; £2,000 to Ehenside Health and Fitness Centre; £1,000 to The National Trust for Highway Centre, Cumbria; £1,000 to Mountain Bothies Association

FINANCES *Year* 1998 *Income* £175,000

TRUSTEES R A Morris (Chairman), A T Morris, W Rathbone, O Turnbull

PUBLICATIONS A leaflet setting out the aims and objectives of the Trust (available on request)

HOW TO APPLY Please write for an application form and further details. Applicants are asked to provide a copy of their latest accounts and will be sent an application form for completion. The Trustees like to monitor the progress of successful grants. All applications will be acknowledged

WHO TO APPLY TO M E Hope, The Hadfield Charitable Trust, c/o Rathbone Bros & Co Ltd, Port of Liverpool Building, Pier Head, Liverpool L3 1NW *Tel* 0151-236 6666 *Fax* 0151-243 7001
CC NO 1067491 **ESTABLISHED** 1998

■ The Hadrian Trust

WHAT IS FUNDED Social welfare and other charitable projects within the boundaries of the old counties of Northumberland and Durham (this includes Tyne and Wear). The main headings under which applications are considered are: social welfare; youth; women; the elderly; the disabled; ethnic minorities; the arts; the environment; education; religion; accommodation and housing; infrastructure, support and development; and health

WHAT IS NOT FUNDED General applications from large national organisations are not considered nor from smaller bodies working outside the beneficial area

WHO CAN BENEFIT Organisations benefiting people of all ages; unemployed people; volunteers; those in care, fostered and adopted; one parent families; widows and widowers and Christians. Beneficiaries may be suffering from various diseases and medical conditions. There are no restrictions on the social circumstances of, or disease or medical condition suffered by, the beneficiaries. Typical grants in 1997 were to: councils for voluntary service, advice and counselling services, women's projects, youth clubs and schools, charities for disabled, and elderly, arts projects, church restoration and block grants for individuals in need

WHERE FUNDING CAN BE GIVEN Within the boundaries of the old counties of Northumberland and Durham (this includes Tyne and Wear and Cleveland north of the Tees)

TYPE OF GRANT Usually one-off for a special project or part of a project. Core funding is rarely considered. The average grant is for £1,000. Buildings, capital, project, research, recurring costs, as well as running costs, salaries and start-up costs. Funding of up to three years will be considered

RANGE OF GRANTS £250–£5,000

SAMPLE GRANTS £6,000 to Newcastle CVS towards the salary of an information officer; £5,000 to Warden and Newbrough Millennium Committee for restoration of Community Centre; £5,000 to St John's College, Durham University for establishment of Outward Bound Youth Training Centre; £5,000 to Northern Sinfonia Development Trust for general financial support for orchestra; £5,000 to Bede's World Jarrow for development of outdoor museum; £5,000 to Brinkburn Summer Music for support of a local music festival; £4,500 to Tyne and Wear Foundation as a contribution towards Millennium Bursary Awards; £3,000 to Funding Information North East towards production of NE Charity Funding Directory; £3,000 to Greggs Charitable Trust as block grant for individuals in need; £2,500 to Institute for the Health of the Elderly

FINANCES *Year* 1997 *Income* £190,976 *Grants* £196,750

TRUSTEES P R M Harbottle, B J Gillespie, J B Parker

PUBLICATIONS Information sheet

NOTES Trustees meetings are held in January, April, July and October

HOW TO APPLY By letter to the address under Who To Apply To. There is no application form but information sheet will be sent if requested. The letter of application should set out concise details of the project, the proposed funding and list any other applications being made, with results if known. Eligible applications will be acknowledged and the acknowledgement will give the date when the application will be considered. Cheques are sent out to successful applicants within two weeks of the meeting, but no further correspondence is sent to unsuccessful applicants. Applications from individuals in need are now referred to Greggs Charitable Trust to whom a block grant is now made. The address is Fernwood House, Clayton Road, Newcastle upon Tyne NE2 1TL

WHO TO APPLY TO John Parker, The Hadrian Trust, 36 Rectory Road, Gosforth, Newcastle upon Tyne NE3 1XP *Tel* 0191-285 9553 (only for specific enquiries)
CC NO 272161 **ESTABLISHED** 1976

■ The Nancy Hadwen Charitable Trust

WHAT IS FUNDED Quaker charities and charities supporting classical music (orchestral and opera) and hospices in the Home Counties. Infrastructure and technical support and support to voluntary and community organisations will be considered

WHAT IS NOT FUNDED Expeditions, scholarships and other projects for the benefit of individuals

WHO CAN BENEFIT Registered charities benefiting older people, retired people, musicians and Quakers

WHERE FUNDING CAN BE GIVEN London and the South East of England

TYPE OF GRANT One-off, preferably for specific projects, core costs, and running costs will be considered. Funding can be given for up to two years

RANGE OF GRANTS £500–£1,000

SAMPLE GRANTS £3,450 to English Sinfonia for general administration/accommodation; £1,500 to Trinity Hospice for general purposes; £1,500 to Wimbledon Guild of Social Welfare for general purposes; £1,000 to BIA Quaker Social Action for general purposes; £1,000 to British Red Cross for general purposes

FINANCES *Year* 1996–97 *Income* £18,740 *Grants* £19,900

TRUSTEES Mrs E N A Hadwen, D J R Wells

HOW TO APPLY By Letter. There is no application form. Applications are considered four times a year. Enclose sae if you require acknowledgement

WHO TO APPLY TO D J R Wells, The Nancy Hadwen Charitable Trust, Arthur Andersen, 20 Old Bailey, London EC4M 7AN

CC NO 291992   **ESTABLISHED** 1985

■ The Haemophilia Society

WHAT IS FUNDED Grants are, in the main, made to individuals in need who suffer from haemophilia, on the recommendation of a health professional affiliated to their haemophilia centre

WHAT IS NOT FUNDED Applications for research grants must be such that they will benefit those with haemophilia. It should be noted that such grants are currently restricted due to financial pressure with preference being given to improving treatment and care facilities

WHO CAN BENEFIT Research workers and individuals in need who suffer from haemophilia

WHERE FUNDING CAN BE GIVEN UK

TYPE OF GRANT Research is considered

FINANCES *Year* 1997 *Income* £675,121 *Grants* £10,418

TRUSTEES Board of Trustees

PUBLICATIONS Annual Report

HOW TO APPLY Write to the Haemophilia Society requesting an application form. Grants applications are considered bi-monthly and the forms must be completed in conjunction with a health professional at their haemophilia centre

WHO TO APPLY TO Joan Doyle, The Haemophilia Society, Chesterfield House, 358 Euston Road, London NW1 7HR *Tel* 0171-380 0600

CC NO 288260   **ESTABLISHED** 1950

■ The Alfred Haines Charitable Trust

WHAT IS FUNDED Christian social action. The Trustees prefer to support specific projects rather than giving for general running costs. They concentrate mainly on smaller West Midlands based charities

WHAT IS NOT FUNDED No church renovations or new buildings. No hospital or medical research projects. No animal charities. No electives or short-term overseas trips. The Trust does not normally support individuals, and prefers smaller, local charities

WHO CAN BENEFIT Christian-based community action including homelessness and young people

WHERE FUNDING CAN BE GIVEN Birmingham and West Midlands

TYPE OF GRANT Normally project-based

SAMPLE GRANTS In 1997 grants were made in the following categories:; Youth workers and support activities; Family support and counselling; Humanitarian and Christian overseas aid; Care for the elderly and disabled; Holidays for disadvantaged children and teenagers; Work with the homeless; Activities for care of underprivileged children; Support for mentally disadvantaged

FINANCES *Year* 1997 *Income* £118,520 *Grants* £208,009

TRUSTEES W I Jollie, A L Gilmour

HOW TO APPLY Applications should be in writing, explaining clearly the project for which funding is required and the current financial position. Applications are not acknowledged. Applications are reviewed bi-monthly. Applicants please quote reference: DGMT

WHO TO APPLY TO The Trustees, The Alfred Haines Charitable Trust, c/o Bloomer Heaven, 33 Lionel Street, Birmingham B3 1AB

CC NO 327166   **ESTABLISHED** 1986

■ The Hale Trust

WHAT IS FUNDED Tend to support local efforts where they can see the use the money is put to. Donations mainly to organisations for deprived or disabled children for capital works. Education is also funded

WHAT IS NOT FUNDED Grants to individuals cannot exceed £1,200 pa or last for more than three years and the total amount allocated from the income of the Trust for this purpose in any one year is strictly limited. The Trust will not fund: unspecified expenditure; deficit funding or the repayment of loans; projects which take place before applications can be processed; projects which are unable to start within 12 months; distribution to other organisations; general or nationwide appeals; on-going salaries; second degrees or postgraduate work

WHO CAN BENEFIT Individuals and registered charities in the area Where Funding Can Be Given. Students for recognised courses. Children and young adults who are disabled, and students who are disadvantaged by poverty, unemployed people and volunteers will be considered

WHERE FUNDING CAN BE GIVEN Surrey, Sussex, Kent and Greater London area

TYPE OF GRANT One-off grants funded for up to one year

SAMPLE GRANTS £1,800 to Edenbridge Holiday Activities Scheme; £1,000 to Hindlap Warren for Equipment; £1,000 to London Federation of Boys Clubs

FINANCES *Year* 1997–98 *Income* £33,000 *Grants* £28,000

TRUSTEES Mrs J M Broughton (Secretary), K F H Hale, Mrs S A Henderson, Mrs C Lemon, N K Maitland, OBE, Capt M T Prest, MBE, RN (Retd) (Chairman), J A Stephens, J E Tuke, FCA (Treasurer)
WHO TO APPLY TO Mrs J M Broughton, Secretary, The Hale Trust, Rosemary House, Woodhurst Park, Oxted, Surrey RH8 9HA
CC NO 313214   **ESTABLISHED** 1970

■ John Robert Halkes Settlement

WHAT IS FUNDED Any charity which furthers the objects of the Methodist church (one half of the income). Benefit of citizens of Lincoln (one half of income). Particularly: infrastructure, support and development; the advancement of religion; arts, culture and recreation; health care; conservation and environment; schools and colleges; and community facilities
WHAT IS NOT FUNDED No grants to individuals
WHO CAN BENEFIT Organisations only. There are no restrictions on the age; professional and economic group; family situation; religion and culture; and social circumstances of; or disease or medical condition suffered by, the beneficiaries
WHERE FUNDING CAN BE GIVEN Lincolnshire preferred (Methodist half), City of Lincoln only (Lincoln half)
TYPE OF GRANT For one-off capital expenditure rather than running costs, including buildings. Funding is for one year or less
RANGE OF GRANTS £250–£2,500
SAMPLE GRANTS £2,500 to St Mary Magdalene Church, Lincoln towards building works; £2,352 to NSPCC for child protection work in Lincoln; £2,000 to Lincoln YMCA towards work with disadvantaged young people; £2,000 to Schidlof Quartet to provide concerts in Lincoln; £1,000 to Methodist Church Louth Circuit for North Somercotes kitchen
FINANCES Year 1997 Income £23,503 Grants £20,827
TRUSTEES P H Race, D C Strange, Mrs E Bennett, Mrs J Davies
HOW TO APPLY By letter with cost of project, annual accounts, proposed contribution of applicant
WHO TO APPLY TO Mrs J Davies, John Robert Halkes Settlement, Messrs Andrew & Co, St Swithins Square, Lincoln LN2 1HA Tel 01522 512123 Fax 01522 546713
CC NO 237710   **ESTABLISHED** 1962

■ The Susan Hall 1995 Charitable Trust

WHAT IS FUNDED General charitable purposes
WHO CAN BENEFIT There are no restrictions on the age; professional and economic group; family situation; religion and culture; and social circumstances of; or disease or medical condition suffered by, the beneficiaries
WHERE FUNDING CAN BE GIVEN UK
RANGE OF GRANTS £50–£250
TRUSTEES Ms C Hall, Ms S S Hall, Ms S V Hall, T A J Hall
HOW TO APPLY By post or fax
WHO TO APPLY TO Ms S Hall, Trustee, The Susan Hall 1995 Charitable Trust, Charnes Hall, Eccleshall, Stafford ST21 6NP Fax 01630 620205
CC NO 1051595   **ESTABLISHED** 1995

■ The Edith Winifred Hall Charitable Trust

WHAT IS FUNDED General charitable purposes
WHO CAN BENEFIT There are no restrictions on the age; professional and economic group; family situation; religion and culture; and social circumstances of; or disease or medical condition suffered by, the beneficiaries
WHERE FUNDING CAN BE GIVEN UK
TRUSTEES D Endicott, Ms E W Hall, J R N Lowe, D Reynolds
WHO TO APPLY TO D Endicott, The Edith Winifred Hall Charitable Trust, 52–54 The Green, Banbury, Oxfordshire OX16 9AD
CC NO 1057032   **ESTABLISHED** 1996

■ Robert Hall Charity

WHAT IS FUNDED General at Trustees' discretion, including charities working with hospices and hospitals, medical research, conservation and campaigning, education and various community services and facilities
WHAT IS NOT FUNDED No grants to individuals
WHO CAN BENEFIT Institutions benefiting children and young adults, there is no restriction on the disease or medical condition suffered by the beneficiaries
WHERE FUNDING CAN BE GIVEN West Walton and St Augustine's area of Wisbech
TYPE OF GRANT Range of grants including buildings, capital, recurring costs and start up costs. Funding for up to three years may be available
RANGE OF GRANTS £500–£5,000
FINANCES Year 1997–98 Income £27,165 Grants £23,550
TRUSTEES Steven Whitteridge, Colin Arnold, David Ball, David Burall
HOW TO APPLY In writing to the address under Who To Apply To
WHO TO APPLY TO David Ball, Robert Hall Charity Frasers, Solicitors, 29 Old Market, Wisbech, Cambridgeshire PE13 1ND
CC NO 1015493   **ESTABLISHED** 1992

■ Hallam Money Mountain Trust

WHAT IS FUNDED Children and youth charities and organisations in South Yorkshire and the North Midlands, also individual children and young people
WHO CAN BENEFIT Individuals, and organisations benefiting children and young adults
WHERE FUNDING CAN BE GIVEN South Yorkshire and North Midlands
FINANCES Year 1996–97 Income £43,906 Grants £43,264
TRUSTEES Bill MacDonald, Tony Parsons, Andrew Darwin, Surriya Falconber, Lisa Roseby, Brendan Moffett, Anthony McKenzie, Peter Flint
HOW TO APPLY To the address under Who To Apply To in writing for consideration at quarterly meetings
WHO TO APPLY TO Lisa Roseby, Hallam Money Mountain Trust, 900 Herries Road, Sheffield S6 1RH
CC NO 513377   **ESTABLISHED** 1982

■ The Hamamelis Trust

WHAT IS FUNDED (a) Medical research in the UK; (b) specific projects for conservation of the countryside in the UK

WHAT IS NOT FUNDED The Trustees will rarely fund more than 50 per cent of the cost of a project

WHO CAN BENEFIT UK charities involved in medical research or conservation projects. There is no restriction on the disease or medical condition suffered by the beneficiaries

WHERE FUNDING CAN BE GIVEN UK but with a special interest in the Godalming and Surrey areas

TYPE OF GRANT Project – cash sums usually in units of £2,500

SAMPLE GRANTS £10,000 to MRI Critical Care Appeal; £5,000 to BCTV; £5,000 to British Heart Foundation; £5,000 to Cancer Relief Macmillan Fund; £5,000 to Godalming Museum Trust; £5,000 to Hereford Nature Trust; £5,000 to Meningitis Research Foundation; £5,000 to Research into Ageing; £5,000 to National Asthma Campaign; £5,000 to The Woodland Trust

FINANCES *Year* 1996–97 *Income* £90,000 *Grants* £103,000

TRUSTEES M Fellingham, C I Slocock, Dr L Martin, D Stewart

HOW TO APPLY To the address under Who To Apply To. All applications are asked to include a short synopsis of the application along with any published material and references. Unsuccessful appeals will not be replied to. The Trustees usually meet twice a year to consider applications. (Medical applications are assessed by Dr Martin, who is medically qualified)

WHO TO APPLY TO Mrs F Collins, The Secretary, The Hamamelis Trust, c/o Penningtons, Highfield, Brighton Road, Godalming, Surrey GU7 1NS

CC NO 280938   **ESTABLISHED** 1980

■ The Hamer Charitable Trust

WHAT IS FUNDED General charitable purposes

WHO CAN BENEFIT There are no restrictions on the age; professional and economic group; family situation; religion and culture; and social circumstances of; or disease or medical condition suffered by, the beneficiaries

WHERE FUNDING CAN BE GIVEN UK and overseas, although charities with connections in the Powys area are of interest to the Settlor

TYPE OF GRANT Payments to be made on a six monthly basis to various charities, as preferred by Settlor. Predominately income payments, although there is power to release capital. All requests from various charities will be considered

TRUSTEES Natwest Investments

HOW TO APPLY The Trustees meet half-yearly to distribute money

WHO TO APPLY TO C L Pemberton, The Hamer Charitable Trust, Natwest Investments Chester, Eden Lakeside, Chester Business Park, Wrexham Road, Chester CH4 9QT *Tel* 01244 683366 *Fax* 01244 682282

CC NO 1070683   **ESTABLISHED** 1998

■ Eleanor Hamilton Educational Trust

WHAT IS FUNDED Persons under the age of 30 whose parents/guardians are unable to pay for their education

WHO CAN BENEFIT Organisations benefiting children and young adults up to the age of 30, and students

WHERE FUNDING CAN BE GIVEN UK

FINANCES *Year* 1997 *Income* £141,362

TRUSTEES Lady Hamilton, CBE, G Miskin, Mrs J N Nyiri, R D D Orr, E S Higgins, OBE, E Ribchester, The Hon William Brandon

HOW TO APPLY By written application to the address under Who To Apply To

WHO TO APPLY TO Mrs A Khadr, Eleanor Hamilton Educational Trust, 43 Lancaster Close, St Petersburgh Place, London W2 4JZ

CC NO 309997   **ESTABLISHED** 1957

■ The Hamilton Trust

WHAT IS FUNDED General charitable purposes but particularly in association with the office of the Chief Rabbi

WHAT IS NOT FUNDED No grants to individuals

WHO CAN BENEFIT There are no restrictions on the age; professional and economic group; family situation; religion and culture; and social circumstances of; or disease or medical condition suffered by, the beneficiaries. However, preference is given to organisations associated with the office of the Chief Rabbi

WHERE FUNDING CAN BE GIVEN UK

RANGE OF GRANTS £200–£29,500

SAMPLE GRANTS £29,500 to the Office of the Chief Rabbi; £13,500 to United Synagogue; £4,000 to Women in the Community; £3,428 to Jews College; £2,500 to National Jewish Chaplaincy

FINANCES *Year* 1995 *Income* £18,316 *Grants* £54,175

TRUSTEES M D Paisner, C Marks, A Grabiner, S Frosh, L Swift

WHO TO APPLY TO M D Paisner, The Hamilton Trust c/o Messrs Paisner & Co, Bouverie House, 154 Fleet Street, London EC4A 2DQ

CC NO 264092   **ESTABLISHED** 1972

■ The Hamilton Trust

WHAT IS FUNDED Education

WHO CAN BENEFIT At the discretion of the Trustees. Organisations benefiting children, young adults and students may be considered

WHERE FUNDING CAN BE GIVEN UK

TYPE OF GRANT At the discretion of the Trustees

FINANCES *Year* 1997 *Income* £54,543 *Grants* £352,010

TRUSTEES Michael R H J O'Regan, Kenneth W Brooks, Elizabeth J O'Regan, Gordon J McMillan

WHO TO APPLY TO M O'Regan, The Hamilton Trust, 6 Northmoor Road, Oxford OX2 6UP

CC NO 1004205   **ESTABLISHED** 1988

■ The Helen Hamlyn Foundation

WHAT IS FUNDED (a) Support of frail, elderly people living at home within their community, through the development and promulgation of Elderly People's Integrated Care Systems (EPICS). (b) Promotion of better design of housing, furniture and equipment for older people, which can also benefit everyone. No grants available outside existing work

WHAT IS NOT FUNDED Organisations working outside the areas outlined above with not be funded. No grants to individuals

WHO CAN BENEFIT Organisations of national significance with whom the Foundation has been working, benefiting elderly people

WHERE FUNDING CAN BE GIVEN Primarily UK

RANGE OF GRANTS £2,500–£57,500

Does the trust you have chosen match your needs? Haphazard applications waste postage and time

273

SAMPLE GRANTS £57,500 to Design Age; £14,911 to BASE – EPICS 2; £5,000 to Centre for Policy and Ageing; £3,000 to Hornsey Housing Trust; £2,500 to Crich Glebe Field Trust Ltd

FINANCES *Year* 1997 *Income* £256,539 *Grants* £82,911

TRUSTEES Paul Hamlyn, CBE, Helen Hamlyn, Rt Hon The Lord Owen, Prof Kevin M Cahill, MD

PUBLICATIONS *New Design for Old*, *Lifetime Homes*, *Elderly People's Integrated Systems*

NOTES It would be counter productive for any organisation not involved in the above work to apply

HOW TO APPLY The Foundation welcomes correspondence from organisations doing similar work

WHO TO APPLY TO The Helen Hamlyn Foundation, Sussex House, 12 Upper Hall, London W6 9TA

CC NO 802628   **ESTABLISHED** 1984

■ B Hammer Charitable Trust

This trust did not respond to CAF's request to amend its entry and, by 30 June 1998, CAF's researchers did not find financial records for later than 1995 on its file at the Charity Commission. Trusts are legally required to submit annual accounts to the Charity Commission under section 42 of the Charities Act 1993

WHAT IS FUNDED General charitable activities

WHO CAN BENEFIT There are no restrictions on the age; professional and economic group; family situation; religion and culture; and social circumstances of; or disease or medical condition suffered by, the beneficiaries

WHERE FUNDING CAN BE GIVEN UK and overseas

TRUSTEES B Hammer

HOW TO APPLY To the address below in writing

WHO TO APPLY TO B Hammer, B Hammer Charitable Trust, 47 Highfield Avenue, London NW11 9EU

CC NO 270093   **ESTABLISHED** 1975

■ The Sue Hammerson Foundation

WHAT IS FUNDED General charitable purposes

WHO CAN BENEFIT There are no restrictions on the age; professional and economic group; family situation; religion and culture; and social circumstances of; or disease or medical condition suffered by, the beneficiaries

WHERE FUNDING CAN BE GIVEN UK

RANGE OF GRANTS £50–£1,200

SAMPLE GRANTS £1,200 to L W Hammerson Memorial Home; £500 to Royal Academy Trust; £300 to Distressed Gentlefolk's Aid Association; £250 to Research into Ageing; £200 to Musicians Benevolent Association; £100 to British Kidney Patients Association; £100 to British Red Cross; £50 to Cystic Fibrosis Trust

FINANCES *Year* 1997 *Income* £105,711 *Grants* £2,700

TRUSTEES D B Hammerson, P A Beecham, P S Hammerson, Sir Gavin Lightman

WHO TO APPLY TO The Sue Hammerson Foundation, Messrs H W Fisher & Co, Acre House, 11–15 William Road, London NW1 3ER

CC NO 262580   **ESTABLISHED** 1971

■ Sue Hammerson's Charitable Trust

WHAT IS FUNDED General charitable purposes. Particular consideration is given to the advancement of medical learning and research and to the relief of sickness and poverty. The Trustees give particular attention to benefiting The Lewis W Hammerson Memorial Home

WHAT IS NOT FUNDED No grants to individuals. The Trust is presently fully committed

WHO CAN BENEFIT Registered charities benefiting: those disadvantaged by poverty; medical professionals; research workers and scientists. There is no restriction on the disease or medical condition suffered by the beneficiaries

WHERE FUNDING CAN BE GIVEN UK

RANGE OF GRANTS £10–£202,200

SAMPLE GRANTS £202,200 to Lewis W Hammerson Memorial Home; £5,000 to Heart Disease and Diabetic Research; £3,000 to Royal Opera House Trust; £2,000 to B'nai B'rith Hillel Foundation Special Needs Fund; £1,200 to New Shakespeare Co Ltd; £1,000 to B'nai B'rith Hillel Foundation General Fund; £950 to Queen Mary's Clothing Guild; £820 to Royal Albert Hall; £750 to West London Synagogue of British Jews; £600 to Lord Mayor's Appeal – St John Ambulance

FINANCES *Year* 1997 *Income* £263,620 *Grants* £242,160

TRUSTEES Sir Gavin Lightman, A J Thompson, A J Bernstein, Mrs P A Beecham

WHO TO APPLY TO A J Bernstein, Sue Hammerson's Charitable Trust, H W Fisher & Co, Acre House, 11–15 William Road, London NW1 3ER

CC NO 235196   **ESTABLISHED** 1957

■ Hammond Suddards Charitable Trust

WHAT IS FUNDED Health and welfare, the elderly, disability

WHO CAN BENEFIT Individuals, local and regional organisations benefiting: the elderly; disabled people; at risk groups; those disadvantaged by poverty; socially isolated people; and the sick. There is no restriction on the disease or medical condition suffered by the beneficiaries

WHERE FUNDING CAN BE GIVEN West Yorkshire

RANGE OF GRANTS £25–£4,000

SAMPLE GRANTS £4,000 to St Ann's PCC; £2,100 to Childline; £2,000 to Royal British Legion; £1,775 to Ilkley Candlelighters Ball; £1,500 to Nell Bank Centre; £650 to Solicitors Benevolent Association; £500 to Assisted Conception Unit Trust Fund; £500 to Jayne Sampson Memorial Trust; £500 to Rotarsport '96; £500 to Bradford Girls Grammar School

FINANCES *Year* 1997 *Income* £38,176 *Grants* £37,590

TRUSTEES M L Shepherd, C N Hutton, C Marks, A H McDougall, M S Henley

HOW TO APPLY To the address under Who To Apply To in writing

WHO TO APPLY TO Mrs F Jackson, Hammond Suddards Charitable Trust, Hammond Suddards, 2 Park Lane, Leeds LS3 1ES

CC NO 1000869   **ESTABLISHED** 1989

■ Hampshire and the Islands Historic Churches Trust

WHAT IS FUNDED The restoration, preservation, repair, maintenance and improvement of churches, including monuments, fittings and furniture, in the area Where Funding Can Be Given

WHERE FUNDING CAN BE GIVEN Hampshire, the Isle of Wight and the Channel Islands

SAMPLE GRANTS £3,000 to All Saints Church, Headley; £2,000 to St Stephen's, Sparsholt; £2,000 to St Andrew the Apostle, Hamble; £1,000 to St Mary's, Hayling Island; £1,000 to St John's, Hartley Wintney

FINANCES *Year* 1997 *Income* £17,000 *Grants* £5,000

TRUSTEES Sir Hugh Beach (Chairman), Corine Bennett, Ven Alan Clarkson, Canon Nicholas France, John Steel

HOW TO APPLY To the address under Who To Apply To in writing

WHO TO APPLY TO The Hon Secretary, Hampshire and the Islands Historic Churches Trust, 19 St Peter Street, Winchester, Hampshire SO23 8BU

CC NO 299633   **ESTABLISHED** 1988

■ The Hampton Wick United Charity

WHAT IS FUNDED Approximately two thirds of the Trust's expenditure is directed towards relief in need, the remainder to the promotion of education, both in the area Where Funding Can Be Given

WHO CAN BENEFIT Some individuals though primarily local organisations benefiting children, young adults and those in need

WHERE FUNDING CAN BE GIVEN Hampton Wick, South Teddington

SAMPLE GRANTS £2,102 to Teddington School for equipment for music studio and prizes; £2,000 to MENCAP as a contribution for holidays; £1,604 to hire a hall for old people's social meetings; £1,000 to Hampton Wick Infants School towards books for the library; £1,000 to Kingston Grammar School for school fees; £1,000 to Hampton Wick Royal Cricket Club for four practice wickets; £1,000 to St John the Baptist PCC; £630 to Hampton Wick and Teddington Old People's Welfare Charity; £487 to St John the Baptist School for grants; £454 to St John the Baptist School for awards and prizes

FINANCES *Year* 1996–97 *Income* £34,024 *Grants* £20,116

TRUSTEES Cllr A F Arbour, Dr P J Butterworth, Miss M E E Kearn, Cllr M H McDougall, Mrs C S M Shaw, J G Sinclair, Rev P Warne

HOW TO APPLY To the address under Who To Apply To in writing

WHO TO APPLY TO R R H Ellison, Clerk, The Hampton Wick United Charity, Stone Cottage, Westlands, Birdham, Chichester, West Sussex PO20 7HJ

CC NO 1010147   **ESTABLISHED** 1990

■ The Ray Hancock Memorial Charity

WHAT IS FUNDED General charitable purposes

WHO CAN BENEFIT There are no restrictions on the age; professional and economic group; family situation; religion and culture; and social circumstances of; or disease or medical condition suffered by, the beneficiaries

WHERE FUNDING CAN BE GIVEN UK

FINANCES *Year* 1997 *Income* £15,056 *Grants* £12,131

TRUSTEES A D Hancock, A P Hancock, A Wheldon

WHO TO APPLY TO Ms A Scragg, The Ray Hancock Memorial Charity, Hancock Holdings Ltd, 25 Jubilee Drive, Loughborough, Leicestershire LE11 5TX

CC NO 1043163   **ESTABLISHED** 1994

■ Hand In Hand In Union

WHAT IS FUNDED General charitable purposes, in particular, to relieve poverty, sickness and distress for the benefit of persons in Romania

WHO CAN BENEFIT There are no restrictions on the age; professional and economic group; family situation; religion and culture; and social circumstances of; or disease or medical condition suffered by, the beneficiaries. However, particular favour is given to those disadvantaged by poverty, the sick, at risk groups and the socially isolated of Romania

WHERE FUNDING CAN BE GIVEN Romania

FINANCES *Year* 1996 *Income* £38,590

WHO TO APPLY TO Mrs V Stratton, Hand In Hand In Union, 2 New Street, Chase Terrace, Walsall, West Midlands WS7 8BS

CC NO 1041740   **ESTABLISHED** 1994

■ Handicapped Children's Aid Committee

WHAT IS FUNDED To assist disabled children by means of equipment and services

WHAT IS NOT FUNDED No bequests of money are made. Building projects will not be funded

WHO CAN BENEFIT Support is given to individual children and their families. Beneficiaries suffering from various diseases and medical conditions will be considered

WHERE FUNDING CAN BE GIVEN UK and overseas

TYPE OF GRANT Capital and one-off grants will be considered. Funding may be given for up to one year

RANGE OF GRANTS Maximum of £2,000 for individuals

FINANCES *Year* 1997 *Income* £360,737 *Grants* £171,978

TRUSTEES The Committee

HOW TO APPLY No initial telephone calls from applicants are welcome. Application forms and guidelines are available

WHO TO APPLY TO Paul Maurice, Handicapped Children's Aid Committee, Amberley Lodge, 13 Beechwood Avenue, Finchley, London N3 3AU

CC NO 200050   **ESTABLISHED** 1961

■ W A Handley Charity Trust

WHAT IS FUNDED General charitable purposes with preference for: alleviation of distress and youth and uniformed groups umbrella bodies

WHAT IS NOT FUNDED Grants will be made to registered charities only. No grants will be made to individuals

WHO CAN BENEFIT Registered charities benefiting: children and young adults; at risk groups; those disadvantaged by poverty; homeless people; victims of abuse and domestic violence

WHERE FUNDING CAN BE GIVEN Preference for Northumberland and Tyneside

TYPE OF GRANT Buildings, capital, core costs, endowments, feasibility studies, one-off, project, research, running costs, recurring costs, salaries and start-up costs. Funding is available for up to one year

SAMPLE GRANTS £25,000 to Newcastle Preparatory School; £10,000 to Kings School, Tynemouth; £10,000 to Lindisfarne Church Heating Appeal; £10,000 to La Sagesse High School; £5,000 to Northumberland Coalition Against Crime; £5,000 to Newburn District Sea Cadets Corps; £5,000 to Save the Children Fund, Newcastle; £5,000 to SSAFA Tyne and Wear for emergency cases

FINANCES *Year* 1997 *Income* £242,000 *Grants* £243,000

TRUSTEES A A E Glenton, MBE, FCA, D Milligan, FCA, D W J Errington

HOW TO APPLY Applications must be in writing, quoting the applicant's official charity number and providing full back-up information. Grants are made quarterly in June, September, December and March

WHO TO APPLY TO Ryecroft Glenton, Accountants, W A Handley Charity Trust, 27 Portland Terrace, Newcastle upon Tyne NE2 1QP

CC NO 230435   **ESTABLISHED** 1963

■ Beatrice Hankey Foundation Ltd

WHAT IS FUNDED Advancement of Christian religion especially training missionaries. To support study and training courses in Eastern Europe

WHO CAN BENEFIT Institutions benefiting Christians

WHERE FUNDING CAN BE GIVEN UK and overseas

TYPE OF GRANT Recurrent

RANGE OF GRANTS £50–£5,000

SAMPLE GRANTS £5,000 to Lagan College; £3,000 to Nairobi Hospice; £2,000 to Buck for counselling and research; £1,000 to Cwmavon Boys' Club; £1,000 to Feed the Minds; £1,000 to Medical Foundation; £1,000 to Nordoff Rubin Music Therapy Centre; £1,000 to St Alfege Community Project; £1,000 to SWS Filtration; £1,000 to UWESCO UK Trust

FINANCES *Year* 1995 *Income* £32,301 *Grants* £19,705

TRUSTEES Prof E G Wedell, Mrs A M Dawe, Rev J Elliott, Mrs C Lethbridge, Mrs I Mentincke-Zuiderweg, Mrs N Starosta, Mrs H Pawson, Rev Mother L Morris, Rev D Savill, Rev Canon J W D Simonson, Mrs D Simpson, Pfarner V Gürke

WHO TO APPLY TO Mrs S M Legge, Secretary, Beatrice Hankey Foundation Ltd, 6 Arundel Place, Farnham, Surrey GU9 7HQ

CC NO 211093   **ESTABLISHED** 1949

■ The Hanley Trust (1987)

WHAT IS FUNDED Social welfare/disadvantaged

WHAT IS NOT FUNDED No grants to individuals

WHO CAN BENEFIT Registered charities benefiting at risk groups, those disadvantaged by poverty and socially isolated people

WHERE FUNDING CAN BE GIVEN UK

TYPE OF GRANT Various

RANGE OF GRANTS £200–£5,000

SAMPLE GRANTS £5,000 to Shelter; £2,500 to Bulter Trust; £2,000 to Irene Taylor Trust; £1,000 to Amnesty (UK); £1,000 to Bourne Trust; £1,000 to Disability Aid Fund; £1,000 to Help the Hospices; £1,000 to Howard League; £1,000 to Mental Health Foundation; £1,000 to MIND

FINANCES *Year* 1997 *Income* £33,348 *Grants* £27,900

TRUSTEES Hon Mrs S T M Price, N W Smith, Hon S J Butler

HOW TO APPLY Preferably in writing

WHO TO APPLY TO The Hon Mrs S Price, The Hanley Trust (1987), Brook House, Spring Back Way, Uppingham, Leicestershire LE15 9TT *Tel* 01572 821831

CC NO 299209   **ESTABLISHED** 1987

■ The Lennox Hannay Charitable Trust

WHAT IS FUNDED This Trust will consider funding accommodation and housing; community development; health professional bodies; volunteer bureaux; churches; health; conservation; animal welfare; agriculture; ecology; endangered species; environmental issues; heritage; special needs education; speech therapy; training for community development; medical research and research institutes; and social care and development

WHAT IS NOT FUNDED No grants to individuals or non-registered charities

WHO CAN BENEFIT Registered charities benefiting people of all ages; ex-service and service people; medical professionals; retired people; those in care, fostered and adopted; parents and children; widows and widowers; at risk groups; disabled people; homeless people; those living in rural areas; disaster victims; and victims of domestic violence. Those suffering from various diseases and medical conditions

WHERE FUNDING CAN BE GIVEN UK

TYPE OF GRANT Capital, core costs, one-off and research

RANGE OF GRANTS £200–£23,000

SAMPLE GRANTS £23,000 to Countryside Foundation; £16,000 to Sue Ryder Foundation; £15,000 to Save the Children Fund; £14,000 to British Deaf Association; £12,000 to Barnardo's; £12,000 to Royal Commonwealth Society for the Blind; £10,000 to Royal London Society for the Blind; £10,000 to Ex-services Mental Welfare for the Blind; £9,000 to Tibet House Trust; £8,000 to Help the Aged

FINANCES *Year* 1996–97 *Income* £316,373 *Grants* £267,950

TRUSTEES Robert Fleming Trustee Co Ltd, W L Hannay, Caroline F Wilmot-Sitwell

HOW TO APPLY In writing. No guidelines or application forms issued

WHO TO APPLY TO Robert Fleming Trustee Co Ltd, The Lennox Hannay Charitable Trust, 25 Copthall Avenue, London EC2R 7DR

CC NO 299099   **ESTABLISHED** 1988

■ Kathleen Hannay Memorial Charity

WHAT IS FUNDED General charitable purposes but Trustees favour religious causes. The Trust will consider funding: community development; support to voluntary and community organisations; support to volunteers; social care professional bodies; the advancement of the Christian religion; churches; Anglican and Free Church umbrella bodies; music; health; the conservation of church buildings; church schools; special schools; education and training; medical research; religion; social sciences; specialist research; and social care and development

WHAT IS NOT FUNDED No grants to individuals or non-registered charities

WHO CAN BENEFIT Registered charities benefiting: people of all ages; clergy; medical professionals; musicians; those in care, fostered and adopted;

parents and children; one parent families; widows and widowers. Baptists, Christians, Church of England, evangelists and Methodists. At risk groups, disabled people and those suffering from mental illness

WHERE FUNDING CAN BE GIVEN UK, Europe and Africa
TYPE OF GRANT Capital, core costs, one-off, project and research. All funding is for one year or less
RANGE OF GRANTS £300–£13,000
SAMPLE GRANTS £13,000 to NSPCC; £11,000 to SANE (Schizophrenia. A National Emergency); £11,000 to Friends of Russian Children; £11,000 to Christian Aid Direct; £10,000 to The Radcliffe Medical Foundation for research; £9,000 to The Samaritans; £9,000 to Childline Charitable Trust; £8,000 to The Treloar Trust; £7,000 to Wiltshire Air Ambulance Appeal; £7,000 to Helen House Hospice
FINANCES *Year* 1997 *Income* £171,528 *Grants* £165,800
TRUSTEES Rev R F Hannay, E A C Hannay, S P Weil
NOTES Donations made in March of each year
HOW TO APPLY In writing only. No application forms or guidelines issued
WHO TO APPLY TO G Fincham, Kathleen Hannay Memorial Charity, Robert Fleming Trustee Co, 25 Copthall Avenue, London EC2R 7DR *Tel* 0171-638 5858
CC NO 299600   **ESTABLISHED** 1988

■ The Hanover Charitable Trust

WHAT IS FUNDED Support for a wide range of charitable causes especially Jewish
WHO CAN BENEFIT Organisations, particularly those benefiting Jewish people
WHERE FUNDING CAN BE GIVEN UK
RANGE OF GRANTS £50–£15,000
SAMPLE GRANTS £15,000 to Joint Jewish Charitable Trust; £10,400 to Ann Frank Educational Trust; £5,000 to Mr and Mrs I S Klug Welfare Foundation; £5,000 to Elsie and Barnett Janner Charitable Trust; £4,500 to Wessex Healthy Living Foundation; £2,500 to Carmel College Scholarship; £2,200 to British Friends of Haifa University; £2,000 to Tel Aviv University Drama Society; £2,000 to Telhai Fund; £1,000 to YAA Society
FINANCES *Year* 1996 *Income* £50,411 *Grants* £58,910
TRUSTEES Mrs B Klug, Mrs P Sumeray, Midland Bank Trust Co Ltd
WHO TO APPLY TO S T Howells, The Hanover Charitable Trust, Midland Trusts, Cumberland House, 15–17 Cumberland Place, Southampton SO15 2UY
CC NO 266343   **ESTABLISHED** 1973

■ The Happold Trust

WHAT IS FUNDED The creation, maintenance and funding of grants, bursaries, scholarships, prizes and rewards for higher education, research and training fields applicable to the construction industry
WHO CAN BENEFIT People working in the construction industry, students and teachers are supported
WHERE FUNDING CAN BE GIVEN Bath and north east Somerset
WHO TO APPLY TO David A Reed, The Happold Trust, Cleveland House, Sydney Road, Bath BA2 6NR
CC NO 1050814   **ESTABLISHED** 1995

■ The Haramead Trust

WHAT IS FUNDED Relief of hardship and distress; the relief of the suffering of animals; provision of facilities for children's welfare and the advancement of education about health
WHO CAN BENEFIT Organisations benefiting children, at risk groups, those disadvantaged by poverty and socially isolated people
WHERE FUNDING CAN BE GIVEN UK and overseas
RANGE OF GRANTS £5,000–35,000
SAMPLE GRANTS £35,000 to Royal Leicestershire Rutland and Wycliffe; £25,000 to Society for the Blind; £25,000 to Catholic Fund for Overseas Students; £20,000 to Leicester Children's Holiday Centre; £15,000 to Rainbows; £10,000 to Children of the Andes; £1,000 to Shelter; £10,000 to LOROS; £5,000 to The Salvation Army; £5,000 to Action Aid
FINANCES *Year* 1997 *Income* £165,992 *Grants* £170,000
TRUSTEES Mrs W M Linnett, M J Linnett, R H Smith, D L Tams
WHO TO APPLY TO D L Tams, Trustee, The Haramead Trust, c/o Crane and Walton, 113–117 London Road, Leicester LE2 0RG
CC NO 1047416   **ESTABLISHED** 1995

■ The Harari Foundation

WHAT IS FUNDED General charitable purposes at the discretion of the Trustees
WHAT IS NOT FUNDED No grants to individuals
WHO CAN BENEFIT At the discretion of the Trustees, but mainly other charitable institutions. There are no restrictions on the age; professional and economic group; family situation; religion and culture; and social circumstances of; or disease or medical condition suffered by, the beneficiaries
WHERE FUNDING CAN BE GIVEN UK and overseas
TYPE OF GRANT At the discretion of the Trustees
RANGE OF GRANTS £20–£7,625
SAMPLE GRANTS £7,625 to JNF; £1,000 to North London Collegiate School; £536 to Stanmore Synagogue; £100 to Norwood Ravenswood; £500 to SAGE; £420 to GAP; £250 to JPAIME; £250 to Spanish and Portuguese Synagogue; £230 to Jewish Care; £200 to Lupus UK
FINANCES *Year* 1997 *Income* £38,983 *Grants* £13,591
TRUSTEES Victor Harari, Jennifer Harari, Michael Dunitz
HOW TO APPLY Please send an sae
WHO TO APPLY TO V Harari, The Harari Foundation, 28 Ashburton Grove, London N7 7AA *Tel* 0171-609 2222
CC NO 1002834   **ESTABLISHED** 1991

■ Miss K M Harbinson's Charitable Trust

WHAT IS FUNDED General charitable purposes
WHO CAN BENEFIT There are no restrictions on the age; professional and economic group; family situation; religion and culture; and social circumstances of; or disease or medical condition suffered by, the beneficiaries
WHERE FUNDING CAN BE GIVEN Scotland
TRUSTEES G A Maguire, G C Harbinson, R Harbinson
WHO TO APPLY TO Miss K M Harbinson's Charitable Trust, Miller, Beckett & Jackson, 190 St Vincent Street, Glasgow G2 5SP *Tel* 0141-221 9005
SC NO SCO 15248

■ The Harborne Parish Lands Charity

WHAT IS FUNDED Charities working in the fields of: accommodation and housing; infrastructure and technical support; infrastructure development; health care; health facilities and buildings; physical and mental disability organisations; schools and colleges; education and training; purchase of books; community centres and village halls; playgrounds and community services; individual need and other charitable purposes will be considered

WHO CAN BENEFIT All grants must benefit those living within the Parish. Local organisations, local branches of national organisations benefiting: students; unemployed people; at risk groups; carers; disabled people; those disadvantaged by poverty; disaster victims; ex-offenders and those at risk of offending; homeless and socially isolated people; those living in urban areas; victims of abuse, crime and domestic violence. There is no restriction on the age or family situation of, or the disease or medical condition suffered by the beneficiaries

WHERE FUNDING CAN BE GIVEN The Ancient Parish of Harborne, comprising parts of Harborne, Bearwood, Quinton and Smethwick

TYPE OF GRANT Buildings, capital, core costs, interest free loans, one-off, project, research, running costs, salaries and start-up costs. Funding for up to one year will be considered

RANGE OF GRANTS £200–£10,000

SAMPLE GRANTS £7,000 to Little Sisters of the Poor for furniture for elderly residents; £5,000 to Raglan Road Christian Fellowship towards minibus; £5,000 to St Marks Community Project towards renovation of Lunch Club kitchen; £5,000 to St John's Community Project towards minibus; £3,000 to Birmingham Royal Institution for the Blind for equipment; £3,000 California Chapel for building work for youth activities; £2,622 to Midland People with Cerebral Palsy for repair work to drains; £2,600 to Cape Primary School for specialist play equipment; £2,000 to Sandwell Multi Handicap Group towards extra care for certain families; £2,000 to St John's Family Centre for staffing of playground

FINANCES *Year* 1996–97 *Income* £350,258 *Grants* £62,517

TRUSTEES J E C Alden, G W B Austin, W Edis, S Gregory, Mrs G Hayes, P Hollingworth, S Josan, P W Lawrence, H W Lovell, I McArdle, D McKerracher, Miss N M Williams

HOW TO APPLY To the address under Who To Apply To in writing

WHO TO APPLY TO L J Bending, Clerk, The Harborne Parish Lands Charity, 7 Harborne Park Road, Harborne, Birmingham B17 0DE *Tel* 0121-426 1600

CC NO 219031 **ESTABLISHED** 1699

■ The Harbour Charitable Trust

WHAT IS FUNDED Child care, education and health research, and various other charitable organisations

WHO CAN BENEFIT Organisations benefiting children, young adults and students. Support may also be given to teachers and governesses, medical professionals, research workers, parents and children and one parent families. There is no restriction on the disease or medical condition suffered by the beneficiaries

WHERE FUNDING CAN BE GIVEN UK

SAMPLE GRANTS £40,800 to L'Chaim Society; £28,421 to other organisations; £25,900 to educational organisations; £16,000 to Jewish Care; £8,650 to childcare organisations; £7,000 to healthcare organisations

FINANCES *Year* 1997 *Income* £218,406 *Grants* £126,771

TRUSTEES B B Green, Z S Blackman, J F Avery Jones

NOTES Time Charity

WHO TO APPLY TO Mrs B Green, The Harbour Charitable Trust, 22 York Terrace East, Regent's Park, London NW1 4PT

CC NO 234268 **ESTABLISHED** 1962

■ The Harbour Foundation Ltd

WHAT IS FUNDED (a) The relief of poverty, suffering and distress amongst refugees, homeless and displaced persons throughout the world. (b) The advancement of education, learning and research of persons and students of all ages and nationalities throughout the world and to disseminate the results of this research. (c) General charitable purposes

WHO CAN BENEFIT There are no restrictions on the age; professional and economic group; family situation; religion and culture; and social circumstances of; or disease or medical condition suffered by, the beneficiaries. However, particular favour is given to at risk groups; those disadvantaged by poverty; the homeless; refugees and socially isolated people. Support may also be given to research workers and students

WHERE FUNDING CAN BE GIVEN UK and overseas

TYPE OF GRANT Recurring costs

FINANCES *Year* 1997 *Income* £349,868 *Grants* £196,384

TRUSTEES Council of Management

NOTES The charity has entered into certain commitments which absorb most of its funds on an advanced basis

WHO TO APPLY TO The Harbour Foundation Ltd, 8–10 Half Moon Court, Bartholomew Close, London EC1A 7HE

CC NO 264927 **ESTABLISHED** 1970

■ The Harding Charitable Trust

WHAT IS FUNDED General charitable purposes

WHO CAN BENEFIT Grants are only made to charities known to the Settlors. There are no restrictions on the age; professional and economic group; family situation; religion and culture; and social circumstances of; or disease or medical condition suffered by, the beneficiaries

WHERE FUNDING CAN BE GIVEN UK

SAMPLE GRANTS £4,969 to G E Harding Fund

FINANCES *Year* 1996 *Income* £17,811 *Grants* £17,811

TRUSTEES Liverpool Council of Social Services, D Bebb, His Honour Judge Duncan, C Feeny, N Frayling, W Fulton, A Hannay, Mrs M Hickland, Ms S Mashiane-Talbot, N Mellor, R Morris, A Smith

HOW TO APPLY This Trust states that it does not respond to unsolicited applications

WHO TO APPLY TO E Murphy, The Harding Charitable Trust, Liverpool Cncl of Social Service, 14 Castle Street, Liverpool, Merseyside L2 0NJ

CC NO 1046728 **ESTABLISHED** 1995

■ The Matthew Harding Charitable Trust

WHAT IS FUNDED General charitable purposes

WHO CAN BENEFIT There are no restrictions on the age; professional and economic group; family situation; religion and culture; and social circumstances of; or disease or medical condition suffered by, the beneficiaries

WHERE FUNDING CAN BE GIVEN UK

FINANCES *Year* 1995 *Income* £152,022

WHO TO APPLY TO R Eaglesfield, The Matthew Harding Charitable Trust, The Charity Service, Gaddom House, 6 Great Jackson Street, Manchester M15 4AX

CC NO 1041224   **ESTABLISHED** 1994

■ The Harding Trust

WHAT IS FUNDED To give to smaller rather than larger charities. Charities supported are in most cases connected with music and the arts but local welfare charities are also given support

WHO CAN BENEFIT To benefit actors and entertainment professionals; musicians; textile workers and designers; writers and poets; at risk groups, those disadvantaged by poverty and socially isolated people. Consideration will be given to national charities if there is a good reason for doing so

WHERE FUNDING CAN BE GIVEN Mainly North Staffordshire

TYPE OF GRANT One-off gifts can be made in any area at the Trustees' discretion

RANGE OF GRANTS £500–£8,000

SAMPLE GRANTS £8,000 to the Stoke and Newcastle Festival; £3,000 to Lichfield Festival; £3,000 to English Haydn Festival, Bridgnorth; £3,000 to BBC Philharmonic Education Project; £2,000 to Clonter Farm Music Trust; £1,500 to Douglas Macmillan Hospice; £1,500 to Katherine House Hospice; £1,000 to Keele Concerts Society; £1,000 to British Diabetic Association (North Staffordshire); £1,000 to Orchestra da Camera

FINANCES *Year* 1997 *Income* £34,417 *Grants* £33,000

TRUSTEES M E Harding, J S McAllester, G G Wall, J P C Fowell, M N Lloyd

PUBLICATIONS Annual Accounts

HOW TO APPLY Generally the Trustees meet in the autumn to distribute income arising in previous fiscal year. Where charities are supported on a regular basis, the Trustees may ask to see the Annual Accounts

WHO TO APPLY TO Lace Mawer, Solicitor, The Harding Trust, Castle Chambers, 43 Castle Street, Liverpool L2 9SU

CC NO 328182   **ESTABLISHED** 1989

■ The Hare of Steep Charitable Trust

WHAT IS FUNDED Charities which benefit the community, in particular the advancement of social, cultural, medical, educational and religious projects

WHAT IS NOT FUNDED No funding for overseas charities, students, visits abroad or political causes

WHO CAN BENEFIT Registered charities. There are no restrictions on the age; professional and economic group; family situation; religion and culture; and social circumstances of; or disease or medical condition suffered by, the beneficiaries

WHERE FUNDING CAN BE GIVEN Mainly Petersfield and East Hampshire

TYPE OF GRANT Mainly annual contributions but grants are made for special projects

RANGE OF GRANTS £250–£2,500

SAMPLE GRANTS £2,500 to Army Benevolent Fund; £1,500 to Alzheimer's Disease Society; £1,500 to Royal Star and Garter Home; £1,500 to the Abbeyfield Liss Society; £1,500 to Arthritis and Rheumatism Council, Petersfield; £1,500 to Le Court; £1,500 to Ex-services Mental Welfare Society; £1,500 to Rainbow House Trust; £1,250 to Soldiers, Sailors and Airmen's Family Association; £1,250 to British Heart Foundation

FINANCES *Year* 1997 *Income* £54,855 *Grants* £45,550

TRUSTEES P L F Baillon, R J de C Glover, V R Jackson, A H Marshall, J R F Fowler

NOTES The Trust's funds are distributed twice a year and the Trust has its own waiting list

HOW TO APPLY **This Trust states that it does not respond to unsolicited applications**

WHO TO APPLY TO Mrs M E Jackson, Secretary, The Hare of Steep Charitable Trust, Island Millstone, Steep, Petersfield, Hampshire GU32 1AE

CC NO 297308   **ESTABLISHED** 1987

■ The Harebell Centenary Fund

WHAT IS FUNDED Providing scholarships and bursaries for young people in need of help to further their studies; neurological research; and the relief of sickness and suffering in animals. Including charities working in fields of: health; medical studies and research; conservation; heritage; special needs education and holidays and outings

WHAT IS NOT FUNDED Inrastructure. No grants to individuals

WHO CAN BENEFIT National and small charitable organisations benefiting children; older people; carers; disabled people; disaster victims and victims of war. There are few restrictions on the disease or medical condition suffered by the beneficiaries

WHERE FUNDING CAN BE GIVEN UK

TYPE OF GRANT One-off, core costs, research, recurring costs, running costs and funding for one year or less will be considered

RANGE OF GRANTS £500–£2,500

FINANCES *Year* 1996–97 *Income* £66,530 *Grants* £53,630

TRUSTEES J M Denker, M I Goodbody, F M Reed

NOTES **The Trustees are unlikely to respond to unsolicited applications or to individuals**

HOW TO APPLY To the address under Who To Apply To in writing

WHO TO APPLY TO Ms P J Chapman, The Harebell Centenary Fund, 20 Blackfriars Lane, London EC4V 6HD *Tel* 0171-248 4282

CC NO 1003552   **ESTABLISHED** 1991

■ Lord Harewood's Charitable Settlement

WHAT IS FUNDED To consider local and particular areas of interest that are registered charities and are known personally to the Trustees especially in the field of music and the arts

WHAT IS NOT FUNDED No reply will be made to speculative applications

WHO CAN BENEFIT Organisations benefiting: actors and entertainment professional; musicians; textile workers and designers; and writers and poets

WHERE FUNDING CAN BE GIVEN North of England

RANGE OF GRANTS Typically £50–£200

FINANCES *Year* 1995 *Income* £14,000
Grants £14,000

TRUSTEES C A Ussher

HOW TO APPLY No telephone calls and no speculative applications

WHO TO APPLY TO The Estate Office, Lord Harewood's Charitable Settlement, Harewood Yard, Harewood, Leeds LS17 9LF

CC NO 243591   **ESTABLISHED** 1964

■ Harford Charitable Trust

WHAT IS FUNDED Support is given to sheltered accommodation; voluntary organisations; hospices; special needs education; environmental issues; nature reserves and woodlands. Funding may be given towards homelessness, unemployment, care in the community, holidays and outings

WHAT IS NOT FUNDED No grants to individuals or students

WHO CAN BENEFIT Small local projects, innovative projects, new established and national organisations. Funding is given to children; young adults; those in care, fostered and adopted; at risk groups; disabled people; homeless people; refugees and victims of abuse. Beneficiaries suffering from Alzheimer's disease, arthritis, rheumatism and head and other injuries will be considered

WHERE FUNDING CAN BE GIVEN UK, with preference to Worcestershire, and overseas

TYPE OF GRANT One-off and recurrent range of grants

RANGE OF GRANTS £150–£600

SAMPLE GRANTS £600 to Children's Family Trust; £600 to Willow Trust (local); £600 to Acquired Aphasia Trust (local); £600 to Crisis; £600 to Emmaus UK

FINANCES *Year* 1997 *Income* £15,500
Grants £14,600

TRUSTEES Sir Timothy Harford, Lady Harford, Mrs Clatworthy, M Harford, S Harford

NOTES Preference for small charities

HOW TO APPLY In writing, preferably enclosing latest audited accounts

WHO TO APPLY TO Sir T Harford, Harford Charitable Trust, South House, South Littleton, Evesham, Worcestershire WR11 5TJ

CC NO 299945   **ESTABLISHED** 1988

■ The Kenneth Hargreaves Trust

WHAT IS FUNDED Currently the main areas of interest are medical research, education, environmental resources, arts and community projects, particularly organisations in which people help voluntarily

WHAT IS NOT FUNDED No grants to individuals

WHO CAN BENEFIT Registered charities benefiting children, young adults, students, medical professionals, research workers, teachers and governesses. There is no restriction on the disease or medical condition suffered by the beneficiaries

WHERE FUNDING CAN BE GIVEN UK. Preference is given to charities local to Wetherby in Yorkshire

FINANCES *Year* 1997 *Income* £36,130
Grants £25,754

TRUSTEES Dr Ingrid Roscoe, Mrs Sheila Holbrook, P Chadwick, Mrs Margret Hargreaves-Allen

PUBLICATIONS Annual Report

WHO TO APPLY TO Mrs Sheila Holbrook, Hon Treasurer, The Kenneth Hargreaves Trust, Bridge End Cottage, Linton, Wetherby LS22 4JB

CC NO 223800   **ESTABLISHED** 1957

■ The Harpenden Trust

WHAT IS FUNDED To provide relief in need, especially for children and older people

WHO CAN BENEFIT Primarily individuals and other good causes benefiting children, older people and those disadvantaged by poverty

WHERE FUNDING CAN BE GIVEN Harpenden and district only

FINANCES *Year* 1996–97 *Income* £48,865
Grants £37,485

TRUSTEES The Management Committee

HOW TO APPLY To the Chairman at the Trust Office in writing

WHO TO APPLY TO The Chairman, The Harpenden Trust, 90 Southdown Road, Harpenden, Hertfordshire AL5 1PS *Tel* 01582 460457

CC NO 212973   **ESTABLISHED** 1948

■ R J Harris Charitable Settlement

WHAT IS FUNDED To make grants of a general charitable nature to registered charities or for charitable purposes in the United Kingdom as the Trustees in their discretion think fit. Applications are generally categorised under the following headings: education; the arts; medical and mental health; young people's projects; conservation; and social welfare

WHO CAN BENEFIT Local organisations within the area Where Funding Can Be Given precedence. There are no restrictions on the age; professional and economic group; family situation; religion and culture; and social circumstances of; or disease or medical condition suffered by, the beneficiaries

WHERE FUNDING CAN BE GIVEN Precedence to North and West Wiltshire with emphasis on the Trowbridge area

FINANCES *Year* 1997 *Income* £65,931
Grants £72,685

TRUSTEES T C M Stock, H M Newton-Clare, J L Rogers, A Pitt

HOW TO APPLY Application by letter – no form. Sae ensures reply

WHO TO APPLY TO J Thring, R J Harris Charitable Settlement, Messrs Thrings and Long, Solicitors, Midland Bridge Road, Bath, Avon BA1 2HQ *Tel* 01225 448494 *Fax* 01225 319735

CC NO 258973   **ESTABLISHED** 1969

■ The John Harris Charitable Trust

WHAT IS FUNDED General charitable purposes

WHO CAN BENEFIT Registered charities. There are no restrictions on the age; professional and economic group; family situation; religion and culture; and social circumstances of; or disease or medical condition suffered by, the beneficiaries

WHERE FUNDING CAN BE GIVEN UK

FINANCES *Year* 1997 *Income* £16,772
Grants £31,250

TRUSTEES J E Harris, D B Harris, A J Kaye, J A Williams

HOW TO APPLY To the address under Who To Apply To, no special date. No saes please. Applications will not necessarily be acknowledged – small Trust with few facilities to do so

WHO TO APPLY TO A J Kaye, The John Harris Charitable Trust, Regent House, 235–241 Regent Street, London W1R 8PS
CC NO 327699   ESTABLISHED 1988

■ The Richard Harris Charitable Trust

WHAT IS FUNDED General charitable purposes
WHO CAN BENEFIT There are no restrictions on the age; professional and economic group; family situation; religion and culture; and social circumstances of; or disease or medical condition suffered by, the beneficiaries
WHERE FUNDING CAN BE GIVEN UK
TRUSTEES R M Harris, D Walsh
WHO TO APPLY TO D Walsh, The Richard Harris Charitable Trust, 54–62 Regent Street, London W1R 5PJ
CC NO 1068254   ESTABLISHED 1998

■ The Harris Charity

WHAT IS FUNDED Charities benefiting young persons under 25
WHO CAN BENEFIT Children and young adults under 25 in the Lancashire area
WHERE FUNDING CAN BE GIVEN Lancashire, preference to Preston area
TYPE OF GRANT Prefer capital projects and provision of equipment
FINANCES Year 1997 Income £114,977
Grants £61,773
TRUSTEES Mrs C Marshall, Mrs S Jackson, W S Huck, E J Booth, J Cotterall, T W S Croft, E C Dickson, S R Fisher, Mrs A Scott, Mrs R Jolly, S Huck, S B R Smith
HOW TO APPLY Half yearly by 30 September and 31 March
WHO TO APPLY TO P R Metcalf, FCA, The Harris Charity, Richard House, 9 Winckley Square, Preston, Lancashire PR1 3HP
Tel 01772 821021 *Fax* 01772 259441
CC NO 526206   ESTABLISHED 1883

■ The Harris Family Charitable Trust

WHAT IS FUNDED General charitable purposes
WHO CAN BENEFIT There are no restrictions on the age; professional and economic group; family situation; religion and culture; and social circumstances of; or disease or medical condition suffered by, the beneficiaries
WHERE FUNDING CAN BE GIVEN UK
TRUSTEES Ms E R Harris, R M Harris
WHO TO APPLY TO R M Harris, Trustee, The Harris Family Charitable Trust, 8–10 Bulstrode Street, London W1M 6AH
CC NO 1064394   ESTABLISHED 1997

■ The John Harrison Charitable Trust

WHAT IS FUNDED General charitable purposes
WHO CAN BENEFIT There are no restrictions on the age; professional and economic group; family situation; religion and culture; and social circumstances of; or disease or medical condition suffered by, the beneficiaries
WHERE FUNDING CAN BE GIVEN UK

FINANCES Year 1997 Income £22,730
Grants £1,000
TRUSTEES M Sebba, J A Garden, J C Sebba
NOTES Funds available are fully committed to specific charities which the Trust supports regularly and the Trustees are unable to entertain other applications. No individual applications should therefore be submitted until further notice
WHO TO APPLY TO M Sebba, The John Harrison Charitable Trust, 465 Salisbury House, London Wall, London EC2M 5RQ
CC NO 277956   ESTABLISHED 1979

■ Harrisons & Crosfield Charitable Fund

This trust did not respond to CAF's request to amend its entry and, by 30 June 1998, CAF's researchers did not find financial records for later than 1995 on its file at the Charity Commission. Trusts are legally required to submit annual accounts to the Charity Commission under section 42 of the Charities Act 1993

WHAT IS FUNDED To support charities assisting disadvantaged people
WHAT IS NOT FUNDED Applications are not invited from charities and are not considered from individuals. Requests for advertising in souvenir brochures are never considered. Telephone or written requests from professional fund raisers are discouraged
WHO CAN BENEFIT Headquarters of organisations benefiting those disadvantaged by poverty
WHERE FUNDING CAN BE GIVEN UK
TYPE OF GRANT Mostly one-off or recurrent for up to four years and some annual donations
TRUSTEES G W Paul, W J Turcan, P D Brown
NOTES Our existing list is constantly under review and rather than add new charities we are more inclined to increase the donations to those already listed. During the last few years we have added some local charities
HOW TO APPLY **This Trust states that it does not respond to unsolicited applications**
WHO TO APPLY TO The Secretary, H & C Charitable Fund, One Great Tower Street, London EC3R 5AH
CC NO 277899   ESTABLISHED 1979

■ Harrogate St Andrew's Players

WHAT IS FUNDED To advance the education of pupils in the arts, in particular, the art of musical drama; other general charitable purposes
WHO CAN BENEFIT Organisations promoting the arts to children and young adults
WHERE FUNDING CAN BE GIVEN UK
FINANCES Year 1995 Income £15,341
WHO TO APPLY TO Mrs M Bell, Harrogate St Andrew's Players, The Hollies Cottage, Walshford, Weatherby, West Yorkshire LS22 5HT
CC NO 1057953   ESTABLISHED 1996

■ The Harrow Community Trust

WHAT IS FUNDED General charitable purposes for the benefit of the community, in particular, the advancement of education, the protection of mental and physical health and the relief of poverty and sickness
WHAT IS NOT FUNDED No grants to individuals
WHO CAN BENEFIT Local organisations benefiting: unemployed people and volunteers of many different social circumstances. There is no restriction on the age, or family situation of, or the

Does the trust you have chosen match your needs? Haphazard applications waste postage and time

281

disease or medical condition suffered by, the beneficiaries

WHERE FUNDING CAN BE GIVEN London Borough of Harrow

TYPE OF GRANT One-off, capital, core costs, feasibility studies, project, recurring costs and start-up costs. Funding will be given for up to one year

RANGE OF GRANTS £250–£1,000

SAMPLE GRANTS £1,000 to Reach Out for core costs/ helpline for sufferers from abuse; £1,000 to Perriwells Riding for the Disabled for equipment for indoor riding centre; £1,000 to Choices 4 All for set up costs of training in catering for those with learning disabilities; £500 to KUFI Education Service for summer school for Afro Caribbean children; £500 to Harrow Crossroads for social outreach feasibility study; £500 to Harrow Stroke Club for core costs and social events; £500 to Women's Aid for training care workers for women's refuge; £500 to BIAS Irish Travellers for extra education project; £500 to MENCAP Harrow for after school club; £500 to St Mary's Music Festival for the costs of free concerts, particularly for the elderly

FINANCES *Year* 1997–98 *Income* £42,000 *Grants* £20,000

TRUSTEES R Funk, R Preston, I Sommerschield, Mrs M Nunn, S Klarfeld, Mrs C Bagnald, P Lomax, S Flash, M Shah, Ms Z Stavrinidis, I Farrell, S Bantin

HOW TO APPLY Initial telephone calls from applicants are welcome. An application form and guidelines are available, there are deadlines for applications. No sae is required

WHO TO APPLY TO M Churchill, Director, The Harrow Community Trust, Unit 4, Forward Drive, Wealdstone, Harrow, Middlesex HA3 8NT *Tel* 0181-424 1167 *Fax* 0181-909 1407

CC NO 299491   **ESTABLISHED** 1988

■ Mrs D L Harryhausen's 1969 Trust

WHAT IS FUNDED Grants are made to a number of specific animal welfare charities in connection with David Livingstone. At present these exhaust the income and the Trustees are not inviting applications

WHO CAN BENEFIT Animal charities

WHERE FUNDING CAN BE GIVEN UK, particularly Scotland

TRUSTEES Simon Mackintosh, George Menzies, Vanessa Harryhausen

PUBLICATIONS Accounts are available from the Trust

NOTES At present the commitments are exhausting the income available

HOW TO APPLY Applications should be made in writing to the address under Who To Apply To but at present no new applications are being invited

WHO TO APPLY TO The Correspondent, Mrs D L Harryhausen's 1969 Trust, Tuncan Connell, Saltire Court, 20 Castle Terrace, Edinburgh EH1 2EF *Tel* 0131-228 8111

SC NO SCO 15688

■ The Hart Charitable Trust

WHAT IS FUNDED For relief of residents in the County of East Sussex who are in conditions of need, hardship or distress

WHO CAN BENEFIT Individuals and organisations benefiting: at risk groups; those disadvantaged by poverty; homeless people; the socially isolated; victims of abuse, crime and domestic violence

WHERE FUNDING CAN BE GIVEN East Sussex

TYPE OF GRANT One-off to relieve immediate need, or meet a particular problem

RANGE OF GRANTS Up to £200

FINANCES *Year* 1995–96 *Income* £20,909 *Grants* £12,272

HOW TO APPLY Application forms are available from the address under Who To Apply To upon written request, and must be completed by a third party such as a social worker who can vouch for the information supplied

WHO TO APPLY TO Michael R Bugden, The Hart Charitable Trust, 2 Eversley Road, Bexhill on Sea, East Sussex TN40 1EY *Tel* 01424 730945

CC NO 801126   **ESTABLISHED** 1989

■ The Spencer Hart Charitable Trust

WHAT IS FUNDED General charitable purposes

WHO CAN BENEFIT Registered charities. There are no restrictions on the age; professional and economic group; family situation; religion and culture; and social circumstances of; or disease or medical condition suffered by, the beneficiaries

WHERE FUNDING CAN BE GIVEN UK and overseas

SAMPLE GRANTS £5,500 to The League of the Helping Hand; £2,000 to Ravenswood; £1,000 to The National Appeal for Music Therapy; £1,000 to Lord Williams' Association; £1,000 to Norwood Ravenswood; £1,000 to The Wigmore Hall Trust; £500 to Garsington Opera; £250 to British Friends of Haifa University; £100 to Friend of the Earth; £100 to Cancer Research Campaign

FINANCES *Year* 1997 *Income* £27,305 *Grants* £12,550

TRUSTEES J S Korn, I A Burman

WHO TO APPLY TO J S Korn, The Spencer Hart Charitable Trust, c/o Beechcroft Stanleys, 20 Furnival Street, London EC4A 1BN

CC NO 800057   **ESTABLISHED** 1988

■ The Hartley Charitable Trust

WHAT IS FUNDED General charitable purposes including medicine and health, welfare, education, sciences, humanities and religion, and environmental resources

WHAT IS NOT FUNDED No grants to individuals or students

WHO CAN BENEFIT Small local projects, innovative projects, new established and national organisations. There are no restrictions on the age; professional and economic group; family situation; religion and culture; and social circumstances of; or disease or medical condition suffered by, the beneficiaries

WHERE FUNDING CAN BE GIVEN UK, especially Yorkshire and Nottinghamshire, and overseas

TYPE OF GRANT One-off and recurrent range of grants

FINANCES *Year* 1995 *Income* £32,858 *Grants* £13,978

TRUSTEES Richard Hartley, Jane Hartley, Peta Hyland

NOTES Aggressive or expensive 'glossy' funding requests are not considered

HOW TO APPLY In writing only. Telephone requests not considered

WHO TO APPLY TO Mrs P Hyland, The Hartley Charitable Trust, 42 Hallfields, Nottingham NG12 4AD

CC NO 800968   **ESTABLISHED** 1989

■ The N and P Hartley Memorial Trust

WHAT IS FUNDED For the benefit of the elderly, children, the disabled and the provision of medical facilities and care for all age groups. Particular attention given to smaller charities and individuals in need

WHO CAN BENEFIT Individuals and community organisations benefiting: disabled people, the elderly and young; and the sick. There is no restriction on the disease or medical condition suffered by the beneficiaries

WHERE FUNDING CAN BE GIVEN West Yorkshire principally, but will consider causes in the remainder of Yorkshire and the Northern counties of England

RANGE OF GRANTS £340–£5,500

SAMPLE GRANTS £5,500 to Kisiizi Hospital; £5,000 to Caring for Life; £2,220 to Winged Fellowship; £2,000 to Leeds and Bradford Asbah; £2,000 to Communication for the Disabled; £1,000 to West Riding Care; £1,000 to Beecroft After School Club; £1,000 to Serious Fun; £1,000 to Disability Aid Fund; £500 to National Asthma Campaign

FINANCES *Year* 1997 *Income* £47,712 *Grants* £21,920

TRUSTEES Mrs V B Procter, J J Procter, J E Kirman

NOTES The Trustees meet three times each year to discuss requests. Pleased to support old and new causes alike and welcome re-applications from those they have helped in the past

HOW TO APPLY By letter outlining your need. Suitable applicants will be invited to complete a questionnaire for the Trustees' consideration at their bi-annual meeting

WHO TO APPLY TO Mrs V Beryl Procter, The N and P Hartley Memorial Trust, 51 Uppleby, Easingwold, Yorkshire YO6 3BD

CC NO 327570　　　**ESTABLISHED** 1987

■ The Hartnett Charitable Trust

WHAT IS FUNDED Mental health research and welfare only

WHAT IS NOT FUNDED No grants to individuals. Only mental health research need apply

WHO CAN BENEFIT To benefit those suffering from mental illness

WHERE FUNDING CAN BE GIVEN UK

TYPE OF GRANT Capital

RANGE OF GRANTS £200–£5,000

SAMPLE GRANTS £5,000 to Cumnor House School Trust; £2,500 to National Missing Persons Helpline; £2,000 to Woodgate Farm Appeal; £200 to Combat Stress

FINANCES *Year* 1997 *Income* £31,573 *Grants* £9,700

TRUSTEES M R N Hartnett, D W Hartnett, J A Hartnett

NOTES Time Charity: 40 years from date of the Deed of Settlement

HOW TO APPLY Brief letter with sae

WHO TO APPLY TO J A Hartnett, The Hartnett Charitable Trust, Belmoredean, Maplehurst Road, West Grinstead, Horsham, West Sussex RH13 6RN

CC NO 276460　　　**ESTABLISHED** 1978

■ The Harvest Seed Trust

WHAT IS FUNDED The advancement of the Christian faith

WHO CAN BENEFIT Organisations benefiting Christians

WHERE FUNDING CAN BE GIVEN UK

WHO TO APPLY TO D G Clapp, Professional Advisor, The Harvest Seed Trust, Sully & Co, 21 Boutport Street, Barnstaple, Devon EX31 1AP *Tel* 01271 42233

CC NO 1064765　　　**ESTABLISHED** 1997

■ Gordon Harvey Charitable Trust

WHAT IS FUNDED General charitable purposes, including the upkeep, repair, etc of any holiday homes for children, the poor and the elderly. Support is given to universities and hospitals

WHO CAN BENEFIT Individuals and organisations benefiting children, the elderly and those disadvantaged by poverty. Grants are usually made to universities and hospitals. Otherwise, there are no restrictions on the age; professional and economic group; family situation; religion and culture; and social circumstances of; or disease or medical condition suffered by, the beneficiaries

WHERE FUNDING CAN BE GIVEN UK

SAMPLE GRANTS £5,900 to The London Lighthouse; £5,400 to the Royal Marsden Hospital; £2,400 to St Barnabas Hospital Trust; £2,400 to British Hospital for Neuro-Disability; £2,400 to Royal Hospital and Home for Incurables

FINANCES *Year* 1997 *Income* £18,327 *Grants* £20,900

TRUSTEES J M P Bishop, H K Harvey

NOTES Support limited mainly to national organisations. The Trust usually supports the same organisations from year to year, and those that are known to the Trustees

WHO TO APPLY TO J M P Bishop, Gordon Harvey Charitable Trust, Messrs E C Brown & Batts, Hearts of Oak House, 84 Kingsway, London WC2B 6NF

CC NO 210976　　　**ESTABLISHED** 1946

■ William Geoffrey Harvey's Discretionary Settlement

WHAT IS FUNDED Animal facilities and services to promote the well-being of and prevent cruelty to animals and birds

WHAT IS NOT FUNDED New causes not likely to receive help. No grants to individuals

WHO CAN BENEFIT Registered charities

WHERE FUNDING CAN BE GIVEN UK

TYPE OF GRANT Running costs

RANGE OF GRANTS £1,000–£5,000

SAMPLE GRANTS £5,000 to PDSA; £5,000 to Redwings Horse Sanctuary; £4,000 to Care for the Wild; £3,500 to National Canine Defence League; £3,500 to Wildfowl and Wetlands Trust; £3,000 to Donkey Sanctuary; £3,000 to Wildlife Hospital Trust; £1,000 to Three Owls Bird Sanctuary

FINANCES *Year* 1997 *Income* £29,085 *Grants* £28,000

TRUSTEES F R Shackleton, F A Sherring

NOTES Trustees make decisions after 5 April every year

HOW TO APPLY **This Trust states that it does not respond to unsolicited applications**

WHO TO APPLY TO F A Sherring, William Geoffrey Harvey's Discretionary Settlement, 1A Gibsons Road, Stockport SK4 4JX

CC NO 800473　　　**ESTABLISHED** 1968

■ The Lord and Lady Haskel Charitable Foundation

WHAT IS FUNDED The Charity is currently funding projects concerned with social policy research and Jewish communal life

WHO CAN BENEFIT To benefit Jews and research workers

WHERE FUNDING CAN BE GIVEN UK

RANGE OF GRANTS £1,000–£40,000

SAMPLE GRANTS £40,000 to Institute of Jewish Policy Research

FINANCES *Year* 1996 *Income* £17,999 *Grants* £47,000

TRUSTEES A Davis, J Haskel, M Nutman

HOW TO APPLY **This Trust states that it does not respond to unsolicited applications**

WHO TO APPLY TO J Lent, The Lord and Lady Haskel Charitable Foundation, Averbach Hope, 58–60 Berners Street, London W1P 4JS *Tel* 0171-637 4121

CC NO 1039969   **ESTABLISHED** 1993

■ Lady Elizabeth Hastings' Estate Charity

WHAT IS FUNDED Grants are distributed to specific schools and individuals in the area Where Funding Can Be Given and to churches, clergy and their dependants and to people in need in the area Where Funding Can Be Given

WHO CAN BENEFIT Individuals, schools and churches benefiting: children; clergy; those disadvantaged by poverty; at risk groups; and socially isolated people

WHERE FUNDING CAN BE GIVEN The parishes of Bardsey with East Keswick, Burton Salmon, Collingham with Harewood, Shadwell and Ledsham with Fairburn, Thorp Arch

FINANCES *Year* 1997 *Income* £327,300

TRUSTEES The vicars of: Collingham with Harewood, Ledsham with Fairburn and Thorp Arch. The owner of Ledston Hall, Cllr Mrs Linda Middleton, C Wilton

HOW TO APPLY To the address under Who To Apply To in writing

WHO TO APPLY TO E F V Waterson, Clerk, Lady Elizabeth Hastings' Estate Charity, Carter Jonas, 82 Micklegate, York YO1 1LF *Tel* 01904 627436

CC NO 224098   **ESTABLISHED** 1964

■ The Maurice Hatter Foundation (227)

This trust failed to supply a copy of its annual report and accounts to CAF as required under section 47(2) of the Charities Act 1993. The information held on file at the Charity Commission was insufficient to enable CAF's researchers to write a substantive commentary on the trust's activities. Accordingly, despite its size, we are unable to list this trust in Spotlight on Major Trusts.

WHAT IS FUNDED General charitable purposes

WHAT IS NOT FUNDED Unsolicited requests are not considered

WHO CAN BENEFIT Voluntary organisations and charitable groups. There are no restrictions on the age; professional and economic group; family situation; religion and culture; and social circumstances of; or disease or medical condition suffered by, the beneficiaries

WHERE FUNDING CAN BE GIVEN UK and overseas

FINANCES *Year* 1997 *Income* £1,313,009 *Grants* £429,373

TRUSTEES M Hatter, N Freeman, H I Connick, J Newman, R Hatter

HOW TO APPLY **This Trust states that it does not respond to unsolicited applications**

WHO TO APPLY TO J S Newman, The Maurice Hatter Foundation, Messrs BDO Stoy Hayward, 8 Baker Street, London W1M 1DA

CC NO 298119   **ESTABLISHED** 1987

■ The Hattori Foundation

WHAT IS FUNDED At present, to give financial assistance to outstanding young musicians

WHO CAN BENEFIT British nationals or persons ordinarily resident in the UK and foreign nationals who are studying in the UK, individual musicians. Less likely to be organisations

WHERE FUNDING CAN BE GIVEN UK and overseas

TYPE OF GRANT Up to £6,000 for advanced tuition and financial support in musical education

FINANCES *Year* 1996–97 *Income* £87,464 *Grants* £44,983

TRUSTEES The Hattori Trust Co Ltd – Directors: E Gruenberg, OBE (Chairman), J Hattori, Mrs T Hattori, Lady Barbirolli, Lord Birkett, J V Hughes, R Jackson, MP, J Seiger, L Howard, P Jones, R Masters, Dr M Lovett OBE

PUBLICATIONS Brochures

NOTES 23 grants were made to individuals during the year

HOW TO APPLY In writing to the address under Who To Apply To

WHO TO APPLY TO John V Hughes, Solicitor/Director, The Hattori Foundation, 4th Floor, 154 Fleet Street, London EC4A 2HX

CC NO 1014709   **ESTABLISHED** 1992

■ Hatzola Northwest Trust

WHAT IS FUNDED General charitable purposes, in particular the protection and preservation of health; the relief of sickness especially the provision of first aid relief assistance to persons who are ill or sick or otherwise in need of medical care and attention; or hospital or clinical nursing services and the provision of first aid cover at public events

WHO CAN BENEFIT Organisations benefiting sick people. There is no restriction on the disease or medical condition suffered by the beneficiaries

WHERE FUNDING CAN BE GIVEN London

SAMPLE GRANTS £2,517 for medical supplies; £371 for training costs

FINANCES *Year* 1997 *Income* £29,441 *Grants* £2,888

TRUSTEES H Frydenson, S C Heller, J Jackson, S Klein, B Liebermann, A R Ormande

WHO TO APPLY TO H Frydenson, Hatzola Northwest Trust, 28 The Grove, London NW11 9SH

CC NO 1041441   **ESTABLISHED** 1994

■ Havering Council for Voluntary Services

WHAT IS FUNDED General charitable purposes for the benefit of the community in the local government district of Havering; in particular, the advancement of education, the protection of health and the relief of poverty, distress and sickness

WHO CAN BENEFIT Organisations benefiting children, young adults, students and those disadvantaged by poverty. Medical professionals and research workers may also be supported. There is no

restriction on the disease or medical condition suffered by the beneficiaries

WHERE FUNDING CAN BE GIVEN District of Havering
RANGE OF GRANTS £507–£19,807
SAMPLE GRANTS £19,807 to Barking and Havering Health Authority; £4,964 to Community Development Foundation; £2,979 to Bridge House Estates Trust Fund; £1,781 to East Thames Side PArtnership; £507 to TSB Foundation for England and Wales
FINANCES *Year* 1997 *Income* £80,699 *Grants* £30,038
TRUSTEES J Atkins, J Hooper, B Norton, A Rushworth, B Walker
NOTES The majority of the Council's income is used to fund the running of the service, ie salaries, expenses and training, etc
WHO TO APPLY TO R Money, Havering Council for Voluntary Services, 9 Tadworth Parade, Elm Park, Hornchurch RM12 5AS
CC NO 1040745   **ESTABLISHED** 1993

■ The M A Hawe Settlement

WHAT IS FUNDED Welfare of the aged, women and children. Education, disability, homelessness and other charitable purposes
WHO CAN BENEFIT National and local organisations and schemes benefiting: people of all ages; women; students; disabled people; at risk groups; socially isolated people; homeless people; and those disadvantaged by poverty.
WHERE FUNDING CAN BE GIVEN UK, with a preference for Lancashire
TYPE OF GRANT One-off, some recurrent
RANGE OF GRANTS Below £100–£174,230
SAMPLE GRANTS £174,230 to Kensington House Trust Limited for welfare purposes; £7,900 to Children in Need; £1,404 to Holy Cross Church and Soup Kitchen; £586 to Old Folks Home; £380 as 12 miscellaneous donations of under £100; £250 to Motability NW; £180 to Jubilee Trust; £100 to an individual; £50 to Hall Park School
FINANCES *Year* 1995–96 *Income* £440,043 *Grants* £185,080
TRUSTEES M A Hawe, Mrs G Hawe, Mark G Hawe
HOW TO APPLY To the address under Who To Apply To in writing
WHO TO APPLY TO M A Hawe, The M A Hawe Settlement, 94 Park View Road, Lytham St Annes, Lancashire FY8 4JF
CC NO 327827   **ESTABLISHED** 1988

■ Harry Fieldsend Hawley Residuary Fund

WHAT IS FUNDED Relief of sickness or suffering in children's hospitals and in children's wards in any hospital, nursing homes, clinics or other like medical institutions anywhere in the United Kingdom but, as far as is practicable, for the benefit of such hospitals, nursing homes, clinics and like medical institutions situated within a radius of five miles or thereabouts from the centres of the towns of Sheffield and Barnsley, South Yorkshire to which children from the Penistone area are customarily sent
WHAT IS NOT FUNDED It is not the policy of the Trustees to supply equipment which should be supplied by the Local Authority or Area Health Authority
WHO CAN BENEFIT Hospitals and like institutions benefiting children, young adults and medical professionals. There is no restriction on the

disease or medical condition suffered by the beneficiaries
WHERE FUNDING CAN BE GIVEN South Yorkshire
TYPE OF GRANT Research and equipment
FINANCES *Year* 1997 *Income* £14,117
TRUSTEES Midland Bank Trust Company Ltd, at address below
HOW TO APPLY At any time to Midland Trusts at address under Who To Apply To
WHO TO APPLY TO Colin Bould, The Trust Manager, Harry Fieldsend Hawley Residuary Fund, Midland Trusts, Cumberland House, 15–17 Cumberland Place, Southampton SO15 2UY
Tel 01703 531348
CC NO 507974   **ESTABLISHED** 1978

■ The Hawthorne Charitable Trust

WHAT IS FUNDED The Trustees make donations, generally on an annual basis, to a large number of charities mainly concerned with the care of the elderly and the young, the relief of pain, sickness and poverty, the advancement of medical research, particularly into the various forms of cancer, research into animal health, the arts and preservation of ancient buildings
WHAT IS NOT FUNDED It is not the Trustees' policy to make grants to individuals
WHO CAN BENEFIT Organisations benefiting: the young and the elderly; medical professionals; and those disadvantaged by poverty. There is no restriction on the disease or medical condition suffered by the beneficiaries
WHERE FUNDING CAN BE GIVEN UK
SAMPLE GRANTS £10,000 to the Haven Trust; £5,000 to Dyson Perrins Museum; £5,000 to Edwards Trust; £5,000 to Macmillan Cancer Relief; £5,000 to Society of Friends of Little Malvern Priory; £3,000 to Downside Abbey (St Wulstans); £3,000 to Malvern Hills Citizens Advice; £2,500 to Alzheimer's Disease Society; £2,500 to Crusaid; £2,500 to Imperial Cancer Research
FINANCES *Year* 1998 *Income* £151,100 *Grants* £145,600
TRUSTEES Mrs A Berington, R J Clark
WHO TO APPLY TO The Hawthorne Charitable Trust, Messrs Baker Tilly, Chartered Accountants, 2 Bloomsbury Street, London WC1B 3ST
CC NO 233921   **ESTABLISHED** 1964

■ The Douglas Hay Trust

WHAT IS FUNDED Grants are primarily given to individuals but are occasionally made to organisations dedicated to helping the disabled
WHAT IS NOT FUNDED Beneficiaries must be under 18
WHO CAN BENEFIT Physically disabled children under the age of 18. A wide range of physical disabilities are considered for funding
WHERE FUNDING CAN BE GIVEN Scotland
RANGE OF GRANTS £50–£2,000, typical grant £35
SAMPLE GRANTS £4,000 to Capability Scotland Western School for general expenses; £4,000 to Trefoil Holiday Centre for general expenses; £2,000 for a hydrotherapy pool-hoist
FINANCES *Year* 1996–97 *Income* £32,000 *Grants* £27,230
TRUSTEES L R S Mackenzie, WS, James Robb, FRCS, Robert P White, CA, Dr John Ross, MD, ChB
HOW TO APPLY Applications are invited from social workers and other officials
WHO TO APPLY TO The Secretary, The Douglas Hay Trust, Tigh Na H'ath, Dulnain Bridge, Morayshire PH26 3NU *Tel* 01479 851266
SC NO SCO 14450   **ESTABLISHED** 1948

■ Hayle's Charity

WHAT IS FUNDED Education and general social needs in Lambeth

WHAT IS NOT FUNDED Beneficiaries must be residents in the London Borough of Lambeth

WHO CAN BENEFIT To benefit children, young adults and students

WHERE FUNDING CAN BE GIVEN London Borough of Lambeth and the Ancient Parish of Lambeth

RANGE OF GRANTS Organisations: £1,000–£5,000

SAMPLE GRANTS £5,000 to St Mary's Family Centre for family support service; £4,140 to Lambeth Chinese Community Association for Luncheon Club running costs; £4,000 to Lambeth CDA for Community Forum Development costs; £3,500 to British Home and Hospital for patient hoist; £3,500 to St Stephen's Neighbourhood for costs of part-time co-ordinator; £3,350 to Kairos Community Trust for building refurbishment of hostel; £3,000 to Chatsworth Family Centre for outdoor play area; £3,000 to Lambeth Mencap Club 25 for social club and activities project; £3,000 to Lambeth MIND for mental health sufferers helpline; £3,000 to Lambeth Vietnamese Community for basic skills training course

FINANCES *Year* 1997 *Income* £207,404 *Grants* £144,765

TRUSTEES Dr C Gerada, Mrs M T Porter, B M Vinter, · Dr J Weddell, Mrs I Allen, MBE, D P de Laszlo, J R D Korner, D Slack, Ms M Evans

NOTES The Hayle's Educational Branch made two grants totalling £860. 185 grants were made to individuals totalling £26,488 and the total paid to projects and organisations was £110,458

HOW TO APPLY Applications must be on a form available on request. Trustees meet quarterly, usually in March, June, October and December and applications must be received at least six weeks before the date of the meeting

WHO TO APPLY TO Robert Dewar, Director and Clerk to Trustees, Hayle's Charity, 127 Kennington Road, London SE11 6SF

CC NO 206462   **ESTABLISHED** 1990

■ Haymills Charitable Trust

WHAT IS FUNDED The Trust seeks to support projects which are not widely known, and therefore likely to be inadequately funded. Main support is to registered charities operating in areas lying in and to the west of London and in Suffolk. Grants fall into four main categories: (a) education: schools colleges and universities; (b) medicine: hospitals, associated institutions and medical research; (c) welfare: primarily to include former Haymills' staff, those who are in necessitous circumstances, or who are otherwise distressed or disadvantaged; and (d) youth: support for schemes to assist in the education, welfare and training of young people. Limited number of applicants will be considered who can show they are committed to further education and training, preferably for employment in the construction industry

WHAT IS NOT FUNDED No personal applications will be considered unless endorsed by a university, college or other appropriate authority

WHO CAN BENEFIT Organisations benefiting children and young adults; former employees of Haymills; at risk groups, those disadvantaged by poverty and socially isolated people

WHERE FUNDING CAN BE GIVEN West of London and Suffolk

RANGE OF GRANTS £300–£10,000

SAMPLE GRANTS £10,000 to Merchant Taylors' Company for Dudley Cox Bursary Awards; £6,000 to Thames Valley University for general grants; £4,000 to Thames Valley for the Haymills Chair of Accountancy; £3,500 to Raleigh Trust; £2,500 to Inter Action, HMS President; £2,500 to Middlesex Young People's Clubs; £2,000 to Central Middlesex Hospital League of Friends; £2,000 to Ealing Hospital League of Friends; £2,000 to Royal College of Physicians; £2,000 to Project Trust

FINANCES *Year* 1997 *Income* £209,927 *Grants* £65,350

TRUSTEES G A Cox, E F C Drake, A M H Jackson, K C Perryman, J A Sharpe, J L Wosner, I W Ferres

NOTES The Trustees meet twice a year, usually in March and October

HOW TO APPLY The Trustees are unable to acknowledge applications made to them

WHO TO APPLY TO I W Ferres, Secretary, Haymills Charitable Trust, c/o Haymills, Empire House, Hanger Green, London W5 3BD

CC NO 277761   **ESTABLISHED** 1979

■ Haywood Charitable Trust

WHAT IS FUNDED Medicine and health

WHO CAN BENEFIT Registered charities. There are no restrictions on the age; professional and economic group; family situation; religion and culture; and social circumstances of; or disease or medical condition suffered by, the beneficiaries

WHERE FUNDING CAN BE GIVEN Hampshire

TYPE OF GRANT Range of grants

RANGE OF GRANTS £100–£1,600

SAMPLE GRANTS £1,600 to Winchester Cathedral Trust; £1,600 to Cancer Research Campaign; £1,600 to Cancer Relief Macmillan Fund; £1,600 to North Hampshire Medical Trust; £1,600 to Motor Neurone Disease Association

FINANCES *Year* 1996 *Income* £16,596 *Grants* £15,500

TRUSTEES D Saunders, Mrs M Saunders, Miss K Saunders, N Saunders, A Brooking

WHO TO APPLY TO A Brooking, Haywood Charitable Trust, Brooking Knowles & Lawrence, Clifton House, Bunnian Place, Basingstoke, Hampshire RG21 1JE

CC NO 1001982   **ESTABLISHED** 1990

■ The Heald Charitable Trust

WHAT IS FUNDED General charitable purposes

WHO CAN BENEFIT There are no restrictions on the age; professional and economic group; family situation; religion and culture; and social circumstances of; or disease or medical condition suffered by, the beneficiaries

WHERE FUNDING CAN BE GIVEN UK

FINANCES *Year* 1996 *Income* £13,819

TRUSTEES K F B O'Kelly

WHO TO APPLY TO NatWest Trustees Ltd, The Heald Charitable Trust, National Westminster Bank plc, Natwest Investments, 67 Maple Road, Surbiton, Surrey KT6 4QT

CC NO 1045914   **ESTABLISHED** 1995

■ The Heart of England Community Foundation

WHAT IS FUNDED General charitable purposes in particular for the benefit of the handicapped or disabled, to promote social and economic development. This includes: residential facilities and services; community arts and recreation; respite care and care for carers; support and self help groups; community services; social issues advice and information; and health advocacy

WHAT IS NOT FUNDED Grants not likely to be made to individuals, educational or religious organisations, medical research, organisations outside the area Where Funding Can Be Given

WHO CAN BENEFIT Groups and activities benefiting a wide range of social circumstance. There is no restriction on the age; family situation; religion and culture of; and disease or medical condition suffered by, the beneficiaries

WHERE FUNDING CAN BE GIVEN Warwickshire and the City of Coventry

TYPE OF GRANT Buildings, capital, core costs, feasibility studies, one-off, project, research, recurring and running costs, salaries, and start-up costs. Funding is available for up to one year

RANGE OF GRANTS £100–£2,000

SAMPLE GRANTS £2,500 to Wood End and Bell Green Truancy and Exclusion Group for pastoral work with truants and excluded children; £2,000 to Centre AT7 for activities with vulnerable young people; £2,000 to Crusader Foundation for basketball camp with vulnerable young people; £2,000 to Leamington Boys Club for outward bound activities; £2,000 to Furnace Fields Parents Centre for Saturday activities for disadvantaged children; £2,000 to Relate Warwickshire for anti-violence course for perpetrators of domestic violence; £2,000 to Coventry Panaghar for play area for children of Asian families experiencing domestic violence; £1,786 to Coventry Cyrenians 'Survivors' Course for women experiencing domestic violence; £1,000 to Rugby MIND for support group for carers of elderly people with dementia; £1,000 to Sanatan Dharm Bridh Sabha support group for Asian elders

FINANCES *Year* 1997–98 *Income* £152,778 *Grants* £44,185

TRUSTEES Margaret Backhouse, Margaret Dorman-Frost, John Purser, Ian Smith, Roger Smith, Andrew McLaren, Peter Bell, Richard Drew, Spencer Fenn, Lady Jean Higgins, Michael Paget-Wilkes, Beth Towers, John Towers, Tom White

NOTES The priorities of the Trustees are reviewed annually, applicants are encouraged to contact by telephone to obtain up-to-date information on current priorities

HOW TO APPLY To the address under Who To Apply To in writing, or telephone with initial enquiry

WHO TO APPLY TO The Director, The Heart of England Community Foundation, Aldermoor House, PO Box 227, Aldermoor Lane, Coventry CV3 1LT *Tel* 01203 884386 *Fax* 01203 884726 *Web Site* http://www.covnet.co.uk/hecf

CC NO 1045304 **ESTABLISHED** 1995

■ Heart of England Radio Charitable Trust

WHAT IS FUNDED Local charities providing help in the areas of: fertility; foetal well being; babies and very young children

WHO CAN BENEFIT Predominantly female and aged between 25–44. Pre-school children, at risk groups, disabled people, those disadvantaged by poverty, those living in urban areas and victims of abuse, crime and domestic violence

WHERE FUNDING CAN BE GIVEN Warwickshire and the West Midlands

TYPE OF GRANT One-off, capital and buildings will be considered. Funding may be given for up to one year

RANGE OF GRANTS £1,000–£75,000

SAMPLE GRANTS £100,000 to Birmingham Children's Hospital for the main appeal; £14,500 to Walsall Hospital NHS Trust for purchase of Propaq Encore monitor; £10,000 to Children's Liver Disease Foundation for purchase of ten home feeding pumps; £5,000 to Birmingham St Mary's Hospice for their main appeal; £3,000 to Redditch Play Council for the purchase of play equipment for pre-school children

HOW TO APPLY Phone or write with basic details

WHO TO APPLY TO Phil Riley, Heart of England Radio Charitable Trust, 1 The Square, 111 Broad Street, Birmingham B15 1AS *Tel* 0121-626 1007 *Fax* 0121-696 1007

CC NO 1054689 **ESTABLISHED** 1996

■ The Mrs C S Heber Percy Charitable Trust

WHAT IS FUNDED General charitable purposes

WHO CAN BENEFIT There are no restrictions on the age; professional and economic group; family situation; religion and culture; and social circumstances of; or disease or medical condition suffered by, the beneficiaries

WHERE FUNDING CAN BE GIVEN UK and overseas

FINANCES *Year* 1995 *Income* £65,364 *Grants* £107,865

TRUSTEES Mrs C S Heber Percy, Mrs S Prest

WHO TO APPLY TO The Secretary, The Mrs C S Heber Percy Charitable Trust, c/o Kleinwort Benson Trustees Ltd, PO Box 191, 10 Fenchurch Street, London EC3M 3LB

CC NO 284387 **ESTABLISHED** 1981

■ Percy Hedley Will Trust

WHAT IS FUNDED General charitable purposes, particularly in the North East of England

WHAT IS NOT FUNDED No grants to individuals. The Trustees will not consider applications for minibuses or similar vehicles, or from students for overseas visits

WHO CAN BENEFIT There are no restrictions on the age; professional and economic group; family situation; religion and culture; and social circumstances of; or disease or medical condition suffered by, the beneficiaries. Priority is given to registered charities in the North East of England

WHERE FUNDING CAN BE GIVEN UK. The Trustees give preference to registered charities in the North East of England

RANGE OF GRANTS £100–£10,000

SAMPLE GRANTS £10,000 to Royal Grammar School 450 Appeal; £5,000 to St Oswald's Hospice for building programme; £3,000 to Percy Hedley Centre for Spastics; £1,000 to Macmillan Nursing Fund; £1,000 to Northumberland Association of Boys Clubs; £1,000 to Newcastle Preparatory School; £1,000 to Wylam Community Playing Fields Association; £1,000 to British Red Cross; £500 to Marie Stopes International; £500 to The Salvation Army

FINANCES *Year* 1996 *Income* £47,719 *Grants* £40,200

TRUSTEES J S Armstrong, G W Meikle

WHO TO APPLY TO G W Meikle (Trustee), Percy Hedley Will Trust, c/o Messrs Dickinson Dees, St Annes Wharf, 112 Quayside, Newcastle upon Tyne NE99 1SB

CC NO 212637   **ESTABLISHED** 1942

■ The H J Heinz Company Limited Charitable Trust

WHAT IS FUNDED Donations are made across the board within the scope permitted by the Trust Deed, typically medical, welfare, education (food technology and nutrition in particular), conservation, community relations, arts. National bodies are more likely to be favoured than local groups unless local applicants operate in the immediate vicinity of the Company's main operating locations

WHAT IS NOT FUNDED No grants to individuals. No political or denominational requests considered. No requests for advertising considered

WHO CAN BENEFIT Organisations benefiting children and young adults, at risk groups, those disadvantaged by poverty and socially isolated people. There is no restriction on the disease or medical condition suffered by the beneficiaries. Those involved in the arts and students may be considered for funding

WHERE FUNDING CAN BE GIVEN Mainly UK but also overseas

TYPE OF GRANT Mainly one-off

SAMPLE GRANTS £20,000 to Holding Hands Appeal; £15,000 to Royal College Paediatrics and Child Health; £10,000 to the Wildlife Trust; £5,000 to Diana, Princess of Wales Memorial Fund; £5,000 to ICAN; £3,525 to Lennard Associates (Wooden Spoon Rugby Society); £3,500 to National Grocers' Benevolent Fund; £3,412 to American Ireland Fund; £2,937 to Royal Academy of Arts; £1,420 to Ireland Fund of Great Britain

FINANCES *Year* 1997 *Income* £115,000 *Grants* £83,571

TRUSTEES A J F O'Reilly, A Beresford, Mrs D Heinz, B R Purgavie, M Cook, A G M Ritchie

HOW TO APPLY Written applications, no follow-up telephone calls. Applications considered once or twice a year. Applicants whether successful or unsuccessful are informed of the Trustees' decisions

WHO TO APPLY TO Mrs Ann Banks, The H J Heinz Company Limited Charitable Trust, H J Heinz Co Ltd, Hayes Park, Hayes, Middlesex UB4 8AL

CC NO 326254   **ESTABLISHED** 1982

■ The Michael Heller Charitable Foundation

WHAT IS FUNDED Medical; education; scientific research

WHAT IS NOT FUNDED No grants to individuals

WHO CAN BENEFIT To benefit: children and young adults; research workers and students. There is no restriction on the disease or medical condition suffered by the beneficiaries

WHERE FUNDING CAN BE GIVEN UK and overseas

RANGE OF GRANTS £5,000–£50,000

SAMPLE GRANTS £31,568 to St Catherine's College; £17,500 to University College, London; £10,500 to the Spiro Institution; £10,000 to Sheffield Hallam University; £6,021 to Friends of the Hebrew University; £5,000 to Gauchers Association; £5,000 to British ORT; £1,000 to the Bruce House Appeal; £1,000 to Wellbeing; £1,000 to British Emunah

FINANCES *Year* 1997 *Income* £154,016 *Grants* £109,967

TRUSTEES Michael Heller, Morven Heller, Pearl Livingstone

HOW TO APPLY To the address under Who To Apply To in writing

WHO TO APPLY TO Doris Carroll, The Michael Heller Charitable Foundation, 8–10 New Fetter Lane, London EC4A 1NQ

CC NO 327832   **ESTABLISHED** 1988

■ The Simon Heller Charitable Settlement

WHAT IS FUNDED Medical research, scientific and educational research

WHAT IS NOT FUNDED No grants to individuals

WHO CAN BENEFIT Organisations benefiting: academics; medical professionals; research workers; scientists; students and teachers. There is no restriction on the disease or medical condition suffered by the beneficiaries

WHERE FUNDING CAN BE GIVEN UK and overseas

RANGE OF GRANTS £5,000–£50,000

FINANCES *Year* 1997 *Income* £250,000 *Grants* £180,000

TRUSTEES S H Trust Co Ltd, Michael Heller, Morven Heller

HOW TO APPLY To the address under Who To Apply To in writing

WHO TO APPLY TO Doris Carroll, Admin, The Simon Heller Charitable Settlement, 8–10 New Fetter Lane, London EC4A 1NQ

CC NO 265405   **ESTABLISHED** 1972

■ Help a London Child Appeal Fund

WHAT IS FUNDED To help disadvantaged and deprived children living in the Greater London area

WHAT IS NOT FUNDED Grants can only be made to organisations with charity status or endorsed by a registered company for the benefit of children 18 or under and living in the Greater London area. No grants to individuals

WHO CAN BENEFIT Children. There are few restrictions on the family situation or social circumstances

WHERE FUNDING CAN BE GIVEN Greater London, within Capital Radio's transmission area

TYPE OF GRANT Capital, core costs, one-off, project, recurring costs, running costs and salaries. Funding is available for one year or less

RANGE OF GRANTS £250–£15800, typical grant £2,000

SAMPLE GRANTS £15,800 to Children's Country Holiday Fund for summer camp; £10,000 to Whiz Kidz for mobility equipment; £8,000 to Emery Theatre for three week theatre tour; £8,000 to Friends of Dulwich Wood Nursery for special needs room; £7,200 to Kids and Co for Operation Outreach; £7,000 to Community Links for children's resource centre; £7,000 to Tower Hamlets Opportunity Centre for escorted travel facility; £6,000 to Friends of Reflection for Saturday club for disabled children; £6,000 to The London Connection for winter programme for the newly homeless

FINANCES *Year* 1997 *Income* £1,000,000

TRUSTEES R Eyre, M King, R Park, A Schaffer

HOW TO APPLY Application forms are available from January and require an A4 sae. Closing date for applications is the end of May. Successful applicants will receive grants by the end of November

WHO TO APPLY TO Adam Findley, Administrator, Help a London Child Appeal Fund, c/o Capital Radio, 29–30 Leicester Square, London WC2H 7LE *Tel* 0171-766 6203 *Fax* 0171-766 6195

CC NO 276543   **ESTABLISHED** 1978

■ Help the Aged

WHAT IS FUNDED Lunch clubs; day centres; transport; capital needs; some revenue costs; refurbishment costs; hospices; respite care for carers; support and self help groups; publishing and printing; support to voluntary and community organisations; charity or voluntary umbrella bodies; transport and alternative transport; equal opportunities; advice centres; community services; community centres; village halls; equal opportunities campaigning; and advice centres for social issues

WHAT IS NOT FUNDED Statutory agencies, private enterprises, loans funding shortfalls due to under-bidding for service agreements, long term revenue. No grants to individuals

WHO CAN BENEFIT Voluntary and charitable groups offering a range of resources to support frail, isolated and poor older people to live independently in their communities. This includes: ethnic minority groups; carers; those disadvantaged by poverty; homeless people; those living in urban and rural areas; and those suffering from Alzheimers disease

WHERE FUNDING CAN BE GIVEN UK

TYPE OF GRANT Funding for both capital needs, one-off, start-up costs, salaries and running costs. Funding is available for up to three years

RANGE OF GRANTS Grants range from £100–£60,000. Typical grant is around £20,000 for a variety of purposes

SAMPLE GRANTS £35,000 to COATS Crowthorne, Berkshire for refurbishing premises including kitchen; £26,000 to Indian Senior Citizens Centre, Manchester for a complete refurbishment of the day centre; £25,813 to Wai Yin Chinese Women's Society, Manchester for establishing development and cooks post; £25,000 to SERVE, Rushden, Northamptonshire for the conversion of property to extend facilities; £24,000 to Arbroath Town Mission, Tayside to complete the extension to the centre; £21,530 to St Anne's Shelter and Housing Action, Leeds for an over 55's homeless project; £20,000 to Fold Housing Association, County Down for establishing a development officer's post; £20,000 to Providence Row, Tower Hamlets, London to provide emergency bedspace for over 50's homeless; £19,336 to Care and Repair, Cymru for establishing a regional officers post; £19,081 to Furnival Methodist Church, Sheffield to establish development workers salary and kitchen equipment

FINANCES *Year* 1997–98 *Income* £56,000,000 *Grants* £1,100,884

TRUSTEES John D Mather (Chairman), Phillip Ashfield, Henry Bowrey, Peter Bowring, CBE, Priscilla Campbell Allen, Jo Connell, Dudley Fisher, CBE, DL, Vera Harley, MBE, Anne Harris, CBE, Dr William Hastings, OBE, Prof Kay-Tee Khaw, Trevor Larman, Ian Mcleod, Lady Jean Macpherson, Hugh Peppiatt, Christopher Woodbridge, Angus Young, Kevin Williams

PUBLICATIONS *A Life Worth Living*-The independence and inclusion of older people. *Challenge on Care*-Challenging the myths around homeless older people. *Coming Home*-A guide to good practise for projects working with homeless older people. *Growing Old in the Countryside*-A case study practise manual

NOTES The grants programme is only one aspect of Help the Aged's work which can include seconding trained fundraisers to projects needing to raise large capital sums from £100,000–several millions

HOW TO APPLY By letter in the first instance to the UK Grants Department at the address below

WHO TO APPLY TO Michael Lake OBE, Director General, Help the Aged, (Care Services Division), St James's Walk, Clerkenwell Green, London EC1R 0BE *Tel* 0171-253 0253 *Fax* 0171-250 4473 *E-mail* hta@dial.pipex.com *Web Site* http://www.helptheaged.org.uk

CC NO 272786   **ESTABLISHED** 1977

■ Help the Homeless

WHAT IS FUNDED To help any voluntary residential project which has made every endeavour, unsuccessfully, to raise funds from other known sources

WHAT IS NOT FUNDED Grants made only for capital expenditure. No grants to individuals

WHO CAN BENEFIT Voluntary agencies benefiting the homeless

WHERE FUNDING CAN BE GIVEN UK

TYPE OF GRANT Usually one-off for buildings, capital and projects. Funding is available for up to one year

FINANCES *Year* 1997–98 *Income* £149,746 *Grants* £20,796

TRUSTEES F J Bergin, L A Bains, T S T Cookson, M McIntyre, T Rogers

PUBLICATIONS Annual audited accounts

HOW TO APPLY By written application to the address under Who To Apply To. Trustees meet quarterly

Does the trust you have chosen match your needs? Haphazard applications waste postage and time

289

WHO TO APPLY TO P Wallace, Secretary, Help the Homeless Ltd, 78 Quaker Street, London E1 6SW
CC NO 271988   ESTABLISHED 1975

■ Help the Hospices

WHAT IS FUNDED Grants to local voluntary hospices, in-patient, day care and home care teams, for equipment for patient care and improved services; training for hospice staff (NHS and voluntary); research funding and advisory services to hospices

WHAT IS NOT FUNDED No grants for major capital costs

WHO CAN BENEFIT Organisations benefiting disabled people and medical professionals in hospices. There is no restriction on the disease or medical condition suffered by the beneficiaries

WHERE FUNDING CAN BE GIVEN UK and overseas

TYPE OF GRANT One-off and recurrent

RANGE OF GRANTS £75–£15,000

SAMPLE GRANTS £16,600 to St Nicholas Hospice, Bury St Edmunds; £15,600 to St Catherines Hospice, Crawley; £12,005 to Butterwick Hospice, Stockton on Tees; £8,695 to Garden House Hospice, Letchworth; £6,115 to St Christophers Hospice, Sydenham; £5,995 to St Michael's Hospice, Harrogate; £5,000 to Hope House Children's Hospice, Oswestry; £4,984 to Luton and South Bedfordshire Hospice, Luton; £4,966 to St Giles Hospice, Lichfield; £4,598 to Trinity Hospice, London

FINANCES Year 1996–97 Income £1,406,765 Grants £468,250

TRUSTEES Rt Hon Lord Hayhoe (President), Sir Leslie Fletcher, DSG (Vice President), Martyn Lewis, CBE (Vice President), Duchess of Norfolk (Chairman), Michael Bayley, Philip Byam-Cook, Ronald Griffin, Dr Peter Griffiths, Dr Andrew Hoy, Dr George Mitchell, Mrs Hilary McNair, Prof Peter Quilliam, OBE, Mick Thorpe, Sam Wills

HOW TO APPLY Support for training on forms available from Grants Administrator, these applications are considered every six weeks. All other applications for support in writing to the Chief Executive in the first instance

WHO TO APPLY TO David Praill, Chief Executive, Help the Hospices, 34–44 Britannia Street, London WC1 9JG Tel 0171-278 5668
CC NO 1014851   ESTABLISHED 1984

■ The Hemby Trust

WHAT IS FUNDED This Trust will consider funding: social needs; community facilities and services; youth and employment; schools and colleges; help for the aged; health; the arts, culture and recreation; the environment; and church buildings

WHAT IS NOT FUNDED No grants will be made for political, religious (except churches), pressure groups, sponsorships or to individuals

WHO CAN BENEFIT There are no restrictions on the age; family situation of; or disease or medical condition suffered by, the beneficiaries; and few restrictions on the social circumstances

WHERE FUNDING CAN BE GIVEN The County of Merseyside and Wirral

TYPE OF GRANT Capital grants

TRUSTEES R A Morris, P T Furlong, A T Morris, N A Wainwright

NOTES The Trustees meet four times a year. Applications need to be received one month prior to the meeting

HOW TO APPLY To the Secretary at the address under Who To Apply To

WHO TO APPLY TO M E Hope, Secretary, The Hemby Trust, c/o Rathbone Bros & Co Ltd, Port of Liverpool Building, Pier Head, Liverpool L3 1NW Tel 0151-236 6666 Fax 0151-243 7001
CC NO Pending   ESTABLISHED 1998

■ The Christina Mary Hendrie Trust for Scottish and Canadian Charities

WHAT IS FUNDED Charities connected with youth and elderly people

WHAT IS NOT FUNDED No grants to individuals

WHO CAN BENEFIT Charities benefiting the young and the elderly

WHERE FUNDING CAN BE GIVEN Scotland and Canada

RANGE OF GRANTS Typical grants £1,000–£10,000

FINANCES Year 1997 Grants £80,000

TRUSTEES C R B Cox, G A S Cox, R N Cox, Mrs A D H Irwin, Maj Gen A S H Irwin, Miss C Irwin, J K Scott Moncrieff, Anthony G Cox

HOW TO APPLY To the address under Who To Apply To in writing

WHO TO APPLY TO G R Russell, The Christina Mary Hendrie Trust, Anderson Strathern WS, 48 Castle Street, Edinburgh EH2 3LX
SC NO SCO 014514   ESTABLISHED 1975

■ The Henley Educational Charity

WHAT IS FUNDED Grants are given to alleviate financial hardship; to support particular educational initiatives and courses and to help meet the cost of educational visits, books and equipment at a local school or college

WHAT IS NOT FUNDED Applicants must be under 25 years of age, be resident in the area Where Funding Can Be Given or attending a publicly maintained school in the area and must have been in attendance for at least two years

WHO CAN BENEFIT Individuals and organisations benefiting children, young adults and those disadvantaged by poverty. Publicly maintained schools and colleges in the area Where Funding Can Be Given

WHERE FUNDING CAN BE GIVEN Henley-on-Thames, the Parish of Remenham in Berkshire, Bix and Rotherfield Greys in Oxfordshire

FINANCES Year 1997–98 Income £92,000 Grants £84,000

TRUSTEES Mayor of Henley, Rector of Henely, A R Austin, R H Brackston, Dr T K Clarke, Mrs S M Dickie, Cllr B M Edwards, Cllr A J Follett, Mrs M S T Hall, Maj J D J Howard, Mrs R G Whittaker

HOW TO APPLY Application forms are available from the address under Who To Apply To upon written request. Potential applicants are advised to consult with the head of their school or college to determine whether their application may be successful

WHO TO APPLY TO Mrs M Clarke, Clerk, The Henley Educational Charity, 6 Berkshire Road, Henley-on-Thames, South Oxfordshire RG9 1NB Tel 01491 575252
CC NO 309237   ESTABLISHED 1604

■ Esther Hennell Charitable Trust

WHAT IS FUNDED General charitable purposes

WHAT IS NOT FUNDED Individuals, students and registered charities

WHO CAN BENEFIT Organisations. There are no restrictions on the age; family situation; religion

and culture; and social circumstances of; or disease or medical condition suffered by, the beneficiaries. There may be few restrictions on their professional and economic group
WHERE FUNDING CAN BE GIVEN UK
TYPE OF GRANT Range of grants
FINANCES *Year* 1997 *Income* £20,935
Grants £13,650
TRUSTEES Mrs E J Hennell, N W Smith, Mrs J A Hunt
HOW TO APPLY **This Trust states that it does not respond to unsolicited applications**
WHO TO APPLY TO Mrs E J Hennell, Esther Hennell Charitable Trust, 46 Church Road, Wimbledon, London SW19 5AN
CC NO 261477   **ESTABLISHED** 1970

■ The Anne Herd Memorial Trust

WHAT IS FUNDED Grants are given to organisations which are dedicated to visually impaired people. Projects that could improve their quality of life have been supported
WHAT IS NOT FUNDED No grants to individuals
WHO CAN BENEFIT Organisations benefiting visually impaired people
WHERE FUNDING CAN BE GIVEN Scotland, particularly Tayside, the City of Dundee and Broughty Ferry
TRUSTEES B N Bowman, P M M Bowman, Mrs E N McGillivray
PUBLICATIONS Accounts are available from the Trust
HOW TO APPLY Applications should be made in writing to the address below
WHO TO APPLY TO B N Bowman, The Anne Herd Memorial Trust, Messrs Bowman Gray Robertson & Wilkie Solicitors, 27 Bank Street, Dundee DD1 1RP
SC NO SCO 14198

■ The Herefordshire Historic Churches Trust

WHAT IS FUNDED The restoration, preservation, repair, maintenance and improvement of churches, their contents and their churchyards in the area Where Funding Can Be Given
WHERE FUNDING CAN BE GIVEN Herefordshire
TYPE OF GRANT Buildings
RANGE OF GRANTS £500–£5,000
SAMPLE GRANTS £5,000 to Brilley; £5,000 to Dilwyn; £5,000 to Kimbolton; £4,000 to Llanveynoe; £3,000 to Wigmore; £2,000 to Stanford Bishop; £1,500 to Mathon; £1,500 to Pudleston; £1,250 to St Weonards; £1,000 to Bishops Frome
FINANCES *Year* 1995 *Income* £61,006
Grants £35,500
HOW TO APPLY To the address under Who To Apply To in writing
WHO TO APPLY TO A P Hollingsworth, Treasurer, The Herefordshire Historic Churches Trust, 68 Hinton Road, Hereford HR2 6BN
CC NO 511181   **ESTABLISHED** 1954

■ Hereward FM, Q.103 FM and Classic Gold Helping Hands Appeal

WHAT IS FUNDED Organisations working with the disabled in the Peterborough area. Particularly charities working in the fields of: special needs education; support to voluntary and community organisations; health professional bodies; social care professional bodies; health care; hospices and various community services

WHO CAN BENEFIT Individuals and organisations benefiting at risk groups; carers; disabled people; those disadvantaged by poverty; homeless and socially isolated people; victims of abuse, crime and domestic violence. There is no restriction on the disease or medical condition suffered by the beneficiaries
WHERE FUNDING CAN BE GIVEN Greater Peterborough (Hereward FM, Q.103 FM and Classic Gold transmission areas)
TYPE OF GRANT Various types of grants are made
SAMPLE GRANTS £5,000 to Open Doors for child wheelchair for local disabled child; £2,500 to NSPCC East Peterborough for group therapy and safety awareness for sexually abused children; £2,000 to Peterborough Hospitals Trust for equipment for young diabetics; £1,500 to Family Welfare Association for support for children from broken homes; £1,000 to Haematology Research Fund PDH for flow cytometer; £750 to Sue Ryder Foundation, Thorpe Hall for Kings Fund Bed, special mobile tilting bed for terminally ill patients; £500 to Orton Family Centre for equipment; £445 to Dial Peterborough for replacement fax machine; £400 to St Johns Church, Orton Goldham for mobile basketball stands; £300 to British Polio Fellowship, Peterborough for cost of hiring bus for a week's annual holiday to Worthing
FINANCES *Year* 1996–97 *Income* £83,039
Grants £19,795
TRUSTEES D M J Ball (Chairman), Mrs L B Couch-Smith, D A Laking, N Sinclair-Brown, D A Wayne
HOW TO APPLY To the address under Who To Apply To in writing
WHO TO APPLY TO Anne Fife, Appeals Co-ordinator, Hereward FM, Q.103 FM and Classic Gold Helping Hands Appeal, PO Box 225, Queengate Centre, Peterborough PE1 1XJ *Tel* 01733 460460
CC NO 801876   **ESTABLISHED** 1989

■ The Heritage of London Trust

WHAT IS FUNDED The restoration of buildings of architectural importance. Grants are mainly given for skilled restoration of notable features of listed buildings, generally (though not exclusively) external work. Examples of buildings assisted are Churches, community centres, almshouses, theatres, hospitals, museums and educational establishments
WHO CAN BENEFIT Listed buildings in London
WHERE FUNDING CAN BE GIVEN The Greater London area
RANGE OF GRANTS Grants rarely exceed £5,000
FINANCES *Year* 1997 *Income* £168,865
Grants £92,230
TRUSTEES Board of Management: William Bell (President), Sir John Lambert, KCVO, CMG (Vice-President); Giles Shepard, CBE (Chair), Sir Hugh Cubitt, CBE, JP, DL, FRICS (Vice-Chair), Miss Sophie Andreae, Ronald Barden, Ashley Barker, OBE, FSA, FRIBA, Alistair Buchanan, FCA, Mrs Bridget Cherry, R Chitham, RIBA, Sir Robin Dent, KCVO, Martin Drury, Kevin Gardner, Cllr R C Harris, Norman Howard, Cllr W Leadbitter, Michael Medlicott, Ron Peet, CBE, Sir Michael Pike, KCVO, CMG, Robert Vigars, Sir William Whitfield, CBE, Julian Spicer (Director), Peter Wise (Hon Secretary), Mrs Diana Beattie (Hon Treasurer), Hon Nicholas Assheton, Jonathan Sestetner
PUBLICATIONS Map: *Historic Buildings in Covent Garden*
HOW TO APPLY In writing to the Director
WHO TO APPLY TO The Director, The Heritage of London Trust, 23 Savile Row, London W1X 1AB
CC NO 280272   **ESTABLISHED** 1980

■ Herne Bay Community Church Trust

WHAT IS FUNDED To advance the Christian religion; to relieve persons who are in conditions of need, hardship or distress or who are aged or sick; other general charitable purposes

WHO CAN BENEFIT Organisations benefiting: older people; Christians; at risk groups; those disadvantaged by poverty and socially isolated people. There is no restriction on the disease or medical condition suffered by the beneficiaries

WHERE FUNDING CAN BE GIVEN Kent, particularly Herne Bay, and elsewhere in the UK or overseas

FINANCES *Year* 1997 *Income* £20,679
Grants £13,450

TRUSTEES P Hulks, S Hulks, D Judd, Ms M Brunt

WHO TO APPLY TO D S Judd, Herne Bay Community Church Trust, 3 Greenhill Gardens, Herne Bay, Kent CT6 8NU

CC NO 1046824   **ESTABLISHED** 1995

■ The William Heron Welfare Trust

WHAT IS FUNDED To provide support for education; health and medicine; social welfare; children and young adults within the area Where Funding Can Be Given

WHAT IS NOT FUNDED No grants to individuals

WHO CAN BENEFIT Grants in response to appeals from registered charitable organisations operating for the benefit of inhabitants of the London Boroughs of Camden and Islington. Organisations benefiting: children and young adults; students; at risk groups; those disadvantaged by poverty; and socially isolated people. There is no restriction on the disease or medical condition suffered by the beneficiaries

WHERE FUNDING CAN BE GIVEN The London Boroughs of Islington and Camden

TYPE OF GRANT One-off and capital grants

RANGE OF GRANTS £1,000–£10,000

FINANCES *Year* 1997 *Income* £44,937
Grants £56,000

TRUSTEES The Clothworkers' Foundation

HOW TO APPLY To the address under Who To Apply To in writing, including the most recent Annual Report and audited Accounts

WHO TO APPLY TO M G T Harris, Secretary, The William Heron Welfare Trust, The Clothworkers' Foundation, Clothworkers' Hall, Dunster Court, Mincing Lane, London EC3R 7AH *Tel* 0171-623 7041

CC NO 264619   **ESTABLISHED** 1961

■ The Hertfordshire Community Trust

WHAT IS FUNDED To support the work of local charities and voluntary groups for the benefit of the community, with the following particular concerns: disadvantaged children and families; developing young people; access to education, training and employment; the needs of older people. This includes: residential facilities and services; infrastructure, support and development; religious ancillary buildings; pre-school education; special schools; education and training; community centres and village halls; playgrounds; recreation grounds; community services; equal opportunities; and social advice and information

WHAT IS NOT FUNDED No major appeals, endowment funds, research, sponsored events, promotion of religion. Grants may be made to individuals only

within specific areas of need. Arts, sport and the environment are normally supported only when there is a benefit to disadvantaged people

WHO CAN BENEFIT Individuals and organisations benefiting: children; young adults; older people; parents and children; one parent families; widows and widowers. There are few restrictions on the social circumstances of the beneficiaries. Any locally based charity or voluntary group benefiting local people. Many are smaller, less well known groups or less 'popular' causes that often find it extremely difficult to obtain funds elsewhere

WHERE FUNDING CAN BE GIVEN Hertfordshire

TYPE OF GRANT Major grants, revenue or capital, not long term funding or as part of a large building project. Maximum £5,000 one-off or £15,000 over three years; usually smaller amounts. Project grants up to £500 for specific purpose, start-up or development. Small grants up to £200 for urgent needs, training bursaries, individual grants within very specific areas. Also considered are research grants and salaries

RANGE OF GRANTS £100–£5,000 pa for up to three years

SAMPLE GRANTS £15,000 to Relate to develop relationship training in schools; £10,000 to Ravidassia Community Centre for free legal advice at multicultural facility; £9,000 to Groups of Elderly Members Meeting Socially (GEMMS) for friendship scheme for those with dementia and their carers; £9,000 to Guideposts Trust for friendship scheme for adults with learning difficulties; £7,500 to Women's Aid, Broxbourne for support for children who have left refuge; £6,000 to Community Care Trust to set up homesharing schemes in Hertfordshire; £5,000 to Hertfordshire MS Therapy Centre to extend facilities for treatment; £5,000 to Design and Manufacture for Disability (DEMAND) for personalised service offered by designer to disabled people; £4,000 to Stevenage Business Initiative for unemployed disabled people to set up their own businesses; £4,000 to St Albans Women's Refuge for new playroom and resource room

FINANCES *Year* 1998 *Income* £762,000
Grants £114,000

TRUSTEES P Burgin, Prof N Buxton, Ms P Calvert, D Cansdale, R Everington, Mrs B Goble, P Groves, Miss C McCaffrey, M Osbaldeston, R Richardson, N Rossiter, D Thomson, A Tucker, J Usher

PUBLICATIONS Annual Review, leaflets, newsletter, guidelines for applicants

HOW TO APPLY An informal discussion, often by telephone, is encouraged first. An application form and guidelines may then be issued. Deadlines for return are the end of February, May, August and November for major grants. All applicants are advised within eight weeks of these dates. Project grants of up to £500 are made monthly. Applications to either Kate Baldwin, Grants Manager, or Christine Mills, Grants Officer, at the address below

WHO TO APPLY TO Kate Baldwin, Grants Manager, The Hertfordshire Community Trust, 2 Townsend Avenue, St Albans, Hertfordshire AL1 3SG *Tel* 01727 867906 *Fax* 01727 867491

CC NO 299438   **ESTABLISHED** 1988

■ The Hesed Trust

WHAT IS FUNDED Christian charitable purposes. The Trust will consider funding the advancement of religion; and the Free church umbrella bodies

WHAT IS NOT FUNDED Expeditions, individual requests

WHO CAN BENEFIT Christian charities benefiting children, young adults, older people, clergy, students, Christians and evangelists
WHERE FUNDING CAN BE GIVEN UK and overseas
TYPE OF GRANT One-off grants, for one year or less
RANGE OF GRANTS Not exceeding £500
FINANCES *Year* 1997–98 *Income* £48,026
Grants £49,034
TRUSTEES G Rawlings, B Shutt, R J Aubrey
HOW TO APPLY To the the address under Who To Apply To in writing. Written applications only, no telephone calls
WHO TO APPLY TO G Rawlings, Secretary, The Hesed Trust, 14 Chiltern Avenue, Cosby, Leicestershire LE91UF *Tel* 0116-286 2990
CC NO 1000489   **ESTABLISHED** 1990

■ The Hesslewood Children's Trust (Hull Seamen's and General Orphanage)

WHAT IS FUNDED To provide aid for young individuals in need, also youth organisations for holidays. Particularly charities working in the fields of education, housing and accommodation, and arts, culture and recreation
WHAT IS NOT FUNDED No grants to benefit people over the age of 25 will be made
WHO CAN BENEFIT Individuals and organisations benefiting children and young adults under 25. Support will be given to: those in care, fostered and adopted; disabled people; those disadvantaged by poverty; ex-offenders and those at risk of offending; homeless people; those living in both rural and urban areas; socially isolated people; and victims of abuse and crime
WHERE FUNDING CAN BE GIVEN Humberside and North Lincolnshire
TYPE OF GRANT One-off. Funding may be given for up to one year
SAMPLE GRANTS £15,000 to Hull Compact Ltd for grants and bursaries to 16–18 year olds in need; £10,000 to The Sobriety Project for refurbishing 'Audry' a sailing barge; £5,000 to The Dyslexia Institute for provision of lessons to young people in financial need; £3,000 to Riding for the Disabled to help young disabled riders
FINANCES *Year* 1997 *Income* £76,845
Grants £71,029
TRUSTEES Dr J Alexander, R M S Allenby, Dr G Cameron, A C Croft, Rev Canon K David, Mrs M Fox, I J Gillespie, I D Graham, Capt E Howlett, Mrs G Munn, Dr D P Nicholas, Mrs F J Turner
HOW TO APPLY To the address under Who To Apply To in writing or telephone requesting an application form. Deadlines for applications are 16 February, 16 June and 16 September
WHO TO APPLY TO Mrs J A Roberts, Secretary, The Hesslewood Children's Trust, 1 Sandringham Close, Cottingham, East Yorkshire HU16 5QZ *Tel* 01482 843559
CC NO 529804   **ESTABLISHED** 1982

■ The Bernhard Heuberger Charitable Trust

WHAT IS FUNDED Jewish charitable purposes
WHO CAN BENEFIT Jewish organisations benefiting Jewish people
WHERE FUNDING CAN BE GIVEN UK and overseas, preference for UK
FINANCES *Year* 1995–96 *Income* £127,438
TRUSTEES B Heuberger, D H Heuberger, S N Heuberger

HOW TO APPLY To the address under Who To Apply To in writing
WHO TO APPLY TO B Heuberger, Secretary, The Bernhard Heubergr Charitable Trust, 12 Sherwood Road, London NW4 1AD
CC NO 294378   **ESTABLISHED** 1986

■ The Hewett/Driver Education Trust

WHAT IS FUNDED Education, with an emphasis on projects directly related to further and higher education. Educational professional bodies and educational voluntary bodies
WHAT IS NOT FUNDED Finance for students' further and higher education
WHO CAN BENEFIT Other voluntary organisations and charities whose projects conform to the objects of the Trust; young teachers and members of NATFHE who may apply for travelling scholarships
WHERE FUNDING CAN BE GIVEN UK and a very limited number of international grants in Africa
TYPE OF GRANT One-off, project and recurrent grants of £1,000 or less. Funding is available for one year or less
RANGE OF GRANTS £50–£1,000
FINANCES *Year* 1997 *Income* £11,159
Grants £4,150
NOTES Do not make grants to individuals beyond those identified under Who Can Benefit
HOW TO APPLY In writing at any time with an sae for the reply
WHO TO APPLY TO D Betts, The Secretary, The Hewett/Driver Education Trust, NATFHE, 27 Britannia Street, London WC1X 9JP *Tel* 0171-837 3636 *Fax* 0171-837 4403
CC NO 1025394   **ESTABLISHED** 1993

■ Hickinbotham Charitable Trust

WHAT IS FUNDED Generally to support local (Leicester and Leicestershire) charities and Quaker activities in a wider field
WHAT IS NOT FUNDED No grants made in response to large national appeals. No grants for travel bursaries
WHO CAN BENEFIT Registered charities only. There are no restrictions on the age; professional and economic group; family situation; religion and culture; and social circumstances of; or disease or medical condition suffered by, the beneficiaries. However favour is given to Quakers
WHERE FUNDING CAN BE GIVEN Leicester, Leicestershire and UK
TYPE OF GRANT Usually one-off grants
FINANCES *Year* 1997–98 *Income* £54,550
Grants £11,100
TRUSTEES Mrs C R Hickinbotham, P F J Hickinbotham, R P Hickinbotham
NOTES Replies may not be sent to unsuccessful applicants
HOW TO APPLY To the address under Who To Apply To in writing
WHO TO APPLY TO Mrs Catherine R Hickinbotham, Hickinbotham Charitable Trust, 69 Main Street, Bushby, Leicester LE7 9PL
CC NO 216432   **ESTABLISHED** 1947

Does the trust you have chosen match your needs? Haphazard applications waste postage and time

293

■ Higgs and Cooper's Educational Charity

WHAT IS FUNDED Educational purposes in the area Where Funding Can Be Given for the benefit of young people under the age of 25 including the purchase of books

WHAT IS NOT FUNDED No grants to people over 25 years old

WHO CAN BENEFIT Individuals and organisations benefiting children, young adults, students and one parent families

WHERE FUNDING CAN BE GIVEN Charlton Kings

RANGE OF GRANTS £50–£1,000

FINANCES *Year* 1996–97 *Income* £33,836 *Grants* £23,592

TRUSTEES K Buckland, Mrs J Collins, Mrs S C Cranna, P L Ginns, D G Masling, J V Miller, C J Morris, D N Perry, Mrs J M Whiteman

HOW TO APPLY To the address under Who To Apply To in writing. The Trustees meet about six times a year. Initial telephone calls are welcome and application forms are available

WHO TO APPLY TO M J Mitchell, Clerk, Higgs and Cooper's Educational Charity, 11 Chestnut Terrace, Charlton Kings, Cheltenham, Gloucestershire GL53 8JQ *Tel* 01242 572810

CC NO 311570   **ESTABLISHED** 1976

■ Higgs and Hill plc Charitable Trust (also known as Swan Hill Group Charitable Trust)

WHAT IS FUNDED To support causes either connected with the construction industry, local to a permanent Higgs and Hill establishment or major appeals of national interest

WHAT IS NOT FUNDED No grants to individuals

WHO CAN BENEFIT There are no restrictions on the age; professional and economic group; family situation; religion and culture; and social circumstances of; or disease or medical condition suffered by, the beneficiaries

WHERE FUNDING CAN BE GIVEN UK

TYPE OF GRANT One-off grants

FINANCES *Year* 1995 *Income* £17,845 *Grants* £26,993

TRUSTEES R W Gale, D Helsen, A C Ackerman, N J Beale, A G Confavreux

PUBLICATIONS Annual Report

NOTES Sponsorship of individuals is not usually considered

HOW TO APPLY To the Secretary at the address under Who To Apply To at any time. There is no application form. Unsolicited applications which cannot be entertained will not normally be acknowledged. All applications must be made in writing

WHO TO APPLY TO A G Confavreux, Higgs and Hill plc Charitable Trust, Cygnet Court, Portsmouth Road, Esher, Surrey KT10 9SG

CC NO 295106   **ESTABLISHED** 1986

■ The Higgs Charitable Trust

WHAT IS FUNDED Largely in support of research into deafness carried out by private charitable foundations. Charities working in the fields of: religious buildings; housing and accommodation; conservation; animal facilities and services; conservation and campaigning; and education and training will also be considered

WHO CAN BENEFIT Mostly medical research trusts or foundations. Organisations benefiting: children,

young adults; older people; those disadvantaged by poverty; and homeless people. There are no restrictions on the disease or medical condition suffered by the beneficiaries

WHERE FUNDING CAN BE GIVEN UK

TYPE OF GRANT One-off and research. Funding for more than three years will be considered

SAMPLE GRANTS £25,000 to TWJ Foundation for general purposes; £10,000 to Skinners Company (Lord Mannesbury Bounty) for general purposes; £2,000 to Jobson Foundation for general purposes; £1,000 to Farnborough RCC for Church Appeal; £1,000 to Linton Lock Supporters Club for general purposes; £1,000 to Salmsford Canal Trust for general purposes; £1,000 to Talent To Work for general purposes; £1,000 to Upper Avon Navigation Trust for general charitable purposes; £500 to SSAFA for general purposes; £500 to Severn Navigation Restoration on Trust to general purposes

FINANCES *Year* 1997 *Income* £51,767 *Grants* £53,881

TRUSTEES D W H Campbell, T W Higgs, Mrs L Humphris

WHO TO APPLY TO A C Nash, The Higgs Charitable Trust, Messrs Moger & Sparrow, 24 Queen Square, Bath, Avon BA1 2HY

CC NO 267036   **ESTABLISHED** 1982

■ The Walter Higgs Charitable Trust

WHAT IS FUNDED General charitable purposes

WHAT IS NOT FUNDED No grants to individuals

WHO CAN BENEFIT There are no restrictions on the age; professional and economic group; family situation; religion and culture; and social circumstances of; or disease or medical condition suffered by, the beneficiaries

WHERE FUNDING CAN BE GIVEN UK

FINANCES *Year* 1998 *Income* £28,000

TRUSTEES D C Y Higgs, Mrs A J Higgs, Lady E P Higgs, Miss C A Higgs, K Knott, Mrs Knott

NOTES **The available funds for 1999 and 2000 are fully committed.** Applications are not answered to minimise on costs

WHO TO APPLY TO D C Y Higgs, The Walter Higgs Charitable Trust, 12 Heaton Drive, Edgbaston, Birmingham B15 3LW

CC NO 229861   **ESTABLISHED** 1952

■ Highcroft Charitable Trust

WHAT IS FUNDED Advancement and study of the Jewish faith and the Torah. Relief of poverty and advancement of education amongst people of the Jewish faith

WHO CAN BENEFIT Organisations benefiting Jewish people, especially those disadvantaged by poverty

WHERE FUNDING CAN BE GIVEN UK and overseas

RANGE OF GRANTS £148–£5,000

SAMPLE GRANTS £5,000 to Gateshaed Talmudical College; £5,000 to Yehiva Gedolah Lubavitch; £5,000 to Yad Eliezer; £4,500 to Academy of Rabbinical Research; £2,567 to Friends of Beth Eliyahu Trust; £2,000 to Union of Orthodox Hebrew Congregations; £1,800 to North West London Talmudical College; £1,600 to HTVC; £1,500 to the Friends of the Bobov Foundation; £1,500 to London Academy for Jewish Studies

FINANCES *Year* 1994–95 *Income* £41,603 *Grants* £39,855

TRUSTEES Rabbi R Fischer, S L Fischer

WHO TO APPLY TO Rabbi R Fischer, Highcroft Charitable Trust, 15 Highcroft Gardens, London NW11 0LY *Tel* 0181-458 5382
CC NO 272684   ESTABLISHED 1975

■ Highfield Charities Limited

WHAT IS FUNDED General charitable purposes
WHAT IS NOT FUNDED No grants to individuals, including students. No grants made in response to general appeals from large national organisations nor to smaller bodies not already on our lists
WHO CAN BENEFIT There are no restrictions on the age; professional and economic group; family situation; religion and culture; and social circumstances of; or disease or medical condition suffered by, the beneficiaries
WHERE FUNDING CAN BE GIVEN UK and overseas
FINANCES *Year* 1997 *Income* £19,847
  Grants £12,707
TRUSTEES The Governors: S Eisenthal, M Schussheim, V Schussheim, A Gelles
WHO TO APPLY TO Highfield Charities Limited, c/o 276 York Way, London N7 9PH
CC NO 254293   ESTABLISHED 1967

■ Highmoor Hall Charitable Trust

WHAT IS FUNDED Christian mission societies and relief agencies
WHO CAN BENEFIT Registered charities benefiting: Christians; at risk groups; victims of famine, man-made and natural disasters and war
WHERE FUNDING CAN BE GIVEN UK and overseas
TYPE OF GRANT One-off donations
FINANCES *Year* 1997 *Income* £172,247
  Grants £185,310
TRUSTEES P D Persson (Settlor), Mrs A D Persson, J P G Persson, A S J Persson
HOW TO APPLY **This Trust states that it does not respond to unsolicited applications.** Telephone calls are not welcome
WHO TO APPLY TO P D Persson, Highmoor Hall Charitable Trust, Highmoor Hall, Highmoor, Henley-on-Thames, Oxfordshire RG9 5DH *Tel* 01491 641543
CC NO 289027   ESTABLISHED 1984

■ Joseph and Mary Hiley Trust

WHAT IS FUNDED Grants are made to a wide variety of charitable organisations operating in the areas of medicine, youth work, religion, caring agencies, community services; conservation; and other charitable purposes
WHAT IS NOT FUNDED No individuals, expeditions or travel bursaries
WHO CAN BENEFIT Organisations benefiting: people of all ages; clergy; ex-service and service people; volunteers; those in care, fostered and adopted; Church of England; disabled people; carers; victims of abuse and crime; victims of man-made or natural disasters; victims of war; and those suffering from Alzheimer's disease
WHERE FUNDING CAN BE GIVEN UK and overseas, with preference for Yorkshire (West Riding)
TYPE OF GRANT Capital, core costs, research and recurring costs
RANGE OF GRANTS Usually £100–£250

SAMPLE GRANTS £2,500 to Sprintmount, Bradford for care of Alzheimer sufferers; £2,500 to Sprintmount, Bradford for care of Alzheimer sufferers; £250 to RNLI for life saving at sea; £250 to Action Research for all aspects of crippling; £250 to Headingley Operatic Society supports local charities
FINANCES *Year* 1995 *Income* £20,934
  Grants £43,815
TRUSTEES Mary Hiley, E M Hjort, Mrs M B Browning, Mrs A B Palmer
HOW TO APPLY An sae will ensure a reply
WHO TO APPLY TO Mrs A B Palmer, Joseph and Mary Hiley Trust, Old Vicarage House, Vicarage Lane, Bramham, Wetherby LS23 6QG
CC NO 248301   ESTABLISHED 1966

■ David Hill Charitable Trust

WHAT IS FUNDED General charitable purposes
WHO CAN BENEFIT There are no restrictions on the age; professional and economic group; family situation; religion and culture; and social circumstances of; or disease or medical condition suffered by, the beneficiaries
WHERE FUNDING CAN BE GIVEN UK
TRUSTEES D Gurney, R Meere
WHO TO APPLY TO Mrs S Comrie, Solicitor, David Hill Charitable Trust, St Paul's Chamber's, 6–8 Hatherton Road, Walsall, West Midlands WS1 1XS
CC NO 1068238   ESTABLISHED 1997

■ The Edwin and Joyce Hill Charitable Trust

WHAT IS FUNDED Willing to provide funding for the arts, museums, libraries and music; also projects for children and young people
WHO CAN BENEFIT Organisations benefiting children, young adults and those involved in the arts
WHERE FUNDING CAN BE GIVEN Devon
RANGE OF GRANTS £300–£6,000
SAMPLE GRANTS £6,000 to Sidmouth College for an extension; £1,500 to Sidmouth Guides and Brownies; £1,000 to Sidmouth College for Sixth Form study facilities; £1,000 to St Nicholas Church of England Junior School for improvement of the playground; £1,000 to Sidmouth Scouts and Cubs; £800 to Sidmouth College for colours system; £500 to Sidmouth Playgroup; £500 to Sidmouth's Infants School for Over 4s Group; £500 to All Saints Church of England Infants School for a four year olds group; £500 to WRVS for a cedar shed
FINANCES *Year* 1997 *Income* £28,763
  Grants £13,600
TRUSTEES Mrs E M Atkinson, Mrs B M Michelmore, K J Woodsford
HOW TO APPLY To the address under Who To Apply To in writing
WHO TO APPLY TO The Edwin and Joyce Hill Charitable Trust, Ford Simmey Daw Roberts, Warwick House, 30 High Street, Sidmouth, Devon EX10 8EA
CC NO 276849   ESTABLISHED 1978

■ The Geoff Hill Charitable Trust

WHAT IS FUNDED General charitable purposes
WHO CAN BENEFIT There are no restrictions on the age; professional and economic group; family situation; religion and culture; and social circumstances of; or disease or medical condition suffered by, the beneficiaries

WHERE FUNDING CAN BE GIVEN UK
TRUSTEES G Hill, Ms M Hill, R E Hill
WHO TO APPLY TO G Hill, Trustee, The Geoff Hill
Charitable Trust, Tinkers Cottage, Lawnswood,
Stourbridge, West Midlands DY7 5QP
CC NO 1067258   ESTABLISHED 1997

■ Holly Hill Charitable Trust

WHAT IS FUNDED Medicine and health; welfare;
education; sciences
WHO CAN BENEFIT Organisations benefiting
academics, chemists, medical professionals,
research workers and scientists. Support is given
to students, teachers, at risk groups, those
disadvantaged by poverty and socially isolated
people. There is no restriction on the disease or
medical condition suffered by the beneficiaries
WHERE FUNDING CAN BE GIVEN South East England
and UK
TYPE OF GRANT Range of grants
SAMPLE GRANTS £28,000 to Imperial College;
£10,000 to Devon Wildlife; £10,000 to Stoke
Mandeville NHS; £10,000 to University College,
London; £3,500 to North Westminster Community
School; £2,500 to Safe Ground
FINANCES Year 1997 Income £57,542
Grants £64,000
TRUSTEES M D Stanley, A Lewis
NOTES Most grants are made directly to educational
institutions which accounts for most of the income
– little is available for other applications
WHO TO APPLY TO M D Stanley, Holly Hill Charitable
Trust, Flat 5, 89 Onslow Square, London SW7 3LT
CC NO 1044510   ESTABLISHED 1994

■ L E Hill Memorial Trust

WHAT IS FUNDED Cancer, Aids and palliative care
charities operating in Scotland. Particularly
charities working in the fields of: hospices and
hospice at home; cancer research and
conservation and campaigning
WHAT IS NOT FUNDED No grants to individuals
WHO CAN BENEFIT UK registered charities benefiting:
victims of famine, man-made or natural disasters;
and beneficiaries suffering from cancers, HIV and
AIDs, and the terminally ill
WHERE FUNDING CAN BE GIVEN Tayside
TYPE OF GRANT Buildings and research funded for one
year or less will be considered
RANGE OF GRANTS £200–£2,000. £5,000 in
exceptional cases
FINANCES Year 1997 Income £23,500
Grants £25,000
TRUSTEES Turcan Connell (Trustees) Limited, M H J
Hill, OBE, J Ivory, CA
HOW TO APPLY Applications, which should be in
writing, are considered at quarterly intervals
WHO TO APPLY TO D A Connell, L E Hill Memorial
Trust, Messrs Turcan Connell, Saltire Court, 20
Castle Terrace, Edinburgh EH1 2EF Tel 0131-
228 8111
SC NO SCO 03454   ESTABLISHED 1989

■ The Charles Littlewood Hill Trust

WHAT IS FUNDED General charitable purposes.
Particularly sympathetic consideration will be given
to applications by charities concerned with the
welfare of Service and ex-service personnel and
their dependants

WHAT IS NOT FUNDED Grants are seldom made for
repairs of Parish Churches outside
Nottinghamshire. No grants to individuals
WHO CAN BENEFIT Preference will be given to
applications relating to projects and activities in
Norfolk and Nottinghamshire, and to projects
concerned with the welfare of service and ex-
service personnel and their dependants
WHERE FUNDING CAN BE GIVEN UK but preference for
Nottinghamshire and Norfolk
TYPE OF GRANT Applications for starter finance
encouraged. Grants seldom made to endowment
or capital funds
FINANCES Year 1997 Income £137,982
Grants £122,000
TRUSTEES C W L Barratt, W F Whysall, N R Savory,
T H Farr
HOW TO APPLY Applications must be in writing and
accompanied by audited accounts dated within
twelve months of application. All applications
considered at meetings held in March, July and
November. Unsuccessful applicants not notified
WHO TO APPLY TO The Trustees, The Charles
Littlewood Hill Trust, Eversheds, 1 Royal Standard
Place, Nottingham NG1 6FZ Tel 0115-950 7000
Fax 0115-950 7111
CC NO 286350   ESTABLISHED 1978

■ Gay & Peter Hartley's Hillards Charitable Trust

WHAT IS FUNDED To give aid to those poor, needy and
sick who live in the areas which were served by a
Hillards store. Churches, community centres and
schools within those areas may also be
beneficiaries but it is preferable if they have
charitable status themselves. The Trust will
consider funding: advice and information on
housing; emergency and short term housing;
respite; community development; support to
voluntary and community organisations; support to
volunteers; Councils for Voluntary Service (CVS);
Christian education; religious ancillary buildings;
religious umbrella bodies; arts education; health
care; ambulances and mobile units; hospices;
cancer research; health related volunteer
schemes; church buildings; historic buildings;
animal homes; animal welfare; schools and
colleges; special needs education; speech
therapy; community services; and other charitable
purposes
WHAT IS NOT FUNDED Personal applications are not
usually granted unless they come through another
charity. As a body, the Trustees do not give to
national charities but the individual Trustees have
some discretion in that respect
WHO CAN BENEFIT Local and regional organisations
benefiting children; young adults, older people;
clergy; ex-service and service people; seafarers
and fishermen; students; volunteers; those in
care, fostered and adopted; parents and children;
one parent families; widows and widowers;
Baptists; Christians; Church of England;
Methodists; Quakers; Roman Catholics;
Unitarians; at risk groups; carers; disabled people;
those disadvantaged by poverty; ex-offenders and
those at risk of offending; homeless people; those
living in urban areas; victims of abuse; victims of
crime; and victims of domestic violence. There are
few restrictions on the disease or medical
condition suffered by the beneficiaries
WHERE FUNDING CAN BE GIVEN Areas served by
Hillards stores, mainly the North of England,
especially Yorkshire

TYPE OF GRANT Buildings, capital, core costs, one-off, project, research, running costs and start up costs. All funding is for one year or less

FINANCES *Year* 1996 *Income* £82,861
Grants £82,355

TRUSTEES P A H Hartley, CBE, Mrs G Hartley, MBE, S R H Hartley, ASVA, Miss S Hartley, BA, MBA, A C H Hartley, MA, MBA, MSc, Miss A Hartley

HOW TO APPLY Application forms are available from the Secretary to the Trustees upon written request and should be returned before 1st November for consideration in December. Applicants are told if they have not been successful

WHO TO APPLY TO Mrs R C Phillips, Secretary to the Trustees, Gay & Peter Hartley's Hillards Charitable Trust, 400 Shadwell Lane, Leeds LS17 8AW
Tel 0113-266 1424 *Fax* 0113-237 0051

CC NO 327879   **ESTABLISHED** 1988

■ Hillingdon Partnership Trust

WHAT IS FUNDED The Trust aims to build links between the local community and the business sector to secure funding for community initiatives and projects. To relieve those resident in Hillingdon who are suffering from sickness, disability, old age, poverty or other social and economic circumstances. To provide, or assist in providing, equipment and facilities not normally provided by the local authority for the purpose of advancing education or relieving those in need

WHO CAN BENEFIT Organisations benefiting people of all ages, at risk groups, those disadvantaged by poverty and socially isolated people. There is no restriction on the disease or medical condition suffered by the beneficiaries

WHERE FUNDING CAN BE GIVEN Borough of Hillingdon

FINANCES *Year* 1996 *Income* £73,426
Grants £14,282

TRUSTEES Cllr E G Boff, J H Crowe, M Elms, G Gray, G B Parker, M J Roberts, M J H Sterling, M J Taylor, J A Watts, MP, M A Wisdom, H S Wolff, A R Woodbridge

HOW TO APPLY To the address under Who To Apply To in writing

WHO TO APPLY TO J Mathews, Marketing Executive, Hillingdon Partnership Trust, Building 219, Epsom Square, London Heathrow Airport, Hillingdon, Hounslow TW6 2BW

CC NO 284668   **ESTABLISHED** 1982

■ Hillside Charitable Trust

WHAT IS FUNDED Advancement of Christian religion and public benefit of religious or other education. The relief of the aged, poor, sick and disabled

WHO CAN BENEFIT Organisations benefiting children, young adults and elderly people, Christians, disabled people and those disadvantaged by poverty. There is no restriction on the disease or medical condition suffered by the beneficiaries

WHERE FUNDING CAN BE GIVEN UK and overseas

TYPE OF GRANT At the discretion of the Trustees

RANGE OF GRANTS £25–£2850

SAMPLE GRANTS £2,850 to St Paul's Church for missionary fund; £2,575 to Crosslinks; £508 to Henham PCC; £500 to Christian Ministries; £500 to TEAR Fund

FINANCES *Year* 1997 *Income* £16,136
Grants £9,541

TRUSTEES Timothy P Houghton, Dorothy M Houghton, David P Houghton

WHO TO APPLY TO T P Houghton, FCA, Hillside Charitable Trust, 28 Warren Avenue, Cheam, Surrey SM2 7QN

CC NO 297494   **ESTABLISHED** 1987

■ Hilmarnan Charitable Trust

WHAT IS FUNDED The welfare of the elderly, poor and infirm in the area Where Funding Can Be Given

WHO CAN BENEFIT Organisations benefiting elderly people, those disadvantaged by poverty and infirm people

WHERE FUNDING CAN BE GIVEN Within a ten mile radius of Moot Hall, Main Street, Keswick

FINANCES *Year* 1995–96 *Income* £18,445
Grants £5,100

HOW TO APPLY To the address under Who To Apply To in writing. Applications are normally made to the Trustees via local doctors who may highlight a particular person in need

WHO TO APPLY TO G W B Mendus, Trustees Solicitor, Hilmarnan Charitable Trust, c/o Ogelthorpe & Broatch, 6 Borrowdale Road, Keswick CA12 5DB

CC NO 500918   **ESTABLISHED** 1971

■ Hinchley Charitable Trust

WHAT IS FUNDED General charitable purposes, with particular reference to evangelical Christian work

WHAT IS NOT FUNDED Replies will rarely, if ever be made to applications for grants by post or on the telephone as existing funds are all fully committed to charities which are regularly supported

WHO CAN BENEFIT There are no restrictions on the age; professional and economic group; family situation; religion and culture; and social circumstances of; or disease or medical condition suffered by, the beneficiaries

WHERE FUNDING CAN BE GIVEN UK and overseas

TYPE OF GRANT One-off and recurring

RANGE OF GRANTS £50–£6,000

SAMPLE GRANTS £6,500 to Purby Baptist Church for general and home and overseas mission; £2,750 to Crusaders; £2,250 to Africa Evangelical Fellowship; £2,000 to Moucecore for Rwanda relief; £2,000 to Spurgeons College; £2,000 to Castle Hill Baptist Church, Warwick for rebuilding; £1,500 to Hildenborough Evangelist Trust; £1,500 to Church Pastoral Aid Society; £1,500 to Trinity College Bristol; £1,500 to Reach for Rwanda for relief work

FINANCES *Year* 1997 *Income* £36,721
Grants £35,625

TRUSTEES R H Stanley, Mrs M B Stanley, Dr B Stanley, Mrs B Levick, J D Levick, Mrs R Stanley

WHO TO APPLY TO R H Stanley, Hinchley Charitable Trust, 26 Rose Walk, Purley, Surrey CR8 3LG

CC NO 281178   **ESTABLISHED** 1973

■ Lady Hind Trust

WHAT IS FUNDED General charitable purposes

WHAT IS NOT FUNDED Grants are rarely made for the repair of Parish Churches outside Nottinghamshire. No grants to individuals

WHO CAN BENEFIT There are no restrictions on the age; professional and economic group; family situation; religion and culture; and social circumstances of; or disease or medical condition suffered by, the beneficiaries. Preference is given to applications relating to projects and activities in Nottinghamshire and Norfolk

WHERE FUNDING CAN BE GIVEN England and Wales only. Preference is given to applications relating to

Does the trust you have chosen match your needs? Haphazard applications waste postage and time

297

projects and activities in Nottinghamshire and Norfolk

FINANCES *Year* 1997 *Income* £295,153 *Grants* £292,863

TRUSTEES C W L Barratt, W F Whysall, N R Savory, T H Farr

HOW TO APPLY Applications must be in writing and accompanied by audited accounts dated within twelve months of application. All applications considered at meetings held in March, July and November. Unsuccessful applicants not notified

WHO TO APPLY TO Lady Hind Trust, Eversheds, 1 Royal Standard Place, Nottingham NG1 6FZ

CC NO 208877   **ESTABLISHED** 1951

■ The Margaret Jeannie Hindley Trust

WHAT IS FUNDED Wide range of charitable causes for the relief of men and women in reduced or destitute circumstances

WHO CAN BENEFIT Young adults and older people diadvantaged by poverty

WHERE FUNDING CAN BE GIVEN Mainly local to Surrey and Hampshire

TYPE OF GRANT One-off and regular grants

RANGE OF GRANTS £40–£10,000

SAMPLE GRANTS £7,500 to Age Concern, Waverley for local projects for the elderly; £2,500 to Haslemere and District Volunteer Bureau for accident prevention for children; £1,061 to an individual for purchase of specially designed chair; £1,000 to Winged Fellowship for Christmas project; £1,000 to Milford Ex-servicemen's Association for needy members

FINANCES *Year* 1996–97 *Income* £18,101 *Grants* £8,429

TRUSTEES D A S Dear, B Kilburn

HOW TO APPLY By letter to the Trustees quoting circumstances and requirements

WHO TO APPLY TO Messrs Marshalls, The Margaret Jeannie Hindley Trust, 102 High Street, Godalming, Surrey GU7 1DS

CC NO 272140   **ESTABLISHED** 1976

■ The W C M Hines Charitable Foundation

This trust did not respond to CAF's request to amend its entry and, by 30 June 1998, CAF's researchers did not find financial records for later than 1995 on its file at the Charity Commission. Trusts are legally required to submit annual accounts to the Charity Commission under section 42 of the Charities Act 1993

WHAT IS FUNDED General charitable purposes

WHO CAN BENEFIT There are no restrictions on the age; professional and economic group; family situation; religion and culture; and social circumstances of; or disease or medical condition suffered by, the beneficiaries

WHERE FUNDING CAN BE GIVEN UK

TYPE OF GRANT Recurrent and one-off

TRUSTEES Mrs W C M Hines, Mrs A P Hines

WHO TO APPLY TO Mrs W C M Hines, The W C M Hines Charitable Foundation, 5 The Grove, London N6 6AU

CC NO 275377   **ESTABLISHED** 1978

■ The Hinrichsen Foundation

WHAT IS FUNDED Assisting contemporary composition and its performance, and musicological research. The Trustees are aware that financial assistance

is often necessary to create the opportunities for both composition and research. They are equally aware that the results of composition or research need to be made known and that financial assistance is often necessary for the production of performance materials, for the publication of the results of research and for performances of new compositions to take place

WHAT IS NOT FUNDED Grants are not given towards recording costs, for funding commissions, for degree or other study courses nor for the purchase of instruments or equipment. No grants made in response to general appeals

WHO CAN BENEFIT Organisations benefiting musicians

WHERE FUNDING CAN BE GIVEN UK

TYPE OF GRANT Usually one-off for a specific project or part of a project

FINANCES *Year* 1996 *Income* £82,639 *Grants* £59,854

TRUSTEES Mrs C E Hinrichsen, P Strang, K Potter, Dr A Whittall, P Standford, S Walsh, J Dyer, J Hosier, Dr J Cross, L Hirst

HOW TO APPLY Standard application form must be submitted, including clear details of the project plus detailed budget. Two independent references required. Trustees meet quarterly

WHO TO APPLY TO The Secretary, The Hinrichsen Foundation, 10–12 Baches Street, London N1 6DN

CC NO 272389   **ESTABLISHED** 1976

■ His Grace World Outreach Trust

WHAT IS FUNDED General charitable purposes; to advance the Christian faith; to relieve persons in need, hardship, who are aged or sick; and to advance education

WHO CAN BENEFIT Organisations benefiting people of all ages, students, Christians, at risk groups, those disadvantaged by poverty and socially isolated people. There is no restriction on the disease or medical condition suffered by the beneficiaries

WHERE FUNDING CAN BE GIVEN UK with preference for London

TRUSTEES P O Fadeyi, E A Onifade, J Nwokoye

WHO TO APPLY TO Rev P K Fadeyl, His Grace World Outreach Trust, 49 Greenwich High Street, Station House, Unit 0203, London SE10 8JL

CC NO 1059112   **ESTABLISHED** 1996

■ The Hiscox Foundation

WHAT IS FUNDED Charities only known to the Trustees

WHAT IS NOT FUNDED Funds fully committed. No applications

WHO CAN BENEFIT Registered charities or individuals. There are no restrictions on the age; professional and economic group; family situation; religion and culture; and social circumstances of; or disease or medical condition suffered by, the beneficiaries

WHERE FUNDING CAN BE GIVEN Worldwide

TYPE OF GRANT Usually one-off

SAMPLE GRANTS £2,000 to Prostate Research Cancer Funds; £1,100 to NSPCC; £1,000 to Prince's Youth Business Trust; £540 to National Childrens Safety Books; £350 to an individual

FINANCES *Year* 1998 *Income* £29,876 *Grants* £10,878

TRUSTEES R R S Hiscox, A N Foster, R Barker

PUBLICATIONS Annual Report

HOW TO APPLY **This Trust states that it does not respond to unsolicited applications**

WHO TO APPLY TO A N Foster, The Hiscox Foundation, 52 Leadenhall Street, London EC3A 2BJ
CC NO 327635   **ESTABLISHED** 1987

■ The Hishtadlut Charitable Trust

WHAT IS FUNDED General charitable purposes
WHO CAN BENEFIT There are no restrictions on the age; professional and economic group; family situation; religion and culture; and social circumstances of; or disease or medical condition suffered by, the beneficiaries
WHERE FUNDING CAN BE GIVEN UK
TRUSTEES Bernhard Metals (UK) Ltd, H Epstein, S Heuberger, D Holt
WHO TO APPLY TO Stephen Heuberger, The Hishtadlut Charitable Trust, 20 Woodlands, London NW11 9QL
CC NO 10572⬤   **ESTABLISHED** 1996

■ The Historic Churches Preservation Trust

WHAT IS FUNDED To assist with grants and loans, the efforts of congregations, mostly in rural areas, with the carrying out of essential repairs to the fabric of historic churches
WHAT IS NOT FUNDED Beneficiaries must be churches and chapels in regular use as places of public worship and over 100 years old. Grants are not made towards electric wiring, lighting, heating, organs, bells, clocks, ornaments or significant alterations. Repairs should be carried out where possible in traditional material
WHO CAN BENEFIT Any church which has historic associations or architectural features which in the opinion of the Trustees are worthy of preservation is eligible for consideration, subject to funds being available
WHERE FUNDING CAN BE GIVEN Currently restricted to England and Wales
FINANCES *Year* 1996 *Income* £900,000
Grants £800,000
TRUSTEES The Archbishops of Canterbury, York and others
WHO TO APPLY TO Wg Cdr Michael Tippen, RAF (Retd), Secretary, Historic Churches Preservation Trust, Fulham Palace, London SW6 6EA
CC NO 207402   **ESTABLISHED** 1953

■ The Historical Research Trust and the Modern Architecture and Town Planning Trust *(in connection with the Royal Institute of British Architects)*

WHAT IS FUNDED To make grants mainly to architects and students for specific research projects
WHAT IS NOT FUNDED The awards are not available for the support of students on taught courses
WHO CAN BENEFIT Architects and students
WHERE FUNDING CAN BE GIVEN UK
TYPE OF GRANT Grants to cover all aspects of research work (including the time cost of the researcher, the hire of research assistants and travel)
RANGE OF GRANTS Up to £5,000
FINANCES *Year* 1997 *Income* £40,000
Grants £30,000
TRUSTEES Royal Institute of British Architects
NOTES As considerable detail is requested and evidence of satisfactory supervision required,

candidates are advised to obtain the application form and conditions as early as possible
HOW TO APPLY Application forms are available in October each year and must be returned by the middle of the following January. Please send applications to RIBA Research Awards Secretary at the above address
WHO TO APPLY TO Education Department, The Historical Research Trust, Royal Institute of British Architects, 66 Portland Place, London W1N 4AD
CC NO 314248   **ESTABLISHED** 1964

■ The Hitachi Charitable Trust

WHAT IS FUNDED Activities are concentrated in the following areas: child and youth development, education and training, medicine and health, social welfare, the arts, the environment and communication disability
WHAT IS NOT FUNDED No individuals, students, political or religious organisations
WHO CAN BENEFIT Local charities where Hitachi has offices benefiting: children; young adults; actors and entertainment professional; musicians; textile workers and designers; writers and poets; at risk groups; those disadvantaged by poverty; and the socially isolated. There are no restrictions on the disease or medical condition suffered by the beneficiaries
WHERE FUNDING CAN BE GIVEN Mainly Berkshire, Windsor and Maidenhead
TYPE OF GRANT One-off
SAMPLE GRANTS £8,955 to Brunel University; £6,856 for arts projects; £3,388 for health/medicine projects; £2,030 for child/youth development projects; £1,781 for education/training projects; £1,762 for social welfare projects; £1,716 for recreation/leisure projects; £1,063 for heritage/environment/community projects
FINANCES *Year* 1996 *Income* £123,055
Grants £27,551
TRUSTEES A Koizumi, M Aso, A Tolan, K Fujita
PUBLICATIONS Annual Report
NOTES Direct one-off donations only. No advertising to support charitable activities
HOW TO APPLY In writing
WHO TO APPLY TO M Takebayashi, Senior Corporate Manager, The Hitachi Charitable Trust, Hitachi Europe Ltd, Whitebrook Park, Lower Cookham Road, Maidenhead, Berkshire SL6 8YA
CC NO 1006169   **ESTABLISHED** 1991

■ Hitchin Education Foundation

WHAT IS FUNDED To advance education and training
WHO CAN BENEFIT Individuals and local organisations benefiting children, young adults and students
WHERE FUNDING CAN BE GIVEN The former urban district of Hitchin and the parishes of Holwell, Ickleford, Lower Stondon and Pirton
TYPE OF GRANT One-off
RANGE OF GRANTS £50–£200
FINANCES *Year* 1995–96 *Income* £65,145
Grants £53,165
TRUSTEES Mrs Dorothy S Haigh, Frederick G Peacock, D Hitchcock, Derrick Ashley, J Banks, Ms J Marr, Mrs Beryl F Wearmouth, Mrs Mary C Goldsmith, Mrs Audrey E Carss, Paul Clark, Mrs J Kirby, Archie F Kingston-Splatt, Mrs Margaret S Anderson, Canon Leslie Ogelsby, John Elliott, Mrs Diane Burleigh, Mrs J Reid
NOTES Applicants must have lived in Hitchin or attended a Hitchin school for at least two years
HOW TO APPLY Application forms are available from the address under Who To Apply To upon written

request and are available at the Citizens Advice Bureau

WHO TO APPLY TO J C Coxall, Clerk, Hitchin Education Foundation, 7 South View, Letchworth, Hertfordshire SG6 3JH *Tel* 01462 487061

CC NO 311024   **ESTABLISHED** 1965

■ The Hobart Charitable Trust

WHAT IS FUNDED To advance education and religion, the relief of poverty and charitable purposes for the benefit of the community

WHO CAN BENEFIT Children; young adults; students and those disadvantaged by poverty. There is no restriction on the religion or culture of the benficiaries

WHERE FUNDING CAN BE GIVEN UK

SAMPLE GRANTS £30,000 to Saint Petersburg Trust; £500 to Cliddesden Parish Church Council; £350 to Herriard Parish Church Council

FINANCES *Year* 1997 *Income* £58,515
Grants £30,850

TRUSTEES Rt Hon Baron Hartwell, C H Rawlings

HOW TO APPLY To the address under Who To Apply To in writing

WHO TO APPLY TO C H Rawlings, Company Secretary, The Hobart Charitable Trust, 140 Trustee Company, 36 Broadway, London SW1H 0BH

CC NO 800750   **ESTABLISHED** 1986

■ Lillian Hobbs Trust

WHAT IS FUNDED Advancement of Christian religion

WHO CAN BENEFIT To benefit Christians

WHERE FUNDING CAN BE GIVEN UK

HOW TO APPLY Application are not invited

WHO TO APPLY TO A E Wakeling, Lillian Hobbs Trust, c/o Stewardship Services (UKET), PO Box 99, Loughton, Essex IG10 3QJ *Tel* 0181-502 5600

CC NO 1066782   **ESTABLISHED** 1997

■ The Hobson Charity Limited

WHAT IS FUNDED Relief of poverty, suffering and distress among the aged, impotent and poor. The provision of recreation and leisure facilities. The advancement of education and other charitable purposes

WHO CAN BENEFIT Registered charities only, particularly those benefiting people of all ages, students, teachers, at risk groups, those disadvantaged by poverty and socially isolated people. Otherwise, there are no restrictions on the age; professional and economic group; family situation; religion and culture; and social circumstances of; or disease or medical condition suffered by, the beneficiaries

WHERE FUNDING CAN BE GIVEN UK

RANGE OF GRANTS £300–£34,000

SAMPLE GRANTS £34,000 to British School of Osteopathy; £33,333 to Tate Gallery; £25,000 to Royal Academy of Music; £25,000 to John Grooms Association; £10,000 to The Howard League; £10,000 to British Youth Orchestra; £10,000 to British Youth Opera; £5,000 to RNLI; £3,500 to Friends of John Grooms; £3,000 to Submarine Museum

FINANCES *Year* 1997 *Income* £139,152
Grants £176,633

TRUSTEES R F Hobson, P M Hobson, Sir Donald Gosling, D Clarke

WHO TO APPLY TO A E Bromfield, The Hobson Charity Limited, 21 Bryanston Street, Marble Arch, London W1A 4NH

CC NO 326839   **ESTABLISHED** 1985

■ Hockerill Educational Foundation

WHAT IS FUNDED In the application of income the Trustees will act in such a manner as will advance education in accordance with the doctrines, rites and practices of the Church of England. Persons who intend to become engaged as teachers or otherwise in work connected with religious education; young persons in need of financial assistance to attend an establishment of higher or further education; bodies engaged in research and development of religious education, the provision of chapels and chaplaincy for students, the provision of instruction, classes, lectures, books, libraries and reading rooms

WHAT IS NOT FUNDED Travel bursaries, funding of courses outside UK

WHO CAN BENEFIT Organisations benefiting: young adults; older people; academics; students; teachers and governesses; Christians and Church of England

WHERE FUNDING CAN BE GIVEN UK. Dioceses of Chelmsford and St Albans. Only Anglican dioceses supported

TYPE OF GRANT For individuals, assistance with fees or maintenance. Corporate bodies, one-off. Only or annual grant for a limited period. Research and funding of up to three years will be considered

RANGE OF GRANTS £500–£10,000

SAMPLE GRANTS £53,080 to various individual applications for teaching qualifications; £52,000 to Diocese of St Albans for various educational projects; £52,000 to Diocese of Chelsford for various educationl projects; £5,000 to University College, Chester for distance learning programme; £2,000 to Nationl Society RE Centre for part-funding of salaried post

FINANCES *Year* 1997 *Income* £210,444
Grants £164,080

TRUSTEES Rt Rev The Lord Bishop of Chelmsford, Dr S Hunter (Chair), Rt Rev The Lord Bishop of St Albans, Rev Canon P Hartley, Rt Rev The Bishop of Bedford, Rt Rev The Bishop of Bradwell, Ven D W M Jennings, Archdeacon of Southend, Mrs M L Helmore, R Wood, Mrs H Potter, Ven T P Jones, Archdeacon of Hertford, Prof B J Aylett

PUBLICATIONS Annual Hockerill Lecture

NOTES Teachers and prospective teachers of RE given preference

HOW TO APPLY An official form is provided. Applications to reach the Secretary by 1 March. Initial telephone calls from applicants are welcome. Application form and guidelines are available. Sae required

WHO TO APPLY TO D J Newman, Secretary, Hockerill Educational Foundation, Ingrebourne, 51 Pole Barn Lane, Frinton-on-Sea, Essex CO13 9NQ *Tel* 01255 676509 *Fax* 01255 851529

CC NO 311018   **ESTABLISHED** 1977

■ The Sir Julian Hodge Charitable Trust

WHAT IS FUNDED General charitable purposes, especially medical research in cancer, polio, tuberculosis and diseases of children. General advancement of medical and surgical science, the advancement of education, the advancement of religion, and the relief of the aged and disabled

300

Think carefully about every application. Is it justified?

WHO CAN BENEFIT Registered charities benefiting people of all ages. Support may also be given to the disabled; medical professionals; research workers; scientists; students and teachers and governesses. Funding may be given to those suffering from cancers, paediatric diseases, polio and tuberculosis

WHERE FUNDING CAN BE GIVEN UK

RANGE OF GRANTS £5,000–£6,500

SAMPLE GRANTS £6,500 to Diocese of Portsmouth; £5,000 to St Gregory's Charitable Trust; £5,000 to Cardiff Eglwys Dewi Sant; £5,000 to Christian Lewis Trust

FINANCES *Year* 1996 *Income* £25,298 *Grants* £21,500

TRUSTEES Sir Julian Hodge, Lady Moira Hodge, J J Hodge, R J Hodge, Joyce Harrison, Derrek L Jones

WHO TO APPLY TO The Secretary, Sir Julian Hodge Charitable Trust, Ty Gwyn, Lisvane Road, Lisvane, Cardiff, South Wales CF4 5SG

CC NO 234848   **ESTABLISHED** 1964

■ Bill & May Hodgson Charitable Trust

WHAT IS FUNDED General charitable purposes

WHO CAN BENEFIT Registered charities only. There are no restrictions on the age; professional and economic group; family situation; religion and culture; and social circumstances of; or disease or medical condition suffered by, the beneficiaries

WHERE FUNDING CAN BE GIVEN UK and Tyne & Wear

RANGE OF GRANTS £100–£1,000

SAMPLE GRANTS £1,000 to the British Red Cross; £400 to Crisis; £400 to Durham Cathedral; £400 to Gosforth Sea Cadets – Geordie Jaunts; £350 to National Missing Persons Helpline

FINANCES *Year* 1996 *Income* £20,164 *Grants* £15,350

TRUSTEES R M Wilson, H Straker, Col G S May

WHO TO APPLY TO Bill & May Hodgson Charitable Trust, Dickinson Dees, Solicitors, Cross Hours, Westgate Road, Newcastle upon Tyne NE99 1SB

CC NO 295313   **ESTABLISHED** 1986

■ The J G Hogg Charitable Trust

WHAT IS FUNDED Humanitarian causes, worldwide, wild and domestic animals welfare causes

WHO CAN BENEFIT To benefit those from varying social circumstances

WHERE FUNDING CAN BE GIVEN UK and overseas

FINANCES *Year* 1996 *Income* £178,841

TRUSTEES Joanne W Hogg, Sarah J Houldsworth

HOW TO APPLY To the address under Who To Apply To in writing

WHO TO APPLY TO C M Jones, Trustee's Accountant, The J G Hogg Charitable Trust, Chantrey Vellacott, Russell Square House, 10–12 Russell Square, London WC1A 5LF

CC NO 299042   **ESTABLISHED** 1987

■ E S Hogg Charity Trust

WHAT IS FUNDED Service and ex-service organisations, conservation, welfare, disability and medical charities

WHO CAN BENEFIT Individuals and organisations benefiting: ex-service and service people; at risk groups; disabled people; those disadvantaged by poverty; and socially isolated people. There is no restriction on the disease or medical condition suffered by the beneficiaries

WHERE FUNDING CAN BE GIVEN UK

TYPE OF GRANT Buildings, capital, one-off, project, research and recurring costs funded for one year or less will be considered

FINANCES *Year* 1996–97 *Income* £61,000 *Grants* £121,500

HOW TO APPLY To the address under Who To Apply To in writing

WHO TO APPLY TO The Sectretary, E S Hogg Charity Trust, Messrs Hoare Trustees, 37 Fleet Street, London EC4P 4DQ *Tel* 0171-353 4522

CC NO 280138   **ESTABLISHED** 1980

■ The Holden Charitable Trust

WHAT IS FUNDED Jewish charitable purposes with emphasis on the advancement of education

WHO CAN BENEFIT Organisations benefiting Jewish people. Children, young adults and students may benefit

WHERE FUNDING CAN BE GIVEN UK, especially Manchester and the surrounding area

FINANCES *Year* 1997 *Income* £75,948 *Grants* £59,523

TRUSTEES D Z Lopian, Ms M Lopian

HOW TO APPLY To the address under Who To Apply To in writing

WHO TO APPLY TO The Clerk, The Holden Charitable Trust, Lopian, Gross, Barnett & Company, 1st Floor, Harvester House, 37 Peter Street, Manchester M2 5QD

CC NO 264185   **ESTABLISHED** 1972

■ The Holford Charitable Foundation

This trust did not respond to CAF's request to amend its entry and, by 30 June 1998, CAF's researchers did not find financial records for later than 1995 on its file at the Charity Commission. Trusts are legally required to submit annual accounts to the Charity Commission under section 42 of the Charities Act 1993

WHAT IS FUNDED General charitable purposes

WHO CAN BENEFIT There are no restrictions on the age; professional and economic group; family situation; religion and culture; and social circumstances of; or disease or medical condition suffered by, the beneficiaries

WHERE FUNDING CAN BE GIVEN Devon

TRUSTEES F R Holford, A W M Miller, S R Thomas, Mrs J Holford

WHO TO APPLY TO A W M Miller, Trustee and Solicitor, The Holford Charitable Foundation, 5 Barnfield Crescent, Exeter EX1 1RF

CC NO 1049719   **ESTABLISHED** 1995

■ John Holford's Charity

WHAT IS FUNDED The Trust is concerned mainly with aiding individuals, though small grants may also be given to local schools and youth organisations. This Charity will consider funding holiday accommodation; support to voluntary and community organisations; social care and professional bodies; council for voluntary service; and the purchase of books for education

WHO CAN BENEFIT Primarily individuals of all ages who are: at risk, disabled; disaster victims; ex-offenders and those at risk of offending; homeless; socially isolated or living in urban areas

WHERE FUNDING CAN BE GIVEN Astbury, the Parish of Clutton, the Borough of Congleton, the Parish of Middlewich

Does the trust you have chosen match your needs? Haphazard applications waste postage and time

301

TYPE OF GRANT Capital, interest free loans and one-off funding

FINANCES *Year* 1996 *Income* £45,000

HOW TO APPLY To the address under Who To Apply To in writing

WHO TO APPLY TO The Clerk, John Holford's Charity, Birch Cullimore, Friars, White Friars, Chester CH1 1XS *Tel* 01244 321066

CC NO 223046   **ESTABLISHED** 1984

■ Maria Holland and St Joseph's Charity

WHAT IS FUNDED The elderly, sick and disabled; schools and local churches, especially Catholic

WHO CAN BENEFIT Regional and local organisations benefiting: persons under the age of 25; the elderly, sick and disabled; and Catholics

WHERE FUNDING CAN BE GIVEN Preston

RANGE OF GRANTS £114–£10,000

SAMPLE GRANTS £10,000 to Catholic Caring Services; £8,000 to Sacred Heart and RC Primary School; £6,000 to Preston and North Lancashire Blind Society; £6,000 to an individual; £5,000 to Age Concern; £5,000 to an individual; £2,697 to an individual; £2,000 to Christ The King High School; £114 to St Wilfrid's RC Primary School

FINANCES *Year* 1995 *Income* £28,739 *Grants* £46,811

TRUSTEES Mrs G R Vernon, M G Sherry

HOW TO APPLY To the address under Who To Apply To in writing

WHO TO APPLY TO M J Belderbos, Trustees' Solicitor, Maria Holland and St Joseph's Charity, Messrs Oswald Goodier & Co, 10 Chapel Street, Preston PR1 8AY

CC NO 223547   **ESTABLISHED** 1990

■ The Dorothy Holmes Charitable Trust

WHAT IS FUNDED Charities working in the fields of: advice and information on housing; emergency and short-term housing; residential facilities; respite and sheltered accommodation; information technology and computers; civil society development; support of voluntary and community organisations; health professional bodies; and religion will be considered. Support is also given to healthcare; hospices and hospitals; cancer research; church buildings; heritage; secondary schools and special schools; counselling on social issues; and income support and maintenance

WHO CAN BENEFIT UK registered charities benefiting: young adults and older people; clergy; ex-service and service people; legal professionals; unemployed people; volunteers; parents and children; one parent families; widows and widowers; at risk groups; carers; and disabled people. Support will also be given to those suffering from various diseases and medical conditions. There is no restriction on the religion or culture of the beneficiaries

WHERE FUNDING CAN BE GIVEN UK, with preference for Poole and District (Dorset)

TYPE OF GRANT Buildings, capital, core costs, one-off, project, research, recurring costs, running costs, salaries and start-up costs. Funding for up to and over three years will be considered

RANGE OF GRANTS £300–£1,000

SAMPLE GRANTS £1,000 to St Wilfrids Hospice, Chichester; £750 to Crisis at Christmas; £700 to Friends of Stansted School; £700 to St Johns School, Wallingford

FINANCES *Year* 1998 *Income* £32,766 *Grants* £31,700

TRUSTEES D S Roberts, B M Cody, M E A Cody, S C Roberts

HOW TO APPLY By letter to the address under Who To Apply To

WHO TO APPLY TO The Dorothy Holmes Charitable Trust, c/o Smallfield, Cody & Co, 5 Harley Place, Harley Street, London W1N 1HB *Tel* 0171-631 4574

CC NO 237213   **ESTABLISHED** 1964

■ Godfrey Holmes Foundation

WHAT IS FUNDED Medical research into multiple sclerosis and schizophrenia

WHO CAN BENEFIT Registered charities benefiting: research workers; medical professionals; and those suffering from multiple sclerosis and schizophrenia; and occasionally individuals

WHERE FUNDING CAN BE GIVEN The scheduled territories and Europe

SAMPLE GRANTS £3,000 to Missing Persons Helpline

FINANCES *Year* 1997 *Income* £19,968 *Grants* £18,038

TRUSTEES J L Curtis, Mrs A Sparkes, Miss M C V Holmes

HOW TO APPLY In writing to Coutts & Co

WHO TO APPLY TO J L Curtis, Godfrey Holmes Foundation, Hall Drive, Canwick, Lincoln LN4 2RG

CC NO 267921   **ESTABLISHED** 1974

■ The Holos Charitable Trust

WHAT IS FUNDED General charitable purposes

WHO CAN BENEFIT There are no restrictions on the age; professional and economic group; family situation; religion and culture; and social circumstances of; or disease or medical condition suffered by, the beneficiaries

WHERE FUNDING CAN BE GIVEN UK

TRUSTEES S V Froud, G J Simpson, D W Taylor

WHO TO APPLY TO Miss S Froud, Professional Advisor, The Holos Charitable Trust, Simpson Froud, 2nd Floor, 207 High Street, Orpington, Kent BR6 0PF *Tel* 01689 896147 *Fax* 01689 898333

CC NO 1069290   **ESTABLISHED** 1998

■ The Holst Foundation

WHAT IS FUNDED To promote public appreciation of the musical works of Gustav and Imogen Holst; to encourage the study and practice of the arts including: music; instrumental; voice and operatic art; drama; dancing; mime; the visual arts; and literature and poetry

WHAT IS NOT FUNDED No support for the recordings or works by the Holsts that are well supported

WHO CAN BENEFIT Actors and entertainment professionals, musicians, and writers and poets

WHERE FUNDING CAN BE GIVEN UK and overseas

FINANCES *Year* 1996 *Income* £282,883 *Grants* £206,307

TRUSTEES Noel Peritan, Rosamund Strode, Prof Arnold Whitall, Peter Carter, Andrew Clements

HOW TO APPLY To the address under Who To Apply To in writing

WHO TO APPLY TO Peter Carter, Secretary, The Holst Foundation, Messrs Forsythe Kerman, 79 New Cavendish Street, London W1M 8AQ *Tel* 0171-637 8566
CC NO 283668   **ESTABLISHED** 1981

■ P H Holt Charitable Trust

WHAT IS FUNDED General charitable purposes in Merseyside and abroad, particularly when original work or work of special excellence is being undertaken

WHAT IS NOT FUNDED No grants to individuals

WHO CAN BENEFIT There are no restrictions on the age; professional and economic group; family situation; religion and culture; and social circumstances of; or disease or medical condition suffered by, the beneficiaries

WHERE FUNDING CAN BE GIVEN Merseyside and overseas

WHO TO APPLY TO The Secretary, P H Holt Charitable Trust, c/o Ocean Transport and Trading plc, India Buildings, Liverpool L2 0RB
CC NO 217332   **ESTABLISHED** 1955

■ The Edward Holt Trust

WHAT IS FUNDED Primarily maintaining block of 10 flats in Didsbury, Manchester, for retired gentlefolk. Preference to charities of which the Trustees have special interest, knowledge or association including cancer, neurological and ageing research

WHAT IS NOT FUNDED None per Trust Deed but administratively no grant applications to be made

WHO CAN BENEFIT Individuals and organisations benefiting older people and those suffering from: Alzheimer's disease; autism; cancers; epilepsy; head and other injuries; mental illness; motor neurone disease and muscular dystrophy

WHERE FUNDING CAN BE GIVEN Bolton, Bury, Manchester, Oldham, Rochdale, Salford, Stockport, Tameside and Trafford

TYPE OF GRANT Buildings, capital, project and research. Funding is available for up to two years

FINANCES *Year* 1997 *Income* £250,000 *Grants* £100,000

TRUSTEES P Kershaw (Chair), H M Fairhurst, R Kershaw, H W E Thompson, FCA, D J Tully

WHO TO APPLY TO J P Sandford, The Edward Holt Trust, KPMG, St James' Square, Manchester M2 6DS *Tel* 0161-838 4000
CC NO 224741   **ESTABLISHED** 1955

■ The Holywood Trust

WHAT IS FUNDED The Trust is particularly keen to provide grants to young people, within the target group of approximately 15 to 25 years of age, who produce proposals aimed at setting up self help activities which contribute to their personal development or training, help other young people and benefit the wider community. Projects which involve or help the young single homeless, the unemployed and those living in urban or rural settings which lack provision, will be of interest to the Trust

WHAT IS NOT FUNDED Grants are not awarded to political parties or projects which are eligible for statutory funding

WHO CAN BENEFIT Young people resident in Dumfries and Galloway who are mentally, physically or socially disadvantaged. Support may be for homeless and unemployed young people and those living in rural and urban areas

WHERE FUNDING CAN BE GIVEN Dumfries and Galloway

TYPE OF GRANT One-off, capital and recurring (usually limited to three years) depending on need

RANGE OF GRANTS Up to £500 for individuals and up to £1,000 for organisations, unless special case

FINANCES *Year* 1996–97 *Grants* £189,000

TRUSTEES J J G Brown, C A Jencks, A M Macleod, E Nelson, A D Scott

PUBLICATIONS An information leaflet and application forms (personal, student and project) are available from the Trust

HOW TO APPLY Applications, containing an outline of the project, should be made in writing to the address below and should be no more than two pages of A4 in length

WHO TO APPLY TO Peter Robertson, Director, The Holywood Trust, Mount St Michael, Craigs Road, Dumfries DG1 4UT *Tel* 01387 269176
SC NO SCO 09942   **ESTABLISHED** 1981

■ Home Housing Trust

WHAT IS FUNDED Relief of persons who by reason of poverty, age, disability or infirmity are in necessitous circumstances and, in particular, by the provision of treatment, care, housing and associated amenities

WHO CAN BENEFIT Individuals, and organisations benefiting older people, disabled people and those disadvantaged by poverty. There is no restriction on the disease or medical condition suffered by the beneficiaries

WHERE FUNDING CAN BE GIVEN UK

RANGE OF GRANTS £68–£14,630

SAMPLE GRANTS £14,630 to National Disabled Persons Housing Scheme; £5,906 to National Wheelchair Housing Association Group for research programme to produce a design for wheelchair housing; £5,000 to Sparrowmire Residents Association for work on the Hallgarth Community Centre; £3,000 to Ford and Pennywell Advice Centre; £2,622 to Peterborough Time Stop; £500 to CHAR; £500 to Arthur's Hill Research Project; £500 to Octavia Hill Birthplace Museum Trust; £500 to Charlotte Straker Trust; £68 to Northbourne Street Area Tenants Group

FINANCES *Year* 1997 *Income* £53,151 *Grants* £33,226

TRUSTEES A F C Hunter, CBE, B Wilson, Mrs M R Hall, R N D Stephenson, OBE, J W Stevens, P M Shirley, P F Tinnion, Mrs A Ward, Mrs M R O Kemp, J K Dumigan, Sir A Pearce, CBE, D L Robinson

WHO TO APPLY TO L Dent, Company Secretary, Home Housing Trust, Ridley House, Regent Centre, Gosforth, Newcastle upon Tyne NE3 3JE
CC NO 327036   **ESTABLISHED** 1985

■ Homelands Charitable Trust

WHAT IS FUNDED General charitable purposes in accordance with the Settlor's wishes. Special emphasis is given to the General Conference of the New Church, medical research and the care and protection of children. Animal welfare is also supported

WHAT IS NOT FUNDED No grants to individuals

WHO CAN BENEFIT Registered charities benefiting children, particularly those in at risk groups, or who are victims of abuse or domestic violence. Support may also be given to clergy, medical professionals and research workers. There is no

restriction on the disease or medical condition suffered by the beneficiaries

WHERE FUNDING CAN BE GIVEN UK

RANGE OF GRANTS £500–£18,500

SAMPLE GRANTS £26,500 to General Conference of the New Church; £18,500 to Bournemouth Society of the New Church; £5,000 to Broadfield Memorial Trust; £5,000 to National Children's Homes; £4,750 to Oxfam; £4,000 to NSPCC; £3,000 to Association for Spina Bifida and Hydrocephalus; £3,000 to Christian Aid; £3,000 to Church of England Children's Society; £3,000 to Friends of the Earth

FINANCES *Year* 1997 *Income* £448,635 *Grants* £158,900

TRUSTEES D G W Ballard, Rev C Curry, N J Armstrong

HOW TO APPLY In writing to the address under Who To Apply To

WHO TO APPLY TO N J Armstrong, FCA, Homelands Charitable Trust, Messrs Alliotts, 5th Floor, 9 Kingsway, London WC2B 6XF

CC NO 214322   **ESTABLISHED** 1962

■ Homeless International

WHAT IS FUNDED International poverty relief. Long term community housing and housing related projects in Asia, Africa, Latin America and the Caribbean

WHAT IS NOT FUNDED No grants to individuals

WHO CAN BENEFIT International organisations, local community organisations and non-governmental organisations benefiting children, young adults, older people, homeless people and those disadvantaged by poverty

WHERE FUNDING CAN BE GIVEN Overseas particularly Asia, Africa, Latin America and the Caribbean

TYPE OF GRANT Range of grants

SAMPLE GRANTS £92,792 to South India Low Cost Shelter Network; £82,940 to PROHABITAT, Bolivia for Housing Improvement and Chagas Disease Control; £72,428 to YCO, Yellamanchili, India for Guarantee Fund Scheme; £49,480 to CERES, Bolivia for Water Extension Project; £47,363 to SPARC, Mumbai, India for Building Centre Project; £44,913 to SPARC, Mumbai, India for Street Children Project; £38,476 to COBIJO, Chile for Housing and Public Spaces Improvement; £32,615 to FVC, Argentina for Housing Project Revolving Loan Fund; £26,853 to Peoples Dialogue, South Africa for South Africa Exchange and Training Project; £26,279 to CRDC, Jamaica for Caribbean Information and Dissemination Programme

FINANCES *Year* 1996–97 *Income* £1,041,000 *Grants* £956,080

TRUSTEES Members of the Council of Management

PUBLICATIONS Annual Report, Guidelines

NOTES Application form available

HOW TO APPLY Initial letter

WHO TO APPLY TO Mrs R McLeod, Homeless International, Guildford House, 20 Queens Road, Coventry CV1 3EG *Tel* 01203 632802 *Fax* 01203 632911 *E-mail* rm@homeint-win-uk.net

CC NO 1017255   **ESTABLISHED** 1989

■ The Homestead Charitable Trust

WHAT IS FUNDED Medical, health and welfare, animal welfare, Christianity and the arts

WHO CAN BENEFIT Actors and entertainment professionals; musicians; textile workers and designers; writers and poets; Christians; at risk groups; those disadvantaged by poverty; and

socially isolated people. There is no restriction on the disease or medical condition suffered by the beneficiaries

WHERE FUNDING CAN BE GIVEN UK

TYPE OF GRANT Some recurring

RANGE OF GRANTS £100–£10,000

SAMPLE GRANTS £10,000 to the Cambridge Foundation; £6,000 to St Cyprians Roman Catholic Church; £6,000 to Carmelite Fathers, Kensington; £1,000 to Dilhurst School, Bombay; £100 to the Donkey Sanctuary

FINANCES *Year* 1997 *Income* £106,880 *Grants* £23,100

TRUSTEES Sir C Bracewell-Smith, Lady N Bracewell-Smith, R Carr

HOW TO APPLY To the address under Who To Apply To in writing

WHO TO APPLY TO D J Clark, Correspondent, The Homestead Charitable Trust, MacIntyre & Co, 28 Ely Place, London EC1N 6RL

CC NO 293979   **ESTABLISHED** 1986

■ Mary Homfray Charitable Trust

WHAT IS FUNDED General charitable purposes

WHO CAN BENEFIT Registered charities. There are no restrictions on the age; professional and economic group; family situation; religion and culture; and social circumstances of; or disease or medical condition suffered by, the beneficiaries

WHERE FUNDING CAN BE GIVEN UK

SAMPLE GRANTS £2,000 to NSPCC to fund children protection services; £2,000 to South Glamorgan Macmillan Nurses Appeal; £2,000 to Help the Aged; £2,000 to Age Concern; £2,000 to British Heart Foundation for research and general funds; £2,000 to Army Benevolent Fund; £2,000 to Imperial Cancer Research; £2,000 to Shelter Cymru; £2,000 to YMCA; £2,000 to The National Memorial Arboretum Appeal

FINANCES *Year* 1997 *Income* £42,995 *Grants* £44,851

TRUSTEES A M Homfray, G C S Gibson

WHO TO APPLY TO Miss K M Griffin, Mary Homfray Charitable Trust, Deloitte and Touche, Blenheim House, Fitzalan Court, Newport Road, Cardiff CF2 1TS *Tel* 01222 481111

CC NO 273564   **ESTABLISHED** 1977

■ The Homfray Trust

WHAT IS FUNDED To assist the families of former or retired employees of Homfray & Co Ltd in financial difficulty. To help certain charitable and other organisations who assist children and the aged, usually in West Yorkshire and particularly in Halifax and Sowerby Bridge. Donations recently included many other charitable funds and organisations, such as health charities, animal welfare, cancer relief and crime prevention schemes

WHAT IS NOT FUNDED No grants to individuals or for expeditions, scholarships or further education

WHO CAN BENEFIT Organisations benefiting children and older people, ex-employees of Hamfray and Co Ltd and those disadvantaged by poverty. Beneficiaries suffering from various diseases and medical conditions will also be considered

WHERE FUNDING CAN BE GIVEN England with preference for West Yorkshire

TYPE OF GRANT One-off donations, but this can often be made year after year in many instances. Core costs are also considered

RANGE OF GRANTS Normally £200–£400

304

Think carefully about every application. Is it justified?

SAMPLE GRANTS £400 to Calderdale Society for Continuing Care (Overgate Hospice); £400 to RSPCA, Halifax Branch; £400 to White Windows Cheshire Home; £400 to Halifax YMCA; £400 to Police Dependants' Trust

FINANCES *Year* 1997 *Income* £17,225 *Grants* £14,182

TRUSTEES H J H Gillam, G S Haigh, D Murray Wells, M Hartley

NOTES Grants unlikely to be given to restore historic buildings or improve the environment

HOW TO APPLY Telephone calls not welcome. No application forms used. Sae from applicants useful, but not essential. No guidelines or deadlines

WHO TO APPLY TO G S Haigh, The Homfray Trust, Newlands House, Warley, Halifax, West Yorkshire HX2 7SW

CC NO 214503   **ESTABLISHED** 1928

■ Honourable Society of Gray's Inn Trust Fund

WHAT IS FUNDED To support organisations concerned with legal matters, and other charitable purposes particularly: legal education; bursaries and fees; and scholarships

WHO CAN BENEFIT Institutions and individuals. There are no restrictions on the age; professional and economic group; family situation; religion and culture; and social circumstances of; or disease or medical condition suffered by, the beneficiaries

WHERE FUNDING CAN BE GIVEN UK

SAMPLE GRANTS £335,833 to Gray's Inn Scholarship Trust for scholarships

FINANCES *Year* 1997 *Income* £1,200,000 *Grants* £335,833

TRUSTEES A J Butcher,QC, M A Simmons,QC, C Sparrow,QC, DL, FSA, The Right Hon Sir A Ward

WHO TO APPLY TO W P Courage, Director of Finance, Honourable Society of Gray's Inn Trust Fund, 8 South Square, Gray's Inn, London WC1R 5EU *Tel* 0171-405 8164

CC NO 1014798   **ESTABLISHED** 1972

■ The Robin Hood Charity Trust

WHAT IS FUNDED The support of Nottingham CVS and general charitable purposes in Nottinghamshire. Charities and voluntary organisations in the fields of: accommodation and housing; infrastructure support and development; religion; arts, culture and recreation; health; conservation and environment; education and training; and social care and development

WHAT IS NOT FUNDED No grants to individuals

WHO CAN BENEFIT There are no restrictions on the age; professional and economic group; family situation; religion and culture; and social circumstances of; or disease or medical condition suffered by, the beneficiaries

WHERE FUNDING CAN BE GIVEN Nottinghamshire

TYPE OF GRANT Buildings, capital, core costs, endowments, feasibility studies, interest free loans, one-off, project, research, recurring costs, running costs, salaries and start-up costs. Grants are for one year or less

SAMPLE GRANTS £8,500 to Nottingham Council for Voluntary Service for general support of running costs

FINANCES *Year* 1997–98 *Income* £30,234 *Grants* £8,500

HOW TO APPLY In writing to the address under Who To Apply To

WHO TO APPLY TO Steve Allen, Secretary, The Robin Hood Charity Trust, 33 Mansfield Road, Nottingham NG1 3FB *Tel* 0115-947 6714

CC NO 501848   **ESTABLISHED** 1972

■ Sir Harold Hood's Charitable Trust

WHAT IS FUNDED Charities dealing with the advancement of the Roman Catholic religion through religious buildings, religious umbrella bodies and other Roman Catholic organisations

WHAT IS NOT FUNDED Only recognised Roman Catholic charities will be considered

WHO CAN BENEFIT Roman Catholic charities in UK and overseas. There are no restrictions on the age; professional and economic group; family situation; religion and culture; and social circumstances of; or disease or medical condition suffered by, the beneficiaries

WHERE FUNDING CAN BE GIVEN UK and overseas

TYPE OF GRANT Recurring

SAMPLE GRANTS £50,000 to Diocese of Aberdeen for maintenance fund of Diocese; £30,000 to Bourne Trust for help to prisoners and their families; £15,000 to Hospital of St John and St Elizabeth, NW8 for St John's Hospice; £10,000 to Downside Settlement, SE1 for boy's club; £8,000 to Housetop Centre, NW1; £7,000 to Trustees' Roman Catholic Charities (RN); £6,000 to Handicapped Pilgrimage Tour, Sutton to send handicapped children to Lourdes; £6,000 to Franciscan Fathers for St Anthony's Orphanage, South Africa; £6,000 to St Elizabeth's Home, Much Hadham for epilepsy; £6,000 to Jesuit Fathers, W1 for a language school, Natal, South Africa

FINANCES *Year* 1996–97 *Income* £94,808 *Grants* £246,000

TRUSTEES Sir Harold Hood, BT, TD, GCSG, The Hon Lady Hood, Kevin P Ney, FCA, Mrs M M E F Gresslin, Nicholas E True, CBE

HOW TO APPLY To the address under Who To Apply To

WHO TO APPLY TO Sir Harold Hood, Bt, Sir Harold Hood's Charitable Trust, 31 Avenue Road, St John's Wood, London NW8 6BS *Tel* 0171-722 9088

CC NO 225870   **ESTABLISHED** 1962

■ The Hoover Foundation

WHAT IS FUNDED Wide range of charities including education (mainly supported through grants to universities, normally for research in the engineering subjects), welfare, medical research and small local charities

WHAT IS NOT FUNDED The Trustees do not make grants to individuals, including students

WHO CAN BENEFIT National registered charities, universities and small local charities working in the areas outlined in the area Where Funding Can Be Given benefiting young adults and students. There is no restriction on the disease or medical condition suffered by the beneficiaries

WHERE FUNDING CAN BE GIVEN Biased towards South Wales, Glasgow and Bolton

TRUSTEES A Bertali, D Lunt

NOTES This Trust replied to CAF's mailing. However, by 30 June 1998, CAF's researchers did not find financial records for later than 1994 filed at the Charity Commission

Does the trust you have chosen match your needs? Haphazard applications waste postage and time

305

WHO TO APPLY TO Mrs Marion Heeffey, The Hoover Foundation, Pentrebach, Merthyr Tydfil, Mid Glamorgan CF48 4TU *Tel* 01685 721222 *Fax* 01685 725667

CC NO 200274 **ESTABLISHED** 1961

■ Charity Known as the Hop Market

WHAT IS FUNDED Community projects and facilities in the fields of voluntary work, counselling and advisory services. For the benefit of persons who for reason of poverty, sickness or infirmity are in need of financial assistance, care or attention whether young or old

WHO CAN BENEFIT People of all ages; volunteers; disabled people; and those disadvantaged by poverty. There are no restrictions on the disease or medical condition suffered by the beneficiaries

WHERE FUNDING CAN BE GIVEN The City of Worcester

RANGE OF GRANTS £500–£11,500

SAMPLE GRANTS £17,000 to Welfare Rights Centre; £15,000 to Worcester Action for Youth; £11,500 to Worcester Play Council; £11,000 to Citizens' Advice Bureau; £5,000 to Perdiswell Young People's Club; £1,980 to Worcester MIND; £500 to Turning Point; £1,000 to People's Dispensary for Sick Animals

FINANCES *Year* 1997 *Income* £100,841 *Grants* £62,080

TRUSTEES The City Council

HOW TO APPLY Application forms are available from the address under Who To Apply To upon written request

WHO TO APPLY TO David Clifford, Community Leisure Officer, Charity Known as the Hop Market, Worcester City Council, Guildhall, Worcester WR1 2EY

CC NO 244569 **ESTABLISHED** 1964

■ Hope House and Gippeswyk Educational Trust

WHAT IS FUNDED To promote the education of persons who are under the age of 21, are in need of financial assistance and are resident in the area of benefit; the relief of such persons who are in need, hardship or distress

WHO CAN BENEFIT Children and young adults under 21 years of age, especially those in need, hardship or distress

WHERE FUNDING CAN BE GIVEN Former County Borough of Ipswich and the surrounding area

TRUSTEES A Coe, E P Grimwade, J F M MacEwan, E C Nicholls, J E Philpot, W L Pipe, M W Piper, N A Ridley, V B Short

HOW TO APPLY Initial telephone call welcomed

WHO TO APPLY TO Mrs S Maskell, Clerk, Hope House and Gippeswyk Educational Trust, St Mildreds Chambers, 6 Cornhill, Ipswich, Suffolk IP1 1DE *Tel* 01473 258581

CC NO 1068441 **ESTABLISHED** 1998

■ Hope Trust

WHAT IS FUNDED The provision of education and the distribution of literature to combat the misuse and effects of drink and drugs and to promote the principles of Reformed Churches. Charities working in the field of: the advancement of the Christian religion; Anglican bodies; free Church; rehabilitation centres; and health education

WHAT IS NOT FUNDED Building, refurbishment

WHO CAN BENEFIT Individuals and organisations benefiting: Christians; Church of England; Evangelists; Methodists; Quakers; Unitarians and beneficiaries suffering from substance addiction

WHERE FUNDING CAN BE GIVEN UK and overseas, with a preference for Scotland

TYPE OF GRANT Core costs, one-off funding, project, research, recurring costs, running costs, salaries, start-up costs and funding for more than three years will be considered

RANGE OF GRANTS £100–£6,000

FINANCES *Year* 1997 *Income* £110,000 *Grants* £87,000

TRUSTEES Rev G R Barr, Rev Prof A C Cheyne, Prof D A S Ferguson, Very Rev Dr W J G McDonald, Prof M Newlands, Rev Prof D W D Shaw

HOW TO APPLY To the address under Who To Apply To in writing

WHO TO APPLY TO Miss Carole Hope, Secretary, Hope Trust, Drummond Miller, 31–32 Moray Place, Edinburgh EH3 6BZ *Tel* 0131-226 5151

CC NO 800462 **ESTABLISHED** Late nineteenth century

■ The Hope Trust

WHAT IS FUNDED The Trust promotes its ideals of temperance and protestant church reform through education and the distribution of literature. The Trust also supports individuals and organisations who are dedicated to the same aims as itself. Support may also be given to hospices, rehabilitation centres, self help groups and towards counselling on health and social issues

WHAT IS NOT FUNDED No grants for building projects

WHO CAN BENEFIT Organisations benefiting: people of all ages; academics; Baptists; Christians; Church of England; Evangelists; Methodists and those suffering from HIV and AIDs.

WHERE FUNDING CAN BE GIVEN UK and overseas with a particular interest in Scotland

TYPE OF GRANT Capital, core costs, one-off, project, research, recurring costs, running costs, salaries, start-up costs and scholarships for postgraduate research in theology will be considered. Funding may be given for up to two years or over three years

RANGE OF GRANTS £100–£6,000, typical grant £500

SAMPLE GRANTS £14,100 to postgraduate theology students; £10,800 to support field worker in schools for lectures and sports activities: anti drugs/drink; £8,500 to World Alliance of Reformed Churches; £5,500 to Leith Drug Prevention Groups towards running a drop in centre; £5,000 to Church of Scotland towards the Priority Area Fund; £3,870 to Scottish Reformation Society for various publications, postage, etc; £2,000 to National Bible Society; £2,000 to Presbyterian Church of East Africa

FINANCES *Year* 1997 *Income* £119,000 *Grants* £88,000

TRUSTEES Rev G R Barr, Rev Prof A C Cheyne, Prof D A S Ferguson, Very Rev Dr W J G McDonald, Prof G M Newlands, Rev Prof D W D Shaw

PUBLICATIONS Accounts are available from the Trust. Professor J H S Burleigh: *A Church History of Scotland*

HOW TO APPLY Applications should be made in writing to the address under Who To Apply To

WHO TO APPLY TO Miss Carole Hope, Secretary, The Hope Trust, 31–32 Moray Place, Edinburgh EH3 6BZ *Tel* 0131-226 5151 *Fax* 0131-225 2608

SC NO SCO 00987

■ The Sir Anthony Hopkins Charitable Foundation

WHAT IS FUNDED Hostels; personnel and human resource services; support to voluntary and community organisations; film, video, multimedia broadcasting; theatre; theatrical companies, theatre groups; support and self help groups; rehabilitation centres; nature reserves; acting schools; professional, specialist training; bursaries and fees; and social counselling

WHO CAN BENEFIT Organisations and individuals benefiting: children; young adults; older people; actors and entertainment professionals; students of accredited drama schools; unemployed people; volunteers; those in care, fostered and adopted; ex-offenders and those at risk of offending; and those suffering from alcohol and drug addiction

WHERE FUNDING CAN BE GIVEN UK

TYPE OF GRANT One-off, recurrent and project grants. Funds are available for up to three years

RANGE OF GRANTS Usually £250–£2,000

SAMPLE GRANTS £12,987 to Drama Centre London towards fees of school selected students; £10,000 to RAPt (Rehabilitation for Addicted Prisoners Trust) for Hardship Fund for released offenders; £2,000 to Clouds (rehab) House for Alcohol Counselling Course for specific person; £2,000 to National Film School towards production costs of graduation film for a specific student; £2,000 to Bristol Old Vic Theatre School towards fees of a specific student; £2,000 to LAMDA towards fees of a specific student; £2,000 to RADA towards fees of a specific student; £2,000 to East 15 Acting School towards fees of a specific student; £2,000 to Mountview Theatre School towards fees of a specific student; £2,000 to Art Educational School towards fees of a specific student

FINANCES *Year* 1998 *Income* £162,338 *Grants* £158,187

TRUSTEES Sir Anthony Hopkins, Lady Jennifer Hopkins, M J Musgrave, Mrs B Simpson

HOW TO APPLY In writing, all applications acknowledged (where possible). The Trust has set guidelines (available on request) to consider making grants

WHO TO APPLY TO Lady Katherine Lambart, The Sir Anthony Hopkins Charitable Foundation, 25 St George's Court, Brompton Road, London SW3 2AT *Tel* 0171-589 2827 *Fax* 0171-589 9770

CC NO 1018638   **ESTABLISHED** 1993

■ The Charity of Joseph Hopkins

WHAT IS FUNDED Relief of persons resident in the City of Birmingham who are in conditions of need, hardship or distress. To support small local charities

WHO CAN BENEFIT Organisations relieving need particularly for the elderly and children

WHERE FUNDING CAN BE GIVEN City of Birmingham

TYPE OF GRANT Cash

RANGE OF GRANTS £75–£1,500

SAMPLE GRANTS £1,500 to Open Door; £1,500 to St Martin's Youth and Community Centre; £1,000 to Birmingham Christian Centre; £1,000 to Birmingham Rathbone Society; £1,000 to Cotteridge Church; £1,000 to Elizabeth Fitzroy Homes; £1,000 to Get a Head Charity Appeal; £1,000 to HALOW; £1,000 to Harvest Trust; £1,000 to Jericho Community Project

FINANCES *Year* 1997 *Income* £68,292 *Grants* £58,035

TRUSTEES A T Argyle, Miss K Baldwin, A V Blakemore, R Blyth, Miss A Cook, Miss A M Grove, Mrs P B Hodder, A C S Hordern (Bailiff), Miss J Hunter, Mrs J R Jaffa, R Sheldon, R J Sarjeant, R M Woodgate

NOTES In 1997, £11,475 worth of clothing vouchers were distributed, £56,960 was given to organisations and £1,175 was given to individuals

WHO TO APPLY TO H B Carslake, The Clerk to the Trustees, The Joseph Hopkins Charity, Martineau Johnson, St Philip's House, St Philip's Place, Birmingham B3 2PP

CC NO 217303   **ESTABLISHED** 1681

■ The Cuthbert Horn Trust

WHAT IS FUNDED (a) Welfare and support in illness/ old age. (b) Ecology/environmental organisations. We usually approach donees ourselves and do not encourage direct applications

WHAT IS NOT FUNDED No grants to individuals

WHO CAN BENEFIT Registered charities only benefiting older people who are at risk, those disadvantaged by poverty and socially isolated people. There is no restriction on the disease or medical condition suffered by the beneficiaries

WHERE FUNDING CAN BE GIVEN UK

TYPE OF GRANT Starter finances. Single projects. Support for continuing operations

RANGE OF GRANTS £2000–£15000

SAMPLE GRANTS £15,000 to Council and Care for the Elderly; £5,000 to The National Trust for Enterprise Neptune; £5,000 to the Soil Association; £4,000 to COMPAID Trust; £4,000 to the SAFE Charitable Trust; £3,000 to Elm Farm Research Centre; £3,000 to Cotswold Canals Trust; £3,000 to the Island Trust; £3,000 to Pesticide Trust; £2,500 to Schumacher College

FINANCES *Year* 1996 *Income* £77,638 *Grants* £65,500

TRUSTEES Alliance Assurance Company Ltd, A H Flint

HOW TO APPLY No applications will be answered as the Trust is fully committed with projects and pledges for some years to come. Grants are made annually in the Autumn

WHO TO APPLY TO H C D Matthews, The Cuthbert Horn Trust, Sun Alliance Trust Co Ltd, 40 Chancery Lane, London WC2A 1JN

CC NO 291465   **ESTABLISHED** 1985

■ The Antony Hornby Charitable Trust

WHAT IS FUNDED Flexible, but mainly medical research, and the arts. Also help for the aged and sick, and disabled, disadvantaged youth, homes and holidays

WHAT IS NOT FUNDED No longer consider appeals outside London and the Home Counties unless they have a particular connection with one of the Trustees. No grants to individuals. No grants to localised building projects for the arts, etc

WHO CAN BENEFIT Organisations benefiting people of all ages, medical professionals, those involved in the arts and disabled people

WHERE FUNDING CAN BE GIVEN London and the Home Counties

FINANCES *Year* 1997 *Income* £40,060

TRUSTEES Mrs M A Hall, Miss J King, M A Loveday, D M Wentworth-Stanley

WHO TO APPLY TO Miss Fiona Grainger, The Antony Hornby Charitable Trust, Deloitte & Touche, Leda House, Station Road, Cambridge CB1 2RN

CC NO 263285   **ESTABLISHED** 1971

◼ Miss D Hornby Charitable Trust

WHAT IS FUNDED Aged, cancer, children's charities and the arts

WHAT IS NOT FUNDED No grants are made to individuals, students, religious denominations, churches

WHO CAN BENEFIT Organisations benefiting: children and the aged; actors and entertainment professionals; musicians; textile workers and designers; writers and poets; and those suffering from cancer

WHERE FUNDING CAN BE GIVEN UK

FINANCES *Year* 1997 *Income* £14,542
Grants £12,850

TRUSTEES Mrs Timothy Cobb, Lady Holland-Martin, DBE, DL

WHO TO APPLY TO Mrs Timothy Cobb, Miss D Hornby Charitable Trust, Horsemoor House, Chieveley, Newbury, Berkshire RG20 8XE

CC NO 266001   **ESTABLISHED** 1973

◼ Mrs E G Hornby's Charitable Settlement

WHAT IS FUNDED General charitable purposes, with particular interest in the fields of animal welfare, the disabled, the elderly and hospices

WHO CAN BENEFIT Registered charities only. There are no restrictions on the age; professional and economic group; family situation; religion and culture; and social circumstances of; or disease or medical condition suffered by, the beneficiaries. However, particular favour is given to the elderly and disabled people

WHERE FUNDING CAN BE GIVEN UK

RANGE OF GRANTS £200–£10,000

SAMPLE GRANTS £10,000 to Countryside Foundation; £5,000 to Romanian Challenge Appeal; £4,000 to Cancer Relief Macmillan Fund; £3,800 to St Christopher's Hospice; £3,800 to St Michael's Hospice Development Fund; £3,800 to St Richard's Hospice; £3,000 to Queen Elizabeth's Foundation for the Disabled; £3,000 to St Mungo's Association Charitable Trust; £2,000 to Martin House Children's Hospice; £2,000 to People's Dispensary for Sick Animals

FINANCES *Year* 1997 *Income* £56,287
Grants £59,800

TRUSTEES Kleinwort Benson Trustees Limited, N J M Lonsdale, Mrs P M W Smith-Maxwell

NOTES New donations are normally considered only for national charities, and the Trustees usually only support charities already known to them

HOW TO APPLY Appeal in writing to the address under Who To Apply To. Only successful applications will be notified of the Trustees' decision

WHO TO APPLY TO Mrs E G Hornby's Charitable Settlement, Kleinwort Benson Trustees Limited, PO Box 191, 10 Fenchurch Street, London EC3M 3LB

CC NO 243516   **ESTABLISHED** 1965

◼ The Hornsey Parochial Charities

WHAT IS FUNDED General benefit of poor persons residing in Old Hornsey

WHAT IS NOT FUNDED Residential qualification needed. No commitment to continuous grants

WHO CAN BENEFIT Individuals and organisations benefiting those disadvantaged by poverty

WHERE FUNDING CAN BE GIVEN The Ancient Parish of Hornsey (North London)

FINANCES *Year* 1997 *Income* £50,000
Grants £42,700

TRUSTEES Chairman and 12 other Trustees

HOW TO APPLY In writing

WHO TO APPLY TO Clerk to the Trustees, The Hornsey Parochial Charities, 47 The Chine, London N10 3PX

CC NO 229410   **ESTABLISHED** 1890

◼ The Hornton Charity

WHAT IS FUNDED General charitable purposes in the West Midlands area, particularly in the arts and medicine

WHO CAN BENEFIT There are no restrictions on the age; professional and economic group; family situation; religion and culture; and social circumstances of; or disease or medical condition suffered by, the beneficiaries. However, particular favour is given to medical professional, arts practitioners and the sick

WHERE FUNDING CAN BE GIVEN The Midlands

RANGE OF GRANTS £250–£2,000

SAMPLE GRANTS £2,000 to Schools Outreach; £2,000 to St Martin's Restoration Fund; £1,200 to PHAB Camps; £1,000 to Adullam House; £1,000 to Birmingham City Mission; £1,000 to Birmingham Royal Institute for the Blind; £1,000 to Children Nationwide; £1,000 to Cruse; £1,000 to Edgbaston High School; £1,000 to Evangelical Alliance

FINANCES *Year* 1996 *Income* £51,209
Grants £42,190

TRUSTEES A C S Hordern, S M Wall, S W B Landale, A R Collins

WHO TO APPLY TO Price Waterhouse, The Hornton Charity, Cornwall Court, 19 Cornwall Street, Birmingham B3 2DT

CC NO 266352   **ESTABLISHED** 1973

◼ The Hospital of God at Greatham

WHAT IS FUNDED Preference is given to projects involving accommodation, the elderly, local initiatives aimed at the disadvantaged, needy and oppressed, particularly charities working in the fields of social care professional bodies, respite care, nursing homes, rehabilitation centres and various community services

WHAT IS NOT FUNDED Grants are not made to CAB's and similar organisations, nor for pure youth work, capital building costs, repairs to buildings or purely medical related issues

WHO CAN BENEFIT Charities, voluntary organisations and individuals. Note: Grants are only made to individuals when the application originates from Social Service offices and other Agencies with which the Charity has established arrangements. Children; young adults; older people; at risk groups; carers; disabled people; those disadvantaged by poverty; the homeless; the socially isolated; victims of abuse and domestic violence; and those suffering from Alzheimer's disease; epilepsy and hearing loss will be considered

WHERE FUNDING CAN BE GIVEN Darlington, Durham, Gateshead, Hartlepool, Newcastle upon Tyne, Northumberland, North Tyneside, South Tyneside, Stockton on Tees and Sunderland

TYPE OF GRANT One-off, capital, core funding, running costs and salaries. Funding for one year or less will be considered

SAMPLE GRANTS £12,000 to Cleveland Alzheimer's Society; £8,000 to Baby Equipment Loan Service, Newcastle; £6,500 to Coatham House, Redcar; £5,000 to Cleveland Youth Association, Middlesbrough; £5,000 to Caring Hands, Newcastle; £4,000 to Shopmobility, Hartlepool; £3,000 to Hartlepool Centre for the Deaf; £3,000 to Blyth Detached Project; £3,000 to Manor Residents Association, Hartlepool; £3,000 to MIND, Hartlepool

FINANCES *Year* 1997 *Income* £1,000,000 *Grants* £100,000

TRUSTEES N D Abram, Rev D C Couling, Ven P Elliott, Dr R Etchells, P Jackson, A A Kennedy, C Porter, R N Spark, Mrs J T Thomas, Dr H Welsh, Ven T Willmott

HOW TO APPLY No application form. Applications to the Correspondent with budgets and accounts. Grants are awarded quarterly in January, April, July and October. The Correspondent is happy to answer initial telephone queries

WHO TO APPLY TO H Cartwright, The Hospital of God at Greatham, Estate Office, Hartlepool TS25 2HS *Tel* 01429 870247 *Fax* 01429 871469

CC NO 228571   **ESTABLISHED** 1273

■ The Hospital Saturday Fund Charitable Trust

WHAT IS FUNDED The support of hospitals, hospices and medical charities for care and research; to aid individuals whose poor health has entailed financial hardship. Various residential facilities and services will also be considered

WHO CAN BENEFIT Charities; hospitals and hospices; individuals. There is no restriction on the disease or medical condition of the beneficiaries

WHERE FUNDING CAN BE GIVEN UK and Ireland

TYPE OF GRANT One-off grants

RANGE OF GRANTS £500–£1,000 for an organisation, usually up to £150 for an individual

SAMPLE GRANTS £1,000 to Sue Ryder Foundation; £1,000 to St John Ambulance; £1,000 to Glasgow Royal Infirmary

FINANCES *Year* 1996–97 *Income* £105,049 *Grants* £108,158

TRUSTEES Mrs P Shaw (Chairperson), L Fellman, A Tierney, K R Bradley, K Fleming Roberts, H Palma, E W Smith

HOW TO APPLY Only from those outlined under What Is Funded; organisations are invited to write detailed letters or send a brochure and accompanying letter. Individuals can obtain a form from the Personal Assistant to be addressed to the Trust Administrator

WHO TO APPLY TO K R Bradley, Administrator, The Hospital Saturday Fund Charitable Trust, 24 Upper Ground, London SE1 9PD *Tel* 0171-928 6662

CC NO 327693   **ESTABLISHED** 1987

■ Hospital Saving Association Charitable Trust

WHAT IS FUNDED The relief of sickness and the furtherance of medical research

WHAT IS NOT FUNDED Only applications in the areas covered by What Is Funded will be considered

WHO CAN BENEFIT Medical professionals, nurses and doctors; research workers. There is no restriction on the disease or medical condition surrered by the beneficiaries. Preference will be given to smaller charities and locally based charities

WHERE FUNDING CAN BE GIVEN UK

TYPE OF GRANT Grants for capital and project costs

RANGE OF GRANTS £500–£10,000

SAMPLE GRANTS Kent Association for the Blind, Maidstone; Age Concern, Coventry; Huddersfield Epilepsy Group; Children's Liver Disease Foundation, Birmingham; Wirral Rehab Mental Health, Birkenhead

FINANCES *Year* 1997–98 *Income* £1,064,000

TRUSTEES P S Howard (Chairman), I D Adam, P Benner, R H Crawford, J A Elliott, Mrs C G Lemon

PUBLICATIONS *Hospital Saving Association Charitable Trust* Information Brochure

HOW TO APPLY In writing to the Secretary to the Trustees at the address under Who To Apply To, including a copy of the most recent audited accounts

WHO TO APPLY TO James Young, Secretary to the Trustees, Hospital Saving Association Charitable Trust, Hambleden House, Andover, Hampshire SP10 1LQ *Tel* 01264 353211

CC NO 263521   **ESTABLISHED** 1972

■ Houblon-Norman Fund

WHAT IS FUNDED Research into the interaction and function of financial and business institutions and the economic conditions affecting them – dissemination of knowledge thereof. In considering applications the Trustees will pay particular regard to the relevance of the research to current problems in economics and finance

WHAT IS NOT FUNDED Grants are not awarded. Fellowships are tenable at the Bank of England. The research work to be undertaken is intended to be whole-time work, and teaching or other paid work must not be undertaken during the tenure of the Fellowship, without the specific consent of the Trustees

WHO CAN BENEFIT Organisations benefiting academics, research workers and students

WHERE FUNDING CAN BE GIVEN UK

TYPE OF GRANT Research

FINANCES *Year* 1996–97 *Income* £80,953 *Grants* £26,667

TRUSTEES Deputy Governor of The Bank of England, Sir Jeremy Morse, C J Allsopp

WHO TO APPLY TO Ms M F Wilson, Houblon-Norman Fund, c/o Secretary's Department, HO-1, Bank of England, Threadneedle Street, London EC2R 8AH *Tel* 0171-601 4751 *Fax* 0171-601 3668

CC NO 213168   **ESTABLISHED** 1944

■ The Howard Charitable Trust

WHAT IS FUNDED To make grants to selected causes and to provide finance for recreation for the elderly and handicapped, general religious purposes and education

WHAT IS NOT FUNDED No restrictions except as far as funds are concerned

WHO CAN BENEFIT Individuals and organisations benefiting: people of all ages; students and disabled people. There is no restriction on the religion or culture of the beneficiaries

WHERE FUNDING CAN BE GIVEN UK with preference for Midlands

TYPE OF GRANT Buildings, capital, core costs, endowments, feasibility studies, interest free loans, one-off, project, research, recurring costs, running costs, salaries and start-up costs. Funding can be given for up to or more than three years

RANGE OF GRANTS Typical grant £100–£200

FINANCES *Year* 1997 *Income* £15,854 *Grants* £14,873

TRUSTEES K H A Smith, Mrs B M Hodgskin-Brown, D P Ensell, M J W Hodgskin-Brown, A J Parker

Does the trust you have chosen match your needs? Haphazard applications waste postage and time

309

HOW TO APPLY In writing please
WHO TO APPLY TO K H A Smith, The Howard Charitable Trust, 1 Sherbourne Road, Acocks Green, Birmingham B27 6AB
CC NO 274309   **ESTABLISHED** 1977

■ John & Ruth Howard Charitable Trust

WHAT IS FUNDED Advancement of public education in archaeology; preservation of historical and religious buildings; choir schools; community arts and recreation; and architecture
WHAT IS NOT FUNDED No grants to individuals
WHO CAN BENEFIT Organisations benefiting young adults and students
WHERE FUNDING CAN BE GIVEN England and Wales
TYPE OF GRANT Funding for single project; maximum grant is £5,000
FINANCES *Year* 1995 *Income* £88,796
Grants £54,998
TRUSTEES A S Atchison, Miss N O Feldman, J H Hillier, R N Hobson
HOW TO APPLY In writing to A S Atchison at address below. Trustees meet every three to six months
WHO TO APPLY TO A S Atchison, John & Ruth Howard Charitable Trust, 111 High Road, Willesden Green, London NW10 2TB
CC NO 1005072   **ESTABLISHED** 1991

■ The Reta Lila Howard Foundation

WHAT IS FUNDED General charitable purposes
WHO CAN BENEFIT There are no restrictions on the age; professional and economic group; family situation; religion and culture; and social circumstances of; or disease or medical condition suffered by, the beneficiaries
WHERE FUNDING CAN BE GIVEN UK
FINANCES *Year* 1997 *Income* £504,105
HOW TO APPLY **This Trust states that it does not respond to unsolicited applications**
WHO TO APPLY TO Jamestown Investments Limited, The Reta Lila Howard Foundation, 4 Felstead Gardens, Ferry Street, London E14 3BS
CC NO 1041634   **ESTABLISHED** 1994

■ Clifford Howarth Charity Trust

WHAT IS FUNDED General charitable purposes
WHAT IS NOT FUNDED No grants to individuals, for scholarships or non-local special projects
WHO CAN BENEFIT Local and national registered charities which were supported by the Founder. There are no restrictions on the age; professional and economic group; family situation; religion and culture; and social circumstances of; or disease or medical condition suffered by, the beneficiaries
WHERE FUNDING CAN BE GIVEN Within Burnley or Rosensdale areas of Lancashire
TYPE OF GRANT One-off
SAMPLE GRANTS £1,000 to local church; £1,000 to RSPCA
FINANCES *Year* 1998 *Income* £37,700
Grants £37,000
TRUSTEES M Fenton, J Howarth, E Howarth
NOTES Grants are distributed annually in February and March
WHO TO APPLY TO The Trustees, Clifford Howarth Charity Trust, c/o Lambert Howarth & Sons Ltd, Healey Royd Works, Healey Royd Road, Burnley, Lancashire BB11 2HL
CC NO 264890   **ESTABLISHED** 1972

■ The James Thom Howat Charitable Trust

WHAT IS FUNDED Grants are given to a range of organisations, including universities, cultural bodies and those caring for the sick. Support may also be given to charities working in the fields of: community services; community centres and village halls; special needs education; voluntary and community organisations; and volunteers
WHO CAN BENEFIT Individuals and organisations benefiting: ex-service and service people; musicians; research workers; seafarers and fishermen; sportsmen and women; students; unemployed people, volunteers; writers and poets. Funding may also be given to at risk groups, carers and disabled people, those disadvantaged by poverty, homeless people, refugees, victims of abuse, crime and domestic violence. There is no restriction on the age or the disease or medical condition suffered by the beneficiaries
WHERE FUNDING CAN BE GIVEN Scotland, especially Glasgow
TYPE OF GRANT Some grants are made to individuals for educational purposes. Core costs, one-off, project, research, running costs and start-up costs will be considered
SAMPLE GRANTS £10,000 to Crossroads (Scotland) Care Attendant Scheme; £10,000 to Eastpark Home for Infirm Children; £8,000 to University of Glasgow for needy students; £8,000 to University of Strathclyde for needy students; £5,000 to Royal Blind Asylum and School; £5,000 to Yorkhill Hospital for Sick Children; £4,250 to National Blind/Deaf Rubella Association; £4,000 to Aged in Distress; £4,000 to Alzheimer's Scotland; £4,000 to Capability Scotland
FINANCES *Year* 1996–97 *Income* £223,000
Grants £199,750
TRUSTEES Leslie Duncan, Christine Howat, James Howat, Russell Howat, Gordon Wyllie
PUBLICATIONS Accounts are available from the Trust
HOW TO APPLY Applications should be made in writing to the address under Who To Apply To and must include an explanation of the scheme as well as the most recent Report and Accounts. Applications are considered quarterly
WHO TO APPLY TO Mrs Lane, The James Thom Howat Charitable Trust, Biggart, Baillie, Dalmore House, 310 St Vincent Street, Glasgow G2 5QR
Tel 0141-228 8000
SC NO SCO 000201

■ The Hubert Charitable Trust

WHAT IS FUNDED General charitable purposes
WHO CAN BENEFIT There are no restrictions on the age; professional and economic group; family situation; religion and culture; and social circumstances of; or disease or medical condition suffered by, the beneficiaries
WHERE FUNDING CAN BE GIVEN UK
TRUSTEES W I Hubert, M L Hooper
WHO TO APPLY TO The Hubert Charitable Trust, Messrs Porter, Matthews & Marsden, Chartered Accountants, Oakmount, 6 East Park Road, Blackburn, Lancashire BB1 8BW
CC NO 264028   **ESTABLISHED** 1971

■ The Walter Hubert Charitable Trust

WHAT IS FUNDED Jewish educational institutions
WHO CAN BENEFIT Jewish educational institutions benefiting children, young adults and students
WHERE FUNDING CAN BE GIVEN Israel
RANGE OF GRANTS £160–£48,503
SAMPLE GRANTS £48,503 to College of Judea and Samaria; £35,366 to Mechinat School; £32,911 to Beth Shammai Grammar School; £25,000 to Sde Chemea Children's Village; £21,004 to Yeshivat Zville, Jerusalem
FINANCES *Year* 1995 *Income* £21,488 *Grants* £255,664
TRUSTEES W Herbert, M L Hooper
HOW TO APPLY **Trust fully committed. No further applications to be made until further notice**
WHO TO APPLY TO The Walter Hubert Charitable Trust, Messrs Porter Matthews & Marsden, Oak Mount, 6 East Park Road, Blackburn, Lancashire BB1 8BW
CC NO 266759   **ESTABLISHED** 1973

■ The Huddersfield Common Good Trust

WHAT IS FUNDED Youth and community groups, children, the elderly and general welfare organisations
WHAT IS NOT FUNDED Applications for funding for religious bodies, central/local government departments, individuals or national organisations will not be considered
WHO CAN BENEFIT Organisations benefiting: people of all ages; at risk groups; carers; disabled people; those disadvantaged by poverty; homeless people and victims of domestic violence.
WHERE FUNDING CAN BE GIVEN The old County Borough of Huddersfield
TYPE OF GRANT Buildings and capital grants will be considered
FINANCES *Year* 1998 *Income* £33,000 *Grants* £28,000
TRUSTEES R Butterworth, J M Fryer, G C Grimwood, Miss V Javin, J A Russell, Miss S Stott, Dr L Sykes, P J Hoyle
PUBLICATIONS Information leaflet
HOW TO APPLY To the address under Who To Apply To in writing
WHO TO APPLY TO A Haigh, Secretary, The Huddersfield Common Good Trust, PO Box 382, Huddersfield HD1 2YN
CC NO 2231096   **ESTABLISHED** 1964

■ The Huddersfield Medical Trust Fund

WHAT IS FUNDED The treatment and care of the sick and infirm within the area Where Funding Can Be Given
WHO CAN BENEFIT There is no restriction on the disease or medical condition suffered by the beneficiaries
WHERE FUNDING CAN BE GIVEN The Huddersfield district of Kirklees Area Health Authority
FINANCES *Year* 1994–95 *Income* £23,288
HOW TO APPLY To the address below in writing
WHO TO APPLY TO Dr M G Miller, The Huddersfield Medical Trust Fund, c/o Huddersfield Royal Infirmary, Acre Street, Lindley, Huddersfield HD3 3EA
CC NO 512734   **ESTABLISHED** 1982

■ The Huddersfield War Memorial Trust Fund

WHAT IS FUNDED Service charities, related organisations working with the elderly
WHAT IS NOT FUNDED No grants for expeditions or scholarships
WHO CAN BENEFIT Local organisations or national organisations with local branches benefiting: people of all ages; those disadvantaged by poverty; and at risk groups
WHERE FUNDING CAN BE GIVEN Huddersfield only
TYPE OF GRANT Recurrent, occasionally one-off
RANGE OF GRANTS £500–£5,000
FINANCES *Year* 1995 *Income* £18,386 *Grants* £19,225
TRUSTEES D P Crowther (Chairman), P Broadbent (Vice Chairman), J R Sugden (Secretary), C Russell, S M Armitage, R A Hawkins, C Brook, W Sack, S Rothery, I Fillan
NOTES Grants only paid to Huddersfield based services charities or Huddersfield based convalescent home caring for those in necessitous circumstances
HOW TO APPLY To the address under Who To Apply To in writing
WHO TO APPLY TO J R Sugden, Trustee and Secretary, The Huddersfield War Memorial Trust Fund, 17 Foxglove Road, Huddersfield HD5 8LW *Tel* 01422 832501
CC NO 220016   **ESTABLISHED** 1922

■ The Huggard Charitable Trust

WHAT IS FUNDED Advancement of religion, the relief of poverty, and the relief of people incapacitated by old age or disability
WHO CAN BENEFIT Older people, disabled people and those disadvantaged by poverty. There is no restriction on the religion or culture of the beneficiaries
WHERE FUNDING CAN BE GIVEN UK
FINANCES *Year* 1996 *Income* £746,493 *Grants* £40,918
TRUSTEES G J Davies, Mrs E M Huggard, R J Huggard
WHO TO APPLY TO G J Davies, The Huggard Charitable Trust, Coopers & Lybrand, Princess House, Princess Way, Swanley SA1 5LH
CC NO 327501   **ESTABLISHED** 1987

■ The Geoffrey C Hughes Charitable Trust

WHAT IS FUNDED Essentially interested in two areas: nature conservation/environment and performing arts, particularly ballet or opera with a bias towards modern work
WHAT IS NOT FUNDED No grants to individuals
WHO CAN BENEFIT Actors and entertainment professionals and musicians
WHERE FUNDING CAN BE GIVEN UK
TYPE OF GRANT Small and large grants
FINANCES *Year* 1995 *Income* £47,522
TRUSTEES J R Young, P C M Solon, R Hillman
HOW TO APPLY Initial applications in writing, prefer details if possible
WHO TO APPLY TO P C M Solon, Trustee, The Geoffrey C Hughes Charitable Trust, Beachcroft Stanleys, 20 Furnival Street, London EC4A 1BN
CC NO 1010079   **ESTABLISHED** 1992

■ The Hull & East Riding Charitable Trust

WHAT IS FUNDED Charitable purposes in Hull and East Riding of Yorkshire

WHAT IS NOT FUNDED No organisations/causes of political nature or for religious purposes. Unlikely to support individuals

WHO CAN BENEFIT There are no restrictions on the age; professional and economic group; family situation; religion and culture; and social circumstances of; or disease or medical condition suffered by, the beneficiaries

WHERE FUNDING CAN BE GIVEN Hull and East Riding of Yorkshire

TYPE OF GRANT Prefer to fund capital costs of a project but will consider funding revenue costs over a limited period of time

SAMPLE GRANTS £10,000 to Hull YWCA; £7,900 to Raleigh International Youth Development Programme; £6,750 to University of Hull for equipment for cancer research; £5,000 to Barnardo's; £5,000 to Bishop Burton Riding for the Disabled Association for an extension to premises; £5,000 to British Red Cross, Humberside Branch for expansion of transport and escort service to rural areas; £5,000 to Girascope Limited; £5,000 to Hull Compact Limited; £5,000 to Hull Independent Housing Aid Centre; £5,000 to Lifestyle Rock Challenge

FINANCES *Year* 1997 *Income* £230,102 *Grants* £144,305

TRUSTEES M J Hollingbery, Mrs M R Barker, A M Horsley, JP

PUBLICATIONS Annual accounts. Trust guidelines

HOW TO APPLY Donations considered at meetings in May and November. Applications must be received by 30 April and 31 October

WHO TO APPLY TO H C Palmer, Queen Victoria House, Guildhall Road, Hull HU1 1HH
Tel 01482 224111 *Fax* 01482 327479
CC NO 516866   **ESTABLISHED** 1985

■ The Rudi and Resi Hulse Charity

WHAT IS FUNDED Health, disability and Jewish charitable purposes

WHO CAN BENEFIT Organisations benefiting Jewish people, the disabled, medical professionals, carers and rabbis. There is no restriction on the disease or medical condition suffered by the beneficiaries

WHERE FUNDING CAN BE GIVEN UK and overseas

RANGE OF GRANTS £25,000–£100,000

SAMPLE GRANTS £100,000 to B B Administration Company Ltd; £75,000 to Cancerkin (RFH); £75,000 to Friends of Shaare Zedek Medical Centre; £50,000 to Friends of the Israeli War Disabled; £50,000 to Jewish Childs Day; £25,000 to British Technion Society; £25,000 to Friends of the Hebrew University; £25,000 to Friends of Jerusalem College of Technology; £25,000 to Tel Aviv University Trust; £25,000 to Weizmann Institute Foundation

FINANCES *Year* 1995 *Income* £553,046 *Grants* £475,000

TRUSTEES A C Kaufman, H Rothenberg, OBE, W D Rothenberg, P W Summerfield

HOW TO APPLY To the address under Who To Apply To in writing

WHO TO APPLY TO Robin Marks, The Rudi and Resi Hulse Charity, Messrs Blick Rothenberg, 12 York Gate, Regents Park, London NW1 4QS
CC NO 282135   **ESTABLISHED** 1981

■ Human Relief Foundation

WHAT IS FUNDED General charitable purposes for the relief of poverty, sickness and to protect and preserve good health and advance education of those in need from impoverished countries in particular Somalia, Bosnia, Iraq, Bangladesh and Lebanon. Infrastructure, support and development and cultural activity are also funded

WHAT IS NOT FUNDED No grants to individuals, or for medical expenses, tutors or examination fees

WHO CAN BENEFIT Organisations benefiting: at risk groups; carers; disabled people; those disadvantaged by poverty; refugees; victims of famine, man-made or natural disasters and war. Medical professionals, scientists, unemployed people and volunteers will be supported. There is no restriction on the age or family situation of, or disease or medical condition suffered by, the beneficiaries

WHERE FUNDING CAN BE GIVEN Somalia, Bosnia, Iraq and other regions requiring urgent relief/aid

FINANCES *Year* 1996 *Income* £131,956

WHO TO APPLY TO Dr N S Al-Ramadhani, Human Relief Foundation, PO Box 194, Bradford, West Yorkshire BD7 1YW *Tel* 01274 392727
CC NO 1043676   **ESTABLISHED** 1995

■ The Humanitarian Trust

WHAT IS FUNDED Main fields of support are educational, medical and social welfare. Individual applicants for educational grants must hold a basic grant. Particularly charities working in the fields of: hospices, medical centres; schools and colleges; speech therapy; bursaries and fees; archaeology; economics; engineering; law; medicine; physics; and libraries and museums

WHAT IS NOT FUNDED The Trustees do not fund overseas courses, fieldwork or travel or any arts subject such as music, dance, theatre, journalism, film, etc

WHO CAN BENEFIT At the discretion of Trustees. Organisations benefiting: young adults; academics; students; (graduate and postgraduate level only); disabled people; refugees; and beneficiaries suffering from diabetes, mental illness and spina bifida and hydrocephalus

WHERE FUNDING CAN BE GIVEN UK and overseas, with preference to London

TYPE OF GRANT One-off grants

RANGE OF GRANTS £200

FINANCES *Year* 1997 *Income* £31,444 *Grants* £33,328

TRUSTEES M Jacques Gunsbourg, Pierre Halban, Lord Rothschild

HOW TO APPLY No application form or deadline for applications

WHO TO APPLY TO Mrs M Myers, The Humanitarian Trust, 36–38 Westbourne Grove, London W2 5SH
CC NO 208575   **ESTABLISHED** 1946

■ Humber Power Charitable Trust

WHAT IS FUNDED General charitable purposes

WHO CAN BENEFIT There are no restrictions on the age; professional and economic group; family situation; religion and culture; and social circumstances of; or disease or medical condition suffered by, the beneficiaries

WHERE FUNDING CAN BE GIVEN UK and overseas

TRUSTEES S Jackson, P Evans, J Groves, D Keedy

WHO TO APPLY TO S Jackson, Humber Power Charitable Trust, South Humber Bank Power Station, Stallingborough, North East Lincolnshire DN41 8BZ
CC NO 1064339   **ESTABLISHED** 1997

■ The Michael and Shirley Hunt Charitable Trust

WHAT IS FUNDED Relief of need, hardship or distress of prisoners and/or their families; relieving the suffering of animals
WHAT IS NOT FUNDED No grants for fines, bail and legal costs, etc
WHO CAN BENEFIT To benefit prisoners and/or their families; those charged with criminal offences and held in custody; unwanted, sick or ill-treated animals of any species
WHERE FUNDING CAN BE GIVEN UK and overseas
TYPE OF GRANT One-off
RANGE OF GRANTS £100–£5,300, typical grant £2,100
SAMPLE GRANTS £5,300 to Brighton YMCA for one year's funding for emergency accommodation for East Sussex Probation Service; £3,300 to an individual for five months employment sponsorship; £3,000 to NACRO as a donation to welfare fund; £1,000 to Federation of Prisoners' Families Support Group as a donation; £100 to an individual for the transportation of clothing from Norwich to Bristol
FINANCES *Year* 1997–98 *Grants* £12,800
TRUSTEES W J Baker, C J Hunt, S E Hunt, D S Jenkins, K D McMullen
HOW TO APPLY In writing
WHO TO APPLY TO Mrs D S Jenkins, Trustee, The Michael and Shirley Hunt Charitable Trust, Ansty House, High Street, Henfield, West Sussex BN5 9DA *Tel* 01273 492233 *Fax* 01273 492273
CC NO 1063418   **ESTABLISHED** 1997

■ The Albert Hunt Trust

WHAT IS FUNDED Projects concerned with homelessness, the elderly, youth, health, medical research and rehabilitation
WHO CAN BENEFIT Large national charities benefiting people of all ages, homeless people, medical professionals and research workers. There is no restriction on the disease or medical condition suffered by the beneficiaries
WHERE FUNDING CAN BE GIVEN UK
RANGE OF GRANTS Typical grant £3,000
SAMPLE GRANTS £3,000 to Aid to the Church in Need; £3,000 to British Heart Foundation; £3,000 to Catholic Children's Society; £3,000 to Greater London Fund for the Blind; £3,000 to Help the Aged; £3,000 to Leukaemia Research Fund; £3,000 to Little Sisters of the Poor; £3,000 to Providence Row (Night Refuge and Home); £3,000 to Shelter; £3,000 to St Christopher Hospice
FINANCES *Year* 1997 *Income* £8,194,816 *Grants* £156,000
TRUSTEES Miss M K Coyle, Mrs McGuire, Coutts & Co
NOTES Only successful applications will be acknowledged. Please note that the above income figure is unusually large due to the addition of a legacy to the Trust's capital assets
HOW TO APPLY To the address under Who To Apply To in writing

WHO TO APPLY TO R J Collis, Trust Manager, The Albert Hunt Trust, Messrs Coutts & Co, Trustee Department, 440 Strand, London WC2R 0QS
CC NO 277318   **ESTABLISHED** 1979

■ The Patrick Mitchell Hunter Fund

WHAT IS FUNDED To support charities or philanthropic institutions operating in the city of Aberdeen
WHAT IS NOT FUNDED No grants to individuals
WHO CAN BENEFIT All types of deserving charities based in Aberdeen. There are no restrictions on the age; professional and economic group; family situation; religion and culture; and social circumstances of; or disease or medical condition suffered by, the beneficiaries
WHERE FUNDING CAN BE GIVEN City of Aberdeen only
TYPE OF GRANT Discretionary
FINANCES *Year* 1997 *Income* £15,800 *Grants* £10,000
TRUSTEES J T C Gillan, W Howie
PUBLICATIONS Accounts are available from the Trust
HOW TO APPLY Contact the address below for further details
WHO TO APPLY TO The Patrick Mitchell Hunter Fund, Wilsone & Duffus, PO Box No 81, 7 Golden Square, Aberdeen, Scotland AB10 1EP *Tel* 01224 641065 *Fax* 01224 647329 *E-mail* info@wilsoneduffus.co.uk
SC NO SCO 17380   **ESTABLISHED** 1954

■ Miss Agnes H Hunter's Trust

WHAT IS FUNDED Charities assisting blind people in Scotland; disabled people; training and education for disadvantaged people; those working towards an established cause, relief or cure for cancer; tuberculosis or rheumatism. These aims are also pursued in the fields of children and family support; youth development; the elderly; homelessness; and mental illness
WHAT IS NOT FUNDED Applications for funding for government organisations are not considered. No grants to individuals
WHO CAN BENEFIT Organisations benefiting people of all ages; unemployed; volunteers; those in care, fostered and adopted; parents and children; and one parent families will be considered. Carers, disabled people, those disadvantaged by poverty, and homeless and socially isolated people may be supported, as well as those suffering from a variety of diseases or medical conditions
WHERE FUNDING CAN BE GIVEN Scotland with a preference for Edinburgh
TYPE OF GRANT Mainly one-off, buildings, capital, core costs, feasibility studies, projects, research and start-up costs will be considered. Funding is available for up to two years
RANGE OF GRANTS £1,000–£8,000, typical grant £2,500–£3,000

Does the trust you have chosen match your needs? Haphazard applications waste postage and time

313

SAMPLE GRANTS £10,750 to Youth Clubs Scotland for an allocation scheme to assist local youth clubs undertake new activities and attend events; £10,000 to Princess Royal Trust for Carers towards two carers centres in Dumfries and Paisley; £10,000 to Scottish Housing Association Charitable Trust towards housing projects for disabled people; £8,000 to Arthritis Research Campaign for rheumatological research; £8,000 to Bethany Christian Trust for life skills and independent living courses and a supported housing team; £8,000 to Cancer Research Campaign for cancer research in Dundee; £8,000 to Shelter, Scotland for the Edinburgh Housing Aid Centre; £7,500 to Alzheimer, Scotland, Action on Dementia for a carer education programme; £7,000 to Macmillan Cancer Relief for Macmillan services in the Highlands

FINANCES *Year* 1997–98 *Income* £267,000
Grants £223,750

TRUSTEES W F MacTaggart, WS, N D S Paterson, WS

PUBLICATIONS An explanatory leaflet is available from the address under Who To Apply To

HOW TO APPLY To the address under Who To Apply To in writing. Closing dates for applications: 1 September and 15 January each year

WHO TO APPLY TO Mrs Jane Paterson, Grants Administrator, Miss Agnes H Hunter's Trust, Robson McLean WS, 28 Abercromby Place, Edinburgh EH3 6QF

SC NO SCO 004843   **ESTABLISHED** 1954

■ The Huntingdon Foundation Limited

WHAT IS FUNDED Jewish organisations

WHO CAN BENEFIT Organisations benefiting Jewish people

WHERE FUNDING CAN BE GIVEN UK and overseas

TYPE OF GRANT One-off

FINANCES *Year* 1995–96 *Income* £1,700,000
Grants £677,000

TRUSTEES B Perl, S Perl, Mrs S Perl

NOTES Grants are usually considered in March, June, September and December

HOW TO APPLY To the address under Who To Apply To in writing

WHO TO APPLY TO Mrs S Perl, Secretary, The Huntingdon Foundation Limited, Forframe House, 35–37 Brent Street, London NW4 2EF

CC NO 286504   **ESTABLISHED** 1984

■ Huntingdon Freemen's Charity

WHAT IS FUNDED General charitable purposes for the benefit of the inhabitants of Huntingdon in particular, paying pensions, relief in need, promotion of education, support in the interests of social welfare by providing facilities for recreation

WHO CAN BENEFIT Organisations benefiting: children, young adults and students; at risk groups; those disadvantaged by poverty and socially isolated people

WHERE FUNDING CAN BE GIVEN Huntingdon

FINANCES *Year* 1997 *Income* £481,367
Grants £279,217

TRUSTEES M A Bloomfield, E G Bocking, P C Booth, E G T Cooper, J R Hough, R D Lamb, B Robertson

NOTES In 1997 grants were totalling: £158,278 for Relief in Need; £97,979 for education; £22,958 for recreation; and £38 for pensions

WHO TO APPLY TO C Jackson, Huntingdon Freemen's Charity, 3 Lansdowne Road, Cambridge CB3 0EU

CC NO 1044573   **ESTABLISHED** 1993

■ Hurdale Charity Limited

WHAT IS FUNDED Jewish organisations that promote the Orthodox Jewish way of life

WHO CAN BENEFIT Organisations benefiting Jews

WHERE FUNDING CAN BE GIVEN UK and overseas

FINANCES *Year* 1997 *Income* £523,982
Grants £342,765

TRUSTEES Mrs E Oestréicher, M Oestréicher

HOW TO APPLY To the address under Who To Apply To in writing

WHO TO APPLY TO The Trustees, Hurdale Charity Limited, 54–56 Euston Street, London NW1 2ES
Tel 0171-387 0155

CC NO 276997   **ESTABLISHED** 1978

■ Arthur Hurst Will Trust

WHAT IS FUNDED Certain charitable allowances are given to distressed gentlewomen and needy clergy who have had to give up their work due to ill health. Support is given to widows of poor clergy for the education of their children. Grants are made either directly to the individual or through an existing society

WHO CAN BENEFIT Individuals and organisations benefiting needy clergy and distressed gentlewomen who have had to give up work due to ill health. Support may also be given to the widows and children of clergy who are at risk, disadvantaged by poverty or socially isolated. There is no restriction on the disease or medical condition suffered by the beneficiaries

WHERE FUNDING CAN BE GIVEN UK

RANGE OF GRANTS Up to £1,850 for organisations

SAMPLE GRANTS £1,850 to Friends of the Elderly and Gentlefolks; £1,750 to Distressed Gentlefolk's Aid Association; £1,150 to Royal United Kingdom Beneficent Association; £1,050 to Counsel and Care for the Elderly; £850 to Church of England Pensions Board; £300 to Home Warmth for the Aged Benevolent Fund; £15 to Wilberforce Home for Multiple Handicap; £15 to North Yorkshire County Council

FINANCES *Year* 1996 *Income* £25,188
Grants £19,282

TRUSTEES The Public Trustee

NOTES Grants to individuals are not included in the Sample Grants list

WHO TO APPLY TO The Trust Officer, (Ref:P647/A9), Arthur Hurst Will Trust, Public Trustee Office, Kingsway, London WC2B 6JX

CC NO 207991   **ESTABLISHED** 1935

■ The Hussey Trust

WHAT IS FUNDED Care and relief of crippled, disabled or deprived children and of the aged

WHO CAN BENEFIT Individuals and institutions benefiting crippled, disabled or deprived children and the aged

WHERE FUNDING CAN BE GIVEN UK and overseas

TYPE OF GRANT One-off grants

SAMPLE GRANTS £6,109 to the Evelyn Hussey Trust

FINANCES *Year* 1997 *Income* £27,362
Grants £6,109

TRUSTEES Mrs E G Hussey, Mrs B M Chandler, R H Chandler, P S Tanswell, FCA, Miss K S E Chandler, P M Hussey

NOTES Annual donations are made to the Evelyn Hussey Trust to cover the deficit on a property
WHO TO APPLY TO P S Tanswell, The Hussey Trust, 32–36 Bath Road, Hounslow, Middlesex TW3 3EF
CC NO 261425   **ESTABLISHED** 1970

■ **E B Hutchinson Charitable Trust** (formerly E B Hutchinson Trust)

WHAT IS FUNDED Preference to charities concerned with specific cancer research projects
WHAT IS NOT FUNDED Applications from individuals will not be acknowledged or considered
WHO CAN BENEFIT Teaching hospitals and local research projects benefiting: medical professionals; research workers; scientists; students and those suffering from cancer
WHERE FUNDING CAN BE GIVEN Kent
TYPE OF GRANT Cash payment
SAMPLE GRANTS £12,000 Pembury Hospital towards cancer research project
FINANCES *Year* 1997 *Income* £24,295 *Grants* £22,000
TRUSTEES R A H Simpson, F J Goulding, T Bates
WHO TO APPLY TO E B Hutchinson Charitable Trust, Messrs Finn-Kelcey & Chapman, Ashford House, County Square, Ashford, Kent TN23 1YB
CC NO 255644   **ESTABLISHED** 1956

■ **The P Y N and B Hyams Trust**

WHAT IS FUNDED General charitable purposes
WHO CAN BENEFIT There are no restrictions on the age; professional and economic group; family situation; religion and culture; and social circumstances of; or disease or medical condition suffered by, the beneficiaries
WHERE FUNDING CAN BE GIVEN UK
FINANCES *Year* 1997 *Income* £73,513 *Grants* £70,887
TRUSTEES N Hyams, Mrs M Hyams, D Levy
WHO TO APPLY TO N J Hyams, Co-Trustee, The P Y N and B Hyams Trust, 3 Carlton Hill, St John's Wood, London NW8 0JX
CC NO 268129   **ESTABLISHED** 1974

■ **Hyde Charitable Trust**

WHAT IS FUNDED The Trust works closely with organisations providing housing for homeless and badly housed people
WHO CAN BENEFIT Homeless people, and those disadvantaged by poverty
WHERE FUNDING CAN BE GIVEN England
TYPE OF GRANT At the discretion of the Trustees
FINANCES *Year* 1996–97 *Income* £92,124 *Grants* £269,750
TRUSTEES D Small (Chairman), B Bishop, E Epson, A Gibbs, M Grinfeld, Cllr Man Mohan, A Morris, H Rose, F Best, J Walker, K Barefoot, Cllr P Coleman, K Cooper, M Davis, A Murphie, V Stead, H Webb
WHO TO APPLY TO Caroline Titley, Company Secretary, Hyde Charitable Trust, Leegate House, Burnt Ash Road, Lee Green, London SE12 8RR *Tel* 0181-297 1500
CC NO 289888   **ESTABLISHED** 1984

■ **The Hyde Park Place Estate Charity**

WHAT IS FUNDED Community facilities and services; advice and information provision; residential and housing services; education and training, particularly books, equipment and travel costs; conservation; health care and medical research; community development and support to voluntary and community organisations
WHAT IS NOT FUNDED Grants will not be given in aid of campaigning activities, academic research, animal charities, furtherance of religious causes
WHO CAN BENEFIT Individuals and voluntary organisations benefiting children; young adults and students; volunteers; at risk groups; those disadvantaged by poverty; homeless and socially isolated people. There is no restriction on the disease or medical condition suffered by the beneficiaries
WHERE FUNDING CAN BE GIVEN Westminster
TYPE OF GRANT One-off or recurring. Will consider capital costs, core costs, start-up costs, running costs, salaries or project costs
FINANCES *Year* 1996–97 *Income* £434,093 *Grants* £458,709
TRUSTEES The Rev W M Atkins, plus eight others, including (ex officio) the Rector and Churchwardens of St George's Hanover Square
HOW TO APPLY By letter to the address under Who To Apply To
WHO TO APPLY TO Miss L McClure, The Hyde Park Place Estate Charity, St George's Vestry, 2a Mill Street, London W1R 9LB
CC NO 212439   **ESTABLISHED** 1914

■ **David Hyman Charitable Trust**

WHAT IS FUNDED Children, especially those who are disabled in any way. Some medical research is funded. Support may also go to sheltered accommodation, dance and ballet, fine art, theatres and opera houses, arts galleries, cultural centres and cultural activities, and holidays and outings
WHO CAN BENEFIT Children and older people, adults who are confined to wheelchairs, severely disabled students, Jewish people, those disadvantaged by poverty and homeless people. Support may be given to those suffering from Alzheimer's disease, cancers, heart disease, mental illness, and hearing or sight loss
WHERE FUNDING CAN BE GIVEN UK
TYPE OF GRANT One-off
TRUSTEES D Hyman, B A Hyman, J D Hyman
HOW TO APPLY In writing only, an self-addressed envelope is requested (not necessarily stamped)
WHO TO APPLY TO David Hyman Charitable Trust, 16 Mulberry Walk, London SW3 6DY
CC NO 274072   **ESTABLISHED** 1977

■ IBC Vehicles Ltd Employees Charity Fund

WHAT IS FUNDED The elderly, physically and mentally disabled and the homeless

WHAT IS NOT FUNDED No grants to political or denominational organisations

WHO CAN BENEFIT Registered charities or charitable organisations benefiting older people, physically and mentally disabled people and homeless people

WHERE FUNDING CAN BE GIVEN Within a 25 mile radius of Luton

RANGE OF GRANTS £50–£900

SAMPLE GRANTS £900 to Cancer Research Campaign; £600 to Contact the Elderly; £500 to Livingstone Family Centre; £500 to Moorings Family Centre; £500 to Manor Family Centre

FINANCES *Year* 1997 *Income* £14,524 *Grants* £16,524

TRUSTEES M Ashley, D Chapman, E Harris, Miss A K Viccars

HOW TO APPLY To the address under Who To Apply To in writing

WHO TO APPLY TO M Ashley, Chairman, IBC Vehicles Ltd Employees Charity Fund, IBC Vehicles Ltd, PO Box 163, Kimpton Road, Luton, Bedfordshire LU2 0TY

CC NO 800728   **ESTABLISHED** 1988

■ IBM United Kingdom Trust

WHAT IS FUNDED IBM United Kingdom Ltd provides support through the donation of resources via the IBM United Kingdom Trust. Its contributions mainly take the form of information technology equipment, software and consultancy, cash, employee time and the use of IBM facilities. Its focus areas for community investment are the use of IT in education and training, and to promote social inclusion in the Information Society. The majority of IBM's community support is given through specific programmes developed with identified partner organisations. Very few unsolicited requests can be considered

WHAT IS NOT FUNDED IBM does not provide core funding or contribute to appeals for building projects, political, religious or sectarian organisations, animal charities, individuals (including students), overseas activities or expeditions, recreational and sports clubs or appeals by third parties on behalf of charities or individuals. The Company does not currently offer full-time secondments of employees to voluntary organisations

WHO CAN BENEFIT Organisations operating within the areas of interest listed in this entry especially those disadvantaged by poverty and those at risk of social exclusion

WHERE FUNDING CAN BE GIVEN Anywhere in the UK, but preference is given to organisations which operate where the Company is based, and/or where there is employee involvement

TYPE OF GRANT Generally our support will be pilot projects developed in partnership with not-for-profit organisations, which demonstrate innovative and replicable uses of IT that will be of benefit to the wider community

SAMPLE GRANTS £175,000 to Brunel University Centre for Lifelong Learning, in the form of equipment and consultancy, for vocational training of local unemployed adults; £117,000 to Knowsley Community College, Merseyside, in the form of equipment and consultancy, to set up multi-media training programme for young unemployed; £35,000 to Albion Trust, in the form of equipment and consultancy, shared computer facilities for charities in Edinburgh; £30,000 to King Alfred's College of Teacher Training, providing equipment for use by trainee primary school teachers; £15,000 to Gateway Training Centre for Young Homeless People, in the form of cash and equipment, for training in the use of IT

FINANCES *Year* 1997 *Income* £588,000 *Grants* £1,800,000

PUBLICATIONS *Living in the Information Society, Social Exclusion, Technology and the Learning Society, The Net Result (Social Inclusion in the Information Society), Down-to-Earth Vision (Community Based IT Initiatives and Social Inclusion).* For copies of the above please contact Marite Stragier, Corporate Affairs, IBM United Kingdom Limited, 76 Upper Ground, London SE1 9PZ Tel: 0171–202 5146

NOTES IBM's total contribution in the UK for 1997 was valued at £1.8 million, offered through a combination of all the resources at its disposal, from equipment and software to consultancy, employee involvement, student placements and financial donations. The cash and IT hardware and software component, donated through the IBM Trust, was £511,000

HOW TO APPLY As previously stated the majority of IBM's community support is given through specific programmes developed with identified partner organisations. Very few unsolicited requests can be considered. There is no formal application process. All requests should be in writing and include a brief resume of the aims of the organisation as well as details of what assistance is required. Cultural and sports sponsorship enquiries should be sent to the address below

WHO TO APPLY TO IBM United Kingdom Trust, c/o Peter Wilkinson Associates, PO Pox 9108, London SW14 8ZN *Web Site* http://www.uk.ibm.com/community/comm2.html

CC NO 290462   **ESTABLISHED** 1984

■ IFAW Charitable Trust (The International Fund for Animal Welfare Charitable Trust)

WHAT IS FUNDED (a) To educate the public in animal welfare; (b) to conserve and protect animals including wildlife and its habitats and the natural environment; and (c) the prevention of cruelty to and suffering of animals including wildlife. To give active consideration to all requests for assistance within the Trust's budget

WHERE FUNDING CAN BE GIVEN UK

FINANCES *Year* 1997 *Income* £631,223 *Grants* £209,536

TRUSTEES Gregory P McEwen, Frederick O'Regan, Eileen B Wilson

HOW TO APPLY To the address under Who To Apply To

WHO TO APPLY TO Gregory Paul McEwen, Solicitor/Trustee, IFAW Charitable Trust, 55A Welbeck Street, London W1M 7HD

CC NO 1024806   **ESTABLISHED** 1992

■ INTACH (UK) Trust

WHAT IS FUNDED Postgraduate study by UK nationals in India, the preservation of the art, cultural and national heritage of India; conservation projects in India and funding for British postgraduate students to study in India

WHAT IS NOT FUNDED No funding for expeditions, undergraduates, school projects or UK charities

WHO CAN BENEFIT UK postgraduates and university projects in India

WHERE FUNDING CAN BE GIVEN UK and India. Grants to be used in India

TYPE OF GRANT One-off and recurring, some to individuals to visit India in connection to projects relating to the Trust's aims. Research is funded

RANGE OF GRANTS £500–£6,000

SAMPLE GRANTS £35,106 to Lucknow; £6,383 to Listing; £5,000 to Calcutta Trecentary Trust; £1,277 to Artist Exchange; £1,060 to Charles Wallace Collection

FINANCES *Year* 1996 *Income* £87,616 *Grants* £67,053

TRUSTEES Martand Singh (Chair), Sir B M Fielden, Sir J Thomson, R W Skelton, Cyrus Guzder, Dr D W MacDowell, Dr R Thapar

PUBLICATIONS Annual Report

NOTES INTACH stands for the Indian National Trust for Art and Cultural Heritage

HOW TO APPLY To the address under Who To Apply To in writing. Applications are considered in January and June each year

WHO TO APPLY TO Dr Philip Whitburn, Secretary, INTACH (UK) Trust, 10 Barley Mow Passage, London W4 4PH *Tel* 0181-994 6477

CC NO 298329 **ESTABLISHED** 1987

■ IOR Stakeholder Fund

WHAT IS FUNDED Grants to universities for the rejuvenation and building of laboratories and provision of audio visual and other equipment in connection with the study of oil recovery

WHO CAN BENEFIT Universities benefiting students

WHERE FUNDING CAN BE GIVEN UK

TRUSTEES More Oil and Gas Resource Management plc, A Gregory, Ms S Gregory, T Young

WHO TO APPLY TO T Cripps, Secretary to the Trustees, IOR Stakeholder Fund, 1 Snow Hill, London EC14 2EN

CC NO 1064065 **ESTABLISHED** 1997

■ The ISA Charity

WHAT IS FUNDED General charitable purposes

WHAT IS NOT FUNDED All funds have been allocated for several years ahead and no applications can be considered

WHO CAN BENEFIT There are no restrictions on the age; professional and economic group; family situation; religion and culture; and social circumstances of; or disease or medical condition suffered by, the beneficiaries

WHERE FUNDING CAN BE GIVEN UK

FINANCES *Year* 1995 *Income* £25,457 *Grants* £25,951

TRUSTEES R Paice, Mrs M Paice, P A Lintott

HOW TO APPLY **This Trust states that it does not respond to unsolicited applications**

WHO TO APPLY TO R Paice, The ISA Charity, ISA (Holdings) Ltd, 29–35 Rathbone Street, London W1P 1AG

CC NO 326882 **ESTABLISHED** 1985

■ The ITF Seafarers Trust

WHAT IS FUNDED Seafaring organisations, the social welfare of seafarers of all nations, their families and dependants

WHO CAN BENEFIT Seafarers of all nations and their dependants

WHERE FUNDING CAN BE GIVEN UK and overseas

RANGE OF GRANTS £5,000–£2,500,000, typical grants £5,001–£20,000

FINANCES *Year* 1997 *Income* £4,448,892 *Grants* £10,145,699

TRUSTEES J Bowers, D Cockroft, J Coombs, E Eulen, J Fay, J Knapp, W M Morris, F Ross, T R M Thomas

HOW TO APPLY To the address under Who To Apply To in writing. Applications must be supported by ab ITF affiliated Seafarers' or Dockers' Trade Union

WHO TO APPLY TO General Secretary, The ITF Seafarers Trust, 49–60 Borough Road, London SE1 1DS

CC NO 281936 **ESTABLISHED** 1981

■ The Ibbett Trust

WHAT IS FUNDED General charitable purposes to favour local causes

WHO CAN BENEFIT Registered charities. There are no restrictions on the age; professional and economic group; family situation; religion and culture; and social circumstances of; or disease or medical condition suffered by, the beneficiaries

WHERE FUNDING CAN BE GIVEN UK and overseas, in particular Bedford

TYPE OF GRANT Cash

FINANCES *Year* 1997 *Income* £82,824 *Grants* £17,070

TRUSTEES C J C Ibbett, J C Ibbett, Mrs S Ibbett, Mrs B Plumbly

NOTES Accruing funds for local home for the aged

WHO TO APPLY TO Mrs B Plumbly, The Ibbett Trust, Estate Office, Milton House, Milton Ernest, Bedford MK44 1YU

CC NO 234329 **ESTABLISHED** 1964

■ The Idlewild Trust

WHAT IS FUNDED (a) Advancement of education and learning and the encouragement of music, drama and the fine arts; (b) Preservation for the benefit of the public of lands, buildings and other objects of beauty or historic interest of national importance. To make grants to registered charities in Great Britain only. Particularly charities working in the fields of: publishing and printing; arts, culture and recreation; church buildings; historic buildings; memorials and monuments; waterways and woodlands; horticulture; heritage; textile and upholstery; bursaries, fees and scholarships; archaeology; architectural research and various community facilities

WHAT IS NOT FUNDED The following categories are excluded: repetitive nationwide appeals, those where all or most of the beneficiaries are outside the UK, appeals in respect of buildings with no distinctive outstanding merit, parochial appeals, appeals for research projects, endowment and deficit funding, appeals received within 12 calendar months of a previous grant. No grants to individuals

WHO CAN BENEFIT Registered charities benefiting: children and young adults; actors and entertainment professionals; musicians; students; textile workers and designers; and writers and poets

WHERE FUNDING CAN BE GIVEN UK

TYPE OF GRANT Buildings, core costs, endowments, feasibility studies, one-off, projects, research and start-up costs. Funding of up to three years will be considered

RANGE OF GRANTS Average grant £2,000

SAMPLE GRANTS £5,000 to Maritime Museum for restoration of Royal Barge; £5,000 to Royal Pavilion, Brighton for Indian Gate; £5,000 to Cotswolds Canal Trust for restoration of canal at Saul Junction; £5,000 to Hereford Cathedral for choral bursaries; £5,000 to Ironbridge Gorge Museum to purchase a Godden Collection; £5,000 to Peterborough Cathedral Trust for restoration of Knave Ceiling; £5,000 to Hestercombe Gardens Project Ltd for restoration of Mausoleum seat; £5,000 to Buildings Books Trust towards 'Pershers' Westminster; £5,000 to St Giles Cathedral Renewal Appeal; £5,000 to Tate Gallery towards purchase of Gawen Hamilton Painting

FINANCES *Year* 1996 *Income* £188,623 *Grants* £217,550

TRUSTEES Dr G W Beard (Chairman), Mrs F L Morrison-Jones, Mrs A C Grellier, Lady Goodison, M H Davenport, Mrs A S Bucks, J C Gale

PUBLICATIONS Guidelines leaflet available

NOTES Trustees regret it is impossible to acknowledge all applications because of the number and expense involved unless an sae is enclosed

HOW TO APPLY To the address under Who To Apply To. Considered in April, August and December each year. No formal application form. Full details of appeal and latest audited accounts required

WHO TO APPLY TO Angela Freestone, The Idlewild Trust, 54–56 Knatchbull Road, London SE5 9QY *Tel* 0171-274 2266 *Fax* 0171-274 5222

CC NO 268124   **ESTABLISHED** 1974

■ The Iliffe Family Charitable Trust

WHAT IS FUNDED Community development, welfare, children and general charitable purposes

WHAT IS NOT FUNDED Grants are not made to individuals

WHO CAN BENEFIT Organisations benefiting people of all ages, at risk groups, those disadvantaged by poverty and socially isolated people

WHERE FUNDING CAN BE GIVEN UK

FINANCES *Year* 1996–97 *Income* £168,000 *Grants* £153,000

TRUSTEES N G E Petter, J R Antipoff, Lord Iliffe

HOW TO APPLY To the address under Who To Apply To in writing

WHO TO APPLY TO J R Antipoff, The Iliffe Family Charitable Trust, Barn Close, Yattendon, Newbury, Berkshire RG18 0UX *Tel* 01635 201255

CC NO 273437   **ESTABLISHED** 1977

■ Inchcape Charitable Trust Fund

WHAT IS FUNDED Inchcape concentrates the majority of its donations budget on one international charity which it plans to support on a long-term basis. In addition, it will also make a limited number of substantial donations to carefully targeted charities which are generally relevant to the Group's businesses, principals and worldwide operations

WHAT IS NOT FUNDED Appeals unrelated to our policy will not be considered

WHO CAN BENEFIT International charities. The majority of the Trust's funds go to Raleigh International which benefits children and young adults

WHERE FUNDING CAN BE GIVEN UK and overseas

RANGE OF GRANTS £125–£122,000

SAMPLE GRANTS £122,000 to Raleigh International; £10,000 to Home Farm Trust; £10,000 to the Maritime Trust; £6,000 to World Fellowship Duke of Edinburgh's Award; £5,000 to Charities Aid Foundation

FINANCES *Year* 1996 *Income* £20,972 *Grants* £160,735

TRUSTEES R C O'Donoghue, J Duncan, C D MacKay, Sir D Plastow

NOTES The Trust's support to Raleigh International totals around £1.25 million. Consideration is being given to winding up the Trust and operating directly through the Charities Aid Foundation

WHO TO APPLY TO Mary MacLennan, Inchcape Charitable Trust Fund, 33 Cavendish Square, London W1M 9HF

CC NO 200234   **ESTABLISHED** 1961

■ The Inchrye Trust

WHAT IS FUNDED Grants are given to cultural, social and humanitarian organisations. Charities working in the fields of: accommodation and housing; arts and arts facilities; arts education; music groups; health care and hospices will be considered. Funding may also be given to special schools, care in the community, counselling on social issues and crime prevention schemes

WHAT IS NOT FUNDED No funding for expeditions, scholarships, large existing charities, animal charities or campaigns

WHO CAN BENEFIT Small projects starting up. Organisations benefiting: people of all ages; at risk groups; carers; disabled people; those disadvantaged by poverty; ex-offenders and those at risk of offending; those living in rural areas; socially isolated people; and victims of man-made or natural disasters

WHERE FUNDING CAN BE GIVEN Primarily Scotland

TYPE OF GRANT One-off grants and recurring funding may be considered

RANGE OF GRANTS £100–£5,000

SAMPLE GRANTS £5,000 to Child Psychotherapy Trust – Scotland; £3,600 to Leith School of Art for courses for disadvantaged children; £3,500 to 'Milan' Senior Welfare Council for a dementia/physical disabilities pilot project (multi-racial); £3,000 to Prison Phoenix Trust for yoga and meditation in Scottish prisons; £2,500 to Pain Association Scotland for teaching pain control without drugs

FINANCES *Year* 1996–97 *Grants* £33,000

TRUSTEES Mrs J David, Miss R Finlay

PUBLICATIONS Accounts are available from the Trust

HOW TO APPLY Applications should be made in writing to the address under Who To Apply To

WHO TO APPLY TO The Trustees, The Inchrye Trust, Messrs Turcan Connell WS, Saltire Court, 20 Castle Terrace, Edinburgh EH1 2EN *Tel* 0131-228 8000

SC NO SCO 13382

■ The Incorporated Church Building Society

WHAT IS FUNDED To make grants and interest free loans repayable over four years, to eligible churches. Larger loans may be made towards the building of Anglican churches

WHAT IS NOT FUNDED Aid is limited to actual church and chapel buildings. Repairs are limited to essential fabric repairs. Enlarging is restricted to the worship area

WHO CAN BENEFIT Living churches benefiting Christians

WHERE FUNDING CAN BE GIVEN England and Wales

FINANCES *Year* 1997 *Income* £52,500 *Grants* £22,750

TRUSTEES The Committee of Clergy and Laymen

WHO TO APPLY TO Wg Cdr Michael Tippen, RAF (Retd), Secretary, Incorporated Church Building Society, Fulham Palace, London SW6 6EA *Tel* 0171-736 3054

CC NO 212752   **ESTABLISHED** 1818

■ The Incorporated Leeds Church Extension Society

WHAT IS FUNDED Capital projects, major repairs and re-ordering of churches and church halls. Outreach; stipends; community projects of the Church of England; church schools; and community centres and village halls are also considered for funding

WHAT IS NOT FUNDED No grants to individuals. Needs outside Archdeaconry of Leeds and organ appeals will not be considered

WHO CAN BENEFIT Church of England. Churches and community projects. All ages and conditions are considered

WHERE FUNDING CAN BE GIVEN Archdeaconry of Leeds

TYPE OF GRANT Buildings, capital, feasibility studies, low costs loans, one-off and project. Funding is available for one year or less

SAMPLE GRANTS £5,500 to St Mary's Church Hall/ Parish Centre, Garforth; £5,000 to St James Church Hall/Parish Centre, Woodside; £3,500 to Middleton St Cross for church restoration and maintenance; £3,000 for clergy stipends; £2,850 to St Paul Church Hall/Parish Centre, Ireland Wood; £2,500 to St Mary, Whitkirk for church restoration and maintenance; £2,500 to St Wilfrid, Halton for church restoration and maintenance; £1,500 to St Philip, Osmondthorpe for mission partner; £1,500 to St Philip, Osmondthorpe for church restoration and maintenance; £1,000 to St Saviour, Richmond Hill for church restoration and maintenance

FINANCES *Year* 1997 *Income* £50,402 *Grants* £33,907

TRUSTEES Rev Canon G C M Smith, Miss C E Walker, Ven J M Oliver, G D Breton, FCA, A B Menzies, FCA

HOW TO APPLY By letter. Application form will be supplied for completion and return together with latest accounts and evidence of cost of project

WHO TO APPLY TO G D Breton, FCA The Incorporated Leeds Church Extension Society, 38c Heathfield, Leeds LS16 7AB *Tel* 0113-267 1098

CC NO 504682   **ESTABLISHED** 1863

■ India Development Group (UK) Limited

WHAT IS FUNDED Relief of poverty, distress and sickness in India; the advancement of education and the promotion of research into poverty in India, particularly rural poverty

WHO CAN BENEFIT Children, young adults, students and research workers, at risk groups, those disadvantaged by poverty, socially isolated people and those living in rural areas. There is no restriction on the disease or medical condition suffered by the beneficiaries

WHERE FUNDING CAN BE GIVEN India

TYPE OF GRANT Research is considered

SAMPLE GRANTS £24,000 to Women and Rural Development; £20,000 to Rural Development and Training Schumacher Institute; £3,000 to Wealth from Waste, ODA JFS:847; £2,206 for monitoring and consultancy; £346 for social security payments on behalf of an employee in India

FINANCES *Year* 1996–97 *Income* £79,218 *Grants* £49,552

WHO TO APPLY TO Suru Hoda, India Development Group (UK) Limited, 68 Downlands Road, Purley, Surrey CR8 4JF

CC NO 291167   **ESTABLISHED** 1985

■ The Ingram Trust

WHAT IS FUNDED General charitable purposes. Prefer to support specific projects including special services and equipment. Support major national charities together with some local ones in the County of Surrey

WHAT IS NOT FUNDED No charities specialising in overseas aid are considered except those dedicated to encouraging self help or providing more permanent solutions. No animal charities except those concerned with wildlife conservation

WHO CAN BENEFIT There are no restrictions on the age; professional and economic group; family situation; religion and culture; and social circumstances of; or disease or medical condition suffered by, the beneficiaries

WHERE FUNDING CAN BE GIVEN Surrey, UK and overseas

SAMPLE GRANTS £6,600 to NSPCC to cover the cost of rent and service charges for the Tottenham Child and Family Centre; £6,000 to LEPRA to buy a four-wheel drive vehicle to function as a mobile treatment unit in India; £5,361 to Shelter; £5,000 to Royal National Theatre for improvements to its South Bank location; £3,000 to Action Aid; £2,500 to WWF-UK; £2,000 to RNIB towards purchase of equipment for Redhill College's Resource Centre; £1,500 to RNID towards a new Tinnitus Retraining Therapy Project in the Feren's Unit at Middlesex Hospital; £1,500 to Queen Elizabeth's Foundation; £1,000 to Cherry Trees towards an additional playroom and meeting room for children with learning or physical disabilities

FINANCES *Year* 1997 *Income* £42,317 *Grants* £35,961

TRUSTEES C J Ingram, Ms J E Ingram, Ms C M Maurice

WHO TO APPLY TO Ms C Maurice, The Ingram Trust, PO Box 63, East Horsley, Surrey KT24 6YP

CC NO 1040194   **ESTABLISHED** 1994

■ The Inland Waterways Association

WHAT IS FUNDED Projects to restore and develop the inland waterways. This Trust will consider funding: historic buildings; memorials and monuments; transport and alternative transport; and arts, culture and recreation, as long as they are linked to inland waterways

WHAT IS NOT FUNDED No grants to individuals

WHO CAN BENEFIT Organisations involved in waterway restoration and development

WHERE FUNDING CAN BE GIVEN UK and Ireland

TYPE OF GRANT Feasibility studies, one-off, project and start-up costs. Funding can be given for up to one, two or three years, and over three years

RANGE OF GRANTS Usually up to £1,000 maximum

FINANCES *Year* 1996 *Income* £335,594

TRUSTEES The Council of the Association

HOW TO APPLY To the address under Who To Apply To in writing, initially giving brief details and applicants latest Annual Reports and Accounts
WHO TO APPLY TO The Executive Director, The Inland Waterways Association, 114 Regents Park Road, London NW1 8UQ *Tel* 0171-586 2510/2556
CC NO 212342   **ESTABLISHED** 1946

■ Inlight

WHAT IS FUNDED To make donations on an undenominational basis to charities providing valuable contributions to spiritual development and charities concerned with spiritual healing and spiritual growth through religious retreats. The Trustees of the Inlight Trust are only allowed under their Trust Deed to give donations for the advancement of a religion
WHAT IS NOT FUNDED Registered charities only. Applications from individuals, including students, are ineligible. No grants made in response to general appeals from large national organisations. Grants seldom available for church buildings
WHO CAN BENEFIT Registered charities benefiting people from many different religions
WHERE FUNDING CAN BE GIVEN UK
TYPE OF GRANT Usually one-off for a specific project or part of a project. Bursary schemes eligible. Core funding and/or salaries rarely considered
FINANCES *Year* 1997 *Income* £27,411 *Grants* £50,000
TRUSTEES Sir Thomas Lucas, Bt (Senior Trustee), Michael Collishaw, Michael Meakin, Alan Thompson (Hon Treasurer), Richard Wolfe, Wendy Collett
HOW TO APPLY At any time. Trustees meet four times a year. Applications should include details of the need the intended project is designed to meet plus an outline budget and the most recent available annual accounts of the charity. **Applications must be accompanied by a copy of the applicant's Trust Deed or a copy of the applicant's entry in the Charity Commissioner's Register.** Only successful applicants will be informed
WHO TO APPLY TO Mrs Judy Hayward, Inlight, P O Box 2, Liss, Hampshire GU33 6YP
CC NO 236782   **ESTABLISHED** 1957

■ The Inman Charity

WHAT IS FUNDED Main areas of interest are the elderly, hospices and social welfare
WHAT IS NOT FUNDED Applications from individuals are not considered
WHO CAN BENEFIT Registered charities benefiting older people. Beneficiaries of most social circumstances
WHERE FUNDING CAN BE GIVEN UK
FINANCES *Year* 1996 *Income* £227,743 *Grants* £217,500
TRUSTEES Inman Charity Trustees Ltd
PUBLICATIONS Annual Accounts filed with Charity Commission
HOW TO APPLY Written – Trustees meet half-yearly in March and September. Applications only considered if supported by a copy of the latest report and accounts
WHO TO APPLY TO Messrs Payne Hicks Beach, The Inman Charity, 10–11 New Square, Lincoln's Inn, London WC2A 3QG
CC NO 261366   **ESTABLISHED** 1970

■ Innes Memorial Fund

WHAT IS FUNDED (a) The relief of sickness in the area of Horsham, Lower Beeding, Horsham Rural and neighbourhood. (b) Support of Roffey Institute. (c) The benefit of general and medical charities in the same area. Particularly charities working in the field of: residential facilities and services; health professional bodies and health
WHO CAN BENEFIT Residents of the Horsham area. There is no restriction on the disease or medical condition suffered by the beneficiaries
WHERE FUNDING CAN BE GIVEN Horsham
TYPE OF GRANT Buildings, capital, core costs, feasibility studies, interest free loans, one-off funding, project, research, recurring costs, running costs, salaries, start-up costs and funding for more than three years will be considered
RANGE OF GRANTS £100–£7,500
SAMPLE GRANTS £5,500 to the elderly for chiropody service; £1,500 to Horsham Mobile Physiotherapy Association for general purposes; £1,000 to St Catherine's Hospice for general purposes; £1,000 to Queen Elizabeth II School for Disabled for general purposes; £1,000 to a patient in NHS Trust Hospital for purchase of a special mattress
FINANCES *Year* 1997–98 *Income* £18,000 *Grants* £14,000
TRUSTEES Lt Col J R Innes, I Innes, Dr J Heatley, Dr C Heath, S B I Lacy
NOTES Applications from outside the Horsham area will not be considered
WHO TO APPLY TO Lt Col J R Innes, Innes Memorial Fund, Romanys, Lawbrook Lane, Peaslake, Surrey GU5 9QW *Tel* 0171-702 3636 *Fax* 0171-702 9333 *E-mail* James.innes@easynet.co.uk
CC NO 212936   **ESTABLISHED** 1913

■ The General Charitable Trust of the Institute of Child Health

WHAT IS FUNDED General charitable purposes
WHO CAN BENEFIT There are no restrictions on the age; professional and economic group; family situation; religion and culture; and social circumstances of; or disease or medical condition suffered by, the beneficiaries
WHERE FUNDING CAN BE GIVEN UK
FINANCES *Year* 1996 *Income* £530,339
WHO TO APPLY TO S O'Brien, Secretary, The General Charitable Trust of the Institute of Child Health, Institute of Child Health, 30 Guilford Street, London WC1N 1EH
CC NO 1053611   **ESTABLISHED** 1996

■ Integreat

WHAT IS FUNDED The relief of young people aged five to 15 who have a disability by bringing them into closer association with able-bodied people. The provision, or assistance in the provision, in the interests of social welfare, of facilities for recreation for young people with and without disabilities. The advancement of education by bringing young people who have a disability into closer association and integration with able-bodied people so that the former will have opportunities for overcome their disabilities and the latter will benefit from such association and integration
WHO CAN BENEFIT Organisations benefiting children and young adults, especially those who are disabled
WHERE FUNDING CAN BE GIVEN UK and Northwest

TRUSTEES P Bailey, BA, MSoc, ScDipEd, Ms S Bell, Ms S Coulter, BA, CQSW, Ms J Crombleholme, MA, MIHSM, R Kapoor, BA, DMS, LIPD, Dr C Sayers, MBChB
WHO TO APPLY TO J P Bailey, Secretary, Integreat, 93 Cheadle Road, Stockport, Cheshire SK8 5DW
CC NO 1064187 **ESTABLISHED** 1997

■ International Arab Women's Council Charities Fund

WHAT IS FUNDED To further among persons whether or not temporarily resident in the United Kingdom and in particular citizens of Arab countries: (a) The relief of poverty. (b) The relief of all persons who have suffered as a result of local, national or international disasters and are thereby in need. (c) The advancement of the education of the public and in particular by assisting in the provision of Arabic classes and the presentation of Arabic art to the public. (d) The relief in cases of need of those who are sick, convalescent, disabled or infirm
WHO CAN BENEFIT Organisations benefiting Arab people, disabled people, those disadvantaged by poverty and victims of man-made or natural disasters. There is no restriction on the disease or medical condition suffered by the beneficiaries
WHERE FUNDING CAN BE GIVEN UK and Arab countries
TYPE OF GRANT One-off payments
FINANCES *Year* 1996 *Income* £36,927 *Grants* £25,366
TRUSTEES Board of Administration
WHO TO APPLY TO Dr Said, International Arab Women's Council Charities Fund, 8 Redcliffe Square, London SW10 9JZ
CC NO 275862 **ESTABLISHED** 1978

■ International Bar Association Educational Trust

WHAT IS FUNDED To advance legal education, to promote the study of law, to promote research into common legal problems and disseminate useful results
WHAT IS NOT FUNDED No grants to individuals
WHO CAN BENEFIT Organisations benefiting legal professionals, law students, teachers and young people
WHERE FUNDING CAN BE GIVEN UK and developing countries
FINANCES *Year* 1996 *Income* £60,474 *Grants* £16,360
TRUSTEES Desmond Fernando, PC (Chairman)
HOW TO APPLY To the address under Who To Apply To in writing
WHO TO APPLY TO P Hoddinot, International Bar Association Educational Trust, 271 Regent Street, London W1R 7PA
CC NO 287324 **ESTABLISHED** 1983

■ The International Foundation for Arts and Culture

WHAT IS FUNDED To advance the education of the public in music
WHO CAN BENEFIT Organisations that benefit musicians and educate members of the public in music
WHERE FUNDING CAN BE GIVEN UK
TRUSTEES A Rutland, J Whelan

WHO TO APPLY TO T G J Tress, Director and Company Secretary, The International Foundation for Arts and Culture, The Red House, 29 Palace Road, East Molesey, Surrey KT8 9DJ
CC NO 1064735 **ESTABLISHED** 1996

■ The International Missions UK Trust

WHAT IS FUNDED Advancement of the Christian religion in the UK by supporting the work of the International Missions Inc
WHO CAN BENEFIT Organisations benefiting Christians, including Baptists, Anglicans, Methodists and Roman Catholics. Support may be given to clergy
WHERE FUNDING CAN BE GIVEN UK
TYPE OF GRANT Recurring
WHO TO APPLY TO Rev Goetsch, The International Missions UK Trust, 48 Kirkstone Drive, Loughborough, Leicestershire LE11 3RW
CC NO 328321 **ESTABLISHED** 1989

■ International Spinal Research Trust

WHAT IS FUNDED Medical research into the cure of paralysis caused by spinal cord injury. Direct grants are made to assist scientifically respectable work to cover salaries, consumables or equipment for qualified scientific personnel
WHAT IS NOT FUNDED Only those projects deemed by our Scientific Committee to be directly relevant to meeting our objective will be funded
WHO CAN BENEFIT Research scientists
WHERE FUNDING CAN BE GIVEN UK and overseas
TYPE OF GRANT For scientific assistants (technical, pre-doctorate and post doctorate), equipment and for collaboration between laboratories. Research, salaries and funding of up to three years will be considered
FINANCES *Year* 1997 *Income* £2,310,447 *Grants* £528,270
TRUSTEES Dr H L Frankel, OBE, MB, FRCP, Dr Paul Sharpe, MD, J W A Hick, P Edmond, CBE, TD, FRCS, Dr L S Illis, MD, BSc, FRCP, S Yesner, (Founder), M P Curtis, Sir Christopher Laidlaw, Philippa Herbert, Prof P D Wall, FRS, DM, FRCP, LLB, H Faulls, BA, Andrew Walker
PUBLICATIONS Review, Report and Accounts, Medical Research Intelligence Summary, Quarterly Newsletters and Bi-Annual Research Digest
HOW TO APPLY No unsolicited applications will be considered by the Trustees since the Trust's present commitments exhaust the income of the Trust
WHO TO APPLY TO Mrs S Astley, International Spinal Research Trust, 8a Bramley Business Centre, Station Road, Bramley, Guildford, Surrey GU5 0AZ
CC NO 281325 **ESTABLISHED** 1981

■ The Inverclyde Bequest Fund

WHAT IS FUNDED Grants are given to seamen's charities
WHAT IS NOT FUNDED No grants to individuals
WHO CAN BENEFIT Merchant seamen
WHERE FUNDING CAN BE GIVEN UK and USA
TRUSTEES The Directors of the Merchants House of Glasgow
HOW TO APPLY Contact the address below for further details

Does the trust you have chosen match your needs? Haphazard applications waste postage and time

321

WHO TO APPLY TO The Collector, The Inverclyde Bequest Fund, Merchants House of Glasgow, 7 West George Street, Glasgow G2 1BA

■ The Inverforth Charitable Trust

WHAT IS FUNDED To support smaller national charities, in the areas of physical and mental health; hospices; youth and education; handicapped and aged. Also specialist caring charities; music and the arts and heritage. Happier with running costs than with projects and able to contribute towards core costs

WHAT IS NOT FUNDED No small or localised charities, churches, village halls, schools, etc. No animal charities. No branches, affiliates or subsidiary charities. Charities only, no individuals. No repeat applications at less than annual intervals. These guidelines are strictly enforced, and non-qualifying applications are not reported to the Trustees. It is therefore likely that any charity with a relevant location or the word 'community' in its title will be excluded. No sponsorship or advertisements

WHO CAN BENEFIT National charities benefiting children, young adults and older people; seafarers and fishermen; carers; homeless people and victims of abuse and crime. There is no restriction on the disease or medical condition suffered by the beneficiaries, however funding is only given to national charities

WHERE FUNDING CAN BE GIVEN UK with a preference for London

TYPE OF GRANT Buildings of national importance, core costs, one-off, research, running costs, recurring costs and salaries. All funding for one year or less. The Trust is willing to support administrative costs. Gifts are made in units of £500–£1,000–£1,500, (and not linked to requests or project size), with a few larger gifts deriving from long standing connections from a list which is reviewed annually. Repeat donations are more common than to new applicants, but there is no commitment beyond current grant

SAMPLE GRANTS £15,000 to National Asthma Campaign; £12,500 to Aldeburgh Foundation for Music/Arts Festival in Suffolk; £5,000 to Diana, Princess of Wales Memorial Fund; £2,500 to British Lung Foundation; £2,500 to Centre Point, Soho for London homeless; £2,500 to Macmillan Cancer Relief; £2,500 to St Mungo Association for London homeless; £2,500 to Shelter, Picadilly Advice Centre for London homeless; £2,000 to The Samaritans; £2,000 to Terrence Higgins Trust

FINANCES *Year* 1997 *Income* £156,000 *Grants* £201,500

TRUSTEES Elizabeth Lady Inverforth, Lord Inverforth, The Hon Mrs Jonathan Kane, Michael Gee

PUBLICATIONS Annual Report, to Charity Commission

NOTES Please do not write if you do not qualify

HOW TO APPLY To the address under Who To Apply To in writing. Initial telephone calls are strongly discouraged. No special forms are necessary, although accounts are desirable. A summary is prepared for the Trustees, who meet quarterly. Replies are normally sent to all applicants; allow up to four months for answer or grant. The Correspondent receives well over 1,000 applications a year, and advises of a high failure rate for new applicants. No need for an sae

WHO TO APPLY TO E A M Lee, FCIB, Barrister-at-Law, The Inverforth Charitable Trust, The Farm, Northington, Alresford, Hampshire SO24 9TH

CC NO 274132   **ESTABLISHED** 1977

■ The Ireland Fund of Great Britain

WHAT IS FUNDED Peace, reconciliation, cultural activity and the alleviation of poverty among Irish communities north and south of the border and in Great Britain

WHAT IS NOT FUNDED No grants to individuals

WHO CAN BENEFIT Organisations benefiting those disadvantaged by poverty

WHERE FUNDING CAN BE GIVEN Ireland and UK

TYPE OF GRANT Annual disbursement

FINANCES *Year* 1997 *Income* £479,977 *Grants* £201,000

TRUSTEES B Hayes, Dr A O'Reilly, J Riordan, G O'Reilly, Ms J Hart, The Hon K Pakenham

HOW TO APPLY British-based applications to be submitted in August, Irish-based applications to be submitted in January

WHO TO APPLY TO Mrs Jacqueline Dutton, The Ireland Fund of Great Britain, 8–10 Greyfriars Road, Reading, Berkshire RG1 1QE *Tel* 0118-956 9111 *Fax* 0118-950 5519

CC NO 327889   **ESTABLISHED** 1988

■ The Ireland Funds

WHAT IS FUNDED The Fund's aim is to promote peace and reconciliation, community development and cultural excellence in Ireland

WHAT IS NOT FUNDED In view of limited resources, some areas of activity, whilst very worthwhile, will not be given consideration. In particular, grants will not be given for: general appeals; individuals; one-off events; purchase of buildings or land; major reconstruction or repairs to buildings; capital costs for video equipment; lighting, costumes, etc; other grant-making Trusts; purchase of vehicles; debt repayment; tuition or student expenses; travel or transport costs; choirs and bands; commercial trading businesses; projects not based in Ireland; replacement of statutory funding; general administration of National or Provincial organisations

WHO CAN BENEFIT There are no restrictions on the age; professional and economic group; family situation; religion and culture; and social circumstances of; or disease or medical condition suffered by, the beneficiaries

WHERE FUNDING CAN BE GIVEN Ireland

TYPE OF GRANT Most grants will be of a one-off nature. However, the Funds may, in certain circumstances, consider supporting a project over three years which can clearly demonstrate the need for sustained assistance. Over that period, the project would be subject to monitoring by The Ireland Funds

RANGE OF GRANTS Typical grants £500–£30,000

TRUSTEES The Advisory Board

NOTES The Ireland Funds is one of the world's leading private sector foundations providing assistance to Ireland. The funds operate in Australia, Canada, France, Germany, Great Britain, Japan, New Zealand, South Africa and the United States. It raises monies in these countries directly from donors or through holding fund-raising events. Last year, for instance, The Funds held 52 events involving 25,000 people which raised over £5 million and supported 250 projects. The Funds, founded in 1976 by Dr Tony O'Reilly, are growing rapidly into the primary network for those interested in Ireland around the world

HOW TO APPLY Applications will only be accepted on an official application form obtainable from the address under Who To Apply To. Before a grant can be made the applicant will have to satisfy The Funds of their status and submit copies of their constitution and accounts. It will also be a condition of grant aid that projects make regular reports of progress, are monitored and provide promotional material and publicity. Notification of outcome will come by letter, meantime we would ask you to contact the office. Lobbying will disqualify

WHO TO APPLY TO Kieran McLoughlin, Director Ireland, The Ireland Funds, Oscar Wilde House, 1 Merrion Square, Dublin 2

CC NO 160956   **ESTABLISHED** 1976

■ Ironmongers' Quincentenary Charitable Fund

WHAT IS FUNDED The Trust supports community work, iron work, research connected to ferrous metallurgy and crafts

WHO CAN BENEFIT Organisations benefiting research workers. There are no restrictions on the age and family situation though there may be a few restrictions on their social circumstances

WHERE FUNDING CAN BE GIVEN UK

TYPE OF GRANT One-off

RANGE OF GRANTS £500–£5,000

FINANCES *Year* 1996–97 *Income* £147,682 *Grants* £63,687

TRUSTEES Worshipful Company of Ironmongers

HOW TO APPLY To the address under Who To Apply To in writing. Application form and guidelines available. Sae required

WHO TO APPLY TO J A Oliver, Clerk, Ironmongers' Quincentenary Charitable Fund, Ironmongers' Hall, Barbican, London EC2Y 8AA *Tel* 0171-606 2725

CC NO 238256

■ Irshad Trust

This trust did not respond to CAF's request to amend its entry and, by 30 June 1998, CAF's researchers did not find financial records for later than 1995 on its file at the Charity Commission. Trusts are legally required to submit annual accounts to the Charity Commission under section 42 of the Charities Act 1993

WHAT IS FUNDED General charitable purposes, in particular, the establishment of a College of Islamic Studies to study Islamic ideology and carry out scientific research in all areas of the Islamic religion. Establishment of educational institutions of different levels such as nursery, primary and secondary schools

WHO CAN BENEFIT Organisations benefiting Muslim children and young adults

WHERE FUNDING CAN BE GIVEN UK

TRUSTEES Dr W Al-Shahib Al-Hilli, M Araki, Prof A Ezzati, Dr S N H Kirmani, M Y Mazaal

WHO TO APPLY TO M J Elmi, Secretary, Irshad Trust, No 1 Stafford House, 1 Maida Avenue, London W2 1TE

CC NO 1056468   **ESTABLISHED** 1996

■ The Charles Irving Charitable Trust

WHAT IS FUNDED The Trust targets Cheltenham and Gloucestershire to benefit the following causes: disabled, mental health, elderly in the community, local community projects, homelessness, victim support

WHAT IS NOT FUNDED Research, expeditions, computers or equipment, unless benefiting disabled

WHO CAN BENEFIT Older people; disabled people, homeless people; victims of abuse, crime and domestic violence; and those suffering from mental illness

WHERE FUNDING CAN BE GIVEN Gloucestershire

TYPE OF GRANT Capital, project and recurring

RANGE OF GRANTS £50–£5,000

FINANCES *Year* 1997 *Income* £88,454 *Grants* £48,207

TRUSTEES Mrs J E Lane, D J Oldham, LLB, P Shephard, A P Hilder

HOW TO APPLY To the address under Who To Apply To in writing

WHO TO APPLY TO Mrs J E Lane, The Charles Irving Charitable Trust, Wood End, Sandy Lane Road, Charlton Kings, Cheltenham, Gloucestershire GL53 9DA *Tel* 01242 572116

CC NO 297712   **ESTABLISHED** 1987

■ Isaacs Charitable Trust

WHAT IS FUNDED General charitable purposes. To support favoured projects

WHO CAN BENEFIT Registered charities. There are no restrictions on the age; professional and economic group; family situation; religion and culture; and social circumstances of; or disease or medical condition suffered by, the beneficiaries

WHERE FUNDING CAN BE GIVEN UK

TYPE OF GRANT Recurrent and single donations

RANGE OF GRANTS £250–£6,500

SAMPLE GRANTS £6,500 to Jewish Care; £2,500 to British Friends of Laniado Hospital; £2,000 to British Heart Foundation; £1,500 to Scope; £1,500 to the Marie Curie Foundation; £1,500 to Scopus; £1,500 to the Child Resettlement Fund; £1,500 to Nightingale House; £1,500 to Ravenswood Foundation; £1,000 to Friends of Magen David Adom

FINANCES *Year* 1997 *Income* £35,394 *Grants* £31,500

TRUSTEES J E Isaacs, N D Isaacs, M C Sefton-Green

WHO TO APPLY TO Trustee Department, Isaacs Charitable Trust, Messrs Osmond Gaunt and Rose, Winston House, 349 Regents Park Road, Finchley, London N3 1DH *Tel* 0181-349 0321

CC NO 264590   **ESTABLISHED** 1972

■ The Edward Isaacs Charitable Trust

WHAT IS FUNDED General charitable purposes

WHO CAN BENEFIT There are no restrictions on the age; professional and economic group; family situation; religion and culture; and social circumstances of; or disease or medical condition suffered by, the beneficiaries

WHERE FUNDING CAN BE GIVEN UK

TRUSTEES A E Isaacs

NOTES Please note that the funds of this Trust are fully committed

WHO TO APPLY TO A E Isaacs, Trustee, The Edward Isaacs Charitable Trust, 276 Ecclesall Road South, Sheffield S11 9PS

CC NO 1047771   **ESTABLISHED** 1995

■ Isle of Dogs Community Foundation

WHAT IS FUNDED Organisations working in the fields of: community development; education, training and employment; and social care and development. Support may also be given to arts activities and education; voluntary organisations; cultural activities; health counselling; support and self help groups; health education and health promotion

WHAT IS NOT FUNDED No grants to individuals. No grants to organisations without a clear local focus

WHO CAN BENEFIT Community organisations serving the defined area or having direct impact on the defined area. Organisations benefiting people of all ages, unemployed people, volunteers, parents and children and those living in urban areas

WHERE FUNDING CAN BE GIVEN Blackwall and Millwall wards of the London Borough of Tower Hamlets

TYPE OF GRANT The Foundation's current policy is to offer: (a) 'Small' grants (up to £400 – normally for one-off projects or capital needs) and (b) 'Standard' grants (up to £5,000 per annum for three years – normally for revenue costs) depending on funds available

RANGE OF GRANTS £200–£5,000, typical grant £2,000

SAMPLE GRANTS £4,000 to Poplar Play Centre for running costs of a project; £2,000 to Alpha Grove Community Centre for weekend youth club; £2,000 to Alpha Grove Playgroup for cost of rent; £2,000 to Cedar Centre for extra places at the after school club; £2,000 to Cubitt Town Youth Project for youth work on the Isle of Dogs; £2,000 to East London Schools Fund for home support work at Woolmore School; £2,000 to George Green's School towards a basket ball court and posts; £2,000 to London Docklands Singers (LDC) for a recruitment drive; £2,000 to Neighbours in Poplar for bereavement training; £2,000 to St Paul's Art Centre towards the cost of an amateur community theatre programme

FINANCES *Year* 1997–98 *Income* £7,460,330 *Grants* £204,131

TRUSTEES NCC Property Ltd, Credit Suisse First Boston, Mirror Group plc, Morgan Stanley & Co Limited, Christ Church, London Borough of Tower Hamlets (2), Splash, AIC, Poplar Play, British Waterways, Bethnal Green and Victoria Park Housing Association, Tower Hamlets Healthcare NHS Trust

PUBLICATIONS Annual Report and financial statements

HOW TO APPLY There are normally three grant rounds each year. Please enquire for further details of current policy. Welcome discussion before applications are submitted and preference will be given to projects which work in partnership with others

WHO TO APPLY TO Project Co-ordinator, Isle of Dogs Community Foundation, PO Box 10449, London E14 8XT *Tel* 0171-531 1200 *Fax* 0171-538 0593 *E-mail* figtree@dircon.co.uk

CC NO 802942   **ESTABLISHED** 1990

■ Islington Chinese Association

WHAT IS FUNDED General charitable purposes for the benefit of the community and in particular members of the Chinese community within the Borough of Islington

WHO CAN BENEFIT Chinese people. There are no restrictions on the age; professional and economic group; family situation; religion and culture; and social circumstances of; or disease or medical condition suffered by, the beneficiaries

WHERE FUNDING CAN BE GIVEN Islington, Greater London

FINANCES *Year* 1997 *Income* £96,312

WHO TO APPLY TO Ms K Blair, Islington Chinese Association, 33 Giesbach Road, London N19 3DA

CC NO 1042435   **ESTABLISHED** 1994

■ JAR Charitable Trust

WHAT IS FUNDED The advancement of the Roman Catholic religion, the provision of education in schools, the provision of food, clothing and accommodation for needy persons over 50

WHAT IS NOT FUNDED No grants to individuals

WHO CAN BENEFIT Organisations benefiting older people, students, Roman Catholics and those disadvantaged by poverty

WHERE FUNDING CAN BE GIVEN UK and overseas

TYPE OF GRANT One-off and recurring

FINANCES *Year* 1997 *Income* £50,000 *Grants* £50,000

TRUSTEES The Rt Rev P J Casey, P R Noble, Rev W Young

NOTES The Trust's income is usually fully committed

WHO TO APPLY TO P R Noble, JAR Charitable Trust, c/o Messrs Vernor Miles & Noble, 5 Raymond Buildings, Gray's Inn, London WC1R 5DD

CC NO 248418   **ESTABLISHED** 1966

■ The J and J Charitable Trust

WHAT IS FUNDED General charitable purposes

WHO CAN BENEFIT There are no restrictions on the age; professional and economic group; family situation; religion and culture; and social circumstances of; or disease or medical condition suffered by, the beneficiaries

WHERE FUNDING CAN BE GIVEN UK

TRUSTEES J Green, Ms J Green

WHO TO APPLY TO S Jaffe, The J and J Charitable Trust, c/o Hazlems Fenton, 1/4 Argyll Street, London W1V 2LD

CC NO 1065660   **ESTABLISHED** 1997

■ JI Charitable Trust

WHAT IS FUNDED General charitable purposes

WHO CAN BENEFIT There are no restrictions on the age; professional and economic group; family situation; religion and culture; and social circumstances of; or disease or medical condition suffered by, the beneficiaries

WHERE FUNDING CAN BE GIVEN UK

TRUSTEES J Isaacs, Ms J Isaacs

WHO TO APPLY TO J Isaacs, Trustee, JI Charitable Trust, 18 Cobden Hill, Radlett, Herfordshire WD7 7JR

CC NO 1059865   **ESTABLISHED** 1996

■ JJCT Charity

WHAT IS FUNDED Jewish charitable purposes

WHO CAN BENEFIT Jewish people

WHERE FUNDING CAN BE GIVEN UK and overseas

SAMPLE GRANTS £1,531,050 to Jewish Continuity; £938,138 to Jewish Philanthropic Association for Israel and the Middle East; £290,547 to Synagogues Sharing in Kol Nidre Appeal; £280,000 to Foundation for Education; £254,654 to information, education and communal activities; £160,000 to Scopus Jewish Educational Trust; £139,516 to Joint Committee for Youth Affairs; £15,000 to Reform Synagogues

of Great Britain; £5,000 to Holocaust Educational Trust; £2,000 to Israel Folk Dance Institute
FINANCES *Year* 1996 *Income* £4,188,619
Grants £3,616,905
TRUSTEES Sir T Chinn, CVO, A Fisher, B Kerner, G Ognall, R Preston, L Shebson, H Stanton, M Ziff
WHO TO APPLY TO Eldred Kraines, JJCT Charity, Balfour House, 741 High Road, Finchley, London N12 0BQ
CC NO 1043047   **ESTABLISHED** 1994

■ The JJ Charitable Trust

WHAT IS FUNDED Literacy: To improve the effectiveness of literacy teaching in the primary education sector for children with general or specific learning difficulties, including dyslexia. To do the same through agencies working with ex-offenders or those at risk of offending. Environment UK: To support environmental education in schools; to support sustainable transport schemes and demonstration projects; to support tree planting and rural conservation. Environment Overseas: To support practical conservation projects, for example helping small farmers to improve productivity by environmentally sustainable means, or helping communities to improve management of local environmental resources
WHAT IS NOT FUNDED No grants to individuals, expeditions or travel bursaries
WHO CAN BENEFIT Organisations benefiting children with learning difficulties particularly dyslexia, ex-offenders and those at risk of offending, and farmers
WHERE FUNDING CAN BE GIVEN UK and overseas (mainly Africa)
RANGE OF GRANTS £500–£32,515
SAMPLE GRANTS £32,515 to Institute of Education; £15,000 to British Dyslexia Association towards running costs of the director's office at BDA; £15,000 to Youth at Risk to support a special needs teacher and assistants for pilot literacy project; £10,300 to New Assembly of Churches towards providing literacy support to young people at risk of offending; £10,000 to Open School Trust towards production of promotional and training videos; £10,000 to Reading Recovery Programme; £10,000 to Council for the Protection of Rural England; £10,000 to FARM Africa; £9,897 to Tavistock Institute to cover work on the production of teaching resources on energy efficiency by a group of teachers; £9,168 to Helen Arkell Dyslexia Centre
FINANCES *Year* 1997 *Income* £2,140,462
Grants £182,006
TRUSTEES J J Sainsbury, M L Sainsbury, Miss J Portrait
NOTES The Trustees meet six times a year to make grants
HOW TO APPLY To the address under Who To Apply To in writing. All applications acknowledged but unsolicited applications are rarely successful. Guidelines are not issued by the Trust
WHO TO APPLY TO M A Pattison, The JJ Charitable Trust, 9 Red Lion Court, London EC4A 3EF
CC NO 1015792   **ESTABLISHED** 1992

■ The JL Charity Trust

WHAT IS FUNDED Primarily Jewish charities
WHAT IS NOT FUNDED No grants to individuals
WHO CAN BENEFIT Jewish charities
WHERE FUNDING CAN BE GIVEN UK
TYPE OF GRANT One-off

SAMPLE GRANTS Grants of general donations:; £7,000 to Jewish Care; £3,000 to Nightingale House; £1,000 to British Retinitis Pigmentosa Society; £1,000 to Children in Crisis
FINANCES *Year* 1998 *Income* £16,421
Grants £15,000
TRUSTEES R A Barsham, Mrs J M Symons, A H Behrens
HOW TO APPLY Applications not normally considered
WHO TO APPLY TO R A Barsham, The JL Charity Trust, Barsham Bradford & Hamilton, 1 Lincoln's Inn Fields, London WC2A 3AA *Tel* 0171-242 5671 *Fax* 0171-831 0699
CC NO 219231   **ESTABLISHED** 1962

■ JMK Charitable Trust

WHAT IS FUNDED Tend to favour charities supporting healthcare and children
WHO CAN BENEFIT Registered charities benefiting children and the sick. There is no restriction on the disease or medical condition suffered by the beneficiaries
WHERE FUNDING CAN BE GIVEN UK and overseas
RANGE OF GRANTS £100–£10,986
SAMPLE GRANTS £10,986 to John Coler School; £10,000 to Theodora's Children's Trust; £9,500 to West London Synagogue; £2,000 to Reading Community Welfare Rights Unit; £1,500 to Tower Hamlets Old People's Welfare Trust; £1,000 to Special Trustees of St George's Hospital; £1,000 to Art Museum of Israel; £1,000 to NSPCC; £910 to Sheperders Trust; £500 to Macmillan Nurses
FINANCES *Year* 1997 *Income* £69,209
Grants £41,017
TRUSTEES Mrs J M Karaviotis, R S Parker, J Karaviotis
HOW TO APPLY By letter to the address under Who To Apply To, but no acknowledgement of receipt will be given
WHO TO APPLY TO R S Parker, JMK Charitable Trust, Messrs Chantrey Vellacott, 23–25 Castle Street, Reading, Berkshire RG1 7SB
CC NO 274576   **ESTABLISHED** 1977

■ The JMR Charitable Trust

WHAT IS FUNDED Charities undertaking general charitable purposes and in whom the Trustees have special interest, knowledge, association or experience
WHAT IS NOT FUNDED No grants to individuals or to registered charities whose work falls outside Trustees' policy
WHO CAN BENEFIT There are no restrictions on the age; professional and economic group; family situation; religion and culture; and social circumstances of; or disease or medical condition suffered by, the beneficiaries. However, grants are only made to pre-selected charitable organisations and institutions already known to the Trustees
WHERE FUNDING CAN BE GIVEN UK
FINANCES *Year* 1996 *Income* £23,247
Grants £43,881
TRUSTEES M Kennedy, Mrs C M Ried, Mrs P R Fernando
WHO TO APPLY TO B F Lowe, Secretary to the Trustees, The JMR Charitable Trust, c/o Herbert Reeves and Co, 44 Great Eastern Street, London EC2A 3EP
CC NO 273546   **ESTABLISHED** 1975

■ JNF Charitable Trust

WHAT IS FUNDED Relief of poverty in Israel and other charitable purposes in the prescribed regions beneficial to persons who are of Jewish religion, race or origin

WHAT IS NOT FUNDED No grants to individuals

WHO CAN BENEFIT Organisations benefiting Jewish people and those disadvantaged by poverty

WHERE FUNDING CAN BE GIVEN Restricted to Israel and other Middle Eastern regions

SAMPLE GRANTS £4,164,258 to Keren Kayemeth Leisrael

FINANCES *Year* 1996 *Income* £4,946,808 *Grants* £2,743,895

TRUSTEES Board of Management: S D Kibel, S Lovatt, Mrs H Rosen, G Seal, R Simmons, J D Zinkin

WHO TO APPLY TO H Bratt, Company Secretary, JNF Charitable Trust, 58–70 Edgware Way, Edgware, Middlesex HA8 8GQ *Tel* 0181-421 7600 *Fax* 0181-905 4299

CC NO 225910 **ESTABLISHED** 1939

■ The JRSST Charitable Trust

WHAT IS FUNDED General charitable purposes. To work in close association with the Joseph Rowntree Reform Trust Ltd which is a non-charitable Trust of which all the Trustees of The JRSST Charitable Trust are Directors

WHAT IS NOT FUNDED No direct applications to The JRSST Charitable Trust. No student grants are funded

WHO CAN BENEFIT Bodies or individuals undertaking research or action in fields which relate directly to the non-charitable work of the Joseph Rowntree Reform Trust Ltd. Academics and research workers may benefit

WHERE FUNDING CAN BE GIVEN UK

TYPE OF GRANT Specific project finance in particular fields of Trust interest. Research is considered

RANGE OF GRANTS £50–£26,448

SAMPLE GRANTS £26,448 to Birkbeck College for the Anthony Barnett Research Fellowship; £26,250 to Unit for the Study of Government in Scotland for research on Democratic Participation and the Scottish Parliament; £12,500 to European Policy Forum; £12,375 to Institute of Community Studies for research; £12,300 to Democratic Dialogue, Northern Ireland; £5,000 to John Smith Memorial Trust; £1,250 to London School of Economics; £750 to Patients Association; £700 to Congregational Church, Hawick; £500 to Gladstone Benevolent Fund

FINANCES *Year* 1996 *Income* £95,234 *Grants* £101,123

TRUSTEES T A Smith (Chairman), D A Currie, C J Day, C J Greenfield, A J Kirkwood, D T Shutt, Ms D E Scott

HOW TO APPLY **This Trust states that it does not respond to unsolicited applications**

WHO TO APPLY TO Ms L Jefferson, The JRSST Charitable Trust, The Garden House, Water End, York YO3 6LP

CC NO 247498 **ESTABLISHED** 1955

■ John D Jackson Charitable Foundation

WHAT IS FUNDED General charitable purposes. Yorkshire based charities working in the fields of welfare and disability, community development and some Jewish causes

WHO CAN BENEFIT Individuals and organisations benefiting those in the Yorkshire area including people with disabilities

WHERE FUNDING CAN BE GIVEN UK, with a preference for West Yorkshire or at the Trustees discretion

TYPE OF GRANT One-off, project funded for one year or less

RANGE OF GRANTS £150

FINANCES *Year* 1996 *Income* £17,197 *Grants* £7,790

TRUSTEES J D Jackson, H A Jackson, S J L Novick, J D Jackson, J D Jackson, J D Jackson

HOW TO APPLY To the address under Who To Apply To in writing

WHO TO APPLY TO John D Jackson, CBE, The John D Jackson Charitable Foundation, Red Oaks, Manor House Lane, Wigton Moor, Leeds LS17 9JD

CC NO 1000457 **ESTABLISHED** 1990

■ The Frank Goddard Jackson Charitable Trust

WHAT IS FUNDED General charitable purposes

WHO CAN BENEFIT There are no restrictions on the age; professional and economic group; family situation; religion and culture; and social circumstances of; or disease or medical condition suffered by, the beneficiaries

WHERE FUNDING CAN BE GIVEN UK

TRUSTEES J B Farnsworth, A G Jackson, O E Tebbs

WHO TO APPLY TO O E Tebbs, Trustee, The Frank Goddard Jackson Charitable Trust, Rustons and Lloyd, Solicitors, 136 High Street, Newmarket, Suffolk CB8 8NN

CC NO 1048409 **ESTABLISHED** 1995

■ The Sir Barry Jackson County Fund

WHAT IS FUNDED Drama and theatrical production, including all the behind-the-scenes skills associated with theatre production

WHAT IS NOT FUNDED No grants to individuals, only established companies are supported

WHO CAN BENEFIT Organisations benefiting actors and entertainment professionals and those involved in theatre production

WHERE FUNDING CAN BE GIVEN West Midlands

RANGE OF GRANTS £14,000–£42,500

SAMPLE GRANTS £42,500 to Birmingham Repertory Theatre Limited; £14,000 to Big Brum TIE Company Limited

FINANCES *Year* 1997 *Income* £59,361 *Grants* £56,500

TRUSTEES Cllr J Alden, P Baird, R S Burman, L A Chorley, D B Edgar, Ms K Horton, I A King, Dr R Leach, D Waine, C R G Winteringham

HOW TO APPLY To the address under Who To Apply To in writing

WHO TO APPLY TO I A King, The Sir Barry Jackson County Fund, Kidsons Impey, Bank House, 8 Cherry Street, Birmingham B2 5AD

CC NO 517306 **ESTABLISHED** 1985

■ The Dorothy Jacobs Charity

WHAT IS FUNDED General charitable purposes

WHO CAN BENEFIT There are no restrictions on the age; professional and economic group; family situation; religion and culture; and social circumstances of; or disease or medical condition suffered by, the beneficiaries

WHERE FUNDING CAN BE GIVEN UK

Have you read How to use the DGMT *on page xvi?*

SAMPLE GRANTS £4,000 to Leukaemia Research; £4,000 to Jewish Care; £4,000 to Imperial Cancer Research; £4,000 to Oxfam; £4,000 to Scope; £4,000 to BBC Children in Need; £4,000 to Royal Marsden Cancer Fund; £4,000 to Great Ormond Street Children's Hospital Fund; £4,000 to Moorfields Eye Hospital; £4,000 to Norwood Child Care

FINANCES *Year* 1997 *Income* £93,055
Grants £60,000

TRUSTEES R H Moss, A M Alexander

WHO TO APPLY TO Trustee, The Dorothy Jacobs Charity, Heywards, St Georges House, 15 Hanover Square, London W1R 0HE

CC NO 328430   **ESTABLISHED** 1989

■ Jacobsen Foundation Limited

WHAT IS FUNDED Relief and assistance to aged, sick or needy persons, employees and past employees of Waldorf Stationery & Greeting Cards Ltd, Hyde, and others elsewhere connected with the printing, bookbinding and stationery trades. Pensions, payments, allowances, medical attendance, funeral expenses. Equipment for hospitals, ambulances and almshouses

WHO CAN BENEFIT Individuals, and organisations benefiting long serving employees and retired ex-employees of Waldorf Stationery & Greeting Cards Ltd, Hyde. Support is also given to at risk groups, those disadvantaged by poverty and socially isolated people. There is no restriction on the disease or medical condition suffered by the beneficiaries

WHERE FUNDING CAN BE GIVEN UK

TYPE OF GRANT Monetary allowances

FINANCES *Year* 1997 *Income* £18,401
Grants £69,429

TRUSTEES Council of Management or Governing Body of the Association, including: H Barlow, J W Coates, J C Seddon, D H Sanderson

HOW TO APPLY At retirement age

WHO TO APPLY TO Mrs Amy Scanes, Secretary, Jacobsen Foundation Limited, 21 Hillcrest, Gee Cross, Hyde, Cheshire SK14 5LJ

CC NO 244774   **ESTABLISHED** 1934

■ The Ruth & Lionel Jacobson Charitable Trust (No 2)

WHAT IS FUNDED Only such bodies of person and trust as are established for charitable purposes, including those working in the fields of: holiday accommodation and residential facilities; support for voluntary organisations; the Jewish religion; arts; health; historic buildings; animal/bird sanctuaries and nature reserves; special needs education and speech therapy and various community facilities and services

WHAT IS NOT FUNDED No individual cases. Registered charities only

WHO CAN BENEFIT Organisations benefiting: people of all ages; medical professionals; parents and children; disabled, stroke victims and terminally ill people; homeless people; refugees and victims of famine. Those suffering from various diseases and medical conditions will also be considered

WHERE FUNDING CAN BE GIVEN British Isles, but especially the North East of England

TYPE OF GRANT One-off, buildings, project and research. Funding is available for one year or less

RANGE OF GRANTS £50–£10,000, typical grant £100–£500

SAMPLE GRANTS £5,200 to the Speech and Language Learning Centre; £5,000 to the Joel Intract House Fund Appeal; £2,000 to St Oswalds Hospice; £1,000 to The Centre for Advanced Rabbinics; £1,000 to the Friends of the Laing Art Gallery; £1,000 to the Society of Friends of the Torah; £500 to Gateshead Jewish High School for Girls; £500 to Geordie Jaunts; £500 to Haskel; £500 to Marbei Torah Trust

FINANCES *Year* 1997 *Income* £64,677
Grants £37,357

TRUSTEES Mrs I R Jacobson, M D Jacobson

HOW TO APPLY Letters of application are considered bi-monthly

WHO TO APPLY TO Mrs I R Jacobson, The Ruth & Lionel Jacobson Charitable Trust, High Wray, 35 Montagu Avenue, Newcastle upon Tyne, Tyne and Wear NE3 4JH

CC NO 326665   **ESTABLISHED** 1984

■ The Yvette and Hermione Jacobson Charitable Trust

WHAT IS FUNDED Youth, disability and charities working with elderly people

WHAT IS NOT FUNDED Under terms of Trust donations are only made to registered charities not to individuals

WHO CAN BENEFIT Registered charities working with young people, disabled people and the elderly

WHERE FUNDING CAN BE GIVEN London, North Yorkshire

FINANCES *Year* 1997 *Income* £26,493

TRUSTEES Mrs H Allen, Miles Allen

HOW TO APPLY At any time to the address below by letter. Trust income required to meet our present commitments

WHO TO APPLY TO Mrs Hermione Allen, The Yvette and Hermione Jacobson Charitable Trust, 5 Cotman Close, London NW11 6QD

CC NO 264491   **ESTABLISHED** 1972

■ John James Charitable Trust

WHAT IS FUNDED Advancement of Christian religion and physical education amongst children and young people so as to develop their physical, mental and spiritual capacities

WHAT IS NOT FUNDED No funding for sabbaticals

WHO CAN BENEFIT Individuals, and organisations benefiting children, young adults and Christians

WHERE FUNDING CAN BE GIVEN UK

TYPE OF GRANT One-off and recurrent, project, salaries and start-up costs

FINANCES *Year* 1996 *Income* £22,613

HOW TO APPLY All applications will be acknowledged

WHO TO APPLY TO D K Runton, Chairman of the Trustees, John James Charitable Trust, Orchard Hill, Cragg Wood Drive, Rawdon, Leeds LS19 6LG

CC NO 328359   **ESTABLISHED** 1989

■ John James Educational Trust

This trust did not respond to CAF's request to amend its entry and, by 30 June 1998, CAF's researchers did not find financial records for later than 1995 on its file at the Charity Commission. Trusts are legally required to submit annual accounts to the Charity Commission under section 42 of the Charities Act 1993

WHAT IS FUNDED Principally to assist the advancement of education among independent schools in Bristol, on application from schools

WHAT IS NOT FUNDED No grants to individuals. Grants at present restricted to existing beneficiaries

WHO CAN BENEFIT Girls and boys from 10 independent schools in Bristol

WHERE FUNDING CAN BE GIVEN Bristol

TYPE OF GRANT Confined to travel and general awards to 10 schools for educational purposes, reviewed annually and increased when appropriate

TRUSTEES J Gordon (Chairman) and others

NOTES To avoid fruitless correspondence, intending applicants should telephone before writing

HOW TO APPLY Applications can at present only be considered from Independent Schools in Bristol

WHO TO APPLY TO J Cottrell, Treasurer, John James Educational Trust, 90 Redland Road, Redland, Bristol BS6 6QZ *Tel* 0117-924 6712

CC NO 279610   **ESTABLISHED** 1980

■ The James Trust

WHAT IS FUNDED To direct the giving of a limited number of donors to the churches, Christian organisations and individuals of their choice. Support is primarily to Christian causes; the advancement of Christian religion; and Anglican diocesan and Free Church umbrella bodies

WHAT IS NOT FUNDED No grants to individuals not known personally to the Trustees

WHO CAN BENEFIT Principally Christian organisations benefiting: Christians; young adults and older people; those disadvantaged by poverty; disaster victims; refugees; and those suffering from leprosy

WHERE FUNDING CAN BE GIVEN UK and overseas

TYPE OF GRANT One-off, capital, core costs, project, recurring costs, salaries and start-up costs. Funding is available for up to three years

SAMPLE GRANTS £10,000 to B and J Leppard for the support of a dermatologist in Tanzania; £3,650 to Highfield Church, Southampton for church funds; £3,200 to Tear Fund for the relief of poverty; £3,122 to Asthma and Allergy Information Research for equipment for B and J Leppard; £2,600 to Christian Aid for the relief of poverty; £2,171 to Above Bar Church, Southampton for church funds; £1,700 to New Life Christian Centre, Croydon for church funds; £1,480 to St John's, Copthorne for church funds; £1,350 to Frontier Youth Club for Christian youth work; £1,275 to Crusaders Union for Christian youth work

FINANCES *Year* 1998 *Income* £56,435 *Grants* £41,557

TRUSTEES R J Todd, P Smith

NOTES No acknowledgements given to unsolicited applications

HOW TO APPLY To the address under Who To Apply To

WHO TO APPLY TO R J Todd, The James Trust, 27 Radway Road, Upper Shirley, Southampton, Hampshire SO15 7PL

CC NO 800774   **ESTABLISHED** 1989

■ The James Trust

WHAT IS FUNDED Charities working with disabled people and the homeless. At present the Trust is fundraising with the ultimate aim to provide accommodation for those with handicaps and those who are homeless through poverty. However, the Trustees are currently looking for ways to improve the quality of lifestyle for these people through arts and crafts. Funds are not currently available

WHO CAN BENEFIT Organisations benefiting disabled and homeless people

WHERE FUNDING CAN BE GIVEN UK

TRUSTEES Ms J Butterworth, D Harvey, R James

WHO TO APPLY TO R James, Trustee, The James Trust, 4 Crossways, Sutton, Surrey SM2 5LB *Tel* 0181-642 3354

CC NO 1049787   **ESTABLISHED** 1995

■ The Janes Pantyfedwen Foundation

WHAT IS FUNDED Church buildings, religious purposes, students (mainly for post graduate study), registered charities, local Eisteddfodau and Sunday Schools. Charities working in the field of Christian education; religious umbrella bodies; infrastructure, support and development; cultural activity; academic research and various community services and facilities will be considered

WHO CAN BENEFIT Institutions based in Wales and individuals who are deemed to be Welsh. Organisations benefiting: children; young adults; clergy; musicians; students; Christians; at risk groups; those disadvantaged by poverty and homeless people

WHERE FUNDING CAN BE GIVEN Wales

TYPE OF GRANT Variable, one-off for registered charities and churches; recurrent for students. Buildings, capital, interest free loans, projects, start-up costs and funding from one year or less up to two years will also be considered

RANGE OF GRANTS Up to a maximum of £8,000 in special cases lower maximum in other cases

FINANCES *Year* 1996–97 *Income* £261,445 *Grants* £205,699

TRUSTEES Prof Graham L Rees, MA (Chair)

PUBLICATIONS Annual report

HOW TO APPLY Applications may be submitted at any time, but not later than 31 July for the following year (for students)

WHO TO APPLY TO Richard H Morgan, Executive Secretary, The Janes Pantyfedwen Foundation, 9 Market Street, Pantyfedwen, Aberystwyth, Wales SY23 1DL *Tel* 01970 612806 *Fax* 01970 612806

CC NO 1069598   **ESTABLISHED** 1998

■ Peter Jansen Charitable Trust

WHAT IS FUNDED The Trustees favour music and education charities

WHO CAN BENEFIT To benefit children, young adults, musicians and students

WHERE FUNDING CAN BE GIVEN UK and overseas

SAMPLE GRANTS £11,000 to Royal Opera House Trust; £10,000 to St Edmund Hall Oxford Development Fund; £6,693 to University of Cape Town; £5,000 to London Business School Foundation for Entrepreneurial Management; £2,010 to Crash Ltd; £1,340 to Royal Opera House Trust and Development Appeal; £1,132 to St George's College, Weybridge; £1,000 to Cancer Relief Macmillan Fund; £1,000 to Garsington Opera

FINANCES *Year* 1997 *Income* £69,203 *Grants* £66,212

TRUSTEES P J Jansen, Mrs F Jansen

WHO TO APPLY TO Peter Jansen Charitable Trust, Messrs MacFarlanes, 10 Norwich Street, London EC4A 1BD

CC NO 328035   **ESTABLISHED** 1988

■ The Jarman Charitable Trust

WHAT IS FUNDED To support welfare work, Church building extension schemes and general social services in Birmingham District. This includes: convalescent homes; hospices; hospitals; nursing homes; rehabilitation centres; cancer research; community centres and village halls; day centres; holidays and outings; and playschemes

WHAT IS NOT FUNDED The Trust does not give grants to individuals. Holders of Charity Number preferred

WHO CAN BENEFIT Organisations benefiting: children; young adults; older people; one parent families; at risk groups; disabled people; and homeless people. Those suffering from Alzheimers's disease; arthritis and rheumatism; asthma; autism; cancers; cystic fibrosis; diabetes; head and other injuries; heart disease; multiple sclerosis; muscular dystrophy; spina bifida and hydrcepholus; and strokes

WHERE FUNDING CAN BE GIVEN Birmingham and District

TYPE OF GRANT Annual donations and one-off payments

RANGE OF GRANTS £50–£275

FINANCES *Year* 1998 *Income* £34,620
Grants £31,040

TRUSTEES G M Jarman, B J Jarman, I J Jarman, S Chilton

HOW TO APPLY In February and September. Telephone calls and sae not required. Application forms not used. Applications not acknowledged. Statement of account if possible. Applications reviewed in April and November

WHO TO APPLY TO Mrs B J Jarman, The Jarman Charitable Trust, 50 Shakespeare Drive, Shirley, Solihull, West Midlands B90 2AN

CC NO 239198   **ESTABLISHED** 1964

■ John Jarrold Trust Ltd

WHAT IS FUNDED General charitable purposes of all kinds and in particular of education and research in all or any of the natural sciences. Funds fully committed for a long time ahead

WHAT IS NOT FUNDED No grants to individuals

WHO CAN BENEFIT Organisations benefiting academics, research workers and students

WHERE FUNDING CAN BE GIVEN Norwich and East Anglia

TYPE OF GRANT One-off

SAMPLE GRANTS £25,000 to H J Sexton Norwich Arts Trust for refurbishment of Assembly House; £7,000 to Theatre Royal (Norwich) Trust for support for Norwegian Opera (The Ring); £7,000 to Norfolk Heritage Fleet Trust for the preservation of historic sailing boats; £5,000 to Friends of Easton College for educational development; £5,000 to Multiple Sclerosis Society for research; £5,000 to British Heart Foundation for research; £4,175 to Norfolk and Norwich Festival for a concert in Norwich Cathedral; £3,500 to Norwich Playhouse for support for theatre; £2,500 to Queens' Heritage Fund for the Queens' College, Cambridge appeal; £2,500 to Queens' Development Fund for the Queens' College, Cambridge appeal

FINANCES *Year* 1997 *Income* £159,175
Grants £182,738

TRUSTEES R E Jarrold (Chairman), A C Jarrold, P J Jarrold, Mrs D J Jarrold, Mrs J Jarrold, Mrs A G Jarrold, Mrs W A L Jarrold

HOW TO APPLY Applications are reviewed at six monthly intervals. No application form is used

WHO TO APPLY TO B Thompson, John Jarrold Trust Ltd, Messrs Jarrold & Sons Ltd, Whitefriars, Norwich, Norfolk NR3 1SH *Tel* 01603 660211

CC NO 242029   **ESTABLISHED** 1965

■ The Jane Jason Charitable Trust

This trust did not respond to CAF's request to amend its entry and, by 30 June 1998, CAF's researchers did not find financial records for later than 1995 on its file at the Charity Commission. Trusts are legally required to submit annual accounts to the Charity Commission under section 42 of the Charities Act 1993

WHAT IS FUNDED Medical research, education and religious institutions

WHAT IS NOT FUNDED Not individuals. Registered charities only

WHO CAN BENEFIT Registered charities benefiting children and young adults, medical professionals, and students. There are no restrictions on the religion and culture of, or disease or medical condition suffered by, the beneficiaries

WHERE FUNDING CAN BE GIVEN UK only

TYPE OF GRANT One-off

TRUSTEES P L Levy, J Jason

HOW TO APPLY By post only to address below – will not be acknowledged

WHO TO APPLY TO P Levis, The Jane Jason Charitable Trust, 71 New Bond Street, London W1Y 9DE

CC NO 275800   **ESTABLISHED** 1978

■ The Jay Foundation

WHAT IS FUNDED For the benefit of children and young people up to and including the age of 25 with the aim to relieve poverty, combat the effects of deprivation, relieve human suffering and distress, advance education and to support their families, legal guardians, carers or educators

WHO CAN BENEFIT Children and young people with disabilities who are victims of abuse, crime or domestic violence. Victims of famine, man-made or natural disasters and war will be considered. Support goes also to carers, at risk groups and those disadvantaged by poverty

WHERE FUNDING CAN BE GIVEN UK and overseas

TYPE OF GRANT One-off or recurring

RANGE OF GRANTS Up to £500

TRUSTEES P C Jackson, S E Jackson, P C Jackson, O J L Jackson

HOW TO APPLY In writing

WHO TO APPLY TO P C Jackson, Chairman, The Jay Foundation, 12 The Mount, Billericay, Essex CM11 1HD *Tel* 01277 633738

CC NO 1068304   **ESTABLISHED** 1998

■ The Jayrose Charitable Trust

WHAT IS FUNDED General charitable purposes

WHO CAN BENEFIT There are no restrictions on the age; professional and economic group; family situation; religion and culture; and social circumstances of; or disease or medical condition suffered by, the beneficiaries

WHERE FUNDING CAN BE GIVEN UK

TRUSTEES J Halpen, R Halpen, S Yodaiken

WHO TO APPLY TO The Jayrose Charitable Trust, 14 Castlefield Avenue, Salford, Manchester M7

CC NO 1067980   **ESTABLISHED** 1997

■ The Jeffrey Charitable Trust

WHAT IS FUNDED Primarily this Trust is concerned with medical research, and carer organisations. It also considers holiday and respite accommodation; health; conservation; independent and special schools, tertiary, higher and special needs education; community facilities and transport; and emergency care for refugees and their families.

WHAT IS NOT FUNDED Projects which are eligible for statutory support and animal charities are not considered

WHO CAN BENEFIT Organisations benefiting: seafarers and fishermen; volunteers; and those in care, fostered and adopted. There are no restrictions on the age of, or disease and medical condition suffered by, the beneficiaries. A wide range of social circumstances are considered for funding

WHERE FUNDING CAN BE GIVEN Scotland, Asia and Africa

TYPE OF GRANT One-off and recurring grants are most commonly made for capital, buildings, core costs, endowment, project, research, running costs, salaries and start-up costs. Funding is available for up to three years

RANGE OF GRANTS £250–£20,000, typical grant £1,000–£1,500

SAMPLE GRANTS £30,000 to Diabetes Centre, Glasgow Royal Infirmary for fundamental research on diabetes

FINANCES *Year* 1998 *Income* £58,000
Grants £44,250

TRUSTEES R B A Bolton, R S Waddell, Mrs M E Bolton

HOW TO APPLY Applications may be made in writing to the address under Who To Apply To. The Trust's long-standing commitment to certain organisations, however, reduces the scope for entirely new grants

WHO TO APPLY TO R B A Bolton, The Jeffrey Charitable Trust, 29 Comrie Street, Crieff, Perthshire PH7 4BD *Tel* 01764 652224

SC NO SCO 15990 **ESTABLISHED** 1972

■ Rees Jeffreys Road Fund

WHAT IS FUNDED The Trustees will consider funding university teaching and postgraduate bursaries; research projects; roadside rests; and transport and alternative transport. Only subjects directly related with road and transportation will be considered

WHO CAN BENEFIT Universities, research bodies, academic staff and students, as well as proposers of roadside rest projects

WHERE FUNDING CAN BE GIVEN UK

TYPE OF GRANT Some are one-off capital, some bursaries and others for research and lectureships include salaries and, in some cases, running costs and endowments. Funding is available for up to three years

FINANCES *Year* 1996 *Income* £252,054
Grants £247,248

TRUSTEES M Milne, CB, BSc, FEng, Dr S Glaister, MSc(Econ), P W Bryant, OBE, MRTPI, M N T Cottell, OBE, FEng, FICE, FIHT, Mrs J Bridgeman, CB, BA, Sir James Duncan, CA, FCIT, CBIM, FRSA, Hon FIRTE

HOW TO APPLY A preliminary telephone call is helpful but not essential. The Trustees meet five times in the year, usually in January, April, July, September and November

WHO TO APPLY TO The Secretary, Rees Jeffreys Road Fund, 13 The Avenue, Chichester, West Sussex PO19 4PX *Tel* 01243 787013
Fax 01243 787013

CC NO 217771 **ESTABLISHED** 1950

■ The M E and J E Jenner Charitable Trust

This trust did not respond to CAF's request to amend its entry and, by 30 June 1998, CAF's researchers did not find financial records for later than 1995 on its file at the Charity Commission. Trusts are legally required to submit annual accounts to the Charity Commission under section 42 of the Charities Act 1993

WHAT IS FUNDED General charitable purposes

WHO CAN BENEFIT There are no restrictions on the age; professional and economic group; family situation; religion and culture; and social circumstances of; or disease or medical condition suffered by, the beneficiaries

WHERE FUNDING CAN BE GIVEN UK and overseas

TRUSTEES Ms J E Jenner, M E Jenner, J T W Martin

WHO TO APPLY TO N Cohen, Solicitor, The M E and J E Jenner Charitable Trust, Messrs Trowers & Hamlins, 6 New Square, Lincoln's Inn, London WC2A 3RP

CC NO 1049767 **ESTABLISHED** 1995

■ The Jenour Foundation

WHAT IS FUNDED General charitable purposes. Preference to local charities

WHAT IS NOT FUNDED Donations to registered charities only

WHO CAN BENEFIT Registered charities only. There are no restrictions on the age; professional and economic group; family situation; religion and culture; and social circumstances of; or disease or medical condition suffered by, the beneficiaries

WHERE FUNDING CAN BE GIVEN UK with preference to Cardiff

TYPE OF GRANT At Trustees' discretion

SAMPLE GRANTS £8,000 to British Red Cross for overseas work; £7,000 to Cancer Research Wales for research and general funds; £4,000 to British Heart Foundation for research; £3,500 to Save the Children; £3,000 to SCOPE; £3,000 to The National Trust for Enterprise Neptune; £2,000 to Barnardos; £2,000 to The Prince's Trust for developing training programme; £2,000 to George Thomas Hospice Care; £1,500 to Cardiff and District Branch of BLESMA

FINANCES *Year* 1997 *Income* £84,025
Grants £83,750

TRUSTEES P J Phillips, MA, G R Camfield, FCA, B G Barry

HOW TO APPLY Deadline for applications is January each year

WHO TO APPLY TO Miss K M Griffin, The Jenour Foundation, Blenheim House, Fitzalan Court, Newport Road, Cardiff CF2 1TS
Tel 01222 481111

CC NO 256637 **ESTABLISHED** 1968

■ The Jephcott Charitable Trust

WHAT IS FUNDED Currently the main areas of interest are the improvement of the quality of life of the poor and developing countries. Priority is given to population control and its achievement through education, health and the environment. The Policy is reviewed regularly. Other charitable purposes will be considered

WHAT IS NOT FUNDED Applications from individuals, including students, are ineligible. No grants made in response to general appeals from large, national organisations nor from organisations concerning themselves with poverty and education in the UK

WHO CAN BENEFIT Organisations benefiting: people of all ages; academics; clergy; legal and medical professionals; research workers; carers; disabled people; those disadvantaged by poverty; those living in rural areas; victims of domestic violence and victims of war. There is no restriction on the disease or medical condition suffered by the beneficiaries. Preference to the smaller concerns/ projects (ie under £500,000)

WHERE FUNDING CAN BE GIVEN UK and overseas

TYPE OF GRANT Usually one-off for a specific project or part of a project. Core funding and/or salaries rarely considered. Monitoring of grant expenditure usually required. Start-up costs and funding of up to three years will be considered

SAMPLE GRANTS £100,000 to Plymouth and District Leukaemia Fund, Devon for equipment; £12,000 to Water Aid, Mozambique to provide a water supply; £10,000 to Friends of ADESA for family centre; £9,489 to Thonh Hoa Maternity Hospital for equipment; £7,000 to Bridgets Trust, Cambridge to help a disabled person; £5,000 to Arpana for Lanes and Drains Project; £5,000 to Feedback Madagascar for Fitekoloha Project; £5,000 to Scott Polar – Russian Academy of Science for research into pollution of the Russian north; £5,000 to University of Cape Town for outreach; £3,413 to L'Arche Brecon, Wales to purchase an estate car

FINANCES *Year* 1996 *Income* £145,571 *Grants* £127,634

TRUSTEES N W Jephcott, MA, (Chair), Mrs A Morgan, MBA, Dr P Davis, MPhil, A T North, LLB, District Judge, Mrs M F Jephcott

HOW TO APPLY At any time in writing to the Secretary. Trustees meet twice a year. Applications should include clear details of the need the intended project is designed to meet plus an outline budget. Only applications from eligible bodies are acknowledged, when further information about the project may be requested. Guidelines are available upon request. Please enclose a sae

WHO TO APPLY TO Mrs Meg Harris, Secretary, The Jephcott Charitable Trust, Gappers Farm, Membury, Axminster, Devon EX13 7TX

CC NO 240915   **ESTABLISHED** 1965

■ The Jerusalem Academy Trust

WHAT IS FUNDED General charitable purposes

WHO CAN BENEFIT There are no restrictions on the age; professional and economic group; family situation; religion and culture; and social circumstances of; or disease or medical condition suffered by, the beneficiaries

WHERE FUNDING CAN BE GIVEN UK

SAMPLE GRANTS £29,724 to Jerusalem Academy Jewish Studies

FINANCES *Year* 1996 *Income* £32,882 *Grants* £29,724

TRUSTEES A Hubert, W Hubert, J Gradel, M Gradel, E Koppenheim, S Mocton

WHO TO APPLY TO Barry Cohen, The Jerusalem Academy Trust, 30 Roston Road, Salford M7 0FS

CC NO 262716   **ESTABLISHED** 1971

■ Jesus Hospital in Chipping Barnet

WHAT IS FUNDED This Trust will consider funding: almshouses; support to voluntary and community organisations; support to volunteers; respite care and care for carers; support and self help groups; ambulances and mobile units; special needs education; training for work; costs of study; academic subjects, sciences and research; and community services

WHAT IS NOT FUNDED No grants for relief of rates, taxes or other public funds

WHO CAN BENEFIT Individuals and local organisations benefiting: people of all ages; academics; research workers; scientists and students. Unemployed people and volunteers; all types of family situation; at risk groups; carers; disabled people; those disadvantaged by poverty and socially isolated; victims of abuse, crime and domestic violence. Also those suffering from a variety of diseases and medical conditions will be considered

WHERE FUNDING CAN BE GIVEN The former Urban Districts of Barnet and East Barnet and Friern Barnet as constituted prior to 1 April 1965

TYPE OF GRANT Capital and one-off. Funding is available for one year or less. Each case is considered on its merits

RANGE OF GRANTS Up to £10,350

FINANCES *Year* 1997 *Income* £278,290 *Grants* £65,089

TRUSTEES M Boyes, A Brum, W S Carrington, Rev Canon A G K Esdaile, J R Hease, M Holford, J Liming, Rev Father R Marriott, P J Mellows, A Pares, M L Slack, F N Wilshire

HOW TO APPLY To the address under Who To Apply To in writing. Relief in Need applications for individuals are normally through recognised organisations

WHO TO APPLY TO Mrs Elaine Huxtable, Clerk to Visitors, Jesus Hospital in Chipping Barnet, Ravenscroft Lodge, 37 Union Street, Barnet EN5 4HY *Tel* 0181-440 4374

CC NO 210151   **ESTABLISHED** 1679

■ Jewish Child's Day

WHAT IS FUNDED To consider applications from organisations in Great Britain and elsewhere for grants for specific purposes of direct benefit to Jewish children. Accounts for the past year must be furnished

WHAT IS NOT FUNDED Grants are made to registered charities only. Applications from individuals, including students, are not normally supported. No grants are made in response to general appeals from large national organisations nor to smaller bodies working in areas other than those set out above

WHO CAN BENEFIT Organisations caring for Jewish children

WHERE FUNDING CAN BE GIVEN UK and overseas

TYPE OF GRANT For medical or scientific equipment, educational material, playthings, clothing, medical supplies, etc of direct benefit to Jewish children with special needs. Grants are not made towards salaries or capital costs

RANGE OF GRANTS £1,000–£133,800

SAMPLE GRANTS £133,800 to Children of Chernobyl; £15,387 to Children's Education Programme for support costs; £14,150 to Youth Aliya; £10,000 to Lubavitch School; £9,425 to Eliya; £5,600 to Shalva; £5,000 to Alyn Orthopaedic Hospital; £3,700 to Micha Society for Deaf Children, Tel Aviv; £3,700 to British Friends of Assaf Harofeh Medical Centre; £3,050 to Israel Sport Centre for the Disabled

FINANCES *Year* 1996–97 *Income* £608,943 *Grants* £269,605

TRUSTEES Rev S Amias, MBE, D Band, Mrs D Birk, Mrs V Campus, D Clayton, S Cohen, Mrs W Cohen, J Davis, H Gosen, Mrs J Halperin, A Handler, Miss N Hurstbourne, Mrs A Ingram, Mrs J Jacobs, Lady

Jakobovitz, Mrs J Karsberg, Mrs T Kling, Mrs S Lurie, S Medhi, Mrs J Moss, S Moss, MBE, L de Rothschild, CBE, R Silverman, Miss J Stiebel, MBE, N Temko, M Worth

PUBLICATIONS Newsletter published two or three times per annum, *50th Anniversary Commemorative Book*

HOW TO APPLY Applications need to be received by January and July for consideration at Allocations Meetings in March and September

WHO TO APPLY TO P Shaw, Executive Director, Jewish Child's Day, 707 High Road, London N12 0BT

CC NO 209266 **ESTABLISHED** 1947

■ Jewish Continuity (formerly the Jewish Educational Development Trust

WHAT IS FUNDED Jewish education to create a vibrant community of proud, knowledgeable and committed Jews

WHO CAN BENEFIT Educational institutes, colleges and schools benefiting Jewish children, young adults and students

WHERE FUNDING CAN BE GIVEN UK

TYPE OF GRANT Recurring and one-off

RANGE OF GRANTS Under £8,000–£223,750

SAMPLE GRANTS £223,750 to JCYA; £150,200 to REQUJE; £103,146 to ULIE (RESQUJE); £88,227 to School J-Link; £58,000 to Union of Jewish Students; £41,000 to B'nai B'rith Enterprise Ltd (database); £40,000 to National Jewish Chaplaincy Board; £33,096 to Glasgow Jewish Continuity; £30,000 to National Jewish Chaplaincy Board (Cambridge Chaplain) (JCAB); £27,000 to Chief Rabbinate Bursary Fund

FINANCES *Year* 1996 *Income* £1,957,300 *Grants* £1,732,005

TRUSTEES The Chief Rabbi, Dr J Sacks, Dr M Sinclair, V Blank, Sir T Chinn, CVO, S S Cohen, C Corman, Mrs R Deech, R Dorfman, Sir M Gilbert, CBE, M Goldmeier, Dr N D Khalili, M Levy, A Loftus, G Ognall, M L Phillips, S Rubin, Sir H Solomon, C Stein, The Rt Hon The Lord Woolf, The Rt Hon The Lord Young of Graffham, PC

HOW TO APPLY To the address under Who To Apply To in writing

WHO TO APPLY TO Lady Winston, Secretary, Jewish Continuity, Balfour House, 741 High Street, London N12 0BQ

CC NO 1024140 **ESTABLISHED** 1993

■ The Jewish Educational Development Trust

WHAT IS FUNDED The promotion of the Jewish Faith and the advancement of education amongst the Jews of Great Britain. In furtherance of the above object, the Trustees may promote or assist in the promotion of Jewish Day Schools, educational resource centres, the training of teachers, etc

WHAT IS NOT FUNDED Grants are rarely given to individuals

WHO CAN BENEFIT Mainly to schools and institutions benefiting Jewish people

WHERE FUNDING CAN BE GIVEN UK

TYPE OF GRANT Grants for building, teacher training, educational resources

SAMPLE GRANTS £12,500 to Immanuel College

FINANCES *Year* 1996 *Income* £232,525 *Grants* £13,103

TRUSTEES Lord Jakobovits (Hon Life President), The Chief Rabbi, Dr Jonathan Sacks (President), Sir Trevor Chinn, CVO (Vice President). Members: M L Phillips, S Kalms, H Knobil, R Metzger, A Millet, C

Morris, M Paisner, B Rix, QC, Sir H Solomon, C Stein. M Teacher, F Worms

PUBLICATIONS *Securing our Future* Think Tank Report

HOW TO APPLY To the address under Who To Apply To

WHO TO APPLY TO R Metzger, The Jewish Educational Development Trust, 44 Albert Road, London NW4 2SJ

CC NO 313443 **ESTABLISHED** 1971

■ Jewish Religious Education Supporters Fund

This trust did not respond to CAF's request to amend its entry and, by 30 June 1998, CAF's researchers did not find financial records for later than 1995 on its file at the Charity Commission. Trusts are legally required to submit annual accounts to the Charity Commission under section 42 of the Charities Act 1993

WHAT IS FUNDED Jewish religious education

WHO CAN BENEFIT Jewish children and young adults

WHERE FUNDING CAN BE GIVEN UK

TRUSTEES A Pfeffer, J Sanger, A Smith, L W Grosshoph

HOW TO APPLY All funds fully committed. No further applications considered

WHO TO APPLY TO A Pfeffer, Jewish Religious Education Supporters Fund, 21 Brant wood Road, Salford M7 0EN

CC NO 249973 **ESTABLISHED** 1966

■ The Jewish Youth Fund (incorporating the Jewish Tercentenary Commemoration Fund)

WHAT IS FUNDED To assist, normally by way of loan, towards the cost of building schemes for Jewish youth clubs and centres

WHO CAN BENEFIT Jewish youth clubs and centres

WHERE FUNDING CAN BE GIVEN UK

TYPE OF GRANT By loan primarily, but also in exceptional circumstances by grants, for special purposes (not maintenance). Buildings may be considered

RANGE OF GRANTS £1,500–£10,000

SAMPLE GRANTS £10,000 to Association for Jewish Youth; £10,000 to Jewish Programme Materials Project; £10,000 to Edgware Masorti Youth Centre; £10,000 to SPEC Jewish Youth and Community Centre; £5,000 to Habomm Dror; £5,000 to Redbridge Jewish Youth and Community Centre; £5,000 to Bushey Youth Scene; £5,000 to Jewish Lads' and Girls' Brigade; £5,000 to Union of Maccabi Associations; £3,000 to Noam Masorti Youth

FINANCES *Year* 1997 *Income* £114,571 *Grants* £77,090

TRUSTEES Judge Israel Finestein, QC, J Gestetner. Lady Morris of Kenwood, P L Levy, OBE

HOW TO APPLY Considered by the Jewish Youth Fund Advisory Committee

WHO TO APPLY TO Peter Shaw, Secretary, The Jewish Youth Fund, 5th Floor, 707 High Road, London N12 0BT

CC NO 251902 **ESTABLISHED** 1937

■ The Harold Joels Charitable Trust

WHAT IS FUNDED General charitable purposes

WHO CAN BENEFIT Registered charities only. There are no restrictions on the age; professional and economic group; family situation; religion and culture; and social circumstances of; or disease or medical condition suffered by, the beneficiaries.

332

Think carefully about every application. Is it justified?

However, particular favour is given to Jewish organisations
WHERE FUNDING CAN BE GIVEN UK and overseas
RANGE OF GRANTS £10–£15,000
SAMPLE GRANTS £15,000 to the Jonathan Joels Charitable Trust; £5,018 to Women's American ORT; £5,000 to World Jewish Relief; £2,913 to Temple Beth Sharon; £1,325 to Women's Resource Centre of Sarasota; £1,100 to Jewish Community Centre of Sarasota; £1,000 to United States Holocaust Memorial Museum; £1,000 to Jewish Care; £850 to Friends of the Royal Academy; £768 to United Synagogue
FINANCES *Year* 1997 *Income* £32,709 *Grants* £33,037
TRUSTEES H Joels, Dr N Joels, Mrs V Joels, N E Joels
HOW TO APPLY In writing to the address under Who To Apply To
WHO TO APPLY TO M S Zatman & Co, Accountants, Refuge House,The Harold Joels Charitable Trust, 311 Ballards Lane, Finchely, London N12 8LY
CC NO 206326   **ESTABLISHED** 1957

The Jacob & Lena Joels Charitable Trust

WHAT IS FUNDED General charitable purposes
WHO CAN BENEFIT Registered charities only. There are no restrictions on the age; professional and economic group; family situation; religion and culture; and social circumstances of; or disease or medical condition suffered by, the beneficiaries
WHERE FUNDING CAN BE GIVEN UK
SAMPLE GRANTS £785,934 to Friends of the Hebrew University
FINANCES *Year* 1996 *Income* £643,677 *Grants* £785,934
TRUSTEES H Joels, Dr N Joels, N E Joels, Ms J L Joels
HOW TO APPLY In writing only
WHO TO APPLY TO The Jacob & Lena Joels Charitable Trust, M S Zatman & Co, 311 Ballards Lane, Finchley, London N12 8LY
CC NO 206328   **ESTABLISHED** 1959

The Jonathan Joels Charitable Trust

WHAT IS FUNDED General charitable purposes
WHO CAN BENEFIT Registered charities only. There are no restrictions on the age; professional and economic group; family situation; religion and culture; and social circumstances of; or disease or medical condition suffered by, the beneficiaries
WHERE FUNDING CAN BE GIVEN UK and overseas
RANGE OF GRANTS $5–$7,661
SAMPLE GRANTS $7,661 to VJC of Bergen County; $6,207 to Moriah School; $1,902 to Congregation Ahavath Torah; $870 to Jewish Community Centre, Palisades; $472 to Moriah Auxiliary Parents; $360 to Sinai Special Needs Institute; $250 to Friends of the IDF; $219 to AMIT Women; $190 to Friends of Lubavitch; $108 to the Orthodox Union
FINANCES *Year* 1996 *Income* £32,470 *Grants* £11,922
TRUSTEES J Joels, N E Joels, H Joels
NOTES The figures in the Range of Grants and Sample Grants are in US dollars
HOW TO APPLY In writing only
WHO TO APPLY TO The Jonathan Joels Charitable Trust, Messrs M S Zatman & Co, 311 Ballards Lane, Finchley, London N12 8LY
CC NO 278408   **ESTABLISHED** 1978

The Nicholas Joels Charitable Trust

WHAT IS FUNDED General charitable purposes
WHO CAN BENEFIT Registered charities only. There are no restrictions on the age; professional and economic group; family situation; religion and culture; and social circumstances of; or disease or medical condition suffered by, the beneficiaries
WHERE FUNDING CAN BE GIVEN UK and overseas
RANGE OF GRANTS £10–£2916
SAMPLE GRANTS £2,916 to Norwood Ravenswood; £2,000 to R F Lamont Florence Fund; £1,500 to Mike Liberman Memorial; £1,250 to Joint Jewish Charitable Trust; £1,115 to CBF World Jewish Relief
FINANCES *Year* 1997 *Income* £22,407 *Grants* £15,819
TRUSTEES N E Joels, J J Joels, H Joels
HOW TO APPLY In writing only
WHO TO APPLY TO M S Zatman & Co, The Nicholas Joels Charitable Trust, 311 Ballards Lane, Finchley, London N12 8LY
CC NO 278409   **ESTABLISHED** 1978

The Norman Joels Charitable Trust

WHAT IS FUNDED General charitable purposes
WHO CAN BENEFIT Registered charities only. There are no restrictions on the age; professional and economic group; family situation; religion and culture; and social circumstances of; or disease or medical condition suffered by, the beneficiaries
WHERE FUNDING CAN BE GIVEN UK
RANGE OF GRANTS £5–£4,000
SAMPLE GRANTS £4,000 to JPAIME; £1,140 to New London Synagogue; £500 to Jewish Care; £400 to Ravenswood; £350 to Youth Aliyah; £300 to World Jewish Relief; £280 to Jewish Deaf Association; £200 to Friends of the Federation of Women Zionists; £200 to Hill Homes Development Appeal; £130 to Assembly of Masorti Synagogues
FINANCES *Year* 1997 *Income* £41,932 *Grants* £10,461
TRUSTEES N Joels, H Joels, Mrs M Joels, Miss J Joels
HOW TO APPLY In writing only to the address under Who To Apply To
WHO TO APPLY TO The Norman Joels Charitable Trust, M S Zatman & Co, 311 Ballards Lane, Finchley, London N12 8LY
CC NO 206325   **ESTABLISHED** 1957

J G Joffe Charitable Trust

WHAT IS FUNDED General charitable purposes. Funds are fully committed to charities of special interest to the Trustees. There is no intention to widen the range and no applications either from organisations or individuals will be considered
WHAT IS NOT FUNDED No applications will be considered
WHO CAN BENEFIT There are no restrictions on the age; professional and economic group; family situation; religion and culture; and social circumstances of; or disease or medical condition suffered by, the beneficiaries
WHERE FUNDING CAN BE GIVEN UK
TYPE OF GRANT One-off
FINANCES *Year* 1997 *Income* £360,000 *Grants* £420,000
TRUSTEES V L Joffe, J G Joffe
HOW TO APPLY **This Trust states that it does not respond to unsolicited applications**

WHO TO APPLY TO J Joffe, J G Joffe Charitable Trust, Liddington Manor, Liddington, Swindon, Wiltshire SN4 0HD
CC NO 270299   **ESTABLISHED** 1968

■ Miss A M Johns Charitable Trust

WHAT IS FUNDED General charitable purposes with special consideration to missionary work
WHO CAN BENEFIT There are no restrictions on the age; professional and economic group; family situation; religion and culture; and social circumstances of; or disease or medical condition suffered by, the beneficiaries
WHERE FUNDING CAN BE GIVEN In practice, mainly within a five mile radius of Beckenham
TRUSTEES S J Fraser and the Partners of Williams de Broe Hill Chaplin and Company
WHO TO APPLY TO P J Castledine, Miss A M Johns Charitable Trust, c/o Thackray Wood, 233–235 High Street, Beckenham, Kent BR3 1BN
CC NO 1060135   **ESTABLISHED** 1997

■ The N B Johnson Charitable Settlement

WHAT IS FUNDED General charitable purposes. Each case considered on its merits. Particularly Jewish charities
WHAT IS NOT FUNDED Generally registered charities only. Individuals only considered in very special cases
WHO CAN BENEFIT Registered charities benefiting Jewish people
WHERE FUNDING CAN BE GIVEN Bias to local causes (Manchester area)
TYPE OF GRANT Cash
FINANCES *Year* 1995 *Income* £31,228 *Grants* £32,496
TRUSTEES N B Johnson, Mrs S J Johnson, L Hyman
HOW TO APPLY At any time to the address under Who To Apply To, but will only be dealt with when Trustees meet every three months and grants are not made in the intervening months
WHO TO APPLY TO L Hyman, The N B Johnson Charitable Settlement, Pannone & Partners, 123 Deansgate, Manchester M3 2BU
CC NO 277237   **ESTABLISHED** 1978

■ The Johnson Foundation

WHAT IS FUNDED Medicine and health, welfare, education, environmental resources, infrastructure development and professional bodies
WHAT IS NOT FUNDED No grants to individuals or students
WHO CAN BENEFIT Registered charities benefiting: medical professionals; carers; disabled people; those disadvantaged by poverty; and victims of abuse. Those suffering from various diseases and medical conditions will also be considered
WHERE FUNDING CAN BE GIVEN Merseyside
TYPE OF GRANT One-off, recurrent, core costs, project and research. Funding is available for up to two years
RANGE OF GRANTS £100–£25,000, typical grant £500

SAMPLE GRANTS £25,000 to Age Concern for a Devonshire Centre; £1,000 to Shaftesbury Youth Centre for youth club facilities; £1,000 to Barnstondale for holiday scheme for underprivileged children
FINANCES *Year* 1997–98 *Income* £721,689 *Grants* £76,208
TRUSTEES P R Johnson, S E Johnson, C W Johnson
PUBLICATIONS Annual Report
HOW TO APPLY To the address under Who To Apply To in writing at any time. Trustees meet monthly
WHO TO APPLY TO P R Johnson, The Johnson Foundation, Westmount, Vyner Road South, Birkenhead, Merseyside L43 7PN *Tel* 0151-653 0566
CC NO 518660   **ESTABLISHED** 1987

■ Johnson Group Cleaners Charity

WHAT IS FUNDED Support of Merseyside charities which feature poverty, underprivileged, relief of suffering. This includes: Councils for Voluntary Service; care in the community; and holidays and outings
WHAT IS NOT FUNDED No grants to national charities or individuals
WHO CAN BENEFIT Registered local charities benefiting children, young adults and older people; at risk groups; carers; those disadvantaged by poverty; ex-offenders and those at risk of offending; homeless people; victims of abuse and domestic violence and those suffering from substance misuse
WHERE FUNDING CAN BE GIVEN Merseyside
TYPE OF GRANT Core costs, one-off, project and running costs. All funding is for up to two years
SAMPLE GRANTS £9,000 to Victims of Violence to assist with essential running costs; £5,000 to Acorn Venture Urban Farm to assist with essential running costs; £5,000 to Merseyside Council for Voluntary Services to assist with essential running costs; £5,000 to Sefton Young Carers to assist with essential running costs; £2,500 to Sail Training Association berths for underprivileged children in Merseyside; £2,000 to Liverpool Motorists Annual Outing for deprived children's day out at Southport; £1,500 to Ocean Youth Club for berths for underprivileged children in Merseyside; £650 to Sefton Women's and Children's Aid to assist with essential running costs; £302 to Marsh Lane Boxing Club for equipment; £250 to Pacific Celtic Boys Foot Ball Club for jerseys
FINANCES *Year* 1998 *Income* £102,145 *Grants* £113,640
TRUSTEES Johnson Group Cleaners Trustee Company (No 1) Ltd
HOW TO APPLY To Charity Administrator in writing
WHO TO APPLY TO Miss A F Smith, Charity Administrator, Johnson Group Cleaners Charity, Mildmay Road, Bootle, Merseyside L20 5EW
CC NO 216973   **ESTABLISHED** 1990

■ The Johnson Matthey plc Educational Trust

WHAT IS FUNDED With particular application to persons connected with or sons or daughters of persons connected with any business, trade, or industry involving the use or processing of precious metals, for first degrees
WHO CAN BENEFIT Individuals and institutions benefiting students, especially those who have

connections with the precious metal business, trade or industry

WHERE FUNDING CAN BE GIVEN UK

FINANCES *Year* 1996 *Income* £22,872

TRUSTEES Johnson Matthey (Nominees) Ltd

PUBLICATIONS Advertisements appear in relevant trade journals

HOW TO APPLY Applications to the address under Who To Apply To, annually by 1 November

WHO TO APPLY TO Mrs D Barnes The Johnson Matthey plc Educational Trust, The Beeches, Thamesdale, London Colney, Hertfordshire AL1 1TB

CC NO 313576   **ESTABLISHED** 1967

■ Johnnie Johnson Trust

WHAT IS FUNDED Heritage and training/adventure breaks for children, youth and welfare organisations

WHO CAN BENEFIT To benefit children and young adults

WHERE FUNDING CAN BE GIVEN West Midlands

SAMPLE GRANTS £51,500 to Johnnie Johnson Adventure Trust; £350 to Young Enterprise; £200 to St Matthew's Church; £100 to 1st Shirley Scouts; £100 to NW District Scout Association

FINANCES *Year* 1996 *Income* £82,895 *Grants* £52,500

TRUSTEES S B Benbow, J S Fordham, G P Green, P E T Johnson, P V Johnson

HOW TO APPLY To the address under Who To Apply To in writing

WHO TO APPLY TO P V Johnson, Johnnie Johnson Trust, Newton House, Hewell Road, Enfield, Reditch, Worcestershire B97 6AJ

CC NO 200351   **ESTABLISHED** 1961

■ The Joicey Trust

WHAT IS FUNDED This Trust will consider funding activities within the following fields: residential facilities and services; a range of infrastructure, technical support and development; charity or voluntary umbrella bodies; religious buildings; music, dance and theatre; health care, facilities and buildings; conservation; education and training and community facilities and services. National appeals are not normally supported unless there is specific evidence of activity benefiting the local area

WHAT IS NOT FUNDED Excluded from consideration are: (a) bodies not having registered charitable status, (b) personal applications, and (c) applications on behalf of individuals, and (d) applications from groups that do not have an identifiable project within the area Where Funding Can Be Given

WHO CAN BENEFIT Registered charities in the North East or groups with a specific project within the area Where Funding Can Be Given. The Trust will consider funding organisations benefiting: people of all ages; seafarers and fishermen; those in care, fostered and adopted; and one parent families. There are no restrictions on the religion or culture of, and the disease or medical condition suffered by, the beneficiaries

WHERE FUNDING CAN BE GIVEN The County of Northumberland and that area of the old metropolitan County of Tyne and Wear. Applications will not be supported outside this area

TYPE OF GRANT The Trustees support both capital and revenue projects but tend to favour discrete projects over the support of general running costs. They do not normally consider recurrent grants but start-up finance is sometimes available, always

providing that the Trustees believe that the project can become viable without the Trust's assistance in a small number of years. Other grants considered are: buildings, core costs, one-off, project and salaries. Funding is available for up to one year

SAMPLE GRANTS £6,298 to Ford Parish Church; £5,000 to Disabled Housing Association; £5,000 to St John the Evangelist, Spittal; £5,000 to Newcastle Diocesan Repair Fund; £3,000 to The Salvation Army, Shiremoor; £2,500 to Calvert Trust, Kielder; £2,500 to Care Fund, Ponteland; £2,000 to Disabled North; £2,000 to Tyne and Wear Foundation; £2,000 to Peabody Trust

FINANCES *Year* 1997 *Income* £171,000 *Grants* £166,000

TRUSTEES Lord Joicey, Lady Joicey, Elizabeth, Lady Joicey, R H Dickinson, Hon A H Joicey

HOW TO APPLY Twice yearly – by end of May and November, in writing to the Appeals Secretary N A Furness at the address below. Applications should include a brief description of the project, together with a copy of the previous years accounts and where possible a copy of the current years projected income and expenditure. Large projects should give an indication from where the major sources of funding are likely to come. There are no formal application forms. Unsuccessful applications are not acknowledged unless an sae is provided with the original application

WHO TO APPLY TO N A Furness, FCA, Appeals Secretary, The Joicey Trust, Messrs Dickinson Dees, St Anne's Wharf, 112 Quayside, Newcastle upon Tyne NE99 1SB *Tel* 0191-279 9679 *Fax* 0191-279 9100

CC NO 244679   **ESTABLISHED** 1965

■ Joint Churches Community Project

WHAT IS FUNDED The relief of poverty and sickness, the advancement of education and the provision of recreational facilities in the interests of social welfare by promoting co-operation between local people and the local authorities

WHO CAN BENEFIT Local people, particularly those disadvantaged by poverty and those who are sick

WHERE FUNDING CAN BE GIVEN Greenbank, Kells, Mirehouse and Woodhouse in Cumbria

FINANCES *Year* 1997 *Income* £20,150

HOW TO APPLY To the address below in writing

WHO TO APPLY TO Fr Tom Singleton, Chairperson, Joint Churches Community Project, St Mary's Presbytery, High Road, Kells, Whitehaven, Cumbria CA28 9PG

CC NO 1064205   **ESTABLISHED** 1997

■ Joint Jewish Charitable Trust

WHAT IS FUNDED General charitable purposes, particularly those benefiting Jewish people

WHO CAN BENEFIT Jewish people. However, there are no restrictions on the age; professional and economic group; family situation; religion and culture; and social circumstances of; or disease or medical condition suffered by, the beneficiaries

WHERE FUNDING CAN BE GIVEN UK

WHO TO APPLY TO Eldred H Kraines, Secretary, Joint Jewish Charitable Trust, Balfour House, 741 High Road, London N12 0BQ

CC NO 1060078   **ESTABLISHED** 1997

■ The Jones 1986 Charitable Trust

WHAT IS FUNDED General charitable purposes primarily to organisations in the Nottingham area

WHAT IS NOT FUNDED No grants to individuals

WHO CAN BENEFIT Registered charities. There are no restrictions on the age; professional and economic group; family situation; religion and culture; and social circumstances of; or disease or medical condition suffered by, the beneficiaries

WHERE FUNDING CAN BE GIVEN UK, with preference for the Nottingham area

SAMPLE GRANTS £186,900 to Nottingham University; £60,000 to Nottinghamshire Wildlife Trust; £55,000 to Riding for the Disabled Association, Highland group; £54,000 to Age Concern, Nottinghamshire; £50,000 to the Nottinghamshire Royal Society for the Blind; £50,000 to Portland College; £40,000 to Cope Children's Trust; £35,000 to Carlton Digby School; £34,000 to the Lord Taverners; £32,000 to Nottinghamshire Leukaemia Appeal

FINANCES *Year* 1997 *Income* £979,895 *Grants* £1,049,551

TRUSTEES J O Knight, R B Stringfellow

HOW TO APPLY The Trustees identify their own target charities and do not wish to receive applications

WHO TO APPLY TO R B Stringfellow, The Jones 1986 Charitable Trust, Messrs Evershed, Royal Standard Place, Nottingham NG1 6FZ

CC NO 327176   **ESTABLISHED** 1986

■ The Marjorie and Geoffrey Jones Charitable Trust

WHAT IS FUNDED General charitable purposes

WHO CAN BENEFIT There are no restrictions on the age; professional and economic group; family situation; religion and culture; and social circumstances of; or disease or medical condition suffered by, the beneficiaries

WHERE FUNDING CAN BE GIVEN UK

RANGE OF GRANTS £1,000–£5,000

SAMPLE GRANTS £5,000 to Cancer Relief Macmillan Fund; £5,000 to The Torquay Museum; £5,000 to Motor Neurone Disease Association; £5,000 to Children's Hospice South West; £5,000 to National Trust for Yealm Estuary; £5,000 to Devon Air Ambulance; £5,000 to Cheshire Homes, Brixham; £5,000 to the Exeter Cystic Fibrosis Research Fund; £5,000 to Ocean Youth Club, Torbay; £3,000 to West of England School for Children

FINANCES *Year* 1997 *Income* £1,353,115 *Grants* £83,000

TRUSTEES W F C Boughey, P M Kay, N J Wollen

WHO TO APPLY TO N J Wollen, Trustee, The Marjorie and Geoffrey Jones Charitable Trust, Carlton House, 30 The Terrace, Torquay, Devon TQ1 1BS

CC NO 1051031   **ESTABLISHED** 1995

■ Edward Cecil Jones Settlement

WHAT IS FUNDED General charitable purposes

WHAT IS NOT FUNDED No grants to individuals

WHO CAN BENEFIT Local registered charities. There are no restrictions on the age; professional and economic group; family situation; religion and culture; and social circumstances of; or disease or medical condition suffered by, the beneficiaries

WHERE FUNDING CAN BE GIVEN County Borough of Southend-on-Sea only

TYPE OF GRANT Recurrent and occasionally one-off

RANGE OF GRANTS Below £1,000–£69,150

SAMPLE GRANTS £69,150 to Essex Community Foundation; £65,000 to Fowler Memorial Trust; £40,000 to CAFOD; £25,319 to Southend YMCA; £15,000 to Christchurch Development; £10,000 to Corporate Action Trust; £5,000 to Ormiston Children's Trust; £3,000 to NSPCC; £2,750 to Queen Elizabeth Foundation for the Disabled; £2,000 to RNIB

FINANCES *Year* 1997 *Income* £123,470 *Grants* £260,594

TRUSTEES J E Tolhurst, J S Cue, W J Tolhurst

HOW TO APPLY The deadline for applications is December. No application form used

WHO TO APPLY TO P J Tolhurst, Edward Cecil Jones Settlement, Tolhurst Fisher Solicitors, 4th Floor, Liverpool Victoria House, New London Road, Chelmsford, Essex CM2 0PP

CC NO 216166   **ESTABLISHED** 1957

■ Cemlyn Jones Trust

WHAT IS FUNDED Medicine and health, welfare, education, sciences, humanities, religion, environmental resources

WHAT IS NOT FUNDED No grants to individuals

WHO CAN BENEFIT Small local projects benefiting: children; young adults; students; at risk groups; those disadvantaged by poverty; homeless people; and socially isolated people. There is no restriction on the disease or medical condition suffered by the beneficiaries

WHERE FUNDING CAN BE GIVEN North Wales

TYPE OF GRANT One-off and recurrent

RANGE OF GRANTS £100 upwards

SAMPLE GRANTS £45,000 to Development Trust, University of Wales, Bangor for marine, environmental and archaeological research; £7,000 to Woodland Trust for Coed Nant General, Snowdonia and a site at Caernarfon; £5,000 to RSPB for emergency bittern programme at Malltraeth Marsh; £1,500 to Council for Music in Hospitals for tour of Anglesey

FINANCES *Year* 1997–98 *Income* £37,300 *Grants* £58,500

TRUSTEES P G Brown, J E Lee, E G Jones

PUBLICATIONS Annual Report

HOW TO APPLY In writing

WHO TO APPLY TO P G Brown, Cemlyn Jones Trust, 59 Madoc Street, Llandudno, County of Conwy LL30 2TW *Tel* 01492 874391 *Fax* 01492 871990

CC NO 1039164   **ESTABLISHED** 1994

■ The Jordan Charitable Foundation

WHAT IS FUNDED General charitable purposes

WHO CAN BENEFIT There are no restrictions on the age; professional and economic group; family situation; religion and culture; and social circumstances of; or disease or medical condition suffered by, the beneficiaries

WHERE FUNDING CAN BE GIVEN UK

TYPE OF GRANT One-off, capital and core costs will be considered

SAMPLE GRANTS £150,750 to Boston Public Library Foundation for the second instalment (of three) for restoration of the library; £100,000 to the National Hospital for Neurology towards the Neuro Rehabilitation Centre Appeal; £65,000 to the Martha Trust, Hereford towards cost of providing therapy garden; £20,000 to Herefordshire Nature Trust; £12,000 to Century Halls for England; £10,000 to the Jersey Wildlife Preservation Trust; £10,000 to St Mary's Hospital, London for an Anniversary Appeal; £8,000 to Whizz Kidz for the purchase of specialist wheelchair via sponsored expedition

FINANCES *Year* 1997 *Income* £932,678 *Grants* £556,250

TRUSTEES Sir R A B Miller, Sir G Russell, R A O Stockwell, Snowport Limited, Parkdove Limited

HOW TO APPLY Postal applications only, with details/costings, etc of any specific projects to be funded. No response will normally be given unless a grant is approved or if the Trustees wish to obtain further information

WHO TO APPLY TO R A Stockwell, Trustee, The Jordan Charitable Foundation, Rawlinson and Hunter, Eagle House, 110 Jermyn Street, London SW1Y 6RH *Tel* 0171-451 9000

CC NO 1051507   **ESTABLISHED** 1995

■ H O Joseph Charitable Trust

This trust did not respond to CAF's request to amend its entry and, by 30 June 1998, CAF's researchers did not find financial records for later than 1995 on its file at the Charity Commission. Trusts are legally required to submit annual accounts to the Charity Commission under section 42 of the Charities Act 1993

WHAT IS FUNDED Principally welfare organisations, although other charitable purposes are considered. Preference to charities of which the Trust has special interest, knowledge or association

WHAT IS NOT FUNDED No grants to individuals

WHO CAN BENEFIT Registered charities only. There are no restrictions on the age; professional and economic group; family situation; religion and culture; and social circumstances of; or disease or medical condition suffered by, the beneficiaries

WHERE FUNDING CAN BE GIVEN Israel

TRUSTEES E W Joseph, OBE, M S Cohen, J Gestetner

HOW TO APPLY In writing to the address below

WHO TO APPLY TO J Gestetner, H O Joseph Charitable Trust, 7 Oakhill Avenue, London NW3 7RD

CC NO 233575   **ESTABLISHED** 1964

■ J E Joseph Charitable Fund

WHAT IS FUNDED For the general relief of poor and needy Jews in certain cities and places in the area Where Funding Can Be Given, priority being given to those of Sephardi extraction. The Trustees respond to all applications which are first vetted by the Secretary

WHAT IS NOT FUNDED Grants to individuals in exceptional cases only and are usually made to assist towards education and in particular further and higher education. No application from an organisation will be considered without a copy of its most recent set of accounts. Only Jewish individuals or organisations need apply

WHO CAN BENEFIT Jewish community organisations, especially those catering for the socially disadvantaged and youth. Only exceptionally individuals

WHERE FUNDING CAN BE GIVEN UK (principally London and Manchester), Near and Far East, Israel, Palestine

TYPE OF GRANT Outright cash grants frequently on an annual basis. Very occasionally loans

RANGE OF GRANTS £500–£10,000

FINANCES *Year* 1998 *Income* £107,098 *Grants* £90,750

HOW TO APPLY To the Secretary by letter

WHO TO APPLY TO Timothy Simon, The Secretary, J E Joseph Charitable Fund, 2 New Square, Lincoln's Inn, London WC2A 3RZ

CC NO 209058   **ESTABLISHED** 1946

■ The Lady Eileen Joseph Foundation

WHAT IS FUNDED Largely welfare and medical causes

WHO CAN BENEFIT National organisations benefiting at risk groups, those disadvantaged by poverty and socially isolated people. There is no restriction on the disease or medical condition suffered by the beneficiaries

WHERE FUNDING CAN BE GIVEN UK

RANGE OF GRANTS £100–£12,000

SAMPLE GRANTS £12,000 to Textile Conservation Centre; £5,000 to Tower Hamlets College Voluntary Fund; £2,500 to Community Security Trust; £2,000 to BACUP; £550 to National Listening Library; £500 to Alzheimer's Disease Society; £500 to Cancer Research Campaign; £500 to Prince's Trust Trading Ltd; £500 to The Samaritans; £300 to Variety Club Events Ltd

FINANCES *Year* 1997 *Income* £50,453 *Grants* £25,200

TRUSTEES A A Davis, Mrs J Sawdy, T W P Simpson, Mrs N J Thornton

HOW TO APPLY To the address under Who To Apply To in writing

WHO TO APPLY TO A A Davis, The Lady Eileen Joseph Foundation, BDO Stoy Hayward, 8 Baker Street, London W1M 1DA

CC NO 327549   **ESTABLISHED** 1987

■ The Joseph Trust

WHAT IS FUNDED General charitable purposes

WHO CAN BENEFIT There are no restrictions on the age; professional and economic group; family situation; religion and culture; and social circumstances of; or disease or medical condition suffered by, the beneficiaries

WHERE FUNDING CAN BE GIVEN UK and overseas

RANGE OF GRANTS £10,000–£72,361

SAMPLE GRANTS £72,361 to Onaway Trust; £10,000 to Friends of the Galilean

FINANCES *Year* 1997 *Income* £190,471 *Grants* £82,361

TRUSTEES A Breslin, Mrs C E Howles, J Morris, Miss B J Pilkington, K Pyrah

HOW TO APPLY To the address under Who To Apply To in writing

WHO TO APPLY TO Miss B J Pilkington, Trustee, The Joseph Trust, 273 Main Street, Shadwell, Leeds LS17 8LH

CC NO 257141   **ESTABLISHED** 1968

■ Harry Josselson & Henrietta Josselson Paradies Charitable Trust

This trust did not respond to CAF's request to amend its entry and, by 30 June 1998, CAF's researchers did not find financial records for later than 1995 on its file at the Charity Commission. Trusts are legally required to submit annual accounts to the Charity Commission under section 42 of the Charities Act 1993

WHAT IS FUNDED General charitable purposes

WHO CAN BENEFIT There are no restrictions on the age; professional and economic group; family situation; religion and culture; and social circumstances of; or disease or medical condition suffered by, the beneficiaries

WHERE FUNDING CAN BE GIVEN UK and overseas

TRUSTEES F Landau, A Fishman

WHO TO APPLY TO M Richman, (Solicitor), Harry Josselson & Henrietta Josselson Paradies Charitable Trust, c/o Asher Fishman & Company, Pearl House, 746 Finchely Road, London NW11 7FH

CC NO 238402   **ESTABLISHED** 1951

■ The Jusaca Charitable Trust

WHAT IS FUNDED Medicine and health; international welfare; education

WHAT IS NOT FUNDED No grants to individuals or students. Registered charities only

WHO CAN BENEFIT Established organisations benefiting children and young adults, at risk groups, those disadvantaged by poverty and socially isolated people. There is no restriction on the disease or medical condition suffered by the beneficiaries

WHERE FUNDING CAN BE GIVEN UK and overseas

TYPE OF GRANT A range of grants

RANGE OF GRANTS £250–£2,500

SAMPLE GRANTS £2,500 to Israel Public Council for Soviet Jewry; £2,500 to British Friends of the Israel Free Loan Society; £2,500 to British Ohim Society; £2,500 to University of Sussex for Centre for German-Jewish Studies; £1,000 to Save the Children Fund

FINANCES *Year* 1996 *Income* £23,164
Grants £20,950

TRUSTEES S Emanuel, C Emanuel, P Rodney

WHO TO APPLY TO Ms C L Emanuel, The Jusaca Charitable Trust, 39 Vesta Road, London SE4 2NJ

CC NO 1012966   **ESTABLISHED** 1992

K

■ The KC Charitable Trust

WHAT IS FUNDED Principally small local charities, preferably concerned with drug abuse, medical research, children/youth (especially the unemployed with special emphasis on re-training schemes and workshops), and the elderly

WHAT IS NOT FUNDED No grants to individuals

WHO CAN BENEFIT Small local organisations benefiting children, young adults and elderly people. Support is also given to those suffering from drug abuse and the unemployed. There is no restriction on the disease or medical condition suffered by the beneficiaries

WHERE FUNDING CAN BE GIVEN Principally Scotland – special emphasis is placed on charities concerned with the Edinburgh area

TYPE OF GRANT The Trustees will consider recurring and one-off grant

RANGE OF GRANTS £25–£5,000

SAMPLE GRANTS £5,000 to The National Trust for Scotland; £500 to the New School Butterstone Ltd

FINANCES *Year* 1997 *Income* £15,617
Grants £5,525

TRUSTEES Kleinwort Benson Trustees Limited, Mrs K Turner, C Turner

NOTES It is not the Trustees' policy to acknowledge appeals and applicants will only receive a communication if their appeal has been successful

HOW TO APPLY Applications in writing to the address under Who To Apply To, which are considered half yearly by the Trustees

WHO TO APPLY TO Kleinwort Benson Trustees Limited, The KC Charitable Trust, PO Box 191, 10 Fenchurch Street, London EC3M 3LB

CC NO 268413   **ESTABLISHED** 1974

■ KFM Charitable Trust

WHAT IS FUNDED General charitable purposes which may have been proposed, suggested or put forward to the Trustees by listeners to the KFM Radio Station

WHO CAN BENEFIT There are no restrictions on the age; professional and economic group; family situation; religion and culture; and social circumstances of; or disease or medical condition suffered by, the beneficiaries

WHERE FUNDING CAN BE GIVEN West Kent and North East Sussex

TRUSTEES C Teacher, A Gemmell-Smith, B Hart

WHO TO APPLY TO B Hart, KFM Charitable Trust, 8A Chestnut Road, Billingshurst, West Sussex RH14 9SY

CC NO 1069083   **ESTABLISHED** 1998

■ The KPMG North East Partners' Charitable Trust

WHAT IS FUNDED General charitable purposes at the discretion of the Trustees

WHO CAN BENEFIT Institutions. There are no restrictions on the age; professional and economic group; family situation; religion and culture; and social circumstances of; or disease or medical condition suffered by, the beneficiaries

WHERE FUNDING CAN BE GIVEN UK and overseas
TYPE OF GRANT At the discretion of the Trustees
FINANCES *Year* 1995 *Income* £23,828
Grants £10,625
TRUSTEES M Lonsborough, Mrs M Ferris, B Bouttel, J G Ridings
HOW TO APPLY **This Trust states that it does not respond to unsolicited applications**
WHO TO APPLY TO Mrs M Ferris, KPMG North East Partners' Charitable Trust, KPMG, The Fountain Precinct, 1 Balm Green, Sheffield, South Yorkshire S1 3AF
CC NO 295478 **ESTABLISHED** 1986

■ Kagyu Dechen Trust

WHAT IS FUNDED The advancement of the Buddhist faith with particular reference to the Karma Kagyu School
WHO CAN BENEFIT Organisations benefiting Buddhists and pupils at the Karma Kagyu School
WHERE FUNDING CAN BE GIVEN North Yorkshire
TRUSTEES R Marshall, C Moss, H Quinn, K Shaw, S Sidwell, G Taylor
HOW TO APPLY To the address under Who To Apply To in writing
WHO TO APPLY TO Patricia Quinn, Chairperson, Kagyu Dechen Trust, 28 Harlow Moor Drive, Harrogate, North Yorkshire HG2 0JY
CC NO 1064198 **ESTABLISHED** 1997

■ Bernard Kahn Charitable Trust

WHAT IS FUNDED Relief of and assistance to Jews to alleviate poverty. The advancement of religion and education
WHO CAN BENEFIT Organisations benefiting Jewish people, children and young adults, those disadvantaged by poverty, teachers, governesses and rabbis
WHERE FUNDING CAN BE GIVEN UK and overseas
RANGE OF GRANTS £100–30,000
SAMPLE GRANTS £30,000 to Telz Academy Trust; £3,000 to Sdei Chemed Children's Village; £25,000 to Jewish Educational Trust; £25,000 to Orthodox Council of Jerusalem; £12,000 to Achisomoch; £10,000 to Hasmonean High School Building Fund; £7,500 to Yeshivat Shaalvim; £5,000 to Friends of Religious Settlements; £5,000 to British Friends of Orot; £3,000 to Yeshivat Har Etzion
FINANCES *Year* 1996 *Income* £207,830
Grants £175,255
TRUSTEES A Bowden, Mrs C Kahn, B Kahn
WHO TO APPLY TO Adolf Bowden, Bernard Kahn Charitable Trust, 62 Gresham Gardens, London NW11 8PD
CC NO 249130 **ESTABLISHED** 1965

■ Kall Kwik Foundation

This trust did not respond to CAF's request to amend its entry and, by 30 June 1998, CAF's researchers did not find financial records for later than 1995 on its file at the Charity Commission. Trusts are legally required to submit annual accounts to the Charity Commission under section 42 of the Charities Act 1993

WHAT IS FUNDED General charitable purposes
WHO CAN BENEFIT There are no restrictions on the age; professional and economic group; family situation; religion and culture; and social circumstances of; or disease or medical condition suffered by, the beneficiaries
WHERE FUNDING CAN BE GIVEN UK
TRUSTEES Kall Kwik Printing Ltd, M Gerstenhaber, M Mendelsohn, N C Toplis
WHO TO APPLY TO A D Fineberg, Company Secretary, Kall Kwik Foundation, 106 Pembroke Road, Ruislip, Middlesex HA4 8NW
CC NO 1051805 **ESTABLISHED** 1995

■ Karate Union of Great Britain Charitable Appeal

WHAT IS FUNDED General charitable purposes. The Trustees select two to three charities each year
WHO CAN BENEFIT Registered charities only. There are no restrictions on the age; professional and economic group; family situation; religion and culture; and social circumstances of; or disease or medical condition suffered by, the beneficiaries
WHERE FUNDING CAN BE GIVEN UK
FINANCES *Year* 1997 *Income* £33,663
TRUSTEES A Sherry, C Naylor, R Poynton
WHO TO APPLY TO R Poynton, Karate Union of Great Britain Charitable Appeal, 20 Waterford Road, Oxton, Wirral, Merseyside L43 6UU
CC NO 1001131 **ESTABLISHED** 1990

■ The Karenza Foundation

WHAT IS FUNDED General charitable purposes
WHO CAN BENEFIT There are no restrictions on the age; professional and economic group; family situation; religion and culture; and social circumstances of; or disease or medical condition suffered by, the beneficiaries
WHERE FUNDING CAN BE GIVEN UK
FINANCES *Year* 1995 *Income* £30,982
Grants £61,000
TRUSTEES Mrs Esme Elvina, Mrs A F Uren, E J Uren
HOW TO APPLY To the address under Who To Apply To in writing
WHO TO APPLY TO G Thornton, The Karenza Foundation, Grant Thornton, Walltree Court, St Peter's Road, Petersfield, Hampshire GU32 3HY
CC NO 264520 **ESTABLISHED** 1972

■ The Boris Karloff Charitable Foundation

WHAT IS FUNDED Arts, culture and recreation, particularly theatre, cinema and stage charities. Health charities will be considered
WHO CAN BENEFIT National and local charities benefiting actors and entertainment professionals and musicians. There is no restriction on the disease or medical condition suffered by the beneficiaries
WHERE FUNDING CAN BE GIVEN UK
RANGE OF GRANTS £100–£10,000
SAMPLE GRANTS £10,000 to Actors Charitable Trust; £10,000 to Cinema and Television Benevolent Fund; £10,000 to Royal Theatrical Fund; £5,000 to Salisbury Samaritans; £5,000 to King Edward VII Hospital; £5,000 to Imperial Cancer Research Fund; £5,000 to Iris Fund for Prevention of Blindness; £5,000 to Help the Aged; £5,000 to Ken Barrington Cricket Centre; £5,000 to Cancer Vaccine Campaign
FINANCES *Year* 1996 *Income* £65,573
Grants £71,100
TRUSTEES I D Wilson, G F Hill

WHO TO APPLY TO I D Wilson, The Boris Karloff Charitable Foundation, Peachey and Co, Solicitors, Arundel House, Arundel Street, London WC2R 3ED
CC NO 326898　　　**ESTABLISHED** 1985

■ The Kathleen Trust

WHAT IS FUNDED General charitable purposes
WHO CAN BENEFIT There are no restrictions on the age; professional and economic group; family situation; religion and culture; and social circumstances of; or disease or medical condition suffered by, the beneficiaries
WHERE FUNDING CAN BE GIVEN Greater London
TRUSTEES E R Haslewood, Lady P A Scott, Sir O C A Scott, Ms C N Withington
WHO TO APPLY TO E R H Perks, Secretary, The Kathleen Trust, Currey and Co, 21 Buckingham Gate, London SW1E 6LS
CC NO 1064516　　　**ESTABLISHED** 1997

■ The Michael and Ilse Katz Foundation

WHAT IS FUNDED Primarily Jewish organisations, also the arts, medical and welfare charities
WHO CAN BENEFIT International and national schemes and organisations benefiting Jews, at risk groups, those disadvantaged by poverty and socially isolated people. There is no restriction on the disease or medical condition suffered by the beneficiaries
WHERE FUNDING CAN BE GIVEN UK and overseas
TYPE OF GRANT One-off and recurring
RANGE OF GRANTS £100–£204,981
SAMPLE GRANTS £204,981 to Federation of Jewish Relief Organisations; £64,156 to Friends of Akim; £15,000 to Jewish Care; £8,000 to Group Relations Educational Trust; £6,500 to Ravenswood; £5,400 to Hillel Foundation; £3,000 to Holocaust Educational Trust; £3,000 per annum to an individual; £2,500 to a Bournemouth school; £1,575 to Worshipful Company of Butchers
FINANCES *Year* 1995–96 *Income* £46,100 *Grants* £339,642
TRUSTEES Norris Gilbert, Osman Azis
HOW TO APPLY To the address under Who To Apply To in writing
WHO TO APPLY TO A D Foreman, Trustees' Accountant, The Michael and Ilse Katz Foundation, New Garden House, 78 Hatton Garden, London EC1N 8JA
CC NO 263726　　　**ESTABLISHED** 1971

■ The Katzauer Charitable Settlement

WHAT IS FUNDED Jewish organisations, predominantly in Israel
WHO CAN BENEFIT Localised schemes benefiting Jewish people
WHERE FUNDING CAN BE GIVEN UK and Israel
SAMPLE GRANTS £10,000 to Spinal Unit Meir Hospital; £5,200 to Moria; £4,000 to S & D Tritsky; £3,750 to Kollel Ra'anana; £3,000 to Lubavitch Ra'anana; £2,500 to British Friends of Yeshivat Ofakim; £2,300 to Mercas Hatoriaus Scholarship; £2,000 to Nachalat Yechiel; £1,000 to Lubavitch Foundation London; £1,000 to World Jewish Relief
FINANCES *Year* 1997 *Income* £47,537 *Grants* £48,245

TRUSTEES A Katzauer, P M Emmanuel, G C Smith
HOW TO APPLY To the address under Who To Apply To in writing
WHO TO APPLY TO P M Emmanuel, The Katzauer Charitable Settlement, Devonshire House, 1 Devonshire Street, London W1N 2DR
CC NO 275110　　　**ESTABLISHED** 1977

■ The C S Kaufman Charitable Trust

WHAT IS FUNDED Mainly Jewish organisations
WHAT IS NOT FUNDED No grants to individuals
WHO CAN BENEFIT Organisations benefiting Jewish people
WHERE FUNDING CAN BE GIVEN UK
RANGE OF GRANTS £25–£11,000
SAMPLE GRANTS £11,000 to Emuno Educational Centre; £100,000 to Friends of Harim Establishments; £7,990 to Society of Friends of Torah; £2,600 to Jewish Teachers Training Centre; £1,250 to Tevini Ltd; £1,150 to Gateshead Foundation for Torah; £1,000 to Friends of Ponevez; £1,000 to Yeshivat Haneger Trust; £1,000 to Toldos Aharon Trust
FINANCES *Year* 1997 *Income* £74,257 *Grants* £54,388
TRUSTEES I I Kaufman, J Kaufman
WHO TO APPLY TO C S Kaufman, The C S Kaufman Charitable Trust, 162 Whitehall Road, Gateshead, Tyne and Wear NE8 1TP
CC NO 253194　　　**ESTABLISHED** 1967

■ Geoffrey John Kaye Charitable Foundation

WHAT IS FUNDED Jewish charitable organisations
WHO CAN BENEFIT To benefit Jewish people
WHERE FUNDING CAN BE GIVEN UK and overseas
TYPE OF GRANT Largely recurrent
RANGE OF GRANTS £400–£15,885
SAMPLE GRANTS £15,885 to Lubavitch Foundation; £9,267 to the Ashken Trust; £6,000 to Tova Trust; £1,000 to Zion Orphanage; £1,000 to Finchley Kosher Lunch Service; £600 to Friends of Nightingale House; £400 to Friends of Immanuel College
FINANCES *Year* 1996 *Income* £37,320 *Grants* £34,152
TRUSTEES G J Kaye, S Rose
HOW TO APPLY To the address under Who To Apply To in writing
WHO TO APPLY TO R J Freebody, Geoffrey John Kaye Charitable Foundation, Messrs Philips Eli & Grass, 54 Welbeck Street, London W1M 7HE
CC NO 262547　　　**ESTABLISHED** 1971

■ The Emmanuel Kaye Foundation

WHAT IS FUNDED Medical research, welfare and Jewish organisations
WHO CAN BENEFIT At the discretion of the Trustees. Organisations benefiting: medical professionals; research workers; scientists; Jews; at risk groups; those disadvantaged by poverty; and socially isolated people. There are no restrictions on the disease or medical condition suffered by the beneficiaries
WHERE FUNDING CAN BE GIVEN UK and overseas
FINANCES *Year* 1996–97 *Income* £146,783
TRUSTEES Sir Emmanuel Kaye, Lady Kaye, John Scriven, Michael Cutler

340

Think carefully about every application. Is it justified?

HOW TO APPLY To the address under Who To Apply To in writing

WHO TO APPLY TO D P H Burgess, The Emmanuel Kaye Foundation, Messrs Gouldens, 22 Tudor Street, London EC4Y 0JJ *Tel* 0171-583 7777

CC NO 280281 **ESTABLISHED** 1980

■ Kejriwal Foundation

WHAT IS FUNDED Primarily for disaster relief, widows and orphan aid and relief of poverty, distress and sickness

WHO CAN BENEFIT To benefit orphans; widows; refugees; the homeless; those disadvantaged by poverty; victims of man-made or natural disasters; at risk groups; and the sick. There is no restriction on the disease or medical condition suffered by the beneficiaries

WHERE FUNDING CAN BE GIVEN UK and overseas, particularly India

TYPE OF GRANT At the discretion of the Trustees

SAMPLE GRANTS £9,345 to Annadana Trust; £8,765 to Tirupatti

FINANCES *Year* 1996 *Income* £17,766
Grants £18,111

TRUSTEES S L Kejriwal, R Meadowcroft, M Kejriwal, G John

WHO TO APPLY TO S L Kejriwal, Kejriwal Foundation, New Park Estate, Kenning Hall Road, London N18 2PE

CC NO 1041639 **ESTABLISHED** 1994

■ Samuel Keller Charitable Trust

WHAT IS FUNDED General charitable purposes. Grant giving priorities include children and the needy elderly

WHAT IS NOT FUNDED No grants made to political causes

WHO CAN BENEFIT Individuals and registered charities benefiting children and elderly people

WHERE FUNDING CAN BE GIVEN UK and overseas

SAMPLE GRANTS £7,750 to an individual for financing of medical treatment; £1,000 to an individual to assist a handicapped child; £1,000 to the Presidents Club for work in connection with children's charities; £1,000 to Nightingale House, Home for Aged Jews

FINANCES *Year* 1997 *Income* £35,582
Grants £11,540

TRUSTEES Mrs S Keller, Mrs S Lennard, Mrs L Gordon

HOW TO APPLY In writing to the address under Who To Apply To

WHO TO APPLY TO I A Gordon, Secretary to the Trustees, Samuel Keller Charitable Trust, c/o Atlantic Estates plc, Cheril House, 181–183 Kings Road, Chelsea, London SW3 5EB *Tel* 0171-351 5353

CC NO 326565 **ESTABLISHED** 1984

■ Kemerton Trustees Ltd

WHAT IS FUNDED The Trust concerns itself primarily with nature conservation on the Kemerton Estate, though small grants may be made to other conservation organisations. Projects currently in operation are: gravel pit nature reserve, the restoring of Kemerton Quarry to a lake and flood meadow as a nature reserve. Invertebrate fauna survey of Kemerton Estate. Planting new trees each year in an arboretum, including exotic and old varieties of apples and pears. Public education through guided walks and open days on the Kemerton Estate. Paying the salaries of the conservation officers

WHERE FUNDING CAN BE GIVEN Gloucestershire, Hereford and Worcester and adjoining counties

FINANCES *Year* 1997 *Income* £30,003
Grants £2,581

TRUSTEES Dr J D S Birks, A M G Darby, M G Darby, P S Doble, R C Knight, C F Nicholson, A J M Teacher, J E J White

NOTES Most of the Trust's income is spent on expenses of running Kemerton Estate, conservation officers costs, etc

HOW TO APPLY To the address under Who To Apply To in writing

WHO TO APPLY TO A M G Darby, Kemerton Trustees Ltd, Kemerton Court, Kemerton, Tewkesbury, Gloucestershire GL20 7HY

CC NO 702488 **ESTABLISHED** 1989

■ The Kemsley Charitable Trust

WHAT IS FUNDED General charitable purposes

WHO CAN BENEFIT There are no restrictions on the age; professional and economic group; family situation; religion and culture; and social circumstances of; or disease or medical condition suffered by, the beneficiaries

WHERE FUNDING CAN BE GIVEN Kent

SAMPLE GRANTS £65,000 to Kent and Canterbury Hospital NHS Trust; £45,000 for medical equipment; £10,000 to the Odyssey Project

FINANCES *Year* 1997 *Income* £145,144
Grants £144,608

TRUSTEES C J G Brown, T W Kemsley, R D Richardson

HOW TO APPLY To the address under Who To Apply To in writing

WHO TO APPLY TO The Secretary, The Kemsley Charitable Trust, Messrs Brachers, 1 Bower Mount Road, Maidstone, Kent ME16 8AX

CC NO 1014991 **ESTABLISHED** 1992

■ William Kendall's Charity

WHAT IS FUNDED Wide range of housing, disabled, educational and health charities supported in Greater London (particularly Bexley). The Trust will consider funding: almshouses; emergency and short-term accommodation; health facilities and buildings, bursaries and fees; and scholarships

WHAT IS NOT FUNDED No grants to individuals or for expeditions

WHO CAN BENEFIT Charitable organisations in Greater London benefiting children and older people

WHERE FUNDING CAN BE GIVEN Greater London with preference for Bexley

TYPE OF GRANT One-off or recurring

RANGE OF GRANTS £500–£23,750, typical grant £2500

SAMPLE GRANTS £23,750 to Bexley United Charities for support of almshouses; £10,700 to Christ's Hospital for support of a scholar; £2,500 to City of London police for support of orphans; £2,500 to City Parochial Foundation for City needy; £2,500 to (City) Sheriff's and Recorders Fund for rehabilitation of prisoners and families; £2,500 to St Botolph's Project, Aldgate for housing; £2,500 to Red Cross, City of London for medical purposes; £2,500 to London City Mission for soup kitchen and missionary; £2,500 to St Bartholomew's Hospital for medical purposes; £2,500 to John Groom's for Housing Project

FINANCES *Year* 1997–98 *Income* £95,000
Grants £95,000

TRUSTEES Worshipful Company of Wax Chandlers

NOTES Most donations are to educational, medical and relief of poverty applicants in London

HOW TO APPLY In writing. Please do not make an initial telephone call. There are no guidelines, application forms or deadlines for applications. No sae required

WHO TO APPLY TO Commander B J Stevens, Clerk to Wax Chandlers, William Kendall's Charity, Wax Chandlers Hall, Gresham Street, London EC2V 7AD *Tel* 0171-606 3591 *Fax* 0171-600 5462

CC NO 228361   ESTABLISHED 1964

■ The Florence Amelia Kendrew Charitable Settlement

WHAT IS FUNDED General charitable purposes

WHO CAN BENEFIT Individuals and registered charities. There are no restrictions on the age; professional and economic group; family situation; religion and culture; and social circumstances of; or disease or medical condition suffered by, the beneficiaries

WHERE FUNDING CAN BE GIVEN UK and overseas

RANGE OF GRANTS £100–£500

SAMPLE GRANTS £500 to St Pauls PCC Building Project Account; £500 to English Heritage; £500 to The English Haydn Festival; £500 to an individual; £500 to Newport News

FINANCES *Year* 1995 *Income* £22,362 *Grants* £13,750

TRUSTEES J Wimbury, Mrs M Wimbury, J Gordon

WHO TO APPLY TO J Wimbury, The Florence Amelia Kendrew Charitable Settlement, 90 Broadway North, Walsall, West Midlands WS1 2QE

CC NO 294473   ESTABLISHED 1986

■ The Kennedy Charitable Foundation

WHAT IS FUNDED General charitable purposes

WHO CAN BENEFIT There are no restrictions on the age; professional and economic group; family situation; religion and culture; and social circumstances of; or disease or medical condition suffered by, the beneficiaries

WHERE FUNDING CAN BE GIVEN UK and overseas

RANGE OF GRANTS £200–£80,000, typical grant £1,000

SAMPLE GRANTS £80,000 to Moy Valley Resources; £50,000 to Restoration Ministries; £46,500 to Diocese of Elphin; £40,000 to Sligo Enterprises; £25,000 to Diocese of Killala; £24,000 to a Reverend; £10,000 to Childline; £10,000 to a Reverend Father; £10,000 to Cregg House; £10,000 to Nazareth House

FINANCES *Year* 1997 *Income* £146,780 *Grants* £474,070

TRUSTEES P J Kennedy, K Kennedy, J G Kennedy, Brown Street Nominees Limited

WHO TO APPLY TO Brown Street Nominees Ltd, Trustee, The Kennedy Charitable Foundation, Deloitte & Touche Private Clients Ltd, PO Box 500, 201 Deansgate, Manchester M60 2AT *Tel* 0161-455 8380

CC NO 1052001   ESTABLISHED 1996

■ The Mathilda and Terence Kennedy Charitable Trust

WHAT IS FUNDED General charitable purposes

WHO CAN BENEFIT There are no restrictions on the age; professional and economic group; family situation; religion and culture; and social

circumstances of; or disease or medical condition suffered by, the beneficiaries

WHERE FUNDING CAN BE GIVEN UK

RANGE OF GRANTS £1,000–£10,000

SAMPLE GRANTS £10,000 to Royal Ballet School; £6,000 to Iris Trust; £6,000 to St Luke's Church, Pinner; £4,000 to WIZO Charitable Foundation; £2,500 to Royal National Theatre; £2,000 to British Friends of the Art Museum of Israel; £2,000 to Mathilda and Terence Kennedy Institute of Rheumatology; £1,500 to Alternative Theatre Company Ltd (Bush Theatre); £1,500 to the Arc Dance Company; £1,500 to Crusaid

FINANCES *Year* 1997 *Income* £51,883 *Grants* £43,000

TRUSTEES Lord Sieff, Mrs L Sieff, J Henderson

NOTES Funds already committed to charities known to Trustees.

HOW TO APPLY Grants are mainly made to charities known personally to the Trustees, rather than as a result of unsolicited applications

WHO TO APPLY TO H W Fisher & Co, The Mathilda & Terence Kennedy Charitable Trust, Acre House, 11–15 William Road, London NW1 3ER

CC NO 206330   ESTABLISHED 1956

■ The Kennel Club Charitable Trust

WHAT IS FUNDED The Trust supports research into canine diseases and disorders and assists charities for disadvantaged dogs and disadvantaged humans aided by dogs

WHO CAN BENEFIT Registered charities benefiting: dogs; research workers; vets; disabled people; those suffering from sight and hearing loss

WHERE FUNDING CAN BE GIVEN UK

TYPE OF GRANT One off and recurring for set periods

SAMPLE GRANTS £25,000 to Animal Health Trust for research; £25,000 to Royal School of Veterinary Surgeons for research; £25,000 to Bristol University for research; £8,050 to PDSA; £6,000 to Royal College of Veterinary Surgeons Trust Fund for veterinary Nursing Bursaries; £5,000 to Blue Cross; £2,500 to Justice for Dogs

FINANCES *Year* 1996–97 *Income* £146,756 *Grants* £108,050

TRUSTEES M T R Stockman, R J Clifford, B J Hall, W R Irwing, M Townsend

HOW TO APPLY To the address under Who To Apply To

WHO TO APPLY TO M C E Quirke, Clerk to the Trustees, The Kennel Club Charitable Trust, 1–5 Clarges Street, Piccadilly, London W1Y 8AB *Tel* 0171-493 6651

CC NO 327802   ESTABLISHED 1988

■ Kennyhill Bequest Fund

WHAT IS FUNDED General charitable purposes. Particularly charities representing people who are deprived

WHAT IS NOT FUNDED No grants to charities outside the Glasgow area

WHO CAN BENEFIT There are no restrictions on the age; professional and economic group; family situation; religion and culture; and social circumstances of; or disease or medical condition suffered by, the beneficiaries

WHERE FUNDING CAN BE GIVEN Glasgow only

TYPE OF GRANT Mainly single projects considered

FINANCES *Year* 1996 *Income* £15,000 *Grants* £10,000

TRUSTEES P J Forrester, P C Paisley, J A M Cuthbert, Mrs Gillian Weir

HOW TO APPLY Considered annually in December

WHO TO APPLY TO J A M Cuthbert, Kennyhill Bequest Fund, Messrs Mitchells Roberton, George House, 36 North Hanover Street, Glasgow G1 2AD
Tel 0141-552 3422 *Fax* 0141-552 2935
E-mail 106017.3412@compuserve.com
SC NO SCO 00122 **ESTABLISHED** 1895

■ The Kensington District Nursing Trust

WHAT IS FUNDED Relief in need, the elderly, housing, disabilities, counselling people with psychiatric problems. Particularly charities working in the fields of: holiday accommodation; support to voluntary and community organisations; volunteer bureaux; healthcare; hospices; and rehabilitation centres

WHAT IS NOT FUNDED Aid will not be given for fines, rent or court orders

WHO CAN BENEFIT Individuals and organisations benefiting: people of all ages; retired people and those disadvantaged by poverty. There is no restriction on the disease or medical condition suffered by the beneficiaries

WHERE FUNDING CAN BE GIVEN The former borough of Kensington

TYPE OF GRANT Usually one-off grants and funding of one year or less

RANGE OF GRANTS For individuals £50–£500, for organisations £500–£2,000

SAMPLE GRANTS £3,500 to Alexander Home for equipment; £3,500 to Harrison Homes for nurse warden; £2,000 to Alan Morkill House for music and movement class; £1,500 to HAPA for hydraulic changing bench; £1,000 to Action for Disability for Polaroid camera; £1,000 to London Cyrenians for resettlement funds; £797 to District Nurses Raymede and Colville Clinics for mobile phones; £746 to Age Concern for bathing equipment; £500 to K & C Mencap for transport costs

FINANCES *Year* 1996–97 *Income* £64,350
Grants £46,771

TRUSTEES Cllr Miss E M Christmas, MBE (Chair), Mrs S Jaffe, M W F Jenkin, K J Kelman, Dr S MacVie, Mrs V Thornhill

NOTES Individuals seeking assistance should be suffering from some medical problem, and should have lived in the former borough of Kensington for at least two years

HOW TO APPLY To the address under Who To Apply To in writing

WHO TO APPLY TO Margaret Rhodes, The Kensington District Nursing Trust, 27a Pembridge Villas, London W11 3EP1 *Tel* 0171-229 3538
CC NO 210931 **ESTABLISHED** 1974

■ The Nancy Kenyon Charitable Trust

WHAT IS FUNDED Primarily for people and causes known to the Trustees

WHAT IS NOT FUNDED No grants to individuals

WHO CAN BENEFIT There are no restrictions on the age, professional and economic group, family situation, religion and culture, and social circumstances of, or disease or medical condition suffered by, the beneficiaries

WHERE FUNDING CAN BE GIVEN UK

TYPE OF GRANT Lump sum

FINANCES *Year* 1997 *Income* £39,409
Grants £28,914

TRUSTEES C M Kenyon, R B Kenyon, R G Brown

NOTES Applications for causes not known to the Trustees are considered annually in December

HOW TO APPLY To the address under Who To Apply To

WHO TO APPLY TO R G Brown, The Nancy Kenyon Charitable Trust, c/o Mercer and Hole, Gloucester House, 72 London Road, St Albans, Hertfordshire AL1 1NS

CC NO 265359 **ESTABLISHED** 1972

■ Keren Association

WHAT IS FUNDED The advancement of education. The provision of religious instruction and training in traditional Judaism. General charitable purposes

WHO CAN BENEFIT Organisations benefiting children, young adults and Jews

WHERE FUNDING CAN BE GIVEN UK

FINANCES *Year* 1996 *Income* £2,497,048
Grants £2,157,232

TRUSTEES The Governors

WHO TO APPLY TO D Segal, Keren Association, 13–17 New Burlington Place, Regent Street, London W1X 2JP

CC NO 313119 **ESTABLISHED** 1961

■ Kermaville Ltd

WHAT IS FUNDED Advancement of religion according to the Orthodox Jewish faith and general charitable purposes

WHO CAN BENEFIT Institutions benefiting Jewish people

WHERE FUNDING CAN BE GIVEN UK

TYPE OF GRANT At the discretion of the Trustees

FINANCES *Year* 1995 *Income* £228,000
Grants £78,000

TRUSTEES S Orenstein, J Orenstein

WHO TO APPLY TO M Frand, Accountant, Kermaville Ltd, 3 Overlea Road, London E5 9BG

CC NO 266075 **ESTABLISHED** 1973

■ The Kessler Foundation

WHAT IS FUNDED General charitable purposes, particularly Jewish

WHO CAN BENEFIT To benefit Jewish people

WHERE FUNDING CAN BE GIVEN UK and overseas

RANGE OF GRANTS Below £50–£5,000

SAMPLE GRANTS £5,000 to the Jewish Museum; £5,000 to UCL; £3,500 to LIMMUD; £2,500 to Jewish Childs Day; £1,554 to Genizah Research Unit; £1,000 to Glasgow Jewish Resource Centre; £1,000 to Jewish Arts; £1,000 to Manchester Jewish Museum; £1,000 to Care for the Needy in Jerusalem; £1,000 to Jewish Deaf Association

FINANCES *Year* 1997 *Income* £45,693
Grants £49,051

TRUSTEES L R Blackstone, R A Fass, Prof M Geller, Mrs J Jacobs, Mrs J F Mayers, P L Morganstern, E J Temko

HOW TO APPLY To the address under Who To Apply To in writing

WHO TO APPLY TO Richard A Fass, Secretary, The Kessler Foundation, 25 Furnival Street, London EC4A 1JT

CC NO 290759 **ESTABLISHED** 1984

■ Keswick Foundation Ltd

WHAT IS FUNDED The advancement of education especially scientific and technical education for Hong Kong residents to help them attend institutions in the UK. The relief of mental illness

WHAT IS NOT FUNDED Any charitable purpose outside of Hong Kong will not be supported

WHO CAN BENEFIT Individuals and registered charities benefiting people of all ages, students suffering from mental illness

WHERE FUNDING CAN BE GIVEN Hong Kong

TYPE OF GRANT One-off, capital, recurring costs, core costs, endowments, project, research, running costs and start-up costs. Funding for up to three years

FINANCES *Year* 1996 *Income* £476,480

TRUSTEES Jeremy J G Brown, Nelson Wing Sun Chow, Caroline P Courtauld, Stacey A Hildebrandt, Charles A Jencks, Sister Helen Kenny, Emma B Keswick, Simon L Keswick, Vicki E Morrison, Christina P Nightingale, Clara M Weatherall, Elizabeth Wong, Myna Wu, Millicent Yung

WHO TO APPLY TO J J Brown, Keswick Foundation Ltd, c/o Matheson & Co Ltd, 3 Lombard Street, London EC3V 9AQ

CC NO 278449   **ESTABLISHED** 1979

■ The Ursula Keyes Trust

WHAT IS FUNDED Ranges from medical research to practical support, eg purchase of equipment, wheelchairs and funding for a hospice to a wide range of activities in the medical/social field with an emphasis on medical research, welfare and care work

WHAT IS NOT FUNDED Students or political groups

WHO CAN BENEFIT Individuals and institutions benefiting: at risk groups; those disadvantaged by poverty; socially isolated people; and the sick. There are no restrictions on the disease or medical condition suffered by the beneficiaries

WHERE FUNDING CAN BE GIVEN Chester primarily, occasionally other areas

TYPE OF GRANT Small and large grants

RANGE OF GRANTS Below £1,000–£30,000

SAMPLE GRANTS £30,000 to Chester Cathedral Development Trust; £27,083 to Liverpool University for a medical research fellowship; £25,000 to Hospice of the Good Shepherd; £10,000 to Chester Area MacMillan Nurse Appeal; £5,000 to Hope House; £3,000 to The Drugwatch Trust; £2,000 to Neuro Muscular Centre; £3,998 to nine individuals; £1,673 in donations of under £1,000 to institutions

FINANCES *Year* 1996 *Income* £252,250 *Grants* £107,754

TRUSTEES Dr A E Elliot, J F Kane, J R Leaman, Dr R A Owen, H M Shaw, P R Wise

HOW TO APPLY Require enquiries and applications in writing

WHO TO APPLY TO P R Wise, Trustee, The Ursula Keyes Trust, 90–92 Telegraph Road, Heswall, Wirral, Merseyside L60 0AQ

CC NO 517200   **ESTABLISHED** 1985

■ The Ronald and Mary Keymer Trust

WHAT IS FUNDED Emphasis on work of Anglican and Presbyterian Churches in Africa and Middle East through their Overseas Missions, particularly Medical Missions, and medical work generally also war service charities

WHAT IS NOT FUNDED No grants to individuals

WHO CAN BENEFIT Mainly headquarters organisations and charities benefiting ex-service and service people. There is no restriction on the disease or medical condition suffered by the beneficiaries

WHERE FUNDING CAN BE GIVEN Mainly Africa

TYPE OF GRANT Recurrent, one-off funding for up to, or more than three years will be considered

SAMPLE GRANTS £1,100 to Church of Scotland World Mission for African mission; £600 to Eygpt Diocesan Association for general purpose and Cairo Deaf Unit; £400 to United Society for Propagation of the Gospel for general funds; £400 to Sudan Church Association for church work in Sudan; £300 to Imperial Cancer Research for cancer research

FINANCES *Year* 1997–98 *Income* £15,919 *Grants* £15,800

TRUSTEES Mrs M Keymer, MBE, MB, ChB, P D Warren, MC, BA, R C Keymer, CBE

HOW TO APPLY Grants mainly made to charities known personally rather than to submissions

WHO TO APPLY TO R C Keymer, CBE, The Ronald and Mary Keymer Trust, 16a Greyfriars Garden, St Andrews, Fife KY16 9HG

CC NO 267310   **ESTABLISHED** 1974

■ Kidderminster New Meeting House

WHAT IS FUNDED To encourage religious observance by Presbyterians

WHO CAN BENEFIT Presbyterians

WHERE FUNDING CAN BE GIVEN Kidderminster

TYPE OF GRANT Recurring

FINANCES *Year* 1996 *Income* £14,514 *Grants* £674

TRUSTEES Mrs E Church, Ms S Dickens, B D Jones, S H Jones, R A Matthews, Mrs M H Phelon

WHO TO APPLY TO B D Jones, Church Treasurer, Kidderminster New Meeting House, 21 Perrin Avenue, Kidderminster, Worcestershire DY11 6LL

CC NO 1045485   **ESTABLISHED** 1784

■ The Michael and Jane Kier Charitable Trust

WHAT IS FUNDED General charitable purposes

WHO CAN BENEFIT There are no restrictions on the age; professional and economic group; family situation; religion and culture; and social circumstances of; or disease or medical condition suffered by, the beneficiaries

WHERE FUNDING CAN BE GIVEN UK

TRUSTEES J E Kier, G I Moscrop

WHO TO APPLY TO M H Kier, The Michael and Jane Kier Charitable Trust, 23 Belmont Road, Twickenham, Middlesex TW2 5DA

CC NO 1064616   **ESTABLISHED** 1997

■ Kilburn Evangelical Church Trust

WHAT IS FUNDED To advance the Christian faith, in particular, in the county of Greater London or elsewhere in the UK or World; to relieve persons who are in conditions of need, hardship, distress or who are elderly or sick and other general charitable purposes

WHO CAN BENEFIT Organisations benefiting elderly people, Christians and those at risk, those disadvantaged by poverty and socially isolated. There is no restriction on the disease or medical condition suffered by the beneficiaries

WHERE FUNDING CAN BE GIVEN UK, with preference for Greater London, and overseas

RANGE OF GRANTS £7–£3,280

SAMPLE GRANTS £3,280 to an individual for employment; £2,860 to an individual for employment; £180 to London Christian Housing Association; £50 to Novi Most International; £50 to Mission without Border

FINANCES *Year* 1996 *Income* £18,467

TRUSTEES R Brown, A Gibbs, J Jolley

NOTES The Trust includes an Employment Fund, Mission Fund, General Fund, Social Fund, Maintenance Fund, Evangelistic Fund, Pastor Fund and Car Fund

WHO TO APPLY TO A J Gibbs, Kilburn Evangelical Church Trust, 53 Elmsleigh Avenue, Kenton, Harrow, Middlesex HA3 8HX

CC NO 1048674   ESTABLISHED 1995

■ Robert Kiln Charitable Trust

WHAT IS FUNDED General charitable purposes with a preference to archaeology, environmental conservation, musical education

WHAT IS NOT FUNDED Grants cannot be made to individuals. Trustees not usually interested in making grants to large or national appeals or large national organisations

WHO CAN BENEFIT Organisations benefiting archaeologists and musicians

WHERE FUNDING CAN BE GIVEN Mainly UK with emphasis on local areas (Hertfordshire and Bedfordshire)

TYPE OF GRANT Usually one-off, or instalments for particular projects. Salaries not considered

RANGE OF GRANTS Smallest £100, average grant £500. Larger amounts for special projects

SAMPLE GRANTS £9,000 to Ver Sur Mer Museum, Normandy for founding of a D-Day Room (the Founder of this Trust, Robert Kiln was involved with the liberation of this village in Normandy in World War 2); £6,250 to British Archaeological Awards various archaeological projects by volunteer groups; £3,000 to Cusichaca Trust for Patacancha Archaeological project which this Trust has supported since 1977; £2,500 to Hertford Museum for Resource Packs for schools; £2,500 to Hertfordshire Yeomanry for help towards the printing of the Regimental History; £2,400 to Hertfordshire Archaeological Trust for community archaeological initiative project; £2,000 to University of Newcastle, Department of Archaeology for Neolithic site Vale of York and Kellah Burn project; £2,000 to University of Sheffield, Department of Archaeology for Hebrides and Frocester projects; £1,500 to Childline

FINANCES *Year* 1997 *Income* £76,000 *Grants* £67,000

TRUSTEES Mrs J Akers, Dr N Akers, Mrs S F Chappell, Mrs B Kiln, S W J Kiln, G M Kiln

PUBLICATIONS Annual Report

HOW TO APPLY In writing. Trustees meet in January and July. Applications should give a clear outline of budgets and purpose of grant. Accounts if available. Applications will no longer be acknowledged

WHO TO APPLY TO Mrs M A Archer, Secretary, Robert Kiln Charitable Trust, 15A Bull Plain, Hertford, Hertfordshire SG14 1DX

CC NO 262756   ESTABLISHED 1970

■ The Kings Medical Research Trust

WHAT IS FUNDED To advance medical research. At the discretion of the Trustees

WHAT IS NOT FUNDED No recurring grants

WHO CAN BENEFIT Medical researchers and PhD students of medicine (postgraduates)

WHERE FUNDING CAN BE GIVEN London SE5 area for the foreseeable future

TYPE OF GRANT Capital, one-off, research and start-up costs

FINANCES *Year* 1994–95 *Income* £268,472 *Grants* £450,000

TRUSTEES J Kemp-Welch, Dr K Zilkha, Sir Simon Hornby, Mrs H Steinberg

PUBLICATIONS Annual Report, Bi-annual Review

WHO TO APPLY TO Ms J Seddon, Kings Medical Research Trust, Rayne Institute, 123 Coldharbour Lane, London SE5 9NU *Tel* 0171-733 9333

CC NO 200539   ESTABLISHED 1959

■ The Kingsgrove Charitable Trust

This trust did not respond to CAF's request to amend its entry and, by 30 June 1998, CAF's researchers did not find financial records for later than 1995 on its file at the Charity Commission. Trusts are legally required to submit annual accounts to the Charity Commission under section 42 of the Charities Act 1993

WHAT IS FUNDED The Trust tends to support evangelical Christian missionary work but sometimes considers other good causes

WHO CAN BENEFIT Registered charities benefiting Christians and Evangelists

WHERE FUNDING CAN BE GIVEN UK

TRUSTEES A Smith, W Smith, R D Smith, R W Smith, S H Smith, H R Barker, R M Barker

WHO TO APPLY TO W Smith, The Kingsgrove Charitable Trust, Odstone, 7 Bridge Farm Close, Grove, Wantage, Oxford OX12 7QF

CC NO 279176   ESTABLISHED 1979

■ The Kingsmead Charitable Trust

WHAT IS FUNDED General charitable purposes

WHO CAN BENEFIT Registered charities. There are no restrictions on the age; professional and economic group; family situation; religion and culture; and social circumstances of; or disease or medical condition suffered by, the beneficiaries

WHERE FUNDING CAN BE GIVEN UK and overseas

RANGE OF GRANTS £25–£2,500

SAMPLE GRANTS £2,500 to Ireland Fund; £1,250 to Child Bereavement Trust; £500 Little Flower Leprosy Welfare Association; £500 Oxford Medical Students Union; £350 to CPRE

FINANCES *Year* 1996 *Income* £16,000 *Grants* £8,977

TRUSTEES D T Puttnam, Mrs P M Puttnam

WHO TO APPLY TO Mrs S A Norris, The Administrator, The Kingsmead Charitable Trust, 13 Queensgate Place Mews, London SW7 5BG

CC NO 1002630   ESTABLISHED 1991

■ The Kingsthorpe Manor and Town Charity

WHAT IS FUNDED Children and youth, the elderly, welfare and schools

WHAT IS NOT FUNDED No grants to individuals

WHO CAN BENEFIT Organisations benefiting children, young adults and elderly people. Support may also be given to organisations benefiting at risk groups, those disadvantaged by poverty and socially isolated people

WHERE FUNDING CAN BE GIVEN The parishes of St David, Northampton and St John the Baptist, Kingsthorpe

Does the trust you have chosen match your needs? Haphazard applications waste postage and time

345

RANGE OF GRANTS Under £1,000–£3,000
SAMPLE GRANTS £3,000 to Kingsthorpe Grove Lower School; £2,000 to St John Ambulance Association; £2,000 to Kingsthorpe Church Handbells Club; £2,000 to St David's Church; £2,000 to St John the Baptist Church
FINANCES *Year* 1996 *Income* £24,781 *Grants* £26,975
TRUSTEES K Baker, B Corrie, B Earl, M A L Holmes, R Johnson, R Liddington
HOW TO APPLY To the address under Who To Apply To in writing
WHO TO APPLY TO The Kingsthorpe Manor and Town Charity, Messrs Wilson Browne, 60 Gold Street, Northampton NN1 1RS
CC NO 239688   **ESTABLISHED** 1975

■ The Kingston Charitable Trust

WHAT IS FUNDED Advancement of Christian religion
WHAT IS NOT FUNDED No grants to individuals
WHO CAN BENEFIT Institutions benefiting Christians
WHERE FUNDING CAN BE GIVEN UK and overseas
TYPE OF GRANT At the discretion of the Trustees
FINANCES *Year* 1997 *Income* £52,764 *Grants* £61,180
TRUSTEES William M Kingston, Mrs Jill M Kingston, Anthony R Collins
HOW TO APPLY This Trust states that it does not respond to unsolicited applications
WHO TO APPLY TO A R Collins, The Kingston Charitable Trust, Messrs Anthony Collins, Solicitors, 5 Waterloo Street, Birmingham B2 5PG
CC NO 1007295   **ESTABLISHED** 1992

■ The Kingston Old People's Home Fund for Ileostomists

WHAT IS FUNDED Elderly ileostomists. The Kingston Trust no longer runs homes of its own. Grants are made at the discretion of the Trustees, either as a one-off payment for a specific need, or, if on a longer term, by routine payments which are reviewed periodically. Generally the Trustees would only consider applications from the UK
WHAT IS NOT FUNDED Aid currently limited by deeds to 'elderly' ileostomists. Advice now being sought to remove 'elderly' from trust deeds to allow wider distribution of aid
WHO CAN BENEFIT Generally to individuals elderly ileostomists
WHERE FUNDING CAN BE GIVEN UK
TYPE OF GRANT Any considered that can be related to relief of ileostomists
FINANCES *Year* 1997 *Income* £328,844 *Grants* £17,973
TRUSTEES G P Wallace, Dr E F Taylor (Chairman), Mrs P A Eades, T K Keily, J G Horrocks
PUBLICATIONS Annual Statement of Accounts (audited) is supplied to the Charities Commission
HOW TO APPLY Applications should be made to the Secretary. Independent corroboration required from responsible person such as GP that applicant is an ileostomist, plus corroboration that a need for financial help exists. Applicant required to supply personal financial statement and personal details. No reply will be sent to unsuccessful applicants
WHO TO APPLY TO Mrs B Kingston, Secretary, The Kingston Trust, The Drove, Fuzzy Drove, Basingstoke, Hampshire RG22 5LU
CC NO 205591   **ESTABLISHED** 1962

■ Kingston-upon-Thames Association for the Blind

WHAT IS FUNDED The welfare of the blind and partially sighted in the area Where Funding Can Be Given
WHO CAN BENEFIT Organisations benefiting blind and partially sighted people
WHERE FUNDING CAN BE GIVEN Kingston-upon-Thames
FINANCES *Year* 1997 *Income* £32,969 *Grants* £666
TRUSTEES K Brown, Mrs J Carpenter, J M Cooper, W Craven, J Davy, Cllr D Fraser, B Gaff, F G J Gaisford, Cllr V Harris, Mrs D Judge, Mrs J Stanley, J Walmsley, Mrs R Walmsley, Mrs E White
NOTES Payments other than grants include rents, contributions to blind clubs' transport costs, outings, donations and resource centres
HOW TO APPLY To the address under Who To Apply To in writing
WHO TO APPLY TO Keith Brown, Hon Secretary, Kingston-upon-Thames Association for the Blind, 1 Albert Cottages, Eastwick Road, Great Bookham, Surrey KT23 4BA
CC NO 249295   **ESTABLISHED** 1966

■ Kinpurnie Charitable Trust

WHAT IS FUNDED General charitable purposes
WHO CAN BENEFIT Registered charities. There are no restrictions on the age; professional and economic group; family situation; religion and culture; and social circumstances of; or disease or medical condition suffered by, the beneficiaries
WHERE FUNDING CAN BE GIVEN Scotland
SAMPLE GRANTS £5,000 to Royal Marsden Hospital Cancer Fund; £4,000 to Puskin Prizes; £3,000 to National Galleries of Scotland; £2,000 to Bells Appeal; £2,000 to Nation Symphony Orchestra of Scotland; £1,500 to New School Butterstone; £1,000 to SSAFA, Dundee Branch; £1,000 to Friends of the Kirov Opera; £1,000 to BRCS, Angus Branch; £1,000 to Tayside Opera
FINANCES *Year* 1996–97 *Income* £42,000 *Grants* £43,500
HOW TO APPLY This Trust states that it does not respond to unsolicited applications
WHO TO APPLY TO J M Haldane, Kinpurnie Charitable Trust, Chiene & Tait, 3 Albyn Place, Edinburgh EH2 4NQ *Tel* 0131-225 7515
SC NO SCO 03986

■ The Kintore Charitable Trust

WHAT IS FUNDED Environmental groups, schemes which involve young people and local projects are all supported by the Trust
WHAT IS NOT FUNDED No grants to individuals
WHO CAN BENEFIT Organisations benefiting young people
WHERE FUNDING CAN BE GIVEN Scotland, particularly Grampian
FINANCES *Year* 1994–95 *Income* £53,000 *Grants* £48,000
TRUSTEES Countess of Kintore, Dundas & Wilson
PUBLICATIONS Accounts are available from the Trust
HOW TO APPLY Applications should be made in writing to the address below
WHO TO APPLY TO The Trustees, The Kintore Charitable Trust, Messrs Dundas & Wilson, Saltire Court, 20 Castle Terrace, Edinburgh EH1 2EN
SC NO SCO 00702

■ The Kirby & West Charitable Trust

WHAT IS FUNDED General charitable purposes
WHAT IS NOT FUNDED No grants to individuals
WHO CAN BENEFIT Registered charities. There are no restrictions on the age, professional and economic group, family situation, religion and culture, and social circumstances of, or disease or medical condition suffered by, the beneficiaries
WHERE FUNDING CAN BE GIVEN Mainly Leicester
FINANCES *Year* 1997 *Income* £19,181 *Grants* £14,625
TRUSTEES I M Grundy, M J Smith, J C Smith
WHO TO APPLY TO J C Smith, The Kirby & West Charitable Trust, Kirby & West Ltd, Richard III Road, Leicester LE3 5QU
CC NO 700119   **ESTABLISHED** 1988

■ Kirkley Poor Lands

WHAT IS FUNDED Welfare and disability. The Trust administers a grocery voucher scheme enabling pensioners in Kirkley to receive a grant each winter to purchase groceries. Co-operates with Kirkley High School to make grants to former pupils whose parents rely on state benefits to help with their expenses at university or other further education establishments. The Trust is applying for the Single Regeneration Budget Grant to be able to make grants to residents whose houses need insulation and draft proofing to improve housing stock of Kirkley
WHO CAN BENEFIT Individuals and organisations benefiting: pensioners; students; former Kirkley High School pupils; at risk groups; disabled people; those disadvantaged by poverty and socially isolated people
WHERE FUNDING CAN BE GIVEN The Parish of Kirkley
RANGE OF GRANTS £10–£5,694
SAMPLE GRANTS £5,694 to the Parish of St Peter and St John; £5,000 to St Nicholas Church, South Cliff; £3,250 to St John Housing Trust; £3,000 to Waveney Women's Aid; £2,400 to St Mary's Day Centre; £1,600 to Harleston House, Church Army; £1,500 to Kirkley Church Hall; £1,400 to Lowestoft Elderly People's Club; £1,200 to Society of St Vincent de Paul; £1,200 to St John Ambulance.
FINANCES *Year* 1997 *Income* £59,714 *Grants* £65,588
TRUSTEES G A Bennett, T M N Carter, Rev J Eyre, Ms J van Pelt, I M Walpole, D G Wharton, R M Wilson
NOTES In 1997, £8,766 was awarded to individuals and £10,750 in grocery vouchers were awarded
HOW TO APPLY To the address under Who To Apply To in writing
WHO TO APPLY TO Ian R Walker, Clerk, Kirkley Poor Lands, Nicholsons, 4 Station Road, Lowestoft, Suffolk NR32 4QF
CC NO 210177   **ESTABLISHED** 1976

■ Richard Kirkman Charitable Trust

WHAT IS FUNDED The Trustees are considering financing various plans for alleviating drug addiction
WHO CAN BENEFIT Registered charities and individuals
WHERE FUNDING CAN BE GIVEN Southampton
RANGE OF GRANTS Below £1,000–£3,000
SAMPLE GRANTS £3,000 to Stroke Association
FINANCES *Year* 1996–97 *Income* £21,874 *Grants* £16,620
TRUSTEES M Howson-Green, FCA, Mrs F O Kirkman

WHO TO APPLY TO M Howson Green, Richard Kirkman Charitable Trust, Charter Court, Third Avenue, Southampton SO15 0AP
CC NO 327972   **ESTABLISHED** 1988

■ The Kirschel Foundation

WHAT IS FUNDED General charitable purposes
WHO CAN BENEFIT There are no restrictions on the age; professional and economic group; family situation; religion and culture; and social circumstances of; or disease or medical condition suffered by, the beneficiaries
WHERE FUNDING CAN BE GIVEN UK
TRUSTEES L G Kirschel, J W Samuels
WHO TO APPLY TO J W Samuels, The Kirschel Foundation, 171 Wardour Street, London W1V 3TA
CC NO 1067672   **ESTABLISHED** 1997

■ Kleinwort Benson Charitable Trust

WHAT IS FUNDED General charitable purposes
WHAT IS NOT FUNDED No grants to individuals
WHO CAN BENEFIT Registered national charities. There are no restrictions on the age; professional and economic group; family situation; religion and culture; and social circumstances of; or disease or medical condition suffered by, the beneficiaries
WHERE FUNDING CAN BE GIVEN UK; local appeals wil only be considered from the City of London or East London boroughs
TYPE OF GRANT One-off or annual grant will be considered
RANGE OF GRANTS £250–£1,000, typical grant £500–£1,000
SAMPLE GRANTS £12,500 to Alzheimer's Disease Society; £12,500 to Child Line; £12,500 to ME Association; £11,000 to Treloar Trust; £10,500 to Hackney Music Development Trust
FINANCES *Year* 1997 *Grants* £247,277
TRUSTEES Kleinwort Benson Trustees Limited
HOW TO APPLY In writing to the Administrator at the address under Who To Apply To for consideration at quarterly meetings
WHO TO APPLY TO Miss J A Emptage, Administrator, Kleinwort Benson Charitable Trust, PO Box 560, 20 Fenchurch Street, London EC3P 3DB *Tel* 0171-623 8000
CC NO 278180   **ESTABLISHED** 1979

■ Knaresborough Relief in Need Charity

WHAT IS FUNDED Institutions and organisations which benefit the local community for general charitable purposes
WHO CAN BENEFIT Individuals and organisations. There are no restrictions on the age; professional and economic group; family situation; religion and culture; and social circumstances of; or disease or medical condition suffered by, the beneficiaries
WHERE FUNDING CAN BE GIVEN The Parish of Knaresborough
RANGE OF GRANTS £12–£4,500
SAMPLE GRANTS £4,500 to Knaresborough Round Table; £1,500 to Links, Knaresborough Club; £1,000 to Knaresborough Old People's Welfare; £500 to Harrogate District Community Transport; £500 to Park Place Social Club
FINANCES *Year* 1996 *Income* £16,564 *Grants* £15,317

TRUSTEES Rev A C Betts, Cllr Mrs E R Ferguson, Cllr Mrs J Dunn, Cllr P D Allott, Cllr Mrs J Gowing, G S Cook, N Willans

HOW TO APPLY To the address under Who To Apply To in writing

WHO TO APPLY TO P R Harris, Clerk, Knaresborough Relief in Need Charity, The Chequers, Boroughbridge Road, Knaresborough HG5 0LX

CC NO 226743   **ESTABLISHED** 1964

■ Knebworth Village Trust

WHAT IS FUNDED Children and schools, youth groups, the terminally ill, provision of village facilities

WHAT IS NOT FUNDED No grants to individuals

WHO CAN BENEFIT Local organisations, particularly those benefiting children, young people and terminally ill people

WHERE FUNDING CAN BE GIVEN Knebworth

RANGE OF GRANTS £249–£4,860

SAMPLE GRANTS £4,860 to Knebworth JMI School for furnishings; £1,984 to Knebworth Scouts and Guides Group towards travel; £1,500 to Knebworth Youth Group towards travel and hall hire; £1,380 to Bereavement Support Group for medical equipment for the Knebworth Surgery to benefit residents in need; £1,133 to Knebworth Nursery school for decorating; £1,046 to Rompers Parent and Toddlers Group for play equipment; £478 to Knebworth Pre-school for play equipment; £294 to Knebworth Parish Council for the War Memorial assessment and cleaning masonry

FINANCES *Year* 1997 *Income* £34,870
Grants £12,675

TRUSTEES R M Tomlinson, J R Plummer (Treasurer), J Bland, G Dumelow, Mrs V Goddard (Chair), R Meredith, M Moult, R Overman, A A Richardson, Rev D Viles, K Williams, Mrs M Young, R Wordsworth, Mrs J Gray

HOW TO APPLY Application forms available from the address under Who To Apply To upon written request. The Trustees meet four times a year, usually in January, April, July and October. Applications are invited from village organisations for capital or revenue projects that will benefit the residents in the Parish of Knebworth

WHO TO APPLY TO Mrs C L Williams, Hon Secretary, Knebworth Village Trust, 3 Bell Close, Knebworth, Hertfordshire SG3 6AJ

CC NO 297228   **ESTABLISHED** 1987

■ The David Knightly Charitable Trust

WHAT IS FUNDED Principally to help improve the built environment for the benefit of the general public. The Trust makes grants under its Pride of Place Awards Scheme for the improvement of the local environment and the provision of amenities. Funding may be given to volunteers, volunteer bureaux, architecture, historic buildings and heritage

WHAT IS NOT FUNDED Applications from individuals, school landscaping, nature trails, projects to improve the natural environment, village halls will not be funded

WHO CAN BENEFIT Voluntary organisations

WHERE FUNDING CAN BE GIVEN England

TYPE OF GRANT Pump-priming, buildings

RANGE OF GRANTS £200–£4,000

SAMPLE GRANTS £1,000 to Rose Road Appeal (Southampton); £1,000 to The Not Forgotten Association; £850 to the Enham Trust; £500 to Crisis Support Centre, Andover; £500 to Canine Partners for Independence

FINANCES *Year* 1998 *Income* £20,662
Grants £14,000

TRUSTEES Mrs M Eve, P G Jessop, C D C Jameson, Miss J K Knightly (Chair), Miss R Knightly, A Lang

HOW TO APPLY To the address under Who To Apply To before the end of February. Guidelines available from this address

WHO TO APPLY TO Gordon Michell, The David Knightly Charitable Trust, 136 The Grove, London W5 3SH

CC NO 277023   **ESTABLISHED** 1978

■ The Knowles Charitable Trust

WHAT IS FUNDED Providing housing and other related amenities for elderly people and people with mental or physical disabilities

WHAT IS NOT FUNDED No grants made for major capital projects, long-term staff posts or individuals

WHO CAN BENEFIT Organisations benefiting: older people; widows and widowers; disabled people; those disadvantaged by poverty; and those suffering from mental illness

WHERE FUNDING CAN BE GIVEN Brent, Camden, Westminster, Barnet, Harrow and Islington

TYPE OF GRANT Generally one-off. Projects and start-up costs will be considered. Funding is available for up to two years

RANGE OF GRANTS £250–£5,000

SAMPLE GRANTS £45,031 to Paddington Churches Housing Association; £5,400 to Umbrella for clothing for mentally ill residents; £2,500 to Brent Crossroads to support the provision of domiciliary respite care; £2,000 to Mind in Camden; £800 to Westminster Association for Mental Health; £400 to Age Concern Westminster; £100 to Camden Family Service Unit

FINANCES *Year* 1997 *Income* £54,859
Grants £56,231

TRUSTEES Jacqueline Cannon, Monica Healy, Margaret Hepburn, Penn Hicks, Alun Jones, Dame Simone Prendergast, Lawrence Wybraniec

HOW TO APPLY To the address under Who To Apply To in writing

WHO TO APPLY TO Dr Alun Jones, Chief Executive, The Knowles Charitable Trust, Paddington Churches Housing Association, Canterbury House, Canterbury Road, London NW6 5SQ *Tel* 0171-372 5671

CC NO 293017   **ESTABLISHED** 1984

■ The Kobler Trust

WHAT IS FUNDED General charitable purposes with emphasis is on the arts, health care and education

WHAT IS NOT FUNDED Grants to individuals are only considered on an exceptional basis

WHO CAN BENEFIT Individuals, and organisations benefiting people of all ages, including actors and entertainment professionals, medical professionals, students, teachers, governesses, writers and poets. There is no restriction on the disease or medical condition suffered by the beneficiaries

WHERE FUNDING CAN BE GIVEN Mainly UK, although donations to organisations within the State of Israel have been made in the past

TYPE OF GRANT No restrictions. These vary from small grants on a one-off basis for a specific project to a continuing relationship

SAMPLE GRANTS £60,000 to Adventures in Motion Pictures; £50,000 to Imperial College; £50,000 to Jewish Care; £35,000 to Beit Issie Shapiro; £20,000 to Chicken Shed Theatre Company; £10,000 to Royal Academy of Music; £8,000 to Federation of Jewish Relief organisations; £8,000 to Federation of Jewish Relief organisations for Tel Aviv Hospital; £3,500 to Jewish Lads and Girls Brigade; £2,500 to British ORT

FINANCES *Year* 1995 *Income* £216,445 *Grants* £267,820

TRUSTEES A A Davis, A Xuereb, A H Stone

NOTES The policy of the Trust is to help where resources are not generally otherwise available. It tends to steer clear of assisting established organisations and prefers to deal with smaller, leaner bodies and, occasionally, individuals

HOW TO APPLY By letter to the address under Who To Apply To

WHO TO APPLY TO A A Davis, The Kobler Trust, BDO Stoy Hayward, 8 Baker Street, London W1M 1DA

CC NO 275237   **ESTABLISHED** 1963

■ The Kurt Olga Koerner Charitable Trust

WHAT IS FUNDED The relief of poverty, the advancement of education, the advancement of religion and other general charitable purposes, including cultural activity

WHAT IS NOT FUNDED No grants to individuals

WHO CAN BENEFIT Children, young adults and older people

WHERE FUNDING CAN BE GIVEN UK

TRUSTEES Ms L Koerner, J L Koerner, S Hotz, M Rausing

NOTES Trustees meet twice a year, in April and September

HOW TO APPLY By invitation from the Trustees only. **This Trust states that it does not respond to unsolicited applications**

WHO TO APPLY TO Mrs E Owen, The Kurt Olga Koerner Charitable Trust, 132 Sloane Street, London SW1X 9AR *Tel* 0171-259 9466 *Fax* 0171-259 9477

CC NO 1067133   **ESTABLISHED** 1998

■ The C D Korn Charitable Trust

WHAT IS FUNDED Registered Jewish and Israeli charities, UK cancer and other health charities will be supported. Education may be considered

WHAT IS NOT FUNDED No grants to individuals. No funding for local charities, scholarships, expeditions or animal charities. No overseas charities other than those in Israel

WHO CAN BENEFIT Registered charities benefiting people of all ages, ex-service and service people, and Jewish people will be considered. Support is also given to disabled people, those disadvantaged by poverty and those suffering from Alzheimer's disease, cancers, hearing loss, kidney disease and multiple sclerosis

WHERE FUNDING CAN BE GIVEN UK, with preference for London, and Israel

TYPE OF GRANT Buildings, capital, core costs, one-off, project and research will be considered. Funding may be given for over three years

RANGE OF GRANTS £36–£25,500

SAMPLE GRANTS £25,500 to Jewish Philanthropic Association for Israel and the Middle East; £7,500 to Masorti Synagogue Assembly; £2,421 to New London Synagogue; £2,000 to Jewish Care; £2,000 to Edgware Masorti Synagogue; £1,000 to Spiro Institute; £500 to Nightingale House; £400 to Shaare Zedek; £200 to Imperial Cancer Research Fund; £200 to Macmillan Cancer Relief

FINANCES *Year* 1997 *Income* £126,220 *Grants* £42,857

TRUSTEES C D Korn, K L Levine

NOTES Income is fully committed

HOW TO APPLY Initial telephone calls are not welcome. No application forms or guidelines are issued, there are no deadlines for applications and an sae is not required

WHO TO APPLY TO C D Korn, The C D Korn Charitable Trust, 30 Harman Drive, London NW2 2ED

CC NO 327834   **ESTABLISHED** 1988

■ The Kramer Charitable Trust

WHAT IS FUNDED General charitable purposes. Trustees consider applications from a wide range of causes

WHO CAN BENEFIT There are no restrictions on the age; professional and economic group; family situation; religion and culture; and social circumstances of; or disease or medical condition suffered by, the beneficiaries

WHERE FUNDING CAN BE GIVEN UK

RANGE OF GRANTS £10–£2,500

SAMPLE GRANTS £2,500 to Foundation for Education; £1,000 to Balfour Diamond Jubilee Trust; £968 to United Synagogue; £500 to Society of Friends of Women Zionists; £500 to Shalom Foundation; £400 to Ajex Charity; £250 to Northwood Liberal Synagogue; £200 to Hampstead Garden Suburb Jewish Youth Centre; £100 to Institute of Jewish Affairs; £100 to GRET

FINANCES *Year* 1995 *Income* £75,908 *Grants* £8,698

TRUSTEES A Kramer, Mrs D Kramer, J M Kramer

WHO TO APPLY TO A Kramer, The Kramer Charitable Trust, 29 Weymouth Street, London W1N 3AF

CC NO 254403   **ESTABLISHED** 1966

■ Kreditor Charitable Trust

WHAT IS FUNDED Jewish organisations working in education and social and medical welfare

WHO CAN BENEFIT Jewish organisations and national welfare organisations benefiting: Jews; at risk groups; those disadvantaged by poverty; and socially isolated people. There is no restriction on the disease or medical condition suffered by the beneficiaries

WHERE FUNDING CAN BE GIVEN UK (London and the North-East of England)

FINANCES *Year* 1994–95 *Income* £65,555 *Grants* £61,690

TRUSTEES Gerald Kreditor, Merle Kreditor

HOW TO APPLY To the address under Who To Apply To in writing

WHO TO APPLY TO G Kreditor, Kreditor Charitable Trust, Gerald Kreditor & Co, Chartered Accountants, Tudor House, Llanvanor Road, London NW2 2AQ

CC NO 292649   **ESTABLISHED** 1985

■ The Heinz & Anna Kroch Foundation

WHAT IS FUNDED This Foundation exists to further medical research and to relieve suffering in cases of injustice and individual hardship

WHAT IS NOT FUNDED No grants are made to students or for holidays

WHO CAN BENEFIT Organisations benefiting: carers; disabled people; those disadvantaged by poverty; homeless people; victims of abuse and domestic violence; victims of war. There are no restrictions on the age or family situation of, or disease or medical condition suffered by the beneficiaries

WHERE FUNDING CAN BE GIVEN UK and Ireland

TYPE OF GRANT Grants do not exceed £15,000. Research and funding of up to three years will be considered

RANGE OF GRANTS £50–£15,000

FINANCES *Year* 1995 *Income* £115,000 *Grants* £79,000

TRUSTEES Ms A C Kroch, H J Kroch, P A English, C T Richardson, D Kroch-Rhodes

NOTES No grants for holidays or education. Individuals must apply through social services, CAB, welfare rights or other recognised organisations

HOW TO APPLY Throughout the year. No application form. Information by letter. Happy to discuss applications on phone prior to applying

WHO TO APPLY TO Mrs H Astle, Administrator, The Heinz & Anna Kroch Foundation, PO Box 17, Worsley, Manchester M28 2SB *Tel* 0161-793 4201

CC NO 207622   **ESTABLISHED** 1962

■ Kulmis Advisory Services

This trust did not respond to CAF's request to amend its entry and, by 30 June 1998, CAF's researchers did not find financial records for later than 1995 on its file at the Charity Commission. Trusts are legally required to submit annual accounts to the Charity Commission under section 42 of the Charities Act 1993

WHAT IS FUNDED (a) To relieve persons in need from the Horn of Africa and Yemen countries, particularly through the provision of information and advice. (b) To protect and preserve health. (c) To advance education, particularly through training adults so they may secure employment

WHO CAN BENEFIT Young adults, at risk groups, those disadvantaged by poverty and socially isolated people. There is no restriction on the disease or medical condition suffered by the beneficiaries

WHERE FUNDING CAN BE GIVEN Horn of Africa and Yemen countries

WHO TO APPLY TO A A Madar, Chairman, Kulmis Advisory Services, 52 Conduit Way, Stonebridge, London NW10 0SS

CC NO 1047761   **ESTABLISHED** 1994

■ The Harry Kweller Charitable Trust

WHAT IS FUNDED Medical, Jewish, educational, animal charities

WHAT IS NOT FUNDED The Trustees will not respond to applications from students, individuals or those seeking to join expeditions

WHO CAN BENEFIT Organisations benefiting children, young adults, Jewish people and the sick. There is no restriction on the disease or medical condition suffered by the beneficiaries

WHERE FUNDING CAN BE GIVEN UK and overseas

RANGE OF GRANTS £100–£1,000

SAMPLE GRANTS £1,000 to Imperial Cancer Research; £1,000 to the Winnicott Foundation; £750 to Jewish Care; £750 to British ORT Charity; £600 to North London Collegiate School for Girls

FINANCES *Year* 1996–97 *Income* £16,020 *Grants* £11,100

TRUSTEES G J West, Ms V Z Brecher

WHO TO APPLY TO Rhodes and Rhodes, The Harry Kweller Charitable Trust, 42 Doughty Street, London WC1N 2LY

CC NO 277474   **ESTABLISHED** 1979

■ Kylsant Charitable Trust

WHAT IS FUNDED General charitable purposes

WHO CAN BENEFIT There are no restrictions on the age; professional and economic group; family situation; religion and culture; and social circumstances of; or disease or medical condition suffered by, the beneficiaries

WHERE FUNDING CAN BE GIVEN UK

TRUSTEES Lady A D Coventry, The Rt Hon Countess of Coventry, P J Miller Scott

WHO TO APPLY TO P J Miller Scott, Kylsant Charitable Trust, 1 Bedford Row, London WC1R 4BZ

CC NO 1069345   **ESTABLISHED** 1997

■ The Kyte Charitable Trust

WHAT IS FUNDED Medical research, community services

WHO CAN BENEFIT Organisations benefiting medical professionals and research workers. Support may go to at risk groups, those disadvantaged by poverty and socially isolated people

WHERE FUNDING CAN BE GIVEN UK

TYPE OF GRANT At the discretion of the Trustees

FINANCES *Year* 1996 *Income* £28,556 *Grants* £53,299

TRUSTEES D M Kyte, T M Kyte, A H Kyte

HOW TO APPLY In writing at any time

WHO TO APPLY TO A Kyte, The Kyte Charitable Trust, 2nd Floor, Walbrook House, Walbrook, London EC4N 8LA

CC NO 1035886   **ESTABLISHED** 1994

■ LSA Charitable Trust

WHAT IS FUNDED Agricultural research, the promotion of agricultural knowledge, relief of poverty

WHO CAN BENEFIT Individuals and institutions benefiting agricultural researchers, farmers and those working in agriculture, and those disadvantaged by poverty

WHERE FUNDING CAN BE GIVEN UK

RANGE OF GRANTS For institutions £2,490–£20,000

SAMPLE GRANTS £20,000 to Department of Plants Sciences, Cambridge University for a project into the causes of certain tomato crop diseases; £6,932 to Nuffield Farming Scholarships Trust to support a scholar; £4,500 to Northern Horticultural Society to recruit a sandwich student to carry out vegetable crop experiments; £3,000 to Food and Farming information Service to improve their literature for schools; £2,490 to Wye College for a student to undertake a project in sustainable agriculture

FINANCES *Year* 1997 *Income* £62,434 *Grants* £53,154

TRUSTEES A R Eden, B E G Howe, P Hadley, C F Woodhouse, A M M Ross

NOTES Grants for individuals made through the Royal Agricultural Benefit Institution

WHO TO APPLY TO C F Woodhouse, LSA Charitable Trust, Messrs Farrer & Co, 66 Lincoln's Inn Fields, London WC2A 3LH

CC NO 803671   **ESTABLISHED** 1989

■ The Labone Charitable Trust

WHAT IS FUNDED Preference is given to the advancement of education, religion and the relief of the effects of poverty

WHO CAN BENEFIT Organisations benefiting children, young adults, students, teachers, clergy and those disadvantaged by poverty

WHERE FUNDING CAN BE GIVEN UK

TRUSTEES A A Stiegler, A B Stiegler, C J Young

WHO TO APPLY TO Mrs Stiegler, Trustee, The Labone Charitable Trust, 17 Eskdale Drive, Aspley, Nottingham, Nottinghamshire NG8 5GZ

CC NO 1042836   **ESTABLISHED** 1994

■ The Lacims-Maclis Trust (formerly the Maclis Trust)

WHAT IS FUNDED General charitable purposes. Funds are strictly limited and already wholly committed to certain charities

WHAT IS NOT FUNDED Expeditions, scholarships, buildings

WHO CAN BENEFIT There are no restrictions on the age; professional and economic group; family situation; religion and culture; and social circumstances of; or disease or medical condition suffered by, the beneficiaries

WHERE FUNDING CAN BE GIVEN UK

FINANCES *Year* 1997 *Income* £16,666 *Grants* £22,150

TRUSTEES R P Tullett, R Leigh Wood, A H Bartlett, M Kerr-Dineen

HOW TO APPLY **Funds wholly committed**

WHO TO APPLY TO Lacims-Maclis Charitable Trust, c/o R P Tullett, Broadwalk House, 5 Appold Street, London EC2A 2DA

CC NO 265596   **ESTABLISHED** 1973

■ The Late Sir Pierce Lacy Charity Trust

WHAT IS FUNDED Medicine and health, welfare, education, religion and general charitable purposes. Particularly charities working in the field of: infrastructure development; residential facilities and services; Christian education; Christian outreach; Catholic bodies; charity or voluntary umbrella bodies; hospices; rehabilitation centres; advocacy; education and training; community services and community issues

WHAT IS NOT FUNDED Only supports the Roman Catholic Church or associated institutions

WHO CAN BENEFIT Newly established and national organisations benefiting: children; young adults; older people; Roman Catholics; at risk groups; carers; disabled people and those disadvantaged by poverty

WHERE FUNDING CAN BE GIVEN UK and overseas

TYPE OF GRANT Recurrent small grants of £1,000 or less, buildings, capital, core costs, project, research, start-up costs and funding for more than three years may be considered

FINANCES *Year* 1998 *Income* £19,000 *Grants* £17,335

TRUSTEES General Accident and Life Assurance Corporation plc

PUBLICATIONS Annual Report

HOW TO APPLY In writing at any time

WHO TO APPLY TO R G Bell, The Late Sir Pierce Lacy Charity Trust, General Accident Trustee Department, Pitheavlis, Perth, Scotland PH2 0NH *Tel* 01738 895394

CC NO 1013505   **ESTABLISHED** 1992

■ Mrs A Lacy Tate Trust

WHAT IS FUNDED Welfare, disability and medical charities

WHO CAN BENEFIT Individuals and organisations benefiting: at risk groups; disabled people; those disadvantaged by poverty and socially isolated people. There is no restriction on the disease or medical condition suffered by the beneficiaries

WHERE FUNDING CAN BE GIVEN East Sussex

TYPE OF GRANT Often recurrent

SAMPLE GRANTS £5,890 to Queen Alexandra Cottage Hospital; £3,000 to East Sussex Care for Carers Council; £3,000 to Citizens Advice Bureau; £2,000 to St Michael's Hospice; £2,000 to Surviving Christmas Appeal; £2,000 to Battle Social Services – Christmas Fund; £2,000 to Fellowship of St Nicholas; £1,000 to Xtract; £1,000 to Elim After School Care Scheme; £1,000 to Hope in the Valley Riding School

FINANCES *Year* 1997 *Income* £43,195 *Grants* £51,166

TRUSTEES Ms L A Burgess, Ms L A Macy, Ms J Roberts, I Stewart

NOTES £35,300 was donated to institutions, £15,866 was donated to individuals

HOW TO APPLY To the address under Who To Apply To in writing

WHO TO APPLY TO I Stewart, Mrs A Lacy Tate Trust, 39 Gilredge Road, Eastbourne, East Sussex BN21 4RY

CC NO 803596   **ESTABLISHED** 1990

■ The Ladybird Trust

WHAT IS FUNDED General charitable purposes, in particular the relief of the sick, mentally or physically handicapped and the disabled. Emphasis is given to the assistance of people suffering from cerebal palsy

WHO CAN BENEFIT Organisations benefiting the disabled, in particular those suffering from cerebal palsy. otherwise there is no restriction on the disease or medical condition suffered by the beneficiaries

WHERE FUNDING CAN BE GIVEN UK

FINANCES *Year* 1996 *Income* £34,946 *Grants* £20,715

TRUSTEES G Arter, Ms G Jones

WHO TO APPLY TO N H Jones, Trustee, The Ladybird Trust, The Ridgeway, Ibstone Lane, Stokenchurch, Buckinghamshire HP14 3XR

CC NO 1044742   **ESTABLISHED** 1994

■ The David Laing Charitable Trust

WHAT IS FUNDED The policy is to support charities aiding: children; broken homes; physically and mentally disabled; with further donations to bodies supporting the improvement of the environment; the arts and animal welfare

WHAT IS NOT FUNDED The Trustees do not make grants to individuals unless they act in a capacity representing a larger body for which a donation is applicable

WHO CAN BENEFIT Organisations benefiting: children, those in care, fostered and adopted; one parent families and disabled people

WHERE FUNDING CAN BE GIVEN UK

TYPE OF GRANT Grants are not normally recurrent on a regular annual basis unless forming phases of a larger donation. Some charities are closely associated with the foundation and would benefit more frequently. Starter finance, recurring expenses or single projects. Sometimes a small grant plus an interest free loan

RANGE OF GRANTS £250–£55,000

SAMPLE GRANTS £55,000 to Charities Aid Foundation; £10,500 to Help the Aged; £6,000 to Abbot's Hill School; £3,500 to International Students House; £2,500 to MacIntyre; £250 to St John Ambulance

FINANCES *Year* 1995 *Income* £126,983 *Grants* £77,750

TRUSTEES D E Laing, R F D Barlow, J S Lewis, Mrs F M Laing

NOTES Where supporting larger charities, the support will be at both headquarters and local levels, as for instance in support of Save the Children Fund where donations to headquarters will aid the African Famine appeal, but support is also given to local branches

HOW TO APPLY Applications will be considered by the Trustees at any time. Applications basically considered between March and September

WHO TO APPLY TO D E and Mrs F M Laing, The David Laing Charitable Trust, c/o Messrs Ernst & Young, Accountants, 400 Capability Green, Luton, Bedfordshire LU1 3LU

CC NO 278462   **ESTABLISHED** 1979

■ Hilda Laing Charitable Trust

WHAT IS FUNDED Grants fall into three main categories: advancement of Christianity and Christian education; relief of poverty in the UK with emphasis on projects run by Christian organisations; relief of poverty overseas, with particular interest in population issues, street children and Christian run projects

WHAT IS NOT FUNDED No gifts to individuals for education or travel purposes, nor towards the individual needs of volunteers. No grants to groups or individuals to cover cost of attendance at conferences or participation in overseas exchange programmes. The Trustees rarely make contributions to the running costs of local organisations

WHO CAN BENEFIT No restrictions, but work with children and young people in particular, but older people; clergy; Christians; Evangelists; disabled people and those disadvantaged by poverty will be considered. Support will also be considered for victims of disasters and famine, refugees, homeless people and ex-offenders and those at risk of offending

WHERE FUNDING CAN BE GIVEN UK and overseas

TYPE OF GRANT A number of annual donations for core funding of national organisations. Most grants are one-off for specific capital projects, eg building or start-up costs

RANGE OF GRANTS In the Trust's first 16 months: £40–£250,000, typical grants £1,000–£10,000

SAMPLE GRANTS £250,000 to Lambeth Fund; £100,000 to The Salvation Army UK HQ; £75,000 to London Christian Radio Ltd; £50,000 to Bible Society; £50,000 to Dorothy Kerin Trust for Burrswood Healing Centre; £50,000 to Friends of Uganda Martyrs University; £45,000 to Evangelical Alliance; £35,000 to Crusaders Union; £30,389 to National Evangelical Church of Beirut; £25,000 to Aids Care Education and Training

FINANCES *Year* 1997 *Income* £1,708,834 *Grants* £1,388,597

TRUSTEES R M Harley, P J Harper, Sir Maurice Laing, Lady Hilda Laing, T D Parr

NOTES The Trust is administered alongside the Maurice Laing Foundation and Beatrice Laing Trust and an application to one is treated as an application to all. The Trusts rarely duplicate gifts

HOW TO APPLY The Trust does not issue application forms. Applications should be by letter giving up to date details of the project for which funding is sought, its total cost, the amount raised and some indication of how the balance is to be raised. A copy of the organisation's Annual Report and Accounts should be enclosed, together with an sae if a response is required. Applicants are asked to accept non-response as a negative reply

WHO TO APPLY TO Miss E A Harley, Hilda Laing Charitable Trust, Box 1, 133 Page Street, London NW7 2ER

CC NO 1058109   **ESTABLISHED** 1996

■ The Christopher Laing Foundation

WHAT IS FUNDED General charitable purposes. Covers specific requests from charity organisations and in addition is aimed at giving benefit to preferred and local bodies

WHAT IS NOT FUNDED Grants will normally be made to organisations

WHO CAN BENEFIT Applications from headquarters organisations and local organisations will be considered. There are no restrictions on the age; professional and economic group; family situation; religion and culture; and social circumstances of; or disease or medical condition suffered by, the beneficiaries

WHERE FUNDING CAN BE GIVEN UK

TYPE OF GRANT Recurrent and one-off

RANGE OF GRANTS £1,000–£55,000

SAMPLE GRANTS £55,000 to National Playing Fields Association; £40,000 to Charities Aid Foundation; £12,000 to Lords Taverners; £10,275 to The Prince's Trust Events Ltd; £10,000 to NSPCC; £7,500 to Simona Trust; £5,000 to Chester Cathedral Development Trust; £5,000 to White Lodge Appeal; £2,500 to British Heart Foundation; £1,000 to Ayot St Lawrence Church

FINANCES *Year* 1997 *Income* £159,474 *Grants* £160,275

TRUSTEES C M Laing, D G Stradling, P S Jackson, Mrs D C Laing

HOW TO APPLY Applications are invited at any time of the year

WHO TO APPLY TO The Christopher Laing Foundation, Messrs Ernst & Young, 400 Capability Green, Luton, Bedfordshire LU1 3LU

CC NO 278460　　　**ESTABLISHED** 1979

■ The Martin Laing Foundation

WHAT IS FUNDED General charitable purposes

WHO CAN BENEFIT There are no restrictions on the age; professional and economic group; family situation; religion and culture; and social circumstances of; or disease or medical condition suffered by, the beneficiaries

WHERE FUNDING CAN BE GIVEN UK

RANGE OF GRANTS £2,500–£50,000

SAMPLE GRANTS £50,000 to Charities Aid Foundation; £25,000 to Princess Helena College; £10,000 to Business in the Community; £10,000 to Westminster Pastoral Foundation; £5,000 to NSPCC; £2,500 to Laing Charitable Trust (The Prince of Wales Business and Environment Programme)

FINANCES *Year* 1997 *Income* £169,492 *Grants* £102,200

TRUSTEES Sir Martin Laing, CBE, D G Stradling, B O Chilver, E C K Laing

WHO TO APPLY TO The Martin Laing Foundation, Ernst & Young, 400 Capability Green, Luton, Bedfordshire LU1 3LU

CC NO 278461　　　**ESTABLISHED** 1979

■ Lajpal International Welfare Trust

WHAT IS FUNDED To help and provide support to victims of injustice, harassment and intimidation and to address issues likely to cause injustice in the hope of influencing policy affecting different groups of people. In particular: (a) to help people who are unlawfully detained or imprisoned; (b) to help parents who lose their children to relatives; (c) to gather information to support victims of injustice; and (d) to work for the general welfare of victims of injustice

WHO CAN BENEFIT Organisations benefiting victims of injustice, those who are unlawfully detained and parents who lose their children to relatives

WHERE FUNDING CAN BE GIVEN UK and overseas

TRUSTEES M Ajaib, J Ackroyd, S Anjum, T Ali, B Brown, U Riaz, B Jago

HOW TO APPLY To the address under Who To Apply To in writing

WHO TO APPLY TO Mohammed Ajaib, Chairperson, Lajpal International Welfare Trust, Cedar House, Lawkholme Lane, Keighley BD21 3DD

CC NO 1064188　　　**ESTABLISHED** 1997

■ The Lambert Charitable Trust

WHAT IS FUNDED Annually, one half of income to organisations in Israel, one third to Jewish organisations based in the UK, one sixth to general charitable purposes in the UK

WHO CAN BENEFIT Particular favour is given to Jewish people, otherwise, there are no restrictions on the age; professional and economic group; family situation; religion and culture; and social circumstances of; or disease or medical condition suffered by, the beneficiaries

WHERE FUNDING CAN BE GIVEN UK and Israel

RANGE OF GRANTS £250–£5,400

SAMPLE GRANTS £5,400 to Five Bridges; £3,783 to London Philharmonic Orchestra; £3,750 to Jewish Care; £2,500 to Royal Opera House Trust; £2,500 to Wentworth Golf and Tennis Scholarship; £1,500 to Ben Gurion University Foundation; £1,500 to Friends of Magen David Adom; £1,500 to Redbridge Jewish Youth and Community Centre; £1,250 to British Friends of the Rambah Medical Centre; £1,200 to Kiryat Sanz Medical Centre

FINANCES *Year* 1996 *Income* £105,732 *Grants* £92,883

TRUSTEES M Lambert, Dr H P Lambert, H Alexander-Passe

WHO TO APPLY TO M Lambert, The Lambert Charitable Trust, 18 Hanover Street, London W1R 9HG

CC NO 257803　　　**ESTABLISHED** 1968

■ Charity of John Lambert

WHAT IS FUNDED Individuals in need and youth organisations

WHO CAN BENEFIT Individuals and organisations benefiting young adults, at risk groups, those disadvantaged by poverty and the socially isolated

WHERE FUNDING CAN BE GIVEN Shepshed

FINANCES *Year* 1996 *Income* £17,680

HOW TO APPLY Applications should be made on a form available from the the address under Who To Apply To. The Trustees meet to consider applications in March, June, September and December

WHO TO APPLY TO G S Freckelton, Charity of John Lambert, 1 Leicester Road, Loughborough, Leicestershire LE11 2AE

CC NO 233664　　　**ESTABLISHED** 1964

■ The John and Rosemary Lancaster Charitable Foundation

WHAT IS FUNDED General charitable purposes

WHO CAN BENEFIT There are no restrictions on the age; professional and economic group; family situation; religion and culture; and social circumstances of; or disease or medical condition suffered by, the beneficiaries

WHERE FUNDING CAN BE GIVEN UK and overseas

TRUSTEES Ms J R Broadhurst, J E Lancaster, Mrs R Lancaster, S G Isherwood

WHO TO APPLY TO Mrs R Lancaster, Chairperson, The John and Rosemary Lancaster Charitable Foundation, c/o Forbes & Partners, Carter House, 28 Castle Street, Clitheroe, Lancashire BB7 2EH

CC NO 1066850　　　**ESTABLISHED** 1997

■ Bryan Lancaster's Trust

WHAT IS FUNDED A Quaker Trust. Helps towards setting up, repairs, running costs and new ventures. Priority is given to projects with Quaker involvement. Preferably for smaller and newer charities in the north-west. Particularly charities working in the fields of: accommodation and housing; infrastructure, support and development; Quaker umbrella bodies; alternative health care, health counselling; respite care, care for carers; support and self help groups; Quaker church buildings; historic buildings; professional and specialist training; bursaries and fees; purchase of books; peace campaigning; advice centres; law centres; and various community facilities and services

WHAT IS NOT FUNDED Applications from students and large medical charities are not considered

WHO CAN BENEFIT Organisations benefiting people of all ages, unemployed people and Quakers. There are few restrictions on the social circumstances of the beneficiaries

WHERE FUNDING CAN BE GIVEN UK with preference towards North West England

TYPE OF GRANT Usually one-off grants towards a specific object and to local, not national, bodies. Buildings, capital, core costs, feasibility studies, running costs and start-up costs. Funding for one year or less will be considered

RANGE OF GRANTS £200–£2,000

FINANCES *Year* 1995 *Income* £39,400
Grants £24,500

TRUSTEES D M Butler, A LeMare, C Cathrow

HOW TO APPLY At any time by letter, no application form. Trustees meet about every two months. No telephone calls. Please enclose sae; no acknowledgement without one

WHO TO APPLY TO David M Butler, Bryan Lancaster's Trust, 9 Greenside, Kendal, Cumbria LA9 5DU

CC NO 222902   **ESTABLISHED** 1719

■ The Landale Charitable Trust

WHAT IS FUNDED This Trust will consider funding: respite accommodation; publishing and printing; Christian education and outreach; churches; arts, culture and recreation; hospice at home; health facilities and buildings; medical studies and research; conservation; agriculture; art galleries and cultural centres; libraries and museums; and other charitable purposes

WHAT IS NOT FUNDED No grants to individuals or students

WHO CAN BENEFIT Registered charities benefiting: people of all ages; research workers; Christians; the terminally ill; and those suffering from cancers and heart disease

WHERE FUNDING CAN BE GIVEN UK

TYPE OF GRANT Recurrent, buildings, capital, core costs, one-off, project and research. Funding is for more than three years

SAMPLE GRANTS £16,444 to Kirkmahoe Barony Church for refurbishment; £6,000 to Kirkmahoe Parish Church as a Deed of Covenant; £3,000 to Yorkhill Hospital for Growth Fund; £2,500 to Scaitcliffe Centenary Appeal; £1,000 to Malcolm Sargent Cancer Fund

FINANCES *Year* 1997 *Income* £18,236
Grants £31,594

TRUSTEES Sir David Landale, KCVO, William Landale, James Landale, Lady Landale, Peter Landale

PUBLICATIONS Annual Report

HOW TO APPLY In writing

WHO TO APPLY TO Jane Clark, The Landale Charitable Trust, Price Waterhouse Coopers, PO Box 90, Erskine House, 68–73 Queen Street, Edinburgh EH2 4NH

CC NO 274722   **ESTABLISHED** 1978

■ Langdale Trust

WHAT IS FUNDED To assist the infirm, youth organisations, the poor and needy of all ages

WHO CAN BENEFIT Support will be given to people of all ages of varying social circumstance. There is no restriction on the disease or medical condition suffered by the beneficiaries

WHERE FUNDING CAN BE GIVEN UK

TYPE OF GRANT Annual for general and specific use

FINANCES *Year* 1995 *Income* £101,245
Grants £90,000

TRUSTEES T R Wilson, M J Woodward, Mrs T M Elvin

HOW TO APPLY Apply by March

WHO TO APPLY TO M J Woodward, Langdale Trust, Messrs Lee Crowder, 39 Newhall Street, Birmingham B3 3DY

CC NO 215317   **ESTABLISHED** 1960

■ Richard Langhorn Trust

WHAT IS FUNDED Sporting opportunities for underprivileged and disabled particularly in the areas of rugby, sailing, basketball and skiing

WHO CAN BENEFIT Underprivileged and disabled children

WHERE FUNDING CAN BE GIVEN UK

TYPE OF GRANT Buildings, interest free loans, one-off and recurring costs will be considered. Funding may be given for more than three years

FINANCES *Year* 1997 *Income* £150,000
Grants £50,000

TRUSTEES Ms G Bell, K Bray, S Langhorn, P Winterbottom, T York

PUBLICATIONS *Forward* published twice a year

HOW TO APPLY Through Harlequins RFC at the address under Who To Apply To

WHO TO APPLY TO Ms A Elliot, Administration, Richard Langhorn Trust, Harlequins Rugby Football Club, Stoop Memorial Ground, Langhorn Drive, Twickenham, Middlesex TW2 7SQ *Tel* 0181-892 0822

CC NO 1046332   **ESTABLISHED** 1995

■ The Langley Charitable Trust

WHAT IS FUNDED Advancement of the gospel and Christianity, welfare and health

WHAT IS NOT FUNDED Trustees will not consider applications from animal or bird charities

WHO CAN BENEFIT Individuals and groups benefiting: Christians, at risk groups, those disadvantaged by poverty, socially isolated people and the sick. There is no restriction on the disease or medical condition suffered by the beneficiaries

WHERE FUNDING CAN BE GIVEN UK and overseas

RANGE OF GRANTS £20–£3,000

SAMPLE GRANTS £3,000 to Holy Trinity Church; £2,295 to Birmingham Bible Institute; £1,000 to London Bible College; £1,000 to Send a Cow; £1,000 to London Bible College; £600 to Teen Challenge; £500 to Canwell Church; £500 to Phoenix Worship; £400 to Sutton Coldfield Baptist Church; £300 to Soapbox

FINANCES *Year* 1995 *Income* £145,387
Grants £12,479

TRUSTEES J P Gilmour, Mrs S S Gilmour

HOW TO APPLY The Trustees only reply where they require further information, etc. No telephone calls or correspondence will be entered into for any proposed or declined applications

WHO TO APPLY TO J P Gilmour, The Langley Charitable Trust, Wheatmoor Farm, 301 Tamworth, Sutton Coldfield, West Midlands B75 6JP

CC NO 280104   **ESTABLISHED** 1980

■ The Langtree Trust

WHAT IS FUNDED General charitable purposes. Trustees' policy is to consider requests only from within the County of Gloucestershire

WHAT IS NOT FUNDED No grants to individuals for training for higher qualifications. Occasional grants to students on, eg Outward Bound, Operation Raleigh. No grants in response to general appeals from large national organisations

WHO CAN BENEFIT The local community. There are no restrictions on the age; professional and economic group; family situation; religion and culture; and social circumstances of; or disease or medical condition suffered by, the beneficiaries

WHERE FUNDING CAN BE GIVEN Gloucestershire only

TYPE OF GRANT Usually one-off for a specific project

RANGE OF GRANTS £100–£1,000

SAMPLE GRANTS The following grants were for church repairs and improvements; £1,000 to High Cross, Avening; £1,000 to St Stephen's, Cheltenham; £750 to Littledean Reformed Church; £750 to Lydney United Reformed Church; £750 to St Ethelbert's Church, Littledean; £750 to St George's Church, Cam; £750 to St Mary the Virgin, Berkeley; £500 to Trinity Baptist Church, Gloucester; £500 to The Haven Trust Gloucester for refuge for battered wives/children; £460 to Lady Hoare Trust for expenses for the seriously disadvantaged

FINANCES *Year* 1997 *Income* £52,383
Grants £41,915

TRUSTEES R H Mann, Col P Haslam, Mrs J Humpidge, G J Yates, Mrs A M Shepherd, Mrs M Hood

HOW TO APPLY To the address under Who To Apply To at any time for consideration at meetings held about every three months. No form is used: application is by simple letter. National appeals are not acknowledged unless there is a specific relevance to Gloucestershire. Relevant details of the sums required and annual finances will assist judgement of grants

WHO TO APPLY TO The Secretary, The Langtree Trust, c/o Randall & Payne, Rodborough Court, Stroud, Gloucestershire GL5 3LR

CC NO 232924   **ESTABLISHED** 1963

■ The Lant Trust

WHAT IS FUNDED To aid welfare organisations and individuals in need. To encourage the study of new treatments in various medical conditions associated with diseases of blood vessels

WHO CAN BENEFIT Individuals and organisations benefiting at risk groups, those disadvantaged by poverty and socially isolated people. Support for medical professionals and research workers investigating treatment of medical conditions related to blood vessel diseases, and those who are suffering from the same

WHERE FUNDING CAN BE GIVEN The ecclesiastical parish of St Peter's, Balsall Common; St John the Baptist, Berkswell; St Mary's, Temple Balsall

SAMPLE GRANTS £6,089 to Charing Cross and WMS Therapeutics Research Fund

FINANCES *Year* 1996 *Income* £60,799
Grants £6,089

TRUSTEES Prof Ariel Lant, A C D Lang, Dr R Zeegen

NOTES The majority of the Trust's income covers salaries and laboratory investigations

HOW TO APPLY To the address under Who To Apply To in writing

WHO TO APPLY TO Prof A F Lant, The Lant Trust, Department of Therapeutics, Chelsea and Westminster Hospital, Fulham Road, London SW10 9NH

CC NO 286065   **ESTABLISHED** 1983

■ Lanvern Foundation

WHAT IS FUNDED Trustees favour medical and educational registered charities

WHO CAN BENEFIT Children, young adults and students. There are no restrictions on the disease or medical condition suffered by the beneficiaries

WHERE FUNDING CAN BE GIVEN UK

TYPE OF GRANT Single projects preferred. Capital expenditure

RANGE OF GRANTS All grants are of £1,000

SAMPLE GRANTS £1,000 to North Hampshire Medical Fund; £1,000 to Children in Hospital; £1,000 to LOROS; £1,000 to Wexham Gastrointestinal Trust; £1,000 to Elizabeth FitzRoy Homes; £1,000 to Music Therapy Charity; £1,000 to Brainwave; £1,000 to RADAR; £1,000 to British Wireless for the Blind; £1,000 to British Heart Foundation

FINANCES *Year* 1996 *Income* £40,163
Grants £30,000

TRUSTEES J C G Stancliffe, R A Stancliffe, A H Isaacs

WHO TO APPLY TO J C G Stancliffe, Lanvern Foundation, PO Box 7017, Hook, Hampshire RG29 1UL

CC NO 295846   **ESTABLISHED** 1986

■ The R J Larg Family Trust

WHAT IS FUNDED Grants are made for cancer research, amateur music and youth organisations including university students' associations. Funding may also be given to churches, conservation, respite care, hospices, MS and neurological research, care in the community and other community facilities. Other charitable purposes will be considered

WHAT IS NOT FUNDED Grants are not made to individuals

WHO CAN BENEFIT Organisations benefiting children, young adults, students and disabled people. Those suffering from various diseases and medical conditions are also considered

WHERE FUNDING CAN BE GIVEN UK

TYPE OF GRANT Generally one-off, some recurring. Buildings, core costs, running costs, salaries and start-up costs will be considered. Funding may be given for up to two years

RANGE OF GRANTS £250–£5,000, typical grant £1,000–£2,000

SAMPLE GRANTS £6,000 to High School, Dundee for the cadet force; £5,500 to Whitehall Theatre Trust for renovations and upkeep; £5,000 to Dundee Industrial Heritage for renovations and upkeep; £5,000 to High School, Dundee for the Larg Scholarship Fund; £5,000 to Children's Hospice Scotland; £4,500 to Scottish Wildlife Trust (Angus and Dundee); £4,000 to University of Dundee for the student hardship fund; £4,000 to Dundee Parish Church, St Mary's for renovation; £4,000 to Multiple Sclerosis (Dundee Branch); £3,500 to City of Dundee Scouts Association

FINANCES *Year* 1997–98 *Income* £124,300
Grants £126,300

TRUSTEES D A Brand, R W Gibson, S A Stewart

HOW TO APPLY Applications should be made in writing to the address under Who To Apply To. Initial telephone calls are not welcome

WHO TO APPLY TO Mrs S A Stewart, The R J Larg Family Trust, Messrs Thorntons WS, 50 Castle Street, Dundee DD1 3RU *Tel* 01382 229111
SC NO SCO 04946   **ESTABLISHED** 1970

■ Largsmount Ltd

WHAT IS FUNDED Jewish charitable purposes
WHO CAN BENEFIT Jewish people
WHERE FUNDING CAN BE GIVEN UK and overseas
FINANCES *Year* 1997 *Income* £323,941 *Grants* £135,647
TRUSTEES C S Kaufman, Mrs I R Kaufman, Z M Kaufman
HOW TO APPLY To the address under Who To Apply To in writing
WHO TO APPLY TO Z M Kaufman, Trustee, Largsmount Ltd, Cohen Arnold & Co, Accountants, 13–17 New Burlington Place, Regent Street, London W1X 2JP *Tel* 0171-734 1362
CC NO 280509   **ESTABLISHED** 1979

■ The Lark Trust

WHAT IS FUNDED Support in the areas of counselling, psychotherapy and the arts. Charities working in the fields of: welfare, children and fine arts are considered. Quaker charities may be funded
WHAT IS NOT FUNDED No grants to individuals
WHO CAN BENEFIT Registered charities benefiting people of all ages and Quakers
WHERE FUNDING CAN BE GIVEN UK with preference for Bristol
TYPE OF GRANT Funding for more than three years will be considered
RANGE OF GRANTS £500–£3,500
SAMPLE GRANTS £3,500 to Actionaid overseas for children in third world countries; £2,000 to The Harbour for HIV counselling service; £1,500 to Artspace for artists studios; £1,500 to Barnardos for work with children; £1,500 to The Salvation Army for work with drop outs; £1,000 to Bedminster Wheels Project for work with offenders of car theft, etc; £1,000 to Bristol Nightstop for homeless women; £1,000 to RNA Artists Awards; £1,000 to Society of Wood Engravers; £1,000 to Walsingham House for work with alcoholics
FINANCES *Year* 1996–97 *Income* £39,042 *Grants* £21,300
TRUSTEES G Tute, I Tute, M Mitchell
NOTES Most grant money goes to projects the Trust is already committed to
HOW TO APPLY To the address under Who To Apply To in writing
WHO TO APPLY TO W T Cardale, The Lark Trust, Burges Salmon, Narrow Quay House, Prince Street, Bristol BS1 4AH *Tel* 0117-939 2000
CC NO 327982   **ESTABLISHED** 1988

■ L'Arome Charitable Trust Company Limited

WHAT IS FUNDED Education and care, upbringing and establishment in life of children and young people. The relief of suffering of animals and the support of animal welfare
WHO CAN BENEFIT Children, young adults and their parents
WHERE FUNDING CAN BE GIVEN UK
TYPE OF GRANT One-off. As determined by the needs of the project
TRUSTEES A Jones, Mrs B Lidford, J Moore
HOW TO APPLY To the address below

WHO TO APPLY TO P J Langton, L'Arome Charitable Trust Company Limited, 28 Parkway, Deeside Ind Park, Deeside, Clwyd CH5 2NS
CC NO 801714   **ESTABLISHED** 1988

■ Felix Laski Foundation

WHAT IS FUNDED To advance, in the UK, Polish dramatic literature and Polish dramatic arts. To further education and cultural activities of the Polish ethnic minority in the UK. To relieve poverty and sickness in Poland and to relieve poor, sick or aged Poles in the UK
WHO CAN BENEFIT Polish peoples born outside the UK who are aged, disadvantaged by poverty or involved in the Polish arts. There is no restriction on the disease or medical condition suffered by the beneficiaries
WHERE FUNDING CAN BE GIVEN UK and overseas
RANGE OF GRANTS £100–£9,140
SAMPLE GRANTS £9,140 to Polish Social and Cultural Association Ltd (POSK); £4,000 to Polish Cultural Foundation (PFK); £2,000 to Polish Cultural Institute; £900 to Polish Heart Club; £100 to Sokowski Institute
FINANCES *Year* 1997 *Income* £16,000 *Grants* £16,140
TRUSTEES F Laski, P D Laski, S R Laski
WHO TO APPLY TO Felix Laski Foundation, 96 Berkeley Court, Baker Street, London NW1 5ND
CC NO 291253   **ESTABLISHED** 1985

■ Lasletts (Hinton) Charity

WHAT IS FUNDED Church repairs, general in Worcester, general benefit of the poor, homes for aged poor, educating poor children and relief of sickness
WHO CAN BENEFIT Children, the aged and those disadvantaged by poverty. There are no restrictions on the disease or medical condition suffered by the beneficiaries
WHERE FUNDING CAN BE GIVEN City and County of Worcester
SAMPLE GRANTS £20,050 to charities and church repairs; £400 to Rector of Hinton's expenses
FINANCES *Year* 1995 *Income* £141,000 *Grants* £20,450
HOW TO APPLY To the address under Who To Apply To in writing
WHO TO APPLY TO H E Wagstaffe, Lasletts (Hinton) Charity, 3–5 Sansome Place, Worcester WR1 1UQ
CC NO 233696   **ESTABLISHED** 1879

■ Rachel and Jack Lass Charities Limited

WHAT IS FUNDED General charitable purposes, with particular favour given to children's charities
WHAT IS NOT FUNDED No grants to individuals or for educational purposes
WHO CAN BENEFIT There are no restrictions on the age; professional and economic group; family situation; religion and culture; and social circumstances of; or disease or medical condition suffered by, the beneficiaries. However particular favour is given to children
WHERE FUNDING CAN BE GIVEN UK
FINANCES *Year* 1995–96 *Grants* £100,000
TRUSTEES The Directors
NOTES Only registered charities are considered
HOW TO APPLY Grants are paid annually during July/ August/September

WHO TO APPLY TO A Lass, Rachel and Jack Lass Charities Limited, 43 Lindon Lea, London N2 0RF
CC NO 256514   **ESTABLISHED** 1968

■ Peter Lathoms Charity

WHAT IS FUNDED The largest proportion of the grant total is given in grants to individuals for education and relief in need purposes
WHO CAN BENEFIT Individuals and some local organisations benefiting those disadvantaged by poverty and those in need
WHERE FUNDING CAN BE GIVEN The parishes of Bickerstaffe; Bispham and Mawdesley; Burscough; Croston; Dalton and Parbold; Newburgh and Latham; Ormskirk; Rufford; Scarisbrick; Skelmersdale; Ulnes; Walton and Eccleston; Heskin and Wrightington; Welch Whittle
FINANCES *Year* 1996 *Income* £30,397
Grants £15,355
TRUSTEES D B Bennett, A Blundell, W J Brown, Rev R J Brunswick, A Caunce, W M Cox, Mrs D M Gardner, N Johnson, A K Lewis, J N Lucas, R Moss, W Norcross, M Pennington, Mrs M D Rees, A C Richardson, Mrs H Rosbotham, J W Rothwell, P W Scarisbrick, R Shepherd, J W Shufflebothamm, Rev R D Talbot, O Taylor, M Warburton, W Waterworth, L Watson, J Smith
HOW TO APPLY To the address under Who To Apply To in writing
WHO TO APPLY TO C J Byron, Clerk, Peter Lathoms Charity, 15 Railway Road, Ormskirk, Lancashire L39 2DW
CC NO 228828   **ESTABLISHED** 1964

■ Latymer Christian Fellowship Trust

WHAT IS FUNDED To advance the Christian faith in the Royal Borough of Kensington, Chelsea and other parts of the UK and the world; to relieve persons who are in conditions of need, hardship, distress or who are elderly or sick; and any other general charitable purposes
WHO CAN BENEFIT Organisations benefiting Christians and those in conditions of need, hardship, distress or who are elderly or sick
WHERE FUNDING CAN BE GIVEN In practice, North Kensington. UK and overseas may be considered
RANGE OF GRANTS £50–£825
SAMPLE GRANTS £825 to Pioneer Trust; £640 to TEAR Fund; £550 to Eurovangelism; £250 to Pioneer Antioch; £150 to an individual; £100 to Latin Links; £75 to Migrants and Refugees Community Forum; £50 to TFG Youth
FINANCES *Year* 1997 *Income* £25,135
Grants £2,740
NOTES Beneficiaries are identified from within the networks and organisations which the Church operates
HOW TO APPLY **This Trust states that it does not respond to unsolicited applications**
WHO TO APPLY TO S Blanchflower, Latymer Christian Fellowship Trust, Latymer Christian Centre, 116 Bramley Road, North Kensington, London W10 6SU *Tel* 0181-960 0090
CC NO 1047828   **ESTABLISHED** 1995

■ The Lauchentilly Charitable Foundation 1988

WHAT IS FUNDED Advancement of education, religion, relief of poverty and general charitable purposes
WHAT IS NOT FUNDED No grants to individuals or students
WHO CAN BENEFIT Small local projects, national and established organisations benefiting children, young adults and those disadvantaged by poverty. There is no restriction on the religion or culture of the beneficiaries
WHERE FUNDING CAN BE GIVEN UK and overseas
TYPE OF GRANT One-off and recurrent grants usually of £5,000 or less
RANGE OF GRANTS £45–£10,385
SAMPLE GRANTS £10,385 to the Iveagh Trust; £2,000 to St George's Church, Hanover Square; £1,000 to Anglo Russian Opera and Ballet Trust; £1,000 to Friends of St Patrick's Cathedral; £1,000 to The Opera Theatre Company
FINANCES *Year* 1996 *Income* £23,809
Grants £21,190
TRUSTEES The Cowdray Trust Ltd, The Countess of Iveagh
NOTES Acknowledgement of appeals only sent if grant is made
HOW TO APPLY In writing only at any time
WHO TO APPLY TO The Secretary, The Lauchentilly Charitable Foundation, The Cowdray Trust Ltd, Pollen House, 10–12 Cork Street, London W1X 1PD
CC NO 299793   **ESTABLISHED** 1988

■ Laufer Charitable Trust

WHAT IS FUNDED Jewish umbrella bodies. Only charities personally known to the Trustees will be considered. Other applications will not be acknowleged
WHAT IS NOT FUNDED No grants to individuals as grants are only made to registered charities
WHO CAN BENEFIT Only charities personally known to the Trustees will be considered benefiting Jews and those suffering from diabetes
WHERE FUNDING CAN BE GIVEN UK
TYPE OF GRANT Core costs for up to one year
RANGE OF GRANTS Any new grants made would not exceed £50 as the Trust had a number of outstanding commitments which will absorb the income of the Trust for the foreseeable future
SAMPLE GRANTS £22,000 to Jewish Philanthropic Association for Israel and the Middle East; £15,000 to Jewish Care; £5,000 to Lubavitch Foundation; £1,540 to Jews College; £1,500 to Jewish Marriage Council; £1,000 to Marbeth Torah Trust; £1,000 to British Diabetic Association; £1,000 to Board of Deputies Charitable Trust; £800 to British Friends Ramot Shapiro; £670 to United Synagogue
FINANCES *Year* 1997–98 *Income* £64,252
Grants £36,565
TRUSTEES S W Laufer, D D Laufer
NOTES As this is a small charity new beneficiaries are only considered in exceptional circumstances as the income is already allocated for some years to come
HOW TO APPLY In view of the above it is suggested that no applications be made
WHO TO APPLY TO S W Laufer, Laufer Charitable Trust, 343 Regents Park Road, London N3 2LJ
CC NO 275375   **ESTABLISHED** 1961

Does the trust you have chosen match your needs? Haphazard applications waste postage and time

357

■ The Lauffer Family Charitable Trust

WHAT IS FUNDED Education, medical
WHAT IS NOT FUNDED No grants to individuals
WHO CAN BENEFIT Educational and medical charities benefiting students. There are no restrictions on the disease or medical condition suffered by the beneficiaries
WHERE FUNDING CAN BE GIVEN UK and overseas
TYPE OF GRANT Starter finance and recurrent for five years
FINANCES *Year* 1997 *Income* £151,726 *Grants* £179,304
TRUSTEES R R Lauffer, BA, J S Lauffer, MA, G L Lauffer, FRCS, MBBS, BSc (Hons), London
HOW TO APPLY Once a year
WHO TO APPLY TO Mrs R Lauffer, The Lauffer Family Charitable Trust, 15 Wildwood Road, London NW11 6UL
CC NO 251115   **ESTABLISHED** 1965

■ The Mrs F B Laurence 1976 Charitable Settlement

WHAT IS FUNDED Aid and support of the chronically ill; support of justice and human rights organisations; support of disabled people; protection of the environment and wildlife. Charities working in the fields of: accommodation and housing; legal services; publishing and printing; support to voluntary and community organisations; volunteer bureaux; community arts and recreation; community facilities; special schools and special needs education; and literacy will also be considered
WHAT IS NOT FUNDED Applications for grants to individuals will not be considered
WHO CAN BENEFIT Organisations benefiting ex-service and service people; retired people; unemployed people and volunteers. There is no restriction on the age, family situation, social circumstances of, or disease or medical condition suffered by, the beneficiaries
WHERE FUNDING CAN BE GIVEN UK and very occasionally, provided the donation is sought by a UK charity, overseas
TYPE OF GRANT Core costs. one-off, project and start-up costs. Funding is for one year or less
SAMPLE GRANTS £4,000 to Foundation for Communication for the Disabled; £3,500 to Pilton Community Health Project; £3,000 to Macmillan Cancer Relief; £2,500 to Canine Partners for Independence; £2,500 to The Gurka Welfare Trust; £2,500 to Motor Neurone Disease Association; £2,500 to Medical Foundation for Care of Victims of Torture; £2,500 to SSAFA; £200 to Abbeyfield Richmond Thames and District Society; £2,000 to British Red Cross for landmines campaign
FINANCES *Year* 1997–98 *Income* £110,217 *Grants* £115,660
TRUSTEES G S Brown, D A G Sarre, M Tooth
NOTES Only applications supported by financial information will be considered
HOW TO APPLY To the address under Who To Apply To in writing
WHO TO APPLY TO The Trustees, The Mrs F B Laurence 1976 Charitable Settlement, c/o Payne Hicks Beach, 10 New Square, Lincoln's Inn, London WC2A 3QG *Tel* 0171-465 4300
CC NO 296548   **ESTABLISHED** 1976

■ Kathleen Laurence's Trust

WHAT IS FUNDED General charitable purposes at the Trustees' discretion. Particularly favouring smaller organisations and those raising funds for specific requirements such as for the purchase of land, the restoration of cathedrals, etc
WHAT IS NOT FUNDED Must be a registered charity. No donations are made for running costs, management expenses or to individuals
WHO CAN BENEFIT General charities with specific projects and events. There are no restrictions on the age; professional and economic group; family situation; religion and culture; and social circumstances of; or disease or medical condition suffered by, the beneficiaries
WHERE FUNDING CAN BE GIVEN UK
RANGE OF GRANTS £350–£5,000
SAMPLE GRANTS £5,000 to Royal London Society for the Blind; £5,000 to University of Aberdeen; £4,000 to Reed's School; £3,000 to RNID; £3,000 to Ronald Raven Choir; £3,000 to Hodgkins Disease Association; £3,000 to Motor Neurone Disease Association; £3,000 to Roy Castle Cause for Hope; £2,000 to The Field Lane Foundation; £2,000 to Benedictine Monastery
FINANCES *Year* 1996 *Income* £107,595 *Grants* £95,555
TRUSTEES Coutts and Company Trustees
HOW TO APPLY Quarterly in February, May, August, November
WHO TO APPLY TO The Manager, Trustee Department, Kathleen Laurence's Trust, Coutts & Co, 440 The Strand, London WC2R 0QS
CC NO 296461   **ESTABLISHED** 1987

■ The Lawlor Foundation

WHAT IS FUNDED The current emphasis is on education, the principal beneficiaries being Irish educational establishments and individual students, British organisations which support Irish immigrants and vulnerable young people. Particularly charities working in the fields of: advice and information on housing; respite; information technology and computers; infrastructure development; rehabilitation centres; support and self help groups; well women clinics; postgraduate education; secondary schools; tertiary and higher education; training for work; bursaries and fees; and the purchase of books
WHAT IS NOT FUNDED No grants for medical causes, expeditions, environmental projects, the arts or for school fees
WHO CAN BENEFIT Individuals and organisations benefiting: young adults and older people; students, parents and children; at risk groups; those disadvantaged by poverty; ex-offenders and those at risk of offending and victims of domestic violence
WHERE FUNDING CAN BE GIVEN Ireland, London and Essex
TYPE OF GRANT Core costs, feasibility studies, one-off, projects, research, recurring costs, running costs and start-up costs. Funding of up to and over three years will be considered
RANGE OF GRANTS £250–£10,000

SAMPLE GRANTS £10,000 to Brent Advice Centre, London for study and treatment of adolescent breakdown; £10,000 to Jesus College, Cambridge for grants to disadvantaged students from Northern Ireland The following grants were for disadvantaged pupils and ex-pupils:; £10,000 to St Louise's College, Belfast; £6,000 to La Salle Secondary School, Belfast; £6,000 to St Mary's Boys' Christian Brothers' School, Belfast; £6,000 to St Cecilia's College, Derry; £6,000 to St Mary's College, Derry; £4,000 to Irish Studies Centre, University North London for grants to disadvantaged Irish students; £3,000 to Brandon Centre, London for support for pilot mental health service for vulnerable young people; £2,500 to Springhill and Ballysillan Schools, Belfast to enable disadvantaged pupils to take up grammar school places

FINANCES *Year* 1996–97 *Income* £116,513 *Grants* £94,050

TRUSTEES E L Lawlor, V K Lawlor, K K Lawlor, F M Baker, M Spiro

NOTES Grants to students are restricted to those with an Irish background

HOW TO APPLY By letter to the address under Who To Apply To at any time, enclosing the latest accounts and a description of the project. Preliminary telephone calls welcome to Mrs Carley Brown Tel: 01392 252184. Applications form only for students. Trustees meet March, July, October and December

WHO TO APPLY TO Mrs Carley Brown, The Lawlor Foundation, 117 High Street, Epping, Essex CM16 4BD *Tel* 01992 561121 *Fax* 01992 578727

CC NO 297219   **ESTABLISHED** 1987

■ The Lawson Charitable Foundation

WHAT IS FUNDED The advancement of education, religion and the relief of poverty, the support of the arts

WHAT IS NOT FUNDED No grants to individuals

WHO CAN BENEFIT Organisations benefiting children, adults, students and those disadvantaged by poverty. Those involved in the arts and of many religions and cultures will be supported

WHERE FUNDING CAN BE GIVEN The South of England

RANGE OF GRANTS £50–£4,200

SAMPLE GRANTS £4,000 to London String Quartet; £3,414 to Guildhall School of Music; £3,150 to Ravenswood Foundation; £3,058 to Central Synagogue; £2,500 to Arts Education Trust; £2,171 to a Rabbi; £1,750 to Juvenile Diabetes; £1,262 to Jewish Federation; £1,250 to Nightingale House; £1,000 to Joint Jewish Charitable Trust

FINANCES *Year* 1997 *Income* £31,658 *Grants* £36,611

TRUSTEES G C H Lawson, M R Lawson, Mrs C Lawson

NOTES In 1997, grants were distributed under three categories: health and welfare; education and culture; and the arts and humanities

HOW TO APPLY In writing, preferably with an sae

WHO TO APPLY TO G Lawson, The Lawson Charitable Foundation, Stilemans, Munstead, Godalming, Surrey GU8 4AB

CC NO 259468   **ESTABLISHED** 1969

■ Raymond and Blanche Lawson Charitable Trust

WHAT IS FUNDED This Trust will consider funding: churches; Councils for Voluntary Service (CVS); volunteer bureaux; arts activities and education; hospice at home; nursing service; hospices; hospitals; cancer research; community centres and village halls; guide dogs for the blind; care in the community; and holidays and outings. The Trustees support local charities. They discourage applications from outside the area Where Funding Can Be Given

WHAT IS NOT FUNDED Registered charities only. Applications from individuals, including students, are not entertained

WHO CAN BENEFIT Registered charities benefiting: children; young adults; older people; at risk groups; carers; disabled people; those disadvantaged by poverty; disaster victims; homeless people; victims of abuse, crime, war and man made or natural disasters. Those suffering from: arthritis and rheumatism; cancers; diabetes; head and other injuries; heart disease; sight loss; and terminal illness

WHERE FUNDING CAN BE GIVEN Whilst national charities are considered, local charities are favoured in East Sussex and Kent

TYPE OF GRANT One-off, project and research. Funding is available for up to one year

RANGE OF GRANTS £100–£23,500. Typically £1,000

SAMPLE GRANTS £23,500 to Hospice in the Weald for general purposes of the charity; £5,400 to Royal British Legion, Tonbridge for building purposes; Grants for general purposes:; £2,750 to Guide Dogs for the Blind; £2,400 to Parenthood; £2,000 to Heart of Kent Hospice; £2,000 to Keystone Appeal YMCA; £1,750 to Tonbridge War Relief Fund; £1,500 to Compaid Trust; £1,500 to Imperial Cancer Research Fund; £1,440 to Samaritans, Tunbridge Wells

FINANCES *Year* 1997 *Income* £89,236 *Grants* £83,236

TRUSTEES J V Banks, J A Bertram, Mrs P E V Banks

HOW TO APPLY At any time, the Trustees are in regular contact. Applications should include clear details of the need for which assistance is sought

WHO TO APPLY TO Mrs P E V Banks, Raymond and Blanche Lawson Charitable Trust, 28 Barden Road, Tonbridge, Kent TN9 1TX *Tel* 01732 352183 *Fax* 01732 352621

CC NO 281269   **ESTABLISHED** 1980

■ The Carole & Geoffrey Lawson Foundation

WHAT IS FUNDED General charitable purposes

WHAT IS NOT FUNDED Individuals should not generally apply

WHO CAN BENEFIT There are no restrictions on the age; professional and economic group; family situation; religion and culture; and social circumstances of; or disease or medical condition suffered by, the beneficiaries

WHERE FUNDING CAN BE GIVEN South of England

RANGE OF GRANTS £200–£38,000

SAMPLE GRANTS £38,000 to Cancer Relief Macmillan Fund; £30,000 to Young Minds; £12,500 to LSO Endowment Fund; £10,000 to Global Cancer Concern; £10,000 to Jewish Care; £10,000 to London Playing Fields Society; £7,500 to Royal Opera House Trust; £5,000 to Greater London Fund for the Blind; £2,500 to Contact the Elderly; £2,500 to Community Security Trust

FINANCES *Year* 1997 *Income* £43,038
Grants £133,000

TRUSTEES Mrs C Lawson, G C H Lawson

WHO TO APPLY TO G C H Lawson, The Carole & Geoffrey Lawson Foundation, Stilemans, Munstead, Godalming, Surrey GU8 4AB

CC NO 801751 **ESTABLISHED** 1989

■ Lawson-Beckman Charitable Trust

WHAT IS FUNDED General charitable purposes

WHAT IS NOT FUNDED No grants to individuals

WHO CAN BENEFIT Mainly headquarters organisations.There are no restrictions on the age; professional and economic group; family situation; religion and culture; and social circumstances of; or disease or medical condition suffered by, the beneficiaries

WHERE FUNDING CAN BE GIVEN UK

RANGE OF GRANTS £100–£21,375

SAMPLE GRANTS £21,375 to Jewish Care; £6,000 to Ravenswood Foundation; £5,000 to Friends of Emmanuel College; £5,000 to University College Hospital; £4,250 to Community Security Trust; £2,500 to World ORT Trust; £10,900 to British Friends of the Art Museums of Israel; £1,000 to British Technion Society; £1,000 to Chief Rabbinate Charitable Trust; £1,000 to JNF Charitable Trust

FINANCES *Year* 1996 *Income* £116,000
Grants £61,435

TRUSTEES M A Lawson, J N Beckman

NOTES Funds are fully committed to charities which are of special interest to the Trustees

WHO TO APPLY TO Melvin Lawson, Lawson-Beckman Charitable Trust, PO Box 1ED, London W1A 1ED

CC NO 261378 **ESTABLISHED** 1970

■ Lawther Foundation

WHAT IS FUNDED General charitable purposes

WHO CAN BENEFIT There are no restrictions on the age; professional and economic group; family situation; religion and culture; and social circumstances of; or disease or medical condition suffered by, the beneficiaries

WHERE FUNDING CAN BE GIVEN UK

TRUSTEES Professor P J Lawther

WHO TO APPLY TO Professor P J Lawther, Trustee, Lawther Foundation, 13 The Ridge, Purley, Surrey CR8 3PF

CC NO 1046253 **ESTABLISHED** 1995

■ Lazard Charitable Trust

WHAT IS FUNDED Charities working in the fields of: accommodation and housing; supporting volunteers; respite care; support and self help groups; and hospices will be considered. Funding may also be given for special needs education, speech therapy, training for work and various community facilities and services

WHAT IS NOT FUNDED No grant for medical research, overseas charities, animal charities, large national/international charities or to individuals

WHO CAN BENEFIT Small, inner-city self help charities benefiting: people of all ages; those in care, fostered and adopted; those disadvantaged by poverty; homeless people and victims of abuse. Funding may also go to those suffering from various diseases and medical conditions. Prenatal care is considered.

WHERE FUNDING CAN BE GIVEN London

TYPE OF GRANT One-off, capital, recurring, core costs, buildings, project, running costs, salaries and start-up costs will be considered. Funding may be given for over three years

RANGE OF GRANTS £100–£2,500

FINANCES *Year* 1995 *Income* £200,000
Grants £195,000

TRUSTEES M C Baugham, Ms F A Heaton, Ms C Syder

HOW TO APPLY In writing, attaching latest available Report and Accounts. No application form or guidelines available

WHO TO APPLY TO Mrs E D Brown, Secretary, Lazard Charitable Trust, Lazard Brothers & Co Ltd, 21 Moorfields, London EC2P 2HT *Tel* 0171-588 2721

CC NO 1048043 **ESTABLISHED** 1995

■ The Norrice Lea Charitable Settlement

WHAT IS FUNDED Local Jewish groups; the promotion of worship

WHO CAN BENEFIT Organisations benefiting Jewish people

WHERE FUNDING CAN BE GIVEN Greater London

FINANCES *Year* 1997 *Income* £66,100
Grants £8,656

TRUSTEES A Cohen, M Goldstein, D Landau

HOW TO APPLY To the address under Who To Apply To in writing

WHO TO APPLY TO A D Cohen, The Norrice Lea Charitable Settlement, 4 Church Mount, Hampstead Garden Suburb, London N2 0RP *Tel* 0181-458 2831

CC NO 285662 **ESTABLISHED** 1982

■ The Eric and Dorothy Leach Charitable Trust

WHAT IS FUNDED Health, conservation, and animal facilities and services

WHAT IS NOT FUNDED No grants to individuals

WHO CAN BENEFIT Organisations benefiting children, young adults and older people

WHERE FUNDING CAN BE GIVEN Principally the North West and North Wales

TYPE OF GRANT Core costs, one-off, project, research, running costs and start-up costs

HOW TO APPLY In writing only

WHO TO APPLY TO R Chamberlain, The Eric and Dorothy Leach Charitable Trust, c/o Swayne, Johnson & Wight Solicitors, High Street, St Asaph, Denbighshire LL17 0RF *Tel* 01745 582535 *Fax* 01745 584504

CC NO 1070041 **ESTABLISHED** 1998

■ The Leach Fourteenth Trust

WHAT IS FUNDED Charities working in the fields of: residential facilities and services; missionary work; conservation and environment; and community services. Support may be given to information technology and computers; professional bodies; Council for Voluntary Service; hospice at home; respite care; ambulances and mobile units; medical research; professional and specialist training; and special needs education. Trustees mainly seek out their own ventures to support

WHAT IS NOT FUNDED Grants to UK-based registered charities only. No grants to individuals, for 'gap year' or similar projects or for sponsored bike rides, etc

WHO CAN BENEFIT Grants to registered charities only. There is no restriction on the age of, or disease or medical condition suffered by the beneficiaries. People of many social circumstances will be considered

WHERE FUNDING CAN BE GIVEN UK but the South West and Channel Islands and London are favoured

TYPE OF GRANT Buildings, capital, core costs, one-off, project, research, running costs, recurring costs, salaries and start-up costs will be considered. Funding may be given for more than three years

RANGE OF GRANTS £500–£5,000

SAMPLE GRANTS £5,500 to Plan International for a new school building in Uganda; £5,000 to DeafBlind UK for a voluntary worker £5,000 to Changing Faces towards aid for facial disfigurement; £4,000 to Power for mine victim limbs; £4,000 to Winston's Wish supporting child bereavement; £4,000 to Countryside Restoration Trust; £3,000 to Jersey Wildlife Preservation Trust (SAFE); £3,000 to Teenage Cancer Trust; £2,000 to Dorethy House Foundation for hospice

FINANCES *Year* 1997 *Income* £77,185 *Grants* £87,000

TRUSTEES W J Henderson, M A Hayes, R Murray-Leach, Mrs J M M Nash

HOW TO APPLY No application forms. Not all applications acknowledged

WHO TO APPLY TO Mr and Mrs R Murray-Leach, The Leach Fourteenth Trust, Nettleton Mill, Castle Combe, Chippenham, Wiltshire SN14 7HJ

CC NO 204844   **ESTABLISHED** 1961

■ The Leadership Trust

WHAT IS FUNDED To provide education and character training, both physical and mental, for the inhabitants of Great Britain with particular emphasis on the exercise of leadership in British commercial life. Covers courses concerning developing personal leadership ability and subsequent personal development programmes; team building and team leadership; and organisational leadership. Promotion of research and development in leadership and related fields

WHO CAN BENEFIT Organisations benefiting those studying and training with the aim of leadership in British commercial life

WHERE FUNDING CAN BE GIVEN Great Britain

SAMPLE GRANTS The following organisations received grants to enable their representatives to attend the courses run by the Trust:; Ministry of Defence (Army); Strategy PR; HAWTEC; St Margaret's Hospice, Somerset; Scottish Police College; Diamond Cable Communications; CIRIA; St Hilary's School, Godalming; West Midlands Fire Service

FINANCES *Year* 1996 *Income* £2,108,801 *Grants* £67,098

TRUSTEES M P Aiken, S A Bentley, M J Smith, T Walker

NOTES The Trust includes a Development Fund for the future purchase and development of property and equipment for the expansion of charitable activities; and the Gilbert-Smith Endowment Fund

for the benefit of people irrespective of their financial means

WHO TO APPLY TO P K Winter, Chief Executive, The Leadership Trust, Weston-under-Penyard, Ross-on-Wye, Herefordshire HR9 7YH

CC NO 270286   **ESTABLISHED** 1975

■ The Leadership Trust Foundation

WHAT IS FUNDED To advance the education and research in the fields of leadership and management, and the training of effective managers and leaders. To advance the education of the public, in particular in knowledge and understanding of effective leadership. To encourage and support individuals who are or wish to be in positions of leadership to learn about and develop leadership skills

WHAT IS NOT FUNDED Capital projects and on-going revenue costs are not funded

WHO CAN BENEFIT Directors and senior managers of voluntary sector organisations

WHERE FUNDING CAN BE GIVEN UK

TYPE OF GRANT Bursaries

RANGE OF GRANTS Up to £5,000

TRUSTEES M P Aiken (Chairman), S A Bently, W M Colacicchi, M Smith, T Walker

HOW TO APPLY Application forms available from the Grants Administrator. Applications considered quarterly in March, June, September and December

WHO TO APPLY TO Karen Frost, Grants Administrator, The Leadership Trust Foundation, Weston-under-Penyard, Ross-on-Wye HR9 7YH *Tel* 01989 767667

CC NO 1063916   **ESTABLISHED** 1997

■ The David Lean Foundation

WHAT IS FUNDED To promote and advance education; to improve public taste in the visual arts, in particular by stimulating original and creative work in the UK in the field for film production (particularly screenplay writing, film production and film editing). Encouraging a high standard of art and technique of persons involved in such film production, arts sciences and techniques. Other general charitable purposes

WHO CAN BENEFIT To benefit: children; young adults; students and those involved in the arts

WHERE FUNDING CAN BE GIVEN UK

WHO TO APPLY TO Kent Jones and Done, Solicitors, The David Lean Foundation, Churchill House, Regent Road, Stoke on Trent ST1 3RQ *Tel* 01782 202020

CC NO 1067074   **ESTABLISHED** 1997

■ The Paul & Evelyn Leboff Charitable Trust

WHAT IS FUNDED The Trustees favour local appeals and support a limited number of national organisations. Regret no further organisations considered, only the existing ones already receiving support. Funding may be given to synagogues and Jewish umbrella bodies; respite care, hospices, cancer and MS research; and special schools

WHO CAN BENEFIT Registered charities including those benefiting the elderly, disadvantaged youth, handicapped and disabled, blind and deaf people

WHERE FUNDING CAN BE GIVEN Hertfordshire and Manchester

TYPE OF GRANT One-off, recurrent and research grants depending on funds available. Funding is for one year or less

RANGE OF GRANTS £25–£1,000 (approximately)

SAMPLE GRANTS £3,368 to Bushey United Synagogue; £2,220 to B'nei B'rith Hillel Foundation; £1,720 to BFIWD; £1,580 to Habad Orphan Aid Society; £1,225 to Rudolph Steiner

FINANCES *Year* 1997 *Income* £20,008 *Grants* £18,302

TRUSTEES Mrs E Leboff, A B Leboff, Mrs M A Cohen

HOW TO APPLY Reviewed generally April and October each year. No phone calls accepted, no application form used

WHO TO APPLY TO Mrs E Leboff, The Paul & Evelyn Leboff Charitable Trust, 7 Priory Court, 169 Sparrows Herne, Bushey, Watford, Hertfordshire WD2 1EF

CC NO 264707   **ESTABLISHED** 1972

■ The Leche Trust

WHAT IS FUNDED Principally: (a) preservation of buildings and furniture of the Georgian period; (b) assistance to organisations concerned with music and drama; (c) assistance to students from overseas during their final months of PhD study in the UK; (d) assistance to postgraduate music students of outstanding ability; (e) art galleries and cultural centres, libraries and museums and theatre and opera houses

WHAT IS NOT FUNDED The Trustees do not make grants for religion, structural repairs to Church of England churches, any school buildings, public schools, social welfare, animals, medicine, expeditions, British students taking first degrees or postgraduate courses

WHO CAN BENEFIT Individuals and organisations benefiting: actors and entertainment professionals; musicians and students

WHERE FUNDING CAN BE GIVEN UK and overseas

TYPE OF GRANT Grants for a specific purpose and not recurrent including building

RANGE OF GRANTS £500–£5,000

FINANCES *Year* 1997 *Income* £203,682 *Grants* £158,000

TRUSTEES Mrs C J F Arnander (Chairman), Mrs Diana Hanbury, J Porteous, Sir John Riddell, I Bristow, S Jervis, S Wethered

HOW TO APPLY In writing to the address under Who To Apply To. The Trustees meet three times a year in October, February and June

WHO TO APPLY TO Mrs L Lawson, Secretary to the Trustees, The Leche Trust, 84 Cicada Road, London SW18 2NZ *Tel* 0181-870 6233 *Fax* 0181-870 6233

CC NO 225659   **ESTABLISHED** 1963

■ The Arnold Lee Charitable Trust

WHAT IS FUNDED To distribute the Trust's income to established charities of high repute working in the fields of education, health and religious purposes

WHO CAN BENEFIT Organisations benefiting children, young adults and Jewish people. Support may also be given to rabbis, medical professionals, students, teachers and governesses. There is no restriction on the disease or medical condition suffered by the beneficiaries. Very occasional grants may be made to individuals

WHERE FUNDING CAN BE GIVEN UK

RANGE OF GRANTS £50–£42,150

SAMPLE GRANTS £42,150 to Joint Jewish Charitable Trust; £12,500 to Jewish Care; £10,000 to Project Seed; £7,250 to Yesodey Hatorah Schools; £5,000 to Lubavitch Foundation; £3,000 to Nightingale House; £2,500 to Huntingdon Foundation Ltd; £2,500 to Service to the Aged (SAGE); £2,000 to British Friends of Yeshivat Hamivtar and Midreshet Lindenbaum; £1,600 to British Friends of the Art Museums of Israel

FINANCES *Year* 1997 *Income* £92,851 *Grants* £105,695

TRUSTEES A Lee, Mrs H Lee, A L Lee

WHO TO APPLY TO A Lee, The Arnold Lee Charitable Trust, 47 Orchard Court, Portman Square, London W1H 9PD

CC NO 264437   **ESTABLISHED** 1972

■ The Incorporated Leeds Church Extension Society

WHAT IS FUNDED Church community projects; the repair and restoration of churches and church buildings. Church of England only

WHAT IS NOT FUNDED No appeals for church organs, or from other denominations

WHO CAN BENEFIT The Church of England

WHERE FUNDING CAN BE GIVEN The Archdeaconry of Leeds or elsewhere

TYPE OF GRANT Buildings and project funding

RANGE OF GRANTS £50–£5,500

SAMPLE GRANTS £5,500 to St Mary, Garforth for a church hall and parish centre; £5,000 to St James, Woodside for a church hall and parish centre; £3,500 to St John and St Barnabas, Belle Isle Middleton St Cross for church restoration and maintenance; £3,000 for clergy stipends; £2,850 to Church Halls and Parish Centres, St Paul, Ireland Wood; £2,500 to St Wilfrid, Halton for church restoration and maintenance; £2,500 to St Mary, Whitkirk for church restoration and maintenance; £1,500 to St Philip, Osmondthorpe for church restoration and maintenance; £1,500 to St Philip, Orsomdthorpe for a mission partner; £1,500 to St Mary, Garforth for a church hall and parish centre

FINANCES *Year* 1997 *Income* £50,402 *Grants* £33,907

TRUSTEES Rev Canon G C M Smith, Miss C E Walker, Ven J M Oliver, G D Breton, FCA, A B Menzies, FCA, Rev T G Warr, R Hardy, K Endersby, N P Spencer, R W Padgett, Mrs D M Evans, Rev J Saxton, Miss E H Paul, G Bass, A Nicholls

HOW TO APPLY Application forms are available from the address under Who To Apply To and should be accompanied by accounts and project details

WHO TO APPLY TO G D Breton, Hon Secretary, The Incorporated Leeds Church Extension Society, 38c Heathfield, Leeds LS16 7AB

CC NO 504682   **ESTABLISHED** 1905

■ The Leeds Hospital Fund Charitable Trust

WHAT IS FUNDED Hospitals, hospices, medical and disability charities

WHO CAN BENEFIT Organisations involved with hospitals and local health related charities including those working with the disabled. There are no restrictions on the disease or medical condition suffered by the beneficiaries

WHERE FUNDING CAN BE GIVEN Yorkshire

TYPE OF GRANT One-off and recurring

FINANCES *Year* 1997 *Income* £803,618 *Grants* £711,111

TRUSTEES V Barker, C Bell, Mrs P J Dobson, T Hardy, R T Strudwick
HOW TO APPLY The Trustees meet in February, July and November to consider applications
WHO TO APPLY TO M A Romaine, The Leeds Hospital Fund Charitable Trust, 41 St Paul's Street, Leeds LS1 2JL *Tel* 0113-245 0813
CC NO 253861   **ESTABLISHED** 1967

■ Leeds Jewish Community Charitable Trust

WHAT IS FUNDED Jewish charitable purposes
WHO CAN BENEFIT Organisations benefiting Jewish people
WHERE FUNDING CAN BE GIVEN Leeds and the surrounding area
SAMPLE GRANTS £13,811 to Community Development Officer; £6,570 for general educational purposes; £2,999 for general religious purposes; £1,334 for welfare; £600 to Genie's Lamp; £100 to Community Security
FINANCES *Year* 1996 *Income* £28,314 *Grants* £25,414
TRUSTEES The Honorary Officers of the Leeds Jewish Representative Council
HOW TO APPLY Applications should be made on a form available from the address under Who To Apply To
WHO TO APPLY TO D A Friedman, Executive Officer, Leeds Jewish Community Charitable Trust, Leeds Jewish Representative Council, 15 Shadwell Lane, Leeds LS17 8DW
CC NO 517835   **ESTABLISHED** 1986

■ Leeke Church Schools and Educational Foundation

WHAT IS FUNDED The advancement of education
WHAT IS NOT FUNDED Only schools and individuals
WHO CAN BENEFIT Individuals and schools benefiting: young adults; students and volunteers. There are no restrictions on the religion or culture of the beneficiaries, but preference is given to those who conform to the doctrines of the Church of England
WHERE FUNDING CAN BE GIVEN Lincoln residents aged between 16 and 24 inclusive
TYPE OF GRANT One-off, project and research. Funding can be given for any length of time
RANGE OF GRANTS £50–£1,500
SAMPLE GRANTS £10,000 to Lincoln Christ's Hospital School for books; £7,000 to Lincoln Minster School for books and equipment; £5,000 to Bishop King School for books; £5,000 to St Mary's School for books; £900 to a pupil towards the cost of a music degree; £900 to a pupil towards the cost of a course in Palestine; £900 to a pupil towards the cost of a language degree; £800 to a pupil for the airfare to Pacific Islands; £750 to a pupil towards the cost of a Graphic Design HND course; £500 to a pupil for a musical instrument
FINANCES *Year* 1995 *Income* £31,475 *Grants* £29,000
NOTES **Funding to schools is fully committed**
HOW TO APPLY To the address under Who To Apply To in writing. Applications by individuals should be made on a form available from the address under Who To Apply To. The Trustees meet in June and November

WHO TO APPLY TO S Waugh, Hon Grants Officer, Leeke Church Schools and Educational Foundation, 27a Nettleham Road, Lincoln LN2 1RQ *Tel* 01522 529630
CC NO 527654   **ESTABLISHED** 1967

■ Leeside Charitable Trust

WHAT IS FUNDED Jewish charities and those helping the sick
WHO CAN BENEFIT Organisations benefiting Jewish people and the sick. There is no restriction on the disease or medical condition suffered by the beneficiaries
WHERE FUNDING CAN BE GIVEN UK
FINANCES *Year* 1995 *Income* £25,558 *Grants* £30,325
TRUSTEES H Wiesenfeld, I Wiesenfeld
NOTES **Income wholly committed to current beneficiaries**
WHO TO APPLY TO H Wiesenfeld, Leeside Charitable Trust, 130 Bridge Lane, London NW11 9JS
CC NO 293716   **ESTABLISHED** 1985

■ Duncan C Leggat Charitable Trust

WHAT IS FUNDED General charitable purposes
WHO CAN BENEFIT Registered charities. There are no restrictions on the age; professional and economic group; family situation; religion and culture; and social circumstances of; or disease or medical condition suffered by, the beneficiaries
WHERE FUNDING CAN BE GIVEN Mainly Glasgow and West of Scotland
TRUSTEES G A Maguire, Mrs J M L Leggatt
WHO TO APPLY TO Duncan C Leggat Charitable Trust Miller, Beckett & Jackson, 190 St Vincent Street, Glasgow G2 5SP
SC NO SCO 11512

■ Leicester and Leicestershire Historic Churches Preservation Trust

WHAT IS FUNDED The restoration, preservation, repair, maintenance and improvement of churches and chapels, their churchyards and contents in the area Where Funding Can Be Given
WHAT IS NOT FUNDED No grants for new extensions to churches or chapels
WHERE FUNDING CAN BE GIVEN The Diocese of Leicester
FINANCES *Year* 1995 *Income* £37,000 *Grants* £15,500
TRUSTEES Sixteen appointees of the Bishop of Leicester
HOW TO APPLY To the address under Who To Apply To in writing for an application form
WHO TO APPLY TO T Y Cocks, Hon Secretary, Leicester and Leicestershire Historic Churches Preservation Trust, 24 Beresford Drive, Leicester LE2 3LA *Tel* 0116-270 3424
CC NO 233476   **ESTABLISHED** 1964

■ The Leicester Charity Organisation Society

WHAT IS FUNDED The primary function of this Trust is the provision of services to other charities, administering their funds and making links between potential beneficiaries and relevant charities. Grants are, however, made by the Society itself to individuals and some organisations

WHO CAN BENEFIT Individuals and organisations. There are no restrictions on the age; professional and economic group; family situation; religion and culture; and social circumstances of; or disease or medical condition suffered by, the beneficiaries

WHERE FUNDING CAN BE GIVEN Leicester and the surrounding area

FINANCES *Year* 1996 *Income* £918,839 *Grants* £597,840

HOW TO APPLY To the the address under Who To Apply To in writing

WHO TO APPLY TO M A Marvell, Secretary, The Leicester Charity Organisation Society, 18 Friar Lane, Leicester LE1 5RA

CC NO 209464   **ESTABLISHED** 1876

■ Leicester's Bede Island Community Foundation

WHAT IS FUNDED General charitable purposes for the benefit of the community

WHO CAN BENEFIT There are no restrictions on the age; professional and economic group; family situation; religion and culture; and social circumstances of; or disease or medical condition suffered by, the beneficiaries

WHERE FUNDING CAN BE GIVEN Leicester City Ward of Westcotes

TRUSTEES J D Sephton, J R Birks, T F Redman

WHO TO APPLY TO M Gage, Director, Leicester's Bede Island Community Foundation, Bede Island Community Association, 147 Narborough Road, Leicester LE3 0PD *Tel* 0116-254 3249 *Fax* 0116-255 9007 *E-mail* bica@foobar.co.uk

CC NO 1063424   **ESTABLISHED** 1997

■ Sir Geoffrey Leigh Charitable Trust

WHAT IS FUNDED General charitable purposes

WHO CAN BENEFIT There are no restrictions on the age; professional and economic group; family situation; religion and culture; and social circumstances of; or disease or medical condition suffered by, the beneficiaries

WHERE FUNDING CAN BE GIVEN UK

TYPE OF GRANT Specific donations

RANGE OF GRANTS £30–£10,125

SAMPLE GRANTS £10,125 to the Bodleian Library; £10,000 to Museum of British History; £6,484 to St Mary's 150th Anniversary Appeal; £5,000 to Community Security Trust; £3,177 to Friends of the Youth Awards Inc; £2,405 to Wellbeing; £2,330 to Cancer Relief Macmillan Fund; £2,000 to the British Fulbright Scholars Association; £1,200 to Action on Addiction; £1,000 to Imperial Cancer Research

FINANCES *Year* 1997 *Income* £41,566 *Grants* £51,844

TRUSTEES Sir Geoffrey Leigh, A A Davis, M D Paisner

HOW TO APPLY Postal applications will not be considered

WHO TO APPLY TO Sir Geoffrey Leigh, Sir Geoffrey Leigh Charitable Trust, 26 Manchester Square, London W1A 2HU

CC NO 265736   **ESTABLISHED** 1973

■ Gerald Leigh Charitable Trust

WHAT IS FUNDED General charitable purposes

WHO CAN BENEFIT Registered charities. There are no restrictions on the age; professional and economic group; family situation; religion and culture; and social circumstances of; or disease or medical condition suffered by, the beneficiaries

WHERE FUNDING CAN BE GIVEN UK

TYPE OF GRANT Recurrent and single donations

RANGE OF GRANTS £50–£5,000

SAMPLE GRANTS £5,000 to New West End Synagogue; £5,000 to TBA; £1,000 to Boy's Brigade; £1,000 to Liberal Jewish Synagogue; £1,000 to Worshipful Company of Blacksmiths

FINANCES *Year* 1997 *Income* £13,846 *Grants* £16,525

TRUSTEES G W Leigh, Mrs L I Foux

HOW TO APPLY In writing

WHO TO APPLY TO M J W Lunt, Gerald Leigh Charitable Trust, 6 Arlington Street, London SW1A 1RE

CC NO 267325   **ESTABLISHED** 1974

■ The Morris Leigh Foundation

WHAT IS FUNDED General charitable purposes

WHO CAN BENEFIT There are no restrictions on the age; professional and economic group; family situation; religion and culture; and social circumstances of; or disease or medical condition suffered by, the beneficiaries

WHERE FUNDING CAN BE GIVEN UK

TYPE OF GRANT Trustees will consider applications for grants and for long term loans

RANGE OF GRANTS £50–£7,500

SAMPLE GRANTS £7,500 to Chicken Shed Theatre Company; £5,000 to Community Security Trust; £3,000 to The Adler Trust; £2,526 to London Philharmonic Orchestra Ltd; £2,500 to the Chief Rabbinate Charitable Trust; £2,500 to Royal College of Music Development Fund; £2,500 to GRET; £1,945 to United Synagogue; £1,750 to Ravenswood Foundation; £1,250 to Institute of Jewish Affairs

FINANCES *Year* 1995 *Income* £72,485 *Grants* £53,374

TRUSTEES M Leigh, Mrs M Leigh, Mrs E C Greenbury, M D Paisner

WHO TO APPLY TO M D Paisner, The Morris Leigh Foundation, Paisner & Co, Solicitors, Bouverie House, 154 Fleet Street, London EC4A 2DQ

CC NO 280695   **ESTABLISHED** 1980

■ The Leigh Trust

WHAT IS FUNDED Legal services; support to voluntary and community organisations; support to volunteers; health counselling; support and self help groups; drug and alcohol rehabilitation; education and training; social counselling; crime prevention schemes; community issues; international rights of the individual; advice and information (social issues); asylum seekers; racial equality; and other charitable causes

WHAT IS NOT FUNDED Registered charities only

WHO CAN BENEFIT Registered charities benefiting: children; young adults; older people; unemployed people; volunteers; those in care, fostered and adopted; ethnic minority groups; at risk groups; those disadvantaged by poverty; ex-offenders and those at risk of offending; refugees; socially isolated people; those living in urban areas; victims of abuse and crime; and those suffering from substance abuse

WHERE FUNDING CAN BE GIVEN UK (priority) and overseas

TYPE OF GRANT Buildings, capital, core costs, one-off, project, recurring costs, running costs, salaries and start-up costs. Funding is available for up to three years

SAMPLE GRANTS £20,000 to Public Concern at Work for administration; £15,000 to West Glamorgan Council on Alcohol and Drugs for councillor salary; £15,000 to Prisoners Abroad for general funding; £10,000 to Redress Trust for victims of torture; £8,000 to St Luke's Medical Trust for general funding; £8,000 to Hospice of the Marshes for general funding; £7,000 to Pimlico Opera for general funding; £6,000 to Cyswlly Ceredigion Contact for drug and alcohol recovery; £5,500 to Guild of Disabled Homeworkers for general funding; £5,500 to Partnership Trust for general funding

FINANCES *Year* 1997 *Income* £141,576 *Grants* £147,148

TRUSTEES D S Bernstein, Dr R M E Stone

NOTES It is likely that one or more of the Trustees or officers of the Trust will wish to visit the project before and after any grant that is made

HOW TO APPLY In writing to the address under Who To Apply To enclosing most recent accounts and an sae. Applicants should state clearly what they do and what they are requesting funding for. They should provide a detailed budget and show other sources of funding if required

WHO TO APPLY TO C M Marks, FCA, The Leigh Trust, Marks Green & Co, 44a New Cavendish Street, London W1M 7LG

CC NO 275372   **ESTABLISHED** 1976

■ P Leigh-Bramwell Trust 'E'

WHAT IS FUNDED Specific regular allocations, leaving little opportunity to add further charities. Support is particularly given to Methodist churches and the Bolton School Boys' and the Bolton School Girls' Division

WHAT IS NOT FUNDED No allocations can be made for personal applications

WHO CAN BENEFIT Registered charities, schools, universities and churches benefiting children, young adults, students and Methodists

WHERE FUNDING CAN BE GIVEN UK

RANGE OF GRANTS £50–£10,500

SAMPLE GRANTS £10,500 to the Methodist Church: Circuit; £3,400 to the Methodist Church: Breightmet; £3,400 to the Methodist Church: Delph Hill; £2,800 to Leigh-Bramwell Scholarship Fund; £1,360 to Bolton and Rochdale Methodist Church Circuit; £500 to RNLI; £500 to St Anne's Hospice; £500 to Bolton Hospice; 500 to Bolton Lads and Girls Club; £250 to Order of St John

FINANCES *Year* 1996–97 *Income* £28,732 *Grants* £28,760

TRUSTEES B H Leigh-Bramwell, Mrs H R Leigh-Bramwell, Mrs J L Hardyment

WHO TO APPLY TO P Morrison, P Leigh-Bramwell Trust, W & J Leigh & Co, Tower Works, Kestor Street, Bolton BL2 2AL

CC NO 267333   **ESTABLISHED** 1973

■ Mrs Vera Leigh's Charity

WHAT IS FUNDED General charitable purposes

WHAT IS NOT FUNDED No grants to individuals

WHO CAN BENEFIT Charities only. There are no restrictions on the age; professional and economic group; family situation; religion and culture; and social circumstances of; or disease or medical condition suffered by, the beneficiaries

WHERE FUNDING CAN BE GIVEN UK

TYPE OF GRANT One-off

RANGE OF GRANTS £100–£750

SAMPLE GRANTS £750 to British Red Cross; £750 to Arthritis and Rheumatism Council; £750 to British Heart Foundation; £750 to Cystic Fibrosis Research Trust; £750 to Leukaemia Research Fund; £750 to Multiple Sclerosis Society; £750 to Muscular Dystrophy Group of Great Britian; £750 to National Asthma Campaign; £750 to Royal National Lifeboat Institution; £750 to Save the Children Fund

FINANCES *Year* 1997 *Income* £40,927 *Grants* £40,350

TRUSTEES V R de A Woollcombe, E J R Hill, T A Cole

NOTES No replies will be sent to unsolicited applications whether from individuals, charities or other bodies

WHO TO APPLY TO Messrs Walker Martineau, Mrs Vera Leigh's Charity, 64 Queen Street, London EC4R 1AD

CC NO 274872   **ESTABLISHED** 1976

■ The Lelia Charitable Trust

This trust did not respond to CAF's request to amend its entry and, by 30 June 1998, CAF's researchers did not find financial records for later than 1995 on its file at the Charity Commission. Trusts are legally required to submit annual accounts to the Charity Commission under section 42 of the Charities Act 1993

WHAT IS FUNDED General charitable purposes

WHO CAN BENEFIT There are no restrictions on the age; professional and economic group; family situation; religion and culture; and social circumstances of; or disease or medical condition suffered by, the beneficiaries

WHERE FUNDING CAN BE GIVEN UK

TRUSTEES D A Pollak, Ms K B Pollak, G C Smith

WHO TO APPLY TO The Lelia Charitable Trust, Underwood and Co, 40 Welbeck Street, London W1M 8LN

CC NO 1049891   **ESTABLISHED** 1995

■ The LEntA Trust

WHAT IS FUNDED To advance the education and training of young people and adults in Greater London in the awareness and development of commercial and business skills. To relieve poverty by assisting needy persons in Greater London to enable them to set up and run business. To promote industry and commerce

WHO CAN BENEFIT To benefit young adults and those disadvantaged by poverty

WHERE FUNDING CAN BE GIVEN Greater London

SAMPLE GRANTS £152,000 to LEntA Education and Training Programmes for job reach project which provides employment training and the Jobsearch Scheme which operates on inner city housing estates in London; £46,250 to Bruce House Project for both job search and training and the Skills Development Centre; £45,010 to Pathways Towards Working Life Project for school curriculum project to help school children understand the world of work; £34,925 to Volunteer Training Project to train, support and supervise volunteers working with the homeless; £5,000 to Cripplegate Project; £2,500 to Mentoring Projects; £2,000 to Design Export Awards; £1,000 to Disaffected Youth Project Bid; £644 to Mercer's Design Enterprise Loan Fund

FINANCES *Year* 1996 *Income* £288,628 *Grants* £289,329

TRUSTEES T G Evans, A R Heal, M Peters, S J Ward

WHO TO APPLY TO D R Fitzpatrick, Company Secretary, The LEntA Trust, Five Trees Field Way, Burnt Common Lane, Ripley, Surrey GU23 6HJ

CC NO 296521   **ESTABLISHED** 1987

■ Leominster District Development Trust

WHAT IS FUNDED Advancement of education; relief of hardship, need and distress; preservation of historical, architectural and constructional heritage; and protection of the countryside and wildlife

WHO CAN BENEFIT Organisations benefiting at risk groups, those disadvantaged by poverty, the socially isolated and homeless people. Support is given to children, young adults, students and teachers

WHERE FUNDING CAN BE GIVEN The area administered by Leominster District Council

TRUSTEES K Miles, B F Wilcox, T C A Edwards, G J Morris, T M James, I K Clements, M O Harrison, J W G Saunders, A Curless, A Mannin-Cox

WHO TO APPLY TO George Wilkinson, Solicitor, Leominster District Development Trust, c/o Bevan Ashford (Solicitors), Mutley House, Princess Street, Plymouth, Devon PL1 2EX

CC NO 1055757   **ESTABLISHED** 1996

■ The Leonard Trust

WHAT IS FUNDED General charitable purposes

WHO CAN BENEFIT There are no restrictions on the age; professional and economic group; family situation; religion and culture; and social circumstances of; or disease or medical condition suffered by, the beneficiaries

WHERE FUNDING CAN BE GIVEN UK

SAMPLE GRANTS £5,000 to Tear Fund; £3,000 to LEPRA; £3,000 to Church Missionary Society; £3,000 to the Winchester Cancer Research Trust; £2,000 to Westminster Chapel; £2,000 to British Red Cross; £2,000 to The Salvation Army; £2,000 to The Samaritans; £2,000 to the Children's Society; £2,000 to The Bible Society

FINANCES *Year* 1997 *Income* £71,481 *Grants* £70,500

WHO TO APPLY TO Mrs T E Feilden, The Leonard Trust, Manor Farm, Bramdean, Alresford, Hampshire SO24 0JS

CC NO 1031723   **ESTABLISHED** 1993

■ The Erica Leonard Trust

WHAT IS FUNDED General charitable purposes

WHO CAN BENEFIT Registered charities only. There are no restrictions on the age; professional and economic group; family situation; religion and culture; and social circumstances of; or disease or medical condition suffered by, the beneficiaries

WHERE FUNDING CAN BE GIVEN Mainly Surrey

FINANCES *Year* 1995 *Income* £40,000 *Grants* £45,000

TRUSTEES R C E Grey, A C Kemp, J L Cash

WHO TO APPLY TO R C E Grey, The Erica Leonard Trust, The Old Farmhouse, Elstead, Surrey GU8 6DB

CC NO 291627   **ESTABLISHED** 1985

■ The Mark Leonard Trust

WHAT IS FUNDED Education: Extending and adding value to existing use of school buildings and facilities; encouraging greater volunteer involvement in extra curricular activities; encouraging greater involvement of parents and school leavers in daytime and extra curricular activities. Environment: To promote energy efficiency and the sustainable use of renewable energy through education and community projects

WHAT IS NOT FUNDED No grants to individuals, expeditions or travel bursaries

WHO CAN BENEFIT Organisations benefiting children, young adults and volunteers

WHERE FUNDING CAN BE GIVEN UK

RANGE OF GRANTS £500–£11,700

SAMPLE GRANTS £11,700 to Education Extra; £10,000 to Howard League of Penal Reform; £5,000 to Landlife; £4,679 to Environmental Education to provide a budget for a network of schools to make applications for environmental education activities, training and resources; £3,500 to Centre for Sustainable Energy; £3,000 to Latch Self-Build; £2,500 to BTCV; £2,500 to Cumbria Association of Youth Clubs towards the training of youth workers and volunteers; £2,000 to Transport 2000 Trust towards a document, technical report and slide set for a public transport project; £2,000 to Prisoners of Conscience Appeal Fund

FINANCES *Year* 1997 *Income* £1,010,236 *Grants* £52,654

TRUSTEES Mrs S Butler-Sloss, Miss J S Portrait, J J Sainsbury, M L Sainsbury

HOW TO APPLY To the address under Who To Apply To in writing. All applications acknowledged. Guidelines are not issued by the Trust

WHO TO APPLY TO M A Pattison, The Mark Leonard Trust, 9 Red Lion Court, London EC4A 3EF

CC NO 1040323   **ESTABLISHED** 1994

■ Lesley Lesley and Mutter Trust

WHAT IS FUNDED Recipients are named and do not vary from year to year: Parkinson's Disease Association, the Chest Heart and Stroke Association, Multiple Sclerosis Society, the Muscular Dystrophy Group of Great Britain, the Royal National Institute for the Blind, the Rowcroft Hospice for Torbay and the Guide Dogs for the Blind (Devon Area Branch)

WHO CAN BENEFIT Registered charities as listed in What Is Funded

WHERE FUNDING CAN BE GIVEN Devon only

TYPE OF GRANT Recurrent

RANGE OF GRANTS £1,839–£10,730

SAMPLE GRANTS £10,730 to Chest Heart and Stroke Association; £10,730 to Parkinson's Disease Association; £1,839 to Multiple Sclerosis Society; £1,839 to Muscular Dystrophy Group of Great Britain; £1,839 to Royal National Institute for the Blind (RNIB); £1,839 to Guide Dogs for the Blind; £1,839 to Rowcroft Hospice
FINANCES *Year* 1996 *Income* £30,685 *Grants* £30,657
TRUSTEES Lloyds Bank
PUBLICATIONS Four Biennial Progress Reports, 49 occasional papers, a Directory entitled *Professional Organisations in the Commonwealth* (Hutchinson, 1976 – second edition): regional aid directories (Caribbean, African, Asian and South Pacific)
HOW TO APPLY Applications are not welcome
WHO TO APPLY TO A/C 215195, Lesley Lesley and Mutter Trust, Lloyds Private Banking Limited, UK Trust Centre, The Clock House, 22–26 Ock Street, Abingdon, Oxforshire OX14 5SW
CC NO 1018747   **ESTABLISHED** 1989

■ The Letchworth Civic Trust

WHAT IS FUNDED Schools and educational purposes
WHO CAN BENEFIT Individuals and organisations benefiting children and young adults
WHERE FUNDING CAN BE GIVEN Letchworth
SAMPLE GRANTS £7,350 to 42 university students for the cost of books and fees; £5,980 to support 12 local charities for outings and equipment for halls, etc; £3,016 to 40 children for the cost of educational trips; £1,065 to eight North Hertfordshire College students for the cost of books and fees; £575 to two individauls refered by Social Services for invalid equipment
FINANCES *Year* 1997 *Income* £28,949 *Grants* £17,986
TRUSTEES W Armitage, J Cruse, Mrs M Deary, K F Emsall, Mrs J Green, D Haynes, W Heaton, W Miller, Cllr J Winder
HOW TO APPLY Applications should be made on a form available from the address under Who To Apply To
WHO TO APPLY TO P M Jackson, Secretary, The Letchworth Civic Trust, Broadway Chambers, Letchworth, Hertfordshire SG6 3AD *Tel* 01462 482248
CC NO 273336   **ESTABLISHED** 1914

■ The Lethendy Charitable Trust

WHAT IS FUNDED The chief interests of the Trustees are in the development of young people and supporting worthwhile causes in Tayside
WHO CAN BENEFIT Priority is given to children and young adults in Tayside
WHERE FUNDING CAN BE GIVEN Scotland, particularly Tayside
TYPE OF GRANT One-off
RANGE OF GRANTS £100–£10,000
SAMPLE GRANTS £10,000 to University of Dundee – Chair in Accountancy; £10,000 to ICRF Cancer Treatment Appeal; £10,000 to New School Butterstone; £5,000 to Link Overseas; £5,000 to Princess Royal Trust for Carers; £4,450 in grants for the development of young people; £2,363 to Tenovus
FINANCES *Year* 1997 *Income* £40,000 *Grants* £40,000
TRUSTEES W R Alexander, D L Laird, I H K Rae, N M Sharp (Chairman), D B Thomson
PUBLICATIONS Accounts are available from the Trust

HOW TO APPLY Applications should be made in writing to the address under Who To Apply To
WHO TO APPLY TO George Hay, The Lethendy Charitable Trust, Henderson & Loggie, Royal Exchange, Panmure Street, Dundee DD1 1DZ *Tel* 01382 200055 *Fax* 01382 200764
SC NO SCO 03428   **ESTABLISHED** 1979

■ Leukaemia Research Fund

WHAT IS FUNDED Research into leukaemia and related blood diseases benefiting: hospitals; medical centres; postgraduate education; scholarships; and fellowships
WHAT IS NOT FUNDED Research expenditure usually restricted to the UK
WHO CAN BENEFIT Hospitals and university medical centres benefiting: medical professionals, nurses and doctors; students and people with leukaemia
WHERE FUNDING CAN BE GIVEN UK
TYPE OF GRANT Project grants usually reimburse salary, and a make contribution towards equipment. Clinical Fellowships and PhD studentships provide support for postgraduate training
FINANCES *Year* 1997 *Income* £13,750,000 *Grants* £10,000,000
TRUSTEES The Executive Committee
PUBLICATIONS Periodic Newsletter, Annual Report, Directory of Research, patient support publications, etc
NOTES Research projects are funded in hospitals and university medical centres throughout Britain and the Fund has established a major programme of specialist Research Centres. The Fund also promotes lectures, symposia and workshops
HOW TO APPLY On the official application from form, LRF Scientific Office, 43 Great Ormond Street, London WC1N 3JJ
WHO TO APPLY TO Dr David Grant, PhD, Scientific Director, Leukaemia Research Fund, 43 Great Ormond Street, London WC1N 3JJ *Tel* 0171-405 0101 *Fax* 0171-242 1488 *E-mail* info@leukaemia-research.org.uk *Web Site* www.leukaemia-research.org.uk
CC NO 216032   **ESTABLISHED** 1960

■ The Rachel Levene Memorial Trust

WHAT IS FUNDED General charitable purposes
WHO CAN BENEFIT There are no restrictions on the age; professional and economic group; family situation; religion and culture; and social circumstances of; or disease or medical condition suffered by, the beneficiaries
WHERE FUNDING CAN BE GIVEN UK
TRUSTEES D J Levene, W S Starr, R J Green
WHO TO APPLY TO R J Green, The Rachel Levene Memorial Trust, Regina House, 124 Finchley Road, London NW3 5JS
CC NO 1068462   **ESTABLISHED** 1997

■ The Ralph Levy Charitable Co Ltd

WHAT IS FUNDED Advancement of education, especially in the science of medicine, or any charitable purpose
WHO CAN BENEFIT Students and academics
WHERE FUNDING CAN BE GIVEN UK
FINANCES *Year* 1997 *Income* £429,598 *Grants* £57,832
TRUSTEES D S Levy, S M Levy, C J F Andrews

HOW TO APPLY No set application forms. Written applications must be received three clear months before commencement of proposed project

WHO TO APPLY TO Christopher Andrews, Director, The Ralph Levy Charitable Co Ltd, 14 Chesterfield Street, London W1X 7HF

CC NO 200009   **ESTABLISHED** 1961

■ The Levy Charitable Trust

WHAT IS FUNDED General charitable purposes

WHO CAN BENEFIT There are no restrictions on the age; professional and economic group; family situation; religion and culture; and social circumstances of; or disease or medical condition suffered by, the beneficiaries

WHERE FUNDING CAN BE GIVEN UK

SAMPLE GRANTS £200,270 to Morris Feinmann Homes Trust

FINANCES *Year* 1997 *Income* £138,331 *Grants* £200,270

TRUSTEES J S Fiddler, J M Levy, Ms M Levy, R A Levy

WHO TO APPLY TO J M Levy, Trustee, The Levy Charitable Trust, c/o Kuit Steinart Levy Solicitors, 3 St Marys Parsonage, Manchester M3 2RD

CC NO 1048182   **ESTABLISHED** 1995

■ The Robert and Rena Lewin Charitable Trust

WHAT IS FUNDED The advancement of the education of the public in the arts both in the UK and overseas

WHO CAN BENEFIT Institutions who are involved with educating the public in the arts

WHERE FUNDING CAN BE GIVEN UK and overseas

RANGE OF GRANTS £50–£1,050

SAMPLE GRANTS £1,050 to Headley Trust (CCIP); £1,000 to British Friends of Art Museums of Israel; £1,000 to '45 Aid Society Holocaust Survivors; £750 to Ben Uri Art Society; £500 to Northern Centre for Contemporary Art; £250 to Ben Gurion University Foundation; £100 to Aid for ALYN; £50 to Institute of Jewish Affairs; £50 to London Ecology Centre

FINANCES *Year* 1995 *Income* £47,237 *Grants* £4,750

TRUSTEES B B Lewin, M D Paisner, R Lewin

WHO TO APPLY TO M D Paisner, The Robert and Rena Lewin Charitable Trust, Paisner & Co, Bouverie House, 154 Fleet Street, London EC4A 2DQ

CC NO 802163   **ESTABLISHED** 1988

■ The Maisie and Raphael Lewis Charitable Trust

WHAT IS FUNDED General charitable purposes

WHO CAN BENEFIT There are no restrictions on the age; professional and economic group; family situation; religion and culture; and social circumstances of; or disease or medical condition suffered by, the beneficiaries

WHERE FUNDING CAN BE GIVEN In practice London and Home Counties generally, and English based charities

FINANCES *Year* 1997 *Income* £42,090

TRUSTEES J H Zamet, B M Slavin

WHO TO APPLY TO J Lent, The Maisie and Raphael Lewis Charitable Trust, Auerbach Hope, 58–60 Berners Street, London W1P 4JS

CC NO 1041848   **ESTABLISHED** 1993

■ The Sir Edward Lewis Foundation

WHAT IS FUNDED General charitable purposes. Preference to charities of which the Trust has special interest, knowledge or association

WHAT IS NOT FUNDED No grants to individuals

WHO CAN BENEFIT Organisations. There are no restrictions on the age; professional and economic group; family situation; religion and culture; and social circumstances of; or disease or medical condition suffered by, the beneficiaries

WHERE FUNDING CAN BE GIVEN UK

FINANCES *Year* 1995 *Income* £99,068 *Grants* £48,350

TRUSTEES R A Lewis, K W Dent

WHO TO APPLY TO K W Dent, The Sir Edward Lewis Foundation, Messrs Rawlinson and Hunter, Eagle House, 110 Jermyn Street, London SW17 6RH

CC NO 264475   **ESTABLISHED** 1972

■ The John Spedan Lewis Foundation

WHAT IS FUNDED To provide finance for charitable purposes and in the first instance reflecting the particular interests of John Spedan Lewis, namely horticulture, ornithology, entomology and associated educational and research projects. The Trustees will also consider applications from organisations for imaginative and original educational projects aimed at developing serious interest and evident talent particularly among young people

WHAT IS NOT FUNDED Objects must be exclusively charitable according to the law. No grants to individuals or to branches of national organisations or for medical research, welfare projects or building work

WHO CAN BENEFIT Preference is given to small projects and organisations benefiting children, young adults, and research workers dealing with the natural sciences

WHERE FUNDING CAN BE GIVEN UK

TYPE OF GRANT Mostly straight donations which may be repeated. Salaries not funded. Feasibility studies, one-off, project and research. Funding up to three years will be considered

FINANCES *Year* 1998 *Income* £46,000 *Grants* £50,000

TRUSTEES S Hampson, M K J Miller, W L R E Gilchrist, D R Cooper, Miss C Walton

HOW TO APPLY Write to Secretary giving full details and enclosing, where applicable, latest Report and Accounts

WHO TO APPLY TO Ms B M F Chamberlain, Secretary, The John Spedan Lewis Foundation, 171 Victoria Street, London SW1E 5NN *Tel* 0171-828 1000

CC NO 240473   **ESTABLISHED** 1964

■ John Lewis Partnership General Community Fund

WHAT IS FUNDED Medical, welfare and education

WHAT IS NOT FUNDED No sponsorship, advertising or help for individuals

WHO CAN BENEFIT National registered charities benefiting children and young adults, at risk groups, sick and disabled people, those disadvantaged by poverty and socially isolated people. There is no restriction on the disease or medical condition suffered by the beneficiaries. Medical professionals and research workers may be considered for funding

WHERE FUNDING CAN BE GIVEN UK

RANGE OF GRANTS £250 upwards
FINANCES *Year* 1997 *Grants* £1,030,000
TRUSTEES The Central Council
HOW TO APPLY In writing, Annual Report required
WHO TO APPLY TO Mrs D M Webster, Secretary, John Lewis Partnership General Community Fund, Central Charities Committee, 171 Victoria Street, London SW1E 5NN
CC NO 209128   ESTABLISHED 1961

■ The Lewis/Goldberg Charitable Trust

WHAT IS FUNDED Welfare organisations
WHO CAN BENEFIT Organisations benefiting at risk groups, those disadvantaged by poverty and socially isolated people
WHERE FUNDING CAN BE GIVEN UK and overseas
TYPE OF GRANT Range of grants
RANGE OF GRANTS £5–£235
SAMPLE GRANTS £235 to Birmingham Hebrew Congregation; £200 to Beit Issie Shapiro; £200 to Lamado Hospital; £140 to BFIWD; £100 to Agudat Achim; £55 to Lo Lev Charitable Trust; £50 to JNF; £50 to Preston Poor Children's Fund; £50 to Birmingham Central Synagogue; £25 to Toferet Schlomo Boys Home
FINANCES *Year* 1997 *Income* £25,242 *Grants* £10,720
TRUSTEES J A Lewis, Ms R E Lewis, I Lewis
WHO TO APPLY TO I Lewis, The Lewis/Goldberg Charitable Trust, 7 Petersham Place, Edgbaston, Birmingham B15 3RY
CC NO 1017429   ESTABLISHED 1993

■ Lewisham Parochial Charities

WHAT IS FUNDED The primary function of the Trust is the provision of almshouse accommodation; other grants are given to individuals for educational purposes and to organisations for welfare and education. Charities working in the fields of: hospices; support to voluntary and community organisations and volunteers; volunteer bureaux; churches; Anglican and Catholic bodies; heritage; community centres, village halls ands sports centres will also be considered
WHO CAN BENEFIT Individuals and organisations benefiting young adults and older people; academics; sportsmen and women; students; widows and widowers; disabled people and those disadvantaged by poverty. There is no restriction on the religion or culture of the beneficiaries. Applicants for educational grants must be 25 years of age or under
WHERE FUNDING CAN BE GIVEN The Ancient Parish of Lewisham (Deptford and Lee parishes excluded)
TYPE OF GRANT One-off and interest free loans funded for one year or less will be considered
RANGE OF GRANTS £50–£250. Educational grants limited by funds available, normally £1,250 pa
SAMPLE GRANTS £500 to ADIS Trust to assist with work for persons in need living in Lewisham; £500 to National Blind Children's Association to assist with work for needy children in Lewisham; £500 to Sedgehall School to assist underprivileged students with tour cost; £250 to St Saviours Brockley to assist underprivileged students with cost of tour; Grants of £150–£250 to four students for further studies; £150 to Prendergast School to encourage higher education
FINANCES *Year* 1995–96 *Income* £83,869
TRUSTEES A Cornforth, W K Church, J L H Eytle, P M Fitzsimmons, D Garlick, K Gorick, N S Hawkins, O

Jackson, W Lucas, M Nevell, V A Shirfield, A Till, D Whiting
NOTES Trustees meet on three occasions each year to consider applications. Educational grant applicants must give details of existing funding, eg LEA
HOW TO APPLY To the address under Who To Apply To in writing, application and guidelines issued. Applicant normally interviewed by Trustees
WHO TO APPLY TO W R Bell, Clerk, Lewisham Parochial Charities, 27 Ruxley Close, North Cray, Sidcup, Kent DA14 5LS *Tel* 0181-300 3531
CC NO 218260   ESTABLISHED 1963

■ The Licensed Trade Charities Trust

WHAT IS FUNDED General charitable purposes. To support four charities linked to the licensed trade
WHAT IS NOT FUNDED No grants to individuals
WHO CAN BENEFIT Charitable institutions connected to the license trade only. There are no restrictions on the age; professional and economic group; family situation; religion and culture; and social circumstances of; or disease or medical condition suffered by; the beneficiaries
WHERE FUNDING CAN BE GIVEN England and Wales
FINANCES *Year* 1997 *Income* £182,000 *Grants* £140,000
TRUSTEES B G Windsor (Chairman), A Bartlett, C P Breen, W P Catesby, T G Cockerell, C Cox, A G Eadie, C J Eld, D A H Harley, J J Madden, J C Overton, G B Richardson
WHO TO APPLY TO N H Block, The Licensed Trade Charities Trust, The Brows, Sutton Place, Dorking, Surrey RH5 6RL *Tel* 01306 731223 *Fax* 01306 731135
CC NO 282161   ESTABLISHED 1981

■ Lichfield Conduit Lands

WHAT IS FUNDED Schools, community development, health and welfare, children
WHO CAN BENEFIT Some individuals and organisations benefiting children and young adults, at risk groups, those disadvantaged by poverty and the socially isolated. Support may also be given to students, teachers and medical professionals. There is no restriction on the disease or medical condition suffered by the beneficiaries
WHERE FUNDING CAN BE GIVEN The Borough of Lichfield as it was prior to 1974
TYPE OF GRANT Some recurrent
FINANCES *Year* 1995 *Income* £55,911
HOW TO APPLY To the address under Who To Apply To in writing
WHO TO APPLY TO W P Coates, Lichfield Conduit Lands, Hadens, St Mary's Chambers, Breadmarket Street, Lichfield, Staffordshire WS13 6LQ
CC NO 254298   ESTABLISHED 1967

■ The Lifespan Trust

WHAT IS FUNDED To undertake research into the special problems of ageing and age discrimination and to publish the results of such research. To advance public education on all matters concerning age and age discrimination. To preserve and protect the health and relieve the disabilities of people aged fifty or more
WHAT IS NOT FUNDED No grants for revenue funding for existing projects

WHO CAN BENEFIT Individuals or groups of people aged 50 or over. There is no restriction on the disease or medical condition suffered by the beneficiaries

WHERE FUNDING CAN BE GIVEN UK

TYPE OF GRANT Usually one-off grants, but would consider staging a grant, subject to satisfactory achievement of pre-agreed interim outcomes

RANGE OF GRANTS £1,000–£2,000 to a maximum of £5,000

TRUSTEES R Davidson, D J Denyer, T Levenon, R Price, Mrs J Wesson (Chair), P A Wilkie

NOTES Request an application form from the Secretary

WHO TO APPLY TO D W Steele, Secretary, The Lifespan Trust, Greencoat House, Francis Street, London SW1P 1DZ *Tel* 0171-828 0500

CC NO 1051850   **ESTABLISHED** 1996

■ Liffe Benefit

WHAT IS FUNDED Medical charities

WHAT IS NOT FUNDED No grants to architectural/ environmental concerns

WHO CAN BENEFIT There is no restriction on the disease or medical condition suffered by the beneficiaries. Medical professionals and research workers may be considered for funding

WHERE FUNDING CAN BE GIVEN Greater London area

TYPE OF GRANT One-off and recurrent grants will be considered

FINANCES *Year* 1997 *Income* £163,189

TRUSTEES M R Bailey, N J Durlacher, D H Hodson, D A R Morgan, M Stanton, J Wigglesworth, G J Anderson, S Balmford, J Campbell-Gray, S Gatterell

WHO TO APPLY TO Ms S Jackson, Liffe Benefit, Cannon Bridge, London EC4R 3XX

CC NO 1019421   **ESTABLISHED** 1993

■ The Essie Lighthill Charity Trust

WHAT IS FUNDED General charitable purposes

WHO CAN BENEFIT There are no restrictions on the age; professional and economic group; family situation; religion and culture; and social circumstances of; or disease or medical condition suffered by, the beneficiaries

WHERE FUNDING CAN BE GIVEN UK

TRUSTEES B Lighthill

WHO TO APPLY TO B Lighthill, Trustee, The Essie Lighthill Charity Trust, 33 Mount Road, London NW4 3QA

CC NO 1046447   **ESTABLISHED** 1995

■ Lightship 2000

WHAT IS FUNDED General charitable purposes

WHO CAN BENEFIT There are no restrictions on the age; professional and economic group; family situation; religion and culture; and social circumstances of; or disease or medical condition suffered by, the beneficiaries

WHERE FUNDING CAN BE GIVEN Cardiff

FINANCES *Year* 1997 *Income* £50,690

TRUSTEES Rev D W Bale, Rev K J Jordan, Rev D K Smith, Rev J A Stacy-Marks

NOTES £48,416 was spent on wages and salaries, ship expenditure, light and heat, etc

WHO TO APPLY TO C Childs, Lightship 2000, Cartwrights Adams and Black, 36 West Bute Street, Cardiff CF1 5UA

CC NO 1058507   **ESTABLISHED** 1996

■ Lilley Benevolent Trust

WHAT IS FUNDED General charitable purposes. The Trustees consider annually the charities to be supported. Preference is given to registered charities of which they have special interest or association, in particular those with connections with Sussex

WHAT IS NOT FUNDED No grants to individuals – registered charities only

WHO CAN BENEFIT Registered charities. There are no restrictions on the age; professional and economic group; family situation; religion and culture; and social circumstances of; or disease or medical condition suffered by, the beneficiaries

WHERE FUNDING CAN BE GIVEN UK with preference to Sussex

TYPE OF GRANT Mainly recurrent

RANGE OF GRANTS £100–£1,000, average grant £300 (1997)

FINANCES *Year* 1997 *Income* £18,946 *Grants* £17,950

TRUSTEES T J R Lilley, N T Neal, A Osmond, Carole Lilley, J P Merricks, JP

HOW TO APPLY In writing – before October in any one year

WHO TO APPLY TO D W J O'Brien, Lilley Benevolent Trust, Amerique, Castle Street, Winchelsea, East Sussex TN36 4HU

CC NO 232174   **ESTABLISHED** 1961

■ The Thomas Lilley Memorial Trust

WHAT IS FUNDED General charitable purposes at Trustees' discretion

WHO CAN BENEFIT Institutions. There are no restrictions on the age; professional and economic group; family situation; religion and culture; and social circumstances of; or disease or medical condition suffered by, the beneficiaries

WHERE FUNDING CAN BE GIVEN UK

FINANCES *Year* 1996 *Income* £18,523 *Grants* £31,136

TRUSTEES J F Luke, P T A Lilley

WHO TO APPLY TO The Thomas Lilley Memorial Trust, Cooper Lancaster Brewers, Accountants, Aldwych House, 81 Aldwych, London WC2B 4HP *Tel* 0171-242 2444

CC NO 1039529   **ESTABLISHED** 1960

■ The Lincoln General Dispensary Fund

WHAT IS FUNDED To relieve in cases of need, persons resident in Lincoln who are sick, convalescent, disabled, handicapped or infirm

WHAT IS NOT FUNDED The Trustees will not make grants which will relieve public funds, contribute to the fabric of buildings, commit themselves to repeat grants or in general pay debts already incurred

WHO CAN BENEFIT Primarily individuals who are sick, disabled or infirm. There is no restriction on the disease or medical condition suffered by the beneficiaries

WHERE FUNDING CAN BE GIVEN Lincoln

RANGE OF GRANTS £77–£5,000

SAMPLE GRANTS £5,000 to See More Scanner Appeal; £2,240 to WRVS; £1,640 to Age Concern; £1,540 to Lincoln Social Services (Lincoln District); £1,050 to SSAFA

FINANCES *Year* 1997 *Income* £15,989 *Grants* £16,670

TRUSTEES Mrs J Davies, Rev J W Dennis, F R Eccleshare, Rev P Floe, Mrs M J Hodgkinson, Mrs S M Lucas, Mrs S M Peacock, M D Rayner, L A Smith, J Thomas, Mrs J M Walton, Mrs E B H Wellman, D Williams, K Woodall
NOTES Applications for grants are generally only accepted through recognised social or medical agencies
HOW TO APPLY To the address under Who To Apply To in writing
WHO TO APPLY TO M G Bonass, Secretary, The Lincoln General Dispensary Fund, 188 High Street, Lincoln LN5 7BE
CC NO 220159   **ESTABLISHED** 1963

■ Lincoln Municipal Relief in Need Charity

WHAT IS FUNDED Individuals in need through poverty and ill health, organisations working in the interests of such people in the area Where Funding Can Be Given
WHO CAN BENEFIT Primarily individuals, but some organisations benefiting those disadvantaged by poverty. There is no restriction on the disease or medical condition suffered by the beneficiaries
WHERE FUNDING CAN BE GIVEN Lincoln
RANGE OF GRANTS Organisation: £100–£250, individuals: £10–£260
SAMPLE GRANTS £260 to an individual; £250 to Lincoln Toy Library; £200 each to three individuals; £200 to St Luke's Youth Hall; £199 to an individual; £100 each to two individuals; £100 to Lincoln Vega Club for the Blind
FINANCES *Year* 1996–97 *Income* £29,860 *Grants* £3,287
TRUSTEES Cllr Freeborough
HOW TO APPLY To the address under Who To Apply To in writing
WHO TO APPLY TO M G Bonass, Clerk, Lincoln Municipal Relief in Need Charity, 188 High Street, Lincoln LN5 7BE
CC NO 213651   **ESTABLISHED** 1978

■ The Lincolnshire Old Churches Trust

WHAT IS FUNDED The preservation, repair and maintenance of churches over 100 years old in the area Where Funding Can Be Given to exclude wind and weather, achieve safety and security and to ensure the preservation of those features which make old churches unique
WHAT IS NOT FUNDED No grants for heating, lighting, gravestone repair or ritual
WHO CAN BENEFIT Churches, principally Christian churches of any denomination
WHERE FUNDING CAN BE GIVEN Lincolnshire, the Anglican Diocese of Lincoln
RANGE OF GRANTS £500–£2,500
SAMPLE GRANTS £2,500 to St Nicholas, Snitterby; £2,000 to St Thomas of Canterbury, Gainsborough; £2,000 to St Mary, Hatcliffe; £2,000 to St Luke, Stickney; £2,000 to St Nicholas, Deeping; £2,000 to St Mary-le-Wigford, Lincoln; £2,000 to St Lawrence, Sedgebrook; £2,000 to St Michael and All Angels, Stragglethorpe; £1,000 to St Michael and All Angels, Edenham; £1,000 to St Peter, Markby
FINANCES *Year* 1995 *Income* £57,980 *Grants* £28,850
TRUSTEES Bishop of Lincoln, Mrs G Bedford, N J Camamile, Sir P Cormack, MP, FSA, Mrs R Cracroft-Eley, W Drakes, Mrs A Jarvis, Dr C

Knightly, Mrs K Neville, Lt Cmdr C H Rodwell, FSA, P Sandberg, R Stanley, FRIBA, F M Stockdale, Rev T Thorold, FSA, Mrs C Walker, D M Wellman, MA, Lt Cmdr C P N Wells-Cole, Lady Willoughby, Mrs J Dymoke, The Ven Dr D Griffiths, FSA, Mrs R Henson
HOW TO APPLY Applications should be made on a form available from the the the address under Who To Apply To
WHO TO APPLY TO The Secretary, The Lincolnshire Old Churches Trust, PO Box 195, Lincoln LN5 9XN
CC NO 509021   **ESTABLISHED** 1953

■ The Lindale Educational Foundation

WHAT IS FUNDED Charities which aim to advance education in accordance with Christian principles and ideals within the Roman Catholic tradition. Most grants are already allocated to specific charities
WHAT IS NOT FUNDED No grants to individuals
WHO CAN BENEFIT Roman Catholic organisations benefiting children, young adults and students
WHERE FUNDING CAN BE GIVEN UK and overseas
TYPE OF GRANT Recurrent
FINANCES *Year* 1995 *Income* £75,500 *Grants* £74,400
TRUSTEES B D Marsh, P Adams, J Valero
WHO TO APPLY TO J Valero, The Lindale Educational Foundation, 1 Leopold Road, London W5 3PB
CC NO 282758   **ESTABLISHED** 1981

■ The Linden Charitable Trust

WHAT IS FUNDED Trustees favour medical and healthcare charities
WHAT IS NOT FUNDED No grants to individuals
WHO CAN BENEFIT Organisations benefiting medical professionals. There is no restriction on the disease or medical condition suffered by the beneficiaries
WHERE FUNDING CAN BE GIVEN Yorkshire area
FINANCES *Year* 1997 *Income* £17,538
TRUSTEES G H Cox, D R Wood, M H Pearson
HOW TO APPLY To the address below in writing
WHO TO APPLY TO P J Howell, The Linden Charitable Trust, PO Box 8, Sovereign House, South Parade, Leeds LS1 1HQ
CC NO 326788   **ESTABLISHED** 1985

■ The Lindeth Charitable Trust

WHAT IS FUNDED The Trustees propose to make grants to charities operating in the fields of ecological and biological research and related research of an educational nature
WHAT IS NOT FUNDED No grants to individuals, although a piece of research to be carried out by a particular person may be funded if sponsored by a registered charity, university department or similar body, in which case applications should be made through that body
WHO CAN BENEFIT Registered charities benefiting scientists and research workers
WHERE FUNDING CAN BE GIVEN UK and overseas
RANGE OF GRANTS £50–£5,000

SAMPLE GRANTS £5,000 to Tusk Trust; £1,000 to Save the Rhino International for Sumatran Rhino Expedition; £900 to Manchester Metropolitan University; £750 to Frontier; £600 to Roehampton Institute of London; £500 to Falklands Conservation; £500 to Portaro Palateau Forest Conservation Programme Guyana 1997; £500 to BTO; £500 to the Sebakwe Black Rhino Trust; £500 to Harrison Zoological Museum

FINANCES *Year* 1997 *Income* £31,981 *Grants* £14,750

TRUSTEES C J Scott, Mrs E J Scott, E R H Perks

HOW TO APPLY To the address under Who To Apply To

WHO TO APPLY TO Currey & Co, Solicitors, The Lindeth Charitable Trust, 21 Buckingham Gate, London SW1E 6LS

CC NO 802665   **ESTABLISHED** 1989

■ Kathleen and Sydney Linkins Memorial Trust

WHAT IS FUNDED The Trust is concerned with the welfare of people over 60 who are in need and live within the area Where Funding Can Be Given

WHO CAN BENEFIT Individuals over the age of 60 and organisations that benefit them

WHERE FUNDING CAN BE GIVEN Chichester and adjoining parishes of Appledram Donnington and Lavant, also the area known as Fishbourne within the parish of Bosham

RANGE OF GRANTS £250–£9,400

SAMPLE GRANTS The following grants are for 1996–97; £9,400 to Chichester Eventide Housing Association Ltd; £1,000 to Age Concern, Chichester Branch; £520 to Chichester Rotary Club; £471 to an individual

FINANCES *Year* 1996 *Income* £18,745 *Grants* £22,490

TRUSTEES B M Smith, A R T Howes, R B Minton, D S F Thompson, C H Phillips

HOW TO APPLY To the address under Who To Apply To in writing

WHO TO APPLY TO C H Phillips, Trustee, Kathleen and Sydney Linkins Memorial Trust, Lion House, 79 St Pancras, Chichester, West Sussex PO19 4NL

CC NO 801712   **ESTABLISHED** 1988

■ Linmardon Trust (also known as The Wedgewood Trust)

WHAT IS FUNDED General charitable purposes. Periodic exercise by the Trustees of their absolute discretion

WHAT IS NOT FUNDED Donations to registered charities only. No grants to individuals

WHO CAN BENEFIT Registered charities only. There are no restrictions on the age; professional and economic group; family situation; religion and culture; and social circumstances of; or disease or medical condition suffered by, the beneficiaries

WHERE FUNDING CAN BE GIVEN Hampshire, Nottinghamshire and some national charities

TYPE OF GRANT Cash payments at Trustees' discretion. Approximately £1,000

TRUSTEES Midland Bank Trust Co Ltd

HOW TO APPLY To the address below in writing

WHO TO APPLY TO Miss S D'Ambrosio, Trust Manager, Midland Trusts, Cumberland House, 15–17 Cumberland Place, Southampton SO15 2UY Tel 01703 531378

CC NO 275307   **ESTABLISHED** 1977

■ Accrington Lions Club Charity Trust Fund

WHAT IS FUNDED General charitable purposes

WHO CAN BENEFIT There are no restrictions on the age; professional and economic group; family situation; religion and culture; and social circumstances of; or disease or medical condition suffered by, the beneficiaries

WHERE FUNDING CAN BE GIVEN UK

RANGE OF GRANTS £7–£990

SAMPLE GRANTS £990– to Pensioners Party; £560 to Acoustic Society for PA system; £500 to Waterwells LCI; £500 to Peter Pan Club; £400 to Andrew Slater Fund for beds for charities; £400 as sponsorship of WWI Exhibition; £350 to Friends of Chernobyl; £300 to East Lancashire Deaf Society; £250 to Inship League Levens Hall; £203 to Diabetic Screening

FINANCES *Year* 1997 *Income* £28,380 *Grants* £10,143

TRUSTEES D Walken, K Hindle, A Deakin

NOTES In 1997 donations under £50 totalled £730 and those over £50 totalled £9,413

WHO TO APPLY TO A Cooper, Accrington Lions Club Charity Trust Fund, 26 Devonshire Road, Rishton, Blackburn, Lancashire BB1 4BX

CC NO 1035385   **ESTABLISHED** 1993

■ Lions Club Charitable Trust Fund (Blaby and District)

WHAT IS FUNDED General charitable purposes

WHO CAN BENEFIT There are no restrictions on the age; professional and economic group; family situation; religion and culture; and social circumstances of; or disease or medical condition suffered by, the beneficiaries

WHERE FUNDING CAN BE GIVEN Territorial area of the club, (Blaby and District), throughout the UK and elsewhere

TRUSTEES G D Brooks, R A Franklin, M H Prideaux

WHO TO APPLY TO R J Bentley, Lions Club Charitable Trust Fund (Blaby and District), 10 Lena Drive, Groby, Leicester LE6 0FJ

CC NO 1049063   **ESTABLISHED** 1995

■ The Lions Club of Keynsham Trust Fund

WHAT IS FUNDED General charitable purposes

WHO CAN BENEFIT There are no restrictions on the age; professional and economic group; family situation; religion and culture; and social circumstances of; or disease or medical condition suffered by, the beneficiaries

WHERE FUNDING CAN BE GIVEN UK

RANGE OF GRANTS £20–£929

SAMPLE GRANTS £21,772 to the Royal United Hospital, Diabetes Centre for the Retinal Screening Unit; £929 to Christmas Shopping for the Elderly; £500 x 2 to New Opportunity Fund; £486 to Avon Special Olympics; £450 to Monday Club (MENCAP); £300 to NEST Christmas donation; £300 to Kelston Road Primary School; £100 to K & C Soby Vocational Fund; £100 to Malawi Education Project

FINANCES *Year* 1997 *Income* £25,974 *Grants* £4,201

TRUSTEES A D Hale, L Smith, R Watson

NOTES The Trust's support for the Retinal Screening Unit at the Royal United Hospital was a one-off project of this size, and it is unlikely that the Trust will handle such large projects in future

372

Think carefully about every application. Is it justified?

WHO TO APPLY TO L Smith, The Lions Club of Keynsham Trust Fund, 43 Bakersfield, Longwell Green, Bristol, Avon BS30 9YP
CC NO 1044126   ESTABLISHED 1995

■ Scunthorpe Lions Club Charity Trust Fund

WHAT IS FUNDED General charitable purposes
WHO CAN BENEFIT There are no restrictions on the age; professional and economic group; family situation; religion and culture; and social circumstances of; or disease or medical condition suffered by, the beneficiaries
WHERE FUNDING CAN BE GIVEN Scunthorpe area only
TYPE OF GRANT Usually one-off
FINANCES *Year* 1996–97 *Income* £14,625
   Grants £7,856
TRUSTEES All Club Members
HOW TO APPLY By letter to the address under Who To Apply To
WHO TO APPLY TO Scunthorpe Lions Club Charity Trust Fund, c/o The Berkerley Hotel, Doncaster Road, Scunthorpe, North Lincolnshire DN15 7DS
CC NO 1042981   ESTABLISHED 1994

■ Southend on Sea Lions Club Trust Fund

WHAT IS FUNDED General charitable purposes and welfare of the general public
WHO CAN BENEFIT There are no restrictions on the age; professional and economic group; family situation; religion and culture; and social circumstances of; or disease or medical condition suffered by, the beneficiaries
WHERE FUNDING CAN BE GIVEN Southend-on-Sea, Essex
RANGE OF GRANTS £4–£4,313
SAMPLE GRANTS £4,313 to BBC Children in Need Appeal; £1,205 to Great Yarmouth Lions towards holiday for needy families; £1,050 to Macmillan Cancer Relief Fund; £500 to Southend Women's Aid; £500 to Arthritis and Rheumatism Council for Research
FINANCES *Year* 1997 *Income* £19,562
   Grants £14,337
TRUSTEES D R Wetton, N I Grant, R T O'Neill
WHO TO APPLY TO A G Smith, Southend on Sea Lions Club Trust Fund, 107 St Augustines Avenue, Thorpe Bay, Southend on Sea, Essex SS1 3JG
CC NO 1049333   ESTABLISHED 1995

■ Thanet Lions Club Charity Trust Fund

WHAT IS FUNDED General charitable purposes at the Trustees discretion
WHO CAN BENEFIT There are no restrictions on the age; professional and economic group; family situation; religion and culture; and social circumstances of; or disease or medical condition suffered by, the beneficiaries
WHERE FUNDING CAN BE GIVEN UK and the Republic of Eire and overseas
RANGE OF GRANTS £27–£800

SAMPLE GRANTS £800 to Lynton House for a computer; £600 to WRVS; £400 to Sail Training; £302 for pantomime seats; £240 to Medic Alert; £200 to St Christophers; £200 to ARC; £180 to The National Trust; £150 to Age Concern (Norfolk); £140 to Kent Mobility
FINANCES *Year* 1997 *Income* £27,841
   Grants £5,998
TRUSTEES Laurence J Waitt, Peter Dickens, Brian Webb, Leslie Gibbs
WHO TO APPLY TO S Carley, Thanet Lions Club Charity Trust Fund, 81a Grange Road, Ramsgate, Kent CT11 9LP
CC NO 287946   ESTABLISHED 1983

■ The Jackie and Leslie Lipowicz Trust

WHAT IS FUNDED The relief of the elderly or the relief of poverty; the advancement of education; the advancement of religion; other general charitable purposes for the benefit of the community at home and abroad
WHO CAN BENEFIT Organisations benefiting children, young adults, older people, students and those disadvantaged by poverty. People of many different religions and cultures will be supported
WHERE FUNDING CAN BE GIVEN UK and overseas
FINANCES *Year* 1998 *Income* £200,245
   Grants £2,945
TRUSTEES Ms B Lipowicz, J Lipowicz, L Lipowicz, Ms V Lipowicz
WHO TO APPLY TO L Lipowicz, The Jackie and Leslie Lipowicz Trust, 1 Valencia Road, Stanmore, London HAQ7 4JL
CC NO 1066566   ESTABLISHED 1997

■ The Ruth & Stuart Lipton Charitable Trust

WHAT IS FUNDED Jewish charitable purposes
WHO CAN BENEFIT Organisations benefiting Jewish people
WHERE FUNDING CAN BE GIVEN UK and overseas
RANGE OF GRANTS £50–£10,600
SAMPLE GRANTS £10,600 to Jewish Philanthropic Association for Israel and the Middle East; £5,000 to Group Relations Educational Trust/Community Security Trust; £3,000 to Building Experiences Trust; £1,101 to Western Marble Arch Synagogue; £500 to National Art Collections Fund; £500 to Jewish Care; £500 to the Chief Rabbinate Charitable Trust; £400 to Children and Youth Aliyah; £340 to Ravenswood Foundation; £300 to the Philharmonia Trust Appeal
FINANCES *Year* 1995 *Income* £31,549
   Grants £26,372
TRUSTEES N Fetterman, M Gilbert
WHO TO APPLY TO N W Benson, The Ruth & Stuart Lipton Charitable Trust, Lewis Golden & Co, 40 Queen Anne Street, London W1M 0EL
CC NO 266741   ESTABLISHED 1973

■ The Lister Charitable Trust

WHAT IS FUNDED To advance the educational and physical, mental and spiritual development of children (or young persons under the age of 25) by providing or assisting in providing facilities for training in sailing and seamanship of children and young persons who have need of such facilities by reason of poverty, social or economic circumstances (so that they may grow to full maturity as individuals and members of society) and to provide or assist in the provision of facilities for recreation and other leisure time occupation of the general public with the object of improving their conditions of life

WHAT IS NOT FUNDED Registered charities only. Applications from individuals, including students, are ineligible. No grants made in response to general appeals from large, national organisations nor to smaller bodies working in areas other than those set out above

WHO CAN BENEFIT Registered charities working with young people in sailing

WHERE FUNDING CAN BE GIVEN UK

TYPE OF GRANT Usually one-off for specific project or part of a project. Core funding and/or salaries rarely considered. Funding may be given for up to one year

SAMPLE GRANTS £150,000 to UK Sailing Academy for the development of Youth Racing Programme/school bursaries

FINANCES *Year* 1997 *Income* £285,952 *Grants* £152,090

TRUSTEES J C Douglas-Withers, N A V Lister, B J C Hall, D J Lister, D A Collingwood

PUBLICATIONS Annual report

HOW TO APPLY At any time. Applications should include clear details of the need the intended project is designed to meet plus an outline budget. Only applications from eligible bodies are acknowledged, when further information may be requested

WHO TO APPLY TO N A V Lister, The Lister Charitable Trust, Windyridge, The Close, Totteridge, London N20 8PJ *Fax* 0181-446 5658

CC NO 288730   **ESTABLISHED** 1981

■ The Margaret Litchfield Trust

WHAT IS FUNDED To relieve in cases of need, hardship, distress or ill health persons under the age of twenty one years who are resident in England. Help will be given for: schools and collages; costs of study; opera companies and groups; and orchestras

WHO CAN BENEFIT To benefit: children; young adults; students; those disadvantaged by poverty; those living in rural areas and socially isolated people

WHERE FUNDING CAN BE GIVEN South East England

TYPE OF GRANT Capital, core costs, endowments, interest free loans, one-off, recurring costs and salaries. Funding is available for up to three years

HOW TO APPLY Applications by post

WHO TO APPLY TO B J Litchfield, Chairman, The Margaret Litchfield Trust, Round Down Farm, Cole Kitchen Lane, Gomshall, Surrey GU5 9QB

CC NO 1067829   **ESTABLISHED** 1998

■ The Andrew and Mary Little Charitable Trust

WHAT IS FUNDED The sick, elderly, poor, blind or otherwise distressed people

WHO CAN BENEFIT People who are in need

WHERE FUNDING CAN BE GIVEN Glasgow

TYPE OF GRANT The vast majority of grants are awarded to individuals

FINANCES *Year* 1995 *Income* £80,000 *Grants* £70,000

TRUSTEES Andrew Abbot, Dr Robin Green, Col A Lawrie, Dr Maud Menzies, R Munton

HOW TO APPLY Applications should be made in writing to the address below. Individuals wishing to apply must do so through a suitable third party

WHO TO APPLY TO Mrs Joan Wright, The Andrew and Mary Little Charitable Trust, Wilson Chalmers & Hendry, Solicitors, 33a Gordon Street, Glasgow G1 3PH

SC NO SCO 11185

■ Littledown Trust

WHAT IS FUNDED Charities working in the fields of: health; special needs education; speech therapy; advice centres; voluntary organisations and community services will be considered

WHAT IS NOT FUNDED Animal and non-people orientated organisations are not funded

WHO CAN BENEFIT Sick, disabled and socially disadvantaged people

WHERE FUNDING CAN BE GIVEN Mainly but not exclusively Kent, East Sussex, Devon and Edinburgh

TYPE OF GRANT One-off, running costs and start-up costs will be considered

RANGE OF GRANTS £100–£500, typical grant £250

TRUSTEES P G Brown (Chairperson), J I Brown, M K Brown

HOW TO APPLY In writing

WHO TO APPLY TO P G Brown Chairperson, Littledown Trust, Littledown Farmhouse, Lamberhurst, Kent TN3 8HD

CC NO 1064291   **ESTABLISHED** 1997

■ The Second Joseph Aaron Littman Foundation

WHAT IS FUNDED General charitable purposes

WHAT IS NOT FUNDED Funds fully committed, no new applications

WHO CAN BENEFIT There are no restrictions on the age; professional and economic group; family situation; religion and culture; and social circumstances of; or disease or medical condition suffered by, the beneficiaries

WHERE FUNDING CAN BE GIVEN UK

FINANCES *Year* 1994 *Income* £80,000

TRUSTEES Mrs C C Littman

WHO TO APPLY TO Barry Lock, The Second Joseph Aaron Littman Foundation, 190 Strand, London WC2R 1JN *Tel* 0171-395 4645

CC NO 201892   **ESTABLISHED** 1961

■ The George John Livanos Charitable Trust

WHAT IS FUNDED General charitable purposes

WHO CAN BENEFIT Individuals and institutions. There are no restrictions on the age; professional and economic group; family situation; religion and culture; and social circumstances of; or disease or medical condition suffered by, the beneficiaries

WHERE FUNDING CAN BE GIVEN UK

TYPE OF GRANT Range of grants

RANGE OF GRANTS £1,000–£315,838

SAMPLE GRANTS £315,838 to St Mary's Hospital, Paddington for the Department of Child Health; £137,607 to Belford Hospital, Fort William; £50,000 to Abbeyfield Society; £50,000 to Royal Surrey County Hospital for St Luke's Cancer Appeal; £45,666 to Great Ormond Street Children's Hospital; £33,000 to Glasgow University; £25,000 to Crimestoppers; £25,000 to Lord Mayor's Appeal for Cancer Research Campaign; £24,960 to Southend Hospital; £23,660 to University of Nottingham

FINANCES *Year* 1996 *Income* £653,499 *Grants* £846,441

TRUSTEES Mrs S D Livanos, P N Harris, A S Holmes, P D Powell

HOW TO APPLY **This Trust states that it does not respond to unsolicited applications**

WHO TO APPLY TO P N Harris, Secretary, The George John Livanos Charitable Trust, c/o Jeffrey Green Russell, Apollo House, 56 New Bond Street, London W1Y 0SX *Tel* 0171-499 7020

CC NO 1002279   **ESTABLISHED** 1985

■ The Liverpool Queen Victoria District Nursing Association

WHAT IS FUNDED Organisations working with sick, infirm and disabled people

WHO CAN BENEFIT Disabled people. There are no restrictions on the disease and social circumstances of the beneficiaries

WHERE FUNDING CAN BE GIVEN Merseyside

TYPE OF GRANT Primarily one-off

FINANCES *Year* 1997 *Income* £35,879 *Grants* £30,567

TRUSTEES M Rathbone, G F Appleton, R Currie, Miss M J Dyke, Canon N Frayling, Mrs L M Newsome, Mrs I Nightingale, Ms M Rangel, Mrs L Spark, R P Bradshaw, Miss V Selwyn-Smith, Cllr Lady D Jones, Cllr R White, K Wright, Ms A Hogg, N Malley

HOW TO APPLY To the address under Who To Apply To in writing stating the aims and activities of your organisation, the purpose of the grant requested and enclosing a recent copy of accounts. The Trustees meet to consider applications in January, May and September

WHO TO APPLY TO The Secretary, Liverpool Queen Victoria District Nursing Assn, Liverpool Council of Social Service Inc, 14 Castle Street, Liverpool L2 0NJ *Tel* 0151-236 7728

CC NO 501196   **ESTABLISHED** 1971

■ Liverpool R C Archdiocesan Trustees Incorporated Special Trusts

This trust did not respond to CAF's request to amend its entry and, by 30 June 1998, CAF's researchers did not find financial records for later than 1995 on its file at the Charity Commission. Trusts are legally required to submit annual accounts to the Charity Commission under section 42 of the Charities Act 1993

WHAT IS FUNDED The education of students wishing to enter the priesthood, church schools

WHO CAN BENEFIT Roman Catholic children and young adults

WHERE FUNDING CAN BE GIVEN Roman Catholic Archdiocese of Liverpool

WHO TO APPLY TO Aaron Kiely, Dept Finance and Development, Liverpool RC Archdiocesan Trustees Inc Special Trusts, The Archdiocese of Liverpool, 152 Brownlow Hill, Liverpool L3 5RQ

CC NO 526575   **ESTABLISHED** 1933

■ Liverpool Sailors' Home Trust

WHAT IS FUNDED Nautical charities in the area Where Funding Can Be Given

WHAT IS NOT FUNDED No grants to individuals

WHO CAN BENEFIT Organisations benefiting: seafarers and fishermen, and ex-service and service people

WHERE FUNDING CAN BE GIVEN Merseyside

TYPE OF GRANT One-off and capital grants will be considered

RANGE OF GRANTS Variable

SAMPLE GRANTS £10,000 to Mersey Mission to Seamen for refurbishment; £10,000 to Bearwood College for educational grant; £10,000 to Sea Cadet Corps – Black Cap; £7,500 to Apostleship of the Sea for refurbishment; £5,000 to Royal National Lifeboat Association, Hoylake and West Kirby; £5,000 to STA Tall Ships; £4,070 to Sea Cadet Corps, TS Storm; £2,000 to Derbyshire Family Association

FINANCES *Year* 1996–97 *Income* £63,589 *Grants* £56,634

TRUSTEES D G Beazley, P O Copland, M Crowson, F D M Lowry, M A Seaford,

HOW TO APPLY To the address under Who To Apply To in writing. Written applications to be received at latest 20 January of relevant year

WHO TO APPLY TO Mrs L Smith, Secretary, Liverpool Sailors' Home Trust, Unit 3a, Ground Floor, Tower Building, 22 Water Street, Liverpool L2 1AB *Tel* 0151-227 3417 *Fax* 0151-227 3417

CC NO 515183   **ESTABLISHED** 1984

■ Mrs C M Livesley 1992 Charitable Trust

WHAT IS FUNDED Hospices, hospitals, cancer research and animal welfare

WHAT IS NOT FUNDED No grants to individuals, for expeditions or scholarships

WHO CAN BENEFIT Registered charities benefiting those suffering from Alzheimer's disease, arthritis, rheumatism, cancers, diabetes, heart disease, HIV and AIDs, kidney disease and strokes

WHERE FUNDING CAN BE GIVEN UK and overseas

TYPE OF GRANT Core costs

RANGE OF GRANTS £1,000–£2,000

SAMPLE GRANTS £6,000 to Redwings Horse Sanctuary; £5,000 to Great Ormond Street Hospital; £2,000 to Cancer Research; £2,000 to British Heart Foundation; £1,000 to Arthritis and Rheumatism Council

TRUSTEES A J Hawes, Miss S B J Livesley, Mrs P A Clare

HOW TO APPLY In writing. Trustees meet every six months

WHO TO APPLY TO A J Hawes, Mrs C M Livesley 1992 Charitable Trust, Blyth House, Rendham Road, Saxmudham, Suffolk IP17 1EA

CC NO 1014492   **ESTABLISHED** 1992

■ Harry Livingstone Charitable Trust

WHAT IS FUNDED Welfare and Jewish charities

WHO CAN BENEFIT Registered charities benefiting: Jewish people; at risk groups; those disadvantaged by poverty and socially isolated people

WHERE FUNDING CAN BE GIVEN UK

RANGE OF GRANTS £500–£17,000

SAMPLE GRANTS £17,000 to Hannah Bloom Charitable Trust; £17,000 to Jack Livingstone Charitable Trust; £3,243 to Southport New Synagogue; £2,500 to Joel Intract Home Appeal Fund; £2,500 to Southport Jewish Convalescent and Aged Home; £2,000 to the Heathlands Village; £2,000 to JPAIME; £1,500 to Alone in London Service Limited; £1,000 to Sale, Altrincham and District SCOPE; £1,000 to Manchester Jewish Blind Society

FINANCES *Year* 1997 *Income* £58,541
Grants £50,243

TRUSTEES J Livingstone, Mrs H Bloom

HOW TO APPLY **This Trust states that it does not respond to unsolicited applications**

WHO TO APPLY TO Jack Livingstone, Trustee, Harry Livingstone Charitable Trust, Westholme, The Springs, Bowdon, Altrincham, Cheshire WA14 3JH

CC NO 263471   ESTABLISHED 1970

■ Jack Livingstone Charitable Trust

WHAT IS FUNDED Health, welfare, Jewish charities

WHO CAN BENEFIT Registered charities benefiting: Jewish people; at risk groups; those disadvantaged by poverty; socially isolated people and the sick. There is no restriction on the disease or medical condition suffered by the beneficiaries

WHERE FUNDING CAN BE GIVEN UK

RANGE OF GRANTS Below £100–£25,000

SAMPLE GRANTS £25,000 to JPAIME; £2,500 to Community Security Trust; £2,000 to Lancashire County Cricket Club Youth Trust; £1,000 to Alone in London; £6,000 to the Balfour Diamond Jubilee Trust; £250 to World Jewish Relief; £250 to Ravenswood; £210 to R Whiteson Memorial Fund; £200 to Macmillan Cancer Relief; £200 to Delamere

FINANCES *Year* 1997 *Income* £79,920
Grants £33,574

TRUSTEES Mrs J V Livingstone, Mrs H Bloom

HOW TO APPLY **This Trust states that it does not respond to unsolicited applications**

WHO TO APPLY TO Mrs Janice Livingstone, Jack Livingstone Charitable Trust, Westholme, The Springs, Bowdon, Altrincham, Cheshire WA14 3JH

CC NO 263473   ESTABLISHED 1971

■ The Elaine and Angus Lloyd Charitable Trust

WHAT IS FUNDED Health and welfare organisations, churches and education

WHAT IS NOT FUNDED No support for overseas aid

WHO CAN BENEFIT Individuals, local, regional and national organisations benefiting: children, young adults, at risk groups, those disadvantaged by poverty and socially isolated people. There is no restriction on the disease or medical condition suffered by the beneficiaries

WHERE FUNDING CAN BE GIVEN UK, with a possible preference for Surrey and the South of England

TYPE OF GRANT Recurrent and one-off

RANGE OF GRANTS Below £1,000–£6,500

SAMPLE GRANTS £26,180 as grants below £1,000 to organisations; £12,392 as grants to individuals; £6,500 to Crossways; £1,350 to St Clements Church, Sandwich; £1,000 Live Music Now

FINANCES *Year* 1997 *Income* £72,891
Grants £47,422

TRUSTEES Sir M Craig-Cooper, CBE, TD, DL, FCIArb, J S Gordon, A S Lloyd, C R H Lloyd

WHO TO APPLY TO The Trustees, The Elaine and Angus Lloyd Charitable Trust, Tunsgate Square, 98–110 High Street, Guildford, Surrey GU1 3HE

CC NO 237250   ESTABLISHED 1964

■ The W M and B W Lloyd Charity Trust

WHAT IS FUNDED Mixed range of support for individual emergencies, disasters, equipment for schools welfare. The advancement of education, medical science and provision of medical equipment and facilities and the provision and improvement of public amenities

WHO CAN BENEFIT Individuals and organisations benefiting: children; young adults; students; and support for individual emergencies and disasters

WHERE FUNDING CAN BE GIVEN Principally the Old Borough of Darwen

TYPE OF GRANT One-off grants

FINANCES *Year* 1997 *Income* £64,474
Grants £61,708

TRUSTEES J N Jacklin, D G Watson, E Aspin

NOTES The Trust has four committees: emergency, education, social amenities and medical. Each committee consider requests specific to its areas of remit. The Trustees meet four times a year for the consideration of requests

WHO TO APPLY TO J N Jacklin, The W M and B W Lloyd Charity Trust, 10 Borough Road, Darwen, Lancashire BB3 1PL

CC NO 503384   ESTABLISHED 1974

■ The Charles Lloyd Foundation

WHAT IS FUNDED Construction, repair and maintenance of Roman Catholic churches, houses, convents and monasteries. Evidence of hardship required. Applications answered only if a grant is intended

WHAT IS NOT FUNDED Restricted to Roman Catholic organisations only

WHO CAN BENEFIT Parishes and religious orders benefiting Roman Catholics

WHERE FUNDING CAN BE GIVEN North and Central Wales only

TYPE OF GRANT Preference for one-off donations for specific projects. Grants annually in November

SAMPLE GRANTS £10,000 to St Mary Cathedral, Wrexham for renovation

FINANCES *Year* 1996 *Income* £23,500
Grants £19,000

TRUSTEES Rev C D S Lloyd, J P B Martin, T V Ryan, R C A Thorn

NOTES Unsuccessful applications are not acknowledged

HOW TO APPLY Anytime by letter with full details

WHO TO APPLY TO Rev C D S Lloyd, The Charles Lloyd Foundation, Dolobran Isaf, Pontrobert, Meifod, Powys, Wales SY22 6HU

CC NO 235225   ESTABLISHED 1964

■ The Lloyd-Everett Trust

WHAT IS FUNDED General charitable purposes. The income has been allocated on an annual basis to a number of chosen charities

WHAT IS NOT FUNDED No grants to individuals

WHO CAN BENEFIT There are no restrictions on the age; professional and economic group; family situation; religion and culture; and social circumstances of; or disease or medical condition suffered by, the beneficiaries

376

Think carefully about every application. Is it justified?

WHERE FUNDING CAN BE GIVEN UK and overseas
TYPE OF GRANT Mainly recurrent, but one-off grants considered
RANGE OF GRANTS £1,000–2,000
SAMPLE GRANTS £2,000 to Royal National Institute for Deaf People; £1,000 to Cancer Relief Macmillan Fund; £1,000 to Shelter; £1,000 to the Children's Society; £1,000 to the Hunter Trust for Education in Malawi
FINANCES *Year* 1997 *Income* £18,654
  Grants £8,000
TRUSTEES P B Shone, M E Kelly, M H Everett
WHO TO APPLY TO P B Shone, The Lloyd-Everett Trust, Bolinge Hill Farm, Buriton, Petersfield, Hampshire GU31 4NN
CC NO 264919   ESTABLISHED 1972

■ The Lloyd's Support Fund

WHAT IS FUNDED To relieve need, hardship or distress amongst members or former members of Lloyd's and their family and dependents; any other general charitable purposes
WHO CAN BENEFIT To benefit members and ex-members of Lloyd's of London who are at risk, disadvantaged by poverty or socially isolated, and their families
WHERE FUNDING CAN BE GIVEN UK
FINANCES *Year* 1997 *Income* £330,459
  Grants £217,158
TRUSTEES D A Acland, Sir H C P Bidwell, Rt Hon Viscount Chelmsford, M D Martin
NOTES There were 85 beneficiaries in 1997
WHO TO APPLY TO C W Dammerum, The Lloyd's Support Fund, Lloyd's of London, One Lime Street, London EC3M 7HA
CC NO 1049661   ESTABLISHED 1995

■ Lloyds TSB Foundation for Northern Ireland

WHAT IS FUNDED To support underfunded voluntary organisations which enable disabled people and those who are disadvantaged through social and economic circumstances to make a contribution to the community. The Trustees regret that, as the funds available are limited, they cannot support all fields of voluntary and charitable activity. The three main objectives to which funds are allocated: (a) social and community needs; (b) education and training; and (c) scientific and medical research. Charities working in the field of housing and accommodation, infrastructure and technical support, infrastructure development, social care professional bodies, health care, health facilities and buildings, health promotion, social campaigning and advocacy, and advice and law centres may be considered
WHAT IS NOT FUNDED Organisations which are not recognised charities. Individuals, including students. Animal welfare. Environment: geographic and scenic, conservation and protection of flora and fauna. Overseas appeals. Activities which are primarily the responsibility of central or local government or some other responsible body. Mainstream schools, universities and colleges (except for projects specifically to benefit disabled students). Hospitals and medical centres. Capital costs, building appeals and running costs. Sponsorship or marketing appeals. Restoration of buildings. Fabric appeals for places of worship. Promotion of religion. Activities which collect funds for subsequent redistribution to other charities or

individuals. Endowment funds. General appeals. Support for fundraising activities. Corporate affiliation or founder membership of a charity. Loans or business finance. Expeditions or overseas travel
WHO CAN BENEFIT Organisations benefiting children; young adults and older people; research workers; unemployed people; volunteers; the homeless; those in rural communities; disabled people and those disadvantaged by poverty, There are no restrictions on the family situation, religion and culture, or disease or medical condition suffered by, the beneficiaries, however there are a few restrictions on their social circumstances
WHERE FUNDING CAN BE GIVEN Northern Ireland
TYPE OF GRANT Capital, core costs, one-off, project, research, recurring costs, salaries, and start-up cost. Funding of up to three years may be considered
RANGE OF GRANTS Normally a maximum of £5,000, but additional amounts are considered
SAMPLE GRANTS £10,000 to Dean of Belfast towards Christmas sit-out for charity; £10,000 to Industrial Therapy Organisation for an information officer; £8,000 to Muscular Dystrophy Group for family weekend; £8,000 to PHAB for playgroup equipment; £7,000 to Shopmobility for powered scooters; £6,500 to NI Music Therapy Centre towards office equipment; £6,000 to Blind Centre NI for day centre equipment; £6,000 to Women's Aid for volunteer training; £6,000 to Citizens Advice Bureau for computer equipment; £6,000 to Mencap for family adviser service
FINANCES *Year* 1997 *Income* £725,000
  Grants £772,000
TRUSTEES James Grew, CBE, DL, JP (Chair), Mrs B Gadd, Mrs B Callaghan, Mrs D Livingstone, D Wilson, R N MacDougall, Lady Anne McCollum, CBE, JP, D Magill, FCA, Mrs A Shaw, I Doherty, M Bishop (Secretary)
HOW TO APPLY Application form required. Guidelines are issued
WHO TO APPLY TO M Bishop, Lloyds TSB Foundation for Northern Ireland, PO Box 4, 4 Queen's Square, Belfast BT1 3DJ *Tel* 01232 325599 *Fax* 01232 231010
IR NO XN 72216   ESTABLISHED 1986

■ Lloyds TSB Foundation for Scotland

WHAT IS FUNDED The Foundation has three main objectives to which it allocates funds: social and community needs; education and training; and scientific and medical research. Every three years the Trustees establish priorities from within these categories. From 1997–2000 they are: young people; rural deprivation; alleviation of homelessness; drug and alcohol abuse; support for minority groups; elderly people; creating positive opportunities for those mentally or physically disadvantaged. The Trustees are also particularly aware of the need to support projects which improve the voluntary sector infrastructure in Scotland
WHAT IS NOT FUNDED Registered charities only. No grants to individuals, including students; animal welfare; environment, geographic and scenic, conservation and protection of flora and fauna; mainstream activities of schools, universities and colleges; hospitals and medical centres; sponsorship or marketing appeals; activities which collect funds for subsequent redistribution; endowment funds; expeditions or overseas travel; fabric appeals for places of worship, other than

Does the trust you have chosen match your needs? Haphazard applications waste postage and time

377

where such buildings provide accommodation to community groups; or historic restoration

WHO CAN BENEFIT Registered charities which provide support to the Scottish community, enabling people, primarily those in need, to become active members of society and improve their quality of life. These include: research workers; scientists; unemployed people and volunteers. There are no restrictions on the family situation or age; and few restrictions on the social circumstances; or disease or medical condition of the beneficiaries

WHERE FUNDING CAN BE GIVEN Scotland

TYPE OF GRANT The majority of grants are made to small grassroots charities, although larger organisations which provide benefit across Scotland have become part of the Foundation's activities. Most donations are made on a one-off basis, however, the Trustees will consider commitments over two or three years. Donations can be for either capital, buildings, core costs feasibility studies, project, research, recurring costs, running costs, salaries and start-up costs

RANGE OF GRANTS £400–£40,000, average grant £7,000

SAMPLE GRANTS £42,000 to Children 1st for parentline initiative; £40,000 to YCSA – Training and Development agency funding training equipment; £35,000 to Brian Beveridge Adventure for Disabled People for the purchase of a boat; £30,000 to Prince and Princess of Wales Hospice providing an extension of care facilities; £30,000 to Edinburgh Festival Society for the installation of wheelchair lifts; £25,000 to Scottish Adoption Association to develop their young people service; £25,000 to Imperial Cancer Research Fund for genetic susceptibility research; £24,000 to Edinburgh Rape Crisis Centre for salary funding; £23,500 to Cornerstone Community Care for salary funding; £21,500 to YMCA Glasgow for repairs to Stroove House

FINANCES *Year* 1997 *Income* £2,700,000 *Grants* £2,600,000

TRUSTEES J D M Robertson (Chairman), P C Paisley, C D Donald, E A Denholm, R G E Peggie, A J Yerburgh, Prof N Lothian, A Robb, J G Mathieson, A D F Findlay

HOW TO APPLY Application packs, incorporating guidelines, can be requested either by telephone or letter. The Trustees meet six times a year in February, April, June, August, October and December. Closing dates are normally 10–12 weeks prior to the Trustees meeting. This timescale allows a thorough assessment of each application to take place. Applicants must leave at least 12 months between applications

WHO TO APPLY TO Connie Williamson, Administrator, Lloyds TSB Foundation for Scotland, Henry Duncan House, 120 George Street, Edinburgh EH2 4LH *Tel* 0131-225 4555 *Fax* 0131-260 0381 *E-mail* cwilliamso@tsbbank.co.uk

SC NO SCO 09481   **ESTABLISHED** 1968

■ Lloyds TSB Foundation for the Channel Islands

WHAT IS FUNDED The main aims of the Foundation are to assist disadvantaged and disabled people and to promote social and community welfare within the Channel Islands, including support to volunteers; residential facilities and services; respite care; self help groups; hospices; campaigning for health issues; health related volunteer scheme; advice centres and various community services

WHAT IS NOT FUNDED Registered charities only. Applications from individuals, including students, are ineligible

WHO CAN BENEFIT Registered charities benefiting young adults; older people; unemployed people; volunteers; at risk groups; carers; disabled people; those disadvantaged by poverty; homeless people; victims of abuse and domestic violence will be considered

WHERE FUNDING CAN BE GIVEN The Channel Islands

TYPE OF GRANT Depends on merit, but usually one-off for a specific project. Research, salaries and start-up costs. Funding of up to three years may be considered

SAMPLE GRANTS £50,000 to Jersey Women's Refuge for refurbishment of refuge; £35,000 to Order of St John - St John Ambulance Jersey towards new ambulance; £35,000 to Friends of St James Association, Guernsey towards installation of a lift for elderly and disabled; £25,000 to Age Concern, Guernsey towards purchase of a minibus; £23,000 to Grow Limited, Guernsey towards replacement glasshouse; £11,000 to Glanville Home for the Aged, Jersey towards refurbishment of home; £10,000 to Cheshire Home, Jersey towards installation of air conditioning in gym; £10,000 to Shelter Trust, Jersey towards new boiler and central heating; £8,250 to Catholic Pastoral Centre, Jersey towards employment of care officer, first of three donations; £8,000 to Mason St Pierre, Guernsey for core funding, first of three donations

FINANCES *Year* 1997 *Income* £410,201 *Grants* £369,583

TRUSTEES R A Picot (Chair), A J Creasey (Deputy Chair), Mrs C A N Bisson, J E Gready, E A Le Maistre, A L Ozanne, D J Watkins

PUBLICATIONS Annual Report and Accounts

HOW TO APPLY In writing at any time. The Trustees meet three times a year, in February, May and October. Application form and guidelines are available from the Administrator

WHO TO APPLY TO David Beaugeard, Administrator, Lloyds TSB Foundation for the Channel Islands, Island Director's Office, Lloyds TSB House, 25 New Street, St Helier, Jersey JE4 8RG *Tel* 01534 503052 *Fax* 01534 864570

CC NO 327113   **ESTABLISHED** 1986

■ Localtrent Ltd

WHAT IS FUNDED Trustees will consider applications from organisations linked to Orthodox Jewish Faith education and poverty

WHO CAN BENEFIT Charities benefiting Jews, children, young adults, students and those disadvantaged by poverty

WHERE FUNDING CAN BE GIVEN Manchester

FINANCES *Year* 1997 *Income* £65,098 *Grants* £61,244

TRUSTEES Mrs M Weiss, B Weiss, J L Weiss, P Weiss, Mrs S Feldman

HOW TO APPLY In writing. Trustees meet three or four times each year

WHO TO APPLY TO H Weiss, Secretary, Localtrent Ltd, 44 Waterpark Road, Salford, Manchester M7 4ET

CC NO 326329   **ESTABLISHED** 1982

■ The Locker Foundation

WHAT IS FUNDED Jewish charities, Synagogues, schools and colleges, Jewish education studies

WHO CAN BENEFIT Organisations benefiting Jewish people, children and young adults, students and teachers

TYPE OF GRANT For new buildings, schools, etc
FINANCES *Year* 1995 *Income* £98,002
TRUSTEES I Carter, Mrs E Freedman
HOW TO APPLY To the address under Who To Apply To
WHO TO APPLY TO I Carter, The Locker Foundation, 9 Neville Drive, Hampstead Garden Suburb, London N2 0RE
CC NO 264180   ESTABLISHED 1972

■ The Loftus Charitable Trust

This trust did not respond to CAF's request to amend its entry and, by 30 June 1998, CAF's researchers did not find financial records for later than 1995 on its file at the Charity Commission. Trusts are legally required to submit annual accounts to the Charity Commission under section 42 of the Charities Act 1993

WHAT IS FUNDED Jewish organisations working in the areas of welfare, education and religion
WHO CAN BENEFIT Jewish organisations benefiting children, young adults and students
WHERE FUNDING CAN BE GIVEN UK and overseas
TRUSTEES R I Loftus, A L Loftus, A D Loftus
HOW TO APPLY To the address under Who To Apply To in writing
WHO TO APPLY TO A Loftus, The Loftus Charitable Trust, 48 George Street, London W1H 5PG
CC NO 297664   ESTABLISHED 1987

■ The Logie Charitable Trust

WHAT IS FUNDED General charitable purposes. Grants are awarded to a range of institutions, charities and appeals
WHAT IS NOT FUNDED No grants to individuals
WHO CAN BENEFIT There are no restrictions on the age; professional and economic group; family situation; religion and culture; and social circumstances of; or disease or medical condition suffered by, the beneficiaries
WHERE FUNDING CAN BE GIVEN UK, particularly Scotland
TRUSTEES Colin Baxter, W & J Burness (Trustees) Ltd, Mrs Graeme Laing, Rt Hon Earl of Leven and Melville
PUBLICATIONS Accounts are available from the Trust
HOW TO APPLY Applications should be made in writing to the address below
WHO TO APPLY TO The Secretary, The Logie Charitable Trust, W & J Burness, Solicitors, 16 Hope Street, Edinburgh EH2 4DD
SC NO SCO 11176

■ The Lolev Charitable Trust

WHAT IS FUNDED Jewish charitable purposes
WHO CAN BENEFIT Organisations benefiting Jewish people
WHERE FUNDING CAN BE GIVEN UK and overseas
FINANCES *Year* 1995 *Income* £676,706
Grants £680,000
HOW TO APPLY To the address under Who To Apply To in writing
WHO TO APPLY TO A Tager, Trustee, The Lolev Charitable Trust, 14a Gilda Crescent, London N16 6JP
CC NO 326249   ESTABLISHED 1982

■ London Arts Board

WHAT IS FUNDED London Arts Board, both on its own and in partnership with others, promotes and supports artistic excellence and innovation throughout London; develops access to the arts for the enjoyment, education and benefit of all who live and work in, or visit, London; celebrates the richness of London's cultural diversity; seeks to enhance London's quality of life, reputation and economy
WHAT IS NOT FUNDED London Arts Board does not give grants to individual students
WHO CAN BENEFIT Arts organisations, artists, local authorities, local education authorities. Organisations benefiting actors, entertainment professionals, musicians, writers and poets
WHERE FUNDING CAN BE GIVEN 32 boroughs of London and the Corporation of London
TYPE OF GRANT One-off project grants, research and fixed term funding of up to three years will be considered
RANGE OF GRANTS £1,000–£20,000 (project grants)
FINANCES *Year* 1996–97 *Income* £14,500,000
Grants £11,798,000
PUBLICATIONS 1998–99 Funding Programme leaflet
HOW TO APPLY Funding Programme leaflet outlining funds and deadlines available from London Arts Board
WHO TO APPLY TO Sue Robertson, London Arts Board, Elme House, 133 Long Acre, London WC2E 9AF *Tel* 0171-240 1313 *Fax* 0171-670 2400
CC NO 1010905   ESTABLISHED 1991

■ London Baptist Association

WHAT IS FUNDED Baptist church initiatives in Greater London and north and east Kent. Particularly charities working in the field of the advancement of Christianity, and churches
WHO CAN BENEFIT Baptist churches which are members of the London Baptist Association
WHERE FUNDING CAN BE GIVEN Greater London, Kent
FINANCES *Year* 1997 *Income* £254,870
Grants £69,296
TRUSTEES London Baptist Property Board Ltd
PUBLICATIONS Annual Directory. Report of General Purposes and Finance Committee
HOW TO APPLY To the address under Who To Apply To in writing who will forward application form or letter
WHO TO APPLY TO Rev Peter Wortley, Association Secretary, London Baptist Association, 1 Merchant Street, London E3 4LY *Tel* 0181-980 6818
CC NO 249703   ESTABLISHED 1865

■ London Charity Trust

This trust did not respond to CAF's request to amend its entry and, by 30 June 1998, CAF's researchers did not find financial records for later than 1995 on its file at the Charity Commission. Trusts are legally required to submit annual accounts to the Charity Commission under section 42 of the Charities Act 1993

WHAT IS FUNDED General charitable purposes
WHO CAN BENEFIT There are no restrictions on the age; professional and economic group; family situation; religion and culture; and social circumstances of; or disease or medical condition suffered by, the beneficiaries
WHERE FUNDING CAN BE GIVEN Overseas
TRUSTEES S Leaman, H Grodzinski, A D Grodzinski

WHO TO APPLY TO A D Grodzinski, 13 Heathfield Gardens, London NW11
CC NO 802169   ESTABLISHED 1989

■ London Law Trust

WHAT IS FUNDED The prevention and cure of illness and disability in children and young people; the alleviation of illness and disability in children and young people; and the encouragement in young people of the qualities of leadership and service to the community. The Trust may also support charities working in the fields of education and residential facilities and services

WHAT IS NOT FUNDED Applications from individuals, including students, are ineligible. No grants made in response to local appeals from branches of national organisations

WHO CAN BENEFIT Registered charities only, or bodies with charitable status working in the areas outlined under What Is Funded. In the case of research projects, preference is given to seed corn or small projects, and in other cases to new ventures. Organisations benefiting: children and young adults; medical professionals; research workers; volunteers; at risk groups; disabled people; those disadvantaged by poverty and those living in rural areas will be considered. There is no restriction on the disease or medical condition suffered by the beneficiaries

WHERE FUNDING CAN BE GIVEN UK

TYPE OF GRANT Usually one-off grants for or towards specific projects. Buildings, capital, core costs, research, running costs, recurring costs, salaries and start-up costs will also be considered. Funding may be given for up to three years

RANGE OF GRANTS £500–£5,000, typical grant £2,500

SAMPLE GRANTS £5,800 to Atlantic College Appeal Fund for bursary funding; £5,000 to Bristol Wheels Project for project worker scheme; £5,000 to Duke of Edinburgh Award Scheme; £5,000 to Schools Outreach for school youth worker scheme; £5,000 to Scientific Exploration Society in support of Fulcrum Challenge Initiative; £5,000 to Association for Children with Life Threatening Conditions; £5,000 to the Glycobiology Institute for research into new drug treatment in glycolipid storaye disease; £5,000 to British Lung Foundation for research into respiratory infections in children; £5,000 to Katherine Dormandy Trust for laboratory equipment; £3,700 to International Spinal Research Trust for spinal injury research

FINANCES *Year* 1997 *Income* £137,071
Grants £103,000

TRUSTEES Prof A R Mellows, TD, PhD, LLD, Brigadier Sir Jeffrey Darell, Bart, MC, R A Pellant, FCA, ATII

PUBLICATIONS Annual Report & Accounts

HOW TO APPLY Between January and June each year. Further information will be requested from shortlisted applicants. Grant Adviser (Mrs B M Crabbe) may visit applicants

WHO TO APPLY TO G D Ogilvie, Secretary, London Law Trust, c/o Alexanders, Solicitors to Trustees, 203 Temple Chambers, Temple Avenue, London EC4Y 0DB *Tel* 0171-353 6221 *Fax* 0171-583 0662
CC NO 255924   ESTABLISHED 1968

■ London Metal Exchange Benevolent Fund

WHAT IS FUNDED Relief of persons who are or have been connected with the London Metal Exchange, and their families

WHO CAN BENEFIT To benefit at risk groups, those disadvantaged by poverty and socially isolated people

WHERE FUNDING CAN BE GIVEN Greater London

FINANCES *Year* 1996–97 *Income* £23,918
Grants £24,552

TRUSTEES M J Beale, I E J Foster, P G Smith, CBE

HOW TO APPLY To the the address under Who To Apply To in writing

WHO TO APPLY TO The Secretary, London Metal Exchange Benevolent Fund, 56 Leadhall Street, London EC3A 2BJ
CC NO 231001   ESTABLISHED 1900

■ London North East Community Foundation (formerly The Redbridge Community Trust)

WHAT IS FUNDED Projects working with disabled people, the elderly, arts organisations, multi-cultural groups through the development of closer links between corporate supporters and local organisations. The advancement of education, protection of physical and mental health, relief of poverty and sickness are all considered, and other charitable purposes

WHO CAN BENEFIT To benefit the community in North East London, including disabled people, the elderly and those disadvantaged by poverty; students; those involved in arts and cultural activities and multi-cultural groups. There is no restriction on the disease or medical condition suffered by the beneficiaries

WHERE FUNDING CAN BE GIVEN The London Borough of Redbridge and its immediate neighbourhood

FINANCES *Year* 1996–97 *Income* £45,911
Grants £21,520

TRUSTEES M Selmon (Chairman), J d'Abbro, Ms P Ballantine, J Clare, D Harris, J Hogben, Cllr Mrs L Hyams, M Sweetingham

HOW TO APPLY To the address under Who To Apply To in writing

WHO TO APPLY TO Christopher Legge, Director, London North East Community Foundation, PO Box 77, Ilford, Essex IG1 1EB *Tel* 0181-553 9469
CC NO 1000540   ESTABLISHED 1990

■ The London Youth Trust (W H Smith Memorial)

WHAT IS FUNDED The Trustees aim to support projects which: (a) support detached youth workers in the inner city; (b) encourage the development of young people physically, mentally and spiritually through carefully planned experiences which lead to positive achievements and growth skills; (c) take account of individual differences and needs, and give priority to those with learning difficulties, physical disabilities or who suffer from the results of poverty, deprivation, abuse or drugs; (d) allow young people to gain an understanding of issues relating to race, culture, sex and religious beliefs; (e) foster and develop good community relationships; (f) encourage young people to accept responsibility in planning and developing their own programmes. Particularly local community initiatives working with young people to

380

Think carefully about every application. Is it justified?

provide training and an atmosphere in which social development is encouraged

WHAT IS NOT FUNDED No grants to individuals or expeditions

WHO CAN BENEFIT Local community initiatives and street organisations benefiting children and young adults, at risk groups, and those disadvantaged by poverty. There are no restrictions on the culture or religion of the beneficiaries

WHERE FUNDING CAN BE GIVEN Greater London

TYPE OF GRANT Project and salaries. Up to a maximum of £5,000 per annum for three years. Recurring costs, salaries and start-up costs are also considered

RANGE OF GRANTS £100–£5,000

FINANCES *Year* 1996–97 *Income* £78,031 *Grants* £61,637

TRUSTEES Mrs Jean Clay, Roger Cobley (Hon Treasurer), Ian Galbraith, Derek Howe, CBE (Chairman), Sidney Jaque (Vice President), The Rt Hon Sir Geoffery Johnson Smith, PC, DL, MP (President), J W Lockhart, Christopher Miers, Allen Molesworth, Michael Pearce, Brig Philip Wildman, OBE

HOW TO APPLY To the address under Who To Apply To. Initial telephone calls are not welcome. There are application forms and guidelines. There are no deadlines and no sae required

WHO TO APPLY TO Rev Canon Brian Walshe, MBE, AKC, The London Youth Trust, 10 Warrior Court, 16 Warrior Square, St Leonards-on-Sea, East Sussex TN37 6BS

CC NO 224484   **ESTABLISHED** 1909

■ Longley Trust

WHAT IS FUNDED Charities working in the fields of: hospices; woodlands; environmental issues; heritage; the construction industry; and schools and colleges. Preference for involvement of company staff

WHAT IS NOT FUNDED No grants to individuals or students

WHO CAN BENEFIT Small local projects benefiting: children; at risk groups; disabled people; victims of disasters and crime. There is no restriction on the disease or medical condition suffered by the beneficiaries

WHERE FUNDING CAN BE GIVEN Sussex

TYPE OF GRANT One-off and recurrent grants of £1,000 or less. Buildings, core costs, endowments and start-up costs. Funding for more than three years will be considered

RANGE OF GRANTS £50–£1,000

SAMPLE GRANTS £1,000 to local hospice for running costs; £1,000 to Crawley BC for arts sponsorship

FINANCES *Year* 1996 *Income* £13,974 *Grants* £13,875

TRUSTEES P Longley, R P Longley, K F Bergin, J W Ebdon

NOTES National charities can be supported but prefer local charities

HOW TO APPLY In writing at any time

WHO TO APPLY TO P Longley, Longley Trust, Longley House, East Park, Crawley, West Sussex RH10 6AP

CC NO 278615   **ESTABLISHED** 1979

■ William and Katherine Longman Charitable Trust

WHAT IS FUNDED General charitable purposes. The Trustees believe in taking a proactive approach in deciding which charities to benefit and it is their policy not to respond to unsolicited appeals

WHAT IS NOT FUNDED No grants to individuals whose applications will not be acknowledged

WHO CAN BENEFIT Registered charities only. There are no restrictions on the age; professional and economic group; family situation; religion and culture; and social circumstances of; or disease or medical condition suffered by, the beneficiaries

WHERE FUNDING CAN BE GIVEN UK

RANGE OF GRANTS £300–£10,000

SAMPLE GRANTS £10,000 to Care; £10,000 to Cystic Fibrosis Trust; £10,000 to Prison Fellowship; £10,000 to the Lambeth Fund – Springboard; £8,000 to Clan MacKenzie Charitable Trust; £7,000 to Oasis Charitable Trust; £5,000 to Abbeyfield (Chelsea and Fulham); £5,000 to Age Concern, Kensington and Chelsea; £5,000 to Alexandra Rose Day; £5,000 to Kent Foundation

FINANCES *Year* 1997 *Income* £132,720 *Grants* £180,000

TRUSTEES W P Harriman, J B Talbot, MC, A C O Bell

HOW TO APPLY **This Trust states that it does not respond to unsolicited applications**

WHO TO APPLY TO W P Harriman, William and Katherine Longman Charitable Trust, c/o Messrs Charles Russell, 8–10 New Fetter Lane, London EC4A 1RS

CC NO 800785   **ESTABLISHED** 1988

■ John Longwill's Agricultural Scheme

WHAT IS FUNDED The provision of grants and loans to farmers in need, to agricultural colleges to support education and to Young Farmers Clubs to promote agriculture

WHO CAN BENEFIT Individuals and organisations benefiting farmers and students at agricultural colleges

WHERE FUNDING CAN BE GIVEN Leicestershire

RANGE OF GRANTS £100–£6,000

SAMPLE GRANTS £6,000 to an individual; £5,500 to Farming and Wildlife Advisory Group; £5,000 each to two individuals; £5,000 to Brooksby Agricultural College; £100 to an individual

FINANCES *Year* 1995 *Income* £46,415 *Grants* £26,600

HOW TO APPLY To the address under Who To Apply To in writing

WHO TO APPLY TO Mrs H A M Lander, Clerk, John Longwill's Agricultural Scheme, 3 Wycliffe Street, Leicester, Leicestershire LE1 5LR

CC NO 215278   **ESTABLISHED** 1963

■ Lord Mayor of Birmingham's Charity

WHAT IS FUNDED General charitable purposes at Trustees' discretion

WHO CAN BENEFIT Registered charities. There are no restrictions on the age; professional and economic group; family situation; religion and culture; and social circumstances of; or disease or medical condition suffered by, the beneficiaries

WHERE FUNDING CAN BE GIVEN UK and West Midlands

TYPE OF GRANT One-off and recurrent

RANGE OF GRANTS £200–£16483

Does the trust you have chosen match your needs? Haphazard applications waste postage and time

381

SAMPLE GRANTS £16,483 to Greenacres Cheshire Home; £14,984 to Norman Land Centre; £14,484 to RNLI Forward Lifeboat Campaign; £800 to Snow Drop Appeal; £500 to Lady Hoare Trust; £250 to Mobility Advice Line

FINANCES *Year* 1997 *Income* £51,519 *Grants* £47,701

TRUSTEES The Lord Mayor of Birmingham, The Deputy Lord Mayor of Birmingham, Hon Alderman H McCallion

WHO TO APPLY TO Ian Toddhunter, Director of Legal Services, Lord Mayor of Birmingham's Charity, Birmingham City Council, Ingleby House, 11–14 Cannon Street, Birmingham B2 5EN

CC NO 1036968　　　**ESTABLISHED** 1994

■ Lord Mayor of Chester Charitable Trust

WHAT IS FUNDED Local registered charities, particularly those working in the fields of: community arts and recreation; health; conservation; animal welfare; schools and colleges; special needs education; playgrounds; and community services. Support is also given to volunteers, and voluntary and community organisations

WHAT IS NOT FUNDED Non-registered charities are not funded

WHO CAN BENEFIT Registered charities benefiting children and young adults, volunteers, at risk groups and carers. There are no restrictions on the family situation of, or the disease or medical condition suffered by, the beneficiaries

WHERE FUNDING CAN BE GIVEN Chester only

TYPE OF GRANT One-off and capital grants will be considered

RANGE OF GRANTS £25–£1,000

SAMPLE GRANTS £1,000 to Grosvenor Housing Association – Foyer; £650 to Hospice of the Good Shepherd; £650 to Chester and Cheshire Society for the Blind; £500 Chester Gateway – Breaking Down Walls; £500 to Wirral Holistic Care Service

FINANCES *Year* 1998 *Grants* £6,205

TRUSTEES D Areld, E Plenderleath, P F Durham, M A Johnson

HOW TO APPLY In writing. Initial telephone calls are welcome. Deadline for applications is May of each year

WHO TO APPLY TO W Healiss, PA to the Lord Mayor, Lord Mayor of Chester Charitable Trust, Council of the City of Chester, Town Hall, Chester CH1 2HS *Tel* 01244 402126

CC NO 513175　　　**ESTABLISHED** 1982

■ Lord Mayor of Manchester's Charity Appeal Trust

WHAT IS FUNDED General charitable purposes for the benefit of the inhabitants of the City of Manchester

WHO CAN BENEFIT There are no restrictions on the age; professional and economic group; family situation; religion and culture; and social circumstances of; or disease or medical condition suffered by, the beneficiaries

WHERE FUNDING CAN BE GIVEN City of Manchester

TRUSTEES The Lord Mayor of Manchester (Gerard Carroll), A Sandford, D Martin

WHO TO APPLY TO E J Treacy, Solicitor, Lord Mayor of Manchester's Charity Appeal Trust, City Solicitors, Town Hall, Albert Square, Manchester M60 2LA

CC NO 1066972　　　**ESTABLISHED** 1997

■ The Loseley & Guildway Charitable Trust

WHAT IS FUNDED Compassionate causes, mainly local or causes with which the family and members of the Firm are associated, including health and animal welfare

WHAT IS NOT FUNDED Registered charities only, not individuals

WHO CAN BENEFIT Organisations benefiting those suffering from: Alzheimer's disease; cancers; epilepsy; HIV and AIDS; leprosy; mental illness; motor neurone disease; multiple sclerosis; Parkinson's disease; sight loss; spina bifida and hydrocephalus; and terminal illness. Victims of natural disasters are also considered

WHERE FUNDING CAN BE GIVEN England with an emphasis on the South East. Also supports Third World countries and countries affected by natural disasters mainly through Red Cross

RANGE OF GRANTS £25–£5,000. Typically £100

SAMPLE GRANTS £7,885 to Chase for building of new hospice an Loseley Estate; £5,000 to Meath Home for a new building appeal; £5,000 to The Dorothy Kerin Trust; £5,000 to SAYC/PHAB; £5,000 to Harriet Davis Seaside Holiday Trust for a new holiday home; £4,000 to QEF; £1,000 to Parentline, Surrey; £1,000 to The Grange Centre; £700 to The Royal British Legion Poppy Appeal; £500 to the Princess Margarita of Romania Trust

FINANCES *Year* 1997 *Income* £53,110 *Grants* £53,440

TRUSTEES J R More-Molyneux, Mrs S More-Molyneux, M G More-Molyneux, F R Gooch, L G Hodson

HOW TO APPLY Quarterly meetings

WHO TO APPLY TO J R More-Molyneux, The Loseley & Guildway Charitable Trust, Loseley Park, Guildford, Surrey GU3 1HS *Tel* 01483 304440 *Fax* 01483 302036

CC NO 267178　　　**ESTABLISHED** 1973

■ Loughborough University Development Trust

WHAT IS FUNDED To promote any charitable purposes of Loughborough University

WHO CAN BENEFIT To benefit students and academics of Loughborough University

WHERE FUNDING CAN BE GIVEN UK

RANGE OF GRANTS Below £400–£3,100

SAMPLE GRANTS £3,100 to Loughborough University

FINANCES *Year* 1997 *Income* £35,132 *Grants* £3,500

TRUSTEES Prof D J Wallace, Dr S C Miller, Dr D E Fletcher, H M Pearson, S J Gorton

WHO TO APPLY TO H M Pearson, Loughborough University Development Trust, Loughborough University, Loughborough, Leicestershire LE11 3TU *Tel* 01509 222102

CC NO 1057889　　　**ESTABLISHED** 1996

■ The Loughborough Welfare Trusts

WHAT IS FUNDED Various projects are supported, including: education; welfare; almshouses; sickness; individuals; relief of those who are convalescent, disabled, handicapped or infirm; and general charitable purposes

WHO CAN BENEFIT There are no restrictions on the age; professional and economic group; family situation; religion and culture; and social circumstances of; or disease or medical condition suffered by, the beneficiaries. However, particular favour is given to children, young adults, students and teachers. Favour is also given to at risk groups, the disabled, those disadvantaged by poverty, the socially isolated and the sick

WHERE FUNDING CAN BE GIVEN Loughborough

FINANCES *Year* 1995–96 *Income* £17,968

NOTES The Welfare Trusts include 21 different local trusts that are all administered as one

HOW TO APPLY To the address under Who To Apply To in writing

WHO TO APPLY TO J O Fox-Russell, Clerk, The Loughborough Welfare Trusts, 20 Churchgate, Loughborough, Leicestershire LE11 1UD

CC NO 214654   **ESTABLISHED** 1972

■ P and M Lovell Charitable Trust

WHAT IS FUNDED General charitable purposes

WHO CAN BENEFIT There are no restrictions on the age; professional and economic group; family situation; religion and culture; and social circumstances of; or disease or medical condition suffered by, the beneficiaries

WHERE FUNDING CAN BE GIVEN UK

RANGE OF GRANTS £20–£2,200

SAMPLE GRANTS £2,200 to Britain Yearly Meeting; £1,000 to MOSA 1995 Appeal; £980 to Stochfield Preparative Meeting; £750 to Crispin Hall Trust; £500 to BYM Swarthmoor Hall Appeal

FINANCES *Year* 1996 *Income* £13,614 *Grants* £9,345

TRUSTEES W Lovell, J P Lovell, B Lovell, M Lovell

WHO TO APPLY TO A E Hill, Accountant, P and M Lovell Charitable Trust, KPMG, 15 Pembroke Road, Clifton, Bristol BS8 3BG

CC NO 274846   **ESTABLISHED** 1977

■ The Low & Bonar Charitable Fund

WHAT IS FUNDED The Trustees give priority to charities falling into the following categories : (a) medical, encompassing research, treatment and the general welfare of patients including those physically and mentally handicapped (b) the welfare of the old and infirm (c) the protection and welfare of children and young people (d) the relief of human suffering where not otherwise covered under (a) to (c) above. The Trustees also give consideration to charities meeting social, cultural and environmental needs and such other charities whose work they judge to be of value

WHAT IS NOT FUNDED The Trustees are precluded by the Trust Deed from making donations for any purpose other than that which is recognised as a charitable purpose within the meaning of the Income Tax Acts in force from time to time. They do not give grants to individuals nor do they help out with debt, festivals, church restoration

WHO CAN BENEFIT Bodies recognised as having charitable status by the Inland Revenue under the Income Tax Acts benefiting children, young adults, older people, at risk groups, disabled people, those disadvantaged by poverty and homeless people. There is no restriction on the disease or medical condition suffered by the beneficiaries. In the case of National or International charities grants may be either to the Headquarters' organisation or, if there is a Scottish or local branch, to such branch. Donations are principally to established charities but innovatory projects are also considered

WHERE FUNDING CAN BE GIVEN Principally Dundee/ Tayside

TYPE OF GRANT One-off cash grants. A number of charities do receive recurring annual grants, but

these are re-considered each year and there is no commitment to repeat

RANGE OF GRANTS £100–£2,000

SAMPLE GRANTS £2,000 to British Heart Foundation; £2,000 to Cancer Relief Macmillan Fund; £2,000 to Cancer Research Campaign; £2,000 to RNLI; £2,000 to RSSPCC; £1,500 to Frigate Unicorn; £1,500 to Leukaemia Research Fund; £1,500 to National Trust for Scotland; £1,000 to Alzheimer's Scotland; £1,000 to Arthritis and Rheumatism Council for Research

FINANCES *Year* 1997 *Income* £65,781 *Grants* £64,950

TRUSTEES G C Bonar, J L Heilig, N D McLeod, P A Bartlett, R D Clegg, J B Marx, J H Robinson, N R Clark

HOW TO APPLY Meetings held at three-monthly intervals with a principal annual review in March each year. Appeals should be in writing and appellants should provide evidence of charitable status and their latest audited Report and Accounts

WHO TO APPLY TO M G Long, Secretary, The Low & Bonar Charitable Fund, PO Box 51, Dundee, Scotland DD1 9JA *Tel* 01382 818171

SC NO SCO 10837   **ESTABLISHED** 1963

■ Michael Lowe's and Associated Charities

WHAT IS FUNDED Relief in need, hardship or distress of residents of the area Where Funding Can Be Given

WHO CAN BENEFIT Primarily individuals in need, some organisations benefiting those in need, hardship or distress

WHERE FUNDING CAN BE GIVEN Lichfield

RANGE OF GRANTS Organisations: £270–£20,000

SAMPLE GRANTS £20,000 to Guild of St Marys; £1,200 to Relate; £1,000 to Mary Slaters Charity; £1,000 to Burntwood and Lichfield Visually Handicapped Club; £1,000 to South Staffordshire Family Mediation Service; £520 to Lichfield Luncheon Club; £360 to Hawthorn House; £270 to MENCAP

FINANCES *Year* 1997 *Income* £94,575 *Grants* £77,717

TRUSTEES Mrs A Hall, M B Johnson, E J Ashley, D L Bailey, Mrs M K Barratt, P G Boggis, Mrs P Brooks, Rev P H Davis, Mrs D Godfrey, N G Sedgwick, Mrs C Tetley, A D Thompson, Rev E G H Townshend, A Wilson

NOTES In total £52,367 was given to individuals, of which £23,800 was to 476 individuals as fuel grants

HOW TO APPLY To the address under Who To Apply To in writing

WHO TO APPLY TO C P Kitto, Clerk, Michael Lowe's and Associated Charities, Hinckley Birch & Brown, 20 St John Street, Lichfield, Staffordshire WS13 6PD

CC NO 214785   **ESTABLISHED** 1980

■ The Lowestoft Church and Town Educational Foundation

WHAT IS FUNDED Education and training

WHO CAN BENEFIT Local schools. Individuals and organisations benefiting children, young adults and higher education students

WHERE FUNDING CAN BE GIVEN Lowestoft

RANGE OF GRANTS Average student grant in 1997 was £200

FINANCES *Year* 1995–96 *Income* £19,023

HOW TO APPLY To the address under Who To Apply To in writing. Higher education grant forms have to be completed and verified by the applicant's college by the 30 November in each academic year
WHO TO APPLY TO J M Loftus, Clerk, Lowestoft Church and Town Educational Foundation, 148 London Road North, Lowestoft, Suffolk NR23 1HF *Tel* 01502 533015
CC NO 310460   **ESTABLISHED** 1964

■ Lowmoor Church Trust

WHAT IS FUNDED Christian religion
WHO CAN BENEFIT Christians and Evangelists. The name of the Trust has been changed to accommodate the building of an evangelical church in Wigton, Cumbria. The Trust is fully committed
WHERE FUNDING CAN BE GIVEN UK
TYPE OF GRANT At the discretion of the Trustees, but building grants are considered
FINANCES *Year* 1997 *Income* £345,024 *Grants* £357
TRUSTEES E P Stobart, E Stobart, W Stobart, Mrs N Stobart, K Fearon
WHO TO APPLY TO E P Stobart, Lowmoor Church Trust, Hawkesdale House, Dalston, Carlisle, Cumbria CA5 7BJ
CC NO 1003055   **ESTABLISHED** 1991

■ The Vanessa Lowndes Charitable Trust

WHAT IS FUNDED The Trustees are restricted in part to giving to charities in New Zealand and national charities in which New Zealand is interested, particularly handicapped children's charities
WHAT IS NOT FUNDED No grants to individuals. Restricted to certain IR approved registered charities plus those in which New Zealand is particularly interested
WHO CAN BENEFIT Handicapped children in particular
WHERE FUNDING CAN BE GIVEN UK, New Zealand
RANGE OF GRANTS £100–£3,650
SAMPLE GRANTS £3,650 to Diabetes Auckland Inc, New Zealand; £3,650 to The Salvation Army in New Zealand; £2,425 to Alzheimer's Society, New Zealand; £2,425 to the Child Cancer Foundation, New Zealand; £2,425 to New Zealand CCS; £2,425 to New Zealand Riding for the Disabled; £1,000 to The Partially Sighted Society; £700 to Lambeth Wel-Care; £400 to Friends of Winchester College; £300 to Accept Services
FINANCES *Year* 1997 *Income* £38,076 *Grants* £40,800
TRUSTEES Miss V Lowndes, A N Hay, M H Wadsworth, P E Rood, M J Calder
NOTES Restricted to named UK charities by deed
HOW TO APPLY By letter with descriptive pamphlet
WHO TO APPLY TO Calder & Co, The Vanessa Lowndes Charitable Trust, 1 Regent Street, London SW1Y 4NW
CC NO 262166   **ESTABLISHED** 1971

■ The C L Loyd Charitable Trust

WHAT IS FUNDED General charitable purposes. Local charities in the area Where Funding Can Be Given, UK health and welfare charities, UK animal welfare charities
WHAT IS NOT FUNDED No local charities with which the Trust is not already closely associated and familiar

WHO CAN BENEFIT Neighbourhood-based community projects and national organisations benefiting: at risk groups; disabled people; those disadvantaged by poverty; and socially isolated people. There is no restriction on the disease or medical condition suffered by the beneficiaries
WHERE FUNDING CAN BE GIVEN UK, with a preference for Berkshire and Oxfordshire
TYPE OF GRANT One-off and recurring
FINANCES *Year* 1996–97 *Income* £126,110 *Grants* £167,375
TRUSTEES C L Loyd, T C Loyd
HOW TO APPLY To the address under Who To Apply To in writing
WHO TO APPLY TO C L Loyd, The C L Loyd Charitable Trust, Lockinge, Wantage, Oxfordshire OX12 8QL *Tel* 01235 833265
CC NO 265076   **ESTABLISHED** 1973

■ Sidney Ivor Luck Counselling Trust

WHAT IS FUNDED General charitable purposes by way of counselling, or by the advancement of education, the protection of health and the relief of poverty, sickness and distress
WHO CAN BENEFIT To benefit clients of Pathways Counselling Centre, those disadvantaged by poverty, at risk or sick. There is no restriction on the disease or medical condition suffered by the beneficiaries
WHERE FUNDING CAN BE GIVEN In practice, Surrey
FINANCES *Year* 1997 *Income* £18,384
TRUSTEES Mrs A V F Renouf, Miss C M Denneny, Mrs J A Robinson
NOTES In practice the Trust's resources are devoted to Pathways Counselling Centre based at the address under Who To Apply To
WHO TO APPLY TO Mrs A V F Renauf, Sidney Ivor Luck Counselling Trust, 38 Waterloo Road, Epsom, Surrey KT19 8EX *Tel* 01372 743338
CC NO 1040965   **ESTABLISHED** 1994

■ The Ludgate Trust

WHAT IS FUNDED To support schemes offering genuine performance opportunities to young instrumentalists
WHO CAN BENEFIT Individuals and institutions benefiting young adults and musicians
WHERE FUNDING CAN BE GIVEN UK
TYPE OF GRANT One-off
RANGE OF GRANTS £500–£15,000
SAMPLE GRANTS £13,500 to LSO String Experience Scheme for orchestral experience project; £10,000 to Live Music Now for costs of concerts; £1,500 to Society for the Promotion of New Music for a performance workshop; £1,000 to Flute Festival for a performance workshop; £800 to Flute Festival for a performance workshop
FINANCES *Year* 1997 *Income* £18,186 *Grants* £26,800
TRUSTEES The Musicians Benevolent Fund
HOW TO APPLY By written application after initial discussion
WHO TO APPLY TO Helen Faulkner, Secretary to the Trustees, The Ludgate Trust, Musicians Benevolent Fund, 16 Ogle Street, London W1P 8JB *Tel* 0171-636 4481
CC NO 259109   **ESTABLISHED** 1969

384

Think carefully about every application. Is it justified?

■ The Luke Trust

WHAT IS FUNDED Charitable purposes connected with Christian religion

WHO CAN BENEFIT Registered charities and institutions benefiting Christians

WHERE FUNDING CAN BE GIVEN Mainly Bedfordshire

TYPE OF GRANT Capital

FINANCES *Year* 1996 *Income* £20,136
Grants £19,350

TRUSTEES Hon H de B Lawson Johnston, J A P Whinney, D G Ward

WHO TO APPLY TO M W Tippen, The Luke Trust, c/o Historic Churches Preservation Trust, Fulham Palace, London SW6 6EA *Tel* 0171-736 3054

CC NO 1000550   **ESTABLISHED** 1943

■ Paul Lunn-Rockliffe Charitable Trust

WHAT IS FUNDED It is the Trustees' policy not to raise income through public and private appeals. The Trust's sole source of income is the dividends received from the Trust's capital investments. As far as grant making is concerned the Trustees' policy is: (a) to give first but not exclusive consideration to charities likely to further Christianity; (b) to give support to charities concerned with the relief of poverty, help the aged, support the infirm and disaster relief; (c) to consider charities connected with prisons and prisoners, medical research, rehabilitation of drug addicts, and youth organisations; (d) housing and accommodation. Training for work; bursaries and fees; neurological research; and holidays and outings will also be considered. Finally, the Trustees should not accept such new commitments that will significantly dilute the size of current grants

WHAT IS NOT FUNDED At present the Trustees are virtually unable to respond to unsolicited applications. The Trustees will not fund individuals, for example students expenses and travel grants. Repair and maintenance of historic buildings are also excluded for support

WHO CAN BENEFIT Organisations of national significance and charities which may be known to the Trustees, or members of their family, benefiting people of all ages; unemployed people; Christians; at risk groups; carers; disabled people; those disadvantaged by poverty; ex-offenders and those at risk of offending; homeless people; those living in urban areas; victims of famine and disasters; and those suffering from cerebral palsy and Parkinson's disease

WHERE FUNDING CAN BE GIVEN UK with preference to the South East; overseas, mainly third world countries

TYPE OF GRANT Core costs, one-off and start-up costs. Funding for more than three years will be considered

RANGE OF GRANTS £200–£1,000

FINANCES *Year* 1998 *Income* £28,725
Grants £27,000

TRUSTEES Mrs J M Lunn-Rockliffe, V P Lunn-Rockliffe, J W Lunn-Rockliffe

HOW TO APPLY At any time. No special form required. We cannot acknowledge unsolicited applications except those with sae. Latest Annual Report and Accounts are a desirable requirement

WHO TO APPLY TO Mrs Lunn-Rockliffe, Paul Lunn-Rockliffe Charitable Trust, 4A Barnes Close, Winchester, Hampshire SO23 9QX
Tel 01962 852949

CC NO 264119   **ESTABLISHED** 1972

■ C F Lunoe Trust Fund

WHAT IS FUNDED General charitable purposes, with particular emphasis on assistance to ex-employees (and their dependants) in needy circumstances, of Norwest Holst Group Ltd. Otherwise, preference is given to projects in which Trustees have special interest or knowledge

WHO CAN BENEFIT There are no restrictions on the age; professional and economic group; family situation; religion and culture; and social circumstances of; or disease or medical condition suffered by, the beneficiaries. However, particular favour is given to ex-employees (and their dependants) of Norwest Holst Group Ltd, in needy circumstances, such as at risk groups, those disadvantaged by poverty and socially isolated people

FINANCES *Year* 1995 *Income* £48,604
Grants £42,700

TRUSTEES D R Huntingford, J A Bosdet, P H Lunoe, H D Wakeford, A M Harris, R F Collins, J E Ellis, M B Watson

NOTES Almost all the funds of the Trust go to registered charities already known to the Trustees so we have to disappoint almost all applications

WHO TO APPLY TO D R Huntingford, C F Lunoe Trust Fund, 4 Woodstock Road, Walthamstow, London E17 4BJ

CC NO 214850   **ESTABLISHED** 1960

■ The Ruth & Jack Lunzer Charitable Trust

WHAT IS FUNDED Educational institutions. Other charitable purposes will be considered

WHO CAN BENEFIT Organisations benefiting children, young adults and students are given priority

WHERE FUNDING CAN BE GIVEN UK

RANGE OF GRANTS £100–£10,000

SAMPLE GRANTS £10,000 to Labavitch Foundation; £10,000 to Yesodey Hatorah Schools; £7,500 to Glyndebourne Education; £4,500 to World Jewish Relief; £4,250 to British Israel Arts Foundation; £4,000 to Chai Lifeline; £4,000 to Menorah Primary School; £3,000 to Independent Jewish Day School; £3,000 to Keren Hatorah; £2,500 to Community Security Trust

FINANCES *Year* 1996 *Income* £43,750
Grants £83,900

TRUSTEES J V Lunzer, M D Paisner

WHO TO APPLY TO J Lunzer, The Ruth & Jack Lunzer Charitable Trust, 7 Turner Drive, London NW11 6TX

CC NO 276201   **ESTABLISHED** 1978

■ Lutterworth Town Estate

WHAT IS FUNDED Main areas of funding include public buildings and amenities and general charitable purposes in the area Where Funding Can Be Given

WHO CAN BENEFIT Individuals and organisations benefiting the local community

WHERE FUNDING CAN BE GIVEN Lutterworth

FINANCES *Year* 1997 *Income* £64,420
Grants £6,775

TRUSTEES G Jones, J Ackerley, M Ross, A Sykes, J Shaw

HOW TO APPLY To the address under Who To Apply To in writing

WHO TO APPLY TO G Jones, Chairman, Lutterworth Town Estate, 19 Biteswell Road, Lutterworth, Leicestershire LE17 4EL *Tel* 01455 552306

CC NO 217609   **ESTABLISHED** 1983

Does the trust you have chosen match your needs? Haphazard applications waste postage and time

385

■ Lyndhurst Settlement

WHAT IS FUNDED The policy of the Lyndhurst Settlement is to encourage research into social problems with specific emphasis on safeguarding civil liberties, maintaining the rights of minorities and protecting the environment which the Trustees regard as an important civil liberty. The Trustees prefer to support charities (both innovatory and long established) that seek to prevent as well as ameliorate hardship. In response to the pressing needs of today, the continuing policy of the Trustees is to make grants in excess of income. Whilst supporting some larger organisations, the Settlement tries to encourage smaller local groups. It is the view of the Trustees that an essential element in the protection of the environment is the discouragement of population growth. The Settlement was one of the first Trusts to be concerned about the civil rights of prisoners. Minority groups, both here and abroad, are also a continuing concern. This includes: community development; support to voluntary and community organisations; residential facilities and services; family planning clinics; respite care and care for carers; well woman clinics; health education and population control. Libraries and museums; community centres and village halls; parks; community services; campaigning, advocacy advice and information on social issues. Conservation; bird and wildlife sanctuaries; ecology; organic food production; and conservation campaigning

WHAT IS NOT FUNDED Grants only made to registered charities. Grants to individuals are not given. The Trustees do not normally support medical or religious charities

WHO CAN BENEFIT Registered charities benefiting: young adults and older people; those in care, fostered and adopted; one parent families; ethnic minority groups; at risk groups; carers; ex-offenders and those at risk of offending; gays and lesbians; homeless people; immigrants and refugees; travellers; victims of abuse, crime and domestic violence and victims of war. Those suffering from HIV and AIDs and substance misuse

WHERE FUNDING CAN BE GIVEN Usually for work within the UK, but applicants from UK registered charities considered if there is strong civil liberty work in other countries

TYPE OF GRANT Core costs, feasibility studies, one-off, projects, research, running costs, salaries and start-up costs. All funding is for one year or less. They are usually for the general purposes of the registered charities supported

SAMPLE GRANTS £9,000 to Birth Control Trust; £9,000 to Immigrants' Aid Trust; £7,000 to Refugee Arrivals Project; £7,000 to Migrant Helpline; £4,000 to Education for Choice; £4,000 to Crisis; £4,000 to Medical Foundation for Victims of Torture; £4,000 to Parents Against Injustice; £4,000 to Prison Reform Trust; £4,000 to Release

FINANCES *Year* 1997–98 *Income* £89,314 *Grants* £175,000

TRUSTEES Michael Isaacs, Anthony Skyrme, Kenneth Plummer

PUBLICATIONS Full accounts are on file at the Charity Commission

HOW TO APPLY Requests for grants or further information must be in writing (not by telephone) and include a brief description of the aims and objects of the charity. Unsuccessful applications are not acknowledged unless an sae is enclosed

WHO TO APPLY TO Bowker, Orford, Chartered Accountants, Lyndhurst Settlement, 15–19 Cavendish Place, London W1M 0DD

CC NO 256063 **ESTABLISHED** 1968

■ The Lyndhurst Trust

WHAT IS FUNDED 41 per cent to Third world countries, 44 per cent to UK, 15 per cent to Europe and others. The maintenance of any charitable body connected with the propagation of the gospel or the promotion of the Christian religion. The distribution of Bibles and other Christian religious works. The support of Christian missions. The provision of clergy. The maintenance of churches and chapels. Work with the disadvantaged in society

WHAT IS NOT FUNDED Designated Christian organisations, not individuals – not buildings

WHO CAN BENEFIT Evangelistic Christian organisations, especially those operating where people have never had the opportunity of hearing the gospel. Those involved in difficult areas for Christian witness. Charities ministering to the needs of the disadvantaged in society are also funded

WHERE FUNDING CAN BE GIVEN UK and overseas with a preference for the North East of England

TYPE OF GRANT Supportive Christian work – recurrent – as necessary

RANGE OF GRANTS £100–£3,000

SAMPLE GRANTS £3,000 to Teen Challenge UK; £2,000 to Emmanuel Fellowship, Yarm; £1,800 to South Bank Baptist Church; £1,500 to Bible Mission International for work in Tibet and Mongolia; £1,500 to Middle East Christian Outreach in Kurdistan; £1,300 to Christ Church Eston; £1,300 to Eston Community Church; £1,000 to Bible Society in South America; £1,000 to Church Missionary Society in Sudan; £1,000 to European Christian Mission in Eastern Europe

FINANCES *Year* 1997 *Income* £51,083 *Grants* £65,250

TRUSTEES W P C Hinton, J A L Hinton, Dr W J Hinton

HOW TO APPLY By letter – no reply unless sae enclosed. Requests reviewed quarterly

WHO TO APPLY TO W P C Hinton, The Lyndhurst Trust, 66 High Street, Swainby, Northallerton, North Yorkshire DL6 3DG

CC NO 235252 **ESTABLISHED** 1964

■ The Lynn Foundation

WHAT IS FUNDED Promotion and encouragement of music, art, masonic charities, disabled and the aged

WHO CAN BENEFIT Registered charities, institutions benefiting musicians, textile workers and designers and artists. Older people and those who are disabled will also benefit

WHERE FUNDING CAN BE GIVEN UK

FINANCES *Year* 1996 *Income* £45,059 *Grants* £25,105

TRUSTEES S S Lynn, G T E Parsons, M D Johnstone, Sir David Wilson, J F Emmott

WHO TO APPLY TO G T E Parsons, Trustee, The Lynn Foundation, 17 Lewes Road, Haywards Heath, West Sussex RH17 7SP

CC NO 326944 **ESTABLISHED** 1985

■ The Lynwood Charitable Trust

WHAT IS FUNDED Advancement of religion and other charitable purposes including churches and church buildings

WHAT IS NOT FUNDED No grants to individuals

WHO CAN BENEFIT Organisations benefiting children

WHERE FUNDING CAN BE GIVEN Bedfordshire

TYPE OF GRANT Scholarships, bursaries and grants to educational establishments, not individuals. This includes grants for capital goods

FINANCES *Year* 1996 *Income* £27,073

TRUSTEES J S Barling, C R Harmer

WHO TO APPLY TO C R Harmer, The Lynwood Charitable Trust, Jacob Cavenagh & Skeet, Chartered Accountants, 6–8 Tudor Court, Sutton, Surrey SM2 5AE *Tel* 0181-643 1166

CC NO 289535   **ESTABLISHED** 1984

■ The Lyons Charitable Trust

WHAT IS FUNDED Homeless, medical research and children in need

WHO CAN BENEFIT Organisations benefiting; homeless people; research workers; medical professionals and children in need

WHERE FUNDING CAN BE GIVEN UK

TYPE OF GRANT Range of grants

RANGE OF GRANTS £5,000–£12,000

SAMPLE GRANTS £12,000 to Printers Charitable Corporation; £12,000 to the Florence Nightingale Fund; £12,000 to Great Ormond Street Hospital for Sick Children; £12,000 to WWF; £5,000 to Terence Higgins Trust

FINANCES *Year* 1998 *Income* £52,058
Grants £90,000

TRUSTEES M S Gibbon, A H Gillott, N R Noble

WHO TO APPLY TO Mrs H Fuff, The Lyons Charitable Trust, Field Fisher Waterhouse, 41 Vine Street, London EC3N 2AA

CC NO 1045650   **ESTABLISHED** 1995

■ Sir Jack Lyons Charitable Trust

WHAT IS FUNDED Charity for relief, arts, education and humanities

WHAT IS NOT FUNDED No grants to individuals

WHO CAN BENEFIT Charities benefiting: children and young people; actors and entertainment professionals; musicians; students; textile workers and designers; writers and poets; at risk groups; those disadvantaged by poverty; and socially isolated people

WHERE FUNDING CAN BE GIVEN UK and overseas

TYPE OF GRANT At Trustees' discretion

RANGE OF GRANTS £10–£194,046

SAMPLE GRANTS £194,046 to British ORT; £19,100 to Royal Academy of Arts; £13,377 to Mount Sinai Medical Center Trust; £12,500 to London Symphony Orchestra; £10,000 to York University; £6,259 to Greater Miami Jewish Federation; £6,061 to the International Centre for the Enhancement of Learning Potential; £5,500 to Joint Israel Appeal and the Charitable Organisations; £4,095 to Jewish National Fund for Israel; £3,128 to Cancer Association of Florida Inc

FINANCES *Year* 1997 *Income* £129,434
Grants £293,521

TRUSTEES Sir Jack Lyons, CBE, DUniv, Lady R M Lyons, M J Friedman, B Com, FCA, J E Lyons, D S Lyons

NOTES Applications from individuals are not considered

HOW TO APPLY Applications are considered at periodical meetings of the Trustees. No formal application form is issued

WHO TO APPLY TO M J Friedman, Sir Jack Lyons Charitable Trust, Sagar Croudson, 3rd Floor, Elizabeth House, Queen Street, Leeds LS1 2TW

CC NO 212148   **ESTABLISHED** 1960

■ The Malcolm Lyons Foundation

WHAT IS FUNDED General charitable purposes in accordance with the wishes of the Settlor and the Trustees

WHO CAN BENEFIT There are no restrictions on the age; professional and economic group; family situation; religion and culture; and social circumstances of; or disease or medical condition suffered by, the beneficiaries

WHERE FUNDING CAN BE GIVEN UK

SAMPLE GRANTS £16,313 to Mesorah Heritage Foundation; £500 to Joint Jewish Charitable Trust

FINANCES *Year* 1996 *Income* £26,667
Grants £16,813

TRUSTEES Ms Lyons, D Mendoza, J S Newman

WHO TO APPLY TO J S Newman, Trustee, The Malcolm Lyons Foundation, c/o BDO Stoy Hayward, 8 Baker Street, London W1M 1DA

CC NO 1050689   **ESTABLISHED** 1995

■ Sylvanus Lysons Charity

WHAT IS FUNDED Religious and charitable work in the areas of youth; community; relief for widows, clergy and the needy of the area Where Funding Can Be Given

WHAT IS NOT FUNDED No grants will be made for the repair or maintenance of churches or church buildings, except where exceptional circumstances can be demonstrated

WHO CAN BENEFIT Individuals and organisations benefiting: people of all ages; clergy; widows and widowers; and Church of England

WHERE FUNDING CAN BE GIVEN The Diocese of Gloucester

TYPE OF GRANT Buildings, capital, core costs, endowments, feasibility studies, interest free loans, one-off, project, research, recurring costs, running costs, salaries and start-up costs. Funding of up to or more than three years will be considered

SAMPLE GRANTS £21,000 to Glen Fall House, Cheltenham for building; £19,260 to King's School, Gloucester for bursaries; £10,000 to Barnwood Church for Visitor Centre; £5,000 to Matson Youth Centre for running costs; The Gloucester Diocesan Board of Finance received the following grants:; £15,065 for salary (stipend); £14,500 for building; £10,000 for salary (stipend); £9,400 for salary (stipend); £4,500 for ministry training; £3,865 for ordination training

FINANCES *Year* 1996–97 *Income* £144,215
Grants £145,445

TRUSTEES B V Day, G V Doswell, Rev G R H Smith, Ven C J H Wagstaff

HOW TO APPLY To the address under Who To Apply To in writing

WHO TO APPLY TO N A M Smith, Sylvanus Lysons Charity, c/o Messrs Rowberry Morris, Morroway House, Station Road, Gloucester GL1 1DW *Tel* 01452 301903

CC NO 202903   **ESTABLISHED** 1962

■ Lytchett Minster Turbary Allotment

WHAT IS FUNDED Youth, the elderly and community facilities

WHAT IS NOT FUNDED No grants to individuals

WHO CAN BENEFIT Organisations benefiting youth and the elderly of Lytchett Minster parish

WHERE FUNDING CAN BE GIVEN Lytchett Minster parish

SAMPLE GRANTS £9,677 to Lytchett Manor Sports Hall for building extension; £1,780 to Age Concern; £627 to Grove Youth Club; £300 to Darby and Joan Club; £82 to Lytchett Minster Schools for prizes

FINANCES *Year* 1997–98 *Income* £13,730 *Grants* £12,465

TRUSTEES Mrs J Desborough, W C Hancox, Sir T E Lees-Bart, Mrs M Pryor, J Sargeant, J C Small, A P Trickett

HOW TO APPLY To the address under Who To Apply To in writing

WHO TO APPLY TO P S James, Lytchett Minster Turbary Allotment, c/o James Harris, Hedge End Farm, Winterborne, Stickland, Blandford, Dorset DT11 0EB *Tel* 01258 881041 *Fax* 01285 881041

CC NO 264977   **ESTABLISHED** 1979

■ M and C Trust

WHAT IS FUNDED Primarily Jewish and welfare organisations

WHO CAN BENEFIT Mainly Jewish organisations benefiting: Jews; at risk groups; those disadvantaged by poverty and socially isolated people

WHERE FUNDING CAN BE GIVEN UK

TYPE OF GRANT Normally one-off grants

FINANCES *Year* 1995–96 *Income* £162,386 *Grants* £109,500

TRUSTEES A Bernstein, Mrs J B Kemble, A C Langridge

HOW TO APPLY To the address under Who To Apply To in writing

WHO TO APPLY TO A C Langridge, Trustee, M and C Trust, Messrs Chantrey Vellacott, Accountants, Russell Square House, 10–12 Russell Square, London WC1B 5LF

CC NO 265391   **ESTABLISHED** 1973

■ The M & N Foundation

WHAT IS FUNDED General charitable purposes

WHO CAN BENEFIT There are no restrictions on the age; professional and economic group; family situation; religion and culture; and social circumstances of; or disease or medical condition suffered by, the beneficiaries

WHERE FUNDING CAN BE GIVEN UK

TRUSTEES P N Ralph, M Thurman, Ms R Thurman

WHO TO APPLY TO Peter Ralph & Co, Financial Planner, The M & N Foundation, Suite 17, Queens Chambers, Shire Hall Complex, Pentonville, Newport, NP9 5HB

CC NO 1067784   **ESTABLISHED** 1998

■ MB Foundation (also known as Mossad Horav Moshe Aryeh Halevy)

This trust did not respond to CAF's request to amend its entry and, by 30 June 1998, CAF's researchers did not find financial records for later than 1995 on its file at the Charity Commission. Trusts are legally required to submit annual accounts to the Charity Commission under section 42 of the Charities Act 1993

WHAT IS FUNDED General charitable purposes. To judge each item by merit and considering available funds for the time being

WHO CAN BENEFIT There are no restrictions on the age; professional and economic group; family situation; religion and culture; and social circumstances of; or disease or medical condition suffered by, the beneficiaries

WHERE FUNDING CAN BE GIVEN UK

TYPE OF GRANT Donations, subsidies and in some cases loans

RANGE OF GRANTS UK

TRUSTEES Rabbi W Kaufman, Rabbi M Bamberger, S B Bamberger

HOW TO APPLY **Funds fully committed.** Applications will not be acknowledged

WHO TO APPLY TO S B Bamberger, Clark & Terry Ltd, Newhaven Business Park, Barton Lane, Eccles M30 0HH

CC NO 222104   **ESTABLISHED** 1958

388

Think carefully about every application. Is it justified?

■ The M D & S Charitable Trust

WHAT IS FUNDED Trustees are primarily interested in Jewish causes for either the relief of poverty or the advancement of education or religion

WHO CAN BENEFIT Organisations benefiting Jewish people. Support is given to rabbis, children and young adults, students, teachers and those disadvantaged by poverty

WHERE FUNDING CAN BE GIVEN UK

RANGE OF GRANTS Below £1,000–12,500

SAMPLE GRANTS £12,500 to Yeshivat Magen Avrohom; £12,000 to Yeshivat Gan Yaakov; £11,000 to Ponevez Aid and Benevolence Fund; £10,000 to Yeshivat Hechel Shimon Volozhin; £7,000 to Botei Avot Children's Town; £6,000 to Yeshivat Ponevez; £5,000 to Mifal Torah Vechesed Trust; £5,000 to Tifrach Torah Centre; £4,500 to Yeshivat Ofakim; £4,000 to Talmud Torah Tashbar

FINANCES *Year* 1996 *Income* £127,504 *Grants* £100,150

TRUSTEES M D Cymerman, Mrs S Cymerman

WHO TO APPLY TO M D Cymerman, The M D & S Charitable Trust, 22 Overlea Road, London E5 9BG

CC NO 273992   **ESTABLISHED** 1977

■ The MK Charitable Trust

WHAT IS FUNDED Jewish organisations

WHO CAN BENEFIT Organisations benefiting Jewish people

WHERE FUNDING CAN BE GIVEN UK, especially north east of England

FINANCES *Year* 1995–96 *Income* £376,229

TRUSTEES Z M Kaufman, I I Kaufman, J Kaufman

HOW TO APPLY To the address under Who To Apply To in writing

WHO TO APPLY TO The MK Charitable Trust, Cohen Arnold & Co, 13–17 Burlington Place, Regent Street, London W1X 2JP

CC NO 260439   **ESTABLISHED** 1966

■ MKR Charitable Trust (formerly Rose

Charitable Settlement)

WHAT IS FUNDED To assist Israel, support Jewish and other genuine local charities

WHAT IS NOT FUNDED Private schemes not normally sponsored

WHO CAN BENEFIT Both headquarters and local organisations benefiting Jews. There are no restrictions on the age; professional and economic group; family situation; religion and culture; and social circumstances of; or disease or medical condition suffered by, the beneficiaries

WHERE FUNDING CAN BE GIVEN Solihull

TYPE OF GRANT One-off

FINANCES *Year* 1996 *Income* £50,000 *Grants* £50,000

TRUSTEES M K Rose, Mrs I W Rose, H Aron, S Gould

HOW TO APPLY By written application to the address under Who To Apply To

WHO TO APPLY TO M K Rose, MKR Charitable Trust, 20 Coppice Close, Dovehouse Lane, Solihull, West Midlands B91 2ED *Tel* 0121-706 6558

CC NO 256336   **ESTABLISHED** 1968

■ MLC Charitable Trust

WHAT IS FUNDED To advance the education of American college students in England and Europe and other general charitable purposes

WHO CAN BENEFIT American college students

WHERE FUNDING CAN BE GIVEN UK and Europe

FINANCES *Year* 1995 *Income* £435,000

TRUSTEES Ms R A Arthur, Ms K H Burnham, Ms D E Tomlin

NOTES Income pays for tuition and fees, housing, transportation, activities etc. No grants given in 1995

WHO TO APPLY TO R G Lorenz, MLC Charitable Trust, 98 Great Russell Street, London WC1B 3LA

CC NO 1040378   **ESTABLISHED** 1994

■ The MT Trust

WHAT IS FUNDED General charitable purposes.The financial, material, social and psychological support of the needy

WHO CAN BENEFIT There are no restrictions on the age; professional and economic group; family situation; religion and culture; and social circumstances of; or disease or medical condition suffered by, the beneficiaries

WHERE FUNDING CAN BE GIVEN UK

TRUSTEES A Bishop, J H Lieberman, Ms P E Lieberman

WHO TO APPLY TO Dr J Lieberman, Trustee, The MT Trust, 93 Singleton Road, Salford M7 4LX

CC NO 1053270   **ESTABLISHED** 1996

■ MYA Charitable Trust

This trust did not respond to CAF's request to amend its entry and, by 30 June 1998, CAF's researchers did not find financial records for later than 1995 on its file at the Charity Commission. Trusts are legally required to submit annual accounts to the Charity Commission under section 42 of the Charities Act 1993

WHAT IS FUNDED Advancement of Orthodox Jewish religion and education

WHO CAN BENEFIT Children, young adults and Jewish people

WHERE FUNDING CAN BE GIVEN UK and overseas

TYPE OF GRANT At the discretion of the Trustees

TRUSTEES Rabbi A Sternbuch, C Rand, M Rothfeld

WHO TO APPLY TO M Rothfeld, MYA Charitable Trust, 25 Egerton Road, London N16 6UE

CC NO 299642   **ESTABLISHED** 1987

■ The E M MacAndrew Trust

WHAT IS FUNDED Trustees are interested in medical and children's charities primarily

WHO CAN BENEFIT Registered charities benefiting children. There is no restriction on the disease or medical condition suffered by the beneficiaries

WHERE FUNDING CAN BE GIVEN UK

FINANCES *Year* 1998 *Income* £42,427 *Grants* £30,500

TRUSTEES A R Nicholson, E P Colquhoun

HOW TO APPLY **This Trust states that it does not respond to unsolicited applications**

WHO TO APPLY TO J P Thornton, Administrator, The E M MacAndrew Trust, J P Thornton & Co, Accountants, Inglewood, Aylesbury, Buckinghamshire HP22 4HD *Tel* 01296 641858

CC NO 290736   **ESTABLISHED** 1984

Does the trust you have chosen match your needs? Haphazard applications waste postage and time

389

■ MacCabe Family Charitable Trust

WHAT IS FUNDED General charitable purposes

WHO CAN BENEFIT There are no restrictions on the age; professional and economic group; family situation; religion and culture; and social circumstances of; or disease or medical condition suffered by, the beneficiaries

WHERE FUNDING CAN BE GIVEN UK

FINANCES *Year* 1997 *Income* £50,000

WHO TO APPLY TO Mr MacCabe, MacCabe Family Charitable Trust, Masons Farm, Hampstead Marshall, Newbury, Berkshire RG20 0HT

CC NO 1042367   **ESTABLISHED** 1994

■ The Maccabi Foundation

WHAT IS FUNDED To promote the educational, religious and social welfare of youth, in particular but not exclusively Jewish youth

WHAT IS NOT FUNDED No grants to individuals

WHO CAN BENEFIT To benefit children and young adults, those disadvantaged by poverty and at risk groups. There is no restriction on the religion or culture of the beneficiaries, but preference is given to Jewish youth

WHERE FUNDING CAN BE GIVEN UK

TYPE OF GRANT To Maccabi Clubs and Maccabi Union

SAMPLE GRANTS £84,000 to Maccabi Union

FINANCES *Year* 1997 *Income* £85,632
Grants £86,509

TRUSTEES Members of the Council and Directors: F S Worms, FCA, E Rayman, R Glatter, FCA, K J Gradon, M L Phillips, FCA, A P Ohrenstein, FCA, J Barnett

WHO TO APPLY TO The Secretary, The Maccabi Foundation, Gildesgame House, 73A Compayne Gardens, London NW6 3RS

CC NO 306056   **ESTABLISHED** 1961

■ McCallum Bequest Fund

WHAT IS FUNDED Charitable institutions and associations for relief of poverty or disease in Glasgow and/or bursaries or scholarships for law students of Glasgow University. To use the whole income for grants each year to charitable organisations, not to individuals

WHAT IS NOT FUNDED No grants to individuals, organisations of a purely religious, educational or sporting nature or organisations outside Glasgow

WHO CAN BENEFIT Students and those disadvantaged by poverty. There is no restriction on the disease or medical condition suffered by the beneficiaries. Charitable institutions which can benefit Glasgow, mostly operating from Glasgow. Usually the Trustees do not consider for grants organisations which seem to them to be of a purely religious, sporting or educational nature

WHERE FUNDING CAN BE GIVEN Glasgow District

FINANCES *Year* 1995 *Income* £15,000
Grants £15,000

TRUSTEES R W B Morris, G G Morris, Mrs G E Morris

NOTES Few new applications are likely to succeed as it is normally the Trustees' policy to continue nearly all existing grants

HOW TO APPLY To the address under Who To Apply To by 1 December yearly

WHO TO APPLY TO Macdonalds, Solicitors, McCallum Bequest Fund, 1 Claremont Terrace, Glasgow, Scotland G3 7UQ

SC NO SCO 07713   **ESTABLISHED** 1914

■ The Eileen McCamman Trust

WHAT IS FUNDED Christian mission and evangelism

WHAT IS NOT FUNDED No funding for general charity work

WHO CAN BENEFIT Organisations benefiting Christians and Evangelists

WHERE FUNDING CAN BE GIVEN UK and overseas

TYPE OF GRANT Buildings, capital, core costs, one-off, project, running costs, salaries, and start-up costs. Funding is available for one year or less

RANGE OF GRANTS £500–£2,500

SAMPLE GRANTS The following grants were made for Christian Outreach:; £5,500 to Crosslinks; £5,000 to International Federation of Evangelical Students; £2,000 to Church Pastoral Aid Society; £2,000 to TEAR Fund

FINANCES *Year* 1997 *Income* £18,395
Grants £16,550

TRUSTEES Mrs D E Gales, S R Gales, C F Jones

NOTES Funds are fully allocated, therefore no additional grants are available

WHO TO APPLY TO S R Gales, The Eileen McCamman Trust, 137 Knutsford Road, Wilmslow SK9 6EL

CC NO 1005297   **ESTABLISHED** 1991

■ The McCarthy Foundation

WHAT IS FUNDED To help the elderly in need, particularly elderly victims of violence and crime

WHAT IS NOT FUNDED Restricted to registered charities and grants to individuals on low incomes

WHO CAN BENEFIT Elderly on low incomes and organisations helping elderly people who are at risk, those disadvantaged by poverty, socially isolated or victims of crime and violence

WHERE FUNDING CAN BE GIVEN UK

TYPE OF GRANT Starter finances and single donations

RANGE OF GRANTS £25–£20000

SAMPLE GRANTS £20,000 to SHACS; £20,000 to Nottinghamshire Constabulary; £10,000 to Care and Repair Leeds; £10,000 to Care and Repair Newham; £9,000 to G M Shrievalty Police Trust

FINANCES *Year* 1995 *Income* £24,200
Grants £100,495

TRUSTEES Sir Marcus Fox, Prof M Hall, Jane Kerr, M Cato, P Girling, S Metcalf, D Tufts, N Bannister, D Walden

NOTES Grants for individuals are given through organisations

HOW TO APPLY In writing to Company Secretary. Application form and guidelines on request

WHO TO APPLY TO The Administrator, The McCarthy Foundation, Homelife House, 26–32 Oxford Road, Bournemouth, Dorset BH8 8EZ

CC NO 297903   **ESTABLISHED** 1987

■ The McCorquodale Charitable Trust

WHAT IS FUNDED Accommodation and housing; religion; arts,culture and recreation; health; conservation and environment; community services and facilities; professional bodies; charity or voluntary umbrella bodies; and other charitable purposes will be considered

WHO CAN BENEFIT There are no restrictions on the age; professional and economic group; family situation; religion and culture; and social circumstances of; or disease or medical condition suffered by, the beneficiaries

WHERE FUNDING CAN BE GIVEN UK, Scotland

TYPE OF GRANT Buildings, core costs, project and research will be considered

RANGE OF GRANTS £100–£1,000

SAMPLE GRANTS £1,000 to The National Trust for Scotland; £1,000 to the Salisbury Cathedral Trust; £400 to Lincoln Cathedral Fabric Fund; £300 to Mental Health Foundation; £250 to St Paul's Church

FINANCES *Year* 1996 *Income* £14,082
Grants £6,025

TRUSTEES C N McCorquodale, Coutts & Co

WHO TO APPLY TO Mrs R A A Iles, Senior Trust Officer, The McCorquodale Charitable Trust, Coutts & Co, Trustee Dept, 440 Strand, London WC2R 0QS

CC NO 297697 **ESTABLISHED** 1986

■ The McCrone Charitable Trust

WHAT IS FUNDED Funding primarily educational, Christian and welfare organisations

WHAT IS NOT FUNDED No grants to individuals

WHO CAN BENEFIT Organisations benefiting children and young adults, students and Christians. There are few restrictions on the social circumstances of the beneficiaries

WHERE FUNDING CAN BE GIVEN UK and overseas

TYPE OF GRANT An annual award is made to a university. One–off grants are also made

TRUSTEES G A Maguire, D P MacLean, R G S Mackay

HOW TO APPLY Applications should be made in writing to the address below

WHO TO APPLY TO The Secretary, The McCrone Charitable Trust, Hardie Caldwell, Savoy Tower, Third Floor, 77 Renfrew Street, Glasgow G2 3BY

SC NO SCO 15385 **ESTABLISHED** 1977

■ The R S Macdonald Charitable Trust

WHAT IS FUNDED Grants are made to charities which focus on research into the origins, prevention of or alleviation of visual impairment and cerebral palsy; also to those which care for people affected by either or both of those conditions. Grants are also made to charities which work to prevent cruelty to children and animals

WHO CAN BENEFIT People with cerebral palsy and the visually impaired, children and animals at risk of cruelty

WHERE FUNDING CAN BE GIVEN Scotland

TYPE OF GRANT One-off, recurring costs, project and research will be considered. Funding may be given for up to three years

FINANCES *Year* 1998 *Income* £367,205
Grants £177,000

TRUSTEES E D Buchanan, D W A Macdonald, S C Macdonald, D G Sutherland, R K Austin

PUBLICATIONS Information is available from the Trust

HOW TO APPLY Applications should be made in writing to the address under Who To Apply To

WHO TO APPLY TO R K Austin, The R S Macdonald Charitable Trust, 27 Cramond Vale, Edinburgh EH4 6RB *Tel* 0131-312 6766

SC NO SCO 12710 **ESTABLISHED** 1978

■ The Findlay MacDonald Trust

WHAT IS FUNDED The advancement of religion, the advancement of education and the relief of poverty

WHO CAN BENEFIT Organisations benefiting children, young adults, students and those disadvantaged by poverty. People from many different cultures and religions will be considered

WHERE FUNDING CAN BE GIVEN UK

TRUSTEES D J Findlay MacDonald, J B Morris, G O McNair

WHO TO APPLY TO J B Morris, The Findlay MacDonald Trust, Chartered Accountants, 133 Albert Road, Widnes, Cheshire WA8 6LB

CC NO 1064902 **ESTABLISHED** 1997

■ Macdonald-Buchanan Charitable Trust

WHAT IS FUNDED General charitable purposes with a preference for charities of which the Trust has special interest, knowledge or association

WHAT IS NOT FUNDED The Trustees will not normally make grants to individuals

WHO CAN BENEFIT There are no restrictions on the age; professional and economic group; family situation; religion and culture; and social circumstances of; or disease or medical condition suffered by, the beneficiaries

WHERE FUNDING CAN BE GIVEN UK

FINANCES *Year* 1995 *Income* £123,587
Grants £95,100

TRUSTEES All correspondence to be via Kleinwort Benson Trustees Ltd

HOW TO APPLY To the address under Who To Apply To in writing. Appeals will not be acknowledged

WHO TO APPLY TO The Secretary, The Macdonald-Buchanan Charitable Trust, c/o Kleinwort Benson Trustees Ltd, PO Box 191, 10 Fenchurch Street, London EC3M 3LB

CC NO 209994 **ESTABLISHED** 1952

■ The McDougall Trust (registered with the Charity Commission as The Arthur McDougall Fund)

WHAT IS FUNDED To advance the knowledge of and to encourage the study of and research in: political or economic science and functions of government and the services provided to the community by public and voluntary organisations; into methods of election of and the selection and government of representative organisations whether national, civic, commercial, industrial or social; and representative democracy, its forms, functions and development and also its associated institutions. The Trustees consider applications and may make grants and provide financial assistance to any charity or individual having purposes analogous to the above Objects. Special priority is given to electoral research projects. The Trustees have established a library called the Lakeman Library for Electoral Studies at 6 Chancel Street, SE1. This is available for the use of research workers and the public generally on conditions laid down by the Trustees

WHAT IS NOT FUNDED No grants to any political party or commercial organisation or for an individual's education, or general appeals, expeditions, internships or scholarships

WHO CAN BENEFIT Charitable body/bodies benefiting academics and research workers, or individual(s)

WHERE FUNDING CAN BE GIVEN UK and overseas

TYPE OF GRANT Usually one-off for a specific project or part of a project – not usually exceeding £2,000. Applications for small 'pump-priming' grants are favoured over requests for the funding of large-scale projects. Feasibility studies and research grants are also considered. Funding is available for up to one year

RANGE OF GRANTS £250–£750

FINANCES *Year* 1996 *Income* £60,783
Grants £1,050

TRUSTEES One-third appointed every two years. Current Trustees: Tom Ellis (Chairman), Elizabeth Collingridge, Joan D Davies, Dr David M Farrell, Lindsay Mathieson, Michael Meadowcroft, John Ward

PUBLICATIONS *Representation: Journal of Representative Democracy*, (quarterly); *Twelve Democracies: Electoral Systems in the European Community*, (1991, 4th ed); Annual Report and Accounts

NOTES Trustees normally meet quarterly. Applications in writing. No application forms required. Brief details of proposal needed. Initial enquiries by telephone accepted. Two deadlines for receipt of applications: 1 May and 1 October. Applications received after a deadline may be held over for consideration at the Trustees' discretion

HOW TO APPLY To the Executive Secretary. Annual accounts required

WHO TO APPLY TO Paul Wilder, The Executive Secretary, The McDougall Trust, 6 Chancel Street, London SE1 0UX *Tel* 0171-620 1080 *Fax* 0171-928 1528

CC NO 212151   **ESTABLISHED** 1959

■ Macfarlane Walker Trust

WHAT IS FUNDED Grants to former employees and their families of Walker, Crosweller & Co Ltd, provision of educational facilities particularly for scientific research; encouragement of music, drama and appreciation of the fine arts. Also support for charities in the fields of: conservation; bird and wildlife sanctuaries; wildlife parks; environmental issues; transport and alternative transport; libraries and museums; and theatres and opera houses

WHAT IS NOT FUNDED No grants are given for: expeditions; scholarships; fees for specialised training courses in higher or further education; medical expenses or nationwide appeals

WHO CAN BENEFIT Individuals, registered charities and institutions benefiting: former employees of Walker, Crosweller and Co Ltd; musicians; research workers; and scientists. Support is also given to those suffering from mental illness

WHERE FUNDING CAN BE GIVEN Norfolk, Camden, Greenwich, Kensington and Chelsea, and Gloucestershire

TYPE OF GRANT Feasibility studies, one-off, project, research, running costs and start-up costs. Funding for up to and over three years will be considered

RANGE OF GRANTS £100–£3,000

FINANCES *Year* 1997 *Income* £36,714 *Grants* £28,191

TRUSTEES R F Walker, D F Walker, N G Walker

HOW TO APPLY By letter giving reason for appealing, outline of project with financial forecast. Sae must accompany initial application

WHO TO APPLY TO D A Launchbury, Secretary to the Trustees, Macfarlane Walker Trust, 32 Apple Orchard, Prestbury, Cheltenham GL52 3EH *Tel* 01242 521438

CC NO 227890   **ESTABLISHED** 1963

■ The Agnes McGallagley Bequest

WHAT IS FUNDED To maintain the Archbishop of Glasgow's residence and to support organisations concerned with Roman Catholicism, education and social welfare

WHO CAN BENEFIT Organisations benefiting children, young adults, Roman Catholics, at risk groups, those disadvantaged by poverty and socially isolated people

WHERE FUNDING CAN BE GIVEN Glasgow

TYPE OF GRANT Recurring grants are made to the Archbishop of Glasgow's residence

TRUSTEES Cardinal T J Winning

PUBLICATIONS Accounts are available from the Trust

NOTES The funds are fully committed at present and no applications are being considered

HOW TO APPLY Contact the address under Who To Apply To for further details

WHO TO APPLY TO The Chancellor, The Agnes McGallagley Bequest, 196 Clyde Street, Glasgow G1 4JY

SC NO SCO16377

■ The McGill University (Canada) Trust

WHAT IS FUNDED Scholarships, bursaries, maintenance allowances, prizes, grants, fellowships and professorships. Improvements and replacements of buildings

WHO CAN BENEFIT Organisations benefiting students and academics, particularly those at McGill University in Canada

WHERE FUNDING CAN BE GIVEN UK and overseas, in particular Canada

FINANCES *Year* 1996 *Income* £14,547

TRUSTEES J A Royle, G J Wasserman, Mrs L Kitchin, A P F Cumyn, W C Harker, Viscount C H N Hardinge, Hon J J Nelson, Hon F R Noel Paton, Lord Strathcona, V P M Dahdaleh, C A McCrae, M Tredgett

WHO TO APPLY TO Mrs L Kitchin, The McGill University (Canada) Trust, Little Frys, Burwash, East Sussex TN19 7HX

CC NO 1044904   **ESTABLISHED** 1995

■ The Mackaness Family Charitable Trust

WHAT IS FUNDED General charitable purposes

WHO CAN BENEFIT There are no restrictions on the age; professional and economic group; family situation; religion and culture; and social circumstances of; or disease or medical condition suffered by, the beneficiaries

WHERE FUNDING CAN BE GIVEN UK, in practice charities in the Yorkshire and Northamptonshire areas

RANGE OF GRANTS £10–£1,000

SAMPLE GRANTS £1,000 to Bramcote Centenary Foundation; £1,000 to Centenary Appeal Kettering General Hospital; £600 to the Benevolent Society; £600 to Northamptonshire S Charities; £500 to St Botolph's Church Organ Project; £400 to Variety Club of Great Britain; £400 to Mencap Promotions Ltd; £250 to Cancer Relief Macmillan Fund; £250 to Dolphin Society; £250 to Northampton Choral Foundation

FINANCES *Year* 1997 *Income* £43,307 *Grants* £8,190

WHO TO APPLY TO P Hudson, The Mackaness Family Charitable Trust, c/o A J Mackaness Ltd, Billing House, The Causeway, Great Billing, Northampton NN3 9EX

CC NO 1041868   **ESTABLISHED** 1994

Think carefully about every application. Is it justified?

■ The Simon and Suzanne McKenna Charity

WHAT IS FUNDED The relief of poverty, the advancement of education and other charitable purposes

WHAT IS NOT FUNDED Grants will not be made for overseas work, travel overseas, etc

WHO CAN BENEFIT Mainly individuals. Particularly those disadvantaged by poverty, children and young adults

WHERE FUNDING CAN BE GIVEN UK, especially Preston

FINANCES *Year* 1995 *Income* £114,870
Grants £10,000

TRUSTEES J L McKenna, P S McKenna, A M McKenna, J P McKenna, J Clark, M G Said

HOW TO APPLY To the address below in writing

WHO TO APPLY TO D R Hazzard, The Simon and Suzanne McKenna Charity, Messrs Wallwork Nelson and Johnson, Derby House, Lytham Road, Fulwood, Preston PR2 8JE

CC NO 1035881   **ESTABLISHED** 1994

■ J H M MacKenzie Charitable Trust

This trust did not respond to CAF's request to amend its entry and, by 30 June 1998, CAF's researchers did not find financial records for later than 1995 on its file at the Charity Commission. Trusts are legally required to submit annual accounts to the Charity Commission under section 42 of the Charities Act 1993

WHAT IS FUNDED The advancement of education, the relief of poverty, the promotion of religion. General charitable purposes

WHAT IS NOT FUNDED No grants to individuals

WHO CAN BENEFIT Registered charities only. There are no restrictions on the age; professional and economic group; family situation; religion and culture; and social circumstances of; or disease or medical condition suffered by, the beneficiaries

WHERE FUNDING CAN BE GIVEN UK

TRUSTEES J H M Mackenzie, J A H M Mackenzie, Mrs J H M Mackenzie

WHO TO APPLY TO J H M Mackenzie, Trustee, J H M MacKenzie Charitable Trust, Mortlake House, Vicarage Road, London NW14 8RU

CC NO 257936   **ESTABLISHED** 1968

■ The Robert McKenzie Trust

WHAT IS FUNDED General charitable purposes including the advancement of education and the relief of poverty

WHAT IS NOT FUNDED No application from individuals

WHO CAN BENEFIT Registered charities benefiting: children; young people; students; and those disadvantaged by poverty

WHERE FUNDING CAN BE GIVEN England only

TYPE OF GRANT Usually one-off

RANGE OF GRANTS Normally under £500

FINANCES *Year* 1997 *Income* £24,263
Grants £16,510

TRUSTEES M R Le Garst, D Sherborn, E R Waring, D K Wilson

WHO TO APPLY TO Patricia D Donald, The Robert McKenzie Trust, Messrs Underwood & Co, 40 Welbeck Street, London W1M 8LN *Tel* 0171-526 6000 *Fax* 0171-487 8974

CC NO 285586   **ESTABLISHED** 1982

■ McLaren Foundation

WHAT IS FUNDED Animal welfare, war disabled, regimental charities, distressed widows and pensioners, preservation of the national landscape and other general charitable purposes

WHAT IS NOT FUNDED Exclusions: owing to the Policy of Governments of both Parties in providing for political reasons ever-increasing numbers of University places, not only has the quality first of A levels and then of First Degrees (in order to achieve, despite the inevitable lower abilities of a larger intake, no more than a politically-acceptable proportion of failures) been debased, with a multiplication not only of Universities but of Degree Faculties some of which are of an almost farcical nature, but as a result the output of Degree holders much exceeds the number who can find suitable paid employment even in normal times. First Degrees (for which Grants are given) having thus been depreciated to the point at which Graduates find it necessary to attempt at once Second Degrees (for which no Grants are available). It is regretted that through lack of funds the Foundation cannot attempt to remedy the results of Government mismanagement by considering applications in respect of Degree studies. Similarly both the financing and the standards of Primary and Secondary Education have become a political kick-ball, and the Foundation has found it necessary to withdraw from this field in the UK. It is regretted also that no funds can be spared for outward bound schemes. Also enjoyable expeditions overseas for students on the pretext of some scientific investigation of doubtful utility that claims to compress into 2–3 weeks scientific work that would require a period of years, or to assist for a few weeks a native population (whose language usually they cannot speak) to carry out simple construction works that they are far better able to carry out themselves, given for materials even a fraction of the funds spent on the expedition, are not entertained

WHO CAN BENEFIT Individuals and organisations benefiting: ex-service and service people; widows and widowers; and disabled people

WHERE FUNDING CAN BE GIVEN UK

FINANCES *Year* 1997–98 *Income* £20,302
Grants £20,142

TRUSTEES H Arbuthnott, Mrs F S Maclaren Webster

HOW TO APPLY By letter addressed to 'The Trustees'. Sae not required (but if no grant can be made it is regretted that for reasons of economy no reply can be sent when an sae has not been provided). Charities or appeals that are able to state in their application that they do not employ professional fund-raisers or pay senior staff at commercial rates will be given priority for any funds available. The Trustees will use their best endeavours not to be prejudiced against an application that uses the jargon evolved by the new Welfare Industry such as 'caring', 'under-privileged' and 'deprived'

WHO TO APPLY TO Colonel S E Scammell, McLaren Foundation, Clouds Estate Office, East Knoyle, Salisbury, Wiltshire SP3 6BE

CC NO 240425   **ESTABLISHED** 1964

■ The Martin McLaren Memorial Trust

WHAT IS FUNDED Church and mental health

WHO CAN BENEFIT Institutions benefiting Christians and those suffering from mental illness

WHERE FUNDING CAN BE GIVEN UK

TYPE OF GRANT A range of grants

Does the trust you have chosen match your needs? Haphazard applications waste postage and time

393

RANGE OF GRANTS £50–£5,000

SAMPLE GRANTS £5,000 to SANE Research Centre, Oxford; £2,000 to Inkpen Church - St Michael's; £1,000 to Dolphin Society; £1,000 to St John's Church, Smith's Square; £1,000 to Combe Parish Church, St Swithun's

FINANCES *Year* 1995 *Income* £23,831 *Grants* £12,900

TRUSTEES Mrs N G McLaren, M R MacFadyen, Rev R F McLaren, N Durlacher

WHO TO APPLY TO M R MacFadyen, The Martin McLaren Memorial Trust, c/o Charles Russell, 8–10 New Fetter Lane, London EC4A 1RS

CC NO 291609   **ESTABLISHED** 1985

■ Macmillan Cancer Relief (formerly Cancer Relief Macmillan Fund and The National Society for Cancer Relief)

WHAT IS FUNDED Macmillan provides care and support for cancer patients and their carers at every stage of their illness. In partnership with the NHS it 'pump-primes' by grant new posts for specially trained Macmillan Nurses, Doctors, Social Workers and other health care professionals to care for patients in their own homes, in the community and in hospitals. It also builds Macmillan cancer care units which are run by the NHS to provide a comprehensive range of specialist services including day, home and in-patient care. The charity's education programme to train doctors and nurses in the skills of palliative care, particularly pain control, is now well established with a series of Macmillan lectureships in Universities throughout the UK together forming the Macmillan National Institute for Education. In addition, Macmillan gives practical help in the form of cash grants to cancer patients in financial difficulties for a wide range of needs. Finally, Macmillan finances other charities in the field. All offer support and information to people with various types of cancer

WHAT IS NOT FUNDED Very occasionally, studies in cancer and palliative care and related sociological matters and in rehabilitation aimed at improving the lives of cancer patients are supported. No grants will be given for equipment intended primarily to cure cancer

WHO CAN BENEFIT (a) Any cancer patient in need; (b) any NHS authority, hospice or NHS trust or NHS contractor; (c) any NHS authority, University, hospice or NHS trust or NHS contractor with teaching responsibilities for doctors, nurses, social workers and other health care professionals looking after cancer patients

WHERE FUNDING CAN BE GIVEN UK; Republic of Ireland (patient support only)

TYPE OF GRANT Buildings, core costs, feasibility studies, interest free loans, one-off, project, research, recurring costs, running costs, salaries and start-up costs. Funding of up to and over three years will be considered

RANGE OF GRANTS £50 to over £1 million

SAMPLE GRANTS £1,079,000 to King Edward VII Hospital for West Sussex Macmillan Service; £850,000 to Cancerlink for information services to patients; £826,000 to Bridgend and District NHS Trust for construction of hospice; £820,000 to Hinchingbrooke Health Care NHS Trust for construction of chemotherapy unit £728,000 to The Martlets Hospice, Brighton for construction of hospice; £678,000 to Lancaster Acute Hospitals NHS Trust for construction of oncology centre; £607,000 to Royal Surrey County NHS Trust for construction of cancer day centre; £549,000 to Plymouth Hospitals NHS Trust for construction of oncology suite; £509,000 to West Glasgow Hospitals University NHS Trust for construction of oncology centre; £500,000 to Breast Cancer Care for information/support services for patients

FINANCES *Year* 1997 *Income* £53,631,000 *Grants* £24,248,000

TRUSTEES The Members of the Board of Management: R Hambro (Chairman), J Asquith (Treasurer), Sir Christopher Benson, Jame Dundas, Sir Christopher France, Prof Geoffrey Hanks, The Duchessof Kent, David Male, CBE, Anthony Simonds-Gooding, Prof Jenifer Wilson-Barnett

HOW TO APPLY Initially by letter, or for patient welfare grant by standard application form

WHO TO APPLY TO The Secretary, Macmillan Cancer Relief, 15–19 Britten Street, London SW3 3TZ *Tel* 0171-351 7811 *Fax* 0171-376 8098

CC NO 261017   **ESTABLISHED** 1911

■ The Helen Isabella McMorran Charitable Foundation

WHAT IS FUNDED General charitable purposes in accordance with Settlor's wishes, including Girton College, Cambridge

WHAT IS NOT FUNDED No grants to individuals

WHO CAN BENEFIT Registered charities. There are no restrictions on the age; professional and economic group; family situation; religion and culture; and social circumstances of; or disease or medical condition suffered by, the beneficiaries. However, particular favour is given to Girton College, Cambridge

TYPE OF GRANT One-off

RANGE OF GRANTS £725–£1,050

SAMPLE GRANTS £1,050 to Royal Commonwealth Association for the Blind; £1,000 to Friends of Fitzwilliam Museum; £1,000 to Historic Churches Preservation Trust; £1,000 to the Homeless Furniture Project; £1,000 to St Andrew's Hospice; £1,000 to the Dystonia Society; £1,000 to National Ankylosing Spondylitis Society; £900 to Ely Cathedral Restoration Trust; £900 to Cambridge Preservation Society; £900 to St John Ambulance

FINANCES *Year* 1996–97 *Income* £28,112 *Grants* £14,350

TRUSTEES National Westminster Bank plc

WHO TO APPLY TO The Manager, National Westminster Bank Ltd, Helen Isabella McMorran Charitable Foundation, Financial & Investment Service, 62 Green Street, London W1Y 4BA

CC NO 266338   **ESTABLISHED** 1973

■ D D McPhail Charitable Settlement

WHAT IS FUNDED General charitable purposes

WHO CAN BENEFIT There are no restrictions on the age; professional and economic group; family situation; religion and culture; and social

circumstances of; or disease or medical condition suffered by, the beneficiaries

WHERE FUNDING CAN BE GIVEN UK

RANGE OF GRANTS £200–£1,000

SAMPLE GRANTS £1,000 to John Groom's Association for the Disabled; £1,000 to Leonard Cheshire Foundation; £700 to Harrow Blind Social club; £700 to National Society for Epilepsy; £600 to Cancer Relief Macmillan Fund

FINANCES *Year* 1996 *Income* £14,535 *Grants* £16,950

TRUSTEES Mrs P A Cruddas

WHO TO APPLY TO Mrs S Watson, D D McPhail Charitable Settlement, PO Box 285, Pinner, Middlesex HA5 3FB

CC NO 267588   **ESTABLISHED** 1973

■ Mactaggart Third Fund

WHAT IS FUNDED Grants are made to charities which are linked in some way to the family or which are based in Scotland

WHAT IS NOT FUNDED Grants are not made to individuals

WHO CAN BENEFIT Organisations. There are no restrictions on the age; professional and economic group; family situation; religion and culture; and social circumstances of; or disease or medical condition suffered by, the beneficiaries

WHERE FUNDING CAN BE GIVEN Scotland

TYPE OF GRANT Grants are usually one-off, but core funding will occasionally be considered

HOW TO APPLY Applications should be made to the address below in writing and must include details of the project and its budget

WHO TO APPLY TO Mactaggart Third Fund, 74 South Audley Street, London W1Y 5FF

SC NO SCO 14285

■ The Magdalen and Lasher Charity

WHAT IS FUNDED Pensions for the elderly in Hastings; other individuals in need; the elderly, sick and poor; counselling services

WHO CAN BENEFIT Individuals and organisations benefiting elderly people, at risk groups, those disadvantaged by poverty and socially isolated people. There is no restriction on the disease or medical condition suffered by the beneficiaries

WHERE FUNDING CAN BE GIVEN Hastings

SAMPLE GRANTS £30,000 to St Michael's Hospice Day Centre; £5,500 to Hastings Lifeline; £5,000 to Children of the Milky Way for nurses appeal; £3,500 to St Clements with All Saints Poor Fund; £3,500 to Relate; £3,400 to British Red Cross; £1,500 to Salvation Army Citadel, Hastings; £1,500 to Hastings Sea Cadets; £1,416 to HUCAC; £1,352 to All Souls Poor Fund

FINANCES *Year* 1995–96 *Income* £758,402 *Grants* £168,406

TRUSTEES J J Adams, M Cornes, G L Dengate, G R Douglas-Kellie, M J Foster, R J B Guy, N Harris, J S Hayward, D McRoberts, C R Morris, C L Richardson, A Slack, P R Smith, I M Steel, R D Stevens

NOTES £18,311 was donated to individuals and £82,356 to organisations, giving a total of £100,668 in aid grants. A further £58,875 was donated in pensions, £4,517 for pensioners' party and £4,346 in day care payments, giving an overall total of £168,406 in grants

HOW TO APPLY To the address under Who To Apply To in writing

WHO TO APPLY TO Christopher Langdon, Clerk to the Trustees, The Magdalen and Lasher Charity, Langham House, Albert Road, Hastings, East Sussex TN34 1QT

CC NO 211415   **ESTABLISHED** 1951

■ Magdalen Hospital Trust

WHAT IS FUNDED Projects for deprived children and young people

WHAT IS NOT FUNDED Non-registered charities

WHO CAN BENEFIT Organisations benefiting: deprived children and young adults up to 25 years; those in care, fostered and adopted, parents and children; one parent families and those disadvantaged by poverty

WHERE FUNDING CAN BE GIVEN UK

TYPE OF GRANT One-off

RANGE OF GRANTS £100–£3,000; typically £1,000

FINANCES *Year* 1995–96 *Income* £34,626

TRUSTEES Mrs M Gregory, Lady Holderness, Mrs B Lucas, Mrs S Gibson, J Martin, Rev R Mitchell, The Venerable F R Hazell, Miss D Lazenby, Miss W Stone, OBE, The Hon E Wood,

HOW TO APPLY Initial telephone calls from applicants welcome. Application form and guidelines available. Deadlines for applications given. Sae required

WHO TO APPLY TO Magdalen Hospital Trust, Furnham Rectory, Furnham Road, Chard, Somerset TA20 1AE *Tel* 01460 63167

CC NO 225878   **ESTABLISHED** 1963

■ The Miss P M Major Charitable Settlement

WHAT IS FUNDED To apply the Trust fund for the benefit of any of the following charitable purposes as the Trustees shall think fit: mental welfare, medical research and services, children, animals, heritage, the aged, the arts, the needy in any part of the world. The Trustees have regard to the specified objects of the Trust and to areas of interest of the Founder

WHAT IS NOT FUNDED No individuals will be supported

WHO CAN BENEFIT Organisations benefiting children, elderly people and those in need. There is no restriction on the disease or medical condition suffered by the beneficiaries. A wide range of social circumstances is considered for support. Medical professionals, research workers and those involved in the arts may benefit

WHERE FUNDING CAN BE GIVEN UK and overseas

RANGE OF GRANTS £500–£3,000

SAMPLE GRANTS £3,000 to St Michael's Church; £2,000 to St Nicholas Church; £1,900 to King Edward VII Hospital; £1,500 to Hearing Dogs for the Deaf; £1,000 to the Emily Appeal Fund

FINANCES *Year* 1996 *Income* £16,757 *Grants* £9,900

TRUSTEES B N A Weatherill, M Popham, Mrs N Baker

WHO TO APPLY TO Mrs N Baker, The Miss P M Major Charitable Settlement, Stilland, Chiddingfold, Surrey GU8 4SX

CC NO 276465   **ESTABLISHED** 1978

■ The Hugh Markham Trust

WHAT IS FUNDED General charitable purposes

WHO CAN BENEFIT There are no restrictions on the age; professional and economic group; family situation; religion and culture; and social

circumstances of; or disease or medical condition suffered by, the beneficiaries

WHERE FUNDING CAN BE GIVEN UK

FINANCES *Year* 1997 *Income* £132,870

TRUSTEES P W E Fitt, J P Hollington, D J Leatherdale, P A Leatherdale, N R Markham

NOTES It is the Trustees' intention to commence making charitable grants and donations during 1997

WHO TO APPLY TO Miss J P Hollington, The Hugh Markham Trust, Ellison and Co Solicitors, Headgate Court, Colchester, Essex CO1 1NP

CC NO 1052108   **ESTABLISHED** 1995

■ The Malachi Trust

WHAT IS FUNDED General charitable purposes

WHO CAN BENEFIT There are no restrictions on the age; professional and economic group; family situation; religion and culture; and social circumstances of; or disease or medical condition suffered by, the beneficiaries

WHERE FUNDING CAN BE GIVEN UK

TRUSTEES A J Ashton, R J Child, D S Flowers, B D Horner

NOTES The Trust's funds are fully committed at this time

HOW TO APPLY **This Trust states that it does not respond to unsolicited applications**

WHO TO APPLY TO A J Ashton, Trustee, The Malachi Trust, c/o The Investment Practice, 3 Berkeley Square, Clifton, Bristol BS8 1HL *Tel* 0117-929 4900

CC NO 1045939   **ESTABLISHED** 1995

■ The E D & F Man Ltd, Charitable Trust

WHAT IS FUNDED General charitable purposes. Favours causes near to or linked to our business

WHO CAN BENEFIT There are no restrictions on the age; professional and economic group; family situation; religion and culture; and social circumstances of; or disease or medical condition suffered by, the beneficiaries

WHERE FUNDING CAN BE GIVEN UK

FINANCES *Year* 1997 *Income* £277,324

TRUSTEES M J C Stone (Chairman), D Boehm, M W Metcalfe, S Fink, S J Nesbitt, A H Scott

HOW TO APPLY In writing. Trustees meet quarterly

WHO TO APPLY TO D Boehm, Director, The E D & F Man Ltd, Charitable Trust, Sugar Quay, Lower Thames Street, London EC3R 6DU

CC NO 275386   **ESTABLISHED** 1978

■ Man of the People Fund

WHAT IS FUNDED Welfare and care of handicapped children, grossly deprived children, disabled adults, frail elderly, the deaf and the blind, cancer research

WHAT IS NOT FUNDED No grants made to individuals or to charities on behalf of individuals. No part of Trust funds to be applied to or for benefit of Mirror Group Newspapers Ltd

WHO CAN BENEFIT Registered charities concerned with welfare of deprived children, the blind and the deaf, disabled adults and handicapped children (mainly hereditary disorders), the frail elderly. Charities promoting medical research into disorders encountered in UK special schools for the handicapped child, including carers

WHERE FUNDING CAN BE GIVEN UK only

TYPE OF GRANT Mainly one-off sums for capital projects

FINANCES *Year* 1998 *Income* £18,322
Grants £30,000

TRUSTEES The Editor; Chairman; Finance Director; Company Secretary of 'The People'

NOTES Disbursements made only in March when total collected is distributed. No grants made to individuals

HOW TO APPLY Applications must be from registered charities and in writing, accompanied by supporting literature, etc. Applications can be made at any time but grants are given only in March of each year when the entire proceeds of the annual appeal to 'The People' readers is distributed, leaving no residue

WHO TO APPLY TO John Smith, Trust Administrator, Man of the People Fund, The People, Mirror Group, 1 Canada Square, Canary Wharf, London E14 5AP

CC NO 258111   **ESTABLISHED** 1968

■ Foundation for Management Education

WHAT IS FUNDED Improvement of quality and relevance of management education and development by encouraging and supporting innovation in management education in the leading UK business schools and colleges; enhancing the supply and quality of management teachers; encouraging the development of research into management education and teaching methods; and supporting innovative developments in management education for managers operating within a highly competitive environment

WHAT IS NOT FUNDED Individual applications for further studies cannot be entertained

WHO CAN BENEFIT UK business schools and management studies departments benefiting young adults, older people and students

WHERE FUNDING CAN BE GIVEN UK

FINANCES *Year* 1997 *Income* £125,884
Grants £50,248

TRUSTEES Council of Management

HOW TO APPLY **Unsolicited applications not encouraged**

WHO TO APPLY TO P C Farmer, Director & Secretary, Foundation for Management Education, 29 Beaumont Street, Oxford OX1 2NP

CC NO 313388   **ESTABLISHED** 1960

■ The Manchester and Salford Saturday and Convalescent Homes' Fund

WHAT IS FUNDED Priority is given to health authorities and NHS trusts, with hospices, homes for people with disabilities and welfare organisations also within the Trust's scope

WHO CAN BENEFIT Health authorities and welfare charities benefiting: disabled people; at risk groups; those disadvantaged by poverty; and the socially isolated. There are no restrictions on the disease or medical condition suffered by the beneficiaries

WHERE FUNDING CAN BE GIVEN Manchester and surrounding region

RANGE OF GRANTS £400–£9,000

396

Think carefully about every application. Is it justified?

SAMPLE GRANTS £9,000 to Salford Royal Hospitals NHS Trust; £7,345 to South Manchester University Hospitals NHS Trust; £7,000 to Manchester Central Hospitals and Community Care NHS Trust; £6,250 to North Manchester Healthcare Services NHS Trust; £5,280 to Tameside and Glossop Health Services NHS Trust; £4,290 to Blackpool Victoria Hospital NHS Trust; £4,275 to Blackburn, Hyndburn and Ribble Valley Healthcare, NHS Trust; £4,000 to Trafford Healthcare NHS Trust; £3,510 to Bury General Hospital HA Endowment Account; £3,400 to Preston Acute Hospitals NHS Trust

FINANCES *Year* 1995 *Income* £100,000 *Grants* £88,099

TRUSTEES Executive Committee: H Tomlinson, W A B Hargreaves, L Martin, Mrs J W Cameron, Mrs R J Carroll, B Cowman, D J Keeley, L Pattison, J Platt, E Sharples, Mrs S Whittaker, Mrs I Widdowson, Mrs G Workmaster, D Kilgannon, Mrs M Elliot

HOW TO APPLY To the address under Who To Apply To in writing

WHO TO APPLY TO Richard Sear, Executive, The Manchester and Salford Saturday and Convalescent Homes' Fund, 43–45 Lever Street, Manchester M60 7HP

CC NO 260031   **ESTABLISHED** 1969

■ The Manchester Guardian Society Charitable Trust

WHAT IS FUNDED General charitable purposes. The emphasis is very much on helping the Greater Manchester area

WHAT IS NOT FUNDED The Trustees do not give grants to individuals. They very much prefer the applicant to be a registered charity although this is not mandatory

WHO CAN BENEFIT Preference is usually shown to the smaller charity operating within Greater Manchester. There are no restrictions on the age; professional and economic group; family situation; religion and culture; and social circumstances of; or disease or medical condition suffered by, the beneficiaries

WHERE FUNDING CAN BE GIVEN Greater Manchester

TYPE OF GRANT Primarily small single capital projects not exceeding £5,000

RANGE OF GRANTS £200–£5,000

SAMPLE GRANTS £5,000 to the Big Step; £5,000 to Rainbow Family Trust; £2,000 to Dean and Canon of Manchester Cathedral; £2,000 to Emmanuel Community; £1,700 to Rathbone Society; £1,600 to Church Lads and Church Girls Brigade; £1,500 to Daubhill and Derby Churches; £1,500 to Disabled Living Services; £1,500 to FWA Limited; £1,500 to Overward Project

FINANCES *Year* 1997 *Income* £110,707 *Grants* £85,566

TRUSTEES P R Green, G D Thomas, D A Sutherland, W R Lees-Jones, Mrs J Powell, D G Wilson, Mrs J Harrison, Mrs O Haig, W J Smith, P Goddard, J P Wainwright

PUBLICATIONS An Annual Report and Accounts is prepared and the Annual General Meeting is held either at the September meeting or the November meeting of the Trustees

HOW TO APPLY Applications are considered at quarterly meetings of the Trustees which take place on the first Monday in March, June and September and the last Monday in November. Applications should be received at least 14 days before these dates

WHO TO APPLY TO J A H Fielden, The Manchester Guardian Society Charitable Trust, Cobbetts, Ship Canal House, King Street, Manchester M2 4WB

CC NO 515341   **ESTABLISHED** 1984

■ Victor Mann Trust Fund

WHAT IS FUNDED The welfare and provision of accommodation for the aged poor of the area Where Funding Can Be Given

WHO CAN BENEFIT Individuals and local organisations benefiting older people, those disadvantaged by poverty and homeless people

WHERE FUNDING CAN BE GIVEN Wallsend

SAMPLE GRANTS £1,225 to Age Concern; £686 to Diabetes Foundation; £500 to Wallsend Vol Cottee Blind; £200 to Eden Court; £64 to Community Transport

FINANCES *Year* 1996 *Income* £36,417 *Grants* £2,675

HOW TO APPLY To the address under Who To Apply To in writing. Applications are considered in April, July, September and December

WHO TO APPLY TO F Lillie, Secretary, Victor Mann Trust Fund, Care in the Community, Elton Street, Wallsend, Tyne and Wear NE28 6BR

CC NO 215476   **ESTABLISHED** 1956

■ R W Mann Trustees Limited

WHAT IS FUNDED Charities working in the fields of: accommodation and housing; infrastructure, support and development; arts education; cultural activity; health; conservation and environment; education and training; and social care and development. Other charitable purposes will be considered

WHAT IS NOT FUNDED No grants to individuals

WHO CAN BENEFIT Local activities or local branches of national charities benefiting children; young adults; older people; academics; seafarers and fishermen; students; teachers and governesses; unemployed people; volunteers; those in care, fostered and adopted; parents and children; one parent families; widows and widowers; at risk groups; carers; disabled people; those disadvantaged by poverty; homeless people; those living in urban areas; victims of abuse, crime and domestic violence. Beneficiaries suffering from Alzheimer's disease, autism, cancers, cerebral palsy, Crohn's disease, mental illness, motor neurone disease, multiple sclerosis, muscular dystrophy and sight loss will be considered

WHERE FUNDING CAN BE GIVEN Usually Tyne and Wear, occasionally beyond with a preference for North Tyneside

TYPE OF GRANT Recurrent expenditure, capital or single expenditure. Fixed grants out of income. Buildings, core costs, feasibility studies, interest free loans, one-off and project funding for one year or less will be considered

RANGE OF GRANTS £250–£7,000

Does the trust you have chosen match your needs? Haphazard applications waste postage and time

397

SAMPLE GRANTS £7,000 to Rising Sun Farm Trust for consultancy for organic farm and countryside park; £5,000 to Fairbridge Tyne and Wear for young people at risk; £5,000 to Marden Residents' Association for extension to community centre; £5,000 to Tyne and Wear Foundation for Millennium awards; £4,000 to Total Learning Challenge Project for special learning for disturbed children; £4,000 to Newcastle CVS for core funding; £4,000 to Tyne and Wear Foundation for core funding; £3,000 to Barnardos, Whitley Bay for The Base Project – Poverty in North Tyneside; £3,000 to Funding Information North East for advice for charities and voluntary groups

FINANCES *Year* 1997 *Income* £128,915 *Grants* £140,795

TRUSTEES The Directors: Mrs J Hamilton, Mrs A M Heath, G Javens

NOTES Please enclose an sae

HOW TO APPLY At any time in the year subject to funds being available. Trustees' meetings are held approximately at intervals of three months. There are no application forms

WHO TO APPLY TO R W Mann Trustees Limited, PO Box 119, Gosforth, Newcastle upon Tyne NE3 4WF *Tel* 0191-284 2158 *Fax* 0191-285 8617 *E-mail* John.Hamilton@onyx.octacon.co.uk

CC NO 259006   **ESTABLISHED** 1959

■ Leslie & Lilian Manning Trust

WHAT IS FUNDED To assist mainly charities in the North-East – principally those in the field of medicine and health and welfare

WHAT IS NOT FUNDED Applications from individuals including students are ineligible. No educational grants for individuals

WHO CAN BENEFIT Charities or organisations working in the areas outlined under What Is Funded. Principally those with local affinities benefiting at risk groups, those disadvantaged by poverty, socially isolated people, and the sick and disabled. There is no restriction on the disease or medical condition suffered by the beneficiaries

WHERE FUNDING CAN BE GIVEN Principally the North East

TYPE OF GRANT Annual – but not necessarily recurrent

RANGE OF GRANTS £100–£3,500

SAMPLE GRANTS £3,500 to The Salvation Army Special Building Appeal; £2,000 to High Gosforth Youth Centre; £1,200 to Marie Curie Memorial Foundation for Conrad House; £1,000 to Children's Foundation; £1,000 to Save the Children Fund (North East); £1,000 to The Salvation Army; £1,000 to Tyneside Cyrenians; £950 to Dr Barnardos Home; £950 to NSPCC; £to Cancer Relief Macmillan Fund

FINANCES *Year* 1997 *Income* £33,843 *Grants* £33,300

TRUSTEES D J M Wilson, N Sherlock, P Jones, D Jones

HOW TO APPLY Once a year in January. Trustees meet in March

WHO TO APPLY TO D Wilson, Leslie & Lilian Manning Trust, Messrs Eversheds, Milburn House, Dean Street, Newcastle upon Tyne, Tyne and Wear NE1 1NP

CC NO 219846   **ESTABLISHED** 1960

■ Manor House Charitable Trust

WHAT IS FUNDED Very general in type but preference for local charities and projects

WHO CAN BENEFIT All applications considered. There are no restrictions on the age; professional and economic group; family situation; religion and culture; and social circumstances of; or disease or medical condition suffered by, the beneficiaries

WHERE FUNDING CAN BE GIVEN Local to Nottingham

FINANCES *Year* 1997 *Income* £18,550 *Grants* £21,472

TRUSTEES W F Whysall, D W Little, P V Little

HOW TO APPLY Applications in writing and accompanied by audited accounts dated within 12 months of application. Unsuccessful applications not notified

WHO TO APPLY TO The Trustees, Manor House Charitable Trust, Eversheds, 1 Royal Standard Place, Nottingham NG1 6FZ

CC NO 328691   **ESTABLISHED** 1989

■ Maranatha Christian Trust

WHAT IS FUNDED General at Trustees' discretion

WHO CAN BENEFIT Individuals and institutions. There are no restrictions on the age; professional and economic group; family situation; religion and culture; and social circumstances of; or disease or medical condition suffered by, the beneficiaries

WHERE FUNDING CAN BE GIVEN UK

TYPE OF GRANT At the discretion of the Trustees

RANGE OF GRANTS £200–£35,000

SAMPLE GRANTS £35,000 to CARE Trust; £10,000 to Riding Lights; £10,000 to Stewards Trust; £9,000 to Prison Fellowship; £8,000 to Nairobi Cathadral Primary School; £7,500 to Portman House Trust; £7,000 to Ashburnham Thanksgiving Trust; £5,000 to InterHealth; £5,000 to Oasis Media; £5,000 to Kingston Charitable Trust (Ukraine)

FINANCES *Year* 1997 *Income* £62,624 *Grants* £215,450

TRUSTEES A C Bell, Rev L Bowring, Viscount Brentford

WHO TO APPLY TO The Secretary, Maranatha Christian Trust, 68 Roslyn Gardens, Gidea Park, Essex RM2 5RD

CC NO 265323   **ESTABLISHED** 1972

■ The Marchday Charitable Fund

WHAT IS FUNDED Smaller charities where our contribution will make a noticeable difference covering: advice and information (housing); emergency and short term housing; respite; arts education; economic regeneration schemes; support to voluntary and community organisations; support to volunteers; health care; convalescent homes; rehabilitation centres; special schools and special needs education; training for work; vocational training and community services

WHAT IS NOT FUNDED No grants to individuals or for scholarships or expeditions

WHO CAN BENEFIT Organisations benefiting children; young adults and older people; those in care, fostered and adopted; parents and children; one parent families; disabled people; those disadvantaged by poverty; ex-offenders and those at risk of offending; homeless people; immigrants and refugees; victims of famine and war. Those suffering from: Alzheimer's disease; cystic fibrosis; HIV and AIDs; mental illness; paediatric disease; psoriasis; substance abuse and terminal illness

WHERE FUNDING CAN BE GIVEN London and South-East England

TYPE OF GRANT Capital, core costs, one-off, project, recurring costs, salaries and start-up costs. All funding is up to three years

RANGE OF GRANTS £1,000–£6,000

SAMPLE GRANTS £7,000 to The refugee Council for volunteer co-ordinator (part funded); £6,300 to The Core Trust for drug therapy project using non-invasive methods; £6,000 to The Medical Foundation for relief of Victims of Torture for a supervising doctor (part funding); £5,000 to Kith and Kids supporting camp for disabled children and working with families; £4,000 to National Missing Persons Helpline financial support; £4,000 to Red R to support work of engineers, etc on aid projects; £3,500 to Horticultural Therapy to support garden projects for the disabled; £3,000 to Anne Frank Educational Trust to support travelling exhibition in UK; £3,000 to Live Music Now! to support concerts for those with disabilities/learning difficulties; £3,000 to Psoriatic Arthropathy to support annual conference for sufferers

FINANCES *Year* 1995 *Income* £50,000 *Grants* £53,000

TRUSTEES D Goldstein, D Leigh, Mrs R Leigh, A Mann, L Mann, Ms M Quinn

HOW TO APPLY In writing, preferably with budget details

WHO TO APPLY TO Mrs R Leigh, The Marchday Charitable Fund, The Marchday Group plc, Allan House, 10 John Princes Street, London W1M 0AH

CC NO 328438   **ESTABLISHED** 1989

■ Marchig Animal Welfare Trust

WHAT IS FUNDED General animal welfare. Support of those engaged in work aimed at preventing or reducing animal suffering. Promotion of alternative methods to animal experimentation. Promotion and encouragement of practical work in preventing cruelty to animals. Periodic awards, known as the Marchig Animal Welfare Awards are made for outstanding work in the furtherance of the above aims. The awards are worth £8,000 and £16,000 and can be split. The following areas are also supported: animal homes; bird and wildlife sanctuaries; cats and catteries, dogs and kennels other facilities; horses and stables, environmental issues, heritage and wildlife parks may also be considered

WHAT IS NOT FUNDED Applications from students attending courses, going on expeditions, study trips, travel bursaries, etc do not qualify for a grant from the Trust and will therefore not be considered

WHO CAN BENEFIT National and international organisations and individuals working for the protection of animals

WHERE FUNDING CAN BE GIVEN UK and overseas, in Europe, Asia and Africa

FINANCES *Year* 1997 *Grants* £9,590

TRUSTEES Jeanne Marchig, Trevor C Scott, Les Ward

HOW TO APPLY Applications assessed continuously. Trustees meet twice a year. Copy of applicant's annual accounts required

WHO TO APPLY TO Mrs Jeanne Marchig, Chairperson, Marchig Animal Welfare Trust, PO Box 14, 1223 Cologny, Geneva, Switzerland *Fax* ++41 22 349 6458

CC NO 802133   **ESTABLISHED** 1989

■ The Marchon Works Employees Charity Fund

WHAT IS FUNDED Recipients of grants include individuals for wheelchairs and stairlifts, as well as hospitals, community organisations and facilities. Other areas of funding include: residential facilities; respite and sheltered accommodation; infrastructure, support and development; churches; music; health care; schools and colleges; community centres and village halls; recreation grounds; community services; and advice centres

WHAT IS NOT FUNDED No grants for expeditions or scholarships

WHO CAN BENEFIT Individuals and some organisations benefiting: people of all ages; retired people; students; carers; disabled people; those disadvantaged by poverty; ex-offenders and those at risk of offending; and victims of domestic violence. Those suffering from various diseases and medical conditions

WHERE FUNDING CAN BE GIVEN Copeland and Allerdale districts within the County of Cumbria

TYPE OF GRANT One-off donations

RANGE OF GRANTS £10–£1,600

SAMPLE GRANTS The following grants were made to individuals:: £1,492 for a PC and monitor; £1,486 for a stairlift; £1,450 for a stairlift; £1,350 for a stairlift; £962 for bathroom/shower refurbishment; £750 for hydrobath; £567 for a cooker and bath; £500 to West Cumbria Ambulances for Romania as a donation towards fuel costs; £455 for resiting a stairlift

FINANCES *Year* 1996–97 *Income* £35,201 *Grants* £15,860

TRUSTEES M McLaughlin (Chairman), Mrs A Ryan (Secretary), D Smitham, (Treasurer), Miss C Baxter, Mrs L C Jones, D Douglas, Dr M E Thompson, A Monkhouse, J Moore, J Prince, S Tumelty, A Moore

HOW TO APPLY To the address under Who To Apply To in writing. Initial telephone calls are welcome. There are no application forms, guidelines or deadlines, and no sae is required

WHO TO APPLY TO D Smitham, Treasurer, Marchon Works Employees Charity Fund, Albright & Wilson Ltd, Marchon Works, Whitehaven, Cumbria CA28 9QQ *Tel* 01946 68216 *Fax* 01946 68181

CC NO 510504   **ESTABLISHED** 1980

■ The Earl of March's Trust Company Ltd

WHAT IS FUNDED Overseas aid, medical, welfare, Christian, disabled, animal welfare, including emergency and short-term housing and housing associations; community development; economic regeneration schemes and support to voluntary organisations. Funding is given to churches and Christian organisations; the arts; alternative health care, hospices and hospitals. Church and historic buildings, animal welfare and homes, education and training, and social care and development will be supported

WHAT IS NOT FUNDED No grants to individuals, students or overseas expeditions

WHO CAN BENEFIT Organisations benefiting: people of all ages; clergy; retired and unemployed people; those in care, fostered and adopted; one parent families; widows and widowers; Christians, Church of England and ethnic minority groups. Support may be given for disabled people, those disadvantaged by poverty, homeless people, those living in rural areas, victims of disasters, famine and war. Those suffering from mental illness, substance misuse and who are terminally ill

WHERE FUNDING CAN BE GIVEN UK and overseas, with some preference for Sussex especially West Sussex

TYPE OF GRANT Largely one-off, some recurrent for core costs, feasibility studies, interest free loans, project, running costs, salaries and start-up costs. Funding is available for up to three years

RANGE OF GRANTS £250–£1,000

SAMPLE GRANTS **Grants are only made to charities known personally to the Trustees**

FINANCES *Year* 1996–97 *Income* £19,000
Grants £9,000

TRUSTEES Duke of Richmond and Gordon, FCA, Duchess of Richmond, Sir Peter Hordern, MP, Mrs C M Ward

NOTES Criteria are strictly adhered to

WHO TO APPLY TO Duke of Richmond, The Earl of March's Trust Company Ltd, Goodwood House, Chichester, West Sussex PO18 0PX
Tel 01243 755000 *Fax* 01243 755005
CC NO 220116   **ESTABLISHED** 1956

■ The Linda Marcus Charitable Trust

WHAT IS FUNDED Education, welfare, the arts and health

WHO CAN BENEFIT Children; young adults; actors and entertainment professionals; musicians; textile workers and designers; and writers and poets

WHERE FUNDING CAN BE GIVEN UK and overseas

TYPE OF GRANT Recurrent and one-off

FINANCES *Year* 1995–96 *Income* £137,934

TRUSTEES Sir Leslie Porter, Dame Shirley Porter, Mrs Linda Marcus

HOW TO APPLY To the address under Who To Apply To in writing

WHO TO APPLY TO Sarah Saint, Secretary, The Linda Marcus Charitable Trust, 12 Hans Road, London SW3 1RT

CC NO 267173   **ESTABLISHED** 1974

■ The Mardon Charitable Trust

WHAT IS FUNDED General charitable purposes

WHO CAN BENEFIT There are no restrictions on the age; professional and economic group; family situation; religion and culture; and social circumstances of; or disease or medical condition suffered by, the beneficiaries

WHERE FUNDING CAN BE GIVEN UK and overseas

TRUSTEES Mardon Associates Ltd, W D Ashcroft, M M Edwards

WHO TO APPLY TO W Ashcroft, Trustee, The Mardon Charitable Trust, Woodcroft, Seymour Plain, Marlow, Buckinghamshire SL7 3DA

CC NO 1054501   **ESTABLISHED** 1996

■ The Margaret Foundation

WHAT IS FUNDED Medical research, welfare of elderly and children and the general relief of suffering

WHAT IS NOT FUNDED No personal applications please

WHO CAN BENEFIT Organisations benefiting children, older people, retired people, those disadvantaged by poverty, at risk groups, socially isolated people and disabled people. There are no restrictions on the disease or medical condition suffered by the beneficiaries

WHERE FUNDING CAN BE GIVEN UK

TYPE OF GRANT One-off

RANGE OF GRANTS £250–£6,000

SAMPLE GRANTS £6,000 to Parents For Children which funds foster and adoptive families for 'unplaceable' children; £3,000 to Childline to cover the cost of training a new volunteer for Childline; £2,100 to The Starting Point for Information and Youth Training Centre in Liverpool; £1,000 to West London Action for Children for profession Childcare service for abused, neglected or ill treated children; £1,000 to The Toxoplasmosis Trust towards work supporting families affected by Toxoplasmosis

FINANCES *Year* 1996–97 *Income* £18,186
Grants £13,100

TRUSTEES Royal Bank of Canada Trust Corporation Limited

HOW TO APPLY June and December. No application forms. Send your application in under cover of a letter and include latest set of report and accounts

WHO TO APPLY TO Mrs S Tayler, The Margaret Foundation, Royal Bank of Canada Trust Corporation Limited, 71 Queen Victoria Street, London EC4V 4DE

CC NO 1001583   **ESTABLISHED** 1990

■ Margulies Charitable Foundation Ltd

WHAT IS FUNDED Advancement of Orthodox Jewish faith; relief of hardship and distress

WHO CAN BENEFIT Organisations benefiting: Jewish people; at risk groups; those disadvantaged by poverty and socially isolated people

WHERE FUNDING CAN BE GIVEN UK

TRUSTEES E S Margulies, M Margulies

NOTES Trustees are not considering new applications at the moment

WHO TO APPLY TO Casson Beckman, Auditor, Margulies Charitable Foundation Ltd, Hobson House, 155 Lower Street, London WC1E 6BJ

CC NO 299255   **ESTABLISHED** 1983

■ The Stella and Alexander Margulies Charitable Trust

WHAT IS FUNDED Jewish charities

WHO CAN BENEFIT Institutions benefiting Jews. There are no restrictions on the age; professional and economic group; family situation; and social circumstances of; or disease or medical condition suffered by, the beneficiaries

WHERE FUNDING CAN BE GIVEN UK

TYPE OF GRANT A range of grants

FINANCES *Year* 1997 *Income* £244,822
Grants £84,329

TRUSTEES M J Margulies, M D Paisner

WHO TO APPLY TO M J Margulies, The Stella and Alexander Margulies Charitable Trust, 23 Grosvenor Street, London W1X 9FE

CC NO 220441   **ESTABLISHED** 1970

■ The Maristow Trust

WHAT IS FUNDED General charitable purposes including education, youth and welfare

WHAT IS NOT FUNDED No grants to individuals

WHO CAN BENEFIT There are no restrictions on the age; professional and economic group; family situation; religion and culture; and social circumstances of; or disease or medical condition suffered by, the beneficiaries

WHERE FUNDING CAN BE GIVEN Devon and Cornwall

TYPE OF GRANT Funding of up to one year may be considered

FINANCES *Year* 1995–96 *Income* £41,424

HOW TO APPLY To the address under Who To Apply To in writing

WHO TO APPLY TO Miss M Hayward, The Maristow Trust, Maristow Estate Office, Common Lane, Roborough, Plymouth PL6 7BN
Tel 01752 695945

CC NO 250953   **ESTABLISHED** 1967

■ Michael Marks Charitable Trust

WHAT IS FUNDED Conservation and environment, and the arts

WHAT IS NOT FUNDED No grants to individuals

WHO CAN BENEFIT Those involved in the arts, conservation and the environment

WHERE FUNDING CAN BE GIVEN UK and overseas

SAMPLE GRANTS £1,000 to English Bach Festival; £800 to London Hellenic Society; £650 to the Headley Trust; £500 to the Wordsworth Trust; £200 to Greek Orthodox Charity Organisation Ltd; £100 to the Weizmann Institute Foundation

FINANCES *Year* 1997 *Income* £279,837
Grants £3,250

TRUSTEES Lady Marks, Dr D MacDiarmid, Prof C White

HOW TO APPLY Grants mainly made to charities which should be known personally rather than to submissions

WHO TO APPLY TO Michael Marks Charitable Trust, Citroen Wells, Accountants, Devonshire House, 1 Devonshire Street, London W1N 2DR

CC NO 248136   **ESTABLISHED** 1966

■ The Simon Marks Charitable Trust

WHAT IS FUNDED General charitable purposes

WHO CAN BENEFIT There are no restrictions on the age; professional and economic group; family situation; religion and culture; and social circumstances of; or disease or medical condition suffered by, the beneficiaries

WHERE FUNDING CAN BE GIVEN UK

RANGE OF GRANTS £100–£4,000

SAMPLE GRANTS £4,000 to Community Security Trust; £2,500 to Friends of Manchester City Galleries; £1,500 to Institute for Jewish Policy Research; £1,100 to Westminster Synagogue; £1,000 to The Samaritans

FINANCES *Year* 1997 *Income* £18,222
Grants £14,150

TRUSTEES J D Lerner, D P Lerner, M A Wilson

NOTES Funds fully committed to charities known to Trustees

HOW TO APPLY Grants mainly made to charities known personally rather than to submissions

WHO TO APPLY TO The Simon Marks Charitable Trust, M S Zatman & Co, 311 Ballards Lane, Finchley, London N12 8LY

CC NO 206316   **ESTABLISHED** 1953

■ The Ann and David Marks Foundation

WHAT IS FUNDED To provide aid for Jewish charities in personnel and human resource services; Jewish umbrella bodies; and schools and colleges

WHAT IS NOT FUNDED No grants to individuals

WHO CAN BENEFIT To benefit people of all ages; those in care, fostered and adopted; parents and children; one parent families and Jews

WHERE FUNDING CAN BE GIVEN UK and overseas, with a preference for Manchester

TYPE OF GRANT Buildings, capital one-off and start-up costs. Funding is available for more than three years

RANGE OF GRANTS £40–£2,975

SAMPLE GRANTS £2,975 to Joint Jewish Charitable Trust; £2,555 to North Cheshire Jewish Primary School; £1,068 to Jewish Social Services; £600 to WIZO; £500 to Yeshivas Lubavitch Manchester; £225 to CICJS; £219 to Yeshurun Hebrew Congregation; £200 to Institute of Contemporary Jewish Studies, Jewish Cultural Centre; £200 to Lubavitch South Manchester; £200 to Manchester Charitable Trust

FINANCES *Year* 1995–96 *Income* £28,095
Grants £11,365

TRUSTEES Mrs A Marks, D L Marks, L J Marks, Miss G E Marks

HOW TO APPLY To the address under Who To Apply To in writing, though charities known to the Trustees are more likely to be successful as funds are fully committed for the foreseeable future

WHO TO APPLY TO D L Marks, The Ann and David Marks Foundation, Mutley House, 1 Ambassador Place, Altrincham, Cheshire WA15 8DB *Tel* 0161-941 3183

CC NO 326303   **ESTABLISHED** 1983

■ The Hilda and Samuel Marks Foundation

WHAT IS FUNDED The relief and assistance of poor and needy persons. Advancement of education and religion or other purposes beneficial to the community. Otherwise the Trust Fund shall be held upon trust for the Jewish Blind Society

WHAT IS NOT FUNDED No grants given directly to individuals

WHO CAN BENEFIT Organisations benefiting people of all ages with many different social circumstances. Support is given to those helped by the Jewish Blind Society

WHERE FUNDING CAN BE GIVEN UK

FINANCES *Year* 1997 *Income* £163,258

TRUSTEES S Marks, Mrs H Marks, D L Marks, Mrs R D Selby

NOTES The Charity has a number of long-standing and regular commitments and funds are unlikely to be available for unsolicited applications

WHO TO APPLY TO D L Marks, The Hilda and Samuel Marks Foundation, 1 Ambassador Place, Altrincham, Cheshire WA15 8DB

CC NO 245208   **ESTABLISHED** 1965

■ The Erich Markus Charitable Foundation

WHAT IS FUNDED Trustees are primarily interested in social welfare causes

WHAT IS NOT FUNDED Do not consider individuals or salaries

WHO CAN BENEFIT Registered charities and institutions benefiting at risk groups, those disadvantaged by poverty and socially isolated people

WHERE FUNDING CAN BE GIVEN UK

RANGE OF GRANTS £500–£10,000

SAMPLE GRANTS £10,000 to Royal Marsden Hospital; £9,000 to The Samaritans; £8,000 to Royal Star and Garter Home; £6,000 to SSAFA; £5,000 to Jewish Blind and Physically Handicapped Society; £5,000 to Ravenswood Foundation; £5,000 to Spanish and Portuguese Jews Home for the Aged; £4,000 to Imperial Cancer Research Fund; £4,000 to London Association for the Blind; £4,000 to Nightingale House

FINANCES *Year* 1997 *Income* £121,217 *Grants* £115,500

TRUSTEES Erich Markus Charity Trustees

WHO TO APPLY TO A Walker, Trust Manager, The Erich Markus Charitable Foundation, Paynes Hicks Beach, Solicitors, 10 New Square, Lincoln's Inn, London WC2A 3QG

CC NO 283128   **ESTABLISHED** 1981

■ The J P Marland Charitable Trust

WHAT IS FUNDED General charitable purposes, at the discretion of the Trustees

WHO CAN BENEFIT There are no restrictions on the age; professional and economic group; family situation; religion and culture; and social circumstances of; or disease or medical condition suffered by, the beneficiaries

WHERE FUNDING CAN BE GIVEN UK

SAMPLE GRANTS £5,000 to Sandroyd School for playing field

FINANCES *Year* 1997 *Income* £15,779

TRUSTEES Jonathan Marland, Penelope Marland, Carol Felstead

HOW TO APPLY To the address under Who To Apply To in writing

WHO TO APPLY TO J Marland, The J P Marland Charitable Trust, Odstock Manor, Salisbury, Wiltshire SP5 4JA *Tel* 01722 329781

CC NO 1049350   **ESTABLISHED** 1995

■ The Julia Marmor Charitable Trust

This trust did not respond to CAF's request to amend its entry and, by 30 June 1998, CAF's researchers did not find financial records for later than 1995 on its file at the Charity Commission. Trusts are legally required to submit annual accounts to the Charity Commission under section 42 of the Charities Act 1993

WHAT IS FUNDED Relief of poverty and sickness. Advancement of education. Providing for the needs of the physically and mentally handicapped children or orphans and of other children whose parents or guardians are incapable for any reason of properly looking after them

WHO CAN BENEFIT Children; young adults; students; disabled people; and orphans. There are no restrictions on the disease or medical condition suffered by, the beneficiaries

WHERE FUNDING CAN BE GIVEN UK

TRUSTEES B Marmor, R Marmor, A M Cushnir

WHO TO APPLY TO Robin Marmor, The Julia Marmor Charitable Trust, 1 Great Cumberland Place, London W1H 7AL

CC NO 260372   **ESTABLISHED** 1969

■ Marr-Munning Trust

WHAT IS FUNDED Overseas aid projects, particularly those likely to improve economic and educational work. Provision of water supplies and general medical care. Refugee works and language-lab schools are also supported

WHAT IS NOT FUNDED No grants to individuals

WHO CAN BENEFIT Organisations benefiting: refugees; those disadvantaged by poverty; and victims of famine, war and man-made or natural disasters

WHERE FUNDING CAN BE GIVEN Overseas only

TYPE OF GRANT Recurrent and one-off grants

RANGE OF GRANTS £250–£10,000

SAMPLE GRANTS £10,000 to Red Cross; £7,500 to Intermediate Technology; £2,512 to Marr Munning Ashram, India; £2,500 to Books Abroad; £2,262 to Gram Nijoyan, India; £1,512 x 3 to Marr Munning Ashram, India; £1,262 x 2 to Gram Nijoyan, India

FINANCES *Year* 1997 *Income* £266,723 *Grants* £38,106

TRUSTEES Joan Honor, MBE, W Macfarlane, Mary Herbert, J O'Brien, C A Alam, Margaret Lorde

HOW TO APPLY **This Trust states that it does not respond to unsolicited applications**, until further notice. The Trust's income has been allocated for several years ahead

WHO TO APPLY TO Miss J Honor, MBE, Trustee, Marr-Munning Trust, Harcourt Lodge, 9 Madeley Road, Ealing, London W5 2LA

CC NO 261786   **ESTABLISHED** 1970

■ The Marsden Charitable Trust

WHAT IS FUNDED General charitable purposes

WHO CAN BENEFIT There are no restrictions on the age; professional and economic group; family situation; religion and culture; and social circumstances of; or disease or medical condition suffered by, the beneficiaries

WHERE FUNDING CAN BE GIVEN UK

FINANCES *Year* 1997 *Income* £25,624

TRUSTEES D J Ironside

HOW TO APPLY Almost all grants are made to charities known personally to the Trustees. Those who issue appeals should assume that the likelihood of a grant is small

WHO TO APPLY TO Laurence J Pearson, Accountant to the Trustees, The Marsden Charitable Trust, 5 Tweed Street, Berwick upon Tweed TD15 1NG

CC NO 268408   **ESTABLISHED** 1972

■ J and H Marsh and McLennan (Charities Fund) Ltd

WHAT IS FUNDED General charitable purposes. Particularly charities working in the fields of: accomodation and housing; infrastructure, support and development; cathedrals; religious umbrella bodies; arts, culture and recreation; health; conservation and environment; special schools and special needs education; speech therapy; training for community development, work, and vocational training; specialist research; community facilities and services including campaigning and advice information

WHAT IS NOT FUNDED No grants to individuals or individual schools, churches or local scout groups, art organisations

WHO CAN BENEFIT National organisations and special appeals. Organisations benefiting: children; young adults; older people; academics; ex-service and service people; reitred people; seafarers and fishermen; sportsmen and women; students; teachers and governesses; volunteers; at risk groups; carers; disabled people; those disadvantaged by poverty; disaster vistims; homeless people; victims of abuse, crime and domsetic violence. there is no restriction on the religion and culture of the beneficiaries though

there are a few restrictions on thier disease or medical condition
WHERE FUNDING CAN BE GIVEN UK
TYPE OF GRANT Buildings, capital, core costs, one-off, project, research, running costs, salaries and grants of one year or less will be considered
RANGE OF GRANTS £100–£500
FINANCES *Year* 1996 *Income* £150,000 *Grants* £150,000
TRUSTEES The Directors
HOW TO APPLY Letter with report and accounts
WHO TO APPLY TO F R Rutter, Director, J and H Marsh and McLennan (Charities Fund) Ltd, Aldgate House, 33 Aldgate High Street, EC3N 1AQ *Tel* 0171-357 3032
CC NO 261955   **ESTABLISHED** 1970

■ The Michael Marsh Charitable Trust
WHAT IS FUNDED Health and welfare charities, community-based organisations
WHO CAN BENEFIT Organisations benefiting at risk groups, disabled people, those disadvantaged by poverty and socially isolated people. There is no restriction on the disease or medical condition suffered by the beneficiaries
WHERE FUNDING CAN BE GIVEN UK, especially the West Midlands
TYPE OF GRANT Largely recurrent
RANGE OF GRANTS £50–£16,500
SAMPLE GRANTS £16,500 to Birmingham Rathbone Society; £10,000 to Little Sisters of the Poor; £7,300 to BRIB; £5,000 to British Blind Sport; £5,000 to Handsworth Grammar School; £4,300 to The Salvation Army; £4,000 to East Birmingham Family Service Unit; £3,000 to Birmingham Settlement; £3,000 to Acafess Community Trust; £2,500 to Cancer Relief Macmillan Fund
FINANCES *Year* 1997 *Income* £69,418 *Grants* £99,150
TRUSTEES G B G Hingley, L S Woodhead
NOTES The Trust will only accept applications from individuals through charitable institutions on their behalf
HOW TO APPLY To the address under Who To Apply To in writing. The Trustees meet half yearly, usually in June and December
WHO TO APPLY TO The Clerk, The Michael Marsh Charitable Trust, c/o Messrs Wragge & Co, Trustees' Solicitors, 55 Colmore Row, Birmingham B3 2AS
CC NO 220473   **ESTABLISHED** 1958

■ The Marsh Christian Trust
WHAT IS FUNDED General charitable purposes
WHAT IS NOT FUNDED No grants can be made to individuals or for sponsorships. No start-up grants. No building funds. No ordinary schools, colleges, universities or hospitals. No grants for research
WHO CAN BENEFIT Registered charities. There are no restrictions on the age; professional and economic group; family situation; religion and culture; and social circumstances of; or disease or medical condition suffered by, the beneficiaries
WHERE FUNDING CAN BE GIVEN UK
TYPE OF GRANT Annual
RANGE OF GRANTS £10–£10,000

SAMPLE GRANTS £10,000 to Author's Club Literary Award Scheme; £4,150 to Foundation Society; £3,000 to National Portrait Gallery; £2,500 to Natural History Museum; £2,000 to Voluntary Service Overseas; £1,672 to Arts Club; £1,610 to Royal College of Music; £1,600 to Children in Crisis; £1,500 to Latimer House; £1,400 to British Museum
FINANCES *Year* 1997 *Income* £144,053 *Grants* £104,004
TRUSTEES B P Marsh, Mrs M Litchfield, Mrs A B Marsh, R J C Marsh, Miss N C S Marsh
PUBLICATIONS Annual review
HOW TO APPLY By post only. Although applications are welcome, applicants should be aware that most funds are allocated and it is rare that new organisations will be considered
WHO TO APPLY TO The Secretary, The Marsh Christian Trust, Granville House, 132–135 Sloane Street, London SW1X 9AX
CC NO 284470   **ESTABLISHED** 1981

■ The Charlotte Marshall Charitable Trust
WHAT IS FUNDED Trustees prefer educational and religious objects for Roman Catholics
WHO CAN BENEFIT Registered charities, institutions benefiting Roman Catholics, children, young adults and students
WHERE FUNDING CAN BE GIVEN UK
FINANCES *Year* 1995 *Income* £98,499 *Grants* £95,500
TRUSTEES S M Lennard, FCA, K F Menzies, A M Cirket, C C Cirket
WHO TO APPLY TO S M Lennard, The Charlotte Marshall Charitable Trust, Theaklen Drive, Ponswood, Hastings, East Sussex TN34 1YS
CC NO 211941   **ESTABLISHED** 1962

■ The Jim Marshall Charitable Trust
WHAT IS FUNDED General charitable purposes, mainly for the benefit of children, young people, families, and the sick and disabled
WHO CAN BENEFIT Organisations benefiting children, young people, families, the sick and the disabled. There is no restriction on the disease or medical condition suffered by the beneficiaries
WHERE FUNDING CAN BE GIVEN UK
FINANCES *Year* 1997 *Income* £567,954 *Grants* £594,484
TRUSTEES J C Marshall, K W J Saunders, FCA, FTII, L Smith, B Charlton, LLB, S B Marshall
HOW TO APPLY Trust ref no GTL
WHO TO APPLY TO The Jim Marshall Charitable Trust, Simpson Wreford & Co, Chartered Accountants, 62 Bereford Street, London SE18 6BG
CC NO 328118   **ESTABLISHED** 1989

■ The Nora Joan Marshall Charitable Trust
WHAT IS FUNDED Mainly to support missionary and evangelical causes
WHAT IS NOT FUNDED Not usually to individuals
WHO CAN BENEFIT Mostly to missionary and church societies benefiting Evangelists and Christians
WHERE FUNDING CAN BE GIVEN UK
TYPE OF GRANT Some recurrent, some one-off
FINANCES *Year* 1996 *Income* £30,115 *Grants* £32,050
TRUSTEES D H E Kahn, R W J Marshall

HOW TO APPLY In writing to the address under Who To Apply To

WHO TO APPLY TO Miss R J W Marshall, The Nora Joan Marshall Charitable Trust, 30 Manor Road, Worthing, West Sussex BN11 4RU

CC NO 220478 **ESTABLISHED** 1962

■ Charity of William Marshall

WHAT IS FUNDED In previous years the local school, parish church council and widows in the area have received help, as well as community amenities

WHAT IS NOT FUNDED No grants for expeditions or scholarships

WHO CAN BENEFIT Organisations benefiting: children; young adults; older people and widows and widowers

WHERE FUNDING CAN BE GIVEN The Parish of Welney

TYPE OF GRANT Quarterly payments to widows currently £85. Grant to school of approximately £500 per annum. For public purposes of variable amounts

SAMPLE GRANTS £8,424 to Parochial Church Council; £8,240 to widows of the parish; £600 to William Marshall School for computer software

FINANCES *Year* 1997 *Income* £31,066 *Grants* £17,264

TRUSTEES D Booth, Bishop of Ely, M J R Clayton, C J Gilbert, S J Goodger, J Loveday, J A Scott, J Frost, E Hubbard, A B Singleterry, Rev S Tooke

HOW TO APPLY To the address under Who To Apply To in writing

WHO TO APPLY TO R J Brooks, Clerk, Charity of William Marshall, Town Hall, Littleport, Ely, Cambridgeshire CB6 1LU *Tel* 01358 860449

CC NO 202211 **ESTABLISHED** 1962

■ Jordan Marshall Memorial Trust

WHAT IS FUNDED General charitable purposes

WHO CAN BENEFIT There are no restrictions on the age; professional and economic group; family situation; religion and culture; and social circumstances of; or disease or medical condition suffered by, the beneficiaries

WHERE FUNDING CAN BE GIVEN Hertfordshire

WHO TO APPLY TO M Marshall, Chair, Jordan Marshall Memorial Trust, 441 Bamacres Road, Bennetts End, Hemel Hempstead, Hertfordshire HP3 8JS

CC NO 1048085 **ESTABLISHED** 1995

■ The D G Marshall of Cambridge Trust

WHAT IS FUNDED Various welfare, arts and heritage charities and organisations

WHO CAN BENEFIT Community projects, local appeals and national charities benefiting at risk groups, those disadvantaged by poverty and socially isolated people. Actors and entertainment professionals, musicians, textile workers and designers, writers and poets may be considered

WHERE FUNDING CAN BE GIVEN Cambridgeshire

RANGE OF GRANTS £100–£5,000

SAMPLE GRANTS £5,000 to Ely Cathedral Restoration Trust; £3,000 to Chesterton Community College; £2,500 to Food Chain Appeal; £2,500 to Perse School; £2,000 to MAGPAS; £2,000 to St John's College School; £1,800 to Air League Educational Trust; £1,500 to Air League; £1,500 to Ben Appeal; £1,500 to Papworth and Enham Foundation

FINANCES *Year* 1997 *Income* £73,688 *Grants* £46,150

TRUSTEES J D Barker, W C M Dastur, M J Marshall

HOW TO APPLY To the address under Who To Apply To in writing

WHO TO APPLY TO J D Barker, Secretary, The D G Marshall of Cambridge Trust, Airport House, The Airport, Newmarket Road, Cambridge CB5 8RY

CC NO 286468 **ESTABLISHED** 1982

■ Mervyn Martin Charitable Trust

WHAT IS FUNDED General charitable purposes at the Trustees' discretion

WHO CAN BENEFIT Institutions. There are no restrictions on the age; professional and economic group; family situation; religion and culture; and social circumstances of; or disease or medical condition suffered by, the beneficiaries

WHERE FUNDING CAN BE GIVEN UK and overseas

TYPE OF GRANT One-off grants

RANGE OF GRANTS £1,000 or less

FINANCES *Year* 1996 *Income* £45,333 *Grants* £18,520

TRUSTEES M H A Martin, A M Martin

WHO TO APPLY TO N J Barker, Mervyn Martin Charitable Trust, Dawson and Co, 2 New Square, Lincoln's Inn, London WC2A 3RZ

CC NO 327682 **ESTABLISHED** 1987

■ The Sir George Martin Trust

WHAT IS FUNDED Education, social welfare, general charitable purposes, especially in Yorkshire. The Trust assists a very wide range of charitable causes with a number of awards to schools and groups working with young people. Although emphasis is placed on projects located in the County of Yorkshire and in particular Leeds and Bradford, some grants are made in other parts of the North of England and occasionally national appeals are considered

WHAT IS NOT FUNDED The Trust is unable to consider applications from organisations without charitable status. No support for individuals or for post-graduate courses. No support for publishing books or articles or for seminars. The Trust does not like to fund projects that were formerly statutorily funded

WHO CAN BENEFIT Organisations benefiting children and young adults. There are few restrictions on the social circumstances of the beneficiaries

WHERE FUNDING CAN BE GIVEN Mainly Yorkshire, in particular Leeds and Bradford, occasionally national

TYPE OF GRANT Grants for capital rather than revenue projects; reluctant to support general running costs. Grants are not repeated to any charity in any one year; the maximum number of consecutive grants is three, though a one-off approach to grant applications is preferred. Average donation is just over £1,230

SAMPLE GRANTS £15,000 to Kew Gardens; £8,500 to Meanwood Urban Valley Farm; £8,250 to Leeds General Infirmary; £5,000 to St George's Crypt, Leeds; £5,000 to Braithwaite and Guardhouse Community Association; £5,000 to Batley Grammar School; £4,250 to Yorkshire Schools Exploring Society; £4,000 to Yorkshire Ballet Seminars; £3,000 to Yorkshire CCC Charitable Youth Trust; £3,000 to Scarborough Parish Trust

FINANCES *Year* 1998 *Income* £337,626 *Grants* £251,517

TRUSTEES Sir George Martin Trust Company Ltd

NOTES The Trust also supports The United Kingdom Charitable Trusts Initiative, a move to persuade wealthy people in the United Kingdom to create their own charitable Foundations

HOW TO APPLY The Trust meets in December and June each year to consider applications. These should be made in writing to the Secretary. Owing to the increase in costs of postage, unsuccessful applications outside the area of the Trust giving will not now be acknowledged. Relevant applications will be considered at the Trustees meetings but only those successful will be informed. No final response to an application means that the application has been unsuccessful. Telephone calls are not encouraged

WHO TO APPLY TO P J D Marshall, Secretary, Sir George Martin Trust, Netherwood House, Ilkley, Yorkshire LS29 9RP *Tel* 01943 831019

CC NO 223554   **ESTABLISHED** 1956

■ Massada Charitable Trust

WHAT IS FUNDED General charitable purposes for specific projects

WHO CAN BENEFIT There are no restrictions on the age; professional and economic group; family situation; religion and culture; and social circumstances of; or disease or medical condition suffered by, the beneficiaries

WHERE FUNDING CAN BE GIVEN UK and overseas

HOW TO APPLY No postal applications are acknowledged or supported

WHO TO APPLY TO T Freedman, Trustee, Massada Charitable Trust, Elizabeth House, 17 Queen Street, Leeds, West Yorkshire LS1 2TW *Tel* 0113-243 5402

CC NO 1068534   **ESTABLISHED** 1998

■ The Nancie Massey Charitable Trust

WHAT IS FUNDED Income split between five areas: the young; the elderly; education; the arts; and medical research

WHAT IS NOT FUNDED No grants to individuals

WHO CAN BENEFIT Charitable groups only. There is no restriction on the age of, or disease or medical condition suffered by, the beneficiaries

WHERE FUNDING CAN BE GIVEN Edinburgh

TYPE OF GRANT Cash only

RANGE OF GRANTS £100–£25,000, typical grant £1,000–£2,000

SAMPLE GRANTS £25,000 to Marie Curie for Fairmile Hospice; £20,000 to Museum of Scotland; £10,000 to Edinburgh Cyrenians for general funds; £5,000 to Macmillan Chemotherapy for Western General Day Care Appeal; £5,000 to St Mary's Cathedral Workshop for renovations; £5,000 to Edinburgh Handicapped Scout Group for general funds; £5,000 to Waverley Care for general funds; £5,000 to Royal Lyceum for lighting; £4,000 to Barnardos for Edinburgh Home; £2,500 to Turning Point, Leith for general funds

FINANCES *Year* 1998 *Income* £200,000 *Grants* £173,000

TRUSTEES J G Morton, M F Sinclair, P A Trotman

HOW TO APPLY By completing application form

WHO TO APPLY TO J G Morton, The Nancie Massey Charitable Trust, 61 Dublin Street, Edinburgh EH3 6NL

SC NO SCO 08977   **ESTABLISHED** 1989

■ The Leonard Matchan Fund Limited

WHAT IS FUNDED General charitable purposes

WHAT IS NOT FUNDED No grants to individuals

WHO CAN BENEFIT General registered charities. There are no restrictions on the age; professional and economic group; family situation; religion and culture; and social circumstances of; or disease or medical condition suffered by, the beneficiaries

WHERE FUNDING CAN BE GIVEN UK

FINANCES *Year* 1997 *Income* £60,939 *Grants* £60,850

TRUSTEES The Council of Management

HOW TO APPLY By letter to the Secretary

WHO TO APPLY TO Ms J Sutherland, The Leonard Matchan Fund Ltd, c/o 16 The Towers, Lower Mortlake Road, Richmond, Surrey TW9 2JR

CC NO 257682   **ESTABLISHED** 1968

■ The Material World Charitable Foundation Limited

This trust did not respond to CAF's request to amend its entry and, by 30 June 1998, CAF's researchers did not find financial records for later than 1995 on its file at the Charity Commission. Trusts are legally required to submit annual accounts to the Charity Commission under section 42 of the Charities Act 1993

WHAT IS FUNDED Environmental organisations, charities benefiting children

WHAT IS NOT FUNDED Donations given only to registered charities in areas shown under what is funded

WHO CAN BENEFIT Registered charities benefitting children

WHERE FUNDING CAN BE GIVEN UK

RANGE OF GRANTS Donations from £250 to £10,000

TRUSTEES The Directors

HOW TO APPLY In writing to the address below

WHO TO APPLY TO The Secretary, Material World Charitable Foundation Ltd, Becket House, 1 Lambeth Palace Road, London SE1 7EU

CC NO 266746   **ESTABLISHED** 1973

■ The Mathew Trust

WHAT IS FUNDED Grants are given to organisations which provide opportunities for employment

WHO CAN BENEFIT To benefit young adults and older people

WHERE FUNDING CAN BE GIVEN Dundee and district

Does the trust you have chosen match your needs? Haphazard applications waste postage and time

405

TYPE OF GRANT Salaries for up to one year

SAMPLE GRANTS £50,000 to the University of Dundee – Wellcome Science Institute; £50,000 to the University of Dundee – Student Communal Facilities; £50,000 to Ninewells Cancer Appeal; £30,000 to the University of Dundee – Clinical Skills Centre; £10,000 to the University of Dundee – Access Summer School; £9,600 to Prince's Trust Volunteers; £5,500 to Tenovus Tayside; £5,000 to Fair Play Project; £5,000 to Unicorn Preservation Trust; £4,500 to Dundee City Council Multi-Sensory Service

FINANCES *Year* 1996–97 *Income* £203,000 *Grants* £240,000

TRUSTEES Lord Provost of Dundee, Dr D B Grant, Prof G S Lowden, A F McDonald

HOW TO APPLY Applications should be made in writing to the address under Who To Apply To

WHO TO APPLY TO The Mathew Trust, Henderson Loggie, Secretaries, Royal Exchange, Dundee DD1 1DZ *Tel* 01382 201234

SC NO SCO 16284   **ESTABLISHED** 1935

■ The Matthew Trust

WHAT IS FUNDED To assist the mentally ill in the community and in prisons, and victims of aggression

WHAT IS NOT FUNDED We are a 'last-stop' agency and all other areas should have been exhausted before the applicant approaches us through statutory and voluntary agencies

WHO CAN BENEFIT To benefit the mentally ill and victims of aggression

WHERE FUNDING CAN BE GIVEN Throughout the UK and Ireland and international where appropriate

TYPE OF GRANT Financial

FINANCES *Year* 1997 *Income* £157,848 *Grants* £59,222

TRUSTEES Susan Conrad, Gordon Sandreth, Rev Eldin Corsey, Rev Gary Piper

PUBLICATIONS *The Medics and the Mentally Disordered* (1991/92), *Victims of Care* (1995/96), *A Burden Too Many* (1997)

NOTES In 1997, £41,356 was also spent on research, reports literature and public policy

HOW TO APPLY Guidelines are issued when requested. All applications are acknowledged. All agencies and applicants must have exhausted all other areas of support before approaching the Matthew Trust in terms of grants

WHO TO APPLY TO Peter Thompson, The Matthew Trust, PO Box 604, London SW6 3AG *Web Site* http://www.activ-8.com/matthew-trust

CC NO 294966   **ESTABLISHED** 1984

■ The Matthews Wrightson Charity Trust

WHAT IS FUNDED The Trustees favour smaller charitable projects seeking to raise under £25,000, with a bias towards youth, Christian work and organisations helping the disadvantaged re-integrate into the community, including residential facilities and services, crime prevention schemes, and training for community and personal development for individuals such as those going abroad to do charitable work, and other charitable purposes. Unusual ideas within the guidelines often catch the Trustees' eye. About 15 per cent of up to 100 applicants a month receive grants

WHAT IS NOT FUNDED Grants will not be awarded to: unconnected local churches, schools and village halls, etc, or animal charities. Gifts sometimes given to individuals, for example students (from UK and abroad) or participants in expeditions undertaking charitable work might receive funding

WHO CAN BENEFIT Young adults, students, ex-offenders and those at risk of offending, Christians and Church of England - both individually and through organisations

WHERE FUNDING CAN BE GIVEN UK

TYPE OF GRANT One-off cash grants, on annual basis

RANGE OF GRANT Average grant size £400

SAMPLE GRANTS £8,500 to Royal College of Art for about 12 scholarships; £1,500 to Genesis Arts Trust for help for artists (Christian); £1,000 to DEMAND for medical equipment; £1,000 to Disabilities Trust; £1,000 to The Rifleman's Aid Society to help soldiers and their families; £1,000 to an individual for a course in London; £1,000 to Peper Harrow Foundation to rehabilitate young offenders; £700 to Keston Institute for Christian education; £700 to Haggai Institute (NI) for Christian evangelism; £600 to Georgian Group for arts organisation

FINANCES *Year* 1997 *Income* £72,500 *Grants* £71,000

TRUSTEES A H Issacs, G D G Wrightson, Miss P W Wrightson

PUBLICATIONS Annual Report

NOTES Gifts are made in small units (£400 for 1998), with a few larger gifts deriving specifically from old connections. 21 per cent to youth, 15 per cent to Christian work, 13 per cent to rehabilitation, 12 per cent to homeless and handicapped, and 9 per cent to individuals

HOW TO APPLY In writing to the Administrator. Initial telephone calls are discouraged. No special forms: accounts desirable. The Trustees are sent covering letters only (two to three pages) monthly, and meet six-monthly for policy and administrative decisions. No reply to unsuccessful applicants without sae; expect a two month delay if successful. The Administrator receives over 1,000 applications a year

WHO TO APPLY TO Adam Lee, Secretary and Administrator, The Matthews Wrightson Charity Trust, The Farm, Northington, Alresford, Hampshire SO24 9TH

CC NO 262109   **ESTABLISHED** 1970

■ The Barbara Maude Charitable Trust

WHAT IS FUNDED General charitable purposes

WHO CAN BENEFIT There are no restrictions on the age; professional and economic group; family situation; religion and culture; and social circumstances of; or disease or medical condition suffered by, the beneficiaries

WHERE FUNDING CAN BE GIVEN UK

TRUSTEES A S Palmer, Mrs B Marshall

WHO TO APPLY TO A S Palmer, Solicitor/Trustee, The Barbara Maude Charitable Trust, 1 Bower Mount Road, Maidstone, Kent ME16 8AX

CC NO 1064258   **ESTABLISHED** 1997

■ Maulana Nisar Dawah and Community Services Trust

WHAT IS FUNDED General charitable purposes, in particular: advancement of religious and general education; relief of the financial and emotional needs of young women over the age of 16; provision of facilities for recreation and leisure-time; promotion of good race relations; to advance persons attending Islamic schools

WHO CAN BENEFIT Organisations benefiting children and young adults, particularly those attending Islamic schools, and young women over the age of 16. Otherwise, there are no restrictions on the age; professional and economic group; family situation; religion and culture; and social circumstances of; or disease or medical condition suffered by, the beneficiaries

WHERE FUNDING CAN BE GIVEN UK

FINANCES *Year* 1997 *Income* £17,928 *Grants* £633

TRUSTEES Dr A S Abdur Rahim, M Noor, Nazir Ahmed Saghir

WHO TO APPLY TO M Noor, Maulana Nisar Dawah and Community Services Trust, 33 Dolobran Road, Sparkbrook, Brimingham B11 1HL

CC NO 1039524　　　**ESTABLISHED** 1993

■ The Violet Mauray Charitable Trust

WHAT IS FUNDED General at Trustees' discretion

WHO CAN BENEFIT There are no restrictions on the age; professional and economic group; family situation; religion and culture; and social circumstances of; or disease or medical condition suffered by, the beneficiaries

WHERE FUNDING CAN BE GIVEN UK and overseas

TYPE OF GRANT A range of grants

RANGE OF GRANTS £50–£1,500

SAMPLE GRANTS £1,500 to an individual; £1,000 to SCOPE; £750 to Joint Jewish Charitable Trust; £250 to CBF World Jewish Relief Fund; £250 to JAMI; £100 to Jewish Care; £100 to an individual

FINANCES *Year* 1998 *Income* £81,185 *Grants* £4,000

TRUSTEES Mrs J Stephany, Mrs A Karlin, J D Stephany, R K Stephany

WHO TO APPLY TO Mrs J Stephany, Trustee, The Violet Mauray Charitable Trust, c/o Febeson and Arbeid, 3 Albermarle Street, London W1X 4AU

CC NO 1001716　　　**ESTABLISHED** 1990

■ Maxell Educational Trust

WHAT IS FUNDED Research projects by teachers in electronics and technology and the publication of such research; students; general charitable purposes; all within the area Where Funding Can Be Given

WHO CAN BENEFIT Particularly organisations benefiting teachers of electronics and technology, and students

WHERE FUNDING CAN BE GIVEN Telford

TYPE OF GRANT Research

SAMPLE GRANTS £20,000 to Shropshire Campus of the University of Wolverhampton to establish an Electronic Product Design Centre; £20,000 to Ercall Wood School to establish the Maxell Music Technology Centre; £10,000 to Wrockwardine Wood School to establish a Maxell Controlled Technology Centre; £5,143 to Southall Special School for the provision of computers and software to enable the pupils to prepare and produce a school newspaper; £1,000 to several schools for the Design Award Challenge

FINANCES *Year* 1997 *Income* £22,192 *Grants* £56,143

TRUSTEES Lord Northfield (Chairman), G Raxster, A Matsumoto

HOW TO APPLY To the address under Who To Apply To in writing

WHO TO APPLY TO G Bullock, Personnel Director, Maxell Educational Trust, Maxell Europe Ltd, Apley, Telford, Shropshire TF6 6DA

CC NO 702640　　　**ESTABLISHED** 1990

■ The Pamela and Jack Maxwell Foundation

WHAT IS FUNDED General charitable purposes. Donations made purely at the discretion of Trustees

WHAT IS NOT FUNDED No grants to individuals or for expeditions

WHO CAN BENEFIT There are no restrictions on the age; professional and economic group; family situation; religion and culture; and social circumstances of; or disease or medical condition suffered by, the beneficiaries

WHERE FUNDING CAN BE GIVEN UK

RANGE OF GRANTS £20–£3,701

SAMPLE GRANTS £3,701 to Ben-Gurion University Foundation; £2,400 to London Symphony Orchestra; £1,000 to the King's Appeal; £750 to Foundation for Conductive Education; £600 to Ravenswood Foundation; £500 to Jewish Philanthropic Association for Israel and the Middle East; £500 to Friends of the IPO Foundation; £500 to the Duke of Edinburgh's Award; £500 to Group Relations ED; £500 to Jewish Child's Day

FINANCES *Year* 1995 *Income* £67,328 *Grants* £19,879

TRUSTEES Mrs P H Maxwell, J A C Bentall

HOW TO APPLY Only successful applicants will be replied to

WHO TO APPLY TO Mrs P H Maxwell, The Pamela and Jack Maxwell Foundation, c/o Binder Hamlyn, 20 Old Bailey, London EC4M 7BH

CC NO 209618　　　**ESTABLISHED** 1957

■ The Alexander Maxwell Law Scholarship Trust

WHAT IS FUNDED To support research of a practical, rather than theoretical nature leading to publication

WHAT IS NOT FUNDED Work must benefit UK citizens

WHO CAN BENEFIT Individuals and organisations benefiting young adults, older people and legal professionals. Preferably young law practitioners rather than academics

WHERE FUNDING CAN BE GIVEN UK

TYPE OF GRANT Single project scholarships and research. Funding is available for up to three years

SAMPLE GRANTS £10,000 to an individual; £6,000 to an individual; £4,000 to an individual

FINANCES *Year* 1997 *Income* £51,959 *Grants* £20,000

TRUSTEES Mrs K Britten, M Dixon, D Hayton, S Healy, L Browning

PUBLICATIONS Brochure available on request

HOW TO APPLY Applications to be made by 31 August each year for consideration for an award in the following year. Application form and guidelines available

WHO TO APPLY TO The Clerk to the Trustees, Alexander Maxwell Law Scholarship Trust, c/o Sweet & Maxwell Ltd, 100 Avenue Road, Swiss Cottage, London NW3 3PF *Tel* 0171-393 7000 *Fax* 0171-393 7010 *E-mail* dick.greener@swelawpub.co.uk

CC NO 289833　　　**ESTABLISHED** 1984

■ Evelyn May Trust

WHAT IS FUNDED Currently the main area of interest is the elderly and medical projects, but cash donations are made to a variety of registered charities chosen by the Trustees

WHAT IS NOT FUNDED Registered charities only. No grants to individuals, including students. No grants are made in response to general appeals

WHO CAN BENEFIT Mainly headquarters organisations, especially those benefiting the elderly, medical professionals and research workers. There is no restriction on the disease or medical condition suffered by the beneficiaries

WHERE FUNDING CAN BE GIVEN UK

TYPE OF GRANT Often one-off for a specific project but cash donations for general purposes are also made. Donation (personal grants cannot be entertained)

SAMPLE GRANTS £25,000 to St Francis Development Trust education department

FINANCES *Year* 1997 *Income* £23,559
Grants £31,000

TRUSTEES Mrs E M Riddoch, Mrs E Tabersham, J R Seargeant

HOW TO APPLY This Trust states that it does not respond to unsolicited applications

WHO TO APPLY TO J R Seargeant, Evelyn May Trust, c/o Jansons, 7 Portman Street, London W1H 0BA

CC NO 261038   **ESTABLISHED** 1970

■ Robert Mayhew Charitable Trust

WHAT IS FUNDED Human welfare

WHO CAN BENEFIT Organisations benefiting: at risk groups; disabled people; those disadvantaged by poverty and socially isolated people. There is no restriction on the disease or medical condition suffered by the beneficiaries

WHERE FUNDING CAN BE GIVEN UK

TYPE OF GRANT Particular interest in granting money for equipment

RANGE OF GRANTS £15–£2,045

SAMPLE GRANTS £2,045 to New to London Project; £1,875 to Children of Lota (Chile); £1,400 to Macmillan Appeal for Brighton and Hove Hospice; £666 to Uckfield Church; £650 to Prince's Trust

FINANCES *Year* 1997 *Income* £16,932
Grants £9,775

TRUSTEES R C P Mayhew, Mrs L B Mayhew

HOW TO APPLY By invitation only. **This Trust states that it does not respond to unsolicited applications**

WHO TO APPLY TO R C P Mayhew, Robert Mayhew Charitable Trust, Flat 6, 40 Hyde Park Gate, London SW7 5DT

CC NO 277060   **ESTABLISHED** 1978

■ The Mayor of Chorley's Helping Hand Charity

WHAT IS FUNDED Local charities in the Chorley area, according to the wishes of the current Mayor of Chorley. The area of focus for funding varies each year according to the wishes of each new Mayor. Support for 1998–99 is for organisations benefiting young people under the age of 18, who are either resident or studying in Chorely, through provision of area grants or maintenance allowances, to enable them to travel for the furtherance of their education. The area of focus for 1999–2000 is not yet known

WHO CAN BENEFIT In 1998–99, organisations benefiting children, young adults and students under the age of 18

WHERE FUNDING CAN BE GIVEN The Borough of Chorley

TRUSTEES The Mayor of Chorley, the Borough Director of Finance, the Borough Solicitor

HOW TO APPLY To the Mayor's Secretary at the address under Who To Apply To

WHO TO APPLY TO Mayor's Secretary, The Mayor of Chorley's Helping Hand Charity, Town Hall, Chorley, Lancashire PR7 1DP *Tel* 01257 515102

CC NO 1058421   **ESTABLISHED** 1996

■ The Mayor of Croydon's Charity Fund

This trust did not respond to CAF's request to amend its entry and, by 30 June 1998, CAF's researchers did not find financial records for later than 1995 on its file at the Charity Commission. Trusts are legally required to submit annual accounts to the Charity Commission under section 42 of the Charities Act 1993

WHAT IS FUNDED General charitable purposes

WHO CAN BENEFIT There are no restrictions on the age; professional and economic group; family situation; religion and culture; and social circumstances of; or disease or medical condition suffered by, the beneficiaries

WHERE FUNDING CAN BE GIVEN London Borough of Croydon

TRUSTEES P Hecks, Ms A Slipper, D Wechster

WHO TO APPLY TO B Middlemiss, The Mayor of Croydon's Charity Fund, Taberner House, Park Lane, Croydon CR9 3JS

CC NO 1042479   **ESTABLISHED** 1994

■ The Mayor of Knowsley Charity Fund

WHAT IS FUNDED General charitable purposes in the area Where Funding Can Be Given

WHO CAN BENEFIT There are no restrictions on the age; professional and economic group; family situation; religion and culture; and social circumstances of; or disease or medical condition suffered by, the beneficiaries

WHERE FUNDING CAN BE GIVEN Knowsley

SAMPLE GRANTS £20,000 to St Helens and Knowsley Hospice; £1,830 to Musical School for musical scholarships; £607 to Cancer Care; £607 to Sea Cadets; £375 to Roy Castle Fund; £152 to MND

FINANCES *Year* 1996–97 *Income* £28,165
Grants £23,571

TRUSTEES The Mayor, Director of Finance, Knowsley, Borough Solicitor, Knowsley,

NOTES The Mayor of Knowsley Charity Fund is chosen by the Mayor and usually only support one charity per year

HOW TO APPLY To the address under Who To Apply To in writing

WHO TO APPLY TO Paula Deegan, The Mayor of Knowsley Charity Fund, Knowsley MBC, Municipal Buildings, Archway Road, Huyton, Merseyside *Tel* 0151-443 3643 *Fax* 0151-443 3661

CC NO 504656   **ESTABLISHED** 1975

■ **The Mayor of the London Borough of Enfield Appeal Fund**

WHAT IS FUNDED Special needs and welfare organisations

WHO CAN BENEFIT Disabled people; those disadvantaged by poverty; at risk groups; and socially isolated people. Some individuals may receive welfare grants, though primarily local organisations are supported

WHERE FUNDING CAN BE GIVEN Enfield

SAMPLE GRANTS £6,284 to Enfield Talking Newspaper; £6,284 to Enfield Deaf Children's Club; £2,500 to Enfield Carnival Association; £2,500 to London Borough of Enfield; £1,250 to Enfield Vision; £1,000 to Middlesex Association for the Blind; £750 to Geranium Club for the Blind; £750 to Sunshine Club for the Blind; £500 to Enfield Deaf Social Club; £500 to Enfield Highway Deaf OAP Club

FINANCES *Year* 1997 *Income* £27,759
Grants £24,519

TRUSTEES London Borough of Enfield Council

HOW TO APPLY To the adrress under Who To Apply To in writing

WHO TO APPLY TO Director of Corporate Services, FAO Pam Taylor, Mayor of the London Borough of Enfield Appeal Fund, PO Box 50, Civic Centre, Silver Street, Enfield, Middlesex EN1 3XA *Tel* 0181-366 6565

CC NO 283320   **ESTABLISHED** 1981

■ **The Mayor of Poole's Appeal Fund**

WHAT IS FUNDED General charitable purposes. Funding is given to charities chosen by successive mayors at the beginning of their term, therefore priorities change annually

WHAT IS NOT FUNDED No grants to individuals

WHO CAN BENEFIT Voluntary organisations and charitable groups only. There are no restrictions on the age; professional and economic group; family situation; religion and culture; and social circumstances of; or disease or medical condition suffered by, the beneficiaries

WHERE FUNDING CAN BE GIVEN Poole

TYPE OF GRANT Funding is given for one year or less

SAMPLE GRANTS £22,500 to CLAPA for donation; £19,000 to Poole General Hospital for Scanner Appeal

FINANCES *Year* 1996–97 *Income* £41,500
Grants £41,500

TRUSTEES J W Brooks, A Greenwood

HOW TO APPLY To the address under Who To Apply To in writing

WHO TO APPLY TO Mrs D Moore, Secretary to the Mayor, The Mayor of Poole's Appeal Fund, c/o Borough of Poole, Civic Centre, Poole, Dorset BH15 2RU *Tel* 01202 633200

CC NO 1027462   **ESTABLISHED** 1993

■ **The Mayor of Sefton's Charity Fund**

WHAT IS FUNDED General charitable purposes in the Borough of Sefton

WHO CAN BENEFIT There are no restrictions on the age; professional and economic group; family situation; religion and culture; and social circumstances of; or disease or medical condition suffered by, the beneficiaries

WHERE FUNDING CAN BE GIVEN Sefton

FINANCES *Year* 1995–96 *Income* £19,980
Grants £16,100

HOW TO APPLY Applications should be made on a form available from the address under Who To Apply To or from on of the Trustees

WHO TO APPLY TO Mrs E Jones, Secretary, The Mayor of Sefton's Charity Fund, Town Hall, Lord Street, Southport PR8 1DA

CC NO 1026227   **ESTABLISHED** 1993

■ **The Mayor of Southwark's Common Good Trust**

WHAT IS FUNDED General charitable purposes for Southwark residents. Support will be considered for any group or individual who can demonstrate need. Particularly charities working in the fields of education and community services

WHO CAN BENEFIT There are no restrictions on the age; professional and economic group; family situation; religion and culture; and social circumstances of; or disease or medical condition suffered by, the beneficiaries

WHERE FUNDING CAN BE GIVEN Southwark

TYPE OF GRANT Finance (through sponsor); capital goods and one-off funding will be considered

FINANCES *Year* 1996–97 *Income* £15,300
Grants £5,000

TRUSTEES Mayor of London Borough of Southwark, R A Coomber (Chief Executive), J Belvir (Borough Solicitor), P Cather, C Robson, P Sullivan, J Wallington, J B Parker

NOTES Successful applications are usually one-off, with no repetition later

HOW TO APPLY To the address under Who To Apply To in writing giving full details of anticipated recipient, background of support elsewhere and responses received to other requests elsewhere, amounts needed. No formal application form. The Trustees consider applications at monthly meetings (usually first Monday in a month) please send requests well in advance

WHO TO APPLY TO N Hammond, Hon Secretary, The Mayor of Southwark's Common Good Trust, Town Hall, Room 33, West House, 31 Peckham Road, London SE5 8UB *Tel* 0171-525 7347 *Fax* 0171-525 7277

CC NO 280011   **ESTABLISHED** 1980

■ **The Mayoress of Trafford's Charity Fund**

WHAT IS FUNDED The Mayoress chooses a single charity to support the year before she takes office; the charity must benefit the inhabitants of the Borough of Trafford

WHO CAN BENEFIT There are no restrictions on the age; professional and economic group; family situation; religion and culture; and social circumstances of; or disease or medical condition suffered by, the beneficiaries

WHERE FUNDING CAN BE GIVEN The Borough of Trafford

SAMPLE GRANTS £37,000 to Macmillan Cancer Care to furnish and equip the physiotherapy room at the Trafford Macmillan day care centre

FINANCES *Year* 1997–98 *Income* £37,000

HOW TO APPLY To the address under Who To Apply To in writing

WHO TO APPLY TO The Chief Executive, The Mayoress of Trafford's Charity Fund, Trafford Town Hall, Talbot Road, Stretford, Trafford, Manchester M32 0YT *Tel* 0161-912 1212

CC NO 512299   **ESTABLISHED** 1982

Does the trust you have chosen match your needs? Haphazard applications waste postage and time

409

■ Maypride Ltd

WHAT IS FUNDED To advance religion in accordance with the Orthodox Jewish faith, relief of poverty and general charitable purposes

WHO CAN BENEFIT Institutions benefiting Jewish people and those disadvantaged by poverty

WHERE FUNDING CAN BE GIVEN UK

TYPE OF GRANT At the discretion of the Trustees

FINANCES *Year* 1997 *Income* £62,090

TRUSTEES A Sterlicht, Mrs E Sternlicht

WHO TO APPLY TO The Secretary, Maypride Ltd, 55 Wolmer Gardens, Edgware HA8 8QB

CC NO 289394　　**ESTABLISHED** 1984

■ The Robert McAlpine Foundation

This trust did not respond to CAF's request to amend its entry and, by 30 June 1998, CAF's researchers did not find financial records for later than 1995 on its file at the Charity Commission. Trusts are legally required to submit annual accounts to the Charity Commission under section 42 of the Charities Act 1993

WHAT IS FUNDED General charitable purposes continuing support to registered charities personally known to the Trustees. Few outside applications are countenanced

WHAT IS NOT FUNDED No grants to individuals

WHO CAN BENEFIT Registered charities only. There are no restrictions on the age; professional and economic group; family situation; religion and culture; and social circumstances of; or disease or medical condition suffered by, the beneficiaries

TRUSTEES The Hon David M McAlpine, M H D McAlpine, Kenneth McAlpine, Cullum McAlpine, Adrian McAlpine

HOW TO APPLY Considered annually, normally in November

WHO TO APPLY TO The Secretary to the Trustees, The Robert McAlpine Foundation, 40 Bernard Street, London WC1N 1LG

CC NO 226646　　**ESTABLISHED** 1963

■ The McKenna & Co Foundation

WHAT IS FUNDED General charitable purposes, in particular charitable purposes connected with children, the mentally or physically disabled, the aged, the deaf and medical research

WHAT IS NOT FUNDED No grants to organisations that are not registered charities. No grants to individuals

WHO CAN BENEFIT Organisations benefiting older people, deaf and disabled people, medical professionals and research workers

WHERE FUNDING CAN BE GIVEN UK

FINANCES *Year* 1996 *Income* £45,697

TRUSTEES C B Powell-Smith, Mrs C F Woolf, R S Derry-Evans

HOW TO APPLY To the address under Who To Apply To in writing

WHO TO APPLY TO The McKenna & Co Foundation, McKenna & Co, Mitre House, 160 Aldersgate Street, London EC1A 4DD

CC NO 268859　　**ESTABLISHED** 1981

■ The James Frederick and Ethel Anne Measures Charity

WHAT IS FUNDED General charitable purposes. Applicants must usually originate in the West Midlands. Applicants must show evidence of self-help in their application. Trustees have a preference for disadvantaged people. Trustees favour grants towards the cost of equipment. Applications by individuals in cases of hardship will not usually be considered unless sponsored by a local authority, health professional or other welfare agency

WHAT IS NOT FUNDED Trustees have a dislike for students who have a full local authority grant and want finance for a different course of study

WHO CAN BENEFIT All categories within the West Midlands area. There are no restrictions on the age; professional and economic group; family situation; religion and culture; and social circumstances of; or disease or medical condition suffered by, the beneficiaries

WHERE FUNDING CAN BE GIVEN West Midlands or West Midlands branches of national organisations

TYPE OF GRANT Recurrent grants are occasionally considered. The Trustees favour grants towards the cost of equipment

RANGE OF GRANTS £100–£1,600

SAMPLE GRANTS £1,600 to Blue Coat School; £1,500 to City Farm School; £650 to BRIB; £500 to 20th Birmingham Scouts; £500 to Ariel Scout Group; £500 to Beaudesert RC School; £500 to Birmingham Botanical Gardens; £500 to East Birmingham Family Service Unit; £500 to Headway; £500 to Horticultural Therapy

FINANCES *Year* 1997 *Income* £45,023
Grants £43,756

TRUSTEES D J K Nichols, C H Lees, Dr I D Kerr, R S Watkins

HOW TO APPLY By letter to the address under Who To Apply To. No reply to unsuccessful applicants unless sae is enclosed. Trustees' meetings every three months

WHO TO APPLY TO Mrs S E Darby, James Frederick and Ethel Anne Measures Charity, 2nd Floor, 33 Great Charles Street, Birmingham B3 3JN

CC NO 266054　　**ESTABLISHED** 1973

■ Charity of Mary Jane, Countess of Meath

WHAT IS FUNDED Supporting poor persons who are aged, infirm, blind or ill or institutions supporting the same

WHO CAN BENEFIT At the discretion of the Trustees, but organisations benefiting older people, those disadvantaged by poverty, sick and infirm people will be considered

WHERE FUNDING CAN BE GIVEN UK

TYPE OF GRANT At the discretion of the Trustees

RANGE OF GRANTS £1,000–£2,000

SAMPLE GRANTS £2,000 to Age Concern; £2,000 to NSPCC; £2,000 to RUKBA; £2,000 to Royal Society for the Blind; £2,000 to Help the Aged; £2,000 to the Red Cross; £2,000 to Meath Homes; £1,500 to Wireless for the Bedridden; £1,500 to NBFA; £1,500 to Friends of the Elderly

FINANCES *Year* 1996–97 *Income* £26,780
Grants £26,000

TRUSTEES Mrs C E Forrester, Mrs E M Poole

WHO TO APPLY TO Mrs C E Forrester, Charity of Mary Jane, Countess of Meath, Copper Beeches, Sikeside, Kirlington, Carlisle, Cumbria CA6 6OR

CC NO 238101　　**ESTABLISHED** 1919

■ Medical Research Council – Trust Funds

WHAT IS FUNDED The endowment funds are used to supplement existing research carried out by the Council. The Trust's aims are to promote the development of medical and related biological research and to advance knowledge that will lead to its improved health care

WHO CAN BENEFIT Organisations benefiting medical professionals, research workers and scientists. There is no restriction on the disease or medical condition suffered by the beneficiaries

WHERE FUNDING CAN BE GIVEN UK and overseas

TYPE OF GRANT Medical research and fellowships

FINANCES *Year* 1996–97 *Income* £1,546,750 *Grants* £288,301

TRUSTEES Medical Research Council

NOTES Funds are only used to supplement existing activities

HOW TO APPLY **This Trust states that it does not respond to unsolicited applications**

WHO TO APPLY TO Brian Latham, Medical Research Council – Trust Funds, 20 Park Crescent, London W1N 4AL

CC NO 250696   **ESTABLISHED** 1920

Mediterranean Archaeological Trust

WHAT IS FUNDED Promotion of study of archaeology with preference for Mycenean archaeology of Greece and other central and west Mediterranean areas

WHO CAN BENEFIT Archaeologists

WHERE FUNDING CAN BE GIVEN UK, Greece and other places in central and western Mediterranean

RANGE OF GRANTS £4,450–£15,843

SAMPLE GRANTS £15,843 to Mycenae Publication; £4,540 to Ayios Stephanos

FINANCES *Year* 1997 *Income* £29,526 *Grants* £22,383

TRUSTEES Mrs V Clifford-Holmes (Chairman), Lord Renfew of Kaimsthorn, Sir John Boardman, Prof M Robertson, Prof A Snodgrass, Dr F Stubbings, Prof R R R Smith, P Ewart

NOTES Funds are mainly committed for the next few years

HOW TO APPLY Applications must be received by 31 January of any year

WHO TO APPLY TO D W Ewart, Mediterranean Archaeological Trust, c/o Hewitson Becke & Shaw Solicitors, Shakespeare House, 42 Newmarket Road, Cambridge CB5 8EP

CC NO 238967   **ESTABLISHED** 1959

The Meir Golda Trust

WHAT IS FUNDED General charitable purposes

WHO CAN BENEFIT There are no restrictions on the age; professional and economic group; family situation; religion and culture; and social circumstances of; or disease or medical condition suffered by, the beneficiaries, however, particular favour is given to Jewish charities

WHERE FUNDING CAN BE GIVEN UK

RANGE OF GRANTS £18–£40,500

SAMPLE GRANTS £40,500 to British Friends of Laniade Hospital; £2,444 for sundry donations; £1,250 to 24 Hours for Children Foundation; £780 to Sunderland Kollel; £750 to Sage; £360 to Yad Eleyhan; £338 to HKMS; £270 to Obser Gemillins Chasodine; £250 to Sihia Syn; £207 to Ravenswood

FINANCES *Year* 1997 *Income* £61,958 *Grants* £47,676

WHO TO APPLY TO J Glatt, The Meir Golda Trust, 12 Brentwood Lodge, Holmdale Gardens, London NW4

CC NO 1041256   **ESTABLISHED** 1994

The Violet Melchett Children's Trust

WHAT IS FUNDED The provision of assistance and treatment (both ante-natal and post-natal) for poor mothers and young children in any part of London. The Trustees are currently supporting major projects initiated by national charities and no funds are available for other applications at present

WHAT IS NOT FUNDED Only projects benefiting mothers or children in what was the GLC area can be supported; no applications can be considered at present. No grants given in response to general or large scale appeals, and such applications will not be acknowledged. No grants to individuals

WHO CAN BENEFIT Groups, institutions or registered charities benefiting poor mothers, children and one parent families

WHERE FUNDING CAN BE GIVEN London only

TYPE OF GRANT Preferably non-recurring, although requests for regular annual support are occasionally considered

RANGE OF GRANTS £500–£7500

SAMPLE GRANTS £7,500 to HAPA (Handicapped Adventure Playground Association) for consultants and other work related to increasing effectiveness of HAPA; £7,500 to Gingerbread for work with single parents in London; £1,000 to Camden Women's Aid for children's playscheme

FINANCES *Year* 1997–98 *Income* £26,000 *Grants* £20,500

TRUSTEES Peter Mond, Cassandra Wedd

PUBLICATIONS Accounts are on file at the Charity Commission

NOTES Please note What Is Not Funded (London area only) and What Is Funded by the Trustees; no applications can be considered at present

HOW TO APPLY At any time

WHO TO APPLY TO Peter Mond, The Violet Melchett Children's Trust, 14 Falkland Road, London NW5 2PT

CC NO 228197   **ESTABLISHED** 1931

The Anthony and Elizabeth Mellows Charitable Settlement

WHAT IS FUNDED (a) The acquisition of objects to be used or displayed in houses of the National Trust or Churches of the Church of England; (b) the encouragement of hospices and medical research; (c) support of the arts; (d) the training and development of children and young people. The Trustees can only consider projects recommended to them by those national institutions with whom they are in close co-operation

WHAT IS NOT FUNDED Applications from individuals, including students, are ineligible

WHO CAN BENEFIT National bodies benefiting: children and young adults; actors and entertainment professionals; musicians; textile workers and designers; and writers and poets. There is no restriction on the disease or medical condition suffered by the beneficiaries

WHERE FUNDING CAN BE GIVEN UK

TYPE OF GRANT Generally single projects

FINANCES *Year* 1998 *Income* £42,000 *Grants* £31,000

TRUSTEES Prof A R Mellows, TD, PhD, LLD, Mrs E A Mellows

HOW TO APPLY Applications are considered when received, but only from national institutions. No specific date. No application forms are used.

Grants will be made three times a year when the Trustees meet to consider applications

WHO TO APPLY TO Prof A R Mellows, TD, The Anthony and Elizabeth Mellows Charitable Settlement, 22 Devereux Court, Temple Bar, London WC2R 3JJ

CC NO 281229   **ESTABLISHED** 1980

....

■ Melodor Ltd

WHAT IS FUNDED Jewish causes, particularly the advancement of religion in accordance with the Orthodox Jewish faith

WHO CAN BENEFIT To benefit Jewish people

WHERE FUNDING CAN BE GIVEN UK and overseas

FINANCES *Year* 1995–96 *Income* £185,469
Grants £163,758

TRUSTEES B Weiss, M Weiss, P Weiss, S Weiss, J L Weiss, H Weiss, R Sofer, W Neuman, F Newman, H Neuman, M Neuman, E Neuman, M Frielander, E Zimet

HOW TO APPLY To the address under Who To Apply To in writing

WHO TO APPLY TO Henry Neuman, Administrator, Melodor Ltd, 6 Brantwood Road, Salford, Manchester M7 4FL

CC NO 260972   **ESTABLISHED** 1970

....

■ Melton Mowbray Building Society Charitable Foundation

WHAT IS FUNDED General charitable purposes for the benefit of persons resident within the counties of Rutland, Leicester, Lincoln and Nottingham, including residential facilities and services; infrastructure development; charity and voluntary umbrella bodies; Christian outreach; churches; community arts and recreation; and health. Support will also go to conservation; education and training; and social care and development

WHAT IS NOT FUNDED No grants to individuals, political requests, extremist or unethical projects

WHO CAN BENEFIT To benefit children, young adults preparing for adult life, disabled people and those requiring assistance

WHERE FUNDING CAN BE GIVEN Rutland, Leicester, Lincoln and Nottingham

TYPE OF GRANT One-off (may consider recurring), buildings, capital, core costs, running costs and start-up costs. Funding is available for up to one year

RANGE OF GRANTS £1–£150, average grant £100

FINANCES *Year* 1998 *Income* £6,254
Grants £1,477

TRUSTEES R J Green, Canon D E B Law, C E I Thornton, D Twitchen, G F Wells

PUBLICATIONS Leaflet on display in all branches of the Building Society

HOW TO APPLY The Foundation is happy to receive initial telephone calls. There are no application forms, guidelines (except for geographical territory) or deadlines for applications. Sae is not required

WHO TO APPLY TO Lisa Lound, Secretary, Melton Mowbray Building Society Charitable Foundation, 39 Nottingham Street, Melton Mowbray, Leicestershire LE13 1NR *Tel* 01664 563937

CC NO 1067348   **ESTABLISHED** 1998

■ The Melton Trust

WHAT IS FUNDED Residential care and day centres for those with learning disabilities

WHAT IS NOT FUNDED The Trust will not contribute towards administrative costs or to individuals

WHO CAN BENEFIT To benefit young adults and older people with learning difficulties, including those suffering from autism, cerebral palsy, mental illness, multiple sclerosis, muscular dystrophy, spina bifida and hydrocephalus

WHERE FUNDING CAN BE GIVEN UK

TYPE OF GRANT One-off, recurring, buildings, capital, projects, core costs and start-up costs. Funding is available for up to three years

RANGE OF GRANTS £500–£5,000

FINANCES *Year* 1997–98 *Income* £63,312

TRUSTEES D M Melman, J H Moule, M W J Thorne

NOTES This Trust had under £5,000 to give away in 1997, there it is unlikely to be able to support any large projects

HOW TO APPLY To the address under Who To Apply To in writing on no more than two sides of A4 paper

WHO TO APPLY TO Richard J F Martin, Company Secretary, The Melton Trust, c/o Home Farm Trust Ltd, Merchants House, Wapping Road, Bristol BS1 4RW *Tel* 0117-927 3746

CC NO 1060467   **ESTABLISHED** 1997

....

■ Melville Trust for Care and Cure of Cancer

WHAT IS FUNDED To provide financial assistance for scientific or clinical investigations on cancer

WHAT IS NOT FUNDED The Trust does not make contributions to other charities

WHO CAN BENEFIT Universities, medical schools, scientific bodies; research workers; medical professionals; and those suffering from cancer

WHERE FUNDING CAN BE GIVEN Investigations based in Lothian, Borders or Fife only

TYPE OF GRANT Fellowships, Research Assistantships, grants for equipment

FINANCES *Year* 1996 *Income* £120,000
Grants £62,000

TRUSTEES Melville Estate Trustees

NOTES In general the Bawden Fund was set up 'for the purposes of charity and benevolence and the advancement of knowledge especially in aid of human suffering' for the benefit of certain charities and institutions that are specified in the Trust Deed. Therefore the discretion of the trustees to award new grants is extremely limited

HOW TO APPLY Application forms available from Tods Murray WS and must be submitted by not later than 31 May

WHO TO APPLY TO Tods Murray WS, Melville Trust for Care and Cure of Cancer, 66 Queen Street, Edinburgh, Scotland EH2 4NE

SC NO SCO 32409   **ESTABLISHED** 1922

....

■ The Menchester Trust

WHAT IS FUNDED General charitable purposes

WHO CAN BENEFIT There are no restrictions on the age; professional and economic group; family situation; religion and culture; and social circumstances of; or disease or medical condition suffered by, the beneficiaries

WHERE FUNDING CAN BE GIVEN UK and overseas

TRUSTEES M Halpern, C E Halpern, G Siemiatycki

412

Think carefully about every application. Is it justified?

WHO TO APPLY TO M Halpern, Trustee, The Menchester Trust, 31 Leadale Road, London N16 6BZ

CC NO 1053452　　**ESTABLISHED** 1996

■ The Mendlesham Educational Foundation

WHAT IS FUNDED The local schools and other local organisations and amenities receive an annual grant, the rest of the grant total is given to youth organisations and individuals for education

WHO CAN BENEFIT Residents of Mendlesham under the age of 25 years. Schools and organisations benefiting children, young adults and those disadvantaged by poverty

WHERE FUNDING CAN BE GIVEN The Parish of Mendlesham

TYPE OF GRANT One-off and recurrent grants will be considered

RANGE OF GRANTS For individuals £50–£750

FINANCES *Year* 1997 *Income* £29,398 *Grants* £22,973

TRUSTEES J B Baker, R B S Colchester, E H Cutting, R M Fenning, S J Fenning, Rev P Gray, T M Styles, Mrs D Smith

HOW TO APPLY To the address under Who To Apply To in writing. Application from individuals must include educational qualifications, details of courses to be taken, other grants applied for, parents' financial position, other children in the family and estimated expenditure

WHO TO APPLY TO Mrs P Colchester, Clerk, The Mendlesham Educational Foundation, Ashes Farm, Mendlesham, Stowmarket, Suffolk IP14 5TE *Tel* 01449 766330

CC NO 271762　　**ESTABLISHED** 1976

■ The Mental Health Foundation

WHAT IS FUNDED To improve treatment, services and support for people with mental health problems and people with learning disabilities. To support innovative, ground-breaking projects under specific programmes of work

WHAT IS NOT FUNDED Individual grants are not made for students to complete their studies or to obtain a higher degree

WHO CAN BENEFIT Organisations benefiting people suffering from mental illness and learning difficulties. Medical professional and research workers may be considered for funding

WHERE FUNDING CAN BE GIVEN UK

TYPE OF GRANT Grants to innovative projects in mental health and learning disabilities. Research fellowships also given. Applicants are invited to apply only under special programmes, which run for three to five years. A small 'World Mental Health Day' award fund for mental health user groups and small organisations. Scientific research essays are made once a year to students

SAMPLE GRANTS £37,000 to L'Arche, Liverpool, for a supported employment project under the Mental Health Foundation's Learning Disabilities Choice Initiative; £32,000 over three years to a doctor at Llandough Hospital, Wales – determinants of cognitive function in older men in the Caerphilly cohort; £30,000 to Depression Alliance, England to fund post of National Groups Co-ordinator; £30,000 over two years to Glasgow Association for Mental Health to fund post of Employment Development Worker

FINANCES *Year* 1997 *Income* £2,985,232 *Grants* £1,714,784

TRUSTEES Prof Sir Raymond Hoffenberg, KBE (President), Michael S Wilson (Chair), Lady Euston (Vice Chair), Giles Ridley (Vice Chair), C Richard Plummer, CA (Treasurer), Jack Barnes, Marion Beeforth, Jennifer Bernard, Lord Dholakia, OBE, JP, Sue Fraser, Roger Graef, Dr Rachel Jenkins, Lord Ramsey, DL, Prof S P Sashidaran, MB, BS, Mphil, MRCPsych, PhD, Prof Jan Scott, MD, FRCPsych, Prof Chris Thompson, MPhil, MD, FRCPsych, FRCP, AFBPS,

PUBLICATIONS List available from Mental Health Foundation, Sales and Promotions Office

HOW TO APPLY The Mental Health Foundation does not accept general fundraising appeals. Information on future award rounds and application forms can be obtained from Kate Rogers, Grants Administrator at the address under Who To Apply To

WHO TO APPLY TO June McKerrow, Director, The Mental Health Foundation, 20–21 Cornwall Terrace, London NW1 4QL *Tel* 0171-535 7400 *Fax* 0171-535 7474 *E-mail* mhf@mentalhealth.org.uk *Web Site* http://www.mentalhealth.org.uk

CC NO 801130　　**ESTABLISHED** 1949

■ Menuchar Ltd

WHAT IS FUNDED Jewish organisations

WHO CAN BENEFIT Jewish organisations

WHERE FUNDING CAN BE GIVEN UK

TYPE OF GRANT Primarily one-off

FINANCES *Year* 1997 *Income* £57,595 *Grants* £134,334

TRUSTEES M Bude, A E Bude, N Bude, R Bude

HOW TO APPLY To the the address under Who To Apply To in writing

WHO TO APPLY TO The Secretary, Menuchar Ltd, Flack Stetson, Mattey House, 128–136 High Street, Edgeware, Middlesex HA8 7EL

CC NO 262782　　**ESTABLISHED** 1971

■ The Stuart Menzies Memorial Trust

This trust did not respond to CAF's request to amend its entry and, by 30 June 1998, CAF's researchers did not find financial records for later than 1995 on its file at the Charity Commission. Trusts are legally required to submit annual accounts to the Charity Commission under section 42 of the Charities Act 1993

WHAT IS FUNDED General charitable purposes

WHO CAN BENEFIT Individuals and institutions. There are no restrictions on the age; professional and economic group; family situation; religion and culture; and social circumstances of; or disease or medical condition suffered by, the beneficiaries

WHERE FUNDING CAN BE GIVEN UK

TYPE OF GRANT Recurring

WHO TO APPLY TO R J Crawe, The Stuart Menzies Memorial Trust, 9 Cheapside, London EC2V 6AD

CC NO 801839　　**ESTABLISHED** 1989

■ The Mercers' Company Educational Trust Fund

WHAT IS FUNDED (a) To provide bursaries where there is financial hardship to assist in the education of children between the ages of 11 and 18 who are currently receiving full-time education at independent schools recognised by the IAPS or GB Associations, or otherwise of a standard acceptable to the Trustees. Priority is given to

Does the trust you have chosen match your needs? Haphazard applications waste postage and time

413

cases where the family meets unexpected misfortune and where children are in the final two years of their GCSE course or final year of GCE Advanced level course. (b) To provide grants in cases of financial hardship to students in further and higher education. The Company makes bursary awards directly to a number of institutions of further and higher education and consequently applications from individual students cannot be accepted for courses in performing arts, law, business and management studies, journalism, BTEC and City and Guilds, intercalated degrees or elective study. Grants are restricted to students under the age of 25. There are four small funds restricted to helping students at Cambridge and Oxford Universities, the Robinson Exhibition for Divinity at Cambridge, and the North, Barrett and Walthall Exhibitions tenable at Oxford and Cambridge

WHO CAN BENEFIT To benefit those between 11 and 25, including students, who are disadvantaged by poverty

WHERE FUNDING CAN BE GIVEN UK

TYPE OF GRANT Termly payments to the school concerned for a stipulated period. Further/higher education grants to individuals

FINANCES *Year* 1996 *Income* £231,303 *Grants* £256,249

TRUSTEES J P G Wathen, J Ounsted, C C Lane, MBE, G H L Rimbault, Dr D M Watney, JP

HOW TO APPLY On forms obtainable from the address under Who To Apply To

WHO TO APPLY TO The Education and Charities Administrator, The Mercers' Company Educational Trust Fund, The Mercers' Company, Mercers' Hall, Ironmonger Lane, London EC2V 8HE *Tel* 0171-726 4991

CC NO 313222 **ESTABLISHED** 1957

■ Merchant Taylors Charities

WHAT IS FUNDED People or organisations connected with the Merchant Taylors Company and other general charitable purposes in the area Where Funding Can Be Given

WHO CAN BENEFIT There are no restrictions on the age; professional and economic group; family situation; religion and culture; and social circumstances of; or disease or medical condition suffered by, the beneficiaries

WHERE FUNDING CAN BE GIVEN York and suburbs

FINANCES *Year* 1997 *Income* £46,629 *Grants* £2,505

TRUSTEES Principal Officers: T R Bradley (Master), J L Bailey (Clerk), P Smith (Chancellor)

HOW TO APPLY To the address under Who To Apply To in writing

WHO TO APPLY TO The Clerk, Merchant Taylors Charities, Mill House, Topcliffe, York YO7 3RZ

CC NO 229067 **ESTABLISHED** 1945

■ Merchant Taylors' Consolidated Charities for the Infirm

WHAT IS FUNDED Maintaining or subscribing to maintenance of homes, clinics, etc, temporary or permanent, for reception, treatment and benefit of physically or mentally disabled poor persons or aged needing assistance. Maintaining or subscribing to maintenance of any organisation providing assistance to beneficiaries in own homes. Charities working in the field of community services

WHAT IS NOT FUNDED Applications restricted to organisations whose activities are wholly within the objects of the Trust, dealing with the infirm

WHO CAN BENEFIT To headquarters organisations benefiting people of all ages; ex-service and service people; retired people; students; textile workers and designers; unemployed people; disabled people; and those disadvantaged by poverty. There is no restriction on the disease or medical condition suffered by the beneficiaries

WHERE FUNDING CAN BE GIVEN UK

TYPE OF GRANT Buildings, endowments, feasibility studies, one-off, project and start-up costs. Funding for up to three years will be considered

FINANCES *Year* 1997 *Income* £155,800 *Grants* £116,700

TRUSTEES The Master and Wardens of the Merchant Taylors' Company

HOW TO APPLY Applications in writing which will all be acknowledged and considered quarterly

WHO TO APPLY TO The Clerk, Merchant Taylors' Consolidated Charities for the Infirm, Merchant Taylors' Company, Merchant Taylors' Hall, 30 Threadneedle Street, London EC2R 8AY *Tel* 0171-450 4440

CC NO 214266 **ESTABLISHED** 1960

■ Merchants House of Glasgow

WHAT IS FUNDED To pay pensions to pensioners who may or may not have membership qualifications and to provide assistance in the form of grants for projects being undertaken by charitable and other institutions within and around Glasgow. This includes organisations concerned with the disabled, elderly or terminally ill and socially deprived; organisations providing care, advancement and rehabilitation of youth, universities, colleges of further education and schools; organisations connected with the arts, music, theatre and visual arts; organisations of which the Dean of Guild is an Honorary President or Vice President or other office-bearer, or on which the Merchants House is officially represented

WHAT IS NOT FUNDED No grants to: individuals; churches other than Glasgow Cathedral

WHO CAN BENEFIT Registered charities benefiting: people of all ages; at risk groups; disabled people; those disadvantaged by poverty; socially isolated people and those who are terminally ill. Actors and entertainment professionals, musicians, textile workers and designers, writers and poets will be considered

WHERE FUNDING CAN BE GIVEN Glasgow and West of Scotland

TYPE OF GRANT Capital projects

FINANCES *Year* 1995 *Income* £580,000 *Grants* £250,000

TRUSTEES Lord Dean of Guild and Directors

HOW TO APPLY Last completed (audited) accounts. Guidelines as above

WHO TO APPLY TO D A R Ballantine, Merchants House of Glasgow, 7 West George Street, Glasgow G2 1BA

SC NO SCO 08900 **ESTABLISHED** 1605

■ Meridian Broadcasting Charitable Trust

WHAT IS FUNDED General charitable purposes. A different area of funding is chosen each year. Please check time table by contacting the address under Who To Apply To. The Trust will fund communication aids which are accessible to communities and which give more opportunities to find out about local facilities and services

WHAT IS NOT FUNDED No funds for schools, individuals, applications outside annual focus, NHS, fundraising organisations, endowments, salaries, appeals

WHO CAN BENEFIT Local voluntary organisations demonstrating wide community benefit to Meridian viewers. There are no restrictions on the age; professional and economic group; family situation; religion and culture; and social circumstances of; or disease or medical condition suffered by, the beneficiaries

WHERE FUNDING CAN BE GIVEN Meridian Broadcasting broadcast area (South East)

TYPE OF GRANT Capital for one year or less

FINANCES *Year* 1995–96 *Income* £30,941 *Grants* £4,454

TRUSTEES S Albury, Baroness Flather, M McAnally, J Morrell, R Niddrie, C North, G Ward

PUBLICATIONS *Breaking the Sound Barrier, Seeing Things Differently, Ready to Care, Freedom to Choose'* free to Meridian viewers

HOW TO APPLY Trust works proactively

WHO TO APPLY TO Margo Horsley, Director, Meridian Broadcasting Charitable Trust, Television Centre, Southampton SO14 0PZ

CC NO 298643   **ESTABLISHED** 1988

■ Merrill Trust

WHAT IS FUNDED General charitable purposes, in particular, to further the education of children attending Merrill Community School

WHO CAN BENEFIT There are no restrictions on the age; professional and economic group; family situation; religion and culture; and social circumstances of; or disease or medical condition suffered by, the beneficiaries. However, particular favour is given to the children attending Merrill Community School

WHERE FUNDING CAN BE GIVEN UK

FINANCES *Year* 1996 *Income* £32,696

WHO TO APPLY TO Mrs R M Adamson, Trustee, Merrill Trust, Windwhistle, Farley Hill, Farley, Matlock, Derbyshire DE4 3LL

CC NO 1048955   **ESTABLISHED** 1995

■ Mersey Basin Trust

WHAT IS FUNDED To conserve, protect and improve water courses, land and buildings within the Mersey Basin Campaign area, to advance the education of the public with regard to the conservation, protection and improvement of the same. Supports voluntary organisations and schools

WHO CAN BENEFIT Organisations, schools and all those involved in environmental conservation

WHERE FUNDING CAN BE GIVEN Northern Mersey Basin: Merseyside, Cheshire, Greater Manchester, Derbyshire and Lancashire

FINANCES *Year* 1997 *Income* £433,820

TRUSTEES J E Ashworth, J Gittins, C W Hamilton, Ms E M Jones, Ms L Johnson, B Lythgoe, F Lythgoe, K Parry, W J Rhodes, D Roydes, Mrs A Selby, C Selby, F Smith, H C West, B Williams, P H M Wilmers, E Whewll

NOTES The Mersey Basin Trust includes the Stream Care Project, Waterside Revival, ICI Green Action Grants, Green Generation Grants and Greenlink Awards

WHO TO APPLY TO T Jones, Company Secretary, Mersey Basin Trust, Sunley Tower, Piccadilly Plaza, Manchester M1 4AG

CC NO 1005305   **ESTABLISHED** 1991

■ The Mersey Basin Trust – Greenlink Awards

WHAT IS FUNDED Nature conservation, the tackling of pollution, urban dereliction and waste, the preservation of the built environment

WHO CAN BENEFIT Non-profit making organisations

WHERE FUNDING CAN BE GIVEN Northern Mersey Basin: Merseyside, Cheshire, Greater Manchester, Derbyshire and Lancashire

FINANCES *Year* 1997 *Grants* £17,283

HOW TO APPLY To the address under Who To Apply To in writing

WHO TO APPLY TO Carol Worral/Anthony Kelly, The Mersey Basin Trust – Greenlink Awards, Lancashire Enterprise, Enterprise House, 17 Ribblesdale Place, Preston PR1 3NA

CC NO 1005305   **ESTABLISHED** 1991

■ Mersey Basin Trust – ICI Green Action Grants

WHAT IS FUNDED The Trust awards ICI Green Action Grants for environmental projects carried out by voluntary groups and schools in the Runcorn and Northwich areas of Cheshire. The grant is part of the Weaver Valley Initiative. Charities working in the fields of: support to voluntary and community organisations; charity or voluntary umbrella bodies; conservation; ecology; natural history; environmental issues; schools and colleges; and parks will be considered

WHAT IS NOT FUNDED No grants for repairs to buildings, etc

WHO CAN BENEFIT Voluntary, community organisations and schools benefiting people of all ages and students

WHERE FUNDING CAN BE GIVEN Runcorn and Northwich

TYPE OF GRANT Project grants paid retrospectively and funded for up to one year

RANGE OF GRANTS £100–£1,000

SAMPLE GRANTS £1,000 to Witton Area Conservation Group for pond dipping platform; £877 to Witton Area Conservation Group for water level restoration project; £860 to Frodsham Wildlife Conservation Group for woodland sensory trail; £859 to Frodsham Town Council for picnic benches; £677 to Norton Priory Museum Trust for pond dipping platform; £606 to Cloughwood School, Hartford for pondside footpath; £600 to Beechwood Primary School, Runcorn for school nature area; £440 to Frodsham Wildlife Conservation Group for pond creation; £397 to Little Leigh Primary School, Northwich for woodland trail; £350 to Cheshire Countryside Management Service for wildflower meadow creation

FINANCES *Year* 1997–98 *Income* £600,000 *Grants* £7,000

TRUSTEES Keith Noble, Derek Bullock, Michael O'Brian, Edgar Whewell, John Gittins, Charles Hamilton, Brian Lythgoe, Alan Howarth, Mrs Ann Gardiner, Dr Robin Henshaw, Frank Smith, Ben Williams, Anne Selby, Paul Christie, Anthony Bielderman, Roger Hutchins, David A Roydes, Frank Lythgoe, Cedric Selby, Mrs Diane Rhodes, Peter Glover, Bill Rhodes, John Ashworth, Bert Bowles

PUBLICATIONS *The Campaigner* quarterly newsletter

HOW TO APPLY Application should be made on a form available either by writing or telephone call. The awards panel meets quarterly

WHO TO APPLY TO Mark Turner, Mersey Basin Trust – ICI Green Action Grants, Sunley Tower, Piccadilly Plaza, Manchester M1 4AG *Tel* 0161-228 6924

CC NO 1005305 **ESTABLISHED** 1991

■ Mersey Basin Trust – Stream Care Project

WHAT IS FUNDED The care and improvement of local watercourses through the encouragement of the local community. The Trust offers advice and support to local groups

WHERE FUNDING CAN BE GIVEN Mersey Basin Campaign Area (Cheshire, part of Lancashire, Greater Manchester, Merseyside and part of Derbyshire)

FINANCES *Year* 1997 *Income* £36,964 *Grants* £11,103

NOTES In 1997, Stream Care supported 46 groups carrying out practical projects and an additional 25 groups received advice and non-financial support. The Trust also produced a new exhibition for display at various venues and events

HOW TO APPLY To the address under Who To Apply To in writing

WHO TO APPLY TO Mark Turner, Mersey Basin Trust – Stream Care Project, Sunley Tower, Piccadilly Plaza, Manchester M1 4AG

CC NO 1005305 **ESTABLISHED** 1991

■ Mersey Basin Trust – Waterside Revival Grants

WHAT IS FUNDED The conservation and improvement of waterside sites, open to the public by funding local voluntary groups to organise and carry out the improvement and management of such sites

WHO CAN BENEFIT Local, voluntary groups involved in waterside conservation

WHERE FUNDING CAN BE GIVEN Mersey Basin Campaign Area (Cheshire, part of Lancashire, Greater Manchester, Merseyside, High Peak in Derbyshire)

FINANCES *Year* 1998 *Grants* £8,000

HOW TO APPLY Applications should be made on a form available from the address under Who To Apply To, whereupon a visit to the site will be made. At present, there is one grant panel per annum to consider applications, held in July. Telephone enquiries welcomed

WHO TO APPLY TO Gwen White, Mersey Basin Trust – Waterside Revival Grants, Sunley Tower, Piccadilly Plaza, Manchester M1 4AG *Tel* 0161-228 6924

CC NO 1005305 **ESTABLISHED** 1991

■ Merseyside Development Foundation

WHAT IS FUNDED Education, health and welfare

WHO CAN BENEFIT Organisations benefiting: children and young adults; at risk groups; those disadvantaged by poverty and socially isolated people. There is no restriction on the disease or medical condition suffered by the beneficiaries

WHERE FUNDING CAN BE GIVEN Merseyside

FINANCES *Year* 1997 *Income* £62,972 *Grants* £17,540

TRUSTEES Directors: Mrs C R Behrend, A R Dronfield, Mrs C J Murphy, M McDonagh, Mrs E Taylor

HOW TO APPLY The Foundation only considered applications via people known to them. Advice and information is available

WHO TO APPLY TO Dr M A Williams, Merseyside Development Foundation, 2nd Floor, Spinney House, Church Street, Liverpool L1 3AS

CC NO 1002626 **ESTABLISHED** 1990

■ The Zachary Merton and George Woofindin Convalescent Trust

WHAT IS FUNDED Grants to convalescent poor, to convalescent homes, travelling expenses of convalescent poor. Grants for the infirm, the chronically sick, sick persons and community medicine

WHAT IS NOT FUNDED No grants to individuals

WHO CAN BENEFIT Organisations benefiting: carers, disabled people and those disadvantaged by poverty. There is no restriction on the disease or medical condition suffered by the beneficiaries

WHERE FUNDING CAN BE GIVEN Sheffield and Lincoln (Sheffield area includes areas of North Derbyshire, South Yorkshire and North Nottingham)

TYPE OF GRANT Bi-annual

RANGE OF GRANTS £250–£5,500

SAMPLE GRANTS £5,500 to Sheffield and District Association for the Disabled; £3,500 to British Red Cross (Sheffield Branch); £3,000 to Trinity Day Care Trust; £2,000 to Sheffield Churches Council for Community Care; £2,000 MIND; £2,000 to Cavendish Fellowship in Hip Surgery; £1,800 to SHARE Psychotherapy; £1,600 to Multiple Sclerosis Society; £1,200 to Lincoln Area Council for Voluntary Service; £1,000 to Sheffield Alcohol Advisory Service

FINANCES *Year* 1997 *Income* £56,500 *Grants* £33,950

TRUSTEES M G S Frampton, N P Nicholson, J H Osborn, G Connell, Dr G A B Davies-Jones, J S Ibberson, Mrs P M Perrimen, N J A Hutton, C J Jewitt, M P Newton

HOW TO APPLY By 25 March and 25 September

WHO TO APPLY TO G J Smallman, Clerk to the Trustees, The Zachary Merton and George Woofindin Convalescent Trust, Fountain Precinct, Balm Green, Sheffield S1 1RZ

CC NO 221760 **ESTABLISHED** 1956

■ Merton Evangelical Church Trust

WHAT IS FUNDED General charitable purposes in particular to advance the Christian religion and to relieve persons who are in conditions of need, hardship or distress or who are elderly or sick

WHO CAN BENEFIT To benefit: the elderly; Christians; at risk groups; those disadvantaged by poverty; socially isolated people; and the sick. There is no restriction on the disease or medical condition suffered by the beneficiaries

WHERE FUNDING CAN BE GIVEN Merton and elsewhere

RANGE OF GRANTS £45–£874

SAMPLE GRANTS £500 to Hynes Home Fund for emergency relief; £425 to Arab World Ministries; £425 to European Missionary Fellowship; £425 to Latin Link; £425 to London City Mission; £425 to Pocket Testament League

FINANCES *Year* 1996 *Income* £45,322 *Grants* £3,544

WHO TO APPLY TO c/o The Chairman, Merton Evangelical Church Trust, 21 Milner Road, South Wimbledon, London SW19 3AB *Tel* 0181-540 0060

CC NO 1043800 **ESTABLISHED** 1994

416

Think carefully about every application. Is it justified?

■ L Messel & Co Charitable Trust

WHAT IS FUNDED General charitable purposes. At the discretion of the Trustees

WHAT IS NOT FUNDED Not to individuals

WHO CAN BENEFIT At the discretion of the Trustees. There are no restrictions on the age; professional and economic group; family situation; religion and culture; and social circumstances of; or disease or medical condition suffered by, the beneficiaries

WHERE FUNDING CAN BE GIVEN UK

TYPE OF GRANT At the discretion of the Trustees

RANGE OF GRANTS £110–£7,000

SAMPLE GRANTS £7,000 to Charities Aid Foundation; £2,000 to International Scientific Trust; £560 to London Events; £400 Royal British Legion; £110 to Queen Elizabeth Fund for Disabled People

FINANCES *Year* 1996 *Income* £14,514
Grants £10,070

TRUSTEES M C Brooks, D H Hunter

WHO TO APPLY TO W B Owen, L Messel & Co Charitable Trust, Kidson Impey, Chartered Accountants, Ruskin House, 14 St Johns Road, Tunbridge Wells, Kent TN4 9NP

CC NO 287421   **ESTABLISHED** 1983

■ The Metcalfe Charitable Trust

WHAT IS FUNDED The Trust's priority is the upkeep of Metcalfe Recreation Ground and village institute, with grants going to community amenities and development, local schools and clubs for older people

WHO CAN BENEFIT To benefit children, young adults and members of the local community

WHERE FUNDING CAN BE GIVEN Everton and Scaftworth

SAMPLE GRANTS £1,200 to Metcalfe Recreation Committee; £275 to Heds; £160 to Golden Age Club; £65 to Everton Old People's Christmas Party

FINANCES *Year* 1997 *Income* £41,600
Grants £20,397

TRUSTEES G F Webster, H H Simpson, F B Poynter, R S Moore, G S Troop

NOTES Expenditure on let property (Schedule 1) £1,780, on village institution and recreation ground £16,917 and grants to village organisations £1,700

HOW TO APPLY To the address under Who To Apply To in writing

WHO TO APPLY TO R R Kewarth, Secretary, The Metcalfe Charitable Trust, Freshfield, Sluice Lane, Everton, Nottinghamshire DN10 5AX

CC NO 213982   **ESTABLISHED** 1960

■ The Tony Metherell Charitable Trust

WHAT IS FUNDED General charitable purposes, including assisting hospices, cancer charities, care and welfare of the elderly and handicapped

WHO CAN BENEFIT Particularly older people, disabled people and those suffering from cancer. However, there are no restrictions on the age; professional and economic group; family situation; religion and culture; and social circumstances of; or disease or medical condition suffered by, the beneficiaries

WHERE FUNDING CAN BE GIVEN UK

RANGE OF GRANTS £50–£5,000

SAMPLE GRANTS £5,000 to Isabel Hospice; £5,000 to Relate; £5,000 to DGAA; £2,900 to British Legion; £2,000 to Cansearch; £1,000 to Colon Cancer Concern; £500 to Women's Link; £500 to Catch; £500 to ICRF; £500 to Crisis at Christmas

FINANCES *Year* 1997 *Income* £73,684
Grants £25,350

TRUSTEES B R M Fox, Ms C J Good

WHO TO APPLY TO B R M Fox, Trustee, The Tony Metherell Charitable Trust, Jenningsbury, Hertford SG13 7NS

CC NO 1046899   **ESTABLISHED** 1992

■ The Methodist Relief and Development Fund

WHAT IS FUNDED (a) Emergency relief in disasters and long-term refugee assistance. (b) Priorities for overseas development: agroforestry (organic farming, permaculture etc). Literacy (both formal and non-formal education) and water (for drinking and agricultural use). Also covered are; social services (including health), skills and capacity building and economic development.
(c) Development of education in the European Union, including campaigns, publications and support for Development Education Organisations

WHAT IS NOT FUNDED Applications from individuals and organisations without charitable status. Scholarships for studies or voluntary work overseas. Individual development education centres affiliated to the Development Education Association

WHO CAN BENEFIT (a) Emergency relief: Action by Churches Together (ACT), Indigenous NGO's/ religious organisations in the affected country or region, particular projects of international aid organisations. (b) Development: indigenous NGO's/religious organisations in the developing world and international NGO's who work with an indigenous partner to implement a project.
(c) Development Education: Development Education Organisations in the European Union. Organisations benefiting; children; young adults; older people; medical professionals; research workers; unemployed people; volunteers; those in care, fostered and adopted; parents and children; one parent families; widows and widowers; and beneficiaries suffering from cerebral palsy, diabetes, head and other injuries, hearing loss, HIV and AIDS, leprosy, mental illness, muscular dystrophy, paediatric diseases, polio, prenatal conditions, sight loss, tropical disease and tuberculosis. There is no restriction on the religion and culture of the beneficiaries though there may be a few restrictions on their social circumstances

WHERE FUNDING CAN BE GIVEN UK and overseas

TYPE OF GRANT Buildings, capital, core costs, feasibility studies, one-off, project, research, recurring costs, running costs and salaries. Funding for up to three years will be considered

RANGE OF GRANTS £100–£80,000. Average grants: £5,000–£15,000

SAMPLE GRANTS £80,000 to Nijera Shikhi Literacy Programme in Bangladesh for non-formal education in literacy; £60,300 (co funded) to African Water and Agroforestry Programme (AWAP) for agroforestry, organic farming and water projects; £60,000 to Association of Arulagam in India for hospice for AIDS sufferers; £56,200 (co-funded) to United Mission to Nepal, Gorkha Health programme for outreach work on non-formal education, health and water; £25,000 to IMPACT in South Africa for community volunteer organisations; £24,500 to Action by Churches Together (ACT) for emergency relief for Zaire; £20,100 to ADESA and Womankind Worldwide, in Peru for capacity building for NGO involved in agricultural work; £17,000 to Methodist Seva Sevana Community Development in Sri Lanka for business apprenticeship and skills training in urban areas; £15,000 to TWIFO Oil Palm Plantation Hospital for medical aid; £10,300 to UNHCR in Ethiopia for income generation projects for long-term Sudanese refugees

FINANCES *Year* 1996–97 *Income* £843,832 *Grants* £628,468

TRUSTEES J Anderson, Rev G Barnard, Rev E Bellamy, K Cash, H Dalzell, Rev D Halstead, B Hindmarsh, J Hindson, Rev R Jacob, Rev Dr R Jones, Dr J Leitch, D Maidment, Rev F Munce, R Shackleton, S Veagra

PUBLICATIONS Annual Report. *MRDF Policy on Humanitarian Aid and Development. Funds in Focus* (quarterly publication). *Africa Link* (agroforestry publication)

HOW TO APPLY Applications should be sent to the address under Who To Apply To. Applicants should request a copy of the *MRDF Policy on Humanitarian Aid and Development* if they are unsure about their application to the MRDF. The MRDF does not issue guidelines or require applicants to complete a form. Applications must reach the correspondent one month prior to a quarterly Trustees meeting (dates available from the MRDF)

WHO TO APPLY TO Martin Watson, Projects Co-ordinator, The Methodist Relief and Development Fund, 1 Central Buildings, London SW1H 9NH *Tel* 0171-222 8010 *Fax* 0171-799 2153 *E-mail* watson@mrdf.demon.co

CC NO 291691   ESTABLISHED 1985

■ Metro FM Pop Fund

WHAT IS FUNDED General charitable purposes at the discretion of the Trustees

WHO CAN BENEFIT Local groups; local branches of national charities. There are no restrictions on the age; professional and economic group; family situation; religion and culture; and social circumstances of; or disease or medical condition suffered by, the beneficiaries

WHERE FUNDING CAN BE GIVEN The radio transmission area of Metro Radio

TYPE OF GRANT Grants given to 48 local charities for specific capital projects or equipment

RANGE OF GRANTS £50–£3,000

FINANCES *Year* 1997 *Income* £26,974

TRUSTEES Sean Marley, Alan Wilson, Donald Dempsey, Mrs Anne Lowrie, Mrs E Mawston

HOW TO APPLY Applications considered in January each year

WHO TO APPLY TO Mrs E Mawston, Metro FM Pop Fund, Radio House, Swalwell, Newcastle Upon Tyne NE99 1BB *Tel* 0191-420 0971 *Fax* 0191-496 0174

CC NO 1001540   ESTABLISHED 1991

■ The Metropolitan Drinking Fountain and Cattle Trough Association

WHAT IS FUNDED Projects working to provide clean water supplies in developing countries, the provision of drinking fountains in schools and the restoration of disused drinking fountains. The preservation of the Association's archive materials, artefacts, drinking fountains, cattle troughs and other installations

WHERE FUNDING CAN BE GIVEN UK and overseas

FINANCES *Year* 1996 *Income* £27,142 *Grants* £24,109

TRUSTEES Members of the Executive Committee: R P Baber, A E Buxton, M W Elliot, I Evans, J King, J E Mills, Mrs I de Pelet, R Sheridan-White, Sir J Smith, Mrs T Wells

PUBLICATIONS *The Drinking Fountain Association*

NOTES The present total of fountains and troughs supplied, for use both in the UK and overseas, by the Foundation of the Association are as follows: 3,910 drinking fountains; 927 cattle troughs; 3,721 water wells/storage; and 24 tanks

HOW TO APPLY To the address under Who To Apply To in writing

WHO TO APPLY TO R P Baber, Secretary and Treaurer, The Metropolitan Drinking Fountain and Cattle Trough Association, Oaklands, 5 Queensborough Gardens, Chislehurst, Kent BR7 6NP

CC NO 207743   ESTABLISHED 1960

■ Metropolitan Society for the Blind

WHAT IS FUNDED Welfare of blind and partially sighted residents of inner London

WHAT IS NOT FUNDED No grants for education or bad debts

WHO CAN BENEFIT The blind and partially sighted of the 12 inner London boroughs and City of London

WHERE FUNDING CAN BE GIVEN City of London and the 12 inner London boroughs: Camden, Greenwich, Hackney, Hammersmith and Fulham, Islington, Kensington and Chelsea, Lambeth, Lewisham, Southwark, Tower Hamlets, Wandsworth and Westminster

TYPE OF GRANT One-off

RANGE OF GRANTS Individuals: maximum £250. Organisations: maximum £1,000

SAMPLE GRANTS £500 to In Touch, Islington towards the cost of a replacement minibus; £400 to Friends of the Totally Blind towards the costs of organising the annual Totally Blind Bowlers Open; £387 to OBAC towards the cost of audio transcribing equipment; £250 to Tower Hamlets Environment to provide plants for a sensory garden; £250 to Aquabats towards cost of a short club break in Eastbourne; £150 to Sixty Plus for Christmas Party; £147 to Low Vision Aids Clinic for a lockable glass display cabinet; £100 to Disability Advocacy Network for the cost of hiring an Old Time Music Hall; £ 100 to Tower Hamlets Environment for landscaping and painting for a sensory garden; £93 to the Village Club for provision of food and transport

FINANCES *Year* 1997 *Income* £346,232 *Grants* £24,477

TRUSTEES C M Mowll, MA, LLD, Rev B A E Coote, BD, A J Brown, FCA, K D Felton, FCA, Rev M O Berridge, BA, M Gundry, FRCS, M G T Harris, P W Holland, CQSW, B H Horne, J R Orme, D L Osborne, FCIS, A J Parfitt, BSc, FRIBA, FRICS, V J Scarr, FCOptom, DOrth, DCLP

HOW TO APPLY Initial telephone calls are welcome. For individuals there are application forms available.

WHO TO APPLY TO Frank Luck or Roger Thurlow, Metropolitan Society for the Blind, Duke House, 4th Floor, 6–12 Tabard Street, London SE1 4JU *Tel* 0171-403 6184 *Fax* 0171-203 0708

CC NO 262119   **ESTABLISHED** 1971

■ The Mettyear Charitable Trust

WHAT IS FUNDED Housing; homelessness; victims of torture and prisoners of conscience; children and schools in Lewes; local civic amenities society projects working to provide water supplies worldwide, especially Nepal

WHAT IS NOT FUNDED No grants to expeditions, scholarships, any fund of direct benefit to an individual or animal welfare

WHO CAN BENEFIT Organisations benefiting: children; those disadvantaged by poverty; homeless people and victims of crime

WHERE FUNDING CAN BE GIVEN UK, especially Lewes and East Sussex. Overseas, especially Nepal

TYPE OF GRANT One-off and interest free loans

RANGE OF GRANTS £300–£5,000, typical grant £500–£1,000

SAMPLE GRANTS £3,000 to Friends of Lewes; £2,000 to Homeless in Sussex Fund; £1,250 to Bristol Cancer Help Centre; £1,250 to Brighton Housing Trust; £1,000 to Crisis at Christmas

FINANCES *Year* 1996–97 *Income* £18,500 *Grants* £18,500

TRUSTEES Peter Mettyear, Susan Mettyear, Kevin Ardagh

HOW TO APPLY To the address under Who To Apply To in writing

WHO TO APPLY TO Peter Mettyear, Trustee, The Mettyear Charitable Trust, The Garden House, Paines Twitten, Lewes, East Sussex BN7 1UB *Tel* 01273 472386

CC NO 298865   **ESTABLISHED** 1988

■ The Meyrick Charitable Trust

WHAT IS FUNDED General charitable purposes

WHO CAN BENEFIT There are no restrictions on the age; professional and economic group; family situation; religion and culture; and social circumstances of; or disease or medical condition suffered by, the beneficiaries

WHERE FUNDING CAN BE GIVEN UK

TRUSTEES G W O T G Meyrick, Sir G C C T G Meyrick

WHO TO APPLY TO D M Tullie, The Meyrick Charitable Trust, Meyrick Estate Management Ltd, Estate Office, Hinton Admiral, Christchurch, Dorset BH23 7DU

CC NO 1063953   **ESTABLISHED** 1997

■ Col Wilfred Horatio Micholls Deceased Charitable Trust Fund

WHAT IS FUNDED Income is distributed in accordance with the wishes of the late Col W H Micholls as expressed in his will – 45 per cent of income to Jewish charities, 10 per cent to service charities, 45 per cent to other charities

WHAT IS NOT FUNDED (a) No personal grants to individuals. (b) No grants to charities relating to purely local interests. (c) No grants to individual branches of large charitable institutions

WHO CAN BENEFIT Registered charities particularly those benefiting Jewish people. There are no

restrictions on the age; professional and economic group; family situation; and social circumstances of; or disease or medical condition suffered by, the beneficiaries

WHERE FUNDING CAN BE GIVEN UK

SAMPLE GRANTS The following were annual donations:; £4,950 to Jewish Care; £1,650 to Barkingside Jewish Youth Centre; £1,430 to Association for Jewish Youth/Norwood; £1,100 to RNI for Blind

TRUSTEES The Hon Michael Samuel, R B Waley-Cohen

NOTES Funds are tied up for the next two years, funding is very unlikely

HOW TO APPLY To address under Who To Apply To with sae for reply

WHO TO APPLY TO Mrs L Sutton, Secretary to the Trustees, Col W H Micholls Decd Charitable Trust, Dylon House, Worsley Bridge Road, Lower Sydenham, London SE26 5HD *Tel* 0181-663 4801 *Fax* 0181-650 9876

CC NO 267472   **ESTABLISHED** 1972

■ Mickel Fund

WHAT IS FUNDED General charitable purposes including: health professional bodies; hospices; cancer research; immunology, MS and neurological research; health related volunteer schemes; church and historical buildings; zoos; heritage; art galleries, libraries and museums; sports centres; care in the community; and holidays and outings

WHAT IS NOT FUNDED No grants to individuals

WHO CAN BENEFIT Mainly registered charities benefiting people of all ages, especially at risk groups. Prefer local but does give to UK charities

WHERE FUNDING CAN BE GIVEN East Lothian, East Renfrewshire, Edinburgh, Glasgow, Midlothian, North Ayrshire, North Lanarkshire, Renfrewshire, South Ayrshire, West Ayrshire and West Lothian

TYPE OF GRANT One-off and recurring funding buildings, capital, project and research. Funding is available for more than three years

SAMPLE GRANTS £52,000 to Edinburgh Old Town Housing Association for special one-off renovations; £26,200 to Scottish Sports Aid Trust; £10,000 to National Trust for Scotland; £5,000 to Bo'ness Old Kirk; £2,500 to Dumbar John Muir Museum; £1,000 to Cancer Research

FINANCES *Year* 1996–97 *Income* £50,000 *Grants* £124,000

TRUSTEES D W Mickel, D A Mickel, B G A Mickel, J C Craig, J R C Wark

HOW TO APPLY In writing from appropriate charities only

WHO TO APPLY TO J R C Wark, Mickel Fund, McTaggart & Mickel Ltd, 126 West Regent Street, Glasgow G2 2BH *Tel* 0141-332 0001

SC NO SCO 03266   **ESTABLISHED** 1970

■ The Gerald Micklem Charitable Trust

WHAT IS FUNDED Medicine and health, welfare, and other general charitable purposes

WHAT IS NOT FUNDED No grants to individuals or students

WHO CAN BENEFIT National and established organisations benefiting at risk groups, those disadvantaged by poverty and socially isolated people. There is no restriction on the disease or medical condition suffered by the beneficiaries

WHERE FUNDING CAN BE GIVEN UK

TYPE OF GRANT One-off and recurrent

SAMPLE GRANTS £500 to The Project Trust
FINANCES *Year* 1995 *Income* £16,327 *Grants* £500
TRUSTEES S Shone, J Scott-Dalgleish, H Ratcliffe
HOW TO APPLY In writing
WHO TO APPLY TO Ms S J Shone, The Gerald Micklem Charitable Trust, Bolinge Hill Farm, Buriton, Petersfield, Hampshire GU31 4NN
CC NO 802583   **ESTABLISHED** 1988

■ Mid Glamorgan Welsh Church Fund

WHAT IS FUNDED To support churches, youth activities, welfare, in most of the former Mid Glamorgan
WHAT IS NOT FUNDED No grants to students, individuals in need or projects of other local authorities
WHO CAN BENEFIT Churches, youth organisations and musical groups benefiting children, young adults, Christians, at risk groups, those disadvantaged by poverty and socially isolated people
WHERE FUNDING CAN BE GIVEN Rhondda-Cynon-Taff, Bridgend and Merthyr Tydfil County Borough Councils, being the areas comprising the former county of Mid Glamorgan, with the exception of Rhymney Valley which is now outside the area of benefit
SAMPLE GRANTS £6,000 to Apostolic Church (Brackla Tabernacle) assisting with building costs and furnishing; £6,000 to Brackla Baptist Church to help in setting up a new church; £6,000 to Ogwr Transport for the Elderly to provide access and amenity facilities; £6,000 to Rest Bay Lifeguard Club assisting with the cost of lifeguard station; £6,000 to Salem Welsh Presbyterian Church towards the cost of repairing chapel; £6,000 to Tondu Methodist Church towards the costs of general restoration; £6,000 to Highland Place Unitarian Church assisting with costs of Church Building Appeal; £6,000 to Jerusalem English Baptist Church assisting with cost of completing interior walls; £6,000 to St Aloysius Roman Catholic Church assisting with the cost of major ceiling and lighting renovations; £6,000 to Zoar Ynysgau Welsh Congregational Chapel assisting with the cost of repairing chapel
FINANCES *Year* 1996–97 *Income* £360,781 *Grants* £237,000
TRUSTEES Rhondda-Cynon-Taff County Borough Council
HOW TO APPLY On an application form available from the address under Who To Apply To. The closing date is the last day of July each year
WHO TO APPLY TO Gareth Griffiths, Finance Department, Mid Glamorgan Welsh Church Fund, Rhondda-Cynon-Taff County Borough Council, Bronwydd House, Porth, RCT CF39 9DL *Tel* 01443 680578
CC NO 506658   **ESTABLISHED** 1977

■ Middlesex County Rugby Football Union Memorial Fund

WHAT IS FUNDED Poor relief, sick relief, physical education of handicapped children and young persons. Particularly charities working in the fields of: acute health care; support and self help groups; health facilities and buildings; and various community facilities and services
WHO CAN BENEFIT Preference given to participants or former participants in sport. Organisations benefiting: people of all ages; sportsmen and women; at risk groups; disabled people; and those disadvantaged by poverty
WHERE FUNDING CAN BE GIVEN UK
TYPE OF GRANT Mainly one-off sums for capital projects. The grants are normally modest having regard to the resources of the Fund. Project, research, recurring costs and running costs funded for one year or less will be considered
RANGE OF GRANTS £250–£5,000, average grant £500
FINANCES *Year* 1996 *Income* £153,480 *Grants* £109,350
TRUSTEES M J Christie, C D L Hogbin, Sir Peter Yarranton, K L King, R H B Jones, D Wellman
HOW TO APPLY To the address under Who To Apply To
WHO TO APPLY TO C D L Hogbin, Middlesex County Rugby Football Union Memorial Fund, Chestnut Cottage, 20a Stubbs Wood, Chesham Bois, Buckinghamshire HP6 6EY
CC NO 209175   **ESTABLISHED** 1947

■ The Harry Middleton Gift

WHAT IS FUNDED Local schools, clubs and community-based organisations. Including charities working in the fields of: building services; information technology and computers; support to voluntary and community organisations; cemeteries and burial grounds; churches; community arts and recreation and community centres and village halls; and other general charitable purposes
WHO CAN BENEFIT Local organisations benefiting children, young adults and older people
WHERE FUNDING CAN BE GIVEN Newport Pagnell
TYPE OF GRANT Buildings and capital will be considered
FINANCES *Year* 1997 *Income* £15,000
HOW TO APPLY To the address under Who To Apply To in writing
WHO TO APPLY TO D J Kirkbright, Secretary, The Harry Middleton Gift, 71 Lakes Lane, Newport Pagnell, Buckinghamshire MK16 8HT
CC NO 259534   **ESTABLISHED** 1969

■ Midland Bank Charitable Trust

This trust did not respond to CAF's request to amend its entry and, by 30 June 1998, CAF's researchers did not find financial records for later than 1995 on its file at the Charity Commission. Trusts are legally required to submit annual accounts to the Charity Commission under section 42 of the Charities Act 1993

WHAT IS FUNDED General charitable purposes
WHO CAN BENEFIT There are no restrictions on the age; professional and economic group; family situation; religion and culture; and social circumstances of; or disease or medical condition suffered by, the beneficiaries
WHERE FUNDING CAN BE GIVEN UK
TRUSTEES Midland Bank Trust Company
WHO TO APPLY TO R Thompson, Trust Manager, Midland Bank Charitable Trust, Midland Bank Trusts Co Ltd, Cumberland House, 15–17 Cumberland Place, Southampton SO15 2UY
CC NO 296594   **ESTABLISHED** 1986

■ The Migraine Trust

WHAT IS FUNDED The provision of assistance for furthering research into the causes, alleviation and treatment of migraine. The making of grants for research at universities and research institutions. Promotion, assistance and

420

Think carefully about every application. Is it justified?

encouragement of schemes of research, education, technical training and treatment. Exchange of information, advice and counselling

WHO CAN BENEFIT Organisations benefiting those suffering from migraines, medical professionals, research workers and scientists

WHERE FUNDING CAN BE GIVEN UK and overseas

TYPE OF GRANT Funds provide for research into migraine at recognised institutions, eg hospitals and universities

FINANCES *Year* 1997 *Income* £601,473 *Grants* £219,244

TRUSTEES Lady Schiemann (Chair), A Jordan (Hon Treasurer), Prof C Kennard, PhD, FRCP, FRCOphth (Medical Trustee), Rt Hon Sir Philip Otton, Sir R Murley, KBE, TD, MS, FRCS, H Mitchell, QC, J Ames, FCA, D Long, J P S Wolff-Ingham

PUBLICATIONS *Migraine News*, *Understanding Migraine*, *Proceedings of Symposia*

NOTES Holds Migraine Trust International Symposia. Funds research into migraine. Has full sufferer service

HOW TO APPLY By application form available from Trust. Applications will be acknowledged

WHO TO APPLY TO Ann Rush, Director, The Migraine Trust, 45 Great Ormond Street, London WC1N 3HZ

CC NO 244250   **ESTABLISHED** 1965

■ Milbourn Charitable Trust

WHAT IS FUNDED Charities involved in famine relief, medical research, aid to disadvantaged by poverty and other similar humanitarian purposes will be considered

WHAT IS NOT FUNDED No grants for arts activities, animal charities or any beneficiary not itself a charity

WHO CAN BENEFIT Organisations benefiting at risk groups, those disadvantaged by poverty, socially isolated people and victims of famine. Medical professionals and research workers may be considered. There is no restriction on the disease or medical condition suffered by the beneficiaries

WHERE FUNDING CAN BE GIVEN UK and overseas

TYPE OF GRANT One-off, research and recurring costs will be considered

RANGE OF GRANTS £150–£5,000, typical grants £500–£1,000

FINANCES *Year* 1997–98 *Income* £19,000 *Grants* £21,000

TRUSTEES F M Milbourn, M P Milbourn

HOW TO APPLY In writing

WHO TO APPLY TO M P Milbourn, Trustee, Milbourn Charitable Trust, The River House, St Mary's Lane, Hertingfordbury, Hertford, Hertfordshire SG14 2LF *Tel* 01992 551502

CC NO 1059558   **ESTABLISHED** 1996

■ Miles Trust for the Putney and Roehampton Community

WHAT IS FUNDED Schools, youth organisations, social welfare organisations caring for the poor, homeless, elderly and the sick

WHO CAN BENEFIT Organisations benefiting people of all ages, those disadvantaged by poverty and homeless people. There is no restriction on the disease or medical condition suffered by the beneficiaries

WHERE FUNDING CAN BE GIVEN Wandsworth

TYPE OF GRANT Often recurring

RANGE OF GRANTS £100–£6,000

SAMPLE GRANTS £6,000 to Wandsworth MIND; £3,000 to Putney Poor Relief Committee; £3,000 to Wandsworth Bereavement Support Group; £2,300 to St Mary's Church of England School; £2,250 to Age Concern; £2,050 to Our Lady of Victories School; £2,030 to Greenwood School; £2,000 to Friends of All Saints School; £2,000 to St Mary's Church of England School; £1,700 to National Schizophrenic Fellowship

FINANCES *Year* 1996 *Income* £42,445 *Grants* £41,742

TRUSTEES A R Collender (Chairman), Rev Dr J Draper, R J G Holman (Treasurer), T J E Marwood (Vice Chairman), Mrs L P Paiba, Mrs A Raikes, Mrs L Moir, Mrs A Stevens, Mrs J Maxwell, Mrs J Walters, P Kitchen

NOTES The Trust donated £21,600 to community projects; £17,542 to youth causes; and £2,600 to the Church

HOW TO APPLY To the address under Who To Apply To in writing

WHO TO APPLY TO Mrs C V M Davey, Secretary, Miles Trust for the Putney and Roehampton Community, 66 Clarendon Drive, Putney, London SW15 1AW

CC NO 246784   **ESTABLISHED** 1967

■ The Milk and Honey Trust

WHAT IS FUNDED To support advancement of education and religion and the relief of poverty

WHO CAN BENEFIT Organisations benefiting children, young adults and those disadvantaged by poverty

WHERE FUNDING CAN BE GIVEN UK

RANGE OF GRANTS £60–£13,750

SAMPLE GRANTS £13,750 to Christian Community Church – Ireland; £5,266 to Cheam Community Church; £2,500 to Queen Mary's Christian Care Foundation; £1,736 to an individual; £945 to Pioneer Trust for training in evangelism; £670 to RADAR; £600 to Covenant Life Association, Cambridge; £296 to other charitable donations; £250 to London Christian Radio; £229 to National Federation of the Blind

FINANCES *Year* 1996 *Income* £30,713 *Grants* £28,723

TRUSTEES J E Croxson, Mrs C Croxson, A M Giles

WHO TO APPLY TO J E Croxson, The Milk and Honey Trust, 40 Cornwall Road, Sutton, Surrey SM2 6DS

CC NO 288229   **ESTABLISHED** 1983

■ Hugh and Mary Miller Bequest

WHAT IS FUNDED Healthcare, art galleries and cultural centres

WHAT IS NOT FUNDED No grants to individuals

WHO CAN BENEFIT Registered charities. There are few restrictions on the social circumstances of the beneficiaries

WHERE FUNDING CAN BE GIVEN Scotland

TYPE OF GRANT Buildings, capital, core costs, project, research, recurring costs, running costs and salaries. Funding is available for more than three years

FINANCES *Year* 1997–98 *Income* £90,000 *Grants* £67,500

TRUSTEES H C Davidson, G R G Graham

HOW TO APPLY By letter. Initial telephone calls are not welcome. There are no application forms, guidelines or deadlines. No sae required

WHO TO APPLY TO G R G Graham, Hugh and Mary Miller Bequest, Messrs Maclay, Murray & Spens, 151 St Vincent Street, Glasgow G2 5NJ *Tel* 0141-248 5011 *Fax* 0141-248 5819

SC NO SCO 14950

Does the trust you have chosen match your needs? Haphazard applications waste postage and time

421

■ The M Miller Charitable Trust

WHAT IS FUNDED General charitable purposes at the Trustees discretion

WHO CAN BENEFIT Institutions. There are no restrictions on the age; professional and economic group; family situation; religion and culture; and social circumstances of; or disease or medical condition suffered by, the beneficiaries

WHERE FUNDING CAN BE GIVEN UK

TYPE OF GRANT At the discretion of the Trustees

FINANCES *Year* 1997 *Income* £19,573
Grants £18,393

TRUSTEES M Miller, R B Miller, R K Ellis

WHO TO APPLY TO M Miller, The M Miller Charitable Trust, 63 Brampton Grove, Hendon, London NW4 4AH

CC NO 1014957   **ESTABLISHED** 1992

■ The Miller Foundation

WHAT IS FUNDED Grants are given to educational projects, especially at tertiary level. Organisations working for the welfare of humans and animals are also supported as are schemes working with the disabled

WHO CAN BENEFIT To benefit children and young adults; students; at risk groups; disabled groups; those disadvantaged by poverty; and socially isolated people

WHERE FUNDING CAN BE GIVEN Scotland and occasionally other areas

TYPE OF GRANT Flexible

RANGE OF GRANTS £750–£7,500

FINANCES *Year* 1997 *Income* £137,000
Grants £130,000

TRUSTEES C Fleming Brown, G R G Graham, James Simpson, C C Wright

HOW TO APPLY Applications should be made in writing to the address under Who To Apply To

WHO TO APPLY TO G R G Graham, The Miller Foundation, Maclay Murray & Spens, 151 St Vincent Street, Glasgow G2 5NJ *Tel* 0141-248 5019

SC NO SCO 08798   **ESTABLISHED** 1979

■ The Alan and Janet Millett Charitable Trust

WHAT IS FUNDED General charitable purposes. Preference may be given to relief of poverty among employees and former employees of R & A Millett (Holdings) Limited and its subsidiaries and to advancement of education in the area where those companies carry on business

WHO CAN BENEFIT Organisations, particularly those benefiting employees and former employees of R & A Millett (Holdings) Limited who disadvantaged by poverty

WHERE FUNDING CAN BE GIVEN UK

RANGE OF GRANTS £50–£2,500

SAMPLE GRANTS £2,500 to Mill Hill Educational and Amenities Trust; £2,000 to British Friends of Beit L'ohamei Haghe; £1,650 to United Synagogue; £1,500 to Jewish Marriage Council; £1,060 to Jewish Care

FINANCES *Year* 1996 *Income* £22,649
Grants £21,560

TRUSTEES A C Millett, Mrs E Millett, P M Millett

WHO TO APPLY TO A C Millett, The Alan and Janet Millett Charitable Trust, Chestnut, Wills Grove, London NW7 1QL

CC NO 269368   **ESTABLISHED** 1975

■ Millfield House Foundation

WHAT IS FUNDED Proposals with any of the following aims: (a) To contribute the lessons of first-hand experience of social need, or the implications of research in the region, to public debate and the policy-making process at national or local level. (b) To elucidate and tackle the fundamental causes of deprivation in the area, rather than simply alleviating it. (c) To develop activities which have been proven elsewhere but have not been developed in Tyne and Wear, particularly those which empower people and communities to overcome their difficulties and exploit their own resources. Trustees aim to concentrate resources on objects which most other funding bodies cannot or will not support

WHAT IS NOT FUNDED Generally, the MHF does not make grants: (a) Not related to the needs of people in Tyne & Wear. (b) To large well-established national charities, or to general appeals. (c) For work in the arts, medicine or conservation. (d) For buildings, or for purely academic research. (e) To make up deficits already incurred, to replace withdrawn, expired or reducing statutory funding, or to provide what should properly be the responsibility of statutory agencies. (f) To meet the needs of particular individuals. (g) For travel/adventure projects, or educational bursaries. (h) To projects likely to qualify for statutory, European Union or National Lottery funding, or likely to appeal to most local or national charitable trusts or similar sources. (MHF will only consider a contribution in such cases if there is a particular part of the project which such other sources would be unlikely to wish to fund). (i) For the delivery of a service, however great the need, unless it contributes to any of the What is Funded list above

WHO CAN BENEFIT Applicants should preferably be voluntary agencies working with the socially and economically disadvantaged. Bodies undertaking policy research and advocacy should have close links with such voluntary organisations

WHERE FUNDING CAN BE GIVEN Gateshead, Newcastle upon Tyne, Northumberland, North Tyneside, South Tyneside and Sunderland

TYPE OF GRANT Significant and medium-term support (alone or in partnership with other funders) to a relatively few carefully selected projects or organisations. Since MHF can only afford to have six to eight such grants in payment at the same time, it will be able to approve only one or two new applications in any year. In some cases MHF may consider a small grant to support work needed in preparation for an application for a major grant

SAMPLE GRANTS £15,000 to North East Family Centres Network (first of three years) for influencing policies affecting families; £14,890 to Low Pay Research Trust for study of child employment in North Tyneside; £10,000 to Tyne & Wear Foundation as a block grant; £7,500 to Church Action on Poverty, North East (£15,000 over two years) for empowerment and campaigning; £2,000 to Hendon 2000 for community participation in case for funding; £720 to STEPS to Excellence for training in personal development for disadvantaged people; £532 to North East Pensioners Association for attendance at rally

FINANCES *Year* 1997–98 *Income* £127,097
Grants £50,642

TRUSTEES D A McClelland, J McClelland, R Chubb, S McClelland, W G McClelland

PUBLICATIONS Guidelines for Applicants. Report on Grant-making 1989–96. Summary of *Political*

Activities and Campaigning by Charities (CC9, Charity Commission 1995)

HOW TO APPLY In writing to the address under Who To Apply To by the end of March or September. Guidelines are available. Not acknowledged if obviously ruled out by MHF published restrictions (see What Is Not Funded above)

WHO TO APPLY TO Millfield House Foundation, 66 Elmfield Road, Newcastle upon Tyne NE3 4BD

CC NO 271180 **ESTABLISHED** 1976

■ The Millfield Trust

WHAT IS FUNDED Support of religious or other charitable institutions or work. Advancement of the Protestant and Evangelical tenets of the Christian Faith and encouragement of missionary activity. Relief of the poor and needy. Help and comfort of the sick and aged. Preference to charities of which the Trust has special interest, knowledge or association. Funds fully allocated or committed

WHO CAN BENEFIT Individuals and organisations benefiting: the elderly, Christians, and the poor and needy. There is no restriction on the disease or medical condition suffered by the beneficiaries

WHERE FUNDING CAN BE GIVEN UK and overseas

RANGE OF GRANTS £40–£12,300

SAMPLE GRANTS £12,300 to Gideons International; £10,000 to Garston Bridge Centre; £10,000 to London City Mission; £8,000 to Mission to Europe; £6,000 to Bridge Chapel Centre Liverpool; £5,500 to UFM Worldwide; £4,000 to Mark Gillingham Charitable Trust; £3,200 to Ashbury Evangelical Free Church; £2,000 to Overseas Council; £1,900 to OMF International

FINANCES *Year* 1997 *Income* £83,504 *Grants* £81,405

TRUSTEES D Bunce, Mrs R Bunce, P W Bunce, S D Bunce, A C Bunce

NOTES In 1997, £78,865 was given to charitable and religious institutions, £2,200 to individual evangelists and missionaries and £340 as Christmas gifts to old age pensioners and widows

HOW TO APPLY No replies to unsolicited applications

WHO TO APPLY TO D Bunce, The Millfield Trust, Millfield House, Bell Lane, Liddington, Swindon, Wiltshire SN4 0HH

CC NO 262406 **ESTABLISHED** 1971

■ The Millhouses Charitable Trust

WHAT IS FUNDED Overseas aid and social welfare (with a Christian emphasis)

WHAT IS NOT FUNDED No grants to individuals. Non-charitable causes will not be funded

WHO CAN BENEFIT Registered charities benefiting Christians; at risk groups; those disadvantaged by poverty; socially isolated people; victims of famine, disasters and war will be considered

WHERE FUNDING CAN BE GIVEN UK

TYPE OF GRANT Recurring and one-off

RANGE OF GRANTS £250–£5,000

SAMPLE GRANTS £10,000 to Batah Foundation; £500 to Christian Aid; £5,000 to Home Mission; £5,000 to Medical Foundation; £5,000 to NSPCC; £5,000 to Amnesty UK Section; £5,000 to Baptist Missionary Society; £2,000 to Barnston Dale Centre; £1,000 to Bible Society; £1,000 to Child Hope UK

FINANCES *Year* 1997 *Income* £98,695 *Grants* £54,500

TRUSTEES Mrs J S Harcus, Dr A W Harcus

NOTES A preference is shown for Baptist charities

HOW TO APPLY The Trust only supports organisations with which the Trustees have a personal contact

WHO TO APPLY TO J S Harcus, The Millhouses Charitable Trust, 79 Beverly Road, Hull HU3 1XR

CC NO 327773 **ESTABLISHED** 1988

■ The Millichope Foundation

WHAT IS FUNDED Social and health funding which is not covered by government programmes. The arts and conservation

WHAT IS NOT FUNDED Registered charities only. Applications from individuals, including students, are ineligible

WHO CAN BENEFIT Organisations benefiting actors and entertainment professionals; musicians; textile workers and designers; writers and poets; at risk groups; those disadvantaged by poverty; socially isolated people and the sick. There is no restriction on the disease or medical condition suffered by the beneficiaries

WHERE FUNDING CAN BE GIVEN Some grants to national and international organisations. Local applications limited to the West Midlands and Shropshire only

TYPE OF GRANT Straight donation. Normally an annual commitment for a period of five years

RANGE OF GRANTS £25–£21,200

SAMPLE GRANTS £21,200 to Fauna and Flora Preservation Society; £5,000 to The National Trust; £5,000 to Moor Park School; £5,000 to the Save the Children Fund; £3,500 to Royal Opera House Trust; £2,500 to Shrewsbury Abbey Appeal; £2,500 to Moor Park School Scholarship Fund; £2,500 to St Paul's Community Project; £2,500 to St Basil's Centre; £2,500 to Prince's Youth Business Trust, Shropshire

FINANCES *Year* 1997 *Income* £148,395 *Grants* £143,405

TRUSTEES L C N Bury, Mrs S A Bury, Mrs B Marshall, M L Ingall

HOW TO APPLY In writing. In order to keep costs to a minimum we do not enter into correspondence with applicants unless an sae is enclosed

WHO TO APPLY TO Mrs S A Bury, The Millichope Foundation, Millichope Park, Munslow, Craven Arms, Shropshire SY7 9HA

CC NO 282357 **ESTABLISHED** 1981

■ The Mills Charity

WHAT IS FUNDED Relief in need and for the general benefit of the inhabitants of Framlingham

WHO CAN BENEFIT Largely individuals and community projects benefiting: at risk groups, those disadvantaged by poverty and socially isolated people

WHERE FUNDING CAN BE GIVEN Framlingham and immediate area

TYPE OF GRANT Capital, not recurring

FINANCES *Year* 1995–96 *Income* £66,112

HOW TO APPLY To the address under Who To Apply To in writing

WHO TO APPLY TO M E Ashwell, Chairman, The Mills Charity, 38 Pembroke Road, Framlingham, Woodbridge, Suffolk IP13 9HA *Tel* 01728 723525

CC NO 207259 **ESTABLISHED** 1961

■ The Edgar Milward Charity

WHAT IS FUNDED Most support goes to evangelical Christian causes, both well known and less so, at home and abroad. Some support is given to humanitarian causes, and 10 per cent overall for educational purposes within a 15 mile radius of Reading, Berkshire. The Trustees already have contact with an ample number of causes they are pleased to support

WHO CAN BENEFIT Organisations benefiting children, young adults, Christians and evangelists. Individuals are only supported occasionally

WHERE FUNDING CAN BE GIVEN UK and overseas

SAMPLE GRANTS £5,000 to Crusaders Union for Christian youth meetings, holidays, working visits abroad; £3,000 to Greyfriars Missionary Trust for a Reading parish church's missionary support vehicle; £3,000 to The Jonas Trust which provides Christian holidays on a North Yorkshire estate; £2,000 to Christian Bookshop, Pisek, Czech Republic for set up support; £2,000 to Four Lanes County Infants School, Basingstoke (Chineham) for refurbishment, new curtains, etc; £1,000 to Kendrick Trust for Kendrick School, Reading for an appeal for a new vehicle for transporting pupils; £1,000 to Victory Outreach UK supporting drug addicts, etc in rehabilitation; £1,000 to Christians in Sport for Christian information in association with 'World Cup'; £1,000 to Institute for Contemporary Christianity for 'intellectual' Christian promotions; £1,000 to Tear Fund for global relief work

FINANCES *Year* 1998 *Income* £59,323 *Grants* £57,269

TRUSTEES J S Milward, JP (Chairman), T Pittom, FCA, Mrs M V Roberts, G M Fogwill, Mrs J C Austin, Mrs E M Smuts

NOTES The Trustees currently have an established interest in a range of charities. Few new charities will be added to this list

HOW TO APPLY No assurance can be given that all applications can be acknowledged, because the administration of the Charity is arranged to minimise costs, so the maximum can go to actual beneficiaries. In all appropriate cases, charities are advised to send a copy of their latest certified annual accounts with new applications or following a re-issue since last contact

WHO TO APPLY TO G M Fogwill, The Edgar Milward Charity, The Bowery, 34 Churchill Crescent, Headley, Bordon, Hampshire GU35 8ND

CC NO 281018   **ESTABLISHED** 1980

■ The Mary Minet Trust

WHAT IS FUNDED To relieve in cases of need persons resident in the London Boroughs of Lambeth and Southwark who are sick, convalescent, disabled, handicapped or infirm. Determined by provisions of Trust Deed

WHO CAN BENEFIT Recipients must have physical or mental illness or handicap. There is no restriction on the age or social circumstances of the beneficiaries, though there may be a few restrictions on their medical condition

WHERE FUNDING CAN BE GIVEN London Boroughs of Lambeth and Southwark

TYPE OF GRANT Financial or grants in kind, almost always one-off to individual applicants

RANGE OF GRANTS Provision for emergency grants of up to £100 in cases of urgent need

SAMPLE GRANTS £400 to South London Family Housing Association towards a minibus; The following grants are to individuals:; £360 for a cooker; £350 for beds; £300 for a spindryer and bedding

FINANCES *Year* 1997 *Income* £16,553 *Grants* £11,365

TRUSTEES Rev D Wilson, Miss K Escritt, Dr A Clark-Jones, Mrs A Clark-Jones, R Baird, Mrs L Stokes, Ms J Easty, D Martin

HOW TO APPLY Quarterly

WHO TO APPLY TO Dr A Clark-Jones, The Mary Minet Trust, 54 Knatchbull Road, London SE5 9QY *Tel* 0171 733 2725

CC NO 212483   **ESTABLISHED** 1973

■ The Peter Minet Trust

WHAT IS FUNDED Priority to registered charities within the Boroughs of Lambeth and Southwark chiefly supporting youth, sick and disabled, disadvantaged, the elderly, the arts and the environment. Occasional support to capital appeals from national charities with similar aims. Education and training is also considered for funding

WHAT IS NOT FUNDED Registered charities only. Applications from individuals are ineligible. No grants made in response to general appeals from large, national organisations. Exclusions: (a) Appeals from organisations whose sole, or main purpose, is to make grants to other charities. (b) Parochial appeals, other than those within the Trust's immediate locality. In this context, parochial means that all, or most of, the beneficiaries reside within the applicant's immediate locality. (c) Appeals for deficit funding. (d) Appeals received within 12 calendar months of a previous grant

WHO CAN BENEFIT Registered charities benefiting at risk groups, disabled people, the sick, and those disadvantaged by poverty. There is no restriction on the disease or medical condition suffered by the beneficiaries

WHERE FUNDING CAN BE GIVEN UK, but mostly Lambeth and Southwark

TYPE OF GRANT Usually one-off for a specific project or part of a project

RANGE OF GRANTS Average grant £1,000

SAMPLE GRANTS £5,000 to Mana Society for the expansion of services; £5,000 to St Mungo's for furniture for the Cedar Road Hostel; £5,000 to Family Welfare Association for Southwark Family Health Scheme; £4,000 to Kings Medical Research Trust for research into stroke damage; £3,000 to Christchurch United Clubs for multi arts residency with young disabled; £3,000 to Weald and Downland Open Air Museum for Paplans Cottage Appeal; £3,000 to Christ Church, North Brixton for Brixwork CANA Project; £3,000 to Chichester Christian Care Association for the homeless; £3,000 to Woodland Trust for purchase of Deering Wood; £3,000 to Pecan Ltd for expanding the Literacy Project

FINANCES *Year* 1997 *Income* £156,318 *Grants* £154,280

TRUSTEES J C B South (Chair), N McGregor-Wood, Ms P Jones, Mrs R L C Rowan, R Luff, Rev B Stokes

PUBLICATIONS Guidelines leaflet available

NOTES Trustees regret it is impossible to acknowledge all applications because of the number and expense involved

HOW TO APPLY At any time. Trustees meet quarterly. Applications should include clear details of the need the project is designed to meet plus an outline budget and latest audited accounts. Unsuccessful applications will not be acknowledged unless an sae is enclosed

WHO TO APPLY TO Angela Freestone, Administrator, The Peter Minet Trust, 54 Knatchbull Road, London SE5 9QY *Tel* 0171-274 2266 *Fax* 0171-274 5222

CC NO 259963   **ESTABLISHED** 1969

■ Minge's Gift

WHAT IS FUNDED General charitable purposes. The income of Minge's Gift is allocated to the Company's endowments. There is no surplus income available for distribution

WHAT IS NOT FUNDED No grants to individuals

WHO CAN BENEFIT There are no restrictions on the age; professional and economic group; family situation; religion and culture; and social circumstances of; or disease or medical condition suffered by, the beneficiaries

WHERE FUNDING CAN BE GIVEN UK

SAMPLE GRANTS £47,243 to Cordwainers College; £2,500 to Royal London Society for the Blind; £2,000 to Royal Free Hospital Nurses Trust; £1,500 to City & Guilds Institute; £1,500 to City University Music Department for bursary/prizes; £1,500 to Royal Free Hospital School of Medicine Scholarship; £1,300 to St Dunstan-in-the-West Church; £1,000 to Royal Free Hospital Nurses Travel Bursaries; £1,000 to Jubilee Sailing Trust; £1,000 to Fairbridge Trust

FINANCES *Year* 1996 *Income* £80,253 *Grants* £64,665

TRUSTEES The Master and Wardens of the Cordwainers' Company: T C Weber-Brown, R P B Skinner, J G Church

WHO TO APPLY TO J R Blundell, The Clerk, Minge's Gift, The Worshipful Company of Cordwainers, Eldon Chambers, 30 Fleet Street, London EC4Y 1AA

CC NO 266073   **ESTABLISHED** 1972

■ The Minos Trust

WHAT IS FUNDED General charitable purposes. Funds fully committed. The Trustees request no further applications

WHAT IS NOT FUNDED No grants available. Funds fully committed

WHO CAN BENEFIT Organisations. There are no restrictions on the age; professional and economic group; family situation; religion and culture; and social circumstances of; or disease or medical condition suffered by, the beneficiaries

WHERE FUNDING CAN BE GIVEN UK and overseas

RANGE OF GRANTS £25–£2,000

SAMPLE GRANTS £2,000 to Care Trust; £1,600 to Chasah Trust; £1,600 to the TEAR Fund; £1,500 to the Lambeth Fund; £1,500 to Slaugham Parochial Church Council; £1,300 to Church of England Evangelical Council; £1,300 to Christian Fellowship Church; £1,000 to Bible Society; £1,000 to Church Army for Nairobi Training College; £1,000 to Friends of the Elderly

FINANCES *Year* 1996 *Income* £42,297 *Grants* £38,191

TRUSTEES Rev K W Habershon, Mrs K W Habershon, S Midwinter

HOW TO APPLY Funds fully committed. The Trustees request no further applications

WHO TO APPLY TO Mr Midwinter, The Minos Trust, Deloitte & Touche, Leda House, Station Road, Cambridge CB1 2RN

CC NO 265012   **ESTABLISHED** 1972

■ Laurence Misener Charitable Trust

WHAT IS FUNDED General charitable purposes. To distribute net annual income

WHO CAN BENEFIT There are no restrictions on the age; professional and economic group; family situation; religion and culture; and social circumstances of; or disease or medical condition suffered by, the beneficiaries. There is a tendency to benefit those charities in which the Settlor was interested

WHERE FUNDING CAN BE GIVEN UK

RANGE OF GRANTS £1,000–£7,300

SAMPLE GRANTS £7,300 to Richard Dimbleby Cancer Fund; £5,200 to Home for Aged Jews, Nightingale House; £5,200 to Jewish Association for Physically Handicapped; £5,200 to Jewish Care; £3,600 to Devon County Association for the Blind; £3,100 to Imperial Cancer Research Fund; £3,100 to Robert Owen Foundation; £3,000 to Jews Temporary Shelter; £2,800 to Royal College of Surgeons of England; £2,800 to SGHMS Haematology Research Fund

FINANCES *Year* 1997 *Income* £79,155 *Grants* £74,200

TRUSTEES J E Cama, P M Tarsh

WHO TO APPLY TO Laurence Misener Charitable Trust, c/o Messrs Bourner Bullock, Sovereign House, 212–224 Shaftesbury Avenue, London WC2H 8HQ

CC NO 283460   **ESTABLISHED** 1981

■ Victor Mishcon Charitable Trust

WHAT IS FUNDED General charitable purposes. Within the limited funds available each application is considered on its merits with preference given to applications for the relief of poverty from recognised organisations

WHO CAN BENEFIT There are no restrictions on the age; professional and economic group; family situation; religion and culture; and social circumstances of; or disease or medical condition suffered by, the beneficiaries

WHERE FUNDING CAN BE GIVEN UK

TYPE OF GRANT One-off as a rule

FINANCES *Year* 1995 *Income* £87,638 *Grants* £91,941

TRUSTEES Lord Mishcon, Lady Mishcon, P A Cohen

HOW TO APPLY Write to the address under Who To Apply To

WHO TO APPLY TO Miss M Grant, Victor Mishcon Charitable Trust, c/o Mishcon DeReya, 21 Southampton Row, London WC1B 5HS

CC NO 213165   **ESTABLISHED** 1961

■ Missionary Friends Trust

WHAT IS FUNDED The advancement of the Christian faith. Financial and spiritual support is offered to those serving the Lord in missionary situations throughout the world

WHO CAN BENEFIT Registered charities benefiting Christians

WHERE FUNDING CAN BE GIVEN UK, with preference for West Midlands, and overseas

TYPE OF GRANT One-off and recurrent

FINANCES *Year* 1997 *Income* £14,441 *Grants* £13,650

TRUSTEES D B Hill, Mrs P F Seickell, Mrs E M Trude, Mrs J A Pont, Mrs R A Renfrew, B Pont

HOW TO APPLY In writing at any time. Trustees meet twice a year

WHO TO APPLY TO Mrs R Renfrew, Missionary Friends Trust, 18 While Road, Sutton Coldfield, West Midlands B72 1ND

CC NO 228886   **ESTABLISHED** 1960

■ The Mitchell Charitable Trust

WHAT IS FUNDED Jewish organisations, social welfare, child welfare, homelessness, voluntary organisations

WHAT IS NOT FUNDED No grants are made to individuals, or for research, education, overseas appeals or non-Jewish religious appeals. No animal causes or cultural activities

WHO CAN BENEFIT Organisations benefiting: people of all ages; volunteers; Jews; at risk groups; those disadvantaged by poverty; homeless people and victims of abuse and domestic violence.

WHERE FUNDING CAN BE GIVEN London with preference for Camden

TYPE OF GRANT Some recurring

RANGE OF GRANTS £50–£20,000

SAMPLE GRANTS £25,000 to Jewish Care for welfare; £20,000 to CBF World Jewish Relief for international aid; £2,000 to Community Security Trust; £1,500 to British ORT for international training; £1,500 to United Israel Appeal; £1,000 to Mineroa Appeal; £955 to Belsize Square Synagogue for Jewish religion; £701 to North Western Reform Synagogue for Jewish religion; £500 to Ham and High Soup Kitchen for welfare; £500 to National Missing Person's Helpline

FINANCES *Year* 1997–98 *Income* £62,041
Grants £55,429

TRUSTEES Ashley Mitchell, Parry Mitchell, Elizabeth Mitchell, Hannah Lowy

HOW TO APPLY To the address under Who To Apply To in writing

WHO TO APPLY TO Ashley Mitchell, The Mitchell Charitable Trust, 24 Rochester Road, London NW1 9JJ *Tel* 0171-284 1761

CC NO 290273   **ESTABLISHED** 1984

■ Mitchell City of London Charity

WHAT IS FUNDED Aid for the elderly and homeless people in the area Where Funding Can Be Given

WHO CAN BENEFIT Organisations benefiting elderly people and the homeless

WHERE FUNDING CAN BE GIVEN City of London

FINANCES *Year* 1997 *Income* £69,998
Grants £8,250

TRUSTEES R A Ratner (Chairman), W W Archibald (Deputy Chairman), H D Balls, J A Barker, S A Bentley, P E M Borrowdale, Dr Y A Burne, B F Catt, M S Chesterton, Mrs E E Cowie, R M Dancey, K F Dibben, W H Dove, S K Knowles, C R S Link, Mrs M E Ross, J Towey

NOTES In 1997 pensions (paid quarterly) totalled £11,112 to 44 people, with an additional £100 at Christmas and £50 to celebrate the official birthday of Her Majesty the Queen for each pensioner. Also connected to the Charity is the Mitchell City of London Educational Foundation

HOW TO APPLY To the address under Who To Apply To in writing

WHO TO APPLY TO John Keyte, Mitchell City of London Charity, Lower House, Bowley Lane, Bodinham, Hereford HR1 3LF

CC NO 207342   **ESTABLISHED** 1900

■ The Patrick Mitchell Hunter Fund

WHAT IS FUNDED General charitable purposes. Grants are awarded to a range of charities or philanthropic institutions operating in the City of Aberdeen

WHAT IS NOT FUNDED No grants to individuals

WHO CAN BENEFIT There are no restrictions on the age; professional and economic group; family situation; religion and culture; and social circumstances of; or disease or medical condition suffered by, the beneficiaries

WHERE FUNDING CAN BE GIVEN City of Aberdeen only

FINANCES *Year* 1997 *Income* £15,000
Grants £10,000

TRUSTEES J T C Gillan, W Howie

PUBLICATIONS Accounts are available from the Trust

HOW TO APPLY Contact the address under Who To Apply To for further details

WHO TO APPLY TO The Administrator, The Patrick Mitchell Hunter Fund, Wilsone & Duffus, PO Box 81, 7 Golden Square, Aberdeen AB10 1EP *Tel* 01224 641065 *Fax* 01224 647329 *E-mail* info@wilsoneduffus.co.uk

SC NO SCO 17380

■ Esme Mitchell Trust

WHAT IS FUNDED General charitable purposes in Ireland as a whole but principally in Northern Ireland with a particular interest in cultural and artistic objects. Part of the Trust Fund is only available to assist certain heritage bodies as set out in Schedule 3 to the Capital Transfer Act 1984

WHAT IS NOT FUNDED No grants to individuals. As a general rule the Trustees are reluctant to assist bodies with routine annual running costs

WHO CAN BENEFIT It is most unlikely that applications from individuals wishing to undertake voluntary service or further education will be successful. Those involved in the arts and cultural activities will be considered

WHERE FUNDING CAN BE GIVEN Mainly Northern Ireland

TYPE OF GRANT No time limits have generally been set on grants. The Trust has on occasions given grant assistance over a period of two to three years but in general tries not to become involved in commitments of a long term nature

FINANCES *Year* 1995–96 *Income* £100,000

TRUSTEES Trust Advisers: P J Rankin, Commander D J Maxwell, R P Blakiston-Houston

NOTES This is a Northern Ireland Trust with an Inland Revenue registration number: XN48053

HOW TO APPLY No formal application. Applicants should submit: (a) Description of proposed project. (b) A recent statement of accounts and balance sheet if available. (c) A copy of the constitution. (d) Details of tax and legal or charitable status. (e) A copy of the latest annual report. (f) A list of committee officers. (g) Information on other sources of finance. (h) A contact address and telephone number. It would be helpful for administration purposes if three copies of the appeal documentation were to be forwarded. To avoid delay in considering applications, the Trust Advisers require a copy of the most recent financial accounts and balance sheet and the Inland Revenue Charities Division reference number with the original application

WHO TO APPLY TO Northern Bank Executor and Trustee Co Ltd, Esme Mitchell Trust, PO Box 800, Donegall Square West, Belfast BT2 7EB

IR NO XN 48053   **ESTABLISHED** 1965

■ Keren Mitzvah Trust

WHAT IS FUNDED General charitable purposes

WHO CAN BENEFIT There are no restrictions on the age; professional and economic group; family situation; religion and culture; and social circumstances of; or disease or medical condition suffered by, the beneficiaries

WHERE FUNDING CAN BE GIVEN UK

FINANCES *Year* 1996 *Income* £86,797
  Grants £174,926
TRUSTEES C J Smith, M Weiss, M Weisss
WHO TO APPLY TO P Willoughby, Keren Mitzvah Trust,
  c/o Manro Haydan Trading, 1 Knightsbridge,
  London SW1X 7LX
CC NO 1041948   ESTABLISHED 1994

■ Mobbs Memorial Trust Limited

WHAT IS FUNDED St Giles Church and other charitable
  purposes including: almshouses; sheltered
  accommodation; community development;
  support to voluntary and community organisations;
  combined arts; community arts and recreation;
  health; conservation and environment; schools
  and colleges; and community facilities and
  services
WHAT IS NOT FUNDED No grants to individuals
WHO CAN BENEFIT Organisations benefiting: people of
  all ages; ex-service and service people;
  volunteers; unemployed; those in care, fostered
  and adopted; parents and children; at risk groups;
  disabled people; those disadvantaged by poverty
  ex-offenders and those at risk of offending;
  homeless people; those living in rural areas;
  socially isolated people; victims of abuse, crime
  and domestic violence. There is no restriction on
  the disease or medical condition suffered by the
  beneficiaries
WHERE FUNDING CAN BE GIVEN Stoke Poges and
  district within a 35 mile radius of St Giles Church
TYPE OF GRANT Buildings and project. Funding is given
  for up to three years
FINANCES *Year* 1995 *Income* £100,000
HOW TO APPLY To the address under Who To Apply To
  in writing
WHO TO APPLY TO Nick Hamilton, Mobbs Memorial
  Trust Limited, Slough Estates House, 234 Bath
  Road, Slough, Berkshire SL1 4EE
  Tel 01753 537171
CC NO 202478   ESTABLISHED 1963

■ The Modern Architecture and Town Planning Trust (in connection with the Royal Institute of British Architects)

WHAT IS FUNDED To make grants mainly to architects
  and students for specific research projects
WHAT IS NOT FUNDED The awards are not available for
  the support of students on taught courses
WHO CAN BENEFIT Architects and students
WHERE FUNDING CAN BE GIVEN European Community
TYPE OF GRANT Grants to cover all aspects of
  research work (including the time cost of the
  researcher, the hire of research assistants and
  travel) normally to a maximum of £5,000
RANGE OF GRANTS Up to £5,000
FINANCES *Year* 1997 *Income* £27,460
TRUSTEES Royal Institute of British Architects
NOTES As considerable detail is requested and
  evidence of satisfactory supervision required,
  candidates are advised to obtain the application
  form and conditions as early as possible
HOW TO APPLY Application forms are available in
  October each year and must be returned by the
  middle of the following January. Please send
  applications to RIBA Research Awards Secretary at
  the address under Who To Apply To
WHO TO APPLY TO Research Awards Secretary,
  Modern Architecture and Town Planning Trust,
  Royal Institute of British Architects, 66 Portland
  Place, London W1N 4AD
CC NO 314248   ESTABLISHED 1964

■ Modiano Charitable Trust

WHAT IS FUNDED Relief of poverty, advancement of
  the arts and culture including: music, opera,
  theatre and community services
WHAT IS NOT FUNDED No grants to individuals
WHO CAN BENEFIT Registered charities benefiting:
  older people; actors and entertainment
  professionals; musicians; retired people; textile
  workers and designers; Christians and Jews;
  disabled people and those disadvantaged by
  poverty
WHERE FUNDING CAN BE GIVEN London, Bradford City
  and Kirklees
TYPE OF GRANT A range of grants
RANGE OF GRANTS £100–£5,000, typical grant £500
FINANCES *Year* 1996 *Income* £15,271
  Grants £11,035
TRUSTEES G Modiano, Mrs B Modiano, L S Modiano
HOW TO APPLY In writing. Initial telephone calls are
  not welcome. There are no application forms,
  guidelines or deadlines for applications. No sae is
  required
WHO TO APPLY TO G Modiano, Modiano Charitable
  Trust, 6th Floor, Rodwell House, 100 Middlesex
  Street, London E1 7HD *Tel* 0171-377 7550
  Fax 0171-377 6954
CC NO 328372   ESTABLISHED 1989

■ The Moette Charitable Trust

WHAT IS FUNDED The poor and needy for educational
  purposes and other charitable purposes
WHO CAN BENEFIT Children, young adults and those
  disadvantaged by poverty
WHERE FUNDING CAN BE GIVEN UK
TRUSTEES S Lopian, P Lopian
WHO TO APPLY TO S Lopian, The Moette Charitable
  Trust, 1 Holden Road, Salford, Manchester
  M7 4NL
CC NO 1068886   ESTABLISHED 1998

■ Mole Charitable Trust

WHAT IS FUNDED To favour Jewish causes,
  educational institutions and organisations to
  relieve poverty
WHO CAN BENEFIT Individuals, registered charities and
  institutions benefiting children, young adults, Jews
  and those disadvantaged by poverty
WHERE FUNDING CAN BE GIVEN Manchester
RANGE OF GRANTS £200–£54,000
SAMPLE GRANTS £54,000 to Yeshivas Shaarei Torah;
  £17,000 to The Satmar Gemach; £12,000 to
  Vaad Hatzdoko Charitable Trust; £8,000 to Broom
  Foundation; £5,000 to Manchester Charitable
  Trust; £4,700 to Manchester Jewish Grammar
  School; £3,550 to Bikur Cholim and Gemiluth
  Chesed Trust; £3,448 to North Salford Synagogue
  and Beth Hamidrash; £3,000 to Kollel Rabbi
  Yechiel; £2,000 to Manchester Jewish Soup
  Kitchen
FINANCES *Year* 1997 *Income* £80,516
  Grants £128,743
TRUSTEES M Gross, Mrs L P Gross
WHO TO APPLY TO M Gross, Mole Charitable Trust, 2
  Okeover Road, Salford, Manchester M7 4JX
CC NO 281452   ESTABLISHED 1980

■ D C Moncrieff Charity

WHAT IS FUNDED General charitable purposes. Trustees already have list of donees whose requirements outweigh the Trustees' ability to help

WHAT IS NOT FUNDED Registered charities only. Applications from individuals, including students are ineligible

WHO CAN BENEFIT There are no restrictions on the age; professional and economic group; family situation; religion and culture; and social circumstances of; or disease or medical condition suffered by, the beneficiaries

WHERE FUNDING CAN BE GIVEN Emphasis on Suffolk

FINANCES *Year* 1997 *Income* £61,469 *Grants* £61,500

TRUSTEES L G Friston, D J Coleman, A S Cunningham

HOW TO APPLY **This Trust states that it does not respond to unsolicited applications**

WHO TO APPLY TO L G Friston, D C Moncrieff Charity, 14 Stubbs Wood, Gunton, Lowestoft, Suffolk NR32 4TA

CC NO 203919 **ESTABLISHED** 1965

■ Monmouthshire County Council Welsh Church Fund

WHAT IS FUNDED Educational, relief in sickness and need, blind and aged persons, medical and social research, probation, social and recreational, libraries, museums and art galleries and protection of historic buildings relating to Wales, places of worship and burial grounds, emergencies and disasters. The funds available each year for grant purposes are strictly limited and applications are generally only considered from bodies or persons directly connected with Monmouthshire

WHO CAN BENEFIT To benefit students, at risk groups, those disadvantaged by poverty, socially isolated people, disaster victims and the sick. There is no restriction on the disease or medical condition suffered by the beneficiaries

WHERE FUNDING CAN BE GIVEN No restriction – but in practice restricted to beneficiaries connected with Monmouthshire

TYPE OF GRANT The maximum grants paid by the Welsh Church Fund for the main categories of grant are: Religious buildings – £500, community/village/OAP halls, etc – £500. These grants are intended for the provision, upkeep and repair of buildings. Other applications coming within the Scheme are considered individually and the amount of grant, if any, is decided on merit by Committee. Research grants are alsl considered

FINANCES *Year* 1995 *Income* £238,077 *Grants* £99,455

TRUSTEES Monmouthshire County Council

HOW TO APPLY Application form obtainable from the address under Who To Apply To

WHO TO APPLY TO Martin Woodford, Treasurers Dept, Monmouthshire County Council Welsh Church Fund, Monmouthshire County Council, County Hall, Cwmbran, Monmouthshire NP44 2XH

CC NO 507094 **ESTABLISHED** 1977

■ The David Montefiore Trust

WHAT IS FUNDED The Trustees' interest is in giving grants to universities or other organisations, to enable them to give scholarships to students from third world countries. Occasionally other grants are made of particular interest to the Trustees

WHAT IS NOT FUNDED No grants to individuals

WHO CAN BENEFIT Universities, colleges and other charitable trusts to benefit students

WHERE FUNDING CAN BE GIVEN UK and overseas

TYPE OF GRANT A single payment, in time for the start of the academic year. The likely amount of any one payment is £500. In certain cases an indication can be given that similar funding should be available in future years

RANGE OF GRANTS £250–£5,000

SAMPLE GRANTS £5,000 to Africa Educational Trust; £500 to Hammersmith Hospital towards an individual's tuition fees for Diploma course in Internal Medicine; £500 to Liverpool School of Tropical Medicine for financial assistance for an individual; £425 to an individual for PLAB test; £250 to an individual towards PLAB test

FINANCES *Year* 1997 *Income* £14,799 *Grants* £7,425

TRUSTEES Prof D G Montefiore, Miss J M Bogaardt

NOTES Applications should only be made from universities, colleges or other groups who would be able to give scholarships in accordance with the Trustees' policy

HOW TO APPLY Applications should be in writing with details of how any funds given would be applied

WHO TO APPLY TO Miss J M Bogaardt, The David Montefiore Trust, Messrs Poole & Co, Dolphin House, 21 Hendford, Yeovil, Somerset BA20 1TP

CC NO 260452 **ESTABLISHED** 1969

■ Agnes C Montgomerie Charitable Trust

WHAT IS FUNDED To favour medical causes, disability and the elderly.

WHAT IS NOT FUNDED No grants to individuals

WHO CAN BENEFIT Registered charities benefiting disabled people and older people. There is no restriction on the disease or medical condition suffered by the beneficiaries

WHERE FUNDING CAN BE GIVEN Scotland

HOW TO APPLY No applications will be considered in the foreseeable future. This is a private trust and the settlor does not wish to consider any further charities

WHO TO APPLY TO McGrigor Donald, Charities Section, Agnes C Montgomerie Charitable Trust Pacific House, 70 Wellington Street, Glasgow G2 6UA *Tel* 0141-248 6677

SC NO SCO08210

■ The Moody Charitable Trust

WHAT IS FUNDED General charitable purposes

WHO CAN BENEFIT There are no restrictions on the age; professional and economic group; family situation; religion and culture; and social circumstances of; or disease or medical condition suffered by, the beneficiaries

WHERE FUNDING CAN BE GIVEN UK

TYPE OF GRANT Monetary

SAMPLE GRANTS £10,000 to Addenbrookes NHS Trsut Endowment Fund; £2,000 to Ingatestone United Reform Church; £750 to The Sarah Field Fund; £500 to an individual for the Svalbard Expedition; £500 to Wren House Trust

FINANCES *Year* 1996 *Income* £14,426 *Grants* £13,750

TRUSTEES D A Moody, S Moody

WHO TO APPLY TO T J Mines, The Moody Charitable Trust, Thomas David & Co, Mercer House, 10 Watermark Way, Foxholes Business Park, Hertford SG13 7TZ
CC NO 326245   **ESTABLISHED** 1982

■ The Horace Moore Charitable Trust

WHAT IS FUNDED This Trust will consider funding: information technology and computers; Christian education and churches; hospices and hospice at home; conservation and environment; purchase of books for education; community facilities and day centres

WHAT IS NOT FUNDED Donations only to registered charities, long waiting list, owing to small income

WHO CAN BENEFIT Organisations benefiting: children; actors and entertainment professionals; ex-service and service people; musicians; seafarers and fishermen; Church of England; Roman Catholic; disabled people and victims of abuse. There are some restrictions on the disease or medical condition suffered by the beneficiaries

WHERE FUNDING CAN BE GIVEN The South East, Bradford, Calderdale, Norfolk, Northamptonshire, Nottingham, Kensington and Chelsea and Ireland

FINANCES *Year* 1997 *Income* £39,559

TRUSTEES J A G Leighton, J E A Leighton

NOTES Funds fully committed

HOW TO APPLY Donations are only given to charitable organisations and to those of personal interest to the Trustees

WHO TO APPLY TO J A G Leighton, Chairman, The Horace Moore Charitable Trust, Mallows Studio, Warreners Lane, Weybridge, Surrey KT13 0LH *Tel* 01932 710250
CC NO 262545   **ESTABLISHED** 1962

■ The George A Moore Foundation

WHAT IS FUNDED The Trustees select causes and projects from the applications received during the year and also independently research and identify specific objectives where they wish to direct assistance. The type of grants made can vary quite widely from one year to another and care is taken to maintain a rough parity among the various fields covered so that one sphere of activity does not benefit unduly at the expense of another. Areas which are not or cannot be covered by official sources are favoured. Charities working in the fields of: respite and sheltered accommodation; infrastructure development; arts activity; aftercare and respite care; well woman clinics; health facilities and buildings will be considered. Support may also go to historic buildings, memorials, monuments, special schools, care in the community, crime prevention schemes and day centres

WHAT IS NOT FUNDED No assistance will be given to individuals, courses of study, expeditions, overseas travel, holidays or for purposes outside the UK. Because of present long-term commitments and recent grants, the Foundation will not consider appeals for religious property or institutions, or for educational purposes

WHO CAN BENEFIT Only registered charities are considered and the Foundation rarely contributes seedcorn finance to newly established organisations. Projects for young people (teenagers/young adults) are favoured, as are community care projects. Organisations benefiting: ex-service and service people; medical

professionals; seafarers and fishermen; parents and children; widows and widowers; Church of England and Methodists. Support may also be given to carers, disabled people, those living in rural areas, victims of crime and those suffering from various diseases and medical conditions

WHERE FUNDING CAN BE GIVEN Principally Yorkshire and the Isle of Man but consideration may be given to some major national charities under certain circumstances

TYPE OF GRANT Grants are generally non-recurrent and the Foundation is reluctant to contribute to revenue appeals. Approximately 75 per cent of the grants made are £500 or below

RANGE OF GRANTS £20–£100,000, average grant £500

SAMPLE GRANTS £100,000 to York Minster Fund for restoration of Great West Door; £50,000 to Prince's Youth Business Trust; £5,000 to Giggleswick School; £2,500 to Sustrans; £1,000 to Anthony Nolan Bone Marrow Trust; £1,000 to Crimestoppers; £1,000 to Methodist Homes for the Aged; £1,000 to Whizz-Kidz; £1,000 to Yorkshire Spinal Injury Centre Appeal; £1,000 to South Parade Baptist Church

FINANCES *Year* 1998 *Income* £452,922 *Grants* £183,567

TRUSTEES George A Moore, CBE, KStJ, Mrs E Moore, J R Moore, Mrs A L James

HOW TO APPLY Written applications only to the address under Who To Apply To. No guidelines or application forms are issued. The Trustees meet approximately four times a year and an appropriate response is sent out after the relevant meeting

WHO TO APPLY TO Miss L P Oldham, The George A Moore Foundation, Follifoot Hall, Pannal Road, Follifoot, Harrogate, North Yorkshire HG3 1DP
CC NO 262107   **ESTABLISHED** 1970

■ The Moore Stephens Charitable Foundation

WHAT IS FUNDED General charitable purposes. To provide support to such charities as meets the wishes of the partnership

WHAT IS NOT FUNDED Preference is given to charities operating within, or affecting, the City of London

WHO CAN BENEFIT There are no restrictions on the age; professional and economic group; family situation; religion and culture; and social circumstances of; or disease or medical condition suffered by, the beneficiaries

WHERE FUNDING CAN BE GIVEN London

FINANCES *Year* 1997 *Income* £27,573 *Grants* £28,334

TRUSTEES Richard Moore, Gervase Hulbert, Nicholas Hilton, Timothy Cripps

HOW TO APPLY In writing

WHO TO APPLY TO N D Hilton, The Moore Stephens Charitable Foundation, Messrs Moore Stephens, St Paul's House, Warwick Lane, London EC4P 4BN *Tel* 0171-334 9191
CC NO 297194   **ESTABLISHED** 1987

■ The Peter Moores Charitable Trust

WHAT IS FUNDED General charitable purposes

WHO CAN BENEFIT There are no restrictions on the age; professional and economic group; family situation; religion and culture; and social circumstances of; or disease or medical condition suffered by, the beneficiaries

Does the trust you have chosen match your needs? Haphazard applications waste postage and time

429

WHERE FUNDING CAN BE GIVEN UK

TRUSTEES M Johnson, P Moores, P E Warburton

WHO TO APPLY TO A C Taggart, The Peter Moores Charitable Trust, 11–12 Buckingham Gate, London SW1E 6LB

CC NO 1066056   ESTABLISHED 1997

■ The Nigel Moores Family Charitable Foundation

WHAT IS FUNDED Principal objective should be the raising of the artistic taste of the public whether in relation to music, drama, opera, painting, sculpture or otherwise in connection with the fine arts, the promotion of education in the fine arts and academic education, the promotion of the environment, the provision of recreation and leisure facilities and the advancement of religion

WHO CAN BENEFIT Institutions benefiting: children and young adults; actors and entertainment professionals; musicians; students; and textile workers and designers. There is no restriction on the religion or culture of the beneficiaries

WHERE FUNDING CAN BE GIVEN UK and overseas

RANGE OF GRANTS £500–£20,500

SAMPLE GRANTS £20,500 to Tate Gallery, Liverpool; £20,000 to Landlife; £19,150 to the New Contemporaries (1988) Ltd; £15,000 to Massive Video; £4,000 to Llantysilio School Fund; £2,000 to Pentrwf Community Association; £1,000 to Llangollen Pre-school Playgroup; £720 to Wrexham Maela Hospital; £720 to Nightingale Appeal; £500 to Cylch Llangollen

FINANCES Year 1997 Income £91,453
Grants £84,090

TRUSTEES J C S Moores, Mrs L M White, Mrs P M Kennaway

WHO TO APPLY TO P Kurthausen, The Nigel Moores Family Charitable Foundation, c/o Macfarlane & Co, 2nd Floor, Cunard Building, Water Street, Liverpool L3 1DS

CC NO 1002366   ESTABLISHED 1991

■ The Moores Rowland Charitable Trust

This trust did not respond to CAF's request to amend its entry and, by 30 June 1998, CAF's researchers did not find financial records for later than 1995 on its file at the Charity Commission. Trusts are legally required to submit annual accounts to the Charity Commission under section 42 of the Charities Act 1993

WHAT IS FUNDED General charitable purposes

WHO CAN BENEFIT There are no restrictions on the age; professional and economic group; family situation; religion and culture; and social circumstances of; or disease or medical condition suffered by, the beneficiaries

WHERE FUNDING CAN BE GIVEN UK

TRUSTEES N A Eastaway, B M Graham, C A Weeks

WHO TO APPLY TO B M Graham, Trustee, The Moores Rowland Charitable Trust, c/o Messrs Moores Rowland, Clifford's Inn, Fetter Lane, London EX4A 1AS

CC NO 1049326   ESTABLISHED 1995

■ Harold Moorhouse Charity

WHAT IS FUNDED General charitable purposes for the residents of Burnham Market, Norfolk

WHO CAN BENEFIT Individuals and organisations. There are no restrictions on the age; professional and economic group; family situation; religion and culture; and social circumstances of; or disease or medical condition suffered by, the beneficiaries

WHERE FUNDING CAN BE GIVEN Burnham Market, Norfolk

TYPE OF GRANT One-off

RANGE OF GRANTS £50–£2,000

SAMPLE GRANTS £4,600 115 x £40 to residents of Burnham Market towards their winter heating bill of the poor of Burnham Market; £2,500 to The Burnhams Surgery for the Equipment Fund; £2,000 to Friends of Wells Cottage Hospital for their fund; £1,750 to Royal National Institute for the Blind for their fund; £500 to Burnham Market Primary School for books

FINANCES Year 1996–97 Income £15,603
Grants £13,295

TRUSTEES R J Utting, Mrs V A Worship

NOTES Burnham Market, Norfolk residents only

HOW TO APPLY To the address under Who To Apply To in writing

WHO TO APPLY TO R J Utting, Treasurer, Harold Moorhouse Charity, Angles House, Station Road, Burnham Market, Kings Lynn, Norfolk PE31 8HA *Tel* 01328 738232

CC NO 287278   ESTABLISHED 1984

■ Morden College

WHAT IS FUNDED Education

WHO CAN BENEFIT To benefit children, young adults and students

WHERE FUNDING CAN BE GIVEN UK

FINANCES Year 1996 Income £4,468,900

WHO TO APPLY TO Clerk to the Trustees, Morden College, 19 St Germans Place, London SE3 0PW

CC NO 215551   ESTABLISHED 1961

■ The Morel Charitable Trust

WHAT IS FUNDED Support of the arts, in particular drama, organisations working for improved race relations, inner city projects and third world projects. Charities working in the fields of arts, culture and recreation; health; conservation and environment; education and training; and social care and development

WHAT IS NOT FUNDED No grants to individuals

WHO CAN BENEFIT Grants are normally made to projects of which the Trustees have personal knowledge. Organisations benefiting children; young adults and older people; actors and entertainment professionals; musicians; volunteers; disabled people; those disadvantaged by poverty, people living in inner city areas and victims of famine. There is no restriction on the disease or medical condition suffered by the beneficiaries

WHERE FUNDING CAN BE GIVEN UK and overseas

TYPE OF GRANT Project

SAMPLE GRANTS £3,000 to Oxfam; £3,000 to VSO; £3,000 to Child to Child (Ecuador); £3,000 to Christian Aid (Jubilee); £2,000 to Ghana School Aid; £2,000 to Harvest Help; £2,000 to Health Unlimited; £2,000 to SAFAD; £2,000 to Fair Trade Foundation; £2,000 to Book Aid International

FINANCES Year 1996–97 Income £40,000
Grants £40,000

TRUSTEES J M Gibbs, W M Gibbs, S E Gibbs, B M O Gibbs

HOW TO APPLY Applications to the address under Who To Apply To in brief written format

WHO TO APPLY TO S E Gibbs, The Morel Charitable Trust, 34 Durand Gardens, London SW9 0PP

CC NO 268943   ESTABLISHED 1972

■ The Morgan Crucible Company plc Charitable Trust

WHAT IS FUNDED Small, specialist charities preferred in fields: health care, medical research, children, support for disabled or ill. Donations made direct, not through intermediate charities

WHAT IS NOT FUNDED No donations are made to individuals, parish churches or youth clubs. The Trust tends to exclude overseas, armed forces, restoration of buildings, private persons, travel, wildlife, countryside

WHO CAN BENEFIT Physically or mentally disabled people, young people in deprived or undesirable circumstances and those disadvantaged by poverty. There is no restriction on the disease or medical condition suffered by the beneficiaries. Medical professionals and research workers will be considered

WHERE FUNDING CAN BE GIVEN Primarily Wirral, Leeds, South Wales, South London, Worcester, Thames Valley

TYPE OF GRANT Donations are made to the same charities for a period of years. One payment per annum

SAMPLE GRANTS £15,800 to the care, including holidays, of people with mental handicaps; £15,160 to direct sponsorship; £6,178 for medical development and research; £5,850 for the care, including holidays, of young people in deprived or undesirable circumstances; £4,900 to local (Windsor area) good causes; £3,950 for adventure or training holidays or courses for character building; £2,800 to the arts; £2,008 to character reform; £1,900 for education; £1,275 for community services

FINANCES *Year* 1997 *Income* £68,000
Grants £59,821

TRUSTEES Sir James Spooner, Dr E B Farmer

HOW TO APPLY Written only

WHO TO APPLY TO D J Coker, The Morgan Crucible Company plc Charitable Trust, The Morgan Crucible Company plc, Morgan House, Madeira Walk, Windsor, Berkshire SL4 1EP

CC NO 273507   **ESTABLISHED** 1977

■ The Mr and Mrs J T Morgan Foundation

WHAT IS FUNDED Preference is given to the support of charities in Wales and to the promotion of education and religion in Wales

WHAT IS NOT FUNDED No grants to individuals

WHO CAN BENEFIT Churches and national and local charities benefiting: children, young adults, students and Christians

WHERE FUNDING CAN BE GIVEN Mainly Wales

TYPE OF GRANT One-off

FINANCES *Year* 1997 *Income* £25,421
Grants £23,702

TRUSTEES J H T Aylward, J A Lloyd, JP, MA, LLM, J R Morgan

HOW TO APPLY To the address under Who To Apply To

WHO TO APPLY TO J A Lloyd, The Mr and Mrs J T Morgan Foundation, 54 Bishopston Road, Bishopston, Swansea, Wales SA3 3EN
Tel 01792 232142

CC NO 241835   **ESTABLISHED** 1965

■ S C and M E Morland's Charitable Trust

WHAT IS FUNDED Support to Quaker charities and others of which the Trustees have special interest, knowledge or association. Religious groups, relief of poverty and ill-health, promotion of peace and development overseas

WHAT IS NOT FUNDED Animal welfare, medical research and individuals are not usually funded

WHO CAN BENEFIT Quaker, local and national charities which have a strong social bias and also some UK-based international charities. Those disadvantaged by poverty are considered. There is no restriction on the disease or medical condition suffered by the beneficiaries

WHERE FUNDING CAN BE GIVEN UK

TYPE OF GRANT Project

RANGE OF GRANTS Below £1,000–£3,500

SAMPLE GRANTS £3,500 to Britain Yearly Meeting

FINANCES *Year* 1997 *Income* £34,835
Grants £25,800

TRUSTEES J C Morland, Ms J E Morland, Ms E Boyd

NOTES Assets are held in trust

WHO TO APPLY TO J C Morland, S C and M E Morland's Charitable Trust, The Gables, Parbrook, Glastonbury, Somerset BA6 8PB

CC NO 201645   **ESTABLISHED** 1957

■ The Morris Charitable Trust

WHAT IS FUNDED General charitable purposes. National, international and local community projects, particularly causes within the community of the London Borough of Islington

WHAT IS NOT FUNDED No grants to individuals

WHO CAN BENEFIT Small local projects and national organisations. There are no restrictions on the age; professional and economic group; family situation; religion and culture; and social circumstances of; or disease or medical condition suffered by, the beneficiaries

WHERE FUNDING CAN BE GIVEN UK with preference to London, overseas

TYPE OF GRANT One-off and recurring grants of £250–£1,000

RANGE OF GRANTS £50–£35,000, average grant £250

FINANCES *Year* 1996 *Income* £100,000
Grants £57,108

TRUSTEES Mrs G Morris, J A Morris, P B Morris, A R Stenning

PUBLICATIONS Annual Report, information pamphlet

HOW TO APPLY In writing to the address under Who To Apply To

WHO TO APPLY TO The Chairman's Secretary, The Morris Charitable Trust, Management Department, Business Design Centre, 52 Upper Strand, London W1 0QH *Tel* 0171-359 3535 *Fax* 0171-226 0590

CC NO 802290   **ESTABLISHED** 1989

■ The Douglas Morris Charitable Trust

WHAT IS FUNDED Registered charities only. Medicine and health, welfare and international

WHAT IS NOT FUNDED No grants to individuals or students

WHO CAN BENEFIT New, established and national organisations benefiting carers, disabled people and those disadvantaged by poverty. There is no restriction on the disease or medical condition suffered by the beneficiaries

WHERE FUNDING CAN BE GIVEN UK and overseas

TYPE OF GRANT One-off and recurrent small grants of £1,000 or less. Research and core costs will also be considered

SAMPLE GRANTS £2,000 to The Samaritans; £1,000 to Royal Commonwealth Society for the Blind; £1,000 to St Christopher's Hospice; £1,000 to The Big Issue Foundation; £1,000 to National Council of YMCAs

FINANCES *Year* 1996–97 *Income* £14,355 *Grants* £14,150

TRUSTEES Mrs P D Douglas-Morris, Mrs G Lind, C J Douglas-Morris

NOTES Applications should be made in Autumn. Grants are made in November

HOW TO APPLY In writing. Applications not acknowledged. Applications should only be made in the autumn. Grants are only made in November/December

WHO TO APPLY TO Mrs Gay Lind, The Douglas Morris Charitable Trust, 295 Unthank Road, Norwich, Norfolk NR4 7QA

CC NO 275719   **ESTABLISHED** 1978

■ The Peter Morrison Charitable Foundation

WHAT IS FUNDED To support a wide range of social welfare causes

WHO CAN BENEFIT Registered charities benefiting at risk groups, those disadvantaged by poverty and socially isolated people

WHERE FUNDING CAN BE GIVEN UK

RANGE OF GRANTS £25–£5,000

SAMPLE GRANTS £5,000 to Nightingale House; £3,700 to Action for Blind People; £3,100 to Jewish Care; £1,507 to West London Synagogue; £1,000 to Hampstead Theatre Trust; £1,000 to Maccabi Union; £1,000 to Wellbeing; £1,000 to Queen's Park Hebrew Congregation; £1,000 to St Gemma's Hospice; £1,000 to Royal Academy

FINANCES *Year* 1997 *Income* £54,340 *Grants* £47,766

TRUSTEES M Morrison, I R Morrison

WHO TO APPLY TO J Payne, The Peter Morrison Charitable Foundation, Hope Agar, Chartered Accountants, Epworth House, 25 City Road, London EC1Y 1AR

CC NO 277202   **ESTABLISHED** 1978

■ G M Morrison Charitable Trust

WHAT IS FUNDED General charitable purposes. The Trustees expect to give priority to those charities already supported. Very few charities are added to the list each year. Appeals not followed up cannot normally be acknowledged

WHAT IS NOT FUNDED The Trustees have never made grants to individuals. Local charities not normally considered

WHO CAN BENEFIT There are no restrictions on the age; professional and economic group; family situation; religion and culture; and social circumstances of; or disease or medical condition suffered by, the beneficiaries

WHERE FUNDING CAN BE GIVEN UK

TYPE OF GRANT Normally annual

RANGE OF GRANTS £200–£1,000

FINANCES *Year* 1996–97 *Income* £169,456 *Grants* £91,000

TRUSTEES G M Morrison, N W Smith

NOTES The Trustees support a portfolio of charities on a regular annual basis. Very few additional charities are added to the list each year. Appeals not followed up cannot normally be acknowledged

HOW TO APPLY In writing. Telephone applications not considered

WHO TO APPLY TO G M Morrison, G M Morrison Charitable Trust, 11J Stuart Tower, 105 Maida Vale, London W9 1UH

CC NO 261380   **ESTABLISHED** 1970

■ The Stanley Morrison Charitable Trust

WHAT IS FUNDED Welfare; education; sport, especially encouraging youth participation; charities based in the area Where Funding Can Be Given. Primarily where a grant will make a big difference

WHAT IS NOT FUNDED No grants to national charities

WHO CAN BENEFIT Organisations benefiting young adults and sportsmen and women

WHERE FUNDING CAN BE GIVEN The west coast of Scotland, especially Glasgow and Ayrshire

TYPE OF GRANT Buildings, project and recurring costs. Grants and funding for up to and over three years will be considered

RANGE OF GRANTS £1,000–£15,000; typical £3,000

FINANCES *Year* 1995–96 *Income* £161,000 *Grants* £55,000

TRUSTEES A S Dudgeon, J H McKean, Mrs M E Morrison, S W Morrison, T F O'Connell, G L Taylor

HOW TO APPLY To the address under Who To Apply To in writing

WHO TO APPLY TO Jean Scott, Secretary, The Stanley Morrison Charitable Trust, Grant Thornton, Chartered Accountant, 114 West George Street, Glasgow G2 1QF *Tel* 0141-332 7484

SC NO SCO 06610   **ESTABLISHED** 1989

■ Moshal Charitable Trust

WHAT IS FUNDED General charitable purposes

WHAT IS NOT FUNDED No funding for Jewish charities

WHO CAN BENEFIT Registered charities. There are no restrictions on the age; professional and economic group; family situation; and social circumstances of; or disease or medical condition suffered by, the beneficiaries

WHERE FUNDING CAN BE GIVEN UK

FINANCES *Year* 1996 *Income* £81,951 *Grants* £45,449

TRUSTEES D Halpern, L Halpern

WHO TO APPLY TO D Z Lopian, Moshal Charitable Trust, Lopian Gross Barnett & Co, Harvester House, 37 Peter Street, Manchester M2 5QD

CC NO 284448   **ESTABLISHED** 1981

■ The Moss Charitable Trust

WHAT IS FUNDED General charitable purposes. The Trust is established to distribute moneys donated by its contributors. Grants are consequently made on the recommendation of contributors, and unsolicited applications are not considered

WHAT IS NOT FUNDED Available funds fully committed.

WHO CAN BENEFIT Mainly Christian – non Denominational Prostestant

WHERE FUNDING CAN BE GIVEN Mainly local: Hampshire, Dorset, Sussex

TYPE OF GRANT Outright grant or interest free loan

FINANCES *Year* 1997 *Income* £311,936 *Grants* £200,679

TRUSTEES R L Malpas, A W Malpas, J L Simmons, A F Simmons, J H Simmons, P L Simmons

HOW TO APPLY **This Trust states that it does not respond to unsolicited applications**
WHO TO APPLY TO P D Malpas, The Moss Charitable Trust, 7 Church Road, Parkstone, Poole, Dorset BH14 8UF
CC NO 258031   ESTABLISHED 1969

■ Philip Moss Charitable Trust

WHAT IS FUNDED General at Trustees' discretion, but consideration given to charities supported by Settlor during his lifetime and listed in his will. Preference to help charities who help people to help themselves
WHAT IS NOT FUNDED Grants are not normally given to animal charities or individuals
WHO CAN BENEFIT Mainly institutions. There are no restrictions on the age; professional and economic group; family situation; religion and culture; and social circumstances of; or disease or medical condition suffered by, the beneficiaries
WHERE FUNDING CAN BE GIVEN England and Wales
TYPE OF GRANT One-off at the discretion of the Trustees
RANGE OF GRANTS £250–£5,000
SAMPLE GRANTS £5,000 to Jewish Blind Society; £5,000 to St John Ambulance; £5,000 to Stoke Manderville Hospital; £5,000 to Royal National Institute for the Blind; £5,000 to Victoria Hospital, Lewes; £5,000 to Royal Marsden NHS Trust; £3,000 to East Sussex Association for the Disabled; £2,500 to Children's Trust Tadworth; £2,000 to Phoenix Centre League of Friends; £2,000 to Guide Dogs for the Blind
FINANCES Year 1996–97 Income £25,594 Grants £47,000
TRUSTEES John W A Mears, Edward G Walker
HOW TO APPLY In writing only. The Trustees normally make grants once a year in March
WHO TO APPLY TO J W A Mears, Philip Moss Charitable Trust, c/o Myros Smith, Times House, Throwley Way, Sutton, Surrey SM1 4AP
CC NO 1014864   ESTABLISHED 1990

■ The Moss Spiro Will Charitable Foundation

WHAT IS FUNDED General charitable purposes, preferably with some Jewish or Israeli welfare connection
WHO CAN BENEFIT Particularly Jewish or Israeli people. However, there are no restrictions on the age; professional and economic group; family situation; religion and culture; and social circumstances of; or disease or medical condition suffered by, the beneficiaries
WHERE FUNDING CAN BE GIVEN UK and overseas
TRUSTEES G M Davis, T D Spiro
WHO TO APPLY TO T Spiro, Trustee, The Moss Spiro Will Charitable Foundation, Crowndean House, 26 Bruton Lane, London W1X 7LA
CC NO 1064249   ESTABLISHED 1997

■ Mossaic Missions

WHAT IS FUNDED Advancement of the Christian faith; relief of persons in conditions of need, hardship or distress or who are aged or sick; advancement of education through research provision in accordance with Christian principles; and other charitable purposes
WHO CAN BENEFIT To benefit people of all ages and Christians. There are few restrictions on the social circumstances of, and no restriction on the disease or medical condition suffered by, the beneficiaries
WHERE FUNDING CAN BE GIVEN UK and overseas
TRUSTEES M Asare, Ms J Hanson, J Osborn, Ms L Sarpong
WHO TO APPLY TO M Asare, Mossaic Missions, 14c Wordsworth Court, Kings Road, Chelmsford, Essex CM1 4HL
CC NO 1065587   ESTABLISHED 1997

■ The Mosse Charitable Settlement

WHAT IS FUNDED Innovative approaches to problems, rather than relief, both social and medical. Particularly charities working in the fields of: civil society development; medical studies and research; literacy; special needs education; speech therapy; development proposals; campaigning in the areas of racial equality, discrimination and relations, and community services
WHAT IS NOT FUNDED Definitely no scholarships, expeditions or national appeals
WHO CAN BENEFIT Registered charities benefiting disabled people. There is no restriction on the disease or medical condition suffered by the beneficiaries
WHERE FUNDING CAN BE GIVEN Mainly UK, some underdeveloped countries
TYPE OF GRANT Mainly one-off, but form of grant depends on what is likely to be effective. Feasibility studies, interest free loans, project and research will be considered
RANGE OF GRANTS £200–£10,000
FINANCES Year 1997 Income £15,000 Grants £12,000
TRUSTEES R W E Mosse, J A Mosse, C A Mosse
NOTES We have major established channels of giving leaving very little unallocated income
HOW TO APPLY **We very rarely give to unsolicited applications** most likely to consider outline of project funded. No deadline, no sae, no application form
WHO TO APPLY TO R W E Mosse, The Mosse Charitable Settlement, 28 Clifton Hill, London NW8 0QG Tel 0171-624 2022
CC NO 285134   ESTABLISHED 1982

■ Mother Humber Memorial Fund

WHAT IS FUNDED The elderly and infirm; children; organisations working towards racial equality; aiding people with drug problems and counselling organisations
WHO CAN BENEFIT Individuals and organisations benefiting children, older people, substance misusers and ethnic minority groups
WHERE FUNDING CAN BE GIVEN Hull
FINANCES Year 1994–95 Income £23,930 Grants £28,000
TRUSTEES J Rose (Chairman), Mrs J Barnett, Mrs P Ellis, J Haines, Cllr D Hale, M Welford
HOW TO APPLY To the address under Who To Apply To in writing
WHO TO APPLY TO Mrs E M Widdicks, Mother Humber Memorial Fund, 7 Wright Street, Hull HU2 8HU
CC NO 225082   ESTABLISHED 1963

Does the trust you have chosen match your needs? Haphazard applications waste postage and time

433

■ The Moulton Charitable Trust

WHAT IS FUNDED Medicine and health

WHAT IS NOT FUNDED Individuals, students, animal charities

WHO CAN BENEFIT National and established organisations benefiting sufferers of asthma

WHERE FUNDING CAN BE GIVEN UK with preference for Kent

TYPE OF GRANT One-off grants of £5,000 or more. Buildings, capital, core costs, project, research, recurring costs and running costs will be considered

FINANCES *Year* 1995 *Income* £30,000 *Grants* £100,000

TRUSTEES J P Moulton, P M Moulton

HOW TO APPLY In writing

WHO TO APPLY TO J Moulton, The Moulton Charitable Trust, 57 Kippington Road, Sevenoaks, Kent TN13 2LL *Tel* 01732 450025 *Fax* 01732 742436

CC NO 1033119   **ESTABLISHED** 1993

■ Moulton Harrox Educational Foundation

WHAT IS FUNDED Schools in the area Where Funding Can Be Given, some individuals for educational purposes

WHAT IS NOT FUNDED Grants must benefit people under 25 years of age

WHO CAN BENEFIT Individuals and organisations benefiting children, young adults and students

WHERE FUNDING CAN BE GIVEN The district of South Holland

RANGE OF GRANTS £33–£4,000

SAMPLE GRANTS £4,000 to Spalding Grammar School; £2,000 to John Harrox CP School, Moulton; £2,000 to Spalding Parish Church Day School; £1,500 to St John Baptist School, Spalding; £600 to Tydd St Mary School

FINANCES *Year* 1997 *Income* £21,819 *Grants* £16,172

TRUSTEES Mrs D Balchin, Cllr Mrs R F Biggadike, T Bray, R Buck, T H Charlton, D J Grimwood, J Ladbrooke, W Lawes, Cllr D G Mawby, Rev P G F Norwood, Cllr W J Speechley

NOTES £3,322 given to individuals, £12,000 given to schools in 1997

HOW TO APPLY Applications should be made on a form available from the address under Who To Apply To. The Trustees meet annually in September

WHO TO APPLY TO R W Lewis, Solicitor, The Moulton Harrox Educational Foundation, 23 New Road, Spalding, Lincolnshire PE11 1DH

CC NO 527635   **ESTABLISHED** 1963

■ Sir Edmund Moundeford's Educational Foundation

WHAT IS FUNDED Educational purposes in the area Where Funding Can Be Given

WHAT IS NOT FUNDED Beneficiaries must be resident in the area Where Funding Can Be Given

WHO CAN BENEFIT Children, young adults and students

WHERE FUNDING CAN BE GIVEN Feltwell

SAMPLE GRANTS £32,589 to Edmund de Moundeford VC Primary School for a new library

FINANCES *Year* 1995 *Income* £60,128 *Grants* £36,568

TRUSTEES Dr J Burgess (Chairman)

HOW TO APPLY To the address under Who To Apply To in writing

WHO TO APPLY TO B L Hawkins, Sir Edmund Moundeford's Educational Foundation, The Estate Office, Lynn Road, Downham, Norfolk PE38 9NL *Tel* 01366 387180

CC NO 311174   **ESTABLISHED** 1878

■ Mount 'A' Charitable Trust

WHAT IS FUNDED General charitable purposes. Grants made at the request of the Settlor and her family; acknowledgements should be addressed to the Trustee

WHAT IS NOT FUNDED No grants to individuals

WHO CAN BENEFIT Registered charities only benefiting children and young adults

WHERE FUNDING CAN BE GIVEN Bristol and the Channel Islands

TYPE OF GRANT Project, research grants funded for one year or less will be considered

FINANCES *Year* 1996 *Income* £35,372 *Grants* £32,345

TRUSTEES The Barbinder Trust

HOW TO APPLY **This Trust states that it does not respond to unsolicited applications**

WHO TO APPLY TO The Director, Mount 'A' Charitable Trust, The Barbinder Trust, 9 Greyfriars Road, Reading, Berkshire RG1 1JG *Tel* 01734 597111

CC NO 264127   **ESTABLISHED** 1971

■ Mount 'B' Charitable Trust

WHAT IS FUNDED General charitable purposes. Grants made at the request of the Settlor and her family, acknowledgements should be addressed to the Trustee

WHAT IS NOT FUNDED No grants to individuals

WHO CAN BENEFIT Registered charities only benefiting children and young adults

WHERE FUNDING CAN BE GIVEN Bristol and the Channel Islands

TYPE OF GRANT Core costs and project funding for one year or less will be considered

FINANCES *Year* 1996 *Income* £35,372 *Grants* £30,395

TRUSTEES The Barbinder Trust

HOW TO APPLY **This Trust states that it does not respond to unsolicited applications**

WHO TO APPLY TO The Director, Mount 'B' Charitable Trust, The Barbinder Trust, 9 Greyfriars Road, Reading, Berkshire RG1 1JG *Tel* 01734 597111

CC NO 264129   **ESTABLISHED** 1971

■ The Mount Everest Foundation

WHAT IS FUNDED Support of expeditions for exploration and research in high mountain regions only

WHAT IS NOT FUNDED Support is limited to expeditions from Great Britain and New Zealand. Youth, training and commercial expeditions are not eligible

WHO CAN BENEFIT Expeditions for the exploration and research of high mountain regions only, benefiting young adults and older people

WHERE FUNDING CAN BE GIVEN Expedition from only Great Britain and New Zealand

TYPE OF GRANT Project

RANGE OF GRANTS £300 to £1,300 (typical)

Have you read How to use the DGMT *on page xvi?*

SAMPLE GRANTS £1,000 to Changabang North Wall 1997, the first ascent of 1,300m north face of Changabang (6,864m); £900 to Torres del Paine South Tower, capsule ascent South Ridge of Tower of Paine (2,500m); £900 to BMES Chile '97 investigation into function of Diamox; £900 to Brit Thunder Mountain and Mount Hunter 1997, new routes on these mountains (c3,350m and c4,270m); £900 to British Choktoi, first ascents of sub-6,000m peaks in Choktoi area; £900 to 1997 British Bhagirathi III, first free ascent of west face route (6,454m); £900 to British Sepu Kangri in Nyain-Qen-Tanghla, first ascent (6,950m); £900 to New Zealand Aghil 1997, exploration of the Aghil mountains with as many ascents as possible; £900 to Scottish-Australian Broad Peak 97, first ascent of South Ridge (8,047m); £900 to Anglo-American Kokshaal-Too/Ak-Su, first ascents on peaks between 4,000m and 6,000m

FINANCES *Year* 1997 *Income* £32,600
Grants £32,600

TRUSTEES The Committee of Management

PUBLICATIONS Annual Report. A map of Central Asia has been produced in collaboration with the Royal Geographical Society

HOW TO APPLY Applications should be made on the appropriate forms obtainable from the Hon Secretary. Deadlines for receipt of completed application forms: 31 August and 31 December for the following year's expeditions

WHO TO APPLY TO W H Ruthven, The Hon Secretary, The Mount Everest Foundation, Gowrie, Cardwell Close, Warton, Preston PR4 1SH
Tel 01772 635346 *Fax* 01772 635346

CC NO 208206   **ESTABLISHED** 1955

■ The Mountbatten Memorial Trust

WHAT IS FUNDED Grants restricted to technological research in aid of disabled and handicapped people

WHAT IS NOT FUNDED Remaining funds reserved for technological research projects

WHO CAN BENEFIT Registered charities engaged in technological research benefiting disabled people

WHERE FUNDING CAN BE GIVEN UK and overseas

TYPE OF GRANT Technological research projects

RANGE OF GRANTS £5,000–£25,000

FINANCES *Year* 1996 *Income* £23,014
Grants £56,007

TRUSTEES HRH The Prince of Wales, KG, KT, GCB, (Chair), Lord Bradbourne, Lady Pamela Hicks, Hon Michael-John Knatchbull, Countess Mountbatten of Burma, CBE, CD, JP, DL, Lord Romsey

HOW TO APPLY At any time

WHO TO APPLY TO J Moss, Secretary, The Mountbatten Memorial Trust, Estate Office, Broadlands, Romsey, Hampshire SO51 9ZE
Tel 01794 518885

CC NO 278691   **ESTABLISHED** 1979

■ The Edwina Mountbatten Trust

WHAT IS FUNDED The Save the Children Fund (for exceptionally sick, distressed or needy children), the promotion and improvement of the arts and the practice of nursing, and St John Ambulance. To assist specific projects and not to supplement working funds

WHAT IS NOT FUNDED No support can be given for further education of nursing personnel working in the UK

WHO CAN BENEFIT The services of St John Ambulance; sick or needy children (through the Save the Children Fund) and those concerned in the promotion of the art and practice of nursing, midwifery and health visiting. There are no restrictions on the disease or medical condition suffered by the beneficiaries

WHERE FUNDING CAN BE GIVEN UK and overseas

TYPE OF GRANT Project grants normally not recurrent

RANGE OF GRANTS £500–£30,000

FINANCES *Year* 1995 *Income* £83,236
Grants £90,300

TRUSTEES Countess Mountbatten of Burma, CBE, CD, JP, DL (Chairman), Noel Cunningham-Reid, Lord Farringdon (Hon Treasurer), Douglas Fairbanks, KBE, DSC, Lord Romsey, P H T Mimpriss, Mrs Mary Fagan, JP

PUBLICATIONS Annual Report

NOTES Applicants for benefits other than those concerned with the promotion and improvement of the art and practice of nursing, are advised that, with few exceptions, grants are restricted to projects organised by the Save the Children Fund, and St John Ambulance.

HOW TO APPLY To the Secretary of the Trust, at the beginning of the year. In writing

WHO TO APPLY TO The Secretary, The Edwina Mountbatten Trust, Estate Office, Broadlands, Romsey, Hampshire SO51 9ZE
Tel 01794 518885

CC NO 228166   **ESTABLISHED** 1960

■ Gweneth Moxon Charitable Trust

WHAT IS FUNDED General charitable purposes

WHAT IS NOT FUNDED No grants to individuals

WHO CAN BENEFIT There are no restrictions on the age; professional and economic group; family situation; religion and culture; and social circumstances of; or disease or medical condition suffered by, the beneficiaries

WHERE FUNDING CAN BE GIVEN UK

RANGE OF GRANTS £500–£4,000

SAMPLE GRANTS £4,000 to Plymouth Age Concern; £2,000 to Children's Hospice – South West; £2,000 to RNLI; £2,000 to Blond McIndoe Centre; £2,000 to Meningitis Research; £2,000 to RNIB; £2,000 to St Loyes College Foundation; £2,000 to Downs Syndrome Association; £1,000 to HEADWAY; £1,000 to the Stroke Association

FINANCES *Year* 1995 *Income* £31,965
Grants £37,000

TRUSTEES NatWest Investments

WHO TO APPLY TO Ref 3/SW.647028, Gweneth Moxon Charitable Trust, NatWest Investments, South West Region, Trinity Quay, Avon Street, Bristol BS2 0YY

CC NO 266672   **ESTABLISHED** 1971

■ The F H Muirhead Charitable Trust

WHAT IS FUNDED To provide donations of specific items of medical equipment for use in research by hospitals and universities. Priority given to applications from smaller organisations

WHAT IS NOT FUNDED No grants to non-charitable bodies. Grants for equipment for diagnostic or clinical use

WHO CAN BENEFIT Charitable bodies only. Hospitals/ medical research institutes. There are no restrictions on the disease or medical condition suffered by the beneficiaries

WHERE FUNDING CAN BE GIVEN UK

TYPE OF GRANT Capital grant to a maximum of £10,000 per application. Research grants will also be considered

RANGE OF GRANTS Any sum up to a maximum of £10,000 per application
FINANCES *Year* 1996 *Income* £46,000 *Grants* £51,500
TRUSTEES J H Purves, M J Harding, S J Gallico
HOW TO APPLY Initial request for application form to be returned with details of specific items of equipment for which grant required. Trustees meet twice a year in March and October. Application forms to be received at least three weeks before meeting
WHO TO APPLY TO Nicola Dudley, The F H Muirhead Charitable Trust, 26 Farringdon Street, London EC4A 4AQ *Tel* 0171-248 9991 *Fax* 0171-236 4025
CC NO 327605   **ESTABLISHED** 1987

■ The Mulberry Trust

WHAT IS FUNDED General charitable purposes
WHO CAN BENEFIT Charitable organisations. There are no restrictions on the age; professional and economic group; family situation; religion and culture; and social circumstances of; or disease or medical condition suffered by, the beneficiaries
WHERE FUNDING CAN BE GIVEN UK
FINANCES *Year* 1996 *Income* £263,906 *Grants* £284,465
TRUSTEES J G Marks, Ms A M Marks, C F Woodhouse
WHO TO APPLY TO The Mulberry Trust, Messrs Farrer & Co, 66 Lincoln's Inn Fields, London WC2A 3LH
CC NO 263296   **ESTABLISHED** 1971

■ The Mulgrave Charity Trust

WHAT IS FUNDED To support three charities mentioned in the schedule with the balance of annual income applied in support of charities concerned with relief of sickness by the free or aided treatment of people by qualified chiropractics or osteopaths and the care and maintenance of orphans, homeless people or the elderly in need
WHO CAN BENEFIT Organisations benefiting: those in care, fostered and adopted; elderly people in need, homeless people, and those needing chiropractic treatment and osteopathy
WHERE FUNDING CAN BE GIVEN The Borough of Sutton
RANGE OF GRANTS £20–£4224
SAMPLE GRANTS £4,224 to JPA; £1,056 to Youth Aliyah; £1,056 to British Technion; £500 to Marie Curie Cancer Care; £500 to Musicians Benevolent Fund
FINANCES *Year* 1997 *Income* £13,623 *Grants* £9,006
TRUSTEES S Leon, Miss D Aldridge, P O Leon
HOW TO APPLY To the address under Who To Apply To in writing
WHO TO APPLY TO The Mulgrave Charity Trust, 17 Mulgrave Road, Sutton, Surrey SM2 6NH
CC NO 265891   **ESTABLISHED** 1973

■ Multiple Sclerosis Society of Great Britain & Northern Ireland

WHAT IS FUNDED Co-operation with the medical profession to encourage scientific research into the causes of and cure for multiple sclerosis. The aid and amelioration of the conditions of those suffering from multiple sclerosis
WHO CAN BENEFIT Individuals suffering from multiple sclerosis and medical research organisations

benefiting those suffering from MS and medical professionals, research workers and scientists
WHERE FUNDING CAN BE GIVEN UK
TYPE OF GRANT One-off grants to individuals with MS. Grants to scientists carrying out research into MS
TRUSTEES The Council of the Society
PUBLICATIONS *The MS News*, Annual Report and Accounts and *The Messenger*
HOW TO APPLY Throughout the year
WHO TO APPLY TO The Chief Executive, Multiple Sclerosis Society of Great Britain & Northern Ireland, 25 Effie Road, Fulham, London SW6 1EE
CC NO 207495   **ESTABLISHED** 1953

■ Municipal Charities

WHAT IS FUNDED Almshouses and relief in need
WHO CAN BENEFIT Individuals and organisations benefiting at risk groups, those disadvantaged by poverty, homeless people and socially isolated people
WHERE FUNDING CAN BE GIVEN Lichfield
RANGE OF GRANTS £33–£2,000
SAMPLE GRANTS £13,158 distributed among 43 individuals; £2,000 to Michael Loves Charity; £1,500 to an Individual; £1,000 to Lichfield Day Centre
FINANCES *Year* 1997 *Income* £115,349 *Grants* £17,658
HOW TO APPLY To the address under Who To Apply To in writing
WHO TO APPLY TO W P Coates, Municipal Charities, Hadens, St Mary's Chambers, Breadmarket Street, Lichfield, Staffordshire WS13 6LQ
CC NO 254299   **ESTABLISHED** 1955

■ The Municipal General Charities for the Poor

WHAT IS FUNDED Relief in need in the area Where Funding Can Be Given
WHAT IS NOT FUNDED No grants for research, expeditions, scholarships or on-going projects
WHO CAN BENEFIT Primarily individuals. At risk groups, those disadvantaged by poverty and socially isolated people will be considered
WHERE FUNDING CAN BE GIVEN Newark
TYPE OF GRANT One-off only
RANGE OF GRANTS £20–£10,000, average grant £150
SAMPLE GRANTS £10,000 to League of Friends, Newark Hospital for equipment; £5,000 to Newark Emmaus Trust for the homeless; £4,913 to Lilley & Stone Endowment for education; £2,894 to Newark Parish Municipal Church; £1,000 to Think Children for childcare; £1,000 to Newark Homestart for the homeless; £895 to Cue & Jones Ltd for electric mobile chair; £750 to an individual for a stairlift; £600 to Care and Repair for assistance with installation of heating; £550 to Healthcare for assistance with career prospects
FINANCES *Year* 1997 *Income* £55,737 *Grants* £49,000
TRUSTEES T Bickley, R Cope, V Dobson, D Green, A E Healey, Rev R Hill, D Jones, J Moore, P Mumby, V Picker, S Stuart, J Whicher, D Whicher, L Wilkes, J Wilkinson, D Westmorland
NOTES Newark residents only. One-off payments only
HOW TO APPLY To the address under Who To Apply To in writing

WHO TO APPLY TO M Gamage, Clerk, The Municipal General Charities for the Poor, 48 Lombard Street, Newark, Nottinghamshire NG24 1XP
Tel 01636 640649
CC NO 217437   **ESTABLISHED** 1963

■ Edith Murphy Foundation

WHAT IS FUNDED To provide relief for those suffering hardship/distress due to their age, youth, infirmity, disablement, poverty or social and economic circumstances. To provide relief of suffering of animals and provision for the care of unwanted or sick animals. Other general charitable purposes
WHO CAN BENEFIT Organisations benefiting people of all ages and disabled people. Those in need or distress of many social and economic circumstances will be considered
WHERE FUNDING CAN BE GIVEN UK
RANGE OF GRANTS £28,591–£150,000
SAMPLE GRANTS £150,000 to the Winged Fellowship Trust for the modernisation of the Skylarks Care Centre; £28,591 to Manor Physiotherapy Unit for the purchase of equipment needed to set up the unit
FINANCES *Year* 1997 *Income* £133,191
Grants £178,591
TRUSTEES Mrs E A Murphy, D L Tams, Ms P M Breakwell, Ms F Kesterton, J Kesterton
HOW TO APPLY To the address under Who To Apply To in writing
WHO TO APPLY TO D L Tams, Solicitor, Edith Murphy Foundation, Crane & Walton, 113–117 London Road, Leicester, Leicestershire LE3 0RG
CC NO 1026062   **ESTABLISHED** 1993

■ Murphy-Neumann Charity Company Limited

WHAT IS FUNDED Financial relief of aged and of the handicapped and young persons
WHAT IS NOT FUNDED Only registered charities are considered. No grants to individuals
WHO CAN BENEFIT Elderly, very young and handicapped
WHERE FUNDING CAN BE GIVEN UK
RANGE OF GRANTS Maximum usually £2,000
SAMPLE GRANTS £2,500 to Ormiston Trust for the support of children and families in East Anglia; £2,000 to the Haemophilia Society; £2,000 to Malcolm Sargent Cancer Fund for Children; £2,000 to Invalids at Home; £2,000 to NSPCC; £2,000 to British Home and Hospital for Incurables; £2,000 to an individual; £1,500 to Royal National Institute for Deaf People; £1,500 to Norwood Child Care; £1,500 to Contact the Elderly
FINANCES *Year* 1996–97 *Income* £42,601
Grants £34,000
TRUSTEES M J Lockett, T R Lockett, M Richman, FCA
HOW TO APPLY To the address under Who To Apply To in writing. Letter outlining purpose of required charitable donation. Telephone calls are not welcome. There are no application forms, guidelines or deadlines. No sae is required. Grants usually given in November and December
WHO TO APPLY TO M J Lockett, Director, Murphy-Neumann Charity Company Limited, Hayling Cottage, Upper Street, Stratford St Mary, Colchester, Essex CO7 6JW
CC NO 229555   **ESTABLISHED** 1963

■ The Mushroom Fund

WHAT IS FUNDED General charitable purposes. Donations are made only to charities known to the Trustees
WHAT IS NOT FUNDED No grants to individuals
WHO CAN BENEFIT There are no restrictions on the age; professional and economic group; family situation; religion and culture; and social circumstances of; or disease or medical condition suffered by, the beneficiaries
WHERE FUNDING CAN BE GIVEN UK
FINANCES *Year* 1997 *Income* £26,787
Grants £19,700
TRUSTEES Liverpool Council of Social Services (Inc), D F Pilkington, Lady K Pilkington, Mrs R Christian, Mrs J Watling
HOW TO APPLY **This Trust states that it does not respond to unsolicited applications**
WHO TO APPLY TO The Secretary, The Mushroom Fund, Liverpool Council of Social Services (Inc), 14 Castle Street, Liverpool, Merseyside L2 0NJ
CC NO 259954   **ESTABLISHED** 1969

■ The Music Sales Charitable Trust

WHAT IS FUNDED To relieve in cases of need, hardship, distress or illness or infirmity. To further the education of children attending schools in the UK, and other charitable purposes. Trustees are particularly interested in helping to promote music and musical education for young people
WHAT IS NOT FUNDED No grants to individuals
WHO CAN BENEFIT Registered charities benefiting children and young adults, musicians, disabled people and those disadvantaged by poverty. There is no restriction on the disease or medical condition suffered by the beneficiaries
WHERE FUNDING CAN BE GIVEN Preference for Bury St Edmunds
FINANCES *Year* 1996 *Income* £64,451
Grants £24,881
TRUSTEES Music Sales Ltd, Robert Wise, Chris Butler (Director and General Manager), Frank Johnson, Ian Morgan, Malcolm Grabham
WHO TO APPLY TO F Johnson, The Music Sales Charitable Trust, Music Sales Ltd, Newmarket Road, Bury St Edmunds, Suffolk IP33 3YB
CC NO 1014942   **ESTABLISHED** 1992

■ Muslim Hands

WHAT IS FUNDED The relief of poverty and sickness in the event of natural disasters and areas of war. Help to those in need, particularly orphans. Advancement of the Islamic faith and distribution of Islamic literature. Provision of schools, training colleges, safe water schemes, medical centres, and orphan sponsorship schemes
WHO CAN BENEFIT Organisations benefiting: those disadvantaged by poverty; victims of man-made or natural disasters and war; orphans and Muslims. Support is given to children and young adults, medical professionals, students and teachers. There is no restriction on the disease or medical condition suffered by the beneficiaries
WHERE FUNDING CAN BE GIVEN Overseas
RANGE OF GRANTS Large grants of £5,000 or more
SAMPLE GRANTS £53,158 to Qurbani; £43,779 for education; £28,810 for general purposes; £17,236 for emergency aid; £15,502 for health; £12,734 to help orphans; £5,140 for salaries; £3,000 for food; £2,785 for well digging
FINANCES *Year* 1997 *Income* £428,561
Grants £182,144

Does the trust you have chosen match your needs? Haphazard applications waste postage and time

437

TRUSTEES S L Hassanain, N Ahmed, A A Parwaz, K A
Minhas, M I Qureshi, Dr Z Nawaz, Dr M Hussain,
S G Jillani, M Ilyas
WHO TO APPLY TO S L Hassanain, Muslim Hands, 205
Radford Road, Hyson Green, Nottingham NG7 5GT
CC NO 1029742   ESTABLISHED 1993

■ Muslim Welfare Institute

WHAT IS FUNDED To advance the Islamic religion, to
advance education and other general charitable
purposes
WHO CAN BENEFIT Children, young adults and
Muslims
WHERE FUNDING CAN BE GIVEN UK
TRUSTEES Y M Hajat, R I Patel, H Sidat
WHO TO APPLY TO Yusuf Moosa Hajat, Muslim Welfare
Institute, 35 Wellington Street, St Johns,
Blackburn, Lancashire BB1 8AF
CC NO 1066665   ESTABLISHED 1997

■ The Mutual Trust Group

WHAT IS FUNDED General charitable purposes. In
particular, for the relief of poverty and the
advancement of Orthodox Jewish religious
education
WHO CAN BENEFIT Organisations benefiting Jewish
people and those disadvantaged by poverty
WHERE FUNDING CAN BE GIVEN UK
FINANCES Year 1996 Income £69,641
Grants £50,188
TRUSTEES A Weisz, B Weisz, M Weisz
WHO TO APPLY TO B Weitz, The Mutual Trust Group,
12 Dunstan Road, London NW11 8AA
CC NO 1039300   ESTABLISHED 1994

■ The Mycro Trust

WHAT IS FUNDED General charitable purposes
WHO CAN BENEFIT There are no restrictions on the
age; professional and economic group; family
situation; religion and culture; and social
circumstances of; or disease or medical condition
suffered by, the beneficiaries
WHERE FUNDING CAN BE GIVEN UK
FINANCES Year 1997 Income £38,537
NOTES The Trust's funds are already allocated, so
unsolicited applications are not accepted
HOW TO APPLY **This Trust states that it does not
respond to unsolicited applications**
WHO TO APPLY TO Dr J Goodall, The Mycro Trust,
Melton, Burrington Drive, Trentham, Stoke on
Trent, Staffordshire ST4 8SP
CC NO 1061506   ESTABLISHED 1997

■ NABA

WHAT IS FUNDED General charitable purposes for the
benefit of Clydach and surrounding areas,
particularly to provide sheltered accommodation
WHO CAN BENEFIT Organisations, particularly those
benefiting homeless people. Otherwise, there are
no restrictions on the age; professional and
economic group; family situation; religion and
culture; and social circumstances of; or disease or
medical condition suffered by, the beneficiaries
WHERE FUNDING CAN BE GIVEN Clydach and
surrounding areas
FINANCES Year 1997 Income £50,365
TRUSTEES F Barrow, J Griffiths, D H Mosford, M
Winson
NOTES No grants were given in 1997, majority of
income spent on running costs
WHO TO APPLY TO Rev D H Mosford, NABA, The
Vicarage, 1 Woodland Park, Ynystawe, West
Glamorgan SA6 5AF
CC NO 1035752   ESTABLISHED 1994

■ NAM Charitable Trust

WHAT IS FUNDED Mainly on recommendations of
Settlor, particularly charities working in the fields
of health, education, and community arts and
recreation
WHAT IS NOT FUNDED No travel or education bursaries
WHO CAN BENEFIT Medical, educational and cultural
institutions benefiting: children; young adults and
older people; actors and entertainment
professionals; musicians; students; writers and
poets; and disabled people. There is no restriction
on the disease or medical condition suffered by
the beneficiaries
WHERE FUNDING CAN BE GIVEN USA mainly
TYPE OF GRANT Recurring
FINANCES Year 1997 Income £36,292
Grants £27,720
TRUSTEES M Cohen, D S Watson
WHO TO APPLY TO M Cohen, NAM Charitable Trust,
Saffery Champness, Fairfax House, Fulwood
Place, Gray's Inn, London WC1N 6UB Tel 0171-
405 2828
CC NO 265830   ESTABLISHED 1973

■ N and K Charitable Trust

WHAT IS FUNDED Jewish charities, hospices and some
medical research, such as cancer, and emergency
care. Regular beneficiaries receive 75 per cent of
the total funds
WHAT IS NOT FUNDED No grants to individuals
WHO CAN BENEFIT Organisations benefiting Jewish
people, victims of disasters, famine and war.
Research worker, medical professionals and
those suffering from cancer will be considered
WHERE FUNDING CAN BE GIVEN Newcastle upon Tyne
TYPE OF GRANT Primarily recurrent
RANGE OF GRANTS £50–£5,000

SAMPLE GRANTS The following grants were for religion and education:; £4,000 to Reform Foundation Trust; £1,000 to Friends of Progressive Judaism and Education; £1,000 to Newcastle Reform Synagogue; £900 to Leo Boech College
FINANCES *Year* 1995 *Income* £19,300
Grants £28,000
TRUSTEES N Jacobson, C Jacobson, D M Jacobson, M Jacobson
HOW TO APPLY To the address under Who To Apply To in writing. Initial telephone calls are not welcome
WHO TO APPLY TO The Clerk to the Trustees, N and K Charitable Trust, Messrs Robert Miller Tate & Co, 3 Portland Terrace, Jesmond, Newcastle upon Tyne NE2 1QQ *Tel* 0191-281 8816
CC NO 277799   **ESTABLISHED** 1979

■ The NR Charitable Trust

WHAT IS FUNDED Support is only given to projects with which the partners of Neville Russell, Chartered Accountants have personal contact. The Trust will consider funding: residential facilities and services; infrastructure, support and development; the advancement of religion; health; conservation; environmental and animal sciences; environmental issues; heritage; church schools; special schools; literacy; special needs education; training for community development; and community services
WHAT IS NOT FUNDED No grants to individuals
WHO CAN BENEFIT Established agencies benefiting: children; young adults; older people; clergy; ex-service and service people; medical professionals, nurses and doctors; the retired; unemployed people; those in care, fostered and adopted; one parent families; widows and widowers; Baptists; Christians; Church of England; Jews; Evangelists; Methodists; Roman Catholics. There are few restrictions on the social circumstances of, and no restrictions on the disease or medical condition suffered by the beneficiaries
WHERE FUNDING CAN BE GIVEN UK and overseas
TYPE OF GRANT Single strategic projects, one-off, research, buildings and capital. Funding is for one year or less
FINANCES *Year* 1997 *Income* £140,975
Grants £126,750
TRUSTEES J S Mellows, FCA, A N Russell, FCA, D E Ryan, FCA
HOW TO APPLY Applications considered annually, in May. No acknowledgement
WHO TO APPLY TO Andrew N Russell, The NR Charitable Trust, 37 Frederick Place, Brighton BN1 4EA
CC NO 287735   **ESTABLISHED** 1983

■ The Kitty and Daniel Nabarro Charitable Trust

WHAT IS FUNDED Relief of poverty and the advancement of education. This Trust will consider funding: information technology and computers; support and self help groups; nature reserves; environmental issues; IT training; literacy; training for work; vocational training; and crime prevention schemes
WHAT IS NOT FUNDED No grants to individuals
WHO CAN BENEFIT Registered charities benefiting those disadvantaged by poverty and homeless people
WHERE FUNDING CAN BE GIVEN UK
TYPE OF GRANT All funding is for up to three years

FINANCES *Year* 1997 *Income* £24,032
Grants £36,475
TRUSTEES D J N Nabarro, Mrs K Nabarro, E Cohen
HOW TO APPLY To the address under Who To Apply To in writing. The Trustees allocate grants on an annual basis to an existing list of charities. The Trustees do not at this time envisage grants to charities which are not already on the list. **This Trust states that it does not respond to unsolicited applications**
WHO TO APPLY TO D J N Nabarro, The Kitty and Daniel Nabarro Charitable Trust, PO Box 7491, London N20 8LY
CC NO 1002786   **ESTABLISHED** 1991

■ The Willie Nagel Charitable Trust

WHAT IS FUNDED General charitable purposes
WHO CAN BENEFIT Registered charities. There are no restrictions on the age; professional and economic group; family situation; religion and culture; and social circumstances of; or disease or medical condition suffered by, the beneficiaries
WHERE FUNDING CAN BE GIVEN UK
FINANCES *Year* 1997 *Income* £107,110
Grants £131,745
TRUSTEES W Nagel, A L Sober
NOTES Funds fully committed
HOW TO APPLY Funds fully committed, applications are not required
WHO TO APPLY TO A L Sober, Trustee, The Willie Nagel Charitable Trust, Lubbock Fine, Russell Bedford House, City Forum, 250 City Road, London EC1V 2QQ
CC NO 275938   **ESTABLISHED** 1978

■ The Naggar Charitable Trust

WHAT IS FUNDED Jewish, medical, the arts
WHO CAN BENEFIT Actors and entertainment professionals; musicians; writers and poets; and textile workers and designers. There is no restriction on the disease or medical condition suffered by the beneficiaries
WHERE FUNDING CAN BE GIVEN UK and overseas
TYPE OF GRANT Some recurrent
FINANCES *Year* 1995–96 *Income* £340,499
TRUSTEES G A Naggar, M Naggar
HOW TO APPLY To the address under Who To Apply To in writing
WHO TO APPLY TO G A Naggar, The Naggar Charitable Trust, 15 Grosvenor Gardens, London SW1W 0BD
CC NO 265409   **ESTABLISHED** 1973

■ The Eleni Nakou Foundation

WHAT IS FUNDED Advancement of education of the peoples of Europe in each other's culture, history, literature, language, institutions, art, science, religion, music and folklore, to promote the exchange of knowledge about the cultures of Northern and Southern Europe in order to bridge the divide between these cultures and promote international understanding
WHO CAN BENEFIT There are no restrictions on the age; professional and economic group; family situation; religion and culture; and social circumstances of; or disease or medical condition suffered by, the beneficiaries
WHERE FUNDING CAN BE GIVEN Europe
TRUSTEES E Holm, Y A Sakellarakis, T Jackson, L St John, H Moller

WHO TO APPLY TO Dr E Holm, The Eleni Nakou Foundation, c/o Kleinwort Benson Trustees, PO Box 191, 10 Fenchurch Street, London EC3M 3LB

CC NO 803753   **ESTABLISHED** 1990

■ Nantwich and Acton Grammar School Foundation

WHAT IS FUNDED (a) Support of Malbank School and Sixth Form Centre. (b) Promoting the education (including social and physical training) of persons under 25 years of age who are pupils or former pupils of the said school or any other school serving the area. (c) Arts, culture and recreation is also considered for funding

WHAT IS NOT FUNDED No grants for the relief of public funds

WHO CAN BENEFIT To the benefit of young people under 25 years of age who are pupils or former pupils of Malbank School and Sixth Form Centre, or other schools serving the area Where Funding Can Be Given

WHERE FUNDING CAN BE GIVEN UK and overseas with reference to What is Funded

TYPE OF GRANT Interest free loans, one-off, project and research. Funding is available for up to and over three years

FINANCES *Year* 1997 *Income* £16,155 *Grants* £5,875

TRUSTEES Mrs L Brookshaw, M Elliott, T Holman, A Kettleday, D Latham, E W Lighton (Chairman), P Taylor (Treasurer)

NOTES Present funding policy is related to early days of the Foundation when capital is being safeguarded. Therefore, grants are of a small scale. Trustees are keen to go beyond the routine academic and travel requests

HOW TO APPLY To the Clerk to the Trustees, with an sae for application form to be returned by 30 April for May consideration, and 31 October for November consideration

WHO TO APPLY TO The Clerk to the Trustees, Nantwich and Acton Grammar School Foundation, Malbank School and VIth Form Centre, Welsh Row, Nantwich, Cheshire CW5 5HD

CC NO 525965   **ESTABLISHED** 1995

■ The Gordon Napier Charitable Trust

WHAT IS FUNDED General charitable purposes at the discretion of the Trustees

WHO CAN BENEFIT There are no restrictions on the age; professional and economic group; family situation; religion and culture; and social circumstances of; or disease or medical condition suffered by, the beneficiaries

WHERE FUNDING CAN BE GIVEN Greater London

TRUSTEES J G Napier, N J Kirk, J M S Kennedy

WHO TO APPLY TO N J Kirk, Trustee, The Gordon Napier Charitable Trust, Streets & Co, Chartered Accountants, Tower House, Lucy Tower Street, Lincoln LN1 1XW

CC NO 1053345   **ESTABLISHED** 1996

■ James and John Napier's Trust

WHAT IS FUNDED Grants are given to a range of smaller charities which support medical research or are dedicated to helping the ill, the disabled, the elderly, and the young, through respite and holiday accommodation; housing associations; support to voluntary and community organisations; community centres and village halls; and holidays and outing. Historic building will also be funded

WHO CAN BENEFIT Organisations benefiting people of all ages, including ex-service and service people, seafarers and fishermen, those disadvantaged by poverty and homeless people. Beneficiaries suffering from many diseases or medical conditions will be considered

WHERE FUNDING CAN BE GIVEN Glasgow and the West of Scotland

TYPE OF GRANT One-off

SAMPLE GRANTS £1,000 to Riding for the Disabled for work in Glasgow; £1,000 to Camping Holidays for Inner City Kids for work in Scotland; £1,000 to Multiple Sclerosis Society for work in Scotland; £1,000 to Boys Brigade Glasgow Battalion; £1,000 to Beatson Oncology Centre for refurbishment work

FINANCES *Year* 1994–95 *Grants* £16,000

TRUSTEES I Bruce, A S Headrick, N M Headrick

PUBLICATIONS Accounts are available from the Trust

HOW TO APPLY Applications should be made in writing to the address under Who To Apply To

WHO TO APPLY TO Neil M Headrick, James and John Napier's Trust, Headrick Inglis Glen & Co, 48 West Regent Street, Glasgow G2 2QR *Tel* 0141-332 3341

SC NO SCO 21113

■ The Janet Nash Charitable Trust

WHAT IS FUNDED General charitable purposes

WHO CAN BENEFIT Institutions and individuals. There are no restrictions on the age; professional and economic group; family situation; religion and culture; and social circumstances of; or disease or medical condition suffered by, the beneficiaries

WHERE FUNDING CAN BE GIVEN UK

SAMPLE GRANTS £20,000 to Warwick Castle Park Trust; £10,000 to Acorns Children's Hospice; £5,000 to MacMillan Cancer Relief; £4,000 to Dyslexia Institute; £2,500 to Warwickshire Care Services Newlands House

FINANCES *Year* 1997 *Income* £251,543 *Grants* £202,155

TRUSTEES Mrs J M Nash, R Gulliver, M S Jacobs

NOTES 1997: Grants to institutions £41,500. Grants to individuals £160,655

WHO TO APPLY TO R Gulliver, The Janet Nash Charitable Trust, Nabarro Nathanson, The Old Chapel, New Mill, Eversley, Hampshire RG27 0RA

CC NO 326880   **ESTABLISHED** 1985

■ The P Nathan Benevolent Charitable Trust

WHAT IS FUNDED To aid Jewish individuals and organisations

WHO CAN BENEFIT Jewish people

WHERE FUNDING CAN BE GIVEN London and environs

TRUSTEES Ms R Bernstein, A L Nathan, Ms J Rose, Ms L Rose, Ms R Sloam

WHO TO APPLY TO Melvyn Epstein, The P Nathan Benevolent Charitable Trust, 19 Thatcham Gardens, Whetstone, London N20 9QE

CC NO 1053755   **ESTABLISHED** 1996

440

Think carefully about every application. Is it justified?

■ Nathan Charitable Trust

WHAT IS FUNDED That the love and lordship of Jesus Christ be real and powerful in the lives of many. Cultural and religious teaching and missionary work is funded

WHAT IS NOT FUNDED General appeals and church building works are not usually considered. No loans will be funded. No grants to individuals

WHO CAN BENEFIT Organisations benefiting people of all ages, Christians, missionaries and trainees. Those involved in missionary relief work and scripture distribution

WHERE FUNDING CAN BE GIVEN UK and overseas

TYPE OF GRANT Core costs, one-off and project will be considered

FINANCES *Year* 1996 *Income* £20,913

TRUSTEES T R Worth, Mrs P J Worth, Rev A M Roberts, G A Jones

HOW TO APPLY Any time, but please enclose an sae and references. Very little funds are available for non-regular giving in any year

WHO TO APPLY TO T R Worth, Nathan Charitable Trust, Trewardreva Mill, Constantine, Falmouth, Cornwall TR11 5QD

CC NO 251781   **ESTABLISHED** 1967

■ National AIDS Trust

WHAT IS FUNDED Voluntary organisations working in the field of HIV/AIDS, also providing fundraising and management training

WHAT IS NOT FUNDED No grants to individuals or for conferences or videos

WHO CAN BENEFIT Community projects benefiting volunteers and those suffering from HIV and AIDs

WHERE FUNDING CAN BE GIVEN UK

TYPE OF GRANT One-off, fundraising and management training service

RANGE OF GRANTS Below £1,000–£25,000

SAMPLE GRANTS £25,000 to Scottish Forum; £13,445 to Welsh Development Project; £2,500 to Names Project; £1,500 to Aidsline WM

FINANCES *Year* 1997 *Income* £695,221 *Grants* £42,931

TRUSTEES Prof M W Adler, G Barlow, OBE, J M Grimshaw, MBE, J F Mayne, CB, Ms D Platt, CBE, P Westland, J Carrier, E N Law, R Pendlebury, P Ward, I W Williams, R Pauly, B Williams, J Bowis

HOW TO APPLY Application forms may be obtained from the address under Who To Apply To. Dates for funding rounds and applications are available from Davel Patel at the address below

WHO TO APPLY TO A Light, Director of Fundraising and Finance, National AIDS Trust, New City Cloister, 188–196 Old Street, London EC1V 9FR

CC NO 297977   **ESTABLISHED** 1987

■ National Animal Sanctuaries Support League

WHAT IS FUNDED Animal welfare

WHAT IS NOT FUNDED Students

WHO CAN BENEFIT New organisations and innovative projects

WHERE FUNDING CAN BE GIVEN UK

RANGE OF GRANTS £1,000 or less

FINANCES *Year* 1996–97 *Income* £19,420 *Grants* £195

TRUSTEES Mrs P A Wilson, R Mackinlay, Mrs B Lambert

PUBLICATIONS Annual Report

HOW TO APPLY In writing

WHO TO APPLY TO Mrs P A Wilson, National Animal Sanctuaries Support League, PO Box 42, Newton Aycliffe, Co Durham DL5 5JA

CC NO 1024884   **ESTABLISHED** 1993

■ National Art-Collections Fund

WHAT IS FUNDED To support museums, galleries and historic houses open to the public

WHAT IS NOT FUNDED Restoration of works of art or buildings and archaeological excavations are excluded

WHO CAN BENEFIT Public museums, galleries and historic houses

WHERE FUNDING CAN BE GIVEN UK

TYPE OF GRANT Purchase grants and capital. Funding for up to one year will be considered

SAMPLE GRANTS £200,000 to Cambridge, Fitzwilliam Museum for Sebastiano del Piombo *Madonna and Child*; £75,189 to Bedford, Cecil Higgins Museum and Art Gallery for J M W Turner *The Loss of an East Indiaman*; £59,379 to London, Tate Gallery for Dorothea Tanning *Eine Kleine Nachtmusik*; £52,500 to Cambridge, Fitzwilliam Museum for Simon-Louis Boizot *A Poet's Monument*; £51,492 to Edinburgh, National Gallery of Scotland for Gavin Hamilton *Dawkins and Wood Discoverying the Ruins of Palmyra*; £51,250 to Belfast, Ulster Museum for Pompeo Batoni *Portrait of James Stewart*; £50,000 to Aylesbury, Buckinghamshire County Museum for *The Darell-Tucker-Dayrell Cup*; £50,000 to Birmingham, Barber Institute of Fine Arts for Andre Derain *Portrait of Bartolomeo Savona*; £50,000 to London, Tate Gallery for Piet Mondrian *Church at Zoutelande*; £50,000 for collection of works on paper by Francis Bacon

FINANCES *Year* 1997 *Income* £3,990,000 *Grants* £2,407,000

TRUSTEES The Executive Committee

PUBLICATIONS The National Art Collections Fund 'Review' is published annually. *The Art Quarterly* four times a year and the *Members' Guide* once a year. Members receive these by post. Membership is 96,000, the subscription for individual members is £25 and for corporate members from £1,000

HOW TO APPLY The museum, gallery or authority requesting the grant submits a form giving its reasons for wishing to acquire the work of art, with any supporting information and photographs of the work. Applications are considered at the monthly meetings of the Committee held at Millais House. The Committee prefer wherever possible to view the work of art

WHO TO APPLY TO David Barrie, Director, National Art-Collections Fund, Millais House, 7 Cromwell Place, London SW7 2JN *Tel* 0171-225 4800 *Fax* 0171-225 4848 *E-mail* info@nacf.org

CC NO 209174   **ESTABLISHED** 1903

■ National Association for the Care and Resettlement of Offenders

This trust did not respond to CAF's request to amend its entry and, by 30 June 1998, CAF's researchers did not find financial records for later than 1995 on its file at the Charity Commission. Trusts are legally required to submit annual accounts to the Charity Commission under section 42 of the Charities Act 1993

WHAT IS FUNDED Financial assistance to offenders, ex-offenders and their families

WHAT IS NOT FUNDED No grants to individuals. Applications must come via: Probation Service;

Does the trust you have chosen match your needs? Haphazard applications waste postage and time

441

registered charities; Citizens' Advice Bureaux; and Social Service departments

WHO CAN BENEFIT Organisations benefiting offenders, ex-offenders and their families – parents and children, widows and widowers, spouses

WHERE FUNDING CAN BE GIVEN UK

TYPE OF GRANT One-off only

TRUSTEES NACRO National Council

PUBLICATIONS Various

HOW TO APPLY Applications must come from Probation or After-Care Services, registered charities, Citizens' Advice Bureaux and Social Service departments

WHO TO APPLY TO Miss A Smith, Welfare Administrator, National Association for the Care and Resettlement of Offenders, ACRO, 169 Clapham Road, London SW9 0PU

CC NO 226171   **ESTABLISHED** 1925

- - -

■ National Asthma

Campaign (formerly Asthma Research Council)

WHAT IS FUNDED Grants for research into and the provision of information and education on asthma and allied respiratory disorders. To fund grants approved by peer review. Charities working in the fields of: health professional bodies; health care; hospitals; and health issues

WHAT IS NOT FUNDED Grants only for projects in the UK

WHO CAN BENEFIT Organisations benefiting: scientists, clinicians, general practitioners, research workers and those suffering from asthma

WHERE FUNDING CAN BE GIVEN UK

TYPE OF GRANT Project grants

FINANCES *Year* 1997 *Income* £6,038,000 *Grants* £2,438,795

TRUSTEES Sir Peter Emery, MP (Chairman) plus 31 Council Members

NOTES Trust formed by a merger between Asthma Research Council and Asthma Society

HOW TO APPLY Completed application form to be returned by deadline. Contact Hilary Leavy for further details

WHO TO APPLY TO Hilary Leavy, National Asthma Campaign, Providence House, Providence Place, London N1 0NT *Tel* 0171 226 2260 ext 332 *Fax* 0171-704 0740 *E-mail* hleavy@asthma.org.uk *Web Site* www.asthma.org.uk

CC NO 802364   **ESTABLISHED** 1990

- - -

■ National Catholic Fund

WHAT IS FUNDED The National Catholic Fund only makes grants for the national work of the Catholic Church in this country and cannot help individuals from its funds

WHAT IS NOT FUNDED Grants are not made to individuals or to local projects or to projects not immediately advancing the Roman Catholic religion

WHO CAN BENEFIT Organisations and projects which are both national and Catholic benefiting Roman Catholics

WHERE FUNDING CAN BE GIVEN England and Wales only

TYPE OF GRANT To National Catholic commissions and organisations

FINANCES *Year* 1997 *Income* £1,079,651

TRUSTEES The Archbishops of England and Wales and three lay people

NOTES This is not an open trust. The money is contributed each year by the Roman Catholic

Dioceses of England and Wales and used for specific purposes

HOW TO APPLY Please enclose sae

WHO TO APPLY TO Rt Rev Mgr Arthur Roche, National Catholic Fund, Secretary to the Trustees, 39 Eccleston Square, London SW1V 1BX

CC NO 257239   **ESTABLISHED** 1968

- - -

■ The National Committee of The Women's World Day of Prayer for England, Wales and Northern Ireland

WHAT IS FUNDED Charitable Christian educational projects, Christian literature societies, including audio-visual materials

WHAT IS NOT FUNDED Grants limited to the production of the Scriptures and other Christian literature. No grants to individuals

WHO CAN BENEFIT Work of Christian literature societies for the benefit of Christians

WHERE FUNDING CAN BE GIVEN UK and overseas

TYPE OF GRANT Annual, regular or one-off

RANGE OF GRANTS £100–£27,000

SAMPLE GRANTS £27,000 to Feed the Minds; £26,000 to Bible Society; £22,000 to United Society for Christian Literature; £11,000 to Scripture Gift Mission; £8,000 to Society for Promoting Christian Knowledge; £8,000 to International Bible Reading Association; £8,000 to Bible Reading Fellowship; £3,000 to the Salvation Army; £2,030 to Leprosy Mission; £2,000 to Royal National Institute for the Blind

FINANCES *Year* 1997 *Income* £228,909 *Grants* £136,606

TRUSTEES The National Committee

PUBLICATIONS Order of service for the Day of Prayer. Children's service. Bible study notes on theme for year. Annual booklet *Together in Prayer*. Meditation cards, Prayer cards

NOTES We are reluctant to increase the number of beneficiaries, but try to increase grants to maintain real value

HOW TO APPLY Applications to the Secretary before the end of August. Grants are funded in September

WHO TO APPLY TO The Secretary, The National Committee of the Women's World Day of Prayer, Commercial Road, Tunbridge Wells, Kent TN1 2RR *Tel* 01892 541411

CC NO 233242   **ESTABLISHED** 1932

- - -

■ National Heart Research Fund

WHAT IS FUNDED Research institutions, all aspects of heart disease prevention and treatment and research projects

WHO CAN BENEFIT Individuals doing research projects in hospitals benefiting those suffering from a range of diseases and medical conditions, especially heart disease

WHERE FUNDING CAN BE GIVEN UK

TYPE OF GRANT One-off and recurrent grants

SAMPLE GRANTS £79,393 for research projects; £11,009 for medical salaries, etc; £256 for overheads of the Killingbech Cardiac Research Unit; £157 for depreciation of research equipment; £25 for research supplies and project expenses

FINANCES *Year* 1995 *Income* £275,755 *Grants* £90,840

TRUSTEES P O Riordan, E A Blackmore, K Watterson, B J Wood, R C Hemsley, D A Watson, FRCS, J P

- - -

McGoldrick, MB, BCh, BAO, MD, FRSC, Ed, D Dickinson

WHO TO APPLY TO Mrs R M Jenkins, Chief Executive, National Heart Research Fund, 4th Floor, Concorde House, Park Lane, Leeds LS3 1EQ

CC NO 251602 **ESTABLISHED** 1967

■ National Hospital Trust

This trust did not respond to CAF's request to amend its entry and, by 30 June 1998, CAF's researchers did not find financial records for later than 1995 on its file at the Charity Commission. Trusts are legally required to submit annual accounts to the Charity Commission under section 42 of the Charities Act 1993

WHAT IS FUNDED Grants are made for medical, surgical and other equipment, for buildings and facilities for use by the National Health Service or other healthcare organisations

WHERE FUNDING CAN BE GIVEN UK

TYPE OF GRANT One-off

TRUSTEES Sir Adrian Blennerhasset, John Evans, Prof Leslie Reid

HOW TO APPLY To the address below in writing

WHO TO APPLY TO Ms G Catchpole, Administrator, National Hospital Trust, 10 Philpot Lane, Shoreditch High Street, London EC3M 8AA

CC NO 801851 **ESTABLISHED** 1988

■ The National Kidney Research Fund Limited

WHAT IS FUNDED The Trust provides finance for research projects and establish Kidney Council Fellowships and Studentships for the advancement and promotion of medical research into kidney and renal disease generally, into the acute failure of the kidneys and chronic renal failure, including the causes, effects and prevention of such disease and failure; and into the congenital malformations of the kidneys and the bladder. It also promotes and distributes the *Donor Card*

WHO CAN BENEFIT Recognised renal research establishments supporting medical professional, research workers and students for the benefit of those suffering from kidney and renal diseases

WHERE FUNDING CAN BE GIVEN UK

TYPE OF GRANT One to five year financial research grants

FINANCES *Year* 1997 *Income* £1,806,218 *Grants* £781,284

TRUSTEES The Executive Committee

PUBLICATIONS Annual Financial Report and various technical reports

HOW TO APPLY Twice yearly in July and September

WHO TO APPLY TO L Rout, Director General, The National Kidney Research Fund Limited, 3 Archers Court, Stukeley Road, Huntingdon, Cambridgeshire PE18 6XG

CC NO 252892 **ESTABLISHED** 1967

■ The National Manuscripts Conservation Trust

WHAT IS FUNDED Conservation of manuscripts and archives

WHAT IS NOT FUNDED The following are not eligible: public records within the meaning of the Public Records Act; official archives of the institution or authority applying except in the case of some older records; loan collections unless exempt from

capital taxation or owned by a charitable trust; photographic, audio-visual or printed materials

WHO CAN BENEFIT Grants are made to record offices, libraries, other similar publicly funded institutions including local authority, university and specialist record repositories, and owners of manuscript material which is conditionally exempt from capital taxation or owned by a charitable trust: where reasonable public access is allowed, suitable storage conditions are available, and there is a commitment to continuing good preservation practice

WHERE FUNDING CAN BE GIVEN UK

TYPE OF GRANT The grants cover the cost of repair, binding and other preservation measures including reprography, but not cost of equipment. Funding is for up to three years

RANGE OF GRANTS To match the applicant's contribution, up to 50 per cent of the total estimated costs between £500–£37,800, typical grant £10,000–£20,000

SAMPLE GRANTS £17,350 to Berkeley Castle to conserve and microfilm the Berkeley Castle Tudor muniments; £14,000 to The King's School, Canterbury, to conserve the Hugh Walpole literary manuscripts; £10,000 to Courtauld Institute of Art to identify, sort, list and access for conservation the Institute's archives; £8,765 to Durham University Library to conserve 23 selected manuscripts dating from the 12th to the 17th centuries; £7,722 to Lincolnshire Archives for conserving Lincolnshire Diocesan Archives; £7,500 to Surrey Record Office for conserving records of John Broadwood & Sons, piano manufacturers; £6,000 to Dean and Chapter of Ely to conserve the Dean and Chapter archives; £6,000 to City of Westminster Archives Centre, to treat and remount items in the Ashbridge collection; £5,690 to Glasgow University Library to conserve the personal papers of Dr William Hunter (1718–83); £4,500 to The National Trust (Cornwall) and Sir Richard Carew-Pole to conserve the Anthony House archive

FINANCES *Year* 1997 *Income* £65,390 *Grants* £100,956

TRUSTEES L L Golden, OBE, JP, FCA, The Lord Egremont, DL, B Naylor, MA, ALA

PUBLICATIONS Annual Report and Accounts. *Brief Guide for Applicants*

NOTES The grants figure includes an annual subvention from the Department for Culture, Media and Sport

HOW TO APPLY By application form and full description of project. Closing dates are on 1 April and 1 October each year

WHO TO APPLY TO The National Manuscripts Conservation Trust, c/o The British Library, Research and Innovation Centre, 96 Euston Road, London NW1 2DB *Tel* 0171-412 7048 *Fax* 0171-412 7251 *E-mail* stephanie.kenna@bl.uk *Web Site* http://www.bl.uk/services/ric/heritage/

CC NO 802796 **ESTABLISHED** 1990

■ The National Patients Support Trust

WHAT IS FUNDED (a) The relief and assistance of patients and former patients of NHS Hospital Trusts who are in need of financial assistance and who are suffering from disease and from other physical and/or mental disablitiy or is convalescent or infirm; (b) The relief in case of financial distress of the dependents of such persons or deceased persons, in particular regard for the needs of children; (c) Generally to support the charitable work of any NHS Trust

WHO CAN BENEFIT To benefit patients of NHS Hospital Trusts and their dependants. There is no restriction on the disease or medical condition suffered by the beneficiaries

WHERE FUNDING CAN BE GIVEN UK

SAMPLE GRANTS £2,163 to DRI NHS Trust; £1,640 to Fife Council SWD; £640 to Western General Hospital; £530 to Edinburgh CC SWD; £484 to RMCH SWDF; £200 to British Diabetic Association; £200 to RISWF; £150 to Home Link; £150 to Cardiff SWD; £140 to Strathclyde RC NHS Trust

FINANCES *Year* 1997 *Income* £40,089
Grants £19,631

WHO TO APPLY TO R H Morris, The National Patients Support Trust, 29 Pine Bank, Hindhead, Surrey GU26 6SS

CC NO 1043598   **ESTABLISHED** 1995

■ The National Poetry Foundation

WHAT IS FUNDED The support of poetry and publication of books of individual people's poetry

WHAT IS NOT FUNDED Poetry only

WHO CAN BENEFIT Poetry magazines and/or groups and societies benefiting writers and poets

WHERE FUNDING CAN BE GIVEN UK

TYPE OF GRANT Cash and advice on becoming self-sufficient. One-off grants, projects and funding for one year or less will be considered

FINANCES *Year* 1995 *Income* £15,600

TRUSTEES Johnathon Clifford (Founder), Helen Robinson, Hazel Robinson, Althea Lord

PUBLICATIONS 168 (to date May 1998)

HOW TO APPLY In writing to the address under Who To Apply To, with an sae

WHO TO APPLY TO Johnathon Clifford, The National Poetry Foundation, 27 Mill Road, Fareham, Hampshire PO16 0TH *Tel* 01329 822218 *Fax* 01329 822218

CC NO 283032   **ESTABLISHED** 1981

■ The National Power Charitable Trust

WHAT IS FUNDED Medicine, health, welfare, community projects and services. This includes: residential services and facilities; infrastructure, support and development; special schools; special needs education; and community issues; development proposals; and social advice and information

WHAT IS NOT FUNDED No support for advertising, appeals from individuals, religious groups, animal charities or the arts

WHO CAN BENEFIT Institutions benefiting: children; young adults; older people; at risk groups; carers; disabled people; those disadvantaged by poverty; ex-offenders and those at risk of offending; homeless people; those living in rural and urban areas; socially isolated people; victims of abuse, crime and domestic violence. There are no restrictions on the disease or medical condition suffered by the beneficiaries

WHERE FUNDING CAN BE GIVEN England, Wales, Europe, Asia, Africa and America

TYPE OF GRANT Buildings, capital, core costs, one-off, project, research and recurring costs. Funding is available for up to three years

SAMPLE GRANTS £50,000 to Barnardo's; £50,000 to Diana, Princess of Wales Memorial Fund; £25,000 to Wiltshire Community Foundation; £12,500 to British Occupational Health Research Foundation; £10,000 to MENCAP; £10,000 to Princess Royal Trust For Carers; £10,000 to SANE; £10,000 to British Executive Service Overseas; £7,500 to National Institute of Conductive Education; £7,500 to Electrical and Electronics Industries Benevolent Association

FINANCES *Year* 1997 *Income* £617,419
Grants £419,322

TRUSTEES Mrs A Ferguson, J W Baker, G A W Blackman, M G Herbert

PUBLICATIONS Annual Report and Accounts

HOW TO APPLY Applications in writing. No application forms

WHO TO APPLY TO Mrs C Springett, The National Power Charitable Trust, Windmill Hill Business Park, Whitehill Way, Swindon, Wiltshire SN5 6PB

CC NO 1002358   **ESTABLISHED** 1991

■ The National Society (CE) for Promoting Religious Education

WHAT IS FUNDED The promotion, encouragement and support of religious education in accordance with the principles of the Church of England, in England and Wales and in any other part of the world where the Church of England or churches in common with it may be at work

WHO CAN BENEFIT Church of England

WHERE FUNDING CAN BE GIVEN England, Wales and worldwide

SAMPLE GRANTS £12,000 to University College of Ripon and York St John for support of all the work of the York Religious Education Centre

FINANCES *Year* 1997 *Income* £866,505
Grants £12,000

TRUSTEES The Society is a corporate body

PUBLICATIONS Annual Report and Accounts. Education Sunday leaflets. Magazine: *Together with Children.* Books, booklets and pamphlets for all concerned with Christian education in schools, colleges and parishes

WHO TO APPLY TO The General Secretary, The National Society, Church House, Great Smith Street, Westminster, London SW1P 3NZ *Tel* 0171-222 1672

CC NO 313070   **ESTABLISHED** 1811

■ The Nationwide Foundation

WHAT IS FUNDED General charitable purposes

WHO CAN BENEFIT There are no restrictions on the age; professional and economic group; family situation; religion and culture; and social circumstances of; or disease or medical condition suffered by, the beneficiaries

WHERE FUNDING CAN BE GIVEN UK

TRUSTEES Ms P Doble, C Nunneley, J del Storther

WHO TO APPLY TO C Wilson, Secretary, The Nationwide Foundation, Nationwide House, Pipers Way, Swindon, Wiltshire SN38 1NW

CC NO 1065552   **ESTABLISHED** 1997

■ Natwest Group Charitable Trust

WHAT IS FUNDED Primarily committed to Staff Give As You Earn scheme. Limited funding of Community Enterprise projects from community and voluntary organisations engaged in developing suitable responses to poverty, unemployment and social exclusion. This includes: training for community and personal development, and for work; and social counselling

WHAT IS NOT FUNDED No grants to organisations of non-charitable status or to individuals

WHO CAN BENEFIT To benefit: unemployed people; at risk groups; those disadvantaged by poverty; and socially isolated people

WHERE FUNDING CAN BE GIVEN UK

TYPE OF GRANT Various including project. Funding is available for up to three years

RANGE OF GRANTS Regional grants typically £250, largest £40,000 pa up to three years

SAMPLE GRANTS £651,429 to Charities Aid Foundation for a Staff Give As You Earn Programme; £150,000 to Crime Concern for a project looking at the impact of crime on small business community; £95,000 to Centre for Employment and Enterprise Development for Young Entrepreneurs Fund to support young people from ethnic minorities set up and continue in business; £83,000 to CSV for a pilot scheme to encourage 150 volunteers in community setting in Cardiff; £75,000 to Bristol Cyrenians for training, support and mentoring to 50 young homeless people; £74,500 to Bromley by Bow Centre for a personal development and training programme for 12 young entrepreneurs; £70,000 to Ford and Pennywell Advice Centre to support young homeless unemployed in renovating houses in Sunderland; £69,000 to Working Support for employment opportunities project for people with learning difficulties; £64,623 to Rushcliffe CVS for developing young people as Citizens – Youth Action Forum; £60,000 to Markfield Project to equip young people to take up work opportunities in the caring professions

FINANCES *Year* 1997 *Income* £2,500,000
Grants £2,700,000

TRUSTEES A C Blessley, J C Cleverdon, T I Collis, P K Hamzahee, A J Jordan, Sir Sydney Lipworth, QC, M L Trainer

HOW TO APPLY **This Trust states that it does not respond to unsolicited applications**

WHO TO APPLY TO Natwest Group Charitable Trust, Natwest Group Community Relations, 2nd Floor, 41 Lothbury, London EC2P 2BP

CC NO 1033525   **ESTABLISHED** 1994

■ NatWest Staff Samaritan Fund

WHAT IS FUNDED To provide financial resources for the purchase of equipment and facilities which will save lives, enhance recovery or give a greater quality of life to the dying or disabled

WHAT IS NOT FUNDED No grants to individuals or for research/general appeals/salaries/running costs

WHO CAN BENEFIT Hospitals, hospices and other charities associated with the welfare of the physically and mentally disabled and able bodied. There is no restriction on the disease or medical condition suffered by the beneficiaries. Support may be given to medical professionals and carers

WHERE FUNDING CAN BE GIVEN UK

TYPE OF GRANT Cash payments for the purchase of specific items of equipment which will be of direct benefit to those in need

RANGE OF GRANTS Under £1,000–£5,750

SAMPLE GRANTS £5,750 to the Manningford Trust; £4,800 to Northam Lodge Centre for the Handicapped; £4,600 to Quidenham Children's Hospice; £4,230 to the Two Town Talker; £3,750 to Treloar Trust; £3,650 to the Uphill Ski Club; £3,570 to CCHA Extra Care; £3,570 to the Holding Hands Appeal, St Vincents; £3,500 to Support Dogs; £3,494 to the Ethel Trust

FINANCES *Year* 1996 *Income* £174,756
Grants £146,020

TRUSTEES J M Spurr, J M Goodswen, F P Hencken, D W Hewson, Mrs S Martin, P J S Hammonds, J R Smith, M S Walker, C R Bottomley, Mrs S J Law, G Westwell

PUBLICATIONS *Helping Hand*

HOW TO APPLY Recommendations from members of staff of National Westminster Group have priority but other written requests will be considered

WHO TO APPLY TO The Secretary, NatWest Staff Samaritan Fund, 8th Floor, Wettern House, 56 Dingwall Road, Croydon, Surrey CR9 3HB

CC NO 253694   **ESTABLISHED** 1924

■ Nayot Foundation

WHAT IS FUNDED General charitable purposes

WHO CAN BENEFIT There are no restrictions on the age; professional and economic group; family situation; religion and culture; and social circumstances of; or disease or medical condition suffered by, the beneficiaries

WHERE FUNDING CAN BE GIVEN UK

TRUSTEES J A D Weil, Mrs J Weil, M Storfer

WHO TO APPLY TO M Chappell, Nayot Foundation, c/o Kensulat plc, Perl House, 746 Finchley Road, London NW11 7TH

CC NO 1067787   **ESTABLISHED** 1997

■ The Nazareth Trust Fund

WHAT IS FUNDED Churches, Christian missionaries, Christian youth work, and overseas aid. Grants are only made to people or causes known personally to the Trustees

WHO CAN BENEFIT Young adults, Christian missionaries and victims of famine, war, and man-made or natural disasters – both individually and through registered archives and institutions

WHERE FUNDING CAN BE GIVEN UK and overseas

FINANCES *Year* 1995 *Income* £28,870
Grants £22,327

TRUSTEES Dr R W G Hunt, Mrs E M Hunt, Rev D R G Hunt, Mrs E R L Hunt, P R W Hunt, Mrs N M Hunt,

PUBLICATIONS Annual Aaccounts sent to the Charity Commissioners

HOW TO APPLY **This Trust states that it does not respond to unsolicited applications**

WHO TO APPLY TO Mrs E M Hunt, The Nazareth Trust Fund, Kewferry House, 10 Kewferry Road, Northwood, Middlesex HA6 2NY

CC NO 210503   **ESTABLISHED** 1956

■ The Nchima Trust

WHAT IS FUNDED Initiation and help in schemes aimed at advancing education, health, welfare standards and the provision of clean water, with particular emphasis on self-help schemes, assisting the handicapped

WHO CAN BENEFIT Individuals and established local organisations benefiting: children and young adults; at risk groups; those disadvantaged by poverty; those living in rural areas; and the sick.

Does the trust you have chosen match your needs? Haphazard applications waste postage and time

445

There is no restriction on the disease or medical condition suffered by the beneficiaries

WHERE FUNDING CAN BE GIVEN Malawi

TYPE OF GRANT General medical, educational, housing and welfare in rural areas

FINANCES *Year* 1996 *Income* £73,347
Grants £35,369

TRUSTEES Ms M Gardiner, OBE, Ms A Scarborough, OBE, Ms G Legg, Ms R Richards, K Legg

NOTES Time charity. Fixed grants of approx £5,000pa plus other discretionary grants

HOW TO APPLY No regular dates for applications

WHO TO APPLY TO Mrs G M Legg, The Nchima Trust, Tudeley Hall, Tudeley, Tonbridge, Kent TN11 0PQ

CC NO 242546   **ESTABLISHED** 1962

■ The Airey Neave Trust

WHAT IS FUNDED Postgraduate education for refugees or those with exceptional or indefinite leave to remain, resident in the UK and recognised by the Home Office. Refugees needing retraining, teaching English as a second or foreign language, fellowships, refugees bursaries and fees, law research and specialist research will be considered

WHAT IS NOT FUNDED No grants to asylum seekers

WHO CAN BENEFIT Individuals, law faculties and researchers. Organisations benefiting young adults; refugees; academics; legal professionals; post graduate refugees; refugees needing retraining will all be considered

WHERE FUNDING CAN BE GIVEN UK

TYPE OF GRANT Fees for refugees up to £2,000 per annum; research grants up to £20,000 per annum. Feasibility studies. Funding of up to three years is available

SAMPLE GRANTS £31,500 to The Centre for the Study of Terrorism and Political Violence for research into Terrorist Use of Weapons of Mass Destruction; £20,500 to The Queen's University, Belfast for research into Judicial Responsibility in the Criminal Courts; £15,000 to 13 refugees for post-graduate education, subjects covering medicine, law, petroleum geology, telecommunications and business management

FINANCES *Year* 1996–97 *Income* £58,517
Grants £63,500

TRUSTEES Rt Hon Sir Adam Butler, Hugh Tilney, Sir Nigel Mobbs, The Hon Patrick Neave, The Hon Sir William MacAlpine, BT

PUBLICATIONS Among others: *Victims of Terrorism, The International Covenant on Civil and Political Rights and UK Law, The World of Science and The Rule of Law*

NOTES We do not contribute to established institutions

HOW TO APPLY We welcome an initial telephone call. There are application forms for refugees but not for research fellows. There are guidelines for research fellows. There are deadlines, viz: refugees – 31 May, and research – 31 May. We prefer an sae from applicant

WHO TO APPLY TO Mrs Hannah Scott, The Airey Neave Trust, 40 Charles Street, London W1X 7PB
Tel 0171-495 0554 *Fax* 0171-491 1118

CC NO 297269   **ESTABLISHED** 1979

■ The Needham Cooper Charitable Trust

WHAT IS FUNDED Charitable institutions and charitable projects

WHAT IS NOT FUNDED Applications from individuals, including students, are ineligible. No grants made to large national organisations except those with a branch locally

WHO CAN BENEFIT Registered charities. There are no restrictions on the age; professional and economic group; family situation; religion and culture; and social circumstances of; or disease or medical condition suffered by, the beneficiaries

WHERE FUNDING CAN BE GIVEN Bristol and District

TYPE OF GRANT At discretion of Trustees

RANGE OF GRANTS £250–£53,400, normally £500–£20,000, mostly £500–£2,000

SAMPLE GRANTS £53,400 to Bristol Age Care for outreach projects; £25,000 to St John Ambulance for a new HQ; £20,000 to Bristol University Department of Surgery for a new department laboratory; £20,000 to Bristol 2000 for a millennium project; £16,000 to Bristol University Department of Engineering for bursaries; £15,830 to Long Ashton Research Station for two research scholarships; £12,000 to Unity Fund for helping the elderly in the homes; £10,000 to Greater Bristol Foundation for Bristol charities; £10,000 to Anchor Society for helping elderly in their homes; £10,000 to Bristol University Department of Medicine for bursaries

FINANCES *Year* 1996–97 *Income* £228,849
Grants £269,680

TRUSTEES Mrs E J B Cooper, S F T Cox, Mrs J L V Penson, R C Baxter

PUBLICATIONS Annual Report and Accounts to Charity Commission

HOW TO APPLY By writing at any time. Trustees meet half-yearly. Applications should include details of the need the intended project is designed to meet, plus an outline budget and current balance sheet. We acknowledge all applications. The Trust is not accepting any new applications at present

WHO TO APPLY TO Mrs E J B Cooper, The Needham Cooper Charitable Trust, Home Farm, Yate Rocks, Yate, Bristol BS37 7BS

CC NO 327865   **ESTABLISHED** 1988

■ Needham Market and Barking Welfare Charities

WHAT IS FUNDED Projects which benefit the local community especially those in need, hardship or distress

WHO CAN BENEFIT To benefit those in need, hardship or distress in the area Where Funding Can Be Given

WHERE FUNDING CAN BE GIVEN Needham Market and the Parish of Barking

RANGE OF GRANTS £35–£5,000

SAMPLE GRANTS £5,000 to Needham Market Playgroup for building work; £4,500 to Needham Market Parish Council for east window of St John the Baptist Church; £1,295 to an individual with restricted vision for a reading machine; £1,082 to Nursing Care and Relief; £1,000 to MSDC for a wheelchair for use at the lake; £791 to individuals; £350 to Barking 1st Guides; £269 to Barking Parish Council towards mower repairs

FINANCES *Year* 1997 *Income* £35,349
Grants £17,389

TRUSTEES R Burl, J Dickerson, G C Miller, R D Robertson, Mrs E Ruffle, Mrs S C Wright

HOW TO APPLY To the address under Who To Apply To in writing, enclosing audited accounts. Individuals should contact the Clerk requesting an application form

WHO TO APPLY TO R Jolley, Clerk, Needham Market and Barking Welfare Charities, 12 Fairfax Gardens, Needham Market, Suffolk IP6 8AZ

CC NO 217499   **ESTABLISHED** 1961

■ Christopher Needler's Charitable Trust

WHAT IS FUNDED General charitable objectives by the direction of the Founder, with emphasis on the relief of specific illness and disability

WHO CAN BENEFIT There are no restrictions on the age; professional and economic group; family situation; religion and culture; and social circumstances of; or disease or medical condition suffered by, the beneficiaries. However, particular favour is given to the disabled and those with specific illnesses

WHERE FUNDING CAN BE GIVEN UK

TRUSTEES A W M Miller, G C H Needler, J D Shephard

NOTES Applications are not encouraged. The founder has their own information and specific charitable objective

HOW TO APPLY **This Trust states that it does not respond to unsolicited applications**

WHO TO APPLY TO Adrian Miller, Trustee and Secretary, Christopher Needler's Charitable Trust, 5 Barnfield Crescent, Exeter, Devon EX1 1RF *Tel* 01392 411221

CC NO 1051392   **ESTABLISHED** 1995

■ The Neighbourly Charitable Trust

WHAT IS FUNDED General charitable purposes. Trustees tend to support the same charities consistently over the years

WHO CAN BENEFIT Registered charities, institutions. There are no restrictions on the age; professional and economic group; family situation; religion and culture; and social circumstances of; or disease or medical condition suffered by, the beneficiaries

WHERE FUNDING CAN BE GIVEN Mainly Bedfordshire

TYPE OF GRANT Recurrent

RANGE OF GRANTS £1,000–£6,000

SAMPLE GRANTS £6,000 to Outreach Project; £3,000 to Women's Royal Voluntary Service; £2,250 to Bedfordshire County Council Social Services Department; £1,000 to Bedfordshire Victims Support Schemes

FINANCES *Year* 1997 *Income* £25,297 *Grants* £12,250

TRUSTEES B A Allen, J R Sell, D Watts

WHO TO APPLY TO John Byrnes, The Neighbourly Charitable Trust, 8 Upper Marlborough Road, St Albans, Hertfordshire AL1 3UR

CC NO 258488   **ESTABLISHED** 1969

■ J H Neill Charitable Settlement

WHAT IS FUNDED General charitable purposes. It is the policy of the Trustees to give preferential consideration to the needs of charitable bodies operating specifically in South Yorkshire

WHAT IS NOT FUNDED No grants are given to individuals. Grants are only given to registered charities

WHO CAN BENEFIT Registered charities only. There are no restrictions on the age; professional and economic group; family situation; religion and

culture; and social circumstances of; or disease or medical condition suffered by, the beneficiaries

WHERE FUNDING CAN BE GIVEN Principally Sheffield and its immediate surroundings

TYPE OF GRANT Starter finance, normally not exceeding £500, but also maintenance grants, normally not exceeding £500 per annum. One-off grants are also considered

RANGE OF GRANTS £50–£1,250

SAMPLE GRANTS £1,250 to South Yorkshire Community Foundation; £1,000 to Diocese of Hallam, St Joseph's; £1,000 to Sheffield Cathedral; £1,000 to Voluntary Action Sheffield; £1,000 to Weston Park Hospital Cancer Care and Research Fund

FINANCES *Year* 1997–98 *Income* £19,449 *Grants* £17,450

TRUSTEES Sir Hugh Neill, KCVO, CBE, TD, Mrs J P Holah, Mrs S E Browne

HOW TO APPLY In writing to the address under Who To Apply To, to arrive during the month of August

WHO TO APPLY TO Sir Hugh Neill, J H Neill Charitable Settlement, Barn Cottage, Lindrick Common, Worksop, Nottingham S81 8BA

CC NO 243806   **ESTABLISHED** 1964

■ The James Neill Trust Fund

WHAT IS FUNDED Voluntary work for the benefit of people in the area Where Funding Can Be Given

WHO CAN BENEFIT Voluntary organisations benefiting people in the area Where Funding Can Be Given

WHERE FUNDING CAN BE GIVEN Within 20 miles of Sheffield Cathedral

TYPE OF GRANT Ongoing support for established organisations and one-off grants to meet start-up costs or unexpected expenses

RANGE OF GRANTS £175–£15,000

SAMPLE GRANTS £15,529 for Christmas Hampers for old age pensioners; £7,500 to South Yorkshire Community Foundation; £1,250 to South Yorkshire Probation Service; £1,200 to Voluntary Action, Sheffield; £1,200 to South Yorkshire and Hallamshire Club for Young People; £1,100 to Relate – Rotherham Marriage Guidance; £1,100 to Relate – Sheffield Marriage Guidance; £1,000 to Sheffield Scout Resources Charity; £1,000 to Darnall and District Medical Aid Society; £1,000 to Handsworth Community Association

FINANCES *Year* 1997–98 *Income* £41,789 *Grants* £49,972

TRUSTEES Sir Hugh Neill, G H N Peel, Lady Neill

HOW TO APPLY To the address under Who To Apply To in writing during July only

WHO TO APPLY TO Sir Hugh Neill, The James Neill Trust Fund, Barn Cottage, Lindrick Common, Worksop, Nottinghamshire S81 8BA

CC NO 503203   **ESTABLISHED** 1974

■ The Barbara Nelson Memorial Trust

WHAT IS FUNDED To support Jewish causes

WHO CAN BENEFIT Individuals and registered charities benefiting Jewish people

WHERE FUNDING CAN BE GIVEN UK

RANGE OF GRANTS £100–£1,000

SAMPLE GRANTS £1,000 to BDO Stoy Hayward Charitable Trust; £750 to Imperial Cancer Research Fund; £750 to Jewish Care; £500 to Child Accident Prevention Trust; £500 to Friends of the Hebrew University of Jerusalem; £500 to Greater London Fund for the Blind; £500 to Head First; £500 to Help the Aged Appeal; £500 to International Spinal Research Trust; £500 to Jewish Childs Day

FINANCES *Year* 1996 *Income* £30,281 *Grants* £13,710

TRUSTEES M Nelson, Mrs D Austin, Edward Langton

WHO TO APPLY TO M Nelson, The Barbara Nelson Memorial Trust, c/o BDO Stoy Hayward, Accountants, 8 Baker Street, London W1M 1DA

CC NO 280928   **ESTABLISHED** 1980

■ Nesswall Ltd

WHAT IS FUNDED Jewish organisations, including education

WHO CAN BENEFIT Jewish organisations

WHERE FUNDING CAN BE GIVEN UK and overseas

FINANCES *Year* 1997 *Income* £55,383 *Grants* £39,940

TRUSTEES I Teitelbaum, Mrs R Teitelbaum, I Chersky

HOW TO APPLY To the address under Who To Apply To in writing

WHO TO APPLY TO Mrs R Teitelbaum, Nesswall Ltd, 28 Overlea Road, London E5 9BG

CC NO 283600   **ESTABLISHED** 1981

■ Employees of Nestle Rowntree York Community Fund

WHAT IS FUNDED At Trustees' discretion. Health and community services

WHAT IS NOT FUNDED Not political or religious. The Trustees will not considered the following: individuals, capital projects, government funded organisations, umbrella organisations, whose purpose is to collect funds to distribute themselves, research where the work or objectives could raise moral or political issues, charities carrying high funds or with high administration costs, appeals requiring substantial funds where donations would not be used, if at all, for a long period or personal requests for grants

WHO CAN BENEFIT Organisations benefiting: people of all ages; disabled people; homeless people; victims of abuse and crime; victims of famine, man-made or natural disasters and war. There are few restrictions on the disease or medical condition suffered by the beneficiaries

WHERE FUNDING CAN BE GIVEN Mainly the Yorkshire area. The Fund supports charities in other parts of the UK which are involved in supporting the deaf, blind, disabled, disadvantaged children, relief and research organisations and some international relief organisations

TYPE OF GRANT Core costs, one-off, recurring costs, research, running costs and start-up costs will be considered

SAMPLE GRANTS £2,000 to St Leonard's Hospice, York; £1,500 to York Council for Voluntary Services; £1,500 to British Legion Poppy Appeal, York; £1,500 to Confectioners Benevolent Fund; £1,400 to Guide Dogs for the Blind; £1,300 to Christian Aid; £1,200 to Martin House, Children's Hospice; £1,200 to Oxfam; £1,000 to UNICEF; £1,000 to York Age Concern

FINANCES *Year* 1996 *Income* £52,791 *Grants* £44,660

TRUSTEES A E Durham, J S Roberts, Mrs S J Dunnill

HOW TO APPLY Initial telephone calls welcome. The most straight forward applications are the best, ie listing the objectives of the appeal, preferably on one sheet of paper

WHO TO APPLY TO A E Durham, Employees of Nestle Rowntree York Community Fund, Nestle Rowntree, Haxby Road, York YO1 1XY

CC NO 516702   **ESTABLISHED** 1985

■ Netivot Olam Foundation

This trust did not respond to CAF's request to amend its entry and, by 30 June 1998, CAF's researchers did not find financial records for later than 1995 on its file at the Charity Commission. Trusts are legally required to submit annual accounts to the Charity Commission under section 42 of the Charities Act 1993

WHAT IS FUNDED General charitable purposes, in particular, the furtherance of education including education in Jewish religion

WHO CAN BENEFIT There are no restrictions on the age; professional and economic group; family situation; religion and culture; and social circumstances of; or disease or medical condition suffered by, the beneficiaries. However, particular favour is given to Jewish people, children, young adults, students and teachers

WHERE FUNDING CAN BE GIVEN UK

TRUSTEES G Balint, Rabbi A Kimche, C Stein

WHO TO APPLY TO C Stein, Netivot Olam Foundation, 94 Wigmore Street, London W1H 9DR

CC NO 1041852   **ESTABLISHED** 1994

■ The Network Foundation

WHAT IS FUNDED The Network Foundation is the charitable arm of the Network for Social Change which is a group of givers who actively seek out projects which they want to fund, rather than responding to applications, in the areas of peace and preservation of the Earth; human rights and solidarity; health and wholeness; arts and media

WHAT IS NOT FUNDED Relief work is not undertaken. No funding for national schemes or organisations

WHO CAN BENEFIT Smaller schemes. There are no restrictions on the age; professional and economic group; family situation; religion and culture; and social circumstances of; or disease or medical condition suffered by, the beneficiaries. However, particular favour may be given to those working in the arts or media and medical professionals

WHERE FUNDING CAN BE GIVEN UK and overseas

TYPE OF GRANT Smaller projects

SAMPLE GRANTS £279,020 to funding cycle; £74,572 to informal funding cycle; £74,322 to help the homeless; £56,925 to legacy; £36,400 to third world debt; £14,333 to Gaia; £11,516 to New Economics Foundation

FINANCES *Year* 1996 *Income* £496,037 *Grants* £549,388

TRUSTEES Patrick Boase (Chairman), John S Broad, Ingrid Broad, C Carolan, Samuel P Clark, M Freudenberg, Oliver Gillie, C Holden, Hugh MacPherson, I Mulder, Sara Robin

HOW TO APPLY **This Trust states that it does not respond to unsolicited applications**

WHO TO APPLY TO Vanessa Adams, Administrator, The Network Foundation, BM Box 2063, London WC1 3XX

CC NO 295237   **ESTABLISHED** 1986

448

Think carefully about every application. Is it justified?

■ The New Appeals Organisation for the City and County of Nottingham

WHAT IS FUNDED Schools and colleges; disability aids and equipment for individuals and organisations. To provide help where this is not available from any other source

WHAT IS NOT FUNDED Appeals to cover debts or arrears will not be considered

WHO CAN BENEFIT Individuals and organisations benefiting at risk groups, disabled people, those disadvantaged by poverty, and socially isolated people. There is no restriction on the age of the beneficiaries and people suffering from many different diseases or medical conditions will be considered

WHERE FUNDING CAN BE GIVEN Nottinghamshire

TYPE OF GRANT One-off

FINANCES *Year* 1995–96 *Income* £65,434

TRUSTEES Cllr B Bateman, L S Levin, D L Jones

HOW TO APPLY To the address under Who To Apply To in writing. An initial telephone call from applicant is welcome

WHO TO APPLY TO The Clerk, The New Appeals Organisation, Messrs Rotheras, Honoray Solicitors, 2 Kayes Walk, The Lace Market, Nottingham NG1 1PZ *Tel* 0115-910 0600

CC NO 502196   **ESTABLISHED** 1973

■ New Court Charitable Trust

WHAT IS FUNDED General charitable purposes. (a) To maintain existing commitments. (b) Provide limited finance to help small nationally orientated charities to become established. (c) Encourage co-ordination between charities working in related fields. (d) To support projects in which Trustees have a special interest and within policy laid down by the Deed

WHAT IS NOT FUNDED Donations can only be made to registered charities. No grants to individuals

WHO CAN BENEFIT Grants are seldom made to regional branches of national charities, local activities or towards building projects. There are no restrictions on the age; professional and economic group; family situation; religion and culture; and social circumstances of; or disease or medical condition suffered by, the beneficiaries

WHERE FUNDING CAN BE GIVEN UK

TYPE OF GRANT Usually single donation

RANGE OF GRANTS £100–£1,000

FINANCES *Year* 1996 *Income* £18,488
Grants £15,698

TRUSTEES E L de Rothschild, CBE, Sir Evelyn de Rothschild, L D de Rothschild, CBE

HOW TO APPLY In writing only

WHO TO APPLY TO The Secretary, New Court Charitable Trust, New Court, St Swithin's Lane, London EC4P 4DU

CC NO 209790   **ESTABLISHED** 1947

■ The New Durlston Trust (formerly The Durlston Trust)

WHAT IS FUNDED Advancement of the Christian religion, including education, youth projects, and Christian industrial and engineering projects

WHAT IS NOT FUNDED Restricted to Christian based charities only – might exceptionally consider others

WHO CAN BENEFIT Normally charities but might consider individuals. Beneficiaries include: Baptists, Christians, Church of England; Methodists, Quakers and Roman Catholics of all ages

WHERE FUNDING CAN BE GIVEN UK and overseas

TYPE OF GRANT Usually one-off, some recurring. Buildings, capital, core costs, projects, running costs, and start-up costs are also considered

RANGE OF GRANTS £25–£1,000

FINANCES *Year* 1997 *Income* £15,831
Grants £16,550

TRUSTEES H H Pool, N A H Pool

HOW TO APPLY In writing with sae. Individuals should supply confirmation from charity concerned

WHO TO APPLY TO N A H Pool, The New Durlston Trust, c/o Herbert Pool Ltd, 95 Fleet Road, Fleet, Hampshire GU13 8PJ

CC NO 1019028   **ESTABLISHED** 1993

■ The New Horizons Trust

WHAT IS FUNDED Groups of older people proposing to carry out a project that will benefit the community. Particularly charities working in the fields of: arts and arts facilities, conservation and community facilities will be considered

WHAT IS NOT FUNDED Groups must consist of at least ten people, at least half of whom must be aged 60 or more. Proposed project must be new and use the knowledge and experience of the group members

WHO CAN BENEFIT Neighbourhood-based community projects benefiting older people and research workers

WHERE FUNDING CAN BE GIVEN UK

TYPE OF GRANT Capital, running costs for up to 18 months, buildings and start-up costs will be considered

RANGE OF GRANTS £500–£5,000

FINANCES *Year* 1995–96 *Income* £50,150
Grants £25,575

TRUSTEES A M Pilch, CBE, Mrs B C Pilch, A R Neale, P Miles, Ms K Dibley

PUBLICATIONS Leaflet, Annual Report

HOW TO APPLY On a form available from the Administrator. Callers are asked to contact the appropriate Area Officer, details given, who will issue application forms, offer advice and guidance. Send completed forms to Trustees. Do not require sae

WHO TO APPLY TO The Administrator, The New Horizons Trust, Paramount House, 290–292 Brighton Road, South Croydon, Surrey CR2 6AG *Tel* 0181-666 0201 *Fax* 0181-667 0037

CC NO 293777   **ESTABLISHED** 1985

■ New Ingrebourne Trust

WHAT IS FUNDED (a) To relieve poverty; (b) to advance the Christian faith; (c) to advance education; (d) other general charitable purposes, in particular for the benefit of the people of Harold Wood, Essex and beyond in accordance with the word of God

WHO CAN BENEFIT To benefit: children and young adults; those disadvantaged by poverty; and Christians and Evangelists

WHERE FUNDING CAN BE GIVEN Primarily Harold Wood, Essex

FINANCES *Year* 1996 *Income* £26,373

TRUSTEES W P Benn, A A Gillard

WHO TO APPLY TO A Gray, New Ingrebourne Trust, The Laurels, Shepherds Hill, Harold Wood, Essex RM3 0NP

CC NO 1042768   **ESTABLISHED** 1994

■ The New Lease Trust (otherwise known as North West London Trust)

WHAT IS FUNDED Housing and the homeless. Drugs and alcohol rehabilitation and ex-offenders

WHO CAN BENEFIT Ex-offenders, homeless and those suffering from substance misuse

WHERE FUNDING CAN BE GIVEN London

TYPE OF GRANT At the discretion of the Trustees

SAMPLE GRANTS £115,000 to The Tudor Trust; £1,500 to Oliver Borthwich Memorial Trust; £1,000 to The Bertie Watson Foundation; £1,000 to The Star Foundation

FINANCES *Year* 1996 *Income* £138,747 *Grants* £119,150

TRUSTEES Hon Mrs S Baring, Mrs Marion Stowell, Richard Griffiths, Ms Clare Thomas, Colin Crewe

WHO TO APPLY TO M D Levine, The New Lease Trust, 3rd Floor, 293–299 Kentish Town Road, London NW5 2TJ

CC NO 802223   **ESTABLISHED** 1989

■ The New Provincial Benevolent Fund

WHAT IS FUNDED General charitable purposes

WHO CAN BENEFIT There are no restrictions on the age; professional and economic group; family situation; religion and culture; and social circumstances of; or disease or medical condition suffered by, the beneficiaries

WHERE FUNDING CAN BE GIVEN UK

FINANCES *Year* 1997 *Income* £95,000

TRUSTEES Dr J R Allin, G M Cooper, G A Brocklesby, G Ives

WHO TO APPLY TO J G Adams, The New Provincial Benevolent Fund, Masonic Hall, Cambridge Road, Grimsby, Lincolnshire DN34 5SZ *Tel* 01472 870042

CC NO 1060091   **ESTABLISHED** 1997

■ Newby Trust Ltd

WHAT IS FUNDED Within the general objects of the Trust, medical welfare, relief of poverty, training and education, one category for special support is selected each year. 1996–97 inner city communities; 1997–98 education for 16–25 year olds. 1998–99 rural welfare; 1999–2000 the elderly. Alongside the special category, relief of poverty, medical welfare and educational grants are made each year

WHAT IS NOT FUNDED For medical welfare and relief of poverty grants from individuals are not considered (see details under Notes). Educational grants are not provided for CPS law exams, BSc intercalated with a medical degree or postgraduate medical veterinary degrees in the first or second year of study

WHO CAN BENEFIT Registered charities, social services for their clients, hospitals, and students. There are no restrictions on the age; family situation; religion and culture; and social circumstances of; or disease or medical condition suffered by, the beneficiaries. People from differing professional and economic groups, will be considered

WHERE FUNDING CAN BE GIVEN UK

TYPE OF GRANT Usually one-off for part of a project. Buildings, capital, core costs and salaries may be considered. Funding will be given for up to three years

SAMPLE GRANTS £10,000 to Fircroft College (Birmingham Reachout); £10,000 to Merseyside Youth Association; £10,000 to Rathbone Community Industry, Manchester; £8,000 to Imperial College, London (School of Medicine at St Mary's); £7,000 to YMCA of Great Britain (Upstone Centre, Leeds); £5,000 to Bedales School Grants Trust Fund; £5,000 to Cedar Centre, Isle of Dogs, London; £5,000 to Donaldson's College, Edinburgh (National School for Deaf Children); £5,000 to New Assembly of Churches (Feltham Youth Offenders Institution); £5,000 to Scout (and Guide) Association (Eaton Vale Activity Centre, Norwich)

FINANCES *Year* 1997–98 *Income* £332,222 *Grants* £320,260

TRUSTEES J Charlton, Mrs J Gooder, Dr R Gooder, Mrs S Reed

PUBLICATIONS Annual Report

NOTES Medical welfare and relief of poverty grants are made only through applications from health authorities, the NHS, social services or registered charities. Educational grants are normally considered for students undertaking second degrees, training in manual skills and for help in the completion of professional qualifications. Grant cheques are not paid to individuals but paid to social services (or similar) in respect of medical welfare and relief of poverty. Educational grants are made out to the educational institution. Application forms are not supplied

HOW TO APPLY At any time. First applications should be made in writing. Applications from students and trainees should include clear details of the course being undertaken, personal circumstances and financial need. They should be accompanied by a CV, two letters of reference, financial statement (to include fees and living expenses) and a sae. Applications from students are not normally accepted in September and October. Decisions about relief of poverty and most medical welfare applications are made within one month; students should expect to wait about three months; decisions on larger institutional grants are made twice yearly at meetings of the Trustees in November and March. Foreign students are considered if circumstances beyond their control (not an ending of funding by their government at home) have led to a breakdown in funding during their course. The course of study in the UK must have already commenced. Office normally manned Monday, Wednesday and Fridays 09.00–12.00 (holidays excepted)

WHO TO APPLY TO Miss W Gillam, Secretary, Newby Trust Ltd, Hill Farm, Froxfield, Petersfield, Hampshire GU32 1BQ *Tel* 01730 827557 *Fax* 01730 827557

CC NO 227151   **ESTABLISHED** 1938

■ Duke of Newcastle's 1986 Charitable Trust

WHAT IS FUNDED To support youth groups and a range of ex-services personnel relief funds

WHAT IS NOT FUNDED No grants to individuals

WHO CAN BENEFIT Registered charities benefiting children, young adults and ex-service personnel relief funds

WHERE FUNDING CAN BE GIVEN UK

FINANCES *Year* 1996 *Income* £17,317 *Grants* £22,000

TRUSTEES R D Van Oss, J A Anstruther-Gough-Calthorpe, C H B Gisborne

HOW TO APPLY To the address under Who To Apply To in writing. (Unsuccessful applicants will not receive an acknowledgement). Applications may be made throughout the year. Applications should include a list of other grant making bodies approached with results. Applicants should be aware that the majority of distributable income is already earmarked for distribution by the Trustees. Applications only considered if supported by a copy of the latest Report and Accounts

WHO TO APPLY TO N Wingerath, Payne Hicks Beach Solicitors, Duke of Newcastle's 1986 Charitable Trust, 10 New Square, Lincoln's Inn, London WC2A 3QG *Tel* 0171-242 6041

CC NO 1003909   **ESTABLISHED** 1986

■ Newcomen Collett Foundation

WHAT IS FUNDED Education of young people under 25 years of age

WHAT IS NOT FUNDED We can only help young people living in the London Borough of Southwark. People on courses of further education should have lived in Southwark for at least two years before starting their course

WHO CAN BENEFIT Individuals and small local projects benefiting children, young adults and students under 25

WHERE FUNDING CAN BE GIVEN London Borough of Southwark only

TYPE OF GRANT One-off

SAMPLE GRANTS £5,000 to London Coaching Foundation; £4,000 to Southwark Children's Foundation; £4,000 to Thameside District Scouts Council; £3,600 to Southwark Children's Foundation; £3,125 to Young Vic; £3,000 to Only Connect Respite Break; £3,000 to St Mary Magdalene School; £2,500 to Roots and Shoots; £2,500 to Kintore Way Nursery School; £2,500 to Arethusa Venture Centre

FINANCES *Year* 1997 *Income* £190,000 *Grants* £164,000

TRUSTEES List in Accounts filed with Charity Commission

HOW TO APPLY Write to the Clerk for an application form. The Governors consider requests four times a year

WHO TO APPLY TO R Goatcher, Clerk, Newcomen Collett Foundation, Marshall House, 66 Newcomen Street, London SE1 1YT *Tel* 0171-407 2967

CC NO 312804   **ESTABLISHED** 1988

■ Newfield Charitable Trust

WHAT IS FUNDED The support of education and welfare projects to benefit girls and young women in the area Where Funding Can Be Given. Grants for items including school and general clothing, beds and bedding, essential household items including fridges, cookers and washing machines, educational trips both home and abroad, college fees, text books, educational equipment and nursery fees

WHAT IS NOT FUNDED Beneficiaries must be under 30 years of age. Postgraduate education will not be supported

WHO CAN BENEFIT Young women and girls in need in the area Where Funding Can Be Given

WHERE FUNDING CAN BE GIVEN Coventry, Leamington Spa

TYPE OF GRANT Capital and costs of study

FINANCES *Year* 1997 *Income* £51,244 *Grants* £33,265

TRUSTEES E J D Bresnen, Canon J Eardley, Mrs H A A Freeman, Miss M Jones, Mrs E Nicolson, A W Parsons, R Stanley

HOW TO APPLY Application forms are available from the address under Who To Apply To upon written request

WHO TO APPLY TO D J Dumbleton, Clerk, Newfield Charitable Trust, 8 and 9 The Quadrant, Coventry CV1 2EG

CC NO 221440   **ESTABLISHED** 1977

■ Richard Newitt Fund

WHAT IS FUNDED The Trustees have designated a small number of educational institutions and awards will be made direct to their student hardship funds

WHO CAN BENEFIT Organisations and institutions benefiting students who are disadvantaged by poverty. The help is for the advancement of a person's further education rather than the financing of a project

WHERE FUNDING CAN BE GIVEN UK

TYPE OF GRANT Non-recurring bursaries to students

RANGE OF GRANTS £1,500–£55,000

SAMPLE GRANTS £55,500 to Southampton University for bursaries, prize awards, hardship awards, WSA and music grants; The following grants were to hardship grant funds:; £4,000 to City University; £4,000 to University of Durham; £4,000 to University of Newcastle upon Tyne; £2,500 Royal Free Hospital School of Medicine; £2,500 to Charing Cross Medical School; £2,500 to Royal Northern College of Music; £2,500 to the Royal Veterinary College; £2,000 to Bristol Old Vic Theatre; £2,000 to Textile Conservation Centre

FINANCES *Year* 1997 *Income* £73,746 *Grants* £84,500

TRUSTEES Kleinwort Benson Trustees Limited, D A Schofield, Prof D Holt, Mrs D Maddock

HOW TO APPLY Requests for application forms should be submitted by 1 April in any one year; applicants will be notified of the results in August. Unsolicited applications are unlikely to be considered, educational institutional applications by invitation only

WHO TO APPLY TO Chris Gilbert, Richard Newitt Fund, Kleinwort Benson Trustees Ltd, PO Box 191, 10 Fenchurch Street, London EC3M 3LB

CC NO 276470   **ESTABLISHED** 1978

■ The Newman Charitable Trust

WHAT IS FUNDED General charitable purposes. Only support to charities known personally to the Trustees

WHAT IS NOT FUNDED No grants to individuals

WHO CAN BENEFIT Other registered charities. There are no restrictions on the age; professional and economic group; family situation; religion and culture; and social circumstances of; or disease or medical condition suffered by, the beneficiaries

WHERE FUNDING CAN BE GIVEN UK and overseas

TYPE OF GRANT A great majority of the anticipated income from this Trust is committed for some years ahead

Not our policy to make grants to individuals

RANGE OF GRANTS £250–£25,000

SAMPLE GRANTS £25,000 to St Marks Hospital Research Foundation Fund; £2,000 to Amnesty International; £1,250 to Chailey Heritage School; £1,000 to AFASIC; £1,000 to Childline; £1,000 to Crisis; £1,000 to Nairobi Hospice Charity; £1,000 to Oxfam; £1,000 to The Salvation Army; £750 to Ethiopiaid

FINANCES *Year* 1997 *Income* £34,884 *Grants* £36,750

TRUSTEES Newman Trustees Ltd

HOW TO APPLY Grants are not made to individuals, but to charities only

WHO TO APPLY TO C S Jones, Secretary, The Newman Charitable Trust, Newman Trustees Ltd, Irwin House, 118 Southwark Street, London SE1 0SW

CC NO 264032   **ESTABLISHED** 1972

■ Mr and Mrs F E F Newman Charitable Trust

WHAT IS FUNDED Primarily local religious purposes, welfare and educational purposes, and other charitable purposes

WHAT IS NOT FUNDED No grants to individuals

WHO CAN BENEFIT Support is given to children, young adults and the elderly. At risk groups, those disadvantaged by poverty and socially isolated people, clergy, students, teachers and governesses may also be supported

WHERE FUNDING CAN BE GIVEN Republic of Ireland, UK, Channel Islands

RANGE OF GRANTS £30–£2,750

SAMPLE GRANTS £2,750 to TEAR fund; £2,750 to Children's Society; £2,750 to Bible Society; £2,000 to Africa Enterprise; £1,000 to 'Tommy's' Church; £1,000 to CMJ; £1,000 to Traidcraft Exchange; £850 to St John's Church; £700 to Monkton Combe School

FINANCES *Year* 1996–97 *Income* £42,158 *Grants* £36,272

TRUSTEES G S Smith, F E F Newman

WHO TO APPLY TO Manches & Co, Mr and Mrs F E F Newman Charitable Trust, Aldwych House, 81 Aldwych, London WC2B 4RP

CC NO 263831   **ESTABLISHED** 1972

■ Newpier Limited

WHAT IS FUNDED Jewish organisations

WHO CAN BENEFIT To benefit Jewish people

WHERE FUNDING CAN BE GIVEN UK

RANGE OF GRANTS £100–£22,500

SAMPLE GRANTS £22,500 to SOFT; £14,300 to KID; £5,000 to Gateshead Foundation for Torah; £2,700 to Lolev Charitable Trust; £1,800 to YHS; £1,500 to Friends of Biala; £650 to Friends of Ben Yakov; £500 to London Jerusalem Chaim; £500 to Gateshead Yeshiva; £500 to Gur Trust

FINANCES *Year* 1997 *Income* £63,876 *Grants* £53,090

TRUSTEES H Knopfler, C Margulies, R Margulies

HOW TO APPLY To the address under Who To Apply To in writing

WHO TO APPLY TO Charles Margulies, Trustee, Newpier Limited, 235 Old Marylebone Road, London NW1 5QT

CC NO 293686   **ESTABLISHED** 1985

■ The Newstead Charity

WHAT IS FUNDED Health and disability and community facilities

WHAT IS NOT FUNDED No grants to individuals

WHO CAN BENEFIT Organisations benfiting sick and disabled people. There are no restrictions on the disease or medical condition suffered by the beneficiaries

WHERE FUNDING CAN BE GIVEN Liverpool City, Knowsley and North Wales

TYPE OF GRANT One-off, project and research. Funding for up to one year will be considered

RANGE OF GRANTS Range of grants from £500

FINANCES *Year* 1996–97 *Income* £24,000 *Grants* £29,000

TRUSTEES K E B Clayton, G D Tasker, W F Glazebrook

HOW TO APPLY Applications in writing only

WHO TO APPLY TO Roberts Legge & Co, The Newstead Charity, 14 Chapel Lane, Formby, Liverpool, Merseyside L37 4DU *Tel* 01704 834490

CC NO 327244   **ESTABLISHED** 1986

■ Nicholson Leslie Charitable Trust

This trust did not respond to CAF's request to amend its entry and, by 30 June 1998, CAF's researchers did not find financial records for later than 1995 on its file at the Charity Commission. Trusts are legally required to submit annual accounts to the Charity Commission under section 42 of the Charities Act 1993

WHAT IS FUNDED General charitable purposes

WHO CAN BENEFIT There are no restrictions on the age; professional and economic group; family situation; religion and culture; and social circumstances of; or disease or medical condition suffered by, the beneficiaries

WHERE FUNDING CAN BE GIVEN UK

TRUSTEES P J Milton, A A M Pinsent, J V F Roberts

WHO TO APPLY TO Miss L Reynolds, Secretary, Nicholson Leslie Charitable Trust, 6 Braham Street, London E1 8ED

CC NO 1051269   **ESTABLISHED** 1995

■ Nichol-Young Foundation

WHAT IS FUNDED Relief of poverty. Advancement of education. Advancement of religion. General charitable purposes. Grants to organisations in East Anglia especially considered. Present income fully committed

WHO CAN BENEFIT Those who are mainly local, but not exclusively, benefiting: children and young adults; students; at risk groups; those disadvantaged by poverty; and socially isolated people. There is no restriction on the religion or culture of the beneficiaries

WHERE FUNDING CAN BE GIVEN East Anglia especially

TYPE OF GRANT Grants are either one-off or for a limited period only

FINANCES *Year* 1995 *Income* £39,703 *Grants* £22,862

TRUSTEES Rev J D Mitson, Rev Carole M Mitson

HOW TO APPLY To The Trustees at the address under Who To Apply To. Applications may be made at any time but will only be considered periodically. Unsuccessful applications will generally not be acknowledged

WHO TO APPLY TO J D Mitson, Nichol-Young Foundation, Messrs Birketts, 24–26 Museum Street, Ipswich, Suffolk IP1 1HZ

CC NO 259994   **ESTABLISHED** 1969

■ The Joseph Nickerson Charitable Foundation

WHAT IS FUNDED Mainly to support or engage in charitable purposes which are of primary benefit to the old County of Lincolnshire parts of Lindsey, agriculture, conservation and ecology

WHO CAN BENEFIT Applications should only be made if in accordance with What is Funded and only if exceptionally meritorious. There are no restrictions on the age; professional and economic group; family situation; religion and culture; and social circumstances of; or disease or medical condition suffered by, the beneficiaries

WHERE FUNDING CAN BE GIVEN Mainly Lincolnshire
TYPE OF GRANT The Trustees will normally decide which grants to make themselves
FINANCES *Year* 1997 *Income* £35,923 *Grants* £21,969
TRUSTEES M S Edmundson, M Kerrigan, P R C Braithwaite, Lady Nickerson
HOW TO APPLY To the address under Who To Apply To
WHO TO APPLY TO Mrs L E Hodges, The Joseph Nickerson Charitable Foundation, Villa Office, Rothwell, Market Rasen, Lincolnshire LN7 6BJ *Tel* 01472 371371 *Fax* 01472 371545
CC NO 276429   ESTABLISHED 1978

■ Bill and Margaret Nicol Charitable Trust

WHAT IS FUNDED General charitable purposes
WHO CAN BENEFIT Registered charities and individuals. There are no restrictions on the age; professional and economic group; family situation; religion and culture; and social circumstances of; or disease or medical condition suffered by, the beneficiaries
WHERE FUNDING CAN BE GIVEN UK
WHO TO APPLY TO D J C MacRobert, Messrs MacRoberts, 152 Bath Street, Glasgow G2 4TB
SC NO SCO 07516

■ The Laurie Nidditch Foundation

WHAT IS FUNDED Advancement of medical and surgical studies and research, homes for the aged, blind and orphans, education and religious learning. Only applications from registered charities considered
WHAT IS NOT FUNDED Time charity
WHO CAN BENEFIT Registered charities benefiting: children; young adults and the aged; medical professionals; research workers; musicians; students; the blind; and orphans. There is no restriction on the religion or culture of the beneficiaries
WHERE FUNDING CAN BE GIVEN UK
TYPE OF GRANT One-off
SAMPLE GRANTS £13,000 to British Friends Israel Free Loan Association; £5,000 to British Aid Committee Jewish Blind in Israel; £3,750 to Shalom Hartman Educational Institute, Jerusalem; £1,800 to Shaare Zedek Hospital, Jerusalem; £1,350 to United Synagogue
FINANCES *Year* 1997 *Income* £19,154 *Grants* £29,960
TRUSTEES Dr J Saper, Mrs S Saper, K C Keller
WHO TO APPLY TO K Keller, The Laurie Nidditch Foundation, 23 Allum Lane, Elstree, Hertfordshire WD6 3NE
CC NO 209668   ESTABLISHED 1960

■ The Night Asylum Fund

WHAT IS FUNDED Grants are given to organisations which work to preserve the family unit and to prevent delinquency, homelessness and vagrancy among young people
WHAT IS NOT FUNDED No grants to individuals
WHO CAN BENEFIT Organisations benefiting young people, homeless people, and parents and children
WHERE FUNDING CAN BE GIVEN Glasgow
FINANCES *Year* 1996 *Income* £20,000 *Grants* £20,000

HOW TO APPLY Applications should be made in writing to the address below
WHO TO APPLY TO James Smillie, General Secretary, The Night Asylum Fund, The City of Glasgow Society of Social Service, 30 George Square, Glasgow G2 1EG
SC NO SCO 07127   ESTABLISHED 1874

■ The Nikeno Trust

WHAT IS FUNDED General charitable purposes in East Sussex, medical research for skin and facial/body disfigurement. Some children's educational projects. Funding may be given to charities working in the fields of church buildings, nature reserves, woodlands, wildlife parks and sanctuaries and various community facilities
WHO CAN BENEFIT Individuals and organisations benefiting people of all ages with head and other injuries and dermatological conditions.
WHERE FUNDING CAN BE GIVEN Wadhurst and surrounding area in East Sussex
TYPE OF GRANT One-off, core costs and research will be considered. Funding may be given for up to two years
RANGE OF GRANTS £500–£30,000
SAMPLE GRANTS £30,000 to Changing Faces for research into facial disfigurement
FINANCES *Year* 1996 *Income* £19,000 *Grants* £138,430
TRUSTEES A L K Koerner, E L Rausing, M M E Rausing, S M E Rausing
HOW TO APPLY By letter to the Administrator
WHO TO APPLY TO Ms J Major, Administrator, The Nikeno Trust, 132 Sloane Street, London SW1X 9AR *Tel* 0171-259 9466
CC NO 1043967   ESTABLISHED 1995

■ Nilgiris Trust

WHAT IS FUNDED Advancement of the Christian religion
WHO CAN BENEFIT Children; young adults; older people and Christians
WHERE FUNDING CAN BE GIVEN UK and overseas
TYPE OF GRANT One-off and recurrent grants
RANGE OF GRANTS Grants of £1,000 or less
FINANCES *Year* 1997 *Income* £24,161 *Grants* £24,781
TRUSTEES K F Morgan, G Morgan
HOW TO APPLY **This Trust states that it does not respond to unsolicited applications**
WHO TO APPLY TO K F Morgan, Nilgiris Trust, The Dell, Hurst Lane, Egham, Surrey TW20 8QJ *Tel* 01784 465500 *Fax* 01344 844436
CC NO 1019010   ESTABLISHED 1975

■ The Lars-Ake Nilsson Scholarship Fund

WHAT IS FUNDED Advancement of education of the public
WHO CAN BENEFIT Children, young adults, students, teachers and governesses
WHERE FUNDING CAN BE GIVEN UK and overseas
WHO TO APPLY TO The Lars-Ake Nilsson Scholarship Fund, Swedish Chamber of Commerce, 73 Welbeck Street, London W1M 7HA
CC NO 1060165   ESTABLISHED 1997

■ Ninesquare Charitable Trust

This trust did not respond to CAF's request to amend its entry and, by 30 June 1998, CAF's researchers did not find financial records for later than 1995 on its file at the Charity Commission. Trusts are legally required to submit annual accounts to the Charity Commission under section 42 of the Charities Act 1993

WHAT IS FUNDED General charitable purposes
WHO CAN BENEFIT There are no restrictions on the age; professional and economic group; family situation; religion and culture; and social circumstances of; or disease or medical condition suffered by, the beneficiaries
WHERE FUNDING CAN BE GIVEN UK
TRUSTEES A T Clothier, J C Clothier, G O Edwards
WHO TO APPLY TO Ninesquare Charitable Trust, KPMG, Trustees Accountants, Richmond Park House, 15 Pembroke Road, Clifton BS8 3BG
CC NO 1048447   **ESTABLISHED** 1995

■ The 1970 Trust

WHAT IS FUNDED General charitable purposes. Grants have been awarded to organisations which support women and children and to a university
WHAT IS NOT FUNDED No grants to individuals
WHO CAN BENEFIT There are no restrictions on the age; professional and economic group; family situation; religion and culture; and social circumstances of; or disease or medical condition suffered by, the beneficiaries
WHERE FUNDING CAN BE GIVEN UK with an interest in Scotland
TRUSTEES David Rennie
PUBLICATIONS Accounts are available from the Trust
HOW TO APPLY Applications should be made in writing to the address below
WHO TO APPLY TO David Rennie, The 1970 Trust, 12 St Catherine Street, Cupar, Fife KY15 4HN
SC NO SCO 08788

■ Nineveh Charitable Trust

WHAT IS FUNDED To advance education in fields other than social science, arts and related subjects. Owing to a large expenditure of capital in educational fields, the education aspect of the Trust is in eclipse other than for grants already on foot. Once the capital has been recouped the intention is to reconsider our primary aims (apart from the mental health funds which are committed indefinitely)
WHAT IS NOT FUNDED Applicants must make their own appeal and show some special circumstance to distinguish them from the routine ones. Hard options are preferred
WHO CAN BENEFIT Individuals and organisations benefiting: students studying certain disciplines, and those suffering from mental illness
WHERE FUNDING CAN BE GIVEN UK, especially Scotland
TYPE OF GRANT Predominantly by an annual grant by standing order
SAMPLE GRANTS £20,063 to Lothian Health Board for eating disorder clinic at the Royal Edinburgh Hospital
FINANCES *Year* 1997 *Income* £42,166
Grants £50,853
TRUSTEES Mrs M F James (Chairman), Prof T E James, Dr M F James, PhD, Robert G H Lewis, John MacGregor
HOW TO APPLY Please send stamped addressed envelope

WHO TO APPLY TO Professor T E James, Nineveh Charitable Trust, Little Nineveh, Benenden, Cranbrook, Kent TN17 4LG
CC NO 256025   **ESTABLISHED** 1968

■ The Noel Buxton Trust

WHAT IS FUNDED Welfare of disadvantaged families; prevention of crime, especially among young people; the rehabilitation of prisoners and the welfare of their families; education and development in Eastern and Southern Africa
WHAT IS NOT FUNDED Grants are not made for: academic research; animals; the arts; buildings; counselling; drugs and alcohol work; the elderly; the environment; expeditions (eg Operation Raleigh); exchanges; visits; to individuals for educational or any other purposes; human rights; anything medical or connected with mental or physical illness or handicap for adults or children; peace and disarmament; race relations; youth; anywhere abroad except East, Central and Southern Africa
WHO CAN BENEFIT Payment can only be made through a registered charity. Grants are not made to large popular national charities or in response to general appeals. Smaller local bodies and less popular causes are preferred benefiting: young adults; older people; at risk groups; those disadvantaged by poverty; ex-offenders and those at risk of offending; and students
WHERE FUNDING CAN BE GIVEN UK and Eastern and Southern Africa
TYPE OF GRANT One-off or recurrent. Not for buildings or salaries
RANGE OF GRANTS £50–£4,000
FINANCES *Year* 1997 *Income* £86,193
Grants £107,645
TRUSTEES Richenda Wallace (Chairman), David Birmingham, Paul Buxton, Simon Buxton, Angelica Mitchell, Joyce Morton, Jon Snow, Jo Tunnard
PUBLICATIONS Annual list of grants made and guidelines on applications; Annual Report
HOW TO APPLY At any time; no application form; applications are not acknowledged but decision is communicated as soon as possible. To reduce administrative costs and maximise funds available for grant-making, no replies are sent to unsuccessful applicants
WHO TO APPLY TO Margaret Beard, Secretary, The Noel Buxton Trust, 28 Russell Square, London WC1B 5DS
CC NO 220881   **ESTABLISHED** 1919

■ The Noon Foundation

WHAT IS FUNDED General charitable purposes, especially education, poverty, alleviation of racial discrimination, treatment of the sick and infirm
WHO CAN BENEFIT Children, young adults and those disadvantaged by poverty. There are no restrictions on the religion and culture of, or disease or medical condition suffered by, the beneficiaries
WHERE FUNDING CAN BE GIVEN UK
TRUSTEES Z Harnal, J J Mehta, G K Noon, Z Sekhon
WHO TO APPLY TO J J Mehta, Trustee, The Noon Foundation, Mehta and Tengra, 4 Wellington Terrace, Bayswater Road, London W2 4LW
CC NO 1053654   **ESTABLISHED** 1996

■ Norfolk Churches Trust Ltd

WHAT IS FUNDED (a) For the advancement of religion to preserve, repair, maintain, improve, beautify and reconstruct churches or chapels of any Christian denomination in the County of Norfolk or Diocese of Norwich, and the monuments, fittings, fixtures, stained glass, furniture, ornaments and chattels in such churches and chapels; and the churchyards belonging to such churches.
(b) Disused or redundant churches or chapels of historic interest or architectural importance. Priority given to churches still in use as such

WHAT IS NOT FUNDED No grants for heating, interior decoration, organs, or individuals

WHO CAN BENEFIT Churches and places of worship with particular regard to country churches still in the parochial system and needing help. beneficiaries include: Baptists, Christians, Church of England, evangelists, Methodists, Quakers, Unitarians and Roman Catholics

WHERE FUNDING CAN BE GIVEN County of Norfolk and Diocese of Norwich

TYPE OF GRANT Buildings and feasibility studies

SAMPLE GRANTS All the following grants were to Norfolk churches for essential structural repairs:; £6,000 to St Peter's Church, Guestwick; £6,000 to St Mary and St Botolph's Church, Hevingham; £5,500 to St Andrew's Church, Longham; £5,000 to Our Lady and St Margaret's Church, Calthorpe; £5,000 to St Peter's Church, Clippesby; £5,000 to St Peter's Church, Crostwick; £5,000 to St Andrew's Church, Kilverstone; £5,000 to St Margaret's Church, Paston; £5,000 to All Saints' Church, Sharrington; £5,000 to All Saints' Church, Shouldham

FINANCES *Year* 1996–97 *Income* £245,568 *Grants* £161,150

TRUSTEES Council of Management (limit 40): Lady Harrod, OBE (President), R Butler-Stoney, OBE (Vice-President), P de Bunsen (Chair), Mrs T Courtauld (Vice-Chair), P Light (Hon Treasurer)

PUBLICATIONS *The Brasses of Norfolk Churches* by Roger Greenwood and Malcolm Norris. *Sculptured Monuments in Norfolk Churches* by Noel Spencer, ARCA. *Occasional Papers on the Rural Church*, Annual Report

NOTES The Trust is lessee for 99 years of the following redundant Churches: Barmer All Saints, Cockthorpe All Saints, Snetterton All Saints, Dunton St Mary, Illington St Andrew, Hargham All Saints, West Rudham St Peter, Bagthorpe St Mary, Morton-on-the-Hill St Margaret, Rackheath All Saints, West Bilney St Cecilia, for use as a shrine, monument and Christian community purposes

HOW TO APPLY Initial telephone call to The Secretary to discuss the situation and request for application form. Up to date financial situation will be required

WHO TO APPLY TO Malcolm Fisher, Secretary, Norfolk Churches Trust Ltd, 9 The Old Church, St Matthews Road, Norwich NR1 1SP *Tel* 01603 767576 *Fax* 01603 868424

CC NO 271176   **ESTABLISHED** 1976

■ Lavinia Norfolk's Family Charitable Trust

WHAT IS FUNDED General charitable purposes. Preference is given to charities of which the Trustees have special interest, knowledge or association. The funds are fully allocated or committed

WHAT IS NOT FUNDED Grant made only to registered charities. No grants to individuals

WHO CAN BENEFIT Registered charities active in West Sussex. There are no restrictions on the age; professional and economic group; family situation; religion and culture; and social circumstances of; or disease or medical condition suffered by, the beneficiaries

WHERE FUNDING CAN BE GIVEN West Sussex

FINANCES *Year* 1997 *Income* £25,000 *Grants* £25,000

TRUSTEES Lady Sarah Clutton, Lady Mary Mumford

NOTES Formed in 1994 upon amalgamation of Lavinia Duchess of Norfolk's Charitable Trust and the MFH and SFH Charitable Trusts

WHO TO APPLY TO Lady Sarah Clutton, Lavinia Norfolk's Family Charitable Trust, The Dover House, Poling, Arundel, West Sussex BN18 9PX

CC NO 232927   **ESTABLISHED** 1994

■ The Educational Foundation of Alderman John Norman

WHAT IS FUNDED The Trust primarily supports the education of the descendants of Alderman Norman, but also supports young people and local schools and educational establishments in the area

WHO CAN BENEFIT Individuals and organisations benefiting children, young adults and students

WHERE FUNDING CAN BE GIVEN Norwich and Old Catton

RANGE OF GRANTS £500–£11,000

SAMPLE GRANTS £11,000 to the Norfolk Heritage Fleet Trust; £5,000 to Norwich Cathedral Choir Endowment Fund; £5,000 to Quidenham Children's Hospice; £4,730 to Norfolk and Norwich Association for the Blind; £4,000 to the 44th Norwich First Old Catton Scouts; £3,500 to the Education Welfare Service Holiday Fund; £3,000 to Norwich local SPLASH; £2,500 to John Innes Centre; £2,000 to Pilgrims Way; £1,500 to Community Music East

FINANCES *Year* 1997 *Income* £230,041

TRUSTEES G Bennett, Lord Blake, Rev J Boston, C D Brown, G H Drake, Dr W Roy, C I H Mawson, FCA, Rev Canon M Smith

NOTES 491 descendants of Alderman Norman received a total of £135,234. 10 Old Catton residents received £1,791. 20 exhibitions received £7,750. Special Awards totalled £57,591 as shown under Sample Grants

HOW TO APPLY To the address under Who To Apply To in writing. The Trustees meet to consider applications at the end of May and in early September

WHO TO APPLY TO Peter Harbord, Clerk, The Educational Foundation of Alderman John Norman, Old Bank of England Court, Queen Street, Norwich, Norfolk NR2 4TA

CC NO 313105   **ESTABLISHED** 1962

■ The Norman Family Charitable Trust

WHAT IS FUNDED Not to make grants to individuals but to support the relief of suffering and the provision of a better way of life for those needing help (both humans and animals). Also to support the Boy Scouts, Girl Guides and other associations for the benefit of young people. Grants are only made to assist the South West of England with preference given to Devon, Cornwall and Somerset. Charities working in the fields of: residential facilities and services; information technology and computers;

voluntary organisations; social care professional bodies; crafts; and health will be considered. Support may also be given to special needs education, research institutes, medical research and various community facilities and services

WHAT IS NOT FUNDED No support will be given to projects involving experiments on live animals or the maintenance of churches, ancient monuments, etc or to overseas projects. No grants to individuals

WHO CAN BENEFIT Organisations benefiting: those in care, fostered and adopted; one parent families; at risk groups; carers; ex-offenders and those at risk of offending; homeless people; and victims of crime, abuse and domestic violence. Support may be given to ex-service and service people, seafarers and fishermen; students and volunteers. There are no restrictions on the age of the beneficiaries and people suffering from many different diseases and medical conditions will be considered

WHERE FUNDING CAN BE GIVEN Devon, Cornwall and Somerset

TYPE OF GRANT One-off, interest free loans. project, research and start-up costs will be considered. Funding may be given for up to one year

RANGE OF GRANTS £250–£10,000

SAMPLE GRANTS £10,000 to Dr Hadwen Trust for research; £10,000 to Budleigh Salterton Health Centre Charity towards building a new health centre; £7,000 to Humane Research Trust towards research; £5,000 to Bristol Royal Infirmary for magnetic scanner appeal; £5,000 to Bristol Hospital for Sick Children for premature baby unit; £5,000 to Exeter Hospice Endowment Trust; £4,000 to Celia Hammond Trust for animal welfare; £3,000 to Arthritis Care; £3,000 to Community Action Trust Crimestoppers; £2,000 to Children's Hospice South West

FINANCES *Year* 1997 *Income* £252,979
Grants £215,000

TRUSTEES W K Norman, R J Dawe, Mrs M H Evans, M B Saunders, Mrs N J Webb

HOW TO APPLY In writing to the address below stating the registration number of the applicant with the Charity Commissioners. No initial telephone calls are welcome. There is an application form available. Sae required

WHO TO APPLY TO W K Norman, The Norman Family Charitable Trust, Rosemerrin, 5 Coastguard Road, Budleigh Salterton, Devon EX9 6NU
Tel 01395 445177

CC NO 277616   **ESTABLISHED** 1979

■ The Norman Trust

WHAT IS FUNDED To benefit children, human rights and the environment

WHO CAN BENEFIT Large national charities working for the international rights of the individual, and organisations benefiting children

WHERE FUNDING CAN BE GIVEN UK and overseas

TYPE OF GRANT Range of grants of £1,000 or more

FINANCES *Year* 1995 *Income* £189,201
Grants £37,537

TRUSTEES T P A Norman, Mrs E A Norman, K C Barlow, FCA

WHO TO APPLY TO T Norman, The Norman Trust, 62 Gloucester Crescent, London NW1 7EG

CC NO 327288   **ESTABLISHED** 1986

■ The Duncan Norman Trust Fund

WHAT IS FUNDED General charitable purposes. Grants are made only to charities known to the Trustees and unsolicited applications are therefore not considered

WHAT IS NOT FUNDED No grants to individuals

WHO CAN BENEFIT There are no restrictions on the age; professional and economic group; family situation; religion and culture; and social circumstances of; or disease or medical condition suffered by, the beneficiaries

WHERE FUNDING CAN BE GIVEN UK

FINANCES *Year* 1997 *Income* £50,961
Grants £75,163

TRUSTEES J A H Norman, R K Asser, Mrs V S Hilton, Mrs C E Lazar, Liverpool Council of Social Service (Inc)

HOW TO APPLY **This Trust states that it does not respond to unsolicited applications**

WHO TO APPLY TO The Duncan Norman Trust Fund, Liverpool Council of Social Service (Inc), 14 Castle Street, Liverpool L2 ONJ

CC NO 250434   **ESTABLISHED** 1996

■ The North Eastern Prison After Care Society (otherwise known as NEPACS)

WHAT IS FUNDED Organisations that work with former prisoners, individuals who have previously suffered a legal restriction on their liberty. To relieve poverty and advance education and training of such persons and their families. To further the study of and research into the prevention of crime and delinquency

WHO CAN BENEFIT Organisations benefiting ex-offenders and those at risk of offending; young people

WHERE FUNDING CAN BE GIVEN Cleveland, Durham, Northumberland, North Yorkshire, Tyne and Wear

TYPE OF GRANT Capital

FINANCES *Year* 1997 *Income* £48,172
Grants £7,965

NOTES Grants made in 1997 were for material goods such as beds and bedding, clothing and shoes, tools, travel, etc. Also the cost of arranging a conference in Durham on 'The Child and the Prison' concerning the effects on children of parents' absence through imprisonment

HOW TO APPLY To the address under Who To Apply To in writing

WHO TO APPLY TO Mrs R Cranfield, Secreatry, The North Eastern Prison After Care Society, 22 Old Elvet, Durham DH1 3HW

CC NO 225175   **ESTABLISHED** 1963

■ North London Charities Limited

This trust did not respond to CAF's request to amend its entry and, by 30 June 1998, CAF's researchers did not find financial records for later than 1995 on its file at the Charity Commission. Trusts are legally required to submit annual accounts to the Charity Commission under section 42 of the Charities Act 1993

WHAT IS FUNDED General charitable purposes

WHO CAN BENEFIT There are no restrictions on the age; professional and economic group; family situation; religion and culture; and social circumstances of; or disease or medical condition suffered by, the beneficiaries

WHERE FUNDING CAN BE GIVEN North London

TRUSTEES H Fieldman, S Fieldman

HOW TO APPLY To the address below in writing

WHO TO APPLY TO H Fieldman, North London Charities Limited, 23 Overlea Road, Springfield Park, London E5 9BG
CC NO 312740   ESTABLISHED 1964

■ North London Islamic Association Trust

WHAT IS FUNDED The advancement of religion according to the tenets and teaching of Islam and the relief of poverty, sickness and distress, in particular: (a) providing and maintaining premises in or near the Finchley area for Muslims for worship, to provide facilities for children's religious education; (b) teaching and educating young members of the Muslim community the Muslim religion; (c) providing transport for handicapped children attending classes; and (d) providing relief to persons in conditions of need, hardship or distress as a result of local, national or international disaster
WHO CAN BENEFIT To benefit: children and young adults; Muslims; disabled people; those disadvantaged by poverty or victims of famine, and man-made or natural disasters. There is no restriction on the disease or medical condition suffered by the beneficiaries
WHERE FUNDING CAN BE GIVEN Finchley area
FINANCES Year 1997 Income £35,157
    Grants £18,810
TRUSTEES Y K Oguz, F Kaldi
HOW TO APPLY The Trustees may grant relief to such persons through the agency of other charities
WHO TO APPLY TO Y K Oguz, North London Islamic Association Trust, 90 Evelyn Court, Amhurst Road, London E8 2BG
CC NO 1037896   ESTABLISHED 1994

■ North West Arts Board

WHAT IS FUNDED Priorities include maximising access to all artforms throughout the region and encouraging creative and innovative work. The Board works in partnerships to increase the resources in the region's arts economy. Training for community and personal development and training for work may be considered. Publishing and printing may also be funded
WHAT IS NOT FUNDED No grants to profit-making organisations
WHO CAN BENEFIT Arts organisations, groups and individuals who are arts practitioners or wish to promote arts events in the North West of England
WHERE FUNDING CAN BE GIVEN Cheshire, Lancashire, Greater Manchester and Merseyside
TYPE OF GRANT Core costs, feasibility studies, one-off, project, research, recurring costs, running costs and start-up costs will be considered
SAMPLE GRANTS All the following grants were revenue support for core activities:; £1,363,250 to Royal Exchange Theatre Company, Manchester; £430,000 to Liverpool Playhouse Theatre; £425,100 to Manchester Young People's Theatre (Contact Theatre); £255,600 to Bolton Octagon Theatre; £240,550 to Cornerhouse, Manchester (Art Gallery/Cinema); £224,400 to Oldham Coliseum Theatre; £210,000 to New Everyman Theatre, Liverpool; £202,500 to NIA Centre, Manchester (Black Arts Centre); £173,850 to Dukes Playhouse, Lancaster; £148,800 to Chester Gateway Theatre
FINANCES Year 1996–97 Income £9,612,157
    Grants £8,241,405
TRUSTEES The Board

PUBLICATIONS Annual Report and various other publications
NOTES Only writers bursaries are available to students
HOW TO APPLY By application form, timings vary according to artform. Contact Information Unit for details
WHO TO APPLY TO Chief Executive, North West Arts Board, Manchester House, 22 Bridge Street, Manchester M3 3AB *Tel* 0161-834 6644 *Fax* 0161-834 6969 *Minicom* 0161-834 9131 *E-mail* nwarts-info@mcr1.poptel.org.uk
CC NO 251558   ESTABLISHED 1966

■ North West Cancer Research Fund (embodying Friends of Liverpool Radium Institute)

WHAT IS FUNDED Fundamental cancer research including cost of associated equipment
WHAT IS NOT FUNDED No grants made outside North West area. No grants for building projects
WHO CAN BENEFIT All cancer research approved by and under the direction of the University of Liverpool Cancer Research Committee. Work must be for the eventual benefit of cancer sufferers
WHERE FUNDING CAN BE GIVEN Merseyside, North Wales, Cheshire, North Shropshire, Lancashire, Cumbria and the Isle of Man
TYPE OF GRANT Project, research, running costs, salaries and start-up costs. Usually for three to five year periods subject to annual review
SAMPLE GRANTS The following grants were given for fundamental cancer research projects:; £30,000 to researchers at University of Liverpool; £30,000 to researchers at Liverpool John Moores University; £30,000 to researchers at University of Lancaster; £30,000 to researchers at University of Wales, Bangor
FINANCES Year 1997 Income £675,227
    Grants £864,500
TRUSTEES M S Potts, FCA, P F Sutcliffe, P H Kenney, J C Lewys-Lloyd, FCA
PUBLICATIONS Annual Report. Publicity leaflet. Donation leaflet
HOW TO APPLY Telephone the Secretary to obtain an application form and guidelines for the awarding of grants. The Committee meets quarterly. Deadlines for applications will be advised
WHO TO APPLY TO Miss Lorraine Wells, Secretary, North West Cancer Research Fund, The University of Liverpool, Cancer Research Committee, Faculty of Medicine, Duncan Building, Liverpool L69 3BX
CC NO 223598   ESTABLISHED 1948

■ North West Media Charitable Trust Limited

WHAT IS FUNDED General charitable purposes, in particular, the relief of poverty, hardship and distress, the relief of the disabled (including the mentally handicapped); the advancement of education (encouragement of the arts) and research; the provision of facilities for recreation and leisure-time for the benefit of the public
WHAT IS NOT FUNDED Proposals from individuals; proposals for projects abroad; projects that do not fall principally within GTV/Border regions; other categories the Board shall determine
WHO CAN BENEFIT Children and young adults who are homeless; research; mentally or terminally ill; disabled or in need of health care. Research workers and students are also considered

Does the trust you have chosen match your needs? Haphazard applications waste postage and time

457

WHERE FUNDING CAN BE GIVEN Granada and Border TV Regions. This is the North West, including Dumfries and Galloway and Isle of Man

TYPE OF GRANT Capital and/or revenue

RANGE OF GRANTS A ceiling on the cost of projects limits any individual project to £1,000,000

TRUSTEES Lord Thomas of Macclesfield, R Mcloughlin, M Davis, J Hartley, N Robinson, J Macnaught, D Shearer, S Jennings, J Kennedy, J Marsion, S Ingham, D Clark, R Lancaster, R Parry, W Martin, A Benzie

NOTES (a) It is anticipated that the Trust will have a limited life. The Board expects to make its final grants in Spring 1999 (b) For precise details of the legal position grant seekers should examine the Memorandum and Articles of Association of the Company

HOW TO APPLY Initial telephone calls are not welcome. Guidelines are available. An sae would be appriciated

WHO TO APPLY TO Mrs A Weisberg, Charity Coordinator, North West Media Charitable Trust Limited, Granada Television, Quay Street, Manchester M60 9EA *Tel* 0161-832 7211 ext 2446

CC NO 1068308   **ESTABLISHED** 1998

■ Northampton Christadelphian Ecclesia

This trust did not respond to CAF's request to amend its entry and, by 30 June 1998, CAF's researchers did not find financial records for later than 1995 on its file at the Charity Commission. Trusts are legally required to submit annual accounts to the Charity Commission under section 42 of the Charities Act 1993

WHAT IS FUNDED The advancement of the Christadelphian faith

WHO CAN BENEFIT Individuals and general public who are members of the Christadelphian faith

WHERE FUNDING CAN BE GIVEN UK

TRUSTEES P Ormiston, D M Pearce, D S Hague

WHO TO APPLY TO P L Ormiston, Northampton Christadelphian Ecclesia, 46 The Avenue, Cliftonville, Northampton NN1 5BT *Tel* 01604 20100

CC NO 264320   **ESTABLISHED** 1968

■ Northampton Municipal Church Charities

WHAT IS FUNDED The elderly

WHO CAN BENEFIT No grants to individuals

WHERE FUNDING CAN BE GIVEN Northampton

FINANCES *Year* 1994–95 *Income* £96,429 *Grants* £14,050

NOTES £2,249 was given in Christmas vouchers. Grants have not been made to organisations in recent years, although the Trust is still able to do so

HOW TO APPLY To the address under Who To Apply To in writing

WHO TO APPLY TO The Clerk, Northampton Municipal Church Charities, Wilson Browne, 60 Gold Street, Northampton NN1 1RS

CC NO 259593   **ESTABLISHED** 1969

■ The Northampton Queen's Institute Relief in Sickness Fund

WHAT IS FUNDED Youth groups, welfare organisations, hospitals and health organisations

WHO CAN BENEFIT Organisations benefiting: children and young adults; at risk groups; those disadvantaged by poverty and socially isolated people. There is no restriction on the disease or medical condition suffered by the beneficiaries

WHERE FUNDING CAN BE GIVEN Northampton

RANGE OF GRANTS £1,000–£5,000

SAMPLE GRANTS £5,000 to Three Shires Hospital; £4,500 to Industrial Rehabilitation Workshops; £3,000 to St John Ambulance; £3,000 to British Red Cross; £3,000 to Bethany Homestead; £3,000 to CCHA Extra Care; £3,000 to Northamptonshire Association for the Blind; £2,500 to Nazareth House; £1,500 to Northampton PHAB; £1,500 to Northamptonshire Association of Youth Clubs

FINANCES *Year* 1996 *Income* £33,667 *Grants* £35,000

HOW TO APPLY To the address under Who To Apply To in writing

WHO TO APPLY TO Mrs S M Peet, Clerk and Solicitor, The Northampton Queen's Institute Relief in Sickness Fund, c/o Shoesmith & Harrison, The Lakes, Bedford Road, Northampton NN4 7SH

CC NO 208583   **ESTABLISHED** 1971

■ Earl of Northampton's Charity

WHAT IS FUNDED Care for the elderly and disabled in homes and other sheltered housing schemes; pensions where recipient is recommended by statutory authorities

WHO CAN BENEFIT Individuals and housing organisations benefiting elderly people, disabled people and those disadvantaged by poverty

WHERE FUNDING CAN BE GIVEN Greater London

SAMPLE GRANTS £200,000 to Mercers' Company Housing Association Ltd for the development of sheltered housing at Sans Walk; £18,625 to Mercers' Charitable Foundation for sheltered housing at Essex Road; £11,250 for 24 out pensions; £2,500 to Trinity Hospital, Castle Rising; £2,500 to Trinity Hospital, Clun; £2,500 to Lady Micos Almshouses; £1,000 to Jubilee Almshouses, Greenwich

FINANCES *Year* 1994–95 *Income* £454,000 *Grants* £238,375

TRUSTEES Mercer's Company

HOW TO APPLY To the address under Who To Apply To in writing

WHO TO APPLY TO H W Truelove, Education/Charities Adminsitrator, Earl of Northampton's Charity, Mercer's Company, Mercer's Hall, Ironmonger Lane, London EC2V 8HE

CC NO 210291   **ESTABLISHED** 1964

■ Northamptonshire Childminding Association

WHAT IS FUNDED To promote the provision of facilities for the daily care, recreation and education of children under the age of eight and to promote the observance of good standards of childminding by the parents of such children and all persons and organisations providing such facilities. To advance the education and training of childminders and other persons and organisations providing day care facilities for children under the age of eight and to conduct research into all aspects of the care, recreation and education of such children, and publish the useful results of such research

WHO CAN BENEFIT Schools and individuals. Children under the age of eight, childminders and research workers

WHERE FUNDING CAN BE GIVEN Northamptonshire, Northampton, Corby, Wellingborough, Daventry, Towcester, Kettering, Oundle and Rushden

TYPE OF GRANT Recurring costs and research

SAMPLE GRANTS £375 to 15 local groups as seasonal/Christmas grants of £25; £200 to four support groups as start-up grants of £50

FINANCES *Year* 1997–98 *Income* £16,311
Grants £725

TRUSTEES M A Patterson, E F Bell, Mrs J E Dougill

WHO TO APPLY TO Mrs J Dougill, Northamptonshire Childminding Association, 4 Hawkstone Close, Duston, Northampton NN5 6RZ

CC NO 1047565　　**ESTABLISHED** 1991

■ Northamptonshire Historic Churches Trust

WHAT IS FUNDED The preservation, improvement, repair and restoration of churches and their fixtures and fittings

WHO CAN BENEFIT Northamptonshire churches

WHERE FUNDING CAN BE GIVEN Northamptonshire

RANGE OF GRANTS £250–£1,500

SAMPLE GRANTS £1,500 to St Mary Magdalene, Helmdon; £1,500 to St Peter and St Paul, Preston Capes; £1,500 to St Mary the Virgin, Maidwell; £1,500 to St Andrew's, Harlestone; £1,500 to St James, Paulerspury; £500 to All Saints, Naseby; £500 to St Mary the Virgin, Grafton Regis; £250 to St Andrew's, Collyweston; £250 to All Saints, Wilharston

FINANCES *Year* 1996 *Income* £31,630
Grants £9,000

TRUSTEES B Bailey, Mrs M Bland, Bishop of Brixworth, P W Dunn, P F Haddon, M F Hawkins, Rev Canon W Kentigem-Fox, Mrs B Lancaster, J Liell, Sir J Lowther, Rev P Moseling, Bishop of Peterborough, J S Shuttleworth, J A White

HOW TO APPLY To the address under Who To Apply To in writing

WHO TO APPLY TO J A White, Secretary, Northamptonshire Historic Churches Trust, c/o Hewitson Becke & Shaw, 7 Spencer Parade, Northampton NN1 5AB

CC NO 1021632　　**ESTABLISHED** 1993

■ The Northcott Charity Trust

WHAT IS FUNDED Deserving causes in Hampshire particularly in relation to the disabled and disadvantaged. Grants to past or present pupils of Blundells School, Tiverton for or towards their education

WHAT IS NOT FUNDED Registered charities only. Applications from individuals, including students, are ineligible. No grants made in response to general appeals from national organisations

WHO CAN BENEFIT Registered charities benefiting the disadvantaged and disabled

WHERE FUNDING CAN BE GIVEN Preference to Hampshire

TYPE OF GRANT Usually one-off for a specific project or part of a project. Core funding and/or salaries rarely considered

RANGE OF GRANTS £100–£1,000

SAMPLE GRANTS £1,000 to the Elizabeth Foundation; £500 to Disability Aid Fund for an individual; £500 to the Sue Ryder Foundation for Bordean House; £500 to World Gospel Mission for an individual; £500 to Earl Haig Fund

FINANCES *Year* 1996 *Income* £16,001
Grants £11,600

TRUSTEES Mrs R Sharpe, Sir Alfred Blake, KCVO, F R Northcott, Mrs J F Northcott, Mrs K A Northcott

HOW TO APPLY Trustees meet quarterly. Applications should include clear details of the need the intended project is designed to meet plus an outline budget. Only applications from eligible bodies are acknowledged when further information about the project may be requested

WHO TO APPLY TO Charles Toghill, Trustees Administrator, The Northcott Charity Trust, 8 Landport Terrace, Portsmouth, Hampshire PO1 2QW

CC NO 239754　　**ESTABLISHED** 1963

■ Northcott Devon Foundation

WHAT IS FUNDED To individuals or to families living in Devon who are suffering distress and hardship deriving from disability, illness, injury, bereavement or exceptional disadvantage, in circumstances where such assistance offers long-term benefit. To registered charities operating primarily within Devon, whose objects are broadly in sympathy with those of the Foundation, and who seek to improve the living conditions or life experiences of disabled or disadvantaged people living in Devon. To young people of limited means undertaking philanthropic activity which is not part of a formal education or training programme and who live in Devon

WHAT IS NOT FUNDED Successful applications generally result in the making of a single grant. The Foundation is unable to enter into longer term financial commitments. Assistance will not be given to statutory agencies, including self-governing National Health Service Trusts in the performance of their duties. Assistance will not be given to make good any debts owed to statutory agencies or to financial institutions. Other debts will not formally be considered unless agreement has been reached with the creditors for full and final settlement in a substantially reduced sum

WHO CAN BENEFIT Individuals, families or registered charities benefiting: students; unemployed people; volunteers; at risk groups; carers; disabled people; those disadvantaged by poverty; ex-offenders and those at risk of offending; gays and lesbians; those living in rural areas and socially isolated people; victims of abuse, crime and domestic violence; and victims of famine, man-made or natural disasters and war. There is no restriction on the age; family situation; religion and culture of; or the disease or medical condition suffered by the beneficiaries

WHERE FUNDING CAN BE GIVEN County of Devon

TYPE OF GRANT Usually one-off for a specific purpose or project. Research, capital and buildings will be considered. Core funding not considered

RANGE OF GRANTS £40–£25,000, average grant £300

SAMPLE GRANTS £25,000 to St Loyse; £11,500 to Royal West of England School for the Deaf; £10,000 to St Loyse; £5,000 to Rowcroft hospital; £3,773 to Exeter University; £1,000 to St Dunstans; £1,000 to Raleigh International; £1,000 to Mental health Foundation

FINANCES *Year* 1997 *Income* £247,000
Grants £214,176

TRUSTEES P Burdick, OBE, (Chairman), M Horwood

NOTES Assistance will not be given unless applicants or their sponsors have checked thoroughly that assistance or benefit is not available from the Department of Social Security, or from other public funds

HOW TO APPLY At any time, on the official application form. Trustees meet quarterly

WHO TO APPLY TO G G Folland, Northcott Devon Foundation, 1B Victoria Road, Exmouth, Devon EX8 1DL *Tel* 01395 269204

CC NO 201277   **ESTABLISHED** 1960

■ Northcott Devon Medical Foundation

WHAT IS FUNDED Support of postgraduate, medical research and the improvement of medical practice. Provision of schools, research laboratories, libraries, etc for the promotion of medicine, surgery and other subjects. To provide scholarships and promote research

WHO CAN BENEFIT To benefit academics, medical professionals, research workers and postgraduate students

WHERE FUNDING CAN BE GIVEN Devon

FINANCES *Year* 1998 *Income* £52,416 *Grants* £66,855

TRUSTEES Prof R S M Ling, W G Selley, Prof P P Anthony, Prof C R Kennedy

HOW TO APPLY To the address under Who To Apply To in writing

WHO TO APPLY TO R A Boyd, Secretary, Northcott Devon Medical Foundation, 2 Barnfield Crescent, Exeter EX1 1QT

CC NO 204660   **ESTABLISHED** 1961

■ Northern Arts

WHAT IS FUNDED The Arts including: (a) access; (b) education; (c) audience development; (d) the individual artist; (e) the arts economy; and (f) the value of the arts

WHAT IS NOT FUNDED Students

WHO CAN BENEFIT Any one involved in arts including: actors and entertainment professional; musicians; textile workers and designers; writers and poets; artists; ethnic minority groups; and disabled people

WHERE FUNDING CAN BE GIVEN Cumbria, Northumberland, Durham, Teesside, Tyne and Wear

TYPE OF GRANT One-off and recurring

RANGE OF GRANTS £150–£600,000

SAMPLE GRANTS £664,250 to Northern Stage; £346,960 to Northern Sinfonia; £184,800 to Tyneside Cinema; £179,000 to Welfare State International; £140,000 to Live Theatre; £140,000 to NTC; £100,000 to Northern Gallery for Contemporary Arts; £87,000 to Zone Gallery; £82,000 to Grizedale Society; £80,600 to Sunderland City Council

FINANCES *Year* 1997 *Income* £8,082,034 *Grants* £6,700,650

TRUSTEES The Board of Directors

PUBLICATIONS Annual Review and programme specific newsletters

NOTES A menu of projects and schemes with detailed guidelines exists

HOW TO APPLY Varies from art form to art form. Potential applicants are advised to outline their proposal in writing, including a budget, with reference to relevant scheme criterion

WHO TO APPLY TO The Chief Executive, Northern Arts, 9–10 Osborne Terrace, Jesmond, Newcastle upon Tyne NE2 1NZ *Tel* 0191-281 6334 *Fax* 0191-281 3276 *E-mail* nab@norab.demon.co.uk

CC NO 517711   **ESTABLISHED** 1961

■ Northern Dairies Educational Trust

WHAT IS FUNDED Medicine and health, humanities, general welfare, education, science and environmental resources, provision of hostels, granting of scholarships, assistance to those suffering discrimination

WHAT IS NOT FUNDED No grants to school children

WHO CAN BENEFIT Individuals (especially from Africa) and organisations benefiting: children and young adults; actors and entertainment professionals; musicians; scientists; textile workers and designers; writers and poets. Support may go to at risk groups, those disadvantaged by poverty, homeless and socially isolated people. There is no restriction on the disease or medical condition suffered by the beneficiaries

WHERE FUNDING CAN BE GIVEN UK, with preference to local charities, and overseas, especially Africa

TYPE OF GRANT One-off small grants only

SAMPLE GRANTS £60,849 made in grants to individuals; £9,350 made in grants to institutions

FINANCES *Year* 1997 *Income* £72,879 *Grants* £70,199

TRUSTEES Mrs G S Haskins, Mrs V Gribbin, J A Horsley, J Vint, Mrs F S Harris, M J Gold, Ms S T Gribbin

HOW TO APPLY Students to write in with details and complete application form

WHO TO APPLY TO Mrs F S Harris, Northern Dairies Educational Trust, c/o Northern Foods plc, Beverley House, St Stephens Square, Hull HU1 3XG

CC NO 1039416   **ESTABLISHED** 1958

■ The Northern Rock Foundation

WHAT IS FUNDED Only organisations or projects in the North of the UK. This Foundation will consider funding: infrastructure development; charity or voluntary umbrella bodies; respite accommodation and respite care for carers; community arts and recreation; support and self help groups; hospices; literacy training; care in the community; social counselling; individual rights; and advice centres

WHAT IS NOT FUNDED There are certain organisations, projects and proposals that are excluded from consideration. If you or your project fall into one of these categories please do not apply to the Foundation. Organisations which are not registered charities; charities which trade, have substantial reserves (normally over 75 per cent of annual running costs in unrestricted reserves) or are in serious deficit; national charities which do not have a regional office or other physical representation in the North East and the North; national organisations seeking proportionate expenditure for the North East element of nation-wide projects or provisions; open ended funding agreements; general appeals, sponsorship and marketing appeals; Retrospective grants; endowment funds; replacement of statutory funding; activities primarily the responsibility of central or local government; individuals, including students, and organisations that distribute funds to or purchase equipment for individuals; animal

460

Think carefully about every application. Is it justified?

welfare; mainstream educational activity, schools, universities and colleges; curriculum education or equipment to support it; medical research, hospitals (other than hospices) and medical centres, health care treatments and therapies whether provided by statutory authorities or not; environmental projects which do not accord with the main objectives of the Foundation; buildings, fabric appeals for places of worship, etc, except where explicitly invited under the Guidelines in programme descriptions; improvements to buildings owned by local authorities or other statutory bodies where the remaining life of the lease is less than 10 years; promotion of religion; corporate applications for founder membership of a charity; loans or business finance; expeditions or overseas travel; grant-making bodies seeking, to distribute grants on our behalf; academic research unless commissioned by the Foundation; conferences, seminars and other similar activities unless specifically related to an activity supported by the Foundation or of exceptional significance. The following are unlikely to be supported: minibuses and other vehicles (unless a critical part of a bigger project and even then unlikely); holidays and outings; applications for 100 per cent of cost **unless**: (a) all other avenues have been exhausted and (b) the project is unique, experimental, possibly a model for others and has potential for enormous returns if successful and (c) the proposed activity is time-limited or has a credible exit strategy. Applications for very large sums (over £100,000) unless they are for something demonstrably exceptional, experimental or ground-breaking. We will usually prefer applications from organisations that can clearly show management involvement of beneficiaries

WHO CAN BENEFIT Organisations benefiting parents and children as well as one parent families. There is no restriction on age, and a wide range of social circumstances of; and disease or medical condition suffered by, the beneficiaries

WHERE FUNDING CAN BE GIVEN In practice, the North East of England, North West, Cumbria, Yorkshire and Scotland

TYPE OF GRANT Buildings, capital, core costs, one-off, project, recurring costs, running costs, salaries and start-up costs. Funding is available for more than three years

RANGE OF GRANTS £1,000–£150,000, typical grant £5,000–£60,000

SAMPLE GRANTS £150,000 to Percy Hedley Centre towards specialist teaching and therapy facilities for young people with disabilities; £84,557 to Advocacy in Gateshead towards advocacy service for adults with learning difficulties who reside in Gateshead; £83,330 to special needs activities and play provision in York towards a three year lifeskills and work experience programme for young people with disabilities; £79,287 to Carers Support, Derwentside to fund a project providing respite support to carers of people with palliative care needs and core costs; £75,000 to The Princess Royal Trust for Carers to establish the Trust in Newcastle; £71,237 to Hartlepool Voluntary Development Agency towards development of new and existing carers' service in Hartlepool; £69,000 to Disability North to employ a disability equality trainer/consultant; £67,598 to the Neurofibromatosis Association towards the costs of employing family support worker(s) to give specialist support/care to people with neurofibromatosis; £63,000 to Hartlepool MIND towards the establishment of user-led support and information service in Hartlepool; £60,000 to Euryalus Phab Club towards funding an independent living unit in new premises in Jarrow

FINANCES *Year* 1997 *Income* £2,024,000

TRUSTEES W R Atkinson (Chairman), R H Dickinson, Josephine, Lady Bonfield, L P Finn, P R M Harbottle, The Lord Howick of Glendale, A E Kilburn, J A Logan, Dorothy, Lady Russell, Miss E E Slattery, J P Wainwright

NOTES The NR Foundation is new and developing. Things change quickly. Enquire or check our Website

HOW TO APPLY Application pack available, includes essential application form

WHO TO APPLY TO Grants Manager, The Northern Rock Foundation, 21 Landsdowne Terrace, Gosforth, Newcastle upon Tyne NE3 1HP *Tel* 0191-284 8412
Web Site www.northernrockfoundation.org.uk

CC NO 1063906   **ESTABLISHED** 1997

....

■ The Northmoor Trust

WHAT IS FUNDED The relief of poverty, hardship or distress; children; prison reform; education; youth; disability; the homeless and immigrants aid

WHAT IS NOT FUNDED Only applications from organisations which are known to one or more of the Trustees will be considered. No support will be given to organisations concerned with the arts, religion or medicine

WHO CAN BENEFIT Local, regional and national organisations benefiting: children and young adults; disabled people; those disadvantaged by poverty; homeless people and immigrants

WHERE FUNDING CAN BE GIVEN UK

TYPE OF GRANT Some recurrent

RANGE OF GRANTS £2,000–£20,000

SAMPLE GRANTS £20,000 to Legal Assistance Trust; £10,500 to St Michael's Fellowship; £10,000 to Comeback; £10,000 to MRCF; £10,000 to St John's Wood Terrace Adventure Playground; £7,850 to ATD Fourth World; £6,750 to Kings Cross Homeless Project; £5,100 to Vietnamese Mental Health Project; £5,000 to Hospice of St John and St Elizabeth; £5,000 to Prison Reform Trust

FINANCES *Year* 1997 *Income* £134,121 *Grants* £103,000

TRUSTEES F Bennett, Lord Runciman, Ruth Runciman

HOW TO APPLY To the Secretary at the address under Who To Apply To in writing for consideration by the Trustees in April or May

WHO TO APPLY TO Mrs Hilary Edwards, Secretary, The Northmoor Trust, 44 Clifton Hill, London NW8 0QG
CC NO 256818   **ESTABLISHED** 1968

■ Northumberland Masonic Charitable Trust

WHAT IS FUNDED The relief of such poor and distressed brother masons or their poor and distressed widows and children or for the benefit of such masonic charities or other charitable purposes
WHO CAN BENEFIT Masons who are disadvantaged by poverty, their dependants, and masonic charities
WHERE FUNDING CAN BE GIVEN In practice, Northumberland and UK though Grand Lodge
SAMPLE GRANTS £14,000 to Richard Henry Holmes Masonic Benevolent Fund; £14,000 to Northumberland Masonic Charity Association; £1,000 to Scarborough Court
FINANCES *Year* 1997 *Income* £248,830
Grants £29,000
NOTES The Trust comprises two distinct funds: the Northumberland Masonic Charity Association (NMCA), the 'Festival' appeal fund for holding a festival of charity; and the Bartlett Fund which makes donations to the Richard Henry Holmes Masonic Benevolent Fund and to the Trustees of the Scarborough Court Home, Cramlington, a residential home for the elderly
WHO TO APPLY TO B Taylor, Northumberland Masonic Charitable Trust, Neville Hall, Westgate Road, Newcastle upon Tyne NE1 1SY
CC NO 1031299   **ESTABLISHED** 1993

■ Northumberland Rugby Union Charitable Trust

WHAT IS FUNDED The provision of facilities for the training and playing of Rugby Union for children at school or college
WHAT IS NOT FUNDED No grants to benefit those over the age of 21
WHO CAN BENEFIT Children and young adults under the age of 21
WHERE FUNDING CAN BE GIVEN Newcastle, North Tyneside, Northumberland
TYPE OF GRANT Capital, one-off, recurring costs, running costs and salaries will be considered. Funding may be given for up to three years
RANGE OF GRANTS £50–£5,000
FINANCES *Year* 1997–98 *Income* £61,576
Grants £10,000
TRUSTEES R S Appleby, S W Bainbridge, D F Hamilton, W G Miller
HOW TO APPLY To the address under Who To Apply To in writing
WHO TO APPLY TO D F Hamilton, Trustee, Northumberland Rugby Union Charitable Trust, Woodvale, Wylam, Northumberland NE41 8EP
Tel 01661 852017
CC NO 1001976   **ESTABLISHED** 1991

■ The Northumberland Village Homes Trust

WHAT IS FUNDED Education and training of young people under the age of 18, the relief of poverty and sickness of young people
WHAT IS NOT FUNDED Individual applicants must be supported by a letter from a local authority or registered charity

WHO CAN BENEFIT Individuals and youth organisations benefiting those under 18 years of age who are disadvantaged by poverty. There is no restriction on the disease or medical condition suffered by the beneficiaries
WHERE FUNDING CAN BE GIVEN UK, especially North East England
RANGE OF GRANTS £250–£8,000
SAMPLE GRANTS £8,000 to Children North East; £8,000 to Catholic Care North East; £5,000 to NSPCC, North East Area; £2,000 to Norcare; £2,000 to the Children's Society; £2,000 to Barnardo's North East England; £2,000 to NCH Action for Children; £2,000 to Childline North East; £1,000 to KIND (Kids in Need and Distress); £1,000 to Toc H
FINANCES *Year* 1996 *Income* £65,831
Grants £51,700
TRUSTEES Richard Baron Gisborough, K Hunt, Mrs L I Lawrence, J M O'Neill, Mrs J M Paley, B Porter, Mrs E P Savage, D Welch
HOW TO APPLY To the address under Who To Apply To in writing, stating the amount required and its purpose, the object (if a charity), other funding sources and whether the applicant is an individual, private or registered charity
WHO TO APPLY TO Mrs M Criddle, The Northumberland Village Homes Trust, Savage Solicitors, Bellwood Buildings, 36 Moorsley Street, Newcastle upon Tyne NE1 1DG
CC NO 225429   **ESTABLISHED** 1880

■ The Northumbria Historic Churches Trust

WHAT IS FUNDED The restoration, preservation, repair, maintenance, reconstruction, improvement and beautification of churches, their contents and their churchyards in the area Where Funding Can Be Given
WHAT IS NOT FUNDED No grants for bells, organs, toilets or kitchens
WHO CAN BENEFIT Churches that are at least 100 years old
WHERE FUNDING CAN BE GIVEN The dioceses of Durham and Newcastle
TYPE OF GRANT One-off, feasibility studies and buildings. Funding is for one year or less
RANGE OF GRANTS £250–£5,000
SAMPLE GRANTS £5,000 to Holy Trinity, Berwick for general repairs; £5,000 to St Cuthbert's, Bellingham for the restoration of interior stonework; £3,000 to St Batholomew's, Whittingham for alterations to stonework; £2,500 to St Paul's, Whitley Bay for repairs to roof; £2,500 to St Michael, Sunderland for polycarbonate overglazing and ironwork repairs; £1,682 to St Mary's, Woolsingham for repairs to clock; £1,500 to St Andrew's, Aycliffe for restoration to stonework; £1,500 to St John, Chevington for drainage work; £1,000 to Whitworth Parish Church for repairs to tower; £1,000 to St Mary Magdalene, Whalton for general repairs
FINANCES *Year* 1997–98 *Income* £35,000
Grants £30,000
TRUSTEES Rev N Banks, Rt Hon A Beith, G Bell, Mrs A Berriman, P O R Bridgeman, C Downs, T R F Fenwick, L J Heron, G E R Heslop, Mrs W T Hinkley, Lady Howick, J B Kendall, Dr R A Lomas, Mrs B D Napier, Lady Sarah Nicholson, R R V Nicholson, J H N Porter, Canon J E Ruscoe, Canon C P Unwin, Lord Vinson, Mrs G Walker, C H L Westmacott

PUBLICATIONS *The Northumbria Historic Churches Trust – The First Fifteen Years*
HOW TO APPLY To the address under Who To Apply To in writing asking for an application form and guidelines. Initial telephone calls are welcome
WHO TO APPLY TO Canon J E Ruscoe, Secretary, The Northumbria Historic Churches Trust, The Vicarage, South Hylton, Sunderland SR4 0QB
Tel 0191-534 2325
CC NO 511314   **ESTABLISHED** 1980

■ Northumbria Police Charities Fund

WHAT IS FUNDED General charitable purposes within the Northumbria Police Force Area
WHO CAN BENEFIT There are no restrictions on the age; professional and economic group; family situation; religion and culture; and social circumstances of; or disease or medical condition suffered by, the beneficiaries
WHERE FUNDING CAN BE GIVEN Within the Northumbria Police Force Area
RANGE OF GRANTS £50–£3,492
SAMPLE GRANTS £3,492 to Weston Spirit; £2,650 to an individual for a wheelchair; £2,639 to Priory School, Hexham; £2,572 to Glebe School; £2,000 to High Sheriffs Youth Against Crime Initiative; £1,500 to Hadrian Park Middle School; £1,500 to Welsh School for Conductive Education; £1,330 to Forest and Gardens Ltd; £1,000 to Cowie Children; £1,000 to Wooler County First School
FINANCES *Year* 1997 *Income* £53,417
Grants £43,412
WHO TO APPLY TO Miss M Moody, Northumbria Police Charities Fund, Policy Support Unit, Northumbria Police Headquarters, North Road, Ponteland NE20 0BL
CC NO 1055033   **ESTABLISHED** 1996

■ The Northwood Charitable Trust

WHAT IS FUNDED General charitable purposes at the discretion of the Trustees. Grants have been given to a university and to medical and educational projects
WHO CAN BENEFIT There are no restrictions on the age; professional and economic group; family situation; religion and culture; and social circumstances of; or disease or medical condition suffered by, the beneficiaries
WHERE FUNDING CAN BE GIVEN Dundee and Tayside
FINANCES *Year* 1997 *Income* £1,120,000
Grants £800,000
TRUSTEES Prof A J McDonald, A F Thomson, B H Thomson, D B Thomson
PUBLICATIONS Accounts and an Annual Report are available from the Trust
HOW TO APPLY **This Trust states that it does not respond to unsolicited applications**
WHO TO APPLY TO The Secretary, The Northwood Charitable Trust, 22 Meadowside, Dundee DD1 1LN
SC NO SCO 14487   **ESTABLISHED** 1972

■ The Norton Foundation

WHAT IS FUNDED The Trustees will consider applications from individuals in need and from organisations working with young persons in need – only in their primary area, Where Funding Can Be Given, of Birmingham and the county of Warwick.

This includes: infrastructure, support and development; Christian education; religious ancillary buildings; religious umbrella bodies; community arts and recreation; education and training; and social care and development
WHO CAN BENEFIT Children and young persons in need due to any cause. Organisations which help such young persons
WHERE FUNDING CAN BE GIVEN The UK and in particular the Birmingham area and the county of Warwick
TYPE OF GRANT Grants to individuals for specific needs. Grants to suitable organisations for any capital or revenue purpose. This includes buildings, core costs, one-off, running costs, recurring costs, salaries and start-up costs. Funding is available for up to two years
RANGE OF GRANTS Individuals £20–£500, typical grant £100; organisations £300–£20,000
SAMPLE GRANTS £10,000 to Focus Housing Association for foyer project; £5,000 to South Birmingham Young Homeless Project for accommodation and care for vulnerable young people; £2,000 to Cornerstone for living accommodation for 16–24 year olds; £2,000 to Friendship Project for Children for extension of their activities into Coventry; £2,000 to Trescott Primary School for residential courses for children from deprived homes; £2,000 to United Evangelical Project for work with needy young children in Handsworth and Aston; £2,000 to Warwick and Leamington Young Homeless Project for relief of homeless young people; £1,000 to 610 Community Centre for equipment for use by disadvantaged youngsters; £1,000 to Aston Residential Project for work with young people at risk in Birmingham; £1,000 to Asian Resource Centre for equipment for use by children of Asian women who have suffered from domestic violence
FINANCES *Year* 1998 *Income* £151,000
Grants £132,000
TRUSTEES P S Bird, W M Colacicchi, Mrs E Corney, Mrs S V Henderson, Mrs P Francis, H Antrobus, J R Kendrick, B W Lewis, A Newland, D F Perkins, R H G Suggett
HOW TO APPLY To clerk from whom application forms can be obtained. Applications from individuals dealt with when received. Applications from organisations dealt with in May of each year
WHO TO APPLY TO Mrs Jane M Emms, Clerk to the Trustees, The Norton Foundation, PO Box 040, Kenilworth, Warwickshire CV8 2ZR
CC NO 702638   **ESTABLISHED** 1990

■ Norwich Church of England Young Men's Society

WHAT IS FUNDED To promote the welfare of members spiritually, socially, intellectually and physically and to aid missionary work at home or abroad. No fixed policies. Financial restraints on own activities necessitates mainly local grants. The Trust will consider funding: respite; support to voluntary and community organisations; Christian education and outreach; missionaries and evangelicals; churches, religious ancillary buildings; religious umbrella bodies; respite care and care for carers; hospices; church buildings; schools and colleges; cultural and religious teaching; bursaries and fees, the purchase of books; and community facilities and services
WHAT IS NOT FUNDED No grants to individuals
WHO CAN BENEFIT Mainly organisations benefiting children, young adults, older people, Baptists, Christians, Church of England and Methodists

WHERE FUNDING CAN BE GIVEN Mainly Norfolk, but also overseas

TYPE OF GRANT One-off for buildings, core costs, projects and salaries. All are for one year or less

RANGE OF GRANTS £250–£1,000. Average is £500

FINANCES *Year* 1996 *Income* £137,000
Grants £5,943

TRUSTEES J Pidgen, D Pilch, J Copeman, Rev Canon D Sharp

PUBLICATIONS Annual Report

NOTES Grant restriction to Church allied activities and the like

HOW TO APPLY All applications discussed by General Committee and Finance Committee quarterly. Only successful applications acknowledged

WHO TO APPLY TO C J Free, Norwich Church of England Young Men's Society, 3 Brigg Street, Norwich, Norfolk NR2 1QN

CC NO 206425   **ESTABLISHED** 1847

■ The Norwich Historic Churches Trust Ltd

WHAT IS FUNDED The preservation, repair and maintenance of disused churches of all denominations which have particular architectural or historic value

WHO CAN BENEFIT Churches

WHERE FUNDING CAN BE GIVEN Norwich

FINANCES *Year* 1997 *Income* £103,520
Grants £66,830

TRUSTEES C J Pordham (Chairman), Cllr D C Bradford, D B Colman, Cllr S Curran, K S Dugdale, Mrs A V Fenner, Cllr T Gordon, J W Knight, J H Pogson, Cllr R E N Quinn, K Rowe, Mrs E T A Smallpiece, P Tolley, A C Whitwood

HOW TO APPLY To the address under Who To Apply To in writing

WHO TO APPLY TO C D Bodkin, Secretary, The Norwich Historic Churches Trust Ltd, 14 Old Grove Court, Norwich, Norfolk NR3 3NL *Tel* 01603 405455

CC NO 266686   **ESTABLISHED** 1973

■ Norwich Town Close Estate Charity

WHAT IS FUNDED The Charity is primarily for Freemen of Norwich, in educational, pensions, TV licences, relief in need and Doughty's Hospital Residents' Maintenance categories. Particularly chairties working in the fields of: information technology and computers; publishing and printing; civil society development; community development; combined arts; arts education; health education; historic buildings; memorials and monuments; education and training; and various community facilities

WHO CAN BENEFIT Only Charities based in the area Where Funding Can be Given and carrying out educational activities will be supported. Neighbourhood-based community projects benefiting children, young adults, older people and Freemen of Norwich

WHERE FUNDING CAN BE GIVEN Within a 20 mile radius of the Guildhall of the City of Norwich

TYPE OF GRANT Buildings, capital, one-off and project. Funding for up to one year will be considered

RANGE OF GRANTS Various

SAMPLE GRANTS Grants for educational purposes; £50,000 to Memorial Trust of 2nd Air Division USAAF; £50,000 to Horstead Centre; £50,000 to Norwich School; £50,000 to UEA: Centre of East Anglian Studies; £25,000 to Eaton Vale Scout and Guide Association; £15,000 to Hethersett Old Hall School; £15,000 to Norwich High School-Minerva Appeal; £14,000 to Care for Clare Appeal; £10,000 to Inspire; £6,000 to Quidenham Children's Hospice

FINANCES *Year* 1996–97 *Income* £730,000
Grants £472,000

TRUSTEES M G Quinton (Chairman), N B Q Back, P J Colby, T C Eaton, R E T Gurney, A P Hansell, J S Livock, F G Self, H E Boreham, Mrs R Frostick, Mrs S James, R H Pearson, A R Shaw, Mrs A Brown, D H Pardey, R G Round

HOW TO APPLY In writing to the Clerk for grants to charities, to the Administrator for individual grants. Meetings held in February and August for grants to other organisations, in August for educational grants and February, April, June and October for welfare and pensions

WHO TO APPLY TO Mrs S A Franklin, Administrator, Norwich Town Close Estate Charity, 10 Golden Dog Lane, Magdalen Street, Norwich, Norfolk NR3 1BP *Tel* 01603 621023

REGIONAL OFFICES M T Martin, Clerk, Norwich Town Close Estate Charity, 10 Golden Dog Lane, Magdalen Street, Norwich, Norfolk NR3 1BP *Tel* 01603 621023

CC NO 235678   **ESTABLISHED** 1977

■ Norwood and Newton Settlement

WHAT IS FUNDED New building work in Methodist and other Free Churches. Smaller national charities in which the Settlor expressed a particular interest and other charitable causes which commend themselves to the Trustees. Charities working in the fields of Christian outreach, churches and religious ancillary building are funded

WHAT IS NOT FUNDED No grants to individuals

WHO CAN BENEFIT No set policy, however churches benefiting Baptists, Methodists, the United Reformed Church, the Church of England, Evangelists and Quakers will be considered

WHERE FUNDING CAN BE GIVEN Churches throughout the UK, but priority given to Essex and South East England

TYPE OF GRANT Normally one-off

FINANCES *Year* 1997–98 *Income* £275,000
Grants £207,000

TRUSTEES P Clarke, D M Holland, W W Leyland

HOW TO APPLY To the address under Who To Apply To

WHO TO APPLY TO David M Holland, Norwood and Newton Settlement, 126 Beauly Way, Romford, Essex RM1 4XL *Tel* 01708 723670

CC NO 234964   **ESTABLISHED** 1952

■ The Noswad Charity

WHAT IS FUNDED Currently the Trustees are supporting those charitable bodies which they have hitherto supported and are likely only to consider applications from charities in connection with general humanities. Emphasis on the arts and disabled people, particularly ex-service personnel

WHAT IS NOT FUNDED Registered charities operating within the above areas will only be considered and applications from individuals are ineligible

WHO CAN BENEFIT Emphasis is on charities which benefit: actors and entertainment professionals; musicians; textile workers and designers; writers

464

Think carefully about every application. Is it justified?

and poets; ex-service and service people. This Foundation may also support at risk groups, those disadvantaged by poverty and socially isolated people. There is no restriction on the disease or medical condition suffered by the beneficiaries

WHERE FUNDING CAN BE GIVEN UK

TYPE OF GRANT At the discretion of the Trustees

RANGE OF GRANTS £600–£2,600

SAMPLE GRANTS £2,600 to Royal Academy of Music for a scholarship to a postgraduate piano student; £2,600 to Royal College of Music for a scholarship to a postgraduate piano student; £1,636 to Douglas Bader Foundation; £1,636 to Royal Air Force Benevolent Fund; £1,636 to BLESMA; £1,636 to RADAR; £1,636 to National Arts Collections Fund; £1,636 to Imperial Cancer Research Fund; £1,636 to Age Concern; £1,636 to British Kidney Transplant Association

FINANCES *Year* 1997–98 *Income* £25,363 *Grants* £25,000

TRUSTEES J A Mills, C N Bardswell, H E Bromley Davenport

HOW TO APPLY By letter

WHO TO APPLY TO The Noswad Charity, Messrs Belmont & Lowe, Solicitors, Henrietta House, 93 Turnmill Street, London EC1M 5TQ

CC NO 282080   **ESTABLISHED** 1981

■ The Noswal Charitable Trust

WHAT IS FUNDED Generally Jewish charities and synagogues but some general health and welfare will be considered

WHO CAN BENEFIT Organisations benefiting Jewish people. At risk groups, those disadvantaged by poverty, sick people and socially isolated people will be considered

WHERE FUNDING CAN BE GIVEN UK and overseas

TYPE OF GRANT One-off and recurrent grants

RANGE OF GRANTS Below £250–£11,190

SAMPLE GRANTS £11,190 to Ben Gurion University Appeal; £10,000 to Jewish Care; £2,174 to London Philharmonic; £655 to West London Synagogue; £500 to Friends of Hebrew University

FINANCES *Year* 1995 *Income* £19,868 *Grants* £25,879

TRUSTEES S S Lawson, MRCS, LRCP, Ms B V Lawson

WHO TO APPLY TO Dr S S Lawson, The Noswal Charitable Trust, 235–241 Regent Street, London W1R 8JU

CC NO 326341   **ESTABLISHED** 1983

■ The Notgrove Trust

WHAT IS FUNDED The Trust will consider funding sheltered accommodation; infrastructure development; arts, culture and recreation; family planning clinics; agriculture and literacy

WHAT IS NOT FUNDED No grants for individuals or medical research

WHO CAN BENEFIT Local or special interests of the Trustees. There are no restrictions on the age, professional and economic group, family situation, religion and culture, and social circumstances of the beneficiaries

WHERE FUNDING CAN BE GIVEN Primarily Gloucestershire and surrounding area

TYPE OF GRANT Current recipients are regional charities, various benevolent associations and a local church. Except in special circumstances, single donations only will be considered

SAMPLE GRANTS £25,000 to DGAA Homelife for new local nursing home; £10,000 to Cheltenham and Gloucestershire Development Trust for agricultural research; £5,000 to Farms for City Children for new farm project; £5,000 to Wheels Project; £3,000 to Notgrove PCC; £2,500 to St Mary's Lower Slaughter Spire Appeal

FINANCES *Year* 1997 *Income* £81,403 *Grants* £72,250

TRUSTEES D Acland, Elizabeth Acland

NOTES Unsuccessful appeals will not be responded to

HOW TO APPLY In writing, including latest accounts. Initial telephone calls are not welcome. There are no application forms, guidelines or deadlines for applicants. No sae is required

WHO TO APPLY TO Elizabeth Acland, The Notgrove Trust, The Manor, Notgrove, Cheltenham, Gloucestershire GL54 3BT

CC NO 278692   **ESTABLISHED** 1979

■ The Nottingham General Dispensary

WHAT IS FUNDED The alleviation of suffering or aid in recovery through the provision of items and services not readily available from ordinary channels. Charities working in the fields of: respite; professional bodies; the Council for Voluntary Service; and health will be considered

WHO CAN BENEFIT Individuals or other organisations. There is no restriction on the age of the beneficiaries or on their medical condition or disease

WHERE FUNDING CAN BE GIVEN Nottinghamshire

TYPE OF GRANT One-off preferred. Capital, project, research, recurring costs, running costs and salaries. Funding for up to three years will be considered

SAMPLE GRANTS £4,000 to District Nurse Network for miscellaneous items of equipment; £3,000 to Radford Visiting Scheme; £2,500 to Cardiac Surgical Training Appeal; £2,500 to Radford Care Group; £1,750 to Nottingham Vascular Surgery Fund

FINANCES *Year* 1997–98 *Income* £56,000 *Grants* £30,632

TRUSTEES Ingle Dawson (Chairman), W J Bendall, R Batterbury, J Williams, Dr S Harris, A Hopwood

HOW TO APPLY To the address under Who To Apply To in writing

WHO TO APPLY TO D S Corder, Secretary, The Nottingham General Dispensary, Bramley House, 1 Oxford Street, Nottingham NG1 5BH *Tel* 0115-936 9369

CC NO 228149   **ESTABLISHED** 1963

■ Nottinghamshire Constabulary Benevolent Fund

WHAT IS FUNDED To assist members and their dependants, as may be in necessitous or impoverished circumstances. To make grants to Police charities and other charities

WHAT IS NOT FUNDED Grants restricted to members and ex-members of Force, their relatives, widows and orphans

WHO CAN BENEFIT Generally to police widows and orphans in necessitous or impoverished circumstances

WHERE FUNDING CAN BE GIVEN Nottinghamshire

TYPE OF GRANT Cash grants

Does the trust you have chosen match your needs? Haphazard applications waste postage and time

465

SAMPLE GRANTS £56,275 to Northern Police Convalescent Home Contra; £17,666 to widows/children; £15,066 to St George Contra; £11,581 to subscribers; £1,363 in miscellaneous gifts

FINANCES *Year* 1996 *Income* £108,633 *Grants* £101,951

TRUSTEES The Committee

PUBLICATIONS Annual Report

NOTES Personal contact with widows is achieved by appointing officers to be responsible for a few widows within their work area and they are able to assess and report upon the current needs, problems and well-being of each widow and dependant child. This helps the Committee to decide upon the level of help in each individual case. It also provides an established contact for the widow in urgent cases and keeps her in touch with her former husband's colleagues. The policy of the Fund is to spend its income each year and not to increase its assets except by investment of existing assets. Donations from the public and any other source are therefore directed to helping the widows and in particular the fatherless children through their school and higher education

HOW TO APPLY To Secretary/Treasurer

WHO TO APPLY TO J M Moody, Secretary/Treasurer, Nottinghamshire Constabulary Benevolent Fund, 268 Nottingham Road, Selston, Nottinghamshire NG16 6AD

CC NO 256806   **ESTABLISHED** 1968

■ The Nova Charitable Trust

WHAT IS FUNDED General charitable purposes, in particular, to assist children who are in need or suffering hardship

WHO CAN BENEFIT Children in need of medical or social assistance

WHERE FUNDING CAN BE GIVEN UK and overseas

TYPE OF GRANT One-off payments and recurring annual payments

TRUSTEES G J Kneller, H Kneller, R P Turton

HOW TO APPLY Written application to the address under Who To Apply To

WHO TO APPLY TO R P Turton, The Nova Charitable Trust, BDD Stoy Hayward, Mander House, Wolverhampton, West Midlands WV1 3NF *Tel* 01902 714828 *Fax* 01902 711475

CC NO 1068293   **ESTABLISHED** 1998

■ Novi Most International

WHAT IS FUNDED Evangelical Christian ministry to meet physical, spiritual, emotional and social needs. Particular emphasis on long-term support of children and young people traumatised by war. Reconciliation and community development initiatives

WHAT IS NOT FUNDED Grants seldom given to projects not connected with evangelical churches or where our own staff or partners are not involved

WHO CAN BENEFIT To benefit those disadvantaged by poverty, at risk groups or victims of war, especially children and young people. There is no restriction on the religion or culture of the beneficiaries

WHERE FUNDING CAN BE GIVEN Bosnia-Herzegovina and Bosnian people in exile

TYPE OF GRANT One-off and recurring

RANGE OF GRANTS £50–£20,000

FINANCES *Year* 1996–97 *Income* £218,943 *Grants* £158,652

TRUSTEES W Beech, D Birch, R Egner, J Parkin, T Stone

PUBLICATIONS *New Bridge* and *Bosnia Prayer Briefing*

NOTES Funds fully committed for the foreseeable future

HOW TO APPLY Unsolicited applications are not encouraged or acknowledged. No telephone enquiries please

WHO TO APPLY TO P H Brooks, Novi Most International, 78 The Broadway, Chesham, Buckinghamshire HP5 1EG *Tel* 01494 793242 *Fax* 01494 793771

CC NO 1043501   **ESTABLISHED** 1995

■ The Viscount Nuffield Auxiliary Fund

WHAT IS FUNDED Grants are made to organisations who need financial help to investigate, adapt or demonstrate a way of using equipment (mobility aids and communications aids) more effectively. Those in need such aids will benefit

WHAT IS NOT FUNDED No grants to individuals in personal difficulty or distress or for obtaining degrees or other qualifications. No appeals

WHO CAN BENEFIT Voluntary organisations and academic institutions benefiting those who need financial help to investigate, adapt or demonstrate equipment, disabled people and those suffering from sight or hearing loss

WHERE FUNDING CAN BE GIVEN UK

TYPE OF GRANT Usually recurrent, for the lifetime of the project

RANGE OF GRANTS £2,000–£15,000

FINANCES *Year* 1998 *Grants* £138,000

TRUSTEES Dr Onora O'Neill, CBE, FBA (Chairman), Prof Tony Atkinson, The Hon Dame Brenda Hale, Prof Sir Robert May, Prof Sir Michael Rutter, CBE, MD, FRCP, FRCPysch, FRS, Mrs Anne Sofer

NOTES Grant-making is delegated to a Committee

HOW TO APPLY Once a year, in April. Guidelines for applications available from the Fund Administrator in January of each year

WHO TO APPLY TO The Administrator, The Viscount Nuffield Auxiliary Fund, 28 Bedford Square, London WC1B 3EG *Tel* 0171-631 0566

CC NO 200561   **ESTABLISHED** 1961

■ The Nuremberg Trust

WHAT IS FUNDED The relief of poverty, the advancement of education and religion, and other charitable purposes for the benefit of the community

WHO CAN BENEFIT Organisations benefiting children, young adults, students and those disadvantaged by poverty. People of many different religions and cultures will benefit

WHERE FUNDING CAN BE GIVEN UK

TRUSTEES J R Adler, P M Oppenheimer, T H P Oppenheimer

WHO TO APPLY TO P Oppenheimer, Chairperson, The Nuremberg Trust, 6 Linton Road, Oxford OX2 6UG

CC NO 1067752   **ESTABLISHED** 1998

O

■ The Oadby Educational Foundation

WHAT IS FUNDED To provide aid for the education of those in need and to benefit youth in the area Where Funding Can Be Given. Help for the poor of Oadby

WHAT IS NOT FUNDED No grants for buildings

WHO CAN BENEFIT To benefit children, young adults and students. Those disadvantaged by poverty in Oadby

WHERE FUNDING CAN BE GIVEN Oadby

RANGE OF GRANTS £60 to further education students per year. £1,000 to schools per year

SAMPLE GRANTS £8,100 to Oadby schools for educational equipment; £2,500 to St Peters and St Pauls Sunday Schools for youth work; £2,250 to Scouts, Cubs, Beavers and Venture Scouts for youth work; £2,250 to Guides, Brownies, Rainbows and Rangers for youth work; £1,800 to churches in Oadby for Sunday schools and youth clubs; £850 to six students for Operation Raleigh; £800 to Oadby Youth Clubs for youth work; £675 to Leicester's Charity Organisation for the poor of Oadby; £500 to Boys and Girls Brigade for youth work

FINANCES *Year* 1997 *Income* £33,624
Grants £32,736

TRUSTEES Dr Bob Borthwick (Chairman), Cllr M Griffiths (Vice Chairman), Rodger Moodie (Hon Secretary), Cllr Kay Relf, Cllr Michael Thornton, Mrs Audrey Hutchins, Mrs Gillian Austen, Jill Gore, Jim Sawbridge, Mrs Rita Shrigley

HOW TO APPLY Application forms for student grants are available from the address under Who To Apply To upon written request and must be returned by 1 October each year. Other requests by written letter for discussion at meetings in March, June and October

WHO TO APPLY TO Rodger D Moodie, Hon Secretary, The Oadby Educational Foundation, 26 Richmond Way, Oadby, Leicester, Leicestershire LE2 5TR

CC NO 528000 **ESTABLISHED** 1967

■ Oak Tree Charitable Trust

WHAT IS FUNDED General charitable purposes

WHO CAN BENEFIT There are no restrictions on the age; professional and economic group; family situation; religion and culture; and social circumstances of; or disease or medical condition suffered by, the beneficiaries

WHERE FUNDING CAN BE GIVEN Greater London

TRUSTEES L Baikie, M L Clarkson, P J Collis, Ms C M Dunk, S B Garside, Ms C J Nicholson

WHO TO APPLY TO M R Lindley, Solicitor, Oak Tree Charitable Trust, c/o Strethers, Sackville House, 40 Piccadilly, London W1V 9PA

CC NO 1067145 **ESTABLISHED** 1998

■ The Oak Trust

WHAT IS FUNDED General charitable purposes. Preference to charities of which the Trust has special interest, knowledge or association

WHAT IS NOT FUNDED Applications from individuals will not be considered

WHO CAN BENEFIT Registered charities. There are no restrictions on the age; professional and economic group; family situation; religion and culture; and social circumstances of; or disease or medical condition suffered by, the beneficiaries

WHERE FUNDING CAN BE GIVEN UK

TYPE OF GRANT Donations rather than subscriptions

FINANCES *Year* 1997 *Income* £40,696
Grants £40,000

TRUSTEES Rev A C C Courtauld, MA, J Courtauld, Dr E Courtauld

NOTES Postal applications please

HOW TO APPLY To the address under Who To Apply To

WHO TO APPLY TO R R Long, The Oak Trust, Birkett Long, Red House, Colchester Road, Halstead, Essex CO9 2DZ

CC NO 231456 **ESTABLISHED** 1963

■ The Oakdale Trust

WHAT IS FUNDED The Trust gives preference to Welsh charities engaged in social work, medical support groups and medical research. Some support is given to UK charities working overseas and to conservation projects at home and abroad

WHAT IS NOT FUNDED The Trust does not normally give grants to individuals, holiday schemes, sports activities and expeditions or church restoration

WHO CAN BENEFIT Organisations benefiting: at risk groups; carers; disabled people; those disadvantaged by poverty; disaster victims; refugees; victims of crime; and victims of famine and war

WHERE FUNDING CAN BE GIVEN UK, with preference to Wales, and overseas

TYPE OF GRANT Single outright grants averaging £500. Buildings, capital, core costs, feasibility studies, one-off, project, research, recurring costs, salaries and start-up costs will be considered. Funding may be given for up to one year

RANGE OF GRANTS Typical grant £500

FINANCES *Year* 1996–97 *Income* £110,000
Grants £123,000

TRUSTEES B Cadbury, Mrs F F Cadbury, R A Cadbury, F B Cadbury, Dr R C Cadbury, Mrs O H Tatton-Brown

HOW TO APPLY No application form is necessary, but requests should be concise, quoting their charity's registration number, a summary of their achievements, plans and needs and a copy or summary of their most recent annual accounts. The six Trustees meet twice yearly, usually in April and September, and requests should be submitted if possible before the start of these months. Owing to a lack of secretarial help and in view of the numerous requests we receive, no applications are acknowledged even when accompanied by a sae

WHO TO APPLY TO Brandon Cadbury, The Oakdale Trust, Tan y Coed, Pantydwr, Rhayader, Powys LD6 5LR

CC NO 218827 **ESTABLISHED** 1950

■ The Oakley Charitable Trust

WHAT IS FUNDED Predominantly welfare; health; education; arts, culture and recreation; conservation and environment; and churches

WHAT IS NOT FUNDED No grants to individuals will be considered

WHO CAN BENEFIT Grants to registered charities benefiting: children and young adults; actors and entertainment professionals; musicians; students; textile workers and designers; writers and poets; at risk groups; disabled people; those disadvantaged by poverty; and socially isolated people. There is no restriction on the disease or medical condition suffered by the beneficiaries

WHERE FUNDING CAN BE GIVEN West Midlands, South West and Channel Islands

TYPE OF GRANT One-off, core costs, project, research, recurring costs and buildings. Funding is available for one year or less

RANGE OF GRANTS Average grant £500–£1,000

FINANCES *Year* 1997 *Income* £70,240 *Grants* £37,510

TRUSTEES Mrs H L Oakley, G M W Oakley, Mrs C M Airey

HOW TO APPLY Applications by letter only

WHO TO APPLY TO G M W Oakley, The Oakley Charitable Trust, 3rd Floor, York House, 38 Great Charles Street, Birmingham B3 3JU

CC NO 233041   **ESTABLISHED** 1963

■ The Oakmoor Trust

WHAT IS FUNDED General charitable purposes

WHO CAN BENEFIT There are no restrictions on the age; professional and economic group; family situation; religion and culture; and social circumstances of; or disease or medical condition suffered by, the beneficiaries

WHERE FUNDING CAN BE GIVEN UK

FINANCES *Year* 1997 *Income* £51,000 *Grants* £35,000

TRUSTEES Kleinwort Benson Trustees Ltd, P M H Andreae, R J Andreae

HOW TO APPLY **This Trust states that it does not respond to unsolicited applications**

WHO TO APPLY TO Trustee Dept, The Oakmoor Trust, Kleinwort Benson Ltd, PO Box 191, 10 Fenchurch Street, London EC3M 3LB

CC NO 258516   **ESTABLISHED** 1969

■ Oasis Church Chadwell Heath Charitable Trust

WHAT IS FUNDED Welfare, education, Christian religion, international, general

WHO CAN BENEFIT Small local projects and national organisations benefiting: children; young adults; students; Christians; at risk groups; disabled people; and socially isolated people

WHERE FUNDING CAN BE GIVEN Essex, UK and overseas

TYPE OF GRANT One-off and recurrent grants

RANGE OF GRANTS £1,000 or less

FINANCES *Year* 1995 *Income* £136,508 *Grants* £66,276

TRUSTEES J Norton, G R Matthews, A D Southwood

WHO TO APPLY TO Mrs L Hedger, Oasis Church Chadwell Heath Charitable Trust, Oasis House, Essex Road, Chadwell Heath, Romford, Essex RM6 4JA

CC NO 1043748   **ESTABLISHED** 1995

■ The Ofenheim Charitable Trust

WHAT IS FUNDED General charitable purposes, usually in the fields of health, the arts and the environment

WHO CAN BENEFIT There are no restrictions on the age; professional and economic group; family situation; religion and culture; and social circumstances of; or disease or medical condition suffered by, the beneficiaries

WHERE FUNDING CAN BE GIVEN UK

FINANCES *Year* 1996 *Income* £49,091

TRUSTEES R J Clark, R McLeod

NOTES The Trust usually supports nationally known and well established charitable organisations of personal interest and concern to Trustees. At present, funds are fully covered by existing commitments

HOW TO APPLY In writing to the address under Who To Apply To, but current income is fully covered by existing commitments. Unsuccessful applications will not be acknowledged

WHO TO APPLY TO R J Clark, The Ofenheim Charitable Trust, Messrs Baker Tilly, Chartered Accountants, 2 Bloomsbury Street, London WC1B 3ST

CC NO 263751   **ESTABLISHED** 1972

■ The Officers' Association (Officers Benevolent Department of the Royal British Legion)

WHAT IS FUNDED To relieve distress among ex-officers of HM Forces their widows and dependants. To re-establish ex-officers to civilian life helping with housing advice and information; almshouses and residential facilities

WHAT IS NOT FUNDED Major capital projects

WHO CAN BENEFIT Individuals and organisations benefiting: older people; ex-officers of HM Forces, their widows and their dependants

WHERE FUNDING CAN BE GIVEN UK and overseas

TYPE OF GRANT To relieve immediate need and to enable individuals to remain in their own homes for as long as they can manage. To help applicants to find spaces in residential and other homes and, if necessary, help them with the fees. Running costs and recurring costs will be considered

FINANCES *Year* 1997 *Income* £2,498,000 *Grants* £948,000

TRUSTEES The Council established by Royal Charter

PUBLICATIONS Annual Report and sundry pamphlets describing how help can be given

NOTES The Association also runs a residential care home in Bishopsteignton, Devon for elderly ex-officers and a small estate of bungalows at Leavesden near Watford for disabled ex-officers and their families.

HOW TO APPLY Applications should be made in the first instance either by phone or in writing to the address under Who To Apply To

WHO TO APPLY TO The General Secretary, The Officers' Association, 48 Pall Mall, London SW1Y 5JY *Tel* 0171 930 0125 *Fax* 0171-930 9053 *E-mail* ags@oaed.org.uk

CC NO 201321   **ESTABLISHED** 1919

■ Ogilvie Charities (Deed No 1)

WHAT IS FUNDED Chiefly concerned with maintenance of homes and almshouses in Suffolk (at Aldringham) and sheltered housing in Colchester, Essex

WHO CAN BENEFIT People in straitened circumstances (especially living in Ipswich and Leiston); widows having dependent children; former governesses or female teachers in need of assistance; shipwrecked seamen and their families and organisations aiding them. Also those disadvantaged by poverty; disabled people; and disaster victims. There are no restrictions on the age; professional and economic group; religion and culture; or disease or medical condition suffered by, the beneficiaries

WHERE FUNDING CAN BE GIVEN UK

TYPE OF GRANT Usually one-off. Funding is available for up to one year

RANGE OF GRANTS £52–£500

SAMPLE GRANTS £500 to poor people of Ipswich; £500 to people in straitened circumstances; £350 to Widows Fund; £52 to poor people of Leiston   -

FINANCES *Year* 1997 *Income* £239,486 *Grants* £1,402

HOW TO APPLY Applications received through social workers or other official sources, not by personal application. Preliminary telephone enquiries acceptable and may prevent abortive correspondence

WHO TO APPLY TO The General Manager, The Ogilvie Charities, The Gate House, 9 Burkitt Road, Woodbridge, Suffolk IP12 4JJ *Tel* 01394 388746

CC NO 211777   **ESTABLISHED** 1887

■ Ogilvie Charities (Deed No 2)

WHAT IS FUNDED Specific philanthropic work. Assistance to present or former governesses or female teachers in straitened circumstances. Country holidays for London children. Support of Charity's own Homes and Almshouses and residents living in them. Aid to other charitable institutions in Metropolitan London, Essex and Suffolk or, if situated beyond, serving the needs of people living in those areas. Support may also be given to infrastructure and technical support and religious ancillary buildings

WHAT IS NOT FUNDED No payment of debts

WHO CAN BENEFIT Individuals or organisations benefiting female teachers and governesses, homeless people and those disadvantaged by poverty. There are no restrictions on the age of the beneficiaries or on their disease or medical condition

WHERE FUNDING CAN BE GIVEN Essex, Suffolk, London and Greater London

TYPE OF GRANT One-off usually. Grants made through medical and other social workers who are already aware of what is available. Buildings, core costs, project, running costs, salaries and start-up costs will be considered. Funding may be given for up to one year

RANGE OF GRANTS Individual grants £100, organisation grants £5,000

FINANCES *Year* 1997 *Income* £72,679 *Grants* £42,600

TRUSTEES A W Allen, B Aynsley-Smith, J N Braithwaite, A Campbell, I H Gillings, P Grieve, J D S Hall, F A Lowe

NOTES Organisations should send copies of annual accounts

HOW TO APPLY Applications received through social worker or other official sources, not by personal application. Preliminary telephone enquiries acceptable and may prevent abortive correspondence

WHO TO APPLY TO T Last, General Manager, The Ogilvie Charities, The Gate House, 9 Burkitt Road, Woodbridge, Suffolk IP12 4JJ *Tel* 01394 388746

CC NO 211778   **ESTABLISHED** 1890

■ The Ogle Christian Trust

WHAT IS FUNDED The Trust's main concern is the promotion of Biblical Christianity. Currently it includes: new initiatives in evangelism; support for the publishing and distribution of Scriptures and Christian literature; training of Bible students and pastors; and Christian social enterprise and famine relief

WHAT IS NOT FUNDED Grants will not be offered in response to general appeals from large national organisations. Funds are not generally available for church and other building projects. Grants to individuals are rare and will normally be made through the sponsoring organisation

WHO CAN BENEFIT Registered charities benefiting Bible students, pastors, Christians, evangelists and victims of famine

WHERE FUNDING CAN BE GIVEN UK and overseas

TYPE OF GRANT Normally one-off or short-term commitments only. Salaries will not be funded. Grants range from £100–£1,000

RANGE OF GRANTS £100–£1,000

FINANCES *Year* 1997 *Income* £155,000 *Grants* £162,000

TRUSTEES A I Kinnear, D J Harris, C A Fischbacher, S Procter, Miss D M Haile, Mrs F Putley

PUBLICATIONS Annual Report and financial statements

HOW TO APPLY Trustees meet half-yearly. Applications, at any time, should be in writing and consistent with the above criteria, together with documentary support and sae

WHO TO APPLY TO C A Fischbacher (Secretary), The Ogle Christian Trust, 6 Chanctonbury View, Henfield, West Sussex BN5 9TW

CC NO 1061458   **ESTABLISHED** 1938

■ The Oikonomia Trust

WHAT IS FUNDED The Trust is not looking for further outlets but is willing to consider such providing that they conform to the position of accepting the whole of the Bible as the Word of the living God and are motivated thereby

WHAT IS NOT FUNDED No grants made in response to general appeals from large national organisations

WHO CAN BENEFIT Organisations benefiting Evangelists

WHERE FUNDING CAN BE GIVEN UK and overseas

TYPE OF GRANT Evangelical work, famine and other relief through Christian agencies, particularly when accompanied with the offer of the Gospel

SAMPLE GRANTS £50,000 to Bethel Church, Ripon towards site for church building; £8,000 to Leeds City Mission towards rescue work in the name of Christ; £6,900 to Bethel Church, Ripon for Christian work, outreach and church; £3,000 to Africa Inland Mission for Christian outreach work; £3,000 to Association of Evangelists for Christian outreach work; £2,000 to Slavic Gospel Association for Christian outreach work; £2,000 to Cause for Concern towards caring for the disabled; £2,000 to Caring for Life for work (rescue) with needy people; £2,000 to Africa Evangelical Fellowship for Christian outreach work; £2,000 to Japan Mission for Christian outreach work

FINANCES *Year* 1994 *Income* £62,644

TRUSTEES D H Metcalfe, R H Metcalfe, S D Metcalfe, R O Owens, C Mountain

HOW TO APPLY Known needs are greater than the Trust's supplies. If an applicant desires an answer an sae should be enclosed. Applications should arrive in January. In writing to the Secretary

WHO TO APPLY TO D H Metcalfe, The Oikonomia Trust, Westoaks, St John's Close, Sharow, Ripon, North Yorkshire HG4 5BB

CC NO 273481   **ESTABLISHED** 1977

■ The Oil Industry Community Fund

WHAT IS FUNDED Grants are made to charities and other community groups working in the fields of: respite and sheltered accommodation; support to voluntary and community organisations; and various community services

WHAT IS NOT FUNDED Grants are not made to religious groups, national charities, for travel overseas, or bricks and mortar projects. No grants to individuals

WHO CAN BENEFIT To benefit people of all ages

WHERE FUNDING CAN BE GIVEN The Sheriffdom of Aberdeen, Aberdeenshire, Highland and Islands, Moray

TYPE OF GRANT Core costs, one-off and recurring costs will be considered. Funding may be given for up to one year

RANGE OF GRANTS £50–£500

TRUSTEES Representatives from the North Sea oil industry

HOW TO APPLY Applications should be made in writing to the address under Who To Apply To

WHO TO APPLY TO Alex Mair, Chairman, The Oil Industry Community Fund, PO Box 185, Aberdeen AB12 3XD

SC NO SCO 15088   **ESTABLISHED** 1985

■ Old Broad Street Charity Trust

WHAT IS FUNDED General charitable purposes including arts and education. Funding scholarships for persons serving in a bank or financial institution in the UK to spend time in any seat of learning (principally INSEAD) to attain the highest level of executive management

WHAT IS NOT FUNDED No general grants to charities. Not our policy to make grants to individuals

WHO CAN BENEFIT Registered charities benefiting children, young adults, students and those working in a bank or financial institution. Actors and entertainment professionals, musicians, textile workers and designers, writers and poets will be considered

WHERE FUNDING CAN BE GIVEN UK and overseas

RANGE OF GRANTS £1,000–£15,000

SAMPLE GRANTS £10,029 to L'Hopital Intercommunal de Creteil; £10,000 to Les Petits Frères des Pouvres; £10,000 to Opera Circus; £10,000 to Pour Que L'Esprit Vive; £9,307 to Bezirksfusorge, Saanen; £8,250 to Bloomfield Early Learning Centre, Guy's Hospital; £5,000 to University of London, Slade School of Sculpture; £4,653 to International Menuhin Music Academy; £2,500 to Chichester Cathedral Trust; £2,500 to Victoria and Albert Museum Trust

FINANCES Year 1997 Income £108,304 Grants £92,566

TRUSTEES Mrs Louis Franck, P A Hetherington, A T J Stanford, Mme Cartier-Bresson, C J Sheridan

NOTES Charity includes the Louis Franck Scholarship Fund

HOW TO APPLY To the address under Who To Apply To in writing

WHO TO APPLY TO B M Covell, Old Broad Street Charity Trust, c/o Messrs Rawlinson & Hunter, Eagle House, 110 Jermyn Street, London SW1Y 6RH

CC NO 231382   **ESTABLISHED** 1964

■ The Old Enfield Charitable Trust

WHAT IS FUNDED Education, community development and social development for those in need. Particularly: almshouses; support to voluntary and community organisations; training for work; vocational training; costs of study including fees and purchase of books; and travel costs

WHAT IS NOT FUNDED Scholarships and loans

WHO CAN BENEFIT Those in need including: children; young adults and older people; parents and children; one parent families; widows and widowers; disabled people and those disadvantaged by poverty

WHERE FUNDING CAN BE GIVEN The Ancient Parish of Enfield

TYPE OF GRANT One-off, core costs, project, running costs; salaries and start-up costs. Funding is available for up to and over three years and assessed according to need

FINANCES Year 1997–98 Income £480,000 Grants £185,000

TRUSTEES S J Attwood, R Bray, H A Brown, R Cross, W D Day, M M Edge, W R Halsey, R G Kendall, J E H Little, D McKean, CB, P Oborn, C W Parker, A D Thacker, J Wood, I H R Woodrow

NOTES The Enfield Parochial Charity and the Hundred Acres Charity merged in 1994 as one charity - The Old Enfield Charitable Trust

HOW TO APPLY To the address under Who To Apply To in writing. Initial telephone calls welcome. Application forms and guidelines are available. There is no deadline for applications and no sae is required

WHO TO APPLY TO Mrs N D Forkgen, Clerk, The Old Enfield Charitable Trust, 34–38 Church Street, Enfield, Middlesex EN2 6BA Tel 0181-367 8941 Fax 0181-372 8521

CC NO 207840   **ESTABLISHED** 1962

■ The Old Possums Practical Trust

WHAT IS FUNDED General charitable purposes and to further the education of the general public

WHAT IS NOT FUNDED Scholarships and foreign travel. Sports

WHO CAN BENEFIT Children; young adults and students

WHERE FUNDING CAN BE GIVEN UK and overseas

FINANCES Year 1998 Income £91,497 Grants £89,920

TRUSTEES Esme Eliot, C Willett, B Stevens

WHO TO APPLY TO The Secretary, The Old Possums Practical Trust, Baker Tilly, Iveco Ford House, Station Road, Watford, Hertfordshire WD1 1TG

CC NO 328558   **ESTABLISHED** 1990

■ The John Oldacre Foundation

WHAT IS FUNDED Research and education in agricultural sciences

WHAT IS NOT FUNDED No grants for expeditions or for individual tuition fees

WHO CAN BENEFIT Universities, agricultural colleges and innovative projects benefiting students and research workers

WHERE FUNDING CAN BE GIVEN UK

TYPE OF GRANT One-off, recurrent, feasibility, project, research and funding of up to three years will be considered

RANGE OF GRANTS £5,000–£10,000

SAMPLE GRANTS £20,000 to The Royal Agricultural College for a bursary; £10,000 to The Royal Agricultural College for organic wheat studies; £10,000 to Harper Adams Agricultural College for research project; £10,000 to Seale Hayne Agricultural College for research project; £9,900 to University of Newcastle for research project; £7,500 to Nuffield Scholarship Trust; £5,000 to Farm Africa as a donation

FINANCES Year 1996 Income £78,802 Grants £72,500

TRUSTEES W J Oldacre, H B Shonler, S J Charnock

HOW TO APPLY In writing. Application forms available

WHO TO APPLY TO W J Oldacre, The John Oldacre Foundation, Woodlands, New Road, Minchinhampton, Gloucestershire GL6 9BQ
CC NO 284960   **ESTABLISHED** 1981

■ William Older's School Charity

WHAT IS FUNDED To provide financial assistance for educational purposes to applicants residing only in the area Where Funding Can Be Given, including church schools, pre-school education, tertiary and higher education
WHAT IS NOT FUNDED Applications from those outside the Ecclesiastical Parish of Angmering will not be considered
WHO CAN BENEFIT Individuals, local schools, playgroups and other educational establishments in academic or specialised courses of study benefiting children, young adults and students
WHERE FUNDING CAN BE GIVEN Ecclesiastical Parish of Angmering, West Sussex
TYPE OF GRANT For educational purposes
SAMPLE GRANTS £1,309 to St Margaret's Church of England School, Angmering for school visits/transport; £760 to Mother Goose Association, Angmering for nursery nurse wages; £500 to an individual for further education; £300 each to five individuals for further education; £250 to Angmering School Playgroup for help with the rent
FINANCES Year 1996 Income £13,047
TRUSTEES L A Baker, N Hare, G Hobson, Mrs A Wood
HOW TO APPLY Trustees meetings are held quarterly. Applications to be submitted in writing to the address under Who To Apply To giving clear details of financial need plus an outline budget
WHO TO APPLY TO Mrs J Howell, William Older's School Charity, 10 Weavers Ring, Angmering Village, West Sussex BN16 4AJ
CC NO 306424   **ESTABLISHED** 1976

■ The Evelyn Oldfield Unit

WHAT IS FUNDED General charitable purposes in particular to provide information, advice, guidance, training and other educational facilities, technical and professional aid, support and other assistance to charitable organisations especially those which assist refugees
WHO CAN BENEFIT Organisations benefiting young people, students and refugees will be considered
WHERE FUNDING CAN BE GIVEN UK
FINANCES Year 1997 Income £46,254
TRUSTEES K Allen, T S Berhane, T Cook, N Castro, A Ali, G Ejene, A Johnson, E Panahi, P Opendi, V Ly Ung, A Sayed, S Stanislaus
NOTES Expenditure for 1997 involves staff costs, training provided, consultancy. No grants were awarded
WHO TO APPLY TO Tzeggai Yohannes Deres, The Evelyn Oldfield Unit, 356 Holloway Road, London N7 6PA
CC NO 1044681   **ESTABLISHED** 1995

■ Oldham Foundation

WHAT IS FUNDED Main donations to former employees of Oldham Batteries (employed before 1971) and charitable activities where Trustees give personal service or where they know people who do so. Charities working in the fields of: arts, culture and recreation; conservation and environment; and churches will be considered. Support may also be given to hospices, nursing services, cancer research, libraries and museums, day centres, holidays and outings
WHAT IS NOT FUNDED Applications from individuals, including students, are ineligible with the exception of those already selected for schemes like Operation Raleigh. No grants to general appeals from national bodies. Inappropriate appeals are not acknowledged
WHO CAN BENEFIT Organisations benefiting children, young adults, ex-service and service people, Church of England and former employees of Oldham Batteries (employed before 1971). Funding is considered for those disadvantaged by poverty; victims of man-made or natural disasters and those suffering from cancers, HIV and AIDs and mental illness
WHERE FUNDING CAN BE GIVEN North West and South West of England. Charities aided in the area may have objectives overseas
TYPE OF GRANT Annual grant to former employees. Grants usually one-off. Does not provide core funding. General charitable grants with bias towards active participation by Trustees
RANGE OF GRANTS £40–£5,000, typical grant £250/£500/£1,000
SAMPLE GRANTS £5,000 to Sue Ryder Home; £5,000 to Cheltenham Festival of Music; £5,000 to Cheltenham Festival of Literature; £2,000 to Cheltenham Samaritans; £2,000 to 24th Leckhampton Scout Group; £2,000 to Christchurch Cheltenham Hall Appeal; £2,000 to Winstons Wish, Gloucester; £2,000 to CABE; £1,500 to Parnham House for a bursary award; £1,000 to Cheltenham Young Homeless Project
FINANCES Year 1998 Income £77,693 Grants £96,892
TRUSTEES J Bodden, Mrs D Oldham, J Oldham (Chairman), S Roberts, Prof R Thomas, J Sharpe
HOW TO APPLY Any time. Trustees meet twice a year. Applications should include clear details of projects, budgets, and/or accounts where appropriate. Telephone submissions not accepted
WHO TO APPLY TO Mrs D Oldham, Oldham Foundation, King's Well, Douro Road, Cheltenham, Gloucestershire GL50 2PF
CC NO 269263   **ESTABLISHED** 1974

■ The Olga Charitable Trust

WHAT IS FUNDED Health and welfare, youth organisations, children's welfare, carers organisations. All must be known to Trustees
WHO CAN BENEFIT National organisations benefiting: children; young adults; at risk groups; those disadvantaged by poverty; socially isolated people; and carers. There is no restriction on the disease or medical condition suffered by the beneficiaries
WHERE FUNDING CAN BE GIVEN UK
SAMPLE GRANTS £11,100 to Prince's Youth Business Trust; £10,000 to Red Cross
FINANCES Year 1996–97 Income £62,592 Grants £27,580
TRUSTEES HRH Princess Alexandra, Hon Sir Angus Ogilvy
HOW TO APPLY To the address under Who To Apply To in writing. **The Trust funds are fully committed and applications made cannot be acknowledged**
WHO TO APPLY TO A V B Broke, Accountant, The Olga Charitable Trust, Adam Broke & Co, 95 Aldwych, London WC2B 4JF Tel 0171-404 5151
CC NO 277925   **ESTABLISHED** 1979

■ The Oliver Charitable Foundation

This trust did not respond to CAF's request to amend its entry and, by 30 June 1998, CAF's researchers did not find financial records for later than 1995 on its file at the Charity Commission. Trusts are legally required to submit annual accounts to the Charity Commission under section 42 of the Charities Act 1993

WHAT IS FUNDED To select four main charities to give grants to each year

WHO CAN BENEFIT Registered charities. There are no restrictions on the age; professional and economic group; family situation; religion and culture; and social circumstances of; or disease or medical condition suffered by, the beneficiaries

WHERE FUNDING CAN BE GIVEN London

TRUSTEES C P Oliver, Mrs S L P Oliver, S Leaman

WHO TO APPLY TO C P Oliver, The Oliver Charitable Foundation, 82 Mount Street, London W1Y 5HH *Tel* 0171-499 4378

CC NO 1006195   **ESTABLISHED** 1991

■ Kate Wilson Oliver Trust

WHAT IS FUNDED Assistance to deserving gentlefolk and to charitable institutions for the relief of human suffering

WHAT IS NOT FUNDED No grants to individuals

WHO CAN BENEFIT Charitable institutions benefiting: at risk groups; those disadvantaged by poverty; disaster victims, homeless people; victims of abuse, crime and domestic violence. There is no restriction on the disease or medical condition suffered by the beneficiaries

WHERE FUNDING CAN BE GIVEN England and Wales

TYPE OF GRANT Lump sum payments

RANGE OF GRANTS £500–£2,000

SAMPLE GRANTS £2,000 to Grey Gables Home for the Elderly; £2,000 to Birmingham Council for old people; £1,000 to Miss Smallwood's Society for Assistance, Malvern; £1,000 to The Mary Stevens Hospice; £1,000 to Help the Aged

FINANCES *Year* 1997 *Income* £24,000 *Grants* £23,200

TRUSTEES W M Colacicchi, C R S Clutterbuck, Mrs C E V Colacicchi

HOW TO APPLY Twice annually To the address under Who To Apply To

WHO TO APPLY TO Kate Wilson Oliver Trust, Messrs Willcox Lane Clutterbuck, 55 Charlotte Street, St Paul's Square, Birmingham B3 1PX

CC NO 211968   **ESTABLISHED** 1940

■ The Father O'Mahoney Memorial Trust

WHAT IS FUNDED The relief of the impotent and poor in all parts of the world

WHO CAN BENEFIT Organisations benefiting impotent people and those disadvantaged by poverty. There is no restriction on the disease or medical condition suffered by the beneficiaries

WHERE FUNDING CAN BE GIVEN UK and overseas

SAMPLE GRANTS £3,000 to Child in Need Institute, Calcutta; £3,000 to Tuberculosis Research Institute, Calcutta; £3,000 to Bushmen Primary Health Care Development, Namibia; £2,000 to an individual for distribution in Belem, Brazil and Lars das Criancas, Saio Paulo; £2,000 to an individual in Diocese of Butare, Rwanda towards the purchase of a vehicle; £1,594 to an individual for distribution in Kenya; £1,500 to an individual for distribution in Bolivia; £1,500 to an individual for distribution in Ecuador; £1,000 to Mission in Nigeria; £1,000 to CAFOD Appeal for Rwanda/ Zaire

FINANCES *Year* 1997 *Income* £42,713 *Grants* £41,711

TRUSTEES A M Carney, C Carney-Smith, C W Elks, Ms C A Hearn, D M Maclean, M A Moran, Fr G Murray, A H Sanford

WHO TO APPLY TO A M Carney, The Father O'Mahoney Memorial Trust, 566 Stratford Road, Shirley, Solihull, West Midlands B90 4AY

CC NO 1039288   **ESTABLISHED** 1993

■ The Onaway Trust

WHAT IS FUNDED Trustees like to provide seed funds for self generating, self sufficiency projects based upon indigenous traditional beliefs and practices. The Trustees concentrate mainly on native Americans. The Onaway Trust's wide remit is to relieve poverty and suffering. This is expressed in many areas: the environment, child and animal welfare, world refugees and human rights

WHAT IS NOT FUNDED Administration

WHO CAN BENEFIT Registered charities benefiting: children; young adults; older people; at risk groups; those disadvantaged by poverty; refugees, socially isolated and in the main, Native Americans

WHERE FUNDING CAN BE GIVEN UK and overseas

TYPE OF GRANT Small, start-up costs

SAMPLE GRANTS £11,118 to Rainy Mountain Foundation for Land Claim for Native American Peoples; £9,924 to PISIL Project-Honduras for promotion of health among native peoples; £7,683 to Alaska Wildlife Alliance to prevent killing of wild animals; £6,000 The Woodland Trust for woodland management and research; £5,122 to Environmental Magazine for promotion of environmental issues; £5,000 to Oxfam for funds for seeds, medicines and tools; £3,250 to Zoo Animal Rescue for animal sanctuary; £3,201 to Californian Indian Basketweavers to make traditional Californian woven baskets; £3,201 to Plenty USA Pine Ridge Project for gardening and traditional ceremonies; £3,201 to White Earth Land Recovery for promotion of a native American landmark

FINANCES *Year* 1996 *Income* £135,352 *Grants* £100,739

TRUSTEES J Morris, B J Pilkington, A Breslin

PUBLICATIONS Annual Report to members

HOW TO APPLY Funds are fully committed and we regret that no further applications can be considered

WHO TO APPLY TO J Morris, 275 Main Street, Shadwell, Leeds LS17 8LH *Tel* 0113-265 9611

CC NO 268448   **ESTABLISHED** 1974

■ Oppenheimer Charitable Trust

WHAT IS FUNDED General charitable purposes for the well-being and benefit of people living in areas where companies of the De Beers group operate. The following areas are particularly supported:

472

Think carefully about every application. Is it justified?

medicine and health; children and youth; the elderly; general welfare; and the arts

WHAT IS NOT FUNDED Educational grants excluded

WHO CAN BENEFIT Registered charities only. There are no restrictions on the age; professional and economic group; family situation; religion and culture; and social circumstances of; or disease or medical condition suffered by, the beneficiaries. However, particular favour is given to children, young adults and the elderly, the sick, at risk groups, those disadvantaged by poverty and socially isolated people

WHERE FUNDING CAN BE GIVEN UK

FINANCES *Year* 1997 *Income* £60,000
Grants £75,000

TRUSTEES T W H Capon, Sir Christopher Collet, G I Watson

NOTES Grants are made in three ways: (a) by application to the Trustees, (b) by recommendation to the Trustees, and (c) on the initiative of the Trustees themselves

HOW TO APPLY In writing to the address under Who To Apply To. Trustees meet in January, April, July and October each year

WHO TO APPLY TO Alastair Gordon, Oppenheimer Charitable Trust, 17 Charterhouse Street, London EC1N 6RA

CC NO 200395   **ESTABLISHED** 1961

■ The Raymond Oppenheimer Foundation

WHAT IS FUNDED General charitable purposes, including conservation, education, the arts and medical research

WHO CAN BENEFIT National organisations and localised institutions' appeals. There are no restrictions on the age; professional and economic group; family situation; religion and culture; and social circumstances of; or disease or medical condition suffered by, the beneficiaries

WHERE FUNDING CAN BE GIVEN UK

TYPE OF GRANT One-off

RANGE OF GRANTS £500–£66,463

SAMPLE GRANTS £66,463 to Stichting Mario Montessori 75 Fund; £10,000 to Befrienders International; £5,000 to Indo-British Appeal for Cancer Relief; £1,820 to Wexham Gastrointestinal Trust; £1,000 to Commonwealth Jewish Council; £500 to Imperial Cancer Research

FINANCES *Year* 1997 *Income* £44,759
Grants £84,783

TRUSTEES Alec G Berber, David Murphy, C T Elphick

HOW TO APPLY To the address under Who To Apply To in writing

WHO TO APPLY TO D Murphy, The Raymond Oppenheimer Foundation, 17 Charterhouse Street, London EC1N 6RA

CC NO 326551   **ESTABLISHED** 1984

■ Orchard Charity Trust

WHAT IS FUNDED General charitable purposes

WHO CAN BENEFIT There are no restrictions on the age; professional and economic group; family situation; religion and culture; and social circumstances of; or disease or medical condition suffered by, the beneficiaries

WHERE FUNDING CAN BE GIVEN UK

RANGE OF GRANTS £25–£2,200

SAMPLE GRANTS £2,200 to Taunton Shop Mobility; £1,000 to Puriton Village Hall; £1,000 to Dorothy House Foundation – Louis Maxwell's Charity; £850 to Tatworth Memorial Hall; £725 to St Margaret's Hospice

FINANCES *Year* 1996 *Income* £17,760
Grants £10,969

TRUSTEES H Bowles, C E B Clive-Ponsonby-Fane, Ms F Cobbold, P Corrigan, P Easton

WHO TO APPLY TO C Clive-Ponsonby-Fane, Orchard Charity Trust, c/o Orchard FM, Haygrove House, Shoreditch, Taunton TA3 7BT

CC NO 1039900   **ESTABLISHED** 1994

■ The Ordman Family Charitable Trust

This trust did not respond to CAF's request to amend its entry and, by 30 June 1998, CAF's researchers did not find financial records for later than 1995 on its file at the Charity Commission. Trusts are legally required to submit annual accounts to the Charity Commission under section 42 of the Charities Act 1993

WHAT IS FUNDED General charitable purposes

WHO CAN BENEFIT There are no restrictions on the age; professional and economic group; family situation; religion and culture; and social circumstances of; or disease or medical condition suffered by, the beneficiaries

WHERE FUNDING CAN BE GIVEN UK and Israel

TRUSTEES J Ordman, N W Ordman, N Ordman, F Ordman

WHO TO APPLY TO N W Ordman, Trustee, The Ordman Family Charitable Trust, 10 Princes Park Avenue, London NW11 0JP

CC NO 1043518   **ESTABLISHED** 1994

■ Orient Regeneration Trust Ltd

WHAT IS FUNDED To provide facilities for recreation. To provide advice and counselling. To provide education and training opportunities for adults and young children. To relieve those in conditions of poverty, need, hardship and distress. To provide housing for those in need or suffering from a mental or physical handicap. To relieve sickness. To preserve, maintain and repair for the benefit of the public buildings of historical, architectural or constructional interest

WHO CAN BENEFIT Organisations benefiting children, young adults, older people, at risk groups, disabled people, those disadvantaged by poverty and socially isolated people. There is no restriction on the disease or medical condition suffered by the beneficiaries

WHERE FUNDING CAN BE GIVEN London Borough of Waltham Forest

WHO TO APPLY TO S G Cain, Company Secretary, Orient Regeneration Trust Ltd, 7 Kirkdale Road, Leytonstone, London E11 1HP

CC NO 1066883   **ESTABLISHED** 1997

Does the trust you have chosen match your needs? Haphazard applications waste postage and time

473

■ The Ormiston Trust (298 =)

This trust failed to supply a copy of its annual report and accounts to CAF as required under section 47(2) of the Charities Act 1993. The information held on file at the Charity Commission was insufficient to enable CAF's researchers to write a substantive commentary on the trust's activities. Accordingly, despite its size, we are unable to list this trust in Spotlight on Major Trusts

WHAT IS FUNDED General charitable purposes

WHO CAN BENEFIT There are no restrictions on the age; professional and economic group; family situation; religion and culture; and social circumstances of; or disease or medical condition suffered by, the beneficiaries

WHERE FUNDING CAN BE GIVEN UK

FINANCES *Year* 1996 *Income* £567,901

WHO TO APPLY TO The Ormiston Trust, Messrs Kidd Rapinet, 14 and 15 Craven Street, London WC2N 5AD *Tel* 0171-925 0303

CC NO 259334   **ESTABLISHED** 1961

■ Ormonde Foundation

WHAT IS FUNDED Grants are limited to those fields where the Trustees have a personal knowledge of the project or charity concerned with particular emphasis on Church of England churches and charities assisting the blind

WHAT IS NOT FUNDED The Foundation does not consider applications from organisations in the medical field, from individual persons, education, sciences, counselling or from churches other than Church of England churches

WHO CAN BENEFIT Mainly local rather than national charities with emphasis on specific projects, rather than donations to general funds. Organisations benefiting Church of England charities and beneficiaries suffering from sight loss and blindness

WHERE FUNDING CAN BE GIVEN UK

TYPE OF GRANT One-off

RANGE OF GRANTS Approximately 40 grants are made annually with a maximum of £1,000

FINANCES *Year* 1997 *Income* £31,000 *Grants* £23,250

TRUSTEES Lady Martha Ponsonby, L A Ponsonby

HOW TO APPLY Applications considered regularly. No application form required

WHO TO APPLY TO L A Ponsonby, Ormonde Foundation, 12 Tokenhouse Yard, London EC2R 7AN

CC NO 259057   **ESTABLISHED** 1969

■ The Ormsby Charitable Trust

WHAT IS FUNDED Mainly sick, elderly and youth

WHAT IS NOT FUNDED No grants to individuals, religious organisations, animals or overseas charities

WHO CAN BENEFIT Organisations benefiting people of all ages. There is no restriction on the disease or medical condition suffered by the beneficiaries

WHERE FUNDING CAN BE GIVEN UK or specific projects in London and the South East

TYPE OF GRANT Range of grants

FINANCES *Year* 1996–97 *Income* £241,248 *Grants* £489,777

TRUSTEES R O David, A O Chiswell, K O McCrossan

HOW TO APPLY In writing

WHO TO APPLY TO Mrs K O McCrossan, The Ormsby Charitable Trust, 85 Ravenscourt Road, London W6 0NJ

CC NO 1000599   **ESTABLISHED** 1990

■ The Orpheus Trust

WHAT IS FUNDED This Trust will consider funding: arts and arts facilities for the disabled; community arts and recreation for the disabled; and music tuition and music productions for the disabled

WHAT IS NOT FUNDED No grants to individuals

WHO CAN BENEFIT Organisations benefiting the disabled

WHERE FUNDING CAN BE GIVEN UK

TYPE OF GRANT Core costs for up to three years

SAMPLE GRANTS £25,000 to Sounds of Progress a continuation of vital work in Scotland with disabled musicians; £17,000 to Music and the Deaf the continuation of vital work in the deaf community; £10,000 to Drake Research Project to enable the Project to continue its work; £9,000 to Flemming Fulton School, Northern Ireland for specialist teacher; £5,000 to Enabling for Music Project to enable Project to continue its work; £5,000 to Aberdeen International Youth Festival to enable the Festival to take place

FINANCES *Year* 1996–97 *Income* £455,000 *Grants* £80,500

TRUSTEES Rev Donald Reeves, Dr Michael Smith, Esther Rantzen, Alex Armitage, Andrew Murison, Richard Stilgoe, Annabel Stilgoe, Rufus Stilgoe, Dr Jemima Stilgoe, Holly Stilgoe, Jack Stilgoe, Joe Stilgoe

HOW TO APPLY To the address under Who To Apply To in writing

WHO TO APPLY TO Richard Stilgoe, The Orpheus Trust, Trevereux Manor, Limpsfield Chart, Oxted, Surrey RH8 0TL *Tel* 01883 730600

CC NO 292501   **ESTABLISHED** 1985

■ Orr Mackintosh Foundation Limited

WHAT IS FUNDED The Foundation was established to administer SHAREGIFT, the charity share donation scheme. Funds raised are distributed to a range of charitable causes, including charities which help to spread the word about SHAREGIFT

WHAT IS NOT FUNDED No grants to individuals, or organisations not registered with the Charity Commission

WHO CAN BENEFIT Registered charities suggested by share donors. There are no restrictions on the age; professional and economic group; family situation; religion and culture; and social circumstances of; or disease or medical condition suffered by, the beneficiaries

WHERE FUNDING CAN BE GIVEN UK and overseas

TYPE OF GRANT One-off and recurrent

RANGE OF GRANTS £500–£1,000

SAMPLE GRANTS To the Children's Society; To Royal National Institute for the Blind; To Youth Sport Trust; To The Prince's Trust; To Action on Addiction

TRUSTEES The Rt Hon Viscountess Mackintosh of Halifax, M N Orr, C H Moore

NOTES Charities may, if they wish, work with the Foundation by helping to promote SHAREGIFT in their newsletters to supporters and so on. A number of beneficiary charities began their relationship with the Foundation in this way

HOW TO APPLY **This Trust states that it does not respond to unsolicited applications.** There is no point in writing to the Foundation unless the charity is genuinely interested in helping to promote SHAREGIFT

WHO TO APPLY TO Viscountess Mackintosh of Halifax, Orr Mackintosh Foundation Limited, 24 Grosvenor Gardens, London SW1W 0DH

CC NO 1052686   **ESTABLISHED** 1996

■ Orrin Charitable Trust

WHAT IS FUNDED General charitable purposes

WHAT IS NOT FUNDED No grants to individuals

WHO CAN BENEFIT Registered charities. There are no restrictions on the age; professional and economic group; family situation; religion and culture; and social circumstances of; or disease or medical condition suffered by, the beneficiaries

WHERE FUNDING CAN BE GIVEN UK

SAMPLE GRANTS £7,500 to The National Trust for Scotland; £7,000 to Wester Ross Fishing Trust; £5,000 to King George VI and Queen Elizabeth Foundation; £4,000 to Atlantic Salmon Conservation Trust; £3,000 to Patrons of the National Galleries of Scotland; £2,000 to King Edward VII's Hospital for Officers; £2,000 to Royal Academy of Arts; £2,000 to Victim Support, Ross-shire; £1,500 to Ace of Clubs; £1,000 to Ely Stained Glass Museum

FINANCES *Year* 1997 *Income* £51,267 *Grants* £40,500

TRUSTEES Mrs E V Macdonald-Buchanan, A J Macdonald-Buchanan, P H Byam-Cook, H J MacDonald-Buchanan

HOW TO APPLY In writing to the address under Who To Apply To

WHO TO APPLY TO The Secretary, Orrin Charitable Trust, c/o Hedley Foundation Limited, 9 Dowgate Hill, London EC4R 2SU

CC NO 274599   **ESTABLISHED** 1977

■ The Ouseley Trust

WHAT IS FUNDED To promote and maintain to a high standard the choral services of the Church of England, the Church in Wales or the Church of Ireland. To respond to applications on the prescribed application form for grants to help with the attainment of the Trust's objects

WHAT IS NOT FUNDED All applications, including those made on behalf of an individual, must be submitted by an institution. Under normal circumstances, grants will not be awarded for buildings, cassettes, commissions, compact discs, furniture, pianos, robes, tours or visits

WHO CAN BENEFIT Cathedrals, choirs, churches, colleges and choir schools benefiting children and young adults and Christians. Funding may be given to individuals through institutions

WHERE FUNDING CAN BE GIVEN England, Ireland and Wales

TYPE OF GRANT One sum – for specific project or contribution to endowment fund

SAMPLE GRANTS £25,000 to S Woolos Cathedral, Newport as an endowment; £20,000 to Ripon Cathedral as an endowment; £20,000 to Lichfield Cathedral as an endowment; £15,000 to Lincoln Cathedral as an endowment; £10,000 to Wells Cathedral Junior School towards fees; £7,000 to Landaff Cathedral School towards fees; £5,000 to St Martin, Scarborough for the repair of organ; £5,000 to Winchester Cathedral School towards fees; £4,500 to Salisbury Cathedral School towards fees; £4,000 to Reigate St Mary's School towards fees

FINANCES *Year* 1997 *Income* £148,882 *Grants* £135,714

TRUSTEES Prof B W Harvey (Chairman), Dr J A Birch, S J Darlington, Dr L F Dakers, H G Pitt, A Ridley,

C J Robinson, R J Shephard, N E Walker, Rev A F Walters, The Very Rev A G Wedderspoon, Sir David Willcocks

HOW TO APPLY On prescribed form available with guidelines from the address under Who To Apply To. Completed form to be received not later than 31 January for disbursement of grants in April and 30 June for disbursement of grants in October. All applications acknowledged. C5 sae required

WHO TO APPLY TO M Williams, Clerk to the Trustees, The Ouseley Trust, 127 Coleherne Court, London SW5 0EB *Fax* 0171-341 0043 *E-mail* 106200.1023@compuserve.com

CC NO 527519   **ESTABLISHED** 1989

■ Overton Community Trust

WHAT IS FUNDED General charitable purposes in the area Where Funding Can Be Given

WHO CAN BENEFIT There are no restrictions on the age; professional and economic group; family situation; religion and culture; and social circumstances of; or disease or medical condition suffered by, the beneficiaries

WHERE FUNDING CAN BE GIVEN Frodsham in Cheshire and surrounding area

SAMPLE GRANTS £1,514 to the handicapped

FINANCES *Year* 1996–97 *Income* £18,424 *Grants* £2,756

HOW TO APPLY To the address under Who To Apply To in writing

WHO TO APPLY TO Miss K Dower, Secretary, Overton Community Trust, 17 Holly Court, Helsby, Cheshire WA6 0PH

CC NO 1050809   **ESTABLISHED** 1995

■ The Owen Family Trust (formerly New Hall Charity Trust)

WHAT IS FUNDED Mainly support for projects known personally by Trustees. Education, Christian projects, conservation, medical, music and the arts, young people and community facilities

WHAT IS NOT FUNDED Grants to individuals are unlikely

WHO CAN BENEFIT Schools, Christian youth centres, churches, community associations, national schemes and organisations benefiting people of all ages, Christians, and those suffering from Alzheimer's disease, cancers and strokes.

WHERE FUNDING CAN BE GIVEN UK but preference for Midlands, and Gwynedd and Wrexham

TYPE OF GRANT Buildings, capital, and recurring costs will be considered. Funding may be given for more than three years

RANGE OF GRANTS £50–£25,000

SAMPLE GRANTS £6,000 to Bucknall Team Ministry; £5,000 to Lichfield Cathedral; £3,300 to Holy Trinity Church, Sutton Coldfield; £3,000 to YMCA; £3,000 to St Paul's Church, Walsall; £2,000 to Shropshire Archaeological and Historical Society; £2,000 to the Grubb Institute; £2,000 to Sutton Coldfield YMCA; £1,500 to Birmingham Federation of Clubs for Young People; £1,500 to British Youth for Christ

FINANCES *Year* 1997 *Income* £48,008 *Grants* £42,350

TRUSTEES Mrs H G Jenkins, A D Owen

NOTES The Trust is only able to consider about 15 new projects each year. Due to cost it is regretted not all applications will be acknowledged

HOW TO APPLY Send brochures with explanatory letter

WHO TO APPLY TO A D Owen, The Owen Family Trust, Mill Dam House, Mill Lane, Aldridge, Walsall WS9 0NB
CC NO 251975 **ESTABLISHED** 1967

■ Oxfam (GB)

WHAT IS FUNDED Organisations worldwide working for the relief of hunger, disease, exploitation and poverty. Plus organisations working in public education in the UK and Ireland. To use resources with maximum effectiveness in areas of greatest need. Oxfam provides emergency relief in times of crisis, together with long-term sustainable development
WHAT IS NOT FUNDED Grants are not made to individuals
WHO CAN BENEFIT Organisations benefiting: people of all ages; those disadvantaged by poverty; disabled; victims of famine, disasters or war. There is no restriction on the religion and culture of, or the disease or medical condition suffered by the beneficiaries
WHERE FUNDING CAN BE GIVEN Africa, Asia, Latin America and Caribbean, Middle East, Eastern Europe, Former Soviet Union, UK and Ireland
TYPE OF GRANT Majority cash grants
FINANCES *Year* 1996–97 *Income* £91,812,000 *Grants* £26,584,000
TRUSTEES The Council of Trustees
PUBLICATIONS Annual Review, Report and Accounts, Grants List, Oxfam News Magazine (quarterly), *Development in Practice Journal* (quarterly). General and technical publications including *The Oxfam Handbook of Development and Relief*, *Country Profile Series* and Oxfam Working Papers (see Publications Catalogue), Education Material (see Education Catalogue), Audio Visual Resources, Oxfam Trading merchandise catalogue. Variety of free material
NOTES Oxfam's Bridge Programme of Fair Trade markets crafts and goods produced by small community groups in developing countries, by mail order and through Oxfam shops. This programme returns profits to producer groups overseas in the form of dividends or grants. Oxfam is also a founding member of the 'Cafedirect' consortium. Oxfam (GB) is affiliated to Oxfam International, a grouping of international agencies which share a common purpose and beliefs and which co-operate together against hunger, distress, suffering and poverty. The current affiliates are Oxfam (GB), Oxfam Canada, Oxfam Quebec, Oxfam in Belgium, Oxfam Hong Kong, Novib (The Netherlands), Community Aid Abroad (Australia), Intermon (Spain), Oxfam Ireland, Oxfam America and Oxfam New Zealand
HOW TO APPLY To the Oxfam Field Office in the country concerned, or where there is no Field Office to the relevant Area Desk in Oxford
WHO TO APPLY TO The Director, David Bryer, Oxfam (GB), 274 Banbury Road, Oxford, Oxfordshire OX2 7DZ *Tel* 01865 311311 *E-mail* oxfam@oxfam.org.uk
CC NO 202918 **ESTABLISHED** 1942

■ The Oxford Preservation Trust

WHAT IS FUNDED The conservation of the countryside surrounding Oxford; the preservation, repair and restoration of historic buildings in the Oxford Area. Including charities working in the fields of: religious building; support to voluntary and community organisations; support to volunteers; architecture and community facilities

WHAT IS NOT FUNDED No educational grants
WHO CAN BENEFIT Projects must be of public benefit
WHERE FUNDING CAN BE GIVEN Oxford and the surrounding Green Belt
TYPE OF GRANT One-off and recurring grants, interest free loans
FINANCES *Year* 1997 *Income* £368,035 *Grants* £28,588
TRUSTEES Sir David Yardley (Chairman), 26 other Trustees
HOW TO APPLY To the address under Who To Apply To in writing. Initial telephone call welcome. No application form, guidelines or deadlines for application
WHO TO APPLY TO The Secretary, The Oxford Preservation Trust, 10 Turn Again Lane, St Ebbes, Oxford, Oxfordshire OX1 1QL *Tel* 01865 242918
CC NO 203043 **ESTABLISHED** 1927

■ The Oxford Trust

WHAT IS FUNDED Projects in Oxfordshire associated with technology transfer and innovation. Charities working in the fields of: job creation; small enterprises; medical studies and research; and research into science and technology will be considered
WHAT IS NOT FUNDED No grants for further and higher education, medical electives or veterinary studies
WHO CAN BENEFIT At the discretion of the Trustees. Research and education organisations for science and technology only
WHERE FUNDING CAN BE GIVEN Oxfordshire only
TYPE OF GRANT At the discretion of the Trustees
FINANCES *Year* 1998 *Income* £622,601 *Grants* £11,038
TRUSTEES J Welfare, M Lomer, M O'Regan, J Iredale, P Brankin, P Williams
WHO TO APPLY TO Paul Bradstock, the Chief Executive, The Oxford Trust, Oxford Centre for Innovation, Mill Street, Oxford OX2 0JX *Tel* 01865 728953 *Fax* 01865 793165 *E-mail* ocfi@oxtrust.org.uk
CC NO 292664 **ESTABLISHED** 1985

■ The Oxfordshire Community Foundation

WHAT IS FUNDED Community-based non-profit organisations constituted in Oxfordshire for specific projects up to one year with outputs related to poverty, unemployment, education, health promotion, including charities working in the fields of infrastructure and technical support, infrastructure development, charity or voluntary umbrella bodies, residential facilities and services, self help groups, campaigning for health issues, health related volunteer schemes, equal opportunities and various community facilities and services
WHAT IS NOT FUNDED No religious or national appeals will be supported. Annual grants are not given. Medical research, heritage, general building funds, statutory services, core costs and individuals will not be considered
WHO CAN BENEFIT Organisations. There are no restrictions on the age, family situation or disease or medical condition suffered by, the beneficiaries, and very few restrictions on their social circumstances
WHERE FUNDING CAN BE GIVEN Oxfordshire
TYPE OF GRANT One-off, capital. One year start-up for projects, training and equipment
RANGE OF GRANTS £150–£2,500, average £800

SAMPLE GRANTS £2,500 to The Gatehouse, first year salary costs of Food Organiser; £1,500 to Botley Alzheimer's Home, first year project costs for new counselling service; £1,500 to Oxfordshire Association of Young People for new computer for mobile youth project; £1,500 to Willy Freud Centre, first year costs of new voluntary youth centre; £1,000 to Wantage Counselling Service, first year costs of new service for young people; £1,000 to Saneway Credit Union for start-up costs; £1,000 to New Morston Pastoral Centre, first year outreach workers costs; £1,000 to Alsingdon CAB for new photocopier; £1,000 to Cowley and District Credit Union for start-up costs; £1,000 to Dovecote After School Club for start-up costs

FINANCES *Year* 1997–98 *Income* £112,000 *Grants* £22,000

TRUSTEES R Birch, J Bridgeman, Ms L Brighouse, J Harwood, M Smith, D Wood, Sir Martin Wood

PUBLICATIONS *The Other Oxfordshire*

NOTES Total value of open grants for 1998–99 budgeted at £55,000

HOW TO APPLY Via application form. Telephone approaches preferred. Guidelines distributed. Regular deadlines (six monthly)

WHO TO APPLY TO Nick Thorn, Director, The Oxfordshire Community Foundation, 15–19 George Street, Oxford OX1 2AU *Tel* 01865 798666

CC NO 1046432   **ESTABLISHED** 1995

■ Oxfordshire Historic Churches Trust

WHAT IS FUNDED The preservation, repair and restoration of churches in the area Where Funding Can Be Given

WHAT IS NOT FUNDED No grants for fixtures and fittings

WHO CAN BENEFIT Churches and chapels of all denominations which are open for public worship

WHERE FUNDING CAN BE GIVEN Oxfordshire

TYPE OF GRANT One-off grants

RANGE OF GRANTS £500–£7,500

SAMPLE GRANTS £5,000 to St Helen's, Benson for reroofing nave and other repairs; £5,000 to St Michael, Stanton Marcourt for major repairs to roof and walls; £5,000 to St Peter and Paul for repair to infestation damage; £4,000 to St Mary and Edburga, Stratton Andley for reroofing the nave and tower; £3,500 to St Mary the Virgin, Cropredy for roof and drainage repairs; £3,500 to All Saints, Shorthampton for repairs to roof, stonework and gutters; £3,000 to St Giles, Horspath for stonework and general repairs; £3,000 to St Michael and All Angels, Leafield for floor and roof repairs; £3,000 to St Denys, Northmoor for roof repairs and repointing tower; £3,000 to St Mary, Weston-on-the-Green for repairs to tower

FINANCES *Year* 1997–98 *Income* £91,000 *Grants* £70,000

TRUSTEES H L J Brunner, R C Cotton, R H Lethbridge, A H A Sandilands, C Walton

HOW TO APPLY Application forms are available from the address under Who To Apply To. The Trustees usually meet in January, May and September to consider applications

WHO TO APPLY TO R H Lethbridge, Hon Secretary, Oxfordshire Historic Churches Trust, The Dower House, Westhall Hill, Fulbrook, Oxfordshire OX18 4BJ *Tel* 01993 824196

CC NO 235644   **ESTABLISHED** 1964

■ PEAUK (The Physical Education Association of The United Kingdom)

WHAT IS FUNDED To consider all applications from members of the Association related to physical education

WHAT IS NOT FUNDED Grant aid must be related to physical education

WHO CAN BENEFIT PE students, teachers, lecturers

WHERE FUNDING CAN BE GIVEN UK

TYPE OF GRANT Grants for travelling and courses/research related to physical education. Usually to voluntary bodies

FINANCES *Year* 1997 *Income* £222,145 *Grants* £5,000

TRUSTEES The Executive of the Physical Education Association: C Laws (President), Ms M Whitehead (Vice President), J Johnstone (Treasurer), N Armstrong, S Bailey, Ms S Capel, C Casbon, Ms J Elbourn, Ms S Gill, Ms C Jones, B Martin, J Matthews, Ms J Moses, S Poynton, Ms J Tower, P Warburton

PUBLICATIONS *The British Journal of Physical Education*, *Primary Focus*, Annual Report

NOTES The Figure of £5,000 under grants in the Finances relates to research and development costs

HOW TO APPLY In letter form to the General Secretary

WHO TO APPLY TO P Harrison, General Secretary, PEAUK, Suite 5, 10 Church Square, Kings Hill, West Malling, Kent ME19 4DU

CC NO 313647   **ESTABLISHED** 1956

■ PI Global Projects Ltd

WHAT IS FUNDED The training of street children in meaningful skills to become independant adults both socially and economocally. The provision of food, basic education and health care. The provision of a night shelter and building a residential home for children

WHO CAN BENEFIT Street children and young adults

WHERE FUNDING CAN BE GIVEN UK and overseas

TRUSTEES P Fox, Ms D Perreau, M Perreau

WHO TO APPLY TO M Perreau, Chairperson, PI Global Projects Ltd, Croft House, Combe St Nicholas, Taunton, Somerset TA20 3ND

CC NO 1068287   **ESTABLISHED** 1998

■ PPP Healthcare Medical Trust Limited

WHAT IS FUNDED At the time of preparation of the publication the grant-giving programmes and priorities to be adopted by the newly enlarged Trust have yet to be decided, although clearly they will be focused within the objects of the Trust. it is anticipated that they will be announced in January 1999. It should be noted, however, that the registered objects of the Trust are: (a) to promote medical education and training including the education and training of nurses and other persons involved in the provision of healthcare or the management and administration of healthcare providers; (b) to promote medical research and the publication of the useful results of such research; (c) to promote the relief of sickness and disability and the preservation of public health; and (d) to promote the relief of the aged

WHAT IS NOT FUNDED Guidelines will be available in January 1999

WHO CAN BENEFIT Guidelines for applicants will be available in January 1999

WHERE FUNDING CAN BE GIVEN UK and Ireland

TYPE OF GRANT Guidelines will be available in January 1999

FINANCES *Year* 1997 *Income* £34,565,482 *Grants* £295,277

TRUSTEES Sir Peter Gadsden (Chairman), Sir Richard Bayliss, Prof B L Pentecost, Dr R H McNeilly, Dr L T Newman, P H Lord, B H Asher, R B Blaxland, Sir Anthony Grabham, Prof M T Marshall, Sir Peter Morris, Sir Michael Peckham, Sir Keith Peters, D H Probert, Lord Renfrew, M B Sayers, M Sheldon

PUBLICATIONS Annual Report and Accounts

NOTES During the second half of 1998 the Trust has been the subject of a major change as a result of the acquisition of the PPP Healthcare Group by the Guardian Royal Exchange which will eventually result in an endowment in excess of £500 million. Consequently, the Trust has been engaged in restructuring and formulating new policy and procedures

HOW TO APPLY Guidelines for applicants will be available in January 1999

WHO TO APPLY TO The Secretary, PPP Healthcare Medical Trust Limited, 13 Cavendish Square, London W1M 9DA *Tel* 0171-307 2622 *Fax* 0171-307 2623

CC NO 286967   **ESTABLISHED** 1983

■ The Gift of Thomas Packlington

WHAT IS FUNDED Medicine and health, for the research, prevention, alleviation and cure of blindness

WHAT IS NOT FUNDED No grants to students

WHO CAN BENEFIT Established medical research organisations benefiting research workers, medical professionals and those suffering from blindness and sight loss

WHERE FUNDING CAN BE GIVEN UK

TYPE OF GRANT One-off grants

RANGE OF GRANTS £7,294–£51,500

SAMPLE GRANTS £51,500 to an individual at St Thomas's Hospital for work on pathogenesis of proliferative retinopathy; £49,980 to an individual at University of Aberdeen for work on retinal inhibitor of proliferative diabetic retinopathy; £28,191 to an individual at St Thomas's Hospital for work on the role of lasers in vitreous surgery; £15,013 to an individual at Moorfields Hospital for an eye survey of British Asian community; £7,294 to an individual at Heriot Watt University for work on cataract surgery and age-related macular degeneration; £6,733 to an individual at the University of Manchester for work on amoebae in corneal infection

FINANCES *Year* 1997 *Income* £3,529,305 *Grants* £158,711

TRUSTEES R S Powell, B T Gifford, A Aston, M J B Todhunter, J Barrick, Mrs P Powell, Hon Mrs J White

PUBLICATIONS Annual Report

HOW TO APPLY In writing. Application form available

WHO TO APPLY TO P L Quin, The Gift of Thomas Packlington, 5 Castle Row, Horticultural Place, Chiswick, London W4 4JQ

CC NO 205996   **ESTABLISHED** 1935

■ Paddington Charitable Estates Educational Fund

WHAT IS FUNDED The educational benefit of young people under 25 years of age living in Paddington

WHAT IS NOT FUNDED Income not to be applied to relieve public funds

WHO CAN BENEFIT Schools, organisations and individuals under the age of 25 who need assistance in furthering their education

WHERE FUNDING CAN BE GIVEN Former Metropolitan Borough of Paddington

TYPE OF GRANT Buildings and capital

FINANCES *Year* 1996 *Income* £24,881 *Grants* £85,961

TRUSTEES As nominated from time to time by the Westminster City Council, and the Vicars of certain Church of England parishes in Paddington

NOTES The Paddington Charitable Estates contain two branches: the Education branch and the Welfare branch

HOW TO APPLY To the Clerk to the Trustees at the address below

WHO TO APPLY TO The Clerk to the Trustees, Paddington Charitable Estates Educational Fund, 18th Floor, Westminster City Hall, 64 Victoria Street, London SW1E 6QP *Tel* 0171-641 2021

CC NO 212102   **ESTABLISHED** 1934

■ Paddington Relief in Need Charity

WHAT IS FUNDED Relief in need in the area Where Funding Can Be Given

WHO CAN BENEFIT Primarily individuals in need in Paddington

WHERE FUNDING CAN BE GIVEN Paddington

FINANCES *Year* 1995 *Income* £23,360 *Grants* £19,655

HOW TO APPLY To the address under Who To Apply To in writing

WHO TO APPLY TO Miss Sarah Carter, Assistant Clerk, Paddington Relief in Need Charity, 18th Floor, Westminster City Council, 64 Victoria Street, London SW1E 6QP

CC NO 810132   **ESTABLISHED** 1977

■ Paddington Welfare Charities

WHAT IS FUNDED Schools in Paddington, on the basis of the number of Paddington pupils on each school roll. Grants are made to organisations dealing with young adults and children, and to community groups involved in educational activities. Funding may be given for the general benefit of poor and sick people living in Paddington

WHAT IS NOT FUNDED No support for anyone residing outside the former Metropolitan Borough of Paddington. Income not to be applied to relieve public funds

WHO CAN BENEFIT Individuals, and organisations benefiting residents of the former Metropolitan Borough of Paddington. Particular favour may be given to children and young adults and those disadvantaged by poverty. There is no restriction on the disease or medical condition suffered by the beneficiaries

WHERE FUNDING CAN BE GIVEN Former Metropolitan Borough of Paddington

TYPE OF GRANT Cash grants to individuals through local casework agencies and to local charitable or voluntary organisations

FINANCES *Year* 1996 *Income* £17,713
Grants £90,945

TRUSTEES As nominated from time to time by the Westminster City Council, Vicars of certain Church of England parishes in Paddington

HOW TO APPLY To the Clerk to the Trustees at the address under Who To Apply To

WHO TO APPLY TO The Clerk to the Trustees, Paddington Welfare Charities, PO Box 240, Westminster City Hall, Victoria Street, London SW1E 6QP

CC NO 212102   **ESTABLISHED** 1977

■ **The Paget Trust** (also known as the Joanna Herbert-Stepney Charitable Settlement)

WHAT IS FUNDED Sheer need is paramount – and in practice, nothing else can be considered. Preference for the unglamorous, for much achievement with minimal resources. Priorities include Third World, deprived children, old age, 'green' projects, animal welfare. We do sometimes give on-going support, thus leaving fewer funds for new applicants

WHAT IS NOT FUNDED Registered British charities only. We cannot help individuals, students, mental disability, medical research or youth clubs

WHO CAN BENEFIT Normally only British registered charities benefiting: children and older people; at risk groups; those disadvantaged by poverty; socially isolated people; victims of famine, man-made or natural disasters and of war

WHERE FUNDING CAN BE GIVEN UK and overseas, with preference for Loughborough in Leicestershire

RANGE OF GRANTS £200–£7,000

SAMPLE GRANTS £7,000 to Oxfam; £4,000 to Crossroads; £3,000 to Children's Family Trust; £3,000 to Find Your Feet; £3,000 to Leicestershire Care at Home Service; £2,050 to Harvest Help; £2,000 to Impact; £2,000 to John Storer House; £2,000 to Royal Agricultural Benevolent Society; £2,000 to St Petersburg Health Trust

FINANCES *Year* 1997 *Income* £159,597
Grants £129,527

TRUSTEES Joanna Herbert-Stepney, Lesley Rolling, Joy Pollard

HOW TO APPLY Any time – Trustees meet spring and autumn. No application form. Regret we cannot respond to all applications

WHO TO APPLY TO Miss J Herbert-Stepney, The Paget Trust, 41 Priory Gardens, London N6 5QU

CC NO 327402   **ESTABLISHED** 1986

■ **The Palgrave Brown Foundation**

WHAT IS FUNDED Health, education and sports, particularly: medical studies and research; independent schools; costs of study; and sports centres

WHAT IS NOT FUNDED No grants to individuals

WHO CAN BENEFIT Registered charities benefiting: sportsmen and women; students; and those suffering from cancers, sight loss and terminal illness

WHERE FUNDING CAN BE GIVEN National and East Anglia

TYPE OF GRANT Capital, recurring, one-off, endowment and project. Funding is available for up to three years

RANGE OF GRANTS Average £1,000–£2,000. Largest is £85,000

SAMPLE GRANTS £85,000 to Shrewsbury School Foundation for educational scholarship sponsorship; Grants for general purposes:; £3,100 to Marie Curie Cancer Care; £2,100 to Imperial Cancer Research Fund; £2,000 to Kings Lynn and District Headway; £1,000 to Neurofibromatosis Association; £1,000 to Royal National Institute for Blind; £1,000 to Shadingfield Parochial Church Council

FINANCES *Year* 1997 *Income* £76,000
Grants £96,000

TRUSTEES A P Brown, I P Brown

HOW TO APPLY **This Trust states that it does not respond to unsolicited applications**

WHO TO APPLY TO D Dooley, The Palgrave Brown Foundation, 24 Bedford Row, London WC1R 4HA *Tel* 0171-831 6393 *Fax* 0171-831 6393

CC NO 267848   **ESTABLISHED** 1973

■ **Pallant Charitable Trust**

WHAT IS FUNDED Support for the development of choral and organ music within churches in the UK

WHO CAN BENEFIT Christians and musicians

WHERE FUNDING CAN BE GIVEN UK

SAMPLE GRANTS £31,000 to Diocese of Portsmouth for the costs of church music advisor project; £24,000 to Sarum College, Salisbury for the cost of church musician; £14,436 to Prebendal School, Chichester for choristers' scholarship; £2,306 to Dean and Chapter of Chichester for awards to organ scholars

FINANCES *Year* 1996–97 *Income* £59,995
Grants £59,033

TRUSTEES R F Ash, W A Fairbairn

PUBLICATIONS *The Parish Choirbook*

HOW TO APPLY To the address under Who To Apply To in writing

WHO TO APPLY TO The Clerk to the Trustees, Pallant Charitable Trust, 5 East Pallant, Chichester, West Sussex PO19 1TS *Tel* 01243 786111

CC NO 265120   **ESTABLISHED** 1972

■ **The Palmer Foundation**

WHAT IS FUNDED To adhere to triennial grant giving policies. Grants and donations to charitable organisations and payments for educational scholarships, bursaries and prizes at Coopers' Company and Coborn School and Strode's College

WHO CAN BENEFIT Selected registered charities chosen by the Trustees. Children and young adults at Coopers' Company and Coborn School and Strode's College will be considered

WHERE FUNDING CAN BE GIVEN London

TYPE OF GRANT Recurrent grants funded for up to three years will be considered

FINANCES *Year* 1997 *Income* £42,243
Grants £30,411

TRUSTEES The Master Wardens or Keepers of the Commonalty of Freeman of the Mystery of Coopers of the City of London and suburbs (commonly known as the Coopers' Company), including J B Holden, J A Newton, J R Lawes

WHO TO APPLY TO Clerk to the Trustees, The Palmer Foundation, Coopers Hall, 13 Devonshire Square, London EC2M 4TH

CC NO 278666   **ESTABLISHED** 1979

■ **The Eleanor Palmer Trust**

WHAT IS FUNDED Charities working in the fields of: relief of those in need; the provision of almshouses, amenities and grants for its housing association residents; support to voluntary and community organisations; training for personal development; training for work; bursaries and fees; the purchase of books; clubs; day centres; and income support and maintenance

WHO CAN BENEFIT Those living in the area Where Funding Can Be Given. Charities benefiting young adults and older people and those disadvantaged by poverty

WHERE FUNDING CAN BE GIVEN Chipping Barnet, East Barnet, both in Hertfordshire

TYPE OF GRANT One-off, project and capital. Funding for one year or less will be considered

RANGE OF GRANTS £100–£4,000

SAMPLE GRANTS £4,000 to High Barnet Good Neighbour Scheme to help local needy people; £3,550 to The Valley Centre for support to people on a deprived estate; £3,000 to Chipping Barnet Day Centre for running costs of local day centre and mini-bus; £2,840 to own residents for coach outings and towards holiday expenses; £2,500 to Chipping Barnet Poors Trust for electricity vouchers for needy people; £2,500 to Barnet Old People's Welfare Committee; £2,500 to Friend-in-Need for community centre in East Barnet; £2,060 to own residents for Christmas gifts; £1,500 to Barnet Care Attendant Scheme for respite for home carers; £1,500 to Alzheimer's Disease Society (Barnet branch) for rent of hall for day centre

FINANCES *Year* 1998 *Income* £49,000 *Grants* £31,000

TRUSTEES Lawrence Adams, Alan Brown, Pauline Coakley-Webb, Pamela Coleman, Adrian Esdaile, Anthony Grimwade, Stephen Lane, Peter Mellows, Joan Nicholson, Catherine Older, Jan Roethenbaugh

HOW TO APPLY To the address under Who To Apply To in writing

WHO TO APPLY TO R W Peart, Clerk, The Eleanor Palmer Trust, 106b Wood Street, Barnet, Hertfordshire EN5 4BY *Tel* 0181-441 3222

CC NO 220857   **ESTABLISHED** 1558

■ The Gerald Palmer Trust

WHAT IS FUNDED (a) The advancement of the Christian religion more particularly according to the teaching and usage of the Orthodox Churches of the East. (b) The advancement of medical research and the study of medicine. (c) The relief of sickness and/or poverty. (d) General charitable purposes. It is not the policy of the Trustees to grant-aid small local charities geographically remote from the Trust's Estate in Berkshire

WHAT IS NOT FUNDED No grants to individuals

WHO CAN BENEFIT Organisations benefiting: Christians; those disadvantaged by poverty; and the sick. There is no restriction on the disease or medical condition suffered by the beneficiaries

WHERE FUNDING CAN BE GIVEN UK and overseas

RANGE OF GRANTS £100–£11,800

SAMPLE GRANTS £11,800 to Enham Trust; £10,000 to VZV Research Foundation; £9,000 to Winchester College Development Campaign; £6,000 to AMREF; £6,000 to Fight for Sight; £6,000 to FWAG; £6,000 to Oxfordshire Relate; £5,000 to Almshouse Rescue Appeal; £5,000 to GAP; £5,000 to Parkinson's Disease Society

FINANCES *Year* 1997 *Income* £535,950 *Grants* £114,526

TRUSTEES J M Clutterbuck, D R W Harrison, C J Pratt, FRICS, J N Abell

HOW TO APPLY To the address under Who To Apply To

WHO TO APPLY TO C J Pratt, FRICS, The Gerald Palmer Trust, Eling Estate Office, Hermitage, Newbury, Berkshire RG16 9UF

CC NO 271327   **ESTABLISHED** 1968

■ The Rudolph Palumbo Charitable Foundation

WHAT IS FUNDED Advancement of education, conservation of the environment, relief of poverty and general purposes

WHO CAN BENEFIT Registered charities working in the areas outlined. Also appeals of a cultural nature. There are no restrictions on the age; professional and economic group; family situation; religion and culture; and social circumstances of; or disease or medical condition suffered by, the beneficiaries

WHERE FUNDING CAN BE GIVEN UK and overseas

TYPE OF GRANT One-off contributions towards the cost of a project

FINANCES *Year* 1995–96 *Income* £311,663

TRUSTEES Lord Mishcon, T H Tharby, Sir Matthew Farrer, Lady Palumbo, J G Underwood

HOW TO APPLY To the address below in writing

WHO TO APPLY TO T H Tharby, The Rudolph Palumbo Charitable Foundation, 37a Walbrook, London EC4N 8BS

CC NO 801683   **ESTABLISHED** 1989

■ Papua New Guinea Church Partnership *(formerly New Guinea Mission)*

WHAT IS FUNDED Provision of financial assistance to the development of the Anglican Church in Papua New Guinea

WHO CAN BENEFIT People in the Anglican Province of Papua New Guinea

WHERE FUNDING CAN BE GIVEN Papua New Guinea

FINANCES *Year* 1995 *Income* £131,279 *Grants* £55,436

TRUSTEES The members of the United Kingdom Committee for the time being including Most Rev and Rt Hon Dr David Hope, Archbishop of York (President)

PUBLICATIONS Papers, leaflets, etc. *Occasional Paper* published from time to time

NOTES PNGCP assists in the recruitment of missionaries (priests, teachers and administrative staff) mostly for training posts. Contributions are made to the Anglican Province of Papua New Guinea for all aspects of the Church's work

WHO TO APPLY TO Mrs C Luxton, Secretary, Papua New Guinea Church Partnership, Partnership House, 157 Waterloo Road, London SE1 8XA

CC NO 249446   **ESTABLISHED** 1891

■ Paragon Concert Society

WHAT IS FUNDED To promote the knowledge and performance of serious music for small combinations of instruments, for string orchestras, with or without voices and instrumental soloists for the purpose of educating its members and the general public in music of the highest standard the emphasis being on music local to Bristol

WHAT IS NOT FUNDED No grants to individuals

WHO CAN BENEFIT To the benefit of musicians and those with an interest in music

WHERE FUNDING CAN BE GIVEN Only local to the Bristol Area

TYPE OF GRANT Money grants for commissions or the purchase of instruments or guarantees against loss in respect of musical events. Funding is usually one-off grants

RANGE OF GRANTS £5–£1,000, typical grant £300

FINANCES *Year* 1997 *Income* £10,000 *Grants* £10,000

TRUSTEES D F Gibbs, C J Brisley, Mrs J V Prichard, Miss L Leschke, A Tyrrell

NOTES Applications from individual students for tuition fees or maintenance grants will not be considered

HOW TO APPLY At any time by letter with supporting figures. No application form required

WHO TO APPLY TO C J Brisley, Paragon Concert Society, 13 St Edwards Road, Clifton Wood, Bristol BS8 4TS

CC NO 280203   **ESTABLISHED** 1952

■ The Paragon Trust

WHAT IS FUNDED To support a wide range of charitable bodies

WHO CAN BENEFIT Charities and occasionally certain individuals but only those known to the Trustees. There are no restrictions on the age; professional and economic group; family situation; religion and culture; and social circumstances of; or disease or medical condition suffered by, the beneficiaries

WHERE FUNDING CAN BE GIVEN UK

TYPE OF GRANT The majority of donations are standing orders

RANGE OF GRANTS £150–£3,000

SAMPLE GRANTS £3,000 to British Red Cross; £1,100 to Crisis; £1,100 to Newnham College; £1,100 to The Salvation Army; £1,000 to YMCA; £1,000 to Greenpeace Trust; £1,000 to Mildmay Mission Hospital; £1,000 to Cancer Relief Macmillan Fund; £1,000 to National Aids Trust; £1,000 to Action Health

FINANCES *Year* 1997 *Income* £36,034 *Grants* £41,389

TRUSTEES Miss B Whistler, Rt Hon J B B Wrenbury, Rev Canon R F Coppin, Miss L J Whistler, P Cunningham, P Bagwell-Purefoy

HOW TO APPLY **This Trust states that it does not respond to unsolicited applications**

WHO TO APPLY TO Miss B Whistler, c/o Thomson, Snell & Passmore, Solicitors, 3 Lonsdale Gardens, Tunbridge Wells, Kent TN1 1NX *Tel* 01892 510000

CC NO 278348   **ESTABLISHED** 1979

■ The Parham Park Trust (1984)

This trust did not respond to CAF's request to amend its entry and, by 30 June 1998, CAF's researchers did not find financial records for later than 1995 on its file at the Charity Commission. Trusts are legally required to submit annual accounts to the Charity Commission under section 42 of the Charities Act 1993

WHAT IS FUNDED General charitable purposes

WHAT IS NOT FUNDED No grants to individuals

WHO CAN BENEFIT Registered charities only. There are no restrictions on the age; professional and economic group; family situation; religion and culture; and social circumstances of; or disease or medical condition suffered by, the beneficiaries

WHERE FUNDING CAN BE GIVEN UK

TRUSTEES The Cowdray Trust Ltd, N W Smith

WHO TO APPLY TO N W Smith, The Parham Park Trust (1984), 21 Buckingham Gate, London SW1E 6LS

CC NO 288828   **ESTABLISHED** 1984

■ Parish Estate

WHAT IS FUNDED The upkeep of St Michael's Church, Spurriergate and any other Church of England church in York; welfare, health and disability

WHO CAN BENEFIT To benefit Church of England; at risk groups; disabled people; those disadvantaged by poverty and socially isolated people. There is no restriction on the disease or medical condition suffered by the beneficiaries

WHERE FUNDING CAN BE GIVEN York

RANGE OF GRANTS £650–£60,000

SAMPLE GRANTS £60,000 to Confessor Church for an extension; £60,000 to All Saints, Pavement for restoration work; £30,000 to All Saints, North Street for work on the vestry stonework and south boundary wall; £20,000 to Holy Trinity, Heworth for leaded glazing; £15,000 to St Michael-le-Belfrey; £10,434 to St Michael's York Trust; £7,033 to St Bedes Pastoral Centre; £5,351 to York and District Cerebral Palsy Society; £5,000 to St Luke's, Burton Stone Lane for quinquennial work; £4,000 to Age Concern

FINANCES *Year* 1995 *Income* £171,523 *Grants* £220,468

TRUSTEES R C Wheway (Chairman), Miss E M Gladwin, C Henderson, D A G Titchener, E F V Waterson, J I Watson, Miss C H L Woollcombe

HOW TO APPLY To the address under Who To Apply To in writing

WHO TO APPLY TO A B Anderson, Clerk, Parish Estate, c/o Messrs Cowling Swift Kitchin, 8 Blake Street, York YO1 1XJ

CC NO 250552   **ESTABLISHED** 1967

■ Parish Lands

WHAT IS FUNDED The Trust supports church wardens, education and welfare within the area Where Funding Can Be Given

WHO CAN BENEFIT Local organisations benefiting children and young adults; church wardens; at risk groups; those disadvantaged by poverty and socially isolated people

WHERE FUNDING CAN BE GIVEN South Brent

SAMPLE GRANTS £3,000 to South Brent School for education and welfare; £2,000 to Friends of South Brent Health Centre for welfare

FINANCES *Year* 1997 *Income* £37,000 *Grants* £27,000

TRUSTEES Rev J Harper, R E Cockings, B Cockfield, C Wood, G H French, R Savery, Dr J Halliday, Mrs A Collier, Mrs C Pannell

HOW TO APPLY To the address under Who To Apply To in writing

WHO TO APPLY TO J I G Blackler, Clerk, Parish Lands, Luscombe Maye, Manorside, Fore Street, South Brent, Devon TQ10 9BQ *Tel* 01364 73651

CC NO 255283   **ESTABLISHED** 1968

■ Parish Lands Charity (Exclusive of Educational Foundation)

WHAT IS FUNDED To benefit people in the area Where Funding Can Be Given and to maintain Colyton Town Hall

WHO CAN BENEFIT Individuals and organisations in the Parish of Colyton. There are no restrictions on the age; professional and economic group; family situation; religion and culture; and social circumstances of; or disease or medical condition suffered by, the beneficiaries

WHERE FUNDING CAN BE GIVEN Within the Parish of Colyton

Does the trust you have chosen match your needs? Haphazard applications waste postage and time

481

TYPE OF GRANT Buildings, interest free loans, one-off and recurring costs will be considered

SAMPLE GRANTS To Girl Guides Association an interest free loan for new HQ building; To Colyton County Primary School for hosting school children from the US; To Colyton Scouts and Cubs for summer camps; To a single mother for travelling expenses to attend college; To Colyton County Primary School for musical tuition for two pupils; To a local resident for financial assistance during serious illness

FINANCES *Year* 1997–98 *Income* £31,595 *Grants* £1,377

TRUSTEES Colyton Chamber of Feoffees

HOW TO APPLY To the address under Who To Apply To in writing

WHO TO APPLY TO A D Gaines, Parish Lands Charity, Colyton Chamber of Feoffees, Town Hall, Market Place, Colyton, Devon EX13 6JR
Tel 01297 553505

CC NO 243224   **ESTABLISHED** 1546

■ The Parivar Trust

WHAT IS FUNDED Relief of sickness and poverty, provision of education, preservation and protection of good health. Grants are for the benefit of children, young people and women. Charities working in the area of infrastructure development will be considered

WHAT IS NOT FUNDED Donations to individuals for further and vocational courses, or sponsored trips are not funded

WHO CAN BENEFIT Individuals and local projects are priorities, but national organisations are also considered. Support is given to: children; women; those in care, fostered and adopted; and parents and children. At risk groups; disabled people; those disadvantaged by poverty; socially isolated people; and victims of abuse and domestic violence may also be considered

WHERE FUNDING CAN BE GIVEN UK with preference for the West Midlands

TYPE OF GRANT Buildings, capital, core costs, one-off, project, recurring costs, running costs, salaries and start-up costs will be considered. Funding may be given for up to three years

RANGE OF GRANTS £50–£500 in UK

FINANCES *Year* 1997 *Income* £27,695 *Grants* £19,033

TRUSTEES N A Rogers, Dr P Ramani, R O Walters

PUBLICATIONS Annual Report

HOW TO APPLY In writing at any time

WHO TO APPLY TO N A Rogers, The Parivar Trust, 62 Symphony Court, Birmingham B16 8AF

CC NO 1032529   **ESTABLISHED** 1993

■ The Park Hill Trust

WHAT IS FUNDED To encourage imaginative new projects which aim to improve the quality of life of older people in retirement and to relieve loneliness by helping them to use their knowledge and experience for the benefit of the community. Particularly charities working in the fields of: arts and arts facilities; community arts and recreation and community facilities

WHAT IS NOT FUNDED The Trust aims to encourage new ideas rather than existing work. No project will be considered unless older people play an active rather than a passive role

WHO CAN BENEFIT Registered charities, but not major nationally known organisations benefiting older people and retired people

WHERE FUNDING CAN BE GIVEN UK

TYPE OF GRANT One-off for a specific project only. Not to be used for payment of salaries. Start-up costs. Funding for one year or less will be considered

FINANCES *Year* 1996–97 *Income* £46,000 *Grants* £41,000

TRUSTEES A M Pilch, Mrs B C Pilch, J R Pendrigh, Mrs R A Gill, P D Salter

HOW TO APPLY No applications can be considered unless they satisfy both What Is Funded and What Is Not Funded above. Applications falling outside these guidelines will not be acknowledged. Apply in writing. No application forms or guidelines, other than those listed above, are issued

WHO TO APPLY TO A M Pilch, The Park Hill Trust, Miller Centre, 30 Godstone Road, Caterham, Surrey CR3 6RA

CC NO 258420   **ESTABLISHED** 1969

■ C F Parker Charitable Trust

WHAT IS FUNDED General charitable purposes

WHO CAN BENEFIT There are no restrictions on the age; professional and economic group; family situation; religion and culture; and social circumstances of; or disease or medical condition suffered by, the beneficiaries

WHERE FUNDING CAN BE GIVEN UK

WHO TO APPLY TO A Vernon, Secretary, C F Parker Charitable Trust, c/o Manby and Steward, Solicitors, Mander House, Mander Centre, Wolverhampton, West Midlands WV1 3NE

CC NO 1048673   **ESTABLISHED** 1995

■ Parkhill Charitable Trust

This trust did not respond to CAF's request to amend its entry and, by 30 June 1998, CAF's researchers did not find financial records for later than 1995 on its file at the Charity Commission. Trusts are legally required to submit annual accounts to the Charity Commission under section 42 of the Charities Act 1993

WHAT IS FUNDED Relief of poverty, Jewish, education and general charitable purposes

WHO CAN BENEFIT Children, young adults, Jewish people and those disadvantaged by poverty

WHERE FUNDING CAN BE GIVEN Manchester

TRUSTEES Deborah Guttentag, Martin S Caller, Jonathan Guttentag

HOW TO APPLY To the address below in writing

WHO TO APPLY TO J Guttentag, Trustee, Parkhill Charitable Trust, 1 Parkhill Drive, Whitefield, Manchester M45 7PD

CC NO 1019828   **ESTABLISHED** 1993

■ The Frank Parkinson Agricultural Trust

WHAT IS FUNDED To make grants in support of the improvement and welfare of British agriculture, primarily to Agricultural Colleges and affiliated institutions

WHAT IS NOT FUNDED Existing financial commitments are such that the Trustees are unable to consider applications by individuals for financial assistance

WHO CAN BENEFIT Mainly corporate entities benefiting the improvement of agriculture and horticulture

WHERE FUNDING CAN BE GIVEN UK

TYPE OF GRANT Short term: two to four years preferred. One-off will also be considered

RANGE OF GRANTS One-off at Chairman's discretion: smallest £200, largest over three years: £100,000, typical grants (over two years): £40,000

SAMPLE GRANTS £40,000 to Wye College, University of London (part of £100,000) Library and Learning Resources Centre; £6,790 to Nuffield Farming Scholarship Trust for annual travel scholarship; £200 to British Association for the Advancement of Science for lecture costs
FINANCES *Year* 1997 *Income* £59,872
Grants £46,990
TRUSTEES Prof P N Wilson, J S Sclanders, Prof J D Leaver, W M Hudson, C P Bourchier
HOW TO APPLY In advance of annual meeting in April. Guidelines are issued, on application. Applications are acknowledged. Annual accounts are not required
WHO TO APPLY TO A D S Robb Esq CA, Secretary, The Frank Parkinson Agricultural Trust, 33 Prospect Lane, West Common, Harpenden, Hertfordshire AL5 2PL
CC NO 209407   **ESTABLISHED** 1943

■ The Parsonage Trust

WHAT IS FUNDED General charitable purposes
WHO CAN BENEFIT There are no restrictions on the age; professional and economic group; family situation; religion and culture; and social circumstances of; or disease or medical condition suffered by, the beneficiaries
WHERE FUNDING CAN BE GIVEN UK
TRUSTEES Sir M Reid, Ms A Whitten, Ms E Whitten, Ms K Whitten, Mrs J Whitten, K R Whitten, Mrs S Whitten, P J H Whitten
WHO TO APPLY TO Pankaj Shah, Hon Treasurer, The Parsonage Trust, 237 Preston Road, Wembley, Middlesex HA9 8PE
CC NO 1053921   **ESTABLISHED** 1996

■ Thomas Parson's Charity (otherwise
known as Land and Possessions of the Poor of Ely)

WHAT IS FUNDED Primarily concerned with the provision and maintenance of almshouses; grants are also made available to individuals and organisations for welfare purposes
WHO CAN BENEFIT Individuals and organisations benefiting at risk groups, those disadvantaged by poverty, homeless and socially isolated people
WHERE FUNDING CAN BE GIVEN Ely
FINANCES *Year* 1995–96 *Income* £105,945
TRUSTEES Lord Bishop of Ely, Dean of Ely, Archdeacon of Ely, R B Bamford, W Bebbington, J Brand, Dr J Crawford, D A Hughes, Canon F Kilner, D O Morbey, R O Setchell, J E Watterson
HOW TO APPLY To the address under Who To Apply To in writing
WHO TO APPLY TO J M Smith, Secretary, Thomas Parson's Charity, Messrs Hall Ennion & Young, 8 High Street, Ely, Cambridgeshire CB7 4JY
CC NO 202634   **ESTABLISHED** 1972

■ The Parthenon Trust

WHAT IS FUNDED General charitable purposes, with an emphasis on the relief of hardship and the advancement of health (including support for medical research). Interested in helping war and famine victims including refugees, helping the aged, homeless and the long-term unemployed. The Trust supports long-term development in the third world, and medical research, patient care, orphanages, hospices and to help the disabled
WHAT IS NOT FUNDED No grants to individuals

WHO CAN BENEFIT Organisations benefiting the elderly, the sick, those in care, fostered and adopted and those suffering from hardship. There is no restriction on the disease or medical condition suffered by the beneficiaries. Support may be given to medical professionals and research workers
WHERE FUNDING CAN BE GIVEN UK and overseas
TYPE OF GRANT Normally one-off grants made for general purposes. Research will be considered
RANGE OF GRANTS Wide range, no typical grant
FINANCES *Year* 1996 *Income* £7,612,895
Grants £7,142,939
TRUSTEES Dr J M Darmady, Prof C N Hales, Mrs Geraldine Whittaker
HOW TO APPLY The Trustees meet irregularly, but at least twice a year. Applications are not considered or acknowledged, unless the applicant has previously telephoned the Secretary and has been informed that it would be appropriate to make an application
WHO TO APPLY TO John E Whittaker, Secretary, The Parthenon Trust, La Maison de Huite, St Saviour, Guernsey, Channel Islands GY7 9XR
Tel 01481 65177   *Fax* 01481 66590
CC NO 1051467   **ESTABLISHED** 1995

■ Alan Pascoe Charitable Trust

WHAT IS FUNDED Medical and children's charities
WHO CAN BENEFIT Organisations benefiting children and sick people. There is no restriction on the disease or medical condition suffered by the beneficiaries
WHERE FUNDING CAN BE GIVEN UK
TYPE OF GRANT One-off and recurrent
RANGE OF GRANTS £20–£75,000
SAMPLE GRANTS £75,000 to British Athletics Federation; £5,000 to Piers and Ashley Home; £4,000 to Team Solent Young Athletes; £4,000 to Spelthorne Elite Gym Club; £2,694 to the Teenage Cancer Trust
FINANCES *Year* 1996 *Income* £18,449
Grants £102,594
TRUSTEES E P S Leesk, A P Pascoe
WHO TO APPLY TO E P S Leesk, Alan Pascoe Charitable Trust, Messrs Edward Leesk, The Old Treasury, 7 Kings Road, Portsmouth, Hampshire PO5 4DJ
CC NO 296552   **ESTABLISHED** 1986

■ The Constance Paterson Charitable Foundation

WHAT IS FUNDED Medical research, welfare of elderly and children
WHAT IS NOT FUNDED No personal applications please
WHO CAN BENEFIT Organisations benefiting children, older people, retired people, at risk groups, socially isolated people and those disadvantaged by poverty. There is no restrictions on the medical condition suffered by the beneficiaries
WHERE FUNDING CAN BE GIVEN UK
TYPE OF GRANT One-off
RANGE OF GRANTS £250–£5,000

SAMPLE GRANTS £3,000 to Camping Holidays for Inner City Kids for camping holidays for underprivileged children; £3,000 to Dystrophic Epidermolysis Belize Research Association for medical research; £3,000 to Contact The Elderly for companionship groups for isolated elderly; £2,500 to Wheelchair Children provides equipment and specialist training; £2,500 to Leukaemia Research Fund for research project in 'B' cells; £2,500 to Guideposts Trust for Day CAre Service Centres for older and infirm people; £2,500 to DEMAND to fund the employment of craftsmen to design and manufacture for disability; £2,250 to Arthritis Research Centre for The Arthritis Research Centre in Oswestry; £2,250 to Counsel and Care for a free and confidential advice service; £2,000 to the NSPCC for NSPCC Child Projection Helpline

FINANCES *Year* 1996–97 *Income* £40,000 *Grants* £27,500

TRUSTEES Royal Bank of Canada Trust Corporation Limited

HOW TO APPLY June and December. No application forms. Send in application under cover of a letter and include latest set of report and accounts

WHO TO APPLY TO Mrs S Tayler, The Constance Paterson Charitable Foundation, Royal Bank of Canada Trust Corporation Limited, 71 Queen Victoria Street, London EC4V 4DE

CC NO 249556   **ESTABLISHED** 1966

■ Arthur James Paterson Charitable Trust

WHAT IS FUNDED Medical research, welfare of elderly and children

WHAT IS NOT FUNDED No personal applications, please. Purely local appeals unlikely to receive grants

WHO CAN BENEFIT Organisations benfiting children, older people, reitired people, at risk groups and socially isolated people and those disadvantaged by poverty. There is no restriction on the disease or medical condition suffered by the beneficiaries

WHERE FUNDING CAN BE GIVEN UK

TYPE OF GRANT One-off

RANGE OF GRANTS £250–£5,000

SAMPLE GRANTS £7,150 to Glenalmond College for educational assistance; £7,150 to Worcester College for educational assistance; £3,400 to The Jessie May Trust for respite care for families nursing terminally ill children; £2,900 to Myasthenia Gravis Association for medical research - Auto Immune Disease; £2,900 to The Blond McIndoe Research Centre for Medical research - Burns, injuries and nerve restoration; £2,750 to Kings Medical Research for medical research - Strokes; £2,750 to Motor Neurone Disease medical research project; £2,750 to Invalids-at-Home to assist people with disabilities to live at home; £2,750 to The Malcom Sargent Cancer Fund for Children to fund the purchase of a property as a respite holiday home; £2,500 to Deaf Blind UK which looks after the welfare of the elderly who have lost both their sight and hearing

FINANCES *Year* 1996–97 *Income* £49,300 *Grants* £42,500

TRUSTEES Royal Bank of Canada Trust Corporation Ltd

HOW TO APPLY February and August. No application forms. Send your application in under cover of a letter and include latest set of report and accounts

WHO TO APPLY TO Mrs S Tayler, Arthur James Paterson Charitable Trust, Royal Bank of Canada Trust Corporation Ltd, 71 Queen Victoria Street, London EC4V 4DE

CC NO 278569   **ESTABLISHED** 1979

■ Mrs M E S Paterson's Charitable Trust

WHAT IS FUNDED Support to the Church of Scotland and other Christian groups in the maintenance of church buildings and in their work with young people; also other causes

WHO CAN BENEFIT Organisations benefiting Christians and young people

WHERE FUNDING CAN BE GIVEN Scotland

FINANCES *Year* 1997 *Income* £30,000 *Grants* £40,000

TRUSTEES C S Kennedy, M A Noble, J A W Somerville

PUBLICATIONS Accounts are available from the Trust

HOW TO APPLY Applications should be made in writing to the address below

WHO TO APPLY TO C S Kennedy, Mrs M E S Paterson's Charitable Trust, Lindsays Solicitors, 11 Atholl Crescent, Edinburgh EH3 8HE

SC NO SCO 04835   **ESTABLISHED** 1989

■ Patients' Aid Association Hospital and Medical Charities Trust

WHAT IS FUNDED Provision of equipment and patient amenities to NHS hospitals, hospices, convalescent homes and other medically related charities in the area where the parent Association operates. These include: support to volunteers; health professional bodies; Councils for Voluntary Service; advancement of religion; churches; respite; sheltered accommodation; health; special schools; speech therapy; special needs education; scholarships; medical research; specialist research; and community services

WHAT IS NOT FUNDED Appeals must be from Officials of the appealing body and submitted on official stationery. Appeals not accepted from, or on behalf of, individuals or for provision of vehicles

WHO CAN BENEFIT Mainly NHS hospitals and registered, medically related charities benefiting children; young adults; older people; ex-service and service people; medical professionals, nurses and doctors; musicians; research workers; volunteers; those in care; fostered and adopted; at risk groups; carers; disabled people; those disadvantaged by poverty; disaster victims; ex-offenders and those at risk of offending; gays and lesbians; homeless people; victims of abuse and domestic violence; and victims of war. There are no restrictions on the disease or medical condition of the beneficiaries

WHERE FUNDING CAN BE GIVEN Mainly East and West Midlands, Staffordshire and Shropshire areas

TYPE OF GRANT Mainly medical equipment. Grants not made towards running costs or administration

RANGE OF GRANTS £953–£2,600

SAMPLE GRANTS £2,600 to Muscular Dystrophy, Birmingham for wheelchairs; £2,500 to Whizz Kidz, London for a special walker for the disabled; £2,000 to Portland College, Nottingham for two lightwriters; £1,800 to Royal Institute for the Blind, Birmingham for a bath hoist; £1,640 to Wolverhampton Healthcare NHS Trust for physiotherapy equipment; £1,500 to Norton House Community Care, Keele for an industrial cooker; £1,000 to Martha Trust, Hereford for multi-sensory equipment; £990 to Leukemia Unit, Dudley for a special bed; £963 to St Anthony's Cheshire Home, Wolverhampton for two shower chairs; £953 to Cotswold Care Hospice, Gloucester for special chairs

FINANCES *Year* 1997 *Income* £86,278 *Grants* £42,139

TRUSTEES T P Horan (Chairman), E P Booth, G F Lewis, T E Ratcliffe, H Reynolds, D Bradley, J Dickie

PUBLICATIONS Brochure concerning Trust

NOTES The Trustees meet four times a year. All appeals are considered before a decision is reached. Full details of the use to which the donations will be put and the cost of the equipment required must be included with the appeal letter

HOW TO APPLY Grant Application Form available on written request giving brief details of requirements and appellant

WHO TO APPLY TO Mrs Patricia Stokes, Secretary, Patients' Aid Association Hospital and Medical Charities Trust, Paycare House, George Street, Wolverhampton WV2 4DX *Tel* 01902 713131 *Fax* 01902 710361

CC NO 240378 **ESTABLISHED** 1964

■ Andrew Paton's Charitable Trust

WHAT IS FUNDED Grants are given to a range of charitable activities such as Christian missionary and youth work, support for a hospice, for children's charities and for medical research

WHAT IS NOT FUNDED No grants to individuals

WHO CAN BENEFIT Organisations benefiting children and young adults. There is no restriction on the disease or medical condition suffered by the beneficiaries

WHERE FUNDING CAN BE GIVEN UK and overseas, particularly Scotland

TRUSTEES N A Fyfe, G A Maguire

PUBLICATIONS Accounts are available from the Trust

HOW TO APPLY Applications should be made in writing to the address below

WHO TO APPLY TO Andrew Paton's Charitable Trust, 190 St Vincent Street, Glasgow G2 5SP

SC NO SCO 17502

■ The Patrick Trust

WHAT IS FUNDED Mainly charities undertaking medical and other work for the disabled, in particular muscular dystrophy

WHAT IS NOT FUNDED No grants to individuals

WHO CAN BENEFIT Registered charities benefiting the disabled, particularly those with muscular dystrophy. Support may also be given to carers and medical professionals

WHERE FUNDING CAN BE GIVEN UK, especially the Midlands area

FINANCES *Year* 1995 *Income* £87,553

TRUSTEES J A Patrick, R L Patrick, M V Patrick, M Kay

NOTES Only registered charities are considered for funding

HOW TO APPLY No specific date. No acknowledgement of unsuccessful applications, unless sae enclosed

WHO TO APPLY TO Alexander Patrick, Chairman, The Patrick Trust, Priory Mill, Castle Road, Studley, West Midlands B80 7AA

CC NO 213849 **ESTABLISHED** 1962

■ The Late Barbara May Paul Charitable Trust

WHAT IS FUNDED Suffolk based charities given priority but national charities considered, with emphasis on care for the elderly and medical research

WHO CAN BENEFIT Registered charities benefiting older people needing care. Research workers and medical professionals will be considered. There is no restriction on the disease or medical condition suffered by the beneficiaries

WHERE FUNDING CAN BE GIVEN Suffolk

TYPE OF GRANT Research funding is considered

RANGE OF GRANTS £150–£10,000

SAMPLE GRANTS £10,000 to British Red Cross; £5,000 to Quidenham Children's Hospice; £5,000 to King George V Memorial Homes; £5,000 to YMCA; £5,000 to East Suffolk MIND; £3,000 to Suffolk Deaf Association; £2,500 to St John the Baptist; £2,500 to Royal Hospital for Neuro-disability; £2,500 to Carousel; £2,000 to St Matthew Society

FINANCES *Year* 1997 *Income* £263,365 *Grants* £124,850

TRUSTEES Lloyds Bank plc

HOW TO APPLY In writing with as much literature as appropriate

WHO TO APPLY TO C Shambrook, Assistant Manager, The Late Barbara May Paul Charitable Trust, Lloyds Private Banking Ltd, Thames Valley Area Office, The Clock House, 22–26 Ock Street, Abingdon, Oxfordshire OX14 5SW

CC NO 256420 **ESTABLISHED** 1968

■ Margaret Jeanne Paul Charitable Trust

WHAT IS FUNDED Suffolk based charities given priority, but national charities considered with emphasis on care for the elderly and medical research

WHO CAN BENEFIT Registered charities benefiting elderly people needing care. Research workers and medical professionals will be considered. There is no restriction on the disease or medical condition suffered by the beneficiaries

WHERE FUNDING CAN BE GIVEN Great Britain with preference for Suffolk

TYPE OF GRANT Research is considered for funding

RANGE OF GRANTS £100–£6,000

SAMPLE GRANTS £6,000 to British Red Cross; £500 to St Elizabeth Hospice; £500 to King George V Memorial Homes; £500 to Children's Hospice for the East Region; £500 to Charter House-in-Southwark

FINANCES *Year* 1997 *Income* £18,324 *Grants* £15,250

TRUSTEES Lloyds Bank plc

HOW TO APPLY In writing with as much literature as appropriate

WHO TO APPLY TO C Shambrook, (Ref 81295/GEW) Margaret Jeanne Paul Charitable Trust, Lloyds Private Banking Ltd, S Midlands Area Office, The Clock House, 22–26 Ock Street, Abingdon, Oxfordshire OX14 5SW

CC NO 256418 **ESTABLISHED** 1968

Does the trust you have chosen match your needs? Haphazard applications waste postage and time

485

■ The Paul Foundation

WHAT IS FUNDED To aid and fund research into improving health care and general charitable purposes at Trustees' discretion

WHO CAN BENEFIT Institutions benefiting research workers. There is no restriction on the disease or medical condition suffered by the beneficiaries

WHERE FUNDING CAN BE GIVEN UK and overseas

TYPE OF GRANT At the discretion of the Trustees

SAMPLE GRANTS £5,000 to Cavendish Memorial Fund

FINANCES *Year* 1997 *Income* £110,531
Grants £5,000

TRUSTEES P R D Paul, D Harvey, Ms N Michaelis

WHO TO APPLY TO P R D Paul, The Paul Foundation, Haycroft, Sherborne, Gloucestershire GL54 3NB

CC NO 1003143 **ESTABLISHED** 1991

■ The Payne Charitable Trust

WHAT IS FUNDED To support religious and charitable objects. The main area of interest is the support of Evangelical Christians in the promotion and proclamation of the Christian gospel

WHAT IS NOT FUNDED Grants are not given for the preservation of historic buildings, including churches, nor to individuals seeking assistance in their further education or research

WHO CAN BENEFIT Missionaries, churches, and people engaged in the propagation of the Gospel

WHERE FUNDING CAN BE GIVEN UK and overseas

TYPE OF GRANT Cash aid

RANGE OF GRANTS £75–£23,595

SAMPLE GRANTS £23,595 to the Andrew League Trust; £2,725 to Crusaders; £2,250 to SASRA; £2,000 to Association of Military Christian Fellowship; £1,655 to TEW Poland; £1,000 to Love Russia; £600 to Bloomsbury Evangelical Church; £250 to St George's Church; £75 to National Truss and Surgical Appliance

FINANCES *Year* 1997 *Income* £75,474
Grants £34,150

TRUSTEES John Payne, Eric Payne

NOTES Due to the large number of applications, some considerable time can elapse before communication can be sent. Grants are not made to individuals

HOW TO APPLY Applications should be made in the period 1 January to 21 March for grants from the following 1 May. An sae should be included if reply is required

WHO TO APPLY TO J Payne, The Payne Charitable Trust, Copthorne House, The Broadway, Abergele LL22 7DD

CC NO 241816 **ESTABLISHED** 1965

■ The Harry Payne Trust

WHAT IS FUNDED To give priority to charitable work in Birmingham, where the trust was founded, in response to appeals. Funding may be given to: churches and religious ancillary buildings; family planning and well woman clinics; hospices and hospitals. Support may also go to woodlands, pre-school ands special needs education, advice centres and community services

WHAT IS NOT FUNDED No grants made to individuals or to any political party or to projects outside geographical area of support. Applications from individuals or outside geographical area will not be acknowledged

WHO CAN BENEFIT Organisations benefiting: those in care, fostered and adopted; parents and children; Baptists; Christians; Church of England; Methodists and Quakers. Support will be considered for many different social circumstances of, and for a variety of diseases or medical conditions suffered by the beneficiaries

WHERE FUNDING CAN BE GIVEN Birmingham and the West Midlands

TYPE OF GRANT Buildings, capital, one-off, research, running costs, recurring costs and start-up costs will be considered. Funding may be given for up to three years

RANGE OF GRANTS £100–£6,000, typical grant £250

SAMPLE GRANTS £6,000 to Care of Elderly Service, Balsall Heath; £2,000 to Birmingham Settlement; £1,500 to MSA; £1,500 to St Mary's Hospice; £1,000 to Woodbrooke College; £750 to HARP; £750 to Birmingham Phab Lamps; £400 to CRUSE; £400 to Selly Oak Nursery School; £400 to Aquarius

FINANCES *Year* 1997–98 *Income* £40,031
Grants £38,800

TRUSTEES Mrs A K Burnett, R King, BEM (Chair), D F Dodd, R C King (Secretary), R I Payne, Mrs B J Major, OBE, D J Cadbury

PUBLICATIONS Notes on the Trust are available from the Secretary

NOTES Applications must be accompanied by an up-to-date copy of audited accounts and should aim to arrive, at latest, by mid-May or mid-October to be considered at the next meeting

HOW TO APPLY By application form available from the Secretary. The Trustees meet twice a year in June and December

WHO TO APPLY TO R C King, Secretary, The Harry Payne Trust, 1 Matthews Close, Rushton, Kettering, Northamptonshire NN14 1QJ
Tel 01536 418905 *E-mail* Robcking@aol.com

CC NO 231063 **ESTABLISHED** 1939

■ The Peabody Donation Fund

WHAT IS FUNDED Community support or development, employment training and urban regeneration. The Trust funds a wide range of activities in support of Londoners in need, especially the disadvantaged in the London area. Grants must benefit those born or currently living in London and the project must help people with low incomes

WHAT IS NOT FUNDED No grants are made for political or religious purposes, for purposes already catered for by statutory bodies, for general appeals, to individuals, to the arts or to medical charities. Donations only to those born, or currently resident in London

WHO CAN BENEFIT Those born or currently resident in London. Organisations benefiting: unemployed people; at risk groups; those disadvantaged by poverty; homeless and socially isolated people

WHERE FUNDING CAN BE GIVEN UK with preference to London

FINANCES *Year* 1997 *Income* £43,810,000
Grants £951,000

TRUSTEES Sir W Benyon, DL, D A Pease, Admiral W J Crowe Jr (US Ambassador), The Hon Albemarle Bowes Lyon, Sir H Cubitt, CBE, JP, DL, J Hambro, M Haines, Prof V Karn, Sir I Pearce, CBE, TD, DL

PUBLICATIONS Peabody Trust Annual Report and Accounts

NOTES Trustees meet in March, June and October

HOW TO APPLY To the Peabody Donation Fund Administrator: E Counsell at the address under Who To Apply To

WHO TO APPLY TO H Doe, Secretary, The Peabody Donation Fund, 45 Westminster Bridge Road, London SE1 7JB

CC NO 206061 **ESTABLISHED** 1948

■ The Michael Peacock Charitable Foundation

WHAT IS FUNDED Support of services for the elderly. Support of research into the causes and treatment of addictions. Provision of scholarships at the London School of Economics for postgraduate students from the former Soviet Union and eastern Europe. Grants are only considered for projects of national or international significance in which the Trustees can be closely involved and monitor results. The Foundation's funds are heavily committed to our current programme of research fellowships and scholarships

WHAT IS NOT FUNDED Financial assistance to individual students is not given by the Foundation

WHO CAN BENEFIT Organisations benefiting young adults and older people, research workers and postgraduate students from the former Soviet Union and eastern Europe

WHERE FUNDING CAN BE GIVEN UK

TYPE OF GRANT Project and research grants will be considered

SAMPLE GRANTS £53,234 to LSE Foundation for postgraduate scholarships at the LSE; £43,493 to Action on Addiction for research fellowship at National Addiction Centre; £3,500 to Counsel and Care for 1996 Graham Lecture; £2,000 to Age Concern

FINANCES *Year* 1996 *Income* £206,625 *Grants* £102,227

TRUSTEES M Peacock (Chair), G Baverstock, M Croft Baker, Sir J Maddox, D Peacock, R Wheeler-Bennett (Hon Treasurer)

HOW TO APPLY In writing

WHO TO APPLY TO The Michael Peacock Charitable Foundation, 21 Woodlands Road, London SW13 0JZ

CC NO 801441   **ESTABLISHED** 1989

■ The Susanna Peake Charitable Trust

WHAT IS FUNDED General charitable purposes

WHO CAN BENEFIT There are no restrictions on the age; professional and economic group; family situation; religion and culture; and social circumstances of; or disease or medical condition suffered by, the beneficiaries

WHERE FUNDING CAN BE GIVEN UK

TYPE OF GRANT Usually one-off grants

FINANCES *Year* 1995 *Income* £63,080 *Grants* £53,530

TRUSTEES Mrs S Peake, D Peake

WHO TO APPLY TO The Susanna Peake Charitable Trust, Kleinwort Benson Trustees Ltd, PO Box 191, 10 Fenchurch Street, London EC3M 3LB

CC NO 283462   **ESTABLISHED** 1981

■ The Sebastian Pearson Charitable Trust

WHAT IS FUNDED General charitable purposes

WHO CAN BENEFIT There are no restrictions on the age; professional and economic group; family situation; religion and culture; and social circumstances of; or disease or medical condition suffered by, the beneficiaries

WHERE FUNDING CAN BE GIVEN In practice UK and Europe

TRUSTEES Rathbone Trust Co Ltd

HOW TO APPLY By letter

WHO TO APPLY TO P J Pickford, Secretary, The Sebastian Pearson Charitable Trust, 159 New Bond Street, London SW1Y 9PA *Tel* 0171-399 0000

CC NO 1051206   **ESTABLISHED** 1995

■ Hon Charles Pearson Charity Trust

WHAT IS FUNDED Registered charities undertaking general charitable purposes

WHAT IS NOT FUNDED No grants to individuals

WHO CAN BENEFIT Registered charities only. There are no restrictions on the age; professional and economic group; family situation; religion and culture; and social circumstances of; or disease or medical condition suffered by, the beneficiaries

WHERE FUNDING CAN BE GIVEN UK

TYPE OF GRANT Mainly one-off

RANGE OF GRANTS £200–£30,000

SAMPLE GRANTS £30,000 to Game Conservancy Scottish Research Trust; £10,000 to Population Concern; £10,000 to University of Aberdeen Quincentenary Appeal; £5,000 to Robert Gordon University, Aberdeen; £5,000 to St Richard's Hospital Appeal; £2,000 to Scottish Country Life Museums Trust; £2,000 to the Liver Group, Gastroenterology Unit; £2,000 to St George's Hospital, Cancer Vaccine Campaign; £1,000 to Echt Church; £1,000 to Geoffery De Havilland Flying Foundation

FINANCES *Year* 1996 *Income* £759,808 *Grants* £69,200

TRUSTEES The Cowdray Trust Limited

NOTES Applications for grants will only be acknowledged if a donation is to be sent

HOW TO APPLY Appeal letters should be sent to the address under Who To Apply To

WHO TO APPLY TO The Secretary, Hon Charles Pearson Charity Trust, The Cowdray Trust Limited, Pollen House, 10–12 Cork Street, London W1X 1PD

CC NO 275821   **ESTABLISHED** 1978

■ The Frank Pearson Foundation

WHAT IS FUNDED General charitable purposes. Emphasis is placed on local use of grants for the elderly, poor and children

WHAT IS NOT FUNDED No grants to individuals

WHO CAN BENEFIT Registered charities. There are no restrictions on the age; professional and economic group; family situation; religion and culture; and social circumstances of; or disease or medical condition suffered by, the beneficiaries. However, particular favour is given to the elderly, the poor and children

WHERE FUNDING CAN BE GIVEN UK

TYPE OF GRANT Where possible, specific projects

RANGE OF GRANTS £250–£1,500

SAMPLE GRANTS £1,500 to Botton Village; £1,100 to National Kidney and Lung Fund; £1,000 to Multiple Sclerosis Society; £1,000 to NSPCC; £1,000 to Plastic Surgery and Burns Research Unit

FINANCES *Year* 1996 *Income* £22,982 *Grants* £20,000

TRUSTEES Mrs I I Pearson, D A F Pearson, Wheawill & Sudworth Trustees Ltd

HOW TO APPLY In writing to the address under Who To Apply To

WHO TO APPLY TO R G Warrington, The Frank Pearson Foundation, c/o 35 Westgate, Huddersfield HD1 1PA
CC NO 278884 **ESTABLISHED** 1979

■ The Pearson plc Charitable Trust

WHAT IS FUNDED General charitable purposes at the discretion of the Trustees
WHAT IS NOT FUNDED No grants to individuals
WHO CAN BENEFIT There are no restrictions on the age; professional and economic group; family situation; religion and culture; and social circumstances of; or disease or medical condition suffered by, the beneficiaries
WHERE FUNDING CAN BE GIVEN UK
RANGE OF GRANTS £50–£100,000
SAMPLE GRANTS £100,000 to Bodleian Library; £30,750 to British Dyslexia Association; £20,000 to National Literacy Trust; £14,000 to National Manuscripts Conservation Trust; £12,500 to Harlow Council; £10,000 to London School of Economics; £10,000 to Institute for Public Policy Research; £10,000 to Demas; £10,000 to British Film Institute; £10,000 to Atlantic College
FINANCES Year 1995 Income £468,975 Grants £479,372
TRUSTEES Pearson plc, The Dickinson Trust Ltd
NOTES The Pearson plc Charitable Trust is part of the Dickinson Trust Ltd
WHO TO APPLY TO R E Webb, The Pearson plc Charitable Trust, Pollen House, 10-12 Cork Street, London W1X 1PD
CC NO 1045393 **ESTABLISHED** 1995

■ Rosanna Pearson's 1987 Charity Trust

WHAT IS FUNDED General charitable purposes
WHAT IS NOT FUNDED No grants to individuals
WHO CAN BENEFIT Registered charities only. There are no restrictions on the age; professional and economic group; family situation; religion and culture; and social circumstances of; or disease or medical condition suffered by, the beneficiaries
WHERE FUNDING CAN BE GIVEN UK
SAMPLE GRANTS £32,000 to Pearson Taylor Trust; £10,000 to Charities Aid Foundation
FINANCES Year 1996 Income £31,830 Grants £42,000
TRUSTEES The Cowdray Trust Ltd
WHO TO APPLY TO A J Winborn, Secretary, Rosanna Pearson's 1987 Charity Trust, Pollen House, 10–12 Cork Street, London W1X 1PD
CC NO 297210 **ESTABLISHED** 1987

■ The Peckitt Charitable Trust

WHAT IS FUNDED General charitable purposes
WHO CAN BENEFIT Registered charities. There are no restrictions on the age; professional and economic group; family situation; religion and culture; and social circumstances of; or disease or medical condition suffered by, the beneficiaries
WHERE FUNDING CAN BE GIVEN Cambridgeshire
FINANCES Year 1996 Income £19,431 Grants £9,593
TRUSTEES T D La Touche
WHO TO APPLY TO P Clayton, The Peckitt Charitable Trust, Messrs Clarke Brownscombe & Co, 33 Cliffe High Street, Lewes, East Sussex BN7 2AN
CC NO 282066 **ESTABLISHED** 1980

■ Pedmore Sporting Club Trust Fund

WHAT IS FUNDED General charitable purposes in response to applications only
WHO CAN BENEFIT There are no restrictions on the age; professional and economic group; family situation; religion and culture; and social circumstances of; or disease or medical condition suffered by, the beneficiaries
WHERE FUNDING CAN BE GIVEN Local West Midlands causes as general rule
TYPE OF GRANT Capital projects not general funding
SAMPLE GRANTS £5,000 to Elizabeth Attwood Refuge for transit van; £2,647 to an individual for wheelchair; £2,400 to Penn Hall School for specialist communication equipment; £1,322 to St John Ambulance HQ, Lye for decorating HQ; £1,260 to local senior citizens for Easter food parcels; £1,100 to Blakebrook Special School, Kidderminster for wheelchair lift in minibus; £1,100 to Kate Wellings Trust 'Sparks' for maintenance of narrow boat; £650 to Norton Scouts and Guides for refurbishment of HQ; £609 to Stourbridge Sons of Rest for HQ repairs; £544 to 1st Wombourne Scouts for five tents
FINANCES Year 1997 Income £36,000 Grants £20,000
TRUSTEES P Pioli, N A Hickman, C Cooper, R Herman-Smith
HOW TO APPLY Written applications to the Secretary
WHO TO APPLY TO B W J Mann, Pedmore Sporting Club Trust Fund, Pedmore House, Ham Lane, Pedmore, Stourbridge, West Midlands
CC NO 263907 **ESTABLISHED** 1973

■ Pedmore Trust

WHAT IS FUNDED Advancement of the Christian Gospel
WHAT IS NOT FUNDED Students on short term projects (gap years)
WHO CAN BENEFIT Causes related to the Christian faith benefiting Christians
WHERE FUNDING CAN BE GIVEN UK and overseas
TYPE OF GRANT Capital and recurring grants, and loans in exceptional circumstances
FINANCES Year 1996–97 Income £153,354 Grants £35,750
TRUSTEES W R Cossham, D R Meek, J Hutchison, D M John, L R Meek, W E John
NOTES Only support causes related to the Christian faith
HOW TO APPLY The Trust is only prepared to consider applications personally recommended by individual Trustees. Applications to the Secretary cannot be considered
WHO TO APPLY TO L R Meek, Secretary, Pedmore Trust, Fallow Croft, Meadow Road, Torquay, Devon TQ2 6PR Tel 01803 606210
CC NO 266644 **ESTABLISHED** 1961

■ The Peel Medical Research Trust

WHAT IS FUNDED (a) Making grants of money to assist medical research being carried out in teaching hospitals and by individual practitioners, including a contribution to the salaries of technical assistants and the purchase of equipment. (b) The award of an annual travelling fellowship which aims to provide one year of post-graduate study in medicine or allied subjects abroad
WHAT IS NOT FUNDED Grants shall not be made to or in aid of any society, organisation, institution or

trust which shall for the time being: (a) be primarily devoted to children, or (b) be wholly or substantially under the control of the central or any local government

WHO CAN BENEFIT Individuals and organisations benefiting: academics; medical professionals; research workers; and students

WHERE FUNDING CAN BE GIVEN UK

TYPE OF GRANT Research grants which average £500 to £3,000 annually in January or February. A travelling fellowship to provide one year of postgraduate study or allied subjects at centres abroad. Contributions to salaries also considered

SAMPLE GRANTS £30,000 to an individual for a travelling fellowship award; £18,000 to an individual for a travelling fellowship award; £3,200 to an individual for a grant; £3,000 to an individual for research; £2,500 to an individual for a travelling grant; £2,280 to an individual for research; £1,950 to an individual for research; £1,800 to an individual for research; £1,800 to an individual for research; £1,675 to an individual for research

FINANCES *Year* 1997 *Income* £90,150
Grants £84,817

TRUSTEES R L Rothwell-Jackson, MCh, FRCS, A G Trower, Dr G Jackson, FRCP

HOW TO APPLY Applications should be made only in response to an advertisement published in the medical journals in September of every year. Grants are awarded the following January

WHO TO APPLY TO L A Valner, The Peel Medical Research Trust, Sceptre Court, 40 Tower Hill, London EC3N 4BN *Tel* 0171-423 8000 *Fax* 0171-423 8001

CC NO 214683   **ESTABLISHED** 1954

■ The J B Pelly Charitable Trust

(formerly The Joanne Pelly Charitable Settlement)

WHAT IS FUNDED Tree planting; organic gardening; nature conservation and environment; natural health promotion; crafts; rehabilitation centres; training for community development; training for personal development; vocational training; support to voluntary and community organisations; crafts; visual arts; arts activities; arts education; cultural activity; recreation grounds; and community issues

WHAT IS NOT FUNDED Illness, disease and Church of England

WHO CAN BENEFIT Young adults; Buddhists and Jainists; and Quakers

WHERE FUNDING CAN BE GIVEN South Devon

TYPE OF GRANT One-off, project, research, and start-up costs. Funding is available for up to three years

RANGE OF GRANTS £50–£1,000

SAMPLE GRANTS £25,000 to Cathy Pelly Maungaronga Trust; £4,000 to CPRE; £3,000 to Community Creation; £2,000 to Willian Cookworthy Museum Society; £2,000 to Friends of the Earth Trust; £1,500 to Sustrans; £1,000 to Intermediate Technology; £1,000 to Volunteer Centre UK; £1,000 to Glebe House; £1,000 to PHAB Wales

FINANCES *Year* 1997 *Income* £65,260
Grants £45,800

TRUSTEES Miss H G Pelly, A J R Pelly

HOW TO APPLY Written applications (with supporting information if available)

WHO TO APPLY TO The J B Pelly Charitable Trust, c/o Bromhead & Co, Britton House, 10 Fore Street, Kingsbridge, Devon TQ7 1NY
Tel 01548 852599 *Fax* 01548 854082

CC NO 285565   **ESTABLISHED** 1987

■ Penny in the Pound Fund Charitable Trust

WHAT IS FUNDED Pay out to NHS hospitals amenities for patients

WHAT IS NOT FUNDED No grants towards medical equipment

WHO CAN BENEFIT NHS hospitals and health authorities. There is no restriction on the disease or medical condition suffered by the beneficiaries

WHERE FUNDING CAN BE GIVEN North East England, North West England, North Wales, Midlands and Scottish regions

TYPE OF GRANT Capital

FINANCES *Year* 1995 *Income* £92,165
Grants £92,203

TRUSTEES P B Teare, K W Monti, H F Settle, K Arnold, B E Straveley

HOW TO APPLY Annually in August

WHO TO APPLY TO K Arnold, Finance Officer, Penny in the Pound Fund Charitable Trust, Merseyside Health Benefits Council, 7 Sir Thomas Street, Liverpool L1 6HE

CC NO 257637   **ESTABLISHED** 1968

■ The Pennycress Trust

WHAT IS FUNDED General charitable purposes. Makes distributions to a restricted list of registered charities only, principally in Cheshire and Norfolk

WHAT IS NOT FUNDED No grants to individuals or large national bodies

WHO CAN BENEFIT There are no restrictions on the age, professional and economic group, family situation, religion and culture, and social circumstances of, or disease or medical condition suffered by, the beneficiaries

WHERE FUNDING CAN BE GIVEN Principally Cheshire and Norfolk

TYPE OF GRANT Recurrent and one-off

RANGE OF GRANTS £300–£500

FINANCES *Year* 1997 *Income* £67,000
Grants £63,000

TRUSTEES A J M Baker, Lady Aline Cholmondeley, C G Cholmondeley

HOW TO APPLY Once yearly. Reviewed June/July and December. Sae appreciated

WHO TO APPLY TO A J M Baker, The Pennycress Trust, Heron Place, 3 George Street, London W1H 6AD

CC NO 261536   **ESTABLISHED** 1970

■ Pen-Y-Clip Charitable Trust

WHAT IS FUNDED Medical and health, welfare, education, sectarian and humanism religion, environmental research

WHAT IS NOT FUNDED No grants to individuals

WHO CAN BENEFIT Small local projects benefiting people of all ages; at risk groups; those disadvantaged by poverty; and socially isolated people. There is no restriction on the disease or medical condition suffered by the beneficiaries

WHERE FUNDING CAN BE GIVEN North Wales

TYPE OF GRANT One-off and recurring

RANGE OF GRANTS £100 upwards

SAMPLE GRANTS £15,000 to Development Trust, University of Wales, Bangor for research studentship in marine archaeology

FINANCES *Year* 1997–98 *Income* £19,400
Grants £25,492

TRUSTEES P G Brown, Mrs J E Lea

PUBLICATIONS Annual Report

HOW TO APPLY In writing

Does the trust you have chosen match your needs? Haphazard applications waste postage and time

489

WHO TO APPLY TO P G Brown, Pen-Y-Clip Charitable Trust, 59 Madoc Street, Llandudno, Gwynedd LL30 2TW *Tel* 01492 874391
Fax 01492 871990
CC NO 519715　　　ESTABLISHED 1987

■ People's Voices

WHAT IS FUNDED To relieve persons who are in a condition of need through disability, ill health or other social or economic circumstances by provision of advocacy services; any other general charitable purposes

WHO CAN BENEFIT Organisations benefiting the disabled, at risk groups, those disadvantaged by poverty and socially isolated people. There is no restriction on the disease or medical condition suffered by the beneficiaries

WHERE FUNDING CAN BE GIVEN In practice, Buckinghamshire and neighbouring areas

FINANCES *Year* 1997 *Income* £27,431

WHO TO APPLY TO E Newhouse, People's Voices, 1 King George V Road, Amersham, Buckinghamshire HP6 5TT

CC NO 1051952　　　ESTABLISHED 1996

■ Perks Trust

WHAT IS FUNDED Medicine, health, welfare and religion

WHAT IS NOT FUNDED No grants to individuals or students

WHO CAN BENEFIT Small local projects and national organisations benefiting at risk groups, those disadvantaged by poverty and socially isolated people. There is no restriction on the disease or medical condition suffered by the beneficiaries. People from many different religions may be supported

WHERE FUNDING CAN BE GIVEN UK

TYPE OF GRANT Range of recurrent grants will be considered

FINANCES *Year* 1994–95 *Income* £15,409
Grants £13,850

TRUSTEES John Gilbert Perks, Michael Stokes, John R Bettingdon

NOTES **This Trust states that it does not respond to unsolicited applications**

WHO TO APPLY TO J G Perks, Perks Trust, 7 Tudor Court, Midland Drive, Sutton Coldfield, West Midlands B72 1TU

CC NO 280544　　　ESTABLISHED 1980

■ Personal Assurance Charitable Trust

WHAT IS FUNDED Medicine and health, welfare, education, environmental resources and general charitable purposes. This includes: residential facilities and services; infrastructure, support and development; religion; arts, culture and recreation; conservation and environment; and social care and development

WHO CAN BENEFIT Health and related charities preferred. There are no restrictions on the age, professional and economic group, family situation, religion and culture, and social circumstances of, or disease or medical condition suffered by, the beneficiaries who are policyholders of Personal Assurance plc or their employers

WHERE FUNDING CAN BE GIVEN Mainly UK, will consider overseas

TYPE OF GRANT Buildings, capital, core costs, endowments, feasibility studies, interest free loans, one-off, project, research, running costs, recurring costs, salaries and start-up costs. Funding is for up to and over three years

SAMPLE GRANTS £14,940 to BBC Children in Need; £10,000 to Kings College, London for Haemochromatosis research; £7,500 to Safety Centre, Milton Keynes for road safety and accidents in the home awareness programme; £5,300 to NSPCC; £5,000 to Milton Keynes Community Trust for various projects in Milton Keynes; £2,625 to Milton Keynes Christmas Day Party Appeal for a Christmas Day Lunch for elderly people in Milton Keynes; £2,500 to TeGWU Yorkshire Show for under privileged children and disabled people to attend the Show; £1,200 to Hammersmith Hospital for kidney research; £1,100 to Mary Stevens Hospice

FINANCES *Year* 1997 *Income* £87,280
Grants £63,150

TRUSTEES C W T Johnston, J Barber

NOTES Applications restricted to policyholders of Personal Assurance plc or their employers

WHO TO APPLY TO Dr J Barber, Personal Assurance Charitable Trust, Personal Assurance plc, Bank House, 171 Midsummer Boulevard, Central Milton Keynes MK9 1EB

CC NO 1023274　　　ESTABLISHED 1993

■ The Persula Foundation

WHAT IS FUNDED Support of (particularly small) groups working in the field of: homelessness; disabled people; human and animal welfare; charities using music in their work

WHAT IS NOT FUNDED No grants to individuals, for buildings/building works or to statutory bodies

WHO CAN BENEFIT Organisations, preferably local, benefiting: musicians; at risk groups; those disadvantaged by poverty; socially isolated and homeless people

WHERE FUNDING CAN BE GIVEN Internationally, but predominantly UK

TYPE OF GRANT Grants for all requirements considered, core costs, one-off projects, recurrent, etc

FINANCES *Year* 1996 *Income* £120,236

TRUSTEES Julian Richer, John Currier, David Robinson, David Highton, David Clark, Mrs R Richer, Mrs H Oppenheim, Rev Peter Timms, Miss Nicola Phillips

PUBLICATIONS Information leaflet, Annual Report, Financial Accounts

HOW TO APPLY Flexible and varied

WHO TO APPLY TO John Currier, Company Secretary, Persula Foundation, Richer House, Hankey Place, London SE1 4BB

CC NO 1044174　　　ESTABLISHED 1994

■ The Pestalozzi Overseas Children's Trust

WHAT IS FUNDED General charitable purposes, in particular, to advance the education of children of any nationality, to provide and maintain assistance and care for those who are orphans, children of broken homes or poor parents or guardians, or refugee children who are in need, particularly in Asia and Africa

WHAT IS NOT FUNDED No grants for UK

WHO CAN BENEFIT To benefit children who are orphans, from broken homes or whose parents or guardians are poor and refugee children in need

WHERE FUNDING CAN BE GIVEN Overseas, particularly Asia and Africa

TYPE OF GRANT Sponsorship of education fees and/or accommodation or subsistence

FINANCES *Year* 1995 *Income* £185,341 *Grants* £700

WHO TO APPLY TO Valerie Deacon, The Pestalozzi Overseas Children's Trust, 51 Thurloe Square, London SW7 2EX *Tel* 0171-581 0101 *Fax* 0171-581 9069 *E-mail* valerie@ladybird.demon.co.uk

CC NO 1046599   **ESTABLISHED** 1995

■ Pet Plan Charitable Trust

WHAT IS FUNDED Veterinary research, animal welfare, education in animal welfare. Other charitable purposes

WHO CAN BENEFIT Animal charities and organisations benefiting students, research workers and veterinarians

WHERE FUNDING CAN BE GIVEN UK

RANGE OF GRANTS £1,000–£77,950

SAMPLE GRANTS £77,950 to Animal Health Trust for research into brain tumours in dogs; £50,000 to Blue Cross for their centenary year; £48,818 to University of Edinburgh for research into hyperthyroidism in cats; £29,050 to University of Liverpool for research into kennel cough; £20,050 to University of Glasgow for research into FIV disease; £7,000 to Feline Advisory Bureau for a cat rescue manual; £6,000 to University of Edinburgh for research into canine atophy; £3,000 to Blue Cross for an intensive care stable; £2,000 to HAPPA for a heat therapy unit; £1,000 to Blue Cross for puppy pens

FINANCES *Year* 1996 *Income* £406,013 *Grants* £245,161

TRUSTEES Patsy Bloom (Chairman), Clarissa Baldwin, John Bower, I Brecher, Dr Andrew Higgins, Denis Loretto, David Simpson

NOTES Before being recommended to the Trustees, veterinary grant applications pass through rigorous processes, including interviews before the Scientific Awards Committee. Welfare and educational applications are scrutinised by a panel of experts with the objective of addressing the root of the problem of disadvantaged and unwanted animals, ie grants for neutering projects

HOW TO APPLY To the address under Who To Apply To in writing

WHO TO APPLY TO Roz Hayward-Butt, Administrator, Pet Plan Charitable Trust, West Cross House, 2 West Cross Way, Brentford, Middlesex TW8 9EG

CC NO 1032907   **ESTABLISHED** 1994

■ Peugeot Motor Company plc Charity Trust (formerly Talbot Motor Company Charity Trust Fund)

WHAT IS FUNDED General charitable purposes. Causes are often associated with the motor industry

WHAT IS NOT FUNDED No grants to individuals

WHO CAN BENEFIT Only local organisations. There are no restrictions on the age; professional and economic group; family situation; religion and culture; and social circumstances of; or disease or medical condition suffered by, the beneficiaries

WHERE FUNDING CAN BE GIVEN West Midlands, in particular Coventry

RANGE OF GRANTS £10–£20,000

SAMPLE GRANTS £20,000 to BEN; £5,000 to Coventry Cyrenians; £4,500 to Belgrade Theatre; £2,500 to Coventry Common Purpose; £500 to Birmingham Children's Hospital; £500 to Ellys Extra Care; £500 to Valley House Association; £500 to Rugby MENCAP hostel; £500 to St Lawrence Church Hall; £500 to Cradle Appeal

FINANCES *Year* 1996 *Income* £46,296 *Grants* £49,008

TRUSTEES R D Parham, R A Lilley, M A B Judge

WHO TO APPLY TO The Secretary, Peugeot Motor Company plc Charity Trust, PO Box 227, Aldermoor Lane, Coventry CV3 1LT

CC NO 266182   **ESTABLISHED** 1970

■ Pewterers' Charity Trust

WHAT IS FUNDED This Trust will consider funding a wide range of charitable bodies in the fields of: infrastructure, support and development; residential facilities and services; religion; arts, culture and recreation; health; conservation and environment; community facilities and services; and other charitable purposes

WHAT IS NOT FUNDED Expeditions and further education for individuals will not be funded

WHO CAN BENEFIT Organisations benefiting: academics; clergy; ex-service and service people; medical professionals; retired people students; and unemployed people. There is no restriction on age, family situation or religion and culture, however, there are some restrictions on the social circumstances of, and the disease or medical condition suffered by, the beneficiaries

WHERE FUNDING CAN BE GIVEN UK

TYPE OF GRANT General charitable grants, including core costs, one-off, project, research, running costs and start-up costs. Funding is available for up to three years

RANGE OF GRANTS £500–£4,000

SAMPLE GRANTS £4,000 to Fairbridge for youth adventure training and outward bound; £3,000 to Whirlow Farm for youth holidays for inner city children; £3,000 to Royal Hospital for Neurodisability for general funds and medical research; £3,000 to Lynda Jackson Macmillan Nurses; £3,000 to Prince's Youth Business Trust for start-up help; £2,000 to Dulwich School for a scholarship; £1,600 to Pewterers' Fellowship for a business school; £1,000 to Universal Beneficent Society for help to elderly people; £1,000 to Arkwright Scholarships for assisted places; £500 to Guildhall Library

FINANCES *Year* 1997–98 *Income* £26,000 *Grants* £22,800

TRUSTEES The Worshipful Company of Pewterers

HOW TO APPLY At any time. Trustees meet half yearly in June and November. This Trust passes on the bulk of claims to the Company's general charity Trustees who can disburse donations of a few hundred pounds. The Seahorse Trustees select a few charities for support for three or more years with £3,000–£4,000 per annum

WHO TO APPLY TO The Clerk to the Trustees, Pewterers' Charity Trust, Pewterers Hall, Oat Lane, London EC2V 7DE

CC NO 261889   **ESTABLISHED** 1974

■ Anshel Pfeffer Trust (1962)

WHAT IS FUNDED General charitable purposes

WHO CAN BENEFIT There are no restrictions on the age; professional and economic group; family situation; religion and culture; and social

---

circumstances of; or disease or medical condition suffered by, the beneficiaries

WHERE FUNDING CAN BE GIVEN UK

SAMPLE GRANTS £18,000 to Anshel Pfeffer Memorial Fund; £5,000 to Society of Friends of Torah

FINANCES *Year* 1995 *Income* £292,767 *Grants* £23,000

TRUSTEES Mrs C Pfeffer, A D Pfeffer

WHO TO APPLY TO E R Epstein, Anshel Pfeffer Trust (1962), Lopian Barnett & Co, Harvester House, 37 Peter Street, Manchester M2 5QD

CC NO 214388 **ESTABLISHED** 1962

■ Brigadier and Mrs D V Phelps Charitable Trust (formerly D V Phelps Charitable Trust)

WHAT IS FUNDED General charitable purposes

WHAT IS NOT FUNDED The Trustees do not make grants to individuals

WHO CAN BENEFIT There are no restrictions on the age; professional and economic group; family situation; religion and culture; and social circumstances of; or disease or medical condition suffered by, the beneficiaries

WHERE FUNDING CAN BE GIVEN UK and overseas, with special preference to Merseyside and Norfolk

RANGE OF GRANTS Below £500–£5,950; £500 is usually the upper limit

SAMPLE GRANTS £5,950 to Liverpool Council of Social Service (Inc); £1,000 to Royal Liverpool University Hospital; £500 to ADAPT; £500 to Assembly House Appeal Fund; £500 to Burlingham House; £500 to CHATTERBOX; £500 to Hillside Animal Sanctuary; £500 to IRIS Fund; £500 to Northern Norfolk Resource Centre – rural

FINANCES *Year* 1997 *Income* £143,388 *Grants* £21,875

TRUSTEES M A F Leather, M Freeth

NOTES Also includes funds from the Hon Mrs H R Phelps Charitable Trust (now wound up)

HOW TO APPLY Write to the Secretary for application form. Closing date is beginning of March. No acknowledgement given to applications

WHO TO APPLY TO Brigadier and Mrs D V Phelps Charitable Trust, c/o KPMG, Holland Court, The Close, Norwich NR1 4DY

CC NO 249047 **ESTABLISHED** 1966

■ Phibes Charitable Trust

WHAT IS FUNDED General charitable purposes

WHO CAN BENEFIT There are no restrictions on the age; professional and economic group; family situation; religion and culture; and social circumstances of; or disease or medical condition suffered by, the beneficiaries

WHERE FUNDING CAN BE GIVEN UK

FINANCES *Year* 1997 *Income* £300,333

TRUSTEES Ms R V Gammon, M G D Giedroyc, W M Heath, M J F Hudson, Lord R W Kerr, P J Parham

WHO TO APPLY TO A Gammon, Secretary, Phibes Charitable Trust, Gammon Holdings, 14 Copthall Avenue, London EC2R 7DJ

CC NO 1047129 **ESTABLISHED** 1995

■ The Philanthropic Trust

WHAT IS FUNDED Projects to alleviate homelessness in the UK and poverty in the developing world. The Trust also has an interest in fauna, wildlife parks and conservation

WHAT IS NOT FUNDED No grants to individuals, for education or the arts

WHO CAN BENEFIT Registered charities benefiting unemployed people and volunteers of all ages, and those from a wide range of social circumstances. Overseas projects must apply through UK registered charities

WHERE FUNDING CAN BE GIVEN UK, Asia and Africa

TYPE OF GRANT Recurring, core costs and projects

RANGE OF GRANTS £500–£2,000

FINANCES *Year* 1997 *Income* £239,672 *Grants* £109,000

TRUSTEES Paul H Burton, Jeremy J Burton, Amanda C Burton

HOW TO APPLY To the address under Who To Apply To in writing, there are no application forms or guidelines, no application deadlines and sae is not required. No telephone calls please

WHO TO APPLY TO Trust Administrator, The Philanthropic Trust, Trustee Management Limited, 27 East Parade, Leeds LS1 5SX

CC NO 1045263 **ESTABLISHED** 1995

■ Reginald M Phillips Charitable Foundation

WHAT IS FUNDED Medical research, scientific study. Majority of funds are utilised in the field of research at Sussex University in cell cultures and ageing diseases (Alzheimer's and Parkinson's)

WHAT IS NOT FUNDED The majority of our income is committed

WHO CAN BENEFIT Registered charities benefiting researchers and scientists. There is no restriction on the disease or medical condition suffered by the beneficiaries, but preference is given to those suffering from Alzheimer's and Parkinson's diseases

WHERE FUNDING CAN BE GIVEN Uk

TYPE OF GRANT Research

RANGE OF GRANTS £1,000–£11,000

SAMPLE GRANTS £110,000 to Trafford Foundation; £2,000 to Brighton West Pier Trust; £2,000 to RAFA Wings Appeal; £1,500 to Brighton Sea Cadets; £1,500 to Impact Foundation; £1,000 to Torah Academy; £1,000 to Rocking Horse Appeal

FINANCES *Year* 1997 *Income* £146,430 *Grants* £119,000

TRUSTEES National Westminster Bank plc

NOTES The majority of the Foundation's funds are committed to the research programme for the next five years

WHO TO APPLY TO The Manager, Reginald M Phillips Charitable Foundation, National Westminster Bank, Brighton Branch, 153 Preston Road, Brighton, East Sussex BN1 6BD

CC NO 245232 **ESTABLISHED** 1965

■ The Phillips Charitable Trust

WHAT IS FUNDED General charitable purposes at the discretion of the Trustees

WHO CAN BENEFIT There are no restrictions on the age; professional and economic group; family situation; religion and culture; and social circumstances of; or disease or medical condition suffered by, the beneficiaries

WHERE FUNDING CAN BE GIVEN UK and overseas

TRUSTEES N Q Grazebrook, J C Keevil, D H Phillips

HOW TO APPLY This Trust states that it does not respond to unsolicited applications

■ The Phillips Family Charitable Trust

WHAT IS FUNDED General charitable purposes
WHAT IS NOT FUNDED No grants to individuals
WHO CAN BENEFIT Registered charities. There are no
restrictions on the age; professional and
economic group; family situation; religion and
culture; and social circumstances of; or disease or
medical condition suffered by, the beneficiaries
WHERE FUNDING CAN BE GIVEN UK
RANGE OF GRANTS £50–£5,000
SAMPLE GRANTS £5,000 to JPS; £1,500 to JIA;
£1,000 to Jaffa Institute; £1,000 to Jewish Care;
£1,000 to Nightingale House; £1,000 to ORT;
£750 to Community Security Trust; £600 to
Medical Foundation for the Care of Victims of
Torture; £500 to Aish Hatorah; £500 to CIS
Development
FINANCES *Year* 1997 *Income* £34,487
Grants £13,850
TRUSTEES M D Paisner, M L Phillips, Mrs R Phillips,
P S Phillips, G M Phillips
WHO TO APPLY TO M D Paisner, The Phillips Family
Charitable Trust, Paisner & Co, Solicitors,
Bouverie House, 154 Fleet Street, London
EC4A 2DQ
CC NO 279120   ESTABLISHED 1979

■ Philological Foundation

WHAT IS FUNDED Individuals may receive grants for
educational expenses and tuition fees; while
schools in the area Where Funding Can Be Given
may benefit over a wide range of purposes
WHAT IS NOT FUNDED No grants for capital works,
buildings, text books (in schools), furniture,
scholarships, loans or expeditions
WHO CAN BENEFIT Schools and individuals for
educational purposes. Organisations benefiting
children, young adults and students
WHERE FUNDING CAN BE GIVEN The City of
Westminster and the Borough of Camden
RANGE OF GRANTS £300–£2,500
SAMPLE GRANTS £2,065 to special school for
playground improvement; £2,000 to a student for
legal fees; £2,000 to secondary school for library
books; £2,000 to primary school for library books;
£2,000 to primary school for library books;
£1,968 to secondary school for information
technology; £1,875 to primary school for gym and
outdoor play improvements; £1,736 to primary
school for information technology; £1,699 to
primary school for information technology; £1,000
to a student for medical elective overseas
FINANCES *Year* 1996–97 *Income* £63,000
Grants £59,000
TRUSTEES P Sayers (Chairman), S Briddes, Mrs R
Brightman, MBE, Mrs G Hampson, D Jones, CBE,
Mrs J Keen, E McNeal, Dr R Philpot
PUBLICATIONS Annual Report
NOTES One application per student or school. Can
apply again after one year
HOW TO APPLY By letter to the Clerk. Trustees meet
typically in January, March, June, September and
December. Apply several weeks before

■ The George and Jessie Pick Charitable Trust

WHAT IS FUNDED Health, homelessness, hospices,
relief of the poor
WHO CAN BENEFIT Institutions benefiting homeless
people amd those disadvantaged by poverty.
There are no restrictions on the disease or
medical condition suffered by the beneficiaries
WHERE FUNDING CAN BE GIVEN UK
TYPE OF GRANT One-off and recurrent
RANGE OF GRANTS £33–£1,000
SAMPLE GRANTS £1,000 to Rural Windsor Trust;
£800 to Imperial Cancer Research Fund; £400 to
Arthritis Care; £400 to Bolton Village Appeal Fund;
£400 to Child Psychotherapy Trust
FINANCES *Year* 1997 *Income* £14,357
Grants £13,883
TRUSTEES G S Pick, P R Holgate, A Parry-Williams, N
Pick
WHO TO APPLY TO P R Holgate, The George and Jessie
Pick Charitable Trust, c/o Kingston Smith,
Devonshire House, 60 Goswell Road, London
EC1M 7AD
CC NO 264732   ESTABLISHED 1972

■ The David Pickford Charitable Foundation

WHAT IS FUNDED Support of a residential Christian
youth centre in Kent for those in the 15 to 25 age
group and other similar activities
WHAT IS NOT FUNDED No grants to individuals. No
building projects
WHO CAN BENEFIT Mainly, but not solely, youths and
Christian evangelism
WHERE FUNDING CAN BE GIVEN Kent and London
TYPE OF GRANT Mainly for Christian youth work
SAMPLE GRANTS To CARE; To Youth with a Mission; To
Philo Trust; To Pickford Trust
FINANCES *Year* 1997 *Income* £52,825
Grants £49,900
TRUSTEES D M Pickford, Mrs E G Pickford
NOTES Applications will not be acknowledged. Those
falling outside What is Funded and Who Can Be
Funded mentioned above will be ignored
HOW TO APPLY In writing at any time
WHO TO APPLY TO D M Pickford, The David Pickford
Charitable Foundation, Elm Tree Farm, Mersham,
Ashford, Kent TN25 7HS *Tel* 01233 720200
Fax 01233 720522
CC NO 243437   ESTABLISHED 1965

■ Bernard Piggot Trust

WHAT IS FUNDED Church of England; Church of Wales;
education; medical charities, both care and
research; drama and the theatre; youth and
children
WHAT IS NOT FUNDED Grants will not be made to
individuals
WHO CAN BENEFIT Organisations benefiting: children;
young adults; actors and entertainment
professionals; and Church of England and Wales.
There are no restrictions on the disease or
medical condition suffered by the beneficiaries
WHERE FUNDING CAN BE GIVEN City of Birmingham and
certain areas in North Wales

TYPE OF GRANT One-off capital

RANGE OF GRANTS £250–£2,000

FINANCES *Year* 1997 *Income* £43,759
Grants £41,500

TRUSTEES D M P Lea, M St George Arrowsmith, The Ven W Thomas

NOTES Cannot deal with applications from individuals

HOW TO APPLY To the address under Who To Apply To in writing, enclosing detailed accounts and details of the proposed project, including projected costs

WHO TO APPLY TO Derek M P Lea, Trustee, Bernard Piggot Trust, 20 Mease Lane, Barnt Green, Birmingham B45 8HW *Tel* 0121-744 1695

CC NO 260347 **ESTABLISHED** 1970

■ C D and M Pike Charity Trust

WHAT IS FUNDED General charitable purposes to support charitable work in Devon. Particularly by making small donations to many people to encourage and advance their leadership qualities and gain experience through organisations such as the Projects Trust, Operation Raleigh, British Schools Exploration Society and the Duke of Edinburgh; Gold Award Scheme

WHO CAN BENEFIT Individuals and organisations in Devon. There are no restrictions on the age; professional and economic group; family situation; religion and culture; and social circumstances of; or disease or medical condition suffered by, the beneficiaries

WHERE FUNDING CAN BE GIVEN Devon only

TYPE OF GRANT One-off grants

SAMPLE GRANTS £3,500 to Torbay Hospital League of Friends MIR Scanner Appeal; £2,500 to Society of Mary and Martha; £1,600 to Exeter College to support 16 students in their Duke of Edinburgh's Gold Award Project; £1,125 to Wolborough PCC; £1,000 to Madison Roadford Church Council; £1,000 to Newton Abbot Citizens' Advice Bureau; £800 to the Cot Death Society; £500 to Devon Historic Churches Trust; £500 to an individual to support their MSc course at Exeter University

FINANCES *Year* 1998 *Income* £74,461
Grants £38,912

TRUSTEES C D Pike, J D Pike, Dr P A D Holland

NOTES No appeals from outside Devon will be considered

WHO TO APPLY TO C D Pike, OBE, DL, C D and M Pike Charity Trust, Dunderlane Lawn, Penshurst Road, Newton Abbot, Devon TQ12 1EN

CC NO 247657 **ESTABLISHED** 1965

■ Claude & Margaret Pike Woodlands Trust

WHAT IS FUNDED (a) To protect, improve or foster an appreciation of the landscape, natural beauty and amenity of woodlands, copses or other areas of land in the UK and the flora and fauna therein for the benefit of the public. (b) To foster the growth of specimen trees and shrubs and the establishment of woodlands or copses which by their location will be an inspiration to man in the environment in which he lives and a demonstration of man's faith in nature

WHAT IS NOT FUNDED No appeals from outside Devon will be considered

WHO CAN BENEFIT Children, young adults and older people living in Devon

WHERE FUNDING CAN BE GIVEN Devon only

SAMPLE GRANTS £5,000 to The Royal Horticultural Society Appeal for the Woods at Rosemoor; £2,500 to Craigencalt Farm Ecology Centre; £1,000 to The Society of Mary and Martha; £1,000 to The MED Theatre; £1,000 to The Young People's Development from Chagford, Devon; £1,000 to Devon County Agricultural Association; £750 to The Newton Abbot Town Council for Russian Youth Visit; £750 to Forde Primary School; £500 to Okehampton Table Tennis Centre; £500 to RSPB

FINANCES *Year* 1998 *Income* £94,543
Grants £17,631

TRUSTEES C D Pike, J D Pike, Dr P A D Holland

HOW TO APPLY In writing to the address below

WHO TO APPLY TO C D Pike, OBE, DL, Claude & Margaret Pike Woodlands Trust, Dunderdale Lawn, Penshurst Road, Newton Abbot, Devon TQ12 1EN

CC NO 266072 **ESTABLISHED** 1973

■ The Pilgram Band Trust

WHAT IS FUNDED Tuition fees for talented young musicians in need of financial help may be paid. Grants are made to schools to purchase musical instruments. A particular focus has been assistance for disabled children. The Trust is the main financial support for the Reigate and Redhill Music Festival

WHO CAN BENEFIT Some individuals and organisations benefiting children, young adults, musicians and disabled people

WHERE FUNDING CAN BE GIVEN Reigate, Surrey

TYPE OF GRANT Scholarships and donations

FINANCES *Year* 1997 *Income* £65,214
Grants £11,283

TRUSTEES K B Donachie, F W Harrison, M Jarvis, M Hensor, Ms A Smith

HOW TO APPLY To the address under Who To Apply To in writing

WHO TO APPLY TO Keith Donachie, Trustee, The Pilgram Band Trust, Faith Lee, 8 Ridgeway Road, Redhill, Surrey RH1 6PH *Tel* 01737 763865

CC NO 277449 **ESTABLISHED** 1979

■ The Cecil Pilkington Charitable Trust

WHAT IS FUNDED Environmental and conservation projects; advancement of education in agriculture and forestry. The arts and humanities. Other charitable purposes will be considered

WHAT IS NOT FUNDED Religious or sporting projects will not be considered. No grants to individuals

WHO CAN BENEFIT Registered charities only. No restrictions as to size. Those involved in the arts will be considered. Support may be given to agricultural students

WHERE FUNDING CAN BE GIVEN UK, though some third world projects considered

TYPE OF GRANT Mostly project grants. Some of these may be recurring

SAMPLE GRANTS £29,788 to Forestry Commission; £17,042 to Conifer Conservation Programme; £10,000 to York University; £10,000 to RSNC; £10,000 to Intermediate Technology; £10,000 to Citadel Arts Centre; £5,000 to BTCV; £5,000 to CAFOD; £5,000 to Ness Botanica Gardens; £3,000 to Sutton Manor Primary School

FINANCES *Year* 1996 *Income* £169,193
Grants £137,830

TRUSTEES Sir Anthony Pilkington, A P Pilkington, R F Carter Jonas

HOW TO APPLY This Trust states that it does not respond to unsolicited applications
WHO TO APPLY TO The Cecil Pilkington Charitable Trust, 9 Greyfriars Road, Reading, Berkshire RG1 1JG
CC NO 249997   **ESTABLISHED** 1966

■ The Roger and Ingrid Pilkington Charitable Trust

WHAT IS FUNDED Costs of study
WHO CAN BENEFIT Organisations benefiting young adults, academics and students
WHERE FUNDING CAN BE GIVEN England
SAMPLE GRANTS £3,000 to Prisoners of Conscience Appeal Fund; £2,000 to an individual for education; £1,500 to a family for education; £1,000 each to three individuals for education; £1,000 each to two individuals
FINANCES *Year* 1997 *Income* £18,050 *Grants* £14,500
TRUSTEES R O Bernays, J Drury, R Horwood-Smart, QC
WHO TO APPLY TO J Fagan, The Roger and Ingrid Pilkington Charitable Trust, c/o Brabner Holden Banks Wilson, 1 Dale Street, Liverpool L2 2ET *Tel* 0151-236 5821
CC NO 1038361   **ESTABLISHED** 1994

■ Pilkington Charities Fund

WHAT IS FUNDED Welfare, illness and disability; a high priority for funding is the C & A Pilkington Trust Fund, which benefits employees and ex-employees of Pilkington. Charities working in the fields of: accommodation and housing; infrastructure, support and development; churches; health; research into medicine, science and technology, and social science; advice and information an social issues; and community facilities and services will be considered
WHAT IS NOT FUNDED Applications from individuals cannot be considered
WHO CAN BENEFIT Local and national organisations benefiting: research workers; retired people; seafarers and fishermen; unemployed people; volunteers; at risk groups; carers; disabled people; those disadvantaged by poverty; disaster victims; homeless people; socially isolated people; victims of abuse, crime and domestic violence; victims of famine, man-made or natural disasters and war. There are no restrictions on the age or family situation of, or the disease or medical condition suffered by the beneficiaries
WHERE FUNDING CAN BE GIVEN UK with preference for Merseyside and St Helens; Overseas
TYPE OF GRANT Buildings, capital, core costs, one-off, project, research, recurring costs. Funding for more than three years will be considered
RANGE OF GRANTS £250–£30,000
SAMPLE GRANTS £30,000 to Intermediate Technology for research; £20,000 to Jefferiss Research Trust for research; £15,000 to St Helens and Knowsley Hospice for general purposes; £10,000 to NSPCC, St Helens for general purposes; £10,000 to Bath Inst, Rheumatic Diseases for general purposes; £10,000 to Human Ageing Trust for research; £10,000 to Liverpool Family Service Units for general purposes; £7,500 to St Helens Housing Association for general purposes; £4,000 to Liverpool School of Tropical Medicine for research; £4,000 to Childrens Society for general purposes
FINANCES *Year* 1996–97 *Income* £487,000 *Grants* £450,000

TRUSTEES A P Pilkington, Dr L H A Pilkington, Hon Mrs J M Jones,
HOW TO APPLY To the address under Who To Apply To in writing
WHO TO APPLY TO Pilkington Charities Fund, Roberts Legge & Co, 14 Chapel Lane, Formby, Liverpool L37 4DU *Tel* 01704 834490
CC NO 225911   **ESTABLISHED** 1964

■ The C F Pilkington Charity

WHAT IS FUNDED General charitable purposes
WHO CAN BENEFIT There are no restrictions on the age; professional and economic group; family situation; religion and culture; and social circumstances of; or disease or medical condition suffered by, the beneficiaries
WHERE FUNDING CAN BE GIVEN UK
RANGE OF GRANTS £50–£7,000
SAMPLE GRANTS £7,000 to Cancer Help Centre; £4,500 to RAF Benevolent Fund; £4,000 to Didsbury Trust; £1,100 to RT Trust; £1,000 to Actors Institute
FINANCES *Year* 1997 *Income* £21,823 *Grants* £15,375
TRUSTEES D F Pilkington, Mrs F A Biggart, W M Pattison
WHO TO APPLY TO W M Pattison, The C F Pilkington Charity, Duncan Sheard Glass & Co, Castle Chambers, 43 Castle Street, Liverpool L2 9TL
CC NO 281996   **ESTABLISHED** 1968

■ The Sir Harry Pilkington Fund

WHAT IS FUNDED General charitable purposes. Grants are made only to charities known to the Settlor and unsolicited applications are therefore not considered
WHO CAN BENEFIT There are no restrictions on the age; professional and economic group; family situation; religion and culture; and social circumstances of; or disease or medical condition suffered by, the beneficiaries
WHERE FUNDING CAN BE GIVEN UK
FINANCES *Year* 1997 *Income* £110,517 *Grants* £82,000
TRUSTEES Liverpool Council of Social Service (Inc)
HOW TO APPLY This Trust states that it does not respond to unsolicited applications
WHO TO APPLY TO The Secretary, The Sir Harry Pilkington Fund, Liverpool Council of Social Service (Inc), 14 Castle Street, Liverpool, Merseyside L2 ONJ
CC NO 206740   **ESTABLISHED** 1962

■ The Austin and Hope Pilkington Trust

WHAT IS FUNDED The Trust decides on new areas of funding for each year. 1998 was for youth and children, elderly and medical causes. 1999 the Trust will support music and art, famine and overseas charities. In 2000, support will be for community projects, relief of poverty and religious causes. Please do not apply for funding for projects that do not fall into these categories
WHAT IS NOT FUNDED No grants to individuals. Travel bursaries and education fees will not be funded
WHO CAN BENEFIT Registered charities only; national organisations preferred. For 1999 victims of famine and those overseas, as well as participants in the arts and music will benefit. In 2000 communities and those disadvantaged by

poverty and in needy circumstances will be supported.

WHERE FUNDING CAN BE GIVEN UK and overseas

TYPE OF GRANT Core costs, one-off, project, research, running costs and start-up costs will be considered. Funding may be given for up to three years

RANGE OF GRANTS Up to £5,000, occasional grants of £10,000–£20,000

SAMPLE GRANTS £530,900 to the Purcell School; £10,000 to Age Concern St Helens; £10,000 to The National Trust, Lake District Appeal Phase II; £10,000 to YMCA Lakeside National Centre; £6,000 to United Reform Church St Helens; £5,000 to Asthma Research; £5,000 to City of Oxford Orchestra; £3,000 to Children's Classic Concerts; £3,000 to Intermediate Technology; £2,000 to Chetham's School of Music

FINANCES *Year* 1996 *Income* £266,369 *Grants* £594,750

TRUSTEES Mrs J Jones, Dr L H A Pilkington, Mrs P Shankar

HOW TO APPLY Payments likely to be in June and November; please include copy of accounts plus project budget. Unsuccessful applicants will not be acknowledged. There is no application form

WHO TO APPLY TO P Jones, The Austin and Hope Pilkington Trust, PO Box 124, Stroud, Gloucestershire GL6 7YM

CC NO 255274   **ESTABLISHED** 1967

■ Dr L H A Pilkington's Charitable Trust

WHAT IS FUNDED General charitable purposes. To grant donations to applicants who they consider suitable, but normally to organisations within the British Isles and Canada and not to individuals

WHAT IS NOT FUNDED Registered charities only. No individual grants

WHO CAN BENEFIT Registered charities. There are no restrictions on the age; professional and economic group; family situation; religion and culture; and social circumstances of; or disease or medical condition suffered by, the beneficiaries

WHERE FUNDING CAN BE GIVEN UK and Canada

TYPE OF GRANT Cash

RANGE OF GRANTS £500–£7,500

SAMPLE GRANTS £7,500 to the Bertram Trust Fund Queens Mechanical, Canada; £7,500 to Hospice Peterborough, Canada; £7,500 to Showplace Peterborough, Canada; £2,000 to NSPCC, St Helens Centenary Appeal; £2,000 to Save the Children, Guernsey Appeal; £1,000 to Christ Church Centre; £1,000 to Imperial Chemical Research Fund; £1,000 to Intermediate Technology; £1,000 to Leprosy Mission; £1,000 to Marie Curie Cancer Care

FINANCES *Year* 1997 *Income* £34,556 *Grants* £38,000

TRUSTEES Mrs Isabel Henniger, P L Henniger, Mrs Eleanor Bankes, T A Bankes

HOW TO APPLY Applications in writing to the Trustees at any time outlining the purposes for which the donation is requested and any supporting literature. No formal application forms. UK distribution in August, deadline 30 June. Canadian distribution in February, deadline 31 December

WHO TO APPLY TO Mrs E Bankes, Dr L H A Pilkington's Charitable Trust, PO Box 122, Stroud, Gloucestershire GL6 7YL

CC NO 241296   **ESTABLISHED** 1964

■ Pirate Trust

WHAT IS FUNDED General charitable purposes for the benefit of the inhabitants of Cornwall, West Devon and Plymouth

WHO CAN BENEFIT There are no restrictions on the age; professional and economic group; family situation; religion and culture; and social circumstances of; or disease or medical condition suffered by, the beneficiaries

WHERE FUNDING CAN BE GIVEN Cornwall and Devon

SAMPLE GRANTS £8,000 to Hall for Cornwall for installation of infra red loop for hard of hearing; £1,500 to 16 year old blind student for specialist computer equipment to enable further education; £700 to West Cornwall Mine Rescue to purchase specialist stretcher; £500 to single mother of three children to replace lost possessions due to house fire; £500 to Double Trees Hostel for equipment for children with severe hearing difficulties

FINANCES *Year* 1997 *Income* £21,954 *Grants* £9,791

TRUSTEES A Merrick, Mrs A Egerton, R Clifford, T Sharp, J Whiting, Miss C Dale, J Coggins, G Haines, T Robinson, N Lake, D Warren, Mrs E Lillicrap

WHO TO APPLY TO Ms Y Clayton, Pirate Trust, Carn Brea Studios, Wilson Way, Redruth, Cornwall TR15 3XX *Tel* 01209 314480

CC NO 1032096   **ESTABLISHED** 1994

■ The John Pitman Charitable Trust

WHAT IS FUNDED Grants to charities which provide services to individuals, to enable the individuals to live their life more fully. Particularly charities working in the fields of: accommodation and housing; infrastructure and technical support; Anglican bodies; healthcare; health facilities and buildings; community facilities and various community services

WHAT IS NOT FUNDED Registered charities only. No grants to individuals, research bodies or education or sponsorship

WHO CAN BENEFIT Organisations benefiting: Christians; at risk groups; carers; disabled people; those disadvantaged by poverty; and the socially isolated. There is no restriction on the disease or medical condition suffered by the beneficiaries

WHERE FUNDING CAN BE GIVEN UK with a preference for London and the South East

TYPE OF GRANT No restriction – either capital or revenue. Buildings, core costs, endowments, one-off, recurring costs and running costs. Funding of up to three years will be considered

RANGE OF GRANTS £250–£2,500; typical grant £1,000

SAMPLE GRANTS £5,000 to Roy Kinnear Charitable Foundation to establish accommodation for physically and mentally handicapped people; £2,000 to VSO to provide facilities and assistance in third world; £1,000 to Pearsons Holiday Fund for children's holidays; £1,000 to John Grooms for facilities for physically handicapped; £1,000 to Cancer Relief Macmillan for carers; £1,000 to Farm Africa for assistance and improvement in agriculture; £1,000 to Ramblers Association for recreational facilities for the able bodied; £1,000 to Church Housing Trust for accommodation; £1,000 to The Samaritans for assistance to the distressed; £1,000 to Holy Trinity, Hounslow for provision of facilities for young people

FINANCES *Year* 1997 *Income* £31,622 *Grants* £25,000

TRUSTEES J M Pitman, N A R Winckless, B Hong Tan, V N C S Browne, J L L McKenzie

NOTES The Trust has no staff and therefor no correspondence can be entered into

HOW TO APPLY Periodically, but no set dates. Applications by post only. All applications are considered but those not met are **not** informed on the grounds of costs. There is no application form

WHO TO APPLY TO J M Pitman, The John Pitman Charitable Trust, Messrs Pitman Power & Co, Parkgate House, 27 High Street, Hampton Hill, Middlesex TW12 1NB

CC NO 803018   **ESTABLISHED** 1988

■ Headley Pitt Trust

WHAT IS FUNDED To administer the old peoples' bungalows which it has built, and to build up reserves for further building. The Trustees also make certain grants to charities, primarily connected with the aged

WHO CAN BENEFIT Organisations benefiting elderly people

WHERE FUNDING CAN BE GIVEN Mainly in the vicinity of Ashford

FINANCES *Year* 1997 *Income* £51,761
Grants £18,400

TRUSTEES Henry C Pitt, Mrs Stella D Pitt, Mrs Deborah B Salino, D H Pitt

HOW TO APPLY No specific dates. No formal application form used

WHO TO APPLY TO Mrs S D Pitt, Headley Pitt Trust, Maybank, Ulley Road, Kennington, Ashford, Kent TN24 9HX

CC NO 252023   **ESTABLISHED** 1955

■ Richard Platt's Relief in Need Charity

WHAT IS FUNDED Relieving persons in conditions of need, hardship or distress. This includes: almshouses; housing associations; respite accommodation; acute health care; aftercare; and income support and maintenance

WHO CAN BENEFIT Individuals and organisations benefiting: young adults and older people; those in care, fostered and adopted; one parent families; parents and children; widows and widowers; those disadvantaged by poverty; refugees; victims of abuse crime and domestic violence. There is no restriction on the disease or medical condition suffered by the beneficiaries

WHERE FUNDING CAN BE GIVEN The Parish of Aldenham

TYPE OF GRANT Buildings, capital, core costs, endowments, feasibility studies, interest free loans, one-off, project, research, recurring costs, running costs, salaries and start-up costs. Funding is for up to and three years

SAMPLE GRANTS £90,000 to Howard Cottage Society Ltd for purchase of land for six affordable housing units; £500 to Letchmore Heath Welcome Committee for Christmas Party for elderly people

FINANCES *Year* 1997 *Income* £26,700
Grants £90,500

TRUSTEES The Brewers Company

HOW TO APPLY To the address under Who To Apply To in writing

WHO TO APPLY TO The Clerk to the Brewers Company, Richard Platt's Relief in Need Charity, Brewers Hall, Aldermanbury Square, London EC2V 7HR *Tel* 0171-606 1301

CC NO 215544   **ESTABLISHED** 1597

■ G S Plaut Charitable Trust Limited

WHAT IS FUNDED Grants to charities considered worthwhile

WHAT IS NOT FUNDED No grants to individuals

WHO CAN BENEFIT There are no restrictions on the age; professional and economic group; family situation; religion and culture; and social circumstances of; or disease or medical condition suffered by, the beneficiaries

WHERE FUNDING CAN BE GIVEN UK

TYPE OF GRANT Some annual, others one-off donations

RANGE OF GRANTS £50–£750

SAMPLE GRANTS £750 to C M Jacobs Home; £750 to WRVS, Liverpool; £600 to Nightingale Home for Aged Jews; £600 to St Dunstans; £500 to AJR Charitable Trust; £500 to Army Benevolent Fund, Northern Region; £500 to Muscular Dystrophy; £500 to North Humberside Hospice Project; £500 to Oxfam; £500 to RAF Benevolent Fund

FINANCES *Year* 1997 *Income* £35,661
Grants £34,520

TRUSTEES The Directors: Dr G S Plaut, T N Wheldon, Mrs I M A Plaut, Mrs A D Wrapson, Dr H M Liebeschuetz, K A Sutcliffe

NOTES All correspondence to the Secretary

HOW TO APPLY In writing to Secretary at the address under Who To Apply To. Applications reviewed twice each year. Sae should be enclosed. Applications will not be acknowledged

WHO TO APPLY TO Dr G G Plaut, G S Plaut Charitable Trust Limited, 18 North Mill PLace, Mill Chase, Halstead, Essex CO9 2FA

CC NO 261469   **ESTABLISHED** 1970

■ The Pleasance Trust

WHAT IS FUNDED Grants are awarded to youth clubs and other voluntary organisations which work with disadvantaged young people

WHAT IS NOT FUNDED Grants are not given to individuals or to national organisations (unless involved in local projects)

WHO CAN BENEFIT To benefit disadvantaged young people in the less well-off areas of Edinburgh

WHERE FUNDING CAN BE GIVEN Edinburgh

TYPE OF GRANT Usually one-off or project

FINANCES *Year* 1996 *Income* £20,000
Grants £30,000

TRUSTEES N Campbell, J Henderson, F Ivory, S Marshall

PUBLICATIONS Accounts are available from the Trust

HOW TO APPLY Applicants should write to the Secretary giving details of project/scheme/reasons for applying plus costs

WHO TO APPLY TO The Secretary, The Pleasance Trust, 45 Charlotte Square, Edinburgh EH2 4HW *Tel* 0131-226 3271

SC NO SCO 00309

■ Harry Plotnek Charitable Trust

This trust did not respond to CAF's request to amend its entry and, by 30 June 1998, CAF's researchers did not find financial records for later than 1995 on its file at the Charity Commission. Trusts are legally required to submit annual accounts to the Charity Commission under section 42 of the Charities Act 1993

WHAT IS FUNDED General charitable purposes. To distribute to charities selected by the Settlor

WHO CAN BENEFIT There are no restrictions on the age; professional and economic group; family

Does the trust you have chosen match your needs? Haphazard applications waste postage and time

497

situation; religion and culture; and social circumstances of; or disease or medical condition suffered by, the beneficiaries

WHERE FUNDING CAN BE GIVEN UK and overseas

TRUSTEES A E Plotnek, H Plotnek

HOW TO APPLY This Trust states that it does not respond to unsolicited applications

WHO TO APPLY TO Maurice Putsman & Co, Britannia House, 50 Great Charles Street, Birmingham B46 2AE

CC NO 260076   **ESTABLISHED** 1969

■ Plymouth Public Dispensary

WHAT IS FUNDED The poor, who are sick, elderly or disabled and residents of Plymouth. Particularly charities working in the fields of: holiday accommodation; respite; acute health care; after care; respite care; care for carers; convalescent homes and hospitals

WHAT IS NOT FUNDED Applications for grants for the relief of taxes and rates will not be considered

WHO CAN BENEFIT Individuals and local organisations; local branches of national organisations benefiting: at risk groups; carers; disabled people; those disadvantaged by poverty; socially isolated people; those living in urban areas; victims of abuse and domestic violence. There is no restriction on the disease or medical condition suffered by the beneficiaries

WHERE FUNDING CAN BE GIVEN Plymouth

TYPE OF GRANT One-off and running costs

FINANCES *Year* 1997 *Income* £46,604 *Grants* £39,920

TRUSTEES Two representatives of the local authority, two representatives of the local health authority, five co-opted

NOTES Grants to individuals are generally made through the social services or related organisations

HOW TO APPLY To the address under Who To Apply To in writing

WHO TO APPLY TO T J Stark, Chairman, Plymouth Public Dispensary, 19 College Avenue, Mannamead, Plymouth, Devon PL4 7AL *Tel* 01752 663951

CC NO 267658   **ESTABLISHED** 1798

■ Podde Trust

WHAT IS FUNDED Welfare and religion, including Christian education and outreach, missionaries and evangelicals

WHO CAN BENEFIT Christian individuals and institutions

WHERE FUNDING CAN BE GIVEN UK

TYPE OF GRANT One-off and recurrent

RANGE OF GRANTS £25–£2,000, typical grant £250

SAMPLE GRANTS £5,100 to Vine Evangelical Church; £3,250 to Family Foundations Trust; £1,000 to Overseas Missionary Fellowship; £650 to Echoes of Service; £560 to Hildenborough Evangelistic Trust

FINANCES *Year* 1997 *Income* £22,680 *Grants* £16,290

TRUSTEES P B Godfrey, Mrs P E Godfrey, Dr D F Maxted

PUBLICATIONS Annual Report

HOW TO APPLY In writing at any time

WHO TO APPLY TO P B Godfrey, Podde Trust, 68 Green Lane, Hucclecote, Gloucester GL3 3QS

CC NO 1016322   **ESTABLISHED** 1993

■ The P H Pointer Charitable Trust

This trust did not respond to CAF's request to amend its entry and, by 30 June 1998, CAF's researchers did not find financial records for later than 1995 on its file at the Charity Commission. Trusts are legally required to submit annual accounts to the Charity Commission under section 42 of the Charities Act 1993

WHAT IS FUNDED Youth and community, health and welfare and heritage

WHAT IS NOT FUNDED No grants to individuals

WHO CAN BENEFIT Local and regional organisations benefiting children and young adults. There are no restrictions on the disease or medical condition suffered by the beneficiaries

WHERE FUNDING CAN BE GIVEN South East England

SAMPLE GRANTS £1,200 to the Salvation Army

TRUSTEES D N Howard, G J R Isbell, Mrs M L Pointer

HOW TO APPLY To the address below in writing

WHO TO APPLY TO Mrs M L Pointer, Trustee, The P H Pointer Charitable Trust, 186 Newmarket Road, Norwich, Norfolk NR4 6AR

CC NO 266365   **ESTABLISHED** 1973

■ Carew Pole Charitable Trust

WHAT IS FUNDED General charitable purposes principally in Cornwall

WHAT IS NOT FUNDED No donations made to individuals for full-time education

WHO CAN BENEFIT Donations normally made only to registered charities, but applications will be considered from individuals for non-full-time education purposes. There are no restrictions on the age; professional and economic group; family situation; religion and culture; and social circumstances of; or disease or medical condition suffered by, the beneficiaries

WHERE FUNDING CAN BE GIVEN National, but in practice Cornwall and in the case of donations to churches and village halls donations are in practice only made to those in the immediate vicinity to Antony House, Torpoint or to those with connections to the Carew Pole Family

TYPE OF GRANT The Trustees have no particular policy

SAMPLE GRANTS £10,000 to The National Trust; £1,000 to St John's Ambulance Brigade; £600 to Sherioch Parochial Church Council; £600 to Maryfield Parochial Church Council; £600 to Antony Parochial Church Council; £500 to Falmouth Citizens Advice Bureau; £300 to British Legion Cornwall Division; £250 to Churchtown Field Studies Centre; £250 to Penzance Sea Cadets; £250 to Truro District Scout Council

FINANCES *Year* 1997 *Income* £26,047 *Grants* £14,850

TRUSTEES J R Cooke-Hurle, J C Richardson

NOTES This Charitable Trust was founded by Sir John Gawen Carew Pole, Bt, DSO, whose family has both lived in and been connected with Cornwall for many years

HOW TO APPLY Applications are considered six-monthly in March and September

WHO TO APPLY TO J C Richardson, Carew Pole Charitable Trust, Messrs Dawson & Co, 2 New Square, Lincoln's Inn, London WC2A 3RZ

CC NO 255375   **ESTABLISHED** 1968

■ The Polehampton Eleemosynary Charity

WHAT IS FUNDED Schools and individuals for education; local youth and community groups; people in need

WHO CAN BENEFIT Individuals and organisations benefiting: children; young adults; students; and people in need

WHERE FUNDING CAN BE GIVEN The Parish of St Mary, Twyford and Ruscombe

TYPE OF GRANT One-off, some recurring. Limited interest free loans to local organisations

RANGE OF GRANTS £50–£5,000, typical grants £100 or £200

FINANCES *Year* 1997 *Income* £57,700
Grants £42,000

TRUSTEES The Rector of Twyford and Ruscombe and ten others

HOW TO APPLY To the address under Who To Apply To in writing

WHO TO APPLY TO Peter M Hutt, Clerk, The Polehampton Eleemosynary Charity, 1 London Street, Reading RG1 4QW *Tel* 01189 391011

CC NO 202514 **ESTABLISHED** 1957

■ George and Esme Pollitzer Charitable Settlement

WHAT IS FUNDED General charitable purposes

WHO CAN BENEFIT There are no restrictions on the age; professional and economic group; family situation; religion and culture; and social circumstances of; or disease or medical condition suffered by, the beneficiaries

WHERE FUNDING CAN BE GIVEN UK

TYPE OF GRANT Normally for single, specific projects

RANGE OF GRANTS £500–£10,000

SAMPLE GRANTS £10,000 to Nightingale House; £10,000 to Norwood Child Care; £10,000 to Royal College of Surgeons; £7,000 to Prince's Youth Business Trust; £5,000 to Abbeyfield West London Society; £5,000 to Royal Hospital for Neuro-Disability; £5,000 to World Jewish Relief; £2,000 to the National Hospital; £2,000 to BHHI; £2,000 to Barnardos

FINANCES *Year* 1997 *Income* £80,223
Grants £98,000

TRUSTEES B G Levy, R F C Pollitzer, Jeremy Barnes

WHO TO APPLY TO J Barnes, George and Esme Pollitzer Charitable Settlement, Saffrey Champness, Fairfax House, Fulwood Place, Gray's Inn, London WC1V 6UB

CC NO 212631 **ESTABLISHED** 1960

■ J S F Pollitzer's Charitable Settlement

WHAT IS FUNDED General charitable purposes including the Arts

WHAT IS NOT FUNDED No grants to individuals or students, ie those without charitable status

WHO CAN BENEFIT There are no restrictions on the age; professional and economic group; family situation; religion and culture; and social circumstances of; or disease or medical condition suffered by, the beneficiaries. However, particular favour is given to neighbourhood-based community projects

TYPE OF GRANT One-off

RANGE OF GRANTS £250–£2,000, typical grant £1,000

SAMPLE GRANTS £2,000 to Anglo Israel Association; £2,000 to Sadler's Wells; £1,000 to British Heart Foundation; £1,000 to Heritage of London Trust Ltd; £1,000 to National Asthma Campaign; £1,000 to Parents at Work; £500 to ASBAH; £500 to Alexandra Rose Day; £500 to Baby Lifeline; £500 to Blond McIndoe Centre

FINANCES *Year* 1997 *Income* £36,483
Grants £37,750

TRUSTEES Mrs J Davis, J Challis, Mrs S O'Farrell, R F C Pollitzer

WHO TO APPLY TO J Challis, J S F Pollitzer's Charitable Settlement, H W Fisher & Co, Acre House, 11–15 William Road, London NW1 3ER

CC NO 210680 **ESTABLISHED** 1960

■ The Pontin Charitable Trust

WHAT IS FUNDED General charitable purposes. The Trustees are already in touch with the organisations which they wish to support and further applications are not applicable

WHO CAN BENEFIT The beneficiary is almost always an organisation well known to the Trustees. There are no restrictions on the age; professional and economic group; family situation; religion and culture; and social circumstances of; or disease or medical condition suffered by, the beneficiaries

WHERE FUNDING CAN BE GIVEN Bristol area with negligible support to national charities

TYPE OF GRANT Buildings, capital, core costs, endowments, feasibility studies, interest free loans, one-off, project, research, running costs, recurring costs, salaries and start-up costs will be considered. Funding may be given for more than three years

RANGE OF GRANTS £500–£25,000

SAMPLE GRANTS £25,000 to Bristol Initiative Charitable Trust for general funds; £5,000 to Bristol Initiative Charitable Trust for Hartcliffe project; £4,640 to Natural Step in Britain; £2,000 to Choices for Bristol; £2,000 to St Andrew's Church, Chew Magna; £2,000 to Environmental Research Association Ltd to assist with the Schumacher lecture programme; £1,500 to Business in the Community; £1,374 to Darlington Hall Trust for a new computer and printer for the Schumacher College; £1,000 to Bristol Energy and Economy Trust; £1,000 to Small School

FINANCES *Year* 1997 *Income* £38,207
Grants £47,519

TRUSTEES D W R Johnstone, R W A Mortimer, C Zealley

HOW TO APPLY No further applications are sought

WHO TO APPLY TO C B Zealley, The Pontin Charitable Trust, Sneydhurst, Broadhempston, Totnes, Devon TQ9 6AX

CC NO 271409 **ESTABLISHED** 1976

■ The Ponton House Trust

WHAT IS FUNDED Grants are given mainly to support small charities working with young people, elderly people and disadvantaged groups

WHAT IS NOT FUNDED No grants to individuals or non-charitable organisations

WHO CAN BENEFIT Organisations benefiting disadvantaged groups, the young and the elderly

WHERE FUNDING CAN BE GIVEN Edinburgh and Lothian

TYPE OF GRANT One-off cash grants

RANGE OF GRANTS £250–£2,000

FINANCES *Year* 1997 *Income* £32,000
Grants £30,000

TRUSTEES A Dobson, G Gemmell, Mrs J Gilliat, Lord Grieve, Mrs F Meikle, Rev J Munro, Mrs G Russell

HOW TO APPLY Applications should be made to the address under Who To Apply To in writing

WHO TO APPLY TO David S Reith, Secretary, The Ponton House Trust, 11 Atholl Crescent, Edinburgh EH3 8HE   *Tel* 0131-477 8708

SC NO SCO 21716   **ESTABLISHED** 1993

■ The Valentine Poole Charity

WHAT IS FUNDED The welfare of the young, elderly, disabled and otherwise disadvantaged people in the area Where Funding Can Be Given

WHO CAN BENEFIT Individuals and local organisations benefiting children, young adults, older people, disabled people and those disadvantaged by poverty

WHERE FUNDING CAN BE GIVEN Barnet and East Barnet

FINANCES *Year* 1997 *Income* £55,776 *Grants* £38,449

TRUSTEES Laurence Adams (Chairman), Adrian Esdaile, Elaine Huxtable, Margaret Jamieson (Vice Chairman), Cllr Anne Jarvis, Stephen Lane, Joan Levinson, Ronald Neil, Brenda Sandford, June Hughes, Alan Brown, JP

NOTES £14,820 was paid out in the form of weekly pensions

HOW TO APPLY To the address under Who To Apply To in writing

WHO TO APPLY TO Mrs M G Lee, Clerk, The Valentine Poole Charity, The Forum Room, Ewen Hall, Wood Street, Barnet, Hertfordshire EN5 4BW

CC NO 220856   **ESTABLISHED** 1624

■ The Karl Popper Charitable Trust

WHAT IS FUNDED The promotion of the philosophy, ideas and writings of Karl Popper – scientific method, critical rationalism and the virtues of open society

WHO CAN BENEFIT Young adults, older people, academics, research workers, scientists, students and scholastic bodies

WHERE FUNDING CAN BE GIVEN UK and overseas

TYPE OF GRANT One-off grants

SAMPLE GRANTS £12,500 to Karl Popper Institut, Vienna, Austria for a microfilm copy of Karl Popper's papers in the archives of the Hoover Institution in Stanford, Califonia, USA

FINANCES *Year* 1997 *Income* £160,424

TRUSTEES A R Mew, Mrs M A Mew, B R Mew, D Miller

NOTES The centenary of Karl Popper's birth will be in 2002 and events will be organised as this year approaches to commemorate his ideas and contributions to philosophy that will provide opportunities for the Trust to help in endowing scholarships in universities and finance other projects

HOW TO APPLY By letter

WHO TO APPLY TO A R Mew, Chairman, The Karl Popper Charitable Trust, 9 High Beech, South Croydon, Surrey CR2 7QB   *Tel* 0181-686 1918

CC NO 1059495   **ESTABLISHED** 1996

■ John Porter Charitable Trust

WHAT IS FUNDED General charitable purposes

WHO CAN BENEFIT There are no restrictions on the age; professional and economic group; family situation; religion and culture; and social circumstances of; or disease or medical condition suffered by, the beneficiaries

WHERE FUNDING CAN BE GIVEN UK

FINANCES *Year* 1997 *Income* £201,523

TRUSTEES L Porter, Mrs S Porter, J R Porter

WHO TO APPLY TO Peter Green, Trustee, John Porter Charitable Trust, 12 Hans Road, London SW3 1RT

CC NO 267170   **ESTABLISHED** 1974

■ The Mason Porter Charitable Trust

WHAT IS FUNDED General charitable purposes. Grants are made only to charities known to the settler

WHO CAN BENEFIT There are no restrictions on the age; professional and economic group; family situation; religion and culture; and social circumstances of; or disease or medical condition suffered by, the beneficiaries

WHERE FUNDING CAN BE GIVEN UK

FINANCES *Year* 1997 *Income* £106,391 *Grants* £40,610

TRUSTEES Liverpool Council of Social Service (Inc)

HOW TO APPLY **This Trust states that it does not respond to unsolicited applications**

WHO TO APPLY TO The Secretary, The Mason Porter Charitable Trust, Liverpool Council of Social Service (Inc), 14 Castle Street, Liverpool, Merseyside L2 ONJ

CC NO 255545   **ESTABLISHED** 1968

■ The Portishead Nautical Trust

WHAT IS FUNDED Disadvantaged young people, also educational support, young offenders; counselling services; youth groups and people with addictions

WHO CAN BENEFIT People under 25 years of age who are disadvantaged or at risk

WHERE FUNDING CAN BE GIVEN Bristol and North Somerset

TYPE OF GRANT One-off, project, recurring costs and running costs will be considered. Funding may be given for up to three years

SAMPLE GRANTS £20,500 to Portishead Dyslexia Centre; £2,700 to The Jungle Book Project for youth activities in deprived area; £2,500 to the Jessie May Trust giving care for terminally ill children; The following grants were for projects to help deprived or disadvantaged children and young people:; £2,500 to Avon Outward Bound Association; £1,000 to Bristol Mediation; £1,000 to Fairbridge in Avon; £1,000 to Felix Road Adventure Playground Association; £1,000 to the Pride of Bristol Trust; £1,000 to the Wheels Project; £1,000 to Totterdown Children's Community Workshop

FINANCES *Year* 1996–97 *Income* £69,137 *Grants* £42,777

TRUSTEES Miss S Belk, H J Crossman, Mrs S O L Haysom, Mrs M Hosking, Dr R B Pardoe, Rev T White, D W Williams, G Russ, Mrs T J F Kirby, Mrs D P Netcott, M R Cruse, Mrs A F Kay

HOW TO APPLY To the address under Who To Apply To in writing

WHO TO APPLY TO P C Dingley-Brown, Secretary, The Portishead Nautical Trust, 108 High Street, Portishead, Bristol BS20 6AJ

CC NO 228876   **ESTABLISHED** 1964

■ The Portrack Charitable Trust

WHAT IS FUNDED Charities working in the fields of: accommodation and housing; Christian education; churches; Anglican and Catholic bodies; arts, culture and recreation; health; conservation; wildlife sanctuaries; endangered species; environmental issues; heritage; and various community facilities and services. Grants are only made to charities or individuals known to the Trustees

WHAT IS NOT FUNDED No expeditions or travel bursaries

WHO CAN BENEFIT Organisations benefiting children; young adults and older people; ex-service and service people; medical professionals, nurses and doctors; musicians; seafarers and fishermen; unemployed people; volunteers; those in care, fostered and adopted; widows and widowers; Christians; Church of England and Roman Catholics; carers; disabled people; homeless people; victims of crime; and victims of man-made or natural disasters. Also sufferers of Alzheimer's disease, blood disorders and haemophilia, cancers, cerebral palsy, cystic fibrosis, hearing loss, heart disease, kidney disease, mental illness, multiple sclerosis, Parkinson's disease and sight loss

WHERE FUNDING CAN BE GIVEN England and Scotland

TYPE OF GRANT Buildings, core costs, one-off, research and recurring costs. Funding of up to three years will be considered

RANGE OF GRANTS £50–£4000

SAMPLE GRANTS £2,500 to Architectural Association for Foundation campaign; £6,500 to Maggie Jencks Cancer Caring Centre to help care for cancer patients; £400 to St Teresa's Church, Dumfries for restoration; £350 to SANE for general appeal; £300 to Shelter towards Scottish campaign for Homeless; £300 to Musicians Benevolent Fund for general appeal; £300 to St David's Home, Ealing for general appeal; £200 to Cancer Relief Macmillan Fund for general appeal; £200 to Great Ormond Street Children's Hospital for 'Gosh' Appeal; £200 to Child Poverty Action Group for general appeal

FINANCES *Year* 1995 *Income* £26,979 *Grants* £25,004

TRUSTEES Clare, Lady Keswick, C A Jencks

HOW TO APPLY Trustees consider applications in June and December

WHO TO APPLY TO The Portrack Charitable Trust, Matheson Bank Ltd, St Helens, I Undershaft, London EC3A 8JX

CC NO 266120   **ESTABLISHED** 1973

■ The J E Posnansky Charitable Trust

WHAT IS FUNDED Primarily Jewish charitable organisations, some in the medical and education fields; also child health; homelessness; AIDS charities; work with victims of torture and freedom for people unjustly imprisoned

WHAT IS NOT FUNDED No grants to individuals

WHO CAN BENEFIT Predominantly Jewish organisations; international and national charities. Beneficiaries include: Jews and those suffering from a range of diseases and medical conditions, especially HIV and AIDs. At risk groups and the homeless are also considered

WHERE FUNDING CAN BE GIVEN UK and overseas

TYPE OF GRANT One-off

RANGE OF GRANTS £500–£30,000

SAMPLE GRANTS £30,000 to British Council of Shaare Zedek Medical Centre; £25,000 to JPAIME; £15,000 to Friends of Alyn Hospital; £15,000 to the Society of Friends of the Federation of Women Zionists; £13,500 to Jewish Care; £13,000 to Friends of the Hebrew University of Jerusalem; £10,000 to General Jewish Hospital Mijgav Ladach; £10,000 to Ravenswood; £10,000 to Save the Children Fund; £7,000 to Central British Fund for World Jewish Relief

FINANCES *Year* 1997–98 *Income* £289,249 *Grants* £292,050

TRUSTEES Phillip A Cohen, Beryl Inglis, Lord Mishcon, Anthony V Posnansky, Gillian Raffles

HOW TO APPLY To the address under Who To Apply To in writing. The Trustees meet annually in May

WHO TO APPLY TO P A Cohen, The J E Posnansky Charitable Trust, Baker Tilly, 2 Bloomsbury Street, London WC1B 3ST *Tel* 0171-413 5235

CC NO 210416   **ESTABLISHED** 1962

■ Ann Potter Memorial Trust

This trust did not respond to CAF's request to amend its entry and, by 30 June 1998, CAF's researchers did not find financial records for later than 1995 on its file at the Charity Commission. Trusts are legally required to submit annual accounts to the Charity Commission under section 42 of the Charities Act 1993

WHAT IS FUNDED General charitable purposes

WHO CAN BENEFIT There are no restrictions on the age; professional and economic group; family situation; religion and culture; and social circumstances of; or disease or medical condition suffered by, the beneficiaries

WHERE FUNDING CAN BE GIVEN UK and Europe

TRUSTEES I C Brookman, P Harvey, G R Jay, Ms J E Shell

WHO TO APPLY TO P Harvey, Solicitor, Ann Potter Memorial Trust, c/o Harvey, Son and Filbey, 231 Foxhall Road, Ipswich, Suffolk IP3 8LF

CC NO 1044580   **ESTABLISHED** 1995

■ Mrs Ruth Powdrill's Charitable Trust

This trust did not respond to CAF's request to amend its entry and, by 30 June 1998, CAF's researchers did not find financial records for later than 1995 on its file at the Charity Commission. Trusts are legally required to submit annual accounts to the Charity Commission under section 42 of the Charities Act 1993

WHAT IS FUNDED General charitable purposes

WHO CAN BENEFIT There are no restrictions on the age; professional and economic group; family situation; religion and culture; and social circumstances of; or disease or medical condition suffered by, the beneficiaries

WHERE FUNDING CAN BE GIVEN UK

TRUSTEES Mrs R M Powdrill, I P Milner Payne, C S Flanagan, B Powdrill

WHO TO APPLY TO I P Milner Payne, Mrs Ruth Powdrill's Charitable Trust, 29 Upper Parliament Street, Nottingham NG1 2AQ

CC NO 1065613   **ESTABLISHED** 1995

■ The Powell Foundation

WHAT IS FUNDED To make grants for the benefit of the elderly and mentally and physically disabled people. Localised charities working in the fields of community development including supporting voluntary organisations, community arts and

Does the trust you have chosen match your needs? Haphazard applications waste postage and time

501

recreation, community facilities and services for the disabled, healthcare and special needs education

WHO CAN BENEFIT Individuals and local organisations benefiting older people and disabled people of any age will be considered

WHERE FUNDING CAN BE GIVEN Within the boundaries of the area covered by Milton Keynes Council

TYPE OF GRANT One-off grants up to £5,000. Longer term funding for specific projects can be considered. Buildings, capital, feasibility studies, project and start-up costs. One, two and three year funding will also be considered

RANGE OF GRANTS £350–£18,000

SAMPLE GRANTS £75,000 to Community Trust – Milton Keynes for projects to benefit elderly or disabled people; £16,854 to The Pace centre to enable children from Milton Keynes to attend this special school; £14,000 to MK MIND for running costs of family and children's centre; £8,500 to Dorngate Pantomime Trip to give elderly and disabled people a free trip to the pantomime; £6,000 to Christmas Donations, small grants given to charities for parcels and parties; £4,590 to Stantonbury Campus Theatre for infra-red sound transmission system for hard of hearing; £1,000 to a severely disabled man to go to New Zealand for Test Matches; £235 to an individual for telephone installation; £200 to SSAFA and FHS Milton Keynes Branch to help ex-servicemen and women who have disabilities

FINANCES *Year* 1996–97 *Income* £184,000 *Grants* £126,000

TRUSTEES R W Norman, R Hill

HOW TO APPLY All grant applications are handled by the Community Trust – Milton Keynes on behalf of the Foundation

WHO TO APPLY TO Powell Grants Co-ordinator, The Powell Foundation, Community Trust - Milton Keynes, Acorn House, 381 Midsummer Boulevard, Central Milton Keynes MK9 3HP *Tel* 01908 690276 *Fax* 01908 233635

CC NO 1012786   **ESTABLISHED** 1992

························

■ Powys Welsh Church Fund

WHAT IS FUNDED Community facilities; various community services; advice and information on social issues; health facilities and buildings; and health advocacy. Arts and arts facilities; community arts and recreation; cultural heritage; the conservation of church and historical buildings; and the purchase of educational books are also considered. Community development; support to voluntary and community organisations; and charity or voluntary umbrella bodies may also be considered. The Fund provides grant-aid to assist organisations, bodies and individuals within Powys or providing services or facilities of benefit to its residents in accordance with these areas of interest

WHAT IS NOT FUNDED Grants are not made to organisations outside Powys or to those which provide services or benefit to residents outside the County. Individuals may only apply if resident in, or natives of, Powys

WHO CAN BENEFIT Charitable organisations, churches, chapels, students and apprentices within or having some connection with the County of Powys. There are no restrictions on the age; professional and economic group; family situation; religion and culture; and social circumstances of; or disease or medical condition suffered by, the beneficiaries. Particular favour is given to children and young adults

WHERE FUNDING CAN BE GIVEN Powys

TYPE OF GRANT Cash payments paid on a pro rata basis of estimated expenditure. Donations of income of charity only – mainly one-off for a specific project (or part). Core funding rarely considered

SAMPLE GRANTS £5,000 to Dolau Recreation Association for new community hall; £3,000 to Castle Caerinion Recreation Association for land purchase for multi-sports area; £3,000 to Guides Cymru for improvements to Welsh Guide Centre; £3,000 to Hope House for children's hospice playroom extension; £3,000 to Clyro Community Hall for improvements; £3,000 to Trefeglwys Community Hall for new building; £3,000 to Llangorse Community Hall for new building; £3,000 to Llanrhaedr Ym Community Hall for improvements; £2,000 to St Peter's Church, Machynlleth for church restoration and repairs; £2,000 to Llanbister Church for church restoration and repairs

FINANCES *Year* 1997 *Income* £88,445

TRUSTEES The Welsh Church Acts Sub Committee of the Community Committee of Powys County Council

NOTES Commencement of projects/building works: the Committee will very rarely consider applications which are submitted after the project/building works have been commenced. Churches and Chapels: repair and restoration work of the main fabric of the building of places of worship will be considered for grant-aid but day to day running costs, constituting maintenance, interior work, including redecoration and repair/ installation of heating systems, will not be grant aided. Applications in respect of Churches and Chapels used for public worship and wider community purposes will be considered separately, and on the same basis as applications in respect of village halls/community centres. The Trustees will not make grants to organisations which are not registered as a charity with the Charity Commissioners

HOW TO APPLY By completion of official application forms which are considered by the Committee quarterly

WHO TO APPLY TO Director of Community, Leisure and Recreation, Powys Welsh Church Fund, Powys County Council, Powys County Hall, Llandrindod Wells, Powys LD1 5LG *Tel* 01597 826000

CC NO 507967   **ESTABLISHED** 1974

························

■ Prairie Trust

WHAT IS FUNDED (a) Overseas development and advocacy. (b) Corporate social responsibility and new economic paradigms. (c) Conflict prevention, conventional and nuclear weapons. (d) Environmental issues. (e) Health issues and emotional literacy. (f) UK poverty advocacy

WHAT IS NOT FUNDED No grants to individuals, for expeditions or capital projects

WHO CAN BENEFIT Organisations benefiting those disadvantaged by poverty and victims of war

WHERE FUNDING CAN BE GIVEN UK and overseas

TYPE OF GRANT Core costs and project funding for up to three years will be considered

RANGE OF GRANTS £250–£10,000. Typical grants £1,000–£5,000 rarely more

············

Have you read How to use the DGMT *on page xvi?*

SAMPLE GRANTS £10,000 to Results Education for citizens' advocacy work on international poverty; £8,750 to Network Foundation for human rights, environmental issues, health issues, arts for social change; £3,250 to New Economics Foundation for corporate social responsibility, new economic paradigms, expenses of Peoples' Summit (G8 Meetings); £3,000 to Oxfam matching funding for sponsored events; £2,500 to Pilotlight for advocacy and policy work on UK and international poverty; £2,500 to Oxford Research Group for the abolition of nuclear weapons, for a non-proliferation treaty; £2,500 to Forum for the Future for environmental issues; £2,500 to Squiggle Foundation for psychotherapy work with the ideas of D W Winnicott; £1,000 to Gaia Foundation for work on biotechnology and genetic patenting; £1,000 to Saferworld for control of the arms trade

FINANCES *Year* 1997–98 *Income* £54,774
Grants £54,774

TRUSTEES Dr R F Mulder, James S Taylor

NOTES The Trust chooses the projects it wishes to support and does not solicit applications. Unfortunately it will not be able to respond to unsolicited applications

HOW TO APPLY **This Trust states that it does not respond to unsolicited applications**

WHO TO APPLY TO Mrs C Nonweiler, Prairie Trust, 83 Belsize Park Gardens, London NW3 4NJ
Tel 0171-722 2105

CC NO 296019   **ESTABLISHED** 1987

■ The W L Pratt Charitable Trust

WHAT IS FUNDED Overseas: to help the Third World by assisting in food production and relief of famine and disease. In Britain: to support religious and social objectives with priority for York and district including health and community services

WHAT IS NOT FUNDED National and foreign grants are restricted to well-known charities. No grants to individuals. No grants for buildings or for the upkeep and preservation of places of worship

WHO CAN BENEFIT (a) Organisations with worldwide scope (b) National welfare organisations; national organisations for handicapped people; (c) Certain local religious and social organisations. Those benefiting children, young people, older people, the terminally ill, disabled people, those disadvantaged by poverty, homeless people, victims of man-made and natural disasters, war and famine and those suffering from arthritis and rheumatism, Alzheimer's disease and cancers

WHERE FUNDING CAN BE GIVEN York, North Yorkshire, UK and overseas

TYPE OF GRANT One-off lump sum grants made out of annual income for core costs, project and research which are funded for up to one year

RANGE OF GRANTS £100–£4,600. Average grant £800

FINANCES *Year* 1997 *Income* £62,415
Grants £50,088

TRUSTEES J L C Pratt, R E Kitching, C C Goodway

HOW TO APPLY In writing to the address under Who To Apply To at any time. Applications will not be acknowledged unless an sae is enclosed

WHO TO APPLY TO C C Goodway, The W L Pratt Charitable Trust, Messrs Grays, Duncombe Place, York, North Yorkshire YO1 7DY

CC NO 256907   **ESTABLISHED** 1968

■ Premierquote Ltd

WHAT IS FUNDED Jewish charitable purposes, relief of poverty, general charitable purposes

WHO CAN BENEFIT To benefit Jews and those disadvantaged by poverty

WHERE FUNDING CAN BE GIVEN UK and overseas

FINANCES *Year* 1996 *Income* £783,474
Grants £157,536

TRUSTEES D Last, H Last, Mrs L Last, M Weisenfeld

HOW TO APPLY To the address under Who To Apply To in writing

WHO TO APPLY TO D Last, Trustee, Premierquote Ltd, 18 Green Walk, London NW4 2AJ

CC NO 801957   **ESTABLISHED** 1985

■ Premishlaner Charitable Trust

WHAT IS FUNDED (a) To advance Othodox Jewish education, (b) to advance the religion of the Jewish faith in accordance with the Orthodox practice, (c) to relieve poverty, (d) other general charitable purposes

WHO CAN BENEFIT To benefit Jewish people and those disadvantaged by poverty

WHERE FUNDING CAN BE GIVEN UK

RANGE OF GRANTS Below £5,000–£25,000

SAMPLE GRANTS £25,000 to Deedpride; £24,500 to Society of Friends of the Torah; £10,275 to Yesodey Hatorah Schools; £10,000 to Jewish Educational Trust; £10,000 to American Friends of Torah Institutions in the Netherlands

FINANCES *Year* 1997 *Income* £40,333
Grants £119,225

TRUSTEES H C Freudenberger, S Honig, C M Margulies

WHO TO APPLY TO C M Margulies, Trustee, Premishlaner Charitable Trust, 186 Lordship Road, London N16 5ES

CC NO 1046945   **ESTABLISHED** 1995

■ The Simone Prendergast Charitable Trust

WHAT IS FUNDED No specific policy merely suitable type of application. Particularly charities working in the fields of religion; arts, culture and recreation; hospices; immunology; historic buildings; pre-school education; theatres and opera houses; crime prevention schemes; play schemes; and campaigning for racial equality, discrimination and relations

WHAT IS NOT FUNDED Registered charities only. No grants to individuals

WHO CAN BENEFIT Registered charities benefiting: children; older people; ex-service and service people; medical professionals; Christians; Jews; ethnic minority groups; disabled people; victims of abuse and those suffering Alzheimer's disease, cancers, diabetes, HIV and AIDs, Parkinson's disease and strokes

WHERE FUNDING CAN BE GIVEN UK, Israel

TYPE OF GRANT Core costs, one-off and research. Funding of up to three years will be considered

SAMPLE GRANTS £4,000 to British Diabetic Association for twins research; £4,000 to East Grinstead Medical Research Trust for research into wound healing; £3,000 to Westminster Children's Society for under five's care; £3,000 to World Jewish Relief for working with refugees/Jews in Eastern Europe; £2,500 to Society of Friends of Federation of Women Zionists for welfare for women and children in Israel; £2,000 to Jewish Lads and Girls Brigade for general youth activities; £2,000 to Age Concern Westminster for general funding; £1,000 to Anglo-Israel Association for general funds; £1,000 to Council of Christians and Jews for general funding; £1,000 to Duke of Edinburgh Award World Fellowship for general funding

FINANCES *Year* 1996 *Income* £36,431 *Grants* £26,165

TRUSTEES Dame Simone Prendergast, C H Prendergast, Mrs J Skidmore

HOW TO APPLY Personal letter to Dame Simone Prendergast. At any time. Trustees meet half yearly. Clear details of project required – no acknowledgements

WHO TO APPLY TO Dame Simone Prendergast, The Simone Prendergast Charitable Trust, Flat C, 52 Warwick Square, London SW1V 2AJ

CC NO 242881   **ESTABLISHED** 1961

■ The Nyda and Oliver Prenn Foundation

WHAT IS FUNDED Arts; education; health. The Trustees prefer to make donations to charities whose work they have come across through their own research

WHAT IS NOT FUNDED Local projects outside London unlikely to be considered

WHO CAN BENEFIT Registered charities benefiting children and adults; actors and entertainment professionals; musicians; students; textile workers and designers; writers and poets; and the sick. There is no restriction on the disease or medical condition suffered by the beneficiaries

WHERE FUNDING CAN BE GIVEN London, UK

TYPE OF GRANT Various

RANGE OF GRANTS £250–£100,000

SAMPLE GRANTS £100,000 to Royal National Theatre; £12,000 to the Speech Language and Hearing Centre; £10,000 to Rambert Dance Company; £4,000 to Parnham Trust; £3,000 to KIDS; £2,500 to Hearing Dogs for the Deaf; £2,000 to Age Concern; £2,000 to Amadeus Scholarship Fund; £2,000 to MIND; £2,000 to Notting Hill Housing Trust

FINANCES *Year* 1997 *Income* £326,078 *Grants* £151,487

TRUSTEES O S Prenn, Mrs N M McDonald Prenn, A D S Prenn, Miss N C N Prenn, S Lee, Mrs C P Cavanagh

HOW TO APPLY Unsolicited applications are not acknowledged

WHO TO APPLY TO T Cripps, The Nyda and Oliver Prenn Foundation, Moore Stephens, Chartered Accountants, 1 Snow Hill, London EC1A 2EN

CC NO 274726   **ESTABLISHED** 1977

■ The Douglas P Prestwich Charitable Trust

WHAT IS FUNDED Help to the elderly especially through hospices and help for the disabled especially through mechanical and other aids

WHO CAN BENEFIT Hospices and other organisations benefiting elderly and disabled people

WHERE FUNDING CAN BE GIVEN Kent, Sussex, Essex and London

RANGE OF GRANTS Grants of £5,000 or more

SAMPLE GRANTS £50,000 to St Wilfrid's Hospice, Chichester for Day Centre Appeal; £25,000 to Hospice in the Weald for 16 bed hospice

FINANCES *Year* 1995–96 *Income* £25,307 *Grants* £40,000

TRUSTEES D P Prestwich, D J Duthie, D D C Monro

WHO TO APPLY TO D D C Monro, The Douglas P Prestwich Charitable Trust, 8 Great James Street, London WC1N 3DA *Fax* 0171-323 1134

CC NO 1017597   **ESTABLISHED** 1993

■ The William Price Charitable Trust

WHAT IS FUNDED Schools, for educational benefits not normally provided by the local education authority and individuals for help with fees, travel, outfits, clothing, books, etc. Also promoting education in the doctrines of the Church of England

WHO CAN BENEFIT Individuals and schools benefiting children, young people and Church of England

WHERE FUNDING CAN BE GIVEN The area of benefit consists of Fareham town parishes (not Fareham Borough)

TYPE OF GRANT One-off

SAMPLE GRANTS £8,600 to Fareham Welfare Trust for poor relief in Fareham; £8,320 to Oak Meadow Primary School for computers, books and toys, etc; £7,925 to Henry Cort School for playground and food tech area; £6,800 to Wykeham House School for nursery/cloakroom/bursary; £6,133 to Cams Hill School for re-surfacing tennis court and for bibles; £5,820 to Neville Lovett School for ground improvements and for bibles; £5,290 to Fareham College School for brailling equipment and for a wheelchair desk; £5,016 to Harrison Primary School for computers, books and toys, etc; £4,867 to Ranvilles Junior School for computers, grounds and sports; £4,850 to Uplands Primary School for PE equipment and stage lighting

FINANCES *Year* 1997–98 *Income* £129,556 *Grants* £108,254

TRUSTEES William Price Trust Company

HOW TO APPLY Whenever possible through the establishment concerned. Application forms can be sent on request. Closing dates for larger grants (above £200) 1 March and 1 September. Smaller grants can be considered at any time

WHO TO APPLY TO Cmdr J A Bagg, Clerk, The William Price Charitable Trust, 59 Kiln Road, Fareham, Hampshire PO16 7UH *Tel* 01329 280636

CC NO 307319   **ESTABLISHED** 1989

■ The Lucy Price Relief in Need Charity

WHAT IS FUNDED Student grants; other education and training grants not subject to statutory funding; support for children, youth clubs and groups

WHO CAN BENEFIT Individuals and organisations benefiting children, young adults and students

WHERE FUNDING CAN BE GIVEN The Parish of Bagington, Warwickshire

FINANCES *Year* 1997 *Income* £44,964 *Grants* £34,985

TRUSTEES A J Brown, Cllr J Coggins, Cllr M F Dash, Cllr D Eastham, Mrs J E Fawcett, G R Yates

504

Think carefully about every application. Is it justified?

HOW TO APPLY To the address under Who To Apply To in writing. Initial telephone calls are welcome. Application forms are available. There are no guidelines or deadlines for applications. No sae is required

WHO TO APPLY TO G Meredith, Clerk, The Lucy Price Relief in Need Charity, 7 St Martins Road, Coventry CV3 6ET *Tel* 01203 413181

CC NO 516967 **ESTABLISHED** 1985

■ Sir John Priestman Charity Trust

WHAT IS FUNDED The Trust includes a clothing fund to provide clothing for poor children resident in Sunderland who attend churches and Sunday School; and a general fund to provide for the relief of the poor, elderly and infirm. The establishment of hospitals and convalescent homes; the advancement of education of candidates for Holy Orders who after ordination will work in Durham for not less than six years. For the benefit of the Church of England

WHO CAN BENEFIT Local organisations benefiting children and older people, clergy, people of the Church of England and those disadvantaged by poverty. There is no restriction on the disease or medical condition suffered by the beneficiaries

WHERE FUNDING CAN BE GIVEN County Borough of Sunderland and Historic Counties of Durham and York

TYPE OF GRANT Usually lump sum payment

SAMPLE GRANTS £10,000 to St John Ambulance Co Durham; £5,000 to Durham Association of Boys Clubs; £5,000 to Herrington (1st) Scout Group; £5,000 to St Clare's Hospice, Jarrow; £5,000 to St Cuthbert's Hospice, Durham; £5,000 to St Teresa's Community Hartlepool; £5,000 to Ascension Church, Middlesbrough; £4,992 to Outward Bound Trust; £4,900 to Durham Diocesan Board of Finance; £4,100 to Governors of Durham School

FINANCES *Year* 1997 *Income* £288,584 *Grants* £264,960

TRUSTEES J R Heslop, J R Kayll, R W Farr, T R P S Norton, P W Taylor

NOTES Grants for clothing £6,500; for the aged and infirm £3,800; establishment and maintenance of hospitals for the poor of Durham £2,000; charitable organisations £151,050; maintenance of churches and church buildings £56,430; relief and maintenance of clergy £23,930; and other £21,250

HOW TO APPLY Applications should include clear details of the need the project is designed to meet plus estimates, where appropriate, and details of amounts subscribed to date. The Trustees meet quarterly, generally January, April, July and October

WHO TO APPLY TO Richard Wilfred Farr, Sir John Priestman Charity Trust, Messrs McKenzie Bell, Solicitors, 19 John Street, Sunderland SR1 1JG

CC NO 209397 **ESTABLISHED** 1931

■ S H and E C Priestman Trust

WHAT IS FUNDED Children, elderly people, disabled people, overseas and home missions

WHAT IS NOT FUNDED No grants to individuals, national societies (except for work in North Humberside area) or professional 'appeals' (where agents and appeal staff are employed or paid)

WHO CAN BENEFIT Organisations benefiting children, elderly people, disabled people and missionaries

WHERE FUNDING CAN BE GIVEN North Humberside (East Riding of Yorkshire and Kingston upon Hull)

TYPE OF GRANT For specific needs rather than regular income support

RANGE OF GRANTS £50–£1,000

SAMPLE GRANTS £1,000 to Michael White Centre for Diabetes and Endocrinology; £750 to Hull and East Yorkshire Institute for the Deaf; £750 to Horder Centre for Arthritis; £750 to National Listening Library; £750 to St Leonard's Hospice

FINANCES *Year* 1997 *Income* £14,931 *Grants* £11,200

TRUSTEES P A Robins, Mrs J A Collier

HOW TO APPLY To the Trustees at any time by post. Grants are normally made in March and September

WHO TO APPLY TO Mrs J A Collier, S H and E C Priestman Trust, 40 Braids Walk, Kirkella, Hull HU10 7PD

CC NO 224581 **ESTABLISHED** 1960

■ The Primrose Trust

WHAT IS FUNDED General charitable purposes. The Trustees make their own decisions regarding donations

WHO CAN BENEFIT Registered charities. There are no restrictions on the age; professional and economic group; family situation; religion and culture; and social circumstances of; or disease or medical condition suffered by, the beneficiaries

WHERE FUNDING CAN BE GIVEN UK

TYPE OF GRANT At Trustees' discretion

RANGE OF GRANTS £1,000–£15,000

SAMPLE GRANTS £15,000 to United Bristol Hospitals; £15,000 to Dorothy House Foundation; £10,000 to The Woodlands Trust; £10,000 to Victim Support; £7,000 to Gloucestershire Wildlife Centre; £5,000 to NSPCC; £5,000 to Tenovus; £5,000 to Tregenys; £5,000 to Army Benevolent Fund; £5,000 to St John's

FINANCES *Year* 1997 *Income* £164,023 *Grants* £220,000

TRUSTEES M G Clark, G E G Daniels, Janet Clark

HOW TO APPLY **This Trust states that it does not respond to unsolicited applications**

WHO TO APPLY TO G E G Daniels, The Primrose Trust, Westgate House, Wananby Street, Cardiff CF1 2UD

CC NO 800049 **ESTABLISHED** 1986

■ The Norah and Leslie Prince Charitable Trust

WHAT IS FUNDED General charitable purposes

WHAT IS NOT FUNDED No grants to individuals. No new applications will be considered as funds are fully committed

WHO CAN BENEFIT Headquarters organisations. There are no restrictions on the age; professional and economic group; family situation; religion and culture; and social circumstances of; or disease or medical condition suffered by, the beneficiaries

WHERE FUNDING CAN BE GIVEN UK

TYPE OF GRANT Recurrent

RANGE OF GRANTS £10–£4,025

SAMPLE GRANTS £4,025 to Liberal Jewish Synagogue; £1,375 to St Michael's Church; £500 to GSMD Foundation; £300 to Brantwood Trust; £250 to Great Ormond Street Children's Hospital Fund

FINANCES *Year* 1997 *Income* £13,368 *Grants* £9,346

TRUSTEES M E G Prince, Mrs L N Lewisohn

NOTES Funds are fully committed to the support of charities which are of special interest to the Trustees

Does the trust you have chosen match your needs? Haphazard applications waste postage and time

505

HOW TO APPLY **This Trust states that it does not respond to unsolicited applications**
WHO TO APPLY TO M E G Prince, The Norah and Leslie Prince Charitable Trust, 5 Knott Park House, Wrenshill, Oxshott, Leatherhead, Surrey KT22 0HW
CC NO 257184   ESTABLISHED 1968

■ The Prince Foundation

WHAT IS FUNDED General charitable purposes. Particularly charities working in the fields of: churches, cancer research and training for community development
WHAT IS NOT FUNDED No grants to individuals
WHO CAN BENEFIT Organisations benefiting people suffering from cancers and heart disease
WHERE FUNDING CAN BE GIVEN Southern England
TYPE OF GRANT Capital, core costs and research. Funding for up to and over three years will be considered
SAMPLE GRANTS £6,000 to All Saints Church, Minstead for church repairs; £5,000 to Minstead Training Project for general costs; £2,000 to IABC Project for research; £997 to Minstead Training project for maintenance of churchyard
FINANCES *Year* 1997 *Income* £54,646
    Grants £15,147
TRUSTEES A C Prince, Mrs S Prince, D L Morgan
HOW TO APPLY Almost all of the Charity's funds are committed for the foreseeable future and the Trustees therefore do not invite applications from the general public
WHO TO APPLY TO D L Morgan, The Prince Foundation, Rothman Pantall & Co, 10 Romsey Road, Eastleigh, Hampshire SO50 4AL
CC NO 328024   ESTABLISHED 1988

■ The Priory Foundation

WHAT IS FUNDED General charitable purposes
WHO CAN BENEFIT There are no restrictions on the age; professional and economic group; family situation; religion and culture; and social circumstances of; or disease or medical condition suffered by, the beneficiaries
WHERE FUNDING CAN BE GIVEN UK
FINANCES *Year* 1995 *Income* £56,921
    Grants £105,019
TRUSTEES N W Wray, L E Wray, T W Bunyard, M Kelly
WHO TO APPLY TO Michael Kelly, The Priory Foundation, The Priory, 54 Totteridge Village, London N20 8PS
CC NO 295919   ESTABLISHED 1986

■ The Prisoners' Education Trust

WHAT IS FUNDED To advance the education of persons who are in custody in prison in England and Wales by: (a) providing a suitable education course for those who have sufficient need for such a course and are unable to pay for it, (b) providing suitable text books, art and craft materials and other materials and educational needs
WHO CAN BENEFIT People in custody wishing to further their education
WHERE FUNDING CAN BE GIVEN England and Wales
FINANCES *Year* 1995 *Income* £51,541
    Grants £23,446
TRUSTEES Lady Andrew, R Boden, D Burton, V Cocking, Ms A Grieves, Ms P Gulliver, P Holborn, D McGovern, M Melman, K Nockels

WHO TO APPLY TO Ms T Smith, Secretary, The Prisoners' Education Trust, Suite 39, Argyll House, All Saints Passge, Wandsworth, London SW18 1EP
CC NO 328098   ESTABLISHED 1989

■ The Privy Purse Charitable Trust (formerly The January 1987 Charitable Trust)

WHAT IS FUNDED General charitable purposes
WHO CAN BENEFIT There are no restrictions on the age; professional and economic group; family situation; religion and culture; and social circumstances of; or disease or medical condition suffered by, the beneficiaries
WHERE FUNDING CAN BE GIVEN UK
FINANCES *Year* 1996–97 *Income* £330,279
    Grants £251,674
TRUSTEES Sir Michael Peat, CVO, G N Kennedy, CVO, J C Parsons, LVO
NOTES **The Trust, which makes donations to a wide variety of national charities, does not respond to appeals**
WHO TO APPLY TO J C Parsons, Trustee, The Privy Purse Charitable Trust, Buckingham Palace, London SW1A 1AA
CC NO 296079   ESTABLISHED 1987

■ Pro-Bio Foundation

WHAT IS FUNDED The advancement of the study, composition and performance of contemporary music, in particular chamber music for viola and other instruments; the encouragement and advancement of the study of philosophy; the advancement of Jewish causes and progressive Jewish religious institutions; other general charitable purposes
WHO CAN BENEFIT To benefit musicians, students and Jewish people
WHERE FUNDING CAN BE GIVEN UK
TRUSTEES J Goumal, L Hepner
WHO TO APPLY TO Dr Leo Hepner, Chairman, Pro-Bio Foundation, c/o C Hepner and Association, Entrance B, Tavistock House North, Tavistock Square, London WC1H 9HX
CC NO 1065640   ESTABLISHED 1997

■ The Albert Edward Proctor Charitable Trust

WHAT IS FUNDED Relief of pain and suffering; the young and elderly; and ecclesiastical organisations
WHO CAN BENEFIT Registered charities benefiting children, young adults and the elderly. Support is also given to at risk groups, those disadvantaged by poverty and socially isolated people. Support may be given to the homeless, immigrants and refugees. There is no restriction on the disease or medical condition suffered by the beneficiaries
WHERE FUNDING CAN BE GIVEN Blackpool area only
SAMPLE GRANTS £2,500 to NSPCC, Acorn Centre, Blackpool
FINANCES *Year* 1996 *Income* £18,860
    Grants £2,500
TRUSTEES The Royal Bank of Scotland plc
WHO TO APPLY TO Royal Bank of Scotland plc, Trustees, The Albert Edward Proctor Charitable Trust, Preston Trustee Office, 2nd Floor, Guildhall House, Guildhall Street, Preston PR1 3NU
CC NO 295913   ESTABLISHED 1984

■ The Proven Family Trust

WHAT IS FUNDED Charities working in the fields of: holiday and respite accommodation; volunteer bureaux; religious and historic buildings; health; and community facilities and services. Other charitable purposes will be considered

WHAT IS NOT FUNDED No grants to individuals

WHO CAN BENEFIT Organisations benefiting children and older people; those in care, fostered and adopted. Support will be given to at risk groups, disabled people, those disadvantaged by poverty, homeless people, and victims of abuse and domestic violence

WHERE FUNDING CAN BE GIVEN Cumbria, Halton, Knowsley, Liverpool, St Helens, Sefton, Warrington, Wigan and Wirral

TYPE OF GRANT One-off

FINANCES *Year* 1998 *Income* £37,180
Grants £32,318

TRUSTEES G R Quigley, Ms D R Proven, M C Taxman, C J Worthington

NOTES The Trustees meet quarterly

HOW TO APPLY In writing at any time

WHO TO APPLY TO Dorothy Proven, Trustee, The Proven Family Trust, 35 The Mount, Papcastle, Cockermouth, Cumbria CA13 0JZ

CC NO 1050877   **ESTABLISHED** 1995

■ Province of Cambridgeshire Masonic Benevolent Association

WHAT IS FUNDED General masonic charitable purposes

WHAT IS NOT FUNDED No grants to individuals

WHO CAN BENEFIT There are no restrictions on the age; professional and economic group; family situation; religion and culture; and social circumstances of; or disease or medical condition suffered by, the beneficiaries

WHERE FUNDING CAN BE GIVEN UK with preference for Cambridgeshire

RANGE OF GRANTS £50–£56,209

SAMPLE GRANTS £56,209 to Royal Masonic Benevolent Institution; £5,770 to New Masonic Samaritan Fund; £2,430 to Multiple Sclerosis Society; £500 to Provincial Charity for Care and Relief; £175 to MAGPAS; £175 to Camsight; £125 to Cancer Research Campaign; £75 to Cornwallis Court; £50 to Trinity Hospice

FINANCES *Year* 1996 *Income* £67,245
Grants £65,509

WHO TO APPLY TO A T Pearce Higgins, Province of Cambridgeshire Masonic Benevolent Association, 147 Huntingon Road, Cambridge, Cambridgeshire CB3 0DH

CC NO 1056195   **ESTABLISHED** 1996

■ The Provincial Grand Charity

WHAT IS FUNDED To provide assistance to masons and their dependants and other charitable purposes in the provincial area. Particularly charities working in the fields of: respite accommodation; religious buildings; religious umbrella bodies and health

WHO CAN BENEFIT Masons, masonic organisations and non-masonic organisations benefiting children, young adults and older people. There is no restriction on the disease or medical condition suffered by the beneficiaries

WHERE FUNDING CAN BE GIVEN The North and East Ridings of Yorkshire

TYPE OF GRANT One-off, capital and funding for one year or less

RANGE OF GRANTS £250–£5,000, typical grant £500–£1,000

FINANCES *Year* 1996–97 *Income* £99,382
Grants £61,635

TRUSTEES J M Raylor, J M Broderick, D E Davinson, K Boaz

NOTES All applications must be sponsored by a masonic lodge in the Province

HOW TO APPLY To the address under Who To Apply To in writing

WHO TO APPLY TO The Provincial Grand Charity, Crown Buildings, Duncombe Place, York YO1 2DX
Tel 01904 624365

CC NO 517923   **ESTABLISHED** 1986

■ Provincial Grand Charity of Northamptonshire and Huntingdonshire

WHAT IS FUNDED Masonic charities, individuals in need, disabled people, homeless people, community groups, family welfare organisations

WHO CAN BENEFIT Individuals, local and regional organisations benefiting: at risk groups; disabled people; those disadvantaged by poverty; and socially isolated people. Those of different family situations will also be considered

WHERE FUNDING CAN BE GIVEN Northamptonshire and Huntingdonshire

FINANCES *Year* 1996 *Income* £36,414
Grants £24,024

NOTES In 1997, £10,000 were awarded to petitioners, £8,800 was awarded to other Masonic donations, £4,500 was awarded for non-masonic donations

HOW TO APPLY To the address under Who To Apply To in writing

WHO TO APPLY TO J R Lowe, Secretary, Provincial Grand Charity of Northamptonshire and Huntingdonshire, 206 Ryeland Road, Old Duston, Northampton NN5 6XF

CC NO 1028243   **ESTABLISHED** 1993

■ The Provincial Grand Master for Yorkshire West Riding Charity Fund

WHAT IS FUNDED To provide benefit to masons and their dependants; masonic charities; other general charitable purposes

WHO CAN BENEFIT Individuals and organisations benefiting masons and their dependants

WHERE FUNDING CAN BE GIVEN West Yorkshire

FINANCES *Year* 1995 *Income* £19,324
Grants £34,740

TRUSTEES G C Barrett, J T Broadley, B Dale, R Howarth, G O Roberts, T G Turnbull, D J Welsh, C J Wilkins, G Wilkinson

HOW TO APPLY To the address under Who To Apply To in writing

WHO TO APPLY TO R M Wellock, Provincial Grand Secretary, The Provincial Grand Master for Yorkshire West Riding Charity Fund, Masonic Hall, Spring Bank Place, Bradford BD8 7BX
Tel 01274 481242

CC NO 518824   **ESTABLISHED** 1987

■ The John Pryor Charitable Trust

WHAT IS FUNDED At present the Trustees are concentrating on a number of charities personally known to them. These include medical research and homeless charities. No new applications can therefore be entertained

WHAT IS NOT FUNDED No grants to individuals. No religious institutions

WHO CAN BENEFIT Medical research and homeless charities. There are no restrictions on the disease or medical condition suffered by the beneficiaries

WHERE FUNDING CAN BE GIVEN UK and overseas

TYPE OF GRANT Recurrent and one-off

SAMPLE GRANTS £10,000 to Help the Hospices; £5,000 to Whale and Dolphin Conservation Society; £1,000 to Research into Ageing; £1,000 to Institute of Orthopaedics; £1,000 to National Osteoporosis Society; £1,000 to Marie Curie Cancer Care; £1,000 to Imperial Cancer Research Fund; £1,000 to Multiple Sclerosis Research Trust; £1,000 to The Multiple Sclerosis Society; £1,000 to Liverpool School of Tropical Medicine

FINANCES *Year* 1995 *Income* £144,988 *Grants* £74,500

TRUSTEES Mrs J H Pryor, M F Cook, A W Cook, Mrs J Dixon

HOW TO APPLY To Mrs J H Pryor. No initial telephone calls are welcome. There are no application forms, guidelines or deadlines. No sae is required from applicants

WHO TO APPLY TO Mrs J H Pryor, The John Pryor Charitable Trust, The Old Cricketers, Passfield, Nr Liphook, Hampshire GU30 7RU

CC NO 275605   **ESTABLISHED** 1977

■ The Ronald & Kathleen Pryor Charity

WHAT IS FUNDED Sick, disabled, youth institutions, cancer research. Particularly charities working in the fields of: music; acute healthcare; hospices and hospitals; conservation; zoos and parks; care in the community; crime prevention schemes; and holidays and outings

WHAT IS NOT FUNDED No grants to individuals

WHO CAN BENEFIT Registered charities only. Organisations benefiting: children and older people; victims of crime and beneficiaries suffering from: arthritis and rheumatism; cancers; cerebral palsy and sight loss

WHERE FUNDING CAN BE GIVEN Sheffield and surrounding area

TYPE OF GRANT One-off funding for up to three years will be considered

RANGE OF GRANTS £250–£5,000

SAMPLE GRANTS £1,250 to The Prince's Youth Business Trust to assist unfortunate young people; £1,000 to the Samaritans of Sheffield to help distressed of all ages; £1,000 to Sheffield Family Service Unit for child and family centre; £1,000 to South Yorkshire Police 'Lifestyle 97' a youth project; £1,000 to Weston Park Hospital for cancer research; £1,000 to Sheffield Children's Hospital for research into special diseases in children; £1,000 to EEF Sheffield Centenary Scholarship (Engineering Employers' Federation) for engineering education; £500 to Victim support Sheffield to help victims of crime; £500 to Rotherham Hospital for community care; £500 to Sheffield and District Association for the Disabled for social activities

FINANCES *Year* 1997 *Income* £33,000 *Grants* £37,000

TRUSTEES P W Lee, CBE, Miss M Upton, J D Grayson

NOTES Trustees meet in January and July each year

HOW TO APPLY By letter to Miss M Upton. Sae not required

WHO TO APPLY TO Miss M Upton, The Ronald & Kathleen Pryor Charity, Edward Pryor & Son Ltd, Egerton Street, Sheffield S1 4JX *Tel* 0114-276 6044 *Fax* 0114-276 6890 *E-mail* enquiries@Pryormarking.com

CC NO 276868   **ESTABLISHED** 1979

■ Public School Lodges Council Benevolent Fund

This trust did not respond to CAF's request to amend its entry and, by 30 June 1998, CAF's researchers did not find financial records for later than 1995 on its file at the Charity Commission. Trusts are legally required to submit annual accounts to the Charity Commission under section 42 of the Charities Act 1993

WHAT IS FUNDED The education and advancement in the life of the children of distressed or deceased freemasons who have been members of one of the public schools. To relieve all poor and distressed freemasons of the public schools and their wives, widows, children or dependents

WHO CAN BENEFIT Children, young adults and older people, widows and those disadvantaged by poverty

WHERE FUNDING CAN BE GIVEN UK

WHO TO APPLY TO F J Blowfield, Treasurer, Public School Lodges Council Benevolent Fund, Beech Hanger, Bell Lane, Little Chalfont, Buckinghamshire HP6 6PQ

CC NO 227058   **ESTABLISHED** 1932

■ The Puebla Charitable Trust Limited

WHAT IS FUNDED The Puebla Charitable Trust was established to make grants for charitable purposes. Priority is given to organisations which seek to help the poorest sections of the population of both Britain and overseas. Priority is also given to organisations involved in community development work. A wide range of organisations are supported and the Trustees try to adopt a flexible approach, making grants to projects in both urban and rural areas. It is the normal policy of the Trustees only to make grants to recognised charities

WHAT IS NOT FUNDED The Trust does not normally give money for capital projects, for religious institutions, for research or for institutions for the disabled. Neither is it usual to sponsor individuals or provide scholarships

WHO CAN BENEFIT Organisations benefiting those disadvantaged by poverty living in both urban and rural areas

WHERE FUNDING CAN BE GIVEN UK and overseas

FINANCES *Year* 1997 *Income* £114,669 *Grants* £85,000

TRUSTEES J Phipps, M A Strutt

HOW TO APPLY Applications are considered periodically but may be submitted at any time. Applications should be addressed to the address under Who To Apply To, only successful applications will be acknowledged

WHO TO APPLY TO The Puebla Charitable Trust Limited, Ensors, Chartered Accountants, Cardinal House, 46 St Nicholas Street, Ipswich, Suffolk IP1 1TT

CC NO 290055   **ESTABLISHED** 1984

■ The Pukaar Foundation

WHAT IS FUNDED The Foundation funds charitable purposes, mainly in inner city areas across Yorkshire. Our primary areas of concern are infrastructure development, poverty, education, social exclusion, poor health and homelessness and enterprise opportunities for young people

WHAT IS NOT FUNDED No grants to individuals

WHO CAN BENEFIT Organisations and groups carrying out charitable work that addresses the Foundation's areas of concern. These include: young adults; children; teachers; those disadvantaged by poverty; homeless people; socially isolated people; those living in inner city areas; and those suffering from poor health. There is no restriction on the disease or medical condition suffered by the beneficiaries

WHERE FUNDING CAN BE GIVEN Yorkshire, with an emphasis on West Yorkshire

TYPE OF GRANT One-off, buildings, capital, core costs, endowments, feasibility studies, project, research, recurring costs, running costs, salaries and start-up costs. Funding is available for up to one year

RANGE OF GRANTS £250–£1,000

SAMPLE GRANTS £1,000 to Bradford Community School for tuition fees; £500 to Bradford Scanner Appeal to purchase a body scanner for the hospital; £300 to an individual to travel to Pakistan for teaching experience in deprived areas; £150 to Asian Women's Resource Association for purchase of educational toys; £150 to Scotchman Middle School for purchase of books

TRUSTEES Dr Mohammed Ali, Miss Adeeba Malik, Mussadik Hussain, Tim Ratcliffe, Nisar Raja, Nazir Hussain

NOTES The Pukaar Foundation is an independent grant-giving charitable trust, set up by Quest for Economic Development, QED in 1990. It is the only known trust in the UK that seeks and distributes funds primarily from the wealthy Asian Business Sector. The Foundation is at present working with Bass in the Community to assist their grant-making programme in West Yorkshire

HOW TO APPLY Applications in writing. Applications are considered when Trustees meet, usually five times a year

WHO TO APPLY TO Dr Mohammed Ali/Zulfiquar Ahmed, The Pukaar Foundation, c/o QED, West Bowling Centre, Clipstone Street, Bradford BD5 8EA *Tel* 01274 735551 *E-mail* z.ahmed@qued-limited.demon.co.uk

CC NO 1056702   **ESTABLISHED** 1996

■ The Purey-Cust Trust

WHAT IS FUNDED To promote the advancement of health and healing in the area of Greater York

WHAT IS NOT FUNDED York area only

WHO CAN BENEFIT Individuals and registered charities benefiting children, young adults and older people. There are no restrictions on the disease or medical condition suffered by the beneficiaries

WHERE FUNDING CAN BE GIVEN York area

TYPE OF GRANT Capital, one-off, running costs, start-up costs and funding for one year or less will be considered

RANGE OF GRANTS £100–£5,000

SAMPLE GRANTS £5,000 to York District Hospital for scanner; £3,000 to Fulford School for lift for disabled children; £3,000 to North Yorkshire Health Authority for electronic patients file; £3,000 to Abbeyfield Nursing Home for disabled people equipment; £2,500 to St Johns Ambulance for ambulance; £2,065 to Our Celebration for training to staff to assist mentally ill persons; £1,500 to Glen Family Resource for special wheelchair for individual; £450 York Rape Crisis; £350 to Breast Cancer Care for set-up assistance; £300 to Accessable Arts for medical health education

FINANCES *Year* 1995 *Income* £26,000 *Grants* £25,000

TRUSTEES Dr A Hunter, Mrs A Pugh, Mrs P Sessions, N A McMahon-Turner, C Tetley

HOW TO APPLY Write in first instance for a grant application form to the address under Who To Apply To. Initial telephone calls welcome

WHO TO APPLY TO N A McMahon-Turner, The Purey-Cust Trust, Stockton Hermitage, Malton Road, York YO3 9TL *Tel* 01904 400177 *Fax* 01904 400070

CC NO 516030   **ESTABLISHED** 1984

■ The Puri Foundation

WHAT IS FUNDED Welfare, community centres, the furtherance of Hinduism. The Trust aims to relieve those in conditions of need, hardship or distress; to advance education; to provide facilities for recreation; to relieve and rehabilitate young unemployed people in the Nottinghamshire area

WHO CAN BENEFIT Organisations benefiting: children; young adults; students; Hindus; at risk groups; those disadvantaged by poverty; and socially isolated people

WHERE FUNDING CAN BE GIVEN Nottinghamshire, India (particularly the towns of Mullan Pur near Chandigarh and Ambala)

FINANCES *Year* 1997 *Income* £66,685 *Grants* £13,122

TRUSTEES J E Philpotts, A Puri, N R Puri, U Puri

HOW TO APPLY To the address under Who To Apply To in writing

WHO TO APPLY TO N R Puri, Trustee, The Puri Foundation, Environment House, 6 Union Road, Nottingham NG3 1FH

CC NO 327854   **ESTABLISHED** 1988

■ The Pye Christian Trust

WHAT IS FUNDED To support Christian evangelistic social and relief work in UK and abroad including: support of local (Lancaster area) churches; Christian outreach and education; missions and evangelists; diocesan boards; Free Church umbrella bodies; and local hospices

WHAT IS NOT FUNDED Campaigning; advocacy; arts; educational training; travel

WHO CAN BENEFIT Registered charities benefiting: people of all ages; Baptists; Christians; evangelists; methodists; those disadvantaged by poverty; and victims of abuse. Those suffering from: kidney disease; sight loss and terminal illness

WHERE FUNDING CAN BE GIVEN UK, mainly North Lancashire. Overseas also considered

TYPE OF GRANT Mainly recurring. Some capital, project and one-off

RANGE OF GRANTS £25–£1,000. Typical grants are £100

Does the trust you have chosen match your needs? Haphazard applications waste postage and time

509

SAMPLE GRANTS £4,700 to The Methodist Church for local church expenses Home and Overseas mission, University Chaplaincy, Methodist Homes; £1,750 to The Baptist Church for local and mission work; £1,500 to North West Evangelical Trust for work (Christian) in schools; £1,200 to Tear Fund for overseas relief work; £1,000 to North West Kidney Research; £1,000 to Dayspring Trust for overseas missions; £1,000 to Operation Mobilisation for overseas missions; £800 to Active Service Trust providing services to missionaries; £750 to Water Aid for provision of clean water to villages in third world

FINANCES *Year* 1997 *Income* £26,661 *Grants* £33,215

TRUSTEES J A Pye, Mrs M Pye

NOTES Income likely to be considerably less for foreseeable future. Therefore grants will be restricted. Preference will be given to many of the causes already supported

HOW TO APPLY By letter with information. No initial telephone calls welcome. There are no application forms, guidelines or deadlines. Sae would be appreciated but not required

WHO TO APPLY TO J A Pye, The Pye Christian Trust, W & J Pye Ltd, Fleet Square, Lancaster, Lancashire LA1 1HA *Tel* 01524 597200

CC NO 501654   **ESTABLISHED** 1972

■ The Pye Foundation

WHAT IS FUNDED Youth; the elderly; welfare; housing; Christian education and outreach; hospices; libraries and museums; day centres; and other charitable purposes

WHAT IS NOT FUNDED No grants to individuals and students or overseas organisations

WHO CAN BENEFIT Organisations benefiting: older people; ex-service and service people; retired people; Christians; those disadvantaged by poverty; homeless people; and those living in rural areas. Those suffering from: arthritis and rheumatism; blood disorders and haemophilia; cancers; cerebral palsy; heart disease and multiple sclerosis

WHERE FUNDING CAN BE GIVEN Cambridgeshire

TYPE OF GRANT Buildings, capital, one-off, project, running costs, recurring costs and start-up costs. Funding is available for up to three years

RANGE OF GRANTS £50–£5,000, typical grant £1,500

FINANCES *Year* 1997 *Income* £74,000 *Grants* £76,257

TRUSTEES P M Threlfall (Chairman), D M J Ball, A B Dasgupta, J A House, F Keys, R R Pascoe

HOW TO APPLY To the address under Who To Apply To in writing. There are no application forms or guidelines

WHO TO APPLY TO M R Hensby, Secretary, The Pye Foundation, PO Box 24, St Andrews Road, Cambridge CB4 1DP *Tel* 01223 877317

CC NO 267851   **ESTABLISHED** 1974

■ Pyke Charity Trust

WHAT IS FUNDED The Foundation operates in four general areas to which it allocates funds: education and training, disabled welfare, social and community needs, medical welfare but not research. The Trustees give grants only to recognised charities. Overall the policy of the Trustees is to support underfunded voluntary organisations to enable the disabled and those who are disadvantaged through social or economic circumstances to make a contribution to the community. (a) Education and training. Projects for disabled people which offer employment training, life skills and independent living. Projects which enhance educational opportunities for children up to secondary school level. (No adult or tertiary education.) Projects to enhance the wider education, understanding and promotion of life skills for young people. In very few, very exceptional cases help may be given to stabilise the education and home life of children. Only the most exceptional cases of need are investigated. We are only able to help where there is a genuine charitable need and where the child's physical/mental well-being is in danger. Full disclosure of all the circumstances leading to the application is required and a home visit will be necessary. (b) Disabled welfare. Projects for all types of disabled welfare are considered, preference is given to physical disabilities. (c) Social and community needs. Projects which assist the disabled and disadvantaged to play a part in the community. Community centres for all ages – family centres, youth clubs, elderly people's clubs, child care provision and drop in clubs. Any project that will enhance the quality of life for disabled people. Promotion of health, home nursing schemes, day care centres for the disabled and elderly. The Trustees support projects which encourage respect for the local community and environment, crime prevention. (d) Medical welfare. The Trust does not fund medical research. It may support medical welfare schemes where equipment can enhance the lives of individual disabled people or families

WHAT IS NOT FUNDED The following lie outside our current guidelines: medical research, postgraduate studies, individual sponsorship, drug or alcohol related charities, HQs of national charities, holiday groups, national and local government responsibilities, organisations which are not recognised charities, activities which collect funds for subsequent redistribution, expeditions or overseas travel, animal charities, promotion of religion, fabric appeals for places of worship, loans and business finance, salaries/wages and general running costs

WHO CAN BENEFIT Help only given to registered charities benefiting people of all ages, and disabled people. There is no restriction on the disease or medical condition suffered by the beneficiaries

WHERE FUNDING CAN BE GIVEN UK only

TYPE OF GRANT One-off only. Usually for a specific project. Core funding, running costs and salaries are not considered. No grants are awarded to groups who request specific amounts

RANGE OF GRANTS Usually £500–£5,000

FINANCES *Year* 1997 *Income* £109,887 *Grants* £156,509

TRUSTEES R J van Zwanenberg, N J van Zwanenberg, J Macpherson, C Marris, T Harrie-Clark

HOW TO APPLY These should be made in good time for the Trustees' meetings in February, June and October. Guidelines for applicants can be sent on request. Applications must include: (a) Full up to date accounts (to the year ending not more than 15 months before the application). (b) Details of what the charity is and does. (c) What the appeal is for and what it will achieve/for who. (d) Details of amounts required and raised so far. (e) Who else they have applied to. (f) How much they expect to receive from other sources. (g) Any other information that will help the Trustees. (h) Details of any application that is likely to fund all or most of the requirements in the application, eg Lottery, etc

WHO TO APPLY TO The Trust Secretary, Pyke Charity Trust, Barlocco Farm, Auchencairn, Castle Douglas, Dumfries, Scotland DG7 1RQ
CC NO 296418   ESTABLISHED 1960

■ QAS Charitable Trust

WHAT IS FUNDED To promote any one or more of the following: (a) The relief of poverty; (b) The relief of sickness; (c) The advancement of education; (d) The promotion of music, art, literature and science; (e) Such other purposes as are charitable according to the law for the time being in force in England and Wales. Trustees' income in the foreseeable future will not exceed existing commitments

WHAT IS NOT FUNDED No grants to individuals

WHO CAN BENEFIT Organisations benefiting those disadvantaged by poverty and sick people. There is no restriction on the disease or medical condition suffered by the beneficiaries. Scientists and those involved in the arts may benefit

WHERE FUNDING CAN BE GIVEN England and Wales

FINANCES *Year* 1997 *Income* £20,000

TRUSTEES A P Ohrenstein, W Sharron

HOW TO APPLY No surplus funds in foreseeable future

WHO TO APPLY TO A P Ohrenstein, QAS Charitable Trust, Messrs Casson Beckman, Hobson House, 155 Gower Street, London WC1E 6BJ

CC NO 277186   ESTABLISHED 1978

■ The Quaker Peace Studies Trust

WHAT IS FUNDED The advancement of learning and knowledge by the study of the nature of peace and the methods by which it can be developed, in particular, by the establishment of a chair of peace studies and by financing research into, and the teaching of, peace studies at the University of Bradford and other institutions of higher education in the UK

WHO CAN BENEFIT Organisations and institutions benefiting students of peace studies

WHERE FUNDING CAN BE GIVEN UK

FINANCES *Year* 1996 *Income* £75,209
          Grants £34,801

TRUSTEES O Claxton, J Geale, J A Horsley, K A Lee, R A McKinley, H Miall, Ms E Pinthus, C A B Smith, A Wilson

WHO TO APPLY TO Owen Claxton, Joint Secretary, The Quaker Peace Studies Trust, Horsley House, 6 Ashgrove, Great Horton Road, Bradford, West Yorkshire BD7 1BN

CC NO 529095   ESTABLISHED 1972

■ Quazi Family Charitable Foundation

WHAT IS FUNDED The advancement of education, advancement of religion and the relief of poverty

WHO CAN BENEFIT To benefit children, young adults and those disadvantaged by poverty. There is no restriction on the religion and culture of the beneficiaries

WHERE FUNDING CAN BE GIVEN UK and overseas

TRUSTEES Dr M A Khawaja, L J Khawaja, M N Khawaja, A W Quazi, Mrs J Quazi

WHO TO APPLY TO A W Quazi, Quazi Family Charitable Foundation, 21 Deerings Drive, Pinner, Middlesex HA5 2NZ

CC NO 1067880   ESTABLISHED 1997

■ Queendeans Association

WHAT IS FUNDED General charitable purposes, including physically disabled, mentally disabled, blind, deaf and local children's charities

WHAT IS NOT FUNDED Anyone outside the area Where Funding Can Be Given should not apply, and such applications will not receive a response

WHO CAN BENEFIT Solely at the discretion of the Committee. Particularly organisations benefiting: children; disabled people; blind and deaf people

WHERE FUNDING CAN BE GIVEN Blackpool and Fylde areas only

TYPE OF GRANT The Trustees do not make cash grants but donate equipment and goods in lieu

RANGE OF GRANTS £214–£10,000

SAMPLE GRANTS £10,000 to Scanner Appeal for medical equipment; £4,135 to South Shore Hospital for a hoist and related equipment; £3,415 to Abbeyfield Home for decor; £2,000 to Guide Dogs for the Blind for two dogs; £1,865 to Schools Safety Campaign for posters, printing, etc

FINANCES *Year* 1997 *Income* £24,513 *Grants* £31,659

TRUSTEES The Association Committee

HOW TO APPLY At any time to the address under Who To Apply To in writing. Telephone contacts are neither accepted or permitted

WHO TO APPLY TO The Secretary, Queendeans Association, Queens Hotel, 469 South Promenade, Blackpool FY4 1AY

CC NO 236277 **ESTABLISHED** 1964

■ The Benevolent Fund of The Queen's Own Buffs, The Royal Kent Regiment

WHAT IS FUNDED (a) For the benefit of any person or persons who owing to poverty are in need of pecuniary assistance and who have served in The Queen's Own Buffs, The Royal Kent Regiment, The Buffs (Royal East Kent Regiment), The Queen's Own Royal West Kent Regiment, or who are the dependents, widows or orphans of persons who have served in those regiments. (b) Making grants to such charitable institutions as the Trustees see fit

WHAT IS NOT FUNDED Expeditions, bursaries, scholarships

WHO CAN BENEFIT Former members and dependents of the above named regiments

WHERE FUNDING CAN BE GIVEN UK and overseas

TYPE OF GRANT One-off

RANGE OF GRANTS £50–£250; typical £150

FINANCES *Year* 1995–96 *Income* £16,775 *Grants* £16,522

TRUSTEES Colonel C G Champion, Colonel K Dodson, OBE, Colonel G D Mullins, DL, Major W D Marshall, Major H C L Tennent

PUBLICATIONS Association newsletter

NOTES Direct applications cannot be accepted

HOW TO APPLY Applicants are advised to make contact with SSAFA Forces Help (listed in local telephone directory) who will assist in completion of application form

WHO TO APPLY TO Major W D Marshall (Retd), The Benevolent Fund of The Queen's Own Buffs, The Royal Kent Regiment, RHQ PWRR, Howe Barracks, Canterbury, Kent CT1 1JY *Tel* 01227 818052 *Fax* 01227 818057

CC NO 201474 **ESTABLISHED** 1972

■ Quercus Trust

WHAT IS FUNDED Mainly the arts. Charities working in the fields of: the advancement of the Jewish religion; Jewish umbrella bodies and cancers

WHAT IS NOT FUNDED Funds are fully committed for the next five years. No grants to individuals

WHO CAN BENEFIT Established organisations and registered charities benefiting: older people; actors and entertainment professionals; musicians; Jews and beneficiaries suffering from cancers

WHERE FUNDING CAN BE GIVEN UK

TYPE OF GRANT One-off and recurring grants

SAMPLE GRANTS £45,000 to Royal National Theatre; £39,500 to The Jerusalem Foundation; £25,000 to Institute for Public Policy Research; £20,000 to Open College of the Arts; £20,000 to The Rambert Dance Company; £6,000 to Institute for Jewish Policy Research; £5,000 to Yitzhak Rabin Fellowship Foundation; £5,000 to The Royal Court Theatre; £2,500 to Royal College of Art; £2,500 to University of Manchester

FINANCES *Year* 1996–97 *Income* £59,067 *Grants* £194,668

TRUSTEES Alexander Bernstein, Thomas H R Crawley, Alan C Langridge, and others

WHO TO APPLY TO T H R Crawley, Quercus Trust, Radcliffes Crossman Block, 5 Great College Street, Westminster, London SW1P 3SJ *Tel* 0171-222 7040 *Fax* 0171-222 6208

CC NO 1039205 **ESTABLISHED** 1993

■ The Second Quothquan Charitable Trust

WHAT IS FUNDED Usually to support Christian projects known to the Trustees

WHAT IS NOT FUNDED Activities which are primarily the responsibility of central or local government or some other responsible body are not considered. Animal welfare is not funded, nor are: church buildings – restoration, improvements, renovations, or new churches; environmental – conservation and protection of wildlife and landscape; expeditions; hospitals and health centre; loans and business finance; medical research projects; national charities; overseas appeals; promotion of any religion other than Christianity; schools, universities and colleges

WHO CAN BENEFIT Not normally to individuals; usually to projects known to the Trustees. Organisations benefiting Christians

WHERE FUNDING CAN BE GIVEN Birmingham and surrounding area – West Midlands

TYPE OF GRANT Not normally for recurrent operational expenses, or for educational purposes

RANGE OF GRANTS £50–£5,000

FINANCES *Year* 1996 *Income* £151,598 *Grants* £63,833

TRUSTEES A L Gilmour, Mrs J A Gilmour

PUBLICATIONS Information sheet available

NOTES No appeals acknowledged or replies made unless grants made

HOW TO APPLY At any time To the address under Who To Apply To

WHO TO APPLY TO The Trustees, The Second Quothquan Charitable Trust, 277 Monmouth Drive, Sutton Coldfield, West Midlands B73 6JU *Tel* 0121-354 7133 *Fax* 0121-603 7135 *E-mail* Quothquan@aol.com

CC NO 273229 **ESTABLISHED** 1977

The RAC Foundation for Motoring and the Environment Ltd

WHAT IS FUNDED Research projects undertaken so far include examining the concept of 'car dependence', the impact of traffic on the North York Moors National Park. Research programme undertaken to examine the impacts of the Okehampton Bypass

WHO CAN BENEFIT Organisations benefiting academics and research workers

WHERE FUNDING CAN BE GIVEN UK

TYPE OF GRANT Research

FINANCES *Year* 1995 *Income* £47,187

TRUSTEES J D Rose, N A Johnson, Sir D G T Williams, Sir Christopher Foster, Prof T M Ridley

NOTES Charitable expenditure concerns consultancy fees for the research projects. No grants were given in 1995

HOW TO APPLY To the address under Who To Apply To in writing

WHO TO APPLY TO H Kemlo, Secretary, The RAC Foundation for Motoring and the Environment Ltd, M1 Cross, Brent Terrace, London NW2 1LT

CC NO 1002705 **ESTABLISHED** 1991

RAMC Charitable Fund 1992

WHAT IS FUNDED Charities working in the fields of: building services; information technology and computers; legal services; and personnel and human resource services. Hospice at home, respite care; hospices and nursing homes will be considered

WHAT IS NOT FUNDED At the discretion of the Trustees

WHO CAN BENEFIT Past and present members of the RAMC, their dependants, orphans, widows and widowers of many different social circumstances will be considered

WHERE FUNDING CAN BE GIVEN UK and overseas

TYPE OF GRANT Buildings, capital, one-off, recurring costs and running costs will be considered. Funding may be given for more than three years

FINANCES *Year* 1997 *Income* £174,720 *Grants* £114,842

HOW TO APPLY Through SSAFA (Soldiers, Sailors, Airmen's Families Association), TRBL (The Royal British Legion), WPA (War Pensions Agency), BCExSL (British Commonwealth Ex-Services League)

WHO TO APPLY TO Lt Col (Retd) T A Reeves, RAMC Charitable Fund 1992, RHQ RAMC, Keogh Barracks, Ash Vale, Aldershot GU12 5RQ

CC NO 1045301 **ESTABLISHED** 1995

R S Charitable Trust

WHAT IS FUNDED General charitable purposes

WHO CAN BENEFIT There are no restrictions on the age; professional and economic group; family situation; religion and culture; and social circumstances of; or disease or medical condition suffered by, the beneficiaries

WHERE FUNDING CAN BE GIVEN UK

WHO TO APPLY TO Max Freudenberger, Trustee, R S Charitable Trust, 138 Stamford Hill, London N16 6QT

CC NO 1053660 **ESTABLISHED** 1996

The RT Trust

WHAT IS FUNDED To back up the relief of cancer sufferers and those with mentally disabilities within the area Where Funding Can Be Given

WHAT IS NOT FUNDED Expeditions

WHO CAN BENEFIT Organisation benefiting disabled people and sufferers of cancers and cerebal palsy

WHERE FUNDING CAN BE GIVEN Oswestry in Shropshire

TYPE OF GRANT One-off, core costs and project. Funding for up to one year will be considered

RANGE OF GRANTS £200–£3,000; typical £300

FINANCES *Year* 1995 *Income* £64,929 *Grants* £38,316

TRUSTEES Mrs E W Moss, G M Humphreys, A J Moss, Mrs N R Bayley

HOW TO APPLY At present, the Trust is over-committed. A sae is required from applicants

WHO TO APPLY TO Mrs E W Moss, The RT Trust, The Postings, Pant Glas, Oswestry, Shropshire SY10 7HS

CC NO 328121 **ESTABLISHED** 1989

Rachel Charitable Trust

WHAT IS FUNDED General charitable purposes at Trustees' discretion

WHO CAN BENEFIT There are no restrictions on the age; professional and economic group; family situation; religion and culture; and social circumstances of; or disease or medical condition suffered by, the beneficiaries

WHERE FUNDING CAN BE GIVEN UK and overseas

TYPE OF GRANT At the discretion of the Trustees

TRUSTEES L Noe, S Noe

WHO TO APPLY TO D Sassoon, Rachel Charitable Trust One Bridge Lane, London NW11 0EA

CC NO 276441 **ESTABLISHED** 1961

The Mr and Mrs Philip Rackham Charitable Trust

WHAT IS FUNDED Trustees' discretion with particular interest in support and relief of asthma sufferers, asthma research and The Samaritans

WHAT IS NOT FUNDED No grants to individuals

WHO CAN BENEFIT Registered charities only, particularly those benefiting asthma sufferers

WHERE FUNDING CAN BE GIVEN Norfolk and Suffolk

TYPE OF GRANT At the discretion of the Trustees

TRUSTEES N G Sparrow, C W L Barratt, C E J Gaze, A E S Rush

WHO TO APPLY TO N G Sparrow, The Mr and Mrs Philip Rackham Charitable Trust, Paston House, 13 Princes Street, Norwich, Norfolk NR3 1BD

CC NO 1013844 **ESTABLISHED** 1992

Richard Radcliffe Trust

WHAT IS FUNDED General charitable purposes; hospice care; help for the severely disabled and those who are deaf and blind; and technical training for young people

WHO CAN BENEFIT Individuals and organisations benefiting: young people; disabled people; the deaf and blind; and those requiring hospice care

Does the trust you have chosen match your needs? Haphazard applications waste postage and time

513

WHERE FUNDING CAN BE GIVEN UK, with a preference for Southern England

TYPE OF GRANT One-off, recurring and projects. Funding is available for more than three years

RANGE OF GRANTS Anticipated £1,000–£5,000 a year

TRUSTEES A M Bell, Miss I M R Radcliffe, Miss P Radcliffe

HOW TO APPLY Written applications only

WHO TO APPLY TO A Bell, Richard Radcliffe Trust, Griffith Smith, Solicitors, 47 Old Steyne, Brighton, East Sussex BN1 1NW *Tel* 01273 324014

CC NO 1068930   **ESTABLISHED** 1998

■ Dr Radcliffe's Trust

WHAT IS FUNDED The Trustees sponsor, in particular, a music scheme and a scheme for the encouragement of the crafts.

WHAT IS NOT FUNDED No grants to individuals or social welfare. Applications for construction and conversion of buildings for medical research or for individual students undergoing courses of education not considered

WHO CAN BENEFIT Organisations and schemes benefiting musicians and those involved in the crafts

WHERE FUNDING CAN BE GIVEN UK and overseas

TYPE OF GRANT The Trustees do not make grants for longer than a three year period except in very exceptional circumstances

RANGE OF GRANTS £15–£15,000

SAMPLE GRANTS £15,000 to Trinity College of Music; £12,500 to St Edwards School, Oxford; £10,819 to Allegri String Quartet; £8,000 to Council for the Care of Churches; £7,979 to an individual at University of Oxford for a Philosophy Fellowship; £7,400 to The National Trust for Scotland; £7,347 to an individual for a Musicology Fellowship; £7,000 to Birmingham Conservatoire; £6,500 to Scottish Maritime Museum; £6,300 to St Mary's Cathedral Workshop

FINANCES *Year* 1997 *Income* £319,493 *Grants* £205,859

TRUSTEES The Rt Hon Lord Cottesloe, DL, JP, The Rt Hon Lord Balfour of Burleigh, FIEE, The Rt Hon Lord Quinton, FBA, C J Butcher, I F Guest

PUBLICATIONS *Dr John Radcliffe and his Trust* by Ivor Guest

HOW TO APPLY There is no application form, but to be considered by the Trustees at their meetings June and December, applications in musical field should be submitted by 1 February and 1 August; applications for other fields by 1 April and 1 October respectively to give time for investigation, where appropriate

WHO TO APPLY TO John Burden, Dr Radcliffe's Trust, c/o Messrs Tweedie & Prideaux, 5 Lincoln's Inn Fields, London WC2A 3BT

CC NO 209212   **ESTABLISHED** 1714

■ Radio Forth Help a Child Appeal

WHAT IS FUNDED Grants are given to local children's charities and needy children in East Central Scotland. Support will be given to children requiring healthcare

WHO CAN BENEFIT Children only. There is no restriction on the family situation of the beneficiaries. Support is especially given to those suffering from paediatric diseases

WHERE FUNDING CAN BE GIVEN East Central Scotland

FINANCES *Year* 1998 *Grants* £72,000

TRUSTEES A Wilson, T Gallagher, T Steele, J Crawford, M Scott, Lady Dunpark, M Gulliver

HOW TO APPLY Applications should be made in writing to the Secretary, Tracy Gallagher. Initial telephone calls are welcome and application forms and guidelines are available. Sae is not required

WHO TO APPLY TO Tracy Gallagher, Secretary, Radio Forth Help a Child Appeal, Forth House, Forth Street, Edinburgh EH1 3LF *Tel* 0131-556 9255 *Fax* 0131-558 3277 *E-mail* forth@srh.co.uk

SC NO SCO 05626   **ESTABLISHED** 1980

■ Radio Tay-Caring for Kids (Radio Tay Listeners Charity)

WHAT IS FUNDED Grants are given to a range of organisations which are concerned with children's education, disabilities and recreation

WHAT IS NOT FUNDED No grants for staff wages

WHO CAN BENEFIT Individuals and organisations benefiting children and young people, especially those from one parent families, and those who are at risk, disabled, disadvantaged by poverty, socially isolated and victims of abuse

WHERE FUNDING CAN BE GIVEN Tayside and North East Fife

SAMPLE GRANTS £25,000 to Ninewells Hospital towards new children's hospital; £5,000 to Armistead Child Development; £5,000 to The Brae (Riding for the Disabled); £5,000 to Fife Attention Deficit Disorder; £5,000 to Perth College Nursery for equipment

TRUSTEES A Ballingall, K Codognato, A Coupar (Chairman), M Laird, M Naulty, A Wilke

HOW TO APPLY Applications should be made in writing to the address under Who To Apply To. Grants are decided in February and March

WHO TO APPLY TO Lorraine Stevenson, Co-ordinator, Radio Tay-Caring for Kids, PO Box 123, Dundee DD1 9UF *Tel* 01382 200800

SC NO SCO 08440

■ The Mark Radiven Charitable Trust

WHAT IS FUNDED General charitable purposes

WHO CAN BENEFIT There are no restrictions on the age; professional and economic group; family situation; religion and culture; and social circumstances of; or disease or medical condition suffered by, the beneficiaries

WHERE FUNDING CAN BE GIVEN UK

FINANCES *Year* 1997 *Income* £11,353

TRUSTEES M Radiven, S Friedland

WHO TO APPLY TO The Mark Radiven Charitable Trust, Charles Frieze & Co, Chartered Accountants, 12 Charlotte Street, Manchester M1 4HP

CC NO 267000   **ESTABLISHED** 1974

■ Radley Charitable Trust

WHAT IS FUNDED To help small organisations that are unlikely to have wide appeal or support and, through them, individuals dependent on them. Particularly charities working in the fields of: infrastructure, support and development; religion; community arts and recreation; campaigning for health issues; landscapes, nature reserves, woodlands and ecology, organic food production, conservation and campaigning; professional specialist training; the purchase of books; research into medicine and social science; community issues; the international rights of the individual; penal reform; advice centres and various community services

WHAT IS NOT FUNDED No grants for electives, for doctorates, for travel bursaries or for expeditions

WHO CAN BENEFIT Organisations (Quaker or other) devoted to peace work, conflict resolution, racial equality, community work, education, social service, conservation, and individuals recommended by these bodies. Also organisations benefiting: medical professionals, unemployed people, disabled people, those disadvantaged by poverty, homeless people, immigrants, refugees, victims of famine, man-made or natural disasters and war, and those suffering from various diseases and medical conditions will be considered

WHERE FUNDING CAN BE GIVEN UK, with preference for Cambridgeshire, and overseas

TYPE OF GRANT Normally one-off grants. Buildings, capital, core costs, project, research, running costs, recurring costs and start-up costs. Funding of one or less will be considered

RANGE OF GRANTS £50–£1,300, typically £150–£500

SAMPLE GRANTS £1,000 to Cheltenham and Gloucester College of Higher Education for fees and maintenance for mature student (rehabilitated drug addict) in last year of three year course; £500 to Hull University Union for payment of final examination fees for Kenyan mature student who had no other sources of finance; £500 to Disability Aid Fund as part payment of expensive computerised machine for sufferers; £500 to Medical Foundation for aid to victims of torture; £500 to Manor House Agricultural Fund for aid for education in farming in Kenya

FINANCES *Year* 1996–97 *Income* £22,568 *Grants* £17,580

TRUSTEES C F Doubleday, I R Menzies, I O Palmer, P F Radley, J J Wheatley

NOTES Meetings of the Trustees to consider applications are held at two-monthly intervals

HOW TO APPLY Letters with details, enclosing sae, to the Correspondent. The name of a referee who is in a position to support the application should be included. Priority will normally be given to individual applications

WHO TO APPLY TO Patrick Radley, Radley Charitable Trust, 12 Jesus Lane, Cambridge CB5 8BA

CC NO 208313   **ESTABLISHED** 1951

■ The Rainford Trust

WHAT IS FUNDED To consider applications from organisations that aim to enhance the quality of community life. To help initiate and promote special projects by charitable organisations which seek to provide new kinds of employment. To assist programmes whose objects are the provision of medical care, including holistic medicine, the advancement of education and the arts, and the improvement of the environment. Applications from religious bodies and individuals will be considered if they fall within the scope of these aims

WHAT IS NOT FUNDED Funding for the arts is restricted to St Helens only. Applications from individuals for grants for educational purposes will be considered only from applicants who are normally resident in St Helens

WHO CAN BENEFIT Individuals, charitable and voluntary organisations benefiting people of all ages. However, some restrictions on the social circumstances of, and disease and medical conditions suffered by the beneficiaries may be applied

WHERE FUNDING CAN BE GIVEN UK and overseas, with a preference for areas where Pilkington plc have works and offices, especially St Helens,

Doncaster, Kings Norton (Birmingham) and St Asaph (Denbighshire)

TYPE OF GRANT Buildings, capital, core costs, project, research, salaries and start-up costs will be considered. Only exceptionally will grants be given in consecutive years, up to a maximum of three years

SAMPLE GRANTS £25,000 to St Helens and Knowsley Hospice towards the building fund; £12,955 to Citadel Arts Gallery, St Helens for revenue funding; £10,000 to Rainford Art Gallery, St Helens for improving the infrastructure of relocated gallery; £3,000 to St Helens Choral Society as two grants (£1,000 and £2,000) for revenue funding; £2,000 to Campaigners for the salary of a youth worker; £2,000 to Age Concern, St Helens towards a music project for the elderly; £2,000 to Allanson Street Primary School, St Helens for the redesign of the playground to make more environmentallly friendly; £2,000 to St Helens Music Centre Association for a summer school workshop

FINANCES *Year* 1997 *Income* £157,912 *Grants* £130,920

TRUSTEES R E Pilkington, Lady Pilkington, R G Pilkington, Mrs I Ratiu, I S Ratiu, A L Hopkins, Mrs J Graham

HOW TO APPLY At any time. Applications should be accompanied by latest accounts and cost data on projects for which funding is sought. Only successful applications will be acknowledged

WHO TO APPLY TO George Gaskell, Secretary, The Rainford Trust, c/o Pilkington plc, Prescot Road, St Helens WA10 3TT

CC NO 266157   **ESTABLISHED** 1973

■ The Peggy Ramsay Foundation

WHAT IS FUNDED For writers and writing causes, relief of poverty for writers families. The assistance of writers for the theatre and the creation of new playwriting

WHAT IS NOT FUNDED Theatrical production and writing in fields other than theatre

WHO CAN BENEFIT Individuals and organisations benefiting playwrights. Also playwrights family members disadvantaged by poverty

WHERE FUNDING CAN BE GIVEN UK

RANGE OF GRANTS £500–£50,000

SAMPLE GRANTS £50,000 to Stellar Quine Theatre Company for Peggy Ramsay, Peay Award for Janet Paisley's play 'Refuge'

FINANCES *Year* 1996 *Income* £255,000 *Grants* £217,000

TRUSTEES G Laurence Harbottle, S P H Callow, J Welch, M V Codron, D Hare, J Tydeman

HOW TO APPLY Applications by short letter

WHO TO APPLY TO G Lawrence Harbottle, The Peggy Ramsay Foundation, Harbottle & Lewis Solicitors, Hanover House, 14 Hanover Square, London W1R 0BE *Tel* 0171-667 5000

CC NO 1015427   **ESTABLISHED** 1992

■ The Ramsden Hall Trust

WHAT IS FUNDED General charitable purposes for the benefit of the inhabitants of Barrow-in-Furness

WHO CAN BENEFIT There are no restrictions on the age; professional and economic group; family situation; religion and culture; and social circumstances of; or disease or medical condition suffered by, the beneficiaries

WHERE FUNDING CAN BE GIVEN Barrow-in-Furness

WHO TO APPLY TO T J H Bodys, Borough Solicitor, The Ramsden Hall Trust, Town Hall, Duke Street, Barrow-in-Furness, Cumbria LA14 2LD
CC NO 1064867   ESTABLISHED 1997

■ The Helen Randag Charitable Foundation

This trust did not respond to CAF's request to amend its entry and, by 30 June 1998, CAF's researchers did not find financial records for later than 1995 on its file at the Charity Commission. Trusts are legally required to submit annual accounts to the Charity Commission under section 42 of the Charities Act 1993

WHAT IS FUNDED General charitable purposes
WHO CAN BENEFIT There are no restrictions on the age; professional and economic group; family situation; religion and culture; and social circumstances of; or disease or medical condition suffered by, the beneficiaries
WHERE FUNDING CAN BE GIVEN UK and overseas
TRUSTEES Ms H L A Randag, J D Rothwell
WHO TO APPLY TO J D Rothwell, Trustee, The Helen Randag Charitable Foundation, Messrs Enersheds, Senator House, 85 Queen Victoria Street, London EC4V 4JL
CC NO 1048227   ESTABLISHED 1995

■ The Joseph and Lena Randall Charitable Trust

WHAT IS FUNDED General charitable purposes, with particular interest in relieving suffering and hardship in the Jewish community. It also supports many non-denominational projects
WHAT IS NOT FUNDED No grants to individuals
WHO CAN BENEFIT Registered charities (mainly headquarters organisations) benefiting at risk groups, those disadvantaged by poverty and socially isolated people. Jewish people are favoured, but support is given to non-Jewish beneficiaries. Otherwise, there are no restrictions on the age; professional and economic group; family situation; religion and culture; and social circumstances of; or disease or medical condition suffered by, the beneficiaries
WHERE FUNDING CAN BE GIVEN UK and overseas
TYPE OF GRANT Recurrent and capital grants
RANGE OF GRANTS Not less than £500 in 1997
FINANCES Year 1997 Income £159,721
Grants £156,289
TRUSTEES D A Randall, Mrs B Y Randall
NOTES All income is allocated or promised so it is regretted we cannot extend our list of charities at present
HOW TO APPLY No further applications can be considered except in special circumstances
WHO TO APPLY TO R E Downhill, Solicitor, The Joseph and Lena Randall Charitable Trust, Berwin Leighton, Adelaide House, London Bridge, London EC4R 9HA
CC NO 255035   ESTABLISHED 1967

■ The Lord Rank 1958 Charity

WHAT IS FUNDED Housing, the elderly, disabled and poor
WHO CAN BENEFIT Organisations benefiting older people, retired people, disabled people and those disadvantaged by poverty. At the discretion of the Trustees
WHERE FUNDING CAN BE GIVEN UK
TYPE OF GRANT At the discretion of the Trustees

FINANCES Year 1997 Income £79,387
Grants £106,628
TRUSTEES R F H Cowen, The Hon Mrs S M Cowen, R H Cowen, J A Wheeler
NOTES **This Trust states that it does not respond to unsolicited applications**
WHO TO APPLY TO J A Wheeler, The Lord Rank 1958 Charity, 11a Station Road West, Oxted, Surrey RH8 9EE *Tel* 01883 717919
CC NO 252676   ESTABLISHED 1958

■ Joseph Rank Benevolent Fund

WHAT IS FUNDED (a) Payments of allowances for the benefit of poor senior citizens of good character who due to age, ill-health, accident or infirmity are wholly or in part unable to maintain themselves by their own exertions. (b) Grants to local charities only, limited to £3,000 per annum (total) made during December each year
WHAT IS NOT FUNDED Restricted to persons residing in Kingston upon Hull and two miles outside boundary
WHO CAN BENEFIT Poor and aged persons. Minimum age limits 60 years for women, 65 years for men. These people must reside within the City of Kingston Upon Hull and within two miles outside the city boundary. There is no restriction on the disease or medical condition suffered by the beneficiaries
WHERE FUNDING CAN BE GIVEN Residents of Kingston upon Hull and the area two miles outside its boundary
TYPE OF GRANT Monthly payments in cash
SAMPLE GRANTS £80,912 to individuals for allowance or other periodical payments; £3,000 to local charities
FINANCES Year 1997 Income £136,172
Grants £83,912
TRUSTEES Mrs J Shepherd (Chair), T H Jackson, OBE, MA, (Hon Secretary), C R Palmer, J R Matthews, I D Wilkinson, I V Askew, P A Robins
PUBLICATIONS Annual Report to the local press
NOTES 50th Anniversary of Trust celebrated in November 1984
HOW TO APPLY To the Clerk to the Trustees
WHO TO APPLY TO Mrs M Burman, Clerk to the Trustees, Joseph Rank Benevolent Fund, The Avenue, Bishop Lane, Hull HU1 1NP
Tel 01482 225542
CC NO 225318   ESTABLISHED 1934

■ Fanny Rapaport Charitable Trust

WHAT IS FUNDED General charitable purposes
WHAT IS NOT FUNDED No grants to individuals
WHO CAN BENEFIT Registered charities only. There are no restrictions on the age; professional and economic group; family situation; religion and culture; and social circumstances of; or disease or medical condition suffered by, the beneficiaries
WHERE FUNDING CAN BE GIVEN North West England favoured

SAMPLE GRANTS £17,000 to donations to 60 charities; £10,000 to the Heathlands Village; £4,250 to the Jewish Philanthropic Association for Israel and the Middle East; £4,000 to Morris Feinmann Homes Trust; £2,000 to Christie Hospital NHS Trust; £1,900 to Manchester Jewish Federation (incorporating Jewish Social Services and Manchester Jew's Benevolent Society); £1,000 to Brookvale towards caring for people with special needs; £1,000 to Community Security Trust; £1,000 to Delamere Forest School; £1,000 to Jewish Child's Day

FINANCES *Year* 1997 *Income* £43,257
Grants £44,150

TRUSTEES J S Fidler, N Marks

HOW TO APPLY Trustees hold meetings twice a year in March/April and September/October with cheques for donations issued shortly thereafter. If applicant does not receive a cheque in April/October, application may be assumed to be unsuccessful. No applications acknowledged. Copy of applicant's annual accounts not necessary (unless it forms part of a package)

WHO TO APPLY TO J S Fidler, Fanny Rapaport Charitable Trust, Kuit Steinart Levy, 3 St Mary's Parsonage, Manchester M3 2RD

CC NO 229406　　**ESTABLISHED** 1963

■ The Ratcliff Charity for the Poor (also known as the Ratcliff Pension Charity)

WHAT IS FUNDED The welfare of elderly people, general welfare and community organisations in the area Where Funding Can Be Given. For relief of need

WHO CAN BENEFIT Individuals and organisations benefiting: older people; at risk groups; those disadvantaged by poverty; socially isolated people and those in need

WHERE FUNDING CAN BE GIVEN Tower Hamlets, especially the Stepney area

FINANCES *Year* 1997 *Income* £49,019
Grants £41,287

TRUSTEES The Coopers' Company

HOW TO APPLY To the address under Who To Apply To in writing

WHO TO APPLY TO J A Newton, Clerk, The Ratcliff Charity for the Poor, Cooper's Hall, 13 Devonshire Square, London EC2M 4TH

CC NO 234613　　**ESTABLISHED** 1967

■ The Ratcliff Foundation

WHAT IS FUNDED General charitable purposes, any balance to the Coventry Diocese Layman's Appeal Fund. To support registered charities only, rather than individuals, which operate in the Birmingham and West Midlands area, or local branches only of national organisations

WHAT IS NOT FUNDED No grants to individuals

WHO CAN BENEFIT Any organisation which is itself of charitable status for tax purposes. There are no restrictions on the age; professional and economic group; family situation; religion and culture; and social circumstances of; or disease or medical condition suffered by, the beneficiaries

WHERE FUNDING CAN BE GIVEN Birmingham and West Midlands

TYPE OF GRANT Cash

RANGE OF GRANTS £500–£25,000

SAMPLE GRANTS £25,000 to CBSO Development Trust; £5,000 to Cancer Research (Kemberton) Campaign; £5,000 to Birmingham Voluntary Service Council; £4,250 to Riding for the Disabled Association; £4,250 to Veterinary Benevolent Fund; £4,000 to St Nicholas Church, Kemerton; £4,000 to Relate; £4,000 to Beacon Centre for the Blind; £3,700 to Phoenix; £3,500 to the West Midlands Wildlife Campaign

FINANCES *Year* 1996 *Income* £222,521
Grants £198,243

TRUSTEES E H Ratcliff, D M Ratcliff, C M Ratcliff, G M Thorpe, J M G Fea, J B Dixon

HOW TO APPLY Should be in hands of Secretary by 30 November for consideration by Trustees in following January. Grants made once per year only by 31 March

WHO TO APPLY TO J B Dixon, The Ratcliff Foundation, Ernst & Young, PO Box 1, One Colmore Row, Birmingham B3 2DB

CC NO 222441　　**ESTABLISHED** 1959

■ The Eleanor Rathbone Charitable Trust (formerly Miss E F Rathbone Charitable Trust)

WHAT IS FUNDED Preference to charities of which the Trust has special interest, knowledge or association. Interest in charities benefiting women and neglected causes, social work charities, arts and education

WHAT IS NOT FUNDED No grants to individuals or causes with a sectarian interest. No support is given to any activity which relieves a statutory authority of its obligations

WHO CAN BENEFIT Organisations benefiting: children and young adults; women; actors and entertainment professionals; musicians; textile workers and designers; students; writers and poets; at risk groups; those disadvantaged by poverty; and socially isolated people

WHERE FUNDING CAN BE GIVEN UK and overseas, but mainly Merseyside

RANGE OF GRANTS £100–£12,000

SAMPLE GRANTS £12,000 to EFR Holiday Fund; £10,000 to London School of Economic and Political Science; £8,600 to LCSS; £5,676 to Rathbone CI; £5,000 to RUKBA; £5,000 to Bryson House; £5,000 to NMGM; £4,000 to Womankind Worldwide; £4,000 to St Johns Playgroup; £3,750 to Sheila Kay Fund

FINANCES *Year* 1997 *Income* £256,977
Grants £224,004

TRUSTEES Dr B L Rathbone, W Rathbone Jnr, Miss J A Rathbone, P W Rathbone

HOW TO APPLY By letter

WHO TO APPLY TO Lindsay Keenan, The Eleanor Rathbone Charitable Trust, 3 Sidney Avenue, Wallasey, Merseyside L45 9JL

CC NO 233241　　**ESTABLISHED** 1947

■ The Elizabeth Rathbone Charity

WHAT IS FUNDED General charitable purposes, especially social work charities. Preference to charities of which the Trust has special interest, knowledge or association

WHAT IS NOT FUNDED No grants to individuals seeking support for second degrees

WHO CAN BENEFIT To benefit at risk groups, those disadvantaged by poverty and socially isolated people

WHERE FUNDING CAN BE GIVEN UK, mainly Merseyside

TYPE OF GRANT Mainly donations

Does the trust you have chosen match your needs? Haphazard applications waste postage and time

517

RANGE OF GRANTS £85–£5,000
SAMPLE GRANTS £5,000 to National Museums and Galleries; £3,000 to Liverpool Family Service Unit; £3,000 to Glaxo Neurological; £2,500 to Rathbone CI; £2,000 to Research into Ageing; £2,000 to St Helen's and Knowsley Macmillan Nurse Appeal; £2,000 to Garston Adventure Playground; £2,000 to Macmillan Cancer Information Centre; £1,000 to Petrus Community Ltd; £1,000 to Blue Coat School
FINANCES *Year* 1997 *Income* £91,607 *Grants* £57,021
TRUSTEES S A Cotton, Ms S K Rathbone, Mrs V P Rathbone, R S Rathbone
HOW TO APPLY By letter
WHO TO APPLY TO The Elizabeth Rathbone Charity, Rathbone Bros & Co, Port of Liverpool Building, 4th Floor, Pier Head, Liverpool L3 1NW
CC NO 233240   ESTABLISHED 1921

■ Marit and Hans Rausing Charitable Foundation

WHAT IS FUNDED Medical research, handicapped children, science and economics. This includes architecture and social science. Also the conservation of fauna, flora and nature reserves are considered for funding
WHAT IS NOT FUNDED No grants to individuals
WHO CAN BENEFIT Organisations benefiting: children; medical professionals; researchers; scientists; and disabled people
WHERE FUNDING CAN BE GIVEN Europe and UK, especially Brighton and Hove, Sussex and Kent
TYPE OF GRANT Buildings, endowments, one-off, project and research
SAMPLE GRANTS £67,000 to Institute of Economic Affairs; £25,000 to Michael von Clemm Charitable Trust; £2,500 to LSE; £1,340 to Sense; £1,500 to Brainwave
FINANCES *Year* 1997 *Income* £200,000 *Grants* £100,000
HOW TO APPLY By letter to the Trustees
WHO TO APPLY TO Miss J Major, Marit and Hans Rausing Charitable Foundation, 132 Sloane Street, London SW1X 9AR *Tel* 0171-468 2561
CC NO 1059714   ESTABLISHED 1996

■ The Ruben and Elizabeth Rausing Trust

WHAT IS FUNDED Preference for charities concerned with women's issues, self reliance and substainability, arts and media organisations. Charities working in the fields of: human rights; campaigning on health and social issues; health professional bodies; the advancement of religion; health care; conservation; ecology; environmental issues; and transport and alternative transport will be considered
WHAT IS NOT FUNDED No grants to individuals
WHO CAN BENEFIT Organisations benefiting women will be supported. People of many religions and cultures may benefit
WHERE FUNDING CAN BE GIVEN UK, with preference for London, and overseas
TYPE OF GRANT One-off, buildings, core costs, project, research, recurring costs, salaries, and start-up costs. Funding may be given for up to one year
RANGE OF GRANTS £250–£500,000, average grant £20,000

SAMPLE GRANTS £500,000 to Human Rights Watch (USA); £200,000 to International Women's Health Coalition; £200,000 to Global Fund for Women; £100,000 to Marie Stopes International; £100,000 to Women, Law and Development; £80,000 to Womankind; £75,000 to Center for Women's Global Leadership; £50,000 to Amnesty International; £50,000 to International Gay and Lesbian Human Rights; £35,000 to Equality Now
FINANCES *Year* 1997 *Income* £2,845,995 *Grants* £2,314,239
TRUSTEES L Koerner, S Rausing, J Mailman, T Kaufman
NOTES Trustees meet in June to consider existing donations and in September to consider new applications and proposals
HOW TO APPLY By invitation from individual Trustees only
WHO TO APPLY TO Ms J Major, Administrator, The Ruben and Elizabeth Rausing Trust, 132 Sloane Street, London SW1X 9AR *Tel* 0171-259 9466
CC NO 1046769   ESTABLISHED 1995

■ The Ravensdale Trust

WHAT IS FUNDED The Trustees' policy is to make donations to such charitable institutions as they believe the Settlor, the late Miss M Pilkington would have wished with particular reference to charities dealing with education, health, the arts, religion, social welfare and the environment
WHAT IS NOT FUNDED No grants to individuals
WHO CAN BENEFIT Registered charities benefiting: people of all ages; Christians, Church of England and Unitarians; at risk groups; disabled people; those disadvantaged by poverty; homeless people, victims of abuse, crime and domestic violence. There are few restrictions on the disease or medical condition suffered by the beneficiaries
WHERE FUNDING CAN BE GIVEN UK, with preference for Merseyside and the North West
TYPE OF GRANT Grants are made at the discretion of the Trustees, though generally one-off
RANGE OF GRANTS £100–£3,000
SAMPLE GRANTS £21,000 to Scarisbrick Girl Guides for building project; £3,000 to St Helens URC; £1,500 to YMCA Lakeside; £1,000 to Girl Guides Heritage Centre; £1,000 to Great Ormond Street Hospital; £1,000 to Liverpool Philharmonic; £1,000 to Save the Children Fund, St Helens; £1,000 to Youth Clubs UK; £1,000 to YMCA St Helens; £1,000 to Purcell School
FINANCES *Year* 1996–97 *Income* £151,020 *Grants* £100,900
TRUSTEES Dr L H A Pilkington, Mrs J M Wailing, Mrs J L Fagan
HOW TO APPLY By letter. No application form. No acknowledgement of applications. Donations are made in June and October of each year
WHO TO APPLY TO Mrs J L Fagan, The Ravensdale Trust, Brabner Holden Banks Wilson, 1 Dale Street, Liverpool L2 2ET *Tel* 0151-236 5821 *Fax* 0151-227 3185
CC NO 265165   ESTABLISHED 1973

■ The Rawdon-Smith Trust

WHAT IS FUNDED The preservation of the area called the 'Bed of Coniston Water' for the benefit of the public; other charitable purposes including education, welfare, animal welfare, preservation of churches
WHAT IS NOT FUNDED Applications for grants for individuals will not be supported

WHO CAN BENEFIT Local organisations benefiting: children; young adults; students; at risk groups; those disadvantaged by poverty and socially isolated people

WHERE FUNDING CAN BE GIVEN Coniston and the areas surrounding Coniston Water

FINANCES *Year* 1996 *Income* £94,394 *Grants* £28,797

HOW TO APPLY To the address under Who To Apply To in writing. The Trustees meet to consider applications in February, May and November

WHO TO APPLY TO I Stancliffe, Secretary, The Rawdon-Smith Trust, Campbell House, Coniston, Cumbria LA21 8EF

CC NO 500355   **ESTABLISHED** 1964

■ The Robert Rawstone Trust Fund

WHAT IS FUNDED Churches, clubs, community centres and youth groups in the area Where Funding Can Be Given

WHO CAN BENEFIT The community of Freckleton

WHERE FUNDING CAN BE GIVEN Freckleton

TYPE OF GRANT One-off grants

RANGE OF GRANTS £50–£1,600

SAMPLE GRANTS £3,150 to Rawstone Sports Centre; £1,600 to Freckleton C of E Church; £1,600 to Freckleton Methodist Church; £1,600 to Holy Family Church; £1,500 to Freckleton Village Hall

FINANCES *Year* 1995–96 *Income* £17,370 *Grants* £16,000

TRUSTEES 12 members of the Parish Council

HOW TO APPLY To the address under Who To Apply To in writing

WHO TO APPLY TO Mrs M Macdonald, Clerk, The Robert Rawstone Trust Fund, Harford, Preston New Road, Freckleton, Preston PR4 1HN *Tel* 01772 634871

CC NO 508396   **ESTABLISHED** 1979

■ The Roger Raymond Charitable Trust

WHAT IS FUNDED General charitable purposes

WHAT IS NOT FUNDED No grants to individuals

WHO CAN BENEFIT There are no restrictions on the age; professional and economic group; family situation; religion and culture; and social circumstances of; or disease or medical condition suffered by, the beneficiaries. Grants are mainly made to headquarters organisations

WHERE FUNDING CAN BE GIVEN UK

TYPE OF GRANT Various

FINANCES *Year* 1997 *Income* £207,627 *Grants* £212,071

TRUSTEES P F Raymond, R W Pullen, M G Raymond

NOTES Funds already allocated

HOW TO APPLY Unsolicited applications are not welcomed by the Trust

WHO TO APPLY TO Roger Raymond Charitable Trust, Sayers Butterworth, 18 Bentinck Street, London W1M 5RL

CC NO 262217   **ESTABLISHED** 1971

■ Roger Raymond Charitable Trust No 2

WHAT IS FUNDED General charitable purposes. Funds already allocated

WHAT IS NOT FUNDED Grants fully allocated each year in advance

WHO CAN BENEFIT Chosen by Trustees. There are no restrictions on the age; professional and economic group; family situation; religion and culture; and social circumstances of; or disease or medical condition suffered by, the beneficiaries

WHERE FUNDING CAN BE GIVEN UK

FINANCES *Year* 1997 *Income* £32,113 *Grants* £64,781

TRUSTEES R W Pullen, P F Raymond, M G Raymond

WHO TO APPLY TO R W Pullen, Roger Raymond Charitable Trust No 2, Sayers Butterworth, 18 Bentinck Street, London W1M 5RL

CC NO 267029   **ESTABLISHED** 1974

■ The Rayne Trust *(formerly the Rayne Charitable Trust)*

WHAT IS FUNDED Relief of distress, welfare of the aged and young and the advancement of learning and religion

WHAT IS NOT FUNDED No grants to individuals

WHO CAN BENEFIT Registered charities benefiting children, the elderly and young people. Support is given to at risk groups, those disadvantaged by poverty and socially isolated people. Support may also be given to students, teachers, governesses and clergy

WHERE FUNDING CAN BE GIVEN UK

TYPE OF GRANT Capital expenditure and recurrent expenses

RANGE OF GRANTS Under £1,000–£35,500

SAMPLE GRANTS £35,500 to Home for Aged Jews; £29,500 to West London Synagogue; £20,000 to Kids Scrap Bank; £10,000 to Community Security Trust; £7,200 to Childeric Primary School; £7,000 to Holocaust Educational Trust; £6,040 to Jewish Care; £5,962 to Open University Psychological Society; £5,000 to Oxford Centre for Hebrew Studies; £5,000 to Manor House Trust

FINANCES *Year* 1997 *Income* £186,615 *Grants* £174,197

TRUSTEES Lord Rayne (Chairman), Lady Rayne (Director), Hon R A Rayne (Director)

NOTES Grants are only made to national headquarters of multiple (registered) charities

HOW TO APPLY At any time

WHO TO APPLY TO R D Lindsay-Rea, MA, The Rayne Trust, Carlton House, 33 Robert Adam Street, London W1M 5AH

CC NO 207392   **ESTABLISHED** 1958

■ The John Rayner Charitable Trust

WHAT IS FUNDED The Charity was formed to apply its income and capital in whole or in part towards the furtherance of such charitable purposes as the Trustees' shall from time to time think fit. Currently the Trustees' policy is to distribute the income of the Trust annually. The range of charities to benefit shall be at the Trustees discretion, with a preference for small charities in the UK to receive the largest donations. The Trustees will divide the annual income between a small number of charities, sometimes committing funds over a period of years. Charities working in the fields of: accommodation and housing; arts, culture and recreation; health; and community facilities and services. Support may also be given to voluntary and community organisations, special schools, and English as a second or foreign language

WHAT IS NOT FUNDED Applications from anyone other than a registered charity. No grants to individuals

WHO CAN BENEFIT Charities, especially those supporting children, medical research, youth projects, drug addiction. The Trust will also consider charities benefiting: people of all ages; ex-service and service people; musicians; seafarers and fishermen; unemployed people; and volunteers. Support may be given to carers; disabled people; those disadvantaged by poverty; homeless and socially isolated people; those living in urban areas and the victims of abuse, crime and domestic violence. There are few restrictions on the disease or medical condition suffered by the beneficiaries

WHERE FUNDING CAN BE GIVEN UK with preference for the North West of England, Yorkshire and Humberside, Hampshire, London, Swindon and Wiltshire

TYPE OF GRANT Single donations given annually in February/March for buildings, capital, core costs, one-off, project, research and start-up costs. Funding may be given for up to three years

SAMPLE GRANTS £5,000 to Live Music Now! North West towards sponsoring concerts in special schools; £5,000 to The Samaritans for general purposes and a project for the aged; £4,000 to Inspire for work with patients with spinal injuries; £4,000 to Whizz-Kidz towards mobility for disabled children; £3,000 to Demand for design and manufacture for disability; £3,000 to ICRF for cancer research; £2,000 to Merseyside Drugs Council working with drug addiction; £2,000 to Headway for people suffering from head injuries; £2,000 to Children Nationwide for intensive care cots; £2,000 to Guildhall School of Music and Drama for small concerts and a bursary

FINANCES *Year* 1997 *Income* £39,000 *Grants* £37,000

TRUSTEES Mrs J Wilkinson and others

HOW TO APPLY To the address under Who To Apply To

WHO TO APPLY TO Mrs J Wilkinson, The John Rayner Charitable Trust, 37 Burns Road, London SW11 5GX *Tel* 0171-223 2779 *Fax* 0171-223 2779

CC NO 802363 **ESTABLISHED** 1989

······································

■ The Nathaniel Rayner Trust Fund

WHAT IS FUNDED The promotion of evangelical Christianity and also general charitable purposes, particularly the advancement of Christian religion and Christian religious buildings

WHAT IS NOT FUNDED No grants for education, scholarships or expeditions

WHO CAN BENEFIT Registered charities and Christian organisations helping children, young adults, older people, clergy, Baptists, Church of England, Christians, Evangelists and Methodists

WHERE FUNDING CAN BE GIVEN Liverpool

RANGE OF GRANTS £200–£3,000

SAMPLE GRANTS £3,375 to Allerton United Reformed Church; £3,000 to St Columbia United Reformed Church; £3,000 to Lancashire and Cheshire Baptist Association; £2,500 to Highfield United Reformed Church; £1,500 to Northern College; £1,500 to Council for World Mission; £1,125 to St Georges United Reformed Church; £1,000 to Maghill Baptist Church; £1,000 to Dovedale Road Baptist Church; £1,000 to Laird Street Baptist Church

FINANCES *Year* 1996–97 *Income* £41,166 *Grants* £32,000

TRUSTEES C G Dickie, D E G Faragher, W B Howarth, G C Lindsay, K W Paterson, Miss M Proven, J R Watson

HOW TO APPLY To the address under Who To Apply To in writing

WHO TO APPLY TO G Barrie Marsh, Secretary, The Nathaniel Rayner Trust Fund, Drury House, 19 Water Street, Liverpool L2 0RP *Tel* 0151-236 8989

CC NO 226319 **ESTABLISHED** 1965

······································

■ The Reader's Digest Trust

WHAT IS FUNDED Education and learning difficulties, arts, culture, science, medicine and conservation

WHAT IS NOT FUNDED UK registered charities only; political and sectarian bodies excluded. Funding of individuals excluded as are expeditions, purchase and maintenance of vehicles, etc

WHO CAN BENEFIT UK registered charities benefiting: children; young adults; actors and entertainment professionals; medical professionals; students; textile workers and designers; musicians; writers and poets; and people with learning disabilities. There are no restrictions on the disease or medical condition suffered by the beneficiaries

WHERE FUNDING CAN BE GIVEN UK

TYPE OF GRANT Financial donations (usually not recurring). Advertising support, product donations

FINANCES *Year* 1997 *Income* £101,000 *Grants* £75,000

TRUSTEES R G Twisk, P Brady, A R Clayton

NOTES In preparing appeals, an initial telephone call to the Trust is advisable, since funds may already have been committed to another charity with similar aims. A special application form is used and mailed on request. All applications are acknowledged. Documents accompanying applications (advisable length 1 page only) should be relevant, and not too bulky as they need to be circulated

HOW TO APPLY In brief, written details and specific projects must be outlined. Trustees meet quarterly

WHO TO APPLY TO The Charity Administrator, The Reader's Digest Trust, The Reader's Digest Association Ltd, 11 Westferry Circus, Canary Wharf, London E14 4HE *Tel* 0171-715 8000 *Fax* 0171-715 8759

CC NO 283115 **ESTABLISHED** 1981

······································

■ The Reading Dispensary Trust

WHAT IS FUNDED Charities working with the sick, convalescent, disabled, handicapped, or infirm with holidays, items, services and facilites

WHAT IS NOT FUNDED Anything where statutory funding is available

WHO CAN BENEFIT Individuals, local organisations, local branches of national organisations benefiting: children; young adults; older people; at risk groups; carers; disabled people; and those disadvantaged by poverty. There are no restrictions on the disease or medical condition suffered by the beneficiaries

WHERE FUNDING CAN BE GIVEN Reading and district (within a 7 mile radius)

TYPE OF GRANT One-off, buildings and capital. Funding for one year or less will be considered

RANGE OF GRANTS £50–£5,000; typical £200

SAMPLE GRANTS £4,000 to Berkshire Multiple Sclerosis towards new centre; £2,500 to an individual for house extension for handicapped child; £2,000 to Abbeyfield, Reading for Residential Home appeal; £2,000 to Berkshire St John for Community Care appeal; £1,000 to Breakthrough Trust for Mobile Advisory Service; £1,000 to Cancer Relief Macmillan Fund for nurses etc; £990 to Thames Valley Association for Mental Health for holidays; £900 to Hampshire St Johns Ambulance for holidays-children from Reading area; £550 to Berkshire Red Cross for holidays-children from Reading area; £500 to DEBRA Research for research re children in area

FINANCES *Year* 1997 *Income* £49,000 *Grants* £38,000

TRUSTEES G A Burrows, Dr J Cahill, H A Finch, L F Fundell, I G Hammond, I G Highley, Rev M Jackson, P N Johnson, D L Jones, M L Richards, L Silver, F E Thomas, J M Warren, D E Lawrence

PUBLICATIONS Leaflet *Can we help you?*

NOTES Applications for individuals generally accaepted via Health and Welfare workers

HOW TO APPLY To the address under Who To Apply To. Initial telephone calls are welcome. Application forms and guidelines are available. Deadlines for applications are monthly. Sae is not required

WHO TO APPLY TO W E Gilbert, Clerk, The Reading Dispensary Trust, 16 Wokingham Road, Reading RG6 1JQ *Tel* 0118-926 5698

CC NO 203943   **ESTABLISHED** 1802

■ Maurice Benington Reckitt Charitable Discretionary Trust

WHAT IS FUNDED General charitable purposes to charitable institutions only

WHAT IS NOT FUNDED The funds of the Trust are fully committed for the foreseeable future and no applications can be considered. No grants to individuals

WHO CAN BENEFIT Charitable Institutions accepted as such by the Charity Commissioners and Commissioners of Inland Revenue. There are no restrictions on the age; professional and economic group; family situation; religion and culture; and social circumstances of; or disease or medical condition suffered by, the beneficiaries

WHERE FUNDING CAN BE GIVEN UK

TYPE OF GRANT Cash grants for the general purposes of the charity

FINANCES *Year* 1997 *Income* £16,400 *Grants* £12,000

TRUSTEES Barclays Bank Trust Company Limited, 54 Lombard Street, London EC3P 3AH

NOTES Trust reference: W0419

HOW TO APPLY **No applications can be considered as the funds are fully committed**

WHO TO APPLY TO The Manager, Maurice Benington Reckitt Charitable Discretionary Trust, Barclays Bank Trust Co Ltd, Box 15, Northwich, Cheshire CW9 7UR

CC NO 262181   **ESTABLISHED** 1971

■ The Albert Reckitt Charitable Trust

WHAT IS FUNDED General charitable purposes (excluding political or sectarian) including charities connected with the Society of Friends

WHAT IS NOT FUNDED Registered charities only. Applications from individuals are ineligible

WHO CAN BENEFIT National organisations including those which benefit the Society of Friends

WHERE FUNDING CAN BE GIVEN Great Britain

TYPE OF GRANT Donations or yearly subscriptions, to registered charities

FINANCES *Year* 1998 *Income* £71,500 *Grants* £65,760

TRUSTEES Sir Michael Colman, Bt, Mrs M Reckitt, Mrs G M Atherton, Mrs S C Bradley, D F Reckitt, J Hughes-Reckitt, P C Knee, Dr A Joy

HOW TO APPLY By 31 March

WHO TO APPLY TO J Barrett, Secretary, The Albert Reckitt Charitable Trust, Southwark Towers, 32 London Bridge Street, London SE1 9SY

CC NO 209974   **ESTABLISHED** 1946

■ Eva Reckitt Trust Fund

This trust did not respond to CAF's request to amend its entry and, by 30 June 1998, CAF's researchers did not find financial records for later than 1995 on its file at the Charity Commission. Trusts are legally required to submit annual accounts to the Charity Commission under section 42 of the Charities Act 1993

WHAT IS FUNDED Overseas relief, housing trusts, discharged prisoners societies, educational, publications and general

WHAT IS NOT FUNDED No grants for people wishing to obtain second qualifications

WHO CAN BENEFIT Specific projects through headquarters and local organisations and individuals. Children, young adults; ex-offenders and those at risk of offending; homeless people; and victims of famine, war, and man-made or natural disasters

WHERE FUNDING CAN BE GIVEN North London

TYPE OF GRANT One-off and recurrent (limited to three years)

TRUSTEES A R H Birch, G Bunney, Mrs D Holliday, C Whittaker

NOTES The Trustees are not able to respond to all unsolicited applications as they receive more than their financial resources can support

HOW TO APPLY Meetings approximately every two months

WHO TO APPLY TO George Bunney, Eva Reckitt Trust Fund, 24 Mitchell Walk, Amersham, Buckinghamshire HP6 6NW

CC NO 210563   **ESTABLISHED** 1940

■ The Red Arrows Trust

WHAT IS FUNDED To Royal Air Force causes and other charitable institutions and appeals

WHO CAN BENEFIT Ex-service and service people

WHERE FUNDING CAN BE GIVEN UK

FINANCES *Year* 1996–97 *Income* £36,471 *Grants* £33,750

TRUSTEES Air Commodore H G Mackay, R Bowder, K R Harkness, FCA, Wing Commander J R Lees, Wing Commander R T Johnston, Squadron Leader H M Willams

WHO TO APPLY TO R Bowder, The Red Arrows Trust, Harvey Ingram Solicitors, 20 New Walk, Leicester LE1 6TX

CC NO 283461   **ESTABLISHED** 1961

■ The Red Rose Charitable Trust

WHAT IS FUNDED General charitable purposes

WHO CAN BENEFIT There are no restrictions on the age; professional and economic group; family situation; religion and culture; and social circumstances of; or disease or medical condition suffered by, the beneficiaries

WHERE FUNDING CAN BE GIVEN UK

RANGE OF GRANTS £250–£1,350

SAMPLE GRANTS £2,208 to Islington Council; £2,000 to Royal Hospital for Neuro-disability; £1,350 to the Harvest Trust Holidays for Children; £1,000 to Barnston Dale Centre; £1,000 to Henshaw's Society for the Blind; £1,000 to Elms Bank High School for access for the disabled; £1,000 to Royal Alfred Seafarers' Society; £1,000 to RAF Benevolent Fund; £1,000 to CCH – Extra Care; £1,000 to Dale Farm Social Development Association

FINANCES *Year* 1997 *Income* £40,375 *Grants* £32,847

TRUSTEES Miss Olwen Seddon, James N L Packer

WHO TO APPLY TO Mrs L E Allison, The Red Rose Charitable Trust, Nigel Packer and Company, 3rd Floor, Royal Liver Building, Pier Head, Liverpool, L3 1JH

CC NO 1038358   ESTABLISHED 1994

■ The Red Socks Charitable Trust

WHAT IS FUNDED Children's welfare, youth organisations, health and welfare organisations

WHO CAN BENEFIT Organisations benefiting: children and young adults; at risk groups; those disadvantaged by poverty; socially isolated people; and the sick. There is no restriction on the disease or medical condition suffered by the beneficiaries

WHERE FUNDING CAN BE GIVEN UK

RANGE OF GRANTS £500–£2,000

SAMPLE GRANTS £2,000 to Prince's Trust; £2,000 to Norfolk Boats; £1,040 to Chernobyl Children's Life Line; £1,000 to Holidays for Children with Special Needs; £734 to Britannic Company, Norfolk Army Cadet Force

FINANCES *Year* 1997 *Income* £23,961 *Grants* £7,274

TRUSTEES H M C Coghill, C H W Holloway, B J Landale, I D R MacNicol

HOW TO APPLY To the address under Who To Apply To in writing

WHO TO APPLY TO C H W Holloway, The Red Socks Charitable Trust, Eversheds, Holland Court, The Close, Norwich, Norfolk NR1 4DX

CC NO 326965   ESTABLISHED 1985

■ C A Redfern Charitable Foundation

WHAT IS FUNDED General charitable purposes

WHAT IS NOT FUNDED No grants for building works or individuals

WHO CAN BENEFIT Registered UK charities. There are no restrictions on the age; professional and economic group; family situation; religion and culture; and social circumstances of; or disease or medical condition suffered by, the beneficiaries

WHERE FUNDING CAN BE GIVEN England

TYPE OF GRANT Core costs, one-off, project and research. Funding is available for one year or less

SAMPLE GRANTS £32,000 to South Buckinghamshire Riding for the Disabled; £20,000 to Saints and Sinners Club

FINANCES *Year* 1996 *Income* £167,923 *Grants* £160,500

TRUSTEES Sir Robert Clark, C A G Redfern, D S Redfern, T P Thornton, S R Ward

NOTES Most of the available capital and income already distributed – further distribution unlikely for some years

HOW TO APPLY **This Trust states that it does not respond to unsolicited applications**

WHO TO APPLY TO C A Redfern Charitable Foundation, Pricewaterhouse Coopers, 9 Greyfriars Road, Reading RG1 1JG

CC NO 299918   ESTABLISHED 1989

■ Reed Charity

WHAT IS FUNDED Relief of poverty and distress for women in the third world

WHO CAN BENEFIT Organisations benefiting those disadvantaged by poverty, victims of famine, war and disasters, particularly women in need

WHERE FUNDING CAN BE GIVEN Third world

RANGE OF GRANTS £500–£156,220

SAMPLE GRANTS £156,220 to Ethiopiaid; £93,338 to Reed Educational Trust; £44,890 to Womankind; £21,412 to an individual for legal costs; £10,000 to Upton House School; £5,000 to Refugee Council; £4,684 to Management Forum; £2,500 to Amnesty International; £2,277 to Trustee Register; £2,000 to St Denys PCC

FINANCES *Year* 1996 *Income* £305,700 *Grants* £348,258

TRUSTEES A E Reed, J A Reed, R A Reed, A M Reed

HOW TO APPLY **This Trust states that it does not respond to unsolicited applications**

WHO TO APPLY TO The Secretary, Reed Charity, Bedford House, Madria Walk, Windsor SL4 1EU

CC NO 264728   ESTABLISHED 1972

■ R A & V B Reekie Trust

WHAT IS FUNDED Donations are only given to registered charitable organisations. We prefer to support organisations concerned with medical projects, social work projects, the arts, local history and conservation

WHAT IS NOT FUNDED No individual applicants

WHO CAN BENEFIT Headquarters organisations plus local branches. There are no restrictions on the age; professional and economic group; family situation; religion and culture; and social circumstances of; or disease or medical condition suffered by, the beneficiaries

WHERE FUNDING CAN BE GIVEN UK, with preference for Wiltshire

TYPE OF GRANT One-off. In exceptional circumstances grant commitments may be recurring

SAMPLE GRANTS £5,000 to Almeida Theatre; £3,000 to Health Plan; £2,000 to East Birmingham Family Service Unit; £2,000 to South Birmingham Family Service Unit; £1,500 to Musica Nel Chiostra

FINANCES *Year* 1998 *Income* £24,216 *Grants* £23,857

TRUSTEES Mrs V B Reekie, R A Reekie, J A J Reekie

PUBLICATIONS Annual Report is included in the Accounts from 1996 onwards

HOW TO APPLY None required. Applications will not be acknowledged

WHO TO APPLY TO Mrs V B Reekie, R A & V B Reekie Trust, c/o Roger Harriman, New Guild House, 45 Great Charles Street, Queensway, Birmingham B3 2LX *Tel* 0121-212 2222

CC NO 274388   ESTABLISHED 1977

■ The Christopher H R Reeves Charitable Trust

WHAT IS FUNDED The Trustees are holding approximately 75 per cent of the Trust's income and capital for application in the limited area of food allergy and related matters. Nearly all the income in this sector has already been committed to 'The Centre for Allergy Research and Environmental Health' at University College, London and to the production and distribution of a database of research references under the title of 'Nutritional and Environmental Medicine and Allergies Database'. New appeals related to food allergy and intolerance are invited and a response will be made to the applicants. The remaining 25 per cent of the Trust's income and capital will be held for general donations. The Trust's main area of interest is in disability. Donations will largely be made to charities already associated with this Trust. Only successful applicants will receive a response

WHAT IS NOT FUNDED In particular, the Trust does not wish to receive appeals relating to: individuals; overseas travel and expeditions; animal charities; church/community hall/schools appeals outside North Bedfordshire area; overseas aid; children's charities; drugs and alcohol; mental health charities and education

WHO CAN BENEFIT Organisations benefiting young adults and older people, academics, research workers, students and those with special dietary needs

WHERE FUNDING CAN BE GIVEN UK

TYPE OF GRANT Income and capital

FINANCES *Year* 1997 *Income* £137,415 *Grants* £110,800

TRUSTEES E M Reeves, M Kennedy, V Reeves

HOW TO APPLY To the Trustees in writing. Replies are only sent to successful applicants

WHO TO APPLY TO E M Reeves, The Christopher H R Reeves Charitable Trust, Hinwick Lodge, Wellingborough, Northamptonshire NN29 7JQ

CC NO 266877   **ESTABLISHED** 1973

■ Reeve's Foundation

WHAT IS FUNDED Priority given to cases of acute need and special educational requirements; there is a long standing connection with Christ's Hospital. Trustees also give consideration to help with vocational training courses preparing people for work

WHO CAN BENEFIT Principally individuals. Applicants or their parent(s) must have lived or worked for the last twelve months, or for at least two of the last ten years, in the area Where Funding Can Be Given. Occasionally schools substantially serving the area. Children, young adults, students and those disadvantaged by poverty may benefit

WHERE FUNDING CAN BE GIVEN Ecclesiastical parish of St Sepulchre or the ancient parishes of Clerkenwell and St Andrew, Holborn, the City of London and the London Boroughs of Camden & Islington

TYPE OF GRANT For individuals, bursaries, maintenance allowances, grants for school clothing, equipment, books and travel costs. For organisations, educational projects benefiting a significant number of students

RANGE OF GRANTS Individuals: £75–£2,000, organisations: £500–£10,000

SAMPLE GRANTS £23,010 to students in need attending Christ's Hospital; £20,000 to students in need attending Birkbeck College; £12,000 to students in need attending the London School of Economics; £8,000 to students in need attending the Guildhall School of Music and Drama; £3,000 to Community Service Volunteers

FINANCES *Year* 1997 *Income* £272,736 *Grants* £104,677

TRUSTEES Rector of St Sepulchre's, 12 others appointed by various bodies, C Brown, K Downham, Mrs E Hoodless, Dr C Mabey, R C

Martin, G D Shelley, G Wheeler, Dr G G Wilson, W P Wright

HOW TO APPLY Meetings normally in March, June, September and December. Initial telephone calls from applicants are welcome. An application form and guidelines are available. Deadlines are two weeks before Governors' meeting. Sae appreciated

WHO TO APPLY TO C J Matthews, Clerk to the Governors, Reeve's Foundation, 90 Central Street, London EC1V 8AQ *Tel* 0171-250 4144 *Fax* 0171-251 8689

CC NO 312504   **ESTABLISHED** 1702

■ Refson-Essoldo Charitable Foundation

WHAT IS FUNDED General charitable purposes

WHO CAN BENEFIT There are no restrictions on the age; professional and economic group; family situation; religion and culture; and social circumstances of; or disease or medical condition suffered by, the beneficiaries

WHERE FUNDING CAN BE GIVEN UK and overseas

TRUSTEES Mrs D P Refson, P S Refson, P A Kraus

NOTES No grants are being made at present time

WHO TO APPLY TO Miss E Grey, Refson-Essoldo Charitable Foundation, Essoldo Ltd, 119–120 High Street, Stourbridge, West Midlands DY8 1DT

CC NO 251624   **ESTABLISHED** 1966

■ The Max Reinhardt Charitable Trust

WHAT IS FUNDED Medical schools and research, the arts, heritage

WHO CAN BENEFIT Actors and entertainment professionals; medical professionals; musicians; students; textile workers and designers; and writers and poets

WHERE FUNDING CAN BE GIVEN UK

FINANCES *Year* 1997 *Income* £128,734 *Grants* £140,875

TRUSTEES Alexandra Reinhardt, Joan D Reinhardt, Max Reinhardt, Veronica Reinhardt

HOW TO APPLY To the address under Who To Apply To in writing

WHO TO APPLY TO The Max Reinhardt Charitable Trust, c/o BSG Valentine, Lynton House, 7–12 Tavistock Square, London WC1H 9BQ

CC NO 264741   **ESTABLISHED** 1973

■ Relief Fund For Romania Limited

WHAT IS FUNDED The relief of poverty, sickness, suffering and distress amongst those permanetly or temorarily resident in Romania who are victims of civil unrest or other social or economic circumstances

WHO CAN BENEFIT Organisations benefiting those people in Romania who are at risk, disadvantaged by poverty, refugees, socially isolated people or victims of war

WHERE FUNDING CAN BE GIVEN In practice, Romania

SAMPLE GRANTS £132,934 for medical and associated purchases

FINANCES *Year* 1997 *Income* £201,158 *Grants* £132,934

WHO TO APPLY TO E Parry, Relief Fund For Romania Limited, 54–62 Regent Street, London W1R 5PJ

CC NO 1046737   **ESTABLISHED** 1995

■ The Remainders Charitable Trust

WHAT IS FUNDED General charitable purposes

WHO CAN BENEFIT There are no restrictions on the age; professional and economic group; family situation; religion and culture; and social circumstances of; or disease or medical condition suffered by, the beneficiaries

WHERE FUNDING CAN BE GIVEN UK

TRUSTEES J P Crossley, M A Crossley, M R Garner, D R Thomas, J P Tucki

WHO TO APPLY TO Mrs J P Crossley, Secretary, The Remainders Charitable Trust, c/o Remainders Ltd, 13–19 Gate Lane, Boldmere, Suton Coldfield, West Midlands B73 5TR

CC NO 1055663   **ESTABLISHED** 1996

■ Rescue - The Foundation for the Brain Injured Infant

WHAT IS FUNDED Research addressing the nature and causes of brain injury in neonates resulting in cerebral palsy and other neurological disorders. Research is sponsored, fostered and carried out into the causes and prevention of neonatal brain injury, its detection, early diagnosis, subsequent treatments, therapies and management

WHO CAN BENEFIT Support is given to medical professionals, research workers, scientists and academics researching into cerebral palsy and neonatal brain injury, and to children (new born) suffering from cerebral palsy and neonatal brain injury

WHERE FUNDING CAN BE GIVEN UK

FINANCES *Year* 1995 *Income* £804,137

TRUSTEES G M Lewis, P C W Muscutt, C H Pittaway, Prof C M Turner

NOTES No grants were given in 1995. Income was spent on research and information costs, ie salaries and wages, travel and subsistence, equipment, etc

WHO TO APPLY TO H Williams, Company Secretary, Rescue, Portland House, Trefin, Haverfordwest, Dyfed SA44 6AF

CC NO 1003037   **ESTABLISHED** 1991

■ The Rest-Harrow Trust

WHAT IS FUNDED Main areas of interest are aged, education, disability, housing, poverty, youth

WHAT IS NOT FUNDED Registered charities only. Applications from individuals are not considered. Grants are usually made to national bodies rather than local branches, or local groups. Mainly UK charities

WHO CAN BENEFIT Registered charities benefiting: people of all ages; disabled people; those disadvantaged by poverty; and the homeless

WHERE FUNDING CAN BE GIVEN Preference for Cheltenham and Warwick

TYPE OF GRANT Usually modest donations. Occasionally one-off for part or all of a particular project

RANGE OF GRANTS £100–£2,000

SAMPLE GRANTS £2,000 to Institute for Jewish Policy Research; £2,000 to Nightingale House; £1,400 to Friends of the Hebrew University of Jerusalem for the Jewish Botanical Gardens Group (The Writtle Scholarship); £1,250 to Lilian Faithfull Homes; £1,000 to Assembly of Masorti Synagogues; £1,000 to Cambridge Foundation; £1,000 to Jewish Care; £1,000 to Jewish Museum; £1,000 to Oxford Centre for Hebrew and Jewish Studies; £500 to CCIP

FINANCES *Year* 1997 *Income* £47,807 *Grants* £21,600

TRUSTEES Miss E R Wix, HON & V Trustee Limited

PUBLICATIONS Annual Report filed at Charity Commission

HOW TO APPLY At any time. Considered quarterly. Only applications from eligible bodies acknowledged. Frequent appeal material, ie several times a year from a single charity, deprecated

WHO TO APPLY TO Portrait Solicitors, The Rest-Harrow Trust, 1 Chancery Lane, London WC2A 1LF

CC NO 238042   **ESTABLISHED** 1964

■ The Reuter Foundation

WHAT IS FUNDED Charities working in the fields of: information technology and computers; support to volunteers and voluntary and community organisations; health professional bodies; charity or voluntary umbrella bodies; film, video, multimedia; community arts and recreation; health; conservation; environmental issues; education and training; and social care and development

WHAT IS NOT FUNDED Will not support political, religious, sports or animal causes. No grants to individuals

WHO CAN BENEFIT Registered charities benefiting: people of all ages; research workers; volunteers; those in care, fostered and adopted; one parent families; disabled people; those disadvantaged by poverty, disaster victims; homeless people; those living in urban areas; and beneficiaries suffering from cancers, diabetes, heart disease, multiple sclerosis, sight loss and tropical diseases

WHERE FUNDING CAN BE GIVEN UK and overseas

TYPE OF GRANT One-off, recurring costs, project, research and start-up costs will be considered

FINANCES *Year* 1997 *Income* £3,121,555 *Grants* £2,794,150

TRUSTEES P Job, D G Ure, M W Wood

PUBLICATIONS *Annual Review, Reuterlink, Reuterlink Extra, Contacts Directory*

NOTES Applications must be supported by a member of Reuters staff

HOW TO APPLY In writing at any time, application form available

WHO TO APPLY TO S Somerville, The Reuter Foundation, 85 Fleet Street, London EC4P 4AJ *Tel* 0171-542 7015 *Fax* 0171-542 8599 *E-mail* rtrfoundation@easynet.co.uk *Web Site* www.foundation.reuters.com

CC NO 803676   **ESTABLISHED** 1982

■ Joan K Reynall Charitable Trust

WHAT IS FUNDED Nature reserves, woodlands, animal welfare, agriculture, children, sight loss and deafness

WHAT IS NOT FUNDED No grants to individuals

WHO CAN BENEFIT Registered charities benefiting children, victims of famine, and those suffering from sight loss and hearing loss

WHERE FUNDING CAN BE GIVEN UK and overseas

TYPE OF GRANT One-off and project, up to one year

524

Think carefully about every application. Is it justified?

RANGE OF GRANTS Up to £500
FINANCES *Year* 1998 *Income* £17,000
TRUSTEES Midland Bank Trust Company Ltd, J K
Reynell, A C Reynell
HOW TO APPLY In writing to the address under Who To
Apply To
WHO TO APPLY TO The Trust Manager, Joan K Reynall
Charitable Trust, Midland Bank Private Banking,
Cumberland House, 15–17 Cumberland Place,
Southampton, Hampshire SO15 2UY
Tel 01703 531396 *Fax* 01703 531341
CC NO 1069397   **ESTABLISHED** 1997

■ Rhema Christian Ministries

WHAT IS FUNDED (a) Advancement of the Christian
faith; (b) relief of persons who are in conditions of
need and suffering, hardship or distress or who
are elderly or sick; (c) advancement of education,
in particular of Christian values; (d) any other
charitable purposes. However the following ares
are particularly favoured: establishment of
Christian churches and training and support of
church leaders and local members; development
and support of the promotion of the Christian
gospel through music and worship; support of
Christian missions and missionaries; advising and
assisting charitable community centred projects,
schemes and initiatives, to care for the young,
elderly and others in need
WHO CAN BENEFIT Organisations benefiting children,
young adults and elderly people. Support is given
to Christians, including Baptists, Anglicans,
Methodists and Roman Catholics. Support may
also be given to clergy and Christian missionaries.
At risk groups, those disadvantaged by poverty,
homeless and socially isolated people are also
supported. There is no restriction on the disease
or medical condition suffered by the beneficiaries
WHERE FUNDING CAN BE GIVEN UK
TRUSTEES R Anderson, Ms J Dublin, Ms J Goodridge,
M Goodridge, D C Williams
WHO TO APPLY TO Ms J Dublin, Office Administrator,
Rhema Christian Ministries, 99 Church Road,
Upper Norwood, London SE19 2PR
CC NO 1061736   **ESTABLISHED** 1997

■ The Rhododendron Trust

WHAT IS FUNDED Overseas charities, UK social
welfare charities and UK cultural charities
WHAT IS NOT FUNDED No grants to individuals, or for
expeditions, scholarships or research work
WHO CAN BENEFIT Registered charities. There are few
restrictions on the social circumstances of the
beneficiaries
WHERE FUNDING CAN BE GIVEN UK and overseas
TYPE OF GRANT Preferably project-based
RANGE OF GRANTS £250–£1,000
FINANCES *Year* 1997 *Income* £35,000
Grants £32,000
TRUSTEES P E Healey, Dr R Walker, S Ray, Dr D M
Smith
HOW TO APPLY Applications are not acknowledged.
Donations made once a year, usually in February.
There is no application form
WHO TO APPLY TO P E Healey, The Rhododendron
Trust, 7–9 Irwell Terrace, Bacup, Lancashire
OL13 9AJ *Tel* 01706 873213
Fax 01706 874211
CC NO 267192   **ESTABLISHED** 1974

■ The Rhondda Cynon Taff Welsh Church Acts Fund (297) (formerly

known as The Mid Glamorgan Welsh Church Acts
Fund)
*This trust failed to supply a copy of its annual report and
accounts to CAF as required under section 47(2) of the
Charities Act 1993. The information held on file at the
Charity Commission was insufficient to enable CAF's
researchers to write a substantive commentary on the
trust's activities. Accordingly, despite its size, we are
unable to list this trust in Spotlight on Major Trusts*

WHAT IS FUNDED General charitable purposes. Grants
distributed locally to Rhondda, Cynon, Taff,
Bridgend and Merthyr. No contribution given
towards running expenses (capital only)
WHAT IS NOT FUNDED No grants to other local
authorities' projects, clubs with a liquor licence,
individuals, students
WHO CAN BENEFIT Local activities. (Applications will
be considered from organisations outside
Rhondda Cynon Taff provided that the work of the
organisation is of local significance). There are no
restrictions on the age; professional and
economic group; family situation; religion and
culture; and social circumstances of; or disease or
medical condition suffered by, the beneficiaries
WHERE FUNDING CAN BE GIVEN Rhondda Cynon Taff
TYPE OF GRANT Capital expenditure (vast amount of
grants devoted to maintenance of church
buildings)
FINANCES *Year* 1994–95 *Income* £386,000
Grants £290,000
TRUSTEES Rhondda Cynon Taff County Borough
Council
PUBLICATIONS Annual statement of accounts
HOW TO APPLY New grants distributed annually.
Application forms must be received at the address
below by 31 July
WHO TO APPLY TO The Treasurer's Dept, The Rhondda
Cynon Taff Welsh Church Acts Fund, Rhondda
Cynon Taff County Borough Council, County Hall,
Cathays Park, Cardiff CF1 3NE
CC NO 506658   **ESTABLISHED** 1961

■ The Tim Rice Charitable Trust

WHAT IS FUNDED General charitable purposes
WHO CAN BENEFIT There are no restrictions on the
age; professional and economic group; family
situation; religion and culture; and social
circumstances of; or disease or medical condition
suffered by, the beneficiaries
WHERE FUNDING CAN BE GIVEN UK
RANGE OF GRANTS £240–£10,000
SAMPLE GRANTS £10,000 to Countryside Movement;
£10,000 to England School's Cricket Association;
£5,000 to Save the Children towards Equality
Learning Centre; £2,700 to Institute for the
Advancement of Journalism; £2,500 to Sir
Geoffrey de Havilland Memorial Fund; £2,500 to
the Peter May Memorial Appeal; £2,000 to Nelson
Mandela's Children's Fund; £1,800 to Saints and
Sinners Trust Ltd; £1,000 to Child Bereavement
Trust; £550 to Phoenix Players Ltd
FINANCES *Year* 1997 *Income* £42,207
Grants £40,990
TRUSTEES N W Benson, Ms E Heinink, Sir T M B Rice
WHO TO APPLY TO Mrs E Heinink, The Tim Rice
Charitable Trust, 31 The Terrace, Barnes, London
SW13 0NR
CC NO 1049578   **ESTABLISHED** 1995

Does the trust you have chosen match your needs? Haphazard applications waste postage and time

525

■ The Cliff Richard Charitable Trust

WHAT IS FUNDED General charitable purposes. To reflect the support, Christian commitment and interest of Sir Cliff Richard

WHAT IS NOT FUNDED No grants to individuals or to church building projects

WHO CAN BENEFIT A broad spectrum but the smaller, grass-roots project is often preferred. Registered charities only. There are no restrictions on the age; professional and economic group; family situation; religion and culture; and social circumstances of; or disease or medical condition suffered by, the beneficiaries

WHERE FUNDING CAN BE GIVEN UK

TYPE OF GRANT Usually small one-off sums for operational needs

FINANCES *Year* 1997 *Income* £27,574
Grants £117,550

TRUSTEES P J Gormley, P P Parker, W O Latham, M C Smith

HOW TO APPLY To the address under Who To Apply To for quarterly consideration. Applications by mail only. All requests acknowledged. Sae helpful

WHO TO APPLY TO Bill Latham, The Cliff Richard Charitable Trust, Harley House, 94 Hare Lane, Claygate, Esher, Surrey KT10 0RB

CC NO 259056   **ESTABLISHED** 1969

■ The Clive Richards Charity

WHAT IS FUNDED To favour the assistance of social welfare, the disabled, the arts and religion mostly in the county of Herefordshire, especially in church schools

WHAT IS NOT FUNDED No grants for political causes

WHO CAN BENEFIT Individuals and registered charities benefiting musicians; Roman Catholics; disabled people; and those disadvantaged by poverty

WHERE FUNDING CAN BE GIVEN Herefordshire

SAMPLE GRANTS £14,500 to Bishop Vessey's School for educational purposes; £13,734 to Lord Mayor's Appeal for Cancer Research for medical research; £5,000 to Hereford Cathedral School for educational purposes; £5,000 to Christ College, Brecon for educational purposes; £3,500 to Royal Opera House for cultural purposes; £3,498 to St Joseph's Church for religious purposes; £2,500 to Hereford Perpetual Trust for religious purposes; £2,500 to Guildford Cancer Self Help for social purposes; £2,500 to Aid in Action, Porthcawl for social purposes; £2,500 to Save the Children Fund for social purposes

FINANCES *Year* 1997 *Income* £78,972
Grants £92,633

TRUSTEES W S C Richards, Mrs S A Richards

WHO TO APPLY TO D H Carter, The Clive Richards Charity, 40 Great James Street, London WC1N 3HB

CC NO 327155   **ESTABLISHED** 1986

■ The Violet M Richards Charity

WHAT IS FUNDED The relief of the aged, the relief of sickness and the advancement of medical education to support particularly: medical research and research into geriatric problems, homes for sick, facilities for the relief of elderly and medical education. The Trustees would prefer to be associated with a programme of research and are prepared to commit themselves to support over a given period

WHAT IS NOT FUNDED No individuals will be supported

WHO CAN BENEFIT Organisations benefiting: the aged; medical professionals; researchers; medical students; and the sick. There is no restriction on the disease or medical condition suffered by the beneficiaries

WHERE FUNDING CAN BE GIVEN UK

RANGE OF GRANTS £7,500–£21,750

SAMPLE GRANTS £21,750 to Miscarriage Association; £7,500 to United Medical and Dental Schools of Guy's and St Thomas's Hospitals

FINANCES *Year* 1996 *Income* £126,382
Grants £29,250

TRUSTEES Mrs E H Hill, Miss M Davies, G R Andersen, C A Hicks

HOW TO APPLY To the address under Who To Apply To, enclosing full details in writing of specific project. Applications will not be acknowledged. Applications are considered around April of each year

WHO TO APPLY TO C A Hicks, The Violet M Richards Charity, Wedlake Bell, 16 Bedford Street, Covent Garden, London WC2E 9HF

CC NO 273928   **ESTABLISHED** 1977

■ The Richardson Family Charitable Trust

WHAT IS FUNDED Charities working in the fields of: accommodation and housing; arts, culture and recreation; infrastructure support and development. Funding may be given for respite care, medical research, adoption and fostering services, counselling on social issues and emergency care

WHAT IS NOT FUNDED No grants to individuals

WHO CAN BENEFIT Organisations benefiting: people of all ages; actors and entertainment professionals; musicians; textile workers and designers; writers and poets; medical professionals; and research workers; and those from many different social circumstances. Funding may also be given to children in care, fostered and adopted

WHERE FUNDING CAN BE GIVEN UK, with preference to Lambeth and Southwark, and overseas

TYPE OF GRANT Feasibility studies, project, research, recurring costs, running costs, salaries and start-up costs. Funding may be given for over three years. Loans are not encouraged

RANGE OF GRANTS Not less than £1,000, typically £5,000

TRUSTEES S D Fish, B E Richardson, J A M Richardson, P Tranter

HOW TO APPLY This Trust states that it does not respond to unsolicited applications

WHO TO APPLY TO J A M Richardson, Trustee, The Richardson Family Charitable Trust, 143 Rosendale Road, London SE21 8HE *Tel* 0181-670 3153

CC NO 1064262   **ESTABLISHED** 1997

■ Miss Maria Susan Rickard Animals' Charity

WHAT IS FUNDED Animal welfare charities

WHO CAN BENEFIT Registered charities

WHERE FUNDING CAN BE GIVEN UK and overseas

RANGE OF GRANTS £10–£550

SAMPLE GRANTS £550 to West Norfolk Seal Rescue; £300 to Cares Wildlife Hospital; £250 to Wood Green Animals Shelter; £209 to British Chelonia Group; £200 to Donkey Sanctuary

FINANCES *Year* 1996 *Income* £14,130
Grants £4,375

TRUSTEES Miss M S Rickard, G E Smart, J T Dean

■ Muriel Edith Rickman Trust

WHAT IS FUNDED Emphasis on cancer, blindness but other areas not excluded. Normally research equipment is funded

WHAT IS NOT FUNDED The Trustees will not respond to individual students, clubs, community projects or expeditions

WHO CAN BENEFIT Hospitals and research organisations benefiting those suffering from cancers and sight loss

WHERE FUNDING CAN BE GIVEN UK

TYPE OF GRANT Research and one-off payments on specified equipment

RANGE OF GRANTS £250–£14,000

SAMPLE GRANTS £14,000 to the Anthony Nolan Bone Marrow Trust; £11,200 to the Epilepsy Research Foundation; £10,791 to Tommy's Campaign; £9,007 to Muscular Dystrophy Group; £7,153 to British Friends of Rambam Medical Centre; £5,145 to Guy's and St Thomas's Medical and Dental School; £1,400 to South Hampstead High School Scholarship; £278 to Alzheimer's Disease Society; £250 to Guide Dogs for the Blind

FINANCES *Year* 1997 *Income* £112,763
Grants £59,224

TRUSTEES H P Rickman, M D Gottlieb, M W Warner

HOW TO APPLY There are no guidelines for applications and we only reply if we have a prima facie interest and then ask for further details. Trustees meet as required

WHO TO APPLY TO H P Rickman, Muriel Edith Rickman Trust, 12 Fitzroy Court, 57–59 Shepherds Hill, London N6 5RD

CC NO 326143   **ESTABLISHED** 1982

■ R G Riddell Charitable Trust

This trust did not respond to CAF's request to amend its entry and, by 30 June 1998, CAF's researchers did not find financial records for later than 1995 on its file at the Charity Commission. Trusts are legally required to submit annual accounts to the Charity Commission under section 42 of the Charities Act 1993

WHAT IS FUNDED Support given to specific Missionary works and organisations and other Evangelical Missionary causes

WHAT IS NOT FUNDED Trust funds can only be distributed to registered charities. Individuals should not apply

WHO CAN BENEFIT Registered charities benefiting Evangelists

WHERE FUNDING CAN BE GIVEN UK

TRUSTEES R G Riddell, L J Voke, J C M Riddell

WHO TO APPLY TO L J Voke, R G Riddell Charitable Trust, Oakview, High Ridge Close, Arundel, West Sussex BN18 9ES

CC NO 267998   **ESTABLISHED** 1974

■ The Riddon Trust

WHAT IS FUNDED General charitable purposes. Local and smaller charities

WHAT IS NOT FUNDED No grants to individuals

WHO CAN BENEFIT Registered charities only. There are no restrictions on the age; professional and economic group; family situation; religion and culture; and social circumstances of; or disease or medical condition suffered by, the beneficiaries

WHERE FUNDING CAN BE GIVEN Hertfordshire and Scotland

TYPE OF GRANT Cash

RANGE OF GRANTS £1,000–£2,000

SAMPLE GRANTS £2,000 to Friends of Harpenden Memorial Hospital; £1,500 to Action for Dysphasic Adults; £1,500 to Cancer Relief Macmillan Fund; £1,500 to Community Meeting Point, Harpenden; £1,500 to Harpenden Mencap – Stairways; £1,500 to Harpenden Trust; £1,500 to the Hertfordshire Charity for Deprived Children; £1,500 to Hertfordshire Autistic Community Trust Appeal; £1,500 to Hospice of St Francis; £1,000 to Abbeyfield (Wheathampstead) Society Ltd

FINANCES *Year* 1997 *Income* £70,815
Grants £53,000

HOW TO APPLY To the address under Who To Apply To in writing in October/November

WHO TO APPLY TO A B Higgs, The Riddon Trust, Cooper Lancaster, 33–35 Bell Street, Reigate, Surrey RH2 7AW

CC NO 228334   **ESTABLISHED** 1962

■ The Ridgmount Foundation

WHAT IS FUNDED General charitable purposes

WHO CAN BENEFIT Registered charities. There are no restrictions on the age; professional and economic group; family situation; religion and culture; and social circumstances of; or disease or medical condition suffered by, the beneficiaries

WHERE FUNDING CAN BE GIVEN South East England

TYPE OF GRANT One-off

FINANCES *Year* 1997 *Income* £16,182
Grants £8,000

TRUSTEES J S Cox, L Jones, Mrs M H Jones, J J Jones, W P Jones, R D Walley

WHO TO APPLY TO R D Walley, The Ridgmount Foundation, Mundays, Solicitors, Crown House, Church Road, Claygate, Surrey KT10 0LP

CC NO 1016703   **ESTABLISHED** 1992

■ Pat Ripley's Charitable Trust

WHAT IS FUNDED General charitable purposes selected at the discretion of the Trustees

WHAT IS NOT FUNDED Overseas applications not considered

WHO CAN BENEFIT Local applicants only. There are no restrictions on the age; professional and economic group; family situation; religion and culture; and social circumstances of; or disease or medical condition suffered by, the beneficiaries

WHERE FUNDING CAN BE GIVEN South West and Channel Islands

TYPE OF GRANT Buildings, capital, one-off and start-up costs. Funding is for up to three years

RANGE OF GRANTS £100–£5,000

FINANCES *Year* 1997 *Income* £22,648
Grants £29,369

TRUSTEES Mrs C A Cameron, E J H Cameron, M Vaughan-Lee

NOTES The Trust's funds are fully committed forward. Priority in appointing any available balance shall be given to applications from local charities. Applicants by circular or from outside the South West region shall not be acknowledged

HOW TO APPLY Applications invited in September/ October for November meeting, May/June for July meeting. Please enclose sae for reply/ acknowledgement. Where appropriate, applicants annual accounts should be enclosed

WHO TO APPLY TO Caroline Cameron, Trustee, Pat Ripley's Charitable Trust, Whitelackington Manor, Ilminster, Somerset TA19 9EG
CC NO 290179 **ESTABLISHED** 1984

■ **The Ripple Effect Foundation**

WHAT IS FUNDED General charitable purposes
WHAT IS NOT FUNDED Appeals restricted to charitable institutions only. No mailshots or telephone appeals
WHO CAN BENEFIT There are no restrictions on the age; professional and economic group; family situation; religion and culture; and social circumstances of; or disease or medical condition suffered by, the beneficiaries
WHERE FUNDING CAN BE GIVEN UK
SAMPLE GRANTS £23,700 to Network Foundation for various projects; £12,150 to Ashoka (UK) Trust for supporting social entrepreneurs in developing countries
FINANCES *Year* 1995 *Income* £82,193 *Grants* £86,900
TRUSTEES Miss Caroline D Marks, I R Marks, Miss Mary E Falk, I S Wesley
HOW TO APPLY **This Trust states that it does not respond to unsolicited applications**
WHO TO APPLY TO Farrer & Co, 66 Lincoln's Inn Fields, London WC2A 3LH
CC NO 802327 **ESTABLISHED** 1989

■ **The Risley Educational Foundation**

WHAT IS FUNDED The teaching of the subjects not on the National Curriculum, mainly music, especially in Church of England schools; students from the area Where Funding Can Be Given studying for degrees at university. Also: Christian education; Anglican bodies; and education and training
WHO CAN BENEFIT Individuals and schools, especially children, young adults, students, musicians and Church of England
WHERE FUNDING CAN BE GIVEN The parishes of Breaston, Church Wilne, Dale Abbey, Draycott, Hopwell, Risley, Sandiacre and Stanton by Dale
FINANCES *Year* 1996–97 *Income* £34,559 *Grants* £16,412
HOW TO APPLY To the address under Who To Apply To in writing
WHO TO APPLY TO Mrs V A Lewis, Clerk, The Risley Educational Foundation, 100 Douglas Road, Long Eaton, Nottingham, NG10 4BD
Tel 0115 9725385
CC NO 702720 **ESTABLISHED** 1990

■ **The Rivendell Trust**

WHAT IS FUNDED To assist small charities that benefit people, particularly children, the sick or disabled, the mentally ill and those with family problems. Consideration will also be given to applications from individuals for educational purposes – particularly music
WHAT IS NOT FUNDED (a) Applications for the construction, restoration or purchase of buildings are not normally considered and (b) Grants to individuals are limited to (i) those in the above categories (ii) children and bona fide students within the UK in connection with education in music. (c) Further grants to charities or individuals will normally be considered once every three years

WHO CAN BENEFIT Individuals and organisations benefiting children, young adults and students, the mentally ill, families in need and disabled people. There is no restriction on the disease or medical condition suffered by the beneficiaries
WHERE FUNDING CAN BE GIVEN UK and overseas
TYPE OF GRANT Usually single cash payments, although more than one will be considered, depending on the circumstances of the grantee. Monthly allowance
RANGE OF GRANTS Individuals: £100–£500, organisations: £50–£1,000
SAMPLE GRANTS £1,000 to Birmingham Conservatoire to assist two students; £400 to Dream holidays for children with cystic fibrosis; The following grants were to individuals:; £500 for a music course; £500 for school fees; £500 for special equipment; £500 for general funding for history course; £350 for sign language course fees; £350 for computer equipment
FINANCES *Year* 1996 *Income* £48,592 *Grants* £20,864
TRUSTEES Mrs S D Caird, G Caird, Miss M J Verney, E R Verney, A Layton, J W Dolman, Dr I Laing
NOTES All applications from individuals should include: (a) their Curriculum Vitae/purpose of grant, (b) an analysis of costs, (c) details of any other grants or funding they may have received, (d) a brief summary of their own and/or parents' financial position, (e) sae. Because of the number of grants received, failure to supply the above could result in an application failing
HOW TO APPLY Charities: Comprehensive details should include a statement of the previous two years' accounts. Individuals apply in writing to Mrs T Burrell, 1 Dean Farrar Street, London SW1H 0DY for application form
WHO TO APPLY TO M J Day, The Rivendell Trust, 1 Dean Farrar Street, Westminster, London SW1H 0DY
CC NO 271375 **ESTABLISHED** 1976

■ **The River Island Trust**

WHAT IS FUNDED To provide for recreation, leisure opportunities for those whose age, youth, disablement or social circumstances have need, including respite and holiday accommodation; arts activities, dance groups, holidays and outings will be considered
WHAT IS NOT FUNDED Buildings, infrastructure, animals, environment and education will not be funded. Those who already have alternative funding will not be considered
WHO CAN BENEFIT Individuals and small groups, who otherwise are not eligible for funding elsewhere, benefiting people of all ages, carers, disabled people and those disadvantaged by poverty. Those in care, fostered and adopted, parents and children, and one parent families will be considered
WHERE FUNDING CAN BE GIVEN South of England, East of England, Midlands, Yorkshire and Humberside and Oxfordshire
TYPE OF GRANT Small one-off grants
RANGE OF GRANTS £25–£200
FINANCES *Year* 1996 *Income* £15,423 *Grants* £3,834
TRUSTEES S F Beaumont, S A Reily-Collins, Ingrid Palmer, G Turner
HOW TO APPLY In writing (with an sae would be appreciated), an application form may be required. All applications are considered at periodic meetings of the Trustees

WHO TO APPLY TO S Beaumont, Chairman, The River Island Trust, Rye Farm, Culham, Abingdon, Oxfordshire OX14 3NN *Tel* 01235 464673
CC NO 1057858 **ESTABLISHED** 1996

■ The River Trust

WHAT IS FUNDED Christian charities
WHO CAN BENEFIT Organisations benefiting Christians
WHERE FUNDING CAN BE GIVEN UK, with preference for Sussex, and overseas
TYPE OF GRANT Certain charities are supported for more than one year
RANGE OF GRANTS £18–£33,000
SAMPLE GRANTS £33,000 to Care Trust; £26,700 to Youth with a Mission; £11,000 to Timothy Trust; £10,000 to Challenge 2000; £8,000 to Genesis Arts Trust; £8,000 to Scripture Union; £6,500 to St Stephen's Society; £6,000 to Indian Christian Mission Centre; £5,100 to Dolphin School Trust; £5,000 to Marriage Resource
FINANCES *Year* 1997 *Income* £208,790 *Grants* £191,218
TRUSTEES The Directors of Kleinwort Benson Trustees Limited: D H Benson, D V Clasper, K W Hotchkiss, D J McGilvray
HOW TO APPLY To the address under Who To Apply To
WHO TO APPLY TO The River Trust, Kleinwort Benson Trustees Ltd, PO Box 191, 10 Fenchurch Street, London EC3M 3LB
CC NO 275843 **ESTABLISHED** 1977

■ Riverside Charitable Trust Limited

WHAT IS FUNDED Relief for the poor, aged, the sick and infirm and for educational and other charitable purposes, including health care and health buildings and facilities
WHAT IS NOT FUNDED Political in any form debarred
WHO CAN BENEFIT Individuals and organisations benefiting people of all ages and those who are retired, including those disadvantaged by poverty. There is no restriction on the disease or medical condition suffered by the beneficiaries. Priority to old age pensioners of the Companies that raised the cash and shares. Minimal hard cases as affected by redundancy, and youth education
WHERE FUNDING CAN BE GIVEN Lancashire
TYPE OF GRANT Recurring costs
RANGE OF GRANTS £100–£2,000
SAMPLE GRANTS £8,000 to British Heart Foundation; £7,750 to Cancer Research – Macmillan Fund; £6,000 to Cancer Research; £6,000 to Rossendale Valley Mencap; £6,000 to St Mary's Hospice; £5,000 to Derwen College for the Disabled; £5,000 to Paramedic Bike Appeal Fund; £4,000 to Rossendale Society for the Blind; £3,500 to RNLI; £3,000 to Cancer Chemotherapy
FINANCES *Year* 1997 *Income* £185,720 *Grants* £180,026
TRUSTEES I B Dearing, Mrs J A Davidson, F Drew, H Francis, Mrs A Higginson, B J Lynch, G Maden
HOW TO APPLY Prefer a request in writing initially
WHO TO APPLY TO Barry J Lynch, Chairman, Riverside Charitable Trust Limited, 20 Dobbin Close, Rossendale, Lancashire BB4 7TH
CC NO 264015 **ESTABLISHED** 1972

■ Otto Rix Memorial Trust

This trust did not respond to CAF's request to amend its entry and, by 30 June 1998, CAF's researchers did not find financial records for later than 1995 on its file at the Charity Commission. Trusts are legally required to submit annual accounts to the Charity Commission under section 42 of the Charities Act 1993

WHAT IS FUNDED General charitable purposes
WHO CAN BENEFIT Registered charities only. There are no restrictions on the age; professional and economic group; family situation; religion and culture; and social circumstances of; or disease or medical condition suffered by, the beneficiaries
WHERE FUNDING CAN BE GIVEN UK
TRUSTEES Hon K D Rix, Mrs S Rix, M D Paisner
WHO TO APPLY TO The Hon Mr Justice Rix, Otto Rix Memorial Trust, The Royal Courts of Justice, Strand, London WC2A 2LL *Tel* 0171-936 7135
CC NO 327399 **ESTABLISHED** 1987

■ The E E Roberts Charitable Trust

WHAT IS FUNDED Education and medical, especially for children with disabilities or from deprived areas. Farming and wildlife including environmental issues
WHAT IS NOT FUNDED No support for large national charities, church or village appeals outside the area or for animal charities
WHO CAN BENEFIT Registered charities benefiting children, young people
WHERE FUNDING CAN BE GIVEN East Sussex and Kent
TYPE OF GRANT Chiefly recurring payments from income. Occasional one-off capital grants and research. Funding is available for more than three years
RANGE OF GRANTS Capital grants: £2,000, recurring grants: £1,000pa
SAMPLE GRANTS £2,953 to Kent Music School; £1,350 to DGAA (Tunbridge Wells); £1,350 to British Red Cross; £1,350 to Church of England Children's Society; £1,350 to local hospice; £1,350 to Sunfield School (for Handicapped); £1,350 to Chailey Heritage School (for handicapped); £1,350 to SANE; £1,350 to John Grooms Association for the Disabled; £1,350 to Fairbridge Trust
FINANCES *Year* 1997 *Income* £34,617 *Grants* £36,603
TRUSTEES Mrs E E Roberts, C S Hall, N B C Evelegh
HOW TO APPLY In writing to the address under Who To Apply To. The Trustees meet twice a year in January and July. Applications will not be acknowledged
WHO TO APPLY TO C Hall, The E E Roberts Charitable Trust, Messrs Cripps Harries Hall, Solicitors, 6–10 Mount Ephraim Road, Tunbridge Wells, Kent TN1 1EE *Tel* 01892 515121
CC NO 273697 **ESTABLISHED** 1977

■ The Thomas Roberts Charitable Trust

WHAT IS FUNDED General charitable purposes, in particular, the relief of need, poverty and distress of past and present employees of the Thomas Roberts (Westminster) Ltd group of companies and their families
WHO CAN BENEFIT There are no restrictions on the age; professional and economic group; family situation; religion and culture; and social circumstances of; or disease or medical condition suffered by, the beneficiaries. Particular favour is

Does the trust you have chosen match your needs? Haphazard applications waste postage and time

529

given to past and present employees of the Thomas Roberts (Westminster) Ltd group of companies, and their families, who are in need, poverty or distress. Support is given to at risk groups and the socially isolated

WHERE FUNDING CAN BE GIVEN UK

TRUSTEES R E Gammage, J Roberts, Ms P M Roberts

WHO TO APPLY TO J Roberts, Trustee, The Thomas Roberts Charitable Trust, 5–6 The Square, Winchester, Hampshire SO23 9WE

CC NO 1067235   **ESTABLISHED** 1997

■ Robinson Brothers (Ryders Green) Ltd, Charitable Trust

WHAT IS FUNDED Maintenance of funding to current beneficiaries

WHAT IS NOT FUNDED The Trust will not fund individuals, nor animal charities

WHO CAN BENEFIT Registered charities. There are no restrictions on the age, professional and economic group, family situation, religion and culture, and social circumstances of, or disease or medical condition suffered by, the beneficiaries

WHERE FUNDING CAN BE GIVEN The Black Country and Newcastle upon Tyne

TYPE OF GRANT Recurring

FINANCES *Year* 1997–98 *Income* £26,500 *Grants* £23,000

TRUSTEES J H M Robinson, F D Robinson, E R Grey, Mrs S M Jones

NOTES The funds of the charity are committed in the main, from year to year and therefore fresh applications will only be considered for minor grants to local charities. Any other applications will not normally be acknowledged

HOW TO APPLY In writing by October each year with accounts

WHO TO APPLY TO J H Robinson, Robinson Brothers Ltd, Charitable Trust, Phoenix Street, West Bromwich, West Midlands B70 0AH

CC NO 1011423   **ESTABLISHED** 1992

■ Sir Edward Robinson Charitable Trust

WHAT IS FUNDED The chief object of the Trust is to support Numismatics. The Trustees seek out projects themselves

WHAT IS NOT FUNDED Registered charities only

WHO CAN BENEFIT Numismatics

WHERE FUNDING CAN BE GIVEN UK

FINANCES *Year* 1995 *Income* £26,000 *Grants* £26,000

TRUSTEES V H Robinson, O H Robinson, Gillian Maude, Sophia Heseltine, K Balston

HOW TO APPLY No further applications can be considered

WHO TO APPLY TO Mrs K Balston, Sir Edward Robinson Charitable Trust, 14 Mercers Road, London N19 4JP

CC NO 211848   **ESTABLISHED** 1956

■ The Edwin George Robinson Charitable Trust

WHAT IS FUNDED For the benefit of any trust, institution or organisation in the UK which provides care for the disabled or aged, provided that they have exclusively charitable objects

WHO CAN BENEFIT Organisations benefiting the aged and disabled people

WHERE FUNDING CAN BE GIVEN UK

TRUSTEES E C Robinson, S C Robinson

WHO TO APPLY TO E C Robinson, Trustee, The Edwin George Robinson Charitable Trust, 71 Manor Road South, Hinchley Wood, Esher, Surrey KT10 0GB

CC NO 1068763   **ESTABLISHED** 1998

■ The J C Robinson Trust No 3

WHAT IS FUNDED (a) The erection, equipping and maintaining of a village hall and reading room in Iford. (b) The foundation, setting up and maintenance of a home for orphans or destitute children at Chailey or any place in the county of Sussex. (c) To help people to develop their maximum potential. (d) Any other charitable purpose. Particularly charities working in the fields of: infrastructure development; charity or voluntary umbrella bodies; conservation; primary schools and community facilities and services

WHAT IS NOT FUNDED No grants made for historic buildings or village halls except in Sussex, Bristol and South Gloucestershire

WHO CAN BENEFIT Individuals in need and registered charities benefiting children; those in care, fostered and adopted; at risk groups; carers; disabled people; those disadvantaged by poverty; ex-offenders and those at risk of offending; homeless people; immigrants and refugees; those living in rural areas; and volunteers

WHERE FUNDING CAN BE GIVEN England

TYPE OF GRANT Recurrent or one-off

SAMPLE GRANTS £3,000 to Lewes and District Scout and Guide HQ for improvements to building; £1,000 to Lewes YMCA for running costs; £1,000 to 133 Bristol Scout Group for Disabled Boys; £1,000 to Whitley Bay Boys Club for repairs to premises; £1,000 to Hastings and Rother Crossroads for care scheme to support carers

FINANCES *Year* 1997 *Income* £17,771 *Grants* £18,973

TRUSTEES Miss C M Howe, Dr C J Burns-Cox

HOW TO APPLY By post only

WHO TO APPLY TO Dr C Burns-Cox, The J C Robinson Trust No 3, Southend Farm, Wotton-under-Edge, Gloucestershire GL12 7PB

CC NO 207294   **ESTABLISHED** 1931

■ Mrs B L Robinson's Charitable Trust

WHAT IS FUNDED The primary recipients of funding are Luton and South Bedforshire Hospice, St Margaret's Church, Streatley and Luton South Girl Guides; small grants may be made in the area of Streatley village

WHO CAN BENEFIT Organisations benefiting children, young adults and Christians. There is no restriction on the disease or medical condition suffered by the beneficiaries

WHERE FUNDING CAN BE GIVEN Bedfordshire (in practice South Bedfordshire)

FINANCES *Year* 1997–98 *Income* £44,000

TRUSTEES P G Brown, D N Cheetham, M I Robinson, Rev R W Wood

HOW TO APPLY To the address under Who To Apply To in writing

WHO TO APPLY TO D N Cheetham, Clerk, Mrs B L Robinson's Charitable Trust, Holywell Lodge, 41 Holywell Hill, St Albans, Hertfordshire AL1 1HD *Tel* 01727 865765

CC NO 802552   **ESTABLISHED** 1990

■ Philip & Marjorie Robinson's Charitable Trust

WHAT IS FUNDED General charitable purposes. Trustees policy is for themselves to seek out projects for benefit. No letters, please, as none can be dealt with or acknowledged

WHO CAN BENEFIT There are no restrictions on the age; professional and economic group; family situation; religion and culture; and social circumstances of; or disease or medical condition suffered by, the beneficiaries

WHERE FUNDING CAN BE GIVEN Mainly London

FINANCES *Year* 1998 *Income* £13,756
Grants £12,700

TRUSTEES D E Brewster, Mrs M Robinson

HOW TO APPLY None required. **This Trust states that it does not respond to unsolicited applications**

WHO TO APPLY TO D E Brewster, Philip & Marjorie Robinson's Charitable Trust, Messrs Pridie Brewster, Chartered Accountants, 29–31 Greville Street, London EC1N 8RB *Tel* 0171-831 8821

CC NO 276761   **ESTABLISHED** 1978

■ The Rochdale Fund for Relief in Sickness

WHAT IS FUNDED Health and welfare charities benefiting the people of Rochdale

WHO CAN BENEFIT Individuals and organisations benefiting sick and disabled people and those disadvantaged by poverty. There is no restriction on the disease or medical condition suffered by the beneficiaries

WHERE FUNDING CAN BE GIVEN Rochdale

RANGE OF GRANTS £150–£2,802 to organisations

SAMPLE GRANTS £2,802 to Innes School; £1,000 to Cancer Relief Macmillan Fund; £1,000 to Turning Point; £750 to Crossroads Care Attendant Scheme; £750 to Riding for the Disabled; £500 to Winged Fellowship, Southport; £500 to Petrus Community; £500 to Marie Curie Memorial Foundation; £500 to Multiple Sclerosis Society; £500 to Family Service Unit

FINANCES *Year* 1997 *Income* £35,657
Grants £13,973

TRUSTEES J G D Chapple (Chairman), Mrs H E Collins, E T Gartside, J M Porritt, Mrs P S Porritt, Mrs B A Lois Rigg, J M Rigg, A Shackleton

HOW TO APPLY To the address under Who To Apply To in writing

WHO TO APPLY TO The Clerk, The Rochdale Fund for Relief in Sickness, Jackson Brierley Hudson Stoney, Old Parsonage, 2 St Mary's Gate, Rochdale OL16 1AP

CC NO 222652   **ESTABLISHED** 1964

■ The Rochester Bridge Trust

WHAT IS FUNDED The maintenance of the Rochester bridges, also any other crossings of the River Medway. Other charitable purposes, including hospitals, conservation and higher education

WHAT IS NOT FUNDED Revenue

WHO CAN BENEFIT Charitable bodies. There are no restrictions on the age; professional and economic group; family situation; religion and culture; and social circumstances of; or disease or medical condition suffered by, the beneficiaries

WHERE FUNDING CAN BE GIVEN Kent

TYPE OF GRANT Capital including equipment, buildings and one-off. Funding is available for one year or less

RANGE OF GRANTS Largest grant £50,000

FINANCES *Year* 1995–96 *Income* £1,800,000
Grants £125,000

TRUSTEES The Court of Wardens and Assistants of Rochester Bridge; 17 members who hold office for three year terms

PUBLICATIONS Policy synopsis available on request

HOW TO APPLY To the address under Who To Apply To in writing. Applications considered annually only in June and July. Determined in October

WHO TO APPLY TO Michael Lewis, Bridge Clerk, The Rochester Bridge Trust, The Bridge Chamber, 5 Esplanade, Rochester, Kent ME1 1QE *Tel* 01634 846706/843457

CC NO 207100   **ESTABLISHED** 1399

■ Rock House Foundation

WHAT IS FUNDED General charitable purposes, in particular, the relief of poverty and sickness, the advancement of religion, the advancement of education and the preservation and protection of mental and physical health

WHO CAN BENEFIT Children, young adults and those disadvantaged by poverty. There are no restrictions on the disease or medical condition suffered by the beneficiaries

WHERE FUNDING CAN BE GIVEN UK

TRUSTEES M E Rossiter, F G Tovee, W G Hilton

WHO TO APPLY TO M Rossiter, Chair, Rock House Foundation, Rock House, Byrons Lane, Gurnett, Macclesfield SK11 0HA

CC NO 1068343   **ESTABLISHED** 1998

■ Rockwell UK Charitable Trust

WHAT IS FUNDED General charitable purposes at Trustees' discretion

WHO CAN BENEFIT At the discretion of the Trustees. There are no restrictions on the age; professional and economic group; family situation; religion and culture; and social circumstances of; or disease or medical condition suffered by, the beneficiaries

WHERE FUNDING CAN BE GIVEN UK

TYPE OF GRANT At the discretion of the Trustees

RANGE OF GRANTS £150–£30,000

SAMPLE GRANTS £30,000 to University of Reading; £16,000 to De Montford University of Leicester; £15,000 to University of Birmingham; £3,040 to Tenovus; £2,200 to New Birmingham Women's Hospital; £1,500 to Foundation for Study of Infant Deaths; £1,500 to Engineering Education Scheme in Wales; £1,500 to Macmillan Cancer Relief Fund; £1,500 to Radio 210 Give a Local Child a Chance; £1,315 to County Air Ambulance

FINANCES *Year* 1997 *Income* £80,768
Grants £95,915

TRUSTEES Rockwell Charitable Trustees Ltd

NOTES Grants are allocated at the discretion of local subsidiary company management

WHO TO APPLY TO D L Williams, Rockwell UK Charitable Trust, Rockwell International Corporation, 600 Anton Boulevard, Suite 700, Costa Mesa, CA 92628-5090 USA

CC NO 1000940   **ESTABLISHED** 1990

■ The Roddick Foundation

WHAT IS FUNDED The promotion of any charitable purposes benefiting the community including relief of poverty, advancement of education and social welfare

WHO CAN BENEFIT There are no restrictions on the age; professional and economic group; family situation; religion and culture; and social

circumstances of; or disease or medical condition suffered by, the beneficiaries

WHERE FUNDING CAN BE GIVEN UK

TRUSTEES Ms A L Roddick, Ms J Roddick, Ms S Roddick, T G Roddick

WHO TO APPLY TO Ms J Roddick, Secretary, The Roddick Foundation, 6 Howitt Road, Belsize Park, London NW3 4LL

CC NO 1061372   **ESTABLISHED** 1997

■ The Richard Rogers Charitable Settlement

WHAT IS FUNDED General charitable purposes. The Trustees are particularly interested in the homeless and housing

WHO CAN BENEFIT Registered charities. There are no restrictions on the age; professional and economic group; family situation; religion and culture; and social circumstances of; or disease or medical condition suffered by, the beneficiaries. TheTrustees are particularly interested in the homeless

WHERE FUNDING CAN BE GIVEN London

TYPE OF GRANT Regular maintenance support for a small list of registered charities plus occasional capital grants for major one-off projects

TRUSTEES R G Rogers, R Rogers, G H Cammamile

WHO TO APPLY TO K A Hawkins, The Richard Rogers Charitable Settlement, Lee Associates, 5 Southampton Place, London WC1A 2DA

CC NO 283252   **ESTABLISHED** 1981

■ Rokeby Charitable Trust

WHAT IS FUNDED Charities working in the fields of: charity or voluntary umbrella bodies; small enterprises; support to voluntary and community organisations; Christian education; schools and colleges and scholarships at Rugby School

WHAT IS NOT FUNDED No grants for buildings

WHO CAN BENEFIT Local charities and local voluntary agencies. Individuals and organisations benefiting young adults, students, at risk groups and those disadvantaged by poverty

WHERE FUNDING CAN BE GIVEN Rugby area

TYPE OF GRANT One-off, core costs and research may be considered. Funding may be given for up to one year

RANGE OF GRANTS £50–£1,000

FINANCES *Year* 1997 *Income* £22,000 *Grants* £9,000

TRUSTEES P A Batt (Chairman), A Lee, J C Marshall, R M Furber, J R Frankton, R D Montgomerie

HOW TO APPLY By letter to the address under Who To Apply To throughout the year, only from local charities

WHO TO APPLY TO Mrs M Sherman, Rokeby Charitable Trust, 283 Alwyn Road, Bilton, Rugby, Warwickshire CV22 7RP

CC NO 257600   **ESTABLISHED** 1968

■ The Helen Roll Charitable Trust

WHAT IS FUNDED General charitable purposes particularly education, especially higher education; libraries and museums; the arts; and health and welfare

WHAT IS NOT FUNDED Applications from individuals are not considered. The Trust only works through registered charities

WHO CAN BENEFIT Registered charities benefiting: actors and entertainment professionals;

musicians; students; textile workers and designers; writers and poets; at risk groups; those disadvantaged by poverty; and socially isolated people. There is no restriction on the disease or medical condition suffered by the beneficiaries. Preference is given to institutions where funding for specific purposes is difficult to secure from other sources

WHERE FUNDING CAN BE GIVEN UK

TYPE OF GRANT Generally one-off for specific projects but within a framework of charities whose work is known to the Trustees

RANGE OF GRANTS £500–£8,000

SAMPLE GRANTS £8,000 to Oxford University Bodleian Library for four separate projects for which other funding not available; £8,000 to Pembroke College, Oxford for security system; £6,500 to Trinity College of Music to support students; £6,500 to Oxford University Ashmolean Museum for three projects for which other funding is not available; £6,000 to Friends of Home Farm Trust for development of Day Services for residents; £6,000 to Purcell School for student awards; £5,500 to Stroud Court Community Trust for activity holidays for residents; £5,000 to Sick Children's Trust for sponsorship of a room at Eckersly House, Leeds; £5,000 to Nuffield Department of Surgery for research into diabetes; £5,000 to Persistent Virus Disease Foundation for research into ME

FINANCES *Year* 1996–97 *Income* £90,415 *Grants* £97,000

TRUSTEES Christine Chapman, Terry Jones, Paul Strang, Dick Williamson, Jennifer Williamson

HOW TO APPLY To the address under Who To Apply To in writing

WHO TO APPLY TO F R Williamson, Trustee, The Helen Roll Charitable Trust, Manches & Co, 3 Worcester Street, Oxford OX1 2PZ

CC NO 299108   **ESTABLISHED** 1988

■ The Vera Kaye Rollit's Trust

WHAT IS FUNDED Animal welfare charities

WHO CAN BENEFIT Local organisations, local branches of national organisations

WHERE FUNDING CAN BE GIVEN Hull and East Riding of Yorkshire

TYPE OF GRANT Buildings, capital, core costs, endowments, feasibility studies, one-off, project, research, recurring costs, running costs, salaries and start-up costs. Funding from less than one year to more than three will be considered. No loans

RANGE OF GRANTS £500–£5,000, typical £500–£1,000

SAMPLE GRANTS £6,000 to PDSA for refurbishment of Hull clinic; £2,000 to Hull Animal Welfare Club for general animal welfare; £1,000 to Cats Protection League for general animal welfare; £1,000 to Hessle Dog Rescue Services for general animal welfare; £500 to Hedgehog Hospital for general animal welfare

FINANCES *Year* 1996–97 *Income* £16,370 *Grants* £13,000

TRUSTEES J W Brennand, D J Bowes, S J Trynka

HOW TO APPLY To the address under Who To Apply To in writing. No formal application form is available

WHO TO APPLY TO The Vera Kaye Rollit's Trust, Wilberforce Court, High Street, Hull HU1 1YJ *Tel* 01482 323239 *Fax* 01482 326239

CC NO 500391   **ESTABLISHED** 1970

■ The Roman Research Trust

WHAT IS FUNDED Excavation, recording, analysis and publication of Romano-British archaeological research not otherwise funded or for which existing funds are insufficient. Romano-British archaeological exhibitions in museums and other places accessible to the public; educational programmes related to Roman Britain

WHO CAN BENEFIT Individuals and organisations benefiting postgraduate students, professional archaeologists and non-professionals of equivalent standing

WHERE FUNDING CAN BE GIVEN UK, but preference given to Wiltshire and neighbouring counties to the west

TYPE OF GRANT Project and research. Funding is for one year or less

RANGE OF GRANTS £200–£10,000. Typical grant £1,000

SAMPLE GRANTS £5,000 to an individual for Corpus of Mosaics of Roman Britain; £5,000 to an individual for study of rural landscapes of Hampshire chalkland; £2,000 to an individual for publication on Roman Public Baths in Lincoln; £1,500 to an individual for excavation of Flavian Fort at Hayton; £1,400 to an individual for excavation of Roman Camp at Alchester; £1,000 to Oglander Roman Trust for the publication of Brading Villa guidebook; £1,000 to an individual for excavation of Fishbourne Roman Palace; £1,000 to an individual for Primary Latin Project; £1,000 to East Dorset Antiguaria Society for excavation of Roman Villa at Minchington; £850 to an indidivual for analysis of Iron Age pottery from Navenby

FINANCES *Year* 1997 *Income* £47,000
Grants £27,000

TRUSTEES A K Bowman (Chairman), P Johnson, A C King, R R Paling, T W Potter, Joan Pye, P Salway, Sir John Sykes, Bt, M Todd

PUBLICATIONS The Roman Research Trust Annual Report 1996

HOW TO APPLY By 15 November and 15 April annually. Application forms and guidelines available from Hon Secretary

WHO TO APPLY TO Dr Lynn Pitts, Hon Secretary, The Roman Research Trust, 34 Mowbray Road, Didcot, Oxfordshire OX11 8SU *Tel* 01235 817127

CC NO 800983   **ESTABLISHED** 1990

■ Rooke Atlay Charitable Trust

WHAT IS FUNDED Young people, the elderly and health

WHO CAN BENEFIT Young people, the elderly and the sick. There are no restrictions on the disease or medical condition suffered by the beneficiaries

WHERE FUNDING CAN BE GIVEN North Yorkshire (Northallerton and its surrounding districts)

TYPE OF GRANT At the discretion of the Trustees

SAMPLE GRANTS £27,000 to Northallerton College; £7,380 to Friarage Hospital; £6,500 to Hurworth Hunt Pony Club; £2,259 to ICAN; £890 to Allertonshire School; £311 to Northallerton Town Council; £90 to CATCH

FINANCES *Year* 1998 *Income* £44,547
Grants £49,112

TRUSTEES R H Renwick, D R Moore, C M Lund

NOTES £4,682 was given to six individual beneficiaries

WHO TO APPLY TO R P Place, Rooke Atlay Charitable Trust, Messrs Place Blair & Hatch, 240 High Street, Northallerton, North Yorkshire DL7 8UL

CC NO 1032546   **ESTABLISHED** 1993

■ C A Rookes Charitable Trust

WHAT IS FUNDED Medicine and health, welfare, humanities

WHAT IS NOT FUNDED No funding for fees and other costs of education and training

WHO CAN BENEFIT Small local projects, innovative projects and national organisations benefiting children, young adults and older people. There is no restriction on the disease or medical condition suffered by the beneficiaries

WHERE FUNDING CAN BE GIVEN Warwickshire/Stratford upon Avon

TYPE OF GRANT One-off and recurrent

RANGE OF GRANTS Grants of £5,000 or less

FINANCES *Year* 1995 *Income* £50,000
Grants £30,000

TRUSTEES C J B Flint, C Ironmonger

HOW TO APPLY In writing at any time

WHO TO APPLY TO C J B Flint, C A Rookes Charitable Trust, 10 Bennetts Hill, Birmingham B2 5RS

CC NO 512437   **ESTABLISHED** 1980

■ The Ropner Centenary Trust

WHAT IS FUNDED Pensions; maritime charities; health and welfare; youth; the relief of poverty or distress, the advancement of education

WHO CAN BENEFIT Individuals, national and local charities benefiting: children and young adults; seafarers and fishermen; students; at risk groups; those disadvantaged by poverty; socially isolated people; and the sick. There is no restriction on the disease or medical condition suffered by the beneficiaries

WHERE FUNDING CAN BE GIVEN County Durham

SAMPLE GRANTS £3,500 to Tyne Mariners Benevolent Institution; £3,500 to Sailors Families Society; £2,000 to the Missions to Seamen, South Shields; £2,000 to the Missions to Seamen, Redcar; £2,000 to Royal Alfred Seafarers Society; £2,000 to Shipwrecked Mariners Society

FINANCES *Year* 1997 *Income* £67,755
Grants £44,195

TRUSTEES M J Kingshott, Sir John Ropner, J V Ropner, A P Theakston

NOTES In 1997, £22,310 was distributed to 97 individuals

HOW TO APPLY To the address under Who To Apply To in writing

WHO TO APPLY TO P C Scott, The Ropner Centenary Trust, 6 Stratton Street, London W1X 5FD

CC NO 269109   **ESTABLISHED** 1975

■ Rosca Trust

WHAT IS FUNDED The Rosca Trust can only make donations to registered charities and it is the fixed policy of the Trustees only to make donations to charities operating within the Boroughs of Southend-on-Sea,Castle Point and Rockford District Council. Applications from outside this area will not receive any response. Preference is given to charities catering for the needs of those under the age of 20, or over the age of 65 or to medical (in the widest sense) charities, or religious charities

WHAT IS NOT FUNDED No grants to individuals

WHO CAN BENEFIT Registered charities benefiting: one parent families; parents and children; those of various religions; ethnic minorities; at risk groups; disabled people; those disadvantaged by poverty; and victims of domestic violence. There is no restriction on the disease or medical condition suffered by the beneficiaries

Does the trust you have chosen match your needs? Haphazard applications waste postage and time

533

WHERE FUNDING CAN BE GIVEN Southend, Castle Point and Rockford local authority areas only

TYPE OF GRANT Special consideration is given to one-off donations for capital projects. Regular donations are also given to other local charities for projects, buildings and start-up costs

SAMPLE GRANTS £1,000 to Southend CAB for office equipment; £1,000 to Nazareth House for Voluntary Elderly Persons for running costs; £1,000 to Lulworth Court Holiday Home for Physically Handicapped for acquiring additional property; £1,000 to RNLI for a new lifeboat; £1,000 to Southend Relate for additional counsellors; £1,000 to Women's Aid Dove Project for new preventive abuse counselling; £1,000 to the Warehouse Project, Rayleigh for premium of youth activity facilities; £1,000 to Christ Church, Thorpe Bay for a new community hall; £1,000 to John Grooms, Dolphin Court for equipment for disabled residents; £1,000 to 4th Canvey Island Sea Scout Group for a new headquarters

FINANCES *Year* 1996–97 *Income* £72,383 *Grants* £39,550

TRUSTEES K J Crowe, T T Ray, Mrs D A Powell, Mrs E J Uren

NOTES Applications reviewed in May – no application form. Sae appreciated. Preliminary telephone calls considered unnecessary. Local branches preferred, both innovatory or long established

HOW TO APPLY To the address under Who To Apply To

WHO TO APPLY TO K J Crowe, Rosca Trust, 19 Avenue Terrace, Westcliff-on-Sea, Essex SS0 7PL

CC NO 259907   **ESTABLISHED** 1966

■ Ian Rose Charitable Foundation

This trust did not respond to CAF's request to amend its entry and, by 30 June 1998, CAF's researchers did not find financial records for later than 1995 on its file at the Charity Commission. Trusts are legally required to submit annual accounts to the Charity Commission under section 42 of the Charities Act 1993

WHAT IS FUNDED Welfare, general charitable purposes

WHO CAN BENEFIT There are no restrictions on the age; professional and economic group; family situation; religion and culture; and social circumstances of; or disease or medical condition suffered by, the beneficiaries

WHERE FUNDING CAN BE GIVEN Blackpool, the Fylde coast area

TRUSTEES K Philbin, I P Rose, J D Rose

HOW TO APPLY To the address below in writing

WHO TO APPLY TO I P Rose, Trustee, Ian Rose Charitable Foundation, 49 Newton Drive, Blackpool, Lancashire FY3 8EW

CC NO 1017911   **ESTABLISHED** 1993

■ The M K Rose Charitable Trust

WHAT IS FUNDED Jewish organisations, medical and welfare charities

WHO CAN BENEFIT To benefit Jews, at risk groups and those disadvantaged by poverty. There is no restriction on the disease or medical condition suffered by the beneficiaries

WHERE FUNDING CAN BE GIVEN Israel and West Midlands

FINANCES *Year* 1995–96 *Income* £60,040 *Grants* £50,000

TRUSTEES Henry Aron, Sharon Gould, Isabel Rose, Martin Rose

HOW TO APPLY To the address under Who To Apply To in writing

WHO TO APPLY TO Mrs S Gould, The M K Rose Charitable Trust, c/o 20 Coppice Close, Dovehouse Lane, Solihull B91 2ED

CC NO 1039857   **ESTABLISHED** 1994

■ Teresa Rosenbaum Golden Trust

WHAT IS FUNDED Medical research only

WHAT IS NOT FUNDED No grants to individuals, or for non-medical research

WHO CAN BENEFIT Independent vetted research projects, especially if departmentally backed and peer reviewed. Organisations benefiting research workers and medical professionals. There may be some restrictions on the disease or medical condition suffered by the beneficiaries

WHERE FUNDING CAN BE GIVEN UK

TYPE OF GRANT Project and research funding for up to three years will be considered

RANGE OF GRANTS £100–£43,000

SAMPLE GRANTS £43,000 to Research into Ageing for Alzheimer's Disease Fellowship; £17,000 to Research into Ageing for mental illness – depression research; £10,000 to Parkinson's Disease Society for research; £6,000 to Kings Medical Research Trust for cancer immune gene therapy research; £5,000 to Kings Medical Research Trust for stroke research; £5,000 to Alzheimer's Disease Society for research; £5,000 to Motor Neurone Disease Association for research; £5,000 to Migraine Trust for research; £5,000 to JAMI for day care centre for mentally ill; £5,000 to Shaare Zedek Medical Centre for women and children's centre in hospital

FINANCES *Year* 1995–96 *Income* £137,000 *Grants* £136,336

TRUSTEES R Ross, T Rosenbaum, R M Abbey

NOTES Six monthly progress reports in layman's terms are a condition of any grant made

HOW TO APPLY Annual report and accounts preferred and a clear concise lay summary of project, stating cost, duration, support and objective

WHO TO APPLY TO R Ross, Trust Administrator, Teresa Rosenbaum Golden Trust, 140 High Street, Edgware, Middlesex HA8 7LW *Tel* 0181-951 1996 *Fax* 0181-952 9414

CC NO 298582   **ESTABLISHED** 1987

■ The Rosenfeld Family Charitable Trust

WHAT IS FUNDED General charitable purposes

WHO CAN BENEFIT There are no restrictions on the age; professional and economic group; family situation; religion and culture; and social circumstances of; or disease or medical condition suffered by, the beneficiaries

WHERE FUNDING CAN BE GIVEN UK

RANGE OF GRANTS £80–£9,350

SAMPLE GRANTS £9,350 to Jewish Care; £6,200 to Foundation for Education; £600 to Wellbeing; £500 to Israel Music Foundation; £500 to Royal Academy of Music Alexander Technique Fund

FINANCES *Year* 1995 *Income* £11,414 *Grants* £20,880

TRUSTEES G Rosenfeld, J S Rosenfeld

WHO TO APPLY TO P P Rough, The Rosenfeld Family Charitable Trust, Roseidimond House, 11 Hatton Garden, London EC1N 8AH

CC NO 229039   **ESTABLISHED** 1961

■ Rotary Club of Barnsley Rockley Trust Fund

This trust did not respond to CAF's request to amend its entry and, by 30 June 1998, CAF's researchers did not find financial records for later than 1995 on its file at the Charity Commission. Trusts are legally required to submit annual accounts to the Charity Commission under section 42 of the Charities Act 1993

WHAT IS FUNDED General charitable purposes, in particular, the relief of the poor and needy

WHO CAN BENEFIT There are no restrictions on the age; professional and economic group; family situation; religion and culture; and social circumstances of; or disease or medical condition suffered by, the beneficiaries. However, particular favour is given to to at risk groups, those disadvantaged by poverty and the socially isolated

WHERE FUNDING CAN BE GIVEN UK and overseas

TRUSTEES R C Watkinson, W B Gaimster, B Farmer, G Day

WHO TO APPLY TO G Day, Rotary Club of Barnsley Rockley Trust Fund, 82 High Street, Clayton West, Huddersfield HD8 9NS

CC NO 1041608   **ESTABLISHED** 1994

■ Rotary Club of Bush Hill Park Trust Fund

WHAT IS FUNDED The relief of the poor and needy and other general charitable purposes

WHO CAN BENEFIT Organisations, particularly those benefiting at risk groups, those disadvantaged by poverty and socially isolated people

WHERE FUNDING CAN BE GIVEN UK

RANGE OF GRANTS £178–£2,000

SAMPLE GRANTS £2,000 to Macmillan Nurses; £2,000 to Life Education; £1,800 to Enterprise Boxing Club; £1,645 to Chase Farm Hospital Diabetes Unit; £1,000 to Faulkner Trust

FINANCES *Year* 1995 *Income* £14,922
Grants £12,152

WHO TO APPLY TO A Spencer, Rotary Club of Bush Hill Park Trust Fund, 69 Pine Grove, Brookmans Park, Hatfield, Hertfordshire AL9 7BL

CC NO 1049166   **ESTABLISHED** 1995

■ Rotary Club of Carshalton Beeches Trust Fund

WHAT IS FUNDED General charitable purposes, in particular, the relief of poverty and the advancement of education

WHO CAN BENEFIT Children, young adults and those disadvantaged by poverty. There are no restrictions on the professional and economic group; family situation; religion and culture; and social circumstances of; or disease or medical condition suffered by, the beneficiaries

WHERE FUNDING CAN BE GIVEN Sutton

SAMPLE GRANTS £3,500 to PHAB; £3,500 to Hand of Hope; £2,000 to Community Drug Helpline

FINANCES *Year* 1997 *Income* £44,457
Grants £9,000

TRUSTEES D Haine, I Benson, J Foxford, K Lohmann, J Izard

WHO TO APPLY TO K M Lohmann, Rotary Club of Carshalton Beeches Trust Fund, 19 Southway, Carshalton Beeches, Surrey SM5 4HP

CC NO 1035610   **ESTABLISHED** 1993

■ Rotary Club of Chesham Trust Fund

WHAT IS FUNDED The relief of poverty, the advancement of education and other general charitable purposes

WHO CAN BENEFIT Organisations, particularly those benefiting at risk groups, those disadvantaged by poverty and socially isolated people. Otherwise, there are no restrictions on the age; professional and economic group; family situation; religion and culture; and social circumstances of; or disease or medical condition suffered by, the beneficiaries

WHERE FUNDING CAN BE GIVEN In practice, Chesham and surrounding area

RANGE OF GRANTS £25–£1,527

SAMPLE GRANTS £1,527 to Rotary Foundation; £1,500 to Heritage House Hydrotherapy Pool; £1,010 to Riding for the Disabled; £500 to Ian Rennie Hospice; £500 to Georgescu-Roman

FINANCES *Year* 1997 *Income* £15,431
Grants £10,336

TRUSTEES A Curtis, L Lee, B H Pritchard, L H Procter

WHO TO APPLY TO L H Procter, Rotary Club of Chesham Trust Fund, Beeches, 1 Lycrome Lane, Chesham, Buckinghamshire HP5 3JY

CC NO 1032366   **ESTABLISHED** 1993

■ Rotary Club of Cuckfield and Lindfield Trust Fund

WHAT IS FUNDED Relief of the poor and needy and other general charitable purposes

WHO CAN BENEFIT Organisations, particularly those benefiting at risk groups, those disadvantaged by poverty and socially isolated people. Otherwise, there are no restrictions on the age; professional and economic group; family situation; religion and culture; and social circumstances of; or disease or medical condition suffered by, the beneficiaries

WHERE FUNDING CAN BE GIVEN UK

RANGE OF GRANTS £18–£3,000

SAMPLE GRANTS £3,000 to St Peters and St James Trust; £432 to Kids Out Day; £250 to Riding for the Disabled; £179 to Blackthorns for a televison set; £148 to Seniors Out Day

FINANCES *Year* 1995 *Income* £14,483
Grants £4,197

WHO TO APPLY TO M Wyaes, Rotary Club of Cuckfield and Lindfield Trust Fund, Little Croft, Gravelye Lane, Lindfield, West Sussex RH16 2SL

CC NO 1032500   **ESTABLISHED** 1994

■ Rotary Club of the Deepings Charitable Trust

WHAT IS FUNDED The relief of the poor and needy and other general charitable purposes

WHO CAN BENEFIT Organisations, particularly those benefiting at risk groups, those disadvantaged by poverty and socially isolated people. Otherwise, there are no restrictions on the age; professional and economic group; family situation; religion and culture; and social circumstances of; or disease or medical condition suffered by, the beneficiaries

WHERE FUNDING CAN BE GIVEN UK

FINANCES *Year* 1995 *Income* £13,407

WHO TO APPLY TO C A Martin, Rotary Club of the Deepings Charitable Trust, 8 Deeping St James Road, Deeping Gate, Peterborough PE6 9AS

CC NO 1031334   **ESTABLISHED** 1993

■ Rotary Club of Didbury and District Trust Fund

WHAT IS FUNDED The relief of the poor and needy and other general charitable purposes

WHO CAN BENEFIT Organisations, particularly those benefiting at risk groups, those disadvantaged by poverty and socially isolated people. Otherwise, there are no restrictions on the age; professional and economic group; family situation; religion and culture; and social circumstances of; or disease or medical condition suffered by, the beneficiaries

WHERE FUNDING CAN BE GIVEN UK and overseas

RANGE OF GRANTS £10–£2,000

SAMPLE GRANTS £2,000 to New Heart New Start; £653 to Parrawood Rural Trust; £300 to Didabury Civic Society; £300 to Rotary Ambassadorial Scholar; £195 to Adopt a Child

FINANCES *Year* 1995 *Income* £13,897 *Grants* £4,988

WHO TO APPLY TO R J Welsh, Rotary Club of Didbury and District Trust Fund, 25 Morville Road, Chorlton, Manchester M21 0UG

CC NO 1039690　　　　　**ESTABLISHED** 1982

■ Rotary Club of Elthorne-Hillingdon Trust Fund

WHAT IS FUNDED The relief of the poor and needy and other general charitable purposes

WHO CAN BENEFIT Organisations, particularly those benefiting at risk groups, those disadvantaged by poverty and socially isolated people. Otherwise, there are no restrictions on the age; professional and economic group; family situation; religion and culture; and social circumstances of; or disease or medical condition suffered by, the beneficiaries

WHERE FUNDING CAN BE GIVEN UK

SAMPLE GRANTS £11,000 to Harefield Hospital; £1,000 to Crossroads; £600 to Rotary Foundation; £329 to RYLA; £250 to Christian Lewis Trust

FINANCES *Year* 1997 *Income* £15,532 *Grants* £13,979

TRUSTEES M Christy, A J Lane, D Thorpe

WHO TO APPLY TO Harry A Scott, Rotary Club of Elthorne-Hillingdon Trust Fund, 14 Kent Close, Uxbridge, Middlesex UB8 1XR

CC NO 1032574　　　　　**ESTABLISHED** 1993

■ Rotary Club of Ewell Trust Fund

WHAT IS FUNDED The relief of the poor and needy and other general charitable purposes

WHO CAN BENEFIT Organisations, particularly those benefiting at risk groups, those disadvantaged by poverty and socially isolated people. Otherwise, there are no restrictions on the age; professional and economic group; family situation; religion and culture; and social circumstances of; or disease or medical condition suffered by, the beneficiaries

WHERE FUNDING CAN BE GIVEN UK and overseas

SAMPLE GRANTS £4,533 to Community Service Committee

FINANCES *Year* 1997 *Income* £18,090 *Grants* £7,795

TRUSTEES G J Ross, A F Heath, S C Reece

WHO TO APPLY TO A F Heath, Rotary Club of Ewell Trust Fund, Fitzalan House, 70 High Street, Ewell, Epsom, Surrey KT17 1RQ

CC NO 1034669　　　　　**ESTABLISHED** 1992

■ Rotary Club of Grantham Trust Fund

WHAT IS FUNDED The relief of the poor and needy and other general charitable purposes

WHO CAN BENEFIT Organisations, particularly those benefiting at risk groups, those disadvantaged by poverty and socially isolated people. Otherwise, there are no restrictions on the age; professional and economic group; family situation; religion and culture; and social circumstances of; or disease or medical condition suffered by, the beneficiaries

WHERE FUNDING CAN BE GIVEN UK, with preference for Lincolnshire, and overseas

FINANCES *Year* 1997 *Income* £22,272 *Grants* £20,679

TRUSTEES C R Lunn, J E Morris, B R Phillips, B Millhouse

WHO TO APPLY TO B Millhouse, Rotary Club of Grantham Trust Fund, 1 Hillside Drive, Grantham, Lincolnshire NG31 7EZ

CC NO 1035902　　　　　**ESTABLISHED** 1993

■ Rotary Club of Hadleigh Charitable Trust Fund

WHAT IS FUNDED The relief of the poor and needy through almshouses, holiday and respite accommodations, and community services. Voluntary organisations and support for volunteers; community arts and recreation; conservation and wildlife sanctuaries; health; and education and training are also considered for funding

WHAT IS NOT FUNDED Endowments, research and on-going projects will not be considered for funding

WHO CAN BENEFIT Individuals and organisations benefiting: people of all ages; academics and students; musicians; unemployed people; volunteers; parents and children; and one parent families. People from many different social circumstances, and those suffering from a variety of diseases and medical conditions will be considered

WHERE FUNDING CAN BE GIVEN Mainly Hadleigh (within a 10 mile radius). Also limited funds for worldwide charitable causes

TYPE OF GRANT One-off, capital and buildings. Funding is available for up to one year

RANGE OF GRANTS £20–£3,000, typical grant £100–£300

SAMPLE GRANTS £1,000 to Stephen Kirby Skin Bank for the provision of a national skin bank; £220 to Hadleigh Elderly People's Welfare Committee to assist with financing a summer outing for the over 60s; £200 to RSPB, Eastern Region towards building rotary hide at Snettisham Reserve; £110 to Hadleigh Guides; £110 to 1st Hadleigh Scouts

FINANCES *Year* 1997 *Income* £16,860 *Grants* £2,435

TRUSTEES D P Stokes, W D Yorke Edwards, I M Burne

HOW TO APPLY By letter giving full details of requirement

WHO TO APPLY TO D P Stokes, Rotary Club of Hadleigh Charitable Trust Fund, Ravenbank, Upper Street, Layham, Ipswich IP7 5JZ *Tel* 01473 827226

CC NO 1049781　　　　　**ESTABLISHED** 1995

■ Rotary Club of Heathrow Airport Trust Fund

WHAT IS FUNDED The relief of the poor and needy and other general charitable purposes

WHO CAN BENEFIT Organisations benefiting at risk groups, those disadvantaged by poverty and socially isolated people. Otherwise, there are no restrictions on the age; professional and economic group; family situation; religion and culture; and social circumstances of; or disease or medical condition suffered by, the beneficiaries

WHERE FUNDING CAN BE GIVEN UK

SAMPLE GRANTS £7,000 to Travelcare; £2,000 to Thame Valley Hospice; £500 to Spelthorne Farm; £500 to St John Ambulance, Hounslow; £500 to Harlington Hospice Association

FINANCES *Year* 1997 *Income* £21,080 *Grants* £14,743

WHO TO APPLY TO John Barker, Rotary Club of Heathrow Airport Trust Fund, 6 Sherwood Close, Bracknell, Berkshire RG12 2SB

CC NO 1032357   **ESTABLISHED** 1993

■ The Rotary Club of Ilfracombe Trust Fund

WHAT IS FUNDED General charitable objects in particular for the relief of the poor and needy

WHO CAN BENEFIT Organisations benefiting in particular at risk groups, those disadvantaged by poverty and socially isolated people

WHERE FUNDING CAN BE GIVEN UK

RANGE OF GRANTS £18–£7,500

SAMPLE GRANTS £7,500 to Children's Hospice South West; £7,500 to North Devon Hospice Care Trust; £3,000 to ND Cancer Care Trust; £2,000 to Jubilee Sailing Trust; £1,000 to Ilfracombe Museum; £850 to Battri Car; £800 to Ilfracombe School Holidays; £795 to Rotary Foundation; £750 to Ilfracombe and District Youth Band; £600 to Exmoor Search and Rescue

FINANCES *Year* 1997 *Income* £33,911 *Grants* £33,494

WHO TO APPLY TO S D Long, The Rotary Club of Ilfracombe Trust Fund, Ashleigh, St Brannocks Park Road, Ilfracombe, Devon EX34 8HX

CC NO 1037348   **ESTABLISHED** 1994

■ The Rotary Club of Kingston Upon Thames

WHAT IS FUNDED The relief of the poor and needy and other general charitable purposes

WHO CAN BENEFIT To benefit at risk groups, those disadvantaged by poverty and socially isolated people

WHERE FUNDING CAN BE GIVEN Kingston

TYPE OF GRANT One-off

RANGE OF GRANTS £50–£1,500

FINANCES *Year* 1997 *Income* £18,052 *Grants* £19,311

WHO TO APPLY TO P Jarvis, Hon Secretary, The Rotary Club of Kingston Upon Thames, Molehills, Mill Lane, Byfleet, Surrey KT14 7RR *Tel* 0181-547 1888

CC NO 1034645   **ESTABLISHED** 1994

■ Rotary Club of Kirby-in-Ashfield Trust Fund

WHAT IS FUNDED The relief of the poor and needy and other general charitable purposes

WHO CAN BENEFIT Organisations, particularly those benefiting at risk groups, those disadvantaged by poverty and socially isolated people. Otherwise, there are no restrictions on the age; professional and economic group; family situation; religion and culture; and social circumstances of; or disease or medical condition suffered by, the beneficiaries

WHERE FUNDING CAN BE GIVEN UK and overseas

SAMPLE GRANTS £1,050 to DARE; £900 to KM Children's Appeal; £625 to RIBI Foundation Fellowship; £571 to OAP Concert Festival Hall; £500 to Railway Signs sponsorship

FINANCES *Year* 1997 *Income* £18,885 *Grants* £8,595

TRUSTEES E Thompson, J K Jones, W Edge, J M McKinley

NOTES £6,736 donated in the UK and £1,859 overseas

WHO TO APPLY TO John D Peacock, Rotary Club of Kirby-in-Ashfield Trust Fund, 15 Forest Road, Annesley Woodhouse, Nottingham NG17 9BE

CC NO 1037261   **ESTABLISHED** 1993

■ Rotary Club of Lowestoft South Trust Fund

WHAT IS FUNDED The relief of the poor and needy and other general charitable purposes

WHO CAN BENEFIT Organisations benefiting people of all ages, those suffering from Alzheimer's disease, epilepsy, leprosy and polio will be considered

WHERE FUNDING CAN BE GIVEN Norfolk and Suffolk

TYPE OF GRANT One-off grants

RANGE OF GRANTS £100–£350

FINANCES *Year* 1997 *Income* £13,367 *Grants* £8,289

WHO TO APPLY TO K H Reeve, Rotary Club of Lowestoft South Trust Fund, 8 Cliftonville Road, Lowestoft, Suffolk NR33 7AY *Tel* 01502 567068

CC NO 1030514   **ESTABLISHED** 1994

■ Rotary Club of Nuneaton Trust Fund

WHAT IS FUNDED The relief of the poor and needy and other general charitable purposes

WHO CAN BENEFIT The poor and needy

WHERE FUNDING CAN BE GIVEN UK

FINANCES *Year* 1996–97 *Income* £16,631

WHO TO APPLY TO P A Jordan, Rotary Club of Nuneaton Trust Fund, 55 Church Lane, Nuneaton, Warwickshire CV10 0EY

CC NO 1036325   **ESTABLISHED** 1994

■ St Austell Rotary Club Charity Trust Fund

This trust did not respond to CAF's request to amend its entry and, by 30 June 1998, CAF's researchers did not find financial records for later than 1995 on its file at the Charity Commission. Trusts are legally required to submit annual accounts to the Charity Commission under section 42 of the Charities Act 1993

WHAT IS FUNDED The relief of the poor and needy and other charitable purposes

WHO CAN BENEFIT There are no restrictions on the age; professional and economic group; family situation; religion and culture; and social circumstances of; or disease or medical condition suffered by, the beneficiaries

WHERE FUNDING CAN BE GIVEN UK

TRUSTEES D J Forty, M T Harper, H L Rosevear, J C Worrow

WHO TO APPLY TO W C Geake, The Secretary, St Austell Rotary Club Charity Trust Fund, Crinnis House, Crinnis Close, Carlyon Bay, St Austell, Cornwall PL25 3SE

CC NO 1037000   **ESTABLISHED** 1994

■ The Rotary Club of Thornbury Trust Fund

WHAT IS FUNDED The relief of the poor and needy and other general charitable purposes including: support to voluntary and community organisations; hospices and medical research; conservation and environment; special needs education, training and costs of study; and community facilities and services

WHO CAN BENEFIT Individuals and organisations benefiting: people of all ages; academics; ex-service and service people; students; volunteers; those in care, fostered and adopted; disabled people; those disadvantaged by poverty; disaster victims and ex-offenders and those at risk of offending. There are some restrictions on the disease or medical condition suffered by the beneficiaries

WHERE FUNDING CAN BE GIVEN South Gloucestershire, UK and overseas

TYPE OF GRANT One-off and start-up costs will be considered

RANGE OF GRANTS £25–£5,000

SAMPLE GRANTS £5,000 to St Peter's Hospice for equipment; £2,500 to Special Care Baby Unit for equipment; £2,500 to University of Bristol Rheumatology Unit for research; £1,708 to 'The Club' Thornbury for equipment; £1,000 to Bristol Oncology Unit for equipment

FINANCES *Year* 1997 *Income* £19,883 *Grants* £10,619

TRUSTEES L Hales, J Massie, S Crawford, J Gibbon

HOW TO APPLY Initial telephone calls welcome

WHO TO APPLY TO S Crawford, The Rotary Club of Thornbury Trust Fund, 30 Cleveland Close, Thornbury, Bristol BS35 2YD *Tel* 01454 413106 *Fax* 01454 413406

CC NO 1035557   **ESTABLISHED** 1982

■ The Rotary Club of Titsey and District Trust Fund

WHAT IS FUNDED General charitable purposes

WHO CAN BENEFIT There are no restrictions on the age; professional and economic group; family situation; religion and culture; and social circumstances of; or disease or medical condition suffered by, the beneficiaries

WHERE FUNDING CAN BE GIVEN Surrey or overseas

TYPE OF GRANT One-off

RANGE OF GRANTS £50–£2,000

SAMPLE GRANTS £2,000 to St Piers Lingfield for equipment; £2,000 to League of Friends, Queen Victoria Hospital, East Grinstead for equipment; £2,000 to Grove Park Association for equipment; £2,000 to Surrey and Sussex Healthcare NHS Trust for equipment; £900 to Rotary Foundation towards Hope and Homes for children and polio plus

FINANCES *Year* 1997–98 *Income* £17,510 *Grants* £15,810

TRUSTEES The officials of the club - President, Vice President, Secretary, Treasurer

HOW TO APPLY By letter to the address under Who To Apply To

WHO TO APPLY TO M Flather, The Rotary Club of Titsey and District Trust Fund, Whiteoaks, 15 Chalkpit Lane, Oxted, Surrey RH8 0NF *Tel* 01883 712508

CC NO 1032237   **ESTABLISHED** 1994

■ The Rotary Club of Waltham Abbey Charity Trust Fund

WHAT IS FUNDED The relief of the poor and needy and other general charitable purposes

WHO CAN BENEFIT Organisations, particularly those benefiting at risk groups, those disadvantaged by poverty and socially isolated people. Otherwise, there are no restrictions on the age; professional and economic group; family situation; religion and culture; and social circumstances of; or disease or medical condition suffered by, the beneficiaries

WHERE FUNDING CAN BE GIVEN In practice, Waltham Abbey or overseas

FINANCES *Year* 1997 *Income* £13,474 *Grants* £6,456

TRUSTEES D Ingrey, P Johnson, F Rudgley, M Spall

NOTES During 1997, the main objective was to purchase a replacement Trimaran sailing craft, specially designed for the use of disabled persons

WHO TO APPLY TO D I Ingrey, The Rotary Club of Waltham Abbey Charity Trust Fund, 55 St Catherine's Road, Broxbourne, Hertfordshire EN10 7LB

CC NO 1032483   **ESTABLISHED** 1993

■ The Rotary Club of Widnes Trust Fund

This trust did not respond to CAF's request to amend its entry and, by 30 June 1998, CAF's researchers did not find financial records for later than 1995 on its file at the Charity Commission. Trusts are legally required to submit annual accounts to the Charity Commission under section 42 of the Charities Act 1993

WHAT IS FUNDED General charitable purposes

WHO CAN BENEFIT There are no restrictions on the age; professional and economic group; family situation; religion and culture; and social circumstances of; or disease or medical condition suffered by, the beneficiaries

WHERE FUNDING CAN BE GIVEN UK

WHO TO APPLY TO S R Jones, The Rotary Club of Widnes Trust Fund, 21 Upton Bridle Path, Widnes, Cheshire WA8 9HB

CC NO 1043861   **ESTABLISHED** 1994

■ The Rotary Club of Wigan Trust Fund

WHAT IS FUNDED The relief of the poor and needy and other general charitable purposes

WHO CAN BENEFIT Organisations, particularly those benefiting at risk groups, those disadvantaged by poverty and socially isolated people. Otherwise, there are no restrictions on the age; professional and economic group; family situation; religion and culture; and social circumstances of; or disease or medical condition suffered by, the beneficiaries

WHERE FUNDING CAN BE GIVEN UK and overseas

RANGE OF GRANTS £11–£2,424

SAMPLE GRANTS £2,424 to Rotary Foundation District 1280; £2,000 to Wigan Hospice New Start; £1,020 to The Samaritans; £1,000 to Life Education Trust; £1,000 to Comet Youth Club

FINANCES Year 1997 Income £16,408 Grants £13,442

TRUSTEES P Eastwood, D H Mellows, J J Crawford, P Catlow

NOTES £8,569 was donated in the UK and £4,873 overseas

WHO TO APPLY TO Platt and Fishwick, The Rotary Club of Wigan Trust Fund, The Old Bank, 47 King Street, Wigan WN1 1DB

CC NO 1037625   **ESTABLISHED** 1993

■ Wolverhampton Rotary Club Charitable Trust

WHAT IS FUNDED To support Rotary or Rotary sponsored charities, or direct payments to individuals in necessitous circumstances, or by the advancement of education

WHO CAN BENEFIT Only local organisations usually. Schools, elderly, Sea Cadets, Blind Eye Camp, Wolverhampton Probation and After Care Service

WHERE FUNDING CAN BE GIVEN Mainly Wolverhampton area

TYPE OF GRANT Preferably one-off

SAMPLE GRANTS £5,465 to Energy Stamps; £4,500 to Good Shepherd Trust; £2,036 to elderly persons and handicapped persons events; £1,866 to matching grant for a generator in Nepal; £1,500 to Prince's Youth Business Trust; £1,365 to Rotary Foundation; £750 to Beacon Centre for the Blind; £750 to Compton Hospice; £620 to Wolverhampton Eye Infirmary; £600 to St Peter's Collegiate School

FINANCES Year 1996 Income £26,401 Grants £26,401

TRUSTEES President, Secretary and Treasurer

PUBLICATIONS Local monthly bulletin for members only

HOW TO APPLY To the address under Who To Apply To for consideration by Governing Council

WHO TO APPLY TO P Gough, Wolverhampton Rotary Club Charitable Trust, 9 Beech Drive, Shifnal, Shropshire TF11 8HF

CC NO 220492   **ESTABLISHED** 1959

■ Rotary Club of Bishop's Waltham Charity Trust Fund

WHAT IS FUNDED The relief of the poor and needy and other general charitable purposes

WHO CAN BENEFIT Organisations, particularly those benefiting at risk groups, those disadvantaged by poverty and socially isolated people

WHERE FUNDING CAN BE GIVEN UK

SAMPLE GRANTS £793 to Kids Out; £618 to Water Aid; £597 to Nantes Jules Verne; £535 to Sight Savers; £511 to Bishop's Waltham House

FINANCES Year 1997 Income £13,345 Grants £7,473

WHO TO APPLY TO P Clarke, Rotary Club of Bishop's Waltham Charity Trust Fund, 10A Upper Basingwell Street, Bishops Waltham, Hampshire SO32 1AL

CC NO 1032602   **ESTABLISHED** 1993

■ The Rothenberg Charitable Foundation (formerly The Helma Charitable Trust)

This trust did not respond to CAF's request to amend its entry and, by 30 June 1998, CAF's researchers did not find financial records for later than 1995 on its file at the Charity Commission. Trusts are legally required to submit annual accounts to the Charity Commission under section 42 of the Charities Act 1993

WHAT IS FUNDED General charitable purposes. All applications considered on their own merit

WHO CAN BENEFIT Registered charities, institutions and individuals. There are no restrictions on the age; professional and economic group; family situation; religion and culture; and social circumstances of; or disease or medical condition suffered by, the beneficiaries

WHERE FUNDING CAN BE GIVEN UK and overseas

TRUSTEES E Wix, H Rothenberg, H S Garfield, R M Rothenberg

WHO TO APPLY TO R M Rothenberg, The Rothenberg Charitable Foundation 12 York Gate, London NW1 4QS

CC NO 248663   **ESTABLISHED** 1966

■ The Rothermere Foundation

WHAT IS FUNDED Establishment and maintenance of 'Rothermere Scholarships' to be awarded to graduates of the Memorial University of Newfoundland to enable them to undertake further periods of study in Britain; support of general charitable causes

WHO CAN BENEFIT Individual graduates of the Memorial University of Newfoundland who wish to undertake further study in Britain. Otherwise there are no restrictions on the age; professional and economic group; family situation; religion and culture; and social circumstances of; or disease or medical condition suffered by, the beneficiaries

WHERE FUNDING CAN BE GIVEN UK and overseas

TYPE OF GRANT Fellowship grants, scholarships, other educational grants

FINANCES Year 1994–95 Income £382,000

TRUSTEES Rt Hon Viscount Rothermere, G B W Walsh, V P W Harmsworth, J Harmsworth, J G Hemingway

HOW TO APPLY To the address under Who To Apply To in writing

WHO TO APPLY TO G B W Walsh, The Rothermere Foundation, Sweptone Walsh, Ref: GBWW, 9 Lincoln's Inn Fields, London WC2A 3BP

CC NO 314125   **ESTABLISHED** 1964

■ The Rotherwick Foundation

WHAT IS FUNDED (i) The provision of scholarships, bursaries and maintenance allowances and educational grants tenable at any school, university or other educational establishment to people under 25 who or whose parents or guardians are resident in the specified localities or have for not less than five years attended a school or other educational establishment within those localities. (ii) The provision of financial assistance, equipment, books and clothing to such people on leaving school, university or other educational establishment for entry into a trade or profession. (iii) The provision of amenities and facilities including public recreation and sports grounds for public benefit. (iv) The advancement of religion and other charitable works of, and the maintenance of, Protestant churches. (v) The provision, maintenance, improvement and equipment of hospitals, nursing homes, hospices and clinics. (vi) Such other charitable purposes as the Trustees in their absolute discretion think fit to support or establish

WHO CAN BENEFIT Individuals and organisations benefiting students and Protestant Christians. There are no restrictions on the age or, or disease or medical condition suffered by, the beneficiaries

WHERE FUNDING CAN BE GIVEN Within a 20 miles radius of wither Ashdown Park Hotel, Wych Cross, East Sussex or Tynley Hall Hotel, Rotherwick, Hampshire

FINANCES *Year* 1996 *Income* £300,000

WHO TO APPLY TO G C Bateman, Trustee and General Manager, The Rotherwick Foundation, Ashdown Park, Wych Cross, Forest Row, East Sussex RH18 5JR

CC NO 1058900   **ESTABLISHED** 1996

■ The Rothley Trust

WHAT IS FUNDED Children, community, education including school fees, handicapped, medical, religion, third world and youth. Apart from a few charities with which the Trust has been associated for many years, its activities are now directed exclusively towards North East England (Northumberland to North Yorkshire inclusive). Third world appeals, arising from this area only, will be considered

WHAT IS NOT FUNDED No grants outside the area Where Funding Can Be Given or for further education or for the repair of buildings used primarily for worship. Organisations for the elderly, ex-services, the arts and wildlife will not be considered. No grants to individuals

WHO CAN BENEFIT Registered charities benefiting: those in care, fostered and adopted; parents and children; and one parent families. There is no restriction on age, and few on social circumstances of the beneficiaries considered for funding

WHERE FUNDING CAN BE GIVEN Northumberland, North and South Tyneside, Newcastle upon Tyne, Gateshead, Durham and Cleveland

TYPE OF GRANT Mainly one-off donations towards specific projects and not running costs. Start-up costs, buildings and capital grants will be considered. Funding is available for up to one year

FINANCES *Year* 1997 *Income* £164,000 *Grants* £144,000

TRUSTEES Dr H A Armstrong, R P Gordon, R R V Nicholson, C J Davies, Mrs R Barkes, Mrs A Galbraith, C J Pumphrey

HOW TO APPLY No forms issued. Write to the address under Who To Apply To. Applications from the area Where Funding Can Be Given only will be acknowledged

WHO TO APPLY TO Mrs Diane Lennon, Secretary, The Rothley Trust, Mea House, Ellison Place, Newcastle upon Tyne NE1 8XS *Tel* 0191-232 7783 *Fax* 0191-232 7783

CC NO 219849   **ESTABLISHED** 1959

■ J Rothschild Assurance Foundation

WHAT IS FUNDED 1999 theme: 'Cherishing the Children'. 2000 theme: to be decided

WHAT IS NOT FUNDED No grants for research, scholarships, expeditions, individuals, political or religious organisations

WHO CAN BENEFIT Registered charities supporting children suffering from mental or physical handicaps, life threatening or degenerative illnesses

WHERE FUNDING CAN BE GIVEN UK

TYPE OF GRANT One-off

RANGE OF GRANTS £500–£8,000, average grant £3,600

SAMPLE GRANTS £7,216 to National Meningitis Trust for equipment/therapy for four children; £6,505 to British Deaf Association for the production of a children's video translated into sign language; £6,000 to Northway School for a multi sensory room for autistic children; £5,000 to Ladybird Development Group for multi sensory equipment; £5,000 to Mental Health Foundation towards their Children and Young Peoples' Mental Health Initiative; £5,000 to Wheelchair Fund for two wheelchairs; £4,943 to Whizz Kidz for two wheelchairs; £4,582 to Devizes and District Opportunity Group for a soft play area; £4,500 to Chernobyl Children Lifeline for 14 children from Belarus to visit UK for four weeks; £4,000 to Lister Lane Special School for specially adapted computers/electronic aids

FINANCES *Year* 1997 *Income* £123,018 *Grants* £94,921

TRUSTEES M Cooper-Smith, J Newman, Sir Mark Weinberg, M Wilson

HOW TO APPLY Initial telephone calls are welcome. There are guidelines and an application form available. Meetings are quarterly

WHO TO APPLY TO M Cooper-Smith, J Rothschild Assurance Foundation, J Rothschild House, Dollar Street, Cirencester, Gloucestershire GL7 2AQ *Tel* 01285 640302

CC NO 1031456   **ESTABLISHED** 1994

■ The Jacob Rothschild GAM Charitable Trust

WHAT IS FUNDED The preservation of heritage sites in the British Isles and the rest of the world for the benefit of the public; museums and galleries

WHERE FUNDING CAN BE GIVEN UK and overseas

FINANCES *Year* 1995–96 *Income* £1,300,000 *Grants* £1,607,500

TRUSTEES Hannah Brookfield, M E Hatch, Serena Rothschild, Nils Taube, Beth Tomassini, Lord Rothschild

HOW TO APPLY To the address under Who To Apply To in writing

WHO TO APPLY TO Miss S A Gallagher, Secretary, The Jacob Rothschild GAM Charitable Trust, 14 St James' Place, London SW1A 1NP *Tel* 0171-493 8111

CC NO 293647   **ESTABLISHED** 1986

■ The J Rothschild Group Charitable Trust (formerly The St James's Place Capital Charitable Trust)

WHAT IS FUNDED To select each year a limited number of areas for support. In 1998 support was for the protection of youth

540

Think carefully about every application. Is it justified?

WHAT IS NOT FUNDED Registered charities only. No grants to individuals. No overseas causes

WHO CAN BENEFIT In 1998, organisations benefiting the protection of youth

WHERE FUNDING CAN BE GIVEN UK

SAMPLE GRANTS £3,000 to East London Schools Fund for school home support services; £2,500 to Just Ask to provide counselling for homeless, unemployed and low waged young people in London; £2,500 to The Salvation Army; £2,500 to Life Education Centres for drug abuse prevention centres; £2,000 to the Field Lane Foundation for a drop-in centre for those families living in temporary accommodation near Kings Cross; £1,500 to Cautioning Support Project working with youth crime; £1,500 to Church Housing Trust working with young people aged 16–25; £1,500 to Wildside Trust to educate young people from urban areas; £1,000 to Capital Housing Project for homeless people in London; £1,000 to Eaves Housing for Women for homeless women

FINANCES *Year* 1997 *Income* £44,853 *Grants* £55,650

TRUSTEES Lord Rothschild, J W P Johnston, A D Loehnis (Chairman)

PUBLICATIONS Annual Report prepared

HOW TO APPLY Considered quarterly

WHO TO APPLY TO Mrs D R Lovegrove, (Administrator), The J Rothschild Group Charitable Trust, 27 St James's Place, London SW1A 1NR *Tel* 0171-493 8111

CC NO 298238   **ESTABLISHED** 1987

■ The Roughley Charitable Trust

WHAT IS FUNDED General charitable purposes. Funds fully committed to projects known to the Trustees

WHO CAN BENEFIT There are no restrictions on the age; professional and economic group; family situation; religion and culture; and social circumstances of; or disease or medical condition suffered by, the beneficiaries

WHERE FUNDING CAN BE GIVEN Mainly Midlands

FINANCES *Year* 1997 *Income* £111,569 *Grants* £76,800

TRUSTEES Mrs M K Smith, G W L Smith, Mrs D M Newton, M C G Smith, J R L Smith

HOW TO APPLY **This Trust states that it does not respond to unsolicited applications**

WHO TO APPLY TO Mrs M K Smith, The Roughley Charitable Trust, 2B Bracebridge Road, Sutton Coldfield, West Midlands B74 2SB

CC NO 264037   **ESTABLISHED** 1972

■ Alnwick and District Round Table Charity Fund

WHAT IS FUNDED General charitable purposes

WHO CAN BENEFIT Individuals and organisations. There are no restrictions on the age; professional and economic group; family situation; religion and culture; and social circumstances of; or disease or medical condition suffered by, the beneficiaries

WHERE FUNDING CAN BE GIVEN Alnwick and District

RANGE OF GRANTS £50–£1,519

SAMPLE GRANTS £1,519 to Old Folks Christmas Parcels; £1,500 to NCC Community Safety Strategy; £600 to British Red Cross; £500 to Alnwick Christmas Lights; £500 to Coquet Shorebase Trust

FINANCES *Year* 1996–97 *Income* £20,371 *Grants* £7,144

TRUSTEES S Cairns (Treasurer)

HOW TO APPLY Contact any member of the Round Table

WHO TO APPLY TO S Cairns, Alnwick and District Round Table Charity Fund, St Aidan's, 43 Swansfield Park Road, Alnwick, Northumberland NE66 1AR

CC NO 1049316   **ESTABLISHED** 1995

■ Barking Round Table Charitable Trust Fund

WHAT IS FUNDED General charitable purposes for the general benefit of the residents of Barking and Dagenham

WHO CAN BENEFIT To benefit the residents of the London Borough of Barking and Dagenham. There are no restrictions on the age; professional and economic group; family situation; religion and culture; and social circumstances of; or disease or medical condition suffered by, the beneficiaries

WHERE FUNDING CAN BE GIVEN London Borough of Barking and Dagenham

FINANCES *Year* 1997 *Income* £29,576 *Grants* £3,947

TRUSTEES A Ford, J O'Neill, M Reed

WHO TO APPLY TO A Ford, Barking Round Table Charitable Trust Fund, 98 Argyle Road, Custom House, London E16 3NE

CC NO 1047096   **ESTABLISHED** 1995

■ Bath and District Round Table No 91 Charity Account

WHAT IS FUNDED General charitable purposes

WHO CAN BENEFIT Local charities. There are no restrictions on the age; professional and economic group; family situation; religion and culture; and social circumstances of; or disease or medical condition suffered by, the beneficiaries

WHERE FUNDING CAN BE GIVEN Bath and District

RANGE OF GRANTS £100–£3,200

SAMPLE GRANTS £3,200 to Bath City Farm; £3,000 to Bath Opportunity Group

FINANCES *Year* 1998 *Income* £18,864 *Grants* £6,300

TRUSTEES W Long, J Richards, S Stafford

WHO TO APPLY TO G Barber, Bath and District Round Table No 91 Charity Account, 28 Bloomfile Avenue, Bath, Somerset BA2 3AB

CC NO 1049162   **ESTABLISHED** 1995

■ Berkhamsted Round Table Charitable Trust

WHAT IS FUNDED Charities working in the fields of: education and training; community facilities and services; community development; and support to volunteers and voluntary and community organisations

WHO CAN BENEFIT Individuals and organisations benefiting at risk groups, carers, disabled people, those disadvantaged by poverty, socially isolated people and victims of abuse. There is no restriction on the age or family situation of the beneficiaries

WHERE FUNDING CAN BE GIVEN In practice, Berkhamsted and District

TYPE OF GRANT Usually one-off grants only. Capital and project will be considered. Funding is available for up to one year

Does the trust you have chosen match your needs? Haphazard applications waste postage and time

541

SAMPLE GRANTS £15,000 for Berkhamsted Community Minibus; £3,000 for Outward Bound holidays for local needy children; £1,000 to local playgroup for equipment
FINANCES *Year* 1997 *Income* £26,264 *Grants* £3,544
HOW TO APPLY Written application
WHO TO APPLY TO John Ward, Berkhamsted Round Table Charitable Trust, 50 Woodlands Avenue, Berkhamsted, Hertfordshire HP4 2JQ
Tel 01831 141919
CC NO 1048981   **ESTABLISHED** 1995

■ Bicester Round Table Trust Fund

WHAT IS FUNDED General charitable purposes
WHO CAN BENEFIT There are no restrictions on the age; professional and economic group; family situation; religion and culture; and social circumstances of; or disease or medical condition suffered by, the beneficiaries
WHERE FUNDING CAN BE GIVEN UK
RANGE OF GRANTS £100–£2,000
SAMPLE GRANTS £2,000 for adapted showers; £1,980 for Christmas vouchers; £1,500 to Bullingdon Playscheme; £410 to Disability Serv's Bike; £300 to St Mary's
FINANCES *Year* 1997 *Income* £20,600 *Grants* £7,736
WHO TO APPLY TO C A Watkins, Bicester Round Table Trust Fund, Bicester, 10 Park Close, Middleton Stoney, Oxfordshire OX6 8ST
CC NO 1051326   **ESTABLISHED** 1995

■ Round Table Charitable Trust Fund

WHAT IS FUNDED General charitable purposes
WHO CAN BENEFIT There are no restrictions on the age; professional and economic group; family situation; religion and culture; and social circumstances of; or disease or medical condition suffered by, the beneficiaries
WHERE FUNDING CAN BE GIVEN In practice, Kenilworth and surrounding areas
SAMPLE GRANTS £15,945 to Waverley Day Centre; £3,500 to Warwick Hospital for a paediatric gastroscope; £1,000 to Kenilworth Alzheimer's; £600 to Radio Warnford; £500 to Kenilworth Youth for Christ; £500 to Children in Need; £420 to Child Development Visit; £400 to Dunblane Round Table; £345 to an individual for a wheelchair battery; £300 to Kenilworth Talking News
FINANCES *Year* 1997 *Income* £31,141 *Grants* £25,360
TRUSTEES R Anderson, J Higgitt, M McGuire, D Plant, M Tyrer
WHO TO APPLY TO A C Appleton, Round Table Charitable Trust Fund, 106 Marlborough Road, Coventry CV2 4ER
CC NO 1044955   **ESTABLISHED** 1995

■ Dorchester Round Table Charitable Trust Fund

WHAT IS FUNDED General charitable purposes
WHO CAN BENEFIT There are no restrictions on the age; professional and economic group; family situation; religion and culture; and social circumstances of; or disease or medical condition suffered by, the beneficiaries
WHERE FUNDING CAN BE GIVEN Dorset

FINANCES *Year* 1996 *Income* £14,079 *Grants* £4,606
WHO TO APPLY TO J Downes, Dorchester Round Table Charitable Trust Fund, 137 Damers Road, Dorchester, Dorset DT1 2JP
CC NO 1047361   **ESTABLISHED** 1995

■ Henleaze Round Table Charity Account

WHAT IS FUNDED General charitable purposes
WHO CAN BENEFIT There are no restrictions on the age; professional and economic group; family situation; religion and culture; and social circumstances of; or disease or medical condition suffered by, the beneficiaries
WHERE FUNDING CAN BE GIVEN UK
FINANCES *Year* 1997 *Income* £20,924 *Grants* £5,716
TRUSTEES A Andrews, C Bray, K Tucker
WHO TO APPLY TO Philip L C Burke, Henleaze Round Table Charity Account, 10 Theresa Avenue, Bristol BS7 9EP
CC NO 1050002   **ESTABLISHED** 1995

■ Reading Round Table Charitable Trust

WHAT IS FUNDED General charitable purposes
WHO CAN BENEFIT There are no restrictions on the age; professional and economic group; family situation; religion and culture; and social circumstances of; or disease or medical condition suffered by, the beneficiaries
WHERE FUNDING CAN BE GIVEN UK and overseas
RANGE OF GRANTS £38–£3,300
SAMPLE GRANTS £3,300 to the Duchess of Kent House; £1,100 to Give a Child a Chance; £1,100 to Brain Injured Children; £741 to Food Hampers for the Old and Needy in Reading; £500 to British Red Cross; £500 to an individual; £150 to the Child Injury Prevention Service; £51 to Food Hampers for Shinfield Infants School; £50 to Norcot Residents' Association; £38 to Trinity Day Centre
FINANCES *Year* 1997 *Income* £25,194 *Grants* £7,532
TRUSTEES A Johnson, C Long, G Robinson
WHO TO APPLY TO W Gornall-King, Reading Round Table Charitable Trust, 56 Allcroft Road, Reading, Berkshire RG1 5HN
CC NO 1055361   **ESTABLISHED** 1996

■ Stafford and District Round Table Charitable Trust

WHAT IS FUNDED General charitable purposes
WHO CAN BENEFIT There are no restrictions on the age; professional and economic group; family situation; religion and culture; and social circumstances of; or disease or medical condition suffered by, the beneficiaries
WHERE FUNDING CAN BE GIVEN UK and overseas
SAMPLE GRANTS £5,000 to Genesis Orthotics
FINANCES *Year* 1997 *Income* £19,597 *Grants* £8,760
WHO TO APPLY TO P M M Farrington, Stafford and District Round Table Charitable Trust, 6 Boardman Crescent, Castlefields, Stafford, Staffordshire ST16 1AF
CC NO 1064080   **ESTABLISHED** 1997

■ Tenby Round Table Charitable Trust Fund

WHAT IS FUNDED General charitable purposes

WHO CAN BENEFIT There are no restrictions on the age; professional and economic group; family situation; religion and culture; and social circumstances of; or disease or medical condition suffered by, the beneficiaries

WHERE FUNDING CAN BE GIVEN In practice Tenby and Saundersfoot District

RANGE OF GRANTS £50–£1,000

SAMPLE GRANTS £1,000 to Friends of Community; £600 to Gateway Club; £400 to Friends of Tenby Hospital; £200 to RNLI; £200 to the Fire Brigade

FINANCES *Year* 1997 *Income* £14,755 *Grants* £3,150

WHO TO APPLY TO J Boot, Tenby Round Table Charitable Trust Fund, Home Farm Cottage, Lydstep, Tenby, Pembrokeshire

CC NO 1051284 **ESTABLISHED** 1995

■ Tettenhall Round Table Charitable Trust

WHAT IS FUNDED General charitable purposes

WHO CAN BENEFIT There are no restrictions on the age; professional and economic group; family situation; religion and culture; and social circumstances of; or disease or medical condition suffered by, the beneficiaries

WHERE FUNDING CAN BE GIVEN UK and overseas

FINANCES *Year* 1997 *Income* £15,978

WHO TO APPLY TO S Maddox, Tettenhall Round Table Charitable Trust, Amberley, Great Moor Road, Pattingham, Wolverhampton, Staffordshire WV6 7AU *Tel* 01902 741144

CC NO 1051226 **ESTABLISHED** 1995

■ Totnes Round Table Charitable Trust Fund

WHAT IS FUNDED General charitable purposes

WHO CAN BENEFIT There are no restrictions on the age; professional and economic group; family situation; religion and culture; and social circumstances of; or disease or medical condition suffered by, the beneficiaries

WHERE FUNDING CAN BE GIVEN UK

FINANCES *Year* 1997 *Income* £34,343 *Grants* £27,988

WHO TO APPLY TO Mike Shires, Totnes Round Table Charitable Trust Fund, 10 Sherwell Close, Staverton, Devon TQ9 6PH

CC NO 1044409 **ESTABLISHED** 1995

■ Worcester Round Table Charity Account

WHAT IS FUNDED General charitable purposes

WHO CAN BENEFIT There are no restrictions on the age; professional and economic group; family situation; religion and culture; and social circumstances of; or disease or medical condition suffered by, the beneficiaries

WHERE FUNDING CAN BE GIVEN UK

SAMPLE GRANTS £1,843 to purchase an electric wheelchair

FINANCES *Year* 1996 *Income* £14,252 *Grants* £2,650

TRUSTEES K P Ruff, T J Young

WHO TO APPLY TO A Smith, Worcester Round Table Charity Account, Mabs Cottage, Trotshill, Worcester WR4 0AQ

CC NO 1049042 **ESTABLISHED** 1995

■ The Row Fogo Charitable Foundation

WHAT IS FUNDED Grants are given to organisations which carry out medical research, particularly in the field of neuroscience; also to local charity projects and to small charities

WHAT IS NOT FUNDED Grants are not awarded to individuals

WHO CAN BENEFIT Funding primarily goes to research workers and those suffering from neurological diseases, but other medical research and charitable purposes are considered

WHERE FUNDING CAN BE GIVEN Edinburgh, Lothian and Dunblane

FINANCES *Year* 1996–97 *Income* £111,000 *Grants* £89,000

TRUSTEES Dr C Brough, E J Cuthbertson, A W Waddell

PUBLICATIONS Accounts and an Annual Report are available from the Trust

HOW TO APPLY Applications should be made in writing to the address under Who To Apply To

WHO TO APPLY TO Andrew M C Dalgleish, The Row Fogo Charitable Foundation, Messrs Brodies WS, 15 Atholl Crescent, Edinburgh EH3 8HA *Tel* 0131-228 3777

SC NO SCO 09685 **ESTABLISHED** 1970

■ The Christopher Rowbotham Charitable Trust

WHAT IS FUNDED To support selected national charities with branches in the North West and North East, and local charities, as stated below. Priority given to smaller charities with low overheads. This Trust will consider funding: infrastructure and development; health care; health education; education and training; and community services

WHAT IS NOT FUNDED Registered charities only. Applications from individuals, including students, are ineligible. No grants made in response to general appeals from large national organisations. No grants overseas. No grants for capital projects

WHO CAN BENEFIT Organisations benefiting: children; young adults; older people; ex-service and service people; medical professionals; retired people; seafarers and fishermen; disabled sportsmen and women; teachers and governesses; unemployed people; and volunteers' There are few restrictions on the social circumstances of, or disease and medical condition suffered by the beneficiaries

WHERE FUNDING CAN BE GIVEN NE England, NW England

TYPE OF GRANT Capital, core costs, one-off, recurring costs, running costs and start-up costs. Funding can be given for up to and over three years. Salaries never considered

RANGE OF GRANTS £100 to £750. Largest grant £3,500

SAMPLE GRANTS £3,500 to Shiplake College; £2,000 to Winged Fellowship for general purposes and respite holidays; £2,000 to Royal Commonwealth Society for the Blind for eye treatment programmes; £1,000 to RUKBA for annuities for retired professionals; £1,000 to Royal Star and Garter Home for disabled ex-service men and women; £1,000 to Instant Muscle for helping unemployed gain employment; £1,000 to Disabled Living Foundation for aids to inform and advise the disabled; £750 to Calvert Trust, Kielder for activities and respite care; £750 to Calvert Trust, Keswick for holidays; £750 to Fairbridge, Tyne and Wear to help young disadvantaged people gain further learning

FINANCES *Year* 1997 *Income* £50,000 *Grants* £48,000

TRUSTEES Mrs C A Jackson, Mrs E J Wilkinson

NOTES Appeals from the North East should be sent to Mrs Jackson at address below. Appeals from the North West should be sent to Mrs Wilkinson: PO Box 43, Bolton, Lancashire BL1 5EZ

HOW TO APPLY At any time. Trustees meet annually in May. No applications acknowledged. Initial telephone calls are not welcome. There are no application forms, guidelines or deadlines, and no sae is required

WHO TO APPLY TO Mrs C A Jackson, The Christopher Rowbotham Charitable Trust, 18 Northumberland Square, North Shields NE30 1PX

CC NO 261991 **ESTABLISHED** 1970

■ The Rowlands Trust

WHAT IS FUNDED Medical and scientific research; the welfare of the elderly, infirm, poor and handicapped; support for the arts and conservation; the encouragement of education and training for individuals to better themselves

WHAT IS NOT FUNDED No grants to be made in areas where statutory funding is available

WHO CAN BENEFIT People of all ages, research workers, disabled people and those disadvantaged by poverty

WHERE FUNDING CAN BE GIVEN West and South Midlands, including Gloucester, Birmingham, Hereford and Worcester, and Shropshire

TRUSTEES C P Harris, G B G Hingley, A C S Horden

HOW TO APPLY Application forms are available from the address below. Trustees will not consider letters or proposals without an application form

WHO TO APPLY TO Miss L S Woodhead, Professional Adviser, The Rowlands Trust, c/o Wragge & Co, Solicitors, 55 Colmore Row, Birmingham B3 2AS

CC NO 1062148 **ESTABLISHED** 1997

■ The Rowley Trust

WHAT IS FUNDED Charities working for the benefit of women and girls

WHO CAN BENEFIT Individuals, registered charities and organisations benefiting women and girls. There are no restrictions on the age; professional and economic group; family situation; religion and culture; and social circumstances of; or disease or medical condition suffered by, the beneficiaries

WHERE FUNDING CAN BE GIVEN Staffordshire and adjacent counties

FINANCES *Year* 1997 *Income* £52,413 *Grants* £40,811

HOW TO APPLY Application form and guidelines can be obtained from the Clerk of the Trust, J G Langford

WHO TO APPLY TO J G Langford, The Clerk, The Rowley Trust, 25 Greengate Street, Stafford ST16 2HU *Tel* 01785 252377

CC NO 508630 **ESTABLISHED** 1988

■ The Royal Botanical & Horticultural Society of Manchester and the Northern Counties

WHAT IS FUNDED Financial assistance to local gardens or projects of horticultural interest and local horticultural societies in the North West

WHO CAN BENEFIT Horticultural societies, shows and gardens of horticultural interest

WHERE FUNDING CAN BE GIVEN North West

TYPE OF GRANT Cash payment towards prize money or specific expenditure

RANGE OF GRANTS £25–£2,000

FINANCES *Year* 1997 *Income* £17,831 *Grants* £16,560

TRUSTEES Incorporated Governors of the Society

HOW TO APPLY Annual by 31 October each year in writing

WHO TO APPLY TO A Pye, MA, FCA, The Royal Botanical & Horticultural Society, PO Box 500, 201 Deansgate, Manchester M60 2AT *Tel* 0161-455 8380 *Fax* 0161-829 3803

CC NO 226683 **ESTABLISHED** 1827

■ The Royal British Legion (incorporated by Royal Charter)

WHAT IS FUNDED The welfare of men and women who have served in the Armed Forces, as well as those who have served in the Mercantile Marine during hostilities afloat, the Allied Civil Police Forces, the Home Guard and Voluntary Aid Societies and their widows, children and dependants. All eligible applications considered on their merits

WHO CAN BENEFIT Those who have served in HM Forces, their widows and dependants, this includes those who have served in the Mercantile Marines, the Allied Civil Police forces, the Home Guard and Voluntary Aid Society

WHERE FUNDING CAN BE GIVEN UK

TYPE OF GRANT Recurrent or one-off

SAMPLE GRANTS £861,000 to Royal British Legion Industries Ltd; £785,000 to the Officers Association; £102,000 to St Dunstans; £30,000 to Ex-Service Mental Welfare Society; £24,000 to British Commonwealth Ex-Services League; £23,000 to Earl Haig Fund – Scotland; £20,000 to Haig Homes; £15,000 to Not Forgotten Association; £15,000 to Ex-Service Fellowship Centres

FINANCES *Year* 1997 *Income* £42,967,000 *Grants* £7,039,000

TRUSTEES National Executive Council: J F Ashworth, J J Brookes, C W Broughton, Lt Col T B Buckby, I P Cannell, J G H Champ, G G Downing, F D C Duff, R I Glendinning, J Hawthornthwaite, N Rogers, D P Smith, B C N Soffe, F Sowden, J A Tedder, M E W Tidnam, J B Tuckley, J E Williamson

PUBLICATIONS *The Legion* magazine, Annual Report

HOW TO APPLY At any time. Individual applicants to branches; other Societies to the Secretary General

WHO TO APPLY TO I Townsend, Secretary General, The Royal British Legion, 48 Pall Mall, London SW1Y 5JY

CC NO 219279 **ESTABLISHED** 1921

■ Royal London Aid Society

WHAT IS FUNDED Prisoners, ex-prisoners and young people at risk. Funding is given for care in the community and crime prevention schemes

WHO CAN BENEFIT Largely individuals and organisations benefiting ex-offenders and those at risk of offending

WHERE FUNDING CAN BE GIVEN England

TYPE OF GRANT Core costs and recurring costs. Funding may be given for up to one year

SAMPLE GRANTS £5,000 to London Prison Community Links for a support grant; £3,000 to Prison Video Trust for a support grant; £2,400 to Shechem House Trust; £2,400 to Barking and Dagenham Befrienders towards additional staff support; £1,500 to Blantyre House Prison Fund for education; £1,500 to Streatham Youth; £1,500 to Koestler Art Awards; £1,000 to Meridan Youth Trust towards equipment; £1,200 to Prisoners Families and Friends Services for family support; £1,000 to CCTL for development support

FINANCES *Year* 1997 *Income* £68,000
Grants £35,000

TRUSTEES D H Kirk, MBE, FCA (Chairman), Miss I O D Harrison, MBE, JP (Vice Chairman), A G F Young, MA (Secretary), I R C Bieber, JP, Miss E A Day, I M Kirk, G E Mitchell, JP, Rev P Timms, OBE, FIMgt

HOW TO APPLY Application forms are available from the address under Who To Apply To upon written request. Applications considered each quarter: March, June, September and December

WHO TO APPLY TO G McCarthy, General Administrator, Royal London Aid Society, 84 Upney Lane, Barking, Essex IG11 9LR *Tel* 0181-594 2168

CC NO 214695   **ESTABLISHED** 1863

■ The Royal Society of St George Charitable Trust

WHAT IS FUNDED To support patriotic causes (non-political)

WHAT IS NOT FUNDED No grants to non-political and unsectarian causes

WHO CAN BENEFIT English organisations and individuals. There are no restrictions on the age; professional and economic group; family situation; religion and culture; and social circumstances of; or disease or medical condition suffered by, the beneficiaries

WHERE FUNDING CAN BE GIVEN England

SAMPLE GRANTS £1,000 to Westminster Branch RSSG; £750 to Westminster Abbey Charity Fund; £750 to Guide Association Seaton, Devon for HQ refurbishment; £500 to 261 (Guildford) Squadron Air Training Corps for new Hut 3; £500 each to four individuals for Raleigh International to Zimbabwe

FINANCES *Year* 1995 *Income* £18,062
Grants £10,625

TRUSTEES G A R Andrews (Chairman), Mrs G Bailey, W R Firth, K A Heywood

PUBLICATIONS *England* (annually)

WHO TO APPLY TO K A Heywood, FCA, The Royal Society of St George Charitable Trust, Dartmouth House, 37 Charles Street, London W1X 8AB

CC NO 263076   **ESTABLISHED** 1971

■ The Royal Theatrical Fund

WHAT IS FUNDED Since the granting of a new Charter in 1974 The Board of Directors through it's Grants Committee are able to offer aid to all applicants who are, or have been, members of the Entertainment Industry. Charities working in the fields of: hospice at home; respite care; and care for carers will be considered

WHAT IS NOT FUNDED We do not fund school fees, or course fees

WHO CAN BENEFIT Individuals. Occasionally to theatrical charities benefiting: young adults; older people; actors and entertainment professionals; musicians; writers and poets

WHERE FUNDING CAN BE GIVEN UK and international, if applicants UK nationals

TYPE OF GRANT One-off. Can be paid monthly on review. Shares with other charities. Capital, running costs with funding for up to or more than three years considered

SAMPLE GRANTS £5,600 to a director for nursing home fees; £4,200 to a dancer for residential homes fees; £3,700 to a pianist for home care nursing; £2,500 to an actor for rent arrears; £1,000 to an actress (share) for a special wheelchair; £840 to a stage manager for domestic bills; £720 to a singer as a monthly allowance; £720 to a circus artiste for winter bills; £600 to an actor (shared) for a hearing aid; £520 to a blind variety artiste as a monthly allowance

FINANCES *Year* 1996 *Income* £366,550

TRUSTEES Annuity Fund – Chairman and Vice Chairman, General Fund – Chairman and Board of Directors

PUBLICATIONS *Backstage* - newsletter

NOTES The Association was formed to provide pensions for actors. In 1974 a new Royal Charter was granted to extend the Board's powers to make grants to those coming within its orbit as laid down under What is Funded

HOW TO APPLY By post or telephone. Application form then sent to be signed and completed

WHO TO APPLY TO Mrs R M Foster, The Royal Theatrical Fund, 11 Garrick Street, London WC2E 9AR *Tel* 0171 836 3322

CC NO 222080   **ESTABLISHED** 1839

■ The Royal Victoria Hall Foundation

WHAT IS FUNDED Encouragement of organisations devoted to the development of and education in theatrical pursuits, infrastructure and technical support, opera and theatre

WHAT IS NOT FUNDED Grants made for theatrical pursuits only, not for the fine arts or music and dance which is not in a theatrical context. Applications from individuals (eg students) not accepted, no retrospective grants made so applications must be timed to coincide with twice yearly Trustees' meetings, no repeat grants within two years

WHO CAN BENEFIT Theatre groups, youth and children's theatre benefiting children; young adults; older people; actors and entertainment professionals who by reason of their social and economic circumstances have a genuine need

WHERE FUNDING CAN BE GIVEN Greater London only

TYPE OF GRANT Buildings, capital, feasibility studies, one-off, projects, recurring costs, running costs and salaries are all considered for one year or less

RANGE OF GRANTS Usually between £500 and £1,000

Does the trust you have chosen match your needs? Haphazard applications waste postage and time

545

SAMPLE GRANTS £2,000 to Chicken Shed for stagecraft needs; £2,000 to Polka Children's Theatre for technical improvements; £1,500 to Graeae Theatre Company for their youth and community programme; £1,000 to Southwark Festival to stage a community event; £1,000 to Operate Theatre Company towards their production 'Miss Julie'; £1,000 to Battersea Arts Centre towards the Sam Shepherd Festival; £1,000 to Serio Ensemble for lighting; £1,000 to Theatre Pur for publicity for production at Young Vic; £1,000 to Ideal Theatre Company towards their production 'Haven'; £1,000 to Perfect Fool Theatre Company towards their production 'The Sentence'

FINANCES *Year* 1997 *Income* £57,460 *Grants* £35,050

TRUSTEES Miss D Gane (Chairman), Ms V Colgan, D Collier, P Heritage, P Hiley, D Russell, M Redington, Miss A Stanesby, S Walters

PUBLICATIONS Annual Report and financial statements

HOW TO APPLY By 1 February and 1 August (to coincide with Trustees' April and October meetings). No replies without a stamped addressed envelope

WHO TO APPLY TO Mrs C A Cooper, The Royal Victoria Hall Foundation, 111 Green Street, Sunbury-on-Thames, Middlesex TW16 6QX

CC NO 211246   **ESTABLISHED** 1891

■ The Alfred and Frances Rubens Charitable Trust

WHAT IS FUNDED General charitable purposes

WHO CAN BENEFIT Restricted to registered charities. There are no restrictions on the age; professional and economic group; family situation; religion and culture; and social circumstances of; or disease or medical condition suffered by, the beneficiaries

WHERE FUNDING CAN BE GIVEN UK

TYPE OF GRANT Recurrent

RANGE OF GRANTS £25–£5,000

SAMPLE GRANTS £5,000 to Jewish Board of Deputies Charitable Fund; £5,000 to League of Jewish Women; £3,375 to West London Synagogue; £3,345 to Jewish Museum; £2,025 to National Council of Women of Great Britain; £2,000 to Jewish Care; £2,000 to World Jewish Relief; £1,068 to Nightingale House (Home for Aged Jews); £1,000 to Jewish Historical Society; £1,000 to Norwood Child Care

FINANCES *Year* 1996 *Income* £36,762 *Grants* £31,313

TRUSTEES F Rubens, K D Rubens, A Rubens, J F Millan

HOW TO APPLY **This Trust states that it does not respond to unsolicited applications**

WHO TO APPLY TO A Rubens, Trustee, The Alfred and Frances Rubens Charitable Trust, 16 Grosvenor Place London SW1X 7HH

CC NO 264430   **ESTABLISHED** 1972

■ The Rubin Foundation

WHAT IS FUNDED Primarily, but not exclusively, Jewish charities. Also, medical charities, museums and universities

WHO CAN BENEFIT Organisations benefiting Jewish people, students and the sick. There is no restriction on the disease or medical condition suffered by the beneficiaries. Medical professionals and research workers may be supported

WHERE FUNDING CAN BE GIVEN UK

RANGE OF GRANTS Below £250–£150,000

SAMPLE GRANTS £150,000 to the Jewish Philanthropic Association; £150,000 to Joint Jewish Charitable Trust; £51,000 to The Reform Foundation Trust; £25,000 to British ORT; £25,000 to University of Oxford; £22,000 to Imperial War Museum; £20,000 to Yigal Allon Education Trust; £20,000 to The Holocaust Educational Trust; £15,850 to World Jewish Relief; £10,025 to West London Synagogue

FINANCES *Year* 1997 *Income* £328,190 *Grants* £568,167

TRUSTEES R S Rubin, A K Rubin, Mrs A Rubin, Ms C Kubetz, Mrs A J Mosheim

HOW TO APPLY The Trust does not normally deal with unsolicited applications. It prefers to support a few known areas

WHO TO APPLY TO Alison McMillan, Secretary to the Trustees, The Rubin Foundation, The Pentland Centre, Lakeside, Squires Lane, Finchley, London N3 2QL

CC NO 327062   **ESTABLISHED** 1986

■ Rudabede

WHAT IS FUNDED General charitable purposes for the benefit of the community and in particular the advancement of Christian religion, Christian education, the relief of poverty and sickness either at home or overseas. Trustees will consider applications only from Christian charities

WHO CAN BENEFIT Individuals and institutions benefiting Christians

WHERE FUNDING CAN BE GIVEN UK and overseas

RANGE OF GRANTS £250–£4,200

SAMPLE GRANTS £4,200 to Lansdowne Baptist Church; £1,200 to Strete Chapel

FINANCES *Year* 1997 *Income* £20,814

TRUSTEES D M N Reeve, Mrs R Reeve, A F Simmons

NOTES The majority of charitable donations distributed in 1997 were to individuals, mainly Reverends

WHO TO APPLY TO D Reeve, Rudabede, 25 Roslin Road South, Talbot Woods, Bournemouth, Dorset BH3 7EF

CC NO 802280   **ESTABLISHED** 1988

■ Carrie Rudolf Charitable Trust

WHAT IS FUNDED At the discretion of the Trustees, however charities working in the fields of infrastructure development, sheltered accommodation, the advancement of the Jewish religion, synagogues, religious umbrella bodies, health, conservation, special schools, education and training, campaigning and various community facilities and services will be considered

WHO CAN BENEFIT Beneficiaries may include: unemployed people, ethnic minority groups, Jews, at risk groups, carers, disabled people, those disadvantaged by poverty, ex-offenders and those at risk of offending, immigrants, the socially isolated, victims of abuse, sufferers of Alzheimer's disease, arthritis and rheumatism, autism, HIV and AIDS, mental illness, multiple sclerosis, Parkinson's disease, strokes and the terminally ill. There is no restriction on the age of the beneficiaries

WHERE FUNDING CAN BE GIVEN UK

TYPE OF GRANT One-off project and research. Funding of up to three years will be considered

SAMPLE GRANTS £52,875 to Jewish Social Services for disabled access to building; £40,000 to Lambeth Wel-Care for building of a creche
FINANCES *Year* 1996–97 *Income* £120,000 *Grants* £92,875
TRUSTEES A L Jarvis, P Feinstein, D Loewe, R Loewe
WHO TO APPLY TO A Jarvis, Carrie Rudolf Charitable Trust, 1 Fleet Place, London EC4M 7WS
CC NO 1050887   **ESTABLISHED** 1995

■ The Rugby Football Union Charitable Fund

WHAT IS FUNDED The advancement of education. The relief of persons in necessitous circumstances and of persons suffering from sickness. The Fund will make donations or subscriptions to any charitable society, institution, trust or organisation which will further the objects of the charity. To relieve the need, sickness or distress of persons injured while participating in any sport and the dependants of persons killed while participating in any sport. Preference is given to persons who have participated in amateur sport
WHO CAN BENEFIT Individuals and organisations benefiting children, young adults and sportsmen and women. The disabled, those disadvantaged by poverty, parents and children, one parent families and widows and widowers. There is no restriction on the disease or medical condition suffered by the beneficiaries
WHERE FUNDING CAN BE GIVEN UK
TYPE OF GRANT One-off payments to persons injured while participating in any sport and of any dependent of any persons who may be killed while participating in any sport. Preference is given to people who have participated in amateur sport. Donations from time-to-time to other registered charities, which assist persons who suffer physical disabilities
RANGE OF GRANTS Organisation: £200–£500, individuals: £250–£3,000
SAMPLE GRANTS The following list is grants to organisations, larger grants were made to some individuals; £500 to British Wheelchair Sports Foundation; £500 to Aidis Trust; £250 to National Institute of Conductive Education; £250 to David Tolkien Trust; £250 to Gloucester Disabled Afloat Riverboats Trust; £250 to The Lady Hoare Trust for Physically Disabled Youth; £250 to The Snowden Award Scheme; £250 to DEMAND; £250 to National Star Centre for Disabled Youth; £250 to Disabled Housing Trust
FINANCES *Year* 1996 *Income* £593,609 *Grants* £70,895
TRUSTEES J H Addison, A E Agar, I D S Beer, CBE, JP, W J Bishop, OBE, JP, Dr J D Carroll, MD, FRCP, FRCPE, FRCPI, M J Christie, Dr T A Kemp, MD, FRCP, M S Phillips, J R Simpson, TD, DL, M R Steele-Bodger, CBE, By Office: The President and Honorary Treasurer of The Rugby Football Union
NOTES Total grants made to individuals was £67,495 and to organisations £3,400
HOW TO APPLY To the address under Who To Apply To
WHO TO APPLY TO Michael J Christie, The Rugby Football Union Charitable Fund, 41 Station Road, North Harrow, Middlesex HA2 7SX
CC NO 209012   **ESTABLISHED** 1958

■ The Runciman Charitable Trust

WHAT IS FUNDED The Trustees principally make grants for the relief of hardship, poverty or distress to projects or bodies of which one pr more of the Trustees have first hand knowledge
WHAT IS NOT FUNDED No grants for religion, medicine, arts, or to individuals
WHO CAN BENEFIT Registered charities benefiting: at risk groups; those disadvantaged by poverty; homeless people; and socially isolated people
WHERE FUNDING CAN BE GIVEN UK
RANGE OF GRANTS £1,000–£10,000
SAMPLE GRANTS £5,000 to Prison Reform Trust; £5,000 to St John's Hospice; £5,000 to British Academy; £1,000 to Ocean Youth Club
FINANCES *Year* 1997 *Income* £39,739 *Grants* £16,000
TRUSTEES Rt Hon Walter Garrison, The Hon Lisa Runciman, The Hon David W Runciman, The Hon Catherine Runciman
WHO TO APPLY TO Mrs H Edwards, Secretary to the Trustees, The Runciman Charitable Trust, 44 Clifton Hill, London NW8 0QG *Tel* 0171-372 0698
CC NO 1002450   **ESTABLISHED** 1991

■ Runcorn Community Action Trust

WHAT IS FUNDED General charitable purposes for the benefit of the community, in particular, the relief of poverty, distress, sickness and the protection of health and the advancement of education
WHO CAN BENEFIT Organisations benefiting children, young adults, students, at risk groups, those disadvantaged by poverty and socially isolated people. There is no restriction on the disease or medical condition suffered by the beneficiaries
WHERE FUNDING CAN BE GIVEN Borough of Halton South of the River Mersey
RANGE OF GRANTS Below £1,000–£8,000
SAMPLE GRANTS £8,000 to Brookvale Residents Association; £5,100 to Halton Disability Information Service; £3,216 to The Park CP School; £2,812 to Runcorn and District Mencap; £2,800 to Halton Age Concern; £2,500 to Priory Credit Union; £1,580 to Brookvale United Junior FC; £1,500 to Runcorn Under 8's; £1,222 to Brookvale Community Centre Management Board; £1,140 to Hallwood Park Junior Club
FINANCES *Year* 1997 *Income* £73,234 *Grants* £59,530
TRUSTEES Rev D Felix, Rev T Barker, Ms D Houghton, B Porter, W Thompson, Ms N Rimmer, Ms E Gwynne, J Patten, D Thomas, J McDonagh, Ms N Hardy, Mrs J Turner
WHO TO APPLY TO Ms J Wood, Runcorn Community Action Trust, 1 Great Ashfield, Hough Green, Widnes, Cheshire WA8 4SA
CC NO 1046581   **ESTABLISHED** 1995

■ Barbara Russell Charitable Trust

WHAT IS FUNDED General charitable purposes at the discretion of the Trustees
WHO CAN BENEFIT There are no restrictions on the age; professional and economic group; family situation; religion and culture; and social circumstances of; or disease or medical condition suffered by, the beneficiaries
WHERE FUNDING CAN BE GIVEN UK, with a strong preference for the Bristol area
RANGE OF GRANTS £500–£35,000

SAMPLE GRANTS £35,000 to Bristol Age Concern; £35,000 to St Peter's Hospice

FINANCES *Year* 1997 *Income* £129,918 *Grants* £135,500

TRUSTEES Mrs A Castle, Ms G Davies, D S Russell

NOTES The Trustees meet only once a year to discuss their grant making. The Trustees have decided that the Charity should ideally have a finite life of approximately five years

HOW TO APPLY Applications should include a project outline with any supporting information. Requests should be submitted to the address under Who To Apply To in May–June for consideration at the yearly meeting

WHO TO APPLY TO David Russell, Trustee, Barbara Russell Charitable Trust, Wheelwrights, Pershore Road, Upton Snodsbury, Worcestershire WR7 4NR

CC NO 1057700   **ESTABLISHED** 1995

■ The Willy Russell Charitable Trust

WHAT IS FUNDED General charitable purposes

WHO CAN BENEFIT Registered charities and individuals. There are no restrictions on the age; professional and economic group; family situation; religion and culture; and social circumstances of; or disease or medical condition suffered by, the beneficiaries

WHERE FUNDING CAN BE GIVEN UK

RANGE OF GRANTS Organisations: £100–£2,500, student sponsorship: £250–£5,200

SAMPLE GRANTS £2,500 to Brother Paul Zapallal Peru; £2,000 to KIND; £1,000 to Amnesty; £1,000 to the Palmist; £1,000 to Merseyside Drugs Council

FINANCES *Year* 1997 *Income* £24,713 *Grants* £11,700

TRUSTEES W M Russell, A Russell, J C Malthouse, FCA

NOTES During 1996–97 eight students were sponsored at theatre and drama schools and at university, amounting to £12,050 (not included in the Grants figure in Finances)

WHO TO APPLY TO J Malthouse, The Willy Russell Charitable Trust, Malthouse and Co, Chartered Accountants, America House, Rumford Court, Rumford Place, Liverpool L3 9DD

CC NO 1003546   **ESTABLISHED** 1991

■ The Russian European Trust

WHAT IS FUNDED To relieve poverty, advance education and other charitable purposes, in particular to advance academic and/or vocational training to protect and preserve good health whether physical or mental and to relieve and rehabilitate persons suffering from any form of physical or mental handicap in Russia and the Republics

WHO CAN BENEFIT Children and young adults; those disadvantaged by poverty; disabled people and those suffering from mental illness

WHERE FUNDING CAN BE GIVEN Russia and the Republics

FINANCES *Year* 1997 *Income* £120,728

TRUSTEES D Wright, Brig J Davies, Lady Braithwaite, H Bellingham, MP, A Longley, OBE, C Wolstenholme, A Woodruff, OBE

WHO TO APPLY TO M Butcher, The Russian European Trust, 5 Tavistock Place, London WC1H 9SN

CC NO 1039251   **ESTABLISHED** 1994

■ Frank Russon Charitable Trust

WHAT IS FUNDED General charitable purposes. Trustees consider applications from UK and Birmingham charities

WHO CAN BENEFIT There are no restrictions on the age; professional and economic group; family situation; religion and culture; and social circumstances of; or disease or medical condition suffered by, the beneficiaries

WHERE FUNDING CAN BE GIVEN UK with preference for Birmingham and Warwickshire

RANGE OF GRANTS £25–£1,572

SAMPLE GRANTS £1,572 to Youth Afloat; £1,000 to Macmillan Nurses Cancer Appeal Fund; £600 to Stonehouse Gang; £575 to NSPCC; £550 to British Legion

FINANCES *Year* 1996 *Income* £21,205 *Grants* £14,822

TRUSTEES F M Russon, P D Russon, E M Russon, P C Russon

HOW TO APPLY In writing to the address under Who To Apply To, to arrive during the month of June

WHO TO APPLY TO F M Russon, Frank Russon Charitable Trust, Marchwood, 51 Lovelace Avenue, Solihull, West Midlands B91 3JR

CC NO 237598   **ESTABLISHED** 1964

■ Rutland Historic Churches Preservation Trust

WHAT IS FUNDED Within the boundaries of the old county of Rutland only, to help work to be carried out on Parish Churches, especially that arising in connection with Quinquennial Surveys, and to assist Christian places of worship of all denominations in other authorised repairs

WHAT IS NOT FUNDED No work in any church or chapel outside Rutland

WHO CAN BENEFIT Christian places of worship in Rutland only

WHERE FUNDING CAN BE GIVEN Rutland only

TYPE OF GRANT Fixed sum and/or interest-free loan repayable over five years, buildings

RANGE OF GRANTS £100–£6,000, typical grant £2,500

SAMPLE GRANTS £6,000 to St Mary's, South Luffenham for heating system; £5,000 to St Mary's, Greetham for re-wiring; £2,000 to All Saints, Braunston for roof repairs; £1,500 to St Andrew's, Hambleton for roof repairs; £1,500 to SS Peter and Paul, Uppingham for woodwork repairs following woodworm attack; £1,000 to Morcott and Barrowden Baptist Chapel for roof repair and ceiling renewal; £500 to Oakham Meeting House for repointing walls; £500 to St Mary's, Ayston for re-wiring; £500 to St Andrew's, Lyddington for churchyard wall repairs

FINANCES *Year* 1997 *Income* £31,798 *Grants* £18,500

TRUSTEES R J A Adams, D Atkinson, Sir David Davenport-Handley, The Ven B Fernyhough, J Gammell, Col T C S Haywood, OBE, Mrs M Norton-Fagge, A C Southern, Mrs L Taylor, G Turner, The Bishop of Peterborough

PUBLICATIONS Annual Report and Statement of Accounts

HOW TO APPLY Contact the Hon Secretary at the address under Who To Apply To

WHO TO APPLY TO Hon Sec, Mrs L I Worrall, Rutland Historic Churches Preservation Trust, 6 Redland Close, Barrowden, Oakham, Rutland LE15 8ES *Tel* 01572 747302

CC NO 211068   **ESTABLISHED** 1954

■ Rycroft Children's Fund

WHAT IS FUNDED Welfare of children and young adults

WHO CAN BENEFIT Individuals and organisations benefiting children and young adults

WHERE FUNDING CAN BE GIVEN Cheshire, Derbyshire, Greater Manchester, Lancashire, Staffordshire, South and West Yorkshire. Preference for those resident in the cities of Manchester, Salford and the Borough of Trafford

FINANCES *Year* 1996–97 *Income* £41,275 *Grants* £39,620

TRUSTEES C P Lees-Jones (Chair), I H D Brown, Mrs J Dixon, Miss M R Mason, A Maddocks, Dr A Robinson

HOW TO APPLY To the address under Who To Apply To in writing

WHO TO APPLY TO J N Smith, Secretary, Rycroft Children's Fund, 10 Heyridge Drive, Northenden, Manchester M22 4HB

CC NO 231771   **ESTABLISHED** 1985

■ Ryder Tremberth Trust

WHAT IS FUNDED (a) Journeys to third world or Eastern Europe. (b) Attempts to write or otherwise present to UK audiences understanding gained of Eastern Europe or the third world

WHAT IS NOT FUNDED Travel which is not focused on a tangible output in some communication

WHO CAN BENEFIT People aged 18–25 who have, or wish to travel to the third world or Eastern Europe

WHERE FUNDING CAN BE GIVEN UK

TYPE OF GRANT Support for journeys abroad, or support while writing or devising other presentations about journeys abroad. Funding is one-off for up to one year

FINANCES *Year* 1998

TRUSTEES Ms Terry Marsh, Ken Durham, Michael Tremberth, Ms Alex Runswick, Neil Ryder

HOW TO APPLY By application form available by post or e-mail

WHO TO APPLY TO Neil Ryder, Ryder Tremberth Trust, 1A Bittacy Park Avenue, Mill Hill, London NW7 2HA *Tel* 0181-349 4607 *Fax* 0181-346 2925 *E-mail* NeilRyder@btinternet.com

CC NO 1003121   **ESTABLISHED** 1991

■ The Rydon Charitable Trust

WHAT IS FUNDED General charitable purposes. Trustees have a preference for local causes

WHO CAN BENEFIT Registered charities. There are no restrictions on the age; professional and economic group; family situation; religion and culture; and social circumstances of; or disease or medical condition suffered by, the beneficiaries

WHERE FUNDING CAN BE GIVEN Kent, Sussex and Surrey

FINANCES *Year* 1997 *Income* £34,476

TRUSTEES Rydon Holdings Ltd, G N Turner, D D Dennard, M W Gearon

WHO TO APPLY TO G N Turner, The Rydon Charitable Trust, Rydon House, Forest Row, Sussex RH18 5DW

CC NO 1017492   **ESTABLISHED** 1992

■ The J S and E C Rymer Charitable Trust

WHAT IS FUNDED Housing for retired people who have spent the major part of their working lives in rural industry or agriculture; general charitable purposes in the area Where Funding Can Be Given

WHO CAN BENEFIT To benefit people who have retired from rural industry or agriculture

WHERE FUNDING CAN BE GIVEN East Yorkshire

SAMPLE GRANTS £3,000 to Sparsholt College; £1,035 to Game Conservancy Trust; £750 to NSPCC; £560 to Dove House Hospice; £500 to Driffield School; £500 to HCC Garton School for Infants; £485 to Cancer Relief; £450 to Merchant Adventurers of York; £300 to Campus Children's Holidays; £300 to Chippenham Cricket Club

FINANCES *Year* 1996 *Income* £58,603 *Grants* £10,917

HOW TO APPLY To the address under Who To Apply To in writing

WHO TO APPLY TO D Milburn, Treasurer, The J S and E C Rymer Charitable Trust, Southburn Offices, Southburn, Driffield, East Yorkshire YO25 9ED

CC NO 267493   **ESTABLISHED** 1974

■ SCK Charitable Trust

This trust did not respond to CAF's request to amend its entry and, by 30 June 1998, CAF's researchers did not find financial records for later than 1995 on its file at the Charity Commission. Trusts are legally required to submit annual accounts to the Charity Commission under section 42 of the Charities Act 1993

WHAT IS FUNDED General charitable purposes
WHO CAN BENEFIT There are no restrictions on the age; professional and economic group; family situation; religion and culture; and social circumstances of; or disease or medical condition suffered by, the beneficiaries
WHERE FUNDING CAN BE GIVEN UK
TRUSTEES S Kaufman, Z Kaufman
WHO TO APPLY TO Z M Kaufman, Trustee, S C K Charitable Trust, 267 Durham Road, Gateshead, Tyne & Wear NE5 8AD
CC NO 1049159 **ESTABLISHED** 1992

■ SCOPE (formerly The Spastics Society)

WHAT IS FUNDED To promote conduct and engage in research and experimental work calculated to be of benefit to people with cerebral palsy and the prevention of cerebral palsy. To provide financial assistance, to make grants and donations to, and to provide equipment and apparatus for, people with cerebral palsy, to provide such other assistance to local or central authorities or other bodies or persons calculated to be of benefit collectively or individually to people with cerebral palsy
WHAT IS NOT FUNDED Grants not made to individuals for masters degree courses or training courses
WHO CAN BENEFIT To benefit those suffering from cerebral palsy
WHERE FUNDING CAN BE GIVEN England and Wales
TYPE OF GRANT Medical and educational research grants. Grants to groups working on behalf of cerebral palsy and related disabilities, grants to individual people with cerebral palsy. Capital grants are considered
SAMPLE GRANTS £469 to people with cerebral palsy; £228 to Opportunity for Volunteers; £194 to South East local support group; £152 to Midlands local support group; £134 to London local support group; £124 to North East local support group £122 to East local support group £115 to West local support group; £105 to North West local support group; £97 to medical and research
FINANCES *Year* 1997 *Income* £85,724
Grants £1,965
TRUSTEES The Executive Council: D G H Ashcroft, A R Berry, P J Clery, A S Drane, P Fiddler, A P M Hewson, S M Hughes, J Kelly, K Mackenzie, G McCarthy, P J McHale, J Rawlinson, P Roberts, P J Roper, J Rowe, A Townsend, G Vernon
PUBLICATIONS *Disability Now* (free). A wide range of leaflets about the Society and for parents of handicapped children. Full publications list available from the Librarian. Produces *Developmental Medicine and Child Neurology*
HOW TO APPLY Medical research applications and educational research applications may be made to the Committee Secretary at any time

WHO TO APPLY TO Christina Semple, The Secretary, SCOPE, 6 Market Road, London N7 0PW
CC NO 208231 **ESTABLISHED** 1953

■ SEM Charitable Trust

WHAT IS FUNDED Mainly recommendations of Settlor particularly charities working in the field of the education of disabled people
WHAT IS NOT FUNDED No grants to individuals
WHO CAN BENEFIT Mainly educational institutions benefiting disabled people, children and young adults
WHERE FUNDING CAN BE GIVEN UK, Israel and South Africa
TYPE OF GRANT Recurring
FINANCES *Year* 1997 *Income* £35,754
Grants £38,933
TRUSTEES Mrs S E Radonir, M Cohen
WHO TO APPLY TO M Cohen, SEM Charitable Trust, Saffery Champness, Fairfax House, Fulwood Place, Gray's Inn, London WC1V 6UB
CC NO 265831 **ESTABLISHED** 1973

■ S Group Charitable Trust

WHAT IS FUNDED To encourage co-operation and practical self-help
WHAT IS NOT FUNDED Grants are not made to overseas aid agencies, animal charities, bricks and mortar appeals, religious causes, research, or to individuals
WHO CAN BENEFIT Registered charities. Preference is given to local voluntary organisations in London benefiting: the homeless; children and young people; the elderly; people with disabilities and mental health problems; and local communities
WHERE FUNDING CAN BE GIVEN Mainly Greater London
TYPE OF GRANT All donations are one-off
RANGE OF GRANTS £500–£7,000
SAMPLE GRANTS £7,000 to NABS; £4,500 to homeless; £2,500 to handicap/disability; £2,250 to elderly; £2,245 to mental health
FINANCES *Year* 1996 *Income* £20,424
Grants £22,245
TRUSTEES R Baird, Miss M A Castle, Mrs W Smyth, Miss G B Matthews
HOW TO APPLY To the address under Who To Apply To. At any time. Trustees meet quarterly. Applications should include clear details of the need the intended project is designed to meet, plus an outline budget
WHO TO APPLY TO Miss K S Brown, S Group Charitable Trust, Saatchi & Saatchi Advertising Ltd, 80 Charlotte Street, London W1A 1AQ
CC NO 291392 **ESTABLISHED** 1985

■ The SMB Trust

WHAT IS FUNDED The advancement of the Christian religion and the relief of suffering
WHAT IS NOT FUNDED Grants to individuals not normally considered
WHO CAN BENEFIT Mainly to bodies for advancement of Christian religion and relief of suffering. There is no restriction on the disease or medical condition suffered by the beneficiaries
WHERE FUNDING CAN BE GIVEN UK
TYPE OF GRANT Most on annual basis; others non-recurring
RANGE OF GRANTS £500–£4,000

SAMPLE GRANTS £4,000 to London City Mission; £4,000 to Pilgrims Homes; £3,000 to The Salvation Army; £2,000 to The British Red Cross; £1,500 to TEAR Fund (Rwanda); £1,500 to Mencap; £1,500 to Scripture Union; £1,500 to Shaftesbury Society; £1,250 to Boys' Brigade
FINANCES *Year* 1997 *Income* £186,664
Grants £106,550
TRUSTEES Miss K E Wood, E D Anstead, P J Stanford, Mrs B O'Driscoll
HOW TO APPLY To the address under Who To Apply To – Trustees meet quarterly
WHO TO APPLY TO E D Anstead, The SMB Trust, Grosvenor Lodge, 72 Grosvenor Road, Tunbridge Wells, Kent TN1 2AZ
CC NO 263814　　　　　**ESTABLISHED** 1962

■ SO Charitable Trust

WHAT IS FUNDED Jewish causes in Gateshead
WHO CAN BENEFIT Jewish people
WHERE FUNDING CAN BE GIVEN Gateshead
RANGE OF GRANTS £1,000–£32,500
SAMPLE GRANTS £32,500 to Gateshead Foundation for Torah; £19,000 to Beis Hatalmud; £3,000 to Centre for Advance Rabbis; £2,800 to Sunderland College; £1,500 to Paslia Ltd; £1,000 to Gateshead Jewish Primary School
FINANCES *Year* 1995 *Income* £65,438
Grants £59,800
TRUSTEES S O'Hayon, N O'Hayon, Mrs S O'Hayon
WHO TO APPLY TO S O'Hayon, SO Charitable Trust, 19 Oxford Terrace, Gateshead, Tyne and Wear NE8 1RQ
CC NO 326314　　　　　**ESTABLISHED** 1982

■ The Audrey Sacher Charitable Trust

WHAT IS FUNDED General charitable purposes
WHAT IS NOT FUNDED No grants are made to private individuals. Grants will be made only to registered charities known personally to the Trustees
WHO CAN BENEFIT There are no restrictions on the age; professional and economic group; family situation; religion and culture; and social circumstances of; or disease or medical condition suffered by, the beneficiaries
WHERE FUNDING CAN BE GIVEN UK
TYPE OF GRANT Grants mainly made as per restrictions and only against personal requests
RANGE OF GRANTS £25–£25,000
SAMPLE GRANTS £25,000 to English National Ballet Ltd; £21,793 to Royal College of Music; £15,600 to Birmingham Royal Ballet Trust; £13,680 to Royal Opera House; £12,000 to English National Ballet School Ltd; £10,200 to Cancer Relief Macmillan Fund; £10,000 to the Anna Freud Centre; £5,000 to London Contemporary Dance School; £5,000 to Yvonne Arnauld Theatre; £2,500 to Chicken Shed Theatre
FINANCES *Year* 1997 *Income* £83,473
Grants £141,025
NOTES Grants mainly made as per restrictions and only against personal requests
HOW TO APPLY Personal submissions only
WHO TO APPLY TO H W Fisher & Co, The Audrey Sacher Charitable Trust, Acre House, 11–15 William Road, London NW1 3ER
CC NO 288973　　　　　**ESTABLISHED** 1984

■ The Michael Sacher Charitable Trust

WHAT IS FUNDED General charitable purposes
WHO CAN BENEFIT There are no restrictions on the age; professional and economic group; family situation; religion and culture; and social circumstances of; or disease or medical condition suffered by, the beneficiaries. However, non-Jewish organisations will only receive mall grants
WHERE FUNDING CAN BE GIVEN UK
FINANCES *Year* 1996 *Income* £121,253
Grants £99,480
TRUSTEES S J Sacher, J M Sacher, M H Sacher
HOW TO APPLY Grants are mainly made to charities known personally rather than to submissions and funds are already committed to charities known to the Trustees
WHO TO APPLY TO Mrs Irene Bailey, Secretary, The Michael Sacher Charitable Trust, Michael House, 57 Baker Street, London W1A 1DN
CC NO 206321　　　　　**ESTABLISHED** 1957

■ The Dr Mortimer and Theresa Sackler Foundation

WHAT IS FUNDED Arts, hospitals
WHO CAN BENEFIT Large institutions benefiting: actors and entertainment professionals; musicians; textile workers and designers; writers and poets. There is no restriction on the disease or medical condition suffered by the beneficiaries
WHERE FUNDING CAN BE GIVEN UK and overseas
TYPE OF GRANT Some recurring, other one-off
FINANCES *Year* 1995 *Income* £1,112,372
Grants £120,950
TRUSTEES Dr Mortimer Sackler, Theresa Sackler, Christopher Mitchell, Robin Stormouth-Darling, Raymond Smith
NOTES With the expiry of the original deed of covenant, donations are likely to fall so that the Foundation's previously large commitments must be curtailed. New applicants are unlikely to be successful
HOW TO APPLY To the address under Who To Apply To in writing
WHO TO APPLY TO C B Mitchell, The Dr Mortimer and Theresa Sackler Foundation, 15 North Audley Street, London W1Y 1WE
CC NO 327863　　　　　**ESTABLISHED** 1988

■ The Ruzin Sadagora Trust

This trust did not respond to CAF's request to amend its entry and, by 30 June 1998, CAF's researchers did not find financial records for later than 1995 on its file at the Charity Commission. Trusts are legally required to submit annual accounts to the Charity Commission under section 42 of the Charities Act 1993

WHAT IS FUNDED Preference to Jewish charities
WHO CAN BENEFIT Charities benefiting Jewish people
WHERE FUNDING CAN BE GIVEN UK and overseas
TYPE OF GRANT At the discretion of the Trustees
TRUSTEES I M Friedman, S Friedman
WHO TO APPLY TO I M Friedman, The Ruzin Sadagora Trust, 32 Overlea Road, Clapton, London E5 9BG
CC NO 285475　　　　　**ESTABLISHED** 1982

■ The Saffron Walden United Charities

WHAT IS FUNDED General charitable purposes

WHO CAN BENEFIT Individuals and organisations. There are no restrictions on the age; professional and economic group; family situation; religion and culture; and social circumstances of; or disease or medical condition suffered by, the beneficiaries

WHERE FUNDING CAN BE GIVEN Saffron Walden

SAMPLE GRANTS £24,582 as gifts; £761 for milk

FINANCES *Year* 1995 *Income* £33,098 *Grants* £25,343

TRUSTEES Mrs J Bailey, Mrs C Blackwell, Mrs B Bronet, J Golding, Mrs F M Gray, Mrs M Green, Mrs E M Harris, Mrs D J Hawkins, Mayor of Saffron Walden, Vicar of the Parish of St Mary the Virgin, Saffron Walden

HOW TO APPLY To the address under Who To Apply To in writing

WHO TO APPLY TO G R Lord, Secretary, The Saffron Walden United Charities, Adams Harrison Solicitors, 14 and 16 Church Street, Saffron Walden, Essex CB10 1JW

CC NO 210662   **ESTABLISHED** 1962

■ Leonard Sainer Charitable Trust

WHAT IS FUNDED General charitable purposes. The funds of this Charity are usually committed long in advance to specific charitable purposes in which the Settlor was interested. Appeals from other charities will not be acknowledged

WHAT IS NOT FUNDED No grants to individuals

WHO CAN BENEFIT Registered charities only. There are no restrictions on the age; professional and economic group; family situation; religion and culture; and social circumstances of; or disease or medical condition suffered by, the beneficiaries

WHERE FUNDING CAN BE GIVEN UK and overseas

TYPE OF GRANT Various

RANGE OF GRANTS £100–£20000

SAMPLE GRANTS £7,568 to British Council; £2,850 Western Marble Arch Synagogue; £5,000 to Nightingale House; £2,500 to Council of Christians and Jews; £2,500 to Jewish Care; £2,500 to Leonard Sainer Legal Education Foundation; £2,000 to British Israel Arts Foundation; £2,000 to Friends of Israel Cancer Association; £1,290 to Royal Opera House; £1,000 to The Weitzmann Institute Foundation

FINANCES *Year* 1996–97 *Income* £40,000 *Grants* £34,300

TRUSTEES S Krendel, A P Sainer, C L Corman, G M Walters

HOW TO APPLY **This Trust states that it does not respond to unsolicited applications**

WHO TO APPLY TO Leonard Sainer Charitable Trust, Titmuss Sainer Dechert, 2 Serjeants' Inn, London EC4Y 1LT *Tel* 0171-583 5353

CC NO 210984   **ESTABLISHED** 1960

■ Jean Sainsbury Animal Welfare Trust (formerly Jean Sainsbury Charitable Trust)

WHAT IS FUNDED To support smaller charities concerned with animal welfare and wildlife

WHAT IS NOT FUNDED No grants to non-registered charities or individuals

WHO CAN BENEFIT National and international animal welfare organisations

WHERE FUNDING CAN BE GIVEN UK and overseas

TYPE OF GRANT Buildings, capital, core costs, project, running costs and recurring costs. Funding for up to one year is available

RANGE OF GRANTS £250–£10,000, typical grant £500

SAMPLE GRANTS £10,000 to Blue Cross Animals' Hospital for Centenary Appeal to rebuild hospital; £8,500 to Animals in Need for flooring in new kennels; £6,600 to Sussex Horse Rescue for cost of new stables; £6,000 to Brent Lodge Bird and Wildlife Trust; £6,000 to Animals in Distress, Manchester; £6,000 to North Clwyd Animal Rescue; £6,000 to Three Owls Bird Sanctuary; £5,000 to Animal Care for refurbishment of grooming/shower room; £5,000 to Faith Animal Rescue for rebuilding kennels; £5,000 to Greenacres Animal Rescue for converting barn unto a cattery

FINANCES *Year* 1997 *Income* £286,457 *Grants* £180,447

TRUSTEES Mrs J Sainsbury, C H Sainsbury, C P Russell, Mrs G Tarlington, J A Keliher, M Spurdens, MRCVS, Miss J Winship, SRN, Mrs A Lowrie

PUBLICATIONS Accounts prepared to December 31, 1997

HOW TO APPLY Three Trustees' meetings yearly. Approximately March, July and November (submissions eight weeks earlier)

WHO TO APPLY TO Miss A Dietrich, Administrator, Jean Sainsbury Animal Welfare Trust, PO Box 469, London W14 8PJ *Fax* 0171-371 4918

CC NO 326358   **ESTABLISHED** 1982

■ The Sainsbury Charitable Fund Ltd

WHAT IS FUNDED Donations to community groups in trading areas, particularly those of a caring nature, children, disabled and the family

WHAT IS NOT FUNDED Grants are not made for expeditions, travel bursaries, sport, individuals, restoration/upkeep of buildings, National Health projects, political or religious causes

WHO CAN BENEFIT Registered charities and self-help groups. National, regional and local organisations benefiting: children; young adults; older people; parents and children; one parent families; widows and widowers; carers; disabled people; victims of man-made and natural disasters; and beneficiaries suffering from asthma, cerebral palsy, cystic fibrosis and diabetes

WHERE FUNDING CAN BE GIVEN UK trading area (England, Aberdeen, Dundee, Edinburgh, Fife, Glasgow, Midlothian, Wrexham, Bridgend, Cardiff, Merthyr Tydfil, Newport, Swansea, Ballymena, Belfast, Coleraine, Craigavon, Derry, Newry and Maine)

TYPE OF GRANT Generally up to £5,000 per project, but smaller grants considered all year round. Project. Funding for one year or less will be considered

RANGE OF GRANTS £200–£5,000

SAMPLE GRANTS £5,000 to Common Purpose for Northern Ireland Bursary; £1,600 to Victims Support London for Volunteers' Conference; £1,500 to Brownlow Community Trust for Northern Ireland Womens Training Scheme; £1,000 to Coleraine Business Education Partnership for Northern Ireland Community Project; £1,000 to Southwark Crossroads for Carers IT Project; £1,000 to Durham Area Disabled Leisure Group for outing for local people; £1,000 to Life Education Centres Swindon for mobile unit for local schools; £550 to Hallam Diocesan Caring Service for parenting scheme; £450 to Cambridge House and Talbot for Southwark Disabled Project; £400 to Ryder-Cheshire Foundation for Swadlincote Disabled Swimming Club

FINANCES *Year* 1998–99 *Income* £125,000

TRUSTEES Ms R Thorne, T Wigley, C J Leaver, N F Matthews, M Pattison, D Fry

NOTES All Sainsbury's stores have a community budget to support local fundraising efforts with raffle prizes. Please write to the Store Manager

HOW TO APPLY At any time. Trustees meet quarterly, but grants up to £1,000 considered weekly. No published guidelines. All applications receive a reply. Information required includes aims and objectives, target audience and links with at least one Sainsbury store

WHO TO APPLY TO Mrs S L Mercer, The Sainsbury Charitable Fund Ltd, Stamford House, Stamford Street, London SE1 9LL *Tel* 0171-695 7390 *Fax* 0171-695 0097 *E-mail* slme@tao.j-sainbury.co.uk

CC NO 245843   **ESTABLISHED** 1965

■ The Robert and Lisa Sainsbury Charitable Trust

WHAT IS FUNDED Medical research charities and caring charities. education in art, the humanities and other branches of learning; general charitable purposes

WHAT IS NOT FUNDED No grants to individuals

WHO CAN BENEFIT Organisations benefiting: students; actors and entertainment professionals; textile workers and designers; musicians; and writers and poets. There are no restrictions on the disease or medical condition suffered by the beneficiaries

WHERE FUNDING CAN BE GIVEN UK and overseas

TYPE OF GRANT Largely capital

FINANCES *Year* 1996–97 *Income* £304,403 *Grants* £466,017

TRUSTEES Sir Robert Sainsbury, Lady Lisa Sainsbury, C T S Stone, HON & V Trustee Ltd

HOW TO APPLY To the address under Who To Apply To in writing, with no supporting material

WHO TO APPLY TO D J Walker, The Robert and Lisa Sainsbury Charitable Trust, c/o Horwath Clark Whitehill, 25 New Street Square, London EC4A 3LN *Tel* 0171-353 1577

CC NO 276923   **ESTABLISHED** 1978

■ St Andrew's Conservation Trust

WHAT IS FUNDED The conservation, restoration and preservation of monuments, sculptures and artefacts of historic or public interest which are upon or attached to property owned by any charitable organisation

WHAT IS NOT FUNDED No support is given for conservation or restoration of churchyard table tombs

WHERE FUNDING CAN BE GIVEN South West England

RANGE OF GRANTS £100–£7,500

SAMPLE GRANTS £7,500 to Wells Cathedral, Somerset for the conservation of 19th century decorations by Burges; £3,000 to Chew Magna, Somerset for the conservation of the Baber Monument (1601); £3,000 to Exeter, St Petrock for the conservation of two 18th century monuments; £3,000 to East Pennard, Somerset for the conservation of box pews; £3,000 to Arlington, Devon for the conservation of two wall monuments; £2,640 to Glastonbury Abbey (Othery, Somerset) for a 15th century Cope made into Altar Frontal; £2,500 to Cydiard Tregoz, Wiltshire for the conservation of two Hatchments; £2,000 to East Holme, Dorset for the conservation of wall paintings; £2,000 to Abergavenny, Monmouthshire for the conservation of Monastic Choir Stalls; £1,500 to Wells - St Thomas, Somerset for the conservation of Tower Statues

FINANCES *Year* 1997 *Income* £28,816 *Grants* £21,688

HOW TO APPLY To the address under Who To Apply To in writing

WHO TO APPLY TO Mrs B Wooster, Secretary, St Andrew's Conservation Trust, 4 Mount Hey, Somerton, Somerset TA11 7PG

CC NO 282157   **ESTABLISHED** 1980

■ St Anthony's Trust

WHAT IS FUNDED Trustees particularly support the advancement of education in accordance with the teachings of Rudolf Steiner

WHO CAN BENEFIT Anthroposophical institutions benefiting young adults and students interested in the teachings of Rudolf Steiner

WHERE FUNDING CAN BE GIVEN UK

TYPE OF GRANT To aid specific capital development and institutional bursary funds

FINANCES *Year* 1997 *Income* £41,683

TRUSTEES R Wills, W Ashe

WHO TO APPLY TO D Donahaye, St Anthony's Trust, 9 Michael Fields, Forest Row, East Sussex RH18 5BH

CC NO 264626   **ESTABLISHED** 1972

■ St Clement Danes Parochial Charities

This trust did not respond to CAF's request to amend its entry and, by 30 June 1998, CAF's researchers did not find financial records for later than 1995 on its file at the Charity Commission. Trusts are legally required to submit annual accounts to the Charity Commission under section 42 of the Charities Act 1993

WHAT IS FUNDED The relief of poverty and the advancement of religion

WHO CAN BENEFIT Those who are disadvantaged by poverty. There is no restriction on the religion or culture of the beneficiaries

WHERE FUNDING CAN BE GIVEN The Parishes of St Clement Danes and St Mary le Strand, London

HOW TO APPLY To the address under Who To Apply To in writing

WHO TO APPLY TO F Brenchley-Brown, St Clement Danes Parochial Charities, St Mary Le Strand Office, 171 Strand, London WC2R 1EP

CC NO 204344   **ESTABLISHED** 1965

Does the trust you have chosen match your needs? Haphazard applications waste postage and time

553

■ Saint Edmund King and Martyr Trust

WHAT IS FUNDED The advancement of religion of the Church of England

WHAT IS NOT FUNDED Applicants must be connected to the Church of England

WHO CAN BENEFIT Organisations benefiting the Church of England

WHERE FUNDING CAN BE GIVEN London

TYPE OF GRANT One-off and recurrent grants

RANGE OF GRANTS £150–£7,650

SAMPLE GRANTS £7,650 to St Edmund King and Martyr and St Mary Woolnoth PCC; £4,500 to All Saints Church, Islington; £3,300 to the Archdeacon of London Float Account; £3,000 to an individual; £2,800 to the Lord Bishop of London Float Account; £2,500 to Emmanuel Church, Southall; £2,000 to an individual; £2,000 to the Barnabas Centre, Homerton; £1,000 to All Souls Clubhouse, Langham Place; £1,000 to Caris Haringey

FINANCES *Year* 1996 *Income* £56,657 *Grants* £48,639

TRUSTEES The Rt Rev and Rt Hon Lord Bishop of London, The Archdeacon of London, Andrew Buxton, James Barclay, The Rector of St Edmund King & Martyr & St Mary Woolnoth

HOW TO APPLY In writing at any time

WHO TO APPLY TO Mr J F Kennedy, Saint Edmund King and Martyr Trust, c/o 2 Amen Court, Warwick Lane, London EC4M 7BU

CC NO 1032116   **ESTABLISHED** 1963

■ St Francis Leprosy Guild

WHAT IS FUNDED The relief of leprosy sufferers throughout the world in centres run or aided by Catholic missionaries or diocesan personnel

WHAT IS NOT FUNDED Centres not run by Catholic missionaries – priests, sisters, volunteers – or not approved by the local bishop will not receive funding

WHO CAN BENEFIT Leprosy sufferers at centres mainly administered or assisted by Catholic missionaries

WHERE FUNDING CAN BE GIVEN Third world countries

TYPE OF GRANT Money for recurrent operational expenses and for specific projects. Capital grants

FINANCES *Year* 1996 *Income* £343,799 *Grants* £308,778

TRUSTEES The Committee

PUBLICATIONS Annual Report

HOW TO APPLY Applications should be made annually, in December. Applications for revenue grants should enclose most recent accounts. Applications for capital grants should specify the total cost and anticipated start date. In all cases, charity registration title and number should be given. The committee regret applications cannot be acknowledged

WHO TO APPLY TO SR Eleanor Marshall FMM, The Hon Secretary, St Francis Leprosy Guild, 26 Inglis Road, Ealing, London W5 3RL

CC NO 208741   **ESTABLISHED** 1895

■ St Gabriel's Trust

WHAT IS FUNDED Higher and further religious education with the purpose of training RE teachers and encouraging good practice in RE

WHAT IS NOT FUNDED Projects which should be subject to statutory funding, or funding by the church will not be supported. No theological study, parish or missionary work, unless schools religious education is involved. No long-term research projects where benefit will be slow to manifest itself in RE teaching will be considered for funding. In general grants cannot be made to schools – higher or further education must be involved

WHO CAN BENEFIT Institutions engaged in higher or further RE, with a view to training school RE teachers. Young adults and members of the Church of England may benefit

WHERE FUNDING CAN BE GIVEN UK, especially the boroughs of Lambeth and Lewisham

TYPE OF GRANT Recurring, one-off, project, research and start-up will be considered

SAMPLE GRANTS £93,294 to the St Gabriel's Programme for pro-active training in school RE; £11,535 to Stapleford Institute to develop new courses for teachers in Christian values; £10,300 to North of England Institute for Christian Education for research into student's motives for choosing Christian theology or religious studies; £10,000 to Southwark Diocesan Board of Education for further education research and development project; £10,000 to South London Multi-Faith Centre for RE teaching materials; £8,000 to the National Society for Promoting RE for RE resources centre; £8,000 to Chester College of HE for development of MA course in Church School Education; £3,400 to Culham Education Foundation for exchange of information in RE; £3,000 to Southwark Cathedral Education Centre for RE; £3,000 to St Pierre International Youth Trust for exchange visits for students following Church Colleges Certificate course

FINANCES *Year* 1997 *Income* £189,000 *Grants* £200,000

TRUSTEES General Secretary of the National Society for Promoting Religious Education, Warden of Goldsmith's College, Vicar of St John the Divine, Kennington, six co-optative trustees

HOW TO APPLY To the address under Who To Apply To in writing

WHO TO APPLY TO Peter Duffell, Clerk, St Gabriel's Trust, Ladykirk, 32 The Ridgeway, Enfield, Middlesex EN2 8QH *Tel* 0181-363 6474

CC NO 312933   **ESTABLISHED** 1977

■ St George the Martyr Charity

WHAT IS FUNDED Holidays and pensions for individuals in need and the elderly in the area Where Funding Can Be Given. Making grants or providing services to relieve individually or generally people in Southwark who are in need, hardship or distress

WHO CAN BENEFIT Individuals and local charities benefiting elderly people and those in need, hardship or distress

WHERE FUNDING CAN BE GIVEN Southwark

SAMPLE GRANTS £96,386 for summer holiday benefits; £47,655 for pensions; £11,761 for Christmas parcels/parties

FINANCES *Year* 1995–96 *Income* £174,585 *Grants* £154,802

TRUSTEES As appointed by London Borough of Southwark, other co-optative trustees: G Stevens, J Hawley, E J Hall, Mrs A Hall, Rev A S Lucas, C Ruddock, B E Stevens, Ms S Harding, Mrs M Ives, Mrs H Robertson

HOW TO APPLY To the address under Who To Apply To in writing

WHO TO APPLY TO D Morley, St George the Martyr Charity, St Georges Rectory, Manciple Street, London SE1 4CW

CC NO 208732   **ESTABLISHED** 1899

■ The St George's Trust

WHAT IS FUNDED This Trust will consider funding the advancement of the Christian religion, churches and Anglican umbrella bodies. The Trustees are not able to subscribe regularly to any cause or project, nor is it their practice to vote money for ordinary church expenses. They are, however, ready to make modest grants to help forward imaginative developments, as well as towards the assistance of individuals in the service of the Church

WHO CAN BENEFIT Church of England, clergy, and those in the service of the Church

WHERE FUNDING CAN BE GIVEN UK

TYPE OF GRANT Project, research and buildings

SAMPLE GRANTS £500 to an individual; £500 to an individual for counselling; £450 to an individual for a sabbatical; £300 to Sully Church/Community Hall; £300 to Mission Aviation Fellowship

FINANCES *Year* 1995 *Income* £15,500
Grants £13,300

TRUSTEES Rev A Cotgrove, SSJE, Rev Aidan Mayoss, CR, Mrs C F Fenn

HOW TO APPLY In writing, to the Hon Secretary, giving details of the project, its likely cost and with a note of any funds available toward it. Applications should be submitted, as far as possible, during March or September in each year. An sae would be appreciated for reply

WHO TO APPLY TO Mrs C F Fenn, The St George's Trust, 7 Brookside, Hornchurch, Essex RM11 2RR

CC NO 253524   **ESTABLISHED** 1924

■ St Giles Charity Estates

WHAT IS FUNDED The elderly, community welfare, disability

WHO CAN BENEFIT Organisations benefiting elderly people, disabled people, those at risk, disadvantaged by poverty and socially isolated

WHERE FUNDING CAN BE GIVEN The Ancient Parish of St Giles in Northampton

RANGE OF GRANTS Below £1,000–£5,000

SAMPLE GRANTS £5,000 to St Giles Church; £1,000 to Northampton Health Care; £1,000 to Council for Voluntary Services; £1,000 to Marie Curie Cancer Research

FINANCES *Year* 1996 *Income* £312,560
Grants £18,687

TRUSTEES D O Michel, OBE, B A Schanschieff, FCA, D Miles, J D Perkins, LLB, Dr R L Sutcliffe, MB, FRCP, B J Clayton, JP, FSVA, Miss M E Coombe, OBE, RGN, SCM, J A Cooper, FCA, Miss M W Blake, MBE, Dr M L Gillian, MA, BMBCH, J Frampton, FRICS, Dr R Sheppard, MB, FRS Path, Mrs A Marrum

NOTES Application forms are available from the address under Who To Apply To in writing. The Trustees meet every February, May, August and November

WHO TO APPLY TO Wilson Brown, Clerk, St Giles Charity Estates, 60 Gold Street, Northampton, Northamptonshire NN1 1RS

CC NO 202540   **ESTABLISHED** 1802

■ St Helens United Voluntary Organisations Community Trust

WHAT IS FUNDED The provision of welfare through charities in the area Where Funding Can Be Given, especially youth and community organisations, disability groups, victim support schemes and senior citizens' clubs

WHAT IS NOT FUNDED Branches of UK charities may only apply if they are financially independent of a national organisation

WHO CAN BENEFIT Young adults, older people and disabled people

WHERE FUNDING CAN BE GIVEN St Helens

FINANCES *Year* 1994–95 *Income* £13,519
Grants £16,200

TRUSTEES W K Atherton, W H Darlington, Lady M Pilkington, S Warren

NOTES Interested charities may apply for membership of the scheme, which is funded by payroll giving of employees of local companies

HOW TO APPLY To the address under Who To Apply To in writing

WHO TO APPLY TO S Warren, Hon Secretary, St Helens United Voluntary Organisations Community Trust, c/o St Helens YMCA, North Road, St Helens, Merseyside WA10 2TJ

CC NO 235214   **ESTABLISHED** 1964

■ St Hilda's Trust

WHAT IS FUNDED The Trust's main areas of concern within its overall objects are: young people generally and in particular today's equivalent of the original clientele of St Hilda's School (an approved school and community home) and those whose needs are not yet met by state social welfare provisions. However, the Trustees do not necessarily limit themselves to these areas

WHO CAN BENEFIT To benefit the young and those whose needs are not yet met by state social welfare provisions

WHERE FUNDING CAN BE GIVEN Diocese of Newcastle (Newcastle upon Tyne, North Tyneside and Northumberland)

TYPE OF GRANT Wide-ranging but seldom recurring. The Trustees prefer to support projects involving the employment of staff qualified to provide care and support to those in need rather than to provide buildings, equipment or motor vehicles

FINANCES *Year* 1995 *Income* £56,498
Grants £51,567

TRUSTEES Bishop of Newcastle, Archdeacon of Northumberland, R P Gordon, Dr R Nicholson, Dr M J Wilkinson, E Wright

HOW TO APPLY Completed application forms should be received no later than the last day of March, June, September or December for consideration at the Trustees' meeting in the following months

WHO TO APPLY TO Col Michael Craster, St Hilda's Trust, Diocese of Newcastle, Church House, Grainger Park Road, Newcastle upon Tyne, NE4 8SX

CC NO 500962   **ESTABLISHED** 1904

■ The St James's Trust Settlement

WHAT IS FUNDED Residential facilities and services; legal services; personnel and human resource services; community development; support to voluntary and community organisations; pre-school education; bursaries and fees; day centres; international rights of the individual; racial equality, discrimination and relations; and other charitable purposes

WHAT IS NOT FUNDED No grants to individuals

WHO CAN BENEFIT Registered charities benefiting: children; young adults; older people; parents and children; ethnic minority groups; homeless people; and immigrants

WHERE FUNDING CAN BE GIVEN UK and overseas

TYPE OF GRANT Core costs, one-off, project, research, recurring costs, salaries and start-up costs. Funding is for up to three years

SAMPLE GRANTS £30,534 to Trevor Day School for education - special needs; £30,000 to Institute for Public Policy Research for Attitudes to Race survey; £22,186 to Theatre For A New Audience for youth; teaching/education; £20,000 to Shelter for staff costs; £15,000 to Association for Gr. London Older Women for staff costs; £15,000 to Charta Mede for anti-discrimination; £15,000 to Exploring Parenthood for workshops for families; £15,000 to Shelter (Bayswater Project) for refugee support; £10,000 to Jewish Council for Racial Equality for inter-race work; £10,000 to One World Action for third world action

FINANCES *Year* 1997 *Income* £129,517 *Grants* £115,328

TRUSTEES Mrs Jane Wells, Dr R M E Stone, Mrs C Ingram

HOW TO APPLY Absolutely no personal callers or telephone enquiries. Applications to be made in writing enclosing sae but it is unlikely that unsolicited applications will be successful

WHO TO APPLY TO Clive M Marks, FCA, The St James's Trust Settlement, Marks Green & Co, 44a New Cavendish Street, London W1M 7LG

CC NO 280455   **ESTABLISHED** 1980

■ Sir Walter St John's Educational Charity

WHAT IS FUNDED The development of new educational initiatives and projects, curriculum enrichment programmes and short holiday projects. This includes: support to voluntary and community organisations; support to volunteers; volunteer bureaux; religion umbrella bodies; arts education; crime prevention schemes; holidays and outings; playschemes; and advice centres (social issues)

WHAT IS NOT FUNDED Applications for grants to pay salaries are not normally considered

WHO CAN BENEFIT Individuals and organisations benefiting: children; young adults; students; unemployed people; volunteers; those in care, fostered and adopted; parents and children; one parent families; those disadvantaged by poverty; ex-offenders and those at risk of offending; refugees; and those living in urban areas

WHERE FUNDING CAN BE GIVEN The boroughs of Wandsworth and Lambeth, especially Battersea

TYPE OF GRANT One-off, buildings, capital, projects and start-up costs. Funding is for up to three years

RANGE OF GRANTS £200–£30,000. Typically less than £5,000

SAMPLE GRANTS £50,000 to Shaftesbury Homes & Arethusa for an Education Support Team; £30,273 to Balham Family Centre for a Home-School Support Service; £10,000 to Bolingbroke School for a Community Playground-Entrance Playground; £7,500 to Home-School Support Service providing Consultancy for Home-School Support; £5,000 to African Caribbean Family Mediation Service for a Home/School Mediation Service; £5,000 to Lambeth Parent Advocacy for School-Based Support Groups; £4,995 to Lambeth Pre-School Learning Alliance for Book Babes-Storytelling for Under Fives; £4,500 to The Children's Society (SHINE) which gives a Voice to Excluded Pupils; £4,056 to The Trojans Scheme to Support Creation & Development of After School Clubs; £3,900 to Marcus Garvey Saturday School for a Homework Club

FINANCES *Year* 1996–97 *Income* £149,000 *Grants* £112,000

TRUSTEES Dr D Lewis (Chair), Lord Dubs, C Blackwood, Ms J Chegwidden, A Cole, A Crellin, Ms D Daytes, Rev Dr T Gaden, N Lucas, J O'Malley, Prof M Naylor, Cllr G Passmore, C Pinnell, Ms S Rackham, Ms J Scribbins, A Smith, M A Tuck, T Wallace

NOTES Office open on Tuesday, Wednesday morning and Thursday

HOW TO APPLY To the address under Who To Apply To by letter or telephone. Guidelines and application forms are available. No sae is required

WHO TO APPLY TO Philip Banard, Administrator, Sir Walter St John's Educational Charity, Unit 11, Culvert House, Culvert Road, London SW11 5AP *Tel* 0171-498 8878

CC NO 312690   **ESTABLISHED** 1992

■ The St John's Wood Trust

WHAT IS FUNDED Promotion of research in biological husbandry and alternative technology, particularly the advancement of organic and experimental farming. Income is currently wholly committed

WHO CAN BENEFIT Organisations benefiting: academics; scientists; research workers and students

WHERE FUNDING CAN BE GIVEN UK

TYPE OF GRANT Research grants

FINANCES *Year* 1997 *Income* £134,377 *Grants* £63,600

TRUSTEES S G Kemp, Hon F D L Astor, Mrs B A Astor, R D L Astor

HOW TO APPLY Since all income is committed for the foreseeable future, no applications can be considered

WHO TO APPLY TO S G Kemp, The St John's Wood Trust, Sayers Butterworth, Chartered Accountants, 18 Bentinck Street, London W1M 5RL

CC NO 281897   **ESTABLISHED** 1980

■ St Jude's Trust

WHAT IS FUNDED Relief of poverty. The advancement of religion and education. Other charitable purposes

WHO CAN BENEFIT Organisations, both local and national, benefiting: children; young adults; students; and those disadvantaged by poverty. There is no restriction on the religion or culture of the beneficiaries. Exceptionally funding will be given to individuals

WHERE FUNDING CAN BE GIVEN UK

TYPE OF GRANT Both recurrent and one-off. Grants made towards both capital and revenue expenditure. May be recurrent for up to 10 years

RANGE OF GRANTS £100–£3,000

SAMPLE GRANTS £3,000 to Compaid; £2,500 to St John Ambulance; £2,000 to NSPCC; £1,000 to NSPCC Berkshire Appeal; £1,000 to Foundation Committee for the Disabled; £1,000 to PACE Centre; £600 to Fund for Epilepsy; £600 to Order of St John; £600 to St Nicholas Remenham

FINANCES *Year* 1997 *Income* £28,820 *Grants* £23,700

TRUSTEES J M Patterson, Mrs R K Duckett

NOTES Funds fully allocated or committed but all applications considered

HOW TO APPLY No application forms, reviews normally twice yearly. No acknowledgements

WHO TO APPLY TO R G Millman, St Jude's Trust, Messrs Arnold, Fooks, Chadwick & Co, 15 Bolton Street, Piccadilly, London W1Y 8AR

CC NO 222883   **ESTABLISHED** 1961

■ St Katharine & Shadwell Trust

WHAT IS FUNDED Priority is given to education and training of children and adults living in one small area of the London Borough of Tower Hamlets only. This includes: arts; culture and recreation; schools and colleges; education and training; purchase of books; playschemes; and advice centres; support to voluntary and community organisations; and support to volunteers

WHAT IS NOT FUNDED The Trust will not normally: (a) Make grants to individuals. (b) Fund travel or study outside the area. (c) Fund what could be paid for by statutory sources. (d) Fund the purchase, repair or maintenance of buildings or vehicles. (e) Support religious groups or political groups. (f) Fund research. (g) Sponsor fundraising. (h) Make retrospective grants or pay off mortgages, deficits, etc

WHO CAN BENEFIT Organisations providing a benefit for residents of the St Katharine and Shadwell wards of the London Borough of Tower Hamlets only, including: children; young adults; older people; actors and entertainment professionals; musicians; textile workers and designers; writers and poets

WHERE FUNDING CAN BE GIVEN St Katharine and Shadwell wards of the London Borough of Tower Hamlets only

TYPE OF GRANT Capital (not vehicles), core costs, one-off, project, running costs, salaries, and start-up costs. Funding is available for up to and over three years

RANGE OF GRANTS Variable

SAMPLE GRANTS £35,305 Parental Involvement in the Core Curriculum for over three years funding to continue project at Cyril Jackson School; £22,500 to London Borough of Tower Hamlets, £7,500 pa for three years for youth apprenticeship scheme; £15,000 to Bishop Challower School to equip new library; £13,000 to Shaowell Basin Outdoor Activity Centre towards costs; £10,500 to Chinese Association of Tower Hamlets £3,500 pa for three years towards employment and guidance and Chinese IT Training project; £10,071 Foundation for Young Musicians; £3,317pa for three years to assist three students; £10,000 to Tower Hamlets Education Business Partnership towards core and development costs; £10,000 to Tower Hamlets Summer University towards core and development costs; £9,159 to Workers Educational Association for over two years towards family literacy and numeracy programmes; £7,858 to Tower Hamlets Community Transport for shopping bus service for elderly and disabled people

FINANCES *Year* 1997 *Income* £371,884
Grants £257,467

TRUSTEES Sir David Hancock, Sir David Hardy, Mrs S McAtee, Ian McDonald, Mrs M Nepstad, Ms J Reed, R Roberts, E Sorensen, P Stehrenberger, Cllr Abdul Asad, Cllr Abdus Shukur, Rev R Swan, L Hinton, Mrs V Ocuneff

PUBLICATIONS Annual Report and accounts, *Artists in Residence: A Teacher's Handbook*, *A New Perspective*

HOW TO APPLY Applications should be made in writing. Telephone enquiries are welcomed. Trust meets four times a year. All applications will be acknowledged

WHO TO APPLY TO Jenny Dawes, Director, St Katharine & Shadwell Trust, PO Box 1779, London E1 9BY *Tel* 0171-782 6962 *Fax* 0171-782 6963

CC NO 1001047   **ESTABLISHED** 1990

■ St Laurence Charities for the Poor

WHAT IS FUNDED The provision of specialist equipment for hospitals and hospices. Health and welfare

WHAT IS NOT FUNDED Grants will not be made to individuals outside of the Parish of St Laurence

WHO CAN BENEFIT Organisations benefiting at risk groups, those disadvantaged by poverty and socially isolated people. There is no restriction on the disease or medical condition suffered by the beneficiaries

WHERE FUNDING CAN BE GIVEN The Ancient Parish of St Laurence and the Borough of Reading

FINANCES *Year* 1994–95 *Income* £87,057

HOW TO APPLY To the address under Who To Apply To in writing

WHO TO APPLY TO J M James, Treasurer, St Laurence Charities for the Poor, Vale and West, Victoria House, 26 Queen Victoria Street, Reading, Berkshire RG1 1TG

CC NO 205043   **ESTABLISHED** 1941

■ St Luke's College Foundation

WHAT IS FUNDED Encouraging original work and imaginative new projects with a religious connection, particularly through the advancement of religion, education, cultural and religious teaching, postgraduate education and various costs of study

WHAT IS NOT FUNDED Grants not made for first degree courses, buildings or schools (except indirectly through research projects). Block grants to support schemes or organisations are not made. Grants are not normally made for periods in excess of three years

WHO CAN BENEFIT Individual or corporate applications benefiting young adults and older people. Some preference for Dioceses of Exeter and Truro and University of Exeter

WHERE FUNDING CAN BE GIVEN UK and overseas, with some preference for Exeter and Truro

TYPE OF GRANT Normally one-off for a specific project or part of a project, and research. Grants can be made for periods of up to three years

FINANCES *Year* 1997 *Income* £158,218
Grants £89,661

TRUSTEES The Bishop of Exeter, The Dean of Exeter, Diocesan Director of Education, Chairman of Diocesan Board of Finance, one nominated by the Bishop of Exeter, three nominated by the University of Exeter, four co-optative trustees

PUBLICATIONS Triennial Report

NOTES The scheme of trust requires that the first charge on the Foundation's income is the maintenance of a Chapel and a Chaplaincy: from the residue grants can be made

HOW TO APPLY Applications considered twice a year: should be received by 1 February and 1 September. Apply in writing only to Prof M Bond

WHO TO APPLY TO Professor M Bond, St Luke's College Foundation, Heathayne, Colyton, Devon EX13 6RS *Tel* 01297 552281 *Fax* 01297 552281

CC NO 306606   **ESTABLISHED** 1977

■ St Mark's Foundation

WHAT IS FUNDED For religious or educational purposes

WHO CAN BENEFIT At present all benefits are committed almost entirely for upkeep of

Does the trust you have chosen match your needs? Haphazard applications waste postage and time

557

Southwark Diocesan Conference Centre, Wychcroft, Blechingley. Organisations benefiting children, young adults and students may be considered

WHERE FUNDING CAN BE GIVEN UK with preference for local charities

FINANCES *Year* 1997 *Income* £24,000 *Grants* £12,000

TRUSTEES Mrs S J F Goad, Miss M S Lambert, S U Lambert

HOW TO APPLY **This Trust states that it does not respond to unsolicited applications**

WHO TO APPLY TO Mrs S J F Goad, St Mark's Foundation, South Park, Blechingley, Redhill, Surrey RH1 4NG

CC NO 262346   **ESTABLISHED** 1970

■ St Martin's Trust

WHAT IS FUNDED The relief of the poor, disabled and elderly; the advancement of education and religion; and other general charitable purposes for the benefit of the community

WHO CAN BENEFIT Organisations benefiting people of all ages, students, disabled people and those disadvantaged by poverty. There are no restrictions on the religion or culture of the beneficiaries

WHERE FUNDING CAN BE GIVEN UK

TRUSTEES D J Ayton, R P Booth, A Harrington

WHO TO APPLY TO Dr R P Booth, St Martin's Trust, Cheyham Cottage, Higher Street, Norton-sub-Hamdon, Somerset TA14 6SN

CC NO 1065584   **ESTABLISHED** 1997

■ St Marylebone Educational Foundation

WHAT IS FUNDED The education of young people between the ages of eight and 25, resident in the City of Westminster, including school and colleges and bursaries and fees

WHO CAN BENEFIT Children, young adults and students

WHERE FUNDING CAN BE GIVEN City of Westminster

TYPE OF GRANT Percentage of fees

FINANCES *Year* 1996–97 *Income* £81,000 *Grants* £76,000

HOW TO APPLY To the address under Who To Apply To in writing

WHO TO APPLY TO Mrs P J le Gassick, Clerk, St Marylebone Educational Foundation, c/o St Peter's Church, 119 Eaton Square, London SW1W 9AL

CC NO 312378   **ESTABLISHED** 1750

■ The St Mary-le-Strand Charity

WHAT IS FUNDED Relief of need, community development, health projects, youth clubs and educational institutions, including accommodation and housing; infrastructure, support and development; Christian outreach; religious ancillary buildings; religious umbrella bodies; arts education; health; schools and colleges; education and training; community centres and village halls; community services and advice centres

WHAT IS NOT FUNDED No grants for expeditions, electives, non-residents of Westminster or asylum-seekers

WHO CAN BENEFIT Residents of Westminster who are in need and have lived in the area for at least one

year. Also to organisations benefiting these residents. This includes those who are unemployed; volunteers; parents and children; one parent families; widows and widowers from a wide range of social circumstances

WHERE FUNDING CAN BE GIVEN City of Westminster

TYPE OF GRANT One-off grants for capital, buildings, core costs, feasibility studies, projects, running costs, salaries and start-up costs. Funding is available for up to one year

RANGE OF GRANTS Organisations: £500–£5,000, individuals: £100

SAMPLE GRANTS £5,500 to St Marylebone Health Society for grants to those in need; £500 to St Saviours Church of England Primary School for rebuilding project, nursery unit; £5,000 to Westminster Society for children with special needs project; £4,000 to House of St Barnabas in Soho for accommodation; £2,500 to Soho Family Centre; £2,000 to Paddington Youth Point; £2,000 to Westminster Sports Unit for disabled sporting event; £1,827 to Terrance Higgins Trust for volunteer training; £1,500 to North Westminster Victim Support; £1,500 to St Johns Hospice for on-going work

FINANCES *Year* 1997 *Income* £76,000 *Grants* £57,000

TRUSTEES M F Cayley, D J Harvey, S Harrow, M Dennison, A Kavanagh, P Maplestone, J d'A Maycock, T Sheppard, J Stevenson, P Symmons, D White

NOTES Residency qualification of one year

HOW TO APPLY To the address under Who To Apply To in writing. Applications for individuals to be made via sponsoring organisations (social services, CAB, etc). Guidelines and application forms available to sponsors

WHO TO APPLY TO The Clerk, The St Mary-le-Strand Charity, The St Mary-le-Strand Office, 171 Strand, London WC2R 1EP

CC NO 208631   **ESTABLISHED** 1962

■ St Mary's Development Trust

WHAT IS FUNDED General charitable purposes

WHO CAN BENEFIT There are no restrictions on the age; professional and economic group; family situation; religion and culture; and social circumstances of; or disease or medical condition suffered by, the beneficiaries

WHERE FUNDING CAN BE GIVEN UK and overseas

SAMPLE GRANTS £685,905 to Imperial College in research grants; £204,530 to Imperial College as other grants; £5,000 as miscellaneous grants

FINANCES *Year* 1995 *Income* £1,589,310 *Grants* £895,435

TRUSTEES Sir E de Rothschild, Sir R Powell, C Thornton, Sir R Bannister, Prof P Richards

WHO TO APPLY TO P V Blissett, St Mary's Development Trust, Norfolk Place, Praed Street, London W2 1PG

CC NO 1041737   **ESTABLISHED** 1984

■ St Olave, St Thomas and St John United Charity

WHAT IS FUNDED Relief in need, pensions, education for people under 24 years of age, general welfare purposes amongst poor people and other worthwhile organisations

WHO CAN BENEFIT To benefit: pensioners; students; at risk groups; those disadvantaged by poverty and socially isolated people. There is no

restriction on the disease or medical condition suffered by the beneficiaries

WHERE FUNDING CAN BE GIVEN Bermondsey

SAMPLE GRANTS £136,193 for holidays and outings; £36,400 for educational foundation grants; £26,175 for Christmas gifts; £8,600 for individual grants

FINANCES *Year* 1997 *Income* £424,034 *Grants* £207,368

TRUSTEES R Doyle, J Burke (Chair), J Chandler, Mrs E Brown, Mrs R Phipps, A Waterfield, J Donovan, Mrs M White (Vice Chair), J O'Grady, C Bennett, D Braiser, H Young, Rev J Bradshaw

HOW TO APPLY To the address under Who To Apply To in writing

WHO TO APPLY TO Mrs S Broughton, Secretary, St Olave, St Thomas and St John United Charity, 6–8 Druid Street, Tooley Street, London SE1 2EU

CC NO 211763   **ESTABLISHED** 1892

■ St Pancras Church Lands Trust

WHAT IS FUNDED Repairs to or the expenses of performing Divine Worship in churches or chapels within the original limits of the Parish of St Pancras and having District Parishes assigned to them which are wholly within such limits

WHAT IS NOT FUNDED Any other matters

WHERE FUNDING CAN BE GIVEN Churches and chapels within the original limits of the Parish of St Pancras

TYPE OF GRANT Repairs to qualiyfying churches or chapels, in cases of extreme need only

RANGE OF GRANTS £5,000–£20,000

SAMPLE GRANTS £12,927 to St Pancras Church for repairs to Church car park

FINANCES *Year* 1997 *Income* £281,134 *Grants* £12,927

TRUSTEES D Brewer, Dr D Brown, Rev B Clover, B Leverton, L Lewis JP, The Very Rev Dr J Moses, M Ogden, A Rouse, Prof D Severin

NOTES Only churchwardens of qualyfying churches or chapels should apply

HOW TO APPLY To the address under Who To Apply To in writing

WHO TO APPLY TO C L Jesson, Clerk, St Pancras Church Lands Trust, 22 South Road, Baldock, Hertfordshire SG7 6BY *Tel* 0171-606 9000

CC NO 212006   **ESTABLISHED** 1962

■ St Peter's Aid for the Needy

WHAT IS FUNDED General charitable purposes, in particular, the relief of poverty, the preservation and promotion of good health

WHO CAN BENEFIT Organisations benefiting those disadvantaged by poverty. There is no restriction on the disease or medical condition suffered by the beneficiaries

WHERE FUNDING CAN BE GIVEN UK and overseas

RANGE OF GRANTS £200–£4,050

SAMPLE GRANTS £4,200 to Starving in Africa; £3,500 to Concern Universal; £2,527 to Nyenga Leprosy Hospital; £2,204 to UK appeals and local needs; £2,108 Appeals for Far and Middle East

FINANCES *Year* 1997 *Income* £20,423 *Grants* £22,124

TRUSTEES J Beaver, Ms J Davison

WHO TO APPLY TO J E Francis, St Peter's Aid for the Needy, Highfield House, Loxley, Warwick CV35 9LB

CC NO 1040252   **ESTABLISHED** 1994

■ St Peters Saltley Trust

WHAT IS FUNDED The advancement of education and religion via projects in the area Where Funding Can Be Given. Infrastructure development will also be considered

WHAT IS NOT FUNDED No grants to individuals

WHO CAN BENEFIT Organisations benefiting people of all ages, teachers, governesses, unemployed people and volunteers. There may be a few restrictions on the religion of the beneficiaries

WHERE FUNDING CAN BE GIVEN The dioceses of Birmingham, Coventry, Hereford, Lichfield and Worcester

TYPE OF GRANT Project funding for up to three years will be considered

FINANCES *Year* 1995–96 *Income* £127,844

TRUSTEES The Lord Bishop of Worcester, The Lord Bishop of Hereford, The Lord Bishop of Lichfield, The Lord Bishop of Birmingham, The Lord Bishop of Coventry, T W Bayliss, P Middlemiss, T D R Jenkins, Rev P Lister, Ven J Duncan, Rev Canon J Eardley, H B Oxenham, Prof J M Hull, Miss H Haines, Rev Jackie Hughes, Mrs J E Jones

HOW TO APPLY To the address under Who To Apply To in writing

WHO TO APPLY TO Mrs J E Jones, Clerk, St Peters Saltley Trust, Grays Court, 3 Nursery Road, Edgbaston, Birmingham B15 3JX *Tel* 0121-427 6800

CC NO 528915   **ESTABLISHED** 1980

■ Saint Sarkis Charity Trust

WHAT IS FUNDED Primarily charitable objectives with an Armenian connection including Armenian religious buildings; and other small charities catering for disadvantaged groups in response to applications

WHAT IS NOT FUNDED No grants to individuals

WHO CAN BENEFIT Smaller registered charities benefiting Christians, disabled people and victims of abuse

WHERE FUNDING CAN BE GIVEN Mainly UK

TYPE OF GRANT Mainly confined to one-off grants for capital projects or operational expenses. Cash donation

SAMPLE GRANTS £58,000 to Armenian Church, London for general fund; £24,000 to Garnahovit Church, Armenia for weatherproofing roof and buildings; £20,000 to Armenian Roots for 4WD Vehicle for project; £11,085 for Gandzasar Theological Centre, Armenia for research for Armenian Hymnal; £10,000 to Centre for Armenian Information and Advice for general fund; £8,000 to Gulbenkian Library, Jerusalem for general fund; £7,000 to Armenia Aid for childrens hospital; £4,000 to London Armenian Poor Relief Society for general fund; £2,000 to Victim Support (N. Ireland) for support work; £2,000 to British Stammering Association for Life Without Stammering appeal

FINANCES *Year* 1997–98 *Income* £291,620 *Grants* £172,276

TRUSTEES M Essayan, B P Gulbenkian, P A Curno, R B Todd

HOW TO APPLY Through the address under Who To Apply To, by letter (sae not required), enclosing financial statements. All applications will be acknowledged

WHO TO APPLY TO P A Lovatt, The Secretary, Saint Sarkis Charity Trust, c/o Economic & General Secretariat Ltd, 98 Portland Place, London W1N 4ET

CC NO 236583   **ESTABLISHED** 1954

■ St Teilo's Trust

This trust did not respond to CAF's request to amend its entry and, by 30 June 1998, CAF's researchers did not find financial records for later than 1995 on its file at the Charity Commission. Trusts are legally required to submit annual accounts to the Charity Commission under section 42 of the Charities Act 1993

WHAT IS FUNDED General charitable purposes

WHO CAN BENEFIT There are no restrictions on the age; professional and economic group; family situation; religion and culture; and social circumstances of; or disease or medical condition suffered by, the beneficiaries

WHERE FUNDING CAN BE GIVEN Dyfed

FINANCES *Income* £13,507

TRUSTEES P C A Mansel Lewis, Mrs C M Lewis, W A Strange, Mrs F J Strange

WHO TO APPLY TO P Mansel Lewis, St Teilo's Trust, Capel Isaf, Manordeilo, Llandeilo SA19 7BS

CC NO 1032405   **ESTABLISHED** 1993

■ St Thomas Ecclesiastical Charity

WHAT IS FUNDED The religious and charitable work of the Church of England, including social welfare and community projects

WHAT IS NOT FUNDED No grants for scholarships or expeditions or to individuals

WHO CAN BENEFIT Charities benefiting the Church of England in the City of Bristol

WHERE FUNDING CAN BE GIVEN Bristol, especially the parishes of St Mary, Redcliffe with Temple and St John the Baptist, Bedminster

TYPE OF GRANT One-off, recurring costs, project, salaries and start-up costs. Funding for up to and over three years will be considered

SAMPLE GRANTS £12,500 to Bishop's Urban Fund, Withywood Project for church and community worker; £11,500 to Bristol Diocese - Industrial and Social Responsibility for commercial sector chaplaincy; £7,200 to Easton Christian Family Centre for youth and administrative workers; £5,000 to St Stephen's Community Work Project, Southmead for administrative worker; £650 to Caring at Christmas for shelter for the homeless at Christmas

FINANCES *Year* 1997 *Income* £62,194
Grants £36,850

TRUSTEES D J Yabsley (Chairman), Ven D J Banfield, Mrs J Bone, N Croucher, Canon S A N Darley, B B Richards, K F Shattock, J Smith, C Tippetts

HOW TO APPLY To the address under Who To Apply To in writing

WHO TO APPLY TO J M Haddrell, Clerk to the Trustees, St Thomas Ecclesiastical Charity, Diocesan Registry, 14 Market Place, Wells, Somerset BA5 2RE *Tel* 01749 674747
Fax 01749 676585

CC NO 229807   **ESTABLISHED** 1989

■ St Vincent De Paul Society (England and Wales)

WHAT IS FUNDED General charitable purposes. Projects include residential care activities involving hostels for the homeless, mentally afflicted, probationers and ex-offenders and women at risk; day care centre provisions and soup runs; holidays for needy adults and families; furniture units; charity shops; pilgrimages for the deaf and sick; support and training for the homeless and unemployed; audio cassettes for the blind and partially sighted; pensioners clubs and meals clubs; prison visitations; and support for refugees. The core activity of the Society is visiting those in need, on a person to person basis, either in their own homes, hospitals or other places of care. These works are undertaken by local groups called 'Conferences' whose members are largely drawn from the Catholic parishes

WHO CAN BENEFIT Organisations benefiting elderly people. Women at risk, the unemployed and the homeless. Those disadvantaged by poverty, socially isolated or who are refugees may also be supported. Funding may be given to organisations benefiting offenders, probationers, ex-offenders and those at risk of offending. There is no restriction on the disease or medical condition suffered by the beneficiaries, but particular favour is given to those suffering from hearing and sight loss or mental illness, or disabled people with physical, sensory or learning impairments

WHERE FUNDING CAN BE GIVEN UK, particularly England and Wales, and overseas

SAMPLE GRANTS £679,306 for residential care; £524,427 for others in need; £348,394 for families; £234,259 for probation hostels; £232,888 for holiday centre and camps; £213,705 for thrift shops and furniture stores; £212,432 in support for the elderly; £90,105 for the homeless and unemployed; £86,489 for single parent families; £68,236 for the handicapped

FINANCES *Year* 1997 *Income* £4,557,762
Grants £3,819,991

TRUSTEES A Abel, Dr P Holland, T Mackin, J O'Connor, Miss C St John-Maurer, L Smith, B Thurlow, D A Williams

PUBLICATIONS *The New Vincentian* quarterly

WHO TO APPLY TO The Secretary, St Vincent De Paul Society (England and Wales), 14 Blandford Street, London W1H 4DP *Tel* 0171-935 9126

CC NO 1053992   **ESTABLISHED** 1996

■ The Saintbury Trust

WHAT IS FUNDED General charitable purposes at the discretion of the Trustees

WHAT IS NOT FUNDED No animal charities

WHO CAN BENEFIT There are no restrictions on the age; professional and economic group; family situation; religion and culture; and social circumstances of; or disease or medical condition suffered by, the beneficiaries

WHERE FUNDING CAN BE GIVEN UK

TYPE OF GRANT At the discretion of the Trustees

RANGE OF GRANTS £200–£50,000

SAMPLE GRANTS £50,000 to University of Birmingham for two research grants of £25,000; £10,000 to University of Birmingham for The Great Hall Campaign; £1,000 to Bloomsbury Church Centre; £1,000 to CCHA Extra Care; £1,000 to the Police Convalescence and Rehabilitation Trust; £1,000 to West House School Centenary Appeal; £500 to the Multiple Sclerosis Society; £500 to the Soho House Archives Appeal; £200 to Theatre Room, Bretform

FINANCES *Year* 1995 *Income* £159,207
Grants £65,200

TRUSTEES A C Bryant, J M Bryant, V K Haughton, A R Thomas, J P Lewis, A E Atkinson-Willes, H O Forrester

WHO TO APPLY TO Mrs V K Houghton, The Saintbury Trust, Hawnby House, Hawnby, York YO62 5QS

CC NO 326790   **ESTABLISHED** 1985

■ The Saints and Sinners Trust Limited

WHAT IS FUNDED General charitable purposes. To give priority to requests for grants sponsored by members of Saints and Sinners

WHAT IS NOT FUNDED No grants to individuals

WHO CAN BENEFIT There are no restrictions on the age; professional and economic group; family situation; religion and culture; and social circumstances of; or disease or medical condition suffered by, the beneficiaries

WHERE FUNDING CAN BE GIVEN UK

TYPE OF GRANT Cash

RANGE OF GRANTS £100–£4,000

SAMPLE GRANTS £4,000 to South Buckinghamshire Riding for the Disabled; £3,000 to Crusaid; £3,000 to Foundation for the Study of Infant Deaths; £3,000 to Manor House Trust; £3,000 to Motor and Allied Trades Benevolent Fund; £3,000 to Reform Foundation Trust; £3,000 to the White Ensign Association Ltd; £2,141 to Help the Aged; £2,000 to Bud Flanagan Leukaemia Fund; £2,000 to Charterhouse in Southwark

FINANCES *Year* 1995 *Income* £74,081
Grants £66,241

TRUSTEES Council of Management: N W Benson, P Moloney, I A N Irvine

HOW TO APPLY To the address under Who To Apply To in writing

WHO TO APPLY TO N W Benson, The Saints and Sinners Trust Limited, Lewis Golden & Co, 40 Queen Anne Street, London W1M 0EL

CC NO 200536   **ESTABLISHED** 1961

■ The Salamander Charitable Trust

WHAT IS FUNDED Concerned with the advancement of education, religion, relief of poverty or physical disability

WHAT IS NOT FUNDED No grants to individuals

WHO CAN BENEFIT Registered charities benefiting children, young adults, those disadvantaged by poverty and disabled people

WHERE FUNDING CAN BE GIVEN UK

TYPE OF GRANT Mostly modest

SAMPLE GRANTS £5,000 to St James' Church, Poole for Restoration Fund; £5,000 to St Peter's Church, Maney, Sutton Coldfield for Restoration Fund; £1,000 to Christian Aid; £1,000 to St James' Church, Poole for general funds; £1,000 to Birmingham Bible Institute for students in need; £1,000 to Churches Commission on Overseas Students for students in need; £1,000 to FEBA Radio for missionary work; £1,000 to Glasgow Bible College for students in need; £1,000 to London Bible College for students in need; £1,000 to Mattersey Hall Bible College for students in need

FINANCES *Year* 1995 *Income* £96,510
Grants £95,435

TRUSTEES J R T Douglas, OBE, Mrs S M Douglas

HOW TO APPLY **This Trust states that it does not respond to unsolicited applications**

WHO TO APPLY TO J R T Douglas, The Salamander Charitable Trust, Threave, 2 Brundenell Avenue, Canford Cliffs, Poole, Dorset BH13 7NW

CC NO 273657   **ESTABLISHED** 1977

■ The Salisbury Pool Charity

WHAT IS FUNDED General charitable purposes. A restricted number of charities primarily those already being funded. Particularly Christian entities, the Armed Forces, gardens and local charitable work

WHAT IS NOT FUNDED No grants to individuals and most national charities

WHO CAN BENEFIT Local organisations particularly those benefiting Christians and ex-service and service people

WHERE FUNDING CAN BE GIVEN Primarily Hertfordshire and Dorset

TYPE OF GRANT One-off and recurring costs may be considered

FINANCES *Year* 1995–96 *Income* £16,500
Grants £10,900

TRUSTEES The Marquess of Salisbury, Viscount Cranborne

HOW TO APPLY To the address under Who To Apply To in writing. Sae from applicants required

WHO TO APPLY TO M R Melville, The Salisbury Pool Charity, Hatfield House, Hatfield, Hertfordshire AL9 5NF

CC NO 272626   **ESTABLISHED** 1976

■ Harold Joseph Salmon Charitable Settlement

WHAT IS FUNDED General charitable purposes. To fund existing commitments

WHAT IS NOT FUNDED No grants to individuals

WHO CAN BENEFIT Registered charities only, long established organisations including local branches. There are no restrictions on the age; professional and economic group; family situation; religion and culture; and social circumstances of; or disease or medical condition suffered by, the beneficiaries

WHERE FUNDING CAN BE GIVEN UK

RANGE OF GRANTS £22–£2,500

SAMPLE GRANTS £2,500 to North London Hospice; £2,000 to Genetic Interest Group; £1,650 to Gaia House Trust; £1,500 to Tower Hamlets Old People's Trust; £1,100 to BDA (Initiatives) Ltd; £1,000 to St John's Hospice; £1,000 to Norwood Ravenswood; £500 to St Merrin PCC; £500 to Friends of the Hebrew University; £500 to Amnesty International British Section Charitable Trust

FINANCES *Year* 1997 *Income* £51,865
Grants £23,772

TRUSTEES R J Gluckstein

HOW TO APPLY To the address under Who To Apply To. New applications not encouraged

WHO TO APPLY TO H J Salmon, Harold Joseph Salmon Charitable Settlement, Warwick House, 181–183 Warwick Road, London W14 8PU

CC NO 207153   **ESTABLISHED** 1955

■ The Guy Salmon Charity

WHAT IS FUNDED The Trustees favour a wide variety of human causes

WHO CAN BENEFIT There are no restrictions on the age; professional and economic group; family situation; religion and culture; and social circumstances of; or disease or medical condition suffered by, the beneficiaries

WHERE FUNDING CAN BE GIVEN UK

RANGE OF GRANTS £5–£1,000

SAMPLE GRANTS £1,000 to The Mayors Charity Fund re:Hospice; £1,000 to The Princess Alice Hospice; £120 to Ben (raffle tickets for staff); £100 to donation to student; £100 to SSFA

FINANCES *Year* 1997 *Income* £15,636
Grants £10,005

TRUSTEES G F Salmon, A D R Owen

Does the trust you have chosen match your needs? Haphazard applications waste postage and time

561

WHO TO APPLY TO R Morgan, The Guy Salmon Charity, Messrs Bells, Solicitors, Eagle Chambers, 16–18 Eden Street, Kingston upon Thames, Surrey KT1 1RD
CC NO 327778   **ESTABLISHED** 1988

....

■ The Salt Foundation

WHAT IS FUNDED To advance education. Funding can also be given for community centres and village halls
WHAT IS NOT FUNDED Benefits of any kind which are normally provided by the local education authority
WHO CAN BENEFIT Individuals and schools benefiting children, young adults, older people and students
WHERE FUNDING CAN BE GIVEN Saltaire and Shipley
TYPE OF GRANT One-off grants (although applicants may reapply), capital, project and recurring costs for funding of one year or less
RANGE OF GRANTS £50–£1,000
SAMPLE GRANTS £3,144 to Woodend Middle School for equipment; £2,000 to North East Windhill Community Centre for Homework Club; £2,000 to St Peters Church for Homework Club; £1,000 to Nab Wood Middle School for textbooks; £1,000 to Low Ash First School for computer equipment; £1,000 to Shipley College for a Student Hardship Fund; £1,000 to Wycliffe Middle School for equipment; £800 to High Crags First School for music equipment; £700 to Greenfield Special School to send a teacher on a course to benefit a Shipley boy; £620 to Glenaire First School for a field trip
FINANCES *Year* 1997–98 *Income* £78,982 *Grants* £41,090
TRUSTEES Mrs J B Evans, N Free, A Law, Mrs G Lister, W Nunn, M W Poole, N Roper, J E Watson, M J Whitaker
HOW TO APPLY To the address under Who To Apply To in writing
WHO TO APPLY TO The Clerk, The Salt Foundation, Room 112, First Floor, City Hall, Bradford BD1 1HY *Tel* 01274 754287
CC NO 511978   **ESTABLISHED** 1981

....

■ George and Thomas Henry Salter Trust

WHAT IS FUNDED Individuals may receive grants for both education and relief in need purposes. Organisations supporting work in the areas of youth, disability and the arts
WHAT IS NOT FUNDED Holidays for individuals
WHO CAN BENEFIT Some individuals, local schools and organisations benefiting: children, young adults, disabled people and those disadvantaged by poverty
WHERE FUNDING CAN BE GIVEN Sandwell only
TYPE OF GRANT One-off. Funding for up to one year will be considered
RANGE OF GRANTS £50–£2,500
SAMPLE GRANTS £1,000 to Stuart Bathurst Roman Catholic School for educational purposes; £1,000 to Alexander High School for educational purposes; £1,000 to Menzies School for purchase of software; £1,000 to WRVS for Christmas hampers; £1,000 to West Bromwich School Football Association for educational purposes
FINANCES *Year* 1997 *Income* £53,945 *Grants* £22,500
TRUSTEES Mayor of Sandwell, P J Elliott, Mrs A F Maybury, R J E Norris, T Turner
HOW TO APPLY To the address under Who To Apply To in writing. Please request application form for

educational grants, or apply through DSS for individual grants for the relief of poverty giving income amd expenditure details
WHO TO APPLY TO Mrs J S Styler, Clerk, George and Thomas Henry Salter Trust, Lombard House, Cronehills Linkway, West Bromwich, West Midlands B70 7PL *Tel* 0121-553 3286
CC NO 216503   **ESTABLISHED** 1963

....

■ Salters Charities

WHAT IS FUNDED General charitable purposes. The Company's charity is spread as widely as possible over the charitable fields. Smaller contributions to major charities will be discontinued and larger sums will be donated to a smaller number of charities
WHAT IS NOT FUNDED As far as possible the charities selected should be nationwide in their application except for those connected with the City of London
WHO CAN BENEFIT As a matter of general policy, the Company should support those charities where Salters are involved. As part of the need to take a more detailed interest in those charities which are supported, Liverymen should be encouraged to make personal enquiries regarding charities which they had initially nominated prior to a subsequent donation being considered. Visits should also be made to supported charities by Liverymen and members of staff. There are no restrictions on the age; professional and economic group; family situation; religion and culture; and social circumstances of; or disease or medical condition suffered by, the beneficiaries
WHERE FUNDING CAN BE GIVEN UK, City of London
RANGE OF GRANTS In the range of £500 to £2,000, usually £1,500
SAMPLE GRANTS £12,500 to Christ's Hospital; £5,000 to The World Conservation Monitoring Centre; £2,500 to Cancer Research Campaign for Lord Mayor's Appeal; £2,000 to The Promis Recovery Centre; £1,600 to Cancer Relief Macmillan Fund; £1,600 to The College of St Barnabas; £1,500 to Starlight Foundation; £1,500 to NCH Action for Children; £1,500 to TEAR Fund; £1,500 to CARE - Christian Action Research and Education
FINANCES *Year* 1996–97 *Income* £127,669 *Grants* £109,257
TRUSTEES The Salters' Company
HOW TO APPLY Monitored monthly, considered by the Company twice per year in May and November. Applications by letter only with sae
WHO TO APPLY TO The Clerk or Charities Administrator, Salters Charities, The Salters' Company, Salters' Hall, 4 Fore Street, London EC2Y 5DE *Tel* 0171-588 5216
CC NO 328258   **ESTABLISHED** 1989

....

■ The Andrew Salvesen Charitable Trust

WHAT IS FUNDED Grants are made to a variety of charitable organisations who work for sick children, the disabled, the homeless and a range of other causes
WHAT IS NOT FUNDED No grants to individuals
WHO CAN BENEFIT Organisations benefiting sick children, disabled people and homeless people
WHERE FUNDING CAN BE GIVEN UK, particularly Scotland
FINANCES *Year* 1996 *Income* £50,000
TRUSTEES V Lall, A C Salvesen, Ms K Turner
PUBLICATIONS Accounts are available from the Trust

HOW TO APPLY This Trust states that it does not respond to unsolicited applications
WHO TO APPLY TO Mark Brown, The Andrew Salvesen Charitable Trust, Meston Reid & Company, 12 Carden Place, Aberdeen AB1 1UR
SC NO SCO 08000 **ESTABLISHED** 1989

■ The Sammermar Trust

WHAT IS FUNDED General charitable purposes
WHO CAN BENEFIT There are no restrictions on the age; professional and economic group; family situation; religion and culture; and social circumstances of; or disease or medical condition suffered by, the beneficiaries
WHERE FUNDING CAN BE GIVEN UK and overseas
SAMPLE GRANTS £15,000 to St Katherine's House; £8,000 to St Clement Danes Resident Chaplain's Discretionary Fund; £5,000 to Parkhouse Award; £4,500 to Spitfire Society; £3,700 to Sparsholt Parochial Church Council; £2,500 to Design Museum; £2,000 to Suttleworth Collection – Hurricane Fund; £1,500 to Wycombe Air Centre Ltd; £1,500 to DGAA Homelife
FINANCES *Year* 1997 *Income* £69,189 *Grants* £53,286
WHO TO APPLY TO B N Swire, Trustee, The Sammermar Trust, c/o John Swire & Sons Ltd, Swire House, 59 Buckingham Gate, London SW1E 6AJ
CC NO 800493 **ESTABLISHED** 1988

■ Coral Samuel Charitable Trust

WHAT IS FUNDED General charitable purposes. Grants made at the discretion of the Trustees
WHAT IS NOT FUNDED Grants can be made to registered charities only
WHO CAN BENEFIT Registered charities only. There are no restrictions on the age; professional and economic group; family situation; religion and culture; and social circumstances of; or disease or medical condition suffered by, the beneficiaries
WHERE FUNDING CAN BE GIVEN UK
RANGE OF GRANTS £250–£50,000
SAMPLE GRANTS £50,000 to the Racing Welfare Charities; £27,000 to University of York; £25,000 to Emmanuel College, Cambridge; £25,000 to the Tate Gallery; £10,000 to Burlington Magazine; £10,000 to the Wallace Collection; £10,000 to Dulwich Picture Gallery; £10,000 to the Natural History Museum; £5,000 to Royal Opera House Trust; £5,000 to Cancer Relief Macmillan Fund
FINANCES *Year* 1997 *Income* £219,239 *Grants* £201,450
TRUSTEES Mrs C C Samuel, CBE, P J Fineman, BSc, FRICS
NOTES Grants of £10,000 or more go to educational, cultural and socially supportive charities and smaller donations are made to other charities
HOW TO APPLY At any time
WHO TO APPLY TO Mrs B Samuel, Coral Samuel Charitable Trust, Messrs Basil & Howard Samuel, Knighton House, 56 Mortimer Street, London W1N 8BD
CC NO 239677 **ESTABLISHED** 1962

■ M J Samuel Charitable Trust

WHAT IS FUNDED Trustees favour a wide range of causes, many of them Jewish, mental health and environmental, particularly in the fields of: the advancement of the Jewish religion; synagogues;

Jewish umbrella bodies; the Council for Voluntary Service; health counselling; self help groups; hospices; cancer research; neurological research; special schools and special needs education
WHAT IS NOT FUNDED No grants given to individuals
WHO CAN BENEFIT Registered charities benefiting children and Jews
WHERE FUNDING CAN BE GIVEN UK and overseas
TYPE OF GRANT Core costs, project and research. Funding of up to two years will be considered
SAMPLE GRANTS £30,000 to PIPPIN for further development of project; £8,000 to Anna Freud Centre for further development of project; £2,500 to Chicken Shed for further development of project; £1,935 to Portobello Trust for further development of project; £1,200 to Barlingside Jewish Youth Centre for general funding; £500 to the Michael Palin Centre for general funding; £500 to Dulwich Picture Gallery for general funding; £500 to Wellbeing for general funding; £500 to Imperial Cancer Fund for general funding; £250 to Cosmic for general funding
FINANCES *Year* 1996 *Income* £31,251 *Grants* £27,482
TRUSTEES The Hon Michael Samuel, J A Samuel, Viscount Bearsted
WHO TO APPLY TO Lindsay Sutton, M J Samuel Charitable Trust, Mayborn Group plc, Dylon House, Worsley Bridge Road, London SE26 5HD
CC NO 327013 **ESTABLISHED** 1985

■ Peter Samuel Charitable Trust

WHAT IS FUNDED Medical sciences, the quality of life in local areas, heritage and land/forestry restoration
WHAT IS NOT FUNDED (a) No grants to individuals. (b) No grants to charities relating to purely local interests other than in Berkshire and Hampshire
WHO CAN BENEFIT Registered charities benefiting: medical professionals; scientists; at risk groups; and those disadvantaged by poverty
WHERE FUNDING CAN BE GIVEN Berkshire and Hampshire
TYPE OF GRANT Single and annual donations
FINANCES *Year* 1995 *Income* £161,142 *Grants* £124,545
TRUSTEES The Rt Hon The Viscount Bearstead, MC, TD, The Hon Nicholas Samuel, The Hon Michael Samuel
HOW TO APPLY Any time to the address under Who To Apply To
WHO TO APPLY TO Rachel Stafford, Peter Samuel Charitable Trust, Farley Farms, Bridge Farm, Reading Road, Arborfield, Berkshire RG2 9HT
CC NO 269065 **ESTABLISHED** 1975

■ The Camilla Samuel Fund

WHAT IS FUNDED The promotion, encouragement, assistance, support, conduct and accomplishment of any research or inquiry into any matters relating to the causes, prevention, diagnosis, incidence, treatment, cure or effects of any form of illness; injury or disability requiring medical or dental treatment; mental defectiveness
WHAT IS NOT FUNDED No grants to individuals, general appeals or any other charitable institution
WHO CAN BENEFIT Medical research projects in a discipline agreed by the Trustees at their annual meetings. Funding may be given to medical professionals, and research workers. There is no restriction on the disease or medical condition to which funding is given
WHERE FUNDING CAN BE GIVEN UK

TYPE OF GRANT Agreed expenses of research only. Maximum period three years, subject to satisfactory annual report and review by Trustees

FINANCES *Year* 1995 *Income* £40,111
Grants £10,947

TRUSTEES Sir Ronald Grierson, The Hon Mrs Waley-Cohen, Dr The Hon J P H Hunt, J Grierson

NOTES As all the money available, together with the Fund's future income, has been earmarked, for four years for an important research project, the Fund will not be in a position to consider any applications for grants during this period

HOW TO APPLY The Trustees will request written applications following the recommendation of a suitable project by the Medical Trustees

WHO TO APPLY TO The Secretary to the Trustees, Camilla Samuel Fund, Upton Viva, Banbury, Oxfordshire OX15 6HT

CC NO 235424 **ESTABLISHED** 1964

■ The Sandford Trust

WHAT IS FUNDED General charitable purposes

WHO CAN BENEFIT Registetred charities. There are no restrictions on the age; professional and economic group; family situation; religion and culture; and social circumstances of; or disease or medical condition suffered by, the beneficiaries

WHERE FUNDING CAN BE GIVEN In practice North Oxfordshire and surrounding area

RANGE OF GRANTS £100–£1,000

SAMPLE GRANTS £1,000 to Teenage Cancer Trust; £1,000 to Oxford Home Start; £1,000 to Farm Africa; £1,000 to Oxfordshire Family Mediation Service; £1,000 to the Society for Mubopolysaccharide Diseases; £1,000 to Hanborough Freeland Scout Group; £735 to Kingham Hill School; £500 to Oxford Community Mediation; £500 to Chicks; £500 to British Blind Spot

FINANCES *Year* 1997 *Income* £26,063
Grants £10,835

TRUSTEES Mrs S K A Lodev, C A Ponsonby, Lady E H M Wills (Chair)

WHO TO APPLY TO Lady Wills, Trustee, The Sandford Trust, Sandford Park, Sandford St Martin, Chipping Norton, Oxfordshire OX7 7AJ

CC NO 1044615 **ESTABLISHED** 1995

■ Sandra Charitable Trust

WHAT IS FUNDED Medical research, hospitals, welfare charities, veterinary colleges

WHO CAN BENEFIT Organisations benefiting: medical professionals; research workers; at risk groups, those disadvantaged by poverty; socially isolated people and veterinary students

WHERE FUNDING CAN BE GIVEN UK, especially South East England

SAMPLE GRANTS £35,364 to SPARKS; £30,000 to Lord Mayor's Appeal for the Cancer Research Campaign; £20,000 to League of Friends Royal Marsden Hospital Trust; £10,000 to Florence Nightingale Foundation; £5,750 to Cancer Relief Macmillan Fund; £5,000 to The Hyperbaric Oxygen Trust; £5,000 to Greek Orthodox Charity Organisation Ltd; £5,000 to Thoroughbred Breeders Society Equine Fertility Unit; £4,000 to NCH Action for Children; £4,000 to Loche Animal Sanctuary

FINANCES *Year* 1997 *Income* £272,563
Grants £226,259

TRUSTEES R Moore, M Macfadyen

HOW TO APPLY To the address under Who To Apply To in writing

WHO TO APPLY TO R Moore, Sandra Charitable Trust, Moore Stephens, St Paul's House, Warwick Lane, London EC4P 4BN *Tel* 0171-248 4499

CC NO 327492 **ESTABLISHED** 1987

■ Sandringham Estate Cottage Horticultural Society Trust

WHAT IS FUNDED The promotion of horticulture and floriculture by the holding of an annual show on the Sandringham Estate for the benefit of the public for the exhibition of flowers, fruit and vegetables and by such other means and other charitable purposes

WHO CAN BENEFIT The people of Kings Lynn and the West Norfolk area

WHERE FUNDING CAN BE GIVEN Kings Lynn and the West Norfolk area

SAMPLE GRANTS £2,500 to QE Hospital, Kings Lynn, Children's Ward; £2,440 to MIND Heacham Branch; £1,700 to Kings Lynn Hospital talking newspaper; £1,000 to Victim Support Scheme, Kings Lynn; £550 to National Deaf Children's Society, West Norfolk; £500 to Norfolk Association for Gardening with Disabled; £500 to Heacham Group Medical Practice; £500 to St John Ambulance Brigade, Kings Lynn; £500 to Springwood School Band, Kings Lynn

FINANCES *Year* 1997 *Income* £59,157
Grants £18,485

TRUSTEES C Davidson, Sir Edmund Grove, Mrs J Jackson, M O'Lone, D Reeve, F Waite

HOW TO APPLY To the Hon Treasurer, C Davidson in writing

WHO TO APPLY TO C Davidson, LVO, Hon Treasurer, Sandringham Estate Cottage Horticultural Society Trust, Farm Cottage, West Newton, Kings Lynn, Norfolk PE31 6AY

CC NO 1037268 **ESTABLISHED** 1994

■ The Sandwich Toll Bridge Fund

WHAT IS FUNDED The maintenance and running costs of the 16th Century Guildhall and general charitable purposes in Sandwich. The fund shall be paid out and applied in any public works for the advantage of the Town of Sandwich

WHO CAN BENEFIT There are no restrictions on the age; professional and economic group; family situation; religion and culture; and social circumstances of; or disease or medical condition suffered by, the beneficiaries

WHERE FUNDING CAN BE GIVEN Sandwich

TYPE OF GRANT One-off, capital, interest free loans, buildings and start-up costs. All funding is for one year or less

RANGE OF GRANTS £50–£10,000

FINANCES *Year* 1996–97 *Income* £126,677
Grants £5,000

TRUSTEES Sandwich Town Council

HOW TO APPLY To the address under Who To Apply To in writing

WHO TO APPLY TO The Town Clerk, The Sandwich Toll Bridge Fund, Sandwich Town Council, Guildhall, Cattle Market, Sandwich, Kent CT13 9AH *Tel* 01304 617197 *Fax* 01304 620170

CC NO 266738 **ESTABLISHED** 1974

■ The Sangster Charitable Trust

This trust did not respond to CAF's request to amend its entry and, by 30 June 1998, CAF's researchers did not find financial records for later than 1995 on its file at the Charity Commission. Trusts are legally required to submit annual accounts to the Charity Commission under section 42 of the Charities Act 1993

WHAT IS FUNDED General charitable purposes with special interest in welfare of the elderly

WHO CAN BENEFIT There are no restrictions on the age; professional and economic group; family situation; religion and culture; and social circumstances of; or disease or medical condition suffered by, the beneficiaries

WHERE FUNDING CAN BE GIVEN UK and overseas

TRUSTEES R E Sangster, K A Paul, G E Sangster

WHO TO APPLY TO H R Sarsfield, The Sangster Charitable Trust Manton House, Manton House Estate, Marlborough, Wiltshire SN8 1PN

CC NO 802386   **ESTABLISHED** 1989

■ G K N Sankey Employees' Charity Trust

WHAT IS FUNDED General charitable purposes

WHO CAN BENEFIT There are no restrictions on the age; professional and economic group; family situation; religion and culture; and social circumstances of; or disease or medical condition suffered by, the beneficiaries

WHERE FUNDING CAN BE GIVEN UK, with a possible preference for Kent

FINANCES *Year* 1996 *Income* £47,790
Grants £56,543

TRUSTEES R J Clowes, V N Corbett, J Shanahan, C Sylvester

HOW TO APPLY To the address under Who To Apply To in writing

WHO TO APPLY TO Jill Stanley, Secretary, G K N Sankey Employees' Charity Trust, 46 Bettescombe Road, Rainham, Kent ME8 9AY

CC NO 1003217   **ESTABLISHED** 1991

■ The Saranda Charitable Trust

WHAT IS FUNDED General charitable purposes

WHAT IS NOT FUNDED No grants to individuals

WHO CAN BENEFIT There are no restrictions on the age; professional and economic group; family situation; religion and culture; and social circumstances of; or disease or medical condition suffered by, the beneficiaries

WHERE FUNDING CAN BE GIVEN UK

TYPE OF GRANT Grants to recognised charities

FINANCES *Year* 1997 *Income* £32,209
Grants £14,900

TRUSTEES Ms S C Dangerfield, D J Humphreys, M C McWhirter

HOW TO APPLY Applications not acknowledged

WHO TO APPLY TO R J A Furneaux, The Saranda Charitable Trust, KPMG, Richmond Park House, 15 Pembroke Road, Clifton, Bristol BS8 3BG

CC NO 328654   **ESTABLISHED** 1990

■ Sargent Charitable Trust

WHAT IS FUNDED The Trustees favour conservation and the environment

WHERE FUNDING CAN BE GIVEN UK

FINANCES *Year* 1996 *Income* £39,701

TRUSTEES R A Oury, N G Sargent, W A Sargent, J G Wesley

WHO TO APPLY TO R A Oury, FCA, Sargent Charitable Trust, Messrs Clarks, PO Box 150, Cippenham Court, Cippenham Lane, Slough, Berkshire SL1 5AT

CC NO 328596   **ESTABLISHED** 1990

■ Sarnia Charitable Trust

WHAT IS FUNDED Interest in wildlife and conservation projects in the Channel Islands especially Guernsey

WHAT IS NOT FUNDED Expeditions and scholarships. No grants to individuals

WHO CAN BENEFIT Registered charities only

WHERE FUNDING CAN BE GIVEN UK and The Channel Islands, especially Guernsey

RANGE OF GRANTS £100–£10,000

SAMPLE GRANTS £10,000 to George Adamson Wildlife Trust; £10,000 to Norfolk Naturalists Trust; £5,000 to Norfolk and Norwich Naturalists Trust; £5,000 to SOF Guernsey Meeting

FINANCES *Year* 1998 *Income* £30,401
Grants £37,500

TRUSTEES Dr T N D Peet, R Harriman, Mrs C V E Benfield

HOW TO APPLY As it is currently fully committed, **this Trust states that it does not respond to unsolicited applications**

WHO TO APPLY TO R Harriman, Sarnia Charitable Trust, New Guild House, 45 Great Charles Street, Queensway, Birmingham B3 2LX
Tel 0121 212 2222

CC NO 281417   **ESTABLISHED** 1979

■ The Sarum St Michael Educational Charity

WHAT IS FUNDED Advancement of education in accordance with the principles and doctrines of the Church of England

WHAT IS NOT FUNDED No grants for buildings, fixtures or fittings. No contribution to the general funds of any organisation

WHO CAN BENEFIT Individuals, parishes, schools and corporate bodies benefiting young adults and Christians

WHERE FUNDING CAN BE GIVEN The Diocese of Salisbury and adjoining dioceses

TYPE OF GRANT One-off, project and research will be considered. Funding may be given for up to three years

SAMPLE GRANTS £28,597 to Salisbury Diocesan Board of Education for Young Sarum Project, new computer and Church School headship training course; £24,900 to Sarum College towards the Principal's salary; £4,000 to Weymouth College Chaplain for part funding of the chaplain's salary; £2,500 to Cotswold Community for play equipment for home for emotionally damaged boys; £2,000 to St John the Baptist Church, Broadstone for parish youth pilgrimage to the Holy Land; £1,632 to Wren Hall Education Centre for a computer and printer; £1,500 to Flame Committee towards expenses for family life project worker; £1,500 to Bridge Project, Salisbury for Sound Nation Project; £1,500 to Splash, Wiltshire for vouchers for summer holiday holiday activity scheme; £1,300 to St Andrew's and St Philip's, Kinson for a community worker

FINANCES *Year* 1997 *Income* £155,000
Grants £160,000

TRUSTEES Lt Col C C G Ross, J Jarvis, M Marriott, J Roseaman, Mrs J Smith. Ex Officio: The Bishop of Salisbury, The Dean of Salisbury Cathedral, The

Does the trust you have chosen match your needs? Haphazard applications waste postage and time

565

Chapter Clerk of Salisbury Cathedral, Diocesan Director of Education

HOW TO APPLY On forms available from the Charity. Considered at five annual meetings

WHO TO APPLY TO The Clerk to the Governors, The Sarum St Michael Educational Charity, 2nd Floor, 13 New Canal, Salisbury, Wiltshire SP1 2AA *Tel* 01722 422296

CC NO 309456   **ESTABLISHED** 1980

■ The Saunderson Foundation

WHAT IS FUNDED Christian outreach

WHO CAN BENEFIT Small local projects, innovative projects, new established and national organisations and overseas work benefiting Christians

WHERE FUNDING CAN BE GIVEN London, UK and overseas

TYPE OF GRANT One-off

FINANCES *Year* 1996–97 *Income* £21,600 *Grants* £16,400

TRUSTEES D J Saunderson, Dr P R Saunderson

HOW TO APPLY Applications by post only

WHO TO APPLY TO D J Saunderson, The Saunderson Foundation, Saunderson House, 20 Long Lane, London EC1 9HL *Tel* 0171-315 6500 *Fax* 0171-315 6550 *E-mail* shl@saunderson-house.co.uk

CC NO 284775   **ESTABLISHED** 1982

■ Save a Child

WHAT IS FUNDED To provide for the care, housing and education of young children in India

WHO CAN BENEFIT Institutions and charitable organisations benefiting destitute children

WHERE FUNDING CAN BE GIVEN India

TYPE OF GRANT Recurring

SAMPLE GRANTS £43,591 to Divya Chaya Trust, India to help destitute children

FINANCES *Year* 1995–96 *Income* £49,902 *Grants* £36,511

TRUSTEES Louise Nicholson, Jean Bond, Barbara Lloyd, Gerald Sanctuary, Ann Chisholm

WHO TO APPLY TO G Sanctuary, Save a Child, 99 Beechwood Drive, St Albans, Hertfordshire AL1 4XU *Tel* 01727 842666

CC NO 328218   **ESTABLISHED** 1989

■ Save & Prosper Foundation

WHAT IS FUNDED General charitable purposes but with a strong interest in education particularly special needs education. Charities working in the fields of: charity or voluntary umbrella bodies; arts, culture and recreation; hospices; hospitals; medical studies and research; playschemes; art galleries and cultural centres; libraries and museums; theatres and opera houses and other general charitable purposes will be considered

WHAT IS NOT FUNDED No grants in response to general appeals from national charities

WHO CAN BENEFIT Individuals and organisations benefiting: children; young adults; older people; at risk groups; disabled people; those disadvantaged by poverty; ex-offenders and those at risk of offending; homeless people and victims of abuse. There are no restrictions on the disease or medical condition suffered by the beneficiaries

WHERE FUNDING CAN BE GIVEN UK with very modest amounts overseas

TYPE OF GRANT Capital, one-off, projects and start-up costs. Funding of up to two years will be considered

SAMPLE GRANTS £20,000 to Glyndebourne Trust; £10,000 to Koppie Goodman Project; £10,000 to St Francis Hospice; £10,000 to Wooden Spoon Society; £8,000 to University of Nottingham; £7,000 to Royal Navy and Marine Sports; £6,000 to Quidenham Hospice; £5,000 to Barbican Art Gallery; £5,000 to Commonwealth Youth Exchange Council; £5,000 to Multiple Sclerosis Trust

FINANCES *Year* 1997 *Income* £214,000 *Grants* £178,000

TRUSTEES Save & Prosper Group Limited

HOW TO APPLY No application form. Initially, a fairly short letter describing the project together with basic supporting material, if appropriate. Large quantities of back-up material are not required

WHO TO APPLY TO D Grant, Director, Save & Prosper Foundation, Finsbury Dials, 20 Finsbury Street, London EC2Y 9AY *Tel* 0171-417 2332

CC NO 291617   **ESTABLISHED** 1985

■ Henry James Sayer Charity

WHAT IS FUNDED General charitable purposes. To support small local charities who make application to the Trustees for financial help for specific projects

WHAT IS NOT FUNDED Birmingham charities only

WHO CAN BENEFIT Charitable organisations and, but only in exceptional cases, individuals. There are no restrictions on the age; professional and economic group; family situation; religion and culture; and social circumstances of; or disease or medical condition suffered by, the beneficiaries

WHERE FUNDING CAN BE GIVEN Birmingham

TYPE OF GRANT Cash – normally not recurrent

FINANCES *Year* 1996 *Income* £27,884 *Grants* £21,970

TRUSTEES M B Shaw, T Sloan, Alderman Shepherd, Alderman Jarvis, Miss A M Grove

HOW TO APPLY Application form from the address under Who To Apply To by 1 April and 1 October each year – audited accounts are required

WHO TO APPLY TO D J Nightingale, Henry James Sayer Charity, Martineau Johnson, Solicitors, St Philips House, St Philips Place, Birmingham B3 2PP *Tel* 0121-200 3300

CC NO 222438   **ESTABLISHED** 1944

■ The Rosemary Scanlan Charitable Trust

WHAT IS FUNDED General charitable purposes

WHO CAN BENEFIT There are no restrictions on the age; professional and economic group; family situation; religion and culture; and social circumstances of; or disease or medical condition suffered by, the beneficiaries

WHERE FUNDING CAN BE GIVEN Glasgow

FINANCES *Year* 1996 *Income* £60,000 *Grants* £80,000

TRUSTEES Rosemary McKenna, K Sweeney, Cardinal T J Winning

PUBLICATIONS Accounts are available from the Trust

HOW TO APPLY Contact the address below for further details

WHO TO APPLY TO The Correspondent, The Rosemary Scanlan Charitable Trust, Messrs Grant Thornton, Chartered Accountants, 112 West George Street, Glasgow G2 1QF

SC NO SCO 00360

■ The Borough of Scarborough Mayoress's Community Fund

WHAT IS FUNDED The arts; welfare; youth and children; medical and disability charities

WHO CAN BENEFIT Organisations benefiting: people of all ages who are homeless; living in rural areas; socially isolated and victims of abuse. People suffering from Alzheimer's disease, asthma, diabetes, motor neurone disease, sight loss and strokes will be considered

WHERE FUNDING CAN BE GIVEN The Borough of Scarborough

TYPE OF GRANT One-off capital

RANGE OF GRANTS £200–£500

SAMPLE GRANTS The following grants of £300 each were made to help with work in the community:; To Edgehill Community Association; To Scarborough Stroke Club; To Caring Support; To Scarborough Volunteer Stroke Scheme

FINANCES *Year* 1996–97 *Income* £13,442 *Grants* £12,500

TRUSTEES 26 wives of councillors or ex-councillors of Scarborough Council

HOW TO APPLY To the address under Who To Apply To in writing in October of each year. Payments are made to the chosen Beneficiaries at the end of April

WHO TO APPLY TO Mrs B B Rayner, Treasurer, The Borough of Scarborough Mayoress's Community Fund, 67 Pickering Road, West Ayton, North Yorkshire YO13 9JE *Tel* 01723 863225

CC NO 509918   **ESTABLISHED** 1980

■ The Scarfe Charitable Trust

WHAT IS FUNDED This Trust will consider funding: conservation; environmental interests; medical research into MS; hospices; arts and arts facilities; arts activities; churches; religious ancillary buildings; art galleries and cultural centres; libraries and museums; and theatres and opera houses

WHAT IS NOT FUNDED Consideration is given primarily to Suffolk charities and individuals

WHO CAN BENEFIT Individuals and organisations benefiting: actors and entertainment professionals; musicians; writers and poets; Christians; and multiple sclerosis sufferers

WHERE FUNDING CAN BE GIVEN Mainly Suffolk

TYPE OF GRANT Capital, core costs, one-off, project, research, recurring costs and running costs. Funding is for one year or less

SAMPLE GRANTS £23,400 to Institute of Neurology; £5,000 to Aldeburgh Foundation; £3,882 to University of London; £1,245 to University of East Anglia; £1,200 to Trinity College; £1,100 to County History Society; £1,000 to Magdalen College; £1,000 to Thornham Parva PCC; £630 to Institute of Psychiatry; £500 to River Stour Trust

FINANCES *Year* 1996–97 *Income* £51,997 *Grants* £45,407

TRUSTEES N Scarfe, E E Maule

HOW TO APPLY No specific meeting dates. In writing to the address under Who To Apply To

WHO TO APPLY TO E E Maule, The Scarfe Charitable Trust, 1 Gainsborough Road, Felixstowe, Suffolk IP11 7HT *Tel* 01394 285537 *Fax* 01394 670073

CC NO 275535   **ESTABLISHED** 1978

■ ScargillsEducationalFoundation

WHAT IS FUNDED Local schools and youth organisations in the area Where Funding Can Be Given. Awarding exhibitions, financial assistance to enter profession, bursaries for educational travel, finance for study of music or the arts

WHO CAN BENEFIT Children and young adults under 25 years of age

WHERE FUNDING CAN BE GIVEN The parishes of Dale Abbey, Mapperley, Stanley (including Stanley Common) and West Hallam

FINANCES *Year* 1997 *Income* £50,111

TRUSTEES Dr K Adey, Rev J Clarke, N Futers, Rev I E Goodings, Mrs C Hart, D Hartley, Rev E C Lyons, K Massey, M Renger, D Stone

NOTES Foundation supports Scargill Church of England VA School, West Hallam and the parishes of West Hallam, Dale Abbey, Stanley and Mapperley

HOW TO APPLY To the address under Who To Apply To in writing

WHO TO APPLY TO S F Marshall, Clerk, Scargills Educational Foundation, 3–5 Mundy Street, Heanor, Derbyshire DE75 7EB

CC NO 527012   **ESTABLISHED** 1982

■ The Scarr-Hall Memorial Trust

WHAT IS FUNDED Education and training of students; general charitable purposes

WHO CAN BENEFIT Individuals and institutions benefiting in particular young adults and students

WHERE FUNDING CAN BE GIVEN England and Wales

TYPE OF GRANT At the discretion of the Trustees

FINANCES *Year* 1997 *Income* £44,249 *Grants* £4,775

TRUSTEES Ian Scarr-Hall, Ruth Scarr-Hall, Gavin Scarr-Hall, Rev Margaret Hall, Duncan Scarr-Hall, Kirsteen Scarr-Hall

WHO TO APPLY TO C Kane, The Scarr-Hall Memorial Trust, Downward Plumb & Colclough, Vernon Road, Stoke on Trent, Staffordshire ST4 2QY

CC NO 328105   **ESTABLISHED** 1988

■ The Schapira Charitable Trust

WHAT IS FUNDED Jewish charitable purposes

WHO CAN BENEFIT Organisations benefiting Jewish people

WHERE FUNDING CAN BE GIVEN UK

SAMPLE GRANTS £10,500 to Keren Association; £6,000 to Gur Trust; £3,000 to BHHT; £2,000 to Ruzin Sadagora Trust

FINANCES *Year* 1995 *Income* £71,900 *Grants* £85,000

TRUSTEES Issac Y Schapira, Michael Neuberger, Suzanne L Schapira

WHO TO APPLY TO The Trustees, The Schapira Charitable Trust, c/o BDO Stoy Haward, 8 Baker Street, London W1M 1DA

CC NO 328435   **ESTABLISHED** 1989

■ The Annie Schiff Charitable Trust

WHAT IS FUNDED For the relief of poverty generally and in payment to needy individuals of the Jewish faith, for the advancement of education and religion. General charitable purposes

WHO CAN BENEFIT Individuals and organisations benefiting children, young adults, students, those disadvantaged by poverty and Jewish people

WHERE FUNDING CAN BE GIVEN UK

SAMPLE GRANTS £50,000 to Menorah Grammar School Trust; £10,000 to Huntingdon Foundation Limited; £7,500 to Bais Yakov Institutions; £7,350 to Emuno Educational Centre Limited; £7,300 to Beth Hamedrash Yisochor Dov; £5,000 to Friends of Harim Establishments; £5,000 to Friends of Nachalat Osher Charitable Trust; £5,000 to Institute for Halachic Studies Be'er Avrohom; £4,000 to Gur Trust; £3,600 to Yeshiva Horome Talmudical (Centre) College

FINANCES *Year* 1997 *Income* £178,211 *Grants* £139,290

TRUSTEES Mrs R Pearlman, J Pearlman

WHO TO APPLY TO J Pearlman, Trustee, The Annie Schiff Charitable Trust, 8 Highfield Gardens, London NW11 9HB

CC NO 265401   **ESTABLISHED** 1973

■ The Schmidt-Bodner Charitable Trust

This trust did not respond to CAF's request to amend its entry and, by 30 June 1998, CAF's researchers did not find financial records for later than 1995 on its file at the Charity Commission. Trusts are legally required to submit annual accounts to the Charity Commission under section 42 of the Charities Act 1993

WHAT IS FUNDED General charitable purposes

WHO CAN BENEFIT There are no restrictions on the age; professional and economic group; family situation; religion and culture; and social circumstances of; or disease or medical condition suffered by, the beneficiaries

WHERE FUNDING CAN BE GIVEN UK

TRUSTEES B Schmidt-Bodner, Mrs E Schmidt-Bodner, M Diner, L Rosenblatt

WHO TO APPLY TO Mr & Mrs B Schmidt-Bodner, The Schmidt-Bodner Charitable Trust, Flat 36, St James's Close, Prince Albert Road, London NW8 7LQ

CC NO 283014   **ESTABLISHED** 1981

■ The R H Scholes Charitable Trust

WHAT IS FUNDED Preference is given to charities in which the Trustees have special interest, knowledge or association. New charities to be supported will be in the fields helping disadvantaged and handicapped children and young people. Particularly charities working in the fields of: residential facilities; respite and sheltered accommodation; Anglican bodies; music and opera; special schools and special needs education; training for community development; care in the community; day centres; holidays and outings; playschemes; and research into medicine

WHAT IS NOT FUNDED Grants only to registered charities. No grants to individuals, animal charities, expeditions or scholarships

WHO CAN BENEFIT Registered charities benefiting children and young adults, Church of England, disabled people and those disadvantaged by poverty

WHERE FUNDING CAN BE GIVEN England

TYPE OF GRANT Both recurrent and one-off grants are made depending upon needs of beneficiary. Core costs, project and research. Funding for more than three years will be considered

RANGE OF GRANTS £100–£1,000, average grant £250

SAMPLE GRANTS £1,000 to Children's Family Trust; £1,000 to Church of England Pensions Board; £1,000 to friends of Lancing Chapel; £1,000 to Horsham PCC; £750 to Camphill Village Trust; £750 to Home Farm Trust; £750 to St Luke's Hospital for the Clergy; £600 to Historic Churches Preservation Trust; £500 to Church Army; £500 to London Clergy Holiday Fund

FINANCES *Year* 1997–98 *Income* £30,300 *Grants* £22,300

TRUSTEES R H C Pattison, Mrs A J Pattison

NOTES Each application is considered but we only reply to successful applicants. Funds available for new applicants are very limited. The Trustees prefer to increase grants to existing beneficiaries when funds are available rather than take on new charities

HOW TO APPLY Applications should be in writing, **no telephone calls**, explaining the need and amount of funds to be raised, supported by the latest Annual Report and Accounts. We do not issue guidelines or have application forms. Applications are considered on a regular basis (1–3 monthly)

WHO TO APPLY TO R H C Pattison, The R H Scholes Charitable Trust, Fairacre, Bonfire Hill, Southwater, Horsham, West Sussex RH13 7BU *E-mail* roger_pattison@msn.com

CC NO 267023   **ESTABLISHED** 1974

■ The Schreib Trust

WHAT IS FUNDED Relief of poverty and advancement of religious education of Jewish people

WHO CAN BENEFIT Jewish people especially those disadvantaged by poverty

WHERE FUNDING CAN BE GIVEN UK

FINANCES *Year* 1996 *Income* £361,913 *Grants* £249,081

TRUSTEES Irene Schreiber, Jacob Schreiber, David Schreiber

HOW TO APPLY To the address under Who To Apply To in writing

WHO TO APPLY TO David Schreiber, The Schreib Trust, 3rd Floor, 5–13 Hatton Wall, London EC1N 8HX

CC NO 275240   **ESTABLISHED** 1977

■ The Schreiber Charitable Trust

WHAT IS FUNDED To prefer Jewish causes

WHO CAN BENEFIT Registered charities benefiting Jewish people

WHERE FUNDING CAN BE GIVEN UK

RANGE OF GRANTS £1,000–£13,000

SAMPLE GRANTS £13,000 to British Friends of JCT; £12,000 to Jewish Philanthropic Association; £8,000 to British Friends of Kol Torah; £7,375 to Gateshead Talmudical College; £4,000 to Friends of the Rabbinical College Kol Torah; £3,672 to Finchley Road Synagogue; £3,500 to Child Resettlement Fund; £2,138 to Society of Friends of the Torah; £1,300 to Project Seed; £1,000 to Yeshiva Horomo

FINANCES *Year* 1997 *Income* £51,891 *Grants* £74,805

TRUSTEES G S Morris, D A Schreiber, Mrs S Schreiber

WHO TO APPLY TO G S Morris, The Schreiber Charitable Trust, 9 West Heath Road, London NW3 7UX

CC NO 264735   **ESTABLISHED** 1972

■ Schroder Charity Trust

WHAT IS FUNDED Medical, international relief, social welfare (including aged), heritage, environment, arts. Preference to national registered charities and charities in which the Trust has a special interest

WHAT IS NOT FUNDED National and registered charities only, no grants to individuals

WHO CAN BENEFIT Organisations benefiting elderly people, at risk groups, those disadvantaged by poverty, socially isolated people, and victims of famine, war and man-made or natural disasters. There is no restriction on the disease or medical condition suffered by the beneficiaries. Support may also be considered for actors and entertainment professionals, musicians, textile workers and designers, writers and poets

WHERE FUNDING CAN BE GIVEN UK, occasionally overseas

TYPE OF GRANT Single payments or regular recurrent payments with preference given to headquarters organisations and established charities

SAMPLE GRANTS £16,700 to Jewish Aid Committee; £13,000 to Old People's Home; £8,800 to Water Aid; £8,334 to Westminster Cathedral; £8,000 to Duke of Edinburgh's Award; £7,500 to Bodleian Library; £6,333 to Motivation; £6,000 to Friends of the ELderly; £6,000 to RNLI; £6,000 to Silver Trust

FINANCES *Year* 1996 *Income* £694,826 *Grants* £587,545

TRUSTEES Directors: Mrs C L Fitzalan Howard, Mrs C B Mallinckrodt, B L Schroder, J H R Schroder, T B Schroder

HOW TO APPLY Monthly. At any time to the address under Who To Apply To

WHO TO APPLY TO B V Tew, Secretary, Schroder Charity Trust, 120 Cheapside, London EC2V 6DS

CC NO 214050   **ESTABLISHED** 1944

■ The Schuster Charitable Trust

WHAT IS FUNDED General charitable purposes. Preference for small, local charities: children and youth; health and welfare; wildlife; conservation and environment; professional bodies; charity or voluntary umbrella bodies; schools and colleges; special needs education and community services

WHAT IS NOT FUNDED No grants to individuals. This includes students on award schemes; expeditions; scholarships

WHO CAN BENEFIT Registered charities benefiting: children; young adults; older people; medical professionals, doctors and nurses; volunteers; those in care, fostered and adopted; parents and children; at risk groups; carers; disabled people; those disadvantaged by poverty; disaster victims; the homeless; refugees; those living in rural areas; victims of abuse; the terminally ill; stroke victims; prenatal patients and those suffering from blood disorders and haemophilia; cancer; head and other injuries; heart disease; kidney disease; mental illness; multiple sclerosis; paediatric diseases; psoriasis; sight loss and substance abuse

WHERE FUNDING CAN BE GIVEN UK and overseas, though principally UK and especially Oxfordshire, Buckinghamshire and Gloucestershire

TYPE OF GRANT Mainly one-off grants, buildings, capital, core costs, project, running costs and start-up costs. Funding can be for more than three years

RANGE OF GRANTS £250–£3,000. Average grant £500–£1,000

SAMPLE GRANTS £2,750 to Wortons PCC for upkeep of church in Oxfordshire; £1,000 to Marie Curie Cancer Care funding of nurses in Oxfordshire area; £1,000 to IMPS for health and safety education for children in Oxfordshire; £1,000 to Katherine House Hospice for hospice care in Oxfordshire; £1,000 to NCH Action for Children for a children's home in Oxfordshire

FINANCES *Year* 1996–97 *Income* £20,263 *Grants* £20,900

TRUSTEES Mrs J V Clarke, P J Schuster, R D Schuster

HOW TO APPLY At all times, no application form used. Trustees meet twice annually, normally June and December

WHO TO APPLY TO Mrs J V Clarke, The Schuster Charitable Trust, Nether Worton House, Middle Barton, Chipping Norton, Oxfordshire OX7 7AT

CC NO 234580   **ESTABLISHED** 1964

■ Richard and Jennifer Schuster Charitable Trust

WHAT IS FUNDED General charitable purposes

WHO CAN BENEFIT There are no restrictions on the age; professional and economic group; family situation; religion and culture; and social circumstances of; or disease or medical condition suffered by, the beneficiaries

WHERE FUNDING CAN BE GIVEN UK

TRUSTEES J W D Hewitt, Ms J C Schuster, R D Schuster

WHO TO APPLY TO Mrs R D Schuster, Trustee, Richard and Jennifer Schuster Charitable Trust, The Grange, Over Worton, Chipping Norton, Oxfordshire OX7 7ES

CC NO 1049096   **ESTABLISHED** 1995

■ Scopus Jewish Educational Trust (formerly Friends of the Zionist Federation Educational Trust)

WHAT IS FUNDED To advance and maintain Jewish day schools and Jewish education in any part of Great Britain and Northern Ireland

WHAT IS NOT FUNDED As per the Trust's Constitution

WHO CAN BENEFIT Jewish day schools, associations, societies and institutions, calculated to benefit directly or indirectly Jewish education

WHERE FUNDING CAN BE GIVEN UK

SAMPLE GRANTS £23,977 to JFS Comprehensive School; £18,500 to North Cheshire Jewish Primary School; £2,000 to King David, Birmingham

FINANCES *Year* 1997 *Income* £1,485,422

TRUSTEES J Kramer, P Ohrenstein, S Cohen, S Ronson

PUBLICATIONS *Scopus Nation Jewish Studies Curriculum, Scopus National Hebrew Curriculum*

WHO TO APPLY TO Maurice Garfield, Chief Accountant, Scopus Jewish Educational Trust, 741 High Road, Finchley, London N12 0BQ *Tel* 0181-343 9228 *Fax* 0181-343 7309

CC NO 313154   **ESTABLISHED** 1956

■ The Scotbelge Charitable Trust

WHAT IS FUNDED Charities working in the fields of: accommodation and housing; arts, culture and recreation; health; conservation; and community facilities

WHAT IS NOT FUNDED No expeditions or travel bursaries. No grants to individuals

WHO CAN BENEFIT Registered charities benefiting: people of all ages; medical professionals; musicians; research workers; scientists; seafarers and fishermen; teachers and governesses; unemployed people; volunteers; parents and children; Christians; at risk groups; carers; disabled people; disaster victims; victims of abuse, crime and domestic violence. Those suffering from various diseases and medical conditions

WHERE FUNDING CAN BE GIVEN Scotland

TYPE OF GRANT Buildings, core costs, one-off and recurring costs. funding of up to three years will be considered

RANGE OF GRANTS £500–£5,000

SAMPLE GRANTS £5,000 to The Princess Royal Trust for work in Scotland; £5,000 to Oriental Museum for a new gallery; £5,000 to Maggie Jenks Cancer Caring Centre for a new cancer centre at Western General Hospital, Edinburgh; £2,000 to National Trust for Scotland for new building project; £2,000 to Museum of Scotland for new building project

FINANCES *Year* 1996–97 *Income* £24,715 *Grants* £25,000

TRUSTEES Mrs A Weatherall, S L Keswick, K H Galloway, A T J Stanford

HOW TO APPLY Applications in writing to the address under Who To Apply To. No telephone calls

WHO TO APPLY TO K H Galloway, The Scotbelge Charitable Trust, Matheson Bank Limited, St Helens, 1 Undershaft, London EC3A 8JX *Fax* 0171-816 8207

CC NO 802962   **ESTABLISHED** 1990

■ Joanna Scott and Others

WHAT IS FUNDED Educational support for people under the age of 25 in the Norwich area

WHAT IS NOT FUNDED Grants are not made towards holidays, nor for people over 25 years old

WHO CAN BENEFIT Individuals and organisations benefiting children; young adults; academics and students below the age of 25 resident in the area Where Funding Can Be Given for the last two years; those in care, fostered and adopted; parents and children and one parent families

WHERE FUNDING CAN BE GIVEN Within a five mile radius of Norwich City Hall

TYPE OF GRANT One-off and recurring costs. Funding of one year or less will be considered

RANGE OF GRANTS £10–£2,000, average grant £100

FINANCES *Year* 1996–97 *Income* £67,669 *Grants* £52,462

TRUSTEES P Buttle, Mrs M Clarke, M Millson, Mrs M Rae, R S Rathbone, Mrs I Voegeli

HOW TO APPLY Application forms are available from the address under Who To Apply To upon receipt of an sae

WHO TO APPLY TO G H Smith, Clerk, Joanna Scott and Others, Hansell Stevenson Solicitors, 13 Cathedral Close, Norwich, Norfolk NR1 4DS *Tel* 01603 624228

CC NO 311253   **ESTABLISHED** 1963

■ The Scott Bader Commonwealth Ltd

WHAT IS FUNDED Assistance of distressed and needy persons of all nationalities. Establishment and support of charitable institutions whose objects may include the advancement of education. The Commonwealth looks for projects, activities or charities which: respond to the needs of those who are most underprivileged, disadvantaged,

poor or excluded; encourage the careful use and protection of the earth's resources (those which assist poor rural people to become self reliant are particularly encouraged); or promote peace-building and democratic participation. The commonwealth also supports the research, development and advancement of education and advancement of education in industrial participation of a nature beneficial to the community

WHAT IS NOT FUNDED The Commonwealth does not support charities concerned with the well being of animals, individuals in need or organisations sending volunteers abroad. It does not respond to general appeals or support the larger well-established national charities. It does not provide educational bursaries or grants for academic research. It does not support projects which should properly be the responsibility of the State or make grants to replace withdrawn or expired statutory funding, or to make up deficits already incurred. It does not support the arts, museums or travel/adventure

WHO CAN BENEFIT Projects, activities or charities which: find difficulty raising funds; are innovative, imaginative and pioneering; or are initiated and/or supported by local people. Organisations benefiting children, young adults, students and teachers. Support is also given to at risk groups, those disadvantaged by poverty, socially isolated people and may be given to the homeless

WHERE FUNDING CAN BE GIVEN UK and overseas

TYPE OF GRANT One-off usually

SAMPLE GRANTS £7,000 to British Kidney Patient Association; £5,500 to Community Creation; £5,400 to UWESO UK; £5,400 to Rowan Gate Primary School; £5,116 to Peper Harow Foundation; £5,000 to Salt of the Earth; £5,000 to Riverpoint (Broadway Project); £5,000 to English Churches Housing Project; £5,000 to Accommodation Concern; £5,000 to Caring and Sharing Trust

FINANCES *Year* 1996 *Income* £150,067 *Grants* £194,985

TRUSTEES The Board of Management: G Skinner, E Lancaster, R Bailey, R Mayhew, Ms C Riddle, D Seear, A Green, D Muir

HOW TO APPLY No application form. Any time. Trustees meet monthly

WHO TO APPLY TO M Jones, Secretary, Scott Bader Commonwealth Ltd, Wollaston, Wellingborough, Northamptonshire NN29 7RL

CC NO 206391   **ESTABLISHED** 1951

■ The Frieda Scott Charitable Trust

WHAT IS FUNDED A very wide range of registered charities concerned with social welfare, community arts projects, church restoration and upkeep of village halls, within the area Where Funding Can Be Given. Charities working in the fields of: infrastructure support and development; health; conservation; animal welfare; literacy; training for community development; training for work; vocational training; equal opportunities; individual rights; advice centres; and law centres will also be considered

WHAT IS NOT FUNDED No grants to individuals or school appeals. No grants to charities outside the stated geographical area

WHO CAN BENEFIT Small local charities, church restoration, parish halls, youth groups and occasionally locally based work of larger charities. Organisations benefiting: ex-service and service people; medical professionals; retired people; unemployed people; volunteers; and writers and poets. There are no restrictions on the age; family situation; religion and culture; or social circumstances of; or on the disease or medical condition suffered by, the beneficiaries

WHERE FUNDING CAN BE GIVEN The old County of Westmorland and the area covered by South Lakeland District Council

TYPE OF GRANT Buildings, capital, core costs, endowments, feasibility studies, one-off, project, research, recurring costs, running costs, salaries and start-up costs. Funding of up to three years will be considered

RANGE OF GRANTS £200–£5,000 with occasional much larger grants

SAMPLE GRANTS £60,000 to Brewery Arts Centre, Kendal for revenue funding; £20,000 to Cancer Care Lakes Appeal for development of day support centre; £10,000 to Council for Voluntary Action, South Lakeland for core funding; £10,000 to St Martin's Church, Windermere towards appeal funds; £7,500 to Kendal Civic Society, Castle Centenary; £7,000 to Westmorland Music Council for support of local music students; £5,000 to Ambleside and Windermere Methodist Circuit for building repairs for project with young seasonal workers; £5,000 to Carlisle Cathedral Development Trust for disabled access at cathedral; £5,000 to MacMillan Appeal for Royal Lancaster Infirmary for Cancer Treatment Unit; £5,000 to National Trust Lake District Appeal for footpath repairs

FINANCES *Year* 1997 *Income* £315,196 *Grants* £199,870

TRUSTEES Mrs C Brockbank (Chairman), Mrs J H Barker, Mrs O Clarke, OBE, R A Hunter, Miss C R Scott, P R W Hensman, Mrs M G Wilson

HOW TO APPLY Applications by letter with accompanying Accounts considered three times a year in February, May and October. Initial telephone calls about applications are welcome

WHO TO APPLY TO D J Harding, Secretary, The Frieda Scott Charitable Trust, Sand Aire House, Kendal, Cumbria LA9 4BE *Tel* 01539 723415

CC NO 221593   **ESTABLISHED** 1962

■ **The Storrow Scott Charitable Will Trust**

WHAT IS FUNDED General charitable purposes

WHAT IS NOT FUNDED Only registered charities, no grants to individuals

WHO CAN BENEFIT Registered charities. There are no restrictions on the age; professional and economic group; family situation; religion and culture; and social circumstances of; or disease or medical condition suffered by, the beneficiaries

WHERE FUNDING CAN BE GIVEN The North of England preferred

RANGE OF GRANTS £150–£2,750

SAMPLE GRANTS £2,750 to Northumberland Association of Boys' Clubs; £1,500 to Camphill Village Trust; £1,500 to the Anaphylaxis Campaign; £1,000 to the Percy Hedley Centre; £750 to St Oswald's Hospice, Gosforth

FINANCES *Year* 1996 *Income* £14,944 *Grants* £10,150

TRUSTEES G W Meikle, J S North Lewis

WHO TO APPLY TO G W Meikle, The Storrow Scott Charitable Will Trust, Dickinson Dees, Solicitors, Cross House, Westgate Road, Newcastle upon Tyne NE99 1SB

CC NO 328391   **ESTABLISHED** 1989

■ **Sir James & Lady Scott Trust**

WHAT IS FUNDED To support Settlor's servants and dependants or others connected with him and his family and who are in need, and local charities. This includes residential facilities and services; infrastructure development; charity or voluntary umbrella bodies; religion; arts, culture and recreation; health care; conservation; animal welfare; environmental issues; heritage; education and training; social care and development; and other charitable purposes

WHAT IS NOT FUNDED No schools or medical appeals

WHO CAN BENEFIT Individuals and registered charities benefiting: retired people; unemployed people; and volunteers. There are no restrictions on the age; family situation; religion and culture; the social circumstances of; or disease or medical condition suffered by, the beneficiaries

WHERE FUNDING CAN BE GIVEN Mainly Bolton

TYPE OF GRANT Recurring costs, one-off, buildings, capital, core costs, endowment, feasibility studies, project research, running costs, salaries and start-up costs. Funding is available for one year or less

RANGE OF GRANTS £200–£5,000

SAMPLE GRANTS £6,000 to Octagon Theatre Trust, Bolton for appointment of youth theatre director; £5,000 to North West Life Education Trust for preventive drug and health education; £2,707 to Bolton YMCA for a children's day camp project; £2,500 to Woodside School PTA towards a minibus; £2,000 to Society of St Vincent de Paul, Bolton for a holiday project for needy families; £2,000 to Relate – Bolton Marriage Guidance for training costs for a counsellor

FINANCES *Year* 1997 *Income* £114,098 *Grants* £41,170

TRUSTEES P F Scott, W L G Swan, C J Scott

HOW TO APPLY By application form accompanied by latest set of audited accounts. An initial telephone call from applicant is welcome

WHO TO APPLY TO D J Harding, The Sir James & Lady Scott Trust, Sand Aire House, Kendal, Cumbria LA9 4BE *Tel* 01539 723415

CC NO 231324   **ESTABLISHED** 1907

■ **The John Scott Trust**

WHAT IS FUNDED Grants are awarded to a variety of organisations whose concerns include Scotland's heritage, recreation for young people and care for the disadvantaged

WHAT IS NOT FUNDED No grants to individuals

WHO CAN BENEFIT Registered charities benefiting children and young adults, at risk groups, those disadvantaged by poverty and socially isolated people

WHERE FUNDING CAN BE GIVEN Scotland

FINANCES *Year* 1996 *Income* £60,000 *Grants* £60,000

TRUSTEES J D Scott

PUBLICATIONS Accounts are available from the Trust

HOW TO APPLY **This Trust states that it does not respond to unsolicited applications**

WHO TO APPLY TO J D Scott, The John Scott Trust, Parkview, 63 Loudoun Road, Newmilns KA16 9HG

SC NO SCO 03297

◾ The Scottish Chartered Accountants' Trust for Education

WHAT IS FUNDED Grants are awarded for the Scottish Institute's research conferences and for publications arising from them; also for research projects which are related to the field of accountancy such as: methods of teaching accountancy and research on accountancy and related subjects. Grants are also available to facilitate visits to the Institute by academics and professionals from overseas to the benefit of Members and students alike

WHO CAN BENEFIT Organisations benefiting students, academics and research workers

WHERE FUNDING CAN BE GIVEN UK

TYPE OF GRANT Recurring and one-off

FINANCES *Year* 1996 *Income* £90,000
Grants £40,000

TRUSTEES J B Cowan, Mrs V A Dickson, J M Haldane, A M Hawthorn, F F Kidd, H M M Johnston, Prof N Lothian, C H Ross, I M Stubbs

PUBLICATIONS Accounts and an outline of the Trust's policies are available upon request

HOW TO APPLY Applicants should contact the address below

WHO TO APPLY TO A G Guest, The Scottish Chartered Accountants' Trust for Education, 27 Queen Street, Edinburgh EH2 1LA

SC NO SCO 08368   **ESTABLISHED** 1977

◾ The Scottish Churches Architectural Heritage Trust

WHAT IS FUNDED To care for Scottish church buildings in use for public worship, principally by raising funds for their repair and restoration and by acting as a source of technical advice and assistance on maintenance and repair

WHERE FUNDING CAN BE GIVEN Scotland

TYPE OF GRANT Buildings

SAMPLE GRANTS £6,500 to Buckie St Peter's Moray for repairs to the bell; £5,000 to Glasgow St Aloysius for Phase Two of general repairs; £5,000 to Symington Parish Church, Ayrshire for roof and rainwater goods; £5,000 to Cockpen and Carrington, Midlothian for repairs to tower; £4,500 to Greenock, Finnart St Pauls for roof repairs; £4,000 to Glasgow St Andrew's East for general repairs; £4,000 to Fortrose St Andrew's Easter Ross for repairs to pinnacles; £4,000 to Stirling, Holy Trinity for repairs to fleche and roof; £4,000 to South Queensferry Priory of St Mary of Mount Carmel for general repairs; £4,000 to Stonehaven, St James the Great for repairs to stonework

FINANCES *Year* 1997 *Income* £120,000
Grants £112,000

TRUSTEES Lord Penrose (Chairman), Donald Erskine, Magnus Magnusson, The Very Rev Robin Barbour, Sir Jamie Stormonth Darling, Lady Fraser, John Gerrard, The Very Rev Malcolm Grant, Mrs Mary Millican, Ivor Guild, Rev Kenneth Nugent, Prof Frank Willett

HOW TO APPLY To the address under Who To Apply To in writing, after which an application form will be sent

WHO TO APPLY TO Mrs Florence MacKenzie, Director, Scottish Churches Architectural Heritage Trust, 15 North Bank Street, The Mound, Edinburgh EH1 2LP *Tel* 0131-225 8644

SC NO SCO 00819   **ESTABLISHED** 1978

◾ The Scottish Community Foundation

WHAT IS FUNDED Organisations aiming to build a bridge between small, local charities who provide essential services but who do not have the local knowledge to know where their help is most needed

WHAT IS NOT FUNDED No grants to individuals

WHO CAN BENEFIT Organisations. There are no restrictions on the age; and social circumstances of; or disease or medical condition suffered by, the beneficiaries

WHERE FUNDING CAN BE GIVEN Scotland

FINANCES *Year* 1996 *Income* £670,000
Grants £110,000

HOW TO APPLY For further information contact the Secretary at the address below

WHO TO APPLY TO The Secretary, The Scottish Community Foundation, 27 Palmerston Place, Edinburgh EH12 5AP *Tel* 0131-225 9804 *Fax* 0131-225 9818
E-mail caledonianfound@msn.com

SC NO SCO 22910   **ESTABLISHED** 1995

◾ The Scottish Homoeopathic Research and Education Trust

WHAT IS FUNDED Grants are given to organisations concerned with research into and education about homoeopathy

WHO CAN BENEFIT Organisations involved with: alternative health care, particularly homoeopathy; health education concerning homoeopathy; medicine; and specialist research. There is no restriction on the disease or medical condition suffered by the beneficiaries. Support may also be given to medical professionals

WHERE FUNDING CAN BE GIVEN UK, particularly Scotland

TRUSTEES Dr R H Baxendale, Dr H W Boyd, W M L Cameron, W A Cuthbertson, C J Davison, Dr R G Gibson, R G Hood, J McKechnie, Dr A D MacNeill, Dr H MacNeill, B B Morrison, Dr D T Reilly, Miss M A Shields, M G Taylor

HOW TO APPLY Applications should be made in writing to the address below

WHO TO APPLY TO D McVicar, The Scottish Homoeopathic Research and Education Trust, 7 Henderland Road, Bearsden, Glasgow G61 1JQ

SC NO SCO 06557

◾ The Scottish Hospital Endowments Research Trust

WHAT IS FUNDED Grants are awarded for individual or group research, scholarships and fellowships, travel and visitors

WHAT IS NOT FUNDED Grants are only awarded for projects carried out in Scotland

WHO CAN BENEFIT Organisations benefiting research workers

WHERE FUNDING CAN BE GIVEN Scotland

FINANCES *Year* 1996 *Income* £1,820,000
Grants £550,000

TRUSTEES Lord Kilpatrick of Kincraig, CBE (Chairman), Prof Margaret Alexander, CBE, Prof W Bowman, Pro G Colle, CBE, Prof G Forwell, OBE, Prof P Griffith, CBE, Dr Janet Morgan, Brenda Rennie

HOW TO APPLY Contact the address below for further information

WHO TO APPLY TO W & J Burness, Secretaries to the Trust, The Scottish Hospital Endowments Research Trust, W & J Burness Solicitors, 16 Hope Street, Edinburgh EH2 4DD
SC NO SCO 14959 **ESTABLISHED** 1953

■ The Scottish Housing Association Charitable Trust (SHACT)

WHAT IS FUNDED Grants are given for projects encompassing homelessness (especially young homeless); housing for people with special needs; for the elderly; care and repair charitable funds; rural projects; community regeneration projects; projects to benefit people of ethnic minorities

WHAT IS NOT FUNDED No grants or loans to be made to individuals, or large national organisations

WHO CAN BENEFIT Organisations benefiting people of all ages, ethnic minority groups, people with special needs, homeless people and those living in rural areas

WHERE FUNDING CAN BE GIVEN Scotland

RANGE OF GRANTS Mostly under £5,000

TRUSTEES Andrew Robertson, Ronald Ironside, David Harley, Gordon Woods, Harry Muligan, Gavin McCrone, Anne Yanetta, Susan Torrence, Paul Farrell, Robert McDowell, Margaret Richards, David Chalmers

NOTES The Trustees meet four times a year

HOW TO APPLY An application form and guidance notes are available from the address under Who To Apply To

WHO TO APPLY TO The Scottish Housing Association Charitable Trust, Messrs Kidsons Imprey, 23 Queen Street, Edinburgh EH2 1JX

SC NO SCO 06002 **ESTABLISHED** 1979

■ The Scottish Housing Associations Charitable Trust

WHAT IS FUNDED Grants and interest free loans are made to voluntary organisations including housing associations, for new/development work. Grants are also made to housing associations for community projects. Priority is for small or underfunded organisations. Organisations must demonstrate good equal opportunities practice and user involvement. Support may also be given to charities working in the fields of: infrastructure development and technical support; art activities; renewable energy and power; and other energy saving projects

WHAT IS NOT FUNDED No grants to individuals, large capital costs; vehicles or holidays

WHO CAN BENEFIT Older people, single homeless, people with disabilities, people in housing need in rural areas or of ethnic minorities; tenants, especially of housing associations, in areas of need or high unemployment. Funding will be given to people with many different social circumstances

WHERE FUNDING CAN BE GIVEN Scotland

TYPE OF GRANT Usually one-off although sometimes an organisation will be encouraged to apply again in the following year. Normally only one grant for an organisation in a financial year. Grants are normally made for start-up or new revenue costs. Interest free loans may be made for revenue or small capital costs. Core costs, feasibility studies, project, research, running costs and salaries may also be considered. Funding may be given for up to two years

RANGE OF GRANTS Average size grant is £2,000. Grants are rarely more than £5,000 or under £500. We prefer to give a grant that will make a sizeable contribution to a moderately-sized project

SAMPLE GRANTS £6,000 to Scottish Human Services for the development of new type of supported housing for people with learning disabilities; £5,000 to Orkney Care and Repair for the extension of handyperson services to outlying islands; £5,000 to Lorn and the Isles Housing Association, Argyll towards community lounge in sheltered housing project; £4,000 to Gryffe Women's Aid, Glasgow towards set-up cost for new supported flats; £3,810 to Valves into Action, Scotland for work on involvement of tenants with support needs; £3,000 to Rosebery Centre, Livingston, West Lothian for the development of drop-in information centre for dementia sufferers and carers; £3,000 to Perth YMCA for the development of service for young homeless people; £3,000 to Anderston Mel-Milaap Centre, Glasgow towards outreach housing advice for older people by volunteers; £3,000 to West End Churches Key Fund, Glasgow towards salary of co-ordinator for rent guarantee scheme; £3,000 to Fourwalls Housing Cooperative, Glasgow towards office and play materials for new women's housing development

FINANCES *Year* 1997–98 *Income* £112,400 *Grants* £87,900

TRUSTEES D W P Chalmers, C Cunningham, P Farrell, May Fong, N Hall, D A H Harley, R G L McCrone, R McDowell, H Mulligan, Sheena Munro, Margaret Richards, A O Robertson (Convener), Anne Yanetta

PUBLICATIONS Annual Reviews from 1993

NOTES As a fund-raising trust, SHACT occasionally has funds available for specific areas of work which may fall outwith the priorities listed above. Thus, grant making in a particular area in one year does not necessarily mean that such grants will always be available. Initial enquiries should always be made. Trustees meet quarterly. Please note that staff are part-time

HOW TO APPLY Applicants should telephone or fax before applying. A completed application form is required with copy of accounts. Guidelines are available, setting out criteria, deadlines and dates of meetings. All applicants will be informed of the outcome after the Trustees meeting

WHO TO APPLY TO Alison Rigg Campbell, Director, The Scottish Housing Associations Charitable Trust, 38 York Place, Edinburgh EH1 3HU *Tel* 0131-556 5777 *Fax* 0131-557 6028 *E-mail* shact@sfha.co.uk

SC NO SCO 24763 **ESTABLISHED** 1979

■ The Scottish International Education Trust

WHAT IS FUNDED Grants are given to organisations and individuals whose concerns lie in education, the arts or the areas of economic or social welfare

WHAT IS NOT FUNDED Grants are not made to commercial organisations or to fund capital costs or the maintenance expenditure of other organisations

WHO CAN BENEFIT Scots (by birth or upbringing) taking advanced studies for which support from public funds cannot be provided. Funding may also be given to children; young adults; students; actors and entertainment professionals; musicians; textile workers and designers; writers and poets; at risk groups, those disadvantaged by poverty and socially isolated people

WHERE FUNDING CAN BE GIVEN Scotland

TYPE OF GRANT One-off

RANGE OF GRANTS £50–£5,000, average grant £1,500

FINANCES *Year* 1997 *Income* £81,000 *Grants* £103,000

TRUSTEES Menzies Campbell, Sean Connery, Sir Alistair Dunnett, Tom Fleming, Lady Gibson, Alexander Goudie, Sir Norman Graham, J D Houston (Chairman), Andy Irvine, Prof Alistair Macfarlane, Kenneth McKellar, Jackie Stewart

PUBLICATIONS A brochure is available from the Trust

HOW TO APPLY Applications should be made in writing to the address under Who To Apply To

WHO TO APPLY TO John F McClellan, The Scottish International Education Trust, 22 Manor Place, Edinburgh EH3 7DS *Tel* 0131-225 1113

SC NO SCO 09207   **ESTABLISHED** 1970

■ The Scottish Slimmers Charitable Trust

WHAT IS FUNDED Most grants are made to major national healthcare charities but funds are also given to smaller, locally based organisations including several hospices

WHAT IS NOT FUNDED No grants to individuals. Grants are not given to overseas organisations or animal charities

WHO CAN BENEFIT Organisations benefiting medical professionals. There is no restriction on the disease or medical condition suffered by the beneficiaries

WHERE FUNDING CAN BE GIVEN UK, particularly Scotland

TRUSTEES Mrs A W Lewis, Ms C H Polson, J L Reid

PUBLICATIONS An information leaflet is available from the Trust

HOW TO APPLY Applications should be made in writing to the address below

WHO TO APPLY TO The Scottish Slimmers Charitable Trust, 151 Vincent Street, Glasgow G2 5NJ

SC NO SCO 21002

■ The Scouloudi Foundation

WHAT IS FUNDED The present policy is to distribute the whole of each year's income among three different categories of grants: (a) An annual donation to the Institute of Historical Research, University of London, to sponsor historical research, publications and fellowships, 'Historical Awards'. (b) Annual donations to a regular list of national charities, 'Regular Donations'. (c) Single donations in connection with capital projects and extraordinary appeals; 'Special Donations'

WHAT IS NOT FUNDED No Regular or Special donations to individuals or local organisations. Historical research awards are not available to those registered for undergraduate or postgraduate courses. Special donations are not made towards the day to day fundraising of charities. The Regular donations list is reviewed regularly but no new recipients are envisaged in the near future

WHO CAN BENEFIT Organisations benefiting graduates with honours degrees in History and research workers. For regular and 'Special' donations there are no restrictions on the age; professional and economic group; family situation; religion and culture; and social circumstances of; or disease or medical condition suffered by, the beneficiaries

WHERE FUNDING CAN BE GIVEN UK

TYPE OF GRANT There are three categories of grant: (a) an annual donation for historical research and fellowships to the Institute of Historical Research

at the University of London; (b) recurring grants to a regular list of charities; and (c) 'special' donations which are one-off grants in connection with capital projects

RANGE OF GRANTS To institutions: £500–£5,000

SAMPLE GRANTS £5,000 to University of London; £2,500 to Alzheimer's Research Trust; £2,500 to Cerebral Palsy Care; £2,500 to Children's Trust, Tadworth; £2,500 to Derbyshire Children's Hospital Kite Appeal; £2,500 to Lasers for Life; £2,500 to the Leopold Muller Arthritis Research Centre; £2,500 to Psychiatry Research Trust; £2,500 to St Vincent's Orthopaedic Hospital; £2,000 to Lincoln Cathedral Library

FINANCES *Year* 1997 *Income* £199,467 *Grants* £196,506

TRUSTEES M E Demetriadi, Miss B R Masters, OBE, BA, FSA, J D Marnham, FCA, Miss S E Stowell, MA

PUBLICATIONS Notes for the Guidance of Applicants for Special Donations and Historical Awards are available on request from the address under Who To Apply To

NOTES The Scouloudi Foundation Historical Awards total for 1997 was £66,000

HOW TO APPLY For Historical Awards, by 20 March each year to the Secretary, The Scouloudi Foundation Awards Committee, Institute of Historical Research, Senate House, University of London WC1E 7HU. For all other purposes, at any time, to the address under Who To Apply To with full but concise details of the appeal. The Trustees decide upon grants once a year in April

WHO TO APPLY TO The Administrators, The Scouloudi Foundation, Hays Allan Accountants, Southampton House, 317 High Holborn, London WC1V 7NL

CC NO 205685   **ESTABLISHED** 1962

■ The Diana Seabrooke Trust

WHAT IS FUNDED Support for Ashford Citizens Advice Bureau, for organisations working in the fields of care, disability and counselling

WHO CAN BENEFIT Organisations benefiting disabled people and those needing counselling. There is no restriction on the disease or medical condition suffered by the beneficiaries, however, there are some restrictions on the social circumstances that will be considered

WHERE FUNDING CAN BE GIVEN Ashford and Kent

RANGE OF GRANTS £100–£3,000

SAMPLE GRANTS £3,000 to Demelza House; £2,000 to Willesborough and District Community Project; £500 to Cancer Day Centre; £500 to League of Friends; £361 to Ashford Citizens Advice Bureau; £250 to Brainwave; £250 to East Kent Hospice; £250 to Ashford Samaritans; £250 to the Friends of Ashford Hospital; £250 to Medicins sans Frontieres

FINANCES *Year* 1996–97 *Income* £46,657 *Grants* £8,551

TRUSTEES J R Bell, P J Laker, C J M Parker

HOW TO APPLY To the address under Who To Apply To in writing

WHO TO APPLY TO P J Laker, Hon Secretary, The Diana Seabrooke Trust, 54 Grasmere Road, Kennington, Ashford, Kent TN24 9BG

CC NO 272406   **ESTABLISHED** 1976

■ Seagram Distillers Charitable Trust

WHAT IS FUNDED Support to the disadvantaged. Preference given to local rather than national charities

WHAT IS NOT FUNDED No grants to individuals, for medical research, the arts or overseas projects

WHO CAN BENEFIT Registered charities benefiting the disadvantaged

WHERE FUNDING CAN BE GIVEN Scotland and Greater London

TYPE OF GRANT Usually one-off cash donations, to enhance revenue rather than capital projects

FINANCES *Year* 1997 *Income* £4,201,000 *Grants* £4,198,000

HOW TO APPLY No specified format. All applications to be made in writing

WHO TO APPLY TO A McWatters, Seagram Distillers Charitable Trust, 111–113 Renfrew Road, Paisley PA3 4DY *Fax* 0141-531 1804

SC NO SCO 05704

■ Search

WHAT IS FUNDED Medicine and health. Provide relief, equipment, materials or grants for persons suffering from disabling conditions or diseases and to give discretionary financial support to educational projects

WHAT IS NOT FUNDED No grants to individuals or students

WHO CAN BENEFIT Established organisations benefiting sick and disabled people. Children and young adults may be considered

WHERE FUNDING CAN BE GIVEN UK

TYPE OF GRANT One-off grants

RANGE OF GRANTS £1,500–£60,000

SAMPLE GRANTS £60,000 to University of Bath; £33,000 to BIB; £25,000 to Stanmore; £20,000 to White Lodge Centre; £20,000 to SPARKS; £20,000 to Snowdon Award Scheme; £10,000 to Institute of Child Health; £8,000 to ACT Bristol; £5,000 to Wingrave School, Aylesbury; £5,000 to Spinal Injuries Association

FINANCES *Year* 1996 *Income* £266,619 *Grants* £210,000

TRUSTEES Dr R Leach, DPhil, Prof H Wolff, BSc, Dr S Glickman, FRCS

PUBLICATIONS Annual Report

NOTES All funds currently fully committed

HOW TO APPLY Application form available

WHO TO APPLY TO A Farquhar, Search, 22 City Business Centre, 6 Brighton Road, Horsham, West Sussex RH13 5BA *Tel* 01403 211252

CC NO 1038477 **ESTABLISHED** 1994

■ The Searchlight Electric Charitable Trust

WHAT IS FUNDED General charitable purposes

WHO CAN BENEFIT There are no restrictions on the age; professional and economic group; family situation; religion and culture; and social circumstances of; or disease or medical condition suffered by; the beneficiaries

WHERE FUNDING CAN BE GIVEN UK

SAMPLE GRANTS £37,300 to JPAIME; £5,000 to Heathlands Home for the Aged; £2,500 to Shaare Torah Yeshiva; £1,250 to VHT; £1,174 to Holy Law Synagogue; £1,000 to Prestwich Women's Zionist Society; £1,000 to New Synagogue, Netanya; £600 to British Friends Israel War Disabled; £600 to Friends of Hebrew University; £600 to Community Security Office

FINANCES *Year* 1997 *Income* £59,345 *Grants* £59,976

TRUSTEES H E Hamburger, D M Hamburger, M E Hamburger, J S Fidler

HOW TO APPLY To the address under Who To Apply To in writing

WHO TO APPLY TO H E Hamburger, Trustee, The Searchlight Electric Charitable Trust, Searchlight Electric Ltd, Water Street, Manchester M3 4JU

CC NO 801644 **ESTABLISHED** 1988

■ The Searle Charitable Trust

WHAT IS FUNDED Projects/organisations connected with sailing for youth development

WHAT IS NOT FUNDED Applications from individuals and non-sailing related requests will not be considered

WHO CAN BENEFIT Established youth organisations benefiting those disadvantaged by poverty

WHERE FUNDING CAN BE GIVEN UK only

TYPE OF GRANT One-off, recurring costs, project and core costs. Funding is available for up to three years

SAMPLE GRANTS £51,657 to London Sailing Project for annual funding for the 'Donald Searle' sail training yacht

FINANCES *Year* 1996–97 *Income* £124,450

TRUSTEES Andrew D Searle, Victoria C Searle

NOTES The Trust funds the 'Donald Searle' sail training yacht which is part of a fleet of vessels run and operated by the London Sailing Project based at Southampton. The main aim of the Trust is youth development within a nautical environment

HOW TO APPLY To the address under Who To Apply To in writing

WHO TO APPLY TO Andrew D Searle, The Searle Charitable Trust, 20 Kensington Church Street, London W8 4EP *Tel* 0171-761 7200 *Fax* 0171-761 7201

CC NO 288541 **ESTABLISHED** 1982

■ The Sears Foundation

WHAT IS FUNDED General charitable purposes. To provide support for charities which are relevant to the needs of Sears customers and the staff and environment in which they operate

WHO CAN BENEFIT There are no restrictions on the age; professional and economic group; family situation; religion and culture; and social circumstances of; or disease or medical condition suffered by, the beneficiaries

WHERE FUNDING CAN BE GIVEN UK

RANGE OF GRANTS £50–£34,354

SAMPLE GRANTS £34,354 to Save the Children; £10,000 to Action on Addiction; £9,910 to Breakthrough Breast Cancer; £4,000 to Police Foundation; £1,691 to Terence Higgins Trust; £1,500 to British Museum Society; £1,250 to Business in the Community; £1,000 to Cottage Homes; £1,000 to Institute of Economic Affairs; £500 to Action Research

FINANCES *Year* 1997 *Income* £74,584 *Grants* £72,496

TRUSTEES Sears Nominees Limited Directors: D A Defty, J D F Drum, Sir B Reid

NOTES The Foundation's main fund raising event of 1997 was Fashion Action Week, which raised money for: Save the Children, Shelter, Breakthrough Breast Cancer and Teenage Cancer Trust

HOW TO APPLY To the Trustees. All income of the Foundation is fully committed

WHO TO APPLY TO Allison Kappes, Secretary, The Sears Foundation, 40 Duke Street, London W1A 2HP

CC NO 283532   **ESTABLISHED** 1981

■ The Helene Sebba Charitable Trust

WHAT IS FUNDED General charitable purposes

WHO CAN BENEFIT There are no restrictions on the age; professional and economic group; family situation; religion and culture; and social circumstances of; or disease or medical condition suffered by, the beneficiaries

WHERE FUNDING CAN BE GIVEN UK

TYPE OF GRANT One-off

RANGE OF GRANTS £100–£2,500

SAMPLE GRANTS £2,500 to Norwood Ravenswood; £2,500 to Jewish Care; £2,500 to Scope; £2,500 to MENCAP; £1,000 to Nightingale House

FINANCES *Year* 1997 *Income* £19,923 *Grants* £20,854

TRUSTEES M Sebba, N C Klein, J C Sebba, L Sebba

HOW TO APPLY Funds available are fully committed to specific charities which the Trust supports regularly and the Trustees are unable to entertain other applications. No individual applications should therefore be submitted until further notice

WHO TO APPLY TO M Sebba, The Helene Sebba Charitable Trust, 465 Salisbury House, London Wall, London EC2M 5RQ

CC NO 277245   **ESTABLISHED** 1978

■ Leslie and Doris Seccombe Charitable Trust

WHAT IS FUNDED General charitable purposes. Local charities through personal connections with the Trustees

WHAT IS NOT FUNDED Registered charities only

WHO CAN BENEFIT There are no restrictions on the age; professional and economic group; family situation; religion and culture; and social circumstances of; or disease or medical condition suffered by, the beneficiaries

WHERE FUNDING CAN BE GIVEN Warwickshire

TYPE OF GRANT Usually one-off for a specific project or part

RANGE OF GRANTS £250–£1,500

SAMPLE GRANTS £1,500 to Devon Horse and Pony Sanctuary; £1,000 to Anglo Italian Society for Animals; £1,000 to Animals in Distress; £1,000 to Animal Samaritans; £1,000 to Battersea Dogs Home

FINANCES *Year* 1997 *Income* £19,503 *Grants* £33,750

TRUSTEES B M Abercrombie, H L Seccombe, J G Lindsay, P S Seccombe

WHO TO APPLY TO Clement Keys, Accountants, Leslie and Doris Seccombe Charitable Trust, Dartmouth House, Sandwell Road, West Bromwich B70 8TH

CC NO 217988   **ESTABLISHED** 1959

■ The Securicor Charitable Trust

WHAT IS FUNDED General charitable purposes. The Trustees prefer to support specific charitable projects rather than large general appeals

WHAT IS NOT FUNDED No educational grants, expeditions, wildlife. No advertising

WHO CAN BENEFIT There are no restrictions on the age; professional and economic group; family situation; religion and culture; and social circumstances of; or disease or medical condition suffered by, the beneficiaries

WHERE FUNDING CAN BE GIVEN Mainly UK but occasionally overseas where the Group has local operations

RANGE OF GRANTS Typical grant £250. Occasionally up to £1,000

FINANCES *Year* 1997 *Income* £54,496 *Grants* £53,200

TRUSTEES Mrs A Munson (Chairman), Mrs I Cowden, A J Gribbon, R K Davies, L K Gateson

HOW TO APPLY Trustees meet every two months. They consider only written applications. No application form. No telephone calls please

WHO TO APPLY TO The Chairman, Securicor Charitable Trust, Sutton Park House, 15 Carshalton Road, Sutton, Surrey SM1 4LD *Fax* 0181-661 0204

CC NO 274637   **ESTABLISHED** 1977

■ The Sedbury Trust

WHAT IS FUNDED General welfare especially concerned with children and young people who have been in care

WHO CAN BENEFIT At the discretion of the Trustees. Organisations benefiting those who have been in care, at risk groups, those disadvantaged by poverty and socially isolated people will be considered

WHERE FUNDING CAN BE GIVEN Gloucestershire

FINANCES *Year* 1998 *Income* £83,750 *Grants* £44,517

TRUSTEES N F C Smith, Miss J Trotter, D Morris, Mavis Lady Dunrossil, K Edwards

WHO TO APPLY TO Mrs J Lane, The Sedbury Trust, Wood End, Sandy Lane Road, Cheltenham, Gloucestershire GL53 9DA *Tel* 01242 572116

CC NO 1012875   **ESTABLISHED** 1992

■ The Seedfield Trust

WHAT IS FUNDED To support the preaching and teaching of the Christian faith throughout the world, including publication and distribution of Scripture, Christian literature and audio-visual aids. To assist in the relief of human suffering and poverty, including retired ministers and missionaries

WHAT IS NOT FUNDED Registered charities only. No grants to individuals

WHO CAN BENEFIT Organisations benefiting: people of all ages; Christians; evangelists; Victims of famine, man-made and natural disasters; those disadvantaged by poverty; and retired clergy

WHERE FUNDING CAN BE GIVEN UK and overseas

TYPE OF GRANT Capital, interest free loans, one-off, project and start-up costs. Funding is for up to three years

RANGE OF GRANTS £100–£10,000

SAMPLE GRANTS £10,000 to Dorothea Trust for retired Christian workers; £10,000 to European Christian Mission; £10,000 to Overseas Missionary Fellowship; £7,500 to Restorer Fund for support to New English Orchestra; £6,000 to Gideons International for bible distribution worldwide; £5,000 to Mullers Homes for social and Christian work with children; £5,000 to Active Service Trust for Wellsprings – Christian workers rehabilitation; £4,300 to ECM – Greece for the establishment of Christian Centre in Larissa; £4,000 to Operation Mobilisation for sowing project (evangelism in Spain); £3,000 to Pentecostal Child Care Association for social and Christian work with children

FINANCES *Year* 1997 *Income* £100,000 *Grants* £106,050

TRUSTEES J Atkins, K Buckler, D Ryan, D Heap, Mrs J Buckler, L E Osborn

HOW TO APPLY Applications should be addressed to the address under Who To Apply To for consideration by the Trustees who meet twice yearly. Please enclose an sae for acknowledgement

WHO TO APPLY TO K Buckler, The Seedfield Trust, Withybank, 3 Woodland Vale, Lakeside, Ulverston, Cumbria LA12 8DR

CC NO 283463   **ESTABLISHED** 1981

■ Sefton Community Foundation

WHAT IS FUNDED General charitable purposes for the benefit of the community, in particular, the advancement of education, the protection of mental and physical health and the relief of poverty and sickness

WHO CAN BENEFIT Children, young adults, disabled people and those disadvantaged by poverty. There are no restrictions on the disease or medical condition suffered by the beneficiaries

WHERE FUNDING CAN BE GIVEN Sefton

TRUSTEES C A Batchelor, Cllr W Burke, J Flynn, G Kaye, Cllr P J McVey, M J O'Brien, M J Swift, A White

WHO TO APPLY TO Mrs A White, Sefton Community Foundation, c/o The Old Museum, Church Road, Waterloo, Liverpool L22 5NB

CC NO 1068887   **ESTABLISHED** 1998

■ Segal Charitable Trust

WHAT IS FUNDED General charitable purposes

WHO CAN BENEFIT There are no restrictions on the age; professional and economic group; family situation; religion and culture; and social circumstances of; or disease or medical condition suffered by, the beneficiaries

WHERE FUNDING CAN BE GIVEN UK

FINANCES *Year* 1994 *Income* £22,287 *Grants* £30,394

TRUSTEES P B Marber, I G Wilder

WHO TO APPLY TO Ian Wilder, 223–237 Old Marylebone Road, London NW1 5QT

CC NO 272295   **ESTABLISHED** 1976

■ Selby Feoffee and Welfare Charity

WHAT IS FUNDED Relief of the aged, poor, sick and those in distress. Improving the conditions of life for the inhabitants of Selby in the interests of social welfare, providing facilities for recreation and leisure time. The income may also be used for the provision and support of educational purposes

WHO CAN BENEFIT Individuals and organisations benefiting older people, at risk groups, those disadvantaged by poverty and socially isolated people. There is no restriction on the disease or medical condition suffered by the beneficiaries

WHERE FUNDING CAN BE GIVEN Selby

SAMPLE GRANTS £12,167 to Feoffe Estate Church Charity; £12,167 to Selby Almshouse and Poors Charity; £12,167 to Welfare Branch; £5,025 to local charitable purposes; £541 to Selby Town Mission; £119 to Selby Sick Poor Fund

FINANCES *Year* 1996 *Income* £38,402 *Grants* £36,501

TRUSTEES The Vicar and Churchwardens of the Parish of Selby Abbey, H F Croxford, T Crossley, N Currey, Cllr Mrs D Davies, Cllr Mrs M Davies, Cllr S Davis, W L L Farman, J M Garnett, Mrs J Hedge, Dr A Robson, J Stevens, A G Tomblin, Cllr J Wetherell, Mrs M G Wetherell

NOTES The Trust is part of Selby United Charities which includes Selby Almshouse and Poors Charity and Selby Estate Church Charity. Income is distributed between these two additional charities and the Welfare Branch distributes money to the Town Mission and Selby Sick Poor Fund

HOW TO APPLY To the address under Who To Apply To in writing

WHO TO APPLY TO W L L Farman, Hon Treasurer, Selby Feoffee and Welfare Charity, Three Greens, The Green, Gateforth, Selby, North Yorkshire YO8 9LF

CC NO 810060   **ESTABLISHED** 1963

■ Leslie Sell Charitable Trust

WHAT IS FUNDED Assistance for Scout and Guide Associations mainly but not exclusively in Bedfordshire, Hertfordshire, and Buckinghamshire area

WHAT IS NOT FUNDED No grants made in response to general appeals from large national organisations nor to smaller bodies working in areas other than those set out in What Is Funded

WHO CAN BENEFIT Scout and Guide Associations

WHERE FUNDING CAN BE GIVEN Bedfordshire, Buckinghamshire and Hertfordshire

TYPE OF GRANT Usually single cash payments for a specific project. Core funding and salaries not considered

RANGE OF GRANTS £100–£24,699

SAMPLE GRANTS £24,699 to Studham, Kensworth and Markyate Scout Groups for the acquisition of a campsite; £6,500 to Cottlesloe School; £3,500 to Guide Association, Hertfordshire; £3,000 to Devere 604 Group Council; £1,000 to 1st Ashstead (Selham) Scouts; £1,000 to 1st Bilston Scouts; £1,000 to 1st Chalfont St Giles Scouts; £1,000 to 1st Chippenham Scouts; £1,000 to 1st Colyton Guides; £1,000 to 1st Feltham Scouts

FINANCES *Year* 1997 *Income* £160,108 *Grants* £104,588

TRUSTEES Mrs M R Wiltshire, P S Sell, D Watts, FCA

HOW TO APPLY Generally by letter to the address under Who To Apply To at any time. Applications should include clear details of the project or purpose for which funds are required, together with estimate of total costs and total funds raised by group or individual for project

WHO TO APPLY TO John Byrnes, Leslie Sell Charitable Trust, The Estate Office, 8 Upper Marlborough Road, St Albans, Hertfordshire AL1 3UR

CC NO 258699   **ESTABLISHED** 1969

■ The Selwood Charitable Trust

WHAT IS FUNDED General charitable purposes

WHO CAN BENEFIT There are no restrictions on the age; professional and economic group; family situation; religion and culture; and social circumstances of; or disease or medical condition suffered by, the beneficiaries

WHERE FUNDING CAN BE GIVEN UK

SAMPLE GRANTS £4,000 to an individual

FINANCES *Year* 1997 *Income* £77,761
Grants £4,000

TRUSTEES M Howson-Green, Mrs M A Selwood, S P Selwood

NOTES Funds are fully committed

HOW TO APPLY **This Trust states that it does not respond to unsolicited applications**

WHO TO APPLY TO T J Selwood, The Selwood Charitable Trust, c/o Stone Osmond Ltd, 75 Bournemouth Road, Eastleigh, Hampshire SO53 3AP

CC NO 265974   **ESTABLISHED** 1973

■ The Selwyn Demmy Charitable Trust

WHAT IS FUNDED General charitable purposes

WHO CAN BENEFIT There are no restrictions on the age; professional and economic group; family situation; religion and culture; and social circumstances of; or disease or medical condition suffered by, the beneficiaries

WHERE FUNDING CAN BE GIVEN UK

WHO TO APPLY TO M Gross, Trustee, The Selwyn Demmy Charitable Trust, c/o Lopian Gross Barnett & Co, 37 Peter Street, Manchester M2 5QD

CC NO 1049032   **ESTABLISHED** 1995

■ The Ayrton Senna Foundation

WHAT IS FUNDED Education, healthcare and medical support for children

WHAT IS NOT FUNDED No grants to individuals

WHO CAN BENEFIT Small local projects, new and established organisations benefiting children and young adults. There is no restriction on the disease or medical condition suffered by the beneficiaries

WHERE FUNDING CAN BE GIVEN UK and overseas

FINANCES *Year* 1995 *Income* £2,328,717
Grants £438,965

TRUSTEES Milton Guerado Theodoro da Silva, Neyde Joanna Senna da Silva, Leonardo Senna da Silva, Brian Stephen Clark, Viviane Lalli, Fabio da Silva Machado, Julian Alexander Robert Jakobi

HOW TO APPLY To the address under Who To Apply To in writing

WHO TO APPLY TO J Jakobi, The Ayrton Senna Foundation, 74 Wimpole Street London W1M 7DD

CC NO 1041759   **ESTABLISHED** 1994

■ The Seven Fifty Trust

WHAT IS FUNDED Trustees mainly give to Christian evangelical causes

WHO CAN BENEFIT Registered charities, particularly those benefiting Christians and Evangelists

WHERE FUNDING CAN BE GIVEN UK

RANGE OF GRANTS £350–£7110

SAMPLE GRANTS £7,110 to All Saints, Crowborough; £3,000 to St Matthew's, Fulham; £2,400 to International Fellowship of Evangelical Students; £2,159 to Coalition for Christian Outreach; £1,900 to Universities and Colleges Christian Fellowship; £1,900 to TEAR Fund; £1,500 to CMS; £1,500 to Overseas Missionary Fellowship; £1,200 to Sokoto Diocese; £1,100 to the Langham Trust

FINANCES *Year* 1996 *Income* £74,404
Grants £28,930

TRUSTEES A C J Cornes, Mrs K E Cornes, P N Collier, Mrs S M Collier

HOW TO APPLY **This Trust states that it does not respond to unsolicited applications**

WHO TO APPLY TO The Rev A C J Cornes, The Seven Fifty Trust, All Saints Vicarage, Chapel Green, Crowborough, East Sussex TN6 1ED

CC NO 298886   **ESTABLISHED** 1988

■ The Severn Trent Water Charitable Trust Fund

WHAT IS FUNDED The relief of those in need, poverty, hardship or distress and are unable to pay for the supply of water and/or sewerage services provided to premises used or occupied by them

WHO CAN BENEFIT Householders unable to meet charges for water or sewerage services provided by Severn Trent Water

WHERE FUNDING CAN BE GIVEN Area where Severn Trent Water is provided

TYPE OF GRANT (a) To individuals towards water charges and some other household charges. (b) To organisations towards the funding of debt counselling/money advice for householders falling into Who Can Benefit category

RANGE OF GRANTS For individuals average grant £340, no upper or lower limit for water debt. For funding debt counselling typically two to three year award of up to £30,000

FINANCES *Year* 1997–98 *Income* £2,000,000
Grants £909,000

TRUSTEES Hon Alderman Mrs Majorie Brown, CBE, JP, J R A Crabtree, Mrs Liz Pusey, BA, CCAW, Mrs Edna Sadler, JP, Roy Simpson

PUBLICATIONS None as yet except newsletter introducing the Trust, for copies please write to the Trust

HOW TO APPLY By application form for grants to individuals, usually with support/help from money advisor. By application form for grants to fund money advice within the Severn Trent Water geographical area

WHO TO APPLY TO S Braley, Chief Executive, The Severn Trent Water Charitable Trust Fund, Ground Floor, Hammond House, 2259–2261 Coventry Road, Birmingham B26 3PA *Tel* 0121-742 1376

CC NO 1064005   **ESTABLISHED** 1997

■ The Cyril Shack Trust

WHAT IS FUNDED General charitable purposes

WHAT IS NOT FUNDED No grants for expeditions, travel bursaries, scholarships or to individuals

WHO CAN BENEFIT There are no restrictions on the age; professional and economic group; family situation; religion and culture; and social circumstances of; or disease or medical condition suffered by, the beneficiaries

WHERE FUNDING CAN BE GIVEN UK

TYPE OF GRANT Capital, recurring

FINANCES *Year* 1997 *Income* £60,252
Grants £50,000

TRUSTEES J Shack, C C Shack
WHO TO APPLY TO The Cyril Shack Trust, c/o Lubbock Fine, 250 City Road, London EC1V 2QQ
CC NO 264270　　**ESTABLISHED** 1972

■ The Shadworth Hodgson Bequest

WHAT IS FUNDED General charitable purposes. Particularly charities working in the fields of: ambulances and mobile units; hospices; and nursing services
WHAT IS NOT FUNDED No projects
WHO CAN BENEFIT There are no restrictions on the age; professional and economic group; family situation; religion and culture; and social circumstances of; or disease or medical condition suffered by, the beneficiaries
WHERE FUNDING CAN BE GIVEN London, with preference to the south west area
TYPE OF GRANT Research grants
SAMPLE GRANTS £9,310 to Rustington Convalescent Home for sponsorship of bed and patients of Brompton Hospital, London; £700 to Trinity Hospice; £500 to Help the Aged; £500 to Marie Curie Cancer Care; £500 to National Institute for the Blind
FINANCES *Year* 1997 *Income* £24,268
Grants £15,750
TRUSTEES C Y Mills, D S Mills, W S Parker
WHO TO APPLY TO Frederick Saffery, Secretary, The Shadworth Hodgson Bequest, Hightrees, 11A Rickards Close, Ditton Hill, Surbiton, Surrey KT6 6RN *Tel* 0181-399 8511
CC NO 1054512　　**ESTABLISHED** 1947

■ Shaftoe Educational Foundation

WHAT IS FUNDED Schools serving the area Where Funding Can Be Given, local organisations and individuals for educational purposes
WHO CAN BENEFIT Residents of Haydon Parish. Schools serving Haydon children
WHERE FUNDING CAN BE GIVEN Haydon
TYPE OF GRANT Usually one-off revenue support
RANGE OF GRANTS £30–£2,000; typical size of grant £200–£500
SAMPLE GRANTS £10,000 to Northumberland County Council for specialist reading tuition in the schools; £6,700 to Shaftoe Trust First School for special equipment and 300th anniversary; £4,400 to Haydon Bridge High School for out of school music/drama; £4,300 to Allendale Middle School for special equipment; £1,800 to an individual student for a scholarship at Edinburgh University in honour of the Founder; £1,700 to Almshouse Charity of John Shaftoe - mandatory grants under Charity Scheme; £1,000 to Waite Travel Scholarship Fund for travel fund for high school pupils
FINANCES *Year* 1998 *Income* £67,919
Grants £44,730
TRUSTEES W J Drydon (Chairman), T A Bates, J W Clarkson, Mrs L A Philip, G M Rowarth, Mrs L A Gilhespy, Mrs E Garrow, T J Stephenson, J C Wardle
HOW TO APPLY To the address under Who To Apply To in writing. Guidance will be given by telephone. Applications are dealt with at regular meetings in March, July and November
WHO TO APPLY TO J P Richardson, Clerk, Shaftoe Educational Foundation, Shaftoe Terrace, Haydon Bridge, Hexham NE47 6BW *Tel* 01434 684298
CC NO 528101　　**ESTABLISHED** 1685

■ The Dr N K Shah Trust

WHAT IS FUNDED Theological related and spiritual studies, especially the causes of Jain studies. Activities to promote Jain values of non-violence, vegetarianism, ecology, animal welfare and human welfare
WHAT IS NOT FUNDED Empirical education not funded, only theological and spiritual studies
WHO CAN BENEFIT Any person or organisation. There are no restrictions on the age; professional and economic group; family situation; and social circumstances of; or disease or medical condition suffered by, the beneficiaries
WHERE FUNDING CAN BE GIVEN Mainly UK, but overseas also considered
TYPE OF GRANT May be project related
RANGE OF GRANTS Depends on the project
FINANCES *Year* 1997 *Income* £15,482
Grants £22,719
TRUSTEES Dr N K Shah, Mrs B N Shah, Dr S N Shah, L N Shah
NOTES Only persons studying theology, spiritual education or research and study related to Jain values may apply
HOW TO APPLY In writing
WHO TO APPLY TO Dr N K Shah, The Dr N K Shah Trust, 20 James Close, London NW11 9QX
CC NO 327291　　**ESTABLISHED** 1986

■ The Shalom Christian Trust

WHAT IS FUNDED To support their church and other charitable purposes known personally to the Trustees
WHAT IS NOT FUNDED All unsolicited requests for grants will not be considered
WHO CAN BENEFIT Individuals and organisations benefiting Christians
WHERE FUNDING CAN BE GIVEN UK and overseas
FINANCES *Year* 1996 *Income* £37,346
Grants £2,412
TRUSTEES R W Borlase, Miss N J Boulton, A L Perry, K Wright
NOTES In 1997, gifts to organisations totalled £2,100 and gifts to individuals totalled £100, allocations from Fellowship Fund totalled £212
HOW TO APPLY **This Trust states that it does not respond to unsolicited applications**
WHO TO APPLY TO A L Perry, The Shalom Christian Trust, 2 Holt Avenue, Moreton, Wirral, Merseyside L46 0SS
CC NO 1000362　　**ESTABLISHED** 1990

■ The Jean Shanks Foundation

WHAT IS FUNDED Medical research and education, scholarships and grants awarded to scientists and other persons engaged in research in medical and related sciences, the establishment of libraries and collections of books, and films and sound recordings relating to such research and education
WHO CAN BENEFIT Individuals and organisations benefiting chemists, research workers, students and medical professionals
WHERE FUNDING CAN BE GIVEN UK
RANGE OF GRANTS £3,750–£28,316

SAMPLE GRANTS £28,316 to The Royal Free Hospital; £28,200 to University College Hospital; £8,000 to Queen Mary and Westfield College; £4,000 to UMDS; £3,750 to University of Birmingham; £3,750 to University of Bristol; £3,750 to University of Leeds; £3,750 to University of Southampton; £3,750 to University of Leicester; £3,750 to University of Manchester

FINANCES *Year* 1997 *Income* £153,157 *Grants* £94,766

TRUSTEES Sir Richard Bayliss, Eric Rothbarth, Dr Jean Shanks, Prof T P Whitehead

HOW TO APPLY To the address under Who To Apply To in writing

WHO TO APPLY TO Dr Jean Shanks, Trustee, The Jean Shanks Foundation, 8 South Eaton Place, London SW1W 9JA

CC NO 293108   **ESTABLISHED** 1985

■ The Michael Shanly Charitable Trust

WHAT IS FUNDED General charitable purposes

WHO CAN BENEFIT There are no restrictions on the age; professional and economic group; family situation; religion and culture; and social circumstances of; or disease or medical condition suffered by, the beneficiaries

WHERE FUNDING CAN BE GIVEN UK

TRUSTEES M J Shanley, J L Meyer

WHO TO APPLY TO J L Meyer, Professional Adviser, The Michael Shanly Charitable Trust, 19/21 Bull Plain, Hertford, Hertfordshire SG14 1DX

CC NO 1065044   **ESTABLISHED** 1997

■ Shanti Charitable Trust

WHAT IS FUNDED General charitable purposes

WHO CAN BENEFIT There are no restrictions on the age; professional and economic group; family situation; religion and culture; and social circumstances of; or disease or medical condition suffered by, the beneficiaries

WHERE FUNDING CAN BE GIVEN UK

TRUSTEES Ms J B Gill, T F X Parr, R K Hyett

WHO TO APPLY TO J E Brown, Solicitor, Shanti Charitable Trust, 53 Kirkgate, Silsden, West Yorkshire BD20 0AQ

CC NO 1064813   **ESTABLISHED** 1997

■ The Shark Trust

WHAT IS FUNDED The advancement for the public benefit of the conservation of sharks, rays and chimaeras in the UK, European and International waters through education and the promotion and dissemination of research into such conservation

WHAT IS NOT FUNDED No grants for expeditions, scholarships, meetings or training

WHO CAN BENEFIT Individuals and organisations working with and benefiting sharks, rays and chimaeras

WHERE FUNDING CAN BE GIVEN UK and overseas

TYPE OF GRANT One-off and recurring for projects and research

RANGE OF GRANTS £100–£500

FINANCES *Year* 1997–98 *Income* £60,000

TRUSTEES G S Croft, I K Fergusson, J Stafford-Deitsch, G Swinney

PUBLICATIONS *Shark Focus* – newsletter

HOW TO APPLY To the address under Who To Apply To in writing

WHO TO APPLY TO Ms S Fowler, Secretary, The Shark Trust, 36 Kingfisher Court, Hambridge Road, Newbury, Berkshire RG14 5SJ *Tel* 01635 551150

CC NO 1064185   **ESTABLISHED** 1997

■ The Sharon Trust

WHAT IS FUNDED To help where needed, especially Christian work and missions. Cultural and religious teaching will be considered. Printing Gospel tracts

WHAT IS NOT FUNDED No grants to individuals

WHO CAN BENEFIT Christian missions, Christian camps, elderly Christian rest homes and organisations benefiting young Christians

WHERE FUNDING CAN BE GIVEN England, Scotland and overseas

TYPE OF GRANT Generally recurrent

FINANCES *Year* 1996 *Income* £51,215 *Grants* £33,223

TRUSTEES J F Warnes, F W Warnes, Mrs H G Taylor, Miss M H Warnes, W R Warnes

HOW TO APPLY About January each year. No application form. No applications considered from individuals

WHO TO APPLY TO The Sharon Trust, c/o Mrs H G Taylor, 3 Mount Pleasant, Lowestoft, Suffolk NR32 4JB *Tel* 01502 560602

CC NO 268742   **ESTABLISHED** 1974

■ The Christopher Sharples Charitable Settlement

WHAT IS FUNDED General charitable purposes

WHO CAN BENEFIT There are no restrictions on the age; professional and economic group; family situation; religion and culture; and social circumstances of; or disease or medical condition suffered by, the beneficiaries

WHERE FUNDING CAN BE GIVEN UK and overseas

TRUSTEES The Hon C J Sharples, The Hon Ms S J Sharples

WHO TO APPLY TO The Hon Christopher Sharples, Trustee, The Christopher Sharples Charitable Settlement, 72 Elm Park Road, London SW3 6AU

CC NO 1064301   **ESTABLISHED** 1997

■ The Linley Shaw Foundation

WHAT IS FUNDED To make grants out of income to charities whose purpose or object or one of whose purposes or objects is, or includes, the conservation, preservation and restoration of the natural beauty of the countryside of the UK for the public benefit. In particular to benefit charities which organise voluntary workers to achieve these objectives

WHAT IS NOT FUNDED Registered charities only. No grants to individuals. Must be rural locations

WHO CAN BENEFIT Volunteers may benefit

WHERE FUNDING CAN BE GIVEN UK

RANGE OF GRANTS £500–£8,000

SAMPLE GRANTS £8,000 to Groundwork, South Tyneside; £7,700 to World Wildlife Fund; £6,500 to Groundwork, Islwyn and Rymney; £6,000 to British Trust for Conservation Volunteers; £5,000 to Groundwork, Plymouth Area; £4,000 to Groundwork, East Lancashire; £4,000 to The NAtional Trust; £3,600 to Warwickshire Wildlife Trust; £3,500 to Badminton Trust; £3,000 to Groundwork, Rochdale and Oldham

FINANCES *Year* 1996 *Income* £134,941 *Grants* £62,335

TRUSTEES National Westminster Bank, London Branch

NOTES The ref no is: 4WE 678982

WHO TO APPLY TO Gavin Cansdale, Financial Services Officer, The Linley Shaw Foundation, NatWest Investments, London Branch, 62 Green Street, London W1Y 4BA

CC NO 1034051　　　**ESTABLISHED** 1993

■ The Shaw Lands Trust

WHAT IS FUNDED Educational bursaries for individuals; youth groups; welfare organisations. In awarding to beneficiaries scholarships, bursaries, maintenance allowances or grants at any place of learning, and in providing financial assistance, outfits, clothing, tools, instruments or books to help beneficiaries on leaving school, a university or other educational establishments

WHO CAN BENEFIT Organisations and individuals who have not attained the age of 25 years, who are resident within the former County Borough of Barnsley, or are or have been for not less than two years been in attendance at any school within the said former borough and who in the opinion of the Trustees are in need of financial assistance

WHERE FUNDING CAN BE GIVEN Barnsley

SAMPLE GRANTS £1,875 to Barnsley Association of Scouts; £1,875 to Air Training Corp; £1,875 to Barnsley Sea Cadets Corp; £1,875 to Barnsley Girl Guides; £1,875 to Army Cadets; £1,125 to The Samaritans (Barnsley Branch); £675 to Barnsley and District Dyslexia Association; £675 to MIND; £675 to Barnsley Blind and Partial Sight Association

FINANCES *Year* 1996–97 *Income* £34,427 *Grants* £28,477

NOTES £11,917 was donated to 32 individuals in educational awards

HOW TO APPLY To the address under Who To Apply To in writing

WHO TO APPLY TO Mr MacDonald, The Shaw Lands Trust, 35 Church Street, Barnsley, South Yorkshire S70 2AP

CC NO 224590　　　**ESTABLISHED** 1915

■ The Shears Charitable Trust

WHAT IS FUNDED Funding may be given to health education; children's charities; arts, culture and recreation; heritage; conservation and environment

WHAT IS NOT FUNDED No grants for domestic animal welfare

WHO CAN BENEFIT Organisations benefiting people of all ages and those suffering from hearing loss will be considered

WHERE FUNDING CAN BE GIVEN Northumberland, Tyne and Wear, Durham, West Yorkshire, Dorset and Isle of Wight

TYPE OF GRANT One-off

RANGE OF GRANTS Up to £5,000, typical grant £1,000

SAMPLE GRANTS £26,000 to National Tramway Museum; £250 to St Oswalds Hospice; £250 to MS Society; £250 to The National Trust; £250 to National Children's Society; £250 to Marie Curie Cancer Care; £250 to Scope; £250 to RNIB; £250 to Barnardos; £250 to Save the Children Fund

FINANCES *Year* 1997 *Income* £49,316 *Grants* £31,150

TRUSTEES Ms L G Shears, T H Shears, P J R Shears

WHO TO APPLY TO T H Shears, Trustee, The Shears Charitable Trust, 35 Elmfield Road, Gosforth, Newcastle upon Tyne NE3 4BA

CC NO 1049907　　　**ESTABLISHED** 1994

■ The Sheepdrove Trust

WHAT IS FUNDED General charitable purposes

WHAT IS NOT FUNDED No grants to individuals

WHO CAN BENEFIT There are no restrictions on the age; professional and economic group; family situation; religion and culture; and social circumstances of; or disease or medical condition suffered by, the beneficiaries

WHERE FUNDING CAN BE GIVEN UK

TYPE OF GRANT One-off and recurrent

FINANCES *Year* 1997 *Income* £413,749 *Grants* £293,616

TRUSTEES Mrs J E Kindersley, P D Kindersley, Miss H R Kindersley, B G Kindersley

HOW TO APPLY In writing at any time. No grants to individuals

WHO TO APPLY TO The Trustees, The Sheepdrove Trust, 2 Methley Street, London SE11 4AJ

CC NO 328369　　　**ESTABLISHED** 1989

■ The Sheffield Bluecoat and Mount Pleasant Educational Foundation

This trust did not respond to CAF's request to amend its entry and, by 30 June 1998, CAF's researchers did not find financial records for later than 1995 on its file at the Charity Commission. Trusts are legally required to submit annual accounts to the Charity Commission under section 42 of the Charities Act 1993

WHAT IS FUNDED Church and public schools, other independent schools, individuals for maintenance allowances, bursaries and scholarships

WHO CAN BENEFIT Individuals and schools benefiting children and young adults

WHERE FUNDING CAN BE GIVEN Sheffield

HOW TO APPLY To the address below in writing

WHO TO APPLY TO P W Lee, Secretary, Sheffield Bluecoat & Mount Pleasant Ed Foundation, c/o Dibb Lupton Broomhead Solicitors, Fountain Precinct, Balm Green, Sheffield, South Yorkshire S1 1RZ

CC NO 529351　　　**ESTABLISHED** 1962

■ Sheffield Town Trust

WHAT IS FUNDED General charitable purposes in the Sheffield area

WHAT IS NOT FUNDED Non-denominational. No applications will be considered from charities without connections in the stated area Where Funding Can Be Given

WHO CAN BENEFIT Mainly local charities. There are no restrictions on the age; professional and economic group; family situation; religion and culture; and social circumstances of; or disease or medical condition suffered by, the beneficiaries

WHERE FUNDING CAN BE GIVEN Sheffield and District

TYPE OF GRANT Charitable and public uses within the city

RANGE OF GRANTS £250–£6,000

SAMPLE GRANTS £6,500 to Voluntary Action, Sheffield; £6,000 to Youth Association South Yorkshire; £6,000 to Manor Reborn Project; £5,000 to Norfolk Park Child Protection Network Development Group; £5,000 to Cavendish Hip Fellowship Appeal; £5,000 to SADACCA Day Centre Appeal; £5,000 to Sheffield Volunteer Bureau; £5,000 to YMCA; £4,000 to Boys Clubs of South Yorkshire and Humberside; £3,600 to Family Service Unit (Sheffield)

FINANCES *Year* 1997 *Income* £327,000 *Grants* £245,000

TRUSTEES C G Murray, MBE, DL, JP, The Rt Hon Robert Arthur Baron Riverdale of Sheffield, DL, G F Young, CBE, DL, JP, LLD, S M de Bartolome, CBE, LLD, R G Grayson, MA, LLB, W R Jenkinson, JP, FCA, C H Talbot, MA, MB, MChir, FRCS, J H Neill, CBE, TD, LLD, C S Barker, DL,BA, A M C Staniforth, BA, FCA, J W Stephenson, JP, FRICS, J R Brayshaw, LLB, Mrs J A Lee

HOW TO APPLY First weeks in January, April, July and October. Applications are normally considered on a quarterly basis

WHO TO APPLY TO G Connell, The Law Clerk, Sheffield Town Trust, Clerk's Office, Old Cathedral Vicarage, St James Row, Sheffield, South Yorkshire S1 1XA *Tel* 0114-272 2061

CC NO 223760   **ESTABLISHED** 1297

■ The Sheldon Trust

WHAT IS FUNDED The funding priorities of the Trustees are the relief of poverty and distress in society, concentrating on community projects. Aftercare, hospice at home, respite care, self help and support groups, and rehabilitation centres are also considered

WHAT IS NOT FUNDED No grants to individuals

WHO CAN BENEFIT Facilities for the deprived and handicapped. Encouragement of local voluntary groups, recreational facilities, youth, community, rehabilitation for drugs, alcohol, and solvent abuse, religion, the elderly, mental health, mental handicap. Organisations benefiting: people of all ages; at risk groups; carers; those disadvantaged by poverty; homeless people; refugees; socially isolated people and substance misusers.

WHERE FUNDING CAN BE GIVEN UK with preference to Warwickshire and Midlands

TYPE OF GRANT Core costs, project, running costs, salaries and start-up costs will be considered. Funding may be given for up to two years

SAMPLE GRANTS £11,000 to Birmingham – Money Advice towards grants for individuals; £8,000 to SENSE for family support worker; £5,500 to Institute of Family Therapy for a clinical director's salary; £5,500 to BCAT towards running costs; £3,000 to Nuneaton Boys' Club for general purposes; £3,000 to Coventry City Farm for equipment; £3,000 to Human City Institute for running costs; £3,000 to Highball Trust for building repairs; £3,000 to John Grooms for housing; £2,500 to Foundation for Communication for the Disabled for assessments

FINANCES *Year* 1997–98 *Income* £125,822 *Grants* £93,700

TRUSTEES Rev R Bidnell, R V Wiglesworth, J C Barratt, R Bagshaw, R England

HOW TO APPLY May, October, February

WHO TO APPLY TO The Sheldon Trust, Box S, White Horse Court, 25c North Street, Bishop's Stortford, Hertfordshire CM23 2LD

CC NO 242328   **ESTABLISHED** 1965

■ The Shelroy Charitable Trust

WHAT IS FUNDED The Trust will in the main support Norfolk bodies or individuals with particular consideration for the elderly, disabled or disadvantaged. It does not, however, rule out donations to overseas projects or charities with Christian or medical aims where local people (Norwich area) are actively involved

WHAT IS NOT FUNDED The Trust does not support large charities with mass circulation

WHO CAN BENEFIT Registered charities in the areas outlined in Funding Priorities, Christian churches or organisations, medical bodies, individuals on Christian/medical youth projects overseas. Disabled people, those suffering from substance misuse, the elderly and children. Must be Norfolk residents

WHERE FUNDING CAN BE GIVEN Norwich and Norfolk only

TYPE OF GRANT Usually one-off for a specific project. Core funding and/or salaries rarely considered

SAMPLE GRANTS £3,000 to lonely elderly and disadvantaged people for Christmas hampers and support for local grouped homes; £2,000 to Crusaders for financial support; £1,475 to students in midwifery at University of East Anglia for midwifery studies; £750 to Norwich Youth for Christ as continuing support for their work; £500 to Cooper Atkinson Trust for India for medical and Christian work in southern India (locally run)

FINANCES *Year* 1996–97 *Income* £17,291 *Grants* £17,580

TRUSTEES A Callf, N F R Jones, R D Kinsley, R C Snelling, D A Varvel, R C Wiltshire

HOW TO APPLY At any time. Trustees meet quarterly. Applications should include clear details of the need the intended project is designed to meet, plus an outline budget. Individuals applying for grants must provide full information and two referees are required. We regret that it is not possible to reply to unsuccessful applicants unless an sae is provided

WHO TO APPLY TO R C Wiltshire, The Shelroy Charitable Trust, 4 Brandon Court, Brundall, Norwich, Norfolk NR13 5NW

CC NO 327776   **ESTABLISHED** 1988

■ The Patricia and Donald Shepherd Charitable Trust

WHAT IS FUNDED General charitable purposes. To donate only to local charities or charities of which the Trustees have personal knowledge, interest or association.

WHAT IS NOT FUNDED No grants to individuals

WHO CAN BENEFIT Mainly local organisations – those in the North of England and Scotland

WHERE FUNDING CAN BE GIVEN North of England and Scotland with preference for the York area

TYPE OF GRANT Mainly one-off

FINANCES *Year* 1995 *Income* £85,595 *Grants* £63,197

TRUSTEES D W Shepherd, Mrs P Shepherd, Mrs J L Robertson, Patrick M Shepherd, D R Reaston

HOW TO APPLY Applications acknowledged on receipt. No application form is used

WHO TO APPLY TO The Trustees, The Patricia and Donald Shepherd Charitable Trust, PO Box 10, York YO1 1XU

CC NO 272948   **ESTABLISHED** 1973

The Sylvia and Colin Shepherd Charitable Trust

WHAT IS FUNDED In the medium term policy is to build up the Trust's capital base. Currently the main areas of interest are community initiatives, care of the elderly, child care, the mentally or physically disabled, conservation, and medical support and equipment

WHAT IS NOT FUNDED Registered charities only. Applications from individuals not considered, neither are applications relating to overseas activities or in the UK areas outside the defined area Where Funding Can Be Given. Preference is given to smaller organisations in the area Where Funding Can Be Given

WHO CAN BENEFIT Registered charities benefiting children and older people, retired people and disabled people. There is no restriction on the disease or medical condition suffered by the beneficiaries

WHERE FUNDING CAN BE GIVEN The Trust's priority is to assist charitable organisations in Greater York, North Yorkshire, and East and West Yorkshire within a 25 mile radius of York only

TYPE OF GRANT Usually for specific projects on an enabling basis. Core funding or ongoing support will not normally be provided

RANGE OF GRANTS £50–£2,500, typically £250–£1,000

SAMPLE GRANTS £2,500 to The National Trust towards local projects; £2,000 to York Against Cancer; £1,000 to Marrick Priory Appeal; £1,000 to Abbeyfield York Society; £1,000 to York Cemetery Trust; £1,000 to York University Young Musicians Fund; £1,000 to Friends of York Hospitals; £1,000 to St Leonards Hospice, York; £1,000 to York Civic Trust; £1,000 to the Macmillan East Yorkshire Appeal

FINANCES *Year* 1998 *Income* £74,000 *Grants* £63,000

TRUSTEES Mrs S Shepherd, Mrs S C Dickson

HOW TO APPLY Applications in writing only, to the address under Who To Apply To. At any time. The Trustees meet frequently and aim to acknowledge all requests for support. Applicants should include details of the need to be met and their achievements in their field of work and enclose a copy of their annual accounts

WHO TO APPLY TO S C Dickson, The Sylvia and Colin Shepherd Charitable Trust, 15 St Edward's Close, York YO24 1QB

CC NO 272788   **ESTABLISHED** 1973

The David Shepherd Conservation Foundation

WHAT IS FUNDED The conservation of endangered mammals worldwide. Particular focus is given to direct funding for field work for tigers, elephants and rhinos in Africa and Asia. The Foundation assists official law enforcement agencies to combat wildlife crime

WHAT IS NOT FUNDED No grants to anything unrelated to critically endangered mammals

WHO CAN BENEFIT Endangered wild flora and fauna and their dependent species including people

WHERE FUNDING CAN BE GIVEN UK and overseas. Any area in which endangered mammals occur is considered

TYPE OF GRANT Direct grants to field projects

RANGE OF GRANTS £200–£20,000

FINANCES *Year* 1996 *Income* £261,651 *Grants* £219,473

TRUSTEES Sir Robert Clark, Anthony Athaide, Peter Giblin, David Gower, OBE, Avril Shepherd, David Shepherd, OBE, FRSA

PUBLICATIONS Bi-annual membership magazine *Wildlife Matters*

HOW TO APPLY On-going

WHO TO APPLY TO Melanie Shepherd, Director, The David Shepherd Conservation Foundation, 61 Smithbrook Kilns, Cranleigh, Surrey GU6 8JJ

CC NO 289646   **ESTABLISHED** 1984

The Sir Peter Shepherd Family Charitable Trust (formerly The Patricia & Peter Charitable Trust)

WHAT IS FUNDED Financial support to organisations established to improve the quality of life of those less fortunate in society, or are of benefit to society. Those involved with health care, medical research, education, the preservation of our heritage and the care of those who have served their country

WHAT IS NOT FUNDED No grants to individuals

WHO CAN BENEFIT To benefit children and young adults; research workers; students; those who have served their country; at risk groups; disabled people; those disadvantaged by poverty; and socially isolated people. There is no restriction on the disease or medical condition suffered by the beneficiaries

WHERE FUNDING CAN BE GIVEN York

RANGE OF GRANTS £50–£1,576

SAMPLE GRANTS £1,576 to the Merchant Adventurers of the City of York; £750 to York Guild of Building; £500 to Abbeyfield Society; £307 to York Civic Trust; £300 to National Asthma Campaign

FINANCES *Year* 1997 *Income* £16,387 *Grants* £8,458

TRUSTEES Lady Shepherd, P M Shepherd, P N Shepherd, P W Shepherd, A M Shepherd

WHO TO APPLY TO Nicholas Shepherd, The Sir Peter Shepherd Family Charitable Trust, Galtres House, Rawcliffe Lane, York YO3 6NP

CC NO 272949   **ESTABLISHED** 1973

Sherburn House Charity

WHAT IS FUNDED Provision of residential care and sheltered housing for elderly residents and former residents of the area Where Funding Can Be Given. Relief of need, hardship and distress within the area Where Funding Can Be Given

WHAT IS NOT FUNDED All applications considered

WHO CAN BENEFIT Residents and former residents of the area Where Funding Can Be Given, either suffering need, hardship or distress, or in need of care or sheltered accommodation. There is no restriction of the age or family situation of the residents

WHERE FUNDING CAN BE GIVEN The boundaries of the Ancient Diocese of Durham, between the River Tweed and the River Tees

TYPE OF GRANT Buildings, capital, core costs, one-off, running costs, salaries and start-up costs will be considered. Funding may be given for more than three years

RANGE OF GRANTS Individual: £100–£1,000, typical grant £400. Organisations: £175–£15,000, typical grant £5,000

FINANCES *Year* 1997–98 *Income* £1,525,595 *Grants* £85,727

TRUSTEES A Beeton, Ven M E Bowering, M Bozic, W Brooks, M Crathorne, C Dickinson, L A F Farthing, W Firby, D Gibson, D Hale, M R Hawgood, J

Mackintosh, J R Marsden, H L Perks, Dr G E Rodmell, L B Smith, Ven T Wilmott, R Wilson

NOTES Grant applications are considered monthly

HOW TO APPLY An application form is available. Applications on behalf of individuals should be submitted by a statutory or voluntary body. Organisations should submit applications on their own behalf

WHO TO APPLY TO S P Hallett, Chief Officer, Sherburn House Charity, Sherburn Hospital, Sherburn House, Durham DH1 2SE *Tel* 0191-372 2551 *Fax* 0191-372 0035

CC NO 217652 **ESTABLISHED** 1181

■ Amardeep Singh Shergill Memorial Charitable Trust

WHAT IS FUNDED The advancement of education and religion according to the tenets of Sikhs and to promote such charitable purposes in the UK and overseas

WHO CAN BENEFIT Organisations benefiting Sihks

WHERE FUNDING CAN BE GIVEN UK and overseas

TRUSTEES G S Gill, J S Sangera, J S Atwal

WHO TO APPLY TO Gurcharan Singh Gill, Chairperson, Amardeep Singh Shergill Memorial Charitable Trust, 215 Jiggins, Bartley, Birmingham B32 3EP

CC NO 1066517 **ESTABLISHED** 1997

■ The Archie Sherman Cardiff Charitable Foundation

WHAT IS FUNDED General charitable purposes within the Scheduled Territories

WHAT IS NOT FUNDED Not able to make donations to private individuals

WHO CAN BENEFIT There are no restrictions on the age; professional and economic group; family situation; religion and culture; and social circumstances of; or disease or medical condition suffered by, the beneficiaries

WHERE FUNDING CAN BE GIVEN UK, Canada, Australia, New Zealand, Pakistan, Sri Lanka, South Africa, India, Israel, USA and other parts of the British Empire or Commonwealth

RANGE OF GRANTS £1,394–£36,000

SAMPLE GRANTS £36,000 to the British Council of the Shaare Zedek Medical Centre; £1,394 to the Joint Jewish Charitable Trust

FINANCES *Year* 1997 *Income* £129,052 *Grants* £37,394

TRUSTEES Rothschild Trust Corporation Ltd Directors: D L Harris, D N Allison, R F A Balfour, A J H Penney, Hon J B Soames

WHO TO APPLY TO Michael J Gee, The Archie Sherman Cardiff Charitable Foundation, 27 Berkeley House, Hay Hill, London W1X 7LG

CC NO 272225 **ESTABLISHED** 1976

■ R C Sherriff Rosebriars Trust

WHAT IS FUNDED Particularly charities working in the fields of: arts, culture and recreation; cultural and religious teaching; training for community and personal development; bursaries and fees; research into the arts and community facilities. Visual arts and crafts, published artwork and the performing arts

WHAT IS NOT FUNDED No grants for long-term education or projects outside Elbmidge

WHO CAN BENEFIT Local individuals and organisations benefiting: people of all ages; actors and entertainment professionals; musicians;

students; textile workers and designers; and writers and poets. There is no restriction on the religion and culture of the beneficiaries

WHERE FUNDING CAN BE GIVEN Elmbridge

TYPE OF GRANT Capital, feasibility studies, one-off, project and schools funds. Funding of up to three years will be considered

RANGE OF GRANTS £95–£12,000, typical grant £1,000

SAMPLE GRANTS £10,632 to Mole Valley Community Trust; £9,000 to River House Barn Theatre; £5,000 to Painshill Park; £5,000 to Elmbridge Day Centres; £3,750 to Princess Alice Hospice; £3,000 to The Barn Theatre Club; £2,567 to Arts in the Suburbs; £2,500 to Brooklands Museum; £2,000 to Surrey Dance Project; £2,000 to DIY Theatre Company

FINANCES *Year* 1997 *Income* £157,277 *Grants* £56,985

TRUSTEES Rosebriars Committee, Elmbridge Borough Council

PUBLICATIONS Grant Pack

HOW TO APPLY Application forms available from the address under Who To Apply To

WHO TO APPLY TO Director, The R C Sherriff Rosebriars Trust, Civic Centre, High Street, Esher, Surrey KT10 9SD *Tel* 01372 474566

CC NO 272527 **ESTABLISHED** 1991

■ The Dr Florence Sherry-Dottridge Trust

This trust did not respond to CAF's request to amend its entry and, by 30 June 1998, CAF's researchers did not find financial records for later than 1995 on its file at the Charity Commission. Trusts are legally required to submit annual accounts to the Charity Commission under section 42 of the Charities Act 1993

WHAT IS FUNDED General charitable purposes

WHO CAN BENEFIT There are no restrictions on the age; professional and economic group; family situation; religion and culture; and social circumstances of; or disease or medical condition suffered by, the beneficiaries

WHERE FUNDING CAN BE GIVEN UK and overseas

TRUSTEES Mrs G R Vernon, M G Sherry

WHO TO APPLY TO R A Hulett, The Dr Florence Sherry-Dottridge Trust, Park House, London Road, High Wycombe, Buckinghamshire HP11 1BZ

CC NO 1041081 **ESTABLISHED** 1994

■ Sherwood and Waudby Charity

WHAT IS FUNDED Youth groups, holiday playschemes, Age Concern, primary schools, community centres, village halls and sports centres, hospices, and local newsletters

WHO CAN BENEFIT Residents of Walkington of all ages and who are disadvantaged by poverty

WHERE FUNDING CAN BE GIVEN Walkington

TYPE OF GRANT Usually yearly grants to village organisations with occasional one-off grants

RANGE OF GRANTS £13–£536, typical grant £175

SAMPLE GRANTS £536 to Walkington Playscheme for hire of minibus; £500 to Walkington School; £300 to Walkington newsletter for the cost of production; £300 to Walkington Guides towards the cost of the annual camp; £200 to Dove House Hospice towards running costs

FINANCES *Year* 1997 *Income* £24,811 *Grants* £4,577

TRUSTEES C G Drew, D Drew, K L Hearne, J F D Johnson, M A Morrill

HOW TO APPLY To the address under Who To Apply To in writing

WHO TO APPLY TO D Henderson, Sherwood and Waudby Charity, 5 Meadow Way, Walkington, Beverley, East Yorkshire HU17 8SD
Tel 01482 868404

CC NO 224209   **ESTABLISHED** 1981

■ Sherwood Coalfield Community Foundation

WHAT IS FUNDED Support to community resource centres in North Nottinghamshire

WHO CAN BENEFIT The communities of North Nottinghamshire

WHERE FUNDING CAN BE GIVEN Ashfield, Bassetlaw, Mansfield, Newark and Sherwood

TRUSTEES Rt Rev Alan Morgan (Chairman), Cllr Joyce Bosnjak, Tony Bostock, Roger Healey, Cllr Sally Higgins, Karen Medhurst, Julie Wagstaff

WHO TO APPLY TO T J Nash, Company Secretary, Sherwood Coalfield Community Foundation, The Old Town Hall, Market Place, Mansfield, Nottinghamshire NG18 1HX *Tel* 01623 429753

CC NO 1069538   **ESTABLISHED** 1998

■ The Mary May Sheward Charitable Trust

WHAT IS FUNDED General charitable purposes

WHO CAN BENEFIT There are no restrictions on the age; professional and economic group; family situation; religion and culture; and social circumstances of; or disease or medical condition suffered by, the beneficiaries

WHERE FUNDING CAN BE GIVEN Shropshire, Hereford and Worcester, West Midlands

TRUSTEES Ms C Brinsdon, Ms S Sherry, David C Bishop (Solicitor)

WHO TO APPLY TO D Bishop, Solicitor, The Mary May Sheward Charitable Trust, Morton Fisher, 18 Lord Street, Bewdley, Worcestershire DY12 2AE

CC NO 1068078   **ESTABLISHED** 1997

■ The Barnett and Sylvia Shine No 1 Charitable Trust

WHAT IS FUNDED General charitable purposes. The Trustees make cash donations to a variety of charitable organisations but do not entertain applications made by or on behalf of individuals

WHAT IS NOT FUNDED No grants to individuals

WHO CAN BENEFIT A range of charitable organisations are considered. There are no restrictions on the age; professional and economic group; family situation; religion and culture; and social circumstances of; or disease or medical condition suffered by, the beneficiaries

WHERE FUNDING CAN BE GIVEN UK

TYPE OF GRANT One-off cash donations

SAMPLE GRANTS £250 to JIA

FINANCES *Year* 1997 *Income* £73,358 *Grants* £250

TRUSTEES M D Paisner, Sybil Shine

WHO TO APPLY TO M D Paisner, The Barnett and Sylvia Shine No 1 Charitable Trust, Messrs Paisner & Co, Bouverie House, 154 Fleet Street, London EC4A 2DQ

CC NO 270025   **ESTABLISHED** 1975

■ The Barnett and Sylvia Shine No 2 Charitable Trust

WHAT IS FUNDED The Trustees make small cash payments for specific purposes to voluntary education and welfare groups. They do not entertain applications made by or on behalf of individuals

WHAT IS NOT FUNDED Applications not made by official personnel

WHO CAN BENEFIT Mainly London local organisations benefiting children and young adults

WHERE FUNDING CAN BE GIVEN London

TYPE OF GRANT One-off cash donations

SAMPLE GRANTS £5,000 to Canon Collins Educational Fund; £4,500 to NHS Support Federation; £2,000 to Oxfam

FINANCES *Year* 1997 *Income* £54,580 *Grants* £14,049

TRUSTEES R Grahame, M D Paisner, Mrs B Grahame

HOW TO APPLY At any time

WHO TO APPLY TO M D Paisner, The Barnett and Sylvia Shine No 2 Charitable Trust, Messrs Paisner & Co, Bouverie House, 154 Fleet Street, London EC4A 2DQ

CC NO 281821   **ESTABLISHED** 1980

■ Thomas Stanley Shipman Charitable Trust

WHAT IS FUNDED General charitable purposes, including relief of poverty by grants and otherwise. To primarily restrict support to those charities operating for the benefit of the citizens of the City and County of Leicester

WHO CAN BENEFIT There are no restrictions on the age; professional and economic group; family situation; religion and culture; and social circumstances of; or disease or medical condition suffered by, the beneficiaries

WHERE FUNDING CAN BE GIVEN City and County of Leicester

TYPE OF GRANT Buildings, capital, core costs, endowment, feasibility studies, interest free loans, one-off, projects, research, recurring costs, running costs, salaries and start-up costs. Funding can be given for any length of time

FINANCES *Year* 1997 *Income* £71,000 *Grants* £55,000

TRUSTEES Mrs J Cartwright, E Watts, M T Newby

HOW TO APPLY Applications may be made at anytime, although the Trustees usually meet in November and May. There is no application form. Applications may be in the form that suits the applicant, but must be accompanied by Annual Reports and audited Accounts

WHO TO APPLY TO A R York, FCA, Thomas Stanley Shipman Charitable Trust, 18 Friar Lane, Leicester LE1 5RA *Tel* 0116-251 6229 *Fax* 0116-253 8115

CC NO 200789   **ESTABLISHED** 1961

■ Bassil Shippam Trust

WHAT IS FUNDED General charitable purposes. Support is concentrated on local charities located in West Sussex rather than on national appeals, with emphasis on Christian objects and youth

WHAT IS NOT FUNDED Individuals are only funded in exceptional cases where there are strong Christian links

WHO CAN BENEFIT Organisations benefiting children, young adults and Christians

WHERE FUNDING CAN BE GIVEN Mainly West Sussex

TYPE OF GRANT General but emphasis on youth

SAMPLE GRANTS £5,000 to West Sussex Association for the Blind; £5,000 to Chichester Eventide Housing; £5,000 to Outset Youth Action South West Sussex; £2,500 to St Wilfred's Hospice (the Dunhill Medical Trust); £2,080 to Holbrook County Primary School; £2,000 to Vision Tesco Rural Development Organisation; £2,000 to West Sussex County Council Voluntary Fund; £1,800 to Chichester District Council for the Elderly; £1,500 to Sailing Centre Ltd; £1,500 to Chichester Youth Wing Mobile Youth Project

FINANCES *Year* 1997 *Income* £50,302
Grants £73,035

TRUSTEES D S Olby, S W Young, M Hanwell, S Trayler, R Tayler, J H S Shippam, C W Doman

HOW TO APPLY To the address under Who To Apply To

WHO TO APPLY TO C W Doman, Bassil Shippam Trust, 5 East Pallant, Chichester PO19 1TS

CC NO 256996   **ESTABLISHED** 1967

■ The Shipwrights Charitable Fund

WHAT IS FUNDED Maritime training, sailors' welfare, maritime heritage. Charities working in the fields of churches and Anglican bodies

WHAT IS NOT FUNDED Applications must have a clear maritime/waterborne connection

WHO CAN BENEFIT Individuals and organisations benefiting children; young adults and older people; ex-service and service people; seafarers and fishermen; parents and children; and victims of war

WHERE FUNDING CAN BE GIVEN UK, with a preference for the London area

TYPE OF GRANT Annual donations, general donations and outdoor activity bursaries. Buildings, capital, core costs, one-off, project and start-up costs. Funding for one year or less will be considered

RANGE OF GRANTS £250–£4,000

SAMPLE GRANTS £4,000 to Royal Merchant Navy School Foundation for education of children of Merchant Navy people; £2,500 to Missions to Seamen for helping distressed marines; £2,500 to National Maritime Museum for 'Maritime London' exhibit, Neptune Hall; £2,500 to Discovering Dockland Trust for the purchase of sailing equipment; £2,500 to George Green's School in the Isle of Dogs for general purposes; £2,000 to City of London Outward Bound Association for outward bound courses for inner London young people; £2,000 to Ocean Youth Club for sailing for young people; £2,000 to City of London Sea Cadets Unit; £2,000 to Docklands Sailing Centre for part-purchase of boat for the use by George Green's School

FINANCES *Year* 1996–97 *Income* £120,000
Grants £67,000

TRUSTEES Changes annually

HOW TO APPLY To the address under Who To Apply To in writing

WHO TO APPLY TO The Clerk, The Shipwrights Charitable Fund, The Worshipful Company of Shipwrights, Ironmongers Hall, Barbican, London EC2Y 8AA *Tel* 0171-606 2376

CC NO 262043   **ESTABLISHED** 1971

■ The Shirley Foundation

WHAT IS FUNDED Projects involving learning disability (particularly autism), information technology and care in the community

WHAT IS NOT FUNDED No grants to individuals

WHO CAN BENEFIT Registered charities benefiting disabled people and those suffering from autism

WHERE FUNDING CAN BE GIVEN UK

TYPE OF GRANT One-off, buildings, core costs, feasibility studies, project, research, and start-up costs. Funding is available for more than three years

TRUSTEES M R MacFadyen, Mrs A M Menzies, Mrs V S Shirely, OBE

NOTES The resources of the Foundation are, for the time being, fully committed to existing projects

HOW TO APPLY Applications are unwelcome at present

WHO TO APPLY TO Mrs V S Shirley, The Shirley Foundation, North Lea House, 66 Northfield End, Henley on Thames, Oxfordshire RG9 2BE *Tel* 01491 572565

CC NO 1057662   **ESTABLISHED** 1996

■ J A Shone Memorial Trust

WHAT IS FUNDED General charitable purposes. Funds directed to organisations known to the Trustees

WHO CAN BENEFIT There are no restrictions on the age; professional and economic group; family situation; religion and culture; and social circumstances of; or disease or medical condition suffered by, the beneficiaries

WHERE FUNDING CAN BE GIVEN UK

SAMPLE GRANTS £15,000 to MAF in Kenya for a new hangar; £5,000 to Philarmonic Endowment Fund; £5,000 to MAF in Tanzania; £5,000 to TEAR Fund – UK Action; £5,000 to St Luke's Hospital for the Clergy; £5,000 to Winged Fellowship; £5,000 to LPSS; £5,000 to All Nations Christian College; £3,000 to Liverpool Diocese; £2,500 to Brentwood School for hymn books

FINANCES *Year* 1997 *Income* £63,267
Grants £77,000

TRUSTEES A W Shone, P S Shone, Mrs S J Gilchrist

HOW TO APPLY **This Trust states that it does not respond to unsolicited applications**

WHO TO APPLY TO A W Shone, J A Shone Memorial Trust, c/o Wilson Foods Ltd, 412 Corn Exchange, Fenwick Street, Liverpool L2 7QS

CC NO 270104   **ESTABLISHED** 1974

■ Shropshire Historic Churches Trust

WHAT IS FUNDED The restoration, preservation, repair, maintenance and improvement of churches and their contents in the area Where Funding Can Be Given

WHO CAN BENEFIT Churches

WHERE FUNDING CAN BE GIVEN Shropshire

TYPE OF GRANT Buildings

FINANCES *Year* 1996 *Income* £28,374
Grants £3,650

HOW TO APPLY To the address under Who To Apply To in writing

WHO TO APPLY TO Archdeacon of Salop, Shropshire Historic Churches Trust, Tong Vicarage, Shifnal, Shropshire TF11 8PW

CC NO 1010690   **ESTABLISHED** 1991

■ The Shuttlewood Clarke Foundation

WHAT IS FUNDED Charitable purposes for the relief of need, hardship, suffering or distress. Funding is given to the Foundation's two day centres. Particularly charities working in the fields of: personnel and human resource services; support to voluntary and community organisations; and support and self help groups

Have you read How to use the DGMT *on page xvi?*

WHO CAN BENEFIT Individuals and organisations benefiting children, older and retired people, widows and widowers, housebound people and disabled people

WHERE FUNDING CAN BE GIVEN UK, with preference to Leicestershire

TYPE OF GRANT One-off

FINANCES *Year* 1996–97 *Income* £258,000 *Grants* £34,000

TRUSTEES D A Clarke, M Freckleton, D N Murphy, K P Byass

HOW TO APPLY Preliminary written enquiry to the address under Who To Apply To

WHO TO APPLY TO D A Clarke, The Shuttlewood Clarke Foundation, Ulverscroft Grange, Ulverscroft, Leicester LE67 9QB *Tel* 01530 244914

CC NO 803525   **ESTABLISHED** 1990

■ Barbara A Shuttleworth Memorial Trust

WHAT IS FUNDED Mental illness, disability, children charities and general charitable purposes

WHO CAN BENEFIT Organisations benefiting, in particular, children, disabled people and those suffering from mental illness

WHERE FUNDING CAN BE GIVEN UK with a preference to West Yorkshire

TYPE OF GRANT At the discretion of the Trustees

SAMPLE GRANTS £14,524 to Heaton Royds School; £3,853 to Shipley Leisure; £2,895 to an individual for a wheelchair; £2,496 to Friends of Airedale Child Development Centre; £2,000 to Meanwood Valley Urban Farm

FINANCES *Year* 1997 *Income* £16,056 *Grants* £27,168

TRUSTEES Miss B A Shuttleworth, J A Baty, C J Eaton, F R Fenton

WHO TO APPLY TO J Baty, Barbara A Shuttleworth Memorial Trust, Baty Cosson Long, Provincial House, 26 Albion Street, Leeds, West Yorkshire LS1 6HX

CC NO 1016117   **ESTABLISHED** 1992

■ Second Sidbury Trust

WHAT IS FUNDED Education, poor relief, relief of sickness especially arthritis and rheumatic diseases

WHAT IS NOT FUNDED No grants to individuals

WHO CAN BENEFIT Organisations benefiting: people of all ages; those disadvantaged by poverty. There is no restriction on the disease or medical condition suffered by the beneficiaries, although priority is given to those suffering from arthritis and rheumatism

WHERE FUNDING CAN BE GIVEN UK

TYPE OF GRANT Recurrent

FINANCES *Year* 1997 *Income* £20,000 *Grants* £26,000

TRUSTEES Lady W M Hamilton, OBE, G F H Glover, J C Vernor Miles, G W S Miskin, Mrs J N Nyiri

NOTES The Trust income is fully committed for the foreseeable future and applications therefore are not welcome

HOW TO APPLY In about April. No form of application

WHO TO APPLY TO J C Vernor Miles, Second Sidbury Trust, Messrs Vernor Miles & Noble, 5 Raymond Buildings, Gray's Inn, London WC1R 5DD

CC NO 239432   **ESTABLISHED** 1964

■ The Mary Elizabeth Siebel Charity

WHAT IS FUNDED Hospice at home; respite care for carers and care in the community

WHO CAN BENEFIT Individuals and some organisations benefiting: the elderly, disabled people and those disadvantaged by poverty as well as their carers

WHERE FUNDING CAN BE GIVEN Within a 12 mile radius of Newark Town Hall

TYPE OF GRANT Flexible, but one-off grants preferred for buildings, capital and core costs

RANGE OF GRANTS £50–£15000

FINANCES *Year* 1996–97 *Income* £77,015 *Grants* £57,078

TRUSTEES P Blatherwick, A E Hine, O Millard, S Watson, R White

NOTES The Trustees have a policy to prefer to assist those who wish to continue to live independently in their own homes

HOW TO APPLY To the address under Who To Apply To in writing, who will supply a formal application form

WHO TO APPLY TO Andrew J Fearn, The Mary Elizabeth Siebel Charity, 3 Middlegate, Newark, Nottinghamshire NG24 1AG *Tel* 01636 671881

CC NO 1001255   **ESTABLISHED** 1990

■ The Julius Silman Charitable Trust

WHAT IS FUNDED Grants are directed to the relief of the disadvantaged, and assistance of individuals coming within this category. Support of humanitarian causes

WHAT IS NOT FUNDED National institutions other than those with local appeal will not be extended beyond existing list

WHO CAN BENEFIT At risk groups, those disadvantaged by poverty and socially isolated people

WHERE FUNDING CAN BE GIVEN Wiltshire area

TYPE OF GRANT Recurrent to established institutions. One-off to individuals, but large-scale sponsorships are not available

FINANCES *Year* 1996 *Income* £28,995 *Grants* £25,051

TRUSTEES J Silman, S A Silman, C Smith

HOW TO APPLY To the address under Who To Apply To by post only. No application form. Applications will not be acknowledged if a grant is not made

WHO TO APPLY TO J Silman, The Julius Silman Charitable Trust, Courtlands, Corsham, Wiltshire SN13 9QJ

CC NO 263830   **ESTABLISHED** 1971

■ The Leslie Silver Charitable Trust

WHAT IS FUNDED Medicine and health, welfare, sciences, humanities, including: the advancement of the Jewish religion; synagogues; Jewish religious umbrella bodies; arts, culture and recreation; and community facilities, and other charitable purposes

WHAT IS NOT FUNDED No grants to individuals or students

WHO CAN BENEFIT Small local projects, new organisations and established organisations benefiting: children and young adults; Jews; at risk groups; those disadvantaged by poverty and socially isolated people. There is no restriction on the disease or medical condition suffered by the beneficiaries

WHERE FUNDING CAN BE GIVEN Charities and appeal funds primarily in the Leeds area. However, the largest donations are made to charitable trusts providing aid in Israel

TYPE OF GRANT One-off, non-recurring grants

RANGE OF GRANTS £300–£10,000

FINANCES *Year* 1996–97 *Income* £64,070
Grants £176,620

TRUSTEES Leslie H Silver, Mark S Silver, Ian J Fraser

HOW TO APPLY Prior telephone call and then in writing to I J Fraser or G Wainwright (Trust Manager)

WHO TO APPLY TO I J Fraser, The Leslie Silver Charitable Trust, Wilson Braithwaite Scholey, 21–27 St Paul's Street, Leeds LS1 2ER
Tel 0113 244 5451

CC NO 1007599   **ESTABLISHED** 1991

■ The Bishop Simeon CR Trust

WHAT IS FUNDED To provide aid and support for the education of young South Africans in the UK and South Africa. Grants normally go to projects in South Africa where the aim is to work with local initiatives in the Dioceses of SE Transvaal and Klerksdorp

WHO CAN BENEFIT Young South Africans and organisations primarily in South Africa

WHERE FUNDING CAN BE GIVEN UK and South Africa, particularly SE Transvaal and Klerksdorp

FINANCES *Year* 1997 *Income* £37,211
Grants £37,403

WHO TO APPLY TO Mrs J A Scott, Director, The Bishop Simeon CR Trust, South Looseland, Cruwys Morchard, Tiverton, Devon EX16 8QS

CC NO 802639   **ESTABLISHED** 1989

■ Simest Charitable Trust

WHAT IS FUNDED General charitable purposes

WHO CAN BENEFIT There are no restrictions on the age; professional and economic group; family situation; religion and culture; and social circumstances of; or disease or medical condition suffered by, the beneficiaries

WHERE FUNDING CAN BE GIVEN UK and overseas

TRUSTEES S Fulda, E Fulda, C Y Fulda

WHO TO APPLY TO Simcha Fulda, Simest Charitable Trust, 42 Waterpark Road, Salford, Manchester M7 4ET

CC NO 1064457   **ESTABLISHED** 1997

■ The Simon Population Trust

WHAT IS FUNDED To promote the relief of poverty and improvements of standards of health throughout the world by promoting a better understanding of the problems of world population and resources

WHO CAN BENEFIT Individuals and institutions benefiting those disadvantaged by poverty. There are no restrictions on the disease or medical condition suffered by the beneficiaries

WHERE FUNDING CAN BE GIVEN UK and overseas

TYPE OF GRANT At the discretion of the Trustees

RANGE OF GRANTS £500–£30,000. Typical grants are about £5,000

FINANCES *Year* 1996–97 *Income* £15,274
Grants £107,283

TRUSTEES Dr Kathleen Kiernan, Tim Dyson, Dr John McEwan, Dilys Cossey, Sir Richard King, KCB, Madeleine Simms, Dr Alan G Hill, John Smithard, Penny Kane, Wendy Savage

WHO TO APPLY TO The Simon Population Trust, 49–51 Bedford Square, London WC1B 3DP

CC NO 290455   **ESTABLISHED** 1984

■ Miss D B Simpson Charitable Trust

WHAT IS FUNDED General charitable purposes

WHAT IS NOT FUNDED No grants to individuals

WHO CAN BENEFIT Registered charities only. There are no restrictions on the age; professional and economic group; family situation; religion and culture; and social circumstances of; or disease or medical condition suffered by, the beneficiaries

WHERE FUNDING CAN BE GIVEN UK but with preference for West Sussex

TYPE OF GRANT One-off grants

RANGE OF GRANTS Typical grant £250

SAMPLE GRANTS £1,000 to Richmond Fellowship; £1,000 to Age Concern Hove and Portslade; £1,000 to Spadework; £750 to Lionel House Trust; £750 to APA Community Drug and Alcohol; £750 to Action for Blind People; £750 to Fellowship of St Nicholas; £750 to SAABAH; £750 to St Thomas Fund for Homeless; £750 to RUKBA

FINANCES *Year* 1997 *Income* £27,000
Grants £18,000

TRUSTEES Barclays Bank Trust Co Ltd

HOW TO APPLY Applications considered at Trustee meetings held four times a year

WHO TO APPLY TO Barclays Bank Trust Company Limited, Miss D B Simpson Charitable Trust, Executorship and Trustee Service, Osborne Court, Gadbrook Park, Rudheath, Northwich, Cheshire CW9 7UE

CC NO 263919   **ESTABLISHED** 1972

■ The Simpson Foundation

WHAT IS FUNDED The support of charities favoured by the Founder in his lifetime and others with similar objects – in the main Catholic charities

WHAT IS NOT FUNDED No grants to individuals

WHO CAN BENEFIT Registered charities particularly those benefiting Roman Catholics

WHERE FUNDING CAN BE GIVEN UK and overseas

RANGE OF GRANTS £200–£1,000

SAMPLE GRANTS £1,000 to Providence (Row) Night Refuge and Home; £1,000 to Sisters of Charity of Jesus and Mary; £1,000 to Stonyhurst Charitable Fund 1992 Appeal; £900 to Von Hugal Institute; £800 to Cardinal Hume Centre

FINANCES *Year* 1997 *Income* £22,509
Grants £22,000

TRUSTEES C E T Bellord, P J M Hawthorne, P J O Herschan

NOTES Funds fully committed already

HOW TO APPLY By written application to the address under Who To Apply To at any time. No telephone applications will be considered

WHO TO APPLY TO C E T Bellord, The Simpson Foundation, Messrs Witham Weld, 70 St George's Square, London SW1V 3RD

CC NO 231030   **ESTABLISHED** 1961

■ The Huntly and Margery Sinclair Charitable Trust

WHAT IS FUNDED To benefit well-established charities in particular

WHAT IS NOT FUNDED Grants are rarely made to individuals

WHO CAN BENEFIT Generally to registered charities. There are no restrictions on the age; professional and economic group; family situation; religion and culture; and social circumstances of; or disease or medical condition suffered by, the beneficiaries

WHERE FUNDING CAN BE GIVEN UK

RANGE OF GRANTS £500–£85,000

SAMPLE GRANTS £85,000 to Rendcomb College; £4,000 to Kings School, Gloucester; £2,500 to St George's Cancer Vaccine Campaign; £1,000 to CARE; £1,000 to SPECAL; £500 to British Liver Trust; £500 to British Red Cross Society; £500 to Colesbourne Church PCC; £500 to Turkdean Church Fabric Fund

FINANCES *Year* 1996 *Income* £59,068 *Grants* £95,500

TRUSTEES Mrs M A H Windsor, Mrs A M H Gibbs, Mrs J Floyd

WHO TO APPLY TO The Huntly and Margery Sinclair Charitable Trust, Messrs Trowers & Hamlins, 6 New Square, Lincoln's Inn, London WC2A 3RP

CC NO 235939   ESTABLISHED 1964

■ Singer Foundation

WHAT IS FUNDED To sponsor projects that encourage individual effort and enterprise: to encourage people, especially the young, to help themselves by helping others in any way that is acceptable to the Trustees and the Charity Division of the Inland Revenue. Youth clubs, the Scout and Guide Associations and voluntary work are supported

WHO CAN BENEFIT Local organisations – scouts, guides, youth clubs, etc. Self-help work and sponsorship for voluntary charitable work. Individual sponsorship for unpaid voluntary charitable work under-taken in the British Isles only

WHERE FUNDING CAN BE GIVEN UK

TYPE OF GRANT One-off – for each project

RANGE OF GRANTS £10–£250

SAMPLE GRANTS £250 to 10th Worcester Scouts; £250 to Chawn Hill Christian Centre; £250 to St Peters Church, Pembury; £250 to Church Army; £250 to Horticulture Therapy; £250 to Corbridge Scouts and Guides; £250 to Caring and Sharing; £250 to Coventry Sea Scouts; £250 to 1st Blackhall Guides and Brownies; £250 to Cesrean Scout Group

FINANCES *Year* 1995 *Income* £38,305 *Grants* £5,585

TRUSTEES D A Day, B J Scandrett, J F Woolgrove, J Day

NOTES Grants are only made when the projects or voluntary unpaid charitable work has been satisfactorily carried out. Written confirmation is requested from a third party

HOW TO APPLY Requests for application forms and details by letter only to the address under Who To Apply To

WHO TO APPLY TO Mrs J Day, Singer Foundation, North Farm, Cherington, Shipston on Stour, Warwickshire CV36 5HZ

CC NO 277364   ESTABLISHED 1960

■ Sino-British Fellowship Trust

WHAT IS FUNDED Scholarships to Chinese subjects to enable them to pursue their studies in Britain. Grants to British subjects in China to educate/train Chinese subjects in any art, science, profession or handicraft. Grants to Chinese subjects associated with charitable bodies to promote their education and understanding of European methods. Applications are received by Established Committees overseas. The final Awards are made in the United Kingdom

WHO CAN BENEFIT Institutions benefiting individual postgraduate students

WHERE FUNDING CAN BE GIVEN UK and China

TYPE OF GRANT Fees, fares and allowance at the discretion of the Trustees

SAMPLE GRANTS £90,000 to UK institutions for students support; £38,000 to Hong Kong institutions for student support; £317 directly to students

FINANCES *Year* 1995 *Income* £283,509 *Grants* £128,317

TRUSTEES Dr V E Frankland Moore, OBE, LLD, K H Mostyn, Prof M N Naylor, RD, BSc, BDS, PhD, FDS, RCS, Dr the Hon Harry S Y Fang, CBE, MChOrth, FRCSE, FACS, FRACS, LLD, JP, Prof C F Cullis, Mrs A Ely, Lady P Youde

PUBLICATIONS Trust Report

NOTES Grants listed do not include those made to individuals

HOW TO APPLY Spring and Autumn. Application forms are used

WHO TO APPLY TO Mrs Elizabeth Ely, Sino-British Fellowship Trust, 23 Bede House, Manor Fields, London SW15 3LT

CC NO 313669   ESTABLISHED 1948

■ The Sirrom Charitable Trust

This trust did not respond to CAF's request to amend its entry and, by 30 June 1998, CAF's researchers did not find financial records for later than 1995 on its file at the Charity Commission. Trusts are legally required to submit annual accounts to the Charity Commission under section 42 of the Charities Act 1993

WHAT IS FUNDED General charitable purposes. To support charities of which they have special knowledge or association

WHAT IS NOT FUNDED No grants to individuals

WHO CAN BENEFIT Mainly headquarters organisations. There are no restrictions on the age; professional and economic group; family situation; religion and culture; and social circumstances of; or disease or medical condition suffered by, the beneficiaries

WHERE FUNDING CAN BE GIVEN UK

TYPE OF GRANT Largely recurrent. The Trustees do not consider grants for salaries or running costs

TRUSTEES J S T Morris, D P Morris

NOTES No telephone calls. Distributions in December yearly, or when there is a disaster needing support

HOW TO APPLY Applications not sought as the Trustees prefer to decide for themselves

WHO TO APPLY TO The Trustees of the Sirrom Charitable Trust, Pottersfields, Potter Row, Great Missenden, Buckinghamshire HP16 9RU

CC NO 262156   ESTABLISHED 1970

■ Bequest of Harry Skells

WHAT IS FUNDED The improvement of streets and roads, and the provision and improvement of park and recreation grounds, public buildings and other public areas in the area Where Funding Can Be Given. Particularly charities working in the fields of: almshouses; building services; religious buildings; religious umbrella bodies; church buildings; historic buildings; memorials and monuments; woodlands and various community services

WHAT IS NOT FUNDED No grants to individuals

WHO CAN BENEFIT Local organisations

WHERE FUNDING CAN BE GIVEN Stamford

TYPE OF GRANT Buildings and project funding for one year or less will be considered

FINANCES *Year* 1995–96 *Income* £20,390

TRUSTEES Stamford Town Council

HOW TO APPLY Application forms are available from the address under Who To Apply To

Does the trust you have chosen match your needs? Haphazard applications waste postage and time

589

WHO TO APPLY TO A Wain, Clerk, Bequest of Harry Skells, Town Hall, Stamford, Lincolnshire PE9 2DR *Tel* 01780 53808
CC NO 239573   ESTABLISHED 1965

■ The Skelton Bounty

WHAT IS FUNDED Restricted to Lancashire charities (not national ones unless operating in Lancashire from a permanent establishment within the County predominantly for the benefit of residents from that County) assisting youth, the aged and infirm
WHAT IS NOT FUNDED Religious charities, medical and scientific research and minibus appeals are not encouraged. Grants can only be made to registered charities
WHO CAN BENEFIT Organisations benefiting young and elderly people and the infirm
WHERE FUNDING CAN BE GIVEN Lancashire – meaning the geographical County as it existed in 1934
TYPE OF GRANT Capital expenditure preferred
RANGE OF GRANTS £200–£7,000
SAMPLE GRANTS £7,000 to Rainbow Family Trust, Stretford; £5,000 to Ocean Youth Club, Denton; £3,500 to Old Swan Youth Club, Liverpool; £3,000 to Carleton Community Association, Poulton-le-Fylde; £3,000 to Christ Church Centre, Netherley; £3,000 to Henshaw's Society for the Blind; £2,500 to Royal School for the Blind, Liverpool; £2,312 to Mawdesley Village Hall; £2,000 to Liverpool Personal Service Society Inc; £2,000 to Merseyside Council for Voluntary Service
FINANCES *Year* 1997 *Income* £70,646 *Grants* £64,352
TRUSTEES G P Bowring, S R Fisher, Mrs A Fishwick, K A Gledhill, Lord Shuttleworth, DL, FRICS, Sir Kenneth M Stoddart, KCVO, AE, LLD, JP, DL, Lady Towneley, A W Waterworth, Sir William L Mather, CVO, OBE, MC, TD, DL
NOTES The Charity comprises three former charities founded by members of the Shelton Family. Each member by their wills founded a charitable trust, all of which were amalgamated into one charity in 1991
HOW TO APPLY Between 1 January and 31 March on form obtainable from the address under Who To Apply To
WHO TO APPLY TO Messrs Cockshott Peck Lewis, The Skelton Bounty, 24 Hoghton Street, Southport PR9 0XH
CC NO 219370   ESTABLISHED 1934

■ Skerritt Trust

WHAT IS FUNDED Trustees consider applications for housing and amenities for the aged including: various residential facilities and services; Council of Voluntary Services; nursing homes; care in the community; and day centres
WHO CAN BENEFIT The elderly
WHERE FUNDING CAN BE GIVEN Ten mile radius from Nottingham Market Square
TYPE OF GRANT Capital, core costs, interest free loans; one-off, project, research, recurring and running costs, salaries and startup costs
FINANCES *Year* 1997 *Income* £60,366 *Grants* £49,285
TRUSTEES Mrs P Davies, J Corder, Mrs C Moore, D Hughes, I W Dawson, H Vernon, Mrs J Kingdon, D Hancock, N Cutts, Mrs J Cursham, R Costa, Canon E Neale, Mrs A Arey
HOW TO APPLY Applications acknowledged, no application form. Meetings approximately every

three months. To the address under Who To Apply To in writing
WHO TO APPLY TO D S Corder, Clerk, Skerritt Trust, Bramley House, 1 Oxford Street, Nottingham NG1 5BH *Tel* 0115-936 9369 *Fax* 0115-936 9370
CC NO 1016701   ESTABLISHED 1992

■ The Charles Skey Charitable Trust

WHAT IS FUNDED General charitable purposes
WHAT IS NOT FUNDED No written or telephoned requests for support will be entertained
WHERE FUNDING CAN BE GIVEN UK
SAMPLE GRANTS £15,000 to St Georges Hospital Special Trustees for research; £10,000 to Lloyds Patriotic Fund; £2,000 to Seeability; £2,000 to Caseforce; £2,000 to Stepping Stones Trust; £1,500 to Camphill Village Trust; £1,500 to Joint Educational Trust; £1,500 to LOROS; £1,000 to Army Benevolent Fund; £1,000 to Activity Centre
FINANCES *Year* 1996–97 *Income* £67,864 *Grants* £48,500
TRUSTEES C H A Skey (Chairman), J M Leggett, C B Berkeley, D C Paul
HOW TO APPLY **This Trust states that it does not respond to unsolicited applications**
WHO TO APPLY TO J M Leggett, The Charles Skey Charitable Trust, Flint House, Park Homer Road, Colehill, Wimborne, Dorset BH21 2SP
CC NO 277697   ESTABLISHED 1979

■ Edward Skinner Charitable Trust

WHAT IS FUNDED Support of the West Watch Trust which provides facilities for Christian groups and organisations running house parties, camps, retreats, etc at West Watch, Chelwood Gate and other Christian organisations
WHAT IS NOT FUNDED Not able to support individuals
WHO CAN BENEFIT Organisations benefiting Evangelical missions and Christians
WHERE FUNDING CAN BE GIVEN UK and overseas
TYPE OF GRANT Core costs, for one year or less
FINANCES *Year* 1997 *Income* £36,826 *Grants* £33,500
TRUSTEES E D Anstead, L W Richards, P J Stanford, Mrs B M O'Driscoll
NOTES Main object of the Trust is to support West Watch Trust, Chelwood Gate
HOW TO APPLY To the address under Who To Apply To
WHO TO APPLY TO Mrs B M O'Driscoll, Edward Skinner Charitable Trust, 15 Wilman Road, Tunbridge Wells, Kent TN4 9AJ
CC NO 258519   ESTABLISHED 1968

■ Skinners' Company Lady Neville Charity

WHAT IS FUNDED This Trust will consider funding: religious and historic buildings; memorials and monuments; arts, culture and recreation; art galleries and museums; cultural centres; libraries and museums; theatres and opera houses; and disability
WHAT IS NOT FUNDED Grants will not be made to: (a) organisations whose work falls outside of the above; (b) large general appeals from national charities; (c) medical research, hospice or hospital activities; (d) organisations working in similar areas as the Skinners' Company. These

are: schools and education; care of elderly people; sheltered housing; (e) individuals

WHO CAN BENEFIT Registered charities benefiting: young adults; actors and entertainment professionals; musicians; and disabled people

WHERE FUNDING CAN BE GIVEN UK

TYPE OF GRANT Usually single donations in the order of £1,000

RANGE OF GRANTS £500–£1,000

FINANCES *Year* 1995 *Income* £179,000 *Grants* £174,000

TRUSTEES The Worshipful Company of Skinners

PUBLICATIONS Leaflet available

NOTES (a) Applications must include copy of latest accounts. (b) Applications are not acknowledged. (c) Successful applicants will be notified normally in January or July of each year. (d) Successful applicants should not apply again for at least 12 months

HOW TO APPLY In writing to the address under Who To Apply To at any time

WHO TO APPLY TO The Charities Officer, Skinners' Company Lady Neville Charity, Skinners' Company, Skinners' Hall, 8 Dogate Hill, London EC4R 2SP *Tel* 0171-236 5629

CC NO 277174   **ESTABLISHED** 1978

■ The John Slater Foundation

WHAT IS FUNDED The relief of suffering

WHAT IS NOT FUNDED No grants to individuals

WHO CAN BENEFIT Registered charities. There is no restriction on the disease or medical condition suffered by the beneficiaries

WHERE FUNDING CAN BE GIVEN West Lancashire

SAMPLE GRANTS £10,000 to Trinity Hospice, Blackpool; £10,000 to Blackpool Ladies' Sick and Poor; £9,000 to St Gemma's Hospice, Leeds; £8,500 to Supt Geral Richardson Memorial Fund; £6,000 to Manorlands Home, Oxenhope; £6,000 to Bury Grammar School; £5,000 to Blackpool and Flyde Society for the Blind; £5,000 to Mission to Deep Sea Fishermen; £5,000 to Church Road Methodist Day Care Unit; £4,500 to Fleetwood and Wyre Mentally Handicapped

FINANCES *Year* 1995 *Income* £500,334 *Grants* £316,422

TRUSTEES Midland Bank Trust Company Limited

HOW TO APPLY Half-yearly – 1 May and 1 November by letter to the address under Who To Apply To

WHO TO APPLY TO The Secretary to the Trustees, The John Slater Foundation, Midland Private Banking, 4 Dale Street, Liverpool L69 2BZ

CC NO 231145   **ESTABLISHED** 1963

■ The Slater Trust Limited

WHAT IS FUNDED Only local applications considered for new grants. Charities working in the fields of: community arts and recreation; community facilities; clubs; charity or voluntary and religious umbrella bodies

WHAT IS NOT FUNDED No new grants to individuals. No new grants at present

WHO CAN BENEFIT Local organisations benefiting people of all ages

WHERE FUNDING CAN BE GIVEN West Cumbria

TYPE OF GRANT Recurrent

RANGE OF GRANTS £15–£550

SAMPLE GRANTS £550 to Boat Trade Benevolent Society; £300 to Cumbria Association of Clubs for Young People for running costs; £250 to The Methodist Church, Cockermouth; £250 to Life Education Centre for Cumbria for abuse of drugs awareness and education campaign; £200 to Mines Advisory Group, Cockermouth for land mine clearance

FINANCES *Year* 1997 *Income* £15,975 *Grants* £11,460

TRUSTEES The Council

NOTES Present commitments restrict availability of new grants

HOW TO APPLY Applications by letter, which are not responded to unless a grant is made

WHO TO APPLY TO The Secretary, The Slater Trust Limited, PO Box No 2, Cockermouth, Cumbria CA13 0NP

CC NO 230099   **ESTABLISHED** 1963

■ The Ernest William Slaughter Charitable Trust

WHAT IS FUNDED General charitable purposes, mainly the elderly and chronically sick

WHAT IS NOT FUNDED No funding for explorations or expeditions. Members should be able to obtain their own financial backers

WHO CAN BENEFIT Organisations benefiting the elderly and chronically sick

WHERE FUNDING CAN BE GIVEN UK

RANGE OF GRANTS £500–£5,000

SAMPLE GRANTS £5,000 to Little Sisters of the Poor; £5,000 to Foetal Medicine Foundation; £4,000 to Vision Aid; £4,000 to Medical Foundation Victims of Torture; £4,000 to Tommies Campaign; £4,000 to Medicines sans Frontiere; £4,000 to Medilink; £3,000 to Motivation; £2,000 to The Passage; £2,000 to Environmental Investigation Agency

FINANCES *Year* 1997 *Income* £58,510 *Grants* £39,000

TRUSTEES A F Moulton, Mrs F S J Slaughter, Mrs J Harris

WHO TO APPLY TO Mrs Jenny Harris, Trustee, The Ernest William Slaughter Charitable Trust, c/o Ozannes, PO Box 186, 1 Le Marchant Street, St Peter Port, Guernsey GY1 4HP

CC NO 256684   **ESTABLISHED** 1968

■ Slimmers Making It a Little Easier For Someone (SMILES)

WHAT IS FUNDED Charities concerned with women and health

WHAT IS NOT FUNDED No grants to individuals

WHO CAN BENEFIT Charities benefiting women. There is no restriction on the age of, or disease or medical condition suffered by, the beneficiaries

WHERE FUNDING CAN BE GIVEN UK

TRUSTEES Miles-Bramwell Executive Services Ltd, D Rathbone, Ms M G Whittaker, R A Whittaker

HOW TO APPLY To the address below in writing

WHO TO APPLY TO D Rathbone, Chartered Accountant, Slimmers Making It a Little Easier For Someone, Clover Nook Industrial Estate, Clover Nook road, Somercoates, Alfreton, Derbyshire DE55 4RF

CC NO 1061429   **ESTABLISHED** 1997

■ The Sloane Street Trust

WHAT IS FUNDED General charitable purposes

WHO CAN BENEFIT There are no restrictions on the age; professional and economic group; family

situation; religion and culture; and social circumstances of; or disease or medical condition suffered by, the beneficiaries

WHERE FUNDING CAN BE GIVEN UK

RANGE OF GRANTS £25–£600

SAMPLE GRANTS £600 to Royal Opera House; £520 to Royal Academy Trust; £500 to British Friends of the Art Museum of Israel; £500 to Institute for Jewish Policy Research; £500 to Joint Jewish Charitable Trust

FINANCES *Year* 1997 *Income* £24,552
Grants £8,888

TRUSTEES K P Green, B H Sandelson, Mrs R Sandelson

HOW TO APPLY To the address under Who To Apply To. Trustees meet January and June

WHO TO APPLY TO B H Sandelson, The Sloane Street Trust, 23 Denbigh House, Hans Place, London SW1X 0EX

CC NO 245176   ESTABLISHED 1965

■ Rita and David Slowe Charitable Trust

WHAT IS FUNDED General charitable purposes

WHO CAN BENEFIT There are no restrictions on the age; professional and economic group; family situation; religion and culture; and social circumstances of; or disease or medical condition suffered by, the beneficiaries

WHERE FUNDING CAN BE GIVEN UK and overseas

FINANCES *Year* 1998 *Income* £34,825
Grants £14,000

TRUSTEES R L Slowe, Ms E H Slowe, J L Slowe, G Weinberg

WHO TO APPLY TO R L Slowe, Rita and David Slowe Charitable Trust, 338 Euston Road, London NW1 3AB

CC NO 1048209   ESTABLISHED 1995

■ The Smallpeice Trust

WHAT IS FUNDED Currently to provide courses on Design for Production, Design for Technology and CAD/CAM Appreciation. Also to promote the challenge of design and problem solving in schools, and engineering as a career

WHAT IS NOT FUNDED Educational grants are not made to individuals or for building projects

WHO CAN BENEFIT Children, young adults, students and industry

WHERE FUNDING CAN BE GIVEN UK

TYPE OF GRANT For promotion of design education across a spectrum of education and industry

FINANCES *Year* 1997 *Income* £1,200,000
Grants £22,000

TRUSTEES Dr A E Moulton, CBE,RDI,FEng, Dr J B Kurtz, MPCP, MRCPath, D C M Prichard, MA, FCP, FBIM, FRSA, Dr W Rizk, CBE, FEng, V J Osola, CBE, FEng, FIMechE, Prof M J French, MA, MSc, CEng, FIMechE, J R Appleton, BSc(Eng), CEng, FIMechE

PUBLICATIONS *Smallpeice News*

NOTES The Trust operates its own training centre in Leamington Spa

HOW TO APPLY On ad hoc basis

WHO TO APPLY TO The Company Secretary, The Smallpeice Trust, Smallpeice House, 27 Newbold Terrace East, Leamington Spa, Warwickshire CV32 4ES

CC NO 313719   ESTABLISHED 1966

■ Mrs Smiley's Second Charity Trust

WHAT IS FUNDED General charitable purposes

WHO CAN BENEFIT Registered charities only. There are no restrictions on the age; professional and economic group; family situation; religion and culture; and social circumstances of; or disease or medical condition suffered by, the beneficiaries

WHERE FUNDING CAN BE GIVEN UK

TYPE OF GRANT Registered charities only. Income deficits, special objectives or capital schemes

FINANCES *Year* 1996 *Income* £13,289

TRUSTEES The Cowdray Trust Limited

PUBLICATIONS Annual Report and Accounts to 30 September

NOTES Applications for grants will only be acknowledged if a donation is to be sent

HOW TO APPLY Appeal letters should be sent to the address under Who To Apply To

WHO TO APPLY TO The Secretary, Mrs Smiley's Second Charity Trust, The Cowdray Trust Limited, Pollen House, 10–12 Cork Street, London W1X 1PD

CC NO 265129   ESTABLISHED 1972

■ The Mrs Smith & Mount Trust

WHAT IS FUNDED The Trust aims by way of a one-off grant to support: (a) The successful continuity of family life by offering appropriate funding to the central carer. The concept of the family is wider than the single household, and, may include other dependants for whom the carer takes responsibility. Note: The Trustees will consider applications in respect of lone parents, or couples, who have more than one child or other dependent kin who have a disability or long term illness, who are in receipt of Invalidity Benefit or have been on long term benefit. (b) Those who have formerly been in care who are entering independent life in the community. (c) Individuals who have needed short term residential care upon their return to the community

WHO CAN BENEFIT Individuals and organisations benefiting families, children, carers and those who have been in care

WHERE FUNDING CAN BE GIVEN UK

TYPE OF GRANT Single payments

SAMPLE GRANTS £81,993 to 582 individuals on low income; £10,000 to Institute of Family Therapy; £8,000 to National Foster Care Association; £7,000 to St Mungos; £6,000 to Compass Trust; £5,000 to CARIS; £5,000 to Mencap for Blue Sky Appeal; £5,000 to the Who Cares Trust; £5,000 to St Mary's Family Centre; £5,000 to Pecan; £5,000 to Watford New Hope Trust

FINANCES *Year* 1997 *Income* £280,194
Grants £266,333

TRUSTEES J C Barratt, R S Fowler, D J L Mobsby, Mrs G M Gorell Barnes

HOW TO APPLY Fortnightly. The Trust provides a Guide to Applicants and application form. Their use is recommended before making an application to the Trust. The Guide will be forwarded upon written request. NB: Only qualified social workers should apply to the Trust as sponsor for an individual, family etc

WHO TO APPLY TO The Trust Administrator, The Mrs Smith & Mount Trust, Box MST, White Horse Court, 25c North Street, Bishop's Stortford, Hertfordshire CM23 2LD

CC NO 1009718   ESTABLISHED 1992

■ The N Smith Charitable Settlement

WHAT IS FUNDED General charitable purposes. All appellants must be of registered charitable status

WHAT IS NOT FUNDED No applications from individuals will be considered

WHO CAN BENEFIT There are no restrictions on the age; professional and economic group; family situation; religion and culture; and social circumstances of; or disease or medical condition suffered by, the beneficiaries

WHERE FUNDING CAN BE GIVEN UK

TYPE OF GRANT Appeals for capital equipment preferred over salary costs

RANGE OF GRANTS £100–£1,000

SAMPLE GRANTS £1,000 to the Rossendale Trust; £1,000 to The Royal Exchange Theatre Company; £1,000 to Action Research; £1,000 to Brainwave (formerly the Kerland Foundation); £1,000 to British Heart Foundation; £1,000 to British Society for Clinical Cytology; £1,000 to Cancer Studies Unit; £1,000 to Cystic Fibrosis Trust; £1,000 to the Foundation for Integrated Medicine; £1,000 to Great Ormond Street Children's Hospital

FINANCES *Year* 1997 *Income* £115,720

TRUSTEES J S Cochrane, T R Kendal, P R Green, J H Williams-Rigby

WHO TO APPLY TO The N Smith Charitable Settlement, Bullock, Worthington & Jackson, 1 Booth Street, Manchester M2 2HA

CC NO 276660   **ESTABLISHED** 1978

■ The Smith Charitable Trust

WHAT IS FUNDED General charitable purposes. To favour National charities

WHAT IS NOT FUNDED No grants to individuals

WHO CAN BENEFIT Registered charities. There are no restrictions on the age; professional and economic group; family situation; religion and culture; and social circumstances of; or disease or medical condition suffered by, the beneficiaries

WHERE FUNDING CAN BE GIVEN UK and overseas

RANGE OF GRANTS £2,500–£7,950

SAMPLE GRANTS £7,950 to Sue Ryder Foundation; £2,850 to the Sea Cadets Association; £2,850 to the Salvation Army; £2,850 to National Children's Homes; £2,850 to Royal National Lifeboat Institute; £2,500 to Royal Commonwealth Society for the Blind; £2,500 to Artist Benevolent Fund; £2,500 to Royal National Institute for the Blind; £2,500 to Research Institute for the Care of the Elderly

FINANCES *Year* 1995 *Income* £28,270 *Grants* £29,350

TRUSTEES A G F Fuller, J W H Carey, C R L Coubrough, R I Turner

NOTES **Please note: no further applications are being considered at present, although existing commitments are to be continued**

WHO TO APPLY TO Mrs C M Livingston, The Smith Charitable Trust, Messrs Moon Beever, Solicitors, 24 Bloomsbury Square, London WC1A 2PL

CC NO 288570   **ESTABLISHED** 1983

■ Amanda Smith Charitable Trust

WHAT IS FUNDED General charitable purposes

WHO CAN BENEFIT Registered charities. There are no restrictions on the age; professional and economic group; family situation; religion and culture; and social circumstances of; or disease or medical condition suffered by, the beneficiaries

WHERE FUNDING CAN BE GIVEN UK

SAMPLE GRANTS £25,000 to the Friends of the Children of Great Ormond Street

FINANCES *Year* 1996 *Income* £693,631 *Grants* £25,000

TRUSTEES P Bennett, Ms A Smith, C Smith

WHO TO APPLY TO M Winter, Secretary, Amanda Smith Charitable Trust, 1 Knightsbridge, London SW1X 7LX

CC NO 1052975   **ESTABLISHED** 1996

■ The E H Smith Charitable Trust

WHAT IS FUNDED Children/youth; medical; welfare; arts; disability and environment/conservation

WHO CAN BENEFIT National organisations and local causes benefiting: children and young adults; at risk groups; disable people; those disadvantaged by poverty and socially isolated people. Actors and entertainment professionals; musicians; textile workers and designers; writers and poets may be considered. There is no restriction on the disease or medical condition suffered by the beneficiaries

WHERE FUNDING CAN BE GIVEN UK, with some preference for the Midlands

TYPE OF GRANT Most grants are small, in the region of £100; some large and a few recurrent grants are given

RANGE OF GRANTS £25–£5,000

SAMPLE GRANTS £5,000 to Sunderland Ecclesia; £464 to Great Ormond Street Hospital; £400 to Watford Christadelphians (Keiv); £347 to Millgate Centre; £311 to Vision Homes Association; £229 to Radar; £182 to BPSO Concert, Enterprise; £150 to the Royal British Legion; £150 to the Roy Castle Cause for Hope Foundation; £150 to Sports Aid Foundation

FINANCES *Year* 1997 *Income* £49,038 *Grants* £13,297

TRUSTEES K H A Smith, Mrs B M Hodgskin-Brown, D P Ensell

HOW TO APPLY To the address under Who To Apply To in writing

WHO TO APPLY TO K H A Smith, The E H Smith Charitable Trust, 1 Sherbourne Road, Acocks Green, Birmingham B27 6AB *Tel* 0121-706 6100

CC NO 328313   **ESTABLISHED** 1989

■ Dorothy Pamela Smith Charity

WHAT IS FUNDED Charitable institutions or purposes concerned with the relief of mental disorder or impairment, including research into their antenatal causes and the cure; and treatment and care of the young suffering from disorders and impairments

WHAT IS NOT FUNDED Grants are not made for administrative expenses

WHO CAN BENEFIT Local organisations and small organisations benefiting those suffering from mental illnesses or disorders, including Alzheimer's disease, autism, epilepsy, Parkinson's disease and strokes. Support is also given to the disabled, children, young adults, medical professionals, research workers and scientists

WHERE FUNDING CAN BE GIVEN UK

TRUSTEES Ms J M Ford, P M Harris, A H B Jones, Ms D P Smith

HOW TO APPLY To the address under Who To Apply To in writing, including details of how much you require and for what purpose, with a short description of what difference a grant would make

Does the trust you have chosen match your needs? Haphazard applications waste postage and time

593

to your work. Include as much as necessary to meet the criteria under What is Funded

WHO TO APPLY TO Nick Stone, Administrator, Dorothy Pamela Smith Charity, 81 Chancery Lane, London WC2A 1DD

CC NO 1061756   **ESTABLISHED** 1995

■ The Leslie Smith Foundation

WHAT IS FUNDED Preference to charities in which the Trust has special interest, knowledge or association but with emphasis on research and the treatment of addiction; arthritis/rheumatism and asthma. Child care treatment and the care of the aged and bereaved is also a special interest as are child and youth charities, including schools. Marriage guidance charities are also favoured. Historic buildings; nature reserves; playgrounds; theatre and opera houses; film, video and multi media broadcasting; hospices, rehabilitation centres and counselling are all considered for funding

WHAT IS NOT FUNDED Registered charities. Applications from individuals are not normally eligible

WHO CAN BENEFIT Small, local charities benefiting: unemployed people; volunteers; writers and poets; clergy; at risk groups; carers; disabled people; and those living in rural areas. Those suffering from arthritis and rheumatism, asthma and addiction. There is nor restriction on the age or the family situation of the beneficiaries

WHERE FUNDING CAN BE GIVEN UK

TYPE OF GRANT Buildings, capital, one-off, research and recurring costs. Funding is available for up to one year

RANGE OF GRANTS £1,000–£100,000, typical grant £3,000–£5,000

SAMPLE GRANTS £35,000 to Music for Living; £30,000 to Paul Strickland Scanner Appeal; £10,000 to CHA Scotland; £10,000 to Wessex Children's Hospice Trust; £10,000 to College of St Barnabas; £10,000 to Joseph Weld Hospice; £5,000 to Norwich Theatre; £4,000 to Suffolk Wildlife Trust; £3,000 to Relate

FINANCES *Year* 1998 *Income* £221,000 *Grants* £130,000

TRUSTEES M D Willcox, Mrs E A Furtek

HOW TO APPLY At any time. Only successful appeals will be acknowledged

WHO TO APPLY TO M D Willcox, The Leslie Smith Foundation, The Old Coach House, Bergh Apton, Norwich, Norfolk NR15 1DD

CC NO 250030   **ESTABLISHED** 1964

■ The Martin Smith Foundation

WHAT IS FUNDED General charitable purposes which may include education, sport, the arts, ecology or the environment, in particular music schools and colleges

WHO CAN BENEFIT Individuals and organisations benefiting: people of all ages; actors and entertainment professionals; musicians; sportsmen and women; and beneficiaries suffering from Alzheimer's disease

WHERE FUNDING CAN BE GIVEN UK

TYPE OF GRANT Buildings, capital, core costs, one-off, project, recurring costs, salaries and start-up costs will be considered. Funding may be given for up to three years

RANGE OF GRANTS Typically £2,500

TRUSTEES E Buchanan, M MacFadyen, E B Smith, J Smith, K Smith, M G Smith

HOW TO APPLY Write to the Administrator with brief description of purpose of application and a form will be sent. Trustees meet once a quarter

WHO TO APPLY TO Mrs G Goodrich, The Martin Smith Foundation, PO Box 22507, London W8 7ZF

CC NO 1066587   **ESTABLISHED** 1997

■ The Stanley Smith General Charitable Trust

WHAT IS FUNDED General charitable purposes

WHO CAN BENEFIT There are no restrictions on the age; professional and economic group; family situation; religion and culture; and social circumstances of; or disease or medical condition suffered by, the beneficiaries

WHERE FUNDING CAN BE GIVEN UK

SAMPLE GRANTS £12,000 to British Red Cross; £10,000 to NSPCC; £5,000 to Pestalozzi Children's Village; £2,500 to NICHS; £2,500 to Rainer Foundation; £2,500 to the Samaritans; £2,500 to the Uphill Ski Club; £2,500 to Victims Support London; £500 to Carr-Gomm Society; £500 to Sense

FINANCES *Year* 1997 *Income* £76,972 *Grants* £42,000

TRUSTEES J L Norton, J J Dilger, A de Brye

WHO TO APPLY TO J Norton, Trustees Accountant, The Stanley Smith General Charitable Trust, Mercer and Hole Trustees Ltd, Gloucester House, 72 London Road, St Albans, Herfordshire AL1 1NS

CC NO 326226   **ESTABLISHED** 1982

■ W H Smith Group Charitable Trust

WHAT IS FUNDED Two-thirds of net annual income is allocated to a 'charity of the year' nominated by W H Smith staff. The remaining one-third is used to support members of staff directly involved in their local community

WHAT IS NOT FUNDED Unsolicited requests are not considered

WHO CAN BENEFIT Local charities in which members of W H Smith staff are directly involved. There are no restrictions on the age; professional and economic group; family situation; religion and culture; and social circumstances of; or disease or medical condition suffered by, the beneficiaries

WHERE FUNDING CAN BE GIVEN UK

FINANCES *Year* 1997 *Income* £160,620 *Grants* £141,207

TRUSTEES P T Blythe, A Forrester, J Hardie, L Harlow, R Howe, M Idle, C Orr

HOW TO APPLY This Trust states that it does not respond to unsolicited applications

WHO TO APPLY TO Andy Finch, W H Smith Group Charitable Trust, W H Smith Group plc, Nations House, 103 Wigmore Street, London E1H 0WH

CC NO 1013782   **ESTABLISHED** 1992

■ The Smith (Haltwhistle and District) Charitable Trust

WHAT IS FUNDED General charitable purposes. Primary purpose to support local charities

WHAT IS NOT FUNDED No grants to individuals

WHO CAN BENEFIT Local organisations and charities together with national charities primarily with local interest. No grants to individuals unless directed through a specific charity

WHERE FUNDING CAN BE GIVEN Primarily Northumberland, the Parish of Haltwhistle

TYPE OF GRANT Recurrent and capital expenditure

SAMPLE GRANTS £2,860 to Beltingham with Henshaw PCC; £990 to Samaritans of Tyneside; £840 to Society of St Francis, Alnmouth; £750 to SSAFA; £750 to St Oswald's Hospice; £680 to Holy Cross PCC; £670 to the Salvation Army; £600 to Women's Royal Voluntary Service for Haltwhistle Over 60's; £600 to Friends of Queens Hall, Hexham; £570 to Royal National Lifeboat Institute

FINANCES *Year* 1997 *Income* £47,351 *Grants* £34,110

TRUSTEES Mrs I M Smith, Dr F G Pattrick, Dr R A D Pattrick, J M Clark, N C N Clayburn, Rev K Fletcher, D G Pattrick, Rev Vincent Ashwin

HOW TO APPLY Allocations to be made annually in July

WHO TO APPLY TO J Y Luke, The Smith Charitable Trust, Messrs Wilkinson Maughan, Sun Alliance House, 35 Mosley Street, Newcastle upon Tyne NE1 1XX

CC NO 200520   **ESTABLISHED** 1961

■ The Albert & Florence Smith Memorial Trust

WHAT IS FUNDED Churches, limited national, overseas

WHAT IS NOT FUNDED No grants to individuals

WHO CAN BENEFIT New grants limited to Essex based projects. There are no restrictions on the age; professional and economic group; family situation; religion and culture; and social circumstances of; or disease or medical condition suffered by, the beneficiaries

WHERE FUNDING CAN BE GIVEN UK, overseas, Essex

TYPE OF GRANT One-off and limited recurrent

SAMPLE GRANTS £20,000 to St Mary's Church; £15,000 to Rayleigh International; £12,000 to Royal Hospital of St Bartholomew; £11,750 to Uttlesford Council Voluntary Service; £10,000 to Langham Support Trust; £10,000 to Mencap; £10,000 to EVAB; £5,000 to SCOPE; £5,000 to Royal British Legion; £5,000 to Barnardos

FINANCES *Year* 1997 *Income* £307,380 *Grants* £168,416

TRUSTEES W J Tolhurst, P J Tolhurst

HOW TO APPLY June and December. No application form used

WHO TO APPLY TO P J Tolhurst, Messrs Tolhurst & Fisher, Greenwood House, New London Road, Chelmsford, Essex CM2 0PP

CC NO 259917   **ESTABLISHED** 1969

■ The Griffith Smith Trust Fund

This trust did not respond to CAF's request to amend its entry and, by 30 June 1998, CAF's researchers did not find financial records for later than 1995 on its file at the Charity Commission. Trusts are legally required to submit annual accounts to the Charity Commission under section 42 of the Charities Act 1993

WHAT IS FUNDED General charitable purposes

WHAT IS NOT FUNDED No grants to individuals or students

WHO CAN BENEFIT Small local projects. There are no restrictions on the age; professional and economic group; family situation; religion and culture; and social circumstances of; or disease or medical condition suffered by, the beneficiaries

WHERE FUNDING CAN BE GIVEN East Sussex

TYPE OF GRANT One-off small grants of £1,000 or less

TRUSTEES I W Dodd, R A Stewart, D J Williams, R J C Fry, R Hinton, L A Padgett, P Goldsmith

NOTES **Unsolicited applications are not often considered**

WHO TO APPLY TO I W Dodd, The Griffith Smith Trust Fund, 47 Old Steyne, Brighton, East Sussex BN1 1NW

CC NO 1018774   **ESTABLISHED** 1993

■ Metcalfe Smith Trust

WHAT IS FUNDED Convalescent holidays for individuals or groups, capital costs, running costs, to alleviate hardship connected with ill-health, assistance with purchase of equipment for people with disabilities

WHAT IS NOT FUNDED No grants for research costs, general appeals or to finance fundraising initiatives

WHO CAN BENEFIT Some individuals and organisations benefiting disabled people and those disadvantaged by poverty. There is no restriction on the disease or medical condition suffered by the beneficiaries

WHERE FUNDING CAN BE GIVEN Leeds, Harrogate, other parts of West Yorkshire

TYPE OF GRANT Capital and running costs will be considered

RANGE OF GRANTS £250–£2,000

SAMPLE GRANTS £2,500 to Harrogate Citizens Guild of Help; £2,195 to Shopmobility, Harrogate for a 25th Anniversary presentation; £1,500 to Saint Michael's Hospice, Harrogate; £1,500 to Voluntary Action Leeds for an emergency fund; £1,200 to Leeds MIND; £1,000 to Alzheimer's Disease Society, Leeds; £1,000 to Friends of PHAB, Leeds; £1,000 to Leeds General Infirmary Children's Centre Appeal; £1,000 to Model Farm Project, Meanwood; £600 to Live Music Now – Yorkshire

FINANCES *Year* 1997 *Income* £28,094 *Grants* £25,547

TRUSTEES Mrs J Boyle, Dr A Clark, M J Dodgson, K Goddard, A Goldthorpe, OBE, Ms D Green, Rev J Hamilton, Mrs M Hirst, Mrs A Mackenzie, Ms A Morris, D Naylor, Ms J Pickard, Mrs J M Wainwright, J D Wilks

HOW TO APPLY To the address under Who To Apply To in writing, enclosing recent accounts. The Trustees meet to consider applications in March and October

WHO TO APPLY TO The Secretary, Metcalfe Smith Trust, c/o Voluntary Action Leeds, 34 Lupton Street, Leeds LS10 2QW

CC NO 228891   **ESTABLISHED** 1868

■ Stanley Smith (UK) Horticultural Trust

WHAT IS FUNDED Grants are made to individual projects which involve the advancement of amenity horticulture and horticultural education. In the past assistance has been given to the creation, preservation and development of gardens to which the public is admitted, to the cultivation and wider distribution of plants derived by breeding or by collection from the wild, to research and to the publication of books with a direct bearing on horticulture

WHAT IS NOT FUNDED Grants are not made to individual students for fees, subsistence, etc relating to any academic or diploma course

WHO CAN BENEFIT Grants are made to individuals or to institutions benefiting students of botany and horticulture, as appropriate

WHERE FUNDING CAN BE GIVEN UK and overseas

TYPE OF GRANT Buildings, capital, core costs, feasibility studies, interest free loans, one-off, research and start-up costs. Grants are normally made as a contribution to cover the costs of identified projects. In exceptional cases grants are made over a three-year period

RANGE OF GRANTS £500–£2,000–£10,000

SAMPLE GRANTS £7,500 to University of Bristol; £7,500 to University of Cambridge; £7,500 to University of Reading; £5,000 to BGCI; £4,941 to University of Bangalore; £4,500 to Chelsea Physic Garden; £4,000 to Castle Bromwich Hall Garden Trust; £3,000 to NCCPG; £2,000 to National Pelargonium Collection; £2,000 to an individual

FINANCES *Year* 1997 *Income* £142,439 *Grants* £63,280

TRUSTEES C D Brickell, J J Dilger, J L Norton, Lady J Renfrew, J B E Simmons

HOW TO APPLY To the Director (address below). Applications are considered twice a year: spring (closing date for the receipt of applications 15 February) and autumn (closing date 15 August). Copies of annual accounts are generally required. Guidelines for applicants are available from the Director

WHO TO APPLY TO James Cullen, DSc, Director, Stanley Smith (UK) Horticultural Trust, Cory Lodge, PO Box 365, Cambridge CB2 1HR *Tel* 01223 336299 *Fax* 01223 336278

CC NO 261925   **ESTABLISHED** 1970

■ Philip Smiths Charitable Trust

WHAT IS FUNDED Conservation and heritage, costs of study, and community facilities and services are considered for funding

WHO CAN BENEFIT National and local charities benefiting: people of all ages; those disadvantaged by poverty; ex-offenders and those at risk of offending; and homeless people

WHERE FUNDING CAN BE GIVEN UK, with preference for Gloucestershire

RANGE OF GRANTS From £1,000

SAMPLE GRANTS The following grants were made in 1998:; £5,000 to Shakespeare Hospice Appeal; £5,000 to NSPCC; £4,040 to Hanford Schoolfor general purposes; £2,019 to Hanford School for general purposes; £2,000 to WHS for shaping the future; £2,000 to Highland Hospice; £2,000 to Gloucester Association for Mental Health; £2,000 to Home Farm Trust; £1,919 to Hanford School for school fees; £1,000 to Gloucestershire Society

FINANCES *Year* 1997 *Income* £323,075 *Grants* £34,836

TRUSTEES Hon P R Smith, Mrs M Smith

WHO TO APPLY TO M Wood, Philip Smiths Charitable Trust, 1 Dean Farrar Street, Westminster, London SW1H 0DY *Tel* 0171-222 8044

CC NO 1003751   **ESTABLISHED** 1991

■ Thomas Herbert Smith's Trust Fund

WHAT IS FUNDED Welfare

WHO CAN BENEFIT Individuals and organisations benefiting people of all ages

WHERE FUNDING CAN BE GIVEN The Parish of Groby in Leicestershire

TYPE OF GRANT One-off grants

RANGE OF GRANTS £50–£10,000, typical grant £250

SAMPLE GRANTS £4,500 to 73rd Leicester (Groby) Scouts; £4,050 in grants to individuals

FINANCES *Year* 1997 *Income* £20,662 *Grants* £12,550

TRUSTEES Mrs F A J Gill, Mrs P Hall, P Griffin, R G Shooter, C D Waterfield

HOW TO APPLY To the address under Who To Apply To in writing

WHO TO APPLY TO D H Cooper, Clerk, Thomas Herbert Smith's Trust Fund, The Administrator's Office, Wyggeston Hospital, Hinckley Road, Leicester, Leicestershire LE3 0UX *Tel* 0116-255 9174

CC NO 701694   **ESTABLISHED** 1989

■ Snipe Charitable Trust

WHAT IS FUNDED Education, arts, culture and recreation. Have established an endowment fund for students of the drama college LAMDA

WHO CAN BENEFIT Theatre production try-outs, and organisations benefiting: drama students, actors and entertainment professionals, musicians, textile workers and designers, writers and poets

WHERE FUNDING CAN BE GIVEN England

TYPE OF GRANT Recurrent

RANGE OF GRANTS £250–£5,000

SAMPLE GRANTS £5,000 to The Poetry Society; £3,000 to LAMDA; £1,000 to an individual; £500 to an individual; £250 to an individual

FINANCES *Year* 1997 *Income* £22,353 *Grants* £9,750

TRUSTEES Timothy Lancaster West, James Sharkey, Richard James Midgley

HOW TO APPLY In writing at any time

WHO TO APPLY TO Midgley Snelling, Snipe Charitable Trust, 6th Floor South, Brettenham House, Lancaster Place, London WC2E 7EW

CC NO 1000810   **ESTABLISHED** 1990

■ The Snowball Trust

WHAT IS FUNDED The provision of ambulances and mobile units for sick and disabled children

WHAT IS NOT FUNDED Beneficiary must live in Coventry or Warwickshire and must be 18 years of age or younger

WHO CAN BENEFIT Either an individual or an institution for the benefit of: children up to 18 years of age who are disabled. There are few restrictions on the disease or medical condition suffered by the beneficiaries

WHERE FUNDING CAN BE GIVEN Coventry and Warwickshire

TYPE OF GRANT Capital and one-off

FINANCES *Year* 1997 *Income* £115,154 *Grants* £47,430

TRUSTEES Celia Grew (Chairman), D Mason, A Rhodes, I Rufus, M Tracey

HOW TO APPLY Application form from the Clerk at the address under Who To Apply To

WHO TO APPLY TO Mrs Pauline Blackham, Clerk to the Trustees, The Snowball Trust, 11 Rotherham Road, Holbrooks, Coventry CV6 4FF

CC NO 702860   **ESTABLISHED** 1989

■ The Society of Friends of the Torah (37)

This trust declined to meet CAF's researchers and failed to supply a copy of its annual report and accounts to CAF as required under section 47(2) of the Charities Act 1993. The information held on file at the Charity Commission was insufficient to enable CAF's researchers to write a substantive commentary on the trust's activities. Accordingly, despite its size, we are unable to list this trust in Spotlight on Major Trusts

WHAT IS FUNDED General charitable purposes especially relief of poverty and advancement of education amongst persons of the Jewish faith

WHO CAN BENEFIT Charities benefiting Jewish people, children, young adults, students, and those disadvantaged by poverty

WHERE FUNDING CAN BE GIVEN UK and overseas

FINANCES *Year* 1994 *Income* £3,610,698 *Grants* £3,420,843

HOW TO APPLY In writing to the address below

WHO TO APPLY TO The Secretary, The Society of Friends of the Torah, 97 Stamford Hill, London N16 5DN

CC NO 238230   **ESTABLISHED** 1960

■ The Society of Motor Manufacturers and Traders Charitable Trust Fund

This trust did not respond to CAF's request to amend its entry and, by 30 June 1998, CAF's researchers did not find financial records for later than 1995 on its file at the Charity Commission. Trusts are legally required to submit annual accounts to the Charity Commission under section 42 of the Charities Act 1993

WHAT IS FUNDED The relief of poor people who are former senior executive employees in the motor industry and their dependants. The support of othercharities with similar objectives. To give sympathetic consideration and all possible assistance to qualifying applicants

WHAT IS NOT FUNDED Other charities or persons having no motor industry relationship

WHO CAN BENEFIT Former motor industry senior executives or their dependants both individually and through registered charities

WHERE FUNDING CAN BE GIVEN UK

TYPE OF GRANT Weekly cash grant or occasional gift

TRUSTEES The Management Trustees

HOW TO APPLY By invitation following introduction from motor industry source

WHO TO APPLY TO The Secretary, The Society of Motor Manufacturers & Traders Charitable Trust Fund, Forbes House, Halkin Street, London SW1X 7DS

CC NO 209852   **ESTABLISHED** 1932

■ Sodality of St Peter Claver

WHAT IS FUNDED The promotion of religion and education and relief of poverty and sickness in accordance with the doctrines of the Roman Catholic Church and other charitable purposes being carried on, directed or supported by the Sodality of St Peter Claver

WHO CAN BENEFIT Organisations benfiting children and young adults, Roman Catholics and those disadvantaged by poverty. There is no restriction on the disease or medical condition suffered by the beneficiaries

WHERE FUNDING CAN BE GIVEN UK and overseas

SAMPLE GRANTS £16,894 for missionaries in Musoma, Tanzania; £14,059 for missionaries in Nairobi, Africa; £13,256 for missionaries in Embu, Kenya; £11,020 for missionaries in Meru, Africa; £9,000 for missionaries in Ngong, Karen, Kenya; £8,411 for missionaries in Kakamega, Kenya; £7,117 for missionaries in Kisii, Kenya; £6,677 for missionaries in Moshi, Tanzania; £6,600 for missionaries in Embu, Kenya; £6,470 for missionaries in Masen, South Africa

FINANCES *Year* 1997 *Income* £245,421 *Grants* £218,023

TRUSTEES Ms M Gancarczk, Ms M Giertych, Ms P James, Ms E Kenny, Ms A Tully

WHO TO APPLY TO D J Clark, Sodality of St Peter Claver, MacIntyre and Co, 28 Ely Place, London EC1N 6RL

CC NO 1048906   **ESTABLISHED** 1995

■ The Frederick Soddy Trust

WHAT IS FUNDED To assist expeditions carrying out the study of the whole life of an area, with major emphasis on the human community. General educational purposes

WHAT IS NOT FUNDED Grants made to groups only. No grants to individuals working alone, or to individuals to join group expeditions. Must be major emphasis on the human community of the area stated – no grants for studies of the physical environment alone

WHO CAN BENEFIT Priority is given to teachers, students and young people generally to enable them to carry out group studies that come within the terms of the Trust

WHERE FUNDING CAN BE GIVEN UK

TYPE OF GRANT One-off. In addition, the Trustees normally provide one Frederick Soddy Fellowship or Studentship at Sussex University

RANGE OF GRANTS £150–£400

SAMPLE GRANTS £400 to Girton College, Cambridge for Project Kamchatka 98; £300 to UCL Costa Rica Expedition to study traditions and change in the Tolamanea Highlands; £300 to Tewkesbury School for expedition to Peru; £200 to University of Eastern Africa, Baraton for research into Luhya and Luo communities in Kenya; £200 to Oxford University for Peru Expedition to study Carhuahuran community

FINANCES *Year* 1997 *Income* £16,449 *Grants* £400

TRUSTEES P J Bunker, OBE, MA, LL M, FRGS (Chairman), W R Mead, FBA, DSc (Econ), FilDr, FRGS, D N Hall, OBE, FCIS, FRGS, C M Harrison, BSc, PhD, FRGS, A R Hanbury-Tenison, OBE, FRGS

PUBLICATIONS Eight Reports of the Trust. *A World Made New* by Linda Mericks

HOW TO APPLY By letter to the address under Who To Apply To at any time

WHO TO APPLY TO H M Crudgel, OBE, The Frederick Soddy Trust, 25 Henry Burt Way, Burgess Hill, West Sussex RH15 9UX

CC NO 313379   **ESTABLISHED** 1956

■ Solev Co Limited

WHAT IS FUNDED Principally Jewish causes

WHO CAN BENEFIT Individuals and organisations benefiting Jewish people

WHERE FUNDING CAN BE GIVEN UK

TYPE OF GRANT Recurrent

RANGE OF GRANTS £25–£100,000

SAMPLE GRANTS £100,000 to Dina Perelman Trust Limited; £40,000 to Songdale Limited; £20,100 to Finchley Road Synagogue; £15,000 to Sage; £10,000 to Jewish Education Foundation for the Torah; £9,000 to Torah Terimah Primary School; £8,500 to Beis Yacov Institution

FINANCES *Year* 1997 *Income* £488,524 *Grants* £313,074

TRUSTEES The Governors: M Grosskopf, A E Perelman, R Tager, QC

WHO TO APPLY TO M Grosskopf, Solev Co Limited, 6 Spring Hill, London E5 9BE

CC NO 254623   **ESTABLISHED** 1967

■ The Solo Charitable Settlement

WHAT IS FUNDED Jewish organisations, medical research and disability

WHO CAN BENEFIT Organisations benefiting: Jewish people; disabled people; research workers and medical professionals

WHERE FUNDING CAN BE GIVEN UK and Israel

TYPE OF GRANT Mostly recurrent

RANGE OF GRANTS £80–£25,953

SAMPLE GRANTS £25,953 to Ashken Trust; £2,500 to Joint Israel Appeal; £6,050 to Jewish Care; £5,000 to Foundation for Education; £1,250 to Joint Jewish Charitable Trust; £1,200 to Ravenswood Foundation; £1,000 to Friends of Hebrew University; £1,000 to Spiro Institute; £810 to Celebrities Guild of Great Britain; £500 to Carmel College

FINANCES *Year* 1996 *Income* £115,820
Grants £72,048

TRUSTEES P D Goldstein, Edna Goldstein, R Goldstein, H Goldstein

HOW TO APPLY To the address under Who To Apply To in writing

WHO TO APPLY TO B W Ellison, Accountant, The Solo Charitable Settlement, Deloitte & Touche, Hill House, 1 Little New Street, London EC4A 3TR *Tel* 0171-936 3000

CC NO 326444   **ESTABLISHED** 1983

■ The Solomon Family Charitable Trust

WHAT IS FUNDED General charitable purposes

WHO CAN BENEFIT There are no restrictions on the age; professional and economic group; family situation; religion and culture; and social circumstances of; or disease or medical condition suffered by, the beneficiaries

WHERE FUNDING CAN BE GIVEN UK

FINANCES *Year* 1995 *Income* £171,150
Grants £130,502

TRUSTEES Sir Harry Solomon, Lady Judith Solomon, Raymond Taylor

HOW TO APPLY Applications must come through social workers, health visitors, etc who complete an application form obtainable from the address under Who To Apply To. Beneficiaries may not apply directly

WHO TO APPLY TO Sir Harry Solomon, The Solomon Family Charitable Trust, 3 Coach House Yard, Hampstead High Street, London NW3 1QD

CC NO 326556   **ESTABLISHED** 1984

■ David Solomons Charitable Trust

WHAT IS FUNDED Trustees consider applications for assistance in capital projects from charities concerned with mental handicap. Particularly charities working in the fields of: residential facilities and services; infrastructure development; charity or voluntary umbrella bodies and health

WHAT IS NOT FUNDED No grants to individuals

WHO CAN BENEFIT organisations benefiting: carers; disabled people; and those suffering from Alzheimer's disease, autism, cerebral palsy, epilepsy and mental illness

WHERE FUNDING CAN BE GIVEN UK

TYPE OF GRANT Buildings, capital, feasibility studies, one-off, project, research and start-up costs. Funding for up to or more than three years will be considered

RANGE OF GRANTS £500–£5,000

FINANCES *Year* 1995 *Income* £46,530
Grants £51,350

TRUSTEES Sir Michael Clapham, Mrs B J Taylor, Dr W A Heaton-Ward, J J Rutter, W McBryde, J Chadwick, J L Drewitt

HOW TO APPLY In writing. Trustees meet in May and November

WHO TO APPLY TO N Duffy, Administrator, David Solomons Charitable Trust, 81 Chancery Lane, London WC2A 1DD *Tel* 0171-911 7149

CC NO 297275   **ESTABLISHED** 1986

■ Dr Richard Solomons' Charitable Trust

WHAT IS FUNDED General charitable purposes. All resources fully committed

WHAT IS NOT FUNDED No grants to individual students, scholarships or animal charities

WHO CAN BENEFIT There are no restrictions on the age; professional and economic group; family situation; religion and culture; and social circumstances of; or disease or medical condition suffered by, the beneficiaries

WHERE FUNDING CAN BE GIVEN UK

SAMPLE GRANTS £21,000 to Instituto de Desarollo Popular for rural development

FINANCES *Year* 1997 *Income* £18,718

TRUSTEES Dr R E B Solomons, Mrs D J Huntingford, Mrs S N Solomons, Dr A M Sepping

NOTES Funds are fully committed

HOW TO APPLY None required

WHO TO APPLY TO Dr R E B Solomons, Dr Richard Solomons' Charitable Trust, Fell Edge Farm, Straight Lane, Addingham, Moorside, West Yorkshire LS29 9JY

CC NO 277309   **ESTABLISHED** 1978

■ Somerfield Community Charity

WHAT IS FUNDED Support of small local causes and individuals and sporting and activity groups across the country as nominated by Somerfield customers

WHAT IS NOT FUNDED Selected causes must be nominated via voting cards in each store

WHO CAN BENEFIT Neighbourhood-based community projects or individuals. There are no restrictions on the age; professional and economic group; family situation; religion and culture; and social circumstances of; or disease or medical condition suffered by, the beneficiaries

WHERE FUNDING CAN BE GIVEN UK – all Somerfield fascia stores

TYPE OF GRANT One-off, capital donations raised in-store via scratchcard sales

RANGE OF GRANTS £500 to £4,000

TRUSTEES Somerfield Stores Ltd, S M Grant, Ms S P Jepson, P Thompson

HOW TO APPLY **This Trust states that it does not respond to unsolicited applications.** Charitable organisations will only be selected by Trustees following in-store nomination by customers

WHO TO APPLY TO Ms Jepson, Trustee, Somerfield Community Charity, Somerfield House, Whitchurch Lane, Whitchurch, Bristol BS14 0TJ

CC NO 1060297   **ESTABLISHED** 1996

■ The Dorothy Somerfield Curtis Will Trust

WHAT IS FUNDED Religion and music. The work of the Methodist Church locally, the Jubilee Trust and through the Epworth Choir, the Macmillan Nurses Appeal and the Woking Hospice Appeal

WHAT IS NOT FUNDED No individuals or students

WHO CAN BENEFIT Small local projects benefiting the elderly and infirm; Methodists; musicians; and medical professionals

WHERE FUNDING CAN BE GIVEN UK

TYPE OF GRANT One-off and recurrent

RANGE OF GRANTS £1,000–£9,465

SAMPLE GRANTS £9,465 to Trinity Methodist Church

FINANCES *Year* 1997 *Income* £17,889
Grants £16,916

TRUSTEES H W James, W Deakin, M S Lee

WHO TO APPLY TO H W James, The Dorothy Somerfield Curtis Will Trust, Links House, Golf Club Road, Hook Heath, Woking, Surrey GU22 0LU

CC NO 1044208 **ESTABLISHED** 1994

■ Songdale Limited

WHAT IS FUNDED All which is in accordance with the Orthodox Jewish faith. Jewish general charitable purposes

WHO CAN BENEFIT To benefit Orthodox Jews

WHERE FUNDING CAN BE GIVEN UK

TRUSTEES M Grosskopf, Mrs M Grosskopf, Y Grosskopf

WHO TO APPLY TO M Grosskopf, Governor, Songdale Limited, 6 Spring Hill, London E5 9BE

CC NO 286075 **ESTABLISHED** 1961

■ The E C Sosnow Charitable Trust

WHAT IS FUNDED Education and Jewish causes; medical; emergency overseas aid; disability; the arts; the underprivileged

WHO CAN BENEFIT Large institutions, national and international organisations benefiting: children, young people and students; Jews; musicians; actors and entertainment professionals; Writers and poets; textile workers and designers; and those disadvantaged by poverty. There is no restriction on the disease or medical condition suffered by the beneficiaries

WHERE FUNDING CAN BE GIVEN UK and overseas

TYPE OF GRANT One-off

RANGE OF GRANTS £50–£15,000

SAMPLE GRANTS £15,000 to London School of Economics; £2,500 to JJCT; £2,500 to Redbridge Community Centre; £1,500 to St Mary's Save the Baby Fund; £15,000 to The Chicken Shed; £1,200 to Jewish Care; £1,000 to British Friends of Art Museums; £1,000 to Friends of the Hebrew University; £1,000 to Hadassah Medical Unit; £1,000 to Imperial War Museum

FINANCES *Year* 1996–97 *Income* £71,955
Grants £37,145

TRUSTEES E Birk, E R Fattal, Mrs F J M Fattal

HOW TO APPLY To the address under Who To Apply To in writing

WHO TO APPLY TO E S Birk, The E C Sosnow Charitable Trust, PO Box 13398, London SW3 6ZL

CC NO 273578 **ESTABLISHED** 1977

■ Souldern Trust

WHAT IS FUNDED The advancement of education and general charitable purposes

WHO CAN BENEFIT Small local projects, innovative projects. There are no restrictions on the age; professional and economic group; family situation; religion and culture; and social circumstances of; or disease or medical condition suffered by, the beneficiaries

WHERE FUNDING CAN BE GIVEN Oxfordshire

TYPE OF GRANT A range of grants

FINANCES *Year* 1997 *Income* £24,244
Grants £8,500

TRUSTEES Joseph C Pillman, Dr Rosemary S Sanders

PUBLICATIONS Annual Report

HOW TO APPLY Initially by letter giving brief outline of reasons for donation and amount required. No telephone requests

WHO TO APPLY TO Dr R Sanders, Trustee, Souldern Trust, Souldern Manor, Souldern, Bicester, Oxfordshire OX6 9LF *Tel* 01869 346644

CC NO 1001488 **ESTABLISHED** 1990

■ The Souter Foundation

WHAT IS FUNDED Projects engaged in the relief of human suffering particularly those with a Christian emphasis, including charities working in the fields of: the advancement of Christianity; health care; health campaigning; adoption and fostering services; care in the community; emergency care for refugees and famine; and playschemes

WHAT IS NOT FUNDED No building projects, expeditions or personal educational grants

WHO CAN BENEFIT Various charities and organisations benefiting: people of all ages; those in care, fostered and adopted; Christians; Evangelists; carers; those disadvantaged by poverty; refugees; victims of famine; man-made or natural disasters and war. There is no restriction on the disease or medical condition suffered by the beneficiaries

WHERE FUNDING CAN BE GIVEN UK, with a preference for Scotland; developing countries

TYPE OF GRANT Core costs, projects, running costs and salaries. Funding for one year or less will be considered

RANGE OF GRANTS £200–£500

SAMPLE GRANTS £123,000 to Church of the Nazarene; £113,000 to Strathclyde House Development Trust; £50,000 to Turning Point; £35,000 to Princess Royal Trust for Carers; £30,000 to Bethany Christian Trust; £30,000 to Oasis Trust; £30,000 to Scottish Business Achievement Awards; £30,000 to Storykeepers; £25,000 to Mission Scotland (Release the Power); £25,000 to Save the Children

FINANCES *Year* 1997 *Income* £1,773,000
Grants £761,000

TRUSTEES Brian Souter, Elizabeth Souter, Linda Scott

NOTES Trustees meet quarterly

HOW TO APPLY Applicants should apply in writing, setting out a brief outline of the project for which funding is sought

WHO TO APPLY TO Linda Scott, Secretary, The Souter Foundation, 21 Auld House, Wynd, Perth PH1 1RG *Tel* 01738 634745
Fax 01738 440275

SC NO SCO 10310 **ESTABLISHED** 1991

■ South Africa Housing Education Project

WHAT IS FUNDED The relief of poverty, in particular the provision of good quality housing to the people of South Africa. The promotion of education, in particular teaching practical skills to people and training teachers so that people can be taught, in South Africa

WHO CAN BENEFIT Organisations benefiting children, young adults, those disadvantaged by poverty, homeless people and trainee teachers

WHERE FUNDING CAN BE GIVEN South Africa

TRUSTEES J R Akker, M C Fletcher, J A Graystone, S Hill, K J Scribbins, M D B Simon

WHO TO APPLY TO C Matheson, South Africa Housing Education Project, 32 Ickburgh Road, London E5 8AD

CC NO 1059493   **ESTABLISHED** 1996

■ South East Arts Board *(formerly South East Arts Association)*

WHAT IS FUNDED South East Arts provides financial support, information and practical advice for those involved or interested in the arts in Kent, Surrey, East Sussex, West Sussex and the unitary authorities of Brighton & Hove and Medway. This includes: community facilities; schools and colleges; the printing and publishing of material; community development; support to voluntary and community organisations; and social advocacy

WHAT IS NOT FUNDED Financial support likely to focus upon the professional element of an event/project for non-profit distrubuting organisations only

WHO CAN BENEFIT Arts organisations and individuals. Actors and entertainment professionals; musicians; research workers; textile workers and designers; writers and poets; retired people; disabled people; gays and lesbians; and those living in both rural and urban areas will be considered

WHERE FUNDING CAN BE GIVEN Kent, Surrey, East Sussex and West Sussex and the unitary authorities of Brighton & Hove and Medway

TYPE OF GRANT Revenue grants for annual programmes, one-off projects, schemes for educational work, commissions and residencies. Capital grants, feasibility studies, research and start-up costs are also funded

FINANCES *Year* 1997 *Income* £3,472,668

TRUSTEES The Board comprises of 18 members which include representatives from local authorities, arts organisations, arts practitioners, commerce and industry

PUBLICATIONS Annual Report. Apply directly for full publications list

NOTES South East Arts works strategically in partnership with other funding agencies, local authorities, educational establishments and commercial sponsors to fund initiatives in the region

HOW TO APPLY Telephone main switchboard number for a copy of *Arts Resources* a leaflet explaining the grants available and the deadlines for applying by

WHO TO APPLY TO The Chief Executive, South East Arts Board, Union House, Eridge Road, Tunbridge Wells, Kent TN4 8HF *Tel* 01892 507200 *E-mail* info@seab.co.uk

CC NO 1008053   **ESTABLISHED** 1991

■ South East London Community Foundation

WHAT IS FUNDED Community based projects actively enhancing the quality of life of people in the community and addressing discrimination and disadvantage. Also the provision or enhancement of community facilities in areas of real need. To provide supplementary and special needs education, as well as training for community development and for work. Campaigning on social and health issues; cultural activities, health counselling; and support and self help groups are also considered for funding

WHAT IS NOT FUNDED No grants to individuals

WHO CAN BENEFIT Community-based groups benefiting: unemployed people; volunteers; at risk groups; those disadvantaged by poverty; refugees and those living in urban areas

WHERE FUNDING CAN BE GIVEN Greenwich, Lambeth, Lewisham, Southwark

TYPE OF GRANT Normally one-off for core costs, feasibility studies, project, running costs, salaries and start-up costs. Funding is available for up to one year or less

RANGE OF GRANTS Normally to a maximum of £2,000

FINANCES *Year* 1997–98 *Income* £189,503 *Grants* £106,478

TRUSTEES Suhail Aziz, Ms Virginia Caldwell-McNay, Canon Peter Challen, David Chiesman, Mrs Gillian Davies, OBE, Lady Hart, Peter Jefferson Smith, CB, Prof Michael Kelly, Ms Vashti Ledford-Jobson, Judge Crawford Lindsay, QC, Ian Mills, Colin Roberts, Ms Carole Souter

HOW TO APPLY Guidelines and application forms are available from the address under Who To Apply To upon written request

WHO TO APPLY TO Kevin Ireland, Director, South East London Community Foundation, Room 6, Winchester House, Cranmer Road, London SW9 6EJ *Tel* 0171-582 5117

CC NO 1047594   **ESTABLISHED** 1995

■ South East Wales Community Foundation

WHAT IS FUNDED The promotion of any charitable purposes for the benefit of Mid and South Glamorgan and its immediate neighbourhood and in particular the protection of good health both mental and physical and the relief of poverty and sickness. Projects providing worthwhile service to the community. Particularly voluntary groups working with: disability; elderly people; children; substance misuse; social deprivation and environmental issues

WHAT IS NOT FUNDED No grants to individuals

WHO CAN BENEFIT Organisations benefiting: people of all ages; volunteers; at risk groups; disabled people; those disadvantaged by poverty; socially deprived people; homeless people and substance misusers. There is no restriction on the disease or medical condition suffered by the beneficiaries

WHERE FUNDING CAN BE GIVEN South East Wales

TYPE OF GRANT One-off, capital and start-up grants

RANGE OF GRANTS £50–£165,000

600

Think carefully about every application. Is it justified?

SAMPLE GRANTS £166,150 to Merthyr Safer Cities for Regeneration Programme – Gurnos Estate; £80,000 to Taff Ely Drug Support for home detoxification service; £59,000 to Pathfinder Project for employment opportunities for long-term unemployed; £50,808 to Merthyr Tydfil Town Centre Project for Drop-in Centre for young people and counselling service; £37,685 to Arts Factory for employment/training/regeneration; £25,114 to Cynon Action for Single Homeless for development of services for young homeless people; £1,000 to Pençywaun Young People's Task Force for equipment for Regeneration Programme; £375 to Children's Festival for one day festival for children with learning disabilities; £300 to Cadaxton House Playgroup for equipment for playgroup; £250 to National Pyramid Trust for project with low achievers

FINANCES *Year* 1997–98 *Income* £567,701

TRUSTEES Keith Arnold, OBE, John Curteis, RD, DL, Jeff Lane, Charles Middleton, John Pathy, OBE, Don Ramsay, Andrew Reid, Tony Roberts, OBE, D Hugh Thomas, CBE, CStJ, DL, MA, R T John Tree, MBE, DL

PUBLICATIONS Brochure *Making More Out of Giving*

HOW TO APPLY Initial enquiries by telephone or letter. Application forms and guidelines available. No deadline. Sae not required

WHO TO APPLY TO Irene John, South East Wales Community Foundation, 14–16 Merthyr Road, Whitchurch, Cardiff CF4 1DG *Tel* 01222 520250 *Fax* 01222 521250

CC NO 519795   **ESTABLISHED** 1987

■ South Glamorgan Welsh Church Fund

WHAT IS FUNDED Restoration of churches and memorials; education, community groups

WHO CAN BENEFIT Organisations benefiting children, young adults and students may be considered

WHERE FUNDING CAN BE GIVEN Wales, with a preference for South Glamorgan

FINANCES *Year* 1997 *Income* £33,431 *Grants* £11,480

HOW TO APPLY On an application form from the address under Who To Apply To

WHO TO APPLY TO Director of Finance and Info Technology, South Glamorgan Welsh Church Fund, Vale of Glamorgan Council, Civic Offices, Holton Road, Barry, Vale of Glamorgan CF63 4RU *Tel* 01446 709250

CC NO 506628   **ESTABLISHED** 1975

■ South Lakeland Communities Charitable Trust

WHAT IS FUNDED Small local initiatives towards sustainable communities, eg in accord with Local Agenda 21 of the 1992 Earth Summit – a document which outlines a local community's vision for an environmentally and socially sustainable and desirable future

WHAT IS NOT FUNDED To be decided

WHO CAN BENEFIT To be decided

WHERE FUNDING CAN BE GIVEN District of South Lakeland

TYPE OF GRANT One-off contributions towards start-up costs

RANGE OF GRANTS To be decided

TRUSTEES J Jeffers, G Henson, L Smyth, E Straughton

WHO TO APPLY TO G Henson, Trustee, South Lakeland Communities Charitable Trust, 22 Castle Garth, Sedbergh, Cumbria LA10 5AN *Tel* 01539 621495

CC NO 167740   **ESTABLISHED** 1998

■ South Leicestershire Council for Voluntary Service

WHAT IS FUNDED General charitable purposes for the benefit of the community in the district of Harborough and in particular, community development, support to voluntary and community organisations, self-help groups and care in the community

WHAT IS NOT FUNDED No grants to individuals. Larger, well funded voluntary agencies are not funded

WHO CAN BENEFIT Small, existing or new community groups benefiting children, older people, carers, disabled people and those living in rural areas

WHERE FUNDING CAN BE GIVEN Harborough district

TYPE OF GRANT One-off and start-up costs will be considered. Funding may be given for up to one year

RANGE OF GRANTS £60–£100

FINANCES *Year* 1996 *Income* £50,665

PUBLICATIONS There is a leaflet explaining the criteria for the Fund

NOTES There are no trustees for this Fund which is not a trust, CVS Trustees administer the Fund

HOW TO APPLY Directly to the CVS for an application form

WHO TO APPLY TO Ms J Shorley, South Leicestershire Council for Voluntary Service, The Settling Rooms, St Marys Place, Springfield Street, Market Harborough, Leicestershire LE16 7DR *Tel* 01858 433232

CC NO 1040677   **ESTABLISHED** 1994

■ South Square Trust

WHAT IS FUNDED Annual income primarily allocated for bursaries and art or humanitarian donations to registered charities, working in the fields of: arts, culture and recreation; health; conservation and environment; community facilities and services will be considered. Support may also be given to almshouses, respite accommodation, infrastructure development and churches. Postgraduate education, tertiary and higher education will be funded with bursaries and books

WHAT IS NOT FUNDED No grants made for expeditions and travel bursaries. No courses outside the UK will be funded

WHO CAN BENEFIT Students and to a limited degree graduates of recognised fine and applied arts disciplines only, particularly those related to silver and gold work. Preference is given to students commencing undergraduate studies, of UK nationality. Young adults and older people; Christians; at risk groups; carers; disabled people; those living in rural areas and victims of abuse will also be considered. People suffering from various diseases and medical conditions will benefit

WHERE FUNDING CAN BE GIVEN UK

TYPE OF GRANT Single donations concerned with art educational purposes preferred. Buildings, capital, core costs, one-off, project, research and recurring costs will be considered. For individual students funding may be given for up to three years

RANGE OF GRANTS £100–£1,000

FINANCES *Year* 1996–97 *Income* £188,264 *Grants* £222,000

Does the trust you have chosen match your needs? Haphazard applications waste postage and time

601

TRUSTEES C R Ponter, A E Woodall, W P Harriman, C P Grimwade, D B Inglis

HOW TO APPLY Applications from individual students are acknowledged. Telephone or write to the Clerk for standard application form for individual students, by the end of April. Charities apply by letter, enclosing accounts. General donations considered three times a year

WHO TO APPLY TO Mrs N Chrimes, Clerk to the Trustees, South Square Trust, PO Box 67, Heathfield, East Sussex TN21 9ZR *Tel* 01435 830778 *Fax* 01435 830778

CC NO 278960 **ESTABLISHED** 1979

■ **The South Staffordshire Water Disconnections Charitable Trust**

WHAT IS FUNDED To relieve those who are in conditions of need, hardship, poverty or distress and are unable to meet or pay for charges for their water supply

WHAT IS NOT FUNDED Anything other than water debt

WHO CAN BENEFIT Customers of South Staffordshire Water plc

WHERE FUNDING CAN BE GIVEN Areas supplied by South Staffordshire Water plc

TYPE OF GRANT Running costs will be considered

FINANCES *Year* 1997–98 *Income* £55,000 *Grants* £67,000

TRUSTEES J Doyle, Cllr F S Hunt, Cllr Mrs E Matthews, J Thompson, B H Whitty

WHO TO APPLY TO M Swallow, South Staffs Water Disconnections Charitable Trust, South Staffordshire Water plc, Green Lane, Walsall, West Midlands WS2 7PD *Tel* 01922 638282

CC NO 1043177 **ESTABLISHED** 1995

■ **South Yorkshire Community Foundation** (formerly South Yorkshire Foundation)

WHAT IS FUNDED Policy is reviewed annually; current priorities are: Neighbourhood based community development initiatives; the education and training needs of voluntary community groups; voluntary sector housing and homelessness initiatives; community information and advice services; community based health projects. Preference is given to projects where a grant of a few hundred pounds will make a significant difference, meaning that most projects helped are small ones

WHAT IS NOT FUNDED Unlikely to receive support (unless fitting strongly with the above priority categories): arts projects, environmental projects, bands, sports clubs, uniformed youth groups, minibuses. No grants are made for holidays, trips and excursions, repayment of debts, academic research, or to individuals. Capital projects costing more than £50,000 are most unlikely to receive funding from the Foundation

WHO CAN BENEFIT Community organisations benefiting those disadvantaged by poverty, the homeless and the sick. There is no restriction on the disease or medical condition suffered by the beneficiaries

WHERE FUNDING CAN BE GIVEN South Yorkshire

TYPE OF GRANT A small number of large grants are made each year but most grants are for amounts under £1,000. Applications are encouraged from small, local groups who find it hard to raise money elsewhere for projects. Capital and revenue

RANGE OF GRANTS £25–£2,000

SAMPLE GRANTS £2,000 to Woodseats Neighbourhood Advice Centre, Sheffield; £1,400 to Birdwell Community Association, Barnsley; £1,050 to Stanham Housing Association Ltd, Barnsley; £1,000 to Grimethorpe Electronic Village Hall, Barnsley; £1,000 to Hexthorpe Community Project, Doncaster; £1,000 to Doncaster HIV Project; £1,000 to Dearne Valley Victim Support Scheme, Rotherham; £1,000 to Work Ltd, Sheffield; £1,000 to Sheffield Common Purpose; £990 to Ward Green Community Association, Barnsley

FINANCES *Year* 1997 *Income* £106,154 *Grants* £68,860

TRUSTEES R Darlison (Chair), T Hale, P Lee, Lord Scarborough, B Upton, I Aiken, B Willis, D Clark, J H Neill, CBE, TD, LLD (President), C J Jewitt, J Clark, R Wheeler

HOW TO APPLY Application forms are available from the Foundation. The Trustees meet quarterly in January, April, July and September. Applications must reach the Foundation six weeks before these meetings. When your application arrives at the Foundation office, as long as it meets the stated guidelines, it goes out to one of the four District Advisory Committees (DACs). The Committees are made up of local people with an interest in the voluntary sector. A member of the committee may want to visit you before your application is discussed. The DACs meet quarterly, about two weeks before the Trustees, and send recommendations about each application to the Trustees' meeting

WHO TO APPLY TO Tony Blackett, South Yorkshire Community Foundation, Heritage Park, 55 Albert Terrace Road, Sheffield S6 3BR

CC NO 517714 **ESTABLISHED** 1986

■ **South Yorkshire Historic Buildings Trust Limited**

WHAT IS FUNDED The renovation and preservation of historic buildings

WHERE FUNDING CAN BE GIVEN South Yorkshire

TYPE OF GRANT Buildings

SAMPLE GRANTS £5,000 to Reachout Christian Fellowship for renovation of Christ Church, Doncaster

FINANCES *Year* 1996–97 *Income* £20,528

TRUSTEES J G Binfield, E L Braim, R Harman, J Hawley, R M Hudson, A R McDool, P O'Brien, P Senior, C Stocks, K S Swinburn

HOW TO APPLY To the address under Who To Apply To in writing

WHO TO APPLY TO P Senior, Trustee, South Yorkshire Historic Buildings Trust Ltd, Whitegates, Middle Street, Misson, Doncaster, South Yorkshire DN10 6EA *Tel* 01709 813561

CC NO 501220 **ESTABLISHED** 1971

■ **Kenneth and Phyllis Southall Charitable Trust**

WHAT IS FUNDED For the relief of the aged, impotent and poor people and for the advancement of education

WHAT IS NOT FUNDED No gifts made to individuals

WHO CAN BENEFIT Registered charities benefiting people of all ages, students, Quakers, disabled people and those disadvantaged by poverty.

WHERE FUNDING CAN BE GIVEN Mostly national with an interest in the West Midlands

TYPE OF GRANT Normally single payments

RANGE OF GRANTS £300–£2,500

SAMPLE GRANTS £2,500 to WNCT; £2,000 to John Muir Trust for Bla Bheinn Appeal; £1,250 to Selly Wood House Bursary Fund; £1,000 to FWAG; £1,000 to Friends of the Earth
FINANCES *Year* 1995 *Income* £19,595 *Grants* £23,900
TRUSTEES Daphne Maw, C M Southall, D H D Southall
HOW TO APPLY To the address under Who To Apply To
WHO TO APPLY TO S T Rutter, Kenneth and Phyllis Southall Charitable Trust, Messrs Rutters, Solicitors, 2 Bimport, Shaftesbury, Dorset SP7 8AY
CC NO 259814   **ESTABLISHED** 1968

■ The Stephen R and Philippa H Southall Charitable Trust

WHAT IS FUNDED General charitable purposes. No applications will be considered whether from organisations or individuals
WHAT IS NOT FUNDED No clerical help, so no replies sent to applications which are thus discouraged. No grants to individuals
WHO CAN BENEFIT Registered charities. There are no restrictions on the age; professional and economic group; family situation; religion and culture; and social circumstances of; or disease or medical condition suffered by, the beneficiaries
WHERE FUNDING CAN BE GIVEN UK, especially Hereford
RANGE OF GRANTS £10–£12,700
SAMPLE GRANTS £12,700 to Hereford Waterworks Museum Trust; £2,140 to Relate; £500 to Alzheimer's Disease Society; £470 to Clifford Church Council; £250 to League of Friends – County Hospital; £250 to Oxfam; £250 to Society of Friends for Almeley Quaker Meeting Fund; £250 to St Michael's Hospice Development Trust; £200 to Hereford Friends of The Samaritans; £150 to National Federation of Women's Institute
FINANCES *Year* 1995 *Income* £61,866 *Grants* £20,245
TRUSTEES S R Southall, Mrs P H Southall
NOTES Funds are fully committed to charities in which the Trustees have a personal interest
HOW TO APPLY **This Trust states that it does not respond to unsolicited applications**
WHO TO APPLY TO Mrs P H Southall, Stephen and Philippa Southall Charitable Trust, Porking Barn, Clifford, Hereford HR3 5HE
CC NO 223190   **ESTABLISHED** 1947

■ W F Southall Trust

WHAT IS FUNDED Society of Friends (Quakers), peace, education, alcohol and drug addiction, social welfare and related charities
WHAT IS NOT FUNDED No grants to individuals
WHO CAN BENEFIT Registered charities benefiting children, young adults and students, Quakers, at risk groups, those disadvantaged by poverty and socially isolated people
WHERE FUNDING CAN BE GIVEN UK
TYPE OF GRANT Normally one-off payments
FINANCES *Year* 1997 *Income* £315,013 *Grants* £223,700
TRUSTEES Mrs Daphne Maw, C M Southall, D H D Southall, Mrs Annette Wallis, M Holtom, Ms J Engelkamp
NOTES Gifts to registered charities only
HOW TO APPLY To the address under Who To Apply To

WHO TO APPLY TO S T Rutter, W F Southall Trust, Messrs Rutters, Solicitors, 2 Bimport, Shaftesbury, Dorset SP7 8AY
CC NO 218371   **ESTABLISHED** 1937

■ Southern Arts

WHAT IS FUNDED To foster and promote the development and appreciation of the arts. The Board makes grants and guarantees and offers an advisory service. Financial assistance is confined in the main to professional activities
WHAT IS NOT FUNDED Grants for students following courses of full-time education are not considered
WHO CAN BENEFIT Individual artists and craftspeople. Arts organisations including galleries, orchestras, dramatic and lyric performing companies. Film workshops, arts centres, studios, festivals. Organisations benefiting actors and entertainment professionals, musicians, textile workers and designers, writers and poets
WHERE FUNDING CAN BE GIVEN Berkshire, Buckinghamshire, Hampshire, Isle of Wight, Oxfordshire, Wiltshire and parts of Dorset (Bournemouth, Christchurch and Poole)
TYPE OF GRANT Core funding to a limited number of organisations within the region meeting detailed criteria. Development grants towards regional programmes/projects (not of a capital nature)
FINANCES *Year* 1996–97 *Income* £4,433,275 *Grants* £3,409,478
TRUSTEES Southern Arts Board
PUBLICATIONS Various – relating to specific arts issues/needs
NOTES The Board works in close co-operation with County and District Councils and with the Arts Council of England, the British Film Institute and the Crafts Council
HOW TO APPLY Core funding: September each year; development funding: check with information department for guidelines and deadlines on specific schemes
WHO TO APPLY TO The Information Officer, Southern Arts, 13 St Clement Street, Winchester, Hampshire SO23 9DQ *Tel* 01962 855099 *Fax* 01962 861186 *E-mail* info@southernarts.co.uk
CC NO 800120   **ESTABLISHED** 1968

■ The Southon Charitable Trust

WHAT IS FUNDED Alzheimer's disease
WHAT IS NOT FUNDED No grants to individuals
WHO CAN BENEFIT Voluntary organisations caring for sufferers of Alzheimer's disease. Support to research workers and medical professionals working in the field of Alzheimer's disease.
WHERE FUNDING CAN BE GIVEN Southern England
TYPE OF GRANT Small capital grants
FINANCES *Year* 1998 *Income* £58,872
TRUSTEES N A V Lister, N R Bowman, F J Cuthbertson
HOW TO APPLY In writing detailing size and type of organisation and enclosing annual accounts. Applications will not be acknowledged
WHO TO APPLY TO Mrs S J Sharkey, The Southon Charitable Trust, Windyridge, The Close, Totteridge, London N20 8PJ *Tel* 0181-446 7281 *Fax* 0181-446 5658
CC NO 296423   **ESTABLISHED** 1986

■ Southover Manor General Education Trust Ltd

WHAT IS FUNDED Education of boys and girls under 25 years of age

WHAT IS NOT FUNDED No funding for bursaries or scholarships

WHO CAN BENEFIT Schools, colleges and individuals under the age of 25

WHERE FUNDING CAN BE GIVEN Sussex only

TYPE OF GRANT Capital, projects

FINANCES *Year* 1996 *Income* £156,774

WHO TO APPLY TO The Secretary, Southover Manor General Education Trust Ltd, Old Vicarage Cottage, Newhaven Road, Iford, Lewes, Sussex BN7 3PL

CC NO 299593 **ESTABLISHED** 1988

■ The Paul Southworth Charitable Trust

WHAT IS FUNDED General charitable purposes

WHO CAN BENEFIT There are no restrictions on the age; professional and economic group; family situation; religion and culture; and social circumstances of; or disease or medical condition suffered by, the beneficiaries

WHERE FUNDING CAN BE GIVEN UK

FINANCES *Year* 1997 *Income* £13,251 *Grants* £3,000

TRUSTEES Ms P M Southworth, B J Mitchell, P Southworth

WHO TO APPLY TO B J Mitchell, Secretary and Treasurer, The Paul Southworth Charitable Trust, Round Oak, Old Station Road, Wadhurst, East Sussex TN5 6TZ

CC NO 1049365 **ESTABLISHED** 1995

■ Spalding Trust

WHAT IS FUNDED Preference for projects which widen the knowledge of one religion among adherents of another, and for applicants intending to put their knowledge to early use rather than to engage in protracted research. Charities working in the fields of: publishing and printing; the advancement of any major world religion; religious umbrella bodies; postgraduate education; tertiary and higher education; cultural and religious teaching; field trips and study trips; research into religion; and libraries and museums

WHAT IS NOT FUNDED Grants are not normally made to students studying their own religion

WHO CAN BENEFIT Colleges, academic research projects, and organisations benefiting; young adults; older people; academics; clergy; research workers; students; teachers and governesses; Buddists and Jainists; Christians; Hindus; Jews; Muslims; and beneficiaries of any other major world religion

WHERE FUNDING CAN BE GIVEN UK and overseas

TYPE OF GRANT One-off, project and research. Funding for up to three years

RANGE OF GRANTS £150–£5,000. Typical grant £750–£1,000

SAMPLE GRANTS £2,000 to research student on life and thought of Mahmud Muhammed Taha; £1,660 to Muslim student studying Christian theology; £1,600 to Leo Baeck College to support conference on Jainism, Christianity and Islam; £1,250 to student for comparative study of free will and predestination in Islam and Christianity; £1,000 to research student on purity and pollution in Zoroastrianism and Jainism; £1,000 to Inter Faith Network for the UK for research on Higher Education and student religious identity; £800 to The Hidden legacy Foundation towards Exhibition 'The Jews of South West England'; £750 to Inter Faith Centre and Library for books on religions other than Christianity; £700 to University lecturer for researching religious identity and co-existence among Hindus and Muslims in Bengal; £300 to UK Association for Buddhists Studies towards publication costs of Journal

FINANCES *Year* 1997 *Income* £62,403 *Grants* £44,422

TRUSTEES J M K Spalding, DM, FRCP (Chairman), Prof C E Bosworth, MA, PhD, FBA, Prof J A Emerton, DD, FBA, Humphrey J Fisher, AB, MA, DPhil, Prof E D A Hulmes, KHS, MA, BD, DPhil, Julius J Lipner, MA, PhD, Michael Loewe, PhD, Mrs E de C Spalding, MB, MRCP, DCH, Miss A C Spalding, BA

NOTES Detailed aims of Trust sent to all applicants

HOW TO APPLY At any time. Information requested includes research proposal, CV, budget including other sources of possible funding and references, sae appreciated. Applications take at least two months from receipt of all information requested

WHO TO APPLY TO Mrs T Rodgers, Spalding Trust, PO Box 85, Stowmarket, Suffolk IP14 3NY *Fax* 01359 240739

CC NO 209066 **ESTABLISHED** 1923

■ The Spandex Foundation (otherwise known as the Starfish Trust)

WHAT IS FUNDED (a) To provide funding for research and development for incurable diseases such as cancer and meningitis. (b) To provide funding for the welfare of sufferers of such illnesses. (c) To provide funding for the development and provision of augmented communication systems, using mainstream technologies, to allow sufferers of conditions such as cerebral palsy and the after effects of strokes to communicate with the outside world. In respect of the the third objective the Foundation has sourced a software package known as 'GUS' which has the ability to transform a portable or desktop PC into a reliable dynamic display augmented communication system

WHO CAN BENEFIT Individuals and organisations benefiting research workers, medical professionals. People suffering from many diseases and medical conditions will be considered

WHERE FUNDING CAN BE GIVEN UK

TYPE OF GRANT Recurring

SAMPLE GRANTS £13,623 to three beneficiaries £5,000 to Cancer Care Appeal; £1,330 to CLIC; £1,194 to Madeline Harding Appeal Fund; £250 to Chernobyl – Children Cancer Care

FINANCES *Year* 1995–96 *Income* £103,822 *Grants* £21,397

TRUSTEES C E Dobson, M Dobson

NOTES During the year 1995–96 GUS software and the associated hardware was presented to ten beneficiaries

WHO TO APPLY TO Mr & Mrs C E Dobson, The Spandex Foundation, Rambles, Knowle Park, Almondsbury, Bristol BS12 4BS *Tel* 01454 616444
CC NO 800203   **ESTABLISHED** 1988

■ Spar Charitable Fund

WHAT IS FUNDED To provide financial assistance at the discretion of the Spar guilds. In practice, grants are only made to beneficiaries connected with the grocery industry
WHO CAN BENEFIT Beneficiaries should be connected with the grocery industry
WHERE FUNDING CAN BE GIVEN UK
FINANCES *Year* 1996 *Income* £47,185
  Grants £100,000
TRUSTEES The National Guild of Spar Ltd, R Harvey, P Marchant
HOW TO APPLY By private arrangement
WHO TO APPLY TO P W Marchant, Spar Charitable Fund, Spar Landmark Ltd, 32–40 Headstone Drive, Harrow, Middlesex HA3 5QT
CC NO 236252   **ESTABLISHED** 1964

■ The Eric F Sparkes Charitable Trust

WHAT IS FUNDED General charitable purposes. To support other charities where Trustees are satisfied assistance is of significant benefit
WHAT IS NOT FUNDED Generally no grants to individuals
WHO CAN BENEFIT Local charities in Devon and special cases known to Trustees. There are no restrictions on the age; professional and economic group; family situation; religion and culture; and social circumstances of; or disease or medical condition suffered by, the beneficiaries
WHERE FUNDING CAN BE GIVEN Mainly Warwickshire and Devon
TYPE OF GRANT General one off for specific projects or support of national charitable organisations. Capital grants are also considered
RANGE OF GRANTS £100–£3,000
FINANCES *Year* 1997 *Income* £21,092
  Grants £16,410
TRUSTEES J M Davies, H M Turner, Mrs K A Davies
HOW TO APPLY Individual applications are considered but distribution normally made only in the autumn. Applications for revenue grants should enclose most recent accounts. For capital, total cost and anticipated start date. Charity registration number should be given. Regret applications cannot be acknowledged
WHO TO APPLY TO H M Turner, The Eric F Sparkes Charitable Trust, 2 Vaughan Parade, Torquay, Devon TQ2 5EF *Tel* 01803 296221
CC NO 233085   **ESTABLISHED** 1963

■ The Sparkhill Trust

WHAT IS FUNDED To further the objects of the Balsall Heath Church Centre (Birmingham) and for other religious and charitable work for the benefit of the inhabitants of Balsall Heath, Sparkhill and the surrounding districts in the West Midlands. Charities working in the fields of: accommodation and housing; Christian religion; hospices and community services will be considered
WHO CAN BENEFIT Christians (principally non-conformist). Individuals and organisations benefiting: Baptists; Church of England; Methodists; Unitarians; at risk groups; carers;

disabled people; those disadvantaged by poverty, the homeless; those living in urban areas; victims of abuse, crime and domestic violence
WHERE FUNDING CAN BE GIVEN Balsall Heath, Sparkhill and surrounding districts in West Midlands
TYPE OF GRANT Single grants for capital or non-recurrent expenditure. Buildings, project, one-off and start-up costs. Funding of one year or less will be considered
SAMPLE GRANTS £2,000 to Balsall Heath Church Centre; £2,000 to Lighthouse Rescue Mission; £1,000 to Wellclose Trust; £1,000 to The Salvation Army; £500 to '870' House
FINANCES *Year* 1997 *Income* £17,553
  Grants £11,000
TRUSTEES P J Maskell, D J Laugharne, Mrs M I Perry, B A Jones, Mrs S A Maskell, D H Clement
HOW TO APPLY Applications must be in writing setting out clearly the objectives and financial considerations, including an outline budget if possible
WHO TO APPLY TO P J Maskell, Chairman, The Sparkhill Trust, Cropthorne, 64 Dovehouse Lane, Solihull, West Midlands B91 2EE
CC NO 511666   **ESTABLISHED** 1981

■ Sparks Charity (Sport Aiding Medical Research For Kids)

WHAT IS FUNDED To support medical research for children
WHO CAN BENEFIT To support researchers and benefit those suffering from paediatric diseases
WHERE FUNDING CAN BE GIVEN UK
RANGE OF GRANTS £5,300–£301,360
SAMPLE GRANTS £301,360 to University College London; £127,679 to University of Newcastle; £108,748 to University of Nottingham; £102,109 to Institute of Child Health London; £59,544 to Royal Post-Grad Medical School, London; £32,869 to Charing Cross and Westminster; £23,019 to Babraham Institute; £9,000 to Cambridge University; £5,300 to Manchester University
FINANCES *Year* 1997 *Income* £1,268,004
  Grants £768,741
TRUSTEES T Brooke-Taylor, J Buddle, Ms T Cash, B Cribbins, R Hadingham, J Hill, K Hopkins, D Lockyear, D Metcalfe, D Mills, G Morgan, R Pierce, K Tubby, R Uttley, M Stephens
NOTES For the purposes of selecting research projects the Charity has entered into an agreement with Action Research. They select from a list of grants administered by Action Research for support by SPARKS
WHO TO APPLY TO The Director, Sparks Charity, Francis House, Francis Street, London SW1P 1DE
CC NO 1003825   **ESTABLISHED** 1991

■ The Spear Charitable Trust

WHAT IS FUNDED Welfare of employees and former employees of J W Spear & Sons plc, their families and dependants; also general charitable purposes
WHO CAN BENEFIT Individuals and organisations, particularly employees and former employees of J W Spear & Sons plc, their families and dependants
WHERE FUNDING CAN BE GIVEN UK

Does the trust you have chosen match your needs? Haphazard applications waste postage and time

605

SAMPLE GRANTS £47,683 to Rhode Island Hospital; £21,630 to the Spear Games Archive Trust; £15,187 to Royal Society for the Prevention of Cruelty to Animals; £9,779 welfare grants and sundry donations; £6,752 to Wellington Hospital; £6,032 to an individual; £5,000 to Institute of Cancer Research; £5,000 to Hanover Band Trust; £4,000 to to the Friends of Wildershausen

FINANCES *Year* 1995 *Income* £180,766 *Grants* £121,063

TRUSTEES P N Harris, K B Stuart Crowhurst, F A Spear, Mrs H E Spear

HOW TO APPLY To the address under Who To Apply To in writing

WHO TO APPLY TO Mrs H E Spear, Secretary, The Spear Charitable Trust, Roughground House, Old Hall Green, Ware, Hertfordshire SG11 1HB

CC NO 1041568   **ESTABLISHED** 1962

■ Special Nursery Trust

WHAT IS FUNDED Grants are given to research projects and any other needs associated with neonatal care in the region

WHO CAN BENEFIT Babies who require special care. Support will also be given to medical professionals and research workers concerned with the advancement of neonatal care

WHERE FUNDING CAN BE GIVEN Grampian Region, Orkney and Shetland

TYPE OF GRANT One-off, capital and 1–2 years funding for research project will be considered

RANGE OF GRANTS Up to £25,000

SAMPLE GRANTS £14,000 to Woman and Child Health Endowment Fund for research funding of the Neonatal Data Bank

FINANCES *Year* 1997 *Income* £24,561 *Grants* £27,579

TRUSTEES Mrs F Burnett, Ms C Barron, M U L Hutton, Dr D J Lloyd

HOW TO APPLY In writing by January

WHO TO APPLY TO Mrs F Burnett, Special Nursery Trust, 68 Station Road, Banchory, Kincardineshire AB31 5YJ

SC NO SCO 14910   **ESTABLISHED** 1987

■ The Jessie Spencer Trust

WHAT IS FUNDED General charitable purposes

WHO CAN BENEFIT There are no restrictions on the age; professional and economic group; family situation; religion and culture; and social circumstances of; or disease or medical condition suffered by, the beneficiaries

WHERE FUNDING CAN BE GIVEN UK

TYPE OF GRANT Grants made towards both capital and revenue expenditure. May be recurrent for up to 10 years

RANGE OF GRANTS For 1995–96: £100–£1,800

SAMPLE GRANTS Grants for 1995–96:; £1,800 to Magdo Szpala; £1,250 to DARE; £1,250 to Winged Fellowship Trust; £1,000 to Childline Midlands; £1,000 to Ex-Services Mental Welfare Society; £1,000 to Matthew Fell Appeal; £1,000 to the Guide Association, Ratcliffe-on-Trent; £500 to Abbeyfield Nottingham Society Limited; £500 to Age Concern; £500 to All Hallows Church, Gedling

FINANCES *Year* 1997 *Income* £108,614 *Grants* £86,675

TRUSTEES V W Semmens, Mrs E K M Brackenbury, R S Hursthouse

NOTES Grants are rarely made for the repair of parish churches outside Nottinghamshire. The list of Top Ten Grants has been compiled using data from the

financial year 1995–96, during which the total charitable grants amounted to £76,025

HOW TO APPLY In writing to the address under Who To Apply To accompanied by audited accounts dated within 12 months of the application. Unsuccessful applicants are not notified

WHO TO APPLY TO The Jessie Spencer Trust, Eversheds, 1 Royal Standard Place, Nottingham NG1 6FZ

CC NO 219289   **ESTABLISHED** 1962

■ W W Spooner Charitable Trust

WHAT IS FUNDED The Trustees invite appeals which broadly fall within the following selected fields: (a) Youth – welfare, sport and education including school appeals and initiatives, clubs, scouting, guiding and adventure training. Individual voluntary service overseas and approved expeditions. (b) The Community – including churches, associations, welfare and support groups. (c) Healing – care of the sick, handicapped and underprivileged. Welfare organisations, victim support, hospitals, hospices and selected medical charities and research. (d) The Countryside – protection and preservation of the environment including rescue and similar services. Preservation and maintenance of historic buildings. (e) The Arts – including museums, teaching, performing, musical and literary festivals. Selective support for the purchase of works of art for public benefit

WHAT IS NOT FUNDED No grants for high profile appeals seeking large sums, most donations made are less than £500

WHO CAN BENEFIT Preference for local activities benefiting: people of all ages; actors and entertainment professionals; ex-services and service people; musicians; volunteers; writers and poets; Christians; disabled people; those disadvantaged by poverty; and victims of abuse, crime and domestic violence. There is no restriction on the disease or medical condition suffered by the beneficiaries

WHERE FUNDING CAN BE GIVEN The County of Yorkshire

TYPE OF GRANT Recurring annual donations to a hard core list of charities. One-off response to 25–30 single appeals

RANGE OF GRANTS £200–£2,000, average £200–£500

SAMPLE GRANTS £3,500 to New College, Oxford; £2,000 to National Arts Collection Fund; £2,000 to New Hall, Cambridge; £1,500 to Courtauld Institute; £1,500 to St Margaret's, Ilkley; £1,100 to Guide Dogs for the Blind; £1,000 to Ilkley Parish Church; £1,000 to Leith School of Art; £1,000 to Yorkshire Ballet Seminar

FINANCES *Year* 1997 *Income* £60,004 *Grants* £52,400

TRUSTEES M H Broughton, Sir James F Hill, Bt, T J P Ramsden, R Ibbotson, J H Wright, Mrs J M McKiddie

NOTES Preference given to Yorkshire-based appeals

HOW TO APPLY By letter to the address under Who To Apply To

WHO TO APPLY TO Messrs Addleshaw Booth & Co, W W Spooner Charitable Trust, Sovereign House, PO Box 8, Sovereign Street, Leeds LS1 1HQ

CC NO 313653   **ESTABLISHED** 1961

■ Stanley Spooner Deceased

WHAT IS FUNDED General charitable purposes, in particular the Metropolitan Police Courts Poor Boxes (Drinan Bequest), the Docklands

Settlements, and the Church of England Children's Society

WHO CAN BENEFIT Organisations, particularly those benefiting children and those disadvantaged by poverty. Otherwise, there are no restrictions on the age; professional and economic group; family situation; religion and culture; and social circumstances of; or disease or medical condition suffered by, the beneficiaries

WHERE FUNDING CAN BE GIVEN UK

SAMPLE GRANTS £10,174 to Church of England Children's Society; £10,174 to Metropolitan Police Courts Poor Boxes (Drinan Bequest); £10,174 to The Docklands Settlements; £1,695 to Barnardos; £1,695 to National Children's Home

FINANCES *Year* 1996 *Income* £38,856 *Grants* £33,914

NOTES Included in the Trust's objective are percentages of the Trust income to go to: the Drinan Bequest, the Dockland Settlements, the Church of England Children's Society

WHO TO APPLY TO M E Mills, Stanley Spooner Deceased, The Public Trust Office, Trust Division (Ref G5361/A5), Stewart House, 24 Kingsway, London WC2B 6JX

CC NO 1044737   **ESTABLISHED** 1995

■ The Spoore, Merry & Rixman Foundation

WHAT IS FUNDED Generally to help young persons resident in the area Where Funding Can Be Given shown below to further their education and to assist schools and institutions providing such education and in particular to assist beneficiaries to study music or other arts. The award of scholarships, bursaries and maintenance allowances tenable at approved places of education and also for scholarships or maintenance allowances for study abroad. Provision of financial assistance, outfits, clothing, instruments, books, etc to enable persons to enter a trade or profession. Provision of recreation, social training or athletic facilities

WHO CAN BENEFIT Residents of Maidenhead and Bray under 25 years of age

WHERE FUNDING CAN BE GIVEN Maidenhead and Bray only

FINANCES *Year* 1996 *Income* £72,350 *Grants* £54,000

TRUSTEES B Hedley, Miss S K Beedell, M W Braxton, Mrs P E Flew, Mrs J K Fotherby, Mrs K Newbound, S Platt, F A Robinson, J Powell (Chair), R H Thomas, G Mair

HOW TO APPLY In writing to the address under Who To Apply To named below. Trustees meet three or four times each year

WHO TO APPLY TO M J Tanner, BSocSc, Clerk, The Spoore, Merry & Rixman Foundation, 25 York Road, Maidenhead, Berkshire SL6 1SQ

CC NO 309040   **ESTABLISHED** 1958

■ The Sportsman's Charity

WHAT IS FUNDED Money is distributed to charities across Scotland, especially those which are successful in their aims, are perhaps less well known, or which focus on the disadvantaged, particularly children, or the needs of the disabled in sport. Infrastructure development, education and training, and community facilities and services will be considered

WHAT IS NOT FUNDED Grants are not made to cover running costs. No grants to individuals

WHO CAN BENEFIT Sportsmen and women of all ages and family situations. However, there are some restrictions on the social circumstances of the beneficiaries

WHERE FUNDING CAN BE GIVEN Scotland

TYPE OF GRANT Capital, one-off and project will be considered. Funding may be given for up to two years

TRUSTEES A Cubie, J Frame, D McLean

PUBLICATIONS Accounts are available from the Charity

HOW TO APPLY Applications should be made in writing to the address under Who To Apply To and must include details of the aims of the organisation and an analysis of costs

WHO TO APPLY TO John Frame, The Sportsman's Charity, 30 Murrayfield Road, Edinburgh EH12 6ER

SC NO SCO 15424   **ESTABLISHED** 1983

■ The Sharon Spratt Trust

WHAT IS FUNDED Research into cancer and its treatment. The relief of patients suffering from cancer; the provision of recreational facilities for such patients and their carers

WHO CAN BENEFIT Beneficiaries suffering from cancer and their carers

WHERE FUNDING CAN BE GIVEN UK

TYPE OF GRANT Project and recurring costs will be considered

FINANCES *Year* 1995 *Income* £14,679 *Grants* £6,600

TRUSTEES Christopher Spratt, Caroline Broadbent, Timothy C Martin, Sally Kalman, Robin Light

WHO TO APPLY TO C T Spratt, The Sharon Spratt Trust, 61 Tarrant Street, Arundel, West Sussex BN18 9DJ *Tel* 01903 234343

CC NO 1039356   **ESTABLISHED** 1994

■ The Rosalyn and Nicholas Springer Charitable Trust

WHAT IS FUNDED General charitable purposes with emphasis on children, medical charities, special needs education and the advancement of the Jewish religion (not Orthodox)

WHAT IS NOT FUNDED No funding is given to animal charities, expeditions or scholarships

WHO CAN BENEFIT Organisations benefiting at risk groups, carers and disabled people. Funding will also be considered for beneficiaries suffering from various diseases and medical conditions

WHERE FUNDING CAN BE GIVEN UK

TYPE OF GRANT One-off, capital, endowments and research will be considered. funding may be given for up to one year

HOW TO APPLY In writing

WHO TO APPLY TO N Springer, Trustee, The Rosalyn and Nicholas Springer Charitable Trust, 27 Berkeley House, Hay Hill, London W1X 7LG *Tel* 0171-493 1904

CC NO 1062239   **ESTABLISHED** 1997

■ Spurgeon Oaklands Charitable Trust

WHAT IS FUNDED The provision of residential accommodation for the occupants; the provision of financial assistance and support to such persons as are or were occupants of Oaklands, and other general charitable purposes

WHO CAN BENEFIT Those seeking residential accommodation, and occupants or former occupants of Oaklands who are disadvantaged by poverty

WHERE FUNDING CAN BE GIVEN UK

FINANCES *Year* 1995 *Income* £14,559

TRUSTEES G D Rattue, D A Chilvers, M Ray-Smith, K J Shield, M A Sippitt, G W Thomas, J A Spurgeon

NOTES No grants were made in 1995, the Trust's income was spent on repairs and service charges

WHO TO APPLY TO M A Sippitt, Spurgeon Oaklands Charitable Trust, c/o Messrs Clarks, Great Western House, Station Road, Reading, Berkshire RG1 1SX

CC NO 1039625 **ESTABLISHED** 1994

■ The R H S Spurgin Charitable Trust

WHAT IS FUNDED General charitable purposes

WHO CAN BENEFIT There are no restrictions on the age; professional and economic group; family situation; religion and culture; and social circumstances of; or disease or medical condition suffered by, the beneficiaries

WHERE FUNDING CAN BE GIVEN Greater London and UK

RANGE OF GRANTS £500

SAMPLE GRANTS £500 to Camphill Village Trust; £500 to Youth Link, Dundee; £500 to Enable; £500 to Northern Ireland Children's Holiday Scheme; £500 to Penumbra

FINANCES *Year* 1996 *Income* £13,761
Grants £11,000

TRUSTEES G G MacMillan, Mrs L Richardson

WHO TO APPLY TO George G MacMillan, Trustee, The R H S Spurgin Charitable Trust, Finlaystone, Langbank, Renfrewshire PA14 6TJ

CC NO 210562 **ESTABLISHED** 1962

■ The Square Mile Charitable Trust

This trust did not respond to CAF's request to amend its entry and, by 30 June 1998, CAF's researchers did not find financial records for later than 1995 on its file at the Charity Commission. Trusts are legally required to submit annual accounts to the Charity Commission under section 42 of the Charities Act 1993

WHAT IS FUNDED General charitable purposes

WHO CAN BENEFIT There are no restrictions on the age; professional and economic group; family situation; religion and culture; and social circumstances of; or disease or medical condition suffered by, the beneficiaries

WHERE FUNDING CAN BE GIVEN UK

TRUSTEES R N Hambro, Viscount Weir, J R A East, P Pottinger, Hambros Bank Executor & Trustee Co,

WHO TO APPLY TO The Square Mile Charitable Trust, Hambros Trust Co Ltd, 41 Tower Hill, London EC3N 4HA

CC NO 293363 **ESTABLISHED** 1985

■ Stafford Educational Endowment Charity

WHAT IS FUNDED Secondary schools for equipment not provided for by statutory funding, and individual students

WHO CAN BENEFIT Some individual students, and schools benefiting children, young adults and students. Teachers may also benefit

WHERE FUNDING CAN BE GIVEN Stafford

FINANCES *Year* 1995–96 *Income* £14,709
Grants £20,000

HOW TO APPLY To the address under Who To Apply To in writing

WHO TO APPLY TO The County Treasurer, Stafford Educational Endowment Charity, Staffordshire County Council, County Buildings, Eastgate Street, Stafford, Staffordshire ST16 2NF

CC NO 517345 **ESTABLISHED** 1986

■ Staffordshire Historic Churches Trust

WHAT IS FUNDED The preservation, improvement, repair, restoration and maintenance of church fabric in the area Where Funding Can Be Given

WHAT IS NOT FUNDED No grants for work on organs, bells, re-ordering, redecoration or church halls

WHO CAN BENEFIT Churches and chapels of all denominations

WHERE FUNDING CAN BE GIVEN Staffordshire including that which now forms part of West Midlands

TYPE OF GRANT One-off grants for buildings

RANGE OF GRANTS £500–£2,500

SAMPLE GRANTS All the following grants were for restoration and maintenance of the church:; £2,500 to St Michael and All Angels, Hamstall Ridware; £2,000 to St Peter, Norbury; £1,250 to St Luke, Onclote; £1,000 to St Anne, Chasetown; £1,000 to St Anne, Weston-on-Trent; £1,000 to St Leonards, Ipstones; £1,000 to St Leonards, Clifton Campville; £700 to St Chad, Slindon; £500 to All Saints, Alrewas; £500 to All Saints, Dilhorne

FINANCES *Year* 1997–98 *Income* £25,000
Grants £15,000

TRUSTEES R D Birch, P B Clarke, D J Simkin

NOTES Grants are offered only for work in connection with the repair, maintenance, restoration of the fabric of the church

HOW TO APPLY To the address under Who To Apply To in writing requesting an application form. When writing please give an outline of the work for which a grant may be requested

WHO TO APPLY TO Dr Jane Benton, Secretary, Staffordshire Historic Churches Trust, 1 Yew Tree Cottage, Slindon, Stafford, Staffordshire ST21 6LX *Tel* 01782 791514

CC NO 240854 **ESTABLISHED** 1953

■ Miss Doreen Stanford Trust

WHAT IS FUNDED General charitable purposes

WHO CAN BENEFIT There are no restrictions on the age; professional and economic group; family situation; religion and culture; and social circumstances of; or disease or medical condition suffered by, the beneficiaries

WHERE FUNDING CAN BE GIVEN UK

FINANCES *Year* 1997 *Income* £49,019
Grants £16,417

TRUSTEES J S Borner, R S Borner, T Borner

WHO TO APPLY TO Mrs G M B Borner, Secretary, Miss Doreen Stanford Trust, 26 The Mead, Beckenham, Kent BR3 5PE

CC NO 1049934 **ESTABLISHED** 1995

■ Stanhope-Palmer Charity

WHAT IS FUNDED Charities working in the fields of: cancer research; hospices; community care; health care; medical research generally; arts facilities; and conservation. Support may be given to zoos; management services; personnel and human resource services; small enterprises; and support to voluntary and community organisations

WHAT IS NOT FUNDED No grants to individuals
WHO CAN BENEFIT Registered UK charities benefiting: children and young adults; disabled people; victims of abuse and disasters. Support for those suffering from Alzheimer's disease, cancers, cystic fibrosis, kidney disease, motor neurone disease, psoriasis, sight loss, tropical diseases and those who are terminally ill
WHERE FUNDING CAN BE GIVEN UK
TYPE OF GRANT One-off, core costs and research grants funded for up to three years will be considered
RANGE OF GRANTS £250–£15000
SAMPLE GRANTS £15,000 to Leonora Children's Cancer Fund; £2,500 to London Playing Fields Society for the Peter May Memorial; £2,000 to Cotswold Care Hospice; £2,000 to Cancer Relief Macmillan Fund; £1,500 to Access Theatre Company
FINANCES *Year* 1997 *Income* £19,238 *Grants* £38,000
TRUSTEES Stanhope-Palmer Charity Trustees Ltd
HOW TO APPLY Please include latest report and accounts with application
WHO TO APPLY TO A B V Hughes, Stanhope-Palmer Charity, Payne Hicks Beach, Solicitors, 10 New Square, Lincolns Inn, London WC2A 3QG *Tel* 0171-465 4401
CC NO 326447   **ESTABLISHED** 1983

■ **The Stanley Charitable Trust**

This trust did not respond to CAF's request to amend its entry and, by 30 June 1998, CAF's researchers did not find financial records for later than 1995 on its file at the Charity Commission. Trusts are legally required to submit annual accounts to the Charity Commission under section 42 of the Charities Act 1993

WHAT IS FUNDED Jewish religious charities
WHAT IS NOT FUNDED Grants are only made to projects and charities known to the Trustees
WHO CAN BENEFIT Charities benefiting Jewish People
WHERE FUNDING CAN BE GIVEN UK, especially Greater Manchester
TRUSTEES A M Alder, I Alder, J Alder
HOW TO APPLY To the address below in writing
WHO TO APPLY TO A M Alder, The Stanley Charitable Trust, 8 Stanley Road, Salford M7 0EG
CC NO 326220   **ESTABLISHED** 1982

■ **Stanley Foundation Limited**

WHAT IS FUNDED Medical, the arts, youth/education
WHAT IS NOT FUNDED No grants to individuals
WHO CAN BENEFIT Organisations benefiting children and young adults, students, actors and entertainment professionals, musicians, students, textile workers and designers, writers and poets, and the sick. There is no restriction on the disease or medical condition suffered by the beneficiaries
WHERE FUNDING CAN BE GIVEN UK, especially London
FINANCES *Year* 1997 *Income* £100,374 *Grants* £110,414
TRUSTEES Council of Management: C O N Stanley, D J Aries, S R Stanley, Mrs E Stanley, C Shale
WHO TO APPLY TO C Shale, The Secretary, Stanley Foundation Limited, Flat 3, 19 Holland Park, London W11 3TD
CC NO 206866   **ESTABLISHED** 1962

■ **Morgan Stanley International Foundation**

WHAT IS FUNDED General charitable purposes with a focus on education and training
WHAT IS NOT FUNDED No grants to individuals or for fundraising events
WHO CAN BENEFIT The communities of Tower Hamlets, Newham and Hackney. Organisations benefiting: unemployed people; at risk groups; carers; disabled people; those disadvantaged by poverty; homeless people and victims of crime, abuse and famine
WHERE FUNDING CAN BE GIVEN London Boroughs of Tower Hamlets, Newham and Hackney only
TYPE OF GRANT Buildings, capital, core costs, one-off, project, recurring costs, running costs and salaries will be considered, but not loans. Funding may be given for more than three years
RANGE OF GRANTS £500–£30,000, average grant £4,500
SAMPLE GRANTS £87,500 to NSPCC for Charity of the Year (employee matching); £31,000 to Community Links for director of children's youth work's salary; £15,000 to De Paul Trust for the part funding of director's salary; £12,900 to Royal London Hospital for equipment; £12,000 to London Chest Hospital for equipment; £10,000 to Mudchute Park and Farm for the part funding of nature study worker's salary; £10,000 to Spitalfields Festival for an education programme; £10,000 to Whitechapel Art Gallery for an education programme; £10,000 to Woodland Centre Trust for a summer holiday programme; £10,000 to Bromley By Bow Centre for core funding
FINANCES *Year* 1997 *Income* £545,000 *Grants* £498,000
TRUSTEES K Brown, J Chenenix-Trench, A Fawcett, J Johansson, P Kellner, D Nicol, T Rowe, C Stott, P Stott, J Studzinski, J Tanner, R Whitehand
HOW TO APPLY Initial telephone call welcomed and encouraged. Deadline for applications – new grants: four weeks prior to next Trustees' meeting. (Five meetings/year.) Deadline for applications – renewals: two weeks before Trustees' meeting. All applications for new grants should be accompanied by a copy of the charity's latest annual report and accounts
WHO TO APPLY TO Mrs H Bird, Morgan Stanley International Foundation, 25 Cabot Square, Canary Wharf, London E14 4QA *Tel* 0171-425 8021 *Fax* 0171-425 4949
CC NO 1042671   **ESTABLISHED** 1994

■ **The Star Foundation Trust**

This trust did not respond to CAF's request to amend its entry and, by 30 June 1998, CAF's researchers did not find financial records for later than 1995 on its file at the Charity Commission. Trusts are legally required to submit annual accounts to the Charity Commission under section 42 of the Charities Act 1993

WHAT IS FUNDED General charitable purposes. Preference to charities of which the Trust has special interest, knowledge or association
WHO CAN BENEFIT There are no restrictions on the age; professional and economic group; family situation; religion and culture; and social circumstances of; or disease or medical condition suffered by, the beneficiaries
WHERE FUNDING CAN BE GIVEN UK
TRUSTEES A C Wilson, Dr Elizabeth Frankland Moore, OBE, LLD, J Crawford, Mrs J S McCreadie, Mrs J Cameron

Does the trust you have chosen match your needs? Haphazard applications waste postage and time

609

WHO TO APPLY TO M S Stewart, Solicitor, The Star Foundation Trust, Farrer and Co, Lincoln's Inn Fields, London WC2A 3LH

CC NO 257711　　**ESTABLISHED** 1968

■ Starkie Bence Charitable Trust

WHAT IS FUNDED General charitable purposes. Trustees consider all applications, but most of the funds are allocated to regular commitments

WHAT IS NOT FUNDED Trustees do not support political activities

WHO CAN BENEFIT Registered charities and institutions. There are no restrictions on the age; professional and economic group; family situation; religion and culture; and social circumstances of; or disease or medical condition suffered by, the beneficiaries

WHERE FUNDING CAN BE GIVEN England and Wales

TYPE OF GRANT Recurrent and single donations

RANGE OF GRANTS £1,000–£3,000

SAMPLE GRANTS £3,000 to Charities Aid Foundation; £1,000 to Arthritis Care; £1,000 to British Red Cross; £1,000 to Camphill Trust; £1,000 to Church of England Pensions Board

FINANCES *Year* 1997 *Income* £20,309 *Grants* £19,000

TRUSTEES A M Ross, Kleinwort Benson Trustees Ltd

NOTES No fund raising is undertaken to support the work of the Charity

WHO TO APPLY TO C Gilbert, Trustees Department, Starkie Bence Charitable Trust, Kleinwort Benson Trustees Ltd, PO Box 191, 10 Fenchurch Street, London EC3M 3LB

CC NO 282541　　**ESTABLISHED** 1981

■ The Stathern Chapel Close Trust

WHAT IS FUNDED Advancement of religion, relief of poverty, education, promotion of Christian gospel

WHO CAN BENEFIT Organisations benefiting Christians, children, young adults and those disadvantaged by poverty

WHERE FUNDING CAN BE GIVEN Fifty mile radius of the address under Who To Apply To

FINANCES *Year* 1997 *Income* £20,310 *Grants* £20,180

TRUSTEES I C Jesson, J L E Jesson, J Stanley

WHO TO APPLY TO I C Jesson, The Stathern Chapel Close Trust, 14 Chapel Lane, Hose, Melton Mowbray, Leicestershire LE14 4JG

CC NO 269010　　**ESTABLISHED** 1973

■ The Peter Stebbings Memorial Charity

WHAT IS FUNDED General charitable purposes

WHAT IS NOT FUNDED Funds fully committed. No new applications considered

WHO CAN BENEFIT Registered charities. There are no restrictions on the age; professional and economic group; family situation; religion and culture; and social circumstances of; or disease or medical condition suffered by, the beneficiaries

WHERE FUNDING CAN BE GIVEN UK

TYPE OF GRANT Annual grants

FINANCES *Year* 1996 *Income* £31,366 *Grants* £20,258

TRUSTEES Mrs P M Cosin, N F Cosin, Mrs J A Clifford, A J F Stebbings

HOW TO APPLY Funds fully committed. **This Trust states that it does not respond to unsolicited applications**

WHO TO APPLY TO Andrew Stebbings, Secretary to the Trustees, The Peter Stebbings Memorial Charity, 45 Pont Street, London SW1X 0BX

CC NO 274862　　**ESTABLISHED** 1977

■ The Steebek Charitable Trust

WHAT IS FUNDED General charitable purposes

WHO CAN BENEFIT There are no restrictions on the age; professional and economic group; family situation; religion and culture; and social circumstances of; or disease or medical condition suffered by, the beneficiaries

WHERE FUNDING CAN BE GIVEN UK

FINANCES *Year* 1997 *Income* £21,000 *Grants* £41,000

TRUSTEES D R L Jones, Ms J Jones, K R Whyman

WHO TO APPLY TO D R L Jones, Trustee, The Steebek Charitable Trust, Garsdon Mill, Garsdon, Malmesbury, Wiltshire *Tel* 0467 491000

CC NO 1049874　　**ESTABLISHED** 1995

■ The Steene Charitable Foundation

WHAT IS FUNDED Reducing the need, hardship or distress of people by making grants or loans of money or providing or paying for items, services or facilities

WHO CAN BENEFIT To benefit those in need, hardship or distress

WHERE FUNDING CAN BE GIVEN UK

FINANCES *Year* 1997 *Income* £49,133

TRUSTEES D A Steene, D K Steene

NOTES Grants were not awarded for the year 1997

WHO TO APPLY TO M J Harbottle, Professional Adviser, The Steene Charitable Foundation, No 2, Kentish Buildings, 125 Borough High Street, London SE1 1NP *Tel* 0171-234 0002

CC NO 1058707　　**ESTABLISHED** 1996

■ The Cyril and Betty Stein Charitable Trust

WHAT IS FUNDED Predominantly Jewish causes, including education, the advancement of the Jewish religion and welfare

WHO CAN BENEFIT Jewish organisations

WHERE FUNDING CAN BE GIVEN UK and Israel

TYPE OF GRANT One-off and recurring

SAMPLE GRANTS £67,167 to the Institute for the Advancement of Education in Jaffa; £43,977 to Friends of Hebrew University in Jerusalem; £16,750 to L'Chaim Independent Charitable Trust; £15,950 to Carmel College; £15,000 to Joint Jewish Charitable Trust; £14,382 to the Sinclair Charitable Trust; £5,264 to the Da'at Foundation; £5,200 to Lubavitch Foundation

FINANCES *Year* 1997 *Income* £340,193 *Grants* £256,173

TRUSTEES C Stein, Mrs B Stein, D Clayton

HOW TO APPLY To the address under Who To Apply To in writing

WHO TO APPLY TO D Clayton, The Cyril and Betty Stein Charitable Trust, 94 Wigmore Street, London W1H 9DR

CC NO 292235　　**ESTABLISHED** 1985

■ The Jack Steinberg Charitable Trust

This trust did not respond to CAF's request to amend its entry and, by 30 June 1998, CAF's researchers did not find financial records for later than 1995 on its file at the Charity Commission. Trusts are legally required to submit annual accounts to the Charity Commission under section 42 of the Charities Act 1993

WHAT IS FUNDED The Trustees only support registered charities who are personally known to them
WHO CAN BENEFIT There are no restrictions on the age; professional and economic group; family situation; religion and culture; and social circumstances of; or disease or medical condition suffered by, the beneficiaries
WHERE FUNDING CAN BE GIVEN UK, Israel, USA, France
TRUSTEES Mrs H A Steinberg, Mrs R J Jay, Mrs K L Palmer
WHO TO APPLY TO Casson Beckman, Chartered Accountant, The Jack Steinberg Charitable Trust, Hobson House, 155 Gower Street, London WC1E 6BJ
CC NO 222383   **ESTABLISHED** 1962

■ The Steinberg Family Charitable Trust

WHAT IS FUNDED General charitable purposes
WHO CAN BENEFIT There are no restrictions on the age; professional and economic group; family situation; religion and culture; and social circumstances of; or disease or medical condition suffered by, the beneficiaries
WHERE FUNDING CAN BE GIVEN UK
FINANCES *Year* 1995 *Income* £36,626
          Grants £11,362
TRUSTEES Ms B Steinberg, L Steinberg, J Steinberg, Ms L R Ferster, D K Johnston
WHO TO APPLY TO L Steinberg, Trustee, The Steinberg Family Charitable Trust, c/o Stanley House, 4–12 Marybone, Liverpool L3 2BY
CC NO 1045231   **ESTABLISHED** 1995

■ The Hugh Stenhouse Foundation

WHAT IS FUNDED Nature reserves; woodlands; and bird sanctuaries. Grants are given for general charitable purposes
WHAT IS NOT FUNDED No grants for expeditions, etc
WHO CAN BENEFIT To benefit: children; young adults; those in care, fostered and adopted; and those disadvantaged by poverty
WHERE FUNDING CAN BE GIVEN West of Scotland
TYPE OF GRANT Recurring, one-off and core costs. Funding is available for more than three years
RANGE OF GRANTS £50–£24,000, typical grant £750
SAMPLE GRANTS £24,000 to Maxwelton House Trust for a historic house; £500 to an individual for the relief of poverty; £200 to Ingliston Development Trust for the enhancement of Royal Highland Showground; £75 to Social Iceberg Foundation towards Hogmanay hospitality for the homeless
FINANCES *Year* 1997–98 *Income* £28,500
          Grants £25,000
TRUSTEES Mrs P R H Irvine Robertson, M R L Stenhouse, P H A Stenhouse, R G T Stenhouse, Mrs R C L Stewart
HOW TO APPLY Applications should be made in writing to the address under Who To Apply To

WHO TO APPLY TO P D Bowman, Secretary and Treasurer, The Hugh Stenhouse Foundation, Lomynd, Knockbuckle Road, Kilmalcolm PA13 4JT *Tel* 01505 872716
CC NO CR 40289   **ESTABLISHED** 1968

■ Will Trust of Edgar John Henry Stephenson (Deceased)

WHAT IS FUNDED Welfare, medical, wildlife and arts charities
WHAT IS NOT FUNDED No grants to individuals
WHO CAN BENEFIT Registered charities only, either national organisations or organisations local to Hampshire and Dorset benefiting at risk groups, those disadvantaged by poverty and socially isolated people. There is no restriction on the disease or medical condition suffered by the beneficiaries
WHERE FUNDING CAN BE GIVEN UK, especially Hampshire and Dorset
RANGE OF GRANTS £5–£6,000
SAMPLE GRANTS £6,000 to Lymington Detached Youth Work Project; £5,000 to New Forest Council of Community Service Volunteer Bureau; £5,000 to Prince's Youth Trust; £1,602 to Brockenhurst Gateway Club; £1,500 to Lymington and District Round Table; £1,245 to RLYC for a children's sail training project; £1,000 to New Forest Romanian Medical Appeal; £1,000 to Children's Hospice Appeal; £1,000 to Artsway; £784 to Oakhaven Fundraisers Account
FINANCES *Year* 1996–97 *Income* £33,786
          Grants £45,368
TRUSTEES A M B Butterworth, M T James
HOW TO APPLY To the address under Who To Apply To in writing
WHO TO APPLY TO A M B Butterworth, Will Trust of Edgar John Henry Stephenson, 48 High Street, Lymington, Hampshire SO41 9ZQ
CC NO 295065   **ESTABLISHED** 1985

■ Stepney Relief in Need Charity

WHAT IS FUNDED The relief, generally or individually, people living in the area Where Funding Can Be Given who are in conditions of need, hardship or distress. This includes: holiday accommodation; respite; social care professional bodies; purchase of books; health care; care in the community; holidays and outings; meals provisions; and community transport
WHO CAN BENEFIT Individuals and organisations benefiting: people of all ages; those in care fostered and adopted; children and parents; one parent families; widows and widowers; retired people; at risk groups; carers; disabled people; those disadvantaged by poverty; homeless people; and socially isolated people. There are no restrictions on the disease or medical condition suffered by the beneficiaries
WHERE FUNDING CAN BE GIVEN Former Metropolitan Borough of Stepney
TYPE OF GRANT One-off
RANGE OF GRANTS £5–£500. Could be larger in special circumstances
FINANCES *Year* 1996–97 *Income* £14,045
          Grants £3,678
HOW TO APPLY Written applications only
WHO TO APPLY TO Mrs J Partleton, Stepney Relief in Need Charity, Rectory Cottage, 5 White Horse Lane, Stepney, London E1 3NE
CC NO 250130   **ESTABLISHED** 1977

■ C E K Stern Charitable Trust

WHAT IS FUNDED General charitable purposes
WHO CAN BENEFIT There are no restrictions on the age; professional and economic group; family situation; religion and culture; and social circumstances of; or disease or medical condition suffered by, the beneficiaries
WHERE FUNDING CAN BE GIVEN UK
WHO TO APPLY TO Z M Kaufman, Trustee, C E K Stern Charitable Trust, 267 Durham Road, Gateshead, Tyne and Wear NE58 5AD
CC NO 1049157   **ESTABLISHED** 1995

■ The Sir Sigmund Sternberg Charitable Foundation

WHAT IS FUNDED To support education and health and related projects
WHAT IS NOT FUNDED No grants to individuals
WHO CAN BENEFIT Registered charities benefiting: children; young adults; students and the sick. There is no restriction on the disease or medical condition suffered by the beneficiaries
WHERE FUNDING CAN BE GIVEN UK
TYPE OF GRANT Usually one-off
RANGE OF GRANTS £15–£29,515
SAMPLE GRANTS £29,515 to Manor House Trust; £9,000 to Institute for Archaeo-Metallurgical Studies; £6,345 to Reform Synagogues of Great Britain; £2,772 to Jewish Music Heritage Trust; £2,500 to the Holocaust Educational Trust; £2,100 to Leo Baeck College; £2,084 to the Reform Foundation Trust; £2,000 to Institute for Jewish Affairs; £2,000 to Friends of the Hebrew University of Jerusalem; £2,000 to St Andrews Trust
FINANCES *Year* 1996 *Income* £226,047 *Grants* £96,064
TRUSTEES Sir Sigmund Sternberg, KCSG, JP, Lady Hazel Sternberg, JP, M V Sternberg, MA, LLM (Cantab)
WHO TO APPLY TO The Sir Sigmund Sternberg Charitable Foundation, 5th Floor, Charles House, 108–110 Finchley Road, London NW3 5JJ
CC NO 257950   **ESTABLISHED** 1968

■ Stervon Ltd

WHAT IS FUNDED Jewish and general charitable purposes in the area Where Funding Can Be Given
WHO CAN BENEFIT Jewish people
WHERE FUNDING CAN BE GIVEN UK
FINANCES *Year* 1996 *Income* £89,226 *Grants* £192,049
TRUSTEES A Reich, G Rothbart
HOW TO APPLY To the address under Who To Apply To in writing
WHO TO APPLY TO A Reich, Trustee, Stervon Ltd, c/o Stervon House, 1 Seaford Road, Salford, Manchester M6 6AS *Tel* 0161-737 5000
CC NO 280958   **ESTABLISHED** 1980

■ The Stevenage Community Trust

WHAT IS FUNDED General charitable purposes
WHAT IS NOT FUNDED Appeals of a political nature are not supported
WHO CAN BENEFIT There are no restrictions on the age; professional and economic group; family situation; religion and culture; and social circumstances of; or disease or medical condition suffered by, the beneficiaries
WHERE FUNDING CAN BE GIVEN Stevenage and the surrounding areas
FINANCES *Year* 1997 *Income* £103,180 *Grants* £23,497
TRUSTEES Lord D Cobbold (Chairman), M Addison, R Ball, J Bentley, P Drury, J Elmore, R Gochin, G Gorham, Dr R Gomm, S Hollingsworth, Mrs M Hurle, Cllr Mrs H Lawrence, A Martin, D Ronksley, M Simpson, D Wall, Cllr R Woodward
HOW TO APPLY Application forms are available. The Trustees meet to consider grants quarterly
WHO TO APPLY TO M Addison, The Stevenage Community Trust, Howe Roche Waller Solicitors, Mindenhall Court, High Street, Stevenage, Hertfordshire SG1 3AY
CC NO 1000762   **ESTABLISHED** 1990

■ The Arthur Stevens Charitable Trust

WHAT IS FUNDED General charitable purposes
WHO CAN BENEFIT There are no restrictions on the age; professional and economic group; family situation; religion and culture; and social circumstances of; or disease or medical condition suffered by, the beneficiaries
WHERE FUNDING CAN BE GIVEN UK and overseas
TRUSTEES R E Stevens, G J Field, Ms V J Clifton-Brown, Ms C M Gleed
WHO TO APPLY TO G J Field, Trustees' Solicitor, The Arthur Stevens Charitable Trust, c/o Longmores, 24 Castle Street, Hertford, Hertfordshire SG14 1HP
CC NO 1058317   **ESTABLISHED** 1996

■ The June Stevens Foundation

WHAT IS FUNDED Trustees have a particular interest in animals and children
WHAT IS NOT FUNDED Grants normally not paid to individuals
WHO CAN BENEFIT Charitable organisations benefiting children and animals
WHERE FUNDING CAN BE GIVEN UK but with preference for Gloucestershire
TYPE OF GRANT At Trustees' discretion
RANGE OF GRANTS £200–£1,000
SAMPLE GRANTS £1,500 to National Canine Defence League; £1,500 to Brooke Hospital for Animals; £1,500 to Greek Animal Welfare Fund; £1,100 to Costwold Victim Support; £1,000 to World Society for Protection of Animals
FINANCES *Year* 1997–98 *Income* £21,000 *Grants* £21,800
TRUSTEES J D Stevens, A J Quinton, A R St C Tahourdin
HOW TO APPLY No formal applications procedure. Applications considered bi-annually, usually in June/July and November/December. Applications are not normally acknowledged
WHO TO APPLY TO A Tahourdin, The June Stevens Foundation, 13 Bedford Row, London WC1R 4BU
CC NO 327829   **ESTABLISHED** 1988

■ The Stevenson Family's Charitable Trust

WHAT IS FUNDED Medical and welfare, arts and heritage
WHAT IS NOT FUNDED No grants to individuals
WHO CAN BENEFIT National, international and local charitable organisations benefiting: actors and entertainment professionals; musicians; textile

workers and designers; writers and poets; at risk groups; disabled people; disadvantaged by poverty and socially isolated people. There are no restrictions on the disease or medical condition suffered by the beneficiaries

WHERE FUNDING CAN BE GIVEN UK and overseas

TYPE OF GRANT Some recurrent

FINANCES *Year* 1997 *Income* £203,000
Grants £226,000

TRUSTEES H A Stevenson, Mrs C M Stevenson, J F Lever

HOW TO APPLY To the address under Who To Apply To in writing

WHO TO APPLY TO H A Stevenson, The Stevenson Family's Charitable Trust, 23 St Mary Axe, London EC3A 8LL

CC NO 327148   **ESTABLISHED** 1986

■ Steventon Allotment and Relief in Need Charity

WHAT IS FUNDED Projects benefiting the local community, churches, schools, the elderly and the maintenance of the allotments and St Michael's House

WHO CAN BENEFIT Individuals and local organisations benefiting people of all ages and Christians in the Parish of Steventon

WHERE FUNDING CAN BE GIVEN Steventon

FINANCES *Year* 1997 *Income* £103,322
Grants £32,739

TRUSTEES R J Dunsdon, H I Fuller, Ms M E Ireson, D M Otterburn, E N Brind, J E Jarvis, S A F Ward

PUBLICATIONS *Steventon News* monthly

HOW TO APPLY To the address under Who To Apply To in writing. All applicants for assistance will be required to complete a form detailing income and expenditure

WHO TO APPLY TO Mrs C Rogers, Steventon Allotment and Relief in Need Charity, Maple Rose Cottage, Milton Hill, Abingdon, Oxfordshire OX1 6AG

CC NO 203331   **ESTABLISHED** 1987

■ The Stewards' Charitable Trust

WHAT IS FUNDED Support of rowing at all levels, from grass roots upwards, among those in full time education or training

WHAT IS NOT FUNDED Grants are rarely made to individuals

WHO CAN BENEFIT Organisations and clubs benefiting sportsmen and women

WHERE FUNDING CAN BE GIVEN Generally within UK

FINANCES *Year* 1995 *Income* £181,536
Grants £60,000

TRUSTEES M A Sweeney, C G V Davidge, W A D Wadham, R C Lester

NOTES Applications are usually first vetted by Amateur Rowing Association

WHO TO APPLY TO R S Goddard, Secretary, The Stewards' Charitable Trust, Regatta Headquarters, Henley-on-Thames, Oxfordshire RG9 2LY

CC NO 299597   **ESTABLISHED** 1988

■ The Stewards' Trust

WHAT IS FUNDED The promotion and encouragement of the Christian faith

WHAT IS NOT FUNDED The Trustees are not able to respond to new appeals or to make any grants for the time being

WHO CAN BENEFIT Organisations benefiting Christians

WHERE FUNDING CAN BE GIVEN UK

FINANCES *Year* 1997 *Income* £69,687
Grants £11,540

TRUSTEES Viscount Brentford, Mrs H C Metters, M Hopkins

NOTES The trust no longer has any surplus funds or income. No applicants can be accepted for the foreseeable future

WHO TO APPLY TO J M Kilbee, Treasurer, The Stewards' Trust, St James the Less School, Moreton Street, London SW1V 2PT

CC NO 238227   **ESTABLISHED** 1956

■ The Stewardship Trust Ripon

WHAT IS FUNDED General charitable purposes at discretion of Trustees, whose main object is to give to Evangelical Christian work including literature, local and missionary workers but funds are virtually all committed to established outlets

WHAT IS NOT FUNDED No support given to theologically liberal organisations

WHO CAN BENEFIT Organisations benefiting Christian Evangelists

WHERE FUNDING CAN BE GIVEN UK

TYPE OF GRANT Recurrent and one-off grants will be considered

RANGE OF GRANTS £2–£3,000

SAMPLE GRANTS £3,000 to United Beach Missions; £2,500 to Ryedale Evangelical Church; £2,000 to Gideons International; £2,000 to Geneva Road Baptist Church; £2,000 to Caring for Life; £2,000 to Leeds City Mission; £1,500 to Leeds City Evangelical Church; £1,500 to Garforth Evangelical Church; £1,000 to Zion Evangelical Baptist Church; £1,000 to Stanton Lees Chapel

FINANCES *Year* 1997 *Income* £32,416
Grants £31,855

TRUSTEES W B Metcalfe, Prof V Wright, G A Vasey, Mrs A Metcalfe, Mrs R M Fay

HOW TO APPLY 1 January: very exceptional cases dealt with between annual meeting of Trustees. Not all applications will be acknowledged

WHO TO APPLY TO W B Metcalfe, The Stewardship Trust Ripon, Hutton Hill, Ripon, North Yorkshire HG4 5DT

CC NO 224447   **ESTABLISHED** 1958

■ Sir Iain Stewart Foundation

WHAT IS FUNDED Grants are made to charities which the Trustees judge the Founder would have wished to benefit

WHAT IS NOT FUNDED No grants to individuals

WHO CAN BENEFIT Registered charities. There are no restrictions on the age; professional and economic group; family situation; religion and culture; and social circumstances of; or disease or medical condition suffered by, the beneficiaries

WHERE FUNDING CAN BE GIVEN UK

HOW TO APPLY Charitable organisations wishing to make an application must submit full accounts

WHO TO APPLY TO P C H Younie WS, Sir Iain Stewart Foundation, Pearsons WS, 23 Alva Street, Edinburgh EH2 4PU

SC NO SCO 13800

Does the trust you have chosen match your needs? Haphazard applications waste postage and time

613

■ The Bill Stickland Fund

This trust did not respond to CAF's request to amend its entry and, by 30 June 1998, CAF's researchers did not find financial records for later than 1995 on its file at the Charity Commission. Trusts are legally required to submit annual accounts to the Charity Commission under section 42 of the Charities Act 1993

WHAT IS FUNDED General charitable purposes, relief of persons in need

WHO CAN BENEFIT There are no restrictions on the age; professional and economic group; family situation; religion and culture; and social circumstances of; or disease or medical condition suffered by, the beneficiaries. However, particular favour is given to people in need

WHERE FUNDING CAN BE GIVEN Wimborne and Ferndown

HOW TO APPLY To the address below in writing

WHO TO APPLY TO J N Sorton, Trustee, The Bill Stickland Fund, Allin Sorton Solicitors, 523 Ringwood Road, Ferndown, Dorset BH22 9BJ

CC NO 801076 **ESTABLISHED** 1989

■ Still Waters Charitable Trust

WHAT IS FUNDED At Trustees' discretion having regard to the wishes of the Settlor

WHAT IS NOT FUNDED No grants to individuals, eg student projects, or for primary medical charities or objects

WHO CAN BENEFIT There are no restrictions on the age; professional and economic group; family situation; religion and culture; and social circumstances of; or disease or medical condition suffered by, the beneficiaries

WHERE FUNDING CAN BE GIVEN UK and overseas

TYPE OF GRANT Normally one-off

RANGE OF GRANTS £500–£2,000, typical grant £750

FINANCES *Year* 1998 *Income* £16,892
Grants £20,125

TRUSTEES P C Glazebrook, R H Kendall, J E Viles

HOW TO APPLY Applications from individuals are not generally accepted. By letter please

WHO TO APPLY TO R H Kendall, Still Waters Charitable Trust, 10 Greenhurst Lane, Oxted, Surrey RH8 0LB

CC NO 802703 **ESTABLISHED** 1989

■ The Leonard Laity Stoate Charitable Trust

WHAT IS FUNDED The broad categories we are supporting at present (in decreasing order of amount spent in 1997–98) are: medical and disablement; youth and children; churches (almost exclusively Methodist in the specified counties); disadvantaged; community projects; environment

WHAT IS NOT FUNDED No grants to individuals unless supported by a registered charity. Large projects (over £500,000) or general appeals mailed out by national charities are unlikely to be successful. Grants are not usually given towards general running expenses of charities

WHO CAN BENEFIT Organisations benefiting children and young adults, Methodists disabled people and those disadvantaged by poverty. There is no restriction on the disease or medical condition suffered by the beneficiaries. Small local innovatory projects with a good measure of self-help are preferred

WHERE FUNDING CAN BE GIVEN England and Wales, but preference for West of England: Bristol, Cornwall, Devon, Dorset and Somerset (especially West Somerset). Although we do not want to rule out anywhere in England and Wales we are a comparatively small trust and are forced to be very selective. Therefore, the further you are from our core area the less likely you are to be successful

TYPE OF GRANT Usually one-off for a specific project or part of a project

RANGE OF GRANTS £100–£5,000

SAMPLE GRANTS £6,000 to a holiday centre for the disabled to equip a sports hall; £5,000 to a disadvantaged family support project connected with a Methodist church for new premises; £2,500 to a Methodist church for redevelopment scheme; £2,000 to a Methodist church for a redevelopment scheme; £2,000 to a hospice for building a new unit; £2,000 to a holiday charity for the disabled for a new canal boat; £2,000 to a village hall for refurbishment; £1,750 to a scout group for an electric wheelchair; £1,500 to a horticultural enterprise for the disabled for new plant house; £1,000 to a local search and rescue service for a new Landrover

FINANCES *Year* 1997–98 *Income* £73,000
Grants £45,000

TRUSTEES D L Stoate, G L Stoate, S R Duckworth, S J Harnden, C Stoate, P C Stoate, P J Stoate

HOW TO APPLY To the address under Who To Apply To in writing. Grants can be considered at any time but the best time for submission is April/May and October/November. No special application form. Accounts or budget should be attached where possible, together with clear details of the need the intended project is designed to meet and of the amount raised so far. We tend not to come in at the early stages of fundraising. No telephone applications please. We regret that unsuccessful applications cannot be acknowledged unless sae supplied

WHO TO APPLY TO Geoffrey L Stoate, LLB, The Leonard Laity Stoate Charitable Trust, Combe House, Hill Lane, Bicknoller, Taunton, Somerset TA4 4EF

CC NO 221325 **ESTABLISHED** 1950

■ The Stobart Newlands Charitable Trust

WHAT IS FUNDED General charitable purposes at the discretion of the Trustees

WHO CAN BENEFIT Institutions. There are no restrictions on the age; professional and economic group; family situation; religion and culture; and social circumstances of; or disease or medical condition suffered by, the beneficiaries

WHERE FUNDING CAN BE GIVEN UK and overseas

TYPE OF GRANT At the discretion of the Trustees

FINANCES *Year* 1996 *Income* £727,838
Grants £486,060

TRUSTEES R J Stobart, M Stobart

WHO TO APPLY TO Mrs M Stobart, The Stobart Newlands Charitable Trust, Mill Croft, Hesket Newmarket, Wigton, Cumbria CA7 8HP

CC NO 328464 **ESTABLISHED** 1989

■ The Stock Aitken & Waterman Charitable Trust

This trust did not respond to CAF's request to amend its entry and, by 30 June 1998, CAF's researchers did not find financial records for later than 1995 on its file at the Charity Commission. Trusts are legally required to submit annual accounts to the Charity Commission under section 42 of the Charities Act 1993

WHAT IS FUNDED General charitable purposes
WHO CAN BENEFIT There are no restrictions on the age; professional and economic group; family situation; religion and culture; and social circumstances of; or disease or medical condition suffered by, the beneficiaries
WHERE FUNDING CAN BE GIVEN UK
TRUSTEES M J Aitken, M Stock, P A Waterman, D A Lester
WHO TO APPLY TO Philip John Newhouse, The Stock Aitken & Waterman Charitable Trust, 50 Victoria Embankment, Blackfriars, London EC4R 0DX
CC NO 328048   **ESTABLISHED** 1988

■ The Stoke Mandeville and Other Parishes Charity

WHAT IS FUNDED General charitable purposes. For the benefit of the people living in the area Where Funding Can Be Given, though primarily those in Stoke Mandeville
WHO CAN BENEFIT Individuals and local organisations. There are no restrictions on the age; professional and economic group; family situation; religion and culture; and social circumstances of; or disease or medical condition suffered by, the beneficiaries
WHERE FUNDING CAN BE GIVEN Great Hampden, Great Missenden, Little Hampden, Stoke Mandeville, Prestwood
SAMPLE GRANTS £27,495 to a school in Stoke Mandeville; £23,515 to a Parish Council in Stoke Mandeville; £11,785 to students in Stoke Mandeville; £7,500 to Sea Scouts in Stoke Mandeville; £5,350 as Christmas grants in Stoke Mandeville; £3,774 towards a newsletter in Stoke Mandeville; £3,562 to a community centre in Great Missenden; £3,000 to a village hall in Great Missenden; £2,883 as welfare grants in Stoke Mandeville; £1,750 to churches in The Hampdens
FINANCES *Year* 1996 *Income* £69,003
Grants £97,560
TRUSTEES N V Stratton, Ms B Ezra, S Allen, R Hunt, S Lee, E G Dell, G Read
HOW TO APPLY To the address under Who To Apply To in writing
WHO TO APPLY TO G Crombie, The Stoke Mandeville and Other Parishes Charity, Blackwells, Great Hampden, Great Missenden, Buckinghamshire HP16 9RJ
CC NO 296174   **ESTABLISHED** 1986

■ Stokenchurch Educational Charity

WHAT IS FUNDED Local nursery, primary and middle schools, students and pupils under the age of 25 residing in the Parish of Stokenchurch
WHAT IS NOT FUNDED No grants to applicants from outside the Parish of Stokenchurch
WHO CAN BENEFIT Local schools, children, young adults and students under the age of 25 residing in the Parish of Stokenchurch
WHERE FUNDING CAN BE GIVEN The Parish of Stokenchurch

RANGE OF GRANTS £5–£500 per academic year
FINANCES *Year* 1998 *Income* £80,000
Grants £60,000
TRUSTEES Rev C Chadwick, Dr A McClelland, A Palmer, Cllr A Plumridge, A Saunders, Mrs M Shurrock
NOTES Educational applications to be received before 31 December of each academic year. Charitable applications by 30 September of each year
HOW TO APPLY An advertisement inviting applications is placed in the local press and two public places in the area Where Funding Can Be Givenannually
WHO TO APPLY TO The Secretary, Stokenchurch Educational Charity, Kinda Cool, Wycombe Road, Stokenchurch, High Wycombe, Buckinghamshire HP14 3RR
CC NO 297846   **ESTABLISHED** 1987

■ F C Stokes Trust

WHAT IS FUNDED General charitable purposes
WHO CAN BENEFIT There are no restrictions on the age; professional and economic group; family situation; religion and culture; and social circumstances of; or disease or medical condition suffered by, the beneficiaries
WHERE FUNDING CAN BE GIVEN West Midlands
RANGE OF GRANTS £200–£5000
SAMPLE GRANTS £5,000 to Barnardos; £5,000 to Coventry Society for the Blind; £1,000 to Coventry Boys Club; £1,000 to NSPCC; £1,000 to the National Deaf, Blind and Rubella Association
FINANCES *Year* 1995 *Income* £18,280
Grants £17,200
TRUSTEES D Baume, R J Brown
WHO TO APPLY TO D Baume, Secretary and Trustee, F C Stokes Trust, c/o Payne Skillington, Lex House, 12 Manor Road, Coventry CV1 2LG
CC NO 289255   **ESTABLISHED** 1962

■ The Stoller Charitable Trust

WHAT IS FUNDED Health care, health facilities and buildings. Other charitable purposes will be considered
WHAT IS NOT FUNDED No grants to individuals
WHO CAN BENEFIT Established national charities and local causes benefiting children and young adults. There is no restriction on the disease or medical condition suffered by the beneficiaries
WHERE FUNDING CAN BE GIVEN UK, with a preference for the North West of England
TYPE OF GRANT Buildings, capital, one-off, project, research, recurring costs and start-up costs will be considered. Funding may be given for up to three years
FINANCES *Year* 1997–98 *Income* £130,000
Grants £130,000
TRUSTEES Norman Stoller, Diane Stoller, Roger Gould, Jan Fidler
HOW TO APPLY To the address under Who To Apply To in writing
WHO TO APPLY TO Roger Gould, The Stoller Charitable Trust, c/o Seton Healthcare Group plc, Tubiton House, Oldham, Lancashire OL1 3HS *Tel* 0161-652 2222
CC NO 285415   **ESTABLISHED** 1982

■ The M J C Stone Charitable Trust

WHAT IS FUNDED Children; medicine and welfare; education and conservation
WHO CAN BENEFIT National charities, smaller scale local organisations benefiting: children and young

adults; at risk groups; those disadvantaged by poverty and socially isolated people. There is no restriction on the disease or medical condition suffered by the beneficiaries. Medical professionals, research workers and students may benefit

WHERE FUNDING CAN BE GIVEN UK

TYPE OF GRANT At the discretion of the Trustees

RANGE OF GRANTS £100–£101,750

SAMPLE GRANTS £101,750 to Bradfield Foundation; £36,410 to National Hospital Development Foundation; £25,120 to Anne Bearpacker Almshouses; £11,900 to UWCA Scholarship; £10,000 to E D and F Man Charitable Trust; £10,000 to Friends of Tetbury Hospital; £2,000 to BTCV Lifestyle; £1,500 to Bournstream Trust for Disabled; £1,250 to World Pheasant Association; £1,100 to Cancer Relief Macmillan Fund

FINANCES *Year* 1996–97 *Income* £287,286 *Grants* £218,010

TRUSTEES M J C Stone, Louisa Stone, C R H Stone, Ms N J Stone, A J Stone

HOW TO APPLY To the address under Who To Apply To in writing

WHO TO APPLY TO M J C Stone, The M J C Stone Charitable Trust, Estate Office, Ozleworth Park, Wotton-under-Edge, Gloucestershire GL12 7QA

CC NO 283920   **ESTABLISHED** 1981

■ The Stone Foundation

WHAT IS FUNDED Charities dealing with drug and alcohol dependency. Supports 'Stone Workshops', which is committed to out patient therapeutic groups and educational workshops. Provides funding for the clinical application of Standards of Practice in treatment centre via EATA

WHO CAN BENEFIT Organisations benefiting substance misusers

WHERE FUNDING CAN BE GIVEN UK

SAMPLE GRANTS £11,200 to EATA; £10,000 to Chemical Dependency Centre; £500 to Life Anew Centre

FINANCES *Year* 1996 *Income* £139,763 *Grants* £26,200

TRUSTEES Lady Shauna Gosling, Dr R I Wolman, M Kirkwood

NOTES In 1997 direct charitable expenditure consisted of donations £26,200; project related consultancy £16,549 and Stone Workshops £63,547

HOW TO APPLY None required at present

WHO TO APPLY TO Lady Gosling, Chairman/Secretary, The Stone Foundation, 20 Wilton Row, The Courtyard, London SW1X 7NS *Tel* 0171-235 4871

CC NO 327998   **ESTABLISHED** 1988

■ The Alexander Stone Foundation

WHAT IS FUNDED Grants are awarded to charitable organisations which work to relieve poverty and distress and to promote art, religion and the common good. Special appeals in response to natural disasters and other catastrophes overseas are also eligible for help. Educational grants and scholarships are also awarded if applied for by recognised organisations or educational institutions

WHAT IS NOT FUNDED Grants are not awarded to: individuals; organisations which waste income on administration instead of fulfilling their charitable objectives; nor generally to charities which distribute money to other charitable organisations. Travel costs and expenses incurred in arranging or

attending conferences will not be met by the Foundation

WHO CAN BENEFIT Organisations benefiting at risk groups; disabled people; those disadvantaged by poverty; disaster victims and victims of famine. Also young adults; students; musicians; artists; and writers and poets. There are no restrictions on the religion or culture of the beneficiaries

WHERE FUNDING CAN BE GIVEN Scotland, particularly Glasgow, the rest of the UK, EU and overseas

HOW TO APPLY Applications should be made in writing to the Administrator and must be accompanied by the applicant's charity number and most up-to-date balance sheet. Grants are awarded at meetings of the Trustees which usually take place on 31 March, 30 June, 30 September and 31 December each year

WHO TO APPLY TO Robert Black, Administrator, The Alexander Stone Foundation, 36 Renfield Street, Glasgow G2 1LU

SC NO SCO 08261

■ The Stonewall Iris Trust

WHAT IS FUNDED Trustees are interested in a wide range of charitable issues particularly those affecting lesbian and gay communities. The advancement of the education of the public in relation to all aspects of discrimination in society

WHO CAN BENEFIT Organisations, particularly those benefiting gays and lesbians

WHERE FUNDING CAN BE GIVEN UK

FINANCES *Year* 1995 *Income* £26,082 *Grants* £13,278

TRUSTEES P St Clements, O Cole-Wilson, Sir Ian McKellen (Chair), Dr P H Rivas, S Fanshawe

NOTES The Trustees meet twice yearly

HOW TO APPLY Applications may be submitted throughout the year

WHO TO APPLY TO The Stonewall Iris Trust, Derek Rothera & Company, 339–340 Upper Street, London N1 0PD

CC NO 802664   **ESTABLISHED** 1989

■ Storaid Limited

WHAT IS FUNDED The relief of poverty amongst current and past employees of Wickes Group Company and their dependants; the advancement of education; and the relief of need due to age or sickness. Charity or voluntary umbrella bodies will be considered

WHO CAN BENEFIT Individuals and organisations benefiting people of all ages, students, and employees and ex-employees of Wickes Group Company and their dependents. Medical professionals and research workers may be considered. There is no restriction on the disease or medical condition suffered by the beneficiaries

WHERE FUNDING CAN BE GIVEN England, Scotland and Wales

TYPE OF GRANT Core costs, one-off, project, research, recurring costs and start-up costs will be considered. Funding may be given for up to one year

TRUSTEES M Von Brentano, W Grimsey, W J Hoskins

WHO TO APPLY TO K Stokes-Smith, Secretary, Storaid Limited, Wickes House, 120/138 Station Road, Harrow, Middlesex HA1 2QB

CC NO 1067975   **ESTABLISHED** 1998

616

Think carefully about every application. Is it justified?

■ The Samuel Storey Family Charitable Trust

WHAT IS FUNDED General charitable purposes

WHAT IS NOT FUNDED No grants to overseas causes. No grants to individuals

WHO CAN BENEFIT Registered charities. There are no restrictions on the age; professional and economic group; family situation; religion and culture; and social circumstances of; or disease or medical condition suffered by, the beneficiaries

WHERE FUNDING CAN BE GIVEN UK

SAMPLE GRANTS £2,500 to Winchester College; £2,000 to The Multiple Births Foundation; £1,000 to Cambridge Foundation; £1,000 to Countss Mountbatten House Campaign; £1,000 to Jubilee Sailing Trust; £1,000 to Lambeth Partnership; £1,000 to LINK; £1,000 to Ranworth PCC; £500 to Acorn Christian Healing Trust

FINANCES *Year* 1997 *Income* £55,376 *Grants* £21,215

TRUSTEES Sir Richard Storey, Bt, A D W Hoskyns, Hon Mrs J Cator, K Storey

WHO TO APPLY TO G A Toffs, The Samuel Storey Family Charitable Trust, Buckton House, 37 Abingdon Road, London W8 6AH

CC NO 267684   **ESTABLISHED** 1974

■ The Foundation of Edward Storey

WHAT IS FUNDED Individuals in need, the Foundation's almshouses, women's welfare organisations

WHO CAN BENEFIT Projects should primarily benefit women over 40, Church of England and those disadvantaged by poverty

WHERE FUNDING CAN BE GIVEN Cambridge

TYPE OF GRANT Funding for up to one year

FINANCES *Year* 1996–97 *Income* £861,404 *Grants* £151,855

TRUSTEES H Ballinger, N Blanning, P Brook, S Fleet, C Gilbraith, P Hadrill, J Marks, E Walser, S Young

HOW TO APPLY To the address under Who To Apply To in writing, including a description of the organisation and who their beneficiaries are

WHO TO APPLY TO Mrs D Lindsay, Clerk, The Foundation of Edward Storey, Storey's House, Mount Pleasant, Cambridge CB3 0BZ *Tel* 01223 364405 *Fax* 01223 321313

CC NO 203653   **ESTABLISHED** 1693

■ Peter Stormonth-Darling Charitable Trust

WHAT IS FUNDED Preference for heritage, education, health care and sports facilities

WHAT IS NOT FUNDED No unsolicited applications

WHO CAN BENEFIT Organisations benefiting children, young adults and sportsmen and women. There is no restriction on the disease or medical condition suffered by the beneficiaries

WHERE FUNDING CAN BE GIVEN UK and overseas

FINANCES *Year* 1996 *Income* £20,891 *Grants* £20,000

TRUSTEES J F M Rodwell, D M F Scott, P Stormonth-Darling

HOW TO APPLY **This Trust states that it does not respond to unsolicited applications**

WHO TO APPLY TO P Stormonth-Darling, Peter Stormonth-Darling Charitable Trust, 33 King William Street, London EC4R 9AS *Tel* 0171-280 2625

CC NO 1049946   **ESTABLISHED** 1995

■ The Stowmarket Relief Trust

WHAT IS FUNDED To provide assistance to people in conditions of need, hardship or distress, either generally or individually, who live in the town of Stowmarket, and, subject to the availability of income, people who live in the Civil Parishes of Stowupland, Creeting St Peter, Badley, Combs, Great Finborough, Onehouse, Haughley, and Old Newton with Dagworth, all in the county of Suffolk

WHAT IS NOT FUNDED Persons in full-time employment will not normally qualify for financial assistance, but there are possible exceptions, eg very large families, and low paid workers. Persons with capital in excess of the limit to qualify for Income Support benefit are normally ineligible

WHO CAN BENEFIT Persons in need of an item, service or facility, who, after receiving all the statutory benefits available to them, do not have the financial resources to meet the cost involved. There are no restrictions with regard to age or occupation of the prospective beneficiary, nor is there a limit in the amount or value of the grant which may be awarded to any beneficiary

WHERE FUNDING CAN BE GIVEN Stowmarket and surrounding parishes only

TYPE OF GRANT In cash or in kind. Normally one-off, but recurrent grants have been made in exceptional circumstances. Core costs, interest free loans, running costs and start-up costs are also considered. Funding is available for up to one year

RANGE OF GRANTS £20–£500, typical grant £250

SAMPLE GRANTS £1,800 towards the cost of an acting course; £1,575 for the purchase of an electric wheelchair; £1,550 for the purchase of an electric wheelchair; £1,000 as a donation to a special needs children playgroup; £1,000 towards living and educational expenses; £1,000 towards the cost of a handicapped children's pilgrimage; £1,000 towards the running expenses of a Good Neighbour Scheme; £940 towards the costs and expenses of a medical student; £650 for the purchase of a riser/recliner armchair; £600 towards the cost of purchasing an electric wheelchair

FINANCES *Year* 1996–97 *Income* £53,584 *Grants* £52,720

TRUSTEES The Committee: E Jones (Chairman), Mrs A V Lower, Mrs A B Moore, D H Hopgood, Rev T C Jones, W P Smith, R D Snell, R A Taylor

PUBLICATIONS General information sheet

NOTES An initial telephone call is advisable

HOW TO APPLY On a formal Application Form obtainable from, and returnable to the address under Who To Apply To. Unless there are exceptional circumstances, Applications will only be accepted from formal organisations or individuals, on behalf of the prospective beneficiary, who have knowledge of his/her needs, and family, and financial, circumstances, eg social workers; probation officers; Citizens' Advice Bureaux; GPs; welfare organisations, etc. Applications are dealt with expeditiously, and a decision can, usually, be expected within seven days of receipt of a fully completed Application Form

WHO TO APPLY TO R J James, The Stowmarket Relief Trust, 5 Oak Road, Stowmarket, Suffolk IP14 4DP *Tel* 01449 615657

CC NO 802572   **ESTABLISHED** 1986

■ Sir Henry Strakosch Memorial Trust

WHAT IS FUNDED To strengthen the bonds of unity between South Africa and the UK

WHAT IS NOT FUNDED By nomination only following invitations issued to specified universities

WHO CAN BENEFIT Graduates of Universities in the UK and South Africa

WHERE FUNDING CAN BE GIVEN The Republic of South Africa and UK

TYPE OF GRANT Scholarships at Cambridge University for graduates of South African Universities. Travel grants to enable Post Graduate Students of UK Universities to visit South Africa for educational purposes

RANGE OF GRANTS Individuals: £750–£10,608, organisations: £15,000–£215,000

SAMPLE GRANTS £215,000 to University of Western Cape; £215,000 to Wits Foundation; £15,000 to Link Africa; £14,250 to individuals, each receiving a grant of £750 for medical school electives; £10,608 to an individual for maintenance and travel grant to Cambridge University; £1,000 to an individual for special travel grant to South Africa

FINANCES *Year* 1996 *Income* £25,899
Grants £470,858

TRUSTEES K H Wallis, E Pavitt, I C Gray, H J Gaylard

NOTES The De Montfort University was due to receive £25,000 in both 1997 and 1998

HOW TO APPLY As advertised by the Universities or to the address under Who To Apply To

WHO TO APPLY TO Miss S A Butcher, Sir Henry Strakosch Memorial Trust, 1–3 Strand, London WC2N 5HA

CC NO 314135   **ESTABLISHED** 1950

■ The Strangward Trust

WHAT IS FUNDED Funding for care and treatment of physically and mentally handicapped people, particularly charities working in the field of the nursing service, hospice in the home, special schools, and holidays and outings

WHO CAN BENEFIT Small local projects, national organisations and individuals. Charities benefiting: children; young adults; disabled people and those suffering from arthritis and rheumatism; asthma; blood disorders and haemophilia; cancers; cerebral palsy; Crohn's disease; cystic fibrosis; hearing loss; mental illness; motor neurone disease; multiple sclerosis; muscular dystrophy; paediatric diseases; polio; spina bifida and hydrocephalus

WHERE FUNDING CAN BE GIVEN National, with preference to Lincolnshire, Northamptonshire, Bedfordshire, Cambridgeshire, Peterborough and Suffolk

TYPE OF GRANT One-off, capital, core costs. Funding is for one year or less

SAMPLE GRANTS £5,000 to RNIB - Rushton Hall for the purchase of equipment; £3,000 to an individual for the cost of specially adapted vehicle for disabled son; £3,000 to SCOPE for computer equipment; £2,500 to Northamptonshire Association for the Blind for Wardington Court hall project; £2,500 to The David Tolkien Trust for Stoke Mandeville, a donation towards National Spinal Injuries Centre; £2,500 to Hinwick Hall College of Further Education for Capital Appeal; £2,500 to Spadework for development of horticultural training centre; £2,000 to The Craft Community, a donation to assist in work being done; £2,000 to Lincolnshire County Council to provide an electrically operated bed, mattress, cover and bedding for an individual; £2,000 to BREAK for holiday and respite care

FINANCES *Year* 1995 *Income* £68,294
Grants £14,000

TRUSTEES Mrs T A Strangward, M Measures, J Higham

NOTES The founders intend to make donations from income generated by the Trust, preferably to smaller charities caring for physically or mentally handicapped people

HOW TO APPLY In writing

WHO TO APPLY TO J Higham, The Strangward Trust, Vincent Sykes, Solicitors, Montague House, Chancery Lane, Kettering, Northamptonshire NN14 4LN

CC NO 1036494   **ESTABLISHED** 1993

■ The Strasser Foundation

WHAT IS FUNDED General charitable purposes, at discretion of the Trustees

WHO CAN BENEFIT Organisations and individuals. There are no restrictions on the age; professional and economic group; family situation; religion and culture; and social circumstances of; or disease or medical condition suffered by, the beneficiaries

WHERE FUNDING CAN BE GIVEN Preferably Staffordshire and environs

TYPE OF GRANT One-off

RANGE OF GRANTS £100–£1,110

SAMPLE GRANTS £1,110 to Resettlement Project North Staffordshire for special needs; £1,000 to Ida Lees Welfare Centre for ambulance fund; £1,000 to Action Research for local project; £1,000 to Hearing Research Trust for research at Keel University; £800 to an individual for specialist tuition fees; £705 to Newcastle College for student support fund; £500 to Raleigh International for educational expeditions; £500 to Crackley Bank School for library books; £500 to Elizabeth Trust for emergency packs; £500 to Stafforshire University for contribution to a student

FINANCES *Year* 1996 *Income* £28,253
Grants £23,222

TRUSTEES A F Booth, FCA, A P Bell, MA, LLB

HOW TO APPLY No fixed dates. Acknowledged only with sae

WHO TO APPLY TO A F Booth, The Strasser Foundation, 28 Highway Lane, Keele, Newcastle-under-Lyme, Staffordshire ST5 5AN

CC NO 511703   **ESTABLISHED** 1978

■ The Street Foundation

WHAT IS FUNDED Profound and multiple learning disabilities in West Midlands only. This includes: respite care and care for carers; neurological research; special needs education; and study in engineering and science and technology

WHAT IS NOT FUNDED Generally projects that are not personally known to the Trustees. No grants to individuals

WHO CAN BENEFIT Children; young adults; disabled people; and those suffering from cerebral palsy

WHERE FUNDING CAN BE GIVEN Herefordshire and West Midlands

TYPE OF GRANT One-off for buildings and research. Funding is available for up to one year

RANGE OF GRANTS General grants less than £5,000

FINANCES *Year* 1996 *Income* £87,500
Grants £82,850

TRUSTEES R E L Smith, H R Smith, Ms M C Smith, Ms S J S Smith

NOTES Unsolicited telephone calls not welcome

HOW TO APPLY Write to address under Who To Apply To

WHO TO APPLY TO R E L Smith, Trustee, The Street Foundation, Kingsland House, Kingsland, Herefordshire HR6 9SG *Tel* 01568 708744 *Fax* 01568 708768

CC NO 1045229 **ESTABLISHED** 1995

■ Streynsham's Charity

WHAT IS FUNDED To advance education and welfare

WHO CAN BENEFIT Individuals and organisations benefiting: children and young adults; students; at risk groups; those disadvantaged by poverty; and socially isolated people

WHERE FUNDING CAN BE GIVEN Those residing in the Parish of St Dunstan and Holy Rood, Canterbury

FINANCES *Year* 1995–96 *Income* £24,804

TRUSTEES Thirteen trustees

HOW TO APPLY To the address under Who To Apply To in writing

WHO TO APPLY TO Mrs J McCulloch, Clerk, Streynsham's Charity, Langley, 13 South Canterbury Road, Canterbury, Kent CT1 3LH *Tel* 01227 761624

CC NO 214436 **ESTABLISHED** 1550

■ The Michael and Lotti Sturge Charitable Trust

WHAT IS FUNDED General charitable purposes

WHO CAN BENEFIT There are no restrictions on the age; professional and economic group; family situation; religion and culture; and social circumstances of; or disease or medical condition suffered by, the beneficiaries

WHERE FUNDING CAN BE GIVEN UK and overseas

TRUSTEES J C Dennis, Ms C M Sturge, Ms L Sturge, M W Sturge, N W Sturge

WHO TO APPLY TO M Sturge, Trustee, The Michael and Lotti Sturge Charitable Trust, 27 Hobgate, Acomb, York YO2 4HE

CC NO 1055618 **ESTABLISHED** 1996

■ The Sudborough Foundation

WHAT IS FUNDED Charitable grants or bursary grants to educational establishments for the benefit of students, or the establishment or maintenance of scholarship awards

WHAT IS NOT FUNDED The Trustees will not consider grants for expeditions or drama and dance courses or make grants to individuals

WHO CAN BENEFIT Organisations benefiting students

WHERE FUNDING CAN BE GIVEN UK

SAMPLE GRANTS £1,500 to the Gordon Robinson Memorial Trust; £1,500 to Leicester University; £1,500 to Peterborough Cathedral; £1,000 to Dennyside Bowling Association; £1,000 to Royal College of Music

FINANCES *Year* 1997 *Income* £21,981
Grants £17,250

TRUSTEES M D Engel (Chairman), R E Engel, LIB, Sir J Lowther, KCVO, CBE, JP, Mrs S E Markham, ACA, ATII, G Pollard, W M Reason, FCA, I E W Robinson, MRCS, LRCP

HOW TO APPLY Applications should be supported with an sae

WHO TO APPLY TO Max D Engel, The Sudborough Foundation, 4 York Road, Northampton NN1 5QG

CC NO 272323 **ESTABLISHED** 1976

■ Sudbury Common Lands Charity

WHAT IS FUNDED The support of Freemen of Sudbury, their widows/widowers and general charitable purposes benefiting the inhabitants of the town of Sudbury. In particular the support of voluntary and community organisations; churches; religious umbrella bodies and the provision of facilities for recreation

WHAT IS NOT FUNDED Relief of public funds and no grants to individuals

WHO CAN BENEFIT Local organisations benefiting young adults; older people; and widows and widowers

WHERE FUNDING CAN BE GIVEN Sudbury

TYPE OF GRANT One-off grants for buildings and other capital costs

RANGE OF GRANTS £500–£10,000

SAMPLE GRANTS £10,000 to Sudbury Christian Youth for Christian Youth Centre, a meeting place for young people; £9,330 to Sudbury Freemen's Trust, 25 percent of disposable income as per scheme; £7,500 to All Saints Church towards the Fabric Fund - new roof for the church hall; £6,089 to Sudbury Freemen's Society, 50 per cent grazing income as per scheme; £4,500 to Sudbury Municipal Charities to carry out scheme requirements; £1,500 to Helping Hands for wheelchair access ramp at resource centre; £1,000 to Sudbury Wanderers Football Club for goal posts/nets for boys and girls teams

FINANCES *Year* 1995 *Income* £63,243
Grants £17,000

TRUSTEES Cllr B Cann, G W Challacombe, Cllr J Frankham, M R Hills, Cllr N Irwin, D Kisby, Canon J Nurser, I C Parsonson, Mrs S Prior, P Richardson, P Scott, Cllr R Titmus, J Wardman, V Waters, Cllr Mrs E Wiles, A Wheeler

NOTES The Charity aims to 'top-out' projects and not start them

HOW TO APPLY To the address under Who To Apply To in writing by 1 October, including recent accounts

WHO TO APPLY TO A C Walters, Clerk, Sudbury Common Lands Charity, Longstop Cottage, The Street, Lawshall, Bury St Edmunds, Suffolk IP29 4QA *Tel* 01284 828219

CC NO 212222 **ESTABLISHED** 1897

■ Sueberry Ltd

WHAT IS FUNDED Jewish organisations, medical, educational and welfare charities

WHO CAN BENEFIT Jewish organisations, national welfare and medical organisations benefiting: children and young adults; Jewish people; at risk groups; those disadvantaged by poverty and socially isolated people. There is no restriction on the disease or medical condition suffered by the beneficiaries

WHERE FUNDING CAN BE GIVEN UK and overseas
TYPE OF GRANT Largely recurrent
FINANCES *Year* 1997 *Income* £46,649 *Grants* £31,273
TRUSTEES J Davis, Mrs M Davis, Mrs H Davis
HOW TO APPLY To the address under Who To Apply To in writing
WHO TO APPLY TO Mrs M Davis, Sueberry Ltd, 11 Clapton Common, London E5 9AA
CC NO 256566 **ESTABLISHED** 1968

■ Suffolk Historic Churches Trust

WHAT IS FUNDED The preservation, repair, maintenance, restoration and improvement of churches in the area Where Funding Can Be Given
WHO CAN BENEFIT Churches
WHERE FUNDING CAN BE GIVEN Suffolk
TYPE OF GRANT Buildings
FINANCES *Year* 1997 *Income* £151,679 *Grants* £141,265
TRUSTEES The Lord Tollemache, DL (Chairman), Mrs H Agate, OBE, A Barker, Ven Archdeacon J Cox, Hon J Ganzoni, DL, P Hickie, Mrs D Hunt, Miss M MacRae, DL, Mrs F Parkinson, Mrs J Rowe, Mrs C van Melzen, B Walker, R Williams, J Wolton
HOW TO APPLY To the address under Who To Apply To in writing
WHO TO APPLY TO M Favell, Suffolk Historic Churches Trust, Mayfields, Holton St Mary, Colchester, Essex CO7 6NL
CC NO 267047 **ESTABLISHED** 1973

■ Sulgrave Charitable Trust

WHAT IS FUNDED To assist the Sulgrave Boys' Club and other young people's clubs in the London area
WHAT IS NOT FUNDED Cash grants to young people's clubs in the London area only. No grants to individuals
WHO CAN BENEFIT Young people's clubs
WHERE FUNDING CAN BE GIVEN London area
TYPE OF GRANT Buildings, capital, core costs and running costs. Funding available for up to one year
SAMPLE GRANTS £35,529 to Sulgrave Club for running costs
FINANCES *Year* 1997 *Income* £35,529 *Grants* £35,529
TRUSTEES M B Fellingham, P J Grant, London Federation of Clubs for Young People Incorp
HOW TO APPLY Grants to Sulgrave Boys' Club and London Federation of Clubs for Young People Incorp only – no other applications considered
WHO TO APPLY TO M B Fellingham, Sulgrave Charitable Trust, Penningtons, Solicitors, Highfield, Brighton Road, Godalming, Surrey GU7 1NS
CC NO 231952 **ESTABLISHED** 1930

■ The Late Misses A N Summer's and I May's Charitable Settlement

WHAT IS FUNDED Four named ecclesiastic, children and animal societies and to institutions and societies for promoting research into and relief of cancer, rheumatism and blindness and for promoting the relief of hunger in any part of the world, institutions and societies for promoting the welfare of clergy and ex-servicemen and their families and dependants. Funds are fully committed to the support of charities whose aims are either set out in the Trust Deed or for which the Trustees feel would have been those supported by the Settlors

WHO CAN BENEFIT There are no restrictions on the age; professional and economic group; family situation; religion and culture; and social circumstances of; or disease or medical condition suffered by, the beneficiaries
WHERE FUNDING CAN BE GIVEN UK and overseas
TYPE OF GRANT Varying cash distributions
SAMPLE GRANTS £3,000 to the St George's Music Trust; £750 to Additional Curates Society; £750 to NSPCC; £750 to RSPCA; £750 to USPG
FINANCES *Year* 1996 *Income* £18,529 *Grants* £26,000
TRUSTEES Lloyds Bank plc, D J Bellew
HOW TO APPLY Applications received in writing are considered half yearly in March and September
WHO TO APPLY TO The Late Misses Summer's and May's Charitable Settlement, UK Trust Centre, Lloyds Private Banking Ltd, The Clock House, 22–26 Ock Street, Abingdon, Oxfordshire OX14 5SW
CC NO 239980 **ESTABLISHED** 1964

■ Sir John Sumner's Trust

WHAT IS FUNDED Mainly (a) grants to persons in necessitous circumstances and (b) donations to charitable organisations in the fields of community facilities and services, art, literature, archaeology and research (other than experiments involving animals). Some grants may be made for education in nursing and mental care
WHAT IS NOT FUNDED Party politics, religion are not funded, though purely social efforts connected with religious denominations are not excluded. Research where vivisection is involved
WHO CAN BENEFIT There are no restrictions on the age; professional and economic group; family situation; religion and culture; and social circumstances of; or disease or medical condition suffered by, the beneficiaries
WHERE FUNDING CAN BE GIVEN UK but prefer Midlands
TYPE OF GRANT One-off grants to individuals plus occasional quarterly to fund education. Normally one-off amounts to charitable organisations
FINANCES *Year* 1996 *Income* £33,820 *Grants* £26,558
TRUSTEES J B Sumner, JP (Chairman), Mrs E J Wood, J M G Fea, Lady Richard Wellesley, A B Sumner
NOTES Grants for education are only made in exceptional circumstances and generally to those who are undertaking courses concerned with nursing or mental care
HOW TO APPLY Personal applications from students or organisations by letter giving details of requirements and finances. All other applications from individuals must be completed on pro-forma supplied at request and generally supported by social services departments, hospital officials or the Probation Service
WHO TO APPLY TO The Secretary, Sir John Sumner's Trust, 8th Floor, Union Chambers, 63 Temple Row, Birmingham B2 5LT
CC NO 218620 **ESTABLISHED** 1927

■ The Sumray Charitable Trust

WHAT IS FUNDED Principally Jewish charities
WHO CAN BENEFIT To benefit Jewish people
WHERE FUNDING CAN BE GIVEN UK
RANGE OF GRANTS Below £250–£10,000

SAMPLE GRANTS £10,000 to Jewish Care; £1,000 to Friends of the Art Museum of Israel; £1,000 to Friends of Hebrew University; £500 to Institute of Jewish Policy Research; £500 to the Board of Deputies Charitable Trust; £500 to Nightingale House; £500 to Maccabiah

FINANCES *Year* 1997 *Income* £33,533 *Grants* £18,620

TRUSTEES M Sumray, Mrs C Sumray, M M Davis, M D Frankel

WHO TO APPLY TO P Emanual, The Sumray Charitable Trust, c/o Citroen Wells & Co, Devonshire House, 1 Devonshire Street, London W1N 2DR

CC NO 270270   ESTABLISHED 1975

■ The Sunflower Trust

WHAT IS FUNDED Mental health. Most grants are awarded to individuals but support has also been given to organisations

WHO CAN BENEFIT Those suffering from mental illness

WHERE FUNDING CAN BE GIVEN Scotland

TRUSTEES I R Clark, J Fenston, Mrs S M Rankin

PUBLICATIONS Accounts are available from the Trust

HOW TO APPLY Applications should be made in writing to the address below

WHO TO APPLY TO The Secretary, The Sunflower Trust, Messrs Dundas & Wilson, Saltire Court, 20 Castle Terrace, Edinburgh EH21 2EN

SC NO SCO 20645

■ The Surrey Historic Buildings Trust Limited

WHAT IS FUNDED The restoration and conservation of significant architectural features through the provision of small grants to individuals and small organisations

WHAT IS NOT FUNDED Grants will not be given for buildings owned by local authorities or for the upkeep of places of worship

WHO CAN BENEFIT Local organisations and individuals

WHERE FUNDING CAN BE GIVEN Surrey

TYPE OF GRANT One-off and project

RANGE OF GRANTS Up to £1,000 per project

SAMPLE GRANTS £1,000 to firm of architects for repairs to a mediaeval wall painting; £1,000 to Brooklands Museum, Weybridge for building restoration; £1,000 to Farnham Trust for feasibility study of the Farnham Pottery Project; £1,000 to Watts Chapel, Compton for restoration of Aldershot Chapel Altarpiece; £1,000 to Painshill Park, Cobham for repair and restoration of the Grotto

FINANCES *Year* 1996–97 *Income* £20,606 *Grants* £9,600

TRUSTEES Mrs P Adamson, Mrs J Ash, M Blower, H P Chetwynd-Stapylton, Mrs A Fraser, M Gammon, Mrs C Gerrard, P J Gray, J Griffiths, A Hayes-Allen, R Kelsall, D Morris, R Rothwell, D J Turner

PUBLICATIONS *The Surrey Style* by Roderick Gradidge

HOW TO APPLY Application forms are available from the Conservation Officer at The Surrey Historic Buildings Trust Limited, County Hall, Kingston-upon-Thames, Surrey KT1 2DN **Tel**: 0181–541 9476 or 9181–541 9419. Completed forms should be accompanied by two copies of the estimated cost of the work and a photograph

WHO TO APPLY TO Conservation Officer, The Surrey Historic Buildings Trust Limited, County Hall, Kingston-upon-Thames, Surrey KT1 2DN *Tel* 0181-541 9001/9019

CC NO 279240   ESTABLISHED 1980

■ Surrey Voluntary Service Council

WHAT IS FUNDED Advancing education; furthering health; relieving poverty, distress or sickness; improving the skill of country craftsmen; and other charitable purposes

WHO CAN BENEFIT To benefit: those in education; country craftsmen; the sick; at risk groups; those disadvantaged by poverty; and socially isolated people

WHERE FUNDING CAN BE GIVEN Surrey

FINANCES *Year* 1998 *Income* £299,509 *Grants* £1,700

TRUSTEES Ms A Cooper, MBE, Terry Daly, FCA, JP, T Allenby, D Beazley, L Clark, FCA, Ms M Kearney, JP, Cllr B Oswald, T Prideaux, JP, Ms C Stevens, CC

PUBLICATIONS Annual Review

WHO TO APPLY TO Miss M Foyster, Surrey Voluntary Service Council, Astolat, Coniers Way, New Inn Lane, Burpham, Guilford, Surrey GU4 7HL

CC NO 1056527   ESTABLISHED 1996

■ The Ann Susman Charitable Trust

WHAT IS FUNDED General charitable purposes. Funds already committed to charities known to Trustees

WHO CAN BENEFIT There are no restrictions on the age; professional and economic group; family situation; religion and culture; and social circumstances of; or disease or medical condition suffered by, the beneficiaries

WHERE FUNDING CAN BE GIVEN UK

RANGE OF GRANTS £100–£1,000

SAMPLE GRANTS £1,000 to Anglo Israel Association; £1,000 to Beth Shalom; £1,000 to British Friends of Neve Shalom; £1,000 to CBF World Jewish Relief; £1,000 to GRET

FINANCES *Year* 1998 *Income* £15,586 *Grants* £13,850

TRUSTEES Mrs A Susman, D R Susman, S N Susman, Mrs J Skidmore

HOW TO APPLY Trustees prefer submissions from those known to them personally

WHO TO APPLY TO The Ann Susman Charitable Trust, H W Fisher & Co, Acre House, 11–15 William Road, London NW1 3ER

CC NO 240469   ESTABLISHED 1963

■ The Sussex Historic Churches Trust

WHAT IS FUNDED The preservation, repair, maintenance and restoration of churches in the area Where Funding Can Be Given

WHAT IS NOT FUNDED Modifications, improvements, additions and internal decorations will not be considered

WHO CAN BENEFIT Churches of any denomination over 100 years old and of some architectural or historical significance

WHERE FUNDING CAN BE GIVEN Sussex

TYPE OF GRANT Interest free loans and buildings will be considered

RANGE OF GRANTS £1,000–£10,000, typical grant £5,000

SAMPLE GRANTS The following grants were for fabric preservation:; £5,000 to St Paul, Elsted; £5,000 to St Mary, Iping; £5,000 to St Margaret, Warnham; £5,000 to St Mary, Westham; £4,000 to St Mary the Virgin, Burpham; £4,000 to St Mary the Virgin, Fittleworth; £4,000 to Christ Church, Fairwarp; £4,000 to St Pancras, Kingston; £3,000 to St Mary the Virgin, Shipley; £3,000 to St Peter, Southease

FINANCES *Year* 1997 *Income* £85,500 *Grants* £56,500

HOW TO APPLY To the address under Who To Apply To in writing

WHO TO APPLY TO The Secretary, The Sussex Historic Churches Trust, Canon Gate House, Canon Lane, Chichester, West Sussex PO19 1PU

CC NO 282159   **ESTABLISHED** 1981

■ Adrienne & Leslie Sussman Charitable Trust

WHAT IS FUNDED General charitable purposes

WHAT IS NOT FUNDED Grants will not be made to: individuals; local branches of national charities, except within London Borough of Barnet

WHO CAN BENEFIT Registered charities only. There are no restrictions on the age; professional and economic group; family situation; religion and culture; and social circumstances of; or disease or medical condition suffered by, the beneficiaries

WHERE FUNDING CAN BE GIVEN Will consider England, but prefer London and London Borough of Barnet

SAMPLE GRANTS £10,425 to Children and Youth Aliyah; £4,000 to Norwood Ravenswood; £3,000 to Sidney Sussex CLL; £2,515 to Child Resettlement; £2,485 to Finchley Synagogue; £2,060 to Jewish Care; £1,500 to Nightingale House; £1,110 to Chai – Lifeline; £1,050 to B'nai B'rith Hillel Fund; £750 to BF Shvut Ami

FINANCES *Year* 1997 *Income* £48,814 *Grants* £40,310

TRUSTEES L Sussman, Mrs A H Sussman, M Paisner, MA, LLM

WHO TO APPLY TO Mrs A H Sussman, Adrienne & Leslie Sussman Charitable Trust, 25 Tillingbourne Gardens, London NW3 3JJ

CC NO 274955   **ESTABLISHED** 1977

■ The Sutasoma Trust

WHAT IS FUNDED Assisting students with the cost of one-off projects related to their studies in the fields of the social sciences and humanities; general charitable purposes

WHO CAN BENEFIT Individuals and organisations benefiting students

WHERE FUNDING CAN BE GIVEN UK and overseas

TYPE OF GRANT Some recurrent, other one-off

RANGE OF GRANTS £500–£10,000

SAMPLE GRANTS £10,000 to Lucy Cavendish College Research Fellowship; £10,000 to University College London Research Fellowship; £3,000 to Emslie Horniman Anthropological Scholarship Fund; £3,000 to Haverford College; £3,000 to Merhamet; £2,618 to Collegio Papio; £2,000 to the Cambodia Trust; £2,000 to Pestalozzi Children's Trust; £2,000 to Radcliffe Brown Trust Fund for Social Anthropological Research; £2,000 to Universitas Udayana

FINANCES *Year* 1996 *Income* £77,155 *Grants* £57,229

TRUSTEES J H R Carver, M K Hobart, Dr A R Hobart, M A Burgaver, J M Lichenstein

NOTES The Trust incorporates the Sutasoma Small Projects Award Fund, small single payments to full time students for one-off projects related to their studies

HOW TO APPLY To the address under Who To Apply To in writing

WHO TO APPLY TO Miss Lynn Wickes, Trust Administrator, The Sutasoma Trust, Palmer Wheeldon, Daedalus House, Station Road, Cambridge CB1 2RE *Tel* 01223 355933

CC NO 803301   **ESTABLISHED** 1990

■ Sutton Nursing Association

WHAT IS FUNDED Community nursing, including care in the community and day centres; medical equipment for hospitals; and grants for charities working with mentally and physically handicapped people. Individuals who are sick and in need. Professional and voluntary umbrella bodies

WHAT IS NOT FUNDED No grants for expenditure not associated with sickness and need

WHO CAN BENEFIT Individuals, local and national organisations benefiting disabled people and those disadvantaged by poverty. There is no restriction on the age, or disease or medical condition suffered by the beneficiaries

WHERE FUNDING CAN BE GIVEN Sutton only

TYPE OF GRANT One-off grants only

RANGE OF GRANTS Usually not more than £3,000

FINANCES *Year* 1997 *Income* £38,656 *Grants* £24,939

TRUSTEES Committee: Mrs M Gordon-Jones (Chairman), J R Mott (Vice Chairman), Dr F R Assinder, Mrs J Alexander, Mrs S Anderson, Miss I Boreham, Mrs M Finnegan, Dr P E Heywood, S R Hobbs, D N Skingle (Secretary/Treasurer), R B Whellock

NOTES Our area is restricted to the London Borough of Sutton

HOW TO APPLY To the address under Who To Apply To in writing giving details of funds raised towards expenditure and, if relevant, individual's circumstances

WHO TO APPLY TO D N Skingle, Secretary/Treasurer, Sutton Nursing Association, 3 Glebe Road, Cheam, Sutton, Surrey SM2 7NS *Tel* 0181-770 1095 *Fax* 0181-770 1094

CC NO 203686   **ESTABLISHED** 1925

■ The Sutton Trust

WHAT IS FUNDED (a) Educational opportunities for young people in the state sector with a particular emphasis on recognising the special needs of academically able young people from non-privileged backgrounds. To this end, the Trust will support projects that are concerned with raising their aspirations and developing their potential within a formal education setting. (b) Projects which address the issue of widening access to universities. (c) Experimental schemes addressed to problems of early learning in the under three age group and including involvement of parents in stimulating their children's early mental development

WHAT IS NOT FUNDED Scholarships, assisted places replacement schemes, sports and arts projects, and individuals are not considered for funding

WHO CAN BENEFIT Children to the age of three and their parents/carers. Young people from eight to eighteen years of age. Academics, students, and teachers and governesses are considered

WHERE FUNDING CAN BE GIVEN UK only

TYPE OF GRANT Core costs, feasibility studies, interest free loans, one-off, project, research, recurring costs, running costs, salaries and start-up costs. Funding is available for up to three years. Capital and equipment grants are not considered

RANGE OF GRANTS First year of Trust, average grant not yet established

TRUSTEES P Lampl, K Lampl

HOW TO APPLY Initial telephone calls are welcome. Guidelines are available. There is no application form

WHO TO APPLY TO Ms L Barbour, Administrator, The Sutton Trust, 5 Lower Belgrave Street, London SW1W 0NR *Tel* 0171-730 5600 *Fax* 0171-730 1209 *E-mail* suttontrust@compuserve.com

CC NO 1067197   **ESTABLISHED** 1998

■ Swan Mountain Trust

WHAT IS FUNDED To support organisations catering for ex-offenders, offenders and mentally ill people. Also training for personal and community development, vocational training and health education

WHAT IS NOT FUNDED No grants to national or large organisations, or to large appeals. No grants for debt repayment or running costs

WHO CAN BENEFIT Small and new organisations and projects benefiting ex-offenders, offenders and those who are mentally ill

WHERE FUNDING CAN BE GIVEN UK

TYPE OF GRANT Usually one-off for specific activity or item of equipment

RANGE OF GRANTS Up to £500

FINANCES *Year* 1997 *Income* £18,085 *Grants* £16,877

TRUSTEES Ms D Carter, Mrs J R Hargreaves, C Younger

NOTES Please telephone on Wednesday afternoons if possible

HOW TO APPLY To the address under Who To Apply To. Telephone calls to discuss possible application welcome. All applications should include annual report and accounts and outline budget if possible. All appropriate applications will be acknowledged

WHO TO APPLY TO Mrs J R Hargreaves, Swan Mountain Trust, 7 Mount Vernon, London NW3 6QS *Tel* 0171-794 2486 *Fax* 0171-794 2486

CC NO 275594   **ESTABLISHED** 1977

■ The Swan Trust

WHAT IS FUNDED General charitable purposes

WHO CAN BENEFIT Registered charities. There are no restrictions on the age; professional and economic group; family situation; religion and culture; and social circumstances of; or disease or medical condition suffered by, the beneficiaries

WHERE FUNDING CAN BE GIVEN UK

RANGE OF GRANTS £5–£5,000

SAMPLE GRANTS £5,000 to Magdalen College Development Trust; £4,000 to Dorothy Kerin Trust; £3,000 to British Museum Development Trust; £1,500 to The National Trust; £1,000 to London City Ballet; £1,000 to Painshill Park Trust; £1,000 to Soane Monuments Trust; £750 to Kensington Day Centre; £6,000 to Royal National Theatre; £500 to Hospice in the Weald

FINANCES *Year* 1996 *Income* £42,950 *Grants* £26,085

TRUSTEES The Committee

WHO TO APPLY TO The Secretary, The Swan Trust, The Cowdray Trust Ltd, Pollen House, 10–12 Cork Street, London W1X 1PD

CC NO 261442   **ESTABLISHED** 1970

■ The Swann-Morton Foundation

WHAT IS FUNDED The advancement of education and the relief of poverty and suffering. Particularly: arts, culture and recreation; health; conservation and environment; and various community services

WHAT IS NOT FUNDED No grants are given for payment of household costs

WHO CAN BENEFIT Individuals and organisations benefiting: children; young adults; medical professionals, nurses and doctors; students; disabled people; and those disadvantaged by poverty. There is no restrictions on the disease or medical condition suffered by the beneficiaries

WHERE FUNDING CAN BE GIVEN UK

RANGE OF GRANTS £50–£4,000. Average £750

SAMPLE GRANTS £4,000 to Royal Hallamshire Hospital, Sheffield for medical equipment; £4,000 to Weston Park Hospital, Sheffield for medical equipment; £4,000 to Northern General Hospital, Sheffield for medical equipment; £4,000 to St Lukes Hospice, Sheffield for medical equipment; £4,000 to Sheffield Children's Hospital for medical equipment; £4,000 to The Jessop Hospital for Women, Sheffield for medical equipment; £2,500 to Sheffield Macmillan Support Team for medical equipment; £2,500 to Sheffield University for student grants; £2,000 to Crown Hill Workshops, Sheffield for general equipment

FINANCES *Year* 1997 *Income* £66,364 *Grants* £68,381

TRUSTEES J P Barker, R Fell, M J McGinley

HOW TO APPLY Applications in writing only to the address under Who To Apply To

WHO TO APPLY TO R Fell, Swann-Morton Foundation, Owlerton Green, Sheffield S6 2BJ *Tel* 0114-234 4231 *Fax* 0114-231 4966

CC NO 271925   **ESTABLISHED** 1976

■ Swansea and Brecon Diocesan Board of Finance Ltd

WHAT IS FUNDED To promote, aid and assist the work of the Church in Wales in general and in particular within the Diocese of Swansea and Brecon

WHAT IS NOT FUNDED Grants or donations are generally restricted to parishes of the Diocese of Swansea and Brecon, to Diocesan and Provincial activities generally and to certain overseas Christian charities and missions. Grants are made to secular charities only in exceptional circumstances

WHO CAN BENEFIT Parochial and other organisations of the Diocese of Swansea and Brecon. Overseas Christian missions may also benefit

WHERE FUNDING CAN BE GIVEN Mainly within the Diocese of Swansea and Brecon, and Christian missions overseas

TYPE OF GRANT One-off or recurrent as appropriate

FINANCES *Year* 1996 *Income* £1,080,193

TRUSTEES Executive Committee

PUBLICATIONS Annual Report and Accounts

NOTES Most of the annual income is reserved to support the ministry of the Church in Wales and Diocesan activities and administration

WHO TO APPLY TO The Secretary to the Board, Swansea and Brecon Diocesan Board of Finance Ltd, The Diocesan Centre, Cathedral Close, Brecon, Powys LD3 9DP

CC NO 249810   **ESTABLISHED** 1967

■ Swaziland Charitable Trust

WHAT IS FUNDED To further settlement in Swaziland of local farmers

WHO CAN BENEFIT Organisations benefiting farmers in Swaziland

WHERE FUNDING CAN BE GIVEN Swaziland

TYPE OF GRANT One-off for a specific project

SAMPLE GRANTS £4,500 to Swaziland Benevolent Trust for the settlement of local farmers

FINANCES *Year* 1996 *Income* £18,672
Grants £4,500

TRUSTEES The Barbinder Trust

WHO TO APPLY TO Gordon Lawrence, Swaziland Charitable Trust, 30 The Pound, Bromham, Chippenham SN15 2HF

CC NO 257666   **ESTABLISHED** 1968

■ The Walter Swindon Charitable Trust

WHAT IS FUNDED General charitable purposes. The Trust makes contributions to charities and worthy causes

WHO CAN BENEFIT There are no restrictions on the age; professional and economic group; family situation; religion and culture; and social circumstances of; or disease or medical condition suffered by, the beneficiaries

WHERE FUNDING CAN BE GIVEN UK

SAMPLE GRANTS £500 to Alzheimer's Disease Society; £250 to The Story of Christmas 1993; £50 to Scottish Children's Hospital; £50 to Ezunah

FINANCES *Year* 1997 *Income* £34,881

TRUSTEES W Swindon, Mrs S R Swindon

WHO TO APPLY TO W Swindon, The Walter Swindon Charitable Trust, 34 Hampstead Grove, London NW3 6SR

CC NO 273105   **ESTABLISHED** 1977

■ The Swinfen Broun Charitable Trust

WHAT IS FUNDED Support for public buildings and facilities and general charitable purposes in Lichfield

WHAT IS NOT FUNDED No grants for the benefit of relief of poverty or ecclesiastical charities

WHO CAN BENEFIT Those living in Lichfield

WHERE FUNDING CAN BE GIVEN Lichfield

SAMPLE GRANTS £12,500 to National Arboretum; £5,000 to Lichfield Mysteries; £3,991 to Stowe Teaching Unit; £3,250 to Clinton House; £3,150 to Lichfield Festival; £2,000 to King Edward VI School; £1,615 to Lichfield RUFC; £800 to Lichfield Saracens Skater Hockey Club; £799 to Lichfield Arts Centre; £750 to Lichfield District Arts Association

FINANCES *Year* 1997 *Income* £27,324
Grants £39,862

TRUSTEES D L Bailey, Mrs M Barratt, J R Brooks, G W Deacon, Mrs A Hall, J A Hopping, Mrs A H R Johnson, J R T Mercer, A O'Donnell, B M Pretty, J N Wilks, W J Wilson

HOW TO APPLY To the address under Who To Apply To in writing

WHO TO APPLY TO J A Haggett, Clerk, The Swinfen Broun Charitable Trust, Moseley Chapman & Skemp, 18 Bore Street, Lichfield, Staffordshire WS13 6LW

CC NO 503515   **ESTABLISHED** 1973

■ John Swire 1989 Charitable Trust

WHAT IS FUNDED General charitable purposes

WHO CAN BENEFIT There are no restrictions on the age; professional and economic group; family situation; religion and culture; and social circumstances of; or disease or medical condition suffered by, the beneficiaries

WHERE FUNDING CAN BE GIVEN UK

FINANCES *Year* 1996 *Income* £153,224
Grants £113,739

TRUSTEES Sir John Swire, B N Swire, J S Swire, Lady Swire, M C Robinson

WHO TO APPLY TO B N Swire, John Swire 1989 Charitable Trust, c/o John Swire and Sons Ltd, Swire House, 59 Buckingham Gate, London SW1E 6AJ

CC NO 802142   **ESTABLISHED** 1989

■ The Swire Educational Trust

WHAT IS FUNDED The Trust supports a variety of scholarship schemes for overseas students to study at universities and colleges in the UK and elsewhere

WHO CAN BENEFIT Institutions and overseas students

WHERE FUNDING CAN BE GIVEN Overseas

FINANCES *Year* 1997 *Income* £355,297
Grants £473,832

TRUSTEES Sir Adrian Swire, Sir John Swire, G D W Swire, C J M Hardie, G C Docherty, M J B Todhunter, B N Swire, Baroness Dunn

NOTES Total grants awarded in 1997 were: for tuition fees £226,633; for allowances £190,588; for sundry expenses £36,632; and for sundry grants £19,979

HOW TO APPLY Applications are not sought

WHO TO APPLY TO G C Pope, Secretary, The Swire Educational Trust, c/o John Swire & Sons Ltd, Swire House, 59 Buckingham Gate, London SW1E 6AJ

CC NO 328366   **ESTABLISHED** 1989

■ The Hugh and Ruby Sykes Charitable Trust

WHAT IS FUNDED Principally to support local charities but some major national charities are supported and the Trust has major commitments with several medical charities. It is the policy of the Trust to distribute income and preserve capital

WHO CAN BENEFIT To benefit sick people. There is no restriction on the disease or medical condition suffered by the beneficiaries

WHERE FUNDING CAN BE GIVEN Principally South Yorkshire and Derbyshire

FINANCES *Year* 1997 *Income* £149,595
Grants £275,335

TRUSTEES Sir H Sykes, Lady Sykes

HOW TO APPLY To the address under Who To Apply To in writing. In order to save administration costs, negative replies are not sent. If the Trustees are able to consider a request for support, it is intended to express interest within one month

WHO TO APPLY TO Hugh Sykes, The Hugh and Ruby Sykes Charitable Trust, Bamford Hall, Bamford, Hope Valley, Sheffield, South Yorkshire S30 2AU
CC NO 327648   **ESTABLISHED** 1987

■ The Verden Sykes Trust

WHAT IS FUNDED Grants are awarded to organisations across a broad range of causes: Christian mission and churches; pensions for retired ministers; work with young people; religious education and music; education for adults and children; the welfare of the elderly and infirm; research into physical and mental instability and disease; the relief of poverty; and the victims of natural disasters worldwide
WHAT IS NOT FUNDED No grants to individuals. Grants are only made to registered charities
WHO CAN BENEFIT Charities benefiting children, young adults and older people, clergy, musicians, Christians, those disadvantaged by poverty, and victims of natural disasters. There is no restriction on the disease or medical condition suffered by the beneficiaries
WHERE FUNDING CAN BE GIVEN UK, particularly Scotland
FINANCES *Year* 1996 *Income* £20,000
         Grants £20,000
TRUSTEES R Ellis, Mrs A McCallum, Rev J R McLaren, Mrs I Merrilees, Mrs P G Robbie, N Wilson, A J Winfield
HOW TO APPLY Applications should be made on a form which is available from the Administrator at the address below
WHO TO APPLY TO Mrs Irene Merrilees, Administrator, The Verden Sykes Trust, 20 Forvie Circle, Bridge of Don, Aberdeen AB22 8TA
SC NO SCO 07281   **ESTABLISHED** 1982

■ The Sylvanus Charitable Trust

WHAT IS FUNDED The traditional Catholic church and animal welfare, including wildlife sanctuaries
WHAT IS NOT FUNDED The Trust does not give grants to expeditions, scholarships or individuals
WHO CAN BENEFIT Organisation benefiting Roman Catholics
WHERE FUNDING CAN BE GIVEN Overseas
TYPE OF GRANT One-off and recurring
FINANCES *Year* 1997 *Income* £63,000
         Grants £68,000
TRUSTEES J C Vernor Miles, A D Gemmill
NOTES The income of this Trust is normally fully committed
WHO TO APPLY TO J C Vernor Miles, The Sylvanus Charitable Trust, Vernor Miles & Noble, 5 Raymond Buildings, Grays Inn, London WC1R 5DD
CC NO 259520   **ESTABLISHED** 1968

■ The Stella Symons Charitable Trust

WHAT IS FUNDED To provide assistance to organisations operating in fields where specific identifiable needs can be shown and which are in the opinion of the Trustees not adequately catered for or likely to have large scale popular appeal. Charities working in the fields of: residential facilities and services; infrastructure, support and development; the advancement of religion; arts, culture and recreation; health; conservation and environment; education and training; and social care and development will be considered
WHAT IS NOT FUNDED The Trustees do not normally favour projects which substitute the statutory obligations of the state or projects which in their opinion should be commercially viable operations per se. No grants to individuals or politically biased organisations
WHO CAN BENEFIT There are no restrictions on the age; professional and economic group; family situation; religion and culture of; or disease or medical condition suffered by, the beneficiaries. There may be few restrictions on their social circumstances
WHERE FUNDING CAN BE GIVEN UK and international projects with some funds reserved for projects and organisations local to Shipston on Stour
TYPE OF GRANT Outright gifts and larger sums on loan on beneficial terms. Buildings, capital, core costs, one-off, project, research, recurring and running costs, salaries, and start-up costs. Funding for up to and over three years will be considered
RANGE OF GRANTS £10–£5,000; average grant £200
FINANCES *Year* 1997 *Income* £54,518
         Grants £55,600
TRUSTEES M E Bosley, J S S Bosley, K A Willis
NOTES The Trustees will consider all applications submitted but regrettably will not be able to support all that they might wish to
HOW TO APPLY By post to address under Who To Apply To with no follow-up, please
WHO TO APPLY TO J S S Bosley, The Stella Symons Charitable Trust, 20 Mill Street, Shipston on Stour, Warwickshire CV36 4AW
CC NO 259638   **ESTABLISHED** 1968

■ The Synthite Charities Fund

WHAT IS FUNDED General charitable purposes
WHO CAN BENEFIT There are no restrictions on the age; professional and economic group; family situation; religion and culture; and social circumstances of; or disease or medical condition suffered by, the beneficiaries
WHERE FUNDING CAN BE GIVEN Mold, Flintshire
TRUSTEES B Chitty, Ms F E Hughes, G Roberts, Ms J Taylor, G D Williams
WHO TO APPLY TO G D Williams, Treasurer, The Synthite Charities Fund, Synthite Limited, Denbigh Road, Mold, Flintshire CH7 1BT
CC NO 1057395   **ESTABLISHED** 1996

■ The TFM Cash Challenge Appeal

WHAT IS FUNDED General charitable purposes
WHO CAN BENEFIT There are no restrictions on the age; professional and economic group; family situation; religion and culture; and social circumstances of; or disease or medical condition suffered by, the beneficiaries
WHERE FUNDING CAN BE GIVEN Teeside, North Yorkshire and County Durham (South) bounded by Peterlee to the North, Thirsk to the South, Barnard Castle to the West and East Coast
TRUSTEES G Ledger, S Aitchson, B Storey, V Bryden, N Irving, A Ford
WHO TO APPLY TO G Ledger, Chairman, The TFM Cash Challenge Appeal, Yale Crescent, Stockton, Cleveland TS17 6AA
CC NO 1065727   **ESTABLISHED** 1997

■ TG No 1 Charitable Trust

This trust did not respond to CAF's request to amend its entry and, by 30 June 1998, CAF's researchers did not find financial records for later than 1995 on its file at the Charity Commission. Trusts are legally required to submit annual accounts to the Charity Commission under section 42 of the Charities Act 1993

WHAT IS FUNDED General charitable purposes
WHO CAN BENEFIT There are no restrictions on the age; professional and economic group; family situation; religion and culture; and social circumstances of; or disease or medical condition suffered by, the beneficiaries
WHERE FUNDING CAN BE GIVEN UK
TRUSTEES M D Paisner, J F de Botton, L H Townsley
WHO TO APPLY TO M D Paisner, TG No 1 Charitable Trust, Paisner & Co, Solicitors, Bouverie House, 154 Fleet Street, London EC4A 2DQ
CC NO 277928   **ESTABLISHED** 1979

■ The TUUT Charitable Trust

WHAT IS FUNDED General at Trustees' discretion, with an overriding priority to charities with strong trade union connections or interests
WHAT IS NOT FUNDED No grants to individuals
WHO CAN BENEFIT Those supported by, or having close associations with, trade unions
WHERE FUNDING CAN BE GIVEN UK and developing world
TYPE OF GRANT One-off, recurrent, research and capital. Funding is for up to three years
FINANCES *Year* 1996–97 *Income* £72,000
Grants £57,100
TRUSTEES A M G Christopher, J Knapp, J Monks, A Tuffin, M Walsh
PUBLICATIONS Annual Report, Guidelines and Newsletter
NOTES The Trust was set up primarily to benefit charities with a strong trades union connection. Funds are likely to be applied towards those causes which can demonstrate a direct or close link with the trades union movement
HOW TO APPLY In writing at any time. Trustees meet three times a year. Applicants should submit latest accounts, purpose for donation and details of trade union links

WHO TO APPLY TO J Wallace, The TUUT Charitable Trust, Congress House, Great Russell Street, London WC1B 3LQ *Tel* 0171-637 7116 *Fax* 0171-637 7087
CC NO 258665   **ESTABLISHED** 1969

■ The Tabeel Trust

WHAT IS FUNDED Christian charitable purposes, where Trustees have an existing interest
WHO CAN BENEFIT Christians
WHERE FUNDING CAN BE GIVEN UK
FINANCES *Year* 1995–96 *Income* £142,811
HOW TO APPLY To the address under Who To Apply To in writing
WHO TO APPLY TO D K Brown, Secretary, The Tabeel Trust, Dairy House Farm, Great Holland, Frinton-on-Sea, Essex CO13 8EX *Tel* 01255 812130
CC NO 266645   **ESTABLISHED** 1974

■ The Tajtelbaum Charitable Trust

WHAT IS FUNDED (a) Orthodox synagogues and education establishments generally in the UK and Israel, and (b) hospitals and old age homes generally in the UK and Israel
WHO CAN BENEFIT Jewish organisations benefiting children, young adults and students will be considered. Support may be given to elderly and sick people. There is no restriction on the disease or medical condition suffered by the beneficiaries
WHERE FUNDING CAN BE GIVEN UK and Israel
RANGE OF GRANTS £1,000–£112,000
SAMPLE GRANTS £112,000 to Friends of Arab; £27,700 to Gur Trust; £25,000 to Friends of Horim; £17,500 to Huntingdon Foundation; £11,000 to Beth Hamedrash Gur; £11,000 to Friends of Nachalas David; £10,000 to Jewish Education Fund; £10,000 to Mercaz Hatorah; £6,800 to Pardes House School; £5,100 to Emunah Education Centre
FINANCES *Year* 1997 *Income* £426,702
Grants £282,044
TRUSTEES Mrs I Tajtelbaum, I Tajtelbaum, M Tajtelbaum, E Tajtelbaum, E Jaswon, H Frydenson
WHO TO APPLY TO Mrs I Tajtelbaum, The Tajtelbaum Charitable Trust, 17 Western Avenue, London NW11 9HE
CC NO 273184   **ESTABLISHED** 1974

■ The Elsie Talbot Bridge Will Trust

WHAT IS FUNDED Wildlife, the arts, education, museums and galleries, medical care
WHO CAN BENEFIT Local and regional organisations benefiting children, young adults, students and sick people. There is no restriction on the disease or medical condition suffered by the beneficiaries. Those involved in the arts may benefit
WHERE FUNDING CAN BE GIVEN Southport
FINANCES *Year* 1996 *Income* £20,145
TRUSTEES D T Bushell, J Kewley
HOW TO APPLY To the Trustees in writing
WHO TO APPLY TO The Elsie Talbot Bridge Will Trust, 11 St George's Place, Lord Street, Southport, Lancashire PR9 0AL
CC NO 279288   **ESTABLISHED** 1961

■ The Talbot Trusts

WHAT IS FUNDED Items, services or facilities which are calculated to relieve suffering or assist recovery

WHAT IS NOT FUNDED Registered charities only, no grants outside the area Where Funding Can Be Given. No grants to individuals

WHO CAN BENEFIT Organisations benefiting medical professionals, disabled people and carers. There is no restriction on the disease or medical condition suffered by the beneficiaries

WHERE FUNDING CAN BE GIVEN Sheffield, South Yorkshire and North Derbyshire

TYPE OF GRANT One-off, capital, core costs, running costs, salaries and start-up costs. Funding may be given for up to one year

SAMPLE GRANTS £5,000 to Sheffield Family Service Unit; £4,500 to North Sheffield Federation for the Disabled; £4,000 to Macmillan Cancer Relief; £3,600 to Turning Point; £3,000 to Sheffield AIDs Support Group; £3,000 to St Luke's Hospice; £3,000 to Sheffield MIND; £3,000 to Multiple Sclerosis Therapy Centre; £3,000 to Trinity Day Care Trust

FINANCES *Year* 1997–98 *Income* £116,829
Grants £109,110

TRUSTEES C S Barker, R P Harper, Miss B P Jackson, Dr L C Kershaw, Sir John Osborn, Mrs A J Riddle

NOTES Applications must be received by 31 May for consideration in July, and by 31 October for consideration in December

HOW TO APPLY Application forms are available from the address under Who To Apply To

WHO TO APPLY TO Ronald Jones, Clerk, The Talbot Trusts, c/o Sheffield Health Authority, Fulwood House, 5 Fulwood Road, Sheffield S10 3TG

CC NO 221356   **ESTABLISHED** 1928

■ Talbot Village Trust

WHAT IS FUNDED Youth, the elderly and church related charities

WHAT IS NOT FUNDED No grants are made to individuals

WHO CAN BENEFIT Organisations benefiting Children, young adults and students, at risk groups, those disadvantaged by poverty and socially isolated people. There is no restriction on the disease or medical condition suffered by the beneficiaries

WHERE FUNDING CAN BE GIVEN The pre 1997 administrative boroughs of Bournemouth, Christchurch, East Dorset, Poole, Isle of Purbeck

SAMPLE GRANTS £58,000 to East Holton Charity for Phase III Assistance; £50,000 to Victoria School Appeal for Carmel House Project; £20,000 to Alder Road Baptist Church for development/ extension; £9,500 to Boscombe Family Drop In for garden/back room improvements; £5,000 to College Foundation for improvements to library facilities; £5,000 to Sheltered Work for glasshouse shading; £5,000 to Winton Steel Band for equipment; £5,000 to Holy Epiphany Church for hall refurbishment; £5,000 to Corfe Castle Nursery towards equipping nursery; £2,953 to Project Christchurch for library aids

FINANCES *Year* 1997 *Income* £3,488,593
Grants £371,000

TRUSTEES Sir T E L Bart, H W Drax, Sir G C Bart, Sir T M J S Bart, J R G Fleming, C J Lees

HOW TO APPLY To the address under Who To Apply To in writing

WHO TO APPLY TO G S Cox, Clerk, Talbot Village Trust, Dickinson Manser Solicitors, 5 Parkstone Road, Poole, Dorset BH15 2NL

CC NO 249349   **ESTABLISHED** 1867

■ The Talmud Torah Machzikei Hadass Trust

WHAT IS FUNDED The furtherance of the Orthodox Jewish Religion

WHO CAN BENEFIT Organisations benefiting Orthodox Jews

WHERE FUNDING CAN BE GIVEN UK and overseas, with a preference for the London Borough of Hackney

FINANCES *Year* 1997 *Income* £13,047
Grants £12,985

TRUSTEES J Moskovitz, Y M Sternlicht

HOW TO APPLY To the address under Who To Apply To in writing

WHO TO APPLY TO Y M Sternlicht, The Talmud Torah Machzikei Hadass Trust, 28 Leadale Road, Hackney, London N16 6DA

CC NO 270693   **ESTABLISHED** 1975

■ Talteg Ltd

WHAT IS FUNDED To support the advancement of religion, especially Jewish and the relief of poverty. Also supports educational and other charitable purposes

WHO CAN BENEFIT Registered charities benefiting Jewish people, children, young adults and those disadvantaged by poverty

WHERE FUNDING CAN BE GIVEN UK

FINANCES *Year* 1996 *Income* £169,868
Grants £140,963

TRUSTEES Governors: A Berkley, A N Berkley, Miss D L Berkley, F S Berkley, M Berkley, M Berkley

HOW TO APPLY Can be made at any time by letter to the Registrar. In writing only

WHO TO APPLY TO F S Berkley, Governor, Talteg Ltd, 90 Mitchell Street, Glasgow G1 3NQ

CC NO 283253   **ESTABLISHED** 1981

■ Tangent Charitable Trust

WHAT IS FUNDED General charitable purposes

WHO CAN BENEFIT There are no restrictions on the age; professional and economic group; family situation; religion and culture; and social circumstances of; or disease or medical condition suffered by, the beneficiaries

WHERE FUNDING CAN BE GIVEN UK

FINANCES *Year* 1995 *Income* £28,476
Grants £17,700

TRUSTEES M P Green, Mrs J de Moller, Mrs T M Green

WHO TO APPLY TO The Secretary, Tangent Charitable Trust, 25 Knightsbridge, London SW1X 7RZ

CC NO 289729   **ESTABLISHED** 1984

■ The Tangley Trust

WHAT IS FUNDED General charitable purposes

WHO CAN BENEFIT There are no restrictions on the age; professional and economic group; family situation; religion and culture; and social circumstances of; or disease or medical condition suffered by, the beneficiaries

WHERE FUNDING CAN BE GIVEN UK

FINANCES *Year* 1997 *Income* £75,472
Grants £1,000

WHO TO APPLY TO The Chairman, The Tangley Trust, PO Box 302, Guildford, Surrey GU4 8YG

CC NO 1052674   **ESTABLISHED** 1996

■ Tanner Trust

WHAT IS FUNDED General charitable purposes

WHO CAN BENEFIT Foundations, schools, societies, charities, projects. There are no restrictions on the age; professional and economic group; family situation; religion and culture; and social circumstances of; or disease or medical condition suffered by, the beneficiaries

WHERE FUNDING CAN BE GIVEN UK

FINANCES *Year* 1995–96 *Income* £103,021 *Grants* £88,810

TRUSTEES Mrs Lucie M Nottingham, MA, Mrs Alice P Williams, BA, Peter A Youatt, LLB

WHO TO APPLY TO Mrs Lyn Hamilton, Tanner Trust, Hedgerley, 28 Tamarisk Way, East Preston, West Sussex BN16 2TE

CC NO 1021175   **ESTABLISHED** 1993

■ The Tanyard Trust

This trust did not respond to CAF's request to amend its entry and, by 30 June 1998, CAF's researchers did not find financial records for later than 1995 on its file at the Charity Commission. Trusts are legally required to submit annual accounts to the Charity Commission under section 42 of the Charities Act 1993

WHAT IS FUNDED Education; medical research; preservation of historic buildings and artefacts; promotion of the arts

WHO CAN BENEFIT Children and young adults, artists, musicians, textile workers and designers, and writers and poets. There is no restriction on the disease or medical condition suffered by the beneficiaries

WHERE FUNDING CAN BE GIVEN Stowemarket, Suffolk and elsewhere

TRUSTEES J G W Portway, Ms J P Portway, N W Portway

WHO TO APPLY TO N W Portway, Trustee, The Tanyard Trust, Dennys Farmhouse, Combs, Stowmarket, Suffolk IP14 2EN

CC NO 1050683   **ESTABLISHED** 1995

■ The Lili Tapper Charitable Foundation

WHAT IS FUNDED The Trustees give preference to charitable purposes or institutions which are for the benefit of the Jewish people

WHAT IS NOT FUNDED No grants to individuals

WHO CAN BENEFIT Organisations benefiting Jewish people

WHERE FUNDING CAN BE GIVEN UK

RANGE OF GRANTS £32–£2,500

SAMPLE GRANTS £2,500 to British ORT; £2,500 to CBF World Jewish Relief; £2,500 to Jewish Association for the Mentally Ill; £2,500 to Jewish Blind and Disabled; £2,500 to Jewish Care

FINANCES *Year* 1997 *Income* £20,143 *Grants* £17,432

TRUSTEES Mrs L Tapper, M Webber

HOW TO APPLY **This Trust states that it does not respond to unsolicited applications**

WHO TO APPLY TO Edna Rowland, The Lili Tapper Charitable Foundation, Binder Hamlyn, 9 Charlotte Street, Manchester M1 4EU

CC NO 268523   **ESTABLISHED** 1974

■ The D N and C H Tarsh Charitable Trust

WHAT IS FUNDED The Trust favours charities connected with Israel, health or education

WHO CAN BENEFIT Organisations benefiting Jewish people, children, young adults and students. There is no restriction on the disease or medical condition suffered by the beneficiaries

WHERE FUNDING CAN BE GIVEN UK

RANGE OF GRANTS £24–£12,500

SAMPLE GRANTS £12,500 to Joint Philanthropic Association for Israel and Middle East; £10,000 to Polack's House Educational Trust; £2,500 to National Society for Epilepsy; £650 to Tel Aviv University Trust; £400 to Jewish Women's Aid

FINANCES *Year* 1998 *Income* £22,239 *Grants* £31,584

TRUSTEES D N Tarsh, C H Tarsh

HOW TO APPLY It is unlikely that any new organisations can be supported

WHO TO APPLY TO D N Tarsh, The D N and C H Tarsh Charitable Trust, Wentworth House, The Green, Richmond-on-Thames, Surrey TW9 1PB *Tel* 0181-948 1701

CC NO 293281   **ESTABLISHED** 1985

■ The Tay Charitable Trust

WHAT IS FUNDED General charitable purposes in the fields of: residential facilities; infrastructure support and development; Christian religion; arts, culture and recreation; health; conservation and environment; education and training; and community facilities and services

WHAT IS NOT FUNDED No grants to individuals

WHO CAN BENEFIT Registered charities benefiting: young adults and older people; Christians; Church of England and Unitarians. A wide range of professional and economic groups are considered. There is no restriction on the family situation of, or on the disease or medical condition suffered by, the beneficiaries

WHERE FUNDING CAN BE GIVEN UK, particularly Scotland, with a preference for Tayside

TYPE OF GRANT One-off and recurring

RANGE OF GRANTS £250–£10,000

SAMPLE GRANTS £15,000 to Dundee Comfort and Support Centre for shelter for homeless people; £10,000 to Museum Scotland Project towards a museum; £7,000 to Little Sisters of the Poor for a home for poor elderly; £5,000 to RNLI for lifeboats; £3,000 to Ward 10 Endowment Fund for medical equipment; £2,000 to The National Trust for Scotland for Scottish heritage; £2,000 to John Muir Trust for Scottish Heritage

FINANCES *Year* 1997–98 *Income* £116,554 *Grants* £99,000

TRUSTEES Mrs E A Mussen, Ms Z C Mussen, G C Bonar

NOTES Recipients must be registered charities

HOW TO APPLY Applications should be made in writing to the address under Who To Apply To and must include full financial information. Initial telephone called are not welcome. There are no application forms or guidelines or application deadlines. Please enclose an sae

WHO TO APPLY TO Mrs Elizabeth A Mussen, The Tay Charitable Trust, 6 Douglas Terrace, Broughty Ferry, Dundee DD5 1EA *Tel* 0132 779923

SC NO SCO 01004   **ESTABLISHED** 1951

■ A R Taylor Charitable Trust

WHAT IS FUNDED Preference is given to charities in which the Trustees have special interest, knowledge or association, particularly service charities and educational organisations. Funds are fully committed or allocated

WHAT IS NOT FUNDED Registered charities or similar bodies only. Applications from individuals for assistance with education or personal projects for themselves or members of their family will not be considered

WHO CAN BENEFIT Registered charities or similar bodies benefiting children, young adults and students

WHERE FUNDING CAN BE GIVEN UK

TYPE OF GRANT Both one-off and recurrent grants. There is no formal limit to the length of time for recurrent grants

RANGE OF GRANTS £50–£7,000

SAMPLE GRANTS £7,000 to Ex-services Mental Welfare Society; £4,000 to Winchester College; £2,500 to Regimental HQ First or Grenadier Regiment of Foot Guards; £2,000 to the Dever Society; £1,600 to Princes Mead School; £1,250 to RUKBA; £1,000 to Bighton Church; £1,000 to Princes Mead School Trust; £1,000 to the Peter May Memorial Appeal; £750 to British Kidney Patient Association

FINANCES *Year* 1998 *Income* £42,183
Grants £27,775

TRUSTEES A R Taylor, Mrs E J Taylor

NOTES Funds are fully committed or allocated

HOW TO APPLY Applications may be made at any time but will only be considered periodically. The trust does not use an application form. Unsuccessful applications will generally not be acknowledged

WHO TO APPLY TO J Bristol, A R Taylor Charitable Trust, Birketts, Solicitors, 24–26 Museum Street, Ipswich, Suffolk IP1 1HZ

CC NO 275560   **ESTABLISHED** 1978

■ The Cyril Taylor Charitable Trust

WHAT IS FUNDED General charitable purposes; to advance the education of the students of Richmond College and the American International University in London

WHO CAN BENEFIT Organisations benefiting students

WHERE FUNDING CAN BE GIVEN In practice, mainly Greater London

SAMPLE GRANTS £10,000 to British Friends of Harvard Business School; £5,000 to Trinity Hall, Cambridge; £2,000 to Institute of Economic Affairs

FINANCES *Year* 1997 *Income* £26,060
Grants £17,000

TRUSTEES Sir Cyril Taylor, Clifford D Joseph, Robert W Maas, Peter A Tchereprine, M Stephen Rasch

WHO TO APPLY TO C D Joseph, The Cyril Taylor Charitable Trust, 8 Grays Inn Square, Grays Inn, London WC1R 5AZ

CC NO 1040179   **ESTABLISHED** 1994

■ A P Taylor Fund

WHAT IS FUNDED For the use of the inhabitants of the Parishes of Hayes and Harlington (as they existed on 9.1.1953) without distinction of political, religious or other opinion

WHO CAN BENEFIT There are no restrictions on the age; professional and economic group; family situation; religion and culture; and social circumstances of; or disease or medical condition suffered by, the beneficiaries

WHERE FUNDING CAN BE GIVEN Hayes and Harlington

SAMPLE GRANTS £3,000 to Charville Community Association; £2,500 to Hayes End Community Association; £2,000 to Judge Health 2000 Gymnastics Club; £2,000 to Brookside Community Association; £2,000 to Hayes and Harlington Community Association; £2,000 to Yeading Community Association; £2,000 to Barnhill Community Association; £2,000 to Bourne Circle Sports and Social Club; £2,000 to Hayes and Harlington Arts Council; £1,000 to Harlington Hospice Association

FINANCES *Year* 1997 *Income* £48,681
Grants £51,800

TRUSTEES A J Tyrrell, A Woodhouse, W C Palmer, H B Clarke, M J Fitzpatrick

WHO TO APPLY TO M J Fitzpatrick, Treasurer, A P Taylor Fund, Homeleigh, 68 Vine Lane, Hillingdon, Middlesex UB10 0BD

CC NO 260741   **ESTABLISHED** 1969

■ C B and H H Taylor Trust

WHAT IS FUNDED General charitable purposes particularly: religious buildings; arts and arts facilities; healthcare; medical studies and research; conservation; environmental and animal sciences; education and training; and community facilities and services

WHAT IS NOT FUNDED Grants are not made to individuals or for university expeditions

WHO CAN BENEFIT Organisations benefiting Christians, ethnic minority groups and Quakers. Approximately 75 per cent of funds available are currently given to the work and concerns of the Religious Society of Friends. The remaining funds are allocated to those charities in which the Trustees have a special interest, particularly in the Midlands

WHERE FUNDING CAN BE GIVEN Birmingham area and some charities operating overseas

TYPE OF GRANT Regular annual donations and some single donations to special appeals

SAMPLE GRANTS £28,000 to Society of Friends, local and national; £3,000 to Bryony House, Birmingham for sheltered accommodation; £2,500 to Birmingham Family Service Unit South; £2,500 to Cape Town Quaker Peace Centre (overseas) for reconciliation; £2,000 to the Salvation Army (Birmingham); £2,000 to Responding to Conflict (national) for reconciliation; £2,000 to Margery Fry Memorial Trust (national); £2,000 to Ulster Quaker Service (Northern Ireland); £1,000 to Wildfowl and Wetlands Trust (national); £1,000 to Friends of Swanivax (India) for education

FINANCES *Year* 1997 *Income* £120,000
Grants £118,000

TRUSTEES Mrs C H Norton, Mrs E J Birmingham, J A B Taylor, W J B Taylor, Mrs C M Penny

NOTES Grants should be acknowledged by an official receipt made out to C B & H H Taylor Trust

HOW TO APPLY Applications for grants made annually should be submitted when due with a copy of accounts for the previous year – other applications can be submitted for consideration at April and November Trust meetings

WHO TO APPLY TO C B and H H Taylor Trust, c/o Home Farm, Abberton, Pershore, Worcestershire WR10 2NR

CC NO 213628   **ESTABLISHED** 1946

■ The Gail Taylor Trust

WHAT IS FUNDED The care and support of people with disabilities, especially cerebral palsy; to make donations to related trusts, societies or institutions

WHO CAN BENEFIT Organisations benefiting disabled people

WHERE FUNDING CAN BE GIVEN UK

FINANCES *Year* 1998 *Income* £38,000

WHO TO APPLY TO Stephen Pritchard, Trustee, The Gail Taylor Trust, 3 Downing Street, Farnham, Surrey GU9 7PA

CC NO 1059891   **ESTABLISHED** 1996

■ Horace Taylor Trust

This trust did not respond to CAF's request to amend its entry and, by 30 June 1998, CAF's researchers did not find financial records for later than 1995 on its file at the Charity Commission. Trusts are legally required to submit annual accounts to the Charity Commission under section 42 of the Charities Act 1993

WHAT IS FUNDED To support needy OAP's, people in sickness and need, youth clubs of the Methodist and Elim chapels and other charitable causes

WHO CAN BENEFIT Children, young adults and older people, and those disadvantaged by poverty. There is no restriction on the disease or medical condition suffered by the beneficiaries

WHERE FUNDING CAN BE GIVEN Driffield and area only

TRUSTEES P S Atkinson, Canon L W Chidzey, Rev M A Simons, A J Barnard, Mrs H H Nelson

WHO TO APPLY TO D E Lundy, Horace Taylor Trust, 17 Exchange Street, Driffield, North Humberside Y025 7LA

CC NO 509182   **ESTABLISHED** 1974

■ Taylor Woodrow Charity Trust

WHAT IS FUNDED General charitable purposes

WHO CAN BENEFIT There are no restrictions on the age; professional and economic group; family situation; religion and culture; and social circumstances of; or disease or medical condition suffered by, the beneficiaries

WHERE FUNDING CAN BE GIVEN UK

TRUSTEES Ms R C Barber, M Beard, G B Borwell, G T Janes, R I Morbey

WHO TO APPLY TO R I Morbey, Taylor Woodrow Charity Trust, 4 Dunraven Street, London W1Y 3FG

CC NO 1064162   **ESTABLISHED** 1997

■ The M and S Teacher Charitable Trust

WHAT IS FUNDED General charitable purposes

WHO CAN BENEFIT There are no restrictions on the age; professional and economic group; family situation; religion and culture; and social circumstances of; or disease or medical condition suffered by, the beneficiaries

WHERE FUNDING CAN BE GIVEN UK

TRUSTEES M J Teacher, Ms S Teacher, D J Teacher

WHO TO APPLY TO M Teacher, Trustee, The M and S Teacher Charitable Trust, 18 Valencia Road, Stanmore, Middlesex HA7 4JH

CC NO 1030233   **ESTABLISHED** 1995

■ Tear Fund

WHAT IS FUNDED Evangelical Christian ministry to meet all needs – physical, mental, social and spiritual

WHO CAN BENEFIT Christian Evangelical organisations benefiting: at risk groups; disabled people; those disadvantaged by poverty; socially isolated people; and victims of famine, man-made or natural disasters and war will be considered. There is no restriction on the disease or medical condition suffered by the beneficiaries

WHERE FUNDING CAN BE GIVEN UK and overseas, but mainly in poorer countries

SAMPLE GRANTS £3,609,000 to Compassion International partners in childcare programmes; £1,777,000 in India; £705,000 in Afghanistan; £595,000 in Rwanda; £581,000 in Zambia; £544,000 in Eritrea; £427,000 in Sudan; £419,000 in Zaire; £409,000 in Kenya; £378,000 in Bangladesh

FINANCES *Year* 1996–97 *Income* £24,212,000 *Grants* £13,259,000

TRUSTEES D P Malton, J K Harvey, B O Chilver, R H Northcott, J S Hughesdon, S Hingston

PUBLICATIONS *Tear Times*

HOW TO APPLY In writing to the Overseas Director. Applications must meet the criteria indicated under What Is Funded

WHO TO APPLY TO The General Director, Tear Fund, 100 Church Road, Teddington, Middlesex TW11 8QE

CC NO 265464   **ESTABLISHED** 1968

■ The Tejani Charitable Trust

WHAT IS FUNDED General charitable purposes

WHO CAN BENEFIT There are no restrictions on the age; professional and economic group; family situation; religion and culture; and social circumstances of; or disease or medical condition suffered by, the beneficiaries

WHERE FUNDING CAN BE GIVEN UK

RANGE OF GRANTS £765-£5,000

FINANCES *Year* 1997 *Income* £13,339 *Grants* £580

TRUSTEES F G Tejani, H G Tejani, N G Tejani, Z G Tejani

WHO TO APPLY TO H Tejani, Trustee, The Tejani Charitable Trust, 47–48 Piccadilly, 4th Floor, Albany Court Yard, London W1V 0LR

CC NO 1046962   **ESTABLISHED** 1995

■ Telford and Wrekin Community Trust

WHAT IS FUNDED Youth and children; community; disability groups in the area Where Funding Can Be Given. The advancement of education, the protection of good health both mental and physical and the relief of poverty, distress, disability or sickness

WHO CAN BENEFIT Local organisations benefiting children, young adults and students, at risk groups, those disadvantaged by poverty and socially isolated people. There is no restriction on the disease or medical condition suffered by the beneficiaries

WHERE FUNDING CAN BE GIVEN Telford and Wrekin in Shropshire

FINANCES *Year* 1996–97 *Income* £32,909 *Grants* £9,204

TRUSTEES B Andrews, Prof G Bennett, Mrs K Bennett, D Chiva, J Cuffley, D A Drew, R Hamilton, J Howard, D Jeffries, P J Kenny, L G Reedman, D A

Rogers, N R Rozzell, Mrs D Walder, C B Waterson, Mrs E Woods, Miss E Yates

HOW TO APPLY To the address under Who To Apply To in writing

WHO TO APPLY TO Mrs P Bradburn, Development Oficer, Telford and Wrekin Community Trust, Meeting Point House, Southwark Square, Telford TF3 4HS

CC NO 1012215 **ESTABLISHED** 1992

■ Templeton Goodwill Trust

WHAT IS FUNDED General charitable purposes. The Trust will considered funding: Christian education and outreach; Catholic umbrella bodies; cultural activity; ambulances and mobile units; convalescent homes; rehabilitation centres; cancer research; and historic buildings

WHAT IS NOT FUNDED No grants to individuals

WHO CAN BENEFIT Scottish registered charities benefiting: people of all ages; ex-service and service people; seafarers and fishermen; Baptists, Christians, Methodists, Quakers and Roman Catholics. Those suffering from various diseases and medical conditions will be considered

WHERE FUNDING CAN BE GIVEN Glasgow and West of Scotland

TYPE OF GRANT Discretionary – both continuing annual sums and 'one-off', support grants

RANGE OF GRANTS £350–£2,500

FINANCES *Year* 1997 *Income* £90,000 *Grants* £90,000

TRUSTEES A D Montgomery, OBE, J H Millar, W T P Barnstaple, B Bannerman

HOW TO APPLY Initial telephone calls are welcome. Guidelines are issued on request. Sae required from applicants

WHO TO APPLY TO W T P Barnstaple, Templeton Goodwill Trust, 12 Doon Street, Motherwell, Lanarkshire ML1 2BN *Tel* 01698 262202

SC NO SCO 04177

■ Tenby Romanian Children Support Group

WHAT IS FUNDED To relieve poverty, sickness and distress, and to promote education among children in or from Romania

WHO CAN BENEFIT Individuals and organisations benefiting children and young adults; those in care, fostered and adopted; parents and children; one parent families; at risk groups; those disadvantaged by poverty; homeless people; victims of abuse and domestic violence; and victims of famine. There is no restriction on the disease or medical condition suffered by the beneficiaries

WHERE FUNDING CAN BE GIVEN Romania

TYPE OF GRANT Recurring costs will be considered

RANGE OF GRANTS £5–£12,000

SAMPLE GRANTS £10,689 for the purchase of a four-room apartment in Bucharest, Romania to provide a home for boys leaving Number 10 Orphanage; £6,609 to provide a holiday in Pembrokeshire, Wales for 44 children and three adults from Number 8 and Number 10 Orphanages

FINANCES *Year* 1996–97 *Income* £18,643 *Grants* £18,408

TRUSTEES C R Jameson, T C A Keohone, P Davies, C Millward

PUBLICATIONS Illustrated brochure on the work of the Charity 1992–1998

HOW TO APPLY By telephone or in writing

WHO TO APPLY TO C R Jameson, Tenby Romanian Children Support Group, Ferry Wood House, Pembroke Ferry, Pembrokeshire SA72 6UD *Tel* 01646 622560 *Fax* 01646 622560

CC NO 1021952 **ESTABLISHED** 1992

■ Tennison Charitable Trust

WHAT IS FUNDED Religious charitable purposes

WHO CAN BENEFIT There are no restrictions on the religion or culture of the beneficiaries

WHERE FUNDING CAN BE GIVEN UK

HOW TO APPLY **This Trust states that it does not respond to unsolicited applications**

WHO TO APPLY TO A E Wakeling, Tennison Charitable Trust, Stewardship Services, PO Box 99, Loughton, Essex IG10 2QJ

CC NO 1069776 **ESTABLISHED** 1998

■ Tenovus – Scotland

WHAT IS FUNDED To 'prime the pump' especially for new and innovative research projects across the full spectrum of medicine

WHAT IS NOT FUNDED Grants are not made to individuals other than as members of institutions engaged in research approved by such institutions and by the Scientific Advisory Committee of Tenovus-Scotland

WHO CAN BENEFIT Individuals and institutions benefiting young adults and older people; academics; medical professionals; research workers and students

WHERE FUNDING CAN BE GIVEN Scotland

TYPE OF GRANT Usually a single grant with the emphasis on equipment and consumables. Only in exceptional circumstances would funding be considered for salaries and then only for a period of up to 12 months. One-off, project, research and start-up costs. Funding for up to three years will be considered

SAMPLE GRANTS £49,800 to an individual doctor in Tayside for work on a molecular analysis of the mechanisms controlling thyroid hormone function in early human development; £14,500 to an individual doctor in Strathclyde for work on the effect of universal childhood vaccination on the selection of hepatitis B virus immune escape variants in a developing country; £10,218 to a research team in Strathclyde for work on immunocytochemical and chromosonal characterisation of tophoblast cells; £10,000 to a team of two doctors in Grampian for work on PH regulation in human airway epithelial cells and its involvement in airway disease; £10,000 to a team of doctors in Grampian for work into the late effects of hypertensive disease in pregnancy on haemostatic marker of cardiovascular MSR; £10,000 to an individual in Grampian for work on purification and characterisation of a manganese-sensitive triacylglycerol and cholesterol esterhydrolase activity; £9,830 to a research team in Edinburgh for work on histological characterisation of known and novel genes involved in eye development and disease

FINANCES *Year* 1996–97 *Income* £377,774 *Grants* £356,931

TRUSTEES The Committee: D G Browm, B Cutler, Dr S Duncan, Sir Malcolm MacNaughton, W M Mann, Mary Marquis, W A R Munro, G M Philips, M Philips, G Paton, Prof I H Stevenson

PUBLICATIONS Annual Report, Six-monthly Newsletter and a video *Today's Research-Tomorrow's Health*

HOW TO APPLY At any time on a Tenovus-Scotland application form, available from the address under

Who To Apply To. Regional Committees meet quarterly

WHO TO APPLY TO E R Read, General Secretary, Tenovus – Scotland, 234 St Vincent Street, Glasgow G2 5RJ *Tel* 0141-221 6268 *Fax* 0141-221 1804

SC NO SCO 09675   **ESTABLISHED** 1967

■ Tenovus – The Cancer Charity

This trust did not respond to CAF's request to amend its entry and, by 30 June 1998, CAF's researchers did not find financial records for later than 1995 on its file at the Charity Commission. Trusts are legally required to submit annual accounts to the Charity Commission under section 42 of the Charities Act 1993

WHAT IS FUNDED Currently Tenovus funds cancer research projects and programmes designed to support cancer patients

WHAT IS NOT FUNDED No grants to individuals. Cancer research projects outside the UK are not funded

WHO CAN BENEFIT Mainly Tenovus Research Centres in Cardiff and Southamption, and organisations benefiting people suffering from cancer. Support may also be given to academics, medical professionals, research workers and scientists

WHERE FUNDING CAN BE GIVEN UK, particularly Cardiff and Southampton

TYPE OF GRANT Research project grants of three or five year duration, hardship grants one-off

TRUSTEES Executive Committee of ten

PUBLICATIONS Annual Report

HOW TO APPLY A brief letter outlining the project and financial requirements will ascertain the current position. Trustees meet quarterly to assess full applications. Research projects are subject to Peer review

WHO TO APPLY TO The Organising Secretary of Tenovus – The Cancer Charity, Tenovus, 11 Whitchurch Road, Cardiff, Wales CF4 3JN

CC NO 223648   **ESTABLISHED** 1940

■ Noel Goddard Terry Charitable Trust

WHAT IS FUNDED Grants mainly for the preservation and restoration of historic buildings in the City of York

WHAT IS NOT FUNDED No grants are made to individuals

WHO CAN BENEFIT Charities concerned with historic buildings

WHERE FUNDING CAN BE GIVEN City of York

SAMPLE GRANTS £4,000 to The National Trust; £2,980 to York Civic Trust for Annual Report colourwork; £2,000 to York Minster Fund; £1,000 to York Civic Trust for 50th Anniversary Dinner

FINANCES *Year* 1997 *Income* £43,326 *Grants* £9,980

TRUSTEES P N L Terry, J Shannon, A K N Terry, M Shannon, J M Hargreaves

NOTES Primary object of grants in recent years has been York Civic Trust

HOW TO APPLY By letter to the address under Who To Apply To

WHO TO APPLY TO Noel Goddard Terry Charitable Trust, Messrs Harland & Co, 18 St Saviourgate, York, North Yorkshire YO1 2NS

CC NO 209203   **ESTABLISHED** 1962

■ Tesco Charity Trust

WHAT IS FUNDED Main areas of interest are: the arts, sporting facilities, the promotion of health and care for the disabled, education and support for work in the community

WHAT IS NOT FUNDED No grants to political organisations, individuals or towards new buildings. The Trust will not make donations to other trusts or charities for onward transmission to other charitable organisations

WHO CAN BENEFIT National and local charity appeals benefiting at risk groups, disabled people, children, young adults, those disadvantaged by poverty and socially isolated people. Actors and entertainment professionals, musicians, textile workers and designers, writers, poets, and sportsmen and women may be considered

WHERE FUNDING CAN BE GIVEN UK

SAMPLE GRANTS £10,000 to Age Concern; £10,000 to Hospice Care Service for East Hertfordshire; £6,000 to National Grocers Benevolent Fund; £5,000 to Age Concern Scotland; £5,000 to Crimestoppers Trust; £5,000 to Cystic Fibrosis Trust; £5,000 to Hertfordshire Young Mariners Base Development Fund; £5,000 to York Minster

FINANCES *Year* 1996 *Income* £766,287 *Grants* £640,312

TRUSTEES R S Ager, A J Elmer, K Doherty, Sir I MacLaurin, Miss F Elliott

NOTES For the year1996, major donations were awarded to 21 charities concerning health and care; one charity concerning the arts; six charities concerning education and youth and seven charities concerning other fields

WHO TO APPLY TO Mrs L Marsh, Tesco Charity Trust, Tesco House, Delamare Road, Cheshunt, Hertfordshire EN8 9SL

CC NO 297126   **ESTABLISHED** 1987

■ The Tesler Foundation

WHAT IS FUNDED To advance education in and the religion of the Orthodox Jewish faith and for such other purposes as are recognised by English law as charitable

WHO CAN BENEFIT Jewish people

WHERE FUNDING CAN BE GIVEN Greater London and the UK

TYPE OF GRANT One-off and recurrent

FINANCES *Year* 1997 *Income* £65,609 *Grants* £16,284

TRUSTEES J Tesler, M W Tesler, Mrs M Gutfreund

WHO TO APPLY TO J Tesler, The Tesler Foundation, Kaye Tesler, Equity House, 86 West Green Road, London N15 5NS

CC NO 1030939   **ESTABLISHED** 1992

■ The C P Thackray General Charitable Trust

WHAT IS FUNDED The Trustees areas of interest in Yorkshire are the care, rehabilitation and education of those with special needs and complementary medicine and the protection of the local environment. International interests lie in training and technology for developing countries, simple medical assistance of mass benefit, the protection of human rights, ecology and conservation

WHAT IS NOT FUNDED Grants are not made for disaster appeals, appeals for medical or educational equipment, charities for domestic pets, politics, religion, the arts and heritage or unregistered charities. No grants to individuals

WHO CAN BENEFIT Organisations benefiting those with special needs, those from developing countries and the sick. There is no restriction on the disease or medical condition suffered by the beneficiaries

WHERE FUNDING CAN BE GIVEN Yorkshire and overseas

TYPE OF GRANT Recurrent grants are made, although this list is reviewed annually and capital projects are considered and allocated a small proportion of the total funds available. Unfortunately, this leaves little funding for new applicants

RANGE OF GRANTS £400–£18,750

SAMPLE GRANTS £18,750 to Age Concern, Leeds; £2,000 to Marie Stopes International; £1,800 to Marie Curie Cancer Care; £1,500 to Swarthmore Educational Centre; £1,200 to Camphill Village Trust; £1,200 to NSPCC; £1,000 to British Red Cross; £1,000 to Dogs for the Disabled; £1,000 to Hearing Dogs for the Deaf; £1,000 to the Howard League for Penal Reform

FINANCES *Year* 1998 *Income* £98,256
Grants £48,150

TRUSTEES C P Thackray, Mrs L T Thackray, R C Gorospe, W M Wrigley, Mrs R L Lockie

HOW TO APPLY Administration is carried out voluntarily. For this reason no further guidance can be given to applicants and only successful applications are acknowledged, following the Trustees' annual meeting

WHO TO APPLY TO Mrs Ramona Lockie, The C P Thackray General Charitable Trust, PO Box 2002, Pulborough, West Sussex RH20 2FR

CC NO 328650   **ESTABLISHED** 1990

■ Thames Community Foundation (formerly Richmond upon Thames Community Trust)

WHAT IS FUNDED Encouraging links between the local communities of the area Where Funding Can Be Given and the business sector

WHO CAN BENEFIT To the benefit of businesses and members of the community

WHERE FUNDING CAN BE GIVEN The Borough of Richmond-upon-Thames and the Royal Borough of Kingston-upon-Thames

FINANCES *Year* 1997 *Income* £69,660
Grants £26,876

TRUSTEES Anne Bogod, Malcolm Childs, Rod Cooke, Anthony Everett, Hilary Garner, Grant Gordon, Serge Lourie, David Nagli, Adrian Parsons, Philip Ralph, Carolyn Rampton, Sylvan Robinson, Martin Westward

HOW TO APPLY To the address under Who To Apply To in writing

WHO TO APPLY TO A C Gilmour, Director, Thames Community Foundation, LGC, Victoria House, Queens Road, Teddington, Middlesex TW11 0LY *Web Site* http://ourworld.compuserve.com/homepages/thamescomfoundation

CC NO 1001994   **ESTABLISHED** 1990

■ The Thames Wharf Charity

WHAT IS FUNDED Financial problems of all kinds except those in connection with purchase of property, motor vehicles or holidays

WHO CAN BENEFIT There are no restrictions on the age; professional and economic group; family situation; religion and culture; and social circumstances of; or disease or medical condition suffered by, the beneficiaries

WHERE FUNDING CAN BE GIVEN UK

RANGE OF GRANTS £21–£9,100

SAMPLE GRANTS £9,100 to Shelter; £4,781 to IUR; £4,000 to Architectural Association; £3,344 to Kent Air Ambulance; £2,770 to World Wildlife Fund; £2,180 to Satya SAI UK; £2,043 to National Meningitis Fund; £2,043 to Clinical Science Foundation; £2,035 to Queen Charlotte's Hospital; £2,020 to Motivation

FINANCES *Year* 1997 *Income* £54,772
Grants £67,633

TRUSTEES G H Camamile, P H Burgess, J M Young, A Lotay

WHO TO APPLY TO K Hawkins, The Thames Wharf Charity, Lee Associates, 5 Southampton Place, London WC1A 2DA

CC NO 1000796   **ESTABLISHED** 1990

■ Trust Thamesmead Limited

WHAT IS FUNDED Community-based organisations working in the field of social welfare in the area Where Funding Can Be Given

WHO CAN BENEFIT Local organisations benefiting at risk groups, those disadvantaged by poverty and socially isolated people

WHERE FUNDING CAN BE GIVEN Thamesmead and surrounding district

RANGE OF GRANTS £40–£300

SAMPLE GRANTS £300 to TCNA; £250 to Abbey Wood Brownies; £233 to St Pauls Playgroup; £225 to Crossways Gym; £150 to Archway Project; £150 to Bubbles Parent and Toddler Group; £150 to Friends of Bishop John Robinson School; £150 to Jon Lever Playgroup; £150 to Neutral group; £150 to Nippers Playgroup

FINANCES *Year* 1995–96 *Income* £32,949
Grants £4,176

TRUSTEES Management Committee: E Claridge, J J Faulkner, G Reynolds, OBE, A Taylor

HOW TO APPLY To the address under Who To Apply To in writing

WHO TO APPLY TO Mrs M J Chambers, Company Secretary, Trust Thamesmead Limited, Thamesmere Leisure Centre, Thamesmere Drive, London SE28 8RE

CC NO 271731   **ESTABLISHED** 1976

■ The Margaret Thatcher Charitable Trust

WHAT IS FUNDED General charitable purposes

WHO CAN BENEFIT There are no restrictions on the age, professional and economic group, family situation, religion and culture, and social circumstances of, or disease or medical condition suffered by, the beneficiaries

WHERE FUNDING CAN BE GIVEN UK and overseas

FINANCES *Year* 1996 *Income* £36,300
Grants £34,800

TRUSTEES The Rt Hon Baroness Thatcher, LG, OM, FRS, Mrs Cynthia M Crawford, MBE, Philip J Gee, FCA

HOW TO APPLY No specific date. No application form

WHO TO APPLY TO Mrs C M Crawford, The Margaret Thatcher Charitable Trust, 73 Chester Square, London SW1W 1DU

CC NO 800225   **ESTABLISHED** 1988

■ The Theatres Trust Charitable Fund

WHAT IS FUNDED Grants are made only to charitable institutions or trusts and in respect of buildings only, and concentrating on professional theatres or those adapted for professional use

WHAT IS NOT FUNDED Grants are not made to students for any part or full time study

WHO CAN BENEFIT Charitable bodies whose objects are similar to the Trust, principally ones which own or manage theatre buildings

WHERE FUNDING CAN BE GIVEN UK

TYPE OF GRANT For the purchase, preservation, restoration or repair of theatre buildings only. Feasibility studies will be considered

FINANCES *Year* 1996–97 *Income* £352,000
Grants £4,500

TRUSTEES Sir J Drummond, CBE (Chairman), A Bernstein, Y Brewster, OBE, D Brierley, CBE, A Burrough, Sir G Cass, M Heighton, P Iles, J S Lane, Sir M Marshall, J Muir, A Riches, Sir S Waley-Cohen, Bt

PUBLICATIONS The Trust's Annual Report is available from the Director

NOTES A very limited number of grants are made. Most are below £2,500

HOW TO APPLY At any time

WHO TO APPLY TO Peter Longman, Director, The Theatres Trust Charitable Fund, 22 Charing Cross Road, London WC2H 0HR *Tel* 0171 836 8591

CC NO 274697   **ESTABLISHED** 1977

■ Loke Wan Tho Memorial Foundation

WHAT IS FUNDED Medical studies and research; conservation and environment; and other charitable purposes

WHAT IS NOT FUNDED No grants to individuals

WHO CAN BENEFIT Registered charities only. Preference for Far East, ornithology and environment. There are no restrictions on the disease or medical condition suffered by the beneficiaries

WHERE FUNDING CAN BE GIVEN UK and overseas

TYPE OF GRANT Project and research. Funding can be given for up to one year

SAMPLE GRANTS £20,717 to Asian Wetlands Bureau; £18,960 to Worldwide Fund for Nature 'Malaysia'; £5,000 to Worldwide Fund for Nature 'Chitral'; £5,000 to Sight Savers International; £5,000 to Marie Stopes International; £5,000 to Liverpool School of Tropical Medicine; £5,000 to Jersey Wildlife Preservation Trust; £2,000 to Intermediate Technology; £2,000 to Diane Fossey Gorilla Fund; £2,000 to Oriental Birds Club

FINANCES *Year* 1996 *Income* £91,917
Grants £78,677

TRUSTEES Lady McNeice, Mr Tonkyn, Mrs Tonkyn

WHO TO APPLY TO The Administrator, Loke Wan Tho Memorial Foundation, Coopers & Lybrand, 9 Greyfriars Road, Reading, Berkshire RG1 1JG *Tel* 0118-959 7111

CC NO 264273   **ESTABLISHED** 1972

■ Thompson Charitable Trust

WHAT IS FUNDED This is a family trust and only finances charities connected with, or introduced by, members of the family

WHO CAN BENEFIT There are no restrictions on the age; professional and economic group; family situation; religion and culture; and social circumstances of; or disease or medical condition suffered by, the beneficiaries

WHERE FUNDING CAN BE GIVEN South-East London

FINANCES *Year* 1997 *Income* £32,000
Grants £60,000

TRUSTEES P J Leslie, A R Way, A P Thompson, J M Thompson

NOTES The income reported refers to the net available income

HOW TO APPLY **This Trust states that it does not respond to unsolicited applications**

WHO TO APPLY TO A P Thompson, Thompson Charitable Trust 13A Pond Road, Blackheath, London SE3 0SL

CC NO 291759   **ESTABLISHED** 1985

■ The Thompson Charitable Trust

WHAT IS FUNDED Preference for donations to lesser known charities in the fields of medicine, welfare and education

WHAT IS NOT FUNDED No fixed restrictions but the Trustees would tend to avoid giving to the major established national charities

WHO CAN BENEFIT All registered charities and charitable purposes subject to What Is Funded above. Organisations benefiting: children, young adults and students; at risk groups; those disadvantaged by poverty; and socially isolated people. There is no restriction on the disease or medical condition suffered by the beneficiaries

WHERE FUNDING CAN BE GIVEN UK

RANGE OF GRANTS £100–£16,545

SAMPLE GRANTS £16,545 to Special Trustees for St Thomas; £1,906 to Sidcot School; £1,100 to Redmaids School; £500 to the Salvation Army; £500 to SCARF; £500 to Eccleshall All Saints Church; £300 to BRACE; £100 to Cancer Care Appeal

FINANCES *Year* 1996–97 *Income* £43,796
Grants £21,451

TRUSTEES T P Thompson, Mrs J M Thompson, J W Sharpe

HOW TO APPLY All applications to the address under Who To Apply To in writing. Applications will not be acknowledged unless successful. No telephone applications

WHO TO APPLY TO J W Sharpe, The Thompson Charitable Trust, Osborne Clarke, 50 Queen Charlotte Street, Bristol BS1 4HE

CC NO 1003013   **ESTABLISHED** 1991

■ The Thompson Family Charitable Trust

WHAT IS FUNDED General charitable purposes. All application are considered on their merits. Only in very exceptional cases would donations be given to entities other than Registered Charities

WHO CAN BENEFIT There are no restrictions on the age; professional and economic group; family situation; religion and culture; and social circumstances of; or disease or medical condition suffered by, the beneficiaries

WHERE FUNDING CAN BE GIVEN UK

RANGE OF GRANTS Largest Grant has been £1,450,000 (1995 Haileybury School/Vivat Appeal)

SAMPLE GRANTS £100,000 to Save the Children; £24,000 to Vivat Appeal; £11,200 to Spinal Injuries Association; £10,167 to Curedley Charitable Trust; £10,000 to King Edward VI Aston Appeal; £5,000 to Alcohol Helpline; £5,000 to Thoroughbred Breeders' Association Equine Fertility Unit; £5,000 to One to One Project; £3,000 to Bramley Educational Trust; £2,500 to Great Ormond Street Children's Hospital Fund

FINANCES *Year* 1997 *Income* £2,475,282 *Grants* £782,702

TRUSTEES D B Thompson, Mrs P Thompson

HOW TO APPLY In writing to the address under Who To Apply To

WHO TO APPLY TO Mrs P Thompson, The Thompson Family Charitable Trust, Hillsdown Court, 15 Totteridge Common, London N20 8LR *Tel* 0181-445 4343

CC NO 326801   **ESTABLISHED** 1985

■ The Thompson Fund

WHAT IS FUNDED Medical education, hospitals, medical welfare and care

WHAT IS NOT FUNDED Grants are not made to individuals

WHO CAN BENEFIT Regional and local organisations benefiting medical students. There is no restriction on the disease or medical condition suffered by the beneficiaries

WHERE FUNDING CAN BE GIVEN UK, especially Brighton and Hove

TYPE OF GRANT Some recurrent grants

RANGE OF GRANTS £250–£5,000

SAMPLE GRANTS £5,000 to Age Concern, Hove and Portslade; £5,000 to Institute of Neurology, University of London; £3,000 to Royal National Institute for the Blind; £3,000 to The Stroke Association; £2,750 to Brighton Heart Support Trust; £2,500 to Motor Neurone Disease Association; £2,500 to NSPCC; £2,500 to Sussex Emmaus; £2,250 to Ovingdean Hall School; £2,000 to WRVS (Hove) Caravan Account

FINANCES *Year* 1997 *Income* £56,181 *Grants* £51,400

TRUSTEES M H de Silva, P G Thompson, P J Thompson

HOW TO APPLY To the address under Who To Apply To in writing

WHO TO APPLY TO The Trustees, The Thompson Fund, 1st Floor, 83 Church Road, Hove, East Sussex BN3 2BB

CC NO 327490   **ESTABLISHED** 1987

■ Thompson Pritchard Trust

WHAT IS FUNDED Community care, disability and children, including the provision of convalescent homes and holiday accommodation, healthcare and the provision of holidays and outings for sick people

WHAT IS NOT FUNDED No grants for buildings and recurring expenses

WHO CAN BENEFIT Individuals and local organisations, local branches of national organisations benefiting disabled people and those disadvantaged by poverty. There is no restriction on the age or family situation of, or disease or medical condition suffered by, the beneficiaries

WHERE FUNDING CAN BE GIVEN Shropshire

TYPE OF GRANT One-off grants. Funding is available for up to one year

RANGE OF GRANTS £50–£300. Rarely above £1,000

FINANCES *Year* 1996 *Income* £15,811

HOW TO APPLY To the address under Who To Apply To in writing. However, initial telephone calls are welcome. An application form is available

WHO TO APPLY TO P L Boardman, Thompson Pritchard Trust, 3 Mayfield Park, Shrewsbury SY2 6PD *Tel* 01743 232768

CC NO 234601   **ESTABLISHED** 1964

■ The Arthur Thomson Charitable Trust

WHAT IS FUNDED To benefit the staff and students of the Medical School and Dental School of the University of Birmingham

WHAT IS NOT FUNDED Restricted to the above purpose

WHO CAN BENEFIT Staff and students of the Medical School and Dental School of the University of Birmingham

WHERE FUNDING CAN BE GIVEN Birmingham

TYPE OF GRANT Mostly one-off. A few recurrent for three years

FINANCES *Year* 1996 *Income* £41,723

TRUSTEES Prof O L Wade, CBE, MD, FRCP, FRCPI(Hon), C M Priddey, D Dodd, Prof A S McNeish, MD, FRCP

PUBLICATIONS Annual Report and Accounts – year end 31 December

NOTES The Trust was set up, by the wishes of its founder, to benefit the University of Birmingham Medical School and Dental School. The Trustees have adhered to this policy and intend to continue to do so in the future

HOW TO APPLY Applications in writing to the correspondent. Grants are considered in March and October

WHO TO APPLY TO Prof A S McNeish, MD, FRCP, The Arthur Thomson Charitable Trust, The Medical School, The University of Birmingham, Edgbaston, Birmingham B15 2TT

CC NO 233005   **ESTABLISHED** 1963

■ The D C Thomson Charitable Trust

WHAT IS FUNDED General charitable purposes. Grants have been made to organisations which are concerned with the arts, disabled people, social welfare and young people

WHAT IS NOT FUNDED No grants to individuals

WHO CAN BENEFIT There are no restrictions on the age; professional and economic group; family situation; religion and culture; and social circumstances of; or disease or medical condition suffered by, the beneficiaries

WHERE FUNDING CAN BE GIVEN Dundee and Tayside

TRUSTEES D C Thomson & Co Ltd, W D C & F Thomson Ltd

PUBLICATIONS Accounts and an Annual Report are available from the Trust

HOW TO APPLY **This Trust states that it does not respond to unsolicited applications**

WHO TO APPLY TO William Thomson & Sons, The D C Thomson Charitable Trust, 22 Meadowside, Dundee DD1 1LN

SC NO SCO 18413

■ The Len Thomson Charitable Trust

WHAT IS FUNDED Young people, local communities and organisations undertaking medical research

WHO CAN BENEFIT Young people. There is no restriction on the disease or medical condition suffered by the beneficiaries

WHERE FUNDING CAN BE GIVEN Scotland

TRUSTEES D A Connell, S Leslie, Mrs E Thomson

HOW TO APPLY Applications should be made in writing to the address below

WHO TO APPLY TO The Secretary, The Len Thomson Charitable Trust, Messrs Dundas & Wilson, Saltire Court, 20 Castle Terrace, Edinburgh EH21 2EN

SC NO SCO 00981

■ The Scott Thomson Charitable Trust

WHAT IS FUNDED Grants are awarded to organisations which advance Christianity and education and work to combat poverty

WHO CAN BENEFIT Organisations benefiting children and young adults, Christians, and those disadvantaged by poverty

WHERE FUNDING CAN BE GIVEN Scotland

TRUSTEES R H Craig, Ms M B Thomson, R Scott Thomson

PUBLICATIONS Accounts are available from the Trust

HOW TO APPLY Applications should be made in writing to the address below

WHO TO APPLY TO R Scott Thomson, The Scott Thomson Charitable Trust, R Scott Thomson Chartered Accountant, 36 Northwood Drive, Glasgow G46 7LS

SC NO SCO 04071

■ The Thomson Corporation Charitable Trust

WHAT IS FUNDED General charitable purposes

WHAT IS NOT FUNDED No grants for advertisements in souvenir brochures and expeditions or to individuals

WHO CAN BENEFIT Registered charities only. There are no restrictions on the age; professional and economic group; family situation; religion and culture; and social circumstances of; or disease or medical condition suffered by, the beneficiaries

WHERE FUNDING CAN BE GIVEN UK

RANGE OF GRANTS £250–£2,000

SAMPLE GRANTS £2,000 to the Arthritis and Rheumatism Council; £2,000 to British Heart Foundation; £2,000 to Derwent House; £2,000 to the Hearing Research Trust; £2,000 to Marie Curie Cancer Care; £2,000 to MIND; £1,500 to the PACE Centre; £1,350 to Northgate School; £1,000 to BACUP; £1,000 to Breast Cancer Care

FINANCES *Year* 1996 *Income* £103,276 *Grants* £95,300

TRUSTEES H B Bateson, S J H Coles

HOW TO APPLY In writing, Trustees meet on an ad hoc basis

WHO TO APPLY TO Ms A Russell, The Thomson Corporation plc, The Thomson Corporation Charitable Trust, 1st Floor, The Quadrangle, 180 Wardour Street, London W1A 4YG

CC NO 1013317   **ESTABLISHED** 1992

■ The Sue Thomson Foundation

WHAT IS FUNDED Advancement of education, especially of children in need. Trustees' main interest is in Christ's Hospital School, Horsham, and its children, especially those in need

WHAT IS NOT FUNDED No large charities or individuals, except as part of a specific scheme

WHO CAN BENEFIT Small, usually self-help, low overhead organisations benefiting children and young adults

WHERE FUNDING CAN BE GIVEN UK

TYPE OF GRANT Very few apart from Christ's Hospital, one-off grants

RANGE OF GRANTS £100–£1,000 for other than Christ's Hospital

SAMPLE GRANTS £57,921 to Christ's Hospital for the education of children in need; £1,000 to Liver Research Trust for medical research; £1,000 to an individual for education, part of a STF scheme; £500 to The Stationers' Company Charity; £600 to Royal Society of Arts for RSA Appeal; £500 to Handicapped Children's Aid Committee for purchasing special equipment for handicapped children; £500 to Lewis and Harris Youth Clubs to support young people in Lewis and Harris; £300 to RNLI for lifeboats; £263 to British Israel Arts Foundation as a contribution to administration; £250 to Discovery Docklands Trust for young people in London's Docklands

FINANCES *Year* 1996–97 *Income* £111,323 *Grants* £65,099

TRUSTEES Mrs S M Mitchell, C L Corman, J Gillham

HOW TO APPLY No guidelines. Applications acknowledged only if an sae enclosed

WHO TO APPLY TO Mrs S M Mitchell, The Sue Thomson Foundation, Furners Keep, Furners Lane, Henfield, West Sussex BN5 9HS *Tel* 01273 493461

CC NO 298808   **ESTABLISHED** 1988

■ Thoresby Charitable Trust

WHAT IS FUNDED Nottinghamshire based charities with the exception of a few national charities. Particularly those working in the fields of: churches; Anglican bodies; arts, culture and recreation; health facilities and buildings; medical studies and research; conservation and environment; education and training; and transport and community services. Other charitable purposes will be considered

WHAT IS NOT FUNDED No grants to individuals

WHO CAN BENEFIT Organisations, often local branches, usually well established, but innovatory appeals considered. Not normally to individuals. Organisations benefiting those suffering from a range of diseases and medical conditions

WHERE FUNDING CAN BE GIVEN UK with preference to Nottinghamshire

TYPE OF GRANT One-off and project. Funding for one year or less will be considered

RANGE OF GRANTS £100–£1,000

FINANCES *Year* 1997 *Income* £13,700 *Grants* £19,320

TRUSTEES Lady F R R Raynes, H P Matheson, I D P Thorne

HOW TO APPLY Donations decided in January of each year for distribution in March. No application form, if acknowledgement required send sae

WHO TO APPLY TO Mrs R P H McFerran, Thoresby Charitable Trust, Century House, Thoresby Park, Newark, Nottinghamshire NG22 9EH

CC NO 277215   **ESTABLISHED** 1978

■ Thorngate Relief in Need and General Charity

WHAT IS FUNDED Welfare, health, disability and community organisations

WHO CAN BENEFIT Local organisations, local branches of national organisations benefiting: at risk groups; disabled people; those disadvantaged by poverty and socially isolated people. There is no restriction on the disease or medical condition suffered by the beneficiaries

WHERE FUNDING CAN BE GIVEN Hampshire, especially Gosport

RANGE OF GRANTS £14–£500

SAMPLE GRANTS £500 to FORT; £500 to Fareham and Gosport Family Aid Group; £400 to Weekly Club for the Blind; £250 to NSPCC; £250 to Rainbow Centre

FINANCES *Year* 1997 *Income* £14,862
Grants £4,875

HOW TO APPLY To the address under Who To Apply To in writing

WHO TO APPLY TO A E Donnelly, Clerk, Thorngate Relief in Need and General Charity, 16a Palmerston way, Gosport, Hampshire PO12 2LZ

CC NO 210946   **ESTABLISHED** 1981

■ The Thornton Foundation

WHAT IS FUNDED General charitable purposes

WHO CAN BENEFIT There are no restrictions on the age; professional and economic group; family situation; religion and culture; and social circumstances of; or disease or medical condition suffered by, the beneficiaries

WHERE FUNDING CAN BE GIVEN UK

RANGE OF GRANTS £1,000–£100,000

SAMPLE GRANTS £100,000 to St Pauls, Knightsbridge for Capital Appeal; £6,079 to Glyndebourne Productions Ltd for the 1990 Building Fund; £6,000 to St Paul's, Knightsbridge for a music tour; £5,000 to Helen House; £5,000 to Worth School; £3,123 to Bermuda National Trust for Capital Campaign; £1,500 to SCOPE; £1,000 to BREAK – Parents of Handicapped Children; £1,000 to St Mary's Church, Tatsfield; £1,000 to Internal Spinal Research

FINANCES *Year* 1997 *Income* £75,566
Grants £132,702

TRUSTEES A H Isaacs, J G Powell, H D C Thornton, R C Thornton, S J Thornton

WHO TO APPLY TO A H Issacs, The Thornton Foundation, Stephenson Harwood, 1 St Paul's Churchyard, London EC4M 8SH

CC NO 326383   **ESTABLISHED** 1983

■ The Thornton Fund

WHAT IS FUNDED To make grants in connection with advancement of liberal religion and in particular to help Unitarian Ministers and families and students at Unitarian Colleges

WHAT IS NOT FUNDED Grants to persons and causes outside the Unitarian Denomination are made only in exceptional circumstances. No grants to national charities nor for buildings, construction or repair

WHO CAN BENEFIT Students, colleges and ministers within the Unitarian Denomination

WHERE FUNDING CAN BE GIVEN UK

TYPE OF GRANT One-off or recurrent, as appropriate

SAMPLE GRANTS £7,400 as individual grants to students

FINANCES *Year* 1996 *Income* £15,377
Grants £14,352

TRUSTEES S A Woolven, Dr R W Smith, Prof R T Booth, J J Teagle

HOW TO APPLY No application form, total costs and funding required, applications acknowledged

WHO TO APPLY TO S A Woolven, The Thornton Fund, Ironstones, 20 Regent Avenue, Lytham St Annes, Lancashire FY8 4AB

CC NO 226803   **ESTABLISHED** 1918

■ The Thornton Trust

WHAT IS FUNDED Promoting and furthering education and the evangelical Christian faith and assisting in the relief of sickness, suffering and poverty

WHAT IS NOT FUNDED No grants to individuals, nor in response to general appeals

WHO CAN BENEFIT Organisations benefiting Christians, Evangelists, at risk groups, disabled people, those disadvantaged by poverty, and socially isolated people. There is no restriction on the disease or medical condition suffered by the beneficiaries

WHERE FUNDING CAN BE GIVEN UK

FINANCES *Year* 1997–8 *Grants* £193,000

TRUSTEES D H Thornton, Mrs B Y Thornton, J D Thornton

NOTES The funds of the Trust are fully committed and applications are unlikely to be considered

HOW TO APPLY To the address under Who To Apply To in writing. Applications will not be acknowledged

WHO TO APPLY TO D H Thornton, The Thornton Trust, Hunters Cottage, Hunters Yard, Saffron Walden, Essex CB11 4AA

CC NO 205357   **ESTABLISHED** 1962

■ The Thornton-Smith Trust

WHAT IS FUNDED The Trustees concentrate on assisting the elderly persons of the business and professional classes by devoting the income to such individuals through charitable organisations whose aims and objectives are to provide the elderly with a better quality of life. The associated charities are the Thornton Smith Young Peoples Trust and the Wilfred Maurice Plevins Charity, and provide assistance for education

WHAT IS NOT FUNDED Applications from individuals which are not from charities on their behalf will not be considered

WHO CAN BENEFIT Organisations benefiting elderly people. Children and young adults may be given support for education

WHERE FUNDING CAN BE GIVEN UK

FINANCES *Year* 1996 *Income* £30,511
Grants £27,000

TRUSTEES Sir Richard Pease, Bart, C Badcock, Hon H A D Cairns, J H L Norton, J S Varley, Mrs F Tennick, R C Gray, P S Larkman

NOTES £24,000 was given through charitable bodies to elderly people and £3,000 was given directly to retired people

HOW TO APPLY In writing to the Grants Secretary

WHO TO APPLY TO Mrs Emma Hobbs, The Thornton-Smith Trust, 38 Old Bath Road, Charvil, Twyford, Berkshire RG10 9QR

CC NO 306144   **ESTABLISHED** 1965

Does the trust you have chosen match your needs? Haphazard applications waste postage and time

637

■ Dame Margaret Thorold Educational Foundation

WHAT IS FUNDED Schools operating in the area Where Funding Can Be Given

WHO CAN BENEFIT Schools benefiting children and young adults

WHERE FUNDING CAN BE GIVEN The parishes of Cranwell, Marston and Sedgebrook

FINANCES *Year* 1995 *Income* £13,338

HOW TO APPLY To the address under Who To Apply To in writing

WHO TO APPLY TO T S Kelway, Clerk, Dame Margaret Thorold Educational Foundation, Messrs Tallents Godfrey & Co, Solicitors, 3 Middlegate, Newark, Nottinghamshire NG24 1AQ *Tel* 01636 71881

CC NO 527666　　　　　　**ESTABLISHED** 1989

■ The 3i Charitable Trust

WHAT IS FUNDED 3i prefers to support the fundraising efforts of its staff and charities with which staff are involved, together with charities local to any of the 3i offices. Particularly charities working in the fields of: respite and sheltered accommodation; conservation; business schools; and social care and development

WHAT IS NOT FUNDED No grants to individuals

WHO CAN BENEFIT Registered charities only. There is no restriction on the age, or social circumstances of, or the disease or medical condition suffered by the beneficiaries

WHERE FUNDING CAN BE GIVEN Newcastle upon Tyne, Liverpool City, Manchester City, Birmingham City, Solihull, Leeds, London, Aberdeen, Edinburgh, Glasgow and Cardiff

TYPE OF GRANT One-off and project will be considered

SAMPLE GRANTS £100,000 to INSEAD Trust for European Management Education; £50,000 to Royal Opera House Development Appeal; £50,000 to Understanding Industry Trust for education; £25,000 to Cambridge Foundation for education; £13,000 to Birkbeck College for education; £11,450 to Business in the Community for education; £10,000 to London Business School Anniversary Trust for education; £10,000 to North Lambeth Day Centre for homelessness; £7,100 to Percy Hedley Centre for education; £5,422 to NSPCC for support for children in the community

FINANCES *Year* 1998 *Income* £310,000 *Grants* £466,550

TRUSTEES 3i Trustee Company Limited

PUBLICATIONS Report & Accounts

HOW TO APPLY The meetings of the Board of Directors of 3i Trustee Company Limited are held approximately every three months

WHO TO APPLY TO Company Secretary's Office, The 3i Charitable Trust, 3i plc, 91 Waterloo Road, London SE1 8XP *Tel* 0171-928 3131 *Fax* 0171-928 0058

CC NO 1014277　　　　　　**ESTABLISHED** 1988

■ Thriplow Charitable Trust

WHAT IS FUNDED Advancement of higher and further education,the promotion of research and the dissemination of the results of such research

WHAT IS NOT FUNDED No grants to individuals

WHO CAN BENEFIT Universities, university colleges, polytechnics and other places of learning benefiting young adults and older people, academics, research workers and students

WHERE FUNDING CAN BE GIVEN UK

TYPE OF GRANT At the discretion of the Trustees. Buildings, capital, feasibility studies, one-off, project, research, and start-up costs will be considered

RANGE OF GRANTS £500–£10,000

SAMPLE GRANTS £20,000 to Carl Baron Memorial Fund (an ex-Trustee) for student support in the Department of English at the University of Hull; £15,000 to Leeds University Union for student hardship; £12,500 to University College, London – Observatory, for the restoration of the Fry Telescope; £10,000 to University of East Anglia, Overseas Development Group for computer equipment; £10,000 to Bridget's Hostel for a handicapped university student; £10,000 to Girton College, Cambridge for computer equipment; £10,000 to Neil Wiseman Memorial Fund for Research Studentship Fund; £5,000 to Courtauld Institute of Art for scholarships

FINANCES *Year* 1996–97 *Income* £88,000 *Grants* £79,000

TRUSTEES Dr H E W Crawford, Dr K I B Sparck-Jones, Prof C A Bayly, Sir P Swinnerton-Dyer

NOTES Two Trustee meetings per year, spring and autumn

HOW TO APPLY There is no application form. Please state purpose of project, costings and degree of supervision

WHO TO APPLY TO Mrs E Mackintosh, Thriplow Charitable Trust, PO Box 243, Cambridge CB3 9PQ

CC NO 1025531　　　　　　**ESTABLISHED** 1993

■ William Thyne Trust

WHAT IS FUNDED Financial assistance to charitable organisations of Edinburgh (Lothian). All organisations must be recognised as charitable by the Inland Revenue

WHAT IS NOT FUNDED No applications outside Edinburgh (Lothian) will be considered or acknowledged whatever their worth

WHO CAN BENEFIT Local organisations/residents. There are no restrictions on the age; professional and economic group; family situation; religion and culture; and social circumstances of; or disease or medical condition suffered by, the beneficiaries

WHERE FUNDING CAN BE GIVEN Edinburgh (Lothian) exclusively

TYPE OF GRANT One-off

TRUSTEES Rev Jack Orr (Chairman), R Graeme Thom, M J Malcolm

PUBLICATIONS Incorporated in Annual Report of Edinburgh Council of Social Service

HOW TO APPLY Applications for large grants (over £200) are considered quarterly. Forms are available from the Trust Fund Administrator. Applications for small grants (under £200) must be made on form available through social workers, health visitors, etc who work in welfare agencies, either local authorities or voluntary bodies

WHO TO APPLY TO The Trust Fund Administrator, William Thyne Trust, 11 St Colme Street, Edinburgh EH3 6AG *Tel* 0131-225 4606

SC NO SCO 15853　　　　　　**ESTABLISHED** 1936

■ The Tillett Trust

WHAT IS FUNDED Funds are in general directed towards assisting outstanding young professional musicians at the start of their careers and in the main for opportunities offering important performing experience. It is not normally available for those at student level, either undergraduate or postgraduate

WHAT IS NOT FUNDED Funding purchase of musical instruments not included; study courses; commercial recordings; commissioning of new works

WHO CAN BENEFIT To benefit young musicians of outstanding talent

WHERE FUNDING CAN BE GIVEN Musicians wishing to base their career in the UK

TYPE OF GRANT Non-recurrent

RANGE OF GRANTS £200–£2,000

SAMPLE GRANTS £10,000 to Young Concert Artists' Trust for the funding of performances/ management of young artists; £9,000 to Young Artists Platform, the Trust's own scheme for providing concerts for auditions and sponsorship of concerts for those on the scheme; £4,000 to Young Song makers for auditions and concerts; £2,000 to an individual for specialist training in Germany; £1,000 to a trio to travel to New York for YCA auditions; £1,000 to an individual for study under Prof Musin in St Petersburg; £600 to an individual for a Park Lane concert at Purcell Room; £500 to an individual for a recital tour of China

FINANCES *Year* 1998 *Income* £50,000
Grants £35,000

TRUSTEES Paul Strang (Chairman), D L Booth, Miss Fiona Grant, Miss Yvonne Minton, CBE, David Stiff (Hon Treasurer), Miss Clara Taylor

HOW TO APPLY No deadlines. Application by letter. No form used. Enclose CV or biography and references, also performance cassette if available and budget for project

WHO TO APPLY TO Miss K Avey, Secretary to the Trust, The Tillett Trust, Courtyard House, Neopardy, Crediton, Devon EX17 5EP *Fax* 01363 777845

CC NO 257329   **ESTABLISHED** 1963

■ The Tisbury Telegraph Trust

WHAT IS FUNDED Most distributions are to charities of which the trustees have personal knowledge. Other applications are unlikely to be successful. Particularly charities working in the fields of: charity or voluntary umbrella bodies; the advancement of Christianity; Anglican bodies and Free Church; dance and ballet; hospices; MS research; flora and fauna, waterways, wildlife parks and sanctuaries, zoos; ecology, environmental issues, renewable energy and power; transport and alternative transport; church schools, pre-school education; special schools and special needs education and playgrounds. Other charitable purposes will be considered

WHAT IS NOT FUNDED No grants to individuals

WHO CAN BENEFIT Registered charities only benefiting: children and young adults; medical professionals; those in care, fostered and adopted; parents and children; one parent families; Christians and Evangelists; disaster victims; homeless people; refugees and victims of war. Those suffering from various diseases and medical conditions will also be considered

WHERE FUNDING CAN BE GIVEN UK and the developing world

TYPE OF GRANT Core costs, one-off, project, research and running costs will be considered

RANGE OF GRANTS £100–£4,000. Any unsolicited applications will not receive more than about £400

SAMPLE GRANTS £4,600 to Community of Celebration; £4,100 to St Mary Magdalene PCC; £2,010 to World Vision UK; £1,900 to St Paul's Church Harvest Appeal for Romania; £1,800 to Post Green Community; £1,500 to Church Mission Society; £1,400 to Christian Aid; £1,200 to Shelter; £1,120 to The National Trust; £1,000 to Help the Aged

FINANCES *Year* 1997 *Income* £57,618
Grants £34,918

TRUSTEES J Davidson, A Davidson, E Orr, R Orr, S Phippard

HOW TO APPLY Applications only acknowledged if sae enclosed. No telephone applications please

WHO TO APPLY TO Mrs E Orr, The Tisbury Telegraph Trust, 35 Kitto Road, Telegraph Hill, London SE14 5TW *E-mail* rogero@howzatt.demon.co.uk

CC NO 328595   **ESTABLISHED** 1990

■ The Tobit Trust (formerly known as The Ault-Ohea Charitable Trust)

WHAT IS FUNDED Welfare, education, humanities and religion

WHO CAN BENEFIT Children, young adults and students; at risk groups; those disadvantaged by poverty; and socially isolated people. There is no restriction on the religion or culture of the beneficiaries

WHERE FUNDING CAN BE GIVEN UK and overseas

TYPE OF GRANT One off range of grants

RANGE OF GRANTS £99–£2,250

SAMPLE GRANTS £2,250 to Ellel Ministries; £1,200 to Royal Academy of Music; £750 to Cormac O'Duffy; £500 to National Viewers and Listeners Association; £500 to Aid to Russian Christians

FINANCES *Year* 1997 *Income* £16,027
Grants £9,299

TRUSTEES Mary Ault, Timothy J Ault, R P Ault, Katherine Knollys

HOW TO APPLY In writing. The Trustees meet as required

WHO TO APPLY TO P D Ault, FCA, The Tobit Trust, 12 Weybridge Park, Weybridge, Surrey KT13 8SQ

CC NO 1026112   **ESTABLISHED** 1993

■ The Tolkien Trust

WHAT IS FUNDED General charitable purposes

WHO CAN BENEFIT There are no restrictions on the age; professional and economic group; family situation; religion and culture; and social circumstances of; or disease or medical condition suffered by, the beneficiaries

WHERE FUNDING CAN BE GIVEN UK

RANGE OF GRANTS £250–£12,000

SAMPLE GRANTS £12,000 to Find Your Feet Ltd; £5,500 to University of Oxford Bodleian Library; £5,000 to Shelter; £5,000 to Medical Foundation for the Victims of Torture; £3,500 to Social Care Unit St Martin in the Fields; £3,000 to Gatehouse, Oxford; £2,520 to Amnesty International; £2,000 to the Tablet Trust; £2,000 to CAFOD; £2,000 to the Samaritans

FINANCES *Year* 1997 *Income* £78,995
Grants £73,500

TRUSTEES J F R Tolkien, C R Tolkien, Ms P M A R Tolkien, F R Williamson

WHO TO APPLY TO Mrs Cathleen Blackburn, The Tolkien Trust, 3 Worcester Street, Oxford OX1 2PZ

CC NO 273615   **ESTABLISHED** 1977

■ Tollemache (Buckminster) Charitable Trust

WHAT IS FUNDED General charitable purposes

WHAT IS NOT FUNDED No grants to individuals

WHO CAN BENEFIT There are no restrictions on the age; professional and economic group; family situation; religion and culture; and social circumstances of; or disease or medical condition suffered by, the beneficiaries

WHERE FUNDING CAN BE GIVEN UK

FINANCES *Year* 1997 *Income* £22,000
Grants £22,000

TRUSTEES Sir Lyonel Tollemache, Bt, H M Neal, W H G Wilks

HOW TO APPLY To Secretary, no acknowledgements sent

WHO TO APPLY TO The Secretary, Tollemache (Buckminster) Charitable Trust, Estate Office, Buckminster, Grantham, Lincolnshire NG33 5SD

CC NO 271795　　　**ESTABLISHED** 1976

■ Tomchei Torah Charitable Trust

WHAT IS FUNDED Jewish causes

WHO CAN BENEFIT Jewish people

WHERE FUNDING CAN BE GIVEN UK and overseas

TYPE OF GRANT At the discretion of the Trustees

RANGE OF GRANTS £50–£10,500

SAMPLE GRANTS £10,500 to Chesed Charity Trust; £6,600 to Woodstock Sinclair Trust; £5,800 to Gateshead Talmudical College; £3,000 to TTE Yetev Lev; £2,500 to Gateshead Foundation for Torah; £1,250 to Support; £1,180 to Torah Temimah Primary School; £1,000 to Yeshivas Shaarei Torah; £750 to Yeshivah L'zeirim Tiferes Yaacov; £610 to Chevras Ezras Nitrichim

FINANCES *Year* 1996 *Income* £77,985
Grants £40,537

TRUSTEES I J Kohn, S M Kohn, A Frei

WHO TO APPLY TO A Frei, Tomchei Torah Charitable Trust, Harold Everett Wreford, Harford House, 101–103 Great Portland Street, London W1N 6BH　*Tel* 0171-637 8891　*Fax* 0171-580 8485　*E-mail* hew@dial.pipex.com

CC NO 802125　　　**ESTABLISHED** 1989

■ Torchbearer Trust

WHAT IS FUNDED For the promotion and encouragement of the Christian faith: (a) enabling or assisting persons who are professing Christians by the provision of bursaries or grants to obtain full-time instruction and training; (b) supporting people engaged in full-time Christian or Missionary work. Mainly grants given to students or ex-students of Torchbearer. Also, support of those in full-time Christian work

WHO CAN BENEFIT Young adults; students; volunteers; Christians and evangelists

WHERE FUNDING CAN BE GIVEN UK and overseas

TYPE OF GRANT Single and recurring as required by the project. Funding is available for up to one year

SAMPLE GRANTS £26,325 to Ethiopia Farm Mission Support and others; £19,688 to students attending Capernwray Bible Schools for full-time courses

FINANCES *Year* 1997 *Income* £179,695
Grants £46,013

TRUSTEES Ms A Mills, Ms J Thomas, M Thomas, J C Nodder

PUBLICATIONS Annual Report

HOW TO APPLY As received. No form required

WHO TO APPLY TO The Secretary, Torchbearer Trust, Capernwray Hall, Carnforth, Lancashire LA6 1AG　*Tel* 01524 733908

CC NO 253607　　　**ESTABLISHED** 1956

■ The Tory Family Foundation

WHAT IS FUNDED General charitable purposes. To support local needs in preference to national appeals

WHAT IS NOT FUNDED No grants for further education

WHO CAN BENEFIT There are no restrictions on the age; professional and economic group; family situation; religion and culture; and social circumstances of; or disease or medical condition suffered by, the beneficiaries

WHERE FUNDING CAN BE GIVEN Mainly Kent but also overseas

SAMPLE GRANTS £8,000 to St Ethelburga's, Lyminge, Kent for heating system; £5,800 to Metropole Arts Centre for music and children's festival; £5,000 to Battle of Britain Memorial Trust for awning at Hawkinge Memorial; £5,000 to Museum of Kent Life for a farmhouse project; £5,000 to Kent Trust for Nature Conservation; £3,000 to St Radigund's, Capel-le-Ferne for rebuilding project; £2,750 to an individual for coursework and accommodation; £2,000 to Buckmore Park for renovation of buildings; £2,000 to Canterbury Volunteer Bureau for gardening project; £2,000 to Marie Stopes for an appeal

FINANCES *Year* 1997 *Income* £83,314
Grants £67,562

TRUSTEES P N Tory, J N Tory, Mrs S A Rice

HOW TO APPLY To the address under Who To Apply To

WHO TO APPLY TO P N Tory, The Tory Family Foundation, The Estate Office, Etchinghill Golf, Folkestone, Kent CT18 8FA

CC NO 326584　　　**ESTABLISHED** 1984

■ The Tower Hill Improvement Trust

WHAT IS FUNDED Organisations working for the relief of need or sickness; to provide leisure and recreation facilities for social welfare and in support of education and to provide and maintain gardens and open spaces

WHO CAN BENEFIT Community-based organisations and appeals benefiting children and young adults, at risk groups, those disadvantaged by poverty and socially isolated people. There is no restriction on the disease or medical condition suffered by the beneficiaries

WHERE FUNDING CAN BE GIVEN The east end of London – Great Tower Hill, Tower Hill, St Katherines Ward in the London Borough of Tower Hamlets

RANGE OF GRANTS £1,000–£19635

SAMPLE GRANTS £19,635 to St Botolph's Project; £4,550 to Ensign Youth Club; £1,000 to Tower Hamlets Youth Exchange

FINANCES *Year* 1997 *Income* £168,517
Grants £25,185

TRUSTEES C G A Parker, JP, MA, DL, D V Palmer, DL, Capt J Cloke, Mrs J Walter, Maj Gen C Taylor, CB

NOTES The Trustees meet to consider applications every three months

HOW TO APPLY To the address under Who To Apply To in writing

WHO TO APPLY TO James Connelly, Secretary, The Tower Hill Improvement Trust, Atlee House, 28 Commercial Street, London E1 6LR

CC NO 206225　　　**ESTABLISHED** 1938

■ The Fred Towler Charity Trust

WHAT IS FUNDED To provide holidays for aged (one-third of income). To support charities devoted to sick, aged and youth (two-thirds of income) and other charitable purposes

WHAT IS NOT FUNDED Gifts are to local charities or local branches of national societies; no grants to individuals

WHO CAN BENEFIT Local charities or local branches of national societies benefiting: children and older people; retired people; those disadvantaged by poverty and those living in urban areas

WHERE FUNDING CAN BE GIVEN Bradford

TYPE OF GRANT For recurrent operational expenses. Funding of up to three years will be considered

SAMPLE GRANTS £7,000 to Craig Convalescent Home; £5,800 to Tradesmen's Homes; £1,250 to Catholic Housing; £1,250 to Spinsters Endowment; £1,250 to Methodist's Homes; £1,050 to Martin House; £1,050 to Bradford Sea Cadets; £700 to the Salvation Army; £520 to Riding for the Disabled; £420 to Bradford Nightstop

FINANCES *Year* 1998 *Income* £38,854
Grants £34,740

TRUSTEES Ten professional and business men in Bradford District

HOW TO APPLY April and October annually

WHO TO APPLY TO P G Meredith, The Fred Towler Charity Trust, Howarth Clark Whitehill, Chartered Accountants, Pelican House, 10 Currer Street, Bradford, West Yorkshire BD1 5BA
Tel 01274 732522 *Fax* 01274 390154

CC NO 225026   **ESTABLISHED** 1939

■ The Town Lands (also known as The Utility Estate)

WHAT IS FUNDED Welfare and general charitable purposes in the Beneficial Area

WHO CAN BENEFIT Individuals and organisations. There are no restrictions on the age; professional and economic group; family situation; religion and culture; and social circumstances of; or disease or medical condition suffered by, the beneficiaries

WHERE FUNDING CAN BE GIVEN Tysoe

FINANCES *Year* 1995 *Income* £29,812

HOW TO APPLY To the address under Who To Apply To in writing

WHO TO APPLY TO Mrs J Walton, Secretary, The Town Lands, Lane End Farm, Lower Tysoe, Warwick, Warwickshire CV35 0BZ *Tel* 01295 680289

CC NO 241493   **ESTABLISHED** 1965

■ Town Lands Charity

WHAT IS FUNDED The maintenance of Cheddington Parish Church, the poor people in the parish and provision of public amenities

WHO CAN BENEFIT Local individuals and local organisations. There are no restrictions on the age; professional and economic group; family situation; religion and culture; and social circumstances of; or disease or medical condition suffered by, the beneficiaries. However, particular favour is given to those disadvantaged by poverty in the Parish of Cheddington, and to Christians

WHERE FUNDING CAN BE GIVEN Cheddington in Bedfordshire

SAMPLE GRANTS To Cheddington PCC for upkeep and operation of the church; To Cheddington Village Hall to subsidise hall for use by local groups; To summer playscheme; To Baby and Toddler Group; To Pentanque Club; To Luncheon Club

FINANCES *Year* 1997 *Income* £26,494
Grants £24,404

TRUSTEES Mrs P Banister, Rev R A Hale, J Hance, Mrs A Mayes, Mrs J Roff

HOW TO APPLY To the address under Who To Apply To in writing

WHO TO APPLY TO W G King, Treasurer, Town Lands Charity, 5 Chaseside Close, Cheddington, Leighton Buzzard, Bedfordshire LU7 0SA

CC NO 235076   **ESTABLISHED** 1964

■ The Towry Law Charitable Trust

WHAT IS FUNDED For the support of education of young people and general charitable purposes. Approximately 55 per cent of the 1997 grant total, was given to charities which specialise in helping or caring for children, or assisting children and young people with their education. In addition over 34 per cent of the total represented grants made to charitable bodies specialising in medical research or assisting disabled or elderly people

WHO CAN BENEFIT Organisations benefiting people of all ages and disabled people. Medical professionals, research workers and students may be considered

WHERE FUNDING CAN BE GIVEN UK

TYPE OF GRANT At the discretion of the trustees

FINANCES *Year* 1997 *Income* £724,991
Grants £266,000

TRUSTEES Hon C T H Law, K H Holmes, D G Ainslie

WHO TO APPLY TO D G Ainslie, The Towry Law Charitable Trust, 57 High Street, Windsor, Berkshire SL4 1LX

CC NO 278880   **ESTABLISHED** 1979

■ The Toy Trust

WHAT IS FUNDED General charitable purposes for children and young people

WHO CAN BENEFIT Children and young adults

WHERE FUNDING CAN BE GIVEN UK and overseas

TYPE OF GRANT Substantial donations to about three charities each year

SAMPLE GRANTS £20,000 to HAPA; £15,000 to Toy Box for Street Children of Guatemala; £7,000 to Hope House Children's Hospice; £5,000 to Constable Educational Trust; £5,000 to Essex Association for Spina Bifida

FINANCES *Year* 1997 *Income* £261,549
Grants £191,343

TRUSTEES The British Toy and Hobby Association, I H Scott, A Munn, M Butcher, N Austin, D L Hawtin

HOW TO APPLY Applications to Anil Vidyarthi, Accountant, or Ms Karen Baxter at the address below

WHO TO APPLY TO The Toy Trust, BTHA Ltd, 80 Camberwell Road, London SE5 0EG

CC NO 1001634   **ESTABLISHED** 1990

Does the trust you have chosen match your needs? Haphazard applications waste postage and time

641

■ Trades Union Congress Educational Trust (108)

This trust declined to meet CAF's researchers and failed to supply a copy of its annual report and accounts to CAF as required under section 47(2) of the Charities Act 1993. The information held on file at the Charity Commission was insufficient to enable CAF's researchers to write a substantive commentary on the trust's activities. Accordingly, despite its size, we are unable to list this trust in Spotlight on Major Trusts

WHAT IS FUNDED Restricted to courses provided at Colleges of Further Education and by the WEA for the TUC for trade union members and at specified Adult Education Colleges listed below. No grants are made in respect of graduate or postgraduate courses

WHAT IS NOT FUNDED Generally available only to the members of trade unions affiliated to the TUC

WHO CAN BENEFIT Members of trade unions affiliated to TUC

WHERE FUNDING CAN BE GIVEN UK

TYPE OF GRANT (a) Tutorial and resource costs of courses provided directly by the Trust.
(b) Bursaries of £800 each tenable at Ruskin, Northern and Hillcroft Colleges and Coleg Harlech for 1 year course of study only

FINANCES *Year* 1996 *Income* £256,020

TRUSTEES J Knapp, J Monks, Rita Donaghy, Nigel de Gruchy, John Edmonds, Barry Reamsbottom, A F Grant (Secretary),

HOW TO APPLY By 1 June each year for the following academic year

WHO TO APPLY TO Paul Clark, Centre Manager, Trades Union Congress Educational Trust, TUC National Education Centre, 77 Crouchend Hill, London N8 8DG

CC NO 313741   **ESTABLISHED** 1946

■ Trafalgar Street Church

WHAT IS FUNDED To advance the Christian faith; to relieve persons who are in conditions of need, hardship or distress and who are aged or sick; other general charitable purposes

WHO CAN BENEFIT Organisations benefiting Christians, those in conditions of need, hardship or distress, sick and elderly people. There is no restriction on the disease or medical condition suffered by the beneficiaries

WHERE FUNDING CAN BE GIVEN UK, with a preference for Hull, and overseas

SAMPLE GRANTS £11,125 to Church missionaries

FINANCES *Year* 1997 *Income* £35,240
Grants £11,125

TRUSTEES M Bradshaw, A Couper, T Kelsey, L Pickering, M Rattenbury, A Smith, D Smith

WHO TO APPLY TO A Smith, Trafalgar Street Church, 250 Ings Road, Hull HU8 0LZ

CC NO 1058354   **ESTABLISHED** 1996

■ The Training For All Foundation

WHAT IS FUNDED Education and training

WHO CAN BENEFIT Organisations benefiting children, young adults and students. Support may also be given to teachers

WHERE FUNDING CAN BE GIVEN UK

FINANCES *Year* 1995–96 *Income* £159,431
Grants £100,270

TRUSTEES B V Cleaver, Ms S A King, G Sehint, B A Darby

WHO TO APPLY TO Ms H Blewitt, The Training For All Foundation, 1st Floor, Daviot House, Lombard Street West, West Bromwich B70 8EG

CC NO 1056953   **ESTABLISHED** 1995

■ Annie Tranmer Charitable Trust

WHAT IS FUNDED General charitable purposes

WHAT IS NOT FUNDED No grants to individuals or students

WHO CAN BENEFIT Small local projects. There are no restrictions on the age; professional and economic group; family situation; religion and culture; and social circumstances of; or disease or medical condition suffered by, the beneficiaries

WHERE FUNDING CAN BE GIVEN South Suffolk

TYPE OF GRANT One-off

FINANCES *Year* 1995 *Income* £158,603

TRUSTEES J F F Miller, V A Lewis

PUBLICATIONS Annual Report

NOTES Trust confines its activities almost entirely to causes within South Suffolk

HOW TO APPLY In writing

WHO TO APPLY TO Mrs M R Kirby, Clerk to the Trustees, Annie Tranmer Charitable Trust, 51 Bennett Road, Ipswich, Suffolk IP1 5HX

CC NO 1044231   **ESTABLISHED** 1995

■ The Trans-Antarctic Association

WHAT IS FUNDED To award grants to assist applicants with projects to support and promote Antarctic research and exploration

WHAT IS NOT FUNDED Projects proposed for support must be directly related to furthering knowledge or exploration of the Antarctic by nationals of UK, Australia, South Africa and New Zealand only

WHO CAN BENEFIT Citizens and research workers of UK, Australia, South Africa and New Zealand

WHERE FUNDING CAN BE GIVEN Nationals of UK, Australia, South Africa and New Zealand for research and exploration of Antarctica only

TYPE OF GRANT Research grants

FINANCES *Year* 1995 *Income* £13,618
Grants £7,949

TRUSTEES The Committee of Management: Dr J A Heap, Dr H H Atkinson, W G Lowe, Dr G de Q Robin (Chairman)

HOW TO APPLY To Grants Secretary by 31 January each year

WHO TO APPLY TO E M Dunmore, Company Secretary, Trans-Antarctic Association, 28 Ely Place, London EC1N 6RL

CC NO 205773   **ESTABLISHED** 1962

■ Constance Travis Charitable Trust

WHAT IS FUNDED General causes. Must be registered charities. Priority is given to work in Northamptonshire

WHAT IS NOT FUNDED No grants to individuals for education, travel, etc

WHO CAN BENEFIT General causes. There are no restrictions on the age; professional and economic group; family situation; religion and culture; and social circumstances of; or disease or medical condition suffered by, the beneficiaries

WHERE FUNDING CAN BE GIVEN Anywhere in the UK, but priority is given to Northamptonshire

TYPE OF GRANT One-off

RANGE OF GRANTS £500–£5,000

FINANCES *Year* 1998 *Income* £173,000
Grants £136,000
TRUSTEES C M Travis, E R A Travis
HOW TO APPLY There are no application forms, guidelines or application deadlines. No sae is required
WHO TO APPLY TO E R A Travis, Constance Travis Charitable Trust, Quinton Rising, Quinton, Northampton NN7 2EF
CC NO 294540 ESTABLISHED 1986

■ Trial Charitable Trust

WHAT IS FUNDED General charitable purposes
WHO CAN BENEFIT There are no restrictions on the age; professional and economic group; family situation; religion and culture; and social circumstances of; or disease or medical condition suffered by, the beneficiaries
WHERE FUNDING CAN BE GIVEN UK
WHO TO APPLY TO R Brown, Trial Charitable Trust, 10 Acacia Road, Balham, London SW12 4AY
CC NO 1051205 ESTABLISHED 1995

■ The Trinity House Charities

WHAT IS FUNDED Seafarers charities, almshouses, the upkeep of Trinity House and chapel, Trinity House School
WHO CAN BENEFIT Local organisations benefiting seafarers and fishermen, those disadvantaged by poverty and children and young adults of the Trinity House School
WHERE FUNDING CAN BE GIVEN Kingston-upon-Hull
TYPE OF GRANT Some recurrent (all those going to seafarers charities)
SAMPLE GRANTS £481,249 to almshouses and pensioners; £18,258 to Trinity House School; £400 to Sailors' Families Society; £400 to Missions to Seamen; £300 to Shipwrecked Fishermen and Mariners' Royal Benevolent Society
FINANCES *Year* 1997 *Income* £1,626,012
Grants £500,607
TRUSTEES Wardens: Capt K Balland, FNI, J W Waldie. Elder Brethren: Capt D Stokes, OBE, Capt N Sharp, MBE, Capt G V Barnes, Capt W V Hopper, Capt W White, Capt N O Cook, Capt W Patch, FIMgt, Capt M D Whiteley, FNI, Capt J Gordon, Capt E Howlett
HOW TO APPLY To the address under Who To Apply To in writing
WHO TO APPLY TO W E Rutter, Secretary to the Trustees, The Trinity House Charities, The Hull Trinity House, Trinity House Lane, Hull HU1 2JG
CC NO 220331 ESTABLISHED 1962

■ Triodos Foundation

WHAT IS FUNDED International and general charitable purposes. The objectives of the Triodos Foundation are to support charitable needs which have been identified through, but which are unable to be fully supported by, the work of Triodos Bank in the UK. Considerable experience in this activity has already been built up through our work in the Netherlands, where Triodos Bank has been involved in grant-making since 1971 through Stichting Triodos (Triodos Foundation). Triodos Foundation brings this grant-making experience together with Triodos Bank's experience in the charitable and community sector in the UK over more than 22 years. Triodos Foundation is a registered charity and, as the UK counterpart of the Stichting Triodos, it received charitable registration in March 1996. Triodos Foundation is working closely with individuals, organisations and depositors of the bank to support projects which work in charitable areas. The Foundation is integrating the services it offers with those offered by Triodos Bank. The Foundation is also offering a separate range of administrative services for donors and charities, including covenant and gift aid processing. The work of the Foundation enables many more valuable projects to stand alongside those already supported by Triodos Bank
WHAT IS NOT FUNDED No grants to individuals or students
WHO CAN BENEFIT Registered charities. There are no restrictions on the age; professional and economic group; family situation; religion and culture; and social circumstances of; or disease or medical condition suffered by, the beneficiaries
WHERE FUNDING CAN BE GIVEN UK and overseas
TYPE OF GRANT A range of grants
FINANCES *Year* 1997 *Income* £136,000
Grants £36,000
TRUSTEES M Robinson, P Blom, G Saunders
NOTES Please phone for advice if any organisation wishes to apply to the foundation
HOW TO APPLY At any time
WHO TO APPLY TO M Robinson, Triodos Foundation, c/o Triodos Bank, Brunel House, 11 The Promenade, Bristol BS8 3NN *Tel* 0117-973 9339 *Fax* 0117-973 9303
CC NO 1052958 ESTABLISHED 1996

■ The Joanna Trollope Charitable Trust

WHAT IS FUNDED To promote welfare of young people suffering from mental and physical disabilities; to promote the education especially of poor, sick or disabled young people; to help the homeless and to provide recreation for poor, sick or needy individuals. Also interested in supporting research into the causes of cancer
WHO CAN BENEFIT Individuals, and organisations benefiting children, young adults, disabled people, and those disadvantaged by poverty and homeless people. There is no restriction on the disease or medical condition suffered by the beneficiaries. Medical professionals, doctors, nurses and research workers may be considered
WHERE FUNDING CAN BE GIVEN County of Gloucestershire and the South West of England
TYPE OF GRANT One-off and research will be considered
TRUSTEES I B Curteis, Ms J Curteis
WHO TO APPLY TO A Cowgill, Solicitor, The Joanna Trollope Charitable Trust, Godwin, Bremridge and Clifton, 12 St Thomas Street, Winchester, Hampshire SO23 9HF *Tel* 01962 841484
CC NO 1049190 ESTABLISHED 1995

■ Mrs S H Troughton Charity Trust

WHAT IS FUNDED General charitable purposes
WHO CAN BENEFIT Individuals and organisations. There are no restrictions on the age; professional and economic group; family situation; religion and culture; and social circumstances of; or disease or medical condition suffered by; the beneficiaries
WHERE FUNDING CAN BE GIVEN UK
RANGE OF GRANTS £400–£12,000

SAMPLE GRANTS £12,000 to West Heath School; £5,000 to Charities Aid Foundation
FINANCES *Year* 1996 *Income* £23,425
Grants £18,940
TRUSTEES The Dickinson Trust Ltd
WHO TO APPLY TO The Secretary, Mrs S H Troughton Charity Trust, The Dickinson Trust Ltd, 10–12 Cork Street, London W1X 1PD
CC NO 265957   **ESTABLISHED** 1972

■ Truedene Co Ltd

WHAT IS FUNDED Educational, religious and other charitable institutions, principally Jewish
WHO CAN BENEFIT Organisations benefiting children, young adults, students and Jewish people
WHERE FUNDING CAN BE GIVEN Great Britain and overseas
FINANCES *Year* 1995 *Income* £512,296
Grants £461,133
TRUSTEES The Governors: H Laufer, M Gross, S Berger, S Laufer, S Berger
WHO TO APPLY TO Truedene Co Ltd, Cohen Arnold & Co, 13–17 New Burlington Place, London W1
CC NO 248268   **ESTABLISHED** 1966

■ The Truemark Trust

WHAT IS FUNDED Small organisations more likely to be favoured. Innovatory projects preferred. Current main areas of interest are the disabled, the elderly and those otherwise disadvantaged and include counselling and community support groups in areas of unrest or deprivation, alternate health projects
WHAT IS NOT FUNDED Registered charities only. Applications from individuals, including students, are ineligible. No grants are made in response to general appeals from large national organisations. Grants are seldom available for churches or church buildings or for scientific or medical research projects
WHO CAN BENEFIT Registered charities with preference for neighbourhood-based community projects and innovatory work with less popular groups. Older people; at risk groups; disabled people; those disadvantaged by poverty; socially isolated people; and those living in deprived areas will be considered
WHERE FUNDING CAN BE GIVEN UK only
TYPE OF GRANT Usually one-off for a specific project or part of a project. Core funding and/or salaries rarely considered
RANGE OF GRANTS Average grant £1,000
FINANCES *Year* 1997 *Income* £160,802
Grants £149,480
TRUSTEES Sir Thomas Lucas, Bt (Senior Trustee), Michael Collishaw, Michael Meakin, Alan Thompson, Richard Wolfe, Wendy Collett
HOW TO APPLY At any time. Trustees meet four times a year. Applications should include clear details of the need the intended project is designed to meet plus an outline budget and the most recent available annual accounts of the charity. Only successful applications are informed
WHO TO APPLY TO Mrs Judy Hayward, The Truemark Trust, PO Box 2, Liss, Hampshire GU33 6YP
CC NO 265855   **ESTABLISHED** 1973

■ Trumros Limited

WHAT IS FUNDED Jewish religious and educational institutions
WHO CAN BENEFIT Jewish institutions
WHERE FUNDING CAN BE GIVEN UK
FINANCES *Year* 1995 *Income* £597,877
Grants £72,558
TRUSTEES Mrs H Hofbaner, R S Hofbaner, M Kahn
HOW TO APPLY To the address under Who To Apply To in writing, though the Trust has more applications than it can give proper consideration
WHO TO APPLY TO R S Hofbaner, Trustee, Trumros Limited, 11 Basing Hill, London NW11 8TE
CC NO 285533   **ESTABLISHED** 1982

■ Trust Sixty Three

WHAT IS FUNDED General charitable purposes
WHO CAN BENEFIT There are no restrictions on the age; professional and economic group; family situation; religion and culture; and social circumstances of; or disease or medical condition suffered by, the beneficiaries
WHERE FUNDING CAN BE GIVEN UK
FINANCES *Year* 1997 *Income* £34,520
Grants £30,020
TRUSTEES M W Tait, Mrs A F Tait, C G Nott, Mrs J Hobbs, Mrs D Staines
WHO TO APPLY TO Mrs A F Tait, Trustee, Trust Sixty Three, 3 The Compasses, High Street, Clophill, Bedfordshire MK45 4AF *Tel* 01582 881999
CC NO 1049136   **ESTABLISHED** 1995

■ The Trusthouse Charitable Foundation

WHAT IS FUNDED General charitable purposes
WHO CAN BENEFIT There are no restrictions on the age; professional and economic group; family situation; religion and culture; and social circumstances of; or disease or medical condition suffered by, the beneficiaries
WHERE FUNDING CAN BE GIVEN UK
TRUSTEES Hon Lord H W Astor, A Bernstein, Rt Hon Lord J A Boyd-Carpenter, Rt Hon Lord L J Callaghan of Cardiff, Rt Hon Earl A G E Noel of Gainsborough, Most Noble J G V H Spencer-Churchill, Duke of Marlborough, Hon O Pollizzi, Rt Hon Lord J W W Peyton of Yeovil, Sir H A L Rossi, Sir P H G Wright
WHO TO APPLY TO Derek P Harris, The Trusthouse Charitable Foundation, 41 Tower Hill, London EC3N 4HA
CC NO 1063945   **ESTABLISHED** 1997

■ The Tryst Settlement

This trust did not respond to CAF's request to amend its entry and, by 30 June 1998, CAF's researchers did not find financial records for later than 1995 on its file at the Charity Commission. Trusts are legally required to submit annual accounts to the Charity Commission under section 42 of the Charities Act 1993

WHAT IS FUNDED General charitable purposes at Trustees' discretion
WHO CAN BENEFIT Institutions. There are no restrictions on the age; professional and economic group; family situation; religion and culture; and social circumstances of; or disease or medical condition suffered by, the beneficiaries
WHERE FUNDING CAN BE GIVEN UK and overseas
TYPE OF GRANT Range of grants

644

Think carefully about every application. Is it justified?

TRUSTEES S W Urry, P M Urry, D B Greenwood

WHO TO APPLY TO S W Urry, The Tryst Settlement, Old House, Ewhurst Green, Cranleigh, Surrey GU6 7SE

CC NO 327909 **ESTABLISHED** 1988

■ The Roy Tucker Charitable Settlement

This trust did not respond to CAF's request to amend its entry and, by 30 June 1998, CAF's researchers did not find financial records for later than 1995 on its file at the Charity Commission. Trusts are legally required to submit annual accounts to the Charity Commission under section 42 of the Charities Act 1993

WHAT IS FUNDED General charitable purposes

WHO CAN BENEFIT There are no restrictions on the age; professional and economic group; family situation; religion and culture; and social circumstances of; or disease or medical condition suffered by, the beneficiaries

WHERE FUNDING CAN BE GIVEN UK

TRUSTEES K R Tucker, Mrs A H Tucker

WHO TO APPLY TO Mrs A H Tucker, The Roy Tucker Charitable Settlement, Nettlestead Place, Nettlestead, Maidstone ME18 5HA

CC NO 269888 **ESTABLISHED** 1975

■ Tudor Rose Ltd

WHAT IS FUNDED Advancement of religion (Orthodox Jewish) and relief of poverty and other charitable purposes. Trustees have very limited funds available

WHO CAN BENEFIT Registered charities benefiting Jewish people and those disadvantaged by poverty

WHERE FUNDING CAN BE GIVEN UK

FINANCES *Year* 1997 *Income* £88,559 *Grants* £87,250

TRUSTEES S Feldman, H F Feldman

WHO TO APPLY TO Martin and Heller, Accountants, Tudor Rose Ltd, 5 North End Road, London NW11 7RJ *Tel* 0181-455 6789

CC NO 800576 **ESTABLISHED** 1987

■ The Tufton Charitable Trust

WHAT IS FUNDED Christian activity supporting evangelism

WHAT IS NOT FUNDED No grants for repair or maintenance of buildings

WHO CAN BENEFIT Individuals and organisations benefiting Christians, Jews and Evangelists

WHERE FUNDING CAN BE GIVEN England

TYPE OF GRANT One-off and project related but not grants for repair or maintenance of buildings

SAMPLE GRANTS £15,500 to London Goodenough Trust; £10,000 to William Wates Memorial Trust; £2,500 to the Institute of Economic Affairs; £350 to Streatham and Clapham High School; £300 to Acton Institute for the Study of Religion and Liberty; £250 to Rehabilitation for Addicted Prisoners Trust

FINANCES *Year* 1997 *Income* £216,814 *Grants* £47,455

TRUSTEES Sir Christopher Wates, Lady Wates, J R F Lulham

HOW TO APPLY In writing enclosing an sae for a reply

WHO TO APPLY TO The Tufton Charitable Trust, Wates Charitable Trustees Limited, 7 St James's Square, London SW1Y 7JU

CC NO 801479 **ESTABLISHED** 1989

■ The John Tunnell Trust

WHAT IS FUNDED Fees are paid to proven chamber music groups in order to encourage the development of chamber music in Scotland

WHAT IS NOT FUNDED Awards are not made to singers, soloists, or to groups who are non-British or whose average age exceeds 27 years. (Awards are not grants but fees paid for engagements arranged by the Trust throughout Scotland)

WHO CAN BENEFIT Young British-based professional chamber music groups. We do not pay money to Scottish Music Clubs but provide them with free concerts

WHERE FUNDING CAN BE GIVEN Scotland, England and Wales

RANGE OF GRANTS Up to approximately £5,000

SAMPLE GRANTS £7,100 to Gilliver/Jones Duo for recital fees; £4,800 to Leopold String Trio for recital fees

FINANCES *Year* 1996–97 *Income* £14,921 *Grants* £11,900

TRUSTEES S Brown, O W Tunnell, J Hogel, C J Packard, K M Robb, D W S Todd, J C Tunnell, Mrs W Tunnell

PUBLICATIONS The Annual Report is available from the Trust

HOW TO APPLY Applications, which should be made on a form obtainable from the Secretary, must be accompanied by references from two musicians of standing and a tape including two or three contrasting pieces or movements. Applications must be made by mid-June; auditions for those shortlisted will be held in London in October

WHO TO APPLY TO Kenneth M Robb, Secretary, The John Tunnell Trust, 4 Royal Terrace, Edinburgh EH7 5AB *Tel* 0131-556 4043

SC NO SCO 18408 **ESTABLISHED** 1988

■ Turkish Women's Philanthropic Association of England

WHAT IS FUNDED (a) To assist financially and otherwise charitable societies and institutions which provide help and assistance to poor, sick, old-aged and destitute persons; (b) provide financial help to students; (c) provide help to those effected by natural disasters and who are in need of assistance; and (d) to promote Turkish culture and social standards

WHO CAN BENEFIT Organisations of national significance only. Any Turkish person(s) or Turkish organisation benefiting older people, students, those disadvantaged by poverty, and victims of man-made or natural disasters

WHERE FUNDING CAN BE GIVEN England

TYPE OF GRANT Capital expenditure of the beneficiary. Hospital and student tuition fees

SAMPLE GRANTS £5,000 to Northern Cyprus Fire Disaster Aid

FINANCES *Year* 1996–97 *Income* £19,059 *Grants* £5,076

TRUSTEES The Executive Committee: Serife Sahir, Gohmen Beha, Semahat Mustafa, Termis Ahmet, Sevtap Kemal, Ruzin Yalcin, Amber Mustafa, Emine Aghdiran, Meral Hussein, Hulya Degirmenciogln, Sevilay Direkogln

NOTES No funds at present as we have just purchased the above premises as our base to work from

HOW TO APPLY Applications should be made in writing to the chairman and should include brief background details about the student, his annual income (including sources), the purpose of the grant, how much assistance is sought from the

Does the trust you have chosen match your needs? Haphazard applications waste postage and time

645

Association, details of any other applications for such aid, any other information which may be of assistance to the Trustees. Applications should be made by January of each academic year

WHO TO APPLY TO The Secretary, Turkish Women's Philanthropic Association of England, 4 Willoughby Road, Turnpike Lane, London N8 0HR

CC NO 271146   **ESTABLISHED** 1976

■ H H Turner Charitable Trust

WHAT IS FUNDED General charitable purposes

WHO CAN BENEFIT There are no restrictions on the age; professional and economic group; family situation; religion and culture; and social circumstances of; or disease or medical condition suffered by, the beneficiaries

WHERE FUNDING CAN BE GIVEN UK

TRUSTEES H H Turner, S V Turner

WHO TO APPLY TO R E Barker, H H Turner Charitable Trust, 41 Barrack Square, Martlesham Heath, Ipswich, Suffolk IP5 3RF

CC NO 1069374   **ESTABLISHED** 1997

■ The Joseph and Hannah Turner Charitable Trust

WHAT IS FUNDED All Jewish causes

WHO CAN BENEFIT Range of Jewish organisations and individual fellowships

WHERE FUNDING CAN BE GIVEN UK and overseas

RANGE OF GRANTS £25–£1,750

SAMPLE GRANTS £1,750 to Bachad Fellowship; £1,100 to Jewish Community Exhibition Centre; £1,000 to Norwood Child Care; £1,000 to Hannah and Joseph Turner Charitable Trust, Israel; £764 to United Synagogue

FINANCES *Year* 1995 *Income* £24,284 *Grants* £11,464

TRUSTEES A Turner, D Turner, H Kaufman

WHO TO APPLY TO H Kaufman, The Joseph and Hannah Turner Charitable Trust, 21 Dorset Square, London NW1 6PX

CC NO 278985   **ESTABLISHED** 1979

■ The R D Turner Charitable Trust

WHAT IS FUNDED Registered charities for general charitable purposes

WHAT IS NOT FUNDED No grants to individuals

WHO CAN BENEFIT There are no restrictions on the age; professional and economic group; family situation; religion and culture; and social circumstances of; or disease or medical condition suffered by, the beneficiaries

WHERE FUNDING CAN BE GIVEN UK, mainly West Midlands

TYPE OF GRANT Mainly recurring

RANGE OF GRANTS £750–£10,000

SAMPLE GRANTS £10,000 to Ironbridge Gorge Museum; £9,000 to British Red Cross, Kidderminster; £5,000 to Kings College, Cambridge; £4,000 to The National Trust; £4,000 to The National Trust for Scotland; £2,255 to Paltaya Orphanage, Thailand; £2,000 to Cancer Resource Centre, Kidderminster; £2,000 to KEMP Hospice, Kidderminster; £2,000 to Friends of Kidderminster Hospital; £1,750 to St John Ambulance, Kidderminster

FINANCES *Year* 1998 *Income* £59,093 *Grants* £52,600

TRUSTEES W S Ellis, J R Clemishaw, D P Pearson, T M Lunt

NOTES The Trust has for many years been fully committed to existing beneficiaries

HOW TO APPLY The Trust is at present fully committed. Initial telephone calls are welcome. There are no application forms, guidelines or deadlines. Please send a sae

WHO TO APPLY TO J E Dyke, The R D Turner Charitable Trust, 1 The Yew Trees, High Street, Henley-in-Arden, Solihull B95 5BN *Tel* 01564 793085

CC NO 263556   **ESTABLISHED** 1971

■ The Florence Turner Trust

WHAT IS FUNDED Local educational establishments, health and welfare, especially the elderly, youth and community

WHAT IS NOT FUNDED No educational, professional, vocation applications from individuals

WHO CAN BENEFIT Local charities and local branches of national charities benefiting: people of all ages; at risk groups; those disadvantaged by poverty; disabled people; and socially isolated people. There is no restriction on the disease or medical condition suffered by the beneficiaries

WHERE FUNDING CAN BE GIVEN Leicestershire and Rutland (but not exclusively)

TYPE OF GRANT Largely recurrent. No loans

SAMPLE GRANTS £17,280 to Leicester Grammar School for bursaries; £16,960 to St John Ambulance, Leicestershire and Rutland for ambulance; £15,000 to Queensmead Junior School for minibus; £9,450 to Leicester Charity Organisation Society; £6,925 to Age Concern, Leicester; £5,000 to LOROS for Leicestershire Hospice; £2,925 to Leicester YMCA; £2,200 to Leicester and Leicestershire Historic Churches Preservation Trust; £2,000 to University of Leicester for medical library; £1,925 to Leicester Society for Mentally Handicapped Children

FINANCES *Year* 1996–97 *Income* £170,970 *Grants* £160,666

TRUSTEES Roger Bowder, Caroline A Macpherson, Allan A Veasey

HOW TO APPLY To the address under Who To Apply To in writing. The Trustees meet every eight to nine weeks

WHO TO APPLY TO The Secretary, The Florence Turner Trust, c/o Harvey Ingram Owston, 20 New Walk, Leicester LE1 6TX *Tel* 0116-254 5454 *Fax* 0116-255 4559

CC NO 502721   **ESTABLISHED** 1973

■ Miss S M Tutton Charitable Trust

WHAT IS FUNDED To provide awards and grants for postgraduate opera studies and grants to music colleges, charities and opera companies

WHAT IS NOT FUNDED Applications for grants are not encouraged. The Trust does have some funds available for occasional discretionary grants but the amounts are very limited and assistance is generally provided only in the case of students who are recommended by organisations with which it has a close working relationship

WHO CAN BENEFIT The Trust provides financial support to young singers through the Sybil Tutton Awards. In addition the Trust makes grants to selected music colleges and training opera companies benefiting adults from 20 to 30, students and musicians

WHERE FUNDING CAN BE GIVEN UK

TYPE OF GRANT Awards and grants. The Trust has only limited funds available for discretionary awards or grants and thses are made only to gifted students with positive expectation of a singing career, supported by references from recognised centres of excellence

FINANCES *Year* 1997 *Income* £45,355
Grants £28,560
TRUSTEES S M Tutton, Chiswell Trustee Co Ltd
WHO TO APPLY TO Moores Rowland Accountants, Miss S M Tutton Charitable Trust, Applemarket House, 17 Union Street, Kingston upon Thames KT1 1RP *Tel* 0181-549 6399
CC NO 298774   **ESTABLISHED** 1988

■ The Edwin Henry Tutty Charitable Trust

This trust did not respond to CAF's request to amend its entry and, by 30 June 1998, CAF's researchers did not find financial records for later than 1995 on its file at the Charity Commission. Trusts are legally required to submit annual accounts to the Charity Commission under section 42 of the Charities Act 1993

WHAT IS FUNDED General charitable purposes
WHAT IS NOT FUNDED No grants to individuals
WHO CAN BENEFIT Registered charities only. There are no restrictions on the age; professional and economic group; family situation; religion and culture; and social circumstances of; or disease or medical condition suffered by, the beneficiaries
WHERE FUNDING CAN BE GIVEN UK
TRUSTEES E H Tutty and two others
WHO TO APPLY TO E H Tutty, The Edwin Henry Tutty Charitable Trust, Richmond, West Drive, Sudbrooke, Lincoln LN2 2RA
CC NO 253124   **ESTABLISHED** 1967

■ The Two Coats Charitable Trust

This trust did not respond to CAF's request to amend its entry and, by 30 June 1998, CAF's researchers did not find financial records for later than 1995 on its file at the Charity Commission. Trusts are legally required to submit annual accounts to the Charity Commission under section 42 of the Charities Act 1993

WHAT IS FUNDED Mainly to fund medical needs and welfare (not research), poverty
WHAT IS NOT FUNDED All funds fully committed and no new applications can be considered
WHO CAN BENEFIT Preference to physically or mentally handicapped (and their carers). Also those disadvantaged by poverty
WHERE FUNDING CAN BE GIVEN UK only
TRUSTEES Mrs E Cockburn, R Cockburn, P Regan
HOW TO APPLY March, June, October. No new applications will be considered
WHO TO APPLY TO R Cockburn, Trustee, The Two Coats Charitable Trust, 30 Southway, London NW11 6RU
CC NO 299137   **ESTABLISHED** 1988

■ Tyneside Charitable Trust

WHAT IS FUNDED Trustees tend to support the relief of former employees of Swan Hunter Group Ltd, or its subsidiary companies or their dependants in necessitous circumstances or such charitable bodies or institutions as the Trustees may in their absolute discretion determine
WHAT IS NOT FUNDED No grants to individuals
WHO CAN BENEFIT Registered charities. There are no restrictions on the age; professional and economic group; family situation; religion and culture; and social circumstances of; or disease or medical condition suffered by; the beneficiaries
WHERE FUNDING CAN BE GIVEN North Tyneside

TYPE OF GRANT Mostly one-off but have some recurrent commitments
RANGE OF GRANT Average gift £1,000
SAMPLE GRANTS £2,250 to St Oswalds Hospice; £2,000 to Marie Curie Memorial Foundation; £2,000 to British Red Cross; £1,500 to Age Concern, North Shields; £1,250 to Northumberland Association of Boys Clubs; £1,000 Mental Health Foundation; £1,000 to SSAFA; £1,000 to British Heart Foundation; £1,000 to Alzheimer's Disease Society, North Shields; £750 to Samaritans of Tyneside
FINANCES *Year* 1997 *Income* £26,350
Grants £22,250
TRUSTEES R H Dickinson, J M Jardine
WHO TO APPLY TO S Lamb, Tyneside Charitable Trust, 43 Fairfield Drive, Cullercoats, North Shields, Tyne and Wear NE30 3AG *Tel* 0191-252 0663
CC NO 505758   **ESTABLISHED** 1976

■ The Tyneside Leukaemia Research Association

WHAT IS FUNDED Research into causes and treatment of leukaemia and to assist organisations with a similar object
WHO CAN BENEFIT To benefit research workers and those suffering from leukaemia
WHERE FUNDING CAN BE GIVEN North East England
TYPE OF GRANT Usually one-off for a specific project or part of a project
SAMPLE GRANTS £147,027 to Newcastle University
FINANCES *Year* 1995 *Income* £170,785
Grants £147,027
TRUSTEES The Executive Committee
NOTES The assets are earmarked for projects at the Royal Victoria Infirmary, Newcastle and the University of Newcastle Medical School
HOW TO APPLY All applications are made to ourselves via The Tyneside Leukaemia Research Fund Committee, University of Newcastle upon Tyne, Department of Medicine
WHO TO APPLY TO Mrs P J Harrison, Hon Treasurer, The Tyneside Leukaemia Research Association, 44 Newlyn Drive, Cramlington, Northumberland NE23 9RR
CC NO 202047   **ESTABLISHED** 1964

■ Trustees of Tzedakah

WHAT IS FUNDED Funds fully committed. Ensure funding is available for religious educational facilities. Provide funding for poor families to supply their day to day facilities
WHAT IS NOT FUNDED Grants only to registered charities. No grants to individuals
WHO CAN BENEFIT Mainly Jewish religious institutions and those disadvantaged by poverty
WHERE FUNDING CAN BE GIVEN UK
TYPE OF GRANT Cash
FINANCES *Year* 1995 *Income* £262,784
Grants £303,155
TRUSTEES Trustees of Tzedakah Ltd
HOW TO APPLY **This Trust states that it does not respond to unsolicited applications**
WHO TO APPLY TO C Hollander, Trustees of Tzedakah, Brentmead House, Britannia Road, London N12 9RU
CC NO 251897   **ESTABLISHED** 1966

■ The Udall Charitable Trust

WHAT IS FUNDED General charitable purposes
WHO CAN BENEFIT There are no restrictions on the age; professional and economic group; family situation; religion and culture; and social circumstances of; or disease or medical condition suffered by, the beneficiaries
WHERE FUNDING CAN BE GIVEN UK and overseas
SAMPLE GRANTS £145,000 to Society for Horticultural Therapy for revenue support and capital development
FINANCES *Year* 1997 *Income* £150,485 *Grants* £145,000
TRUSTEES Sir P Barkley, J Campbell, J A Johnsen
WHO TO APPLY TO J A Saunders, The Udall Charitable Trust, Ashcombe House, Queen Street, Godalming, Surrey GU7 1BB
CC NO 1042667   **ESTABLISHED** 1986

■ Ujima International Networking Association

WHAT IS FUNDED To relieve poverty, advance education and religion and other charitable purposes amongst young people aged under 25 in the UK and overseas
WHO CAN BENEFIT Organisations benefiting children and young adults under 25 years of age, especially those who are disadvantaged by poverty. Young people of different cultures and religions will be supported
WHERE FUNDING CAN BE GIVEN UK and overseas
WHO TO APPLY TO A Barnett, Ujima International Networking Association, 12 Walcott Close, Long Sight, Manchester M13 9AP
CC NO 1064908   **ESTABLISHED** 1997

■ The Ullmann Trust (formerly the Isaac and Emilie Ullmann Charitable Foundation)

WHAT IS FUNDED Education and training, disabled groups and the advancement of the Jewish religion
WHO CAN BENEFIT Individuals and organisations benefiting Jews and disabled people
WHERE FUNDING CAN BE GIVEN UK
TYPE OF GRANT Cash payments
RANGE OF GRANTS £200–£2,000
SAMPLE GRANTS £2,000 to St Catherine's College, Oxford; £1,500 to Israel Diaspora Trust
FINANCES *Year* 1995 *Income* £38,706 *Grants* £30,000
TRUSTEES B W Lillyman, M Ullmann, C Ullmann
WHO TO APPLY TO Michael Ullmann, The Ullmann Trust, Lathbury Park, Newport Pagnell, Milton Keynes MK16 8LD *Tel* 01908 610316 *Fax* 01908 216494
CC NO 233630   **ESTABLISHED** 1970

■ Ultach Trust

WHAT IS FUNDED The Trust normally funds new or established groups based in Northern Ireland involved in the promotion of the Irish language. Grants are normally aimed at specific projects and schemes rather than ongoing costs. Particular consideration is given to groups developing inter-community Irish-language activities. The Trustees also, in exceptional cases, support projects aimed at improving the position of Irish in the community and promoting knowledge of the language
WHAT IS NOT FUNDED The Trust does not normally fund individuals, support ongoing running costs, fund major capital programmes, respond to cutbacks in statutory funding, or support travel expenses, publications or videos
WHO CAN BENEFIT Generally voluntary Irish-language or cross-community groups based in Northern Ireland. Irish medium schools benefiting children and young adults
WHERE FUNDING CAN BE GIVEN Northern Ireland only
TYPE OF GRANT Except with regard to Irish-medium education, funding is generally restricted to starter finances and single projects
RANGE OF GRANTS £250–£5,000
FINANCES *Year* 1996–97 *Income* £123,449 *Grants* £86,333
TRUSTEES Ruairí Ó Bleine, Leslie Burnett, Sean Ó Coinn, Robin Glendinning, Barry Kinghan, Ferdia Mac an Fháilí, Risteard Mac Gabhann, Sue McGeown, Séamus de Napier
PUBLICATIONS Title of publications and Irish courses available on request
HOW TO APPLY Application form and guidelines available from office
WHO TO APPLY TO Aodan Mac Póilin, Ultach Trust, Room 202, Fountain House, 19 Donegall Place, Belfast BT1 5AB *Tel* 01232 230749 *Fax* 01232 230749
IR NO XN 83581   **ESTABLISHED** 1989

■ Ulting Overseas Trust

WHAT IS FUNDED Grants to evangelical Christian organisations, only for the further training of Christian workers in the developing world
WHAT IS NOT FUNDED No grants to students and others seeking overseas or home experience. For training other than for Christian ministry
WHO CAN BENEFIT Christians and evangelists
WHERE FUNDING CAN BE GIVEN Asia, Africa and America
SAMPLE GRANTS The following grants were given for training:; £17,500 to International Fellowship of Evangelical Students; £16,000 to Scripture Union; £10,000 to Langham Trust; £8,000 to Interserve; £8,000 to Nairobi Evangelical Graduate School of Theology; £6,000 to Latin Link; £5,000 to Asian Theology Seminary; £5,000 to Discipleship Training College, Singapore; £5,000 to Oxford Centre for Mission Studies; £5,000 to Pan African Christian College
FINANCES *Year* 1997 *Income* £103,690 *Grants* £104,240
TRUSTEES Dr J B A Kessler, Mrs M Kessler, J S Payne, A J Bale, C Harland, Dr D G Osborne, Mrs M Brinkley, D Ford
WHO TO APPLY TO Colin Harland, Ulting Overseas Trust, 41 Rectory Park, South Croydon, Surrey CR2 9JR
CC NO 294397   **ESTABLISHED** 1986

■ The Unemployed Voluntary Action Fund

WHAT IS FUNDED Grants are given to voluntary organisations whose projects use the skills and resources of unemployed people for the benefit of individuals in the community. Projects may include: mutual help schemes, such as carers' support groups; pre-school and family centre developments; home-visiting and escort services for housebound and disabled people; recreational programmes to integrate people with learning difficulties; family advisory services; health related schemes; practical assistance such as community gardens or gardening with older people; volunteer bureau project; neighbourhood care projects

WHAT IS NOT FUNDED Schemes which cannot be considered include: exhibitions; arts clubs and performances; business co-operatives; credit unions; food co-operatives; out of schools care; housing and hostel welfare; formal educational or vocational course and skills training; clean-ups and one-off projects; holidays and camps; conservation schemes; building projects, including playgrounds; social clubs; sports centres and sports activities; campaigning and political activities. No grants to individuals

WHO CAN BENEFIT Beneficiaries by social circumstances. At risk groups; carers; disabled people (physical, sensory, learning impairments); disadvantaged by poverty; ex-offenders and those at risk of offending; gays and lesbians; homeless; refugees; those living in rural and urban areas; socially isolated; travellers; victims of abuse and domestic violence

WHERE FUNDING CAN BE GIVEN Scotland

TYPE OF GRANT Small Grants Scheme: one-off, one year starter grants; Main Grants Programme: three years project grants. Feasibility studies, core costs, running costs and salaries will also be considered

RANGE OF GRANTS Small Grants Scheme: Up to £5,000. Average: around £2350. Main Grants Programme: Up to £31,000 per annum. Average: around £19,560

SAMPLE GRANTS £24,433 to Lothian Community Transport services – Volunteer Drivers Brokerage Project to improve the quality and quantity of voluntary sector transport and passenger care by establishing a volunteer driver training and brokerage project; £24,180 to Aberdeen Cyrenians – Getting Home Project to involve volunteers in providing practical support for homeless people moving into new tenancies and coping with housing problems; and to offer individuals work experience, training and opportunities for personal development through volunteering; £23,858 to Blantyre Volunteer Group – Independence in the Community, Practical Support Scheme to involve volunteers in providing practical assistance to older people, people with disabilities and health related problems, and to promote the benefits of volunteering particularly to people with extra support needs; £23,804 to Voluntary Action Lewis – Befriending Scheme to involve volunteers in befriending and supporting those, in particular older people, who are socially isolated or facing difficulties living independently in the community, and to develop ways of working appropriate to local needs in a rural and widely dispersed environment; £23,454 to Edinburgh Headway Group - Branching Out Project to set up a scheme for volunteer befrienders to offer companionship and support to link people, especially young people, who have suffered traumatic brain injury back into the community; £19,470 to Knowetop Community Farm – Friends of the Farm Project, Dumbarton to establish and develop volunteer involvement, including volunteers with learning disabilities, in the day to day running of the community farm and to help with visitors; £18,422 to Fife Advocacy Project – Volunteer Advocacy Service to develop a volunteer advocacy scheme for mental health services users; £15,981 to Stepping Stones in Scotland – Child Contact Centre, Ruchill, Glasgow to involve volunteers in running a contact centre where children may meet their non-custodial parents in a safe, child-friendly environment; £15,964 to Scotland Yard Adventure Centre – Volunteer Maintenance Team, Edinburgh to involve volunteers in the practical aspects of running the centre, particularly the maintenance of the grounds and equipment, and to increase access to volunteering for adults with disabilities and special needs; £6,000 to New Horizons – Drop-In Project, Borders to involve key volunteers in assisting users of mental health services to operate local self-help drop-in centres in Galashiels, Hawick and Kelso

FINANCES *Year* 1997–98 *Income* £867,600 *Grants* £790,780

TRUSTEES Dorothy Dalton (Convenor), Bob Benson, Rona Connolly, Carol Downie, Patricia Carruthers, Susan Elsley, John Hawthorne, John Knox

PUBLICATIONS Accounts and the Annual Report are available from the Trust which also provides a detailed applicant's guidelines pack

HOW TO APPLY Applicants should request a guidelines pack from the Fund Office. The application should show the need for the service and give a realistic measure of what change can be achieved. Applications for the Main Grants Programme must arrive by 30 June. Small grants are made throughout the year

WHO TO APPLY TO Mrs Sandra Carter, Administrator, The Unemployed Voluntary Action Fund, Comely Park House, 80 New Row, Dunfermline, Fife KY12 7EJ *Tel* 01383 620780

SC NO SCO 05229   **ESTABLISHED** 1982

Does the trust you have chosen match your needs? Haphazard applications waste postage and time

649

■ The Union of Orthodox Hebrew Congregation

This trust did not respond to CAF's request to amend its entry and, by 30 June 1998, CAF's researchers did not find financial records for later than 1995 on its file at the Charity Commission. Trusts are legally required to submit annual accounts to the Charity Commission under section 42 of the Charities Act 1993

WHAT IS FUNDED To protect and to further in every way the interests of traditional Judaism in Great Britain and to establish and support such institutions as will serve this object
WHO CAN BENEFIT Jewish organisations
WHERE FUNDING CAN BE GIVEN UK
FINANCES *Year* 1994 *Income* £83,249
TRUSTEES B S F Freshwater, I Cymerman, C King, Rabbi A Pinter
WHO TO APPLY TO J R Conrad, Acting Administrator, The Union of Orthodox Hebrew Congregation, 140 Stamford Hill, London N16 6QT
CC NO 249892   **ESTABLISHED** 1966

■ United Kingdom Friends for Further Education in Israel

WHAT IS FUNDED Furtherance of the advancement of education, either generally or in any subjects, at the School for Advanced Studies at Beersheba or elsewhere in Israel
WHAT IS NOT FUNDED Restricted to Israel: education, welfare and recreation
WHO CAN BENEFIT Organisations benefiting children, young adults and students
WHERE FUNDING CAN BE GIVEN Israel
FINANCES *Year* 1997 *Income* £32,039
 Grants £90,000
TRUSTEES P Mishon, OBE (Chairman), Lt Cmdr S Brilliant, DSC, L Manuel, P Stern, FCA
NOTES Grants mainly made to charities known personally rather than to submissions
HOW TO APPLY All correspondence to be marked 'For the personal attention of the Chairman'
WHO TO APPLY TO Philip Mishon, OBE, UK Friends for Further Education in Israel, 53 Bolsover Street, London W1P 7HL
CC NO 261087   **ESTABLISHED** 1970

■ United Merseyside Trust

WHAT IS FUNDED To promote, further or support any charitable purpose in the area Where Funding Can Be Given
WHO CAN BENEFIT There are no restrictions on the age; professional and economic group; family situation; religion and culture; and social circumstances of; or disease or medical condition suffered by, the beneficiaries
WHERE FUNDING CAN BE GIVEN Merseyside county
TYPE OF GRANT Core costs. Funding is available for more than three years
RANGE OF GRANTS £100–£1,000
FINANCES *Year* 1997 *Income* £65,754
 Grants £65,158
PUBLICATIONS (1997–98 summary report-Merseyside area)
NOTES Small grants given to local charities benefiting local people. Local committees decide for each borough
HOW TO APPLY Please send accounts and sae. Applications must be received before the end of the calendar year

WHO TO APPLY TO John Pritchard, Administrator, United Merseyside Trust, c/o United Trusts, PO Box 14, 8 Nelson Road, Liverpool L69 7AA
 Tel 0151-709 8252
CC NO 701910   **ESTABLISHED** 1989

■ United St Saviour's Charities

WHAT IS FUNDED General benefit of the poor in the area Where Funding Can Be Given
WHAT IS NOT FUNDED Support will not be given for individual applications, recurrent grants, relief of taxes or rates, running costs or salaries
WHO CAN BENEFIT Organisations benefiting those disadvantaged by poverty
WHERE FUNDING CAN BE GIVEN Northern part of London Borough of Southwark
TYPE OF GRANT Buildings, capital, interest free loans, one-off, project and start-up costs. Funding is for one year or less
RANGE OF GRANTS £300–£4,000
FINANCES *Year* 1997–98 *Income* £625,000
 Grants £32,000
TRUSTEES E Bowman, Mrs H L Bowman, Mrs G Domminney, E A C Tucker, Mrs J M Vigar
NOTES Trustees usually meet monthly
HOW TO APPLY To the address under Who To Apply To in writing. Initial telephone calls are welcome. Application forms are available, but no guidelines. No sae required
WHO TO APPLY TO D M Wilkinson, Clerk, United St Saviour's Charities, The Offices, 8 Southwark Street, London SE1 1TL *Tel* 0171-407 5961
CC NO 206767   **ESTABLISHED** 1960

■ United Society for Christian Literature

WHAT IS FUNDED The promotion of Christian literature in response to requests from the Christian church and its various societies and organisations. Particularly charities working in the fields of the advancement of the Christian religion, Anglican bodies, Catholic bodies, Free Church and theological colleges
WHAT IS NOT FUNDED All grants are handled by Feed The Minds and are normally for work in developing countries and Eastern Europe in accordance with Feed The Minds policy. No grants to individuals
WHO CAN BENEFIT Christian organisations
WHERE FUNDING CAN BE GIVEN Mainly overseas working through Feed the Minds
TYPE OF GRANT Mainly one-off, and usually to initiate a project. Funding of up to three years may be available
SAMPLE GRANTS £105,200 to Feed the Minds, UK for overseas literature grants; £10,000 to Feed the Minds, UK for books for first year theological students in the UK; £1,500 to University of Leeds for religious education books; £840 to Hi, Kids! for evangelistic booklets
FINANCES *Year* 1997 *Income* £266,412
 Grants £56,866
TRUSTEES The Committee, (John Clark (Chairman))
NOTES Grants are mostly one-off and intended to start a new piece of work or a fresh development to something that is already established. Application in the first instance by preliminary letter
HOW TO APPLY In writing to the Secretary

WHO TO APPLY TO Dr A Marriage, The Secretary, United Society for Christian Literature, Albany House, 67 Sydenham Road, Guildford, Surrey GU1 3RY *Tel* 01483 888580 *Fax* 01483 888580
CC NO 226512   **ESTABLISHED** 1799

■ United Society for the Propagation of the Gospel

WHAT IS FUNDED Service to churches in the Anglican Communion in fostering mission worldwide. Primarily to overseas churches and only in consultation with the appropriate authorities in the local church. Based mainly on priorities decided at Partners-in-Mission and other Consultations, but also consist of ad hoc grants for emergencies and development needs, as well as theological or other training and primary healthcare projects

WHAT IS NOT FUNDED Direct applications from individuals

WHO CAN BENEFIT Overseas Anglican provinces and Diocese and churches in communion with the Anglican Church benefiting Christians

WHERE FUNDING CAN BE GIVEN Mainly churches in Africa, West Indies, South Pacific, South America, Pakistan, India, Indian Ocean, Myanmar (Burma), Bangladesh, East Asia

TYPE OF GRANT USPG administers Festina, a revolving loan scheme, financed by money lent for the purpose, for capital-intensive projects. Bursaries are offered for extending the training of personnel as recommended by their churches, and personnel are supported for work or experience overseas. Additional gifts and legacies are always welcome

FINANCES *Year* 1997 *Income* £6,115,886 *Grants* £4,415,122

TRUSTEES Governors: Rev Canon Helen Cunliffe, His Honour Judge Aglionby, Robert Boyd, Douglas Yates, Rev Alan Moses, Rev Canon Ivor Smith-Cameron, Rev David Tuck, Mrs Jane Arden, Dss Diane Clutterbuck, Mrs Sonia Kasibante, William Peters

PUBLICATIONS Annually – *Yearbook*. Also project information, educational books, religious pamphlets and visual aids

HOW TO APPLY To be submitted by Archbishops and Bishops to the USPG Funding Officer

WHO TO APPLY TO The Funding Officer, USPG, Partnership House, 157 Waterloo Road, London SE1 8XA *Tel* 0171-928 8681 *Fax* 0171-928 2371 *E-mail* enquiries@QUSPG.org.uk
CC NO 234518   **ESTABLISHED** 1701

■ United Trusts

WHAT IS FUNDED General charitable purposes. Distribution decisions are made by work place charity committees or local trust committees

WHAT IS NOT FUNDED The donor's committees decide what is not funded

WHO CAN BENEFIT Neighbourhood-based community projects tend to be major recipients. There are no restrictions on the age; professional and economic group; family situation; religion and culture; and social circumstances of; or disease or medical condition suffered by, the beneficiaries

WHERE FUNDING CAN BE GIVEN UK, at present mainly North West England

FINANCES *Year* 1996–97 *Income* £382,000 *Grants* £295,000

TRUSTEES Up to twenty people elected by members

HOW TO APPLY Applications should be made to the Secretary of the local United Trust Fund or Workplace Trust concerned. Applications from charities in Merseyside may be made either direct to the Trust Chairman or to John Pritchard, the Administrator

WHO TO APPLY TO Fred Freeman, Chairman and Hon Director, United Trusts, PO Box 14, 8 Nelson Road, Edge Hill, Liverpool L69 7AA *Tel* 0151-709 8252
CC NO 327579   **ESTABLISHED** 1987

■ Unitek Foundation (formerly Techspan Foundation)

WHAT IS FUNDED Social care and development

WHO CAN BENEFIT Small community-based organisations. People of many different social circumstances will be considered

WHERE FUNDING CAN BE GIVEN UK and overseas

TYPE OF GRANT At the discretion of the Trustees

RANGE OF GRANTS £60–£3,950

SAMPLE GRANTS £3,950 to the Chalfonts Community College; £2,700 to Harvest Trust; £2,000 to Sir Francis Drake Primary School; £1,670 to Regents College of Psychotherapy; £100 to RADAR

FINANCES *Year* 1997 *Income* £19,464 *Grants* £10,580

TRUSTEES Clive Percy Brooks, Richard Alfred Nye, Ann Mary Nye

HOW TO APPLY Require annual accounts from grant applicants

WHO TO APPLY TO C P Brooks, Unitek Foundation, Benacre, Hammerpond Road, Horsham, West Sussex RH13 6PE
CC NO 1029106   **ESTABLISHED** 1991

■ David Uri Memorial Trust

WHAT IS FUNDED Mainly Jewish organisations, also welfare and education charities, which must be registered with the Charity Commission

WHAT IS NOT FUNDED No grants to individuals

WHO CAN BENEFIT Organisations benefiting Jewish people, at risk groups, those disadvantaged by poverty and socially isolated people

WHERE FUNDING CAN BE GIVEN UK and overseas

TYPE OF GRANT One-off, capital, feasibility studies and research grants will be considered. Funding is available for up to three years

RANGE OF GRANTS £250–£1,500

FINANCES *Year* 1997 *Income* £186,809 *Grants* £27,550

TRUSTEES Ms S Blackman, Ms B Green, Ms B Roden

HOW TO APPLY To the address under Who To Apply To in writing

WHO TO APPLY TO Mrs Z S Blackman, Trustee, David Uri Memorial Trust, 48 Avenue Close, London NW8 6DA *Tel* 0171-722 3922
CC NO 327810   **ESTABLISHED** 1988

■ Uxbridge United Welfare Trusts

WHAT IS FUNDED Education, relief of poverty, including the provision of almshouses

WHO CAN BENEFIT Local organisations benefiting children, young adults and those disadvantaged by poverty

WHERE FUNDING CAN BE GIVEN Uxbridge and locality

SAMPLE GRANTS £36,579 to Hardship relief grants; £6,068 to educational grants

FINANCES *Year* 1997 *Income* £313,606 *Grants* £42,647

TRUSTEES P W E Hesford (Chairman), L R Pond (Vice Chairman), Dr D R Copland, G Hooper, J Miles, B Onthwaite, A J Pond, Mrs S M Pritchard, Mrs S Spargo, J Lonsdale, Mrs P Crawley

HOW TO APPLY To the address under Who To Apply To in writing

WHO TO APPLY TO D C Newland, Chairman, Uxbridge United Welfare Trusts, Inglefield Cottage, Hawthorn Lane, Farnham Common, Berkshire SL2 3SW *Tel* 01753 643054

CC NO 217066   **ESTABLISHED** 1991

■ V S & H Charitable Trust

WHAT IS FUNDED Small donations to Jewish causes

WHO CAN BENEFIT Organisations benefiting Jews

WHERE FUNDING CAN BE GIVEN UK and overseas

FINANCES *Year* 1996–97 *Income* £13,459 *Grants* £21,740

TRUSTEES V S Conway, H Conway, S D Conway, F G Hershkorn

HOW TO APPLY **This Trust states that it does not respond to unsolicited applications**

WHO TO APPLY TO V Conway, V S & H Charitable Trust, 6 Imperial Court, 55–56 Prince Albert Road, London NW8 7PT

CC NO 295408   **ESTABLISHED** 1986

■ Vale of Aylesbury Vineyard Christian Fellowship

WHAT IS FUNDED Religious and secular public education; the advancement of the Christian faith and support of missionary activities both in the UK and overseas, including the planting of new churches and organisation of the congregation; the relief of the poor and needy and the sick and elderly; other charitable purposes at the discretion of the committee

WHO CAN BENEFIT Charitable bodies and persons working in the fields described under What Is Funded to benefit people of all ages who are disadvantaged by poverty. There is no restriction on the disease or medical condition suffered by the beneficiaries

WHERE FUNDING CAN BE GIVEN Buckinghamshire and overseas

TYPE OF GRANT At the discretion of the Committee

TRUSTEES M Elias, D Groom, J Van Der Merwe

HOW TO APPLY To the address under Who To Apply To in writing

WHO TO APPLY TO Michael Arthur Elias, Secretary, Vale of Aylesbury Vineyard Christian Fellowship, 45 New Road, Weston Turville, Aylesbury, Buckinghamshire HP22 5RA *Tel* 01296 614768

CC NO 1064215   **ESTABLISHED** 1997

■ The Valentine Charitable Trust

WHAT IS FUNDED Trustees mainly restrict their giving to healthcare and environmental projects

WHAT IS NOT FUNDED Non-charitable gifts will not be considered

WHO CAN BENEFIT Registered charities. There is no restriction on the disease or medical condition suffered by the beneficiaries

WHERE FUNDING CAN BE GIVEN Slight preference for South East Dorset

RANGE OF GRANTS Up to £10,000 or more depending on the Trustees

652

Think carefully about every application. Is it justified?

SAMPLE GRANTS £3,500 to Green Island Holiday Trust; £3,000 to Victoria School Appeal; £3,000 to The Place Next Door (Salvation Army); £2,900 to SSAFA; £2,000 to Cystic Fibrosis Research Trust; £2,000 to HYPED; £2,000 to Demand; £2,000 to Alzheimer's Disease Society; £2,000 to Brooke Hospital for Animals; £2,000 to Leonard Cheshire Homes

FINANCES *Year* 1997 *Income* £48,513
Grants £39,900

TRUSTEES Miss M A Cotton, D J E Neville-Jones, Mrs S F Neville-Jones, Mrs P B N Walker

HOW TO APPLY By letter

WHO TO APPLY TO D J E Neville-Jones, The Valentine Charitable Trust, Preston & Redman, Solicitors, Hinton House, Hinton Road, Bournemouth, Dorset BH1 2EN *Tel* 01202 292424

CC NO 1001782   ESTABLISHED 1990

■ Valley Church Andover Trust

WHAT IS FUNDED To advance the Christian religion; to relieve sickness, poverty, distress and who are in need because of age, social or economic circumstances; to advance education; other general charitable purposes

WHO CAN BENEFIT Any Christian organisation. For individual beneficiaries there are no restrictions on their age, professional and economic group, family situation; religion and culture or social circumstances

WHERE FUNDING CAN BE GIVEN Andover and surrounding area

TYPE OF GRANT One-off grants or loans to individuals. Regular support to Christian organisations or missions. Funding may be given for more than three years

RANGE OF GRANTS £30–£500

SAMPLE GRANTS £31,900 to Waterloo Free Church for the support of staff in Christian church planting in the UK; £5,727 to Valley Church Agape Fund for relief of poor in the Andover area; £1,500 to New Frontiers International towards overseas mission work and church planting; £286 to Jesus Alive Ministries for mission work in Africa; £100 to Evangelical Alliance towards membership of the Alliance

FINANCES *Year* 1997–98 *Income* £61,485
Grants £40,337

TRUSTEES A J Carter, J Davies, N C May, P D E Stagg, A Swatton

HOW TO APPLY In person, in writing or by telephone

WHO TO APPLY TO A T Evans, Valley Church Andover Trust, 31–33 Bridge Street, Andover, Hampshire SP10 1BE *Tel* 01264 335522

CC NO 1056821   ESTABLISHED 1996

■ The Albert Van Den Bergh Charitable Trust

WHAT IS FUNDED Welfare and medical charities, including research charities. Also youth and the elderly

WHO CAN BENEFIT Local and national organisations benefiting people of all ages, at risk groups, those disadvantaged by poverty and welfare. There is no restriction on the disease or medical condition suffered by the beneficiaries

WHERE FUNDING CAN BE GIVEN UK, with some preference for Surrey and the South East, and overseas

RANGE OF GRANTS £500–£2,100

SAMPLE GRANTS £5,000 to United Charities Fund, Liberal Jewish Synagogue; £2,100 to Care for the Elderly; £2,000 to Parentline, Surrey; £1,200 to Riding for the Disabled, Cranleigh Branch; £1,200 to Council and Care for the Elderly; £1,000 to Age Concern; £1,000 to Cancer Research, Macmillan Fund; £1,000 to St John Ambulance; £500 to Alexander Rose Day; £500 to Alzheimer's

FINANCES *Year* 1997 *Income* £75,023
Grants £35,900

TRUSTEES P A Van Den Bergh, G R Oliver, Mrs J M Harvey

HOW TO APPLY To the address under Who To Apply To in writing, enclosing accounts and budgets

WHO TO APPLY TO G R Oliver, Trustee, The Albert Van Den Bergh Charitable Trust, c/o Wilkinsons, Broadoak House, Horsham Road, Cranleigh, Surrey GU6 8DJ

CC NO 296885   ESTABLISHED 1987

■ Baroness Van Heemstra's Charitable Trust

WHAT IS FUNDED General charitable purposes

WHO CAN BENEFIT There are no restrictions on the age; professional and economic group; family situation; religion and culture; and social circumstances of; or disease or medical condition suffered by, the beneficiaries

WHERE FUNDING CAN BE GIVEN UK

SAMPLE GRANTS £30,000 to Ferne Animal Sanctuary

FINANCES *Year* 1996 *Income* £13,400
Grants £30,000

TRUSTEES R E MacWatt, A B V Hughes, Ms M L MacWatt

WHO TO APPLY TO R E MacWatt, Baroness Van Heemstra's Charitable Trust, Paynes Hicks Beach, Solicitors, 10 New Square, Lincoln's Inn, London WC2A 3QG

CC NO 289249   ESTABLISHED 1983

■ The Van Neste Foundation

WHAT IS FUNDED Currently the main areas of interest are: Third World; handicapped and elderly; advancement of religion; community and Christian family life; respect for sanctity and dignity of life

WHAT IS NOT FUNDED Registered charities only. Applications from individuals, including students are ineligible. No grants made in response to general appeals from large, national organisations

WHO CAN BENEFIT Those who fall into the category of What Is Funded including those disadvantaged by poverty, disabled people, elderly people and Christians

WHERE FUNDING CAN BE GIVEN UK and overseas

TYPE OF GRANT Usually one-off for a specific project or part of a project. Core funding is rarely considered

SAMPLE GRANTS £65,258 to Bristol University for Chair in Ethics in Medicine; £31,123 to Downside Abbey for Community and Support Centre, Bristol; £20,000 to Hope and Homes for children orphaned by war; £11,034 to Abufari Brazil for community skills project; £10,000 to Sustrans for adapting cycleways for the elderly and handicapped; £10,000 to Downside Bermondsey Settlement for education for the disadvantaged; £7,750 to Little Brothers of Nazareth for second stage accommodation; £6,495 to Clifton Diocese for parish support; £6,000 to Life for pregnancy counselling service; £6,000 to Redmaids School for education

FINANCES *Year* 1998 *Income* £269,509
Grants £231,709

TRUSTEES M T M Appleby (Chair), G J Walker, MBE, F J F Lyons, KSG (Secretary)

NOTES Finances: The grants figure results from a reservation made for future commitment

HOW TO APPLY At any time. In writing only. Trustees meet quarterly. Applications should include clear details of the need the intended project is designed to meet plus an outline budget. Acknowledgements are only made when an sae is enclosed

WHO TO APPLY TO F J F Lyons, The Van Neste Foundation, 15 Alexandra Road, Clifton, Bristol BS8 2DD

CC NO 201951   **ESTABLISHED** 1959

■ Mrs Maud Van Norden's Charitable Foundation

WHAT IS FUNDED General charitable purposes in particular aid to the elderly, the disabled, preservation of the environment and heritage and animal welfare. Annual review of list of donations with occasional additions and deletions at the discretion of the Trustees

WHAT IS NOT FUNDED No grants to individuals. Registered charities only

WHO CAN BENEFIT Registered charities benefiting mainly older people and disabled people

WHERE FUNDING CAN BE GIVEN UK

TYPE OF GRANT Cash grants of £600 on an annual basis and of £600 to £1,000 on a once only basis. Annual grants can be for running expenses: once only grants are more usually for capital projects and special appeals

FINANCES *Year* 1997 *Income* £44,000 *Grants* £36,200

TRUSTEES F C S Tufton, Mrs E M Dukler, A O Deas, Mrs E A Humphryes

NOTES Applications only considered if supported by a copy of the latest Report and Accounts

HOW TO APPLY In writing to the address under Who To Apply To. No acknowledgement or notification of result unless successful. If a reply is required sae should be sent. Appeals considered once a year in May or June

WHO TO APPLY TO Messrs Payne Hicks Beach, Mrs Maud Van Norden's Charitable Foundation, 10 New Square, Lincoln's Inn, London WC2A 3QG

CC NO 210844   **ESTABLISHED** 1960

■ Vandervell Foundation

This trust did not respond to CAF's request to amend its entry and, by 30 June 1998, CAF's researchers did not find financial records for later than 1995 on its file at the Charity Commission. Trusts are legally required to submit annual accounts to the Charity Commission under section 42 of the Charities Act 1993

WHAT IS FUNDED General charitable purposes

WHO CAN BENEFIT There are no restrictions on the age; professional and economic group; family situation; religion and culture; and social circumstances of; or disease or medical condition suffered by, the beneficiaries

WHERE FUNDING CAN BE GIVEN UK

TYPE OF GRANT Mainly recurrent

TRUSTEES Vandervell Foundation Ltd

WHO TO APPLY TO J L Reed, Vandervell Foundation, Bridge House, 181 Queen Victoria Street, London EC4V 4DD

CC NO 255651   **ESTABLISHED** 1968

■ The Vardy Foundation

WHAT IS FUNDED General charitable purposes

WHO CAN BENEFIT There are no restrictions on the age; professional and economic group; family situation; religion and culture; and social circumstances of; or disease or medical condition suffered by, the beneficiaries

WHERE FUNDING CAN BE GIVEN UK

TYPE OF GRANT Recurrent

SAMPLE GRANTS £125,000 to Emmanuel College; £40,976 to Crusaders in the North East; £25,000 to Butterwick Hospice; £25,000 to Christian missionary charities; £11,000 to YMCA; £5,349 for donations to other Christian charities; £2,000 to British Red Cross; £1,800 to Cancer and AIDs charities; £985 as donations for educational projects

FINANCES *Year* 1995 *Income* £172,589 *Grants* £237,678

TRUSTEES P Vardy, M B Vardy, R H Dickinson

WHO TO APPLY TO P Vardy, The Vardy Foundation, c/o Reg Vardy plc, Houghton House, Wessington Way, Sunderland, Tyne and Wear SR5 3RJ

CC NO 328415   **ESTABLISHED** 1989

■ The Vaux Group Foundation

WHAT IS FUNDED The Trust funds communities and organisations where the company operates. Particularly charities working in the fields of: housing associations; sheltered accomodation; information technology and computers; personnel and human resource services; infrastructure development; charity or voluntary umbrella bodies; architecture; combined arts; visual arts; opera companies and opera groups; theatrical companies and theatre groups; health facilities and buildings; conservation; animal facilities and services; schools and colleges; bursaries and fees; community issues; and various community facilities and services

WHAT IS NOT FUNDED Individuals. National appeals unless there is a local bias towards a Group trading

WHO CAN BENEFIT Small, local groups, local and regional charitable organisations and some national organisations benefiting: children; young adults; older people; actors and entertainment professionals; at risk groups; carers; disabled people; those disadvantaged by poverty; gays and lesbians; those living in rural areas; victims of abuse, crime and domestic violence

WHERE FUNDING CAN BE GIVEN North East and North West England and Yorkshire

SAMPLE GRANTS £15,000 to Durham County Foundation for community issues; £10,000 to Diana, Princess of Wales Memorial Fund for community issues; £75,000 to Midland Enterprise Fund for community issues; £7,000 to Manchester University; £5,000 to Hotel and Catering Benevolent Association; £5,000 to Hospitality Training Foundation; £2,500 to Manor Training and Resource Centre for community issues; £2,500 to Prince's Youth Business Trust for youth appeal; £2,000 to South Yorkshire Foundation for community issues; £2,000 to NE Civic Trust for community issues

FINANCES *Year* 1995–96 *Income* £36,478 *Grants* £127,000

TRUSTEES William P Catesby, Frank Nicholson, Sir Paul Nicholson, Christopher Storey, Neal Gossage

HOW TO APPLY To the address under Who To Apply To in writing

WHO TO APPLY TO Hilary Florek, Administrator, The Vaux Group Foundation, Vaux Group plc, The Brewery, Sunderland SR1 3AN *Tel* 0191-567 6277 *Fax* 0191-514 2488 *Web Site* http://www.vaux.group.co.uk
CC NO 802636   ESTABLISHED 1988

■ The Vec Acorn Trust

WHAT IS FUNDED To help young people between the ages of 16 and 25 who are disadvantaged as a result of the environment in which they live. To assist in developing their potential in skills which otherwise they may not be able to achieve. To give support to projects which reach a number of people but with the emphasis on self help. Particularly charities working in the fields of: schools and colleges; cost of study; counselling on social issues; and holidays and outing

WHAT IS NOT FUNDED Grants are made only to medically or environmentallly disadvantaged young people

WHO CAN BENEFIT Individuals and organisations benefiting young adults; those disadvantaged by poverty and those living in rural and urban areas. The Trustees prefer to support projects not attached to already well established charitable organisations and are willing to consider joint ventures

WHERE FUNDING CAN BE GIVEN South West Hampshire

TYPE OF GRANT The Trustees are prepared to consider applications on their merit as to whether they involve single or recurring grants. Capital, project, salaries and start-up costs. Funding of up to three years will be considered

RANGE OF GRANTS £100–£20,000, average grant £1,000–£5,000

SAMPLE GRANTS £24,740 to Minstead Training Project for salaries for the manager of Sheltered Work Scheme and a Work Experience and Employment Co-ordinator; £19,000 a year for three years to It's Your Choice for salary/costs for Advice and Information Worker; £11,000 to HYPED for purchase of a minibus for young people; £10,000 to Meridan Trust for workshop project at Eastney; £5,000 a year for three years to Artsway for programme development – contemporary and visual arts in the New Forest; £4,860 to Forest Forge Theatre for salary of Associate Director Outreach; £3,800 to the Royal Ballet School to sponsor a student; £3,000 to Lymington Detached Youth Work Project for the salary of Senior Youth Worker; £2,400 to Royal Lymington Yacht Club for sponsorship of two dinghies for the Wednesday Sailing Club; £1,600 to Brockenhurst Gateway Club for young adults with learning difficulties

FINANCES *Year* 1997 *Income* £69,610 *Grants* £94,668

TRUSTEES Mrs V E Coates, K Newman, MBE, D A Rule, ACIB, Mrs P L Youngman

HOW TO APPLY The Trustees meet quarterly

WHO TO APPLY TO Mrs S Leary, Secretary to the Trustees, The Vec Acorn Trust, Pennington Chase, Lower Pennington Lane, Lymington, Hampshire SO41 8AN
CC NO 1002997   ESTABLISHED 1991

■ The Verdon-Smith Family Charitable Settlement

WHAT IS FUNDED This Trust will consider funding: almshouses and respite accommodation; architecture; music; visual arts; arts education; orchestras; cultural activities; religious buildings; acute health care; hospices and hospice at home; respite care for carers; cancer and MS research; conservation; animal welfare; church schools; independent schools; care in the community and day centres. Quarterly review of regular donations with occasional addition of new donations at discretion of Trustees

WHAT IS NOT FUNDED No donations to individuals, no salaries or running costs

WHO CAN BENEFIT Registered charities with emphasis on local activity and needs benefiting: people of all ages; ex-service and service people; seafarers and fishermen; musicians; widows and widowers; Church of England; disabled people; disaster victims; and homeless people

WHERE FUNDING CAN BE GIVEN South West England – new responses increasingly limited to Bristol, Somerset, South Gloucestershire, and Wiltshire

TYPE OF GRANT Recurrent, occasional one-off, buildings, capital, core costs, project and research. Funding is available for one year or less

RANGE OF GRANTS £50–£300, typical grant £140

SAMPLE GRANTS £500 to Bristol Children's Hospital for new building; £250 to Barnardo's, Wales and West; £250 to NSPCC, Salisbury for work with children; £250 to the Salvation Army Western Region for relief of necessitous persons; £250 to Home Farm Trust for support for those with learning difficulties; £250 to St Peters Hospice, Bristol for terminal care; £250 to Bristol Age Care for support and care for the elderly; £250 to Bristol and Avon Federation of Clubs for Young People for youth projects; £200 to Gloucestershire Society for relief of necessitous persons; £200 to Mencap for project in Portishead, Somerset

FINANCES *Year* 1997 *Income* £27,127 *Grants* £20,459

TRUSTEES Lady Verdon-Smith, W G Verdon-Smith, Lady E J White, Mrs D N Verdon-Smith

PUBLICATIONS Annual Report

HOW TO APPLY In writing To the address under Who To Apply To. Applications will not be acknowledged unless successful. No telephone calls

WHO TO APPLY TO Lady White, The Verdon-Smith Family Charitable Settlement, Pypers, Rudgeway, Bristol BS35 3SQ
CC NO 284919   ESTABLISHED 1983

■ The Mr and Mrs Nicholas Verey Charitable Trust

WHAT IS FUNDED The Trustees seek to cover mainly leukaemia and other cancer-based charities

WHAT IS NOT FUNDED No grants to individuals

WHO CAN BENEFIT Organisations benefiting people suffering from cancer, especially leukaemia

WHERE FUNDING CAN BE GIVEN UK and overseas

RANGE OF GRANTS £100–£1,000

SAMPLE GRANTS £1,000 to Qualified Cancer Care Fund; £500 to The Countess of Chester Hospital NHS Trust for Dr Elizabeth Rhodes Leukaemia Lymphoma Fund; £250 to Queen Elizabeth's Foundation for Disabled People; £250 to WellBeing; £250 to Wooden Spoon Society; £100 to Imperial Cancer Research Fund; £100 to MOUF; £100 to Rainbow Trust

FINANCES *Year* 1997 *Income* £72,341 *Grants* £2,550

TRUSTEES A R Beevor, Mrs D V Verey

WHO TO APPLY TO Mrs D V Verey, The Mr and Mrs Nicholas Verey Charitable Trust, 20 Eldon Road, London W8 5PT
CC NO 1047838   ESTABLISHED 1995

■ Veronique Charitable Trust

WHAT IS FUNDED Consideration given annually to distribution of income arising to benefit elderly and blind members of the Jewish faith

WHAT IS NOT FUNDED Registered charities only, applications from individuals, including students, are ineligible

WHO CAN BENEFIT Registered charities benefiting elderly an blind members of the Jewish faith

WHERE FUNDING CAN BE GIVEN UK

TYPE OF GRANT Buildings, capital, one-off, project and research will be considered

SAMPLE GRANTS £7,000 to Jewish Care for Dolly Ross Home in Braemar Royal; £7,000 to Jewish Blind and Physically Handicapped Society; £7,000 to Hannah Levy House Trust; £2,000 to Interlink Foundation for Friends in Deed – to assist elderly Jews; £2,000 to Hull Jewish Community Care; £2,000 to Food Life Line for Pesach Appeal; £2,000 to Yad Voezer Helping Hand Society; £2,000 to Hospital Kosher Meals Service; £2,000 to RUKBA for Jewish beneficiaries; £2,000 to St Dunstans for Jewish men and women in their care

FINANCES *Year* 1998 *Income* £42,895 *Grants* £42,000

TRUSTEES National Westminster Bank plc

HOW TO APPLY These will be received provided they comply with What is Funded stated above

WHO TO APPLY TO National Westminster Bank plc, Veronique Charitable Trust, NatWest Investments, Bournemouth Branch, 1st Floor, Heron House, 10 Christchurch Road, Bournemouth, Dorset BH1 3NH

CC NO 279349   **ESTABLISHED** 1980

■ The Vestey Foundation

WHAT IS FUNDED The relief of poverty, the advancement of public education and the advancement of religion. Other charitable purposes

WHO CAN BENEFIT Organisations benefiting those disadvantaged by poverty, children, young adults and students. People of many religions and cultures will be supported

WHERE FUNDING CAN BE GIVEN UK

TYPE OF GRANT Specific needs rather then regular income support

RANGE OF GRANTS £2,500–£60,000

SAMPLE GRANTS £60,000 to The Royal Veterinary College; £2,500 to Animal Health Trust

FINANCES *Year* 1996 *Income* £85,153 *Grants* £62,500

TRUSTEES E H Vestey, Rt Hon S G Armstrong, Baron Vestey, Rt Hon M W Vestey

WHO TO APPLY TO J R Cuthbert, The Vestey Foundation, 6–9 Middle Street, London EC1A 7JA

CC NO 803468   **ESTABLISHED** 1990

■ Victory Healing Faith Church Trust

WHAT IS FUNDED General charitable purposes, in particular to advance the Christian religion and to relieve sickness by means of spiritual healing

WHO CAN BENEFIT Organisations benefiting Christians. There is no restriction on the disease or medical condition suffered by the beneficiaries

WHERE FUNDING CAN BE GIVEN Staffordshire

FINANCES *Year* 1995 *Income* £34,026 *Grants* £2,863

NOTES The majority of the Trust's income is spent on ministry, rent and book printing, etc

HOW TO APPLY £1,300 to minister; £320 to Hallelujah Israel; £206 to T & F Bantiles; £148 to World Vision; £50 to Mission W/O Border

WHO TO APPLY TO A H Ford, Victory Healing Faith Church Trust, 9 Jean Close, Burslem, Stoke-on-Trent, Staffordshire ST6 7BH

CC NO 1043764   **ESTABLISHED** 1994

■ Eric W Vincent Trust Fund

WHAT IS FUNDED General charitable purposes. Particularly charities working in the fields of: residential facilities and services; infrastructure development; professional bodies; religious umbrella bodies; arts, culture and recreation; education and training; and community facilities and services. Applications considered on merit subject to funds being available

WHAT IS NOT FUNDED The Trust will not fund: second degree students or courses being re-taken due to a previous examination failure. Grants are not made towards salaries or to pay off debts. Vehicles will not be funded

WHO CAN BENEFIT Local activities preferred. There are no restrictions on the age; professional and economic group; family situation; religion and culture; and social circumstances of; or disease or medical condition suffered by, the beneficiaries. Organisations and students must be from an area of a 20-mile radius of Halesowen

WHERE FUNDING CAN BE GIVEN Within a 20-mile radius of Halesowen in the West Midlands

TYPE OF GRANT Mainly one-off and capital grants. Funding is available for up to one year

RANGE OF GRANTS £50–£500; typical grant £200–£250

FINANCES *Year* 1997 *Income* £51,016 *Grants* £48,305

TRUSTEES J M Jennings, K E Symonds, Mrs D Williams, Rev R Morris, C Jordan, A R Birch, P Denner

HOW TO APPLY Trustees meet six times a year. Applications for Holiday Schemes must be received by 1 April and will be considered at May meeting. Applications from organisations should be accompanied by a copy of the latest accounts. Student applications must be received by 1 September and will be considered at the September/October meeting. Applications should be accompanied by a letter from a tutor or other person aware of the student's capabilities and circumstances, to provide the Trustees with an independent viewpoint

WHO TO APPLY TO Mrs J Stephen, Eric W Vincent Trust Fund, 4–5 Summer Hill, Halesowen B63 3BU

CC NO 204843   **ESTABLISHED** 1954

■ Vineyard Christian Fellowship of South West Nottingham

WHAT IS FUNDED The Trustees support general church activities in the community and the training of people involved in the church

WHO CAN BENEFIT Individuals within the church

WHERE FUNDING CAN BE GIVEN South West Nottingham

TYPE OF GRANT One-off and recurrent small grants

FINANCES *Income* £25,000

TRUSTEES G J Smith, D T McNeil, R L Pillar

NOTES As yet the Trust has not supported causes/projects outside the church, although they may do so in the future

WHO TO APPLY TO Gary Smith, Secretary, Vineyard Christian Fellowship of South West Nottingham, 270 Derby Road, Bramcote, Nottingham NG9 3JN
CC NO 1054485   **ESTABLISHED** 1996

■ Nigel Vinson Charitable Trust

WHAT IS FUNDED The encouragement and development of business and industry, the arts and education
WHO CAN BENEFIT Individuals and organisations benefiting: actors and entertainment professionals; musicians; students; textile workers and designers; and writers and poets
WHERE FUNDING CAN BE GIVEN UK, especially the north east of England
TYPE OF GRANT Buildings, capital, one-off, project and research. Funding is for one year or less
FINANCES *Year* 1996–97 *Income* £70,000 *Grants* £35,030
TRUSTEES Rt Hon Lord Vinson of Roddam Dene, P R Fyson, M F Jodrell, Miss Bettina C Vinson
HOW TO APPLY To the address under Who To Apply To in writing
WHO TO APPLY TO Rt Hon Lord Vinson of Roddam Dene, Nigel Vinson Charitable Trust, 37 Fleet Street, London EC4P 4DQ *Tel* 0171-353 4522
CC NO 265077   **ESTABLISHED** 1973

■ The William and Ellen Vinten Trust

WHAT IS FUNDED Training and education of people for industry, scientific and technological training in schools and colleges. Welfare of people in industry
WHO CAN BENEFIT Individuals, schools and colleges and industrial firms and companies
WHERE FUNDING CAN BE GIVEN Bury St Edmunds, Suffolk
FINANCES *Year* 1996–97 *Income* £55,769 *Grants* £112,944
TRUSTEES D J Medcalf, Maj R C Bracewell, J Vinten Crosher
WHO TO APPLY TO T B Catton, The William and Ellen Vinten Trust, Messrs Greene and Greene Solicitors, 80 Guildhall Street, Bury St Edmunds, Suffolk IP33 1QB
CC NO 285758   **ESTABLISHED** 1982

■ Vision Charity

WHAT IS FUNDED General charitable purposes. To benefit blind, visually disabled and dyslexic children
WHO CAN BENEFIT National organisations supporting those suffering from visual disabilities but other applications may also be considered
WHERE FUNDING CAN BE GIVEN UK
FINANCES *Year* 1997–98 *Income* £301,243 *Grants* £104,264
TRUSTEES D Coupe, M Carey, G Davis, P Davies, W Drew, Mrs G Fitzpatrick (Secretary), R Fossett, A Gell, B Gold, C Histed, M Holland, A Knight, K Lowy (Life President), R Morgan (Treasurer), D Pacy, D Reeves, Mrs B Saville, N Simpson, E Taylor, P Thompson, J White, T Wragg
PUBLICATIONS *Vision Charity News* (published twice yearly)
HOW TO APPLY A brief summary of the request should be sent to the address below. If the request is of interest to the Trustees, further details will be requested. If the request has not been

acknowledged within three months of submission, the applicant should assume that it has not been successful. The Charity is interested to receive such applications but regrets that it is not able to acknowledge every unsuccessful submission
WHO TO APPLY TO P H Thompson, Vision Charity, PO Box 10, Princes Risborough, Buckinghamshire HP27 0UA
CC NO 282295   **ESTABLISHED** 1976

■ Vivdale Ltd

WHAT IS FUNDED To advance religion in accordance with the Orthodox Jewish faith and general charitable purposes
WHO CAN BENEFIT Jewish people
WHERE FUNDING CAN BE GIVEN UK and overseas
TYPE OF GRANT At the discretion of the Trustees
FINANCES *Year* 1996–97 *Income* £77,638 *Grants* £34,078
TRUSTEES D H Marks, L Marks, F Z Sinclair
WHO TO APPLY TO D H Marks, Vivdale Ltd, 631 Green Lanes, London N8 0RE
CC NO 268505   **ESTABLISHED** 1974

■ The Viznitz (Keren Nitzchi) Foundation

WHAT IS FUNDED General charitable purposes
WHO CAN BENEFIT There are no restrictions on the age; professional and economic group; family situation; religion and culture; and social circumstances of; or disease or medical condition suffered by, the beneficiaries
WHERE FUNDING CAN BE GIVEN UK
FINANCES *Year* 1994–95 *Income* £114,845
TRUSTEES H Feldman, E Kahan, E S Margulies
HOW TO APPLY To the address under Who To Apply To in writing
WHO TO APPLY TO H Feldman, The Viznitz (Keren Nitzchi) Foundation, 23 Overlea Road, London E5 9BG
CC NO 326581   **ESTABLISHED** 1984

■ The Vodafone Group Charitable Trust

WHAT IS FUNDED Trustees favour applications from projects with a communications bias. They will give their support within the following areas: to voluntary organisations; residential facilities; arts and arts facilities, including arts education; health and medical research; conservation and environment; education and training and community services
WHAT IS NOT FUNDED Funding is not generally given to overseas based charities. No grants to individuals
WHO CAN BENEFIT Registered charities benefiting those involved in: medical research, the socially disadvantaged, education, the disabled, the arts and the environment
WHERE FUNDING CAN BE GIVEN UK and Europe
TYPE OF GRANT Buildings, capital, one-off, project and research will be considered. Funding is available for up to three years
RANGE OF GRANTS £1,000–£20,000, typical grant £10,000

SAMPLE GRANTS £100,000 to Newbury College for a new college development; £30,000 to Variety Club Children's Charity for a minibus; £15,600 to Meridian Broadcasting Charitable Trust for Spotlight on Mental Health Directory; £13,982 to Stroke Association towards funding new merchandise catalogue; £11,800 to Cystic Fibrosis Trust for a research project; £11,750 to Help the Aged for seniorlink telephones; £10,000pa for five years to Ronald Raven Chair in Clinical Oncology to fund research; £10,000 to Cancer BACUP for an employee support scheme; £10,000 to Cancer Research Campaign for the Oxford Appeal; £10,000 to Brain Research Trust for a research appeal

FINANCES *Year* 1997 *Income* £357,031 *Grants* £394,643

TRUSTEES P R Williams, T G Barwick, Sir Alec Broers

HOW TO APPLY Applications in writing with charity registration number. No application form required

WHO TO APPLY TO P R Williams, The Vodafone Group Charitable Trust, Vodafone Group plc, 2–4 London Road, Newbury, Berkshire RG14 1JX

CC NO 1013850   ESTABLISHED 1992

■ Voluntary Action Luton

WHAT IS FUNDED General charitable purposes, in particular the advancement of education and the releif of poverty, sickness and distress

WHO CAN BENEFIT Organisations benefiting children, young adults and students, at risk groups, those disadvantaged by poverty and socially isolated people. There is no restriction on the disease or medical condition suffered by the beneficiaries

WHERE FUNDING CAN BE GIVEN Luton and district

FINANCES *Year* 1997 *Income* £69,089 *Grants* £36,354

TRUSTEES Mrs P Commons, G Dillingham, I Feekins, Mrs C Holmes, J Islam, R Licorish, Mrs N Mitchell, B Moran, D Tsiricos

WHO TO APPLY TO Mrs S Dallimore, Voluntary Action Luton, First Floor, Redcliffe House, Mill St, Luton LU1 2NA

CC NO 1059287   ESTABLISHED 1996

■ Voluntary Action Rutland

WHAT IS FUNDED General charitable purposes in particular the advancement of education, the protection of health and the relief of poverty for the benefit of the community of Rutland. To promote, co-ordinate and support voluntary and community action in Rutland

WHO CAN BENEFIT Organisations benefiting children, young adults, students, volunteers and those disadvantaged by poverty. There is no restriction on the disease or medical condition suffered by the beneficiaries

WHERE FUNDING CAN BE GIVEN Rutland

FINANCES *Year* 1998 *Income* £110,144 *Grants* £6,348

TRUSTEES S E Seabrook, S D Smith, P H Williams

WHO TO APPLY TO Mrs E E Tagg, Secretary, Voluntary Action Rutland, The Rutland Volunteer Centre, Rear of Rutland College, Barleythorpe Road, Oakham, Rutland LE15 6QH

CC NO 1044271   ESTABLISHED 1994

■ Marie-Louise von Motesiczky Charitable Trust

WHAT IS FUNDED Education of the public in painting and sculpture; publication of literary works about the life and work of artists; the assistance of artists with medical expenses incurred where medical conditions have an effect on their vision

WHO CAN BENEFIT Artists, particularly those with medical conditions which have had an affect on their vision

WHERE FUNDING CAN BE GIVEN UK

TRUSTEES J Alder, A M Jaffe, R Karplus, S Rainbird, S Scrase

WHO TO APPLY TO Julian Smith, Marie-Louise von Motesiczky Charitable Trust, Farrer and Co, 66 Lincoln's Inn Field, London WC2A 3LH

CC NO 1059380   ESTABLISHED 1996

■ The W (Double You) Charitable Foundation

WHAT IS FUNDED General charitable purposes

WHO CAN BENEFIT There are no restrictions on the age; professional and economic group; family situation; religion and culture; and social circumstances of; or disease or medical condition suffered by, the beneficiaries

WHERE FUNDING CAN BE GIVEN UK

TRUSTEES D P Woolf, A J Woolf, R E Downhill

WHO TO APPLY TO J Barron, Effective Secretary, The W (Double You) Charitable Foundation, Sanford House, 10 Maynards Close, Kings Road, London SW6 2DB

CC NO 1068539 **ESTABLISHED** 1997

■ WWF UK (World Wide Fund for Nature)

WHAT IS FUNDED Projects which contribute to WWF UKs conservation programme which comprises targeted areas of activity within the broad headings of: living seas, forests, wetlands, species and habitats of special concern, future landscapes, climate change, toxics and sustainable resource use. Applicants should telephone to discuss whether projects would fall within the priority areas

WHAT IS NOT FUNDED No grants to expeditions, university courses, buildings, animal welfare, pure research or school/community conservation areas

WHERE FUNDING CAN BE GIVEN UK and overseas

TYPE OF GRANT Short or long-term grants (maximum usually three years). Interest free loans for 6–12 months. Core costs, one-off, project, running costs, salaries and start-up costs will also be considered

RANGE OF GRANTS £1,000–£50,000, typical grant £10,000

FINANCES *Year* 1996–97 *Income* £26,018,000 *Grants* £13,771,000

TRUSTEES Conservation Committee and UK Project Allocation Group

PUBLICATIONS *WWF-UK Catalogue of Conservation Projects and Report*

HOW TO APPLY By telephone prior to submitting a formal application. Two forms are available, one for the general category and one for land purchase, both include guidance notes. Applications should be completed by the end of each year to be considered for the following year's conservation programme. However, applications may be considered at any time for the uncommitted part of the budget set aside for innovative and urgent projects. It is expected that applicants will also be applying for grants to other bodies such as the Countryside Commission, Countryside Council for Wales, English Nature and Scottish Natural Heritage

WHO TO APPLY TO Bryony Chapman, UK Project Officer, WWF UK (World Wide Fund for Nature), Panda House, Weyside Park, Godalming, Surrey GU7 1XR *Tel* 01483 426444 *Fax* 01483 426409

CC NO 201707 **ESTABLISHED** 1961

■ The Charity of Thomas Wade & Others

WHAT IS FUNDED Provision of open spaces, allotments, playing fields, facilities for recreation, amusement, entertainment, including establishment of community and youth centres and for the general social intercourse of inhabitants of the City of Leeds; or grants to any authority, association or body providing such facilities

WHAT IS NOT FUNDED No grants to individuals. Tend not to support schools or medicine or health orientated bodies

WHO CAN BENEFIT Charities benefiting people of all ages and those living in urban areas. Mainly youth organisations and community centres. Past beneficiaries include YMCA and YWCA, Age Concern, Central Yorks Scout Council, Hunslet Boys' Club, Leeds Children's Holiday Camps Association, South Leeds Youth Theatre

WHERE FUNDING CAN BE GIVEN Leeds (pre-1974 boundary of the City)

TYPE OF GRANT Usually one-off capital grants. Core costs, recurring costs, running costs and start-up costs. Funding for up to three years may be considered

RANGE OF GRANTS £200–£30,000, typical grant £1,000–£2,000

SAMPLE GRANTS £30,000 to Hunslet Club for Boys and Girls for general running costs; £25,000 to YMCA, Leeds Central for general running costs; £19,992 to Western Flatts Park for one-off park improvements including play area; £19,000 to St George's Crypt for redeveloping a centre for the homeless; £6,500 to Age Concern, Leeds; £6,000 to YMCA, Middleton; £5,000 to Central Yorkshire Scout Council; £5,000 to Leeds Children's Holiday Camps Association for holidays for young people; £3,000 to Leeds County Guide Association; £3,000 to parish of St Cross, Middleton for community centre

FINANCES *Year* 1997 *Income* £187,488 *Grants* £163,642

TRUSTEES Lord Mayor, Rector of Leeds, J Roberts, E M Arnold, J Horrocks, P J D Marshall, OBE, Dr A Cooke, M J Dodgson, I A Ziff, J Tinker, J M Barr, CBE, M S Wainwright, B T Braimah, MBE, J D M Stoddart-Scott, J Thorpe (+ three representatives of Leeds City Council)

HOW TO APPLY Trustees meet April, July and November. Applications should reach them at least three weeks before the meeting because applications are checked, applicants visited and the project discussed. Essential to submit accounts and contact telephone number with application. Reports are required from all successful applicants

WHO TO APPLY TO W M Wrigley, The Charity of Thomas Wade & Others, Wrigleys Solicitors, 5 Butts Court, Leeds LS1 5JS

CC NO 224939 **ESTABLISHED** 1530

■ Wade Foundation

WHAT IS FUNDED General charitable purposes. The Wade Foundation as a matter of policy, only makes gifts to registered charities

WHAT IS NOT FUNDED No grants to individuals

WHO CAN BENEFIT There are no restrictions on the age; professional and economic group; family situation; religion and culture; and social circumstances of; or disease or medical condition suffered by, the beneficiaries

WHERE FUNDING CAN BE GIVEN UK

RANGE OF GRANTS £250–£1,500

SAMPLE GRANTS £1,500 to Wessex Children's Hospice Trust; £1,500 to Society of St Dismas; £1,500 to Multiple Sclerosis Society; £1,400 to YMCA Southampton; £1,000 to Alzheimer's Disease Society

FINANCES *Year* 1996 *Income* £16,417 *Grants* £60,775

TRUSTEES H R Heath, G A Harding

WHO TO APPLY TO Wade Foundation, Bennett Welch & Co, Bank Chambers, Upper Norwood, London SE19 1TY

CC NO 260523 **ESTABLISHED** 1969

■ The Scurrah Wainwright Charity

WHAT IS FUNDED At the discretion of the Trustees. With a preference for radical rather than palliative projects relating to the most disadvantaged in society and where possible involving them in management. Particularly charities working in the fields of: infrastructure and technical support; infrastructure development; accommodation and housing; education and training; and social care and development

WHAT IS NOT FUNDED No grants to medical problem-related charities or animal charities

WHO CAN BENEFIT Rarely individuals. Organisations benefiting people of all ages; unemployed people; at risk groups; those disadvantaged by poverty; homeless people; those living in urban areas; those in care, fostered and adopted; one parent families; and widows and widowers

WHERE FUNDING CAN BE GIVEN Yorkshire and Southern Africa

TYPE OF GRANT One-off and recurring grants

RANGE OF GRANTS £100–£50,000

SAMPLE GRANTS £51,000 to Oxfam for Southern Africa drought relief/land reform; £12,000 to Arthur McDougall Foundation for electoral reform research; £10,333 to Ebor Gardens Advice Centre for inner city renewal, Leeds; £10,000 to Gipsil for homeless assisted housing, Leeds; £10,000 to Zimbabwe Educational Trust for educational assistance in Zimbabwe; £8,400 to Foundation for East-West Initiatives for regeneration in Slovakia; £7,500 to Libertarian Research and Education Trust for civil liberties research, UK and EU; £6,000 to Black Mental Health Resource Centre for centre in Leeds; £6,000 to Public Concern at Work for whistleblowers; £5,000 to Caring for Life for rehabilitation project in Leeds

FINANCES *Year* 1996–97 *Income* £88,813 *Grants* £153,653

TRUSTEES R R Bhaskar, H P I Scott, H A Wainwright, J M Wainwright, M S Wainwright (Chair), P Wainwright, R S Wainwright, T M Wainwright

HOW TO APPLY TO In writing to the address under Who To Apply To. Please specify amount required, purpose of grant and, if institution, enclose copy of most recent accounts. If uncertain that objectives are strictly charitable telephone for details of associated, non-charitable Andrew Wainwright Reform Trust

WHO TO APPLY TO G W Falding, Accountant to the Trustees, The Scurrah Wainwright Charity, c/o 5 Tower Place, York YO1 1RZ *Tel* 01904 641971

CC NO 1002755 **ESTABLISHED** 1991

■ Wakefield Covenant Community

WHAT IS FUNDED Advancement of the Christian faith. Relief of persons who are in conditions of need, hardship or distress or who are aged or sick, the advancement of education on the basis of Christian principles

WHO CAN BENEFIT Organisations benefiting: older people; retired people; Christians; at risk groups; those disadvantaged by poverty; and socially isolated people. There is no restriction on the disease or medical condition suffered by the beneficiaries. At the discretion of the Trustees

WHERE FUNDING CAN BE GIVEN UK

TYPE OF GRANT At the discretion of the Trustees

FINANCES *Year* 1995 *Income* £30,000

TRUSTEES Leslie C Tutfield, John C Mellor, Neville J Rigby, Paul Sheffield

WHO TO APPLY TO N J Rigby, IPFA, Wakefield Covenant Community, 141 Wrenthorpe Road, Wakefield WF2 0JN *Tel* 01302 737903

CC NO 1052699

■ Wakefield (Tower Hill, Trinity Square) Trust

WHAT IS FUNDED General charitable purposes for the development of Tower Hill and Trinity Square as a centre from which welfare work can be promoted. In particular, the following area are supported: assistance to hostels for young men giving their time to welfare work; assistance to clubs for youths, boys, young women or girls, living or working in the Trust's area; assistance to educational and recreational associations in connection with hostels or youth clubs

WHAT IS NOT FUNDED No grants to individuals. No grants for: capital expenditure; lobbying (political or otherwise); replacement or the meeting of statutory funding; business schemes; private education; foreign travel; commercial publications; establishing funds for bursaries or loan schemes; or to projects based outside the Trust's one mile area

WHO CAN BENEFIT Registered charities within our one mile beneficial area. Particularly those benefiting children and young adults

WHERE FUNDING CAN BE GIVEN The one mile radius from 41 Trinity Square, London EC3

TYPE OF GRANT General, although preference is given to revenue and salary costs

RANGE OF GRANTS £200–£50,000

SAMPLE GRANTS £50,500 to Toc H; £50,000 to All Hallows Church; £8,625 to Ensign Youth Club; £7,500 to Spitalfields Careworker Service; £6,000 to Winant Clayton Volunteer Association; £6,000 to London Coaching Foundation; £5,700 to YWCA – Avenues Unlimited; £5,450 to Attlee Foundation Adventure Playground; £5,000 to Davenant Centre; £5,000 to Tower Hamlets Old People's Welfare Trust

FINANCES *Year* 1996 *Income* £362,629 *Grants* £171,552

TRUSTEES L J Windridge, FCIS (Chairman), Canon P Delany, T Ahmed, MBE, Prof H Allred, P Bowring, CBE, P Fairclough, OBE, Ms J Harris, K Prideaux-Brune, M Sparks

NOTES In addition to supporting All Hallows Church, Tower Hill and Toc H, the Trust was set up to assist such general charitable purposes as will be most conducive to the development of Tower Hill and Trinity Square, EC3 as a centre from which welfare work can be promoted, in the City of London and within a radius of one mile from Trinity Square, London, EC3. It is hoped that part of future grant-giving will be towards new initiatives. Funding is also available for summer projects. Please note that our income will be severely restricted as from 1997. Please contact the Grant Administrator prior to making an application

660

Think carefully about every application. Is it justified?

HOW TO APPLY Applications are considered twice a year in March and September. Modest applications for summer projects are considered in June each year
WHO TO APPLY TO Barbara Moody, Grant Administrator, Attlee House, 28 Commercial Street, London E1 6LR
CC NO 209123   **ESTABLISHED** 1937

■ The Wakefield Trust

WHAT IS FUNDED Church restoration in Devon. See Notes below
WHAT IS NOT FUNDED No grants to individuals
WHO CAN BENEFIT Those disadvantaged by poverty
WHERE FUNDING CAN BE GIVEN South West
FINANCES *Year* 1997 *Income* £43,554 *Grants* £37,500
TRUSTEES Mrs M P Mitchell, Dr A N Brain, C D Torlesse, M B Shaw
NOTES The Trustees intend to endow further Almshouses in the Totnes area and will not consider new applications for a number of years
WHO TO APPLY TO Michael Fea, The Wakefield Trust, St Philip's House, St Philip's Place, Birmingham B3 2PP
CC NO 800079   **ESTABLISHED** 1988

■ The Wakeham Trust

WHAT IS FUNDED We like to help projects which are: (a) small, so that grants of up to £1,000 will make a real difference; (b) doing something which is new (either in national terms, or in their locality); (c) run by ordinary people, not social work professionals; (d) involving people – especially young people and the elderly – in helping their own communities; (e) (in many cases) unconventional and unlikely to attract funding from more traditional sources; (f) not on the grapevine in terms of having ready access to funding from large foundations. We are especially interested in helping projects making imaginative use of Community Service Volunteers, and in unconventional community arts projects
WHAT IS NOT FUNDED No grants to individuals, national appeals, playgroups, playing fields, or Boy Scouts, etc unless they are doing something very unusual and are helping other people. No consciousness raising. No building or vehicles appeals
WHO CAN BENEFIT Registered charities particularly those benefiting young people, the elderly and volunteers
WHERE FUNDING CAN BE GIVEN Normally UK, but we will consider third world projects meeting our normal criteria, if there is a sponsoring UK charity
TYPE OF GRANT We normally support each project only once. We aim to provide start-up finance, not continuing support. Grants can only be made to registered charities, though we can often help new non-registered groups via grants to an umbrella charity such as a Church or CVS
RANGE OF GRANTS £100–£1,000
SAMPLE GRANTS £4,000 to One25 for helping women working in street prostitution; £2,500 to Rainbow Charity for Homeless Children to provide residential care and education in small villages in India; £1,000 to Halton YMCA to replace and refurbish equipment and facilities; £900 to Katie's Ski Tracks to provide skiing holidays for sick and disabled children; £500 to Aid Workforce to provide a clinic in a village in Romania
FINANCES *Year* 1997 *Income* £20,000 *Grants* £20,000

TRUSTEES H Carter, Mrs A Knight, B Newbolt, Ms S Owen, R Salmon, Ms T Silkstone
HOW TO APPLY At any time. Trustees meet twice a year, usually in October and April. Write to Julie Austin with an outline of why you need help, and how you will spend the money. You should also show what other fund raising you have done, how many people you will actually be helping, and how you will expect to become self-sufficient in terms of fund raising in the future. If you can show evidence of support and interest from your local community (such as press cuttings) this will help your application. Please do include an sae but do not include any precious original material such as photographs, in case we lose them. Please enclose the name and charity registration number of a charity which is willing to accept a grant on your behalf, if your project is not itself registered. Applications can take time to be ready for submission to the Trustees – so please apply early, so that we can tell you if we need more information
WHO TO APPLY TO Mrs Julie Austin, Organiser, The Wakeham Trust, Wakeham Lodge, Terwick Hill, Rogate, Petersfield, Hampshire GU31 5EJ *Tel* 01730 821748
CC NO 267495   **ESTABLISHED** 1974

■ The Princess of Wales' Charities Trust

WHAT IS FUNDED The Princess of Wales' Charities Trust makes donations to charitable bodies and for charitable purposes at the discretion of the Trustees. The Trustees are principally concerned to continue to support charitable bodies and purposes in which Diana, Princess of Wales had a particular interest
WHAT IS NOT FUNDED No grants to individuals
WHO CAN BENEFIT Registered charities only. There are no restrictions on the age; professional and economic group; family situation; religion and culture; and social circumstances of; or disease or medical condition suffered by, the beneficiaries
WHERE FUNDING CAN BE GIVEN UK
SAMPLE GRANTS To St Matthew Society; To the David Tolkien Trust for Stoke Mandeville; To Great Ormond Street Hospital; To PHAB Wales; To Liverpool One Parent Families; To Richmond Fellowship; To Rainbow Appeal Fund; To Cherry Trees; To Calibre; To the Scout Association Trust
FINANCES *Year* 1996 *Income* £54,922 *Grants* £43,649
TRUSTEES Sir Matthew Farrer, GCVO, Angela Hordern
HOW TO APPLY At any time, in writing to the address under Who To Apply To
WHO TO APPLY TO Sir Charles Matthew Farrer, GCVO, The Princess of Wales' Charities Trust, 66 Lincolns Inn Fields, London WC2A 3LH
CC NO 283879   **ESTABLISHED** 1981

■ The Wales Council for the Deaf

WHAT IS FUNDED The relief of those adults and children who are hearing impaired, deaf, deafened, hard of hearing and deaf-blind
WHO CAN BENEFIT Organisations benefiting people who are hearing impaired
WHERE FUNDING CAN BE GIVEN Wales
FINANCES *Year* 1997 *Income* £178,890 *Grants* £634
TRUSTEES Mrs P Brown, W R David, Cllr Miss M H Ellis, H Graham, Mrs D Gunning, D T Harris, MBE, T Jones, R J Lewington, J R Martin, S Parkinson,

Does the trust you have chosen match your needs? Haphazard applications waste postage and time

661

A J Taffurelli, D V Williams, Mrs R Claydon, K
Davies, J L Jones, G Price, E Ross, Mrs O Jones,
Cllr W H Hitchings, G Rosser, W P G Davies, R
Lewington, Pastor B Mort, J Moore, R Williams, K
Davies

NOTES Total charitable expenditure totalled £85,260
WHO TO APPLY TO N B Moore, Wales Council for the
Deaf, Glenview House, Courthouse Street,
Pontypridd, Rhondda-Cynon-Taff CF37 1JY
CC NO 1035893   **ESTABLISHED** 1994

■ Wales Council for Voluntary Action

WHAT IS FUNDED General charitable purposes for the
benefit of the community, in particular, the
advancement of education, the furtherance of
health and the relief of poverty, sickness and
distress
WHO CAN BENEFIT There are no restrictions on the
age; professional and economic group; family
situation; religion and culture; and social
circumstances of; or disease or medical condition
suffered by, the beneficiaries
WHERE FUNDING CAN BE GIVEN Wales
FINANCES *Year* 1997 *Income* £1,595,178
Grants £1,236,084
TRUSTEES Executive Committee: P Barrett, H
Bhamjee, Prof M Broady, Mrs C Davies, Mrs M
Dykins, J Ashton-Edwards, S Etherington, Ms S M
Evans, Ms J Hutt, G Loan, Mrs M Jervis, J R Jones,
W P Kitson, Ms M Knight, Ms J Lewis, The Earl of
Lisburne, Ms R Mark, R Norris, J Payne, D Marc
Phillips, J Puzey, D Reith, Ms J Render, K Savage,
A Tharani, Mrs M Thorne, M Williams, A Wood
PUBLICATIONS *Wales Funding Handbook*, *Directory of
Voluntary Organisations in Wales*. Also other
guides and handbooks, briefing papers, reports
and information sheets
WHO TO APPLY TO D E Morris, Director, Wales Council
for Voluntary Action, Llys Ifor, Crescent Road,
Caerphilly CF83 1XL
CC NO 218093   **ESTABLISHED** 1963

■ Robert & Felicity Waley-Cohen Charitable Trust

WHAT IS FUNDED General charitable purposes
WHO CAN BENEFIT There are no restrictions on the
age; professional and economic group; family
situation; religion and culture; and social
circumstances of; or disease or medical condition
suffered by, the beneficiaries
WHERE FUNDING CAN BE GIVEN England
FINANCES *Year* 1995 *Income* £17,706
TRUSTEES R B Waley-Cohen, The Hon F A Waley-
Cohen
WHO TO APPLY TO R B Waley-Cohen, Robert & Felicity
Waley-Cohen Charitable Trust, 18 Gilston Road,
London SW10 9SR
CC NO 272126   **ESTABLISHED** 1976

■ The Walker 597 Trust

WHAT IS FUNDED Animal welfare and the prevention of
cruelty to animals. To make grants to relatively
small organisations
WHAT IS NOT FUNDED None, but smaller organisations
with low overheads preferred
WHO CAN BENEFIT Animal welfare organisations
WHERE FUNDING CAN BE GIVEN UK and overseas
TYPE OF GRANT Cash – generally not exceeding £200

SAMPLE GRANTS £200 to Animal Concern; £200 to
Friends of Bristol; £200 to Mare and Foal
Sanctuary; £200 to Swan Lifeline; £200 to World
Parrot Trust; £200 to Woodside Animal Welfare
Centre; £200 to Donkey Sanctuary; £200 to Otter
Trust; £200 to People's Trust for Endangered
Species; £200 to Sebakwe Black Rhino Trust
FINANCES *Year* 1996 *Income* £25,740
Grants £18,600
TRUSTEES J C H Walker, Mrs J M Walker, N Q
Grazebrook, Mrs R H Rowett
HOW TO APPLY To the address under Who To Apply To
quoting Ref NQG, preferably in July or December
WHO TO APPLY TO The Walker 597 Trust, Messrs
Shakespeares, Solicitors, 10 Bennetts Hill,
Birmingham B2 5RS
CC NO 278582   **ESTABLISHED** 1979

■ The Walker Trust (known as the Charity of Charles Clement Walker)

WHAT IS FUNDED To operate within the terms of the
Trust in the County of Shropshire only. In the
establishment or towards maintenance of any
hospital, infirmary, convalescent homes or other
institution having for its object the relief of
sickness or promoting convalescence. The
provision of medical or surgical aid or appliance.
Any institution for the maintenance and education
of orphans
WHO CAN BENEFIT Individuals and organisations
benefiting children and young adults who are in
care, fostered and adopted. There is no restriction
on the disease or medical condition suffered by
the beneficiaries
WHERE FUNDING CAN BE GIVEN County of Shropshire
only or Shropshire residents
TYPE OF GRANT Grants made on merit to individuals or
having a direct link with the County
SAMPLE GRANTS £25,000 to Much Wenlock Cottage
Hospital; £15,000 to Shropshire Records and
Research Centre; £10,000 to Shelton Hospital
League of Friends; £5,000 to Mayfair Community
Association; £4,000 to Telford Drive; £3,500 to
Shropshire Regimental Museum; £3,500 to
Shropshire Rural Stress Support Network; £3,000
to Keele University; £2,500 to Ex-service Mental
Welfare Society; £2,000 to the Lyneal Trust
FINANCES *Year* 1997 *Income* £163,336
Grants £160,145
TRUSTEES A E H Heber-Percy, G Raxster, N Bishop,
Mrs C Paton-Smith, P F Phillips
PUBLICATIONS Leaflet on grant policy
NOTES The Trustees personally consider all
applications that come within the objects of the
Charity. They give equal importance to both health
and education. They do not normally assist with
second or post-graduate degrees or with vacation
trips abroad or first degrees where the applicant is
receiving a mandatory or discretionary award. In
1997 a total of £65,683 was donated to 189
individuals and £94,462 to organisations
HOW TO APPLY Applications may be made at any time
to the Administrator of the Trust. Forms are
available for individual applications. All applicants
are informed of the Trustees' decision
WHO TO APPLY TO E Hewitt, Administrator, The Walker
Trust, The Shirehall, Abbey Foregate, Shrewsbury
SY2 6ND
CC NO 215479   **ESTABLISHED** 1897

◼ The Wall Charitable Trust

WHAT IS FUNDED General charitable purposes

WHO CAN BENEFIT There are no restrictions on the age; professional and economic group; family situation; religion and culture; and social circumstances of; or disease or medical condition suffered by, the beneficiaries

WHERE FUNDING CAN BE GIVEN Preference is given to Bristol charities

TYPE OF GRANT Donations

FINANCES *Year* 1995–96 *Income* £123,000 *Grants* £119,400

TRUSTEES P G B Letts and The Orchard Executor and Trustee Company

NOTES Only registered charities are considered for funding

HOW TO APPLY Any applications received will usually be considered on a monthly basis

WHO TO APPLY TO P G B Letts, The Wall Charitable Trust, Meade-King Solicitors, 24 Orchard Street, Bristol BS1 5DF

CC NO 281155   **ESTABLISHED** 1979

◼ The Thomas Wall Trust

WHAT IS FUNDED Grants are given to UK individual students for educational, especially vocational, courses which will lead to paid employment. For medicine, dentistry, law and veterinary science interest-free loans are given, not grants. Grants are only given to schoolchildren if unexpected financial crisis occurs during their final 'A' level year. Grants to charitable organisations in education and social welfare will preferably be made to those which are small or pioneering, and for specific purposes, not for recurrent costs

WHAT IS NOT FUNDED Not for post-graduate study or research for Higher Degrees except short courses of vocational or professional training. Not for travel or study abroad. Not for elective or intercalated courses. Not for attendance at conferences. Not for building projects nor large general appeals

WHO CAN BENEFIT Students needing to gain a skill or qualification to earn a living; community-based organisations with practical schemes for helping the young. Organisations benefiting young adults; older people; those in care, fostered and adopted; parents and children; one parent families; widows and widowers; disabled people and those disadvantaged by poverty

WHERE FUNDING CAN BE GIVEN UK

TYPE OF GRANT For fees or maintenance (students); for non-recurring expenses (charities). Maximum grant £600. Capital, one-off, project and start-up costs. Funding for one year or less will be considered

RANGE OF GRANTS £200–£600

SAMPLE GRANTS £600 each to individual adult students for courses including: MSc in Clinical Communications (Speech Therapy); DipHE in Counselling; Diploma in Dietetics; Practical Boat Building course; Stonecarving Graduateship; National Diploma in Horticulture; and Stage Management and Theatre Production; £600 to Discovery Docklands Trust for cost of new boats; £600 to Crime prevention Panel, Tooting towards their lock/alarm fitting service for local residents; £600 to 3C Teamwork, Crewe towards equipping a furniture restoration workshop

FINANCES *Year* 1997 *Income* £109,700 *Grants* £62,147

TRUSTEES P H Williams, MA, DPhil (Chairman), T Snow, MA, Miss A S Kennedy, MA, P H Bolton, MA, G Copland, MA, DPhil, CPhys, MInstP, FRSA, C R Broomfield, MA, F V McClure, BA, J Porteous,

OBE, One representative from each of Secondary Heads Association and Oxford, Cambridge and London Universities, and five co-opted

HOW TO APPLY Applications from individuals may be made from January onwards preceding the start of the academic year for which the grant is sought, and will be considered for as long as the available funds allow. Eligible charitable organisations may submit applications by mid-May for decisions at the Trustees' meeting in July, and by mid October for December

WHO TO APPLY TO W B Cook, MA, Director, The Thomas Wall Trust, Charterford House, 75 London Road, Headington, Oxford, Oxfordshire OX3 9AA *Tel* 01865 744228

CC NO 206121   **ESTABLISHED** 1920

◼ The A F Wallace Charity Trust

WHAT IS FUNDED Most appeals and charitable causes considered. Currently the main call on the Trust's funds is to provide enhanced housing, welfare and pension facilities for a number of senior citizens in the UK who have been associated over many years with the Wallace family

WHO CAN BENEFIT To benefit senior citizens who have been associated with the Wallace family

WHERE FUNDING CAN BE GIVEN UK, particularly Scotland

TYPE OF GRANT Mainly one-off

RANGE OF GRANTS Registered charities: average £200

SAMPLE GRANTS £18,362 to senior citizens in the upper Donside area of West Aberdeenshire; £14,480 to former employees of the Bombay Burmah Trading Corporation; £3,900 to registered charities; £2,322 as charitable donations; £2,224 as an educational grant to an individual

FINANCES *Year* 1997 *Income* £46,154 *Grants* £41,294

TRUSTEES F A Wallace, A J W F Wallace

HOW TO APPLY To the address under Who To Apply To

WHO TO APPLY TO The A F Wallace Charity Trust, Bartlett House, 9–12 Basinghall Street, London EC2V 5NS

CC NO 207110   **ESTABLISHED** 1912

◼ The Hamilton Wallace Trust

WHAT IS FUNDED General charitable purposes. The Principal is especially interested in benefiting charities working in the areas of medical research, children and hospitals

WHO CAN BENEFIT There are no restrictions on the age; professional and economic group; family situation; religion and culture; and social circumstances of; or disease or medical condition suffered by, the beneficiaries. However, particular favour is given to children, medical professionals, research workers and scientists. Favour is also given to the sick

WHERE FUNDING CAN BE GIVEN UK, with a preference for the London Borough of Hillingdon

NOTES The Trustees meet in July and January

WHO TO APPLY TO Bryan Weir, Secretary, The Hamilton Wallace Trust, c/o Travers Smith Braithwaite, Solicitors, 10 Snow Hill, London EC1A 2AL

CC NO 1052453   **ESTABLISHED** 1996

■ Wallington Missionary Mart & Auctions

WHAT IS FUNDED The Company aims to give financial assistance to missionaries and missionary societies working overseas involved in Christian education and outreach

WHAT IS NOT FUNDED Registered charities only. Applications from individuals only considered if funds will go to a missionary society or Christian charity

WHO CAN BENEFIT Missionary societies working overseas benefiting: Christians, Baptists, Church of England, evangelists and Methodists

WHERE FUNDING CAN BE GIVEN UK and overseas

TYPE OF GRANT Usually one-off grants for core costs. Fully committed for charities selected by the Trustees

SAMPLE GRANTS £18,544 to Feba Radio; £15,341 to OMF International (UK); £13,057 to Action Partners; £12,799 to All Nations Christian College; £11,763 to South American Mission Society; £11,136 to Crusaders; £10,847 to Mid-Africa Ministry; £10,368 to Tear Fund; £9,467 to Church Mission Society; £7,621 to Bible Society

FINANCES *Year* 1997 *Income* £339,465
Grants £259,835

TRUSTEES The Council of Management

NOTES The Company was incorporated in 1984 to take over two charities established since 1965

HOW TO APPLY By letter to Company Secretary with sae. Applications from individuals should give details of the support being received from their home church

WHO TO APPLY TO B E Chapman, Company Secretary, Wallington Missionary Mart & Auctions, 99 Woodmansterne Road, Carshalton Beeches, Surrey SM5 4EG *Tel* 0181-643 3616

CC NO 289030   **ESTABLISHED** 1965

■ The F J Wallis Charitable Trust

WHAT IS FUNDED General charitable purposes. The policy is wide and could be said to be any deserving cause (excluding individuals)

WHAT IS NOT FUNDED No grants to individuals

WHO CAN BENEFIT Can be either HQ or local branches. There are no restrictions on the age; professional and economic group; family situation; religion and culture; and social circumstances of; or disease or medical condition suffered by, the beneficiaries

WHERE FUNDING CAN BE GIVEN UK, Hampshire and Surrey

TYPE OF GRANT Mostly one-off but there are some recurring grants

RANGE OF GRANTS £100–£3,000

SAMPLE GRANTS £3,000 to Age Concern, Winchester; £2,500 to Colden Common Methodist Church; £1,000 to Childline; £1,000 to NSPCC; £1,000 to Roehampton Institute; £1,000 to SANDS; £1,000 to Sports Aid Foundation Charitable Trust; £1,000 to the Multiple Sclerosis Society; £1,000 to the Snowdon Award Scheme; £1,000 to VSO

FINANCES *Year* 1997 *Income* £57,829
Grants £71,450

TRUSTEES Mrs D I Wallis, F H Hughes, A J Hills

HOW TO APPLY Certainly no telephone calls. Brief written details are required. There is no application form and unsuccessful applicants will not be notified unless an sae is provided

WHO TO APPLY TO F H Hughes, The F J Wallis Charitable Trust, 25 Chargate Close, Burwood Park, Walton-on-Thames, Surrey KT12 5DW

CC NO 279273   **ESTABLISHED** 1979

■ The Walsall Town Darts Club Charitable Trust

WHAT IS FUNDED Charities benefiting elderly and disabled people and hospital geriatric wards

WHO CAN BENEFIT Local charities and hospitals benefiting the elderly and disabled

WHERE FUNDING CAN BE GIVEN Walsall, West Midlands

FINANCES *Year* 1997 *Income* £13,753
Grants £18,238

HOW TO APPLY To the the address under Who To Apply To in writing

WHO TO APPLY TO W F Dawson, The Walsall Town Darts Club Charitable Trust, 7 Millfield Avenue, High Heath, Pelsall, Walsall, West Midlands WS4 1DD

CC NO 508058   **ESTABLISHED** 1978

■ The Isidore and David Walton Foundation

WHAT IS FUNDED Charities working in the fields of: religion; health; cancer research; recreation grounds, playgrounds and clubs; and care in the community. Funding may also be given to business schools, pre-school education, cultural and religious teaching, arts and arts facilities. Health and social care professional bodies will be considered

WHAT IS NOT FUNDED Grants are not awarded for political causes nor to individuals

WHO CAN BENEFIT Organisations benefiting: people of all ages; those disadvantaged by poverty; refugees; victims of man-made or natural disasters and those suffering from asthma; cancers; heart disease; mental illness; strokes and terminal illnesses

WHERE FUNDING CAN BE GIVEN West of Scotland, particularly Glasgow

FINANCES *Year* 1996 *Income* £100,000
Grants £40,000

TRUSTEES Prof L Blumgart, E Glen, Prof R A Lorimer, Mrs C Walton, D Walton, J R Walton, M Walton

PUBLICATIONS Accounts are available from Deloitte-Touche & Co Chartered Accountants, 39 St Vincent Place, Glasgow G1 2QQ

HOW TO APPLY Applications should be made in writing to the address under Who To Apply To. **Unsolicited applications are not invited**

WHO TO APPLY TO David Walton, The Isidore and David Walton Foundation, Royal Exchange House, 100 Queen Street, Glasgow G1 3DL *Tel* 0141-248 7333

SC NO SCO 04005

■ War on Want

WHAT IS FUNDED War on Want funds overseas development projects that address the root causes of poverty, oppression and injustice in developing countries The current focus is on workers' rights

WHO CAN BENEFIT Typically War on Want directly funds the work of labour organisations and NGOs in developing countries. These are usually trades unions or similar workers' organisations in both the formal and informal sectors. Assistance is also given to women's organisations

WHAT IS NOT FUNDED War on Want does not make grants to organisations in the UK

WHERE FUNDING CAN BE GIVEN Developing countries

TYPE OF GRANT Continuous project funding

664

Think carefully about every application. Is it justified?

FINANCES *Year* 1996 *Income* £1,165,434
Grants £878,513

TRUSTEES The Council of Management: D Cameron, J Chowcatt, R Gaeton, B Green, T Harding, M Hughes, A Keene, K Khan, M Leutchford, L Philipson

PUBLICATIONS For a publications list please telephone or write to War on Want. Subjects include: Health, Women, Trade, Aid, Asia, Latin America and Africa

HOW TO APPLY Anytime

WHO TO APPLY TO The Director, War on Want, Fenner Brockway House, 37–39 Great Guildford Street, London SE1 0ES

CC NO 208724   **ESTABLISHED** 1959

■ Warbeck Fund Limited

WHAT IS FUNDED General charitable purposes

WHAT IS NOT FUNDED No grants to individuals

WHO CAN BENEFIT Both headquarters and local organisations. There are no restrictions on the age; professional and economic group; family situation; religion and culture; and social circumstances of; or disease or medical condition suffered by, the beneficiaries

WHERE FUNDING CAN BE GIVEN Payments to UK charities only, but ultimate beneficiary anywhere

RANGE OF GRANTS £10–£17,100

SAMPLE GRANTS £17,100 to Royal National Theatre; £16,300 to Weizmann Institute Foundation; £10,000 to the Tate Gallery; £8,605 to Norwood Ravenswood; £5,100 to British ORT

FINANCES *Year* 1998 *Income* £19,726
Grants £129,288

TRUSTEES M B David, J Gestetner, N Sinclair

HOW TO APPLY Funds fully committed

WHO TO APPLY TO J Winskell, The Secretary, Warbeck Fund Limited, 32 Featherstone Street, London EC1Y 8QX

CC NO 252953   **ESTABLISHED** 1967

■ The Ward Blenkinsop Trust

WHAT IS FUNDED General charitable purposes with emphasis on support for medical research

WHAT IS NOT FUNDED No grants to individuals

WHO CAN BENEFIT Mainly research foundations and charitable organisations. There are no restrictions on the age; professional and economic group; family situation; religion and culture; and social circumstances of; or disease or medical condition suffered by, the beneficiaries

WHERE FUNDING CAN BE GIVEN UK. Special interest in the Merseyside area

TYPE OF GRANT Mainly cash

SAMPLE GRANTS £36,650 to Cheshire County Council for youth arts initiative; £25,000 to Chatterbridge Cancer Research Fund for cancer research; £16,400 to Royal Academy of Dancing for special needs programme; £10,000 to St Mary's (Horsham) Restoration Appeal; £8,000 to The CLOD Ensemble; £5,000 to International Spinal Research Trust; £5,000 to Stephen Park Trust; £5,000 to Father Roger Charter Mission; £5,000 to Manchester Youth Theatre; £5,000 to British Sports Association for the Disabled

FINANCES *Year* 1997 *Income* £246,511
Grants £244,935

TRUSTEES J H Awdry, A M Blenkinsop, T R Tilling

HOW TO APPLY In writing from charitable organisations, not individuals

WHO TO APPLY TO J H Awdry, The Ward Blenkinsop Trust, Broxbury, Codmore Hill, Pulborough, West Sussex RH20 2HY

CC NO 265449   **ESTABLISHED** 1972

■ The George Ward Charitable Trust

WHAT IS FUNDED General charitable purposes. For the relief of poverty amongst those in need of assistance who have been employed by the companies of George Ward Holdings Ltd and Ward White Ltd for a period of not less than three consecutive months, between 1 November 1941 and 31 January 1984, and their wives, widows, husbands, widowers, children or other dependants. Consideration given to local causes

WHO CAN BENEFIT Former employees of George Ward Holdings Ltd and Ward White Ltd who are disadvantaged by poverty and their wives, widows, husbands, widowers, children and other dependants

WHERE FUNDING CAN BE GIVEN The area comprised by the Hinckley and Bosworth Borough Council, Leicestershire

FINANCES *Year* 1997 *Income* £50,449
Grants £53,045

TRUSTEES D M Radford, J A Calow, D A Herbert (Chairman), B Smith, B Carnall, H Platts, J Malpas, B Hirons, C Orton, N Grewcock, R Clarke, M Buckle

NOTES Payments to ex-employees of the companies or their dependants – £51,245. Donations to organisations within the Hinckley and Bosworth Borough Council area – £1,800

WHO TO APPLY TO N Lafrenais, The George Ward Charitable Trust, Thomas May & Co, Allen House, Newark Street, Leicester LE1 5SG

CC NO 516954   **ESTABLISHED** 1985

■ The Peter Ward Charitable Trust

WHAT IS FUNDED General charitable purposes in Oxfordshire. Charities already being supported by the Trust

WHAT IS NOT FUNDED Expeditions and scholarships are not funded

WHO CAN BENEFIT There are no restrictions on the age; professional and economic group; family situation; religion and culture; and social circumstances of; or disease or medical condition suffered by, the beneficiaries

WHERE FUNDING CAN BE GIVEN Oxfordshire

TYPE OF GRANT Mainly one-off

RANGE OF GRANTS £100–£10,000

SAMPLE GRANTS £10,000 to Ruskin Mill Educational Charity; £5,000 to Katherine House Hospice Trust; £3,000 to Oxfordshire Association of Young People; £2,500 National Trust; £2,000 to Kingham Community Hall

FINANCES *Year* 1997 *Income* £16,366
Grants £23,885

TRUSTEES A T Grieve, M D Stanford-Tuck

HOW TO APPLY No guidelines or application form. The funds available are limited, and the Trustees are not actively considering any new requests. Unsolicited requests are therefore unlikely to be successful as existing grants use up the available income each year

WHO TO APPLY TO A J Carter, The Peter Ward Charitable Trust, 22b High Street, Witney, Oxfordshire OX8 6HB *Tel* 01993 703414

CC NO 258403   **ESTABLISHED** 1968

Does the trust you have chosen match your needs? Haphazard applications waste postage and time

665

■ The John Warren Foundation

WHAT IS FUNDED Church fabric repairs

WHAT IS NOT FUNDED No grants to individuals

WHO CAN BENEFIT Churches

WHERE FUNDING CAN BE GIVEN Bedfordshire and Lincolnshire

TYPE OF GRANT One-off grants

FINANCES *Year* 1996 *Income* £33,719
Grants £22,000

TRUSTEES J E Lamb and others

WHO TO APPLY TO The John Warren Foundation, Lamb & Holmes, Solicitors, West Street, Kettering, Northamptonshire NN16 0AZ

CC NO 201522 **ESTABLISHED** 1949

■ Warrington Church of England Educational Trust

WHAT IS FUNDED Educational purposes in the area Where Funding Can Be Given, including repairs to school buildings

WHO CAN BENEFIT Schools benefiting children and young adults

WHERE FUNDING CAN BE GIVEN Warrington

FINANCES *Year* 1996 *Income* £46,157
Grants £32,358

TRUSTEES J O Colling (Chairman), J B Naylor (Treasurer)

HOW TO APPLY To the address under Who To Apply To in writing

WHO TO APPLY TO John Naylor, Law Clerk, Warrington Church of England Educational Trust, Ridgway Greenall, 21 Palmyra Square, Warrington, Cheshire WA1 1BW

CC NO 511469 **ESTABLISHED** 1952

■ The Warwick Municipal Charities

WHAT IS FUNDED General charitable purposes in Warwick

WHO CAN BENEFIT There are no restrictions on the age; professional and economic group; family situation; religion and culture; and social circumstances of; or disease or medical condition suffered by, the beneficiaries

WHERE FUNDING CAN BE GIVEN Warwick

FINANCES *Year* 1995 *Income* £1,451,896

TRUSTEES B Brewster, D G Fuller, B Gillit, Mrs M Haywood, J P McCarthy, T K Meredith, Mrs S Rhodes, N F J Thurley, H R C Walden

HOW TO APPLY To the address under Who To Apply To in writing. Trustees meet to consider applications in February, May, October and December

WHO TO APPLY TO P G Butler, Clerk, The Warwick Municipal Charities, 12 Euston Place, Leamington Spa, Warwickshire CV32 4LR

CC NO 232862 **ESTABLISHED** 1964

■ The Warwickshire Masonic Charitable Association Limited

WHAT IS FUNDED Masonic charities, health and welfare causes, especially hospices and disability organisations

WHO CAN BENEFIT Local and regional organisations and local branches of national organisations benefiting masons, at risk groups, disabled people, those disadvantaged by poverty and socially isolated people. There is no restriction on the disease or medical condition suffered by the beneficiaries

WHERE FUNDING CAN BE GIVEN Warwickshire and the Midlands

RANGE OF GRANTS £25–£3,000

SAMPLE GRANTS £3,000 to Birmingham Lord Major's Appeal; £3,000 to Shakespeare Hospice; £2,000 to BBC Children in Need; £2,000 to Grove Residential Home; £2,000 to Royal Warwickshire Regiment Museum Appeal; £1,750 to Greenacres Cheshire Home; £1,500 to Warren Pearl; £1,500 to St Mary's Hospice; £1,500 to James Hiron Home; £1,500 to Myton Hamlet Hospice

FINANCES *Year* 1997 *Income* £507,215
Grants £304,090

TRUSTEES W F Aitken, R E Albutt, M D Arnold, E G Bailey, G G Bissell, J G Blandford, P L Britton, P J Campbell, S W Downes, R Eamonson, W S Ellson, W Forster-Jones. W E Gibbons, A J Hackney, W E Herbaert, D C Hobson, G C Hooker, F Jephcott, I Jones, V W Keene, R Kemp, S A Lates, A D Morris, G E Newby, D J Peachey, R Pullin, M J Price, P G Randon, R A Riley, R G Russell, R G Swain, R V Wallis, D W Yates

HOW TO APPLY To the address under Who To Apply To in writing

WHO TO APPLY TO A J Hackney, Secretary, Warwickshire Masonic Charitable Association Ltd, Warwickshire Masonic Temple, 2 Stirling Road, Edgbaston, Birmingham B16 9SB

CC NO 211588 **ESTABLISHED** 1945

■ The Roger Waters 1989 Charity Trust

WHAT IS FUNDED General charitable purposes

WHO CAN BENEFIT There are no restrictions on the age; professional and economic group; family situation; religion and culture; and social circumstances of; or disease or medical condition suffered by, the beneficiaries

WHERE FUNDING CAN BE GIVEN UK

RANGE OF GRANTS £250–£10,000

SAMPLE GRANTS £10,000 to Children in Crisis; £5,000 to Treloar Trust; £2,000 to The Children's Hospice Appeal; £1,000 to Elizabeth Fitzroy Homes; £1,000 to Variety Club; £350 to Royal Academy Trust; £200 to ICRF; £200 to King George's Fund for Sailors

FINANCES *Year* 1996 *Income* £119,916
Grants £19,750

TRUSTEES G R Waters, A D Russell

WHO TO APPLY TO G R Waters, The Roger Waters 1989 Charity Trust, 31 Ruvigny Gardens, London SW15 1JR

CC NO 328574 **ESTABLISHED** 1989

■ The Neil Wates Charitable Trust

WHAT IS FUNDED Education, environment

WHAT IS NOT FUNDED No grants to individuals

WHO CAN BENEFIT Organisations benefiting children, young adults and students

WHERE FUNDING CAN BE GIVEN The main financial support is given to projects and programmes of activity based at Bore Place, Kent

TYPE OF GRANT One-off

FINANCES *Year* 1997 *Income* £132,541
Grants £82,396

TRUSTEES The Neil Wates Trust Ltd

PUBLICATIONS Annual Report

NOTES Unsolicited applications will not be considered

HOW TO APPLY **This Trust states that it does not respond to unsolicited applications**

WHO TO APPLY TO Mrs J M Oakley, The Neil Wates
Charitable Trust, Bore Place, Chiddingstone,
Edenbridge Kent TN8 7AR
CC NO 247942 **ESTABLISHED** 1966

■ Watford Health Trust

WHAT IS FUNDED Hospices and health organisations
WHO CAN BENEFIT Individuals and organisations.
There are no restrictions on the disease or
medical condition suffered by the beneficiaries
WHERE FUNDING CAN BE GIVEN Watford and
surrounding areas
SAMPLE GRANTS £21,730 to individuals; £10,500 to
organisations
FINANCES *Year* 1995 *Income* £23,536
Grants £32,562
TRUSTEES P E Braybrooke, FCA, G H Hall, LLB, N E
Lane, H Smith, FCA, Mrs J Spivey
HOW TO APPLY To the address under Who To Apply To
in writing
WHO TO APPLY TO P E Braybrooke, Treasurer, Watford
Health Trust, 16 Castle Hill Avenue, Berkhamsted,
Hertfordshire HP4 1HJ
CC NO 214160 **ESTABLISHED** 1982

■ The Wathes Charitable Trust

WHAT IS FUNDED Welfare
WHO CAN BENEFIT To the benefit of at risk groups,
those disadvantaged by poverty and socially
isolated people
WHERE FUNDING CAN BE GIVEN UK
RANGE OF GRANTS £50–£15,000
SAMPLE GRANTS £15,000 to Bendrigg Trust; £10,000
to Croft Care Trust; £3,000 to an individual;
£2,000 to Heartline; £2,000 to Woodland Centre
Trust; £500 to Scottish European Aid; £500 to
Royal School for the Blind, Liverpool; £500 to
SEA/MCE (Romania); £500 to Cancer Care Lakes
Appeal; £200 to Feel the Need (Romania)
FINANCES *Year* 1997 *Income* £87,959
Grants £34,450
TRUSTEES Peter G Thurnham, Sarah J Thurnham,
Michael J Stephenson
HOW TO APPLY To the address under Who To Apply To
in writing
WHO TO APPLY TO M J Stephenson, The Wathes
Charitable Trust, Wathes Holdings Ltd, Wathes
House, Frog Island, Leicester, Leicestershire
LE3 5BG
CC NO 328511 **ESTABLISHED** 1989

■ The Perry Watlington Trust

WHAT IS FUNDED Charities working with the disabled
and the chronically ill
WHO CAN BENEFIT Local and regional organisations,
local branches of national organisations benefiting:
disabled people. There are few restrictions on the
disease or medical condition suffered by the
beneficiaries
WHERE FUNDING CAN BE GIVEN Essex
TYPE OF GRANT Recurrent, occasionally one-off
FINANCES *Year* 1997 *Income* £28,072
Grants £28,250
TRUSTEES Mrs A Ashton, Mrs C Cottrell, Mrs M Judd,
R L H Lyster, R G Newman, T Ruggles-Brise, Sir N
Strutt
NOTES **Funds are fully committed**, grant seekers are
highly unlikely to obtain financial support from the
Trust
HOW TO APPLY To the address under Who To Apply To
in writing

WHO TO APPLY TO R L H Lyster, Chairman, The Perry
Watlington Trust, Malting Green House, Layer De
la Haye, Colchester, Essex CO2 0JE
CC NO 255014 **ESTABLISHED** 1968

■ Watside Charities *(also known as John*

Woodside Ltd)
WHAT IS FUNDED General charitable purposes
WHO CAN BENEFIT There are no restrictions on the
age; professional and economic group; family
situation; religion and culture; and social
circumstances of; or disease or medical condition
suffered by, the beneficiaries
WHERE FUNDING CAN BE GIVEN UK and overseas
FINANCES *Year* 1994–95 *Income* £76,688
TRUSTEES J Reid, C F Eadie
HOW TO APPLY To the address under Who To Apply To
in writing
WHO TO APPLY TO John Rudd, Watside Charities,
Singles House, 32 Galena Road, London E6 0LT
CC NO 326091 **ESTABLISHED** 1982

■ The Bertie Watson Foundation

WHAT IS FUNDED Small hospitals, hospices,
children's health care and welfare, mental illness,
Portuguese charities
WHAT IS NOT FUNDED No grants to individuals,
including students. No grants will be made in
response to general appeals from large
organisations nor to smaller bodies working in
areas other than those set out above
WHO CAN BENEFIT Organisations benefiting children,
medical professionals and those who are sick.
There is no restriction on the disease or medical
condition suffered by the beneficiaries
WHERE FUNDING CAN BE GIVEN UK and Portugal
FINANCES *Year* 1997 *Income* £34,548
Grants £22,600
TRUSTEES N S D Bulmer, J M Robb, Rt Hon
Viscountess Waverley
HOW TO APPLY Trustees meet annually in June to
consider applications. Applications should be
made to the address below in writing and should
include clear details of the need, the project and
the outline budget, including the amount of funds
raised so far. Successful applications only will be
acknowledged
WHO TO APPLY TO N S D Bulmer, The Bertie Watson
Foundation, Messrs Farrer & Co, 66 Lincoln's Inn
Fields, London WC2A 3LH
CC NO 285523 **ESTABLISHED** 1982

■ John Watson's Trust

WHAT IS FUNDED (a) Grants to children and young
persons under 21, physically or mentally
handicapped or socially disadvantaged, for further
education and training, equipment, travel, and
educational, social, recreational and cultural
activities. Grants to charitable organisations and
ad hoc groups in this field and to bodies and
persons for educational experiments and
research. (b) Grants for boarding education to
orphans, children of single-parent families (widely
defined) and children subject to some other
special family difficulty. See the John Watson's
Trust Scheme l984 (SI l984 No l480)
WHAT IS NOT FUNDED No grants to applicants over 21
years of age
WHO CAN BENEFIT Individuals, charitable
organisations, ad hoc groups, research bodies or

persons. Beneficiaries must be under 21 years of age. Those in care, fostered and adopted; children of one parent families; disabled people; and those disadvantaged by poverty will be considered

WHERE FUNDING CAN BE GIVEN For What Is Funded (a) Scotland with preference for Lothian. For What Is Funded (b) Scotland only

TYPE OF GRANT Equipment, small capital expenditure, tuition, student support, personal equipment, (eg special wheelchairs, special typewriters), projects and activities including travel. Grant one year only but can be extended

RANGE OF GRANTS Grants for What Is Funded (a) are likely to be in the main around the £100–£1,000 mark and are unlikely to exceed £10,000 (though some in £5,000 range)

FINANCES *Year* 1997 *Income* £176,700 *Grants* £150,000

TRUSTEES Six representatives of the Society of Writers to Her Majesty's Signet, two representatives from Lothian Regional Council, one from the Merchant Company Education Board, one from the Lothian Association of Youth Clubs, and one additional member

PUBLICATIONS Background Notes and application forms available

NOTES Morning is best time for telephoning

HOW TO APPLY Trustees meet eight times a year

WHO TO APPLY TO I Wilson, Administrator, John Watson's Trust, Grants Committee, HM Signet Library, Parliament Square, Edinburgh EH1 1RF *Tel* 0131-220 1640

SC NO SCO 14004   **ESTABLISHED** 1984

■ The Lady Margaret Watt Charitable Trust

WHAT IS FUNDED Organisations which are concerned with education, religion, combating poverty or illness or contributing to the quality of life in the community

WHAT IS NOT FUNDED Grants are not made to individuals

WHO CAN BENEFIT Organisations benefiting children, young adults and those disadvantaged by poverty. There are no restrictions on the religion and culture of, or disease or medical condition suffered by, the beneficiaries

WHERE FUNDING CAN BE GIVEN Scotland

FINANCES *Year* 1996 *Income* £50,000 *Grants* £40,000

TRUSTEES J C Craig, R S Waddell, The Management Trust Company Ltd

PUBLICATIONS Accounts are available from the Trust

HOW TO APPLY Applications should be made in writing to the address below

WHO TO APPLY TO John C Craig, The Lady Margaret Watt Charitable Trust, KPMG, 24 Blythswood Square, Glasgow G2 4QS

SC NO SCO 11619   **ESTABLISHED** 1976

■ The Wayfarers Charitable Trust

This trust did not respond to CAF's request to amend its entry and, by 30 June 1998, CAF's researchers did not find financial records for later than 1995 on its file at the Charity Commission. Trusts are legally required to submit annual accounts to the Charity Commission under section 42 of the Charities Act 1993

WHAT IS FUNDED General charitable purposes

WHO CAN BENEFIT There are no restrictions on the age; professional and economic group; family situation; religion and culture; and social circumstances of; or disease or medical condition suffered by, the beneficiaries

WHERE FUNDING CAN BE GIVEN UK

TRUSTEES I E Baird, J F Slater, L E Williams

WHO TO APPLY TO I E Baird, Clerk, The Wayfarers Charitable Trust, 16 Ripon Road, Bournemouth, Dorset BH9 1RD

CC NO 1056928   **ESTABLISHED** 1989

■ Waynflete Charitable Trust

This trust did not respond to CAF's request to amend its entry and, by 30 June 1998, CAF's researchers did not find financial records for later than 1995 on its file at the Charity Commission. Trusts are legally required to submit annual accounts to the Charity Commission under section 42 of the Charities Act 1993

WHAT IS FUNDED General charitable purposes

WHO CAN BENEFIT There are no restrictions on the age; professional and economic group; family situation; religion and culture; and social circumstances of; or disease or medical condition suffered by, the beneficiaries

WHERE FUNDING CAN BE GIVEN UK

TRUSTEES M J Worth, M W Fordyce

WHO TO APPLY TO M J Worth, Waynflete Charitable Trust, Carlton Scroop Hall, Carlton Scroop, Grantham, Lincolnshire NG32 3BB

CC NO 1068892   **ESTABLISHED** 1986

■ The Weavers' Company Benevolent Fund

WHAT IS FUNDED Trustees restrict their grants to projects concerned with helping young people at risk from criminal involvement and with the rehabilitation of young prisoners and ex-prisoners

WHAT IS NOT FUNDED Grants restricted to registered charities. No grants to individuals

WHO CAN BENEFIT Registered charities; small, community-based groups, rather than larger, national charities. Benefiting young people at risk from criminal involvement

WHERE FUNDING CAN BE GIVEN UK

TYPE OF GRANT Pump-priming grants for one – three years for new and innovatory projects

RANGE OF GRANTS £1,000–£10,000

SAMPLE GRANTS £10,000 to HOPE for work with offenders and penal affairs in Scotland; £10,000 to Weavers' Youth Forum for job training for Asian young people in Tower Hamlets; £10,000 to Barbara Mclunsky Fund for establishing a youth work training scheme for young people from settled refugee communities; £7,500 to St Alfege School for a pastoral care worker in Greenwich Primary School; £7,500 to Greater Manchester Shrievalty Police Trust for youth mediation scheme; £7,000 to East London Schools Fund for family liaison worker to work with vulnerable children on transfer from primary to secondary school; £6,000 to Open Door towards establishing an advice and information centre in Essex; £6,000 to Bristol Wheels for work with young people based in motorbike workshop; £6,000 to Cinderford Area Neighbourhood Development for outreach provision for young people in isolated rural communities

FINANCES *Year* 1997 *Income* £267,137 *Grants* £194,762

TRUSTEES The Worshipful Company of Weavers

PUBLICATIONS Guidelines

HOW TO APPLY Applications should be made by letter in the first instance and may be made at any time

WHO TO APPLY TO Mrs F Newcombe, Clerk, Weavers' Company Benevolent Fund, Saddlers' House, Gutter Lane, London EC2V 6BR *Tel* 0171-606 1155 *Fax* 0171-606 1119
CC NO 266189　　　ESTABLISHED 1973

■ The Dennis George Webb Charitable Trust

WHAT IS FUNDED General charitable purposes, as directed by the Settlor, at the Trustees' discretion
WHO CAN BENEFIT There are no restrictions on the age; professional and economic group; family situation; religion and culture; and social circumstances of; or disease or medical condition suffered by, the beneficiaries
WHERE FUNDING CAN BE GIVEN UK and overseas
RANGE OF GRANTS £100–£25,000
SAMPLE GRANTS £25,000 to East Midlands Province VRC; £15,000 to Barnes Close; £5,000 to Farnsfield PCC; £2,500 to Castle Hill VRC; £1,000 to Farnsfield Parish Church
FINANCES *Year* 1996 *Income* £19,362 *Grants* £52,500
TRUSTEES J G Webb, Mrs J Bartlett
HOW TO APPLY **This Trust states that it does not respond to unsolicited applications**
WHO TO APPLY TO The Dennis George Webb Charitable Trust, Tallents Godfrey & Co, 2 Westgate, Southwell, Nottinghamshire NG25 0JJ
CC NO 257413　　　ESTABLISHED 1968

■ Ethel Webber Trust Fund

WHAT IS FUNDED For specified charities, general charitable purposes. No laid down policy, considered annually when applications received
WHAT IS NOT FUNDED Restricted to specified charities
WHO CAN BENEFIT Mainly charities located in Exeter/Torbay area of Devon and specified charities. There are no restrictions on the age; professional and economic group; family situation; religion and culture; and social circumstances of; or disease or medical condition suffered by, the beneficiaries
WHERE FUNDING CAN BE GIVEN Exeter/Torbay area of Devon
TYPE OF GRANT Annual
RANGE OF GRANTS £428–£4,500
SAMPLE GRANTS £4,500 to Preston Baptist Church for the repair of a leaking roof; £428 to St Dunstans; £428 to Royal National Institute for the Blind; £428 to Royal National Institute for the Deaf; £428 to Royal National Lifeboat Institute; £428 to Baptist Missionary Society; £428 to Baptist Union of Great Britain; £428 to Barnardos; £428 to Spurgeons Homes; £428 to The Salvation Army
FINANCES *Year* 1996 *Income* £71,558 *Grants* £13,060
TRUSTEES Lloyds Bank plc, 71 Lombard Street, London
HOW TO APPLY No application form. Applications usually considered in May/June
WHO TO APPLY TO Ethel Webber Trust Fund, Lloyds Private Banking Ltd, UK Trust Centre, The Clock House, 22–26 Ock Street, Abingdon, Oxfordshire OX14 5SW
CC NO 258033　　　ESTABLISHED 1966

■ William Webster Charitable Trust

WHAT IS FUNDED General charitable purposes. Generally to fund capital projects
WHAT IS NOT FUNDED Grants are restricted to registered charitable organisations only from the North East of England. No grants to individuals
WHO CAN BENEFIT Registered charitable organisations in the North East of England, or for the benefit of branches in the North East of England. There are no restrictions on the age; professional and economic group; family situation; religion and culture; and social circumstances of; or disease or medical condition suffered by, the beneficiaries
WHERE FUNDING CAN BE GIVEN North East of England
TYPE OF GRANT One-off only
SAMPLE GRANTS £10,000 to Broomley Grange (Prev Committee); £5,000 to Coatham House; £2,000 to Geordie Jaunts; £1,000 to Byker Bridge Housing Association; £1,000 to All Saints Church, Blackwell; £1,000 to St Jane's and St Basil's Restoration Fund; £1,000 to North Shields Methodist Church; £1,000 to Julie Graham Children's Charity; £1,000 to Holy Trinity Church, Whitefield; £1,000 to Heads North
FINANCES *Year* 1997 *Income* £99,000 *Grants* £90,000
TRUSTEES Barclays Bank Trust Company Limited
HOW TO APPLY Details required are: details of the project, the amount of funding required, the funding raised from other sources, and a copy of the last report and accounts of the organisation. Meetings of the Trustees are held in March, July and November
WHO TO APPLY TO Barclays Bank Trust Co Ltd, William Webster Charitable Trust, Executorship & Trustee Service, Osborne Court, Gadbrook Park, Rudheath, Northwich, Cheshire CW9 7RE *Tel* 01606 313173
CC NO 259848　　　ESTABLISHED 1969

■ The Wedge

WHAT IS FUNDED The Trust makes grants only to organisations undertaking play and youth work in Merseyside. It prefers to support small local organisations rather than large or national bodies. Grants are made towards playscheme running costs, play equipment, day trips for playschemes
WHAT IS NOT FUNDED No grants to individuals. No grants are given for holidays, salaries, building costs or to religious organisations
WHO CAN BENEFIT Organisations benefiting children and young adults
WHERE FUNDING CAN BE GIVEN Liverpool
TYPE OF GRANT Grants to small local charities undertaking play and youth work. The Trust prefers to make a larger number of small grants rather than a few large grants. Grants are both single payment and recurrent
RANGE OF GRANTS £50–£500
FINANCES *Year* 1995 *Income* £14,113 *Grants* £17,500
TRUSTEES B Moores, A C McIntyre, A T Mcfarlane
HOW TO APPLY Applications should be in writing including a detailed budget and a copy of the latest available Accounts. Trustees meet quarterly
WHO TO APPLY TO A C McIntyre, The Wedge, South Moss House, Pasture Lane, Formby, Merseyside L37 0AP
CC NO 328382　　　ESTABLISHED 1988

■ The Weetabix Charitable Trust

WHAT IS FUNDED General charitable purposes

WHO CAN BENEFIT There are no restrictions on the age; professional and economic group; family situation; religion and culture; and social circumstances of; or disease or medical condition suffered by, the beneficiaries

WHERE FUNDING CAN BE GIVEN UK

FINANCES *Year* 1997 *Income* £673,798 *Grants* £603,104

TRUSTEES J H Carver, I P Clarke, Sir R W George

WHO TO APPLY TO I P Clarke, The Weetabix Charitable Trust, Weetabix Mills, Burton Latimer, Kettering, Northamptonshire NN15 5JR *Tel* 01536 722181

CC NO 1044949   **ESTABLISHED** 1995

■ The Weinstein Foundation

WHAT IS FUNDED General charitable purposes

WHAT IS NOT FUNDED No grants to individuals

WHO CAN BENEFIT Only local registered charities. There are no restrictions on the age; professional and economic group; family situation; religion and culture; and social circumstances of; or disease or medical condition suffered by, the beneficiaries

WHERE FUNDING CAN BE GIVEN London

TYPE OF GRANT Recurrent

FINANCES *Year* 1995 *Income* £84,654 *Grants* £88,233

TRUSTEES E Weinstein, Mrs S R Weinstein, M L Weinstein, P D Weinstein, Mrs L A F Newman

HOW TO APPLY To the address under Who To Apply To

WHO TO APPLY TO M L Weinstein, Trustee The Weinstein Foundation, 32 Fairholme Gardens, Finchley, London N3 3EB

CC NO 277779   **ESTABLISHED** 1979

■ The Weinstock Fund

WHAT IS FUNDED Nationally constituted charities mainly for children, old and disabled people, social welfare and education

WHAT IS NOT FUNDED Individuals and non-registered organisations will not be funded

WHO CAN BENEFIT Registered charities benefiting people of all ages, at risk groups, disabled people, those disadvantaged by poverty and socially isolated people

WHERE FUNDING CAN BE GIVEN UK

RANGE OF GRANTS £100–£100,000

SAMPLE GRANTS £100,000 to British Museum; £35,972 to Friends of Ravenna Festival; £26,000 to Royal Opera House, Covent Garden; £20,000 to Jewish Philanthropic Association for Israel and the Middle East; £10,000 to Constable Educational Trust; £10,000 to Masorti Organisation of Synagogues; £6,750 to North London Hospice; £5,500 to Jewish Care; £5,000 to British Heart Foundation; £5,000 to British ORT

FINANCES *Year* 1997 *Income* £424,854 *Grants* £503,572

TRUSTEES M Lester, Hon Susan G Lacroix

HOW TO APPLY Annually

WHO TO APPLY TO J Wood, The Weinstock Fund, Messrs Herbert Smith, Exchange House, Primrose Street, London EC2A 2HS

CC NO 222376   **ESTABLISHED** 1962

■ The Alfred and Beatrice Weintrop Charity

WHAT IS FUNDED Cancer, immunology and neurological research. Care of the sick, disabled and elderly. Advancement of the Jewish religion

WHAT IS NOT FUNDED Preference is given to Jewish causes

WHO CAN BENEFIT Older people; disabled people; and Jews. Those suffering from: Alzheimer's disease; arthritis and rheumatism; asthma; blood disorders and haemophilia; cancers; Crohn's disease; diabetes; hearing loss; heart disease; kidney disease; mental illness; motor neurone disease; multiple sclerosis; muscular dystrophy; Parkinson's disease; psoriasis; sight loss; strokes; and terminal illness

WHERE FUNDING CAN BE GIVEN UK

TYPE OF GRANT One-off

RANGE OF GRANTS £1,000–£50,000

SAMPLE GRANTS Grants for general purposes:; £6,000 to British Heart Foundation; £6,000 to British Diabetic Association; £6,000 to Parkinson's Disease Society; £6,000 to Jewish Care; £6,000 to National Asthma Campaign

FINANCES *Year* 1995 *Income* £50,104

TRUSTEES Mrs S Joseph, D Howells

HOW TO APPLY In writing to the address under Who To Apply To

WHO TO APPLY TO Miss K Spicer, The Alfred and Beatrice Weintrop Charity, Fladgate Fielder, Heron Place, 3 George Street, London W1H 6AD

CC NO 296706   **ESTABLISHED** 1987

■ The James Weir Foundation

WHAT IS FUNDED To subscribe to national appeals and to support local Scottish appeals in the Glasgow and Ayrshire area in particular. Hospices, hospice at home, health counselling and self help groups will be considered

WHAT IS NOT FUNDED No covenants. Preferably registered charities. No grants to individuals

WHO CAN BENEFIT Mainly Scottish charities benefiting the sick. There is no restriction on the disease or medical condition suffered by the beneficiaries

WHERE FUNDING CAN BE GIVEN Glasgow and Ayrshire

TYPE OF GRANT Lump sum. Many annually recurrent or one-off

RANGE OF GRANTS £500–£21,809

SAMPLE GRANTS £21,809 to the Royal Society of Edinburgh; £5,000 to University of Strathclyde Engineering Foundation; £2,250 to Royal Air Forces Benevolent Fund; £2,000 to National Galleries of Scotland; £2,000 to Royal Society, Scotland; £2,000 to the Army Benevolent Fund; £2,000 to British Association for the Advancement of Science; £2,000 to Cancer Research Campaign; £2,000 to Care; £1,000 to Ardgowan Hospice

FINANCES *Year* 1995 *Income* £167,959 *Grants* £138,559

TRUSTEES The Hon G Weir, S Bonham, W Ducas, Ms D J Donaldson

NOTES Trustees review appeals twice per year and mutually agree who benefits

HOW TO APPLY To the address under Who To Apply To. No application form required. Trustees meet twice annually May and October. No acknowledgements

WHO TO APPLY TO The James Weir Foundation, Messrs Binder Hamlyn, Trustees Accountants, Victoria Square, Victoria Street, St Albans, Hertfordshire AL1 3TF *Tel* 01727 836363

CC NO 251764   **ESTABLISHED** 1967

■ The Barbara Welby Trust

WHAT IS FUNDED General charitable purposes. Preference given to charities of which the Founder had special knowledge or with the objects of which she was specially associated

WHO CAN BENEFIT Normally limited to established charitable foundations and institutions. There are no restrictions on the age; professional and economic group; family situation; religion and culture; and social circumstances of; or disease or medical condition suffered by, the beneficiaries

WHERE FUNDING CAN BE GIVEN UK

TYPE OF GRANT Donations

RANGE OF GRANTS £250–£5,000

SAMPLE GRANTS £5,000 to British Red Cross for Rwanda Emergency Fund; £3,500 to Branston by Belvoir for Organ Restoration Fund; £1,500 to Newton PCC; £1,250 to Denton PCC for Denton Church Bells Fund; £1,000 to Lincoln Cathedral; £1,000 to The Children's Society; £1,000 to St Andrew's Trust; £500 to The Prince's Youth Trust; £500 to St Wulfram's Church, Grantham; £500 to SSAFA, Lambeth Branch

FINANCES *Year* 1995 *Income* £36,118 *Grants* £24,000

TRUSTEES N J Barker, C W H Welby, C N Robertson

NOTES Applications for individual assistance not normally considered unless made through an established charitable organisation

HOW TO APPLY At any time, by letter to the address under Who To Apply To

WHO TO APPLY TO The Barbara Welby Trust, Messrs Dawson & Co, 2 New Square, Lincoln's Inn, London WC2A 3RZ

CC NO 252973 **ESTABLISHED** 1967

■ The Weldon UK Charitable Trust

WHAT IS FUNDED Trustees fund a very limited number of major projects normally associated with the arts or education

WHAT IS NOT FUNDED No grants to individuals

WHO CAN BENEFIT Arts and educational institutions benefiting children; young adults and older people; academics; students; actors and entertainment professionals; musicians; and writers and poets

WHERE FUNDING CAN BE GIVEN UK

TYPE OF GRANT Capital grant

FINANCES *Year* 1997 *Income* £36,350 *Grants* £171,562

TRUSTEES J M St J Harris, H J Fritze

WHO TO APPLY TO J M St J Harris, The Weldon UK Charitable Trust, 4 Grosvenor Place, London SW1X 7HJ *Tel* 0171-235 6146

CC NO 327497 **ESTABLISHED** 1987

■ Welfare Charity Establishment

This trust did not respond to CAF's request to amend its entry and, by 30 June 1998, CAF's researchers did not find financial records for later than 1995 on its file at the Charity Commission. Trusts are legally required to submit annual accounts to the Charity Commission under section 42 of the Charities Act 1993

WHAT IS FUNDED The relief of poverty and the advancement of the Christian religion, particularly by providing religious instruction to young people, for the general public and for Iraqis living in Great Britain

WHO CAN BENEFIT Children and young adults, Christians and those disadvantaged by poverty

WHERE FUNDING CAN BE GIVEN UK

TRUSTEES B Tuoma and others

WHO TO APPLY TO B Tuoma, Welfare Charity Establishment, 9 Canford Avenue, Northolt, Middlesex UB5 5QF

CC NO 1020182 **ESTABLISHED** 1993

■ Wellfield Trust

WHAT IS FUNDED General welfare purposes in the area Where Funding Can Be Given

WHO CAN BENEFIT To the benefit of at risk groups, those disadvantaged by poverty and socially isolated people

WHERE FUNDING CAN BE GIVEN Hertfordshire, especially Hatfield

SAMPLE GRANTS £22,043 to individuals; £15,653 to organisations and projects

FINANCES *Year* 1996–97 *Income* £62,537 *Grants* £37,696

TRUSTEES A V Ashby, A C Appleby, R Bruce, M Clark, J W Dean, Dr P Dymoke, Mrs S Jones, Mrs M Tyler, G Wenham

HOW TO APPLY To the address under Who To Apply To in writing

WHO TO APPLY TO Mrs K Richards, Wellfield Trust, Birchwood Centre, Longmead, Hatfield, Hertfordshire AL10 0AN

CC NO 296205 **ESTABLISHED** 1987

■ Wellington Foundation

WHAT IS FUNDED Medical education and research

WHO CAN BENEFIT Medical postgraduates and research workers may benefit

WHERE FUNDING CAN BE GIVEN UK

TYPE OF GRANT Projects and research will be considered

FINANCES *Year* 1996 *Income* £32,070 *Grants* £19,200

TRUSTEES Dr A Levin, J Phillips, Mrs B Abela, J Pickle

HOW TO APPLY In writing

WHO TO APPLY TO Ms J Orr, Secretary, The Wellington Foundation, 34 Circus Road, London NW8 9SG

CC NO 274656 **ESTABLISHED** 1977

■ The Wells Charitable Settlement

WHAT IS FUNDED General charitable purposes

WHO CAN BENEFIT There are no restrictions on the age; professional and economic group; family situation; religion and culture; and social circumstances of; or disease or medical condition suffered by, the beneficiaries

WHERE FUNDING CAN BE GIVEN UK, particularly Bristol

TYPE OF GRANT Recurring

RANGE OF GRANTS £2,400–£4,000

SAMPLE GRANTS £4,000 to Bristol Mediation; £2,400 to Community Self Build Agency

FINANCES *Year* 1995–96 *Income* £119,096 *Grants* £6,400

TRUSTEES Avon Executor and Trustee Company, Marion Valiant Wells

WHO TO APPLY TO The Wells Charitable Settlement, Avon Executor and Trustee Co, 15 Pembroke Road, Bristol BS8 3BG

CC NO 283078 **ESTABLISHED** 1981

■ The Wendover Charitable Trust

WHAT IS FUNDED Relief in need, education and general charitable purposes within the area Where Funding Can Be Given

WHO CAN BENEFIT Local individuals and organisations benefiting: children; young adults; students from a wide range of social circumstances

WHERE FUNDING CAN BE GIVEN Wendover

FINANCES *Year* 1996 *Income* £37,756

TRUSTEES T Mogford (Chairperson)

HOW TO APPLY To the address under Who To Apply To in writing. The Trustees meet to consider applications in April or May annually, though urgent applications may be considered as they are received

WHO TO APPLY TO T Mogford, Chairperson, The Wendover Charitable Trust, Bank Farm, Wendover, Aylesbury, Buckinghamshire HP22 6NE

CC NO 274879   **ESTABLISHED** 1977

■ Wentworth Charity

WHAT IS FUNDED Welfare, youth and community organisations in the area Where Funding Can Be Given

WHO CAN BENEFIT Local organisations benefiting children and young adults. At risk groups, those disadvantaged by poverty and socially isolated people are all considered

WHERE FUNDING CAN BE GIVEN Wentworth

TYPE OF GRANT Mainly recurrent

SAMPLE GRANTS All of the following grants were given for the benefit of the local community:; £4,500 to Wentworth Mechanics Institute; £1,940 for Christmas groceries for pensioners; £500 to Wentworth School; £500 to Wentworth Old Age Pensioners Fund

FINANCES *Year* 1996–97 *Income* £20,376

TRUSTEES Guy R Canby

HOW TO APPLY To the address under Who To Apply To in writing

WHO TO APPLY TO Guy R Canby, Secretary and Trustee, Wentworth Charity, Fitzwilliam (Wentworth) Estates, Estate Office, Wentworth, Rotherham S62 7TD *Tel* 01226 742041 *Fax* 01226 350292

CC NO 225243   **ESTABLISHED** 1975

■ The Alexander Pigott Wernher Memorial Trust

WHAT IS FUNDED Research into the causes of blindness and deafness in the Commonwealth. Take advice of Medical Research Council, but conserve capital

WHAT IS NOT FUNDED No grants to individuals

WHO CAN BENEFIT Organisations benefiting research workers and beneficiaries suffering from sight loss and hearing loss

WHERE FUNDING CAN BE GIVEN Commonwealth countries

TYPE OF GRANT Research and travelling fellowships

FINANCES *Year* 1997 *Income* £24,931 *Grants* £16,000

TRUSTEES Major Sir David Butter, KCVO, MC

HOW TO APPLY To Medical Research Council

WHO TO APPLY TO Miss A Snow, The Alexander Pigott Wernher Memorial Trust, 8 Meredyth Road, Barnes, London SW13 0DY

CC NO 261362   **ESTABLISHED** 1946

■ The Wesleyan Charitable Trust

WHAT IS FUNDED Medicine and health, welfare. General preference given to causes associated with the Wesleyan Assurance Society's policy holders and staff

WHAT IS NOT FUNDED No grants to individuals, students or overseas projects

WHO CAN BENEFIT Small local projects, established and national organisations benefiting children and older people; those in care, fostered and adopted; at risk groups; carers; those disadvantaged by poverty; homeless people; victims of abuse, crime and domestic violence. There are a few restrictions on the disease or medical condition suffered by the beneficiaries

WHERE FUNDING CAN BE GIVEN UK

TYPE OF GRANT Buildings, capital, core costs, one-off, project, research, running costs and recurring costs. Funding is for one year or less

RANGE OF GRANTS £50–£15,000, typical grant £250

SAMPLE GRANTS £7,000 to Blue Coat School Sports Centre Account for building appeal; £1,000 to Multiple Sclerosis Resource Centre for research; £1,000 to Birmingham Children's Hospital for building appeal; £775 to Cancer Relief Macmillan Fund for research; £750 to Insurance Benevolent Fund for assistance to the needy; £500 to Sense Midlands for building appeal; £500 to Dodford Children's Holiday Farm for refurbishment appeal; £500 to National Institute for Conductive Education for running costs; £500 to Birmingham Retirement Council for building appeal; £500 to Brainwave for research

FINANCES *Year* 1996–97 *Income* £33,343 *Grants* £30,846

TRUSTEES J Roderick, R F Lowe, C C Ward, D A Byfield, A D Coton

PUBLICATIONS Annual Report

HOW TO APPLY In writing at any time. Annual accounts required

WHO TO APPLY TO N Boast, The Wesleyan Charitable Trust, Wesleyan Assurance Society, Colmore Circus, Birmingham B4 6AR *Tel* 0121-200 9599 *Fax* 0121-200 2971

CC NO 276698   **ESTABLISHED** 1978

■ Charity of John West & Others

WHAT IS FUNDED The income of this charity is, first of all, used to provide pensions to visually handicapped people in need through recognised relief agencies. No new pension obligations are entered into. The balance of the income is used to make grants to charitable organisations concerned with visual handicap

WHAT IS NOT FUNDED Grants to registered charities only. No grants to individuals

WHO CAN BENEFIT Charitable organisations benefiting people of all ages, retired people and those suffering from sight loss and blindness

WHERE FUNDING CAN BE GIVEN UK

TYPE OF GRANT One-off and capital

RANGE OF GRANTS £1,000–£50,000

FINANCES *Year* 1997 *Income* £199,336 *Grants* £180,539

TRUSTEES The Clothworkers' Foundation

WHO TO APPLY TO M G T Harris, The Secretary, The Clothworkers' Foundation, Clothworkers' Hall, Dunster Court, Mincing Lane, London EC3R 7AH *Tel* 0171-623 7041

CC NO 803660   **ESTABLISHED** 1987

■ The West Cumbria Charitable Trust

WHAT IS FUNDED Priority given to urban or rural regeneration, environmental improvements, benefits for children or young people, assistance for the elderly, funding for local projects

WHAT IS NOT FUNDED National charities based in West Cumbria, organisations based outside the area who wish to develop work in West Cumbria, organisations focusing on the unemployed or economic development

WHO CAN BENEFIT People living in West Cumbria whose groups meet Trust guidelines. All applications must have element of self help. Charities benefiting people of all ages and living in both urban and rural areas will be considered

WHERE FUNDING CAN BE GIVEN West Cumbria

TYPE OF GRANT Generally small grants

RANGE OF GRANTS £200–£2,000

SAMPLE GRANTS £2,000 to West Cumbria Gym Club to renovation of derelict area for gym use; £1,530 to Bootle Village Hall for disabled toilets and showers; £1,250 to Turning Point, Workington for furniture for arts project; £1,200 to Netherhall School, Maryport for renovation and environmental work on yard; £1,120 to Cockermouth Mechanics Band towards new instruments; £1,023 to Distington Walled Garden for new polythene tunnel for charitable business; £1,000 to CHILD (Children's Holiday Initiative) for toys for children with learning disabilities; £1,000 to Greysouthen playing field for equipment for the play area; £1,000 to Brigham War Memorial Hall towards a new kitchen; £500 to Haverigg Guides for replacement camping equipment

FINANCES *Year* 1998 *Income* £25,000 *Grants* £17,000

TRUSTEES Rev J Baker, Mrs A Cunningham, Mrs B Ford, B Minto, Mrs H Scott, D Sibbit, Lady Ann Shuttleworth

NOTES Trustees meet in February and July

HOW TO APPLY Leaflet outlining Trust's aims and guidelines available from CVS, Border House, Whitehaven. The CVS will give help and advice to applicants if necessary. All applications to be made in writing

WHO TO APPLY TO Mrs H J Scott, The West Cumbria Charitable Trust, 148 Queen Street, Whitehaven, Cumbria CA28 7AZ

CC NO 1067621   **ESTABLISHED** 1998

■ West Derby Waste Lands Charity

WHAT IS FUNDED Health and welfare; carers organisations; victim support and volunteer organisations

WHAT IS NOT FUNDED Education. No grants for individuals

WHO CAN BENEFIT Local organisations and local branches of national organisations benefiting: volunteers; at risk groups; carers; those disadvantaged by poverty; socially isolated people; victims of abuse; victims of crime; and victims of domestic violence. There is no restriction on disease or medical condition suffered by the beneficiaries

WHERE FUNDING CAN BE GIVEN Only within the ancient township of West Derby

FINANCES *Year* 1997 *Income* £63,435 *Grants* £48,721

TRUSTEES Cllr W Burke, Mrs C Crane, Cllr S Ellison, T B Flynn, Cllr D Gavin, Mrs J Holmes, E J Horton, D Lunt, P H North, R H Owen, J Ruddock,

HOW TO APPLY To the address under Who To Apply To in writing

WHO TO APPLY TO G B Marsh, Secretary, West Derby Waste Lands Charity, Sixth Floor, Drury House, 19 Water Street, Liverpool L2 0RP *Tel* 0151-236 8989

CC NO 223623   **ESTABLISHED** 1964

■ West Lancashire Masonic Educational Trust

WHAT IS FUNDED The relief of poverty and the advancement of education, especially special schools, by: (a) the assistance of such children of any age of freemasons in West Lancashire; (b) the assistance of any children whether or not children of a Freemason; and (c) making grants to other charities registered in England and operating in the same field or relief as the Trust

WHAT IS NOT FUNDED No grant are made for travel bursaries or expeditions

WHO CAN BENEFIT To benefit children, young adults, disabled people and those disadvantaged by poverty. Neighbourhood-based schemes, assistance to any organisation assisting children in educational and/or medical need

WHERE FUNDING CAN BE GIVEN Lancashire and surrounding counties

TYPE OF GRANT Project, capital, recurring costs and one-off. Funding is available for up to and over three years

SAMPLE GRANTS £160,000 to 1997 Festival Masonic Trust for Girls and Boys for maintenance and education; £45,111 to the Royal School for the Blind, Liverpool to provide a mobile training unit

FINANCES *Year* 1997–98 *Income* £80,554 *Grants* £205,000

TRUSTEES C P Wright, K E Moxley, T Hudson

HOW TO APPLY Guideline are issued by the Trust. A copy of the applicant's constitution, annual report, and income and expenditure accounts are required. All applications will be acknowledged

WHO TO APPLY TO Hon Secretary, West Lancashire Masonic Educational Trust, Masonic Hall, 22 Hope Street, Liverpool L1 9BY *Tel* 0151-709 2458 *Fax* 0151-709 6864

CC NO 526574   **ESTABLISHED** 1855

■ West London Synagogue Charitable Fund

WHAT IS FUNDED Grants are made to Jewish, Israeli, Inter-faith and non-Jewish charities for general charitable purposes, at a national level and local level within Westminster and Marylebone

WHAT IS NOT FUNDED No grants to individuals

WHO CAN BENEFIT Registered charities only. There are no restrictions on the age; professional and economic group; family situation; religion and culture; and social circumstances of; or disease or medical condition suffered by, the beneficiaries. However, particular favour is given to Jewish people

WHERE FUNDING CAN BE GIVEN UK, particularly Marylebone and Westminster

FINANCES *Year* 1996 *Income* £65,000 *Grants* £60,000

TRUSTEES Management Committee

NOTES The Fund prefers to be involved with charities which synagogue members are involved with or helped by

HOW TO APPLY Applications are considered annually in December. Grant distributions mid-January. Requests should be received by mid-October

WHO TO APPLY TO Mrs Joella Leaf, Co-ordinator, West London Synagogue Charitable Fund, 33 Seymour Place, London W1H 6AT

CC NO 209778   **ESTABLISHED** 1959

Does the trust you have chosen match your needs? Haphazard applications waste postage and time

673

■ West London Synagogue Endowment Fund

WHAT IS FUNDED General charitable purposes

WHO CAN BENEFIT There are no restrictions on the age; professional and economic group; family situation; religion and culture; and social circumstances of; or disease or medical condition suffered by, the beneficiaries

WHERE FUNDING CAN BE GIVEN UK

FINANCES *Year* 1996 *Income* £169,621

WHO TO APPLY TO M Ross, West London Synagogue Endowment Fund, West London Synagogue of British Jews, 33 Seymour Place, London W1H 6AT

CC NO 1046622   **ESTABLISHED** 1995

■ West Looe Town Trust

WHAT IS FUNDED Projects benefiting the local community, children and youth groups

WHO CAN BENEFIT Individuals, local organisations, local branches of national organisations, particularly those benefiting children and young adults

WHERE FUNDING CAN BE GIVEN The area of Looe administered by the Looe Town Council

RANGE OF GRANTS £15–£986

SAMPLE GRANTS £986 to FSNBF; £750 to Looe in Bloom; £713 to Caradon District Council (Lux Park); £565 to an individual; £500 to Looe Action Group; £348 to ELTT Town Clock; £250 to Torchlight Procession; £250 to Cornish Lugger; £100 to NBCS; £100 to a playgroup

FINANCES *Year* 1997 *Income* £256,914
Grants £5,082

TRUSTEES J Bassett, J R B Dingle, S Gardner, I Jolliff, Mrs G Oliver, K Pengelly

HOW TO APPLY To the address under Who To Apply To in writing

WHO TO APPLY TO Keith Wilson, Clerk, West Looe Town Trust, Cobblers Cottage, Fore Street, West Looe, Cornwall PL13 2HA

CC NO 228167   **ESTABLISHED** 1931

■ West Midlands Regional Arts Board

WHAT IS FUNDED To promote artistic and cultural activity by providing advice and support

WHAT IS NOT FUNDED No capital grants given for buildings

WHO CAN BENEFIT Individuals; arts organisations and community initiatives benefiting: children; young adults; actors and entertainment professionals; musicians; textile workers and designers; writers and poets; ethnic minority groups; disabled people and those living in rural areas

WHERE FUNDING CAN BE GIVEN Herefordshire, Worcestershire, Shropshire, Staffordshire, Warwickshire, Stoke on Trent, Telford and Wrekin, and the metropolitan districts of Birmingham, Coventry, Dudley, Sandwell. Solihull, Walsall and Wolverhampton

TYPE OF GRANT Projects include:Promoters and Presenters; Arts Education Development Fund; Arts in Healthcare; Arts in Surgeries; Go and See Awards; Senior Arts Manager Bursaries; Rural Partnerships; New Work and Commissions Awards; Stagewrite; Professional Development Bursaries in Music; Creative Ambition Awards; Chelsea Crafts Fair Bursaries; Craft Showcase Awards; Photography Portfolio Awards; Film and Video Rsearch and Development Awards;

Storytelling Apprenticeship; Reading Service for Literature and Film

RANGE OF GRANTS £500 and upwards

FINANCES *Year* 1998 *Income* £6,701,950
Grants £5,154,240

TRUSTEES A Board drawn from the arts and business sectors, and local authorities in the region

PUBLICATIONS Annual Report, Monthly Bulletin, Visual Arts Update

NOTES West Midlands Arts also provide advice on the National Arts Lottery

HOW TO APPLY To Financial Services Unit, closing dates available from West Midlands Arts

WHO TO APPLY TO Sally Luton, (Chief Executive), West Midlands Regional Arts Board, WMA, 82 Granville Street, Birmingham B1 2LH *Tel* 0121-631 3121 *Fax* 0121-643 7239
E-mail west.midarts@midnet.com *Web Site* http://www.arts.org.uk/

CC NO 702187   **ESTABLISHED** 1971

■ The Robert Westall Charitable Trust

WHAT IS FUNDED General charitable purposes

WHO CAN BENEFIT There are no restrictions on the age; professional and economic group; family situation; religion and culture; and social circumstances of; or disease or medical condition suffered by, the beneficiaries

WHERE FUNDING CAN BE GIVEN UK

TRUSTEES Ms V Bierman, Ms B E McKinnel, Ms S E McKinnel

WHO TO APPLY TO Miss S McKinnel, The Robert Westall Charitable Trust, The Courtyard, Homesteads Road, Kempshott, Basingstoke RG22 5RP

CC NO 1049805   **ESTABLISHED** 1995

■ Westcroft Trust

WHAT IS FUNDED Currently the Trustees have five main areas of interest: international understanding, including conflict resolution and the material needs of the Third world; religious causes, particularly of social outreach, usually of the Society of Friends (Quakers) but also for those originating in Shropshire; development of the voluntary sector in Shropshire; special needs of those with disabilities, primarily in Shropshire; development of community groups and reconciliation between different cultures in Northern Ireland. Woodlands and medical research into orthopaedics will be considered. Medical education is only helped by support for expeditions abroad which include pre-clinical students. Medical aid, education and relief work in developing countries are helped but mainly through UK agencies; international disasters may be helped in response to public appeals

WHAT IS NOT FUNDED Charitable bodies only. Applications from individuals are not accepted. No grants for medical electives, to sport, the arts (unless specifically for those in Shropshire with disabilities) or to armed forces charities. Requests for sponsorship not supported. Annual grants are withheld if recent accounts are not to hand or do not satisfy the Trustees as to continuing need

WHO CAN BENEFIT Organisations benefiting: people of all ages; medical professionals; Quakers; ex-offenders and those at risk of offending; victims of abuse; victims of famine, man-made or natural disasters and war

WHERE FUNDING CAN BE GIVEN Shropshire, Northern Ireland and overseas

TYPE OF GRANT Single or annual with or without specified time limit. Few grants for capital or endowment. One-off, research, recurring costs, running costs and start-up costs. Funding for up to and over three years will be considered

FINANCES *Year* 1997 *Income* £81,329 *Grants* £71,378

TRUSTEES Edward P Cadbury, Mary C Cadbury, Richard G Cadbury, James E Cadbury, Erica R Cadbury

PUBLICATIONS Annual Accounts and Report on file at the Charity Commission

NOTES The Trustees favour charities which carry low administrative overheads and which pursue clear policies of equal opportunity in meeting need. Printed letters signed by the great and good and glossy literature are wasted on them

HOW TO APPLY In writing to the address under Who To Apply To. No telephone calls or fax. No application form or set format but applications should be restricted to a maximum of three sheets of paper, stating purpose, overall financial needs and resources, together with previous year's accounts if appropriate. No acknowledgement will be given. Applications are dealt with at about two month intervals. Relevant unsuccessful applicants will only be notified if a sae is enclosed with the application. Some annual grants are made by Bank Giro. Details of bank name, branch, sort code and account name and number are needed for these. Time and correspondence can be saved if these are sent

WHO TO APPLY TO Edward P Cadbury, Managing Trustee, Westcroft Trust, 32 Hampton Road, Oswestry, Shropshire SY11 1SJ

CC NO 212931   **ESTABLISHED** 1947

■ The Weston Bampfylde Trust

WHAT IS FUNDED General charitable purposes at the Trustees' discretion

WHO CAN BENEFIT At the discretion of the Trustees. There are no restrictions on the age; professional and economic group; family situation; religion and culture; and social circumstances of; or disease or medical condition suffered by, the beneficiaries

WHERE FUNDING CAN BE GIVEN Somerset and UK

TYPE OF GRANT At the discretion of the Trustees

RANGE OF GRANTS £50–£5,000

SAMPLE GRANTS £5,000 to Weston Bampfylde Church Appeal Fund; £1,500 to Brainwave; £1,000 to Sense; £500 to Woodland Trust; £500 to Botton Village

FINANCES *Year* 1997 *Income* £23,163 *Grants* £9,500

TRUSTEES Justin Crawford, Cynthia Crawford, Victoria Matson

WHO TO APPLY TO J Crawford, The Weston Bampfylde Trust, The Old Rectory, Weston Bampfylde, Yeovil, Somerset BA22 7HT

CC NO 297153   **ESTABLISHED** 1987

■ Mrs S K West's Charitable Trust

WHAT IS FUNDED General charitable purposes. To make grants to registered charities selected by the Trustees

WHO CAN BENEFIT Registered charities. There are no restrictions on the age; professional and economic group; family situation; religion and culture; and social circumstances of; or disease or medical condition suffered by, the beneficiaries

WHERE FUNDING CAN BE GIVEN UK

FINANCES *Year* 1996 *Income* £25,022

TRUSTEES Mrs S K West, P Schoon, J P Burnley

HOW TO APPLY **This Trust states that it does not respond to unsolicited applications**

WHO TO APPLY TO Mrs S K West's Charitable Trust, Messrs Simpson Curtis, Solicitors, 41 Park Square, Leeds LS1 2NS

CC NO 294755   **ESTABLISHED** 1986

■ The Westward Trust

WHAT IS FUNDED General charitable purposes. Funds are fully committed to charities in which the trustees have a personal interest. The trustees do not welcome unsolicited requests for aid, are very unlikely to read them and even less likely to respond

WHO CAN BENEFIT There are no restrictions on the age; professional and economic group; family situation; religion and culture; and social circumstances of; or disease or medical condition suffered by, the beneficiaries

WHERE FUNDING CAN BE GIVEN UK

SAMPLE GRANTS £8,546 to Bath Friends Housing Association and Mount Haviland Appeal Fund; £4,587 to individuals known personally to the Trustees; £5,499 to Society of Friends (Quakers)

FINANCES *Year* 1997 *Income* £29,814 *Grants* £19,041

TRUSTEES B J P Dodd, Mrs R M Dodd, Mrs A R Ironside, D J Ironside, Mrs J Ironside, J M Ironside

HOW TO APPLY **This Trust states that it does not respond to unsolicited applications**

WHO TO APPLY TO Mrs A R Ironside, The Westward Trust, 17 Green Meadow Road, Birmingham B29 4DD

CC NO 260488   **ESTABLISHED** 1970

■ Wheelwright's Charity

WHAT IS FUNDED Projects allowing greater mobility for people with disabilities, relief in need of wheelwrights and general charitable purposes in the City of London

WHO CAN BENEFIT Individuals and organisations benefiting wheelwrights and disabled people

WHERE FUNDING CAN BE GIVEN City of London

RANGE OF GRANTS £100–£9,241

SAMPLE GRANTS £9,241 to Whizz-Kidz towards the provision of wheelchairs for four young people; £1,000 to King Edward's School, Witley; £500 to The Lord Mayor's Charity; £500 to St Bartholomew's Medical School; £300 to Providence Row; £300 to The Salvation Army; £250 to City Red Cross; £250 to City University; £100 to City & Guilds of London; £100 to the Treloar Trust

FINANCES *Year* 1995 *Income* £28,442 *Grants* £12,841

TRUSTEES G R Hart, J A F Taylor, K A Wells, J Holland

HOW TO APPLY To the address under Who To Apply To in writing

WHO TO APPLY TO Brian P Boreham, Hon Treasurer, Wheelwright's Charity, Trenance, Howell Hill, Ewell, Epsom, Surrey KT17 3EL *Tel* 0181-393 3540

CC NO 288173   **ESTABLISHED** 1983

■ The Wheldon Charitable Trust

WHAT IS FUNDED General charitable purposes

WHO CAN BENEFIT There are no restrictions on the age; professional and economic group; family situation; religion and culture; and social

circumstances of; or disease or medical condition suffered by, the beneficiaries

WHERE FUNDING CAN BE GIVEN England and Wales

TRUSTEES Mrs C G Wheldon, Miss J L Wheldon, M D G Wheldon

WHO TO APPLY TO The Wheldon Charitable Trust, Messrs Wilsons, Solicitors, Steyning House, Fisherton Street, Salisbury, Wiltshire SP2 7RJ

CC NO 1068192   **ESTABLISHED** 1998

■ Whinney Banks Parental Support

WHAT IS FUNDED General charitable purposes in particular the relief of poverty, to advance education, to provide support, advice and counselling services in particular for parents, guardians and carers of young children

WHO CAN BENEFIT Organisations benefiting those disadvantaged by poverty and parents, guardians and carers of children

WHERE FUNDING CAN BE GIVEN Ayresome Ward of Middlesbrough

RANGE OF GRANTS £6–£1,032

SAMPLE GRANTS £1,032 to a creche; £884 to a playscheme/children's clubs; £350 for a Christmas party for children; £110 to Composity; £110 for outings

FINANCES *Year* 1995 *Income* £13,653
Grants £9,888

TRUSTEES J Holfores, L Gray, A Fisher

WHO TO APPLY TO Ms M Dales, Support Worker, Whinney Banks Parental Support, Whinney Banks Youth and Community Centre, Harehills Road, Whinney Banks, Middlesbrough, Cleveland TS5 4LL

CC NO 1068374   **ESTABLISHED** 1998

■ Whitaker Charitable Trust

WHAT IS FUNDED The Trust's resources are heavily committed and only very limited funds are available for charities not previously supported by the Trustees. The Trustees are particularly interested in music education, agricultural education, countryside conservation, spiritual matters, prison-related charities and supporting charities in the area Where Funding Can Be Given

WHAT IS NOT FUNDED No grants to individuals or for the maintenance or repair of individual churches

WHO CAN BENEFIT Registered charities benefiting musicians, students and those in prison. There is no restriction on the religion or culture of the beneficiaries

WHERE FUNDING CAN BE GIVEN UK, particularly Nottinghamshire, the East Midlands, Scotland and Northern Ireland

TYPE OF GRANT Cash payments

RANGE OF GRANTS £100–£80,000

SAMPLE GRANTS £80,000 to United World College of the Atlantic; £20,000 to Kopple Goodman Project; £5,000 to Rabbi Hugo Gryn Appeal (c/o the Atlantic College); £4,000 to Marlborough College; £2,000 to Harambee Educational Fund; £2,000 to Bramcote Centenary Foundation; £2,000 to Countryside Foundation; £1,500 to Nottinghamshire Farming and Wildlife Advisory Group; £1,000 to Home Start Bassetlaw; £1,000 to the Willow Trust

FINANCES *Year* 1997 *Income* £189,140
Grants £155,700

TRUSTEES D W J Price, E R H Perks, Mrs E J R Whitaker, Lady M E L Whitaker

HOW TO APPLY To the address under Who To Apply To at any time. Trustees meet half yearly. Applications should include clear details of the

need the intended project is designed to meet plus a copy of the latest accounts available and an outline budget. If an acknowledgement of the application or notification, in the event of the application not being accepted, is required, an sae should be enclosed

WHO TO APPLY TO Currey & Co, Solicitors, Whitaker Charitable Trust, 21 Buckingham Gate, London SW1E 6LS

CC NO 234491   **ESTABLISHED** 1964

■ The Whitbread 1988 Charitable Trust

WHAT IS FUNDED General charitable purposes

WHAT IS NOT FUNDED No support given to individuals

WHO CAN BENEFIT There are no restrictions on the age; professional and economic group; family situation; religion and culture; and social circumstances of; or disease or medical condition suffered by, the beneficiaries

WHERE FUNDING CAN BE GIVEN UK

SAMPLE GRANTS £32,800 to Business in the Community; £25,416 to Charities Aid Foundation; £24,436 to University of Edinburgh Development Trust; £15,000 to National Centre for Volunteering; £13,229 to Luton and Dunstable Irish Care and Advice Association; £10,000 to Bedfordshire Police Partnership; £10,000 to Radio Lollipop; £10,000 to Young Enterprise Record of Achievement; £9,062 to Disability Initiatives; £7,692 to YPT for the E and NC

FINANCES *Year* 1997 *Income* £481,897
Grants £350,722

TRUSTEES S C Barratt, Sir Michael Angus, S J Ward

WHO TO APPLY TO Robert N C Franklin, Administrator, The Whitbread 1988 Charitable Trust, Brewery, Chiswell Street, London EC1Y 4SD

CC NO 800501   **ESTABLISHED** 1988

■ Colonel W H Whitbread Charitable Trust

WHAT IS FUNDED Primarily local health and welfare charities, colleges and to a lesser extent youth, the arts and churches

WHO CAN BENEFIT To benefit: children and young adults; actors and entertainment professionals; musicians; textile workers and designers; writers and poets; at risk groups; those disadvantaged by poverty; and socially isolated people. There is no restriction on the disease or medical condition suffered by the beneficiaries

WHERE FUNDING CAN BE GIVEN UK

RANGE OF GRANTS £500–£7,500

SAMPLE GRANTS £7,500 to Opera Omnibus; £7,000 to Appeal 400 A/C The Aldenham School General Charitable Trust; £5,000 to St John Ambulance Gloucestershire; £3,000 to Malvern Festival Theatre; £2,500 to Forthampton Village Hall; £2,500 to the Trust for Princess Diana; £2,000 to Acorns Children's Hospice; £2,000 to British Red Cross Gloucestershire; £2,000 to the Countryside Foundation; £2,000 to the Leonard Cheshire Homes in West Dorset

FINANCES *Year* 1997 *Income* £186,566
Grants £121,000

TRUSTEES J J Russell, M W Whitbread, R H J Steel

HOW TO APPLY To the address under Who To Apply To in writing. The Trustees meet to consider applications four times a year

676

Think carefully about every application. Is it justified?

WHO TO APPLY TO R H A MacDougald, Colonel W H Whitbread Charitable Trust, Winckworth and Pemberton, 35 Great Peter Street, Westminster, London SW1P 3LR
CC NO 210496 **ESTABLISHED** 1953

■ The Simon Whitbread Charitable Trust

WHAT IS FUNDED General charitable purposes. Preference is given to charities of which the Trustees have special interest, knowledge or association
WHAT IS NOT FUNDED Grants are not often made to individuals
WHO CAN BENEFIT There are no restrictions on the age; professional and economic group; family situation; religion and culture; and social circumstances of; or disease or medical condition suffered by, the beneficiaries
WHERE FUNDING CAN BE GIVEN UK
TYPE OF GRANT Usually one-off, but dependent on circumstances
RANGE OF GRANTS £50–£15,000
SAMPLE GRANTS £15,000 and £10,000 to Christian Family Care; £4,000 to the Countryside Foundation; £2,500 to MIND Bedfordshire; £2,000 to St Luke's Hospital for the Clergy; £2,000 to Royal Anglian Regiment Museum Appeal; £1,000 to Cancer Care; £1,000 to St Etheldreda's Trust (GOLD); £1,000 to Streatham Youth Centre; £1,000 to Charities Aid Foundation for the Tomkinson Trust
FINANCES *Year* 1994–95 *Income* £103,443 *Grants* £80,550
TRUSTEES Mrs H Whitbread, S C Whitbread, E C A Martineau
HOW TO APPLY Applications by letter to the address under Who To Apply To. No sae required nor acknowledgement made
WHO TO APPLY TO E C A Martineau, The Simon Whitbread Charitable Trust, Dawson & Co, 2 New Square, Lincoln's Inn, London WC2A 3RZ
CC NO 200412 **ESTABLISHED** 1961

■ H Whitbread First Charitable Trust

WHAT IS FUNDED Localised charities working in the fields of arts, culture and recreation, churches, religion, residential facilities and services, health, conservation and environment and various community facilities and services. Church schools, information technology and computers, personnel and human resource services, charity or voluntary bodies and support to voluntary and community organisations will also be considered
WHAT IS NOT FUNDED No grants made to individuals or non-registered charities, except churches
WHO CAN BENEFIT Local organisations benefiting children, young adults and older people. There is no restrictions on the family situation or disease or medical condition suffered by, the beneficiaries. There are few restrictions on professional and economic group, religion and culture and social circumstance of the beneficiaries
WHERE FUNDING CAN BE GIVEN UK, particularly the East of England
TYPE OF GRANT Many recurrent, including capital, core costs, one-off and research. Grants can be given for a period of up to or more than three years
RANGE OF GRANTS £50–£5,000, average grant £250
FINANCES *Year* 1995 *Income* £281,207 *Grants* £59,925

TRUSTEES H Whitbread, S C Whitbread, C R Skottowe
HOW TO APPLY To the address under Who To Apply To in writing
WHO TO APPLY TO Mrs Shirley Morrell, H Whitbread First Charitable Trust, Howards House, Cardington, Bedford MK44 3SR
CC NO 210089 **ESTABLISHED** 1949

■ The League of Friends of Whitby Hospital

WHAT IS FUNDED The relief of sick, convalescent, infirm, disabled and needy patients and former patients of the hospital and the support of the charitable work of the hospital
WHO CAN BENEFIT To benefit disabled and sick people who are patients or former patients of Whitby Hospital. There is no restriction on the disease or medical condition suffered by the beneficiaries
WHERE FUNDING CAN BE GIVEN North Yorkshire
TRUSTEES Dr A Brighouse, Mrs S A Gould, Mrs F Coser, Mrs L Hutchinson, Mrs K Turnbull, Mrs W Hall, Mrs N Jackson, Dr L Cooper, Mrs R Clarkson, Mrs T Buckmaster, Mrs V Pain, Mrs J Cooke, P Shelton, Mrs F Shelton, Mrs M Wood, Mrs C Doubleday, Mrs A Hutchinson, Mrs P Greenwood
WHO TO APPLY TO Dr A Brighouse, Chairperson, Whitby Hospital, Spring Hill, Whitby, North Yorkshire YO21 1DP
CC NO 1064194 **ESTABLISHED** 1997

■ The White Foundation Limited

WHAT IS FUNDED The advancement of religion in accordance with the Orthodox Jewish Faith; the relief of poverty and other general charitable purposes
WHO CAN BENEFIT To benefit Jewish people and those disadvantaged by poverty
WHERE FUNDING CAN BE GIVEN UK and Israel
FINANCES *Year* 1996 *Income* £82,000 *Grants* £42,236
TRUSTEES D D Cuby, J Gutstein, J D Hassan, Mrs A V Sternbuch, Mrs E R Gruenburg
WHO TO APPLY TO J Gutstein, The White Foundation Limited, Everjoy House, 84 Hatton Gardens, London EC1N 8JR
CC NO 1041955 **ESTABLISHED** 1994

■ The White Oak Charitable Trust

WHAT IS FUNDED The sick, elderly and children. Catholic umbrella bodies, hospice at home and hospices may be considered
WHAT IS NOT FUNDED No funding for town halls, scholarships, travel or animals
WHO CAN BENEFIT Organisations benefiting: people of all ages; those in care, fostered and adopted; Roman Catholics; disabled people; those disadvantaged by poverty; and homeless people. There are some restrictions on the disease or medical condition suffered by the beneficiaries
WHERE FUNDING CAN BE GIVEN UK
TYPE OF GRANT No loans
RANGE OF GRANTS £100–£500
SAMPLE GRANTS £200 to Catholic Children's Society; £200 to National Deaf Children's Society
FINANCES *Year* 1997 *Income* £22,143 *Grants* £600
TRUSTEES Hon Mrs M H C Czernin, J Czernin, Sir A Mackechnie
NOTES The Trust is small and can, therefore, not easily expand beyond the list of beneficiaries regularly supported

HOW TO APPLY Applications in writing only. No telephone calls please. Unsuccessful applicants cannot be notified owing to volume of requests
WHO TO APPLY TO Hon Mrs M H C Czernin, The White Oak Charitable Trust, 47 Queen's Gate Gardens, London SW7 5ND
CC NO 298781   **ESTABLISHED** 1987

■ White Rose Children's Aid International Charity

WHAT IS FUNDED Helping children with physical and emotional difficulties, those who suffer hardship, poverty, poor conditions, war or disease. The Charity gives help to hospitals, respite homes, special needs schools and youth groups
WHO CAN BENEFIT Organisations benefiting young adults, the disabled, those disadvantaged by poverty and the suffering from emotional difficulties. Support may also be given to the unemployed, homeless, at risk groups and the socially isolated. There is no restriction on the disease or medical condition suffered by the beneficiaries
WHERE FUNDING CAN BE GIVEN UK and overseas
TYPE OF GRANT Small grants of £3,000 or less
RANGE OF GRANTS £10–£1,449
SAMPLE GRANTS 1449 to Hill Top School, Mountby; £1,266 to Crystal Peaks Charity Fund, Sheffield; £1,240 to Rwanda Appeal; £755 to Bents Green School, Sheffield; £725 to The Lodge Youth Club, Sheffield; £706 to The Cygnets Respite Centre, Scunthorpe; £678 to Dr John Worral Special School, Sheffield; £555 to Linden School, Newark; £510 to National Children's Home; £418 to Kirkleatham Hall School, Redcar
FINANCES *Year* 1995 *Income* £31,174
Grants £16,480
TRUSTEES R Brown, J F Buttery, JP, P Johnson, B Knipe, J Nelson, D Rayner, CBE, B Ridley, R Rosser, JP, E Straw, R W Urie, A M Wright
WHO TO APPLY TO A Wright, White Rose Children's Aid International Charity, 23 Teesdale Road, Ridgeway, Sheffield, South Yorkshire S12 3XH
CC NO 1036377   **ESTABLISHED** 1994

■ The Whitecourt Charitable Trust

WHAT IS FUNDED General charitable purposes. Trustees prefer to support Christian projects, especially near Sheffield
WHO CAN BENEFIT Organisations benefiting Christians
WHERE FUNDING CAN BE GIVEN UK with preference to Sheffield
RANGE OF GRANTS £20–£3,500
SAMPLE GRANTS £3,500 to Christ Church Fulwood Missionary Fund; £3,500 to Christ Church – General Fund; £3,003 to an individual for school fees for his daughter with special needs; £1,000 to Christ Church Fulwood for Vicar's Discretionary Fund; £1,000 to Church Mission Society; £1,000 to Evangelical Alliance for a media fund; £1,000 to Christ Church Fulwood for Kendray Fund; £1,000 to South Yorkshire Community Foundation; £1,000 to Sheffield Family Service Unit; £700 to Scripture Union
FINANCES *Year* 1997 *Income* £70,808
Grants £30,256
TRUSTEES P W Lee, Mrs G W Lee, M P W Lee
NOTES The funds of the Trust are fully committed
WHO TO APPLY TO Mrs P W Lee, The Whitecourt Charitable Trust, 48 Canterbury Avenue, Sheffield, South Yorkshire S10 3RU
CC NO 1000012   **ESTABLISHED** 1990

■ J E Whitehead Charitable Trust

WHAT IS FUNDED Main interest in private and independent schools and Methodist churches
WHO CAN BENEFIT Children, young adults and Methodists
WHERE FUNDING CAN BE GIVEN UK and overseas
TYPE OF GRANT A range of grants
RANGE OF GRANTS £5,000 or more
SAMPLE GRANTS £5,200 to Emanuel School; £5,200 to Hulme Grammar School; £5,200 to Mill Hill School; £1,600 to Methodist Church Overseas
FINANCES *Year* 1997 *Income* £29,278
Grants £17,200
TRUSTEES R J Bingle, J O Cretney
WHO TO APPLY TO J O Cretney, J E Whitehead Charitable Trust, Cobbett Leak Almond Solicitors, Ship Canal House, King Street, Manchester M2 4WB
CC NO 260951   **ESTABLISHED** 1970

■ Sydney Dean Whitehead's Charitable Trust

WHAT IS FUNDED The Trustees basically apply their funds towards supporting parents with the educational costs of their children and respond more readily to appeals relating to children with special talents, particularly in the artistic fields. They also respond more readily to appeals which show that there is an element of self-help already in operation and where a lack of finance could preclude children from receiving the type of education their particular 'gift' merits
WHAT IS NOT FUNDED Medical applications are not considered
WHO CAN BENEFIT Children needing help with educational costs
WHERE FUNDING CAN BE GIVEN UK
TYPE OF GRANT Donations
RANGE OF GRANTS Up to £2,000 pa
FINANCES *Year* 1998 *Income* £32,493
Grants £33,050
TRUSTEES Mrs I P Pembroke, Mrs F C P Whitehead, Dr D S Whitehead, P J W Langley
NOTES The Trustees have now approved the format of a questionnaire which most applicants are required to complete to provide the basic information to enable the Trustees to assess the application
HOW TO APPLY The Trustees would like to have some sort of financial statement (as up to date as possible) with applications from charities or where individuals are applying, some sort of guide as to what amount of support is required by the applicant. To Secretary, in writing. An sae would be appreciated
WHO TO APPLY TO Ernst & Young, Sydney Dean Whitehead's Charitable Trust, 100 Barbirolli Square, Manchester M2 3EY *Tel* 0161-952 1000 *Fax* 0161-952 1500
CC NO 207714   **ESTABLISHED** 1946

■ Norman Whiteley Trust

WHAT IS FUNDED To help evangelical Christian causes primarily
WHAT IS NOT FUNDED No grants made in response to general appeals from large national organisations nor to smaller bodies working in areas other than those set out above
WHO CAN BENEFIT Christian charities. Organisations benefiting Christians and Evangelists
WHERE FUNDING CAN BE GIVEN Cumbria only

Have you read How to use the DGMT *on page xvi?*

TYPE OF GRANT One-off, recurrent, capital, running costs
FINANCES *Year* 1997 *Income* £144,000
Grants £101,000
TRUSTEES Mrs B M Whiteley, P Whiteley, W Thomas, J Ratcliff, D Dixon
HOW TO APPLY In writing only – no telephone calls
WHO TO APPLY TO D Foster, Secretary, Norman Whiteley Trust, Fallbarrow, Windermere, Cumbria LA23 3DL
CC NO 226445   **ESTABLISHED** 1963

■ Whitley Animal Protection Trust (275)

This trust failed to supply a copy of its annual report and accounts to CAF as required under section 47(2) of the Charities Act 1993. The information held on file at the Charity Commission was insufficient to enable CAF's researchers to write a substantive commentary on the trust's activities. Accordingly, despite its size, we are unable to list this trust in Spotlight on Major Trusts

WHAT IS FUNDED Animal welfare and protection
WHAT IS NOT FUNDED No grants to individuals
WHO CAN BENEFIT Registered charities only
WHERE FUNDING CAN BE GIVEN UK
FINANCES *Year* 1995 *Income* £300,000
Grants £267,000
TRUSTEES E Whitley, Mrs P A Whitley, E J Whitley, J Whitley
HOW TO APPLY No application form
WHO TO APPLY TO M T Gwynne, Secretary, Whitley Animal Protection Trust, Messrs R Gwynne & Sons, Solicitors, Edgbaston House, Walker Street, Wellington, Telford, Shropshire TF1 1HF *Tel* 01952 641651 *Fax* 01952 247441
CC NO 236746   **ESTABLISHED** 1964

■ Sheila Whitley Trust

WHAT IS FUNDED Assistance to the sick, disabled, elderly or deprived
WHAT IS NOT FUNDED Donations to registered charities only
WHO CAN BENEFIT Registered charities benefiting: the elderly; at risk groups; those disadvantaged by poverty; socially isolated people and the disabled. There is no restriction on the disease or medical condition suffered by the beneficiaries
WHERE FUNDING CAN BE GIVEN UK
TYPE OF GRANT Ad hoc grants to organisations with similar objects
RANGE OF GRANTS £500–£5,850
SAMPLE GRANTS £5,850 to Shropshire Voluntary Association for the Blind; £500 to Fairbridge
FINANCES *Year* 1995 *Income* £14,669
Grants £6,350
TRUSTEES Mrs P A Whitley, E Whitley, Mrs V Thompson, E J Whitley, J Whitley
HOW TO APPLY There is no application form
WHO TO APPLY TO M T Gwynne, Secretary, Sheila Whitley Trust, Messrs R Gwynne & Sons, Solicitors, Edgbaston House, Walker Street, Wellington, Telford, Shropshire TF1 1HF
CC NO 253681   **ESTABLISHED** 1967

■ Sir Richard Whittington Charity

WHAT IS FUNDED Relief in need, including pensions and almshouse provision, homelessness, health and hospitals, youth and elderly people
WHO CAN BENEFIT Local organisations, projects and institutions benefiting those disadvantaged by poverty and homeless people. There is no restriction on the age of the beneficiaries or on their disease or medical condition
WHERE FUNDING CAN BE GIVEN UK, especially London
SAMPLE GRANTS £830,000 to Mercers' Company Housing Association; £75,000 to Lady Miclo's Almshouse, Stepney; £15,000 to Thomas Telford School for needy children, clothing, etc; £15,000 to Bromley by Bow Centre; £10,000 to Christ's Hospital for needy children, clothing, etc; £10,000 to Across Trust; £10,000 to Cancer Research Campaign; £10,000 to London Playing Fields Society; £7,500 to Development Trust for the Mentally Handicapped; £7,500 to Lions Boys' Club
FINANCES *Year* 1997 *Income* £4,287,000
Grants £1,843,000
TRUSTEES Mercers' Company
HOW TO APPLY To the address under Who To Apply To in writing
WHO TO APPLY TO The Charities Administrator, Sir Richard Whittington Charity, Mercers' Hall, Ironmonger Lane, London EC2V 8HE *Tel* 0171-726 4991
CC NO 210293   **ESTABLISHED** 1424

■ The Whittlesey Charity

WHAT IS FUNDED Youth and community organisations, care of the old and infirm in the community, disability, churches and church councils
WHO CAN BENEFIT Primarily local community organisations benefiting people of all ages, Christians and disabled people
WHERE FUNDING CAN BE GIVEN The urban and rural parishes of Whittlesey
SAMPLE GRANTS £11,703 to public purposes; £7,242 to education; £6,196 to Relief in Need; £5,344 to the church
FINANCES *Year* 1997 *Income* £47,199
Grants £15,485
HOW TO APPLY To the address under Who To Apply To in writing. The Trustees meet to consider applications in February, May, August and November
WHO TO APPLY TO P S Gray, The Whittlesey Charity, 36 Gracious Street, Whittlesey, Peterborough PE7 1AR
CC NO 1005069   **ESTABLISHED** 1990

■ The S F Wickham Charitable Trust

This trust did not respond to CAF's request to amend its entry and, by 30 June 1998, CAF's researchers did not find financial records for later than 1995 on its file at the Charity Commission. Trusts are legally required to submit annual accounts to the Charity Commission under section 42 of the Charities Act 1993

WHAT IS FUNDED General charitable purposes
WHO CAN BENEFIT There are no restrictions on the age; professional and economic group; family situation; religion and culture; and social circumstances of; or disease or medical condition suffered by, the beneficiaries
WHERE FUNDING CAN BE GIVEN UK
TRUSTEES D R P Williams-Freeman, C O Motley
WHO TO APPLY TO D R P Williams-Freeman, Trustee and Settler, The S F Wickham Charitable Trust, Bartlet House, 9–12 Basinghall Street, London EC2V 5NS
CC NO 1050393   **ESTABLISHED** 1995

■ The Wicksteed Village Trust

WHAT IS FUNDED Improvement of the conditions of the working classes and prevention of cruelty and unnecessary pain to animals. The running of a leisure and nature park and of the Trust's own Old People's residential establishment

WHAT IS NOT FUNDED No grants to individuals

WHO CAN BENEFIT There are no restrictions on the age; professional and economic group; family situation; religion and culture; and social circumstances of; or disease or medical condition suffered by, the beneficiaries. Particular favour may be given to at risk groups, those disadvantaged by poverty and those who are socially isolated. Favour is also given to local causes

WHERE FUNDING CAN BE GIVEN Mainly Kettering but also elsewhere in the UK

TYPE OF GRANT Cash and kind

FINANCES *Year* 1994 *Income* £95,116

TRUSTEES R J Wicksteed (Chairman), J Brandon-Jones, Mrs C Joynson, Rev Canon F Pearce, J H Wicksteed, P J Wilson

NOTES The principal contribution is the support of our own Old People's Residential Establishment, Barton Memorial Trust, Barton Hall, Kettering

HOW TO APPLY A review of donations made, or to be made by the Trust, takes place annually

WHO TO APPLY TO R W Alderson, General Manager, Wicksteed Village Trust, Wicksteed Park, Kettering, Northamptonshire NN15 6NJ

CC NO 203662　　**ESTABLISHED** 1916

■ Joseph Wiggins Trust

WHAT IS FUNDED Support in general for Evangelical Christian movements

WHO CAN BENEFIT To benefit Christians Evangelist organisations and a printing works in France via the Slavic Gospel Association

WHERE FUNDING CAN BE GIVEN UK and overseas

SAMPLE GRANTS £2,700 to Slavic Gospel Association; £500 to New Life League, Japan; £500 to London Bible College; £300 to Scripture Union; £250 to Protestant Alliance

FINANCES *Year* 1998 *Income* £13,878
Grants £13,878

TRUSTEES J G Wiggins, P D Warren, Mrs J Wiggins, J Sterry

WHO TO APPLY TO J G Wiggins, Joseph Wiggins Trust, The Haven, 32 Park Avenue, Bedford MK40 2LR

CC NO 228033　　**ESTABLISHED** 1962

■ The Gladys Wightwick Charitable Trust

WHAT IS FUNDED General charitable purposes

WHO CAN BENEFIT There are no restrictions on the age; professional and economic group; family situation; religion and culture; and social circumstances of; or disease or medical condition suffered by, the beneficiaries

WHERE FUNDING CAN BE GIVEN UK

TYPE OF GRANT One-off grants

FINANCES *Year* 1997 *Income* £24,801
Grants £27,000

TRUSTEES C A McLintock, K T C Arnold, D Harriss, P Smith

HOW TO APPLY In writing, Trustees meet in Spring and Autumn

WHO TO APPLY TO P Smith, The Gladys Wightwick Charitable Trust, Messrs Bird & Bird, Solicitors, 90 Fetter Lane, London EC4A 1JP *Tel* 0171-415 6000

CC NO 1024622　　**ESTABLISHED** 1969

■ The Felicity Wilde Charitable Trust

WHAT IS FUNDED Children's charities and medical research, particularly into asthma

WHAT IS NOT FUNDED Registered charities only

WHO CAN BENEFIT National organisations benefiting children. Research workers and medical professionals may be supported for research work. There is no restriction on the disease or medical condition suffered by the beneficiaries, however, priority is given to those suffering from asthma

WHERE FUNDING CAN BE GIVEN UK

TYPE OF GRANT Range of grants

RANGE OF GRANTS £1,000

FINANCES *Year* 1997 *Income* £99,935
Grants £27,250

TRUSTEES Barclays Bank Trust Company Ltd

HOW TO APPLY In writing at any time. The Trustees meet quarterly

WHO TO APPLY TO Barclays Bank Trust Company Ltd, The Felicity Wilde Charitable Trust, Executorship and Trustee Centre, Osborne Court, Gadbrook Park, Northwich, Cheshire CW9 7UR

CC NO 264404　　**ESTABLISHED** 1972

■ The Wilde Sapte Charitable Trust

WHAT IS FUNDED General charitable purposes at the Trustees' discretion. Normally to fund registered charities

WHAT IS NOT FUNDED Individuals education and scholarships will not be funded

WHO CAN BENEFIT There are no restrictions on the age; professional and economic group; family situation; religion and culture; and social circumstances of; or disease or medical condition suffered by, the beneficiaries

WHERE FUNDING CAN BE GIVEN UK

TYPE OF GRANT At the discretion of the Trustees

FINANCES *Year* 1996 *Income* £33,333

TRUSTEES A J C Collett, M B Andrews, A S Miles

WHO TO APPLY TO A J C Collett, Partner, The Wilde Sapte Charitable Trust, Wilde Sapte, 1 Fleet Place, London EC4M 7WS *Tel* 0171-246 7000

CC NO 1041204　　**ESTABLISHED** 1994

■ The Wilkinson Charitable Foundation

WHAT IS FUNDED The advancement of scientific knowledge, especially in the fields of chemistry, virology and radiology through research, support of facilities and encouragement of promising students

WHAT IS NOT FUNDED No grants are made to individuals

WHO CAN BENEFIT Academic institutions benefiting young adults and older people, students, research workers and scientists

WHERE FUNDING CAN BE GIVEN UK

FINANCES *Year* 1995–96 *Income* £80,000

TRUSTEES Dr Anne M Hardy, B D S Lock

HOW TO APPLY To the address under Who To Apply To in writing

WHO TO APPLY TO B D S Lock, The Wilkinson Charitable Foundation, 190 Strand, London WC2R 1JN *Tel* 0171-379 4645
CC NO 276214   ESTABLISHED 1978

■ The Ronald Willcox Trust

WHAT IS FUNDED General charitable purposes
WHO CAN BENEFIT There are no restrictions on the age; professional and economic group; family situation; religion and culture; and social circumstances of; or disease or medical condition suffered by, the beneficiaries
WHERE FUNDING CAN BE GIVEN UK
FINANCES *Year* 1996 *Income* £15,644
Grants £5,325
TRUSTEES Miss P J Willcox, R C Lucas, J G Ruffer, P D Warren, MC, BA
NOTES Funds are fully allocated or committed
WHO TO APPLY TO D G Sheppard, Secretary, The Ronald Willcox Trust, 9 Maryland Road, Tunbridge Wells, Kent TN2 5HE
CC NO 245621   ESTABLISHED 1965

■ The Willenhall Area Relief Rehabilitation and Nursing Trust (otherwise known as WARRANT)

WHAT IS FUNDED Care of the elderly, children and the disabled
WHO CAN BENEFIT Children, the elderly and the disabled
WHERE FUNDING CAN BE GIVEN Willenhall and the Borough of Walsall
RANGE OF GRANTS £350–£1,500
SAMPLE GRANTS £1,500 to Rainbow House Childrens Hospice; £1,500 to Compton Hospice; £1,000 to Willenhall Fellowship for the Disabled; £1,000 to Walsall Hospital League of Friends; £1,000 to Communicare Tool Box; £1,000 to Old Hall School; £1,000 to Beacon Centre for the Blind; £500 to Wolverhampton Digestive Foundation; £500 to Walsall Society for the Blind; £500 to Electronic Aids for the Blind
FINANCES *Year* 1997 *Income* £38,381
Grants £11,360
TRUSTEES L T Baddeley, T W Bradley, A E Costin, Mrs M Myatt, Dr S G Phillips, T W Poole, J L Ward, Mrs A Wrighton
HOW TO APPLY To the address under Who To Apply To in writing
WHO TO APPLY TO J L Ward, Clerk, The Willenhall Area Relief Rehabilitation and Nursing Trust, 1 New Road, Willenhall, West Midlands WV13 2AH
CC NO 216097   ESTABLISHED 1981

■ The Kay Williams Charitable Foundation

WHAT IS FUNDED General charitable purposes
WHO CAN BENEFIT There are no restrictions on the age; professional and economic group; family situation; religion and culture; and social circumstances of; or disease or medical condition suffered by, the beneficiaries
WHERE FUNDING CAN BE GIVEN UK
RANGE OF GRANTS £250–£2,000

SAMPLE GRANTS £2,000 to Action for the Blind; £2,000 to BACUP, helping people live with cancer; £2,000 to Cancer Research Campaign; £2,000 to Macmillan Fund (Cancer Relief); £2,000 to MIND; £2,000 to National Institute for Deaf People; £2,000 to Royal National Institute for the Blind; £2,000 to The Samaritans; £2,000 to Voluntary Service Overseas; £2,000 to World Cancer Research Fund
FINANCES *Year* 1996 *Income* £1,055,555
Grants £25,250
TRUSTEES R M Cantor, D W Graham, Mrs M C Williams
WHO TO APPLY TO R M Cantor, Trustee, The Kay Williams Charitable Foundation, BDO Stoy Hayward, Bowman House, 2–10 Bridge Street, Reading, Berkshire RG1 2LU
CC NO 1047947   ESTABLISHED 1995

■ A G Williams Charitable Trust

WHAT IS FUNDED General charitable purposes
WHO CAN BENEFIT There are no restrictions on the age; professional and economic group; family situation; religion and culture; and social circumstances of; or disease or medical condition suffered by, the beneficiaries
WHERE FUNDING CAN BE GIVEN UK
TRUSTEES A G Williams, Ms S Williams
WHO TO APPLY TO G M Catton, Professional Adviser, A G Williams Charitable Trust, 14 Pensioners Court, The Charterhouse Square, London EC1M 6AU
CC NO 1065474   ESTABLISHED 1997

■ Sheelagh Williams Charitable Trust

WHAT IS FUNDED General charitable purposes
WHO CAN BENEFIT There are no restrictions on the age; professional and economic group; family situation; religion and culture; and social circumstances of; or disease or medical condition suffered by, the beneficiaries
WHERE FUNDING CAN BE GIVEN UK
TRUSTEES A G Williams, Ms S Williams
WHO TO APPLY TO G M Catton, Sheelagh Williams Charitable Trust, 14 Pensioners Court, The Chaterhouse, Charterhouse Square, London EC1M 6AU
CC NO 1065465   ESTABLISHED 1997

■ William Williams Charity

WHAT IS FUNDED People in need, youth organisations, schools and welfare charities
WHO CAN BENEFIT Primarily individuals, also some local organisations benefiting: those in need; children, young adults; at risk groups; those disadvantaged by poverty and socially isolated people
WHERE FUNDING CAN BE GIVEN The ancient parishes of Blandford Forum, Shaftesbury and Sturminster Newton
FINANCES *Year* 1996 *Income* £166,348
Grants £120,203
HOW TO APPLY To the address under Who To Apply To in writing
WHO TO APPLY TO O B N Paine, William Williams Charity, 42 High West Street, Dorchester, Dorset DT1 1UU
CC NO 202188   ESTABLISHED 1621

Does the trust you have chosen match your needs? Haphazard applications waste postage and time

681

■ The Williams Family Charitable Trust

WHAT IS FUNDED To support Jewish organisations
WHO CAN BENEFIT Organisations benefiting Jewish people
WHERE FUNDING CAN BE GIVEN UK
RANGE OF GRANTS £50–£108,000
SAMPLE GRANTS £108,000 to Yeshiva Kiryat Arba; £10,250 to Child Resettlement Fund; £8,000 to Haamuta Lkidum Hahinuch; £8,000 to Holon Association for absorption of immigrants; £5,200 to Friends of Ariel; £5,200 to Yesha; £2,250 to Israel Cancer Association; £2,250 to Yeshiva Hazon Elkanan; £2,250 to Yeshiva Or Hevron; £1,500 to Seeing Eyes for the Blind of Israel
FINANCES *Year* 1997 *Income* £94,119 *Grants* £185,780
TRUSTEES H Landy, S Benison, A Levy
HOW TO APPLY To the address under Who To Apply To in writing
WHO TO APPLY TO Harry Landy, Trustee, The Williams Family Charitable Trust, 8 Holne Chase, London N2 0QN
CC NO 255452   **ESTABLISHED** 1959

■ James Williams Trust

WHAT IS FUNDED To make grants to Evangelical Christian work. Preference to charities of which the Trustees have special interest, knowledge or association
WHAT IS NOT FUNDED Grants are restricted to evangelical causes
WHO CAN BENEFIT Individuals, churches and evangelical trusts benefiting evangelists and Christians
WHERE FUNDING CAN BE GIVEN UK and overseas
TYPE OF GRANT Regular grants in furtherance of the objective
FINANCES *Year* 1997 *Income* £24,560 *Grants* £15,525
TRUSTEES G G Brown, W J Capper, B M George, R F Steele, S Burt
HOW TO APPLY The Trustees regret that applications cannot be acknowledged. Funding is restricted
WHO TO APPLY TO R F Steele, James Williams Trust, 21 Wood Crescent, Rogerstone, Newport, Gwent NP1 0AL
CC NO 1000451   **ESTABLISHED** 1990

■ The Neville Williams Trust

WHAT IS FUNDED Provision of old people's homes, care and welfare of the elderly
WHO CAN BENEFIT To the benefit of older and retired people who are at risk, disadvantaged by poverty and socially isolated. There is no restriction on the disease or medical condition suffered by the beneficiaries
WHERE FUNDING CAN BE GIVEN City of Birmingham
SAMPLE GRANTS £1,725 for a pension; £500 to Birmingham Jewish Day Centre
FINANCES *Year* 1997 *Income* £44,003 *Grants* £2,225
TRUSTEES Mrs P M Whitley, J M Baron, J R Crane, R J H Parkes
WHO TO APPLY TO B Glasgow, The Neville Williams Trust, Birmingham Council for Old People, Onneley House, 109 Court-Oak Road, Harborne, Birmingham B17 9AA
CC NO 245209   **ESTABLISHED** 1947

■ Williamson Trust

This trust did not respond to CAF's request to amend its entry and, by 30 June 1998, CAF's researchers did not find financial records for later than 1995 on its file at the Charity Commission. Trusts are legally required to submit annual accounts to the Charity Commission under section 42 of the Charities Act 1993

WHAT IS FUNDED Promotion for the public benefit the relief and treatment of physical, mental or emotional illness, disorder or disability
WHO CAN BENEFIT Disabled people, and those suffering from mental illness
WHERE FUNDING CAN BE GIVEN UK
TYPE OF GRANT At the discretion of the Trustees
TRUSTEES W Salt, S Robinson, J Robinson
WHO TO APPLY TO J Robinson, Williamson Trust, 8 Brackley Road, Eccles, Monton, Manchester M30 9LG
CC NO 327601   **ESTABLISHED** 1987

■ R H Willis Charitable Trust

WHAT IS FUNDED General charitable purposes
WHO CAN BENEFIT There are no restrictions on the age; professional and economic group; family situation; religion and culture; and social circumstances of; or disease or medical condition suffered by, the beneficiaries
WHERE FUNDING CAN BE GIVEN Birmingham
TYPE OF GRANT At the discretion of the Trustees
RANGE OF GRANTS £250–£5,400
SAMPLE GRANTS £5,400 to Acafess Community Trust; £5,200 to St Basil's Centre; £3,000 to Dodford Children's Holiday Farm; £3,000 to Trinity Centre; £2,000 to Birmingham Voluntary Service; £2,000 to CCHA Extra Care; £1,500 to Birmingham Rathbone Society; £1,000 to Birmingham Citizens' Advice Bureau; £1,000 to St Peter's Community Project; £1,000 to the Salvation Army
FINANCES *Year* 1997 *Income* £38,828 *Grants* £35,650
TRUSTEES G B G Hingley, Ms L S Woodhead
WHO TO APPLY TO G B G Hingley, R H Willis Charitable Trust, c/o Messrs Wragge and Co, 55 Colmore Row, Birmingham B3 2AS
CC NO 328525   **ESTABLISHED** 1989

■ Willoughby Memorial Trust

WHAT IS FUNDED The maintenance of a library and art gallery and the promotion of study and greater knowledge of literature and arts in the area Where Funding Can Be Given
WHAT IS NOT FUNDED No grants to individuals
WHO CAN BENEFIT Organisations involved with the arts
WHERE FUNDING CAN BE GIVEN Lincolnshire
SAMPLE GRANTS £1,000 to Grantham Music Festival for repairs to a piano
FINANCES *Year* 1997 *Income* £16,973 *Grants* £1,000
TRUSTEES Lady Willoughby de Eresby, B Chase, M C Hedley Lewis
HOW TO APPLY To the address under Who To Apply To in writing
WHO TO APPLY TO Bernard P Chase, Willoughby Memorial Trust, Glenbourn, 17 South Road, Bourne, Lincolnshire PE10 9JD
CC NO 527647   **ESTABLISHED** 1965

■ The H D H Wills 1965 Charitable Trust

WHAT IS FUNDED Funds are fully committed and donations can only be made to registered charities. Grants are given in seven year cycles to: 1st year Magdalen College, Oxford; 2nd year Rendcomb College Gloucestershire; 3rd and 4th years any registered charity dedicated or primarily dedicated to the conservation of wildlife; 5th year Ditchley Foundation (registered charity no 312911); 6th and 7th years such charitable institutions as the Trustees shall in their absolute discretion think fit

WHAT IS NOT FUNDED No grants to individuals

WHO CAN BENEFIT Organisations benefiting young adults and students

WHERE FUNDING CAN BE GIVEN UK including the Channel Islands and the Irish Republic

SAMPLE GRANTS £200,000 to Martin Wills Wildlife Maintenance Trust; £125,000 to Spey Research Trust; £25,000 to Farm Africa; £20,000 to Royal Botanic Gardens, Kew for Millennium Seed Bank; £20,000 to FWAG – Farming and Wildlife Advisory Group; £20,000 to The Batsford Foundation; £20,000 to Northumberland Wildlife Trust; £17,000 to TUSK; £14,000 to World Pheasant Association; £10,000 to University of Oxford, Botanical Gardens

FINANCES *Year* 1997 *Income* £1,086,917 *Grants* £920,109

TRUSTEES J Kemp-Welch, Lord Killearn, J S B Carson, Lady E H Wills, Dr C M H Wills

NOTES The above figures include the financial details for Knockando Church Fund and Martin Wills Fund

HOW TO APPLY No application form in use. No specific dates for making applications but at present few new applications can be considered

WHO TO APPLY TO Mrs I R Wootton, The H D H Wills 1965 Charitable Trust, 12 Tokenhouse Yard, London EC2R 7AN *Tel* 0171-588 2828 *Fax* 0171-606 9205

CC NO 244610   **ESTABLISHED** 1965

■ Dame Violet Wills Charitable Trust

WHAT IS FUNDED General charitable purposes for Evangelical Associations

WHAT IS NOT FUNDED No grants to individuals

WHO CAN BENEFIT Associations for Evangelical religious purposes

WHERE FUNDING CAN BE GIVEN UK

TYPE OF GRANT One-off

FINANCES *Year* 1997 *Income* £113,935 *Grants* £138,900

TRUSTEES H E Cooper, R D Speare, Dr D Cunningham, S Burton, Rev A Motyer, Prof A Linton, Miss J Guy, G Landreth, D Cleave, A Cooper, J R Dean, Mrs M J Lewis

HOW TO APPLY In January and July

WHO TO APPLY TO H E Cooper, FCA, Dame Violet Wills Charitable Trust, c/o Messrs Ricketts, Cooper & Co, Thornton House, Richmond Hill, Clifton, Bristol BS8 1AT

CC NO 219485   **ESTABLISHED** 1955

■ The Spencer Wills Trust

WHAT IS FUNDED General charitable purposes at the discretion of the Trustees

WHO CAN BENEFIT There are no restrictions on the age; professional and economic group; family situation; religion and culture; and social circumstances of; or disease or medical condition suffered by, the beneficiaries

WHERE FUNDING CAN BE GIVEN UK

TRUSTEES P Williams, M Rudman, C S Wills

NOTES Grants are made wholly at the discretion of the Trustees

HOW TO APPLY **This Trust states that it does not respond to unsolicited applications**

WHO TO APPLY TO A C Gamble, Administrator, The Spencer Wills Trust, 239–241 Shaftesbury Avenue, London WC2H 8EH

CC NO 278023   **ESTABLISHED** 1979

■ Dame Violet Wills Will Trust 1965

WHAT IS FUNDED The support of homes established privately by the late Dame Violet Wills and charities active in Bristol and South Devon

WHAT IS NOT FUNDED Registered charities only and working in the area Where Funding Can Be Given. No grants to individuals

WHO CAN BENEFIT Registered charities benefiting children. There are no restrictions on the professional and economic group, family situation, religion and culture, and social circumstances of, or disease or medical condition suffered by, the beneficiaries

WHERE FUNDING CAN BE GIVEN Bristol and South Devon

TYPE OF GRANT Single donations

SAMPLE GRANTS £3,500 to St John Ambulance, Bristol; £2,000 to Wills and Stickland Homes, Clevedon; £2,000 to Bristol Area Stroke Foundation; £2,000 to John Groom's Association for the Disabled; £2,000 to Jessie May Trust; £2,000 to Macmillan Cancer Relief; £2,000 to Brainwave; £2,000 to DRIB; £2,000 to NSPCC; £2,000 each to RNLI Torbay and Bristol Channel

FINANCES *Year* 1997 *Income* £74,173 *Grants* £63,105

TRUSTEES H J Page, D P L Howe, P J Page

HOW TO APPLY At any time

WHO TO APPLY TO H J Page, Dame Violet Wills Will Trust 1965, 33 Julian Road, Sneyd Park, Bristol BS9 1JY

CC NO 262251   **ESTABLISHED** 1965

■ The Wilmcote Charitrust

WHAT IS FUNDED General charitable purposes. The Trustee's present policy is to restrict grants to charitable bodies: (a) as requested by the donors of the four funds; (b) are of particular interest to individual Trustees. These usually are Birmingham, Warwickshire and Worcestershire orientated

WHAT IS NOT FUNDED No grants to individuals

WHO CAN BENEFIT There are no restrictions on the age; professional and economic group; family situation; religion and culture; and social circumstances of; or disease or medical condition suffered by, the beneficiaries

WHERE FUNDING CAN BE GIVEN Birmingham, Warwickshire and Worcestershire

FINANCES *Year* 1996 *Income* £43,908

TRUSTEES G C Allman, B W Frost, Mrs A L M Murphy, Mrs R J S Whiteside

WHO TO APPLY TO Douglas M King, Clerk, The Wilmcote Charitrust, Warren Chase, Wilmcote, Stratford upon Avon, Warwickshire CV37 9XG *Tel* 01789 298472

CC NO 503837   **ESTABLISHED** 1974

■ The John Wilson Bequest Fund

WHAT IS FUNDED Annual allowance to men over 60 resident in Edinburgh and grants to local charities working with the poor in Edinburgh

WHO CAN BENEFIT Men over 60 in Edinburgh area and local charities for the poor in the Edinburgh area

WHERE FUNDING CAN BE GIVEN Edinburgh area

TYPE OF GRANT Recurrent for individuals: one-off for charities

RANGE OF GRANTS Allowance to men over 60 up to £400 per annum. Grants to local charities for the poor in Edinburgh area: £250–£2,000 each

TRUSTEES A M Bradley, Dr A Currie, A G D Johnston, Dr G M McAndrew, Dr H M MacLeod, D M Nicholson, C F Sleigh, Cllr J C Wilson

HOW TO APPLY To the address under Who To Apply To

WHO TO APPLY TO The John Wilson Bequest Fund, County Buildings, Market Street, Fofar DD8 3LG

SC NO SCO 18661   **ESTABLISHED** 1922

■ Connolly Thomas Wilson Foundation

WHAT IS FUNDED To give a helping hand to youngsters who themselves have made an effort to succeed. Sponsorship of individual sportspeople

WHAT IS NOT FUNDED No grants to people outside the age limit of 14 to 21 years of age

WHO CAN BENEFIT Mainly young people between 14 and 21 years of age, including sportspeople

WHERE FUNDING CAN BE GIVEN Northamptonshire

TYPE OF GRANT Cash contributions towards courses for individuals

FINANCES *Year* 1996 *Income* £20,245 *Grants* £16,743

TRUSTEES L A Wilson, S G Schanschieff, D M Auden, T O'Connor, N C Wilson (Administrative Trustee), C Hayward (Treasurer)

HOW TO APPLY To the address under Who To Apply To in writing

WHO TO APPLY TO N C Wilson, Connolly Thomas Wilson Foundation, 4 St Giles Street, Northampton NN1 1JA *Tel* 01604 623990

CC NO 267063   **ESTABLISHED** 1973

■ The David Wilson Foundation

WHAT IS FUNDED General charitable purposes

WHO CAN BENEFIT There are no restrictions on the age; professional and economic group; family situation; religion and culture; and social circumstances of; or disease or medical condition suffered by, the beneficiaries

WHERE FUNDING CAN BE GIVEN UK

WHO TO APPLY TO J A Gillions, Solicitor to the Charity, The David Wilson Foundation, 6–8 Kilwardby Street, Ashby de la Zouch, Leicestershire LE65 2FU

CC NO 1049047   **ESTABLISHED** 1995

■ J and J R Wilson Trust

WHAT IS FUNDED Grants are given to charitable bodies which are concerned with elderly people, or the care of both domestic and wild animals and birds

WHAT IS NOT FUNDED No grants to individuals

WHO CAN BENEFIT Organisations benefiting elderly people, animals and birds

WHERE FUNDING CAN BE GIVEN Mainly Scotland, particularly Glasgow and the West of Scotland

HOW TO APPLY The Trustees decide which charitable bodies to support and how much funding should be allocated to each

WHO TO APPLY TO The Correspondent, J and J R Wilson Trust, Hugh Macfarlane, Keith Hopkins, Montgomerie & Co, Apsley House, 29 Wellington Street, Glasgow G2 6JA

SC NO SCO 07411

■ The Kit Wilson Trust for Animal Welfare

WHAT IS FUNDED To aid and promote animal welfare

WHO CAN BENEFIT Those with limited income whose animals may breed unwanted litters, feral cat colonies, societies and individuals involved in animal rescue in need of assistance to spay/ neuter cats/dogs

WHERE FUNDING CAN BE GIVEN UK, occasionally overseas

TYPE OF GRANT For spaying and neutering only

FINANCES *Year* 1996 *Income* £131,981 *Grants* £66,733

TRUSTEES Miss C H Marshall (Chair), Mrs M E Alexander (Hon Treasurer), Mrs C A Billings, Mrs S V Hill (Secretary)

PUBLICATIONS Newsletter – three times a year. Information and legacy leaflets

NOTES The purpose of the Trust is to promote the welfare of animals and especially to rescue abandoned, unwanted and ill treated and neglected animals; to care for these animals and provide them with any necessary veterinary attention until they can be rehomed; to spay/ neuter animals in the Trust's care and to give financial help to people of limited means to spay/ neuter their pets to reduce the number of unwanted animals. The figure under Grants in the Finances represents the amount spent on the various aspects of animal welfare and not donations to other organisations or individuals

HOW TO APPLY The Trustees meet every month. Possible grants would be considered at these meetings. Urgent applications are dealt with immediately on application to the Chairman

WHO TO APPLY TO The Kit Wilson Trust for Animal Welfare, Animal Rescue Centre, Stonehurst Lane, Hadlow Down, Uckfield, East Sussex TN22 4ED

CC NO 270419   **ESTABLISHED** 1975

■ Wiltshire Community Foundation

WHAT IS FUNDED Main projects fund: (a) Supporting community care. (b) Tackling isolation. (c) Investing in young people. Community development fund. Initiatives fund. Support may also be given to accommodation and housing, health, infrastructure development and infrastructure and technical support

WHAT IS NOT FUNDED Projects outside Wiltshire, individuals, sponsored events, advancement of religion, medical research and equipment, animal welfare, party political activities and the replacement of previous statutory funding

WHO CAN BENEFIT Voluntary and community groups in Wiltshire benefiting: young adults and older people; one parent families and ethnic minority groups. Funding will be given to people of many different social circumstances

WHERE FUNDING CAN BE GIVEN County of Wiltshire

TYPE OF GRANT Not normally for capital expenditure or to contribute to large appeals. Core costs, feasibility studies, project, research, running costs, recurring costs, salaries and start-up costs will be considered. Funding is given for up to three years

RANGE OF GRANTS £200–£3,000pa for three years

SAMPLE GRANTS £9,500 to Salisbury and District CAB for the continued provision of an outreach advice service in the rural villages of Mere and Tisbury; £9,000 to Victim Support to develop the service for victims of sexual violence and to provide practical help, counselling and emotional support; £8,700 to Swindon Advocacy Movement towards office and administration costs for this project enabling people with learning difficulties to speak for themselves; £7,500 to the Greencroft Centre towards transport costs to enable those with continuing mental health problems, living in rural areas to attend the Centre; £6,750 to Home Computer Training for Disabled People to provide software for computers and printers for people with disabilities who wish to undertake computer training at home; £6,675 to Swindon and District MIND towards the cost of establishing a 'drop-in' centre in Swindon for people with mental health problems; £6,000 to New Road Centre to assist with transport costs for people with disabilities living in rural areas who wish to attend the day centre; £6,000 to West Wiltshire CAB to help fund employment costs of a resource worker within the Bureau to support the volunteer advice workers; £5,336 to Zeals Youth Trust to encourage young people in the rural village of Zeals in developing a young persons project within the village; £5,000 to Homestart Kennet to establish a new office in Devizes helping families on low incomes and in difficult circumstances, to cope with children under five

FINANCES *Year* 1997–98 *Income* £566,500 *Grants* £108,595

TRUSTEES David Airey, Mike Ball, Charles Bartholomew, Alice Cleland, John Emmerson, Elinor Goodman, Chapman Harrison, Maj Gen Tony Jeapes, CB, OBE, MC, John Manser, CBE (Chairman), Zandria Pauncefort, Gill Prior, Paula Rudgard, Jeremy del Strother, Sir John Sykes, Bt (Hon Solicitor), Marigold Treloar, Steve Willcox, Ian Wilson

PUBLICATIONS Grants Policy booklet. Annual Report and Accounts. *Communities at Risk in Wiltshire* (needs assessment report) and *The Future We All Want* (developing the strategy for the care of older people in Eastern Wiltshire)

NOTES Applications unlikely to succeed. Wiltshire Community Foundation aims to assist groups that are working very closely with their local community. The Foundation also aims to allocate funds where they will make the most difference. For these reasons the following applications are unlikely to be supported. (a) Applications from national charities where there is no clear management structure based in Wiltshire. (b) Applications from organisation that have access to 'professional fund-raisers'. (c) Applications for services that are closely associated with statutory provision. (d) Applications for contributions towards projects that are not being offered mainly in Wiltshire. (d) Applications for a contribution toward a major item where WCF's contribution would not make a significant difference

HOW TO APPLY On official form following discussions with Project Director. Decisions are made at twice yearly grants meetings

WHO TO APPLY TO Jan Crawley, Project Director, Wiltshire Community Foundation, 48 New Park Street, Devizes, Wiltshire SN10 1DS *Tel* 01380 729284 *Fax* 01380 729772 *Web Site* http://www.moneyshop.co.uk/charity/wiltshire.htm

CC NO 298936 **ESTABLISHED** 1991

··

■ The Wincott Foundation

WHAT IS FUNDED Advancement of education, and promotion of research in economics and finance. Special reference to promotion of highest standards in economic and financial journalism

WHAT IS NOT FUNDED No student maintenance grants

WHO CAN BENEFIT Individuals as well as voluntary and charitable organisations benefiting research workers and academics

WHERE FUNDING CAN BE GIVEN UK and Europe

TYPE OF GRANT Research with funding of up to three years

SAMPLE GRANTS £10,000 to an individual at the Institute of Economic Affairs for Welfare State and Voluntary Action Project; £5,800 to Reuter Foundation to enable financial journalists from Eastern Europe to visit the UK; £5,000 to University of Buckingham for publication of discussion papers; £3,000 to an individual as part payment of book on History of Financial Journalism; £2,500 to an individual at University of Bristol for research on transformation of Labour Party; £2,000 to an individual at University of Nottingham for research on financing public expenditure

FINANCES *Year* 1998 *Income* £33,000 *Grants* £30,000

TRUSTEES W M Clarke, Lord Harris of High Cross, Mrs E Heckett, I Morison, Sir Geoffrey Owen, Prof G Wood, F A Scott, Prof C Robinson, C Williams

HOW TO APPLY At any time, by letter only

WHO TO APPLY TO I M Griffiths, MBE, Secretary, The Wincott Foundation, 326 Hempstead Road, Watford, Hertfordshire WD1 3NA *Tel* 01923 242469

CC NO 313770 **ESTABLISHED** 1969

··

■ The J L Wine Charitable Trust

WHAT IS FUNDED General charitable purposes

WHO CAN BENEFIT There are no restrictions on the age; professional and economic group; family situation; religion and culture; and social circumstances of; or disease or medical condition suffered by, the beneficiaries

WHERE FUNDING CAN BE GIVEN UK

RANGE OF GRANTS £50–£6,800

SAMPLE GRANTS £6,800 to Nightingale House; £600 to Jewish Care; £587 to Royal Court Theatre; £550 to Wimbledon and District Synagogue; £500 to Wigmore Hall Trust

FINANCES *Year* 1997 *Income* £21,474 *Grants* £11,097

TRUSTEES H M Wine, Ms C Goldbart, J S Korn

HOW TO APPLY Trustees do not welcome applications

WHO TO APPLY TO J S Korn, The J L Wine Charitable Trust, c/o Beechcroft Stanleys, 20 Furnival Street, London EC4A 1BN *Tel* 0171-242 1011

CC NO 291209 **ESTABLISHED** 1985

Does the trust you have chosen match your needs? Haphazard applications waste postage and time

··········
685

■ Benjamin Winegarten Charitable Trust

WHAT IS FUNDED Relief of poverty and the advancement of Jewish religion and religious education

WHO CAN BENEFIT Individuals and organisations benefiting Jewish people and those disadvantaged by poverty

WHERE FUNDING CAN BE GIVEN UK

RANGE OF GRANTS £200–£5,000

SAMPLE GRANTS £5,000 to Tiferes Yaakov; £5,000 to Agudas Israel Housing Association Ltd; £5,000 to the Gevurath Ari Torah Academy Trust; £5,000 to the Telz Talmudical Academy and Talmud Torah Trust; £5,000 to an individual; £4,000 to Sunderland Talmudical College; £3,000 to Achiezer; £2,500 to Mericaz Lechinuch Torani Zichron Ya'akov; £2,300 to Yad Leachim Pe'ylim; £2,000 to Talmud Torah Tashbar

FINANCES *Year* 1997 *Income* £70,750
Grants £49,460

TRUSTEES B A Winegarten, Mrs E Winegarten

WHO TO APPLY TO B A Winegarten, Benjamin Winegarten Charitable Trust, 25 St Andrew's Grove, Stoke Newington, London N16 5NF

CC NO 271442   **ESTABLISHED** 1976

■ W Wing Yip and Brothers Charitable Trust

WHAT IS FUNDED Chinese organisations, especially educational. Relief of poverty, Chinese students, education of Chinese children living in the area Where Funding Can Be Given

WHO CAN BENEFIT Chinese organisations benefiting: children, young adults, students and those disadvantaged by poverty

WHERE FUNDING CAN BE GIVEN Birmingham, Manchester, Croydon and Cricklewood

TYPE OF GRANT One-off, project and start-up costs. Funding for up to two years will be considered

RANGE OF GRANTS £50–£1,900; typical £250

FINANCES *Year* 1996–97 *Income* £139,102
Grants £7,200

TRUSTEES R A Brittain, D M King, G Y Yap, L S Yap, W Wing Yip

HOW TO APPLY To the address under Who To Apply To in writing

WHO TO APPLY TO R A Brittain, Trustee, W Wing Yip and Brothers Charitable Trust, 375 Nechells Park Road, Nechells, Birmingham B7 5NT *Tel* 0121-327 6618

CC NO 326999   **ESTABLISHED** 1986

■ Mrs Wingfield's Charitable Trust

WHAT IS FUNDED General charitable purposes. Applications considered on merit and available funds

WHAT IS NOT FUNDED Grants not normally made to individuals, unless case of exceptional merit

WHO CAN BENEFIT Mainly established organisations in charitable or artistic fields. There are no restrictions on the age, professional and economic group, family situation, religion and culture, and social circumstances of, or disease or medical condition suffered by the beneficiaries

WHERE FUNDING CAN BE GIVEN UK, especially Shropshire and The Wrekin

TYPE OF GRANT Single payment, no restriction on capital expenditure or revenue costs. Funding is for one year or less

RANGE OF GRANTS £5–£500

FINANCES *Year* 1997 *Income* £14,052
Grants £14,011

TRUSTEES J M Dodds, D J Onslow

HOW TO APPLY In writing, Trustees meet as and when required. Applications reviewed February, May, August, November. Sae please. Absolutely no personal callers or telephone enquiries

WHO TO APPLY TO Messrs Dyke Yaxley, Mrs Wingfield's Charitable Trust, Abbey House, Abbey Foregate, Shrewsbury, Salop SY2 6BH
Fax 01743 235795
E-mail dykeaxley@dial.pipex.com

CC NO 269524   **ESTABLISHED** 1974

■ The Francis Winham Foundation (225)

This trust failed to supply a copy of its annual report and accounts to CAF as required under section 47(2) of the Charities Act 1993. The information held on file at the Charity Commission was insufficient to enable CAF's researchers to write a substantive commentary on the trust's activities. Accordingly, despite its size, we are unable to list this trust in Spotlight on Major Trusts

WHAT IS FUNDED Organisations, institutions and foundations benefiting older people

WHO CAN BENEFIT Organisations benefiting any aged person in England

WHERE FUNDING CAN BE GIVEN England only

TYPE OF GRANT Discretionary grants

SAMPLE GRANTS Grant made in 1996 included:; £13,359 to Age Concern; £10,000 to Invalids at Home; £3,500 to RNIB; £1,000 to People to Places

FINANCES *Year* 1996 *Income* £475,144
Grants £295,957

TRUSTEES F O Winham, J M N Roberts, G D Winham

HOW TO APPLY By letter, the Trustees regret they cannot send replies to applications outside the area Where Funding Can Be Given

WHO TO APPLY TO The Francis Winham Foundation, 35 Pembroke Gardens, London W8 6HU

CC NO 278092   **ESTABLISHED** 1979

■ Hyman Winstone Foundation

WHAT IS FUNDED General areas of interest – with emphasis on local charities. Particularly charities working in the field of: health care; animal facilities and services and various community facilities and services

WHAT IS NOT FUNDED Registered charities only – no grants to individuals

WHO CAN BENEFIT Registered charities working in the areas outlined above benefiting Jews, disabled people and those disadvantaged by poverty. There is no restriction on the medical condition or disease suffered by the beneficiaries

WHERE FUNDING CAN BE GIVEN UK with preference to Sheffield. Israel

FINANCES *Year* 1997 *Income* £18,900
Grants £17,500

TRUSTEES T B Gee, M H Elliott, R J Elliott, D H Gee

HOW TO APPLY In writing to the address under Who To Apply To below

WHO TO APPLY TO M H Elliott, Hyman Winstone Foundation, Benson Flint, Solicitors, 32 Wilkinson Street, Sheffield S10 2GB

CC NO 224442   **ESTABLISHED** 1956

■ Winterbourne Charitable Trust

WHAT IS FUNDED To support performing arts and ex-service personnel charities

WHO CAN BENEFIT Institutions, registered charities and individuals of outstanding artistic ability seeking aid to take up the opportunity for further education or training. Support also for ex-service people

WHERE FUNDING CAN BE GIVEN UK

FINANCES *Year* 1996 *Income* £17,500

TRUSTEES A S D Barrett

WHO TO APPLY TO A S D Barrett, Winterbourne Charitable Trust, 9 Wilton Row, London SW1X 7NR *Tel* 0171-935 2748

CC NO 282144   **ESTABLISHED** 1981

■ The James Wise Charitable Trust

WHAT IS FUNDED General charitable purposes benefiting a wide range of charitable causes at Trustees discretion

WHO CAN BENEFIT There are no restrictions on the age; professional and economic group; family situation; religion and culture; and social circumstances of; or disease or medical condition suffered by, the beneficiaries

WHERE FUNDING CAN BE GIVEN Mainly Surrey and Hampshire

TYPE OF GRANT Generally one-off or recurrent grants

RANGE OF GRANTS Up to £25,000

SAMPLE GRANTS £25,000 to St Lukes Cancer Wing, Royal Surrey County Hospital for fitting out; £5,000 to Liver Cancer Surgery Appeal for purchase of machine; £2,000 to Godalming Social Services playscheme for provision of playscheme; £2,000 to Kingsley Centre, Bordon; £1,900 to CRUSE for bereavement counselling; £400 to Godalming Volunteer Bureau for funding volunteer service

FINANCES *Year* 1996–97 *Income* £44,646 *Grants* £34,948

TRUSTEES D A S Dear, B Kilburn, S C C Coate

HOW TO APPLY By letter addressed to the Trustees quoting circumstances and requirements

WHO TO APPLY TO L Rabinowitz, The James Wise Charitable Trust, Marshalls, Solicitors, 102 High Street, Godalming, Surrey GU7 1DS *Tel* 01483 416101

CC NO 273853   **ESTABLISHED** 1977

■ The Michael and Anna Wix Charitable Trust

WHAT IS FUNDED Main areas of interest are aged, disability, education, medicine and health, poverty, welfare

WHAT IS NOT FUNDED Registered charities only. Applications from individuals are not considered. Grants are to national bodies rather than local branches or local groups. Mainly UK charities

WHO CAN BENEFIT To benefit students, at risk groups, disabled people, those disadvantaged by poverty and socially isolated people. There is no restriction on the age, disease or medical condition suffered by the beneficiaries

WHERE FUNDING CAN BE GIVEN UK

TYPE OF GRANT Modest semi-regular donations. Also one-off for part or all of a specific project

SAMPLE GRANTS £20,000 to British Technion Society; £2,000 to Nightingale House; £1,500 to the Jewish Museum; £1,250 to Norwood Ravenswood; £1,000 to Institute for Jewish Policy Research; £1,000 to World Jewish Relief; £500 to Jewish Care; £350 to Lilian Faithfull Homes; £250 to Break; £250 to British ORT

FINANCES *Year* 1997–98 *Income* £40,917 *Grants* £27,000

TRUSTEES Miss E Wix, Mrs J B Bloch, Miss J S Portrait

PUBLICATIONS Annual Accounts filed at Charity Commission

HOW TO APPLY At any time. Considered quarterly. Only applications from eligible bodies acknowledged. Frequent appeal material, ie several times a year from a single charity, is not appreciated

WHO TO APPLY TO The Michael and Anna Wix Charitable Trust, Portrait Solicitors, 1 Chancery Lane, London WC2A 1LF *Tel* 0171-320 3883

CC NO 207863   **ESTABLISHED** 1955

■ Woburn 1986 Charitable Trust

WHAT IS FUNDED Provision and maintenance of housing for Woburn estate pensioners in need is the main priority of the Trustees

WHO CAN BENEFIT Promarily pensioners

WHERE FUNDING CAN BE GIVEN Primarily Woburn

TYPE OF GRANT Recurrent and single donations

FINANCES *Year* 1996 *Income* £33,797 *Grants* £37,300

TRUSTEES Most Hon The Marquess of Tavistock, Rt Hon Lord Howland, J A Worrell, D H Fox

WHO TO APPLY TO J A Worrell, Woburn 1986 Charitable Trust, Bedford Office, Woburn Abbey, Woburn, Milton Keynes MK17 9PQ

CC NO 295525   **ESTABLISHED** 1986

■ The Maurice Wohl Charitable Foundation

WHAT IS FUNDED The main areas of interest include medicine and health, including research projects, organisations for the physically and mentally handicapped, sheltered housing, community welfare, including aged and children, education and the Arts

WHAT IS NOT FUNDED The Trustees do not in general entertain applications for grants for on-going maintenance projects. The Trustees do not administer any schemes for individual awards or scholarships and they do not, therefore, entertain any individual applications for grants

WHO CAN BENEFIT Registered charities benefiting: children and the aged; disabled people; at risk groups; those disadvantaged by poverty; socially isolated people; and the sick. There is no restriction on the disease or medical condition suffered by the beneficiaries

WHERE FUNDING CAN BE GIVEN UK and overseas

TYPE OF GRANT Specific projects or part of a project, variable annual donations or one-off donations to a number of different charitable organisations, as defined under What Is Funded, including research

RANGE OF GRANTS £100–£72,000

SAMPLE GRANTS £100,000 to Jewish Care; £72,000 to Royal Postgraduate Medical School; £25,250 to Ravenswood; £15,705 to British Council of the Shaare Zedek Medical Centre; £10,690 to Communaute Israelite de Geneve; £5,000 to Hasmonean High School; £5,000 to Mazkereth Gittel Ltd; £5,000 to Home for Aged Jews, Nightingale House; £4,927 to Conference of European Rabbis, Western Marble Arch Synagogue; £4,000 to Federation of Jewish Relief

FINANCES *Year* 1997 *Income* £801,716 *Grants* £273,326

TRUSTEES M Wohl, CBE, FKC, Mrs V Wohl, Mrs E Latchman, Prof D S Latchman, M Paisner, MA, LLM, D Davis, FCCA

PUBLICATIONS Annual accounts

WHO TO APPLY TO J Houri, The Maurice Wohl Charitable Foundation, 7–8 Conduit Street, London W1R 9TG

CC NO 244519   **ESTABLISHED** 1965

■ The Maurice Wohl Charitable Trust

WHAT IS FUNDED The main areas of interest include medicine and health, including research projects, organisations for the physically and mentally disabled, sheltered housing, welfare of the community, including the aged and children, education and the arts

WHAT IS NOT FUNDED The Trustees do not administer any schemes for individual awards or scholarships, and they do not therefore entertain any individual applications for grants

WHO CAN BENEFIT Registered charities benefiting people of all ages, at risk groups, disabled people, those disadvantaged by poverty, homeless people and socially isolated people. Support may be given to actors and entertainment professionals, medical professionals, research workers, textile workers and designers, writers and poets. There is no restriction on the disease or medical condition suffered by the beneficiaries

WHERE FUNDING CAN BE GIVEN UK and overseas

TYPE OF GRANT Specific projects or part of project; variable annual donations or one-off donations to a number of different charitable organisations, as defined in What Is Funded above. The Trustees do not in general entertain grants for ongoing maintenance projects. Research is considered

RANGE OF GRANTS £25–£10,796

SAMPLE GRANTS £10,796 to Communaute Israelite de Geneve; £6,246 to the Jerusalem Great Synagogue; £2,445 to Society of Friends of the Torah; £2,000 to Yesoday Hatorah Schools; £1,195 to Re'nth, Friends of the Israel Aged; £1,000 to Hammerson Home Charitable Trust Ltd; £1,000 to Keren Klita; £1,000 to Finchley Road Synagogue; £1,000 to Yeshivat Hahotel; £1,000 to Friends of the Sick

FINANCES *Year* 1997 *Income* £187,896 *Grants* £40,173

TRUSTEES M Wohl, CBE, FKC, Mrs V Wohl, Mrs E Latchman, Prof D S Latchman, M D Paisner, D Davis

PUBLICATIONS Annual Accounts

HOW TO APPLY At any time. Trustees meet periodically to consider applications

WHO TO APPLY TO J Houri, The Maurice Wohl Charitable Trust, 1st Floor, 7–8 Conduit Street, London W1R 9TG

CC NO 244518   **ESTABLISHED** 1965

■ The Wolfe Family's Charitable Trust

WHAT IS FUNDED Registered charities catering for: children and elderly (disability/hardship), disablement (blindness/deafness/cancer/mental handicap/ex-service), research and rehabilitation, social hardship, overseas deprivation and disaster, with preference to smaller bodies. Other charitable purposes will be considered

WHAT IS NOT FUNDED No grants to individuals

WHO CAN BENEFIT Organisations benefiting: children; older people; ex-service people; disabled people; disaster victims; and beneficiaries suffering from cancer, hearing loss, mental illness and sight loss

WHERE FUNDING CAN BE GIVEN UK and overseas

TYPE OF GRANT Buildings, capital, core costs, one-off, research, recurring costs. Funding for up to one year will be considered

RANGE OF GRANTS £100–£500. Typically £150

SAMPLE GRANTS £400 to Feed the Children; £200 to Harrison Homes; £150 to BLESMA; £150 to Sight Savers; £150 to Martha Trust

FINANCES *Year* 1997 *Income* £20,600 *Grants* £15,150

TRUSTEES G M Wolfe, A C Wolfe, B F Robinson

HOW TO APPLY By post only. Trustees meet 4 times a year and grants usually made quarterly. No facilities exist for acknowledgement of applications

WHO TO APPLY TO G M Wolfe, The Wolfe Family's Charitable Trust, The Heights, Berghers Hill, Wooburn Common, Nr High Wycombe, Bucks HP10 0JP

CC NO 266242   **ESTABLISHED** 1973

■ Wolff Charity Trust

WHAT IS FUNDED General charitable purposes on behalf of the people of the Jewish faith, with particular favour given to the advancement of education and the advancement of the Jewish faith

WHAT IS NOT FUNDED Restricted to the support of Jewish charities and organisations

WHO CAN BENEFIT Organisations benefiting Jewish people

WHERE FUNDING CAN BE GIVEN UK and overseas

TYPE OF GRANT Cash donations

FINANCES *Year* 1995 *Income* £13,684

TRUSTEES W Wolff, Mrs E Wolff

HOW TO APPLY Written applications only to the address under Who To Apply To

WHO TO APPLY TO W Wolff, Wolff Charity Trust, 96 Lordship Park, London N16 5UB

CC NO 231877   **ESTABLISHED** 1961

■ Peter Wolff Theatre Trust

WHAT IS FUNDED To advance education by improving and extending the appreciation of the public for dramatic works of high quality, in particular, such works by new British playwrights

WHO CAN BENEFIT Organisations benefiting actors, entertainment professionals, writers and poets

WHERE FUNDING CAN BE GIVEN UK

WHO TO APPLY TO B Freedman, Trustee, Peter Wolff Theatre Trust, 13 New Row, London WC2N 4LF *Tel* 0171-497 3320

CC NO 1066835   **ESTABLISHED** 1997

688

Think carefully about every application. Is it justified?

■ The Aviezer Wolfson Charitable Trust

WHAT IS FUNDED Trustees mainly give to Jewish charities and organisations

WHO CAN BENEFIT Registered charities and institutions especially those benefiting Jewish people

WHERE FUNDING CAN BE GIVEN UK

RANGE OF GRANTS £3,000–£10,000

SAMPLE GRANTS £10,000 to Yad Eliezev; £5,000 to British Friends of Laniado Hospital; £4,000 to British Friends of Ezra Lamarpeh; £3,300 to Arachim; £3,000 to British Friends of Yad Sarah

FINANCES *Year* 1997 *Income* £58,609 *Grants* £25,300

TRUSTEES I S J Wolfson, Mrs A Wolfson, D Clayton, Mrs R R Lauffer

WHO TO APPLY TO D Clayton, The Aviezer Wolfson Charitable Trust, c/o Clayton Stark & Co, 5th Floor, Charles House, 108–110 Finchley Road, London NW3 5JJ

CC NO 275927   **ESTABLISHED** 1978

■ Janet Wolfson de Botton Charitable Trust

WHAT IS FUNDED General charitable purposes

WHO CAN BENEFIT There are no restrictions on the age; professional and economic group; family situation; religion and culture; and social circumstances of; or disease or medical condition suffered by, the beneficiaries

WHERE FUNDING CAN BE GIVEN UK

TRUSTEES The Hon J F Wolfson de Botton, M D Paisner, Ms L H Wolfson Townsley

WHO TO APPLY TO Martin Paisner, Trustee, Janet Wolfson de Botton Charitable Trust, Bouverie House, 154 Fleet Street, London EC4A 2DQ

CC NO 1054068   **ESTABLISHED** 1996

■ The Edith & Isaac Wolfson (Scotland) Trust

WHAT IS FUNDED Building and equipment for higher education

WHAT IS NOT FUNDED No grants to individuals

WHO CAN BENEFIT Scottish organisations, especially those benefiting students

WHERE FUNDING CAN BE GIVEN Scotland

TYPE OF GRANT Capital and buildings will be considered

RANGE OF GRANTS £5,000–£50,000

FINANCES *Year* 1997 *Income* £69,000

TRUSTEES Lord Wolfson of Marylebone, FBA (Chairman), Lord Quirk, CBE, FBA, Lord Quinton, FBA

HOW TO APPLY This Trust is administered in conjunction with the Wolfson Foundation (please cross-reference)

WHO TO APPLY TO Dr Victoria Harrison, Executive Secretary, The Edith & Isaac Wolfson (Scotland) Trust, 8 Queen Anne Street, London W1M 9LD

SC NO SCO 06281   **ESTABLISHED** 1976

■ Wolseley-Hughes Charitable Trust

WHAT IS FUNDED General charitable purposes. In the main to local charities in areas where our employees are resident or may be involved. Generally recommended by employees or management of subsidiaries

WHAT IS NOT FUNDED Registered charities only. Applications from individuals, including students, are ineligible. No grants made in response to general appeals from large, national organisations nor to smaller bodies working in areas other than those set out above

WHO CAN BENEFIT Mainly local organisations benefiting employees of Wolseley plc. There is no restriction on the age; family situation; religion and culture; and social circumstances of; or disease or medical condition suffered by, the beneficiaries, though there may be a few restrictions on their professional and economic group

WHERE FUNDING CAN BE GIVEN UK

TYPE OF GRANT One-off cash donation

RANGE OF GRANTS Typical grant £100

FINANCES *Year* 1997 *Income* £21,730 *Grants* £10,323

TRUSTEES Mrs D M Boddington, F C Davies, K H D Jones, R Smith, D A Branson, M R Haines, V McCarthy, V G Nash, J Tredwell, S P Webster

WHO TO APPLY TO The Secretary, Wolseley-Hughes Charitable Trust, Wolseley plc, PO Box 18, Vines Lane, Droitwich, Worcestershire WR9 8ND

CC NO 326607   **ESTABLISHED** 1984

■ Women at Risk

WHAT IS FUNDED The relief of poverty and sickness, the preservation of health and advancement of education among women who are in need

WHO CAN BENEFIT Smaller projects that do not have well developed fundraising campaigns, benefiting: women; those disadvantaged by poverty; research workers; scientists; students; medical professionals and teachers. There is no restriction on the disease or medical condition suffered by the beneficiaries

WHERE FUNDING CAN BE GIVEN UK

FINANCES *Year* 1996 *Income* £100,000

TRUSTEES A Reed, A J Jewitt, Ms M Newham

NOTES The Trust seeks projects that meet their charitable objects, to work in partnership to fundraise and to then distribute the money raised to the partners

HOW TO APPLY To the address under Who To Apply To in writing

WHO TO APPLY TO Alec Reed, Chairperson, Women at Risk, Bedford House, Madeira Walk, Windsor, Berkshire SL4 1EU

CC NO 1059332   **ESTABLISHED** 1996

■ The Women Caring Trust

WHAT IS FUNDED To give practical help to innocent families in the troubled areas of Northern Ireland; to promote integrated education and the support of groups and organisations working for peace and reconciliation among young people. A leg-up, not a hand-out. Trustees are keen to encourage new projects, particularly cross-community, wherever possible

WHAT IS NOT FUNDED No grants to individuals. Holiday schemes outside the island of Ireland are not considered. Core-funding or salaries rarely considered. Applications from mentally or physically disabled support groups are currently rarely accepted

WHO CAN BENEFIT Integrated schools, community playgroups, play buses, youth clubs, women's groups, cross-community holiday schemes benefiting children and young adults

WHERE FUNDING CAN BE GIVEN Northern Ireland

TYPE OF GRANT Recurring costs funded for up to one year

SAMPLE GRANTS £6,000 to 174 Trust, North Belfast to help equip a new building; £3,000 to Plumbridge Community Toy Library for equipment; £2,000 to Suffolk Family Support Unit, Lisburn; £1,000 to Reach-Across, Londonderry for a summer programme; £1,000 to Voluntary Service, Belfast for repairs to a damaged playbus; £1,000 to Wave Belfast for residential course costs; £1,000 to Laurencetown, Lgnadry and Tullyish Youth Group for equipment and furnishings; £1,000 to NI Children's Holiday Scheme for holiday programme running costs; £1,000 to Little Flower Playgroup, Strabane for building renovations

FINANCES *Year* 1997 *Income* £76,036 *Grants* £50,990

TRUSTEES His Honour Judge Hubert Dunn, QC, Mrs G Darling (NI), Mrs M Garland, Mrs J Herdman (NI), Mrs G Moriarty, Mrs D Lindsay (NI), Mrs M Mackie (NI), Mrs A McKenzie-Hill, Mrs C Nelson, S Tester, CA, A Watson

PUBLICATIONS Annual Report, descriptive brochure

HOW TO APPLY Trustees meet quarterly. Grants under £500 can be approved between meetings. Applications should be in writing, with details of the proposed project, Statement of Accounts and an outline budget. All projects are visited and monitored by NI Trustees or their representatives. At any time in writing

WHO TO APPLY TO The General Secretary, Women Caring Trust, 38 Ebury Street, London SW1W 0LU *Tel* 0171-730 8883 *Fax* 0171-730 8885

CC NO 264843   **ESTABLISHED** 1972

■ James Wood Bequest Fund for the Poor

WHAT IS FUNDED General charitable purposes

WHO CAN BENEFIT There are no restrictions on the age; professional and economic group; family situation; religion and culture; and social circumstances of; or disease or medical condition suffered by, the beneficiaries

WHERE FUNDING CAN BE GIVEN Armadale, West Lothian

WHO TO APPLY TO Deputy Director of Finance, James Wood Bequest Fund for the Poor, West Lothian District Council, South Bridge Street, Bathgate, West Lothian EH48 1TS *Tel* 01506 53631

SC NO SCO19709

■ James Wood Bequest Fund

WHAT IS FUNDED General charitable purposes. Church of Scotland, historic buildings and other registered charities based in Scotland with preference being given to the central belt

WHAT IS NOT FUNDED No grants to individuals

WHO CAN BENEFIT Registered charities. There are no restrictions on the age; professional and economic group; family situation; and social circumstances of; or disease or medical condition suffered by, the beneficiaries

WHERE FUNDING CAN BE GIVEN The central belt of Scotland

TYPE OF GRANT Capital

FINANCES *Year* 1995 *Income* £115,254 *Grants* £53,100

HOW TO APPLY Annual distribution list is compiled May/June each year. No application form. Sae not required. Applications not normally acknowledged

WHO TO APPLY TO E H Webster, James Wood Bequest Fund, Messrs Mitchells Roberton, George House, 36 North Hanover Street, Glasgow G1 2AD

SC NO SCO 00459

■ The Sydney Wood Foundation

WHAT IS FUNDED Trustee tends to favour the elderly and medical research

WHAT IS NOT FUNDED No grants to individuals

WHO CAN BENEFIT Registered charities benefiting older people and retired people. There is no restriction on the disease or medical condition suffered by the beneficiaries

WHERE FUNDING CAN BE GIVEN UK

TYPE OF GRANT Donation rather than subscriptions

FINANCES *Year* 1995 *Income* £19,672 *Grants* £10,550

TRUSTEES S T J Wood, Mrs J C Wood, C Ward, D N Kilby

NOTES Please do not apply for grants

HOW TO APPLY **This Trust states that it does not respond to unsolicited applications**

WHO TO APPLY TO C Ward, The Sydney Wood Foundation, Clarks, Solicitors, Great Western House, Station Road, Reading RG6 2UX *Tel* 01734 585321

CC NO 328019   **ESTABLISHED** 1988

■ The Woodcote Trust

WHAT IS FUNDED General charitable purposes. Funds shall be used for the benefit of registered charities and selected individuals and groups with particular reference to needs of Woburn Sands and district

WHO CAN BENEFIT There are no restrictions on the age; professional and economic group; family situation; religion and culture; and social circumstances of; or disease or medical condition suffered by, the beneficiaries

WHERE FUNDING CAN BE GIVEN Preference is given to Woburn Sands and district

RANGE OF GRANTS £100–£5,000

FINANCES *Year* 1997 *Income* £50,588 *Grants* £48,461

TRUSTEES Mrs P A Henstock, M J Summerlin

WHO TO APPLY TO C S J Summerlin, The Woodcote Trust, Woodcote, Woodside, Aspley Guise, Milton Keynes, Buckinghamshire MK17 8EB

CC NO 326090   **ESTABLISHED** 1982

■ Woodlands Green Ltd

WHAT IS FUNDED Jewish charitable purposes worldwide

WHAT IS NOT FUNDED No grants to individuals, or for expeditions or scholarships

WHO CAN BENEFIT Organisations benefiting Jewish people

WHERE FUNDING CAN BE GIVEN UK and overseas

FINANCES *Year* 1995–96 *Income* £202,340

TRUSTEES A Ost, E Ost, D J A Ost, J A Ost

HOW TO APPLY To the address under Who To Apply To in writing

WHO TO APPLY TO A Ost, Woodlands Green Ltd, 19 Green Walk, London NW4 2AZ

CC NO 277299   **ESTABLISHED** 1979

■ Woodlands Trust

WHAT IS FUNDED To support church and missionary work, preaching and teaching the gospel

WHO CAN BENEFIT Organisations benefiting Christians

WHERE FUNDING CAN BE GIVEN Hereford & Worcester

RANGE OF GRANTS £92–£6,000

SAMPLE GRANTS £6,333 to London City Mission; £6,000 to Wigton Evangelical; £2,500 to North of England Ministry; £2,000 to Temple Sowerby School; £2,000 to Houghton School; £2,000 to Gideons International; £2,000 to Lighthouse Fellowship Stockton Project; £1,500 to CUMNISCU; £1,500 to Northumbria Bible College for a students support allowance; £1,000 to Edinburgh City Mission

FINANCES *Year* 1995 *Income* £140,793
Grants £46,795

TRUSTEES E Stobart, W Stobart, E P Stobart, Rev J McAllen, I B Thomas

WHO TO APPLY TO I B Thomas, Woodlands Trust, 33 Longlands Road, Carlisle, Cumbria CA3 9AD

CC NO 1015942   **ESTABLISHED** 1992

■ Woodlands Trust

WHAT IS FUNDED Preference to charities of which the Trust has special interest, knowledge or association. Particularly charities working in the fields of: hospice at home; respite care, care for carers; support and self help groups; woodlands; and horticulture

WHAT IS NOT FUNDED No grants to individuals

WHO CAN BENEFIT Organisations benefiting young adults and older people; at risk groups; carers, disabled people; those disadvantaged by poverty; ex-offenders and those at risk of offending; homeless people; those living in rural and urban areas, socially isolated people; refugees; victims of abuse, crime and domestic violence

WHERE FUNDING CAN BE GIVEN West Midlands

TYPE OF GRANT Core costs, one-off, project, research, running costs, recurring costs, salaries and start-up costs. Funding of up to three years will be considered

SAMPLE GRANTS £5,000 to Refugee Council for general/travel expenses to day centres; £4,000 to Orbis International for mobile eye hospital; £4,000 to Central Methodist for development; £3,000 to BCAT; £3,000 to Waits Organisation; £3,000 to Institute of Family Therapy; £2,000 to Birmingham Multi-handicapped for holiday scheme; £2,000 to British Trust for Conservation Volunteers; £2,000 to Magic Me; £2,000 to Henry Doubleday for leaflet/establishment of agro-forestry demonstrations and seed collection in Ghana

FINANCES *Year* 1996–97 *Income* £73,369
Grants £55,750

TRUSTEES J D W Field, J C Barratt, Miss J Steele, Mrs R M Bagshaw, Mrs J N Houston

HOW TO APPLY Six monthly. The Trust Administrator will only enter into correspondence if: (a) further information is required concerning the appeal, (b) the appeal has been placed on the Trustees' next agenda. Notification will then be given as to the Trustees' decision

WHO TO APPLY TO The Trust Administrator, Woodlands Trust, Box W, White Horse Court, 25c North Street, Bishop's Stortford, Hertfordshire CM23 2LD

CC NO 259569   **ESTABLISHED** 1969

■ Woodley Carnival Charities Fund

WHAT IS FUNDED Money raised from the Woodley Carnival is used for a wide range of charitable purposes, including disability and children's welfare

WHO CAN BENEFIT There are no restrictions on the age; professional and economic group; family situation; religion and culture; and social circumstances of; or disease or medical condition suffered by, the beneficiaries

WHERE FUNDING CAN BE GIVEN Woodley and district

FINANCES *Year* 1996 *Income* £19,524
Grants £2,800

NOTES The Carnival is held on the first or second Saturday in June

HOW TO APPLY To the address under Who To Apply To in writing. Grant requests should be received by mid-August

WHO TO APPLY TO B D Moore, Hon Treasurer, Woodley Carnival Charities Fund, National Westminster Bank plc, 131 Crockhamwell Road, Woodley, Reading, Berkshire RG5 3JX

CC NO 291732   **ESTABLISHED** 1985

■ The Woodroffe Benton Foundation

WHAT IS FUNDED (a) Financial assistance in times of disaster on behalf of individuals in need within the UK through registered charitable bodies; (b) accommodation and housing; (c) promotion of education - especially at Queen Elizabeth Grammar School in Ashbourne with scholarships, etc; (d) conservation and environment; (e) community services and facilities; (f) general charitable purposes

WHAT IS NOT FUNDED None, provided that the grants are made within the objects of the Foundation. Grants are not made outside the UK. Grants only made to registered national charities, not to individuals

WHO CAN BENEFIT Registered charities only. There are no restrictions on the age; professional and economic group; family situation; religion and culture; and social circumstances of; or disease or medical condition suffered by, the beneficiaries

WHERE FUNDING CAN BE GIVEN UK, Derbyshire (so far as education is concerned)

TYPE OF GRANT Starter finances, recurrent, research, project, one-off, core costs, feasibility studies and running costs. Funding is available for one year or less

RANGE OF GRANTS Normally between £500 and £1,500

FINANCES *Year* 1975 *Income* £159,000
Grants £90,650

TRUSTEES J J Hope (Chairman), C G Russell, FCA, G R Bartlett, Miss C Clout, K P W Stoneley, JP, MSc, FCIS, ATII (Secretary)

PUBLICATIONS None

HOW TO APPLY No application form, but advice given as to how to apply on request. Trustees meet quarterly. If applications have to be handwritten – and typewritten is preferred – then black ink should be used as applications are photocopied for the Trustees. Audited Accounts and Annual Reports are invariably required. All applications are acknowledged but further letters are only sent to successful applicants

WHO TO APPLY TO A F King, MA, FInst HA, Secretary, The Woodroffe Benton Foundation, 16 Fernleigh Court, Harrow, Middlesex HA2 6NA *Tel* 0181-428 7183

CC NO 328011   **ESTABLISHED** 1988

■ Geoffrey Woods Charitable Foundation

WHAT IS FUNDED General charitable purposes, particularly the advancement of education, relief of poverty and advancement of religion anywhere in the world. Mainly support of small localised charities of which the Trustees have personal knowledge and which absorb available income – preference for City beneficiaries. Must be registered charities

WHAT IS NOT FUNDED Time Charity. Applications from individuals, including students, are seldom considered

WHO CAN BENEFIT There are no restrictions on the age; professional and economic group; family situation; religion and culture; and social circumstances of; or disease or medical condition suffered by, the beneficiaries. However, particular favour is given to those disadvantaged by poverty

WHERE FUNDING CAN BE GIVEN UK and overseas

TYPE OF GRANT Specific projects preferred. Core funding and/or salaries rarely considered. One-off and capital grants

RANGE OF GRANTS Under £1,000–£30,000

SAMPLE GRANTS £30,000 to London Federation of Clubs for Young People; £10,000 to Gordon's School; £6,950 to Cancer Relief Macmillan Fund (and branches); £5,480 to Crown and Manor Boys Club; £5,400 to Orbis International; £5,000 to King's College, Cambridge; £5,000 to National Spinal Injuries Unit; £5,000 to Queen Elizabeth Foundation for the Disabled; £5,000 to Resource Information Services Directory; £5,000 to St George's Hospital Cancer Vaccine Campaign

FINANCES *Year* 1996 *Income* £276,795 *Grants* £253,694

TRUSTEES The Girdlers' Company and others

HOW TO APPLY Preferably during February and September to the address under Who To Apply To

WHO TO APPLY TO N H Wyldbore-Smith, Clerk To The Girdlers' Company, Geoffrey Woods Charitable Foundation, Basinghall Avenue, London EC2V 5DD

CC NO 248205   **ESTABLISHED** 1966

■ Miss Hazel Wood's Charitable Trust

WHAT IS FUNDED Grants are given for a specific item rather than to a generalised appeal whenever possible. The main areas of concern to the Trust are: the arts, architecture, the national heritage and social welfare

WHO CAN BENEFIT Arts practitioners and architects. There are few restrictions on the social circumstances of the beneficiaries

WHERE FUNDING CAN BE GIVEN UK

TYPE OF GRANT One-off grants

WHO TO APPLY TO W Brian Robertson WS, Administrator, Miss Hazel Wood's Charitable Trust, Lindsays WS, 11 Atholl Crescent, Edinburgh EH3 8HE

SC NO SCO 03658

■ The Woodstock-Sinclair Trust

This trust did not respond to CAF's request to amend its entry and, by 30 June 1998, CAF's researchers did not find financial records for later than 1995 on its file at the Charity Commission. Trusts are legally required to submit annual accounts to the Charity Commission under section 42 of the Charities Act 1993

WHAT IS FUNDED General charitable purposes

WHO CAN BENEFIT Individuals, general public. There are no restrictions on the age; professional and economic group; family situation; religion and culture; and social circumstances of; or disease or medical condition suffered by, the beneficiaries

WHERE FUNDING CAN BE GIVEN UK and overseas

WHO TO APPLY TO A Galandauer, The Woodstock-Sinclair Trust, 105 Hamilton Road, London NW11 9EE

CC NO 288624   **ESTABLISHED** 1983

■ The Woolf Charitable Trust (formerly the Sir John and Lady Woolf Charitable Trust)

WHAT IS FUNDED To charities selected by Trustees, particularly donations to medical, children's and Jewish causes. Promotion of art through loans for display by museums

WHAT IS NOT FUNDED No grants to individuals or students

WHO CAN BENEFIT Registered charities benefiting children and Jewish people. Research workers and medical professionals may be considered. There is no restriction on the disease or medical condition suffered by the beneficiaries

WHERE FUNDING CAN BE GIVEN UK

FINANCES *Year* 1996 *Income* £38,875

TRUSTEES Sir John Woolf, Jonathan C Woolf

WHO TO APPLY TO Ms Bernadette Curley, Secretary, The Woolf Charitable Trust, 214 The Chambers, Chelsea Harbour, London SW10 0XF

CC NO 261265   **ESTABLISHED** 1970

■ The A & R Woolf Charitable Trust

WHAT IS FUNDED General charitable purposes. Sundry charitable organisations and institutions which are registered charities or of similar standing and which are personally known or of personal interest to the Trustees

WHAT IS NOT FUNDED No grants to individuals

WHO CAN BENEFIT There are no restrictions on the age; professional and economic group; family situation; religion and culture; and social circumstances of; or disease or medical condition suffered by, the beneficiaries

WHERE FUNDING CAN BE GIVEN UK

RANGE OF GRANTS £100–£5,000

FINANCES *Year* 1995–96 *Income* £75,041 *Grants* £39,431

TRUSTEES Mrs J D H Rose, JP, C Rose, Dr G Edmunds, S A Rose, A M Rose

WHO TO APPLY TO Mrs J D H Rose, The A & R Woolf Charitable Trust 38 Main Avenue, Moor Park, Northwood, Middlesex HA6 2LQ *Tel* 01923 821385 *Fax* 01923 840515

CC NO 273079   **ESTABLISHED** 1977

■ The Woolmen's Company Charitable Trust

WHAT IS FUNDED To support charities concerned with the development of wool and of the City of London, eg Inner City farms

WHAT IS NOT FUNDED In accordance with Trustees' policy

WHO CAN BENEFIT There are no restrictions on the age; professional and economic group; family situation; religion and culture; and social circumstances of; or disease or medical condition suffered by, the beneficiaries

WHERE FUNDING CAN BE GIVEN UK

TYPE OF GRANT Usually one-off

RANGE OF GRANTS £50–£1,000

SAMPLE GRANTS £1,000 to Lord Mayor's Appeal; £1,000 to Newfield Charitable Trust; £445 to St Michael's Church for the choir; £300 to BWMB Keep a Sheep; £250 to Hackney City Farm

FINANCES *Year* 1998 *Income* £23,749 *Grants* £4,670

TRUSTEES The Master, Wardens and Court Assistants of the Worshipful Company of Woolmen

HOW TO APPLY In writing

WHO TO APPLY TO F Allen, The Clerk, The Woolmen's Company Charitable Trust, The Worshipful Company of Woolmen, Hollands, Hedsor Road, Bourne End, Buckinghamshire SL8 5EE

CC NO 262211   **ESTABLISHED** 1970

■ **The Woolnoth Society Charitable Trust**

WHAT IS FUNDED Welfare, housing, relief in need, community health groups, facilities for children in their local communities

WHO CAN BENEFIT Local organisations and smaller charities benefiting: children; at risk groups; those disadvantaged by poverty; homeless and socially isolated people. There is no restriction on the disease or medical condition suffered by the beneficiaries

WHERE FUNDING CAN BE GIVEN City of London and the surrounding areas

RANGE OF GRANTS £500–£5,000

SAMPLE GRANTS £5,000 to British Heart Foundation; £3,345 to KIDS, Working for Children with Special Needs; £3,000 to House of St Barnabas in Soho; £3,000 to Whitechapel Mission; £2,035 to Charterhouse in Southwark

FINANCES *Year* 1998 *Grants* £30,000

TRUSTEES Woolnoth Society

HOW TO APPLY To the address under Who To Apply To in writing

WHO TO APPLY TO R Parkinson, The Woolnoth Society Charitable Trust, 54 Tachbrook Street, Pimlico, London SW1V 2NA

CC NO 274008   **ESTABLISHED** 1977

■ **The Woolton Charitable Trust**

WHAT IS FUNDED The current policy of the Trustees is to make one-off grants to Liverpool based charities and charities specialising in research into blindness and other sight disabilities

WHAT IS NOT FUNDED No grants to non-registered charities

WHO CAN BENEFIT Registered charities benefiting medical professionals, research workers and those suffering sight loss and blindness

WHERE FUNDING CAN BE GIVEN Merseyside

TYPE OF GRANT One-off or annual

RANGE OF GRANTS £100–£2000

FINANCES *Year* 1997 *Income* £24,423 *Grants* £20,185

TRUSTEES Rt Hon Simon Frederick, Third Earl of Woolton, Ms J Sandeman-Allen

HOW TO APPLY Applications for grants can be submitted at any time, and suitable applications

are then forwarded to the Trustees for their approval

WHO TO APPLY TO The Trustees of the Woolton Charitable Trust, c/o Nigel Packer & Company, 3rd Floor, Royal Liver Building, Pier Head, Liverpool L3 1JH

CC NO 209931   **ESTABLISHED** 1959

■ **Worcester Consolidated Municipal Charity**

WHAT IS FUNDED The provision of almshouse accommodation, general charitable purposes in the area Where Funding Can Be Given

WHO CAN BENEFIT To benefit, in particular, those disadvantaged by poverty and homeless people

WHERE FUNDING CAN BE GIVEN Worcester

SAMPLE GRANTS £121,519 for relief in need; £23,584 to Worcester Municipal Exhibitions Foundation

FINANCES *Year* 1995 *Income* £393,068 *Grants* £145,103

HOW TO APPLY To the address under Who To Apply To in writing

WHO TO APPLY TO H E Wagstaff, Clerk, Worcester Consolidated Municipal Charity, 4–5 Sansome Place, Worcester, Worcestershire WR1 1UQ

CC NO 205299   **ESTABLISHED** 1977

■ **The Workman Trust**

WHAT IS FUNDED Grants are made to only those charities of which the Trust has special knowledge or association – with preference for those local to Birmingham serving the needs of the elderly and their welfare and accommodation; for medical research

WHAT IS NOT FUNDED Registered charities only. Applications from individuals, including students, are ineligible. No grants are made in response to general appeals from large, national organisations nor to smaller bodies working in areas other than those set out above. No grants for education or sporting activities

WHO CAN BENEFIT To benefit: older people; at risk groups; those disadvantaged by poverty and socially isolated people. There is no restriction on the disease or medical condition suffered by the beneficiaries

WHERE FUNDING CAN BE GIVEN Birmingham

FINANCES *Year* 1995 *Income* £13,825

TRUSTEES J M Baron, B H Singleton, J G Lowe

NOTES Trust set up by the late Mrs Edith Workman of Moseley, Birmingham

HOW TO APPLY Applications including copy of last accounts by March each year

WHO TO APPLY TO The Workman Trust, Messrs Lee, Crowder, 39 Newhall Street, Birmingham B3 3DY

CC NO 228812   **ESTABLISHED** 1963

■ **World in Need** (formerly The Phyllis Trust)

WHAT IS FUNDED To help initiate pioneering projects. Funds are often committed to financing charitable activities in which the Trust has a direct involvement; Trustees often take the initiative in seeking out organisations as well as responding to applications. The emphasis of the Trust is in supporting seed corn projects, compatible with Christian objectives, which are seen to be initiating innovative work, either in promoting the Christian religion or in the area of social welfare

Does the trust you have chosen match your needs? Haphazard applications waste postage and time

693

WHAT IS NOT FUNDED No grants to individuals or for building works

WHO CAN BENEFIT Organisations benefiting: Christians; at risk groups; those disadvantaged by poverty; and socially isolated people

WHERE FUNDING CAN BE GIVEN UK and overseas

TYPE OF GRANT Projects, recurring costs, start-up costs and funding for up to three years will be considered

RANGE OF GRANTS £5,000–£100,000

SAMPLE GRANTS £108,076 to Opportunity Trust; £88,888 to The Catch Up Project; £65,500 to The Spire Trust; £15,300 to Burrswood

FINANCES *Year* 1998 *Income* £384,755 *Grants* £277,764

TRUSTEES R Benson, J Bridgland, J C Cole, M Feilden, A Fitzalan Howard, A Greetham, A Radford, M Robson, D Saint, R Stanley, Mrs S Webster, N K Wright,

HOW TO APPLY In writing to the address under Who To Apply To

WHO TO APPLY TO N Colloff, World in Need, 103 High Street, Oxford OX1 4BW *Tel* 01865 794411

CC NO 243509   **ESTABLISHED** 1965

■ World of Islam Festival Trust

WHAT IS FUNDED Advancing the education of the public in the Islamic and Muslim cultures by means of providing a festival, exhibitions, lectures, conferences, films, books, and other similar contacts

WHO CAN BENEFIT Organisations promoting the Islamic and Muslim cultures

WHERE FUNDING CAN BE GIVEN UK and overseas

SAMPLE GRANTS £4,500 to an individual; £2,000 to Islamic Art Foundation; £1,500 to Welcome Institute – History of Medicine; £750 to Medical Aid/Children of Palestine; £500 to International Conference on Jerusalem; £300 to SPCK; £250 to Glasgow Muslims Islamic Art Leaflet; £250 to Mulberry School for Girls for library fund; £250 to Friends of Betholem University; £250 to ABCD for remedial treatment for juvenile intifada victims

FINANCES *Year* 1995 *Income* £162,737 *Grants* £11,905

TRUSTEES M Ali, Sir H Beeley, A H D Cowan, Dr E Ibrahim, A Jones, Sir J Moberley, M A Sherif, P Tripp

WHO TO APPLY TO A Duncan, World of Islam Festival Trust, 330 Thurloe Place, London SW7 2HQ

CC NO 313799   **ESTABLISHED** 1973

■ World University Service (UK) – WUS (UK)

WHAT IS FUNDED To provide funds and support for international educational and developmental programmes, and to advise refugees and asylum seekers on education and training

WHAT IS NOT FUNDED Grants to individuals can only be given to refugees in certain categories

WHO CAN BENEFIT Individuals and organisations benefiting: academic refugees or exiles, refugee students and victims of war

WHERE FUNDING CAN BE GIVEN The Trust works directly in the UK and with partner organisations in Africa, Latin America and the Middle East

TYPE OF GRANT Small educational awards and project support

RANGE OF GRANTS £20–£400, typical grant £150

SAMPLE GRANTS £500 to an individual for educational grant

FINANCES *Year* 1996 *Income* £1,756,464 *Grants* £38,000

TRUSTEES WUS Honorary Officers: Kay Pole, Matthew Judd, Heather Lamont

PUBLICATIONS Annual Report, *WUS News*, reports and videos on education and development issues

HOW TO APPLY Guidelines are issued in relation to each programme. **This Trust states that it does not respond to unsolicited applications**

WHO TO APPLY TO World University Service, 14 Dufferin Street, London EC1Y 8PD *Tel* 0171-426 5800/20 *Fax* 0171-251 1314/1315

CC NO 1003323   **ESTABLISHED** 1951

■ The Fred and Della Worms Charitable Trust

WHAT IS FUNDED General charitable purposes, but primarily the support of educational and youth work

WHAT IS NOT FUNDED No grants to individuals

WHO CAN BENEFIT There are no restrictions on the age; professional and economic group; family situation; religion and culture; and social circumstances of; or disease or medical condition suffered by, the beneficiaries. However, particular favour is given to young adults; Jewish people; teachers and governesses

WHERE FUNDING CAN BE GIVEN UK

TYPE OF GRANT Small one-off grants

RANGE OF GRANTS £20–£18,000

SAMPLE GRANTS £18,000 to Jewish Educational Development Trust; £10,000 to Aleph Society Trust; £7,090 to Friends of Covent Garden; £5,110 to Child Resettlement Fund; £5,000 to B'nai B'rith Hillel Foundation; £5,000 to Jewish Care; £5,000 to European Jewish Publication Society; £3,980 to British Friends of the Arts Museums of Israel; £2,510 to British Friends of the Hebrew University of Jerusalem; £2,000 to Joint Jewish Charitable Trust

FINANCES *Year* 1997 *Income* £110,596 *Grants* £90,537

TRUSTEES Mrs D Worms, M Paisner, MA, LLM

NOTES Trust income committed for some years

WHO TO APPLY TO F S Worms, The Fred and Della Worms Charitable Trust, 58a Crewys Road, London NW2 2AD

CC NO 200036   **ESTABLISHED** 1961

■ Worshipful Company of Builders Merchants

WHAT IS FUNDED General charitable purposes. Charities with some connection with the City of London or the building industry

WHAT IS NOT FUNDED No grants to individuals

WHO CAN BENEFIT There are no restrictions on the age; professional and economic group; family situation; religion and culture; and social circumstances of; or disease or medical condition suffered by, the beneficiaries. However, particular favour is given to beneficiaries within the Builders Merchants trade

WHERE FUNDING CAN BE GIVEN City of London, UK and overseas

SAMPLE GRANTS £2,035 to BMF for cash prizes; £2,000 to Lord Mayor's Appeal; £1,400 to Institute of BM Handbook; £750 to Master's Nomination 1996–97 – Coppercliffe Hospice; £700 as ex-gratia payments to dependants
FINANCES *Year* 1996–97 *Income* £23,072 *Grants* £12,841
TRUSTEES J S Faulder, M H Harris, M A Wright
HOW TO APPLY Telephone calls are not welcome
WHO TO APPLY TO The Clerk, Worshipful Company of Builders Merchants, 4 College Hill, London EC4R 2RA
CC NO 235467   **ESTABLISHED** 1964

■ Worshipful Company of Chartered Accountants in England and Wales General Charitable Trust

WHAT IS FUNDED The Master's Charitable Project is chosen immediately after his installation in October and closes in January. The £25,000 must be sponsored by a Liveryman of the Company. The Trust also supports educational projects in primary schools for numeracy and literacy. For this purpose a total of £20,000 is given in grants and applications must be sponsored by a Liveryman of the Company. Funding is also given to the development of the profession of chartered accountancy in the developing world
WHAT IS NOT FUNDED No casual requests for grants and donations
WHO CAN BENEFIT Those in primary education and chartered accountants in the developing world
WHERE FUNDING CAN BE GIVEN UK and overseas when it is related to the benefit of accountancy
RANGE OF GRANTS £50–£25,000
FINANCES *Year* 1996–97 *Income* £87,000 *Grants* £51,000
TRUSTEES J A Ferguson, R W J Foster, J M Renshall, CBE, G H Kingsmill, MM, D T Young, Sir J Hanley, KCMG
NOTES Casual requests for grants are unlikely to be granted
HOW TO APPLY To the address under Who To Apply To in writing
WHO TO APPLY TO John E Maxwell, Clerk to the Trustees, Worshipful Company of Chartered Accountants, 5 Cliffe House, Radnor Cliff, Folkestone, Kent CT20 2TY
CC NO 327681   **ESTABLISHED** 1988

■ The Worshipful Company of Cutlers

WHAT IS FUNDED Charities connected with cutlery and crafts or Guilds and the City of London. Scholarships given to schools and universities
WHAT IS NOT FUNDED National charities not normally aided
WHO CAN BENEFIT Scholarships given to students and travellers
WHERE FUNDING CAN BE GIVEN UK and overseas
RANGE OF GRANTS Mostly small grants of £250 to a large number of charities, but larger grants can be made at the Master's discretion
FINANCES *Year* 1996–97 *Income* £66,380 *Grants* £37,702
TRUSTEES The Master and Wardens
NOTES Travelling scholarships are given to personal applicants. Otherwise all educational grants are given on the recommendation of schools and colleges

HOW TO APPLY In writing to the address under Who To Apply To. An application form is required for travelling scholarships
WHO TO APPLY TO K S G Hinde, The Worshipful Company of Cutlers, Cutlers Hall, Warwick Lane, London EC4M 7BR *Tel* 0171-248 1866 *Fax* 0171-248 8426
CC NO 283096   **ESTABLISHED** 1961

■ The Worshipful Company of Engineers' Charitable Trust Fund

WHAT IS FUNDED To encourage study and research in engineering with reference to multi-disciplinary projects. Medical research, conservation, art galleries, cultural centres, libraries and museums will be considered. Support may also be given for information technology and computers; personnel and human resource centres; social care professional bodies and rural community councils
WHAT IS NOT FUNDED Local or community-based projects
WHO CAN BENEFIT National organisations or individuals. Funding may be given to young adults, older people and disabled people. Academics, chemists, medical professionals, research workers, scientists, students, and teachers and governesses
WHERE FUNDING CAN BE GIVEN UK
TYPE OF GRANT Bursaries and scholarships, prizes for engineering excellence or achievement
RANGE OF GRANTS £100–£5,000
SAMPLE GRANTS £2,000 to Royal Greenwich Observatory for an exchange of engineers between UK and Australia; £1,000 to an individual – Cadzow Smith Award for final year undergraduate studies; £1,000 to Friends of St Peter's (Tower of London) for the organ fund; £1,000 to Ironbridge Gorge Museum Development Trust; £500 to an individual at City University for MEng bursary; £500 to an individual studying food technology as an award for a paper presented at ICEF–7 Conference; £500 to an individual consulting engineer as a young consulting engineer award; £500 to City and Guilds of London Institute; £500 to Lord Mayor of London Appeal; £500 to Sir Geoffrey de Havilland Memorial Fund
FINANCES *Year* 1997 *Income* £30,443 *Grants* £12,840
TRUSTEES L F Turner, Sir Frederick Crawford, Dr J C Smith, Dr D S Mitchell
HOW TO APPLY To the address under Who To Apply To. Applications at any time for consideration by the Trustees
WHO TO APPLY TO Cdr B D Gibson, Clerk, Worshipful Company of Engineers, Kiln Bank, Bodle Street Green, Hailsham, East Sussex BN27 4UA *Tel* 01323 833554 *Fax* 01323 833979
CC NO 289819   **ESTABLISHED** 1984

■ The Worshipful Company of Founders Charities

WHAT IS FUNDED Connected with Foundry Industry, education and support for the young or the old. Accommodation and housing, infrastructure development, hospice at home. respite care, hospices, holidays and outings will be considered
WHAT IS NOT FUNDED No grants to national appeals and larger charities
WHO CAN BENEFIT Needy dependants of members of the Company or in the Foundry Industry for one trust, open for individual application for the remaining trusts. Individuals and organisations

benefiting: people of all ages; parents and children; widows and widowers will be considered. Ex-service and service people; medical professionals; students; volunteers; Christians; Church of England and Quakers may be supported. Funding may also be given to at risk groups, carers, disabled people, homeless people, and victims of abuse, crime and domestic violence. There is no restriction on the disease or medical condition suffered by the beneficiaries

WHERE FUNDING CAN BE GIVEN England

TYPE OF GRANT One-off. Funding is available for up to three years

RANGE OF GRANTS £200–£1,000

FINANCES *Year* 1997 *Income* £40,000
Grants £40,000

TRUSTEES The Master Wardens and Commonalty of the Founders

NOTES Ten grants of £1,000 each were given as bursaries for studying materials engineering at the universities of Birmingham and Nottingham

HOW TO APPLY Before end of May in each year

WHO TO APPLY TO The Clerk, The Worshipful Company of Founders Charities, Founders' Hall, 1 Cloth Fair, London EC2Y 8DL

CC NO 222905   **ESTABLISHED** 1365

■ The Worshipful Company of Glass Sellers' Charity Trust

WHAT IS FUNDED Support is given particularly to those charities with some connection with the City of London or glass industry, and education specifically related to glass

WHO CAN BENEFIT Adults working in the glass industry and students in education specifically related to glass

WHERE FUNDING CAN BE GIVEN UK

TYPE OF GRANT Charitable donations

FINANCES *Year* 1996 *Income* £21,000
Grants £12,000

TRUSTEES R Long, M R Nathan, A S Miller, R L Thomas

NOTES All figures given in Finances are approximate

HOW TO APPLY To the address under Who To Apply To. Trustees meet at quarterly intervals to consider applications. Appeals must be accompanied by most recently published Annual Report and Accounts. Applications will not be acknowledged

WHO TO APPLY TO Robin Long, Chairman of the Trustees, Worshipful Company of Glass Sellers' Charity Trust, 73 Pilgrims Way, Sevenoaks, Kent TN15 6TD

CC NO 253973   **ESTABLISHED** 1967

■ Worshipful Company of Innholders General Charity Fund

WHAT IS FUNDED General charitable purposes

WHAT IS NOT FUNDED No grants to individuals

WHO CAN BENEFIT There are no restrictions on the age; professional and economic group; family situation; religion and culture; or disease or medical condition suffered of, the beneficiaries

WHERE FUNDING CAN BE GIVEN UK

TYPE OF GRANT Mainly one-off, but also recurrent

FINANCES *Year* 1996 *Income* £78,399
Grants £32,983

TRUSTEES J R Edwardes Jones, N L Hall, MBE, H A Mellery-Pratt, G I M McDonald

WHO TO APPLY TO J R Edwardes Jones, Clerk, Worshipful Company of Innholders General Charity Fund, Druces & Attlee, Salisbury House, London Wall, London EC2M 5PS

CC NO 270948   **ESTABLISHED** 1976

■ The Worshipful Company of Launderers Benevolent Trust Fund

WHAT IS FUNDED General charitable purposes at the Master, Wardens and Court of Assistants of the Company's discretion

WHO CAN BENEFIT Individuals and registered charities normally connected with the laundry and dry cleaning and allied trades. There are no restrictions on the age; professional and economic group; family situation; religion and culture; and social circumstances of; or disease or medical condition suffered by, the beneficiaries

WHERE FUNDING CAN BE GIVEN Mainly London

RANGE OF GRANTS £50–£1,000

SAMPLE GRANTS £1,000 to Launderers and Cleaners Education Trust; £1,000 to Daybrook; £1,000 to Jubilee Sailing Trust; £703 to an individual; £500 to Southward Playgrounds Trust

FINANCES *Year* 1997 *Income* £16,718
Grants £10,492

TRUSTEES The Master and Wardens of the Company

WHO TO APPLY TO The Clerk, Worshipful Co of Launderers Benevolent Trust Fund, Glaziers Hall, 9 Montague Close, London Bridge, London SE1 9DD

CC NO 262750   **ESTABLISHED** 1963

■ Charity Fund of the Worshipful Company of Paviors

WHAT IS FUNDED General charitable purposes. To support and benefit charities, charitable institutions and charitable purposes in or operating principally in the City of London with power to assist work of a national nature

WHO CAN BENEFIT There are no restrictions on the age; professional and economic group; family situation; religion and culture; and social circumstances of; or disease or medical condition suffered by, the beneficiaries

WHERE FUNDING CAN BE GIVEN City of London, occasionally elsewhere in the UK

RANGE OF GRANTS £50–£13,100

SAMPLE GRANTS £13,100 to Charity Fund; £2,027 to Amberley Chalk Pits Museum; £650 to City of London Freemans School for a bursary; £200 to Croydon College for prizes; £50 to City of London Freemans School for prizes

FINANCES *Year* 1995 *Income* £26,024
Grants £16,027

WHO TO APPLY TO R F Coe, Clerk to the Paviors Company, 154 Dukes Avenue, New Malden, Surrey KT3 4HR

CC NO 257671   **ESTABLISHED** 1934

■ Worshipful Company of Pewterers 500th Anniversary Trust

WHAT IS FUNDED To further scientific medical research into the effects of heavy metals on the brain. Funding is given to a Research Fellow at the Institute of Neurology, University of London

696

Think carefully about every application. Is it justified?

WHAT IS NOT FUNDED This charitable Trust is geared specifically to maintaining research at the Institute of Neurology. It is not open to applications for support by other bodies

WHO CAN BENEFIT Research workers

WHERE FUNDING CAN BE GIVEN London

TYPE OF GRANT Research

FINANCES *Year* 1997 *Income* £37,800 *Grants* £25,600

TRUSTEES J D Campling, R G Wildash, J R W Peacock

HOW TO APPLY **This Trust states that it does not respond to unsolicited applications**

WHO TO APPLY TO The Clerk to the Trustees, Worshipful Company of Pewterers 500th Anniversary Trust, Pewterers Hall, Oat Lane, London EC2V 7DE

CC NO 267420   ESTABLISHED 1974

■ The Worshipful Company of Shipwrights Charitable Fund

WHAT IS FUNDED Support confined to charities associated with maritime industry and the City of London, including youth and educational work

WHAT IS NOT FUNDED Donations will only be granted to activities with a waterborne element

WHO CAN BENEFIT Variable, but who are citizens of the United Kingdom of Great Britain and Northern Ireland. This includes children, young adults, students and seafarers and fishermen

WHERE FUNDING CAN BE GIVEN UK

TYPE OF GRANT Recurrent and one-off

SAMPLE GRANTS £4,000 to Royal Merchant Navy School Foundation for the support of pupils; £2,500 to Missions to Seamen; £2,500 to National Maritime Museum; £2,150 to George Green's School, Isle of Dogs for extra-curricular activities/prizes; £2,000 to City of London Outward Bound Association; £2,000 to City of London Sea Cadets Corps; £2,000 to Ocean Youth Club; £2,000 for the purchase of Thames cutter for rowing for George Green's School; £1,500 to Royal National Mission to Deep Sea Fishermen; £1,500 to RYA 'Sailability' for a disabled regatta

FINANCES *Year* 1997–98 *Income* £134,000 *Grants* £79,000

TRUSTEES The Wardens of the Company

HOW TO APPLY In writing to the Clerk, Shipwrights' Company at the address under Who To Apply To

WHO TO APPLY TO The Clerk, The Worshipful Company of Shipwrights Charitable Fund, Ironmonger's Hall, Barbican, London EC2Y 8AA *Tel* 0171-606 2376 *Fax* 0171-600 3519

CC NO 262403   ESTABLISHED 1948

■ The Worshipful Company of Turners

This trust did not respond to CAF's request to amend its entry and, by 30 June 1998, CAF's researchers did not find financial records for later than 1995 on its file at the Charity Commission. Trusts are legally required to submit annual accounts to the Charity Commission under section 42 of the Charities Act 1993

WHAT IS FUNDED Education and other charitable purposes

WHO CAN BENEFIT Children, young adults and students

WHERE FUNDING CAN BE GIVEN London and UK

RANGE OF GRANTS Grants of £1,000 or less

NOTES Support is mainly given to the craft of turning in the form of prizes medals and gifts to schools

HOW TO APPLY To the address under Who To Apply To in writing

WHO TO APPLY TO R S Ouvery, Clerk, The Worshipful Company of Turners, Apothecaries Hall, 33A Hill Avenue, Amersham, Buckinghamshire HP6 5BX

CC NO 267372   ESTABLISHED 1974

■ The Worshipful Company of Weavers Textile Education Fund (formerly The Worshipful Company of Weavers General Charitable Trust Fund)

WHAT IS FUNDED Education in textile subjects, through providing scholarships to weaving students and assisting textile educational establishments to provide the training necessary to equip students to work in the modern textile industry

WHAT IS NOT FUNDED Open only to British subjects

WHO CAN BENEFIT Postgraduate students, educational establishments and textile designers and workers in the textile industry

WHERE FUNDING CAN BE GIVEN UK

TYPE OF GRANT Bursaries, scholarships and awards in connection with textile education, especially woven textiles

FINANCES *Year* 1996 *Income* £48,951 *Grants* £17,700

TRUSTEES The Worshipful Company of Weavers: S A A Block, CC, Rt Hon Lord Gorell, E L Shannon, C M Wigan, Rt Hon Lord Brain, O A E J Makower, J C M Graham, C J Bourne, M A C Winterton, TD, R D N Day, N F Townsend, JP, J G Bevan, Sir B Fairbairn, Bt, G E L Yeandle, Sir R Baker Wilbraham, Bt, DL, J G Y Radcliffe, TD, Hon G W M Chubb, N R Winterton, MP, M C Tubbs, R H W Graham-Palmer, R D B Mynors

HOW TO APPLY Further information obtainable from the Clerk to the Company

WHO TO APPLY TO Mrs Freda Newcombe, The Clerk of the Weavers' Company, Worshipful Company of Weavers Textile Education Fund, Saddlers' House, Gutter Lane, London EC2V 6BR

CC NO 238076   ESTABLISHED 1933

■ Wrexham Foyer

WHAT IS FUNDED General charitable purposes for the benefit of the community of Wrexham, in particular, the advancement of education, the relief of sickness, poverty and distress and the preservation and protection of good health

WHO CAN BENEFIT Organisations benefiting children, young adults, students, at risk groups, those disadvantaged by poverty and socially isolated people. There is no restriction on the disease or medical condition suffered by the beneficiaries. Medical professionals and research workers may be considered

WHERE FUNDING CAN BE GIVEN Borough of Wrexham

FINANCES *Year* 1997 *Income* £42,968

WHO TO APPLY TO J P Lloyd, Wrexham Foyer, Kelso House, 13 Grosvenor Road, Wrexham LL11 1BS

CC NO 1068300   ESTABLISHED 1998

■ The Diana Edgson Wright Charitable Trust

WHAT IS FUNDED General charitable purposes. To support a small number of charities

WHO CAN BENEFIT There are no restrictions on the age; professional and economic group; family

situation; religion and culture; and social circumstances of; or disease or medical condition suffered by, the beneficiaries

WHERE FUNDING CAN BE GIVEN UK

RANGE OF GRANTS £100–£16,000

SAMPLE GRANTS £16,000 to Sustainable London Trust; £3,500 to Red Cross; £2,500 to Marlborough College; £2,000 to Royal British Legion; £2,000 to World Wildlife Fund; £1,500 to Little Chart (Kent) Parochial Church Council; £1,000 to Action Aid; £1,000 to Artists General Benevolent Institution; £1,000 to Ashford Sea Cadets; £1,000 to RNLI

FINANCES *Year* 1996 *Income* £35,889 *Grants* £37,500

TRUSTEES R H V Moorhead, H C D Moorhead, P E Wright

WHO TO APPLY TO R H V Moorhead, The Diana Edgson Wright Charitable Trust, Henry Moorhead and Co, 2 Stade Street, Hythe, Kent CT21 6BD

CC NO 327737   **ESTABLISHED** 1987

■ John William Wright Deceased Trust

WHAT IS FUNDED A proportion of grants is usually given to Methodist charities. Particularly charities working in the fields of: charity or voluntary umbrella bodies; religion; arts, culture and recreation; health facilities and buildings; medical studies and research; conservation and environment; schools and colleges and community services and facilities

WHAT IS NOT FUNDED No grants to individuals

WHO CAN BENEFIT There are no restrictions on the age; professional and economic group; family situation; religion and culture; and social circumstances of; or disease or medical condition suffered by, the beneficiaries

WHERE FUNDING CAN BE GIVEN Preference to Lincoln and Lincolnshire, only very exceptionally are grants made outside this area

TYPE OF GRANT For capital expenditure of a non-recurring nature. The Trust has supported conservation and preservation projects and projects supporting children with special needs. Buildings, one-off and funding for one year or less will be considered

RANGE OF GRANTS £100–£1,000

SAMPLE GRANTS £1,000 to All Saints Church Lincoln for refurbishment and heating of the hall; £750 to Salvation Army for refurbishment of the hall; £500 to NSPCC for Lincoln project; £500 to National Children's Home for Lincolnshire Caring Together Project; £500 to SENSE for contribution to building bungalows

FINANCES *Year* 1997 *Income* £14,417 *Grants* £8,210

TRUSTEES R D Atkinson, P R Strange, Miss M Hall, Mrs G Harrison

HOW TO APPLY By letter with details of cost and applicants contribution and a copy of the accounts. Any application from outside Lincolnshire should telephone first to enquire if there is any probability their application will be considered

WHO TO APPLY TO Messrs Andrew & Co, (Ref JD), John William Wright Deceased Trust, St Swithin's Square, Lincoln, Lincolnshire LN2 1HB *Tel* 01522 512123 *Fax* 01522 546713

CC NO 249619   **ESTABLISHED** 1964

■ Wychdale Limited

WHAT IS FUNDED To advance religion in accordance with the Orthodox Jewish faith and for such other general charitable purposes

WHO CAN BENEFIT Jewish people

WHERE FUNDING CAN BE GIVEN UK and overseas

TYPE OF GRANT At the discretion of the Trustees

FINANCES *Year* 1997 *Income* £114,623 *Grants* £160,661

TRUSTEES C D Schlaff, J Schlaff, Mrs Z Schlaff

WHO TO APPLY TO The Secretary, Wychdale Limited, 89 Darenth Road, London N16 6EB

CC NO 267447   **ESTABLISHED** 1974

■ Wychville Ltd

WHAT IS FUNDED Jewish organisations and general charitable purposes

WHO CAN BENEFIT Organisations benefiting Jewish people

WHERE FUNDING CAN BE GIVEN UK

FINANCES *Year* 1994–95 *Income* £199,137 *Grants* £178,500

TRUSTEES B Englander, Mrs B R Englander, E Englander, Mrs S Englander

HOW TO APPLY To the address under Who To Apply To in writing

WHO TO APPLY TO Berisch Englander, Trustee, Wychville Ltd, 44 Leweston Place, London N16 6RU

CC NO 267584   **ESTABLISHED** 1973

■ The Wyford Charitable Trust

WHAT IS FUNDED At Trustees' discretion – current emphasis on animal welfare and organisations for the elderly. Including charities working in the fields of: accommodation and housing; churches; health facilities and buildings; conservation; endangered species; playgrounds and care in the community

WHAT IS NOT FUNDED No non-registered charities, no grants to individuals

WHO CAN BENEFIT Animal welfare. Organisations benefiting children and older people; retired people; widows and widowers and those suffering from asthma

WHERE FUNDING CAN BE GIVEN UK and Switzerland

TYPE OF GRANT At the discretion of the Trustees. Capital and core costs. Funding of one year or less will be considered

RANGE OF GRANTS £1,000–£2600

SAMPLE GRANTS Grants given for core costs:; £5,000 to Tibet House Trust; £2,600 to Distressed Gentlefolk's Aid Association; £2,500 to St John Ambulance; £2,000 to The Animal Welfare Trust; £2,000 to PDSA; £2,000 to RUKBA; £2,000 to Pine Ridge Dog Sanctuary; £2,000 to London Clinic Diamond Jubilee Fund; £1,500 to Pro Senectute Pour La Vieilesse; £1,400 to National Asthma Campaign

FINANCES *Year* 1996–97 *Income* £28,719 *Grants* £28,428

TRUSTEES Robert Fleming Trustee Co Ltd, Roderick J Fleming, Nicholas R D Powell

HOW TO APPLY In writing. No application forms or guidelines issued

WHO TO APPLY TO The Trust Manager, The Wyford Charitable Trust, Robert Fleming Trustee Co Ltd, 25 Copthall Avenue, London EC2R 7DR

CC NO 298093   **ESTABLISHED** 1987

■ The Anthony and Gwendoline Wylde Memorial Charity

WHAT IS FUNDED General charitable purposes

WHO CAN BENEFIT There are no restrictions on the age; professional and economic group; family situation; religion and culture; and social circumstances of; or disease or medical condition suffered by, the beneficiaries

WHERE FUNDING CAN BE GIVEN Preference for Stourbridge and Kinver

RANGE OF GRANTS £50–£3,000

SAMPLE GRANTS £3,000 to St Thomas Organ Fund for organ repairs; £1,000 to County Air Ambulance; £1,000 to the Stourbridge Navigation Trust for restoration of offices; £1,000 to Kinver Community Bus Ltd; £1,000 to WHAT Centre; £600 to RNIB talking books services; £520 to Old Park School for equipment; £500 to Kinver Methodist Church for building work; £500 each to two individuals for educational purposes

FINANCES *Year* 1997 *Income* £53,870 *Grants* £34,036

WHO TO APPLY TO Mrs P I Gardener, The Anthony and Gwendoline Wylde Memorial Charity, Remlane House, 25–27 Hagley Road, Stourbridge, West Midlands DY8 1QH *Tel* 01384 342075

CC NO 700239   **ESTABLISHED** 1988

■ The Wyndham Charitable Trust

WHAT IS FUNDED General charitable purposes

WHAT IS NOT FUNDED No grants to individuals

WHO CAN BENEFIT Recognised charities. There are no restrictions on the age; professional and economic group; family situation; religion and culture; and social circumstances of; or disease or medical condition suffered by, the beneficiaries

WHERE FUNDING CAN BE GIVEN UK and overseas

TYPE OF GRANT One-off (often recurring)

RANGE OF GRANTS £10–£5,000; typical £100

SAMPLE GRANTS £4,200 to Anti-Slavery International; £1,000 to Christain Aid; £590 to PCC of St Mary, Bryanston Square with St Mark's St Marylebone; £500 to International Glaucoma Association to help establish a Research Chair; £500 to Imperial Cancer Research Fund

FINANCES *Year* 1997–98 *Income* £15,000 *Grants* £15,160

TRUSTEES J Gaselee, J Gaselee

NOTES The Trustees decide on all grants and do not consider applications

HOW TO APPLY **This Trust states that it does not respond to unsolicited applications**

WHO TO APPLY TO J S Gaselee, Trustee, The Wyndham Charitable Trust, 16 Shouldham Street, London W1H 5FG

CC NO 259313   **ESTABLISHED** 1969

■ Wyre Animal Welfare

WHAT IS FUNDED The Trust supports the rehousing of homeless animals and gives financial assistance to low income families to neuter and spay animals

WHO CAN BENEFIT Individuals or families, animal welfare organisations. All individuals and families must be on income support

WHERE FUNDING CAN BE GIVEN UK with preferences to Lancashire, and if funds are sufficient, overseas

TYPE OF GRANT Very small grants, eg for OAP's vets fees, a few to animal charities, and medical fees for animal rescue. Running costs are considered

RANGE OF GRANTS £200–£250

FINANCES *Year* 1997 *Income* £16,283 *Grants* £650

TRUSTEES Mrs Evans, R A Dodd, Mrs Brown

NOTES Majority of income spent on running costs, ie pet food, veterinary fees, cleaning, etc

HOW TO APPLY In person at the Wyre Animal Welfare Shop, otherwise in writing

WHO TO APPLY TO R A Dodd, Wyre Animal Welfare, 87 Poulton Road, Fleetwood, Lancashire FY7 6TQ

CC NO 1025042   **ESTABLISHED** 1993

■ The Wyseliot Charitable Trust

WHAT IS FUNDED Medical, especially cancer research and care, welfare, arts organisations including music, visual arts and literature

WHAT IS NOT FUNDED New charities sending circular appeal and large national charities are not supported. Charities with large reserves or high administrative costs

WHO CAN BENEFIT Actors and entertainment professionals; medical professionals, nurses and doctors; musicians and writers and poets. There are few restrictions by social circumstances, or disease or medical condition suffered by the beneficiaries

WHERE FUNDING CAN BE GIVEN UK. Charities working in a specific location, except in London, will not be supported

FINANCES *Year* 1995–96 *Income* £54,374

TRUSTEES A E G Raphael, E A D Rose, J H Rose

NOTES Charities researching cancer care are welcome to send information to the Trust

HOW TO APPLY To the address under Who To Apply To in writing, but note Restrictions. Also be aware that new charities are supported each year

WHO TO APPLY TO J H Rose, Trustee, The Wyseliot Charitable Trust, 17 Chelsea Square, London SW3 6LF

CC NO 257219   **ESTABLISHED** 1968

■ The Wyvill Charitable Trust

This trust did not respond to CAF's request to amend its entry and, by 30 June 1998, CAF's researchers did not find financial records for later than 1995 on its file at the Charity Commission. Trusts are legally required to submit annual accounts to the Charity Commission under section 42 of the Charities Act 1993

WHAT IS FUNDED General charitable purposes

WHAT IS NOT FUNDED No grants to individuals or for travel bursaries

WHO CAN BENEFIT Registered charities only. There are no restrictions on the age; professional and economic group; family situation; religion and culture; and social circumstances of; or disease or medical condition suffered by, the beneficiaries

WHERE FUNDING CAN BE GIVEN Mainly Northamptonshire

TRUSTEES A F Saxby, J F Mereweather, M W Saxby

WHO TO APPLY TO J F Mereweather, The Wyvill Charitable Trust, 14 Wold Road, Burton Latimer, Northamptonshire NN15 5PN

CC NO 266936   **ESTABLISHED** 1973

■ The Xerox (UK) Trust

WHAT IS FUNDED The advancement of equality of opportunity, the cause of the disabled and disadvantaged or terminally ill and youth

WHAT IS NOT FUNDED No grants to individuals, religious organisations or national bodies

WHO CAN BENEFIT Usually local mid-sized organisations benefiting: children; young adults; at risk groups; disabled people; those disadvantaged by poverty and socially isolated people

WHERE FUNDING CAN BE GIVEN UK

TYPE OF GRANT One-off grants

RANGE OF GRANTS £2,500–£5,000

SAMPLE GRANTS £5,000 to St Basil's Centre for Homeless People; £5,000 to Drugsline Chabad; £5,000 to REACT; £5,000 to Royal Academy of Music; £3,300 to Watford Peace Memorial Hospice; £3,200 to the National Information Forum; £2,500 to Jubilee Sailing Trust

FINANCES *Year* 1997 *Income* £69,273 *Grants* £29,000

TRUSTEES S M Cronin, S W Pantling, C J Pinney

HOW TO APPLY Applications are reviewed half yearly

WHO TO APPLY TO S C Dillon, The Xerox (UK) Trust, Bridge House, Oxford Road, Uxbridge UB8 1HS

CC NO 284698   **ESTABLISHED** 1982

■ Yad Voezer Limited

WHAT IS FUNDED (a) The relief of persons with physical, mental or learning disabilities in accordance with the principles of the Orthodox Jewish faith; (b) the relief of poverty; (c) other general charitable purposes

WHO CAN BENEFIT To benefit: disabled people; those suffering from mental illness; those disadvantaged by poverty; and Jewish people

WHERE FUNDING CAN BE GIVEN Stamford Hill

FINANCES *Year* 1997 *Income* £440,142

TRUSTEES R E Landau, R Spitzer, A Singer

WHO TO APPLY TO Mrs Z Landau, Yad Voezer Limited, 80 Queen Elizabeth's Walk, London N16 5UQ

CC NO 1032490   **ESTABLISHED** 1993

■ The Yadiran Trust

WHAT IS FUNDED General charitable purposes

WHO CAN BENEFIT There are no restrictions on the age; professional and economic group; family situation; religion and culture; and social circumstances of; or disease or medical condition suffered by, the beneficiaries

WHERE FUNDING CAN BE GIVEN UK and overseas

TRUSTEES Dr R Rastegor, Mrs S Rastigor, A R Rastigor, A D Kerman

WHO TO APPLY TO A D Kerman, The Yadiran Trust, 79 New Cavendish Street, London W1M 8AQ

CC NO 1069122   **ESTABLISHED** 1997

■ Yamanouchi European Foundation

WHAT IS FUNDED The promotion of medical and related scientific programmes, the integration of science and clinical research, the support of educational lectures and discussions to promote or sponsor exchange of views, to support general charitable purposes

WHO CAN BENEFIT Scientific research institutes, universities, research workers and medical professionals

WHERE FUNDING CAN BE GIVEN UK and overseas, particularly Europe

SAMPLE GRANTS $50,000 to Centro Superior de Investigaciones Científicas; $10,000 to Stichting Cliniclowns Nederland (NL); $10,000 to VIDAS (Italy); $10,000 to ASBL (Belgium); $5,000 to Associacao Sol (Portugal)

FINANCES *Year* 1997 *Income* $9,958,298 *Grants* $100,000

TRUSTEES S Morioka (Chairman), M Onoda, Dr K Takahashi, A Paasman, S Takahashi, H Uchiyama, D H Ferguson, Dr J M Lackie, J F Harford

NOTES All figures in the Finances and Sample Grants are in US Dollars

HOW TO APPLY To the address under Who To Apply To in writing

WHO TO APPLY TO D Ferguson, Trustee, Yamanouchi European Foundation, Yamanouchi House, Pyrford Road, West Byfleet, Surrey KT14 6RA

CC NO 1036344   **ESTABLISHED** 1993

■ The Yapp Education and Research Trust

WHAT IS FUNDED To promote and assist the advancement of education and learning, and of scientific and medical research. In general, the Trustees prefer to fund capital expenditure rather than revenue expenditure. Grants for the advancement of education and learning are normally limited to schools, universities, polytechnic colleges, and similar institutions

WHAT IS NOT FUNDED Grants are made to applicants having charitable status only. Grants are not made to: (a) individuals; (b) applicants who still need to raise over £20,000 in total; (c) university expeditions; (d) school buildings or development funds; (e) applicants who have received a grant from the Trust within the preceding three years

WHO CAN BENEFIT Applicants having charitable status only. Smaller, locally-based charities are preferred. Children, young adults, students, academics, scientists and research workers may benefit

WHERE FUNDING CAN BE GIVEN UK

TYPE OF GRANT Outright grants only, not loans. Recurring grants are not normally made

FINANCES *Year* 1996 *Income* £107,065 *Grants* £81,550

TRUSTEES Rev T C Brooke, Miss A J Norman, M W Rapinet, P M Williams, P G Murray

NOTES The Trustees meet three times a year, usually in March, July and November, to allocate grants. Completed grant application forms need to be submitted at least six weeks before the date of the Meeting at which they are to be considered

HOW TO APPLY Applicants should apply in writing to the address under Who To Apply To giving brief details of the purpose for which a grant is sought and the total amount which the applicant still needs to raise. Eligible applicants are then asked to complete a short grant application form

WHO TO APPLY TO L V Waumsley, Secretary, The Yapp Education and Research Trust, c/o Kidd Rapinet Solicitors, 14–15 Craven Street, London WC2N 5AD

CC NO 257145   **ESTABLISHED** 1968

■ The Yapp Welfare Trust

WHAT IS FUNDED To promote and assist any charitable activity directed to: (a) care and housing of old people, (b) youth clubs, youth hostels, students hostels or like institutions connected with the welfare of youth, (c) care or special education of people who are mentally or physically disabled, (d) advancement of moral welfare

WHAT IS NOT FUNDED Grants are made to applicants having charitable status only. Grants are not made to: (a) individuals, (b) applicants who still need to raise over £10,000 in total, (c) university expeditions, (d) school building or development funds, or (e) applicants who have received a grant from the Trust within the preceding three years. The advancement of religion as such is not regarded as an eligible object of the Trust

WHO CAN BENEFIT Applicants having charitable status only. Smaller locally-based charities are preferred benefiting: children, young adults and the elderly, students, and those who are mentally and physically disabled

WHERE FUNDING CAN BE GIVEN UK

TYPE OF GRANT Outright grants only, not loans. Recurring grants are not normally made. In general, the Trustees prefer to fund capital expenditure rather than revenue expenditure

FINANCES *Year* 1997 *Income* £198,706 *Grants* £184,485

TRUSTEES Rev T C Brooke, Miss A J Norman, M W Rapinet, P M Williams, P G Murray

NOTES The Trustees meet three times a year, usually in March, July and November, to allocate grants. Completed Grant Application Forms need to be submitted at least six weeks before the date of the Meeting at which they are to be considered

HOW TO APPLY Applicants should apply in writing to the address under Who To Apply To giving brief details of the purpose for which a grant is sought and the total amount which the applicant still needs to raise. Eligible applicants are then asked to complete a short Grant Application Form

WHO TO APPLY TO Claire Bowden-Dan, The Yapp Welfare Trust, 14–15 Craven Street, London WC2N 5AD

CC NO 257144   **ESTABLISHED** 1968

■ Yardley Great Trust

WHAT IS FUNDED To relieve either generally or individually persons resident in the area of benefit who are in condition of need, hardship or distress. Projects which benefit the community. Particularly charities working in the fields of: support for voluntary and community organisations; community centres and village halls; community transport; day centres; holidays and outings; meals provision and playschemes

WHAT IS NOT FUNDED Grants will not be paid in relief of rates, taxes or other public funds

WHO CAN BENEFIT Individuals and organisations benefiting people of all ages in the ancient parish of Great Yardley in Birmingham

WHERE FUNDING CAN BE GIVEN The ancient parish of Great Yardley in Birmingham which incorporates Acocks Green, Billesley (part), Brandwood (part), Fox Hollies, Hall Green, Highters Heath, Hodge Hill (part), Moseley (part), Shard End, Sheldon, Small Heath (part), Sparkbrook (part), Sparkhill, Stechford, Yardley, Yardley Wood (part)

TYPE OF GRANT Usually one-off. Buildings, capital, feasibility studies, project and start-up costs funded for one year or less will be considered

RANGE OF GRANTS No limit

SAMPLE GRANTS £10,474 to Hall Green PCC for community hall refurbishment; £10,000 to St Richards PCC for kitchen refurbishment; £5,000 to Victim Support; £4,200 to Immanuel PCC for community hall car park; £4,000 to Yardley PCC for Trust School refurbishment; £3,000 to Youthwise for equipment; £2,468 to Garretts Green Nursery for equipment; £2,000 to Stechford Youth Project for equipment; £2,000 to St Basil's Centre for refurbishment; £1,300 to St Mary's PCC for kitchen refurbishment

FINANCES *Year* 1997 *Income* £133,760 *Grants* £100,490

TRUSTEES 5 Ex-officio (incumbents of 5 Parishes), 2 Nominative (City Council), 7 Lay – Co-optative

HOW TO APPLY Groups/Organisations must apply in writing enclosing a business plan or similar. Individuals must apply on a standard application form via a referral agency (CAB, Social Services, Probation Service, Council Neighbourhood Office, Priest, Doctor, Head Teacher). Trustees meet monthly (except August) to consider grant applications

WHO TO APPLY TO L K Moreton, Clerk to the Trustees, Yardley Great Trust, Old Brookside, Yardley Fields Road, Birmingham B33 8QL *Tel* 0121-784 7889 *Fax* 0121-785 1386

CC NO 216082   **ESTABLISHED** 1300

■ The Dennis Alan Yardy Charitable Trust

WHAT IS FUNDED Medicine and health, welfare, education, humanities, religion, international, general charitable purposes

WHAT IS NOT FUNDED No grants to individuals

WHO CAN BENEFIT Small local projects, national organisations, established organisations. There are no restrictions on the age; professional and economic group; family situation; religion and culture; and social circumstances of; or disease or medical condition suffered by, the beneficiaries. However particular favour is given to children and young adults, students, teachers, medical professionals and clergy. Also favoured are at risk groups, those disadvantaged by poverty and the socially isolated. Preference is given to religious beneficiaries and the sick

WHERE FUNDING CAN BE GIVEN Northamptonshire, UK and overseas

TYPE OF GRANT One-off

FINANCES *Year* 1995 *Income* £439,461 *Grants* £12,000

TRUSTEES C A Yardy, D A Yardy, J Creek

HOW TO APPLY In writing at any time

WHO TO APPLY TO Ms C A Yardy, (Trustee), Grange Farm, Welford Road, Spratton, Northampton NN6 8LA

CC NO 1039719   **ESTABLISHED** 1993

■ The Yates Foundation

WHAT IS FUNDED General charitable purposes

WHO CAN BENEFIT There are no restrictions on the age; professional and economic group; family situation; religion and culture; and social circumstances of; or disease or medical condition suffered by, the beneficiaries

WHERE FUNDING CAN BE GIVEN UK

WHO TO APPLY TO J D Bee, Secretary, The Yates Foundation, Peter Yates House, Manchester Road, Bolton BL3 2PU

CC NO 1061571   **ESTABLISHED** 1997

■ Yeovil Community Church Trust

WHAT IS FUNDED To advance the Christian religion and in particular to support the work of Yeovil Community Church; to advance religious education in accordance with the Chrisitan faith; to maintain the up-keep and repair of the fabric of any buildings in connection with Yeovil Community Church and the maintainance of their services; any other general charitable purposes for the benefit of the local community and other areas

WHAT IS NOT FUNDED No support for activities not connected in some way with the work of Yeovil Community Church

WHO CAN BENEFIT Christian workers connected with Yeovil Community Church in UK and overseas

WHERE FUNDING CAN BE GIVEN In practice Yeovil, Somerset

TYPE OF GRANT As appropriate to the above including buildings

FINANCES *Year* 1997 *Income* £336,597

WHO TO APPLY TO M Nichols, Yeovil Community Church Trust, 164 Preston Road, Yeovil, Somerset BA20 2EQ

CC NO 1039903   **ESTABLISHED** 1994

■ York Children's Trust

WHAT IS FUNDED Voluntary groups helping in the care and development of young people through arts, culture and recreation, healthcare, education and community services; support of individuals with special needs

WHO CAN BENEFIT Individuals, group-based organisations, local groups, schools and benefiting: those under 25 years of age; parents and children; one parent families; at risk groups; disabled people and those disadvantaged by poverty

WHERE FUNDING CAN BE GIVEN The Greater York area (20 mile radius of York)

FINANCES *Year* 1996 *Income* £89,588 *Grants* £70,247

TRUSTEES Ald J P Birch (Chairman), R W Miers (Vice-Chairman), Miss L J Hill, Mrs A Hope, Lady M Fitzalan Howard, Mrs K Lethem, Mrs E M Mungall, Mrs A Smith, Mrs M E Wilkinson, Mrs R Wilson, Dr H J Heggarty, G Hierons, JP, C P Roberts, JP, W M Sessions, Rev G Webster, R Wilkinson

HOW TO APPLY To the address under Who To Apply To in writing

WHO TO APPLY TO H G Sherriff, Secretary, York Children's Trust, 34 Lucombe Way, Hartrigg Oaks, New Barswick, York YO32 4DS *Tel* 01904 750705

CC NO 222279   **ESTABLISHED** 1976

■ York Civic Trust

WHAT IS FUNDED The preservation of natural, cultural and artistic amenities in the area Where Funding Can Be Given for the benefit of the local inhabitants

WHO CAN BENEFIT Local inhabitants

WHERE FUNDING CAN BE GIVEN York

FINANCES *Year* 1995 *Income* £188,338 *Grants* £8,380

TRUSTEES Council of Management: R J Carr-Archer, Miss J M Hargreaves, M W Jones, G Millar, A R Royle, J Shannon, C S Shepherd, R G Sims, M D B Sinclair, P N L Terry, E F V Waterson

HOW TO APPLY To the address under Who To Apply To in writing

WHO TO APPLY TO Peter Brown, Secretary, York Civic Trust, Fairfax House, Castlegate, York YO1 9RN

CC NO 229336   **ESTABLISHED** 1950

■ Yorkshire Agricultural Society

WHAT IS FUNDED (a) Promotion of agriculture and allied industries, related research and education. (b) Protection and safeguarding of the environment. (c) Holding of an annual agricultural show. (d) Appropriate charitable purposes. Priority is given to charities in Yorkshire and former Cleveland, with some activities extending into Durham and Northumberland. Environmental projects normally require relevance to agriculture to attract support. This Trust will consider giving support to religious umbrella bodies; schools and colleges; and rural crime prevention schemes

WHAT IS NOT FUNDED No grants are made for students' fees within higher or further education. Overseas projects are seldom supported

WHO CAN BENEFIT Primarily local individuals, activities and organisations benefiting people of all ages, those in the farming industry and those living in rural areas

WHERE FUNDING CAN BE GIVEN North east England, Yorkshire and Humberside

TYPE OF GRANT At discretion of Council/Executive Committee – most usually once only or starter/pump priming finance. Buildings, capital, core costs, feasibility studies, projects, research, running costs, recurring costs and salaries will be considered. Funding may be given for up to three years
RANGE OF GRANTS £200–£10,000, typical grant £1,000
SAMPLE GRANTS £20,000 for six grants for university research projects relevant to farming and the countryside; £15,000 to Dales Countryside Museum for redevelopment; £6,000 to Farming and Wildlife Advisory Groups (FWAG) for administration costs shared equally between four groups; £2,000 to Durham Wildlife Trust for educational display; £2,000 to 'Dales Watch' for security initiative to combat rural crime; £2,000 to Huddersfield Community Farm for visitors centre; £1,000 to 'Caring for Life' Crag House Farm, Leeds for care and development for those with learning difficulties, farm based; £1,000 to British Isles Bee Breeders Association for research; £1,000 to Rare Breeds Survival Trust for show costs; £1,000 to Northern Horticultural Society for administrative costs
FINANCES Year 1997 Income £2,200,000 Grants £112,500
TRUSTEES Council members of whom there are 38
PUBLICATIONS (a) Annual Report. (b) Quarterly Newsletter
HOW TO APPLY To Chief Executive in writing. Applications considered quarterly. Must include recent accounts (if applicable) and proposed budget together with confirmed and anticipated sources of funding. Details of ongoing management and costs also important
WHO TO APPLY TO R T Keigwin, Chief Executive, Yorkshire Agricultural Society, Great Yorkshire Showground, Harrogate HG2 8PW
Tel 01423 541000 *Fax* 01423 541414
E-mail info@yas.co.uk
CC NO 513238   ESTABLISHED 1837

■ Yorkshire and Humberside Arts

WHAT IS FUNDED Financial support to arts activities and provision of arts services
WHAT IS NOT FUNDED Grants are never awarded retrospectively and are not usually offered for capital purchases or to students for the purpose of study or fund raising events
WHO CAN BENEFIT Individuals and organisations benefiting: children; young adults and older people; actors and entertainment professionals; musicians; textile workers and designers; volunteers; writers and poets; individual artists and non-profit making arts organisations
WHERE FUNDING CAN BE GIVEN West Yorkshire, South Yorkshire, North Yorkshire, Humberside
TYPE OF GRANT Core costs, one-off, project, research, running costs, recurring costs, salaries and start-up costs. All funding is for up to or more than three years
SAMPLE GRANTS £840,750 to West Yorkshire Playhouse; £641,400 to Sheffield Theatres; £392,000 to York Theatre Royal; £278,900 to Yorkshire Sculpture Park; £278,250 to Phoenix Dance Company; £230,000 to Stephen Joseph Theatre; £176,300 to Harrogate Theatre; £170,700 to Hull Truck Theatre; £130,000 to Major Road Theatre; £115,700 to Huddersfield Contemporary Music Festival
FINANCES Year 1996–97 Income £7,561,912 Grants £6,543,122

TRUSTEES The Members (nominated representatives of subscribing local authorities and Board Directors)
PUBLICATIONS Quarterly newsletter, monthly 'What's On' guide and other occasional publications
NOTES Apply at least eight weeks in advance of the activity to be supported
HOW TO APPLY Applications to be made by 1 April or 1 October. Telephone contact welcome. Application forms for some grants. Grants information leaflet available
WHO TO APPLY TO Roger Lancaster, Chief Executive, Yorkshire & Humberside Arts, 21 Bond Street, Dewsbury, West Yorkshire WF13 1AX
Tel 01924 455555 *Fax* 01924 455555
CC NO 1003794   ESTABLISHED 1991

■ The Yorkshire Bank Charitable Trust

WHAT IS FUNDED Charities considered for support include those engaged in youth work, facilities for the less able-bodied and mentally disabled, counselling and community work in depressed areas, with some support also being given for education and for the arts. The Trustees would be unlikely to make more than one donation within any 12 month period
WHAT IS NOT FUNDED Applications from individuals, including students, are ineligible. No grants made in response to general appeals from national organisations
WHO CAN BENEFIT Registered charities benefiting: children and young adults; at risk groups; disabled people; those disadvantaged by poverty; socially isolated people and those involved in the arts
WHERE FUNDING CAN BE GIVEN Within the area covered by branches of the Bank, ie in England from north of the Thames Valley to Newcastle upon Tyne
TYPE OF GRANT Usually one-off for a specific project or part of a project
FINANCES Year 1996 Income £240,439 Grants £122,357
TRUSTEES D T Gallagher, O P Vanzuyden, C Herbert
HOW TO APPLY At any time. Applications should include relevant details of the need the intended project is designed to meet
WHO TO APPLY TO Executive Secretary, The Yorkshire Bank Charitable Trust, Yorkshire Bank plc, 20 Merrion Way, Leeds, West Yorkshire LS2 8NZ
CC NO 326269   ESTABLISHED 1982

■ Yorkshire Building Society Charitable Foundation

WHAT IS FUNDED General charitable purposes
WHO CAN BENEFIT There are no restrictions on the age; professional and economic group; family situation; religion and culture; and social circumstances of; or disease or medical condition suffered by, the beneficiaries
WHERE FUNDING CAN BE GIVEN UK
TRUSTEES C J Faulkner
WHO TO APPLY TO C J Faulkner, Trustee, Yorkshire Building Society Charitable Foundation, Yorkshire House, Yorkshire Drive, Bradford, Yorkshire BD5 8LJ
CC NO 1069082   ESTABLISHED 1998

◼ The Yorkshire County Cricket Club Charitable Youth Trust

WHAT IS FUNDED The provision of facilities for young people in full-time education to play cricket

WHO CAN BENEFIT Schools and colleges benefiting: children and young adults; students; sports people; teachers and coaches

WHERE FUNDING CAN BE GIVEN Yorkshire

FINANCES *Year* 1995 *Income* £69,769

HOW TO APPLY To the address under Who To Apply To in writing

WHO TO APPLY TO J P Honeysett, Secretary, The Yorkshire County Cricket Club Charitable Youth Trust, Stray Putt, 9 St Winifred's Road, Harrogate, North Yorkshire HG2 8LN

CC NO 1001497   **ESTABLISHED** 1991

◼ The Yorkshire Historic Churches Trust

WHAT IS FUNDED The repair, restoration, preservation, maintenance and improvement of churches in the area Where Funding Can Be Given

WHAT IS NOT FUNDED Re-ordering of churches

WHO CAN BENEFIT All Christian churches

WHERE FUNDING CAN BE GIVEN Yorkshire

TYPE OF GRANT Capital building grants. Funding of up to three years will be considered

RANGE OF GRANTS £300–£1,600

SAMPLE GRANTS £1,500 to Barnby Dun, SS Peter and Paul for roof and tower repairs; £1,500 to Leeds, St Saviour for repairs to roof, windows and gullies; £1,500 to Wakefield, Chantry Chapel for roof and heating repairs; £1,250 to South Dalton, St Mary for reroofing and repointing; £1,000 to Londesborough, All Saints to conserve monument; £800 to Badsworth, St Mary for roof repairs; £800 to Beeford, St Leonard for masonry and roof repairs; £800 to Crathorne, St Mary for repairs to windows, gutters and brickwork; £800 to Escrick, St Helen for tower masonry repairs; £800 to Gillingwest, St Agatha for nave roof repairs and repointing

FINANCES *Year* 1997 *Income* £33,452
Grants £17,500

TRUSTEES Dr C Binfield, R Carr-Archer, C L Clarkson, N Forbesadam, W Legard, L Lennox, N McDermid, S Reynolds, D Ryott, B E Smith, W J A Smith, I Watson, Sir M Worsley

HOW TO APPLY To the address under Who To Apply To in writing. Ask for application form. Closing date for grants - 31st March

WHO TO APPLY TO Mrs P Langstaff, The Yorkshire Historic Churches Trust, 430 Bradford Road, Sandbeds, Keighley BD20 5NP
Tel 01274 563277

CC NO 700639   **ESTABLISHED** 1988

◼ Yorkshire Water Community Trust

WHAT IS FUNDED To relieve those who are in conditions of need, poverty, hardship and distress and can not, therefore, meet the charges for the supply of water or sewerage to their residential accommodation, and other charitable purposes

WHO CAN BENEFIT Individuals and organisations benefiting one parent families, those disadvantaged by poverty and disabled people

WHERE FUNDING CAN BE GIVEN West Yorkshire

TYPE OF GRANT Running costs

FINANCES *Year* 1997 *Income* £132,422
Grants £162,360

TRUSTEES Mrs P Marsh, C L Cameron, MBE, J L Dawson, Ms T Flanders, Prof N Jepson, Mrs J Smith, Mrs J Kirkham, D Brimblecombe

NOTES For help with water charges, prime consideration is given to cases where multiple debt exists and where outgoings exceed income. The criteria also includes at least one of the following: the applicant must be claiming income support; be disabled; a one parent family; or have financially dependant relatives

WHO TO APPLY TO D Brimblecombe, Secretary, Yorkshire Water Community Trust, 2 The Embankment, Sovereign Street, Leeds LS1 4BG

CC NO 1047923   **ESTABLISHED** 1995

◼ The John Young Charitable Settlement

WHAT IS FUNDED General charitable purposes

WHO CAN BENEFIT There are no restrictions on the age; professional and economic group; family situation; religion and culture; and social circumstances of; or disease or medical condition suffered by, the beneficiaries

WHERE FUNDING CAN BE GIVEN UK

RANGE OF GRANTS £120–£10,000

SAMPLE GRANTS £10,000 to Heart of Britain Appeal; £7,500 to CAF Mediciens Du Monde; £5,000 to Futures for Children; £5,000 to Population Concern; £2,222 to Architectural Association; £2,000 to Anti-bullying Campaign; £1,500 to SCOPE; £1,500 to The Serious Road Trip; £1,000 to Union of UEA Students; £1,000 to Friends of the Earth

FINANCES *Year* 1997 *Income* £51,476
Grants £39,842

TRUSTEES J M Young, G H Camamile

WHO TO APPLY TO K A Hawkins, The John Young Charitable Settlement, Lee Associates, 5 Southampton Place, London WC1A 2DA

CC NO 283254   **ESTABLISHED** 1981

◼ David Young Charitable Trust

WHAT IS FUNDED General charitable purposes

WHO CAN BENEFIT There are no restrictions on the age; professional and economic group; family situation; religion and culture; and social circumstances of; or disease or medical condition suffered by, the beneficiaries

WHERE FUNDING CAN BE GIVEN UK

RANGE OF GRANTS £30–£20,000

SAMPLE GRANTS £20,000 to Joint Israel Appeal; £12,500 to Joint Jewish Charitable Trust; £7,500 to Community Security Trust; £2,500 to Hamilton Advertising; £1,819 to United Synagogue; £500 to North West London Jewish Day Services Golden Jubilee; £300 to Midhurst Music Society; £200 to Leukaemia Research; £200 to Progress; £150 to Weizman Institute Foundation

FINANCES *Year* 1996 *Income* £54,020
Grants £46,299

TRUSTEES Lord Young, Lady Young, M S Mischon

WHO TO APPLY TO David Young Charitable Trust, Blick Rothenberg, Chartered Accountants, 12 York Gate, Regents Park, London NW1 4QS

CC NO 265195   **ESTABLISHED** 1972

◼ John K Young Endowment Fund

WHAT IS FUNDED Grants are given to support medical and surgical research and research in chemistry as an aid to UK industry. Also to fund charities which are concerned with the physical wellbeing of the youth of Edinburgh or with restoring the sick to health

WHO CAN BENEFIT Organisations benefiting: people of all ages; chemists; research workers and medical professionals. There is no restriction on the disease or medical condition suffered by the beneficiaries

WHERE FUNDING CAN BE GIVEN Scotland, particularly Edinburgh

TYPE OF GRANT One-off grants are awarded. Funding is available for up to one year

RANGE OF GRANTS £500–£2,000

FINANCES *Year* 1997–98 *Income* £40,000 *Grants* £30,000

TRUSTEES T C Foggo, A J R Ferguson, R J S Morton, R I F Macdonald

HOW TO APPLY Applications are considered in the spring and autumn

WHO TO APPLY TO Roin Morton, Partner/Trust Administrator, John K Young Endowment Fund, Skene, Edwards WS, 5 Albyn Place, Edinburgh EH2 4NJ *Tel* 0131-225 6665 *Fax* 0131-220 1015

SC NO SCO 02264

■ The Jonathan Young Memorial Trust

WHAT IS FUNDED Computers and computer equipment

WHO CAN BENEFIT Individuals who fall within the criteria of the Trust or organisations working with them. Particularly disabled people

WHERE FUNDING CAN BE GIVEN Emphasis on Nottinghamshire and other parts of the East Midlands

TYPE OF GRANT One-off. Some second-hand equipment may also be available

RANGE OF GRANTS £50–£2,000

TRUSTEES R Beadles, B Gregson, A H Young, J D C Young, M A Willmot

HOW TO APPLY In writing. Grants are normally made in September/October, but applications may be considered at other times

WHO TO APPLY TO J D C Young, Chairman, The Jonathan Young Memorial Trust, 10 Huntingdon Drive, The Park, Nottingham NG7 1BW *Tel* 0115-947 0493

CC NO 1067619   **ESTABLISHED** 1998

■ Youngs of Stokesley Charitable Trust

WHAT IS FUNDED General charitable purposes

WHO CAN BENEFIT There are no restrictions on the age; professional and economic group; family situation; religion and culture; and social circumstances of; or disease or medical condition suffered by, the beneficiaries

WHERE FUNDING CAN BE GIVEN UK with preference to North East England and North Yorkshire

SAMPLE GRANTS £1,767 for church repairs

FINANCES *Year* 1997 *Income* £29,848 *Grants* £1,767

WHO TO APPLY TO Miss H C Lewis, Youngs of Stokesley Charitable Trust, Messrs Punch Robson, 35 Albert Road, Middlesbrough, Cleveland TS1 1NU

CC NO 1037211   **ESTABLISHED** 1994

■ Youth Appeal for Eastern Europe

WHAT IS FUNDED Strengthening of the development of partner Non Governmental Organisations in Central and Eastern Europe, working with or for children and young people aged between 5–25 years. Grants can be made for the following: to support the delivery of services; to purchase basic equipment; to train staff; to carry out basic research and feasibility studies; to cover travel to and from the region; local translation and interpretation costs; technical assistance; the development of skills; and to help other support programmes

WHAT IS NOT FUNDED Grants will not normally be made for: retrospective funding; the teaching of English as a foreign language; the administration of schemes for UK volunteers (eg working holidays); activities for personal rather than institutional development; in response to general appeals; the provision of direct humanitarian aid; standard socio-cultural and artistic exchanges

WHO CAN BENEFIT Registered charities or organisations within the UK approved for charitable status by the Inland Revenue, which have a partner in Central or Eastern Europe or the newly independent states of the former Soviet Union. The grants are to benefit the partner organisation, not the UK charity. Support is given to organisations benefiting children and young adults between the age of 5 and 25

WHERE FUNDING CAN BE GIVEN UK charities working in partnership with NGOs in Central and Eastern Europe and the newly independent states of the Former Soviet Union

TYPE OF GRANT Small grants

RANGE OF GRANTS Up to £1,000

FINANCES *Year* 1995–96 *Income* £40,000 *Grants* £18,000

HOW TO APPLY On standard application form. Meetings are quarterly in March, June, September and December with a deadline for receipt of applications six weeks before a meeting

WHO TO APPLY TO Judith McQuillan, Grants Administrator, Youth Appeal for Eastern Europe, Charities Aid Foundation, Kings Hill, West Malling, Kent ME19 4TA

CC NO 268369   **ESTABLISHED** 1994

Z

■ The ZSV Trust

WHAT IS FUNDED The relief of poverty and other general charitable purposes

WHO CAN BENEFIT There are no restrictions on the age; professional and economic group; family situation; religion and culture; and social circumstances of; or disease or medical condition suffered by, the beneficiaries

WHERE FUNDING CAN BE GIVEN UK

SAMPLE GRANTS £23,891 to Relief of Poverty

FINANCES *Year* 1997 *Income* £33,719
Grants £23,891

TRUSTEES M Fogel, Z Friedman, A Weinberger

WHO TO APPLY TO Mordechai Fogel, Trustee, The ZSV Trust, 46 Cambridge Court, Amhurst Park, London N16 5AQ

CC NO 1063860 **ESTABLISHED** 1997

■ The Elizabeth and Prince Zaiger Trust

WHAT IS FUNDED Relief for elderly and handicapped persons, advancement of education relief of poverty and general charitable purposes

WHO CAN BENEFIT Registered charities benefiting people of all ages who are mentally and physically disabled and disadvantaged by poverty.

WHERE FUNDING CAN BE GIVEN Somerset, UK

TYPE OF GRANT One-off and recurrent

RANGE OF GRANTS £25–£5,000

SAMPLE GRANTS £5,000 to Children's Unit, Yeovil Hospital; £3,500 to the Spastics Society; £3,500 to Action Research for the Crippled Child; £3,500 to Marie Curie Memorial Foundation; £3,500 to the Royal Institute for the Blind; £3,500 to Association for Spina Bifida and Hydrocephalus; £3,500 to St Margaret's Hospice Limited; £3,500 to the Horder Centre for Arthritics; £3,500 to British Institute for Brain Injured Children; £3,500 to National Deaf, Blind and Rubella Association

FINANCES *Year* 1996 *Income* £148,420

TRUSTEES P J Harvey, D Long, D W Parry

HOW TO APPLY **This Trust states that it does not respond to unsolicited applications**

WHO TO APPLY TO D W Parry, The Elizabeth and Prince Zaiger Trust, 6 Alleyn Road, Dulwich, London SE21 8AL

CC NO 282096 **ESTABLISHED** 1981

■ Zephyr Charitable Trust

WHAT IS FUNDED Housing, health, environment, third world projects

WHAT IS NOT FUNDED No grants to individuals, expeditions or scholarships

WHO CAN BENEFIT National help organisations benefiting: disabled people; homeless people; victims of famine, man-made or natural disasters and war. There is no restriction on the disease or medical condition suffered by the beneficiaries

WHERE FUNDING CAN BE GIVEN UK and overseas

TYPE OF GRANT Range of grants

RANGE OF GRANTS £250–£3,000

SAMPLE GRANTS £3,000 to Intermediate Technology for brickmaking process in Sudan; £2,000 to CRISIS; £2,000 to Medical Foundation for the Care of Victims of Torture; £2,000 to MIND; £1,900 to Shelter; £1,900 Survival International; £1,900 to Voluntary Service Organisation; £1,600 to Pesticides Trust; £1,600 to Womankind

FINANCES *Year* 1998 *Income* £57,645
Grants £25,250

TRUSTEES Elizabeth Breeze, Roger Harriman, David Baldock, Donald I Watson

PUBLICATIONS Annual Report forms part of Accounts

NOTES The bulk of the Trust's annual income is allocated by way of 14 annual subscriptions leaving a very small annual amount of £2,000 available for one-off grants. **Unsolicited applications are therefore unlikely to be successful**

WHO TO APPLY TO R Harriman, Zephyr Charitable Trust, New Guild House, 45 Great Charles Street, Queensway, Birmingham B3 2LX *Tel* 0121-212 2222

CC NO 1003234 **ESTABLISHED** 1991

■ I A Ziff Charitable Foundation

WHAT IS FUNDED General charitable purposes. Value for money; donations which will bring the most benefit to the largest number of people

WHAT IS NOT FUNDED No grants available to individuals

WHO CAN BENEFIT There are no restrictions on the age; professional and economic group; family situation; religion and culture; and social circumstances of; or disease or medical condition suffered by, the beneficiaries

WHERE FUNDING CAN BE GIVEN Leeds, Yorkshire

TYPE OF GRANT One-off, no loans

FINANCES *Year* 1997 *Income* £240,172
Grants £135,985

TRUSTEES I A Ziff, Mrs M E Ziff, M A Ziff, E M Ziff, Mrs A L Manning

NOTES The Charity has undertaken to finance two major projects which will consume its resources for the foreseeable future. It may make token gifts to requests outside its normal range of beneficiaries but the funds available are very strictly limited

HOW TO APPLY Initial telephone calls welcome. Sae ensures a reply

WHO TO APPLY TO K N Riley, I A Ziff Charitable Foundation, Town Centre House, The Merrion Centre, Leeds LS2 8LY *Tel* 0113-245 9172 *Fax* 0113-242 1026

CC NO 249368 **ESTABLISHED** 1964

■ The Stephen Zimmerman Charitable Trust

WHAT IS FUNDED General charitable purposes

WHO CAN BENEFIT There are no restrictions on the age; professional and economic group; family situation; religion and culture; and social circumstances of; or disease or medical condition suffered by, the beneficiaries

WHERE FUNDING CAN BE GIVEN UK

TYPE OF GRANT At the discretion of the trustees

RANGE OF GRANTS £100–£5,000

SAMPLE GRANTS £5,000 to Mowbray Trust; £4,675 to Jewish Care Charity; £3,000 to Joint Jewish Charitable Trust; £1,300 to The Weizmann Institute Foundation; £750 to Sarum Hall School Appeal Fund; £650 to Polack's House Educational Trust; £500 to British Ort Charity; £375 to United Synagogue; £250 to Action and Addiction Charity; £200 to Ravenswood

FINANCES *Year* 1996 *Income* £59,393 *Grants* £16,800

TRUSTEES Stephen A Zimmerman, Laura J Zimmerman, Sidney Houswirth

HOW TO APPLY **This Trust states that it does not respond to unsolicited applications**

WHO TO APPLY TO S Zimmerman The Stephen Zimmerman Charitable Trust, 35 Stormont Road, Highgate, London N6 4NR

CC NO 1038310   **ESTABLISHED** 1994

■ The David Zodelava Charitable Trust

This trust did not respond to CAF's request to amend its entry and, by 30 June 1998, CAF's researchers did not find financial records for later than 1995 on its file at the Charity Commission. Trusts are legally required to submit annual accounts to the Charity Commission under section 42 of the Charities Act 1993

WHAT IS FUNDED (a) To promote and advance the education of gifted children; (b) to advance the education of adult citizens of Georgia or those purposes beneficial to the community; (c) to relieve poverty, advance education and other charitable purposes for the benefit of the community

WHO CAN BENEFIT Children, young adults and those disadvantaged by poverty

WHERE FUNDING CAN BE GIVEN The State of Georgia formerly of the Union of Soviet Socialist Republics (USSR)

TRUSTEES R W J Alexander, D A Baker, D Zodelava

WHO TO APPLY TO The Correspondent, The David Zodelava Charitable Trust, Portner & Jaskel, Solicitors, 8 Welbeck Way, London W1M 7PE

CC NO 1046062   **ESTABLISHED** 1995

■ Victor Zorza Hospice Trust

WHAT IS FUNDED Projects in Russia run by British charitable organisations which promote hospice principles and encourage the development of a Russian hospice network. These may include training and support programmes; educational projects to raise public awareness of the benefits of hospice care, or to give information and assistance in starting a local hospice; provision of medical textbooks and literature relating to palliative care; and the provision of medical equipment under specified conditions

WHAT IS NOT FUNDED Funds are usually required to be spent in the UK. Any grants spent in Russia are to be under the control of the British organisation concerned

WHO CAN BENEFIT Small British charitable organisations with experience of working in Russia in the palliative care field, or similarly experienced individuals using their skills to benefit the Russian hospice movement

WHERE FUNDING CAN BE GIVEN Principally Russia

TYPE OF GRANT Project; possibly recurring. Small ongoing initiatives more likely to be funded than big capital projects

TRUSTEES Mrs Ruth Bradby, Mrs Patricia Cockrell, Mrs Eileen Lerche-Thomsen, Dr John Williams

NOTES Mrs Lerche-Thomsen will be moving to the address under Who To Apply To at the end of March 1999. Until then, applications for funding should be sent to: Mrs Eileen Lerche-Thomsen, The Victor Zorza Hospice Trust, Dairy Cottage, Hitcham Lane, Burnham, Buckinghamshire SLI 7DS

WHO TO APPLY TO Mrs Eileen Lerche-Thomsen, Victor Zorza Hospice Trust, Svendborg, Greve d'Azette, St Clement, Jersey JE2 6PT *Tel* 01534 35616 *E-mail* vzhospicetrust@l-tz.freeserve.co.uk

■ Zurich Financial Services (UKISA) Community Trust Limited

WHAT IS FUNDED The Trust's current programmes are dementia, domestic violence, active citizenship, India and all aspects of employee involvement in the community. Grant and volunteer support may also be available to local voluntary organisations around the Groups companies' main offices (Allied Dunbar, Eagle Star)

WHAT IS NOT FUNDED No grants for educational scholarships; expeditions; medical research; animal charities; religious organisations; sponsorship; publications or to individuals

WHO CAN BENEFIT Voluntary organisations benefiting people with Alzheimer's disease; disabled people; those disadvantaged by poverty; the socially isolated and victims of domestic violence

WHERE FUNDING CAN BE GIVEN UK and developing world

TYPE OF GRANT Recurrent and one-off. Capital, core costs, project, running costs, salaries and start-up costs. Funding for up to three years or more will be considered

SAMPLE GRANTS £1,489,011 to ASPIRE for a training centre; £100,000 to London Connection for refurbishment costs; £80,000 to Citizens Organising Foundation for organiser's core costs; £65,000 to Alzheimer Scotland for early onset support; £62,000 to Alzheimer Scotland for advocacy project; £60,000 to Alzheimer's Disease Society for Care Consortium (training/quality standards); £40,000 to Alzheimer's Disease Society for North Wales development worker; £30,000 to Women's Aid Federation of England for training unit; £29,472 to WAITS, Birmingham for domestic violence development with ethnic groups; £27,500 to Northern Ireland Women's Aid Federation for refuge development

FINANCES *Year* 1997 *Income* £3,293,000 *Grants* £3,374,000

TRUSTEES P Smith, S Leitch, K Baldwin

PUBLICATIONS Annual Report

NOTES **All funds for major programmes are fully committed**

HOW TO APPLY Telephone enquiries are welcome provided the caller has made reasonable efforts to check whether their request is likely to fit our criteria. Application forms and/or guidelines are provided where appropriate

WHO TO APPLY TO J B Bickell, Zurich Finanacial Services (UKISA) Community Trust Limited, PO Box 1288, Swindon, Wiltshire SN1 1FL *Tel* 01793 514514 *Fax* 01793 506982 *E-mail* comm.aff@dial.pipex.com

CC NO 266983   **ESTABLISHED** 1973